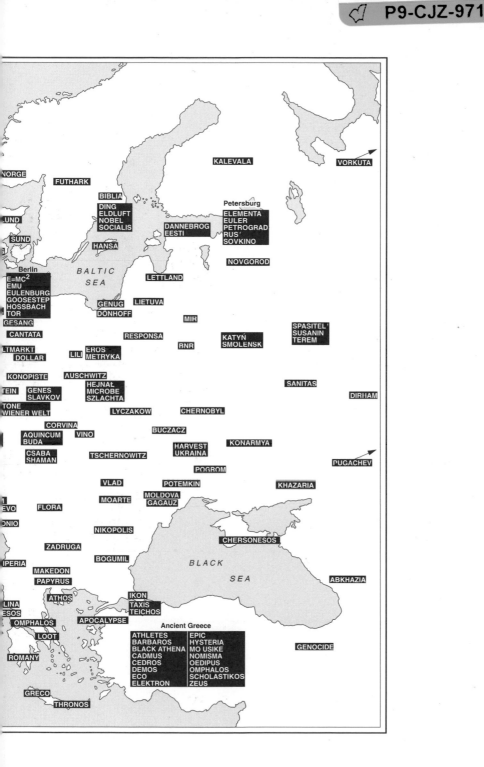

NORGE
FUTHARK
KALEVALA
VORKUTA
BIBLIA
DING
ELDLUFT
NOBEL
SOCIALIS
Petersburg
ELEMENTA
EULER
PETROGRAD
RUS'
SOVKINO
UND
SUND
DANNEBROG
EESTI
HANSA
NOVGOROD
Berlin
E=MC^2
EMU
EULENBURG
GOOSESTEP
HOSSBACH
TOR
GESANG
BALTIC
SEA
LETTLAND
GENUG
DONHOFF
LIETUVA
MIR
SPASITEL'
SUSANIN
TEREM
CANTATA
RESPONSA
KATYŃ
SMOLENSK
LTMARKT
DOLLAR
LILI
EROS
METRYKA
RNR
KONOPISTE
AUSCHWITZ
SANITAS
DIRHAM
TEIN
GENES
SLAVKOV
HEJNAŁ
MICROBE
SZLACHTA
TONE
WIENER WELT
LYCZAKOW
CHERNOBYL
CORVINA
AQUINCUM
BUDA
VINO
BUCZACZ
KONARMYA
CSABA
SHAMAN
TSCHERNOWITZ
HARVEST
UKRAINA
POGROM
PUGACHEV
VLAD
POTEMKIN
KHAZARIA
EVO
FLORA
MOARTE
MOLDOVA
GAGAUZ
ONIO
NIKOPOLIS
CHERSONESOS
ZADRUGA
IPERIA
BOGUMIL
BLACK
SEA
ABKHAZIA
MAKEDON
PAPYRUS
ATHOS
IKON
TAXIS
TEICHOS
LINA
ESOS
OMPHALOS
APOCALYPSE
Ancient Greece
LOOT
ROMANY
ATHLETES
BARBAROS
BLACK ATHENA
CADMUS
CEDROS
DEMOS
ECO
ELEKTRON
EPIC
HYSTERIA
MO USIKE
NOMISMA
OEDIPUS
OMPHALOS
SCHOLASTIKOS
ZEUS
GENOCIDE
GRECO
THRONOS

EUROPE

EUROPE

A HISTORY

Norman Davies

Oxford · New York

OXFORD UNIVERSITY PRESS

1996

Oxford University Press

Oxford   New York
Athens   Auckland   Bangkok   Bogota   Bombay
Buenos Aires   Calcutta   Cape Town   Dar es Salaam
Delhi   Florence   Hong Kong   Istanbul   Karachi
Kuala Lumpur   Madras   Madrid   Melbourne
Mexico City   Nairobi   Paris   Singapore
Taipei   Tokyo   Toronto

and associated companies in
Berlin   Ibadan

Published by Oxford University Press, Inc.,
198 Madison Avenue, New York, New York   10016

Oxford is a registered trademark of Oxford University Press, Inc.

British Library Cataloging in Publication Data
Data available

Library of Congress Cataloging in Publication Data
Data applied for

ISBN 0-19-520912-5

7 9 8 6

Data capture by Pure Tech India Ltd., Pondicherry
Typeset by Hope Services (Abingdon) Ltd.
Printed in the United States of America
on acid-free paper

For Christian
Our Californian

PREFACE

THIS book contains little that is original. Since most aspects of the subject have been thoroughly worked over by previous historians, primary research was rarely required. The book's originality, such as it is, lies only in the selection, rearrangement, and presentation of the contents. The main aim was to map out a grid of time and space for European history and, by introducing a sufficiently comprehensive range of topics into the framework, to convey an impression of the unattainable whole.

The academic apparatus has been kept to a minimum. There are no notes relating to facts and statements that can be found in any of the established works of reference. Among the latter, special mention must be made of my twenty-nine volumes of *The Encyclopaedia Britannica* (11th edn., 1910–11), which far surpasses all its successors. Endnotes are only provided to substantiate less familiar quotations and sources of information beyond the range of the standard textbooks. One should not assume that the text necessarily agrees with interpretations found in the works cited: '*On ne s'étonnera pas que la doctrine exposée dans le texte ne soit toujours d'accord avec les travaux auxquels il est renvoyé en note.*'*

The academic considerations which underlay the writing of the present volume have been set out in the Introduction. But its design may need some explanation.

The text has been constructed on several different levels. Twelve narrative chapters pan across the whole of Europe's past, from prehistory to the present. They gradually zoom in from the distant focus of Chapter I, which covers the first five million years, to the relatively close focus of Chapters XI and XII, which cover the twentieth century at roughly one page per year. Each chapter carries a selection of more specific 'capsules', picked out, as it were, by telephoto, and illustrating narrower themes that cut across the chronological flow. Each chapter ends with a wide-angle 'snapshot' of the whole Continent as seen from one particular vantage-point. The overall effect may be likened to a historical picture album, in which panoramic tableaux are interspersed by a collection of detailed insets and close-ups. One hopes it is understood that the degree of precision attainable at these different levels will vary considerably. Indeed, a work of synthesis cannot expect to match the standards of scientific monographs that have rather different purposes in mind.

The twelve main chapters follow the conventional framework of European history. They provide the basic chronological and geographical grid into which all the other topics and subjects have been fitted. They concentrate on 'event-based

* 'One will not be surprised when the doctrine expounded in the text does not always accord with the works to which reference is made in the notes'; Ferdinand Lot, *La Fin du monde antique et le début du Moyen Âge* (Paris, 1927), 3.

history': on the principal political divisions, cultural movements, and socio-economic trends which enable historians to break the mass of information into manageable (though necessarily artificial) units. The chronological emphasis lies on the medieval and modern periods, where a recognizably European community can be seen to be operating. The geographical spread aims to give equitable coverage to all parts of the European Peninsula from the Atlantic to the Urals—north, east, west, south, and centre.

At every stage, an attempt has been made to counteract the bias of 'Eurocentrism' and 'Western civilization' (see Introduction, pp. 16–19, 19–31). But in a work of this scope it has not been possible to extend the narrative beyond Europe's own frontiers. Suitable signals have been made to indicate the great importance of contingent subjects such as Islam, colonialism, or Europe overseas. East European affairs are given their proper prominence. Wherever appropriate, they are integrated into the major themes which affect the whole of the Continent. An eastern element is included in the exposition of topics such as the Barbarian invasions, the Renaissance, or the French Revolution, which all too often have been presented as relevant only to the West. The space given to the Slavs can be attributed to the fact that they form the largest of Europe's ethnic families. National histories are regularly summarized; but attention has been paid to the stateless nations, not just to the nation-states. Minority communities, from heretics and lepers to Jews, Romanies, and Muslims, have not been forgotten.

In the last chapters, the priorities of the 'Allied scheme of history' have not been followed (see Introduction, pp. 39–42). Nor have they been polemically contested. The two World Wars have been treated as 'two successive acts of a single drama', preference being given to the central continental contest between Germany and Russia. The final chapter on post-war Europe takes the narrative to the events of 1989–91 and the disintegration of the Soviet Union. The argument contends that 1991 saw the end of a geopolitical arena, dubbed 'the Great Triangle', whose origins can be dated to the turn of the twentieth century (see Appendix III, p. 1312), and whose demise offers a suitable hiatus in a continuing story. The approach of the twenty-first century sees the opening of a new opportunity to design a new Europe.

The capsules, of which there are some 300 (see Map 30 and Appendix I), perform several purposes. They draw attention to a wide variety of specifics which would otherwise find no place among the generalizations and simplifications of synthetic history-writing. They sometimes introduce topics which cross the boundaries of the main chapters; and they illustrate all the curiosities, whimsies, and inconsequential sidestreams which over-serious historians can often overlook. Above all, they have been selected to give as many glimpses as possible of 'the new methods, the new disciplines, and the new fields' of recent research. They provide samples from some sixty categories of knowledge, which have been distributed over the chapters in the widest possible scatter of period, location, and subject-matter. For arbitrary reasons of the book's length, the publishers' patience, and the author's stamina, the original capsule list had to be reduced.

None the less, it is hoped that the overall pointilliste technique will still create an effective impression, even with a smaller number of points.

Each capsule is anchored into the text at a specific point in time and space, and is marked by a headword that summarizes its contents. Each can be tasted as a separate, self-contained morsel; or it can be read in conjunction with the narrative into which it is inserted.

The snapshots, of which there are twelve, are designed to present a series of panoramic overviews across the changing map of Europe. They freeze the frame of the chronological narrative, usually at moments of symbolic importance, and call a temporary halt to the headlong charge across enormous expanses of time and territory. They should help the reader to catch breath, and to take stock of the numerous transformations which were progressing at any one time on many different fronts. They are deliberately focused from a single vantage-point, and make no attempt to weigh the multiplicity of opinions and alternative perspectives which undoubtedly existed. To this extent, they are shamelessly subjective and impressionistic. In some instances, they border on the controversial realm of 'faction', combining known events with undocumented suppositions and deductions. Like several other elements in the book, they may be judged to exceed the conventional bounds of academic argument and analysis. If so, they will draw attention not only to the rich variety of Europe's past but also to the rich variety of prisms through which it can be viewed.

The book has been largely written in Oxford. It owes much to the rich and ancient resources of the Bodleian Library, and to that Library's rich and ancient standards of service. It was also helped by scholarships kindly provided by the Institut für die Wissenschaften vom Menschen in Vienna and by Harvard University's Ukrainian Research Institute. It has been coloured by several visits to the mainland of Europe during its writing, notably by impressions garnered in Belarus and Ukraine, on the road from Bavaria to Bologna, in the French and Swiss Alps, in the Netherlands, in Hungary, and in the Vendée.

I wish to acknowledge a period of one year's study leave which was granted by the School of Slavonic and East European Studies, University of London, on the condition that private funds were raised against the cost of replacement teaching. At other times, when leave was not granted, the book has possibly benefited from the discipline of writing in every sort of inspiring locale—on trains, in planes, in canteens, in hospital waiting-rooms, on Hawaiian beaches, on the back row of other people's seminars, even in a crematorium car park. I also acknowledge a special subsidy provided by Heinemann and Mandarin in order to speed the preparation of auxiliary materials.

I wish to express my thanks to colleagues and friends who have served as readers for particular chapters or sections: Barry Cunliffe, Stephanie West, Riet van Bremen, David Morgan, David Eltis, Fania Oz-Salzburger, Mark Almond, and Timothy Garton Ash; to a legion of helpers and consultants including Tony Armstrong, Sylvia Astle, Alex Boyd, Michael Branch, Lawrence Brockliss, Caroline Brownstone, Gordon Craig, Richard Crampton, Jim Cutsall, Rees Davies,

Regina Davy, Dennis Deletant, Geoffrey Ellis, Roger Greene, Hugo Gryn, Michael Hurst, Geraint Jenkins, Mahmud Khan, Maria Korzeniewicz, Grzegorz Król, Ian McKellen, Dimitri Obolensky, Laszlo Peter, Robert Pynsent, Martyn Rady, Mary Seton-Watson, Heidrun Speedy, Christine Stone, Athena Syriatou, Eva Travers, Luke Treadwell, Peter Varey, Maria Widowson, and Sergei Yakovenko; to a team of secretarial assistants, headed by 'Kingsley'; to Sarah Barrett, copy-editor; to Sally Kendall, designer; to Gill Metcalfe, picture researcher; to Roger Moorhouse, indexer; to Ken Wass and Tim Aspen, cartographers; Andrew Boag, illustrator; to my editors at OUP and at Mandarin; to the project manager Patrick Duffy; and especially to my wife, without whose support and forbearance the project could never have come to fruition. There is no prize for finding the black cat.

There is strong reason to believe that European history is a valid academic subject, which is solidly based on past events that really happened. Europe's past, however, can only be recalled through fleeting glimpses, partial probes, and selective soundings. It can never be recovered in its entirety. This volume, therefore, is only one from an almost infinite number of histories of Europe that could be written. It is the view of one pair of eyes, filtered by one brain, and translated by one pen.

NORMAN DAVIES

Oxford, Bloomsday, 1993

In preparing the corrected edition of *Europe: a history*, the amendments have been addressed solely to errors of fact, nomenclature and orthography. No attempt was made to re-enter the realm of historical interpretation. In addition to the original team of consultants, most of whom have offered a second round of advice, I wish to convey my special thanks to:

J. S. Adams, Ann Armstrong, Neal Ascherson, Timothy Bainbridge, Tim Blanning, Tim Boyle, Sir Raymond Carr, James Cornish, J. Cremona, M. F. Cullis, I. D. Davidson, H.E. the Ambassador of Finland, H.E. the Ambassador of Italy, Felipe Fernandez-Armesto, J. M. Forrester, Robert Frost, Michael Futrell, Graham Gladwell, Richard Hofton, Hugh Kearney, Noel Malcolm, Velibor Milovanović, B. C. Moberly, Jan Morris, W. Schulte Nordolt, Robin Osborne, Steven Pálffy, Roy Porter, Paul Preston, Jim Reed, Donald Russell, David Selbourne, Andrew L. Simon, N. C. W. Spence, Norman Stone, Alan H. Stratford, Richard Tyndorf, John Wagar, Michael West, B. K. Workman, Philip Wynn, and Basil Yamey.

NORMAN DAVIES

17 March 1997

CONTENTS

LIST OF MAPS

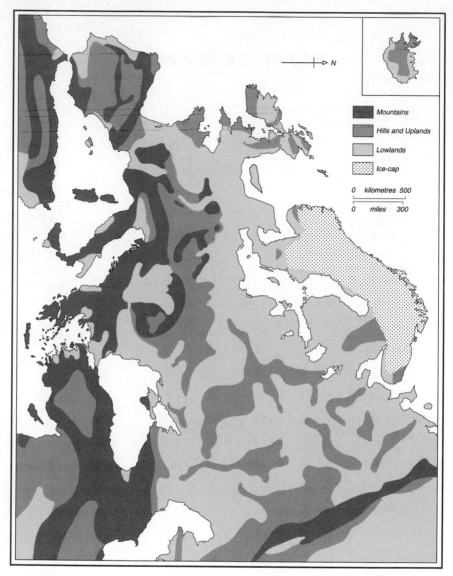

Map 1.
The Peninsula, *c.*10,000 BC

THE LEGEND OF EUROPA

IN the beginning, there was no Europe. All there was, for five million years, was a long, sinuous peninsula with no name, set like the figurehead of a ship on the prow of the world's largest land mass. To the west lay the ocean which no one had crossed. To the south lay two enclosed and interlinked seas, sprinkled with islands, inlets, and peninsulas of their own. To the north lay the great polar ice-cap, expanding and contracting across the ages like some monstrous, freezing jellyfish. To the east lay the land-bridge to the rest of the world, whence all peoples and all civilizations were to come.

In the intervals between the Ice Ages, the Peninsula received its first human set-tlers. The humanoids of Neanderthal, and the cave people of Cromagnon, must have had names and faces and ideas. But it cannot be known who they really were. They can only be recognized dimly from their pictures, their artefacts, and their bones.

With the last retreat of the ice, only twelve thousand years ago, the Peninsula received new waves of migrants. Unsung pioneers and prospectors moved slowly out to the west, rounding the coasts, crossing the land and the seas until the fur-thest islands were reached. Their greatest surviving masterwork, as the Age of Stone gave way to that of Bronze, was built on the edge of human habitation on a remote, offshore island. But no amount of modern speculation can reveal for certain what inspired those master masons, nor what their great stone circle was called.[1]

At the other end of the Peninsula, another of those distant peoples at the dawn of the Bronze Age was founding a community whose influence has lasted to the present day. By tradition the Hellenes descended from the continental interior in three main waves, taking control of the shores of the Aegean towards the end of the second millennium BC. They conquered and mingled with the existing inhab-itants. They spread out through the thousand islands which lie scattered among the waters between the coasts of the Peloponnese and of Asia Minor. They absorbed the prevailing culture of the mainland, and the still older culture of Crete. Their language distinguished them from the 'barbarians'—the 'speakers of unintelligible babble'. They were the creators of ancient Greece. [**BARBAROS**]

Later, when children of classical times asked where humankind had come from, they were told about the creation of the world by an unidentified *opifex rerum* or 'divine maker'. They were told about the Flood, and about Europa.

Europa was the subject of one of the most venerable legends of the classical world. Europa was the mother of Minos, Lord of Crete, and hence the progeni-trix of the most ancient branch of Mediterranean civilization. She was mentioned in passing by Homer. But in *Europa and the Bull*, attributed to Moschus of Syracuse, and above all in the *Metamorphoses* of the Roman poet, Ovid, she is immortalized as an innocent princess seduced by the Father of the Gods. Wandering with her maidens along the shore of her native Phoenicia, she was beguiled by Zeus in the guise of a snow-white bull:

> And gradually she lost her fear, and he
> Offered his breast for her virgin caresses,
> His horns for her to wind with chains of flowers,
> Until the princess dared to mount his back,
> Her pet bull's back, unwitting whom she rode.
> Then—slowly, slowly down the broad, dry beach—
> First in the shallow waves the great god set
> His spurious hooves, then sauntered further out
> Till in the open sea he bore his prize.
> Fear filled her heart as, gazing back, she saw
> The fast receding sands. Her right hand grasped
> A horn, the other lent upon his back.
> Her fluttering tunic floated in the breeze.[2]

Here was the familiar legend of Europa as painted on Grecian vases, in the houses of Pompeii (See Plate no. 1), and in modern times by Titian, Rembrandt, Rubens, Veronese, and Claude Lorrain.

The historian Herodotus, writing in the fifth century BC, was not impressed by the legend. In his view, the abduction of Europa was just an incident in the age-old wars over women-stealing. A band of Phoenicians from Tyre had carried off Io, daughter of the King of Argos; so a band of Greeks from Crete sailed over to Phoenicia and carried off the daughter of the King of Tyre. It was a case of tit for tit.[3]

The legend of Europa has many connotations. But in carrying the princess to Crete from the shore of Phoenicia (now south Lebanon) Zeus was surely trans-ferring the fruits of the older Asian civilizations of the East to the new island colonies of the Aegean. Phoenicia belonged to the orbit of the Pharaohs. Europa's ride provides the mythical link between Ancient Egypt and Ancient Greece. Europa's brother Cadmus, who roamed the world in search of her, *orbe pererrato*, was credited with bringing the art of writing to Greece. [**CADMUS**]

Europa's ride also captures the essential restlessness of those who followed in her footsteps. Unlike the great river valley civilizations of the Nile, of the Indus, of Mesopotamia, and of China, which were long in duration but lethargic in their geographical and intellectual development, the civilization of the Mediterranean Sea was stimulated by constant movement. Movement caused uncertainty and insecurity. Uncertainty fed a constant ferment of ideas. Insecurity prompted energetic activity. Minos was famed for his ships. Crete was the first naval power. The ships carried people and goods and culture, fostering exchanges of all kinds with the lands to which they sailed. Like the vestments of Europa, the minds of those ancient mariners were constantly left 'fluttering in the breeze'—*tremulae sinuantur flamine vestes*.[4]

Europa rode in the path of the sun from east to west. According to another legend, the Sun was a chariot of fire, pulled by unseen horses from their secret stables behind the sunrise to their resting-place beyond the sunset. Indeed, one of several possible etymologies contrasts Asia, 'the land of the Sunrise', with Europa, 'the land of the Sunset'.[5] The Hellenes came to use 'Europe' as a name for their territory to the west of the Aegean as distinct from the older lands in Asia Minor.

At the dawn of European history, the known world lay to the east. The unknown waited in the west, in destinations still to be discovered. Europa's curiosity may have been her undoing. But it led to the founding of a new civilization that would eventually bear her name and would spread to the whole Peninsula.

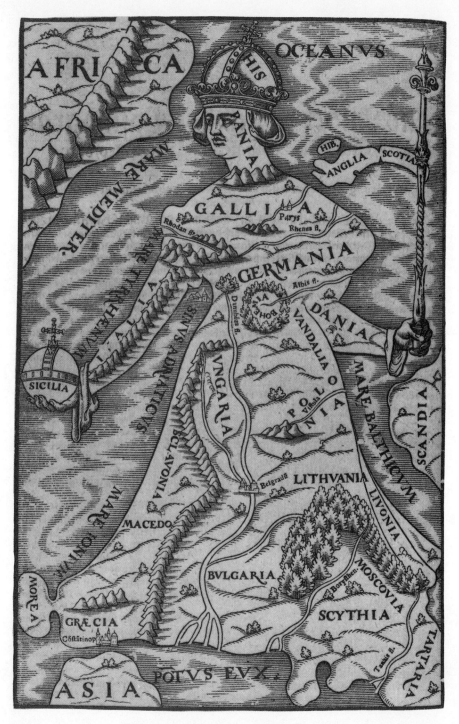

Map 2. Queen Europe (Regina Europa)
An engraving from an edition of Sebastian Müntzer's *Cosmography*
(*Cosmographia Universalis* lib. vi; Basel 1550–4) courtesy of Bodleian Library

INTRODUCTION

History Today

HISTORY can be written at any magnification. One can write the history of the universe on a single page, or the life-cycle of a mayfly in forty volumes. A very senior and distinguished historian, who specializes in the diplomacy of the 1930s, once wrote a book on the Munich Crisis and its consequences (1938–9), a second book on *The Last Week of Peace*, and a third entitled *31 August 1939*. His colleagues waited in vain for a crowning volume to be called *One Minute to Midnight*.[1] It is an example of the modern compulsion to know more and more about less and less.

The history of Europe, too, can be written at any degree of magnitude. The French series *L'Évolution de l'humanité*, whose content was over 90 percent European, was planned after the First World War with 110 main volumes and several supplementary ones.[2] The present work, in contrast, has been commissioned to compress the same material and more between two covers.

Yet no historian can compete with the poets for economy of thought:

> If Europe is a Nymph,
> Then Naples is her bright-blue eye,
> And Warsaw is her heart.
> Sebastopol and Azoff,
> Petersburg, Mitau, Odessa:
> These are the thorns in her feet.
> Paris is the head,
> London the starched collar,
> And Rome—the scapulary.[3]

For some reason, whilst historical monographs have become ever narrower in scope, general surveys have settled down to a conventional magnification of several hundred pages per century. *The Cambridge Mediaeval History* (1936–9), for example, covers the period from Constantine to Thomas More in eight volumes.[4] The German *Handbuch der europäischen Geschichte* (1968–79) covers the twelve centuries from Charlemagne to the Greek colonels in seven similarly weighty tomes.[5] It is common practice to give greater coverage to the contemporary than to the ancient or the medieval periods. For English readers, a pioneering collection such as Rivington's eight-volume 'Periods of European History' moved from the distant to the recent with ever-increasing magnification—442 years at the rate of 1.16 years per page for Charles Oman's *Dark Ages, 476–918* (1919), 104 years at 4.57 pages per year for A. H. Johnson's *Europe in the Sixteenth Century* (1897), 84 years at 6.59 pages per year for W. Alison Phillipps's *Modern Europe, 1815–99* (1905).[6] More recent collections follow the same pattern.[7]

Most readers are most interested in the history of their own times. But not all historians are willing to indulge them. '"Current Affairs" cannot become "History" until half a century has elapsed,' runs one opinion, until 'documents have become available and hindsight [has] cleared men's minds.'[8] It is a valid point of view. But it means that any general survey must break off at the point where it starts to be most interesting. Contemporary history is vulnerable to all sorts of political pressure. Yet no educated adult can hope to function efficiently without some grounding in the origins of contemporary problems.[9] Four hundred years ago Sir Walter Ralegh, writing under sentence of death, understood the dangers perfectly. 'Whosoever in writing a modern history shall follow the Truth too near the heels,' he wrote, 'it may haply strike out his teeth.'[10]

Given the complications, one should not be surprised to find that the subject-matter of studies of 'Europe' or of 'European civilization' varies enormously. Successful attempts to survey the whole of European history without recourse to multiple volumes and multiple authors have been few and far between. H. A. L. Fisher's *A History of Europe* (1936)[11] or Eugene Weber's *A Modern History of Europe* (1971)[12] are among the rare exceptions. Both of these are extended essays on the dubious concept of 'Western civilization' (see below). Probably the most effective of grand surveys are those which have concentrated on one theme, such as Kenneth Clark's *Civilisation*,[13] which looked at Europe's past through the prism of art and painting, or Jacob Bronowski's *The Ascent of Man* (1973),[14] which made its approach through the history of science and technology. Both were the offshoots of opulent television productions. A more recent essay approached the subject from a materialistic standpoint based on geology and economic resources.[15]

The value of multi-volume historical surveys is not in question; but they are condemned to remain works of reference, to be consulted, not read. Neither full-time history students nor general readers are going to plough through ten, twenty, or one hundred and ten volumes of general European synthesis before turning to the topics which attract them most. This is unfortunate. The framework of the whole sets parameters and assumptions which reappear without discussion in detailed works on the parts.

In recent years, the urgency of reviewing the general framework of European history has grown in proportion to the fashion for highly specialized, high-magnification studies. A few distinguished exceptions, such as the work of Fernand Braudel,[16] may serve to prove the rule. But many historians and students have been drawn into 'more and more about less and less' to the point where the wider perspectives are sometimes forgotten. Yet the humanities require all degrees of magnification. History needs to see the equivalent of the planets spinning in space; to zoom in and observe people at ground level, and to dig deep beneath their skins and their feet. The historian needs to use counterparts of the telescope, the microscope, the brain-scanner, and the geological probe.

It is beyond dispute that the study of history has been greatly enriched in recent years by new methods, new disciplines, and new fields. The advent of computers has opened up a whole range of quantitative investigations hitherto beyond the historian's reach. [**RENTES**] Historical research has greatly benefited from the use of techniques and concepts derived from the social and human sciences. [**ARICIA**] [**CEDRA**] [**CHASSE**] [**CONDOM**] [**EPIC**] [**FIESTA**] [**GENES**] [**GOTTHARD**] [**LEONARDO**] [**LIETUVA**] [**NOVGOROD**] [**PLOVUM**] [**PROPAGANDA**] [**SAMPHIRE**] [**VENDANGE.**] A trend pioneered by the French Annales school from 1929 onwards has now won almost universal acclaim. [**ANNALES**] New academic fields such as oral history, historical psychiatry (or 'psycho-history'), or family history, or the history of manners, are now well established. [**BOGEY**] [**MORES**] [**SOUND**] [**ZADRUGA**] At the same time, a number of subjects reflecting contemporary concerns have been given a fresh historical dimension. Anti-racism, environment, gender, sex, Semitism, class, and peace are topics which occupy a sizeable part of current writing and debate. Notwithstanding the overtones of 'political correctness', all serve to enrich the whole. [**BLACK ATHENA**] [**CAUCASIA**] [**ECO**] [**FEMME**] [**NOBEL**] [**POGROM**] [**SPARTACUS**]

None the less, the multiplication of fields, and the corresponding increase in learned publications, have inevitably created severe strains. Professional historians despair of 'keeping up with the literature'. They are tempted to plunge ever deeper into the alleyways of ultra-specialization, and to lose the capacity of communicating with the general public. Much specialization has proceeded to the detriment of narrative history. Some specialists have worked on the assumption that the broad outlines need no revision: that the only route to new discovery lies in digging deep on a narrow front. Others, intent on the exploration of 'deep structures', have turned their backs on 'the surface' of history altogether. They concentrate instead on the analysis of 'long-term, underlying trends'. Like some of their confrères in literary criticism, who hold the literal meaning of a text to be worthless, some historians have seen fit to abandon the study of conventional 'facts'. They produce students who have no intention of learning what happened how, where, and when.

The decline of factual history has been accompanied, especially in the classroom, with the rise of 'empathy', that is, of exercises designed to stimulate the historical imagination. Imagination is undoubtedly a vital ingredient of historical study. But empathetic exercises can only be justified if accompanied by a modicum of knowledge. In a world where fictional literature is also under threat as a respectable source of historical information, students are sometimes in danger of having nothing but their teacher's prejudices on which to build an awareness of the past.[17]

The divorce between history and literature has been particularly regrettable. When the 'structuralists' in the humanities were overtaken in some parts of the profession by the 'deconstructionists', both historians and literary critics looked set not only to exclude all conventional knowledge but also to exclude each other. Fortunately, as the wilder aspects of deconstructionism are deconstructed, there are hopes that these esoteric rifts can be healed.[18] There is absolutely no reason why the judicious historian should not use literary texts, critically assessed, or why literary critics should not use historical knowledge. [**GATTOPARDO**] [**KONARMIYA**]

It would now seem, therefore, that the specialists may have overplayed their hand. There has always been a fair division of labour between the industrious worker bees of the historical profession and the queen bees, the *grands simplifica-teurs*, who bring order to the labours of the hive. There will be no honey if the workers take over completely. Nor can one accept that the broad outlines of 'general history' have been fixed for all time. They too shift according to fashion: and those fixed fifty or one hundred years ago are ripe for revision (see below). Equally, the study of the geological strata of history must never be divorced from doings on the ground. In the search for 'trends', 'societies', 'economies', or 'cultures', one should not lose sight of men, women, and children.

Specialization has opened the door to unscrupulous political interests. Since no one is judged competent to offer an opinion beyond their own particular mine-shaft, beasts of prey have been left to prowl across the prairie unchecked. The combination of solid documentary research harnessed to blatantly selective topics, which a priori exclude a full review of all relevant factors, is specially vicious. As A. J. P. Taylor is reputed to have said of one such work, 'it is ninety per cent true and one hundred per cent useless'.[19]

The prudent response to these developments is to argue for pluralism of interpretation and for 'safety in numbers': that is, to encourage a wide variety of special views in order to counter the limitations of each and every one. One single viewpoint is risky. But fifty or sixty viewpoints—or three hundred—can together be counted on to construct a passable composite. 'There is no one Truth, but as many truths as there are *sensitivities*.'[20]

In Chapter II, below, mention is made of Archimedes' famous solution of the problem of π, that is, of calculating the ratio of a circle's circumference to its diameter. Archimedes knew that the length of the circumference must lie somewhere between the sum of the sides of a square drawn outside the circle and the sum of the sides of a square drawn inside the circle (see diagram). Unable to work it out directly, he hit on the idea of finding an approximation by adding up the length of a 99-sided polygon contained within the circle. The more sides he gave to his polygon, the nearer it would come to the shape of the circle. Similarly, one is tempted to think, the larger the number of sources of illumination, the smaller the gap will be between past reality and historians' attempts to reconstruct it.

Elsewhere, the impossible task of the historian has been likened to that of a photographer, whose static two-dimensional picture can never deliver an accurate representation of the mobile, three-dimensional world. 'The historian, like the camera, always lies.'[21] If this simile were to be developed, one could say that photographers can greatly increase the verisimilitude of their work—where verisimilitude is the aim—by multiplying the number of pictures of the same subject. A large number of shots taken from different angles, and with different lenses, filters, and films, can collectively reduce the gross selectivity of the single shot. As movie-makers discovered, a large number of frames taken in sequence creates a passable imitation of time and motion. By the same token, 'history in the round' can only be reconstructed if the historian collates the results of the widest possible range of sources. The effect will never be perfect; but every different angle and every different technique contributes to the illumination of the parts which together make up the whole.

Distortion is a necessary characteristic of all sources of information. Absolute objectivity is absolutely unattainable. Every technique has its strengths and its weaknesses. The important thing is to understand where the value and the distortions of each technique lie, and to arrive at a reasonable approximation. Critics who object to the historian's use of poetry, or sociology or astrology, or whatever, on the grounds that such sources are 'subjective' or 'partial' or 'unscientific', are stating the obvious. It is as though one could object to X-ray pictures of the skeleton, or ultra-sound scans of the womb, on the grounds that they give a pretty poor image of the human face. Medical doctors use every known device for prying open the secrets of the human mind and body. Historians need a similar range of equipment for penetrating the mysteries of the past.

Documentary history, which has enjoyed a long innings, is simultaneously one of the most valuable and the most risky lines of approach. Treated with incaution, it is open to gross forms of misrepresentation; and there are huge areas of past experience which it is incapable of recording. Yet no one can deny that historical documents remain one of the most fruitful veins of knowledge. [HOSSBACH] [METRYKA] [SMOLENSK]

Lord Acton, founder of the Cambridge school of history, once predicted a specially deleterious effect of documentary history. It tends to give priority to the amassing of evidence over the historian's interpretation of evidence. [We live] 'in a documentary age,' Acton wrote some ninety years ago, 'which will tend to make history independent of historians, to develop learning at the expense of writing.'[22]

Generally speaking, historians have given more thought to their own debates than to the problems encountered by their long-suffering readers. The pursuit of scientific objectivity has done much to reduce earlier flights of fancy, and to separate fact from fiction. At the same time it has reduced the number of instruments which historians can use to transmit their discoveries. For it is not sufficient for the good historian merely to establish the facts and to muster the evidence. The other half of the task is to penetrate the readers' minds, to do battle with all the distorting perceptors with which every consumer of history is equipped. These perceptors include not only all five physical senses but also a complex of pre-set intellectual circuits, varying from linguistic terminology, geographical names, and symbolic codes to political opinions, social conventions, emotional disposition, religious beliefs, visual memory, and traditional historical knowledge. Every consumer of history has a store of previous experience through which all incoming information about the past must be filtered.

For this reason, effective historians must devote as much care to transmitting their information as to collecting and shaping it. In this part of their work, they share many of the same preoccupations as poets, writers, and artists. They must keep an eye on the work of all the others who help to mould and to transmit our impressions of the past—the art historians, the musicologists, the museologues, the archivists, the illustrators, the cartographers, the diarists and biographers, the sound-recordists, the film-makers, the historical novelists, even the purveyors of 'bottled medieval air'. At every stage the key quality, as first defined by Vico, is that of 'creative historical imagination'. Without it, the work of the historian remains a dead letter, an unbroadcast message. [**PRADO**] [**SONATA**] [**SOVKINO**]

In this supposedly scientific age, the imaginative side of the historical profession has undoubtedly been downgraded. The value of unreadable academic papers and of undigested research data is exaggerated. Imaginative historians such as Thomas Carlyle, have not simply been censured for an excess of poetic licence. They have been forgotten. Yet Carlyle's convictions on the relationship of history and poetry are at least worthy of consideration.[23] It is important to check and to verify, as Carlyle sometimes failed to do. But 'telling it right' is also important. All historians must tell their tale convincingly, or be ignored.

'Postmodernism' has been a pastime in recent years for all those who give precedence to the study of historians over the study of the past. It refers to a fashion which has followed in the steps of the two French gurus, Foucault and Derrida, and which has attacked both the accepted canon of historical knowledge and the principles of conventional methodology. In one line of approach, it has sought to demolish the value of documentary source materials in the way that literary deconstructionists have sought to dismantle the 'meaning' of literary texts. Elsewhere it has denounced 'the tyranny of facts' and the 'authoritarian ideologies' which are thought to lurk behind every body of information. At the extreme, it holds that all statements about past reality are 'coercive'. And the purveyors of that coercion include all historians who argue for 'a commitment to human values'. In the eyes of its critics, it has reduced history to 'the pleasure of the historian'; and it has become an instrument for politicized radicals with an agenda of their own. In its contempt for prescribed data, it hints that knowing something is more dangerous than knowing nothing.[24]

Yet the phenomenon has raised more problems than it solves. Its enthusiasts can only be likened to those lugubrious academics who, instead of telling jokes, write learned tomes on the analysis of humour. One also wonders whether conventional liberal historiography can properly be defined as 'modernist'; and whether 'post-modernist' ought not to be reserved for those who are trying to strike a balance between the old and the new. It is all very well to deride the authority of all and sundry; but it only leads in the end to the deriding of Derrida. It is only a matter of time before the deconstructionists are deconstructed by their own techniques. 'We have survived the "Death of God" and the "Death of Man". We will surely survive "the Death of History" . . . and the death of post-modernism.'[25]

But to return to the question of magnification. Any narrative which chronicles the march of history over long periods is bound to be differently designed from the panorama which co-ordinates all the features relevant to a particular stage or moment. The former, chronological approach has to emphasize innovative events and movements which, though untypical at the time of their first appearance, will gain prominence at a later date. The latter, synchronic approach has to combine both the innovative and the traditional, and their interactions. The first risks anachronism, the second immobility.

Early modern Europe has served as one of the laboratories for these problems. Once dominated by historians exploring the roots of humanism, protestantism, capitalism, science, and the nation-state, it then attracted the attention of specialists who showed, quite correctly, how elements of the medieval and pagan worlds had survived and thrived. The comprehensive historian must somehow strike a balance between the two. In describing the sixteenth century, for example, it is as misguided to write exclusively about witches, alchemists, and fairies as it once was to write almost exclusively about Luther, Copernicus, or the rise of the English Parliament. Comprehensive history must take note of the specialists' debate, but it must equally find a way to rise above their passing concerns.

Concepts of Europe

'Europe' is a relatively modern idea. It gradually replaced the earlier concept of 'Christendom' in a complex intellectual process lasting from the fourteenth to the eighteenth centuries. The decisive period, however, was reached in the decades on either side of 1700 after generations of religious conflict. In that early phase of the Enlightenment (see Chapter VIII) it became an embarrassment for the divided community of nations to be reminded of their common Christian identity; and 'Europe' filled the need for a designation with more neutral connotations. In the West, the wars against Louis XIV inspired a number of publicists who appealed for common action to settle the divisions of the day. The much-imprisoned Quaker William Penn (1644–1718), son of an Anglo-Dutch marriage and founder of Pennsylvania, had the distinction of advocating both universal toleration and a European parliament. The dissident French abbé, Charles Castel de St Pierre (1658–1743), author of *Projet d'une paix perpétuelle* (1713), called for a confederation of European powers to guarantee a lasting peace. In the East, the emergence of the Russian Empire under Peter the Great required radical rethinking of the international framework. The Treaty of Utrecht of 1713 provided the last major occasion when public reference to the *Respublica Christiana*, the 'Christian Commonwealth', was made.

After that, the awareness of a European as opposed to a Christian community gained the upper hand. Writing in 1751, Voltaire described Europe as:

a kind of great republic divided into several states, some monarchical, the others mixed . . . but all corresponding with one another. They all have the same religious foundation, even if divided into several confessions. They all have the same principle of public law and politics, unknown in other parts of the world.[26]

Twenty years later, Rousseau announced: 'There are no longer Frenchmen, Germans, and Spaniards, or even English, but only Europeans.' According to one judgement, the final realization of the 'idea of Europe' took place in 1796, when Edmund Burke wrote: 'No European can be a complete exile in any part of Europe.'[27] Even so, the geographical, cultural, and political parameters of the European community have always remained open to debate. In 1794, when William Blake published one of his most unintelligible poems entitled 'Europe: A Prophecy', he illustrated it with a picture of the Almighty leaning out of the heavens and holding a pair of compasses.[28]

Most of Europe's outline is determined by its extensive sea-coasts. But the delineation of its land frontier was long in the making. The dividing line between Europe and Asia had been fixed by the ancients from the Hellespont to the River Don, and it was still there in medieval times. A fourteenth-century encyclopedist could produce a fairly precise definition:

'Europe is said to be a third of the whole world, and has its name from Europa, daughter of Agenor, King of Libya. Jupiter ravished this Europa, and brought her to Crete, and called most of the land after her Europa . . . Europe begins on the river Tanay [Don] and stretches along the Northern Ocean to the end of Spain. The east and south part rises from the sea called Pontus [Black Sea] and is all joined to the Great Sea [the Mediterranean] and ends at the islands of Cadiz [Gibraltar] . . .'[29]

Pope Pius II (Enea Piccolomini) began his early *Treatise on the State of Europe* (1458) with a description of Hungary, Transylvania, and Thrace, which at that juncture were under threat from the Turks.

Neither the ancients nor the medievals had any close knowledge of the easterly reaches of the European Plain, several sections of which were not permanently settled until the eighteenth century. So it was not until 1730 that a Swedish officer in the Russian service called Strahlenberg suggested that Europe's boundary should be pushed back from the Don to the Ural Mountains and the Ural River. Sometime in the late eighteenth century, the Russian government erected a boundary post on the trail between Yekaterinburg and Tyumen to mark the frontier of Europe and Asia. From then on the gangs of Tsarist exiles, who were marched to Siberia in irons, created the custom of kneeling by the post and of scooping up a last handful of European earth. 'There is no other boundary post in the whole world', wrote one observer, 'which has seen . . . so many broken hearts.'[30] By 1833, when Volger's *Handbuch der Geographie* was published, the idea of 'Europe from the Atlantic to the Urals' had gained general acceptance.[31]

None the less, there is nothing sacred about the reigning convention. The extension of Europe to the Urals was accepted as a result of the rise of the Russian Empire. But it has been widely criticized, especially by analytical geographers. The frontier on the Urals had little validity in the eyes of Halford Mackinder, of Arnold Toynbee, for whom environmental factors had primacy, or of the Swiss geographer, J. Reynold, who wrote that 'Russia is the geographical antithesis of Europe'. The decline of Russian power could well invoke a revision—in which

case the views of a Russian-born Oxford professor about a 'tidal Europe', whose
frontiers ebb and flow, would be borne out.[32]

Geographical Europe has always had to compete with notions of Europe as a cultural community; and in the absence of common political structures, European
civilization could only be defined by cultural criteria. Special emphasis is usually
placed on the seminal role of Christianity, a role which did not cease when the
label of Christendom was dropped.

Broadcasting to a defeated Germany in 1945, the poet T. S. Eliot expounded the
view that European civilization stands in mortal peril after repeated dilutions of
the Christian core. He described 'the closing of Europe's mental frontiers' that
had occurred during the years which had seen the nation-states assert themselves
to the full. 'A kind of cultural autarchy followed inevitably on political and economic autarchy,' he said. He stressed the organic nature of culture: 'Culture is
something that must grow. You cannot build a tree; you can only plant it, and
care for it, and wait for it to mature . . .' He stressed the interdependence of the
numerous sub-cultures within the European family. What he called cultural
'trade' was the organism's lifeblood. And he stressed the special duty of men of
letters. Above all, he stressed the centrality of the Christian tradition, which subsumes within itself 'the legacy of Greece, of Rome, and of Israel':

'The dominant feature in creating a common culture between peoples, each of which has
its own distinct culture, is religion. . . . I am talking about the common tradition of
Christianity which has made Europe what it is, and about the common cultural elements
which this common Christianity has brought with it. . . . It is in Christianity that our arts
have developed; it is in Christianity that the laws of Europe—until recently—have been
rooted. It is against a background of Christianity that all our thought has significance. An
individual European may not believe that the Christian Faith is true; and yet what he says,
and makes, and does, will all . . . depend on [the Christian heritage] for its meaning. Only
a Christian culture could have produced a Voltaire or a Nietzsche. I do not believe that the
culture of Europe could survive the complete disappearance of the Christian Faith.'[33]

This concept is, in all senses, the traditional one. It is the yardstick of all other
variants, breakaways, and bright ideas on the subject. It is the starting-point of
what Mme de Staël once called 'penser à l'européenne'.

For cultural historians of Europe, the most fundamental of tasks is to identify
the many competing strands within the Christian tradition and to gauge their
weight in relation to various non-Christian and anti-Christian elements.
Pluralism is de rigueur. Despite the apparent supremacy of Christian belief right
up to the mid-twentieth century, it is impossible to deny that many of the most
fruitful stimuli of modern times, from the Renaissance passion for antiquity to
the Romantics' obsession with Nature, were essentially pagan in character.
Similarly, it is hard to argue that the contemporary cults of modernism, eroticism,
economics, sport, or pop culture have much to do with the Christian heritage.
The main problem nowadays is to decide whether the centrifugal forces of the
twentieth century have reduced that heritage to a meaningless jumble or not. Few

analysts would now maintain that anything resembling a European cultural monolith has ever existed. One interesting solution is to see Europe's cultural legacy as composed of four or five overlapping and interlocking circles[34] (see Appendix III, p. 1238). According to the novelist Alberto Moravia, Europe's unique cultural identity is 'a reversible fabric, one side variegated . . . the other a single colour rich and deep'.[35]

It would be wrong to suppose, however, that 'Europe' was devoid of political content. On the contrary, it has often been taken as a synonym for the harmony and unity which was lacking. 'Europe' has been the unattainable ideal, the goal for which all good Europeans are supposed to strive.

This messianic or utopian view of Europe can be observed as far back as the discussion which preceded the Treaty of Westphalia. It was loudly invoked in the propaganda of William of Orange and his allies, who organized the coalitions against Louis XIV, as in those who opposed Napoleon. 'Europe', said Tsar Alexander I, 'is us.' It was present in the rhetoric of the Balance of Power in the eighteenth century, and of the Concert in the nineteenth. It was an essential feature of the peaceful Age of Imperialism which, until shattered by the Great War of 1914, saw Europe as the home base of worldwide dominion.

In the twentieth century, the European ideal has been revived by politicians determined to heal the wounds of two world wars. In the 1920s, after the First World War, when it could be propagated in all parts of the continent outside the Soviet Union, it found expression in the League of Nations and particularly in the work of Aristide Briand (see pp. 949–51). It was specially attractive to the new states of Eastern Europe, who were not encumbered by extra-European empires and who sought communal protection against the great powers. In the late 1940s, after the creation of the Iron Curtain, it was appropriated by people who were intent on building a Little Europe in the West, who imagined their construction as a series of concentric circles focused on France and Germany. But it equally served as a beacon of hope for others cut off by oppressive communist rule in the East (see p. 13 below). The collapse of the Soviet empire in 1989–91 offered the first glimpses of a pan-European community that could aspire to spread to all parts of the continent.

Yet the frailty of the European ideal has been recognized both by its opponents and by its advocates. In 1876 Bismarck dismissed Europe, as Metternich had once dismissed Italy, as 'a geographical notion'. Seventy years later Jean Monnet, 'the Father of Europe', saw the force of Bismarck's disdain. 'Europe has never existed,' he admitted; 'one has genuinely to create Europe.'[36]

For more than five hundred years the cardinal problem in defining Europe has centred on the inclusion or exclusion of Russia. Throughout modern history, an Orthodox, autocratic, economically backward but expanding Russia has been a bad fit. Russia's Western neighbours have often sought reasons for excluding her. Russians themselves have never been sure whether they wanted to be in or out.

In 1517, for example, the Rector of the Jagiellonian University in Cracow, Maciej Miechowita, published a geographical treatise which upheld the traditional Ptolemeian distinction between *Sarmatia europaea* (European Sarmatia) and *Sarmatia asiatica* (Asian Sarmatia) with the boundary on the Don. So Poland-Lithuania was in and Russian Muscovy was out.[37] Three centuries later, things were not so clear. Poland-Lithuania had just been dismembered, and Russia's frontier had shifted dramatically westwards. When the Frenchman Louis-Philippe de Ségur (1753–1830) passed by on the eve of the French Revolution, he was in no doubt that Poland no longer lay in Europe. 'On croit sortir entièrement de l'Europe,' he wrote after entering Poland; 'tout ferait penser qu'on a reculé de dix siècles.' (One believes oneself to be leaving Europe completely; everything might give the impression of retreating ten centuries in time.) By using economic advancement as the main criterion for European membership, he was absolutely up to date.[38]

Yet this was exactly the era when the Russian government was insisting on its European credentials. Notwithstanding the fact that her territory stretched in unbroken line through Asia to North America, the Empress Catherine categorically announced in 1767 that 'Russia is a European state'. Everyone who wished to do business with St Petersburg took note. After all, Muscovy had been an integral part of Christendom since the tenth century; and the Russian Empire was a valued member of the diplomatic round. Fears of the 'Bear' did not prevent the growth of a general consensus regarding Russia's membership of Europe. This was greatly strengthened in the nineteenth century by Russia's role in the defeat of Napoleon, and by the magnificent flowering of Russian culture in the age of Tolstoy, Tchaikovsky, and Chekov.

Russian intellectuals, divided between Westernizers and Slavophiles, were uncertain about the degree of Russia's Europeanness (see Chapter X, pp. 811–12, 817). In *Russia and Europe* (1871), the Slavophile Nikolay Danilevskiy (1822–85) argued that Russia possessed a distinctive Slavic civilization of its own, midway between Europe and Asia. Dostoevsky, in contrast, speaking at the unveiling of a statue to the poet Pushkin, chose to launch into a eulogy of Europe. 'Peoples of Europe', he declared, 'they don't know how dear to us they are.' Only the small group of *vostochniki* or 'orientals' held that Russia was entirely un-European, having most in common with China.[39]

After 1917 the conduct of the Bolsheviks revived many of the old doubts and ambiguities. The Bolsheviks were widely regarded abroad as barbarians—in Churchill's words, 'a baboonery'—a gang of wild Asiatics sowing death and destruction like Attila or Genghis Khan. In Soviet Russia itself, the Marxist revolutionaries were often denounced as a Western implant, dominated by Jews, backed by Western money, and manipulated by German Intelligence. At the same time, a strong line of official opinion held that the Revolution had severed all links with 'decadent' Europe. Many Russians felt humiliated by their isolation, and boasted that a revitalized Russia would soon overwhelm the faithless West. Early in 1918, the leading Russian poet of the revolutionary years wrote a defiant poem entitled 'The Scythians':

> You're millions; we are hosts and hosts and hosts.
>   Engage with us and prove our seed!
> We're Scythians and Asians, too, from coasts
>   That breed squint eyes, bespeaking greed.
>
> Russia's a Sphinx! Triumphant though in pain
>   She bathes her limbs in blood's dark stream.
> Her eyes gaze on you—gaze and gaze again—
>   With hate and love in a single beam.
>
> Old world—once more—awake! Your brothers' plight
>   To toil and peace, a feast of fire.
> Once more! Come join your brothers' festal light!
>   Obey the call of Barbary's lyre.[40]

Not for the first time, the Russians were torn in two directions at once.

As for the Bolshevik leadership, Lenin and his circle identified closely with Europe. They saw themselves as heirs to a tradition launched by the French Revolution; they saw their immediate roots in the socialist movement in Germany; and they assumed that their strategy would be to join up with revolutions in the advanced capitalist countries of the West. In the early 1920s, Comintern mooted the possibility of a (communist-led) United States of Europe. Only under Stalin, who killed all the old Bolsheviks, did the Soviet Union choose to distance itself spiritually from European affairs. In those same decades, an influential group of emigré Russian intellectuals including Prince N. S. Trubetskoy, P. N. Savitsky, and G. Vernadsky, chose to re-emphasize the Asiatic factors within Russia's cultural mix. Known as *Yevraziytsy* or 'Eurasians', they were fundamentally opposed to Bolshevism, whilst maintaining a sceptical stance to the virtues of Western Europe.

Of course, seventy years of totalitarian Soviet rule built huge mental as well as physical curtains across Europe. The public face of the Soviet regime grew blatantly xenophobic—a posture greatly assisted by experiences during the Second World War, and assiduously cultivated by the Stalinists. In their hearts, however, many individual Russians followed the great majority of non-Russians in the Soviet Bloc in fostering a heightened sense of their European identity. It was a lifeline for their spiritual survival against communism. When the chains of communism melted away, it enabled them to greet, in Vaclav Havel's phrase, 'the Return to Europe'.

None the less, scepticism about Russia's European qualifications continued to circulate both inside and outside Russia. Russian nationalist opinion, which heartily dislikes and envies 'the West', supplied a rallying-point for the Stalinist apparatus, which felt humiliated by the collapse of Soviet power and which wanted nothing more than to get its empire back. As the core of opposition to hopes for a post-communist democracy, the unholy alliance of Russian nationalists and unreformed communists could only look askance at Moscow's growing *rapprochement* with Washington and with Western Europe.

For their part, Western leaders were most impressed by the need for stability.

Having failed to find a lasting partnership with Gorbachev's humanized version of the USSR, they rushed headlong to shore up the Russian Federation. They responded sympathetically to Moscow's requests for economic aid and for association both with NATO and with the European Community. But then some of them began to see the drawbacks. After all, the Russian Federation was not a cohesive nation-state, ripe for liberal democracy. It was still a multinational complex spanning Eurasia, still highly militarized, and still manifesting imperial reflexes about its security. It was not clearly committed to letting its neighbours follow their own road. Unless it could find ways of shedding the imperialist legacy, like all other ex-imperial states in Europe, it could not expect to be considered a suitable candidate for any European community. Such at least was the strong opinion of the doyen of the European Parliament, speaking in September 1993. [EESTI]

Some commentators have insisted that Britain's European credentials are no less ambiguous than Russia's. From the Norman Conquest to the Hundred Years War, the kingdom of England was deeply embroiled in Continental affairs. But for most of modern history the English sought their fortunes elsewhere. Having subdued and absorbed their neighbours in the British Isles, they sailed away to create an empire overseas. Like the Russians, they were definitely Europeans, but with prime extra-European interests. They were, in fact, semi-detached. Their habit of looking on 'the Continent' as if from a great distance did not start to wane until their empire disappeared. What is more, the imperial experience had taught them to look on Europe in terms of 'great powers', mainly in the West, and 'small nations', mainly in the East, which did not really count. Among the sculptures surrounding the Albert Memorial (1876) in London is a group of figures symbolizing 'Europe'. It consists of only four figures—Britain, Germany, France, and Italy. For all these reasons, historians have often regarded Britain as 'a special case'.[41] The initiators of the first pan-European movement in the 1920s (see pp. 944, 1065) assumed that neither Britain nor Russia would join.

In the mean time, a variety of attempts have been made to define Europe's cultural subdivisions. In the late nineteenth century, the concept of a German-dominated *Mitteleuropa* was launched to coincide with the political sphere of the Central Powers. In the inter-war years, a domain called 'East Central Europe' was invented to coincide with the newly independent 'successor states'—from Finland and Poland to Yugoslavia. This was revived again after 1945 as a convenient label for the similar set of nominally independent countries which were caught inside the Soviet bloc. By that time the main division, between a 'Western Europe' dominated by NATO and the EEC and an 'Eastern Europe' dominated by Soviet communism seemed to be set in stone. In the 1980s a group of writers led by the Czech novelist, Milan Kundera, launched a new version of 'Central Europe', to break down the reigning barriers. Here was yet another configuration, another true 'kingdom of the spirit'.[42]

The 'Heart of Europe' is an attractive idea which possesses both geographical and emotional connotations. But it is peculiarly elusive. One author has placed it in Belgium, another in Poland, a third in Bohemia, a fourth in Hungary, and a fifth in the realm of German literature.[43] Wherever it is, the British Prime Minister declared in 1991 that he intended to be there. For those who think that the heart lies in the dead centre, it is located either in the commune of St Clement (Allier), the dead centre of the European Community, or else at a point variously calculated to lie in the suburbs of Warsaw or in the depths of Lithuania, the dead centre of geographical Europe.

During the seventy-five years when Europe was divided by the longest of its civil wars, the concept of European unity could only be kept alive by people of the widest cultural and historical horizons. Especially during the forty years of the Cold War, it took the greatest intellectual courage and stamina to resist not only persistent nationalism but also the parochial view of a Europe based exclusively on the prosperous West. Fortunately, a few individuals of the necessary stature did exist, and have left their legacy in writings which will soon be sounding prophetic.

One such person was Hugh Seton-Watson (1916–84), elder son of the pioneer of East European studies in Britain, R. W. Seton-Watson (1879–1951). As a boy he played at the knee of Thomas Masaryk; he spoke Serbo-Croat, Hungarian, and Romanian as effortlessly as French, German, and Italian. Born in London, where he became Professor of Russian History at the School of Slavonic and East European Studies, he usually described himself as a Scot. He never succumbed to the conventional wisdom of his day. He set out his testament on the concept of Europe in a paper published posthumously. His argument stressed three fundamental points—the need for a European ideal, the complementary role of the East and the West European nations, and the pluralism of Europe's cultural tradition. Each deserves a quotation of some length.

Seton-Watson's first thunderbolt was directed at the low horizons of those who expected European unity to be built on nothing more than the security interests of NATO or the economic interests of the EEC:

Let us not underrate the' need for a positive common cause, for something more exciting than the price of butter, more constructive than the allocation of defence contracts—a need for an European *mystique*.[44]

The second shaft was directed at those who sought to exclude the East Europeans in the name of Western civilization:

The European cultural community includes the peoples living beyond Germany and Italy . . . something in no way annulled by the fact that they cannot today belong to an all-European economic or political community . . . Nowhere in the world is there so widespread a belief in the reality, and the importance, of a European cultural community, as in the countries lying between the EEC and the Soviet Union . . . To these peoples, the idea of Europe is that of a community of cultures to which the specific culture or sub-culture of each belongs. None of them can survive without Europe, or Europe without them. This is of course a myth . . . a sort of chemical compound of truth and fantasy. The absurdities of the fantasy need not obscure the truth.[45]

The third shaft was aimed at those who harbour a simplistic or monolithic view of European culture:

The interweaving of the notions of Europe and of Christendom is a fact of History which even the most brilliant sophistry cannot undo . . . But it is no less true that there are strands in European culture that are not Christian: the Roman, the Hellenic, arguably the Persian, and (in modern centuries) the Jewish. Whether there is also a Muslim strand is more difficult to say.[46]

The conclusion defines the purpose and value of European culture:

[European culture] is not an instrument of capitalism or socialism; it is not a monopoly possession of EEC Eurocrats or of anyone else. To owe allegiance to it, is not to claim superiority over other cultures . . . The unity of European culture is simply the end-product of 3000 years of labour by our diverse ancestors. It is a heritage which we spurn at our peril, and of which it would be a crime to deprive younger and future generations. Rather it is our task to preserve and renew it.[47]

Seton-Watson was one of a select band of lonely runners who carried the torch of European unity through the long night of Europe's eclipse. He was one of the minority of Western scholars who bestrode the barriers between East and West, and who saw Soviet communism for what it was. He died on the eve of the events which were to vindicate so many of his judgements. His intellectual legacy is the one which the present work is honoured to follow most closely.[48]

The writing of European history could not proceed until the concept of Europe had stabilized and the historian's art had assumed an analytical turn. But it was certainly well under way in the early decades of the nineteenth century. The earliest effective attempt at synthesis was by the French writer and statesman François Guizot (1787–1874). His *Histoire de la civilisation en Europe* (1828–30) was based on lectures presented at the Sorbonne.

Thanks to the problems of definition, most historians would agree that the subject-matter of European history must concentrate on the shared experiences which are to be found in each of the great epochs of Europe's past. Most would also agree that it was in late antiquity that European history ceased to be an assortment of unrelated events within the given Peninsula and began to take on the characteristics of a more coherent civilizational process. Central to this process was the merging of the classical and the barbarian worlds, and the resultant assertion of a consciously Christian community—in other words, the founding of Christendom. Later on, all manner of schisms, rebellions, expansions, evolutions, and fissiparities took place, giving rise to the exceedingly diverse and pluralistic phenomenon which is Europe today. No two lists of the main constituents of European civilization would ever coincide. But many items have always featured prominently: from the roots of the Christian world in Greece, Rome, and Judaism to modern phenomena such as the Enlightenment, modernization, romanticism, nationalism, liberalism, imperialism, totalitarianism. Nor should one forget the sorry catalogue of wars, conflicts, and persecutions that have dogged every stage of the tale. Perhaps the most apposite analogy is the musical one. European historians are not tracing the story of a simple libretto. They are out to recapture a complicated score, with all its cacophony of sounds and its own inimitable codes of communication: 'Europe . . . has been likened to an orchestra. There are certain moments when certain of the instruments play a minor role, or even fall silent altogether. But the ensemble exists.'[49] There is much to be said also for the contention that Europe's musical language has provided one of the most universal strands of the European tradition. [**MUSIKE**]

None the less, since Europe has never been politically united, diversity has evidently provided one of its most enduring characteristics. Diversity can be observed in the great range of reactions to each of the shared experiences. There is lasting diversity in the national states and cultures which persist within European civilization as a whole. There is diversity in the varying rhythms of power and of decline. Guizot, the pioneer, was not alone in thinking of diversity as Europe's *prime* characteristic.

Eurocentrism

European history-writing cannot be accused of Eurocentrism simply for focusing its attention on European affairs, that is, for keeping to the subject. Eurocentrism is a matter of attitude, not content. It refers to the traditional tendency of European authors to regard their civilization as superior and self-contained, and to neglect the need for taking non-European viewpoints into consideration. Nor is it surprising or regrettable to find that European history has mainly been written by Europeans and for Europeans. Everybody feels the urge to discover their roots. Unfortunately, European historians have frequently approached their subject as Narcissus approached the pool, looking only for a reflection of his own beauty. Guizot has had many imitators since he identified European civilization with the wishes of the Almighty. 'European civilisation has entered . . . into the eternal truth, into the plan of Providence,' he reflected. 'It progresses according to the intentions of God.'[50] For him, and for many like him, Europe was the promised land and Europeans the chosen people.

Many historians have continued in the same self-congratulatory vein, and have argued, often quite explicitly, that the European record provides a model for all other peoples to follow. Until recently, they paid scant regard to the interaction of European culture with that of its neighbours in Africa, India, or Islam. A prominent American scholar, writing in 1898, who traced European civilization primarily to the work of 'Teutonic tribes', took it as axiomatic that Europe was the universal model:

The heirs of the ancient world were the Teutonic tribes, who . . . gradually formed a new uniform civilisation on the foundation of the classic, and in recent times this has begun to be worldwide and to bring into close relationship and under common influences all the inhabitants of the earth.[51]

When Oxford University Press last dared to publish a one-volume History of Europe, the authors opened their preface with a similar choice sentiment:

Although a number of grand civilisations have existed in various ages, it is the civilisation of Europe which has made the deepest and widest impression, and which now (as developed on both sides of the Atlantic) sets the standard for all the peoples of the earth.[52]

This line of thought and mode of presentation has steadily been losing its attractions, especially for non-Europeans.

Rudyard Kipling (1865–1936) is sometimes regarded as a central figure of the Eurocentric tradition, even as 'an apologist for the civilizing mission of British colonial expansion'. His famous *Ballad of East and West* was composed with India in mind:

Oh, East is East, and West is West, and never the twain shall meet
Till Earth and Sky stand presently at God's great Judgement Seat.
But there is neither East nor West, Border, Breed nor Birth,
When two strong men stand face to face, though they come from the ends of
the Earth.[53]

Kipling shared little of the arrogance which was usually associated with the European attitudes of his day. He did not shrink from the phraseology of his day concerning our 'dominion over palm and pine' or 'the lesser breeds without the Law'. Yet he was strongly attracted to Indian culture—hence his wonderful *Jungle Books*—and he was a deeply religious and humble man:

The tumult and the shouting dies—
The captains and the kings depart—
Still stands Thine ancient sacrifice,
An humble and a contrite heart.
Lord God of Hosts, be with us yet,
Lest we forget, lest we forget.[54]

These words are a standing rebuke to anyone who would lump all 'Western imperialists' into the same gang of arrogants.

Opposition to Eurocentrism comes at present from four main sources. In North America it has emerged from that part of the Black community, and their political sympathizers, who are rebelling against an educational system allegedly dominated by 'white supremacist values', in other words by the glorification of European culture. It has found expression in the Black Muslim movement and, in scholarship, in a variety of Black studies (Afrology) directed against conventional American academia.[55] In its most militant form, it aims to replace Eurocentrism with Afrocentricity—'the belief in the centrality of Africans in post-modern history'.[56] This is based on the contention that European civilization has 'stolen' the birthright of mankind, and of Africans in particular.[57] In the world of Islam, especially in Iran, similar opposition is mounted by religious fundamentalists, who see 'the West' as the domain of Satan. Elsewhere in the Third World, it is espoused by intellectuals, often of a Marxian complexion, who regard Eurocentric views as

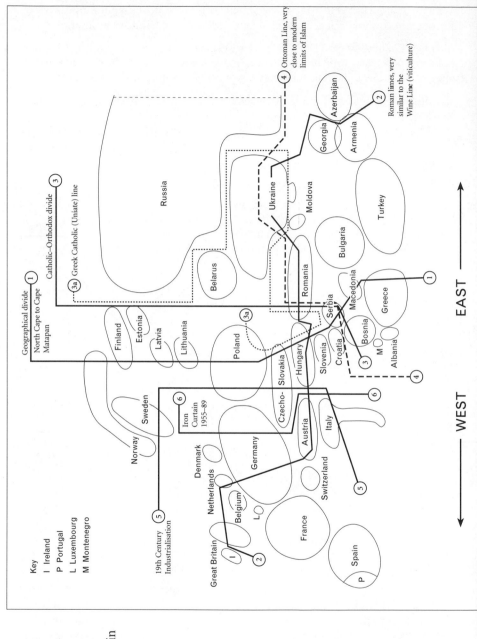

Map 3.
East–West
Fault Lines in
Europe

Key
I Ireland
P Portugal
L Luxembourg
M Montenegro

Geographical divide ①
North Cape to Cape
Matapan

Catholic–Orthodox divide ③

③ₐ Greek Catholic (Uniate) line

④ Ottoman Line, very
close to modern
limits of Islam

② Roman lines, very
similar to the
Wine Line (viticulture)

⑤ 19th Century
Industrialisation

⑥ Iron
Curtain
1955–89

WEST ←   → EAST

Norway Sweden Finland Estonia Latvia Lithuania

Denmark Germany Poland Belarus Russia

Netherlands Belgium L

Great Britain I

France Switzerland Austria Czecho-Slovakia Hungary

Spain P

Italy Slovenia Croatia Serbia Romania Ukraine Moldova Georgia Azerbaijan

Bosnia M Macedonia Bulgaria Armenia

Albania Greece Turkey

part and parcel of capitalist ideology.[58] In Europe it is widespread, though not always well articulated, in a generation which, when they paused to think, have been thoroughly ashamed of many of their elders' attitudes.

One way forward for historians will be to pay more attention to the interaction of European and non-European peoples. [GONCALVEZ] Another is to use non-European sources for the elucidation of European problems. [RUS'] A third is to insist on honest comparisons with Europe's neighbours—comparisons which in many aspects and instances will not be in Europe's favour. Above all, it is essential to modulate the tone. For the last hundred years the conduct of those 'Teutonic tribes', and of other Europeans, has not been much to boast of.

In the end, like all human activities, the European record must be judged on its own merits. It cannot be fairly represented in a list of 'Great Books', which selects whatever is most genial and ignores the dross (see below). It can be viewed with admiration or with disgust, or with a mixture of both. The opinion of one Frenchman strikes an optimistic note: 'After all, crime and western history are not the same thing. Whatever [the West] has given to the world by far exceeds that which it has done against various societies and individuals.'[59] Not everyone would agree.

Western Civilization

For the best part of 200 years European history has frequently been confused with the heritage of 'Western civilization'. Indeed, the impression has been created that everything 'Western' is civilized, and that everything civilized is Western. By extension, or simply by default, anything vaguely Eastern or 'Oriental' stands to be considered backward or inferior, and hence worthy of neglect. The workings of this syndrome have been ably exposed with regard to European attitudes towards Islam and the Arab world, that is, in the tradition of so-called 'Orientalism'.[60] But it is not difficult to demonstrate that it operates with equal force in relation to some of Europe's own regions, especially in the East. Generally speaking, Western civilization is not taken to extend to the whole of Europe (although it may be applied to distant parts of the globe far beyond Europe).

Historians most given to thinking of themselves as from 'the West'—notably from England, France, Germany, and North America—rarely see any necessity to describe Europe's past in its entirety. They see no more reason to consider the countries of Eastern Europe than to dwell on the more westerly parts of Western Europe. Any number of titles could be cited which masquerade as histories of 'Europe', or of 'Christendom', but which are nothing of the sort. Any number of surveys of 'Western civilization' confine themselves to topics which relate only to their chosen fragments of the Peninsula. In many such works there is no Portugal, no Ireland, Scotland or Wales, and no Scandinavia, just as there is no Poland, no Hungary, no Bohemia, no Byzantium, no Balkans, no Baltic States, no Byelorussia or Ukraine, no Crimea or Caucasus. There is sometimes a Russia, and sometimes not. Whatever Western civilization is, therefore, it does not involve an honest attempt to summarize European history. Whatever 'the West' is, it is not just a synonym for Western Europe.[61] This is a very strange phenomenon. It seems to assume that historians of Europe can conduct themselves like the cheese-makers of Gruyère, whose product contains as many holes as cheese.

Examples are legion; but three or four must suffice. A *History of Mediaeval Europe*, written by a distinguished Oxford tutor, has long served as a standard introduction to the subject. Readers of the preface may be surprised to learn, therefore, that the contents do not coincide with the title:

In the hope of maintaining a continuity of theme . . . I have probably been guilty of over-simplifying things . . . The history of mediaeval Byzantium is so different from that of west-ern Europe in its whole tone and tenor that it seemed wiser not to attempt any systematic survey of it; in any case, I am not qualified to undertake such a survey. I have said nothing about the history of mediaeval Russia, which is remote from the themes which I have cho-sen to pursue; and I have probably said less than I should have done about Spain.[62]

The subject, in fact, is defined as 'western Europe (Latin Christendom), the terms being more or less analogous'.[63] One might then think that all would be well if the book were to receive a title to match its contents. 'A History of Medieval Western Europe' or 'A History of Latin Christendom in the Middle Ages' might seem appropriate. But then one finds that the text makes little attempt to address all the parts even of Latin Christendom. Neither Ireland nor Wales, for example, find mention. The realm of the Jagiellons in Poland and Lithuania, which in the latter part of the chosen period was absolutely the largest state in Latin Christendom, merits two passing references. One relates to the policies of the German Emperor Otto III, the other to the plight of the Teutonic Knights. The huge, multinational kingdom of Hungary, which stretched from the Adriatic to Transylvania, gains much less attention than Byzantium and the Greeks, which the author has put a priori out of bounds. The book has many virtues; but, like very many others, what it amounts to is a survey of selected themes from favoured sectors of one part of Europe.

A highly influential *Handbook to the History of Western Civilization* is organized within a similar strange framework. The largest of its three parts, 'European Civilization (*c.*AD 900–Present)', starts with 'The Geographical Setting of European Civilization', and explains how 'the transitions from Oriental to Classical and from Classical to European civilizations each time involved a shift to the periphery of the older society'. The 'original homeland of European Civilization' is described in terms of a plain 'extending from the Pyrenees . . . into Russia', and separated from 'the Mediterranean lands' by an 'irregular mountain barrier'. But there is no attempt in subsequent chapters to map out the history of this homeland. The former lands of the Roman Empire 'came to be di-vided between three civilizations—Islam, Orthodox Christianity, and Latin Christianity'. But no systematic treatment of this threefold division in Europe is forthcoming. One sentence is awarded to pagan Scandinavia, and none to any of the other pagan lands which were later christianized. There is a small subsection on 'The Peoples of Western Europe' in early times (p. 129), including unspecified 'Indo-European tribesmen', but none on the peoples of Eastern Europe in any period. There are scattered references to 'Slavic' or 'Slavic-speaking' peoples, but no indication that they represented the largest of Europe's Indo-European groups. There are major chapters on 'Western Christendom 900–1500'; but no chapter appears on Eastern Christendom. The paragraphs on 'The Expansion of Europe' refer either to German colonization or to ocean voyages outside Europe. Two sentences suddenly inform the reader that Western Christendom in the fourteenth century actually included 'Scandinavia, the Baltic States, Poland, Lithuania, and Hungary' (p. 345). But no further details are given. The largest of all the chapters, 'The Modern World, 1500–Present', deals exclusively with themes shorn of their eastern element until Russia, and Russia alone, appears ready-made under Peter the Great. From then on, Russia has apparently been a fully qualified member of the West. The author apologizes in advance for his 'arbitrary principles of ordering and selection' (p. xviii). Unfortunately, he does not reveal what they are.[64]

The 'Great Books Scheme' is another product of the same Chicago School. It purports to list the key authors and works that are essential for an understanding of Western civilization. It was invented at Columbia University in 1921, used from 1930 at Chicago, and became the model for university courses throughout America. No one would expect such a list to give exact parity to all the regions and cultures of Europe. But the prejudices and preferences are manifest. Of the 151 authors on the amended list, 49 are English or American, 27 French, 20 German, 15 Classical Greek, 9 Classical Latin, 6 Russian, 4 Scandinavian, 3 Spanish, 3 early Italian, 3 Irish, 3 Scots, and 3 East European (see Appendix III, p. 1230).[65]

Political theorists often betray the same bias. It is very common, for example, to classify European nationalism in terms of two contrasting types—'Eastern' and 'Western'. A prominent Oxford scholar, who stressed the cultural roots of nationalism, explained his version of the scheme:

What I call eastern nationalism has flourished among the Slavs as well as in Africa and Asia, and . . . also in Latin America. I could not call it non-European and have thought it best to call it eastern because it first appeared to the east of Western Europe.[66]

He then elucidated his view of Western nationalism by reference to the Germans and the Italians, whom he took, by the time of the onset of nationalism in the late eighteenth century, to have been 'well equipped culturally':

They had languages adapted to the . . . consciously progressive civilisation to which they belonged. They had universities and schools imparting the skills prized in that civilisation. They had . . . philosophers, scientists, artists and poets . . . of 'world' reputation. They had legal, medical and other professions with high professional standards . . . To put themselves on a level with the English and the French, they had little need to equip themselves culturally by appropriating what was alien to them . . . Their most urgent need, so it seemed to them, was to acquire national states of their own . . .

The case with the Slavs, and later with the Africans and the Asians, has been quite different.[67]

It would be difficult to invent a more cock-eyed comment on the geography and chronology of Europe's cultural history. The analysis of 'the Slavs', it turns out, is evidenced exclusively by points relating to Czechs, Slovaks, Slovenes, Serbs, and Croats. Nothing is said about the three largest Slav nations, the Russians, Ukrainians, and Poles, whose experiences flatly contradict the analysis. Who, what, and where, one wonders, did Professor Plamenatz imagine the Slavs to be? Is Eastern Europe inhabited only by Slavs? Did the Poles or the Czechs or the Serbs not feel an urgent need to acquire a state? Did not Polish develop as a language of government and of high culture before German did? Did the universities of Prague (1348) and Cracow (1364) belong to the 'East'? Was Copernicus educated in Oxford?

As it happens, there is much to be said for a typology of nationalism which is based on varying rates of cultural development and on the differing correlations of nationality and statehood. But there is nothing to be said for giving it the labels of 'Eastern' and 'Western'. If one does, one finds that the best candidate for a nationalism of the Eastern type is to be found in the far west of Western Europe, in Ireland. As everyone knows, the Irish are typical products of Eastern Europe (see Chapter X, pp. 820–1, 829–31).

By questioning the framework within which European history and culture is so frequently discussed, therefore, one does not necessarily query the excellence of the material presented. The purpose is simply to enquire why the framework should be so strangely designed. If textbooks of human anatomy were designed with the same attention to structure, one would be contemplating a creature with one lobe to its brain, one eye, one arm, one lung, and one leg.

The chronology of the subject is also instructive. The idea of 'the West' is as old as the Greeks, who saw Free Hellas as the antithesis of the Persian-ruled despotisms to the East. In modern times, it has been adopted by a long succession of political interests who wished to reinforce their identity and to dissociate themselves from their neighbours. As a result, 'Western civilization' has been given layer upon layer of meanings and connotations that have accrued over the centuries. There are a dozen or so main variants:

> *The Roman Empire*, which stretched far beyond the European Peninsula, none the less left a lasting impression on Europe's development. To this day, there is a clear distinction between those countries, such as France or Spain, which once formed an integral part of the Empire, and those, such as Poland or Sweden, which the Romans never reached. In this context, 'the West' came to be associated with those parts of Europe which can claim a share in the Roman legacy, as distinct from those which can not. (See Map 3.)

> *Christian civilization*, whose main base settled down in Europe, was defined from the seventh century onwards by the religious frontier with Islam (see Chapter IV). Christendom was the West, Islam the East.

> *The Catholic world* was built on the divergent traditions of the Roman and the Greek churches, especially after the Schism of 1054, and on the use of Latin as

a universal language. In this version, the West was equivalent to Catholicism, where the frequent divorce of ecclesiastical and secular authority facilitated the rise of successive non-conformist movements, notably the Renaissance, the Reformation, the Scientific Revolution, and the Enlightenment (see Chapter VII). None of these key movements made an early impact on the Orthodox world.

Protestantism gave Western civilization a new focus in the cluster of countries in northern Europe, which broke away from Catholic control in the sixteenth century. The dramatic decline of major Catholic powers such as Spain or Poland was accompanied by the rise of the United Provinces, England, Sweden, and later Prussia, where naval or military pre-eminence was underpinned by economic and technological prowess.

The French variant of Western civilization gained prominence in the seventeenth and eighteenth centuries. It found expression in the secular philosophy of the Enlightenment and in the ideals of the Revolution of 1789—both of which have had a lasting influence. The French language was adopted by the educated élites of Germany and Eastern Europe, making French still more universal than the earlier reign of Latin.

The imperial variant of Western civilization was based on the unbounded self-confidence of the leading imperial powers during the long European Peace prior to 1914. It was fired by a belief in the God-given right of the 'imperial races' to rule over others, and in their supposedly superior cultural, economic, and constitutional development. Germany, England, and France were the clear leaders, whose prejudices could be impressed on the rest. Other major empire-owners, such as Portugal or the Netherlands, were minor players within Europe. Russia and Austria were impressive imperial powers, but fell short on other qualifications. For the rich imperial club in the West was marked by its advanced industrial economies and sophisticated systems of administration; the East by peasant societies, stateless nations, and raw autocracy.

The Marxist variant was a mirror image of the imperial one. Marx and Engels accepted the premiss that the imperialist countries of Western Europe had reached a superior level of development; but they believed that the precocity of the West would result in early decadence and revolution. Their opinions carried little weight in their own day, but for a time gained greatly in importance thanks to the unexpected adoption of Marxism-Leninism as the official ideology of the Soviet empire.

The first German variant of Western civilization was encouraged by the onset of the First World War. It was predicated on German control of *Mitteleuropa* (Central Europe), especially Austria, on hopes for the military defeat of France and Russia, and on future greatness to be shared with the Anglo-Saxon powers. Its advocates harboured no doubts about Germany's civilizing mission in Eastern Europe, whilst their rivalry with France, and their rejection of liberalism and 'the ideas of 1789', led to a distinction between *Abendlich* (Occidental) and *Westlich* (Western) civilization. The political formulation of the scheme was most closely associated with Friedrich Naumann. Its demise was assured by Germany's defeat in 1918, and was mourned in Spengler's *Der Untergang des Abendlandes* (1918–22). In the sphere of secular culture, the ethos of Mitteleuropa owed much to the influx of a strong Jewish element, which had turned its back on the East and whose assimilation into German life and language coincided with the peak of Germany's imperial ambitions.[68] [**WIENER WELT**]

The WASP* variant of Western civilization came to fruition through the common interests of the USA and the British Empire as revealed during the First World War. It was predicated on the anglophile tendencies of America's then élite, on the shared traditions of Protestantism, parliamentary government, and the common law; on opposition to German hegemony in Europe; on the prospect of a special strategic partnership; and on the primacy of the English language, which was now set to become the principal means of international communication. Despite American contempt for the traditional forms of imperialism, it assumed that the USA was the equal of Europe's imperial powers. Its most obvious cultural monuments are to be found in the 'Great Books Scheme' (1921) and in the takeover of the *Encyclopaedia Britannica*. Its strategic implications were formulated, among others, by the 'father of geopolitics', Sir Halford Mackinder,[69] and found early expression in the Washington Conference of 1922. It was revived at full strength after the USA's return to Europe in 1941 and the sealing of the Grand Alliance. It was global in scope and 'mid-Atlantic' in focus. It inevitably faded after the collapse of the British Empire and the rise of American interests in the Pacific; but it left Britain with a 'special relationship', that helped NATO and hindered European unification; and it inspired a characteristic 'Allied Scheme of History' which has held sway for the rest of the twentieth century (see below).

The second German variant, as conceived by the Nazis, revived many features of the first but added some of its own. To the original military and strategic considerations, it added 'Aryan' racism, Greater German nationalism, pagan mythology, and anti-Bolshevism. It underlay Germany's second bid for supremacy in Europe, which began in 1933 and ended in the ruins of 1945. It specifically excluded the Jews.

The American variant of Western civilization coalesced after the Second World War, around a constellation of countries which accepted the leadership of the USA and which paid court to American ideas of democracy and capitalism. It grew from the older Anglo-Saxon variant, but has outgrown its European origins. It is no longer dependent either on WASP supremacy in American society or on Britain's pivotal role as America's agent in Europe. Indeed, its centre of gravity soon moved from the mid-Atlantic to 'the Pacific Rim'. In addition

---

* White Anglo-Saxon Protestant—the dominant social and cultural group during the formative years of US history.

to NATO members in Western Europe, it is supported by countries as 'Western' as Japan, South Korea, the Philippines, Australia, South Africa, and Israel, even Egypt, Syria, and Saudi Arabia. Through forty years of the Cold War, it was fired by perceptions of the worldwide threat of communism. One wonders how long it can continue to call itself 'the West'.

The Euro-variant of Western civilization emerged in the late 1940s, amidst efforts to forge a new (West) European Community. It was predicated on the existence of the Iron Curtain, on Franco-German reconciliation, on the rejection of overseas empires, on the material prosperity of the EEC, and on the desire to limit the influence of the 'Anglo-Saxons'. It looked back to Charlemagne, and forward to a federal Europe united under the leadership of its founding members. So long as the community confined its principal activities to the economic sphere, it was not incompatible with the Americans' alternative vision of the West or with American-led NATO, which provided its defence. But the accession of the United Kingdom, the collapse of the Iron Curtain, plans for closer political and monetary union, and the prospect of membership spreading eastwards all combined to cause a profound crisis both of identity and of intent.

From all these examples it appears that Western civilization is essentially an amalgam of intellectual constructs which were designed to further the interests of their authors. It is the product of complex exercises in ideology, of countless identity trips, of sophisticated essays in cultural propaganda. It can be defined by its advocates in almost any way that they think fit. Its elastic geography has been inspired by the distribution of religions, by the demands of liberalism and of imperialism, by the unequal progress of modernization, by the divisive effects of world wars and of the Russian Revolution, and by the self-centred visions of French *philosophes*, of Prussian historians, and of British and American statesmen and educators, all of whom have had their reasons to neglect or to despise 'the East'. In its latest phase it has been immensely strengthened by the physical division of Europe, which lasted from 1947–8 to 1991. On the brink of the twenty-first century, one is entitled to ask in whose interests it may be used in the future.

A set of assumptions recurs time and again. The first maintains that West and East, however defined, have little or nothing in common. The second implies that the division of Europe is justified by natural, unbridgeable differences; the third that the West is superior; the fourth that the West alone deserves the name of Europe. The geographical assumptions are abetted by selective constructs of a more overtly political nature. Every variant of Western civilization is taken to have an important core and a less important periphery. Great powers can always command attention. Failing powers, lesser states, stateless nations, minor cultures, weak economies do not have to be considered even if they occupy a large part of the overall scene.

Four mechanisms have been employed to achieve the necessary effect. By a process of reduction, one can compress European history into a tale which

illustrates the origins of themes most relevant to present concerns. By elimination, one can remove all contradictory material. By anachronism, one can present
the facts in categories which suggest that present groupings are permanent
fixtures of the historical scene. By the emphases and enthusiasms of language, one
can indicate what is to be praised and what deplored. These are the normal mechanisms of propaganda. They devalue the diversity and the shifting patterns of
European history; they rule out interpretations suggested by the full historical
record; and they turn their unwitting readers into a mutual admiration society.

Anachronism is particularly insidious. By taking transient contemporary divisions, such as the Iron Curtain, as a standing definition of 'West' or 'East', one is
bound to distort any description of Europe in earlier periods. Poland is neatly
excised from the Renaissance, Hungary from the Reformation, Bohemia from
industrialization, Greece from the Ottoman experience. More seriously, one
deprives a large part of Europe of its true historical personality, with immeasurable consequences in the miscalculations of diplomats, business people, and academics.

As for the products of European history, which the propagandists of Western
civilization are most eager to emphasize, everyone's list would vary. In the late
twentieth century many would like to point to religious toleration, human rights,
democratic government, the rule of law, the scientific tradition, social modernization, cultural pluralism, a free market economy and the supreme Christian
virtues such as compassion, charity, and respect for the individual. How far these
things are truly representative of Europe's past is a matter for debate. It would not
be difficult to draw up a matching list which starts with religious persecution and
ends with totalitarian contempt for human life.

If mainstream claims to European supremacy have undoubtedly come out of
the West, it should not be forgotten that there has been no shortage of counter-
claims from the East. Just as Germany once reacted against the French
Enlightenment, so the Orthodox Church, the Russian Empire, the pan-Slav
movement, and the Soviet Union have all reacted against the more powerful
West, producing theories which claim the truth and future for themselves. They
have repeatedly maintained that, although the West may well be rich and powerful, the East is free from moral and ideological corruption.

In the final years of communist rule in Eastern Europe, dissident intellectuals
produced their own variation on this theme. They drew a fundamental distinction
between the political regimes of the Soviet bloc and the convictions of the people.
They felt themselves less infected by the mindless materialism of the West, and
argued that communist oppression had strengthened their attachment to
Europe's traditional culture. They looked forward to a time when, in a reunited
Europe, they could trade their 'Europeanness' for Western food and technology.
Here was yet another exercise in wishful thinking.

In determining the difference between Western Civilization and European
History, it is no easy task to sift reality from illusion. Having discovered where the

distortions of Western civilization come from, the historian has to put something in their place. The answer would seem to lie in the goal of comprehensiveness, that is, to write of Europe north, east, west, and south; to keep all aspects of human life in mind; to describe the admirable, the deplorable, and the banal.

None the less no historian could deny that there are many real and important lines on the map which have helped to divide Europe into 'West' and 'East'. Probably the most durable is the line between Catholic (Latin) Christianity and Orthodox (Greek) Christianity. It has been in place since the earliest centuries of our era. As shown by events during the collapse of Yugoslavia, it could still be a powerful factor in the affairs of the 1990s. But there are many others. There is the line of the Roman *limes*, dividing Europe into one area with a Roman past and another area without it. There is the line between the western Roman Empire and the eastern Roman Empire. In more modern times there is the Ottoman line, which marked off the Balkan lands which lived for centuries under Muslim rule. Most recently, until 1989, there was the Iron Curtain (see Map 3).

Less certainly, social scientists invent divisions based on the criteria of their own disciplines. Economic historians, for example, see a line separating the industrialized countries of the West from the peasant societies of the East. [CAP-AG] Historical anthropologists have identified a Leningrad–Trieste line, which supposedly separates the zone of nuclear families from that of the extended family. [ZADRUGA] Legal historians trace a line separating the lands which adopted forms of Roman law and those which did not. Constitutional historians emphasize the line dividing countries with a liberal, democratic tradition from those without. As mentioned above, political scientists have found a line dividing 'Western' and 'non-Western' forms of nationalism.[70]

All these lines, real and imagined, have profoundly affected the framework within which European history has been conceived and written. Their influence is so strong that some commentators can talk disparagingly of a 'White Europe' in the West and a 'Black Europe' in the East. The division of Europe into two opposing halves, therefore, is not entirely fanciful. Yet one has to insist that the West–East division has never been fixed or permanent. Moreover, it rides roughshod over many other lines of division of equal importance. It ignores serious differences both within the West and within the East; and it ignores the strong and historic division between North and South. Any competent historian or geographer taking the full range of factors into consideration can only conclude that Europe should be divided, not into two regions, but into five or six.

Similarly, no competent historian is going to deny that Europe in its various guises has always possessed a central core and a series of expanding peripheries. European peoples have migrated far and wide, and one could argue in a very real sense that Europe's periphery lies along a line joining San Francisco with Buenos Aires, Cape Town, Sydney, and Vladivostok. Yet, once again, there can be no simple definition of what the core consists of. Different disciplines give different analyses. They have based their findings on the geographical Peninsula of Europe; on the ethnic heritage of the European branch of the Indo-European peoples; on the cultural legacy of Christendom; on the political community which grew from 'the Concert of Europe'; or, in the hands of the economists, on the growth of a world economy.

For the purposes of comprehensive treatment, however, the important thing about all these definitions is that each and every one contains a variety of re-gional aspects. Wherever or whatever the core is taken to be, it is linked to the Ebro, the Danube, and the Volga as well as the Rhône and the Rhine; to the Baltic and the Black Seas as well as the Atlantic and the Mediterranean; to the Balts and the Slavs as well as the Germanics and the Celts; to the Greeks as well as the Latins; to the peasantry as well as the proletariat. Despite their differences, all the regions of Europe hold a very great deal in common. They are inhabited by peoples of predominantly Indo-European culture and related kin. They are co-heirs of Christendom. They are connected by every sort of political, economic, and cultural overlap and interaction. Despite their own antagonisms, they share fears and anxieties about influences from outside—whether from America, from Africa, or from Asia. Their fundamental unities are no less obvious than their manifest diversity.

Western supremacy is one of those dogmas which holds good at some points in European history and not at others. It does not apply in the earlier centuries, when, for example, Byzantium was far more advanced than the empire of Charlemagne (which explains why Byzantium is often passed over). It has applied in many domains in recent times, when the West has clearly been richer and more powerful than the East. Yet as many would argue, the criminal conduct of Westerners in the twentieth century has destroyed the moral basis to all former claims.

The title of 'Europe', like the earlier label of 'Christendom', therefore, can hardly be arrogated by one of its several regions. Eastern Europe is no less European for being poor, or undeveloped, or ruled by tyrants. In many ways, thanks to its deprivations, it has become more European, more attached to the values which affluent Westerners can take for granted. Nor can Eastern Europe be rejected because it is 'different'. All European countries are different. All *West* European countries are different. And there are important similarities which span the divide. A country like Poland might be very different from Germany or from Britain; but the Polish experience is much closer to that of Ireland or of Spain than many West European countries are to each other. A country like Greece, which some people have thought to be Western by virtue of Homer and Aristotle, was admitted to the European Community; but its formative experiences in modern times were in the Orthodox world under Ottoman rule. They were considerably more distant from those of Western Europe than several countries who found themselves on the wrong side of the Iron Curtain.

The really vicious quality shared by almost all accounts of 'Western civilization' lies in the fact that they present idealized, and hence essentially false, pictures of past reality. They extract everything that might be judged genial or impressive; and they filter out anything that might appear mundane or repulsive. It is bad enough that they attribute all the positive things to the 'West', and denigrate the 'East'. But they do not even give an honest account of the West: judging from some of the textbooks, one gets the distinct impression that everyone in the 'West' was a genius, a philosopher, a pioneer, a democrat, or a saint, that it was a world inhabited exclusively by Platos and Marie Curies. Such hagiography is no longer credible. The established canon of European Culture is desperately in need of revision. Overblown talk about 'Western civilization' threatens to render the European legacy, which has much to be said in its favour, disreputable.

In the United States the debate about Western civilization has centred on the changing requirements of American education. In recent years, it seems to have been driven by the needs of a multiethnic and multicultural society, and by concern for Americans whose origins lie neither in Europe nor in Europe's Christian-based culture. Generally speaking, it has not re-examined the picture of the European heritage as marketed by the likes of the 'Great Books Scheme'; and it has not been disturbed by demands from Americans of European descent for a fairer introduction to Europe. Where courses on Western civilization have been abandoned, they have been rejected for their alleged Eurocentrism, not for their limited vision of Europe. In very many cases, they have been replaced by courses on world history, which is judged better suited to America's contemporary understanding of the 'West'.

   One well-publicized reaction against the shortcomings of 'Western civilization' was to abolish it. Stanford University in California took the lead in 1989, instituting a 'Culture, Ideas and Values' course in place of the former foundation course in 'Western Culture' that had hitherto been compulsory for all freshpersons. According to reports, the university authorities surrendered to chants of 'Hey-ho, Hey-ho, Western Culture has to go!' Readings in Virgil, Cicero, Tacitus, Dante, Luther, Aquinas, More, Galileo, Locke, and Mill were replaced by excerpts from Rigoberta Manchu, Frantz Fanon, Juan Rulfo, Sandra Cisneros, and Zora Neale Hurston (none of whom suffered the stigma of being 'Dead White European Males').[71] This event was excessively satirized. Stanford can take some pride from seeing a problem and trying to tackle it. The trouble is that the cure may prove worse than the malady. In theory, there is much to be said for introducing 'multiculturalism' and 'ethnic diversity' into American academe. It is unfortunate that there is no known Tibetan Tacitus, no African Aquinas, no Mexican Mill for students to study. Indeed, there is nothing very much in any of the recorded non-European cultures that might illustrate the roots of America's supposedly liberal traditions.[72]

   At the time of the furore over Stanford's program on Western Culture, its parallel courses on European History escaped the spotlight. But they were cast in the same mould. The choice of 39 set readings for the program in 'Europe I, II, and III', for example, revealed a brand of selectivity with far-reaching implications. Apart from Joseph Conrad (Korzeniowski), there was no single author from Eastern Europe. (Conrad was included for his novels about Africa, such as *Heart of Darkness*, not for his writings on Eastern Europe.) Apart from Matthew Arnold, there was no single author with any sort of connection with the Celtic world. (Arnold was included as English critic and poet, not as Professor of Celtic Literature.) There was no single Italian author more modern than Baldassare Castiglione, who died in 1528. There was one novelist from South Africa, but no one from Ireland, no one from Scandinavia, no one but Germans from central Europe, no one from the Balkan countries, no one from Russia. Most curiously, from a history department, there was no historical text more modern than one from Herodotus.[73]

To be fair, selection is always necessary, always difficult, and always unsatisfactory: Stanford's quandary is not unique. But the particular form of selection practised by one of the world's most expensive seats of learning is indicative of wider concerns. It purports to introduce 'Europe', but introduces only a small corner of the European continent. It purports to introduce 'the Western Heritage'—the title of its textbook—but it leaves much of the West untouched. It purports to give emphasis to Europe's 'literary and philosophical aspects', but emphasises only a partial slice of European culture. It mentions neither Joyce nor Yeats, neither Andersen, Ibsen, nor Kirkegaard, neither Kafka, Koestler, nor Kundera, neither Solzhenitzyn nor even Dostoevsky. No Trades Description Act could ever sanction a product whose list of ingredients lacked so many of the basic items.

No zoo can contain all the animals. But, equally, no self-respecting collection can confine itself to monkeys, vultures, or snakes. No impartial zoologist could possibly approve of a reptile house which masquerades as a safari park and which contains only twelve crocodiles (of both sexes), eleven lizards, one dodo, and fifteen sloths. In any case, Stanford was hardly alone. By 1991, the National Endowment for the Humanities was quoted with an assessment that students could graduate from 78 per cent of US colleges and universities without ever taking a course in Western civilization.[74] One suspects, in fact, that the problem lies less in the subject-matter of European studies than in the outlook of those who present them. Many American courses, like the Great Books Scheme, were directed at a particular generation of young Americans, who were desperately eager to learn a simplified version of the lost heritage of their immigrant forebears. Nowadays, they obviously need to be modified to match a new generation, with different perceptions. Readings about Europe might arouse less resentment if they were laced with some of its less savoury aspects. Intelligent students can always sense when something is concealed, when they are not expected to understand, but to admire.

Some of America's minorities may indeed have a case for contesting Eurocentrism. If so, America's majority, who are overwhelmingly European in their origins, may choose to challenge 'Western civilization' on other grounds. Many of America's most numerous communities—Irish, Spanish, Polish, Ukrainian, Italian, Greek, Jewish—came from regions of Europe which find little place in existing surveys of 'Western civilization'; and they have every reason to expect an improvement.

The great paradox of contemporary American intellectual life, however, lies in the fact that the virtues most prized by the American version of Western civilization—tolerance, freedom of thought, cultural pluralism—now seem to be under attack from the very people who have benefited from them most. Critics have observed 'the Closing of the American Mind'.[75] Self-styled 'liberals' have been shown to be pursuing an 'Illiberal Education'.[76] Sixty years on, the author of the Great Books Scheme, still proud of 'The Opening of the American Mind', prefers to lambast his colleagues at the University of Chicago rather than to modify his prescription.[77] The wrangles may be over-reported. But America's historic drive towards a unified language and culture looks to be losing out to those lobbies and pressure groups who shout loudest.

It is an understatement to say that history did not quite work out as the devotees of 'Western civilization' would have wished. All of them were believers in one or another form of European domination. Spengler was as right to record the West's decline as he was wrong to believe in the future supremacy of Russia. But the ideas linger on, and their final defeat has not yet occurred. For most Europeans, they have lost their former vitality. They have been shattered by two World Wars and by the loss of overseas empires. They will obviously make their last stand in the USA.

For only in the USA do the true well-springs of 'Western civilization' still flow. Since the collapse of the Soviet empire in 1991, the USA is the sole heir of European imperialism, and has inherited many of its attitudes. It may not be an empire of the old sort; but it has been left with 'the white man's burden'. Like imperial Europe before it, the USA struggles to police the world, whilst battling the ethnic and racial conflicts within its own borders. Like Europe today, it is in urgent need of a unifying mystique to outreach the dwindling attractions of mere democracy and consumerism. Unlike Europe, it has not known the lash of war on its own face within living memory.

An absolute majority of Americans have European roots. They have adopted and adapted the English language and the European culture of the founding fathers, often in creative ways. Yet those Euro-Americans will never draw their main inspiration from Asia or Africa, or from studying the world in general. In order to cope with themselves, they have a profound need to come to terms with Europe's heritage. In order to do so successfully, they must liberate their view of Europe's past from its former limitations. If the European example shows anything at all, it shows that belief in the divisive propositions of 'Western civilization' is a sure road to disaster.

The greatest minds in Europe's past have had no truck with the artificial divorce of East and West:

> Gottes ist der Orient!
> Gottes ist der Okzident!
> Nord- und südliches Gelände
> Ruht im Frieden seiner Hände.

(God's is the East; God's is the West. Northern and southern lands rest in the peace of His hands.)[78]

National Histories

In modern times, almost every European country has devoted greater energy and resources to the study of its own national history than to the study of Europe as a whole. For reasons that are very understandable, the parts have been made to seem more significant than the whole. Linguistic barriers, political interests, and the line of least resistance have helped to perpetuate the reigning citadels of national historiography, and the attitudes which accompany them.

The problem is particularly acute in Great Britain, where the old routines have never been overturned by political collapse or national defeat. Until recently, British history has generally been taken to be a separate subject from European history—requiring a separate sort of expertise, separate courses, separate teachers, and separate textbooks. Traditional insularity is a fitting partner to the other widespread convention that equates British History with English History. (Only the most mischievous of historians would bother to point out that his *English History* referred only to England.)[79] Politicians have accepted the misplaced equation without a thought. In 1962, when opposing British entry to the European Economic Community, the leader of HM Opposition felt able to declare quite wrongly that such a step would spell 'the end of a thousand years of British history'.[80] The English are not only insular; most of them have never been taught the basic history of their own islands.

Similar attitudes prevail in universities. Honourable exceptions no doubt exist; but Britain's largest history faculty did not start teaching 'British history' until 1974; and even then the content remained almost entirely English. The students rarely learn anything about Ireland, Scotland, or Wales. When they take examinations in 'European history', they are faced with a few optional questions about Eastern Europe and none about Britain. The net result can only be a view of the world where everything beyond England is alien.[81] The basic, and fallacious, assumption, writes one dissenter, 'is that everything important in British History can be explained in terms of British causes'. Or again: 'The deeply ingrained and undiminished segregation of "British"—in reality English—history from European history . . . creates a narrowness of vision that has become a powerfully constricting cultural factor.'[82] According to another harsh critic, a combination of traditional structures, arcane research, and excessive professionalization has reduced British history to 'incoherence'. 'At the universities as in the schools,' he wrote before sensibly emigrating, 'the belief that history provides an education . . . has all but vanished.'[83]

Cultural history as taught at Britain's universities often clings to a narrow, national focus. There is a marked preference for the old-style study of national roots, over broad international comparisons. At the University of Oxford, for example, the one and only compulsory subject for all students of the English Faculty remains the Anglo-Saxon text of *Beowulf*.[84] Until very recently in Oxford's Faculty of Modern History (*sic*), the one and only compulsory reading was the Latin text of the seventh century, 'History of the English Church and People' by the Venerable Bede.[85]

Curiosities of the same order no doubt exist in all countries. In Germany, for instance, universities suffer from the ramifications of the Humboldtian principle of 'academic freedom'. German history professors are reputedly free to teach whatever they like. German history students are free to learn whatever they choose from the menu served up by their professors. In most universities, the only rule is that each student must choose at least one course from ancient history, one from medieval, and one from modern. At times of great pressure from the German state, therefore, professors sympathetic to official ideology were free to load the menu with a heavy dose of German national history. (Back to the Teutonic tribes, once again.) In more recent times, when the state has been loath to interfere, they have been free to devise a menu where German national history can be completely avoided by any student so inclined.

The problem of national bias is probably best observed in the realm of school textbooks and popular histories. The more that historians have to condense and to simplify their material, the harder it is to mask their prejudices. A few comments are called for.

In the first place, it may be taken for granted that historical education in most European countries has traditionally possessed a strong nationalistic flavour. In its origins in the nineteenth century, history-teaching was recruited to the service of patriotism. In its most primitive form, it consisted of little more than a rota of the names, dates, and titles of the ruling dynasty. From that it progressed to a recital of the nation's heroes, victories, and achievements. [BOUBOULINA] In its most extreme form, it deliberately set out to condition schoolchildren for their future role as killers and casualties in the nation's wars.[86] On the other hand, it is not right to assume that nationalistic history-teaching has passed unchallenged. There has been a long countercurrent of trying to inculcate an awareness of wider horizons; and practices changed radically after 1945, at least in Western Europe.[87]

A remarkable textbook on 'modern history', published in Austrian Galicia in 1889, directly confronted the assumptions of the age of nationalism. The book was designed for Polish-language secondary schools. Its author, a historian from Warsaw, who could not publish freely in his home city, then under Russian rule, explained the priorities:

In the struggles and achievements of the modern era, nations do not act on their own, but collectively. They are joined together in a variety of interrelated groupings and alliances. For this reason, we are obliged to use the 'synchronic method', that is, to speak of all the nations who participated in the events of any given time. Such general history cannot present a complete picture of all the nations involved; and . . . their individual histories . . . must be consigned to (the category) of special, national histories.[88]

The result was a book where, in volume I, covering the period from the Renaissance to 1648, Habsburg and Polish events occupy exactly 71 and 519 pages respectively. The author makes a careful distinction between 'Poland' and 'the Polish-Lithuanian-Ruthenian-Prussian state'. The student could learn in some detail about 'the Catholic and the Lutheran Reformations', as about Islam and the

Ottomans. The geographical range stretched from the Portuguese voyages of discovery to Ivan the Terrible's conquest of the Khanate of Kazan, from Mary Stuart's overthrow in Edinburgh to Charles V's expedition to Tunis.[89] This volume would rate more highly on the non-nationalist scale than many still emanating from member states of the European Community.[90]

It is also fair to say that concerted attempts have been made in recent years to purge educational materials of the grosser forms of misinformation. Bilateral textbook commissions have worked long and hard on such matters as militarism, place-names and historical atlases, and one-sided interpretations. Scholars and teachers are possibly more aware of the problems than previously.[91] In the last analysis, two extremes can be observed. At one extreme is the cosmic approach, where historians are expected to write, and students to learn, about all parts of the world in all ages. At the other extreme lies the parochial approach, where attention is reserved for one country in one short period of time. The cosmic approach has breadth, but lacks depth. The parochial approach has the chance of depth, but lacks breadth. The ideal must be somehow to strike a balance between breadth *and* depth.

On this score, one has to admit that the centrally planned syllabuses and textbooks of Soviet bloc countries were sometimes more successful than those of their Western counterparts. Though the actual content tended to be horrendously chauvinist and ideological, the chronological and geographical framework was often admirably comprehensive. All Soviet schoolchildren had to work their way through the five stages of historical development, gaining some knowledge of primitive society, classical antiquity, 'feudalism', 'capitalism', and from 1917 so-called 'socialism'. Courses on the history of the USSR insisted on giving priority to the leading historical role of Russia and the Russians. At the same time, even in the worst years of Stalinism, any standard Soviet textbook would devote space to the ancient Greeks, Scythians, and Romans, to the history of the Caucasus, to the empires of Genghis Khan and Tamerlane, and to the Muslim states of Kazan or Crimea. One would look in vain for such things in most general histories of Europe.

In England, in contrast—where the syllabus of history-teaching has largely been left to individual schools and teachers—the chronological and geographical framework tends to be extremely narrow. Even senior pupils studying history at advanced level are often confined to standard courses such as 'The Tudors and Stuarts' or 'Britain in the Nineteenth Century'.[92]

Local history provides an interesting solution to some of these dilemmas. It draws on the familiar and the down-to-earth, encourages individual exploration and research, and is relatively resistant to nationalistic or to ideological pressures. It is well suited to subjects such as the family, which is readily understood by schoolchildren, whilst being used by specialists as the basis for far-flung international theorizing.[93] At the other end of the scale world history has been developed, both at schools and universities. It has strong arguments in its favour for the education of a generation which must take their place in 'the global village'.[94] Its critics would argue, as some argue about European history, that the sheer size of its content condemns all but its most able practitioners to deal in worthless generalities.

Naturally, narrowness of one kind provides an opportunity for breadth of a different kind. The narrowing of chronological and geographical parameters enables teachers to widen the variety of techniques and perspectives that can be explored within the chosen sector. Generally speaking, English pupils are relatively well grounded in the study of sources, in causational problems, in the connections between political, socio-economic, and cultural factors, and in the art of thinking for themselves. Here, their historical education has strength. On the other hand, there really must be something wrong if their studies are limited to 5 or 10 per cent of the span of only one-third of just one of the 38 sovereign states of the world's smallest continent.

The problem of national bias will only disappear when historians and educators cease to regard history as a vehicle for state politics. More than 1,800 years ago the Greek writer Lucian (AD 120–80) advised that 'the historian among his books should forget his nationality'. It was sound advice. In the longer term, the definitive history of Europe will probably be written by a Chinese, a Persian, or an African. There are some good precedents: a Frenchman once wrote the best introduction to Victorian England; an Englishman is now established as the leading historian of Italy, and the only survey of British History to give proportionate weight to all four nations was written by an exile in the USA.[95]

So far, none of the experiments aimed at writing history 'from the European point of view' has met with general acclaim. Some historians, such as Christopher Dawson, have made the attempt by appealing to Europe's Christian foundations.[96] But Dawson's Catholic thesis did not illuminate the pluralism of recent centuries, and did not convince his predominantly WASP readership. Others have taken the task of tracing the drive for European unity.[97] The trouble here is that the list of contents is exceedingly short. Nation-states and national consciousness have been dominant phenomena throughout the era when history has been written as a systematic science. To a large extent, national histories have been allowed to predominate through the lack of alternatives. This may be regrettable; but it reflects the true condition of a Europe that has been deeply divided over recent centuries. Ever since the fragmentation of Christendom during the Renaissance and the Reformation, Europe has had no unifying ideal; historians cannot pretend otherwise. As some analysts have realized about the United States, the mosaic of Europe is every bit as important as the melting-pot.

In all probability, therefore, it is still too early for a satisfactory European synthesis to be conceived and accepted. National sensitivities still abound. National histories cannot simply be abandoned; and it would be a gross distortion if the differences between Europe's nations were to be wilfully submerged 'in some bland Eurohistory':

European history may be more than the sum of its parts; but it cannot be built except by studying those parts in their full idiosyncrasies . . . It seems that . . . we cannot be content with national history; but 'pan-European history' cannot be easily achieved.[98]

This is wise counsel. The implication is that the reformulating of European history must inch forward alongside the gradual construction of a wider European community. Neither will be built in a day.

Unfortunately, national bias dies slowly. In April 1605, soon after England and Scotland were joined in personal union, Sir Francis Bacon wrote to the Lord Chancellor recommending that 'one just and complete history be compiled of both nations'. His wish has not yet been granted. In the words of one of the few British historians who are trying to address the problem of British identity, 'the ingrained reluctance to ask fundamental questions about the nature of Britain remains constant.'[99]

Two Failed Visions

The prevalence of nationalism in the twentieth century has not encouraged internationalist history. But two forceful attempts were made to overcome prevailing divisions, and to provide the ideological framework for a new, universal vision of Europe's past. Both attempts failed, and deserved to fail.

Of the two, the Marxist-Leninist or Communist version of European history started first and lasted longest. It grew out of Marxism, whose spirit and intentions it ignored, and in the hands of the Bolsheviks became one of the coercive instruments of state policy. In the initial phase, 1917–34, under enthusiasts such as M. N. Pokrovsky (1868–1932), it was strongly internationalist in flavour. Pokrovsky fully accepted that history was 'politics turned towards the past'; and he threw himself with gusto into the fight against chauvinism. 'Great Russia was built on the bones of the non-Russian nations,' he wrote. 'In the past, we Russians were the greatest robbers on earth.' Yet for Stalin the rejection of Russia's imperial traditions was anathema; and from 1934, when Stalin's decrees on history-teaching took effect, the direction changed abruptly. Pokrovsky died, and most of his unrecanting colleagues were shot. Their textbooks were suppressed. In their place there appeared a virulent brew of vulgar Marxism and extreme Russian imperialism that was served up by all the ideological agencies of the USSR for the next fifty years.[100]

The twin elements of communist history were at bottom contradictory. They were held together by the messianic dogma of an ideology that no one could openly question. The pseudo-Marxist element was contained in the famous Five-Stage Scheme, that led from prehistory to the Revolution of 1917. The Russian element was predicated on the special mission awarded to the Russian nation as the 'elder brother' of the Soviet peoples and the 'vanguard' of the world's proletariat. By Lenin's own admission, Soviet Russia was not yet as advanced as Germany and the other industrialized countries. But the 'world's first socialist state' had been created to sow the seeds of the world revolution, to hold the fort of socialism during capitalism's terminal decline, and to inherit the earth at the end. In the meantime, superior Soviet methods of social organization and economic planning would soon ensure that the capitalist world was rapidly overtaken. Indeed, as the final chapter of the textbooks always stressed, the Soviet Union was surging ahead in everything from military might to living standards, technology, and environmental protection. The final victory of socialism (as communism was always called) was taken to be scientifically proved and *inevitable*.

Despite its lip-service to 'socialist internationalism', the historical thinking of the Soviets paid homage both to 'Eurocentrism' and, in a backhanded way, to 'Western civilization'. Its Eurocentrism found expression in the fund of European examples on which Marxist-Leninist argument was based, and in the mania for European-style industrialization. It was specially blatant in the emphasis placed on the historic destiny of the Russians. Soviet assumptions on this last score caused offence to the European members of their empire, had an unsettling effect on the comrades of the communist movement in the Third World, and was the principal cause of the Sino-Soviet split. In Chinese eyes, the droves of Soviet advisers and technicians who appeared in China in the 1950s gave a worse display of European arrogance (and bad machinery) than any previous wave of 'foreign devils' they had known. For the Chinese, as for Balts, Poles, or Georgians, the Russians' belief in their own superiority was bizarre. If Russians were accustomed to think of themselves as 'Westerners' in relation to China, they were obviously 'Easterners' in relation to the main body of Europeans.

There is no doubt that Soviet communism proclaimed 'the West' to be the ideological enemy. At the same time it did not deny that its own roots lay in Europe, and that Lenin's dearest wish had been to link the revolution in Russia with the expected revolution in Germany. So 'Western civilization' was not all bad. Indeed, so long as they were dead, leading Western figures could be readily admired. The point was: the West had grown decadent; the East, in the hands of the heroic proletariat, had stayed vigorous and healthy. Sooner or later the capitalist regimes would fade, the socialist fatherland would give them a final push, the frontiers would fall, and East would be rejoined with the West under Soviet Russian leadership in a new revolutionary brotherhood. This is what Lenin had dreamed of, and what Leonid Brezhnev would have in mind when he talked of 'a common European home'.[101] This view of the communists' messianic mission was exported, with local variations, to all the countries which the Soviet Union controlled. In its strictly historical aspect it sought to instil two cardinal dogmas—the primacy of 'socio-economic forces' and the benign nature of Russia's expansion. It was greatly boosted by the Soviet defeat of Germany in 1941–5, and was still being taught as gospel to tens of millions of European students and schoolchildren in the late 1980s. Right at the end of communism's career, the General Secretary of the CPSU, Mikhail Gorbachev, revived the slogan of 'a common European home'.[102] It was seized on by many foreign commentators and widely welcomed; but Gorbachev never had time to explain what he meant. He was dictator of an empire from Kaliningrad to Kamchatka—a peninsula as remote, and as European, as neighbouring Alaska. Could it be possible that Gorbachev's dream was of a Greater Europe, stretching right round the globe?

The rival, fascist version of history started later, and flourished more briefly. To some extent it grew up in response to Communism, and in the hands of the Nazis became one of the instruments of their New Order. In the initial phase, 1922–34, it contained a certain socialist flavour both in Germany and Italy, but was dominated by the Italian variant and by Mussolini's dream of a restored Roman Empire. From 1934, when Hitler began to remodel Germany, the direction changed abruptly. The socialist element of National Socialism was purged. The German variant of fascism took the driving seat, and overtly racial theories came to the fore. As a result, there appeared a virulent brew of racism and German imperialism that was served up by all the ideological agencies of the Nazi Reich as long as it lasted.[103]

Despite Nazi–Soviet hostility, Nazi ideology was not so completely different from that of Stalinism. The racial element was predicated on the special mission supposedly awarded to the German nation as the most vigorous and healthy branch of the white Aryan race. The German imperial element was predicated on the criminal 'Diktat' of Versailles, and on Germany's supposed right to recover its leading position. Together, they formed the basis of a programme which assumed that Nazi power would spread across Europe, and eventually beyond it. There were serious incompatibilities with fascist ideologies elsewhere in Europe, especially in Italy, whose nationalism had always possessed strong anti-Germanic overtones. But these did not have the time to ferment.

The historical thinking of the Nazis contained the most extreme versions of 'Eurocentrism' and 'Western civilization' that have ever existed. The 'Master Race' was identified with Aryan Europeans, wherever they lived in the world. They were the only true human beings, and were credited with all the most important achievements of the past. All non-Aryans (non-whites and non-Europeans) were classed as genetically inferior, and were placed in descending categories of *Untermenschen* or 'subhumans'. A parallel hierarchy of biological merit was established within Europe, with the tall, slim, blond, Nordic type—as tall as Goebbels, as slim as Goering, as blond as Hitler—considered superior to all others. The Slavs of the East (Poles, Russians, Serbs, etc.), who were wrongly classified as a racial subgroup, were declared inferior to the dominant Germanic peoples of the West, and were treated on a level with various non-Aryan subhumans. The lowest categories of European inhabitants were those of non-European origin—principally gypsies and Jews—who were blamed for all the evils of European history, and were deprived of the right to life.

Nazi strategy was largely constructed from these absurdities, where the distinction between 'West' and 'East' was paramount. Beyond the removal of recalcitrant governments, Hitler harboured few designs against Western Europe, of which he felt himself to be the champion. He despised the French, whose Frankishness had been much diluted, and whose historic hatred for Germany had somehow to be cured. He disliked the Italians and their Roman connections, and felt them to be unreliable partners. He respected the Spaniards, who had once saved Europe from the Blacks, and was puzzled by Franco's reluctance to co-operate. With the exception of certain degenerate individuals, he admired the 'Anglo-Saxons', and found their persistent hostility towards him distressing. In his own terms, their behaviour could only be explained as that of fellow Germanics who were preparing to compete for mastery of the Master Race. All he wanted from them was that they should leave him alone.

All of the Nazis' most radical ambitions were directed against the East. *Mein Kampf* clearly identified Eastern Europe as the site of Germany's *Lebensraum*, her future 'living space'. Eastern Europe was inhabited by an assortment of inferior Slavs and Jews; its genetic stock had to be improved by massive German colonization. The 'diseased elements' had to be surgically removed, that is, murdered. Eastern Europe was also the sphere of Soviet power; and the 'nest of Jewish Bolshevism' had to be smashed. When the Nazis launched the German invasions of Eastern Europe, first against Poland and then against the Soviet Union, they felt they were launching a 'Crusade'. And they said so explicitly. They were told by their history books that they were marching in the glorious steps of Henry the Fowler, the Teutonic Knights, and Frederick the Great. They claimed to be speeding to the ultimate showdown of 'a thousand years of history'.

Unlike Communism, Nazism was not granted seventy-five years in which to elaborate its theory and practice. It was destroyed by the combined efforts of its neighbours, before the Greater Reich could be consolidated. It never reached the point where a Nazi-run Europe would have been obliged to articulate its posture towards the other continents. Yet if the Soviets had succumbed, as they very nearly did in 1941–2, Nazism would have become the driving force of a Eurasian power of immense size; and it would have had to prepare for a global confrontation against rival centres in the USA and Japan. Conflict would surely have ensued. As it was, Nazidom was kept within Europe's bounds. Hitler was not given the chance to operate beyond the world of his fellow Aryans. Both as theorist and as political leader, he remained to the end a European.

Though Nazidom once stretched from the Atlantic to the Volga, the Nazi version of history was only free to operate for a very brief interval. In Germany itself, its career was limited to a mere twelve years—less than the school days of one single class. Elsewhere, it could only sow its poison for a matter of weeks or months. Its impact was intense, but fleeting in the extreme. When it collapsed in disgrace in 1944–5, it left a gaping vacuum that could only be filled by the historical thoughts of the victorious powers. In Eastern Europe, occupied from 1944–5 by the Soviet army, the Soviet version was imposed without ceremony. Western Europe, liberated by the Anglo-Americans, was left open for 'the Allied Scheme of History'.

The Allied Scheme of History

Contemporary views of Europe have been strongly influenced by the emotions and experiences of two World Wars and especially by the victory of the 'Grand Alliance'. Thanks to their triumphs in 1918, in 1945, and at the end of the Cold War in 1989, the Western Powers have been able to export their interpretation of events worldwide. They have been particularly successful in this regard in Germany whose receptiveness was heightened by a combination of native guilt and Allied re-education policies.

The priorities and assumptions which derive from Allied attitudes of the wartime vintage are very common in accounts of the twentieth century; and are sometimes projected back into more remote periods. They may be tentatively summarized as follows:

—The belief in a unique, secular brand of Western civilization in which 'the Atlantic community' is presented as the pinnacle of human progress. Anglo-Saxon democracy, the rule of law in the tradition of Magna Carta, and a capitalist, free-market economy are taken to be the highest forms of Good. Keystones in the scheme include the Wilsonian principle of National Self-determination (1917) and the Atlantic Charter (1941).

—The ideology of 'anti-fascism', in which the Second World War of 1939–45 is perceived as 'the War against Fascism' and as the defining event in the triumph of Good over Evil. Opposition to fascism, or suffering at its hands, is the over-riding measure of merit. The opponents or the victims of fascists deserve the greatest admiration and sympathy.

—A demonological fascination with Germany, the twice-defeated enemy. Germany stands condemned as the prime source both of the malignant imperialism which produced the First World War, and of the virulent brand of fascism which provoked the Second. Individuals and nations who fought on the German side, especially in 1939–45, bear the stigma of 'collaboration'. (N.B. German culture is not to be confused with German politics.)

—An indulgent, romanticized view of the Tsarist empire and the Soviet Union, the strategic ally in the East, commonly called 'Russia'. Russia's manifest faults should never be classed with those of the enemy. For Russia is steadily converging with the West. Russia's great merits as a partner in the 'anti-fascist' alliance, whose huge sacrifices brought fascism to its knees, outweigh all the negative aspects of her record.

—The unspoken acceptance of the division of Europe into Western and Eastern spheres. Whereas 'Atlantic values' are expected to predominate in the more advanced West, Russia's understandable desire for security justifies its domination over the backward East. It is natural for the Western Powers to protect themselves against the threat of further Russian expansion, but they should not interfere in Russia's legitimate sphere of influence.

—The studied neglect of all facts which do not add credence to the above.

The Allied scheme of history grew naturally out of the politics and sympathies of two world wars, and has never been consciously or precisely formulated. In the hurly-burly of free societies it could never establish a monopoly; nor has it ever been systematically contested. Yet half a century after the Second World War it was everywhere evident in academic discussions and, perhaps unknowingly, in the conceptual framework which informs the policy decisions of governments. It was the natural residue of a state of affairs where Allied soldiers could be formally arrested for saying that Hitler and Stalin 'are equally evil'.[104]

In the academic sphere, the Allied scheme can be seen at work in institutional priorities and structures, as well as in debates on particular issues. It has contributed to the crushing preponderance of research in history and political science that is devoted to Nazi or Nazi-related themes, and to the prominence of German studies, especially in the USA. It helps explain why the analysis of East European affairs continues to be organized in separate institutes of 'Soviet' or 'Slavonic' studies, and why the sovietological profession was notoriously reluctant to expose the realities of Soviet life.[105] It was responsible in part for the excessive emphasis on Russian within the Soviet and Slavic field, often to the total exclusion of non-Russian cultures. It was present, above all, in the assumptions and illusions surrounding views on the Second World War. Half a century after that war was fought, the majority of episodes which contradict the Allied myth continued to be minimized or discounted. [**ALTMARKT**] [**KATYŃ**] [**KEELHAUL**]

Many wartime stereotypes have been perpetuated, especially regarding Eastern Europe. One can observe a clear-cut hierarchy of perceptions at work which are related to the degree of subservience of various nations to the Allied cause. The Czechs and Serbs, for example, who had a long tradition of co-operation with Russia and of hostility towards Germany, fitted well into the Allied scheme. So they could be hailed as 'brave', 'friendly', and 'democratic'—at least until the wars in Bosnia. The Slovaks, Croats, and Baltic nations, in contrast, who were thought to have rejected the friends of the West or to have collaborated with the enemy, deserved no such compliments. The Poles, as always, fitted no one's scheme. By resisting German aggression, they were obviously fighting staunchly for democracy. By resisting Soviet aggression, they were obviously 'treacherous', 'fascistic', 'irresponsible', and 'anti-democratic'. The Ukrainians, too, defied classification. Although they probably suffered absolutely the largest number of civilian casualties of any European nation, their main political aim was to escape from Soviet and Russian domination. The best thing to do with such an embarrassing nation was to pretend that it didn't exist, and to accept the old Tsarist fiction about their being 'Little Russians'. In reality they were neither little nor Russians. [**UKRAINA**]

In the political sphere, the Allied scheme has been the foundation stone of the USA's supposed 'special relationship' with the United Kingdom, and one source for the exclusion of democratic Germany and democratic Japan from bodies such as the UN Security Council. It was explicit when a British Prime Minister scolded the French President over the relative merits of Magna Carta and the 'Rights of Man', or when the prospect of a European 'superstate' was blasted in tones reminiscent of Pitt or Churchill. It underlay the vote in the British House of Commons in favour of a War Crimes Bill which limits those crimes to offences committed 'in Germany or in German-controlled territory'—as if no other war crimes count. Arguably, it was present when a national Holocaust Memorial Museum was opened in Washington.[106]

The hold of the Allied scheme was perhaps most strongly evident, however, in reactions to the collapse of communism after 1989. The outburst of 'Gorbymania', the priority given to the integrity of wartime allies (first the USSR and then Yugoslavia), and the wilful confusing of patriotism with nationalism in Eastern Europe can only be explained in terms of pre-set historical reflexes. It was only by a slow process of readjustment that Western opinion learned that 'Russia' and the 'Soviet Union' were not the same thing; that Gorbachev headed a deeply hated regime; that the Yugoslav Federation was a communist front organization; that the most extreme nationalism was emanating from the communist leadership of Serbia; or that Lithuania, Slovenia, Ukraine, or Croatia were distinct European nations legitimately seeking statehood. The realization that 'the West' had been misled on so many basic issues was bound to swell demands for the revision of European history.

Eurohistory

The movement for European unity which began in Western Europe after 1945 was fired by an idealism that contained an important historical dimension. It aimed to remove the welter of ultra-nationalistic attitudes which had fuelled the conflicts of the past. All communities require both a sense of present identity and the sense of a shared past. So historical revision was a natural requirement. The first stage sought to root out the historical misinformation and misunderstandings which had proliferated in all European countries. The second stage was to build a consensus on the positive content of a new 'Eurohistory'.

The Council of Europe provided the forum within which most early discussions took place. As an organization supported by twenty-four governments in Western Europe, it was never bounded by the political horizons either of the EEC or of NATO; and in the cultural field it gained the co-operation of four non-member countries from the Soviet bloc, Poland, Czechoslovakia, Hungary, and the USSR. Its input ranged from the Vatican to the Kremlin. From the first colloquium, which was organized at Calw in 1953 on 'The European Idea in History Teaching', the Council organized at least one major international meeting on historical matters every year for forty years. A 1965 symposium on 'Teaching History' at Elsinore and a 1986 seminar on 'The Viking Age' emphasized the desirability both of broad-based themes and of a generous geographical and chronological spread.

Apart from historical didactics, and the problems of introducing a skills-based 'new history' into school-teaching, the main focus lay on the elimination of national bias and religious prejudice from European education. Special attention was given to the shortcomings of national history textbooks. Numerous bilateral commissions were established for examining the sins of omission and commission of which all European educators were guilty in the presentation of their own and their neighbours' past. In this the Georg Eckert Institute for International

Textbook Research, established at Braunschweig in West Germany played a pioneering role.[107]

The obstacles to creating a consensus about European history, however, were legion. One line, following the Gaullist concept of a *Europe des patries*, might have contented itself with an amalgam of national histories shorn of all offensive material. Others have sought to fuse the national elements into a more coherent whole. A major obstacle lay in shifting political realities, and the expanding membership of the (West) European Community. It was one thing to imagine a history which might reconcile the historical perceptions of the original 'Six'; it was a much greater task to anticipate the sensitivities of the Twelve, the Nineteen, or even the Thirty-Eight. By the 1990s the notion of European unity could no longer be confined to Western Europe. 'Modern History syllabuses will have to abandon the old bifocal view of Europe in favour of an all-embracing concept.'[108] In the mean time, brave souls had not been deterred from attempting a new synthesis.

One history project that was financially supported (though not originated) by the European Commission in Brussels was conceived prior to the political deluge of 1989–91. Labelled 'An Adventure in Understanding', it was planned in three stages: a 500-page survey of European history, a 10-part television series, and a school textbook to be published simultaneously in all eight languages of the EC. Its authors were quite open about their 'political quest': their aim was to replace history written according to the ethos of the sovereign nation-state:

Nationalism, and the fragmentation of Europe into nation-states, are relatively recent phenomena: they may be temporary, and are certainly not irreversible. The end of Empires and the destruction wrought by nationalism have been accompanied by the defeat of totalitarianism and the triumph of liberal democracy in Western Europe, completed in 1974–5. This has enabled people to begin to rise above their nationalistic instincts.[109]

'Nationalistic instincts' was an unfortunate phrase. But the principal author, who had published both on early Christianity and on *L'Idée de l'Europe dans l'histoire* (1965), was convinced of Europe's basic 'unity in diversity': 'There are solid historic reasons for regarding Europe not only as a mosaic of cultures but as an organic whole.'

The timing of the venture was unfortunate, since it reached the market at the very time when its geographical frame of reference had just collapsed. It had defined 'Europe' as the territory of the member states of the EC, with Scandinavia, Austria, and Switzerland thrown in. The status of Finland, Poland, Hungary, and Bohemia, it had intimated, was not clear. So here was yet another exercise in Western civilization. Several of the critics were not kind. Its moral tone was likened by one reviewer as 'reminiscent . . . of Soviet-bloc historiography'. Elsewhere its approach was summed up in the headline 'Half-truths about half of Europe'.[110]

The Greeks in particular were incensed. Although Greece had been a member state of the EC since 1981, Duroselle had largely omitted the contributions of ancient Greece and Byzantium. Letters of protest were addressed to the European

Commission by several Greek MEPs, the Archbishop of Athens, and others. The text was likened to the *Satanic Verses*. Attention was drawn to the opinion of the French historian, Ernest Renan: 'L'Europe est grecque par la pensée et l'art, romaine par le droit, et judéo-chrétienne par la religion.' (Europe is Greek in its thought and its art, Roman in its law, and Judaeo-Christian in its religion.) A British correspondent invoked the Greek origins of the words *Europa* and *Istoria*. If the Greek contribution is to be denied, he asked, one wonders what this book ought to be called. In due course the European Commission was obliged to dissociate itself from the project.[111]

The most telling observation was made amongst remarks originating in the Academy of Athens. It concerned M. Duroselle's concept of 'a European history of Europe'. If a study addressed almost exclusively to Western Europe was to be categorized as 'European', it followed that the rest of Europe was somehow not European. ' "Non-western" is made to mean "non-European"; "Europe" equals "West" in everything but simple geography.'[112] Eastern Europe—whether Byzantine Europe, Orthodox Europe, Slavic Europe, Ottoman Europe, Balkan Europe, or Soviet Europe—was to be permanently beyond the pale. Here was the fundamental fallacy which led M. Duroselle to discuss 'the ancient peoples of Europe' without mentioning either the Greeks or the Slavs. The author's attempts to defend himself were not always felicitous. Charged that his book did not mention the Battle of Marathon, he was said to have countered with the news that it did not mention the Battle of Verdun either—in which case it must be judged as weak on West European history as on European history as a whole.[113]

The project's textbook, composed by twelve historians from twelve different countries, appeared in 1992. The text had been established by collective discussion. A French account of 'the Barbarian Invasions' was changed to 'the Germanic Invasions'. A Spanish description of Sir Francis Drake as a 'pirate' was overruled. A picture of General de Gaulle among the portraits on the cover was replaced by one of Queen Victoria. For whatever reason, *The European History Book* did not find a British publisher, and was judged unlikely to pass the strict authorization criteria of the sixteen German *Länder*.[114]

Eurohistory, however, was not engaged on frivolous business. Its strong point lay in the search for a dynamic vision of a European community that would be capable of creating its own mystique. In its initial form, that vision was of necessity stunted. After all, it saw its origins in the middle of the Cold War. But it may have grasped an essential truth—that sovereign national states do not offer the sole form of sound political community. National states are themselves 'imagined communities': they are built on powerful myths, and on the political rewriting of history:

All communities larger than the primordial villages of face-to-face contact (and perhaps even these) are imagined. . . . members of even the smallest nation will never know their fellow members . . . and yet in the mind of each lives the image of their communion.[115]

Europeans need that same imagination. Sooner or later, a convincing new picture of Europe's past will have to be composed to accompany the new aspirations for Europe's future.

The European movement of the 1990s may succeed or it may fail. If it succeeds, it will owe much to the historians who will have helped to give it a sense of community. They will have helped to provide a spiritual home for those millions of Europeans whose multiple identities and multiple loyalties already transcend existing frontiers.

European History

When asked to define 'European history', many professional historians cannot give a clear answer. They do not usually concern themselves with such matters. If pressed, however, most of them would contrast the certainties of past assumptions with the confusions of the present. An enquiry organized by a historical journal in 1986 brought some revealing replies. One distinguished scholar said:

When I was a schoolboy in France in the 1930s, the answer to . . . 'What is European History?' seemed simple and obvious . . . ; any place, event, or personality that has a relationship to France belongs to European History (nay, to History *tout court.*) . . . [But now], there is no single European history, but rather many.[116]

A second respondent delivered a homily about Europe's traditional parochialism and the need for world-wide horizons:

The concept of European History, indeed the History of Europe, was but history seen with the eyes of Europe and with a European vision of History . . . This kind of presentation is indefensible today.[117]

The implication seemed to be that the Eurocentric attitudes of his misguided predecessors had somehow invalidated the entire subject.

A Hungarian contributor pointed to the eccentric British habit of distinguishing 'European' from 'British' history.[118] Through this distinction, 'European' is made to mean 'Continental', and the British part is made to appear as something completely unique.

Yet another contributor offered an analysis of three separate definitions of European History. He listed 'the geographical', 'the cultural or civilizational', and a category which he described as 'a convenient shorthand for the central zone of the capitalist world-economy as it has developed since the sixteenth century'.[119]

In Magdalen College, one was used to more incisive opinions. Mr A. J. P. Taylor produced an inimitable sample for the benefit of the journal's enquiry:

European History is whatever the historian wants it to be. It is a summary of the events and ideas, political, religious, military, pacific, serious, romantic, near at hand, far away, tragic, comic, significant, meaningless, anything else you would like it to be. There is only one limiting factor. It must take place in, or derive from, the area we call Europe. But as I am not sure what exactly that area is meant to be, I am pretty well in a haze about the rest.[120]

As usual, my old tutor was more than half-right, and completely amusing. But he put himself in the company of those who imply that European history, even if it exists, is not a subject worth worrying about.

In the end, therefore, intellectual definitions raise more questions than they answer. It is the same with European history as with a camel. The practical approach is not to try and define it, but to describe it.

I

PENINSULA

Environment and Prehistory

THERE is a marked determinism about many descriptions of Europe's environmental history. Many Europeans have assumed that their 'continent' was so magnificently endowed that it was destined by Nature for world supremacy. And many have imagined that Europe's good fortune would somehow last forever. 'The empire of climate', wrote Montesquieu in 1748, 'is the first of all empires'; and he proceeded to show that the European climate had no rival. For Montesquieu, as for his many successors, Europe was synonymous with Progress.[1]

There has also been a good deal of national parochialism. Even the founder of human geography, the great Paul Vidal de la Blache (1845–1918), one of the intellectual ancestors of the *Annales* school, was not above a touch of Gallic chauvinizing. The geography of France, he stressed, was marked by the keynote of variety. 'Against the diversities which assail her', he wrote, 'France sets her *force d'assimilation*, her power of assimilation. She transforms everything that she receives.' On Britain, in contrast, he quotes the doggerel lines about 'this paltry little isle, I with acres few and weather vile'. One hundred years later one finds Fernand Braudel doing similar things.[2] Variety is indeed a characteristic of France's superb make-up. But it is not a French monopoly; it is a hallmark of Europe as a whole.

In fact, the Peninsula of Europe is not really a 'continent' at all: it is not a self-contained land mass. At *c.*10 million km² (3.6 million square miles), it is less than one-quarter the size of Asia, one-third of Africa, one-half of each of the Americas. Modern geographers classify it, like India, as a subcontinent of Eurasia: 'a cape of the old continent, a western appendix of Asia'. Even so, it is impossible to deny that Europe has been endowed with a formidable repertoire of physical features. Europe's landforms, climate, geology, and fauna have combined to produce a benign environment that is essential to an understanding of its development.

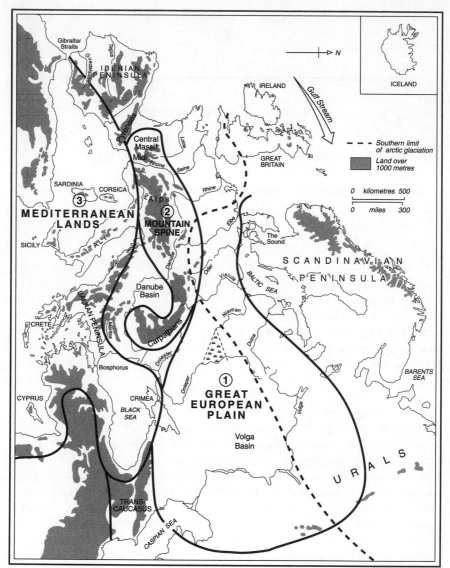

Map 4. Europe: Physical Regions

Europe's landforms do not resemble those of any other continent or subcontinent. The depressions to north and south have been flooded by the ocean to
form two parallel sea-chains which penetrate deep into the interior. In the north,
the North Sea–Baltic sea lane stretches 1,500 miles (2,500 km) from the Atlantic to
Russia. In the south, the Mediterranean–Black Sea system stretches over 2,400
miles (4,000 km) from Gibraltar to the Caucasus. Within these protected seas lie

a vast complex of lesser gulfs and a huge spangle of islands. As a result, the ratio of shoreline to landmass is exceptionally high: at *c.*37,000 km, or more than 23,000 miles, the European shoreline is almost exactly the length of the Equator. For early Man, this was perhaps the most important measure of accessibility.

What is more, since the shores of the Peninsula lie in the temperate latitudes of Eurasia's western extremity, they are served by a user-friendly climate. Prevailing ocean winds blow westerly; and it is the western coasts of the great continents that stand to benefit most from the moderating influx of sea air. Yet few other west-facing continental coasts can actually enjoy the advantage. Elsewhere, if the western shore is not blocked by towering peaks or icy currents, it is lined by deserts such as the Sahara, the Kalahari, or the Atacama.

The climate of Europe, therefore, is unusually temperate for its latitude. Generally speaking, under the influence of the Gulf Stream, northern Europe is mild and moist; southern Europe is relatively warm, dry, and sunny. Central and eastern Europe enjoy elements of a true continental climate, with clear, cold winters and baking hot summers. But everywhere the weather is changeable. Extremes are usually avoided. Even in European Russia, where the difference between the mean temperatures of January and July can approach 45 °C, the range is only half what it is in Siberia. The wettest district in Europe is in western Norway, with an average annual precipitation of 3,500 mm (138 inches). The dryest district surrounds the Caspian Sea, with less than 250 mm (9 inches) per annum. The coldest spot is Vorkuta, with a mean January chill of −20 °C; the hottest is disputed between Seville and Astrakhan, both with mean July roasts of +29 °C. These extremes do not compare with their counterparts in Asia, Africa, or the Americas.

Europe's temperate climate favoured the requirements of primitive agriculture. Most of the Peninsula lies within the natural zone of cultivable grasses. There were abundant woodlands to provide fuel and shelter. Upland pasture often occurs in close proximity to fertile valleys. In the west and south, livestock can winter in the open. Local conditions frequently encouraged special adaptations. The extensive coastline, combined with the broad Continental Shelf, gave fishermen rich rewards. The open plains, especially of the Danube Basin, preserved the nomadic horse-rearing and cattle-driving of the Eurasian steppes. In the Alps—which take their name from the high pastures above the tree-line—transhumance has been practised from an early date.

Europe's climate was probably also responsible for the prevalent skin-colour of its human fauna. Moderate levels of sunshine, and hence of ultra-violet radiation, meant that moderate levels of pigmentation came to be encoded in the Peninsula's gene pool. Certainly, in historic times pale faces have predominated, together with blond or golden hair and blue eyes in the northern regions. The great majority of Europeans and their descendants can be easily recognized as such from their looks.

Until recently, of course, it was impossible to take anything but the most superficial racial factors into consideration. The analysis of blood groups, body tissues, and DNA imprints, for example, was unknown until the late twentieth century; and it was not realized just how much genetic material all human beings have in common. As a result, racial theorists were apt to draw conclusions from external criteria such as skin colour, stature, or skull form. In reality, the racial make-up of Europe's population has always displayed considerable variety. The tall, blue-eyed, fair-skinned, platinum blonds of the so-called 'Nordic race' which established itself in Scandinavia forms the only group remotely qualified for the label of 'white'. They bore little resemblance to the squat, brown-eyed, swarthy-skinned and black-haired people of the so-called 'Mediterranean' or 'Indo-Mediterranean Race' which dominated large parts of the south. Between the two extremes there were numerous gradations. Most of the Peninsula's population can be clearly distinguished from the Mongoloid, Indoid, and Negroid races, but not from other groups predominating in the Near East and North Africa.

Some of the most promising advances in the field of prehistory are now being made through modern genetic research. The refinement of serology, the discovery of DNA (1953), and the subsequent operation of mapping the 3,000 million 'letters' on human genes permit investigations of a very sophisticated nature. The correlation of genetic and linguistic records now suggests that the patterns of biological and cultural evolution may be closer than imagined. Recent studies show that the movement of genetic material into prehistoric Europe corresponded with parallel cultural trends. 'Genes, peoples, and languages have . . . diverged in tandem,' writes a leading scholar.[3] Local studies show that isolated cultural communities, such as the non-Indo-European Basques, possess recognizable genetic traces of their own. There are no general conclusions. But the study of Europe's genetic inheritance, once a pseudo-science, is now a respectable pursuit. At last, 'we are beginning to read the messages left to us by distant ancestors'.[4] [CAUCA-SIA] [TAMMUZ]

From the psychological point of view, the Peninsula presented early man with a stimulating blend of opportunity and challenge. It created a degree of stress that demanded enterprise but was still manageable. Life was hard but rewarding. Seasonal rhythms fostered activities which required routine and foresight. The changeable weather stimulated flexibility. There were plenty of natural hazards to be overcome—ocean gales, winter snows, summer droughts, and disease; yet the prospects for health and survival were good. One may surmise that the primitive settlers of prehistoric Europe felt less at risk than their descendants on the eastern seaboard of North America several millennia later.

It would be rash to state that the European Peninsula was the only location where human civilization could have developed as it did; yet most of the alternative locations had their drawbacks. Compared to the sub-tropical river valleys where mankind first flourished, the seasonal rhythms and benign moderation of the Peninsula provided an altogether more receptive setting for sustained development. The geological and biological environment is rich and varied. There are 'young' alpine mountains, ancient primary hills, active volcanoes; deep gorges and wide plains; racing upland torrents, broad rivers, lakes by the thousand; subarctic tundra, permafrost, glaciers; rocky coasts, sandy beaches, and spreading delta. There are open grasslands, spacious deciduous woods, gloomy pine-forests, and sub-tropical palms; leached, semi-desert soils, vast marshes, and zones of deep loess and 'black earth'. The range of plant life and fauna is large. Enough of Europe's wildernesses have survived to show what the primeval habitat would have resembled.

Importantly, however, the scale of heights and distances is far less forbidding than elsewhere. Europe's localities are linked by a network of natural pathways which primitive man must have found more of an invitation than a barrier. Just as one could paddle round most of the inland coasts in a dugout, one could float down any number of rivers in almost any direction. The Seine, the Rhine, the Elbe, Oder, Vistula, Niemen, and Dvina all flow to the north; the Ebro, the Rhône, the Maritsa, the Dnieper, and the Volga to the south. Tagus, Loire, and Severn flow to the west; Thames, Danube, Po, and Dniester to the east. Between them, there is an endless series of short walks and easy porterages. In the district of Auxois in upper Burgundy, for instance, one can stroll in the course of a few hours between waters that take one to the Mediterranean, the Atlantic, or the English Channel. In the central Alps, the sources of the Rhine and the Rhône rise side by side near Andermatt before flowing north and south respectively. On the Dvina–Dnieper porterage, in the vicinity of Vitebsk, one can easily haul a boat which has come from Sweden to a point that will take it to Egypt.

One should not underestimate the lengthy process whereby the highways and byways of Europe were opened up to human movement and settlement. On the other hand, there is no comparison between the relative ease of travel in Europe and that in the greater continents. Caravans on the ancient silk route from China needed a year or more to cross the body of Asia. Yet from time immemorial any fit and reasonably enterprising traveller has been able to move across Europe in a matter of weeks, if not days.

The division of Europe into 'natural' or 'historic' regions has long provided an intellectual exercise that is as entertaining as it is inconclusive. Attempts to define 'Western Europe', as distinct from 'Eastern Europe', have been as numerous as the criteria used to fix the dividing lines. (See Map 3, and Introduction, pp. 22–5.) The distinction between 'Northern Europe' and 'Southern Europe' is clear and permanent in the Peninsula's central alpine sector. But it does not hold good to the same extent either in Europe's far west, in Iberia, or in Europe's far east, in the hinterland of the Black Sea. The arguments advanced to prove the pedigree of regions such as 'Central Europe' or 'East Central Europe' are as ingenious as they are contorted.[5] One stands on safer ground dividing Europe into regions based on physical and geographical features.

The European Peninsula is constructed from five natural components. In historical times, these geographical units have remained largely constant, whilst the political units surmounting them have come and gone with great fickleness.

'Earth's proud empires' are constantly passing away. But the plains and the mountains, the seas, peninsulas, and islands, apparently go on forever.

1. *The Great European Plain* stretches without interruption for over 2,400 miles (4,000 km) from the Atlantic to the Urals. It is Europe's dominant territorial feature. Indeed, since the Urals form little more than a gentle bridge, the plain may be regarded as an extension of the still greater expanse of lowland stretching to the Verkhoyansk Ridge of eastern Siberia. At the longitude of the Urals it spans the 1,200 miles (2,000 km) between the Barents Sea and the Caspian. Between the coast and the hills in the Low Countries, it narrows to less than 200 km. Almost all the major rivers of the plain flow on a north–south axis, thereby creating a series of natural breaks to east–west traffic and dividing the traverse of the plain into six or seven easy stages. East of the Vistula, the impenetrable Pripet Marshes split the plain into two natural pathways—a northerly one, which skirts the Baltic lakeland, and a southerly one, serving as the highroad to and from the steppes. [**UKRAINA**]

The Plain is at its most vulnerable in the section between the Rhine and the Oder. Here, it is overborne by ranges of impenetrable, forested hills. The Ardennes, the Teutoburger Wald, and the Harz remain formidable barriers even today. They inhibit movement both laterally along the Plain and vertically from the Plain to the Alps. The map of modern Germany shows how almost all the country's development has been channelled either onto the Plain or into the four river basins of the Rhine, Main, Neckar, and Danube.

The peoples who settled on the Plain suffered from one permanent disability: they could find no natural limits to the territory which they chose to occupy. They had to fight for it. Lowlanders tend to think of themselves as docile tillers of the soil in contrast to the ferocious, predatory men from the hills. In reality, it was the plainsmen who had to learn the arts of systematic military organization and occupation. On the plain, one learned to strike first or to be struck down oneself. It is perhaps no accident that the Plain long resisted the onset of settlement; also that in due course it nourished the most formidable military powers of European history. France, Prussia, and Russia—all grew strong from the interminable wars of the plains, and all developed a martial tradition to match their predicament. The lowlands provided the setting for many of their most titanic encounters: at Kunersdorf and Kursk, at Leipzig and Tannenberg, at Waterloo and Stalingrad.

The physical gradients of the European Plain are tipped in two different directions—on the one hand from the alpine ridge to the shore of the northern seas, and, on the other hand, from east to west, from the peak of the Urals (1,894 m) to France's Atlantic coast. On average, the main east–west gradient falls by 6,000 ft over almost 3,000 miles, or 26 inches per mile—a gradient of only 0.04 per cent.

The idea of 'cultural gradients', which run across the European Plain in the opposite direction to the physical ones, developed in response to Europe's particular patterns of settlement and of political evolution. It so happened that permanent settlement occurred first in the south and the west, later in the north and centre, and last in the east. Hence for much of the last 4,000 years, to cross the mountains

UKRAINA

UKRAINE is the land through which the greatest number of European peoples approached their eventual homeland. In ancient times it was variously known as Scythia or Sarmatia, after the peoples who dominated the Pontic steppes long before the arrival of the Slavs. [**CHERSONESOS**] It occupies the largest sector of the southern European plain, between the Volga crossing and the Carpathian narrows; and it carries the principal overland pathway between Asia and Europe. Its modern, Slavonic name means 'On the Edge', a close counterpart to the American concept of 'the Frontier'. Its focal point at the rapids of the Dnieper, where the steppe pathway crosses the river trade-route, was fiercely contested by all comers, for it provided the point of transition between the settled lands to the West and the open steppes to the East. Ukraine is rich in mineral resources—such as the coal of the 'Donbass' and the iron of Krivoi Roh. The loess of its famous 'black earth' underlies Europe's richest agricultural lands, which in the years prior to 1914 were to become the Continent's leading exporter of grain.

Yet apart from the peninsula of Crimea and the main river valleys—the Dnistro, the Dnipro, and the Din, which had served as the focus both for [**KHAZARIA**] and for the first East Slav state (see Appendix III, p. 1249)—much of Ukraine was only systematically settled in modern times. Until then, the wide open spaces of the 'wild plains' were ruled by the raids of pagans and nomads and by the wars of Cossacks and Tartars. Ottoman rule in the 15th–18th centuries drew it closer to the Black Sea and the Muslim world. Polish rule after 1569 brought in many Polish landowners and Polish Jews. Russian rule, which was steadily extended in stages between 1654 and 1945, brought in Russians and russification. The 'Sich' of the Zaporozhian Cossacks, on an island in the Dnieper, was destroyed by the Russian army in 1775; the Tartar Khanate of Crimea in 1783. Under the Tsars, the whole country was officially named 'Little Russia'. The southern provinces designated for new colonization were called 'New Russia'.

Not surprisingly, after so many twists and turns of fortune, Ukraine's modern inhabitants are fiercely attached to their land. It features prominently in their plaintive poetry:

ЗАПОВІТ

Як умру, то поховайте
Мене на могилі,
Серед степу широкого,
На Вкраїні милій,
Щоб лани широкополі,
І Дніпро, і кручі
Було видно, було чути,
Як реве ревучий.
Як понесе з України

У синєє море
Кров ворожу... отоді я
І лани і гори —
Все покину і полину
До самого бога
Молитися... а до того
Я не знаю бога.
Поховайте та вставайте,
Кайдани порвіте
І вражою злою кров'ю
Волю окропіте.
І мене в сім'ї великій,
В сім'ї вольній, новій,
Не забудьте пом'янути
Незлим тихим словом.

As it bears away to the far blue sea
Our oppressors' blood.
Then will I leave hills and fields for eternity
To stand before God Almighty
And to make my peace in prayer.
Till that time, it's my destiny
To know nothing of God.
First make my grave. Then arise
To sunder your chains
And bless your freedom
In the flux of evil foemen's veins!
At last, in that great family
Young and free,
Do not forget. But with good intent
Speak quietly of me.

However, since the plain has always been the playground of power politics, the Ukrainians have rarely been allowed to control their destiny. In
the twentieth century they were repeatedly suppressed. Their short-lived
Republic, which in 1918–20 served as one of the main battlegrounds for
Russia's Reds and Whites, was crushed by the victorious Red Army (see
pp. 928–9). They were victims of some of the Continent's most terrible
man-made disasters, and of wholesale genocide. Their casualties during
the wars of 1918–20, the collectivization campaign of the 1930s, the terror-
famine of 1932–3, and the devastations of the Second World War must
have approached 20 million. [**CHERNOBYL**] [**HARVEST**] Some among them,
frustrated by their impotence in face of Russians, Poles, and Germans,
and unable to reach the source of their oppression, struck out in desperate violence against their neighbours. [**BUCZACZ**] [**POGROM**] Their population is similar in size to that of England or France, and contains important
minorities; but the Ukrainians find very little place in the history books. For
many years, they were usually presented to the outside world as
'Russians' or 'Soviets' whenever they were to be praised, and as
'Ukrainians' only when they did evil. [**LETTLAND**] They did not recover a
free voice until the 1990s. The Republic of Ukraine eventually reclaimed its
independence in December 1991, facing an uncertain future.[2]

from the Plain and to descend to the Mediterranean was actually to undertake a
'cultural ascent'. Similarly, in modern times, to move along the European Plain
from west to east was widely considered to involve a 'cultural descent'.

This concept of the *Kulturgefälle* or 'cultural gradient' was implicit in the ideology of German nationalism, which reacted against the cultural dominance of the
West whilst laying claim to the East. It can be observed in some aspects of French
attitudes to Belgium and Germany, of German attitudes to the Slavs, of Polish attitudes to Russia and Ukraine, of Russian attitudes to the peoples of Central Asia.
Human nature always tempts people to imagine that they inhabit the cultural
upland whilst their neighbours inhabit the Styx. In the British Isles, for example, the

English majority are apt to perceive all cultural gradients sloping steadily downhill from the Himalayan peaks of Oxford or Hyde Park Corner to the 'Celtic fringe', the 'Scotch mist', the 'Irish bogs', and the 'Channel fog'. The English saying that 'wogs begin at Calais' is very close in spirit to France's *histoires belges*, to Metternich's most Viennese remark that 'Asia begins at the Landstrasse', or to the Polish proverb 'Na Rusi się musi' (in Russia, one has to). The prejudices inherent in their elastic cultural geography have undoubtedly been strengthened by fears of the instability of life on the Plain.

Thanks to the configuration of its approaches, one small branch-line of the European Plain has assumed special importance. The plain of Pannonia, now in modern Hungary, is the only extensive stretch of grassland south of the mountain chain. It is protected in the north by the main Carpathian ridge, and is bounded to the south by the middle reaches of the Danube. It has three natural gateways—one at Vienna from the west, another through the Iron Gates from the east, and a third through the Moravian Gap from the north. Its well-watered pastures offered a natural terminus for nomads moving from east to west, and a convenient springboard for many a barbarian tribe preparing to invade the Roman Empire. It was the home successively of the Gepids, the Huns (from whom it took the name of Hungaria), the Avars, the Cumans, the Slavs, and eventually the Magyars. The Magyars call it the *Alföld* (Lowland), and sometimes the *puszta*, a word of Slav origin meaning 'the wilderness'.

2. *The Mountains.* The central feature of the Peninsula is to be found in the majestic chain of mountains which curve in two elegant arcs from the Maritime Alps in Provence to the Carpathian Alps in Transylvania. This impressive barrier forms the Peninsula's backbone, creating a watershed which divides the northern Plain from the Mediterranean lands. The highest peaks in the westerly sections—Mont Blanc (4,807 m), the Matterhorn (4,478 m), or Gran Paradiso (4,061 m)—are significantly higher than those in the more easterly ranges—Triglav (2,863 m) in the Julian Alps, Gerlach (2,655 m) in the Tatras, or Moldoveanu (2,543 m) in Romania. Even so, with the eternal snows lying above the 3,200-m line on the south-facing *Sonnenseite* or 'sunshine side', and above the 2,500-m contour on the north-facing slopes, the upper ridges are impassable almost everywhere. Continental Europe's largest glacier, the Aletsch, which runs beneath the Jungfrau in the Bernese Oberland, has no equivalent in the East. But all the highest passes are closed by snow during the winter months. For well over 1,200 miles there are only three significant gaps in the chain—the Danube Gap in Bavaria, the Elbe Gap in Bohemia, and the Moravian Gap which links Silesia with Hungary.

For obvious reasons, the peoples who settled in the high valleys kept themselves aloof from the turbulent affairs of the lowlands, regarding their mountain home as a refuge and fortress to be defended against all intruders. Switzerland, which emerged in the thirteenth century as a confederation of mountain cantons (see p. 404), has retained something of this outlook to the present day. [**ALPI**]

The mountains, however, have had a unifying as well as a divisive function. The critical distances across them are not very great. Bourg St Maurice on the Isère and Martigny on the Rhône are, respectively, only 62 and 88 km (39 and 55 miles) from Italian Aosta. Austrian Innsbruck is 68 km from Bressanone (Brixen) in South Tirol; Sambor on the Dniester is 105 km from Uzhgorod, on a tributary of the Danube. Once the high alpine passes were tamed, the lands on either side of the ridge acquired common links, common interests, and to a large degree a common culture. Turin, for example, is much closer to Lyons and Geneva than it is to Rome. Milan or Venice have had stronger ties with Zurich, Munich, or Vienna than with distant Sicily. Bavaria, which was long cut off from the north by the vast forests and hills of central Germany, has shared much with nearby Lombardy. The old province of Galicia on the northern slopes of the Carpathians had much to do with Hungary over the ridge to the south. As any tourist can see, the worlds of the *Alpenraum* or of the Carpathians have survived, notwithstanding the barriers created by modern national states. [GOTTHARD]

The presence of the mountains gave special significance to the three major gaps between them. The Bavarian Gap, which follows the corridor of the middle Danube from Passau to Krems, became a capital link between north and south. The Elbe Gap opened Bohemia to the German influences which the Böhmer Wald might otherwise have impeded. Of equal importance, especially in earlier times, was the Moravian Gap, which formed a natural south-bound funnel for many of the peoples coming from the steppes. In early medieval times it provided the site of the first Slav state, the Great Moravian Empire (see Chapter IV). In historic times it has provided a pathway for innumerable armies, for Sobieski bound for the Turkish Wars or for Napoleon bound for Austerlitz. It ultimately leads, like the routes through the Bavarian and the Elbe Gaps, to the Danube near Vienna, 'the heart of the heart of Europe'. [SLAVKOV]

Of course, Europe possesses many mighty mountain chains in addition to its central spine. Mulhacen (3,487 m) in the Sierra Nevada, Le Pic de Néthou or d'Aneto (3,404 m) in the Pyrenees, Mt Etna (3,323 m) in Sicily, Monte Corno (2,912 m) in the Apennines, Musala (2,925 m) in Bulgaria, Korab (2,764 m) in Albania, and Olympus itself (2,917 m) are all peaks of alpine proportions. Not all Europeans are aware that the supreme summit of the Peninsula is to be found, not on Mont Blanc, but on the Elbrus Massif (5,642 m) in the Greater Caucasus.

3. *The Mediterranean*, that marvellously secluded sea which laps Europe's southern coastline, forms the basis of a self-contained geographical unit. Its sea lanes provide a ready channel for cultural, economic, and political contacts. It supplied the cradle for the classical world. Under the Caesars it became in effect a Roman lake. In the Renaissance and after, it was the focus of an interwoven civilization with important material as well as cultural dimensions.[6] Yet significantly, since the decline of Roman power, the Mediterranean has never been politically united. Seapower has never been sufficient to overcome the land-based empires which established themselves on its perimeter. Indeed, once the Muslim states took root in the Levant and in Africa, the Mediterranean became an area of permanent

ALPI

CONTRARY to first appearances, the high alpine valleys provided an excellent environment for early colonization and primitive agriculture. They possessed an abundance of sunshine, fresh water, fuel, building materials, pasture, and most importantly, security. Their remoteness was one of their assets. They were inhabited from the earliest times, and, as Hannibal discovered in the fourth century BC, fiercely defended. Traces of hearths found in the Drachenloch cave at 2,445 m in Switzerland's Tamina Valley date from the Riss–Wurm interglacial. Evidence of transhumance goes back 12,000 years. Roman building works and settlements were well established, especially in Val d'Aosta and the mining district of Noricum.[1] Villages perched on impregnable rocks, such as those in the Alpes Maritimes and Haute-Provence, were immune from bandits, invaders, and tax-collectors.

In medieval times, many alpine communities established a distinct political independence. The Swiss cantons are not the only example. The 52 communes of Briançon obtained a charter of liberties in 1343, six years before the Dauphin of Vienne sold the rest of his patrimony and his title to the King of France. They maintained their self-government until the Revolution.

Other districts avoided close control by the lack of communications. Barcelonnette, founded by the Counts of Provence and Barcelona, was ceded to France with the Pays d'Ubaye by the Treaty of Utrecht. But it could only be approached by a 15-hour mule trek until the permanent road was built in 1883. The villages of the Gorges du Verdon were not linked to the outside world until 1947. The lowest pass in the western Alps, the Col de l'Échelle, still does not possess an all-weather road on both sides.

Many roads were built for strategic reasons. An obelisk atop the Montgenèvre (1,054 m) announces in French, Latin, Italian, and Spanish that the route was opened for carriages in 1807 'while the Emperor Napoleon was triumphing over his enemies on the Oder and Vistula'. The highest road in Europe, over the Col du Galibier (3,242 m) was built in the 1930s as part of France's frontier defences.

The *Alpenraum* was exploited most intensively in the second half of the nineteenth century, when mixed farming was pushed to high altitudes, and the rural population rose dramatically. Yet the advent of modern communications provoked a mass exodus, reflected in the old Savoyard complaint: *Toujours ma chèvre monte et ma femme descend.* (My goat is always going up, and my wife going down.) The trend was reaching crisis proportions in many localities until the growth of hydroelectricity and mass tourism, especially winter skiing, after 1945.[2]

The antiquity and peculiarities of alpine life have inspired a wealth of specialized museums. The doyen is the Museo della Montagna, founded in 1874 in Turin. The Ethnographic Museum at Geneva, like many smaller ones, specializes in the tools, buildings, ceramic stoves, and folk art of alpine communities.

GOTTHARD

THE St Gotthard Pass commands the shortest passage across the central Alps. It can fairly claim to be Europe's most vital artery. By joining the valley of the Reuss, which flows northward into the Rhine, and the valley of the Ticino, which flows southwards into the Po, it provides the most direct link between southern Germany and northern Italy. At 2,108 m. it is significantly lower than its main rivals, which stay closed for longer periods during winter and bad weather. (See Appendix III, p. 1219.)

It is interesting that the St Gotthard route did not become a major thoroughfare until relatively late. It was not developed by the Romans, who preferred the more westerly passes, especially the Great St Bernard, the *Mons Jovis*. Nor was it used during the centuries after the fall of the Roman Empire in the West, despite the constant migrations from north to south. The problem lay with a short section of the upper Reuss valley, which for some three miles north of the modern Andermatt enters a precipitous rocky canyon. This Schollenen Gorge, whose upper entrance is lined with sheer cliffs, was sufficient to defy all traffic until extensive engineering works were undertaken. The works began some time after AD 1200. The entrance to the gorge was spanned by the magnificent single arch of the Devil's Bridge, whose lofty construction must have been no less demanding than the vault of a Gothic cathedral. At the steepest passage of the defile, rock-steps known as *scaliones* or *Schollen* were cut into the cliff, together with supports for the wooden platforms which were suspended alongside the overhangs. By AD 1300, when the hospice at the summit of the pass was dedicated to St Gotthard, Bishop of distant Hildesheim, it is clear that the flow of travellers had become steady and regular.

For nearly 600 summers the St Gotthard road served from June to November as Europe's premier north–south trail. From Altdorf at the head of Lake Lucerne to Biasca at the head of the Levantina, the stream of pilgrims, merchants, and soldiers faced 60 miles of rough climbing over four or five stages. The southern approach, through the eerie Valle Tremola or 'Valley of Trembling', the source of the translucent mineral called tremolite, was hardly less daunting than the Devil's Bridge. The zigzag path could only be negotiated by pack mules, by litters, and by foot travellers. Before the widening of the track in 1830, the only person to cross the pass in a wheeled vehicle was the Englishman Charles Greville, who won a bet in 1775 by paying a team of Swiss guides to carry his phaeton on their shoulders all the way.

The opening of the St Gotthard had important strategic consequences. It gave a particular stimulus to the Swiss district of Uri, the guardian of the pass, and hence to the Swiss Confederation as a whole. It enabled armies to march swiftly from Germany to Lombardy and back, a facility exploited by numerous emperors, and most notably by General Suvorov's Russians in 1799.

The construction of the St Gotthard railway in 1882 was no less remarkable than that of the St Gotthard road. It required a main tunnel of 15 km. under the summit, together with 80 others. At the famous *Pfaffensprung* or 'Parson's Leap' above Goschenen, trains enter the spiral trackway travelling right and emerge several hundred feet higher up travelling left. It cost the lives of many workmen, among them its designer. The railway tunnel has been joined since 1980 by a 16.5 km motorway tunnel, which carries six lanes of vehicles in all weathers and all seasons. Motor cyclists, who hug their machines as they themselves are hugged by leather-suited pillionesses, scream over the pass in minutes.

Yet modern travellers who stop by the Devil's Bridge can see a curious monument built into the rock beneath the modern viaduct. The inscription, in Tsarist Cyrillic, may be translated: TO THE VALIANT COMPANIONS OF FIELD MARSHAL COUNT SUVOROV-RIMNITSKY, PRINCE OF ITALY, WHO LOST THEIR LIVES DURING THE MARCH ACROSS THE ALPS IN 1799.[2] Raised on the centenary of that march, it is a suitable reminder both of the unity of Europe and of the grandeur of its mountains.

political division. Maritime and commercial powers such as Venice were incapable of uniting the whole. The European powers of the nineteenth century founded colonies from Syria to Morocco; but they were prevented by their rivalries from destroying the principal Muslim bastion in Turkey, and hence from creating a general hegemony.

Political disunity may well explain some of the cultural unities which persist across state frontiers in the Mediterranean. One deep-rooted feature has been found in the existence of 'parallel authorities', such as that of the Mafia in southern Italy, which defy all efforts to suppress them.[7] For most of recorded history, the peoples inhabiting the northern shores of the Mediterranean have outnumbered their southern neighbours by at least two to one, and hence have played a dominant role. A demographic explosion in North Africa promises to upset the traditional balance. In any case, the 'Mediterranean lands' have never been confined to the countries on the immediate shoreline. In Europe, the Mediterranean watershed lies far to the north, taking in Bavaria, Transylvania, and Ukraine. No power or culture, not even Rome, has ever united all of these.

Similar patterns are observable in the history of Europe's other enclosed seas—the Baltic and the Black Sea. The Baltic came to prominence at a relatively late date. It was the focus in Hansa times for German commercial expansion, and in the seventeenth century for Sweden's bid for glory. Yet no single Baltic power ever achieved the long dreamt-of *dominium maris*. German, Swedish,

Danish, Polish, and Russian rivalry has kept the Baltic disunited to the present day.[8] [**HANSA**]

The Black Sea—first known to the ancients as the *Axenos* or 'Inhospitable', later as the *Euxine* or 'Hospitable' and then as the *Pontus*—is the Mediterranean's siamese twin. It has passed through phases of Greek, Roman, Byzantine, and Ottoman dominance. Yet there again, the rise of a major landpower in Russia led to lasting divisions. Until the 1990s, the Soviet Union and its satellites faced NATO's southern flank in Turkey across hostile waters. More seriously, perhaps, much of the Black Sea is anoxic—that is, it is so heavily impregnated with hydrogen sulphide (H_2S) that 'its depths form the largest mass of lifeless water in the world'. If 'turnover' of the water strata were to occur, it would provoke 'the worst natural cataclysm to strike the earth since the last Ice Age'.[9]

Since undisputed command of Europe's seas has proved impossible, special attention has inevitably been given to their three strategic gateways. The Straits of Gibraltar, the Dardanelles, and the Danish Sound have handed inordinate power and influence to the states that control them. [**SUND**]

4. *The mainland trunk* of the Peninsula is amplified by several large sub-peninsulas which protrude into the surrounding seas. One such mountainous promontory, Scandinavia, adjoins the Baltic. Three others—Iberia, Italy, and the Balkan massif—adjoin the Mediterranean. Two more—Crimea and Caucasus—adjoin

---

SUND

LIKE its southern counterpart at the Straits of Gibraltar, the Danish Sound has been called Europe's jugular vein. Controlling the sole point of entry to a major sea, it possessed immense strategic and commercial value.[1] Its potential was first realized in 1200, when King Canute VI of Denmark imprisoned some Lübeck merchants until they paid for the right of passage into the Baltic herring grounds. From then on, the Sound Dues were exacted for as long as the Danes could enforce them. They were accepted by other medieval Baltic powers such as Poland, the Teutonic State, and the Hansa, and survived Sweden's challenge in the seventeenth century. They declined after 1732, but continued in being until the Redemption Treaty of 1857 when British naval power finally persuaded the Danes to commute their ancient interest. Even then, the Sound remained important until Prussia acquired Kiel in 1866 and by-passed the Sound by building the Kaiser Wilhelm Canal (1895). Once aeroplanes could overfly them, all maritime straits, including the English Channel, lost much of their strategic significance. All that is left is the memory of greatness, a ferry crossing, and the shade of Hamlet's Ghost on the battlements at Elsinore.

the Black Sea. Each of them, though physically joined to the Continent, has more readily been approached by sea than by land.

Scandinavia, once the site of the shrinking European ice-cap, could never support a large population. But its wild, western fiords are tempered by the Gulf Stream; the mountains are rich in minerals; and the morainic lakes left by the retreating ice are abundant in fish. What the Scandinavians lack in terms of climate, they have gained from a secure home base.

The Iberian Peninsula consists largely of a lofty tableland, separated from the rest of the Continent by the high peaks of the Pyrenees. Its eastern seaboard forms part of the Mediterranean world, and in early times was drawn successively into the Carthaginian, Roman, and Muslim spheres. But much of the arid interior is drawn through the valleys of the Douro, the Tagus, and the Guadalquivir towards the Atlantic. Hence, in modern times whilst Aragon expanded eastward into the Mediterranean, Portugal and Castile moved confidently to the western ocean. They were Europe's first colonial powers, and they once divided the world between them.

Italy is the most perfect of peninsulas. The alpine barrier to the north is seamless. The plain of the Po forms a rich natural larder. The long, craggy 'leg and toe' shelter a large number of fertile, impregnable valleys with ready access to the sea. Some of these Italian localities have been rich and extrovert; one of them, Rome, gave rise to the largest empire of the ancient world. But after Rome's decline they could so defend their independence that Italy was not reunited again for almost 2,000 years.

The Balkan Peninsula is far less welcoming than Italy. Its interior is more arid; the mountains, from the Dinaric Alps to the Rhodopes, more stony; the valleys more remote, the sea less accessible. Its main function in history has been to preserve the tenacious communities which cling to its soil, and which block the direct passage between the Mediterranean and the Danube Basin.

The peninsularity of *Crimea*—formerly known as Taurus—was emphasized by its hinterland on the Ukrainian steppe, which was not permanently settled until recent times. It looks to the sea, the sun, and the south, and formed part of successive east Mediterranean civilizations until conquered by the Russian Empire in 1783. [CHERSONESOS]

The Caucasus, too, has many peninsular characteristics. Although it is physically joined to land at both ends, to Europe in the north and to Asia in the south, the mountains which ring it on the landward side are so massive that its activities have inevitably been channelled seawards. The ridge of the Greater Caucasus, which tops 18,000 ft (5,486 m), is significantly higher than the Alps or the Carpathians. The Lesser Caucasus to the south attains a similar elevation on Mt Ararat (16,786 ft or 5,165 m). The inhabitants of the Caucasus are Eurasians in more senses than one. [CAUCASIA]

5. Europe was endowed by Nature with ten thousand islands. The largest of them—Iceland, Ireland, Great Britain, Corsica, Sardinia, Sicily, and Crete—have been able at various times to develop distinct cultures and political entities of their own. One sceptred isle, in exceptional circumstances and for a very brief

period, was able to amass the largest empire in world history. They are all part of Europe, yet physically and psychologically separate. As the twin slots on the post-boxes in Messina and Syracuse rightly indicate, there are two different worlds—*Sicilia* and *Continente*.

Many of the lesser islands, from Spitzbergen to Malta, stand like watchmen in the lonely sea. But others are grouped in comforting archipelagos that support a sense of mutual interest and identity. The Shetlands, Orkneys, and Hebrides off Great Britain; the Balearics off Catalonia, and, above all, the Ionians, the Sporades, the Cyclades, and the Dodecanese off Greece all have their collective as well as their individual characters. [FAROE]

Nowadays, however, insularity is shrinking fast. Great Britain, for example, built its overseas empire in an era when naval power could provide effective insulation from continental affairs. But the same degree of separation is no longer possible. Naval power has been superseded by aeroplanes, and aeroplanes by ICBMs, that render surface features such as the English Channel almost irrelevant. The British Empire has disappeared, and Britain's dependence on her continental neighbours has correspondingly increased. The opening of the Channel Tunnel in 1994 was an event of more than symbolic importance. It marked the end of Britain's island history.

Given the principal divisions of the Peninsula, three sub-regions have gained functions of particular importance: the Midi, the Danube Basin, and the Volga corridor.

The Midi or 'South' of modern France abuts the Mediterranean coast between the Pyrenees and the Alps. For anyone cruising the Mediterranean, it offers the only painless passage to the northern Plain. A landing in the Midi offers the immediate prospect of an easy journey to the main part of the Continent. From ancient Marseille, or from Arles at the mouth of the Rhône, one can move without hindrance either across the lowland of Languedoc to the Atlantic or round the flank of the Massif Central to the headwaters of the Loire and the Seine. The Rhône's main tributary, the Saône, leads straight to the Belfort Gap and a gentle descent to the Rhine. At every other point between Gibraltar and the Dardanelles, the early northbound traveller would be faced with alpine passes, dead ends, or lengthy detours.

The felicitous location of the Midi, bridgeland between the Mediterranean and the Plain, had important consequences. It provided the most effective setting for the fusion of the ancient civilization of the south with the 'barbarian' cultures of the north. For the Romans it offered, as Cisalpine Gaul, the first major province beyond Italy. For the Franks, the first of the barbarians to establish a major empire of their own, it offered the promise of the sun, and of high culture. They established a foothold in AD 537, a century after the fall of Roman power, and never let go. The resultant Kingdom of France, partly northern, partly Mediterranean, developed the most influential and the most universal culture of the Continent.

The Danube Basin, like the Midi, links the Plain with the Mediterranean; but in this case the link lies west–east. The Danube rises in the Black Forest, crosses

---

FAROE

OF all Europe's many islands, none can match the lonely grandeur of the Faroes, whose high black basalt cliffs rise from the stormy North Atlantic midway between Iceland, Norway, and Scotland. Seventeen inhabited islands, centred on Stremoy and the principal harbour of Tórshavn, support a modern population of 45,464 (1984), mainly from fishing. Descended from Norsemen who settled in the eighth century, the Faroese answered to the *Gulating*, the assembly of western Norway, and to their own local *Loegting*. [**DING**] Their language is a dialect of Norwegian; but they have their own sagas, their own poets and artists, their own culture. Yet from 1814, when Norway was annexed to Denmark, 'Europe's smallest democracy' was subjected to a Danish governor and to Danish interests.

As a result, the Faroese national movement came to be directed against Denmark, 'the one Scandinavian country with which they have least in common'.[1] In this the Faroese followed in the steps of Iceland, aiming above all to preserve their identity. The big moment came in June 1940, when, with Copenhagen under Nazi occupation, a British warship ordered a Torshavn skipper to hoist the Faroese flag in place of the Danish one. The referendum of 1946, which opted for unlimited sovereignty, preceded the compromise settlement of 1 April 1948. Faroe accepted home rule within the Danish realm. In 1970 it was granted independent membership of the Nordic Council. The *Norðurlandahusið* or 'Nordic House' in Tórshavn was built with Swedish wood, Norwegian slate, Danish glass, and Icelandic roofing, and was equipped with Finnish furniture.

---

the mountain line in the Bavarian Gap at Passau, and flows east for 1,500 miles to the Black Sea. For peoples approaching from the east it offered the simplest route to the interior; for the peoples of the Plain, the most tempting itinerary to the southern seas. For most of its length, it constituted the principal frontier line of the Roman Empire and hence of 'civilization'. In modern times, its catchment area supplied the territorial base for the great multinational empire of the Habsburgs, and the scene for the principal confrontation in Europe between Christianity and Islam. [**DANUBIUS**]

Of all the bridgelands, however, none is more vital than that through which the Volga flows. By modern convention, the Continental divide is taken to lie on the line of the Ural Mountains and the Ural River. To the west of the Ural, in the Volga Basin, one is in Europe; to the east of the Ural, in Siberia or Kazakhstan, one is in Asia. On the banks of the Volga, therefore, at Saratov or Tsaritsyn, one stands truly at the gate. For the Volga marks the first European station on the highroad of the steppe; and it fills the corridor which joins the Baltic with the

DANUVIUS

IN ancient times, the River Danube represented one of the great dividing
lines of the European Peninsula. Established as the frontier of the
Roman Empire in the 1st century AD, the Latin *Danuvius*, or Greek *Ister*
divided civilization from barbarity.

In later times, however, the Danube was to develop into one of Europe's
major thoroughfares, an open boulevard linking West and East.[1] In
Bernini's famous composition for the Fountain of the Four Rivers in the
Piazza Navona in Rome, it is the Danube which is taken to personate
Europe alongside Africa's Nile, Asia's Ganges, and America's Plate.

In its upper reaches, as the Donau, the river flows through the heart of
the Germanic world. A plaque in the Fürstenberg Park at Donaueschingen
in the Black Forest marks its source: *HIER ENTSPRINGT DIE DONAU.*
Passing the castle of Sigmaringen, home of the Hohenzollerns, the river
passes Ulm and Regensburg, chief cities of the Holy Roman Empire, and
after Passau enters the 'eastern realm' of Oesterreich. In Austria, it guided
the route of the [**NIBELUNGEN**]. It passes Linz, where the Emperor Frederick
III was buried under his motto of *A-E-I-O-U*, meaning *Austria erit in orbe
ultima*; Amstetten, where Franz Ferdinand is buried; Kierling, where
Kafka died; and Eisenstadt, which is Haydn's last resting-place:

> *Himmel habe Dank!*   (Heaven, receive our thanks!
> *Ein harmonischer Gesang*   My life's course
> *War mein Lebenslauf*   Was one harmonious hymn.)

Vienna, as Metternich remarked, is where 'Europe' meets 'Asia'.

In its middle reaches as the Duna, the broadening stream enters
Hungary, the land of the Magyars driven like a wedge through the lands of
the Slavs on either side. At Bratislava/Pozsony/Pressburg, it laps the
sometime capital of 'Upper Hungary', now the capital of the Slovakian
Republic. Fertoód was the site of the Eszterházy's 'second Versailles';
Esztergom, the home of the Hungarian Primates. Szentendre (St Andrew),
once a refuge for Serbian exiles, is now a mecca for bohemian artists. At
Buda and Pest, a Turkish Castle on one bank faces an English-style
Parliament on the other. [**BUDA**]

In the lower reaches, beyond the Iron Gates, the river flows from
Catholicism into Orthodoxy. [**NIKOPOLIS**] is where Wulfila translated the
Greek bible into Gothic, 'the starting-point of Germanism'. [**BIBLIA**]
Romania on the left side claims to be a descendant of Trajan's Dacia.
Serbia and Bulgaria on the right bank, long occupied by the Ottomans
(who called it the Tuna), were founded on top of Byzantine provinces.
Chileavecche was once a Genoese outpost. The last landing-stage is at
Sulina in the Delta, in Europe's largest bird reserve, in a world not of civi-
lization but of eternal Nature.[2]

Rivers to the geographer are the bearers of sediment and trade. To the historian they are the bearers of culture, ideas, and sometimes conflict.[3] They
are like life itself. For 2,888 kilometres from Donaueschingen to the Delta,
the flow never stops.

Caspian. Until the seventeenth century the Volga also happened to coincide with the limit of Christian settlement, and hence with an important cultural boundary. It is Europe's largest river, and a worthy guardian of the Peninsula which stretches 'from the Atlantic to the Urals'.

Environmental change is taken for granted in all aspects of physical geography. Yet traditional disciplines such as geology give the impression that the pace of change is so slow as to be marginal within the human time-frame. Only recently has the realization dawned that the modern environment is far less fixed than was once supposed.

Climate, for example, is constantly on the move. In *Civilisation and Climate* (1915), the American scholar Ellsworth Huntington published the fruits of his ingenious research into the giant redwoods of California. It was the starting-point of historical climatology. Since the redwoods can live for more than 3,000 years, and since the annual rings of their trunks vary in size according to the warmth and humidity of every year that passes, the cross-section of a redwood trunk provides a systematic record of climatic variations over three millennia. Huntington's technique, now called dendrochronology, inspired a 'pulsatory theory' of alternating climatic phases which could be applied to the past of all the continents. This in turn produced a special brand of environmental determinism. The growth of classical civilization in the Mediterranean could be attributed to the onset of a moist phase which permitted the cultivation of wheat in North Africa, for instance, whilst northern Europe floundered under an excessive deluge of rain, fog, and frost. The decline of the ancient world could be attributed to a climatic shift in the opposite direction, which brought Mediterranean sunshine north of the Alps. The migrations of the Mongols, which directly affected the history both of China and of Europe (see pp. 364–6), could be attributed to an extended drought in the oases of Central Asia. In his later work, *The Mainsprings of Civilisation* (1945), Huntington explored other factors of the physical environment such as diet and disease, and their interplay with human heredity.[10] Crude linkages gave the subject a bad name, and attempts have since been made to refine the earlier findings.

Nevertheless, periodicity theories continue to have their advocates. 'Cyclomania' is not yet dead: the rise and fall of civilizations has been linked to everything from sunspots to locust swarms. Whatever their particular preference, scholars are bound to be drawn to the phenomenon of environmental variation, and to its impact on human affairs. After all, it is a matter of simple fact that climate *does* vary. Parts of the Roman world which once supported a flourishing population now find themselves in desert wasteland. Viking graves were once dug in plots in Iceland and Greenland, which permafrost renders impenetrable to pick or shovel. In the seventeenth century, annual fairs were held on the winter ice of the Thames in London; and armies marched across the frozen Baltic in places where similar ventures would now be suicidal. The European environment is not a fixed entity, even if its subtler rhythms cannot always be exactly measured.

[VENDANGE]

Arnold Toynbee's *A Study of History* (1933–9), which offered a comprehensive theory of the growth, breakdown, and disintegration of civilizations, is but the most prominent of environmental histories. After discussing the genesis of civilizations in terms of mankind's response to the 'challenge of the environment', he propounds his law on 'the virtues of adversity'. The Roman Campagna, the semi-desert of Judah, the sandy wastes of Brandenburg, and the hostile shore of New England are all cited as dour environments that have generated a vigorous response. One might add the backwoods of Muscovy. After outlining 'the stimuli of blows, pressures, and penalisations', he comes to the concept of the 'golden mean.' If the Slavs in Eastern Europe suffered from a lack of early stimuli, the Celts and the Scandinavians suffered from excessive adversity. According to Toynbee, the nearest thing to ideal conditions was experienced by the Hellenic civilization of ancient Greece—'the finest flower of the species that has ever yet come to bloom'.[11]

Nowadays, though the impact of the environment on man is by no means discounted, special attention is also paid to the impact of man on the environment. [ECO] Historical ecology emerged as an academic subject well before the onset of the 'greenhouse effect' alerted everyone to its importance. It calls on a wide range of technological wizardry. Aerial archaeology has revolutionized our knowledge of the prehistoric landscape. Sedimentology, which studies the patterns of riverine deposits, and glaciology, which studies the patterns of ice formation in glaciers, have been mobilized to give new precision to environmental change over centuries and millennia. Geochemical analysis, which measures tell-tale phosphates in the soil of ancient habitations, has given archaeologists another potent tool. Palynology, or pollen analysis, which analyses ancient grains preserved in the earth, permits the reconstruction of former plant-life spectra. Specialists debate the evidence for 'the great elm decline', for the crops of prehistoric agriculture, or for the chronology of forest clearances. Peat analysis, which depends on the composition and rate of accumulation of peat bogs, has identified five major climatic 'deteriorations' in the period between 3000 BC and AD 1000. The science of prehistory has moved far from the time when archaeologists could only dig objects out of the earth, and struggle to match their finds with fragmentary references in the writings of the ancients. [C14]

Today's prehistorians also place great emphasis on the processes of prehistoric social change. Time was when almost all new cultural phenomena were explained in terms of human migration. The emergence of new burial practices, of new rites, of new artefacts, or of a new language group was automatically linked to the presumed arrival of new peoples. Now, though prehistoric migrations are not discounted, it is well understood that material and cultural changes can be explained in terms of evolution within existing populations. Technological advances, religious conversions, and linguistic evolutions must all be taken into consideration.

European prehistory has to be related to two chronologies of entirely different orders of magnitude. Geological time, which spans the estimated 4,550 million

VENDANGE

HISTORICAL climatology relies on records preserved in books, and on records preserved by nature herself. The former include diaries, travellers' tales, and weather data kept by estate managers, grain merchants, or wine-growers. The latter involves the study of tree-rings, fossils, sediments, stalactites, and glaciers.[1]

The precision of Nature's own records is amazing, even within historical times. The annual deposits of the great Salt Lake in Crimea have been logged to 2294 BC. Some of the great stalagmites, such as that in the cave of Aven d'Orgnac in the Jura, are over 7,000 years old. Variations in the density of their calcite deposits faithfully reflect historical rainfall patterns.

Phenology is the study of fruit-ripening, and has been widely exploited in relation to the history of wine-harvests. Every year for centuries, many French vineyards issued a public proclamation of the date for commencing the collection of grapes. An early date signified a sunny growing season; a late date signified a cool season. By listing the dates of the *première cuvée* in a particular location, historians can produce complete 'phenological series' over very long periods. By collating the phenological series for different locations, they can work out the mean seasonal date for each region. These *courbes de vendanges* or 'wine-harvest curves' present precise indications of climatic change.[2] (See Appendix III, p. 1220.)

The movement of glaciers provides another source of information. Glaciers advance in periods of cold, and retreat in periods of relative warmth. What is more, the length of Europe's alpine glaciers in any particular year can often be established from eyewitness accounts, from old prints, or from official records. Archives such as those of the Chambre des Comptes de Savoie contain inspectors' reports on glacial advances which destroyed villages or prevented the inhabitants from paying their tithes and taxes. In 1600, for example, a year of disaster at Chamonix, people on both the French and Italian side of Mont Blanc lived in fear for their future. Detailed studies of the *Mer de Glace*, of the *Rhonegletscher* in the Valais, or the *Vernagt* in Tyrol, all of whose termini in the late sixteenth century stood several kilometres below their current position, demonstrate the reality of Europe's 'Little Ice Age'. Periods of glacial maxima peaked in 1599–1600, 1640–50, 1680, 1716–20, and 1770. In 1653 local people defiantly placed a statue of St Ignatius at the base of the Aletsch glacier; and the glacier stopped. The contemporary glacial retreat has continued since 1850.[3]

Climatic data are most convincing when different sources produce the same results. Wildly fluctuating weather in the 1530s, for example, is confirmed both by tree-rings from Germany, and by the Franco-Swiss vendanges (see Appendix III). The coldest year for Europe's vineyards occurred in 1816. Collection of the ruined grapes began in eastern France on All Saints Day (1 November). Mary Shelley, vacationing in nearby Switzerland, could not even go out for walks. Instead, she stayed indoors, and invented Frankenstein.

C14

4 0,000 years is the length of time within which isotopes of Carbon14 show measurable signs of radioactivity. This means that radiocarbon dating methods can be applied to organic materials from the late palae-olithic to the recent past. 35,000 BC is approximately the date when the Neanderthals died out and when humans lived at Cromagnon.

The value of C14, whose exploitation gave rise to a Nobel prize for chemistry in 1960, derives from the spontaneous and steady rate of its decay. It is the only one of three carbon isotopes to be radioactive, and it accumulates in all living matter through the action of cosmic rays on the atmosphere. It is present in bones, body tissue, shells, meat, hair, rope, cloth, wood, and many other materials which abound on archaeological sites. It starts to decay as soon as the organism dies, and continues to do so over a half-life of 5,730 years and a mean life of c.8,033 years. A 1 per cent decrease can be measured to c.80 years.

The calibration of results is fraught with variables. But it has been greatly improved in recent years by the discovery of complementary techniques that provide a basis for comparison. Thermoluminescence (TL) and electron spin resonance (ESR), for example, detect minute changes caused by natural radioactivity in the crystal lattice of minerals, and are specially effective in dating ceramics. The examination of carbon isotopes by Accelerator Mass Spectrometry (AMS) has extended the chronological range to c.100,000 years, throwing doubt on previous age estimates of the oldest humanoid remains.[1]

After three decades of development, radiocarbon dating has been used to construct impressive data collections. Archaeologists of the mesolithic, for instance, can consult catalogues which list the dates of finds from all over Europe. A piece of linear beaded pottery from Eitzum in Lower Saxony is dated 6480 ± 210; charcoal from a site at Vlasać in Serbia, 7930 ± 77; a charred pine-branch from Calowanie near Warsaw, 10,030 ± 120.[2] Every new measurement consolidates the overall picture.

The most sensational challenge for C14, however, arose with the dating of the Turin Shroud. Supposedly brought to Europe from the Holy Land in the fourteenth century, the shroud bears the faint impression of a dead man's face and body, and had been venerated as a relic of the Crucifixion. Tests undertaken in 1988–9 showed that the cloth of the shroud had been manufactured between AD 1260 and 1390. But they did not explain the dead man's image.[3]

years since the formation of the earth, is divided into eras, periods, and epochs from the Azoic to the Holocene. Human life, in contrast, is confined to the terminal tip of geological time. Its earliest origins occur in Africa in the middle of the Pliocene. It reaches Europe in the middle of Pleistocene. It does not move into the stage called 'Civilization' until after the end of the Quaternary. Europe in its present form is no more than five million years old; and the human presence in Europe has not lasted for more than one million years (see Appendix III, p. 1215).

On the scale of geological time, the formation of the European Peninsula must be counted as a recent event. Eighty million years ago most of the land that was destined to constitute Europe lay half-submerged in a scattered archipelago of mid-ocean islands. After that, as the Atlantic opened up to its fullest extent, the drifting African plate closed the ocean gap from the south. Five million years ago Africa was still directly joined to Eurasia, with the Alps and the Atlas mountains piled high on either side of the dry Mediterranean trench. But then 'the natural dam at Gibraltar broke'. 'A gigantic waterfall of sea-water, one hundred times the size of Victoria Falls' rushed in, and completed the Peninsula's familiar outline.[12] Two final afterthoughts less than ten thousand years ago opened up the English Channel and the Danish Sound, thereby creating first the British Isles and then the Baltic Sea.

Over the last million years, the young Peninsula lived through seventeen ice ages. At its greatest extent, the ice sheet reached to a line joining North Devon, Hanover, Cracow, and Kiev. Humanoid visitors made their appearance during the warmer interglacials. The earliest traces of Man in Europe have been found at sites near Vertesszölös in Hungary and at Isernia in Italy, both dated 850–700,000 BC. At Isernia, *Homo erectus* ate a varied diet from the fauna of a savannah-type countryside. At Terra Amata, on the beach near Nice, a human footprint 400,000 years old was found in hard-baked fireside clay. In 1987 a cache of fossilized human remains was discovered deep in a cave chamber at Atapuerca near Burgos in Spain.

In the course of the ice ages, human evolution progressed though the stages of *homo erectus, homo sapiens,* and *homo sapiens sapiens* (modern humankind). The remains of a transitional creature were found in a quarry in the Neanderthal Valley near Dusseldorf in 1856, thereby provoking the public debate on human origins that has continued ever since. [MONKEY] The Neanderthals, with massive bones and short limbs, are thought to have been a specifically European variant adapted to glacial conditions. They used flint tools, understood the secret of fire, buried their dead, and cared for the living. Their particular brand of 'Mousterian' stone technology was named after a site in Dordogne. They hunted in organized collectives, as shown by the sites at La Cotte de St Brelade on the island of Jersey, or more recently at Zwoleń in Poland, which was used over many millennia for the entrapment of stampeding horses and mammoths. They passed away some 40–35,000 years ago, during the last interglacial. Recent finds at St Césaire have suggested that they survived for a time alongside new immigrants who were arriving from Africa and the Middle East.[13]

The newcomers were slight in build, but much more dexterous, possessing finger-bones only half as thick as those of their predecessors. As shown by remains from Sungir in northern Russia, they could thread very fine bone needles and could sew clothes. They are widely known as 'cavemen', but caves were only one of their habitats. They roamed the plains, hunting bison and mammoth and gathering wild plants. At Mezirich in Ukraine, one ice-age encampment has survived intact. Its spacious huts were built from hundreds of mammoth bones covered with hides. [**GAT-HUNTER**]

The end of the last ice age was preceded by the daddy of all volcanic explosions. The pressure of the African plate had opened a fault-line running along the bed of the Mediterranean; and it created a string of volcanoes, which still exist. Some 36,000 years ago the largest of these volcanoes blew its cone, leaving a trail of volcanic ash that reached to the Volga. At Pozzuoli, near Naples, it left a *caldera* or crater ring some seven miles wide. It was the forerunner of all the great eruptions of historic times—at Thera in 1628 BC (see pp. 93–4), at Vesuvius in AD 79 [**PANTA**], at Etna in 1669. It is a sobering reminder that mankind has always been skating on the fragile crust of its geological heritage.

By convention, the human sector of European prehistory is usually related to the 'Three-Age System' of Stone, Bronze, and Iron. The system was first set out in 1836 by a Danish antiquary, Christian Thomsen; and it provides a framework of time based on the changing implements of primitive man. Hence, the palaeolithic (Old Stone Age) refers to the vast period before the end of the ice ages when Man worked with chipped stone tools. The mesolithic (Middle Stone Age) refers to the much more recent period following the last of the ice, c.8000–3000 BC. The two millennia which preceded the Christian or Common Era, which forms our own, arbitrary scheme of chronology [**ANNO DOMINI**], were taken up successively by the neolithic (New Stone Age), the Bronze Age, and the Iron Age. Each of these technological 'Ages' can be subdivided into early, middle, and late phases. It is essential to remember, however, that the Three-Age System is *not* based on any absolute scale of time. At any given moment, one place might have lingered in the neolithic whilst others had reached the Iron Age. In any given region, there could be peoples living at different stages of development, or using different forms of technology simultaneously.

The Old Stone Age reached back for a million years. It overlapped with the penultimate era of quaternary geological time, the Pleistocene, and with the last great glaciations—known respectively as Mindel, Riss, and Würm. Apart from Neanderthal and Le Moustier, invaluable finds have been made at Cromagnon (1868), Grimaldi (1874), Combe-Capelle (1909), Chancelade (1888), and at all points between Abbeville and Ojców, each associated with particular humanoid types, periods, or cultures. At Aurignac, Solutré, and Abri La Madeleine, sculptures of the human form first appeared in the shape of figurines such as the 'Venus of Willendorf' or the 'Venus of Laussel'. With the Magdalenian period, at the end of the palaeolithic age when bone tools were in fashion, under the shadow of the last ice cap, the high point of cave art was reached. Magnificent

---

GAT-HUNTER

THE origins of organized political communities, or 'states', have rarely been sought before the neolithic period. Some theorists, including Marxists, have looked to the tribes and tribal chiefdoms of the Bronze and Iron Ages. Others have looked to the neolithic revolution in agriculture and to the associated growth of fixed settlement. According to V. Gordon Childe, for instance, the preconditions for a state organized on residence, not kinship, required territorial authority, surplus capital, symbolic monuments, long-distance trade, labour specialization, stratified society, scientific knowledge, and the art of writing. Such preconditions were first met in Egypt and Mesopotamia, and in Europe, in the city-states of ancient Greece (see Chapter II).

Analysis of the complex society of hunter-gatherers, however, projects the topic much further back in time. Hunter-gatherers or gatherer-hunters, it seems, were not saved by the advent of agriculture from the immemorial threat of extinction. On the contrary, they enjoyed many millennia of 'unending leisure and affluence'. They were not unfamiliar with agriculture when it arose, but rejected it, except as a marginal or supplementary activity.

What is more, in the later stages of prehistory they developed social structures which permitted differentiated specialization. In addition to the far-roaming hunter-warriors and the home-based gatherers, some groups could specialize in the new labour-intensive processes of fishing, seafood collection, harvesting wild grass and nuts, or bird-trapping. Others were free to specialize as organizers or as negotiators in the formation of federations and regional alliances. In other words, the hunter-gatherer bands possessed an embryonic representative and political class. The historical problem can be addressed by analogy with the native peoples of North America, Australia, or New Guinea.

The big question about the hunter-gatherers, therefore, does not seem to be 'How did they progress towards the higher level of an agricultural and politicised society?' but 'What persuaded them to abandon the secure, well-provided and psychologically liberating advantages of their primordial lifestyle?'.[1]

---

subterranean galleries have survived at Altamira in Spain (1879) and at Lascaux in Dordogne (1940), leading some commentators to talk of a 'Franco-Cantabrian School'. In a cave near Menton on the Riviera, a hoard of *Cassis rufa* shells from the Indian Ocean was found. The shells were thought to possess life-giving powers, and their presence would seem to confirm both a sophisticated religious system and a far-flung trading network.[14] [**LAUSSEL**]

LAUSSEL

T HE 'Venus of Laussel' dates from c.19000 BC. It is a bas-relief, sculptured on the inner wall of a cave in the Dordogne, and painted with red
ochre. It shows a seated female figure with no surviving facial features,
but with a large coiffe of hair drawn behind the shoulder, long pendulant
breasts, and knees opened wide to display the vulva. The left hand rests
on a pregnant belly. The crooked right arm holds aloft a crescent-shaped
bison horn.

Like most of the human images of earliest European art, covering over
90 per cent of human history, the manifestly female gender of this artefact
is both striking and eloquent. It is widely taken to represent the palaeolithic Godhead, a variant of the 'Great Cosmic Mother', whose cult dominated the rites of a matriarchal community. According to one interpretation, it would have presided over masked ritual dancing, where women,
men, and children sought mystical communion with the animal spirits.
Less certainly, it formed the pinnacle of cave-life imagery where the
cave was the 'Womb-tomb-maze of the Great Earth Mother' and where
'blood–woman– moon–bison horn–birth–magic–the cycle of life are analo-
gised in a continuous resonance, or harmony, of sacred energies.'[1]

The matriarchal, or 'matrifocal' character of prehistoric society has
been accepted by most theorists, from Marx and Engels onwards.
However the assumption that matriarchy only operated at the most 'primitive' level is not now regarded as valid. In his work on myths, the poet
Robert Graves explored the origins and fate of matrifocal culture in
Europe, tracing the decline of woman's status from ancient divinity to
classical slavery.[2]

Others have considered the female origins of speech, and hence of conscious culture. In humanity's long 'nursery age', women and children may
conceivably have learned to talk whilst the menfolk were away hunting. If
so, the gender difference can only have been one of degree, since boy-
children must surely have learned to verbalize alongside their sisters.

More convincing is the strong possibility that matriarchal and patriarchal societies overlapped, creating a wide range of hybrid forms. If the
Gimbutas theory is correct (see p. 86), the advance on to the Pontic
Steppes of the late neolithic 'Kurgan peoples' marked the arrival not only
of the Indo-Europeans but also of warlike, patriarchal traditions. On the
other hand, after the subsequent arrival of the Sauromatians—the first
wave of the Irano-Sarmatian confederation—the matriarchal newcomers
began to mingle c.3000 BC with their patriarchal predecessors. In this connection, Herodotus retailed a curious story how Amazon warriors fled the
southern shores of the Black Sea and, after mating with Scythian braves,
set up a new homeland 'three days march from the Maeotian Lake'. The

story was rejected as sheer invention until archaeologists began to uncover the skeletons of female warriors in Sauromatian graves. A Sarmatian princess of a still later vintage, whose tomb was found at Kolbiakov on the Don, had been buried with her battle-axe.[3]

Like every committed doctrine, the feminist approach to 'preherstory' has its extravagances. But it is not entirely implausible:

Because we have separated humanity from nature, subject from object, . . . and universities from the universe, it is enormously difficult for anyone but a poet or a mystic to understand . . . the holistic and mythopoeic thought of Ice Age humanity. The very language we use . . . speaks of tools, hunters, and men, when every statue and painting we discover cries out that this Ice Age humanity was a culture of art, the love of animals, and women . . . Gathering is as important as hunting, but only hunting is discussed. Storytelling is discussed, but the storyteller is a hunter rather than an old priestess of the moon. Initiation is imagined, but the initiate is not the young girl in menarche about to wed the moon, but a young man about to become a great hunter.[4]

Western civilization, however defined, is generally thought to have its roots in the Judaeo-Christian tradition and in the Classical World. Both those source cultures, whether of Yehovah or of Zeus-Jupiter, were dominated by male Godheads. Yet one should not forget that through eons of earlier time the Godhead was female. One can only presume that humankind, so long as it was a tiny vulnerable species, was more moved by the feminine role of generation and birth than by the male role of killing and death.

All sorts of people have dreamed of a long-lost paradise in the remote past. Romantics, nationalists, and Marxists have all had their idealized Gardens of Eden, their semi-mythical Golden Ages. Now feminists are doing the same.[5] One thing is certain. The Venus of Laussel, and others like her, was no sex object of male gratification. In fact, she was no Venus at all.

The Middle Stone Age or mesolithic represents a transitional era when Man was adapting to rapidly improving climatic conditions. The terminal moraine of the last Finno-Scandinavian ice sheet has been dated to 7300 BC. Technological advance was characterized by the appearance of microliths—very small, pointed or bladed flints. Greatly increased supplies of fish and shellfish encouraged settlement along the lakes, rivers, and coasts. Earlier cultures identified in the south, as at Mas d'Azil in the Pyrenees, were complemented by more northerly ones, such as Maglemose in Zealand or Ertebølle in Jutland, where deep-sea fishing emerged. For the first time, the mesolithic stone axe was capable of felling the largest trees.

The New Stone Age, or neolithic, was marked by the transition from food-gathering to food production. The domestication of plants and animals, otherwise known as agriculture, was accompanied by further improvements in stone technology, where grinding, polishing, and boring produced implements of far superior quality. This 'Neolithic Revolution' began in the Middle East in the eighth millennium BC, in northern parts of Europe as late as the second. It saw the beginnings of cattle, sheep, and pig-farming; of horse-breeding and of hybridization to produce mules; of systematic cereal production; of ploughing, weaving, pottery, mining. It also saw the principal drive for the comprehensive colonization of the Peninsula, where previously only scattered settlements had existed.

Two main lines of neolithic advance have been identified. One, which is associated with the *Linearbandkeramik* or 'linear pottery', moved rapidly up the Danube Valley into central Europe. In a brief spurt of perhaps 700 years in the fifth millennium, it crossed the 1,500 miles between present-day Romania and the Netherlands. The pioneer settlements clustered round great communal long-houses built from the largest timbers of the newly cleared forest. Problems of agricultural over-exploitation and of manpower shortages led to temporary retreats, followed by the characteristic reoccupation of abandoned sites. A second line of advance, associated with the spread of a 'stamped-pottery' culture, moved westwards round the Mediterranean shore. In the fourth millennium there were further extensions of agricultural settlement into the Peninsula's western and northern extremities—into Iberia, France, and Switzerland, the British Isles, Scandinavia, and eastern parts of the Great Plain. By c.3200 BC the whole of the Peninsula below latitude 62 °N was occupied by various types of a food-producing economy.[15] [GAT-HUNTER] [TAMMUZ] [VINO]

In this era lake villages were built such as those at Charavines near Grenoble, at Chalain in the Jura, on the Federsee in Württemberg, or on Lake Zurich. They are particularly valuable to archaeologists, since the mud of the lake has acted as an almost perfect preservative of everything from kitchen utensils to half-eaten apple-cores. [TOLLUND]

Overall, six principal neolithic zones have been established: an east Mediterranean and Balkan zone, under strong influences from the Levant; the Tripol'ye–Cucuteni zone on the Ukrainian steppe; the Baltic–Black Sea zone of cord-impressed ceramics and of the 'battle-axe' people; the central zone of linear ceramics, with its heartland in Bohemia but with outposts west of the Rhine and east of the Vistula; the northern zone of the Great Plain, dominated by funnel-necked beaker ware; and the western zone of the 'bell beaker' people, stretching from southern Spain to the British Isles and Scandinavia. Late neolithic cultures were often connected with vast megalith constructions varying from simple dolmens or menhirs to huge chambered tombs, stone avenues, and stone circles. The principal sites are at New Grange (Ireland) and Maes Howe in the Orkneys, at Carnac in Brittany, and at Avebury and Stonehenge in Wiltshire. The risky suggestion has been made that they owe their

TAMMUZ

TAMMUZ, son of Ishtar or Ashetar, Mother of the Universe, was the Corn God of ancient Babylon. At the end of the harvest, the stalks of the last sheaves were plaited into straw fans or cages, in which the god could take refuge until the next season.

These corn idols or 'dollies' have continued to be made wherever wheat is cultivated. In the Balkans a dolly known as the Montenegrin Fan is still fashioned in the shape of its predecessors on the Nile. In Germany and Scandinavia straw stars and straw angels are popular items of Christmas decoration.

In England a vast repertoire of corn dollies was saved by rural conservationists when the art began to die out in the 1950s. Simple designs such as the Neck and the Horseshoe, the Knot and the Cat's Paw, the Bell and the Lantern, can be found in all the wheat-growing counties. Local specialities include the Shropshire Mare, the Derbyshire Crown, and the Cambridge Umbrella. The Kern Babby of Northumberland and the Ivy Girl of Kent are nothing other than modern versions of 'Mother Earth', distant daughters of Egyptian Ishtar, of Demeter of the Greeks, and of Roman Ceres.[1]

The world knows three major staple cereals: rice, maize, and wheat. Of the three, 'Europe chose wheat.' Wheat came to Europe from Mesopotamia, and wherever Europeans have settled in force, they have taken their wheat with them—first to the empty lands of the neolithic north-west, more recently to the virgin prairies of America, Australia, and southern Siberia. The process whereby 'the choice' was made involved an endless series of experiments over several millennia. Although the rival cereals of rye, barley, oats, buckwheat, and millet have continued to exist in Europe, the triumphal march of King Wheat is uncontestable.[2]

Wheat—the genus *Triticum* of the grain-bearing grass family—is known in more than 1,000 varieties. Its grain is extremely nutritious. It consists on average of 70 per cent carbohydrate, 12 per cent protein, 2 per cent fat, 1.8 per cent minerals. The protein content is markedly higher than that of rice, 1 lb yielding up to 1,500 calories. Wheat-based nutrition is one of the factors which has given most Europeans a clear advantage in bodily stature over most rice-eaters and corn-eaters. Wheat is a seasonal crop, which only requires intensive labour at the spring sowing and the autumn harvest. Unlike the rice-growers, who had to tend the paddy-fields in disciplined brigades throughout the year, the wheat farmer was granted time and freedom to branch out, to grow secondary crops, to reclaim land, to build, to fight, to politicize. This conjunction may well contain the preconditions for many features of Europe's social and political history, from feudalism and individualism to warmongering and imperialism. Wheat, however, quickly exhausts the soil. In ancient times, the land could only retain its fertility if the wheat fields were regularly left fallow and manured by domestic animals. From this there arose the traditional European pattern of mixed arable and livestock farming, and the varied diet of cereals, vegetables, and meat.

In bread-making, wheat proteins have the unique property of forming gluten when mixed with water to form dough. In turn, the gluten retains carbon dioxide emitted from the fermentation of yeast. The net result is a wheaten loaf that is lighter, finer, and more digestible than any of its competitors.[3] 'Give us this day our daily bread' is a sentiment which European civilization could share with some of its Middle Eastern neighbours, but not with Indians, Chinese, Aztecs, or Incas.

development to international enterprise, even to contact with Egyptian, or possibly Minoan, metal-prospectors. [DASA] [GGANTIJA]

The Chalcolithic Age is a term used by some prehistorians to describe the long transitional phase when Stone and Bronze overlapped.

The Bronze Age was marked by the manufacture of a new alloy through the admixture of copper with tin. Its onset began in the Middle East c.3000 BC, in northern Europe perhaps a thousand years later. Especially in the Mediterranean, it saw the growth of urban culture: written records, specialized crafts, widespread trade. Its greatest achievements were found at Mycenae, unearthed by Heinrich Schliemann from 1876 and at Cnossos in Crete, excavated by Sir Arthur Evans in 1899–1930. These sites are roughly contemporary with the stone circles at Stonehenge, whose three phases of construction began c.2600 BC. Charcoal from the 'Aubrey Holes' of Phase I at Stonehenge has been carbon-dated to 1848 BC ± 275 years; an antler pick from a stone socket of Phase III to 1710 BC ± 150 years. Hence, whilst advanced civilizations akin to those of the Middle East were developing in the Aegean, the peoples of the north-west were passing through the transition from Neolithic to Bronze. [SAMPHIRE]

However, talk of 'advanced' or 'backward' cultures might well be inhibited by the skills of the engineers of Stonehenge, who contrived to transport eighty bluestones weighing over fifty tons apiece from the distant Prescelly Mountains of South Wales, and to erect them with such precision that awestruck observers have imagined them to be the working parts of a sun-computer.[16] Indeed, carvings at Stonehenge of axes and daggers resembling objects found in the shaft-graves at Mycenae gave rise once again to speculation about direct contacts with the Mediterranean.

Interregional trade, especially in minerals, is one of the important features of Bronze Age Europe. The Peninsula's mineral resources were rich and varied, but their distribution was uneven; and a widespread network of trade-routes grew up

VINO

WINE is no ordinary beverage. It has always been associated with love and religion. Its name, like that of Venus, is derived from the Sanskrit *vêna*, 'beloved'. Coming from the Caucasus, it featured in both the daily diet and the religious ceremonies of the ancient world. First cultivated by Noah (*Genesis* ix. 20), it inspired not only pagan bacchanalia but also the communion cup of Christianity.[1]

Saint Martin of Tours, born at Sabaria (modern Szombathely) near the Danube, was the first patron saint of wine-drinkers. St Urban and St Vincent (whose name offers a play on 'reeking of wine'), became the principal patrons of wine-growers and vintners.

Commercial wine-growing in medieval Europe was pioneered by the Benedictines at Château-Prieuré in the Bordeaux region, and at locations such as the Clos Vougeot on the Côte de Beaune in Burgundy. The Cluniacs on the Côte d'Or near Macon, and the Cistercians at Nuits St Georges, extended the tradition. According to Froissart, England's possession of Bordeaux demanded a fleet of 300 vessels to carry the vintage home. *Bénédictine* (1534) from the Abbey of Fécamp, and *Chartreuse* (1604) from the Charterhouse in Dauphiné, pioneered the art of fortified wine.

Europe's wine zone cuts the Peninsula in two. Its northern reaches pass along a line stretching from the Loire, through Champagne to the Mosel and the Rhineland, and thence eastwards to the slopes of the Danube, and on to Moldavia and Crimea. There are very few wine-growing districts which did not once belong to the Roman Empire. Balkan wines in Serbia, Romania, Bulgaria, and Greece, inhibited by the anti-alcoholic Ottomans, are every bit as ancient as those of Spain, Italy, or France.

The consumption of wine has far-reaching social, psychological, and medical consequences. It has been invoked as a factor in religious and political groupings, such as the Protestant–Catholic divide in Germany, and even in the fate of battles. 'It was wine and beer that clashed at Waterloo. The red fury of wine repeatedly washed in vain against the immovable wall of the sons of beer . . .'[2]

Nor has St Martin's homeland lost its viticultural excellence. The volcanic soil on the slopes above Tokay, the hot summer air of the Hungarian plain, the moisture of the Bodrog River, and the most nobly rotten of 'Aszu' grapes, form a unique combination. The pungent, velvety, peach-like *essencia* of golden Tokay is not to everyone's taste; and has rarely been well produced in recent decades. But it was once laid down for 200 years in the most exclusive cellars of Poland, and kept for the death-bed of monarchs. A bottle of 'Imperial Tokay' from the days of Francis-Joseph is still one of the connoisseur's most prized ambitions.[3]

ĠGANTIJA

THE islands of Malta present two historic puzzles—their language and their megaliths. The former is Semitic, of mediaeval Arab provenance. It is the only Semitic tongue to be written in the Latin script. (Romantic philologists once linked it with ancient Phoenician.) The megaliths are far older. The principal sites at the temple of Ġgantija on Gozo Island, and at the unique subterranean *hypogeum* or 'collective burial chamber' at Hal Saflieni, dating from *c*.2400 BC. The earliest rock-cut monuments were constructed a millennium before.[1]

The procession of civilizations through Malta reads like a shorthand guide to European history.[2] After the neolithic cave-dwellers, who built the megaliths, and the Bronze Age Beaker Folk, came the Carthaginians (from the seventh century BC) and then the Romans (from 218 BC). Gozo is often identified as 'Calypso's Isle', where Odysseus was stranded. St Paul was shipwrecked in a bay named after him, north of Valetta, in AD 60. Allocated to the Eastern (Byzantine) Empire in 395, Malta was then ruled successively by Arabs (from 870), by Normans (from 1091), by the Knights Hospitallers (from 1530), by the French (from 1798), by the British (from 1802)—and from 1964, belatedly, by the Maltese themselves.

in response to the imbalances. Salt had been sought from the earliest times, either by mining rock-salt or by evaporating brine from seaside salt-pans. Huge rock-salt mountains occur naturally in several locations, from Cardona in Catalonia to the Salzkammergut in Austria or Wieliczka in Poland. Primitive salt-pans or *salinae* were located all along the hot southern coast, from the Rhone to the Dnieper. Now, permanent 'salt roads' began to function. Best known among them was the ancient Via Salaria, which linked Rome with the salt-pans of the Adriatic coast. Amber, which can be found both on the western shore of Jutland and on the Baltic shore east of the Vistula, was greatly prized as jewellery. The ancient 'amber road' ran down the valley of the Oder, through the Moravian Gap to the Danube, and over the Brenner Pass to the Adriatic. Obsidian and lapis lazuli were also in great demand. Copper and tin were the staples. Copper came first from Cyprus—whence its name—later from the Dolomites, and above all from the Carpathians. Carpathian copper found its way northwards at an early date to Scandinavia, and was later sent south to the Aegean. Tin, which was not always distinguished by the ancients from lead, was brought from distant Cornwall. The search for copper and tin seems to have stimulated transcontinental contacts more effectively than the subsequent search for iron, which was found much more readily.

Special prominence accrued to those districts where several of the desired commodities could be found in close proximity. One such district was the Salzkammergut (Noricum), where the salt mountains of Ischl and Hallstatt lay alongside the metal mines of Noriae. Another lay in the vicinity of Cracow, where

DASA

A POPULAR history of mathematics states that the advance of the Beaker Folk into neolithic Europe was accompanied by the spread both of the Indo-European languages and of the decimal system. The statement is supported by lists of number words from a selection of Indo-European languages which use the Base-10 or decimal method of numeration. The implication is that prehistoric Europe was familiar with Base-10 counting three millennia before its introduction in written form.[1]

It is intriguing, of course, to think that one might reconstruct modes of counting in a remote and illiterate society, for which no direct evidence is available. Yet there can be no certainty that numbers used today have remained constant since prehistoric times; and one must be careful to test the hypothesis against all the most relevant languages:

	Celtic (Welsh)	German		Latin	Ancient Greek	Slavonic (Russian)	Sanskrit
1.	un	eins	I	unus	heis	odin	eka
2.	dau	zwei	II	duo	duo	dva	dvi
3.	tri	drei	III	tres	treis	tri	tri
4.	pedwar	vier	IV	quattuor	tessares	chetyre	katur
5.	pump	fünf	V	quinque	pente	piat'	panka
6.	chwech	sechs	VI	sex	hex	shest'	shash
7.	saith	sieben	VII	septem	hepta	syem'	sapta
8.	wyth	acht	VIII	octo	octo	vosyem'	ashta
9.	naw	neun	IX	novem	ennea	devyat'	nava
10.	deg	zehn	X	decem	deka	decyat'	dasa

Sanskrit, meaning 'perfect speech', is the second oldest of the recorded Indo-European languages. It was the language of ancient India and, in Hindu tradition, of the Gods. It was employed c.1500 BC for the composition of Vedic literature. Its prime followed shortly after the fall of the Indus civilization, which invented the decimal system.

Sanskrit's number words were definitely based on decimal counting. Its units 1–10 corresponded with those found in other Indo-European languages. Its teens were simple combinations of units with the word for ten, hence ekadasa (1 + 10 = 11) or navadasa (9 + 10 = 19). Its tens were combinations of units with the collective numeral for a 'decade', dasat(i), hence vimsati or dvimdesati (2 x 10 = 20) or trimsati (3 x 10 = 30). Its word for 1,000, dasasata, meaning 'ten hundreds', stood alongside sa-hasra, a variation used in the formation of still higher numbers. It had a single word, crore for '10 million', and another, satam, to express 'percentage'.[2] Latin numbers, too, are essentially decimal. But their structure bears no relation to Roman numerals, which are based on conglomerates of units, fives, and tens.

The Celtic languages, of which Welsh is the most active modern survivor, once stretched across much of Europe. They belong to the most
ancient Indo-European forms in the West. Yet Celtic numerals have preserved elements of counting in Base-5, Base-10, and especially Base-20.
Modern Welsh, like Sanskrit, uses decimal units for 1–10; but in the teens
it uses numbers similar in structure to Roman numerals. Sixteen is *un ar
bymtheg* or 'one over five and ten' (XVI); and nineteen is *pedwar ar bymtheg*
or 'four over five and ten'. Above nineteen, Base-20 counting takes over.
Ugain is the base, and *deugain* (40), *trigain* (60), and *pedwar gain* (80) are all
multiples of twenty. Thirty, seventy, and ninety are expressed as 'ten over'
a multiple of twenty. Fifty, *hanner cant*, means 'half of a hundred'.

	Welsh		Latin	Sanskrit
11	*un ar ddeg*	XI	*undecim*	*ekadasa*
20	*ugain*	XX	*viginti*	*vimsati*
30	*deg ar hugain*	XXX	*triginta*	*trimsati*
40	*deugain*	XL	*quadraginta*	*katvarimsati*
50	*hanner cant*	L	*quinquaginta*	*pankasati*
60	*trigain*	LX	*sexaginta*	*shashti*
70	*deg ar thrigain*	LXX	*septuaginta*	*septati*
80	*pedwar ugain*	LXXX	*octoginta*	*ashiti*
90	*deg ar phedwar ugain*	XC	*nonaginta*	*navati*
100	*cant*	C	*centum*	*sata*
1,000	*mila*	M	*mille*	*dasasata/sa-hasra*

Base-20 counting, which started by using toes as well as fingers, is preserved in the English word 'score', which derives from the mark cut into
counting-sticks. It is also reflected in French *quatre-vingt*, meaning 'four
times twenty', which is probably a relic of Celtic Gaul.

In all probability, therefore, Europe's early peoples counted in twos,
fives, tens, dozens, or scores as they thought fit. At some point they must
also have encountered the Babylonian system of Base-60, which was
adopted for counting minutes and seconds. There is little reason to
assume that Indo-Europeans in general, or the Beaker Folk in particular,
were decimalized from the start.

In fact, Europe had to wait until the thirteenth century AD before Base-
10 numbers were widely introduced. The key step, the use of 0 for 'zero',
had first been taken in India. From there, the decimal system found its way
into the Muslim world, and through Arabic Spain into Christendom. For
several centuries it operated alongside the much clumsier Roman numerals, which could not even be used for addition or multiplication. When it
finally triumphed, many Europeans did not realize that their numbers
were not European at all.[3] (See Appendix III, p. 1242.)

silver, lead, iron, and salt could all be found within a stone's throw of the upper Vistula. Most productive of all, however, were the islands of the Aegean. Melos yielded obsidian; Paros yielded pure white marble; Kythnos yielded copper; Siphnos, and Laurion on the coast of Attica, yielded silver and lead. The wealth and power of Crete, and later of Mycenae, was clearly connected with the command of these Aegean resources and with their role as the termini of the transcontinental trade routes. They were the focus of what has been called the 'international spirit' of the Bronze Age.

Neither Crete nor Mycenae were known to the early classicists who first formed our view of the ancient world. But it is now generally accepted that Minoan culture on Crete, and Mycenean culture on mainland Greece, formed the twin peaks of 'Europe's first civilization'. From the day when Schliemann found a golden death-mask in one of the royal shaft-graves at Mycenae, and telegraphed the mistaken news: 'Today I have looked on the face of Agamemnon', it was clear that he was opening up something far more significant than just another rich prehistoric grave. [**LOOT**] Both the palace sites on Crete, at Cnossos, Phaestus, and Mallia, and the mainland sites at Mycenae, Tiryns, and Pylos have yielded abundant proof of art, religion, technology, and social organization of a far more sophisticated kind than anything known before. The golden age of Minoan life, in the so-called 'palatial period', began c.1900 BC. That of the more warlike Mycenaeans, whose fortresses commanded the Plain of Argos and the Gulf of Corinth, began three or four centuries later. Together with the Trojans, who commanded the Dardanelles, the Minoans and the Mycenaeans brought European history out of the realm of faceless archaeology. [**TRONOS**]

In the late Bronze Age of central Europe, a widespread group of 'Urnfield cultures' was characterized by cemeteries where the cremated remains of the dead were buried in urns together with elaborate grave goods. Important Bronze Age sites have been found at Terramare (Italy), El Argar (Spain), Leubingen, Buchau, Adlerberg (Germany), Unětice near Prague in Czechoslovakia, and at Otomani in Romania.

In the last quarter of the second millennium, c.1200 BC, Bronze Age Europe suffered an unexplained breakdown from which it never recovered. Archaeologists write of a 'general systems collapse'. Trade was disrupted; cities were abandoned; political structures were destroyed. Waves of invaders descended on the remnants. Crete, having barely withstood a series of terrible natural catastrophes, had already fallen to the Mycenean Greeks, before Mycenae itself was destroyed. Within the space of a single century, many established centres passed into oblivion. The Aegean was overrun by tribes from the interior. The Hittite Empire in Asia Minor came to an end. Egypt itself was besieged by unidentified 'sea peoples'. The Urnfield People survived in Central Europe relapsing into a long passive era which ended with the appearance of the Celts. Greece was plunged into its archaic Dark Age which separated the legendary era of the Trojan Wars from the recorded history of the later city-states.

SAMPHIRE

Boiled Samphire. . . . Pick marsh samphire during July or August at low tide. It should be carefully washed soon after collection and is best eaten very fresh. Tie the washed samphire with its roots still intact in bundles, and boil in shallow unsalted water for 8–10 minutes. Cut the string, and serve with melted butter. Eat the samphire by picking each stem up by the root and biting lightly, pulling the fleshy part away from the woody core.[1]

Prehistoric food has long since perished, and cannot easily be studied. Modern attempts to reconstruct the menus and the gastronomic techniques of the neolithic period rely on six main sources of information. Prehistoric rubbish tips present the archaeologists with large collections of meatbones, eggshells, and shellfish remains. The kitchen areas of hut sites often reveal seeds and pollen grains which can be identified and analysed. Implements for fishing and hunting and utensils for preparing, cooking, and eating food have survived in large numbers. (Cauldrons for boiling were common; ovens for baking were not.) The total food resources of the past can be assessed by subtracting modern items—such as yeast, wine, or onions—from the vast repertoire of edible plants and fauna living in the wild. All sorts of delicacies no longer in the cookbooks are known to have been eaten: guillemots, seakale, hedgehogs, beechmast, sloes. Much may also be learned by analogy with the food technology of primitive or pre-industrial societies, whose skills in everything from wild herbs to wind-drying, salting, and preserving are by necessity very considerable. Finally, modern techniques have permitted the analysis of the stomach contents of prehistoric corpses. The Tollund Man, for example, had eaten linseed, barley, and wild plants. [**TOLLUND**] [**VINO**]

Whether, in the end, one can ever recreate an authentic neolithic meal is a matter for debate, preferably pursued whilst chasing the samphire with marrow-bones served with virpa:

Marrow-Bones. (8 oz/225 g. marrow-bones, flour, salt, dry toast) Scrape and wash the bones, and saw in half across the shaft . . . Make a stiff paste of flour and water, and roll it out. Cover the ends of the bones with the paste to seal in the marrow, and tie the bones in a floured cloth. Stand upright in a pan of boiling salted water and simmer slowly for about 2 hours . . . Untie the cloth, and remove the paste from each bone. Fasten a paper napkin round each one and serve with dry toast.[2]

Sowans or Virpa. (1 lb/450 g. fine oatmeal, 3 lb. wheatmeal, 16 pt./ 9 l. water) Put both meals into a stone crock. Stir in 14 pints or 8 litres of lukewarm water, and let it stand for 5–8 days until sour. Pour off the clear liquid . . . This is the swats, which makes a refreshing drink. The remainder in the crock will resemble thick starch. Add about 2 pints or 1 litre water to give the consistency of cream. Strain through a cheesecloth over a colander. The liquid . . . will contain all the nutritious properties of oatmeal . . . Gentle rubbing with a wooden spoon, and a final squeezing of the cloth . . . will hasten the process.[3]

Reconstructing the past is rather like translating poetry. It can be done, but never exactly. Whether one deals in prehistoric recipes, colonial settlements, or medieval music, it needs great imagination and restraint if the twin perils of artless authenticity and clueless empathy are to be avoided. Did neolithic cooks really serve marrow-bones in a paper napkin, or strain their virpa through a cheesecloth? And were there prehistoric Augusts, when samphire could be picked?

THRONOS

THE throne in the Palace of Knossos in Crete has been described as 'Europe's oldest chair'. The claim is unlikely to be correct. What *is* certain is that high-backed chairs with arm-rests were reserved in ancient times for ceremonial purposes. They enabled rulers and high priests to assume a relaxed, dignified, and elevated position, whilst everyone else stood at their feet. From the royal throne, the concept of the chair as a symbol of authority has passed to the *cathedra* or See of bishops and to the Chairs of professors.

Furniture for everyday sitting is a relatively modern, European invention. When not standing, primitive peoples sat, squatted, or lay on the floor. Many Asian nations, including the Japanese, still prefer to do so. Ancient Greeks and Romans reclined on couches. The medievals used rough-hewn benches. Individual chairs were first introduced into monastic cells, perhaps to facilitate reading. They did not join the standard household inventory until the sixteenth century, nor the repertoire of fine design until the eighteenth. They were not widely used in schools, offices and workplaces until the end of the nineteenth.

Unfortunately, flat-bottomed chairs do not match the requirements of the human anatomy. Unlike the horse-saddle, which transfers much of the rider's body-weight onto the stirrup, leaving the natural curvature of the spine intact, chairs lift the thighs at right-angles to the trunk and disrupt the equilibrium of the skeleton. In so doing, they put abnormal stress on the immobilized pelvis, hip-joints, and lumbar regions. Chronic backache is one of the many self-inflicted scars of modern progress.[1]

The Iron Age brings prehistory within range of regular historical sources. Iron-working is usually thought to have been initiated by the Hittites of Asia Minor. A gold-hilted dagger with an iron blade, unearthed from the royal tombs at Alaca Hüyük, may originate from the end of the third millennium BC. From there, the use of iron spread first to Egypt c.1200 BC, to the Aegean c.1000 BC, and to the Danube Basin c.750 BC. [**TOLLUND**]

On the mainland of the Peninsula, the prehistoric Iron Age is customarily divided into two successive periods—that of Hallstatt (*c.*750–400 BC) and of La Tène (*c.*400–50). Hallstatt, a site in the Saltzkammergut first explored in 1846, gave its name to a period and culture which blended the traditions of the former Urnfield people with fresh influences coming from the East. La Tène, a site on Lake Neuchâtel in Switzerland discovered in 1858, gave its name to the second period, where iron-working reached a very high level of competence. Longswords, beautifully wrought from a hard iron core and a soft iron cutting edge which could be fearfully sharpened, were the hallmark of a warrior society, living in great hill forts. These people were familiar with the potter's wheel, with horse-drawn chariots, with the minting of coins, and with highly stylistical art forms that combine native, Mediterranean, and even nomadic elements. At Rudki in the Holy Cross Mountains near Cracow in southern Poland, they left traces of the most extensive iron-workings in prehistoric Europe. They were active traders, and the tombs of their princes have yielded up Celtic jewellery, Etruscan vases, Greek amphorae, Roman artefacts. Not without dissenting voices, they have been widely identified with the Celts, 'the first great nation north of the Alps whose name we know'. Apart from La Tène itself, important sites are located at Entremont in Provence, at Alesia in Burgundy, and at Villanova in Emilia.

With the appearance of Celts, European prehistory reaches the knottiest of all problems—the matching of the material cultures defined by archaeologists with the ethnic and linguistic groupings known from other sources. Most prehistorians do indeed accept that those iron-workers of the La Tène period were Celts, that they derived from the formation or influx of Celtic tribes in the first millennium BC, and that they were one and the same group whom Greek and Roman literary records refer to as *Keltoi* or *Celtae*. But the most recent survey of the matter maintains that the origin of the Celtic languages may lie much further back, in the neolithic era.[17] One thing is certain: modern linguistic research has proved beyond doubt that the languages of the Celts are cognate both to Latin and to Greek, and to most of the languages of modern Europe. The Celts were the vanguard of a linguistic community that can be more clearly defined than the archaeological communities of prehistory. The Celts stand at the centre of the Indo-European phenomenon.

As long ago as 1786 Sir William Jones, a British judge serving in Calcutta, made the epoch-making discovery that the main languages of Europe are closely related to the principal languages of India. Jones saw the link between classical Latin and Greek and ancient Sanskrit. It subsequently turned out that many modern Indian languages formed part of the same family as their counterparts in Europe, namely the Romance, Celtic, Germanic, Baltic, and Slavonic groups (see Appendix III, p. 1232).

At the time, no one had any idea how this family of 'Indo-European' languages could have found its way across Eurasia, though it came to be assumed that they must have been carried to the West by migrating peoples. In 1902, however, a German archaeologist, Gustav Kossinna, linked the Indo-Europeans with a

TOLLUND

TOLLUND is the name of a marsh near Aarhus in Denmark, where in 1950 the whole body of a prehistoric man was discovered in a state of remarkable preservation. It is displayed in the Silkeborg Museum. The tannic acid of the peat had mummified him so perfectly that the delicate facial features were quite intact, as were the contents of his stomach. Except for a pointed leather cap and waistband, he was naked, and had been strangled with a braided leather rope, apparently the victim of ritual murder some two thousand years ago. His strange fate can evoke a haunting sense of compassion, even today:

> Something of his sad freedom
> As he rode the tumbril
> Should come to me, driving,
> Saying the names
>
> Tollund, Grauballe, Nebelgard,
> Watching the pointing hands
> Of country people,
> Not knowing their tongue.
>
> Out there in Jutland
> In the old, man-killing parishes
> I will feel lost,
> Unhappy, and home.[1]

Yet Tollund Man is not alone. Similar discoveries were made thirty years later at Lindow Moss in Cheshire (England); and a particularly interesting corpse came to light in September 1991 in a glacial pocket near the Similaun Ridge of the Otztaler Alps in South Tirol. The body appeared to be that of a pre-Bronze Age hunter, fully dressed and equipped. He was 5 feet (152 cm) in height, 120 lb (54.4 kg), perhaps twenty years old, with blue eyes, a shaven face, and even a complete brain. He was very thoroughly clad in tanned leather tunic and leggings, a cap of chamois fur, birchbark gloves, and hay-lined, thick-soled boots. His skin was tattooed with blue tribal markings in four places, and he was wearing a necklace made from 20 sunray thongs and one stone bead. He was carrying an empty wooden-framed rucksack, a broken 32-inch (975 cm) bow, a quiver of 14 bone-tipped arrows, a stone-bladed axe tipped with pure copper, a short flint knife, and a body belt containing flints and tinder. He apparently froze to death whilst crossing the pass in a blizzard. Rigor mortis fixed his outstretched arm, still trying to shield his eyes. Dated to 2731 BC ± 125, he finally reached an unintended destination in the deep-freeze at Innsbruck University with some 5,000 years' delay.[2]

Prehistoric bodies are clearly a valuable source of scientific information. Recent advances in 'prehistoric pathology' have facilitated detailed analysis of the bodies' tissues, diseases, bacteria, and diet. But no one can entirely forget the case of Piltdown Man, whose bones were unearthed at a quarry in Sussex in 1908. In the same year that Tollund Man was discovered, Piltdown Man was shown to be one of the great master forgeries.

specific type of corded ware pottery, that was widely distributed in sites through-out northern Germany. Kossinna's conclusions indicated that an 'Indo-European homeland' could have existed in the north European Iron Age. The idea was developed by the prominent Australian archaeologist Vere Gordon Childe (1892–1957), whose synthesis, *The Dawn of European Civilisation* (1925), was one of the most influential books of its day. Most recently the Lithuanian-American archaeologist Marija Gimbutas has confirmed his placement of the Indo-European homeland on the steppelands of Ukraine by identifying it with the widespread Kurgan culture of barrow-burials in that area:

Constantly accumulating archaeological discoveries have effectively eliminated the earlier theories of Indo-European homelands. . . . The Kurgan culture seems the only remaining candidate for being Proto-Indo-European. There was no other culture in the neolithic and chalcolithic periods which would correspond with the hypothetical mother culture of the Indo-Europeans as reconstructed with the help of common words; and there were no other great expansions and conquests affecting whole territories where the earliest historic sources and a cultural continuum prove the existence of Indo-European speakers.[18]

The essential point here is that Gordon Childe and his successors were using the term 'culture' in relation to human groups defined both by material and by lin-guistic criteria. Yet on reflection there seems no good reason why archaeological cultures should necessarily be correlated with linguistic groups in this way. The Indo-European enigma is not really solved. It is particularly exciting to realize that languages evolve by ceaseless mutation just as living organisms do. In this case, it may become possible to correlate the chronology of language change in Europe with that of genetic change. By comparing the time-trace of 'linguistic clocks' with that of our 'molecular clocks', the story of the origins of the European peoples and their languages may one day be unravelled.[19]

Europe's place-names are the product of thousands of years. They form a deep resource for understanding its past. The names of rivers, hills, towns, provinces, and countries are often the relics of bygone ages. The science of onomastics can delve beneath the crust of historical records.[20] By common consent the names of rivers are among the most ancient and persistent. They are frequently the only surviving links with the peoples who preceded the present population. By a process of accretion, they can sometimes preserve a record of the successive waves of settlement on their banks. The 'River Avon', for example, combines two syn-onyms, one English, the other the older Welsh. Five Celtic root words connected with water—*afon, dwr, uisge, rhe*, and possibly *don*—supply the commonest ele-ments in river-names right across Europe. Scholars endlessly disagree, of course. But among the best-known candidates would be the Inn and the Yonne, Avignon on the Rhodanus ('Watertown' on the 'Swift River'), the Esk, the Etsch (or Adige), the Usk, and the Danube.

Celtic names abound from Portugal to Poland. The modern Welsh *dŵr*, 'water', for example, has its cognates in Dee, Douro, Dordogne, Derwent (Clear

Water), Durance, and Oder/Odra. *Pen*, meaning 'head' and hence 'mountain', appears in Pennine, Apennine, Pieniny, and Pindus; *ard*, 'high', in Arden, Ardennes, Lizard (High Cape), and Auvergne (*Ar Fearann*, 'High Country'); *dun*, 'fort', in Dunkeld (Fort of the Celts), Dungannon, London, Verdun, Augustodunum (Fort Augustus, Autun), Lugdunum (Lyons), Lugodinum (Leyden), Thun in Switzerland, and Tyniec near Cracow. All attest to the far-flung presence of the Celts.[LLANFAIR] [LUGDUNUM]

Similar exercises can be undertaken with Norse roots, Germanic roots, Slavonic roots, even Phoenician and Arabic roots. *Etna* is a very suitable Phoenician name meaning 'the furnace'. Elsewhere in Sicily, *Marsala* has a simple Arabic name meaning 'Port of God'. Trajan's bridge across the upper Tagus in Spain is now known as *La puente de Alcantara*—*al cantara* being the exact Arabic equivalent of the Latin *pons*.

Slavonic place-names spread much further west than the present-day Slavonic population. In northern Germany, for example, they are common in the region of Hanover. In Austria, names such as *Zwettl* (Světlý, 'Bright Spot'), *Doebling* (Dub, 'Little Oak'), or *Feistritz* (Bystřice, 'Swift Stream') can be encountered from the environs of Vienna to Tyrol. In Italy, they overlap with Italian in the province of Friuli.

The names of towns and villages frequently incorporate a record of their origins. Edinburgh was once 'Edwin's fort'; Paris, the city of the Parisii tribe; Turin (Torino), the city of the Taurini; Göttingen, the 'family home of the Godings'; Kraków (Cracow), the seat of good King Krak. Elsewhere, they record the attributes or function of the place. *Lisboa/Lisbon* means 'Good Spot'; *Trondheim* means 'Home of the Throne'; *Munich/München*, 'Place of the Monks'; *Redruth* 'Place of the Druids'; *Novgorod*, 'New City'. Sometimes they recall distant disasters. *Ossaia* in Tuscany, meaning 'Place of Bones', lies on the site of Hannibal's victory at Trasimeno in 217 BC. *Pourrières* in Provence, originally 'Campi Putridi' (Putrid Fields), marks the slaughter of the Teutons by Marius in 102 BC; *Lechfeld* in Bavaria, the 'Field of Corpses', the scene of the Magyars' defeat in AD 955.

The names of nations frequently reflect the way they saw themselves or were seen by others. The west Celtic neighbours of the Anglo-Saxons call themselves *Cymry* or 'Compatriots', but were dubbed *Welsh* or 'Foreigners' by the Germanic intruders. Similarly, French-speaking Walloons are known to the Flemings as *Waalsch*. The Germanic peoples often call themselves *Deutsch* or *Dutch* (meaning 'germane' or 'alike'), but are called *Niemtsy*, 'the Dumb', by their Slavonic neighbours. The Slavs think of each other as the people of the *Slovo* or 'common word', or as *Serb* (kinsman). They often call the Latins *Vlachy*, *Wallachs*, or *Włochy*— which is another variation on the 'Welsh' theme. The assorted Vlachs and Wallachians of the Balkans tend to call themselves *Romani*, *Rumeni*, or *Aromani* (Romans).

The names of countries and provinces frequently record the people who once ruled them. The Celtic root of Gal-, indicating 'Land of the Gaels or Gauls', occurs in Portugal, Galicia in Spain, Gallia (Gaul), Pays des Galles (Wales), Cornwall,

Donegal, Caledonia (later Scotland), Galloway, Calais, Galicia in southern Poland, even in distant Galatia in Asia Minor.

Place-names, however, are infinitely mobile. They change over time; and they vary according to the language and the perspective of the people who use them. They are the intellectual property of their users, and as such have caused endless conflicts. They can be the object of propaganda, of tendentious wrangling, of rigid censorship, even of wars. In reality, where several variants exist, one cannot speak of correct or incorrect forms. One can only indicate the variant which is appropriate to a particular time, place, or usage. Equally, when referring to events over large areas of time and space, the historian is often forced to make a choice between equally inappropriate alternatives.

Yet historians must always be sensitive to the implications. One easily forgets that 'Spain', 'France', 'England', 'Germany', 'Poland', or 'Russia' are relatively recent labels which can easily be used anachronistically. It is clearly wrong to talk of 'France' instead of 'Gaul' in the Roman period, as it is dubious to speak of 'Russia' prior to the state in Muscovy. Writing in English, one automatically writes of the 'English Channel', ignoring that 'La Manche' is at least half French. Writing in Polish, one automatically writes 'Lipsk' for Leipzig, without laying claim to the Polishness of Saxony, just as in German one says 'Danzig' for Gdańsk, or 'Breslau' for Wrocław, without necessarily implying the exclusive Germanity of Pomerania or Silesia. One forgets that official language, which presents place-names in forms preferred by the bureaucracy of the ruling state, does not always concur with the practice of the inhabitants. Above all, one forgets that different people have every reason to think of place-names in different ways, and that no one has the right to dictate exclusive forms. One man's *Derry* is another man's *Londonderry*. This person's *Antwerpen* is the other person's *Anvers*. For them, it was *East Galicia* or *Eastern Little Poland*; for others, it is 'Western Ukraine'. For the ancients, it was the Borysthenes: for the moderns, it is the Dnipr, the Dnepr, or the Dnieper. For them, it is *Oxford*, or even *Niu-Jin*: for us, forever *Rhydychen*.

'European History' has always been an ambiguous concept. Indeed, both 'Europe' and 'History' are ambiguous. Europe may just refer to that Peninsula whose landward boundary for long stayed undefined—in which case historians must decide for themselves where the arbitrary bounds of their studies will lie. But 'European' can equally apply to the peoples and cultures which originated on the Peninsula—in which case the historian will be struggling with the world-wide problems of 'European Civilization'. History may refer to the past in general; or else, in distinction to prehistory, it may be confined to that part of the past for which a full range of sources are extant. With prehistory, one is dealing with the evidence of myth, of language, and above all of archaeology. With history in the narrower sense, one is also dealing with literary records, with documents, and above all with the work of earlier historians. In either case, whether one is beckoned by the ends of prehistory or the beginning of history proper, one is brought to the terminus of Europa's ride, to the island of Crete.

1628 BC, Cnossos, Crete. Standing on the high northern terrace of the palace, the courtiers of Minos looked out to the distant sea over the shimmering groves of olive and cypress. They were the servants of the great Priest-King, masters of the Cretan *thalassokratia*, the world's first 'seaborne empire'. Supported by the trade of their far-ranging ships, they lived a life of comfort, of ritual, and of administrative order. Their quarters were supplied with running water, with drainage, and with flushed sewers. Their walls were covered with frescos—griffins, dolphins, and flowers, painted onto luminous settings of deep blue and gold. Their spacious courtyards were regularly turned into arenas for the ceremonial sport of bull-leaping. Their underground storehouses were packed with huge stone vats filled with corn, wine, and oil for 4,000 people. Their domestic accounts were immaculately kept on soft clay tablets, using a method of writing which progressed over the centuries through hieroglyphic, cursive, and linear forms. Their craftsmen were skilled in jewellery, metalwork, ceramics, faience. They were so confident of their power and prosperity that none of their palaces was fortified (see Appendix III, p. 1217).

Religion played a vital role in the life of the Minoans. The central object of their worship was probably the great Earth Goddess, later known as Rhea, mother of Zeus. She was revealed in many forms and aspects, and was attended by a host of lesser deities. Her sanctuaries were placed on mountain-tops, in caves, or in the temple-chambers of the palaces. Surviving sealstones portray naked women embracing the sacred boulders in ecstasy. Sacrifices were surrounded by the Cult of the Bull, by orgies, and by a mass of ritual paraphernalia such as altar tables, votive containers, blood-buckets, and wasp-waisted statuettes of fertility goddesses. The ubiquitous symbols of bulls' horns and of the *labrys* or double-headed axe were carried on high poles in procession. In times of danger or disaster, the sacrifice of animals was supplemented by the sacrifice of human children, even by cannibalistic feasts. (After all, Rhea's husband, Cronus, was remembered as a devourer of children, and but for a timely ruse would have eaten the infant Zeus.) Minoan ritual, therefore, was intense. But it was an important ingredient in the social cement which held a peaceable society together for centuries. Some observers have remarked on the absence of modern masculinity in representation of Minoan males.[21] These remarks necessarily prompt questions about the island's role in the transition from 'primitive matriarchy', and the onset of 'patriarchal warfare'. (See Plates 3, 4.)

Minoan civilization flourished on Crete for the best part of a thousand years. According to Sir Arthur Evans, the excavator of Cnossos, it passed through nine distinct phases, each identified with a particular ceramic style, from Early Minoan I to Late Minoan III. The zenith was reached somewhere in the middle of Minoan II, in the second quarter of the second millennium BC. By that time, unbeknown

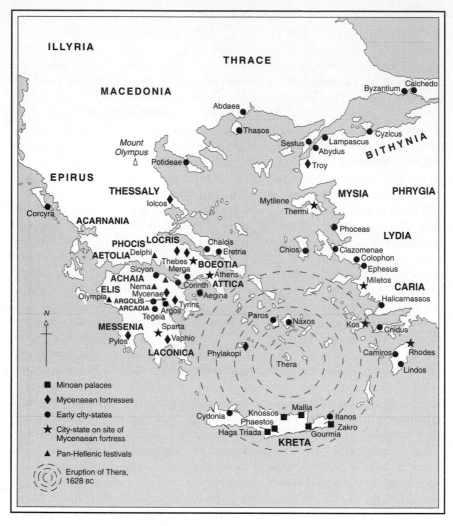

Map 5.
The Ancient Aegean: 2nd Millennium BC

to the courtiers on the terrace, the first of the 'great catastrophes' was upon them.

The ethnic identity of the Minoans is the subject of considerable controversy. The old assumption that they were Hellenes is no longer widely accepted. The Linear A script, which might unlock the language of the earlier periods, has not been deciphered; whilst Linear B, which was definitively identified as Greek in 1952, clearly belongs only to the final phase. Arthur Evans was convinced not only of a strong Egyptian influence on Crete but also of the possibility of Egyptian colonization. 'It may well be asked whether, in the times . . . that marked the triumph of the dynastic element in the Nile Valley, some part of the older population . . . may not have made an actual settlement on the soil of Crete.'[22] However, in the course of the second millennium Crete seems to have been invaded by several waves of migrants. It can reasonably be supposed that the hellenization of the island began with one of the later waves some time after the 'great catastrophes'.

Another possibility is that the Minoans of the middle period were Hittites from Asia Minor. The Hittites were Indo-Europeans, and spoke a language called Kanesian. Their great confederation was centred on what is now Hattusas in Anatolia, and mounted a major challenge both to Mesopotamia and to Egypt. In the fourteenth century BC their greatest ruler, Suppiluliumash or Shubbiluliuma (c.1380–1347 BC), extended his sway as far as Jerusalem. In 1269 BC they entered a treaty of alliance with Egypt. (The bilingual text of the tablet recording this event, the oldest diplomatic document in existence, is now displayed in the foyer of the United Nations Building in New York.) In 1256 BC the Hittite King Khattushilish III travelled to Egypt to attend the wedding of his daughter with the Pharaoh Rameses II. So, if Hittite influence had been spread so widely over the Middle East, there is every likelihood that it could also have been projected from the mainland to Crete. More specifically, the discovery of a bull cult at the Hittite centre of Çatal Huyuk in Anatolia suggests a connection of much greater intimacy. But nothing is certain.

According to later Greek legend, Crete was the birthplace both of Zeus and of the dreaded Minotaur. Zeus, after abducting Europa, had simply brought her to his island home. A cave on Mount Ida is still shown to tourists as the site of his birth. The Minotaur, on the other hand, was the product of a stranger passion. Pasiphaë, the queen of Minos, was said to have taken a liking to a sacrificial bull presented by the sea-god, Poseidon, and, with the assistance of Daedalus, the architect of Cnossos, had succeeded in having intercourse with it. For this purpose, Daedalus devised a hollow wooden cow, within which the intrepid queen had presumably struck a suitable pose. The resultant offspring was the monstrous Minotaur—half-man, half-beast, *l'infamia di Creti*. Whereupon Daedalus was ordered to devise a labyrinth in which to keep it.

At that point, the plot thickened with the arrival of Theseus, hero of Athens. Theseus' obsession with killing the Minotaur may well be explained by the fact that he was the child of yet another mother who had dallied with a bull. At all events, having joined the annual transport of seven boys and seven maidens which Athens paid to Crete as tribute, he managed to reach Cnossos; and, mastering the labyrinth by means of a ball of thread provided by Ariadne, Pasiphaë's daughter, he slew the Minotaur and escaped. He then fled with Ariadne to Naxos, where he deserted her. By another lamentable lapse, on approaching Athens he forgot to give the agreed signal of success, which was to change the colour of his sail from black to white. His despairing father, Aegeus, threw himself into the sea, which was henceforth named after him. These stories clearly date from an era when Crete was the great power, and the Greek communities of the mainland were dependent tributaries.

Daedalus is also credited by legend with mankind's maiden flight. Barred by Minos from leaving Crete, he fashioned two pairs of wings from wax and feathers and, in the company of his son Icarus, soared from the slopes of Mount Ida. Icarus flew too close to the sun, and plunged to his death. But Daedalus flew on to complete his escape to the mainland. 'Minos may own everything,' wrote Ovid, 'but not the air' (*Omnia possideat, non possidet aera Minos*).

Mount Ida stands 8,000 ft (2,434 m) above the sea, and one can well imagine how the thermal currents would have carried those human birds to a height where the whole of Aegean civilization was laid out like a map beneath them. Crete itself, a rocky strip some 130 miles in length, faced south to the shore of Africa and north across the Aegean. Its dominion stretched to Sicily in the west and to Cyprus in the east. To the north-west lay the Peloponnese, dominated by the city of Mycenae with its royal 'beehive' tombs, and its Lion Gate. To the north-east, in the angle of Asia Minor, stood the ancient city of Troy. In the centre lay the scattered islands of the Cyclades, Crete's first colonies. Nearest of all, set like a jet-black diamond in the deep blue sea, beautiful and ominous, rose the perfect cone of the island of Thera.

It is doubtful that the Minoans knew much about the lands and peoples beyond the range of their ships. They knew North Africa, of course, especially Egypt, with which they traded: Cretan envoys are depicted on the temple walls at Thebes. Cnossos at the height of its magnificence in Late Minoan II coincided with the close of the 18th Dynasty of Aminhotep III, and hence with the accession of Tutankhamun. The Minoans knew the cities of the Levant—Sidon, Tyre, and Jericho—which were already ancient, and through them the countries of the Near East. In the seventeenth century BC the Hebrews were still kept captive in Egypt. The Aryans had recently migrated from Persia to India. The Babylonians ruled over the Land of the Two Rivers, united by Hammurabi the Lawgiver. Hammurabi's Code, based on the principle of 'an eye for an eye, a tooth for a tooth', was the civilizational high point of the age. The Assyrians had recently become the vassals of Babylon. The Hittites, having formed the strongest state in western Asia, were starting to press into Palestine. (See Appendix III, p. 1216.)

The Minoans may well have had dealings with the pre-Latin peoples of Italy. There was no obstacle to their ships cruising into the western Mediterranean. They could also have met the Bell-Beaker People and the Megalith-Builders of Malta and southern Spain, and have sailed into the Black Sea, where they could have encountered the Tripolye People. The latter could have acted as middlemen on the last, southern leg of the trade routes which led from the dominant Unětice and Tumulus peoples of the interior. The prime commodity was copper, its main source the mines of the Dolomites and the Carpathians.

Beyond that, the veil of the Minoans' direct knowledge would have been firmly drawn. Whilst they basked in the Bronze Age, the northern lands lingered in the later stages of the neolithic. The westward march of the Indo-Europeans had undoubtedly begun. It is sometimes associated with the advent of a male-dominated warrior culture, which subdued both its peaceable predecessors and its own women. The advance guard of the Celts was already on station in central Europe. The Germanic, Baltic, and Slavonic tribes rested somewhere in the rear. The first northern trappers and merchants from beyond the 'frontier' may well have reached the Aegean. Both amber and jade had found their way to Crete.

The eruption of Thera (Santorini) was one of the greatest events of European prehistory. In one crack of doom, like that at Krakatoa in modern times, 30 cubic kilometres of rock, fire, and sulphuric acid were blown twenty miles into the stratosphere. At a distance of only one hundred miles, the watchers at Cnossos could not have failed to see the plume and the flashes, and then the pillar of fiery ash. With nine minutes' delay they would have heard the boom, the rumbles, and the thuds. They would have seen the sea recede as it rushed to fill the gash in the seabed, only to recover with the dispatch of a mighty tidal wave that swamped the Cretan shore under a hundred feet of brine.

High above Cnossos, on the northern slopes of Mount Juktas, the priests of the mountain shrine busied themselves with the human sacrifice which the disaster demanded. On this occasion, the everyday offerings of fruit, seeds, or wine, or even the slaughter of a prime bull, would not suffice. In the dark central chamber of the temple, one man prepared a blood-bucket adorned with the figure of a bull in white relief. At the inner end of the western chamber, a young woman lay face down, legs apart. On a low table, a young man lay with his feet bound—on his chest a bronze-bladed knife engraved with a boar's head. Beside him stood a powerful man of status, who wore a precious iron ring and an agate sealstone engraved with the figure of a god punting a boat. But the earthquake triggered by the eruption of Thera struck first. The temple roof collapsed. The sacrifice was never completed. The bodies of the participants remained where they lay, to be discovered three and a half millennia later.[23]

The dating of Thera's eruption has largely been achieved by dendrochronology. In 1628 BC the rings of trees as far apart as the bristle-cone pines of California and the bog oaks of Ireland entered a period of stunted growth. Temperatures evidently plummeted throughout the northern hemisphere, probably in response to the 'veil effect' of high-floating volcanic dust. Confirmation of a world-wide disaster in the period 1645 BC, ± 20 years, comes from sulphuric acid deposits in the relevant ice-layers in Greenland. Recent carbon-dating at Thera itself also suggests an eruption date at least a century earlier than the original estimate of 1500 BC. Scientific doubts remain, of course; but 1628 BC is clearly 'the best working hypothesis'.[24]

The palace at Cnossos escaped the later fate of Pompeii and Herculaneum. A westerly wind happened to be blowing on the day of the eruption, and the heaviest deposits of ash fell on the coast of Asia Minor. Even so, Cnossos was rocked by the quake that felled walls and pillars; and one has to assume that damage to the vital Minoan navy was extensive, if not total. In the space of a few hours the cone of Thera was reduced to a smouldering ring of black basalt cliffs round an eerie, sulphurous lagoon. Like the stump of rock in the centre of that lagoon, Crete must have been left marooned at the centre of a blasted empire.

Archaeological layering on eastern Crete shows that a clear interval of time separated the Thera eruption from a subsequent, and still unexplained, disaster which left the palace of Cnossos in ruins, with the clay tablets baked so hard by fire that they can still be read today. Thera did not destroy Cnossos, as was once proposed. But it certainly delivered the first of the blows which spelled the end of Minoan civilization. Material destruction and population loss must have been enormous, the disruption of trade crippling. A weakened Crete was left open to the mercy of Dorian warriors, and in due course was thoroughly hellenized.

The violent end of Europe's first civilization inevitably prompts thoughts about the rise and fall of civilizations in general. One wonders whether the Minoan survivors would have blamed their misfortunes on their own shortcomings. One wonders whether the Catastrophe Theory that applies to various branches of the physical sciences can equally be applied to the long-term patterns of human affairs. One wonders whether the mathematical Theory of Chaos can somehow explain why long, tranquil periods of growth and development can be suddenly interrupted by intervals of confusion and disorder. Is it conceivable that the eruption of Thera was provoked by the fluttering wings of some prehistoric butterfly?

Archaeologists and prehistorians think in large spans of time. For them, the prehistoric, Bronze Age civilization which came to an end with Cnossos and Mycenae was but the first of three great cycles of European history. The second cycle coincided with the classical world of Greece and Rome. The third cycle, which began with the 'systems collapse' at the end of the Roman Empire, coincides with the rise of modern Europe. It is still with us.

Almost 3,500 years have passed since the destruction of Cnossos. In that time the face of Europe has been transformed many times over. Just as Greece succeeded to the glory that was Crete, so Rome was built on Greek foundations, and 'Europe' on the relics of Rome. Vigorous youth, confident maturity, and impotent age all seem to be encoded into the history of political and cultural communities as they are in the lives of individuals. Europe has no shortage of successors to the fate of Crete—of states and nations that once were strong and now are weak. Europe itself, which once was strong, is now weaker. The nuclear explosion at Chernobyl in April 1986 alerted people to the possibility of a continental disaster of Theran proportions; whilst in 1989 the explosive liberation of the nations of Eastern Europe inspired hopes of greater peace and unity. The watchers of late European III worry whether their fate will be one of terminal decline, of invasion by some new barbarians, or perhaps of catastrophic destruction. Or perhaps they will live to see the last golden summer of Late European IV.

II

HELLAS

Ancient Greece

THERE is a quality of excellence about Ancient Greece that brooks few comparisons. In the same way that the quality of Greek light enables painters to see form and colour with exceptional precision and intensity, so the conditions for human development in Greece seem to have favoured both the external environment and the inner life of mankind. Indeed, high-intensity sunlight may well have been one of the many ingredients which produced such spectacular results—in which case Homer, Plato, and Archimedes may be seen as the product of native genius plus photochemistry.

Certainly, in trying to explain the Greek phenomenon, one would have to weigh a very particular combination of factors. One factor would have to be that sun-drenched but seasonal climate which provided optimal encouragement for a vigorous outdoor life. A second factor would be the Aegean, whose islands and straits provided an ideal nursery in the skills of seafaring, commerce, and colonization. A third factor would be the proximity of older, established civilizations whose achievements were waiting to be imported and developed. There were other parts of the world, such as present-day California or southern Australia, which possessed the same favourable climate. There were other enclosed seas, such as the Baltic or the Great Lakes of North America, which were suited to primitive navigation. There were numerous regions adjacent to the great River Valley civilizations that were perfectly habitable. But nowhere—with the possible exception of the Sea of Japan—did all three factors coincide as they did in the eastern Mediterranean. The rise of Ancient Greece often strikes its many awestruck admirers as miraculous; but it may not have been entirely fortuitous.

No doubt a touch of caution should be added to prevailing comment on 'the most amazing period of human history'. Modern opinion has been so saturated by the special pleading both of the Enlightenment and of Romanticism that it is often difficult to see ancient Greece for what it was. Johann Joachim Winckelmann (1717–68), 'The Discoverer', sometime Prefect of Antiquities at Rome, invented an aesthetic scheme which has deeply affected European attitudes

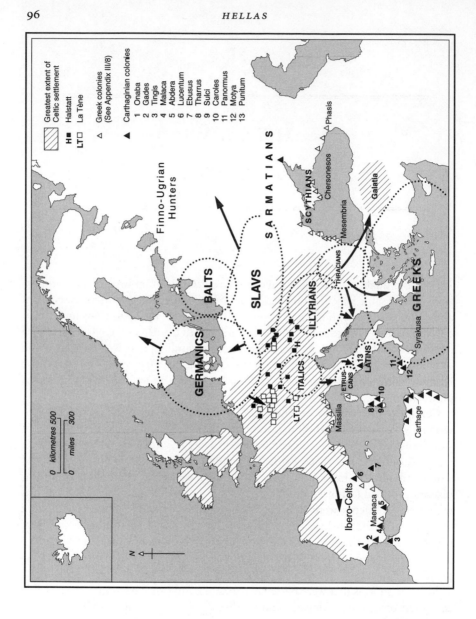

Map 6.
Prehistoric Europe

to Greece ever since. In his *Thoughts on the Imitation of Greek Works . . .* (1755) and his *History of Art Among the Ancients* (1764), he wrote of 'the noble simplicity and serene greatness' and 'the perfect law of art' which supposedly infused everything Greek.[1] The motto was taken to be 'Nothing in excess' or 'Moderation in all things'. One can now suspect that many classical scholars have imposed interpretations which owed more than they knew to the rationalism and restraint of Winckelmann's era. It was not the fashion to give emphasis either to the irrational element in Greek life or to its sheer *joie de vivre*. The philhellenic Romantics of the nineteenth century held priorities of their own. First there came John Keats with his 'Ode on a Grecian Urn':

> O Attic shape! fair attitude! with brede
> of marble men and maidens overwrought,
> With forest branches and the trodden weed:
> Thou silent form! dost tease us out of thought
> As does eternity. Cold Pastoral!
> When old age shall this generation waste,
> Thou shalt remain, in midst of other woe
> Than ours, a friend to man, to whom thou say'st,
> 'Beauty is truth, truth beauty,—that is all
> Ye know on earth, and all ye need to know.'

Then there is Shelley enthusing on 'Hellas':

> The world's great age begins anew,
> The golden years return,
> The earth doth like a snake renew
> Her winter weeds outworn.
> Heaven smiles, and faiths and empires gleam
> Like wrecks of a dissolving dream.

Above all, there was the young Lord Byron dreaming about 'The Isles of Greece':

> Place me on Sunium's marbled steep
> Where nothing save the waves and I
> May hear our mutual murmurs sweep.
> There, swan-like, let me sing and die.[2]

The Romantics wrote on Greece with beguiling genius; and it is not surprising that they can 'tease us out of thought'. Even the most distinguished critics can lose their critical faculties. One of them can be found writing on Greek literature about 'results so satisfactory in form and so compelling in substance that their work has often been held up as a type of perfection'. Another can be found waxing on the joys of digging 'at any classical or sub-classical site in the Greek world . . . where practically every object you find will be beautiful'. Yet another claimed that 'the spirit of Ancient Greece . . . hath so animated universal nature that the very rocks and woods, the very torrents and wilds burst forth with it'. It may be that moderns are fired by nostalgia for a time when the world was young, or moved by a misplaced desire to prove the uniqueness of ancient Greece. Or perhaps, in marvelling at the surviving masterpieces, they forget the dross which has not survived. It was 'a liberal education even to walk in the streets of that wonderful city', wrote a popular historian of Athens, 'to worship in her splendid shrines, to sail the Mediterranean in her fleets'.[3]

Negative aspects can undoubtedly be found by those who seek them. Those noble Greeks, who are so admired, were none the less surrounded by 'degrading superstitions, unnatural vices, human sacrifice, and slavery'.[4] Many commentators compare the high-minded vigour of the early period with the violence and decadence of later centuries. Still, the facts remain. When the civilization of Ancient Greece first came into focus, its links to the older worlds of Egypt and Mesopotamia were tenuous. [**BLACK ATHENA**] [**CADMUS**] [**EPIC**] Yet in the space of three or four hundred years it had created breathtaking achievements in almost every field of human endeavour. European history knows no such burst of vital energy until the era of the Renaissance. For Greece, apparently, did not develop slowly and methodically. It blazed.

◁══════▷

The political history of Ancient Greece spanned more than a thousand years, and passed through several distinct ages. The initial prehistoric age, which looked to the twin centres of Minoan and Mycenean civilization, came to an end in the twelfth century BC. In its later stages it coincided to a large extent with the so-called 'Heroic Age' which culminated in the Trojan War, and which later Greek literature peopled with the legendary names of Hercules, Ajax, Achilles, and Agamemnon. Troy was built on the Asian side of the Aegean which, especially in Ionia, supported the major centres of Greek settlement for centuries. The traditional date for Troy's fall is 1184 BC. Excavations have shown that the historical basis of the legends is stronger than was once supposed.

After that, an extended 'Dark Age' ensued, where the historical and even the archaeological record is meagre.

The 'Golden Age' of the Greek city-states lasted from the eighth to the fourth centuries, and itself passed through several distinct periods. The Archaic period reached the historical record with the first Olympiad whose traditional date of 776 BC was to be adopted as the arbitrary starting-point of the Greek chronology. The central period of Greece's greatest glory began in the fifth century and ended in 338 BC, when the Greeks were forced to surrender to the Macedonians. Thereafter, in the period of dependence, the Greek cities laboured under foreign rule, first Macedonian, then Roman. [**ECO**] [**NOMISMA**]

The principal conflicts of this Golden Age were provided by the wars against the empire of Persia, which under Cyrus the Great (558–529) absorbed the eastern half of the Greek world, and later by the Peloponnesian War (431–404), where the Greek cities fought in fratricidal strife. The battles where the invading Persians were held and repulsed, at the Plain of Marathon (490 BC), or at the Pass of Thermopylae and the Bay of Salamis (480 BC) have inspired endless panegyrics. In contrast, Sparta's inglorious victory over Athens in 404 BC, which was

ECO

ECOLOGICAL devastation had already caught the attention of Greek rulers in the early sixth century BC. Solon the Law-giver proposed that the cultivation of steep slopes should be banned to prevent soil erosion; and Pisistratus introduced a bounty for farmers who planted olive trees to counteract deforestation and over-grazing. Two hundred years later Plato noted the damage inflicted on the land in Attica:

What now remains compared with what then existed is like the skeleton of a sick man, all the fat and soft earth having wasted away. . . . There are some mountains which now have nothing but food for bees, but they had trees not long ago . . . and boundless pasturage. Moreover, it was enriched by the yearly rains from Zeus, which were not lost to it, as now . . . [providing] . . . abundant supplies of springwaters and streams, whereof the shrines still remain even now, at the spots where the fountains formerly existed.[1]

From the ecological point of view, 'the adoption of agriculture was the most fundamental change in human history'. It is known as the 'First Transition', since it created the first form of artificial habitat—the cultivated countryside. Europe, in this process, served as a latter-day appendage to the main developments in south-west Asia, moving in parallel with China and Mesoamerica. But it shared all the consequences—a permanent food surplus and hence the potential for demographic growth; an ordered, hierarchical society; an increase in social coercion, both in labour and in warfare; the emergence of cities, organized trade, and literary culture—and ecological disasters.

Above all, particular ways of thinking about mankind's relationship to Nature were engendered. The Judaeo-Christian tradition, which was destined to triumph in Europe, derived from the era of the 'First Transition'. It stressed Man's supremacy over the rest of Creation:

Be fruitful, and multiply, and replenish the earth. And the fear of you and the dread of you shall be upon every beast of the earth, upon every fowl of the air, upon all the fishes of the sea; into your hand are they delivered.
Every moving thing that liveth shall be meat for you; even as the green herb, have I given you all things. (Gen. 9)

For Thou hast made him [Man,] a little lower than the angels, and hast crowned him with glory and honour.
Thou hast made him to have dominion over the works of thy hands; Thou hast put all things under his feet . . . (Ps. 8)

The heavens are the Lord's, but the earth he has given to the sons of man. (Ps. 115)[2]

Dissident thinkers, such as Maimonides or St Francis, who rejected these exploitative nostrums must be counted a distinct minority.

Nor did attitudes change with the emergence of secular thought during the Renaissance and the Scientific Revolution (see Chapter VII). 'Man, if we look to the final causes,' wrote Francis Bacon, 'must be regarded as the centre of the world.' Progress, including open-ended material progress, was one of the ideals of the Enlightenment. Mankind was judged perfectible, among other things through the application of the new science of economics. Yet in the eyes of the true ecologist, 'economics has enthroned some of our most unattractive predispositions: material acquisitiveness, competition, gluttony, pride, selfishness, shortsightedness, and just plain greed'.[3] [**MARKET**]

Of course, by the time of the Enlightenment, the world was moving into the era of the 'Second Transition'. The logic of exploitation was advancing from 'the rape of nature', i.e. of renewable botanical and zoological resources, to the unbridled consumption of non-renewable resources, especially of fossil fuels such as coal and oil. At this stage, Europe definitely took the lead. The Industrial Revolution vastly increased the sheer weight of human numbers, the urban sprawl, the expectation of affluence, and the rate of consumption, pollution, and exhaustion. Above all, it magnified mankind's capacity for causing ecological trauma on a scale which Solon and Plato could never have imagined.

It has taken a long time for people to take the effects of a damaged environment seriously. When the ex-Emperor Napoleon lay dying at Longwood House on St Helena in 1821, his terminal illness aroused much disquiet. A post-mortem stated the cause of death to have been abdominal cancer. But tests conducted in 1840, when the body was returned to France for reburial, revealed traces of arsenic in the hair roots. Earlier suspicions of murder seemed confirmed. Various persons in his entourage were named as the poisoner. Over a hundred years later, however, a fresh suspicion emerged. In the early nineteenth century, arsenic compounds were sometimes used to fix the colours of fabrics; and close examinations at Longwood House showed that a strong constituent of arsenic was present in the wallpaper of the ex-Emperor's specially redecorated rooms. The subject still arouses controversy. But it is not beyond possibility that Napoleon's death was a case not of murder but of environmental pollution.[4] (See p. 762.)

accomplished with Persian support, or the merciless suppression of Sparta by Thebes, have received less attention.

The Persian Wars gave a permanent sense of identity to the Greeks who escaped Persian domination. Free Hellas was seen as the 'Glorious West', 'the Land of Liberty', the home of Beauty and Wisdom. The East was the seat of slavery, brutality, ignorance. Aeschylus put these sentiments into the mouth of the

NOMISMA

NOMISMA, meaning 'coin', was used by both Greeks and Romans. Our own word 'money' derives, via the French *monnaie*, from the Latin *moneta*, meaning the mint, where coins are struck. (In early Rome the mint was situated on the Capitoline Hill in the temple of Juno Moneta.)

Money, in the sense of coinage, began to circulate in the Aegean in the early seventh century BC. According to Herodotus it was the Kingdom of Lydia which minted the first coins. A *stater* or two-drachma piece of electrum, an alloy of gold and silver, struck either in Lydia or in Ionia, is often described as the world's oldest coin.[1] Certainly the kings of Phrygia, from the legendary Midas, whose touch turned everything to gold, to Croesus (r. 561–546 BC), whose name was synonymous with fabulous wealth, were closely connected with the origins of money. They owned the 'golden sands' of the River Pactolus, near the Lydian capital, Sardis.

The island of Aegina also participated in the early days of coinage. Aegina's silver coins, introduced in 670 BC, were certainly the first in Europe. Stamped with the emblem of a sea tortoise, they mark the beginning both of the widespread 'aeginetic' system of weights and measures and of numismatic art.[2] Each of the subsequent mints adopted a similar emblem—the owl or the olive-branch for Athens, the pegasus for Corinth, the Arethusan nymph for Syracuse. From an early date, heads of divinities and inscriptions identifying the mint or the ruling authority were also common. Coins bearing the head of the ruler did not come into fashion until Hellenistic times, but were the norm under the Roman Empire.

Numismatics, the study of coins, is one of history's auxiliary sciences. It deals with some of the most durable evidence of ancient times, and is particularly valuable for dating the layers of archaeological sites. Coins struck in hard metal speak with great precision about time and space. They bear witness not only to material conditions but also to the ramifications of international trade and cultural contacts.

From the seventh century Aegean coins have spread throughout the world. They form the basis of most monetary systems and of most commercial exchange. The right to mint coins has become one of the hallmarks of political sovereignty. 1,500 mints are known from ancient Greece alone. The Lydian *stater* has its descendants in the coinage of Rome, of Christian Europe, and now of all countries. Like the silver drachma of Aegina, some coins have gained currency far beyond the times and the territories for which they were intended. Indeed, the charisma of nomisma became so powerful that many came to fear it. 'The love of money', wrote St Paul from Macedonia in AD 65, 'is the root of all evil.' [**DOLLAR**]

Queen of Persia. The scene is the royal palace at Susa, where news has arrived of her son's defeat at Salamis:

> QUEEN. My friends, where is this Athens said to be?
> CHORUS. Far toward the dying flames of the sun.
> QUEEN. Yet my son lusts to track it down.
> CHORUS. Then all of Hellas would be subject to the King.
> QUEEN. So rich in numbers are they?
> CHORUS. So great a host as dealt to the Persians many woes.
> QUEEN. Who commands them? Who is shepherd to their host?
> CHORUS. They are slaves to none, neither are they subject.[5]

The notion that Greece was all liberty, and Persia all tyranny, was an extremely subjective one. But it provided the foundation of a tradition which has persistently linked 'civilization' with 'Europa' and 'the West' (see Introduction, p. 22). [**BARBAROS**]

The rise of Macedonia, a hellenized country to the north of Greece, reached its peak in the reigns of Philip of Macedon (r. 359–336 BC) and of Philip's son, Alexander the Great (r. 336–323 BC). In a series of campaigns of unparalleled brilliance, which ended only with Alexander's death from fever in Babylon, the whole of Persia's vast domains were overrun and the Greek world was extended to the banks of the Indus. According to one admiring opinion, Alexander was the first man to view the whole known world, the *oikoumene*, as one country. But for the senior English historian of Greece, at the end of his twelfth volume and his 96th chapter, the passing of 'Free Hellas' was to be lamented even more than Alexander was to be praised. 'The historian feels that the life has departed from his subject,' he wrote, 'and with sadness and humiliation brings his narrative to a close.'[6] In the political sense, this Hellenistic Age, which began with the Macedonian supremacy, lasted until the systematic elimination of Alexander's successors by the growing power of Rome. [**MAKEDON**]

The geographical expansion of the Greek world was impressive. The miniature island- and city-states which ringed the stony shore of the Aegean often lacked the resources to support a growing population. Arable land was at a premium. Commercial outlets grew, even without a modern sense of enterprise. Friendly trading-posts were needed for effective contacts with the continental interior. For all these reasons, the foundation of clone colonies offered many attractions. From the eighth century onwards, therefore, several of the most ancient cities of the Greek mainland and of Asia Minor—Chalcis, Eretria, Corinth, Megara, Phocaea, and, above all, Miletus—were engaged in active colonization. The most frequent locations were found in Sicily and southern Italy, in Thrace, and on the coasts of the Euxine or 'Hospitable' Sea—so named, like the Pacific, in the hope that its name might offset its nature. [**CHERSONESOS**]

In time, as the early colonies themselves gave birth to further colonies of their own, whole chains or families of cities were established, each with its lasting devotion to the parent foundation. Miletus constructed the largest of such families, with up to eighty members of various generations. In the west, in Sicily, the first

BARBAROS

Every textbook stresses the formative influence of the Persian Wars in uniting the people of 'Free Hellas' and in fixing their sense of Greek identity. Less obvious is the fact that those same wars set in motion a process whereby the Greeks would define their view of the outside, 'barbarian' world. Yet 'inventing the Hellene' went hand in hand with 'inventing the barbarian'; and Athenian drama of the 5th century provided the medium through which the effect was achieved.[1]

Prior to Marathon and Salamis, the Greeks do not appear to have harboured strong feelings about their neighbours as enemies. Archaic poetry had often made heroes out of supernatural outsiders, including Titans and Amazons. Homer treated Greeks and Trojans as equals. Greek colonies on the Black Sea Coast lived from fruitful co-operation and interchange with the Scythians of the steppe. [CHERSONESOS]

In the 5th century, however, the Greeks became much more self-congratulatory and xenophobic. One finds the ethnic factor raised by Herodotus (b. 484), who, whilst appreciating the older civilizations, especially Egypt, laid great store by the 'shared blood' and common language of the Hellenes.

But the most effective catalysts of changing attitudes were the tragedians, especially Aeschylus (b. 525), who had himself fought at Marathon. In his *Persae*, Aeschylus creates a lasting stereotype whereby the civilized Persians are reduced to cringing, ostentatious, arrogant, cruel, effeminate, and lawless aliens.

Henceforth, all outsiders stood to be denigrated as barbarous. No one could compare to the wise, courageous, judicious, and freedom-loving Greeks. The Thracians were boorish and mendacious. The Macedonians were not *echte hellenisch*. By Plato's time, a permanent barrier had been raised between Greeks and all foreigners. It is assumed that the Greeks alone had the right and the natural disposition to rule. In Athens, it was simply not done to liken the conduct of foreign tyrants to the ways that Athenians could themselves behave towards subject peoples.

The 'superiority complex' of the ancient Greeks inevitably raises questions about similar ethnocentric and xenophobic ideas which surface in Europe at later dates. It was certainly adopted by the Romans, and must be held in the reckoning when one considers the various purveyors of 'Western Civilization' who, like the Romans, have felt such an affinity for ancient Greece. Nor can it be irrelevant to the resentments which combine attacks on 'Western Civilization' with a particular brand of Classical revisionism. [BLACK ATHENA] Some commentators hold that the conclusions which the ancient Greeks drew from their encounter with the otherness of neighbouring peoples have passed into the body of European tradition:

In this particular encounter began the idea of 'Europe' with all its arrogance, all its implications of superiority, all its assumptions of priority and antiquity, all its pretensions to a natural right to dominate.[2]

Chalcidian colonies, Naxos and Messana (Messina), dated from 735 BC. Emporia (Ampurias) in Iberia, Massilia (Marseille), Neapolis (Naples), Syracusae (Syracuse), Byzantium on the Bosporus, Cyrene in North Africa, and Sinope on the southern Euxine shore all date from the same early centuries. At a later date, following the conquests of Alexander the Great, Greek cities arose in the depths of Asia. Foundations which bore the name of the Macedonian conqueror included Alexandria-at-World's-End (Khojent, in Turkestan), Alexandria in Areia (Herat), Alexandria in Arachosia (Kandahar), Alexandria in Syria, and, above all, Alexandria in Egypt (332 BC). From Saguntum (Sagunto near Valencia) in the far west to Bucephala (Jhelum) in the Punjab at the eastern extremity, named after Alexander's faithful charger, the interlinked chains of Greek cities stretched for almost 4,500 miles, that is, for almost twice the distance across North America. [MASSILIA] (See Appendix III, p. 1222.)

Sicily and southern Italy (then known as Magna Graecia or 'Greater Greece') had a special role to play. They developed the same relationship with the Greek mainland that the Americas would develop with Europe. Until the Persian conquest of Asia Minor in the sixth century, the focus had remained very firmly in the Aegean. Miletus had been an even larger and more prosperous city than Athens. But once 'Europa' came under threat, first from Persia and then from Macedonia and Rome, the cities of Magna Graecia assumed a new importance. Sicily, full of luxury and tyrants, thrived on its special symbiosis with the surrounding Phoenician world. Syracuse was for Athens what New York was to be for London. On Greek Sicily and its internecine wars, Michelet waxed specially eloquent:

It grew in gigantic proportions. Its volcano, Etna, put Vesuvius to shame . . . and the surrounding towns responded to its grandeur. The herculean hand of the Dorians can be seen in the remains of Acragas (Agrigentum), in the columns of Posidonia (Paestum), in the white phantom that is Selinonte . . . Yet the colossal power of these cities, their prodigious riches, their naval forces . . . did nothing to retard their ruin. In the history of Magna Graecia, one defeat spelt disaster. Thus Sybaris and Agrigentum passed from the world, the Tyre and the Babylon of the West . . .[7]

Magna Graecia commanded a region of great strategic importance, where the Greek world came into direct contact with the rival spheres first of the Phoenicians and then of Rome.

Phoenicia, homeland of Europa, flourished in parallel to Greece and in similar style. Indeed, Phoenicia's city-states were considerably senior to their Greek counterparts, as were the Phoenician colonies. Sidon and Tyre had risen to prominence at the time when Crete was in terminal decline. *Kart-hadshat*, or 'New City' (Kartigon, Carthago, Carthage) had been founded in North Africa in 810 BC, reputedly by Phoenician colonists led by Pygmalion and his sister Dido. Neighbouring *Atiq* (Utica) was still older. When old Phoenicia was overrun, like Asia Minor, by the Persians, Carthage and Utica were left, like the cities of the Greek mainland, to thrive on their own.

Carthage built a huge empire through naval power, trade, and colonization. Its daughter colonies stretched from beyond the Pillars of Hercules at Gades (Cadiz)

CHERSONESOS

CHERSONESOS, 'Peninsular City', was founded in 422–421 BC by Dorian colonists from Heraclea Pontica. It stood on a headland on the western coast of the peninsula of Taurica,* 3 km beyond modern Sevastopol. It was one of a score of Greek cities on the northern shore of the Euxine Sea, most of them colonies of Miletus—Olbia ('Prosperity'), Panticapaeum on the Cimmerian Bosphorus (The Straits of Kerch), Tanais on the Don, Phanagoria, and others. Its foundation coincided very closely with the visit to neighbouring Olbia of the historian, Herodotus, who recorded the first description of the Scythian and Tauric peoples inhabiting the Pontic steppes. Like its neighbours, it lived from commerce with the inland tribes, and from the resulting seaborne trade in wheat, wine, hides, and salted fish. Its population of perhaps 20,000 inhabited a typical grid of straight stone streets, replete with the usual agora, acropolis, theatre, and port.[1]

Exceptionally, Chersonesos survived all the turbulence of the next 1,700 years, passing through successive Greek, Sarmatian, Roman, and Byzantine phases. After its initial period as a solitary Greek outpost, it was absorbed in the 2nd century BC by the growing 'Kingdom of the Bosphorus', based at nearby Panticapaeum. The Kingdom, whose huge wealth grew from the grain trade, especially with Athens, was dominated by the latest wave of immigrants from the steppe, the Iranic Sarmatians, whose ability to assimilate into preceding Greek civilization created a brilliant new synthesis. Its goldsmiths, who worked to order for the Scythian chiefs of the interior, produced some of the most magnificent artistic jewellery of the ancient world. Its Spartocid dynasty, which was not Greek, eventually sought the protection of Mithridates VI Eupator, King of Pontus—the subject of Mozart's early opera, *Mitridate, Re di Ponto*—who died in Panticapaeum in 63 BC (the acropolis at Kerch is still called Mount Mithridates). The Roman garrison, installed at that time, did not impose full imperial rule for nearly two centuries.

Despite repeated invasions, particularly by the Goths, Huns, and Khazars, the late Roman/early Byzantine period saw some fifty Christian churches built at Chersonesos. In one of them, in 988 or 991, the latest barbarian visitor, Prince Wolodymyr (or Vladimir) of Kiev, stepped into the marble pool of the baptistery to be christened before his marriage to the Byzantine Emperor's sister. By that time, Khazar overlordship had waned, and the Byzantines were able to re-establish Chersonesos as capital of the Theme of Klimata.[2] The final destruction of the 'Peninsular City' came in 1299 at the hands of the Mongol Tartars, who were busy turning Crimea

* The Tauric Peninsula's modern name, *Krym* or *Crimea*, derives from the Turkish word *kerim* meaning 'fortress', and dates only from the 15th century.

into their homeland. It lived to see neither the arrival of the Ottomans in the fifteenth century nor the Russian conquest of 1783.

Excavations at Chersonesos began in 1829. They were intensified before the First World War, and resumed in the 1920s by a Soviet Archaeological Commission. The Tsarists were mainly looking for evidence of St Vladimir's baptism. In 1891 they erected a vast domed basilica, now shattered, on the wrong spot. The Soviets were looking for remains of the material culture of a slave-owning society.[3]

Possession of the classical Black Sea sites gave their modern owners a strong sense of historical pride. The naval port of Sevastopol was founded beside the ruins of Chersonesos with an appropriate Greek name meaning 'City of Glory'. The Tauride Palace in St Petersburg, built for the conqueror of Crimea, Prince Potemkin, started Russia's 'native classical style'. After the attack of the British and French in 1854–6, and the heroic Russian defence, the Crimean coast became a favourite resort for the summer palaces of tsarist courtiers and Soviet Party bosses. They all justified their presence through the dubious Russian Version of History that starts with St Vladimir. In 1941–2, after a second heroic siege of Sevastopol, the Crimea was briefly occupied by the Nazis, whose 'Gotland Project' would have returned the peninsula into the hands of German colonists. In 1954, on the tercentenary of another dubious event, the Soviet Government in Moscow presented Crimea to Ukraine. The gift was intended to symbolize the indissoluble links of Crimea and Ukraine with Russia. Instead, on the collapse of the USSR, it had exactly the opposite effect. In August 1991, the last Soviet General Secretary was caught holidaying in his villa at Foros, along the coast from Sevastopol, when the abortive coup in Moscow brought the Soviet era to an end.[4] (See p. 1126.)

In recent times, the great variety of Crimea's native population has all but disappeared. The ancient Tauri and Tauro-Scythians were long since over-run. The Crimean Goths defended their inland stronghold of Mangup until 1475. The Tartars were deported en masse by Stalin in 1942.[5] The Pontic Greeks survived until their deportation in 1949. A handful of Jews, who had escaped the Nazis, left for Israel in the 1980s. Russians and Ukrainians were left in an absolute majority.

In 1992, as families of the ex-Soviet military from Sevastopol shared the pebbly beach with the tourists, seeking their suntans beneath the ruined clifftop columns of Chersonesos, they looked on anxiously at the returning Tartars, at Ukrainian claims to the Black Sea Fleet, and at Russian demands for an autonomous Crimean republic. No location could have reminded them more of the impermanence of glory.

MASSILIA

MASSILIA (Marseille) was founded c.600 BC by Greeks from Phocaean Asia Minor. According to legend Photis, their leader, sailed his galley into the harbour just as the chieftain of the local Ligurian tribe was holding a betrothal ceremony for his favourite daughter. When the girl was invited to hand the cup of betrothal to one of the assembled warriors, she handed it instead to the handsome Greek. Thus began one of the richest and most dynamic of all Greek colonies.

Surrounded by high white-stone crags and guarded by an offshore island, the magnificent harbour of ancient Massilia has served as a major centre of commercial and cultural life for more than 2,500 years. The government was a merchant oligarchy. A Great Council of 600 citizens, elected for life, appointed a smaller Council of Fifteen, which formed the executive. The trade and exploration of the Massiliots spread far and wide. They dominated the sea from Luna in Tuscany to the south of Iberia, and they set up trading-posts at Nicaea (Nice), Antipolis (Antibes), Rhoda (Arles), and distant Emporia, all dedicated to their own patron goddess, the Ephesian Artemis. Their sailors did not fear the ocean beyond the Pillars of Hercules, and were reputed to have reached Iceland in the north, and what is now Senegal in the south. One daring fourth-century Massiliot, Pytheas, navigated the northern coasts of Europe including the 'Tin Islands' (as Herodotus called Britain). His lost 'Survey of the Earth' was known to Strabo and Polybius.

Faced with the jealous rivalry of the Phoenicians and Carthaginians, Massilia had often appealed to Rome for support. But they did so once too often. In 125 BC when they called for military aid against the Gauls, the Roman legions overran the entire country, thereby creating the Province of Transalpine Gaul (Provence). From this a trilingual community grew up, speaking Greek, Latin, and Celtic. Thereafter, the city's life mirrored all the changes of Mediterranean politics—Arabs, Byzantines, Genoans, and, from 1481, the French. The greatest days of Marseilles's prosperity started in the nineteenth century, with the opening of French interests in the Levant. Napoleon's expedition to Egypt, and the building of the Suez Canal by de Lesseps, were key episodes.

Modern Marseilles, like ancient Massilia, is still ruled by the sea. Le Vieux Port, immortalized by the dramatic trilogy of Marcel Pagnol, has been superseded by the vast Port Autonome beyond the digue. But the turbulent emotions of Fanny, Marius, and César, hopelessly torn by the tearful departures and arrivals of the ships, are constantly repeated:

FANNY. Et toi, Marius, tu ne m'aimes pas? [*Il se tait*] . . .
MARIUS. Je te l'ai déjà dit, Fanny. Je ne peux pas me marier.

FANNY. Alors, c'est quelque vilaine femme des vieux quartiers. . . . Dis-le moi. Marius . . .

MARIUS. J'ai confiance en toi. Je vais te le dire. Je veux partir.[1]

(Marius, don't you love me? / I've told you already, Fanny, I can't marry you. / Oh, I see: it's one of those nasty women from the old town . . . Go on, say it. / No. I trust no-one but you, Fanny. I'm about to tell you. I want to leave./)

From the terrace of Notre Dame de la Garde, perched high on the site of a Greek temple, one can still gaze down on the ships slipping into the harbour like the galleys of Photis. Or, like the Count of Monte Cristo in the Château d'If, or like Marius, one can dream of escape across the sea.[2]

---

and Tingis (Tangier) to Panormus (Palermo) on Sicily. In its heyday it was probably most prosperous of all city-states, dominating all the islands and coasts of the western Mediterranean. From the fifth century onwards, it fought and destroyed many of the Greek cities of Sicily, where its ambitions were cut short only by the arrival of Roman power.

The Phoenicians and Carthaginians, like Jews and Arabs, were Semites. As the ultimate losers in the struggle for supremacy in the Mediterranean, they did not enjoy the sympathy either of the Greeks or of the Romans. As idolators of Baal, the ultimate graven image, they have always been singled out for derision by followers of the Judaeo-Christian tradition, which the Graeco-Roman world eventually adopted. Though Europa's Phoenician kinsfolk held sway for a millennium and more, their civilization is very little known or studied. Their story may have suffered from yet another variant of antisemitism.

Greek religion progressed from early animism and fetishism to a view of the world seen as 'one great City of gods and men'. The Olympian pantheon was already extant in the late prehistoric age. Zeus, Father of the Gods, and Hera, his consort, ruled over the headstrong family of Olympians—Apollo, Artemis, Pallas Athene, Ares, Poseidon, Hermes, Dionysus, Demeter, Pluto, and Persephone. Their home on the summit of Mount Olympus was generally taken to stand on the northern frontier of the Greek homeland. They were joined by a rich gallery of local deities, satyrs, shades, nymphs, furies, sibyls, and muses, to whom the Greeks paid their oblations. The ritual sacrifice of animals remained the normal practice. Though it was the prerogative of the gods to be capricious, and though some, such as Ares, God of War, or Poseidon, God of the Sea, could be vengeful, there was no Devil, no power of darkness or sin to prey on people's deeper fears. Man's supreme fault was *hubris* or overweening pride, commonly punished by *nemesis*, the wrath of the gods. [**SPICE-OX**]

A thousand myths, and a dazzling choice of cults and oracles, proliferated. They fostered an outlook where courage and enterprise, tempered by respect,

SPICE-OX

PYTHAGORAS (*fl. c.*530 BC) gave voice to two well-known maxims: 'Everything is numbers' and 'Eating beans is a crime equal to eating the heads of one's parents'. Scholars concerned with the origins of modern science study his mathematics. Those concerned with the working of the Greek mind study his ideas on gastronomy. (See Appendix III, p. 1221.)

Like the Pilgrim Fathers of a later age, Pythagoras was a religious dissenter, and sailed away from his native Samos to found a sectarian colony in Magna Graecia. There he found the freedom to apply his religious theories, among other things to food and diet. His central contention sprang from the concept of metempsychosis, 'the transmigration of souls', which could pass after death from person to person, or from persons to animals. As a result, he was opposed in principle to the custom of animal sacrifices, and held that the perfume of heated herbs and spices was a more fitting offering to the gods than the stench of roasted fat.

But if spices formed the link with Heaven, beans were the link with Hades. Broad beans, whose nodeless shoots relentlessly push their way to the sunlight, were thought to act as 'ladders for the souls of men' migrating from the underworld. Beans propagated in a closed pot produced a seething mess of obscene shapes reminiscent of sexual organs and aborted foetuses. Similar taboos were placed on the consumption of the noble meats, especially of beef. Some creatures like the pig and the goat, which root around and damage nature, were judged harmful, and hence edible. Others, like the sheep, which gives wool, and the 'working ox', man's most faithful companion, were judged useful, and hence inedible. Joints of ignoble meat could be eaten, if necessary, but the vital organs such as the heart or the brain could not. According to Aristoxenos of Tarentum, the resultant diet consisted of *maza* (barley meal), wine, fruit, wild mallow and asphodel, *artos* (wheatbread), raw and cooked vegetables, opson seasoning, and, on special occasions, suckling pig and kid. Once, an ox rescued by Pythagoras from a beanfield was given a lifelong pension of barley meal in the local Temple of Hera.

More famously, when Pythagoras' disciple, Empedocles of Acragas, won the chariot race at Olympia in 496 BC, he refused to offer up the customary sacrifice of a roasted ox. Instead, he burned the image of an ox made from oil and spices, saluting the gods amidst a billowing cloud of frankincense and myrrh. The Pythagoreans believed that diet was an essential branch of ethics. 'So long as men slaughter animals,' the master said, 'they won't stop killing each other.'[1] [**KONOPIΠTE**]

were thought to be rewarded by health and fortune. The cult of Zeus, centred at Olympia, which hosted the Olympic Games, was universal, as was the combination of piety and competitive endeavour. The widespread cult of Apollo, God of Light, was centred at his birthplace on the island of Delos, and at Delphi. The Mysteries of Demeter, Goddess of the Earth, at Eleusis, and the still more ecstatic Mysteries of Dionysus, God of Wine, developed from ancient fertility rites. The cult of Orpheus the Singer, who had pursued his dead love, Eurydice, through the underworld, turned on a belief in the existence and purification of souls. Orphism, which lasted from the seventh century until late Roman times, inspired endless poetic comment, from Plato and Virgil onwards:

> Nur wer die Leier schon hob
> auch unter Schatten,
> darf das unendliche Lob
> ahnend erstatten.
>
> Nur wer mit Toten vom Mohn
> aß, von dem ihren
> wird nicht den leisesten Ton
> wieder verlieren.
>
> Mag auch die Spieglung im Teich
> oft uns verschwimmen:
> *Wisse das Bild.*
>
> Erst in dem Doppelbereich
> werden die Stimmen
> ewig und mild.

(Only he who has raised the lyre even among the shades can dispense the infinite praise. Only he who ate of their poppy with the Dead will never lose even the softest note. Though the reflection in the pond may often dissolve before us—*Know the image!* Only in the double realm will the voices be lasting and gentle.)[8]

All these cults, as well as the Hellenistic cults of Mithras and Isis, were still in full circulation when Christianity arrived in the period after the 200th Olympiad (see Chapter III). [**OMPHALOS**]

Greek philosophy, or 'love of wisdom', grew up in opposition to conventional religious attitudes. Socrates (469–399 BC), son of a stonemason, was sentenced in Athens to drink hemlock for 'introducing strange gods' and 'corrupting youth'. Yet the Socratic method of asking penetrating questions in order to test the assumptions which underlie knowledge provided the basis of all subsequent rational thought. It was used by Socrates to challenge what he regarded as the specious arguments of the earlier Sophists or 'sages'. His motto was 'Life unexamined is not worth living'. According to his disciple Plato, Socrates said: 'All I know is that I know nothing.' It was the perfect start for epistemology.

Plato (*c.*429–347 BC) and Plato's own disciple Aristotle (384–322 BC) together laid the foundations of most branches of speculative and natural philosophy.

Plato's Academy or 'Grove' and Aristotle's Lyceum, otherwise known as the Peripatetic School, were the Oxford and Cambridge (or Harvard and Yale) of the ancient world. With them in mind, it has been said: 'the legacy of the Greeks to Western Philosophy was Western Philosophy'.[9] Of the two Plato was the idealist, creating the first imaginary utopias, fundamental theories of forms and of immortality, an influential cosmogony, a far-ranging critique of knowledge, and a famous analysis of love. Nothing in intellectual history is more powerful than Plato's metaphor of the cave, which suggests that we can only perceive the world indirectly, seeing reality only by means of its firelit shadows on the wall. Aristotle, in contrast, was 'the practitioner of inspired common sense', the systematizer. His encyclopedic works range from metaphysics and ethics to politics, literary criticism, logic, physics, biology, and astronomy.

Greek literature, initially in the form of epic poetry, was one of those wonders which apparently came into being in a mature state. Homer, who probably lived and wrote in the middle of the eighth century BC, was exploiting a much older oral tradition. He may or may not have been the sole author of the works attributed to him. But the first poet of European literature is widely considered to have been the most influential. The *Iliad* and the *Odyssey* have few peers, and no superiors. Homer's language, which classicists call 'sublime', proved to be infinitely flexible and expressive. [EPIC]

Written literature depends on literacy, whose origins go back to the importation of an alphabet in the eighth century. The art of letters was greatly encouraged by the urban character of Greek life, but the extent of its penetration into the various social strata is a matter of some controversy. [CADMUS]

Homer's successors—his fellow epicists from Hesiod (*fl. c.*700 BC) to the unknown author(s) of the so-called 'Homeric Hymns'; the elegists from Callinus of Ephesus (*fl.* from 690 BC) to Xenophanes of Colophon (*c.*570–480 BC); the lyricists from Sappho (b. 612 BC) to Pindar (518–438 BC), from Anacreon (*fl. c.*530 BC) to Simonides of Ceos (556–468 BC)—have attracted countless imitators and translators. Theocritus the Syracusan (*c.*300–260 BC) wrote idylls of nymphs and goatherds which became the model for a pastoral tradition stretching from Virgil's eclogues to *As You Like It*. But none sang so sweet as the 'tenth muse' of Lesbos:

> Some say that the most beautiful thing on this dark earth
> Is a squadron of cavalry; others say
> A troop of infantry, others a fleet of ships;
> But I say that it is the one you love.[10]

Poetry-reading was closely allied to music; and the melody of a seven-stringed lyre served as a common accompaniment to the declaimed hexameters. The Greek word *musike* encompassed all melodious sounds, whether words or notes. Poetry was to be found in the simplest inscriptions, in the widespread art of epigrams:

OMPHALOS

DELPHI, in the view of the Greeks, lay at the exact centre of the world. Its *omphalos* or 'navel stone' marked the meeting-place of two of Zeus's eagles, one sent from the east and one from the west. Here, too, in a deep valley ringed by the dark pines and rose-tinted cliffs of Mt Parnassus, Apollo had slain the snake-god Python and, in a steam-filled cave above a gaseous chasm, had established the most prestigious of oracles. In historic times, the Temple of Apollo was built alongside a theatre, a stadium for the Pythian Games, and the numerous treasuries of patron cities. In 331 BC Aristotle and his nephew drew up a list of all the victors of the Pythian Games to date. Their findings were inscribed on four stone tablets, which survived to be found by modern archaeologists.[1]

The procedures of the oracle followed a timeless ritual. On the seventh day of each month the high priestess, Pythia, freshly purified in the Castalian Spring, would seat herself on the sacred tripod above the chasm and, locked in an ecstatic trance among the vapours, would await her petitioners' enquiries. The petitioners, having watched the customary sacrifice of a goat, would await her notoriously ambiguous responses, delivered in hexameters.[2]

Theseus, the legendary slayer of the Minotaur and founder of Athens, was given this comfort:

> THESEUS, SON OF AEGEUS . . . DO NOT BE DISTRESSED. FOR AS A LEATHERN BOTTLE YOU WILL RIDE THE WAVES EVEN IN A SWELLING SURGE.

The citizens of Thera, worried by their failing colony on the African coast, were told to reconsider its location:

> IF YOU KNOW LIBYA, THE NURSE OF FLOCKS, BETTER THAN I DO, WHEN YOU HAVE NOT BEEN THERE . . . I ADMIRE YOUR WISDOM.

Moved to the mainland from its offshore island, Cyrene prospered.

King Croesus of Lydia wanted to know whether to make war or to keep the peace. The Oracle said: 'GO TO WAR AND DESTROY A GREAT EMPIRE.' He went to war, and *his* empire was destroyed.

Before Salamis in 480 BC, an Athenian delegation implored the aid of Apollo against the Persian invaders:

> PALLAS IS NOT ABLE TO APPEASE ZEUS . . . BUT WHEN ALL ELSE HAS BEEN CAPTURED . . . YET ZEUS OF THE BROAD HEAVEN GIVES TO THE TRITON-BORN A WOODEN WALL . . . TO BLESS YOU AND YOUR CHILDREN.

Themistocles, the Athenian admiral, rightly deduced that the key to victory lay with his wooden ships.

Lysander, the Spartan general who had entered Athens in triumph at the end of the Peloponnesian War, was warned:

I BID YOU GUARD AGAINST A ROARING HOPLITE AND A SNAKE, CUNNING SON OF THE EARTH, WHICH ATTACKS BEHIND THE BACK.

He was killed by a soldier with the emblem of a snake on his shield.

Philip of Macedon, notorious for his bribery, was reputedly told 'TO FIGHT WITH SILVER SPEARS'. More authentically, on preparing to fight the Persians, he received this prophecy: 'THE BULL IS GARLANDED. THE END IS COME. THE SACRIFICER IS NIGH.' Shortly afterwards he was murdered.

The Roman, Lucius Junius Brutus, consulted the Oracle with two companions, and asked about their future:

YOUNG MEN, HE AMONG YOU WHO FIRST SHALL KISS HIS MOTHER WILL HOLD THE HIGHEST POWER IN ROME.

Brutus' companions took the hint literally, whilst Brutus bent down to kiss the earth. In 509 BC Brutus became Rome's first Consul.

Four centuries later, Cicero asked the Oracle how one achieved the highest fame. He was told:

MAKE YOUR OWN NATURE, NOT THE OPINION OF THE MULTITUDE, THE GUIDE OF YOUR LIFE.

The Emperor Nero, fearing death, was told: 'EXPECT EVIL FROM 73'. Encouraged, he thought that he might live to be 73. In the event he was overthrown and forced to kill himself at the age of 31. Seventy-three turned out to be the age of his successor, Galba.

Most famously, perhaps, when Alexander the Great consulted the Oracle, it remained silent.[3]

Belief in the omniscience of the Delphic Oracle is almost as great among enthusiastic moderns as it was among the superstitious Greeks of old. For scholars, however, the problem lies in distinguishing the Oracle's real achievements from its limitless reputation. Sceptics point out that none of the alleged predictions was ever recorded in advance of the events to which they referred. The amazing powers of the Oracle could never be tested. A powerful cult, an efficient publicity machine, and a gullible public were all essential elements of the operation.

Many of the oracle's most famous sayings were inscribed on the walls of the Temple of Apollo. These included 'Nothing in Excess' and 'Know Thyself'.[4] They became the watchwords of Greek civilization.

EPIC

HOMER'S *Iliad* and *Odyssey* were traditionally regarded in Europe not merely as the oldest examples of European literature but as the earliest form of high literature anywhere. In 1872, however, following excavations of clay tablets from the palace library of Assurbanipal at Nineveh, the capital of ancient Assyria, the world was introduced to the *Epic of Gilgamesh*.

Gilgamesh was already venerable by the time that Homer's poems were composed. Indeed, it can be traced back through a Mesopotamian literary tradition into the third millennium BC. It begins:

> [Of him who] found out all things, I shall tell the land,
> [Of him who] experienced everything, [I shall teach] the whole.
> He searched [?] lands [?] everywhere.
> He who experienced the whole gained complete wisdom.
> He found out what was secret, and uncovered what was hidden.
> He brought back a tale of times before the flood.
> He had journeyed far and wide, weary and at last resigned,
> He engraved all his toils on memorial tablets of stone.[1]

Initial interest in the Babylonian epic centred on its biblical connections, notably on its narration of the Flood and the Ark and the story of Creation. But it was not long before scholars noticed echoes of Homer. After all, the chronological coincidence was close enough. Assurbanipal was building his library at Nineveh in the last quarter of the seventh century BC; Nineveh was destroyed in 612, in much the same era that the Homeric poems must have found their final form. (See Appendix III, p. 1216.)

Many textual similarities can be explained by the oral conventions practised by all pre-literate epic poets. But many things cannot be so easily explained. The opening invocation of *Gilgamesh* resembles the opening lines of the *Odyssey* both in tone and sentiment:

Goddess of song, teach me the story of a hero. This was the man of wide-ranging spirit who had sacked the sacred city of Troy and who had wandered afterwards long and far. Many were those whose cities he viewed and whose minds he came to know, many the trouble that vexed his heart . . . Goddess, daughter of Zeus, impart to me in turn some knowledge of all these things, beginning where you will.[2]

Stronger still is the case that can be made for the influence of *Gilgamesh* on the *Iliad*. Both epics turn on a dramatic twist of the plot which occurs with the death of one of two inseparable friends. Gilgamesh mourns for Enkidu as Achilles mourns for Patroclus. Other episodes, such as that where the gods draw lots for the division of the earth, sea, and sky, are strikingly similar. What was once rated as 'a possible Greek debt to Assyria' must now be upgraded to a probability.[3] If this supposition is correct, the Homeric epics not only supply a link between Classical Letters and the countless generations of *aoidoi*, the unlettered bards of the immemorial tradition. They also span the gap between the conventional western literary canon and the far more ancient writings of non-European literature.

πάντα γέλως καὶ πάντα κόντα τὸ μηδέν·
πάντα γὰρ ἐξ ἀλόγων ἐστὶ τὰ γιγνόμενα.

(Everything's laughter, everything dust, everything nothing. | Out of unreason comes everything that exists.)[11]

and of epitaphs:

ὦ ξεῖν', ἄγγειλον Λακεδαιμονίοις ὅτι τῆδε
κείμεθα τοῖς κείνων ῥήμασι πειθόμενοι.

(Tell them in Lakedaemon, passer-by. | That we kept the rules, resolved to die.)[12]

Greek drama evolved out of the ceremonies of religious festivals. The concept of *tragodia*, literally 'goat-song', was originally connected with ritual sacrifice. The first Athenian dramas were performed at the festival of Dionysus. Like the Games, they were staged in the spirit of competition. The stylized dialogue between the players and the chorus provided a vehicle for exploring the most terrible psychological and spiritual conflicts. Between them the triad of tragedians, Aeschylus (525–456), Sophocles (c.496–406), and Euripides (c.480–406), turned tribal myth and legend into the foundation-stones of world literature. *Seven Against Thebes*, the *Oresteia*, and *Prometheus Bound*; *Oedipus the King*, *Electra*, and *Antigone*; *Iphigenia among the Taurians*, *Medea*, and *Hippolytus*, represent the remnants of a much larger repertoire. [OEDIPUS]

Only thirty-two tragedies have survived; but they continue to be performed the world over. They are specially needed by the horror-struck twentieth century. 'Tragedy enables us to live through the unbearable.' 'The greatest Greek tragedies are a constant education in [the] nightmare possibility . . . that we will all end in darkness and despair and suicide.' 'Having boldly looked right into the terrible destructiveness of so-called World History, as well as the cruelty of nature, the Greek comforts himself. . . . Art saves him, and through art—life.'[13]

The comedians, led by Aristophanes (c.450–385), felt free to poke fun at everyone from philosophers to politicians. *The Knights*, *The Birds*, *The Clouds*, *The Wasps*, *The Frogs*, whose fantastic plots are laced with lavatorial and sexual humour, still raise roars of laughter from audiences the world over. Aristophanes had a matchless talent for coining unforgettable phrases. He is the inventor of *Nephelokokkugia*, 'Cloudcuckooland'. [SCHOLASTIKOS]

It is no exaggeration to say that Greek letters form the launch-pad of the

CADMUS

CADMUS, son of Agenor, King of Phoenicia, and brother of Europa, features in numerous Greek myths. He was honoured as founder of Boeotian Thebes, and as importer of the alphabet. Wandering the earth in search of his abducted sister, Cadmus consulted the oracle at Delphi. He was told to build a city 'wherever a cow would rest'. So he followed a likely bovine from Phocis into the plain of Boeotia. He marked the spot where it finally lay down beside a hillock, and started to build the *Cadmea*, the oval acropolis of Thebes. The city's inhabitants were born from the teeth of a dragon which Cadmus had slain on the advice of Athena. Athena made him their governor, and Zeus gave him a wife, Harmonia.

Birthplace of Dionysus and Hercules, of the seer, Tiresias, and of the magical musician, Amphion, Thebes was also the scene of the tragedy of *Oedipus* and of the *Seven Against Thebes*. It was the neighbour and hereditary rival of Athens; it was the ally and then the destroyer of Sparta; and it was destroyed itself by Alexander. [**OEDIPUS**]

The Phoenician alphabet, which Cadmus reputedly brought to Greece, was phonetic but purely consonantal. It is known in its basic form from before 1200 BC, having, like its partner, Hebrew, supplanted the earlier hieroglyphs. A simple system, easily learned by children, it broke the monopoly in arcane writing which had been exercised for millennia by the priestly castes of previous Middle Eastern civilizations. The names of the letters passed almost unchanged into Greek: *aleph* (*alpha*) = 'ox', *beth* (*beta*) = 'house'; *gimel* (*gamma*) = 'camel'; *daleth* (*delta*) = 'tent door'. The old Greek alphabet was produced by adding five vowels to the original sixteen Phoenician consonants. It also doubled for use as numerals. In due course, it became the ancestor of the main branches of European writing—modern Greek, Etruscan, Latin, Glagolitic, and Cyrillic.[1] (See Appendix III, p. 1218)

The earliest manifestations of the Latin alphabet date from the sixth century BC. It was based on a script found in the Chalcidian colonies, such as Cumae, in Magna Graecia. It was subsequently adopted and adapted by all the languages of western Christendom, from Irish to Finnish, and in recent times for many non-European languages, including Turkish.

The Glagolitic and Cyrillic alphabets were developed from the Greek in Byzantine times for the purpose of writing certain Slavonic languages. In Orthodox Serbia, 'Serbo-Croat' is written in Cyrillic; in Croatia the same language is written in the Latin alphabet. [**ILLYRIA**]

The angular style of Phoenician, Greek, and Roman scripts was dictated by the art of the stone-chisel. The gradual evolution of cursive styles was made possible by use of the stylus on wax and of quill on parchment.

> Latin minuscules, which are the basis of modern 'small letters', emerged around AD 600, although the Roman majuscules, or 'capitals', have also been retained. [**PALAEO**]
>
> Letters and literature are one of the glories of European civilization. The story of Cadmus hints that their roots lay in Asia.

humanist tradition. 'Wonders are many,' wrote Sophocles; 'but nothing more wonderful than man':

> CHORUS. Wonders are many on earth, and the greatest of these
> Is man, who rides the ocean . . .
> He is master of the ageless earth, to his own will bending
> The immortal mother of gods . . .
> He is lord of all living things . . .
> The use of language, the wind-swift motion of brain
> He learnt; found out the laws of living together
> In cities . . .
> There is nothing beyond his power . . .[14]

Greek oratory was an art fostered both by the theatre and by the tradition of open-air law-courts and political assemblies. Rhetoric, first expounded in *The Art of Words* by Corax of Syracuse (*fl. c.*465 BC), was studied as a formal subject. Of the 'Ten Attic Orators' from Antiphon to Dinarchus of Corinth, none matched the skill of Demosthenes (384–322). In his youth an orphan and a stammerer, he overcame all difficulties, drove his arch-rival Aeschines (389–314) into exile, and became the acknowledged master both of public speaking and of prose style. His series of *Philippics* argued eloquently and passionately for resistance to Philip of Macedon. His oration *On the Crown*, delivered in his defence at a trial in 330 BC, was modestly described by Macaulay as 'the ne plus ultra of human art'.

Greek art, too, experienced its great awakening—what one leading scholar has dared to call 'the greatest and most astonishing revolution in the whole history of Art'.[15] Modern appreciation is influenced no doubt by those forms which have best survived, notably sculpture in stone, architecture, and figure-painting on ceramic vases. Even so, the sudden leap from the stiff and gloomy styles of older antiquity, the explosive flowering which took place in the sixth and fifth centuries, is remarkable. Strongly inspired by spiritual and religious motives, Greek artists paid special attention to the human body, seeking, as Socrates urged, 'to represent the workings of the soul' by observing the effect of people's inner feelings on the body in action. The two most celebrated statues of Phidias (*c.*490–415 BC) are only known from later copies; but the Parthenon friezes, dubiously salvaged by Lord Elgin, speak for themselves. [**LOOT**] A century later Praxiteles (*fl. c.*350 BC), a sculptor of almost ethereal ease and grace, was no more fortunate than Pheidias

MOUSIKE

THE Greek term *mousike* embraced both poetry and the art of contrived sound. Both have a long history.

Ancient Greek music was built on 'modes'. A musical mode, like a scale, is a fixed sequence of notes whose intervals provide the basis for melodic invention. The Greeks were familiar with six of them; and Pythagorean mathematicians correctly calculated the frequencies which underlie their component tones, semitones and quarter-tones. The modal system, however, does not operate in quite the same manner as the later system of keys and scales. A change of mode alters the configuration of the intervals in a melodic line, whilst a change of key only alters the pitch.

In the fourth century St Ambrose selected four so-called 'authentic modes' for ecclesiastical use, to which Gregory the Great added four more so-called 'plagal modes', making eight 'church modes' in all. These formed the basis of plainsong [CANTUS]. In the sixteenth century the Swiss monk Henry of Glarus (Glareanus) set out a full table of twelve modes, giving them a confusing series of names which, with one exception, did not coincide with the ancient originals:

No.	Glareanus	Greek name	Range	Final	Dominant
I	Dorian	Phrygian	D–D	D	A
II	Hypodorian	—	A–A	D	F
III	Phrygian	Dorian	E–E	E	C
IV	Hypophrygian	—	B–B	E	A
V	Lydian	Syntonolydian	F–F	F	C
VI	Hypolydian	—	C–C	F	A
VII	Mixolydian	Ionian	G–G	G	D
VIII	Hypomixolydian	—	D–D	G	C
IX	Aeolian	Aeolian	A–A	A	E
X	Hypoaeolian	—	E–E	A	G
XI	Ionian	Lydian	C–C	C	C
XII	Hypoionian	—	G–G	C	E[1]

The development of modern harmony rendered most of the ancient modes redundant. But two of them, XI and IX, the Lydian and the Aeolian, survived. Known from the seventeenth century onwards as the major and the minor variants of the twelve key scales, they supply the twin aspects, the 'joyful' and the 'mournful', of the melodic system on which most European 'classical music' is based. Together with time and harmony, they constitute one of three basic grammatical elements in the musical language which marks Europe off from its Asian and African neighbours.

Given that Europe has never acquired a universal spoken language, i.e. a common verbal *musike*, Europe's musical idiom, its non-verbal *musike*, must be reckoned the longest and strongest thread of its common culture. Indeed, since it extends from Spain to Russia but not to India or to the Islamic world, one is tempted to suggest that it is the only universal medium of pan-European communication.

in the survival of his masterworks, though the Hermes of Olympia and the Aphrodite of Arles attest to his talent. These, together with figures of the later period such as the bronze Apollo Belvedere, or the Aphrodite of Melos, better known as the 'Venus de Milo', have often been taken as ideal models for male and female beauty. By the era of Alexander the Great, the Greeks had created 'the pictorial language of half the world'.[16]

Greek architecture succeeded in harnessing immense technical skill to exquisite sensibility. The art of building, which in Mesopotamia and in Egypt had largely sought to impress by means of its colossal scale, now aimed to exhibit more spiritual values. The finely proportioned harmonies of the Doric temples, with their subtly tapered colonnades and sculptured plinths and pediments, could convey either heavyweight muscular power, as at the Temple of Poseidon at Posidonia (Paestum), or effortless elegance, as in the white Pentelic marble of the Athenian Parthenon. The tone and the mood of the temple could be tuned to the special characteristics of whatever deity inhabited the enclosed *cella* or 'sanctuary' behind the soaring columns. Of the 'Seven Wonders of the World', as listed in the second century BC by Antipater of Sidon for the first generation of classical tourists, five were masterpieces of Greek architecture. After the Pyramids of Egypt and the Hanging Gardens of Semiramis at Babylon, these were: the statue of Zeus at Olympia, the (third) Temple of Artemis at Ephesus, the Mausoleum of Halicarnassus, the Colossus of Rhodes, and the Pharos or Lighthouse of Alexandria. [ZEUS]

Greek science was simply a branch of general philosophy. Most philosophers were concerned with both the physical and the abstract sciences. Thales of Miletus (c.636–546), who held that everything derived from water, died fittingly by falling down a well. He measured the flood levels of the Nile, the distances between ships, and the height of mountains, and he was credited with predicting solar eclipses. Heraclitus of Ephesus (fl. c.500), in contrast, considered fire to be the primary form of all matter, which was constantly in flux. Anaxagoras of Clazomenae (c.500–428), the teacher of Pericles, argued for the existence of a supreme Mind or *nous* which animated all living things and which, by exerting its force on infinitely divisible 'seeds', enabled them to combine into all forms of matter. He claimed that the planets were stones torn from the earth, and that the sun was red-hot through motion.

Empedocles of Acragas (c.493–433) proposed that the earth is made of four 'elements': fire, earth, air, and water, and that these elements are constantly merging and separating under the contrary stresses of love and strife. He reputedly leapt into the crater of Mount Etna in order to test his capacity for reincarnation. But the volcano obliged by returning only one sandal. Democritus of Abdera (c.460–361) refined the atomic theory of Leucippus, holding that all physical matter could be explained in terms of the random collisions of tiny particles which he called *atoma* or 'unbreakables'. He was popularly known as the laughing philosopher, because of his amusement at human folly.

OEDIPUS

O EDIPUS 'the Swollen-Foot', King of Thebes, is one of the most ubiquitous characters of ancient Greek myth and literature. He also fur-
nishes a prime illustration of the Classical Tradition which derives from
them.

The story of Oedipus is that of a Theban outcast who, being rejected by
his royal parents, is doomed to take the most terrible, though involuntary,
revenge. Exposed to die as an infant because his father, King Laius,
feared a bad omen about him, he is saved by a shepherd and is fostered in
nearby Corinth by people unaware of his origins. Consulting the oracle at
Delphi, he is told that he will kill his father and marry his mother. For
which reason he flees Corinth and comes again to Thebes. He kills Laius
during a chance meeting; solves the riddle of the Sphinx; rids the city
of its terror, and as a reward, is given the King's widow, Jocasta, his own
mother, to wife. After fathering four children through this unwittingly incestuous union, he discovers the truth, and sees Jocasta hang herself
in despair. Thereon he blinds himself, and is led into exile by his daughter, Antigone. His end comes, at Colonus in Attica, where the tragic wanderer disappears into a sacred grove.

Homer mentions Oedipus in both *Iliad* and *Odyssey*. But it is the lost
epic, *Thebais*, which was probably the main source of the later story. It
then becomes the centrepiece of the Theban trilogy of Sophocles, and the
background to Aeschylus' *Seven Against Thebes* and to Euripides'
Suppliants and *Phoenician Women*.

Oedipus recurs throughout subsequent European literature. The Roman
poet Statius wrote an epic *Thebaid* which in turn was the model for
Racine's first play *La Thébaide* (1665). The Roman tragedian Seneca composed a variation on Sophocles' *Oedipus*, inspiring further versions by
Corneille (1659) and by André Gide (1950) and a loose adaptation by the
contemporary poet, Ted Hughes. Sophocles' *Oedipus at Colonnus* provides the basis both for T. S. Eliot's verse drama *The Elder Statesman* (1952)
and Jean Cocteau's *Infernal Machine* (1934). His *Antigone* has been
followed by dramas of the same name and subject by Cocteau, Jean
Anouilh (1944), and Brecht (1947). Anthony Burgess wrote an Oedipus
novel entitled *MF* (1971). There are two paintings of *Oedipus and the Sphinx*
(1808) by Ingres. There is an opera-oratorio *Oedipus-Rex* (1927) by
Stravinsky set to Cocteau's Latin libretto, and a film, *Oedipus-Rex* (1967)
by Pasolini.[1]

By far the best known use of the legend, however, was made by
Sigmund Freud who gave the label of 'Oedipus Complex' to the repressed
hostility of boys to their fathers. Deriving from the rivalry of father and son

for the mother's affection, the syndrome can lead in later life to a pathological mother-fixation.

The Classical Tradition, which may be defined as the creative reworking
of ancient themes for contemporary purposes, draws on thousands of
such examples. Nourished since the Renaissance by five centuries of education in Greek and Latin, it has supplied a body of knowledge with which
all educated Europeans have been familiar. Together with Christianity, it
has provided a stream within 'the bloodstream of European Culture' and
'a code of instant recognition'. Its decline in the late 20th century has been
precipitated by changing social and educational priorities. Its advocates
argue that its survival is essential if European civilization is not to wither
from alienation.

SCHOLASTIKOS

THE *Philogelos* or 'Love of Laughter', once attributed to Philagrius of
Alexandria and the fifth century AD, is a collection of much older Greek
witticisms. It features the original *scholastikos* or 'absent-minded professor', together with the men of Abdera and Cumae, butts of early forms of
the Irish (or Polish) joke.

● A *scholastikos* who wanted to see what he looked like when asleep stood in
front of a mirror with his eyes shut.

● A *scholastikos* met a friend and said, 'I heard you'd died.' 'But you see I'm
alive.' 'Yes, but the man who told me was much more reliable than you.'

● A Cumaean went to the embalmer's to collect the body of his dead father.
The embalmer, looking for the right corpse, asked if it had any distinctive
features. 'A bad cough.'

● A Cumaean was selling honey. A passer-by tasted it, and found it excellent.
'Yes,' said the Cumaean, 'I wouldn't be selling it at all if a mouse hadn't
fallen into it.'

● A Scottish *scholastikos* decided to economize by training his donkey not to
eat, so he gave it no food. When the animal had starved to death, the owner
complained, 'And just when it was learning to live without eating.'[1]

Collectors of folk-tales have recorded versions of the last story in Estonian,
Latvian, Lithuanian, Swedish, English, Spanish, Catalan, Walloon,
German, Italian, Slovene, Serbo-Croat, Russian, and Greek. Malcolm
Bradbury uses it in *Rates of Exchange*, as part of the heritage of his imagi-
nary East European country, 'Slaka'.[2]

Hippocrates of Cos (*c.*460–357) took medicine out of the realm of religion and magic. Numerous treatises on public health, hygiene, patient care, and surgery were attributed to him. The Hippocratic Oath, whereby doctors dedicated their lives to the welfare of their patients, remained the corner-stone of medical practice until quite recently. His book of aphorisms begins with the line: 'Life is short, Art is long.' [**HYSTERIA**]

Eudoxus of Cnidus (*fl. c.*350) taught the motions of the planets round the sun, whilst inventing the sundial. Aristotle wrote systematic works in both physics and biology. His classification of animal species forms the basis of all subsequent zoology. His *Politics* begins with the inimitable remark: 'Man is above all a political animal.' Aristotle's pupil, Theophrastus of Lesbos (*c.*370–288), applied the same methods of classification to botany. His treatise on *Characters* can be seen as the founding text of analytical psychology.

From the historian's point of view, Heraclitus was probably the most important of these pioneers. Heraclitus reasoned that everything in the world is subject to perpetual change and decay: also that change is caused by the inevitable clash of opposites—in other words, by dialectics. In so doing he unwrapped the two basic ideas of the historian's trade: change over time, and causation. His favourite aphorism was: 'You cannot step into the same river twice.' [**ELEKTRON**]

Greek mathematics developed under the influence both of speculative thought and of religious mysticism. Thales had supposedly learned the rudiments of arithmetic and geometry in Egypt. But it was Pythagoras of Samos (*c.*572–497) who, in addition to compiling the results of his predecessors, made a number of original advances. He launched the Theory of Numbers, formulated the theorem about the square of the hypotenuse of the right-angle triangle, and, most interestingly, worked out the mathematical basis of musical harmony. He may be the author of the beautiful but mistaken theory of 'the music of the spheres'. Eudoxus discovered the Theory of Proportions, and the method of exhaustion for measuring curvilinear surfaces. His disciple, Menaechmus, discovered conic sections.

All these researches prepared the way for Euclides of Alexandria (*fl. c.*300), whose *Elements* is said to have reigned supreme for longer than any book save the Bible. Euclid was the great mathematical systematizer, who set out to provide lasting proofs for all existing knowledge. When asked by the ruler of Egypt whether geometry could not be made more simple, he replied that there was 'no royal road'. The next generation was dominated by Archimedes and by Eratosthenes of Cyrene (276–196), who, in calculating the earth's diameter at 252,000 stades or 7,850 miles, erred by less than 1 per cent. Lastly there was Apollonius of Perge (*fl. c.*220 BC), who wrote a vast eight-volume study of Conics and found an approximation for *pi* that was even closer than that of Archimedes. [**ARCHIMEDES**]

Greek moral philosophy, divided in the later centuries into several rival schools, greatly modified the teachings of traditional religion. The Sceptics, founded by Pyrrho of Elis, whose dates are not known, asserted that it is not possible to attain

HYSTERIA

A CCORDING to various Hippocratic treatises on medicine, hysteria was exclusively a woman's disease associated with uterine disorders. *Hystera* in Greek meant 'womb'; and the state of nervous agitation was caused when menstrual blood was unable to escape:

Whenever the menses are suppressed or cannot find a way out, illness results. This happens if the mouth of the womb is closed or if some part of [the] vagina is prolapsed . . . Whenever two months' menses are accumulated in the womb, they move off into the lungs where they are prevented from exiting.[1]

In another variant, the womb itself was thought to become displaced and to wander round the body cavity. By pressing on the heart or brain, it provoked anxiety and eventually uncontrollable panic. Religious taboos forbade human dissection; and the internal workings of women's (and of men's) bodies were not understood until modern times. In the view of one analyst, however, ancient attitudes to women survived even when ancient anatomical theories had been discounted. 'The notion persisted that women's minds could be adversely affected by their reproductive tracts.'[2]

The history of women's bodies is a complicated subject. Over the ages, their size, weight, shape, muscular development, menstruation, child-bearing capacity, maturing, ageing, and disease patterns have varied considerably, as have their symbolism, their religious connotation, their aesthetic appreciation, their decoration, clothing, and display. Women's awareness of their physical potential has been particularly constrained. So much so that a standard textbook on the subject can seriously ask: 'Could any woman enjoy sex before 1900?'[3] Histories of the male body do not ask such things.

As for the wonderful workings of the womb, modern research suggests that the interdependence of the female nervous and reproductive systems is extremely sophisticated. A survey of women's health conducted during the prolonged Siege of Budapest in 1944–5, for example, revealed unusually high levels of *amenorrhea*. Menstruation was suspended through well-grounded anxieties, not through hysteria. The womb does not need to be told that a minimal birthrate makes very good sense in times of maximum danger.

ELEKTRON

ELEKTRON, 'bright stone', was the ancient Greek name for amber. The Greeks knew that, when rubbed, it generated a force which attracted other objects, such as feathers. Thales of Miletus said it had 'psyche'. Electra, 'the Bright One', was the name given to two women prominent in Greek myth. One, the daughter of Atlas, was a favourite paramour of Zeus. The other, daughter of Agamemnon and Clytemnestra and sister to Orestes, figures in the tragedies of Aeschylus, Sophocles and Euripides.

The invisible physical force which repels and attracts had no name until William Gilbert, the 'father of magnetism', called it 'electric' in his treatise *De Magnete* (1600). 'Earth', he wrote, 'is nothing but a large magnet.'

Advances in the study of electricity and magnetism were made by A. M. Ampère, H. C. Oersted, and Michael Faraday, until J. C. Maxwell (1831–79) combined the two into the theory of electromagnetic force. H. R. Hertz (1857–94) demonstrated the existence of electromagnetic waves filling a spectrum of different frequencies. Application of electricity had moved on from the dynamo and the electric motor to radio and X-rays. Finally, in 1891, the British physicist J. D. Stoney needed a label for the negatively charged particles which constitute the smallest component of matter and which, in the company of positively charged protons and non-charged neutrons, orbit round the nucleus of an atom on the scale of a pinhead in St Peter's dome. He called them electrons.[1] (See Appendix III, p. 1272.)

certain knowledge about anything, and hence that man's sole object should be the pursuit of virtue. He was an anti-speculative speculator, who exerted an important influence on the Athenian Academy after Plato's death.

The Cynics were founded by Diogenes of Sinope (*c.*412–323), who held a Tolstoyan sort of belief in the value of freeing oneself from desire. Their name meant literally 'the dogs'. Diogenes was a noted eccentric, who lived in a barrel as a gesture of renouncing the world's comforts, and walked the streets of daytime Athens with a lantern, 'looking for honest men'. In a meeting with Alexander the Great in Corinth, he is said to have told the King to 'stop blocking my sunshine'.

The Epicureans, named after Epicurus of Samos (342–270), taught that people should devote themselves to the pursuit of happiness, fearing neither death nor the gods. (It is a thought which found its way into the constitution of the USA.) They gained an undeserved reputation for mere pleasure-seeking; in reality, they held that the road to happiness lay through self-control, calm, and self-denial.

The Stoics, founded by Zenon of Cyprus (335–263), took their name from the Athenian *Stoa poikile* or 'painted porch', where the group first gathered. They followed the conviction that human passions should be governed by reason and (like the Sceptics) that the pursuit of virtue was all. Their vision of a universal

ARCHIMEDES

ARCHIMEDES of Syracuse (287–212 BC) was the mathematicians' mathematician. He possessed a childlike delight in solving problems for their own sake. Not that he was averse to practical matters. After studying in Alexandria, he returned to Sicily as adviser to King Hiero II. There he invented the 'Screw' for raising water; he built a planetarium, later carried off to Rome; and he designed the catapults and grapnels which held off the final Roman siege of Syracuse (see pp. 143–4). He launched the science of hydrostatics, and is best known for running naked into the street, shouting *Heureka, heureka* ('I've found it'), after supposedly working out the 'Archimedes Principle' in his bath. The Principle states that an object immersed in water apparently loses weight equal to the weight of the water displaced. The volume of the object can then be easily calculated. On the subject of levers, he said: 'Give me a place to stand, and I will move the earth.'

His greatest enthusiasm, however, was reserved for purely speculative problems:

1. *The Sand-reckoner.* Archimedes set himself the task of calculating how many grains of sand would be needed to fill the universe. To deal with the vast numbers involved, and since decimals were not yet in existence, he came up with the original concept of 'a myriad myriad', i.e. 10,000 x 10,000 or $10,000^2$. Given that he assumed the universe to be equivalent to the galaxy of the sun, his answer of $10,000^{37}$ was entirely respectable.

2. *Measuring the Circle.* Archimedes worked out the ratio of the circumference to the diameter by starting from the upper and lower limits of the perimeter of a 96-sided polygon. He took certain known approximations, and went on to find approximations for the square roots of the necessary seven-digit numbers. He had to work, of course, in the clumsy alphabetic system of numeration. But his answer for what is now called *pi* (π) lay between the limits of $3\frac{1}{7}$ (= 3.1428571) and $3^{10}/_{71}$ (3.140845). (The accepted modern value is 3.14159265.)

3. *Problema Bovinum.* Archimedes thought up a seemingly straightforward teaser about the God Apollo having a herd of cattle, bulls and cows together, some black, some brown, some white, some spotted. Among the bulls, the number of white ones was half plus one-third of the number of the black ones, greater than the brown . . . etc., etc. Among the cows, the number of white ones was one-third plus one-quarter the number of the total black cattle . . . etc., etc. What was the composition of the herd? The answer comes to a total of more than 79 billion, which is far in excess of the number of beasts that could possibly find standing-room on the island of Sicily. (Sicily's 25,000 km^2 can only accommodate 12.75 billion cattle at 2 m^2 per head, not excepting those which would have to stand in the boiling crater of Mount Etna.)[1]

brotherhood of mankind, their sense of duty, and their disciplined training,
designed to insure them against pain and suffering, proved specially attractive to
the Romans. [**ATHLETOS**]

Greek sexuality is a subject for which fashionable scholarship would prefer
monographs to paragraphs. What for scholars of an older vintage was 'unnatural vice' has now been upgraded to personal 'orientation' or 'preference'; and
homosexuality is widely considered to occupy a central position in an ancient
code of social manners which, as now presented, has very modern overtones.
'The Greek vice' did not generate guilt: for a man to pursue young boys was no
more reprehensible than to pursue young girls. Young Greek males, like English
public schoolboys, had presumably to take sodomy in their stride. Parents
sought to protect their sons in the same ways that they protected their daughters. Female homosexuality was in evidence alongside its male counterpart,
though the island of Lesbos, home of the poetess Sappho and her circle, did not
lend its name to the phenomenon in ancient times. Incest, too, was clearly an
issue. The tragic fate of the legendary Oedipus, who killed his father and married his mother by mistake, was proof of divine wrath. Generally speaking, the
Greeks do not appear either licentious or puritanical so much as practical and
open-minded. Their world was full of explicit erotica, about which they were
sublimely unembarrassed.[17]

One must not imagine, however, that Greek assumptions about sexuality resembled those of contemporary California. A slave-owning society, for example,
assumed that the bodies of the unfree were available for the uses and abuses of the
free. Sexual activity thus became a function of social status. Mutuality in sexual
relations did not have to be taken into account, still less shared feelings.
Satisfaction was mainly associated with the phallic pleasure of the active male who
imposed himself and his organ on its passive recipients. Despite legal constraints
men of superior status often took it for granted that they could penetrate their
inferiors at will; and inferiors included women, boys, servants, and foreigners. This
assumption, if correctly identified, would render the modern distinction between
homo- and heterosexuality largely irrelevant. Similarly, the distinction between
pederast and *philerast* was less dependent on personal proclivities than on the age
at which the growing male could assert himself.[18]

The classic text for the study of such matters—Aristophanes' myth in Plato's
Symposium—mentions a number of sexual practices that appear to foreshadow
familiar modern categories. Yet closer inspection suggests that the Greeks may have
followed a system of values that are very alien to our own. According to the myth,
human beings were originally eight-limbed, two-faced creatures, each with two sets
of genitals front and back. They came in three varieties—male, female, and andro-
gynous. Zeus later cut them in half, and invented sexual intercourse for the benefit
of the separated halves. People possessed assorted sexual desires in line with the type
of ancestor from whom they were descended. Hence the binary opposition of male
and female would seem to have been lacking; and pluralist sexuality, present to

ATHLETES

ATHLETIC games were an essential part of Greek life. Every self-respecting city had its stadium. The pan-hellenic games at Olympia were but the most prestigious of more than a hundred such festivals.[1] The common devotion to athletics, and to the gods, whose patronage the games celebrated, gave a strong sense of cultural unity to a politically divided country. The athletes, all male, competed in ten well-established disciplines. From the seventh century onwards, when one competitor accidentally lost his shorts, they customarily performed naked. They were not amateurs, being accustomed to arduous training and expecting handsome rewards. The tariff of prizes (in denarii) awarded at a minor festival at Aphrodisias in the first century indicates the status of particular events:

long-distance race: 750; pentathlon: 500; race in armour: 500; sprint (1 stade): 1,250; pankration: 3,000; wrestling: 2,000; foot race (2 stades): 1,000; boxing: 2,000.

The standard *stade*, or stadium length, was about 212 metres. Runners turned round a post at the end opposite the start. The *pentathlon* consisted of five events: long jump, discus, javelin, foot race, wrestling. In the *pankration*, a form of all-in combat, one aimed as in judo to force one's opponent into submission. Quoit-throwing and chariot-racing were also important.[2]

Athletes and their home cities gained great renown from their triumphs at the Olympiads. Sparta was prominent. Athens during its golden age gained only four victories out of a possible 183. But the most successful district was Elis in the Peloponnese, home of the first recorded victor, Coroebus, in 776 BC, and site of Olympia itself.

The all-time champion athlete was Milo of Croton, who won the prize for wrestling in five successive Olympiads between 536 and 520 BC. On the last occasion he carried the sacrificial ox round the stadium on his shoulders, before sitting down to eat it. [**SPICE-OX**]

Most of Pindar's surviving odes are devoted to the games:

> Single is the race, single
> Of men and of gods;
> From a single mother we both draw breath.
> But a difference of power in everything
> Keeps us apart.
> For the one thing is Nothing, but the brazen sky
> Stays a fixed habitation for ever.
> Yet we can in greatness of mind
> Or of body be like the Immortals,
> Though we know not to what goal
> By day or in the nights
> Fate has written that we shall run.[3]

The ethos of the games lasted well into Christian times. St Paul was surely a fan, if not a competitor. 'I have fought a good fight,' he wrote. 'I have run the course. I have kept the faith.'[4] The sentiment was quintessentially Greek.

The last ancient games at Olympia took place either in AD 389 or 393. The last known *victor ludorum*, in 385, was an Armenian. There is no evidence that the Emperor Theodosius I formally banned the festival. More probably, since Christian opinion had turned against pagan cults of all sorts, it was impossible to revive it after the Visigoths' invasion of Greece in 395. Substitute games continued at Antioch in Asia until 530.[5]

The Olympics were revived at Athens on 6–12 April 1896, after an interval of more than 1,500 years. The initiator and founding president of the International Olympic Committee was the French sportsman Baron Pierre de Coubertin (1863–1937). With the exception of wartime, the games have been held at four-year intervals and at various venues throughout the twentieth century. Women were permitted to compete from 1912. The Winter Olympics were organized as from the 1924 meeting in Chamonix. Appropriately enough, the winner of the first marathon race of the modern series in 1896, Louis Spyridon, was a Greek.

---

different degrees in all individuals, may have been considered the basic condition. Unfortunately, modern scholarly opinion presents no less pluralism than the subject in hand.[19]

Greek social structures do not present a simple picture. There were fundamental differences between the societies of the city-states and those of the remoter mountain areas, such as Arcadia in the Peloponnese, where pastoral, pre-Greek tribes survived into Roman times. Slavery was a general feature, though it did not necessarily form the foundation of all social and economic institutions, as some historians would like to believe. (In the 'five-stage scheme' of Marxism-Leninism, classical slave-holding is taken as the necessary starting-point of all social history.) In Athens, the population was divided between slaves, *metics* or 'resident foreigners', and citizens. The slaves, who were called *andrapoda*, literally 'human feet', were treated as chattels, and could be killed with impunity. They were not allowed to serve in the army. Freed slaves automatically rose to the status of metics, who could be both taxed and conscripted. The citizens (who alone could call themselves 'Athenians') had the right to landed property and the duty of military service. They were divided into ten *phylai* or tribes, and the tribes into smaller groupings called *trittyes* (thirds) and *demes* or parishes. Each of these bodies had its own corporate life, with a role in both civil and military organization.

Greek political organization was characterized by variety and experimentation. Since every *polis* or city-state governed itself, at least in theory, a wide range of political traditions developed, each with its variants, derivatives, and imitations. There were monarchies, like Samos under the pirate-king Polycrates. There were despotisms, especially among the cities of Asia Minor influenced by the Persian example. There were oligarchies of various types like Corinth, Sparta, or Massilia. There were democracies, like Athens in its prime. Yet incessant wars, leagues, and confederations caused constant interaction; and each of the different polities was subject to drastic evolutions.

The Athenian system itself underwent many changes, from its earliest known manifestations in the seventh century under Draco, author of the first 'draconian' law-code, and the sixth-century reforms of Solon and the benevolent despotism of Pisistratus. Two hundred years after Draco, Athens's defeat in the Peloponnesian War ushered in the episode of the 'Thirty Tyrants' and the rule of the radical Cleon, Pericles's chief critic. Even in the central decades of Athenian democracy in the fifth century, modern scholarship is far from unanimous about the true extent of participation by the citizens. Elaborate controversies take place over the size of the slave population, the role of the city mob, the degree of land-holding among the citizens, the place of the citizen-peasant, and, above all, the operations of various city assemblies—the *Boule* or 'Council of 500', the *Ecclesia*, which was the main legislative assembly, and the jury courts. It turns out that the *demos* or 'people', which is thought to have consisted of up to 50,000 exclusively male freemen, is no easier to define than the democracy. Nor is it easy to recon-cile the fact that Pericles or Demosthenes, the great Athenian democrats, were (like Washington and Jefferson) slave-owners, or that the democratic Athens exercised a tyrannical hold over the city's lesser dependencies. [**DEMOS**]

Not surprisingly, the extreme complications of Greek political practice offered fertile ground for the growth of political theory. Plato's *Republic*, which advocates the rule of the Guardians—a somewhat totalitarian breed of so-called philosopher-kings—and Aristotle's *Politics*, with its categoric statement about man being *zoon politikon*, offer two opposing approaches to the subject. The basic political vocab-ulary of the modern world, from 'anarchy' to 'politics' itself, is largely a Greek invention.

Greek history-writing, like the theatre, had its triad of giants. Herodotus of Halicarnassus (484–420) is commonly known as the 'Father of History', but his keen interest in foreign lands earned from his more chauvinistic compatriots the label of 'Father of Lies'. He wrote from eyewitness reports and from personal observation on his far-flung travels. He saw the past in terms of the titanic con-test between Europe and Asia, and his nine books culminate in the Graeco-Persian wars. Thucydides (455–*c*.401 BC) the Athenian, in the opinion of Thomas Hobbes and many others, was quite simply 'the most Politick Historiographer that ever writ'. He introduced the systematic analysis of causation and conse-quence; he quoted documents and treatises at length; and in the set-piece orations

DEMOS

S OME people believe that in 507 BC a lasting tradition of popular sovereignty was launched by Cleisthenes the Alcmaeonid. In AD 1993 they
were moved to celebrate 'the 2,500th anniversary of the birth of democracy'. To this end, a lavish banquet in London's Guildhall was addressed
by the President of the Classical Society.[1] In fact, the seeds of Athenian
democracy had been sown some time before Cleisthenes. The Assembly
of Citizens, the *Ecclesia*, which met in the meeting-ground of the Pnyx
alongside the Acropolis, was established by Solon. But it was easily
manipulated by aristocratic leaders such as Pisistratus and his sons, who
used it to bolster their fifty-year tyranny from 560 to 510 BC.

Cleisthenes belonged to a rich family which tried to share power with
Pisistratus, then chose exile. He was probably responsible for refacing the
Temple of Zeus at Delphi with Parian marble to atone for a massacre committed by his kin. He led an abortive invasion of Attica in 513, possibly
seeking Persian aid. But it was the Spartans not Cleisthenes who drove
out the last of the Pisistratids three years later.

Cleisthenes is said to have invoked the power of the people in order to
undermine the old tribal organizations on which his predecessors had
relied. By proposing sovereign power for the *Ecclesia*, he gained the
authority to instigate still wider reforms. He replaced the four old tribes
with ten new ones, each with its own shrine and hero-cult. He greatly
strengthened the *demes* or 'parishes' into which the tribes were divided,
and extended the franchise to all freemen resident on Athenian territory.
Above all, he instituted the *Boule*, which functioned as a steering committee for the Assembly's agenda. He also initiated legal ostracism. He has
been called 'the founder of the art of organizing public opinion'.

Athenian democracy, which lasted for 185 years, was far from perfect.
The sovereignty of the people was limited by the machinations of the
Boule, by the waywardness of the *deme*, and by the continuing influence
of wealthy patrons and demagogues. To ensure a quorum of 6,000 at meetings of the *Ecclesia*, the citizens were literally 'roped in' from the streets,
with a rope dipped in red paint. The extent of participation, both in the
central and the district bodies, is a matter of intense scholarly debate.[2]
And yet the citizens really did rule. They enjoyed equality before the law.
They elected the ten top officials, including the *Strategos* or military commander. They drew lots for distributing hundreds of annual administrative
posts among themselves. Most importantly, they held public servants to
account. Dishonest or bungling officials could be dismissed, or even executed.

Not everyone was impressed. Plato thought that democracy meant the rule of the incompetent. Aristophanes made fun of 'that angry, waspish, intractable old man, Demos of Pnyx'. At one point he asked, 'So what's the solution?' and replied, 'Women'.

Unfortunately, the link between the democracy of ancient Athens and that of contemporary Europe is tenuous. Democracy did not prevail in its birthplace. It was not admired by Roman thinkers; and it was all but forgotten for more than a millennium. The democratic practices of today's Europe trace their origins as much to popular assemblies of the Viking type [**DING**], to the diets convened by feudal monarchs, and to medieval city republics. The Athenian notion of a sovereign assembly consisting of all qualified citizens found its counterparts in medieval Novgorod, Hungary, and Poland—in political systems which spawned no heirs. The theorists of the Enlightenment blended classical knowledge with an interest in constitutional reform; and a romanticized vision of ancient Athens played a part in this among classically educated liberals. But liberals could themselves be critical. De Tocqueville inveighed against 'the tyranny of the majority'. Edmund Burke called democracy on the French model 'the most shameless thing in the world'. Democracy has rarely been the norm.

Nowadays there is little consensus about the essence of democracy. In theory, it promotes all the virtues, from freedom, justice, and equality to the rule of law, the respect for human rights, and the promotion of political pluralism and of civil society. In practice, 'rule by the people' is impossible. There is much to divide the Continental brand of popular sovereignty from the British brand of parliamentary sovereignty (see p. 631). And all brands have their faults. Winston Churchill once said that 'democracy is the worst of political systems, except for all the others'. What does exist, as always, is almost universal abhorrence of tyranny. And this is what propels all newly liberated nations in the direction of democracy, irrespective of previous realities. 'Our whole history inclines us towards the democratic Powers', declared the President of newborn Czechoslovakia in 1918.[3] In 1989–91, similar sentiments were echoed by leaders of all the countries of the ex-Soviet bloc.

This is not to deny that democracy, like any other movement, needs its founding myth. It needs an ancient pedigree and worthy heroes. And who could be more ancient or more worthy than Cleisthenes the Alcmaeonid?

of his principal protagonists he found a marvellous method for injecting his strictly impartial narrative with subjective opinion. His eight books on the Peloponnesian War were 'not designed', he wrote, 'to meet the taste of an immediate public, but to last for ever'. Xenophon (c.428–354), another Athenian, was author of the *Hellenica* and of *Anabasis*. The *Hellenica* continues the narrative of Greek history from the point where Thucydides had broken off (in 411), just as Thucydides had to some extent carried on from Herodotus. The *Anabasis*, translated as 'The Persian Expedition', describes the long march of 10,000 Greek mercenaries, including Xenophon himself, who went to Mesopotamia and back in the service of a Persian pretender. The shout of *Thalassa! Thalassa!*—'The sea! The sea!'—when, after months of marching, Xenophon's companions caught sight of the coast from the hills behind Trebizond, provides one of the most enthusiastic moments of military chronicles.

By common assent, the zenith of Greek civilization was reached during the Age of Pericles in Athens. In the interval between the city's salvation from the Persian invasion in 480 BC and the onset of the ruinous war with Sparta in 431, the political, intellectual, and cultural energies of Athens peaked. Pericles (c.495–429), general and statesman, was leader of the moderate democratic faction. He had organized the reconstruction of the pillaged Acropolis, and was the friend of artists and philosophers. His funeral oration for the dead of the first year of the Peloponnesian War pulses with pride at the freedom and high culture of his native city:

Our love of what is beautiful does not lead to extravagance; our love of the things of the mind does not make us soft. We regard wealth as something to be properly used, rather than as something to boast about. . . . Here each individual is interested not only in his own affairs, but in the affairs of the state as well. . . . We do not say that a man who takes no interest in politics is a man who minds his own business; we say that he has no business here at all. . . . Others are brave out of ignorance, and, when they begin to think, they begin to fear. But the man who can most truly be accounted brave is he who best knows the meaning of what is sweet in life and what is terrible, and then goes out undeterred to meet what is to come.[20]

The Athenian contemporaries of Pericles gave him good reason to be proud. Anaxagoras and Socrates, Euripides and Aeschylus, Pindar and Pheidias, Antiphon and Aristophanes, Democritus and Hippocrates, Herodotus and Thucydides, all walked the same streets, all watched the Parthenon taking shape for its inauguration in 438. Athens, 'the eye of Greece, Mother of arts and eloquence', had fulfilled the prediction of the Oracle: 'You will become an eagle among the clouds for all time'. Most appropriate perhaps are the words from a fragment of Pindar:

Αἱ τε λιπαραὶ καὶ ἰοστέφανοι καὶ ἀοίδιμοι,
Ἑλλάδος ἔρεισμα, κλειναὶ Ἀθᾶναι, δαιμόνιον προλίεθρον.

(Shining and violet-crowned and celebrated in song, bulwark of Greece, famous Athens, divine city.)[21]

Sparta, otherwise known as Lacedaemon, was Athens's foil and rival. To modern sensibilities it was as ugly as Athens is attractive. Exceptionally, it was a landlocked city, built on the plain of Laconia in the middle of the Peleponnese. It possessed no native navy, and was entirely devoted to the militarism which had enabled it to confront all its immediate neighbours—the Messenians, the Argives, and the Arcadians. Its system of government, bestowed in remote times by the divine Lycurgus, was variously described as a despotic form of oligarchy or an oligarchic form of despotism. A council of *ephors* or magistrates wielded dictatorial powers. They gave orders to the two hereditary 'kings' of Sparta, who acted as high priests and military commanders. Sparta had few colonies, and solved its problems of overpopulation by culling its male infants. Weaklings were ceremonially left to die in the open. All surviving boys were taken by the state at the age of seven to be trained in physical prowess and military discipline. At twenty, they started their forty-year service as citizen-soldiers. They were forbidden to undertake trade or crafts, and were supported by the toil of an underclass of *helots* or slaves. The result was a culture which had little time for the arts and graces, and little sense of solidarity with the rest of Hellas. According to Aristotle, it was also a society in which the number of men began to fall alarmingly, and a large part of the land was held by women. To be 'laconic' was to spurn fine words. When Philip of Macedon sent a threatening letter to Sparta: 'if I enter Lacedaemon, I shall raze it', the ephors sent him a one-word reply, *an*, 'if'. [**MAKEDON**]

The era of hellenism—that is, the era when the world of the Greek city-states was merged into the wider but essentially non-Greek world created by Alexander and his successors—is frequently despised for its decadence. Certainly, in the political sphere, the internecine strife of the dynasties that latched onto Alexander's dismembered empire does not make an edifying story. On the other hand, Greek culture had stamina, and the beneficial effects of a common tradition, through several centuries and in diverse lands, should not be casually dismissed. Greek rulers in the Indus Valley, where the veneer of hellenism was thinnest, held on into the middle of the first century BC. In Macedonia the Antigonid dynasty, founded by Alexander's one-eyed general, Antigonus (382–301), reigned until their defeat by the Romans in 168. In Syria, and for a time in Persia and in Asia Minor, the Seleucid dynasty, founded by Seleucus I Nicator (ruled 280–261), controlled vast if ever-diminishing Asiatic territories. They were active hellenizers, consciously executing Alexander's plans for a network of new Greek colonies in Asia. They surrendered to Rome in 69. The eastern half of the Seleucid realm was seized in 250 BC by Arsaces, the Parthian (d. 248), whose Arsacid dynasty ruled in Persia for nearly 500 years, until the rebirth of a native Persian empire in AD 226. In Egypt the Ptolemaic dynasty launched by Alexander's bastard half-brother, Ptolemaeus Soter, 'the Preserver' (d. 285), reigned until 31 BC.

MAKEDON

To ask whether Macedonia is Greek is rather like asking whether Prussia was German. If one talks of distant origins, the answer in both cases must be 'No'. Ancient Macedonia started its career in the orbit of Illyrian or Thracian civilization. But, as shown by excavation of the royal tombs, it was subject to a high degree of hellenization before Philip of Macedon conquered Greece.[1] [**PAPYRUS**]

The Roman province of Macedonia stretched to the Adriatic [**EGNATIA**], and from the sixth century onwards was heavily settled by migrant Slavs. According to one theory, the Slavs mingled with the residue of the pre-Greek population to form a new, non-Greek Macedonian nation. The Byzantine empire was sometimes dubbed 'Macedonia' because of its Greek connections. But the former province of Macedonia, and much of the Peloponnese, was submerged in 'Sclavonia'.

In medieval times Macedonia was incorporated for a time into the Bulgarian empire, and remained permanently within the exarchate of the Bulgarian Orthodox Church. This strengthened later Bulgarian claims. In the fourteenth century it passed under Serbian rule. In 1346 Stefan Dusan was crowned in Skopje 'Tsar of the Serbs, Greeks, Bulgars and Albanians'. This was to strengthen Serbian claims. Then came the Ottomans.

In the late nineteenth century, Ottoman Macedonia was a typical Balkan province of mixed religious and ethnic composition. Orthodox Christians lived alongside Muslims, and Greeks and Slavs alongside Albanians and Turks. By custom, all Orthodox Christians were counted as 'Greeks' because of their allegiance to the Patriarch of Constantinople.

Throughout the Balkan wars (see p. 874) Macedonia was fought over by Greece, Bulgaria, and Serbia. It was divided into three parts. (See Appendix III, p. 1309.) Southern Macedonia, centred on Thessaloniki, was taken over by Greece. After the Graeco-Turkish population exchange of 1922, and the Slav exodus due to the Civil War in 1949, it came to be dominated by a strong majority of highly patriotic Greeks, 'Alexander's successors', many of them immigrants from Turkey. Eastern Macedonia found itself in Bulgaria, which treated it as synonymous with 'Western Bulgaria'. Northern Macedonia, centred on Skopje and the upper Vardar valley, possessed a mixed Albanian and Slav population living within Serbia.

When this northern section was reconstituted in 1945 as the autonomous republic of 'Makedonija' within Yugoslavia, a determined campaign was launched to simplify history and to transmute the identity of the entire population. The Yugoslav leadership was intent on reversing the effects of wartime Bulgarian occupation, and on resisting the cultural charms of ancient Greece. The Slav dialect of the political élite was declared to be a separate language; Old Church Slavonic was equated with 'Old Macedonian'; and a whole generation was educated according to the 'Great Idea' of a Slav Macedonia stretching back for centuries.[2]

Not surprisingly, when the government of Skopje declared independence in 1992, no one could agree what their republic should be called. A Greek scholar was reported to have received death threats for revealing the existence of a Slavic-speaking minority on the Greek side of Greece's closed northern frontier.[3] Neutral commentators abroad adopted the evocative acronym of FYROM—'Former Yugoslav Republic of Macedonia.' Equally useful was the curious mnemonic of FOPITGROBBSOSY—'Former Province of Illyria, Thrace, Greece, Rome, Byzantium, Bulgaria, Serbia, the Ottoman Empire, Serbia, and Yugoslavia.'

The Ptolemies were noted for their love and patronage of the arts and learning, even when, occasionally, as with Ptolemy VII Physcon ('The Paunch'), they were also noted for the most disgusting perversions. Through a series of matrimonial contortions, Physcon contrived to marry his sister, who was also his brother's widow (and who thereby became simultaneously sister, wife, and sister-in-law); to divorce her in favour of her daughter by a previous marriage (who thereby became simultaneously his second wife, niece and stepdaughter); and to murder his son (who was also a nephew). Incest, to protect the purity of royal blood, was a tradition of the Pharaohs which other cultures have called decadence.

Yet Therme (Thessalonika), Antioch, Pergamum, Palmyra, and above all Alexandria of Egypt became major cultural, economic, and political centres. The blending of Greek and oriental influences, which fermented alongside the decadent dynasties, created that inimitable hellenistic culture which eventually triumphed over its Western, Latin masters. After all, the 'Romans' of Byzantium, who upheld the Roman Empire for a thousand years beyond the fall of Rome, were heirs to the hellenistic Greeks, and in a very real sense the last successors of Alexander. In the words of Horace, *Graecia capta ferum victorem cepit*, 'Captured Greece conquered its fierce conqueror'.

Hellenistic culture, therefore, acquired a much broader base than did its hellenic progenitor. According to Isocrates (436–338), the last of the Attic Orators, 'Athens has brought it to pass that the name of Greek should no longer be thought of as a matter of race, but a matter of intelligence'. As a result, the quantity of Greek writers actually increased. There was a gang of geographers, from Strabo (*c.*63 BC to AD 21) to Pausanias (*fl. c.* AD 150). There was a profusion of poets: Apollonius, Aratus, and Bion, author of *The Lament for Adonis*; Hermesaniax; Moschus, Meleager, and Musaeus; Oppian, Timon, and Theocritus. There was a host of historians: Manetho of Egypt, inventor of the chronological system of kingdoms and dynasties, and Berosus (Bar-Osea) of Babylon; Polybius of Megalopolis (204–122 BC), the Greek apologist for Rome, and Josephus (b. AD 36),

Governor of Judaea and author of *The Jewish War*, Appian, Arrian, Herodian, Eusebius. Galenus (129–99) wrote a shelf of medical textbooks, Hermogenes (*fl. c.* AD 170) the standard treatise on rhetoric. Among philosophers the Neostoics, such as Epictetus of Hierapolis (AD 55–135), vied with the Neoplatonists: Plotinus (205–70), Porphyry (232–305), Proclus (412–88). The *Enchiridion* or 'Manual' of Stoicism, written by Epictetus, has been called the guidebook to the morality of the later classical world. Plutarch (*c.*46–126), the biographer and essayist, Lucian of Samosata (*c.*120–80), the satirist and the novelists Longus (late 2nd century) and Heliodorus (3rd century) exemplify the continuing diversity of the Greek prose tradition under Roman rule. [PAPYRUS]

Among the writers of the hellenistic period, many wrote Greek as their second language. Josephus, Lucian, and Marcus Aurelius fit into this category, as do the Christian evangelists Matthew, Mark, Luke, and John, and above all St Paul.

Within the Hellenistic world, Alexandria in Egypt soon gained the pre-eminence that Athens had enjoyed in Greece. Under the rule of the Ptolemies, it grew into the largest and most cultured city of the East, second only to Rome in wealth and splendour. Its multinational and multilingual population consisted of 'Macedonians', Jews, and Egyptians. The decree inscribed on the Rosetta Stone, now in the British Museum, provided the trilingual text which permitted Champollion to decipher its hieroglyphics. The fabulous *Museum* or 'College of the Muses', with its library of 700,000 volumes, was dedicated to the collection, preservation, and study of ancient Greek culture. It was a beacon of learning, illuminating the intellectual life of the later classical world as surely as the great Pharos illuminated the sea lanes of the harbour. Aristophanes of Byzantium (*c.*257–180 BC), one of the early librarians at Alexandria, was responsible both for the first annotated editions of Greek literature and for the first systematic analysis of Greek grammar and orthography. Aristarchus of Samothrace (*fl. c.*150 BC) established the text of the *Iliad* and the *Odyssey*. Philon or Philo Judaeus (30 BC–AD 45), a leader of Alexandria's thriving Jewish community, attempted to reconcile Greek philosophy with traditional Judaic theology. Heron, an Alexandrian engineer of uncertain date, is reputed to have invented, among other things, the steam-engine, the syphon, and a drachma-in-the-slot machine.

Specially important in the history of cultural transmission were the so-called Hermetic Writings. Long attributed to an otherwise unknown author, Hermes Trismegistus (the 'thrice greatest Hermes', scribe of the Gods), this huge collection of Greek texts from Alexandria purports in effect to be an encyclopedia of ancient Egypt. Forty-two sacred books summarize the laws of the Pharaohs, their deities, rituals, beliefs, cosmography, astrology, medicine. Other books dating from the third century contain a strange mixture of Neoplatonic and cabbalistic texts apparently directed against the rise of Christianity. [BLACK ATHENA]

In the long run, however, it is not surprising that Greece's 'shoreline civilization' proved unequal to the massed battalions of the neighbouring land-based powers.

PAPYRUS

IN 1963 a carbonized papyrus from the fourth century BC was unearthed at Derveni near Thessaloniki in Macedonia. It had either been burned as part of a funeral rite or had possibly been used as a firelighter. But it was still readable. Deciphered by Dr Faekelmann of Vienna, who separated the layers of the reheated roll with static electricity, it was shown to carry a commentary on the Orphic poems. It replaced the papyrus of Timotheus' *Persae* (P. Berol. 9875), unearthed at Abusir in Egypt, as the oldest Greek papyrological discovery.[1] In 1964 a similar papyrus roll was found in the hand of a man buried in the fourth century BC at Callatis on the Black Sea coast of Romania. But it crumbled to dust on discovery.

The *Cyperus papyrus* plant had been used for writing in Egypt since 3,000 BC. It was laid out in horizontal and vertical strips, which were then pressed flat to form a long *volumen* or scroll. A thick black ink made from soot was applied either by the tip of a sliced reed or by a quill. Papyrus continued to be used in Greek and Roman times, especially in lands close to the source of supply in the Nile delta. The largest find of classical papyri, some 800 in number, was extracted from the lava-sealed ruins of Herculaneum.

Papyrology—the science of papyri—has made an immense contribution to classical studies. Since very few other forms of writing have survived over two millennia, it has greatly advanced knowledge of ancient Palaeography; and it has helped bridge the philological chasm between ancient and medieval Greek. It has supplied many texts from the lost repertoire of classical literature, including Aristotle's *Constitution of Athens*, Sophocles' *Trackers*, and Menander's *The Discontented Man*. It has also played a key role in Biblical studies. Some 7,000 early Greek MSS of various fragments of the Bible are now extant. The Dead Sea Scrolls contained a few Christian as well as Jewish texts. There are two pre-Christian papyrus rolls containing segments of Deuteronomy. A papyrus from AD 125 carrying the Gospel of St John is significantly older than any version on parchment. Some of the oldest papal bulls to survive have done so on papyrus.[2]

As papyrus gave way to parchment, to vellum, and eventually to paper, so too did the roll give way, to the folded pages of the codex. The passing of papyrus, and the advent of the codex, combined to launch the birth of the book. [**BIBLIA**] [**XATIVAH**]

BLACK ATHENA

No thesis has divided the world of classics more profoundly than that associated with the title of *Black Athena*. The traditionalists regard it as freakish; others maintain that it deserves close attention.[1] The thesis has two separate aspects—one critical, the other propositional. The critical part argues with some force that classical studies were moulded by the self-centred assumptions of eighteenth- and nineteenth-century Europeans, and that the cultural debt of Greece and Rome to the older civilizations of the Near East was systematically ignored. The critic's purpose, 'to lessen European cultural arrogance', would seem to be fruitful, though talk of 'the Aryan model of Greek civilization' is provocative.

The main propositions of the thesis centre on the twin notions of Greek civilization being specifically rooted in Egypt and of ancient Egyptian civilization being 'fundamentally African' and created by 'blacks'. This line stands on shakier ground. The Coptic contribution to Greek vocabulary is at best marginal. The skin-colour of the Pharaohs, as portrayed on tomb-paintings, is usually much fairer than that of their frequently negroid servants. Egyptian men were tanned, the women pale. A Nubian dynasty of the seventh century BC is the only one out of thirty-one that can realistically be categorized as 'black'. Sceptics might suspect that scholarship has been hijacked by the racial politics of the USA.

In which case, it is perhaps necessary to re-state the obvious. If one cares to go back far enough, there is no doubt that the origins both of Europeans and of European civilization lie far beyond Europe. The point is: how far back, and to what starting-point, do prehistorians have to go?

[CADMUS] [CAUCASIA] [DASA] [EPIC]

Aristotle's simile of mankind living 'like ants milling on the shore' underlines the strategic problem of concentrating Greek manpower and resources. The thin, extended lines of communication were effective for purposes of economic and cultural expansion, but vulnerable to military attack. In the fifth century BC the Persian challenge had been repulsed with the greatest difficulty. In the fourth century the Macedonians overran the whole of Greece and Persia in the space of thirty years. From the third century onwards, the advance of the Roman legions was unstoppable. At no time could the Greeks ever put more than 50,000 hoplites into the field; yet once the Roman Republic was able to conscript the manpower of the populous Italian peninsula, it had more than half a million soldiers at its disposal. The military contest between Greece and Rome was heavily weighted from the start. The Roman conquest of Magna Graecia was completed at the end of the Pyrrhic Wars in 266 BC. Sicily was annexed following the spirited defence of Syracuse in 212. Macedonia was defeated at the Battle of Pydna in 168.

Mainland Greece, which under the Achaean League had reasserted its independence from Macedonian rule, was subdued by the Consul L. Mummius in 146, and turned into the Roman province of Achaia.

Thereafter, Rome successively reduced all the Greek successor states of the former Macedonian empire. The dramatic end occurred in 30 BC, when Cleopatra, daughter of Ptolemy XII Auletes and the last Queen of Egypt, terminated both a political tradition and her own life by 'pressing the asp to her snow-white breast'. As the lover of both Caesar and Antony, she had done her utmost to control the relentless advance, and advances, of the Romans. But Pascal's *bon mot* that 'the face of the earth would have been different if Cleopatra's nose had been a little shorter' was hardly to the point. The political and military strength of the Greek world was exhausted; the absolute supremacy of Rome was already an established fact.

The resultant fusion of the hellenistic and the Roman world, and the emergence of the hybrid Graeco-Roman civilization, makes it impossible to put a precise date on the death of ancient Greece. But hellenic and hellenistic traditions persisted much longer than is usually supposed. The Delphic Oracle continued to operate until destroyed by marauding barbarians in AD 267. The Olympic Games continued to be held every four years until the 292nd Olympiad in AD 392. The Academy continued to teach its pupils in Athens until closed by the Christian Emperor Justinian in AD 529. The library of Alexandria, though badly burned during Caesar's siege, was not finally closed until the arrival of the Muslim Caliphate in AD 641. By then twenty centuries, or two whole millennia, had passed since the twilight of Crete and the dawn at Mycenae.

Much of Greek civilization was lost. Much was absorbed by the Romans, to be passed by them into the Christian and the Byzantine traditions. Much had to await rediscovery during the Renaissance and after. Yet, one way or another, enough has survived for that one small East European country to be regularly acclaimed as 'the Mother of Europe', the 'Source of the West', a vital ingredient if not the sole fountain-head of Europe.

Syracuse, Sicily, Year 1 of the 141st Olympiad. In the late summer of the sixth year of the Second Punic War, the epic struggle between the Italian city of Rome and the African city of Carthage was balanced on the knife-edge of fate. Hannibal, the Carthaginian general, having annihilated a number of Roman armies sent to halt him, had marched the length of Italy and was campaigning strongly in the south. He had just seized the port and fortress of Tarentum (see Chapter III, p. 155). The Romans, unable to tame him directly, were straining to hold off his allies—the Celts of northern Italy, Philip V of Macedon, who had invaded Illyria, and the Greek city of Syracuse. They were specially eager to subdue Syracuse, since Syracuse held the key both to Hannibal's supply lines from Africa and to their own intentions of re-conquering Sicily. As a result, Syracuse was enduring the second season of a determined siege from a Roman force under M. Claudius Marcellus.

Syrakousai, queen of Greater Greece, was the largest, the most prosperous, and reputedly the most beautiful of all the Greek colonies in the West. Proudly independent in a hellenic age which had seen the subjugation of most city-states, it had asserted its supremacy over Athens long since, and had escaped the attentions of Alexander the Great. It had overhauled its sometime rival, the glorious Acragas, razed by the Carthaginians and never fully restored. In this third century BC it had upheld its profitable role astride the overlapping spheres of Rome and Carthage. It was the last major representative of unconquered Greek civilization.

Situated on the east coast of Sicily, half-way between the snowy slopes of Mt Etna and the island's most southerly point at Cape Pachynum, Syracuse commanded a site of unequalled splendour, security, and convenience. It was the natural entrepôt for trade between the eastern and the western parts of the Mediterranean, and the most usual staging-post between Italy and Africa. Originally founded on a rocky offshore islet, the Ortygia, it had spread upwards onto the neighbouring seaside plateau, which was protected by an almost unbroken ring of cliffs and crags. The grand harbour, which curved southwards for almost five miles in a perfect bay, was screened by lofty mountains. On the other side of the Ortygia, a second harbour could also accommodate the largest fleet of ships. [See Map 7, opposite.]

The island of Ortygia, which served as the city's acropolis, had been joined to the mainland by a fortified causeway in the sixth century. Watered by the marvellous freshwater spring of Arethusa, it was dominated by a huge Temple of Apollo which looked out across the harbour to the matching Temple of Zeus on the opposite headland at Olympieum. In the fifth century the entire plateau had been enclosed within a mighty length of stone walls which ran atop all the natural features. These walls, which stretched for over fifteen miles, were anchored to the castle of Euryalos at the foot of the mountains. They surrounded half a million citizens living in five distinct suburbs. The Achradina or 'Upper City', which possessed its own internal walls, contained the main Agora or Forum. Beyond that lay the residential suburbs of Tyche and Epipolae and, above them, the monumental buildings of Neapolis, the 'New Town', containing a hillside theatre, a nest of temples, and, in Hieron's Altar, the largest sacrificial structure of the ancient world. In all this magnificent site there was only one blemish. An area of marshland astride the River Anapus, which flowed into the Grand Harbour, was a notorious source of summer pestilence. With that one proviso, Syracuse basked in unrivalled favours. According to Cicero, who was to govern there somewhat later, there was never a day when the sun failed to shine. The elevated plateau caught every breeze that blew across the wine-dark waves. Flowers bloomed on the cliffs, and still do, even in winter.

Prior to the arrival of the Roman army, Syracuse could boast more than 500 years of history. Founded by Corinthian colonists in 734 BC, it was only twenty years younger than Rome, and had spread its influence through a network of daughter colonies. In 474, only six years after Salamis, it had been responsible for the destruction of the naval power of the Etruscans, thereby removing one of

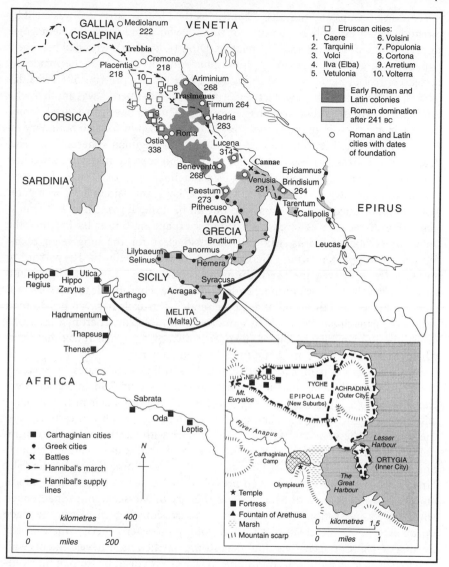

Map 7. Rome—Sicily—Carthage, 212 BC

the early obstacles to Roman fortunes. Like many city-states, it passed through phases of oligarchic, democratic, and monarchical government. It survived its supreme test in the successive sieges of 415–413 and 405–404, the former laid by the Athenians, the latter by the Carthaginians.

For want of better information, the political history of ancient Sicily has to be written in terms of successive Syracusan tyrants, who ruled through a bloody succession of coups and tumults.[22] Dionysius the Elder (r. 405–367) was cited by Aristotle as an example of the type of tyrant 'who gains power by demagogic appeals to the poorer classes'. His relative, Dion (r. 357–354), who had been per-sonally tutored in the ways of a philosopher-king by Plato and the Academy, seized control of Syracuse after sailing from Greece in a pre-run of Garibaldi's Thousand. Timoleon (r. 344–36), the Corinthian 'son of liberty', was another who triumphed with the aid of mercenaries; but he seems to have introduced demo-cratic constitutions in many of the cities, and succeeded in fixing a boundary on the River Halycus between the Greek and the Carthaginian spheres. The cruel Agathocles (r. 317–289) was a plebeian potter who rose by marrying a wealthy widow. In 310 BC he resolved the second Carthaginian siege of Syracuse by carry-ing the war into Africa. This self-styled 'King of Sicily' was said to have been para-lysed by a poisoned toothpick and laid out on his funeral pyre alive. In the next generation Syracuse was saved from Rome's expanding power by Pyrrhus, the adventurer-King of Epirus, who left the field clear for the long reign of his Syracusan supporter, King Hieron II (r. 269–215). Hieron II, patron of Archimedes, preserved the peace through an unbroken treaty with Rome and gave Syracuse its last spell of independent affluence. Hieron's death, however, at a crucial moment in the Punic Wars, precipitated a struggle between pro-Roman and pro-Carthaginian factions. His grandson and successor, Hieronymus, aban-doned the Roman alliance, only to be overthrown by a popular revolt that over-whelmed first the royal family and then the Roman party.

In 215 the election of two Carthaginians as ruling magistrates in Syracuse greatly aroused Roman anxieties. Shortly afterwards four Roman legions were transported to Sicily, and a *casus belli* was found in a border skirmish. Marcellus laid siege to Syracuse, by land and by sea, late in 214 or possibly in early 213. For the besiegers, the year was 538 AUC. Their rivalry with Carthage was the central political feature of the era. It was a natural extension of Rome's earlier conquest of southern Italy. Carthage was the established power, Rome the challenger. The First Punic War (267–241) had been provoked by Roman intervention in a local quarrel between Hieron of Syracuse and the city of Messana; and it had ended with Rome's annexation of all Carthaginian possessions in Sicily. Carthage made up for its loss by the creation of a new colony in eastern Iberia, where in 227 Carthagonova (Cartagena) was founded. Rome watched these developments with intense suspicion; and the Second Punic War was provoked by Roman interven-tion at Saguntum in Iberia, despite a treaty recognizing Carthaginian rule up to the Ebro. Hannibal had then carried the war to the gates of Rome, causing a gen-eral conflagration in which the strategic control of the central Mediterranean was at stake. Syracuse was the pivot.

M. Claudius Marcellus (d. 208), five times consul, was a pious hero-warrior of the old Roman school. In his first consulship in 222 he had slain the King of the Insubrian Gauls in single combat on the plain near Milan, and had dedicated the whole of his Gallic spoils to the temple of Jupiter Feretrius. He was due to die in battle, ambushed by Hannibal. He earned himself a Life by Plutarch. By all accounts, which include those of Livy and Polybius as well as Plutarch, the Roman siege of Syracuse was laid with high hopes of quick success. Marcellus was opposed by the unbreached walls and by confident defenders. Yet, in addition to three legions of perhaps 25,000 men, he was armed with 100 warships, a huge train of siege engines, and by the knowledge that Syracusan counsels were divided. He had reckoned on everything, writes Livy, except on one man.

That man was Archimedes, *unicus spectator caeli siderumque,* 'that unrivalled observer of the heaven and the stars, even more remarkable as the inventor and engineer of artillery and engines of war'.[23] Throughout the reign of Hieron II, Archimedes had been building an arsenal of ingenious anti-siege machines of every range and calibre.

Livy's account of the scene when the Roman troops approached the sea-walls makes good reading:

The wall of Achradina . . . which is washed by the sea, was attacked by Marcellus with sixty-five quinquiremes. From most of the ships, archers and slingers . . . allowed hardly anyone to stand on the wall without being wounded.

Other five-bankers, paired and lashed together . . . and propelled by the outer banks of oars like a single ship, brought up siege-towers several storeys high, together with engines for battering the wall.

Against this naval equipment, Archimedes had lined the walls with artillery of various sizes. Ships lying offshore were bombarded with a regular discharge of stones of great weight. The nearer vessels were attacked with lighter but much more frequent missiles.

Finally, to let his men discharge their bolts without exposure to wounds, he opened up the wall from top to bottom with numerous loopholes about a cubit wide. Through these, without being seen, some shot at the enemy with arrows, others from small protected 'scorpions'.[24]

Polybius relates that the floating siege-towers were called *sambucae,* since their shape resembled that of a musical instrument of that name, no doubt an ancestor of the modern Greek *bouzouki.*

Most disconcerting were Archimedes' devices for lifting the attackers clean out of the water:

Huge beams were suddenly projected from the walls, right over the ships, which could then be sunk by great weights released from on high. Other ships were grabbed at the prow by iron claws, or beaks, like those of cranes, winched up into the air, then dropped stern first into the depths. Others again were spun round and round by means of machinery inside the city, and dashed on the steep cliffs . . . with great destruction of the fighting men on board . . . Frequently, a ship would be lifted into mid-air, and whirled hither and thither . . . until its crew had been thrown out in all directions . . .[25]

Marcellus recognized a superior adversary. 'Let us stop fighting this geometrical giant,' he exclaimed, 'who uses our ships to ladle water from the sea.' Or again, 'Our sambuca band has been whipped out of the banquet.' Plutarch commented, 'The Romans seemed to be fighting against the Gods.'

With the assault abandoned, the siege turned into a blockade that lasted for two years. The Syracusans remained buoyant for many months. A Carthaginian relief force set up camp in the valley of the Anapus, requiring Marcellus to bring a fourth legion from Panormus. A naval sortie left the harbour successfully, and returned with a fleet of reinforcements. In the interior of the island a Roman massacre of the citizens of Henna, a city sacred to Proserpina, turned the Sicilians against them. In the spring of 212 Marcellus mounted a night raid on the Galeagra Tower during the Festival of Artemis, and broke through the Hexapyloi Gate into the suburb of Epipolae. But the main fortresses held firm. In the summer the Carthaginian admiral, Bomilcar, gathered a vast fleet of 700 transports, protected by 130 warships. With clear superiority, he lay in wait for the Roman fleet off Cape Pachynum. At the last moment, for reasons unknown, he declined Marcellus' offer of battle, stood out to sea, and sailed on to Tarentum.

In the end, the outcome of the siege was decided by plague and by treachery. The Carthaginians, who had been struck by the plague when attacking Syracuse two centuries earlier, were now decimated by the same disease when trying to defend it. Then, with parleys in progress, an Iberian captain called Moeriscus, one of three prefects of Achradina, decided to save his skin by letting the Romans in near the Fountain of Arethusa. On the agreed signal, during a diversionary attack, he opened the gate. After setting guards on the houses of the pro-Roman faction, Marcellus gave Syracuse to plunder.

Archimedes was counted among the many victims. Later tradition held that he was killed by a Roman soldier whilst working on a mathematical problem traced in the sand. Plutarch reviewed the various versions in circulation:

As it happened, Archimedes was on his own, working out some problem with the aid of a diagram. Having fixed his mind on his study, he was not aware of the Romans' incursion.

Suddenly, a soldier came upon him with drawn sword, and ordered him to Marcellus. Archimedes refused until he had finished his problem . . . Whereupon the soldier flew into a rage, and despatched him.

Others say that the Roman . . . had threatened to kill him at once, and that Archimedes, when he saw him, had earnestly begged him to wait so that the result would not be left without demonstration. But the soldier paid no attention, and made an end of him there and then.

There is a third story, that some soldiers fell in with Archimedes as he was taking some of his scientific instruments to Marcellus, such as sun-dials, spheres, and quadrants. They slew him, thinking that he was carrying gold.

It is generally agreed, however, that Marcellus was greatly troubled by the death, and shunned the killer, seeking out the relatives of Archimedes and paying them his respects.[26]

Such was the impact when Greek civilization met Roman power.

At his own expressed wish, Archimedes was buried in a tomb designed as a sphere inside a cylinder. He once said that the ratio of 2 : 3, as expressed in a sphere and cylinder of similar length and diameter, offered the most pleasing of proportions.

The fall of Syracuse had immediate consequences. On the cultural front, it underlined Rome's obsession with everything Greek. The artistic loot, wrote Livy, was no less than if Carthage itself had been sacked. It created the fashion for Greek artefacts and Greek ideas which henceforth became the norm for all educated Romans. It was probably the single most powerful stimulus in the growth of a shared Graeco-Roman culture. On the strategic front, it completed the Roman hold on Sicily. It cut off Carthage from a major source of trade and food, and deprived Hannibal of his principal source of logistical support. Before Syracuse, Rome was an equal player in the three-sided Greek–Carthaginian–Roman power game. After Syracuse, Rome held the initiative in all directions.

In the longer term, the Romans' success in Sicily encouraged their further embroilment in Greek affairs. During the siege of Syracuse, Rome had just opened an alliance with the Aetolian League in central Greece, in order to outflank Carthage's other ally, Macedonia. From then on, Rome had Greek clients to be satisfied and interests to be protected. Three Macedonian Wars (215–205, 200–197, and 171–168), and the struggle against Macedonia's chief associate, Antiochus III of Syria, brought the Romans into Greece with a vengeance. In the end, as in Sicily, Rome decided to terminate the complications by turning the whole of Macedonia and the Peloponnese into Roman provinces.

At the time, the fall of Syracuse must have been soon forgotten, even by the Syracusans. They were lucky to escape the fate of other defeated cities, where the whole of the surviving population was habitually sold into slavery. After all, it was just one event in the endless series of campaigns and battles that accompanied the rise of Rome and the demise of Greece. On consideration, however, it may be seen to be symptomatic of shifts and changes that were to affect a much wider con- stituency than that of central Mediterranean politics.

Historians who look back at Rome's triumphant expansion are locked into the knowledge of subsequent developments. They are fully aware that the resultant Graeco-Roman culture was destined to dominate the whole of the classical world, and to exert a lasting influence as one of the pillars of 'Western civilization'. Their antennae are less sensitive to other trends and prospects which existed alongside it. Equally, fully equipped with a knowledge of Greek and Latin, the standard vehicles of higher education in modern Europe, they have sometimes been slow to relate the growth of the Graeco-Roman sphere to the full panorama of con- temporary events. No one could fairly deny that the fusion of the Greek and Roman worlds, in which the fall of Syracuse was a signal moment, was a process of capital importance. The difficulty is to see what other perspectives were in the offing.

No record has survived of Syracusan reflections at the time of the siege. But many of the citizens of a merchant city must have travelled widely. They lived on an island which had long been contested between Greeks and Carthaginians and only recently invaded by Romans. As a result, whatever side they favoured in the Punic Wars, they must surely have seen the Carthaginians, like themselves, as members of an ancient order challenged by Roman upstarts. Indeed, as a seagoing commercial nation they would probably have felt a deeper affinity with Carthage than with Rome. Certainly, living more than a century after Alexander put the Greeks into intimate contact with Persia and India, they must surely have felt themselves to be part of that Graeco-oriental world of Hellenism than of a Graeco-Roman world which had not yet been delivered. For them, the centre of the world was undoubtedly neither Carthage nor Rome, but Alexandria.

Modern perspectives have often placed Syracuse as a Greek and therefore a European city whose new bond with European Rome was a natural, if not an inevitable, development. They instinctively avoid the suggestion that the Greeks were more Asiatic than European at this juncture, or that they might well have maintained their oriental connections indefinitely. Few courses on Western civilization which honour Archimedes would point out that the great mathematical genius gave his life opposing the union of his Greek city with Rome.

Four years after the battle of Cannae (see p. 155) Rome's position was still extremely precarious. It would have been entirely reasonable for the Carthaginian party to calculate that Marcellus lacked the strength to take Syracuse by assault; that Roman failure at Syracuse would give heart to Carthage's other allies; that the reassertion of Carthaginian power in Sicily would guarantee proper logistical support for Hannibal; that Hannibal, effectively supplied, would break the stalemate in Italy; that Rome, in other words, had every chance of being defeated. There was no Cato in Syracuse; but the razing of troublesome cities was an established practice. In the long watches on the Syracusan walls, it was entirely possible that some of Archimedes' men, if not Archimedes himself, could have realistically mused: *Roma delenda est*—that is, until the plague struck and Moeriscus opened the gate.

The Syracusans' knowledge of the world would have been largely confined to the Great Sea, and to the countries of the East. The science of geography had made great advances in classical Greece, although the frontiers of the world directly known to the ancients had not radically changed. A contemporary of Archimedes, Eratosthenes of Cyrene (276–196), librarian at Alexandria, had concluded that the world was a sphere; and his work was known to Ptolemy and Strabo. But, apart from the Phoenician route to the Tin Islands, little progress was made in practical exploration. No known contact was ever made with West Africa, with the Americas, or with the more distant parts of northern Europe. The rigid division between the 'civilized' world of the Mediterranean shoreline and the 'barbarian' wilderness beyond was not overcome.

In the late third century Mediterranean civilization was still made up of three major spheres of influence: Carthaginian in the West, Romano-Italic in the centre, Greek-Hellenic in the East. Thanks to Alexander's conquests, it was more closely tied than previously to the oriental empires from Egypt to India. Along the fragile tracks of Central Asia, it had some slight link with the Empire of China which at that very moment had begun to construct its Great Wall against nomadic incursions.

Over the previous centuries, the barbarian wilderness of northern and central

Europe had begun the slow transition from the Bronze to the Iron Age. It had been strongly marked by the dominant influence of the Celts, whose culture had taken hold, whether by migration or osmosis, at most points from the middle Vistula to Iberia, Gaul, and Britain. The Celts had stormed Rome in 387, and had moved in force into northern Italy. Celtic hill-forts had created a permanent network of urban stations, and their commercial activities formed an important intermediary for the Germanic, Slavic, and Baltic tribes further afield. In the late third century one branch of the Celts, the Galatians, who were established in their kingdom of Tyle in Thrace (on the territory of modern Bulgaria), were facing revolt by their Thracian subjects and preparing the move to neighbouring Asia Minor, where they lingered until medieval times. Their sojourn in Thrace has been confirmed by the recent discovery of inscriptions at Seuthopolis and Messembria (Nesebar).[27]

In the third century BC, however, many historians would consider that the European Peninsula was at least 1,000 years away from anything recognizable as European civilization. In particular, the Europeanness of ancient Greece is being questioned as an anachronistic, intellectual construction of latter-day Europeans. Which is all very proper.

Yet the two most striking processes of that age—the fusion of Graeco-Roman civilization in the Mediterranean and the supremacy of the Celts across much of the interior—put two essential building-blocks into place for the developments of the future. There was little trace of a common culture or common ideology, though both Graeco-Romans and Celts were Indo-Europeans (see Chapter IV). There was absolutely no inkling of a common identity. None the less, one has to concede that these were the peoples whose descendants and traditions were to find themselves at the core of later European history. It is one thing to correct the excessively Eurocentric interpretations of the ancient world, which have prevailed for too long. It is quite another to go to the other extreme, and to maintain that Greeks and Romans hold little or no relevance to the later European story.

There are certain events which happened, and whose consequences are still with us. One cannot pretend otherwise. If Moeriscus had *not* opened the gate; if Syracuse had resisted the Romans as it once resisted the Athenians; if Hannibal had destroyed Rome as Rome would soon destroy Carthage; if, as a result, the Greek world had eventually fused with semitic Carthage, then history would have been rather different. The point is: Moeriscus *did* open the gate.

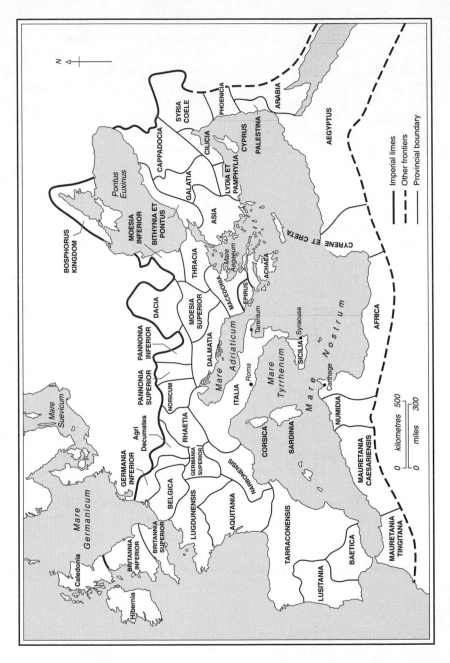

Map 8.
The Roman
Empire, 1st
Century AD

Imperial limes
Other frontiers
Provincial boundary

Caledonia

Hibernia

BRITANNIA
INFERIOR

BRITANNIA
SUPERIOR

Mare
Germanicum

Mare
Suevicum

GERMANIA
INFERIOR

Agri
Decumates

GERMANIA
SUPERIOR

BELGICA

LUGDUNENSIS

AQUITANIA

NARBONENSIS

RHAETIA

NORICUM

PANNONIA
SUPERIOR

PANNONIA
INFERIOR

DACIA

MOESIA
SUPERIOR

MOESIA
INFERIOR

BOSPHORUS
KINGDOM

Pontus
Euxinus

BITHYNIA ET
PONTUS

CAPPADOCIA

GALATIA

THRACIA

MACEDONIA

EPIRUS

ACHAEA

Mare
Aegaeum

ASIA

LYDIA ET
PAMPHYLIA

CILICIA

SYRIA
COELE

PHOENICIA

CYPRUS

PALESTINA

ARABIA

AEGYPTUS

CYRENE ET CRETA

DALMATIA

Mare
Adriaticum

ITALIA

Roma

Tarentum

Mare
Tyrrhenum

Mare Nostrum

SICILIA

Syracuse

Carthage

AFRICA

NUMIDIA

SARDINIA

CORSICA

MAURETANIA
CAESARIENSIS

MAURETANIA
TINGITANA

BAETICA

LUSITANIA

TARRACONENSIS

N

0   kilometres   500
0   miles   300

III

ROMA

Ancient Rome, 753 BC–AD 337

THERE is a quality of cohesiveness about the Roman world which applied neither to Greece nor perhaps to any other civilization, ancient or modern. Like the stones of a Roman wall, which were held together both by the regularity of the design and by that peculiarly powerful Roman cement, so the various parts of the Roman realm were bonded into a massive, monolithic entity by physical, organizational, and psychological controls. The physical bonds included the network of military garrisons which were stationed in every province, and the network of stone-built roads which linked the provinces with Rome. The organizational bonds were based on the common principles of law and administration, and on the universal army of officials who enforced common standards of conduct. The psychological controls were built on fear and punishment—on the absolute certainty that anyone or anything that threatened the authority of Rome would be utterly destroyed.

The source of the Roman obsession with unity and cohesion may well have lain in the pattern of Rome's early development. Whereas Greece had grown from scores of scattered cities, Rome grew from one single organism. Whilst the Greek world had expanded along the Mediterranean sea lanes, the Roman world was assembled by territorial conquest. Of course, the contrast is not quite so stark: in Alexander the Great the Greeks had found the greatest territorial conqueror of all time; and the Romans, once they moved outside Italy, did not fail to learn the lessons of sea power. Yet the essential difference is undeniable. The key to the Greek world lay in its high-prowed ships; the key to Roman power lay in its marching legions. The Greeks were wedded to the sea, the Romans to the land. The Greek was a sailor at heart, the Roman a landsman.

Certainly, in trying to explain the Roman phenomenon, one would have to place great emphasis on this almost animal instinct for the 'territorial imperative'. Roman priorities lay in the organization, exploitation, and defence of their territory. In all probability it was the fertile plain of Latium that created the habits and skills of landed settlement, landed property, landed economy, landed administration, and a land-based society. From this arose the Roman genius for military organization and orderly government. In turn, a deep attachment to the land, and to the stability which rural life engenders, fostered the Roman virtues: *gravitas*, a sense of responsibility, *pietas*, a sense of devotion to family and country, and *iustitia*, a sense of the natural order. 'Tillers of the soil make the strongest men and the bravest soldiers,' wrote the Elder Cato.[1]

Modern attitudes to Roman civilization range from the infinitely impressed to the thoroughly disgusted. As always, there are the power-worshippers, especially among historians, who are predisposed to admire whatever is strong, who feel more attracted to the might of Rome than to the subtlety of Greece. They admire the size and strength of the Colosseum with never a thought for the purposes to which it was put. The Colosseum, in fact, became the symbol of Roman civilization. It became a commonplace: 'When falls the Colosseum, Rome shall fall; and when Rome falls—the World.'[2] At the same time there is a solid body of opinion which dislikes Rome. For many, Rome is at best the imitator and the continuator of Greece on a larger scale. Greek civilization had quality, Rome mere quantity. Greece was original, Rome derivative. Greece had style, Rome had money. Greece was the inventor, Rome the Research and Development division. Such indeed was the opinion of some of the more intellectual Romans. 'Had the Greeks held novelty in such disdain as we,' asked Horace in his *Epistles*, 'what work of ancient date would now exist?' What is more, the Romans vulgarized many of the things which they copied. In architecture, for example, they borrowed the heavy and luxurious late Corinthian order, but not the Doric or the Ionian. 'The whole fabric of Greek art goes to pieces', writes one critic, 'when it is brought into contact with a purely utilitarian nation like Rome.'[3]

Rome's debt to Greece, however, was enormous. In religion, the Romans adopted the Olympians wholesale—turning Zeus into Jupiter, Hera into Juno, Ares into Mars, Aphrodite into Venus. They adopted Greek moral philosophy to the point where Stoicism was more typical of Rome than of Athens. In literature, Greek writers were consciously used as models by their Latin successors. It was absolutely accepted that an educated Roman should be fluent in Greek. In speculative philosophy and the sciences, the Romans made virtually no advance on earlier achievements.

Yet it would be wrong to suggest that Rome was somehow a junior partner in Graeco-Roman civilization. The Roman genius was projected into new spheres—especially into those of law, military organization, administration, and engineering. Moreover, the tensions which arose within the Roman state produced literary and artistic sensibilities of the highest order. It was no accident that many leading Roman soldiers and statesmen were writers of high calibre. Equally, the long list of Roman vices cannot be forgotten. Critics have pointed to a specially repulsive brand of slavery, to cruelty beyond measure, and, in time, to a degree of decadence that made hellenism look puritanical.

In its widest definition, from the founding of the 'Eternal City' in 753 BC to the final destruction of the Roman Empire in AD 1453, the political history of ancient Rome lasted for 2,206 years. In its more usual definition, from the founding of the city to the collapse of that western segment of the Roman Empire of which Rome was the capital, it lasted for barely half that time. It is customarily divided into three distinct periods: the Kingdom, the Republic, and the Empire. [AUC]

The semi-legendary Roman Kingdom corresponds in many ways to the earlier 'Heroic Age' of Greece. It begins with the tale of Romulus and Remus, the orphaned twins, reputedly descendants of Aeneas, who were suckled by a she-wolf, and it ends with the expulsion of the last of the seven kings, Tarquin the Proud, in 510 BC. Those two-and-a-half centuries lie long before the era of recorded history. Romulus, the founder of Rome, supposedly organized the Rape of the Sabine Women, who helped to populate the new city. Numa Pompilius, a Sabine, introduced the calendar and the official religious practices. He founded the Temple of Janus in the Forum, whose doors were opened in time of war and closed in times of peace. Tullius Hostilius, the third king, a Latin, razed the neighbouring city of Alba Longa and deported its population. Ancus Marcius created the order of *plebs* or 'common people' from imported captives. Servius Tullius, the sixth king, granted Rome its first constitution, giving the plebs independence from the patricians or 'elders', and created the Latin League. The fifth and seventh kings, Tarquinius Priscus and Tarquinius Superbus, were of Etruscan descent. The former undertook the first public works in Rome, including the vast sewer named after him. The latter was expelled, following the Rape of Lucretia organized by his son. [ETRUSCHERIA]

Rome, with its seven hills commanding the strategic crossing-point of the River Tiber, was but one of several cities of Latium that spoke the 'Latin' tongue. In those early years it was dominated by more powerful neighbours, especially by the Etruscans to the north, whose fortified city of Veii lay only 16 km from the Forum. The remains of the 'Etruscan Places' at Vulci, Tarquinia, and Perugia attest to an advanced but mysterious civilization. Rome borrowed much from them. According to Livy, the city only survived the Etruscan attempt to storm it and to reinstate the Tarquins after the one-eyed Horatius Cocles had held the Sublician Bridge:

> Then out spake brave Horatius
>   The Captain of the Gate:
> 'To every man upon this earth
>   Death cometh soon or late;
> And how can man die better
>   Than facing fearful odds,
> For the ashes of his fathers
>   And the temples of his Gods?
>
> Hew down the bridge, Sir Consul,
>   With all the speed ye may:

AUC

ROMAN chronology was based on the conventional date for the founding of the city. Zero year was long taken to be equivalent to 750 BC. All subsequent dates were calculated AUC, *ab urbe condita*, 'from the founding of the city'. A modified scheme came into being in the first century BC, when the computations of M. Terentius Varro (636–725 AUC), 'the most learned of the Romans', made the city's foundation equivalent to 753 BC.

By Varro's time, however, most Romans had also become accustomed to an alternative system, which referred not to the date of the year but to the names of the annual consuls. Both in official records and in everyday conversations, they talked of 'the year of C. Terentius Varro and L. Aemilius Paulus' (216 BC), or of 'the seven consulships of C. Marius' (107, 104, 103, 102, 101, 100, and 86 BC). One needed a detailed grasp of Roman history to follow the references. Few educated people would not have known that the elder Varro and Aemilius Paulus had commanded the Roman army at the disaster of Cannae.

Fortunately, the two systems were compatible. Each of them could be invoked to support the other. For example, the rise and fall of G. Iulius Caesar could be calculated with reference to the following:

AUC	Consulship	BC
695	M. Calpurnius Bibulus and C. Iulius Caesar (I)	59
705	C. Claudius Marcellus and L. Cornelius Lentulus Crus	49
706	C. Iulius Caesar (II) and P. Servilius Vatia Isauricus	48
707	Q. Rufius Calenus and P. Vatinius	47
708	C. Iulius Caesar (III) and M. Aemilius Lepidus	46
709	C. Iulius Caesar (IV) Sole Consul	45
710	C. Iulius Caesar (V) and M. Antonius	44
711	C. Vibius Pansa and A. Hirtius, both killed; replaced by the Triumvirate of M. Antonius, G. Octavianus, and M. Aemilius Lepidus.	43

It was Caesar who realized that the existing calendar was becoming inoperable. The old Roman year contained only 304 days divided into 10 months, beginning on xi Kal. Maius or 21 April. The extra months of *Ianuarius* and *Februarius* had been invented as stop-gaps. In 708 AUC, therefore, during Caesar's third consulship, drastic reforms were introduced. The current year was prolonged by 151 days so that the New Year could begin on 1 January 707 AUC/45 BC and run over twelve months of 365 days until 31 December. Further adjustments were made under Augustus in 737 AUC/AD 4, when the old fifth and sixth months, *Quintilis* and *Sextilis*, were renamed *Julius* (after Caesar) and *Augustus*, and the four-yearly *bis-sextile* or 'leap-day' was introduced. The resultant Julian Year of 365¼ days was misaligned with the earth only by the tiny margin of 11 minutes 12 seconds, and remained in universal use until AD 1582.

None the less, consuls continued to be appointed throughout the Principate; and the custom of counting years by consulships was preserved with them. The regnal years of the emperors were not usually invoked. In the later Empire, when consulships were abolished, the AUC system was supported by references to the fifteen-year tax cycle of 'Indictions'. When the Christian era finally came into use in the mid-sixth century AD, the Roman era had been in operation for thirteen centuries.[1] [**ANNO DOMINI**]

I, with two more to help me,
　Will hold the foe in play.
In yon straight path a thousand
　May well be stopped by three.
Now who will stand on either hand
　And keep the bridge with me?'

'Horatius', quoth the Consul,
　'As thou sayest, so let it be.'
And straight against that great array
　Forth went the dauntless Three.
For Romans in Rome's quarrel
　Spared neither land nor gold,
Nor son nor wife, nor limb nor life,
　In the brave days of old.[4]

The Roman Republic presided over the city's growth from provincial obscurity to mastery of the whole Mediterranean. The process began in 509 BC with the first election of the ruling consuls, and ended 478 years later, when Octavian established the first imperial dynasty. It was an epoch of incessant conquest. In the fifth century, **Rome gained a hold over its immediate neighbours and a territory of 822 km²** (314 square miles). In one famous episode, in 491 BC, the Roman exile G. Marcius Coriolanus, who had led an all-conquering Volscian army to the gates of Rome, was persuaded to desist by the tearful entreaties of his mother. In the fourth century Rome recovered from its sack by the Gauls in 390 BC, and in the three fierce Samnite Wars established its supremacy over central Italy. In the third century Rome undertook the conquest of the Greek south, first in the war against Pyrrhus, King of Epirus (282–272 BC), who came to the aid of his compatriots, and later in successive campaigns ending with the annexation of Sicily (see pp. 138–47, above). These campaigns provoked extended conflict with Carthage, and the three Punic Wars.

Of all Rome's wars it was the hundred years' conflict with Carthage that best demonstrated that famous Roman combination of stamina and ruthlessness. Older than Rome, African Carthage had been founded by migrants from Phoenicia, in Latin *Punica* (see pp. 104–8). Relations between them had traditionally been pacific, protected by a treaty contained in the oldest known

ETRUSCHERIA

A͏T Santa Severa, ancient Pyrgi, near Rome, archaeologists have uncovered two Etruscan temples overlooking the sea. The find, made in 1957–64, was exceptional. It was the first Etruscan site that offered something other than tombs. Dated c.500 BC, it yielded three wafer-thin gold tablets, with inscriptions in Punic and Etruscan:

To the lady Astarte. This is the sacred place made and given by Thefarie Velianas, king of Cisra, in the month of the Sacrifice of the Sun . . . in the third year of his reign, in the month of Kir, of the Day of the Burial of the Divinity. And the years of the statue of the goddess [are as many] as these stars.[1]

Pyrgi served as harbour to the nearby town of Cisra (modern Cerveteri); and King Thefarie or 'Tiberius' had chosen to worship a Carthaginian Goddess. [TAMMUZ] The temples must have been dedicated some time after the abortive Etruscan raid on Greek Cumae on the Bay of Naples, perhaps within a decade of the revolt of Rome against Etruscan overlordship.

The Etruscans flourished in Tuscany and Umbria from 700 to 100 BC. They claimed to be immigrants from Asia Minor. Their alphabet, derived from the Greek, is easily read, but their language has not been fully deciphered. After the initial era of princes, they passed in the sixth century into the era of mercantile city-states on the Greek model. Their grave-chambers are covered in fine, stylized, pictorial murals often depicting banquets of the dead (see Plate 5). The little that is known about them derives either from archaeology or from hostile Roman accounts of a later age, when they are painted as gluttons, lechers, and religious devotees. From the first Etruscan exhibition in London in 1837 to its most recent successor in Paris in 1992,[2] many attempts have been made to interest the European public in Etruscology. The greatest stimulus came in 1828–36, from the opening of tombs at Vulci, Caere, and Tarquinia, then in the Papal States.

But the dominant mode has been one of Romantic speculation. The Medici, who organized the first investigations, claimed to be of Etruscan descent. In the eighteenth century, Josiah Wedgwood named his pottery 'Etruria' unaware that the fashionable 'Etruscan Style' was of Greek, not Etruscan, origin. Prosper Mérimée was beguiled by the mystery of the Etruscans, as was the Victorian pioneer George Dennis. And so was D. H. Lawrence:

The things [the Etruscans] did in their easy centuries were as natural as breathing. And that is the true Etruscan quality: ease, naturalness, and an abundance of life . . . And death was just a natural continuance of the fullness of life.[3]

This is not Etruscology; it is *Etruscheria*, or, as the French would say, *étruscomanie*.

document of Roman history. Dated in the first year of Republic, the treaty enjoined each side to respect the other's sphere of influence. The peace was kept for nearly three centuries before Roman forces crossed the Straits of Messina.

In the First Punic War (264–241) Carthage itself remained relatively immune from Roman landpower, although its hold on Sicily was lost. Rome learned the arts of naval warfare. In the Second Punic War (218–201), which followed Hannibal's spectacular expedition across the Alps from Spain to Italy, Rome recovered by sheer persistence from the brink of annihilation. The Celts of northern Italy were in revolt, as was much of Sicily; and the road to Rome was left almost undefended. The two battles of Lake Trasimeno (217) and Cannae (216) belong to Rome's most crushing defeats. Only the tactics of Q. Fabius Maximus 'Cunctator', 'The Delayer', the dogged nursing of resources, and the capture of Syracuse (see pp. 142–4) enabled Rome to survive. Hannibal's brother Hasdrubal was thwarted in a second attempt to invade Italy from Spain, and in 203 Hannibal himself was forced to withdraw. He was followed to Africa by the young Publius Cornelius Scipio 'Africanus', survivor of Cannae, conqueror of Cartagena. At Zama in 202, Hannibal met his match. Taking refuge with the enemies of Rome in Greece, he was eventually harried to suicide.

Carthage, deprived of its fleet and paying heavy tribute, survived for sixty years more. But in the Third Punic War (149–146 BC) the elder Cato raised the call for the enemy's complete destruction. *Carthago delenda est*. The deed was carried out in 146. The city was razed, the population sold into slavery, the site ploughed, and salt poured into the furrow. In Tacitus' words on another occasion, the Romans 'created a desert and called it peace'. Scipio Aemilianus, watching the scene in the company of the historian Polybius, was moved to quote the words of Hector in the *Iliad*: 'The day shall come when sacred Troy shall fall.' When asked what he meant he replied: 'This is a glorious moment, Polybius, yet I am seized with foreboding that some day the same fate will befall my own country'.[5]

As the challenge of Carthage was neutralized, and then removed, the triumphant legions of the Republic began to pick off the remaining countries of the Mediterranean. Cisalpine Gaul was conquered between 241 and 190. Iberia and much of northern Africa came as a prize in 201. Illyria was conquered between 229 and 168. Macedonia, together with mainland Greece, was taken over by 146. Transalpine Gaul was invaded in 125 BC, and finally subdued by Caesar in 58–50 BC. The independent kingdoms of Asia Minor were annexed in 67–61 BC, Syria and Palestine by 64 BC. [EGNATIA]

In the last hundred years of the Republic's existence the foreign campaigns became entangled in a series of civil wars. Successful generals sought to control the central government in Rome, whilst would-be reformers sought to satisfy the demands of the lower orders. The resultant strife led to intermittent periods of chaos and of dictatorial rule. In 133–121 BC the popular tribunes Tiberius Sempronius Gracchus and his brother, G. Sempronius Gracchus, attempted to allocate public lands to displaced peasants who had served in the Republic's conquests. Both were opposed by the ruling oligarchy, and both were slain. In 82–79

EGNATIA

O F all the Roman roads, the Via Egnatia proved to be one of the most vital. Built in the second century BC, it linked Rome with Byzantium and hence, in a later age, the Western with the Eastern Empire. It took its name from the city of Egnatia in Apulia, the site of a miraculous fiery altar and a main stage between Rome and the Adriatic port of Brindisium. In Italy it provided an alternative route to the older Via Appia, which reached the same destination through Beneventum and Tarentum. On the eastern Adriatic shore, its starting-point was at Dyracchion (Durres), with a feeder road from Apollonia. It crossed the province of Macedonia, passing Lychnidos (Ochrid) and Pella to reach Thessalonika. It skirted the Chalkidike peninsula at Amphipolis and Philippi, before terminating at Dypsela on the Hebros (Maritsa) in Thrace.[1]

The final section into Byzantium did not originally carry the name of Egnatia, and made a long inland detour to avoid the coastal lagoons. The direct route between Rhegion and Hebdomon was only paved by Justinian I, bringing the traveller to the Golden Gate of Constantinople after twenty days and over 500 miles. It was proverbial that 'all roads lead to Rome'. But all roads led away from Rome as well.

L. Sulla Felix declared himself Dictator after defeating the partisans of G. Marius (157–86), the greatest soldier of his age. In 60 BC three rival soldier-politicians, M. Licinius Crassus, Pompeius Magnus, and C. Iulius Caesar, formed the first ruling triumvirate. But in 48 BC Caesar claimed the title of *Imperator* after crushing the faction of the remaining triumvir, Pompey. Finally, in 31 BC, after the fall of the second triumvirate, Octavian brought the civil wars to a close. His victory at Actium brought about the surrender of Egypt, the death of Antony and Cleopatra, the end of opposition, and his assumption of the title of 'Augustus'. In this way the last gasp of the Roman Republic coincided with the capture of the last piece of the Mediterranean coast which had remained at least nominally independent. In almost 500 years the gates of the Temple of Janus had been closed on only three occasions. [AQUILA]

The civil strife was the outward expression, above all, of a shift in political attitudes, which is well illustrated from the careers of the two Catos, both of whom supported the losing side. Marcus Porcius Cato, 'The Censor' (234–149 BC), became a byword for the old Roman virtues of austerity and puritanism. After twenty-seven years of soldiering he retired to his farm to write books on history and agriculture. He railed against the wave of hellenistic luxury and sophistication, and in particular against the unprincipled careerism, as he saw it, of the Scipios. In his last years he called unrelentingly for the annihilation of Carthage. His great-grandson M. Porcius Cato Uticensis (95–46 BC) showed the same

AQUILA

THE eagle's ranking as 'king of the birds' is as ancient as the lion's as 'king of the beasts'. In Roman lore, it was Jupiter's 'storm-bird', carrier of the thunderbolt. Eagles figured as emblems of power and majesty in Babylon and Persia, and were adopted by the Roman general, Marius, after his oriental conquests. The legions of the Roman Empire marched behind eagle ensigns; and Roman consuls carried eagle-tipped sceptres.[1] (See Appendix III, p. 1228.)

In Slavonic folklore, the three brothers, Lekh, Chekh, and Rus, set out to find their fortune. Rus went to the east, Chekh to the south to Bohemia, whilst Lekh crossed the plain to the west. Lekh stopped beside a lake under a great tree where a white eagle had built its nest. He was the father of the Poles; and Gniezno, the 'eagle's nest', was their first home.

In Wales, too, the peak of Mount Snowdon, the heart of the national homeland, is called *Eryri*, 'the place of eagles'.

In Christian symbolism the eagle is associated with St John the Evangelist (alongside the Angel and Axe of St Matthew, the Bull of St Luke, and the Lion of St Mark). It appears on the lecterns of churches, upholding the Bible on its outspread wings to repel the serpent of falsehood. According to St Jerome, it was the emblem of the Ascension.

Throughout European history, the imperial eagle has been co-opted by rulers who claimed superiority over their fellow princes. Charlemagne wore an eagle-embossed cloak; and Canute the Great was buried in one.[2] Both Napoleon I and Napoleon III used eagle symbolism with relish. Napoleon's heir, the King of Rome, received the sobriquet of *aiglon* or 'eaglet'. Only the British, to be different, betrayed no aquiline interests.

Eagles recur throughout European heraldry, having been present at an earlier date in Islamic insignia.[3] Both Serbia and Poland boast a white eagle, the Polish one crowned (and temporarily uncrowned by the Communist regime). Both Tyrol and Brandenburg-Prussia sported a red eagle, the Swedish province of Varmland a blue one. The Federal Republic of Germany took a single stylized black eagle from the city arms of Aachen. Under the dynasty of the Palaeologues, the Byzantine Empire took on the emblem of a black, double-headed spread eagle, symbol of the Roman succession in East and West. In due course this passed to the Tsars of Moscow, 'the Third Rome', to the Holy Roman Emperors in Germany, and to the Habsburgs of Austria.

Ein Adler fängt keine Mücken, runs the German proverb: 'an eagle catches no midges'.

rectitude and obstinacy of character. A Stoic by training, he joined Pompey in the campaign to check the dictatorial ambitions of Caesar. When Pompey's cause was lost, he killed himself rather than submit, after a heroic journey across the Libyan desert which led only to encirclement in the town of Utica. He had spent his last night reading Plato's *Phaedo*, on the immortality of the soul. In this way he became a symbol of republican opposition to tyranny, of principled opposition. Cicero praised him. Caesar, in his *Anticato*, tried meanly to discredit him. The poet Lucan (AD 39–65), who also committed suicide rather than submit to a despot, makes him the champion of political freedom. Dante, after Lucan, makes him the guardian of Mount Purgatory, and hence of the path to spiritual liberty.

C. Iulius Caesar (100–44 BC) led the decisive attack on the established procedures of the Republic. A successful general and administrator, he shared the first triumvirate from 60 BC with Pompey and Crassus, served as Consul and, from 59, Proconsul of the two Gauls. Caesar's enemies were disgusted by his shameless bribing of the Roman populace, by his manipulation of politicians, by the 'smash-and-grab' policy of his military campaigns. Cicero's protest—'O tempora! O mores!'—is still with us. On 10 January 49 BC, when Caesar crossed the frontier of the province of Italia on the River Rubicon, he declared war on Rome. He shunned the outward trappings of monarchy, but his dictatorship was a reality; his name became synonymous with absolute power. He even succeeded in changing the calendar. He was assassinated on the Ides of March, 44 BC, by a group of republican conspirators headed by M. Brutus and C. Cassius Longinus, whom admirers have called the 'Liberators'. Brutus was a descendant of Rome's first Consul, who overthrew the Tarquins. Shakespeare called him 'the noblest Roman of them all'. Dante put him in the lowest circle of Hell for his betrayal of Caesar's friendship.

After Caesar's death, the leadership of the Caesarian party was assumed by his nephew, Octavian. C. Octavius (b. 63 BC), whose name had been changed to C. Iulius Caesar Octavianus, when he was adopted as Caesar's official heir, was to change it again when all the battles were won. He served for twelve years in a second, shaky triumvirate with M. Aemilius Lepidus and M. Antonius (*c.*82–30 BC), who together at Philippi suppressed the republican faction of Brutus and Cassius. But then he turned on his partners, and attacked the dominant Mark Antony. Octavian was master of the west, Mark Antony of the east; and the naval battle of Actium was a rather tame conclusion to a confrontation in which the combined forces of almost all the Roman world were ranged. But Actium was decisive: it ended the civil wars, finished off the Republic, and gave Octavian the supreme title of Augustus.

The Empire, whose early years are widely referred to as 'the Principate', begins with the triumph of Augustus in 31 BC. It saw the marvellous *Pax Romana*, the 'Roman Peace', established from the Atlantic to the Persian Gulf. Although turbulent politics and murderous intrigues continued, especially in Rome, the provinces were firmly controlled, and wars were largely confined to the distant frontiers. A few new territories were acquired—Britannia in AD 43, Armenia in 63,

---

AQUINCUM

L IKE neighbouring Carnuntum, Aquincum started life as a legionary
camp on the Danube in the reign of Tiberius. It soon attracted a cluster of *canabae* or 'informal settlements', and in the second century AD was
given the formal status of *municipium*. As a gateway to the Empire from
the plains of Pannonia, it thrived mightily, both as a legionary base and as
a commercial centre. Its prosperity is reflected in its twin amphitheatres,
military and civilian, and the mural paintings which adorned its more opulent houses.[1]

The ruins of Aquincum lie in the suburbs of modern Budapest [**BUDA**].
Like the English, the Hungarians had no direct experience of the Roman
world, having migrated to their present homeland after the Empire's fall.
But they cherish their 'Roman heritage' all the more.[2] [**BARBAROS**]

Dacia in 105. But in the main the Empire was content to protect itself in Europe
behind the *limes* or 'frontier line' from Hadrian's Wall to the Danube delta, and
to fight in Asia against Rome's most formidable enemies—the Parthians and
Persians. [**AQUINCUM**]

Eventually, the imperial retreat had to begin. And retreat led to crumbling at
the edges and demoralization at the centre. Already in the third century AD a rash
of short-lived emperors signalled the weakening of the monolith. A partial recovery was staged by ordering the division of the Empire into East and West. But in
the fourth century a marked shift of resources in favour of the East was accompanied by the decision to transfer the capital from Rome to Byzantium. That was
in AD 330. Rome had reached its term as a political centre. The 'eternity' of its rule
over Kingdom, Republic, and Empire lasted exactly 1,083 years.

The motor of Roman expansion was far more powerful than that which had
fuelled the growth of the Greek city-states or of Macedonia. Although the overall
dimensions of Alexander's empire may briefly have exceeded those of the later
Roman world, the area of land which Rome systematically settled and mobilized
was undoubtedly the larger. From the outset Rome applied a variety of legal,
demographic, and agrarian instruments which ensured that an incorporated territory contribute to the overall resources of the Roman war-machine. According
to circumstance, the inhabitants of conquered districts would be granted the status either of full Roman citizenship, or of half-citizenship (*civitas sine suffragio*),
or of Roman allies. In each case their duty to contribute money and soldiers was
carefully assessed. Loyal soldiers were rewarded with generous grants of land,
which would be surveyed and divided into regular plots. The result was a growing territory that needed ever more troops to defend it, and a growing army that
needed ever more land to support it. A militarized society, where citizenship was
synonymous with military service, developed an insatiable agrarian appetite.

A fund of state land, the *ager publicus*, was held back to reward the state's most devoted servants, especially senators.

Within this overall strategy, political arrangements could be extremely flexible. The introduction of uniform administration was not an immediate priority. Peninsular Italy, which was united under Roman rule at the end of the third century BC, had to wait 200 years for its reorganization into regular provinces. Local rulers were frequently left in place. Those who resisted, or rebelled, risked annihilation. In Greece, for example, resistance was undermined when in 146 BC the Roman general appeared at the Isthmian Games and announced that the city-states would be allowed to retain their autonomy. Corinth, which declined the offer, suffered the same fate as Carthage (and in the same year).

Roman religious life was amazingly eclectic. Over the centuries the Romans came into contact with virtually all the gods of the Mediterranean, each of whose cults they added to their collection. In the early days, the devotion of a Roman family was centred on the household deities of hearth and barn. Civic life centred on a series of guardian cults, such as that of the Vestal Virgins, who tended the eternal flame, and on a complicated calendar of festivals presided over by the Pontifex Maximus. Later, the proximity of Magna Graecia led to the wholesale adoption of the Olympian pantheon. The first temple of Apollo was consecrated in Rome in 431 BC. The Epicureans, and especially the Stoics, also found many adherents. In late republican times, oriental mystery cults were popularized—among them that of Atargatis from Syria, of Cybele, the 'Magna Mater' of Asia Minor, and of Egyptian Isis. In imperial times, official religion shifted to the obligatory cult of recent or reigning emperors. Christianity took hold at a time when the Persian sun-god Mithras was increasingly cultivated, especially in the army. The gospel of love had to contend with the dualist doctrine of light and darkness, whose initiates bathed in bull's blood and celebrated the birth of their god on 25 December. Their subterranean oblations are imagined in the 'Hymn of the XXX Legion':

> Mithras, God of the Morning, our trumpets waken the Wall!
> Rome is above the nations, but Thou art over all!
> Now as the names are answered, and the guards are marched away,
> Mithras, also a soldier, give us strength for this day!

> Mithras, God of the Sunset, low on the western main—
> Thou descending immortal, immortal to rise again!
> Now when the watch is ended, now when the wine is drawn,
> Mithras, also a soldier, keep us pure till the dawn!

> Mithras, God of the Midnight, here where the great Bull dies,
> Look on Thy children in darkness. O take our sacrifice!
> Many roads Thou hast fashioned—all of them lead to the Light!
> Mithras, also a soldier, teach us to die aright![6]   [ARICIA]

The Roman economy combined a large measure of self-sufficiency in the inland areas with extensive trade and commerce in the Mediterranean. Overland

ARICIA

A DOZEN miles to the south of Rome, in a crater amidst the Alban hills, lies Lake Nemi, the 'lake of the grove'. In imperial times, the nearby village of Nemi was called Aricia; and throughout the Roman era the woods beside the lake sheltered the sacred Arician Grove, home of *Diana nemorensis*, 'The Diana of the Grove'.

The Arician cult is known both from the writings of Strabo and from modern archaeology. In many ways, it was unremarkable. It involved the worship of a sacred oak, whose boughs were not to be broken, and a sanctuary of perpetual fire. Apart from Diana, it addressed two minor deities— Egeria, a water nymph, and Virbius, a fugitive from the wrath of Zeus. As shown by the surviving mounds of votive offerings, its main devotees were women who hoped to conceive. On the day of the annual summer festival, the grove was lit up by myriad torches, and women all over Italy burned fires in gratitude.

In one respect, however, the cult was exceptional. The Chief Priest of Aricia, who bore the title of *Rex Nemorensis* or 'King of the Grove', was obliged to win his position by slaying his predecessor. At one and the same time he was priest, murderer, and prospective murder victim. Stalking the grove with drawn sword, even at dead of night, he awaited the hour when the next contestant would appear, break off a twig of the Oak, and challenge him to mortal combat.

In recent times, the Arician Grove is notable as the starting-point of James Frazer's *The Golden Bough* (1890), one of the founding works of modern anthropology. Frazer ranks alongside Marx, Freud, and Einstein as a pioneer who changed the thinking of the world. Frazer posed himself two simple questions: 'Why had the priest to slay his predecessor?' and 'Why, before he slew him, had he first to pluck the Golden Bough?'[1]

In search of possible answers, he set off on an investigation of supernatural beliefs in every conceivable culture, ancient or modern. He examines rain-making in China; priest-kings from the Pharaohs to Dalai Lama; tree-spirits from New Guinea to the Cedar of Gilgit, corn-spirits from the Isle of Skye to the Gardens of Adonis; May-Day festivals, summer Fire Festivals, and harvest Festivals. He describes belief in the internal Soul among the Hawaiians and in the external Soul among the Samoyeds of Siberia: in the transference of evil and the expulsion of spirits. He outlines a great range of sacrificial ceremonies from sacrifices among the Khonds of Bengal, to 'eating the God' in Lithuania and 'crying the neck' by the reapers of Devon.

Frazer was making two assumptions, which in his own day were revolutionary. On one hand, he insisted that so-called 'primitive' or 'savage' practices were based on serious ideas, and hence, despite their grotesque appearances, were worthy of respect. At the same time, he showed that the supposedly advanced religions of the civilized world, including Christianity, owed much to their pagan predecessors. 'The life of the old kings and priests teems with instruction', he wrote. 'In it, was summed up all that passed for wisdom when the world was young'.[2] Or again:

Our resemblances to the savage are still far more numerous than our differences. . . . We are like heirs to a fortune which has been handed down for so many ages that the memory of those who built it up has been lost. . . . Their errors were not wilful extravagances or the ravings of insanity. . . . We shall do well to look with leniency upon their errors as inevitable slips made in the search for truth and to give them the benefit for that indulgence which we may one day stand in need of ourselves: *cum exclusione itaque veteres audiendi sunt.*[3]

Frazer's universal tolerance was one of the principal means whereby the European humanities were able to escape from their narrow Christian strait-jacket, and open themselves up to all times and all peoples. His demonstration that many of the customs of Christian peoples had their roots in pagan practices was particularly shocking:

At the approach of Easter, Sicilian women sow wheat, lentils and canary-seed in plates which are kept in the dark and watered. . . . The plants soon shoot up: the stalks are tied together with red ribbons and the plates containing them are placed on the sepulchres which with effigies of the dead Christ, are made up in . . . churches on Good Friday. . . . The whole custom—sepulchres as well as plates of sprouting grain—is probably nothing but a continuation, under another name, of Adonis worship.[4]

Returning to the Arician Grove, Frazer concluded that the King of the Grove personified the tree with the Golden Bough, and that the rite of his death had parallels among many European peoples from Gaul to Norway. The Golden Bough, he claimed, was none other than the mistletoe, whose name he derived from the Welsh, meaning 'tree of pure gold'. 'The King of the Wood lived and died as an incarnation of the supreme Aryan God, whose life was in the mistletoe or Golden Bough.'[5]

To be safe, he added a final paragraph saying that nowadays the visitor to Nemi's woods can hear the church bells of Rome 'which chime out from the distant city, and die lingeringly away across the wide Campagnan marshes. . . . *Le Roi est mort, vive le roi!*'[6] In other words, the pagan King of the Grove has gone; the Christian 'King of Heaven' reigns supreme. He didn't care to mention that the Christian King, too, was born to be slain.

transport costs were high, despite the main roads, so provincial cities did not look beyond the surrounding districts for most commodities. But the seaborne traffic, first developed by Greeks and Phoenicians, was increased still further. Wine, oil, furs, pottery, metals, slaves, and corn were the standard cargoes. [CEDRA]

The growing population of Rome was fed on state-supplied corn, the *frumentum publicum*, which was imported initially from Latium and later from Sicily and North Africa. But the Romans were also wedded to luxuries, and were able to pay for them. The 'silk route' was opened to China, and the 'spice lanes' to India. Roman traders, the notorious *negotiatores*, moved freely round the Empire after the armies, taking valuables, styles, and expectations with them. [SAMOS]

A common currency was introduced in Italy in 269 BC and in Roman territories as a whole in 49 BC. In the imperial period there were gold, silver, brass, and copper coins. The brass *sestertius* became the basic unit of currency. The gold *aureus* was worth 100s., the silver *denarius* 4, the copper *as* one quarter. Local currencies

---

CEDROS

THE fact that the Greeks and Romans had only one word—either *kedros* or *cedros*—to describe the two different species of juniper and cedar merits a nine-page appendix. On the scale of scholarship demanded by a genuine specialist, a subject such as *Trees and Timber in the Ancient Mediterranean World* needs a volume as large as the one you are reading.[1]

And it is worth every page. It shows what a dedicated scholar can do by applying a very narrow instrument to a very broad front—in other words, if one is permitted the only appropriate metaphor, to saw a cross-section through the trunk of the classical world. Like other such works, it starts with a meticulous examination of the different sources of evidence: archaeology, literary references, inscriptions, temple commissioners' accounts and reports, dendrochronology. It then surveys the subject-matter—from the cedar floorbeams at Cnossos to the ash spear of Achilles, from the 220 Roman ships built in 45 days for the First Punic War to the bridge over the Rhine built in ten days for Julius Caesar.

Greece and Rome were not timber-based civilizations, like those of the far north. [NOVGOROD] But their knowledge of timber was renowned, and the timber trade well developed. After reading up on the subject, one can never see a fir tree without thinking of the Athenian fleet at Salamis, nor pass a larch without imagining the 100-foot mast of a Roman trireme. Every bare hillside is a reminder of the Romans' deforestation of southern Italy and of northern Africa. [ECO]

History demands sympathetic historians. There has never been a finer dovetail than that which joined classical trees and timber to the son of a timber merchant from New York State.

SAMOS

S AMIAN ware, the everyday 'red-gloss pottery' of the Roman Empire, probably originated on the island of Samos, but the great mass of it was not manufactured there. From an important factory at Arretium (Arezzo), which was most active AD 30–40, its production was moved to a number of large-scale potteries in Gaul. Forty-five main centres are known; but the major ones from the first century were located at sites at La Graufesenque (Aveyron) and Banassac (Lozère), from the second century at Les Martres de Veyre and Lezoux (Puy-de-Dôme), and from the third century at Trier and at *Tabernae Rhenanae* (Rheinzabern) in Germany. The full geographical range stretches from Spain and North Africa to Colchester and Upchurch in England and Westerndorff on the River Inn in Austria.[1]

Ceramology seeks the triumph of ingenuity and pedantry over the remains of millions of archaeologists' pots and shards; and Samian ware has offered the most extensive challenge. Since studies began in 1879, over 160 kilns have been identified, together with over 3,000 individual potters' marks. Hans Dragendorff (1895) classified 55 standard forms of vessel (D1–D55). Others have catalogued standard decorative motifs, analysed technical aspects such as the gloss, the clay, and the texture of the *terra sigillata*, or established the colour spectrum from the characteristic orange-pink of Banassac to the deep orange-brown of Les Martres de Veyre. Pioneer collections at the British Museum and the Musée Carnavalet led the way for numerous studies from Toronto to Ljubljana.[2]

Potters' marks are specially revealing. Often preceded by the letter *f* (= *fecit*, made by), *m* (= *manu*, by the hand of), or *of* (-*officina*, by the factory of), they bring to life the craftsmen who fed the most widespread commodity of imperial trade. The working lives of 51 central Gaulish potters have been exactly charted. Cocatus Idenalis and Ranto worked throughout the reign of Trajan (98–117); Cinnamus of Lezoux was active *c.*150–90; Banuus, Casurius, and Divixtus spanned the five reigns from Antoninus Pius (138–61) to Albinus (193–7).[3]

The net result is a corpus of information that is so sophisticated that the date and provenance of the smallest fragment of Samian ware can be precisely established. For archaeologists, it is a research aid of inestimable value. A crate of Samian ware from Gaul was found, unopened, at Pompeii. Similar consignments were sent to every town and settlement of the Empire.

continued alongside, however, and the right to mint was an important mark of status. [NOMISMA]

Roman society was built on fundamental legal distinctions between the citizen and the non-citizen and, among the non-citizens, between the free and the unfree. It was a strict system of hereditary social 'orders' or estates. Practices which began in ancient Latium were modified over the centuries until they encompassed the vast and variegated populations of all the Empire's provinces. In early republican Rome, the *patres* or city fathers were set apart from the *plebs* or common people, with whom they were forbidden to intermarry. The patrician clans dominated both the political life of the city in the Senate and economic life through their hold on the distribution of land; and they fought a long rearguard action against the plebeian challenge. But eventually their privileges were undermined. In 296 BC, by the *Lex Ogulnia*, the plebs were to be admitted to the sacred colleges of pontifices and augurs. In 287 BC, by the *Lex Hortensia*, the laws of the plebeian assembly became binding on all citizens. The plebs had become part of the Establishment. In the so-called 'Social War' of 90–89 BC, Rome's Italian allies successfully claimed the rights of full citizenship. But it was not until AD 212 that the *Constitutio Antoniniana* gave citizenship to all free-born male subjects of the Empire.

Important distinctions developed within the patrician oligarchy of the later Republic. A handful of the most ancient and senior clans, the *gentes maiores*, formed an aristocracy among the patricians—the Valerii, Fabii, Cornelii, Claudii, and others. The *nobiles* were a wider but still senatorial group, consisting of all who could claim descent from a consul. They possessed the highly valued right of displaying in public the waxen portraits of their ancestors. The *equites* or 'knights' formed a sub-senatorial propertied class which possessed the means to belong to the cavalry. They had the right to wear a toga edged with two thin purple stripes, the *angusticlavia*, as opposed to the senator's toga with broad purple stripes, the *laticlavia*. In the theatre, they sat in the first fourteen rows, immediately behind the *orchestra*, reserved for senators. They were the chief beneficiaries of promotions under Augustus, when they largely displaced the nobiles as the backbone of the ruling class.

The strong contrast between city and countryside persisted. Like Rome itself, the provincial cities developed into major urban centres, characterized by imposing public works—paved streets, aqueducts, baths, theatres, temples, monuments—and by the growth of merchant, artisan, and proletarian classes. The city mob—constantly pacified, in Juvenal's words, 'through bread and circuses', *panem et circenses*, became a vital social factor. In the countryside, the villas of local dignitaries stood out above the toiling mass of slaves who worked the great latifundia. An intermediate and, in the nature of things, enterprising group of *libertini* or 'freed slaves' grew in importance, as the import of fresh slave populations tailed off with the end of the Republic's conquests. [SPARTACUS]

Despite the extreme contrasts of Roman society—between the vast power and

SPARTACUS

SPARTACUS (d. 71 BC) was a gladiator, and the leader of the ancient world's most extensive slave uprising. A Thracian by birth, he had served in the Roman army before deserting and being sold into slavery to the gladiatorial school in Capua. In 73 BC, he broke out, and with a band of fellow fugitives set up camp on Mount Vesuvius. For the next two years he defied all attempts to catch him. His army swelled to almost 100,000 desperate men, who marched the length and breadth of Italy, to the Alps and the straits of Messina. In 72 BC he defeated each of the reigning consuls in turn in pitched battles. He was finally cornered at Petelia in Lucania, separated from his Gallic and German allies, and annihilated by the forces of the praetor, M. Licinius Crassus. Spartacus died sword in hand, having first killed his horse to render further flight impossible.[1]

Appropriately enough, Crassus was one of the wealthiest slave-owners in Rome. He had benefited from the estates sequestered from the faction of Marius, and grew vastly rich by training his slaves in lucrative trades and by mining silver. Known as 'Dives', he was Consul in 70 with Pompey, and triumvir with Pompey and Caesar in 60. He celebrated his victory over Spartacus by lining 120 miles of the road from Capua to Rome with crucified prisoners, and by treating the Roman populace to a banquet of ten thousand tables. He enriched himself further as Governor of Syria, only to be killed in 53 BC by the Parthians. His head was cut off, the mouth stuffed with molten gold. The accompanying notice from the Parthian king read: 'Gorge yourself in death with the metal you so craved in life.'

Slavery was omnipresent in Roman society, and in some estimations the key institution of the economy. It provided the manpower for agriculture and industry, and underpinned the luxury of the cities. It involved the total physical, economic, and sexual exploitation of the slaves and their children. It was supported by the wars of the Republic, which brought in millions of captives, and in later centuries by systematic slave-raiding and slave-trading. Julius Caesar sold off 53,000 Gallic prisoners after one battle alone, at Atuatia (Namur). The island of Delos served as the principal entrepôt for barbarians brought from the East, and from beyond the Danube.

Slavery continued to be a feature of European life long after Roman times—as it was in most other cultures. It persisted throughout medieval Christendom, though it was gradually overtaken by the institution of serfdom. It was generally permitted among Christians so long as the slaves themselves were not Christian. It was still common enough in Renaissance Italy, where Muslim slaves were treated much as in their countries of origin. In more modern times, the European powers only tolerated it in their overseas colonies, where it survived the conversion of the slaves to Christianity.

The abolition of slavery was one of the chief social products of the European Enlightenment. It progressed through three main stages. The outlawry of slave-owning in the home countries was followed by the suppression of the international slave trade and then of slave-owning in the overseas colonies. In Britain's case, these stages were reached in 1772, 1807, and 1833. Abolition did not occur, however, through revolts such as that of Spartacus. It occurred, as Emerson remarked, 'through the repentance of the tyrant'.[2]

In modern times, Spartacus was adopted as a historical hero by the communist movement. His name was borrowed by the forerunner of the KPD, the Spartakusbund of 1916–19; and it was used by Arthur Koestler for the protagonist of his novel *The Gladiators* (1939). Slave revolts, in the Marxist view, were a necessary feature of ancient society, and were given suitable prominence in communist textbooks. A partner for Spartacus was found in Saumacus, leader of an earlier revolt among the Scythian slaves of Crimea, i.e. on 'Soviet territory'. Soviet historians did not care to emphasize the parallels between the world of Spartacus and Crassus and that of the Gulag, forced collectivization, and the *nomenklatura*.[3] [**CHERSONESOS**]

wealth of the patricians and the lot of their slaves, between the opulence of many city-dwellers and the backwardness of the desert tribes and barbarian settlers on the periphery—it is a tribute to the flexible paternalism of the Roman social tradition that the outbreaks of class conflict were relatively few and far between. Blood relations carried great weight in Rome, where elaborate kinship groups proliferated. The patriciate presided over society at large just as the *paterfamilias* presided over every extended family. The patricians were originally divided into three tribes; the tribes into thirty *curiae* or parishes; and the parishes into *gentes* or clans and families. In later times the *gens* was composed of persons boasting the same remote male ancestor, whilst the *familia* was narrowed to mean 'household group'. The absolute rights of fathers over all members of their family, the *patria potestas*, was one of the corner-stones of family law. [**NOMEN**]

There was a profusion of popular assemblies in Rome, which had both social and political functions. The patricians met on their own in the *comitia curiata*, their 'parish meetings', where, among other things, they ratified the appointment of the consuls. The plebeians, too, met regularly in the *comitia tributa* or 'tribal meetings', where they discussed their communal affairs and elected their officials—the tribunes, or 'spokesmen of the tribes', the *quaestores*, and the *aediles*, the plebeian magistrates. After 449 BC they could be summoned by the consuls as well as by the tribunes. They met in the Forum; and in the *plebiscita*, or 'voting of the plebs', they gave their opinion on any matter put to them.

For military purposes, patricians and plebeians met together in the *comitia centuriata* or the 'meetings of the centuries'. They assembled outside the city, on

NOMEN

CLAN and family provided the basis for the Roman system of personal names. All patrician males had three names. The *praenomen* or forename was generally chosen from a short list of twelve, usually written in abbreviated form:

C(G) = Gaius, Gn = Gnaeus, D = Decimus, Fl = Flavius, L = Lucius, M = Marcus, N = Numerius, P = Publius, Q = Quintus, R = Rufus, S = Sextus, T = Titus

The *nomen* indicated a man's clan, the *cognomen* his family. Hence 'C. Julius Caesar' stood for Gaius, from the *gens* or clan of the Julii, and the *domus* or family of Caesar.

All men belonging to the same patrician clan shared the same *nomen*, whilst all their paternal male kin shared both *nomen* and *cognomen*. At any one time, therefore, there were several 'Julius Caesars' in circulation, each distinguished by his *praenomen*. The famous general's father was L. Iulius Caesar. When several members of the same family had all three names in common, they were differentiated by additional epithets:

P. Cornelius Scipio, tribune 396–395 BC
P. Cornelius Scipio Barbatus ('the Beard'), dictator 306
P. Cornelius Scipio Asina ('the She-Ass'), consul 221
P. Cornelius Scipio, consul 218; father of Africanus
P. Cornelius Scipio Africanus Maior ('the Elder African' 236–184), general, consul 205, 194, victor over Hannibal
L. Cornelius Scipio Asiaticus ('the Asian'); brother of Africanus
P. Cornelius Scipio Africanus Minor ('the Younger African'); son of Africanus Maior
P. Cornelius Scipio Aemilianus Africanus Minor Numantinus ('the Numantian', 184–129 BC); adopted son of Africanus Minor, destroyer of Carthage
P. Cornelius Scipio Nasica ('the Nose'), consul 191
P. Cornelius Scipio Corculum ('Little Heart'), pontifex maximus 150

Plebeians, like G. Marius or M. Antonius, possessed no *nomen*.

Women, in contrast, were given only one name—either the feminine *nomen* of the clan for patricians or the feminine *cognomen* of the family for plebeians. Hence all the daughters of the Julii were called 'Julia', or of the Livii 'Livia'. Sisters were not differentiated. The two daughters of Mark Antony were both called 'Antonia'. One became the mother of Germanicus, the other the grandmother of Nero. All the daughters of Marius were called 'Maria'. It is a sign of Roman women's lowly standing that they were denied a full individual identity.[1]

As Roman practice shows, multiple names were only required by citizens with independent legal status. For much of European history, therefore, most people made do with much less. All they had was a forename, or 'Christian name', together with a patronymic or adjectival description. All the languages of Europe had their counterparts for 'Little John, son of Big Tom'. In addition to a personal name, women often used a term denoting whose wife or daughter they were. In the Slavonic world, this took the form of the suffixes -ova or -ovna. 'Maria Stefanowa' (Polish) stood for 'Stephen's wife, Mary'; 'Elena Borisovna' (Russian) for 'Helen, daughter of Boris'. Well-known people and foreigners often acquired names indicating their place of origin.

In the Middle Ages, the feudal nobility needed to associate themselves with the fief or landed property which justified their rank. As a result, they adopted place-based surnames using either a prefix, such as von, or di, or suffix, such as -ski. Hence, the French prince Charles de Lorraine would be known in German as 'Karl von Lotharingen' or in Polish as 'Karol Lotariński'. Members of guilds adopted names denoting their craft or trade. The ubiquitous Bakers, Carters, Millers, and Smiths belonged to the largest group to fix on the custom of family surnames. More recently, state governments have turned custom into a legal requirement, bringing individuals into the net of censuses, tax-collecting, and conscription.[2]

The Gaels of Scotland and the Jews of Poland were two ancient communities who long escaped surnames. Both had enjoyed communal autonomy, surviving for centuries with traditional name forms using either patronymics (such as the Jewish 'Abraham Ben Isaac', i.e. Abraham, son of Isaac) or personal epithets. The famous Highland outlaw, whom the English-speaking Lowlanders called Rob Roy MacGregor, c.1660–1732, was known to his own as Rob Ruadh (Red Robert) of Inversnaid. Both the Gaelic and the Jewish nomenclatures fell victim to state bureaucracies in the late eighteenth century. After the Jacobite defeat, the Scottish Highlanders were registered according to clan names which they had previously rarely used, thereby giving rise to thousands upon thousands of MacGregors, MacDonalds, and MacLeods. After the Partitions of Poland, Polish Jews in Russia usually took the names of their home towns or of their noble employers. In Prussia and Austria they were allotted German surnames by state officials. From 1795 to 1806, the Jewish community of Warsaw found itself at the mercy of E. T. A. Hoffmann, then chief Prussian administrator of the city, who handed out surnames according to his fancy. The lucky ones came away with Apfelbaum, Himmelfarb, or Vogelsang: the less fortunate with Fischbein, Hosenduft, or Katzenellenbogen.[3]

the vast Campus Martius, the Field of Mars, where they were drawn up in their thirty-five tribes. Each tribe was divided according to wealth into five classes, with the *equites* or 'knights of the cavalry' at the top and the poorest of the *pedites* or 'infantry' at the bottom. In time, there was also an unpropertied class of *proletarii* or 'proles'. Each of the classes was organized in turn into *centuriae* or 'centuries', and each century into 'seniors' (men aged between 45–60, on the reserve list) and 'juniors' (men aged between 17–45, liable for active service). The census of 241 BC showed a total of 260,000 citizens in 373 centuries, which works out at almost 700 men per century. Here was the whole of Roman (male) society in full view. These *comitia centuriata* gradually assumed the functions once reserved for the patricians, including the elections of the chief magistrates, the conferment of the *imperium* or 'right of command' on military leaders, the ratification of laws, and decisions of war and peace. They voted by dropping clay tablets into one of two baskets as they filed out of their century enclosures. Their proceedings were required to be completed within one day.

Within these assemblies, patronage groups played a vital role. In a hierarchical and highly compartmentalized society it was natural, indeed essential, for wealthy patricians to manipulate the activities of the lower orders and thereby to influence the decisions of popular institutions. To this end each *patronus* retained a following of dependent *clientes*. The patron expected his followers to support his policies and his preferred candidates. The clients expected a reward of money, office, or property. Serving a wealthy patron was the best road to social advancement. It was patronage that gave Roman government its characteristic blend of democratic forms and oligarchic control.

The network of assemblies, the rotation of offices, and the need for frequent meetings created a strong sense of belonging. Every Roman citizen knew exactly where he stood with regard to his tribe, his clan, his family, his century, and his patron. Participation and service were part of the accepted ethos. In formal terms, it was the popular assemblies which appointed the chief officials, and the officials who appointed the Senate. In reality, it was the senators who made all other institutions function to their advantage. Whoever dominated the Senate ruled the Republic.

The Senate, which held centre stage under both Republic and Empire, had a membership which fluctuated between 300 and 600 men. Its members were appointed by the consuls, whom it was called on to advise. But since the consuls were required to give preference to 'experienced men', and since senatorial patrons controlled all the major offices of state, the Senate could blithely perpetuate its hold on government. It was the core of a self-perpetuating élite. The dominant element within the Senate at any particular moment depended on the delicate balance of power between competing individuals, clans, and *clientelae* or 'client groups'. But the same patrician names are repeated over and over through the centuries, until a tidal wave of upstarts finally swept them away.

With time, the efficiency of senatorial control declined in proportion to the growth of factionalism. When the Senate was paralysed through civil strife, the only ways to keep the system running were either for a dictator to be installed by common consent or for one faction to impose its will through force of arms. This was the source of the string of dictators in the first century BC. In the end, the faction led by Octavian Caesar, the future 'Augustus', imposed its will on all the others. Octavian became the patron of patrons, holding the fate of all the senators in his hands.

The two consuls, the joint chief executives of Rome, held office for one year from 1 January. In its origins, their office was essentially a military one. They were proposed by the Senate and appointed by the *comitia centuriata*, which gave them the *imperium* or 'army command' for specific tasks. But they gradually assumed additional functions. They presided over the Senate, and, in conjunction with the Senate, held responsibility for foreign affairs. They supervised the management of the city's internal affairs under the *praetores*, the 'chief judges' who ran the judicial system, the *censores*, who controlled taxation and the registration of citizens, the *quaestores*, who ran public finance, the *aediles*, who policed the city and ran the Games, and the *pontifex*, the high priest. In conjunction with the tribunes, they were expected to keep the peace between the Senate and the people. It is a measure of the consuls' importance that Romans kept the historical record of the city, not in terms of numbered years, but in terms of the consulships. [AUC]

Thanks to the reforms of Marius and Sulla, the profile of the consulship changed. The practice of administering the provinces through *proconsules*, or consular deputies, extended its range of powers. On the other hand, direct control of the army was lost.

Roman government seems to be the subject of many misconceptions. It was in constant flux over a very long period of time, and did not attain any great measure of homogeneity, except, perhaps, briefly in the age of the Antonines. Its undoubted success was due to the limited but clearly defined goals that were set. It provided magistrates to settle disputes and to exact tribute. It provided an army for external defence, law enforcement, and internal security. And it supported the authority of approved local or regional élites, often through their participation in religious rites and civic ceremonies. The magic combination involved both great circumspection, in the degree of the state's encroachment on established rights and privileges, and utter mercilessness, in defending lawful authority. In Virgil's words:

> Tu regere imperio populos, Romane, memento
> (hae tibi erunt artes), pacisque imponere morem
> parcere subiectis et debellare superbos.

(Make it your task, Roman, to rule the peoples by your command; and these are your skills: to impose the habit of peace, to spare those who submit, and to conquer the proud.)[7]

Yet Roman institutions seen through modern concepts can be deceptive. Under the Roman kingdom the monarchy was not hereditary, and it was limited by the Senate of the patricians which eventually overthrew it. Under the early

Republic the two consuls, elected annually by the patrician Senate, received the full 'power to command'. But they were closely constrained both by the dual nature of the office and by the right of veto established in 494 by the tribunes of the plebs. Hence the famous formula of SPQR—*Senatus Populusque Romanus*, 'the Senate and People of Rome'—in whose name all authority was exercised. Under the late Republic and early Empire, most of the traditional magistracies and legislative bodies survived; but they were subordinated to the increasingly dictatorial pretensions of the executive.

Roman political culture determined how changing institutions actually worked. Political and religious life were always closely interwoven. The reading of the auguries accompanied all decision-making. Strong emphasis was placed on family or local authority. As a result, civic responsibility, the demands of military service, and respect for the law were deeply ingrained. Rotating offices demanded a high degree of lobbying and initiative. Under the Republic consensus was always sought through the taking of *consilium* (advice). Under the Principate (or early Empire), it was obedience that counted.

Roman law has been described as the Romans' 'most enduring contribution to world history'.[8] Its career began with the Twelve Tables of 451–50 BC, which were thenceforth regarded as the fount of 'equal law', the ideas that were equally binding on all citizens. It distinguished two main components, the *ius civile* (state law) regulating the relations between citizens, and the *ius gentium* (international law). It developed through the agglomeration of accepted custom and practice, as determined by *prudentia* or 'legal method'. Over the years every point of law was tested, amended, or expanded. The praetors were the main source of this type of law-making until the 'Perpetual Edict' of the Emperor Hadrian put a stop to further amendments. Laws initiated by magistrates, the *leges rogatae*, were differentiated from the *plebiscita* or 'popular judgements' initiated by one or other of the assemblies.

The complexity and antiquity of legal practice inevitably gave rise to the science of jurisprudence, and to the long line of Roman jurists from Q. Mucius Scaevola (Consul in 95 BC) onwards. It was a sign of deteriorating times that two of the greatest jurists, Aemilius Papinianus (Papinian, d. 213), a Greek, and Domitius Ulpianus (Ulpian, d. 223), were both put to death. [**LEX**]

The Roman army was the product of a society nurtured in perpetual warfare. Its logistical support system was as remarkable as its technical skills and its corporate ethos. For half a millennium, from the Second Punic War to the disasters of the third century, it was virtually invincible. Its victories were endless, each marked by the pomp of a Triumph and by a vast collection of monuments on the model of Titus' Arch or Trajan's Column. Its defeats were all the more shocking for being exceptional. The annihilation of three Roman legions in the German backwoods in AD 9 was a sensation unparalleled until the death of the Emperor Decius in battle against the Goths in 251, or the capture of the Emperor Valerian by the Persians in 260. The Latin proverb *si vis pacem, para bellum*, 'if you want peace, prepare for war', summarized a way of life. [**HERMANN**]

LEX

I T is often said that Roman law is one of the pillars of European civilization. And so, indeed, it is. Latin *lex* means 'the bond', 'that which binds'.
The same idea underlies that other keystone of Roman legality, the *pactum*
or 'contract'. Once freely agreed by two parties, whether for commercial,
matrimonial, or political purposes, the conditions of the contract bind the
parties to observe it. As the Romans knew, the rule of law ensures sound
government, commercial confidence, and orderly society.

Yet it must not be imagined that the legal traditions of Rome were
bequeathed to modern Europe by any simple line of direct inheritance.
Most of the Empire's law codes fell into disuse with the disintegration of
the Empire, and had to be rediscovered in the Middle Ages (see Chapter
V). They survived longest in Byzantium, but did not by that route strongly
influence modern law-making. Indeed, in terms of direct example, they
probably most immediately affected the formulation of Catholic canon
law.

What is more, even in the secular sphere the revival of Roman traditions
had to compete with other non-Roman, and often contradictory, legal practices. Rome was only one of several sources of European jurisprudence.
Customary law, in all its diversity, was equally important. In some countries,
such as France, a balance was achieved between Roman and customary
traditions. In most of Germany, the Roman law arrived in the
fifteenth century, at a very late date. In England, exceptionally, the common
law, modified by the principles of equity, was to gain a virtual monopoly.

Even so, the Roman distinction between the public and the private
domains was to suit the purposes of Europe's growing polities; and civil
law in most European countries was to be based on codified principles in
the Roman fashion (as opposed to the Anglo-American concept of legal
precedent). In this regard, the single most influential institution came to
be the French *Code Napoléon* (1804).

Whatever their connections, all educated European lawyers acknowledge their debt to Cicero and to Cicero's successors. It was Cicero, in *De
legibus*, who wrote: *Salus populi suprema lex*, 'the safety of the people is
the highest law'.[1] One could equally say that the rule of law provides the
people with the highest degree of safety.

During the *Pax Romana*, the Empire's fortresses and frontiers were maintained
by a standing force of some thirty legions. Many legions became closely associated with the provinces in which they were permanently stationed for generations,
or even for centuries—the 'II Augusta' and the 'XX Valeria Victrix' in Britain, the
'XV Apollinaris' in Pannonia, or the 'V Macedonica' in Moesia.

Each legion counted c.5–6,000 men, and was commanded by a senator. It consisted of three lines of infantry—the *hastati, principes*, and *triarii*, each made up
of ten maniples commanded by a 'prior' and a 'posterior' centurion; a body of
velites or 'skirmishers'; the *iustus equitatus* or 'complement of cavalry', consisting
of ten *turmae* or 'squadrons'; and a train of engineers. In addition, there were a
large number of auxiliary regiments made up of allies and mercenaries, each organized in a separate cohort under its own prefect.

With time, the percentage of citizen-soldiers declined disastrously; but the
backbone of the system continued to rest on the middle-ranking Roman officer
caste, who served as centurions. Distinguished service was rewarded with medals,
or with crowns for the generals; and loyal veterans could expect a grant of land in
one of the military colonies. Discipline was maintained by fierce punishments,
including flogging and (for turncoats) crucifixion. In later times, the decline of
civilian institutions gave the military their chance to dominate imperial politics.
The *gladius* or 'thrusting sword', first adopted from the Iberians during the
Second Punic War, became, in the hands of the gladiators, the symbol of Rome's
pleasures as well as her invincibility.

Roman architecture had a strong proclivity for the utilitarian. Its achievements
belong more to the realm of engineering than to design. Although the Greek tradition of temple-building was continued, the most innovative features were concerned with roads and bridges, with urban planning and with secular, functional
buildings. The Romans, unlike the Greeks, mastered the problem of the arch and
the vault, using them as the basis for bridges and for roofs. The triumphal arch,
therefore, which adorned almost all Roman cities combined both the technical
mastery and the ethos of Roman building. The Pantheon, first built by Agrippa in
27 BC in honour of 'all the gods' and the Battle of Actium, carries a vaulted dome
that is 4 ft 6 in (1.5 m) wider than St Peter's. (It is now the Church of Santa Maria
Rotunda ad Martyres.) The Colosseum (80 AD), more correctly the Flavian
Amphitheatre, is a marvellous amalgam of Greek and Roman features, and has
four tiers of arches interspersed with columns. It seated 87,000 spectators. The
vast brick-built Baths of Caracalla or Thermae Antoninianae (AD 217)—where
Shelley composed his *Prometheus Unbound*—are a monument to the Roman lifestyle, 360 yards (330 m) square. They contained the usual sections graded by temperature—the *frigidarium, tepidarium*, and *caldarium*, a *piscina* or pool for 1,600
bathers, a stadium, Greek and Latin libraries, a picture gallery, and assembly
rooms. The Baths of Diocletian (AD 306) were even more sumptuous. The
grandiose Circus Maximus was devoted to chariot-racing; it was enlarged until it
could accommodate 385,000 spectators. [EPIGRAPH]

Roman literature is all the more attractive for challenging the prevailing ethos of
a military and, to a large extent, a philistine society. The Roman literati obviously
had their clientele, especially among the leisured aristocracy of late Republican
and early imperial Rome. But somehow they did not blend into the landscape so

EPIGRAPH

EPIGRAPHY, the study of inscriptions, is one of the important auxiliary sciences in exploring the classical world. Since so much material and cultural evidence has perished, the inscriptions which have survived on stone or on metal provide an invaluable source of information. The careful study of tombstones, dedicatory tablets, statues, public monuments, and the like yields a rich harvest of intimate details about the people whom the inscriptions commemorate—their family life, their names and titles, their writing, their careers, their regiments, their laws, their gods, their morality. The great epigraphic collections, such as the *Corpus Inscriptionum Latinarum* (CIL) and the *Corpus Inscriptionum Graecarum* (CIG), both produced in nineteenth-century Berlin, are as solid and as durable as the monuments which they record.

The most famous of Roman epigraphs—the Twelve Tables of the Law, which stood for centuries in the Forum—did not survive; but the variety of the extant material is extraordinary.

Roman tombstones frequently bore a poetic description of the dead person's life and career. A stone from Moguntium (Mainz) carried a protest over the manner of the dedicatee's death:

> Jucundus M Terenti I(ibertus) pecuarius
> Praeteriens quicumque legis consiste viator
> Et vide quam indigne raptus inane queror.
> Vivere non potui plures XXX per annos
> Nam erupuit servus mihi vitam et ipse
> Praecipitem sese dejecit in amnem:
> Apstulit huic Moenus quod domino eripuit.
> Patronus de suo posuit.[1]

(Jucundus, shepherd, a free slave of Marcus Terentius. Traveller, whoever you are, stop and peruse these lines. Learn how my life was wrongly taken from me, and listen to my vain laments. I was not able to live for more than 30 years. A slave took my life, then threw himself in the river. The Man took his life, of which his master was deprived. (My) patron has raised (this stone) at his own expense.)

Dedications to the gods were a usual feature of public monuments. An inscription discovered in the Circus Maximus, and now placed on an obelisk in the Piazza del Popolo, was originally erected in 10–9 BC by the Emperor Augustus in honour of the conquest of Egypt:

> IMP . CAESAR . DIVI . F
> AUGUSTUS
> PONTIFEX . MAXIMUS
> IMP XII . COS XI . TRIB POT XIV
> AEGYPTO . IN POTESTATEM
> POPULI ROMANI REDACTA
> SOLI . DONUM . DEDIT.[2]

(The Emperor Caesar Augustus, son of the divine (Julius), Supreme Priest, twelve times Commander, eleven times Consul, fourteen times Tribune, Egypt having passed to the control of the Roman people, has offered this gift to the Sun.)

Objects of a much more humble nature often bear interesting inscriptions. Vases and pottery carried marks of manufacture. Metal stamps, for imprinting a name or advertisement onto clay, were in common use. A whole series of such stamps, from the bottles of an optician, were found at Reims:

D CALLISEST FRAGIS ADASPRITVDI

D(ecimi) Gall Sest(i) [s] frag(is) ad aspritudi(nem)
(Decimus Gallius Sestus' Eye-Wash for Granulous Pupils)[3]

naturally as their Greek counterparts. There was always tension between the sophisticated world of letters and the stern Roman world at large. This tension may well explain why Latin literature developed so late, and why it received such a hostile reception from those who, like Cato, saw it as a mere aping of decadent Greek habits. It may also explain why dramatic comedy was the first genre to be imported, and why satire was the only medium which the Romans could honestly call their own. Of the thirty or so masters of the Latin repertoire, Virgil, Horace, Ovid, and Cicero have gained universal recognition. But anyone who recoils from the luxury, gluttony, and cruelty of Roman living must surely feel an affinity for the sensitive souls who reacted most strongly against their milieu— for the exquisite lyrics of Catullus, the biting wit of Juvenal, the epigrams of Martial.

The first Roman writers wrote in Greek. Livius Andronicus (*c.*284–204), who translated Homer into Latin verse, was an educated Greek slave brought to Rome after the sack of Tarentum in 272 BC. Serious Latin literature appeared in the second half of the third century BC, with the plays of Cn. Naevius (d. *c.*200 BC), T. Maccius Plautus (*c.*254–184 BC), and P. Terentius Afer, 'Terence' (b. 185 BC). All three made brilliant adaptations of the Greek comedies; with them, the theatre became a central institution of Roman culture. Native Latin poetry begins with Q. Ennius (239–169 BC), a prime literary innovator. He introduced tragedy, launched the art of satire, and fashioned the Latin hexameter which provided the basic metre of many later poets.

Oratory held a prominent place in Roman life, as it did in Greece. Its greatest practitioner, M. Tullius Cicero (106–43 BC), spoke and wrote in a polished style which has been taken ever since as the model for Latin prose. A 'new man', Cicero rose to the highest office of consul in 63, only to be banished and, after a second spell of political activity, to be proscribed and beheaded. His writings, which included moral philosophy and political theory as well as the orations, had an immense influence both on Christian and on rationalist thinking. He was a champion of the rule of law, and of republican government. His successor, the elder

Seneca (*c*.55 BC–*c*.AD 37), a rhetorician from Cordoba, compiled a great anthology of oratory.

History writing had much to feed on. Titus Livius, 'Livy' (59 BC–AD 17), wrote a history of Rome in 142 books, 35 of which are extant. He idealized the Roman Republic, and impresses more by style than by analysis. 'I shall find satisfaction, not I trust ignobly,' Livy began, 'by labouring to record the story of the greatest nation in the world.' C. Iulius Caesar (100–44 BC) was both the supreme maker and recorder of Roman history. His accounts of the Gallic War and of the civil war against Pompey are masterpieces of simplicity, once known to every European schoolboy. C. Sallustius Crispus or 'Sallust' (86–34 BC) followed Caesar both in his political and his literary interests. Cornelius Tacitus (AD 55–120) continued the annals of Livy through the first century of the Empire, and not with any great enthusiasm for the emperors. His inimitably astringent style can also be seen in monographs such as the *Germania*. 'The revolution of the ages may bring round the same calamities,' wrote Gibbon in a footnote, 'but the ages may revolve without a Tacitus to describe them.'[9]

The art of biography also flourished. The supreme exponent was C. Suetonius Tranquillus (AD *c*.69–140), sometime secretary of the Emperor Hadrian. His racy *Lives of the Twelve Caesars* is a mine of information and entertainment, outshone only by Tacitus' study of his father-in-law Agricola, Governor of Britain.

Latin literature undoubtedly reached its heights with the poets of the Augustan Age—Virgil, Horace, and Ovid, the lyricist C. Valerius Catullus (*c*.84–54), the elegiac poet Albius Tibullus (*c*.55–19 BC), and the aptly named Sextus Propertius (*c*.50–15 BC), whose love poems to the exasperating Cynthia match those of Catullus to his Lesbia. 'Cupid is naked', wrote Propertius, 'and does not like artifice contrived by beauty.'

P. Vergilius Maro, 'Virgil' (70–19 BC), created language that rarely palls, even with the most mundane of subject-matter. His *Eclogues* or 'Selections' are pastoral poems; his *Georgics* eulogize farming. The *Aeneid*, or 'Voyage of Aeneas', is an extended allegorical epic which celebrates the Roman debt to Homer and to Greece. Recounting the adventures of Aeneas, a survivor of Troy and ancestor both of Romulus and of the *gens Iulia*, Virgil provided the mythical pedigree with which educated Romans wished to identify. His infinitely precise hexameters are not really translatable. They were written at the rate of one line a day for ten years, and sing in inimitable tone—serene, sustained, subtle, sad:

> FELIX QUI POTUIT RERUM COGNOSCERE CAUSAS,
> (Happy is he who could learn the causes of things.)

> SED FUGIT INTEREA, FUGIT IRREPARABILE TEMPUS.
> (But meanwhile time is flying, flying beyond recall.)

> OMNIA VINCIT AMOR; ET NOS CEDAMUS AMORI.
> (Love conquers all, so let us yield to Love.)

> ET PENITUS TOTO DIVISOS ORBE BRITANNOS
> (And Britons wholly separated from all the world.)

SUNT LACRIMAE RERUM ET MENTEM MORTALIA TANGUNT.
(There are tears shed for things, and mortality touches the mind.)[10]

For Dante, Virgil was *il maestro di lor che sanno* (the master of those who know), and 'the fount which spilt such a broad river of words'. For the early Christians he was the pagan poet who, in the fourth Eclogue, was thought to have forecast the birth of Christ. For the moderns he was 'lord of language . . . poet of the poet-satyr . . . wielder of the stateliest measure ever moulded by the lips of man'. He probably composed his own epitaph, seen at Pozzuoli by Petrarch:

MANTUA ME GENUIT: CALABRI RAPUERE: TENET NUNC
PARTHENOPE. CECINI PASCUA, RURA, DUCES.

(Mantua bore me; Calabria carried me away; Naples now holds me. I sang of pastures, fields, and lords.)[11]

Q. Horatius Flaccus, 'Horace' (65–8 BC), Virgil's friend and contemporary, was the author of *Odes* and *Satires*, *Epodes* and *Epistles*. He had studied in Athens, commanded a legion, and fought at Philippi before retiring to his Sabine farm under the protection of his patron Maecenas. He was a gentle, tolerant soul. His Epistle to the Pisos, otherwise the *Ars Poetica*, was much admired by later poets. His Satires were directed at human folly, not evil. His Odes shine with translucent clarity, and with *curiosa felicitas*, a 'marvellous felicity of expression':

DULCE ET DECORUM EST PRO PATRIA MORI.
(It is sweet and fitting to die for one's country.)
PARTURIENT MONTES, NASCETUR RIDICULUS MUS.
(The mountains will give birth, and a silly mouse will be born.)
ATQUE INTER SILVAS ACADEMI QUAERERE VERUM.
(And seek for truth even in the groves of Academe.)
EXEGI MONUMENTUM AERE PERENNIUS . . . NON OMNIS MORIAR.
(I have created a monument more lasting than bronze . . . I shall
not die completely.)[12]

Horace is the most imitated, and the most translated of poets.

P. Ovidius Naso, 'Ovid' (43 BC–17 AD), was a leading figure of Roman society until banished to the Black Sea coast by the Emperor Augustus. The causes of his exile, he says, were 'a poem and an error'. The poem was undoubtedly his *Ars amatoria*, 'The Art of Love'; the error probably involved the Emperor's daughter Julia, who was also banished. Ovid's *Metamorphoses* or 'Transformations', which rework over two hundred Greek and Roman myths and legends, has been rated the most influential book of the ancient world. It has provided the favourite reading not only of the Romans but of people as different as Chaucer, Montaigne, and Goethe. It has inspired a torrent of creative works from Petrarch to Picasso. *Si vis amari*, wrote Ovid, *ama* (If you wish to be loved, you, too, must love).[13]

The Silver Age of Latin literature, which lasted from the death of Augustus to perhaps the middle of the second century, contained fewer giants. Apart from

Tacitus and Suetonius, there gleamed the talent of the Stoic philosopher Seneca II, of the two Plinys, of the poet Lucan, the rhetorician Quintilian, the novelist Petronius, and, above all, of the satirist D. Iunius Iuvenalis, 'Juvenal' (c.47–130). *Difficile est saturam non scribere*, wrote Juvenal (it is difficult *not* to write satire).

The calculated violence of Roman life was proverbial. The butcheries of the foreign wars were repeated in the civil strife of the city. Livy's catch-phrase, *Vae victis!* (Woe to the vanquished) was no empty slogan. In 88 BC, when the so-called 'Vespers of Ephesus' saw perhaps 100,000 Romans massacred in one day on the orders of King Mithridates, Sulla, leader of the aristocratic 'Optimates', marched on Rome and proscribed the rival followers of Marius. The head of the Tribune, P. Sulpicius Rufus, was exhibited in the Forum. The urban Praetor, preparing to conduct a sacrifice before the Temple of Concord, was sacrificed himself. In 87 BC, when Rome opened its gates to Marius, it was the turn of the Optimates to be slaughtered. Marius' legions of slaves and his Dalmatian Guard struck down every senator whom the general did not salute. Among his victims were names of later importance—Gn. Octavius, the reigning consul, M. Crassus, M. Antonius, L. Caesar, all ex-consuls. In 86, after the sudden death of Marius, the general's associate, Q. Sertorius, summoned the executioners on the pretext of distributing their pay, then cut them down *en masse* to the number of some 4,000. In 82, when the Optimates finally triumphed, they too massacred their prisoners: 'the clatter of arms and the groans of the dying were distinctly heard in the Temple of Bellona, where Sulla was just holding a meeting of the Senate'.[14]

Thereafter, to avoid such scenes, the procedure of proscription was formalized. Victorious factions would post a list of names in the Forum to summon the leaders of the defeated faction to stand trial or risk confiscation. Men on the list who killed themselves in time, usually by opening their veins in a warm bath, could save their families from ruin. Those who failed to do so found their names on a new list, carved in marble, declaring their lives and the property of their kin to be forfeit. In 43, for example, the proscription of the second triumvirate caused the deaths of at least 300 senators and 2,000 knights. Among them was Cicero, whose head and hands, severed from the corpse, were exhibited on the rostra of the Forum. Where the ruling class of Rome set an example, the populace followed. [**LUDI**]

'The Roman Revolution' is not a term that was used in ancient times. But it has been widely accepted by historians who see the transition from Republic to Principate as the product of profound social transformations. In other words, it is not an established historical event so much as the subject of modern sociological theorizing. 'The period witnessed the violent transfer of power and property,' wrote its chief interpreter, 'and the Principate of Augustus should be regarded as the consolidation of the revolutionary process.'[15] In this scenario the chief victim was the old Roman aristocracy. The chief revolutionary was Caesar's heir, the young Octavius—a 'chill and mature terrorist', a gangster, a 'chameleon' who

LUDI

'THE people who have conquered the world', wrote Juvenal, 'now have only two interests—bread and circuses.' 'The art of conversation is dead!' exclaimed Seneca. 'Can no one today talk of anything else than charioteers?' The *Ludi* or 'Games' had become a central feature of Roman life. Originally staged on four set weeks during the year in April, July, September, and November, they grew to the point where the Circus Maximus and the Colosseum were in almost permanent session. At the first recorded Games in 264 BC, three pairs of slaves had fought to the death. Four centuries later, the Emperor Trajan laid on a festival where 10,000 persons and 11,000 animals perished.[1]

Professional gladiators provided shows of mortal combat. Marching in procession through the Gate of Life, they entered the arena and addressed the imperial podium with the traditional shout: AVE, CAESAR! MORITURI SALU-TAMUS (Hail Caesar! We, who are about to die, greet thee). Nimble *retiarii* with net and trident faced heavily armed *secutores* with sword and shield. Sometimes they would join forces against teams of captives or exotic barbarians. The corpses of the losers were dragged out on meat hooks through the Gate of Death. If a gladiator fell wounded, the emperor or other president of the Games would signal by 'thumbs up' or 'thumbs down' whether he should be reprieved or killed. Promoters exploited the rivalry of gladiatorial schools, and advertised the feats of famous performers.

One programme which has survived listed a fight between *T. v Pugnax Ner III* and *M. p Murranus Ner III*, i.e. two fighters from the Neronian school in Capua, each with three wins, one fighting with (T)hracian arms—small shield and curved sword—and the other in Gallic (M)yrmillo style. Pugnax came out v(ictor), whilst Murranus ended up p(eritus), dead.[2]

The thirst for grand spectacles gradually led to the practice where gladiatorial shows were interspersed with *venationes* or 'wild-beast hunts', by full-scale military battles, and even by naval contests in a flooded arena. In time, acts of gross obscenity, bestiality, and mass cruelty were demanded. Popular stories elaborated scenes of spreadeagled girls smeared with the vaginal fluid of cows and raped by wild bulls, of Christian captives roasted alive, crucified, set alight or thrown to the lions, or of wretches forced to paddle in sinking boats across water filled with crocodiles. These were only passing variations in an endless variety of victims and torments. They continued until the Christian Emperor Honorius overruled the Senate and put an end to the Games in AD 404.

Nothing, however, roused such passions as chariot-racing, which began in Rome and continued in Byzantium. Traditionally, six teams of four horses careered seven times round the spine of the circus, competing for vast prizes. Sensational spills and fatal crashes were routine. Huge bets were placed. Successful charioteers became idols of the mob, and as wealthy as senators. Successful horses were commemorated by stone statues: 'Tuscus, driven by Fortunatus of the Blues, 386 wins.'

Racing was in the hands of the four corporations—Whites, Reds, Greens, and Blues, who supplied the competing stables, teams, and drivers. The 'factions' of circus supporters were responsible for many a riot. In Byzantine times they were institutionalized, and were once thought to have formed the basis for incipient political parties. This theory is now largely abandoned; but faction-like associations were still performing in late Byzantine ceremonies. The Christian Church always frowned. 'Some put their trust in chariots and some in horses; but we will remember the Name of the Lord Our God.'[3]

presented himself in turns as bloodthirsty avenger or moderate peacemaker. The resultant changes included the ruin of the established governing class, the promotion of new social elements, the domination of Rome by ambitious Italian outsiders, and, with their support, the emergence of a *de facto* monarchy. The key to Roman politics lay in the patronage of the rival dynasts—especially Caesar, Pompey, Mark Antony, and Octavius. The key to understanding the essential mechanisms lies in the art of prosopography—which analyses the detailed careers of a class in order to uncover the inducements which animate them. (Syme, relying heavily on the work of Münzer, did for Roman history what Lewis Namier did for Georgian England.) 'Political life', he wrote, 'was stamped and swayed not by the parties and programmes of a modern parliamentary character, not by the ostensible opposition of Senate and People . . . but by the struggle for power, wealth, and glory.'[16] Particularly important in an age of civil war was a politician's ability to control the army and to satisfy the soldiers with lands, money, and respect. Fighting, it would seem, was only a secondary preoccupation for successful generals.

Overall, it is a cynical picture. Shifting alliances of convenience predominate over parties of principle. Political concepts—Cicero's *libertas populi, auctoritas Senatus, concordia ordinum, consensus Italiae*—are presented as mere slogans and catchwords. The Roman constitution was 'a screen and a sham, a mere façade for men's baser instincts'. The old aristocracy could be bought. The new men were driven by greed and vanity. They were the 'trousered Senators', the 'ghastly and disgusting rabble' of Caesar's provincial dependants; the 'thousand creatures' installed in the Senate by the second triumvirate; the servile apologists and propagandists whom Octavius hired to win public opinion and to distort history. Behind the scenes lurked the bankers, the millionaire paymasters, the adventurers—C. Maecenas, L. Cornelius Balbus from Gades, C. Rabirius Posthumus, treasurer of Alexandria.

In this scenario, therefore, the turning-point occurred already in 43 BC, during the proscriptions of the second triumvirate which followed Caesar's death and in which, to his discredit, Octavian took the lead:

> The Republic had been abolished . . . Despotism ruled, supported by violence and confiscation. The best men were dead or proscribed. The Senate was packed with ruffians. The Consulate, once the reward of civic virtue, now became the recompense of craft or crime. *Non mos, non ius* . . . The Caesarians claimed the right and duty of avenging Caesar . . . Out of the blood of Caesar the monarchy was born.[17]

The rest was an epilogue. All cried 'Liberty', and all longed for peace. 'When peace came, it was the peace of despotism.'

None the less, it is not possible to dismiss all the works of Augustus (r. 31 BC–AD 14) as the fruits of propaganda. He undoubtedly had a seamier side but, importantly for the Romans, the omens were with him. Suetonius tells the story how the future Emperor's mother had been entered by a serpent during a midnight service in the Temple of Apollo nine months before his birth. But then a comet had appeared in the sky when he first celebrated the *Ludi Victoriae Caesaris*. And on the eve of Actium, where he left the battle to subordinates like Agrippa, he met a Greek peasant driving an ass along the shore. 'I am Eutyches [Prosper],' said the peasant, 'and this is my ass Nikon [Victory].'[18] [CONDOM]

The nature of the early Empire, or Principate, is particularly deceptive. The Emperor Augustus achieved lasting power for himself and his successors, not by the abolition of republican institutions, but by collecting all the offices that controlled them. He made himself *Imperator* or 'Supreme Commander', Consul, Tribune, Censor, *Pontifex Maximus*, and Proconsul of Spain, Gaul, Syria and Cilicia, etc. As a result, he possessed powers as extensive as many an autocrat; but he did not exercise them through centralized autocratic channels. He replaced the pseudo-republic of the senatorial oligarchy with a quasi-empire, whose old institutions were obliged to work in a new way. As *Princeps senatus*, a new office, he acted as chairman of the Senate, whose membership was drawn either from ex-magistrates, whom he would have appointed, or from imperial nominees. He left the Senate in charge of roughly half the provinces, into which all the Empire was now divided; but he subjected their deliberations to an imperial veto. Dictatorial powers were delegated to former municipal offices such as those of the *Praefectus Urbi*, in charge of criminal jurisdiction, or of the *Praefectus Annonae*, in charge of trade, markets, and the corn dole. Similarly, numerous boards of *Curatores* or Commissioners, overseeing everything from roads and rivers to the repair of public buildings, now answered solely to the Emperor. The growth of a more formal autocracy was a development of Christian times, especially in the Eastern Empire, where Persian influences were strong. (See Appendix III, p. 1223.)

The main law-making procedures of the Republic were gradually abandoned.

CONDOM

IN 18 BC, and again in AD 9, Emperor Augustus attempted to increase the fertility of the Empire's population through decrees curbing abortion and infanticide. From this and other sources it is clear that the Romans were familiar with many methods of contraception, including herbs: spermicidal douches containing cedar gum, vinegar or olive oil, vaginal pessaries soaked in honey, and condoms fashioned from goats' bladders. One Roman writer advised: 'Wear the liver of a cat in a tube on the left foot . . . or part of the womb of a lioness in a tube of ivory.'[1]

Research into medieval practices once suggested that the necessary mentality for 'diverting nature' was simply not present.[2] But this view has been revised. Examination of church penitentials shows that the subject was much discussed, especially since the 'sins of Onan' can reasonably be taken to include *coitus interruptus*.[3] Dante's hints in *Paradiso* xv (106–9) about Florence's 'empty family houses' and about 'what was possible in the bedchamber' leave little to the modern imagination. The increase of urban prostitution increased an interest in avoiding pregnancy. The Cathars, too, were notoriously non-pro-life. In the 1320s, the inquisitors succeeded in persuading a Cathar priest's lover to reveal their techniques:

When [the priest] wanted to know me carnally, he used to wear this herb wrapped up in a piece of linen . . . about the size of the first joint of my little finger. And he had a long cord which he used to put round my neck when we made love; and this thing or herb at the end of the cord used to hang down as far as the opening of my stomach . . . It might happen that he might want to know me carnally twice or more in a single night. In that case, the priest would ask me before uniting his body with mine: Where is the herb? . . . I would put the herb in his hand and then he himself would place it at the opening of my stomach, still with the cord between my breasts.

The only detail missing was the name of the herb.[4]

Historical demographers studying Italian merchant families and English villages have concluded that births must have been kept artificially low in both the medieval and modern periods.[5] In the eighteenth century, lechers like James Boswell made no secret of using 'armour'. Their Continental counterparts talked of 'English overcoats' or 'umbrellas'. Their hero was the mysterious Captain Condom, said to have been either physician or commander of the guard at the Court of Charles II.[6] The first pope to have condemned contraceptive practices was supposedly Clement XII in 1731.

Modern campaigners for birth control did not advocate contraception in the cause of permissiveness. Marie Stopes, though packed with nymphomaniac drive, was also an old-fashioned romantic. In *Married Love and Wise Parenthood*, she was arguing to give women the chance of relief from

child-bearing and of enjoyable love-making within marriage.[7] Military
authorities who distributed 'French letters' to troops on the Western Front
were concerned both for the soldiers' health and for civilian relations.
Abortion remained the principal technique in the Communist world, as in
the Roman Empire. In the West, contraception was not linked to changing
sexual mores until the availability of 'the Pill' and of free clinical advice for
unmarried adolescents in the 1960s. Yet, as a jingle of the 1920s recalls,
success was nowhere guaranteed:

> Jeanie, Jeanie, full of hopes
> Read a book by Marie Stopes.
> But, to judge from her condition,
> She must have read the wrong edition.[8]

But many of its statutes remained. The *comitia tributa* was occasionally summoned to confirm laws passed by other bodies; and the *senatus consulta* or 'decisions of the Senate' were still issued. From the second century AD, however, the Emperor became the sole source of new law—through his edicts, or ordinances, his rescripts or 'written judgements' on petitions, his *decreta* or rulings on judicial appeals, and his mandates or administrative instructions. By that time the Senate had been replaced as the supreme court of appeal by the Emperor's praetorian prefect.

With the passage of time, the vast corpus of Roman law had to be repeatedly codified. There were three such partial attempts in the Codex Gregorianus (AD *c.*295), the Codex Hermogenianus (*c.*324), and the Codex Theodosianus (438). Similarly, in the Edict of Theodoric (before 515), the so-called Breviary of Alaric (506), and the Burgundian Code (516), barbarian rulers attempted to summarize the law which they found in provinces captured from Rome. Yet the main work of systematization was undertaken under the Emperor Justinian. Between them, the fifty Decisions (531), the Institutes (533), the Digest of the Jurists (534), the Revised Code (534), and the Novels (565) covered every aspect of public and private, criminal and civil, secular and ecclesiastical law. It was through the Justinian law-books that this huge heritage was transmitted to the modern world. [**LEX**]

The term *provincia*, 'sphere of action', originally referred to the jurisdiction of magistrates sent to govern conquered lands. Under the Empire, it came to refer to the lands themselves. Each province was given a charter, the *lex provincialis*, which determined its limits, its subdivisions, and its privileges. Each was entrusted to a governor, either a proconsul or a propraetor, who raised troops, collected tribute, and through 'edicts' spoke with the force of law. Each governor was accompanied by a staff of legates appointed by the Senate, by a military guard, and by an army of clerks. A distinction was made between imperial provinces, which the Emperor retained under his direct control, and senatorial provinces, which were left to the Senate. The creation of provinces had far-reaching consequences both for Rome and for the fate of the Empire. In the short run, Rome thrived mightily from the vast influx of tribute and from the constant traffic in people and goods. In the long run, through the steady internal consolidation of the provinces, the capital city was squeezed from the sources of wealth and power. Over four centuries, 'Mother Rome' was gradually rendered redundant by her own children.

As Rome waned, the provinces waxed. In the first stage, provincial élites supplied the droves of newcomer knights and senators who swamped the traditional oligarchy and ran the Empire. In the second stage, when the military forces were concentrated on an increasingly self-sufficient periphery, provincial cities such as Lugdunum (Lyons) or Mediolanum (Milan) flourished in competition with Rome. Political life was plagued by the rivalries of provincial generals, many of whom became emperors. In the third stage, the links between the periphery and Rome were weakened to the point where the provinces began to claim autonomous status. Especially in the West, the fruit was ready to fall from the tree. The centrifugal shift of power and resources was one of the underlying causes of the Empire's later distress. [**ILLYRICUM**] [**LUGDUNUM**]

The Empire's finances, like its provinces, were split into two sectors. The *Aerarium* of the Senate was the successor to the Republican Treasury in the Temple of Saturn and Ops. The imperial *Fiscus* was an innovation of Augustus. In theory, it was separate from the Emperor's private property, the *patrimonium Caesaris*; in practice, the boundaries were not respected. The main items of income included rent from the state lands in Italy, tribute from the provinces, *portaria* or 'gate dues', the state monopoly in salt, the mint, direct taxes on slaves, manumissions and inheritance, and extraordinary loans. Apart from the army, the main items of expenditure included religious ceremonies, public works, administration, poor relief and the corn dole, and the imperial court. In time, imperial agents took over all tax-collecting outside Rome.

The army was gradually increased in size and strength, reaching a maximum in 31 BC of almost sixty legions. After Actium, the Empire's permanent defence force consisted of 28 legions of *c*.6,000 professionals apiece. The Navy maintained squadrons on the Rhine and the Danube, as well as in the Mediterranean. From 2 BC Augustus initiated the nine cohorts of the élite praetorian lifeguard, based in Rome. The soldiers were paid 720 d. per annum for a praetorian, 300 d. for a cavalryman, 225 d. for a legionary; and they served for twenty years.

The legions were known by number and by name. Augustus retained the sequential numbering used both by his own and by Mark Antony's army, awarding distinctive names to legions with the same number. Hence there was a Legio III Augusta and a Legio III Cyrenaica, a Legio VI Victrix and a Legio VI Ferrata. Several legions possessed the number I, since emperors liked to give seniority to units raised by themselves. Legions which were destroyed in battle, such as the XVII, XVIII, and XIX lost in Germany, or the Legio IX Hispana wiped out in Britain in AD 120, were never restored.

The *limes*, the 'frontier line', was a vital feature of the Empire's defence. It was not, as is sometimes supposed, an impenetrable barrier. From the military point

ILLYRICUM

THE Roman province of Illyricum occupied the eastern shore of the Adriatic between the Italian district of Istria and the Greek province of Epirus. It was bounded to the north by Pannonia beyond the river Dravus and to the east by Moesia and Macedonia. It was known to the Greeks as *Illyris Barbara*, being the part of ancient Illyria which had remained free from the conquests of Philip of Macedon. In imperial times it was divided into three prefectures—Liburnia and Dalmatia on the coast and Iapydia in the interior. Apart from Siscia (modern Zagreb) and Narona (Mostar), its principal cities were all seaports—Tartatica, Ader (Zadar), Salonae (Split), Epidaurum. The southernmost fortress city of Lissus had been founded by Syracusan colonists in 385 BC. (See Appendix III, p. 1231.)

Illyricum was subdued in stages. It first paid tribute to Rome in 229 BC, and was twice overrun during the Macedonian Wars of the second century. It was fully incorporated under Augustus in 23 BC. Having participated in the great Pannonian revolt of AD 6–9, it remained in the Empire until Byzantine times.

Little is known of the ancient Illyrians. Their language was Indo-European, and probably supplied an underlying stratum to modern Albanian. Their material culture was renowned for its sophisticated metalwork. From the sixth century their 'Situla art' was distinguished by fine repoussé figures set on bronze wine-buckets amidst scenes of feasting, racing, and riding. A silver coinage was minted in the third century. Illyrian warriors fought in chain-mail like the Scythians, but not in chariots like the Celts.[1]

Illyricum gave birth to two Roman emperors and to St Jerome. The Emperor Diocletian retired to a grandiose palace built on the seafront of his native Salonae. His octagonal mausoleum survived as a Christian church—an ironic fate for the resting-place of the Christians' last great persecutor. St Jerome was born at nearby Strido in AD 347, more than 200 years before the first appearance of the Slavs who were to lay the foundations of the future Croatia, Bosnia, and Montenegro.

Illyricum, like Britannia, belongs to a group of Roman provinces whose ethnic and cultural connections were totally transformed by the great migrations (see Chapter IV). But the memory of the Illyrians was cherished by their successors. Their legacy is very different from that bequeathed to those parts of Europe which never knew Rome at all.
[ILLYRIA]

LUGDUNUM

IN 43 BC the Proconsul Muniatus Plancus drew the centre-line of a new city overlooking the confluence of the Rhône and the Saône. Lugdunum was to be the principal city of Roman Gaul, the meeting-point of a star-like network of paved roads. Its amphitheatres can still be seen on the hill of Fourvières. It commanded not only the Rhône–Rhine corridor but the route leading north-west from Italy to the Channel.[1]

The Rhône, though navigable, was a swift and turbulent river. Downstream, ships risked being wrecked on numerous reefs and islands; upstream, they could only make headway against the current with the help of horses. In the decades before the arrival of steamboats in 1821, 6,000 horses worked the towpath, hauling cargoes up to Lyons before floating back down on rafts.

From 1271 to 1483, the lower Rhône constituted an international frontier. The left bank, known as *l'Empi*, lay in the Holy Roman Empire. The right bank, *le Riaume*, and all the islands, belonged to the Kingdom of France. Fifteen stone bridges were built between Geneva and Arles; and several sets of twin towns, such as Valence and Beaucaire, grew up on opposing banks.

In that same era, Lyons recovered the economic pre-eminence which it had once commanded in ancient Gaul. It was annexed to France by Philippe le Bel, who entered the city on 3 March 1311, after which it headed 'the French isthmus' linking France's northern and southern possessions. From 1420 it hosted four international fairs annually; from 1464 it received privileges aimed at subverting the commerce of Geneva; and from 1494 to 1559 it supplied the logistical base for France's Italian wars. Its merchant élite was distinguished by many Italian families, including the Medici, the Guadagni (Gadagne), and numerous Genoese. This 'lively, determined and secretive city', 'caught up in whirlpools and rhythms of a very particular kind', made itself 'the leading centre of the European economy.'[2]

'Vieux Lyons', the old quarter nestling beside the Saône, recalls the city's golden decades. A hillside warren of narrow streets connected by tunnel-like *traboules* or 'transambulant passage-ways', it is crowded with highly ornamented Gothic and Renaissance hotels, courtyards, squares, and churches. Its names, from the *Manécanterie* or 'cathedral choir-school' to the *Hôtel de Gadagne* on the *Rue Juiverie* or 'Jewry Street', ring with the memory of colourful bygone inhabitants. The Place Bellecour was laid out under Louis XIV on the interfluvial plain. Its statue of the Sun King, which had been shipped from Paris by sea, came to grief in transit and had to be fished from the river.

Given Lyons's strategic location, and its industrial prowess based on silk

[**JACQUARD**], geographers have wondered why it never ousted Paris as France's capital. The prospect has remained an unrealized possibility. From 1311 Lyons has had to be content as France's second city. For geography only determines what is possible; it does not determine which possibility will triumph. 'A country is a storehouse of dormant energies', wrote the master, 'whose seeds have been planted by nature but whose use depends on man.'[3]

of view it was more of a cordon, or series of parallel cordons, which, whilst deterring casual incursions, would trigger active counter-measures as soon as it was seriously breached. It was a line which normally could only be crossed by paying *portaria* and by accepting the Empire's authority. It was, above all, a marker which left no one in doubt as to which lands were subject to Roman jurisdiction and which were not. Its most important characteristic was its continuity. It ran up hill and down dale without a break, and along all frontier rivers and coasts. In places, as in Britain, it took the form of a Great Wall on the Chinese model. Elsewhere it might carry a wooden stockade atop earthworks, or a string of linked coastal forts, or, as in Africa, blocks of fortified farmhouses facing the desert interior. Its guarded crossing-points were clearly marked with gates and roadways. They naturally became the focus for towns and cities which grew round the military camps and markets which the upkeep of the frontier required.

Thanks to the *limes*, Rome could manage its relations with the barbarians in an orderly fashion. Throughout the Empire, barbarian officers and auxiliaries served with the Roman army, and barbarian tribes were settled by agreement in the imperial provinces. The romanization of barbarians, and the barbarization of Romans, were processes that had been operating since the earliest conquests of the Republic in Italy. After all, Caesar's 'trousered senators' were Romans of Celtic origin who still liked to wear their native leggings under their togas.

Societies, it has been said, rot from the head down, like dead fish. Certainly, the list of early emperors contains more than its share of degenerates.

The Emperor Tiberius (r. AD 14–37), adopted son of Augustus, left Rome for Capri, to practise his cruelties and perversions. Under him, mass proscriptions returned to fashion, fuelled by the deadly work of the *delatores* or informers. Caligula (r. 37–41) ordered himself deified in his lifetime, and appointed his horse to a consulship. 'It was his habit to commit incest with each of his three sisters in turn,' Suetonius wrote; 'and, at large banquets when his wife reclined above him, he placed them all in turn below him.' 'Because of his baldness and hairiness, he announced that it was a capital offence for anyone to mention goats in any context.'[19] He succumbed to an assassin who struck, appropriately, at his genitals. Claudius (r. 41–54), who married two murderous wives, Messalina and Agrippina, was poisoned by a toadstool sauce mixed with his mushrooms.[20]

The Emperor Nero (r. 54–68), an obsessive aesthete and sybarite, disposed of his mother by having her stabbed (after an attempted drowning miscarried). He murdered his aunt by administering a laxative of fatal strength, executed his first wife on a false charge of adultery, and kicked his pregnant second wife to death. 'Not satisfied with seducing free-born boys and married women,' wrote Suetonius, 'he raped the Vestal Virgin Rubria.' Then:

Having tried to turn the boy Sporus into a girl by castration, he went through a wedding ceremony with him—dowry, bridal veil and all—which the whole Court attended; then brought him home and treated him as a wife . . . The world would have been a happier place had Nero's father Domitius married the same sort of a wife.[21]

In the end, he committed suicide with the words *Qualis artifex pereo* (what an artist perishes in me).

The Emperor Galba (r. 68–9), a military man, was killed by the mutinous military in 'the year of the four emperors', as were his successors Otho and Vitellius. Vespasian (r. 69–79), son of a provincial tax-gatherer, succeeded in his main aim—'to die on his feet'. His last words were 'Dear me, I must be turning into a god.'[22] Titus (r. 79–81) was supposedly poisoned by his brother, after a reign of unusual felicity marred only by the eruption of Mt Vesuvius. The supposed poisoner, the Emperor Domitian (r. 81–96), was stabbed to death by his wife and her accomplices. Eight of the ten immediate successors of Augustus had died a nasty death. [**PANTA**]

Yet Rome's Indian summer still lay ahead. 'If a man were called to fix the period in the history of the world, during which the condition of the human race was most happy and prosperous,' wrote Gibbon, 'he would, without hesitation, name that which elapsed from the death of Domitian to the accession of Commodus.'[23] Under the emperors Nerva (r. 96–8), Trajan (r. 98–117), Hadrian (r. 117–38), Antoninus Pius (r. 138–61), and Marcus Aurelius (r. 161–80), the Empire not only reached its greatest geographical extent but enjoyed an unrivalled era of calm and stability. Nerva initiated the tradition of poor relief; Trajan was an honest, indefatigable soldier; Hadrian a builder and patron of the arts. Of Antoninus Pius, Gibbon wrote: 'His reign is marked by the rare advantage of furnishing very few materials for history, which is, indeed, little more than the register of the crimes, follies, and misfortunes of mankind.'[24]

The minutiae of imperial administration during its heyday have survived in the voluminous correspondence of the Emperor Trajan with Pliny the Younger, administrator of Bithynia-Pontus:

PLINY. Nicaea has expended 10,000,000 sesterces on a theatre that was tottering and great sums on a gymnasium that was burned . . . At Claudiopolis, they are excavating a bathhouse at the foot of the mountain . . . What am I to do?

TRAJAN. You are on the spot, decide for yourself. As for architects, we at Rome send to Greece for them. You should find some where you are.

PLINY. The money due to the towns of the province has been called in, and no

PANTA

WHEN the city of Colonia Cornelia Veneria Pompeiana was buried under five metres of volcanic ash on 24 August AD 79, all forms of human life were extinguished—the elegant, the mundane, and the seamy. Yet when Pompeii was excavated, mainly from 1869 onwards, one aspect of its former life, its dedication to Venus, was officially concealed. A huge collection of objects which offended against the nineteenth century's fear of obscenity were kept for decades in the *stanze proibiti* or 'prohibited sections' of the National Museum in Naples.[1]

The sexual commerce of Pompeii, in contrast, was plied without shame or hypocrisy. Brothels or *lupinari* were located in all parts of the town, and openly advertised their menus and their tariffs. The cheapest girls, such as Successa or Optata, charged 2 *assi*; Speranza charged 8, Attica 16. Outside brothels, there were notices to discourage eavesdroppers. One notice read: 'No place for idlers . . . Clear off'. Inside, there were pictures to encourage the customers. Paintings and sculptures of sexual subjects were common, even in private houses. Murals portraying the 'mysteries' of the city's cults had a semi-sacred character. Phalluses of gigantic proportions were on frequent display. They served as the flame-holders of oil-lamps, as the centrepiece of comic drawings, even as the spouts of drinking cups. Humorous trinkets showing male gods with divine equipment, or the god Pan plunging an upturned she-goat, were commonplace.

Many of the city's whores are known by name or, like actresses, by their *noms de scène*: hence Panta (Everything), Culibonia (Lovely Bum), Kallitremia (Super Crotch), Laxa (Spacious), Landicosa (Big Clit), or Extaliosa (Back Channel). Their clients are also known by name or nickname. One was Enoclione (Valorous Toper), another Skordopordonikos (Garlic Farter). The chief ponce of Pompeii's largest brothel died shortly before the volcano erupted. His servant had scratched an obituary on the gate: 'For All Who Grieve. Africanus Is Dead. Rusticus Wrote This.' The trade was both bisexual and bilingual: rent boys were available for both sexes, and the language of the game was either Greek or Latin. The essential vocabulary included *futuere, lingere, fellare*; *phallus, mentula, verpa*; *cunnus* or *connos* (m.) and *lupa*.

Most expressive are the graffiti, ancient moments of triumph and disaster recorded for all time:

FILIUS SALAX QUOT MULIERUM DIFUTUISTI[2]
AMPLIATE, ICARUS TE PEDICAT[3]
RESTITUTA PONE TUNICAM ROGO REDES PILOSA CO[4]
DOLETE PUELLAE PEDI— . . . CUNNE SUPERBE VALE . . . AMPLIATUS TOTIES . . .
HOC QUOQUE FUTUTUI . . .[5]
IMPELLE LENTE[6]
MESSIUS HIC NIHIL FUTUIT[7]

borrowers at 12 per cent are to be found. Ought I to reduce the rate of interest . . . or compel the decurions to borrow the money in equal shares?

TRAJAN. Put the interest low enough to attract borrowers, but do not force anyone to borrow . . . Such a course would be inconsistent with the temper of our century.

PLINY. Byzantium has a legionary centurion sent by the Legatus of Lower Moesia . . . to watch over its privileges. Juliopolis . . . requests the same favour.

TRAJAN. Byzantium is a great city . . . But if I give such help to Juliopolis, all small towns will want the same thing.

PLINY. A great fire has devastated Nicomedia. Would it be in order to establish a society of 150 firemen?

TRAJAN. No. Corporations, whatever they're called, are sure to become political associations . . .

PLINY. I have never been present at the resolutions concerning the Christians, therefore I know not for what causes . . . they may be objects of punishment . . . Are those who retract to be pardoned? Must they be punished for their profession alone?

TRAJAN. The Christians need not be sought out. If they are brought into your presence and convicted, they must be punished. But anonymous information against them should not carry any weight in the charges.[25]

With Marcus Aurelius (r. 161–80) Rome received a true philosopher-king. A disciple of Epictetus, he trained himself to withstand the rigours of constant campaigning, the burdens of office, and the demands of a profligate family. His notes 'To Myself', known as his *Meditations*, exude all the higher sentiments:

What peculiar distinction remains for a wise and good man, but to be easy and contented under every event of human life . . .? Not to offend the divine Principle that resides in his soul, nor to disturb the tranquillity of his mind by a variety of fantastical pursuits . . . To observe a strict regard to truth in his words and justice in his actions; and though all mankind should conspire to question his integrity and modesty . . . he is not offended at their incredulity, nor yet deviates from the path which leads him to the true end of life, at which everyone should endeavour to arrive with a clear conscience, undaunted and prepared for his dissolution, resigned to his fate without murmuring or reluctance.[26]

Marcus Aurelius had a marvellous sense of who, and where, he was:

As the Emperor Antoninus, Rome is my city and my country; but as a man, I am a citizen of the world . . . Asia and Europe are mere corners of the globe, the Great Ocean a mere drop of water, Mount Athos is a grain of sand in the universe. The present instant of time is only a point compared to eternity. All things here are diminutive, subject to change and decay; yet all things proceed from . . . the one Intelligent Cause.[27]

By the mid-third century the Roman Empire was showing all the outward symptoms of an inner wasting disease. Political decadence was apparent in the lack of resolve at the centre, and in disorder on the periphery. In the ninety years from AD 180 no fewer than eighty short-lived emperors claimed the purple, by right or by usurpation. 'The reign of Gallienus', wrote Gibbon, 'produced only nineteen pretenders to the throne . . . The rapid and perpetual transitions from the cottage to the throne, and from the throne to the grave, might have amused an indifferent philosopher.'[28] The army dictated to its civilian masters with impunity. The barbarians flooded over the *limes*, often unchecked. The raids of the Goths turned into permanent occupations. In 268 they sacked Athens. One breakaway 'Empire', under a certain Postumus, appeared in central Gaul, and another in Palmyra. The difficulty of enforcing the cult of worthless or transient emperors led to recurrent persecution of the growing Christian sect. From 250 to 265, plague raged in many regions: for a time, 5,000 people a day were dying in Rome alone. Famine followed the plague. Severe price inflation set in, accompanied by a seriously debased coinage. Marcus Aurelius had issued an imperial silver coin of 75 per cent purity. Under Gallienus (r. 260–8), a century later, it was 95 per cent impure. Tax revenues slumped; the imperial authorities concentrated resources in the frontier provinces; elsewhere, many provincial centres declined; amphitheatres were demolished to provide stone for defensive walls.

Even under Diocletian (r. 284–305), whose twenty-one years have been seen as the 'founding of a new empire', all was far from well. The tetrarchy, or 'rule of four', which divided the Empire into two halves, each with its own Augustus and its own deputy Caesar, facilitated administration and frontier defence. The army was greatly increased—but so was the bureaucracy. The rise in prices was controlled—but not the fall in population. The Christian persecutions continued. In 304 a great Triumph was organized in Rome; but it was the last. One year later, Diocletian abdicated, retiring to his native Dalmatia.

Flavius Valerius Constantinus (r. 306–37), later called 'Constantine the Great', was born at Naissus in Moesia Superior (i.e. Nis, in modern Serbia, not, as Gibbon says, in Dacia). His father, Constantius Chlorus, Diocletian's Western Caesar, died at Eboracum (York) soon after succeeding to the purple. His mother, Helena, was a British Christian, revered in legend as the discoverer of the True Cross. Constantine reunited the two parts of the divided Empire and, in the Edict of Milan, proclaimed general religious toleration. At two crucial moments of his career he claimed to have had a vision. Initially, the vision was said to have been of Apollo, later of a Cross, together with the words 'By this you will conquer'. He quarrelled with the citizens of Rome, and determined to move his capital to the shores of the Bosphorus. On his deathbed he was formally baptized into Christianity. In this way, at the moment of its Emperor's Christian conversion, Rome ceased to be the centre of the Empire which it had created.

Christianity

In its origins, Christianity was not a European religion. Like Judaism and Islam, to which it is related, it came from Western Asia; and Europe did not become its main area of concentration for several centuries.

Jesus of Nazareth (*c.*5BC–35AD), Jewish nonconformist and itinerant preacher, was born in the Roman province of Judaea in the middle of the reign of Augustus. He was executed in Jerusalem, by crucifixion, during the reign of Tiberius (14–37AD) and the procuratorship of Pontius Pilatus, praenomen unknown, a Roman knight who may later have served at Vienna (Vienne) in Gaul. Reportedly, though no fault was found in him, the procurator acquiesced in the demands of the Jewish Sanhedrin to put him to death. [**CRUX**]

Apart from four short gospels, whose evidence is partly repetitive and partly contradictory, few facts are known about the life of Jesus. There is no historical document which mentions him, and there is no trace of him in Roman literary sources. He did not even attract major notice from the Jewish writers of the period such as Josephus or Philo. His personal teaching is known only from a score of parables, from his sayings during the various incidents and miracles of his ministry, from his talks with the apostles, and from a handful of key pronouncements: his Sermon on the Mount, his answers in the Temple and at his trial, his discourse at the Last Supper, his words on the Cross. He claimed to be the 'Messiah', the long-foretold saviour of the Jewish scriptures; but he reduced the vast corpus of those scriptures to two simple commandments:

Jesus said unto him, Thou shalt love the Lord thy God with all thy heart, with all thy soul and with all thy mind. This is the first and greatest commandment. And the second is like unto it, Thou shalt love thy neighbour as thyself. (Matt. 22: 37–9)

Jesus did not challenge the secular authorities, stressing on several occasions, 'My kingdom is not of this world'. When he died, he left no organization, no church or priesthood, no political testament, no Gospel, indeed; just the enigmatic instruction to his disciples:

If any man will come after me, let him deny himself, and take up his cross, and follow me. For whosoever will save his life shall lose it: and whosoever will lose his life for my sake shall find it. (Matt. 16: 24–5)

That Christianity should have become the official religion of the Roman Empire could hardly have been foreseen. For generations of Christian believers in later times, the triumph of Christianity was simply the will of God. It was not seriously questioned or analysed. But for many Romans in the early centuries it must have presented a real puzzle. Jesus was long regarded as an obscure, local phenomenon. His followers, whose beliefs were confused by outsiders with Judaism, were unlikely candidates to found a religion of universal appeal. The faith of slaves and simple fishermen offered no advantage for class or sectional interest. Their gospel, which made such a clear distinction between the spiritual 'Kingdom of God' and the rule of Caesar, seemed to have resigned in advance from all secular ambitions. Even when they became more numerous, and were repressed for refusing to participate in the imperial cult, Christians could hardly be seen as a general menace. [**APOCALYPSE**]

Of course, one may see with hindsight that Christianity's emphasis on the inner life was filling a spiritual void to which the Roman lifestyle gave no relief; also that the Christian doctrine of redemption, and the triumph over death, must have exerted great attractions. But one can also understand the bafflement of imperial officials, like Pliny the Younger in Bithynia (see p. 191 above). It is one thing to decide that the ancient world was ripe for a new 'salvationist' religion; it is quite

CRUX

L IKE the square, the circle, the triangle, the arrow, and the notch, the cross is one of the irreducible, primary signs that recur throughout human history. Sometimes called 'the sign of signs', it is used in science to denote 'add', 'plus', and 'positive'. Owing to the crucifixion of Christ, however, it was adopted at an early stage as the prime symbol of Christianity.

The Cross is omnipresent in the Christian World—in churches, on graves, on public monuments, in heraldry, on national flags. Christians are baptized with the sign of the Cross; they are blessed by their priests with the sign of the Cross; and they cross themselves—Catholics and Orthodox in opposite directions—when they implore divine assistance or when they listen to the Gospel. Medieval crusaders wore the Cross on their surcoats. The Christian Cross can be found in any number of variants, each with a specific symbolic or ornamental connotation.[1] (See Appendix III, p. 1229.) [**DANNEBROG**]

Yet pre-Christian signs have long existed in Europe alongside their Christian counterparts. Best known is the age-old *swastika* or 'crooked cross', whose name derives from a Sanskrit phrase for 'well-being'. In ancient Chinese lore, it signified 'bad luck' when the hooks were turned down to the left, and 'good luck' when they were turned up to the right. In its Scandinavian form, it was thought to represent two crossed strokes of lightning giving light or two crossed sticks making fire. In its rounded Celtic form, common in Ireland, it was made to represent the sun.[2] It had several millennia behind it before the pagan Nazis chose a modern version of the *hakenkreuz* as their party emblem.

Another example of the transmission of oriental and non-Christian insignia concerns the *tamgas* or 'pictorial charges' of the ancient Sarmatians. The *tamgas*, which occasionally resemble some of the more simple Chinese ideographs, reappeared in the tribal signs of the Turkish tribes, who advanced into the Near East in early medieval times. By this route, they are thought to have contributed to the system of Islamic heraldry which western crusaders were to encounter in the Holy Land.[3] At the same time, they bear a striking resemblance to signs which emerged at a somewhat later period in the unique heraldic system of Poland. As a result, scholars have been tempted to speculate that the familiar claim about the Polish nobility being descended from ancient Sarmatian ancestors may not be entirely fanciful. Their so-called 'Sarmatian Ideology', their heraldic clans, and their remarkable cavalry tradition have all been linked to the long-lost oriental horsemen of the steppes. One hypothesis holds that Poland's Sarmatian connection may best be explained as a legacy of the Sarmatian Alans who disappeared into the backwoods of Eastern Europe in the 4th century AD.[4]

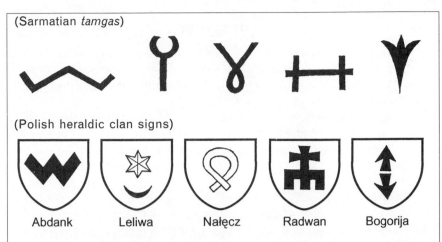

(Sarmatian *tamgas*)

(Polish heraldic clan signs)

| Abdank | Leliwa | Nałęcz | Radwan | Bogorija |

Symbols can arouse the deepest emotions. When the International Red Cross was founded in 1863, few Europeans realized that its emblem could be other than a universal symbol of compassion. But in due course it had to be supplemented with the Red Crescent, the Red Lion, and the Red Star. Similarly, when a Christian cross was raised on the site of the former Nazi Concentration Camp at Auschwitz, it caused bitter controversy, especially among those who were not aware that the victims of the camp included large numbers of Christians as well as Jews. In 1993, nine years of accusations and broken agreements were ended with the creation of an ecumenical memorial centre.[5] [**AUSCHWITZ**]

to explain why the void should have been filled by Christianity rather than by half a dozen other candidates. Of all the sceptics writing about the rise of the Christian Church, none was more sceptical than Edward Gibbon. Gibbon's *Decline and Fall* contains on the one hand the most magnificent historical prose in the English language and on the other hand the most sustained polemic against the Church's departure from Christian principles. He conducted what he called 'a candid but rational enquiry into the progress and establishment of . . . a pure and humble religion [which] finally erected the triumphant banner of the Cross on the ruins of the Capitol'.[29] (See Appendix III, p. 1236.)

The spread of Christianity was greatly facilitated by the *Pax Romana*. Within three decades of Christ's crucifixion, Christian communities were established in most of the great cities of the eastern Mediterranean. St Paul, whose writings constitute the greater part of the New Testament, and whose journeys were the first pastoral visit of a Christian leader, was largely concerned with the Greek-speaking cities of the East. St Peter, Christ's closest disciple, is said to have sailed to Rome and to have been martyred there *c.* AD 68. From Rome, the gospel travelled to every province of the Empire, from Iberia to Armenia.

The key figure was without doubt Saul of Tarsus (d. *c.*65), known as St Paul.

APOCALYPSE

Patmos is Europe's last island, hard by the Aegean's Asian shore. In the first century AD it was used as a penal colony for the nearby Roman city of Ephesus. It was a fitting place to compose the last book of the canon of Christian scripture.

The author of the Book of Revelation, the Apocalypse, was called John. He never claimed what later tradition assumed, that he was St John the Apostle; and neither his style nor his outlook matches those of the Fourth Gospel. He had been exiled for religious offences, and was probably writing between AD 81 and 96.

The Apocalypse of St John the Divine records a series of mystical visions which, like Jewish apocalyptic literature of the same vintage, foretell the end of the existing order. The interpretation of its wondrous symbolism—of the Lamb, the Seven Seals, the Four Beasts and the Four Horsemen, the Great Whore of Babylon and the Red Dragon, and many more—has kept Christians puzzled and entranced ever since. The central chapters deal with the struggle with Anti-Christ, supplying a rich fund of demonology. [**DIABOLOS**] The concluding section, chapters 21–2, presents a view of 'a new heaven and a new earth':

'And God shall wipe away all tears from their eyes: and there shall be no more death neither sorrow nor crying; neither shall there be any more pain: for the former things have passed away.

And He that sat upon the throne said, Behold I make all things new. And He said unto me, Write: for these words are true and faithful.

And He said unto me, It is done. I am Alpha and Omega, the beginning and the end.'[1] (Rev. 21: 4–6)

Born a Jew and educated as a Pharisee, he took part in early Jewish persecutions of Christ's followers. He was present at the stoning of the first Christian martyr, Stephen, in Jerusalem *c.*35. But then, after his sudden conversion on the road to Damascus, he received baptism and became the most energetic proselyte of the New Way. His three missionary journeys were the single most important stimulus to its growth. He met with varying success. In Athens, in 53, where he found an altar 'To the Unknown God', he was received with hostility by the Jews and with suspicion by the Greeks:

Then certain philosophers of the Epicureans and the Stoics encountered him. And some said, What will this babbler say? other-some, He seemeth to be a setter forth of strange Gods: because he preached unto them Jesus and the resurrection. And they took him and brought him to Areopagus, saying May we know what this new doctrine . . . is? . . . For the Athenians . . . spent their time in nothing else, but either to tell or to hear some new thing. (Acts 17: 18–21)

He sojourned twice in more congenial company at Corinth, where he probably wrote the Epistle to the Romans. On returning to Jerusalem he was accused of transgressing the Jewish Law, but as a Roman citizen appealed for trial in Rome. He is generally thought to have perished in Rome during the persecutions of Nero.

St Paul's contribution was crucial on two separate counts. On the one hand, as the Apostle of the Gentiles, he established the principle that the New Way was not the tribal preserve of Jews, that it was open to all comers. 'There shall be neither Jew nor Gentile, neither bond nor free.' On the other hand, he laid the foundations of all subsequent Christian theology. Sinful humanity is redeemed by Divine Grace through Christ, whose Resurrection abrogated the Old Law and ushered in the new era of the Spirit. Christ is more than the Messiah: He is the Son of God, identified with the Church in His mystical Body, which is shared by the faithful through Repentance and the Sacraments until the Second Coming. Jesus was uniquely the source of its inspiration; but it was St Paul who founded Christianity as a coherent religion. [**CHASTITY**]

The Jewish origins of Christianity have had lasting consequences, especially on relations between Christians and Jews. Following the Jewish Revolt of AD 70, the Jewish diaspora began to spread far and wide through the Empire. Judaism ceased to be concentrated in Judaea, and 'the People of the Book' became a religious minority in many parts of Europe and Asia. For them, Jesus Christ was a false messiah, a usurper, a renegade. For them, the Christians were a threat and a menace: dangerous rivals who had hijacked the scriptures and who broke the sacred taboos dividing Jew from Gentile. For the Christians, the Jews were also a threat and a challenge. They were Christ's own people who had none the less denied his divinity, and whose leaders had handed him over for execution. In popular legend, and eventually for a time in official theology, they became the 'Christ-killers'.

The schism within the Judaeo-Christian tradition has been generated on both sides by intense feelings of betrayal. It was inevitably more bitter than the conflicts of Christians with other religions. It is an unresolved, and unresolvable, quarrel within the family. From the hard-line Jewish perspective, Christianity is by nature antisemitic; and antisemitism is seen as a Christian phenomenon *par excellence*. From the hard-line Christian perspective, Judaism is by nature the seat of the antichrist, a bad loser, the perpetual source of smears, blasphemy, and insults. Notwithstanding the doctrine of forgiveness, it is the hardest thing in the world for Christians and Jews to see themselves as partners in the same tradition. Only the most Christian of Christians can contemplate calling the Jews 'our elder brethren'.

Christianity, however, did not draw on Judaism alone. It was influenced by various oriental religions current in the Empire, and especially by Greek philosophy. The Gospel of St John, which begins 'In the beginning was the Word, and the Word was with God, and the Word was God', stands in marked contrast to the other three gospels, where this manifestly Greek doctrine of the *Logos* is

CHASTITY

C HASTITY—in the sense of the permanent renunciation of sexual
activity—was adopted by the early Christians as a central feature of
their moral code. It was not unknown among the ancients, although
Juvenal hinted that it had not been seen since 'Saturn filled the throne'. It
was practised by pagan priestesses, such as the vestal virgins of Rome, on
pain of death, and in the Jewish world by some of the all-male sects. But
it had never been upheld as a universal ideal.

Indeed, the wholesale pursuit of the virgin life had serious social implications. It threatened the family, the most respected institution of Roman
life, and it undermined marriage. In a world where infant mortality was
high, and average life expectancy did not exceed 25 years, the average
household needed five pregnancies from each of its adult women to maintain numbers. Celibacy among adults seriously endangered the reproduction of the species.

Yet the Christians cherished chastity with unremitting ardour. From St
Paul onwards, they increasingly condemned the 'bondage of the flesh'.
'For I delight in the law of God after the inward man,' wrote St Paul. 'But I
see another law in my members, warring against the law of my mind, and
bringing me into captivity to the law of sin which is in my members. . . . For
to be carnally minded is death; but to be spiritually minded is life and
peace.'[1]

The appeal of these Pauline teachings can only be partly explained in
terms of the life of the spirit demanding freedom from all worldly preoccupations. The belief in the imminence of the 'Second Coming' may also
have played a part, since it was thought to have rendered procreation
superfluous. Sexual orgasm was condemned because it involved the ultimate loss of free will. Many people believed that the character of a child
was determined by the parents' humour during intercourse. This created
further inhibitions, since lovers would fear that impure sexual feelings
might deform their offspring. Galen reports an erroneous medical notion
to the effect that semen was produced from the froth of agitated blood. For
men, sex was linked with physical as well as with spiritual disorder. For
women, lifelong virginity was seen as the surest means of liberation from
the tyranny of husbands and of traditional domestic duties. In general,
therefore, sex was seen to be the mechanism whereby 'the sins of the
fathers' were transmitted from generation to generation.

In August 386 there occurred in Milan one of the most famous conversions of a self-confessed fornicator. St Augustine's *Confessions* provide a
vital insight into the considerations involved in his acceptance of chastity.
By that time, however, three hundred years had passed since St Paul.
Established Christian communities were feeling the need to multiply.

Hence the secondary ideal of Christian marriage was revived alongside the primary ideal of Christian chastity. In this, marriage officially remained a stop-gap measure, a guard against lust and fornication for those too weak to abstain. 'For it is better to marry', St Paul had written to the Christians of Corinth, 'than to burn.'[2]

This 'rout of the body' continued to hold sway in the Middle Ages. The secular Latin clergy joined the monks in celibacy. The 'Virgin Saints' were universally revered. The cult of the Virgin Mary, immaculate notwithstanding both conception and childbirth, was given a status similar to that accorded to the creed of the Trinity. Christian ascetics practised every form of mental and physical restraint, self-castration not excepted.

The history of chastity is one of those topics in the study of *Mentalités* which best help modern readers to penetrate the mind of the ancients. It serves as a point of entry to what has been called 'a long extinct and deeply reticent world'. The magisterial study, which traces the debates on chastity among the Church Fathers of both Greek and Latin traditions, does not comment on present-day sexual attitudes, which the early Christians must surely have seen as a form of tyranny. But it undertakes the task of every good historian—to signal the differences between the past and the present, where chastity, to borrow a phrase, is often seen as the most unnatural of sexual perversions. 'To modern persons', Peter Brown concludes, '. . . the early Christian themes of sexual renunciation, continence, celibacy and the virgin life have come to carry with them icy overtones. . . . Whether they say anything of help or comfort for our own times, the readers . . . must decide for themselves.'[3]

---

not present. Modern scholars stress the hellenistic as well as the Judaic context. Philo of Alexandria, a hellenized Jew who sought to reconcile the Jewish scriptures with Platonism, holds a prominent place in this regard. [**DIABOLOS**]

The most recent research tends to suggest that Christianity and Judaism did not completely part company for perhaps two centuries. For many decades, the two overlapping communities may have shared the same messianic hopes. Judaic texts from the period 200 BC–AD 50, located in newly released sections of the Dead Sea Scrolls, bear a striking resemblance to the Christian gospels. One assessment maintains that the final break between Christians and Jews occurred in AD 131, when the leader of the second Jewish revolt against Rome, Simon Bar-Kokhba, proclaimed himself the Messiah, thereby severing the bond.[30] [**PASQUA**]

Whatever the date of the final split, the Jewish presence alongside Christianity has never been extinguished. Every week for two millennia, the celebration of the Jewish Sabbath on Friday evening has always preceded the Christian Sabbath on Sundays. After the lighting of the candles and the prayers for peace, the service culminates in the opening of the Ark of the Covenant and a reading from the Book of the Law, the *Torah*:

The Ark is Opened

The Torah is a tree of life to those
who hold it fast, and those who
cling to it are blessed. Its ways
are ways of pleasantness, and all
its paths are peace.

ETZ CHA-YIM HI   עֵץ־חַיִּים הִיא לַמַּחֲזִיקִים
LA-MA-CHA-ZI-KIM BA
V'TOM-CHE-HA M'U-SHAR.   בָּהּ וְתֹמְכֶיהָ מְאֻשָּׁר:
D'RA-CHE-HA DAR-CHEY NO-AM,   דְּרָכֶיהָ דַרְכֵי נֹעַם וְכָל־
V'CHOL N'TI-VO-TE-HA SHA-LOM.
                                  נְתִיבוֹתֶיהָ שָׁלוֹם:

The Ark is closed; Congregation is seated [31]

Early Christianity had many rivals. In the first two centuries of the Empire the mystery cults of Isis, Cybele, and the Persian sun-god Mithras were thriving. They shared several important traits with early Christianity, including the ecstatic union with the divinity, the concept of a personal Saviour or Lord, and initiation rites akin to baptism. The anthropological approach to religion would stress these similarities.

Gnosticism, too, had much in common with Christianity. In origin the Gnostics were philosophers, 'seekers after knowledge', but they attracted a following of a more religious character. They borrowed heavily from both Judaism and increasingly from Christianity, to the point where they were sometimes regarded as a Christian sect. They held to a distinction between the Creator or *Demiurge*, who was responsible for an evil world, and the Supreme Being; also, in the nature of Man, to a distinction between his vile, physical existence and the spark of divine essence which gives people the capacity to reach for the heavenly spheres. Simon Magus is mentioned in the New Testament. Valentinus was active in Rome, *c.*136–65, Basilides in Alexandria. Marcion (d. 160) founded a gnostic sect that lasted until the fifth century. He taught that Christ's body was not real, and hence that the Resurrection could not have taken place in any physical sense; and he rejected the Old Testament, holding that the Jewish Jehovah was incomplete without the God of Love as revealed by Jesus. This 'Docetism' launched the long-running christological debate about the true nature of Christ.

The disputes between Christians and Gnostics revealed the need for a recognized canon of scripture. Which of the holy writings were God-given, and which were merely man-made? This question preoccupied Christians at the turn of the second and third centuries, though the definitive statement was not made until the *Festal Letter* of Athanasius in 367. The core of the New Testament—the four Gospels and the 13 letters of St Paul—was accepted *c.*130, and the Old Testament—that is, the Hebrew canon less the Apocrypha—*c.*220. Other

PASCHA

EASTER is the prime festival of the Christian calendar. It celebrates Christ's resurrection from the dead. It is preceded by the forty days of the Lenten fast, and culminates in the eight days of Holy Week, starting on Palm Sunday. It reaches its most sombre point during Passiontide, which begins at the hour of the Crucifixion at noon on Good Friday, only to erupt in an outburst of joy on the Third Day, on Easter Morning, when the Tomb was found empty.

In most European languages Easter is called by some variant of the late Latin word *Pascha*, which in turn derives from the Hebrew *pesach*, 'passover'. In Spanish it is *Pascua*, in French *Pâques*, in Welsh *Pasg*, in Swedish *Pask*, in Russian and Greek *Paskha*. In German, however, it is *Ostern*, which derives, like its English equivalent, from the ancient Germanic goddess of springtime Eostro (Ostara). From this it appears that the Christians adapted earlier spring festivals marking the renewal of life after winter. They also appropriated the Jewish symbolism of Passover, with the crucified Christ becoming the 'Paschal Lamb'.

The difference in names also recalls ancient controversies over the date of Easter. Those early Christians who followed the practices of the Jewish Passover fixed Easter on the fourteenth day of the moon following the vernal equinox. In 325 the Council of Nicaea decided that Easter day should fall on the first Sunday after the full moon following the vernal equinox.

But the matter could not rest there, since several rival astronomical cycles were in existence for calculating solar years and lunations. Originally the great observatory at Alexandria was charged with the mathematics; but soon important discrepancies crept in between the Greek and Latin Churches, and between different provinces within the Latin Church. In 387 Easter was held in Gaul on 21 March, in Italy on 18 April, and in Egypt on 25 April. Subsequent attempts at standardization succeeded only partially, though 21 March and 25 April have remained the extreme limits. The Orthodox and Catholic Easters were never harmonized. Since Easter is a movable feast, all other festivals in the annual Christian calendar which depend on it, from Whitsun (Pentecost) to Ascension Day must move with it.[1] Easter finds no mention in the Bible, except for an isolated mistranslation in the English Authorized Version of 1613 where, in Acts 12: 4, 'Easter' appears in place of 'Passover'.

For nearly two millennia Christendom has resounded at Easter-time to triumphal hymns about Christ's 'victory over Death'. For non-Christians these hymns can sound threatening. For the faithful, they express the deepest sense of their existence. The ancients sang the fourth-century *Aurora Lucis rutilat* ('The day draws on with golden light'), *Finita iam sunt proelia* ('The strife is o'er, the battle done' or *Victimae Paschali Laudes*). The best known Easter hymns, including *Salve, festa dies* ('Welcome, happy including *Salve, festa dies* ('Welcome, happy morning'), *Vexilla regis* ('The royal banners forward go'), and *Pange lingua gloriosi proelium certaminis* ('Sing, my tongue, the glorious battle') were composed by Venantius Fortunatus (*c.*530–610), sometime Bishop of Poitiers. The best Greek counterparts, such as *Anastaseos Imera* ('The day of resurrection'), sometimes sung to the melody of 'Lancashire', were composed by St John of Damascus (*c.*675–749). Germans sing the *Jesus lebt!* of Christian Furchtegott Gellert; the French, *À Toi la gloire, O résuscité!*; the Poles, *Chrystus zmartwychstan jest*; the Greeks, *Hristos Anesti!* The English-speaking world sings 'Christ the Lord is risen today' to words by Charles Wesley:

> Vain the Stone, the watch, the seal;
> Christ has burst the gates of hell.
> Death in vain forbids his rise.
> Christ has opened Paradise.
> Lives again our Glorious King;
> Where, O Death, is now thy sting?
> Once he died, our souls to save;
> Where thy victory, O grave?
> *Hallelujah!*[2]

DIABOLOS

A LL the main traditions from which European civilization was fused were strongly conscious of the Evil One. In prehistoric religion, as in pagan folklore, he often took the form of a horned animal—the dragon, the serpent, the goat-man of the witches' sabbath, the seductive Gentleman who could not quite conceal his horns, his tail, and his hooves. In classical mythology he was a lord of the underworld, with a pedigree that can be traced to the encounter of Gilgamesh with Huwawa. [EPIC] In the Manichean tradition [BOGUMIL], he was the Prince of Darkness. To Aristotle, he may have been no more than the absence of the Good. But to the Platonists, he was already the *diabolos*, the opponent, the Old Enemy. In the Old Testament, especially in the Book of Job, he was the agent of sin and inexplicable suffering. In Christian lore, the tempter of Christ in the wilderness becomes the Satan and the Lucifer of the Fall. He finds a central place in medieval demonology and in St Augustine's discussion of free will and of God's licence for evil, as in the master-works of Milton and Goethe. In recent times Europeans have dropped their guard. But a history of Europe without the Devil would be as odd as an account of Christendom without Christ.[1]

books, especially the Apocalypse or Revelation, were disputed much longer. [APOCALYPSE]

Theological disputes foreshadowed the need for some form of ecclesiastical authority to resolve them. One solution was provided by Clement of Rome (d. c.90), who furthered the doctrine of the apostolic succession. Christian leaders had authority if they could trace their appointment to one of the twelve apostles, or to the apostles' recognized successors. Clement himself, who was probably third in line to St Peter as 'bishop' at Rome, based his own claim on the text 'Thou art Peter, and on this rock I shall build my church'. The same point was made with greater force by Bishop Irenaeus of Lyons (c.130–200), in his writings against the Gnostics:

The greatest and most ancient of churches, known to all, [is that] established at Rome by the apostles Peter and Paul . . . Every other church, that is, the faithful from all other parts, ought to be harmonized [with Rome], by virtue of the authority of its origins. And it is there that Tradition, derived from the apostles, has been preserved . . .[32]

Here already was the essence of the Roman Catholic tradition. (See Appendix III, p. 1224.)

For the time being, several competing authorities prevailed, and the apostolic succession, as interpreted in Rome, never gained universal acceptance. Direct contact with Christ's apostles, however, obviously carried kudos. Apart from St Clement, the Apostolic Fathers included Ignatius of Antioch, Papias of Hierapolis, and St Polycarp of Smyrna (c.69–155), who was burned at the stake.

The persecution of early Christians is a matter of some controversy, and its true extent cannot be disentangled from the martyrology of the most interested party. 'The ecclesiastical writers of the fourth and fifth centuries', wrote Gibbon, 'ascribed to the magistrates of Rome the same degree of implacable and unrelenting zeal which filled their own breasts.'[33] Still, fitful repressions did occur. Nero made Christians into scapegoats for the great fire of Rome in 64. This was contrary to the general toleration extended to national cults, such as Judaism, to which Christianity was judged to belong. Domitian, who demanded that he be worshipped as *Dominus et Deus*, executed Christian recalcitrants for 'atheism'. Marcus Aurelius sanctioned a severe repression at Lyons in 177. But it was not until 250 that the Emperor Decius (249–51) ordered that all his subjects sacrifice to the state gods on pain of death. After another interval, Diocletian ordered in 303 that all Christian churches be destroyed and all bibles burnt. This Great Persecution lasted thirteen years, and was the prelude to the general toleration proclaimed in the following reign. Excessive repression had proved counterproductive. The Roman Empire's surrender to Christianity was irrigated by the blood of martyrs. [CATACOMBI]

The growth of clergy—as a separate estate from the laity—seems to have been a gradual matter. The offices of *Episcopos* or 'bishop' as communal leader, and of *diaconus* or 'deacon', preceded that of the *presbyter* or 'priest' with exclusive sacerdotal functions. The title of Patriarch, the 'Father' of the bishops in any particular province or country, was long used very inconsistently. No special status

CATACOMBI

BELIEF in the resurrection of the dead gave burial a special role in the early Christian community; and two miles beyond Rome's Aurelian Walls, in the vicinity of the Appian Way, lay a district, *Ad Catacumbas*, where for safety early Christians buried their dead in underground galleries. Forty-two such catacombs have been identified since their rediscovery in the sixteenth century, each of them a warren of tunnels on five or six levels linking the maze of chambers and family *loculi* or 'notches'. The earliest tombs, such as that of Flavia Domitilla, wife of the consul for AD 95, date from the end of the first century. But the greatest number date from the era of persecutions in the third century. The catacombs were never lived in; but later, under Christian rule, they became a favourite meeting-ground, where festivals were held and chapels built in honour of the popes and martyrs. Most of the inscriptions were cut at that time. For example, in the Catacomb of Praetextus, there is an inscription to one of Pope Sixtus' martyred deacons, St Ianuarius, arrested with him on 6 August 258: BEATISSIMO MARTYRI IANUARIO DAMASUS EPISCOP FECIT (Bishop Damasus made [this monument dedicated] to the Blessed Martyr Ianuarius).

The largest complex, the Catacomb of St Callistus, was built by the ex-slave who became pope in 217–22. It includes the papal chamber, containing burials up to Pope Miltiades (d. 314), the crypt of St Cecilia, and in the Crypt of the Sacraments an extraordinary collection of mural paintings. Catacomb art was highly symbolic of the spiritual life and the world to come. Its favourite motifs included the dove, the anchor, the dolphin, the fisherman, the Good Shepherd, and Jonah, precursor of the Resurrection.

Pillaging by Goths and Vandals in the fifth century caused many relics to be withdrawn to churches within the city; and the postponement of the Second Coming caused the gradual abandonment of underground burial. St Sebastian's crypt was one of the few sites to remain frequented. It was sought out by medieval pilgrims seeking protection from the plague.

Beside the Catacomb of Basileo stands a church which marks Rome's most famous Christian legend. Fleeing from persecution along the Appian Way, St Peter met Christ on the road and asked him *Domine, quo vadis?* (Lord, where are you going?) Christ answered, 'To Rome, for a second crucifixion.' Peter turned back, and was martyred.

Three of the forty-two catacombs—at Villa Torlonia, at Vigna Randatini, and at Monte Verde—are Jewish.[1]

was accorded to the bishop of Rome. The prestige which accrued from leading the Christian community in the capital of the Empire was diminished when the imperial government ceased to reside there. And it exposed the Christians of Rome to greater persecution. Throughout the early centuries there was a line of bishops on the 'throne of St Peter'; but they did not emerge as a leading force in the Church until the fifth or, some might reckon, the seventh century.

The 'Fathers of the Church' is a collective label which was used from the fourth century onwards for the Christian leaders of the preceding period. The Apologists, from Aristides of Athens to Tertullian (155–255), clarified what ultimately became orthodox beliefs. Others, including Hippolytus (165–236), Clement of Alexandria (c.150–215), Origen (185–250), and Cyprian of Carthage (d. 258), were revered for their defence of the faith against pagans and heretics. The body of Patristics or 'writings of the Fathers' is not judged to end before those of St John Chrysostom (347–407).

Heresy, of course, is a tendentious concept. It is an accusation levelled by one group of believers against another; and it can only exist if the accusers believe in their own dogmatic monopoly of the truth. In Christian history, it only emerges in the second and third centuries as the general consensus solidified. Most of the Church's Fathers were heretical in varying degrees. The chief heresies, as defined by later orthodoxy, included Docetism, Montanism, Novatianism, Apollinarianism, Nestorianism, Eutychianism, Arianism, Pelagianism, Donatism, Monophysitism, and Monothelitism. Of these, Arianism was specially important because it won the adherence of many communities both inside and outside the Empire. Founded by Arius (c.250–336), a priest of Alexandria, it held that Christ, as Son of God, could not share the full divinity of God the Father. It provoked the first ecumenical Council of the Church, where it was condemned. But it re-emerged through the support of the Emperor Constantius II, and its acceptance by several barbarian peoples, notably the Goths. It even split into three main sub-heresies: the Anomoeans, the Homoeans, and the Semi-Arians. It did not die out until the sixth century. [**BRITO**]

Christian monasticism was entirely oriental in its beginnings. St Antony of the Desert (c.251–356), an opponent of Arius and founder of the first anchorite community, was yet another Alexandrian.

The Christian concepts and practices, therefore, which in due course were pronounced Catholic (universal) and orthodox (correct) were the fruit of many years of debate and dispute. Their final definition awaited the work of four Doctors of the Church, who were active in the late fourth century—SS Martin, Jerome, Ambrose, and Augustine. Apart from the debate on the *Logos*, which soon gave precedence to the christological issue, they centred on the doctrines of Grace, Atonement, and the Church; on the Sacraments, Baptism and Eucharist; and above all on the Trinity. In 325, when the Emperor Constantine convened the first General Council of the Church at Nicaea in Asia Minor, the 300 delegates were asked to summarize the articles of basic Christian belief. They were dominated by the party from Alexandria, especially by the anti-Arian or Trinitarian group led by Athanasius (*c.*296–373). There were only a handful of bishops from the West, including Cordoba and Lyons. The absent Bishop of Rome, Sylvester I, was represented by two legates. What they produced was a combination of a baptismal formula used in Jerusalem with the famous idea of *homoousios* or 'consubstantiality'. The Nicene Creed has been binding on all Christians ever since:

> We believe in one God, the Father Almighty,
> Maker of all things both visible and invisible;
> And in one Lord Jesus Christ, the Son of God,
> Begotten of the Father, Only-begotten,
> That is, of one substance with the Father;
> By whom all things both in heaven and earth were made;
> Who for us men and our salvation
> Came down and was incarnate, became man,
> Suffered and rose again the third day;
> Ascended into the heavens;
> Cometh to judge the quick and the dead;
> And in the Holy Spirit.[34]

It was three hundred years since Christ had walked in Galilee.

The Bosporus, 4 November 1079 AUC. Shortly after ordering the execution of his heir apparent, the Emperor Constantine conducted a ceremony to mark the foundation of his new capital city. He laid the first stone of the western wall, at the point where it meets the sea. He was attended by the neoplatonist philosopher Sopater, who was acting as *telestes* or 'magician' and who cast the spells to secure the city's good fortune. Also present was Praetestatus, a pontifex from Rome, who was said to have brought the most sacred of Roman talismans, the Palladium, to be buried at the base of the founder's statue in the new forum. 'The sun was in the sign of Sagittarius, but the Crab ruled the hour.'[35]

Four years later, on 11 May 1083 (AD 330), fresh ceremonies inaugurated the life of the new foundation. Shortly after the execution of Sopater, and of another pagan philosopher, Canonaris, who had shouted out: 'Do not raise yourself against our ancestors', Constantine presided at a grand inaugural festival. The city was officially named 'Constantinopolis' and 'Roma Nova'. Prayers to the goddess Tyche, or 'Fortune', the city's tutelary genius, mingled with the Christian chant of *kyrie eleison*. In the Circus, by the Temple of Castor and Pollux, sumptuous games were held, but no gladiatorial contests. In the Forum, the oversize statue of the Emperor was unveiled. It had been made by mounting Constantine's head on an ancient Colossus of Apollo, and it stood on a huge porphyry column. In all probability, a smaller gilded statue of Constantine, carrying a tiny Tyche on its outstretched hand, was paraded in torchlight procession. Certainly a procession of that sort soon became an annual tradition in Constantinople on Founder's Day. The Tyche carried a Cross welded to her forehead. All subsequent emperors were expected to rise and to prostrate themselves before it. New coins and medals were

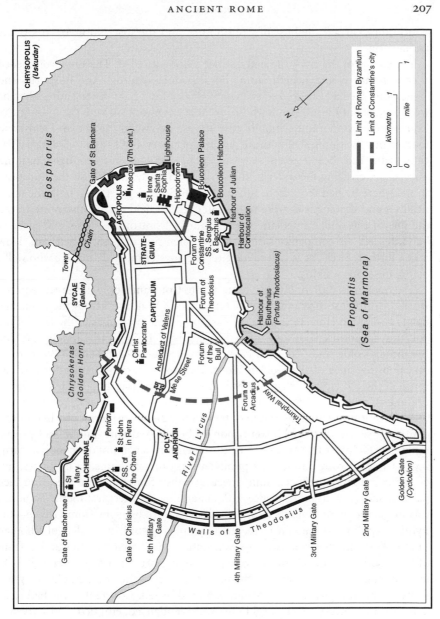

Map 9.
Constantinople

struck: they carried the bust of Constantine, and the inscription TOTIUS ORBIS IMPERATOR.

The choice of the city's site had not been easily decided. The Emperor needed a capital that would benefit from the sea routes through the Bosporus and Hellespont. He had first looked at ancient Chalcedon on the Asian shore. Then he went for ancient Ilium (Troy), whose legendary connections with the founding of Rome offered important symbolic advantages. He visited the Trojan Fields, and marked out the outlines of a future city at a place revered as Hector's Grave. The gates had already been erected (they can still be seen), before he changed his mind once again, crossing the water to the small town of Byzantium on the European shore, where he had recently conducted a victorious siege. At last, both the practicalities and the auguries were right. Later legend held that Constantine traced the line of the walls in person. Striding out in front of the surveyors, spear in hand, he left his companions far behind. When one of them called out, 'How much further, Sire?', he is said to have replied mysteriously, 'Until He who walks before me stops walking.'

The transformation of little Byzantium into Constantinople the Great required works of immense size and speed. Constantine's Wall ran across the peninsula from the Golden Horn to the Sea of Marmora, some two miles to the west of the ancient acropolis. Constantine's Forum was built immediately outside Byzantium's older wall. The separate suburbs of Sycae (Galata) and of Blachernae, on opposing sides of the Golden Horn, received separate fortifications; whilst much of the old city was stripped or demolished. The graceful granite column of Claudius Gothicus, erected in AD 269 after a famous victory, was left on the point of the promontory, looking out over the sea to Asia. Constantinople, like Rome, contained seven hills, which were soon to be covered with public and private buildings. Eighty years later, a description mentions a Capitol or school of learning, a Circus, two theatres, eight public and 153 private baths, 52 porticoes, five granaries, eight aqueducts, four meeting-halls, fourteen churches, fourteen palaces, and 4,388 listed residences of outstanding architectural merit. To adorn this megalopolis, vast numbers of art treasures were brought from Greece—the Pythian Apollo, the Samian Hera, the Olympian [ZEUS], the Pallas of Rhodian Lindos. Four hundred and twenty-seven statues were assembled to stand in front of Saint Sophia alone. Colonists were forcibly imported from all the neighbouring settlements. In order to feed them, and to supply the annual dole, the grain fleets of Egypt, Syria, and Asia Minor were redirected. Constantinople had to be launched in record time; its neighbours were vandalized, emptied, and starved.

The character of Constantine has attracted much speculation. As the first Christian emperor, he became the subject of shameless hagiography. 'Speech and reason stand mute', wrote Eusebius of Caesarea, the first biographer, 'when I gaze in spirit upon this thrice-blessed soul, united with God, free of all mortal dross, in robes gleaming like lightning, and in ever radiant diadem.'[36] Yet to his detractors he was an odious hypocrite, a tyrant and murderer, whose reputation was only burnished by a deathbed conversion and by the forgeries of the subsequent era. Gibbon, who was allergic to Christian legends, none the less preferred a generous interpretation, stressing talents marred only by the extravagances of his old age. Constantine was 'tall and majestic, dexterous . . . intrepid in war, affable in peace . . . and tempered by habitual prudence . . . He *deserved* the appellation of the first Emperor who publicly professed the Christian religion.'[37]

Despite his mother's example, it is a moot point how far Constantine was a practising Christian. He publicly confessed his debt to the One God; but most of his actions, including the Edict of Toleration, could equally be explained by the policy of a tolerant pagan. During the festivities at Constantinople, he was most interested in promoting the worship of himself. At the same time, he was a devoted patron of church-building, not least in Rome, where both St Peter's and the Basilica Constantiniana (St John Lateran) were his foundations. In 321 he enforced the general observance of Sunday as a day of rest. As was common, he long deferred his formal baptism, being christened by Bishop Eusebius of Nicomedia, an Arian, on his deathbed. He gave no special favours to the Bishop of Rome. Constantine basked in the deepening theatricality of the late imperial cult. As the *Sol Invictus* (the Unconquered Sun), he inherited Diocletian's practice of the *adoratio purpurae*, the adoration of the purple, and he surrounded himself with the obsequious language of oriental despotism. Public art, as illustrated on the friezes of the Arch of Constantine in Rome, was growing more stiff and formal. Intellectual life at Constantine's court was dominated by the drive to reconcile the rising tide of Christianity with traditional culture. Constantine relied on the convert rhetorician Lactantius, whom he had known at Trier, both to teach his son Crispus and, in the *Divinae Institutiones*, to set out a systematic account of the Christian world view.

The state of the Christian religion in Constantine's reign must be nicely gauged. After the Edict of Milan (313) the Church benefited from official toleration and a stable revenue and, with the Nicene Creed, from a coherent doctrine. Yet it was still little more than a minority sect in the early stages of institutional growth. There was no supreme ecclesiastical authority. The scriptural canon was not fully agreed. None of the greatest of the Church Fathers, from John Chrysostom to Augustine, had yet been born. The greatest of the heresiarchs, Arius, enjoyed considerable influence at the imperial court, being recalled from exile in 334. Indeed, Arianism was destined to become dominant in the succeeding reign. The Donatists in Africa had recently been suppressed. The only countries where Christianity was growing beyond the Empire were Armenia and Abyssinia. The age of sporadic persecutions was past; but 'the divisions of Christendom suspended the ruin of Paganism'.

In 330 the Empire was in healthier shape than for many decades. East and West had been reunited. The general peace held. Constantine's reforms have been dismissed as 'a timid policy, of dividing whatever is united, of reducing whatever is eminent, of dreading every active power, of expecting that the most feeble will prove the most obedient'. At least they gave the Empire a breathing space. The army was brought under control by dividing the jurisdiction of the praetorian prefects into rival masterships of cavalry and infantry; by distinguishing the élite palatine troops from the second-rate forces on the frontier; and by the widespread introduction of barbarian officers and auxiliaries. The Emperor's lavish building projects, and his repair of the road and postal system, was paid for by an oppressive land tax. A far-flung network of imperial messengers, who acted as official spies, kept potential opponents in fear.

Constantine had no plan for avoiding the perennial problems of succession. He had killed his eldest son, Crispus, on rumours of a Roman plot. But this still left him with three more sons—Constantine, Constantius, and Constans—a favoured nephew, and three brothers. Two years before his death he divided the Empire between them, raising his sons to the rank of Caesar. They ill repaid his generosity. Constantine II was killed whilst invading the territory of Constans. Constans was killed by the usurper, Maxentius. Constantius II, having initiated a massacre of his remaining relatives, was left to win the Empire from Maxentius.

Following the chaos of the previous century, the economy of the Empire was restored to a modicum of prosperity and stability. Civic munificence was diminished from earlier levels; but provincial cities, especially on the frontier zones of central Europe, retained a solid measure of pride in their public works. Diocletian's tax reforms, based on assessments of agricultural labour, had provided the basis for regular budgetary planning. They also swelled the imperial bureaucracy. Complaints were heard about tax-collectors outnumbering tax-payers. The gold coinage, struck at the rate of 60 coins per pound of bullion, offset the debasement of copper coins and laid the foundations of Byzantium's stable currency.

The Empire's frontiers were holding firm; in fact, for a time they were slightly expanded. The valuable province of Armenia had been wrested from Persia in 297, and through romanization and christianization was laying the basis of a permanent and distinctive culture. To facilitate administration, the Empire was divided into the four prefectures of Oriens (Constantinople), Illyricum (Sirmium), Italia et Africa (Milan), and Gaul (Trier). In the West, in Britain, the depredations of the Picts and Scots had been held at bay by the expedition of Constantine's father. The separatist 'emperors of Britain', Carausius and Alectus, had been brought to heel. In the East, Sassanid Persia threatened, but did not overrun. In the south, Moorish tribes were pressing on Roman Africa.

The most important changes to Europe's political and ethnic map were proceeding beyond the Empire's limits and beyond the reach of documentary history. The huge region of Celtic supremacy was dwindling fast. The Celts' western strongholds in Britain and Gaul were heavily romanized. Their homelands in the centre were being overrun, absorbed, or destroyed by the movement of Germanic and Slavonic tribes (see Chapter IV). The Franks were already settled on either side of the Rhine frontier. The Goths had completed their Long March from the Vistula to the Dnieper. The Slavs were drifting westwards towards the centre, where Celtic Bohemia was heading for slavicization. The Balts already lived on the Baltic. The Finno-Ugrians, long since divided, were well on their way to their future territories. The Finns were on station on the Volga–Baltic bridge; the

Magyars were settled at one of their many halts along the southern steppes. The nomads and the sea-raiders remained for the time being along the outer periphery. The Scythians were no more than a distant memory. The Huns were still in Central Asia. The Norsemen were already in Norway, as shown by the oldest of their runic inscriptions.

Constantine's view of the outside world would have been governed by the state of Roman communications. China, which was still disunited by the chaos of the recent 'Three Kingdom Period', was known through the fragile contacts of the silk route. It had been visited in AD 284 by the ambassadors of Diocletian. It was nominally subject to the Chin dynasty, whose influence was slowly spreading from north to south. It had largely abandoned the philosophy of Confucius and, through the flowering of Buddhism, was building strong cultural ties with India. India, whose northern region had just come under the rule of the Gupta emperors, the greatest patrons of Hindu art and culture, was much closer to Rome and was much better known. News of the crowning of Chandragupta I at Magadha in 320 would almost certainly have reached Constantinople via Egypt. Egypt was also the source of news from Abyssinia, which was the target of Christian missions from Syria and Alexandria. The Sassanid Empire of Persia, which shared a long and fragile frontier with Rome, was the object of intense interest. It had rejected the hellenism of the previous era and passed into a phase of militant Zoroastrianism. Mani, the prophet of dualist Manichaeanism, who had sought to marry Zoroaster's principles with those of Christianity, had been executed some sixty years before. The boy-king Shapur II (310–79) was still in the power of his priests and magnatial guardians, who, apart from completing the compilation of the holy scriptures, the *Avesta*, were conducting a thorough persecution of all dissenters. The Roman–Persian peace, which had not been broken for thirty-three years, was due to hold until Constantine's death.

The founding of Constantinople in 330, which was a clear-cut event, seems to support the widespread practice of taking the reign of Constantine as the dividing line between the ancient and the medieval periods. In this, it has to vie with a number of competing dates: with 392 and the accession of Theodosius I, the first emperor whose empire was exclusively Christian; with 476 and the collapse of the Roman Empire in the West (see p. 240); with 622 and the rise of Islam, which divided the former Roman world into Muslim and Christian spheres (see pp. 251–8); and with 800 and Charlemagne's restoration of a Christian empire in the West (see pp. 298–306). If this sort of dividing line were to be taken seriously, there is a danger that the young Constantine might be judged an ancient and the older Constantine a medieval.

Much more important is the overall balance at any given time between the legacy of the past and the sum total of innovations—what professional historians sometimes call the 'continuities' and the 'discontinuities'. On this basis, one can state with some confidence that no such tipping of an important balance occurred in Constantinople in AD 330.

The city of Rome was inevitably diminished, not least when Constantine abolished the praetorian guard and razed their Roman headquarters. But Rome's practical importance had declined long since. In the long run it actually benefited: by losing control of an empire which was set to crumble, it ensured that it would not be linked to the Empire's fate. It was to find a new and lasting role as the home of Christianity's most powerful hierarch. The current Bishop of Rome, however, was far from assertive. Sylvester I (314–35) attended neither the Council of Arles, which Constantine convened in 314 to end the Donatist quarrel, nor the General Council of Nicaea.

Most historians would agree that the core of Graeco-Roman civilization, as solidified in the later phases of the ancient world, lay first and foremost in the Empire and secondly in the complex cultural pluralism which it patronized and tolerated. The core of medieval civilization, in contrast, lay in the community of Christendom and its exclusively Christian culture. It developed through the mingling of ex-Roman and non-Roman peoples on a territorial base that coincided with that of the former Empire only in part. In 330, very few of the processes which led from the one to the other had even begun. Constantine himself was no European.

One must not forget the sequence of events. The span of time which separated Constantine from Charlemagne was greater than that which separated Constantine from Caesar and Augustus. It was equal to the span which encompasses the whole of modern history, from the Renaissance and Reformation to the present.

Yet Constantine did plant the seed of one historic notion—that the Christian religion was compatible with politics. Christ himself had categorically rejected political involvement; and prior to Constantine, Christians had not sought to assume power as a means of furthering their cause. After Constantine, Christianity and high politics went hand in hand. This, in the eyes of the purists, was the moment of corruption.

Appropriately enough, therefore, Constantinople soon became the founding seat of Christian power. It was made the official capital of the Roman Empire in 331, on the first anniversary of its inauguration, and it retained the distinction for more than a thousand years. Within one or two generations it assumed a predominantly Christian character, with the churches outnumbering the temples, until the temples were eventually banned. It was the source, and later the heart, of the 'Byzantine' state—the senior branch of medieval Christendom, and, despite the devotees of 'Western Civilization', an essential constituent of European history.

IV

ORIGO

The Birth of Europe, AD c.330–800

THERE is a sense of impending doom about most modern attempts to describe the late Roman Empire. The fact of the Empire's decline and fall is known in advance to virtually everyone, and it is all but impossible to recreate the perspectives of those long centuries when the eventual outcome was a mystery. Voltaire dismissed the history of the late Empire as 'ridiculous'; Gibbon wrote that he had described 'the triumph of barbarism and religion'.

Yet contemporaries could hardly have shared the viewpoint of the Enlightenment. True enough, they were very conscious of living through difficult times. Nothing is more redolent of the age than the melancholy reflections of the late Roman philosopher Boethius (c.480–525). 'The most unfortunate sort of misfortune', he wrote in his *Consolations of Philosophy*, 'is once to have been happy.' On the other hand, if they watched the Empire's decline, they did not necessarily foresee its fall. For many Christians, the end of the Empire came to be synonymous with Christ's Second Coming, with Doomsday itself. But Doomsday was so often postponed that it ceased to play a part in practical considerations. What is more, it is doubtful whether the barbarians, whose incursions were the most visible symptom of the Empire's weakness, had any intention of destroying it. On the contrary, they wanted to share in its benefits. The shocking sack of Rome in AD 410 occurred because the Emperor had refused to settle Alaric's Goths in the Empire. From the modern vantage-point, the real marvels to contemplate are the longevity of the Roman Empire, and the growing interdependence of the ex-Roman and the ex-barbarian worlds. In the long run, this was the interaction which gave birth to the entity called 'Christendom', the foundation of European civilization.

At the death of Constantine, the division of the 'known world' into two simple parts, the Roman and the barbarian, generally still stood. On one side of the frontier the reunited Roman Empire held firm; on the other a restless mass of peoples, largely in the tribal stage of development, tilled the forest clearings or roamed the plain. Understandably enough, most Romans saw this division in terms of black and white. For them, the Empire was 'civilized'—that is, subject to ordered government; the barbarians were, by definition 'uncivilized'. Though the concept of the 'noble savage' certainly existed—as when the captive British chief, Caractacus, had been paraded through Rome—the crossing from the Empire to the uncharted lands beyond was seen as a step from sunlight into shade.

In reality, the distinction between the Roman and the non-Roman world could never have been so stark. Roman armies regularly fought under barbarian generals, who used barbarian auxiliaries to help repel the Empire's barbarian foes. The countries adjacent to the frontier had been exposed to Roman influence for centuries. Roman traders and artefacts penetrated far beyond the imperial frontiers. Roman coins have been unearthed throughout Germany and eastern Europe. Hoards and graves have yielded stunning Roman gold, bronze, and silver ware, at Hildesheim near Hanover, at Lubsow in Pomerania, at Trondheim in Norway, at Klajpeda in Lithuania, even in Afghanistan. Important Roman trading-stations operated as far afield as south India.[1]

It is equally hard to be precise about the tempo of the Roman Empire's decline. Three grand historical processes which begin to take centre stage after Constantine were already in motion; and each of them lasted for many centuries. The first was the relentless westward drive of the barbarian peoples from Asia into Europe (see pp. 215–38). The second was the growing rift between the Western and the Eastern halves of the Roman world (see pp. 239–51). The third was the steady export of Christianity to the pagan peoples (see pp. 275–82). These three processes dominated the period which were later to be dubbed 'the Dark Ages'. A fourth, the rise of Islam (see pp. 251–8), exploded out of distant Arabia in the seventh century, and rapidly set the southern and eastern limits within which the others could interact.

For modern readers, one main problem lies with the traditional romanocentric and christianophile perceptions of European historians whose approach to 'the Dark Ages' has strongly reflected both their classical education and their religious beliefs. Of course, there is no reason why one should not put oneself in the shoes of a Boethius or a Gregory of Tours, and empathize with their gloomy judgements. If one does, the sense of impending doom can only be reinforced. On the other hand, there is no reason why one perspective should be accepted to the exclusion of all others. If only the sources were more abundant, one could empathize no less properly with the experiences of the advancing barbarians, of the pagans, or of the Muslim warriors. In which case the prevailing air would probably become one of excitement, of expectation, and of promise. According to Salvian of Marseilles, many Romans of good birth and education took refuge among the Goths and the Franks, 'seeking a Roman humanity among the barbarians, because they could no longer support barbarian inhumanity among the Romans'.[2]

⊂———⊃

Migrations and Settlement

In the early centuries of the first millennium, few parts of the Peninsula were inhabited by the peoples who would later settle there permanently in well-defined national 'homelands'. Much of the population beyond the Roman frontier was on the move. Tribes and federations of tribes, large and small, conducted an unending search for better land. From time to time the pace of their wanderings would be quickened by dearth, or by the violent arrival of nomadic horsemen, in which case, having tarried for decades or even centuries in one location, they would suddenly move on to the next.

The irregular rhythms of migration depended on a complex equation involving climatic changes, food supply, demographic growth, local rivalries, distant crises. For the Romans watching anxiously on the frontier, they were entirely unpredictable. Pressures would accumulate imperceptibly, until some unforeseen event would snap the restraints. Long intervals of quiescence would alternate with short, intense surges. As always, the act of migration depended on the delicate balance between the forces of inertia, the 'push' of local difficulties, and the 'pull' of greener grass over the horizon. The critical cause of any particular displacement might lie far away on the steppes of central Asia; and a 'shunting effect' is clearly observable. Changes at one end of the chain of peoples could set off ripples along all the links of the chain. Like the last wagon of a train in the shunting yards, the last tribe on the western end of the chain could be propelled from its resting-place with great force.

In this regard, the Huns caused ripples in the West long before they themselves appeared. A Hunnic Empire had been destroyed by the Chinese c.36/35 BC. Thereafter the Hunnic hordes, and the herds of cattle from which they lived, were based in what is now Turkestan. Their raiding parties could easily cover a couple of thousand miles a month. Mounted on swift Mongolian ponies and armed with bows and arrows, they could ride deep into Europe or the Far East and return in the course of a single summer. Like all the true nomads, they generated a huge motive force on the agricultural or semi-nomadic peoples with whom they came into contact. In the second century AD their base shifted to the north of the Caspian Sea; in the fourth century it was shifting towards what is now Ukraine. There, in 375, they encountered the Ostrogoths, a Germanic people who, exceptionally, had been moving in the opposite direction. The resultant clash pushed the Ostrogoths, and the neighbouring Visigoths, into the Roman Empire. Within fifty years another of the associated tribes, the Alans, appeared in what is now southern Portugal—almost 3,000 miles away. The Huns did not attack the Empire themselves until 441. The rate of migration, of course, was extremely slow. The Alans, who crossed the Dnieper c.375 and the Rhine in 406, and reached the Atlantic in the 420s, averaged perhaps 5 miles per year. The 'sudden irruption' of the Vandals, who shared part of the Alans' journey (see below), maintained a mean speed of 2 km per week. Tribal columns weighed down with carts, livestock, and supplies could not hope to compete with the nomads.

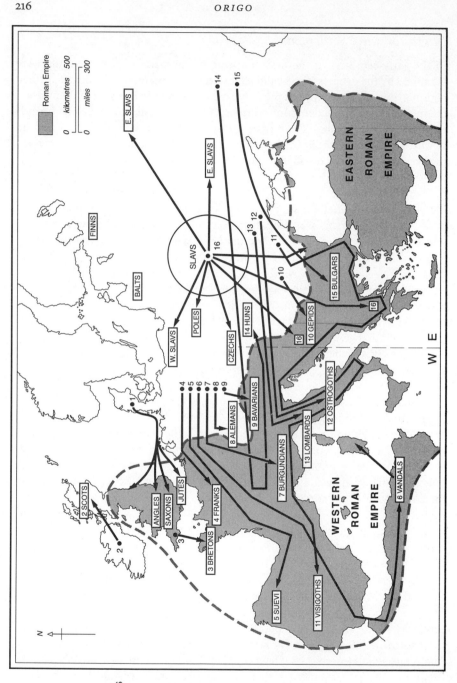

Map 10.
Europe:
Migrations

Geographical considerations played a central role. The main obstacle to the free movement of peoples was not the imperial frontier but the mountains. All the tribes following the prehistoric trail across the Eurasian steppes, if they did not turn immediately south along the Black Sea shore, were automatically channelled to the north along the European plain. After that, there were only two possible southbound turns, through the Moravian or the Bavarian Gaps. To take the southerly route involved an early military confrontation with imperial forces on the Danube. To pass along the northerly route was to follow the line of least resistance, where inertia would carry the migrants directly to the Rhine. For these reasons, pressure steadily mounted on the Rhine barrier, until in the third and fourth centuries a veritable traffic jam of tribes was produced. The passage through the mountains into the Danube basin was impractical for the larger convoys. But it became the chosen route of the nomads; and the lush plains of Pannonia—later named 'Hungaria' after the Huns—formed their natural terminus. (See pp. 232, 296, 316.) [CSABA]

Another obstacle lay with tribes that were blocking the path ahead. True enough, the Peninsula had many open spaces: the density of population was very low, even in the Empire. But much was wilderness. The dense forests, sandy heaths, and sodden valleys could neither be cultivated nor easily crossed; and the migrants had to compete for finite areas of cleared or cultivable land. It was difficult for the tribes to move without coming into contact, and potential conflict, with their predecessors on the trail. As a result, the bunching and mingling of tribes in some of the choicer locations of the European plain was inevitable. There is absolutely no reason to suppose that Celts, Germans, Slavs, and others did not overlap, and sometimes intermingle. The idea of exclusive national homelands is a modern fantasy.

The fluidity of migrant tribal groupings, and the chaotic nature of their movements, did not suit the purposes of those who tried to make sense of the migrations in later times. Chroniclers and historians were tempted to write in terms of discrete, permanent, and self-conscious tribes where no such entities had necessarily existed. It is far from certain, for example, whether the Angles, Saxons, and Jutes who ended up in England were quite as distinct as the Venerable Bede portrayed them (see below). Yet once they were settled, all the peoples were keen to invent a unique pedigree for themselves. All have suffered, too, from the attentions of nationalist historians in our own day, who think nothing of projecting modern identities backwards into prehistory. In the absence of alternatives, it is difficult to know how one can describe the migrations except in terms of the traditional tribes. But some awareness of the drawbacks is necessary.

Such, then, was the setting for the massive historical process which, from the standpoint of the Empire, has been called 'the Barbarian Invasions' and which, from the parochial standpoint of Western Europe, has often been reduced to 'the Germanic Invasions'. To the Germans it is known as the *Völkerwanderung*, the 'Wandering of Peoples'—an apt term which could well be applied to its Germanic and non-Germanic participants alike. In reality, it engulfed the greater part of the

CSABA

'IN the vast plains of Asia—he began—lived two brave, wild tribes. They were called Huns and Magyars. When their people grew numerous, the Huns set out for a new place to settle. After many hardships, they came to a land that was green with pastures, blue with swift-flowing rivers, rich with wooded mountains. But the land was not free. It belonged to the Romans, who called it Pannonia.

The bravest of the Huns was a young prince, Attila, so they made him their king. He took more and more land, and ruled his people with an iron hand. When his wife died, leaving him with two sons, Csaba and Aladar, he boldly demanded the daughter of the Roman Emperor for his wife [and] half the Empire for the dowry.

Finally, they clashed at Katalaun. The light cavalry of the Huns swept down on the Roman army like a furious whirlwind, only to be battered to pieces on their iron-clad ranks. . . . Placid rivers turned into rivers of blood. The "Scourge of God" was broken. . . . Old in spirit, he died shortly afterwards.

Then Csaba decided to take the strongest men and return to far Asia . . . to the Magyars. He called his people together. "Dead or alive," he promised, "we will come to your aid if you are in danger."

When he had left, yet another vast army of foes marched against the Huns. Endless columns of ruthless warriors swept into their stronghold. The Huns fell on their knees and prayed for Csaba. Thunder, long, deep, ever increasing thunder answered them . . . A sparkling white streak appeared among the stars, forming a great arch like a rainbow. With the flashing swords and battlecries of thousands of men, and the clattering hoofbeats of thousands of horses, Csaba and his warriors swept down from the sky, scattering the terror-struck enemy.

Csaba and his army of spirits came back one last time, leading the Magyars to rejoin their brothers in this beautiful land of ours. After that, he never came back. But the sparkling skyway, "the skyway of the warriors", has remained there forever.'[1]

Folk tales are the repository of collective memory. They were designed to entertain, but also to reinforce tribal identity. Five hundred years separated the exploits of Huns and Magyars in Hungary. Yet the latter continued to feel an affinity for their predecessors and fellow nomads. In modern times, none but a Magyar family would dream of calling their son Attila.

European Peninsula, East and West, and continued throughout the first millennium AD and beyond, until all the wanderers had found a permanent abode. Its main events are only known from Roman sources, since the illiterate wanderers left few records of their own. Yet here is the process from which most of the later national groupings must trace their origins. To parody a phrase from a later age, it could well be called the *Drang nach Westen*, the Drive to the West, the road to permanent settlement. Without it, any concept of 'Europe' or of 'Europeans' would be unrecognizable. Anthropological analysis suggests that three main types of population were involved: the settled inhabitants of the Empire, living in cities or on rural estates; the barbarian tribes, living from primitive arable or pastoral farming; and the true nomads. One must also add the sea raiders, who, like the nomads, lived largely from plunder, and who operated over huge distances in the northern seas.

From the technological standpoint, it is important to note that Iron Age agriculture was reaching the point where more was to be gained by tilling the same patch of ground than by constantly moving on. The barbarians were not simply seeking an adventure in the sun. They were looking for somewhere to put down roots.

From the ethnic standpoint, the peoples of the Peninsula possessed the most variegated connections. Subject to certain reservations, however, one can say that the Indo-European element already predominated by the first half of the first millennium. The majority of inhabitants of the Empire, though not Latins or Hellenes by origin, were thoroughly latinized in the West and hellenized in the East. With some notable exceptions, the barbarian migrants belonged to one of the other main Indo-European families (see Appendix III, pp. 1232–3).

Apart from the nomads, the non-Indo-Europeans would have included members of the Uralian-Finnic group; pockets of the original Iberian tribes of Spain; remnants of the pre-Latin population in the remoter parts of Italy; and unassimilated elements among the Illyrians, Dacians, and Thracians of the Balkans. The Jews had spread to all the major cities of the Mediterranean. The Uralian-Finnic group of peoples had already split into its component parts. The Finns, or *Suomalainen*, had trekked across the subarctic taiga from their starting-point in Siberia. They occupied the lands between the end of the Baltic and the upper Volga, which would later become the heart of Russia. Ethnically, they were related both to the Huns and the Magyars and to several smaller units—the Cheremiss, Mordvins, Permians, Voguls, and Ostyaks—who stayed behind in the Ural region. More distantly, they were also related to the Altaic Group which includes Turks, Mongols, and Tartars. Their neighbours, the Lapps, were already engaged in their timeless peregrinations with the arctic reindeer. The Lapps called themselves 'Sameh'; but, in the interests of confusion, the Nordic nations usually called them 'Finns'. Hence the later Swedish province of Finnmark.

In the Caucasus, two other fragmented groups of peoples had few known connections. The north Caucasians are made up from the Abkhaz, Chechens, and Avars; the south Caucasians from the Laz, Mingrelians, and Georgians. In the 1920s an amateur linguist of Scottish origin, who assumed the russianized name of Nikolai Yakovelitch Marr (1864–1934), invented a theory which linked these Caucasian languages with Basque, Etruscan, and ancient Hebrew, thereby tying up all the loose ends of the European ethnic scene. Unfortunately, though patronized by the greatest of all Georgians, Marr's theory has been comprehensively disproved.

The Asian nomads penetrated the Peninsula in waves that are spread over most

of recorded history. The Huns, who appeared in the fifth century AD, were successors to earlier hordes who had ridden the same steppes, notably the ancient
Scythians and the Irano-Sarmatians, whom Ptolemy reported as the overlords of
the steppelands in the second century AD. They were the predecessors of the
Avars, the Magyars, and the Mongols, who were all to reach central Europe. Other
nomads restricted their movements to the vicinity of the Black Sea. One branch
of the Turkic Bulgars had established a kingdom on the middle Volga. Another
branch settled near the mouth of the Danube in the seventh century AD. The
Khazars followed traces of the Bulgars, creating a kingdom stretching from
the north Caucasus to the Dniester. The Patzinaks (Pechinegs) advanced into the
Balkans in the wake of the Khazars. After them, another ephemeral state was built
on the Black Sea steppes by the Cumans. The gypsies or 'Romanies' reached
Europe from India in the eleventh century. One branch of the Turks impinged on
the Caucasus about the same time; the main branch conquered the Balkans in the
fourteenth century.

Of all these non-Indo-Europeans, few were to leave a lasting mark. The Basques
and the Maltese have weathered the centuries, speaking languages unrelated to any
of their neighbours. The Jews, too, kept their separate identity. The Finns and
Estonians on the Baltic, and Magyars in 'Hungaria', succeeded in founding modern nations. The Lapps still follow the reindeer. The Tartars, last descendants of the
Mongols, have survived in 'Tatarstan' on the Volga and, despite modern deportations, in the Crimea. Gypsies are still spread all over Europe. The Turks, who won
and lost a vast empire, have kept a precarious toehold in Europe in the immediate
vicinity of Istanbul. The Balkan Bulgars have so identified with the Slav world that
the communist regime could persecute its Turkish minority in the 1980s, on the
grounds that their victims were not 'true Turks' but turkicized Slavs. If Bulgarian
officialdom were consistent, it would have to recommend the mass expulsion of all
Bulgarians on the grounds that they themselves are not 'true Slavs', but slavicized
Turkics. [**GAGAUZ**]

'Indo-European', it must be emphasized, refers essentially to a linguistic category (see Chapter I, pp. 49–50), and only by extension to the peoples who have
used those languages as their native tongue. All the languages which belong to the
group can be traced back to a common proto-Indo-European language spoken
somewhere in Eurasia over 5,000 years ago. Since then the group has spread over
a wide area stretching from Iceland to Ceylon and, through modern colonization,
to all continents of the world. It has been said that 'language is the single most
valuable possession of the human race'; and there can be no doubt that the 'Indo-
Europeans' form one of the most important linguistic communities of human
history.[3] (See Appendix III, p. 1232.)

The real problem, however, is to determine what, apart from their linguistic
heritage, the Indo-Europeans may have in common. The old idea that language is
necessarily linked to race has been discredited. Languages can be easily transferred
from one racial group to another. Over a period of time, there need be no correlation whatsoever between a people's 'native language' and their racial origins.

(This can be easily demonstrated from the English-speaking world, where English has been adopted by millions of Afro-Americans and Afro-Caribbeans.) In the case of Eurasia, it is by no means clear whether the brown-skinned Indo-element exported their language to their paler 'European' neighbours, or vice versa, or whether both adopted it from a third party. There is a popular tradition in Afghanistan that all Indo-Europeans came from there. By the same token, even if it exists, the so-called 'European', 'Caucasian', or 'Aryan' race group does not coincide with the Indo-European languages. The majority of Turks, for example, seem to be Caucasian by race but are manifestly non-European by language. [**CAUCASIA**]

Certainly, racial purity is a non-starter when applied to the European peoples in historic times. The population of the Roman Empire contained a strong admixture of both north African negroids and west Asian semitics. The barbarian tribes were constantly replenishing their genetic stock from captive women and prisoners. Though any visit to Ireland or to Scandinavia can easily demonstrate that racial types are no fiction of the imagination, language, culture, religion, and politics have been more powerful determinants of ethnicity than race. What *is* true is that any tribal or social grouping which lives together for any length of time needs to adopt a common language. Equally, to protect its sense of identity, it will often erect formal or informal barriers against interbreeding. In some cases, where membership is defined by criteria of kinship backed by religious taboos, miscegenation can be punished by expulsion. In this way, language and kinship do become intimately intertwined.

The Celts, who were the avant-garde of the Indo-Europeans on the northern plain, had moved well to the west by Roman times. They had founded some of the most advanced archaeological cultures (see p. 84). They had been associated with the spread of metal-working, and their possession of iron weapons may well explain their dramatic expansion. Celts stormed Rome in 390 BC and Greece in 279 BC, terrifying their victims by their huge stature, their red hair and ferocious temperament, and by their sickening habit of head-hunting. For twenty years at the close of the second century BC, in the shape of the Cimbri, who set off from Jutland in the company of the Teutons, they caused immense havoc in Gaul and Spain until caught by the Consul Marius. Having annihilated the Teutons at Campi Putridi (see p. 87), Marius annihilated the Cimbri at Campi Raudii, near Verona, in 101 BC. One or two setbacks, however, did not stem the tide. The Celtic Bohemii were known in 'Bohemia'. Other Celts had settled in force in northern Italy, creating Cisalpine Gaul. They occupied the whole of the land to the west and north-west of the Alps, creating Transalpine Gaul. They crossed the Pyrenees, creating, among other things, Galicia: and they moved into the Rhineland. Already in the eighth century BC they had invaded the offshore islands, thereby creating the 'British' Isles.

Hence, when the Roman legions conquered much of Western Europe in the late Republican era, it was the Celts who provided the native resistance. During the Empire, they constituted the basic demographic stock of romanized

Celto-Iberians in Spain, of Gallo-Romans in Gaul, of Romano-Britons in Britain. Many of their tribal names are recognizable in modern places that have entirely lost their Celtic connections—*Boii* (Bohemia), *Belgae* (Belgium), *Helvetii* (Switzerland), *Treveri* (Trier), *Parisi* (Paris), *Redones* (Rennes), *Dumnonii* (Devon), *Cantiaci* (Kent), *Brigantes* (Brigsteer). In due course, overwhelmed in many parts by the next influx of Germanic peoples, they set up their permanent strongholds in the far north-west, on the 'Celtic fringe' of Britain—in Ireland, western Scotland, Wales, and Cornwall. In the fourth century AD, under pressure from the Anglo-Saxons, Celtic migrants from Cornwall crossed into ' Finisterre', thereby creating Brittany. Of the six Celtic languages which have survived into contemporary times, three belong to the Goidelic or Q-Celtic group, and three to the Brythonic or P-Celtic group. *Cymru am byth!* One branch of the Celts departed for Asia Minor. 'O foolish Galatians,' exclaimed St Paul when he visited these 'Gauls of the East' in AD 52 (Gal. 3: 1). Three hundred years later St Jerome, who came from Trier, correctly noted that the Galatians spoke essentially the same tongue as the Gauls of his native Rhineland. [**TRISTAN**]

The Germanic peoples probably formed the largest barbarian population of the Roman period. First identified in southern Scandinavia, they were designated as *Germani* by Posidonius in 90 BC, by which time they were well into the task of settling the lands that have borne their name ever since. In the west they overlapped with the Celts, so that tribes such as the Cimbri and the Teutons have been variously designated as Celtic, Germanic, or germanized Celts. In the east they overlapped with the Slavs, so that controversies have raged over whether tribes such as the *Venedi*, who were mentioned by Tacitus, were Slavonic Wends, Germanic Vandals, or perhaps germanized Slavs.

The Germanic peoples are generally classified in three groupings. The Scandinavian group gave rise to the later Danish, Swedish, Norwegian, and Icelandic communities. The West Germanic group, centred on the North Sea coast, included Batavians, Frisians, Franks, Alamans, Jutes, Angles, and Saxons. They are the principal ancestors of the later Dutch, Flemish, English, and lowland Scots communities; also, in part, of the French. The East Germanic group, to the east of the Elbe, included Swabians, Lombards, Burgundians, Vandals, Gepids, Alans, and Goths. They were largely responsible for the tribal traffic jam on the northern plain, and were among the principal actors in the crisis of the Western Empire. [**FUTHARK**]

The *Germania* of Tacitus provides a detailed survey of the customs, social structure, and religion of the Germanic tribes. They had traded with the Mediterranean world since Bronze Age times, and were adopting Roman farming methods, even viticulture. Their clans were united by kinship, and ruled in conjunction with a democratic assembly of warriors, the [**DING**] or 'Thing'. Their religion centred on the fertility gods Njordr (Nerthus) and Freyr, on Wodin (Odin), the master of magic and god of war, and on Thor (Donar), protector of the farmers against giants, fairies, and evil of all sorts. There was no priesthood, since their war-leaders, who often took the title of king, combined both military and religious functions. They long resisted Christianity, though the Goths adopted Arianism at an early date (see below).

TRISTAN

B Y the roadside at Menabilly, two miles north of Fowey in Cornwall, stands a tapering stone column some seven feet high. It bears a faint inscription, in sixth-century Roman letters: 'DRUSTANS HIC IACET CUNOMORI FILIUS' (Here lies Tristan [or Tristram], son of Quonimorius). The earthworks of an Iron Age fort, Castle Dôr, rise in the vicinity. Excavations within its perimeter have uncovered evidence of its reoccupation in early medieval times. The neighbouring farm of Lantyan also suggests that here stood ancient *Lancien*—the palace of 'King Mark, called Quonimorius'. The Forest of *Moresk* or Morrois, the Evil Ford of *Malpas*, and the manor of *Tir Gwyn* or *La Blanche Lande*, and the monastery of St Sampson-in-Golant, all with names which recur in the later texts, are to be found nearby. There is little reason to doubt that the tombstone belongs to the historic Tristan.[1]

According to legend, Tristan, prince of the lost land of Lyonesse, fell passionately in love with Isolt, princess of Ireland, whom he had conveyed by sea to her marriage with his kinsman, King Mark. Fired by a secret love potion, their passion condemns them to a lifetime of illicit trysts and elopements. It ends when Tristan is mortally wounded by the King's poisoned spear, and Isolt casts herself in death into their last embrace.

Centuries later, the tragic Celtic love story was versified in courtly romance throughout Europe. The earliest French fragment, like that in Rhenish German by Eilhardt, dates from 1170. The fullest German version, by Gottfried von Strassburg (*c*.1200), provided the main source for the libretto of Wagner's opera (1859). There were early Provençal and early English versions. In the fifteenth century Sir Thomas Malory's *Morte D'Arthur*, like the French prose *Roman de Tristan*, combines the Tristan story with that of King Arthur. A copy of the French version, with magnificent illuminated miniatures, is preserved as Vienna MS Codex 2537 in the Austrian National Library.[2] A Byelorussian Tristan composed in the sixteenth century, and now preserved in Poznań, constitutes the earliest item of secular Belarus literature.[3] By then, the story was already 1,000 years old:

And then, anon, Sir Tristan took the sea, and La Beale Isoud. . . . in their cabin, it happed that they were thirsty, and they saw a little flacket of gold, and it seemed it was noble wine . . . Then they laughed and made good cheer, and either drank to other freely . . . But by that the drink was in their bodies, they loved either other so well that never their love departed for weal neither for woe. . . .[4]

Like Tristan, the central figure of the Arthurian cycles remains a historical enigma. Most scholars agree that Arthur, 'the once and future king', must have been a Christian British warlord battling the tide of Anglo-Saxon invaders. But no one has identified him with certainty. The eighth-century chronicler, Nennius, called Arthur the *dux bellorum*, who had crushed the Saxons at 'Mount Badon'. Welsh sources called him *amheradawr* or 'emperor'. In the twelfth century, Geoffrey of Monmouth said that he was born on the stupendous island fortress of Tintagel on the coast of Cornwall, and that he died at Glastonbury, by the shrine of the Holy Grail. Modern archaeology, which has discovered a late Roman monastic community at Tintagel, has strengthened the Cornish claims. But another study connects him with a Welsh leader, Owain Ddantgwain, King of Gwynedd and Powys, son of the Head Dragon, also known as 'the Bear', who died in 520.[5] Somerset tradition holds that the hillfort at Cadbury Castle sheltered Arthur's court at Camelot, whilst Glastonbury was the 'Avalon' where he died. In 1278 King Edward I ordered a tomb at Glastonbury to be opened, and found the caskets of a warrior and a lady. He took them to contain the remains of Arthur and Guinevere. A cross on the tomb, since lost, was said to bear the inscription HIC IACET SEPULTUS INCLITUS REX ARTURIUS IN INSULA AVALONIAE (Here lies buried the famous King Arthur in the Isle of Avalon).[6]

Ancient legends constantly renew their purposes. Just as medieval England's Anglo-Norman Kings liked to link themselves with the pre-Saxon rulers of the conquered land, so Romantic Victorians sought to reinforce their sense of modern British unity by pondering the fate of the Ancient Britons. Alfred, Lord Tennyson (1809–92) spent forty-two years as Poet Laureate and fifty-five working on his much-admired, and much-derided, Arthurian epic, *The Idylls of the King*. It was an extended allegory of the eternal struggle between spirituality and materialism:

> . . . their fears
> Are morning shadows huger than the shapes
> That cast them, not those gloomier which forego
> The darkness of that battle in the west
> Where all of high and holy dies away.[7]

The Germanic peoples were on the move throughout the imperial period. The Gothic federation left its resting-place on the lower Vistula in the second century AD, drifting slowly south-eastwards against the main migratory current. Two hundred years later, the Visigoths were established on the Black Sea coast north of the Danube delta. The Ostrogoths lay further east, in the Crimea and on the Dnieper steppes, precariously close to the advancing Huns. In that fourth century, some of the Frankish tribes were invited into the Empire as imperial *foederati*, and charged with the defence of the Rhine.

The Slavonic peoples pressed hard on the heels of their Germanic neighbours. Their prehistory is less well documented, since they had fewer contacts with the

Empire, and has become the subject of many modern musings. The ancient 'Slavonic homeland' has often been viewed as a fixed reservation. The Polish 'aboriginal school' of prehistorians insists that it extended over the territory between the Oder and the Vistula *ab origine*, although it is more convincingly designated to a wooded zone further east, on the slopes of the Carpathians. For some inexplicable reason Western scholars love to relegate the proto-Slavs to the least likely and least comfortable of locations, in the middle of the Pripet Marshes. Whatever its bounds, the Slavonic homeland straddled the main prehistoric trail. It must have been overrun, and probably subordinated, by each of the great nomadic incursions. A Scythian chieftain was buried with all his treasures at Witaszkowo on the western Neisse. The memory of the Sarmatians lingered for 2,000 years, so that Polish nobles would claim Sarmatian pedigree. [CRUX] The migrating Goths and Gepids drifted slowly past, to no known ill effect. In the fifth century AD the passage of the Huns left few traces except for a tantalizing phrase in an Anglo-Saxon poem, the *Widsith*, which tells how 'the Hraede with their sharp swords must defend their ancient seat from the people of Aetla by the Wistla wood'.[4] The Huns' successors, the Avars, created some sort of Slavo-Avaric confederation that first enters the historical record from Byzantine sources in the sixth century.

It is doubtful whether the proto-Slavonic language could have been deeply differentiated until the main migrations began in the middle of the first millennium. It is only known from scholarly reconstructions. Like Greek and Latin, it was marked by highly complex declensions and conjugations and by free word order. The Slavonic tribes are often thought to have developed a characteristic social institution, the [ZADRUGA] or 'joint family', where all the relatives of the chieftain lived together under fierce patriarchal discipline. They worshipped numerous deities such as Triglav, the Three-Headed One, Svarog, the Sun-Maker, and Perun, the God of the Thunderclap. Interestingly enough, much of their religious vocabulary, from *Bog* (God) to *raj* (Paradise), is Sarmato-Iranian in origin; just as many of their words relating to primitive technology, such as *dach* (roof in Polish) or *plug* (plough in Russian) is Germanic. Isolated though they were, they had clearly benefited from contact with their neighbours. (See Appendix III, p. 1223.)

A taste of the shaky sources, and of the scepticism, of Western historians may be drawn from the following description of the Slavs, which was compiled, with some poetic licence, 'from the evidence of Procopius and of the Emperor Mauritius':

The Sclavonians used one common language (it was harsh and irregular) and were known by the resemblance of their form which deviated from the swarthy Tartar and approached, without attaining, the lofty stature and fair complexion of the German. Four thousand six hundred villages were scattered over the provinces of Russia and Poland, and their huts were hastily built of rough timber ... We may, not perhaps without flattery, compare them to the architecture of the beaver ...

FUTHARK

RUNES or 'matchstick signs' form the basis of an alphabet which was used by the Vikings and which, from its first six letters, was known as 'Futhark'. Runes were chiselled into wood or stone, often in long, snake-like inscriptions. There were two main variants—Common or Danish Futhark, and Swedo-Norwegian, each with sixteen basic signs:

ᚠᚢᚦᚨᚱᚴ᛭ᚼᛁᚤ᛫ᛏᛒᚤᛌ

Runic inscriptions have been found in great numbers, especially in central Sweden and in Denmark. They record voyages, legal agreements, and deaths, sometimes in skaldic verse. A silver neck-ring from Troons in northern Norway tells how the silver was won:

Forum drengia Frislands a vit	We went to the lands of Frisia
ok vigs fǫtum ver skiptum	And we it was who split the spoils of war.

At Gripsholm in Sodermanland, a mother mourns her sons, Ingmar and Harald, who perished on an expedition to the Mediterranean:

peir fóru drengila fiarri et gulli	Like men they journeyed for gold,
ok austarla arne gáfu	And in the east they feasted the eagle,
dóu sunnarla á Serklandi	And in the south they died in Serkland.

There is a runic graffito in a gallery of St Sophia's in Istanbul, and another on one of the lions of St Mark, brought to Venice from Athens.[1]

Runes, however, were not just used for writing. The 16-sign Futhark of the Vikings, which dates from AD *c*.350, had been condensed from the much more extensive *Hallristningar* or 'Rune Hoard', which was used from the Bronze Age onwards for the purposes of occult divination:

The *Germania* of Tacitus describes the reading of the runes:

They break off a branch from a fruit tree, and slice it into strips; they distinguish these by certain runes and throw them, as fortune will have it, onto a white cloth. Then the state priest . . . or the family father . . . after praying to the gods . . . picks up three of them, one at a time, and reads their meaning from the runes carved on them.[3]

In later times, among many variants, the 33-sign series found in Anglo-Saxon England and the 18-sign series of Armanen Runes found in the German-speaking world had much in common (see Appendix III, pp. 1234–5). Runes provide a gateway to the mysterious and strangely beautiful aesthetic world of the vikings.

Ogham, or Ogams, were a Celtic counterpart of Scandinavian runes, being used both for writing and for divination, especially in Ireland. Each sign consisted of simple vertical staves cut against a horizontal or slanting baseline. Each was primarily associated with a tree and with a letter corresponding to the tree's name, but also, by alliteration, with birds and animals, with colours, with periods of the year, and with days of the week:

B L F   S N H D T   C Q M G Ng   ST   R   A O U E   I   Ea Oi Ui Ia Ao

Europe's native writing systems were an essential adjunct to pagan religion. Ogam and Runes, like the North Italic and the Etruscan, were rooted in times when the divination of Nature lay at the heart of all knowledge and understanding. Even so much of the associated lore and magic has survived the advent of classical and Christian civilization.

The fertility of the soil, rather than the labour of the natives, supplied the rustic plenty of the Sclavonians . . . The field which they sowed with millet and panic afforded, in the place of bread, a coarse and less nutritive food . . . As their supreme God, they adored an invisible master of the thunder . . .

The Sclavonians disdained to obey a despot . . . Some voluntary respect was yielded to age and valour; but each tribe or village existed as a separate republic, and all must be persuaded where none could be compelled . . . They fought on foot, almost naked . . . They swam, they dived, they remained under water, drawing breath through a hollow cane. But these were the achievements of spies or stragglers. The military art was unknown to the Sclavonians. Their name was unknown, and their conquests obscure.[5]

The Baltic peoples lived in still greater isolation. The Prussians to the east of the Vistula delta, the Lithuanians in the valley of the Niemen, and the Letts on the western Dvina spoke languages that scholars regard as the least evolved of all. They were once thought, erroneously, to form part of the Slavonic group, but are now judged closer to proto-Indo-European even than Sanskrit. Like all Indo-Europeans, the Balts must surely have migrated from the East at some point in prehistory, but nothing is known of their movements. They settled on the morainic debris of the last Ice Age, and stayed there among the dark pines and the shimmering lakes. Like the Finns and the Estonians, they seem to have been left alone until the tide of the peoples turned in the opposite direction in the first half of the second millennium. [LIETUVA]

LIETUVA

THERE is no shortage of authorities to confirm that the Lithuanian language is 'the most archaic of all Indo-European tongues,'[1] or that 'it
has better preserved its archaic forms . . . than have other contemporary
Indo-European languages'.[2] Ever since Karl Brugmann published
his *Grundriss*, or outline, of comparative Indo-Germanic languages in
1897, Lithuanian has been a favourite among etymologists of the Romantic
persuasion.

It is true that the Lithuanian lexicon contains a core of words that any
classicist would recognize: *vyras* 'man', *saulē* 'sun', *mēnuo* 'moon', *ugnis*
'fire', *kalba* 'language'. Lithuania has kept dual as well as plural number,
long vowels of nasal origin, seven-case declensions, and a verb system of
tenses, conjugations, and moods not dissimilar to Latin's. On the other
hand, the Slavonic element in the Lithuanian lexicon is also very large:
galva 'head' (Russian *golova*), *ranka* 'hand' (Polish *ręka*), *paukštis* 'bird',
žiema 'winter', and *sniegas* 'snow' (Polish *ptaszek*, *zima*, and *śnieg*). Polish,
too, has plural number, nasal vowels, and seven cases. Unlike Lithuanian
(or French), most Slavonic languages have not lost the neuter form. In
reality, Lithuanian is mainly characterized by features common to both the
Baltic and the Slavonic language groups. Anyone who imagines that it is
a close relative to Sanskrit is in for a disappointment.

None the less, the survival of Lithuanian is remarkable. It remained a
local peasant vernacular throughout the long centuries of the Grand
Duchy of Lithuania (see p. 392), and was never used as a language of high
culture or government. The Lithuanian Statutes, written in *ruski* or
'Ruthenian' were translated into Latin (1530) and Polish (1531), but not into
Lithuanian. Starting with the Catechism (1547) of M. Mazvidas, however,
Lithuanian was used for religious purposes. In the nineteenth century,
Russian educators tried printing it in Cyrillic. But the Polish bishops of
Wilno (Vilnius) successfully countered the ploy by supporting Lithuanian
primary education in the Roman alphabet, thereby cementing Lithuania's
deep attachment to Catholicism. This makes it entirely appropriate for
amateur linguists to cut their teeth on a scriptural text:

> Ir angēlas
> tare jiems:
> 'Nesibijokties!
> Štay!'
> Apsakau jums didj dźaugsmą
> kurs nusidůs
> vissiems źmonems. (Luke 2: 10)[3]

Despite Western conventions, it is important to view the barbarian migrations as a whole. They were *not* confined to the Germanic peoples, nor to the Roman frontline in the West. What appeared in the West as a sudden deluge at the end of the fourth century was just one act in a drama that was far more extensive both geographically and chronologically.

The first sign of the coming deluge occurred in 376, when the Ostrogoths, pressed by the Huns, petitioned the Emperor Valens to settle in Moesia. Some of them were allowed to cross the Danube, but were required to surrender both their arms and their children. Two years later, in August 378, they fought a pitched battle at Hadrianopolis (Edirne) in which the Emperor was killed. Thanks to the heavy cavalry of the Goths' allies, the Sarmatian Alans, Rome's invincible legions were decisively beaten. (In military history, that demonstration of the power of Sarmatian-style lances and their oversize chargers marks the debut of the most characteristic features of medieval warfare.) Four years after that it was the turn of the Visigoths. Their king and war-leader, Alaric, cannot have been indifferent to the Ostrogoths' success. He was given the title of *magister militum illyricorum* as a sop. But in the course of a thirty-year adventure his imperial office did not restrain him from sacking first Athens (396) and then Rome (410). The immediate cause of Alaric's wrath lay in the Empire's refusal to accept the Visigoths for settlement in Noricum. Thereafter, he conceived a plan to take them to Africa. But his death at Cosenza caused yet another change of direction. Alaric's successor, Athaulf, married the captured stepsister of the Emperor Honorius, whilst his brother Wallia gave the Visigoths respite by settling them in Aquitaine. The Visigoth kingdom of Tolosa (Toulouse) was short-lived. But it provided the springboard from which, some time after 507, the Visigoths set out to create their most enduring legacy in Spain.

The rampage of the Visigoths provided an opening for three more huge invasions. When the legions of Gaul were withdrawn to protect Constantinople from Alaric, the garrison of the Rhine was dangerously thinned. Some time around 400 the Burgundians took their chance to move into the area at the confluence of Rhine and Main. Thirty years later they were challenged by the Roman general Aetius, whose Hunnish auxiliaries drove them off. But in 443 they were back to settle permanently in the vicinity of Lyons. Henceforth the Burgundian Kingdom developed in the valleys of the Rhone and Saône, controlling the principal Alpine passes. [NIBELUNG]

At Christmas 406 a vast horde of barbarians crossed the frozen Rhine near Coblenz. Vandals, Suevi, and Alans poured into Gaul. The Vandals took a roundabout route to Alaric's original destination in Africa. They crossed the Pyrenees in 409, the Straits of Gibraltar in 429, and the gates of Carthage in 439. They took 33 years to cover the 2,500 miles from the Rhine. From their Carthaginian base they took to the sea, seizing the Balearic Islands and Sardinia. In 455, under Genseric, they imitated Alaric and sacked Rome. The Vandal kingdom in Africa remained a major force until the restoration of imperial power in the following century. The Vandals parted company with their original companions, the Suevi

NIBELUNG

FOR several decades at the turn of the fifth century, the Burgundian court stood at Worms on the Rhine, the ancient *Civitas Vangionum*. Known as Nibelungs after a former chief, the Burgundians had been brought in as auxiliaries on the imperial frontier. They were to be driven out in 435–6 during battles with the Roman general Aetius and the advancing Huns. The names of three royal brothers Gundharius (Gunther), Gislaharius (Giselher), and Godomar (Gemot) are known from the later *Lex Burgundiorum*. After halting at Geneva, they moved on to Lyons, where in 461 they set up the first Kingdom of Burgundy. [**LUGDUNUM**] A plaque on the site of the former palace at Worms recalls that city's distinctions:

Here Was
The Holy Temple Area of the Romans
The Royal Castle of the Nibelungen
The Imperial Residence of Charlemagne
The Court of the Prince-Bishop of Worms
Destroyed by the French in the Years 1689 and 1745.
More than One Hundred Imperial and Princely Diets
Took Place Here.
Here, Before Emperor and Empire, Stood
Martin Luther[1]

Further north, near the present frontier of the Netherlands, stands the cathedral of St Victor at Xanten (*Ad Sanctos*). St Victor, a Christian martyr of the late Roman era, is taken to be the prototype of the legendary warrior Siegfried (Victory-Peace).

At the time of the Burgundians' sojourn at Worms, the Huns of Attila were still camped on the plains of the Middle Danube. They too form one of the many historical elements which, interwoven with the fantasies of myth and saga, form the basis for the most famous Germanic legends.

The *Nibelungenlied* is an epic poem of some 2,300 rhyming stanzas written in Austria in the early thirteenth century. Of 34 extant manuscripts, MS A is kept at Munich, MS B at St Gall, and MS C at Donaueschingen. All variants relate the adventures of the Burgundian court following the arrival of the invincible Prince Siegfried—dragon-slayer, guardian of the Nibelungs' treasure, and owner of the magic cape of darkness. Siegfried saves the country from a Saxon army, overpowers the Icelandic princess Brunhild, who will only submit to a man that can defeat her in athletic contest, and, after ceding Brunhild to King Gunther, wins the hand of Gunther's sister, Krimhild. The harmony of the two couples cools when Brunhild learns the secret of her defeat. Gunther's retainer Hagen discovers Siegfried's one point of weakness, kills him with a spear as he is drinking at a spring, and casts his treasure into the Rhine.[2] (See Plate 9.)

Just as the unknown author of the *Nibelungenlied* transposed these pagan tales into the courtly and Christian idiom of medieval Germany, so Richard Wagner would transpose them, embellished, into the idiom of Romantic opera in *Das Rheingold* (1869), *Die Walküre* (1870), *Siegfried* (1872), and *Götterdämmerung* (1876). The first complete performance of the Ring Cycle took place at the Festspielhaus, Bayreuth, in August 1876.

In the second part of the *Nibelungenlied*, the widowed Krimhild leaves Germany to marry the heathen Etzel (Attila). In due course, she invites her Burgundian relatives to visit her at Etzelburg/Gran (the modern Esztergöm). Her aim is to avenge her beloved Siegfried. After cutting off Hagen's head with Siegfried's faithful sword, she leads all the poem's principal personalities into a bloodbath of common hatred.

Modern literary pilgrims can trace the road of the Burgundian party from Worms to 'Hunland'. They go from the 'See of the Three Rivers' at Passau, where Krimhild's brother was bishop, to the seat of Count Rudiger at Bechlaren (Pochlärn), and on to the fortress of Melk, to the Roman gate of Traismauer, to Tulln, where Etzel awaited his bride, and to Vienna, where the seventeen-day wedding banquet was held. Yet at the end all is sorrow:

Hier hat die Mär ein Ende.
Diz ist der Nibelunge Not.

(Here the tale has its end. This is the Nibelung's downfall)

and the Alans, in Spain. The Suevi created a kingdom in the far north-west, in Galicia; the western Alans went for the valley of the Tagus.

In Britain, the departure of the legions in 410 gave a signal for the onslaught of the sea raiders. For more than a century, the Roman governors had sought to hold the forts of the 'Saxon Shore'. Now the Romano-Britons were left to their own devices. Some Roman troops may possibly have returned for a decade or two after 418; but a vain appeal for assistance was made to Aetius in 446. Soon afterwards, all regular contact between Britain and the Empire was severed. Henceforth, the Anglo-Saxon longships brought not just raiders but mercenaries and colonists. In 457 Kent was surrendered to Hengest's Jutes, a tribe that had worked its way from 'Jutland' in Denmark via Frisia. The Angles, who left a sign of their earlier abode in the district of 'Angeln' in Schleswig, took over Britain's eastern coastlands. They sailed into the Humber, founding communities which underlay the expansive kingdom of Mercia, meaning the March or 'Frontier'. The Saxons, under Aelle, first landed on the south coast, laying the foundation of the kingdom of the south Saxons (Sussex). Others—the middle Saxons (Middlesex) and the east Saxons (Essex)—moved up the valley of the Thames.

Thus began the long conquest and settlement of eastern Britain which resulted in the emergence of 'England'. For three centuries and more, hundreds of local chieftains controlled their own minuscule statelets, until by a process of merger and annexation the larger groupings emerged. The most powerful of the later Anglo-Saxon principalities, that of the West Saxons (Wessex), did not eliminate its rivals until 940—five hundred years after the first Anglo-Saxon raids. In the meantime the hard-pressed Britons struggled to stem the tide. Their victory under the semi-legendary King Arthur at Mons Badonicus c.500 served to hold the Anglo-Saxons back, and to preserve the Celts of the West. [TRISTAN]

Whilst the Germanic tribes overran the Empire's western provinces, the instigators of the cataclysm, the Huns, finally made their appearance in Pannonia. They built their tented capital on the plains of the Tisza (Theiss) in 420. In 443 they came under the rule of Attila (c.404–53). His was a name that became a byword for wanton destruction: 'The grass never grew where his horse had trod.' For several seasons this 'Scourge of God' wreaked havoc in the Empire's Danubian provinces. In 451 he rode to the north and west, collecting assorted barbarian allies, including Gepids and Burgundians. He spared Paris, protected by the prayers of St Geneviève. But on the Catalaunian Plains near Châlons, on grassland well suited to his cavalry, he met bloody defeat at the hands of a coalition formed by Aetius from Theodoric's Ostrogoths and the Salian Franks under the 'Sea-born' Merovig. 'His retreat beyond the Rhine comprised the last victory achieved in the name of the western Empire.'[6] Attila then turned on Italy. Turin, Padua, and Aquileia suffered the earlier fate of Metz. 'The succeeding generation could scarce discover the ruins of Aquileia.' At Milan, Attila was offended by a mural in the royal palace which showed the princes of Scythia prostrate before the imperial throne. He commanded a painter to reverse the roles. In 452, on the shores of Lake Bolsena, he was somehow persuaded to withdraw by the Patriarch of Rome, Leo I. Suitably enough, having retired to the Tisza with an item of female loot called Ildico, he expired during the nuptial night from a burst artery, 'suffocated by a torrent of blood . . . which regurgitated into his stomach and lungs'. The horsemen of the Hunnic horde dispersed as quickly as they had appeared. Shattered by the treacherous attack of their former allies, they were forced to cede their hold on the Pannonian station to the Gepids and the Ostrogoths. [CSABA] [EPIDEMIA]

Attila's death gave the Ostrogoths the chance to assert their independence to the full. Advancing from Pannonia, they launched into a campaign of rapine in the Eastern Empire which did not cease until Theodoric received the usual prize, together with the titles of *magister militum* and *patricius* of Italy. Unfortunately for him, another barbarian warlord was in the field. Having casually deposed the last of the Western emperors, Odoacer had won his position at the head of a mercenary army operating in Sicily, Dalmatia, and even beyond the Alps. A fight to the finish was inevitable. The end came after a three-year siege of Ravenna and Odoacer's murder by Theodoric. It was 493. The way was now open for the establishment of an Ostrogothic kingdom in Italy.

Similarly, Merovig's grandson, Hlodwig or Clovis (c.466–511), king of the Salian Franks, was able to exploit his status as a Roman *foederatus* and to multiply his dominions in the disputed province of Gaul. Starting from the old Salian capital

EPIDEMIA

BY all accounts, many of Attila's warriors were already stricken by a violent illness on the eve of their defeat by Aetius in 451. Some historians
have concluded that it was the Huns who added smallpox to Europe's pool
of diseases.[1] Others report that smallpox was alreeady raging during the
Roman plaugue of 165–80. It was certainly still killing large numbers in the
eighteenth century. It claimed 14,000 in Paris in the epidemic of 1719,
which preceded the discovery of vaccination by a couple of years. Even so,
it killed Louis XV in 1774, and possibly Joseph II in 1790.

From time immemorial, all feared the shadow of pestilence. Russian
folklore included the tale of the ghostly Pest Maiden, whom villagers
kissed at their peril. In the Book of Revelation, there was the Fourth
Horseman on his 'pale horse', 'and his name that sat on him was Death'.

For the long-term historian, as for the epidemiologist, the crucial problem is to know why certain diseases, which exist in mild form for generations, can suddenly explode with devastating virulence. Environmental
shifts, a mutant strain, or a fresh human habitat may all be contributing
factors. Smallpox, for instance, was well known to medieval Europe without ever being the worst scourge of its kind. Yet on reaching the Americas
it wreaked unparalleled havoc, virtually annihilating Aztec civilization,
decimating the native Americans, turning 20 per cent of mankind into 3
per cent, 'singlehandedly establishing and sustaining slavery'.[2] Syphilis,
'the Americans' Revenge', followed a similar career in reverse. In the
Americas it had caused minor skin irritations; in Europe it killed and disfigured millions. [**SYPHILUS**]

Malaria was exceptional. Endemic since ancient times, when it had
claimed Alexander the Great, it was never responsible for sensational epidemics. But it killed steadily and ceaselessly, especially in districts like the
Campagna marshes near Rome, where the *plasmodium* parasite could
breed in warm, stagnant water. Cumulatively, it 'caused the greatest harm
to the greatest number'.[3]

Every deadly disease has had its day, and every age its particular plague.
Leprosy reached its peak in the thirteenth century. The Black Death cut its
swathe in the fourteenth century (See Chapter VI) and several times later.
Syphilis raged during the Renaissance and Reformation, and on into the
Enlightenment. Tuberculosis reaped its crop among the Romantics, claiming Chopin, Słowacki, Keats, and countless others. Cholera was the
scourge of Europe's early industrial cities, and influenza the unlikely reaper
of the early twentieth century. AIDS, the leprosy of the late twentieth century, arrived to shake the complacency of a scientific age, and to show that
plagues were not just a curiosity of the past. [**LEPER**] [**SANITAS**]

at Tournai, Clovis defeated the last 'Roman' general of Gaul, Syagrius, before conquering the rival Riparian Franks (in modern 'Franconia'), the Alamanni, the
Burgundians, and in 507 the Visigoths of Aquitaine. Putting all the lesser Frankish
princes to death, and taking a Christian wife, Clotilda, he was baptized at Rheims,
possibly at Easter 496. The result was a huge 'Merovingian' realm stretching from
the Pyrenees to Bavaria. Clovis reputedly received a diadem from the Emperor in
Constantinople, together with the honorific title of Consul. He died in his new
capital, Paris, after a reign of thirty years. Without knowing it, he had founded
what Lavisse called 'not a nation, but a historical force'—a force which was destined to give rise both to France and to the German Empire.

In that sixth century, the barbarian conquests were consolidated despite the
brief reassertion of the Empire under Justinian (see below). The Visigothic kingdom flourished in Spain, unlike its predecessor in southern Gaul. Under
Leovigild, who made his capital at Toledo, it absorbed the Suevian realm. The
Ostrogothic kingdom, which included several of the Danubian provinces as well
as Italy, was taken over by the last of the east Germanic tribes to migrate, the
Lombards. The Lombards, or Langobardi, 'Long Beards', had spent the century
since the dispersal of Huns mastering the Gepids and the Avars beyond the
Danube. But in 568 they turned south, and established a new hegemony centred
on Pavia. Henceforth, the Italian peninsula was to be contested between the
Lombards, the Byzantines in the south, and the ever-growing power of the
Franks. The Franks, in fact, were expanding in all possible directions. They displaced a party of Saxons which had established itself on the northern coast of
Gaul. On their eastern marches they were pressing on the main body of Saxons,
and on the Thuringians. It was the Franks who contained the Avars in the
Bavarian Gap, and then sent Germanic colonists to their *Ostland* or 'Austria' on
the middle Danube. It was the resultant collapse of the Avars in the Danube basin
which paved the way for the advances of the Slavs.

The western Slavs marched across the plain, up the Elbe, and up the Danube.
The Wends or Sorbs of Lusatia, to the west of the Oder, and the Kashubs of
Pomerania are still extant. Czech tribes took over Bohemia, the Slovaks the southern slopes of the Carpathians. These were the founders of the Great Moravian
Empire which flourished in the eighth and ninth centuries. The Poles, or *Polanie*,
the 'people of the open plains' first appeared on the Warta, an eastern tributary of
the Oder. Related tribes occupied virtually the whole of the Vistula basin.

Płynie Wisła, płynie
Po polskiej krainie,
Po polskiej krainie,
I dopóki płynie
Polska nie zaginie,
Polska nie zaginie.

(Flows the Vistula, flows I Across the Polish land, I Across the Polish land, I So long as she keeps flowing, I Poland still shall stand, I Poland still shall stand.)

The eastern Slavs gradually moved north and east from the Dnieper into Baltic and Finnic territory, and into the forests of the upper Volga. Their centrifugal movements created divergences that underlay the later division between Ruthenians and Russians. If the Poles sang of the Vistula, the Russians were to sing of the Volga, which was to become their 'native mother'.

The southern Slavs invaded the Empire in the sixth century, crossing the Danube in many places. In 540 they laid siege to Constantinople. They were to slavicize Illyria, Bulgaria, Macedonia [**MAKEDON**], and most of mainland Greece. The Croats, a people first mentioned in what is now southern Poland, colonized the upper Sava and the Dalmatian coast. Another group which settled on the upper Drava became known as Slovenes. The Serbs took over the region at the confluence of the Drava, the Sava, and the Danube.

The dynamism of the migrant tribes had serious implications for all their neighbours. Where the preceding population was not overwhelmed or absorbed, it was frequently shunted into motion. In the West, the Celts were swamped in Gaul and corralled in Britain. Only the Irish were secure from invasion. A Celtic people from Ireland, the Scots, migrated to the highlands of Caledonia and, by subjugating the native Picts, laid the foundations of Gaelic Scotland. In the same period, a migration of Celts from Cornwall laid the foundations of Celtic Brittany. Elsewhere, the Celtic Britons were pushed back by the Anglo-Saxons into the fastnesses of Wales.

In the East, in one of the darkest periods of the Dark Ages, the confusion in the Danube basin was not resolved for almost three centuries. The Slavs still evaded literary sources, and their struggles with the Avars and with the Germanic outposts are not well documented. The last piece of the jigsaw did not fall into place until the irruption of the nomadic Magyars in the ninth century (see p. 296). On the Pontine steppes, a jumble of peoples passed under the hegemony of yet another tribe of Asian adventurers—the Khazars. They in their turn submitted in the early seventh century to the overlordship of a Turkic dynasty from the North Caucasus. Though Indo-European Slavs were present within the jumble, they would not begin to form the dominant element until the founding of the Kievan state in the ninth century. [**KHAZARIA**]

The effect of the migrations on the ethnic and linguistic make-up of the Peninsula was profound. They radically changed the ethnic mix of the population in several

KHAZARIA

O F all the transient realms of the European plain, none has aroused more controversy than that of the Khazars. Yet from AD c.630, when it was taken over by the Turkic dynasty of Ashihna, to 970, when it was conquered by Prince Svyatoslav of Kiev, it played a vital role in the contacts between East and West.

The administrative organization of Khazaria reflected the variety of its subject peoples. The Khazar *kagan* or khan ruled over three principal provinces, seven dependent kingdoms, and seven tributary tribes. The chief province, Kwalis, was centred on the twin cities of Amol-Atil on the Lower Volga (the site of the future Tsaritsyn). Semender on the River Terek had been the dynasty's earlier refuge after their expulsion from Turkestan. Šarkel was centred on the River Don, west of the Volga bend. It was ruled from a stone city of the same name built by ninth-century Byzantine engineers.

Of the dependent kingdoms, by far the most important was Khotzir in Crimea, the Khazars' new headquarters. It had succeeded the realm of the Goths, who in turn had conquered the ancient Hellenistic 'Kingdom of the Bosphorus'. [**CHERSONESOS**] It was ruled from Phullai, modern Planerskoe, on the coast; and it possessed a strong Jewish community active in the Black Sea trade. Other dependencies included Hun on the River Sulak (home of Attila's descendants), Onogur on the Kama, Turkoi or Levedia on the Donets (home of the future Magyars), and three divisions of the Volga Bulgars. Of the tributary tribes in the northern forest zone, three were ethnically Slavic, three Finnic, and one unidentified.

Khazaria was famed for its commerce and for its religious tolerance. It was the traditional supplier of Slav slaves to the Mediterranean market (see p. 257); and in the tenth century an overland trade route began to develop along the line of Regensburg–Vienna–Cracow–Kiev–Atil.

Muslim, Christian, Jewish, and pagan religions all flourished under their own communal judges. The Khazar army was largely drawn from Iranian Muslims from the eastern province; and in 737 the Khan himself adopted Islam. But some time soon afterwards his successors converted to Judaism and made it the state religion. This conversion, surprisingly, finds no echo in contemporary Byzantine, Arabic, or Jewish sources; but it was already known to the monk Druthmar of Aquitaine, writing at Corvey in Westphalia in 864:

For in the lands of Gog and Magog, who are a Hunnish race and call themselves Gazari, there is one tribe, a very belligerent one . . . and all of them profess the Jewish faith.[1]

During the period of Arab expansion in the seventh to ninth centuries, Khazaria generally allied itself with Byzantium against the Arabs. During the Viking era, Scandinavians opened up the Baltic–Dnieper route, mastered Kiev, and possibly took over the khanate as a whole. [**RUS'**]

Jewish historians have naturally shown immense interest in Khazaria's conversion to Judaism. Judah Halevi (1075–1141), writing in Toledo, idealized the Khazar Khan as a hero of the faith. The Karaites of Crimea called the Khazars *mamzer*, meaning 'bastard' or 'false Jews'. But the Karaite scholar Abraham Firkovich (1785–1874) claimed that the Khazars had been Karaites. Arthur Koestler, writing in the 1970s, claimed that migrant Jewish Khazars begat the main body of Ashkenazy Jewry in Central Europe.[2] The Khazar puzzle is still not fully solved.

Yet Khazaria lives on. In Greece, children do not wait at Christmas time for Santa Claus bringing gifts from Lapland. They wait for St Basil, coming from Khazaria.

countries, and in some parts introduced completely fresh ingredients. If in AD 400 the population of the Peninsula had been clearly divided between 'Romans' and 'barbarians', by 600 or 700 it was inhabited by a far more complex mix of semi-barbarized ex-Romans and semi-romanized ex-barbarians.

In Spain, for example, the romanized Celto-Iberians received a significant injection of Germanics—with important Moorish and Jewish layers to follow. In Gaul, the Gallo-Romans received a stronger but uneven Germanic overlay—heavy in the north-east, light in the south-west. In Italy, too, the latinized Celto-Italics and Greeks imbibed a strong Germanic element, that was predominant in the north. In Britain, the Romano-British population was either absorbed or displaced, leaving two distinct communities—Celtic in the west, Germanic in the east, centre, and south. Caledonia (Scotland) was divided between the Germanic lowlanders and the Celtic highlanders. In Germany, the balance between west Germanic and east Germanic tribes shifted decisively in the former's favour, since most of the latter had migrated. The Slavonic peoples took decisive control not only of the largest sector of the northern plain but also of the Balkans. Within the new Slavonic homelands, however, many non-Slavonic peoples, including the Vlachs, remained.*

Ethnic changes were inevitably reflected in language. The vulgar Latin which had been the lingua franca of the late Western Empire, was gradually broken down into a bevy of bowdlerized neo-latinate idioms—from Portuguese to Romanian. Latin *pater* drifted towards *padre* in Spanish and Italian, towards *père* in French, towards *tata* in Romanian.

---

* 'Vlach' or 'Wloch' is the old Slavonic word for Latin. It gave rise to a number of Vallachias—Old Vallachia in Serbia, Vallachia Major in Thessaly, Vallachia Minor in northen Romania, Wallachia in southern Romania, and Maurovallachia, the land of the *Negrolatini* or 'Black Vlachs' in the Dinaric Alps. *Włochy* is still the usual Polish word for 'Italy'.

The linguistic transitions were very slow. In the case of French, the vulgar Latin vernacular *romanz* of Gaul passed through three distinct phases—(eighth century), Old French (eleventh), Middle French (fourteenth)—before a recognizable variety of modern French was achieved. New grammar and new word-forms evolved as the old Latin declensions, conjugations, and inflexions were dropped. *Bonum, bonam, bonas* moved towards *bon, bonne, bonnes. Rex* became *le roi; amat* changed to *aime, regina* to *la reine.* The earliest text in 'Roman', the Strasbourg Oath, dates from 843—by which time the kings of France had stopped speaking Germanic Frankish altogether. Britain was one of several ex-Roman provinces where Latin was completely wiped out.

Greek persisted in the Eastern Empire, both as the official language and in many places, especially in Asia Minor, as the vernacular. But several areas, including the Peloponnese, were for a period wholly or partly slavicized. One should be wary of oversimplification. But the thesis advanced by the Bavarian scholar, Jakub Fallmerayer (1790–1861), in *Ueber die Entstehung der Neugriechen* (1835), merits attention. Fallmerayer's work, which caused deep trauma amidst the Greeks of his day, argued that the Greek nation of modern times was largely descended from hellenized Albanians and Slavs, 'with hardly a drop of true Greek blood in their veins'. This may have been an exaggeration; but it is less absurd than the notion that every modern Greek is a direct ethnic descendant of the inhabitants of ancient Greece. No modern European nation can lay reasonable claim to undiluted 'ethnic purity'. [**MAKEDON**]

The dispersal of the Slavs encouraged the evolution of the three main Slavonic linguistic groups, and the well-springs of a dozen Slavonic languages. (See Appendix III, p. 1233.)

By the eighth century, therefore, the ethnic settlement of the Peninsula was beginning to achieve a lasting pattern. The eighth century, indeed, was the point when important social crystallizations occurred. Yet five more major migrations had to happen before all the basic population of the future Europe was complete. One of these five later migrant groups, the Vikings, were sea-raiders (see p. 293). Two more, the Magyars and the Mongols, were nomads (see pp. 296–8). Two others, the Moors and the Turks, were warriors of a new religion (see pp. 253, 386). Europe was conceived from the most diverse elements, and her birth was painfully protracted.

The Empire: From Rome to Byzantium, 330–867

From 330 onwards, ruled from the Bosporus, the Roman Empire changed its character. The *Romanitas*, the 'Latinity', of the empire was inevitably reduced. But political priorities shifted as well: henceforth the heartland lay not in Italy but in the Balkans and in Asia Minor. The provinces which lay nearest to the emperors' concerns were not Gaul or Spain or Africa, but Egypt, Syria, even Armenia. Increasingly, the frontier to be defended at all costs lay not on the Rhine but on the lower Danube and the Pontic shore. Recognizing the shift, most historians drop the title of 'Roman Empire' in favour of 'Byzantine Empire'. The emperors and their subjects, however, continued to think of themselves as 'Romans'. Constantine had no intention of abandoning anything but a decayed capital city. The growing divergence of East and West was so slow that it was virtually imperceptible to contemporaries. For them, it was far less impressive than the sturdy strands of continuity.

What is more, there is no general consensus about the point where 'Rome' was truly supplanted by 'Byzantium'. In its origins, the split can be traced back to Octavius and Mark Antony, whose rivalry had briefly divided the Roman world for the first time. In which case the gradual emergence of Byzantium, and the supremacy of the East, might be seen as belated compensation for the tragedy of Antony and Cleopatra. Diocletian, who deliberately chose the Eastern half of the Empire for himself, has been proposed as 'the first Byzantine Emperor'. Other obvious contenders for the title would be Constantine, founder of Constantinople, Justinian, and Heraclius. At the other extreme, some historians might withhold the 'Byzantine' label until the Empire's last links with the West were severed. In which case one would be talking of the ninth century, or even of the eleventh, when the Greek Church of the East finally parted company with the Latin Church of Rome. In this view, 'Byzantium' is not the foil to the Rome of late antiquity but rather to the 'Holy Roman Empire' of the Middle Ages.

This period of transition lasted for half a millennium. In the fourth and fifth centuries, the Empire's links with the Western provinces were weakened to the point where imperial rule in the West was abandoned. The last remnants of ancient paganism were suppressed. In the sixth century there was a concerted attempt under Justinian (r. 527–65) to restore the Western connection, but it ended in failure. Then, with the influx of Bulgars and Slavs, the remnants of the Empire's Latin-speaking population were overwhelmed. Byzantium was left entirely Greek. In the seventh century, the valuable Eastern provinces were overrun by the Arabs; and the territorial base of the Empire shrank to something remarkably akin to that of the ancient Greek world prior to Alexander's conquests (see Map 5). In the eighth century, when the Arab tide was ebbing, the Empire was shaken by an amazingly protracted religious furore over icons, which was one of the sources of the schism between Eastern and Western Christianity. Protracted wars with the fearsome Bulgars were not damped down before a Bulgar khan had quaffed his wine from an emperor's skull. The Iconoclast controversy came to an end in 842–3. Relations with Bulgars reached an important turning-point in 865, when their warleader was baptized by the Patriarch of Constantinople. Five hundred years of turmoil were moving to a close. At that date, the Roman Empire stood within two years of the founding of the great Macedonian dynasty, whose emperors were to bring it to a new apogee. Over the previous five centuries, the long procession of external and internal crises had changed the political, social, religious, and cultural life of the Empire out of all recognition. By then, if not before, Byzantium had truly succeeded the Roman world in every sense.

The fifth-century collapse of the Empire's Western provinces came as the result

of long decay. It is doubtful whether the barbarian invasions did more than cata-
lyse a process which was already well advanced. Some, like Gibbon, have stressed
the decadent luxury of the ruling class. Others have stressed socio-economic factors—monetary and price inflation, over-taxation, bureaucracy, agricultural
decline, which in turn produced what Ferdinand Lot called 'a regime of castes'.
Ossification of the social strata was accompanied by 'a total transformation of
human psychology'.[7] Here above all was the classic case of imperial 'overstretch':
the Empire could not sustain the military effort indefinitely. The imperial armies
were so saturated by barbarian soldiers and ex-barbarian generals that the old distinction between Roman and non-Roman became increasingly irrelevant.

Yet the moment of truth was slow in coming. In the fourth century,
Constantine's successors were at least as alarmed by the Persians as by the western barbarians. Julian (r. 361–3), having spent many years in Gaul restoring the
Rhine garrisons, was slain in Mesopotamia. Valentinian I (r. 364–75) again divided the Empire in order to continue Julian's work in Gaul. Theodosius I
(r. 378–96), son of a general, managed the crisis caused by the Ostrogothic invasion (see p. 229), and was the last to restore imperial unity. After his death, the
division between East and West was made permanent, and the Western provinces
were allowed to drift away. Of Honorius (r. 395–423), who ruled in Milan, at first
under the regency of Stilicho the Vandal, it was said that he knew nothing of
'Roma' beyond the fact that it was the name of his pet chicken.

The last act of the Empire in the West, in 476, is instructive. A boy-emperor
with the symbolic name of Romulus Augustulus was the latest puppet to be elevated to the imperial dignity by the squabbling army factions. But a delegation of
the Roman senate, which travelled to Constantinople to obtain the usual agreement from the Eastern Emperor, did not ask for Romulus Augustulus to be
confirmed. Instead, they begged the Emperor Zeno (474–91) to accept the overlordship of the West for himself, whilst granting the title of Patrician to Odoacer,
the barbarian general who actually controlled Italy at the time. In this way the
principle of imperial rule was upheld in theory, though all practical government
was surrendered. For centuries after 476, therefore, the emperors in Constantinople were able to maintain their claim to supreme authority in the West. None
of the barbarian rulers in the ex-imperial provinces paid much attention to the
claim. But its existence may explain why any alternative source of supreme
authority was so slow to develop. [**PALAEO**]

Overall, therefore, the Empire's strategy was more to absorb the barbarian challenge than to attempt any decisive solution. The problem was too large to be
neatly solved. The emperors exacted tribute, both in money and in recognition,
from the invaders. They settled them where possible in the lands they demanded,
or acquiesced where necessary. They employed a whole gallery of barbarian generals—from Stilicho the Vandal to Odoacer of the Heruli—and recruited masses
of barbarian soldiery, which steadily subverted political life in the Western
provinces. In the end, it was largely immaterial whether the emperor gave his
blessing to a puppet Caesar elected by barbarian troops or to a barbarian king. Yet

PALAEO

IN the fourth century a form of *uncials* or 'inch-high letters' made their appearance in the writing of the late Roman Empire. They were generally smaller, rounder, and more suited to the requirements of pen than imperial forms had been. They long coexisted with the traditional Latin script which used 'square' and later 'rustic' capitals without punctuation or gaps between words. But it was the start of the long process of evolution of Latin writing which led from the uncial and half-uncial stage, through Caroline minuscule and Gothic to the humanistic italic of the Renaissance period. [**CADMUS**]

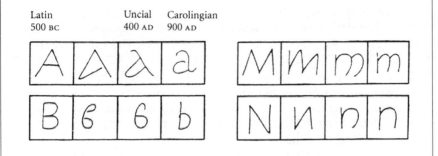

Latin 500 BC — Uncial 400 AD — Carolingian 900 AD

Palaeography, the study of ancient writing, is one of the auxiliary sciences vital to the historian's and archivist's craft. It often provides the only means for judging where, when, and by whom a document was written. Every period, every location, and every scribe reveal their own peculiarities.[1] Greek, Cyrillic, and Arabic scripts passed through similar evolutions to those of Latin. All moved away from early formal styles to the cursive forms of later times. The records of the Ottoman chancelleries, written in an eccentric Turkish variant of Arabic, have the reputation of being unusually hard to decipher. (See Appendix III, p. 1227.)

Though the invention of printing, and later of typewriters, greatly facilitated the deciphering of documents, palaeography never became redundant. Many letters and diaries continued to be written by hand. In 1990 a team of German tricksters almost convinced the world that they had found the long-lost diaries of Adolf Hitler. The palaeographical skills of the forger exceeded those of the distinguished English professor who was hired to check his work.[2]

it is important to realize that the Roman Empire was not destroyed by the barbarian invasions. It reeled under the blows and suffered great losses, both in territory and influence. But it held together for almost a thousand years after 476,
and it succeeded in reasserting itself on several notable occasions. To suggest
otherwise is simply to succumb to Western prejudice. [TEICHOS]

Justinian (r. 527–65) is mainly remembered for his codification of Roman law,
and for a determined attempt to reassert imperial rule over the lost Western
provinces. His legal reforms were certainly a lasting achievement; but from the
standpoint of the Empire as a whole his preoccupations in the West must have
seemed something of a diversion from more pressing matters. Justinian's reign
saw the Slavs appear on the Adriatic, and the Persians on the Mediterranean shore
of the Levant. Constantinople was decimated by plague, and by the strife of the
hippodrome factions, the Blues and the Greens. It was besieged by the Slavs in 540
and by the Avars in 562. Justinian caused an early scandal by marrying a so-called
dancer called Theodora, the daughter of a Cypriot manager of the Greens.
According to the *Secret History* attributed to Procopius, Theodora once regretted
'that God had not endowed her with more orifices to give more pleasure to more
people at the same time'. But she turned out to be an active and intelligent consort; it was a famous partnership. (See Appendix III, p. 1237.)

Justinian's reconquest of the West centred on the exploits of his general,
Belisarius, who set out on his first expedition to Africa in 533. His surprising success in destroying the Vandal kingdom at a stroke encouraged him to attack the
Ostrogoths in Sicily and Italy. An isolated army of 7,500 men advanced on a realm
which boasted 100,000 Germanic warriors. In 535 Belisarius took Palermo as
reigning consul, and on 9 December 536 he entered Rome at the request of its
frantic bishop. There, in 537–8, he withstood a mighty siege, where the walls of
Aurelian held off the horde. At the critical moment, the defenders broke the heads
of the Goths by hurling down the marble statues of gods and emperors ripped
from Hadrian's mausoleum. In 540 Belisarius took the Gothic capital of Ravenna.
But thirteen years of war remained. Rome was subjected to two more punishing
sieges. The occupation by Totila in 546 proved far more destructive than anything
inflicted by Alaric or Genseric. The Gothic troops breached the walls, burned the
gates, and deported the citizens. Most ominously, they smashed the arches of the
aqueducts. 'For forty days the imperial city was given up to the wolf and the owl.'[8]
Then fortunes were reversed once more. In 553 the campaign of Narses, an ageing
eunuch of the Palace, completed what Belisarius had begun: Italy was restored as
an imperial province with a governor at Ravenna; the Ostrogoths and their horde
were dispersed. In 554, the imperialists attacked Spain, driving the Visigoths into
the central plateau and re-establishing a Roman province in the south.

On the face of it, Justinian had restored the Empire to much of its former glory.
The Mediterranean, once again, was a Roman lake. Yet the glory was superficial:
'Reste une grandeur caduque, même malfaisante' (the grandeur which remained
was decrepit, even noxious).[9] Italy in particular was so ruined by Justinian's
wars, so oppressed by his governors and tax-collectors, that the inhabitants soon

TEICHOS

A N inscription on the Porta Rhegium records the reconstruction of the Land Walls of Constantinople in AD 447. A recent earthquake had seriously damaged the third line of the city's fortifications, which had been built by the Regent Artemius, thirty years earlier; and repairs and renovations were urgently required. The Huns were on the Danube frontier, and had already made one successful sortie to the Bosporus. As a result, a magnificent, multi-tiered system of defences was erected in the last years of Theodosius II, all the way from the Golden Gate to the Golden Horn. The main rampart of the Artemesian Wall was raised to a height of 100 feet above the surrounding countryside; a massive, battlemented protective wall was erected in front of it, providing a high terraced walkway; an outer esplanade guarded by a third line of battlements separated the walls from a broad, brick-lined moat. The whole was equipped with ninety-six major bastions, a host of lesser watch-towers, and a maze of traps, dams, sally-points, and false approaches. Though numerous extensions and alterations were made to the city's defences at other more vulnerable points, it was the main Theodosian Walls, the great *Teichos*, which withstood the repeated attacks of the barbarians for more than a thousand years.[1] (See Map 9.)

There is no scene more redolent of Christendom's early centuries than this great fortress of the Christian empire, magnificently impregnable against the puny attempts of all attackers. The Visigoths came and went empty-handed in 378, the Huns in 441, the Ostrogoths in 476. The Slavs tried and failed in 540, the Persians in 609–10, 617–26, and again in 781, the Avars in 625. The Arabs laid unsuccessful siege in 673–8, and 717–18, the Bulgars in 813 and 913, the Rus in 865 and 904, the Pechenegs in 1087, and the Venetians in 1203. The Crusaders broke into Constantinople in April 1204 from the seaward side (see p. 360). But the Theodosian Walls remained intact until the Ottoman siege of 1453. Their fall was to mark not only the end of the Roman Empire but the beginning of modern military history. Gunpowder seriously modified the art of fortification. (See pp. 448–50).

To stand by the Golden Gate at sunset is one of the most moving of experiences for any historian. Originally built by Theodosius I as a threefold triumphal arch beyond the city, the *Porta Aurea* was incorporated into the Walls in 417; but it continued to serve as the starting station of the imperial processional route. (It is now the *Yedi Kuleh*, the Fortress of the Seven Towers, at the entrance to Istanbul.) In the eyes of the defenders, the barbarians, like the last rays of the setting sun, always came from the West.

regretted the restoration. The Patriarch of Rome, resentful of interference in his ecclesiastical freedom, was driven to think of permanent separation. What is more, with the destruction of the Gothic horde, Italy had lost its defences. It fell an easy prey to the next wave of invaders—the Lombards. Apart from the lonely exarchate of Ravenna, the only parts to remain in imperial hands were in the south and in Sicily. Meanwhile all sorts of other enemies were looming on the horizon. In the fifth, sixth, and seventh centuries Constantinople was repeatedly attacked. Huns, Ostrogoths, Avars, Slavs, Persians, and Arabs all made their bid for the ultimate prize. The Huns under Attila had ridden for the Bosporus on their outward journey. They reached the walls of Constantinople in 441. The Ostrogoths under Theodoric arrived after their victory at Adrianople. They reached the walls in 476.

Seen from Constantinople, the Slavs must have raised excitements like the Celtic and Germanic tribes had once raised in Rome. Though less well reported, their crossing of the Danube in 551 must have resembled the earlier surge of the Germanics across the Rhine. The impact was certainly similar. Whole provinces of the Empire—Illyria, Dalmatia, Macedonia, and Thrace—were turned into one vast *Sclavinia* or 'Slavdom'. They so overwhelmed the Latin-speaking population that only small pockets were left—as Daco-Romans (Romanians) north of the Danube, or as scattered communities of 'Vlachs' to the south. They provided the main ethnic component of three later principalities carved out of former imperial territory—Croatia, Serbia, and greater Bulgaria. Sailing on primitive one-log boats, they even penetrated the Greek islands. They reached the walls of Constantinople in 540.

Persia had seen a major revival of its fortunes since the days of Alexander's successors. Under the Sassanid dynasty, the eastern frontiers of Rome were ceaselessly contested. Under Ardashir I (r. 227–41) and again under the two Khosrus (also known as Chosroes)—Khosru I (r. 531–79) and Khosru II (r. 590–628), Persian resurgence reached the point where the latter could claim possession of the Mediterranean in a 'ceremony of the sea' performed near Antioch. They reached the walls in 609–10 and again in 625–6. The Avars made for the Bosporus, having been driven down the Danube by the Franks. They joined the Persians at the walls in 625. The Arabs poured out of the east like a desert sandstorm (see p. 253). They reached the walls in 673, and again in 717. [TEICHOS]

Heraclius (575–641) is the best-backed candidate for the title of 'first of the Byzantines'. He had none of Justinian's Western interests, and he gave the state a distinctly oriental flavour. He spent most of his reign dealing with one great enemy, only to find another more formidable to hand. In 617 the Persian host of Chosroes II marched to the Hellespont and called on Constantinople to surrender. They had already captured Damascus and Jerusalem (614), where they had seized the True Cross; and by occupying Egypt they had cut off the Empire's corn dole—another relic of Roman times. It was a confrontation between Europe and Asia worthy of Herodotus:

Chosroes, greatest of Gods, and master of the earth, to Heraclius, his vile and insensate slave. Why do you still . . . call yourself a king? But I will pardon your faults if you submit . . . Do not deceive yourself with vain hope in that Christ, who was not able to save himself from the Jews, who killed him by nailing him to a cross. Even if you take refuge in the depths of the sea, I will stretch out my hand and take you . . .[10]

At which point the Avars rode in to landward and, having ambushed the Emperor before the walls, had to be bought off.

Yet in 622 Heraclius was able to launch a series of masterful campaigns that have been called the 'first crusade'. A great Christian army marched to Jerusalem. Leaving Constantinople to the Perso-Avar siege, he led his troops into the heart of Persia, plundered the palace of Chosroes at Dastager, near Ctesiphon, and, as the crowning clause of the Peace in 628, recovered the True Cross. He was hailed in Constantinople as 'the new Scipio'. If he had died then, he would have gone down in history as the greatest Roman general since Caesar.

In fact, Heraclius had softened up both the Roman and the Persian empires for the Muslim onslaught. When the armies of Islam appeared in the 630s, he could do nothing to hold them. Jerusalem, saved from the Persians, fell to the Arabs in 638. Three years later, with Heraclius on his death bed, the Empire's wealthiest province in Egypt was on the point of falling. The first round in Byzantium's 800-year war with Islam had been lost. None the less, all the main outlines of Byzantine identity were present. The Empire's territory was reduced to its Greek heartland. The Greek language was the sole vehicle of culture. And the Patriarch of Constantinople, after the loss of his colleagues in Jerusalem, Antioch, and Alexandria, was left as the unchallenged leader of the Greek Church. The initial conflict with the Arabs raged for decades. There were two more great sieges of Constantinople, each broken by the supremacy of the imperial fleet and the 'Greek fire'. There were numberless skirmishes and rearguard actions in the islands and the provinces. Roman Armenia was lost in 636, Cyprus in 643, Rhodes in 655, Carthage in 698. The Saracen wars of Justinian II (r. 685–95 and 705–11) reflected the general chaos of the age. After one battle, he ordered his guards to slaughter the only unit of his troops who had not deserted, to prevent them from deserting in the next. After the fall of Rhodes, the remains of the fallen Colossus were sold to a Jewish dealer for scrap. It was a sign of the times.

Iconoclasm—'image-breaking'—was a movement which gripped the Empire in the eighth and early ninth centuries, and which in some respects was a sympathetic reaction to the puritanical values of Islam. At one level it involved a purely religious controversy over the place of images in Christian worship. The Iconoclasts followed the Muslim example in banning all representational art, accusing their opponents of iconoduly—'idolatry'. An edict of Leo I the Isaurian in 726 decreed that the crucifix be everywhere replaced by a plain Cross. And in due course the order was given for all images of the saints, and especially of the Virgin Mary, to be whitewashed. At another level, however, a deep social and political struggle was in progress. By attacking iconodulous monasteries and sequestrating their considerable properties, the Iconoclast emperors were strengthening the hold of the State over the Church. Equally, they could be seen to be asserting Constantinople's control over wayward provinces, especially in Europe. The chief Iconoclast, Constantine Copronymos (r. 740–75), 'hammer of the monks', was confirmed in his position in 754 by the packed Council of Constantinople, which was roundly anathematized by Rome. At one point all the monks and nuns of Thrace were assembled, and given the choice between instant marriage or exile in Cyprus. The Emperor survived open rebellion, engaging himself in victorious campaigns in Mesopotamia and in public works. [IKON]

The war of the images, however, was far from finished. Both the Empress Irena (r. 797–802) and Theodora, wife of Theophilus (r. 829–42), were ardent iconodules. Theodora's son, Michael III (r. 842–67), among many scandalous acts, exhumed and burned the body of Constantine Copronymos. Iconoclasm was proscribed. Religious peace had to await the murder of Michael, and the emergence of the Macedonian dynasty in 867. By that time, much damage had been done. Iconoclasm must be seen as one of the key factors which disrupted the bond between the Patriarchs of Constantinople and Rome, and which drove the Latin Church into the arms of the Franks.

In that same era, the Bulgars rose to a position of great power in the Balkans. Their ancestral chieftain, Kourat, had been an ally of Heraclius; and some time later they were settled on the Black Sea coast south of the Danube. In 717–18 they helped the Empire repel the Arab siege. They conquered seven Slav tribes of the locality, only to adopt the language and customs of the conquered. In the ninth century the warlike Krum declared war on the Empire and on Christianity. It was he, having slain the Emperor Nicephorus in 811, who toasted his victory in the emperor's skull. He forced Byzantium to build the 'Great Fence'—a new Roman *limes*. His successor, Boris, though baptized in Constantinople, was balancing his loyalties between the Greek and the Roman Churches. (See Appendix III, p. 1245.)

Byzantine civilization, as established by the ninth century, possessed several inimitable features which set it apart both from contemporary states in the West and from the earlier Roman Empire. The state and the church were fused into one indivisible whole. The Emperor, the *autokrator*, and the Patriarch were seen as the secular and the ecclesiastical pillars of divine authority. The Empire defended the Orthodox Church, and the Church praised the Empire. This 'Caesaropapism' had no equal in the West, where secular rule and papal authority had never been joined. [TAXIS]

The imperial court was the hub of a vast centralized administration run by an army of bureaucrats. Heraclius had taken the Persian title of *Basileus*, and the despotic nature of the state machine was self-evident in its oriental ceremonies. 'Byzantium' became a byword for total subservience, secretiveness, and intrigue. The shell of some of the old Roman institutions was retained but was completely subordinated. The senate was an assembly of office-holders, organized in a strict table of ranks. The chief ministers of state under the *eparchos* (prefect), *symponus* (chancellor), and *logothete* (chief justice) were offset by the chief officers of the

IKON

RELIGIOUS icons form the most enduring genre of European Art. But they were never painted primarily as artistic works. They are aids to devotion. They are 'gates of mystery', 'doors of perception' into the spiritual world beyond the images. Their appreciation depends on the theological knowledge and the emotional receptiveness of the viewer.[1] The Byzantine Empire long protected the leading centres, though the medieval West later produced important schools of its own.

The posture demanded from the venerator of icons is summed up by the Greek word *hesychia* or 'watchful calm'. It requires patience, detachment, humility, and prayerful concentration. The *Philokalia*, a 5th-century Byzantine treatise and anthology of texts on 'the Love of the Beautiful', likens it to a cat transfixed by the task of catching a mouse.

Legend holds that St Luke was the first icon-painter, his subject the Virgin and Child. (See Plate 22.) Together with 'Christus Pantokrator', the Virgin always headed the repertoire. She appeared in three standard positions—the *eleus*, where She holds the Child to her face; the *odititria*, where She holds the Child on her outstretched arm; and the *orakta*, where her arms are raised and the Child is in her womb.[2]

During the long *Iconomachia*, the 'War of the Icons', St John Damascene (675–749) was the greatest of the Iconophiles or 'Iconodules', i.e. 'slaves of the Icon'. Yet he stressed the distinction between the veneration of icons and the more profound adoration of God which icons facilitate. He also defined the three-level theological theory of images. Christ became Man; Man was made in the image of God; icons, therefore, were true images of the Godhead and the Saints.

Icons have always held a central place in Orthodox churches. The *iconostasis* or 'icon screen' separates the congregation from the church's sanctuary, reserved for the clergy. It traditionally carried four rows of icons which represent, respectively, the company of saints at the top, the twelve feasts of the Church, the Twelve Apostles, and the twelve prophets. In the centre, the double doors are covered by six panels representing the Archangel Gabriel, the Mother of God, and the Four Evangelists. In Greece, they are 'The Gates of Beauty', in Russia 'the Imperial Gates'. They are surmounted by the three larger icons of God in Judgement, the Trinity, and the Crucifixion. During an Orthodox service, an icon is often paraded through the Church to be kissed by the faithful.

Icons are painted on portable wooden boards. The painters use pure egg tempera colours on a white or gilded surface. Stylized postures, gestures, and faces convey the requisite air of reverence.[3] The disregard for perspective is characteristic. [FLAGELLATIO]

Orthodox icon-painting passed through several distinct periods. The first 'Golden Age' ended with the Iconoclast controversy. Few specimens survive. The second period ended with the Latin conquest of Byzantium in 1204. The late Byzantine period saw the growth of national schools in Bulgaria, Serbia, and Russia. Novgorod, Belarus, and Pskov all possessed their own traditions until the latterday Russian Orthodox Church imposed an obligatory Muscovite style. Since then, Orthodox iconography has been remarkably insulated from developments in Catholic art. None the less, some important cross-fertilization did take place. A unique 'composite Veneto-Byzantine style' emerged in Crete. A similar blend of Catholic and Orthodox imagery can be observed in Ukrainian Uniate Art.⁴ [**GRECO**]

Despite the Church Schism (see pp. 328–32), Orthodox icons continued to be highly valued in the West. All the famous 'Black Madonnas' of Catholic Europe derive from Byzantine sources. [**MADONNA**] So, too, does the 'Holy Face' of Laon in Picardy, another extraordinary black icon, this time of Christ. Strongly reminiscent of 'The Shroud of Turin', the *Sainte-Face* is classed as a *mandylion*, that is, an image produced without human hands. Though painted on pineboards, it bears an incongruous Slavonic inscription—OBRAS' GOSPODEN NAUBRUS' (The Image of Our Lord on Cloth), probably of Serbian origin. It could be a copy of the Holy Shroud once displayed in Byzantium. At all events, it was obtained by Jacques de Troyes, archdeacon of Laon and the future Pope Urban IV, from 'certain pious men' at the Serbian monastery in Bari in southern Italy. According to a surviving letter dated 3 July 1249, the archdeacon sent it as a gift to his sister Sibylle, abbess of the Cistercian convent of Montreuil, whence it duly found its way to the Cathedral at Laon.⁵

Icons are honoured in all devout Orthodox households. Maxim Gorky recalled his grandparents' house in Nizhny Novgorod in the 1870s:

When [my Grandmother] talked about God, her face regained its youth. . . . I took the heavy locks of her hair in my hands, and wound them round my neck. 'Man can't see God,' she said 'if he did, he'd go blind. Only the Saints can look him full in the face.' To see her wipe the dust from the icons and clean the chasubles was very interesting. . . . She would nimbly pick an icon up, smile at it, and say with great feeling 'What a lovely face!' Then she would cross herself, and kiss the icon.⁶

court, all eunuchs, under the *Paracomoenus* (high chamberlain). By castrating its leading courtiers, the Empire protected itself neatly from the possibility of hereditary power in the palace, as often happened in the West. Military defence was divided between a central imperial reserve and guard of foreign mercenaries, commanded by the *domestikos*, and a system of *themes* or 'military regions', each commanded by its *strategos*.

TAXIS

IN September 641 Constans II was crowned by the Patriarch of Constantinople in the ambo of St Sophia, 'the Great Church'. The old Roman practice of acclaiming a new emperor in the Hippodrome was abandoned. The most important politico-religious ceremony in the Byzantine repertoire was finding its final form. Henceforth a diadem was laid on the Emperor's head, instead of the traditional torque round his neck. Largesse was distributed; coins were struck. Co-emperors were crowned by emperors, empresses by their husbands. Conventional iconographic representations of the ceremony showed the emperors being crowned by Christ.

Political ritual played a central role in Byzantine life. Its aim was to reinforce the ideal of *taxis*, the changeless, harmonious, and hierarchical 'order of things'. Elaborate spectacles were designed with immense concern for symbolic detail. Processions and public parades were organized on the slightest pretext, above all on Christian feast days. Imperial acclamations were accompanied by the chanting of Biblical texts and political slogans, by the declamation of poems and panegyrics, and by mighty shouts, which contrasted with the total silence that the Emperor's presence otherwise required. Imperial bride-shows, weddings, and funerals were orchestrated with suitable shows of joy or lamentation. Imperial audiences were meticulously graded according to the status of the visitor. The exact distance between the throne and the prostrations of the visitor was prescribed in advance. The imperial *Adventus* or 'arrival' demanded calibration of the rank of the delegates sent out to meet him, the site and form of the greeting, the route into the city, the choice of church for the thanksgiving service, and the menu for the banquet. The imperial *Profectio* or 'departure', especially for battle, was marked by the distribution of alms, by the veneration of the Standard of the True Cross, and by the consecration of the army and the fleet. The *Thriambus* or 'Imperial Triumph', as inherited from Rome, involved displays of troops, captives, and booty, games and races in the Circus and Hippodrome, and the *trachelismos* or ritual trampling of the defeated enemy or usurper. The promotions of high officials were staged in a manner that left no doubt of the source of their success.

On all occasions, great attention was paid to clothing, to the insignia of office, to colour, and to gesture. Robing and disrobing ceremonies opened and closed all processions. The imperial crown, orb, sceptre, and *akakia*, the 'pouch of dust' symbolizing mortality, were always given prominence. The wearing of the purple was reserved for the Emperor and, in iconography, for Christ and the Virgin Mary. Byzantine body language stressed the ideal of *agalma* or 'statuesque calm'.[1]

The most complete compendium of Byzantine ritual is to be found in the tenth-century manuscript *De Ceremoniis aulae byzantinae* or 'The Book of Ceremonies of the Byzantine Court'.[2] It contains 153 chapters or dossiers of instructions relating to practices and procedures over 600 years. It prescribes everything from the rules of dance and address to the length of the Emperor's haircut.[3] Imperial ceremonial was imitated and adapted by Patriarchs, by provincial administrators, by generals, by bishops, and eventually by rulers throughout the Christian world. In time, it supplied the basis for all sorts of monarchical and ecclesiastical symbolism far beyond the Empire. Charlemagne, for example, copied much from Byzantium, just as other Western sovereigns copied much from Charlemagne.[3] [**KRAL**]

Not all, however, was one-way traffic. The practice of raising the Emperor aloft on the shields of his troops was borrowed from the Germanic tribes. It was first used by Julian in Paris in 361, and lasted, with intervals until the eighth century. The ceremony of *chrisma*, 'anointment with holy oil', seems to have been first adopted by the Franks and introduced to Constantinople by Crusaders in the thirteenth century.[4] By that time, the christianization of monarchical ritual in Europe was universal.

Byzantium, however, was primarily a naval power. Its navy of 300 biremes, armed with battering rams and the 'Greek fire', could hold its own against all comers. Despite the great battle with the Arabs off Phoenix in Lycia in 655, Byzantine sea-power continued to dominate the Aegean and the Black Sea.

The Byzantine state practised unremitting paternalism in social and economic affairs. Trade was controlled by state officials, who exacted a straight 10 per cent tax on all exports and imports. State regulations governed all aspects of guild and industrial life. State factories, such as the *gynaceum*, the women's silk-works, guaranteed full employment within the walls. The imperial gold coinage—1 *nomisma* = 12 *milliaressia* = 144 *pholes*—supplied the main international currency of the East. Such was the abundance of the state-run fisheries in the Black Sea that the workers of Constantinople regularly ate caviar.

Under its mantle of Greek culture, Byzantium sheltered a multinational community of the most diverse ethnic origins. Imperial brides could be Khazars, Franks, Rus. The population was Graeco-Slav in the Balkans, post-hellenic and Armenian in the Asian provinces. Beyond the serf villages of the countryside, Byzantine society was highly educated and refined. There was provision for church schools, state universities, academies of law, and for female education. Devotional literature predominated. But the tenth-century *Digenis Akritas* has been described as 'the most splendid *chanson de geste* ever written', and Byzantine historians from Procopius to Anna Porphyrogeneta (1083–1154) as 'the finest school . . . between Ancient Rome and modern Europe'. Byzantine art and architecture developed absolutely inimitable styles. Despite or perhaps because of the iconoclastic restraints, the Byzantine icon made a lasting contribution to European art. Byzantium remained civilized, while most of the countries of the West were, in terms of formal culture, struggling in outer darkness.[11]

The Rise of Islam, 622–778

On 20 September 622 an obscure Arab mystic called Muhammad reached safety in the city of Medina. He had been driven from his native Mecca. He asked that a temple be built on the spot where his anxious disciples had greeted him. Thus, on Day One of Year One of the new religion, the first Muhammadan mosque was erected.

For more than a decade, the former camel-driver had preached his radical ideas without success, having received a vision of his destiny from the archangel Gabriel in a cave on Mount Hira. 'Muhammad, in truth, in real truth, thou art Prophet of the Lord.' Later, after this first Night of Destiny, he had experienced another mystical vision, the Night Journey to Heaven. Riding on a magical steed, he was transported to Solomon's temple in Jerusalem, and thence through the spheres of the sky to the threshold of the Unseen Infinite. In 624 Muhammad armed 300 of his followers and routed an army sent to suppress them. In 628 he rode unopposed into Mecca on his favourite camel, at the head of 10,000 faithful. He struck down the heathen idols in the shrine of the Kaaba, and transformed it into the holiest shrine of his own following. After four more years of teaching at Medina, where the main body of the Prophet's wisdom was recorded for the Holy Book, the *Koran*, he set out once more on the Farewell Pilgrimage to Mecca. In the Valley of Arafat he delivered his last message:

Listen to my words, my people, for in the year to come I shall not be with you . . . Hold your goods, your honour and your lives as sacred . . . until the day you return to God. Aid the poor and clothe them . . . Remember that one day you will appear before the Almighty and that He will ask you the reason for your actions . . . It is true that you have certain rights with regard to your women, but they also have rights with regard to you. Treat them well, for they are your support . . . I have accomplished my mission, and I am leaving you a guide in the shape of the Lord's Book and the example of His Messenger . . . You will not fail if you follow this guide.

As he fell to the ground, God spoke:

This day have I perfected for you your religion, and completed my Favour unto you, and chosen for you as your religion—Islam.[12]

Back in Medina, the Angel of Death entered the Prophet's chamber, and the Prophet said, 'Oh Death, execute your orders'. It was, according to the Christian calendar, 7 June 632.

The desert land of Arabia forms a stepping-stone between the mainlands of Africa and Asia. It had always maintained a fierce independence from the surrounding empires. It faced Egypt and Abyssinia to the west, Mesopotamia and Persia to the north, and India to the east. Notwithstanding its arid wastes and bedouin tribes, it participated in all the great civilizations of the region. The Kaaba at Mecca marked the spot where Adam came after his expulsion from the Garden of Eden and where Abraham rebuilt the sacred shrine. Mecca itself was a wealthy staging-post on the caravan route joining the Mediterranean with East Africa and India. In the early seventh century it was in close contact with the Roman Empire in Egypt and with the rival Sassanid Empire of Persia. It was an unexpected source for a new world religion; but it had many advantages as a secure base for Islam's propagation.

Islam, meaning 'submission', was a universal religion from the start. Although it has always clung to Arabic as the sacred language of the Koran, it appeals to all nations, to all classes, and to both sexes. One of the most basic precepts is that all Muslims are brothers and sisters. In his lifetime Muhammad denounced the economic privileges of the ruling élite, the subordination of women, and the 'blood laws' of the semitic tribes. His call for social, economic, and political equality threatened the foundations of traditional societies. His insistence on the rights of the oppressed and of women, and on the duty of charity and compassion, spelled liberation for the masses. Here was a revolutionary creed, whose almost instantaneous military power derived from the fervent devotion of the faithful. It enjoined that soldiers were the equal of their generals, subjects of their rulers, wives of their husbands. 'Better justice without religion than the tyranny of a devout ruler.' Like Christianity, it professed ideals which often outstripped the practices of its adherents; but the force and purity of those ideals is manifest. 'In the name of Allah, the all-Merciful, the Compassionate', it spread and spread, like wildfire through the deadwood of a *wadi*.

Islam is said to rest on five pillars. The first, the confession of faith, consists of reciting the formula: 'Lā ilāha illā llāh, Muḥammadu 'rasūlu llāh' (There is no God but Allah, and Muhammad is his Messenger). Whoever says these words before witnesses becomes a Muslim. The second, ritual prayer requires the faithful to wash and to touch the ground with their heads turned towards Mecca at daybreak, noon, sunset, and evening. The third, called *Zakat*, involves giving alms to the poor. The fourth is fasting. Every sane and healthy Muslim adult must refrain from food, drink, and sexual intercourse from dawn to dusk throughout the month of Ramadan. The fifth, the *Hadj* obliges every Muslim to make the pilgrimage to Mecca at least once in his or her lifetime. Above all, the loyal Muslim is enjoined to respect the teachings of the Koran, whose 114 *suras* or chapters provide a source of law, a manual of science and philosophy, a collection of myths and stories, and an ethical textbook.

The caliphs, that is 'the successors' of the Prophet, quickly turned a united Arabia into the springboard for a theocratic world-empire. In their day they commanded unrivalled power, and wealth beyond tally, inspiring science, literature, and arts. Under Abu Bakr (r. 632–4), Omar (r. 634–44), and Othman (r. 644–56), their armies conquered Syria, Palestine, Persia, and Egypt in lightning succession.

A fleet was constructed to protect Alexandria, and the Arabs soon became the leading sea-power of the Mediterranean. Under Ali (r. 656–61), a cousin and son-in-law of the Prophet, civil and religious dissension broke out. But under the Omayyad dynasty unity was restored. Mo'awiya (r. 661–80) established the capital in Damascus. Yazid I (r. 680–3) defeated Ali's rebellious son Hussein—the seminal event in the history of the Shi'ite sect. Abdulmalik (r. 685–705) suppressed an anti-Caliph in Mecca. Walid I (r. 705–15) saw the zenith of Omayyad power, before their long rivalry with the Abbasid dynasty ended in the bloodbath on the Zab in 750. Thereafter, under Al-Mansur ('The Victorious', r. 754–75) the Abbasids launched a 500-year reign. For a time, their capital in Baghdad was the centre of the world.

The transfer of Jerusalem from Christian to Muslim hands was an event of immense consequence. The city was, and is, sacred to all three monotheistic religions. But in the centuries since the Roman expulsion of the Jews, the Christians had guarded the Holy Places for themselves:

On a February day in the year AD 638, the Caliph Omar entered Jerusalem riding on a white camel. He was dressed in worn, filthy robes, and the army that followed him was rough and unkempt; but its discipline was perfect. At his side rode the Patriarch Sophronius as chief magistrate of the surrendered city. Omar rode straight to the site of the Temple of Solomon, whence his friend Mahomet had ascended into Heaven. Watching him stand there, the Patriarch remembered the words of Christ and murmured through his tears: 'Behold the abomination of desolation, spoken of by Daniel the prophet.'[13]

Henceforth the Holy City was to be held by Islamic authorities. The Patriarch became a hostage to fortune. Christian pilgrims could not easily reach their goal, and chose increasingly to visit Rome instead. Christianity's centre of gravity shifted dramatically westwards.

In that century following the Prophet's death, the armies of Islam marched on relentlessly. Byzantium was unsuccessfully besieged on two occasions, in 673–8 and 717–18. But Kabul, Bokhara, and Samarkand were captured in the East, Carthage and Tangier in the west. In 711 the crossing of the Pillars of Hercules by Al-Tariq—henceforth called Jebel al-Tariq, or Gibraltar—brought the Muslims into Europe, overwhelming Visigothic Spain and breaching the Pyrenees. In 732, on the centenary of Muhammad's death, they reached Tours on the Loire, a couple of days' ride from Paris, in the heart of the Frankish kingdom.

As a result of these far-flung conquests, autonomous Islamic states, paying no more than nominal service to the distant Caliphs, emerged in Spain, in Morocco, in Tunisia, in Egypt, in Persia, and in Transoxania. Islam progressed as far in one century as Christianity in seven. In Iberia the Muslim conquerors remembered their history and called the country *El-Andalus*, the 'Land of the Vandals', creating many new principalities. The emirate of Cordova, founded shortly after Al-Tariq's arrival, established the most durable Muslim presence on the European continent. Together with its successors, the Almoravid empire and the emirate of Granada, it was to last for nearly eight centuries. At its height under Abd al-Rahman (r. 912–61), it covered the greater part of the Iberian peninsula, and claimed the caliphate of all Islam. It brought civilization of the highest order, and a major demographic influx of Arabs, Moors, Berbers, and Jews. There were repeated injections of North Africans into Spain from the eighth to the twelfth centuries. [MEZQUITA]

From that point on, Islam has had a permanent presence in Europe. First in the south-west, in Iberia, and later in the south-east, in the Balkan and Black Sea regions (see Chapter VII). The interaction of Christians and Muslims has provided one of the most enduring features of Europe's political and cultural life. From the eighth century onwards there has never been a day when the *adhan*, the call of the muezzin, could not be heard morning and evening, summoning the faithful to prayer:

اذان کا بیان

Allāhu akbar
ašhadu ʾan lā ilāha illā llāh
ašhadu anna Muḥammadu ʾrasūlu ʾllāh
ʿalā ʾl-salāh
hayyā ʿalā ʾl-falāḥ
Allāhu akbar
ašhadu ʿan lā ilāha illā llāh

اَللّٰهُ اَکْبَرُ اَللّٰهُ اَکْبَرُ اَللّٰهُ اَکْبَرُ
اَللّٰهُ اَکْبَرُ اَشْهَدُ اَنْ لَّا اِلٰهَ اِلَّا
اللّٰهُ اَشْهَدُ اَنْ لَّا اِلٰهَ اِلَّا اللّٰهُ اَشْهَدُ
اَنْ مُحَمَّدًا رَّسُوْلُ اللّٰهِ اَشْهَدُ اَنْ
مُحَمَّدًا رَّسُوْلُ اللّٰهِ حَیَّ عَلَی الصَّلٰوةِ
حَیَّ عَلَی الصَّلٰوةِ حَیَّ عَلَی الْفَلَاحِ
حَیَّ عَلَی الْفَلَاحِ اللّٰهُ اَکْبَرُ اللّٰهُ
اَکْبَرُ لَآ اِلٰهَ اِلَّا اللّٰهُ

(God is most great | I testify that there is no god but God | I testify that Muhammad is the prophet of God | To prayer, | Come on, to salvation! | God is most great | I testify that there is no god but God.)[14]

At the dawn call, an extra summons is inserted after the fourth formula, *al-salat khair min al-nawm*, 'Prayer is better than sleep'. All Muslims who hear the call must repeat its words, except after the fourth and fifth formulas, when they recite: 'There is no power nor strength but in Allah', and 'Thou hast spoken truthfully and righteously'. Every adult and healthy Muslim is obliged to perform the *Salat*, or 'ritual prostrations', five times each day.

Meanwhile, with the Arabs on the Loire, the Franks steeled themselves to repel the Muslim advance. Charles Martel (*c.*688–741), mayor of the Merovingian palace, gathered an army which stemmed the tide. The Battle of Poitiers in 732 may well have been exaggerated by Christian apologists: the Arabs may have been obliged to retreat through over-extended lines of communication. They were, after all, more than 1,000 miles out from Gibraltar. But it inspired some magnificent passages:

The repetition of an equal space would have carried the Saracens to the confines of Poland and the highlands of Scotland; the Rhine is not more impassable than the Nile or the Euphrates, and the Arabian fleet might have sailed without a naval combat into the mouth of the Thames. Perhaps the interpretation of the Koran would now be taught in the schools of Oxford, and her pulpits might demonstrate to a circumcised people the sanctity and truth of the revelation of Mohammed.[15]

Thenceforth, in the West, the Muslims were to be held on the line of the Pyrenees. Muslims and Franks were to contest the mountain passes for generations. One such encounter at the Pass of Roncevaux gave rise to the most famous of medieval legends, as celebrated in the *chansons de geste*. Two Frankish knights, variously known as Roland and Oliver or Orlando and Rinaldo, are hard-pressed by the Muslim army as they try to withdraw their forces to safety on the northern side. Oliver urges his companion to sound the signal horn to bring up reinforcements. Roland, more valiant than wise, fails to comply until the battle is already lost. When he finally blows the horn, bursting the veins in his head, it is heard all over Francia. Roland, swooning on his horse, is struck by mistake in the mêlée by the blinded Oliver:

> 'Sir cumpain, faites le vos de gred?
> Ja est co Rollant, ki tant vos soelt amer!
> Par nule guise ne m'aviez desfiet!'
> Dist Oliver: 'Or vos oi jo parler.
> Je ne vos vei, veied vus Damnedeu!
> Ferut vos ai, car le me pardunez!'
> Rollant respunt: 'Jo n'ai nient de mel.
> Jol vos pardains ici e devant Deu.'
> A icel mot l'un a l'altre ad clinet.
> Par tel amur as les vus desevred.

('Companion, Sir, did you intend this stroke? | For I am Roland who loves you so dear, | And you have not defied or challenged me.' | Oliver said: 'Now I can hear you speak | But see you not; God keep you in his sight! | I have struck you? Forgive me then I beg!' | Roland replies: 'I have come to no harm. | You have my pardon here and before God.' | At this, each bows towards the other's breast. | See with what love they to their parting come!)[16]

'Alas, sweet Francia, today you will be shorn of your good vassals.'

In the East, the Christian line was held by the Byzantine forces. But the Muslim presence was felt deep into the Slavonic hinterland. The Muslim world had a growing appetite for slaves, and raw-boned Slavs were a favourite commodity. Jewish traders and Vikings acted as the middlemen and the carriers, especially through Crimea [**KHAZARIA**] [**RUS'**], but later in the Baltic and Central Europe

MEZQUITA

NO building in Europe better illustrates the cycle of civilizations than the Mezquita Aljama, now the cathedral church in Cordoba. Its oldest part dates from the reign of Ab-der-Rahman I (r. 755–88). As a treasure-house of Hispano-Islamic art, it ranks with the Alcazar in Seville or the fabled palace of Alhambra at Granada. But its originality lies in the use of materials taken from the demolished Latin-Byzantine Basilica of St Vincent which stood until 741 on the same site, and which had once been shared by Christian and Moslem congregations. What is more, both mosque and basilica rested on the foundations of a great Roman temple, which in its turn had replaced a Greek or possibly a Phoenician edifice. Only St Sofia in Istanbul can match such varied connections.

The proportions of the Mezquita befit a city which outgrew medieval Rome many times over. Together with its central Orange-Tree Courtyard, it covers an area of 130 m. × 180 m., surrounded by walls and decorated battlements. Most impressive, however, are the many features which combine Islamic and Christian elements. The great nave is filled with a forest of multicoloured marble columns supporting two layers of arches. The columns, topped by variegated capitals, came from the old basilica. The lower, 'horseshoe' arches are made from alternating segments of white limestone and red brick. The upper layer of round arches is pure Roman. The main northern door is covered with metal plates at the centre of which the word DEUS alternates with AL-MULK LILAH ('The empire and power are God's alone'). The exquisite Dove's Door has an ornate Arabian arch embellished by a medieval ogive surround. The *miharab* or 'niche of orientation', indicating the direction of Mecca, was built by Syrian architects, who duly pointed it to the south. It takes the form of a small octagonal room under a single conchshell ceiling. It is entered by an archway in polychrome mosaic and preceded by a vestibule under three Byzantine cupolas. Persian-style cufic inscriptions abound, even in sections such as the Royal Chapel, which was refurbished with gothic ornament and feudal heraldry in the fourteenth century. Christian Baroque inspired the altar and entablature within the mosque, and the Chapel of the Incas.[1]

A few sites in Spain, like the Mezquita of Cordoba or the old city of Toledo, do convey a strong sense of continuity. Modern tourists love to be told that Muslim Spain introduced Europeans to oranges, lemons, spinach, asparagus, aubergines, artichokes, pasta, and toothpaste, together with mathematics, Greek philosophy, and paper. [**XATIVAH**]

But the fact is that the continuities are few. Muslim civilization in Spain was not just superseded; wherever possible it was eradicated (see p. 345). Visitors might get a truer sense of history if they visit the lonely Muslim castle of Trujillo in Extremadura or the deserted walled city of Vascos in

Castille. In Cordoba, one should proceed from the Mezquita to the palace of Madinat al-Zahra (Medina Azahara) outside the city. It was once the residence of a caliph who could contact Egypt within twenty-four hours along a network of sun-mirror stations, and who required foreign ambassadors to approach his throne-room under a canopy three miles long and supported by a double row of his Berber soldiers. It once housed a population of 20,000 including a harem of 6,000. Damaged by the Berber revolt in 1010, its ruins were not rediscovered by archaeologists until 1911.[2]

When Spaniards shout 'Olé', many do not care to remember that they are voicing an invocation to Allah.

[DIRHAM]. Such was the association of Slavs with the slave-trade that the two words 'Slav' and 'slave' have widely been thought to be synonymous. The Arabic word for eunuch, *sakaliba*, is also considered to derive from 'Slav'. It is no accident that the first surviving eyewitness report of the Slavonic lands was written by a Moorish Jew, a merchant from Tortosa (see p. 454).

Islam's impact on the Christian world cannot be exaggerated. Islam's conquests turned Europe into Christianity's main base. At the same time the great swathe of Muslim territory cut the Christians off from virtually all direct contact with other religions and civilizations. The barrier of militant Islam turned the Peninsula in on itself, severing or transforming many of the earlier lines of commercial, intellectual, and political intercourse. In the field of religious conflict, it left Christendom with two tasks—to fight Islam and to convert the remaining pagans. It forced the Byzantine Empire to give lasting priority to the defence of its Eastern borders, and hence to neglect its imperial mission in the West. It created the conditions where the other, more distant Christian states had to fend for themselves, and increasingly to adopt measures for local autonomy and economic self-sufficiency. In other words, it gave a major stimulus to feudalism. Above all, by commandeering the Mediterranean Sea, it destroyed the supremacy which the Mediterranean lands had hitherto exercised over the rest of the Peninsula. Before Islam, the post-classical world of Greece and Rome, as transmuted by Christianity, had remained essentially intact. After Islam, it was gone forever. Almost by default, the political initiative passed from the Mediterranean to the primitive kingdoms of the north, especially to the most powerful of those kingdoms in 'Francia'.

In the course of that eighth century, therefore, when Europe's Christians were digesting the implications of the Islamic conquests, the seeds of a new order were sown. The Patriarch of Rome, deprived of support from Byzantium, was forced to turn to the Franks, and to embark on the enterprise of the 'Papacy'. The Franks saw their chance to back the Pope. Indirectly, Charlemagne was the product of Muhammad (see below, pp. 284–90). According to Henri Pirenne, whose thesis shattered earlier conceptions as surely as Islam shattered the ancient world, 'The

Frankish Empire would probably never have existed without Islam, and Charlemagne without Mahomet would be inconceivable.'[17] The arguments of Pirenne have been diminished on detailed points, especially regarding the alleged break in commercial relations. But they revolutionized the study of the transition from the ancient to the medieval worlds.

To talk of Muhammad and Charlemagne, however, is not enough. Islam affected Eastern Europe even more directly than it affected Western Europe. Its appearance set the bounds of a new, compact entity called 'Christendom', of which Constantinople would be the strongest centre for some time to come. It set a challenge to the pagans on the eastern fringes of Christian–Muslim rivalry, who henceforth faced the prospect of choosing between the two dominant religions. Above all, it created the cultural bulwark against which European identity could be defined. Europe, let alone Charlemagne, is inconceivable without Muhammad.

Christianity's rivalry with Islam raised moral and psychological problems no less profound than those already existing between Christianity and Judaism. Both Christians and Muslims were taught to regard the other as the infidel. Their misunderstandings, antagonisms and negative stereotypes were endless. It was never popular, least of all among the clergy, to stress how much the three great monotheistic religions held in common. As a result, a strong dichotomy developed between the Christian 'West' and the Islamic 'East'. Medieval Europeans commonly referred to Muslims as 'Saracens', an epithet derived from the Arabic word *sharakyoun* or 'easterner'. Among those Westerners who have imagined themselves to be the bearers of a superior civilization, there has been a long tradition of viewing the Muslim East with mindless disdain.

The Christian Church in the Age of the General Councils, 325–787

By the time of the first General Council at Nicaea in 325 (see p. 205), the Christian Church headed the largest religious community in the Empire. Since the Edict of Milan, it benefited from the policy of toleration; and it had the support of the reigning emperor. But its position was not entirely secure. It was not the established state religion, and it had many enemies in high places. It had made few inroads beyond the Empire. Progress, from the Christian point of view, and particularly from that of the 'Orthodox' party led by Athanasius, was going to be bumpy. [IKON]

Under Constantius II (r. 337–61) there was a brief resurgence of Arianism. Not for the last time, Athanasius was banished. In 340, when the Goths were still resident to the north of the Danube delta, they were converted to Christianity in its Arian form. As a result, when the Ostrogoths and the Visigoths invaded the Empire and established their kingdoms in Italy, Gaul, Spain, and Africa, they took their Arianism with them. They presented a major obstacle to the spread of Orthodox Christianity among the barbarians. [BIBLIA] Another change of tack came with the Emperor Julian (r. 361–3), a philosopher-monarch known in the Christian tradition as 'the Apostate'. Educated in the Christian faith by people who had murdered his family, 'he had always declared himself an advocate of Paganism'. The end result was an edict of general toleration, and a last interval of respite for the Roman gods. 'The only hardship which he inflicted on the Christians was to deprive them of the power of tormenting their fellow subjects.' There is no evidence for the legend that his last words were *Vicisti Galilaee*, 'Thou hast conquered, O pale Galilean'.[18]

These experiences shook the Trinitarian party from their complacency. Athanasius in the East and Hilary of Poitiers (315–67) in the West, who had led the opposition to Constantius and Julian, were succeeded by the generation of the Church's most brilliant and commanding Fathers. John Chrysostom (347–407), the 'Golden Mouth', Bishop of Constantinople, was the greatest preacher of the age, who ruffled many feathers in high society. Basil the Great (330–79), Bishop of Caesarea, came from a remarkable family that claimed no fewer than eight saints. He is generally accounted the founder of communal monasticism. His brother, Gregory of Nyssa (335–95), and his friend, Gregory of Nazianus (329–89), were both prominent theologians, who carried the day at the Second General Council at Constantinople (381). In the West, the Pannonian Martin of Tours (315–97) completed the evangelization of Gaul. Ambrose of Milan (c.334–97) was the leading ecclesiastical politician of the age. The Dalmatian Jerome (c.345–420) was the leading biblical scholar of the early church. The African, Augustine of Hippo, was probably the most influential of the Church Fathers.

Their efforts bore fruit in the reign of Theodosius (r. 378–95), who was the last emperor to rule both East and West and who gave his support to the Trinitarian party. Theodosius was a Spaniard, son of a general, and a man of ferocious temper. He turned to the Trinitarians for the simple reason that his predecessor, Valens, had been killed by the Arian Goths. Under his protection the Second General Council ratified the Nicene Creed. Trinitarian Christianity was supported with the force of law; Arianism was banned; paganism was persecuted. This is the point where the Trinitarians could start to enforce their claim to orthodoxy, and to condemn their rivals past and present as 'heretics'. [INDEX] [RUFINUS] [ZEUS]

To many believers in subsequent centuries, this 'triumph of Christianity' was celebrated as a wonderful achievement. Theodosius was awarded the epithet of 'Great'. But there was little in the teaching of Christ to recommend such a close association of spiritual and political authority. Moreover, Theodosius was hardly an example of Christlike virtue. In 388 he killed his co-emperor, Magnus Maximus; and in 390 he wreaked terrible revenge on the city of Thessalonika for daring to permit a rebellious riot. He ordered his officers to invite the whole population to the Circus, as if to the Games, and then to slaughter all 7,000 in cold blood. For this crime he was constrained by Ambrose to perform public penance, and he died in Milan, somewhat better apprised of the religion to which he had given such signal services.

Theologian and bishop, St Augustine (354–430) had trained as a rhetorician, and had once been an advocate of Manichaeanism. He was converted to

INDEX

E ARLY Church tradition credited Pope Innocent I (r. 401–17) with the first list of forbidden books, and Pope Gelasius (r. 492–6) with the first decree on the subject. The Gelasian decree adds lists of recommended and of supplementary reading to its pronouncement on the canon of authentic Scripture. Modern scholarship, though, doubts that the decree had any connection with Gelasius. What is certain is that the Church always guarded its right to pronounce on the propriety, or impropriety, of the written word. From the fifth to the fifteenth centuries, it placed any number of bans on individual authors, from Arius and Photius to Hus and Pico della Mirandola (1486). A further step was prompted by the advent of printing. Though there is some dispute again about precedence, Pope Innocent VIII (r. 1484–92) either initiated or consolidated the rule that all publications should receive a bishop's licence. [**PRESS**]

Thanks to the flood of books produced during the Renaissance and Reformation, the Church hierarchy increasingly sought guidance from the Vatican; and the Council of Trent demanded action. The result was the *Index Librorum Prohibitorum* or 'Guide to Prohibited Books' drawn up by Paul IV in 1557. Owing to dissensions in the Vatican, that first version was suppressed; and it was the second version of 1559 which was eventually published. Revised yet again at the request of the Council, the Tridentine Index of 1564 set the norm for subsequent practice. In addition to the list of authors and works which had earned the Church's disapproval, it set out ten criteria for judging them. Since 1564 Rome's 'Blacklist' has been constantly extended. Its rules were modified in 1596, 1664, 1758, 1900, and 1948. (See Appendix III, p. 1274.)

Over the years the Index has been subject to much criticism. It was always ineffective, in that the prohibited titles could always find a publisher in Protestant states beyond the Vatican's reach. What is more, since forbidden fruits always taste sweeter, the Index could seriously be charged with actively promoting what it sought to suppress. Enemies of the Church were always quick to cite it as proof of Catholic intolerance. From the Enlightenment, liberated intellectuals have never failed to pour ridicule both on the individual decisions of the Index and on its very existence. Given the tally of world-beaters and best-sellers which it has tried to oppose, one can see the reason why.

On the other hand, the Index has to be judged in context. Every authority in modern Europe, whether secular or ecclesiastical, Protestant, Catholic, or Orthodox, has shared the Vatican's desire to control publications. Censors were at work in all European countries until the second half of the twentieth century. Many of those vociferous in condemning the Papal Index have failed to see a contradiction when they themselves seek to suppress books. One has only to look at some of the times and places in which the classics of European literature have been banned by authorities other than the Vatican:

AD 35	Homer	*Opera omnia*	Roman Empire
1497	Dante	*Opera omnia*	City of Florence
1555	Erasmus	*Opera omnia*	Scotland
1660	Milton	*Eikonoklastes*	England
1701	Locke	*Essay on Human Understanding*	Oxford University
1776	Goethe	*Sorrows of Werther*	Denmark
1788–1820	Shakespeare	*King Lear*	Great Britain
1835	Heine	*Opera omnia*	Prussia
1880	Tolstoy	*Anna Karenina,* and others	Russia
1931	Marie Stopes	*Opera omnia*	Republic of Ireland
1939	Goethe	*Opera omnia*	Spain
1928–60	D. H. Lawrence	*Lady Chatterley's Lover*	Great Britain[1]

Of course, there is a fundamental liberal position which holds that all publications should be permitted, even when material is manifestly blasphemous, subversive, incitatory, obscene, or untrue. It demands that people tolerate what they abhor. This position was tested in the 1980s by so-called 'revisionist history', which denies the reality of the Jewish Holocaust, or by the Islamic *fatwah* pronounced on Salman Rushdie's *Satanic Verses*. In practice, many liberals shrink from the application of their own absolute principles. Every society, and every generation, has to determine its stance in relation to the shifting line between the acceptable and the unacceptable.[2] Nor is it appropriate to compare the Papal Index with contemporary totalitarian censorship. In Nazi Germany 1933–45, and in the Soviet world 1917–91, all works were officially considered banned until specifically approved. In this regard, the principle of episcopal licensing might be judged more repressive than the Index.

In 1966 the head of the Vatican's Congregation of the Doctrine of the Faith announced that the prohibition of publications had been suspended. By that time, the Index contained some 4,000 titles.

Much of the above information derives from an impeccable source, each of whose eighteen volumes bears evidence of a favourable episcopal decision—NIHIL OBSTAT (There is no impediment) and IMPRIMATUR (Let it be printed).[3]

RUFINUS

RUFINUS Tyrannius of Aquileia (*c.*340–410), sometime associate of St Jerome, made his name on two related scores—as the Latin translator of Greek theological works, especially by Origen, and as author of the earliest book printed by the Oxford University Press. His commentary on the Apostles' Creed, the *Expositio Sancti Hieronymi in symbolum apostolorum*, was printed in Oxford by Theodoric Rood of Cologne, and completed on 17 December 1478. It began, alas, with a misprint, an 'x' having been lost on the frontispiece, where the publication date appeared (wrongly) as M CCCC LXVIII.[1]

Since then, OUP's list has seen both its ups and its downs:

Charles Butler, *The Feminine Monarchie Or a Treatise Concerning Bees* (1609)
John Smith, *A Map of Virginia* (1612)
Robert Burton, *The Anatomy of Melancholy* (1621)
The Book of Common Prayer, and Administration of the Sacraments (1675–)
The Holy Bible, Containing the Old Testament and the New (1675–)
Edmund Pococke (ed.), *Specimen Historiae Arabum* (1650)
—— Maimonides, *Porta Mosis* (1655)
—— *Greg. Abulfaragii historia compendiosa dynastiarum* (1663)
[Richard Allestree] *The Ladies Calling: by the Author of the Whole Duty of Man* (1673)
Johann Schaeffer, *A History of Lapland* (1674)
H. W. Ludolf, *Grammatica Russica* (1696)
William Blackstone, *Commentaries on the Laws of England* (4 vols., 1765–9)
F. M. Müller, *Rigveda-Sanhita: Sacred Hymns of the Brahmins* (1849–73)
Lewis Carroll, *Alice's Adventures in Wonderland* (1865)
Norman Davies, *God's Playground: A History of Poland* (2 vols., 1981)

Reputedly, OUP's most remarkable feat was in 1914, when a team of Oxford historians went into print in support of Britain's war effort. The manuscript of *Why We Are at War* was delivered on 26 August, barely three weeks after the outbreak of war. The 206-page volume was edited, typeset by hand, printed, bound and ready for distribution by 14 September. Times change.[2]

Christianity in Milan in 386. His willingness to admit to human weaknesses makes him the most appealing writer. His *Confessions*, which recount the emotions of a young man called to renounce the comforts and pleasures of the worldly life, stand in stark contrast to the polemicist disputing with Donatists, Manichaeans, and Pelagians. Yet he analysed and systematized the intricacies of those doctrines with such mastery that he left little to be done until Thomas Aquinas almost 800 years later. He stressed the primacy of love in a way that almost recommends libertinism. *Dilige et quod vis fac* (Love and do what you want) and *Cum dilectione hominum et odio vitiorum* (Love the sinner and hate the sins) were two of his maxims. At the same time, he stressed the necessity of the institutionalized Church. *Salus extra ecclesiam non est* (there is no salvation outside the Church), he wrote; also *Roma locuta est; causa finita.* (Rome has spoken; the case is closed.) The most popular of his 113 books, *De Civitate Dei* (The City of God), was inspired by Alaric's sack of Rome, and describes a spiritual city built on the ruins of the material world. Nothing could be more expressive of the age. Augustine spent over thirty years as Bishop of Hippo in his native Africa, living by an ascetic rule that later inspired a number of Church orders including the Augustinian Canons, the Dominican (Black) Friars, the Praemonstratensians, and the Brigittines. He died in Hippo besieged by the Vandals.

Disturbances in the heart of the Empire inevitably weakened links with the periphery. In the fifth century, important peculiarities developed on the one hand in the 'Celtic fringe', and on the other hand in the Caucasus. The Celtic Church had adopted Christianity from Gaulish, anchorite monks. Its bishops were peripatetic hermits, and through the practice of single-handed consecration, extremely numerous. Ireland, which had never formed part of the Empire, was systematically evangelized by St Patrick (*c.*389–461), a Roman citizen from western Britain who landed in Ulster in 432. In this way Ireland had been secured for Christianity before the blanket of Anglo-Saxon heathenism fell over the rest of the British Isles. The Irish would repay their debt. [**BRITO**]

ZEUS

THE statue of Zeus was transported to Constantinople from the shrine at Olympia following the last Olympiad in AD 396. By then it was over eight centuries old, and had been long established as one of the 'wonders of the world'. Completed *c.*432 BC by the exiled Athenian Pheidias, whose statue of Athena graced the Parthenon, it consisted of a gigantic ivory figure, wreathed and enthroned, some 13 metres high. Plated in part with solid gold, it portrayed the Father of the Gods holding a statuette of Winged Victory in his right hand and an inlaid, eagle-topped sceptre in his left. It had been described in detail both by Pausanias and by Strabo, who said that if the God moved, his head would go through the roof. Suetonius reports that when the Emperor Caligula's workmen had tried to remove it in the first century AD, 'the God cackled so loudly' that the scaffolding collapsed and the workmen fled. So it stayed in situ for three more centuries. When it was finally consumed by the flames of an accidental fire in 462, in the capital of the Christian Emperor, Leo I, Olympia was already deserted. In 1958 German archaeologists excavating the temple workshops at Olympia found a terracotta cup inscribed with the graffito 'I BELONGED TO PHEIDIAS'.[1]

BRITO

PELAGIUS (*c*.360–420) was a Welshman, or at least a Celt from the British Isles ('Pelagius' is a Graeco-Roman calque of his surname, Morgan, meaning 'Son of the Sea'). His friends called him 'Brito'. He was a Christian theologian, and one of the few from Western Europe who participated in the leading doctrinal debates of his day. He lived at a time when orthodox doctrine, as formulated by the Greeks, was beginning to crystallize. Though his views were deemed heretical, he was none the less a vital contributor. He was a contemporary of St Augustine of Hippo, whom he provoked into formulating what became the definitive statements on such central issues as Divine Grace, The Fall of Man, Original Sin, Free Will, and Predestination. Together with another Briton, Celestius, whom he met in Rome, he laid emphasis on man's capacity for virtuous action through the exercise of will, in other words, on responsible conduct. His central concept, known as 'the power of contrary choice', is contained in the formula *Si necessitatis est, peccatum non est; si voluntatis, vitiari potest* (If there be need, there is no sin; but if the will is there, then sinning is possible). He also held that the first step towards salvation must be made by an act of will.

These views were rejected partly because they were thought to minimize God's grace and partly because they attributed sin to individual failings rather than to human nature. The label of Pelagianism is generally attached to theological standpoints which deny or limit Original Sin. They figured strongly in the seventeenth-century debates surrounding Arminius and Jansen. (See pp. 492, 502.)

In 410, having fled the Gothic siege of Rome, Pelagius and Celestius took refuge in North Africa, where further doctrinal charges were laid against them. One of the Councils of Carthage condemned six cardinal errors:

> That Adam would have died even if he had not sinned.
> That Adam injured himself alone, not the human race.
> That new-born children, like Adam at birth, are without sin.
> That the human race does not die through Adam's death or sin.
> That the law, as well as the gospel, gives entrance to Heaven.
> That there were men without sin even before Christ's coming.

Pelagius sailed for Palestine, only to find that Augustine's *De peccatorum meritis* (On the Merits of Sinners) had singled him out for attack. He survived one inquisition; but he was lost when the sympathies of Pope Zosimus were won over by the African bishops. In an edict of 30 April 418 the Emperor Honorius condemned him to confiscation and banishment. The Venerable Bede showed no sympathy for his 'noxious and abominable teaching':

Against the great Augustine see him crawl,
This wretched scribbler with his pen of gall![1]

A movement to reconcile Pelagius with Augustine developed round the works of Bishop Honoratus of Arles (c.350–429). It held that Divine Grace and Human Will are coefficient factors in salvation. This 'semi-Pelagianism' was condemned at the Council of Orange (529). But its home, at the monastery of St Honorat on the Isle de Lerins off the Côte d'Azur, did not close. St Vincent of Lerins (d. 450) invented the famous 'Vincentian Canon' whereby all theological propositions can be tested against the threefold criteria of ecumenicity, antiquity, and consent. The monks of Lerins published the definitive edition of St Hilary's *Life of Honoratus* in 1977.[2]

The Armenian Church came into being when the province still belonged to the Empire. Like its Celtic counterpart, it lost all direct contact with the centre and became eccentric in all senses of the word. When the Celts were turning to Pelagianism, the Armenians were turning to Monophysitism. Christianity had reached Georgia in 330, when the ruling house was converted by a Cappadocian slave-girl. Being one step removed from Armenia, it was less exposed to Asian politics and maintained closer links with Constantinople. (The Georgian Church had a separate and continuous history until forcibly incorporated into Russian Orthodoxy in 1811.) In 431 a third General Council was held at Ephesus, thereby creating a series. The seven General Councils recognized as binding by both East and West were Nicaea I (325), Constantinople I (381), Ephesus (431), Chalcedon (451), Constantinople II (553), Constantinople III (680–1), Nicaea II (787). The Council of Ephesus condemned the Nestorian heresy. Gibbon called it an 'ecclesiastical riot'. Like its predecessors and successors, it was convened by the Emperor in Constantinople, who claimed the highest authority in Church affairs. It was entirely dominated by bishops from the East. The bishops in the West accepted the decisions, but with growing reluctance.

Doctrinal divergences persisted over the seemingly incurable habit of christological hairsplitting: over Christ's nature, over Christ's will, over Christ's role in the genesis of the Holy Ghost. Does Christ have one single nature, that is, divine, or a dual nature both human *and* divine? The Orthodox leaders supported Diophysitism, and in the Definition of Chalcedon (451) affirmed the formula of One Person in Two Natures, 'unconfusedly, unchangeably, indivisibly, and inseparably' united. The Monophysites were condemned; but they continued to flourish in the East. The empress Theodora was a Monophysite, and so were the majority of Christians in Armenia, Syria, and Egypt. Does Christ have one will or two? Pope Honorius carelessly used the phrase 'one will' in a letter to Constantinople in 634. But the Orthodox leaders supported Diothelitism, which they affirmed at the sixth General Council in 681. The Monothelites were condemned, and the delegates of Pope Agatho acquiesced in the Council's ruling. Within the Trinity of Father, Son, and Holy Ghost, does the Holy Ghost proceed from the Father, as the sole fount of divinity, and hence *through the Son*, or does it proceed jointly, from Father *and Son* together? Constantinople held to *per filium* (through the Son); Rome held to *filioque* (and the Son). The matter first surfaced in 589 in Spain, and by the ninth century was causing major ruptures. It has never been resolved.

The attraction of monasticism grew in proportion to political and social disorder. Eastern practices, both anchorite and communal, spread to the West. The earliest communal monasteries preceded the fall of the Western Empire. St Martin founded Ligugé in 360. But the greatest influence was that of Benedict of Nursia (*c.*480–550), who formulated the most widely adopted of all monastic rules. As imperial authority shrank, especially in the former Western provinces, the monasteries increasingly served as oases of classical learning in the barbarian desert. The conjunction of Christian teaching with an appreciation of Greek philosophy and the Latin authors had long been accepted in the East, especially in Alexandria; but in the West it had to be cultivated. The central figure in this regard was Flavius Magnus Aurelius Senator (*c.*485–580), known as Cassiodorus, sometime governor of Italy under Theodoric the Ostrogoth. Retiring to a monastery after the arrival of Belisarius, he advocated a system of education where sacred and profane subjects were seen as complementary; and he started the collection of ancient documents. It was none too soon. [**ANNO DOMINI**] [**BAUME**]

In the seventh century the shock of Islam changed the contours of the Christian world for ever. It ended the cultural unity of the Mediterranean lands and broke the dominance which they had always exercised over the northern outposts. By overrunning Persia, Syria, and Egypt, it determined that three of the five recognized Patriarchs—in Antioch, Jerusalem, and Alexandria—would be forced to operate *in partibus infidelium*. The politics of the Christian Church was reduced from a healthy five-sided arena to a bitter two-sided contest between the Greek Patriarch in Constantinople and the Latin Patriarch in Rome. Before Islam, the Patriarch of Rome spoke with one Latin voice against four Greeks; after Islam, it was one to one. And the Roman Church enjoyed a greater margin for manœuvre. Moreover, the threatening quarrel with the Monophysites in the East was not resolved. The new Muslim rulers proved more tolerant of heresy than Orthodox Christians had been. So the Monophysite Armenian, Syrian, and Coptic Churches were never recalled to the fold.

Most importantly, perhaps, Islam cut Christianity off from the rest of the world. Before Islam, the Christian Gospels had reached both Ceylon and Abyssinia; after Islam, they were effectively excluded for centuries from further expansion into Asia or Africa. Most Christians never saw a Muslim during their lifetime; but all of them lived in Islam's shade. Islam, in fact, provided the solid, external shield within which Christendom could consolidate and be defined. In this sense, it provided the single greatest stimulus to what was eventually called 'Europe'.

ANNO DOMINI

F OR six centuries after the birth of Christ, very few people were conscious of living in 'the Christian Era'. Indeed, the basic chronology of
history since 'Christ walked in Galilee' was not established before the work
of Dionysius Exiguus, a Greek-speaking monk from Scythia Minor and
friend of Cassiodorus who died in Rome c.550. It was the idea of Dionysius
that the counting of years should be based on Christ's Incarnation and
that it should begin on the Day of the Annunciation, when the Virgin Mary
had conceived. He fixed this date, Day One of Year One, at 25 March, nine
months before the birth of Christ on 25 December. All previous years,
counted in receding order, were to be designated *ante Christum* (AC), or
'Before Christ' (BC). All subsequent years were to be 'Years since the
Incarnation', or *Anni Domini*, 'Years of Our Lord' (AD). There was no Zero
Year.[1]

Many more centuries elapsed before the Christian Era, or Common Era,
gradually came into use, first in the Latin Church, later in the East. The
Venerable Bede (673–735), who was the author of a book on chronology, *De
Temporibus*, had fully accepted the new system when he wrote his *History
of the English Church and People* in the early eighth century.

In the mean time, all sorts of local chronologies prevailed. The most
usual system was that of regnal years. Historical time was measured by
reigns and generations. Dates were determined by their point in the reign
of a particular emperor, pope, or prince. The model was in the Old
Testament: 'And it came to pass in the fourth year of King Hezekiah,
which was the seventh year of Hoshea, son of Elah king of Israel, that
Shalmaneser king of Assyria came up against Samaria and besieged it . . .'

The Christian Era had to compete with numerous rival chronological
systems. The table of Greek Olympiads, the four-year cycles between
Olympic Games, which began with the Olympiad of Coroebus on 1 July 776
BC, was continued until the end of the fourth century AD. The Babylonian
Era of Nabonassar, which was used by the Greeks of Alexandria, was
known in medieval times from the works of Ptolemy. Its starting-point was
equivalent to Wednesday, 26 February 747 BC. The Macedonian Era of the
Seleucids, which began with occupation of Babylon by Seleucus Nicator
in 312 BC, was widely used in the Levant. Known to the Jews as 'the era of
contracts', it was used by them until the fifteenth century. The Roman Era
was based on the passage of years since 'the Foundation of the City' [**AUC**].
In Spain, the Era of the Caesars can be traced to the conquest of Iberia by
Octavian in 39 BC. Adopted by the Visigoths, it remained in force in Catalonia till 1180, in Castile until 1382, in Portugal until 1415. The Muslim Era
of Hegira, which marks the flight of the Prophet from Mecca, corresponds
to Friday, 16 July AD 622. It remains in force throughout the Muslim world.

Not surprisingly, given the complications, the calculation of the birth of Christ by Dionysius Exiguus has since turned out to be faulty. Dionysius equated Year One with Olympic Era 195 (1), with 754 AUC, and, mistakenly, with 'the Consulship of C. Caesar, son of Augustus, and L. Aemilius Paullus, son of Paullus'. In reality, there is nothing to show that Christ was actually born in AD 1. According to whether one follows St Luke or St Matthew, the Christian Era began either in the last year of Herod the Great (4 BC) or in the year of the first Roman census in Judaea (AD 6–7).

For Christians as for Jews, the prime historical date was the Year of Creation, or *Annus Mundi*. The Byzantine Church fixed it at 5509 BC, which remained the basis of the ecclesiastical calendar in parts of the Orthodox world, in Greece and in Russia, until modern times. Jewish scholars preferred 3760 BC—the starting-point of the modern Jewish calendar. The Coptic Church, like the Alexandrians, fixed on 5500 BC. The Church of England, under Archbishop Ussher in 1650, picked 4004 BC.

The critical comparison and harmonization of oriental, classical, and Christian chronologies awaited the great Renaissance scholar Joseph Scaliger (1540–1609). Scaliger's *De Emendatione Temporum* (The Reform of Dates, 1583), written with Protestant interests in mind, coincided with the reform of the Julian calendar by Pope Gregory XIII. It marks the beginning of chronological science, and of modern concerns about the standard measurement of historical time.[2]

The Gregorian Calendar, however, known as 'New Style' (NS) and introduced into the Catholic countries of Europe in 1585, was not universally accepted. Most Protestant or Orthodox countries stayed with the Julian 'Old Style'. They adopted the New Style as the spirit moved them: Scotland in 1700, England in 1752, Russia in 1918. So long as the two calendars co-existed, all international correspondence had to be conducted with reference to both. Letters had to carry the two versions of the date— '1/12 March 1734' or '24 October/7 November 1917'.

As a result, numerous curiosities prevailed. Since the discrepancy between the calendars amounted in the seventeenth century to ten or eleven days, it was possible to sail across the English Channel from Dover and arrive in Calais in the middle of the following month. Similarly, since the Old Style year began on 25 March and the New Style year on 1 January, it was possible to leave Calais in one year and to reach Dover in the previous year. Europe did not work in full synchrony until the Bolshevik government abandoned the Old Style. Nothing happened in Russia between 31 January 1918 (OS) and 14 February (NS). From 1918 to 1940, the Soviet communists imitated the French revolutionaries by abolishing the seven-day week, replacing the names of days with numbers, and counting the 'Years of the Revolution' from 1917.[3] [**VENDÉMIAIRE**]

BAUME

THE Abbey of Baume, says the *Guide Michelin*, was founded in the sixth century by the Irish monk, St Colomban. Its name, of Celtic origin, means 'grotto', and it was set in one of Europe's most dramatic locations—at the bottom of an immense limestone gorge, the Cirque de Baume, in the depths of the pine woods of the Jura. Like a convent of the same name, fifty miles away on the River Doubs, where the blind St Odile received her sight, it is said to date from the era when Gallo-Roman civilization had been overrun by the pagan Burgundians, and when Christianity was being rebuilt by anchorite communities in the wilderness. It grew into an institution of great wealth and power, possessing several hundred villages and benefices. Eventually, the chapter turned itself into a secularized community of aristocratic canons. It survived until 1790, when revolutionaries dissolved the abbey, smashed most of its monuments, and changed the name of the town from Baume-les-Moines to Baume-les-Messieurs.[1]

In the history of Christian monasticism, the Burgundian communities like Baume form an important link between the anchorite system of the ancient world, as preserved in Ireland, and the great medieval foundations which appear from the tenth century onwards. After all, it was from Baume that Berno and his companions set out in 910 to found the great abbey of Cluny (see p. 315).

For readers of the *Guide Michelin*, however, it is a disappointment to find that many of these details of Baume's past are at best unauthenticated legends. There is no hard evidence to connect Baume with St Colomban, and there is no reason to suppose that it was founded in the sixth century. In fact, the first definite mention of a *cellula* at Balma dates from 869—which makes it younger than St Odile's convent at Baume-les-Dames. In all probability, the link with St Colomban was invented by the monks of Cluny, who thereby embellished the pedigree of their parent house.[2]

Similar doubts surround Baume's most colourful personality—Jean, Seigneur de Watteville (1618–1702), abbot for forty years during the reign of Louis XIV. Soldier, murderer, and monk, de Watteville had once fled from justice to Constantinople, where he rose to the rank of pasha and governor of Morea, before obtaining a papal absolution. According to Saint-Simon, he was an example of a sinner redeemed by true repentance. According to the record, he was a habitual turncoat whose treachery facilitated the brutal French conquest of his native province of Franche-Comté. His tombstone reads thus:

ITALUS ET BURGUNDUS IN ARMIS
GALLUS IN ALBIS

IN CURIA RECTUS PRESBYTER
ABBAS ADEST.[3]

('Here lies an Italian and a Burgundian soldier, a Frenchman,
when he took the cowl, an upright man in his office, a priest and abbot').

Baume, therefore, provides the stuff of legend as well as history. People
have always had a need to use the past for their own purposes. The writers of scientific monographs are playing a losing game. The past as transmitted to posterity will always be a confused mixture of facts, legends, and
downright lies.

The emancipation of the papacy cannot be pinned on a particular date. The
Patriarchs of Rome possessed a large measure of freedom long before they asserted their claims to supremacy. Growing differences between the Latin and the
Greek parts of the Church led to frequent schisms of a temporary nature, but not
to an irreparable breach. Oddly enough, in the first four centuries, when Rome
was still the heart of the Empire, the Roman Church had often been dominated
by Greeks and by Greek culture. Leo I (440–61) was the first to emphasize its
Latinity. In the same period the Latin Patriarchs broke free from immediate political control, sheltering behind the city of Rome in its many affrays with the civil
power. The resultant separation of ecclesiastical and secular authority, so typical
for the West and so foreign to the East, was an established fact from then on. In
the sixth century the Patriarchs of Rome had to face first the restoration of imperial power under Justinian, and then the Lombards. Two of their number,
Silverius (536–7) and Vigilius (537–55), found themselves under imperial arrest.
The latter was brutally bullied into submission by the imperial authorities on the
Monophysite controversy.

Gregory I (540–604), the first monk to sit on St Peter's throne, is often regarded as the architect of future papal power through both his administrative skills
and his stand on principle. Self-styled 'servant of the servants of God', he ran the
civil affairs of the city of Rome, negotiated a settlement with the Lombard kings,
reorganized the Church's lands and finances, and restored Roman contacts with
Africa, Spain, Gaul, and Britain. His *Regula Pastoralis* (Pastoral Care) quickly
became the handbook for medieval bishops. He repeatedly protested against his
brother of Constantinople using the title of 'Oecumenical Patriarch'. By the time
of his death, the balance was shifting in Rome's favour. Preoccupied by the
Muslim onslaught, the emperors lost almost all influence in Italy, though several
desperate demonstrations of imperial claims were attempted. As a result of the
Monothelite affair, Martin I (d. 655), the last papal martyr, died in exile in Crimea,
having been kidnapped by the Exarch of Ravenna, flogged, and banished by a
court in Constantinople. [**CANTUS**]

CANTUS

THE plainsong of the Latin Church, or *cantus planus*, is often called Gregorian Chant in honour of the Pope who fixed its eight component modes and collected some 3,000 melodies. Together with the related idiom of Byzantium, it is thought to have derived from Greek and especially Jewish traditions of chanting. In turn, it became the foundation on which European music was built. It was used for the unaccompanied singing of psalms, hymns, and antiphons, customarily in unison and in free rhythm. It had four main 'dialects'—Ambrosian, Roman, Gallican, and Mozarabic, though the Roman school gradually gained ascendancy. Initially, it was not written down; and the early forms cannot be reconstructed with certainty. [**MUSIKE**]

The notation developed for plainsong passed through several stages. The Byzantines, like the Greeks, used a literal system to designate notes, supplemented by neums or 'accents' to indicate the movement of the melodic line. The Slavic Orthodox preserved the system long after it was superseded elsewhere:

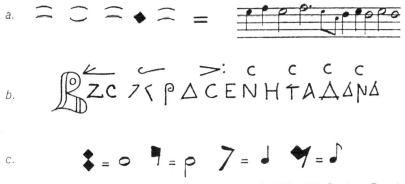

a. 11th Century Kufisma Notation without stave. *b.* 12th–13th Century Russian notation using a Graeco-Byzantine literal system. *c.* 17th–20th Century: musical signs used in Russian Orthodox liturgical notation.
(After Machabey.)

In the West, as expounded in the Frankish treatise *De harmonica institutione* by Hucbald of St Amand (*c.*840–930), a similar convention had been adopted whereby neums were placed over the syllables of the Latin text. Notger Balbulus of St Gall explored *tropes* or 'melodies added to the main chant'. In the eleventh century, the musicologist Guido d'Arezzo (*c.*995–1050) invented a notational system which is the progenitor of the tonic sol-fa.

Taking the initial syllables of the lines of *Ut queant laxis*, the Hymn to St John the Baptist, he established the ascending hexachord of UT-RE-MI-

SOL-LA-FA. The seventh syllable SI, for (S)ancte (I)ohannis, was added later. He also devised a spatial stave of up to ten lines, forerunner of the modern five-line stave. It had a mobile key signature, and carried a 'square notation' of 'points' and 'rods'. It is debatable whether the notes had fixed duration or accentuation:

('Let Thine example, Holy John, remind us | Ere we can meetly sing thy deeds of wonder, | Hearts must be chastened, and the bonds that bind us | Broken asunder.')[3]

From the late twelfth century onwards, Gregorian chant was enriched by the art of polyphony, where two or more independent melodic lines were sung in parallel. The practice encouraged the growth of instrumental accompaniment. The medieval ear only recognized concordance in octaves, fourths, and fifths. But the introduction of fixed measures, perhaps from folksong and dance, and the need for counterpoint where the melodies crossed, encouraged the study of rhythm and harmony. These, together with melody, constitute the basic elements of modern musical form. The art of canon began in the thirteenth century. From then on, a standard vocabulary of musical phrase could communicate a wide range of emotion and meaning. Europe's 'language of music' has a continuous history, therefore, from plainsong to Stravinsky.[4]

In the nineteenth century, the so-called 'Caecilian movement' regarded Gregorian chant as the one true source of European music. The Benedictine monks of Solesmes, near Le Mans, undertook the task of reconstituting its theory and practices. Their work, which inspired among other things Liszt's *Christus*, is regarded as the principal modern authority.

In the eighth century, the Emperor could no longer mount even a demonstration of power in the West. In 710 Emperor Justinian II summoned the Roman Patriarch to Constantinople, and Constantine (708–15), a Syrian, dutifully obeyed. At their meeting—the last, as it proved, between Roman bishop and reigning emperor—the emperor ceremonially kissed the Roman feet, receiving absolution and communion in return. But Constantine was murdered shortly afterwards; and their agreement over Ravenna came to nothing. In 732 Emperor Leo fitted out a fleet to recover Ravenna, which had been conquered by the Lombards, and to arrest Gregory III (731–41) who had defied the edict on Iconoclasm. But the fleet sank in the Adriatic. Thereafter, for all practical purposes, the Roman Patriarchs were totally independent. No subsequent bishop of Rome ever sought the imperial mandate for his election. No imperial officials from Constantinople could ever exert their authority in Rome.

In any case, the Patriarchate of Rome already possessed the means to support its independence. As guardian of the Roman pilgrimage, which grew greatly in importance once Islam sealed off the road to Jerusalem, it attracted huge prestige and a ready income. In the Decretals it had a body of legal decisions that would come to service its wide jurisdiction, especially after the codification of Canon Law (see p. 349). In the Patrimony of St Peter (the Church's landed estates), which would soon be greatly expanded, it possessed a solid basis for temporal power. In its alliances with the Lombards, and then with the Lombards' rivals, the Franks, it had the means to obtain international protection. The unity of the Christian Church still existed in theory; in reality it had gone. The title of *Papa* had once been affectionately applied to all bishops. Henceforth it was reserved exclusively for the bishop of Rome. This was the era when the papacy was born. [**REVERENTIA**]

The seventh General Council (787), the second at Nicaea, was devoted to Iconoclasm. It declared in favour of an opinion sent from Rome by Hadrian I. Images could be venerated, but not with the same adoration due to God. This was to be the last occasion on which Rome and Constantinople were to take common action in matters of faith.

REVERENTIA

ONE day in the sixth century, whilst travelling with his mother between Burgundy and Auvergne, the young Georgius Florentius (the future Gregory of Tours) was caught in a storm. His mother waved a bag of holy relics at the lowering sky, the clouds parted, and the travellers passed on unscathed. At first, the conceited boy took the miracle to be a reward for his own good behaviour, whereupon his horse stumbled and threw him to the ground. It was a lesson in the wages of vanity. On another occasion, whilst visiting the shrine of St Julien at Brioude, Gregory developed a splitting headache. Putting his head into the self-same fountain where the head of the decapitated martyr had once been washed, he found the headache was cured. It was a lesson in *reverentia*—in the precise observation due to hallowed things and places, and in their healing power.

Since the end of the era of persecution, the cult of martyrs and the collection of holy relics was moving into the centre-ground of Christian life. Primary relics were those directly connected with the main figures of the Gospels. Secondary relics, with less immediate links, also came to be accepted. Constantinople became the main collecting and distributing centre. Its prize possessions, apart from two fragments of the True Cross, included the Crown of Thorns, the Sacred Lance, the Virgin's Girdle, and several heads of John the Baptist. After the second Council of Nicaea ruled that all new churches should be consecrated in the presence of relics, a brisk trade developed. The body of St Mark was snatched from Alexandria in 823, and brought to Venice. The body of St Nicholas reached Bari in 1087. Western crusaders were to be the greatest relic-mongers of all.

The reverence for relics, so evident in Gregory of Tours, has often been dismissed as mere credulity. Yet close examination shows that it provided the vehicle not only for an emerging code of personal ethics but also for the more subtle games of social politics and social status. *Reverentia* was the mark of a true believer. Its absence marked the pagan, the illiterate, or the complacent. Clerics who officiated at the translation of relics gained in stature, consolidating the consensus or approbation of the flock. Churches or cities in possession of high-grade relics gained in prestige, in divine protection, and no doubt in the revenue from pilgrims. It is a nice paradox that Christian belief in the soul's departure for Paradise should have been surrounded by the paraphernalia of death, and by special veneration for bones and tombs. It was accompanied by an almost Baroque sensibility which stressed how the very special dead emitted the scent of lilies and roses, the aura of shining lights, and the sound of angelic choirs.[1]

With time, however, relics were necessarily devalued. When all the apostles, martyrs, and fathers of the Church had been claimed, there was a danger that every dead bishop would be declared a saint. Bishop Priscus of Lyons, who was elevated to the see in 573, would have none of it. He buried his predecessor, Nicetius, in a standard tomb, and allowed his deacon to wear Nicetius' chasuble as a dressing-gown. As it happened, both Priscus and Nicetius were canonized, but only in 1308.

The Protestant Reformation waged war on relics, and many shrines were then destroyed. But the Protestant rage affected neither the Orthodox nor the Catholic world. The mummies or skeletons of the Very Special Dead can still be viewed in many an Italian church as in the catacombs of the Pecharskaya Lavra, the 'Monastery of the Caves' in Kiev. One of the most extraordinary collections of relics, the twelfth-century Treasure of the Priory of Oignies, has survived intact at Namur. Twice buried to defy the treasure-hunters of the French Revolution and of the Nazi Occupation, its priceless items include St Peter's Rib, St James's Foot, and the Virgin's Milk. All are encased in dazzling reliquaries, each gruesomely shaped to fit the anatomical form of the contents, and fashioned from gold and silver filigree, gemstones, and silver-on-black *niello*. Designated among 'the Seven Wonders of Belgium', they are kept by the Sisters of Our Lady at 17 rue Julie Billiart, Namur.[2]

The Export of Christianity, 395–785

From the day that Christ said 'Follow me', Christianity has been an evangelical religion. And from St Paul's confirmation that it was open to all comers, there were no limits to its potential constituency. But once the Empire had adopted Christianity as the state religion, religious conversion became a matter of imperial policy. For Christian rulers, the export of the faith was directed not just at individual souls but at whole nations: it was a question of strategic ideology. For the would-be converts, too, the acceptance of Christianity involved political considerations. There was much to be gained in terms of literacy and trade. But the decision to import Christianity from Rome, or from Constantinople, or from neither, involved a crucial political choice.

Ireland came to notice at an early date owing to the apparent spread there of Pelagianism. As a result, Germanus of Auxerre, a Gallo-Roman bishop, took a close interest both in the British Isles and in Brittany. One mission headed by Palladius, the 'first Bishop of the believing Irish', who landed at Wicklow in 432, was fruitless; but a second mission by St Patrick (c.385–461), a British disciple of St Germanus, had lasting results. At Tara in Meath he confronted the High King, Laoghaire, kindled the paschal fire on the hill of Slane, and silenced the Druids. The first episcopal see was established at Armagh in 444.

The Frankish conquest of Gaul was closely bound up with the religious divisions of the province. By the fifth century the Gallo-Roman population had been fully converted to Roman Christianity long since. But the Visigoths, Burgundians, and Alamans who first overran them were Arians, whilst the Franks in the north had remained heathen. Clovis did not accept baptism from the hands of St Rémy, Bishop of Reims, until some point between 496 and 506. But by doing so from one of the Roman bishops, he allied his Merovingian dynasty with the Gallo-Roman populace against their initial barbarian rulers. He is said to have used the Catholic bishops of Aquitaine as a 'fifth column'. The 'Catholic connection' of the Franks, therefore, undoubtedly facilitated the consolidation of their power, and laid the foundation for their special relationship with Rome. Much of our knowledge about early Frankish Christianity derives from the *Historia Francorum* of Gregory of Tours (540–94). Yet Gregory's eulogy of the Merovingians cannot hide the fact that Clovis, his 'New Constantine', was something of a savage. Gregory tells the story of the looted vase of Soissons, which had been smashed to pieces by a Frankish warrior who refused to share the spoil. Clovis waited until the Champ de Mars, the annual parade, of the following spring, where he chided the vase-breaker over the state of his equipment. As the warrior bent down to reach for a weapon, Clovis smashed his skull with a battle-axe, saying, '*Thus didst thou to the vase of Soissons*'.[19]

In the sixth century the Christian world was still reeling from the inroads of the barbarians. One series of counter-measures was undertaken by Irish missionaries. Another was launched by the Emperor Justinian, whose reconquests of Africa, Italy, and Spain were motivated in part by the desire to root out Arianism. A third was the work of Gregory I. The Irish missions, which began in 563 with the arrival of St Columba (*c.*521–97) on Iona, were directed first at northern Britain and then at the Frankish dominions. Twenty years later St Columbanus (*c.*540–615) set out with a band of companions from the great monastery at Bangor, bound for Burgundy. He founded several monasteries, including Luxeuil; sojourned at Bregenz on Lake Constance; offended the Burgundian royals by excoriating their loose living; and died at Bobbio, near Genoa. St Gall (d. 640) missionized what is now Switzerland, giving his name to the great religious centre of St Gallen. St Aidan (d. 651) moved from Iona to Holy Island (Lindisfarne) *c.*635, thereby advancing the conversion of England. In all these instances the Irish monks followed practices that were out of step with Rome. Major problems were to arise in the subsequent period in reconciling the Celtic and the Latin traditions. [IONA]

Iberian Christianity was shaken by the imperial invasion of 554. The Arian Visigoths had lived apart from their subjects, who constantly conspired with the imperials of the south. After decades of convulsion, in which the Visigothic kingdom barely held its own against internal rebellion and external attack, Reccared (r. 586–601)—son of an Arian father and a Roman mother—peacefully accepted Catholicism as an act of policy. The decision was confirmed by the second Council of Toledo (589). [COMPOSTELA]

In Italy, at almost the same moment, the heathen Lombards accepted Christianity on the occasion of the marriage of their King Agilulf with the

---

IONA

ONE evening in May 597, the ageing St Columba expired on the altar steps of his abbey church on the tiny, treeless Hebridean island of Iona. He had been copying the Psalms, and had just transcribed the verse of Psalm 34: 'They that seek the Lord shall want no good thing.' A native of Donegal, he had founded many churches in Ireland, starting with Derry, before landing with twelve brothers on the *Innis Druinidh*, 'The Isle of Druids' in 563. The 'Apostle of Caledonia', who crowned the King of Dalriada in his island church, he was instrumental in the expansion of Celtic Christianity and Gaelic civilization to western Scotland. By its mission to Lindisfarne in Northumbria, his community would also launch the Christianization of northern England. He died in the same year that St Augustine of Canterbury established the Roman mission in Kent.

The fate of the Celtic Church on Iona is instructive. It survived the terrible Viking raid of 806, when the abbot and 68 monks were killed. The monks of St Columba's tradition were driven out *c*.1200, when Reginald, Lord of the Isles, set up a Benedictine monastery and Augustinian convent in their stead. These establishments were already dead or moribund when, in 1560, the reformed Church of Scotland abolished monasticism outright. The island itself passed into the hands of the Campbell Dukes of Argyle, who in 1899 returned it to the Church of Scotland with a view to restoration. The reconstructed cathedral was reconsecrated in 1905. The reconstituted Iona community, dedicated to ecumenical work and prayer, was founded by Dr George Macleod in 1938.[1] Every age has its own brand of Christianity.

Catholic Frank, Theodelinda. At the basilica of Monza, near Milan, which they founded, the iron crown of Lombardy can still be seen with its inscription: AGILULF GRATIA DEI VIR GLORIOSUS REX TOTIUS ITALIAE OFFERT SANCTO IOHANNI BAPTISTAE IN ECCLESIA MODICAE. Conflict between Catholics and Arians persisted until the eventual Catholic victory at Coronate in 689. [LEPER]

England is said to have caught the attention of the Roman Patriarchs when Gregory I saw fair-headed boys for sale in the slave-market. *Non Angli, sed angeli* (not Angles, but angels), he remarked. Shortly afterwards, in 596–7, he dispatched one of his monks, St Augustine of Canterbury (d. 605) to convert the heathen English. Within a short period Ethelbert, King of Kent, was baptized, and sees were set up at Canterbury, Rochester, and London. The complex story of English Christianity forms the life-work of the 'Venerable' Bede (673–735), monk of Jarrow in Northumbria, whose *History of the English Church and People* is one of the monuments of the age. Bede was specially interested in the conflict between the northern and southern missions, with their rival centres at York and

COMPOSTELA

A CCORDING to legend, the body of St James the Apostle, together with its severed head, was brought in a stone boat from Palestine to Galicia some time in the fourth century. The mooring-post to which the boat was tied is preserved in the tiny harbour church at Padrón near Corunna. News of the event began to circulate more widely, and some two hundred years later the site of the saint's shrine at Libredon, or Santiago, attracted a growing stream of pilgrims. In 859, an invocation to St James gave the Christians of Leon a miraculous victory over the Moors. The saint gained the epithet of *Matamoros* or 'Moorslayer'; and Leon grew into a sovereign kingdom. From 899 a new cathedral was built over the saint's tomb as a focus for the pilgrimage. Its emblem was the pilgrim's scrip and the Atlantic starshell, *la compostela*.

Pilgrims' motives were not simple. Some set out from a belief in the power of famous saints to intercede for their souls. Some set out for a cure. Many went for the joy of fellowship, for a rollicking adventure, or for baser reasons of lust, gain, or escape. Santiago was specially attractive because it lay 'as far as one could go', and because it was chosen by the Church as a place of formal penance.

Four long pilgrim trails led half-way across Western Europe to Santiago (see Appendix III, p. 1253). One started at the Church of St Jacques in Paris, and led south via Tours, Poitiers, Saintes, and Bordeaux. The second started at Ste Marie-Madeleine at Vézelay in Burgundy, leading south-west through Bourges and Limoges. The third started at the cathedral of Notre Dame at Le Puy-en-Velay in Auvergne. All three converged at the Pass of Roncevalles in the Pyrenees. A fourth route left St Trophime in Arles, led westwards to Toulouse, crossed the Pyrenees at the Col de Somport, and met the three other routes at Puente la Reina on the River Arga. For the last 250 miles, through the ever-wilder scenery of Asturias, Burgos, and Leon, all pilgrims walked along the same *Camino de Santiago* until they stood before the Portal de la Gloria.

At its height in the fourteenth and fifteenth centuries, the pilgrimage to Santiago was a major transcontinental business. English and Irish pilgrims often made first for Tours, or sailed to Talmont on the Gironde. The Germans and Swiss came down the Rhône to Lyons en route for Vézelay or Le Puy. Italians sailed to Marseilles or direct to Arles. Guide books were written. Abbeys and shrines on the way, such as the Abbey of Ste Foy at Conques, grew rich from pilgrims' donations. The refuge at Roncevalles served 30,000 meals a year. Churchyards along the road received the remains of those who could go no further.

Historians discuss the factors which made for the unity of Christendom. Santiago de Compostela was certainly one of them.[1]

LEPER

I N 643 King Rothar of Lombardy issued a decree: 'If any man become a leper . . . and is expelled from his city or dwelling, let him not donate his possessions to anyone. For on the very day he is expelled, he is considered dead.'[1] This, in itself, is enough to dispel the myth that leprosy came to Europe with the Crusades.

The ostracism of lepers is attested throughout the Middle Ages. Byzantium, which possessed at least one lazar-house in the fifth century, shared the same attitudes. Leviticus 13 offered ample biblical support. Lepers were forced to live beyond town limits; they had to wear a long robe of distinctive colour marked by the letter L; and they had to signal their approach by bell, clapper, or horn, or by shouting, 'Unclean, unclean!' The sixth-century Council of Lyons formally placed them under the care of bishops. In fact, they lived from begging. In 1179 the Third Lateran Council formalized the procedures. Suspect lepers were to be examined before a priest or magistrate and, if found infected, were to be ritually separated from the community through an act of symbolic burial.

A description of this ceremony, the *separatio leprosorum*, was written down at St Algin's in Angers. The penitent leper stood in an open grave with a black cloth over his head. The priest said: 'Be dead to the world, be reborn in God.' The leper said: 'Jesus, my Redeemer . . . may I be reborn in Thee.' Then the priest read the proscription:

I forbid you to enter church, monastery, fair, mill, marketplace or tavern . . . I forbid you ever to leave your house without your leper's costume, or to walk barefoot . . . I forbid you to wash or to drink in the stream or fountain . . . I forbid you to live with any woman other than your own. If you meet and talk with some person on the road, I forbid you to answer before you have moved downwind . . . I forbid you to touch a well, or well cord, without your gloves. I forbid you ever to touch children, or to give them anything . . . I forbid you eating or drinking, except with lepers.[2]

The leper was then led in procession to the place of exile.

Some rulers sanctioned more ferocious methods. In 1318 Philip V of France charged the country's lepers of being in league with 'the Saracens', and of poisoning wells. He ordered them all to be burned, together with Jews who gave them counsel and comfort.[3] In 1371, 1388, 1394, 1402, and 1404 the municipality of Paris vainly called for the leprosy laws to be enforced. The ferocity of their reactions derived from the rooted belief that leprosy was a punishment for sexual depravity. The disease carried a heavy moral stigma, which caused the risk of contagion to be grossly exaggerated.

Even so, leprosy affected high and low. It struck down Baldwin IV, King of Jerusalem, and Hugh d'Orivalle, Bishop of London (d. 1085). Physicians had no clue of its bacterial cause, and few suggestions for its relief. Following Avicenna, they stressed its supposed psychological symptoms of craftiness and lust. The *leprosarium* or lazar-house was a common sight beyond city walls. In England the leper colony at Hambledown, near Canterbury, grew into a sizeable settlement. At Burton Lazar it was located near the healing waters, later used for brewing.

Medieval literature used leprosy as a sensational device. In several versions of Tristan and Isolde, the heroine is saved from burning only to be thrown to the lepers:

> Do sprach der herzoge, ich wil sie
> minen sichen bringen,
> die suln sie alle minnen
> sô stirbet sie lesterlichen.

(The Duke spoke: I will bring her to my sick ones. They will all love her, so that she will die dishonourably.)[4]

By all accounts leprosy greatly declined in sixteenth-century Europe. Its place was taken by syphilis [**SYPHILUS**]. But prejudices did not change. In 1933 the *OED* defined it as 'a loathsome disease', *elephantiasis graecorum*. And in 1959 a popular American novelist could be criticized for repeating all the old degrading stereotypes.[5] Leprosy was the medieval counterpart to AIDS.

Canterbury, and in their eventual reconciliation at the Synod of Whitby (664). He also records the extensive correspondence of Pope Gregory with Augustine:

Augustine's Eighth Question. May an expectant mother be baptised? How soon after childbirth may she enter church? And how soon after birth may a child be baptised if in danger of death? How soon after childbirth may a husband have relations with his wife? And may a woman enter church at certain periods? And may she receive Communion at these times? And may a man enter church after relations with his wife before he has washed? Or receive the sacred mystery of communion? These uncouth English people require guidance on all these matters.[20]

Gregory was specially solicitous to adapt heathen practices to Christian usage.

We have come to the conclusion that the temples of idols . . . should on no account be destroyed. He is to destroy the idols, but the temples themselves are to be aspersed with holy water, altars set up, and relics enclosed in them . . . In this way, we hope that the people may abandon idolatry . . . and resort to these places as before . . . And since they have a custom of sacrificing many oxen to devils, let some other solemnity be substituted in its place . . . They are no longer to sacrifice beasts to the Devil, but they may kill them for food to the praise of God . . . If the people are allowed some worldly pleasures . . . they will come more readily to desire the joys of the spirit. For it is impossible to eradicate all errors from obstinate minds at a stroke; and whoever wishes to climb to a mountaintop climbs step by step . . .[21]

This caution no doubt explains the ultimate success of the missions: but it envisaged an extended period where thinly veiled heathen practices coexisted with a slowly evolving Christianity. Generally speaking, the Church was successful in its evangelical mission because it managed to appeal to the 'barbarian' outlook. It was able to convince its converts that only through baptism could one become part of the civilized order. The interplay of Christian authors with pagan themes, which is evident, for example, in the Anglo-Saxon poem *Beowulf*, provided a central feature of cultural life over a very long period.

In the East, the emperors were too preoccupied with the Muslim onslaught to show much concern for the souls of their non-Christian subjects and neighbours. For the time being, the great *Sclavinia* was largely left to its own devices, as were the Bulgars. In the seventh and eighth centuries Constantinople contented itself with the rehellenization and rechristianization of the Peloponnese and the islands. It is not an episode which commands much comment in modern histories of Greece. Crete remained in Muslim hands until the tenth century.

Despite the example of the Franks, the Germanic tribes to the east of the Rhine held Christianity at arm's length for two centuries more. The task of conversion was left to English missionaries from the north, and to Frankish warriors from the west. St Wilfred of York (634–710), whose Catholic line had been carried at Whitby, began by preaching in Friesland in 678–9. But the central figure was undoubtedly St Boniface of Crediton (*c*.675–755), creator of the first German see at Mainz, founder of the great abbey at Fulda (744), and martyr of the faith at Dokkum in Friesland. Boniface had many close assistants, among them the well-named SS Sturm and Lull, who quarrelled over Fulda, St Willibald of Bavaria (*c*.700–86), the first known English pilgrim to the Holy Land, his brother St Winebald of Thuringia (d. 761), and his sister St Walburga (d. 779), abbess of Heidenheim.

The peaceable work of the English missionaries was complemented, not to say disgraced, by the merciless campaigns of the Franks in Saxony between 772 and 785. Submission to Christianity was an absolute condition of the Frankish conquest, where butchery and treachery were the normal instruments both of attack and resistance. The sacred grove of Irminsul was axed at the outset; and mass baptisms were performed at nearby Paderborn, and again in the Ocker and the Elbe. The Saxon rebels, some 4,500 of whom were beheaded in the massacre of Verden (782), were finally broken when their leader, Witikind, surrendered to the holy water. Missionary bishoprics were created at Bremen, Verden, Minden, Münster, Paderborn, and Osnabrück.

The advance of Christianity into central Germany marked the beginning of a strategic change. Up to that point Christianity had been largely confined to the Roman Empire, or to lands which retained an important leaven of ex-Roman, Christian citizens. To a large extent it was still the 'imperial religion', even in places that had long since severed their imperial links. But now it was edging into countries that had never claimed any sort of connection with the Empire. The Rhineland had once been a Roman province; Saxony had not. Whilst several ex-Roman provinces still awaited the return of the faith, especially in the Balkans, Christianity was starting to creep into untouched heathen territory. After Germany, Slavdom awaited its turn, and beyond the Slavs, Scandinavia and the Balts.

If the first stage of christianization, the conversion of the Empire, had taken 400 years, the second stage, the reconversion of the former Roman provinces, was drawing to a close after another 400. The third stage, the conversion of virgin hea-thendom, was to last for six long centuries after that (see pp. 321–8, 430). [**BIBLIA**]

At first sight it may seem that the processes which provide the main themes of the Dark Ages were not closely related. What is more, none of them came to an end during this period. The long procession of barbarian irruptions continued until the last Mongol raid of 1287 (see pp. 364–6). The split between East and West was projected from the imperial to the ecclesiastical plane, and was not formalized until 1054 (see p. 330). The Christian conversion of Europe's pagans was not completed until 1417 (see p. 430). The soldiers of Islam were still on the march when the

---

BIBLIA

THE 6th century *Codex Argenteus* (Cod. DG 1 fol. 118v) is kept in the University Library at Uppsala. It was brought to Sweden from Prague. Written in silver letters on purple parchment, it is probably the finest early copy of the Gothic translation of the Bible completed by Ulfilas (Wulfilla, c.311–83). Wulfilla, or 'Little Wolf', the Arian grandson of Christian captives, was consecrated 'Bishop of the Goths' during their sojourn on the Danube frontier. His translation of the Bible into Gothic started the long history of vernacular scriptures and of Germanic literature.

The *Codex Amiatinus*, now in the Laurentian Library in Florence, is not quite so old. It was written at Jarrow in Northumbria c.690–700 during the rule of Abbot Ceolfrid. It is the oldest extant copy of the Vulgate, St Jerome's translation of the scriptures into Latin. It was based on an older Vulgate copy by Cassiodorus (see p. 266), and was presented by Abbot Ceolfrid to the Papacy, whence in turn it was lodged in the Abbey of Amiata. The vellum on which it was written was made from the skins of 1,500 animals.

It is worthy of note that Wulfilla completed his Gothic translation prior to St Jerome's translation of the Bible into Latin. Both of them based their translation on older Greek texts, of which there was no single authoritative version. Modern reconstructions of the early Greek scriptures are based on the 4th-century *Codex Vaticanus* from Alexandria, on the 4th-century *Codex Sinaiticus*, brought from Mt. Sinai and sold to the British Museum by a Russian Tsar: on the 5th-century *Codex Alexandrinus*, also in the British Library, which came from Constantinople, and the 5th-century *Codex Ephraemi* in the Bibliothèque Nationale in Paris.

The task of establishing a totally accurate and reliable text of the scriptures, suited to each passing generation, has always been impossible. But the attempt has to be made ceaselessly. The *Old Testament* was written in Hebrew and Aramaic, the *New Testament* in Hellenistic Greek. The former was put into Greek, as the Septuagint, for the use of the Greek-speaking Jews in Alexandria. So, in theory, a complete Greek text of both testaments may be thought to have existed from the 1st century AD onwards.

Those books which make up the present Bible, in its Catholic and Protestant forms, number almost one hundred. They could not be collated into a unified *pandekt* of both Testaments, until the basic canon was established in the 4th century. In the meantime, numerous variations of every book of the Bible, together with the uncanonical apocrypha, circulated separately. They are only known to modern scholarship in the fragments found in ancient papyri, in passages quoted by the Fathers, in various pre-Vulgate 'Old Faith' texts, and in the work of ancient Judaic and Christian critics. Among the latter, by far the most important was the wonderful *Hexapla* of Origen, who wrote out six Hebrew and Greek versions of the Old Testament in six parallel columns. [**PAPYRUS**]

Not even the Vulgate existed in systematic form. As St Jerome completed successive sections of his work, he sent each off to assorted destinations. They, too, have to be unscrambled from the variegated biblical compilations into which they were inserted. What is more, the work of medieval copyists resembled nothing more than the game of 'Chinese Whispers', where errors are compounded at every stage. It is easy to see why the Greek word *biblia* or holy 'books' (pl.) originally existed only in the plural. Uniform biblical texts were not attainable until the age of printing. [**PRESS**]

By then, however, Christendom was on the verge of the Reformation when Protestants would challenge all previous biblical scholarship. Protestant scholars were specially dedicated to vernacular translations for which they needed authoritative texts of the Hebrew and Greek originals. Hence a whole new era of bibliology characterized by Protestant–Catholic rivalry.

In 1907 a Vatican Commission entrusted the preparation of a definitive edition of the Vulgate to the Benedictines. Work has continued throughout the twentieth century. When it may be complete, as one stoical Benedictine remarked, 'God only knows'.[1]

Ottomans landed in Europe in 1354 (see p. 386). Only then was the Roman Empire finally heading for extinction.

None the less, these various processes *did* interact; and the essential effects of their interaction can be identified by the time that most of the Mediterranean was conquered by the armies of the Prophet. It was the four centuries following Constantine that brought Europe into being. This was the period when the majority of the Peninsula's diverse peoples found their way to permanent homelands. This was the period when the rump of the Roman Empire became just one among many sovereign states in a community of 'Christendom' that was consolidating behind the screen of Islam. No one yet used the name of 'Europe' to describe this community; but there can be little doubt that it was already in existence.

Mons Iovis, The Pennine Alps, *c.*25 November AD 753. It was very late in the season, just before the winter snows. Stephen II, Bishop and Patriarch of Rome, was hurrying to cross the Alps before the roads were blocked. He had come from Pavia on the Po, the capital of the Lombard kingdom, and was entering the kingdom of the Franks. He was heading in the first instance for the monastery of St Maurice on the upper Rhône. From there he would make for the royal villa of Ponthion on the Marne—a journey of nearly 500 miles. Averaging ten or twelve miles a day, it would take him six weeks.[22]

The Mons Jovis, 'Jupiter's Mount', carried one of two Roman roads constructed seven centuries earlier to link the provinces of Cisalpine and Transalpine Gaul. Also known as Alpis Poenina or 'Pennine Pass', it had once been the gateway to the lands of the Helvetii. It reached an elevation of 2,476 m or 8,111 ft. The stone-paved roadway, 4 metres wide, had been designed for wheeled traffic, which in the old days would have covered the 55 miles from Augusta Praetoria (Aosta) to Octodorus (Martigny) in one day. In the eighth century the going was harder. The locals would have called it by a name that was part-way between the Latin Mons Jovis and the modern Monte Iove or Montjoux.*

Stephen II had been raised to St Peter's throne in unexpected circumstances twenty months previously. The orphaned son of an aristocratic Roman family, he had been brought up in the patriarchal palace of St John Lateran, and had served Patriarch Zacharias (r. 741–52) as deacon. A career administrator, he had been sufficiently senior to put his signature to the acts of the Roman synod of 743. So a decade later he was probably in middle age. After Zacharias's death he would have been present when an elderly priest, also called Stephen, was chosen to succeed. He would have shared the sense of shock when Priest Stephen died of a stroke, unconsecrated, after only four days; and he must have been totally unprepared when he himself was acclaimed on the same day. Thanks to Priest Stephen's

---

* The name Grand St Bernard was not adopted until after the 11th c., when St Bernard of Montjoux (d. 1008) built hospices on the summits both of the Alpis Poenina and of the Alpis Graia (the Little St Bernard). The breed of huge St Bernard dogs, which were trained to rescue travellers from the snow, dates from the same period, 3 centuries after Stephen II's journey.

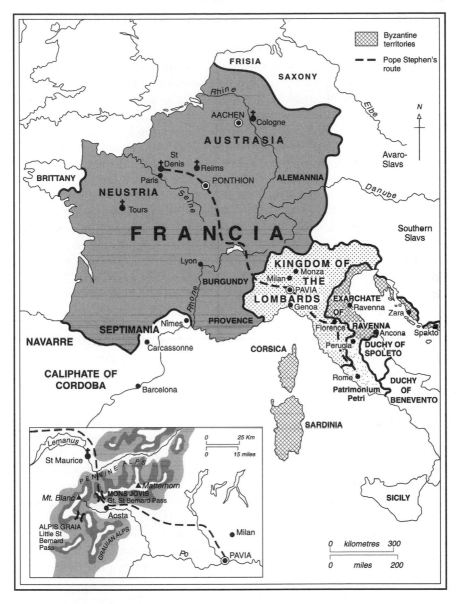

Map 11.
Pope Stephen's Journey, AD 753

uncertain status, Deacon Stephen is variously numbered as Stephen II, Stephen III, or Stephen II (III).[23]

Zacharias, a learned Greek from Calabria, had been pursuing a line of policy established by his predecessors, Gregory II (715–31) and Gregory III (731–41). Whilst resisting the Iconoclastic demands of Emperor Constantine Copronymos, he had taken care not to break with the Empire. At the same time he had followed northern affairs with close interest. He had been in constant touch with St Boniface, whom he commissioned as legate to romanize Frankish church practices. Most importantly, at the request of the Franks, he had issued a formal ruling which stated that it was desirable for royal titles to be held by those who actually exercised power. In effect, he had authorized the deposition of the last Merovingian king. He had signed a twenty-year truce with the Lombards on behalf of the city of Rome, and had tried to mediate in the Lombards' quarrels with the Byzantine Exarch of Ravenna. But in the last year of his life he had been powerless to restrain the Lombards' aggressive new king, Aistulf. In 751 Aistulf seized Ravenna, before marching south. When Lombard agents started to exact an annual tax from Rome, it was clear that the long-established freedoms of the city and the Patriarch were directly threatened. These were the events which had provoked the journey by Zacharias's successor.

Francia or 'Frankland', the largest of the successor states to the western Roman Empire, had been ruled for 300 years by the descendants of Count Merovig (d. 458), grandfather of Clovis I. It stretched from the Pyrenees to the Weser. Of its three constituent parts, Neustria, centred on Paris, and Burgundy on the Rhône were still essentially Gallo-Roman, whilst Austrasia in the East, centred on Reims, was the original Frankish homeland and predominantly Germanic. Over the generations it had frequently been partitioned and reunited. In the eighth century the Merovingian monarchy had lost all but nominal control to Austrasia's hereditary 'mayors of the palace', the Arnulfings, who exercised effective rule over the whole country. In 751 it was the Mayor, Peppin III, Charles Martel's grandson, who had sent envoys to Patriarch Zacharias to ask 'whether it was just for one to reign and for another to rule'. On receiving the desired answer, he had arrested his king, Childeric III, and seized the throne. (See Appendix III, p. 1246.)

As the travellers toiled to the top of the pass, the state of the road amidst the grandiose rigours of the mountains must have made a deep impression. The once smooth pavement was cracked, jagged, overgrown, and in places completely washed away. Its great stone slabs had been left unrepaired for longer than anyone remembered. The imperial posts had ceased to function. In a hollow below the barren, mist-strewn summit, the ruins of the Temple of Jupiter Poeninus stood forlorn beside the frozen lake. Having lived all his life within sight of the decaying Forum, Stephen did not need to be reminded about the passing of Roman glory. But the desolation of the pass must have matched his mood. He cannot have ignored the fact that he was embarking on something that none of his predecessors had risked. Though Gregory II had once prepared a similar journey, it was called off. No bishop of Rome had ever crossed the Alps. When

Stephen started the long descent to St Maurice he must have pondered the implications. He was not acting on impulse. He had sent for assistance to Constantinople, but in vain. He had visited Pavia, and had appealed to King Aistulf in person, but to no effect. He was turning to the Franks in a final, calculated step to avert disaster. If an anachronistic phrase is permitted, he was 'calling in the New World to redress the balance of the Old'.

The Christendom in which the Roman Patriarch was seeking to establish a more central role was smaller than it had been in the past, or was destined to be in the future. It had been greatly diminished by the Arab conquests of the previous century, and had not yet spread to the lands in the centre and east of the Peninsula. The Byzantine Empire had withstood the Arab siege of 718, but was hemmed into the Balkans and Asia Minor. The Muslims had recently won the whole of the western Mediterranean and most of Iberia. Though driven back from the Loire some twenty years before, they still held much of southern Gaul, where the Gothic cities of Nîmes and Beziers were in a state of revolt. If Stephen had crossed the neighbouring pass of the Alpis Graia, some twenty miles to the west, he would have found himself descending into Muslim territory.

At that juncture, Latin Christendom was confined to a narrow corridor running from the British Isles to central Italy. Half-way between the Lindisfarne Gospels and the Book of Kells, the Celtic art of illumination was at its peak. In England, the Venerable Bede had died just eighteen years back. His mantle in Anglo-Saxon scholarship had passed to Alcuin, who was to make his name in Germany. The central part of Germany had only just been converted. Its patron, St Boniface, had passed away only two years before, leaving the Abbey of Fulda and its choir-school in its infancy. The Lombard rulers of Italy had been Catholics since the previous century, but they looked with suspicion on the liberties of Rome. They smelled treason whenever the Patriarchs had sided with the citizens against Pavia. Their control of central and southern Italy, through the duchies of Tuscany, Spoleto, and Benevento, was contested by the Byzantines, whose themes (or provinces) of Sicily, of Calabria, and of Naples were still intact.

By far the greatest part of the European Peninsula was still held by heathen tribes. Scandinavia was fast approaching the point of explosion when its wild Viking raiders would pour out over the northern seas. The heathen Frisians and Saxons had been repeatedly ravaged by the Franks, but had not been finally subdued. At this very moment, the Frankish ruler whom Stephen was going to meet, Peppin the Short (r. 751–68), was resting at Bonn, having just completed the latest of his punitive campaigns into Saxony. Further east, the heathen Slavs held all the lands from the mouth of the Elbe to the Aegean. In addition to the Elbe, they commanded almost all the great rivers—the Oder, the Vistula, the middle Danube, and the Dnieper. Kiev had recently been recorded as a staging-post on the river route from the Baltic to the Black Sea and Mesopotamia.

Fortunately for Christendom, the Muslim world was in turmoil. The Abbasid caliphate was in the early stages of moving its centre of gravity from Arabia to Persia. Al-Mansur was on the march. His son, Harun-al-Rashid, who would be known to history as the hero of the *Thousand and One Nights*, was a young boy. The last of the defeated Omayyads was on his way to Spain to found the emirate of Cordoba.

The events of Patriarch Stephen's journey have to be reconstructed from two main sources—one Roman, the other Frankish. The *Vita Stephani* forms part of the huge compilation known as the *Liber Pontificalis*, which is made up from a long series of biographies and decretals dating from the sixth to the seventeenth centuries.[24] It is at pains to present the episode from the papal point of view. In contrast, the third continuation of the Chronicle of the Pseudo-Fredegar forms an appendix to the main Frankish record of the Merovingian era.[25] It is confined to the reign of Peppin III, and was written on the orders of Peppin's relative Count Nibelung. It is at pains to present the Carolingian point of view. The emphases and omissions of the two sources have given historians a broad range of interpretation.

The sources say little directly about the political bargain which inspired Stephen's journey; yet the outline is clear. Although Peppin had taken the precaution of seeking papal advice before his *coup d'état*, and had probably been consecrated by St Boniface, his right to rule was obviously open to question. Equally, although Stephen II had consulted both the Emperor and the Lombard King, his appeal to the Franks must have been unsettling to both of them. The essence of the deal that was brewing, therefore, was that Rome should provide what Peppin lacked in legitimacy if the Franks would supply what Rome was lacking in force of arms. Stephen II was willing to give his religious sanction to Peppin's rule in return for Peppin restoring political order in Italy.

Later tradition assumed that a sovereign Roman papacy had every right to act without reference to the Byzantine Emperor. But that was to read history backwards. Formally, the Patriarch of Rome *did* owe allegiance to the Empire. His virtual immunity in the Eternal City had been gained without legal sanction. Not that there is reason to suppose that he was deliberately seeking to damage the Empire's interests. After all, he had started out in the company of the imperial ambassador, who accompanied him to Pavia for the interview with Aistulf. In recommending his plan to Peppin he was to use the phrase 'for the cause of St Peter and the Roman Republic'. Prior to the formation of the Papal State, *respublica romanorum* could only have referred to the Byzantine Empire. Calling in one barbarian chief to fight off another was one of the Empire's oldest tactics. So it has to be argued that calling in the Franks was not in itself an act of disloyalty. Stephen II did not breach his faith with the Empire until the end of the story.

The Patriarch's initial progress is recorded in the *Liber Pontificalis*. He leaves Rome on 15 October, and travels to Pavia. The *malignus rex langobardorum*, 'the evil king of the Lombards', hears him out but fails to deflect him from his purpose. He leaves Pavia on 15 November:

Unde et cum nimia celeritate, Deo praevio, ad Francorum coniunxit clusas. Quas ingressus cum his qui cum eo erant, confestim laudes omnipotenti Deo reddidit; et coeptum gradiens iter, ad venerabile monasterium sancti Christi martyris Mauricii . . . sospes hisdem beatissimus pontifex . . . advenit.

(From Pavia, with God's aid, he reached the gates of the Frankish Kingdom with tremendous speed. Having crossed [the pass] with his entourage, he gladly rendered praise to Almighty God. The start of the journey was steep, but the blessed pontifex [came through] unhurt to the venerable monastery of St Maurice, a martyr of Christ.)[26]

He was travelling in the company of a dozen high-ranking priests, and was escorted by the Frankish envoys Duke Aitchar (Ogier) and the Chancellor, Bishop Chrodegang of Metz.

At St Maurice the Patriarch was welcomed into the Frankish realm by Peppin's personal representative, Abbot Fulrad of St Denis. The monastery was built on the site of Agaunum, where five centuries before the Roman centurion Mauricius had met his death, having urged the soldiers of the Theban legion to disobey orders rather than fight their fellow Christians. From there, a message was sent to Peppin to arrange the rendezvous at Ponthion. The messengers found the King in the Ardennes, on his way back from Bonn. Peppin sent instructions for his young son Charles to ride out and meet the visitor on the road. After leaving St Maurice, Patriarch Stephen rounded Lake Lemanus and crossed the Jura. His encounter with the King's son took place somewhere in Burgundy in late December. The twelve-year-old Charles had made a hundred miles south from Ponthion.

Stephen reached Ponthion on 6 January 754. According to the Roman account, the King came to greet him outside the town, dismounted, prostrated himself, and personally held the Patriarch's bridle. At which point, in tears, the Patriarch beseeched the King's aid:

'Beatissimus papa praefatum Christianissimum regem lacrimabiliter deprecatus est, ut per pacis foedera causam beati Petri et republicae Romanorum disponeret.

(The blessed pope tearfully begged the supreme and most Christian king that he would reach agreements in the cause of peace, of St Peter, and of the Roman Republic.)[27]

According to the Frankish account, 'the Pope of Rome came into the King's presence . . . showered rich gifts upon him and his Franks, and asked for his help against the Lombards and their king on account of their double dealing'.[28] Peppin then handed Stephen to the care of Abbot Fulrad, to winter at St Denis.

In the following weeks Peppin exchanged embassies with Aistulf. A Frankish envoy was sent to Pavia, enjoining the Lombards to desist from their seizures of territory and their 'heretical demands'. Aistulf countered by sending Peppin's younger brother, Carloman, as his envoy to the Franks. (Carloman had retired to a monastery in Rome, and was thus a resident of the Lombard realm.) On 1 March the Franks held their annual parade, the Champ de Mars, at Bernacus (Berny-Rivière, Aisne). Then at Cariascum (Quercy), at Easter, on 14 April, they assembled to discuss the destination of the season's campaign. Not without dissent, they decided to march against the Lombards.

Here the sources diverge. The continuator of Fredegard's Chronicle relates how the Frankish army crossed the Alps at Mont Cenis and inflicted a crushing defeat on the Lombards in the Val de Susa. The *Liber Pontificalis*, in contrast, relates how at midsummer Stephen reconsecrated Peppin and his Queen Bertrada at St Denis, anointing them with holy oil and granting them the title of 'Patricians of the Romans'. Peppin's sons and heirs were given the papal blessing to rule in perpetuity. The historicity of these proceedings is confirmed in another contemporary document, apparently an eyewitness account, the *Clausula de Unctione Peppini*. One may surmise that Frankish commentators were embarrassed by the fact that Peppin's desire for reconsecration underlined the impropriety of his earlier coronation.

The consequences took a couple of years to clarify. After the first Frankish victory, Aistulf submitted to Peppin and the Bishop was restored to Rome. Within months, however, the Lombards broke their oath and returned to their attacks. In 756, therefore, Peppin mounted a second campaign against Lombardy, capturing Pavia and crushing all resistance. On this occasion, if not before, the Franks took the former Exarchate of Ravenna away from the Lombards and donated it to the Patriarch. By doing so they created the territorial basis for the Papal State. By accepting it as part of the patrimony of St Peter, in defiance of Byzantine claims, the Bishop revealed that his allegiance to the Emperor had been renounced.

Yet several items remain confused. It seems that many important details were written into the sources after the event. In this kind of operation the papal chancery was specially expert. The *Liber Pontificalis* states, for example, that the 'Donation of Peppin' was made not in 756 but in 753 at Quercy. What is more, it insists that Peppin was merely returning a property to which Rome possessed ancient title. As is now known, the papal chancery was concocting the spurious Donation of Constantine at this very time. Until the forgery was unmasked in the sixteenth century, all loyal Catholics were misled into believing that the Roman Church had received the Exarchate of Ravenna from the hands of the first Christian emperor 400 years before Peppin. It would appear, therefore, that the false 'Donation of Constantine' may have been concocted in order to reinforce the genuine Donation of Peppin. It also appears, in the midst of his chastisement of the Lombards, that Peppin established friendly relations with the Byzantines. The Frankish continuator says that he doesn't know what happened to this friendship except that it didn't flourish.[29] What happened, of course, was that the Byzantines asked for the return of their Exarchate, only to be told that it had recently been given to the Pope. Betrayed by Rome and powerless against the Franks, the Byzantines were left trying to make common cause with the Lombards.

As so often in history, the long-term consequences were not foreseen. The Franks were unable to disentangle themselves from Italy. The Bishop of Rome put himself in a position to be recognized as the supreme Patriarch, 'the Pope'; the papacy gained the territorial basis for a sovereign state; and the Franco-papal alliance became a durable feature of the international scene. By daring to cross the Alps, Stephen II had personally forged the link which gave the north a permanent voice in the affairs of the south. Above all, the authority of the Empire was critically weakened in the West. The boy who had ridden out to greet Bishop Stephen in Burgundy was left with the idea that he might found an empire of his own.

V

MEDIUM

The Middle Age, c.750–1270

THERE is an air of immobility about many descriptions of the medieval world. The impression is created by emphasizing the slow pace of technological change, the closed character of feudal society, and the fixed, theocratic perceptions of human life. The prime symbols of the period are the armoured knight on his lumbering steed; the serfs tied to the land of their lord's demesne; and cloistered monks and nuns at prayer. They are made to represent physical immobility, social immobility, intellectual immobility.

Medium Aevum, 'the Middle Age', was a term first used by devout Christians who saw themselves living in the interval between Christ's first and Second Coming. Much later it was taken up for different purposes. Renaissance scholars began to talk in the fifteenth century of the 'Middle Age' as the interval between the decline of antiquity and the revival of classical culture in their own times. For them, the ancient world stood for high civilization; the Middle Age represented a descent into barbarism, parochiality, religious bigotry. During the Enlightenment, when the virtues of human reason were openly lauded over those of religious belief, 'medievalism' became synonymous with obscurantism and backwardness. Since then, of course, as the 'Modern Age' which followed the Middle Age was itself fading into the past, new terms had to be invented to mark the passage of time. The medieval period has been incorporated into the fourfold convention which divides European history into ancient, medieval, modern, and now contemporary sections. By convention also, the medieval period is often subdivided into early, high, and late phases, creating several successive Middle Ages. Of course, people whom later historians refer to as 'medieval' had no inkling of that designation.

Unfortunately, there are no clear lines which mark the end of the ancient world or the beginning of modern times. The start of the medieval period has been fixed at any number of points from the conversion of Constantine onwards. Its end has variously been fixed at 1453, at 1493, at 1517, or even, by those who use their own definition of feudalism as the touchstone of medievality, at 1917. Almost all medievalists would agree, therefore, that the label which defines their subject is unsatisfactory. Many who base their views on a knowledge of Western Europe alone would stress the contrast between the destructive tendencies of the early medieval phase and the constructive tendencies of the later phase. In this scheme, the 'Dark Ages' of the fifth to eleventh centuries are characterized by the progressive dismemberment of the Roman world; the turning-point is reached with the so-called 'twelfth-century renaissance'; and the peak of 'high' medieval civilization is reached in the thirteenth and fourteenth centuries. These distinctions bear little relation to the East, where the Roman Empire survived until 1453, and where no 'renaissance' in the Western sense was ever experienced.

Most would agree, however, that the unifying feature of the medieval world is to be found in organized Christianity. Here they would accord with the people of medieval Europe, who, if asked, would have seen themselves as Christians, living in the Christian era and in the Christian part of the earth. Yet Christendom itself was an elastic concept. It contracted and expanded over the centuries in response to the wars with Islam and the campaigns against the pagans. It was never exactly coterminous with the Peninsula of 'Europe'. The Christendom known to Stephen II, when he crossed the Alps in 753, was a very different place from the Christendom of 1453, when the Turks scaled the walls of Constantinople.

The vacuum left by the decline of the Roman Empire was filled by the growing awareness of Christendom, not just as a religious community but also as a coherent political entity. Though the Roman Empire ultimately perished, its religion triumphed. The spiritual and temporal leaders of Christianity gradually assumed the mantle of the Caesars. In the West, where the Empire first crumbled, it was the Bishop of Rome who conceived the notion of a new order predicated on the joint authority of the Latin Church and a Catholic Emperor. 'The Papacy', wrote Thomas Hobbes, 'is no other than the Ghost of the deceased Roman Empire sitting crowned upon the grave thereof.'[1] The chosen instrument of the Papacy was found in the new Caesars or 'Kaisers' of Germany. In the East, where the Roman Empire survived far longer, the notion of a substitute order, based on the authority of the Greek Church and of a new Orthodox Emperor, had to await the emergence of the Caesars or 'Tsars' of Moscow.

In this light, if the central theme of the Middle Ages is taken to be the reorganization of Christendom into new imperial systems, a clear chronological framework emerges. The first step may be seen in the coronation of Charlemagne on Christmas Day in the year 800, the last step in the definitive adoption of the title of Tsar by Ivan III, Grand Duke of Moscow, in 1493.

From an early stage, however, the growing community of Christendom was divided against itself. Though the Latin and the Greek Churches shared all their basic beliefs, they often regarded each other as aliens. Though impartial observers might see them as two variants of the same faith, like the Sunnis and the Shiahs of the Muslim world, they were more conscious of their differences than their commonality. In the first millennium they maintained at least a façade of unity; in the second millennium they abandoned the façade. The old crack opened wide after the schism of 1054. Here was proof that even the foundations of Christendom were subject to movement.

◁━━▷

750–1054

From the eighth century onwards, faltering thoughts about a new political order were stimulated by continuing depredations from beyond the fringe of Christendom. The foundation of the Empire of Charlemagne in 800, of the Holy Roman Empire from 962, and eventually of the Tsardom of Moscow can only be understood in conjunction with the activities of the Vikings, the Magyars, the Mongols, and the Turks.

The Vikings or 'Northmen' ravaged the northern coasts for more than 200 years. They were the product of overpopulation in the remote fiords of Scandinavia, whose 'rowmen' took to their longships for plunder, trade, mercenary service, and sheer adventure. From c.700 parties of Vikings would raid isolated settlements in the British Isles or Frisia before sailing home at the end of each season. They ransacked Lindisfarne in 793 and Iona in 795 [IONA]. From the middle of the ninth century, however, huge Viking camps were set up to act as bases for more protracted campaigns of pillage. In several instances these camps led to permanent settlement. The Danish Vikings, for example, created one such 'great army' at the mouth of the Seine, from which they repeatedly looted the defenceless cities of northern France. They captured ports such as Rouen and Nantes, whilst sailing off to Portugal (844), to the Balearic Islands, even to Provence and Tuscany (859–62). In 851 they invaded England, fanning out through the eastern half of the country. From 866 the 'Danelaw' was established from Northumbria to East Anglia. The struggle between the Anglo-Saxons and the Danes dominated the next 150 years of England's history. In 911, tradition holds that the Northmen of the Seine were permanently settled under Rollo, thereby creating 'Normandy'.

The Norwegian Vikings concentrated on the outer islands. They occupied the Orkneys and Shetlands in the eighth century, the Faroes, the Hebrides, and eastern Ireland in the ninth. Their major colony, Iceland, was settled from 874. Dublin was founded in 988. They discovered Greenland; and in all probability, under Eric the Red, they sailed on to North America, which they called Vinland. [EIRIK] The Swedish Vikings operated throughout the Baltic. They established fortified camps at Wolin on the Oder, at Truso on the Vistula, and at Novgorod, whence they penetrated the rivers of the Bay of Riga and the Gulf of Finland. In the ninth century they took hold of the overland route between the Baltic and the Black Sea. Known as Varangians, they controlled the Dnieper, and appeared in Constantinople. [DIRHAM] [FUTHARK]

In the final period, adventurers of Viking origin, who had acquired a veneer of the culture of their adopted countries, created a number of new political states.

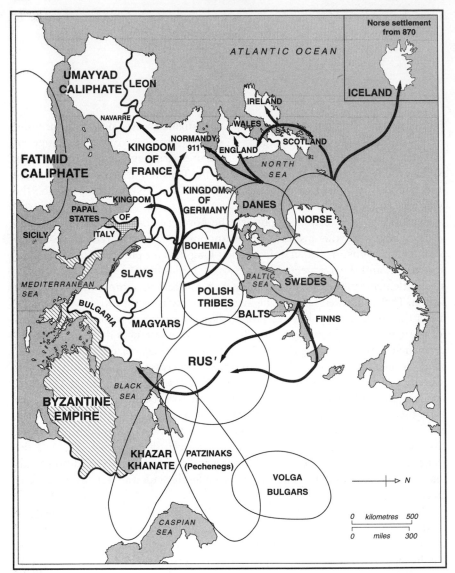

Map 12. Europe, c. AD 900

Rurik the Varangian and his sons organized the first durable principality of the eastern Slavs at Novgorod and Kiev, c.860–80. Knut the Dane or 'Canute the Great' (r. 1016–35) was lord of a vast North Sea empire joining England with Denmark (see p. 308). Robert Guiscard, the Norman, sailed to southern Italy in 1059 (see p. 336). William the Bastard, Duke of Normandy, conquered the kingdom of England in 1066 (see p. 339). Norman rule was destined to last longer in Sicily and in England than in Normandy itself. [**DING**]

DIRHAM

ON 12 May AD 922, a caravan walked into the Bulgar city of Suvar on the Volga. It had been travelling for more than three months from the port of Jurjan on the Caspian Sea. It was led by an Arab merchant, Ibn Fadlhān, who wrote an account of his travels.[1] It is one small incident in the history of commercial contacts between Eastern Europe and the Arab states of Central Asia over five centuries. Ibn Fadlhān was coming to buy furs; and there is no doubt that he was carrying a plentiful supply of dirhams to pay for his purchases.

The dirham or *dirhem* was a coin of pure silver weighing 2.97 grammes, and worth one-tenth of a dinar. It was minted both in North Africa and in Central Asia under various dynasties. It was standard currency in Eastern Europe in the era before local mints existed. Hoards of dirhams have been found all over European Russia, Ukraine, Byelorussia, the Baltic States, Sweden, and northern Poland. The largest of them contained over 50,000 coins. Buried by their owners in times of insecurity, they sometimes remained uncollected until found by modern archaeologists and treasure-hunters. They can be dated quite precisely from the date of the newest coin in any particular lot.

Analysis of dirham hoards indicates four recognizable periods. In the first period, *c*.800–25, the hoards contain Abbasid dirhams, predominantly from North Africa. They may well reflect Khazar–Arab trade links via the Mediterranean [**KHAZARIA**]. In the second period, 825–905, the North African issues disappear, and are replaced by Central Asian coins. In the third period, 905–60, the hoards still consist overwhelmingly of Sāmānid issues, but are joined by large numbers of Buwayhid and Ziyarid issues.[2]

In the Viking Age, when Swedish Vikings controlled the Baltic–Dnieper route, dirhams were taken all over the north. [**FUTHARK**] [**RUS'**] Important finds have been made in Sweden, and especially on the island of Gotland.[3] Indeed, as Ibn Fadlhān recorded when he encountered a party of Swedes, the possession of dirhams had become a matter of status and public ostentation:

'I saw the [Swedes] when they landed and camped beside the Volga. I never saw statelier men. They are as tall as palm-trees, ruddy-cheeked, and with red hair. They wear neither kirtle nor caftan, but the men have a rough cloak which they throw to one side, leaving their hands free . . .

Fastened on the breasts of the women is a capsule of iron, copper, silver or gold according to the wealth of the husband. In the capsule is a ring, and attached to it, a knife . . . Round their necks, they wear gold and silver chains. For when a man owns 10,000 dirhems, he has one chain made for his wife; for 20,000, she has two chains. Thus [an extra] chain is added [to the wife's neck] for each 10,000 dirhems that the husband possesses.'[4]

> The import of Arab silver to Eastern Europe faltered in the late tenth and ended in the early eleventh century. The latest Sāmānid dirham found in Sweden dates from 969, in Russia from 1015. This used to be attributed to a 'silver crisis' in Central Asia. But other factors were at work. The end of the re-export of Arab silver from Rus' to Sweden coincides with the appearance of silver deniers from Western Europe. By the end of the eleventh century, Arab coins had been totally supplanted. The details may be obscure; but the numismatic evidence clearly supports developments known from other sources, namely the reorientation of the Baltic trade and the rise of Novgorod.

The Magyars were the last of the nomads to colonize central Europe. Descendants of the Ugrian branch of the Finno-Ugrian peoples, their earliest known cradle-land lay east of the Urals in the valleys of the Irtysh and Ob. They parted company with their Finnic kinsfolk in the third millennium BC. Thenceforth they occupied successive stations on the southern steppes, gradually adapting themselves to the nomadic life, first in 'Magna Hungaria' between the Kama and Ural rivers, later in 'Lebedia' north of the Sea of Azov, and finally in the land of *Etelkőz* or 'mesopotamia' between the Dnieper and Dniester (see Appendix III, p. 1240). On the steppes of the first millennium, the Magyars were the neighbours of the Scythians, Sarmatians, Alans, Bulgars, Khazars, Uzi, and Pechenegs. They were already divided into their seven tribes: Nyék, Kűrtgyarmat, Tarján, Jenő, Kér, Keszi, and Magyar—the last name being later applied to them all. Byzantine sources speak of their trading in slaves through the Black Sea ports.

The Magyars' decisive move was made at the end of the ninth century. The steppe peoples had been in commotion for several decades. The Arabs dispersed the Uzi and stole their cattle; the Uzi did the same to the Pechenegs. In 894 the Pechenegs made common cause with the Bulgarian Tsar, and together they fell on the Magyars. The time had come for what the Magyars themselves call the *honfoglalás*, 'the occupation of the fatherland'. Overwhelmed by their neighbours, they decided to migrate to the west. For the first time their horsemen, who in recent years had lent their services both to the Franks and the Byzantines, did not return to Etelkoz. Instead, with Arpad at their head, they led the long trains of their people over the Verecke Pass in the Carpathians. It was the spring of 895 at the latest. Perhaps 20,000 warriors and 400,000 tribesfolk had come to found the land of the Magyars on the plains of 'Hungaria'. [**CSABA**] [**SHAMAN**]

The Mongols, or 'Tartars', commanded the greatest of all the nomadic empires. Centred on the arid steppes of central Asia, their fortunes waxed and waned; but they directly impinged on the affairs of the West on two separate occasions. Genghis Khan (r. 1206–27), starting from Karakorum, conquered a territory which stretched from the Pacific to the Black Sea, from Korea to Crimea

DING

THE custom among Germanic tribes of holding popular assemblies was described by Tacitus; and there is little doubt that they had existed since prehistoric times. The earliest such assembly to enter the historical record, in the ninth-century *Legend of Ansgar*, was the *Ding* which met at Birka on the island of Björkö in Sweden. A similar assembly met at a similar period in Denmark.

Iceland's national assembly, the *Althing*, came into being in AD 930 under the Law Rock by the lake at Thingvellir. Thereafter, it met annually 'after ten weeks of summer' and was attended by the island's thirty-six clan chiefs and by their chosen delegates or *thingmen*, who elected the Lawspeaker. It appointed judges, passed laws, and made executive decisions, adopting the principle of majority voting from 1130. Each year, it was preceded by the Maytime *farthings* or 'regional assemblies' of the island's four quarters, and was followed by the *leid*—a meeting when the populace was informed of decisions taken. It was the centrepiece of Iceland's 'free state', which continued until the 'Old Treaty' of 1264 and the Norwegian takeover.[1]

The Manx Assembly on the Isle of Man, the *Tynwald*, like that of the Faroes, dates from a similar early period. [**FAROE**]

Nordic democracy put special emphasis on local assemblies. Every Swedish province had its *ding*, like Iceland's *farthings*, in each of the country's twelve jurisdictions. Denmark had three *landlings*, and Norway its *lögthings*. At the lowest level in Iceland, a system of *hieppar* or 'farmers' gatherings' functioned from the eleventh to the nineteenth centuries. These traditions greatly modified the ambitions of Nordic kingship, and obstructed Scandinavian political union. When the Nordic countries did eventually enter the Union of Kalmar (see p. 431), it was for dynastic reasons that did not last. The Charter of Rights which was forced on the Danish King Erik Glipping in 1282, and the Swedish equivalent of 1319, were more extensive than England's Magna Carta. All had their roots in a much older political culture.[2]

Nor was the influence of Nordic democracy confined to Scandinavia. It had an impact everywhere the Vikings went—in England, in Scotland, in Russian Novgorod, and very probably in Poland, where the same legal right of rebellion took root (see p. 555). Although the Scandinavian countries were due to experience an era of absolute monarchy, the tradition of local democracy may help to explain the strength of constitutionalism and representative government in modern times.

(see p. 364). The renewer of the Mongol empire, Timur or Tamerlane (1336–1405), starting from Samarkand, mastered an area somewhat more to the south, from Delhi to the Aegean. Indirectly, it was the Mongols who set another Central Asian people in motion. The Turks originated in Turkestan, whence they were displaced in the eighth century and where related peoples still live. They were destined to appear on the horizons of the West first with the Seljuk Turks in the eleventh century (see pp. 332–3) and then with the Ottoman Turks in the thirteenth (see p. 386). The story of their epic wanderings encompasses the whole span which in the West separated Charlemagne from the end of the Crusades.

The empire of Charlemagne consummated the alliance between the Roman Papacy and the growing kingdom of the Franks. It was an ephemeral affair, barely surviving its founder's death and disappearing completely within a century. None the less, its impact was profound. Charlemagne, or Charles the Great (r. 768–814), great-grandson of Charles Martel, united the two halves of his forebears' realm, Neustria and Austrasia, in a vast territory from the Atlantic to the Danube, from the Netherlands to Provence. After fifty-three campaigns and a lifetime in the saddle, he succeeded in extending that realm in all directions: to the Kingdom of the Lombards south of the Alps (773–4); to Saxony (775–804), Bavaria (788), and Carinthia (799); to the March of Brittany (786); and to the Spanish March across the Pyrenees (795–7). Having assumed the title of 'King of the Franks and Lombards', and confirmed the grant of the Exarchate of Ravenna to the Papacy, he had clearly outstripped the rival chieftains of his day, and was looking for suitable recognition. For its part, the Papacy had severed its links with the Emperor in Constantinople and was looking for a permanent protector. Pope Leo III (795–816) was tempted to regard the imperial title as vacant after the pathological Empress Irene had seized sole power in Constantinople. Moreover, attacked in Rome by a gang of his predecessor's relatives who had tried to mutilate him, he was forced to take refuge with Charles in Frankland, whither he had earlier sent the keys of St Peter's and the banner of Rome. [**BRIE**]

After Charlemagne's early years, the western borders of Frankland were not seriously disturbed. The line of the Pyrenees was held against major Muslim incursions (see p. 255); and the Caliphate, though prosperous and populous, was preoccupied with the internal strife of its constituent states. The Frankish position was strengthened by allies among the Christian princes who clung tenaciously to the coastland of northern Iberia, first in the Kingdom of Asturias and then in the later Kingdoms of Leon, Castile, and Navarre. On the southern flank, it was protected by the Christian buffer states which took root in Aragon and in the County of Barcelona. Relative security in the west gave Charlemagne and his successors the chance to turn their attention to problems elsewhere, notably in the east and in Italy. [**MADONNA**]

The Franco-papal alliance was consummated in 800, during Charles's fifth journey to Italy. A council of notables had absolved Leo of all crimes, and during Christmas Mass, as Charles rose from prayer before St Peter's tomb, the Pope

BRIE

RETURNING from his campaign against the Lombards in 774, Charlemagne halted on the Plateau de Brie, close to the Abbey of Meaux. The monks served him a Lenten plate of cheese. They insisted that he eat it whole, without removing the crust. Delighted, he promptly ordered two batches of Brie to be sent to Aachen every year. Charlemagne's secretary, Einhard, recorded a similar incident four years later during the Saracen wars. Stopping in the district of Rouergue in the Midi, the King took an instant liking to the local blue cheese of ewes' milk that was known and matured since Roman times in the limestone caves at Roquefort.[1]

Charlemagne's fine cheeses were matched by a cellar of fine wines. He owned many *ouvrées* or 'enclosures' in the Burgundian vineyard at Aloxe-Corton, whose choicest *Grand Cru* white, 'smelling of cinnamon and tasting of gunflint', is still marketed as CORTON-CHARLEMAGNE.[2]

Brie de Meaux, one of France's 500 listed cheeses, dates from the era of early monastic farming. After renneting and airing, the curd is shovelled into a flat, straw-based mould, and left to drain on a sloping stone shelf. Decanted after 24 hours, it is salted, dried, frequently turned, and matured in cellars for 4–7 weeks. The final product measures 37 x 3.5 cm, weighs 3 kg, and will have taken up 23 litres of full-cream milk, preferably from a herd of Normandy cows. It has a golden-roseate crust, a firm, straw-coloured body, and a succulent, ivory *âme* or 'centre'—literally 'the soul'. It should be eaten between thin slices of crusty bread.

For centuries, Brie was shipped along the River Marne to Paris, where the street-sellers shouted *'Fromage de Brye'*. It was a royal favourite with Charles VIII and Henri IV, but cost the life of Louis XVI, who was caught in the tavern at Varennes through tarrying to eat his cheese. Brie was made internationally famous at the Congress of Vienna, where Metternich pronounced it *le prince des fromages*—'the only prince which Talleyrand would never betray'.

The CAP of the European Community is all but killing traditional farmhouse cheese. In 1985, some 6,000 tonnes of Brie ANOC (*Appellation Nationale d'Origine Controllée*) were produced, as against over 18,000 tonnes of 'horrific' industrial Brie.

In August 1792, when many of the monks of Meaux were killed during the revolutionary Terror, one brother, the Abbé Gobert, fled to Normandy en route for England. He stopped long enough in a village near Vimoutiers (Orne) to show a farmer's wife what he knew about cheese-making. The village was called Camembert.[3]

MADONNA

OUR Lady of Monserrat is a statue of indeterminate age, though the monastery which houses her shrine on the 'Saw-Tooth Mountain' in Catalonia was founded in 975. The small wooden figure, which was carved in a seated position, possibly in Byzantium, is crowned, and holds an orb on one side and the Christ-child on the other. The Child, also crowned, raises the right hand in blessing, whilst proffering a pine-cone in the left. The Madonna's face, whose elongated features bear a look of utter serenity, is black.[1]

In 1384 an icon of the Virgin Mother and Child was brought to the Pauline monastery of Jasna Góra, the 'Bright Mountain', near the township of Częstochowa in western Poland. It was donated by the Prince of Opole in Silesia. Legend was to hold that it had been painted by St Luke on boards from the Holy Family's table in Nazareth. More likely, it was copied from a Byzantine original. The head is covered by a dark cape edged with gold, and spangled with fleur-de-lis, and it is crowned beneath a halo. The eyes are half-closed, as if by tears, and a countenance of utter sorrow is emphasized by two long slashes or sabre-cuts which radiate from the right cheek. The face, like that of *la Moreneta*, is black (see Plate 20).[2]

There is a Black Madonna at Notre-Dame de Rocamadour, centrepiece of a group of shrines built in the twelfth century into the cliffs of the Gorge d'Alzou in central France. The figure is said to have been carved by St Amadour or Amateur, whom legend links with Zacchaeus the Publican, a disciple of Christ.[3] Another tiny icon of a black madonna, of Byzantine origin, graces the altar of the crypt of Notre-Dame du Port in Clermont.[4]

In Russia, the Black Virgin of Kazan has long been ascribed miracle-working powers. First discovered in 1579, buried in a field, the icon was installed in the Bogoroditsky convent in Kazan, shortly after the city's conquest by Ivan the Terrible. One copy was taken to Moscow in 1612 to mark the expulsion of the Poles from the Kremlin; another was brought to St Petersburg in 1710 to mark the benediction of Russia's new capital. A grandiose, neo-classical cathedral, completed by Alexander I, was built to house St Petersburg's Virgin, which few people knew to be a copy. In 1904 the original icon was stolen from Kazan. It duly reappeared in Western Europe, and was acquired by the Orthodox Church of the USA—thus avoiding the fate of many famous Russian icons which were either destroyed during the Bolshevik Revolution or deposited in state art galleries.[5]

Monserrat, Częstochowa, Rocamadour, and Kazan are but four of the countless Marian shrines across Europe. In a continent of white faces, the Black Madonnas possess an air of added mystery. *La Moreneta*, patroness of Catalonia, saw the conversion of Ignatius Loyola. She became a focus of attention during the Napoleonic Wars, when the monastery was destroyed. She is well known in Sicily, in Mexico, and in Bohemia. Wallenstein, the Imperial General, was building a chapel in her honour when he was assassinated. The *Matka Boska* or 'Divine Mother' of Częstochowa, the 'Queen of Poland', first attracted pilgrims during the Hussite Wars, before assuming a national role during the seventeenth century (see p. 556). Together with her Lithuanian counterpart, the 'Matka Boska Ostrobramska' in Wilno, she is celebrated by Poles in all their churches, from Irkutsk in Siberia to Doylestown (Pennsylvania). The Virgin of Rocamadour was venerated by St Louis in 1245, by Charles le Bel (1324), and by Louis XI (1463). She inspired the *Litanie de la Vierge Noire* (1936) by Francis Poulenc. The Virgin of Kazan was adopted as the supreme patroness of the Romanov dynasty, a Russian counterpart to the Virgin of Blachernae in Constantinople. Unlike her Catholic counterparts, who receive special adoration during the Feast of the Assumption, her feast-day is held on 8 July (OS).

The cult of the Virgin Mary finds no place in the Bible. It first appears with the doctrine of the *Theotokos* or 'God-bearer' at the Council of Ephesus. It inspired the consecration of S. Maria Maggiore (432) in Rome, of Reims Cathedral about the same time, and of the rededicated Parthenon in Athens. In sixth-century Byzantium it launched the regular celebration of the Feasts of the Annunciation (25 March), the Assumption (15 August), and the Dormition, all favourite themes of iconography. From there, it spread steadily throughout Latin Christendom. In St Mary it presented a divine image of womanhood, the *Mater Misericordiae*, the *Magna Mater*, the spotless Queen of Heaven, the Mother of God—an ideal foil for the older Christian fixation with Eve, the sinner, and with Mary Magdalene, the repentant whore. It was vehemently denounced by Protestants, as by modern feminists.[6] But it did not find formal acceptance until the dogma of Immaculate Conception in 1854. Demands for recognition of 'the Co-redemptress' were rejected at the Second Vatican Council.

Yet the Blessed Virgin does not cease to inspire. She is the foremost subject of Christian art, the recurrent source of mystical visions, [BERNADETTE] [FATIMA], and the recipient of ceaseless prayers [ANGELUS]. The 'fifteen decades' of the Rosary are recited in her honour. Since 1568 the *Ave Maria* or 'Hail Mary' has had a permanent place in the Roman Catholic Breviary:

> Hail Mary, full of Grace, the Lord is with Thee.
> Blessed art Thou among women, and blessed is the fruit of
> Thy womb.
> Holy Mary, Mother of God! Pray for us sinners,
> Now and at the hour of our death.

slipped an imperial crown on his head. The congregation acclaimed him 'Caesar' and 'Augustus', and the Pope knelt in homage before him. Einhard, Charlemagne's biographer, claims that the coronation occurred spontaneously; in all probability it was carefully rehearsed. In terms of tradition it was entirely irregular: Pope Leo had no recognized right to confer the imperial title, and Charlemagne had no right to receive it. But it happened. Henceforth, there was a Catholic Emperor in the West independent of the Byzantine Empire. The barbaric Frankish kingdom was upgraded, dependent on the Pope for its new status (see Appendix III, p. 1239). [**AQUILA**] [**PAPESSA**]

Charlemagne's kingdom and empire were governed by an itinerant court that journeyed incessantly from one domain to the next; by a number of subordinate courts established in Neustria, Aquitaine, and Lombardy; and by a network of perhaps 300 *comitates* or 'counties', each headed by an imperial lieutenant or 'Count'. The work of the Emperor's court was supervised by a staff of clerics, initially by the Arch-Chaplain Fulrad and later by the Emperor's favourite counsellor, the Northumbrian monk Alcuin. Local bishops were often used to supervise the counts, and *missi dominici*, 'royal legates', toured the realm on fixed circuits. Law and order, and all appointments, were administered in the name of the King. A central silver coinage was introduced, with 240 *denarii* to the pound. An international executive class, united by royal favour and often by marriage, made its appearance. A series of capitularies, or collected edicts, strove to encourage uniform rules for both Church and State. The tithe was made obligatory. Murder of a priest was made punishable by death. The clergy could only be judged by a court presided over jointly by count and bishop. Pagan cremations were banned. It may have appeared that a new, centralized political order was in the making. In reality, local customs and leaders retained much of their force.

Charlemagne's court was certainly the focus of continental power and influence. An entry in the royal annals for 798 reveals its far-flung contacts:

A legate came from King Alfonso of Galicia and Asturias, Froia by name, who handed over a tent of marvellous beauty. But at Easter-time the *Nordliudi* across the Elbe rose in rebellion and seized the royal legates residing amongst them to dispense justice . . . The king collected an army and defeated them in battle and took hostages. And proceeding to his palace at Aachen, he received a Greek delegation sent from Constantinople. In this year, the star called Mars was not to be seen anywhere in the heavens from July to July. The Balearic Isles were plundered by Moors and Saracens. King Alfonso, who had plundered Lisbon, sent his legates Froia and Basiliscus in winter-time to the Lord King with breastplates, mules and Moorish prisoners as evidence of his victory. Then Christmas and Easter were celebrated in this place by the King.[2]

It was in the court of Charles the Great that the ancient term of 'Europe' was revived. The Carolingians needed a label to describe that section of the world which they dominated, as distinct from the pagan lands, from Byzantium, or from Christendom as a whole. This 'first Europe', therefore, was an ephemeral Western concept which lasted no longer than Charles himself.

PAPESSA

A CCORDING to persistent medieval tradition, the throne of St Peter was once occupied by a woman. In the commonest version Pope Leo IV, who died in AD 855, was succeeded by one 'Johannes Anglicus.' Leo's successor had greatly impressed the Curia with learned lectures, having studied in Athens, but two years later caused grave scandal by dying in childbirth in a Roman street. This account can be traced to the work of Martinus Polonus of Troppau OP (c.1200–78), who presented the events as proven fact. His *Chronicon summorum pontificum imperatorumque* was a widely used work of reference. A different version made 'Pope Joan' the successor to Victor III, who had died in 1087. In this case, she revealed her sex by giving birth while mounting a horse. She was promptly tied to the horse's tail and stoned to death. That account appeared in the *Universal Chronicle of Mainz* prepared by another inventive Dominican, Jean de Mailly, also in the mid-thirteenth century.

It is not remarkable that medieval chroniclers should have told strange tales; but it *is* remarkable that their fabrications should have passed without question for centuries. Both Petrarch and Boccaccio believed them. A statue of Pope Joan stands alongside those of other popes in the cathedral at Siena. When Jan Hus cited her at the Council of Constance as an instance of ecclesiastical abuse, he was not corrected. An enigmatic monument near the Church of San Clemente in Rome, at the spot where the Pope's child was supposedly delivered, is said to have stood undisturbed until the 1560s. No scholar seems to have doubted the fable until the *Annales* of the Bavarian, 'Aventinus', published in 1554. Its historicity was only demolished definitively in treatises written by the French Protestant, David Blondel, in 1647 and 1657.

Textbooks of medieval history treat Pope Joan, if at all, as a minor curiosity. In fact, she signals a mode of gender image that differed markedly from that of a later age. There must have been something inherently credible in the fable for it to have persisted so long. Joan herself may not have been historical. But the fable certainly was.[1]

Charlemagne, however, was an energetic builder. He built palaces at Nijmegen, Engelheim, and Aachen. He bridged the Rhine at Mainz, and linked the tributaries of the Rhine and Danube with a canal, the *Kaisergrab*. He was the pioneer of romanesque architecture north of the Alps. By reputation, Charlemagne was also a great patron of learning. He himself, though a forceful orator, was illiterate. But he employed scholars of repute—Alcuin of York, Peter of Pisa, Agobard of Lyons. He collected manuscripts, revised the text of the Bible, published grammars, histories, and ballads. His lifestory, the *Vita Karoli* by Abbot Einhard, has been called 'the first secular biography'. Not everyone is impressed: one historian has blamed Charlemagne for 'saddling us with a literary tradition of derivative book-learning which hangs today like a millstone round the neck of our educational system'.[3] [**AGOBARD**] [**PFALZ**]

Charlemagne did not hesitate to govern the Church as an integral part of his domains. At the Council of Frankfurt of 794 he rejected the decrees of the (VIIth) General Council of Nicaea. Bishoprics and abbeys were regarded as feudal benefices and subject to the law of treason. Whilst forbidding his bishops to engage in battle, he spread the Gospel by fire and sword. Whether he grasped the Sermon on the Mount is a moot point. His services to Christianity were eventually rewarded by canonization, though the process was obstructed for 351 years by reports that his sexual conquests were no less extensive than his territorial ones.

Charlemagne died on 28 January 814. On his tomb in Aachen, since lost, a portrait was placed, and an inscription:

Beneath this tomb lies the body of Charles, great and orthodox Emperor, who nobly increased the kingdom of the Franks, and reigned prosperously for forty-seven years. He died in his seventies in the year of our Lord 814, in the seventh indiction, on the fifth of the Kalends of February.[4]

AGOBARD

BY all the omens, 810 was going to be Charlemagne's worst year. There were two eclipses of the sun and two of the moon, all observable in Frankland. And sure enough, the Emperor's pet elephant, a gift from the Caliph, died; there was a widespread outbreak of cattle-plague; and the Duke of Benevento rebelled.

All this, and more, was faithfully recorded by Agobard, Bishop of Lyons (c.779–840). What is more, Agobard found that the common people were drawing superstitious conclusions. They believed that their cattle were dying from a poisonous dust spread by the Duke of Benevento's spies. They also believed that Frankland was being invaded by 'cloud-borne ships' navigated by 'aerial sailors'. The invaders were said to be beating down the harvest of the Franks with hailstones launched from the sky, before carrying it off to the far-away land of 'Magonia'. Agobard was not easily swayed by such stories which, after investigation, he duly refuted. Yet he did appear to believe that the Catholic Church was being invaded by Jews. When his collected works were discovered in 1605, it turned out that he had devoted no fewer than five treatises to the Jewish peril.[1]

Agobard's most remarkable departure, however, was to demand the establishment of a universal Christian law for a universal Christian commonwealth. 'If God has suffered so that all be reconciled in his Body,' he wrote, 'is not the incredible diversity of laws . . . in opposition to this divine work of unity?'[2] Agobard was the first European centralist.

PFALZ

AACHEN takes its name from the Roman spa of Aquisgranium, 'Waters of Apollo-Granus'. Its warm, healing waters explain Charlemagne's choice for the site of his favourite residence, the *Kaiserpfalz*. The French name, Aix-la-Chapelle, marks the famous chapel, now part of Aachen Cathedral, which Charlemagne added to his palace.

Charlemagne's chapel was completed in 805. It is a three-tiered octagon, built in the Byzantine style of San Vitale in Ravenna, which Charlemagne had seen and admired. Its proportions are said to follow the mystical numbers of the seventh vision of St John's Revelation. In its day it was the largest stone building north of the Alps. Round the interior of the octagon, above the first tier of Roman arches, there runs a dedication reputedly composed by Alcuin:

CUM LAPIDES VIVI PACIS CONPAGE LIGANTUR
Since the living stones have been joined in peaceful harmony,
INQUE PARES NUMEROS OMNIA CONVENIUNT
And all numbers and measurements are in agreement
CLARET OPUS DOMINI, TOTAM QUI CONSTRUIT AULAM
The work of the Lord who built this hall will shine brightly.
EFFECTUSQUE PIIS DAT STUDIIS HOMINUM
The completed edifice crowns the pious efforts of the people
QUORUM PERPETUI DECORIS STRUCTURA MANEBIT
Whose work will remain forever as a monument of beauty
SI PERFECTA AUCTOR PROTEGAT ATQUE REGAT.
If the Author of All things protects and rules over it.
SIC DEUS HOC TUTUM STABILI FUNDAMINE TEMPLUM
May God therefore watch over this temple
QUOD KAROLUS PRINCEPS CONDIDIT, ESSE VELIT.
Which Charles the Prince has founded on a solid base.

The decoration of the chapel is heavy with the imperial symbolism which Charlemagne and his successors had revived in a new and naïve Christian setting. A mosaic inside the dome represents the Adoration of the Lamb. The *ambo* or pulpit is encrusted with fragments of Roman pottery, glass, and an eagle cameo. Egyptian columns in green and rose porphyry support the second tier of arches. The *pala d'oro* or altar panel portrays the Passion in classic Roman relief and in solid gold. The *Lotharkreuz* or Cross of Lothar is a magnificent Christian ornament of beaten gold encrusted with antique gems. It is surmounted by a central portrait cameo of the Emperor Augustus. The imperial throne, cut from simple slabs of white marble, looks down from the first-floor gallery as it did during all the 32 coronations of 700 years. The message is clear: the Empire which Charlemagne launched thought of itself both as Holy *and* as Roman.

In the twelfth century, on the orders of Frederick Barbarossa, the chapel was turned into Charlemagne's shrine. In 1165 the body of the newly

canonized saint was transferred to a casket of solid gold. It was surrounded by a collection of suitable relics—the loincloth of Christ, the
Virgin's girdle, a splinter of Charlemagne's skull—all placed in precious
reliquaries. Barbarossa himself donated a huge, wheel-shaped, iron chan-
delier, the 'Crown of Lights', which is suspended in the centre of the octagon and which symbolizes the walls of the New Jerusalem. It bears another long inscription:

Jerusalem, celestial Zion; John, herald of salvation saw Thee . . . Frederick,
Catholic Emperor of the Roman Empire pledged this crown of lights as a
princely gift . . . Now, O Holy Virgin, he dedicates it to Thee. O *Stella Maris*, O
Star of the Sea, take the humble Frederick into Thy care . . . and protect the
Emperor's wife, Beatrix.

Today the imperial chapel at Aachen is ranked among the foremost
wonders of romanesque art. But it is more than that. It provides a history
lesson more vivid than any book can offer. As visitors enter, they pass
through the Wolf's Door—so called after the legend of the wolf who
cheated the Devil for possession of the chapel. It is a dull mind that is not
gripped by the powerful fusion of the barbarian and the classical, of the
Christian and the pagan, which provided the spiritual drive of the age.
Here is Western Europe's greatest memorial to a time when romanesque
was a novelty, and when the centre of civilization still lay in the East.[1]

Charlemagne's lifeblood had been the cement of the realm. His inheritance was
immediately disputed by his son and grandsons. Repeated partitions ensured its
early disintegration. In 817 the partition of Aachen provoked civil war; in 843, following protracted family slaughter, the Treaty of Verdun produced a three-way
split between the surviving grandsons. Charles the Bald received the Western,
Romance sector—Neustria, Aquitaine, western Burgundy, and the Spanish
March. Lothair I, King of Italy, received the title of Emperor together with the
'Middle Kingdom', consisting of Austrasia, eastern Burgundy, Provence, and
Italy. Lewis the German received the bulk of the eastern, solidly Germanic sector
(see Map 12). The Treaty of Verdun created the core of both the future Germany
and the future France. The 'Middle Kingdom' was left a bone of eternal contention between them. Charlemagne's ultimate legacy was not just the example of
fragile unity but, equally, the prospect of unending strife. [KRAL]

The feuding of the Carolingians or 'Karlings' created an opportunity which the
Vikings were quick to exploit. The summer of 841 saw them sailing up the Seine
to plunder Rouen. In 843–4, following the Treaty of Verdun, they wintered on the
island of Noirmoutier. In 854 the new city of Hamburg was burned, and Paris was
sacked while Charles the Bald took refuge on Montmartre. In 847 the ancient city
of Bordeaux was taken hostage for years. In 852 an ominous precedent was set

KRAL

CHARLEMAGNE ravaged the Slavs on at least four fronts. He reduced the Abotrites and Sorbs, to the east of the Elbe, in 789. He forced the Czechs of Bohemia to pay tribute in 805–6, and the Carinthian Slavs of the Sava and Drava likewise. In respect for the great conqueror, the Slavs adopted his name as their word for 'king'. Karol has become *kral* in Czech, *król* in Polish, *korol'* in Russian. The Franks gave the Slavs their first model of Christian kingship. (*Kral* even means 'king' in Turkish.)

In the West, Charlemagne was adopted as the presiding monarch of numerous medieval legends, the supreme hero of the *chansons de geste*.[1] Already in the ninth century, a monk of St Gall composed a largely fabulous chronicle, *De Gestis Karoli Magni*. Soon Charlemagne was to be portrayed by the troubadours as the ubiquitous champion of Christendom, swinging his sacred sword 'Joyeuse', smiting the infidel, riding at the head of his companions—Roland, Ganelon, Naimes of Bavaria, Ogier the Dane, Guillaume of Toulouse, Turpin the battling Archbishop of Reims.

In the French tradition the 'twelve peers' of Charlemagne consisted of the three Dukes of Normandy, Burgundy, and Aquitaine, the three Counts of Champagne, Toulouse, and Flanders, and the six spiritual peers, the Bishops of Reims, Laon, Châlons, Beauvais, Langres, and Noyon.

In the German legends Charlemagne was often said to be sleeping, waiting for the call to wake and save his beloved subjects from their ills. In the Bavarian tale he is seated on a chair in the Untersberg, as on his throne in the chapel at Aachen. The end of the world will be nigh when his beard has grown thrice round the table before him. In the German language, Charlemagne's name has been given to the constellation of the Great Bear—the *Karlswagen*. In Old English, the 'Charles Wain' was an alternative name for the constellation of the Plough.

Later, both in France and Germany, Charles the Great was hailed as the progenitor of the nation's royalty. For the French 'Charlemagne', for the Germans 'Karl der Grosse', he was seen not as a Frank but as a patriotic French or German leader. His example was invoked at Napoleon's imperial coronation in 1804. His portrait occupies the first place in the gallery of the German emperors painted in 1838–52 in the *Kaisersaal* at Frankfurt.[2]

In the twentieth century, Charles the Great has been more regarded as a symbol of Franco-German reconciliation. In 1943, when the Nazis formed a new division of French volunteers for the Waffen SS, or in 1955 when the Council of Europe funded a Prize 'for services to the cause of European unity', the organizers appealed to the same name—to 'Charlemagne'.

when Charles the Bald, having trapped the Viking host in their camp at Jeufosse near the Seine estuary, paid them off with gold and permanent grants of land. He was rewarded by repeated raids which Orléans alone was able to resist.

In 864, by the Edict of Pîtres, Charles the Bald at last gave orders for all localities to build fortifications, and for a task force of cavalry to be on hand. But relief was still far off. Year after year the internecine wars of the Karlings were studded with royal deaths, with temporary partitions, and with Viking raids of ever greater insolence. From 867 to 878 the Danes were preoccupied in England. In 880 they ravaged the valley of the Elbe. In 885–6, 40,000 Vikings poured out of 700 long-ships drawn up on the present-day Champ de Mars, and laid siege to Paris for eleven months. Count Odo conducted a heroic defence, only to find that the King, Charles the Fat, had paid off the Vikings with 700 lb of silver and packed them off into Burgundy.

In the British Isles, which had escaped the attentions of Charlemagne, the impact of the Vikings was particularly severe. The Danish invasions created divisions which persisted for 200 years. Egbert, King of Wessex, had been recognized as *Bretwalda* or overlord of Britain in 828. Within a generation, however, the Danes were challenging the supremacy of Wessex. Alfred the Great, King of Wessex (r. 849–99), spent a lifetime containing them. At one point, in 878, he was forced to hide in the marshes of Athelney in Somerset. But battles in that same year enabled him to partition the country. The Treaty of Wedmore created the *Danelagh*—a vast area subject to Danish rule. From then on, until the fateful year of 1066, England was to be disputed by the English house of Wessex and the Danes. In the tenth century, after the expulsion of Eric Bloodaxe, the last Danish king of York, Viking raids were resumed with a vengeance. In 994 London was beset by a combined force of Danes and Norwegians. From 1017–35 Knut, or Canute, ruled over a vast North Sea empire linking England with Scandinavia. The old Anglo-Saxon kingdom enjoyed a brief respite under Edward the Confessor (r. 1042–66), founder of Westminster Abbey. Edward's death in 1066 prompted a war between three rival claimants—Harold Hardrada of Norway, Harold Godwinson of Wessex, and William the Bastard, Duke of Normandy.

Whilst the English battled the Danes, the rest of the British Isles witnessed a long, complex struggle between Vikings and Celts. Fluctuating federations of Northmen fought fluctuating leagues of Celtic princes. In Ireland, the Celts held the interior against fortified Viking settlements on the coast. After a century of mayhem, they finally gained the upper hand under the much-sung Bhriain Boroimhe (Brian Boru, r. 1002–14), who left the kingdom to be disputed between the O'Brians, the O'Neills, and the O'Connors. There followed an era when the Irish again ruled the whole of Ireland unchallenged for 150 years. An *Ard Rih* or 'High King' of Erin held authority over the lesser kings of the 'Fifths' of Meath, Munster, Leinster, Ulster, and Connaught; the ancient Brehon Laws, which had originated in prehistoric times, were written down to provide a firm framework of administrative practice and social custom; and the traditional life of the *fine* or 'clans' held sway under its assemblies, its judges, and the growing influence of an increasingly institutionalized Church. In Wales, the Celtic principalities were trapped between Vikings on the coasts and unrelenting English pressure on the inland borders. From the eighth century onwards they were held behind the great Dyke built by Offa, King of Mercia, and were largely cut off from their kinsmen in Strathclyde and Cornwall. They found champions and temporary overlords in the much-sung Rhodri Mawr (Roderick the Great, d. 877) and Gruffydd ap Llewellyn (Griffith, d. 1062). [**LLANFAIR**]

In the north of Britain the Gaelic King of Kintyre, Kenneth MacAlpin (d. *c*.860) was the first to join Picts with Scots, and thereby to launch the concept of a united 'Scotland'. After that, a three-sided contest emerged between the Gaels of the highlands, the English of the lowlands, and the Norsemen of the outer isles. It was in 1040 that Macbeth, Lord of Moray, who is said to have made a pilgrimage to Rome, determined to murder Duncan, King of the Scots:

> To-morrow, and to-morrow, and to-morrow,
> Creeps in this petty pace from day to day
> To the last syllable of recorded time,
> And all our yesterdays have lighted fools
> The way to dusty death. Out, out brief candle!
> Life's but a walking shadow, a poor player
> That struts and frets his hour upon the stage
> And then is heard no more; it is a tale
> Told by an idiot, full of sound and fury,
> Signifying nothing.[5]

The history of Britain's Celts was recorded by their bards, and by chroniclers such as Marianus Scotus (*c*.1028–83). It was of little interest to the English, like William Shakespeare, until a much later date.

In the midst of the chaos, five Frankish kingdoms were steadily drifting apart, as each was left to fend for itself. In Neustria, royal authority declined to the point where hereditary fiefs began to emerge in each of the main counties—in Toulouse (862), in Flanders (862), in Poitou (867), in Anjou (870), in Gascony, Burgundy, and Auvergne. These were the kernels of the later French provinces. In 911 Charles the Simple, King of France, lifted the Viking threat by signing the Treaty of Saint-Clair-sur-Epte with the veteran sea-king Hrolfe or Rollo. The origins of 'Normandy' seem to have lain in a French version of the *Danelagh* in England. In the eastern kingdom, Arnulf of Carinthia cleared Germany of Norsemen, but only by importing the Magyars. A kingdom of upper Burgundy had crystallized round the court of Count Rudolf at St Maurice/Moritz, and a kingdom of lower Burgundy under Count Boso at Arles. In Italy, where Moorish 'saracens' from Sicily played Vikings, successive invasions by the Byzantines in 874–95, the Neustrians in 877, and the Austrasians in 894–6 left all political authority in shreds. By 900 Count Berengar of Friuli was left in sole possession through a process of sanguinary elimination. Western historians have often described those final decades of the ninth century as the 'darkest hour' of the Dark Ages.

LLANFAIR

APART from being wonderfully expressive, the place names of medieval Wales provide a point of entry into the study of historical developments, such as land settlement, which took place before the era of documentary records. They are informative as well as curious.

In the centuries prior to the English conquest (see p. 408), the land in Wales was subject to the competing jurisdictions of the native princes, of the Anglo-Norman marcher lords, and of the ecclesiastical hierarchy. The princes, who were entirely Welsh by culture, ruled over the five principalities of Gwynedd, Powys, Deheubarth, Morganwg, and Gwent. The marcher lords, with a mixture of English and French connections, dominated the east and the south. The bishops, who were educated in Church Latin, were based on the four dioceses of Bangor, St Asaph, St David's, and Llandaff. By analysing the interplay of Welsh and non-Welsh names with the intersection of secular and ecclesiastical authority, historians can build up a picture of how, when, by whom, and for what purposes settlements were founded or extended.[1]

Some places in Wales, for example, have names which only exist in the Welsh form and which are clearly ecclesiastical in origin. The commonest of them all is *Llanfair*, meaning 'St Mary's'. Others in this category would be *Betws-y-Coed* (Chapel in the Wood) or *Eglwys Fair* (St Mary's Church). More common are place-names which are obviously ecclesiastical in origin but which have bilingual forms. Such are *Llanbedr*/Lampeter (St Peter's), *Caergybi*/Holyhead in Anglesey, or *Llanbedr Fynydd*/Peterston-super-Montem in Glamorgan. Then there are the places with bilingual names of secular origin. Such are *Abertawe*/Swansea, *Cas Gwent*/Chepstow, and *Y Gelli Gandryll*/Hay-on-Wye in Brecknockshire. Modern 'Hay' derives from the medieval Norman *La Haie Taillée* (Clipped Hedge).

The final category comprises bilingual forms with mixed ecclesiastical and secular associations. This would include *Llanfihangel Troddi*/ Mitchell Troy in Monmouthshire and *Llansanffraid-ar-Ogwr*/St Bride's Minor in Glamorgan.

The most famous of Welsh place names, however, has no medieval origins. When the London–Holyhead railway was opened in 1850, the first station on the Anglesey side of the Menai straits was at the village of Llanfair. Seeking fame and tourists, the station-master decided to improve its name, concocting an 'ancient' Welsh circumlocution which made the station's nameboard longer than the station's platform. What the British Post Office calls Llanfair P. G. 'Jones the Station' called *Llanfairpwllgwyngyllgogerychwerndrobwllllantysiliogogogoch*. Tourists are told that it stands for 'St Mary's in a hollow of white hazel near to a rapid whirlpool and to St Tysilio's Church by the red cave'.[2]

In those Western lands, disorder begat feudalism. One cannot easily distinguish causes from effects; but the fragmentation of political authority and the defence-lessness of the localities encouraged a series of political, legal, social, economic, and military developments which together form what later theoreticians have called 'the feudal regime'. In reality, feudalism was not a uniform system: problems of definition and variation abound. One of the most influential modern summaries of the subject had to be called *Qu'est-ce que la féodalité?*:

Feudalism, in the technical sense, may be regarded as a body of institutions creating and regulating the obligations of obedience and service . . . on the part of one free man (the vassal) towards another free man (the lord), and the obligations of protection and maintenance on the part of the lord with regard to his vassal.[6]

The key elements were heavy cavalry, vassalage, enfeoffment, immunity, private castles, and chivalry.

Heavy cavalry, of a sort which demanded over-sized cataphracts or 'great horses' to carry armoured knights, came to the West from Persia and Byzantium. Charles Martel has been credited not only with their introduction but also with secularizing large amounts of Church land to support their upkeep. For this reason he has been called 'the founder of European feudalism'.[7] The stirrup was invented about the same time. By helping the horseman to stand firmly on his mount, and to carry a lance backed by the full momentum of horse and rider, the stirrup changed cavalry warfare from light, mobile skirmishing into heavyweight offence.[8] The main problem, therefore, was to provide a social framework wherein a sizeable class of knights could permanently support both the psychological demands of their service and training and the enormous costs of their horses, their equipment, and their retinue. The upkeep of the knightly class—*cabalarii, chevaliers, Rittern, szlachta*—where landowning and the cavalry tradition went hand in hand, provided the central rationale of feudal society.

Vassalage grew out of the late Roman practice of *commendatio*, 'commendation', where a patron would seal an offer of protection by clasping the hands of his clients. In Carolingian times the lord began to be tied to his vassals or 'subordinates' by an oath of fealty, and by the act of homage sealed with a kiss. The two men embraced; the vassal knelt, and was invested with the symbols of his new status—a banner, a lance, a charter of agreement, a clod of earth. Thereafter they were bound for life in a mutual contract of reciprocal duties and obligations. The vassal was sworn to serve, the lord to protect and to maintain:

> Berars de Monsdidier devant Karle est venuz;
> A ses piez s'agenouille, s'est ses hom devenuz;
> L'ampereres le baise, si l'a releve suz;
> Par une blanche anisagne, li est ses fiez renduz.

(Berard of Montdidier came before Charlemagne, knelt at his feet, and became his man. The Emperor kissed him, when he had raised him up; and gave him his word by means of a white banner.)[9]

The *feodum* or 'fief', whence feudalism takes its name, grew out of the earlier practice of *beneficium* or 'benefit', where a patron would make a gift of land in vague expectation of some future advantage. In Carolingian times, such land grants began to be made explicitly as the 'fee' for military service. In due course the feudal tariff was refined and extended. It was originally calculated in terms of knight-service, that is, the number of knights to be provided in return for a given area of land. But it was stretched to include castle-guard and escort duties, judicial service in the lord's court, *consilium* or 'advice' rendered in the lord's council, and various forms of *auxilium* or 'assistance'. The lords came to interpret assistance in the sense of financial 'reliefs', including a downpayment equivalent to one year's income plus the 'aids in four kinds' which were payable for the lord's ransom, for the knighting of his eldest son, for the dowry of his eldest daughter, and for crusade. They also reserved their rights of *custodia* (wardship of minors), of *gîte* (lodging), of *marriage* (permission to marry), and of *retrait* (buying out the contract). But in exchange for the dues the vassal or 'tenant' received both the income of the land and the jurisdiction over all its inhabitants. In the case of default, the land and its income reverted to the owner.

In principle the fief was indivisible and inalienable. The contract automatically lapsed on the death of either party—in German *Manfall* or *Herrenfall*. In practice vassals went to great lengths to secure the succession of their relations and the right to divide or dispose of the land. For their part, lords took elaborate precautions to control the succession of women, of minors, or of incompetents. Special terms and eccentric clauses abounded. The chief vassals of the bishop of Paris were contracted to carry the bishop on their shoulders during his consecration. Certain fiefs in Kent were held on condition that their tenant 'held the king's head in the boat' during Channel crossings. The opportunities for financial extortion were enormous. When Ferrand of Portugal contracted with the King of France for the fief of Flanders in 1212, he paid a 'relief' of £50,000 for permission to marry the heiress.

Not surprisingly, legal wrangles were endemic. It was usual practice at an early date for all sovereign territories to create a separate code of feudal law, the *Lehnrecht*, and a separate system of courts, the *Lehnsgericht*, for trying feudal disputes. The prince customarily acted as court president, his chief vassals as assessors. Feudalism is generally judged to have come into operation when the practice of enfeoffment, or infeudation, became hereditary, and when it was merged with vassalage into one coherent whole. 'It was the indissoluble union between the position of a vassal and the possession of a fief that constituted the feudal system.'[10] In the last resort, however, vassalage and enfeoffment were incompatible. As vassals, the members of a knightly family were sworn to pursue the interests of their lord. As possessors of a fief, they were driven to pursue their own interests. Hence the characteristic tensions, and treacheries, of feudal society.

Feudal society consisted of a dense network of contractual relationships which linked the highest to the lowest in the realm. At the highest level, enfeoffment involved a contract between the sovereign and his 'tenants-in-chief', that is, with the barons holding the principal provinces of the kingdom. But through 'sub-infeudation' the tenants-in-chief could enfeoff tenants of their own; and sub-tenants could then enfeoff further tenants; and so on, right down the line. Most men who were vassals in relation to their 'superiors' acted as lords in relation to their 'inferiors'.

Feudal contracts were recorded for posterity in charters and indentures, though few from the early period survive:

In the name of the Trinity . . . Amen. I, Louis, by the Grace of God King of the French, hereby make known to all present and those to come that in our presence Count Henry of Champagne conceded the fief of Savigny to Bartholomew, Bishop of Beauvais, and to his successors. And for that fief, the said bishop has made promise and engagement for one knight, and justice and service to Count Henry . . . and has agreed that bishops to come will do likewise. Done at Mantes, in the year of the Incarnate Word 1167 . . . and given by the hand of Hugh, the chancellor.[11]

At the local level, the fiefs of princes and barons were reflected in the arrange-ments of manorial estates. In this case, the lord of the manor granted a plot of land to each of his serf families in exchange for service in the form of unpaid labour on his demesne. Enserfment, being a bargain between free and unfree, lacked many of the reciprocities of enfeoffment. But in so far that it implied a con-tract trading land for service, and protection for loyalty, it was based on similar principles. It was not to be confused with common slavery. In some parts of Europe—in northern Italy, for instance—serfs swore an oath of loyalty to their master, like knights to their liege-lord.

Given this network of contractual relationships, feudal society became extremely hierarchical. The Treaty of Verdun in 843 had stated the principle that 'every man should have a lord'. In theory at least, the only persons to possess absolute independence were the Pope and the Emperor, and they were vassals of God. Attempts to describe this state of affairs have led to concepts such as the 'feudal ladder' or the 'feudal pyramid', where the ruler of a country sits gaily atop neat layers of tenants and subtenants and subsubtenants . . . right down to the serfs at the bottom. Such models mislead by their artificial neatness and sym-metry. In reality, feudal society was built on a confused mass of conflicting depen-dencies and loyalties, riddled with exceptions and exemptions, where the once clear lines of service were fouled up by generations of contested privileges, dis-puted rights, and half-forgotten obligations. It was certainly hierarchical, but it was anything but neat and regular.

The extent of the survival of *allodium*, 'freehold land', was also very uneven. In some regions, such as the future Switzerland, freehold was common; in others, such as northern France, it virtually disappeared. Most usually there was a terrible tangle of feudal and freehold estates, and of families holding part of their land in fief and part in full ownership. To the feudal mind freehold was an aberration. It was sometimes called *feodum solis*, a 'fief of the sun.' Psychologically, however, the consequences were simple. Almost everyone was conditioned by their position in the social order, hemmed in by their legal and emotional ties of dependence. Those ties gave them a measure of security, and an unquestioned framework of identity; but they also made individuals vulnerable to exploitation, repression, and involuntary ignorance. 'What characterizes mediaeval in contrast to modern society is its lack of individual freedom.'[12]

One might also presume that a feeling of powerlessness over their personal lives added to medieval people's preoccupation with religion—in particular to their strong belief in the afterlife, and to their morbid cult of death.

Immunitas or immunity concerned the granting of exemptions from taxes, or from other impositions due to the central authority. In the early days the Church was the chief beneficiary; but immunities of various sorts were gradually granted to a wide variety of individuals, institutions, and corporations. They stemmed from a recognition that rulers could no longer cope with all their responsibilities; and they fostered the fragmentation of political, jurisdictional, and economic authority. The result was a patchwork of authorities where each locality was governed not by any uniform obligations but by the specific terms of the charters and 'liberties' granted to the particular abbeys, districts, or cities. Particularism was a hallmark of the feudal order.

Stone castles, together with heavy cavalry, were one of the factors which eventually contained the damage inflicted by Viking, Saracen, and Magyar raiders. An impregnable fortress, perched on crag or coast, provided the inhabitants of the district with a place of refuge, and dominated the land over which its garrison could sally forth. Castle-building began in the ninth and tenth centuries, when royal and princely authority had reached its lowest ebb; and castles, once built, could be used to defy the king or prince long after the raiders had departed. In this way private castles became the bastions of local and feudal power, permanent obstacles to the resurgence of a centralized state. Many centuries later, when statesmen such as Cardinal Richelieu set out to break the feudal nobility, their first task lay in the razing of castles. [**MIR**]

Chivalry, which derives from *chevalerie*, 'knightly class', refers in its narrowest sense to the 'code of honour' by which every knight was bound. It encompasses moral values such as honesty, loyalty, modesty, gallantry, fortitude. It commanded the knight to protect the Church, to succour the weak, to respect women, to love his country, to obey his lord, to fight the infidel, to uphold truth and justice, and to keep his word. By extension, chivalry referred to all the customs and practices associated with knighthood—and hence to their titles, orders, ceremonies, heraldry, vocabulary. In its widest sense, however, it refers to the prevailing ethos of feudal society as a whole, which was so completely dominated by the knights and all they stood for. With Christianity, it is one of the twin pillars of 'the medieval mind'.

Although many elements of nascent feudalism were present in Carolingian times, their full fusion into a coherent social order did not really begin until later. The 'classic age of feudalism' is generally located in the tenth to thirteenth centuries. The leading scholar of the subject distinguishes two feudal ages—the first from the ninth to the mid-eleventh centuries, where small-scale, caste-based arrangements prevailed between warlords and peasants, and a 'second feudal age', from the mid-eleventh to the mid-thirteenth century, which saw the flowering of feudal culture and the growth of hereditary nobility.[13] Chivalry, in particular, was slow to emerge: its attitudes were not fully manifest until the era of the twelfth-century renaissance (see pp. 348–50).

Feudalism, rooted in the Carolingian débâcle, remained essentially a Western phenomenon. The Byzantine Empire made provision for hereditary land grants to soldiers; and the system of *pomest'ye* in early eastern Slavdom seems to have involved similar practices. But the state feudalism of the East, if that is what it was, lacked many of the basic ingredients. As far as the countries of central Europe are concerned, historians strongly disagree over the importance of feudal institutions. Marxists assume that feudalism had to be the basis for the social order; others, on the whole, argue that it did not.[14] Everything depends on what definition of feudalism is used.

Feudalism deeply affected the life of the Church. It greatly weakened central ecclesiastical authority. It gave great power to local potentates, and put the clergy at their mercy. Counts and princes became accustomed to making and unmaking bishops at will. Lesser feudatories controlled the lesser clerics. 'Bishops were in danger of becoming barons in mitres; kings looked on prelates as officials bound to do them service; and patrons sold [church] benefices to the highest bidder.'[15] Not even the Papacy was exempt. With limited means of their own, the Popes stood to become puppets either of Roman noblemen, of Italian princes, or, at a later stage, of a reviving Empire.

Thanks to the Benedictine monastery at Cluny in Burgundy, Western monasticism adapted itself to the changing circumstances. Isolated abbeys and hermitages had been specially vulnerable to both raiders and to local barons. They felt a strong need for a collective effort to strengthen their position. Founded in 910 by Guillaume le Pieux, Count of Auvergne, Cluny was the source of reforms which answered that need. The Cluniacs modified the Benedictine rule to include stricter observances and services of inhuman length. More importantly, they raised their abbot to a position of strict authority over all the daughter houses which they founded or co-opted. In effect, they established the first monastic order. Their iron discipline and their independence from local concerns gave them a strong voice in Church politics. Above all, having secured the popes' support for their reforms, they became the unwavering advocates of papal supremacy. Between 910 and 1157 seven long-lived Abbots of Cluny—Berno, Odo, Aymard, Majolus, Odilo, St Hugh, and Peter the Venerable—created a network of 314 monasteries from Spain to Poland. It was no accident that the principal architect of the 'papal monarchy', Urban II, was himself a Cluniac (see below).

Feudalism left a profound legacy in Western culture. It moulded speech and manners; it conditioned attitudes to property, to the rule of law, and to relations between the state and the individual. By its emphasis on contract, and on the balance between rights and obligations, it generated lasting concern for mutual trust and for keeping one's word. These attitudes held implications far beyond the narrow spheres of military service and land-holding.

The military dispositions of the feudal order were put to the test when the fearsome Magyars rode onto the stage at the end of the ninth century (see p. 296). Though not related to the Huns, the Magyars lived by the same predatory habits, and settled on the same plains of 'Hungaria'. For sixty years, from 895 to 955, their annual raiding-parties stormed through the former Carolingian empire. They were every bit as murderous as the Vikings, and far fleeter. They were masters of blackmail, exacting vast sums in tribute or in ransom. In 899 they shattered the host of Italy on the River Brenta. In 904 they overwhelmed Moravia, in 907 Bavaria, in 922 Saxony. By the 940s they felt free to roam at will—to Apulia, to Aragon, to Aquitaine. They finally met their match when the princes and nobles of Germany united to challenge the latest invasion of Bavaria in 955. There, on the Lechfeld near Augsburg on 10–12 August, Otto of Saxony led the Germans to a famous victory in three days of slaughter. The Magyars were tamed. The remnants straggled back, and turned to the arts of tending their herds and ploughing the plain. [BUDA]

For some reason it has been the fashion among some historians to minimize the impact of the Magyars, who 'were not a creative factor in the West'.[16] (All this means is that the Magyars did not reach Cambridge.) They were, indeed, a destructive force. But they furnished the stimulus for developments of profound importance. By destroying Greater Moravia (see p. 321), they recast the ethnic and political patterns of the Danube basin, and determined the future profile of all Central Europe. Their presence was a vital element in the formation not only of Hungary but of Bohemia, of Poland, of Croatia and Serbia, of Austria, and of the German Empire. They created the living barrier which separated the Slavs of the north from the Slavs of the south. They opened the way for German colonists to move down the Danube, and to consolidate their hold on 'Austria'. They drove the princes of Germany to unite, and to accept the victor of the Lechfeld as their emperor. One account relates how the German troops raised Otto of Saxony on their shields at the end of the battle, and acclaimed him emperor on the spot. This may not have been the Magyars' intention. But for seven tribes of refugee nomads to have crossed the Carpathians, and within one lifetime to have provoked the rise of six or seven durable fixtures on the map of Europe, was no mean achievement. Only armchair historians, sitting in a backwater of an offshore island, might judge such developments trivial.

Of course, the elevation of Otto I of Saxony (r. 936–73), who was formally crowned Emperor in Rome in 962, cannot be attributed exclusively to his victory on the Lechfeld. His father, Henry the Fowler (r. 919–36), had already turned Saxony into a formidable power. From his palace at Mamleben in the Harz mountains he had initiated the eastern Marches, building walled towns and planting German settlers against the incursions of Danes, Slavs, and Magyars.

Quedlinburg, Meissen, and Merseburg all date from that reign. So Otto was building on firm foundations. The Marches were consolidated with ecclesiastical help. The archbishopric of Magdeburg (968), the bishoprics of Brandenburg and Havelberg, and the new port of Hamburg could now be safely planted. Three campaigns in Italy, in 951–2, 961–5, and 966–72, ensured that the imperial link between Germany and Italy was restored. A series of civil wars, and of judicious matrimonial alliances, saw the wayward duchies of Franconia, Lotharingia, Swabia, and Bavaria reintegrated.

Henceforth the restored Empire was destined to have a continuous existence until its destruction by Napoleon. The leadership of the house of Saxony naturally turned its centre of gravity to the east, although its economic life was still dominated by the Rhineland. Its kingmaking capital stayed in Aachen; and its possession of Lotharingia, the old 'Middle Kingdom', gave it a permanent stake in western affairs. The Salian dynasty which followed the Saxons from 1024 to 1125 were of Frankish origin. But they no longer ruled the empire of the Franks. They ruled a creature which would grow into the Holy Roman Empire of the German Nation—the launch-pad of 'Germany' (see Appendix III, p. 1246).

In 972, at the end of his last campaign in Italy, Otto I took a momentous step. Having conquered the Byzantines' Italian territories, he offered to return them in exchange for the mutual recognition of titles. He was to defer to the 'Empire of the Romans' if they would recognize his own, equal, imperial status. The agreement was sealed by the marriage of Otto's son to Theophano, daughter of the previous Byzantine Emperor, Romanus II. From then on, there were to be two empires. The dream of one universal empire was lost forever. True enough, Theophano's son, Otto III (r. 983–1002), *did* entertain visions of a wider realm. He made a pilgrimage to Aachen to open Charlemagne's tomb, and he paid an official visit to his eastern Polish neighbours. But his ideas attracted support neither in Germany nor in Constantinople, and he left no heirs. His successor, Henry II (r. 1002–24), the last of the Saxon line, was soon grappling with all the problems which became the Empire's normal burden: civil wars in Germany, frontier wars against the Slavs, expeditions into Italy, sporadic conflict with France.

Otto I had viewed the Papacy with autocratic disdain. He ordered that no pope should be consecrated before swearing allegiance to the Empire. Having hanged the tribunes and Prefect of Rome, he imposed John XIII (965–72) as a prelude to his own coronation. For the time being, the Latin Pope was scarcely more independent than the Greek Patriarch. Generally speaking, the Saxon emperors left the feuding rulers of 'West Francia' to their own devices. In the tenth century, the heirs of the Carolingians were locked in a complicated struggle of rivalry and mutual dependence with the descendants of Robert, Count of Paris, notably with Hugues le Grand, 'Duke of the French', a habitual kingmaker. In the process they lost their stake in Lotharingia, and hence of the old Frankish heartland. In 987, when the last Carolingian king died without heir, the struggle was resolved in favour of the Duke's son, Hugues Capet (r. 987–96)—founder of a dynasty that would reign for nearly 400 years.

Henceforth the kingdom of France was destined to have a continuous exis-tence. The leadership of the house of Capet inevitably turned the centre of grav-ity to the West. Of course, the memory of Charlemagne, and the claims to Lotharingia remained; but the kingdom had lost its essentially Frankish character. Contrary to later assertions, it was not involved in ceaseless warfare with its German neighbours; but its definitive separation from the reconstituted Empire acted as a powerful motor for a new identity. It was the launch-pad of the French nation.

In the period when the Frankish empire waned and the Saxon empire waxed strong, the Byzantine Empire reached its zenith under the Macedonian dynasty. Basil I (r. 867–86), an ex-horsebreaker who took the throne through murder, proved to be an able administrator who initiated 'an age of recovery and consol-idation'. The long reigns of his successors, Leo VI the Wise (r. 886–912) and Constantine VII Porphyrogenitus (r. 913–59), both of them scholars, coincided with a marked upsurge in Constantinople's commercial prosperity. The warrior emperors, John Tzimisces (r. 969–76) and Basil II Bulgaroctone (r. 976–1025), 'the Bulgar-slayer', took the offensive on all fronts. The Empress Zoë (c.978–1050) maintained power for half a century through the manipulation of three imperial husbands. Her portrait in mosaic has survived in Hagia Sophia, flanked on one side by Christ and on the other by an emperor whose inscription has been suit-ably obliterated. Her scheming sister Theodora (r. 1055–6) briefly emerged as sole ruler. [**ATHOS**]

Under the Macedonians, the Byzantine state was able to assert itself both inter-nally and externally. The Patriarchs were kept in abject subservience. The imper-ial court presided over a bureaucracy which introduced uniform practices throughout the provinces. The army was reorganized with professional, knight-like cadres. The aristocratic clans were wedded to state service. The state regulated trade and prices whilst maximizing its own income. With a population counted in six figures, Constantinople served as the leading entrepôt between East and West, by far exceeding all other European cities of the age. Byzantium's territor-ial power was greatly reinforced. Basil I re-established the Byzantine presence in southern Italy with the recapture of Taranto (880). There were two exarchates, in Calabria and in Langobardia, and a *Catapenatus* at Bari. In the East, annual cam-paigns throughout the tenth century were rewarded with the recovery of Syria, Cyprus, Crete, Cilicia, part of Mesopotamia. The Arab advance was checked. Armenia, which in the ninth century had been ruled by the native Bagratid dynasty, was returned to Byzantine vassalage. The Bulgars, who in 924 laid siege to Constantinople, spread their hegemony to the west, but were gradually tamed by baptism and the sword.

Political stability set the stage for a cultural renaissance. Basil I and Leo VI, a philosopher, codified the imperial decrees of recent centuries. Byzantine church architecture acquired harmonious homogeneity. Men of letters crowded the court. Photios (c.810–93), Patriarch and professor, revived the study of antiquity.

ATHOS

IN a chrysobull of 885, the Emperor Basil I formally recognized the 'Holy Mountain' of Athos as a territory reserved for monks and hermits. Henceforth, all civilians and females (human and non-human) were banned from the 360 km² of the 'Garden of the Virgin' on the easternmost of the three sea-girt promontories of Chalkidikës. The first permanent monastery, the Great Laura, was founded in 936. The basic *typikon* or charter dates from 972. The peninsula of Mount Athos, which rises to 2,033 m., was to be ruled by a protos or primate and by a council of abbots meeting in the central town of Karyes.[1]

From the outset, Athonite monasticism had to compromise between the communal and the anchorite traditions. Thirteen of the twenty great monasteries built between the tenth and the sixteenth centuries were purely *coenobitic*, having all activities in common, whilst seven were *idiorhythmic*, allowing monks to eat and work individually. These include the three oldest—the Great Laura, Vatopedi, and the Georgian-founded Iveron. Each of the monasteries is linked to a network of outlying farms, chapels, and anchorite cells. The ultimate sanctuary of the hermits is to be found in the vertigo-defying settlement of Karoulia, at the precipitous end of the peninsula, where the warren of individual huts is approached along a maze of cliff paths, stone steps, and chain ladders.

Over the centuries, Athos came under threat from a succession of invaders, including Arab pirates, Lakh shepherds, and Catalan raiders. In the period of the Latin Empire (1204–61), concerted attempts were made to convert the monks to Catholicism—hence their trenchant opposition to all later movements for East–West union. After that, they found ready patrons in the princes of Serbia, Bulgaria, and Wallachia. When Salonika was captured by the Turks in 1430, the monks secured their privileges from the sultan.

In the eighteenth century, Athos was the centre of an important pan-orthodox movement linked to the Patriarch of Constantinople. The Academy at Vatopedi was a seat of international learning.

In the nineteenth century, Athos was targeted by St Petersburg as an instrument of Russian influence. As many as 5,000 Russian monks took up residence, especially in the *roussikon* of St Panteleimon and in the *skete* of St Andrew. Greek, Serbian, Romanian, and Bulgarian foundations were similarly turned into agencies of their respective national churches. Athos lost its last great benefactor in the Russian Revolution of 1917. Its present constitution was introduced by treaty with Greece in 1926.

After decades of decay, a fresh influx of monks in the 1980s raised total numbers to c.1,500, fuelling demands for reform. Monasteries were repaired, commercial forestry exploited, access roads built, and (male) tourists welcomed. Discussions took place about renewed contacts with Rome. A monk of Athos published his complaints for an international audience.[2] 'The Athonites are famous factionists and gossips,' an observer commented. 'After all, it is the heart of what remains of the Byzantine world.'[3]

Simeon Metaphrastes (d. *c.*1000) composed the *Menologion*, the standard collection of the lives of the Christian saints. His contemporary, the poet John Geometres, wrote hymns, epigrams, and verse with great humanist sensitivity. Michael Psellos (*c.*1018–81), court philosopher and polymath, published a huge range of historical, theological, and literary works. Critics of the 'Macedonian Renaissance' maintain that its achievement was more encyclopedic than creative.

Secure and confident beyond the disasters which beset the West, Byzantium cruised along in style. When Liutprand of Cremona, historian of Otto the Great and ambassador of the King of Italy, visited Constantinople in 949 he was overwhelmed with amazement. His reception by Constantine Porphyrogenitus impressed, and offended, him mightily:

'In front of the emperor's throne stood a tree of gilded iron, whose branches were filled with birds of various kinds, also made of gilded iron, which gave forth a variety of bird-songs. The throne itself was so cunningly constructed that at one moment it looked low . . . and a moment later had risen to a great height. It was guarded on either side by huge lions of gilded metal or wood which lashed their tails on the floor and roared aloud with open mouths and moving tongues.

In this hall, attended by two eunuchs, I was brought before the emperor. At my entrance, the lions roared and the birds sang . . . But after prostrating myself for the third time, when I raised my head, I beheld the emperor, whom I had seen at first seated slightly above me, elevated almost to the roof of the hall and clad in different garments. How this was managed, I do not know . . .'[17]

Liutprand's understandable sense of inferiority aptly reflects Western attitudes towards the East in this period.

Byzantium's principal foe was Islam, against which it stood as Christendom's front-line bastion. But on its Balkan flank it faced a vigorous state that was a major rival for more than two centuries. The first Bulgarian Empire emerged from the tribal adventures of Terbel, Krum, and Omartag (see p. 220) and exercised sway over much of Byzantium's former Danubian provinces. Its adoption of Orthodox Christianity (see pp. 321–4) brought it into the world of Byzantine civilization, but did not prevent intense conflicts. Under Simeon (r. 893–927), who styled himself '*Basileus kai Autokrator* of the Bulgars and Greeks' as well as 'Tsar' (Caesar), Bulgaria sought to assume Byzantium's role in the Balkans, but came to grief in 924 before the walls of Constantinople. In the tenth century Byzantine forces reconquered the eastern heartland of Bulgaria. In this they were helped by the strife surrounding the Bogumil heresy, and by their Magyar and Kievan mercenary allies. In 966–7 Svyatoslav of Kiev attacked and captured the ancient Bulgarian capital, Preslav, in return for 1,800 pounds of Byzantine gold.

Under Tsar Samuel (r. 976–1014) the Bulgarian empire knew a second lease of life. The new capital of Ochrid became the centre of a powerful monastic movement, and of an autocephalous Bulgarian Church that survived the Byzantine reconquest. The political end came in 1014, following the Byzantine victory at Serres in Macedonia. Basil II blinded 14,000 Bulgarian prisoners of war before returning them to their Tsar, who promptly died of shame. Byzantium was still some way from the great crisis of 1071, when the Normans in Sicily, the Seljuks in Asia Minor, and the Pechenegs before the walls of Constantinople combined to provoke the onset of irreversible decline. [**BOGUMIL**]

In the three centuries after Charlemagne the frontiers of Christendom were greatly extended. The countries converted were (in the order of their conversion) Moravia, Bulgaria, Bohemia, Poland, Hungary, and Kievan Rus'. In the north, the steady advance of the Saxon marches was accompanied by forcible christianization; but it was not until the eleventh century that any major advance was made into Scandinavia. Despite considerable friction on the ground, the leadership of the Greek and Latin Churches were still apt to view their missionary work as the common task of Christendom.

Moravia—whose name is related to the German *Mähren*, meaning marchlands—lay on the north bank of the Danube to the east of Charlemagne's empire. It was the first of the Slav lands to emerge as an organized principality. In the seventh century, under one Samo, it is mentioned in Fredegar's chronicle as a territory that had rejected the Frankish obedience. In the eighth century it was evangelized from Bavaria by (among others) the Irish missionary, Virgil of Salzburg. In the ninth century the reigning prince appears to have been baptized by a German bishop, and a church was consecrated at Nitra.

In 862, however, a Moravian approach to the Patriarch of Constantinople was answered by a mission led by two Macedonian brothers, Michael and Constantine, known respectively as SS Methodius (815–85) and Cyril (826–67). Methodius had been governor of one of the Byzantine empire's Slav provinces; and Cyril, a diplomat, had travelled in the Muslim lands and in Khazaria. The purpose of their invitation to Moravia was apparently to check the oppressive influence of German priests, and to enable the country to worship in its own idiom. To this end Cyril devised the Glagolitic alphabet and a Slavonic liturgy, and translated the Bible.

After founding the Moravian mission, it is significant that the brothers travelled to Rome, where Cyril died. He was interred in the crypt of San Clemente. But Methodius returned to exercise his calling as Bishop of Pannonia and Moravia. He died in 885, probably at Velehrad near modern Bratislava. There was clearly much wrangling in Moravia between Latin and Greek clergy; yet Cyril and Methodius, the 'Apostles of the Slavs', enjoyed the patronage both of the Roman Pope and of the Byzantine Patriarch, thereby setting a rare, ecumenical example. Their names are revered by Czechs, Croats, and Serbs, and especially by the Bulgars, among whom the remnants of the mission eventually took refuge. Twenty years after the death of Methodius, Moravia was destroyed by the Magyars; but the memory of the 'co-patrons of Europe' has lingered on.

In Bulgaria, the rivalry of the Latin and the Greek Churches was ultimately resolved in favour of the Greeks. In the mid-ninth century the ruler of Bulgaria,

BOGUMIL

IN 975 the Emperor John Tzimisces transplanted a community of Armenian heretics to the district of Philipopolis (Plovdiv) in Bulgarian Thrace. They were 'Paulicians', remnants of a much larger movement broken by the Byzantines some time earlier. At the same time, the Orthodox Church was showing concern about the followers of an obscure Bulgarian priest, Bogumil, whose errors suspiciously resembled those of the Paulicians. They too were dualists, heirs to a tradition that went back to the Gnostics and the (non-Christian) Manicheans. Merging together, the two groups were to found a faith whose adherents would stretch right across Europe 'from Black Sea to Biscay'.[1]

Bogumilstvo or 'Bogumilism' appealed to the downtrodden Slav peasants of the Balkans, resentful of Greek or Bulgar overlords. It was to develop in two forms, the main, 'Bulgarian' variety and the lesser, 'Dragovitsan' variety, so named after a village on the borders of Macedonia, where a thoroughgoing dualist doctrine of Paulician origin took root. It was brought to Constantinople by a monk called Basil the Bulgar, many of whose unrepentant followers were burned at the stake. But it resurfaced in the mid-twelfth century, when 'false bishops' had to be dismissed and a patriarch retired for Bogumil sympathies.

Bogumil doctrine diverged from Orthodox Christianity on issues derived from their views on the origin of evil. The Bogumils rejected the creation story of the Old Testament, believing that the world was created by Satan, God's elder son. They also rejected Christ's miracles, except as allegorical stories, the Sacraments, icons, feast days, and the entire liturgy and ritual of Orthodoxy. They specially detested the Cross since it was the instrument of Christ's murder. According to one account, they believed that God had tempered his wrath by allowing Satan to keep what was already created, and that he sent Jesus, his second Son, to cure the resultant ills. Jesus, the embodiment of the Word, 'entered the Virgin through her ear, took flesh there and emerged by the same door. The Virgin did not notice, but found Him as an infant in a Cave in Bethlehem. He lived and taught, and by seeming to die, was able to descend into Hell and bind Satan.'[2]

Bogumil practices appeared very strange to contemporaries. Bogumils read only selected parts of the Bible, especially the Psalms, the Prophets, the Gospels, the Epistles, and Revelation. Their only prayer was 'Our Father', which they recited 120 times a day. They practised fasting, discouraged marriage, and trained an élite caste of 'the Elect'. One branch, the followers of Cyril the Barefoot, practised nudism in an attempt to regain the Garden of Eden. Another, following the preacher Theodosius, indulged in orgies, deliberately experiencing sin in order to qualify for repentance. In political matters, all Bogumils presented a front of passive but obdurate nonconformity.

Though Bogumilism was eradicated in Byzantium and Bulgaria during the thirteenth century, it had spread by then to the West (see pp. 361–3), and was taking root in fresh parts of the Balkans. In the fourteenth century it even penetrated the holy mountain of Athos. But its greatest success was to occur in the principalities of Bosnia and Hum (Hercegovina), whose rulers chose to propagate the Bogumil faith as an antidote to the pretensions of their Hungarian Catholic and Serbian Orthodox neighbours. It was in 1199 that the Ban of Bosnia and his court first declared themselves 'Patarenes', as the Bosnian Bogumils were called; and despite many twists of religious fortune, Bosnia remained predominantly Patarene until the Ottoman conquest of 1463. At this point the Bosnian nobility converted promptly to Islam, thereby avoiding the Catholic and Orthodox trap once again. [**SARAJEVO**]

Scholars once believed that the Slavs were predisposed to Bogumilism through the dualist beliefs of Slav paganism. Hetmold of Lübeck reported in the twelfth century that the north German Slavs worshipped a good God and a bad God. If so, the phenomenon was purely local. Pagan Slavs were more likely to have been affected by Bogumilism than vice versa. The same can be said of Balkan folklore.

Dualists of the Bogumil type attracted many labels. Among them, apart from Bogumils, Dragovitsans, and Patarenes, were the *Phundaites* or 'scrip-bearers', *Babuni* (in Serbia), *Runcarii* or *Runkeler* (in Germany), *Kudugers* (in fifteenth-century Macedonia), *Poplicani* (in northern France), and *Bougres*, *Textores* or *Tisserands* or 'weavers', *Albigensians*, and *Cathars* in Languedoc.[3]

Bogumilism has been called 'a hopeless faith'. If so, its adherents showed exceptional perseverance in place of hope.

Boris X (r. 852–88), was toying with a Frankish alliance; and in 862 he met with Louis the German at Tulln on the Danube. But the scheme misfired; and peace with Byzantium in 865 caused Boris to accept baptism from the Patriarch of Constantinople. Boris, however, continued to intrigue with Rome, and a long letter containing 106 questions on Roman practice and theology evoked the famous *Responsa* of Pope Nicholas II. A further Byzantine advance then led to the Bulgarian mission of St Clement Slovensky (840–916) and the final drive to bring Bulgaria into the Orthodox fold. Clement, a fellow Macedonian, had accompanied Cyril and Methodius to Moravia, and was Cyril's principal continuator in his work on the Slavonic liturgy. He was probably the true systematizer both of the Old Church Slavonic liturgical language and of the Cyrillic alphabet. He was the first bishop of the Bulgarian Church, and is buried in the monastery of St Pantaleinion at Ochrid. After 893, when pagan opposition to Christianity was crushed, the court of Tsar Simeon at Preslav hosted a veritable explosion of ecclesiastical learning for which Old Church Slavonic was now the vehicle. The autocephalous Bulgarian Church had seven sees: Ochrid, Pliska, Preska, Nesebar, Sardica (Sofia), Belgrade, and Preslav.

Bohemia, like Bulgaria, balanced for many years between Latin and Greek influences. In the ninth century the loyalties of the princes of Bohemia were pulled in two opposite directions—to the Franks and to the Moravians. Borivoj (r. 855–91) and his consort Ludmila, founders of the Hradčany chapel on the castle hill in Prague, were baptized into the Moravian (Slavonic) rite. Borivoj's successor, Spytygner (r. 893–915), was baptized at Regensburg in Bavaria into the Latin rite. Václav (r. 900–29), better known as St Wenceslas, whose life and death are celebrated in equal measure in Latin and in Slavonic sources, reigned briefly at the height of the Magyar onslaught. He was murdered by his brother Boleslas I (r. 929–67), who was seeking a closer association with Saxony. In due course, as a martyr to growing German influence, he became the national saint of the Czechs. When the bishopric of Prague was founded in 967, it was subordinated to the metropolitan of Mainz, thereby reflecting the power of the new Ottonian empire. St Vojtech or Adalbert (956–97) was its second bishop.

Yet for more than a century, under the protection of the Přemyslid dynasty, the Slavonic rite survived in Bohemia alongside the Latin one. At the monastery of Sazanar in particular a rich school of Slavonic learning flourished, with contacts both in Kiev and in Croatia. In 1091, as an act of defiance, King Vratislav II submitted himself to a second Slavonic coronation by the last abbot of Sazanar. Thereafter, Latinization was virtually complete. Bohemia, a fief of the Empire and a client province of the German Church, was the Slav country most firmly drawn into the German orbit.

Poland, Bohemia's eastern neighbour, edged toward Christendom in a similarly complex and prolonged process. In the ninth century, when the *Wiślanie* or 'Vistulanian tribe' owed allegiance to Moravia, the earliest Christian contacts were made with the mission of Cyril and Methodius. The chief of the Vistulanians appears to have accepted baptism in the Slavonic rite in 875; and traces of several Christian churches from that period have been discovered. The region of the upper Vistula, including Cracow, remained part of Bohemia until 990, and did not finally sever its connections with the Czech world until 1086. Poland's early links with the Slavonic rite have not been emphasized; but it is arguable, as in Bohemia, that they persisted into the twelfth century.[18]

Most of the tribes to the north, who would form the core of the first Polish kingdom, followed a different course. They remained pagan to the middle of the tenth century, after which they were drawn directly into the sphere of the Latin Church. The fullest description of Slavdom in its final pagan days was composed by a Moorish Jew, Ibrahim-Ibn-Jakub, who was sent by the Caliph of Cordova on an embassy to central Europe *c*.965. He visited Prague and possibly Cracow:

The lands of the Slavs stretch from the Syrian Sea to the Ocean in the north . . . At present there are four kings: the king of the Bulgars; Bojeslav, King of Faraga, Boiema and Karako; Mesko, king of the north; and Nakon on the border of the West.

In general, the Slavs are violent and inclined to aggression. If not for the disharmony among them . . . no people could match their strength . . . They are specially energetic in agriculture . . . Their trade on land reaches to the Ruthenians and to Constantinople. . . .

Their women, when married, do not commit adultery. But a girl when she falls in love with some man or other, will go to him and quench her lust. If a husband marries a girl and finds her to be a virgin . . . he says to her, 'If there were something good in you . . . you would certainly have found someone to take your virginity.' Then he sends her back.

The lands of the Slavs are coldest of all. When the nights are moonlit and the days clear, the most severe frosts occur . . . When people breathe, icicles form on their beards, as if made of glass . . .

They have no bath-houses as such, but . . . they build a stone stove on which, when it is heated, they pour water. They hold a bunch of grass in their hands and waft the steam around. Then their pores open, and all excess matter escapes from their bodies. This hut is called al-istba . . . .

Their kings travel in great carriages, on four wheels. From the corners of the carriage a cradle is slung on chains, so that the passenger is not shaken . . .

The Slavs wage war with the Byzantines, with the Franks and Langobards, and with other peoples . . .[19]

Interestingly enough, Ibrahim-Ibn-Jakub did not appear to regard the Rus as Slavs, presumably because they were still seen as Norsemen. What is not in doubt is that this diplomat from Muslim Spain looked on the exotic peoples of the European interior with the curiosity of a modern anthropologist surveying the tribes of Papua (see Appendix III, p. 1264).

In 965, in the same year as Ibrahim-Ibn-Jakub's visit, Mieszko I, prince of the *Polanie* or Polanians, who lived on the River Warta, allied himself with the Czechs. As part of the alliance he married the Czech princess Dubravka and accepted Christian baptism. He was responding to the rise of the Saxon Empire after the defeat of the Magyars, and to pressures for accepting Christianity from Germany. The first Latin missionary bishopric was created at Poznań in succession to an earlier see of the Slavonic rite, probably at Sandomierz. Dependence on the German Empire had been avoided. The ecclesiastical province of 'Polonia' was launched some thirty years later, in conjunction with a rapidly consolidating Polish state. When the Emperor Otto III visited the newly created metropolitan see at Gniezno in AD 1000, and embraced the Polish prince as his 'friend and ally', the *Wielkopolska* (Great Poland) of Mieszko had already been joined to the *Małopolska* (Little Poland) of the south. Benedictine monasteries had been established at Międzyrzecz and at Tyniec. Bolesław Chrobry 'the Brave' (r. 992–1025), who stormed Prague in 1003 and notched his sword on the Golden Gate of Kiev in 1018, was rewarded by the Pope with Poland's first royal crown. In 1037 a great pagan revolt marked the death throes of the old order. Thereafter the royal capital moved to Cracow; and the well-established Piast dynasty slowly turned Poland into the prime bastion of Catholicism in the East.

Hungary followed very closely in the path of Poland. Its first Christian contacts were with Byzantium. A captive Greek monk, Hierothos, was consecrated 'Bishop of Turkia' *c.*950. But the battle of the Lechfeld brought German influence in its wake. The Magyar Prince Géza (r. 972–97) was baptized with all his family into the Latin rite in 975. Géza's son István (St Stephen, r. 997–1038) consolidated the imperial link by marrying a Bavarian princess and by accepting a royal crown from Rome. Stephen's coronation at the new see of Esztergom (Gran) took place in 1001, only one year after Emperor Otto's visit to Gniezno. The abbey at Pannonhalma opened in the same year as its sister house at Międzyrzecz. [**BUDA**]

All these primitive kingdoms were patrimonial states, where all rights and property were held by the ruling prince. The adoption of Christianity, which brought in literate clergy, has to be seen as a move to strengthen the infant monarchies.

Kievan Rus' adopted Christianity from Byzantium in 988 as part of a comprehensive political settlement. Rus' had been growing closer to Byzantium for over a century. Dnieper trade, Varangian raids, and the wars of the steppes had established contacts of all sorts. The Prince of Kiev, Volodymyr or Vladimir (r. 980–1015), was 'a doughty heathen', a fratricide, and a polygamist. But Orthodox baptism, and marriage to Anna, sister of the Emperor Basil II, was the necessary price for persuading the Emperor to hire the 6,000 warriors of the famous Varangian Guard. Though the Prince's grandmother, St Olha (Olga), had been a Christian convert, he had weighed various alternatives before taking the same course. Envoys were sent abroad to report on the competing attractions of Judaism, Islam, and Christianity. The envoys who reported on their impressions from the church of St Sophia in Constantinople carried the day, having been treated to the ecclesiastical equivalent of Liutprand's audience with the Emperor. Only then did the Kievan Prince receive his christening. He ordered his people to the banks of the Dnieper, where they, too, were baptized *en masse*. He took the children of his nobles from their parents, and educated them in the new faith. Missionaries were later sent into the country to teach the variant of Orthodoxy popularized in Bulgaria by St Clement, together with the Old Church Slavonic liturgy, the Cyrillic alphabet, and loyalty to the Patriarch of Constantinople. Churches were built, heathen shrines demolished. Christianity reached Novgorod, Minsk, and Polotsk in the early eleventh century. Henceforth, Rus' was to be an unshakeable member of Christendom. [**NOVGOROD**]

Volodymyr or Vladimir, Prince of Kiev, is frequently likened to Charlemagne, creator of another vast but ephemeral realm.[20] The parallel is apt enough, not least because both men became heroes of later national legends. Of course, Volodymyr the Rus was no more a Russian than Charlemagne the Frank had been a Frenchman. 'Russia' did not exist in his day, any more than 'France' existed in Charlemagne's. Unfortunately, when the Russian Orthodox Church came on to the scene five centuries later, it laid monopoly claims to the Kievan heritage; and modern Russian propaganda has done everything in its power to suppress rival claims and traditions, notably among the Ukrainians. Meanwhile, just as

NOVGOROD

A NCIENT Novgorod lay in the centre of the forest zone, and hence was built almost entirely from wood—with wooden houses, wooden churches, wooden streets, wooden drains, even a wooden, birch-bark writing system. It began life as a trading-post on the banks of the River Volkov, at the northern end of the Baltic–Black Sea and Caspian–Baltic trade routes. Timber must always have been one of its staple commodities.

When Novgorod was comprehensively excavated in 1951–62, in one of the showpieces of medieval archaeology, the science of *dendrochronology* or 'tree-ring dating' was presented with one of its major challenges. The waterlogged ground had preserved the wooden remains in a remarkable state; and in thirteen seasons of excavation the team, led by A. V. Artikhovsky and B. A. Kolchin, opened up a site of 9,000 square metres, uncovering 1,150 log buildings. Most surprisingly, no fewer than 28 layers of wooden street-levels were identified on the former high street, from the top level 1 of AD 1462 to the earliest level 28 of 953. On average, the roadway had been renewed once every 18 years over 5 centuries, simply by laying a new layer of pine logs over the old ones damaged by cart-wheels and sledge runners. Extensive coin hoards, two from eighth-century Central Asia, showed that Novgorod's far-flung trading contacts had never been seriously interrupted, even by the Mongol invasions. [DIRHAM]

Of 400 birch-bark letters, all but one Finnish specimen were written in an early form of Russian. In No. 17, which was found at level 5 (1409–27), the bailiff from an estate outside the city writes to his lord:

Mikhail makes obeisance to his lord, Timothy. The ground is prepared and we must sow. Come, sir, for everyone is ready, but we cannot have rye without your command.[1]

In a fragment of No. 37, found between levels 12 and 13 (1268–99), there is a proposal of marriage:

From Nikita to Ulyanitsa. Marry me. I want you, and you me. And Ignatio will act as witness.[2]

Walking the wooden streets of old Novgorod, whose inhabitants were slaughtered by the agents of Moscow, some people wonder how the world would have changed if Russia could have grown under the leadership of this peaceable republic.[3] A Novgorodian Russia would clearly have been very different from the Muscovite Russia which triumphed over its rivals. But such thoughts are unhistorical. In any case, medieval archaeology offers no clue.

Charlemagne was turned into the national hero of the *chansons de geste*, so the saintly 'Prince Vladimir' was turned into the central figure of medieval Russian *byliny*. Roland, Oliver, and Bishop Turpin have their counterparts in Alyosha Popovich, Dobryna Nikitich, and the valiant peasant Ilya Popovich—the companions of the *Krasnoe Solnyshko*, 'our beloved little Sunshine'. No one would have laughed more rumbustiously at this epithet than the very unsaintly saint himself (see Appendix III, p. 1249).

Scandinavia was not taken into the Christian fold without a struggle. A missionary bishopric, directed to the conversion of Scandinavia, had been active at Bremen since the 780s. But the Vikings' way of life was not readily compatible with the Gospel, and a determined pagan party existed in the court of each of the three kingdoms. In Denmark, Harald Bluetooth (r. 940–86) accepted Christianity *c.*960, only to be expelled after founding the bishoprics of Aarhus and Schleswig. His son, Swein Forkbeard (r. 985–1014), once the leader of the heathen resistance, became the leading christianizer of the Danes. Under Canute the Great (r. 1016–35), who ruled England as well as Denmark, Anglo-Saxon missionaries set sail for Scandinavia.

In Norway, too, the drama took place in two acts. One attempt by Olaf Tryggvason (r. 995–1000) faltered, whilst the second, by Olaf Haraldson (r. 1016–28), succeeded through a mixture of bribery, coercion, and zealotry. This second Olav, who was killed defending his country against the Danes, was buried in the cathedral at Nidaros (Trondheim), and in due course was canonized as the national saint. In Sweden, Olaf Skutkonung (r. 995–1022) was baptized in 1008; but the resultant civil war between Christian and pagan factions continued for more than a century. Like St Olaf, St Eric of Sweden (d. 1160), who died in battle, and St Canute IV of Denmark (d. 1085), who was assassinated, came to be revered as martyrs of the faith. Metropolitan sees were established at Trondheim, Uppsala, and Lund in the 1140s by the then Cardinal-Legate, Nicholas Breakspeare, destined to be the only English Pope. [**EIRIK**]

The unsaintly character of all the national saint-kings from Wenceslas to Eric may well point to the superficiality of the conversions; but it also points to the process whereby Christianity was used to foster a sense of community within the state. Poland alone of the neophyte nations failed to produce a kingly saint or a martyr-king at this stage. Instead, it produced a martyr-bishop. Stanisław Szczepanowski (1030–79), the turbulent Bishop of Cracow, was literally cut to pieces in front of the altar by the knights of the king whom he had defied. His death, which set an uncanny precedent for the better-known martyrdom of St Thomas à Becket in England, indicated the growing power of the Latin Church, and the consequent conflicts between Church and State. In later days it was taken to symbolize the dismemberment of the sinful Polish kingdom into warring feudal fiefs.

Throughout this long second stage of conversions, the Greek and Latin Churches had coexisted in a state of strained separation. There was little co-operation; but

EIRIK

SOMETIME before 1075 King Svein Ulfsson, nephew of Canute the Great, received a man called Audun, who had sailed from Greenland to Denmark to present him with a polar bear. The episode is recalled in a saga called *Audun's Story*. Shortly afterwards, the King received the German priest, Adam of Bremen, who was collecting information for his monumental history of the Archbishopric of Hamburg, under whose juris-diction Scandinavia then fell. According to Adam, the King told him 'that there was another island in that ocean which had been discovered by many and was called *Vinland* because vines grow wild there and yield excellent wine, and moreover, self-grown grain grows there in abun-dance'.[1] It is the earliest European reference to North America. Archaeological evidence, notably from northern Newfoundland, confirms the fact that Norsemen did indeed found transatlantic settlements.[2]

The exploration of 'the Glacial Sea' extended over several centuries. Iceland was known to the Irish in the eighth century. Norse settlement began there *c*.870. Greenland was known some eighty years before it received its earliest colonists, *c*.985/6, the date which is also given to the first sighting of 'Vinland'.[3]

The central figure in the explorations was the adventurer Eirik the Red (*c*.940–1002). Eirik left his home at Jaederen in Norway after a series of murders; but he then started a feud in Iceland when his slaves engineered a landslide to demolish a neighbour's farm. Outlawed by the Icelandic Assembly at Thorness, he sailed away to found a colony on the western coast of an island 'which he called *Greenland*, so that others would be tempted to go there'. This was fifteen years before Iceland officially adopt-ed Christianity in AD 1000. Eirik's younger son, Leif Ericsson 'the Lucky', sailed on from Greenland *c*.1001 to test reports of land to the west, and returned with descriptions of *Helluland* ('Slab-land', probably Baffin Island), *Markland* ('Forest Land', probably Labrador), and the elusive *Vinland*, 'the Land of Grapes'. It was Tyrkir the German, a member of Leif's crew, who found the vines; and it was Thorfinn Karlsefni, the wealthy sec-ond husband of Eirik's daughter-in-law, Gutrid, who twice organized ex-peditions to site permanent settlements on the American shore. Eric's bastard daughter Freydis also visited Vinland twice. On the first occasion, she was said to have repulsed an Indian attack by baring her breasts. On the second, she murdered all her companions. In the autumn of 1009, Gutrid, Karlsefni's wife, and widow of Eirik's elder son, Thorstein, gave birth in Vinland to a boy called Snorri, the first Euro-American.

The exact location of Vinland has caused endless scholarly headaches. The consensus now leans towards Newfoundland and a site at L'Anse-aux-Meadows. The *vinber* or 'wineberries' found by Tyrkir may well have

been wild cranberries and the 'self-sown wheat' lyme grass. The subject
has produced much 'Skandiknavery'. Among the sensations one must list
a runic inscription for M1 or AD 1001 carved by some joker on a boulder at
Martha's Vineyard in 1920, and Yale's Vinland Map produced in 1965.[4]

The main sources remain the Norse sagas, especially *The
Graenlandinga Saga* (c.1190) *Eirik's Saga* (c.1260) and the *Islandingabòk*
(c.1127), a history of the Icelanders commissioned by a bishop who was the
great grandson of Snorri Karsefnisson.[5]

Except for Iceland, the outermost Norse colonies did not last. Vinland
was abandoned after a few decades. Greenland, once prosperous from the
trade in walrus ivory, furs, and snowy falcons, declined in the fourteenth
century. Rickets and a deteriorating climate took their toll. The last ship
from Greenland reached Iceland in 1410. 'The last Norse Greenlander died
some time later, "unknelled, uncoffined, and unknown".'[6] His frozen
remains, or those of one of his last companions, were discovered near the
Greenland shore in 1586 by the Elizabethan explorer John Davys
(1550–1605). Like Eirik the Red and Leif Ericsson exactly 600 years before,
Davys was sailing to the far north-west in search of his fortune in mysterious lands beyond the 'Great Passage'.[7]

equally there was no formal divorce. In the mid-eleventh century, however, the
point of parting was reached. In Constantinople, the Patriarch Michael
Kerullarios, promoted in 1043, entered into a dispute with the Byzantine governor
of southern Italy. In the process he closed all the Latin churches in the capital, and
wrote to the Latin bishops denouncing their schismatic practices, in particular
their use of unleavened bread in the Eucharist. At the same time the Roman
Papacy passed for five dramatic years into the assertive hands of Leo IX (1049–54),
formerly Bruno von Egisheim, Bishop of Toul, and a cousin of the German
emperor. Pope Leo was driven by a strong belief in his own mission, and was no
more inclined to brook the pettiness of the Greek Patriarch than to tolerate the
abuses of the bishops and kings in the West. In January 1054 he dispatched a legation to Constantinople under Cardinal Humbert de Moyenmoutier, and ordered
them to obtain confirmation of his claims to papal supremacy. Not surprisingly,
disaster ensued. The Patriarch refused to recognize the legates' powers and
pressed on with the publication of an aggressive manifesto, notwithstanding news
of Pope Leo's death. On 16 July the legates replied by excommunicating the
Patriarch in a Bull which they placed on the hallowed altar of St Sophia itself. The
insult was unforgivable. A synod of the Greek Church was convened to condemn
the Latin heresies in creed and in practice, and to excommunicate the papal
legates. It was the point of no return. [MISSA]

The schism between East and West, Christendom's major scandal, has never
been repaired. From 1054 onwards there were not only two supposedly universal

MISSA

THE Christian liturgy has never been static. The Divine Office of hymns, psalms, lessons, homilies, responsories, canticles, and collects began to crystallize from the fifth century. The Canonical Hours, which enabled monks to spread out their recital of the 150 psalms, once recited daily, were instituted by St Benedict. Prudentius, Bishop of Troyes (d. 861) is credited with an early Breviary or summary of approved liturgical texts.

The most solemn of the Christian sacraments, the Mass or *missa*, assumed definitive form slightly later. Variously known as the Eucharist or 'Rite of Thanksgiving', as the 'Communion', or as the commemoration of 'the Lord's Supper', it was customarily separated from the rest of the Divine Office. The earliest Missal or 'Order of the Mass' dates from the tenth century. The central act of Communion occurs when the priest consecrates bread and wine, the body and blood of Christ, and offers them to the communicants. From the thirteenth century to 1965, the Roman Church restricted the chalice of wine to the priestly celebrant. But now, as originally, it offers 'Communion in Both Kinds'. The theological implications of the Eucharist, notably the Thomist doctrine of transubstantiation, caused immense controversy during the Reformation.

The custom of setting key parts of the Mass to music had far-reaching consequences. The Propers, or items whose words vary according to the occasion, were usually recited or chanted. They include the Introit, the Gradual, the Offertory, and the Communion Anthem. But the Ordinaries, whose text was invariable, opened the way for elaborate musical inventions. The Ordinaries include: the *Kyrie Eleison* ('Lord Have Mercy'), an ancient imprecation borrowed from sun worship; the *Gloria in Excelsis Deo* ('Glory to God on High'), a hymn usually omitted during Lent; the *Credo* or Nicene Creed; the *Sanctus* ('Holy, Holy, Holy'), an adorational hymn which prefaces the Communion; the *Agnus Dei* ('O Lamb of God, who takest away the sins of the world'); and finally the Dismissal, *Ite, missa est* ('Go in peace; the Mass is ended').

Setting the Ordinaries for two or more voices, and then for choirs with instrumental accompaniment, presented the principal challenge of medieval polyphony. A complete Mass cycle was composed by Guillaume de Machaut (d. 1377), and similar compositions were common by the Renaissance. The supreme masters were undoubtedly Palestrina (d. 1594) and his contemporary, William Byrd (1543–1623), a Catholic in Anglican service. Palestrina's highly original *Missa Papae Marcellae* (1555) followed the instructions of the Council of Trent in giving maximum clarity to the words. [CANTUS]

The impact of the Mass on musical history was incalculable. Just as incantation had transformed the spiritual and aesthetic effect of the

liturgy, so the choral and instrumental arrangements of the Mass profoundly influenced Europe's evolving musical tradition. 'The liturgical text
forms the portal through which music enters into the cultural history of the
Western Christian world.'[1]

The stupendous Mass in B minor (1738) of J. S. Bach initiated a stage
where musical performances of the Mass could be divorced from religious
ceremony. Haydn wrote fourteen such masses, among them the Drum
Mass (1796) and the Wind-Band Mass (1802). Mozart wrote eighteen,
including the sublime, unfinished Requiem (1791). Beethoven's Missa
Solemnis in D (1823) may be regarded as the zenith of the series, to be followed in Romantic style by those of Liszt, Gounod, Bruckner, and Janáček.
In the twentieth century the Mass survived both the dilution of Christian
belief and the disintegration of traditional musical form. Frederick Delius
composed a choral Mass of Life (1909) based on anti-religious texts by
Nietzsche. Stravinsky's Mass for Chorus and Wind Instruments (1948)
experiments with neo-polyphonic techniques modelled on Machaut.[2]

Yet sung and unsung masses can be heard every day in Catholic and
Orthodox churches around the world. Both the religious tradition and the
musical genres descended from it are very much alive.

Christian Empires; there were two supposedly universal and orthodox Christian
Churches. Three hundred years earlier, the principal line of division in Europe lay
between the Christian lands of the south and the heathen lands of the north. From
now on, it lay between the Catholic lands of the West and the Orthodox lands of
the East. (See Map 3.)

1054–1268

Whereas, in the age of the Vikings and Magyars, it was the West and Centre of
Europe that had borne the brunt of the turmoil, it was the East that sustained the
havoc when first the Seljuk Turks and then the Mongols appeared on the scene.
Indeed, from the second half of the eleventh century onwards, Latin Christendom
entered an era of reform and revitalization. In that same period the Eastern
Empire entered a stage of irreversible decline. As shown by the Crusades, the two
movements were not unrelated.

At the time of the Schism between East and West, the Byzantine Empire was
preoccupied with a series of petty upheavals caused by wars on the frontier and
strife in the palace. Indeed, the revolts of generals, the ambitions of the Patriarch,
and the intrigues of the empresses proved no less disruptive than the Normans in
Italy, the Pechenegs on the Danube, and the Seljuk Turks in Armenia. The death

of the ageing Theodora in 1057, which ended the Macedonian dynasty, distracted the Empire at the moment it faced its greatest challenge.

The Saljuqs or Seljuks had crossed the Oxus in 1031, gaining mastery over Persia in the 1040s, Armenia in the 1060s, and Jerusalem in 1070. They came within a hair's breadth of capturing Baghdad. Their sultans, Tughril Beg (r. 1038–63), the 'Reviver of Islam', and Alp Arslan (r. 1063–72), infused the fighting spirit which mobilized a motley following. Their entourage included Persian administrators, Greek advisers, and a rich company of philosophers, mathematicians, and poets:

> Awake! For Morning in the Bowl of Night
> Has flung the Stone that puts the Stars to Flight:
>   And lo! the Hunter of the East has caught
> The Sultan's Turret in a Noose of Light.
>
> Here with a Loaf of Bread beneath the Bough,
> A Flask of Wine, a Book of Verse—and Thou
>   Beside me, singing in the Wilderness—
> And wilderness is Paradise enow.
>
> 'Tis all a chequer-board of Nights and Days
> Where Destiny with Men for pieces plays,
>   Hither and thither moves, and mates, and slays,
> And one by one back in the Closet lays.[21]

Omar Khayyam (1048–1131), whose Persian quatrains would be turned in translation into one of the favourite items of English literature, served as astronomer and calendarist at the Seljuk court under Alp Arslan, the architect of their greatest triumph. On 19 August 1071, at Manzikert near Lake Van, the Seljuks turned a border contest into an imperial rout. The Byzantine army was utterly destroyed. The Emperor, Romanus IV Diogenes, was captured. The Empire's heartland in Asia Minor was overrun, serving thenceforth as the base for the Turkish emirate of Rum. The Empire's population and economic resources were drastically reduced.

Byzantium never fully recovered. From now on, the emperors were seeking to defend the shrinking foreground of Fortress Constantinople. The Seljuks, too, had shot their bolt. They soon lost the guardianship of Jerusalem to the Shi'ite Fatimids of Egypt; and the wars of rival emirs gave the Empire some respite. The energetic young Emperor Alexius I Comnenus (r. 1081–1118) held the line by a mixture of valour and dubious financial expedients, such as seizing the Church's treasure. He repulsed the Normans from Greece, and recovered a valuable stretch of the Pontic and Aegean shore. But a return to the status quo ante was out of the question. Under Manuel I (r. 1143–80), a certain 'Comnenian Renaissance' bloomed, especially in scholarship, theology, and architecture. Grandiose schemes for reuniting with Rome or for conquering Egypt came to nought. The growing influence of the Latins, with whom Manuel packed his court, led to increasing friction, especially with the Venetians. The degenerate Andronicus Comnenus (r. 1183–5) was tortured to death by a mob which followed his own example. The façade of greatness was still intact. Constantinople was still the richest and most civilized city of Christendom: its trade, its ceremonies, its intense religious devotions continued in full swing. But the substance was ebbing away. Its body politic awaited the shock which in 1204 would all but kill it dead.

Byzantium's distress produced serious repercussions in the Orthodox Slav lands. There was neither the will nor the means whereby the Greek Patriarch could exercise the same control over Bulgars, Serbs, or Kievans as the Papacy was now beginning to exercise in the West. In the century after Manzikert, the Balkans descended once more into turmoil. The Pechenegs, who reached the walls of Constantinople for a second time in 1090, were not subdued until 1122. Long campaigns had to be fought in the north-west to hold Serbia from the Magyars. In 1186 the Bulgars broke free once more to found their 'Second Empire'.

Kievan Rus' was largely left to its own devices. Jaroslav the Wise (r. 1019–54), successor to St Volodymyr, had taken Red Ruthenia from the Poles, had defeated the Pechenegs, and had even sent a major naval expedition against Constantinople. But on his death, the state disintegrated into warring principalities—Halicz and Volhynia in the west; Kiev, Turov, Chernigov in the south; Novgorod, Polotsk, and Smolensk in the north; Tver, Vladimir-Suzdal, and Ryazan on the upper Volga. The dissensions of Rus' were cleverly fanned by the Byzantines, and might well have been exploited by the neighbouring Poles had the Polish kingdom itself not fallen likewise into an extended period of fragmentation after 1138. The primitive kingdoms of the Slavs stood in considerable disarray long before the arrival of the Mongols.

Divergences among the east Slavs now became evident. Kiev remained a commercial and religious centre; but it was exposed to the whims of the Pechenegs (Patzinaks) and Polovtsians (Cumans) on the steppes, and had all but lost political control. In the twelfth century the name *Ukraina*, meaning 'On the edge' or 'the frontier', was first applied to the lands round Kiev. Halicz (Galicia), first noted in 1140, and Volhynia passed under the Romanowicz dynasty. Daniel Romanowicz (r. 1235–65) received his crown from a papal legate, but later renounced the Catholic connection. According to one chronicle, he was urged to side with the people in suppressing the boyars. 'You cannot eat the honey', he was told, 'until you have killed the bees.'

The north-eastern principalities of Rus' attracted an important peasant migration into the forest zone of the upper Volga, which helped the growth of cities. The settlement of Moscow on the River Moskva was first recorded in 1146. In 1169 Andrei Bogulyubsky, Prince of Vladimir, was strong enough to sack Kiev. In 1185 Prince Igor of Sever led a famous expedition against the Polovtsians. The city of Novgorod began its career as an independent republic from 1126. Its *veche*, an assembly of its free citizens, elected both the chief administrator and the archbishop. It set the terms of the contract which limited the powers of the ruling prince. Huge territories in the north, as far as the monastery of St Michael the Archangel on the White Sea, were subject to Novgorod's writ. Alexander Nevsky (*c.*1220–63), Prince of Vladimir and Novgorod, repelled both the Swedes on the Neva (1240) and the Teutonic knights on the ice of Lake Peipus. [**NOVGOROD**]

Another clear beneficiary of Byzantium's decline was the fledgeling kingdom of Hungary. Protected to the north by the Carpathians, and safely distanced both from Constantinople and from the German Empire, Hungary could consolidate its hold on the Danube basin without serious opposition. In 1004 it took control of Transylvania, and after 1089 of Croatia and Dalmatia, opening an important corridor to the sea. In the twelfth century it absorbed the beautiful mountain-girt province of Bosnia. In all the peripheral territories, including Upper Hungary (Slovakia), Magyar nobles of the Latin faith were established on vast estates largely inhabited by Slavs, Germans, or Romanians. On the eastern borders, a lengthy military zone was permanently settled by conquered Cumans. Paganism was eradicated. Under the 'soldier king', St Ladislas or Laszlo (r. 1077–95) and his nephew Coloman I or Kálmán (r. 1095–1116), both of whom had close family ties with Constantinople, the pioneering tasks of St Stephen were concluded. As early as 1222, in the 'Golden Bull' of Andreas II, the Hungarian king confirmed the immunity of the nobles and high clergy, who formed a national assembly armed with the formal right of resistance.

The Byzantine retreat also led to important changes in Transcaucasia. The Bagratid state of Greater Armenia, based on Ani near Kars, which had flourished since the ninth century, was submerged by the Seljuks. Many Armenians were driven into exile, some as far afield as Poland. A rump state of 'Little Armenia' was set up in the south, in the former province of Cilicia; and it survived for three centuries more.[22] But Georgia broke free: under David the Renovator (r. 1089–1125), the Seljuks were repulsed from Tbilisi. Under Queen Tamara (r. 1184–1213) a brilliant court culture flourished, the native Christian element blending with Turkish, Persian, and Arab infusions. The poet Shot'ha Rust'aveli, who was educated in Greece, gained international renown. His epic poem, *Knight in a Tiger Skin*, dedicated to Tamara, has been optimistically classified as 'the first breath of the Renaissance'.[23]

Medieval society remained overwhelmingly rural. Life was centred on the feudal estates, and on the timeless relations of lord and serf. The emergence of cities in embryo, therefore, did not change the overall scene; but it was important, not merely for the future but for the organization of trade and the spread of culture.

Walled cities, like walled castles, reflected the insecurities of the countryside. Their ramparts, their gates and towers were designed to protect an oasis of safety. But they also fostered distinct social communities, which increasingly sought to give themselves a separate legal and political identity. They coalesced around ports and river-crossings, around markets, or around the residences of counts and bishops. Many nascent towns failed and relapsed into obscurity; but by the twelfth century several regions of Europe were beginning to show pockets of vigorous urbanization. The Italian port cities of Venice, Pisa, and Genoa led the way. They were soon rivalled by the cities of Lombardy and of the Rhineland, and by clusters of textile towns—Florence and Siena in Tuscany, Ypres, Bruges, and Ghent in Flanders. London and Paris grew for political as well as for economic reasons. The largest of them had populations of 50,000 or more, and rising. [**FIESTA**]

Urban society was marked by the formation of a class of burghers, who organized themselves against the more numerous artisans and rootless elements. The important thing was that most of these city-dwellers in the West freed themselves from the feudal relations prevailing beyond the city walls. 'Freedom became the legal status of the bourgeoisie . . . no longer a personal privilege, but a territorial one, inherent in the urban soil.'[24] Slavery on the Muslim model, however, was common, especially in Italy. Special charters were issued to cope with the influx of Jews brought in by Mediterranean trade. [**GHETTO**]

Trade patterns were determined by a handful of well-tried routes. Venice and Genoa took over from Constantinople as the organizers of trade with the Levant. The North Sea routes were built up in response to the demand for English wool. Lombardy and the Rhineland stood at either end of the transalpine corridor. From 1180 the Counts of Champagne established an early form of free-trade zone, whose fairs became the clearing-house of international commerce. [**GOTTHARD**] [**HANSA**]

In the second half of the eleventh century, in many parts of Western Europe, a series of seemingly unconnected innovations set long-lasting processes in motion. Institutions were starting to gel; temporary expedients turned themselves into plans for a long-term future.

On 14 April 1059 Pope Nicholas II decreed that papal elections should be conducted by the College of Cardinals. The move was designed to assert the independence of the Papacy and to avoid the scenes of the previous year, when two rival popes had been appointed by two rival factions. For centuries, the traditional appointment of popes by 'the people and clergy of Rome' had left them at the mercy of local politics. More recently, the German emperors had assumed the practice of nominating candidates. Now the Papacy was taking the necessary steps to free itself from external control. The Roman Curia, the papal court and government, was first mentioned shortly afterwards. [**CONCLAVE**]

In August 1059, at Melfi in Apulia, Robert Guiscard, fourth of twelve sons of Tancred d'Hauteville, was invested by the Pope with the Duchy of Apulia and Calabria, together with the 'future' Duchy of Sicily. In return, if he could seize the allocated lands, Duke Robert was to pay the Pope a fee of twelve pence per ploughland. At the time, the treaty represented just another twist in the Papacy's tortuous diplomacy. Ever since their arrival in Calabria in 1017, the Norman adventurers had been opposed by Rome; indeed, in the middle of the Schism with Byzantium in 1054, having marched south with a German army, Pope Leo IX had been the Normans' prisoner. But now Nicholas II decided to do business with them. What he could not have foreseen was that the d'Hautevilles would put their plans so promptly into practice. They crossed the Straits of Messina in 1060 and started the systematic conquest of Sicily from the Saracens. Within a decade they had both captured Palermo and driven the Byzantines from their last Italian

FIESTA

IN AD 1000 the Doge of Venice took the title of Duke of Dalmatia after capturing the strongholds of the Adriatic pirates at Curzola and Lagosta. It
was Venice's first step to becoming a naval power. The ceremony of the
Sposalizio del Mar, the 'Wedding of the Doge and the Sea', where a regatta of bedecked gondolas parades down the Grand Canal, began that same
year. It used to be the centrepiece of Venice's annual Ascension Day Fair,
the *Sensa*, but now forms part of the *Regata Storica* in September.

The European calendar is packed with festivals that feature every sort of
procession, masked parade, dance, fair, or games. Many of them, such as
the *Bloemen Curso* in Haarlem, the *Midsommer* in Sweden, or the beer-
swilling *Oktoberfest* in Munich, celebrate the passing of the seasons. The
days of *Fasching* which occur throughout Germany and Austria, like the
fire-burning *Dożynki* in Poland, are pagan survivals. France's *fêtes des
vignerons* are the wine-growers' equivalent of harvest festivals.

Many others have religious connections. The *Carnaval* or 'Farewell to
the Flesh', held on *Mardi Gras* or 'Pancake Tuesday', is best known in Nice.
It marks the last day before the fast of Lent. The Easter *Semana Santa* in
Seville sees penitents parade in high-pointed black hats. Corpus Christi is
another day for general Christian witness, as are Whitsun and the Feast of
the Blessed Virgin (15 August). At Sainte-Marie de la Mer near Arles, gypsies from many countries carry their icon of the Virgin into the sea. The
procession of the Holy Blood at Bruges and the *Ommegang* in Brussels
honour local relics.

Many fiestas take the form of public contests. Such are the highland
games in Scotland, the *course à la cocarde* in the Roman arenas at Arles
and Nîmes, the bull-running at Pamplona, and the magnificent horseback
races of the *Palio* at Siena.

Most often, however, Europeans set out to remember the dramatic
events which, like the *Sposalizio*, pepper the history of their cities:

Moros y Cristianos	Alcoy (Alicante)	the Christian conquest of 1227
Lajkonik	Cracow (Poland)	the Mongol raids (13th c.)
Giostra del Saracino	Arezzo (Italy)	(jousting): the Saracen wars
Jeanne d'Arc	Orléans (France)	the siege of 1428
Fürstenhochzeit	Landshut (Bavaria)	the Bavarian–Polish wedding of 1475
Escalade	Geneva (CH)	the Savoyard assault of 1602
Guy Fawkes	England	Gunpowder Plot, 1605
Up Helly Aa	Lerwick (Shetland)	Viking rule, 751
Meistertrunk	Rothenberg (Germany)	the siege of 1631
Vikingspillene	Frederikssund (Denmark)	discovery of a Viking ship, 1950

Old or new, fiestas are annual events. They cement local pride to the continuity of the passing centuries.[1]

Yet nothing is so grand as the festivals and parades which accompany military victories. In June 1940 the Wehrmacht marched symbolically through the Arc de Triomphe in Paris. Five years later, in Red Square, the Wehrmacht's banners were piled up high at Stalin's feet. In the Allied countries, though not in Germany, 11 November has been honoured for decades with solemn pomp as 'Remembrance Day'.

GHETTO

IN many Italian cities, walled and gated quarters reserved for Jews had existed at least since the eleventh century. They resulted from the concordance of view between the municipal magistrates, who demanded segregation, and the Jews' own religious laws, which forbade residence among Gentiles. In Venice, the Jewish quarter was called *Il Ghetto*, either from a contraction of *borghetto* or 'little town' or from a deformation of the *gietto* or 'foundry' which had once existed there. The name came to be used across Europe. Major ghettos were created in Prague, Frankfurt, Trieste, and in Rome, where the ghetto was maintained from 1536 to 1870.[1]

Formal ghettos were unknown, however, in the Jews' main refuge in Poland-Lithuania, where royal charters of protection were in force from 1265. Several Polish cities, including Warsaw, enforced statutes *de non tolerandis Judaeis*, which excluded Jews from districts under municipal jurisdiction. (Nobles, peasants, and officers of the Crown were similarly excluded.) The effect was to channel Jewish residence on to noble-owned land in the immediate vicinity of the city gates. Small Jewish *shtetln* or 'townlets' also grew up under noble patronage alongside manorial centres in the countryside. The Jews of Poland-Lithuania possessed both local autonomy and, in their Council of the Four Lands, their own central parliament.[2]

No Jews were permitted to reside in Russia prior to the partitions of Poland. After the partitions, Catherine II turned Russia's ex-Polish provinces into the core of a huge Jewish 'pale of settlement' (see Appendix III, p. 1311). But closed ghettos of the Western type did not reach Eastern Europe until the Nazi advance of 1939–41.

To escape from the ghetto was no simple matter. Would-be escapees had to defy the laws and customs both of the Gentile and of the Jewish communities, and to risk dire penalties. Until modern times, formal conversion was often the only practical way out.

foothold at Bari. In due course the Norman conquests in the south were united into one 'Kingdom of the Two Sicilies', which survived until the days of Garibaldi.

Before the conquest of Sicily was complete, the Papacy decided to back another Norman adventurer. In 1066 William the Bastard, Duke of Normandy, was sent the banner of St Peter to bless his expedition against England. From Rome's point of view this was another move to build up a body of papal supporters who were independent of the Empire. From William's point of view it was a means of persuading his troops to fight. (He later repudiated the papal claim to a deal similar to the one agreed over Sicily.) But once again fortune favoured the venture. Having waited many weeks to cross the Channel, the Normans attacked the Anglo-Saxon army waiting at Hastings. Harold of England, having been given the time to return from the north, where he had defeated his other rival, Harold of Norway, was confident of further success. But on 28 September he died in battle, pierced through the eye by a Norman arrow. William, now the Conqueror, was crowned in Westminster Abbey at Christmas. The kingdom of England, like Sicily, was parcelled out among the Norman knights and turned into a model feudal kingdom. (The English claim that it has never been conquered since.)

In March 1075 a new Pope, Gregory VII (1073–85), enunciated the twenty-seven propositions of his *Dictatus Papae* (the Pope's Supremacy). He claimed supreme legislative and judicial power within Christendom, together with the right to depose all princes, both temporal and spiritual. Soon afterwards, in synod, he formally ordered the excommunication of all secular rulers who invested candidates for church appointments without reference to ecclesiastical authority. The Pope, formerly Hildebrand, a Tuscan monk and the principal adviser of the preceding popes, had been elected by the cardinals in the new manner. The Emperor, Henry IV (r. 1056–1106), had not been notified, let alone consulted. A major conflict between Empire and Papacy was unavoidable. It was the start of the Investiture Contest.

Despite the high-flown legal and theological language in which it was conducted, the Investiture Contest was a straightforward struggle for power. Was the Emperor to control the Pope, or the Pope to control the Emperor? The agreed theory was simple: Latin Christendom was supported by two pillars of authority—the temporal, headed by the Emperor, and the spiritual, headed by the Pope. But the relationship between the two was open to interpretation. In the imperial view, the Pope should have confined his attentions to the spiritual sphere. In the papal view, just as earth was below heaven, so the Emperor should submit to the will of the Pope. The propositions of Hildebrand's *Dictatus* were uncompromising:

2. The Roman Pontiff alone merits the Catholic or 'universal' title.
3. The Pontiff alone can depose and absolve bishops.
12. The Pontiff is permitted to depose emperors.
16. The Pontiff alone can convene a General Synod.
20. No one can condemn a decision of the Holy See.

HANSA

As German colonists and crusaders moved eastwards along the Baltic shore, it was natural that commercial interests would follow. Equally, in a region emerging from the Viking Age, it was only to be expected that merchants established in Baltic and North Sea ports would band together for protection. The first such *hansa* or 'commercial association' was established at Wisby on the island of Gotland in 1161 under the name of the 'United Gotland Travellers of the Holy Roman Empire'. Within a century, a far-flung confederation of *am-see staten* or 'free cities of the sea' had developed from the Atlantic to the Gulf of Finland.

The *Bund van der dudeschen hanse* or 'Hanseatic League' rose to the peak of its influence in the course of the 14th century. It comprised a series of constituent leagues, whose delegates met regularly to co-ordinate policy. The most important of these was the 'Wendish-Saxon Quarter' based on Hamburg, Bremen, Lübeck, Wismar, and Rostock. The Westphalian group was headed by Cologne, the Livonian group by Wisby, later by Reval. The three main groups formed the *Drittel* or 'Triangle' at the core of the organization. Each of the member cities possessed dependent towns known as *vororte* or 'suburbs', whilst the League as a whole established a chain of *kontore* or 'foreign offices' from which all members could benefit. Five key offices were maintained: at Bruges—the main terminus of the transalpine trade-route to Venice, at the 'Peterhof' in Novgorod (from 1229), at the 'Steelyard' in London (1237), at the 'German Bridge' in Bergen (1343), and at the annual herring market at Falsterbo in Skania.

Hansa membership was confined neither to Germany nor the littoral. At various times, over two hundred cities belonged to the network. They stretched from Dinant in the West to Oslo in the North and Narva in the East. Major inland members included Brunswick, Magdeburg, Breslau, and Cracow.

The Hanseatic League possessed no formal constitution and no central government. But a body of law and custom accumulated; and from 1373 the Free Imperial City of Lübeck was confirmed as the home of the court of appeal and as the most frequent meeting-place for the League's triennial *Hansetage* or 'General Assemblies'. The Law of Lübeck was adopted by many member cities.

In its early days, the League aimed to consolidate the legal rights of anchorage, storage, residence, and local immunity, which its members required to conduct their business. It was also concerned to stabilize currency and to facilitate the means of payment. (The English word *sterling* derives from 'Easterling', an epithet widely applied to Hansa merchants.)

Yet the pursuit of mercantile interests soon involved politics. The League's original weapon lay in the *Verhansung* or 'commercial boycott' of its enemies. But it was gradually obliged to levy taxes and to raise naval forces, first to suppress pirates and then to contest the policies of established kingdoms, especially Denmark. An alliance between Norway, Sweden, and the Hansa was provoked by the Danish sacking of Wisby in 1361. In that first Danish War, the League was heavily defeated. But in the second war of 1368–9, the troops of the League captured Helsingborg, destroyed Copenhagen, and occupied the Sound. By the Treaty of Stralsund (1370), Denmark was forced to concede that no Danish King could be crowned without the League's approval and the confirmation of its privileges. [**SUND**]

Thereafter, the slow decline of the Hanseatic League was the result both of economic and of political factors. The Baltic herring shoals mysteriously relocated to the North Sea in the fifteenth century. In the same period, northern Europe's centre of commercial gravity was shifting to the Netherlands. The Hansa met increasing difficulty in asserting itself against aggressive modern states such as England, Prussia, and Muscovy. The closing of the Peterhof in Novgorod in 1494 was a sign of the times, as was the closing of the Steelyard in London in 1598. The Hansa received little support from the fragmented authority of the Holy Roman Empire. During the Thirty Years War it was reduced to an active membership of three—Lübeck, Hamburg, and Bremen—who held their last General Assembly in 1669. From then on, the Hansa name was connected only with the independence of those three cities, which stayed apart from the German Customs Union until 1889.[1]

The legacy of the Hansa long outlived its demise. Over the centuries it had created a way of life whose solid virtues were cemented into every stone of its bustling and elegant cities. To be Hanseatic was to belong to an inimitable, international civilization based on shared values and priorities. Great cities such as Hamburg, Danzig (Gdańsk), or Riga were not to share a common political destiny. But they retained a strong sense of their common origins. The citizens of Hamburg still take pride in registering their cars under the ancient municipal formula of 'HH'—*Hansestadt Hamburg*. Bremeners display 'HB'; Lübeckers 'HL', Rostockers 'HRO'.

Nazi ideology naturally made great efforts to appropriate the Hanseatic tradition. In a famous Grotemeyer painting of 1942, for example, a medieval wagon train sets out along the Elbe from Hamburg as if to conquer Germany's *Lebensraum* in the East.[2] But this was a gross distortion. In German History, the Hanseatic tradition stands in stark contrast to the Prussianism, nationalism, and imperialism which supplanted it. In European history, it shines as a beacon for all who seek a future based on sturdy local autonomy, international co-operation, and mutual prosperity.

22. The Church of Rome has never erred, and as Scripture attests, can never err in
    the future . . .
23. No one who opposes the Church of Rome can be considered Catholic.
27. The Pontiff can release the vassals of unjust men from their oath of loyalty . . .[25]

At first sight, since the Pope had no means of enforcement at his command, it appeared that the Emperor's position was the stronger one. In practice, since many bishops resented their dependence on secular patrons, and since many barons resented their dependence on prince or emperor, the centrifugal forces of the feudal order worked to the Pope's advantage. In the long run, the Contest ended in stalemate and compromise; but not before, in the first round, the Emperor suffered comprehensive humiliation.

Hildebrand's challenge provoked an unholy brawl. At the Emperor's command, the bishops of the Empire excommunicated the Pope. The Pope promptly excommunicated the Emperor, releasing the Emperor's subjects from their allegiance. The German barons thereon rebelled, and chose Rudolf of Swabia as their 'anticaesar'. Henry chose penitence. Crossing the Mont Cenis in winter with his wife and child, he sought out Hildebrand in the lonely castle of Canossa. There he stood barefoot for three days in the snow, dressed in rags and begging the Pope for forgiveness. On the fourth day Hildebrand relented, and Henry threw himself at his feet, crying 'Holy Father, spare me!' But the dramatics of Canossa achieved nothing; Henry soon returned to his habit of lay investiture. After a long civil war in Germany, and Henry's second excommunication, a synod of imperial bishops met at Brixen and elected an 'antipope', Clement III. The West now had two Popes and two Emperors. In 1083–4 the imperial party captured Rome, with Hildebrand holed up in the Castel Sant'Angelo. Robert Guiscard saw them off with a Saracen army, which put Rome to the sack. Hildebrand died in exile. Henry died in 1106, but not before his second wife Adelaide had publicly laid charges against him with the Church. The Concordat of Worms in 1122 called a truce in the wrangles, with Pope and Emperor both granted a hand in investiture. [**MARSTON**]

In 1075 the city of Pisa sought papal approval for its municipal code of laws, the *consuetudine di mare*. They were confirmed by an imperial patent six years later. As part of the arrangement, the local Duke of Tuscany renounced all jurisdiction within the city, and undertook to name no new marquis in the region without the Pisans' consent. At the time Pisa was simply taking precautions against the brewing conflict between Pope and Emperor; but it was pioneering the process whereby leading cities could establish communal independence. Pisa had grown rich from the plunder of the campaigns against the Saracens in Sicily and Sardinia, as reflected in the marble splendours of its cathedral with the leaning baptistery tower (*c.*1089). In due course it was subdued by its maritime rival, Genoa, and absorbed by its landward neighbour, Florence. But the growth of wealthy city communes, replete with constitutions, military forces, and civic pride, was a feature of ensuing centuries. In France, Le Mans, St Quentin, and Beauvais were self-regulating cities by the end of the eleventh century. In Flanders, the charter

MARSTON

O LD Marston happens to be the nearest medieval parish to where this book is being written. It has had a continuous history for nearly 900 years. A chapel on the site was granted to the Austin Priory of St Frideswide in Oxford in 1122; and it was raised to the status of a parish in the following century. In 1451 a papal bull joined it to the neighbouring parish of Headington in an arrangement which lasted until 1637. For much of the modern period, the living lay in the gift of the lordship of Headington.

In its long history, Marston has seen few momentous events. This 'marsh village', three miles from the city of Oxford, had no interesting features other than the Marston Ferry, which plied across the River Cherwell from 1279 until the 1960s. At its greatest extent prior to the growth of the modern city suburbs, the village was inhabited by forty or fifty households, who worked some 600 acres of arable land and possessed some 200 horses and cattle and 800 sheep. After 1655, when the two main fields were enclosed for pasture, the population declined. During the English Civil War, Marston was occupied by the Parliamentary forces besieging the King's headquarters in Oxford. The Parliamentary commander, Sir Thomas Fairfax, was billeted in 1643 with the Croke family at Marston Manor House, where he received a visit from Oliver Cromwell. There was no school in the village before 1816, when a boarding-house was established for paying pupils. The elementary school opened in 1851. The only charitable foundation in the parish was created in 1671 by the will of Mary Brett, widow, who left a house and a parcel of land worth 22s. 6d. for providing bread for the poor. The only inhabitant of the parish to achieve national fame was a fox-terrier bitch called 'Trump', who was purchased in the hamlet of Elsfield in 1815. Trump's new master, the sporting parson, Revd. Jack Russell, used her to found the canine breed that bears his name.[1]

The Parish Church of St Nicholas, Marston, built in Late Perpendicular Gothic, is described as 'unpretentious'.[2] There is a low west tower with battlemented parapet. Only tiny portions of the original fabric survive. Most of the stonework dates from the fifteenth century, as restored in 1883. The plain oak furnishing of the interior is largely Elizabethan or Jacobean.

A list of officiating clergy from c.1210 to 1991 hangs on a board in the nave. Despite the interval between 1529 and 1637 when Marston was served by non-resident curates, the list conveys a strong sense of continuity. The name of the earliest recorded priest is Osbert, son of Hereward (c.1210). John de Bradeley (1349) died in the Black Death. Robert Kene (1397–8) was the first priest to use a surname. Thomas Fylldar (1529), a Dominican, was the last Catholic priest before the Reformation. John Allen (1637–85), an appointee of

Archbishop Laud, served the reconstituted parish for forty-eight years. So, too, did his Edwardian successor, John Hamilton Mortimer (1904–52).

All over Europe, tens of thousands of church parishes form a network of territorial authority, which is often much older and more continuous than that of the civil power. They answer to the bishop as opposed to the Crown. In England, they pre-dated the counties. They coincide in large measure with the village communities, where the parish priest has been a central figure of respect and influence regardless of the changes in political regime and land ownership. In recent times, the parish council has provided an element of local democracy and, together with the parish pump and the parish hall, a focus for social life.

Parish registers of births, marriages, and deaths, which in England have been kept since the reign of Elizabeth I, are one of the major sources of genealogical and demographic information. They provide the natural gateway into local history.[3]

Above all, the parish is the corner-stone of the ordered life of Europe's countryside. The villagers' ceaseless toil against the seasons has survived serfdom, plagues, famines, wars, poverty, and the CAP:

> Far from the madding crowd's ignoble strife,
> Their sober wishes never learned to stray;
> Along the cool sequestered vale of life
> They kept the noiseless tenor of their way.[4]

St Omer (1127) led the way for Bruges and Ghent. In north Germany, the self-government of Lübeck (1143) preceded that of Hamburg (1189). Within these communes, merchant associations and craft guilds began to form.

In May 1082 the city of Venice received a charter of liberties from the Byzantine Emperor, guaranteeing freedom of transit and exemption from taxes and duties throughout the Empire west of the Bosporus. Three quays were to be reserved for Venetian use on the Golden Horn. At the time the concessions must have seemed a reasonable price to pay for Venice's help in the Emperor's Norman wars. Trade between Italy and the Levant had been severely restricted since the Muslim conquests of the seventh century, and the merchants of Venice, who had been the Emperor's subjects as well as his allies, were hardly a major power. In the event the 'Golden Bull' of 1082 proved to be a milestone. Granted on the eve of the Crusades and the reopening of the eastern Mediterranean, it turned the Venetian lagoon into the principal emporium between East and West, the home base for a seaborne fortune that was to rival Constantinople itself. Previously the city of St Mark, whose relics had been brought to the Rialto in 828, had been overshadowed by the nearby island of Torcello. The ravages of the Magyars, like the earlier invasion of the Lombards which had propelled the first refugees into the lagoon in the first place, had disrupted contacts with Germany. Henceforth, transalpine trade was to boom. With a chain of forts, trading stations and later colonies at Ragusa, Corfu, Corinth, Crete, and Cyprus, the Venetian galleys could protect the convoys carrying silks, spices, silver and slaves, timber, corn, and salt. The Republic of Venice did not have an easy relationship with Byzantium; in 1182 all its merchants in Constantinople were massacred. But it outlasted the Empire, surviving until destroyed by Napoleon in 1797. [GHETTO] [MORES]

In 1084, at the monastery of Chartreuse near Grenoble, the Carthusian Order was founded by St Bruno of Cologne (1033–1101). Its strict contemplative rules directed the monks to live in silence in closed cells. At the time it must have seemed just an austere variation on the older Cluniac model; in fact it was the sign that the Latin Church was moving into an era of systematic institutionalization. In 1098, at Citeaux in Burgundy, the long career of the Cistercian Order was launched. It owed its main development to St Bernard of Clairvaux (1090–1153). Elsewhere, secular clerics or 'regular canons' entered organized communities governed by the three vows of chastity, poverty, and obedience. Most adopted the Rule of St Augustine, and hence were known as Augustinians. One such group, the Premonstratensians or Norbertines, founded by St Norbert at Prémontré near Laon in 1120, spread widely in Eastern as well as Western Europe. In those same years, the monks at Cluny were building a church which for five centuries remained the largest in Western Christendom.

In the summer of 1085 Alfonso VI of Castile-Leon captured the Muslim city of Toledo. At the time, it appeared to be just one more incident on the Christian–Muslim frontier: Alfonso was in league with the Emir of Seville, and was keeping the Emir's daughter as his concubine. In fact it proved to be the first step in the Christian *Reconquista*—the 400-year-struggle for possession of the Iberian peninsula. Toledo was the largest and most central of some twenty-five *taifa* or 'party' kingdoms into which the old Cordoban emirate had fragmented. Their disunity gave the Christian rulers their chance. Within the decade, Alfonso's champion, Rodrigo Díaz de Vivar, El Cid, had entered Valencia. Within a century, the wars of Christian and Muslim had turned into a general contest of attrition on all fronts. The Moors suffered a decisive defeat at the pass of Las Navas de Tolosa in 1212. The capture of Cordova in 1236, of Seville in 1248, and of Murcia in 1266 put the greater part of the Peninsula into Christian hands. [EL CID]

On 27 November 1095, at the synod of Clermont in Auvergne, Pope Urban II appealed to all Christians to fight for the delivery of Jerusalem. Enthroned on a dais on the hillside below Notre Dame du Port, he addressed a great throng of mitred bishops, knights, and common people. At the time he was seeking to promote the so-called Truce of God, and to bring a halt to the endemic warfare of feudal society. He was also pursuing a policy of reconciliation with the Byzantine Patriarch, wishing to share the Byzantines' distress at the Turkish advance. Yet his appeal struck a chord of popular sympathy: the crowd roared *Dios lo volt*, 'God wishes it'; a cardinal fell on his knees and, in the name of the multitude, seized with convulsive trembling, recited the *Confiteor*. There and then, men jostled to

MORES

I N the late eleventh century, when a Byzantine princess arrived in Venice to marry the Doge, it was found that she ate her food with a golden fork. She was reprimanded by the Bishop for anti-social behaviour. People in the medieval West took meat with their fingers from a common dish. The fork came into general use only during the Renaissance, and only for lifting morsels to one's own plate.[1] The table set of knife, fork, and spoon was an eighteenth-century innovation.

European manners can be thoroughly studied from the stream of manuals written to teach people how to behave. The earliest such manuals, such as *De institutione novitarum* by Hugh St Victor (d. 1141), were addressed to clerics. The thirteenth-century Bavarian *Hofzucht* (Courtly Manners), attributed to Tannhäuser, was directed at boorish courtiers, as was John Russell's fifteenth-century *Book of Courtesye*. The most influential publication of the genre, the *De Civilitate Morum Puerilium* (1530) by Erasmus, ran into 130 editions. It was reprinted in Russia when Peter the Great sought to 'civilize' his court 200 years later.[2] *Il Cortegiano* (The Courtier, 1528), by Baldassare Castiglione, and a similar Latin treatise (1566) by Łukasz Górnicki, enjoyed long-standing international fame. Thereafter, numerous guides to the conduct of 'high society', especially on the French model, were used to spread the cultivation of manners into ever-widening social circles.

At one time, historians treated manners as a subject of passing fashions. But serious analysts have argued that they provide the outward evidence for profound social and psychological changes. Attitudes to every activity can be plotted over time, and related to long-term trends.

Injunctions about spitting, for example, reveal a number of basic shifts:

Do not spit over or on the table. (English *c.*1463)
Do not spit across the table as hunters do. (German, 15th cent.)
Turn away when spitting, lest your saliva fall on someone. If anything purulent falls to the ground, it should be trodden upon. (Erasmus, 1530)
You should abstain from spitting at table, if possible. (Italian, 1558)
Formerly, it was permitted to spit on the ground before people of rank. . . . Today, that is an indecency. (French, 1572)
Frequent spitting is disagreeable. At important houses, one spits into one's handkerchief . . . Do not spit so far that you have to look for the saliva to stamp on it. (Liège, 1714)
It is very ill-mannered to swallow what should be spat . . . After spitting into your handkerchief, you should fold it once, without looking at it, and put it in your pocket. (La Salle, 1729)
It is unpardonably gross for children to spit in the faces of their playmates. (La Salle, 1774)

Spitting is at all times a disgusting habit. Besides being coarse and atrocious, it is very bad for the health. (English, 1859)

Have you noticed that today we [hide] what our fathers did not hesitate to display openly? . . . The spittoon is a piece of furniture no longer found in modern households. (Cabanès, 1910)[3]

It emerges that the need to spit was not challenged until the eighteenth century, although the constraints about where, when, and how to spit had grown steadily. In the nineteenth century, spitting fell into disrepute, perhaps through fear of tuberculosis. Yet a certain hypocrisy separated the rules of good manners and the widespread use of the spittoon—a vessel required by the habit of tobacco-chewing. Only in the twentieth century did a total ban become effective. 'No Spitting' notices were retained on London buses until the 1960s. By that time certain rock groups were urging their fans to spit as a mark of social defiance. Spitting may yet return to respectability.

Just as 'the civilizing process' is seen gradually to build up self-restraint within society as a whole, so the training of infants builds up self-restraint within adults:

Thus the sociohistorical process of centuries, in which the standard of what is shameful and offensive is slowly raised, is re-enacted in abbreviated form in the life of the individual human being . . . One could speak, as a parallel to the laws of biogenesis, of a fundamental law of sociogenesis and psychogenesis.[4]

Critics of this 'civilizing' theory might object to such a narrow definition of civilization. Some might think it a peculiarly German theory—all tidy habits and empty heads. Many would insist that the art of *savoir vivre* demands rather more than the ability to control one's spittle, sphincter, and silverware. The 'civilisation curves' of Norbert Elias and his theory of unilinear progress will not convince everyone. But all would admit to the gulf which separates so-called 'Western civilized man' from medieval modes of behaviour, where modern concepts of hygiene, of individual respect, of privacy, and of 'personal space' were virtually absent. One has only to ponder some other assorted medieval injunctions:

It is bad manners . . . to wear a helmet when serving ladies.
Don't blow your nose with the fingers you hold the meat with.
If you have to scrape [the back of] your throat, do so politely with your
Farts may be concealed by coughing.   [coat
Before you sit down, make sure that your seat has not been fouled.
It is impolite to greet someone who is urinating or defecating.
When you eat, do not forget the poor. God will reward you.[5]

EL CID

THE knight Rodrigo Díaz died in Valencia in 1099. In history he had spent a lifetime fighting both for the Moors and against them. But in legend he was elevated by the Arabic epithet of *al-sayyid* or *El Cid*, 'the Master'; and he was turned into the spotless champion of the Christian cause, the national hero of Castile. The legend was already flourishing a century later, in the epic romance of *El Canto del mío Cid*.[1] (See Appendix III, p. 1241.)

The transformation of historical figures into the special status of national heroes is a much more complicated process than the mere glorification of famous men or women. It is part of the search for a collective identity that can only be defined in distinction to hostile neighbours or oppressors. In England, whose history is peculiarly lacking in external invaders, the only possible candidate was Robin Hood, the shadowy outlaw who defended the common people against the Anglo-Norman barons.[2] Among England's neighbours the national heroes, whether Llewellyn ap Gruffydd, William Wallace the 'Braveheart', Hugh O'Neill, or Joan of Arc, could only be figures who fought the English. In later British history, British national heroes could only be military figures who, like Admiral Nelson or the Duke of Wellington, saved the empire from its foreign foes. In Albania, George Castriota (known as 'Skanderbeg', 1403–67) was seen, like El Cid, as the symbol of resistance to the Ottomans, although he too had both joined and deserted the Ottoman and the Muslim cause.

    The cult of national heroes became obligatory when Romanticism collided with Nationalism in the nineteenth century (see p. 815). Nations who lacked an established ancient champion adopted more recent ones: Kościuszko, Kossuth, and Shamil fought against the Russians; Andreas Hofer in Tyrol against the French; Janosik, the 'Robin Hood of the Tatras', against the Austrians. On the northern side of the Tatras, Janosik is the hero of the Polish highlanders: on the southern side, the national hero of Slovakia.[3] It is fair comment on the state of European identity to recall that, as yet, there is no national hero or heroine of Europe.

join. The proposal for a Crusade, a 'War of the Cross', was taken up throughout the Latin Church. Preachers such as Peter the Hermit spread the word. Henceforth, for six or seven generations, counts, kings, commoners, and even children flocked 'to take the Cross' and to fight the infidel in the Holy Land.

    All these innovations contributed to what scholars have called the 'Twelfth-Century Renaissance'—the moment when, in the setting of enhanced confidence and prosperity, Western Christendom consciously sought to put its ideals into practice. Events such as the Investiture Contest or the Crusades were not just evidence of new energies; they were 'ideological'. A thirst for knowledge was inherent in the new mentality. A marked increase in the production of books and the collection of libraries took place in recognized intellectual centres. The Latin classics were lionized; the Latin language was pruned and refined; Latin poetry came into fashion, high and low:

> Meum est propositum in taberna mori,
> Ut sint vina proxima morientis ori.
> Tunc cantabunt letius angelorum chori:
> 'Sit Deus propitius huic potatori.'

(My resolution is to die in the tavern. May wine be near my dying lips. Then the angelic choirs will gaily sing: 'May God show mercy on this boozer.')[26]

All manner of history-writing was undertaken, from simple annals and lives of the saints to sophisticated treatises such as Guibert de Nogent's *De pignoribus sanctorum* (*c.*1119), William of Malmesbury's *Gesta regum* (1120), or Otto von Freising's *Gesta* (*c.*1156) relating the exploits of Emperor Frederick I. In his fantastic *Historia Regnum Britanniae* (*c.*1136), Geoffrey of Monmouth assembled an imaginative collection of stories and legends from the Celtic past, which would be quarried and embellished by numerous poets and troubadours. The systematization of Canon Law, notably in the *Decretum* (1141) of Gratian of Bologna, accompanied the study of Roman law by a long line of glossators starting with Irnerius (*fl.* *c.*1130). Latin translations from Arabic and ancient Greek proliferated, by such scholars as Adelard of Bath or Burgundio di Pisa. Schools of law, medicine, and general learning flourished at Salerno, Montpellier, and, above all, at Bologna. North of the Alps, cathedral schools, as at Chartres or Paris, competed with the earlier monastic centres, where St Anselm of Aosta (1033–1109), sometime Abbot of Bec and Archbishop of Canterbury, had been a seminal figure. At Palermo in Sicily and Toledo in Spain the wisdom of the ancients, preserved by Arab scholars, was finally transmitted to Christendom. The commentaries of Averroes of Cordoba (Ibn Rushd, 1126–98) turned Aristotle into *the* philosopher of the Middle Ages. Muslim Spain gave Europe decimal numbers and mathematical expertise. [XATIVAH]

Courtly literature was composed in reaction against the boorish lifestyle of the barons and the stifling ethics of the Church. Initially, there were two main centres—at the northern French courts, which popularized the *chansons de geste* celebrating the exploits of Frankish and Arthurian chivalry, and at the court of Aquitaine at Poitiers, which specialized in the *chansons d'amor*, the songs of 'courtly love'. The former, which was most productive in the decades after 1120, depended heavily on the cult of Charlemagne, especially in epics such as *La Chanson de Roland* and its derivatives—the *Pélérinage de Charlemagne* or *La Prise d'Orange*. The latter, which came into prominence after 1170, elaborated a stylized code of behaviour recorded in the thirty-one articles of *De Arte Honeste Amandi*, 'the Art of Honest Love', drawn up by one Andreas Capellanus. These rules, which gave the lead to the *dompna* or 'mistress' of the knight's affections, reversed the accepted gender roles of the day and flouted matrimonial conventions. 'Marriage', said Andreas, 'is no barrier to Love.' The genre may well have had its

XATIVAH

THE art and craft of paper-making was first recorded in Europe in 1144 in the small Moorish town of Xativah, now San Felipe, near Valencia. It had taken 1,000 years to cross Eurasia from China, via Samarkand and Cairo. Important technical developments, including dipping moulds and watermarks, were pioneered a century later in Italy, most probably at Fabriano near Ancona. The first known watermark was a large *F* (for Fabriano).

From there paper spread far and wide, gradually replacing the older writing materials of papyrus, parchment, and pergamon. Early paper-mills were built at Ambert in Auvergne (1326), Troyes (1338), Nürnberg (1390), Leira in Portugal (1411), Hertford in England (mid-fourteenth-century), Constantinople (1453), Cracow (1491), and Moscow (1565). The demand for paper was greatly increased by the arrival of printing. [**PRESS**]

Standard paper sizes were introduced in Bologna in 1389: Imperial (22 x 30 inches), Royal, Medium, and Chancery. Book pages were made by folding sheets double (*folio*), twice (*quarto*), or three times (*octavo*). In 1783 the Montgolfier brothers, who owned a paper-works at Annonay, constructed their hot-air balloon from paper. But paper's supreme contribution lay in the dissemination of knowledge. 'Hail to the inventor of paper,' wrote Herder, 'who did more for literature than all the monarchs on earth.'

Handcrafted paper still has its enthusiasts today. There is an International Association of Paper Historians, with their journal based in Germany, and a score of paper museums. Antique paper-mills still function at Fabriano, at Moulin Ricard-en-Bas in France, at Koog aan de Zaan in the Netherlands, at Niederzwonitz in Germany, at St Alban in Basle, Switzerland, and at Duszniki Zdrój in Silesia.[1]

origins in Muslim Spain; but it was taken up by troubadours across the south, whence it spread to the trouvères of the north and the Minnesingers of Germany. 'Love', wrote one of the authors of *Tristan*, 'is stronger than laws.' The acknowledged master of courtly romance, however, was Chrétien de Troyes (*c*.1135–90), a native of Champagne, author of the Arthurian trilogy—*Yvain, ou le Chevalier au Lion, Lancelot, ou le Chevalier à la Charrette*, and *Perceval, ou le Conte du Graal.* [**TRISTAN**]

The German Empire's struggle with the Papacy had always been complicated by Italian politics. But in the twelfth and thirteenth centuries the problems became hopelessly entangled, and all parties to the conflict were seriously weakened. Apart from the Hildebrandine ideology of the Popes, the German emperors had to contend with the centrifugal tendencies of the tribal duchies, especially Saxony;

with the dynastic rivalries within Germany, especially that of the Guelphs and the Hohenstaufen; with the sturdy independence of the Lombard cities; with the way-ward city of Rome; and with the distant kingdom of the Sicilies. The road to im-perial power, therefore, was strewn with hurdles. Contenders had first to win the support of the German nobles and bishops, and to win election as king in Germany. After that, there was a similar challenge to win the crown of Italy. Only then could they move into the end-game and seek imperial coronation by the Pope. For over a century this obstacle course consumed the energies of three forceful generations from the House of Hohenstaufen von Weiblingen—Frederick I Barbarossa, Henry VI, and the inimitable Frederick II.

Barbarossa (r. 1155–90), son of the Hohenstaufen Duke of Swabia and of a Guelph princess from Bavaria, was married to the heiress of the Franche-Comté and Arles, where he was crowned King. Hence, whilst enjoying an extensive power-base of his own, he was able to reconcile the warring German dukes. His chief Guelph rival, Henry the Lion, Duke of Saxony and Bavaria, was eventually ruined by a trial before the imperial court which stripped him of his main pos-sessions. But a clash at the Diet of Besançon in 1157, where the papal legate described the imperial crown as an ecclesiastical 'benefice', revived the Investiture Contest. And a second clash at the Diet of Roncaglia in 1158, where the imperial party stressed the seniority of the *podestà* or 'imperial governor' over all other officials in the cities of the Empire, fuelled the endless wars of the Lombard leagues. Barbarossa re-enacted all the travails of his predecessors—excommuni-cation by the Pope, the election of an antipope, feudal revolts in Germany, con-flict in Rome, and six wearying Italian expeditions. On 24 July 1177, in the porch of St Mark's, Venice, and on the centenary of Canossa, he fell on his knees before Pope Alexander III and obtained absolution. But, like Canossa, it was just a gesture. His master-stroke was to marry his son and heir, Henry (r. 1190–97), to the Norman heiress of Sicily, Constanza di Apulia. In 1186 he saw the young pair wed in Milan, which he had once reduced in a terrible siege eighteen years before. Confident of splitting the Papacy from its Sicilian allies, he departed with the Third Crusade, and never returned. [**CONSPIRO**]

Barbarossa's grandson, Frederick II (r. 1211–50), was the offspring of the Sicilian connection. He inherited the personal union of Sicily with the Empire as estab-lished by his parents, and so cherished his Sicilian kingdom that he would be accused of neglecting the rest of his realms. Crusader, linguist, philosopher, ornithologist, patron of the arts, protector of Jews, and master of a harem, Frederick II was twice excommunicated by the Pope for disobedience and offici-ally condemned by a General Council as a heretic. He ruled in the south as a despot, imposing an efficient, centralized administration on Church and State alike. He even encouraged an imperial cult of his own person. He presided over a brilliant, cultured court at Palermo—a magnificent blend of Latin, German, Jewish, Greek, and Saracen elements. To his contemporaries he was quite simply the *stupor mundi*, the 'wonder of the age'.

However, to rule the whole of a disparate feudal empire by autocratic means

CONSPIRO

THE League of the Holy Court, or *Heilige Fehme*, has the distinction of being Europe's senior secret society—except for those which remained secret. It came into prominence in Germany, during the disorders which followed the imperial ban placed on Henry the Lion, chief of the Guelph party, in the late twelfth century. Its aim was to administer justice wherever imperial authority had collapsed and, by means of forest tribunals, administered by *Freischöffen* or *francs-juges*, to hold the populace in fear. The League had an élite caste of initiates, the *Wissenden* or 'sages', an elaborate system of oaths, signs, and rituals, and a hierarchical structure headed by the *Oberststuhlherr*—originally the Archbishop of Cologne. By the fourteenth century, it possessed 100,000 members. Its activities in Westphalia were officially recognized. In the fifteenth century, having recruited the Emperor Sigismund himself, its influence did not wane until the legal reforms of the 1490s. Its last meeting was held in 1568.

The *Femgerichte* (forest courts) followed exact procedures, hearing witnesses for prosecution and defence. But death was their only sentence. The condemned person was left hanging from a tree into which was stuck a knife bearing the mystical letters SSGG (standing for *Stein, Strick, Gras, Grün*—'Stone', 'Rope', 'Grass', 'Green').

Secret societies can be classified as political, religious, social, and criminal, though the categories have often overlapped. In the early seventeenth century, the mystical Brotherhood of the Rosicrucians chose to reveal its existence. Its occult theosophy was systematized by the Englishman Robert Fludd (1574–1637). It attracted considerable interest all over northern Europe, from Bacon and Descartes among others, and exercised an important influence on the early stages of Freemasonry [MASON].

Between 1776–85 the short-lived Order of Luminaries of Adam Weishaupt professed very advanced projects of social reform in Bavaria. Its members had close connections both with Freemasons and even with the Jacobins. The early nineteenth century saw the rise of the Carbonari (see p. 823), the Mafia, and the secret societies of Ireland. Some are still in existence.[1] [ORANGE]

Conspiracy theories of history are not fashionable. But European history has never known a shortage of conspiratorial societies, conspiracies, or conspirators.

was impossible, and beyond Naples and Sicily Frederick II was repeatedly obliged to make concessions to keep the imperial party intact. In Germany, after granting a charter of liberties to the Church (1220), he relinquished direct control of ecclesiastical lands in the hope of ruling through prelates such as Archbishop Engelbert of Cologne. As a result, he did succeed in having his son, Henry VII, elected King of the Romans. At the Diet of Worms in 1231 he ordered Henry to promulgate a *Statutum in favorem principum*, whereby the secular princes were granted the same far-reaching liberties as the bishops. In the East, he granted unlimited rights to his old crusading companion, Hermann von Salza, the first Grand Master of the Teutonic Knights, who repeatedly tried to mediate on his behalf in Rome. In northern Italy his attempts to consolidate a dominant Ghibelline party were constantly thwarted by the spoiling tactics of the popes, especially Gregory IX (1227–41), and the league of Lombard cities.

Frederick was living in a maelstrom that was not entirely of his own making. A papal ward in his youth, he had only been given Sicily on papal lease, and he was only raised to the Empire at the end of a twenty-year baronial war in Germany, where the Pope took against the previous incumbent and papal client, Otto of Brunswick. He was not present at the fateful battle of Bouvines in Flanders, when the French crushed Otto's anti-papal coalition. It was an irony of the political carousel that the Papacy would then take against him. In 1235 he restored order in Germany by force, banishing his elder son Henry in favour of the younger Conrad. In 1236–7 he crushed the Lombard cities at Cortenuova and marched through Cremona with a parade of elephants. In 1241, having sunk a papal fleet off Genoa, he took a bevy of hostile archbishops and abbots hostage. But in 1248, after the abortive siege of Parma, he lost his harem. No power on earth, it seems, could have restrained the partisan hatreds of Guelph and Ghibelline.

After Frederick's death, his son, Conrad IV (r. 1250–4), and grandson, Conradin (d. 1268), failed to enforce the Hohenstaufen succession, and the Empire was crippled once again by an extended interregnum (1254–73). The Papacy promptly reclaimed its overlordship of Sicily, which was turned over to the French Angevins. The popes, nominally victorious, were being pushed ever closer towards dependence on the kingdom of France. Under Gregory X (Tedaldo Visconti, 1271–6), arrangements were finalized for ensuring swift and effective papal elections. [**CONCLAVE**]

It was France which benefited most from the Empire's distress. In the eleventh century the Capetian kings had been masters only of the tiny royal domain in the Île de France round Paris; elsewhere, the prerogatives of kingship had been virtually abandoned to the constituent fiefs. But as from Louis VI (r. 1108–37) a series of long-lived monarchs greatly enhanced the substance of France. In this they were assisted by a remarkable demographic boom, especially in the northern provinces, by the growth of prosperous communes, and by important territorial acquisitions, notably in the Midi. Louis VII (r. 1137–80) was strong enough to marshal the entire nobility of France for the Second Crusade, and later to leave the realm in peace during private pilgrimages to Compostela and to Canterbury.

After repudiating his queen, Eleanor of Aquitaine, who promptly married his vassal, Henry II of England, he was mortified to watch the assemblage of a rival Plantagenet realm stretching from the Scottish borders to the Pyrenees. But the crisis passed; and the Capetians were to recover their supremacy. (See Appendix III, p. 1244.) [GOTHIC]

In this period, French and English affairs remained intimately entangled. The Angevin or 'Plantagenet' Dynasty came into being through the Anglo-Norman marriage of William the Conqueror's granddaughter, Matilda, with Geoffrey Plantagenet, Count of Anjou. Their son, Henry II (r. 1154–89) put an end to the prevailing anarchy of Stephen's reign, and stayed long enough with his queen, Eleanor, to procreate a line of monarchs that were to hold the English throne until 1399. His reign was marked by judicial reform, by the English invasion of Ireland, by incessant travelling to all points between Northumberland and Gascony, and by a conflict between Church and State culminating in the murder of Archbishop Becket (1170). His elder surviving son, Richard Cœur de Lion (r. 1189–99) was totally preoccupied with crusading. Richard's brother, John Lackland (r. 1199–1216) lost his subjects' trust through repeated acts of tyranny, lost the Duchy of Normandy through defeat at the Battle of Bouvines (1214), and lost the initiative in English politics through the concessions of *Magna Carta* (1215). John's son, Henry III (r. 1216–72) was a long survivor, relegated by Dante 'to the limbo of ineffectual souls'. (See Appendix III, p. 1252.)

Those early Plantagenet decades also saw the initial English incursions into Ireland. A band of Anglo-Norman adventurers led by Richard 'Strongbow', Earl of Pembroke, conspired to support the deposed king of Leinster. Their mailed knights made such advances following their landings in Wexford in 1169 that Henry II felt obliged to follow them and to receive the joint homage of the leading Irish kings. From then on, the English never left. John Lackland obtained the title of *Dominus Hiberniae*, 'Lord of Ireland', in his father's lifetime. In 1210 he set up a regular English colony at Dublin, forming a cluster of counties governed by English law and by English justiciars. Under Henry III, the first discriminatory moves were made to legally separate the newcomers from the natives and to exclude the Irish from positions of power.

Eleanor of Aquitaine (1122–1204) was perhaps the outstanding personality of the age. She made her mark not only as a woman of remarkable spirit but as a political and cultural patron of immense influence. She was the indomitable heiress to a great duchy. Married at 15, she had to be brought back from the Second Crusade under arrest for defying her royal husband. Divorced at 28, she remarried within two months, having engineered the dynastic coup of the century. Separated in her late forties through her second husband's liaison with the Fair Rosamund of Godstow, she returned to rule in style in her native Poitiers. Among her children and grandchildren, she lived to see one emperor, three kings of England, kings of Jerusalem and Castile, a duke of Brittany, and another queen of France. At Poitiers, at the head of a like-minded band of ladies, she became 'the Queen of the Troubadours':

> Domna vostre sui e serai,
> Del vostre servizi garnitz.
> Vostr'om sui juratz e plevitz,
> E vostre m'era des abans.
> E vos etz lo meus jois primers,
> E si seretz vos lo derrers,
> Tan com la vida m'er durans.

(Lady, I'm yours and yours shall be, I Vowed to your service constantly. I This is the oath of fealty I I pledged to you this long time past. I As my first joy was all in you, I So shall my last be found there too, I So long as life in me shall last.)[27]

Hostile French comment tried to blacken Eleanor's reputation with tales of poisoning and incest. But she stands as the central figure in the cultural history of a land which her enemies were about to destroy.

For Aquitaine formed the central sector of a distinct cultural and linguistic region now known as Occitania. The *langue d'oc*, whose speakers said *oc* for 'yes', was quite separate from the *langue d'oïl*, the 'French' language of northern Gaul. It was spoken right across the Midi from Catalonia to Provence. It transcended all political frontiers from the Kingdom of Aragon to the Arelate (Kingdom of Burgundy-Arles), which still belonged to the Empire. In the twelfth and early thirteenth centuries, on the eve of the French advance, it was the scene of one of Europe's most brilliant civilizations.

Philippe-Auguste (r. 1180–1223) gave the French monarchy its decisive impetus. Whilst tripling the size of the royal domain, he drew great advantage by playing off the rivalries of Empire and Papacy. He laid the foundations of a national army and, through the system of *baillis* or royal bailiffs, of a centralized administration. He was then able to withstand the eternal intrigues of the tenants-in-chief, and to destroy the Plantagenet challenge. Having stripped John Lackland of his legal rights in France through charges of breaching feudal obligation, he followed up the courtroom's decision with the sword. From 1202 he smoothly annexed Normandy, Anjou, Touraine, and most of Poitou. In 1214, at Bouvines, where he was unhorsed and saved by his vassals, he destroyed France's imperial and Plantagenet foes on the same field.

His grandson, Louis IX (r. 1226–70), gave France the moral prestige which military and economic success could not. Having inherited the extended kingdom which his father, Louis VIII, had just secured in Aquitaine and Languedoc, he did not need to wage war on his neighbours. He personified the highest ideals of a Christian king, as then conceived, and his life by Jean, Sire de Joinville, presents an entrancing portrait. 'Mon cher fils,' he told his eldest son, 'I beg you to love the people . . . For in truth, I would prefer that a Scotsman should . . . govern the people well and loyally, than that you should be seen to rule the kingdom badly.'[28] Louis had spent his youth under the regency of his mother, Eleanor's grand-daughter, Blanche of Castile, when

GOTHIC

VISITORS to the abbey of St Denis near Paris are shown the pointed arches in the apse which Abbot Suger completed in 1143 or 1144, and which are said to have initiated the Gothic style. Whether or not the work at St Denis preceded the Gothic vaulting at the cathedral of Sens, which was under construction during the same years, is a matter for debate. But France's senior basilica, the site of numerous royal coronations and burials and home of the *oriflamme*, would be a fitting place for such a momentous event; and it certainly preceded both Notre-Dame de Paris, the masterpiece of the 'transitional style', and the glories of Chartres, Reims, and Amiens.

From its beginnings in France, the Gothic spread far and wide throughout the Catholic world to become the archetypal style for medieval church-building north of the Alps. Scores of Gothic cathedrals were built, from Seville in the west to Dorpat in the east, from Lund in the north to Milan in the south. They were imitated in thousands of parish churches.

Many experts would argue that the ultimate aesthetic effect was achieved at the Sainte-Chapelle, which was completed in Paris on the orders of St Louis on 25 April 1248. Smaller than the great cathedrals, it is an edifice of exquisite delicacy and light, its tall, slender windows filled with brilliant expanses of stained glass.

Far away, the castle chapel of the Holy Trinity in Lublin, between Vistula and Bug, is one of those cultural orientation points which enable one to see Europe as a whole. Built in pure Gothic style by King Władysław Jagiełło (d. 1434), for a Polish-Lithuanian capital that never developed, it is a distant, rustic echo of the Sainte-Chapelle. At the same time, like the neighbouring Gothic cathedral of Sandomierz, its interior walls were painted in rich Byzantine splendour with murals designed by artists imported either from Ruthenia or possibly from Ottoman-occupied Macedonia. It lies at the point where the architecture of the West coincides with the decorative style of the East. The date of its completion is recorded, at the end of a long Cyrillic dedication in Old Church Slavonic, as St Lawrence's Day, 1418.

The career of the Gothic style did not end, however, with medieval church-building. It was revived as the favourite architectural style of the Romantic era, which sought to recover its prestigious aesthetic appeal and to apply it to all manner of secular structures. Manchester City Hall, King Ludwig's fantasy castle at Neuschwanstein in Bavaria, and the Austrian waterworks in Cracow are all descendants of Abbot Suger's apse at the terminus of Metro Line 13.

All modern interpretations of Gothic style are coloured by those nineteenth-century enthusiasms. The theories of Schlegel, Ruskin, and

Viollet-le-Duc were as crude as their propensity for 'improving' the medieval originals, including St Denis. From being a term of 'unmitigated contempt' for 'savageness', to use Ruskin's words, Gothic became the object of unrestrained adulation.[1] Goethe's essay 'Von deutscher Baukunst' (*On German Architecture*), which mythologized the origins of Strasbourg Cathedral and its builder, Erwin von Steinbach, was an inspiration to many others. In due course it tempted German scholars to claim Gothic as their own. In fact, Gothic was one of the most international of styles, with numerous regional variants. It is one of the many strands on which theories about the unity of European culture might easily be built.[2]

a dangerous feudal reaction arose. But his integrity and his limitless bank of marriageable relatives drew the great fiefs back into partnership with the Crown. In an age of intense litigiousness, he was the chosen arbiter of many a royal or feudal dispute, dispensing justice under the Oak of Vincennes. His treatment of the Jews and of the Midi was less than saintly. Yet towards the end of his long reign, St Louis was without contest the first prince of Christendom.

In England, a normal baronial war produced an abnormal outcome. Henry III Plantagenet (r. 1216–72), Lackland's son, had made himself unpopular with his barons by giving preference to his Poitevin, Savoyard, and Lusignan relatives, by an unsuccessful French war, and by extravagant building projects such as the renovation of Westminster Abbey. In 1258 a reforming faction emerged under the leadership of Simon de Montfort, Earl of Leicester, son of the Albigensian crusader (see below). By withholding a grant to solve the King's financial problems, the reformers pushed through the Provisions of Oxford whereby the King's administration was to be supervised by their nominees. When the King reneged, Simon waged war, and in the battle of Lewes succeeded in capturing the King, the King's eldest son, and the King's brother, Richard of Cornwall, King of Germany. In the following year the royal party rallied, and Simon was slain at Evesham (1265). In the interval, in January 1265, a new sort of Parliament had been summoned—not just from the magnates and prelates, but from the knights of the shires and from the burgesses of selected boroughs. For constitutionalists it was an important precedent, a decisive step on the road to limited monarchy—the first appearance of the House of Commons.

Yet it is doubtful whether England or France had any sense of their later national identities. In the thirteenth century the kingdom of England was still bound up with its Continental possessions. Its ruling class was still tied to the culture and ambitions of their French relations. France itself had only just acquired the territorial base, from the Channel to the Mediterranean, on which its future fortunes would be forged. There were many things about England which were considerably more 'French' than many parts of the new France.

The obsession with the recovery of the Holy Land lasted for 200 years and ended in failure. Between 1096 and 1291 there were seven major Crusades and numerous minor ones. The First Crusade (1096–9), led by the barons Godfroi de Bouillon, Raymond de St Gilles, Count of Toulouse, and Hugues de Vermandois, brother of the King of France, succeeded in capturing Jerusalem, massacring its inhabitants, and establishing a Latin kingdom in Palestine. The Second Crusade (1147–9), preached by St Bernard and led jointly by Louis VII of France and Conrad III of Germany, achieved little except the incidental seizure of Lisbon from the Moors by an English fleet. The Third Crusade (1189–92), mounted by the Emperor Frederick Barbarossa, Philippe Auguste of France, and Richard Cœur de Lion of England, failed to retake Jerusalem. The Fourth Crusade (1202–4), diverted by the ambitions of the Doge of Venice, succeeded in capturing Constantinople, massacring its inhabitants, and establishing a Latin empire in Byzantium—which was not the point of the exercise. The Fifth (1218–21), Sixth (1248–54), and Seventh (1270) Crusades ended up in Egypt or in Tunis, where St Louis of France himself died of the plague. When the last Christian stronghold in the Holy Land fell at Acre in 1291, there was no coherent response.

The conduct of the Crusaders was shocking—not only to modern sensibilities, but equally to contemporaries. St Bernard himself was moved to denounce it. They ravaged the countries through which they marched—Bohemia, Hungary, Bulgaria, and Byzantium. In 1096 they killed up to 8,000 Jews in their progress through the Rhineland—the first major series of Europe's pogroms. Their naval expeditions devastated the Mediterranean ports. They fought among themselves no less than against the Infidel. They fleeced their subjects to fill their coffers. 'I will sell the city of London', said Richard Cœur de Lion, 'if I can find a buyer.' The cost in wasted lives and effort was incalculable. One German emperor was drowned in a river in Cilicia; a second held the King of England to ransom; a third was excommunicated as he set sail for Palestine. Murder and massacre in the service of the Gospel were commonplace. Seventy thousand civilians were said to have been butchered in cold blood in the initial sack of Jerusalem. 'The lives and labours of millions who were buried in the East, would have been more profitably employed in the improvement of their native country.'[29] 'Arguably, the only fruit of the Crusades kept by the Christians was the apricot.'[30]

Yet the horrors along the crusaders' road often mask the deeper causes of their motivation. Religious fervour was mixed with the resentments of a society suffering from waves of famine, plague, and overpopulation. Crusading was a means to sublimate the pains of an indigent existence. In this, the well-fed knight with his well-shod retinue was far outnumbered by the hordes of paupers who followed in his wake. The 'People's Crusades' and 'Shepherds' Crusades' continued long after the major expeditions. For them, Jerusalem was the visionary city of Revelation, where Christ beckoned. The Crusades were 'an armed pilgrimage', 'a collective *imitatio Christi*, a mass sacrifice which was to be rewarded by a mass apotheosis at Jerusalem', the inspiration of 'the messianism of the poor'.[31] Successful crusaders of the knightly caste might be portrayed in stone in their parish church, their legs piously crossed in death. Most of their companions never came home, presumed dead. Of course, the concept of crusading was not limited to the Holy Land. The Latin Church gave equal weight to the northern crusades in the Baltic (see pp. 362–4) and to the 'third flank' in the *Reconquista* in Spain (see p. 345).

The impact of the Crusades was profound. The Latin kingdom of Jerusalem (1099–1187) was the first experiment in a 'Europe Overseas'.[32] The eastern Mediterranean was reopened to trade and travel. The Italian cities, especially Venice and Genoa, flourished. The collective identity of the Latin Church was consolidated under papal leadership. The Crusades supplied a vast fund of heroism and curiosity which underlay the growth of medieval romance, philosophy, and literature. Yet the Crusades also served to strengthen the nexus between Western Christendom, feudalism, and militarism. They gave rise to the military orders. Through the misconduct of the Latins, and the disgust of the Greeks who witnessed the misdeeds, they rendered the reunification of Christendom virtually impossible. Above all, they reinforced the barriers between Christianity and Islam, poisoning relations in which Westerners were cast in the role both of aggressors and of losers. In short, the Crusaders brought Christianity into disrepute.

The military orders, especially the Hospitallers and the Templars, were central to the debate on crusading ethics. The 'Knights of the Order of the Hospital of St John of Jerusalem' were created in 1099 after the first Crusade. They included military, medical, and pastoral brothers. After the fall of Acre they escaped to Cyprus, ruled Rhodes (1309–1522), and eventually Malta (1530–1801). The 'Poor Knights of Christ and the Temple of Solomon' came into being in 1118 for the purpose of protecting pilgrims on the road to Jerusalem. They diversified, however, into banking and real estate, growing immensely rich from properties all over Christendom. They were suppressed in 1312 on false charges of magic, sodomy, and heresy brought against them by the King of France. Their emblem, two knights riding on one horse, goes back to the first Master, Hugues de Payens, who was so poor that he shared his horse with a friend. It was a curious bent of the medieval mind that men could reconcile monastic vows with soldiering. Both the Hospitallers and the Templars were international bodies with depots in all the countries of the West. The Teutonic Knights, in contrast, were diverted at an early stage to the Baltic (see below). The military orders of Santiago, Calatrava, and Alcantara did not operate outside Spain.

The double conquest of Constantinople in 1203–4 well illustrates the doubtful virtues of the crusading movement. The army of the Fourth Crusade, which had congregated at Venice, soon fell prey to the schemes of the ageing Doge Enrico Dandolo and of the German King Philip of Swabia, who was married to Irene of Byzantium. The Doge saw a chance to enlarge the Republic's possessions in the Levant; the King saw a chance to restore his exiled nephew to the Byzantine throne. So, in return for the hire of a fleet, the Crusaders had to agree to share their booty with the Venetians and to back the restoration of Alexius IV. In addition, when they failed to pay for their ships, they were obliged to seize the

Hungarian port of Zara in Dalmatia as collateral. In July 1203 they sailed through the Dardanelles without resistance and stormed the sea-walls. But a palace revolution in Constantinople, where Alexius IV was strangled, robbed them of their victory; and in April they had to repeat the exercise. This time the city of Constantine was comprehensively ransacked, the churches pillaged, the citizens butchered, the icons smashed. Baldwin, Count of Flanders, was crowned 'Basileus' in St Sophia by a Venetian Patriarch. The Empire was parcelled out into Venetian colonies and Latin fiefs. At which point, at Adrianople in April 1205, the crusading army was annihilated by the Bulgars. They never came within a thousand miles of Jerusalem. They had committed 'the Great Betrayal'.[33]

The Fourth Crusade left two Roman Empires in the East: the Latin 'Empire of the Straits' at Constantinople and the Byzantine rump ruled from Nicaea in Asia Minor. The former survived for sixty years until, in 1261, in the temporary absence of the Venetian fleet, the latter recovered its position. In the long run, Venice was the sole beneficiary.

None the less, the fiasco of the Fourth Crusade coincided with what many regard as the political apogee of the Latin Church—the Papacy of Innocent III (1198–1216). Born Lotario d'Anagni, Innocent was an instinctive power-broker who came nearest to the ideal of subordinating all rulers to 'theocratic government'. In Germany he contrived both to crown one of the imperial contenders, Otto of Brunswick, and then to depose him. In France he refused to approve Philippe-Auguste's matrimonial arrangements and, having placed the country under interdict, eventually forced the King to restore his Queen after a twenty-year separation. In England, after another lengthy struggle with King John, he again wielded the interdict and forced the King to submit. England joined Aragon, Sicily, Denmark, and even Bulgaria as vassals of the Holy See. The XIIth General Council of the Church, which convened in the Lateran in November 1215, saw 1,500 prelates from all over Christendom meekly adopting the Pope's proposals.

In reality, the Latin Church was rather more influential in high politics than in the lives of ordinary men and women. The hierarchy was often out of touch with the people. Heresy, pagan reversions, fantastic superstitions, and fierce resentments of the Church's wealth were prevalent. To combat the crisis, Innocent III gave his blessing to two new orders of mendicant brothers, who were to live exemplary lives of communal service among the masses. The Order of Preachers (OP), the Black Friars or Dominicans, was founded by a Castilian, St Dominic Guzmán (1170–1221), who fixed their rule in two general Chapters in 1220–1. Ever since they have been specially devoted both to evangelizing and to study. The Order of Friars Minor (OFM), the Minorites or Grey Friars, was founded by St Francis of Assisi (c.1181–1226) and received their papal charter in 1223. Ever since, they have been specially devoted to moral teaching. Both Dominicans and Franciscans accepted men and women, and were sworn to corporate and individual poverty. Until further developments were halted in 1274, they were joined by other mendicants including the Poor Clares, the Carmelites or White Friars, and the Austin Friars. Unlike the monks, whose piety was sometimes suspect, the 'jovial friar' was as popular with the laity as he was unpopular with the high clergy.

St Francis is undoubtedly the most endearing figure of medieval Christianity. Born the son of a rich merchant of Assisi in Umbria, he changed his clothes for those of a beggar and renounced his inheritance. He was the 'husband of Lady Poverty'. He lived for a time as a hermit in a cave above Assisi, but in 1219 accompanied a crusading expedition to Egypt. He had more direct influence on the foundation of the Poor Clares than of the Franciscans. In 1224, when he was praying on Monte Verna, his body was impressed with the Stigmata—scars corresponding to the wounds of the crucified Christ. His legendary ability to commune with Nature is conveyed in his 'Canticle to the Sun' and in the later *Fioretti* (The Little Flowers of St Francis and his Companions). He was the author of hymns and prayers which go to the heart of the Christian ethos:

> Lord, make me an instrument of your peace;
> Where there is hatred, let me sow love,
> Where there is injury, pardon,
> Where there is doubt, faith,
> Where there is despair, hope,
> Where there is darkness, light,
> Where there is sadness, joy.
> O Divine Master, Grant that I may not so much seek
> To be consoled, as to console,
> To be understood, as to understand,
> To be loved, as to love;
> For it is in giving that we receive;
> It is in pardoning that we are pardoned;
> It is in dying that we are born to eternal life.[34]

The friars were instrumental in another development of the age—the rise of universities. The 'twelfth-century renaissance' had established the principle that secular learning had value apart from theology. But it was not acceptable that educational institutions should be set up without licence of the Church. Hence the idea of a *Studium Generale* or 'university', divided into four or five faculties— Theology, Law, Medicine, Arts or Philosophy, and Music—incorporated by charter and regulated by a self-governing academic body. Among Europe's senior universities, after Bologna (1088, refounded 1215) came Paris (c.1150) and then Oxford 1167). By 1300, a score of foundations had proliferated in Italy, France, England, and Spain, with many more to come. (See Appendix III, p. 1248.)

The Albigensian Crusade (1209–29) illustrates a very different aspect of medieval Christianity. In 1199 Innocent III had declared heresy to be 'treason against God'. The target of his fulminations were the Cathars or 'Albigensians' of Languedoc. Spiritual descendants of the ancient Gnostics, Manichaeans, and Bogumils, the Cathars had left traces of an earlier presence in Bosnia and had been the subject of a heresy trial in Milan. They then spread rapidly in the weaving towns of Albi, Agen, Pamiers, Carcassonne, and Toulouse, where they gained the protection of the local counts. They believed that the prevalence of evil contradicted the existence of a sole benign Creator; that good and evil, therefore, must be separate creations. They were vegetarian, ascetic, puritanical; they practised the equality of men and women; and they supported a caste of *perfecti* who administered the rite of *consolamentum*, the 'laying on of hands'. In 1167 they had held a dissident Council, at Saint Félix de Caraman near Toulouse, which was in touch with fellow dissidents of the same persuasion in Asia Minor. The XIth General Council of the Church, called in 1179 to discuss the problem, had made no progress; and the preaching of St Dominic was equally fruitless. In 1209 the murder of a papal legate was used as the pretext for launching a general attack. [BOGUMIL]

Innocent III pronounced a Crusade on the same terms as the Crusades against Islam—the remission of sins and unrestricted loot. In the first phase, between 1209 and 1218, 12,000 knights from France and Burgundy, under Simon de Montfort the Elder, battled the heretics under the Raymonds VI and VII of Toulouse. In the second phase, from 1225 to 1271, the armies of the King of France entered the fray. The Cathars faced the choice between abjuration or death. Many chose death. The Holy Inquisition, led by a Cathar defector, Robert the Bugger,* spread a veritable reign of torture and terror. In 1244, at Montségur, the holy place of the Perfects, 200 recalcitrants were burned alive in one vast pyre. Year by year, village by village, by sword and by trial, the extirpation went on. The castle of Queribus fell in 1255. By the fourteenth century the surviving ex-Cathars found themselves in the Roman Catholic fold. Their province of Languedoc found itself in the kingdom of France. The unity of France was built on the misery of the Midi.[35]

Crusading, however, had further uses. If it could be used against the infidel, it could also be used against the heathen nearer to home. In 1147, at Frankfurt, St Bernard had found that the Saxon nobles were much keener on attacking their Slavonic neighbours than marching to the Holy Land. A papal bull, *Divina dispensatione*, was obtained, and St Bernard urged the northern crusaders 'to fight the heathen until such time as, by God's help, they shall either be converted or wiped out'.[36] The Wendish Crusade (1147–85) saw Saxons, Danes, and Poles reducing the obstinate tribes of Mecklenburg and Lusatia to the Catholic obedience. (See Plate 26.)

In 1198 Hartwig II, Archbishop of Bremen, launched another 'continuous crusade' in Livonia. Assisted by an Order of armed German monks, the Brothers of the Sword, based at Riga, he created an organization which gradually brought all the north-east Baltic under Catholic control. Livonia was subdued by the Order, Estonia by the Danes, and Finland by the Swedes. Their exploits were recorded c.1295 by the nameless author of the *Livlandische Reimchronik*, who describes the urge to kill and burn in the name of the Lord:

* Robert le Bougre. Thanks to their Bogumil connections, the Cathars were widely known as *bougres*, a corruption of 'Bulgars'. Also, since the *perfecti* practised severe sexual celibacy, they were widely accused of sodomy. Hence the evolution in the meaning of 'buggery'.

The first of the fires that burned that day
Was lit by the hand of a Friar Grey,
And a Blackfriar followed after.[37] [**DANNEBROG**]

The Prussian Crusade began in 1230. The Prussians had preserved their independence since the days of St Vojtech, and were worrying the local Polish princes by their incessant raiding. One of those princes, Konrad Mazowiecki (Conrad of Mazovia), determined to solve the problem by calling in a minor military Order, the Teutonic Knights, unemployed since their recent expulsion from the Holy Land. He was sowing the dragon's teeth: instead of completing their contract and departing, the Knights obtained charters of permanent crusading rights from both the Emperor and the Pope, and dug in for the duration. By playing off their various sponsors, they were able to escape the control of all. The bull *Pietati*

DANNEBROG

ON 15 June 1219, the Danish expedition to Estonia faced disaster. The native Estonians had just submitted to King Valdemar the Victorious, who was preparing to baptize them. But they rushed the Danish camp at nightfall, killed the bishop, and drove the crusaders towards the sea. According to legend, the fate of the battle only turned when the heavens let fall a red banner with a white cross, and a voice was heard urging the Danes to rally round it. Valdemar triumphed; the city of Tallin or 'Danish Castle', was founded; and Denmark adopted the *dannebrog* or 'red rag' as the national flag.[1]

Since then, every independent nation has adopted a flag of its own. Many, like the *Dannebrog*, bear a cross—the red cross of St George in England, the diagonal blue cross of St Andrew for Scotland, Sweden's yellow cross on a blue ground. Switzerland adopted Denmark's colours, but a different cross. The Union Jack of the United Kingdom, which combines the crosses of SS George, Andrew, and Patrick, was first flown after the Irish Union on 1 January 1801.

All European monarchies possess a royal standard in addition to the national flag. Denmark's royal standard, which carries three lions statant azure, with hearts gules, on a field or, pre-dates the Dannebrog.

Following the example of the Netherlands (1652), most modern republics have adopted simple tricolours or bicolours. Some of these, like the French (1792), the Italian (1805), or the Irish (1922), are vertical. Others, like those of Germany (1918) or Russia (1917), are horizontal. Most have had to contend with flags of rival regimes. National flags are a focus for patriotism, and a vital symbol of identity. The sequence in which they were adopted is not irrelevant to the uneven maturity of Europe's national communities.

proximum (1234), claiming Prussia as a papal fief, remained a dead letter, as did a similar imperial decree of 1245 claiming Courland, Semigalia, and Lithuania for the Empire. The Knights-Brothers, in their white surcoats with black crosses, pressed on regardless, building forts and trading posts as they went—Thorn (Toruń 1231), Marienwerder (Kwidzyn 1233), Elbing (Elbląg 1237). By 1295, after a final heathen revolt, Prussia had become the Teutonic State, an independent crusading enterprise in the heart of Europe.

The methods and motives of the Teutonic Knights have long been the subject of controversy. Their neighbours in Poland and Pomerania, against whom they fought incessantly, complained bitterly to the Pope, and later brought the matter to the Council of Constance. More sympathetic observers have not seen the discrepancy:

> The dominant motive of the Teutonic Knights, as of all crusaders, was the desire for atonement through sacrifice. The method chosen may seem bizarre, especially when contrasted with the ministry of love carried on by the Franciscans . . . but the Teutonic Knights and the Friars . . . had this in common: they were both trying to achieve redemption and holiness without cutting themselves off from the practical world. . . . they shared a monastic dedication to an unmonastic way of life.[38]

Thus did civilization advance.

In the thirteenth century Eastern Europe was stormed by invaders who made the Teutonic Knights look like laggards. The Mongols of Genghis Khan swept out of the Asian steppes like a whirlwind, first in 1207, when Juji, son of Genghis, subjugated southern Siberia, and then in 1223, when they ravaged Transcaucasia and destroyed a Kievan army on the Kalka River. In 1236–7 Batu Khan, grandson of Genghis, crossed the Urals, ravaged the principalities of Ryazan and Vladimir, and razed Moscow. He took Kiev by siege in 1240 before moving off to the west. In 1241 Galicia was ravaged and Cracow razed. On 9 April 1241 the Polish princes under Henry the Bearded were cut to pieces on the field of Legnica in Silesia. As proof of their victory the Mongols were said to have collected nine sackfuls of right ears from the bodies of the slain. Another column of the horde swept on to Hungary, where a similar fate awaited the Magyar princes under Bela IV on the river Tisza. Batu then returned eastwards, setting up his camp at Saray near the mouth of the Volga. Similar trails of destruction were blazed again in 1259 and in 1287. [HEJNAL]

The Mongol invasions transformed the face of several countries. The horsemen of Batu Khan settled down on the Volga for good. The state of the 'Golden Horde', which they created between Volga and Don, supplanted that of the Volga Bulgars, whose sumptuous capital they razed. The khanates of Kazan and Astrakhan, which were eventually to be annexed by Muscovy in 1552–6, put an Asiatic population in place that is the basis of modern 'Tatarstan'. The Tartars of Crimea established a thriving state from their seat at Bakshishsarai that lived for centuries from their *czambuls* or 'raiding-parties'. Their presence provoked the

HEJNAŁ

HEJNAŁ, which derives from the Hungarian word for the dawn and, by extension for reveille, has passed into the Polish language as a term for the trumpet-call which sounds the alarm on the enemy's approach.

Hejnal krakowski

Today, the *hejnał mariacki* or 'trumpet-call of St Mary's' is one of the many curiosities of old Cracow. It is sounded from the top of the tower of the ancient church which overlooks the city square. It is sounded on the hour, every hour of the day and night, winter and summer; and each time it is repeated four times: to north, south, east, and west. It consists of a simple melody of open chords, which is always cut short in the middle of the final cadence. It commemorates the trumpeter who, whilst raising the alarm in 1241, or perhaps in 1259, was shot through the throat by a Mongol arrow. His call, though interrupted, enabled the burghers to flee. The survivors undertook to endow a town trumpeter in perpetuity.

The ritual has been maintained for over 700 years, with only short interruptions in the nineteenth century, and during the German occupation of 1939–45. It is older than the church from which it is sounded. The melody took its present form in the seventeenth century. After 1945, Polish Radio adopted it as a prelude to its daily time signal at twelve noon. It reminds millions of listeners both of the ancient pedigree of Polish culture and of Poland's exposed location. It is one of the few active mementoes of Genghis Khan, and of the irruption of his horsemen into the heart of Europe.[1]

On 25 October 1405 the Swiss city of Lausanne was ravaged by fire. The Bishop promptly issued an eleven-point edict on fire precautions. Article 5 stated that 'at every hour of the night, one of the watchmen on the tower of the Cathedral is obliged to shout the hour and to call to the watchmen of the city's other wards . . . on pain of 6 deniers for every failing.' Six centuries later, from 10 o'clock every evening, the watchman's call still echoes to the four winds: 'Il a sonné dix!'[2]

At Ripon in Yorkshire, they say that the 'charter horn' has 'sounded the trump' every evening since 886.

The European Ground and Tower Watch Association was founded in 1987 at Ebeltoft in Denmark. Most of its members represent modern revivals. Cracow, Lausanne, and Ripon, together with Annaberg, Celle, and Nordlingen in Germany, and Ystad in Sweden belong to the select company which can claim to have kept the watch 'since the beginning'.

rise of the later Cossack communities of the Dnieper and Don, and long delayed the settlement of adjoining Ukraine.

Poland and Hungary, denuded of much population, were left to recover as best they could. In both cases, since a ready supply of colonists was available in the German Empire, the Mongol invasions accelerated an existing process of migration and colonization. In this period German and Flemish settlers moved into Silesia and Pomerania, and also into Transylvania. The princes' 'locators' offered land on favourable terms of tenure, and persuaded whole convoys of peasant migrants to trek east. At the same time, the cities were rebuilt and provided with charters on the model of the Magdeburg or, less frequently, the Lübeck Law. The cities of that vintage—Breslau (1242), Buda (1244), Cracow (1257) and others— were governed by German law and were full of German merchants. Added to the activities in the Baltic both of the Hanseatic League and of the Teutonic Knights, these changes brought about a massive increase of German influence. [BUDA] [HANSA]

The Mongols destroyed all semblance of unity among the east Slavs whose lands they had subjugated. Some of the princes of Rus' were eventually able to escape by turning to their Lithuanian neighbours (see p. 392). But those in the East were forced, quite literally, to 'bend the neck'. Summoned at regular intervals to the camp of the khan, they were obliged to walk between blazing bonfires, to stoop beneath the proffered yoke, and to prostrate themselves before their master. It was a ritual humiliation whose purpose was not forgotten. Their people were condemned to pay tribute, collected by resident Mongol *baskiki* or 'governors'. But the Orthodox Church was not oppressed. It was the period of 'the Tartar Yoke'.

There is a description of 'the province of Russia' at this time in the travels of the Venetian Marco Polo, whose father had visited the Crimea on a trading venture in 1260:

The province . . . is of vast extent . . . and borders upon that northern tract which has been described as the Region of Darkness. Its inhabitants are Christians, and follow the Greek ritual . . . The men are extremely well-favoured, tall and of fair complexion; the women are also . . . of a good size, with light hair which they are accustomed to wear long. The country pays tribute to the king of the Western Tartars . . . Within it are collected in great abundance the furs of ermines, sables, martens, foxes . . . together with much wax. It contains several [silver] mines . . . [It] is an exceedingly cold region, and I have been assured that it extends even as far as the Northern Ocean, where . . . peregrine falcons are taken in vast numbers.[39]

Contrary to former assumptions, economic life in the Middle Ages was not stagnant. There is a school of thought which holds that 'an agricultural revolution' in northern Europe at this time was 'equally decisive in its historical effects' as 'the so-called Industrial Revolution' of the nineteenth century.[40] The argument centres on new sources of power such as the water-mill and the windmill, on expanded mining activities, on the impact of the iron plough and horsepower, and on crop

BUDA

IN 1244, King Bela IV of Hungary granted a charter of autonomy to the 'free city of Pest' on the Danube. His decision formed part of a wider pro-gramme of reconstruction following the recent Tartar invasions. Henceforth, the city was to govern itself according to the Law of Magdeburg, the king ceding all but residual powers. In due course, simi-lar arrangements would be made for the castle suburb of Buda on the opposite bank of the river, creating two distinct jurisdictional units within the one urban area.[1] Buda, which in German was known as Ofen, suc-ceeded Esztergom as Hungary's royal capital in 1361.

The future life of a city was greatly influenced by the nature of the authority which granted its founding charter. Although municipal char-ters granted by kings and princes were most common, bishops were often active, especially in Germany. Wherever the nobility was strong, as in Hungary and Poland, private cities also sprang up, providing oases of immunity from the long arms of Church and State. The growth of cities greatly strengthened the centrifugal tendencies of late medieval polities. In Hungary, it complemented the existing system of territorial counties and of noble liberties.

A city's adoption of the Magdeburg model does not necessarily mean that it was a German settlement. The Magdeburg Law was adopted all over East and Central Europe by German and by non-German cities alike. None the less, there was always a strong German community both in Pest and in Buda even under Ottoman rule. The twin cities were not joined into one joint municipality until 1872, shortly after Hungary re-asserted its separate existence within the Habsburgs' dual Monarchy. In 1896, they played host to an extravagant festival celebrating the millennium of Hungary's foun-dation.

Hungary's Millennium naturally focused on the person of St Stephen and on the gift of a crown by the Pope. This event, like the founding of Pest, was understood to have cemented the lasting connection with the West. Stephen's queen, Gisella, was sister to Henry of Bavaria (the future German Emperor, who was also canonized). His coronation in AD 1001 helped him oust his Bulgarian- and Orthodox-backed rivals for the throne. From then on, like Poland, Hungary was firmly committed to the Western, Catholic camp.

The crown, which bears St Stephen's name and which is now the prime exhibit in the Hungarian National Museum, came to symbolize Hungary's extraordinary powers of survival. It was supposedly worn by all the Hungarian kings from the Arpads to the Habsburgs, and was a necessary adjunct to all valid coronations. It was many times lost or hidden, but never destroyed. In 1405 it fell unnoticed into an Austrian bog, whilst being illegally exported by Sigismund of Luxembourg, but was recovered when the bog started to glow with heavenly rays. In 1945 it was smuggled out of the country again, taken to the USA, and secretly deposited in Fort Knox. It was returned to Budapest in 1978, even though Hungary was still a communist-ruled country.

It is interesting to find, therefore, that doubts have been raised whether 'St Stephen's Crown' had ever belonged to St Stephen. Nor, despite later attributions, is it likely to have originated in Rome. According to the most recent scholarly opinions, the principal gold band, the *corona graeca*, was made in eleventh-century Byzantium, probably for Synadene, consort to Geza I (r. 1074–7). In the traditional view, this 'Greek Crown' was welded onto an older crown, the *corona latina*, which had been made for Stephen I.[2] In the modern view, its only possible link with St Stephen lies in the original cross, a relic of the True Cross now lost, which once topped the arched bands of the Latin Crown.

Whatever their origins, the two constituent parts of the Crown, the Greek and the Latin, combine to present the aptest of reminders not of Hungary's western connections but of medieval Hungary's location at the heart of Christendom. The Greek Crown carries a ring of alternating gemstones and of small plaques of cloisonné enamel. At the front, above the forehead, stands a raised plaque of Christ Pantokrator: at the rear, a corresponding plaque of the Emperor Michael VII Dukas (r. 1071–8) with green aureole. On either side of the Emperor there are portraits of the emperor's son Constantine and of King Geza. Geza's plaque is accompanied by a Greek inscription: GEOBITZAS PISTOS KRALES TURKIAS (Geza the believer king of Turkia). Elsewhere round the rim runs a circle of Byzantine archangels and saints. The Latin crown, in contrast, carries eight plaques of the apostles, with Christ enthroned at the crossing-point of its bands. A leaning gold cross, which replaced the original in 1551 at the time of the first Habsburg coronation, precariously surmounts the whole.[3]

What is certain is the aptness of the quality with which the Crown is said to be most strongly endowed—its *inadmissibility*, 'its incapacity to be permanently lost'.[4]

rotation and improved nutrition. New techniques sometimes took centuries to be widely applied, but the chain effect over time was decisive. Agriculture moved into the heavier but more fertile soils of the valleys. The increased food supply fuelled a demographic explosion, especially in northern France and the Low Countries. The rising population filled the new towns and released a new labour force. The labour force could be employed in new industrial enterprises such as mining and weaving: specialized textile towns proliferated. Sea trade was steadily expanded. [PLOVUM][MURANO]

MURANO

MURANO is an island in the Venetian lagoon. It is the site of a Romanesque church, Santa Maria e Donato, dating from 999, and the glassworks of the former Venetian Republic.

Glass-making has been practised in Europe since ancient times, but Greek and Roman glass was coarse in texture and opaque in colour. It was only at Murano, near the turn of the thirteenth century, that the glass-masters created a product that was both tough and transparent. For several decades the formula remained secret; but then it leaked to Nuremberg, whence it spread to all corners of the continent.

Transparent glass made possible the science of optics, and was crucial in the development of precision instruments. The principles of the lens and the refraction of light were known by the time, c.1260, that Roger Bacon was credited with designing the first pair of spectacles. (There is a portrait of the Emperor Henry VII (d. 1313) wearing spectacles in one of the stained glass windows of Strasbourg cathedral.) Glass windows gradually came into fashion between the fourteenth and sixteenth centuries, first in churches and palaces and later in more humble dwellings. Glass flasks, retorts, and tubes facilitated the experiments of alchemy, later of chemistry. Glass cloches and greenhouses transformed market-gardening. The microscope (1590), telescope (1608), barometer (1644), and thermometer (1593), all glass-based, revolutionized our views of the world. The silvered mirror, first manufactured at Murano, revolutionized the way we see ourselves.

The social consequences of glass were far-reaching. The use of spectacles extended the reading span of monks and scholars, and accelerated the spread of learning. Windows increased the hours and efficiency of indoor work, especially in northern Europe. Workplaces could be better lit and better heated. Greenhouses vastly improved the cultivation of flowers, fruit, and vegetables, bringing a healthier and more abundant diet, previously known only in the Mediterranean. Storm-proof lanterns, enclosed coaches, and watch-glasses all appeared, whilst precision instruments encouraged a wide range of scientific disciplines, from astronomy to medicine.

The mirror had important psychological consequences. People who could see a sharp image of their own faces developed a new consciousness. They became more aware of their appearances, and hence of clothes, hairstyles, and cosmetics. They were also led to ponder the link between external features and the inner life, in short, to study personality and individuality. They developed interests in portraiture, biography, and fashion. The very unmedieval habits of introspection were strongly reflected in Rembrandt's paintings, for example, and ultimately in the novel. The Galerie des Glaces (Hall of Mirrors) at the palace of Versailles was opened on 15 November 1684. It was a wonder of the age. Spanning the full façade of the central pavilion and overlooking the park, its colossal mirrors reflected the light of seventeen huge windows and seventeen colossal chandeliers. It was the secular counterpart to the medieval stained glass of Chartres.

The ancients had seen through glass darkly. The moderns saw through it clearly, in a shocking, shining cascade of light that reached into their innermost lives.[1]

Other historians would go still further. Compared to previous conditions, the growth of cities was spectacular; and their activities have been seen as evidence for the 'take-off' of a European economy.[41] This is perhaps an exaggeration. The huge annual fairs which were held from 1180 onwards on the plains of Champagne, at Lagny, Provins, Troyes, or Bar-sur-Aube, were indeed a major development. They were located midway between the urban centres in Lombardy, in the Rhineland, in the Low Countries, and in northern France; and they provided the meeting-point for merchants and financiers with international connections. One can say that they were the focus of a Europe-wide, if not an all-European, economic system.

Urban wealth underlay many of the political problems. City corporations were acquiring the means to challenge the authority of the local bishop or count, just as the guilds and merchant associations could press the city fathers. (The first recorded strike was organized by the weavers of Douai in 1245.[42]) The feudal order was weakening from within. In Germany, the sturdy independence of cities such as Cologne or Nuremberg helps to explain why neither the Church nor the barons could reimpose the authority of the Hohenstaufen. In Italy, the colossal resources of Milan, Genoa, Venice, and Florence explain why the wars of Guelphs and Ghibellines were so intractable, why neither Pope nor Emperor would desist. In Flanders, urban overpopulation supplied an important element in the migrations to the East. There were marked contrasts between Eastern and Western Europe—which none the less, and as always, betrayed strong indications of interdependence. Europe was on the move.

Schiedam, County of Holland, 5 December 1262. Hendrik, Bishop of Utrecht, on the Eve of St Nicholas granted a licence to a church built and endowed 'on the new land' at Schiedam by the Countess Aleida van Henegouwen, Regent of Holland and Zeeland:

Henricus Dei Gratia Traiectensis episcopus universis presentes literas inspecturis salutem in Domino sempiternam. Cum illustris domina, dilecta nostra consanguinea domina Aleidis, uxor quondam domini Iohannis de Avennis, Hollandie et Selandie tutrix, in nova

PLOVUM

THE heavy, iron, three-piece plough or *plovum* was a far more sophisti-cated implement than its predecessor, the simple wooden 'scratch-plough' or *aratrum*. Equipped with a vertical sod-cutter or coulter, a horizontal ploughshare, a tilted mouldboard, and usually with wheels, it could turn the heaviest soils. Yet it demanded the sort of tractive power that was rarely available in the ancient world. A thousand years passed between its earliest sighting by Pliny in the Po valley and its general adoption in northern Europe in the eleventh to twelfth centuries. For all that time, the main problem was how to pull it. In the early Middle Ages ox teams were the norm. Land was measured in ox-hides and ox-gangs, i.e. in units of ploughland that could be served by one ox-team. But the ox was painfully slow; and a full team of eight oxen was expensive both to buy and to feed. Horses were only bred in the fast but smaller and less powerful breeds.

Five developments were required before the iron plough could come into its own. First was the breeding of heavy farm-horses—an offshoot of the Carolingian charger. Second was the horse-collar, not noted before AD 800, which enabled the draught animal to haul maximum loads without being throttled. Third was the horseshoe, adopted c.900. Fourth was the cultivation of oats, the workhorse's staple food. Most important of all was the introduction of the three-field system of crop rotation. The change from the two-field to the three-field plan greatly improved crop yields whilst increasing the peasant family's productivity by at least 50 per cent. It permitted the growing of all four cereals, and effectively distributed the peasant's toil between spring and autumn sowing. But it demanded a marked rise in ploughing capacity. (See Plate 29.)

By the twelfth century at the latest, all the elements of the northern agri-cultural revolution were in place from France to Poland. Historians may have modified some of the simpler equations of the subject, such as Meltzen's 'Scratch-plough + cross-ploughing = square fields' or Marc Bloch's famous 'Three-piece plough + wheels = strips = open fields = communal agriculture'. But the main lines are now generally accepted. Square-shaped upland fields, which required cross-ploughing, were often abandoned, whilst long open-strip fields made their appearance in the heavy but fertile lands of the valley bottoms. Europe's landscape was altered once and for all. The fields were adorned with the familiar pattern of ridge-and-furrow. Time saved from ploughing could be used to extend the arable. Forests were felled, marshes drained, polders reclaimed from the sea. Larger villages clustered in the valleys, and the working of the strips was regulated by new forms of communal management. The village council and the manorial economy both went into action. From it all, Europeans gained a growing supply of ever more nutritious food that was to sustain a correspondingly greater population until the dawn of the Industrial Revolution.[1]

terra apud Schiedam in divini honorem nominis de novo ecclesiam construi fecerit et dotaverit eandem, nos ipsius in hac parte piis supplicationibus inclinati ad huiusmodi structuram ecclesiae licentiam concedimus . . .[43]

Two years later, the Countess Aleida ordered a dam and sluice to be built across the stream of the Schie at the point where it flowed into the tidal waters of the Rhine delta. Its purpose was to regulate the channel which linked the nearby town of Delft with its tiny river-port of Delfshaven. It was to be built in conjunction with another dike and dam across a still smaller rivulet, the Rotte, two miles upstream. Three years after that, on 11 August 1270, the young Count Floris V granted privileges to the burghers of Rotterdam.[44] About the same time, construction of a dam began on the River Amstel, 35 miles to the north. Step by step, the Rhine delta was being tamed.

Though not the earliest man-made constructions in the area, the dams were specifically designed to aid commercial navigation in the perilous wastes which stretched in a huge arc over some 25,000 km² (10,000 sq. miles) between the Scheldt and the Ems (see Map 13, opposite). In retrospect, they may be seen as crucial steps in the evolution of Europe's most densely populated country, of the world's largest port, and of one of Europe's most distinctive nations. It could not have seemed so at the time.

The country of Holland was one of the more remote and underdeveloped districts of the Holy Roman Empire. Its name, meaning *Holt-land* or 'Marshland', under-lined the fact that it was entirely dominated by the watery wastes. It was the low-est of all the low countries, the *Nederlanden*. Between the ring of sand islands on the seaward side and the inland terra firma, at least two-thirds of its surface area lay below sea-level. It consisted for the most part of mud-flats, salt-marsh, flood-banks, brackish lakes, and treacherous *wadden* or shallows. Travel was usually by boat, except in the winter when the shallow waters froze solid to form roads across the ice.

The Rhine delta was the most recent and most mobile of Europe's landforms. Created in the few thousand years since the last Ice Age, it had been shaped by the contending forces of three north-flowing rivers—the Scheldt (Escaut), the Maas (Meuse), and the Rijn (Rhine)—and of the westerly winds and tides of the sea. As a result, it was visibly subject to change and movement. The seaborne sand had formed a massive barrier of dunes up to 70 m high and 4 or 5 km wide. Behind this, the river-borne sediment piled up in ever-shifting configurations, whilst the freshwater flow gushed and probed against the points of least resistance in the unceasing battle to force new outlets to the sea. In Roman times, a number of coastal forts had stood on the sand barrier beyond a great inland lagoon, the Fleo Lacus. The main waters of the 'Old Rhine' reached the sea through a channel which still exists in modern Leiden, whilst the 'Old Maas' wound its separate way some twenty miles further south.

But the intervening millennium had wrought several dramatic alterations. In 839 a great flood had diverted the principal Rhine flow into the Maas, creating the

Map 13. The Low Countries, 1265

interlinked channels of Lek, Waal, and 'New Maas'. The freshwater lagoon to the
north, starved of water, partly silted up. Then, in the twelfth and thirteenth centuries, a warmer climatic phase caused a gradual rise in the sea-level. The dune
barrier was breached repeatedly; the estuary of the Scheldt was split into several
channels, opening Antwerp to sea traffic; and islands proliferated. The salt water
rushed in to turn the northern lagoon into a broad sea bay, the Zuider Zee, which
cut Frisia in two. High tides were overrunning the tributaries of the main

channels, threatening the livelihood of the towns on their banks. This was the problem that inspired the construction of the dams.

Prior to the mid-thirteenth century, human habitation in the delta region had been limited to three types of location. There was a string of ancient towns on the edge of the mainland. Arnhem (Arenacum or 'Sandtown'), nearby Nijmegen (Noviomagum or 'New Market'), and Utrecht (Trajectum ad Rhenam or 'Rhine Ford') were all Roman foundations. Antwerp (Aen de Werpen or 'Anchorage') had grown up round the seventh-century church of St Amand on the banks of the Scheldt. There were a few isolated settlements on the sand-dunes, such as the abbey of Middleburg on Walcheren dating from 1120, or the hunting-lodge recently built at s'Gravenhaage or 'Count's Hedge' in 1242. A number of fishing villages had found a precarious foothold in the lee of the dunes. Several of these had reached the status of a formal chartered city—Dordrecht (1220), Haarlem (1245), Delft (1246), and Alkmaar (1254). But none of them contained a fraction of the teeming population of the great textile cities of neighbouring Flanders. For centuries, the bishop of Utrecht exercised the main religious and secular authority. The delta ports had long served as staging posts on the costal trade.

Land reclamation was an ancient and improving art. Holland's characteristic *terpen* or artificial 'mounds', on which houses could be safely built above flood level, dated from time immemorial. They had been mentioned by Pliny. The earliest dikes of the *zeewering* or 'sea-defences' dated from the eighth or ninth century. River dikes began to spread after the perfection of the sluice-gate in the eleventh century. The construction of polders or enclosed 'stake fields' depended on a sophisticated system of drainage which was not mastered until *c.*1150. The dikes had to be built, with back-breaking labour, round lines of stakes driven deep into the soft ground, then filled with rubble and stones and planted with anchor grass. Once enclosed, the field had to be repeatedly flooded with fresh water over ten or fifteen years and repeatedly drained to disperse the salt. Only then could the rich alluvial soil begin to repay the efforts. But its fertility was proverbial: as well as the meat, wool, and leather of sheep and cattle that grazed on the sea-turf pastures, it provided both the life-support system for dense colonization and an abundance of produce for export to the neighbouring towns.

In the thirteenth century the polderization of Holland was in its infancy: it could only nibble at the very edge of the marshes. Before the introduction of wind-driven water-balers, there was no efficient means of draining large enclosures. Immense damage was to be done by the terrible St Elizabeth flood of 1421, which drowned 72 villages and 10,000 people and negated the progress of two centuries. The greater part of the land below sea-level requiring permanent drainage could not be touched until the invention *c.*1550 of windmills with rotating turrets, which could pump non-stop, irrespective of wind direction. No schedule for reclaiming the whole of Holland existed before the Land Reclamation Act of 1918. Another catastrophic flood was needed in 1953 before the grand Delta Plan (1957–86) was brought in to regulate all the rivers and fill the channels to the sea. Eight hundred years of dogged struggle against the elements cannot have failed to leave its mark on the people involved. Some historians have been tempted to see it as the determinant factor in the Dutch character.

The building of the dams marked a special stage in this long history. It launched a system of inland waterways whose operation could be controlled by the keepers of the sluices. Since seagoing ships could not easily pass the narrow locks, entrepôts sprang up round the dams, where shipping could exchange cargoes with those of smaller river barges. Schiedam-Rotterdam and Amsterdam both grew from the junction of the sea trade and the river trade. They would not grow to pre-eminence, however, without a whole series of extraneous developments which resulted in the demise of their principal competitors. Foremost among these, and at a much later date, was the wholly arbitrary ruin of Antwerp, effected through the forcible closure of the Scheldt 1648–1863. (See p. 567.)

Holland's strategic location on the western frontier of the Empire ensured a high degree of political involvement. It had once formed the northern segment of the middle kingdom of 'Lotharingia'. It spent a dozen years in the early tenth century in the sphere of West Francia, before passing definitively into the eastern, imperial sphere in 925. For the next 300 years, as part of the 'Duchy of Lower Lorraine', it was drawn into the endless rivalries of the feudal princes and their manœuvrings between the Empire and the rising kingdom of France.

The counts of Holland traced their pedigree to Dirk I (Dietrich, Thierri, or Theodoric), the descendant of Vikings who had established a base in the delta in the ninth century. Dirk I had been granted lands near Haarlem in 922, in a district then called Kennemerland, where he founded the Benedictine monastery of Egmont. The family's fortunes were assured after 1018 when Count Dirk III, having set up unauthorized tolls on the lower Rhine, repulsed the Duke of Lorraine in a famous battle on the dikes. Dirk III first used the name of Holland in his title. Thereafter, secure in their castle at Haarlem, the counts engaged in ceaseless feudal strife. Holland was one of a dozen counties whose interests straddled the imperial frontier. Neither the Emperor nor the king of France could exert a permanent influence, except by proxy through the shifting combinations of their vassals. For practical purposes the feudal lords of the ill-defined Low Countries, the *Nederlanden*, which stretched from the Rhineland to Picardy, fought it out among themselves. By doing so, they were gradually creating a region with a separate identity and with a destiny that was neither German nor French.

Within this circle, Holland must be counted one of the lesser lights. The mighty bishops of Utrecht and Liège, the dukes of Lorraine and Brabant, and the neighbouring county of Flanders were all much more substantial. Holland's successful contest with Flanders over the control of the islands of Zeeland had run for centuries until the Peace of Brussels in 1253. Her subjugation of the fierce inhabitants of Frisia or Friesland, who remained pagan until Charlemagne's time, had been concluded more by the inundations of the sea than by successful conquest. Together with the excess population of the crowded Flemish cities, distressed Frieslanders supplied one of the largest contingents of emigrants who were colonizing the lands of Germany's eastern marches.

None the less, the counts of Holland were men of considerable political sub-stance. William I (r. 1205–22) fought at Bouvines on the imperial side and was taken prisoner by the French. Like his forebear, who had taken Lisbon from the Saracens, he was a devoted crusader. He died in Egypt after participating in the siege of Damietta. William II (r. 1234–56) aspired to the supreme imperial digni-ty. Succeeding as a minor, he was raised a son of the Church by his guardian, the Bishop of Utrecht, and found himself propelled into the higher realms of Pope Innocent IV's attempts to depose the Hohenstaufen. (See p. 353.) In 1247 he was crowned at Aachen under ecclesiastical sponsorship as King, or anti-King, of the Romans. Married to a Guelph duchess, and allied to the powerful confederation of Rhineland cities, he briefly won the upper hand in Germany's internecine pol-itics. In January 1256 he went home to Holland to deal with a local problem in Frisia before proceeding to his coronation as Emperor in Rome. A crack in the ice, through which armoured horse and armoured rider sank on impact, put an end to a promising career. But for the accident, the Hollander would probably have become Holy Roman Emperor.

Floris V (r. 1256–96), the current Count and the grandson of William II, was to be the penultimate incumbent of Holland's first dynasty. He was the ruler who finally put an end to the Frisian troubles, and who won the acclaim of his lowli-est subjects. Faced by an insurrection of peasants, who joined forces with the mob of Utrecht, he undertook to curb the arbitrary rule of his bailiffs and to introduce a code of written laws. He was remembered in legend as *der keerlen God*, 'the Peasant's God'. For many years he was to enjoy a close alliance with Edward I of England, to whose court he sent his son and heir to be educated and married. This was Count Floris, the hero of Holland's 'Rhyming Chronicle', the *Rijmkronik van Melis Stoke*:

> Tgraefscap ende dat jonghe kynt
> Daer wonder of ghesciede sint.

(So ended the countship of the young man [who] was the wonder of history.)[45]

Aleida van Henegouven was the aunt and guardian of the young Floris V. As Regent of Holland during the Count's minority, she was one of several powerful women who held the reins of state in the Netherlands. Of these, the most prom-inent was her neighbour, the extraordinary Countess Margaret of Flanders. Known as Zwarte Griet or 'Black Meg', Countess Margaret (d. 1280) was caught up in all the feudal fortunes and misfortunes that one could imagine. She was the younger daughter of Count Baldwin IX, the leader of the Fourth Crusade, who took over the Latin Empire of the East. Like her sister Joanna she had been born in Constantinople, whence she had been brought home after her father's death and, together with Joanna, made a pawn of the politics of Innocent III. As a child, she watched her sister married off to Fernando of Portugal, nephew of the King of France, whilst she herself was given as a child bride to Bouchard d'Avesnes, Lord of Hainault. After the battle of Bouvines, which sent Fernando to the dun-geons of the Louvre, she saw her sister married for a second time to Thomas of

Savoy, whilst she herself, on the Pope's insistence, was divorced and remarried to a French knight, Guy de Dampierre. By the time in 1244 that she succeeded Joanna as Countess both of Hainault and of Flanders, she was mother of five sons by two marriages, and already one of the prime survivors of her day. She could not prevent her two eldest sons fighting over her inheritance and was obliged to accept a famous mediation of St Louis, who awarded Hainault to Jean d'Avesnes and Flanders to Guillaume de Dampierre. She would outlive them all.

Flanders, which was torn by the rivalry of Bruges and Ghent, was none the less the richest prize in Netherlands politics. Its fate could not be a matter of indifference to Holland. In the past the counts of Flanders had balanced between the Empire and France and had accepted fiefs from both sides, creating groups of territories known as *Kroon-Vlaanderen* and *Rijks-Vlaanderen*. Since Bouvines, however, French influence had been rising steeply, and would lead to a full-scale French occupation. In 1265 the struggle between Pope and Emperor was fast approaching its nadir. The Papacy had blocked the cause of the Hohenstaufen after Frederick II's death; and the interregnum in the Empire, which Count William's accident left unresolved, was sinking into ever deeper complications. 1257 had brought a double election: one meeting of the imperial Electors produced a decision in favour of Richard, Earl of Cornwall, the younger brother of Henry III of England, a second meeting decided for Alfonso, King of Castile. In contrast to Alfonso, who stayed at home in Toledo, Earl Richard did proceed to his coronation as King of the Romans. But neither of the rival candidates could exercise any authority over Germany as a whole.

Richard of Cornwall (1209–72) was one of the wealthiest and best-connected men of his age.[46] His possession of the Cornish stannaries was worth a second earldom, whilst his management of the Mint and of England's reformed coinage brought him a fabulous cash income. Through his financial adviser, Abraham of Berkhamsted, he was able to make loans to kings and cardinals; and he had no difficulty in finding the 28,000 marks which greased the machinery of his German election. Lord of Corfe, and of Wallingford and Berkhamsted, he had dabbled with the baronial opposition in England, and was known as one of the very few barons who actually spoke English. As titular Count of Poitou, he held strong interests in Gascony, where he had served as royal governor. He had led a Crusade to Acre, but had used the expedition as an occasion for making the personal acquaintance of his two brothers-in-law, first of St Louis in Paris and then of Frederick II in Sicily. He had good relations with the Low Countries, whence Floris V had hastened to London to pay him homage in person. He was due to take as his third wife, after Isabella Marshal and Sanchia of Provence, Beatrice Countess of Falkenburg in Brabant.

For most of 1265, however, Earl Richard's fortunes were at a low ebb. Three visits to Germany had given him no benefit. What is more, having been caught up in his brother's baronial war and captured by de Montfort's men, he was now a prisoner in Kenilworth Castle. His inglorious adventures after the Battle of Lewes, where he hid in a windmill, gave birth to one of England's earliest political satires:

> The King of Alemaigne wende do ful wel
> He saisede the mulne for a castel,
> With hare sharpe swerds he grounde the stel
> He wende that the sayles were mangonel to helpe Wyndesor.
> Richard, thah thou be ever trichard
> trichen shalt thou never more.[47]

At that juncture, the royal party was well and truly hated in England. Simon de Montfort, the *protector gentis Angliae*, was seen as a popular champion against oppression:

> Il est apelé de Montfort,
> Il est el mond et si est fort
> Si ad grant chevalerie.
> Ce voir, et je m'acort,
> Il eime droit, et hete le tort.
> Si avera la mesterie.[48]

(He is called de Montfort / He is our protector (*mund*) and is so strong (*fort*) / And has such great chivalry. / Look here, I quite agree, / He loves right and hates wrong. / Thus he will have the mastery.)

When Simon was killed at Evesham on 4 August 1265, his companions in the emplacement on Green Hill died with him to a man; he was mourned as a saint and a martyr.

That year also saw a papal election. Clement IV was a Frenchman who, as Guy Foulques, had once had a wife and children and had served as legal consultant to St Louis. Rome and parts of northern Italy were still so sympathetic to the Hohenstaufen that Clement, who had been away on legation to England, was obliged to travel home disguised as a monk and to take up residence in Perugia. From there he arranged for Charles of Anjou to be invested with the kingdom of Sicily and Naples, and for finance to be found for the brutal campaigns that were to put an end first to the Emperor's bastard son, Manfred, and then to Manfred's nephew, the young Conradin. From Perugia, he sent a bull to the Abbey of Egmont in Holland confirming its ancient rights and immunities.[49]

Like the Civil War in England, the imperial interregnum in Germany reduced the country to chaos:

Every floodgate of anarchy was opened; prelates and barons extended their domains by war; robber-knights infested the roads and the rivers; the misery of the weak, the tyranny and violence of the strong were such as had not been seen for centuries . . . The Roman Empire ought now to have been suffered to expire.[50]

Less traditional historians do not see the Empire's distress quite so drastically. The absence of an Emperor gave the signal for the rise of several regional and city states, which were destined to play a prominent role in European history. The Netherlands, among others, prospered in the shadow of the Empire's weakness.

Holland, however, was the main focus neither of politics of the Netherlands nor of the Dutch language. Various forms of proto-Middle Dutch were spoken right through the Low Countries as far west as Kortrijk (Courtrai) and Rijsel (Lille). French was dominant in Hainault, Liège, and Namur and in the speech of the nobility in general. Low German overlapped on the eastern borders in Guelders. But the greatest pool of Dutch-speakers was undoubtedly contained in the cities of Flanders. Dialectical nuances between *Vlaams* and *Hollandisch* were not marked. Holland itself was still engaged in assimilating Frisian, Frankish, and Saxon elements. Frisian in particular, which was the closest of the Germanic idioms to English, was still strong in north Holland and the islands. The establishment of Holland as the home of standard Dutch, or *Nederlands*, was the work of a much later age.

Dutch literature, too, was largely written in Flanders. Thirteenth-century Holland did produce a number of valuable texts, including the Egmont Chronicle and an animal fantasy *Van den Vos Reinarde* (*c*.1270), by a certain Willem. But the leading names, such as Jacob van Maerlent (*c*.1235–71), author of *Alexander's Feasts* (1258) and born at Bruges, were Flemings.

Foreign trade flowed as yet quite feebly. Dordrecht, where a castle had been built to owerawe ships plying between the Rhineland and the North Sea, was the only port of substance. It had contacts with England, and hopes of drawing the lucrative English staple from the more prosperous Flemish ports along the coast. There were no regular links with the Baltic, or with Russia.[51] Social conditions in Holland did not conform to the standard structures of the 'age of feudalism'. Feudal institutions, in fact, were weak. Serfdom was rare beyond the estates of the Church, and settlements of free peasants and independent fisherfolk were common. The nobles, though well integrated into the practices and mores of knighthood and landownership, were not subordinated in any systematic way to feudal superiors. The cities, though small, could look to the example of the nearby Rhineland, and were set to play a preponderant role. Religious life in Holland was also somewhat untypical. The bishop of Utrecht was losing much of his former power, and did not exercise the same degree of secular and legal authority that flourished in the neighbouring diocese of Liège. Despite a number of new foundations, neither the friars nor the new monastic orders had impressed their presence very strongly. Frisia was a notorious refuge of pagan survivals; rebellious mystic sects were an established fact.

Any description of Holland's early history belies the popular misconception that Europe's later nations must already have existed in embryo in the medieval period. The thirteenth century marks the mid-point of the span which separates our contemporary age from the so-called 'Birth of Europe' amidst the ruins of the Classical World. One might have expected that the national communities, which came to dominate the end of the story, would at least be discernible, albeit in a half-formed stage of development. Yet this was not so. In the case of the Low Countries, familiar terms such as 'Holland', 'Dutch', and 'Netherlands' all possessed different connotations from those which they later acquired. The modern myth about the permanent union of a 'nation' and its 'soil' was plainly irrelevant.

In the thirteenth century Holland was not the core of a developing Dutch nation. Indeed, much of the soil which 300 and 400 years later would form the central territorial base of Dutch national consciousness had not yet been deposited.

Most of Europe in 1265 displayed the same lack of recognizable national communities. In the middle of the Christian *Reconquista*, the Iberian states of Portugal, Castile, and Aragon had little awareness of a common Spain. In the year of Dante's birth, the defeat of the Hohenstaufen was putting an end to the dream of a united Italy. In the midst of the Mongol invasions and the 'age of fragmentation', a united Poland was no more than a memory. There was no longer any Rus', let alone a sense of Russia. A kingdom of England did exist, on the ruins of the Plantagenet empire; but it still had stronger connections with the Continent, in Gascony and Aquitaine, than with Wales or Ireland. Its French-speaking Anglo-Norman aristocracy did not yet share a common culture with the English people, and the baronial opposition was led by Continental adventurers like de Montfort. There was no concept of Britishness whatsoever. The kingdom of Scotland was still disputing its territory with the Norwegians, who had just invaded the northern isles. Under St Louis, the kingdom of France now stretched from the Channel to the Mediterranean. But it was an amalgam of the most diverse elements that would have to disintegrate before they could be reconstituted for a second time as a more cohesive whole. As the interregnum showed, the German Empire had collapsed in all but name. It was hopelessly rent by the competing interests of its German and its Italian territories on either side of the Alps. There was no such country as Switzerland; and the Habsburgs were yet to move to Austria. The Prussia of the Teutonic Knights was in the earliest decades of its career; but it bore no resemblance to the later Prussia of the Hohenzollerns (who in 1265 were still ensconced in their native castle in Swabia). In Scandinavia, Norway had broken away from Danish control; but the break was not due to last. The Swedes, like the Lithuanians, were embroiled in multinational conquests in the East. Bohemia under Ottokar II (r. 1253–78) was at the pinnacle of its glory, having just annexed Austria and Styria. Hungary was in a state of collapse, following the two Mongol raids, and was facing the end of the native Árpád dynasty. The Byzantine Empire, Europe's oldest polity, had recovered Constantinople four years before, and had driven out the Latin usurpers to their toeholds in Greece. None of these entities was destined to survive into modern times.

It would be problematical, therefore, to talk of national states at any point in the thirteenth century. But if national identities were judged to be developing effectively in any place at the time, it could only have been in some of the small countries who had successfully segregated themselves from their neighbours. Portugal was a candidate for this, as was Denmark, and, in the Balkans, Serbia and Bulgaria. Both Serbia and Bulgaria had re-established their independence from Byzantium in the 1180s. More importantly, they both created their own national Orthodox Churches with their own patriarchs—Bulgaria in 1235, Serbia in 1346. This step gave them a powerful instrument for forging a separate identity, for educating a national élite, for political publicity, and for the sanctification of national institutions. It was a step which none of the countries of Latin Christendom could take until the Reformation, and which Muscovite Russia did not take until 1589. It strengthened the bonds of these two Slav peoples whose cohesion would be tested through 500 years of Ottoman rule.

For Europe was living out its last few decades before the Ottomans, and the second great Muslim advance. The silk road to the East was still open. Christian travellers were reporting on their journeys to Tartary. In the year that a 'Venice of the North' was founded on the Amstel, Marco Polo set out from the Rialto for China.

Dutch historians, like everyone else, have had to contend with the habit of reading history backwards. When national histories were first formulated in the nineteenth century, the Low Countries had just been definitively divided into the kingdoms of Belgium and Holland; and it was accepted form to maintain that separate Flemish and Dutch communities had been present from the earliest times. Great pains were taken to show that the medieval churches of Sluis, for example, on one side of the Scheldt, were pearls of the Hollandish style, while the churches of Damme on the other bank were treasures of the Flemish heritage. It took a great leap of the imagination for historians to demonstrate that separate Dutch and Belgian traditions did not pre-date the Dutch Revolt of 1566–1648 (see pp. 534–9), which put an arbitrary stop on the previous growth of a shared Netherlands consciousness. It was more difficult to suggest in the early chapters of the story that little sense of a common identity existed, and still more that Holland might not have lain at the heart of Dutchness. There were many more twists in the tale, under Burgundian and Habsburg rule, and many fundamental shifts in economic and demographic patterns, before the 'Land of the Dams' could assume its modern form and function. After all, it was not until 1593 that Carolus Clusius (1526–1609), Professor of Medicine at Leiden, received the very first tulip bulbs from Turkey and planted them in the fertile flowerfields between Leiden and Haarlem.

In all these matters of nationality, the key element is consciousness. As one Dutch historian explained, nationality can be observed neither in the blood, nor in the soil, nor even on the tongue:

Nationality exists in the minds of men, . . . its only conceivable habitat . . . Outside men's minds there can be no nationality, because nationality is a manner of looking at oneself not an entity *an sich.* Common sense is able to detect it, and the only human discipline that can describe and analyse it is psychology . . . This awareness, this sense of nationality, this national sentiment, is more than a characteristic of the nation. It is nationhood itself.[52]

In the thirteenth century, in the midst of the feudal strife, it is very doubtful whether the local patriotism of Holland could have started to merge into any sense of general solidarity with the Low Countries as a whole. Three hundred years before the stirring and formative experiences of the Dutch Revolt, it is certain that the half-formed northern provinces, such as Holland, could not have possessed much common consciousness *vis-à-vis* the southern provinces. One can only conclude that the Dutch nation did not then exist. This is an object lesson for the whole of medieval Europe.

After which one may be tempted to enquire as to where, if not in nations, the thirteenth-century consciousness actually resided. The only answer must be 'there was what there was'. Medieval Europeans were conscious of belonging to their native village or town, and to a group possessing a local language whose members could communicate without recourse to Latin or Greek. They were aware of belonging to a body of men and women who acknowledged the same feudal lord; to a social estate, which shared the same privileges; above all, to the great corporation of Christendom. Beyond that, as the greatest son of the 1260s would soon describe, one could only wait for Death and the Day of Judgement. Then at last one could learn to which of the really important social groups one belonged—to the passengers on the ferry of the Damned, to the company of penitents sailing for Purgatory, or perhaps to the choirs of Paradise.

VI

PESTIS

Christendom in Crisis, c.1250–1493

THERE is a sense of fatalism about life in the later Middle Ages. People knew that Christendom was sick; they knew that the ideals of the Gospel of Love were far removed from prevailing reality; but they had little idea of how to cure it. The senior Christian state, the Byzantine Empire, was reduced to a pathetic rump. The Holy Roman Empire could not control its own mighty subjects, let alone exercise leadership over others. The Papacy was falling into the quagmire of political dependence. Feudal particularism reached the point where every city, every princeling, had to fight incessantly for survival. The world was ruled by brigandage, superstition, and the plague. When the Black Death struck, the wrath of God was clearly striking at Christendom's sins. 'According to a popular belief, no-one since the beginning of the great Western Schism had entered Paradise.'[1]

At the same time, 'the violent tenor' of medieval life, its 'vehement pathos', had so intensified the pains and pleasures of living that modern sensibility is said to be barely capable of grasping them. 'The violent contrasts and impressive forms lent a tone of excitement and passion to everyday life, and tended to produce that perpetual oscillation between despair and distracted joy, between cruelty and pious tenderness, which characterises the Middle Ages.'[2]

Johan Huizinga, whose studies have had a powerful impact on perceptions of the period, was talking not only of insecurity in face of constant calamities but also of the 'proud or cruel publicity' which surrounded almost all persons and events—the lepers with rattles, the beggars in churches, the public executions, the hellfire sermons, the processions, the dwarves and magicians, the pageantry, the stark colours of heraldry, the steeple bells and the street-criers, the stench and the perfume:

When the massacre of the Armagnacs was in full swing . . . [in 1418] the Parisians founded a brotherhood of Saint Andrew in the church of Saint Eustache: every one, priest or layman, wore a wreath of red roses, so that the church was perfumed . . . as if washed with rose-water.[3]

Map 14.
Europe, c.1300

This 'extreme excitability of the medieval soul' may owe something to the Gothic enthusiasms of the later Romantics. But it is an essential element to be considered in the impossible task of recapturing the medieval past.

Yet the very brilliance of Huizinga's thesis invites caution. Like most Western historians, he directed his researches to one corner of Western Europe, in his case to France and the Netherlands; and there must be some reluctance to apply the generalizations to Christendom as a whole. More importantly, in portraying the spirit of the declining Middle Ages so vividly, there must be some danger of underplaying the seeds of change and regeneration which were also present. Renaissance scholars have no difficulty in tracing the origins of their subject to the early fourteenth century (see Chapter VII). It stands to reason that there was a very long period when the old coexisted with the new. Historians stress the one or the other according to the burden of their tale. Huizinga suggested that humanist forms did make a late appearance, but without the 'inspiration' of the Renaissance. And he ended with that favourite metaphor of all historians struggling with the rhythms of change: 'the tide is turning'.[4]

In the circumstances, it may be wise to resist the metaphor of the waning medieval twilight. It might be more accurate to think of the period in terms of a prolonged crisis for which contemporaries had no solution. There was no awareness of a dawn to come. In more senses than one, late medieval Europeans were children of the plague.

The Byzantine Empire, as reconstituted after the expulsion of the Latin Emperors, was a mere shadow of a shadow. On the European shore it held little more than the city of Constantinople and the adjacent province of Roumelia. In Asia Minor it held a few towns on the Black Sea, and most of the Aegean coastline. Elsewhere, its former provinces were in the hands of the independent kingdoms of Bulgaria and Serbia; of assorted Frankish princes, displaced crusaders, and Venetian governors; and in Anatolia, of the Turkish sultans of Iconium, the so-called empire of Trebizond, and the kingdom of Lesser Armenia. From 1261 to its eventual destruction in 1453, it was ruled by the dynasty of the Palaeologi, descendants of Michael VIII Palaeologus (1258–82), who had engineered the recapture of Constantinople during the absence of the Venetian fleet. Of this Empire, in its dotage, it has been written:

The Greeks gloried in the name of Romans: they clung to the forms of imperial government without its military power; they retained the Roman code without the systematic administration of justice, and prided themselves on the orthodoxy of a Church in which the clergy ... lived in a state of vassalage to the imperial Court. Such a society could only wither, though it might wither slowly.[5]

The desperate Palaeologi sought aid from all and sundry. To hold off Venice, they turned to the Genoans who at various times possessed Amastris, Pera, and Smyrna and the islands of Lesbos, Chios, and Samos. They allied with Aragon;

and on several occasions they tempted the Papacy with the prospect of ending the Schism. In the Epoch of Civil Wars, 1321–54, they briefly restored their rule as far as Epirus. Until 1382 an anti-emperor maintained his court at Mistra in the Morea. By that time John V (1341–91) had become both a catholic and a vassal of the Turks. In 1399 his successor, Manuel II (1391–1425), set off on a vain journey to raise support in Rome, Paris, and London. [MUSIKE]

The most sensational development of the era was the appearance of a new Turkish warrior tribe that was destined to supplant the Byzantines. The Osmanlis or Ottomans moved into the void left by the Mongols' defeat of the Seljuks. They took their name from Osman I (r. 1281–1326), son of their founder, Ertugrul, who had established an outpost in the Anatolian interior. From that base they raided far and wide, chipping away at the Byzantine frontier, launching fleets of pirates into the Aegean, and crossing over into the Balkans. They first entered Europe in 1308, when a band of Turkish mercenaries was imported by the Byzantines' own mercenary force, the Catalan Grand Company, which had rebelled against its imperial employers. In that year they took Ephesus; in 1326, Bursa—which became their first capital; in 1329, Nicaea; in 1337, Nicomedia. Osman's son, Orkhan (r. 1326–62), established a permanent bridgehead on the Dardanelles, and styled himself Sultan. His grandson, Murad I (r. 1362–89), having set up the second Ottoman capital in Adrianopolis (Edirne), dared to use the old Seljuk title 'Sultan-i-Rum' (Sultan of Rome). Sultan Bayezit (r. 1389–1403), though defeated by Tamerlane, conducted the main conquest of Asia Minor, overwhelming the Greek settlements with Muslim colonists, whilst attacking both the Peloponnese and Wallachia. On his death, Ottoman territory was forty times greater than a century earlier, and Constantinople was surrounded (see Appendix III, p. 1259).

During that century of conquest, the frontier between Christendom and Islam was remade. The Byzantines' former subjects, in Greece, Bulgaria, Serbia, and Bosnia, enjoyed a brief interval of liberty and confusion, before they too were subjugated by the invincible Turk. The Ottomans led a supreme nation of *ghazis*, 'warriors of Islam'—and they knew it. In the old mosque at Bursa, an inscription to Orkhan runs: 'To the Sultan, son of the Sultan of the Ghazis, Ghazi son of Ghazi, Margrave of the horizons, hero of the world.'[6]

Medieval Greece, in the interval between the Latin and the Ottoman conquests, was split into local principalities. The despotate of Epirus, the duchy of Athens, the southern principality of Achaea, and the island duchy of Naxos all passed a couple of centuries in the sun. Their commercial interests were controlled by the Italian cities; their rulers were Latins; the populace Orthodox. [ROMANY]

Bulgaria, too, moved away from the Byzantine orbit. The second Bulgarian empire, which had emerged in the late twelfth century, was a dynamic, multinational realm. From his capital at Trnovo, Ivan Asen (r. 1186–1218), 'Tsar of the Bulgars and Greeks', spread his sway to Belgrade and Skopje. His successor, Ivan Asen II (r. 1218–41), took in Albania, Epirus, Macedonia, and Thrace. Two further dynasties were of Cuman origin. But on 28 June 1330 Tsar Michael Shishman was slain by the Serbians, who thereby established their hegemony. In the following

ROMANY

IN 1378 the Venetian governor of Nauplion in the Peloponnese confirmed privileges already granted to the local community of *atsingani*. It was the first documented record of Romany gypsies in Europe. In 1416 the city of Brasov (Kronstadt) in Transylvania made gifts of silver, grain, and poultry to one 'Emaus of Egypt and his 120 companions'. In 1418 the same group reached Hamburg. In August 1427 a band of some 100 travellers, presenting themselves as victims of persecution in Lower Egypt, were refused entry to Paris and lodged instead at St Denis. The anonymous chronicler of the *Journal d'un bourgeois de Paris* described them as swarthy, poorly dressed, the women with knotted shawls, the children with earrings. They were moved on when the Church authorities protested against their palmistry and fortune-telling.[1]

There is no doubt that the Romanies migrated to Europe from India, although their earlier movements can only be reconstructed from linguistic evidence. Romany is an Indo-European language akin to Hindi, and is spoken all along the trail through the Middle East to Europe. The fact that the European dialects of Romany contain a strong admixture of Slavonic and Greek words indicates a lengthy sojourn in the Balkans.

The long list of names given to Romanies reinforces popular confusion about their origins. The Greek *atsingani*, which gave rise to *gitans* (French), *zingari* (Italian), *gitanos* (Spanish), *zigeuner* (German), and *tsigan* (Russian), derives from the name of a medieval Manichean sect from Asia Minor, and is an obvious misattribution. 'Bohemians' and 'Egyptians'—hence *gyfti* (Greek), *gypsy* (English), and *faraoni* (Hungarian)—are also common. 'Romany' probably derives from their medieval attachment to the Byzantine Empire, rather than to Romania. They call themselves *Rom* (singular) or *Roma* (plural).

Attempts to regulate the presence of nomadic gypsies by law created a wide variety of practices. An English statute of 1596 carefully distinguished between gypsies and common vagabonds. [**PICARO**] A band of gypsies had been apprehended in Yorkshire, and some of them executed for necromancy. But the statute permitted law-abiding gypsies to travel, to pursue their tinker's trade, and to receive victuals in payment. Similar protection was extended in France in 1683. In Austria the statutes of 1761 sought to settle the gypsies in fixed abodes—but to no lasting effect. In Russia, Catherine II sought to protect gypsies by giving them the status of 'Crown slaves' which they had previously been assigned in Moldavia and Wallachia. But, like the Jews, they were forbidden to enter St Petersburg. In the Netherlands and several German states, a policy of total exclusion was pursued.

Throughout the nineteenth and twentieth centuries, European

Romanies have struggled to sustain their nomadic lifestyle, their special-ized trades, their language, and their music [**FLAMENCO**]. Their culture emphasizes the occult, their social organization the importance of extended families and tribes presided over by 'kings' and judges. Their communal activities are centred on annual gatherings which take place at regular venues. Saintes-Maries-de-la-Mer in Camargue, for example, is the scene of a Romany festival and pilgrimage which heads every May to the tomb of their patroness, Sara. According to legend, Sara was a com-panion of Mary Magdalen who saved a party of Christ's relatives and dis-ciples from persecution, and brought them as refugees to Provence.

During the Romantic era, Romanies attracted great artistic and literary attention. Hugo, Mérimée, and Borrow all wrote books on gypsy themes. Henri Murger's *Scènes de la vie de bohème* (1849) enjoyed huge popular suc-cess. Liszt wrote a learned treatise on Romany music, starting a vogue which influenced both the classical repertoire and café entertainment. Bizet's *Carmen* (1875), based on a story by Mérimée, and Puccini's *La Bohème* (1895), based on Murger's *Scènes*, are among the most enduring of operas.

Romanies have always been subject to harassment and to periodic vio-lence.[2] But the Nazis' wholesale genocide of gypsies, which mirrored their extermination of Jews, had no precedent. Communist regimes were gener-ally indifferent. The post-war democracies have attempted to combine regu-lation with humanitarian tolerance. But the stereotype of the rootless, alien gypsy constantly resurfaces, most recently in the ugly campaign in 1993 against asylum-seekers in Germany. It is perhaps inevitable that the conven-tionally settled population of Europe will always feel a mixture of phobia and fascination for a lifestyle which is so fundamentally different from their own:

> Come, let me read the oft-told tale again:
>   The story of that Oxford scholar poor,
> Of pregnant parts and quick inventive brain,
>   Who, tired of knocking at Preferment's door,
>   One summer morn forsook
> His friends, and went to learn the Gipsy-lore,
>   And roam'd the world with that wild brotherhood . . .[3]

decade the Ottomans began to ravish the valley of the Maritsa. By 1366 the last Bulgarian Tsar, Ivan Shishman III, was obliged to send his sister to the Sultan's harem and to declare himself an Ottoman vassal. Trnovo was razed. Bulgaria was starting its 500-year career as an Ottoman province.

Serbia suffered a similar fate. Pressed by the neighbouring kingdom of Hungary, where their south Slav relations had joined the Catholic fold, the Serbs balanced between their Roman and their Orthodox connections. The country was first united under Stefan I Nemanya (1114–1200), who had obliged Byzantium to concede his independence. Nemanya's youngest son, St Sava (1175–1235), a monk of Athos, had emancipated the Serbian Church from the Greek archbishop at Okhrid. He persuaded his brother, Stefan II, to accept a royal crown from the Pope. Medieval Serbia reached its apogee under the ferocious Stefan IV Dushan (1308–55). In 1346, when Dushan was crowned Tsar, Serbia controlled several former Bulgarian and Byzantine provinces in the south; a Serbian Patriarch ruled from Pec (Ipek); and an imperial *Zakonnik* or Codex regulated the administration. Dushan exercised suzerainty over the young Vlach principalities, and even made plans to conquer Constantinople. But Serbia was no match for the advancing Ottomans. On 15 June 1389, at Kosovo, on the 'Field of the Blackbirds', the Serbian host was humbled. The last Serbian king was slain and the Ottoman sultan treacherously murdered. Serbia joined Bulgaria as an Ottoman province. [**ZADRUGA**]

North of the Danube the Latin-speaking Vlachs, strengthened by migrants from the mountains of Transylvania, succeeded in creating independent principalities of their own. Henceforth Wallachia and Moldavia became the frontier posts of Christian rule in the Balkans. The plight of the Balkan Christians reawakened the crusading traditions of the West. In 1344 a naval league headed by Venice and the Hospitallers retook Smyrna from the Ottomans for a season. In 1365 Amadeus VI of Savoy briefly recaptured Gallipoli, and released the emperor imprisoned by the Bulgars. In 1396 a crusading army led by Sigismund of Hungary met disaster at Nikopolis on the Danube. In 1402 a garrison of crusaders under the French knight Boucicault manned the walls of Constantinople, awaiting the Sultan's imminent assault. Beyond the Black Sea, the Orthodox Christians of the former Rus' gradually eased the grip of the Tartar yoke. In this they were assisted by the two rising power-centres of the north-east—the Grand Duchy of Moscow and the Grand Duchy of Lithuania. [**NIKOPOLIS**]

The princes of Moscow grew from obscurity to prominence in the two centuries following the Mongol invasion. First, by a combination of valour and treachery, they established their supremacy over numerous Rurikid princelings in the surrounding region of Vladimir-Suzdal. The hereditary title of Grand Prince of Vladimir was theirs from 1364. Secondly, by currying favour with the Khan of the Golden Horde, they obtained the *yarlyk* to act as the Mongols' chief tribute-gatherers, accepting responsibility for the payments, and arrears, of all other princes. Ivan I (r. 1301–40), known as Kalita or 'the Money-Bag', spent more of his reign on the road to Sarai than he did in Moscow. Karl Marx wrote that he blended 'the characters of the Tartars' hangman, sycophant, and slave-in-chief'.[7] Thirdly, by lavishly patronizing the Orthodox Church they added an aura of religiosity to their political supremacy. In 1300 the Metropolitan Archbishop of Kiev moved to Vladimir, and from 1308 resided in Moscow. Monasteries were planted far and wide in the forest wilderness, forming new centres for commercial and territorial expansion. Despite the Mongol blockade, and a long river and sea journey of two months, close contact was maintained with the Patriarch of Constantinople. Muscovy was a patrimonial state *par excellence*, where the

ZADRUGA

ARTICLE 70 of the law code of Stefan Dushan, published *c.*1349–54, makes a clear reference to the existence of extended families and of joint patrilinear households. '*A father and son, or brothers, who live in the same house and share the same hearth*', it states, '*but who have separate food and property, should work like the other peasants.*' The Serbian Tsar was evidently trying to ensure that every peasant household could be taxed on the same basis.

The Article has been invoked, however, to justify the assumption that the *zadruga* or 'joint patrilinear household' has been the standard form of social organization among the Balkan Slavs since time immemorial. It is now commonplace for overenthusiastic scholars to discuss the role of the *zadruga* in Slavonic kinship patterns at all points between prehistory and contemporary Europe. Yet expert comment has recently exploded some of the grosser generalizations. It turns out that the term *zadruga* is an academic neologism first recorded in a Serbian dictionary in 1818. It has never been current in the speech of the people who are supposed to practise it. Moreover, it is not actually mentioned in the text of Stefan Dushan's law code. Although one may conclude from Article 70 that some form of joint household did exist in medieval Serbia, there is no reason to assume that the *zadruga* was the standard or prevalent form in all parts of the realm.

In modern times, the distribution of the *zadruga* across the Balkans is extremely patchy. It is common in the mountainous stock-breeding zone that runs from Bosnia and Hercegovina to Montenegro, Macedonia, and central Albania. It is frequently encountered in the Rhodopes and the Balkan Range. But it is not known on the Adriatic littoral or in most of Bulgaria. It is present in sectors of the old Military Frontier or *Krajina* settled by Serb immigrants to Croatia in the sixteenth century, and among the non-Slavic Vlachs. It is largely absent from Greece and Romania.

Most seriously, a cursory survey of recent scholarship on the subject, especially in the West, shows that the *zadruga* is employed for any number of contradictory purposes. Above all it is used, with very little foundation of fact or detailed research, to bolster spurious assertions either about the collectivist inclinations of all Slav peoples, or about the uniform structure of a (non-existent) pan-Slav society, or about the backwardness of the Balkans, the *Volksmuseum* of Europe. In short, it is in real danger of becoming a sort of racial myth, a worthy partner to that other figment of the Western imagination, 'the Slav soul'.[1]

NIKOPOLIS

O N the evening of 25 September 1396 a great French champion, the Sire de Coucy, was dragged before the victorious Sultan Bajazet on the field of Nikopolis. Together with some other rich crusaders, including Jean de Nevers, the future Duke of Burgundy, who were being held for ransom, he watched as the scimitars of the Sultan's guards decapitated several thousand lesser Christian captives. (The crusaders had recently treated their Muslim captives likewise.) He was marched in chains over the 350 miles to Gallipoli, then taken to Bursa in Asia, where he wrote his last will and died, heirless.

Nikopolis is forever associated with this last great catastrophe of the crusading movement. The principal fortress of Bulgaria, it commanded the lower Danube; and its capture by the Ottomans had provoked the expedition raised by the King of Hungary. An army of Latin knights had assembled at Buda to avenge the Sultan's boast that he would 'feed his horse oats on the altar of St Peter's'. They brought wine and silks, but no catapults. So the siege of Nikopolis failed; and they had to face the Ottomans in the open. A premature assault by the French, as at Crécy, was exploited by the cavalry of the Sultan's Serbian allies: and the main body of crusaders was encircled. Sigismund of Hungary escaped, and a Polish knight famously swam the Danube in full armour. But most of the survivors were captured. Their defeat left Bulgaria in Muslim hands for 500 years, ended the Latin challenge in the East, and presaged the fall of Constantinople.

Enguerrand de Coucy VII (1340–97), Count of Soissons, has been taken as a man whose biography encapsulates the 'crisis of Christendom'. Lord of the largest castle in Europe, at Coucy in Picardy, and a patron both of Froissart and Chaucer, he was personally involved in almost all the catastrophes of a catastrophic age. His father was probably killed at Crécy. His mother, a Habsburg, died of the Black Death. After Poitiers he spent five years as a hostage in England, where he married the King's daughter. He fought alongside Hawkswood, the *condottiere*, in Savoy, against the 'Free Companies' which infested France, and in the Swiss campaign of 1375–6. He was the first ashore at Tunis (1390). He loyally served a rotten French monarchy in all the contortions of imperial rivalry and the papal schism. When Hungarian envoys arrived in Paris, calling for a crusade 'in the name of kinship and the love of God', he eagerly volunteered.[1]

prince's subjects and their possessions could be treated with total disregard. The hold over the resources of the apanage princedoms inexorably strengthened Muscovite hegemony. In 1327 Ivan Kalita helped the Mongols to suppress a rebellion by his chief rival, the city of Tver' on the Volga. Yet in 1380–2 Prince Dmitri Donskoy (r. 1350–89) challenged the military might of the Mongols for the first time. At Kulikovo, on 8 September 1380, he won a famous victory over the invincible horde, only to see Moscow burned in revenge two years later. In 1408 Dmitri's son, Vasili I (r. 1389–1425), was tempted to withhold the tribute but, with Moscow besieged, relented. The Muscovites were waxing powerful, but were still vassals.

It was in this period that the Muscovites began to call their state by the Greek name for Rus', *Rossiya* (Russia), and to call themselves Russians. These Muscovite-Russians had never ruled over Kiev; but the disability did not prevent them from regarding Moscow as the sole legitimate heir of the Kievan succession. It was their variant of east Slav speech that provided the roots of the modern Russian language. Their tendentious version of history, which persisted in confusing Muscovy-Russia with the whole of Rus', was not accepted by those other east Slavs who remained beyond Moscow's rule for centuries to come.

The Lithuanians were the last pagans of Europe. Secure in their remote Baltic forests, they escaped both the initial advance of the Teutonic Knights and the Mongol conquest. They were ruled by Baltic warrior princes who recognized a historic opportunity in the disintegration of the Kievan state. Hence, at the same time that Moscow was consolidating the northern and eastern remnants of Rus', Lithuania began its takeover of the western and southern remnants. Three great leaders stand out in a state-building exercise that, in the period, outstripped even the Muscovite effort—Grand Duke Gediminas (*c.*1275–1341), his son Algirdas (r. 1345–77), and Jogaila (r. 1377–1434), who launched the historic union with Poland. A century of raiding, castle-building, and tribute-gathering brought spectacular results throughout the vast Dnieper basin. White Ruthenia (now Belarus') was absorbed whole. Red Ruthenia (or Galicia) was carved up in 1349 with the Poles. Kiev was taken in 1362, after Algirdas had broken the Mongol grip at the Battle of the Blue Water in the Dnieper bend. In 1375 he took Polotsk. The Lithuanians were not checked until in 1399 they were defeated by the Tartars in the far south, on the River Vorksla. By that time Lithuania stretched virtually 'from sea to shining sea', from the Baltic to the Black Sea approaches. From 1386 its ruling circles were converted to Roman Catholicism (see p. 430), and were increasingly polonized. But the mass of the population, in White Ruthenia and Ukraine, were Orthodox Slavs. They called themselves *rusini* or 'Ruthenes'; and it is the Ruthenian variants of east Slav speech from the Grand Duchy of Lithuania that provided the roots of the modern Byelorussian and Ukrainian languages. Until 1700 the official language of the Grand Duchy, which was largely administered by literate Christian Slavs, was not Lithuanian but Ruthenian.

At first sight the Orthodox Church was necessarily more passive than its Catholic counterpart. Its head, the Patriarch of Constantinople, was closely bound to the fate of the Byzantine Empire. Yet its role was not trivial. It was the stubborn determination of the Orthodox Church in the East, where Christendom was under attack from Mongols and Turks, which sowed the seeds of modern nationhood among the Serbs, Bulgars, and Romanians of the Balkans, among the Russians of Muscovy, and among the Ruthenes of Lithuania.

At the other end of the Peninsula, in Spain, the *Reconquista* was virtually suspended. (See Appendix III, p. 1241.) After 1248 the Moorish armies had retreated to the Sierra Nevada, in whose shadow the emirate of Granada could flourish for two centuries more. Thenceforth it was the only Muslim-ruled state in Iberia. Beyond its borders local Muslim leaders, notably Ibn-Hud, had overthrown their African Moorish overlords and had established themselves in 'Al-Andaluz' as dependents of Castile. The result was a broad frontier region, whose countryside was dominated by the estates of the military orders and whose towns were swelled by Muslim and Jewish migrants. The majority of the population were Spanish speakers, irrespective of their religion. The kingdom of Portugal, independent since 1179, controlled the Atlantic seaboard, where it conquered the Algarve in 1250. The kingdom of Navarre, which straddled the Basque districts of the northern Pyrenees, was subject from 1234 to French rulers, who maintained their independence until 1516.

The victorious kingdom of Leon and Castile, having swept from the northern to the southern coast, where it surrounded Granada on all sides, was left in a state of internal anarchy. The first race of *conquistadores* grew rich from the plunder of the south and from the establishment of great latifundia. The successors of Ferdinand III the Saint (r. 1217–52), who was eventually canonized for his part in the *Reconquista*, were plagued by disputed successions, by fractious nobles, by the vagaries of the *Cortes* or 'diets', and by the *hermandades* or 'armed leagues' of the cities. Alfonso X (r. 1252–84) competed unsuccessfully for the imperial crown in Germany. In 1340 at Salado, Alfonso XI (r. 1312–50) achieved the first Castilian victory over the Moors for almost a century, and crossed the Straits to Algeciras. Pedro the Cruel (r. 1350–69) deserved the epithet. Henry III (r. 1390–1406) combined a talent for administration with an alliance with the Lancastrian kings of England. But he died young; and Castile passed under the despotic rule of the Constable, and Master of the Order of St James, Alvaro de Luna. Thanks to the sturdy, African merino sheep which grazed on the uplands of the *Meseta* or Plateau, Castile became Europe's principal exporter of wool, which was carried from Bilbao and Santander to Flanders.

The kingdom of Aragon, in contrast, turned to the sea. (See Appendix III, p. 1251.) Forged from the union of the Pyrenean district of Aragon with Catalonia and Valencia, it had gained an early foothold on the coast. James I the Conqueror (r. 1213–76) occupied Minorca and Majorca in the Moorish war, where he magnanimously gave Murcia to Castile. Peter III (r. 1276–85) was given the throne of Sicily in 1282 following the expulsion of the French. Sardinia was taken from the Genoese in 1326. Alfonso V (r. 1416–58) took southern Italy from the Angevins in

1442. Aragon's domination of the western Mediterranean created an inimitable maritime community, based on Barcelona, Palermo, and Naples, where Catalan was the lingua franca and where the nobles enjoyed a regime of remarkable liberality. Disputes between the monarchs and their subjects were referred to the Justiciar of the Cortes, usually a lowly knight who was raised by his peers to the office of supreme arbiter. In 1287, by the Privilege of Union, the nobles were empowered to take up arms against any king who infringed their rights—a liberty unequalled except in Poland. The result was a nation of unusual solidarity. 'It is as hard to divide the nobles of Aragon', said Ferdinand V (r. 1479–1516), 'as it is to unite the nobles of Castile.' In the fifteenth century Aragon controlled both the largest city in Iberia—Barcelona—and the largest city in Europe—Naples.

The cultural synthesis of medieval Spain was something quite inimitable. In the five kingdoms, three main religions were practised: Christianity, Islam, and Judaism; and six main languages were spoken: Castilian, Gallego, Catalan, Portuguese, Arab, and Basque. The Christian population, dominated by the ranchers and soldiers of the central Plateau, was generally much rougher than the more urbanized and civilized Moors of the fertile south. But they were emerging from centuries of isolation, and were now in full commercial and intellectual contact with the rest of Christendom. The Spanish Jews, who had gained a foothold through the tolerance of Muslim rulers, spread throughout the Peninsula and played a prominent part in administration, medicine, learning, trade, and finance. They figured in many roles. The philosopher Maimonides of Cordoba (1135–1204), who had emigrated to Egypt, was long remembered as author of the *Guide to the Perplexed*. Samuel Halevi (d. 1361), chief tax-collector of Pedro the Cruel, who tortured him to death, was a patron of the arts. The convert Pablo de Santa María (Solomon Halevi, b. 1350) served as diplomat, Bishop of Burgos, and notorious antisemite. Earlier, disputations between the religions were popular. Later, and particularly in 1348–51 and 1391, ugly pogroms occurred. In the fifteenth century a large caste of *conversos* or New Christians—the Lunas, Guzmáns, Mendozas, Enríquez—filled the highest offices of Church and State. Nothing conveys the symbiosis more eloquently than Spanish architecture, an exquisite blend of Mediterranean romanesque, Catholic Gothic, and oriental ornament.[8] [CABALA]

In the heart of the Catholic world, politics still revolved round the triangle of rivalries between the Empire, the Papacy, and the kingdom of France. In the course of the fourteenth century, each of the three main parties was subject to such tremendous local stresses that no international victor emerged. Following the interregnum of 1254–73, the Emperors were so absorbed by the internecine affairs of Germany that Italy was abandoned. The Papacy, overwhelmed by the wars of Italy, took refuge in the Midi for nearly seventy years before falling into schism. The kingdom of France, hopelessly overrun by the Hundred Years War against England, did not recover until the middle of the fifteenth century. By 1410, when there were three emperors, three popes, and two kings of France, the leaders of Catholic Christendom were in despair. Such was the chaos in the centre that opportunities arose for the creation of powerful new states. Apart from Aragon, the newcomers were Switzerland, Burgundy, and Poland-Lithuania.

The Holy Roman Empire was permanently weakened by the fall of the Hohenstaufen. The interregnum, which met its nadir with the execution of Conradin at Naples, ushered in decades of chaos (see p. 353). Worse still, there was little prospect that imperial power could be reasserted. By gambling so heavily on their Italian ambitions, the Hohenstaufen had condemned their successors to a position of perpetual subservience in Germany. With the imperial coffers empty, and the imperial domain dispersed, it could hardly have been otherwise. As a result the German princes perpetuated their privileges, and the elective constitution of the Empire became ossified. In 1338 the Electoral College rejected papal claims to confirm Emperors; and in the Golden Bull of 1356 the mechanics of election were fixed for the duration. Henceforth Frankfurt-am-Main was to be the site of imperial elections. A majority of votes among seven named Electors was to be decisive. The seven Electors were to be the archbishops of Mainz, Cologne, and Trier and the princes of Bohemia, the Rhine Palatinate, Saxony, and Brandenburg.* The Emperor Charles IV, who formulated the Golden Bull, was bowing to reality. In Bryce's famous pronouncement, 'He legalised anarchy and called it a constitution.'9

From 1273 onwards the enfeebled Empire struggled to recover. Of the nine emperors from Rudolf von Habsburg (r. 1273–91) to Sigismund of Luxemburg (r. 1410–37), only three attained the dignity of a full imperial coronation. Two— Adolf von Nassau in 1298 and Wenzel of Luxemburg in 1400—were deposed by the Electors. Henry VII (r. 1308–13), Dante's last great hope, aped his forebears by making a progress through Italy; he was shut out of Rome and died ignominiously of fever at Pisa. His successor, Ludwig of Bavaria (r. 1314–47), having fallen foul of the Pope, took Rome by storm in 1328; but his action only provoked yet another round of anti-popes and anti-kings. Charles IV of Luxemburg (r. 1346–78) brought a measure of stability. Upgraded from anti-king to Emperor, he used the Empire to build up his beloved Bohemia. Germany was ruled for a season from the Karlstejn. High politics was disputed between four leading families—the Bavarian-based Wittelsbachs, who also held Hainault and Holland; the Luxemburgs, who held Luxemburg, Brabant, and Bohemia from 1310, Silesia from 1333, and Lusatia and Brandenburg to 1415; the Wettins of Saxony; and the Habsburgs of Austria, whose possessions spread across the south from the Sundgau to Carniola. Local politics were controlled by the ubiquitous predatory prelates, by the powerful imperial cities, or by the seething mass of petty knights. This was the age of the *Raubritter*, the robber barons, and the *Faustrecht*, the law of the fist. Late medieval Germany lacked the confident national monarchies which ruled on either side in France and in Poland. Not until the election of three

---

* The arrangement stayed intact until 1623, when the Palatinate was replaced by Bavaria. In 1648 the Palatinate was reinstated alongside Bavaria, and in 1708 Hanover was raised to the ninth Electorate. Napoleon's extensive amendments were never put into practice.

CABALA

SOME time after 1264 but before 1290, a Hebrew work entitled *Sepher ha-Zohar al ha-Torah*, 'the Book of Splendour on the Law', began to circulate among the Jews of Spain. It purported to be the writings of a revered rabbi of the second century, Simon ben Jochai. In reality, it had been composed by a local scholar, very probably Moses of Leon (1250–1305). It took the form of complex and lengthy commentaries on the Pentateuch, and it was soon known to both Jewish and Christian biblicists. A definitive three-volume edition was printed at Mantua in Italy in 1558–60. It was, and is, the standard textbook of the Cabala.

The word *Cabala* means 'the tradition'. It generally refers to a collection of mystical doctrines and techniques, which had been used for centuries to find hidden meanings beneath the literal text of the scriptures. The basic doctrines of the Cabala probably derived from neo-Platonist and Manichean ideas of the late classical period. They centred on the contending realms of Light and Darkness, the one ruled by God and the other by the Devil. God as well as the Devil consisted of paternal and maternal components, the male being white in colour and active in nature, the female being red and receptive. God's forms could be either *abba* (father/king) or *imma* (mother/queen); those of the Devil could either be Shamael, the poisonous Angel of Death, or Aholah, the Great Harlot. The intercourse of these pairs produced alternatively harmony or disorder.

Since the Godhead and the Devil were judged boundless and invisible, they could only be comprehended by means of their ten emanations. Each emanation corresponded to one of the ten main members of *Adam Kadmon* (Primordial Man) or *Adam Belial* (the Worthless One). The ten divine emanations were: *Kether* (Crown or the head), *Chochma* (Wisdom or the brains), and *Bina* (Comprehension or the heart), which made up 'the intellectual world'; *Chased* (Mercy) and *Din* (Justice), the arms, and *Tephereth* (Beauty or the bosom), which made up 'the moral world'; *Nezach* (Splendour) and *Hod* (Majesty), the legs, and *Jesod* (Foundation or the genitals), which made up 'the material world'; and lastly *Malchuth* (the Kingdom). They could equally be arranged as the ten branches of *Ilan*, 'the cabbalistic tree', or in the Three Pillars:

Comprehension	Crown	Wisdom
Justice	Beauty	Mercy
Splendour	Foundation	Majesty
	The Kingdom	

The Cabalists believed that God created the world after several abortive attempts; that everything real is imperishable; and that souls migrate from body to body. They looked for a Messiah who would come when the seductions of the Devil had been rejected.

The techniques for decoding the Scriptures included *notarikon*, the attribution of words to initial letters within other words, *gematria*, the numerical equivalence of letters, and *temurah* or 'permutation cyphers'.

Examples of *notarikon* would be ADaM, 'Adam, David, Messiah', or the famous Greek Christian ICHTHOS, 'the Fish', meaning 'Jesus Christ, God's Son'.

Gematria operated by calculating sums derived from names and dates. One such sum worked out in the nineteenth century for Emperor Wilhelm I of Germany, born on 22 March 1797, gave: 22 + 3 + 1797 + 7 (letters in his name) = 1829 (his marriage):

1829 + 1 + 8 + 2 + 9 = 1849 (Suppression of Revolution)
1849 + 1 + 8 + 4 + 9 = 1871 (Imperial Coronation)
1871 + 1 + 8 + 7 + 1 = 1888 (Death)

Temurah used twenty-four permutated sequences of the Hebrew alphabet. Its application to the four letters of YaHVeH or 'God', for example, produced 2,112 variations on the divine name.

The Cabala profoundly influenced Judaic thought. It greatly strengthened the religion's mystical aspects, and undermined the rational study of the Torah. It was specially attractive to the Chassidim of a later age, who sang and danced to cabbalistic incantations, and who ascribed infallible truth to the oracular riddles and prophecies of their *zaddiks*.

Many Christian scholars, too, from Raymond Llull to Pico and Reuchlin, were fascinated by the Cabala; and it became a standard ingredient of European magic. A Latin translation of the *Book of Splendour*, published by Baron Rosenroth at Sulzbach in Germany in 1677–8, made its secrets more widely accessible. Its ideas, images, and vocabulary permeated European language and literature, often unannounced and unattributed.[1]

---

successive Habsburgs, in 1438, 1440, and 1486, did the Empire begin to assume the guise of a quasi-hereditary monarchy. And even then the emperors gained little freedom of action. If particularism is the measure of the feudal system, Germany was the most feudal country of all.

In Italy, too, the Hohenstaufen left a bitter legacy. In the north, the warring communes substituted domestic for German oppression. All the cities of Lombardy and Tuscany fell under the control of one or other of the leading contenders—Milan, Florence, or Venice. This was an age of burgeoning commercial wealth and cultural splendour, but also of unending strife. The swordsmen and poisoners flourished alongside the artists and poets. In central Italy, a Concordat signed in 1275 between the Empire and the Papacy abolished all claims to imperial suzerainty over the Patrimony of St Peter. The Papal State, which, in addition to Rome, included the Romagna, the Pentapolis, the March of Ancona, and the

Campagna, found itself free but defenceless. And it was eternally racked by the restless citizens of Rome. In the south, the Papacy's clients, the House of Anjou, which had been imported to replace the Hohenstaufen, became unbearable in their turn. The 'Sicilian Vespers' of 30 March 1282, when the resentful populace of Palermo massacred perhaps 4,000 of their French rulers, led to the introduction of Aragonese rule in Sicily, to the encirclement of the Angevins in Naples, and to a twenty-year war. [CONCLAVE]

The city of Florence stood in the centre of the squalls and sun-shafts of late medieval Italy. Nurtured on the wool of its beautiful Apennine *contado*, it grew in the thirteenth century into a thriving community of perhaps 100,000 turbulent

---

CONCLAVE

THE Roman Catholic Church is not a democracy. But its procedures for electing a pope are based on hard experience. The system of conclave was regularized by Gregory X to avoid the scandalous delays of his own appointment. Meeting at Viterbo at the end of 1268, the cardinals had wrangled for three years. Their prevarication so incensed the town authorities that the doors of the cardinals' residence were locked from the outside, then their roof was removed, and their diet reduced to starvation levels.

Henceforth, the College of Cardinals was to assemble in the Vatican Palace in Rome within fifteen days of the death of an incumbent pope. (Prior to the age of telegraph and rail travel, this rule automatically excluded most cardinals not already in Italy.) The papal chamberlain was then ordered to lock their Eminences into a suitable apartment, usually the Sistine Chapel, and to keep them there *con chiave*—'with his keys'—until they had reached a decision. Voting could be by acclamation, by committee, or, as became customary, by secret ballot. In votes held morning and afternoon, each cardinal placed the name of one preferred candidate in a chalice on the altar. Each day, the chamberlain burned the voting papers of inconclusive rounds, sending a column of black smoke from the chimney of the stove. Voting was to continue until the successful candidate achieved a majority of two-thirds plus one. At which point the chamberlain released the tell-tale signal of white smoke, and the electors cemented their choice of the new pontiff with a sacred vow of homage.

Gregory X's system remains essentially intact, modified only by the constitution *Vacantis apostolicae sedis* (1945). In the twentieth century, the workings of providence overcame a veto from the Emperor Francis-Joseph delivered to the conclave of 1903, and produced a record one-day conclave in 1939. Pope John Paul II was elected in October 1978, apparently at the eighth ballot and with a final vote of support from 103 out of 109 cardinals.[1]

souls. Its gold coin, the florin, became standard currency far beyond Italy. An ambitious bourgeoisie, calling itself the *popolo*, organized in opposition to the traditional *comune* of the castle-based nobles of the contado—the Donati, Uberti, Cerchi, Alberti. The major and minor *arti* or guilds clamoured for a place in the city's elected councils and rotating magistracies; and a lusty mob added to the fray. The *podestà* or governor, once an imperial appointee, was brought under municipal control. Constitutions enacted in 1266, 1295, and 1343 failed to quell the uproar.

Traditionally, Florence was a Guelph city resistant to imperial authority. But the Emperor's absence turned the city's energies in new directions. Relations with the Papacy were strained, and the Florentine Guelphs were themselves riven by faction. Florence gained local supremacy after the Battle of Campaldino, where on 11 June 1289 the forces of Ghibelline Arezzo were overcome following the earlier defeat by the Sienese at Montaperti (1260). But then the feud between 'the Blacks' and 'the Whites' took over. In 1301, after the failure of a papal arbiter in the person of Charles de Valois, the Whites, like the Ghibellines before them, were banished. This factionalism was the sure precursor of despotic power, subsequently exercised by the Medici. Florence was so full of poison, says one of the inhabitants of Dante's Hell, 'that the sack brims o'er . . . Three sparks from Hell— Avarice, Envy, Pride— | In all men's bosoms sowed the fiery seed.'[10]

Yet social and political turbulence seems to have stimulated cultural life. The three great writers of the era—Dante Alighieri, Petrarch, and Boccaccio—were all Florentines. The city's buildings reflected its progress to opulent self-confidence: the Bargello (begun in 1254), the new city walls (1284–1310), the Palazzo Vecchio (begun in 1298), the rebuilt Ponte Vecchio (1345), and the Loggia della Signoria (1381); the palaces of the Arte della Lana or Wool Guild (1300), of the Guelph Party, of the Pazzi, Pitti, Strozzi, Antinori, and Medici-Riccardi (1444); and, above all, the religious art—the romanesque church of San Miniato al Monte, the Gothic Santa Croce (1294), the marble-plated octagon of the Baptistery of St John (1296), the Duomo (begun in 1294), Giotto's Campanile (1339), Brunelleschi's cathedral dome (1436), Ghiberti's baptistery doors (1452), and the frescos of Fra Angelico in the Dominican convent of San Marco.

Dante Alighieri (1265–1321) was the greatest of the poets of Christendom. He was deeply involved in Florentine politics, and walked the city's streets when its finest monuments were under construction. His literary and visionary powers are unsurpassed. As a youth, he had charged in the front ranks at Campaldino. He served as one of the municipal priors in the regime of the White Guelphs, only to be banished for life by the Blacks. Embittered by twenty years in exile, he died in Ravenna at the court of Can Grande da Polenta, who placed the laurel wreath on his fading brow. His *Vita Nuova* (The New Life) makes a rare medieval excursion into a man's internal emotions. His *De Monarchia* (On Monarchy) makes an impassioned plea for the restoration of imperial rule. In *De Vulgari Eloquentia*, his reasoned advocacy of the vernacular makes him the father of modern European literature.

Dante's masterwork, the *Commedia*, a poem of 100 cantos, acquired the epithet of 'Divine' from its admiring readers. It describes the poet's journey through the three realms of the afterlife—through the Pit of Hell in the *Inferno*, the Mount of Expiation in the *Purgatorio*, and the sunlit Circles of Heaven in the *Paradiso*. At one level, like the *Odyssey* or the *Aeneid*, it is a voyage of fictional adventure, where Virgil is Dante's initial guide, and where a convincing setting is created for meeting the shades of people past and present. At another level it is an extended allegory of the spiritual journey of a Christian soul from sin to salvation, rewarded by a blinding vision of God. At yet another level it is an elaborate exercise in moral architecture, whose teeming inhabitants are precisely located according to their vices and virtues among the Damned, the Hopeful, or the Blessed. The language dazzles by its beautiful economy. The tales enrapture both by the quaint detail of the poet's encounters and by the grandeur of the moral landscape in which they occur. Appropriately, the lowest point of human experience is to be found where all Love is lost—in the icy infernal depths round the frozen figure of Judas. The Earthly Paradise is reached in a fragrant grove atop Mount Purgatory, 'where pain gives way to hope'. The ultimate pinnacle is reached beyond the Primum Mobile, in the heart of the heavenly Rose of Light, in ecstasy too intense for words. This is the source of 'the Love that moves the Sun and other stars', 'L'amor che move il sole e l'altre stelle'.

Dante was equally the source of vivid legend. One story tells how the poet heard a donkey-driver singing one of his songs, interspersed with shouts of *Arri, arri!*, 'Giddy-up!' The furious poet then made to strike the donkey-driver, shouting 'Cotesto arri non vi misi io' (That there 'giddy-up' was not put in by *me*!).[11]

Dante's prime overlapped with the youth of Francesco Petrarca (1304–74). Petrarch's exquisite love poems, the *Canzonieri*, echo the spirit of the *Vita Nuova*, just as his devotion to Laura mirrors Dante's devotion to Beatrice. Both looked back to the founders of the *dolce stil nuovo*, such as the Bolognese poet Guido Guinicelli (1230–76), whom Dante called his literary 'father'; and their 'sweet new style' was only one step removed from the troubadours. It is only the pedantry of critics which would categorize Dante as 'profoundly medieval' and Petrarch as 'the harbinger of the Renaissance':

> Di pensier in pensier, di monte in monte,
> mi guida Amor; ch'ogni segnato calle
> provo contrario alla tranquilla vita.
> Se 'n solitaria piaggia, rivo, o fonte,
> Se 'n fra duo poggi siede ombrosa valle,
> ivi s'acquieta l'alma sbigottita;
> e, com'Amor la 'nvita,
> or ride, or piange, or teme, or s'assicura:
> e 'l volto che lei segue, ov'ella il mena
> si turba e rasserena,
> ed in un esser picciol tempo dura;
> onde alla vista uom di tal vita esperto
> diria: questi arde, e di suo stato è incerto.

(From thought to thought, from mountain to mountain, | Love leads me on; since every marked path | I find contrary to a tranquil life. | Where'er a river or fountain [adorns] a lonely slope, | Or 'twixt two hills a shady vale [is hid], | There the disturbed soul can calm itself; | And, as Love bids, | Either laughs or weeps or fears or is assured. | And the face, which follows the soul where'er it leads | Is tormented and serene by turns, | And stays little time in any one state. | Whence, on seeing it, a man learned in such a life | Would say: this one burns, and is unsure of his condition.)[12]

Fourteenth-century Italy provided the breeding-ground both for violent municipal blood-feuds and for Europe's first merchant bankers. The former gave rise to the incessant depredations of the Free Companies—largely foreign mercenaries such as those of Conrad von Wolfort, of the ex-hospitaller Fra Moriale, of the knight errant John of Bohemia, or of the Englishman Sir John Hawkwood. Venice and Genoa were locked in perpetual maritime warfare over the Levantine trade. Rome, shorn of its popes, was racked by the oppression of its aristocratic factions and by the revolts of its citizens, notably in 1347–54 under its visionary popular dictator Cola di Rienzo. Angevin Naples raged through the anarchy presided over by Joanna I (r. 1343–82) and her four husbands.

Italian bankers learned how to profit from the conflicts. They devised all manner of modern financial techniques, from letters of exchange to insurance and accountancy; and by using the network of the Church hierarchy they extended their activities throughout Latin Christendom. Florence was rocked in 1339–49 by the bankruptcy of its leading houses, ruined by overextended credit; but it recovered. Somewhere, in the midst of the wealth and the misery, the world of capitalism was born. [COMPUTIO]

The late medieval Papacy, after a brief paroxysm of self-assertion under Boniface VIII, relapsed into dependency and exile. Boniface VIII (1294–1303) has been described as 'the last medieval pope'. He was elected in succession to the miserable hermit Pietro del Morrone (Celestine V), whom he had advised to abdicate and later imprisoned for life. He was intent on enriching his family, the Gaetani, on beggaring the rival Colonnas, and on restoring the Angevins to Sicily in the endless 'War of the Vespers'. None the less, he was responsible for the *Sextus* (1298), the third part of the corpus of canon law; and in 1300 he launched a jubilee year, with plenary indulgence for the million pilgrims who flocked to Rome. His Bull *Unam Sanctam* (1302) contained an extreme statement of papal supremacy, claiming that no creature could attain salvation without it. However, having picked a quarrel with France, for whose benefit *Unam Sanctam* was framed, he overreached himself. He died from the shock of being kidnapped at his native Anagni by the French King's agent. Dante, who may have met Boniface in person during a Florentine embassy to Rome, was totally unforgiving, calling him 'the prince of the new Pharisees'. In *Inferno* he consigned him to hell for simony. In *Paradiso* he puts the words of denunciation into the mouth of St Peter himself:

> *Quegli ch'usurpa in terra il luogo mio,*
> *il luogo mio, il luogo mio . . .*

COMPUTATIO

IN 1494 Luca Pacioli's *Summa de Arithmetica* was printed and published in Venice. It contained the same author's treatise *Particularis de Computis et Scripturis*, 'On the Particulars of Accounting and Records'. In this work, the modern profession of accountancy received its first textbook.

Pacioli (1447–1517), otherwise known by his religious name of Fra Luca di Borgo San Sepolcro, was a Franciscan friar and a prominent itinerant Florentine professor. His best-known treatise, *De Divina Proportione* (1509), was illustrated by Leonardo da Vinci. Recent authors have dubbed him the 'Father of Accountancy'.[1]

The 'Venetian method' of double-entry book-keeping had grown up in the Italian cities some considerable time before Pacioli described it. It required three books—a memorial book, a journal, and a ledger. The memorial received a note of all transactions as they were made. The journal was made up from the memorial and summarised each day's business in chronological order. It had a left-hand column for debts *in dare*, and a right-hand column for credits, *in havere*. The ledger reserved a double page for each account, debits on the left and credits on the right, together with an index of accounts. It also contained a record of running balances, summaries of the merchant's assets, and lists of various categories of income and expenditure. As each account was closed, the closing profit and loss was entered in the main capital account, where the proprietor's net worth could be seen in the total capital balance.[2]

Systematic accounting methods are often seen as a pre-condition for the growth of capitalism. Their spread across Europe can be traced in the publications which followed Pacioli's. These included: Jan Ympyn Christoffel's *Nieuwe instructie ende biwijs de der loofelijcker consten des rekenboecks* (Antwerp, 1543); Valentin Mennher's *Practique brifue pour cyfrer et tenir livres de coupte* (Antwerp, 1550); James Peele, *The maner and fourme how to kepe a perfect reconying . . .* (London, 1553); Claes Pietersz, *Boeckhouwen op die Italienische maniere* (Amsterdam, 1576); and Simon Stevin's, *Vorsteliche Bouckhouding . . .* (Leyden, 1607) which was written for Prince Maurice of Nassau.

Historians often forget. Even the most mundane of professions have their history.[3] And those mundane professions increasingly run the capitalist world, including academic life.

He who on earth usurps my see,
  my see, my see, which now stands vacant
  before the Son of God
Has made a sewer from my sepulchre
  full of blood and pus—at which the Perverse One,
  who fell from here, takes pleasure down below. . . .

In shepherd's guise, rapacious wolves
  are seen among the pastures. Oh, why
  do God's defenders lie so low?
Gascons and Cahorsines prepare to drink
  our blood. Oh, fine principle,
  to what foul end is it fit for you to fall?[13]

The 'foul end' of the Papacy turned out to be the long exile of the popes in Avignon, begun by the Gascon, Bertrand de Got, who reigned as Clement V (1305–14).

The Babylonish captivity of the Avignon popes lasted from 1309 to 1377. It began at the instigation of Philippe le Bel, who pressured Clement V mercilessly; it ended at the instigation of St Catherine of Siena, who confirmed Gregory IX (1370–8) in his resolve to return to Rome. In the mean time all seven popes were Frenchmen, elected by a French-dominated College of Cardinals. Avignon, on the Rhône, did not lie in French territory but in an enclave of the Venaissin granted to the Papacy by its Angevin clients, and bought outright in 1348 for 80,000 gold crowns. But French influence was paramount; and many acts of policy, such as the dissolution of the Templars, were dictated by it. The authority of the Avignon popes was not accepted in all countries. Latin Christendom was divided against itself in the most blatant manner possible.

The manifest abuses of ecclesiastical power inevitably provoked strong reactions. One such reaction lay in the retreat into mysticism, with its emphasis on religious ecstasy and on the experience of direct communion with God (see pp. 436–7). Another lay in the proliferation of popular sects—all more or less unconventional in their theology. What they shared was a sense of betrayal by the established Church. Such were the *Fraticelli*, or Franciscan Spirituals, who held property to be contrary to salvation, the wandering mendicants, known as 'Beghards and Beguines', the Brethren of the Free Spirit, the German Luciferans, who were Pantheists, the mystical *Gottesfreunde* or Friends of God, and the Lollards in England. All were bitterly persecuted by the Inquisition.

Church reform could not be widely discussed given the political chaos and fear of the Inquisition. It had both theological and organizational aspects. The Englishman John Wyclif (*c*.1330–84), sometime Master of Balliol College, railed against the wealth of the Church, rejected papal supremacy, and denied the doctrine of transubstantiation of the Eucharist. He was burned as a heretic, but only posthumously. The Czech Jan Hus (*c*.1372–1415), sometime Rector of the University at Prague, was much influenced by Wyclif. He stressed the concept of predestination, and the Church of the Elect. In Bohemia he became the focus of

Czech resentment against the largely German hierarchy. Hus, excommunicated, appealed to a General Council of the Church. Though they lacked the name, Wyclif and Hus were the pioneer Protestants. [**MAGIC**]

Switzerland, *die Schweiz*, takes its name from the district of Schwyz on Lake Lucerne, one of three cantons that began to assert their separate political identity against the German Empire in the late thirteenth century. In 1291 Schwyz, Uri, and Unterwalden signed an 'Everlasting League' of self-defence, swearing to assist each other against outside interference. In this way they sought to break free of the local counts, the Habsburgs, who had tried to impose servile judges on the free men of the valleys. In 1315, at the battle of Morgarten, a Habsburg army was routed, and the League became the nucleus for other disaffected districts. The first of these was Luzern (1331) whose advent created the *Vierwaldstaette* of 'Four Forest Cantons'. After that came the Imperial city of Zurich (1351), Glarus (1351), Zug (1352), and the powerful city-state of Bern (1353). Another Habsburg defeat, at Sempach in 1386, where dismounted knights were cut to pieces by Swiss halberdiers, established the cantons' practical independence. (See Appendix III, p. 1257.)

In the mid-fifteenth century the Habsburgs fomented a civil war by supporting Zurich against its neighbours. But a crushing Swiss victory over Burgundy in 1474–6, when the red flag with white cross was first carried, brought another train of members—Fribourg and Solothurn (1481), Basle and Schaffhausen (1501), and Appenzell (1513). By then, Switzerland stretched from the Jura in the west to Tyrol in the east. There were extensive 'subject' and 'protected' territories, including the Vaud round Lake Geneva, the Valais on the upper Rhône, the Ticino as far south as Lake Lugano, and the Graubunden or Grisons, the 'Grey Leagues', to the east. There were German-speakers, French-speakers, Italian-speakers, and speakers of Romansch. Yet apart from the Compact of Stans (1481), which regulated the network of mutual alliances, there were no common institutions. Though the Empire recognized the League's existence by the Treaty of 1499, there had been no formal declaration of independence. The Swiss had proved themselves the finest soldiers in Europe, widely in demand as mercenaries. The Switzers or Swiss Guard of the Vatican, with costumes by Michelangelo, date from 1516.

South and west of Switzerland, the ancient House of Savoy was consolidating its own alpine territories. Amadeus V (r. 1285–1323) reunited the county of Savoy round Chambéry with the principality of Piedmont at Turin. Amadeus VI (r. 1343–83), the *Conte Verde*, a crusader, introduced a system of state-supported poor relief. Amadeus VIII (r. 1391–1440) lived in the hermitage of Ripaille on Lake Geneva. The Emperor made him a Duke, and the Council of Basle elected him the last anti-pope, as Felix V (1439–49).

Given the disarray of the Empire and the Papacy, the kingdom of France faced the first of several historic opportunities to become the dominant power in Europe. As the heirs of St Louis, the last three generations of Capetian kings—Philippe III le Hardi (r. 1270–85), Philippe IV le Bel (r. 1285–1314), and the latter's three sons,

MAGIC

THE 'Twelve Conclusions' of the Lollards of 1395 contains a direct attack on the medieval English Church's involvement with magic. The Protestant movement contained a very strong impulse 'to take the magic out of religion', and this very first manifestation of Protestantism demonstrated the impulse in no uncertain manner:

That exorcisms and hallowings, made in the Church, of wine, bread and wax, water, salt and oil and incense, the stone of the altar, upon vestments, mitre, cross and pilgrims' staves, be the very practice of necromancy, not of holy theology. For . . . we see nothing of change in no such creatures that is so charmed, except by false belief, which is the principle of the devil's craft.[1]

None the less, in the fifteenth, sixteenth, and seventeenth centuries Europe continued to be devoted to every form of magical belief. The landscape was filled with alchemists, astrologers, diviners, conjurers, healers, and witches. [**ALCHEMIA**] [**HEXEN**] [**NOSTRADAMUS**] The countryside was populated with ghosts, fairies, hobgoblins, and elves. Wyclif, the Lollards' guru, translated the Bible into English to make it accessible to all. Yet 300 years later, in Cromwell's Puritan England, the sales charts were topped by William Lilly's astrological almanac, the *Merlinus Anglicus*, and by his *Collection of Ancient and Moderne Prophecies*.[2] Magic and religion were often inseparable. People who venerated the Christian saints also believed in Puck and Queen Mab and Merlin the Magician. Magic held its own throughout the Reformation era.

In this respect, therefore, the Protestant onslaught on magic enjoyed only partial success, even in countries where Protestantism was to be nominally triumphant. But the intentions of the radicals were unmistakable. After Wyclif came Luther's attack on indulgences (see p. 484) and Calvin's dismissal of transubstantiation as 'conjury'. Every aspect of religious life with the slightest supernatural connotation came under suspicion. Protestants abhorred oaths, miracles, consecrations, symbols, images, holy water, saints' days, processions, pilgrimages. Moreover, since Protestant Christianity was supposedly magic-free, Protestantism's enemy, 'Popery', was judged equivalent to black magic; the Pope was a wizard; and the Catholic Mass was a branch of devil-worship.

In reality, such views contained a high dose of hypocrisy. Despite all manner of statutes and reforms, the Protestant clergy could not avoid finding a *modus vivendi* with magic. Anglicans and Lutherans would stay closer to sacramental religion than did Calvinists, Anabaptists, and other evangelicals. But it proved difficult to abandon the sign of the Cross, oaths in court, or the 'churching' of women after childbirth. It proved virtually impossible to abandon the consecration of church buildings, of battle standards, of food, of ships, and of burial grounds. Protestantism was due to create a new form of Christianity, with the emphasis on conscious belief; but magic was never eliminated.

The decline of magic did not really commence until the latter part of the seventeenth century. It has been attributed to the Scientific Revolution (see pp. 507–10), to the consequent rise of rationalism, to modern medicine, to mathematics and a greater understanding of probability, and to a social environment which gradually grew less threatening. [**LLOYD'S**] Yet belief in magic, and its interdependence with religion, has never died out. In the twentieth century, horoscopes are ubiquitous. In the land of the Lollards, sacramental magic was revived in the newfangled rituals of the British monarchy, reaching a pinnacle in the coronation of 1953.[3] In Catholic countries such as Poland and Italy, priests bless everything from motor cars to football mascots. The Vatican still holds with faith-healing and prophecies. [**BERNADETTE**] [**FATIMA**] Even in Russia, where Communism decimated Orthodox religion, belief in astrology and fairies could not be purged.

The study of magic and religion is inevitably coloured by prejudices and preferences. Ever since Frazer's *Golden Bough,* scientific anthropologists have tried to act with impartiality. But scholars cannot always resist the temptation to denigrate other people's magic. That may be a form of superstition in itself. [**ARICIA**]

Louis X (r. 1314–16), Philippe V (r. 1316–22), and Charles IV (r. 1322–8)—ruled a large population which was growing in numbers and prosperity and was well administered. That they failed to press home their advantage can be attributed partly to the disputed succession, partly to their ruinous rivalry with England, and partly to the pestilence.

Philippe le Bel, grandson of St Louis, was fair of face, and unfair by nature. He was notorious for minting debased coinage and for extorting ingenious taxes. His one act of successful territorial aggrandisement—the incorporation of the city of Lyons in 1312—was undertaken by stealth during the absence of the Emperor in Italy. His confrontation with the Papacy, which led to the scandal of Anagni, began over money. When faced with the Bull *Clericis laicos,* whereby Pope Boniface had sought to prevent him taxing the clergy, he simply banned the export of all money. His vendetta against the Templars, which ended with their proscription, was rooted in envy and pursued with malice. Their trial, 1307–12, was marked by fiendish accusations about leagues with the Devil or with the infidel, by confessions extracted under torture, and in the end by legalized murder and state robbery. The death of the last Grand Master, Jacques de Molai, burned at the stake in Paris after retracting all his confessions, left a lasting stain. [**ANGELUS**]

Yet Philippe le Bel was the author of durable institutions. With the aid of his *légistes* or legal counsellors, he found all manner of pretexts to fleece his subjects, to institutionalize his depredations, and to cloak them in the guise of a national consensus. His guiding principle lay in the Roman adage *quod principi placuit legis habet vigorem* (whatever pleases the king has the force of law). The old royal court was divided into three branches: The royal council governed the kingdom; the *chambre des comptes*, or exchequer, managed its finances; the *parlement* was charged with royal justice, and with registering all royal edicts. (It was not a true parliament.) The Estates-General, which first met in 1302, summoned nobles, clergy, and commoners to approve royal policy. Philippe le Bel died opportunely, thereby avoiding a popular outburst; but much of his administrative machinery survived till 1789.

In 1316 the Capetian succession was thrown into confusion. The three sons of Philippe le Bel had produced six daughters between them, but no male heir. When Louis X le Hutin (the Quarrelsome) died suddenly, he left one daughter, a pregnant queen, and an unborn child, who, as Jean I the Posthumous, lived and reigned for less than a week. The ultimate outcome was the so-called Salic Law,

---

ANGELUS

WHILST preaching the First Crusade, Pope Urban II had urged the faithful to recite the 'Angelus' three times daily. The Blessed Virgin was patroness of the Crusaders; and the prayer which begins *Angelus Domini nuntiavit Mariae* ('The Angel of the Lord announced to Mary') was already the standard invocation to the Virgin. The Pope's proposal was largely ignored. But the cathedral church of Saint-Pierre at Saintes in Poitou was an exception. Not only did the clergy of Saintes recite the Angelus regularly; they established the practice of sounding a bell at sunrise, noon, and sunset to announce the commencement of their devotions.

According to local tradition, Pope John XXII renewed the appeal of his predecessor in 1318, ordering the custom of Saintes to be adopted throughout the universal Church.[1] Other authorities point to the pontificate of Callistus III in 1456. At all events, the sound of the angelus bell was to become as characteristic for the towns and villages of Latin Christendom as the sound of the muezzin in Islam. The Middle Ages was a world without background noise. There were no factories, no engines, no traffic, no radio, no musak. Sound had not been devalued. In the narrow, crowded streets of tiny towns, vendors' cries mingled with the bustle of artisans' workshops. But in the vast open countryside, the sounds of nature were largely undisturbed. The only serious competition for the church bell came from the wind in the trees, the lowing of cattle, and the distant clang of the blacksmith's forge. [**SOUND**]

which the lawyers of Louis's brothers devised to exclude their sister (and all subsequent females of the French royal house). But in 1328, when the throne passed to the founder of a new line, Philippe de Valois, the succession was inevitably challenged. The challenger was Philippe le Bel's only surviving grandson, Edward III, King of England. [MONTAILLOU]

England under three Edward Plantagenets—Edward I (r. 1272–1307), Edward II (r. 1307–27), and Edward III (r. 1327–77)—saw only three reigns in more than a century. There was no lack of baronial discontent and foreign wars; and, since the Plantagenets continued to hold Gascony and Guyenne as fiefs of France, the territorial base was still fluid. But the wool trade with Flanders was booming, and the towns were growing. Under Edward I, in particular, there were concerted policies to consolidate the institutions of government, and to secure England's dominant position within the British Isles. The 'model parliament' of 1295, which followed De Montfort's precedent thirty years before, summoned burgesses as well as lords and knights of the shire, thereby laying the foundation of the House of Commons. Magna Carta was reconfirmed. But in an amendment accepted during a parliamentary session on Stepney Green in 1297, the principle of 'no taxation without representation' was established. Thereafter, Westminster Hall became the permanent site of England's Parliament. Edward's writ of *Quo Warranto* (1278) had threatened the barons' landholdings: but the Second Statute of Westminster (1285), which favoured the entailing of estates, benefited both the monarchy and the tenants-in-chief. His conflict with the Church over *Clericis laicos* was controlled by the simple device of outlawing the clergy. His conquest of Wales, 1277–1301, which was held down by the chain of magnificent castles from Harlech to Conway, proved to be permanent. But his invasion of Scotland provoked the Scots' bid for total independence. Edward II, who understood little of his father's motto *Pactum servare*, 'Keep Troth'—was murdered at Berkeley Castle on the orders of his queen. Edward III fell into the endless struggle of the Hundred Years War with France.

Scotland emerged as a nation-state much sooner than England did. The Scots had not been directly overrun by the Norman Conquest; and they reached a *modus vivendi* with the Gaelic clans long before the English came to terms with the Welsh. Scots monarchs and nobles had long been embroiled in English affairs, much as the English were embroiled in France. But they cut themselves free nearly two centuries earlier. The critical moment occurred during the decades of war which followed Edward I's intervention in a disputed succession. One contender, John Balliol (d. 1313), was imprisoned in England, then exiled in France. Another, Robert the Bruce (r. 1306–29), victor of Bannockburn in June 1314, started as England's vassal and finished as Scotland's saviour. But none had a greater impact than William Wallace (1270–1305), who roused the commons of Scotland to resistance. Betrayed, and hanged in London as a common bandit, he was the martyr-hero of Scotland's cause:

> Scots, wha hae wi' Wallace bled,
> Scots, wham Bruce has aften led,

Welcome to your gory bed
Or to victorie.[14]

'We are resolved never to submit to English domination,' the Scots lords informed the Pope in the Declaration of Arbroath (1320); 'we are fighting for freedom, and freedom only.'[15] Their cause was finally vindicated in 1328.

The wars of England and Scotland had direct repercussions in Ireland. In 1297, Edward I's viceroy in Dublin, Sir John Wogan, had set up an Irish parliament in imitation of the 'model parliament' in London. But the English defeat at Bannockburn gave the Irish lords the opportunity to rebel, and for three years, 1315–18, they accepted a Scottish Bruce as king. Subsequent decades of turmoil were not brought to an end until the Statute of Kilkenny (1366) limited English rule and the English language to Dublin and to a surrounding Pale of Settlement.

The 'Black Death' of 1347–50 stopped Europe's petty troubles in their tracks. Here was a pandemic of plague such as the world had not seen since the sixth century and was not destined to see again till the 1890s. It was fuelled by a devastating brew of three related diseases—bubonic plague, septicaemic plague, and pneumonic or pulmonary plague. The first two variants were carried by fleas hosted by the black rat; the third, airborne variant was especially fast and lethal. In its most common bubonic form, the bacillus *pasteurella pestis* caused a boil-like nodule or bubo in the victim's groin or armpit, together with dark blotches on the skin from internal haemorrhage. Three or four days of intolerable pain preceded certain death if the bubo did not burst beforehand.

Medieval medicine, though generally conscious of infection and contagion, did not comprehend the particular mechanisms of the plague's transmission. Doctors watched in anguish. Crowded tenements and poor sanitation, especially in the towns, provided excellent encouragement for the rats. The result was mass mortality. Boccaccio wrote that 100,000 died in Florence alone. Eight hundred corpses a day had to be buried in Paris. 'At Marseilles,' wrote the cynical English chronicler, Henry Knighton, 'not one of the hundred and fifty Franciscans survived to tell the tale. And a good job too.'[16]

The pandemic, which began in central Asia, spread with frightening speed. Initially it had turned east, to China and India; but it was first reported in Europe in the summer of 1346, at the Genoese colony of Caffa in the Crimea, which was under siege by the Tartars. The besiegers catapulted plague-ridden corpses into the city to break its resistance; whereupon the defenders took to the galleys, and rowed for safety. In October 1347 the plague reached Messina in Sicily. In January 1348 it reached Genoa, by way of a well-authenticated galley from Caffa. Expelled from its home port by the terrified citizens, the stricken galley sailed on to Marseilles and to Valencia. That same winter the plague struck Venice and other Adriatic cities, before moving on to Pisa, Florence, and central Italy. By the summer it was in Paris, and by the end of the year it had crossed the English Channel. 1349 saw it march northwards across the British Isles, eastwards across Germany,

MONTAILLOU

BETWEEN 1318 and 1325 Jacques Fournier, Bishop of Pamiers in the Pyrenean county of Foix, conducted a campaign of inquisition into the revival of heresy in his diocese. In 370 sessions he examined 114 suspects, 48 of whom were women, and 25 from the village of Montaillou. All the questions and all the answers were recorded in the Bishop's Register.

Montaillou was a community of some 250 souls drawn from 26 main clans known as *ostal* or *domus*, living in perhaps 50 separate households. It sprawled down the hillside from the castle at the top to the church at the bottom. Its inhabitants were mainly peasant farmers and craftsmen. There was also a strong contingent of transhumant shepherds, who were organized into *cabanes* or 'folds' working the pastures and trails leading into Catalonia. Though officially Catholic, they were in large part secret Cathars, who hid the itinerant *Perfecti* in their barns and cellars. Their natural feuds and rivalries were intensified by fears of the Inquisition, whose arrests during the last visitation in 1308 had turned the village into 'a desert for sheep and children'. The Register has served as a sort of 'historical microscope', revealing every detail of the villagers' lives. 'Montaillou is only a drop in the ocean,' wrote its celebrated historian, 'but we can see the protozoa swimming about in it.'[1]

The twenty-two members of the *ostal* of the Clergues dominated the village. Old Pons Clergue, a die-hard heretic, had four sons and two daughters. One son, Pierre, the priest of Montaillou, was a flagrant womanizer who died in prison. Another son, Bernard, the *bayle* or manorial bailiff, eventually suffered the same fate after elaborate attempts to save his brother by suborning witnesses. Pons's widow, Mengarde, the matriarch of Montaillou's heretics, was none the less buried under the altar of the parish church. One of the priest's many lovers, Béatrice de Planissoles, a noblewoman, was first married to Bérenger de Roquefort, the castellan and agent of the Count of Foix. Twice widowed, she became the accepted concubine of the priest's bastard cousin, Pathaud, who had once raped her. She took numerous bed-partners, even as an old lady, bore four daughters, and revealed all to the Inquisition. In 1322 she was condemned to wear the double yellow cross of the repentant heretic. [**CONDOM**]

The religious practices of the Cathars were heatedly discussed during the long fireside talks of the winter, and during long, intimate delousing sessions. They betrayed a two-tier system of morality—extremely severe for the *Perfecti* and extremely lax for the laity. At the end of their lives the former submitted to the *endura*, a last act of suicidal ritual fasting. The laity sought to be 'hereticated', that is, to receive the ritual *consolamentum* or 'absolution'.

The dilemmas inherent in a part-Cathar and part-Catholic community were illustrated by the incident of Sybille Pierre's infant daughter, who had been administered the *consolamentum*. The *Perfectus* forbade the sick baby to receive milk or meat. 'When [they] had left the house, I could bear it no longer,' the mother related, 'I could not let my daughter die before my eyes. So I put her to the breast. When my husband came back . . . he was very grieved.'[2]

Everyday life in medieval Occitania exuded a special emotional climate. People could weep quite openly. They saw no sin in sexual liaisons that were mutually pleasurable; they were not driven by any developed work ethic; and they had a marked distaste for conspicuous wealth. They had large numbers of children to compensate for high infant mortality; but they were not indifferent to their losses. They lived in a complicated world of belief where magic and folklore mingled with Catholicism and heresy. And they were frequently visited by death.

Bishop Fournier's career was not damaged by his zeal at Pamiers. He rose to Cardinal in 1327, and Pope, as Benedict XII, in 1334. His Register found its way into the Vatican Library. His most lasting monument is the Palais des Papes at Avignon.

---

and south-eastwards into the Balkans. 1350 saw it entering Scotland, Denmark, and Sweden and, via the Hansa cities of the Baltic, Russia. There were few places which stayed inviolate—Poland, the county of Béarn in the Pyrenees, Liège.

One of the best attempts to describe the plague was made by a Welsh poet, Ieuan Gethin, who saw the outbreak in March or April 1349:

We see death coming into our midst like black smoke, a plague which cuts off the young, a rootless phantom which has no mercy for fair countenance. Woe is me of the shilling of the armpit . . . It is of the form of an apple, like the head of an onion, a small boil that spares no-one. Great is its seething, like a burning cinder, a grievous thing of ashy colour . . . They are similar to the seeds of the black peas, broken fragments of brittle sea-coal . . . cinders of the peelings of the cockle weed, a mixed multitude, a black plague like half pence, like berries . . .[17]

Popular reactions to the plague varied from panic and wild debauchery to dutiful fortitude. Many who could flee, fled. Boccaccio's *Decameron* is set among a company of men and women incarcerated in a country castle for the duration of the plague. Others, losing the sense of restraint, indulged in orgies of drink and lechery. The clergy often suffered disproportionately from tending their flock. Elsewhere they left the sick to shrive themselves, the black flag flapping forlornly from the abandoned parish churches. The conviction reigned that God was punishing mankind for its sins.

Calculating the losses is a difficult, and highly technical, task. Contemporary estimates are often, and demonstrably, exaggerated. Boccaccio's report of 100,000 dead in Florence exceeded the total known population of the city; 50,000 may be nearer the mark. Generally speaking, the towns were hit more severely than the countryside, the poor more than the rich, the young and fit more than the old and infirm. No pope, no kings were stricken. In the absence of anything resembling a census, historians have to base their calculations on fragmentary records. In England they use the court rolls, the payment of frank-pledge dues, post mortem inquisitions, or the episcopal register. Specific studies can suggest very high rates of mortality: the manor of Cuxham in Oxfordshire lost over two-thirds of its inhabitants;[18] the parish priests of England were reduced by 45 per cent. But it is hard to extrapolate any general conclusions. Cautious estimates suggest overall losses of one-third. 'That one European in three died during the Black Death . . . cannot be wildly far from the truth.'[19] This works out at 1.4–2 million deaths in England: 8 million in France, perhaps 30 million for Europe as a whole.

The social and economic consequences of such gigantic losses must have been very far-reaching. Indeed, the Black Death was conventionally seen by historians as the decisive point in the decline of the feudal system in Western Europe. The second half of the fourteenth century was clearly a period of manorial dislocation, of languishing trade, of labour shortages, of urban distress. Yet nowadays specialists tend to argue that many of the changes were visible before 1347. Even basic demographic decline had set in at least thirty years before. This means that the Black Death was the accelerator of existing processes rather than their originator. At all events, serfs were increasingly commuting their labour dues for money rents, thereby creating a more mobile, and less dependent, labour force. Feudal vassals were increasingly commuting their military and judicial obligations for cash payments, thereby creating a phenomenon which in England has been called 'bastard feudalism'. Above all, in a labour market deprived at a stroke of manpower, wages were sure to rise with rising demand. The money economy was expanded; social barriers were threatened. [**PROSTIBULA**]

The psychological trauma ran deep. Though the Church as an institution was weakened, popular religiosity increased. Charity foundations proliferated. Intense piety came into fashion: people felt that God's wrath must be placated. In Germany, huge companies of flagellants flourished until suppressed on orders from Avignon. Communal scapegoats were sought. In some places lepers were picked on; elsewhere the Jews were charged with poisoning the water. In September 1348 a trial of Jews at Chillon was supported by evidence extracted by torture. It was the signal for wholesale pogroms: in Basle, all the Jews were penned into wooden buildings and burned alive; similar scenes occurred in Stuttgart, Ulm, Speyer, and Dresden. Two thousand Jews were massacred in Strasburg: in Mainz as many as 12,000. The remnants of German Jewry fled to Poland—henceforth the principal Jewish sanctuary in Europe. [**ALTMARKT**] [**USURY**]

PROSTIBULA

THE terminal period of medieval Europe, from 1350 to c.1480, 'was a golden age of prostitution'.[1] *Prostibula publica*, public brothels, were licensed to operate in most towns. A small place like Tarascon, with 500 or 600 households, supported ten municipal whores. The Church did not protest: since the evil existed, it had to be channelled. Licensed fornication tempered street disorder, diverted young men from sodomy and worse, and broke them in for conjugal duty. After 1480, practice changed. Expensive courtesans served the rich, but many whorehouses were closed down. In Protestant countries, fallen women were liable to re-education.[2]

Throughout history, prostitution circulates through phases of licensed control, futile proscription, and unofficial toleration.

Popular risings were a prominent feature of the period following the Black Death. Demands on the surviving peasants soared, and a decimated labour force resented attempts to hold down wages, as in England's Statute of Labourers (1351). A peasant *jacquerie* ravaged the castles and families of the nobility in the Île de France and Champagne before being cruelly suppressed. But the rash of risings in the years 1378–82, exactly one generation after the plague, does seem symptomatic of some general social malaise. Marxist historians have seized on the events as evidence of the 'timeless characteristics' of class warfare. Others have dismissed them as 'outbursts of anger without a future'.[20]

Yet contemporaries had good reason to take fright when the endemic disorders of the towns were fused with more widespread violence in the countryside. In 1378, during the revolt of the *ciompi* or wool-carders, Florence was taken over for several months by riotous elements. In 1379 the weavers of Ghent and Bruges rose against the Count of Flanders in a vicious outbreak reminiscent of an earlier episode in the 1320s. Both culminated in pitched battles with the royal army; and once again, Ghent held out for six years. In 1381 several counties of England were drawn into the Peasants' Revolt; in 1382 it was the turn of Paris.

The ramifications of the movement were noted by a Florentine merchant, Buonocorso Pitti, who was present at the French court:

The people of Ghent rebelled against their overlord, the Count of Flanders, who was the father of the duchess of Burgundy. They marched in great numbers to Bruges, took the city, deposed the Count, and robbed and killed all his officers . . . Their leader was Philip van Artevelde. As the number of [Flemish rebels] increased, they sent secret embassies to the populace of Paris and Rouen . . . Accordingly, these two cities rebelled against the King of France. The first insurrection of the Paris mob was sparked off by a costermonger, who, when an official tried to levy tax on the fruit and vegetables he was selling, began to roar, 'Down with the *gabelle*'. At this cry, the whole populace ran to the tax-collectors' houses, and robbed and murdered them. . . . The *popolo grasso*, or men of substance, who in French

ALTMARKT

O N Shrove Tuesday 1349, the *Altmarkt* of Dresden, the Old City Square, was filled with the smoke and flames of burning pyres. The Margrave of Meissen had ordered all the city's Jews to be burned, probably on a charge of spreading the plague. This veritable *auto-da-fé* is described in the *Chronicum Parvum Dresdense*.[1]

Six hundred years later, at 10 pm on the evening of another Shrove Tuesday, 13 February 1945, Dresden's Old City was illuminated by a phosphorescent Primary Flare dropped by a high-flying pathfinder plane of 83 Squadron RAF. The *Altmarkt* had been selected as the base-point of the Target Area of the most destructive bombing raid in Europe's history.

Despite the public stance, which affirmed that only military and industrial targets were selected, both the RAF and the USAF had followed the German *Luftwaffe* into a strategy of indiscriminate 'area bombing'. In a bitter controversy over the priorities of the Allied Bombing Offensive, the advocates of area bombing, led by Air Vice-Marshal Arthur Harris, had won out. The technique was to send massed fleets of heavy bombers repeatedly against one city, and to wreak a crescendo effect of devastation.[2] As Harris was to boast: 'We shall take out one German city after another, like pulling teeth.' The first 1,000-bomber Raid was launched against Cologne on 31 May 1942. But the desired effect was not fully achieved until the night raid on Hamburg on 27/28 July 1943, when the resultant firestorm killed over 40,000 people.

Dresden, the capital of Saxony, had reached 1945 virtually intact. The medieval *Altstadt* was ringed by elegant squares and boulevards, lined with Renaissance and Baroque monuments. The Royal Palace, the *Georgenschloss*, dated from 1535. The Catholic *Hofkirche* (1751) commemorated the Saxon Elector's conversion to Catholicism. The Protestant *Frauenkirche* (1742) had been built to deplore it.

Dresden was now selected for a Main Force Raid in response to Soviet requests for Allied air support. The city was the main reception centre for hundreds of thousands of refugees displaced by the Soviet advance, and for their relief teams, mainly young women.

Ten minutes after the Primary Flare was dropped, the first wave of 529 Lancasters began to arrive from the south-west on a flightpath of 68°. Undeterred by flak or fighters, they dropped a lethal cocktail of high-explosive blockbusters and incendiary clusters. Within 45 minutes, the firestorm was raging. Dresden's ancient heart, and everyone in it, was consumed.[3]

In the morning, as relief columns approached on the ground, a second wave of 450 Flying Fortresses of the 1st Air Division of the US Strategic Air Force arrived. Fighter escorts strafed anything that moved.

Huge discrepancies divide estimates of the damage. The British Bombing Survey reported 1,681 acres totally destroyed. The post-war Dresden Planning Report counted 3,140 acres 75% destroyed. The local *Abteilung Tote* or 'Death Bureau' reported 39,773 identified dead by May 1945. This figure did not account for missing or unregistered persons, unrecorded burials, or the contents of numerous mass graves. It must be reckoned an absolute minimum. The chief of the Bureau later ventured an estimated total of 135,000 deaths. A British historian has suggested a range of 120–150,000.[4] No one knows how many uncounted corpses were disposed of behind the SS cordons, as an endless stream of carts fed the pyres blazing once again on the *Altmarkt*.

The strategic impact of the raid appears to have been slight. Trains were running through Dresden within two days. Vital war factories, such as the electronics plant at Dresden-Neusiedlitz, were unscathed. The Red Army did not arrive until 8 May.

An information battle ensued. An Associated Press report, later disowned, announced 'Allied air chiefs have made the long-awaited decision to adopt deliberate terror-bombings of German population centres.' A Nazi communiqué agreed: 'SHAEF war criminals have cold-bloodedly ordered the extermination of the innocent German public.' In the House of Commons, on 6 March 1945, Richard Stokes MP asked 'Was terror-bombing now part of official government policy?' The official reply was: 'We are not wasting time or bombers on purely terror tactics.'[5]

At 10.10 pm on 13 February 1946, church bells tolled in remembrance throughout the Soviet Zone of Germany. Of all Dresden's churches, only the solitary shell of the *Frauenkirche*, with its shattered cupola, was still standing. On that same day, ex-Air Marshal Harris boarded a ship at Southampton in a bowler hat, bound for a civilian career abroad. Though he received a belated knighthood in 1953, he was not honoured like his peers until a monument was unveiled in London's Strand on 31 May 1992. It was the fiftieth anniversary of the raid on Cologne. The Oberbürgermeister of Cologne lodged a public protest: 'In my view, it makes no sense to commemorate war heroes like Arthur Harris', he wrote, 'although he fought on the right side and for the right cause.'[6]

Anticipating Dresden's own anniversary in 1995, Germany's President Herzog reflected further. The bombing of Dresden, he said, 'was an example . . . of the brutalization of man in war . . . History written by individual nations in which each one selects what he has done well cannot be allowed to continue. If we really want to unify this Europe, then history must be unified as well.'[7]

USURY

EARLY in 1317 in Marseilles, a certain Bondavid de Draguignan was charged in court for continuing to demand payment after the capital of his loan to one Laurentius Girardi had already been repaid. Bondavid was a Jew and a moneylender, and was suspected of breaking the laws against usury. Here was one well-documented incident amongst countless others which reinforced the medieval stereotype of the Jew as a heartless swindler. Bondavid was a real precursor of the fictional Shylock, whom Shakespeare immortalized two centuries later in *The Merchant of Venice*.[1]

Usury—the taking of interest, or of excessive interest, on money lent—was regarded in Christian Europe as both a sin and a crime. Churchmen pointed to Christ's teaching: *'But love your enemies, and do good, and lend nothing hoping for nothing again . . . Be ye therefore merciful, as your Father also is merciful'* (Luke 6: 35–6). Repeated attempts were made to ban interest or, later, to limit it to 10 per cent per annum.

Jewish practice, in contrast, whilst forbidding usury between Jews, permitted a Jew to charge interest to a non-Jew: *'unto a stranger thou mayest lend upon interest; but unto thy brother thou shalt not lend on interest'* (Deut. 23: 20). This distinction supposedly gave Jews an edge in the medieval money-markets, and loan business. It also gave rise to one of the sharpest points of antagonism between Christians and Jews, captured in Shylock's provocative aside about his rival, Antonio:

> I hate him for he is a Christian;
> But more for that in low simplicity
> He lends out money gratis, and brings down
> The rate of usance here with us in Venice. . . .
> He hates our sacred nation; and he rails
> Even there where merchants do most congregate,
> On me, my bargains, and my well-won thrift
> Which he calls interest. Cursed be my tribe
> If I forgive him.

> (*The Merchant of Venice*, I. iii. 37–47)

In reality, the laws on usury were observed in the breach. Christian bankers could conceal high interest rates by not recording the sums borrowed, only the sums repaid.[2] Jewish moneylenders probably drew the greatest opprobrium because they concentrated on petty loans with the populace at large. Hypocrisy, and a measure of animosity, were perhaps inevitable, and one of the essential techniques of capitalism was inhibited for centuries. Even so, the prominent role of Jews in European credit and banking is a fact of history.

are called *bourgeois*, fearing lest the mob might rob them, too, took arms and managed to subdue them.[21]

The Peasants' Revolt in England cannot be attributed to the desperate rage of paupers. The chronicler Froissart said that the common people who led it were living in 'ease and riches'. Their demands for an end to servitude were made amidst improving material conditions. They harboured special grievances about a third poll-tax in four years; and they expressed a strong sense of moral protest, as befitted the era of the Lollards. Their fury was directed against the clergy as well as the gentry. Popular preachers, like the rebel priest John Ball, had been spreading egalitarian ideas: 'When Adam delved and Eve span, Who was then the gentleman?'

For a few days in June 1381, therefore, it looked as though the entire social hierarchy was under attack. Wat Tyler and his men poured into London from Kent. Jack Straw marched in from Essex. They burned the home of John of Gaunt at Savoy House. They burned Highbury Manor, and a Flemish brothel by London Bridge. They strung up the Archbishop, and beheaded a number of citizens. At Smithfield they came face to face with the young King and his entourage; and in a scuffle Wat Tyler was killed. After that, they turned into a rabble. The ringleaders were seized and executed. The rest dispersed, to be pursued at assizes through the shires. No one cared to boast of their achievements. Chaucer, who had been present, never raised the subject; nor did Shakespeare in his play *Richard II*. Not till the nineteenth century did the Revolt receive sympathetic consideration.[22]

[TABARD]

The Papal Schism, which lasted from 1378 to 1417, followed hard on the popes' return from Avignon. There had been anti-popes before, of course; but the spectacle of two men, both elected by the same College of Cardinals and each preaching war and anathema against his rival, proved a grave scandal. The two original claimants, Urban VI and Clement VII, could hardly be described as holy men. The former turned out to be a deranged sadist who read his breviary in the Vatican garden whilst supervising the torture of his cardinals. The latter, Robert of Geneva, had once ordered the appalling bloodbath at Cesena. In 1409, when both the Urbanite and the Clementine parties declined to attend a council designed to reconcile them, the College elected a third. The Schism was not ended until the Council of Constance dismissed all three existing pontiffs and unanimously acclaimed Cardinal Odo Colonna as Martin V (1417–31) in their place.

The Council of Constance (1414–17) saw the culmination of the conciliar movement. Professors of the University of Paris had been calling for such an assembly for half a century. It was summoned by the German King, Sigismund of Luxemburg, and invitations were sent to all cardinals, bishops, abbots, princes, friars, teachers. Eighteen thousand clerics, fired with a mission of unity, converged on the tiny lakeside town. Among other things, they were supposed to limit papal power. They ended the Schism by confirming the election of Martin V

TABARD

A STATUTE of Richard II in 1393 made it compulsory for every inn in England to display a sign. The result is a great open-air gallery of picturesque names and signboards.[1]

Medieval inns were often connected with pilgrimages. Chaucer's Canterbury Pilgrims started from the TABARD in Southwark. The TRYPPE TO JERUSALEM, which took its present name in 1189, is still extant in Nottingham. London's inns were decimated by the Great Fire of 1666. The thirteenth-century HOOP AND GRAPES in Aldgate claims to be the oldest survivor.

Very many inn names denote the heraldic arms of their patron. Richard II's arms bore the WHITE HART. The RISING SUN recalls Edward III; the BLUE BOAR, the House of York: the GREEN DRAGON, the Earl of Pembroke; the GREYHOUND, Henry VII. Many others were founded by crafts or guilds, hence the BLACKSMITHS' ARMS or the WEAVERS' ARMS. The BEETLE AND WEDGE or the MAN AND SCYTHE recall craftsmen's tools. Connections with transport were legion. The PACK HORSE, the COACH AND HORSES, and the RAILWAY TAVERN reflect improving means of travel. The BLUE POSTS in St James's, London SW1, marks an eighteenth-century system of litter stops. Sporting connections are also numerous. Some, like the HARE AND HOUNDS or the FALCON, refer to hunting, others, like the DOG AND DUCK, the FIGHTING COCKS, or the BULL, to cruel sports long since banned.

More modern inns have often been dedicated to popular heroes and to literary figures. These include everyone from LILY LANGTRY and LADY HAMILTON (WC2) to the ARTFUL DODGER, ELIZA DOOLITTLE, and, in Bromley, the BUNTER. Historical battles, such as TRAFALGAR, gave frequent inspiration, as did the ROYAL OAK, which hid Charles II in 1651. Less dramatic events find an echo in THE CARDINAL'S ERROR (the suppression of Tonbridge Priory in 1540), THE WORLD TURNED UPSIDE DOWN (the discovery of Australia in 1683), or THE TORCH in Wembley (the Olympic Games of 1948).

Corrupted names abound. The CAT 'N' FIDDLE is reputedly a corruption of 'Caton le Fidèle', a knight who once held Calais for England. BAG O'NAILS comes from the Latin 'Bacchanales' or 'drinkers', the GOAT AND COMPASSES from a Puritan slogan, 'God Encompasses Us'. Patriotic references were popular—hence the ALBION, the ANCIENT BRITON, the BRITANNIA, and the VICTORIA. The ANTIGALLICAN (SE1) was the name of a famous man-of-war of Napoleonic vintage.

But foreign countries are not neglected. The KING OF DENMARK (N1) recalls the visit of Christian IV in 1606. The HERO OF SWITZERLAND commemorates William Tell; the ANGERSTEIN honours the Baltic German who refounded Lloyd's; and the INDEPENDENT (N1) the Hungarian leader Kossuth. The SPANISH PATRIOT in Lambeth was founded by veterans of the International Brigades of the 1930s. [**ADELANTE**]

None the less, an undecipherable residue remains. It is anybody's guess what to make of the MAGPIE AND STUMP (Old Bailey), the WIG AND FIDGET in Boxted, or the GOAT IN BOOTS (NW1).

as sole Pope. But they burned Jan Hus, on the grounds that an imperial safe conduct was not valid in the hands of a manifest heretic; and they did nothing to reform their own abuses. A further conciliar meeting, envisaged at Constance, finally met at Basle under the protection of the Duke of Savoy in 1431, and dragged on for years. But it fell into conflict with Pope Eugene IV, and ended by confirming the Duke himself as anti-pope. Ironically enough, the final outcome of the conciliar movement was to reinforce the conviction that the Church needed a strong Papacy.

Italy evaded all foreign tutelage. In the fifteenth century Italy boiled with great prosperity, great turbulence, and immense cultural energy. It saw the zenith of the city-states, the city despots, the *condottieri*, and the early Renaissance (see Chapter VII). Unending municipal conflicts destroyed the oligarchic communes, giving the opening for local tyrants. Milan under twelve Viscontis (from 1277 to 1447) and five Sforzas (from 1450 to 1535) or Florence under Cosimo and Lorenzo dei Medici (from 1434 to 1494) saw no incompatibility between low politics and high art. Venice rose to the peak of its power and wealth, winning extensive possessions on the mainland, including Padua. Naples was cast into the outer darkness of civil strife. But Rome, in the hands of ambitious and cultured popes such as the Florentine Nicholas V (1447–55), re-emerged into the sunlight. Italy was free to enjoy its own strife and splendours until the reappearance of the French in 1494.

The 'Hundred Years War', whose conventional dates run from 1337 to 1453, was not a formal or continuous war between France and England. It is a historians' label, first used in 1823, for a long period of troubles, 'le temps des malheurs', which were constantly used by the English as an occasion for raids, jaunts, and military expeditions. (It is sometimes called the *Second* Hundred Years War—in succession to the earlier Anglo-French conflict of 1152–1259.) It was, above all, an orgy of what later generations were to judge most despicable about 'medievalism'—endless killings, witless superstition, faithless chivalry, and countless particular interests pursued without regard to the common weal. The scene is strewn with colourful figures. There were great knights such as the Breton Bertrand Duguesclin (*c*.1320–80), Constable of France, or his adversary Edward of Woodstock (1330–76), Prince of Wales and Aquitaine, 'the Black Prince'. There were treacherous barons such as Charles le Mauvais of Navarre, rowdy adventurers such as Sir John Fastolf, and any number of unscrupulous prelates like Pierre Cauchon, Bishop of Beauvais, who would formulate a theological justification of murder or an ecclesiastical show trial to order. Few emerge with much credit. Fittingly enough, the most influential personage of the war was Bishop Cauchon's chief victim Jeanne d'Arc, a blameless peasant girl who had heard mystical voices, who rode to battle in full armour, and who was burned at the stake on false charges of heresy and witchcraft. By that time, in 1430, every memory of the origins of the troubles had been lost. Well might Charles d'Orléans (1394–1465), princely poet and 35 years an English prisoner, lament for his native land:

> Paix est tresor qu'on ne peut trop loer
> Je hé guerre, point ne la doy prisier;
> Destourbe m'a long temps, soit tort ou droit,
> De voir France que mon cœur amer doit.[23]

(Peace is a treasure which cannot be praised too much. / I hate war: one should not hold it in high regard. / I have long been troubled, whether rightly or wrongly, / To see France, that my heart should love.)

France's troubles were rooted partly in the dynastic problems of the House of Valois, partly in the waywardness of the great fiefs—notably Flanders, Brittany, Guyenne (Aquitaine), and Burgundy—and partly in the volatility of Paris. England's interest lay in the Plantagenets' continuing claims to the French throne; in their territorial possessions—notably in Guyenne; in commercial links with Flanders; and, above all, in the conviction of four or five generations of Englishmen that fame and fortune awaited them across the Channel. Potentially, France was always the stronger contestant; but English dominance at sea kept the island safe from all but France's Scots allies; whilst the technical superiority of the English armies repeatedly postponed a clear decision. As a result, virtually all the fighting took place on French soil; and the English were free to keep on trying their luck and their manhood. Even in the 1450s, after a century of adventuring, it is doubtful whether the English would have stayed away if they had not been caught by a great civil war of their own.

Given the vast panorama, one should stress that six major royal expeditions from England, which start with Edward III's landing at Antwerp in July 1338, and end with the death of Henry V at Vincennes in August 1422, are somehow less typical than the smaller but more frequent provincial campaigns, and the rovings of independent war parties. The glorious English victories in the set battles at Crécy (1346), Poitiers (1356), or Agincourt (1415), though sensational, were less illustrative of the whole than the interminable skirmishes and castle-storming of the lesser actions. And they must be set against the shameful massacre of the citizens of Limoges by the Black Prince in 1370, or the wanton *chevauchée* from Calais to Bordeaux by his brother John of Gaunt, Duke of Lancaster, in 1373. They were certainly less decisive than the naval battle off L'Écluse (Sluys), where 20,000 Frenchmen perished in 1340. The short-lived royal armies probably caused less devastation than the freelance war parties, the *Grandes Compagnies* of the nobles, or the murderous banditry of the *routiers* and *écorcheurs*. The major diplomatic events, such as the Peace of Brétigny (1360) or the Congress of Arras (1435), were no more productive than the innumerable minor pacts and broken truces.

The miseries of France form an essential backdrop to the main military and diplomatic events. The plague of 1347–9, which forced the third truce, was an important factor. So, too, were the *jacquerie* of 1358; the exploits of Étienne Marcel, draper of Paris, who took control of the Estates-General; the revolt in 1382 of the *maillotins*, who literally hammered the king's tax-collectors to death; the butchers' mob of Jean Caboche, or the warring factions of the Burgundians and the Armagnacs. Ferocious murders were commonplace: Marcel, who had murdered the royal marshals in their master's presence in the Louvre, was himself murdered. Louis d'Orléans, founder of the Armagnacs, was murdered in 1407, as was the Constable of Armagnac and their chief rival, the ex-crusader Jean Sans Peur of Burgundy, on the bridge at Montereau. The unhappy house of Valois sat uneasily on the throne. With the exception of Charles V le Sage (r. 1364–80), a capable despot, they knew little repose. Jean le Bon (r. 1350–64), captured at Poitiers, died in English captivity. Charles VI (r. 1380–1422) passed thirty years in insanity. Charles VII (r. 1422–61), after years as Dauphin and as the hapless 'King of Bourges', survived decades in the shadow of Armagnacs and Burgundians before emerging as 'the Well-Served' at the head of France's resurgent administration. [CHASSE]

The crux of the conflict was reached in the 1420s, a decade which started with the English rampant and ended with the French resurgent. After Agincourt, the young Henry V was busy organizing a new Anglo-French kingdom. By the Treaty of Troyes (1420) he controlled virtually all of France north of the Loire; and as son-in-law of the French King he was formally recognized as heir apparent to the Valois. After his sudden death at Vincennes his infant son, Henry VI, was proclaimed King under the regency of John, Duke of Bedford. Paris remained in Anglo-Burgundian hands from 1418 to 1436, with an English garrison in the Bastille. In 1428 Bedford laid siege to Orléans, the last royal-Armagnac stronghold in the north, and Valois fortunes were depressed to the point of despair. Yet no one had reckoned with that peasant girl, Jeanne d'Arc, *la Pucelle*, the maiden cavalier, who shamed the hesitant Dauphin into action. On 8 May 1429 she charged across the bridge and broke the Siege of Orléans. She then led her reluctant monarch across Anglo-Burgundian territory to his coronation at Reims. By the time of her death in 1431, tied to an English stake in the market square at Rouen, the English tide was ebbing fast. [RENTES]

Thereafter, the tempo of the conflict gradually declined. Once the Congress of Arras in 1435 had weaned Burgundy from the English alliance, it was unlikely that England's fortunes would revive. The *Ordonnance sur la Gendarmerie* of 1439 at last gave the French kingdom a powerful standing army of cavalry and archers. The suppression of the *Praguerie* revolt ended Armagnac and aristocratic resistance. The last actions took place in 1449–53. When the Earl of Shrewsbury was defeated by artillery fire at Castillon in July 1453, and the gates of Bordeaux

CHASSE

LE LIVRE DE LA CHASSE (The Book of Hunting) by Gaston Phœbus, or, to give its full title, *Les Deduits de la chasse des bestes sauvages et des oiseaulx de proye* (1381), is a remarkable social document, which inspired some of the finest illuminated manuscripts ever produced. It is best known in the version of MS 616 Français in the Bibliothèque Nationale in Paris. Its author, Gaston III, called Phébus, Count of Foix and Seigneur of Béarn (1331–91), was a colourful adventurer from Gascony, who had fought for the French at Crécy and for the Teutonic Knights in Prussia, and who had frequently entertained the chronicler Froissart in his Pyrenean castle at Orthez. It surveys all the species of game and the methods of hunting them: wolf, stag, bear, boar, and badger; bloodhound, greyhound, mastiff, and spaniel: stalking, coursing, trapping, netting, shooting, snaring, even poaching; every step from the scent to the *mort* is expertly described and illustrated.[1] (See Plate 30.)

In the fourteenth century, hunting was still an integral part of the European economy. Game provided an essential supplement to the diet, especially in winter. The weapons of hunting—bow, sword, and pike—the horsemanship, and the psychology of the chase and the kill together formed an essential element of military accomplishment. Forest reserves, protected by fierce laws, provided an important item in royal and noble privilege.

In the East, where both the forests and game were larger, and agriculture more precarious, the art of hunting was still more important. The historian, Marcin Kromer, writing in 1577, described a bison hunt in Podolia on the Dniester in terms very reminiscent of a Spanish *corrida*:

Meanwhile, one of the hunters, assisted by powerful hounds, approaches, and draws the bison round and round the tree, playing it and teasing it until it drops from its wounds or just from sheer exhaustion. Should the hunter . . . be threatened by danger, his colleagues distract the bison by waving large red capes, since red is a colour which drives it to a fury. Thus tormented, the bison releases the first man, and attacks the next one who is then able to finish it off.[2]

The development of firearms, and of agricultural production, gradually transformed the techniques and the social role of hunting. In England, for example, where the last wolf was killed in the eighteenth century, hunting had to centre on the fox, the arch-enemy of farmers. The ancient ritual, with the 'hunting pink', the horns, and the howls of 'Tally-ho', were preserved. But the original utility was lost. In 1893 Oscar Wilde could gaily portray the English country gentleman galloping after a fox as 'the unspeakable in full pursuit of the uneatable'.[3] Hunting and shooting had been reduced to a form of recreation. In the eyes of anti-blood sport

fundamentalists, even angling would be added to the list of cruel barbaric survivals.[4] [**KONOPIŠTE**]

In Eastern Europe, hunting retained its social cachet somewhat longer.
It was adopted as a status symbol by the top communist dignitaries. For
them, as for Reichsmarschall Hermann Goering in the 1930s, shooting
bison was the ultimate prize, the ultimate parody of feudal aristocracy.

thrown open to French rule, Calais alone remained in English hands. In 1475, in a
sort of coda, an English army landed in France expecting the support of the
Burgundians; but it was bought off for a pension of 50,000 crowns per annum,
75,000 crowns down payment, and the promise of the Dauphin's marriage to
Edward IV's daughter.

For France, the Hundred Years War was a sobering experience. The population
had fallen by perhaps 50 per cent. National regeneration began from the lowest
possible point. Under Louis XI (r. 1461–83), the 'universal spider' and master of
diplomacy, it proceeded apace, notably by his removal of the Burgundian menace.

For England, the era of the Hundred Years War was crucial in the formation of
a national community. At the outset, Plantagenet England was a dynastic realm
which in cultural as well as political terms was little more than an outpost of
French civilization. By the end, shorn of its Continental possessions, Lancastrian
England was an island kingdom, secure in its separateness, confident in its new-
found Englishness. The Anglo-Norman establishment had been thoroughly angli-
cized. With Geoffrey Chaucer (c.1340–1400) English literature began its long
career. Under Richard II (r. 1377–99) and the three Lancastrians—Henry IV (r.
1399–1413), Henry V (r. 1413–22), and Henry VI (r. 1422–61)—the wars in France
provided a safety valve for energies left over from the violent struggles of monarchy and barons. Richard II was forced to abdicate, and later murdered at
Pontefract. Henry IV, the usurper son of John of Gaunt, seized the throne with
the aid of a false genealogy. Henry V was cut short in his endeavour to conquer
France. Henry VI, another infant king, was eventually deposed. But underneath
the blood-soaked surface of the political stage a firm sense of patriotism and
national pride was building. No doubt it was anachronistic for William
Shakespeare, writing 200 years later, to put England's finest patriotic eulogy into
the mouth of John of Gaunt, who spent so much time and energy fighting over
the spoils of France. But he was expressing a sentiment that grew from the conflicts of that earlier age:

> This royal throne of kings, this scept'red isle,
> This earth of majesty, this seat of Mars,
> This other Eden, demi-paradise
> This fortress built by Nature for herself
> Against infection and the hand of war,

RENTES

CLIOMETRICS—the science of quantitative history—came into its own through computers. Previously, historians were often deterred by the immensity of surviving data and by the inadequate means for exploring them. Statistical samples were small; time-runs were short; and conclusions were tentative. The arrival of historical number-crunching removed many such inhibitions.

The 'Section Six' of the École Pratique des Hautes Études in Paris, founded in 1947, was among the pioneers. One of their projects sought to establish the growth of Parisian ground-rents from the late Middle Ages to the Revolution.[1] The first stage, using 23,000 sets of institutional and private records, was to calculate average annual rents in livres tournois. The second stage, to compensate for currency deflation, was to convert the monetary figures into a series representing real purchasing power. This was done by relating the rents to mean, three-year cycles of wheat prices, expressed in *setiers* or 'hectolitres' of wheat. The third stage was to plot the deflated 'rent-curve' against sample soundings from a second, independent source—in this case, from the records of the *Minutier Central* or 'Main Notaries' Register', which was available from 1550. The resultant concordance was close (see Appendix III, p. 1263):

Average rents by calculation				*Rents from the* Minutier Central		
	Livres	*Setiers*			*Livres*	*Setiers*
1549–51	64.24	16.77		1550	63.72	16.64
1603–5	168.39	17.81		1604	229.00	24.23
1696–8	481.96	23.41		1697	531.00	25.79
1732–4	835.55	55.70		1734	818.35	54.55
1786–8	1281.04	58.63		1788	1697.65	77.69

The Paris 'rent-curve' reflects both political events and economic trends. The low points, when rents were depressed, occurred, predictably enough, during the 'Joan of Arc Depression' of 1420–3, the 'St Bartélémy Basin' of 1564–75, the 'Slump of the Siege' in 1591–3, and the 'Vale of the Fronde' in 1650–6. The periods of recovery tended to be much longer—in the 'Renaissance' of 1445–1500, in the decades of the Price Revolution after 1500, when the rise in 'real rents' lagged far behind the whirlwind ascent of nominal rents, in the era of Louis XIV's stability up to 1690, and on the steady upward slope of the mid-eighteenth century. According to the computer calculations, the highest peaks were reached in 1759–61 (69.78 *setiers*) and in 1777–82 (65.26 *setiers*). According to the *Minutier*, they were reached in 1788 (77.69 *setiers*).

The ultimate value of this data is open to question. The rent curve offers no insight into many key factors which affected the Paris housing market, let alone the French economy in general. It says nothing about the pressure of population, the size and quality of tenements, or the construction of new dwellings. Yet for the pre-modern age, where historians can only dream of a full range of statistics about prices, wages, costs, and incomes, it provides one modest index against which different sources of information can be gauged. Above all, it illustrates the hopes of economic structuralists, who put their faith in establishing the *conjoncture*, the overall pattern of underlying trends. In their view, the *conjoncture* is the foundation on to which all other historical facts are to be fitted.

> This happy breed of men, this little world,
> This precious stone set in a silver sea,
> . . . This blessed plot, this earth, this realm, this England.[24]

It was in France that the English performed those exploits which cemented the spirit of their common patriotism. Where but before Harfleur, on the eve of Agincourt, could Shakespeare have set the speech which ever since has called on the 'noblest English' to hold the breach?

Within England's island kingdom, the Welsh formed the only community which could not be fully assimilated. In 1400–14, at the height of the French Wars, they staged a promising rebellion with links to the King's other enemies in Northumbria, Ireland, Scotland, and France. Under Owain ap Gruffydd, Lord of Glyndyvrdwy (c.1359–1416), who was known to the English as 'Owen Glendower', they revived the vision of a liberated Wales, and briefly reconstituted an independent principality. In 1404–5 a sovereign Welsh parliament was summoned to Machynlleth. Within a decade, however, the enterprise was crumbling. Its fate was sealed by the English victory at Agincourt. After that, the royal castles in Wales were gradually recovered, and Glendower's son was forced to submit. Henceforth, though culturally and linguistically impervious, Wales was to form an integral part of the English realm.

From 1450 onwards England was laid low by a fratricidal war reminiscent of that between the Burgundians and the Armagnacs. An insane king and a disputed succession set the Lancastrians and the Yorkists at each other's throats. The Wars of the Roses did not leave England free to benefit from its growing prosperity until the rivalries of the three contenders—Edward IV, Richard III, and Henry VII—had been buried by the victorious Tudors.

Again, it was out of place for Shakespeare to describe how 'The Blood of England shall manure the ground . . . the field of Golgotha and dead men's skulls'. In reality, if recent research is to be believed, the fighting was rather gentlemanly.[25] Except at Tewkesbury in 1471, prisoners were not generally slaughtered. Much of the action took place on the Celtic fringe: at St Michael's Mount in Cornwall, and in Wales—at Denbigh, Harlech, Carreg Cennen, and at Pembroke, the birthplace of Henry Tudor, who eventually triumphed. The scene at Bosworth Field on 22 August 1485—with the despairing hunchback, Richard III, crying 'My kingdom for a horse', as his discarded crown hung on a thorn bush—has become a cliché. But it gave a fitting end to English medieval history.

One of the by-products of the Hundred Years War was the rise of Burgundy as a quasi-independent state of great brilliance. The eclipse both of France and of the Empire created the opening for a 'middle kingdom', which played a powerful role in European politics but which, lacking in cohesion, was extinguished as rapidly as it had flared. Though royal status evaded the four great Valois dukes of Burgundy—Philippe le Hardi (1342–1404), Jean sans Peur (1371–1419), Philippe le Bon (1396–1467), and Charles le Téméraire (1433–77)—their wealth and prestige exceeded that of many kings. Their initial holding, the ancient Duchy of Burgundy round Dijon, was granted to Philippe le Hardi by his royal French father in 1361. From then on, it was steadily expanded by the acquisition of numerous territories on either side of the Franco-imperial border (see Appendix III, p. 1281). Philippe remained essentially one of the French 'princes of the lilies', together with his brothers, the Duke of Berry and the Duke of Anjou. But thanks to their English alliance his son and grandson were able to free themselves from their family ties. Philippe's great-grandson, Charles the Rash, overstretched himself in a bid to outsmart his neighbours. Their wealth derived largely from the flourishing northern cities—Bruges, Arras, Ypres, Ghent, and Antwerp. Their court was still itinerant, but apart from the Hôtel d'Artois in Paris and the ducal palace in Dijon, they maintained important residences at Lille, at the Prinsenhof in Bruges, at the Coudenberg in Brussels, and at the castle of Hesdin in Artois (see Appendix III, p. 1260).

The Burgundian court was the focus of an extravagant cult of chivalry, manifest in the ceremonies of the Order of the Golden Fleece and the enthusiastic sponsorship of crusading. Tournaments, jousting, banquets, spectacles, processions of all sorts were the rage. The dukes were lavish patrons of the arts—of sculptors such as Claus Sluter, of artists such as Jan van Eyck and Roger van der Weyden, of poets, musicians, romanciers, and of the famous tapissiers. They bedecked themselves and their courtiers in cloth-of-gold, ermine, jewels—all designed to impress and astonish. They were masters of diplomacy and, above all, of diplomatic marriage. Philippe le Bon once offered refuge to his cousin, the future Louis XI, only to watch the one-time refugee turn bitter adversary. Duke Charles was gradually caught up in Louis's political web, defeated by Louis's Swiss allies at Morat, and killed fighting the Lorrainers at Nancy. The *Burgunderbeute* or 'Booty of Burgundy' fills Swiss museums to the present day.[26] [**CODPIECE**]

Charles's death in 1477 precipitated Burgundy's downfall and partition. Louis XI recovered the original duchy; but the lion's share fell to Mary, Charles's daughter, and thence to her husband, Maximilian von Habsburg. Their part of the Burgundian legacy—Flanders, Brabant, Zeeland, Holland, and Guelders—formed the basis of the future Netherlands, and the fortune of their grandson, Charles V, 'the last of the Burgundians'. Nothing remained of the Burgundian

---

CODPIECE

AFTER their victory at Morat in 1476, the Swiss soldiery plundered the Burgundian camp, captured large chests of elegant clothes, cut them to pieces, and held a mock parade in the tattered garments of their foe. This incident has been taken not only to explain the source of the fashionable 'slashed doublet' of the sixteenth century, but to illustrate the military origins of medieval male fashion in general.[1]

At that time two other items of male garb were in evidence, both with explicitly erotic overtones. The *poulaine or cornadu*, the 'horned shoe', was literally on its last legs. Invented to facilitate standing in stirrups, its upturned point was later thought to demonstrate the prowess of members other than toes. The *braguette* or 'codpiece' was on its way in. Invented, according to Rabelais, to protect the genitals in battle, it was more likely devised to facilitate the armoured knight's call to nature. It has also been said to have protected the wearer's clothes from staining by greasy, antisyphilitic ointments. None of which explains why it had to be flaunted in so exhibitionist a fashion for more than a hundred years. In *As You Like It*, Shakespeare wrote of Hercules, whose codpiece was 'as massive as his club'.

Until recently many intimate garments, especially of underwear, were classed as 'unmentionables'. Polite historians ignored them. Nowadays they are the subject of learned dissertations and of lurid exhibitions.[2]

---

state; not even the magnificent ducal mausoleum at the charterhouse of Champmol, near Dijon, has survived.[27]

Many years later, a monk showed the skull of Jean sans Peur to Francis I, King of France, and reportedly said, 'There is the hole through which the English made their way into France.' One could equally point to the brainless ambitions of Charles the Rash: there was the gap that brought the Habsburgs into western Europe.

For the time being, however, the Habsburgs were still on the make. Though they held the imperial title in Germany without interruption from 1438—Frederick III von Habsburg (1440–93) being the last emperor crowned in Rome—they still had not outgrown their rivals. Indeed, in the fourteenth and fifteenth centuries there was nothing to set them above the other mighty dynasties of the region. In the end, it was only by accident that the Habsburgs succeeded where the Jagiellons failed.

For two centuries the rumbustious nobles of Bohemia, Hungary, and Poland, who held the right of confirming the royal succession in their kingdoms, danced an elaborate gavotte with the representatives of four great central European dynasties. They resembled nothing so much as the shareholders of old-established companies who seek an association with one or more of the stronger multi-national conglomerates. In this, whilst assuring a measure of continuing control over their own affairs, they supposedly obtained both experienced management and effective protection from takeovers and mergers. In all three countries, the opening was created by the extinction of the native ruling house. The Árpád line died out in Hungary in 1301, the Přemyslids in Bohemia in 1306, and the Polish Piasts in 1370. (See Appendix III, p. 1261.)

As a result, east-central Europe passed into a long period of shifting dynastic consortia involving the Habsburgs, the Luxemburgers, the Angevins, and the Jagiellons. At first it seemed that the Luxemburgers would get the upper hand. They held the Empire in 1308–13 and 1347–1437, Bohemia 1310–1437, and Hungary 1387–1437. In the mid-fifteenth century the Habsburgs amassed a similar conglomeration, only to see both Bohemia and Hungary pass back to native rulers. By 1490 the Jagiellons controlled Poland-Lithuania, Bohemia, and Hungary, but not the Empire. Imperial or national histories of the period, written without reference to these wider connections, lack an essential ingredient.

Bohemia was a special prize after its kings became hereditary Electors of the Empire. In their final phase, the Přemyslids had taken hold of Austria-Styria-Carinthia, only to lose them to the Habsburgs at the battle of Dürnkrut in 1278. Later, Vaclav II (r. 1278–1305) obtained the crowns of both Poland and Hungary. After the Přemyslids' demise, Bohemia saw periods of Luxemburg, Habsburg, and Jagiellonian rule. In the fifteenth century, the Bohemian crown was embroiled in extended wars both with the nobles and with the Hussites. The last native King, Jiří z Poděbrad (George of Podiebrady, r. 1458–71), gave his country two decades of fragile independence.

The Hussites, who founded a national Czech Church, survived repeated attempts to suppress them. They appeared at a juncture when the Papal Schism was at its height and when Bohemia was rent by conflicts between Czechs and Germans, between kings and nobles, between the clergy and the Pope, between the University and the Archbishop of Prague. Their demands soon exceeded the theological and political propositions advanced by Hus. They were so infuriated by the news of his death, and by the excommunications hurled at the whole Czech people by the Council of Constance, that they launched what in effect was a national rising and 'the first Reformation'. They were divided into two main groups: the Utraquists, who took over the established Church from its largely German, Catholic hierarchy, and the radical Taborites, who founded separate evangelical communities centred on their fortified camp or 'Tábor'.

Matters came to a head in Prague on 30 July 1419. A Hussite procession was stoned in the New Town, and the German burgomaster was thrown to the crowd from the window of his Rathaus. The Pope responded by announcing a general crusade against the heretics. Thereupon the Utraquists, who held that the bread and wine of the Communion should be dispensed *sub utraque specie*, 'in both kinds', promptly formalized their doctrine in the Articles of Prague (1420), whilst the Taborites took to the field under their marvellous one-eyed captain, Jan Žižka z Torncova (1376–1424). Year after year, huge invading armies of German crusaders were heavily defeated. The Hussites, who carried the struggle into Saxony, into Silesia, and into Hungary, suffered most from their own internal divisions. In 1434 a crushing Utraquist victory over the Taborites at Lipany enabled the victors to make their peace with the Catholic Church. Through the Compacts of Basle, they were able to keep an Utraquist church order in Bohemia until 1620. In the subsequent political settlement the Czech nobles attempted to run their own affairs by choosing a Habsburg infant to succeed the Luxemburgers and, twenty years later, by choosing the forceful Utraquist general, Jiří z Poděbrad. After Jiří's death, the Diet settled for Vladislav Jagiellon (r. 1471–90) to save them from the Hungarians and the Habsburgs.

Hungarian history followed a similar pattern to that of Bohemia. In this case, after a brief interval under the Bavarian Wittelsbachs, Hungary was taken over by the Angevins of Naples. Charles Robert or Carobert (r. 1310–42) and Louis (r. 1342–82), known as Lajos the Great, established a powerful supremacy, only to yield to the Luxemburgers and the Habsburgs. The last prominent native king, Matthias Corvinus, ruled from 1458 to 1490. The first Jagiellon to be invited to rule Hungary, Ladislas of Varna (r. 1440–4), was killed fighting the Turks. The third, Louis II (r. 1516–26), died in the same way at Mohács.

Poland was heading for a grander and more independent destiny. After 182 years of feudal fragmentation, it was reunited as a viable kingdom by Władysław Łokietek (r. 1320–33) who, having visited Rome for the Jubilee, obtained a papal crown. Łokietek's son Casimir the Great (r. 1333–70), the last of the royal Piasts, established an efficient administration, a code of laws, and a coherent foreign policy. By resigning Poland's western provinces, notably Silesia, to the Luxemburgs, he freed himself for expansion to the East. His acquisition of Galicia and the city of Lwów in 1349 was Poland's first major step into the east Slav lands. His reception of Jewish refugees from Germany in that same year laid the foundation of Europe's largest Jewish community. The reign of Louis of Anjou was marked by the Statute of Košice (1374) which gave the Polish nobles similar rights to their brothers in Hungary. Henceforth the power of the Szlachta grew inexorably. Most momentous, however, was the marriage of Louis's daughter Jadwiga, already accepted as *rex* in Poland, to Jogaila, Grand Duke of Lithuania. [SZLACHTA]

The union of Poland and Lithuania had wide international implications. By bringing together two large countries, both in a dynamic stage of development, it fuelled a powerful fusion, almost a new civilization. Its immediate rationale derived from the menace of the Teutonic Knights, whose activities were deplored no less in Cracow than in Vilnius. But much more was involved. Poland, which had recovered from the Mongol invasions and escaped the Black Death, was looking eagerly to the open spaces of the East. Lithuania, still ruled by a pagan élite and anxious about the rise of neighbouring Moscow, was looking for an entrée into the mainstream of Christendom. Both were looking for mutual support. Here was a marriage, therefore, that far transcended the two persons most directly involved.

Jadwiga, a twelve-year-old fatherless girl, bowed to her duty. Jogaila, a forty-year-old warrior-bachelor, whom the Poles called Jagiełło, sensed a historic opportunity, which he could not refuse.

Lithuania's baptism followed decades of vacillation between the Latin and the Orthodox options. Jogaila's father, Grand Duke Algirdas (r. 1341–77), had pursued a policy of 'dynamic balance'. Throughout his reign, he teased both Avignon and Constantinople with the prospects of a conversion. In the 1370s it looked as though he would take the Orthodox path in order to supplant Moscow as leader of the Orthodox Slavs. In 1375 he persuaded the Patriarch of Constantinople to create a separate metropolitan of 'Kiev, Rus' and Lithuania', in opposition to the older metropolitanate of 'Kiev and all Rus'', now controlled by Moscow. Jogaila, too, had leaned towards the Eastern option. In 1382 he was pushed towards Moscow, when his disaffected brother began to consort with the Teutonic Knights. As late as 1384 a provisional treaty was concluded by Jogaila's Christian mother, Juliana of Tver, whereby Jogaila was to be betrothed to a Muscovite princess and Lithuania to Orthodoxy. The plans were probably ruined by the Tartars, who razed Moscow and destroyed the value of a Muscovite alliance. So, when the die was cast in favour of union with Catholic Poland, it was cast very suddenly. Jogaila reached agreement with the Polish and Hungarian-Angevin envoys at Kreva in August 1385. On 15 February 1386 he was baptized in Cracow, receiving the Christian name of Władysław. Three days later he was married to Jadwiga. On 4 March he was crowned co-king of Poland.[28] (See Appendix III, p. 1262.)

Oddly enough, when the sacred oaks were felled in Vilnius in 1387, it was not the last Christian conversion in Europe. At the time, the district of Samogitia or 'Lower Lithuania' was occupied by the Teutonic Knights, who did not care to take the same step. So the district did not receive its baptism until recovered by the Lithuanians in 1417.[29] Eleven centuries after Constantine, the long career of pagan Europe reached its term.

The Jagiellons quickly established themselves as a major force. Their future was assured once the Teutonic Knights were routed at the Battle of Grunwald in 1410. With one branch of the family ruling in Vilnius and the other in Cracow, the Jagiellons ruled the largest realm in Christendom. Though Roman Catholicism was the dominant cultural force, and Polish increasingly the language of the ruling nobility, they presided over a multinational community where Polish, Ruthenian, and Jewish interests were all strongly represented. (Lithuanian culture receded into the peasant mass of the north-east.) Jogaila's son Ladislas/Władysław IV (d. 1444) reigned in Hungary as well as Poland, dying on crusade at distant Varna. His grandson Kazimierz Jagiellończyk (r. 1445–92), who was married to a Habsburg, was known as the 'grandfather of Europe'. Indeed, when Kazimierz died in 1492, his heirs looked set to inherit the earth. Fate intervened in the form of the Turk. When Louis Jagiellończyk, King of Bohemia and Hungary, perished heirless on the field of Mohacs in 1526, his possessions reverted to the Habsburgs. And it was the Habsburgs who inherited central Europe. Even so, the Jagiellons had given rise to a civilization that long outlasted their eclipse. [MICROBE]

1. Europa's Ride

*(For Notes on Illustrations
see pp. 1205-12)*

2. Gatherers and Hunters

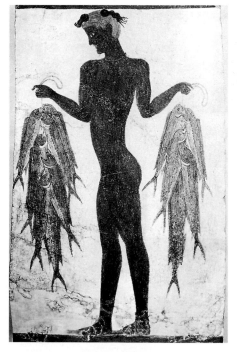

3. Minoan Fisherman

4. Prince of Knossos

5. Symposion—A Banquet

6. Etruscheria

7. Arcadian Idyll

8. Sabine Rape

9. Death of Siegfried

10. Attila invades Rome, AD 452

11. Eastern Orthodoxy

12. Western Monasticism

13. Constantine's Donation

14. The Slavonic Liturgy

15. Catholic Pietism

16. St Augustine

17. St Charlemagne

18. St Matthew

19. SS John the Baptist and Jerome

20. Matka Boska

21. St John the Theologian

22. St Luke—Icon Painter

23. Bogorodica

24. Homage to Otto III

25. England Conquered

26. Wendish Crusade

27. Truce in the Reconquista

28. Tristan's Last Song

29. Iron Plough

30. Scent of the Stag

31. Dante in Love

32. Bartolomea in a Dilemma

33. St Francis blesses the Birds

34. King Casimir greets the Jews

35. Picaro

36. Marco Polo

37. Westerner as Easterner

MICROBE

CASIMIR Jagiellończyk, King of Poland and Grand Duke of Lithuania, was buried in the Holy Cross Chapel of Wawel Cathedral in Cracow in July 1492. In May 1973, 481 years later, the Cardinal-Archbishop of Cracow, Karol Wojtyła, gave permission to a team of conservationists to reopen the tomb, together with that of Casimir's queen, Elizabeth of Austria. The occasion was not unique: the tomb of Casimir the Great (d. 1370) had been reopened in 1869, and the reburial gave occasion for a great Polish patriotic demonstration. The tomb of St Jadwiga (d. 1399) had been reopened in 1949.

Yet the exhumation of 1973 was, in all senses, disturbing. Within a short period of time, no fewer than sixteen persons directly involved had died of uncertain causes. The world's press remembered the 'Curse of the Pharaohs' and speculated about 500-year-old bacilli. A Cracow journalist wrote a best-selling book on *Curses, Microbes and Scholars* which, in the best medieval fashion, reverted its readers' attention to the topic of human mortality.[1]

In late medieval Scandinavia, the three monarchies were overshadowed by the separate interests of a stormy nobility and by the commercial activities of the Hansa. The Viking communities had abandoned their sea-raiding by the thirteenth century, and had settled down to exploit the agriculture of the lowlands, the timber and iron mines, and the rich fishing grounds such as the famous herring-beds off Scania. The Hansa network based at Lübeck and at Visby linked Scandinavia both with Western Europe and with Russia.

In 1397 the remarkable Queen Margaret (1353–1412), who reigned in Denmark by inheritance, in Norway by marriage, and in Sweden by election, succeeded in forging a limited union of the three countries. But this Union of Kalmar was an agglomerate, not a compound; and it was due to disintegrate into its national components. In the favourite saying of Queen Margaret's father, Waldemar IV Atterdag, 'Tomorrow is another day.'

Medieval civilization is frequently called 'theocratic'—that is, it was governed by the all-pervasive concept of the Christian God. God's will was sufficient to explain all phenomena. The service of God was seen as the sole legitimate purpose of all human enterprise. The contemplation of God was the highest form of intellectual or creative endeavour.

It is important to realize, therefore, that much modern knowledge about the Middle Ages has been coloured by the religious perspective of the churchmen who provided the information and wrote the chronicles. To some degree, modern observers may well have been misled 'into supposing that mediaeval civilisation was more intrinsically Christian than was probably the case'.[30] Even so, the central position of Christian belief can hardly be denied. On this point the growing schism between Latin and Orthodox Christianity made little difference. If the West was largely theocratic in outlook, the East was almost completely so. Indeed, the Orthodox world avoided most of the new influences which, from the fourteenth century onwards, made some of the broad generalizations less tenable (see Chapter VII).

There is a distinction to be made, however, between the 'high culture' of the educated élite and the 'low culture' of ordinary people. Recent scholars have contrasted 'clerical culture' with the 'folklore tradition'. Since the educated minority was made up either of clerics or of clerics' pupils, the formal culture of literate circles could be expected to adhere fairly closely to conventional religious teaching. By the same token, since large sectors of the population were illiterate, including untutored women and the unlettered aristocracy, it would not be surprising to find pagan survivals, heretical opinions, or decidedly irreligious viewpoints among them. Traditional medieval scholarship was largely confined to the sphere of high culture. Popular culture is one of the subjects of the 'new Middle Ages', as presented by the latest generation of medievalists.

Imagining the Middle Ages is, indeed, the problem. Historians have to stress not just what the medieval scene contained but also what it lacked. In its physical surroundings, it lacked many of the sights, sounds, and smells that have since become commonplace. There were no factory chimneys, no background traffic noise, no artificial pollutants or deodorants. Tiny isolated settlements existed in an overpowering wilderness of forest and heath, in a stillness where a church bell or the lowing of a cow could carry for miles, amidst a collection of natural but pungent whiffs from the midden and the wood fire. People's perception of those surroundings lacked any strong sense of discrimination between what later times would call the natural and the supernatural, between fact and fiction, between the present and the past. Men and women had few means of verifying the messages of their senses, so all sorts of sensations were given similar credence. Angels, devils, and sprites were as real as one's neighbours. The heroes of yesteryear, or of the Bible, were just as present (or as distant) as the kings and queens of one's own country. Nothing was more fitting, or more obvious, than Dante's story of a living man who could walk through heaven and hell, and who could meet the shades of people from all ages—undecayed, undifferentiated, undivided.

The medieval awareness of time and space was radically different from our own. Time was measured by the irregular motions of day and night, of the seasons, of sowing and reaping. Fixed hours and calendars were in the sacred preserve of the Church. Men travelled so slowly that they possessed no means of testing conventional geographical wisdom. Jerusalem lay at the centre of the three continents—Asia, Africa, and Europe, allocated respectively to the sons of Noah: Shem, Ham, and Japheth. Beyond the continents lay the encompassing ocean, and beyond the ocean the line where heaven and earth merged imperceptibly into one. [TEMPUS]

Medieval interest in the human body was as minimal as the understanding of it. The internal organs were not clearly differentiated, let alone the interdependent workings of the nervous, skeletal, circulatory, digestive, and reproductive systems. Instead, the body was thought to be composed of a marvellous combination of the four elements, the four humours, and the four complexions. Earth, fire, air, and water were matched with black and yellow bile, blood and phlegm, and permed against Man's melancholic, choleric, sanguine, and phlegmatic temperaments. Specialist knowledge grew very slowly. The early fourteenth century saw doctors practising post mortem dissection, and a corresponding improvement in textbooks, notably in the *Anatomia* of Mondini di Luzzi (1316) and of Guido da Vigevano (1345). Surgery benefited from new textbooks such as the *Chirurgica Magna* by Guy de Chauliac (1363). After the experience of the Black Death, quarantine against plague ships was instituted, first at Ragusa (Dubrovnik) in 1377, then at Marseilles in 1383.

Above all, it has been suggested that medieval people lived in a psychological environment of fear and insecurity that inhibited bold and independent thought. Exposure to the forces of nature, incessant warfare, widespread banditry, raids by Vikings, nomads, and infidels, plague, famine, and anarchy—all contributed to the conviction that man was feeble and God was great. Only in the asylum of a monastery could a forceful mind follow its own genius.

Medieval philosophy, therefore, remained essentially a branch of theology. The central task was to accommodate Aristotelian ideas with religious dogma, and more generally to reconcile reason with faith. The greatest of medieval philosophers, the Dominican St Thomas Aquinas (*c.*1225–74), achieved this by saying that human reason was divinely appointed, that faith was rational, and that, properly interpreted, the two could not be contradictory. Related problems were elaborated by three Franciscans, all from Britain: Roger Bacon (1214–92), John Duns Scotus (1265–1308), and William of Ockham (*c.*1285–1349). Bacon, the *doctor mirabilis*, spent fourteen years in prison for his 'suspect novelties'. Duns Scotus, after whom, somewhat quaintly, the English language obtained the word 'Dunce', dissented from Aquinas, arguing that reason could only be applied to the realm of what was immediately perceptible. He was champion of the Immaculate Conception. Ockham, the *venerabilis inceptor*, excommunicated for his pains, was the leader of the so-called Nominalists. His demolition of the reigning Platonic notion of universals—abstract essences that were thought to exist independently of particular objects—undermined the philosophical foundations of many inflexible medieval conventions, including the social orders. 'Ockham's Razor'—the principle that facts should be interpreted with a minimum of explanatory causes—proved a powerful instrument for logical thinking. His complete separation of reason from faith opened the way for scientific and secular investigations. His watchword was *Entia non sunt multiplicanda praeter necessitatem* (entities should not be unnecessarily multiplied). When he was presented to the German Emperor, Lewis of Bavaria, he was supposed to have said, 'If you will defend me with the sword, Sire, I shall defend you with the pen.'

TEMPUS

GIOVANNI DA DONDI (1318–89), Professor of Astronomy at Padua, was by no means the first clockmaker. Dante mentions a clock in his *Paradiso*; and there are records of clocks in London's St Paul's in 1286 and in Milan in 1309. But Dondi's treatise *Il Tractus Astarii* (1364) provides the earliest detailed description of clockwork. It presented a seven-dialled astronomical clock, regulated by an escapement of the crown-wheel-and-verge type. (It has inspired several modern replicas, one of which is displayed in the Science Museum, Kensington, another in the Smithsonian Institution, Washington.)[1] (See Appendix III, p. 1250.)

The original invention of clockwork is usually attributed to an eighth-century Chinese, Liang Lin-son. But practical applications were not made in Europe until the end of the thirteenth century. The first clocks simply struck an hour bell. A machine of this type, built in 1386, still operates in Salisbury cathedral. Later models had dials, showing not only the hours of the day but also phases of the moon, the passage of the planets, even the calendar of saints' days and religious festivals. The finest examples were built at Milan (1335), Strasbourg (1354), Lund (1380), Rouen (1389), Wells (1392), and Prague (1462). Mechanical clocks gradually supplanted earlier types of timepiece such as shadow-clocks, sundials, hourglasses, and clepsydras. They were specially attractive for the northern countries, where sunshine was unreliable. They were constructed in all the great cathedrals, on city squares and gates, and above all in monasteries.

The twenty-four-hour clock, with hours of a fixed duration, revolutionized daily habits of time-keeping. Most people had lived by the variable rhythms of sunrise and sunset. Where systems of hours had been known and used, they varied in length from season to season, and from country to country. Daytime 'temporal hours' differed both from the 'watches' of the night and from the 'canonical hours' of the Church, divided into matins, laude, prime, terce, sext, none, vespers, and compline. Ordinary folk took the idea of a fixed daily routine, regulated by equalized hours, from the medieval monks. These provided the necessary prelude to the later norms of urban life, and to the artificial disciplines of industrialized society. The clock is a 'totalitarian taskmaster' with a powerful socializing influence. Newtonian physics sanctified the idea that the whole universe was one great 'celestial clock'; and it has taken the greatest of modern minds, including Einstein and Proust, to show how unnatural the mechanistic perception of time really is.[2] [**COMBRAY**] [$e = mc^2$]

Landmarks in the evolution of clockwork included miniaturization, which gave rise to domestic clocks in the fifteenth century, and to personal watches in the sixteenth; the pendulum (1657), which greatly increased reliability; the marine chronometer (1761), which solved the long-standing problem of measuring longitude at sea; and the keyless mechanism (1823), which led to popular pocket and wrist watches. The ultimate timepiece, an atomic clock accurate to one second in 3,000 years, was built at Britain's National Physical Laboratory in 1955.

Over the centuries, clockmaking developed from a highly specialized craft to a mass production industry. The early centres were found at Nuremberg and Augsburg, and at Paris and Blois. Switzerland benefited by the influx of Huguenot craftsmen. In the seventeenth and eighteenth centuries England became predominant. France led the field with case design and ornamental clocks. The Black Forest specialized in wooden 'cuckoo clocks'. In the nineteenth century Swiss industry, based at Geneva and at Chaux-les-Fonds in the Jura, gained worldwide supremacy in high-quality machine-made watches.

The craft of clockmakers grew out of the earlier guilds of locksmiths and jewellers. Famous names include Jacques de la Garde of Blois, maker of the first watch (1551); Christian Huygens (1629–95) of the Hague, inventor both of the pendulum and of the spiral-balance hairspring; John Arnold, Thomas Earnshaw, and John Harrison (1693–1776), masters of maritime chronometry; Julien Leroy (1686–1759), clockmaker to Versailles; Abraham-Louis Bréguet (1747–1823), inventor of the self-winding *montre perpetuelle*; and Edward John Dent (1790–1853), designer of Big Ben. Antoni Patek of Warsaw and Adrienne Philippe of Berne joined forces in 1832 to found Patek-Philippe, the leading Swiss firm of the day.

By that time clocks and watches were a universal feature of urbanized Western society. The peasants of Eastern Europe adapted more slowly. For millions of Soviet soldiers, the Red Army's advance into Europe in 1944–5 provided the great chance to 'liberate' and to possess a watch.

Medieval science, too, was inextricably bound up with theology. There was no clear sense of the separation of physical and spiritual phenomena, so that exploring the 'secrets of nature' was frequently seen as immodest prying 'into the womb of Mother Church'. The medieval German language, for example, made no distinction between 'gas' and 'spirit'. Both were *Geist*, the modern equivalent of the English 'ghost'. Scientific experiments often risked charges of sorcery. Alchemy long outpaced physics and chemistry, and astrology outpaced astronomy. The Oxford of Robert Grosseteste (*c.*1170–1253), Chancellor of the University and Bishop of Lincoln, is sometimes taken as the first home of the scientific tradition.

But most of the landmark achievements came from the work of scattered individuals. Roger Bacon's experiments with optics and machines formed part of his general attack on corruption and superstition. He was trying to verify knowledge, in the same way that his unfashionable insistence on Greek was an effort to verify the accuracy of the Latin Scriptures. Bacon's master Pierre de Maricourt (Peter the Stranger) produced a fundamental treatise on magnetism, apparently as he whiled away the time during the Angevin siege of Lucera di Calabria in 1269. Witello, or Vitellon (1230–80), a Silesian, wrote a fundamental treatise on optics, the *Perspectiva*, which, by dividing the mechanical operations of the eye from the co-ordinating function of the mind, opened the way to modern psychology. Nicolas Oresme (*c.*1320–82), Bishop of Lisieux, produced an influential work on the economics of money, and another on astronomy, *De Coelo et Mundo*, which supported the theory of the rotation of the earth. He was an enthusiastic advocate of Reason, a man of the Enlightenment before his time, a denouncer of astrologers and miracle-mongers. 'Everything contained in the Gospels', he argued, 'is *rationabilissima.*' A century later, Cardinal Nicholas Cusanus (1401–64), from Kues on the Moselle, repeated the idea of the earth's rotation, predicted calendar reform, and prophesied the end of the world in 1734. All these men had little difficulty distinguishing the *mirabilia* of nature from the *miracula* of the Church.

Given the gradual accumulation of knowledge, a need was created for ency-clopaedic compendia. Among the most widely distributed were the *Speculum Maius* (1264) of Vincent of Beauvais and the *Opus Maius* (1268) of Roger Bacon.

Religious belief, however, remained surrounded by every form of irrationality and superstition. In the later Middle Ages, Church dogma was still being formulated and systematized. The area of belief which people were ordered to accept unquestioningly was expanding. The Lateran Council of 1215 had made confession and penance obligatory. In 1439 the doctrine of the seven sacraments, from baptism to extreme unction, was regularized. The doctrine of transsubstantiation—the contention that the bread and wine of the Eucharist are miraculously transformed into the blood and body of Christ—was so refined that the priest alone was allowed to drink the wine of the chalice. Lay communicants could only partake of the bread. The separation of the people from the magical, priestly caste was emphasized. Masses were performed on every possible occasion. The cult of the Virgin Mary, the divine mediator with Christ, was officially adopted, the recitation of the *Ave Maria*, 'Hail Mary', being formally added to the order of the Mass after the *Pater Noster*. Every sort of organization, from guilds to chivalric orders, had its patron saint. The veneration of relics was ubiquitous. Pilgrimages were part of everyday life for everyone, not just for the devout. Belief in the super-natural was reinforced by official teaching about an elaborate hierarchy of good and evil angels, and by the universal fear of the Devil. Lucifer, the fallen archangel who once sat beside Gabriel in the empyrean of Heaven, now stalked the world in command of the forces of darkness. The horrors of Hell gave preachers their favourite theme and artists a popular subject.

The mystical tradition, which gave precedence to religious intuition over ra-tional belief, had first found coherent expression in the twelfth century in the Augustinian monastery of St Victor in Paris. It later took deep root among the populace at large. Its leading exponents were headed by St Bonaventura (*c*.1217–74), sometime Master of the Franciscans and author of the influential *Itinerarium Mentis in Deum*; by 'Meister' Johann Eckhart (1260–1327) of Strasbourg, Vicar-General of Bohemia, who reputedly claimed that the world was created by his little finger; by the Fleming Jan van Ruysbroeck (1294–1381), 'the Ecstatic Teacher', author of *De Septem Gradibus Amoris*; by the Englishman Walter Hilton (d. 1396), author of a similar work in the vernacular, *The Ladder of Perfection*; above all by Thomas Hemerken from Kempen, near Cologne, known as Thomas à Kempis (*c*.1380–1471), author of the *Imitatio Christi*. The anonymous Englishman who wrote *The Cloud of Unknowing* was also representative of the genre. Many of the mystics were speculative philosophers; but they taught Christians to cultivate the inner life, and to shun the evil world which they could not control. Their writings helped to fan the embers which eventually fired the Reformation.

Witchcraft developed in parallel to Christian mysticism, and for some of the same reasons. Witches, black and white, were undoubtedly a hangover from the pagan animism of the pre-Christian countryside, as was the firm belief in pixies, elves, sprites, and hobgoblins. Yet the systematic practice of witchcraft seems to have been a product of the late medieval period. What is more, by openly entering into combat with witchcraft, the Church inadvertently fostered the climate of hysteria on which the alleged witches and sorcerers thrived. The crucial Bull *Summis Desiderantes*, which launched the Church's official counter-offensive, was issued by Innocent VIII as late as 1484. The standard handbook for witchhunters, the *Malleus Maleficarum*, was published in 1486 by the Dominicans. If previously there had been reticence about witches' doings, now there could be none. Henceforth all Christendom knew that the legions of the Devil were led by evil women who anointed themselves with grease from the flesh of unbaptized children, who rode stark naked on flying broomsticks or on the backs of rams and goats, and who attended their nocturnal 'sabbaths' to work their spells and copulate with demons. Women were classified as weak, inferior beings, who could not resist temptation. Once the Church gave public credence to such things, the potency of witchcraft was greatly increased. Large sums of money could be obtained by people who undertook to ruin a neighbour's crops or to cause an enemy's wife to miscarry. The frontiers between fact and delusion, between charlatanry and hallucination, were hopelessly blurred.

'It has lately come to our ears', declared Innocent VIII, 'that . . . many people of both sexes have abandoned themselves to devils, *incubi et succubi*, and by their incantations, spells, conjurations and other accursed charms . . . have slain infants in their mother's womb . . . have blasted the produce of the earth, the grapes of the vine, the fruits of the trees . . . These wretches, furthermore, blasphemously renounce the Faith, which is theirs by Baptism, and at the instigation of the Enemy of Mankind they do not shrink . . . from perpetrating the . . . filthiest excesses to the deadly peril of their souls.'[31]

After that, for 300 years and more, witchcraft and witch-hunting were endemic to most parts of Europe. [HEXEN]

Medieval ethics, as expounded by the Church, were governed by hierarchical notions both of the social order and of the moral code. Everyone and everything that was inherently inferior should be subordinated to their superiors: serfs should be obedient to their masters; women should be ruled by men. Venial sins should be distinguished from the seven mortal sins. In those countries where the ancient practice of 'head-money' survived, the murder or rape of a noble person was judged more serious, and hence more costly, than that of ignoble victims. Penitential tariffs emphasized that minor transgressions should not be punished in the same way as major ones. Despite the repressive teaching of St Augustine on sexual matters, sexual peccadilloes were not judged severely. 'Misdirected Love', as Dante put it, could not be compared to sins driven by hatred or betrayal. Adulterers pined in the highest circle of Hell; traitors languished in the Pit. Betrayal of God was the ultimate evil. Blasphemy and heresy carried the greatest opprobrium. The Council of Constance of 1414–17, which burned Jan Hus at the stake, attracted an estimated 700 prostitutes. [**PROSTIBULA**]

Medieval law, too, was governed by a hierarchy of values. In theory at least, human laws were subject to divine law as defined by the Church; in practice, diversity was the norm. A welter of competing jurisdictions—canon law in the ecclesiastical courts, local custom in city or manor courts, royal decrees in the king's courts—were matched by a profusion of legal sources, practices, and penalties. Roman law remained the principal source in southern Europe; Germanic and Slavonic tribal custom were the main source in northern and eastern Europe.

Customary law, however, should not be thought of as the mere survival of primitive practices. It was the product of a long process of detailed bargaining between princes and their subjects, and was often written down in elaborate codes. The *Weistümer*, for example, proliferated throughout Austria and parts of western Germany. In Austria they were known as *Banntaidingen*, in Switzerland as *Öffnungen*. Over 600 have survived from Alsace, where they were known as *Dingofrodeln*. Their existence greatly strengthened the concept of *Gutherrschaft*, as opposed to the prevailing *Grundherrschaft* east of the Elbe, whilst conserving the position of the peasant *Gemeinde* or communes in the countryside. They provide one of the basic explanations why western Germany escaped the tide of 'neoserfdom' which was to occur in the East (see pp. 583–4). In some parts of eastern Europe, such as Bohemia and Silesia, the influx of German settlers led to the merger of German and of local legal customs.

In the later centuries, the revival of classical studies helped Roman law to extend its sphere at the expense of customary law. In 1495, for example, it was admitted to the *Reichskammergericht* or Supreme Court of Justice of the German Empire. Its impact was to be profound. Given the growing fragmentation of sovereignty in the Empire, it encouraged all princes to regard themselves as the sole fount of legislation, and in due course to flood every aspect of life with regulations. The German *Rechtsstaat* or 'state ordered by law' would grow into a land which could produce the famous road sign in Baden: 'It is permitted to travel on this road.'[32]

England alone remained exclusively attached to its common law. In England, as in other countries west of the Rhine, it was assumed that where the law was silent, the citizen was free. France, apart from the growing power of the royal *ordonnances* and of the central *Parlement*, continued to be divided between the sphere of customary law in the north and the sphere of Roman law in the Midi.

Many countries undertook extensive codifications at an early date. In Castile, the *Leyes de las Siete Partidas* (1264–6), which formed the core of later Spanish law, served the same purpose as, for example, the Statutes (1364) of Casimir the Great and the *Dygesta* (1488) in Poland, or the *Sudiebnik* of Casimir Jagiellon in Lithuania. In the absence of police forces, enforcement tended to be weak. Fugitives from justice were ubiquitous. Punishments for those apprehended, therefore, tended to be ferocious and exemplary: hanging was often accompanied by drawing and quartering; mutilation by branding or by amputation was designed to be a social deterrent. Imprisonment and fines, which developed with statute law, led to inhuman conditions for poor prisoners, since little or no provision was made for their upkeep.

Medieval education built on the foundations laid down in the twelfth and thirteenth centuries. Primary learning, of letters and numbers, was largely left to the supervision of the family or the village priest. Secondary learning was supported by the cathedrals and increasingly by city councils. The content, though less so the clientele, was still geared to the training of clergy. The three disciplines of the Trivium—Grammar, Rhetoric, and Logic—were the basic diet. Well-established foundations such as Winchester College (1382) or the Latin School at Deventer enjoyed a national, if not an international, reputation. Several of the large cities in Italy and Germany opened commercial schools. Fourteenth-century Florence possessed six such schools, with over 1,200 pupils. University foundations spread during the fifteenth century to all countries of Latin Christendom: such foundations included Leipzig (1409), St Andrews (1413), and Louvain (1425).

Medieval literature remained predominantly devotional in character, although the secular tradition promoted by the *chansons de geste* and the *byliny* continued to develop. Most books were written in Latin or Greek. Many of them remained within the milieu for which they were written. The fifteenth-century discovery of the works of Hrotswitha of Gandersheim, for instance, a German nun who had written a series of Latin comedies five centuries earlier, suggests that a significant part of medieval literature may never have come into general circulation. An extensive popular literature, however, such as ballads and lives of the saints, was increasingly found in the vernacular, partly because formal education was not available for women. Popular theatre began with the miracle plays staged by the Church. New developments, though pregnant for the future, were confined to narrow circles (see Chapter VII).

Medieval historiography remained the realm of the chroniclers and the annalists—men, often monks, who sought to record the past but not to explain it. Divine Providence was accepted as sufficient causation. The corpus of medieval chronicles contains several hundred major items. Some, such as the early *Anglo-Saxon Chronicle* in England or Nestor's eleventh-century *Primary Chronicle* from Kiev, were written in the vernacular. So too were the great series of French chronicles—Villehardouin (*c.*1150–1212), Joinville (*c.*1224–1317), Froissart (1337–1400), Commynes (1447–1511). Latin or Greek, however, predominated. The chroniclers' bias fell heavily in favour of the Church's view on events, or that of the ruling prince. 'Qui Diex vielt aidier', concluded Villehardouin, 'nuls hom ne li puet nuire' (he whom God wishes to help, no man can harm). Political thought centred on the perennial problem of defining the powers of Church and State. Carolingian thinking had approximated to the Caesaropapism of Byzantium. Feudalism stressed the concept of contract. The investiture dispute and its derivatives produced ardent apologists both for papal supremacy or, like Dante's *De Monarchia*, for the imperial cause. Roman ideas on sovereign monarchy re-emerged with the study of Roman law, especially in France. But nothing was so revolutionary as the anti-papal treatise, *Defensor Pacis*, of Marsilio of Padua (1270–1342), sometime rector of the University in Paris, who dared to propose that supreme authority should be wielded by a sovereign people controlling a secular state.

International relations were governed by St Augustine's idea of a just war. In theory, war could only be just if it satisfied certain conditions. According to Ramón di Peñafort, these were: the desire to redress injury, the exhaustion of alternative means, the use of professional soldiers, the good faith of the instigator, and the approval of the sovereign. In practice, warfare was endemic. Subservient clerics could always be found to confirm the justice of anyone's cause, private or public. Outbreaks of temporary peace punctuated the normal predominance of fighting. And war involved the unbridled licence of the soldiery. Medieval military logistics and technology did not facilitate the rapid settlement of disputes. Armies were tiny, the theatres of operations vast. A defeated enemy could easily retire and recoup. Action was directed at local castles and strong-points. Sieges were more common than set battles. The spoils of war were more desired than mere victory. In the fourteenth and fifteenth centuries mercenary companies, first raised by the Italian cities, were used to supplement the unwieldy feudal hosts. Longbows, and crossbows, greatly improved since their appearance in the twelfth century, increased fire-power. Gunpowder, first used in the fourteenth century, led to artillery, which, in the hands of Hussites or Turks, became a decisive arm. But armoured cavalry remained the backbone of any major fighting force.

Medieval architecture was dominated by two classes of stone building—churches and castles. The late medieval church style, which the nineteenth century was to dub 'Gothic', is widely thought to be essentially aesthetic in inspiration—soaring, as it were, towards Heaven. As such, it is often contrasted with the military functionalism of the turrets, barbicans, and machicolations of the castles. In fact, all the main Gothic features, from the pointed arch to the flying buttress, are no less functional than aesthetic: they were devised for the purposes of efficient vaulting and of large window spaces. From the innovations of Abbot

Suger at St Denis, the Gothic spread all over Latin Christendom. Gothic cathedrals were built from Seville to Dorpat, and at all points in between. The Orthodox world, in contrast, stayed loyal to the Romanesque-Byzantine tradition. East of the Catholic/Orthodox divide there are neither Gothic cathedrals nor private castles. New-found civic pride gave rise to magnificent belfries, city halls, and cloth halls. Fine examples were built at Brussels (1402), Arras, Ghent, Ypres (1302), and Cracow (1392). [GOTHIC]

Most medieval arts developed in the setting of church or cathedral. Painting was directed either to icons and altar-pieces or to the religious scenes of church murals. Book illumination was undertaken to adorn bibles and psalters. Sculpture in stone gloried in the statues and tableaux of cathedral fronts, and in the effigies of tombs and chantries. Sculpture in wood embellished choir stalls or choir screens. Stained glass filled the vast expanses of Gothic church windows. 'All art was more or less applied art.'[33]

Yet the secular element in medieval art, never completely absent, was growing. Princes, and then the rich bourgeois, began to commission their portraits or their statues. The art of illumination was applied to copies of the *chansons de geste* and to the fashion for books of hours, herbaries, and bestiaries. Late medieval dress entered a period of extravagant flamboyance where rich materials, fantastic styles, and brilliant colours were all designed for effect. Green represented love; blue, fidelity; yellow, enmity; white, innocence. Heraldry moved from its original military function into the realm of social ostentation.

Medieval music, too, saw a fruitful blending of the sacred and the profane. The dominant sounds still emerged from the churches; but secular patronage was increasing, notably in Burgundy and the Flemish cities. The *ars nova* style of the fourteenth century enjoyed the same international influence as Gothic architecture. John Dunstable (*c*.1390–1453), court musician to the Duke of Bedford in France, was innovative and influential, as was Guillaume Dufay (*c*.1400–74). Choral polyphony developed, as did instrumental music. The dulcimer has been noted in 1400, the clavichord in 1404, the organ keyboard in 1450, the sackbut or trombone in 1495.

The 'medieval person' is an abstraction, and as such is unhistorical. Individuals are by definition unique, and no one person can possibly reflect all the main social, intellectual, and artistic trends of an age. Yet some attempt must be made to overcome the anonymity which surrounds many medieval endeavours. Individualism was not in fashion. Artists such as Jan Van Eyck might occasionally sign their works—JVE FECIT—but as often as not leading figures remained anonymous. Hence the very great value of modern works which seek to reconstruct the detailed lives of ordinary people. [MERCANTE]

No one is more medieval, however, in the utter conviction of the mission of Christendom, and yet more open to all the rich currents of the age, than the famous Catalan doctor, philosopher, linguist, poet, prodigious traveller and martyr, Ramon Llull (*c*.1235–1315). Born in Palma, Majorca, shortly after the Aragonese conquest, he knew Arabic no less than Latin; and he was raised on the

MERCANTE

IN 1348 or 1349 the young Messer Francesco Datini inherited a small plot of land in the town of Prato, near Florence. Both his parents had died in the Black Death. He sold the land, and used the proceeds to set up business in the papal city of Avignon. There he flourished, importing silk, spices, weapons, and armour from Italy. In due course he was able to transfer the business to Florence, opening branches in Pisa, Genoa, Barcelona, Valencia, Majorca, and Ibiza. He was specially strong in the wool trade, buying fleeces direct from producers in England, Spain, and the Balearics. As he sat at his counter in Florence, he supervised the construction of a splendid *palazzo* in Prato, and the management of his country estate in the Apennine foothills. The *palazzo*, which still stands, was built round an arcaded courtyard and with a marble-panelled frontage. It was run by his wife, Monna Margharita, helped by his bastard daughter Ginevra, and by a large domestic staff, including slaves. It was enlivened by the constant flow of messengers and mule-trains. When Messer Francesco died heirless on 16 August 1410, of the gallstones, he bequeathed his estate, his papers and an enormous endowment of 70,000 gold florins, to the poor people of Prato. Over the door was inscribed:

> Ceppo di Francescho di Marco
> Mercante dei Poveri di Xto
> del quale il Chomune di Prato
> è dispensatore
> lasciato nell'anno MCCCCX.

(Almshouse of Francesco, son of Marco | Merchant of Christ's Poor | Of which the Commune of Prato | is trustee | Bequeathed in the year 1410).

Francesco's will also arranged for the manumission of his slaves, the cancellation of all debts, and payment of a sum for the restitution of profits from usury.[1]

The Datini Archive contains over 150,000 letters, 500 account ledgers, 400 insurance policies, and 300 deeds of partnership. It shows how Messer Francesco, by extraordinary attention to detail, kept the pulse of a multinational operation. It also gave historians an unparalleled picture of a medieval company and household.[2] A typical bill of exchange reads:

In the name of God, 12th February 1399. Pay at usance[3] by this first of exchange to Giovanni Asapardo £306. 13s. 4d. *Barcelonesi*, which are for 400 florins received here from Bartolomei Garzoni at 15s. 4d. per florin. Pay and charge to our account there and reply. God keep you. Francesco and Andrea, greetings from Barcelona. Accepted March 13. Set down in Red Book B, f 97.[4]

Such transactions moved money and credit round Europe effortlessly. But they did not cure Messer Francesco's incurable anxiety:

I dreamed last night of a house that had fallen to pieces . . . and it gives me much to ponder on. For there is no news of a galley that left Venice more than two months ago bound for Catalonia. I had insured her for 300 florins . . . But I am so vexed . . . The more I seek, the less I find. God knows what will happen.[5]

According to Braudel, the world of the *Mercante a taglio* or *Fernhandler*, the rich and powerful 'long-distance merchants', has to be extracted from the petty dealing and intense competition of small-scale, local market economies. The former were the true capitalist pioneers. Thanks to their superior sources of intelligence and their command of large sums of ready cash, they could escape the laws of market competition. By concentrating on single transactions of great promise, this 'small group of large merchants' stood to make exorbitant profits:

From the very beginning, [these men] went beyond national boundaries . . . [They] knew a thousand ways of rigging the odds in their favour: the manipulation of credit, and the profitable game of good money for bad . . . They grabbed up everything worth taking—land, real estate, rents.[6]

Generally speaking, the capitalists did not specialize, and they did not finance manufactures. They put their money promptly wherever the maximum opportunity lay. Money trading was the one area in which they did sometimes concentrate their interest. 'But its success never lasted long, as if the economic edifice could not pump enough nourishment up to this high point of the economy.' From the fourteenth century onwards, therefore, a cavalcade of inordinately wealthy capitalists creamed off the greatest profits of the European economy—the Bardi, the Medici, the Fuggers, the Neckers, and the Rothschilds.

Clearly, the successes and disasters of the capitalists rested on the general movements of the European economy. In the fifteenth century, 'the "ground floor" of economic life recovered', especially in the cities. In the sixteenth century, when Atlantic trade expanded, 'the driving force operated at the level of the international fairs—Antwerp, Frankfurt, Lyons and Piacenza'. The seventeenth century, though often described as a period of stagnation, saw 'the fantastic rise of Amsterdam'. In the 'general economic acceleration' of the eighteenth century, when London supplanted Amsterdam, the uncontrolled private market outperformed the regulated public market. Finally, 'financial capitalism only succeeded . . . after the period 1830–60, when the banks grabbed both industry and merchandise, and when the general economy could support this edifice permanently'.[7]

About that time, in 1870, Messer Francesco's ledgers were found in a pile of sacks under the stairs of his house in Prato. His motto was written inside each ledger: 'In the Name of God and of Profit'.

works of the Moorish and Jewish philosophers. He laboured for many years at the Franciscan monastery at Miramar on Mt Randa, before setting out on his endless tours to persuade popes and princes to adopt the teaching of oriental languages. He taught at various times at Montpellier, Paris, Padua, Genoa, Naples, and Messina, and journeyed as far afield as Georgia and Abyssinia. At the Council of Vienne in 1311 he witnessed the nominal acceptance of his cherished proposals. He made repeated missionary expeditions to Muslim North Africa, where he was tragically stoned to death for his pains. His *Libro del Gentil* (1272) (Book of the Gentile and the Three Sages), first published in Arabic, describes an inconclusive disputation between the three religions. His *Ars Major* and *Ars generalis* contain a mass of speculative philosophy, which impressed thinkers as different as Giordano Bruno and Leibniz but which is largely disregarded. Llull had a vision of universal knowledge:

It took the form of what can only be described as a computing engine, which linked up the basic principles or 'ground-words' of all knowledge by a mechanism consisting of concentric circles segmented by radii and of geometric symbols. It seems to have been what might be called a cybernetic machine, prepared to unravel every problem, every science, even faith itself . . .[34]

His *Blanquerna* (1283) is sometimes cited as the world's first novel, or the first utopian tract. His poetry, in *El Desconort* or *Lo Cant de Ramon*, is beautifully simple and sincere. Llull has been called 'a great European'.

The fifteenth century is generally taken as the century of transition between the medieval and the modern periods. In certain spheres the quickening pace of change led to a decisive break with the medieval tradition. This was true in learning, in the arts, and, to some degree through the rise of national monarchies, in politics (see Chapter VII). In most other spheres, the old order held sway. Huge variations, of course, continued to persist. If life in some of the late medieval cities was precociously developed, especially in Italy and the Low Countries, life in the countryside remained largely unaffected. Old and new lived side by side. [**PRESS**] The gulf between Latin Christendom in the West and Orthodox Christendom in the East was steadily increasing.

   For the fifteenth century saw a momentous shift in the strategic confrontation between Christendom and Islam. In 1400 the European Peninsula was still gripped in the Muslim pincers that had stayed in place for the previous 700 years. One arm of the pincers still held on, ever more precariously, to Granada. The other arm, ever more persistently was throttling Constantinople. Yet by 1500 the pincers had slipped, and the main axis of the confrontation had moved dramatically. Islam, which was finally defeated in the West, was victorious in the East. As the Moors finally faltered, the Ottoman Turks triumphed. At the very time that Western Europe broke free of the Muslim blockade, Eastern Europe was confronted with the Muslim challenge in intensified form. In 1400 the main weight of the Muslim world could be felt along the whole of the traditional southern front.

PRESS

THE printing-press of Johann Gensfleisch zum Gutenberg, which started work c.1450 in the Rhineland city of Mainz, did not initiate the art of printing. It was the successor to an ancient line of Chinese woodblocks, metal engraving plates, and stone lithographs. Even so, it launched a revolution in information technology. Like many inventions, it created an original process through the combination of several existing techniques, including those of the Roman wine-press, the goldsmith's punch, and impressionable paper. Also, through the use of movable metal type cast in replica moulds, it saw the first application of 'the theory of interchangeable parts'—one of the basic principles of a later machine age. It possessed the inestimable facility for the text of a book to be set up, edited, and corrected before being reproduced in thousands of identical copies.

Gutenberg is probably best remembered for his 43-line and 36-line Bibles. But in some ways his printing of the *Catholicon* or 'Book of Universal Knowledge' represents a more distinctive milestone. This encyclopedia had been compiled by the Genoese Giovanni Balbo in the thirteenth century. In Gutenberg's printed edition, it marked the first item of secular literature in mass circulation. It contains a brief preface from the publisher:

With the help of the Most High, at whose will the tongues of infants become eloquent . . . this noble book has been printed and accomplished without the help of reed, stylus, or pen, but by the wondrous agreement, proportion, and harmony of punches and types, in the Year of the Lord's Incarnation 1460, in the notable city of Mainz of the renowned German nation.[1]

Within the period of *incunabula* before 1500, when printing was in its swaddling clothes, the main roman, italic, and gothic type-styles emerged; and the presses spread quickly to Basle (1466), Rome (1467), Pilzno in Bohemia (1468), Paris (1470), Buda (1473), Cracow (1474), Westminster (1476), and Cetinje in Montenegro (1493). Printing reached Moscow in 1555.

The power of the printed word inevitably aroused the fears of the religious authorities. Hence Mainz, the cradle of the press, also became the cradle of censorship. In 1485, the local Archbishop-Elector asked the city council of nearby Frankfurt-am-Main to examine the books to be exhibited at the Lenten Fair, and to help in the suppression of dangerous publications. As a result, in the following year, Europe's earliest censorship office was set up jointly by the electorate of Mainz and the city of Frankfurt. The first edict issued by the Frankfurt censor against printed books banned vernacular translations of the Bible.[2] [INDEX]

In contrast to Christendom, the Islamic world exercised a total ban on printing until the nineteenth century. The consequences, both for Islam and for the spread of knowledge in general, can hardly be exaggerated.[3]

By 1500, though the green flags of the Prophet still waved along the African coast, they were concentrated overwhelmingly in the East. Christians of the Latin West could rejoice; Christians of the Orthodox East could not. [**MATRIMONIO**]

The strategic shift was signalled by two landmark events: the fall of Constantinople to the Turks in 1453 and the fall of Granada to the Spaniards in 1492. The consequences were immense. The shift gave rise in the religious sphere to the last vain attempt to reunite the two divided halves of Christendom; in the economic sphere to the search for new trade routes. In the realm of geopolitics, it ensured that the emergent kingdom of Spain was bathed in Catholic triumphalism, whilst the emergent principality of Moscow was immersed in the resentments of the Orthodox defeat. The liberated West, led by Spain, was preparing for the conquest of new worlds. The embattled Orthodox East, led by Moscow, dug in behind its mental stockade. Each in its own way was preparing a further round in the medieval quest for a Christian empire.

Given the Ottoman encirclement of Constantinople (see p. 386), Christian leaders were driven to reconsider the healing of the Schism between the Greek and Latin Churches. The result was the ill-starred Union of Florence of 1439, one of the most pathetic episodes in the scandalous annals of Christian disunity. The Greeks had been petitioning the Papacy for decades, and a Venetian Pope, Eugene IV (1431–47), finally recognized the emergency. Indeed, being pressured beyond endurance by the reforming Council of Basle, he saw that mending relations with the Orthodox might strengthen his own position. The negotiations which opened in Ferrara in January 1438 and continued in Florence were led by the Pope; by the Byzantine Emperor John VIII Palaeologos (r. 1425–48) and his Patriarch; and by twenty-two bishops, who had deserted their colleagues in Basle to attend. Not surprisingly, the desperate Greeks gave way on all matters of substance, readily accepting the Roman doctrines of papal supremacy, purgatory, the Eucharist, and the *Filioque*. The way was cleared for reinstating the unity of the Church on papal terms. In the decree *Laetantur coeli* of 6 July 1439, the union was formally sealed. The text of the union was read from the pulpit of Santa Croce in Latin by Cardinal Julian and in Greek by Archbishop Bessarion of Nicaea; and the two churchmen symbolically embraced.

Unfortunately, none of the parties to the Union actually possessed the means for putting it into effect. The Pope was bitterly denounced by the rump of the Council of Basle, which moved swiftly to elect the last of the antipopes, Felix V (1439–49). The German bishops stayed aloof. The French bishops, elated by the recent enactment of the antipapal Pragmatic Sanction of Bourges, leaned towards the Council. The attempt to end the Schism with Constantinople had provoked yet another schism within the Roman Church itself. The Orthodox Church was no more enthusiastic. In Constantinople, the clergy who had signed the Union were repudiated. 'We need no Latins,' the mob shouted. 'God and the Madonna who have saved us from Persians and Arabs will save us now from Muhammad.' In Alexandria, a synod convened by the eastern Patriarchs condemned the Union outright. In Moscow, the Metropolitan Isidore returned from Florence wearing a

MATRIMONIO

SIGISMUND DE ZORZI and his wife, patricians of fifteenth-century Ragusa, had twelve children—six boys and six girls. In the order of their birth, c.1427–49, the children were Johannes, Franciscus, Vecchia, Junius, Margarita, Maria, Marinus, Antonius, Helisabeth, Aloisius, Artulina, and Clara.

Three boys and one of the girls did not marry. Even so, finding suitable marriage partners for the other eight must have kept their parents busy over at least two decades. Margarita (No. 5) was the first to be betrothed in 1453, closely followed by Maria (No. 6, 1455) and the eldest daughter, Vecchia (1455). The eldest son, Johannes, did not marry until 1459, when he must have been at least 32 years of age. He was followed the next year by his sister, Helizabeth (No. 9), who was about 16 years his junior. Franciscus (No. 2) waited until 1465, when he was about 36, whilst 1471 saw the betrothals both of Artulina (No. 11), aged about 24, and Junius (No. 4), aged about 38.

The pattern of marriages in this one family was not unusual. They match not only those of other patrician families in Ragusa but also studies from Renaissance Italy. It conforms to what historical demographers have called the Mediterranean Marriage Pattern (MMP), characterized by high levels of celibacy and by a gross discrepancy in the age at marriage of sons and daughters.[1]

Ragusa was a city-republic living from Adriatic shipping and the overland Balkan trade.[2] (It gave its name to the English word 'argosy'.) Its population of c.20,000 was dominated by a score of closely intermarried patrician clans who held all the municipal offices. Marriage in medieval Ragusa was a serious business. Detailed *pacta matrimonialia* were drawn up between the bride's father and the prospective son-in-law. Dowries were fixed on average at 2,600 *hyperi* (866 gold ducats). The standard penalty for not proceeding within the agreed period from betrothal to wedding and consummation was 1,000 gold ducats. The average age at betrothal, usually two to three years before marriage, was 18 for girls, 33.2 for men. As the de Zorzi example shows, brothers usually had to wait until their sisters had been provided for.

The underlying factors of Ragusa's 'marriage culture' were economic, biological, mathematical, and customary. Men held back from matrimony until they could support a family and could expect a share of their father's legacy to augment the wife's dowry. Many waited so long that they never married at all. Women entered matrimony much earlier, but not just to maximize their child-bearing capacity. They had to compete for the pool of reluctant grooms. Families preferred their sons-in-law, who would normally become business partners, to be mature, and to take early responsibility for their daughters' 'honour'.

> The ramifications of marriage strategy in history are so complex that macro-theorizing on the subject has proved less satisfactory than empirical local studies. The theory which divided the whole of Europe into two simple zones of a late-marrying 'European [sic] Marriage Pattern' and an early-marrying 'East European Marriage Pattern'[3] carries much less conviction than the micro-analysis of matrimony in medieval Florence[4] or Renaissance Ragusa. [**ZADRUGA**]
>
> Ragusa retained its independence until 1805, when it was occupied by the French. After a century of Habsburg rule, it was joined in 1918, as Dubrovnik, to Yugoslavia, and to the Republic of Croatia in 1992. The medieval city in which the de Zorzi lived was twice devastated—by the earthquake of 1667 and by the Serbian naval bombardments of 1991–2. Among the many Renaissance buildings in the Stari Grad which took a direct hit was the Sponza Palace, home of the city archives and of the marriage registers.[5]

Latin cross and was promptly imprisoned. His bishops rebelled against the 'treason of the Greeks', and proceeded to elect a new Metropolitan without reference to the Patriarch of Constantinople. This was the start of separate Russian Orthodox tradition.

The Ottomans pressed on. At Varna on the Black Sea coast, in 1444, the Ottoman Sultan Murad II destroyed the last of the crusades which papal money could send against him. In 1448 he crushed the last of the Hungarian expeditions across the Danube. Only in Albania, under Skanderbeg, did resistance to the Sultan flourish. Feeble, friendless, but still defiant, Constantinople awaited its destiny. [**VLAD**]

The final siege of Constantinople began on 2 April 1453, Easter Monday, and lasted for eight weeks. The twenty-year-old Sultan, Mehmet II (r. 1451–81), handsome and secretive, was eager to attack, having been frustrated as a boy, when his plan for a campaign against the Walls had been rejected. The bachelor Emperor, Constantine XI Palaeologos (r. 1448–53), still optimistically searching for a bride, awaited him without illusions. Preparations had been thorough. The cities of Thrace and the Black Sea coast were ravaged to prevent assistance. A fleet of triremes and transport barges was assembled at Gallipoli. A castle was built at the narrowest point of the Bosporus at Rumeli Hisar. A 26-ft (7.9-m) bronze cannon, hurling stone shot of 12 hundredweight (609 kilos) each, had been specially cast by the Sultan's Hungarian engineer, and was pulled from Adrianople by 60 oxen. Inside the city, weapons were collected and money raised to pay the troops. Outside the walls, the ditches were deepened and the moat by the Blachernae Gate flooded. Embassies were duly sent to Venice, to the Vatican, to France and Aragon. A company of 700 men arrived under Giovanni Giustiniani Longo, a Genoese captain who was given command of the land walls. On the day that the

VLAD

VLAD III, Prince of Wallachia (1431–76), otherwise known as 'Dracula' and 'Vlad the Impaler', quickly passed into legend as a byword for cruelty. In recent times, the sexual overtones of his perversion have attracted much notoriety. Yet he was an historical figure, whose birthplace at Sighişoara, and castles at Poenari and Bran, can be visited in present-day Romania. His principality of Wallachia lay on the left bank of the lower Danube, squeezed between the great Kingdom of Hungary, which regarded him as its vassal, and the growing empire of the Ottoman Turks, to whom he paid tribute. During the Crusade of Varna in 1443–4, when he was an adolescent boy, he was sent as a hostage to the court of the Ottoman Sultan, Murad II; and the buggery to which he was subjected can be considered the likely psychiatric source of his later obsessions.

The use of the *pala* or 'pointed stake' was well known to the Turks as a form of punishment. But in the hands of Vlad III it became an instrument of veritable mass terror. In the more refined variant, a needle-thin stake, specially sharpened and greased, was rammed in the victim's rectum and out through the mouth in such a way that the death throes could last for days. Vlad III came to power in 1456, only three years after the Turkish Conquest of Constantinople, and saw himself as champion of the Christian princes confronting the Infidel. One expedition across the Danube reputedly brought him 23,883 prisoners for impaling, not counting those mercifully beheaded or burned alive. At home, his reign began with the mass killing of the Wallachian nobility, perhaps twenty thousand men, women, and children impaled on a forest of stakes beneath the castle window.[1]

Dracula's arrest and imprisonment by Matthias Corvinus, King of Hungary, led in 1463 to the publication in Vienna of a German account of his misdeeds, *Geschichte Dracole Wayde*, which was the basis for all subsequent literature. A Russian version produced in 1488 was certainly known to Ivan the Terrible, who seems to have made use of it. Its pages serve to remind us of the strange connection between religious fanaticism and pathological cruelty which persisted in both East and West. The annals of the Spanish Inquisition, or of the Marian persecution in England as related in John Foxe's *Book of Martyrs* (1563), belong to the same sickening genre as the horrors of the Wallachian vampire-prince.[2] [**LUDI**]

[**TORMENTA**]

first Turkish detachments came into view, a procession of migrating storks flew over the Straits. The city gates were closed. A great iron chain was stretched across the entrance to the Golden Horn. Only 7,000 defenders stood to arms against the onslaught of 80,000.

The progress of the siege at first gave encouragement to the defenders, though the impaling of Christian prisoners in view of the Walls was calculated to cause panic. On 12 April a naval attack on the boom failed. The great cannon, firing once every seven minutes from sunrise to sunset, day after day, reduced large sections of the outer wall to rubble. But the gaps were filled at night with wooden stockades. On 20 April an imperial transport flotilla fought its way into the harbour. Turkish mining operations were betrayed.

But then, in a masterstroke, the Sultan ordered his fleet of galleys to be dragged overland behind Pera and into the Golden Horn. The City lost its harbour. From then on, the defenders had only three options: victory, death, or conversion to Islam. On 27 April an ecumenical mass was celebrated in St Sophia, for Greeks and Italians, Orthodox and Catholics. 'At this moment, there was Union in the Church of Constantinople.'[35]

The decisive assault was launched about half-past one in the morning of Tuesday, 29 May, the fifty-third day of the siege. First came the bashi-bazouk irregulars, then the Anatolians, then the Janissaries:

The Janissaries advanced at the double, not rushing in wildly . . . but keeping their ranks in perfect order, unbroken by the missiles of the enemy. The martial music that urged them on was so loud that the sound could be heard between the roar of the guns from right across the Bosphorus. Mehmet himself led them as far as the fosse, and stood there shouting encouragement . . . Wave after wave of these fresh, magnificent and stoutly armoured men rushed up to the stockade, to tear at the barrels of earth that surmounted it, to hack at the beams that supported it, to place their ladders against it . . . each wave making way without panic for its successor.[36]

Just before sunrise, Giustiniani took a culverin shot on his breastplate and retired, covered in blood. A giant janissary called Hasan was slain after mounting the stockade; but he showed it was possible. A small sally-port, the Kerkoporte, was left open by retreating Greeks, and the Turks swarmed in. The Emperor dismounted from his white Arabian mare, plunged into the fray, and disappeared.

Constantinople was sacked. Gross slaughter and rapine ensued. St Sophia was turned into a mosque:

The *muezzin* ascended the most lofty turret, and proclaimed the *ezan* or public invitation . . . The imam preached; and Mohammed the Second performed the *namaz* of thanksgiving on the great altar, where the Christian mysteries had so lately been celebrated before the last of the Caesars. From St Sophia, he proceeded to the august but desolate mansion of a hundred successors of the great Constantine . . . A melancholy reflection on the vicissitudes of human greatness forced itself on his mind, and he repeated an elegant distich of Persian poetry. 'The spider has woven his web in the Imperial Palace, and the owl hath sung her watch-song on the towers of Afrasiab'.[37]

The Roman Empire had ceased to exist.

In the course of their conquest of the eastern Mediterranean, the Ottoman Turks gradually set the terms of trade in the region, controlling the routes which linked Europe with the Levant and India. In practice the Turks were tolerant to Christian traders, and the reluctance of Venice and Genoa to assist Constantinople can only be explained by the lucrative trade which they already operated in the Ottoman realms. But contemporaries further afield may have judged the situation differently; and the rise of the Ottomans is traditionally associated with the attempts by Christian leaders in the West, led by Portugal, to discover a new route to India. It may well be, of course, that the Portuguese were as unwelcome to the Venetians as to the Turks, or were pulled by the lure of African slaves and beautiful islands.

At all events, for forty years Prince Henry of Portugal (1394–1460), known as 'the Navigator', sent expedition after expedition down the western coast of Africa in the wake of earlier Arab voyagers. His ships found Porto Santo (1419), Madeira (1420), the Canaries (1421), later ceded to Castile, the Azores (1431), Cabo Blanco (1441), and Cape Verde (1446). The fate of the Canaries, where the native Guanche population was annihilated under Spanish rule, gave a foretaste of the instincts of later European colonization. In 1437 the Colonial and Naval Institute at Sagres was founded, the first of its kind. By 1471 the Portuguese were strong enough to wrest Tangier from the Moors. In 1486, sailing from Portuguese settlements on the Gold Coast, Bartholomew Diaz rounded the *Cabo Tormentoso*, subsequently renamed the Cape of Good Hope. In 1497 Vasco da Gama completed an unbroken voyage from Lisbon to Calicut, thereby circumventing the Ottoman sphere. [**GONCALVEZ**]

In neighbouring Spain, that same era was crowned by a famous political union. The two rival kingdoms of Castile and Aragon had long tempered their rivalry with dynastic alliances and marriages. The marriage of Juan I of Trastámara, King of Castile (r. 1379–90), to Eleanora of Aragon produced the protoplasts of both the Castilian and the Aragonese houses of the following century. One son, Henry III (r. 1390–1406), reigned in Castile, whilst the second son, Ferdinand I, was unexpectedly chosen in 1412 for the throne of Aragon in Barcelona. The marriage between Henry III's granddaughter Isabella, Princess of Castile (1451–1504), 'La Católica', and Ferdinand I's grandson, Ferdinand, Prince of Aragon (1452–1516), 'El Católico', which was concluded in 1469 at Valladolid, was not without precedent; but its future implications were immense.

Both bride and groom were heirs to the desperately troubled families, and to viciously disputed kingdoms. They were cousins, and knew well what to expect if their relatives or their nobles were allowed to gain control. Isabella, upright and devout, had been touted for marriage in Portugal, England, and France throughout her childhood, and had only been saved from the altar by the death of an unwanted suitor on his way to the wedding. Her claim to Castile only arose through the unlawful exclusion of her niece; and her accession in 1474 sparked off both a civil and an international war with France and Portugal. Ferdinand, devious and devout, sought her hand as a means of escape from his own miserable

GONCALVEZ

IN 1441 Antam Goncalvez sailed his tiny ship out of Lisbon, edged southwards along the Atlantic coast of Morocco, passed the Canary Islands,
and rounded Cape Bojador. Since the prevailing winds blow northerly off
that part of the African coast, it was only seven years earlier that a similar
Portuguese ship had succeeded in passing the fearful Cape and in returning safely to Europe.

Goncalvez had set out to collect a cargo of blubber and sea-lion skins.
But landing on the shore of the Rio de Oro, he was seized by the idea of
taking a few of the local inhabitants as a prize for his master, Prince Henry.
So the next evening a party of ten sailors marched inland. Returning
empty-handed across the sand dunes at dawn, they spied a naked Berber
walking behind a camel and carrying two spears. The man defended himself with spirit, but was soon wounded, overpowered, and captured.
Together with a luckless black woman, probably a local slave girl, who also
appeared on the scene, he was tied up and carried off. They were the first
recorded victims of a European slave-raid south of the Sahara.[1]

Soon afterwards Goncalvez joined up with another ship commanded by
Nuno Tristao. Their combined crews mounted a night attack on a native
encampment. With wild cries of 'Portugal' and 'Santiago' they fell on the
sleeping villagers, killing three and taking ten prisoner. In all, they
returned to Lisbon with twelve captives. Their exploits were recorded by
the chronicler Zurara, and Prince Henry sent an embassy to Rome to seek
the Pope's blessing for this new sort of crusade. The Pope granted 'complete forgiveness of sins . . . to all engaged in the said war'.[2]

Slave-raiding and slave-trading were an immemorial feature of African
life, but this was the moment when Europeans broke into operations that
had hitherto been handled by African and Muslim traders. It happened
some fifty years before Europe's first contacts with the Americas, and it
put European entrepreneurs into a good position for exploiting the new
opportunities. In 1501 Spain issued a decree to limit the export of Christian
girls to garrison brothels across the Atlantic. In 1515 Spain sent the first
consignment of black slaves directly from Africa to America, whilst receiving the first shipment of slave-grown American sugar.

More than a century after Goncalvez, a fresh stage of the Atlantic slave
trade was reached, when English sea captains broke into the Spanish and
Portuguese monopoly. In October 1562 John Hawkins sailed from
Plymouth for the coast of Guinea with three ships—the *Salomon*, the
Swallow, and the *Jonas*. Variously described as a pirate and an admiral,
Hawkins established the 'Great Circuit', with its threefold profits of
English goods sold in Africa, African slaves sold in the Indies, and
American products sold in England. On that first voyage he took a short

cut by relieving a Portuguese slave ship of its human cargo at sea. On his second voyage, in 1564, he received financial backing from the Queen of England herself, who rewarded him with a knighthood and with a coat of arms bearing 'a demi-Moor, chained'. On a third voyage, in 1567, he obtained 470 slaves as booty after lending his crewmen as mercenaries to the kings of Sierra Leone and of Castros, who were fighting a war against their enemies, Zacina and Zatecama.[3] [**USKOK**]

In this way, European traders entered a lasting and lucrative partnership with their African suppliers. 'The Root of the Evil', writes one historian, lay in 'a demand for slaves on one side, and on the other a monopolist interest among African chiefs in obtaining European consumer goods, especially firearms.'[4] Before the trade was stopped in the nineteenth century, some 15 million Africans had been seized for slavery in the Western hemisphere. Of those, perhaps 11 or 12 million were actually landed alive.[5]

circumstances. His childhood was passed amidst the horrors of a protracted Catalan revolt. His claim to Aragon only arose through the exclusion of his bastard cousin, Ferrante of Naples, and the poisoning of his half-brother, Charles of Viana, Prince of Navarre. Isabella's brother, Henry IV (r. 1454–74), has been described as 'a miserable, abnormal cipher'. Ferdinand's father, John II (r. 1458–79), was the hated poisoner of a son and a daughter. It is not surprising, therefore, that Ferdinand and Isabella, 'the Catholic monarchs', were advocates of strong and orderly government.

For the time being, the union of Castile and Aragon remained a personal one. The two kingdoms retained their separate laws and governments. Isabella had little choice but to attack the nobility of Castile; Ferdinand had no choice but to work with the Cortes of Aragon. Even when he asked for a window to be closed in the debating chamber, he was wont to add: 'if the *fueros* permit'. The sense of common purpose was achieved partly by the introduction of a common currency and the removal of commercial barriers and partly by the enforcement of ultra-Catholic ideology. In 1476 Isabella set up a sinister but efficient law-enforcement agency, initially aimed at the noble brigands of Castile—the *Santa Hermandad* or Holy Brotherhood. In 1483, both Castile and Aragon were required to play host to the first institution of united Spain, a reorganized royal version of the Holy Inquisition under its president, the Queen's confessor, the Dominican Thomas Torquemada (1420–98). Henceforth, treason and heresy were virtually indistinguishable. Non-conformers, Jews, and dissidents were rigorously persecuted. The further existence of the emirate of Granada could not be tolerated. [**DEVIATIO**]

The final conquest of Granada began in 1481 and lasted for ten years. In wealth and population Granada was as superior among the provinces of Spain as Constantinople among the cities of the East. Seventy walled towns, supplied by

DEVIATIO

No medieval institution has attracted greater opprobrium from later ages than the Holy Inquisition. To many modern commentators, the ferocity aroused during the pursuit of heretics, Jews, or witches [**HEXEN**] is often incomprehensible. The inquisitors were simply deranged. Yet a little reflection suggests that the phenomenon is not exclusively medieval. The definition of 'normal' and 'deviant' is always subjective. People whose unconventional conduct threatens entrenched interests can easily be denounced as 'mad' or 'dangerous'. Comparisons have been made between the Inquisition and the contemporary medical establishment's opposition to the Mental Health Movement.[1] They can also be made with the treatment of dissidents to the Soviet regime, who in the 1980s were still regularly consigned to psychiatric clinics, diagnosed as 'schizophrenic', and forcibly disabled with drugs.[2]

the most fertile countryside, might have hoped to resist indefinitely. But the dissensions of the Moorish rulers gave entry to the united Spanish forces. When Granada itself was besieged, a wooden city called Santa Fe or 'Holy Faith' was built to house the besiegers. The capitulation came on 2 January 1492. In the eyes of Christian enthusiasts, Constantinople was avenged.

The conquest of Granada was accompanied by an appalling breach of good faith. Promises of religious toleration were not kept. When Queen Isabella hesitated, the Grand Inquisitor, Torquemada, is said to have held out a cross with the words: 'Judas sold his master for thirty pieces of silver. How many will you take for this cross?' The Jews were then faced with a decree enforcing conversion or banishment.[38] Perhaps 20,000 Sephardic families chose exile—many, ironically, in Smyrna and Istanbul, whence the Sultan sent ships to collect them.[39] The class of *conversos*, many still secretly loyal to Judaism, was greatly enlarged. By a decree of 1502 the Muslims were given the same choice. Many migrated to North Africa; the remainder were left to form a second group of dubious converts, the *moriscos*. Only in Aragon did the Cortes prevent the King from compelling the Muslim serfs, the *mudejares*, to change religion. In a climate of religious hatred and suspicion, the Inquisitors could barely cope. The fires of the *autos-da-fé*, the 'acts of faith', burned all over Spain. Spaniards became obsessed with the *limpieza de sangre*, the 'purity of blood'.

By coincidence, the fall of Granada in 1492 was witnessed by a Genoese sailor who had come to the camp at Santa Fe to seek the Catholic monarchs' patronage. Cristoforo Colombo (*c*.1446–1506), known as Cristóbal Colón, had long been seeking their support for his scheme to sail across the Atlantic Ocean in search of Asia. There, after the fall of Granada, he struck the deal. On 3 August, as 'Admiral of the Ocean', he set sail from the port of Palos in three tiny ships—the *Santa*

María, the *Pinta*, and the *Niña*. Ten weeks later, at two in the morning on 12 (21) October, a crewman sighted land. Columbus landed at daybreak, kissed the ground, named it San Salvador, and laid claim to it for Castile and Leon. He returned to Palos, via the Azores and Lisbon, on 15 March 1493, convinced that he had discovered a route to the (East) 'Indies'.[40]

That same year, after vigorous petitioning by Spain and Portugal, Pope Alexander VI agreed to set a boundary between their respective spheres of over-seas interest. All land discovered to the west of a line lying 100 leagues beyond the Azores was to belong to Spain; everything to the east was to be Portugal's. The world was neatly divided in two on the sole authority of a pope. In 1494, by the Treaty of Tordesillas, the line was moved 250 leagues further west. The event was nicely medieval. Yet it could hardly have taken place, still less been exploited, if the Iberian kingdoms had not been freed from their preoccupations with Islam. After all, Ferdinand and Isabella had stubbornly refused to negotiate with Columbus until the fall of Granada was accomplished. [**STATE**]

Three thousand miles to the east, at the other extremity of Christendom, the shift of the Christian–Moslem frontier was having equally unsettling effects. By 1452, almost the whole of the Orthodox Christian world was subject to foreign rule. The Orthodox of the Greek Rite, with the exception of the tiny Byzantine Empire and its dependencies, had fallen under Ottoman rule. The Orthodox of the Slavonic Rite, with minor exceptions, had all fallen under Tartar, Polish-Lithuanian, or Hungarian rule. So, when Constantinople surrendered, it looked as if the Orthodox of Europe were set to endure the same unending captivity that the Orthodox of Asia and Africa had endured since the seventh century. In one place alone, in the city of Moscow, there were thoughts of a different destiny.

Moscow in the mid-fifteenth century, though nominally subject to the Tartar khan, enjoyed a wide measure of autonomy. It was ruled by the Grand Prince Vassily II (r. 1425–62), who, having lost his sight, relied heavily on his son and heir. Ivan III (r. 1462–1505), therefore, was already an experienced politician when he mounted the throne. The once powerful Tartar Horde was greatly weakened, and Moscow had avoided payment of the annual tribute since 1452. As a result, Ivan had hopes of escaping 'the Tartar yoke' for good. In this, it was obvious that he should stress his role as the champion of the Orthodox Christians against the Muslims of the south and the Catholics of Poland-Lithuania to the west. If only he could gain recognition of his sovereignty, he would then become the one and only independent and Orthodox prince on earth.

Oddly enough, Ivan's ambition was greatly assisted by the schemes of the Roman Pope. After the disaster of 1453 the Papacy had accepted the wardship of Zoe Palaeologos (b. 1445), niece of the last Byzantine Emperor. Zoe, daughter of Thomas, Despot of Morea, had been born in Greece, but had been well educated by tutors in Rome. In 1469 she was a bright young woman of 24, eager to escape her guardians. Pope Paul II, a Venetian, thought that he could revive the union of Florence and forge a Muscovite alliance against the Turks. So, when he heard that

STATE

IN 1493, the year in which Columbus returned to the Kingdom of Castile, the map of Europe from Portugal to the Khanate of Astrakhan contained at least thirty sovereign states. Five hundred years later, if one discounts Andorra and Monaco, the Union of Kalmar and the Swiss Federation, whose independence had been little more than *de facto*, no single one of those thirty states had maintained its separate sovereign existence. Of the sovereign states on the map of Europe in 1993, four had been formed in the sixteenth century, four in the seventeenth, two in the eighteenth, seven in the nineteenth, and no fewer than thirty-six in the twentieth. The rise and fall of states represents one of the most important phenomena of modern Europe (see Appendix III, p. 1268).

State-formation in Europe has been analysed in many ways. The traditional approach was based on constitutional and international law. The aim was to describe the legal framework within which empires, monarchies, and republics organize their government, control their dependencies, and gain recognition. More recently, greater emphasis has fallen on long-term considerations—on statistical calculations of the longevity of states,[1] for example. Norbert Elias viewed state-formation as part of a civilizational process operating since the period of feudal fragmentation through the steady accretion of princely power.[2]

Others have looked more at the interplay of internal structures and external relations. In one view, three types of state have prevailed— tribute-raising empires, systems of fragmented sovereignty, and national states. Their internal life-force has been dominated either by the concentration of capital, as in Venice or the United Provinces, or by the concentration of coercion, as in Russia, or by varying concentrations of the two—as in Britain, France, or Prussia. Money and violence were the prime movers. The performance of states in the international arena depended on their participation in the elaborate multilateral power combinations that have constantly coalesced and recoalesced during more than 100 major wars in Europe since the Renaissance. The key questions were: 'How did states make war?' and 'How did wars make states?'[3] Many of the issues resemble those examined in a more empirical fashion by Paul Kennedy.[4]

The supposedly ultimate destination, the nation-state, has been achieved many times. But the paths leading to that destination have been extremely varied. In the last resort, everything turned on power. '*Qui a la force*', wrote Richelieu, '*a souvent la raison en matière d'État.*'[5] In short, 'might is right'. Which only makes one wonder whether the nation-state should really be the ultimate destination.

Ivan III was recently widowed, he produced the ideal candidate. Papal emissaries appeared in Moscow, and the match was made. Zoe travelled after them via the Baltic port of Reval. She was readmitted to the Orthodox faith, and married to Ivan on 12 November 1472. The prestige which attended Ivan's marriage to a Byzantine princess is hard to exaggerate. Up to then, Moscow had been the most peripheral province of the most downtrodden branch of Christendom. Its princes were barely on the map. But now they were touching the mantle of the Caesars. They were only one step removed from adopting the imperial mantle for themselves.

In 1477–8 Ivan moved against Novgorod the Great, whose five provinces far exceeded the territory of Moscow. Novgorod had recently conceded the secular overlordship of Lithuania and the ecclesiastical authority of the Metropolitan of Kiev. Ivan saw this as a personal affront, and his army soon forced the poorly defended city to capitulate and to switch allegiance. A second visitation was made to suppress sedition, and was followed by mass executions and deportations. Pskov and Vyatka received the same treatment. In the summer of 1480 Ahmad, Khan of the Golden Horde, launched the third of his expeditions to enforce payment of Moscow's tribute. He had counted on the aid of Poland-Lithuania, but it did not materialize. When Ivan held firm, and Ahmad retired empty handed, Moscow's dependence on the Horde was taken to have finally lapsed. Moscow was free. By that time Ivan had started to refer to himself as 'Tsar' and 'Samodyerzhets'—Russian equivalents of Caesar and Autokrator. Like Charlemagne almost 700 years before, a semi-barbarian prince was building his image not as the founder of a modern state, but rather as the reincarnator of the old, dead, and barely lamented empire of the Romans.

The Feast of Epiphany, 6 January 1493, the Kremlin, Moscow. The celebration of the holy day was proceeding amidst the splendours of the Grand Duke's private chapel in the *Blagoveshchensky Sobor*, the Cathedral of the Annunciation. It was the twelfth day of Christmas, the final stage of the season of the Nativity, a remembrance of the time when Christ made himself manifest to the Three Kings. Sonorous voices intoned the Byzantine Rite in words of Old Church Slavonic, which echoed round every corner of the cathedral's domes and frescoed walls. The icon screen, which cut off the inner sanctuary, was far older than the church. It was covered by rows of icons painted by Moscow's greatest medieval artists— Theophanes the Greek, Andrei Rublev, Prokhor of Gorodets. Black-robed and bearded priests moved round the chancel, performing the preliminary ceremonies of vesting, censing, and veiling of the gifts.

This being Epiphany, the alternate liturgy of St Basil the Great took the place of the more usual liturgy of St John Chrysostom.[41] In its Slavonic version, it was essentially the same as that which was used by the Orthodox of the Balkans. Though familiar, it was no more intelligible to the Russian congregation standing patiently before the screen than Latin was to Italians or Spaniards. The public

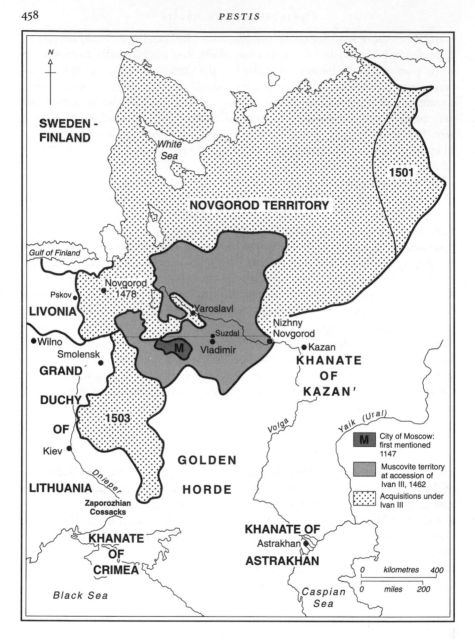

Map 15.

The Growth of Muscovy

service, the *Synaxis* or Assembly, began as the celebrants entered the nave, and a deacon recited the Litany of Peace: 'For peace from on high, and for the salvation of our souls, let us pray to the Lord. For the peace of the whole world . . . ' There followed hymns, ferial anthems, psalms, the Beatitudes, lessons from the Apostles and from the Gospel, prayers, further litanies, and the Cherubic Hymn of the Thrice-Holy. The Gospel reading, introduced by the usual Preface, was taken from the first verses of Matthew 2:

> *The priest*, bowing as he takes up the Book, and coming out of the holy doors preceded by tapers, turns to the west and saith:
> 'Wisdom, be steadfast, let us hear the holy Gospel. Peace be with you all.'
> *Choir*: 'And with thy spirit.'
> *Deacon*: 'The Lesson of the holy Gospel according to St Matthew.'
> *Choir*: 'Glory be to Thee, O Lord.'
> *Priest*: 'Let us give heed.'
> *The deacon* then reads the Lesson:

ГЛАВА̀ в҃.	ГЛАВА 2.
Інсꙋ же рождшꙋсѧ въ ви-дѧлеемѣ і҆ꙋдейстѣмъ во дни и҆рода царѧ, се, волсви ѿ востокъ прїидоша во і҆ерлимъ, глаголюще: в҃. гдѣ є҆сть рождейсѧ црь і҆ꙋдейскїй, видѣхомъ бо звѣздꙋ є҆гѡ на востоцѣ и҆ прїидохомъ поклонитисѧ є҆мꙋ.	Когда же Іисусъ родился въ Виѳлеемѣ Іудейскомъ во дни царя Ирода, пришли въ Іеруса-лимъ волхвы * съ востока и говорятъ: 2. гдѣ родившійся Царь Іудейскій? ибо мы видѣли звѣзду Его на востокѣ и пришли поклониться Ему.

(Now when Jesus was born in Bethlehem of Judaea in the days of Herod the Tsar, behold there came wise men from the east to Jerusalem, saying: Where is he that is born Tsar of the Jews? for we have seen his star in the east, and are come to worship him . . .)[42]

The second part of the service, the *Anaphora* or offering of the gifts, began with the Great Entrance, when priests and deacons processed round the nave with prayers, censers, and candles. There followed the recital of the Creed, the preparation of the bread and the wine, the Lord's Prayer, and the Communion. During Communion, the choir sang 'Receive ye the body of Christ, Taste ye of the fountain of immortal life'. The priest, in the Orthodox tradition, mentioned every communicant by name. 'The servant of God, Ivan, partaketh of the holy precious body and blood of . . . Our Saviour Jesus Christ, unto remission of his sins and unto everlasting life.' After the thanksgiving, the priest distributed the blessed bread, held up the Cross for the people to kiss, then re-entered the chancel before the gates were shut behind him. The closing words of the Dismissal—'Lord, now lettest Thou Thy servant depart in peace'—were accompanied by hymns ending with the Contakion of the Sixth Tone:

> Unshakeable foundation of the Church hast Thou shewn Thyself,
> Unto all mankind bequeathing an assured mastery
> Sealed by Thy ordinances,
> Basil by heaven proven most holy,
> Both now, and for ever and world without end. Amen.

Far away, unbeknown to the people of Moscow, the Admiral of the Ocean was battling at that very time against midwinter gales on the final stage of his return voyage to Spain. He would land at Palos within the week.

That year, the Christmas celebrations in Moscow were coloured by very special emotions. Learned monks had been predicting for some time that no one would live to see the year completed. According to Orthodox calculations, August 1492—the month when Columbus had set sail on his outward voyage—marked the end of the seventh millennium since the Creation; and it had been widely foretold to be the End of the World. Indeed, no steps had been taken to calculate the Church calendar for the following years. Although the Orthodox used the same Julian calendar that was current in the Latin Church, they had a different system for counting the *anni mundi*, the years of creation. Also, as in Byzantium, it was their custom to start the ecclesiastical year on 1 September. So, given their belief that the 'seven days' of creation were a metaphor for seven millennia, and their dating of the Creation to 5509 BC, AD 1492 was reckoned equivalent to 7000 AM, and the likeliest date for Judgement Day. 31 August was the critical date. Failing that, the crack of doom might be delayed until 31 December, the last day of the secular year—and the midpoint of the season of Nativity. When Epiphany was reached without incident, Moscow breathed a sigh of relief.[43]

Moscow, in fact, stood on the brink of a new career. Its Grand Duke, Ivan III, had *not* been counting on the Day of Judgement. He was nearing completion of grandiose plans to remodel the *Kreml* or 'fortified city' of his capital. By symbolic and ideological means, he was preparing to launch the powerful Russian myth which was to be a fitting partner for Moscow's growing political might.

Most of the cities of Rus' had their kremlins. But the Kremlin of Moscow, as redesigned by Ivan III, outshone anything that existed elsewhere. In January 1493 the vast enclosure of its red-brick walls and tall round towers had been completed only a few months earlier. It covered an irregular triangle round a perimeter of 2.5 km, enough to envelop half the City of London. At its heart was the airy expanse of an open square, round which were ranged four cathedrals and the grand ducal residence. The Cathedral of the Annunciation was in pristine state, having received its finishing touches only three years earlier. Its neighbour, the *Uspensky Sobor*, the Cathedral of the Dormition, the seat of the Metropolitan, was now thirteen years old. It had been built by the Bolognese architect Aristotle Firavanti, whose brief was to adapt the ancient Vladimir style to modern uses. It became a standard for Muscovite church architecture. Its interior provided a large open space, without galleries, under matching domed and vaulted compartments. Its frescos were still being painted in the inimitable bright colours and elongated figures of Dionysius the Greek. On the other side the Church of the *Razpolozhenie*, 'of the Deposition of the Robe', was seven years old. The *Archangelsky Sobor*, with its Renaissance façade, was still on the drawing board. The *Granovitaya Palata* or 'Palace of the Facets' by Marco Rulto and Pietro Solano—so called from the diamond-cut stones of its façade—had just been occupied by Ivan's household. They moved in after several years sharing the house of his favourite minister. It replaced the former wooden hall which had served Ivan's predecessors for centuries. Few capitals in Christendom short of Rome or Constantinople could compare with such splendour.

Within the Palace of Facets, Ivan's household was riven by the rivalry of two powerful women—Zoe Palaeologos, his second wife, and Elena Stepanovna, his daughter-in-law. Zoe, the niece of the last Byzantine Emperor, had married Ivan after the death of his first wife, Maria of Tver. Her preoccupation was to protect the interests of her seven children, headed by the thirteen-year-old Vasily. Elena was the daughter of Stephen IV, Hospodar of Moldavia, and widow of Ivan's first heir and successor, Ivan the Younger, who had recently died. Her concern was to preserve the interests of her nine-year-old son, Dmitri. In 1493 Ivan III had not yet decided whether he should name his son Vasily or his grandson Dmitri to succeed him: he was to favour each by turns. The tension beneath the surface in the Kremlin must have been electric.[44]

(1) **Maria of Tver = Ivan III = Zoe Palaeologos** (2)

```
                                    (1440–
                                     1505)        ──  Elena = Alexander, Grand Duke of
                                                          Lithuania
                  Elena = Ivan the Younger
               Stepanovna │ (d. 1490)                    Maria
               of Moldavia │
                          │                       ──  Vasily (Tsar 1505–30)
                        Dmitri                    ──  Yuri
                      (1483–1509)                 ──  Dmitri
                                                  ──  Semen
                                                  ──  Ivan
                                                  ──  Andrei
```

Ivan III is popularly remembered in Russia as the Tsar who threw off the Tartar yoke. He might be better considered as an exponent of Tartar financial, military, and political methods, who used the shifting alliances of khans and princes to replace the Tartar yoke with a Muscovite one. In his struggle with the Golden Horde, whose hegemony he definitively rejected after 1480, his closest ally was the Khan of the Crimea, who helped him to attack the autonomy of his fellow Christian principalities to a degree that the Tartars had never attempted. From the Muscovite point of view, which later enjoyed a monopoly, 'Ivan the Great' was the restorer of 'Russian' hegemony. From the viewpoint of the Novgorodians or the Pskovians he was the Antichrist, the destroyer of Russia's best traditions.

When he came to write his will, he described himself, as his father had done, as 'the much-sinning slave of God'.[45]

Ivan III had first called himself *Tsar* or 'Caesar' twenty years before. He did so in a treaty with the republic of Pskov, presumably to laud his superiority over other local princes; and he repeated the exercise on several occasions in the 1480s. But Tsar, though a cut above Grand Duke, was not the equivalent of the Byzantine title of Basileus. It could not be construed as a full imperial dignity unless accompanied by all the other trappings of Empire. Caesar, after all, was the term that had been used to designate the co-emperors and deputy emperors of the supreme Augustus.

In 1489 Ivan III had considered another proposition. In his dealings with the Habsburgs, he was told that a royal crown could be procured for him from the Pope. His standing in the West would certainly have been enhanced by regal status. But the title of *rex* or *korol'* had connotations that offended Muscovite pride. [KRAL] To accept would be to repeat the alleged treason to the True Faith which the Greeks had committed at Florence. So Ivan refused. 'My ancestors', he explained, 'were friendly with the Emperors who had once given Rome to the Pope.'[46] What he did do, though, was to borrow the Habsburgs' imperial emblem. As from the 1490s, the double-headed eagle began to appear as the symbol of state in Moscow as in Vienna, as indeed in Constantinople. [AQUILA]

Apart from its fears about the end of the world, the Muscovite Church was enduring a period of great uncertainty. It had broken with the Patriarch of Constantinople (see pp. 446–7) without yet finding a fully independent role. Unlike the Metropolitan of Kiev, who was a resident of Lithuania, the Moscow Metropolitan was elected by his bishops, and headed an ecclesiastical organization which admitted no superior. For forty years it had been impossible to reconcile this state of affairs with the absence of an emperor, and hence with the Byzantine tradition that Church and State were indivisible. Just as there could be no emperor without the true faith, there could be no true faith without an Emperor. Some had pinned their hopes on the reconquest of Constantinople for an Orthodox Christian emperor—the so-called 'Great Idea'. Others hoped that some arrangement might be reached with the German Emperor of the Latins. But that was rejected. The one remaining alternative was for Moscow to do what both Serbia and Bulgaria had done in the past—to find an Emperor of their own.

The immediate problem, however, was to draw up a new paschal canon, with its calculations of the Easters for the eighth millennium. This is the task to which Metropolitan Zosimus had been putting his mind in the autumn of 1492. 'We await the Advent of our Lord,' he wrote in the Preface, 'but the hour of his coming cannot be established.' He then appended a brief historical summary. Constantine had founded the New Rome, and St Vladimir had baptized Rus'. Now Ivan III was to be 'the new Emperor Constantine of the new Constantinople—Moscow'.[47] This was the first indirect mention of the pedigree with which Moscow would now be clothed.

Also in 1492, and also for the first time, the 'new Constantinople—Moscow' may have been given its more familiar label of 'the Third Rome'. In that year Archbishop Gennadius of Novgorod supposedly received a translation of the Roman Legend of the White Klobuck, and with it a preface explaining how a manuscript of the legend had been found in Rome. Scholars disagree about the age of this text, parts of which may have been interpolated at a later date. But it is not irrelevant that the Preface contains a clear reference to Moscow as the 'Third Rome'. The author of the Preface is sometimes equated with a known translator who was working on the Apocalypse of Ezra. This work was part of Archbishop Gennadius' project to endow the Muscovite Church with a complete version of the Bible equivalent to the Latin Vulgate.[48]

Once the Russian principalities were brought to heel, Moscow's imperial ambitions would obviously be directed against the Grand Duchy of Lithuania—Muscovy's western neighbour. Lithuania had benefited from the Mongol invasions, using its base on the northern periphery to expand its annexations among the fragments of the former Rus', just as Moscow had done. By the end of the fifteenth century Lithuania, like Muscovy, controlled a huge swathe of territory—essentially the Dnieper basin—which stretched from the shore of the Baltic to the confines of the Black Sea.

Unlike Muscovy, however, Lithuania was open to Western influences. For more than a century the Grand Duchy had flourished under the personal union with Poland (see pp. 429–30). By the 1490s the Lithuanian court at Wilno and the Catholic ruling élite were to a large extent polonized in language and political culture. The Lithuanian dynasty was in possession not only of Poland and Lithuania but of Bohemia and Hungary as well. Unlike Muscovy, Lithuania permitted a wide measure of religious diversity. The Roman Catholic establishment did not impede either the numerical predominance of Orthodox Christianity or the steady influx of a strong Jewish element. Unlike Muscovy, the Orthodox Church in Lithuania had not broken with Constantinople nor with its ancient Byzantine loyalties. The Metropolitan of Kiev had every reason to resist Moscow's separatist line, which was dividing Slavic Orthodoxy and moving inexorably towards the formation of a breakaway Russian Orthodox Church.

In January 1493 Moscow's relations with Lithuania were about to take a new turn. Six months earlier Casimir Jagiellonczyk, King of Poland and Grand Duke of Lithuania, had died, dividing his realm between his second and third sons. The Polish kingdom passed to Jan Olbracht, Lithuania to the unmarried Alexander. (The eldest son was already King of Bohemia and Hungary.) Ivan III had seen the possibilities. On the one hand, he was preparing an embassy which would travel to Wilno, and would launch negotiations leading to a political marriage between Grand Duke Alexander and Ivan's daughter Elena. At the same time, he was setting conditions which would undermine the previous *modus vivendi* of the two states. For the first time in Moscow's history, he armed his ambassador with instructions demanding recognition of the hitherto unknown title of *gosudar' vseya Rusi*—'lord of all-Rus' '.[49] It was a classic diplomatic double hold—one part apparently friendly, the other potentially hostile. Ivan was deliberately pulling

Lithuania into an engagement that called into question the future of all the eastern Slavs.

To make his point, Ivan staged a sensational demonstration. Some time before Christmas he had arrested two Lithuanians employed in the Moscow Kremlin. He charged them with plotting to poison him. The accusations against Jan Lukhomski and Maciej the Pole did not sound very credible; but their guilt or innocence was hardly relevant. They were held in an open cage on the frozen Moskva River for all the world to see; and on the eve of the departure of Ivan's envoy to Lithuania, they were burned alive in their cage.[50] As the ice melted under the fierce heat of the fire and the heavy iron cage sank beneath the water, taking its carbonized occupants down in a great hiss of steam, one could have well imagined that something was being said about Lithuania's political future.

The title 'Lord of All-Rus'' did not possess much basis either in history or in current reality. It came into the same category as that whereby the kings of England laid claim to France. In the 1490s, two-and-a-half centuries after all traces of a united Kievan Rus' had been destroyed, it had the same degree of credibility that the king of France might have enjoyed if, in his struggle with the German Empire, he had proclaimed himself 'Lord of all the Franks'. By that time, it conflicted with the separate identity that the 'Ruthenes' of Lithuania had assumed from the 'Russians' of Moscow. Indeed, it all seemed sufficiently unreal for the Lithuanians to accept it as a small price to pay for Ivan's good humour. They were not to know it, but they were conceding the ideological cornerstone of territorial ambitions that would be pursued for 500 years.

By 1493, therefore, all the main elements of the ideology of the 'Third Rome' were in existence. There was an autonomous branch of the Orthodox Church looking for an emperor; there was a prince, related to the last Byzantine Emperor, who had already called himself Tsar; and there was a claim to the lordship of all-Rus'. All that was lacking was a suitably ingenious ideologue, who could weld these elements into the sort of mystical theory that was demanded by an intensely theocratic state. Such a man was at hand.

Philotheus of Pskov (*c*.1450–1525) was a learned monk of Pskov's Eleazar monastery. He was familiar with the biblical prophecies of Ezra and Daniel, with historical precedents from Serbia and the second Bulgarian Empire, with the Pseudo-Methodius and the Chronicle of Manasses, and with the Legend of the White Klobuck. Such knowledge was not unique. Philotheus was unusual only in his willingness to use these things for the benefit of the Muscovite princes. Pskov, like Novgorod, lived in fear and trembling of Moscow. Most of its monks were fiercely anti-Muscovite. When they made references in their Chronicle to Nebuchadnezzar's Dream, or to the four beasts of Daniel's Vision, they were apt to do so in a manner that identified Nebuchadnezzar with Moscow. For whatever reason, Philotheus was prepared to turn the material round to Moscow's advantage. In 1493, in his early forties, he held no office of authority in the monastery where he would later rule as *hegumen* or abbot; and he had not yet written any of the public Epistles which were to make him famous. But the ferment in the Church which was to shape his views, was already in progress. In due course he was to be the advocate of the total submission of all Christians to the Tsar, and of total opposition to the Latin Church. In his Epistle to Ivan's successor, he enjoins the new Tsar to rule justly, because the world was now entering the terminal phase of history:

And now I say unto Thee, take care and take heed, pious Tsar: all the empires of Christendom are united in thine. For two Romes have fallen, and the Third exists; and there will not be a fourth. Thy Christian Empire, according to the great theologian, will not pass away. And, for the Church, the word of the blessed David will be fulfilled: 'she is my place of eternal rest' . . .[51]

Later, in his Epistle to Munexin, Philotheus would fulminate 'Against the Astrologers and the Latins':

And now, alone, the Holy Catholic and Apostolic Church of the East shines more brightly than the sun in the universe; and only the great Orthodox Tsar of Rome, like Noah saved from the flood in the ark, directs the Church . . .[52]

Here, twenty years after Ivan III's death, but clearly inspired by his policies, was the definitive formulation of an ideology of Church and State that left no inch for compromise.

Later Russian tradition was to hold that Moscow had simply inherited the Byzantine mantle. In reality, whilst Byzantine forms were retained, the essence of the Byzantine ethos was lost. Muscovite ideologues had little interest in the universal and ecumenical ideals of East Roman Christianity. The most distinguished historian of these matters has described the ideology of 'Third Rome' as 'a meretricious substitute'. 'The Christian universalism of Byzantium was being transformed and distorted within the more narrow framework of Muscovite nationalism.'[53]

Muscovite theology was disturbed in Ivan III's later years by a couple of related controversies that would both be settled in favour of the most uncompromising elements. One controversy centred on the views of a sect or tendency known as the *zhidovstvuyushchie* or 'Judaizers'. The other centred on the supposed scandal of Christian monasteries growing rich through the possession of land. Joseph, Abbot of Volokhamsk, was the organizer both of the 'anti-Judaizers' and of 'the possessors'.

Landed property was inseparable from the power of the Muscovite Church. But it was opposed by a company of puritanical monks led by the 'Elders beyond the Volga' who cherished Orthodox monasticism's older, eremitical tradition. Ivan III seems to have prepared a scheme for secularizing monastic wealth, but was persuaded to desist. Matters only came to a head after his death, when his former favourite Patrikeev, now turned monk, published a new edition of the *Nomocanon*, the Orthodox manual of canon law. One of Patrikeev's associates, Maxim the Greek, who offered a 'non-possessorial' interpretation of the Church's landed property, was lucky to escape with his life.

The Judaizers provoked still greater passions. They had emerged in the 1470s in Novgorod, where they were said to have formed an anti-Muscovite faction. Their views were allegedly inspired by Jews from Poland and Lithuania, and their members were said to be clandestine adherents of Judaism. Their activities do not seem to have worried the Tsar, who appointed a suspect Novgorodian to be archpriest of the Uspensky Cathedral; and they may have enjoyed the support of Elena Stepanovna. Despite a Council convened in 1490 to examine charges of anti-trinitarianism and iconoclasm, they continued to circulate in the highest circles. But Abbot Joseph did not give up. In 1497, in his *Prosvetitel'* or 'Enlightener', he named none other than Metropolitan Zosima as the chief 'Judaizer and Sodomizer', 'a foul evil wolf'.[54] Abbot Joseph and his partner, Archbishop Gennadius, were both admirers of the Spanish Inquisition, and their zeal was eventually rewarded by a grand *auto-da-fé*. They had succeeded in persuading their compatriots to believe what would prove a recurrent theme in Russian history—that evil came from the West. In their day, the West meant in the first instance Novgorod, and beyond Novgorod, Poland-Lithuania.

Ivan III's diplomacy was taking the same direction.[55] Diplomacy in those days moved extremely slowly. Muscovite embassies took anything between six months and four years to return and report from foreign countries; and ambassadors often found on arrival that the situation no longer matched their instructions. Even so, it was clear by the 1490s that the encirclement of Lithuania was becoming Moscow's top priority. Ivan's father had kept the peace with Lithuania for decades; and on his death Ivan and his mother had been entrusted to the care of 'my Brother, the King of Poland and Grand Duke of Lithuania, Casimir'.[56] All this was being revised.

By 1493, Ivan III was coming to the end of twenty years of intensive diplomatic activity. The common thread was to check and to encircle the Jagiellons. His treaty with Stephen IV, Hospodar of Moldavia, sealed by the marriage of his son, had tried in vain to prevent Moldavia paying homage to the Polish king. His scheme for an anti-Jagiellonian pact with Hungary was ruined by the sudden death of Matthias Corvinus, and by the subsequent election of Władysław Jagiellon as King of Hungary. He even made contact with the independent dukes of Mazovia. As from 1486, Ivan III repeatedly exchanged embassies with the Habsburgs, who until then had wrongly thought that Muscovy was a fief of Lithuania. In 1491 an Austrian envoy, Jörg von Thurn, outlined plans for a grand anti-Jagiellonian coalition made up of the Empire, the Teutonic Knights, Moldavia, and the Tartars. In January 1493 Ivan's envoy, Yuri Trakhaniot, tracked Maximilian down to Colmar only to find that the Emperor had already made his peace with the Jagiellons and was now more interested in a Crusade. Ivan III's relations with the Crimea included an important anti-Lithuanian component. His main use for them was as allies against the Golden Horde; and in June 1491 he sent three armies to help disperse the camp which the Golden Horde had established at the mouth of the Dnieper. At the same time, he could not fail to notice that the Tartars, when sweetened by Moscow, spent most of their energies raiding Poland and Lithuania.

In the winter of 1492–3 Muscovy was engaged in a desultory frontier war with Lithuania. Several of the border princelings had changed sides. The Prince of Ryazan' was preparing to challenge a punitive incursion mounted by the Lithuanian Voivode of Smolensk. The Muscovite army, which had orders to capture the city of Vyazma on the headwaters of the Dnieper, moved off within a few days of the Muscovite peace mission to Wilno. Whether peace or war was uppermost in Ivan's mind was anyone's guess.

In this age of discovery, therefore, Moscow, though remote, was not totally isolated. Each of the Muscovite embassies returned with foreign engineers, architects, and gunners in tow; and German and Polish merchants came every year to buy large stocks of furs. It is true that there was no direct contact with Tudor England, with Valois France, or with the Spain of Ferdinand and Isabella. The Baltic trade with the Netherlands stopped in Livonia, and the route round the North Cape had not yet been opened. Even so, Moscow had well-established lines of communication with the rest of Europe. In the north, the 'German Road' led through Novgorod to Reval or to Riga, and thence by sea to Lübeck. Overland, the forest trails stretched westwards to the frontier before Smolensk, and thence to Wilno and Warsaw. Ivan III had inaugurated a system of posts and post-horses, whose upkeep he commended in his will.[57] To the south, the ancient rivers carried travellers rapidly to the Caspian or the Black Sea, and thence by ship to all points of the Mediterranean. Despite the Ottoman advance, Moscow was still in close touch with the old Byzantine world—that is, with the Balkans, with Greece, especially Athos, and via Greece with Italy.

Moscow, in any case, was making discoveries of its own. In 1466–72 a merchant of Tver, Afanasii Nikitin (d. 1472), made a six-year journey to Persia and India. He travelled out via Baku and Hormuz, and returned via Trebizond and Caffa. His adventures were written down in an early travel book, *Khozenie za tri moria* (A Journey Beyond the Three Seas). Ten years later the military expedition of Saltyk and Kurbskii crossed the Urals and reached the headwaters of the Irtysk and the Ob (a feat equivalent in scale to that of Lewis and Clark in America 300 years later). In 1491 two Hungarian prospectors had penetrated the Arctic tributaries of the Pechora, where silver and copper had been discovered. This discovery probably explains the arrival in Moscow in January 1493 of an Austrian prospector called Snups, who carried letters from the Emperor Maximilian asking him to be allowed to explore the Ob. Since Ivan's link with the Habsburgs was no longer convenient, Snups was refused.

As for the Admiral of the Ocean, news of his exploits were brought to Moscow with a quarter of a century's delay in the company of Maxim the Greek. Maxim Grek (Michael Trivolis, c.1470–1560) belonged to the dying Byzantine world whose parts still formed one cultural region. He was born at Arta in Epirus under Ottoman rule, whence his family moved to Venetian Corfu. In 1493 he was in Florence, studying with the Platonists and listening with approval to Savonarola's sermons. After further studies at Venice and at Mirandola, where he specialized in the exegesis of Greek texts, he took the vows of the Dominican order in

Savonarola's own monastery of San Marco. Later, as the monk Maximos, he worked for a decade as a translator in the Vatopedi monastery on Mount Athos, in a pan-Orthodox and graeco-Slav environment, where the schism between the Orthodox and Catholic traditions did not apply. He was then invited to Moscow to organize the Tsar's collection of Greek and Byzantine manuscripts, which Muscovite scholars were no longer trained to decipher. He soon fell foul of the hard-line faction of the Muscovite Church, which accused him of sorcery, espionage, and respect for the Patriarch of Constantinople. Yet he survived his lengthy imprisonment, met Ivan IV in person, and enjoyed his patronage. He was 'one of the last of his kind'.[58]

Maxim's writings, which appeared in the 1550s, make mention of 'a large island called Cuba'.[59] There is no doubt that by then he had a firm knowledge of Columbus's landings in the Caribbean. But the chronology of his career is important. Since Maxim spent three decades incarcerated in a Muscovite gaol, it is reasonable to suppose that he brought the information with him when he first travelled to Moscow in 1518, twenty-five years after Columbus's first voyage.

It is one of the wonderful coincidences of history that modern 'Russia' and modern 'America' both took flight in the same year of AD 1493. Europeans learned of the 'New World', as they saw it, at the self-same moment that Muscovites learned that their 'Old World' was not yet coming to an end.

VII

RENATIO

Renaissances and Reformations, c.1450–1670

THERE is a strong sense of unreality about the Renaissance. The mode of thinking which is supposed to distinguish modern European civilization both from medieval Christendom and from other non-European civilizations such as Islam had no clear beginning and no end. For a very long time it remained the preserve of a small intellectual élite, and had to compete with rival trends of thought, old and new. In the so-called 'Age of the Renaissance and Reformation' which conventionally begins c.1450, it can only be described as a minority interest. There were large sectors of European society, and huge areas of European territory, where as yet it wielded no influence whatsoever. It somehow contrived to be the most remarkable feature of the age and yet to be divorced from the main aspects of everyday political, social, and cultural life. It was untypical and unrepresentative, yet immensely significant. Like the wonderful figures of Sandro Botticelli, which are among its most powerful manifestations, whether the exquisite *Primavera* (1478) or the ethereal *Venus Rising from the Waves* (c.1485), its feet somehow did not touch the ground. It floated over the surface of the world from which it arose, a disembodied abstraction, a new energizing spirit.

Faced with the problem, many historians of the period have abandoned their earlier concerns. It is no longer the fashion to write so much about those minority interests. Humanist thought, reformation theology, scientific discovery, and overseas exploration have had to give way to studies of material conditions, of the medieval continuities, and of popular belief (and unbelief) as opposed to high culture. The professionals now like to spotlight magic, vagrancy, disease, or the decimation of colonial populations. This may be a very proper corrective; but it is as odd to forget Leonardo or Luther as it once was to ignore a Nostradamus or the Miller of Friuli. No one who wishes to know why Europe was so different in the mid-seventeenth century from what it had been in the fifteenth can afford to bypass the traditional subjects.

Even so, the incautious reader needs to be reminded. The world of Renaissance and Reformation was also the world of divination, astrology, miracles,

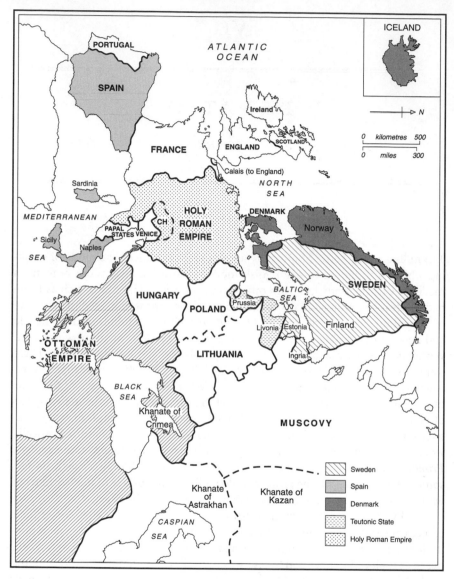

Map 16.
Europe, 1519

conjuration, witchcraft, necromancy, folk cures, ghosts, omens, and fairies. Magic continued to compete, and to interact with religion and science. Indeed, the dominion of magic among the common people held sway through a long period of cohabitation with the new ideas over two centuries or more.[1] One implication is that this 'Early Modern Period' may not be quite so modern after all. Despite the fresh seeds that were sown, it could well have had more in common with the medievalism that preceded it than with the Enlightenment which followed.

◀━━━▶

The Renaissance, therefore, cannot be easily defined. It is easiest to say what it was not. 'Ever since the Renaissance invented itself some six hundred years ago,' complained one American historian, 'there has been no agreement as to what it is.'[2] The Renaissance, for example, did not merely refer to the burgeoning interest in classical art and learning, for such a revival had been gathering pace ever since the twelfth century. Nor did it involve either a total rejection of medieval values or a sudden return to the world-view of Greece and Rome. Least of all did it involve the conscious abandonment of Christian belief. The term *renatio* or 'rebirth' was a Latin calque for a Greek theological term, *palingenesis,* used in the sense of 'spiritual rebirth' or 'resurrection from the dead'. The essence of the Renaissance lay not in any sudden rediscovery of classical civilization but rather in the use which was made of classical models to test the authority underlying conventional taste and wisdom. It is incomprehensible without reference to the depths of disrepute into which the medieval Church, the previous fount of all authority, had fallen. In this the Renaissance was part and parcel of the same movement which resulted in religious reforms. In the longer term, it was the first stage in the evolution which led via the Reformation and the Scientific Revolution to the Enlightenment. It was the spiritual force which cracked the mould of medieval civilization, setting in motion the long process of disintegration which gradually gave birth to 'modern Europe'. [BALETTO]

In that process, the Christian religion was not abandoned. But the power of the Church was gradually corralled within the religious sphere: the influence of religion increasingly limited to the realm of private conscience. As a result the speculations of theologians, scientists, and philosophers, the work of artists and writers, and the policies of princes were freed from the control of a Church with monopoly powers and 'totalitarian' pretensions. The prime quality of the Renaissance has been defined as 'independence of mind'. Its ideal was a person who, by mastering all branches of art and thought, need depend on no outside authority for the formation of knowledge, tastes, and beliefs. Such a person was *l'uomo universale,* the 'complete man'.[3]

The principal product of the new thinking lay in a growing conviction that humanity was capable of mastering the world in which it lived. The great Renaissance figures were filled with self-confidence. They felt that God-given ingenuity could, and should, be used to unravel the secrets of God's universe; and that, by extension, man's fate on earth could be controlled and improved. Here

BALLETTO

D ANCE, having played a central role in pagan religious rites, was largely ignored during the Middle Ages, except for rustic entertainment.
It is generally agreed that the secular dance spectacle performed by
Bergonzio di Botta at the Duke of Milan's wedding, at Tortona in 1489, is
the earliest example of the modern genre on record. From Italy, the *baletto*
was exported in the time of Catherine de' Medici to the French court,
where, under Louis XIV, it became a major art form. Lully's *Triomphe de
l'Amour* (1681) fixed the long-lasting genre of opera-ballet.

The modern theory and practice of ballet were largely developed in mid-
eighteenth-century Paris, especially by the royal ballet master Jean
Georges Noverre (1727–1810). Leading dancers such as Marie Camargo or
Gaetano Vestris, who modestly called himself *le dieu de la danse*, based
their training and performances on the grammar of the five classical positions. At a later stage, the combination of classical technique with
Romantic music, such as the *Coppélia* (1870) of Léo Delibes or the Roy
Douglas fantasia on Chopin tunes, *Les Sylphides* (1909), proved immensely
attractive.

Russia first imported French and Italian ballet under Peter the Great,
but in the nineteenth century moved rapidly from imitation to creative
excellence. Tchaikovsky's music for *Swan Lake* (1876), *Sleeping Beauty*
(1890), and *The Nutcracker* (1892) laid the foundations for Russia's
supremacy. In the last years of peace, the Ballets Russes launched by
Sergei Diaghilev (1872–1929) enjoyed a series of unsurpassed triumphs.
The choreography of Fokine, the dancing of Nizinski and Karsavina, and,
above all, the scores of Stravinsky, brought ballet to its zenith with *The
Firebird* (1910), *Petrushka* (1911), and *The Rite of Spring* (1913). After the
Revolutions of 1917, the Ballets Russes stayed abroad, whilst the Soviet
Bolshoi and Kirov Ballets combined stunning technical mastery with rigid
artistic conservatism.

Modern dance, as opposed to ballet, is older than might be supposed. Its
basic principles, of translating musical rhythm into corresponding bodily
movements, were put forward by the music teacher François Delsarte
(1811–71). Delsarte inspired the two principal practitioners of the art,
the Swiss Jacques Dalcroze (1865–1950), the pioneer of rhythmic gymnastics, and the Hungarian Rodolf Laban (1879–1958). After modern dance in
central Europe fell foul of the Nazis, the centre of gravity moved to North

was the decisive break with the mentality of the Middle Ages, whose religiosity and mysticism were reinforced by exactly the opposite conviction—that men and women were the helpless pawns of Providence, overwhelmed by the incomprehensible workings of their environment and of their own nature. Medieval attitudes were dominated by a paralysing anxiety about human inadequacy, ignorance, impotence—in short, by the concept of universal sin. Renaissance attitudes, in contrast, were bred by a sense of liberation and refreshment, deriving from the growing awareness of human potential. Speculation, initiative, experiment, and exploration could surely be rewarded with success. Intellectual historians examine the Renaissance in terms of new ideas and new forms; psychologists would look more to the conquests of fears and inhibitions which had prevented the new ideas from flourishing for so long (see Appendix III, p. 1269).

No simple chronological framework can be imposed on the Renaissance. Literary historians look for its origins in the fourteenth-century songs and sonnets of Petrarch, who observed human emotions for their own sake (see Chapter VI). Art historians look back to the painters Giotto and Masaccio (1401–28), to the architect Filippo Brunelleschi (1379–1446), who measured the dome of the Pantheon in Rome in order to build a still more daring dome for the cathedral in Florence, or to the sculptors Ghiberti (1378–1455) and Donatello (c.1386–1466). Political historians look back to Niccolo Machiavelli (1469–1527), who first explained the mechanics of politics as power for power's sake. Every one of these pioneers was a Florentine. As the first home of the Renaissance, Florence can fairly lay claim to be 'the mother of modern Europe'. [**FLAGELLATIO**]

In those unmatched generations of versatile Florentines, no one ever outshone Leonardo da Vinci (1452–1519). The painter of perhaps the most celebrated picture in the world, *La Gioconda* (1506), he possessed seemingly limitless talents to pursue his equally limitless curiosity. His notebooks contain everything from anatomical drawings to designs for a helicopter, a submarine, a machine-gun. (Such mechanical inventions had been the rage in Germany at an even earlier period.[4]) His fame is surrounded by the mystery which derives from lost works, from the reputation of wizardry. It is said that, as a young boy in the street market in Florence, he bought cage-birds just to set them free. He did the same for the secrets of art and nature. He lived his last years in France, in the service of Francis I. He died in the Château de Cloux near Amboise on the Loire—in a part of the world which has been called 'an Italy more Italian than Italy itself'.[5] [**LEONARDO**]

The Renaissance was never confined to Italy or to Italian fashions, and its effects were steadily disseminated throughout Latin Christendom. Modern scholars sometimes overlook this fact. Such was the impact of the work of the Swiss historian Jakob Burckhardt, *Die Kultur der Renaissance in Italien* (Basle, 1860) that many people have been left unaware of the wider dimensions. In fact, the intellectual ferment of the period was observable from an early date in northern Europe, especially in the cities of Burgundy and Germany. In France it displayed many native strands in addition to imported Italian fashions. Nor was it confined to Italy's immediate neighbours: it affected Hungary and Poland, for example,

FLAGELLATIO

PIERO DELLA FRANCESCA (*c.*1415–92) painted the small study generally known as *The Flagellation* some time between 1447 and 1460. The picture, now in the Galleria Nazionale at Urbino, is remarkable for its diptych structure, for its architectural detail, for its stunning use of perspective, and, above all, for its enigmatic allegory (see Plate 39).[1] The picture is divided into two distinct zones. On the left, a nocturnal flagellation scene takes place in the pearly interior of an antique courtyard. On the right, three large male figures converse in an open garden. The pale moonlight on the left is diffused by the daylight flooding in from the right.

The architectural elements are strangely ambiguous. The praetorium courtyard is severely classical. The heavy roof panels are supported by two rows of fluted Corinthian columns rising from a marble pavement. In the centre, a prisoner is tied to the column of the *Helia capitolina*, symbol of Jerusalem, surmounted by a golden statue. Yet two medieval houses with an overhanging belvedere appear alongside. Beyond is a patch of greenery and of blue sky. One section of the picture, therefore, was set in the past, the other in the present.

The two groups of figures do not betray any obvious connection. The flogging in the courtyard is watched by a seated official who wears a pointed 'Palaeologi' hat, by a turbaned Arab or Turk, and by an attendant in a short Roman toga. The foreground group in the garden consists of a bearded Greek dressed in round hat, maroon robe, and soft boots, a barefoot youth in red smock and laurel wreath, and a rich merchant dressed in a Flemish-style fur-hemmed brocade.

Piero uses perspective drawing to ensure that the small figure of the prisoner remains the central focus. The convergent lines of the beams, the roof panels and the columns, and the foreshortened marble squares of the pavement constitute a textbook exposition of an architectural setting which emphasizes the action within it.[2]

As for the allegory, a prominent exponent of Piero's art has stated that the conflicting interpretations are too numerous to mention.[3] The conventional view holds that *The Flagellation* portrays the scourging of Christ before Pilate. Many commentators have identified the barefoot youth as Oddantonio di Montefeltro. Yet the Byzantine accents are strong; and they suggest a number of interpretations connected to the Ottoman siege and conquest of Constantinople which dominated the news in the period. In which case, the prisoner may not be Christ, but St Martin, the seventh-century Roman Pope who met martyrdom at Byzantine hands. The presiding official may not be Pilate, but the Byzantine Emperor. The three foreground figures could be participants in the Council of Mantua (1459), where a Greek emissary begs the Western princes to mount a crusade to rescue the Eastern Empire.

A leading British authority, however, is adamant that the picture represents *The Dream of St Jerome*. Jerome once dreamed that he was being flogged for reading the pagan Cicero. This would explain the discordance between the two sections. The three foreground figures—two men and 'a barefoot angel'—'are discussing the relation between classical and patristic literature embodied in the story of St Jerome's dream'.[4]

Linear perspective was the artistic sensation of the era.[5] It so excited Piero's contemporary, Paolo Uccello, that he would wake his wife in bed to discuss it. It was a pictorial system for creating a realistic image of the three-dimensional world on a flat, two-dimensional surface. It set out to present the world as seen by the human eye, and as such marked a fundamental rejection of the hieratical proportions of medieval art. It was first discovered by Brunelleschi in his explorations of classical architecture, and expounded in many theoretical treatises headed by Alberti's *De Pictura* (1435), by Piero's own *De Prospettiva Pingendi* (pre-1475), and by Dürer's *Treatise on Measurement* (1525). Its rules included the pictorial convergence of parallel lines towards an illusory 'vanishing-point' and 'horizon line', the decreasing size of objects in relation to their distance from the 'viewing point', and the foreshortening of features lying along the central line of vision.[6] The pioneering examples of the system are to be found in the bronze panels of Ghiberti's 'Gates of Paradise' (1401–24) in the Baptistery at Florence, and in Masaccio's fresco of the Trinity (c.1427) in the nave of St Maria Novella. Other standard items include Uccello's *Battle of San Romagno* (c.1450), Mantegna's *Lamentation over the Dead Christ* (c.1480), and Leonardo's *Last Supper* (1497).

Perspective was to dominate representational art for the next 400 years. Leonardo called it 'the rein and rudder of painting'.[7] A modern critic was to call it 'a uniquely European way of seeing'.[8] Naturally, when modern artists eventually began to deconstruct traditional methods, linear perspective became one of their targets. Giorgio de Chirico (1888–1978) and his *Scuola Metafisica* explored the effects of dislocated perspective in paintings such as *The Disquieting Muses* (1917), as did Paul Klee in his *Phantom Perspective* (1920). It was left to the Dutchman M. C. Escher (1898–1970) to invent the visual riddles which show that in the last resort all lines on paper deal in illusions. [**IMPRESSION**]

LEONARDO

L EONARDO DA VINCI (1452–1519) was a left-handed, homosexual engineer, best known for his sideline in painting. He was the love-child of a Florentine lawyer and a peasant girl from the village of Vinci. He is widely rated the most versatile of all Europe's 'geniuses'. Only a dozen or so of his paintings have survived, some of them unfinished. But they include a number of supreme masterpieces, including the *Mona Lisa* in Paris, the *Last Supper* in Milan, and the *Lady with Otter* in Cracow. His left-handedness caused him to write backwards, in a script that can only be read with a mirror. His sexual proclivity led him to support a parasitic companion, called Salai, and to live in constant fear of prosecution. His most valuable legacy may well lie in his voluminous scientific notebooks, containing sketches and explanations of thousands of devices and inventions which never saw the light of day.[1] Not surprisingly, he has constantly attracted the attentions of all who try to measure the ingredients of genius. His name features on all sorts of lists of prominent Europeans who have allegedly shared his characteristics:

Left-handedness	*Brain radiation levels*[2]	*Homosexuality*
Tiberius	(on the Brunler Scale	Sappho
Michelangelo	where 500 = 'genius')	Alexander the Great
C. P. E. Bach	Leonardo, 720	Julius Caesar
George II	Michelangelo, 688	Hadrian
Nelson	Cheiro (palmist), 675	Richard Lionheart
Carlyle	Helena Blavatsky, 660	A. Poliziano, scholar
	Titian, 660	Botticelli
Estimated IQ	Frederick the Great, 657	Julius III, Pope
John Stuart Mill, 190	Raphael, 649	Cardinal Carafa
Goethe, 185	Francis Bacon, 640	Henri III
T. Chatterton, 170	Rembrandt, 638	Francis Bacon
Voltaire, 170	Goethe, 608	James VI and I
Georges Sand, 150	Napoleon, 598	Jean-Baptiste Lully
Mozart, 150	Chopin, 550	Queen Christina
Lord Byron, 150	El Greco, 550	Frederick the Great
Dickens, 145	Rasputin, 526	Alexander von Humboldt
Galileo Galilei, 145	Picasso, 515	Hans Christian Andersen
Napoleon, 140	Mussolini, 470	Tchaikovsky
Wagner, 135	Einstein, 469	Wilde
Darwin, 135	Freud, 420	Proust
Beethoven, 135		Keynes
Leonardo, 135		

After Leonardo's death, an experiment was made to replicate his genius. His half-brother, Bartolomeo, sought out a girl from the same village as Leonardo's mother, fathered a son by her, and raised the boy in one of Florence's finest studios. Pierino da Vinci (1530–53) showed great talent: his youthful paintings were good enough to be misattributed to Michelangelo. But he died before his genius matured.[3]

more deeply than Spain; and it met no insurmountable barrier until it reached the borders of the Orthodox world. Traces of the Renaissance were slight in countries absorbed by the Ottoman Empire; and in Muscovy they were limited to a few artistic imitations. Indeed, by giving a new lease of life to the Latin West, the Renaissance only deepened the gulf between East and West.

The causes of the Renaissance were as deep as they were broad. They can be related to the growth of cities and of late medieval trade, to the rise of rich and powerful capitalist patrons, to technical progress which affected both economic and artistic life. But the source of spiritual developments must be sought above all in the spiritual sphere. Here, the malaise of the Church, and the despondency surrounding the Church's traditional teaching, becomes the major factor. It is no accident that the roots of Renaissance and Reformation alike are found in the realm of ideas.

The New Learning of the fifteenth century possessed three novel features. One was the cultivation of long-neglected classical authors, especially those such as Cicero or Homer who had not attracted the medieval schoolmen. The second was the cultivation of ancient Greek as an essential partner to Latin. The third was the rise of biblical scholarship based on the critical study of the original Hebrew and Greek texts. This last activity provided an important bond between the secular Renaissance and the religious Reformation which was to place special emphasis on the authority of the Scriptures. Scholarly criticism of classical texts was growing rapidly long before the advent of printing. The lead, here again, had been given by Petrarch. He was emulated by Boccaccio, by Guarino, Filelfo, Bruni, Aurispa, and by that indefatigable collector and papal secretary G. F. Poggio Bracciolini (1380–1459). Poggio's rival Lorenzo Valla (*c*.1406–57), was responsible both for the treatise *De Elegantiis Latinae Linguae*, which established the superiority of Ciceronian Latin, and for the exposure of the false Donation of Constantine. The Greek tradition, fostered by the Byzantine Manuel Chrysoloras (1355–1415), sometime Professor of Greek at Florence, and by Angelo Poliziano (1454–94), poet and translator of Homer, was boosted by the wave of Greek refugees and their manuscripts after 1453. A later generation of scholars was dominated in Italy by the hellenist and orientalist G. Pico della Mirandola (1463–94), who explored the cabala, and by Marsilio Ficino (1433–99); in France by Jacques Lefèvre d'Étaples (1455–1537) and Guillaume Budé (1467–1540); in Germany by the Hebraist Johann Reuchlin (1455–1522), by the wandering knight Ulrich von Hutten (1488–1523), and by Philip Melanchthon (1497–1560). Particularly relevant for the future of science was Ficino's translation of the Alexandrian Hermes Trismegistus. The printing-machine made its entrée when the movement was well advanced. [CABALA] [PRESS]

Enthusiastic circles of such 'humanists' sprang up at all points, from Oxford and Salamanca to Cracow and Lwów. Their patrons, from Cardinal Beaufort to Cardinal Oleśnicki, were often prominent churchmen. All, in their devotion to the ancients, would have echoed the *cri de cœur* of one of their lesser brethren, Cyriac of Ancona: 'I go to wake the dead.' All paid homage to the greatest of their number—Erasmus of Rotterdam.

Gerhard Gerhards (*c*.1466–1536), a Dutchman from Rotterdam better known by his Latin and Greek pen-names of 'Desiderius' and 'Erasmus', was the principal practitioner of Christian humanism. Scholar at Deventer, chorister at Utrecht, secretary to the Bishop of Cambrai, frequent visitor to London and Cambridge, and long-term resident of Basle, Erasmus 'made himself the centre of the scientific study of Divinity . . . the touchstone of classical erudition and literary taste'.[6] One of the first truly popular authors of the age of printing—his *Moriae Encomium* (Folly's Praise of Folly, 1511) ran into 43 editions in his lifetime—he did more than anyone else to marry the new humanism with the Catholic tradition. His *Enchiridion Militis Christiani* (Handbook of a Christian Soldier, 1503) was another winner. Like his close friend Thomas More, he was no less a Pauline than a Platonist. His publication of the Greek *New Testament* (1516) was a landmark event. Its Preface contained the famous words:

I wish that every woman might read the Gospel and the Epistles of St Paul. Would that these were translated into every language . . . and understood not only by Scots and Irishmen but by Turks and Saracens. Would that the farmer might sing snatches of Scripture at his plough, that the weaver might hum phrases of Scripture to the tune of his shuttle . . .[7]

Most attractive, perhaps, was his beautifully paradoxical temperament. He was a priest with a strong streak of anticlericalism; a scholar with a deep loathing of pedantry; a royal and imperial pensioner who lacerated kings and princes; a true protestant against the abuses of the Church who took no part in the Reformation; a devoted humanist and a devoted Christian. His books remained on the Church's Index for centuries but were freely printed in England, Switzerland, and the Netherlands. He sported both a gentle spirit of moderation and a savage wit. 'What disasters would befall', he asked of the Rome of Julius II, 'if ever the supreme pontiffs, the Vicars of Christ, should make the attempt to imitate His life of poverty and toil?' The answer was that 'thousands of scribes, sycophants . . . muleteers . . . and pimps' would become unemployed.[8] 'Christ too', he wrote to the outrage of the Inquisition, 'was made something of a fool himself, in order to help the folly of mankind.'[9]

Erasmus greatly influenced the language of the age. His collection of annotated *Adagia* (1508) was the world's first bestseller, bringing over 3,000 classical proverbs and phrases into popular circulation:

oleum camino	(to pour) oil on the fire
ululas Athenas	(to send) owls to Athens
iugulare mortuos	to cut the throat of corpses
mortuum flagellas	you are flogging a dead (horse)
asinus ad lyram	(to put) an ass to the lyre
arare litus	to plough the seashore
surdo oppedere	to belch before the deaf
mulgere hircum	to milk a billy goat
barba tenus sapientes	wise as far as the beard.[10]

Humanism is a label given to the wider intellectual movement of which the New Learning was both precursor and catalyst. It was marked by a fundamental shift from the theocratic or God-centred world-view of the Middle Ages to the anthropocentric or man-centred view of the Renaissance. Its manifesto may be seen to have been written by Pico's treatise *On the Dignity of Man*; and, in time, it diffused all branches of knowledge and art. It is credited with the concept of human personality, created by the new emphasis on the uniqueness and worth of individuals. It is credited with the birth of history, as the study of the processes of change, and hence of the notion of progress; and it is connected with the stirrings of science—that is, the principle that nothing should be taken as true unless it can be tried and demonstrated. In religious thought, it was a necessary precondition for Protestant emphasis on the individual conscience. In art it was accompanied by renewed interest in the human body and in the uniqueness of human faces. In politics it gave emphasis to the idea of the sovereign state as opposed to the community of Christendom, and hence to the beginnings of modern nationality. The sovereign nation-state is the collective counterpart of the autonomous human person. [**STATE**]

Both in its fondness for pagan antiquity and in its insistence on the exercise of man's critical faculties, Renaissance humanism contradicted the prevailing modes and assumptions of Christian practice. Notwithstanding its intentions, traditionalists believed that it *was* destructive of religion, and ought to have been restrained. Five hundred years later, when the disintegration of Christendom was far more advanced, it has been seen by many Christian theologians as the source of all the rot. According to one Catholic philosopher:

The difference between the Renaissance and the Middle Ages was not a difference by addition but by subtraction. The Renaissance . . . was not the Middle Ages plus Man, but the Middle Ages minus God.

An American Protestant was no less forgiving: 'The Renaissance is the real cradle of that very un-Christian concept: the autonomous individual.' A Russian Orthodox was the most uncompromising of all:

Renaissance humanism affirmed the autonomy of man, and his freedom in the spheres of cultural creation, science and art. Herein lay its truth, for it was essential that the creative force of humanity should surmount the obstacles and prohibitions that mediaeval Christianity put in its way. Unfortunately, however, the Renaissance also began to assert man's self-sufficiency, and to make a rift between him and the eternal truths of Christianity . . . Here we have the fountain-head of the tragedy of modern history. . . . God became the enemy of Man, and man the enemy of God.[11]

By the same token, many people in recent times who do not hide their contempt for Christianity—Marxists, scientific sociologists, and atheists among them—have welcomed the Renaissance as the beginning of Europe's liberation. Nothing would have horrified the Renaissance masters more. Few of them saw any contradiction between their humanism and their religion; and most modern Christians would agree. All the developments deriving from the Renaissance,

from Cartesian rationalism to Darwinian science, have been judged by fundamentalists to be contrary to religion; yet Christianity has adapted, and has accommodated them. Left to itself, humanism will always find its logical destination in
atheism. But mainstream European civilization did not follow that extreme road.
Through all the conflicts which ensued, a new and ever-changing synthesis was
found between faith and reason, tradition and innovation, convention and conviction. Despite the growing prominence of secular subjects, the overwhelming
bulk of European art continued to be devoted to religious themes; and all the
great masters were religious believers. Suitably enough, at the end of a long life,
Michelangelo Buonarroti (1474–1564)—sculptor of the Florentine *David* (1504),
painter of the Sistine Chapel, and architect of St Peter's dome—turned for consolation to devotional poetry:

> Giunto è già 'l corso della vita mia,
> con tempestoso mar per fragil barca,
> al commun porto, ov'a render si varca
> conto e ragion d'ogni' opra trista e pia.
> Onde l'affettuosa fantasia,
> che l'arte me fece idol' e monarca,
> conosco or ben, com'era d'error carca,
> e quel c'a mal suo grado ogn'uom desia.
> Gli amorosi pensier, già vani e lieti,
> che fien'or, s'a due morti m'avvicino?
> D'una so 'l certo, e l' altra mi minaccia.
> Né pinger né scolpir fia più che quieti
> l'anima volta a quell' Amor divino
> c'aperse, a prender noi, 'n croce le braccia.

(The course of my life has come, | by fragile ship through stormy seas, | to the common
port, where one calls | to give account of all our evil and pious deeds. | Whence the fond
fantasy, | which made Art my idol and monarch, | I now know to have been a cargo of
error, | and see what every man desires to his own harm. | Those thoughts of love, once
light and gay, | what of them if now two deaths beset me? | I know the certainty of one,
whilst the other oppresses. | Nor painting nor sculpture brings real repose; | my soul turns
to that love divine | which, to enfold us, opens its arms on the cross.)[12]

Education played a capital role in Renaissance thinking. The humanists knew
that to create a New Man one had to start from schoolboys and students.
Educational treatises and experiments proliferated—from Vittorino da Feltre to
Erasmus's *Instruction of a Prince*. Their ideal, whilst conserving the bedrock of
Christian instruction, was to develop both the mental and the physical talents of
youth. To this end, gymnastics were taught alongside Greek and Latin. Vittorino's
academy in Mantua is often taken to be the first school of the new type. Later
examples included the refounded St Paul's School (1512) in London.

Renaissance music was marked by the appearance of secular choral music
alongside polyphonic settings for the Mass. The supreme masters, Josquin des
Prés (*c.*1445–1521) and Clément Jannequin (*c.*1485–1558), whose work was much

prized in Italy as well as France, painted panoramas in sound. Pieces such as Jannequin's *Les Oiseaux, Les Cris de Paris,* or *La Bataille de Marignan* abound with joy and energy. The art of the madrigal was widely disseminated, plied by an international school of lutenists.

Textbooks of Renaissance art tend to divide the subject into three neat periods. The Early Renaissance of fifteenth-century 'innovation' is followed by the High Renaissance of 'harmony attained' in the mid-sixteenth century, and by imitative Mannerism thereafter. The great innovative figures include Paolo Uccello (1397–1475), conqueror of perspective, Andrea Mantegna (1431–1506), master of realistic action, and Sandro Botticelli (1446–1510), the magical blender of landscape and human form. The three supreme giants are generally acknowledged to be Leonardo, Raphael Santi (1483–1520), and the mighty Michelangelo. The imitators, of course, were legion. But imitation is a form of flattery; and the treatment of the human face and body, of landscape and light, was transformed. Raphael's Madonnas are a world apart in spirit from medieval icons.

Yet over-neat classifications must be resisted. For one thing, innovation continued. Nothing could be more innovative in the use of form and colour than the daring canvases of Antonio Allegri (Correggio, 1489–1534), of the Venetians Tiziano Vercelli (Titian, 1477–1576) and Jacopo Robusti (Tintoretto, 1518–94), or of the Cretan Domenico Theotocopuli (El Greco, c.1541–1614), who found his way via Venice to Toledo. For another, the art of northern Europe, first prominent in Burgundy, developed strongly and independently. The German school forming around Albrecht Dürer (1471–1528), Lucas Cranach of Nuremberg (1472–1553), the landscapist Albrecht Altdorfer of Regensburg (1480–1538), and the portraitist Hans Holbein of Augsburg (1497–1543), was in contact with the South, but was anything but derivative. Finally, one has to take account of powerful and original artists who were more closely connected with continuing medieval traditions. Such would include the extraordinary altar-carver Veit Stoss or Wit Stwosz (c.1447–1533), who worked in Germany and Poland, the mysterious Master of Grünewald (c.1460–1528), the fantastic Dutchman Hieronymus Bosch (d. 1516), with his visions of Hell, or the Flemish 'peasant genre' painter Pieter Bruegel the Elder (c.1525–69).

Renaissance architecture is usually characterized by reactions against the Gothic style. The Florentine 'classical style', whose earliest example is to be found in the Pazzi Chapel (1430), had many admirers. The classical villas of Andrea Palladio (1518–80) became an obsession with the European nobility. His finely illustrated *Quattro Libri della Architectura* (1570), published in Venice, was placed in all respectable libraries. When gunpowder rendered castles obsolete, building funds were spent on magnificent palaces, notably in the aristocratic residences of the Loire; on the monuments to municipal pride in the burgher houses and arcaded squares of Germany and Holland; and on Italianate city halls from Amsterdam to Augsburg, Leipzig, and Zamość.

Renaissance literature was characterized by an explosion of the vernacular languages, which saw the world afresh in every way. The tentative work of the humanists gave way in the sixteenth century to the launch of full-blown national literatures. Indeed, the possession of a popular literary tradition in the vernacular was to become one of the key attributes of modern national identity. This tradition was established in French by the poets of the *Pléiade*, in Portuguese by Luiz de Camoens (1524–80), in Spanish by Miguel Cervantes (1547–1616), in Dutch by Anna Bijns (*c.*1494–1575) and Joost van den Vondel (b. 1587), in Polish by Jan Kochanowski (1530–84), in English by the Elizabethan poets and dramatists Spenser, Marlowe, and Shakespeare. In Italian, where the tradition was older and stronger, it was consolidated by Ludovico Ariosto (1474–1533) and Torquato Tasso (1544–95). [**SINGULARIS**]

Not all of Europe's linguistic communities produced serious literature. Those who lagged behind, principally in Germany, Russia, and the Balkans, were still preoccupied with religious pursuits. Apart from Luther and the *Narrenschiff* or 'Ship of Fools' (1494) of Sebastian Brant (1457–1527), the poetry of the Silesians, Andreas Gryphius (1616–69) and Martin Opitz (1597–1639), historiographer to the King of Poland, and the picaresque novel *Simplicissimus* of H.J.C. von Grimmelshausen (*c.*1625–76), little of note was published in Germany beyond religious tracts and popular *Volksbücher* such as the story of *Doktor Faustus* (1657) [**FAUSTUS**]. In Central Europe, an important branch of literature continued to be wirtten in Latin. The chief exponents of neo-Latin poetry included the German Conrad Pickel, alias 'Celtis' (1459–1508), first poet laureate of the Holy Roman Empire; Ianus Pannonius (1434–72), the Hungarian; the Italians Fracastorius (1483–1553) and Alciati (1492–1550); and the Poles Dantiscus (1485–1548) and Ianicius (1516–43).

Clearly, the Renaissance had something in common with the older movement for Church reform. Humanists and would-be reformers both fretted against fossilized clerical attitudes, and both suffered from the suspicions of the ruling hierarchy. What is more, by encouraging the critical study of the New Testament, both led the rising generation to dream about the lost virtues of primitive Christianity, much as others had dreamt about the lost age of classical Antiquity. In this connection, but not in the happiest of metaphors, it used to be said that 'Erasmus laid the egg and Luther hatched it'.

The Reformation. None the less, it is not possible to view the Reformation simply as an extension of the Renaissance. Unlike humanism, it appealed to the deepest devotional traditions of the Middle Ages, and it rode on a wave of a religious revival which affected not just the scholars but the masses. It was launched by men who had every intention of keeping the Catholic Church intact, and who only redoubled their campaign for a cleansed and unified religion when one branch of the reforming movement began to break away. It had nothing at all to do with the humanist spirit of tolerance. The common well springs of Renaissance and Reformation, therefore, should not be allowed to conceal the fact that they grew into streams flowing in very different directions. A similar split developed within the movement for Church reform. What started as a broad religious

SINGULARIS

INDIVIDUALISM is widely billed as one of the inherent qualities of 'Western civilization', and Michel de Montaigne could claim to be one of the pioneer individualists:

The greatest thing on earth is to know how to belong to oneself. Everyone looks in front of them. But I look inside myself. I have no concerns but my own. I constantly reflect on myself; I control myself; I taste myself . . . We owe some things in part to society, but the greater part to ourselves. It is necessary to lend oneself to others, but to give oneself only to oneself.[1]

The roots of individualism have been identified in Platonism, in Christian theology of the soul, in the nominalism of medieval philosophy.[2] But the main surge came with the Renaissance, which Burckhardt characterized by its brilliant individuals. The cultural interest in human beings, the religious interest in private conscience, and the economic interest in capitalist enterprise all put the individual centre stage. Starting with Locke and Spinoza, the Enlightenment elaborated the theme until the 'liberty of the individual' and 'human rights' joined the common stock of European discourse.

In the nineteenth century individualist theory developed along several divergent tracks. Kant had remarked that the unrestrained pursuit of self-interest was immoral; and it was left to John Stuart Mill *On Liberty* (1850) to reconcile the conflicting interests of individuals and of society. In *Socialisme et liberté* (1898) Jean Jaurès undertook a similar exercise in socialist terms. Yet there were always people ready to pursue the extremes. In *The Individual and His Property* (1844) Max Stirner condemned all forms of collective, whether 'nation', 'state', or 'society'. In *The Soul of Man under Socialism* (1891) Oscar Wilde defended the absolute rights of the creative artist: 'Art is the most intense mode of individualism that the world has known.'

In the twentieth century, both communism and fascism treated the individual with contempt. Even in democratic states, bloated government bureaucracies often oppressed those whom they were created to serve. The neo-liberal response gathered pace in the 'Vienna School' of the 1920s. Its leaders—Karl Popper (b. 1902), Ludwig von Mises (1881–1973), and Friedrich von Hayek (b. 1899)—all emigrated. Hayek's *Road to Serfdom* (1944) and *Individualism and the Economic Order* (1949) educated the post-war neo-conservatives. A fervent disciple once indignantly proclaimed: 'There is no such thing as society.'[3]

Such excesses tended to present the citizen as a mere consumer of goods, services, and rights. Politics threatened to degenerate into a 'culture of complaint'. At some point, the counter-tendency was due to reassert itself in the equally venerable tradition of Duty.[4]

revival gradually divided into two separate and hostile movements, later known as the Catholic Reformation and the Protestant Reformation.

The religious revival, clearly visible at the end of the fifteenth century, was largely driven by popular disgust at the decadence of the clergy. Despite the declared intention of calling a General Council every ten years, the Church had not called one since the 1430s. The canonization of a long line of saints, from St Vincent Ferrer OP (cd. 1455) and St Bernardino of Siena (cd. 1450) to St Casimir of Poland (1458–84), could not detract from the blatant lack of saintliness in the Church as a whole. Europe was full of tales about simoniac bishops, nepotistic popes, promiscuous priests, idle monks, and, above all, the sheer worldly wealth of the Church.

Once again, the harbinger of things to come appeared in Florence. The ferocious hellfire sermons of a fanatical friar, Fra Girolamo Savonarola (1452–98), raised a revolt in the 1490s which temporarily drove out the Medici and which only ended with the friar's own burning. In Spain, under Cardinal Cisneros, religious discipline was combined with energetic scholarship. The new school of theology at the University of Alcalá, founded in 1498, gave birth to the Polyglot Bible (1510–20). In Italy, under Cardinal Giampietro Carafa (1476–1559), the future Paul IV and co-founder c.1511 of the Oratory of Divine Love, an influential circle of Roman churchmen bound themselves to a regime of intense devotional exercises and practical charity. From them there arose a series of new Catholic congregations of clerks regular, neither monks nor friars—among them the Theatines (1523), the Barnabites (1528), the Jesuits (1540), and the Oratorians (1575).

The stirrings of religious revival coincided with the nadir of the Church's reputation, reached during the papacies of Rodrigo de Borgia (Alexander VI, 1492–1503) and Giuliano della Rovere (Julius II, 1503–13). Alexander's passions were for gold, women, and the careers of his bastard children. Julius gratified 'an innate love of war and conquest': he is remembered as the pope who rode into battle in full armour, the rebuilder of St Peter's, the refounder of the Papal States. In 1509, when he was planning to pay for his wars and for St Peter's through the sale in Germany of 'indulgences'—paper certificates guaranteeing relief from punishment in Purgatory—Rome was visited by a young Augustinian monk from Wittenberg in Saxony. Martin Luther was shocked to the bones by what he saw. 'Even depravity', wrote Ranke, 'may have its perfection.'[13]

Within ten years Luther (1483–1546) found himself at the head of the first 'Protestant' revolt. His lectures as Professor of Theology at Wittenberg show that his doctrine of 'justification by faith alone' had been brewing for some years; and as a man wrestling with his inner convictions, he had little patience with the gentle humanists of the day. He was inordinately rude and bad-tempered. His language was often unrepeatable. Rome, to him, was the seat of sodomy and the Beast of the Apocalypse.

Luther's fury was brought to the boil by the appearance in Germany of a friar, Johann Tetzel, who was selling indulgences. Tetzel had been banned from the territory of the Elector of Saxony, who had no desire to see his subjects pouring large sums into papal coffers. So by challenging Tetzel's theological credentials, Luther was reinforcing the policy of his Prince. On 31 October 1517, All Saints' Eve, he took the fateful step of nailing a sheet of 95 Theses, or arguments against indulgences, to the door of Wittenberg's castle church. Or tradition so insists.

From that famous act of defiance several consequences flowed. First, Luther was embroiled in a series of public disputations, notably the one staged at Leipzig with Dr von Eck which preceded his formal excommunication (June 1520). In the course of his preparations he penned the primary treatises of Lutheranism—the *Resolutions, Liberty of a Christian Man, Address to the Christian Nobility of German Nation, On the Babylonian Captivity of the Church of God*; and he publicly burned the papal Bull of Excommunication, *Exsurge Domine*. Secondly, German politics was split between the advocates and the opponents of Luther's punishment. In 1521 the Emperor Charles V summoned Luther to appear under safe conduct before the Imperial Diet at Worms. Luther, like Hus at Constance, defended himself with fortitude:

I am overcome by the Scriptures I have quoted; my conscience is captive to God's Word. I cannot and will not revoke anything, for to act against conscience is neither safe nor honest . . . *Hier stehe ich. Ich kann nicht anders.* [Here I stand. I cannot do otherwise.]

After that, he was spirited away by the Saxon Elector's men and hidden in the Wartburg Castle. The ban pronounced by the Diet against Luther could not be enforced. Religious protest was turning into political revolt.

Germany in 1522–5 was convulsed by two major outbursts of unrest: the feud of the Imperial Knights (1522–3) at Trier and the violent social disturbances of the Peasants' War (1524–5), which began at Waldshut in Bavaria. Luther's defiance of the Church may have been a factor in the defiance of political authority; but he had no sympathy for the peasants' 'twelve articles' drawn up in Swabia by Christoph Schappeler and Sebastian Lotzer of Memmingen. When fresh rebel bands appeared in Thuringia, Luther published his appeal *Against the Murderous and Thieving Hordes of Peasants*, trenchantly defending the social order and the princes' rights. The peasant rebels were crushed in a sea of blood.

The Lutheran revolt took definite shape during three later sessions of the Imperial Diet. The Emperor's opponents took their chance to consolidate their position whilst he was distracted by the wars against France and the Turks. At Speyer in 1526, in the Recess Declaration of the Diet, they managed to insert a clause for princely liberty in religion anticipating the famous formula: *Cuius regio, eius religio* (whoever rules has the right to determine religion). At the second Diet of Speyer in 1529, they formally lodged the Protest which gave them their name, bemoaning the annulment of the Recess. At Augsburg in 1530, they presented a measured summary of their beliefs. This Confession of Augsburg, composed by Melanchthon, was the Protestant manifesto—after which an adamant Emperor set April 1531 as the deadline for their submission. In response, the Protestant princes formed the armed League of Schmalkalden. From then on, the Catholic and the Protestant camps were clearly defined. [GESANG]

GESANG

MARTIN Luther's paraphrase of Psalm 46—'God is our refuge and strength'—was first set to music in J. Klug's *Gesangbuch* of 1529. It showed that 'the nightingale of Wittenberg' was a poet and composer as well as church reformer and theologian. It turned out to be perhaps the greatest hymn in the Christian repertoire:

EIN' FESTE BURG 8 7 8 7 6 6 6 6 7

Ein' feste Burg ist unser Gott,	A safe stronghold our God is still,
ein gute Wehr und Waffen.	A trusty shield and weapon;
Er hilft uns frei aus aller Not,	He'll help us clear from all the ill
die uns jetzt hat betroffen.	That hath us now o'ertaken.
Der alt boese Feind	The ancient prince of Hell
mit Ernst er's jetzt meint,	Hath risen with purpose fell;
gross Macht und viel List,	Strong mail of craft and power
sein grausam Ruestung ist	He weareth in this hour;
auf Erd ist nich seins gleichen.[1]	On earth is not his fellow.[2]

Luther, as a monk, was familiar with church music. He had a good tenor voice, and wanted all people to share his enjoyment of singing in church. Musical participation was to be the liturgical counterpart to his theological doctrine of the communion of all believers. He gave high priority to congregational music-making. His *Formula Missae* (1523) reformed the Latin Mass, providing a basis for the later Swedish liturgy. The *Geystliche Gesangk Buchlein* (1524), published by his disciple J. Walter, provided an anthology of polyphonic choral settings. In 1525 he brought the world's first musical press to Wittenberg. His *Deutsche Messe und Ordnung Gottesdienst* (1526) supplied a form of the vernacular sung Mass. It concluded with a version of the Hussite hymn 'Jesus Christus, unser Heiland'. Heinrich Lufft's *Enchiridion* (also 1526) constituted the first ever congregational hymn-book. Within five years of the Diet of Worms, Luther's followers were musically fully equipped.

The Lutheran musical tradition had far-reaching consequences. It required every parish to keep its cantor, its organist, its choir school, and its body of trained singers and instrumentalists. As a result, it played a

prominent role in turning Germany into the most musically educated
nation in Europe—the richest resource for Europe's secular music-
making. The genius of J. S. Bach could have found no more fertile soil
than in Lutheranism.

A hypothesis exists which maintains that it was the German language
and its rhythms which lay at the root of Germany's musical pre-eminence.
This may or may not be true. But one can find Luther saying in 1525 that
'both text and notes, accent, melody and performance ought to grow from
the true mother tongue and its reflections'. Luther's emphasis on the use
of the vernacular deeply affected German education. There is a direct link
between the hymns and masses of Luther, Walter, Rhaw, and Heinrich
Schutz (1585–1672), and the later glories of Bach, Haydn, Mozart,
Beethoven, Schubert, and Brahms.[3]

To celebrate the Lutheran tradition in isolation no doubt does a disser-
vice to Catholic music, and to the fruitful interactions of various Christian
traditions. But one only has to compare the sterile music of Calvinism,
whose ban on 'Popish polyphony' reduced the Geneva Psalter (1562) to a
collection of metrical unisons, to see the felicity of Luther's music-making.

In many ways the Church of England shares Luther's musicality, developing a wonderful tradition launched by Tallis, Gibbons, and Byrd. In its
stunning simplicity, Tallis's *Canon*, composed by a monk of Waltham
Abbey who became a gentleman of the Chapel Royal, is the Anglican
equivalent of *Ein' feste Burg*, and an eight-part round to boot:

TALLIS'S CANON 8 8 8 8 (LM)

Glory to thee, my God, this night
For all the blessings of the light.
Keep me, oh keep me, King of Kings
Beneath thine own almighty wings.[4]

Nor should one neglect the magnificent musical tradition of the Orthodox Church, which adopted polyphony as readily as Luther did. In this case the ban on musical instruments inspired a very special expertise in choral part-singing. The Catholic Church always permitted instrumental accompaniment. The earliest surviving church organ, dating from 1320, is still operational at Sion in the Valais. But in Russia and Ukraine the polyphony had to be generated by human voices alone, thereby fostering a culture which is as ready to make music as to appreciate it. In this context, Tchaikovsky was no more of an accident than Bach was.

Meanwhile, the Lutheran protest movement was swelled by a series of parallel events, each of which widened the nature of Protestantism. In 1522 in Switzerland, Huldrych Zwingli (1484–1531), hellenist, correspondent of Erasmus, and 'people's priest' at Zurich, challenged the Roman Church both on ecclesiastical organization and on doctrine. Like Luther, he started by denouncing indulgences; and he shared Luther's concept of justification by faith. But he also rejected the authority of bishops; and he taught that the Eucharist was no more than a simple, symbolic ceremony. He was killed at Kappel in 1531, carrying the Protestant banner in a war against the five Catholic forest cantons that had split the Swiss Confederation. He launched an important Protestant trend, in which local congregations or communities claimed the right to control their affairs. [HOLISM]

In the 1520s radical preachers and sects proliferated in Germany. Andreas Karlstadt (1480–1541), who quarrelled with Luther, went off to Basel. The 'Prophets of Zwickau'—Storch, Stuebner and Thomae—were old-fashioned millenarians. The mystic Thomas Muentzer (1490–1525), possessed both communist and anarchist traits, modelling his group on the Czech Taborites. After many wanderings, he was caught at the head of a band of expropriators during the Peasants' War in Thuringia, and executed at Muhlhausen. The Anabaptists or 'Rebaptisers' emerged among some disgruntled Swiss Zwinglians. Rejecting all established authority, they declared all previous baptisms invalid. They also sought to found an ideal Christian republic on evangelical principles, renouncing oaths, property, and (in theory) all violence. In 1534–5 at Münster in Westphalia under two Dutchmen—Jan Matthijs of Haarlem and Jan Beukelz of Leiden—they briefly created a 'Kingdom of the Elect' that was crushed with great cruelty. The cages which once held the remains of their leaders, still hang from the spire of St. Lambert's Church. The Anabaptists were Christendom's first fundamentalists, persecuted by Protestants and Catholics alike. They recovered as 'Mennonites' under the Frieslander, Menno Simons (1496–1561), sowing a spiritual legacy for later Baptists, Unitarians and Quakers. Christian Spiritualism, in contrast, drew support from Bavarian Denckians, Swabian Franckians and Silesian Schwenkfeldians.

HOLISM

IN February 1528 the wonderful 'Dr Paracelsus' lost his brief appointment as Basle's city physician. He had been barred from the university, had offended the guild of apothecaries, and had sued a prelate for refusing to pay him a full professional fee. When he publicly accused the magistrates of bias, he risked arrest and fled. His ideas were no more acceptable to the scholastic medicine of his day than to the supposedly scientific medicine of a later age.

Philippus Aureolus Theophrastus Bombastus von Hohenheim (1493–1541), known as Paracelsus, was born at Einsiedeln in the canton of Schwyz. He was the contemporary of Luther, Erasmus, and Michelangelo. He graduated from the medical faculty at Ferrara in 1524. But he dropped higher study and spent seven years travelling, learning the lore of herbalists, gypsies, and magicians, and earning his keep at the artisan grade of barber-surgeon. He visited Spain and Portugal, Russia and Poland, Scandinavia and Constantinople, Crimea and possibly Egypt. Formerly a Catholic, he often associated with the radical sects such as the Anabaptists and the Brethren of the Free Spirit. Arrested in Salzburg in 1525 for supporting rebellious peasants, he narrowly escaped execution. Apart from Basle, his longer sojourns were at Strasbourg, Nuremberg, St Gallen, Meran in Tyrol, St Moritz, Bad Pfeifers, Augsburg, Kromau in Moravia, Bratislava, Vienna and Villach. He was a prolific author on everything from theology to magic—the centrepiece being *Opus Paramirium* (1531), his 'Work Beyond Wonders'.

Paracelsus rejected the reigning notion that medical knowledge was to be garnered from ancient texts. At Basle, he had joined some students who were burning the works of Avicenna. Instead, he proposed to learn on the one hand from practical observations and on the other from 'the four pillars'—natural philosophy, astrology, alchemy, and 'Virtue' (by which he meant the innate powers of people, plants, and minerals). His empirical bent led to a series of brilliant treatments and techniques in amputations, antisepsis, homeopathy, and balneology. His other lines led him to an alternative system of biochemistry based on sulphur, salt, and mercury, and gave him a lasting reputation for wizardry. Not for 400 years was even part of Europe's medical profession prepared to consider his holistic precept—that the good doctor seeks the harmony of all factors affecting the patient's well-being, including the environmental, the psychosomatic and the supernatural.

Paracelsus lived at a time when no one understood the workings of the digestive, circulatory, neural, or reproductive systems, let alone genes or chromosomes. Yet many of his insights resonate across the centuries:

Both the man and the woman each have half a seed, and the two together make a whole seed . . . There is in the matrix [womb] an attractive force (like

> amber or a magnet) . . . Once the will has been determined, the matrix draws
> unto itself the seed of the woman and the man from the humours of the heart,
> the liver, the spleen, the bone, the blood . . . and all that is in the body. For
> every part of the body has its own particular seed. But when all these seeds
> come together, they are only one seed.[1]

In 1529 King Henry VIII of England initiated the policy which was to separate
the English Church from Rome. The initial cause lay in Henry's obsessive desire
for a male heir and in the Pope's refusal to grant him a divorce. Henry, who had
earlier earned the title of *Fidei Defensor* for denouncing Luther, had little religious
motivation; but he gained great support in Parliament, and immense material
advantage, by attacking the Church's privileges and property. The Act of Annates
(1532) cut financial payments to Rome. The Act of Appeals (1533) curtailed Rome's
ecclesiastical jurisdiction. The Act of Supremacy (1534) abolished papal authority
completely, raising the King to be Supreme Head of the Church of England.
Subjects such as Thomas More or Cardinal John Fisher, who declined to accede,
were executed for treason. The Ten Articles (1536) and Six Articles (1539) asserted
the inviolability of the Roman Mass and of traditional doctrine. The direct association of Church and State—later called Erastianism—brought Anglicanism
closer to Orthodox than to Catholic practice. [UTOPIA]

In 1541, at the second attempt, Jean Calvin (1509–64) was persuaded to take
control of the church in Geneva. A fugitive Frenchman, more radical than Luther,
Calvin founded of the most widely influential branch of Protestantism. A scholar
raised in the spirit of Lefèvre d'Étaples and a sometime Catholic lawyer, he had
been protected by the circle of Marguerite d'Angoulême. He was converted to the
new thinking after hearing a homily on the sovereignty of the Scriptures by the
Rector of the Sorbonne, Nicholas Cop. Fearing repressions, he resigned his
benefice in his native Noyon and fled to Basle. There, in 1535, he published his
seminal *Institution de la religion chrétienne*.

Calvin expressed original ideas on theology, on the relations of Church and
State, and especially on private morality. He was nearer to Luther than to Zwingli
on the Eucharist; but his revival of the doctrine of predestination proved shocking. He saw humanity to be divided into the Damned and the Elect. By this, he
taught his disciples to think of themselves as an embattled minority, a band of
righteous brothers surrounded by a hostile world, 'Strangers among Sinners':

Ainsi les Bourgeois du Ciel n'aiment point le Monde, ni les choses qui sont au Monde . . .
il s'écrient avec le Sage: 'Vanité des Vanités; tout n'est que vanité et rongement d'Esprit'.

(The inhabitants of the city of Heaven do not love the World, nor the things of the World
. . . They cry with the Prophet, 'Vanity of vanities; everything is nothing but vanity and the
devouring of the spirit.')[14]

On Church organization, too, Calvin's innovations far exceeded those of
Zwingli. He insisted not only on the separation of Church and State but also on

UTOPIA

UTOPIA, meaning 'No Place', was the name coined in 1516 by Sir Thomas More for his book describing his search for an ideal form of government. Translated into English in 1551, after the author's martyrdom, as *A Frutefull, pleasant and wittie worke of the beste state of a publique weale, and of the new yle called Utopia*, and also into French, German, Spanish, and Italian, it became a bestseller. In it More described a land where property was held in common, both men and women benefited from universal education, and all religions were tolerated.[1]

Utopian thinking supplies a deep human need for an ideal vision of a better world. The genre has attracted many practitioners, from Plato's *Republic* to Bacon's *New Atlantis* and Harrington's *Oceana*. Similar effects may be gained by imagining the horrors of *Dystopia* or 'Bad Place'. Such was the intent of Aldous Huxley's *Brave New World* (1932) or of George Orwell's *Nineteen Eighty-Four* (1949). In the twentieth century, utopianism has generally been associated with left-wing thinking. Soviet Russia was widely thought by its admirers to have been a modern utopia, free of the evils of capitalist democracy. 'I have seen the future,' said an American visitor in 1919, 'and it works.' Such opinions have since been disgraced by knowledge of the mass murders committed in the name of 'socialism' and 'progress'. Modern liberals have moved on to the more humdrum task of bettering the lot of individuals.[2] [HARVEST] [VORKUTA]

What is not so readily accepted is that Fascism too had its utopias. After the initial phase of brutal conquest, many Nazis, like many Communists, dreamed of a beautiful, harmonious future. The French writer 'Vercors', for example, recounts the musings of a German officer in occupied France, who looks forward to the glorious future of Franco-German union. 'It will be a replay of Beauty and the Beast'.[3] After the war, in Eastern Europe's Communist prisons, many democrats imprisoned for opposition to Communism had to listen to the broken dreams of their convicted Nazi cell-mates.[4] The Fascist utopia, like that of the Communists, was false, and generated immense suffering. But there were those who dreamed it sincerely. [LETTLAND]

the competence of local congregations. On the other hand, he also expected that the temporal power would be inspired by religious precepts, and by a desire to enforce all judgements of the Church organs. In matters of toleration, therefore, he was no more flexible than the Inquisition or Henry VIII. [**SYROP**]

In ethical matters, Calvin established a new and inimitable code which made his followers instantly recognizable. The good Calvinist family was to abhor all forms of pleasure and frivolity—dancing, songs, drinking, gaming, flirtation, bright clothes, entertaining books, loud language, even vivacious gestures. Their life was to be marked by sobriety, self-restraint, hard work, thrift, and, above all, godliness. Their membership of the Elect was to be manifest in their appearance, in their conduct, in their church-going, and in their worldly success. To the old Catholic burden of sin they added the new burden of keeping up appearances. In art, they were to avoid all direct portrayal of the Deity, all mystical symbols and allegories. They were to find the sole source of joy and guidance in the daily reading of the Bible. Here was what the English-speaking world would come to know as the Puritan.

The full formation of Calvinist principles had to await the definitive publication of the *Institution* in 1559 and the second Helvetic Confession, drawn up by H. Bullinger (1504–75), Zwingli's successor at Zurich, in 1566.

Calvin's successor at Geneva, Theodore Beza (1519–1605), a Greek scholar and theologian, introduced a rigid, determinist view of predestination that was vigorously opposed by the followers of Jakub Hermans (Arminius, 1560–1609), Professor at Leyden in Holland. The Arminians emphasized the doctrine of free will, and the efficacy of Christ's death for all believers, not just for the Elect.

The spread of Protestantism has to be described both in socio-political as well as in geographical terms.

Lutheranism appealed directly to independent-minded princes. It confirmed the legitimacy of their rule whilst maintaining the existing social order. It was quickly adopted in several states—notably in Wurtemberg, Hesse, Anhalt, electoral and ducal Saxony, Neumark, and Pomerania—and in most north German cities from Bremen to Riga. It entered a prolonged crisis in 1540, when Luther condoned the bigamous marriage of Philip of Hesse by advising the new faith's leading patron 'to tell a good strong lie'. Until the Formula of Concord (1580), it survived several decades of schism between the strict 'Gnesio-Lutherans' and the more liberal 'Melanchthonians'. In Denmark and Norway, through the preaching of 'the Danish Luther', Hans Tausen, it became the state religion in 1537. It helped perpetuate Denmark's loss of Sweden, where it was not fully established until 1593; and it accelerated the collapse of the Teutonic States in Prussia (1525) and in Livonia (1561).

Calvinism, in contrast, coincided less with state politics than with the inclinations of particular social groups. In Western Europe it often appealed to the rising urban bourgeoisie, and in France to an impressive cross-section of the nobility. In Eastern Europe, also, it appealed both to the landed gentry and to the magnates. In the kingdom of England, Calvinism began to make an impact after the death

SYROP

O N Saturday, 12 August 1553 a fugitive from the Holy Inquisition rode into the village of Louyset on the French side of Geneva. Four months earlier he had been arrested in Lyons on charges of heresy and, after interrogation by the Inquisitor General, condemned to death. He had escaped from prison, and had been wandering ever since. His aim was to take a boat across the lake from Geneva, and to make for Zurich. Geneva was the stronghold of Calvin, Zurich of the Zwinglians.

Prior to his arrest, the fugitive had been employed as physician to the Archbishop of Vienne. A native of Navarre, he had studied at Toulouse, Paris, Louvain, and Montpellier. He was the author of several medical treatises, of a study of Ptolemy's Geography, and of two anti-trinitarian theological works—De Trinitatis Erroribus (1521) and the anonymous Christianismi restitutio (1553). For the past eight years he had corresponded with some animosity with Calvin, whom he had once met.[1]

On the Sunday, having sold his horse, he walked into Geneva, found a room at La Rose, and went to an afternoon service. In church, he was recognized by someone and denounced to the city authorities. By the next morning he was facing the same questions from a Calvinist interrogator that he had faced from the Catholic Inquisitor. He was Fr. Miguel Serveto de Villanova, otherwise 'Servetus' (1511–53).

Calvin's conduct towards Servetus was, to put it mildly, unchristian. He had once warned him against coming to Geneva. He had even supplied the Inquisition at Lyons with a specimen of his correspondent's handwriting. He now set aside Geneva's laws concerning religious toleration, and recommended that Servetus be beheaded. Instead, by order of the court, he was burned alive at Champel on 27 October.

Nowhere in Europe could radical thinkers feel really safe. The Russian Orthodox Church had burned its 'Judaizers'. Byzantium, too, had its Inquisition. Giordano Bruno (1548–1600), philosopher and renegade Dominican, who was burned at the stake in Rome, was also, it seems, an English spy.[2] Poland-Lithuania was an isolated haven, where from 1565 episcopal courts could not enforce their verdicts. The anti-trinitarians tarried in Transylvania before moving on to Poland. Their leader, the Siennese Fausto Sozzini (1539–1604) to whom Servetus is sometimes compared, had also lived in Lyons and Geneva, where, enrolled in the Italian Church, he had kept quiet.

Long after his death, Servetus was remembered as a symbol of the interdependence of Protestant and Catholic bigotry. Monuments to his memory would be erected in Madrid (1876), Paris (1907), and Vienne (1910). Had he lived longer, he would have enjoyed the success of the four editions of his work on medicinal syrops, Syroporum universa ratio (1537).

of Henry VIII in 1547. The reign of the boy king Edward VI produced much confusion, and the interval of the ultra-Catholic Queen Mary, a crop of Protestant
martyrs, notably at Oxford. Thereafter, under Elizabeth I, the Church Settlement
enshrined in the Act of Uniformity (1559) and the Thirty-Nine Articles (1571)
reached a judicious synthesis of Erastian, Lutheran, Zwinglian, Calvinist, and
traditional Catholic influences. From then on, Anglicanism has always provided
an umbrella for two main political and theological tendencies—the 'High
Church' of Anglo-Catholicism and the 'Low Church' of the Calvinistic evangelicals. Despite merciless persecution under Elizabeth, both recusant Catholics and
non-conformist puritans survived underground. The latter re-emerged in force in
the seventeenth century and, under Cromwell's Commonwealth (1649–58),
briefly controlled the state.

In France the Calvinists were dubbed Huguenots. They spread rapidly in the
former Albigensian lands in the south and west, and in the urban populations of
all provinces. They formed the backbone of the Bourbon Party during the Wars
of Religion, and an essential feature of the French religious scene until their ultimate expulsion in 1685.

Thanks to the efforts of John Knox (1513–72), Calvinism became the sole
established religion in Scotland in 1560, in a form known as Presbyterianism.
Though subject to Anglican influences, the Scottish Kirk stayed apart.

In the Netherlands the rise of Calvinism, especially among the burghers of
Amsterdam, Rotterdam, and Leyden, provided a basic factor in the split between
the Catholic provinces to the west and the United Provinces to the east. The
Dutch Reformed Church has played a central role in the country since its establishment as the state religion in 1622.

In Germany Calvinism was long opposed both by Lutherans and Catholics. It
received its major support from the adherence in 1563 of the Elector-Palatine,
Frederick III, who imposed the Heidelberg Catechism on all his subjects; from
Christian I of Saxony (d. 1591), and in 1613 from the conversion of the
Hohenzollerns of Brandenburg. Brandenburg-Prussia was unusual in tolerating
both Calvinism and Lutheranism. [**FAUSTUS**]

In Poland-Lithuania, Bohemia, and Hungary Calvinism appealed to a wide section of the landed gentry. In some parts, such as Transylvania or the Duchy of
Cieszyn, its presence proved durable. The Hungarian city of Debrecen has been
'the Calvinist Rome' ever since. In Lithuania it claimed the allegiance of many
magnates, including Europe's largest landowners—the Radziwiłłs.

The effects of Protestantism can be observed in every sphere of European life.
By emphasizing the necessity of Bible-reading, it made a major impact on education in the Protestant countries, and hence on popular literacy. In the economic
sphere it made a major contribution to enterprise culture, and hence to the rise
of capitalism. In politics it proved a major bone of contention both between states
and between rival groupings within states. By dividing the Catholic world in two,
it spurred the Roman Church into the Reform which it had repeatedly postponed.
Above all, it dealt a fatal blow to the ideal of a united Christendom. Until the

FAUSTUS

THE real-life 'Dr Faustus' was a vagabond mountebank and fairground conjurer, who died at Staufen in Breisgau in 1541. Supposedly a graduate of Cracow like Copernicus, he frequented numerous German universities, presenting himself as Magister Georgius Sabellicus Faustus Junior. He became notorious for his blasphemies, for his 'miracles' such as changing water into wine, and for his claim to be in league with the Devil. His exploits inspired a stream of so-called *Faustbuchs*. The first of them, compiled at Frankfurt in 1587, was translated into Danish in 1588, into French and Dutch in 1592, into English before 1594, and into Czech in 1602.

As a fictional figure, Faust made his début in 1594 in the play by Christopher Marlowe, where he appears as a man of overweening ambition, striving to become 'great Emperor of the world'. He enjoys a season of power before the Devil reclaims his own. In Germany he featured in a lost drama by Lessing, and in a novel by F. M. Klinger (1791), before being adopted as the central protagonist of Goethe's two-part verse tragedy (1808, 1832). Ferruccio Busoni's opera, *Doktor Faust (1916)* remained unfinished.

Goethe's *Faust* defies easy summary. Faust's pact with Mephisto promises him rejuvenation, and he lives to be a hundred. *Gib meine Jugend mir zurück!* In Part I, which deals with the 'smaller world' of private emotion, Faust wrestles with the conflict between his duty to the Devil and his love for Gretchen. In Part II, which treats the *grosse Welt* of society and politics, he is the minister of a wastrel Emperor. When he dies, Gretchen intervenes, and the Devil is cheated; Heavenly choirs greet the progress of a redeemed soul, as Love triumphs:

> Der früh Geliebte,
> Nicht mehr Getrübt,
> Er kommt zurück!
>
> (The beloved of long ago, no more befogged, is coming back!)[1]

Goethe's masterpiece inspired two operas, by Gounod and Berlioz, and the Faust Symphony (1857) by Liszt. In more recent times, Thomas Mann's novel *Doktor Faustus* (1947) revived the legend for a grim judgement on contemporary Germany. A musician, Adrian Leverkühn, seduced by the works of Wagner and Nietzsche, contracts the diabolical curse of syphilis from a *femme fatale*, and expires after composing a nihilistic cantata, *D. Fausti Weheklag*. At its close, a sustained diminuendo from a solo cello recalls 'the light in the night', hinting that German civilization may not, after all, engender total despair.[2]

1530s, Christendom had been split into two halves—Orthodox and Catholic. From the 1530s onwards it was split into three: Orthodox, Catholic, and Protestant. And the Protestants themselves were split into ever more rival factions. The scandal was so great, and the fragmentation was so widespread, that people stopped talking about Christendom, and began to talk instead about 'Europe'.

The Counter-Reformation was given its name by Protestant historians who assumed that it was born to oppose the Protestant Reformation. Catholic historians see it differently, as the second stage of a movement for Church reform which had a continuous history from the conciliarists of the late fourteenth century to the Council of Trent. One must stress, however, that the Counter-Reformation was not some sort of autarkic historical engine operating in isolation. Like the Renaissance and the Reformation, it interacted with all the other great phenomena of the age.

The paralysis reigning at the centre of the Catholic Church eased during the pontificate of Paul III (Alessandro Farnese, 1534–49). Known as 'Cardinal Petticoat', Paul III was a flagrant nepotist, brother of a papal concubine, and the lavish patron of Michelangelo and Titian. At the same time he saw the urgency of change. He revitalized the Sacred College, commissioned the key inquiry into Church reform, *Consilium de emendanda ecclesia* (1537), patronized the Jesuits, established the Holy Office, and launched the Council of Trent. Until the 1530s the Sacred College of Cardinals, which elected the Popes, was one of the Church's weaker pillars. But with its budget cut, and its numbers increased by several brilliant appointments, it became the Vatican's power-house for change. Its outstanding names included Cardinals Caraffa (later Paul IV, 1555–9), Cervini (later Marcellus II, 1555), and the Englishman Reginald Pole, who missed election in 1550 by one vote. The next run of popes was of a different stamp. Pius IV (1559–65) did not hesitate to condemn to death the criminal nephews of his predecessor. The austere and fanatical Pius V (1566–72), sometime Inquisitor-General who walked barefoot in Rome, was later canonized. Gregory XIII (1572–85), who rejoiced at the massacre of St Bartholomew's Eve, was wholly political.

The Society of Jesus has been called the *corps d'élite* of Catholic Reform. It combined the fierce piety and military lifestyle of its Basque founder, Íñigo López de Recalde (St Ignatius Loyola, 1491–1556), author of the *Spiritual Exercises* (1523). Approved in 1540 by Paul III's Bull *Regimini Militantis Ecclesiae*, it operated under direct papal command. Its members were organized in ranks under their General, and were trained to think of themselves as 'companions of Jesus'. Their aims were to convert the heathen, to reconvert the lapsed, and, above all, to educate. Within a few decades of their formation, their missionaries appeared all over the world from Mexico to Japan. Their colleges sprang up in every corner of Catholic Europe, from Braganza to Kiev. 'I have never left the Army,' said St Ignatius; 'I have only been seconded to the service of God.' And elsewhere: 'Give me a boy at the age of seven, and he will be mine for ever.' At his canonization it was said, 'Ignatius had a heart large enough to hold the universe.'[15]

Despite their successes, the Jesuits aroused immense fear and resentment, among Catholics as well as Protestants. They were famed for their casuistry in dispute, and were widely thought to hold that 'the end justifies the means'. They came to be seen as the Church's secret thought police, accountable to no one. Already in 1612 the forged *Monita Secreta*, published in Cracow, purported to reveal the instructions of their worldwide conspiracy under the formidable General Acquaviva, 'the Black Pope'. The Society was suppressed in 1773 but restored in 1814.

The Holy Office was established in 1542 as the supreme court of appeal in matters of heresy. Staffed by leading cardinals, it assumed supervision of the Inquisition and in 1557 issued the first Index, the list of prohibited books. In 1588 it became one of the nine reorganized Congregations, or executive departments of the Roman Curia. It worked alongside the Office for the Propagation of the Faith, which was charged with converting the heathen and heretics. [**INDEX**] [**INQUISITIO**] [**PROPAGANDA**]

The Council of Trent, which met in three sessions, 1545–7, 1551–2, and 1562–3, was the General Council for which Church reformers had been praying for decades. It provided the doctrinal definitions and the institutional structures which enabled the Roman Church to revive and to meet the Protestant challenge. Its decrees on doctrine were largely conservative. It confirmed that the Church alone could interpret the Scriptures, and that religious truth derived from Catholic tradition as well as from the Bible. It upheld traditional views of original sin, justification, and merit, and rejected the various Protestant alternatives to transubstantiation during the Eucharist. Its decrees on organization reformed the Church orders, regularized the appointment of bishops, and established seminaries in every diocese. Its decrees on the form of the Mass, contained in a new Catechism and a revised Breviary, affected the lives of ordinary Catholics most directly. After 1563 the same Latin Tridentine Mass could be heard in most Roman Catholic churches throughout the world.

Critics of the Council of Trent point to its neglect of practical ethics, its failure to give Catholics a moral code to match that of the Protestants. 'It impressed on the Church the stamp of an intolerant age,' wrote an English Catholic, 'and perpetuated . . . the spirit of an austere immorality.'[16] The Protestant historian Ranke stressed the paradox of a Council which had intended to trim the Papacy. Instead, by oaths of loyalty, detailed regulations, and punishments, the entire Catholic hierarchy was subordinated to the Pope. 'Discipline was restored, but all the faculties of directing it were centred in Rome.'[17] Several Catholic monarchs, including Philip II of Spain, so feared the Tridentine decrees that they curtailed their publication.

The particular religious ethos promoted by the Counter-Reformation emphasized the discipline and collective life of the faithful. It reflected the wide powers of enforcement given to the hierarchy, and the outward show of conformity which believers were now required to display. It insisted on regular confession as a sign of submission. It was supported by a wide range of communal practices—

498 *RENATIO*

INQUISITIO

S IXTEENTH-CENTURY SEVILLE. Jesus Christ has returned to earth, and has been caught performing miracles. He is promptly arrested. The Grand Inquisitor conducts the prisoner's interrogation in person. 'Why have you come to meddle with us?' he asks. And answer received he none.

Among many recriminations, the Inquisitor accuses Christ of misleading people with the gift of Free Will. Man is by nature a rebel and given the choice will always choose the path to damnation. For their own good, he implies, people must be denied their freedom in order to save their souls. 'Did you forget that a tranquil mind, and a tranquil death, is dearer to Man than freedom in the knowledge of Good and Evil?'

Moreover, the Inquisitor claims, the facts of History support his case. People are too weak to resist temptation. For 1,500 years, they have wallowed in sin and suffering, incapable of heeding Christ's behests. 'You promised them bread from Heaven, but can it compare with earthly bread in the eyes of the weak, vicious, and always ignoble race of men? We are more humane than you.'

The Inquisitor charges that Christ did not rebut the Devil's challenge, and did not give proof of his Divinity. He failed the threefold test on Mystery, Miracle, and Authority. The Papacy, in fact, is secretly on the Devil's side. 'We have been with him, and not with you,' the Inquisitor reveals, referring to the Catholic–Orthodox Schism, 'for eight centuries'.

The Inquisitor bitterly foretells the victory of faithless materialism. 'Do you know that centuries will pass, and mankind will proclaim . . . that there is no crime, and therefore no sin, and only starving people? "Feed them first, and then demand virtue!" That's what will be written on the banners with which they will destroy your temple.'

In the Inquisitor's dungeon, the conclusion seems inevitable. 'You have been disgorged from Hell', he tells Christ; 'You are a heretic. Tomorrow I shall burn you!'

At the last moment, Christian forgiveness triumphs. Christ kisses the Inquisitor on the cheek. Overcome by the power of love, the Inquisitor relents, and the prison gate is opened. . . .

Such a summary might serve as introductory student notes on 'The Legend of the Grand Inquisitor'. The creator of 'The Legend' was a young Russian author, Ivan Karamazov, who lived with his father and brothers in the 1860s. The Karamazovs' own saga, like the 'Legend', which forms one of its central episodes, poses the eternal questions of Good and Evil. Father Karamazov is a nasty debauchee, against whom the elder son, Dmitri, has already rebelled. Ivan and Aloysha, Dmitri's half-brothers, are respectively the sceptical atheist and the trusting optimist. But it is the fourth, bastard son, Smyerdyakov or 'Stinker', who kills the Father before killing himself. At the trial, Ivan is racked by guilt for inciting the deed, and

tries to take the blame. But in an atrocious miscarriage of justice, the innocent Dmitri is condemned. In a final scene, the family's children show
their elders how to live in harmony.[1]

The creator of *The Brothers Karamazov* (1880) was Feodor Dostoyevsky.[2]
In it, he re-worked many of the themes and insights of a lifetime's writing.
In the view of Sigmund Freud, it is 'the most magnificent novel ever writ-
ten.' About the Creator of Dostoyevsky, Dostoyevsky had no doubts.

Dostoyevsky invented the Grand Inquisitor's Legend as the vehicle for
European literature's most penetrating critique of the Christian Church.
In it, he presages the moral objections to totalitarianism. He imagines
a fictional event. It well illustrates the author's prejudices against
Catholicism, but also his belief in the essential unity of Christendom.

On the surface, Dostoyevsky was a Russian chauvinist. He disliked 'merciless' Jews; he despised Catholics, especially Poles, whom he often portrayed as criminals; and he hated socialists. He took the Russian Orthodox
Church to be what its name proclaimed—the only True Faith. 'In the
West there is no longer any Christianity', he ranted; 'Catholicism is transforming itself into idolatry, whilst Protestantism is rapidly changing into
atheism and to variable ethics.'[3] Allegedly, his formula was: 'Catholicism
= Unity without Freedom. Protestantism = Freedom without Unity;
Orthodoxy = Freedom in Unity, Unity in Freedom.'

Many critics consider that Dostoyevsky put the Inquisitor's arguments
more forcefully than Christ's. In the confrontation between Church and
Faith, the Faith appears to lose. This was probably his intention, since he
rated logic far lower than belief. 'Even if it were proved to me that Christ
were outside the Truth', he once wrote, 'I would still stay with Christ.'[4]

Dostoyevsky's critique of the West was unremitting (which may explain
his star rating among Western intellectuals). Yet he saw the division of
Christendom as an instance of the Evil which would ultimately be overcome. He believed fervently that evil could be conquered. Sin and suffering precede redemption. The scandals of the Church were a necessary
prelude to Christian harmony. By this reasoning, the horrors of the
Spanish Inquisition were an indication of Christianity's ultimate triumph.
In his heart of hearts, the old reactionary was a universal Christian, and, in
the spiritual sense, a devout European.

Above all, Dostoyevsky believed in the healing power of faith. On the
title-page of *The Brothers Karamazov*, he added the verse 'Verily, verily, I
say unto you, except a grain of wheat fall into the ground and die, it
abideth alone. But if it die, it bringeth forth much fruit.'[5] Those same
words were carved on his tombstone.

PROPAGANDA

Propaganda is the child of conflicting belief, and of people's determination to spread their own doctrines against all others. Its origins undoubtedly lay in the religious sphere. It is in essence biased, being most successful when it appeals to hatred and prejudice. It is the antithesis of all honest education and information.

To be most effective, propaganda needs the help of censorship. Within a sealed informational arena, it can mobilize all means of communication—printed, spoken, artistic, and visual—and press its claims to maximum advantage. To this end, the Roman *Officium de Propaganda Fidei*, from which the term derives, worked alongside the Inquisition. It became one of the Vatican's permanent congregations in 1622.

Propaganda was no less prevalent in Protestant and Orthodox countries, where the Churches were subordinated to state power. Political propaganda, too, had always existed, though without the name. It was boosted by printing, and later by newspapers and broadsheets. It was most in evidence in wartime, especially during civil and religious wars. During the 1790s, French soldiers were given to appearing in the enemy camp armed only with leaflets.

In the twentieth century, the scope for propaganda was dramatically expanded by the advent of new media, such as film, radio, and TV; by the techniques of marketing, mass persuasion, commercial advertising, and 'PR'; by the appearance of utopian ideologies; and by the ruthlessness of the totalitarian state. 'Total propaganda' and the art of 'the Big Lie' was pioneered by the Bolsheviks. Lenin, after Plekhanov, distinguished between the high-powered propagandist, who devised the strategy, and the low-level agitator, who put it into practice. Where Soviet *agitprop* led, the Fascists were quick to follow.

Theorists of propaganda have identified five basic rules:

1. The rule of simplification: reducing all data to a simple confrontation between 'Good and Bad', 'Friend and Foe'.
2. The rule of disfiguration: discrediting the opposition by crude smears and parodies.
3. The rule of transfusion: manipulating the consensus values of the target audience for one's own ends.
4. The rule of unanimity: presenting one's viewpoint as if it were the unanimous opinion of all right-thinking people: drawing the doubting individual into agreement by the appeal of star-performers, by social pressure, and by 'psychological contagion'.
5. The rule of orchestration: endlessly repeating the same messages in different variations and combinations.

In this regard, one of the supreme masters acknowledged his antecedents. 'The Catholic Church keeps going', said Dr Goebbels, 'because it has been repeating the same thing for two thousand years. The National Socialist Party must do likewise.'[1]

One of the more insidious forms of propaganda, however, is that where the true sources of information are hidden from recipients and propagators alike. This genre of so-called 'covertly directed propaganda' aims to mobilize a network of unsuspecting 'agents of influence' who pass on the desired message as if they were acting spontaneously. By feigning a coincidence of views with those of the target society, which it seeks to subvert, and by pandering to the proclivities of key individuals, it can suborn a dominant élite of opinion-makers by stealth.

Such, it seems, was the chosen method of Stalin's propaganda chiefs who spun their webs among the cultural circles of leading Western countries from the 1920s onwards. The chief controller in the field was an apparently harmless German Communist, an erstwhile colleague of Lenin in Switzerland and sometime acquaintance of Dr Goebbels in the Reichstag, Willi Munzenberg (1889–1940). Working alongside Soviet spies, he perfected the art of doing secret business in the open. He set the agenda of a series of campaigns against 'Anti-militarism', 'Anti-imperialism', and above all 'Anti-fascism', homing in on a handful of receptive milieux in Berlin, Paris, and London. His principal dupes and recruits, dubbed 'fellow-travellers' by the sceptics, rarely joined the Communist Party and would indignantly deny being manipulated. They included writers, artists, editors, left-wing publishers, and carefully selected celebrities—hence Romain Rolland, Louis Aragon, André Malraux, Heinrich Mann, Berthold Brecht, Anthony Blunt, Harold Laski, Claud Cockburn, Sidney and Beatrice Webb, and half the Bloomsbury Set. Since all attracted strings of acolytes, dubbed 'Innocents' Clubs', they achieved a ripple effect that was aptly called 'rabbit breeding'. The ultimate goal has been nicely defined; 'to create for the right-thinking, non-communist West the dominating political prejudice of the era: the belief that any opinion that happened to serve . . . the Soviet Union was derived from the most essential elements of human decency.'[2]

Such cynicism has few parallels. It can be judged by the fate which the Great Leader reserved for all his most devoted propagandists such as Karol Radek, and probably Munzenberg himself, who was found mysteriously hanged in the French mountains. Brecht's comment on Stalin's victims was less of a joke than he thought. 'The more innocent they are', he wrote, 'the more they deserve to be shot'.[3]

pilgrimages, ceremonies, and processions—and by the calculated theatricality of the accompanying art, architecture, and music. Catholic propaganda of this vintage was strong both on rational argument, and on devices for impressing the senses. The Baroque churches of the era, crammed with altars, columns, statues, cherubs, gold leaf, icons, monstrances, candelabra, and incense, were designed to leave nothing to the private thoughts of the congregation. Unlike the Protestant preachers, who stressed individual conscience and individual probity, all too often the Catholic clergy seemed to urge their flock to blind obedience.

The Counter-Reformation saw a plentiful harvest of Catholic saints. There were the Spanish mystics: St Teresa of Ávila (1515–82) and St John of the Cross (1542–91); there was a long line of servants of the sick and the poor: St Philip Neri (1515–95), St Camillo de Lellis (1550–1614), St Vincent de Paul (1576–1660), St Louise de Marillac (1591–1660); and there were the Jesuit saints and martyrs: St Francis Xavier (1506–52), St Stanisław Kostka (1550–68), St Aloysius Gonzaga (1568–91), St Peter Canisius (1521–97), St John Berchmans (1599–1621), and St Robert Bellarmine (1542–1621). They won back much lost ground.

The impact of the Counter-Reformation was felt right across Europe. Traditional support for the Church was strongest in Italy and Spain, but pockets of nonconformity had to be smoked out even there. The Spanish Netherlands, trapped between France and the United Provinces, were turned into a hotbed of Catholic militancy in which the University of Louvain (Leuven) and the Jesuit College at Douai took the lead. Yet an important reaction against the prevailing zeal was provoked by Cornelius Jansen (1585–1638), Bishop of Ypres and a fervent critic of the Jesuits. In his digest of the works of St Augustine, the *Augustinus* (1640), Jansen attacked what he took to be the theological casuistry and superficial morality of his day, placing special emphasis on the believer's need for Divine Grace and for spiritual rebirth. Though he never wavered in his loyalty to Rome, and rejected the Protestant doctrine of justification by faith, several of his propositions on the issue of Divine Grace approached the Protestant standpoint, and were duly condemned as such. (See Chapter VIII.)

Switzerland was rent by the hostility of the Catholic and the Protestant cantons. The doctrines of Zurich and Geneva penetrated many of the alpine villages of the surrounding regions. They were eradicated by violent means on the Italian border by St Charles Borromeo, Cardinal-Archbishop of Milan (1538–84), and contested in Savoy by the more gentle persuasion of St Francis de Sales (1567–1622), author of the bestselling *Introduction to the Devout Life* (1609). [MENOCCHI]

In France, many Catholics stood aloof from the new militancy, partly in line with the Gallican tradition and the Concordat of 1516, and partly from France's hostility to the Habsburgs. But a pro-Roman 'ultramontane' party grew in prominence round the faction of the Guises. Their darkest deed was committed at the massacre of St Bartholomew's Eve on 23 August 1572, when 2,000 Huguenots were butchered in Paris—after which the Pope celebrated a *Te Deum* and the King of Spain 'began to laugh'. In the seventeenth century Jansenism offered a middle way, an antidote to the partisanship of contending ultras and Huguenots.

MENOCCHI

IN 1599 a simple miller from Montereale in Friuli, Comenico Scandella, was burned at the stake for heresy, just two years before Giordano Bruno suffered the same penalty in Rome. The papers of his case, which have survived at Udine, open the world of unconventional belief which historians penetrate with difficulty. After two trials, long interrogation, imprisonment, and torture, the Holy Inquisition insisted that he had denied 'the virginity of the Blessed Virgin, the divinity of Christ, and the Providence of God'.

Known as 'Menocchio', the miller of Montereale, sometime village mayor, was father of eleven children, a rampant gossip, an outspoken anti-cleric, and a voracious reader. When he was arrested, his house contained:

a vernacular Italian Bible;
Il Fioretto della Bibbia (a Catalan biblical anthology in translation);
Il Rosario della Madonna by Alberto da Castello, OP;
A translation of the *Legenda Aurea*, 'the Golden Legend';
Historia del Giudicio, in fifteenth-century rhyme;
Il Cavalier Zuanne de Mandavilla (a translation of Sir John Mandeville's *Travels*);
Il Sogno di Caravia (Venice, 1541);
Il Supplemento delle Cronache (a version of Foesti's chronicle);
Lunario al Modo di Italia (an almanac);
an unexpurgated edition of Boccaccio's *Decameron*;
an unnamed book, identified by a witness as the Koran.

Menocchio had talked at length with one Simon the Jew, was interested in Lutheranism, and would not admit the biblical Creation story. Echoing Dante[1] and numerous ancient myths, he insisted that the angels were produced by nature 'just as worms are produced from cheese'.[2]

The Kingdom of England was targeted for reconversion in a campaign that spawned the Forty Catholic martyrs led by St Edmund Campion SJ (1540–81) and many other victims. Ireland was confirmed in its Catholicism, especially after the brutal Elizabethan expedition of 1598. But religious unity in Ireland was shattered by the planting of a Scottish Presbyterian colony in Ulster in 1611, and by the Anglican inclinations of the Anglo-Irish gentry.

In the lands of the Austrian Habsburgs, the Counter-Reformation became inextricably confused with the dynasty and its politics. Indeed, that special brand of Catholicism, the *pietas austriaca*, which emerged at the turn of the seventeenth century became the prime ingredient of a wide cultural community that has outlived Habsburg rule. It was once called 'Confessional Absolutism'. The Collegium Germanicum in Rome played a strategic role. The Jesuits took an unrivalled hold over education in Vienna and Prague through the efforts of the Dutchman, Canisius. Western Hungary, Slovakia, Croatia, Silesia, Bohemia, and, at a later date, western Galicia all belonged to this same sphere. Baroque culture, it has been argued, represented the ivy which not only covered the ramshackle Habsburg edifice but helped to hold it together (see p. 529).

Elsewhere in Germany, an uneasy *modus vivendi* between Catholics and Protestants had been reached in 1555 at the Peace of Augsburg: each prince was to decide on the religion of his subjects; Lutheranism was to be the only Protestant denomination allowed; Lutherans living in Catholic states were to be tolerated. Germany was turned into a religious patchwork where, however, the Catholic princes and emperors, feared a further Protestant advance. As from the 1550s, 'Spanish priests' set up Jesuit centres at Cologne, Mainz, Ingolstadt, and Munich, creating durable Catholic bastions in the Rhineland and Bavaria. Calvinist enclaves, in the Palatinate and Saxony and elsewhere, were not secured until the second half of the century. In December 1607 the Duke of Bavaria provocatively seized the city of Donauwörth in Swabia in order to stop Protestant interference with Catholic processions. Ten Protestant princes thereon convened an Evangelical Union to defend their interests, only to be confronted by the rival activities of a Catholic League. It is difficult to say, therefore, whether the outbreak of the Thirty Years War occurred in 1618 or beforehand.

In this world of growing religious intolerance, Poland-Lithuania occupied a place apart. A vast territory with a very varied population, it had contained a mosaic of the Catholic, Orthodox, Judaic, and Muslim faiths even before Lutheranism claimed the cities of Polish Prussia or Calvinism a sizeable section of the nobility. Such was the position of the ruling *szlachta* that every manor could run its religious affairs with the same liberty as German princedoms. From 1565 the verdicts of ecclesiastical courts could not be enforced on the private estates of noblemen. At the very time that Cardinal Hozjusz, President of the Council of Trent and Bishop of Warmia, was introducing the Jesuits, Poland was receiving all manner of heretics and religious refugees—English and Scottish Catholics, Czech Brethren, Anabaptists from Holland, or, like Faustus Sozzini (Socinius), Italian unitarians. In 1573, with Calvinists commanding a majority in the Senate, the Polish parliament passed a statute of permanent and universal toleration, from which only the Socinians were excepted. Under Sigismund III Vasa (r. 1587–1632), a fervent pupil of the Jesuits, the ultramontane party gradually reasserted the Catholic supremacy. But progress was slow; and non-violent methods alone were available. In this period Poland could rightly boast of its role both as the bulwark of Christendom against Turk and Tartar and as Europe's prime haven of toleration.

Elsewhere in Eastern Europe the Counter-Reformation reverberated far and wide. The Vatican, under Gregory XIII (1572–85), entertained hopes of netting not only Sweden and Poland but even Muscovy. In Sweden those hopes remained high until the victory of the Protestants in the civil war of the 1590s dashed Jesuit plans for good. In Moscow the papal nuncio Possevino was received by Ivan the

Terrible, only to find that the Tsar's main interest in Catholicism lay in the workings of the papal litter. Clumsy pressure from the Catholic side probably pushed Ivan's son, Fedor, into creating the Moscow Patriarchate in 1589, thereby finalizing the emergence of the separate Russian Orthodox Church.

Moscow's *démarche* provoked a crisis among the Orthodox in neighbouring Poland-Lithuania, who till then had always looked to the Patriarch of Constantinople. With the new Muscovite Patriarch claiming jurisdiction over them from across the frontier, many of those Orthodox now sought the protection of Rome. In 1596, at the Union of Brest, the majority of their bishops chose to found a new Uniate communion—the Greek Catholic Church of Slavic Rite. They retained their ritual, and their married clergy, whilst admitting the supremacy of the Pope. Most of the Orthodox churches in Byelorussia and Ukraine, including the ancient cathedral of St Sophia in Kiev, passed into the hands of the Uniates. For a time the old 'disuniate' remnant was officially banned by the state.

Moscow, however, was never reconciled to these developments. The furious determination of the Russian Orthodox Church to punish and forcibly to reconvert the Uniates remained constant throughout modern history. Nowhere has the stereotype of the dastardly, scheming Jesuit remained stronger. The Russo-Polish wars, when in 1610–12 the Poles briefly occupied the Kremlin, only served to cement the religious hatreds. On the great Russian monastery at Zagorsk near Moscow, a commemorative tablet underlines the popular Russian view of the Counter-Reformation: 'Typhus—Tartars—Poles: Three Plagues'.

In Hungary, a similar Uniate communion emerged from the Union of Uzhgorod (1646). In this case, the Orthodox Ruthenes of the sub-Carpathian region chose to seek union with Rome along the lines adopted in neighbouring Ukraine. (Their decision was still causing ructions between Roman Catholic and Uniate Ruthenes in the USA in the 1920s.)

All over Europe, religious fervour profoundly affected the progress of the arts. The more severe forms of Protestantism questioned the very propriety of artistic endeavour. The plastic arts were often channelled into secular subjects, since religious subjects had become suspect. In some countries, such as Holland or Scotland, music was reduced to hymn-singing and metrical psalms. In England, in contrast, Thomas Tallis (*c.*1505–85) and others launched the wonderful tradition of Anglican cathedral music. In the Catholic countries, all branches of the arts were exposed to demands for sumptuous and theatrical displays of the Church's glory and power. The trend is known as 'Baroque'. In music, it was associated with the names of Jan Peterzoon Sweelinck (1562–1621), of Heinrich Schutz (1585–1672), and above all of Giovanni Palestrina (1526–94), magister capellae at St Peter's, whose ninety-four extant masses reveal huge variety and inventiveness. Claudio Monteverdi (1567–1643), pioneer of monody as opposed to polyphony, rediscoverer of dissonance, and proponent of Italy's 'New Music', occupies a special place in the evolution of Europe's secular music. He was largely employed in Venice, as always a counterpoint to the arts of Rome. Baroque painting was dominated by Michelangelo Caravaggio (1573–1610), a pardoned murderer; by the

Fleming Paul Rubens (1577–1640), and by the Spaniard Diego Velázquez (1599–1660). In architecture, the ubiquitous Baroque churches were often modelled on the Jesuit *Gesù* Church (1575) in Rome.

Religious fervour came to the fore in the wars of the sixteenth and seventeenth centuries. Passions and hatreds once reserved for the campaigns against Islam now fired the conflicts between Christians. Protestant fears of Catholic domination surfaced in the Wars of the Schmalkaldic League in Germany, 1531–48, which ended with the Peace of Augsburg; in the French Wars of Religion, 1562–98; in the Swedish civil war, 1598–1604; in the Thirty Years War, 1618–48. Catholic fears of Protestant domination inspired many episodes such as the Pilgrimage of Grace (1536) in England, Irish resistance to Mountjoy and Cromwell, Polish resistance to the Swedes in 1655–60. In the East, the extended campaigns between Russians and Poles—1561–5, 1578–82, 1610–19, 1632–4, 1654–67—took on all the trappings of a Holy War between Catholic and Orthodox. Religious fanaticism could be made to inspire armies. In the sixteenth century the invincible Spaniards were taught to believe that they were fighting for the only true faith. In the seventeenth century the psalm-singing troopers of Gustavus Adolphus, or of Cromwell's marvellous New Model Army, were taught exactly the same.

The French Wars of Religion were spectacularly un-Christian. Persecution of the Huguenots had begun with the *chambre ardente* under Henri II. But the King's sudden death in 1559, and that of the Duke of Anjou, provoked prolonged uncertainty about the succession. [**NOSTRADAMUS**] This in turn enflamed the ambitions of the Catholic faction led by the Guises, and of the Bourbon–Huguenot faction led by the Kings of Navarre. A vain attempt at religious reconciliation at the Colloquy of Passy (1561) was bracketed by two violent provocations—one by the Protestants at Amboise in 1560 and the second by the Catholics at Vassy in 1562. Thereafter the rival factions set at each other's throats with a will, fanned by the schemes of the Queen Mother, Catherine de' Medici. The massacre of St Bartholomew's Eve was but the largest of the series. Vicious skirmishing reminiscent of the earlier English wars produced few set battles, but plenty of opportunity for the dashing adventurers such as the Protestant Baron d'Adrets or the Catholic Blaise de Montluc. Eight wars in thirty years were peppered with broken truces and foul murders. In the 1580s, such was the power of the Guises' Holy League, intent alike on suppressing toleration and on reining in the homosexual king, that the latter ordered the assassination of the Duke and Cardinal de Guise (1588). (Their father, François de Guise, the famous general, had been murdered at Orléans in 1563.) In response, on 1 August 1589 at St Cloud, the King himself was assassinated by a furious monk, Jacques Clément. This left Henri of Navarre as sole contender for the throne. When the Catholic clergy refused to anoint a lapsed heretic, he cynically undertook to reconvert; he was crowned at Chartres in 1594 and entered Paris in triumph. *Paris vaut bien une messe* (Paris is well worth a Mass) sums up the moral tone. The resultant Edict of Nantes (1598) was no better. Having fought all his life in the name of religious liberty, Henri IV now undertook to limit toleration of the Huguenots to aristocratic houses, to two churches per district, and to 120 named strongholds. Intense fears and suspicions remained.

Given the persistence of religious pluralism in Britain, France, the Netherlands, and Poland-Lithuania, it is erroneous to view Europe in this period in terms of a simple division between the 'Protestant North' and the 'Catholic South'. The Irish, the Belgians, and the Poles, among others, have every right to insist that the North was not uniformly Protestant. Both Orthodox Christians and Muslims have good reason to object to the South being classified as uniformly Catholic. The Protestant–Catholic divide was an important feature of Central Europe, and of Germany in particular. But it cannot be applied with any precision to the Continent as a whole. Attempts by Marx or Weber to correlate it with later divisions based on social or economic criteria would seem to be Germanocentric to a fault. One might as well ask why the Protestant God was so successful in endowing his followers with coalfields.

One thing was clear. Senseless bloodletting in the name of religion inevitably sparked off a reaction in the minds of intelligent people. The Wars of Religion offered fertile soil for the fragile seeds of reason and science.

The Scientific Revolution, which is generally held to have taken place between the mid-sixteenth and the mid-seventeenth centuries, has been called 'the most important event in European History since the rise of Christianity'.[18] It followed a natural progression from Renaissance humanism, and was assisted to some extent by Protestant attitudes. Its forte lay in astronomy, and in those sciences such as mathematics, optics, and physics which were needed to collect and to interpret astronomical data. But it changed mankind's view both of human nature and the human predicament. It began with observations made on the tower of the capitular church of Frombork (Frauenburg) in Polish Prussia in the second decade of the sixteenth century; and it culminated at a meeting of the Royal Society at Gresham College in London on 28 April 1686.

The difficulty with the Scientific Revolution, as with any fundamental shift in human thought, lies in the fact that its precepts did not accord with prevailing ideas and practices. The so-called 'age of Copernicus, Bacon and Galileo' is a misnomer: in most respects this was still the age of the alchemists, the astrologers, and the magicians. Nor should modern historians mock the achievements of those whose theories were eventually proved mistaken. It is fair to say that the alchemists misunderstood the nature of matter. It is not fair to say that researchers who have seen the constructive aspects of alchemy are 'tinctured by the lunacy which they try to describe'. It would be hard to find a more 'whiggish interpretation' of scientific history.[19]

Mikołaj Kopernik (Copernicus, 1473–1543), who had studied both at Cracow and at Padua, established that the Sun, not the Earth, lay at the centre of the solar system. His heliocentric ideas coincided with the common astrological habit of using the sun as the symbol of unity. But the point is: he proved the hypothesis by detailed experiments and measurements. Son of a German merchant family from

Thorn (Toruń) and a loyal subject of the King of Poland, whom he had actively defended against the Teutonic Knights, he lived for thirty years in Frombork as a canon of the province of Warmia (Ermeland). He was employed by the King in the pursuit of monetary reform; and his treatise *Monetae cudendae ratio* (1526), about 'bad money driving out good', expounded Gresham's Law thirty years before Gresham. His theory of heliocentrism, first advanced in 1510, was fully supported with statistical data in *De revolutionibus orbium coelestium* (On the Revolutions of the Celestial Spheres, 1543). It was published on the initiative of a mathematical colleague from Lutheran Wittenberg, G. J. von Lauchen (Rheticus), dedicated to Pope Paul III, and delivered to its author on his deathbed. At a stroke it overturned reigning conceptions of the universe, dashing the Aristotelian ideas about a central, immobile, and unplanetlike Earth. Its immediate impact was much reduced because a fearful editor replaced Copernicus's introduction with a misleading preface of his own.

The Copernican theory gestated for almost a century. The Dane Tycho Brahe (1546–1601) rejected heliocentrism; but through observing the pathways of comets he destroyed another ancient misconception, namely that the cosmos consists of onion-like crystalline spheres. Brahe's colleague in Prague, Johann Kepler (1571–1630), established the elliptical shape of planetary orbits, and enunciated the laws of motion underlying Copernicus. But it was the Florentine, Galileo Galilei (1564–1642), one of the first to avail himself of the newly invented telescope, who really brought Copernicus to the wider public. Fortunately for posterity, Galileo was as rash as he was perceptive. Having discovered that 'the moon is not smooth or uniform, but rough and full of cavities, like the earth', he exploded the prevailing theory of 'perfect spheres'. Moreover, he defended his findings with scathing comments on his opponents' biblical references. 'The astronomical language of the Bible', he suggested to the dowager Duchess of Tuscany, was 'designed for the comprehension of the ignorant'. This, in 1616, earned him a summons to Rome, and a papal admonition. And Galileo's praise for Copernicus put Copernicus onto the Index. When Galileo persisted, however, and published his *Dialogo dei due massimi Sistemi del mondo* (Dialogue on the two main world systems, 1632), which expounded the superiority of Copernicus over Ptolemy, he was formally tried by the Inquisition, and forced to recant. His supposed parting comment to the inquisitors, *Eppur si muove* (Yet it does move), is apocryphal. [**LESBIA**]

Practical science remained in its infancy during the era when the Copernican theory was in dispute. Some important assertions were made, however, by the sometime Chancellor of England, Francis Bacon (1561–1626), the father of scientific method. In his *Advancement of Learning* (1605), the *Novum Organum* (1620), and the *New Atlantis* (1627), Bacon stated the proposition that knowledge should proceed by orderly and systematic experimentation, and by inductions based on experimental data. In this he boldly opposed the traditional inductive method, where knowledge could only be established by reference to certain accepted axioms sanctioned by the Church. Significantly, Bacon held that scientific research must be complementary to the study of the Bible. Science was to be kept

---

LESBIA

IN 1622, in a little-publicized ecclesiastical trial, a Florentine abbess called Benedetta Carlini was accused of irregular practices. She had boasted of mystical visions; she had claimed to possess the sacred stigmata; and she had raised suspicions through some form of sexual offence. She was subsequently demoted, and spent forty-five years incarcerated.

In 1985, amidst much greater publicity, a leading American publisher launched an account of the trial under the guise of 'a Lesbian Nun in Renaissance Italy'.[1] Unfortunately, the materials of the trial did not quite coincide with the implications of the title. The post-Renaissance inquisitors had focused on the defendant's religious beliefs. They not only failed to emphasize the lurid details of a lesbian 'lifestyle'; they simply were not interested. One disappointed reviewer commented that at no time before the present century were men capable of comprehending the notion of lesbianism. At the same time, 'the apparently oxymoronic term "lesbian nun" easily tickles the curiosity . . . and guarantees the sale of a certain number of books.'[2]

It is indeed the duty of historians to stress the contrast between the standards of the past and the standards of the present. Some fulfil that duty on purpose, others by accident.

---

compatible with Christian theology. 'The scientist became the priest of God's Book of Nature.' One of Bacon's ardent followers, John Wilkins (1614–72), sometime Bishop of Chester and a founder member of the Royal Society, wrote the curious *Discovery of a World on the Moon* (1638) containing the idea of lunar travel: 'The inhabitants of other worlds are redeemed by the same means as we are, by the blood of Christ.'[20]

Important advances, too, were made by philosophers with a mathematical bent, notably by the two dazzling Frenchmen, René Descartes (1596–1650) and Blaise Pascal (1623–62), and their successor, Benedictus Spinoza (1632–77). Descartes, a soldier-adventurer who witnessed the Battle of the White Mountain (see p. 564), lived much of his life in exile in Holland. He is most associated with the uncompromising rationalist system named after him (Cartesianism) and elaborated in his *Discours sur la méthode* (1637). Having rejected every piece of information which came to him through his senses, or on the authority of others, he concluded that he must at least exist if he was capable of thinking: *Cogito, ergo sum*, 'I think, therefore I am', is the launch-pad of modern epistemology. At the same time, in a philosophy which divided matter from spirit and which delved into everything from medicine to morals, Descartes emphasized the mechanistic view of the world which even then was taking hold. Animals, for example, were viewed as complex machines, as were human beings.

Pascal, a native of Clermont-Ferrand and an inmate of the Jansenist Port-Royal in Paris, took the mechanical ideal to the point where he was able to produce the first 'computer'. His *Lettres provinciales* (1656) are still quoted in Jesuit literature as a cup of poison. Yet his collected *Pensées* (1670) are a delectable blend of the fashionable rationalism and of sound common sense. 'Le cœur a ses raisons', he wrote, 'que la Raison ne connaît point' (the heart has its reasons which Reason cannot know). Or again: 'People are neither angels nor beasts. Yet bad luck would have it that anyone who tries to create an angel creates a beast.' Amidst growing hints about the conflict between science and religion, he proposed his famous gamble in favour of Faith. If the Christian God exists, he argued, believers will inherit everlasting life. If not, they will be no worse off than unbelievers. In which case, Christian belief is worth the risk.

Spinoza, a Sephardic Jew and a lens-grinder by profession, had been expelled from Amsterdam's Jewish community for heresy. He shared Descartes's intensely mathematical and logical view of a universe formed by first principles, and Hobbes's concept of a social contract. He was a pantheist, seeing God and nature as indistinguishable. The highest virtue lay in restraint guided by a full understanding of the world and of self. Evil derived from a lack of understanding. Blind faith was despicable. 'The Will of God' was the refuge of ignorance.

In England, the advocates of 'experimental philosophy' began to organize themselves in the 1640s. An inner circle, led by Dr Wilkins and Dr Robert Boyle (1627–91), formed an 'Invisible College' in Oxford during the Civil War. They joined together in 1660 to found the Royal Society for the Improvement of Natural Knowledge. Their first meeting was addressed by the architect Christopher Wren. Their early membership included a number of magicians, whose influence was not overtaken by the new school of scientists, such as Isaac Newton, for another twenty years. With Newton, modern science came of age (see Chapter VIII); and the example of the Royal Society radiated across Europe.

As always, old ideas mingled with the new. By the second half of the seventeenth century, Europe's leading thinkers were largely agreed on a mechanical view of the universe operating on principles analogous to clockwork. Galileo had divined the principle of force—the basic element of mechanics; and force, as applied to everything from Boyle's Law of Gases to Newton's Laws of Motion, could be precisely calculated. At last, it seemed, the universe and all it contained could be explained and measured. What is more, the laws of nature, which were now yielding their secrets to the scientists, could be accepted as examples of God's will. The Christian God, whom Aquinas had equated with Aristotle's 'first Cause', was now equated with 'the Great Clockmaker'. There was to be no more conflict between science and religion for nearly two hundred years. [MAGIC] [MONKEY]

Europe overseas is not a subject that starts with Columbus or the Caribbean. One experiment, in the crusader kingdoms of the Holy Land, was already ancient history. Another, in the Canaries, had been in progress for seventy years. But once contact had been made with distant islands, Europeans sailed overseas in ever-increasing numbers. They sailed for reasons of trade, of loot, of conquest, and increasingly of religion. For many, it provided the first meeting with people of different races. To validate their claim over the inhabitants of the conquered lands, the Spanish monarchs had first to establish that non-Europeans were human. According to the Requirement of 1512, which the conquistadors were ordered to read out to all native peoples: 'The Lord Our God, Living and Eternal, created Heaven and Earth, and one man and woman, of whom you and I, and all the men of the world, were and are descendants . . .'[21] To confirm the point, Pope Paul III decreed in 1537 that 'all Indians are truly men, not only capable of understanding the Catholic faith, but . . . exceedingly desirous to receive it'.[22] [**GONCALVEZ**]

The earlier voyages of exploration were continued and extended. The existence of a vast fourth continent in the West was gradually established by trial and error, some time in the twenty years after Columbus's first return to Palos. Responsibility for the achievement was hotly disputed. Columbus himself made three more voyages without ever knowing where he had really been. Another Genoese, Giovanni Caboto (John Cabot, 1450–98), sailed from Bristol aboard the *Matthew* in May 1497 under licence from Henry VII; he landed on Cape Breton Island, which he took to be part of China. The Florentine Amerigo Vespucci (1451–1512), once the Medicis' agent in Seville, made three or four transatlantic voyages between 1497 and 1504. He then obtained the post of *piloto mayor* or 'Chief Pilot' of Spain. It was this fact which determined, rightly or wrongly, that the fourth continent should be named after him. In 1513 a stowaway, Vasco Núñez de Balboa (d. 1519), walked across the isthmus of Panama and sighted the Pacific. In 1519–22 a Spanish expedition led by the Portuguese captain Ferdinand Magellan (*c.*1480–1521) circumnavigated the world. It proved beyond doubt that the earth was round, that the Pacific and Atlantic were separate oceans, and that the Americas lay between them. [**SYPHILUS**]

The presence of a fifth continent in the antipodes was not suspected for another century. In 1605 a Spanish ship out of Peru and a Dutch ship out of Java both sailed to the Gulf of Carpentaria. The main outlines of the great *Zuidland* or 'Southland' (Australia and New Zealand) were charted by the Dutch navigator Abel Tasman (1603–59) in 1642–3.

The Portuguese were quickest to exploit the commercial opportunities of the new lands. They claimed Brazil in 1500, Mauritius in 1505, Sumatra in 1509, Malacca and the 'Spice Islands' (Indonesia) in 1511. To protect their trade, they established a chain of fortified stations stretching from Goa in India to Macao in China. The Spaniards, in contrast, did not hesitate to apply their military might. Lured by the dream of El Dorado the *conquistadores*, who had so recently subdued Iberia, now turned their energies to the conquest of America. They settled Cuba in 1511 and used it as a base for further campaigns. In 1519–20 Hernando Cortez (1485–1547) seized the Aztec empire in Mexico in a sea of blood. In the 1520s and 1530s permanent settlements were established in Costa Rica, Honduras, Guatemala, and New Granada (Colombia and Venezuela). From 1532 Francisco Pizarro (*c.*1476–1541) seized the empire of the Incas in Peru.

SYPHILUS

OR many years it had no official name. Italians, Germans, Poles, and
English all called it 'the French disease'. The French called it 'the
Neapolitan disease'. The Neapolitans called it 'the Spanish disease'. The
Portuguese called it 'the Castilian disease' and the Turks 'the Christian
disease'. The Spanish doctor who was one of the first to treat it, Dr Ruy
Diaz de Isla, called it 'the Serpent of Hispaniola'.[1]

Syphilis supposedly made its European début in Barcelona in 1493. Diaz
de Isla later claimed to have treated the master of the *Niña*, Vicente
Pinzon; and it was assumed to have crossed the Atlantic with Columbus's
crew. At all events, whether carried by sailors or slaves, or both, it reached
Naples in 1494 in time to welcome the invading French army. When the
French king's mercenaries dispersed in the following year, they took it
with them to almost every European country. In 1495 the Emperor
Maximilian issued a decree against 'the Evil Pox', taken to be God's punishment for blasphemy. In 1496 the city of Geneva tried to clean out its
syphilitic brothels. In 1497, in distant Edinburgh, a statute ordered suffer-
ers to the island of Inchkeith on pain of branding. Of Charles VIII's campaign in Italy, Voltaire would later write: 'France did not lose all she had
won. She kept the pox.'[2]

For reasons that are unclear, the spirochete microbe, *Treponema pal-
lidum*, which causes syphilis, assumed a specially virulent form when it
reached Europe. It bored into the human genitals, exploiting the scabrous
fissures that were common in the unwashed crotches of the day, forming
highly contagious chancres. Within weeks it covered the body in suppu-
rating pustules, attacked the central nervous system, and destroyed all
hair. It killed within months, painfully. Physicians chose to apply mercury
to the pustules, unwittingly poisoning their patients. Over six or seven
decades, the spirochete created its own resistance and calmed down.
Henceforth, it would be the cause of a common three-stage venereal disease that left its deformed and sterile hosts a longer span. By then,
amongst millions, its victims had included Pope Julius II, Cardinal Wolsey,
Henry VIII, and Ivan the Terrible. It was not tamed until the advent of penicillin. The impact of syphilis was necessarily far-reaching. It has been
linked to the sexual puritanism which took hold on all classes short of the
aristocracy; to the banishment of hitherto popular, and licentious, bath-
houses; to the institution of hand-shaking in place of public kissing; and,
from 1570 onwards, to the growing fashion for wigs.

In 1530 the Italian poet, Girolamo Fracastoro, composed a poem about a
shepherd struck down by the French disease. In due course, this was used
by learned men to give the disease its learned name. The shepherd's
name was Syphilus.[3]

European colonization in North America began in 1536 with the founding of Montreal in Canada by the Breton sailor Jacques Cartier (1491–1557) and in 1565 of St Augustine in Florida by Pedro Menéndez. Menéndez had just destroyed a nearby Huguenot settlement (in the future South Carolina), where he hanged America's first religious exiles 'as Lutherans'. Three years later the Huguenots' compatriot, Dominique de Gourgues, arrived on the same spot and hanged the Spanish garrison 'as robbers and murderers'. Western civilization was on the move.

The Dutch and the English were relative latecomers to colonization, but in the late sixteenth century they both began to reap its benefits. Having founded Batavia in Java in 1597, the Dutch set out to wrest the East Indies from the Portuguese. The English colony of Virginia, discovered in 1598, received its first successful settlement at Jamestown in 1607. The *Mayflower*, carrying 120 puritan 'Pilgrim Fathers' and their families, landed in their Plymouth Colony on 11 (21) December 1620. The Massachusetts Bay Colony followed ten years later. Although religious refugees from England, they did not prove tolerant. The colony of Rhode Island (1636) was founded by dissenters expelled from Massachusetts. By that time the existence of a worldwide network of European colonies, and their seaborne lines of communication, was an established fact.

The international sea trade multiplied by leaps and bounds. To the west, the transatlantic route was long dominated by Spain. By 1600, 200 ships a year entered Seville from the New World. In the peak decade of 1591–1600, 19 million grams of gold and nearly 3 billion grams of silver came with them. The southerly route via the Cape of Good Hope was worked first by the Portuguese and then by the Dutch, who also provided the main commercial link between the North Sea and the Mediterranean. To the east, the Dutch also pioneered a huge trade in Baltic grain. The growing demand for food in West European cities was met by the growing capacity of the Polish producers to supply. This Baltic grain trade reached its peak in 1618, when 118,000 *lasts* or 'boatloads' left Danzig for Amsterdam. The English trade in cloth to the Low Countries had reached record levels somewhat earlier, in 1550. English adventurers launched a Muscovy Company (1565), a Levant Company (1581), and the East India Company (1600).

The nexus of all these activities was located in the Low Countries. Antwerp, which was the main entrepôt of both the Spanish and the English trade, reigned supreme until the crash of 1557–60; thereafter the focus moved to Amsterdam. The year 1602, which saw the foundation both of the Dutch East India Company and of the world's first stock exchange in Amsterdam, can be taken to mark a new era in commercial history. [INFANTA]

As overseas trade expanded, Europe received a wide range of new staple foods, as well as exotic 'colonial' products including pepper, coffee, cocoa, sugar, and tobacco. Europe's diet, cuisine, and palate were never the same again. The haricot bean, which was first recorded in France in 1542, the tomato, which spread far and wide via Italy in the same period, and the capsicum pepper, which was grown throughout the Balkans, were all American in origin.

INFANTA

IN 1572 Martin de Voos painted a family portrait for Antoon Anselme, an Antwerp magistrate. He portrayed the husband and wife seated at a table, one holding their son and the other their daughter. The picture is surmounted by a scrolled inscription which announces that the master of the house was born on 9 February 1536, his wife, Johanna Hooftmans, on 16 December 1545, their son, Aegidius, on 21 August 1565, and their daughter, Johanna, on 26 September 1566. It illustrates the emergence of the modern concept of the family made up of distinct individuals, both children and adults.[1]

In 1579 Sanchez Coello painted a portrait of the Infanta Isabella, daughter of Philip II of Spain, aged thirteen. She was the complete little lady, resplendent in jewelled headdress, curled hair, high ruff, formal gown, and ringed fingers. The tradition would last in the Spanish court until the 1650s, and the famous series by Velazquez of another Infanta, Margharita of Austria, daughter of Philip IV. Once again, the exquisite seven- or eight-year old is shown as a lady in miniature, dressed in corset and crinoline, and topped by the ringlets of a lady's coiffure. Children were still thought of as persons of lesser stature, not fully grown, but not qualitatively different from their parents.[2] (See Plate 51.)

In earlier times, neither the nuclear family nor the age of childhood had been recognized as distinct entities. All generations lived together in large households. Children passed straight from swaddling clothes into adult dress. They participated in all the household's games and activities. In all but the richest classes, they had little or no schooling; if they were taught at all, they were taught together. They were usually put out to work as domestics or apprentices at the age of seven or eight. They died in such numbers that everyone had the greatest incentive for them to grow up fast. Families existed, but they 'existed in silence'. Childhood, too, existed; but it was granted no special status, and it was ended as soon as possible.

The 'discovery of childhood' was a process which took shape between the sixteenth and eighteenth centuries. It can be traced in the dress and iconography of the times, in the invention of toys, games, and pastimes specifically for children, in changing morals and manners; above all, in a radical new approach to education.

Medieval children had largely learned by living, eating, and sleeping with their elders, all of whose activities they observed at first hand. They were not isolated or protected from the adult world. Only boys from higher society attended school, and they did so in all-purpose, all-age groups. One of the earliest instances of a school being divided into classes was recorded at St Paul's School in London in 1519. With age-grouping, and the extension of schooling, came a great increase in imposed discipline. Christian morality, codes of conduct, and humiliating punishments were imposed from above. Schoolboys were the first to be introduced to a prolonged and graduated progression towards adulthood. Girls, sometimes married as early as thirteen, were much more likely to miss out.

Childhood implies innocence. Yet immodesty in children, and in relationships with them, had long been taken as natural. The boyhood conduct of Louis XIII (b. 1601) was observed in every detail by the court physician, Dr Héroard. The Dauphin was not reprimanded for groping his governess in bed, for instance, nor for showing off his first erections, which went up and down 'like a drawbridge'. Married at fourteen, he was placed in the nuptial bed by his mother, to whom he returned 'after about an hour and performing twice', 'with his cock all red'.[3]

The 'ages of Man', as summarized by the soliloquy in *As You Like It*, clearly constituted a well-formed scheme by Shakespeare's time. But every century has made its contribution to generational concepts. If childhood was discovered in early modern Europe, adolescence was discovered by the Romantics, after Goethe's Werther, and 'senior citizens' by the post-industrial era.

Europe's intercourse with America, heretofore a largely hermetic ecological zone, led to a vast Exchange of people, diseases, plants, and animals. This 'Columbian Exchange' worked decidedly in Europe's favour. European colonists braved hardship and deprivation, and in some places faced hostile 'Indians'. But their losses were minuscule compared to the genocidal casualties which they and their firearms inflicted. They brought some benefits, but with them depopulation and despoliation on a grand scale. Europe received syphilis; but its ravages were not to be compared to the pandemics of smallpox, pleurisy, and typhus which literally decimated the native Americans. The Europeans introduced horses; in return they received two foods of capital importance, potatoes and maize, as well as the turkey, the most substantial and nutritious of domestic poultry. Potatoes were adopted in Ireland at an early date, and moved steadily across northern Europe, becoming the staple of Germany, Poland, and Russia. Maize, which was variously known as 'American corn' and 'American fallow', enriched exhausted soil and greatly facilitated both crop rotation and livestock farming. It was well established in the Po valley in the sixteenth century. It was inhibited from crossing the Alps until climatic conditions improved some hundred years later, but its long-term impact was enormous. There is good reason to count American additions to the food supply as one of the major factors underlying the dramatic growth of Europe's population at the end of the early modern period.[23]
[SYPHILUS]

Descriptions of the arrival of Europeans in America have recently undergone fundamental revision. They have been 'decolumbianized'. What was once 'the discovery' is now called an 'encounter' or a 'meeting of cultures'.[24] It would be better to be honest and call it a conquest. Columbus, too, has been downgraded. The primacy of his voyages has been handed to Vikings or Irishmen, or even to a Welshman in a coracle. His landing on San Salvador (Watling Island) has been relocated to Samana Cay in the Bahamas.[25] The 'peerless navigator' is now said to have been a ruthless and rapacious 'colonialist pirate', alternatively a quixotic Jew sailing in search of the lost tribes of Israel.[26] He is even said to have heard about the other continent from American women already in Europe.[27] The sources for Columbus's activities are meagre, the myths abundant.[28] The real discoverers of America are those who went in the steps of the *conquistadores*, often friars like Bernardino de Sahagún, 'the world's first anthropologist', and who tried to understand what was happening.[29]

Intercourse with America had a profound impact on European culture. A gulf began to open between those countries which had ready access to the New World and those which did not. 'Philosophy is born of the merchant. Science is born of commerce. Henceforth, Europe is almost cut into two. The West is preoccupied with the sea. The East is preoccupied with itself.'[30]

Early modern society was not conceived in terms of class, which is a more recent invention, but in terms of social orders or 'estates'—in Latin *status*, in German *Stände*, in French *état*. These basic social groups were defined by their function, by the legal restrictions and privileges which were imposed in order to facilitate that function, and by their corporate institutions. Wealth and income played only a secondary role. Heredity was the main criterion for determining to which estate (save the clergy) any particular family might belong.

The nobility, for example, descendants of medieval knighthood, were defined by their military function and by laws giving them special rights to landownership and to the government of their properties. With the growth of standing armies, their exclusive military function was somewhat diminished, but their position as the backbone of the ruling caste remained. Through their regional assemblies they ran local politics in the countryside, and they usually enjoyed full jurisdiction over the inhabitants of their lands. In most countries they were headed by an upper crust such as the peers of England or the grandees of Spain; or else they were divided, as in Germany, into numerous ranks. The burgher estate, built on the liberties of self-governing cities and of the city guilds, was also stratified between the patricians, the freemen, and the propertyless plebs. It was usually protected by royal charters, and enjoyed full jurisdiction within the city walls. The peasants consisted of an enserfed majority and a minority who remained free or who were emerging from serfdom. The status of the serfs could vary considerably depending whether they lived on church, crown, or noble land.

The existence of many fragmented jurisdictions was incompatible with state despotism, and hence with Muscovite Tsarism or Ottoman rule. Here was the social base which rendered western absolutism rather different from eastern autocracy. It was built on a mass of practices inherited from the earlier period and, despite innovations, was still essentially medieval. In the West as in the East, the social constraints on individuals remained very onerous by modern standards. Everyone, and not just the serf, was expected to belong to a corporate body and to abide by its rules. Renaissance individualism used to be celebrated by historians like Burckhardt exactly because they welcomed the first frail attempts to break free from the prevailing social curbs and compartments. When an exception was made, as when Michelangelo was released from his guild of artisans, it took a Pope to make it.[31]

The price revolution, Europe's first encounter with inflation, was initially attributed to the wickedness of usurers. From the 1550s, through the researches of the University of Salamanca, it was attributed to the influx of Spanish gold and silver. 'What makes Spain poor', wrote a commentator, 'is her wealth.'[32] Although the view of contemporaries was blurred by the wild fluctuation of prices and by governments' repeated attempts to cope by debasing their coinage, it is perfectly clear that the general trend throughout the sixteenth century was for a steady price rise. Grain prices in France, for example, where the supply of coin was relatively scarce, were over seven times higher in 1600 than in 1500.

The cost of living, especially in Western Europe, rose dramatically (see Appendix III, p. 1263). Explaining this, recent scholars have laid less emphasis on bullion and more on population growth, on land hunger, and on rising rents and taxation. In the sixteenth century, Europe's five giant cities of 100,000 + rose to perhaps fourteen: Constantinople, Naples, Venice, Milan, Paris, Rome, Palermo, Messina, Marseilles, Lisbon, Seville, Antwerp, Amsterdam, and Moscow. Peasants flooded into the growing towns; wages lagged behind prices; beggars proliferated. Landowners maximized their profits; governments, constantly hit by the falling value of their income, raised taxes. There was little relief until the early seventeenth century.

The social consequences of the price revolution are the subject of immense controversy. The expansion of the money economy encouraged social mobility, especially in England and Holland. The commercial bourgeoisie was greatly strengthened. Capitalism reached the point of take-off. Yet the growth of cities in the West was closely linked to the parallel growth of 'neoserfdom' in the East. The nobility of Germany, Poland, and Hungary strengthened their position whilst their counterparts further west were thrown into confusion. English historians of the period cannot agree whether the gentry was rising or falling. The English Civil War has been variously attributed to the self-assertion of a confident gentry against a ruined aristocracy and to the desperation of a gentry impoverished by the price revolution.[33] [CAP-AG]

Particularly interesting are the links between economic and religious developments. The Protestant Reformation had always been explained in religious and political terms. But Marxists have not been alone in seeing a correlation between 'the Protestant ethic' and commercial enterprise. Max Weber's *The Protestant Ethic and the Spirit of Capitalism* (1904) and Richard Tawney's *Religion and the Rise of Capitalism* (1926), though much criticized in detail, have inspired a whole school of comment. Capitalism, after all, needed its ideologues as well as its technicians. In this, Protestant writers undoubtedly played an important role in opposing deep-seated attitudes about usury. But they did so at a rather later date than historians once supposed. Tawney relies heavily for evidence on the English Puritan Richard Baxter; Weber, anachronistically, on the eighteenth-century American Benjamin Franklin. It was not until 1658 that the state of Holland ruled that no banker should be denied communion for practising usury. Theory, therefore, lagged well behind practice. [USURY]

In reality, capitalism thrived no less in Catholic than in Protestant cities. Fugger of Augsburg was no Puritan. He thrived because of expanding trade and industry, and because war, for all its destructiveness, stimulated demand for goods and for financial services. Protestant divines were less effective as advocates of capitalist techniques than the numerous refugee entrepreneurs who flooded into Protestant countries.

It was through these migrations that the seeds of medieval capitalism were scattered throughout Europe. The biggest businessman in Geneva, Francesco Turrettini (1547–1628), was a refugee from Lucca. Louis de Geer (1587–1652), financier and industrialist to Gustavus Adolphus in Sweden, came from Liège. Marcus Perez (1527–72), William the Silent's original bankroller, was a Jewish *converso* from Spain.[34]

The military changes of the era—which like most things are now classed as a 'Revolution'—had far-reaching effects. In essence, they involved the introduction of new weaponry, principally the pike, the musket, and improved artillery; the establishment of systematic training, which required professional cadres and instructors; and the growth of standing armies, which only the richest princes could afford.

One thing followed from another. The 16-ft Swiss infantry pike provided the long-desired means for stopping cavalry charges. But it could only be effectively deployed in a mobile square of pikemen, who had to wheel and manœuvre with precision to face the swirling line of attack. As the Spaniards discovered, it was best used in conjunction with muskets, whose firepower could actually bring the attackers down. The musket's accuracy, however, and its reloading rate, left much to be desired. It was only effective when a body of musketeers were trained to fire in unison, moving smartly in and out of the pike square between salvoes. Though it first appeared in 1512 at Ravenna, it was only widely adopted from the 1560s in the wars of the Low Countries. The combination of pike and musket demanded elaborate drill techniques, together with the steadiness and *esprit de corps* of disciplined professionals.

An answer to the pike square was found in the development of massed artillery. The cannon, which was fast rendering medieval fortifications obsolete, now came to be widely used on the battlefield for opening up gaps in the enemy line. Yet expanded artillery trains required complex technical support, an efficient iron industry, high-quality gunpowder, expensive transport, and professional gunners.

In naval warfare, the increased calibre of the cannon stimulated a rapid growth in the size, tonnage, and manœuvrability of ships. Warships had to be turned into floating gun platforms. The increased range of ships stimulated the science of navigation, which depended in turn on precision instruments, on sound astronomical data and cartography, and on advanced mathematics.

On land, great thought was given to rescuing the art of fortification from the effects of artillery bombardment. The *trace italienne*, which appeared in the mid-sixteenth century, set out a sophisticated system of ditches, entrapments, and low, angled bastions, which denied the cannoneers easy targets and access, whilst exposing them to withering counterfire. Antwerp, fortified in this way by Italian engineers in 1568, started a trend which was to bring back the prevalence of siege warfare. By the time of the celebrated Sebastien le Prestre de Vauban (1633–1707), the engineers had regained the advantage over the artillerymen (see p. 619). Cavalry never became obsolete, but was forced to adapt. It was increasingly divided into dedicated regiments; of light horse for reconnaissance and skirmishing; of lancers for battlefield offence; and of mounted dragoons for mobile firepower.

The military commanders who supervised these developments were faced with a welter of unfamiliar technological and organizational problems. Part-time gentlemen soldiers could no longer cope. The emergence of salaried career officers was accompanied by the consolidation of a professional military and naval caste. Military careers offered prospects not only for sons of the old nobility but for all talents. Rulers had to found military academies for their training.

Rulers also had to find new sources of income for their armies, and a new bureaucracy to administer them. Once they had done so, however, they found that they possessed an incomparable political instrument for reducing the power of the nobles and for forcing their subjects to obey. The modern state without the military revolution is unthinkable. The road from the arquebus to absolutism, or from the maritime mortar to mercantilism, was a direct one.

Yet the military revolution is another subject where would-be theorists have been tempted to use their localized studies from parts of Western Europe for making unwarranted generalizations about the whole continent. It is often implied that East European methods of warfare, in which the cavalry did not cede supremacy to the infantry, were somehow retarded. They were not. The armies of Poland or Muscovy needed no lessons from their Western counterparts. They were soon familiar with the latest technical and organizational developments; but fighting across the vast empty expanses of the East, in a harsh climate, they met logistical problems unknown in the battlegrounds of northern Italy or the Netherlands. When Poland's wonderful winged hussars met Western-style infantry, as they did against the Swedes at Kirchholm in 1605, they wreaked terrible slaughter. They repeated the performance when they faced hordes of oriental-style light horse at Klushino in 1610 or at Chocim in 1621 (see below). At the same time, thanks to the flexible, cell-like structure of their units, the *towarzysze* or hussar 'comrades' were able to forage and skirmish and to sustain themselves in hostile country where all less adaptable armies were devoured. In their encounters with the Poles, the Muscovites experienced many decades of failure, often because of ill-conceived Western innovations. But they possessed first-class artillery from an early date; and it was the Russian artillery which finally broke Sweden's military supremacy at Poltava.[35]

'The nation-state' and 'nationalism' are terms which are frequently applied, or misapplied, to the sixteenth century. They are more appropriate to the nineteenth, when they were invented by historians looking for the origins of the nation-states of their own day. They should certainly not be used to convey premature preoccupations with ethnic identity. What they can properly convey, however, is the strong sense of sovereignty which both monarchs and subjects assumed, as the unity of the Middle Ages disintegrated. Their overriding *raison d'état* had an economic dimension associated with mercantilism, as well as the purely political one.

Il Principe (The Prince), written in 1513, served as the handbook for all such rulers who wished to reach a position of untrammelled command. It is often judged to be the starting-point of modern political science. Its author, Niccolò Machiavelli (1469–1527), historian, dramatist, and Florentine diplomat, who had observed Cesare Borgia and Pope Alexander VI, 'the great deceiver', at close quarters, wrote his book in the hope that it would inspire a prince to fulfil Dante's old dream of a unified Italy. But its appeal was universal. By separating politics from moral scruples, it gave voice to the art of *Machtpolitik* or untrammelled power politics. At one level this 'Machiavellianism' caused grave scandal. Concepts such as *frodi onorevoli* (honourable frauds) or *scelleratezze gloriose* (glorious rascalries) became notorious. At a more serious level, if *The Prince* is read in conjunction with the *Discourses* on Livy, Machiavelli can be seen to have been a devoted advocate of limited government, of the rule of law and of liberty. His low view of human nature provides the ground base on which constitutional structures have to be built. But it is his cynical aphorisms that were best remembered. 'The nearer people are to the Church of Rome,' he wrote, 'the more irreligious they are.' 'A prince who desires to maintain his position must learn to be good or not as needs may require.' 'War should be the only study of a prince. He should look upon peace only as a breathing space which . . . gives him the means to execute military plans.' Machiavelli has had no shortage of disciples.

On the subject of the model Renaissance prince, most historians would think in the first place of the Italian despots like Lorenzo the Magnificent or Ludovico Sforza. After that they would probably propose those formidable neighbours and rivals, Francis I and Henry VIII, whose meeting on the 'Field of Cloth of Gold' (1520) exemplified so many quirks and qualities of the age. Yet none deserves more attention than Matthias Hunyadi 'Corvinus', King of Hungary (r. 1458–90).

Corvinus—so called from the raven in his coat-of-arms—was a social upstart, the son of a baron and crusader from Transylvania, Iancu of Hunedoara, (János Hunyadi), who had made his name fighting the Turks. He used his Transylvanian base and a strong mercenary army to subdue the Hungarian magnates, and to initiate a reign where Italian culture was made the mark of political prestige. He had been educated by the humanist Archbishop Vitez; he was married to a neapolitan princess, Beatrice of Aragon; and he succeeded to a royal court which had cultivated its Italian ties since Angevin times. The court at Buda was filled with books, pictures, and philosophers, and was in touch with all the leading scholars of the day, from Poliziano to Ficino. It also boasted a great library, which as a collection of incunabula and manuscripts was the chief rival of the Medicis' library in Florence. In 1485, when Corvinus captured Vienna, he looked to be on the brink of founding a Hungaro-Austrian monarchy that would soon make a solid bid for control of the Empire. In the event, all plans were brought to naught by his sudden death. His scholarly son was rejected by the Hungarian nobles in favour of a Jagiellon. With some small delay, the pickings were taken by the Habsburgs and the Turks. Like the books of the plundered royal library, the traces of Renaissance Hungary were scattered to the winds. [**CORVINA**]

Of course, the strengthening of royal power in some quarters does not mean that one can talk about the general advent of absolutism, except as one of several competing ideals. In France, the restraints on the king were still so great that scholars can debate at length whether, under Francis I, for instance, French government was 'more consultative' or 'less decentralised'.[36] In England, after the assertion of Tudor monarchy, it was Parliament which asserted itself under the subsequent rule of the Stuarts. In the Holy Roman Empire the imperial Diet gained ground against the Emperor. In Poland-Lithuania republicanism triumphed over monarchy.

True enough, some Renaissance scholars, like Budé, looked to the Roman Empire for their views on monarchy; but others like Bishop Goślicki (Goslicius) looked back to the Roman Republic. Of the two most influential political treatises of the period, the *De la République* (1576) of Jean Bodin favoured constitutional monarchy, whilst the *Leviathan* (1651) of Thomas Hobbes made eccentric use of contract theory to favour absolutism. Without much evidence, Hobbes maintained that kings held unlimited rights because at some unspecified time in the past their subjects had supposedly surrendered their own rights. The resultant Leviathan, a 'monster composed of men'—his metaphor for the modern state—was a regrettable necessity, the only alternative to endless conflict:

During the time when men live without a common power to keep them in awe, they are in that condition which is called war . . . where every man is enemy to every man. In such condition, there is no place for industry . . . no navigation . . . no arts, no letters, no society, and . . . continual fear of violent death; and the life of man, solitary, poor, nasty, brutish, and short.[37]

The Renaissance stimulated the study of Roman law; but the period was equally marked by the reinforcement and collation of separate national laws and,

CORVINA

SOME time in the 1460s Matthias Corvinus, King of Hungary, started collecting books. His passion was inspired by his old mentor, Janos Vítez, Bishop of Várad (Oradea), and by the Bishop's nephew, Janos Csezmiczei. Both men were classical scholars, both educated in Italy, and both fervent bibliophiles. The former rose to become Primate of Hungary, the latter, as 'Janus Pannonius', the leading Latin poet of the age. When both were disgraced by a political plot, the Primate retired; the poet committed suicide; and the King added their libraries to his own. In 1476 Matthias married Beatrice of Aragon, who brought her own rich book collection from Naples. In 1485 he captured Vienna, laying plans for a new Hungaro-Austrian monarchy, whose cultural centrepiece was to be the royal library, then under construction in Buda. Staffed by an army of archivists, copyists, translators, binders, and illuminators, and by a transcontinental network of agents, the Biblioteca Corviniana was designed to excel in Europe's 'revival of letters'. It even excelled the magnificent library of Lorenzo the Magnificent in Florence.

None of King Matthias's hopes were realized. When he died in 1490, his son did not succeed him. The Habsburgs recovered Vienna, and the Hungarian nobles rebelled against their taxes. Work on the library stopped. When the Ottoman army captured Buda in 1526, the Library was pillaged. Most of its contents, including 650 ancient manuscripts of unique value, disappeared.

All, however, was not lost. On the quincentenary of King Matthias's death, Hungary's National Library mounted an exhibition to reassemble the surviving treasures. It turned out that Queen Beatrice had contrived to send some prize items back to Naples. Her daughter-in-law had taken others off to Germany. Charles V's sister Mary, sometime Queen of Hungary, brought still more to Brussels. Most importantly, it emerged that the store of looted books in Constantinople had been used over the centuries as a gift fund for favoured foreign ambassadors. The priceless descriptive catalogue of the Corviniana prepared by the King's Florentine agent, Naldo Naldi, had been given by a sultan to a Polish ambassador and preserved at Toruń. Seneca's tragedies, presented to an English ambassador, were preserved in Oxford. The Byzantine 'Book of Ceremonies' was preserved in Leipzig. [**TAXIS**] Twenty-six manuscripts sent to Francis-Joseph were kept in Vienna. Still more found their way into the library of Duke Augustus at Wolfenbüttel. Uppsala was holding pieces which Queen Christina's army had looted from Prague . . . Madrid, Besançon, Rome, and Volterra all contributed.

The 1990 exhibition contained only fragments of the lost collection. But they were enough to show that bibliophilia lay at the heart of the Renaissance urge. In size and variety, the Biblioteca Corviniana had been second only to the Vatican Library. Thanks to the circumstances of its dispersal, its role in the spread of learning was probably second to none.[1]

in the treatise *De jure belli et pacis* (1625) of Hugo De Groot (Grotius, 1583–1645), by the emergence of international law.

Mercantilism, or 'the mercantile system', is a label that had little currency until popularized in the late eighteenth century. [**MARKET**] Yet the set of ideas which Adam Smith was to criticize formed the main stock of economic thought of the early modern period. Mercantilism has meant many things to many men; but in essence it referred to the conviction that in order to prosper, the modern state needed to manipulate every available legal, administrative, military, and regulatory device. In this sense, it was the opposite of the *laissez-faire* system, which Smith would later advocate. In one popular form it consisted of bullionism—the idea that a country's wealth and power depended on amassing gold. In another, it concentrated on improving the balance of trade by assisting exports, penalizing imports, and encouraging home manufactures. In all forms, it was concerned with strengthening the sources of economic power—colonies, manufactures, navies, tariffs—and was expressly directed against a country's commercial rivals. In the Dutch version—where even the navy was controlled by five separate admiralties—policy was largely left to private and to local initiative. In the French, and later the Prussian, version, it was held very firmly in the hands of the king's ministers. In England it depended on a mixture of private and royal initiative. An early exposition can be found in *The Discourse of the Common Weal of this Realm of England* (1549). 'The ordinary means to encrease our wealth and treasure is by Foreign Trade,' wrote Thomas Mun a little later, 'wherein we must ever observe this rule: to sell more to strangers yearly than we consume of theirs in value.'[38]

Diplomatic practice, like mercantilist thought, developed in response to the rise of state power. In the past, monarchs had been content to recall their ambassadors as soon as each mission was concluded. In the fifteenth century, Venice was the only power to maintain a network of permanent embassies abroad, until the papal nunciatures and other Italian cities followed the Venetian lead. From about 1500, however, sovereign rulers gradually saw the appointment of resident ambassadors as a sign of their status and independence. They also valued the influx of commercial and political intelligence. One of the first was Ferdinand the Catholic, whose embassy to the Court of St James dates from 1487 and was originally headed by Dr Rodrigo Gondesalvi de Puebla, later by a woman—Catherine of Aragon, Princess of Wales, the King's daughter. Francis I of France is usually credited with having the first comprehensive royal diplomatic service, including an embassy at the Ottoman Porte from 1526.

Soon, a *corps diplomatique* appeared in every major court and capital. Living in conditions of some danger, the diplomats quickly worked out the necessary rules of immunity, reciprocity, extraterritoriality, credence, and precedence. In 1515 the Pope ruled that the nuncio should act as doyen of the *corps*, that the imperial ambassador should have precedence over his colleagues, and that all other ambassadors should be given seniority according to the date of their country's conversion to Christianity. In practice the arrangement did not work, because Charles V preferred Spanish to imperial diplomats and because, as the 'Most Catholic' King of Spain, he refused to cede precedence to the French. This launched a quarrel where French and Spanish ambassadors stolidly held their ground for 200 years. On one occasion, at the Hague in 1661, when the retinues of the French and Spanish ambassadors met in a narrow street, the diplomats stood rooted to the spot for a whole day, until the city council demolished the railings and enabled them to pass on equal terms. The Muscovites were equal sticklers for form. The Tsar's ambassadors were wont to demand precedence over the Emperor's own courtiers. In Warsaw, one Muscovite ambassador arrived wearing two hats—one to be raised to the King of Poland in the customary greeting, the other to keep his head covered according to the instructions of the Kremlin.

In the age of Machiavelli, diplomats soon gained a reputation for deception. They had to be familiar with codes, ciphers, and invisible ink. 'An ambassador', quipped Sir Henry Wootton, 'is an honest man sent to lie abroad for the good of his country.' None the less, the growth of permanent diplomacy marked an important stage in the formation of a community of nations. In 1643–8, when a great diplomatic conference was convened at Münster and at Osnabrück to terminate the Thirty Years War, the 'Concert of Europe' was already coming into existence.

At the turn of the sixteenth century, the central sensation on the map of Europe came from the sudden rise of the House of Habsburg to a position of immoderate greatness. The Habsburgs' success was not achieved by conquest but by the failure of rival dynasties, by far-sighted matrimonial schemes, and by sheer good fortune. *Fortes bella gerant,* ran the motto, *Tu felix Austria nube.** The emphasis was on *felix*, 'fortunate', and *nube*, 'marry'.

In 1490 Maximilian I of Habsburg, King of the Romans, was still a refugee from Hungarian-occupied Vienna. His hold on the Empire looked precarious; and he was obliged to initiate a series of imperial reforms from a position of weakness. He oversaw the establishment in 1495 of the *Reichskammergericht* (Imperial Court of Justice), in 1500 of the *Reichsregiment* (the permanent Council of Regency), and in 1512 of the *Reichsschlüsse* or 'Mandates' of the Imperial Diet. With the creation of three Colleges of the Diet—Electors, Princes, Cities—and the division of the Empire into ten territorial Circles, each under the *directorium* of two princes charged with administering justice, taxation, and military matters, he effectively surrendered all direct rule of the Empire. He made the House of Habsburg indispensable to the German princes by giving them all they had ever desired.

Simultaneously, Maximilian greatly strengthened the Habsburgs' *Hausmacht*, the dynasty's private power. The early death of his first wife, Mary, had given him the fabulous Duchy of Burgundy; and in 1490 he inherited Tirol, giving him his favourite residence at Innsbruck. One inheritance treaty in 1491 with the Jagiellons gave him the reversion of Bohemia, another in 1515 the reversion of Hungary. Both policies would mature on the death of Louis Jagiellon in 1526, leaving the dynasty

---

* 'Let the strong wage war. You, lucky Austria, marry.' Attributed to Matthias Corvinus, King of Hungary.

with 'the foundations of a Danubian monarchy'.[39] Equally important was the marriage of his son to the heiress of Ferdinand and Isabella, which put a grappling hook onto the Spanish dominions. In 1497 his own second marriage to Bianca Sforza of Milan eased the cash flow and assisted his confirmation as Emperor in 1508. By then this most ideological of the Habsburgs must have felt that his mission was being fulfilled. Shortly afterwards, he was confident enough to propose that he be elected Pope!

When Maximilian died, his grandson Charles of Ghent succeeded to a collection of real estate 'on which the sun never set'. To cap it all, with the help of the Fuggers' ducats, Charles overcame French and papal opposition to be elected Holy Roman Emperor in record time and in immediate succession to his grandfather. (See Appendix III, p. 1270.) [DOLLAR]

DOLLAR

JACHIMOV is a small Bohemian town in the Joachimtal, some 80 km north of Plzen (Pilsen). In 1518 Count von Schlick was granted an imperial patent to mine silver there and to establish a mint. His silver coins were produced by *Walzenwerke* or 'rolling machines', and were formally classed as 'large groats'. Their popular name was *Joachimsthaler*, soon shortened to *thaler*.

By the seventeenth century the thaler had become a unit of currency all over central Europe. It had also been copied in Habsburg Spain, whose *taleros* or 'pieces of eight' circulated throughout the Americas. They were known in English as 'dollars'. The 30 shilling silver piece of James VI of Scotland was dubbed 'the Sword Dollar'. In the eighteenth century silver thalers were widely replaced by copper 'plate money' imported from Sweden, which acquired the Swedish name of *daler*. A copper *daler* of 1720 was equivalent in value to a silver thaler, even though its weight was 250 times greater; and it could only be transported by horse and cart.[1]

The acknowledged masterpiece of the series, however, was the Maria Theresa dollar of 1751. This superb coin bore the bust of the Empress, with the two-headed eagle on the reverse, and the inscription:

R[omae] IMP[eratrix] * HU[ngariae et] BO[hemiae] REG[ina] * M[aria] THERESIA * D[ei] G[ratia] ARCHID[ux] AUST[riae] * DUX BURG[undiae] * COM[es] TUR[olis]*

It continued to be minted in millions throughout the nineteenth century, all posthumous issues bearing the date of the Empress's death in 1780. It was minted by Mussolini in 1936 to finance the invasion of Abyssinia, and by the British in Bombay. Two hundred years later, it still circulates in parts of Asia as an international trade currency.[2]

The dollar was adopted as the currency of the USA in 1787, and of Canada in 1871. But it figures no longer among the currency units of Europe.

Charles V (Emperor 1519–56), whose realms stretched from the Philippines to Peru, was gradually overwhelmed by the multiplicity of competing problems. Physically, he was most unimperial: weak adenoids gave him a whining voice and a permanently drooping mouth, which an insolent Spanish grandee once told him to shut 'to keep the flies out'. Yet he possessed many talents for governing his vast dominions, speaking Flemish by choice, Spanish, French, and Italian to his officials, 'and German to his horse'. And he was not lacking in fortitude. 'Name me an emperor who was ever struck by a cannon-ball,' he retorted when refusing to remain in the rear at Mühlberg. As the accepted leader of the Catholic princes, he headed the strongest cause which might have held Christendom together. Yet the sheer size and complexity of the internal and external crises defied co-ordinated action. In the Church, though successful in launching the General Council, he realized that the deliberations at Trent were only hardening divided opinions. His plans for restoring religious unity in the Empire were disastrously delayed. Despite the victory at Mühlberg, the wars of the Schmalkaldic League ended with the stalemate of the Peace of Augsburg (1555). In Spain, where he reigned as co-king with his mentally disturbed mother, he wrestled with the revolt of the *comuneros* and then with the divergent interests of Castile and Aragon. In the New World he fought a losing battle to protect the Amerindians. In the Netherlands, which he had left in the hands of his aunt, Margaret, he was painfully obliged to suppress the revolt of his native Ghent by force (1540). In the main hereditary Habsburg lands—Austria, Bohemia, and Hungary—which he had consigned to his brother Ferdinand, he faced constant opposition from local leaders, such as Jan Zapolyai in Transylvania, and in 1546–7 the first Bohemian Revolt. Everywhere he had to struggle with provincial diets, fractious nobles, particularist interests. On the strategic scale, he had to cope with the hostility of France, with the expansion of the Turks, and with the threat of Franco-Ottoman co-operation.

Rivalry with France engendered five wars, fought at all the points of territorial contact—in the Netherlands, in Lorraine, in Savoy, in the Pyrenees, and in Italy—and, indirectly, to the great shame of his life, the Sack of Rome (1527). Fear of the Turks led to Habsburg takeovers in Hungary and Bohemia; in the longer run, however, they produced an endless series of exhausting complications, both in the Balkans and in the Mediterranean. [ORANGE]

In his last decade, Charles V might have had some grounds for optimism. But the Peace of Augsburg was a disappointment; and, endlessly frustrated, he abdicated. He left Spain and the Netherlands to his son Philip, the rest to his brother. He died in retreat at Yuste. He was the last Emperor to cherish a dream of universal unity, and has been invoked by some in contemporary times as patron of a united Europe. 'Charles V, once regarded as the last fighter of a rearguard action,' writes an interested party, 'is suddenly seen to have been a forerunner.'[40]

After the abdication, the Austrian Habsburgs forgot Charles's universal vision. Maximilian II (r. 1564–76), grandson of the Jagiellons, gained nothing from his nominal election as King of Poland-Lithuania. His two sons, Rudolf II (r.

ORANGE

IN 1544, at the height of the Franco-Imperial wars, an officer of the Imperial Army, René von Nassau, was killed at St Dizier by a French bullet. His death was to drive events that would affect the history not only of his native Nassau but of Provence, the Netherlands, and Ireland.

Nassau was a small German duchy on the right bank of the middle Rhine. Between the Westerwald forests and the rugged Taunus Mountains north of Wiesbaden, Nassau's fertile Rheingau contained some of Germany's finest vineyards, including Johanisberg and Rudesheim. René's father, Heinrich von Nassau, resided at Siegen, sharing the duchy with the cadet branch of the family at Dillenberg. René's mother, Claudia, was the sister and heiress of an imperial general, Philibert de Châlons, who had led the sack of Rome and who had been richly rewarded by Charles V with lands in Brabant. Moreover, she had taken over Philibert's title to the Principality of Orange. When the heirless René was killed, it emerged that he had bequeathed his collection of lands and titles to his eleven-year-old cousin, William of Nassau-Dillenburg.

Orange was a small sovereign principality on the left bank of the Rhône north of Avignon. (See Appendix III, p. 1254.) Bordered to the east by the heights of Mont Ventoux, it was a rich wine-growing district, several of whose villages, such as Gigondas and Châteauneuf-du-Pape, were to become famous. Its tiny capital, ancient Arausio, was dominated by the huge Roman arch erected by Tiberius. From the twelfth century it was a fief of the counts of Provence, and hence of the Empire. But in 1393 the heiress to Orange, Marie de Baux, was given in marriage to the Burgundian Jean de Châlons; and it was their descendants who thereafter became the principality's absentee rulers. In 1431, when the Count of Provence needed a ransom in a hurry, he agreed to sell off the Châlons' obligation to homage, thereby making them princes of Orange in their own right. As an independent enclave within the Kingdom of France, Orange attracted many Italian and Jewish merchants, and in the mid-sixteenth century it was fast becoming a Protestant bastion.[1] It would eventually be suppressed by Louis XIV, who decided to put an end to this nest of Huguenots in 1703.

Thanks to his inheritances in Germany, Provence, and Brabant, William of Nassau-Dillenburg (1533–84) became one of the richest men in Europe. He even held a claim to the defunct Kingdom of Arles. Born a Lutheran but raised as a Catholic at the imperial court in Brussels, where he called the Regent Margaret 'mother', he set up his own affluent residence at Breda in north Brabant. In 1555 he held the arm of the ailing Charles V during the abdication ceremony; and in 1559 he served as imperial plenipotentiary to the Treaty of Câteau-Cambrésis. He then went to Paris as one of three sureties for the Treaty's implementation. To all appearances he was a pillar of the Catholic, imperial Establishment. But in Paris, he heard of Spanish plans to subdue the Netherlands; and he contracted a lifelong distaste for Spanish machinations. He is known to history as 'William the Silent' (see pp. 536–8).[2]

Despite its subsequent Dutch connections, therefore, the House of Orange-Nassau, which William founded, was not Dutch in origin. It was a typical dynastic multinational amalgam founded by accident and perpetuated by good fortune. Of William's three sons only one was to keep the line intact. That child was conceived by William's fourth wife in between two attempts by Spanish agents to have William murdered. (William had once granted a pardon to his adulterous second wife's lover, who then went off to father Peter Paul Rubens.) William's great-grandson, also William of Orange (1650–1702), who became King William III of England, was born in the middle of a Dutch revolution, eight days after his father had died of smallpox.

The Orange Order was founded in Armagh in 1795. Like the earlier 'Peep o' Day Boys', it aimed to preserve the Protestant (Episcopalian) supremacy in Ireland. Its hero was 'King Billy' (William III): its watchword, 'No Surrender!' At a time when British law discriminated against Catholics and Presbyterians alike, the Order saw itself as the shield of an isolated elite against the growing popularity of Wolfe Tone's United Irishmen. Tone (1763–98), a moderate Protestant, sought the twin goals of universal toleration and a sovereign Irish republic. He had appealed for military aid from France.

In the bitter fighting of 1795–8, the Orange Order played a leading part in British plans to repel invasion and suppress sedition. Faced by incompetent adversaries, it prevailed. The expedition of General Hoche, which sailed from Brest in 1796, came to grief in Bantry Bay. The successful landing by General Humbert at Killala in County Mayo was short-lived. The armed rising in Wicklow and Wexford collapsed after the Battle of Vinegar Hill (June 1798). Tone, captured in French naval uniform, committed suicide.

In these and all subsequent events, the Orangemen followed their own exclusive agenda. They opposed both the Act of Union (1801) and Daniel O'Connell. They were not converted to the Union until the prospect arose after 1829 that an autonomous Ireland might be run by emancipated Catholics. Yet they rejected mainstream British Unionism. In 1912–14, they provided the backbone of the Ulster Volunteers who were training to defy

Westminster and the Irish Home Rule Bill (see p. 831). Their greatest influence was exerted when Northern Ireland ruled itself within the United Kingdom from 1920 to 1976.

For 200 years, the Orange Order has held its annual parades on the anniversary of the Boyne (see p. 631). Marchers in bowler hats and orange sashes tramp defiantly through Catholic quarters to the whistle and beat of fife and drum. And the old toast is raised:

"To the glorious, pious and immortal memory of the great and good King William, who saved us from popery, slavery, knavery, brass money, and wooden shoes. And a fig to the Bishop of Cork!"

1576–1612), the eccentric hermit of Prague, and Matthias (r. 1612–19), were fully absorbed by their mutual suspicions and by religious discord. Over 200 religious revolts or riots took place in the decade after the Donauworth Incident of 1607. Ferdinand II (r. 1619–37), Ferdinand III (r. 1637–57), and Leopold I (r. 1658–1705) were entirely consumed by the Thirty Years War and its aftermath. With the emergence of a permanent and separate Austrian chancellery in Vienna, the centre of gravity of their operation was shifting decisively to the East, whilst the Empire itself seemed to teeter on the edge of imminent dissolution. As the drinkers in the tavern of Goethe's *Faust* were given to singing:

> The dear old Holy Roman Empire,
> How does it hang together?

The answer, in the view of a distinguished British historian, lay less in the political sphere than in a 'civilisation', a set of shared attitudes and sensibilities.[41]

The Emperor Rudolf II assembled a court at Prague that really was a wonderful curiosity. His chosen companions, the most brilliant artists and scientists of the age, were men who took natural and supernatural to be part and parcel of their everyday researches. Apart from Kepler, Brahe, Campion, and Bruno, Giuseppe Arcimboldo (1537–93) achieved fame as the founder of surrealist painting (see Plate 54), and Cornelius Drebber (1572–1633), illusionist and opera designer, as inventor of a perpetual-motion machine. Drebber, who visited London, promised James I a telescope which could read books at a mile's distance. He is thought to have been the model for Prospero, 'rapt in secret studies', in Shakespeare's *Tempest*, just as Rudolf himself may have inspired the Duke in *Measure for Measure*.[42] Rudolf's fabulous art collection became a strategic target of the Swedish army during the latter stages of the Thirty Years' War. [**ALCHEMIA**] [**OPERA**]

Spain passed from grandeur to decline in little more than a century. 'For a few fabulous decades Spain was to be the greatest power on earth' and 'all but the master of Europe.'[43] Under Charles V/Carlos I (r. 1516–56) it lived through the age

ALCHEMIA

IN 1606, the Emperor Rudolph II was the subject of a formal complaint drawn up by the Habsburg Archdukes. 'His Majesty', they wrote in their Proposition, 'is only interested in wizards, alchemists, cabbalists and the like.' Rudolph's court at Prague did indeed house Europe's most distinguished research centre for the occult arts.[1]

In that same year a Hungarian alchemist, Janos Bánffy-Hunyadi (1576–1641), set out from his native Transylvania. He stopped over at the Court of Maurice of Hesse at Cassel, the principal Protestant centre of occultism, before moving on to London.[2] His arrival coincided with the death of the learned Welshman, Dr John Dee (1527–1608), sometime astrologer to Queen Elizabeth I, who once invented the term 'Great Britain' to please his queen and who had spent several years both in Prague and in Poland. Such 'cosmopolitans', as they were called, made their careers on the international circuit of alchemy, the true predecessor of the later scientific community.

Europe was experiencing a veritable 'occult revival', in which alchemy was the most important of several related 'secret arts'. 'Alchemy', writes the historian of Rudolph's world, 'was the greatest passion of the age in Central Europe.'[3] It combined the search for the philosopher's stone, which would transmute base metals into gold, with the parallel search for the spiritual rebirth of mankind. 'What is below is like what is above.'

Alchemists required expertise across a very wide range of knowledge. To conduct their experiments with metals and other substances, they needed to be familiar with the latest technology. To interpret their results, they needed a sound grasp of astrology, of cabbalistic number theory, of lapidarism, of herbalism, and of the 'iatrochemistry' developed by Paracelsus [HOLISM]. Most importantly, in a religious age, they sought to present their findings in the language of mystical Christian symbolism. It was no accident that at this time the secret Rosicrucian Society, the adepts of 'Rose' and 'Cross', chose to come into the open, at Cassel, or that the principal systematizer of Rosicrucian theosophy, Robert Fludd, was also a respectable alchemist. [CONSPIRO]

In later scientific times, the alchemists were seen as an aberrant breed which long delayed the growth of true knowledge. Indeed, in the so-called 'Age of the Scientific Revolution' they have sometimes been seen as 'the opposition'. The most charitable historian of science calls them practitioners of 'technology without science'.[4] Yet in their own eyes, and in the eyes of powerful patrons, there was no such distinction. They were 'white wizards' fighting for the Good; they were reformers; they were engaged in a quest to unlock the secret forces of mind and matter. They would not be overtaken by scientists of the modern persuasion until the end of the following century; and chemistry did not establish itself until still later. [**ELDLUFT**][5]

The Emperor Rudolph's cosmopolitan alchemists often held respons-ible positions. Several, like Michael Maier, who also worked in London, or the Huguenot sympathizer, Nicholas Barnard, held the office of *Leibarzt* or court physician. Others, such as Sebald Schwaertzer, served as imperial controller of mines at Rudolfov and Joachimsthal. [**DOLLAR**] Heinrich Kuhnrath (1560–1605), author of the grandiose *Amphitheatrum Sapientiae Aeternae Christiano-kabalisticum*, came from Leipzig. Michał Sędziwój or 'Sendivogius' (1566–1636), whose *Novum Lumen Chymicum* (1604) ran into 54 editions and would be thoroughly studied by Isaac Newton, came from Warsaw. He was connected to the powerful faction of pro-Habsburg mag-nates in Poland, who had contacts with Oxford and who brought John Dee to Cracow. John Dee's dubious assistant, Edward Kelley, classed as *Cacochimicus*, probably died in prison in Prague. Their company included the ill-fated Giordano Bruno [**SYROP**], the astronomers Kepler and Brahe, and an English poetess called Elizabeth Jane Weston.

There was also a prominent Jewish element. The Chief Rabbi of Prague, Judah Loew ben Bezalel (d. 1609), patronized a revival of the [**CABALA**]. It was fed by the works of Sephardi writers such as Isaac Luria or Moses Cordovero, whose *Pardes Rimmonim* was published in Cracow in 1591. One of the Emperor's closest associates, Mardochaeus the Jew, was a specialist in elixirs of fertility.

For contemporaries, alchemy had the most positive connotations;

> Full many a glorious morning have I seen
> Flatter the mountain tops with sovereign eye,
> Kissing with golden face the meadows green,
> Gilding pale streams with heavenly alchemy.[6]

of the *crucero*, the *conquistadores*, and the *tercio*, there being a clear correlation between the supply of American gold and the upkeep of the finest army in Europe. Under Philip II (r. 1556–98) it stood at the pinnacle of its political and cultural power, until undermined by internal resistance, by the hostility of France and England, and by the revolt of the Netherlands. Under Philip's successors—Philip III (r. 1598–1621), Philip IV (r. 1621–65), and the imbecile Charles II (r. 1665–1700)—it never recovered from a decadent dynasty, from noble faction, or from its debilitating involvement in the Thirty Years War. The fall was so sud-den that Spaniards themselves were apt to wonder: 'was the original achievement no more than an *engaño*—an illusion?'[44] [**FLAMENCO**]

Philip II must be the prototype of all monarchs who have tried to rule without rising from their desks (see Plate 43). Austere, penitential, tireless, ensconced in a solitary study in the gloomy Escorial on the barren plateau outside Madrid,

OPERA

THE composer called it a *favola in musica*, 'a fable set to music'. It was intended as an imitation of ancient Greek drama, and was produced in February 1607 before the Accademia degli Invaghiti in Mantua, probably in the Gallery of the Rivers in the ducal palace of the Gonzagas. Its five acts consisted of a series of madrigal groups and dances linked by instrumental interludes and recitatives. The libretto was written by the poet Alessandro Striggio. The music of the infernal scenes was given to trombones, the pastorals to flutes and recorders. It culminated in the great tenor aria 'Possente spirto' at the end of Act III. It was Claudio Monteverdi's *Orfeo*, 'the first viable opera in the repertoire'.[1]

Since its origins in the court entertainments of late Renaissance Italy, the operatic genre, which combines music, secular drama, and spectacle, has passed through many phases. The *opera seria*, whose most prolific proponent was Pietro Metastasio (1698–1782), author of 800 libretti, was devoted to classical and historical themes. Alongside it, the *opera buffa* launched a long tradition of light-hearted entertainment leading through opéra comique to operetta and musical comedy. Grand Opera, which starts in the late eighteenth century, reached its peaks in the Viennese, Italian, French, German, and Russian schools. Romantic nationalism became a prominent ingredient. The supreme laurels are disputed between the lovers of Verdi and Puccini and the fanatical acolytes of Richard Wagner. Modernist opera began with Debussy's *Pelléas et Mélisande* (1902), the precursor of a rich category including Berg's *Wozzeck* (1925), Britten's *Peter Grimes* (1945), and Stravinsky's *Rake's Progress* (1951) (see Appendix III, p. 1278). [**SUSANIN**] [**TRISTAN**]

The Orphean theme has provided recurrent inspiration. Jacopo Peri's Florentine masque *Euridice* (1600) anticipated Monteverdi's production in Mantua. Gluck's *Orpheus and Eurydice* (1762) opened the classical repertoire. Offenbach's *Orpheus in the Underworld* (1858) is one of the most joyous of the standard operettas. Luciano Berio's *Opera* (1971) puts the traditional story to a serial score.

he strove to enforce a spiritual and administrative uniformity which the variety of his vast dominions would never permit. He ruled through two sets of parallel councils—one set devoted to the main areas of policy, the other to the government of six major territorial units. For, in addition to his father's Castilian, Aragonese, Italian, Burgundian, and American legacies, in 1580 he seized his mother's vast Portuguese inheritance. His disregard for the rights of the various Diets culminated in the hanging of the *Justizar* of Aragon. Yet the dream of 'one monarch, one empire, one sword' was relentlessly pursued under the pretext that

FLAMENCO

ANDALUSIAN gypsy music in the style now known as flamenco has been played and admired since the sixteenth century. The plaintive melodies of the *cante* or 'singing' blend to inimitable effect with the dramatic poses and rhythmic stamping of the *baile* or 'dance'. The dissonances and quarter-tones, the exquisitely raucous vocal delivery, and the pulsating guitars and castanets contribute to a sound that has no counterpart in Europe's musical folklore.

The history of flamenco turns on three separate features—the name, the gypsies, and the music. No scholarly consensus exists about any of them.[1]

Flamenco simply meant 'Flemish'. In the vocabulary of art, it also gained the connotation of 'exotic' or 'ornate'. One theory proposes that Jewish songs banned by the Inquisition found their way back to Spain from Flanders, where many Spanish Jews had taken refuge. Another suggests that *flamenco* derives from the Arabic *fellah-mangu* or 'singing peasant'.

Gypsies reached Spain after the expulsions of the Jews and Moors. They were known as *gitanos* or *egipcianos*. The English traveller and writer George Borrow was the first to record in the 1840s that people were calling them *flamencos*. [**ROMANY**]

Andalusia's long tradition of Moorish music dated back to the eighth and ninth centuries. The Omeyas of Cordoba were entertained by oriental singers accompanied on the lute. One high point was reached in the reign of Abd-er-Rahman (r. 821–52) with the arrival of a singer from Baghdad known as Zoriab. Another occurred at the Sevillian court of the poet-king Al-Motamit (r. 1040–95), where orchestras of more than 100 lutes and flutes are known to have performed. In the twelfth century the philosopher Averroes said: 'When a scholar dies in Seville, his books are sold in Cordoba; when a musician dies in Cordoba, his instruments are sold in Seville.'

It would be rash to speculate on Flamenco's links with the earlier Moorish music of the region. Europe's gypsies had a strong musical tradition of their own, and produced startling results elsewhere—notably in Romania and Hungary. How exactly the music and the musicians came together in Andalusia is a mystery. The psychological traumas of Andalusia undoubtedly set the scene. The ancient *flamenco jondo* or 'deep flamenco', especially the *tonas* or 'unaccompanied melodies', belong to the world of tears and lament. Like the blues of America's deep South, they express the black moods of people in despair: they are the songs of the dispossessed. In this, they differ markedly from the flamboyant style of *flamenco chico*, 'smart flamenco', which swept Spain's café life in the 1860s and which furthered the romantic 'reinvention' of Andalusia. '*Flamenco Jondo*', wrote Federico Garcia Lorca, 'is a stammer, a marvellous buccal undulation that smashes the resonant cells of our tempered scale, eludes the cold rigid staves of modern music, and makes the tightly closed flowers of the semitones blossom into a thousand petals.'[2]

the King knew best how to *trabajar para el pueblo,* 'work for his people'.[45] In the process, he drove his sick, imprisoned son to death; he drove the Inquisition to waves of *autos-da-fé;* and he drove the persecuted Moriscos of Granada to rebel in 1568–9, the offended Dutch to rebel in 1566, the humiliated Aragonese to rebel in 1591–2. His adversaries, like William the Silent, considered him simply 'a murderer and a liar'. Never can an apparently sensitive man have so completely ignored the sensitivities of others. Absolute master of the Church in Spain, he sought to extirpate the Church's enemies across Europe. He swore to avenge his second wife's memory in England. He intervened against the Huguenots in France. He wrongly saw the Dutch Protestants as the source of all discontent in the Netherlands. But God, like Philip II, did not smile on Spain. By the 1590s a general crisis loomed. The Great Armada of 1588 had been dashed by storms. The Dutch held out. Plague swept the Spanish cities. The countryside, drained by taxes and hit by agricultural failures, was beginning to depopulate. The richest coffers in the world were empty. In 1596 Philip II was formally bankrupt for the fourth time. There was misery amidst splendour, and an overpowering sense of disillusionment. Philip, like Don Quixote, had been tilting at windmills. The supremacy of Castile was deeply resented by Spain's other constituent kingdoms. 'Castile has made Spain,' the epitaph reads, 'and Castile has destroyed it.'[46] [INQUISITIO]

After Philip's death the Spanish Habsburgs sought in vain to restore their fortunes. A concerted attempt was made to join forces with their Austrian relations. Gaspar de Guzman, Count of Oliverez and Duke of San Lucar, popularly known as *El Conde Duque,* the 'Count-Duke', who held the reins of policy from 1621 to 1643, applied the principles of earlier Castilian reformers. But his career came to grief amidst the shattering secession of Portugal (1640) and the revolt of Catalonia (1640–8). Spain's involvement in the Thirty Years War ended with the loss of the United Provinces—its richest single asset. The interrelated wars with France were protracted until the Treaty of the Pyrenees (1659). Overwhelmed by the spiralling costs of war, by the multiplicity of fronts, by the absence of any interval of respite, Spain could rescue neither itself nor its Austrian partner. Thanks to the extraordinary problems of 'the Spanish Road', the logistics of supporting an army in the Low Countries became insuperable. *Poner una pica en Flandres* (putting a pikeman into Flanders) became a Spanish idiom for 'attempting the impossible'.[47] 'The Habsburg bloc', writes the historian of political logistics, 'provides one of the greatest examples of strategical overstretch in history.'[48] [PICARO] [VALTELLINA]

The Revolt of the Netherlands, which began in 1566 and ended in 1648, constituted a long-running drama which spanned the transition from the supremacy of the Habsburgs to that of France. At the outset, the seventeen provinces of the imperial Burgundian Circle that were transferred to Spanish rule in 1551 presented a mosaic of local privileges and of social and cultural divisions. The feudal aristocracy of the countryside contrasted sharply with the wealthy burghers and

PICARO

PICARO was the Spanish name given to rogues and vagabonds, that is, to people living beyond the margin of settled and respectable society. It was also given to a genre of popular literature, the picaresque, which flourished across Europe from the sixteenth to the eighteenth centuries in advance of the novel. The archetype of the genre was found in Mateo Alemán's *Guzmán de Alfrache* (1599), whose adventures on the road from Seville to Rome in the company of a dubious lady-friend ran into twenty-six editions. Guzmán revealed how the brotherhood of beggars formed a mutual protection society, revelling in their ingenious schemes to cheat the governing classes.

But Guzmán was one among many. In Spain, a certain Lazarillo had appeared half a century earlier. In Germany, the practical joker Till Eulenspiegel was well known before he first made it into print. In 1523 Luther wrote a preface to the much-reprinted *Liber Vagatorum*, which contains a description of twenty-eight categories of tramp. *Simplicissimus*, the ex-soldier of the Thirty Years War who wandered round the world, was the creation of H. J. C. von Grimmelshausen in 1669. In France, after numerous earlier appearances, *Gil Blas* emerged from the pen of Le Sage in 1715. In Italy, there appeared *Il vagabondo* (1621). In England, many minor references to roguery from Chaucer onwards culminated in John Gay's sensationally popular *The Beggar's Opera* of 1728.[1]

Picaresque literature was clearly responding to a widespread social condition. Vagabondage and beggary filled a large social space, midway between the medieval forest outlaws and the regimented urban poor of the nineteenth century. It was spawned by the disintegration of hierarchical rural society, and encouraged by social policing that combined ferocious punishments with highly incompetent enforcement. Men and women took to the road in droves because they were unemployed, because they were fugitives from justice, above all because they longed to escape the oppressive, dependent status of serfs and servants. The *picaro* was wild but free.

Vagabonds sought protection in numbers, and in social hierarchies of their own. They travelled in bands with families and children, some of them mutilated to excite pity. They had specialized guilds of pickpockets, thieves, burglars, pedlars, beggars, cripples real and feigned, jugglers, entertainers, fortune-tellers, tinkers, whores, washerwomen, chaplains, and musicians—each with rules and guardians. They even developed their own secret language, known as *rotwelsch* or *żargon*. They gathered intermittently for meetings and 'parliaments', where they elected their 'kings' and 'queens'; and they shared the roads with gypsy tribes and gangs of unpaid soldiery:

Hark, hark! the dogs do bark.
The beggars are coming to town.
Some in rags, and some in tags,
And some in a velvet gown.

Social provision for vagrancy was minimal. Only the richest cities could afford charitable refuges—such as those at Bruges from 1565, Milan from 1578, and Lyons from 1613. In any case, 'charity' could be an ill-disguised euphemism for repression. In 1612, when the city of Paris asked its 8–10,000 vagrants to assemble on the Place St Germain to receive assistance, only 91 persons came forward. [**FOLLY**]

Ferocious legislation underlined the authorities' impotence. In Elizabethan England, for example, every parish was given the right to brand 'sturdy beggars' on the shoulder with a letter R for 'rogue', to flog the homeless and to send them 'home': in effect to condemn them 'to be whipped from parish to parish'. Georgian England made an attempt to distinguish 'the deserving poor'. At the same time, the Black Waltham Act of 1713 let suspected highwaymen and their accomplices be hanged without trial. In practice, most countries could only keep vagrancy down by periodic military expeditions into the countryside, where exemplary hangings and press-gangings took place. In Eastern Europe vagrancy was conditioned by a harsher climate and by the persistence of serfdom. But fugitive serfs were a common phenomenon. In Russia the *yurodiv* or itinerant 'holy fool' was traditionally the recipient of hospitality and charity—proof too, perhaps, of more Christian social attitudes.[2]

fishermen of the coastal towns. The francophone and predominantly Catholic Walloons of Hainault, Namur, and Liège contrasted with the Dutch-speaking and increasingly Calvinist population of Holland, Zeeland, and Utrecht. The central provinces of Flanders and Brabant lay across the main religious and linguistic divide. Over 200 cities controlled perhaps 50 per cent of Europe's trade, bringing Spain seven times more in taxes than the bullion of the Indies. Certainly, in the initial stages of Spanish rule, the threat to provincial liberties and to the nobles' control of Church benefices gave greater cause for popular offence than the threat of activating the Inquisition (see Appendix III, p. 1275).

Under the regency of Margaret of Parma, 1559–67, discontent came to a head over a scheme for ecclesiastical reform. Three protesters—William the Silent, Prince of Orange (1533–84), Lamoral, Count of Egmont, and Philip Montmorency, Count of Horn—petitioned the King with the Regent's permission. They were ridiculed as *Geuzen, les Gueux*, 'the Beggars', and in 1565, in the Edict of Segovia, Philip indicated his refusal to authorize change. Following further petitions for reform, and a meeting in 1566 of confederated nobles at St Trond, which demanded religious toleration, there occurred a serious outbreak of

VALTELLINA

IN July 1620 a bloody massacre took place in a remote alpine valley—the Valtellina or Veltlin. The Catholic faction in the valley fell on their Protestant neighbours and, with the aid of a Spanish force from Milan, killed as many as they could seize. This *Veltlinermord*, at the outset of the Thirty Years War, alerted the Powers to the Valtellina's strategic potential.

The Valtellina lies on the southern side of the Bernina section of the main alpine ridge. It was formed by the River Adda, and runs some 74 miles due eastwards from the tip of Lake Como, then north-east to the old Roman spa at Bormio. An important side-valley, the Val di Poschiavo, leads northwards via the Bernia Pass to St Moritz. The main valley leads over the Stelvio Pass or Stilfserjoch (9,055 feet) to southern Tyrol. In 1520 the shrine of the Madonna di Tirano was built where the main road cross-es a north–south track leading down the Val di Poschiavo and over into the Val Camonica. In 1603 a Spanish fortress was built to command the entrance to the valley from Lake Como. A string of villages on the sunny northern terraces of the Adda are famed for their chestnuts, figs, honey, and aromatic 'Retico' wine.[1] (See Appendix III, p. 1219.)

It was political geography, however, that was crucial. By the 1600s almost all the transalpine routes were controlled by the Duke of Savoy, by the Swiss Confederation, or by the Republic of Venice. When the Austrian Habsburgs were looking for support from their Spanish relatives in Italy, the Valtellina had become the sole accessible corridor between the two main blocks of Habsburg territory. Indeed, since the sea-lanes between Spain and the Netherlands were increasingly threatened by Dutch and English warships, the Valtellina became the last sure route for sending gold and troops from Spain and Spanish Italy to the empire. It was the jugular vein of the Habsburgs' body politic.

Yet the columns of marching pikemen, and the mule trains loaded with pieces of eight, remained extremely vulnerable. They were not welcome to the local inhabitants, many of whom had turned to Calvinism; they were open to direct attack from the Swiss Freestate of the *Graubunden* or Grisons, via the Val di Poschiavo; and they were subject to the changing fortunes of complicated proprietorial disputes. Both the Habsburgs and the Grisons had inherited claims to the Valtellina rooted in the medieval wrangles between the Visconti dukes of Milan and the bishops of Chur. Not to be outdone, the French reckoned that Charlemagne had granted the Valtellina in perpetuity to the Abbey of St Denis.

After 1620, the valley became the focus of Richelieu's diplomacy with Venice, Switzerland, and Savoy. Five times in the next twenty years it saw French and Spanish garrisons change places. In 1623 and in 1627 it was handed over during arbitration to papal forces. In 1623–5 it was taken by the Grisons. In 1633 and 1635–7 it was taken by French forces under the Huguenot Duke of Rohan. But the French so offended their Protestant allies that a local pastor, George Jenatsch, changed sides, called in the Spaniards, and converted to Roman Catholicism. By then, having laid hands on the Rhine, the French could safely leave the Valtellina to its Catholic and, ultimately, to its Italian destiny. After a generation of turmoil the valley could return to its vines, to the production of Sassella, Grumello, Valgella, Montagna, and the orange-coloured dessert wine, the *Sfurzat*.

rioting and religious desecrations. The action of the confederates in helping the Regent to quell the disorders did not deter Philip from ordering general repression. Under the regency of the Duke of Alva, 1567–73, a Council of Tumults, the notorious *Bloedraad* or 'Blood-Council' was set up to try the King's opponents. Egmont and Horn were beheaded in the square at Brussels, their severed heads sent to Madrid in a box. William of Orange escaped to lead the continuing fight. With the whole population of the Netherlands condemned to death as heretics by the Church, the south rebelled as well as the north. The 'Sea Beggars' attacked shipping. Haarlem, besieged, capitulated. Spanish garrisons spread fire and plunder. Thousands perished from random arrests, mock trials, and casual violence.

Under the governorships of Don Luis de Requesens, Grand Commander of Castile 1573–6, and of Don John of Austria 1576–8 reconciliation was attempted but failed. Leyden, besieged, survived. The sack of Antwerp during the Spanish Fury of 1576 hardened resistance. Under the regency of the Duke of Parma 1578–92, the split became irreversible. By the Union of Arras (1578) ten southern provinces accepted Spanish terms and recovered their liberties. By the Union of Utrecht (1579) the seven northern provinces resolved to fight for their independence. Thereafter, there was unremitting war. Spanish military resources could never be brought to bear against the Dutchmen's dykes, their money, warships, and allies. In 1581–5 and 1595–8 the Dutch were assisted by the French, in 1585–7 by the English under the Earl of Leicester. In 1609 they enjoyed an eleven-year truce, but were forced to fight on from 1621 to 1648 in the ranks of the anti-imperial coalition. Their steadfastness prevailed. The spirit of a new nation was inscribed on the front of a burgher's house in Zijlstraat, Haarlem: 'INT SOET NEDERLAND; ICK BLYF GETROU; ICK WYCT NYET AF' (To the dear Netherlands. I shall be true. I shall not waver.)[49]

The Dutch Republic of the 'United Provinces of the Netherlands'—misleadingly known in English as Holland—was the wonder of seventeenth-century Europe. It succeeded for the same reasons that its would-be Spanish masters failed: throughout the eighty years of its painful birth, its disposable resources were actually growing. Having resisted the greatest military power of the day, it then became a major maritime power in its own right. Its sturdy burgher society widely practised the virtues of prudent management, democracy, and toleration. Its engineers, bankers, and sailors were justly famed. Its constitution (1584) ensured that the governments of the seven provinces remained separate from a federal council of state at The Hague. The latter was chaired by an executive *Stadholder*, whose office was generally held, together with the offices of Captain-General and Admiral-General, by the House of Orange. [ORANGE]

The Dutch Republic rapidly became a haven for religious dissidents, for capitalists, for philosophers, and for painters. The earlier Flemish school of Rubens (1577–1640) and Van Dyck (1599–1641) was surpassed by the Dutch School of Hals, Ruysdael, Vermeer, and, above all, of Rembrandt (Harmenszoon van Rijn, 1609–66). Nor were the Netherlands blighted by bourgeois dullness. Its religious affairs were enlivened by the Arminian controversy, its military affairs by a vocal element of pacifist opinion, its politics by a party of extreme republicans who in 1651–72, under Jan de Witt (1625–72), succeeded in keeping the Stadholdership vacant. Its political power began to wane with the three English wars of 1651–4, 1665–7, and 1672–4. Even so, despite its peculiar, decentralised constitution, it had every reason to regard itself as the first modern state.[50] [BATAVIA]

France, too, was entering a period of renewed vigour and splendour. Less encumbered by distant colonies, and geographically more compact, she was a worthy rival for the Habsburgs. Yet France was strategically encircled, by the Empire on one side and by Spain on the other, by the Spanish Netherlands in the north and by the Spanish Mediterranean possessions in the south. The French were repeatedly thwarted in their attempts to reach the dominant position to which they felt entitled.

In the century-and-a-half which separated Renaissance France from Louis XIV, French kings repeatedly ran into strangulating complications both at home and abroad. Charles VIII launched the Italian wars in 1494, in romantic pursuit of the Angevin claim to Naples, only to embroil his country in a series of titanic conflicts lasting 65 years. Louis XII (r. 1498–1515), *Père de son Peuple* and heir to the Visconti, did likewise by pursuing his claim to Milan. Francis I (r. 1515–47), born at Cognac, a magnificent knight, cultivated man of pleasure, and Renaissance prince par excellence, met his first setback at the imperial election of 1519 and the second by his capture at Pavia in 1525. 'Tout est perdu,' he wrote to his mother, 'fors l'honneur et la vie.' His release, and marriage to the Emperor's sister, did not restrain him from persisting with the Franco-German feud that henceforth gripped Europe for the rest of modern history. He was a prince of wide horizons: patron of Jacques Cartier's expedition to Canada, as of Rabelais, Leonardo, Cellini; founder alike of Le Havre and of the Collège de France; builder of Chambord, Saint-Germain, Fontainebleau. [ALCOFRIBAS][NEZ][TORMENTA]

In the reigns of the last four Valois—Henry II (r. 1547–59), Francis II (r. 1559–60), the youthful Charles IX (r. 1560–74), and the flagrant Henry III (r. 1574–89)—France gained respite from the Habsburg conflict at the Peace of Câteau-Cambrésis (1559), only to sink into the appalling morass of the Wars of Religion (see above). The cynical Bourbon Henry IV (r. 1589–1610) saved France from religious discord and, with his visionary minister, the Duc de Sully

BATAVIA

IN the mid-seventeenth century, several travellers to Amsterdam record-ed their astonishment at the 'drowning cell' which they had seen, or heard about, in the city's house of correction. In order to teach idle young men to work, the candidates for correction would be cast into a sealed cel-lar furnished only with a running tap and a hand-pump. Whenever they stopped working the pump, they were faced with the imminent prospect of drowning. This installation was a wonderful metaphor for the physical predicament of the Dutch Republic and its dykes. It is also a fine illustra-tion of the country's 'moral geography'—what has been called 'the Batavian Temperament'.[1]

The Dutch Republic in its heyday was famous for its commerce, for its cities, for its seapower, for its canals, windmills, and tulips, for its art, for its religious tolerance, for its black-and-white cattle, and for the puritani-cal culture of its burgher élite. The picture is true enough. But it provokes two major questions. One concerns the ambiguities which abound in the interplay of the component parts, the other concerns the miracle of how it all happened in the first place—'how a modest assortment of farming, fishing and shipping communities, with no shared language, religion or government, transformed itself into a world empire'. A leading historian of the subject stresses that the miracle was not the work of a class, but of a precocious 'community of the nation'.[2]

The central paradox of Dutch culture lies in the strange contradiction between its frugal, hard-working, God-fearing ethos and its 'embarrass-ing' storehouse of riches. The sober, dark-suited Dutch burghers loved feasting, adored tobacco, built sumptuous houses, furnished them lavishly, collected paintings, indulged in the vanity of portraiture, and amassed money. Sexual relations were relaxed. Family life was companionable rather than patriarchal. Women, by the standards of the time, were liber-ated, and children were cherished. The accepted practice for raising funds to help the poor was to organize a municipal lottery or an auction of gold, jewels, and silverware.

Over it all there reigned an inimitable freedom of spirit. It was accepted that wealth and security could only be gained by those who were game for the risk:

Here lies Isaac le Maire, merchant, who during his affairs throughout the world, by the grace of God, has known much abundance and has lost in thirty years (excepting his honour) over 150,000 guilders. Died as a Christian 30 September 1624.[3]

Much of these matters were well known to Dutch scholars. But the task of recreating this distinctive *mentalité* for the world at large fell to a British scholar of Dutch-Jewish parentage. It has reopened the vexed question of whether national character really exists or not.

(1560–1641), prepared plans both for the restoration of prosperity and for international peace. 'There will be no labourer in my kingdom', he promised, 'without a chicken in his pot.' Like his predecessor, he was cut down by an assassin. [DESSEIN]

The long reign of Louis XIII (r.1610–43) and the minority of his son, Louis XIV (1643–51), were overshadowed by the long careers of two formidable churchmen—Armand Duplessis, Cardinal de Richelieu (1585–1642) and Giulio

---

ALCOFRIBAS

THE works of François Rabelais, ex-monk, ex-lawyer, and physician, form one of the richest mines of literary and historical treasure that early modern Europe can offer. But their eccentricity aroused the suspicions of an intolerant age, and were first published under the anagrammic pseudonym of Alcofribas Nasier. Studies by Lucien Febvre and of Mikhail Bakhtin illustrate the breadth of scholarly interest which they still arouse.

Febvre, co-founder of *Annales*, was drawn to Rabelais after learning that specialists were leaning to the notion that the inventor of Pantagruel and Gargantua had been a secret and militant atheist. Having invented the community of Thélème, whose only rule was *Fais ce que voudras* ('Do whatever you would like'), no one could claim that Rabelais was a conventional religious thinker. On the other hand, to charge him with subversion of Christianity was a serious matter. Febvre, in response, produced one of the great surveys of 'collective mentality': *Le Problème de l'incroyance au XVIᵉ siècle* (1942). Having examined all the charges of scandal, and all the possible sources of irregular belief, in radical Protestantism, science, philosophy, and the occult, he concluded that Rabelais had shared 'the deep religiosity' of 'a century which wanted to believe'.[1]

Bakhtin, a distinguished Russian Dostoevskian scholar, turned to Rabelais from an interest in psychology. Rabelais has had the reputation of being the master of the vulgar belly-laugh [NEZ]. But he also enters that profounder realm where laughter mingles with tears. Bakhtin emerged with a hypothesis centred on Rabelais's famous proposition that 'laughter is the mark of humanity'. 'To laugh is human, to be human is to laugh.' *Mieux est de rire que de larmes écrire. Pour ce que rire est le propre de l'homme.*

But Bakhtin suspects that modern civilization has seriously repressed this most human of qualities. Europeans, since Rabelais, have grown so inhibited that they only laugh at trivia. Indeed, they no longer know what is sacred in order to laugh at it. It is a profoundly pessimistic opinion parallel to the social analysis of Michel Foucault. One is left wondering whether Rabelais was not the last European to be truly human.[2] [CARITAS]

NEZ

IN 1532 Rabelais described an imaginary duel of gestures between his fictional hero, Panurge, and an Englishman:

Then the Englishe man made this sign. His left hand all open he lifted into the aire, then . . . instantly shut the foure fingers thereof, and his thumb extended at length he placed upon the gristle of his nose. Presently, he lifted up his right hand all open, putting the thumb [beside] the little finger of his left hand; and the foure right hand fingers he softly moved in the aire. Then contrarily, he did with the right what he had done with the left, and with the left what he had done with the right.

According to a recent study, 'thumbing the nose' or 'cocking a snoot' is the most widespread of all European gestures. It conveys mockery. In France it is known as *le pied de nez* or 'fool's nose', in Italy as *marameo* or 'mewing', in Germany as *die lange Nase*, in Portugal as *tocar tromfete* 'to blow the trumpet', in Serbo-Croat as *sviri ti svode* 'to play the flute'. It is more common and less ambiguous than the Fingertips Kiss, the Temple Screw, the Eyelid Pull, the Forearm Jerk, the Ring, the Fig, the Nose Tap, and the V-sign—all of which have important regional and contextual variations.[1]

It is debatable whether there is a culture of gestures exclusive to Europe or to Christendom. But there is no doubt that gestures change over time. The English, who literally refused to kowtow in China, also abandoned bowing at home in the late eighteenth century, inventing the handshake as an easier form of sexless and classless greeting. 'À l'anglaise donc', said Madame Bovary in 1857 when offered a gentleman's hand. In the twentieth century, however, the English became much more obstinately reticent, frequently refusing to shake hands while Continentals did so routinely.[2] They stand at the opposite end of the European spectrum to the Poles, whose readiness to bow, to embrace both sexes, and to kiss hands in public has survived two world wars, modernization, Fascism, and even Communism.

Mazzarini, Cardinal Mazarin (1602–61). External affairs were entirely preoccupied with the Thirty Years War, internal affairs with the assertion of centralized royal power against the privileges of the provinces and the nobility. The Estates-General was suspended after the session of 1614. The merciless attack by Richelieu on the sources of noble wealth and power in the provinces underlay the desperate rebellions and the Wars of the Fronde, in 1648–53. The sunrise of Louis XIV's mature years burst from very cloudy skies.

The Italian Wars have often been used as the starting-point of modern history, and as the model of a local conflict which became internationalized. (They were

TORMENTA

A T the Midsummer's Fair in mid-sixteenth-century Paris, cat-burning was a regular attraction. A special stage was built so that a large net containing several dozen cats could be lowered onto the bonfire beneath. The spectators, including kings and queens, shrieked with laughter as the animals, howling with pain, were singed, roasted, and finally carbonized. Cruelty was evidently thought to be funny.[1] It played its part in many of Europe's more traditional sports, including cock-fighting, bear-baiting, bull-fighting, and fox-hunting. [**LUDI**]

Two hundred years later, on 2 March 1757, Robert François Damiens was condemned in Paris 'to make honourable amends':

He was brought in a tumbril, naked except for a smock, and carrying a torch of burning wax in his hand. The scaffold stood on the Place de Grève. Pincered at the breasts, arms, thighs and calves, his right hand holding the knife, with which he perpetrated the said act, he was to be burned on the hand with sulphur, to be doused at the pinion points with boiling oil, molten lead, and burning resin, and then to be dismembered by four horses, before his body was burned, reduced to ashes, and scattered to the winds.

When the fire was lit, the heat was so feeble that only the skin on the back of one hand was damaged. But then one of the executioners, a strong and robust man, grasped the metal pincers, each 1½ feet long, and by twisting and turning them, tore out huge lumps of flesh, leaving gaping wounds which were doused from a red-hot spoon.

Between his screams, Damiens repeatedly called out, 'My God, take pity on me!' and 'Jesus, help me!' The spectators were greatly edified by the compassion of an aged curé who lost no moment to console him.

The Clerk of the Court, the Sieur de Breton, went up to the sufferer several times, and asked him if he had anything to say. He said no . . .

The final operation lasted a very long time, because the horses were not used to it. Six horses were needed; but even they were not enough . . .

The executioner asked whether they should cut him in pieces, but the Clerk ordered them to try again. The confessors drew close once more, and he said 'Kiss me, sires', and one of them kissed him on the forehead.

After two or three more attempts, the executioners took out knives, and cut off his legs . . . They said that he was dead. But when the body had been pulled apart, the lower jaw was still moving, as if to speak . . . In execution of the decree, the last pieces of flesh were not consumed until 10.30 in the evening . . .[2]

Damiens was being punished for attempted regicide. His immediate family were banished from France; his brothers and sisters were ordered to change their names; and his house was razed. He had approached Louis XV as the King was entering his carriage, and he had inflicted a small wound with a small knife. He made some sort of complaint about the Parlement. He made no attempt to escape, and said that he only wanted to give the King a fright. Nowadays, he would be assessed as a crank.

Torture had been an established feature both of legal proceedings and of executions since Roman times. St Augustine recognized its fallibility, but admitted its necessity. Torture at executions was thought to have a didactic purpose. Death was the least part of the penalty when the convict was to be impaled, disembowelled, burned at the stake, or broken on the wheel. [**VLAD**]

Damiens's death was the last of its kind in France. The Enlightenment did not approve. Shortly afterwards a Milanese, the Marquis Cesare Beccaria-Bonesana (1735–94), published a tract, *Dei delitti i delle pene* ('On Crimes and Punishment', 1764). It argued that torture was both improper and ineffective. Translated into many languages, with a preface by Voltaire, it was the catalyst of reform across Europe. It is widely seen as the starting-point of a long progressive trend which was to press first for humane methods of execution, and eventually for the abolition of the death penalty. The 'cruelty curve' was to decline until liberal opinion held that torture degrades, not the tortured, but the torturer and the torturer's masters. But that was not the whole story. And torture in Europe did not come to an end.[4] [**ALCOFRIBAS**]

neither.) When French troops crossed the pass of Montgenèvre in September 1494 bound for Naples, they did so by express agreement of the Empire, which had been compensated in advance with Franche-Comté, and of Aragon, which had been bought off with the gift of Roussillon. So the conflict had been 'internationalized' from the start. The result was three French expeditions, each of which provoked a powerful coalition to defeat it. The expedition of Charles VIII 1494–5, after sweeping triumphantly through Milan, Florence, and Rome, captured Naples; but it was forced to retreat with the same speed. The expedition of Louis XII, 1499–1515, captured Milan in similar style—using Leonardo's equestrian statue for target practice; but it aroused the opposition of the Holy League raised by Pope Julius II. The expedition of Francis I 1515–26 began with the stunning victory of Marignano which, among other things, turned the Swiss to permanent neutrality and persuaded the Pope to sign the Concordat of 1516. But it was interrupted by the bitterness of the imperial election, which turned Francis I and Charles V into mortal enemies. At Pavia in 1525 Marignano was avenged and Francis I taken prisoner. Imperial forces pressed on through Provence as far as Marseilles. After his release, Francis persuaded a new Pope to form a new Holy League against an over-mighty Emperor. The fearful Sack of Rome by imperial troops ensued in 1527, this time with the Pope made captive. By then the Italian Wars had become simply one front of a generalized Franco-imperial struggle.

The Franco-imperial wars assumed Continental proportions. In his attempt to break imperial encirclement, Francis I did not hesitate to recruit allies from all quarters. In 1519, he stood in person as candidate for Emperor. Despite the

abortive meeting at the splendiferous Field of Cloth of Gold, he eventually won
Henry VIII of England's sympathies. He laid scandalous plans with the Protestant
princes of Germany; and in 1536, in the famous Capitulations, he made common
cause with the Infidel, Suleiman the Magnificent, and with the Sultan's North
African vassals, including the corsair-king Kair-el-Din Barbarossa. In the shifting
permutations of Italy he was supported both by the Popes and by the Vatican's
chief opponent, the Republic of Venice.

The result was four more wars. In 1521–6 the imperialists first attacked French
Burgundy, before concentrating on the Italian campaign which ended with Pavia
and the Treaty of Madrid (1526). In 1526–9 the Emperor overstretched and disgraced himself, signing the Ladies' Peace at Cambrai (1529). In 1536–8 and 1542–4
he was embroiled with the Turks and the German Protestants as well as the
French, and was constrained to sign the Treaty of Crépy-en-Valois (1544), which
created an interval permitting the opening of the Council of Trent, and the long-
delayed attack on the Schmalkaldic League. In 1551–9, under Henry II, the French
conspired with the German Protestants to occupy the three archbishoprics of
Lorraine—Metz, Toul, and Verdun—thereby launching the 'March to the Rhine'
and a frontier struggle not ended till 1945. (See Appendix III, p. 1281.) The
Habsburgs responded in the Low Countries with the occupation of Artois, and
with an English alliance that instantly inspired the French to forget their religious
differences and to capture Calais (7 January 1558). Mary Tudor, whose proxy marriage to Philip II was the price of this brief Habsburg–Tudor *rapprochement*,
exclaimed: 'When I die, you will find Calais engraved on my heart.' By the general peace of Câteau-Cambrésis, France kept Lorraine and Calais, the Habsburgs
kept Artois, Milan, and Naples. England was shut out of the Continent for good.
The main issue was postponed, not solved. [**NOSTRADAMUS**]

The British Isles, increasingly dominated by the English, were taken closer to the
unification which had beckoned once or twice already. Having lost its foothold on
the Continent, the Kingdom of England turned its energies into the affairs of its
immediate neighbours and into overseas ventures. A typical composite polity of
the era, consisting of England, Wales, and Ireland, it lacked the national cohesion
which Scotland already possessed. But under the Tudors it manifested great
vigour. Notwithstanding the religious conflicts of the age, Henry VIII (r. 1509–47)
and his three children—Edward VI (r. 1547–53), Mary I (r. 1553–8), and Elizabeth
(r. 1558–1603)—created the Church of England, the lasting symbiosis of monarchy
and Parliament, and the Royal Navy. [**BARD**]

The Stuarts, who had ruled in Scotland since 1371, accepted the Personal Union
of Scotland and England (1603) after the Tudors ran out of heirs. They had much
to gain. Deceived by its Continental alliances, Scotland had lived in England's
shadow since the bloody disaster of Flodden Field (1513). Anglo-Scottish relations
were badly shaken by the intrigues of the deposed Mary, Queen of Scots
(1542–87), who died on an English scaffold. But Mary's son, James I and VI
(r. 1567(1603)–1625), succeeded by general consent to the inheritance which had

NOSTRADAMUS

THE royal summons arrived at Salon in Provence early in July 1556. The Queen of France, Catherine de' Medici, wished to speak to the author of a book of prophecies published the previous year. One of its verses appeared to predict the death of the Queen's husband:

> *Le lion jeune le vieux surmontera*
> (The young lion will overcome the older one)
> *En champ bellique par singulier duelle.*
> (In a field of combat, in single fight.)
> *Dans caige d'or les yeux lui crevera.*
> (He will pierce his eyes in their golden cage.)
> *Deux classes une, puis mourir, mort cruelle.*
> (Two wounds in one, then he dies a cruel death.)[1]

Within a month, speeded by royal horses, the author was ushered into the Queen's presence at St Germain-en-Laye. He calmed her fears by saying that he saw four kings among her four sons.

But three years later King Henri II was killed in a tournament. The splintered lance of his opponent, Montgomery, Captain of the Scottish Guard, had split the visor of the King's gilded helmet, piercing eye and throat, and inflicting wounds which caused death after ten days of agony.

Michel de Nostredame (1503–66), called Nostradamus, was well known in the Midi as an unconventional healer. He came from a family of Jewish *conversos* at St Rémy-en-Provence, and had graduated in medicine at Montpellier. He was learned in potions and remedies, concocting an elixir of life for the Bishop of Carcassonne and a diet of quince jelly for the Papal Legate. He worked in plague-stricken Marseilles and Avignon when all other doctors had left, refusing to bleed patients as was customary, and insisting on fresh air and clean water. More than once, as a suspected wizard, he attracted the notice of the Inquisition and fled abroad. On one such journey in the 1540s he is said to have met a young Italian monk and former shepherd, Felice Peretti, whom he addressed without hesitation as 'Your Holiness'. Forty years later, long after Nostradamus's death, Peretti was elected Pope as Sextus V.

The prophecies of Nostradamus were composed late in life with the help of magical, astrological, and cabalistic books. They were written in quatrains and organized in centuries. They were published in two parts, in 1555 and 1568, and were an immediate sensation. One year after their full publication, Catherine de' Medici's eldest son, King Francis II, husband

Mary Queen of Scots, died suddenly at the age of 17 years, 10 months, and 15 days:

> Premier fils, veuve, malheureux mariage
> (The first son, a widow, an unhappy marriage)
> Sans nul enfant; deux isles en discorde,
> (Without children; two islands in discord,)
> Avant dixhuit incompetant eage
> (Before eighteen years of age, a minor)
> De l'autre près plus bas sera l'accord.
> (Still younger than the other will be betrothed.)[2]

In that same year the youngest brother, later Charles IX, aged 11, was betrothed to an Austrian princess.

This posthumous success ensured the reputation of the Prophecies for all time. They have been endlessly reprinted, and applied to almost every known event, from submarines and ICBMs to the deaths of the Kennedys and men on the moon. Nostradamus correctly named the family Saulce, where Louis XVI lodged during the flight to Varennes. He convinced both Napoleon and Hitler, who figures as 'Hister', that their careers had been foreseen in the stars. The quatrains are wonderfully suggestive and obscure, and can be made to fit all manner of coincidences. But many come too close for comfort:

> Quand la licture du tourbillon versée
> (When the litters are overturned by whirlwind)
> Et seront faces de leurs manteaux couvers
> (And faces will be covered by cloaks)
> La République pars gens nouveaux vexée
> (The Republic will be troubled by new people.)
> Lors blancs et rouges jugeront à l'envers.
> (At that time, Whites and Reds will rule inside out.)[3]

In 1792 the Republic did arrive in France, and the Reds did overturn the Whites.

And, as a short description of life in the twentieth century, the following is uncanny:

> Les fléaux passées diminue le monde.
> (Plagues extinguished, the world becomes smaller.)
> Long temps la paix terres inhabitées:
> (For a long time, there is peace in empty lands.)
> Seur marchera par ciel, terre, mer et onde;
> (People will walk safely by air, land, sea, waves.)
> Puis de nouveau les guerres suscitées.
> (Then again wars will be stirred up.)[4]

BARD

SHAKESPEARE wrote his plays in the short interval after post-Reformation England had severed her direct links with the Continent but before she had acquired an overseas empire. His main dramas were written in the same decades when the first English colonies were being founded in America. His voice was to reign supreme in the English-speaking world, and, as far as one knows, he never set foot outside England. The universality of his genius would not be generally recognized in Europe until the Romantic era.

Yet the settings of the plays suggest that the Swan of Avon was in no way a Little Englander. He may even have been a secret Catholic. The Tudor censorship may well have inhibited politically sensitive material. Yet of thirty-seven titles, only ten were set in whole or in part in England; and the historical series has a strong admixture of French locations. *The Merry Wives* is set in Windsor, *As You Like It* in the Forest of Arden. The three dark stories of *Macbeth*, *King Lear*, and *Cymbeline* are placed in ancient Celtic Britain; and eight classical dramas in Athens, Rome, Tyre, or Troy. The fantastic fables of *Twelfth Night, A Winter's Tale*, and *The Tempest* unfold in a mythical Illyria, in a sea-girt Bohemia, and on 'an uninhabited island'. But the rest are manifestly Continental:

Much Ado About Nothing	Messina	*A Midsummer Night's Dream*	Athens
The Merchant of Venice	Venice	*Romeo and Juliet*	Verona
The Taming of the Shrew	Padua	*Hamlet*	Denmark
Measure for Measure	Vienna	*Othello*	Venice
Love's Labour's Lost	Navarre	*All's Well that Ends Well*	Roussillon, Paris, Marseilles, Florence

The countries which Shakespeare avoids are Ireland, Russia, which was barely known, Poland, except for passing references in *Hamlet*, Germany, and England's prime enemy in his day, Spain and the Spanish Netherlands.

As for where exactly these countries lay, Shakespeare, like his contemporaries, was in two minds. Sir John Falstaff wanted to describe himself as 'the most active fellow in Europe'. But Petrucchio, wooing the Shrew, calls her 'The prettiest Kate in Christendom'.[1] 'Christendom' and 'Europe' were still virtually interchangeable.

escaped his mother. He, his son Charles I (r. 1625–49), and his grandson Charles II (r. 1649(60)–85), ruled from Holyrood and from Whitehall in parallel. James I talked to his first Parliament at Westminster of

England and Scotland now in the ... fullness of time united ... in my Person, alike lineally descended of both the Crowns, whereby it has now become like a little World within itself, being fortified round about with a natural, and yet admirable, pond or ditch ...

The integration of the dependent principalities did not proceed so smoothly. Wales, which was shired by Henry VIII, entered the community of English government without demur. The Anglo-Welsh gentry were reasonably content with their lot. But Ireland, whose parliament had virtually broken free of English control since the Wars of the Roses, was only reined in with difficulty. In 1541— after both the Church of England and the counties of Wales had come into being in 1534—Henry VIII declared himself 'King of Ireland'. He was storing up trouble for his successors. The policy of turning Irish chiefs into Earls and Barons was little more than a palliative, especially when Irish customs and language were curtailed. Resentment against the Crown was soon mixed with resentment against the Protestant Reformation, fuelling a series of revolts. The Nine Years' War, 1592–1601, was waged round the Ulster Rising of Hugh O'Neill, Earl of Tyrone. It closed amidst the devastating reprisals of Queen Elizabeth's lieutenant, Lord Mountjoy, who removed the distinction between the Pale and the native lands, abolished Irish law, and started a policy of systematic colonization. A prosperous decade of reconciliation in the 1630s under the Earl of Strafford was to be followed by a further insurrectionary decade in the 1640s, when the Irish profited from England's troubles to introduce religious toleration and an independent parliament. Ireland was brutally conquered by Cromwell in 1649–51, and effectively annexed. (See Appendix III, p. 1279.) [**BLARNEY**]

England's power and prosperity were visibly on the increase, not least through its oceanic adventures. The new colony in Ulster was largely peopled by Scots Presbyterians, seeking the same sort of refuge offered by the English colonies across the Atlantic, in Virginia and New England. The foundation of Maryland (1632) was followed by Jamaica, which was seized from Spain in 1655, the Carolinas (1663), New York, formerly Dutch New Amsterdam (1664), and New Jersey (1665). The Navigation Act of 1651, passed by Cromwell's Rump Parliament in the aftermath of Dutch independence, insisted, among other things, that Dutch ships salute the English flag. It was a sign of England's growing arrogance.

Scotland was the scene of bitter religious and political conflicts which eventually provoked the 'British Civil Wars' of the mid-seventeenth century. Knox's Presbyterian Kirk had been founded on the Genevan model, and was designed by its Calvinist founders as a theocracy. But a resentful court party repeatedly trimmed its aspirations. In 1572, the year of Knox's death, a regent forced the Kirk to accept bishops, thereby causing ceaseless strife between Church and State. In 1610, to safeguard the apostolic succession, James VI had three Scottish bishops consecrated by their English counterparts. In 1618 he imposed his five Articles,

---

BLARNEY

IN 1602 Cormack McCarthy, Lord of Blarney in County Cork, repeatedly delayed the surrender of his castle to the English through an endless series of parleys, promises, queries, and time-wasting speeches. Despite the support of a Spanish landing force, the Irish lords had already been heavily defeated the previous year at nearby Kinsale; and it was only a matter of time before Mountjoy's English army would reduce the whole of Ireland to obedience.[1] But McCarthy's act of defiance gave people a good laugh; and 'Blarney' passed into common parlance as a synonym for 'the miraculous power of speech' or 'the gift of the gab'.[2]

Indeed, since the defeated Irish became famous for their musical and literary skills, Blarney Castle became a symbol of Irishness and of Irish pride. Popularized by the song, 'The Groves of Blarney' (*c.*1798), it became a place of pilgrimage. The castle's foundation-stone, which bears the inscription 'Cormac McCarthy fortis me fieri fecit AD 1446', was taken to possess magical powers; and the perilous ritual of 'kissing the Blarney Stone' under the overhanging battlements is said to reward the pilgrim with the gift of persuasiveness. The interesting thing, historically, is that the language in which the Irish became so proficient and persuasive was not their own.

---

which insisted on a number of practices such as kneeling at communion. At each step he suspended the General Assembly of the Kirk until it submitted, thereby arousing intense popular anger. In 1637 Charles I imposed a modified version of the Anglican liturgy and prayerbook. He did so by personal order, and without reference to a General Assembly, and sparked a rebellion. When the liturgy was first introduced at St Giles's Cathedral in Edinburgh on 23 July, it caused a riot. In due course it led to the formation of 'the Tables', a revolutionary committee of all estates, and in February 1638 to the signing of 'the Covenant'. The covenanters recruited an armed league which was sworn, Polish-style, to defend its statutes to the death. They sought to protect the Presbyterian Kirk from the King and bishops and Scotland from the English. They were soon claiming the allegiance of all true Scotsmen, and set up a parliament without royal warrant. In August 1640 the first of several armies of covenanters crossed the Tweed, and invaded England.

In this way Scotland's religious wars became embroiled with the equally long-running constitutional struggle between King and Parliament in England. Under the Tudors, the partnership between the monarch and the elected representatives of the shires and boroughs did not conceal the fact that England's Parliament was an instrument of royal policy. 'We at no time stand so highly in our estate royal as in the time of Parliament,' declared Henry VIII to a parliamentary delegation, 'wherein we as head and you as members are conjoined and knit together into one body politick.' There were no doubts who was head: parliamentarians had no immunity, and had reason to fear the royal wrath.

The winning of the political initiative by the House of Commons under James I, however, put an end to Parliament's subservience. In the long term, parliamentary control of taxation was to prove decisive. In 1629–40, when Charles I decided to rule without Parliament, no one had the means to oppose him. But in April 1640, when the costs of the Scottish war forced the King to recall the English Parliament and to beg for money, the storm broke. Court talk about the divine right of kings was opposed by parliamentary lawyers quoting Magna Carta. According to the popular dictum of the late Chief Justice, Sir Edward Coke, 'The law of the realm cannot be changed but by parliament'. A Grand Remonstrance (1641) faced the King with a vast catalogue of recriminations. His chief minister, the Earl of Strafford, was impeached by Parliament and, with the King's reluctant consent, sacrificed.

Ireland now entered the equation. Strafford had treated the Presbyterians of Ulster with the same harshness that his predecessors had used towards the Irish Catholics. He had started to raise an Irish army for use against the King's rebellious subjects in England and Scotland; but on quitting Ireland in June 1641 without paying the troops, he left a country in open rebellion. A Scots army arrived in Ireland to support their Protestant co-religionists; and multi-sided warfare proceeded unchecked. Baulked on all sides, Charles I then attempted in good Tudor style to arrest the contumacious members of the English Commons. He failed: 'I see the birds have flown,' he stuttered. There was nothing left for him but to flee London and to call his subjects to arms. Defied by the Parliament which he had not wished to summon, he abandoned the tradition of kings accepting the advice of their councils, and raised his standard at Nottingham. It was the summer of 1642. The conflict was to cost him his life. No satisfactory constitutional equilibrium was reached until 1689.

The 'English Civil War', therefore, is a misnomer which inadequately describes the nature of a very complex conflict. It did not start in England, and was not confined to England. It embraced three separate civil wars in Scotland, Ireland, and England, and involved interrelated developments within all parts of the Stuart realm. The crisis in England in August 1642 cannot be viewed in isolation. The King's edgy conduct towards the Parliament at Westminster was undoubtedly conditioned by his unhappy experiences in Edinburgh. The militancy of English parliamentarians was heightened by their knowledge of the King's despotic policies in Scotland and Ireland, by his proven record of religious impositions, and by the fighting already in progress. Here, above all, was a conflict of political and religious principle. Attempts to explain it in terms of social groups or economic interests, though helpful on some points, have not replaced the older analyses based on a mix of constitutional and religious convictions. Catholics and High Church Anglicans felt the greatest loyalty for the King, whose monarchical prerogatives were under attack. English puritans and Calvinist Scots provided the core support of Parliament, which they saw as a bulwark against absolutism. The gentry was split down the middle.

The English have been taught that their Civil War did not share the religious bigotry and mindless killings of contemporary wars on the Continent. One of the favourite quotations is taken from a letter of the parliamentary major-general, Sir William Waller, which he addressed to the commander of the royalists' western army, Sir Ralph Hopton, on the eve of the battle at Roundway Down in 1643:

My affections to you are so unchangeable that hostility itself cannot violate my friendship to your person, but I must be true to the cause I serve. The great God, who is a searcher of my heart, knows . . . with what perfect hatred I look upon this war without an enemy. We are both upon the stage and we must act the parts assigned to us in this tragedy. Let us do it in a way of honour and without personal animosities.[51]

If such forbearance had prevailed, the wars could never have been sustained.

For there were several key issues on which neither party was prepared to show a margin of tolerance. The 'low-taxation philosophy' of the parliamentarians did not provide the means for the King to govern effectively. Also, the dominant English establishment was only interested in England, and careless of the separate interests of Ireland and Scotland. Above all, in religious matters, both sides were determined to persecute their opponents in the hope of imposing a single religion. The War 'was not fought for religious liberty, but between rival groups of persecutors'.[52] The royalists upheld the Act of Uniformity. The Parliament, in its hour of military triumph, attempted to impose the Presbyterian Covenant. Both found that absolute uniformity could not be enforced.

Nor was the war free of horrors. Well-documented atrocities such as the general massacre at Bolton (June 1644) perpetrated by the troops of Prince Rupert of the Rhine, or the fearful Sack of Drogheda (1649), where Cromwell slaughtered the entire population of an Irish town, were accompanied by the less-publicized practices of killing prisoners and razing villages.

Four years of fighting saw a large number of engagements involving both local and central forces. The royalists, with their headquarters in Christ Church, Oxford, initially held the upper hand in most of the English counties. But the parliamentary forces, aided by the Scots' League of Covenanters, held an impregnable base in London, and hence the organs of central government. In due course they were able to raise a professional New Model Army, whose creator, the formidable Oliver Cromwell (1599–1658), gradually assumed a commanding role in political as well as military affairs. Parliament often controlled the towns and the King the countryside. Neither combatant enjoyed any general advantage, until Parliament slowly reaped the benefits of superior organization, of an invincible general, and of the Scots alliance. After the initial clash at Edge Hill (24 September 1642) north of Oxford, the decisive battles were contested at Marston Moor in Yorkshire (2 July 1644) and at Naseby (14 June 1645). Once the King had surrendered to the Scots at Newark in 1646, all open resistance from the royalists ceased.

As the fighting slowed, the political situation accelerated with revolutionary speed. The parliamentary camp was rapidly radicalized, both in its republicanism and in its association with extreme evangelical sectarians, among them the

Levellers and the Diggers. Unable to pin the King to a firm agreement, Cromwell decided on his execution—which was carried out in front of Whitehall Palace on 31 January 1649, thereby initiating the Commonwealth. Unable to control the Long Parliament, Cromwell purged it. Unable to win over the Irish and the Scots by persuasion, he invaded first Ireland then Scotland. His victory over the Scots at Worcester (1651) left him totally triumphant in the field. Yet he could never engineer a political settlement to match his military triumphs. Unable to carry even the Barebones Parliament of picked supporters, he dissolved it. 'Necessity', he told them, 'hath no law.' Cromwell was left ruling as Lord Protector through the colonels of eleven military districts. The parliamentary cause, having abandoned parliamentary government, was politically bankrupt.

'The Great Oliver' was a man of unparalleled strength of purpose. 'Mr Lely,' he told the portraitist, 'I desire you . . . to paint the picture truly like me, and to remark all these roughnesses, pimples, and warts; otherwise I will never pay you a farthing.' But he devised no lasting solutions, and was apt to attribute everything, even the massacre of Drogheda, to the judgement of God. On his death the royalist cause revived. There was no alternative to a return of the *status quo ante bellum*. Both King and Parliament had to be restored. Charles II returned from exile on 29 May 1660, on the terms of an Act of Indemnity and Oblivion. Both King and Parliament had to relearn the rules of watchful cohabitation.

In some ways the British Civil Wars were symptomatic of strains which surrounded the growth of a modern state in numerous European countries. But they did not inspire any Continental emulators, and must be judged a tragedy of essentially regional significance.

Across the North Sea, the Scandinavian countries were moving in the opposite direction—away from unification. Sweden, in particular, had long fretted against Danish dominance. It had possessed its own *Riksdag* or 'parliament' of four estates since the 1460s, and its own university at Uppsala since 1479. At Christmas in 1520 a revolt broke out in Darlecarlia against the coronation of yet another Danish king. A bloodbath in the city square of Stockholm, where a hundred supporters of the revolt were executed for treason, only fanned the flames. Led by a young nobleman, Gustav Eriksson Vasa, the rebels expelled the Danish army. In 1523 the Union of Kalmar fell apart. Sweden, under Gustavus Vasa (r. 1523–60), went its own way. Denmark and Norway, under Frederick I (r. 1523–33) and his successors, were early recruits to Lutheranism. The resultant rivalry, not least over the disputed province of Halland, remained intense for more than a century.

Sweden's fortunes were tied henceforth to the Vasas, to the search for supremacy in the Baltic, and, with some delay, to the Protestant cause. In 1527, at the Diet of Vasteras, Gustavus created an Erastian Church anticipating that of Henry VIII in England. He abolished the Catholic rite; but by transferring the landed wealth of the Church to his supporters, he created the social base for a powerful monarchy.

His second son, John III (r. 1568–92), married the heiress of the Polish Jagiellons, and his grandson, Sigismund Vasa (r. 1592–1604), was elected King of Poland. Sigismund was seen as the last hope of Sweden's fading Catholic party; and the civil war which flowed from his accession persuaded the majority of the nobles to identify national independence with Protestantism. In 1593 the Synod of Uppsala adopted the Confession of Augsburg for the state religion. Sigismund was deposed in favour of his uncle, Charles IX of Södermanland (r. 1604–11), parent of the Protestant line. Henceforth, in the constant wars with Poland, Sweden added dynastic and religious motives to the conflict of strategic interests in the Baltic.

The young Gustavus Adolphus (r. 1611–32) assumed that attack was the best form of defence. Possessed of immense talent, a secure political base, a navy, and a native army that was to outclass even the Spaniards, he perfected the art of self-financing military expeditions. In 1613 he recovered Kalmar from Denmark; in 1614–17 he intervened in Muscovy's Time of Troubles, coming away with Ingria and Karelia; in 1617–29 he attacked Poland-Lithuania, taking Riga (1621) and besieging Danzig (1626–9). He once escaped capture by Polish hussars by a whisker; but he made so much money milking the Vistula tolls that he could play for still greater stakes. In 1630, with French backing, he made his dramatic entry into Germany. His death in battle at Lützen (see below) cut short a career still full of promise.

Queen Christina (r. 1632–54), who grew up under the regency of Chancellor Oxenstierna, saw Sweden rise to its peak with the conquest of Halland (1645) and the Treaty of Westphalia. But she secretly converted to Catholicism, abdicated, and retired to Rome. Her cousin Charles X (r. 1654–60), worried by the ambitions of Moscow and by the cost of an unemployed army, resorted to the old policy of intervention in Poland-Lithuania. His untimely death gave occasion for the comprehensive settlement at the Treaty of Oliva (1660) (see below).

Sweden never gained complete control of the Baltic, the much-heralded *dominium maris Balticae*. But for half a century she played a disproportionate part in European affairs—the terror of the north, the military wonder of the age, the most active of the Protestant powers.

Poland-Lithuania was another country which experienced its 'Golden Age' during the sixteenth and early seventeenth centuries. The realm of the last Jagiellons was absolutely the largest state in Europe; and it escaped both the religious wars and the Ottoman invasions which beset many of its contemporaries. Under Zygmunt I (r. 1506–48) and Zygmunt-August (r. 1548–72), husband and son of yet another Sforza queen, it enjoyed strong links with Italy, especially with Venice; and Cracow hosted one of the most vibrant of Renaissance courts.

The *Rzeczpospolita*—'Republic' or 'Commonwealth'—which came into being at the Union of Lublin (1569) resulted partly from the lack of a royal heir and partly from the threat of Muscovite expansion. It was an early form of *Ausgleich* between Polish and Lithuanian interests. The *Korona* or Kingdom of Poland accepted the Grand Duchy of Lithuania as an equal partner, though it took over the vast palatinates of Ukraine in compensation. The Grand Duchy retained its own laws, its own administration, and its own army. The dual state was to be governed by a common elective monarchy and by a common *Sejm* or Diet. The ruling *szlachta* who designed this system of noble democracy reserved a dominant role. Through their regional assemblies or *sejmiki* (dietines), which controlled the central Diet, they ran taxation and military affairs. Through the *Pacta Conventa* or 'agreed terms' which they attached to the Coronation Oath, they could hire their kings like managers on contract. Through their legal right of resistance embodied in armed leagues or confederations, they could defend their position against all royal machinations. Through the principle of unanimity, which governed all their deliberations, they ensured that no king or faction could override the common interest. This was not the system of general anarchy which prevailed in the eighteenth century. Whatever its faults, it was a bold experiment in democracy that, in the era of absolutism and religious strife, offered a refreshing alternative. The reputation of the *Rzeczpospolita* among fellow-democrats should not depend on the jaundiced propaganda of its later assassins.

In the eighty years which separated the Union of Lublin from the general crisis of 1648, the *Rzeczpospolita* fared better than its neighbours. Baltic trade brought unaccustomed wealth to many noblemen. The cities, especially Danzig, prospered mightily under their royal charters. The Counter-Reformation, though vigorously pursued, did not cause open strife. The nobles, though they brought government to a halt during the great *rokosz* or 'legal rebellion' of 1606–9, did not usually push the paralysing practices of a later age to extremes. They usually elected kings who were resistant to the bishops and to the ultramontane, pro-Habsburg faction. Foreign wars were fought either on the periphery or on foreign territory.

The monarchy, though run by kings of varying talent, retained its general authority. Admittedly, the first elected king, Henry Valois (r. 1574–5), was an unmitigated disaster; but he fled after four months, to inflict his person on his native France, and was not mourned. The next, the vigorous Transylvanian Stefan Batory (r. 1576–86), reasserted respect and drove the complicated machinery of the state into effective action. His successful war against Ivan the Terrible in 1578–82 brought possession of Livonia. The third king, the Swede Sigismund Vasa (r. 1587–1632), suffered many vicissitudes, but outlived both the *rokosz* and Poland's unsettling intervention in Muscovy in 1610–19. His two sons, Władysław IV (r. 1632–48), the sometime Tsar, and John Casimir (r. 1648–68), the sometime Cardinal, experienced respectively calm and chaos.

The chain reaction of calamities which marked John Casimir's reign erupted from an almost cloudless sky. In 1648–54 the rebellion of the Dnieper Cossacks under Bogdan Chmielnicki (Khmelnytsky), which brought a murderous army of Cossacks and Tartars right up to the Vistula, left a swathe of butchered Catholics and Jews across Ukraine. It linked peasant fury to the very real political, social, and religious grievances of the eastern provinces. It was virtually suppressed by the time a despairing Chmielnicki turned to the Tsar for aid. The Muscovite invasion of 1654–67, which brought death and destruction both to Lithuania and to Ukraine, aroused the strategic anxieties of the Swedes. The double Swedish invasion of 1655–60, which was known in Poland as *Potop* or 'the Deluge', overran both the Kingdom and the Grand Duchy and drove the King into exile and the magnates into treason. Only the monastery of Jasna Góra at Częstochowa, whose Black Madonna deflected Swedish cannon-balls with miraculous ease, was able to resist. The accompanying invasions of the Transylvanians and the Brandenburgers pushed the country close to total collapse. But Poland recovered with marvellous resilience. The Muscovites were halted; the Swedes were rounded up; the Prussians were bought off. In 1658 Hetman Czarnecki could even afford to go campaigning against Sweden in Jutland. The Treaty of Oliva (1660), which settled the demands of the Republic's western neighbours, ended the Vasa feud, confirmed the independence of Ducal Prussia, and promised better times.

Thereafter, the Republic seemed to have been given space to tackle its outstanding problems. In the annual campaigns of the 1660s, the Polish cavalry steadily pushed the Muscovites back towards Russia. Then, with general recovery already in view, the King's programme of constitutional reform aroused a disproportionate and violent reaction from the noble democrats. In 1665–7 the fratricidal strife of Hetman Lubomirski's rebellion put an end to progress on all fronts. It produced political stalemate between the King and his opponents. At the same time it pushed the Republic into the fateful Truce of Andrusovo (1667), which handed Kiev and left-bank Ukraine to the Russians, in theory for twenty years, in practice forever. The King abdicated and retired to France, where he was buried in the church of St Germain-des-Prés. The debased coinage of his reign bore his initials, ICR: Iohannes Casimirus Rex. These were taken to stand for *Initium Calamitatum Reipublicae*, the Beginning of the Republic's Catastrophes.

The beginnings of Poland's distress coincided with the stirrings of power in two of Poland's neighbours—Prussia and Muscovy.

Prussia, which in the early sixteenth century still housed the remains of the Teutonic State, had been wasting away for decades, and stood in desperate need of radical renovation. It had lost its mission for converting the pagans through the conversion of Lithuania, its military supremacy through the defeat at Grunwald (1410), and its commercial prominence through Poland's acquisition of Elbing, Thorn, and Danzig (1466). Its very existence was threatened by the onset of the German Reformation, and it was hurriedly transformed by its last Grand Master, Albrecht von Hohenzollern, into a secular fief of the Kingdom of Poland. A convert to Lutheranism, he dismissed the Teutonic Order, and in 1525 paid homage for his new duchy in the city square of Cracow. From the capital of Königsberg, he laid the strategy which would eventually link his possessions with those of his relatives in Brandenburg. By purchasing the legal reversion of his duchy, he ensured that the failure of his own heirs would automatically give possession to the Hohenzollerns of Berlin. The policy came to fruition in 1618: after that, one and the same Hohenzollern ruler enjoyed the twin titles of Elector of

Brandenburg and Duke of Prussia, and the state of Brandenburg-Prussia was born (see Appendix III, p. 1276).

Frederick-William (r. 1640–88), the Great Elector, who spoke Polish and harboured pretensions of being 'the first prince of Poland', paid homage for his duchy in 1641. Fifteen years later his troops occupied Warsaw, capital of his liege, at the height of the Swedish Deluge. The Prussian army had made its début. All that was needed thereafter was a double diplomatic double-cross which wrested recognition of Prussia's sovereign status first from the Swedes and then from the Poles. It gained formal recognition at Oliva. The Prussian spirit was on the march.

Muscovy, whose strategy of grandeur was launched by Ivan III, held to its course with marvellous tenacity. Ivan IV (r. 1533–84), known as Grozny or 'the Terrible', finalized the patrimonial state which his predecessors had prepared. 'All the people consider themselves to be *kholops*,' wrote one of the earliest Western travellers, 'that is, slaves of their Prince.'[53] By establishing the *oprichnina*—the forerunner of all subsequent Russian security agencies—he was able to set aside whole provinces for his private will and domain, and to unleash a reign of unrestrained terror. By razing Novgorod, and slaughtering almost its entire population in a blood-bath that proceeded for weeks, he affirmed Moscow's supremacy in Russia. By destroying the power of ancient boyar clans and their *zemskii Sobor* or Council he created a thoroughly subservient, hierarchical society. By appointing the first Patriarch of Moscow he completed the separate and dependent nature of the Russian Orthodox Church, henceforth severed from all outside influences. By annexing the khanate of Kazan, where the great Orthodox cathedral of the Annunciation (1562) was raised as a monument to a Christian victory in a Muslim land, he gave notice of unrestrained imperial ambitions. Through the *razryład* or 'service list' and the *pomestnyi prikaz*, the 'bureau of placements', he kept track of all state servants and their appointments: the forerunner of the *nomenklatura*. After such comprehensive socio-political transplants and amputations, it is not surprising that the patient fell sick.

The *Smutnoe Vremya* or 'Time of Troubles' filled the years between the death of Ivan's son Feodor in 1598, and the accession of the Romanovs fifteen years later. With central authority in shreds, the warring boyar factions raised five ill-starred Tsars in succession; there were peasant revolts and Cossack raids; and the country was invaded by Swedes, Poles, and Tartars. Feodor's chief minister, Boris Godunov (r. 1598–1605), a Tartar boyar, was brought down amidst accusations of killing the rightful heir. The False Dmitri I (r. 1605–6), an impostor, claimed to be Ivan's murdered son. Having gained the support of a Polish magnate, Jerzy Mniszek, and of Mniszek's Jesuit friends, he married Mniszek's daughter Marina, and marched on Moscow. His brief, reforming reign came to an explosive end when he was fired from a cannon in Red Square by the followers of the next contestant, Basil Shuiskiy (r. 1605–11). Shuiskiy was in turn overthrown by another impostor, the False Dmitri II, the 'Thief of Tushino', who somehow managed to persuade Marina that he was her resurrected husband. Shuiskiy died in Polish captivity. He was succeeded by the Polish Crown Prince, Władysław Vasa, whose candidature was being pressed by yet another of the boyar factions.

Though many Polish nobles, like Mniszek, had long been privately involved in the Troubles, the official policy of the *Rzeczpospolita* was to stand aloof. The King had declined to back Mniszek's plan—despite Russian rumours to the contrary; and the Diet had warned the King against committing any money or forces beyond the limited objective of recapturing Smolensk. Hence, when the Polish army advanced on Smolensk in 1610, alongside the Swedes already in Novgorod, it had no orders to go further. However, as their commander later explained to an angry Sejm, the Poles pressed on despite instructions. With the Russian army defeated at Klushino and the road to Moscow undefended, they occupied the Kremlin unopposed. A garrison remained for a year until forced to surrender. It set Moscow ablaze before being murdered by a patriotic Russian populace rallying to Minin the butcher, Pozharskiy the prince, and Michael Romanov (r. 1613–45), the new Tsar. The Russians had found their dynasty, and their national identity. It was a ready-made subject for opera. [SUSANIN]

Moscow's recovery was slow but methodical. The Poles were seen off by 1619; Prince Władysław resigned his claim; Smolensk was recovered (1654). Under Alexei Mikhailovitch (r. 1645–76), fundamental reforms caused internal turmoil that was only partly offset by territorial acquisitions. A reform of the law, which led to the *Ulozhenie* or Legal Code of 1649 containing over 1,000 articles, perpetuated and systematized serfdom, creating conditions that underlay the vast peasant rising of Sten'ka Razin. The Church reforms of Patriarch Nikon (1605–81), who aimed both to modernize the rite and to moderate state control, provoked both the defection of the Old Believers and the ire of the Tsar. Military reforms on Western lines preceded the none too successful campaigns against Poland. In this light, the great territorial gains of the Truce of Andrusovo (1667) came as an unexpected bonus (see Appendix III, p. 1277).

Yet the acquisition of Ukraine from Poland cannot be overestimated. It gave Muscovy the economic resources and the geopolitical stance to become a great power. What is more, it came in the same generation that pushed the exploration and conquest of Siberia to the Pacific. The formula Muscovy + Ukraine = Russia does not feature in the Russians' own version of their history; but it is fundamental. In which case the true founder of the Russian Empire was Alexei Mikhailovitch, not his more celebrated son Peter. [TEREM]

The lengthy contest between Russia, Poland, and Sweden was deciding the fate of Eastern Europe. In retrospect, one can see that the Truce of Andrusovo of 1667 tipped the balance of power. Poland-Lithuania was being imperceptibly replaced by Russia as the dominant state of the region. Poland and Russia, however, had one thing in common. Neither allowed itself to be dragged into the Thirty Years War.

The Ottoman Empire, the southern neighbour of Poland and Russia, reached its apogee at the same time as the Habsburgs. From the Muslim perspective, the key

TEREM

SOPHIA ALEXEYEVNA, the sixth child of Tsar Alexei Mikhailovitch, was born in the Moscow Kremlin on 17 September 1657. As a junior princess in a country that had never recognized female succession, her prospects for attaining political power were almost nil.

In Muscovy, high-born ladies were kept in strict seclusion.[1] They lived in separate female quarters, the *Terem*, in Muslim fashion, and only sallied forth either veiled or in closed carriages. A special Terem Palace had been added to the Kremlin in the 1630s to accommodate the ladies. What is more, the sisters and daughters of the Tsars were usually condemned to celibacy. As an official explained, they could not be married to noblemen, since it was a disgrace 'to give a lady to a slave'. And they could not be easily married to foreign princes for fear of contaminating the court with heresy or faction. 'The female sex is not venerated among the Muscovites', reported an Austrian envoy, 'as amongst the majority of the nations of Europe. In this country, they are the slaves of men, who esteem them little.'[2]

None the less, in association with the leading minister, Prince Golitsyn, Sophia came to exercise influence during the reign of her brother Feodor (1676–82). Then, having mediated in a military rebellion, she broke the bounds of the Terem completely, becoming Regent during the minority of the co-Tsars Ivan and Peter, and the first woman ruler of Russia. She personally presided over foreign policy, in particular over the 'Eternal Peace' with Poland, which put Moscow at the head of East European affairs (see p. 657).

Sophia's reputation was blackened by supporters of Peter the Great, who terminated her regency in 1689. Dismissed as an ambitious schemer, she has often been described in the words of a dubious quotation as being 'of monstrous size, with a head as big as a bushel, with hair on her face and growths on her legs'.[3] She lived her last fourteen years as Sister Susanna in the Novodevichy Convent—a foundation which she had earlier endowed in the style of the 'Moscow Baroque'.

Female biography is often inspired by a wish to compensate for the overblown record of male achievers. It is the oldest form of herstoriography, and has been successfully applied to a large number of heroines from Sappho and Boudicca to Eleanor of Aquitaine and Elizabeth of England. But in one sense it can be misleading. The lives of exceptional women cannot fail to emphasize the gulf which separated them from the average woman's lot. Sophia Alexeyevna was a ruler who proved the exception.

development lay in the Ottomans' decision to lead the main Sunni branch of Islam against the Shi'ites. When Sultan Selim I (r. 1512–20) moved against Persia, he ended the sixty-year pause which followed the Fall of Constantinople. Thereafter, the conquest of the former caliphates of Damascus, Cairo, and Baghdad (1534) took place in succession. Suleiman I 'the Magnificent' (r. 1520–66), who added the Prophet's tomb in Mecca to the realm, had good reason to style himself *Padishah-i-Islam*, 'Emperor of Islam'. Many monuments, including the Süleymaniye Mosque in Istanbul, attest to the reality of that magnificence.

From the Christian viewpoint, danger signals began to flash when the Turks used their new-found strength to move westwards. They advanced both up the Danube valley into Hungary, and against the corsair states of the North African coast. The Danubian campaigns began in 1512 with the takeover of Moldavia. Then, when Belgrade was captured (1521), the wide Hungarian plain lay open to the Ottoman advance. After 1526, when the last independent King of Bohemia and Hungary, Louis II Jagiellon, was killed at the Battle of Mohács, Austria itself came under threat. The Turks laid their first unsuccessful Siege of Vienna in 1529, and three years later were still raiding deep into the alpine valleys. The truce of 1533 was only obtained at the price of the partition of Hungary. Western Hungary was left to its new Habsburg rulers; central Hungary, including Budapest, became an Ottoman province; Transylvania became a separate principality subject to Ottoman tutelage. Skirmishing raged all along the new borders until the Peace of Adrianople (1568), when the Habsburgs undertook to pay annual tribute. In 1620–1 the Turks moved up the Dniester beyond Moldavia, only to feel the weight of the Polish hussars at Chocim. [**USKOK**]

In the Mediterranean, renewed Ottoman expansion was signalled by the attack on Rhodes and the capitulation of the Knights Hospitallers (1522). Algiers was captured in 1529, Tripoli in 1551, Cyprus in 1571, Tunis at the second attempt in 1574. Malta survived a grand siege (1565). In the view of the Catholic world, the centrepiece was provided by the naval battle of Lepanto (1571), where Don John of Austria, natural brother of Philip II, succeeded in uniting the combined naval forces of Venice, Genoa, and Spain, and destroying the Ottoman fleet. Here was the last crusade, the last battle of massed galleys, the last significant Ottoman move for many decades. [**GRECO**]

The Ottoman surge had several consequences. First, it revived the old crusading spirit, especially in the Catholic countries. The question posed by Erasmus— 'Is not the Turk also a man and a brother?'—reflected an eccentric response to contemporary passions. Secondly, it helped preserve the division of Christendom by diverting major Catholic forces at the height of the Protestant Reformation. The Sultan was Luther's best ally. Thirdly, on the diplomatic front, it made the Western powers think more closely about Eastern Europe, and to open the first tentative contacts with the East. It underlay France's openings to the Porte and to Poland-Lithuania, and the Empire's missions to Moscow. Lastly, it started a craze for Turkish styles and artefacts—Europe's first experience of 'Orientalism'.

USKOK

IN 1615–17 the Republic of Venice fought an 'Uskok War' in the Adriatic against the Habsburgs. The object, as Venice saw it, was to suppress Habsburg-sponsored piracy. As the Habsburgs saw it, the *uskoki* or 'Corsairs of Senj', were a necessary part of the Empire's defences, and the Venetians were undermining their security.[1]

Senj, now in Croatia, was an Adriatic port situated near the point where Venetian, Habsburg, and Ottoman territory met. Its castle was the coastal anchor of the Habsburgs' *Militärgrenze* or *vojna krajina*, the 'Military Frontier', which had been established in the 1520s and consolidated along its length with fortified settlements. Its harbour provided a base for the pirate-patriots, who lived partly from fishing, but mainly from plundering Venetian ships on the sea and Ottoman towns in the interior.

These *Uskoks*—whose name derives from the Croatian word *uskočiti*, 'to jump in' or 'to board'—lived by a code of honour and vengeance. They were the maritime counterparts of the martial frontiersmen or *grenzer*, many of them refugee Serbs and fugitive serfs, who guarded the length of the inland border and who one day would rise against Croatian rule. Like their brothers on the Ottoman frontier in Poland and Hungary, or the Cossacks of Ukraine, they saw themselves as champions of the faith, defenders of the *antemurale christianitatis*, heroes of the holy war. They were celebrated as such in the epic legends of South Slav literature. Their activities were encouraged and rewarded by the Habsburgs until the middle of the 18th century. The Krajina was not officially abolished until 1881.

Piracy, like banditry, is a relative concept. Early modern Europe was full of *klephts*, *hajduks*, 'corsairs' or 'sea-raiders', whose operations might be approved by one authority whilst being judged illegal by others.

The seadogs of England and France were a case in point. When Francis Drake (1545–95) sailed out of Plymouth to plunder the Spanish Main or to 'singe the King of Spain's beard' at Cadiz, he did so under licence from the English Queen, and was knighted for his services. But when others behaved likewise, they were denounced in England as savages. For a time in the early 17th century, for example, Moslem corsairs from the Barbary Coast set up base on Lundy Island, raiding the ports of Devon and Cornwall and selling their captives into slavery. When Jean Bart of Dunkirk (1650–1702) terrorized shipping in the Channel and the Bay of Biscay under licence from Louis XIV, he was received at Versailles and ennobled. In the eyes of their compatriots, Drake or Bart were 'admirals'. In Spanish eyes, they were international criminals. One man's 'rover' was the next man's 'robber'.

GRECO

TWO prominent Cretan artists were known to their contemporaries as *El*, or *Il, Greco*—'the Greek'. One was the painter Dominikos Theotokopoulos, who settled in Toledo. The other was the musician and composer Frangiskos Leondaritis (*c*.1518–72), sometime Catholic organist at Kastro, cantor at St Mark's Venice, and music master to the Duke of Bavaria. Both were products of the Cretan Renaissance.

Crete, ruled by Venice from 1221 to 1669, was the crossroads of Greek and Latin culture. Its capital had been founded and fortified as 'El Khandak' during the previous Arab occupation of 827–961; but as Candia or Chandax it became the seat of a Venetian Duke. Candia's town square was flanked by a ducal palace, by a cathedral of St Mark with *campanile*, and by a loggia that was the favourite meeting-place of the island's Veneto-Cretan lords. From 1648 to the final capitulation of 16 September 1669, it was the nerve-centre of Duke Morosini's 21-year resistance to the Ottoman siege.

After the fall of Constantinople, Crete had welcomed numerous Byzantine scholars on their way to Italy. It thereby made a contribution to the Greek Revival which formed such an important stimulus to the Renaissance in the West. Its main contribution to the Greek-speaking world, however, lay in influences moving in the opposite direction. A substantial Cretan colony in Venice, centred on the Church of San Giorgio, had long played a prominent part in the history of Greek printing and publishing. A Venetian from Crete, Zacharias Kalliergis, a rival to the Aldine Press of Marucci, produced the first book in demotic Greek in 1509. Yet in the last century of Venetian rule Crete itself witnessed a sunburst of creativity that was to leave its mark far beyond the island's shores. The focus, in addition to painting, music, and architecture, was on vernacular Greek literature. A school of dramatists using the Cretan dialect composed a corpus of works in rhyming couplets that covered a wide range of religious, comic, tragic, and pastoral subjects. The *Erofili* of Georgios Chortasis (1545–1610) is a tragedy set in Egypt. The *Erotokritos* of Vitsentsos Kornaros (*c*.1553–1614) is a romance in the style of Ariosto. The *Cretan War* of Marinos Bounialis is an epic history recounting the events of the Ottoman siege:

> Ω Κάστρο μου περίδοξο, τάχατες όσοι ζούνε,
> τάχατες να σε κλαίσινε και να σ' αναζητούνε;
> Έπρεπε όλ' οι Καστρινοί μαύρα για να βαστούσι,
> να κλαίγουνε καθημερνό κι όχι να τραγουδούσι·
> άντρες, γυναίκες και παιδιά και πάσα κορασίδα,
> να δείχνου πως εχάσανε τέτοιας λογής πατρίδα.

(S. Alexiou 1969a: 229)

(O my glorious Kastro, do they who still live / weep for you and ask after you? / All the people of Kastro should put on black / and weep day after day, and sing no more; / men, women and children and every maiden / should let it be seen what a fatherland they have lost.)[1]

The theatres and academies of Candia, Kastro, and Rhethymno came to a sudden end in 1669. So too did that last fruitful symbiosis of Veneto-Cretan culture, which for a brief moment had reached the status of 'an independent, innovative force'. But Cretan exiles took their literature with them to the mainland, where it soon established itself as popular reading. Though despised by the Athenian élite, eighteenth-century book catalogues show that it enjoyed wide circulation. Indeed, prior to the work of Dionysius Solomos (1798–1857) and the Ionian School, the Cretan dramas formed the sole substantial demotic repertoire. It was the Cretan Renaissance which gave the Greeks their start as a modern, literate nation.[2]

The Thirty Years War (1618–48) may be seen as an episode in the age-old German conflict between Emperor and princes. At another level, it may be seen as an extension of the international wars of religion between Catholic and Protestant; at yet another, as an important stage in a Continental power-struggle involving most of the states and rulers of Europe. It grew from a row in Bohemia between the supporters and opponents of Archduke Ferdinand, and it mushroomed in four distinct phases. 'Almost all [the combatants]', wrote one of its most distinguished historians, 'were actuated by fear rather than by lust of conquest or passion of faith. They wanted peace and they fought for thirty years to be sure of it. They did not learn then, and have not learned since, that war only breeds war.'[54]

The Bohemian phase, 1618–23, began on 23 May 1618, when a delegation of Czech nobles entered the Hradčany Castle in Prague and threw the Habsburg governors, Jaroslav von Martinitz and Wilhelm von Salvata, out of a high window and into a dungheap (which broke their fall). They were protesting against recent attacks on Protestant churches, against Archduke Ferdinand's contested assumption of the Bohemian throne, and against his alleged violations of the Royal Charter of Toleration, the *Majestätsbrief* of 1609. (This defenestration of Prague was a deliberate imitation of the incident that had sparked off the Hussite War 200 years earlier.) At the time, Ferdinand was campaigning for the imperial election, and the religious peace in Germany was wavering. The Lutheran princes were watching uneasily as the Evangelical Union led by Frederick, Elector Palatine, measured up to the Catholic League led by Maximilian, Elector of Bavaria. The Bohemian rebels raided Vienna and started a revolt in Austria. In 1619, when Ferdinand succeeded to the Empire, they formally deposed him as King of Bohemia, choosing the Calvinist Elector Palatine in his place. This meant open war (see Appendix III, p. 1280).

At the great Battle of Bíláhora (Weissenberg, or the White Mountain) near Prague on 7 November 1620, the Bohemian army was crushed by the imperialists. Then, in a terrible revenge, Bohemia's native nobility was suppressed, by execution or confiscation. Czech society was literally decapitated. The country was systematically catholicized and germanized. The Calvinists were expelled. The 'Winter King' fled. His lands in the Palatinate were invaded from the Spanish Netherlands and seized by the Bavarians. The Catholics' general, Count Tilly (1559–1632), victor of Prague, stormed Heidelberg (1622) and criss-crossed northern Germany in pursuit of the Protestant forces headed by Count von Mansfeld (1580–1626). The unprovisioned armies began to live off the land like so many hordes of locusts.

The Danish phase, 1625–9, began when Christian IV of Denmark, Superior of the Imperial Circle of Lower Saxony, entered the fray in defence of his hard-pressed Protestant confrères. Assisted by English, French, and Dutch subsidies, he had to contend with a new imperialist army raised by a Catholic nobleman from Bohemia, Albrecht von Waldstein or 'Wallenstein' (1583–1634). After defeat at the Bridge of Dessau on the Elbe (1626), the Protestant forces attempted to link up with their Transylvanian ally, Bethlen Gábor. Mansfeld marched all the way to the Danube, via Silesia. Then it was the turn of the imperialists, after dealing with Mansfeld at Neuhausel (near Bratislava), to move in strength against the Protestant north. Tilly attacked the Netherlands with the help of the Spaniards. Wallenstein overran Brunswick, Lower Saxony, Mecklenburg, Schleswig, Holstein, Jutland, and the Baltic coast to the outskirts of Stralsund, declaring himself 'Generalissimo of the Baltic and the Ocean Seas'. By the Treaty of Lübeck (1629) the Danes were persuaded to retire on the return of their lost possessions. By the Edict of Restitution the Emperor ordered the Protestants to surrender all the former ecclesiastical lands acquired since the Peace of Augsburg. Wallenstein, whose army contained many non-Catholics, objected and was dismissed.

The Swedish phase, 1630–35, began when Gustavus Adolphus sent a contingent to hold Stralsund. In 1631, fortified by the Treaty of Bärwalde with France, he landed with the main Swedish army and proceeded to restore Protestant fortunes with vigour. In 1631 he failed to relieve Magdeburg before it was mercilessly sacked by the imperialists; but at Breitenfeld he crushed Tilly and moved into the Palatinate. He was joined by John George, Elector of Saxony, a Lutheran who previously had backed the Emperor. In 1632 he entered Bavaria. Munich and Nuremberg opened their gates. With the Swedes preparing to march on Vienna, and the Saxons in Prague, a desperate Emperor was forced to recall Wallenstein. At the furious Battle of Lützen near Leipzig (16 November 1632), the Swedes prevailed. But Gustavus fell; his naked body was discovered under a heap of dead, a bullet hole through his head, a dagger thrust in his side, another bullet, ominously, in his back. The Protestant cause faltered until revived once more by the League of Heilbronn. In 1634 Wallenstein opened negotiations, only to be placed for his pains under the ban of the Empire, and assassinated. After the imperial success at Nordlingen, an ailing Emperor made peace with the Lutheran princes at Prague. The Edict of Restitution was suspended.

One day in 1631, the Bavarian town of Rothenburg-ob-der-Tauber was invested by the imperial army. According to tradition, General Tilly ordered that the town be put to the sack unless one of the citizens could drink up an enormous flagon of wine. Whereon the *Bürgermeister*, Heinrich Toppler, drained the flagon, saved the town, and fell down dead. His feat is commemorated in a play, *Der Meistertrunk*, which is performed to this day every Whit Monday in the Kaisersaal of the Rathaus.

The experience of one village must stand as an example of thousands of others. In January 1634 twenty Swedish soldiers rode into Linden in Franconia, demanding food and wine. They broke into one of the thirteen cottages, belonging to Georg Rosch, raped his wife, and took what they wanted. Shortly afterwards, they were ambushed by the villagers, stripped of their clothes, loot and horses. The next day, they returned with a constable, who arrested four men for assaulting the Swedes. He then made a report to General Horn, naming one of the soldiers, a Finn, as Frau Rosch's rapist. What happened next is not clear; but shortly after the village was registered as uninhabited. Its inhabitants did not return to their pre-war number until 1690.[55] [**HEXEN**]

The French phase, 1635–48, began when France became the protector of the League of Heilbronn, whose remaining Calvinist members had been excluded from the Peace of Prague. Richelieu's strategy now came into the open. France declared war on Spain, took the Swedes into its pay, and invaded Alsace. The war developed on three fronts, in the Netherlands, on the Rhine, and in Saxony. In 1636 the Spaniards advanced towards Paris, but pulled back when threatened from the flank. In 1637 the Emperor Ferdinand died, raising hopes for an eventual peace. From 1638, when Richelieu's German allies presented him with the great fortress of Breisach on the Rhine, French fortunes were mounting. The arrival of the youthful Duc d'Enghien, Prince de Condé (1621–86), gave them the finest general in Europe. His stunning victory at Rocroi in the Ardennes (1643) ended the Spanish military supremacy which had lasted since Pavia in 1525. From 1644 the diplomats were hard at work, shuttling between the Protestant delegates at Osnabrück and the Catholic delegates at Münster. Whilst they argued, the French and the Swedes ravaged Bavaria.

The Treaty of Westphalia, which was arranged simultaneously in its two parts, set the ground plan of the international order in central Europe for the next century and more. It registered both the ascendancy of France and the subordination of the Habsburgs to the German princes. On the religious issue, it ended the strife in Germany by granting the same rights to the Calvinists as to Catholics and Lutherans. It fixed 1624 as the date for ecclesiastical restitution; and it made provision for denominational changes except in the Upper Palatinate and in the hereditary lands of the House of Austria, which were reserved for the Catholic faith. On the constitutional issue, it greatly strengthened the Princes by granting them the right to sign foreign treaties and by making all imperial legislation conditional on the Diet's approval. It proposed that both Bavaria and the Palatinate be made electorates. On the numerous territorial issues, it attempted to give

HEXEN

IN 1635 Dr Benedikt Carpzov (1595–1666), professor at Leipzig and son and brother of Saxony's most celebrated jurists, published his *Practica rerum criminalium* on the conduct of witch trials. Whilst admitting that torture exacted many false confessions, he advocated its use. 'He would live to a ripe old age, and look back on a meritorious life in which he had read the Bible fifty-three times, taken the sacrament every week . . . and procured the death of 20,000 persons.'[1] He was a Protestant, and Europe's leading witch-hunter. Nowadays, historians challenge the numbers.

A few years earlier Johann Julius, burgomaster of Bamberg in Franconia, lay in the town dungeon, condemned to death for attending a witches' sabbath. He had been denounced by the Chancellor of the principality, who had already been burned for showing 'suspicious leniency' in witch trials. But he managed to smuggle out a detailed account of the proceedings to his daughter. 'My dearest child . . . it is all falsehood and invention, so help me God . . . They never cease to torture until one says something . . . If God sends no means of bringing the truth to light, our whole kindred will be burnt.'[2] The Catholic Prince-Bishop of Bamberg, Johan Georg II Fuchs von Dornheim, possessed a purpose-built witch-house, complete with torture-chamber adorned with biblical texts. In his ten-year reign (1623–33) he is said to have burned 600 witches.

The European witch craze had reached one of its periodic peaks. In England, the Pendle Witches of Lancashire were brought to justice in 1612. In Poland, the record of a trial at Kalisz detailed the procedures in the self-same year:

Naked, shaved above and below, anointed with holy oil, suspended from the ceiling lest by touching the ground she summon the Devil to her aid, and bound hand and foot, 'she was willing to say nothing except that she sometimes bathed sick people with herbs. Racked, she said she was innocent, God knows. Burned with candles, she said nothing, only that she was innocent. Lowered, she said that she was innocent to Almighty God in the Trinity. Repositioned, and again burned with candles, she said Ach! Ach! Ach! For God's sake, she did go with Dorota and the miller's wife . . . Thereafter the confessions agreed.'[3]

In the countryside, villagers often took matters into their own hands. If a suspected witch drowned when submerged in a pond on the 'ducking-stool', she was obviously innocent. If she floated, she was guilty.

Many learned treatises were written on the black arts of witchcraft. They included Jean Bodin's *De la démonomanie des sorciers* (1580), the *Daemonolatreia* (1595) of Nicholas Rémy in Lorraine, the massive encyclopaedia of Martin del Rio SJ published at Louvain in 1600, and King James's *Demonologie* (1597) in Scotland. They discussed the mechanics of night-flying on broomsticks, the nature and effect of spells and curses, the menu of witches' cauldrons, and, above all, the sexual orgies organized at witches' sabbaths. The Devil was said to appear either as a bearded black man, or as a 'stinking goat', who liked to be kissed under the tail, or as a toad. He could be an incubus for the benefit of she-witches, or a succubus for the benefit of he-witches. He sometimes summoned his faithful fifth column to crowded general assemblies in notorious locations such as the Blåkulla Meadow in Sweden, the summit of the Blocksberg in the Harz, or to the Aquelarre at La Hendaye in Navarre.

The witch craze poses many problems. Historians have to explain why the age of the Renaissance and the Reformation proved so much more vicious in this regard than the so-called Dark Ages, why superstition came to a head when humanism and the scientific revolution were supposedly working in the opposite direction. They usually attribute it to the pathological effects of religious conflict. They must also explain why certain countries and regions, notably Germany and the Alps, were specially susceptible, and why the most ardent witch-hunters, such as King James VI and I, were among the most learned and, at the conscious level, the most Christian men of their day. And there is an important comparative aspect: the collective hysteria and false denunciations of witch-hunting have much in common with the phenomena of Jew-baiting and of the Communist purges. [**DEVIATIO**] [**HARVEST**] [**POGROM**]

From the papal bull of 1484 to its decline in the eighteenth century, the craze persisted intermittently for 300 years, consuming vast numbers of innocents. Signs of critical protest first emerged among the Jesuits of Bavaria, where persecutions had been especially fanatical, notably with Friedrich Spee's *Cautio criminalis* (1631). Europe's last witch-burnings took place in Scotland in 1722, in Switzerland and Spain in 1782, and in Prussian-occupied Poznań in 1793. By that time, they were all illegal. The last of the Lancashire Witches, Mary Nutter, died naturally in 1828.

something to all the leading claimants. Switzerland and the United Provinces received their independence. The Dutch succeeded in their demand that the Scheldt be closed to traffic. France received a lion's share—sovereignty over Metz, Toul, and Verdun; Pinerolo; the Sundgau in southern Alsace; Breisach; garrison rights in Philippsburg; the *Landvogtei* or 'Advocacy' of ten further Alsatian cities. Sweden received Bremen and Verden, and western Pomerania including Stettin. Bavaria took the Upper Palatinate; Saxony took Lusatia; Brandenburg took the greater part of eastern Pomerania up to the Polish frontier, the former bishoprics of Halberstadt, Minden, and Kammin, and the 'candidacy' of Magdeburg. Mecklenburg-Schwerin, Brunswick-Lüneburg, and Hesse-Cassel were each thrown a morsel. The final signatures were penned on 24 October 1648.

The end came slowly. In Prague, where the war had begun, they were still fighting. Monks, students, and townsmen were manning the Charles Bridge against an
expected Swedish assault. But then, with nine days' delay, news of the Peace
arrived. 'The clanging of church bells drowned the last thunders of the cannon'.[56]
But the troops did not go home. A second congress had to be held at Nuremburg
in 1650 to settle the indemnities claimed by the armies. The Spaniards kept their
garrison at Frankenthal in the Palatinate until 1653, when the Emperor offered
them Besançon in exchange. The last Swedish soldiers did not depart until 1654.
Delegates at Westphalia had already started calling it 'the Thirty Years War'. In
fact, since the first act of violence at Donauworth, it had taken up forty-seven
years.

The Pope, Innocent X, was outraged. A lifelong foe of Cardinal Mazarin, who
had attempted to veto his election, he was offended by the concessions made to
France and to the Protestants; and he ordered the nuncio at Münster to denounce
the settlement. In his brief *Zelus domus Dei* (1650), he described the Treaty as
'null, void, invalid, iniquitous, unjust, damnable, reprobate, inane, and devoid of
meaning for all time'. Behind his anger lay the realization that hopes for a united
Christendom had been dashed for ever. After Westphalia, people who could no
longer bear to talk of 'Christendom' began to talk instead of 'Europe'.

Germany lay desolate. The population had fallen from 21 million to perhaps 13
million. Between a third and a half of the people were dead. Whole cities, like
Magdeburg, stood in ruins. Whole districts lay stripped of their inhabitants, their
livestock, their supplies. Trade had virtually ceased. A whole generation of pillage,
famine, disease, and social disruption had wreaked such havoc that in the end the
princes were forced to reinstate serfdom, to curtail municipal liberties, and to
nullify the progress of a century. The manly exploits of Spanish, Swedish, Italian,
Croat, Flemish, and French soldiers had changed the racial composition of the
people. German culture was so traumatized that art and literature passed entirely
under the spell of foreign, especially French, fashions.

Germany's strategic position was greatly weakened. The French now held the
middle Rhine. The mouths of Germany's three great rivers—Rhine, Elbe, and
Oder—were held respectively by the Dutch, the Danes, and the Swedes. The common interest of the Empire was subject to the separate interests of the larger
German states: Austria, Bavaria, Saxony, and Brandenburg-Prussia. Destitution
was accompanied by humiliation. Some historians have seen it as the soil of despair which alone can have fed the seeds of virulent German pride that sprouted
from the recovery of a later age. Austria, which had begun the period as the
wonder of the age, was reduced to being just one German state among many.

In the years after 1648, however, Germany was not alone in its misery. Spain was
struggling with the revolts of Portugal and Catalonia, whilst still at war with
France. England was in the after-shock of Civil War. France was rocked by the
Fronde. Poland-Lithuania was torn apart by the Cossack revolt, the Swedish
'Deluge', and the Russian wars. This concatenation of catastrophes has led to the

supposition of a general 'seventeenth-century crisis'. Those who believe in the existence of an all-European feudal system tend to argue in favour of an all-European socio-political revolution caused by the growing pains of all-European capitalism. Some argue in contrast in favour of 'a crisis of the modern state', where the peripheries reacted violently against the rising demands of the centre. Others suspect that it may all have been a coincidence.

Rome, 19 February 1667. Gianlorenzo Bernini (1598–1680), the papal architect, submitted his designs for the third and last section of the great colonnade that was nearing completion round the square of St Peter's. He proposed that this *terzo braccio* or third arm of the colonnade should take the form of a detached *propylaeum* or 'gateway' with nine bays surmounted by a clock-tower. It was to be positioned at the entrance to the square directly opposite the centrepoint of St Peter's façade (see Map 17, p. 570).

In the *giustificazione* or 'argument of proposal' which accompanied the original plans a dozen years before, Bernini had explained the design and symbolism of St Peter's Square. The Square was to provide an approachway to the church, a meeting-place for crowds receiving the papal benedictions, and a boundary to the holy space. The colonnade was to be permeable, with more gaps than columns, thereby facilitating the circulation of pedestrians and avoiding the sense of a physical barrier. It was to be covered by a continuous pediment, giving protection to processions in inclement weather; and it was to be graced above the pediment by a ring of statues, illustrating the communion of saints. Its two semicircular arms, which were projected beyond the straight sides of the immediate cathedral forecourt, were specifically likened by Bernini to 'the enfolding arms of Mother Church', offering comfort to all humanity. The proposed propylaeum was to have taken the place of hands clasped in prayer, joining the extremities of the Church's outstretched arms.

As it happened, the cardinals of the *Congregazione della Reverenda Fabbrica*, who managed the building works, had other ideas. They authorized the construction of the Piazza's pavement and of a second fountain, but not the propylaeum. Shortly afterwards Bernini's ailing papal patron died; and no decision was ever made about the *terzo braccio*. The enclosure of 'the amphitheatre of the Christian universe' was left incomplete.[57]

As the size of the church demanded, the dimensions of the Square were grandiose. Its total length, from the main portico to the western entrance, was 339 m (370 yds): the maximum width 220 m (240 yds). It could accommodate a crowd of 100,000 with no difficulty. The shapes of its connected areas, though complex, were brilliantly harmonious. The tapered quadrilaterals in front of the façade opened out into an ellipse between the arms of the colonnade. In all, the colonnade contained 284 Doric columns and 88 rhomboid pilasters arranged in quadruple rows. Its Ionic entablature carried 96 statues, with a further 44 above the galleries of the forecourt. The Obelisk of Heliopolis, 41 m (135 ft) high,

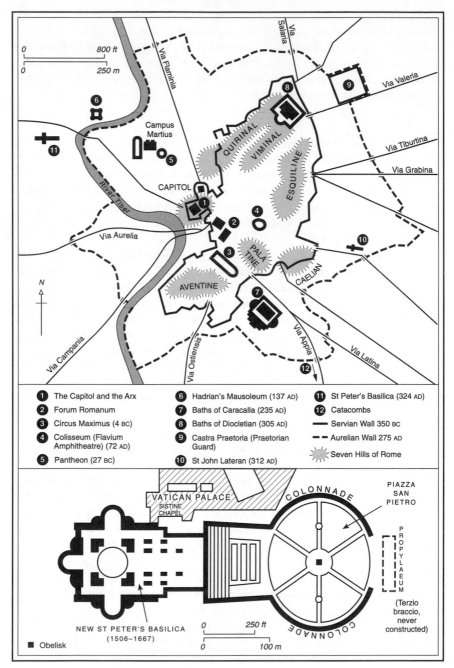

Map 17.
Rome, Ancient and Modern

erected in 1586, was left at the focal point of the ellipse. It was flanked on either side by a circular fountain, one by Maderna (1614), the other added by Bernini in 1667.

The building of Bernini's colonnade terminated a programme of reconstruction that had been in progress at St Peter's for 161 years. It concluded works which had spanned the whole of the Counter-Reformation. Though a start was made in 1506, the greater part of the grand plan drawn up by Bramante, the basilica's first architect, had remained on paper throughout the sixteenth century. Michelangelo's dome was completed in 1590. Even then, there was no nave; and the remnant of Constantine's fourth-century basilica still blocked the old piazza. Not until 1605 was Carlo Maderno authorized to demolish the old basilica, and to erect the new portico and façade in time for a grand opening on Palm Sunday 1615. The young Bernini added two lofty *campanili* or bell-towers to Maderno's façade in the 1620s, only to see them pulled down twenty years later. Nominated as chief architect in 1628, he was not awarded the remaining 'great commissions' until 1655. The *Scala Regia*—the chief staircase to the Vatican Palace—the Throne of St Peter, and the new Piazza with its colonnade, occupied Bernini for the next dozen years.[58]

The Rome of Bernini's lifetime was a hive of intrigue and activity where the art and politics of the Church combined with the ambitions of the great aristocratic clans, the bustling prosperity of traders and artisans, and the grinding misery of the plebs. Bernini would have heard of the burning of Giordano Bruno, and was present during the trials of Galileo. He would have watched the ruin of the Papal States, and the impotence of the popes to intervene in the religious wars. He would have seen the Tiber in flood—which inspired one of his most spectacular tableaux—the visitations of the plague, and the citizens' laments against ever-rising taxes:

> Han' fatto piu danno
> Urbano e nepoti
> Che Vandali e Gothi,
> A Roma mia bella.
> O Papa Gabella!

(This Pope of the Salt Tax, Urban and his 'nephews', have done more harm to my beautiful Rome than the Vandals and the Goths.)[59]

It was a mystery how the Church could support such splendour amidst so much hardship.

At 68, Bernini was at the height of his protean powers, and still had a decade of creativity before him. He was the son of an engineer-architect in the papal service, Pietro Bernino, who among many other things had designed the 'ship fountain' in the Piazza di Spagna. From the day he came to Rome with his father at the age of eight, he had daily contact with the city's monuments, and enjoyed intimate familiarity with cardinals and wealthy patrons. He was personally acquainted with eight popes, from the Borghese, Paul V (1605–21) to the Odaleschi, Innocent XI (1676–89). Paul V told Bernini's father: 'We hope that this boy will become the

Michelangelo of his century.' Urban VIII (1623–44) told him: 'It is your good fortune, Cavaliere, to see that Cardinal Matteo Barberini is now Pope. But our fortune is far greater to see that Cavaliere Bernini lives during our pontificate.' Alexander VII (1655–67) summoned him to the Vatican and commissioned the final works at St Peter's on the very first evening of his reign.

Bernini was well capable of returning the compliments. Pleased by Louis XIV's ability to stand still during modelling, he said: 'Sire, I always knew that you were great in great things. I now know that you are also great in little things.' And he knew how to flatter the ladies. 'All women are beautiful,' he once announced. 'But under the skin of Italian women runs blood, under the skin of French women— milk.'

By profession Bernini was a sculptor. He performed the most prodigious feats of skill and artistry from his earliest years. His first major commissions, such as *Aenea, Anchise e Ascanio* (1618–19), which portrayed a muscular figure carrying an older man across his shoulders, were executed in his teens. His last commissions, such as the extraordinary Tomb of Alexander VII, which portrayed Truth in the daring form of a female nude, were still in the making 60 years later. His work was characterized by the tension produced from the competing qualities of realism and fantasy. His portraits in stone could be shockingly lifelike: at the unveiling of the bust of Monsignor Montoia, the Pope addressed the statue and said, 'Now this *is* the monsignor', then, turning to Montoia, 'and this is a remarkable likeness.' The dramatic poses, the dynamic bodily and facial gestures, and unfailingly original designs brought spiritual power to the most hackneyed subjects.[60]

According to the connoisseur Filippo Baldinucci, who wrote the first biography, Bernini possessed two supreme virtues—ingenuity and audacity. 'His highest merit lay in . . . making beautiful things out of the inadequate and the ill-adapted.' Above all, he betrayed no fear of the unconventional. 'Those who do not sometimes go outside the rules', he once said, 'never go beyond them.'[61]

The catalogue of Bernini's sculptures runs into several hundred items. The best known among them included the portraits of Charles I of England (1638), executed from a painting by Van Dyck, and of Louis XIV of France (1665), *The Rape of Proserpina*, the *David*, who is arched backwards to tense the catapult, *The Ecstasy of Saint Teresa*, *The Death of Beata Albertoni*, *Truth Unveiled by Time*, and the tomb of Urban VIII, where the angel of death is shown writing the book of history.

Sculpture, however, was only Bernini's starting-point. It provided his entrée into artistic compositions which called for the broadest co-ordination of all the arts. His expertise extended to decoration, painting, and architecture as well as sculpture. In St Peter's, it is met at every turn: in the fantastically threaded bronze pillars of the *Baldacchino* (1632) of the high altar; in the decoration of the piers supporting the dome; in the bas-relief over the front door, and the multicoloured marble floor of the arcade; in the bronze and lapis lazuli ciborium of the Chapel of the Sacrament—the 'holiest of holies in the greatest temple of Christendom'.

Bernini's abundant contributions to the city of Rome ran to no fewer than 45 major buildings. He built the stupendous *Fontana del Tritone* (1643), where the

Triton spouts a jet of water from a conch as he sits in a broader shell held aloft by three dolphins; and he was part-author of the *Fontana dei Fiumi* in the Piazza Navona, with its portrayal of the four great rivers of the world—the Nile, Ganges, Danube, and Plate. He built the façade of the College for the Propagation of the Faith, the Jesuit Church of S. Andrea di Monte Cavallo, and the town church of Castelgandolfo. He restored the Quirinal and Chigi palaces, and the Arsenal at Civitavecchia.

In the eyes of contemporaries, Bernini's most appreciated talents lay in the realm of scenography. Posterity is a loser from the fact that much inventive energy was thrown into plays, masques, carnivals, and processions, which were staged on a heroic scale but which left no record. In 1661 he decorated the hill of S. Trinità del Monte for a firework display celebrating the birth of the French Dauphin. In 1669 he organized a famous show to mark the defence of Crete. In the theatre of the Tor' di Nona (1670–6) he worked with playwrights, stage designers, actors, and composers such as Corelli and Scarlatti. Theatricality is often mentioned as the spirit of Baroque. In this respect, Bernini must be described as the most spirited practitioner of the genre.

Bernini's failures were few but wounding. The demolition of his bell-towers at St Peter's must be attributed to the ill will of rival advisers under Innocent X. But the fiasco of his foray into France in 1665 was less explicable. The project started with a flattering invitation from Colbert, who described him in a letter as 'the admiration of the whole world'. He travelled to Paris, taking plans with him for the construction of an amphitheatrical building, based on the Colosseum, to fill the space between the Louvre and the Tuileries. But the plans were rejected, and he returned home six months later, his dismay sweetened only by the memory of the jolly sittings with Louis XIV. At the very end of his career, when cracks appeared in the stonework of the piers under the crossing of St Peter's, Bernini was blamed for the fault. Baldinucci was inspired to write his book in order to disprove these accusations.

In 1667 Pope Alexander VII was almost exactly Bernini's contemporary. As Cardinal Fabio Chigi, he had been a career diplomat. Serving as Nuncio in Cologne throughout the 1640s, he was the Vatican's chief negotiator in the settlement of the Thirty Years War, where he gained the reputation for opposing all concessions to the Protestants. He thoroughly approved of Bernini's quip, 'Better a bad Catholic than a good heretic.' He was a devotee of St Francis de Sales, whom he canonized, was friendly to the Jesuits, and took a harsh line against Jansenism. In short, he was a model Counter-Reformation pope. At the same time he was a man of great literary and artistic refinement. Himself a published Latin poet, he was a collector of books and a determined patron of the arts. He was already employing Bernini on the Chigi residences when still Secretary of State, before summoning him on that first evening of his pontificate.

Alexander's chief rival as Rome's leading patron was undoubtedly ex-Queen Christina of Sweden. Arriving in Rome in the December after Alexander's election, Christina was the most famous Catholic convert of her age. A forceful intellectual, she turned the Palazzo Riario into a salon of wit and taste and, through the *squadro volante* (action group) of Cardinal Azzelino, into a hotbed of ecclesiastical intrigue. Her lesbian leanings, and her longing for the cerebral kind of Catholicism by which Descartes had originally been impressed, made her a poor fit in Alexander's puritanical Rome.

Seen from Rome, Christendom had reached a sorry pass. By the 1660s the long struggle against Protestantism had reached stalemate. Hopes of embracing the Orthodox were lost. With the exception of France, all the leading Catholic powers were in disarray; and France, like Portugal, was in tacit rebellion against the Pope's authority. The Empire under Leopold I was ravaged and depopulated: Poland-Lithuania likewise; Spain was bankrupt.

In northern Europe, all sorts of conflict took place without any reference to Rome. As soon as England made peace with the Netherlands by the Treaty of Breda, the French made war on Spanish Flanders. Restoration England had just survived the plague and the Great Fire of London, celebrated in Dryden's *Annus Mirabilis*. In the East, at Andrusovo, the Orthodox Muscovites were tempting Poland to cede Ukraine, and threatening to tip the balance in perpetuity. Brandenburg Prussia, recently independent, was poised to unseat the Swedes as the leading Protestant military power.

In the Balkans and the Mediterranean, the Turks were in the ascendant. The Venetians were hanging grimly onto their last Cretan stronghold at Candia (Heraklion). The Papal States, like the rest of Italy, were suffering a dramatic economic decline. It was inexplicable how they supplied the revenue to pay for Bernini's extravaganzas, and for the Venetian subsidies. For all its magnificence, Catholic Rome was tangibly reaching the end of its greatest days.

The Vatican's quarrel with France was rooted in the grievances of the late Cardinal Mazarin. Mazarin could not forgive Rome for giving shelter to his *bête noire*, Cardinal de Retz, Archbishop of Paris. He took his revenge by helping the Farnese and the d'Este in their dispute over property in the Papal States. For his trouble, he was excluded from the Conclave of 1655 that elected Alexander VII, on the grounds that cardinals needed the permission of the Curia to assume permanent residence abroad. Louis XIV had chosen to continue the feud after Mazarin's death. On the pretext that the immunity of the French embassy in Rome had been infringed, he expelled the Nuncio from Paris and occupied Avignon. The hapless Alexander was obliged to offer humiliating apologies, and to erect a pyramid in Rome inscribed with an admission of the offences of the Pope's own servants. Relations were not improved by the humiliation felt in the Vatican in 1665 from Bernini's abortive visit to Versailles. Bernini may have scored a great success with Louis: by parting the King's wig during one of the sittings, he inspired an instant hairstyle known as *la modification Bernin*. But no one could fail to see, in taste as in politics and religion, that France was determined to set her own course. Versailles was to take no notice when the Vatican opposed the persecution of the Huguenots.

In literature, 1667 saw the publication both of Racine's *Andromaque* and of Milton's *Paradise Lost*. The former, set in ancient Troy, confirmed the continuing vitality of the classical tradition, as well as the supremacy of French letters. The latter's matchless cadences confirmed the enduring appeal of Christian themes:

> Of Man's first disobedience, and the fruit
> Of that forbidden tree whose mortal taste
> Brought death into the World, and all our woe,
> With loss of Eden, till one greater Man
> Restore us, and regain the blissful seat,
> Sing, Heavenly Muse, . . .
> That to the highth of this great Argument
> I may assert eternal Providence,
> And justifie the ways of God to men.[62]

Bernini's creative contemporaries were at every possible stage in their varied careers. In Amsterdam, with *The Jewish Bride*, Rembrandt was painting his last major canvas. In Madrid, Murillo was engaged on a series of 22 paintings for the Church of the Capuchins. In Paris, Claude Lorrain painted *Europa*. In London, in the wake of the Great Fire, Christopher Wren was planning his spectacular series of churches; and Richard Lower performed the first human blood transfusion. In Cambridge, the young Isaac Newton had just cracked the theory of colours. In Oxford, Hooke was proposing systematic meteorological recordings. In Munich, the Theatinerkirche was in mid-construction. In February 1667 Frans Hals, the portraitist, had just died; Jonathan Swift, the satirist, was being conceived.

There can be no doubt that the protracted reconstruction of St Peter's constituted a central event in the era of Church reform. St Peter's was not just a building; it was the chief temple and symbol of the loyalty against which Luther had rebelled, and to which the Pope's own divisions had rallied. It is also true that the building of Bernini's colonnade marked a definite stage in that story. For the sake of convenience, historians can be tempted to say that it marks the end of the Counter-Reformation. And so, in a sense, it does.

Yet, in reality, the Counter-Reformation did *not* come to an end, just as the colonnade was never really finished. The history of civilization is a continuum which has few simple stops and starts. The Roman Church was already being overshadowed by the rise of the secular powers; but it did not cease to be a prominent feature of European life. The ideals of the Counter-Reformation continued to be pressed for centuries. Its institutions are still in operation nearly 400 years later. Indeed, the mission of the Roman Church will not have ceased so long as the pilgrims crowd into St Peter's Square, pray before St Peter's Throne, and mingle with the tourists under Bernini's Colonnade.

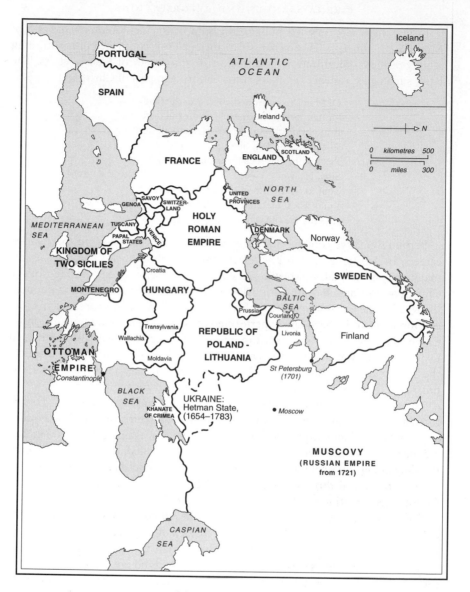

Map 18. Europe, 1713

VIII

LUMEN

Enlightenment and Absolutism, c.1650–1789

THERE is an air of naïvety about the so-called 'Age of Reason'. In restrospect it seems extraordinary that so many of Europe's leading intellects should have given such weight to one human faculty—Reason—at the expense of all the others. Naïvety of such proportions, one might conclude, was heading for a fall; and a fall, in the shape of the terrible revolutionary years, is what the Age of Reason eventually encountered.

In the periods both before and after, the virtues of Reason were much less appreciated. On seeing his father's ghost, Shakespeare's Hamlet had told his doubting companion, 'There are more things in heaven and earth, Horatio, than are dreamt of in your philosophy.' In the nineteenth century, too, rationalism was out of fashion:

ENLIGHTENMENT . . . 2. Shallow and pretentious intellectualism, unreasonable contempt for authority and tradition, etc.; applied *esp.* to the spirit and aims of the French philosophers of the 18th C. 1865.[1]

On the other hand, when judging the period which followed the Reformations, one must remember what Europeans had been contending with for so long. The consensus between Reason and Faith, as promised by the Renaissance humanists, had not prevailed against the world of religious dogma, magic, and superstition. After the Wars of Religion, one can see that the exercise of 'the Light of sweet Reason' was a natural and necessary antidote. Indeed, even the full flood of the Enlightenment may only have washed over the surface of continuing bigotries.

Similar problems surround the label of the 'Age of Absolutism' which political historians apply to this same period. One might easily be led to imagine that most European rulers of the time either enjoyed absolute powers or at least sought to do so. Such, alas, was not the case. Europeans in the Age of Absolutism were no more uniform absolutists than they were uniform rationalists.

In the century and a half between the Peace of Westphalia and the French Revolution, the map of Europe underwent few radical changes. Each of the wars of the period ended with a certain amount of territorial trading. The Treaty of Utrecht (1713), in particular, caused a stir; and the first partition of Poland-Lithuania (1773) signalled the onset of an avalanche. The unification of the island of Great Britain (1707) confirmed the emergence of an important new unit. But most of the main blocs on the map remained essentially intact. France's drive to the Rhine was only partly successful; Prussia had to be content with relatively modest gains; the Ottomans' last great surge was contained and then reversed. Russia alone continued to grow dramatically. None of Europe's invalids actually perished: Spain, the Holy Roman Empire, Sweden, and Poland-Lithuania all ailed, but all survived.

The range of political systems was far greater than most textbooks allow (see Appendix III, p. 1265). In this 'Age of Absolutism', absolutist states actually formed a minority. Between the completely decentralized, constitutional, and republican confederation of Switzerland at one end of the scale and the extreme autocracies in Russia, the Ottoman Empire, and the Papal States at the other, great variety flourished. Europe's republics were represented by Venice, Poland-Lithuania, and the United Provinces; the constitutional monarchies at various times by England, Scotland, and Sweden; the absolutist monarchies by France, Spain, and Austria. The Holy Roman Empire, with monarch both elected and hereditary, fell somewhere between the republics and the constitutional monarchies; Prussia, which operated constitutional structures according to an authoritarian tradition, fell somewhere between constitutionalism and absolutism. Even greater variety can be found among Europe's *Kleinstaaterei*—the hundreds of petty states which the younger Pitt would once call in exasperation 'the swarm of gnats'. There were miniature city-republics like Ragusa (Dubrovnik), Genoa, or Geneva; there were miniature principalities like Courland; ecclesiastical states like Avignon, and curious hybrids like Andorra.

What is more, many European states continued to be conglomerates, where the ruler had to operate a different system within each of the constituent territories. The kings of Prussia had to conduct themselves in one way in Berlin, where they were imperial subjects, in another way in Königsberg, where they were completely independent, and in yet other ways in possessions such as Minden or Neuchâtel. The Habsburgs could be figureheads in the Empire, despots in Prague or Vienna, and constitutional monarchs after 1713 in Brussels. The British kings could be constitutional monarchs at home and autocrats in the colonies.

There were also important variations over time. England, for example, veered in the republican direction under Cromwell, in the monarchical direction after the restoration of the Stuarts, and back to its greatly admired centrist position after the 'Bloodless Revolution' of 1688–9. In the late seventeenth century both the Swedish and the Danish monarchies headed rapidly towards absolutism. In eighteenth-century Sweden the 'Hats' and 'Caps' moved headlong in the opposite direction. Under John Sobieski (r. 1674–96) Poland-Lithuania still functioned according to rules of the noble democracy. After 1717 it could only function as a Russian protectorate. In Russia the Tsars acted as unashamed autocrats; in Poland they posed as the champions of 'Golden Freedom'. Appearances, and simple categories, deceive.

Absolutism, in particular, must be viewed with circumspection. It was something less than the autocracy of tsars and sultans, who faced no institutional obstacle to the exercise of their will. Yet it was something more than the authoritarian spirit which enabled certain monarchs to follow the Prussian example and to dragoon the institutions with which they were supposed to co-operate. It clearly had its roots in the late feudal period, where struggling monarchies had to combat the entrenched privileges both of the provinces and of the nobility, and in the Catholic world, where the Roman Church remained immune from direct political control. It did not usually fit the conditions of either the Protestant or the Orthodox world. At various stages France, Spain, Austria, and Portugal came definitely within its purview. For various reasons Britain, Prussia, Poland-Lithuania, and Russia did not.

Absolutism, one should stress, refers more to an ideal than to the practical realities of government. It was concerned with a set of political ideas and assumptions which came into existence as a corrective to the excessively decentralized institutions left over from the late medieval era. It often stood for little more than the 'personal power' of certain monarchs as opposed to the 'limited powers' of others whose authority was curtailed by Diets, autonomous provinces, municipal charters, exempted nobles, and clergy. It could not be easily defined, and was often justified more in the panegyrical tones of courtiers than in the detailed arguments of philosophers. It had many a Bossuet or a Boileau, but only one Hobbes. It was probably better illustrated in some of its minor examples, such as Tuscany, than in any of the major powers. Nowhere did it achieve complete success: nowhere did it bring a perfectly absolute state into existence. Yet in the sixteenth and seventeenth centuries it certainly provided a radical force for change. In the eighteenth century, when its influence was becoming more diffuse, it was overtaken by new trends for democracy, liberty, and the general will. The age of the 'enlightened despots' was equally the era of British and American constitutionalism.

One must also be aware that shouts of 'absolutism' were frequently raised in a misleading way. When the English gentry complained about the absolutism of the Stuarts, they were less perturbed by the actual balance of power between King and Parliament than by fears of the imposition of French or Spanish practices. When the Polish nobles took to screaming about the 'absolutism' of their Saxon kings, whose position in Poland-Lithuania was more limited than that of any limited monarch, they were simply objecting to change.

The absolutism of France served as the main point of reference. Under Louis XIV (r. 1643–1715), whose reign was the longest in European history, France was far and away Europe's greatest power; and her example excited numerous admirers. Yet the greatest of absolutists died disillusioned, convinced that the ideal lay out of reach.

In the end, therefore, absolutism proved a dismal failure. The Ancien Régime created by Louis XIV was to end in the disaster of a Revolution which, whilst turning France into the apostle of republicanism, brought French supremacy to a close. The ultimate triumph was to be enjoyed by Absolutism's most doughty opponents. British constitutionalism inspired not only the leading power of the nineteenth century but also, via the constitution of Britain's rebel colonies, the world's leading superpower of the twentieth.

Europe's colonies and overseas possessions continued to multiply after 1650, and in some cases reached independent viability. Spain and Portugal had their hands full exploiting their existing possessions. In North America, the Spaniards pressed inland from New Spain (Mexico) to California, Arizona, Colorado. In South America, aided by systematic Jesuit settlements, they concentrated their efforts on Venezuela, on New Granada (Bogotá), on Peru, Paraguay, and La Plata (Córdoba). They attempted to keep all trade to their own ships, until forced by the Asiento Treaty of 1713 to admit foreigners. The Portuguese survived a long campaign by the Dutch to take over the Brazilian coast. After the treaty of 1662, they moved south from São Paulo to the River Plate (1680) and westwards into the gold-rich interior at Minas Geraes (1693) and the Matto Grosso. Apart from the East Indies, the Dutch were left with colonies in Guyana and Curaçao. The Russians, who had discovered what was later to be named the Bering Strait in 1648, occupied Kamchatka (1679) and signed a border treaty with China on the Amur (1689). A century later, after the explorations of the Dane Vitus Bering (1680–1741), they established a fort on Kodiak Island (1783) and claimed Alaska (1791), whence they sent out an offshoot to Fort Ross in northern California (1812).

Most new colonial enterprises, however, were started by the French and the British. France launched the Compagnie des Indes in 1664, establishing stations on the east coast of India at Pondicherry and Karaikal, with staging-posts on the islands of Madagascar and Reunion. In 1682 Louisiana was founded on the Mississippi in honour of Louis XIV, with its capital at New Orleans (1718). England consolidated its American colonies with the foundation of Delaware (1682), of the Quaker colony of Pennsylvania (1683), and of Georgia (1733). In India the East India Company, which now held Bombay and Calcutta as well as Madras, was hard-pressed by French competition. Commercial interests went hand in hand with maritime discovery. In 1766–8 the French admiral Bougainville circumnavigated the globe, as did the three expeditions of Captain James Cook RN between 1768 and 1780. In the circumstances, Franco-British colonial conflicts became almost inevitable. They were settled by superior British naval power. Great Britain took Newfoundland in 1713, French India in 1757, and French Canada in 1759–60, thereby confirming its status as the prime colonial power.

Colonialism was very much confined to those maritime states which first began it. The German states, Austria, and the Italian states did not take part. In this they lagged behind the Polish fief of Courland, whose Duke bought Tobago in 1645 and briefly maintained a trading-post in the Gambia; or Denmark, whose West India Company obtained both St Thomas and St John (1671) and St Croix (1733).

The impact of Europe's growing contacts with distant continents and cultures cannot be exaggerated. Europe had long been shut in on itself. Knowledge of civilizations beyond Europe was meagre. Fantastic tales, like that of 'El Dorado', abounded. But now a steady stream of detailed accounts of India, China, or the American Frontier began to stimulate more serious reflection. *Les Six Voyages* (1676) of J. B. Tavernier (1605–89), who made great wealth in Persia, started a genre written in the same vein as the celebrated *New Voyage round the World* (1697) of the buccaneer William Dampier (1652–1715), the *History of Japan* (1727) by the German surgeon Engelbert Kaempfer (1651–1716), or the later *Travels in Arabia* of the Swiss J. L. Burckhardt (1784–1817), the first European to visit Mecca. *The Strange, Surprizing Adventures of Robinson Crusoe* (1719), the world's first popular novel, was written by the English satirist, Daniel Defoe (1659–1731), on the basis of the real experiences of a Scots sailor marooned on Juan Fernández Island off Valparaíso by Dampier. These works often gave European readers a comparative perspective on the religions, folklore, and culture of the world; and they handed the philosophers of the Enlightenment one of their most effective devices for questioning European or Christian assumptions. It hit Europeans hard to learn that the Siamese might be happier, the Brahmin more sagacious, or the Iroquois less bloodthirsty than they were themselves. It is a curious fact that Jesuit authors, who excelled in travelogues of the ethnological type, provided the very ammunition with which their own intellectual world was most effectively bombarded. Here one would mention the description of Amerindian life in Canada by Fr. J.-F. Lafitau (1670–1740) or the much-translated memoir of Persia by Fr. T. Krusiński SJ (1675–1756), published in 1733.

International relations were clearly affected by the colonial factor. Almost all the wars of the period had naval or colonial theatres which were fought over in parallel to the main military conflict on the Continent. The great land powers—France, Spain, Austria, and increasingly Prussia and Russia—had to take account of the wealthy maritime powers, especially the British and the Dutch, who, whilst possessing few troops of their own, could play a vital role as paymasters, quartermasters, and weavers of diplomatic coalitions.

Diplomacy was increasingly governed by the Balance of Power—a doctrine which viewed any change in one part of Europe as a potential threat to the whole. This was a sure sign that a 'European system' was coming into being. And colonial assets were an integral part of the equation. The system was of particular interest to the British, who instinctively opposed any preponderant Continental power and who made a fine art of maintaining the Balance at minimum cost to themselves. International relations of this sort entirely lacked the moral and religious fervour of previous times. They were often reduced almost to a form of ritual, where the current state of the Balance was tested in set-piece battles fought by small professional armies; where elegant officers of both sides belonged to the

same international confraternity of arms; and where the result was nicely calculated in territory ceded or gained. Territorial possessions were viewed rather like
casino chips that rulers lost or amassed according to the fortunes of war, with no
thought for the interests of the inhabitants. Like Westphalia, all the great congresses of the subsequent era—Utrecht (1713), Vienna (1738), Aix-la-Chapelle
(1748), and Paris (1763)—were conducted in the same spirit of cheerful cynicism.

   Economic life, too, was greatly affected by the colonies. Europe was increasingly divided into countries which could benefit from colonial commerce and
those which could not. Britain benefited most, especially after Utrecht, gaining a
predominant hold on the Atlantic trade in sugar, tobacco, and slaves, from which
Liverpool, Glasgow, and Bristol grew rich. Britain's policy of enforcing a blockade
on enemy ports in time of war led to constant trouble not only with France and
Spain but also with the neutrals—Dutch, Danes, and Swedes—who had specialized in smuggling, raiding, and blockade-running. In Britain, in emulation of the
Dutch, this period saw the growth of all the permanent institutions of public
credit—the Bank of England (1694), the Royal Exchange, and the National Debt.
The first steps of the Industrial Revolution were taken in the 1760s. [**CAP-AG**]

   Britain produced John Law (1671–1729), a racy Scots financier, who invented
the first experiment for harnessing colonial trade to popular capitalism. His grand
'Scheme' and *Banque royale* (1716–20) in Paris, which was patronized by the
Regent, and which coincided with the similarly disastrous South Sea Company in
London, created a veritable fever of speculation by selling paper shares in the
future of Louisiana. The Bubble burst; thousands, if not millions, of investors
were ruined, Law fled, and France was permanently inoculated against credit
operations. Meanwhile, the commercial operations of Law's company
thrived; and the value of French overseas commerce quadrupled between 1716 and
1743.

   In Central and Eastern Europe, few such developments occurred. Land
remained the major source of wealth; serfdom reigned supreme; inland trade
could not compare to its maritime counterpart. Germany's recovery was slow,
Bohemia's somewhat faster; Poland-Lithuania after 1648 experienced an absolute
economic regression from which it never recovered. Baltic trade passed increasingly to Russia, where the foundation of St Petersburg (1701) opened its 'window
to the West'.

   Social life, despite the recurrence of violent outbursts, remained within its
established channels until the opening of the floodgates in 1789. Extremes of
wealth among the aristocracy and of misery among the peasants were normal.
Differences between Western and Eastern Europe were growing, but not dramatic. Even in Britain, where commercial pressures were greatest, the landed aristocracy maintained its supremacy. Indeed since the English lords were not averse
to commercial activities like canal-building or coalmining, their pre-eminence
was prolonged. This was the age of the grandees and the magnates—the Medina
Sidonia and Osuña in Spain, the Brahes and Bondes in Sweden, the
Schwarzenbergs in Austria, the Esterhazy in Hungary, the Lobkowitz in Bohemia,

CAP-AG

IN volume 70 of the journal *Past and Present* (1976), an American historian advanced a hypothesis on 'Agrarian Class Structure and Economic Development in Pre-industrial Europe'. He was questioning the established view which attributed economic change to the pressures of rising population. Starting from contrasts between England and France, he argued that the key to England's precocity and France's retardation lay in their different class structures. Whereas the landlord class in England had created a flourishing system of agrarian capitalism, 'the most complete freedom and property rights for the rural population [in France] meant poverty and a self-perpetuating cycle of backwardness'.[1]

An elaborate historians' debate raged in the journal's next seventeen issues. Volume 78 carried a symposium on 'Population and Class Relations in Feudal Society', a second joint critique of the hypothesis, and an exposition of 'Peasant Organization and Class in East and West Germany'. Volume 79 carried two still more hostile pieces, one lamenting 'the confused view of manorial development' and another, from the star of French rural history, which pummelled the Brenner thesis with a comprehensive eighteen-point 'Reply'. Volume 85 extended the debate to 'Pre-industrial Bohemia'. At last, in volume 97, Professor Brenner's long-awaited rejoinder stretched matters still further by expounding his views on 'the agrarian roots of European Capitalism'.[2]

Debates of this sort are the chosen method for historical specialists to bridge the gaps in existing knowledge. They appear to have two weaknesses. They use tiny samples to make huge generalizations; and they are shamelessly inconclusive. If engineers were to approach their subject in the same spirit, no river would ever be bridged.

A solution of sorts, however, was to hand. In the same year that the Brenner debate was launched, another American scholar took the same subject of 'capitalist agriculture' and used it to explain 'the origins of a world-economy'.[3] By applying the techniques of systems theory, Immanuel Wallerstein was able to locate a 'core' of the European economy in the West and a dependent 'periphery' in the East. In his view, the core region, which consisted of England, the Netherlands, northern France, and western Germany, had possessed only a 'slight edge' in the fifteenth century. But they were able to exploit their advantage through favourable trading relations, and to set up the conditions which transformed the feudal nobilities of Eastern Europe into a capitalist landowning class. They also projected their growing economic power into the New World. As a result, they created the familiar framework where 'coercive, cash-crop capitalism' took hold both of colonial and of East European agriculture. Whilst the core countries flourished, the serfs of Prussia,

Bohemia, Poland, and Hungary were reduced to the status of plantation blacks. Once established, the system could only magnify its imbalances. 'The slight edge of the fifteenth century became the great disparity of the seventeenth and the monumental difference of the nineteenth.'[4]

The hypothesis soon came under fire from the specialists, not least from Brenner. Wallerstein was accused of oversimplification, of overemphasis on trade, even of 'neo-Smithianism'.[5] It turns out that the 'Polish model', which was central to his argument, did not hold good even for the whole of Poland, and was largely invented. The Hungarian beef trade, it seems, was not run by nobles or capitalist middlemen, but by free, wage-earning peasants. The Russian and the Ottoman elements in European trade had been ignored. Instead of a micro-theory which could not sustain generalizations, here was a macro-theory, which could not bear the specifics.

In the end, the most interesting aspect of Wallerstein's work was the light which it shed on the relations of Eastern and Western Europe. Though the postulate of a core and a dependent periphery had not been proved, the interdependence of all parts of Europe had been amply demonstrated.

the Radziwiłł and the Zamoyski in Poland—each with a vast latifundium protected by entail, a princely life-style, and enormous patronial power. [**SZLACHTA**]

In many countries the nobility was now mobilized for the service of the state. In France and in Russia, this was achieved in a formal, systematic way. Louis XIV introduced a hierarchy of ranks and titles, each supported by suitable pensions, starting with the *enfants de France* (royal family) and the *pairs* (princes of the blood, together with 50 dukes and 7 bishops) and ending with the cadres of the *noblesse d'épée* (the old military families) and the *noblesse de robe* (civilian courtiers). Peter the Great introduced a service nobility divided into 14 ranks and even more strictly dependent on state employment. In Prussia the alliance between the Crown and the Junkers was more informal but no less effective. The petty nobility, which was particularly numerous in Spain and in Poland, was squeezed into the retinues of the magnates, into military service, or into foreign employment. In England, in the absence of serfdom, the Enclosure movement could capitalize on landholding most effectively. A prosperous stratum of yeomen and gentleman farmers developed at the expense of peasants driven from the land.

In all the great cities of Europe there was a wealthy commercial and professional class, alongside the artisanate, the urban poor, and, in two or three localities, the beginnings of an industrial work-force. Generally speaking, however, the old institutions of the social Estates remained intact. The nobles kept their Diets, the cities their charters and their guilds, the peasantry their corvées and their famines. Social changes were undoubtedly taking place, but within the established

SZLACHTA

A CCORDING to an inventory of 1739, Stanisław Lubomirski (1719–83) had inherited a latifundium of 1,071 landed estates. They stretched right across the nine southern palatinates of Poland, from the family seat at Wisnicz near Cracow to Tetiev near Kiev in Ukraine, and were worked by close to a million serfs. Grand Marshal of the Crown from 1766, Lubomirski could have laid claim to be Europe's largest private landowner. Allied by marriage and politics to the related clans of the Czartoryski, Poniatowski, and Zamoyski, he certainly belonged to the most powerful circle of magnates in the land. Each of them possessed vast estates, a private army, and an income larger than the king's. They stood at the pinnacle of a social system whose noble estate—the *szlachta*—was the most numerous in Europe.

The magnates, however, were highly untypical of the nobility as a whole. By the mid-eighteenth century an absolute majority of Polish nobles had become landless. They survived by renting properties, by serving the magnates, or even by working the land like peasants. Yet no amount of economic degradation could deprive them of what they prized most—their noble blood, their *herb* or 'coat of arms', their legal status, and their right to bequeath it to their children. [CRUX]

Poland's *drobna szlachta* or 'petty nobility' was absolutely inimitable. In certain provinces, such as Mazovia, they made up a quarter of the population. In some districts, where they built walled villages to separate themselves from the peasantry, the *zaścianki* or 'nobles-behind-the-wall' constituted the whole population. They preserved their way of life with fierce determination, addressing each other as *Pan* or *Pani*, 'Lord and Lady', and the peasants as *Ty*, 'Thou'. They regarded all nobles as brothers, and everyone else as inferiors. They reserved the severest penalties for anyone falsely masquerading as a noble, and jealously guarded the procedures of ennoblement. They engaged in no trade, except for soldiering and land management. They always rode into town, if only on a nag; and they wore carmine capes and weapons, if only symbolic wooden swords. Their houses may have been hovels; but they had to have a porch on which to display the family shield. Above all, they insisted that Prince Lubomirski and his like were their equals.

The most prominent feature of the *szlachta*, therefore, was the tremendous contrast between their economic stratification and their legal, cultural, and political solidarity. Unlike their counterparts elsewhere in Europe, they admitted no native titles. There were no Polish barons, marquises, or counts. The most they would do was to confirm the personal titles which some of their number had gained in Lithuania before the union of 1569 or which, like the Lubomirskis, had been granted by pope or emperor.

In legal terms, Poland's noble estate came to an end when the laws governing its status were abolished by the Partitions. Some, like the Lubomirskis, managed to confirm their nobility in Austria or in Prussia. A few did so in Russia, though 80 per cent of them there lost their status, forming a déclassé reservoir of anti-Russian discontent that raged throughout the nineteenth century. In 1921, when the Polish Republic was restored, a democratic Polish Sejm formally confirmed the abolition of noble privilege. Yet the *szlachta's* consciousness of their special identity survived all manner of catastrophes. As late as the 1950s, sociologists found collective farmers in Mazovia who shunned their 'peasant' neighbours, dressed differently, spoke differently, and observed complex betrothal customs to prevent intermarriage. In 1990, when Poland's Communist regime collapsed, there were still young Poles who would wear a signet ring with a coat of arms, just to show who they were. By then, everyone in Poland addressed each other as *Pan* and *Pani*. The 'noble culture' had become a major ingredient of the culture of the whole nation.

Nobility played a central part in social and political life all over early modern Europe. But the only place where the Polish model was matched, even in part, was in Spain, where the grandees and *hidalgos* of the West resembled the magnates and petty gentry of the East.[1]

framework. When the shell finally cracked, as it did in France in 1789, the social explosion was to be unprecedented. [**PUGACHEV**]

Cultural life burgeoned under royal, ecclesiastical, and aristocratic patronage. The European arts entered the era of Classicism, where, in reaction to the Baroque, rules, rigour, and restraint were the order of the day. Architecture saw a return to the Greek and Roman styles of the Renaissance, with a touch of gaudy or rococo ornamentation. The outstanding buildings were palaces and public offices. Urban planning, formal, geometric gardens, and landscape design gained prominence. The obsession was to reduce the chaos of the natural world to order and harmony. The show cities, after Paris, were Dresden, Vienna, and St Petersburg.

Painting had passed its precocious peak. In France the classical landscapes and mythological scenes of Nicolas Poussin (1594–1665), Claude Lorrain (1600–82), and Charles Le Brun (1619–90) were succeeded by the idyllic frivolities painted by J. A. Watteau (1684–1721) and J.-H. Fragonard (1732–1806). The English school of social portraiture, which began with Godfrey Kneller (1646–1723), culminated in the superlative work of Joshua Reynolds (1723–92) and Thomas Gainsborough (1727–88). The two Canalettos (1697–1768, 1724–80) left realistic panoramas of Venice, London, and Warsaw. Except for occasional figures of stature, such as G. B. Tiepolo (1693–1770) in Venice, religious painting was in decline. Interior

PUGACHEV

SINCE peasants formed by far the largest social class in modern Europe and the Russian empire by far the largest state, it is not surprising to find that the greatest peasant revolts took place in the heartland of Russia. There were four—those of Bolotnikov, 1606–7, of Sten'ka Razin, 1670–1, of Bulavin, 1707–8, and of Pugachev, 1773–4. Equally, the civil war in Soviet Russia, 1917–21[1] contained a major element of peasant unrest.

Emelyan Ivanovich Pugachev (1726–75) was a small Cossack landowner and veteran officer. He had spent years wandering among the monasteries of the Old Believers, storing up his sense of resentment. In 1773 he raised the standard of revolt at Yaitsk on the Ural River, on the very frontier of Europe, declaring himself to be the Emperor Peter III and promising the emancipation of the serfs. Hundreds of thousands joined his cause throughout the Volga provinces. He was acclaimed by peasants, by Cossacks, even by the nomadic Bashkirs and Kazakhs. Lacking co-ordination his supporters deteriorated into rampaging bands.

At first the Empress made light of 'L'affaire du Marquis de Pugachev', setting a modest price of 500 roubles on his head. But the price soon rose to 28,000. At one point, all the Volga forts were in his hands. Pugachev reduced Kazan to ashes, slaughtering all resisters. He maintained a satirical court, mimicking the entourage of Catherine's murdered husband. The end came after two years of mayhem, when Pugachev's main force was cornered at Tsaritsyn. Pugachev was brought to Moscow, and quartered.[2]

At any time until the mid-twentieth century the numerical preponderance of the peasantry was not reflected in historiography. Peasants only found their way into textbooks when their periodic revolts disturbed the political scene. Events such as England's Peasants' Revolt of 1381 or Germany's Peasants' War in 1524–5, were favoured by Marxist history-writing because they were taken to demonstrate the revolutionary potential of the masses.[3] In fact, no peasant rising ever succeeded. Peasants have been shown the most conservative of social forces, deeply attached to religion, to the land, to the family, and to an immemorial way of life. Their periodic *fureurs* were outbursts of desperation. Their revolving cycle of fortune and misfortune was far more important to them than any thought of social revolution.[4]

Peasant studies is one of several flourishing new academic fields. It offers great opportunity to examine the interrelations of social, economic, anthropological, and cultural themes. It was specially suited to comparative analysis—both between European regions and between continents. *A Journal of Peasant Studies* (1973–) grew out of a seminar centred at London's School of Oriental and African Studies. Its editorial statement stressed the sheer size of the world's peasantry and their problems:

Of the underprivileged majority of mankind, [the peasants] are the most under-privileged . . . No social class has a longer history of struggle against such conditions . . . Hitherto, scholarly periodicals have treated peasants in a peripheral way. We offer this journal as one where the peasantry will be central . . . [5]

France, like Russia, has drawn historians to the study of its very substantial peasantry. A multivolume *Economic and Social History of France* was to inspire the second generation of the *Annales* team. The key volume was written by Le Roi Ladurie, whose analysis combines the thematic factors of territory, demography, and economy with chronological periodization over four centuries. The 'Rural Renaissance' of the late fifteenth century followed the earlier 'Destruction of the Full World' and preceded the 'Trauma of Civil Wars' and the 'Drift, Reconstruction and Crisis' of a seventeenth-century Ecosystem which would survive the Revolution.[6]

Numerous studies have been made of revolts in the French countryside—the 'tithe strikes' of the sixteenth century, the revolt of the *Pitauts* against the salt-tax in Guyenne (1548), the *Croquants* and *Nouveaux Croquants* in the Limousin-Perigord (1594, 1636–7),[7] the *Gautiers and Nu-pieds* in Normandy (1594, 1639), the 'Enigma of the Rural Fronde' (1648–9), and the repeated insurrections in Provence (1596–1715). Attempts have been made to link the rhythms of peasant unrest in France to those in Russia, and even China.[8]

The historian of insurrections in Provence demonstrates that peasant revolts were interlaced with other forms of social unrest. He proposes a typology of five categories of revolt:

1. factional struggles within the nobility or bourgeoisie,
2. struggles between the *menu peuple* and the well-to-do,
3. popular action by the peasants against one of the political factions,
4. struggles between different peasant action groups,
5. united struggle of the whole community against outside agencies.[9]

Anthropological studies are specially fruitful. They reveal the universal, immemorial qualities of peasant life. Sicilian reapers sing as peasants sang for centuries from Galway to Galicia:

> Fly, fly sharp sickle
> The countryside is all full,
> All full with goods
> For the joy of the landlords [*bis*]
> How sweet is the good life!
> *Tutrutrù, Tutrutrù,*
> The pig was four scudi [*bis*]
> Rich and poor, we are all cuckolds.[10]

decoration, and furniture in particular, responded to aristocratic demand. The cabinet-makers of Paris, led by A. C. Boulle (1642–1732), took advantage of exotic imports such as ebony, mahogany, and satinwood; Boulle specialized in marquetry and inlaid ebony. Their creations, now instantly recognizable as 'Louis XIV', 'Louis XV', or 'Louis XVI', eventually found their match in the work of Grinling Gibbons (1648–1721) and Thomas Chippendale (d. 1779). Fine porcelain owed much to imports from China. The royal factory at Saint Cloud (1696) and later Sèvres (1756) had counterparts at Meissen (1710) in Saxony, at St Petersburg (1744), at Worcester (1751), and at the 'Etruria' factory (1769) of Josiah Wedgwood (1730–95). Silk, silver, and sumptuous sundries saturated the salons.

European literature entered the phase when the vernacular languages took an irreversible lead over Latin. Drama, in the hands of the French court playwrights—Pierre Corneille (1606–84), Jean-Baptiste Poquelin (Molière, 1622–73) and Jean Racine (1639–99)—adopted forms of language and structure that served as the international model for the next century. The tradition of social and moralizing comedy was extended in England by the Restoration comedians and by Richard Brinsley Sheridan (1751–1816); in France by Pierre Augustin Beaumarchais (1732–99); in Italy by Carlo Goldoni (1707–93).

Poetry was particularly susceptible to the drive for rigorous style and form. In English it is dominated by the triad of John Milton (1608–74), John Dryden (1631–1700), and Alexander Pope (1688–1744). Pope's intellectual discourses, written in the heroic couplets of the *Essay on Criticism* (1711) and the *Essay on Man* (1733), are infinitely expressive of his generation's temper and interests:

> True ease in writing comes from art, not chance,
> As those move easiest who have learned to dance.
> 'Tis not enough no harshness gives offence,
> The sound must seem an echo of the sense.
>
> All nature is but art, unknown to Thee;
> All chance, direction which thou canst not see;
> All discord, harmony not understood;
> All partial evil, universal good.
> And, spite of pride, in erring reason's spite,
> One truth is clear, Whatever is, is right.[2]

Later, lyrical poetry reasserted itself to redress the balance—in the Scots poems of Robert Burns (1759–96), the German of Christian von Kleist (1715–59), F. G. Klopstock (1724–1803), and the young Goethe, and the French of Jean Roucher (1745–94) and André Chénier (1762–94). Prose-writing, though heavily dependent on the non-fictional genres, witnessed the growth of true fiction. Here, the pioneers appeared in England. Apart from *Robinson Crusoe*, the leading titles included Jonathan Swift's *Gulliver's Travels* (1726), Samuel Richardson's *Pamela* (1740), Henry Fielding's *Tom Jones* (1749), and Laurence Sterne's *Tristram Shandy* (1767). In France, both Voltaire and Rousseau, among their other talents, were accomplished novelists (see below).

Although French, English, and German authors predominated, the reading public was by no means confined to their countries of origin. Almost all educated people in Europe read French at this time; and local translations of important titles were widespread. In Poland, for example, which many might mistake for a cultural backwater, the catalogue of translations into Polish included *Robinson Krusoe* (1769), *Manon Lesko* (1769), *Kandyd* (1780), *Gulliwer* (1784), *Awantury Amelii* (1788), *Historia Tom-Dźona* (1793). Some Polish authors, such as Jan Potocki (1761–1825), the orientalist, wrote in French for both a local and an international readership.

European musicians, from J. S. Bach (1685–1750) to W. A. Mozart (1756–91) and Ludwig van Beethoven (1770–1827), consolidated the foundations of the classical repertoire. They worked in each of its main divisions: instrumental, chamber, orchestral, and choral; and they developed a style, which, though often confused with the preceding Baroque, was marked by a very particular rhythmic energy that has given it lasting appeal. [**SONATA**] They also preserved a balance between the sacred and the profane. This may be illustrated from Bach's cantatas, Mozart's *Requiem* (1791) and Beethoven's *Missa solemnis* (1823), and from Bach's concertos, Mozart's forty-one and Beethoven's nine symphonies. Austro-German composers enjoyed a growing preponderance. In addition to Bach, Mozart, and Beethoven, their first rank included Johann Pachelbel (1653–1706), G. P. Telemann (1681–1767), G. F. Handel (1685–1759), and Josef Haydn (1732–1809). Yet music remained essentially international in character. In their day, the Italians J.-B. Lully (1632–87), Arcangelo Corelli (1653–1713), Alessandro Scarlatti (1660–1725), Tomaso Albinoni (1671–1751), and Antonio Vivaldi (1675–1741) were just as influential as the Germans. So, too, were the Dane Dietrich Buxtehude (1637–1707), the Frenchmen François Couperin (1668–1733) and J.-P. Rameau (1683–1764), or the organist of Westminster Abbey, Henry Purcell (*c.*1659–95), in London. The violin, the prime instrument of European music, was perfected by Antonio Stradivari (1644–1737) of Cremona. The pianoforte was invented in 1709 by B. Cristofori of Padua. Opera developed from the early stage of dialogue-with-music to the full-scale musical dramas of W. C. Gluck (1714–87). [**CANTATA**] [**MUSIKE**] [**OPERA**] [**STRAD**]

Formal religion stayed set in the earlier mould. The religious map of Europe did not change significantly. Established Churches continued to operate according to rigorous state laws of toleration and non-toleration. Members of the official religion gained preferment, having sworn oaths and passed strict tests of conformity; non-members and non-jurors, when not actively persecuted, lingered in legal limbo. In Catholic countries, Protestants were generally deprived of civil rights. In Protestant countries, Catholics suffered the same fate. In Great Britain, the Church of England and the Church of Scotland formally barred both Roman Catholics and their respective Protestant dissenters. In Sweden, Denmark and Holland similar proscriptions applied. In Russia, the Russian Orthodox Church enjoyed sole recognition; there were no Jews legally resident. In Poland-Lithuania, where the greatest degree of religious heterodoxy persisted, restrictions

SONATA

IN origin, *sonata* referred to music that was 'sounded', not 'sung'. But in the eighteenth century it was applied to a particular form of composition that came to dominate almost all instrumental music. Sonata form occupies a central place in the work of the classical composers from Haydn to Mahler. It is to be contrasted with the polyphonic style of the preceding era; and it embodied the conventions against which later 'modern' styles were to react. It has two aspects—the division of compositions into a formal sequence of movements and the elaboration of homophonic harmony. [**TONE**]

Sonata form had no single starting-point. An early manifestation was Gabrieli's *Sonata pian e forte* (1597) for violin, cornett, and six trombones. But its codification into four set movements did not occur until the work of Arcangelo Corelli (1653–1713) of Bologna. It was developed in the keyboard compositions of C. P. E. Bach (1714–88), and was brought to perfection by Haydn and Mozart. Its theoretical foundations were foreshadowed in J.-P. Rameau's *Traité d'harmonie* (1722), but were not fully expounded until Carl Czerny's *School of Practical Composition* (1848), twenty years after the death of its greatest exponent—Beethoven.

Conventional sonata form divides the musical work into four contrasting movements. The opening *Allegro*, in fast tempo, has parallels with the operatic overture. The slow second movement grew out of the Baroque *aria da capo*. The third movement, usually minuet and trio, was based on the dance suite. The finale returns to a key and tempo reminiscent of the opening. Each of the four movements follows a standard pattern consisting of the *exposition* of melodic subjects, their harmonic *development*, and, at the end, their *recapitulation*, sometimes with a related *coda* or 'afterthought'.

Homophony is the opposite of polyphony. It is characterized by music based, like hymn tunes, on a progression of chords, whose constituent notes do not possess either melodic or rhythmic independence. Classical harmony, therefore, is the opposite of polyphonic counterpoint. The scene of J. S. Bach composing his '*Art of Fugue*' (1750) in an empty church in Leipzig symbolizes the passing of the polyphonic era. The scene of Beethoven, weary but sublimated, struggling to complete his five last quartets, may be taken as the summit of homophony.

Beethoven considered his *Quartet in C sharp minor, Opus 131* (1826), to be his finest work. In it, he expounds each of the elements from which sonata form had grown—an opening fugue; a single-theme scherzo; a central aria with variations; and a 'sonata within a sonata' on the inverted fugue. It has been called 'a cycle of human experience', and 'a microcosm of European music'.[1]

In that span from 1750 to 1827, Haydn, Mozart, and Beethoven composed between them over 150 symphonies, over 100 piano sonatas, over 50 string quartets, and numerous concertos—all in sonata form. These works form the core of the classical repertoire.

STRAD

LE MESSIE, 'The Messiah', bears the most prestigious of all labels: *Antonius Stradivarius Cremonensis Faciebat Anno 1716*. It was one of ten violins still in the workshop of Antonio Stradivari (*c*.1644–1737) almost forty years after his death, and was sold by his sons to Count Cozio di Salabue in 1775. Apart from a dozen years in the possession of the French music teacher Delphin Alard (1815–88), 'Il Salabue' belonged exclusively to dealers—Tarisio, Vuillaume, and W. E. Hills. Tarisio was always promising to show it to his friends, but never actually did so. 'It's like the Messiah,' one of them said; 'always promised, never produced.'[1]

The instrument, rarely played, sits in virtually mint condition in its humidified case in Oxford's Ashmolean Museum. It is nothing remarkable to look at. Unlike the 'Long Strads' of earlier date, it has the standard body length of 356 mm. It has a straight-grained belly, angular corners, plain purfling, slanting f-holes, and a two-panelled back in flamed walnut. Its pedigree is only revealed by the orange-brown glow of Stradivari's unique varnish. Joachim, who played it once, said that it 'combined sweetness and grandeur'.[2] The key to a string instrument's tonal quality was often thought to lie in its varnish. Too hard a varnish produces an ugly metallic sound; too soft a varnish dampens the resonance. Stradivari, a master in all departments of his trade, found a varnish whose great elasticity was also durable. His reputation is unequalled.

The violin emerged in late Renaissance Italy. It was descended from the family of six-stringed viols, and more particularly from the rebec and the *lira da braccio*. It was extremely versatile. Its fine melodic quality suited it for solo purposes, whilst it was the natural leader of the string group of violin, viola, cello, and double bass. As the common 'fiddle', it was easily adopted for dance music. Small, portable, and relatively inexpensive, it soon became the universal workhorse both of Europe's popular and of its 'classical' music. With the exception of Jacob Stainer (1617–78) in Tyrol, all the master violin-makers, from Maggini of Brescia to Amati and Stradivari of Cremona and Guarneri of Venice, were Italian.

The art of violin-playing was greatly advanced by the development of systematic teaching methods, including those of Leopold Mozart and of G. B. Viotti. The Paris Conservatoire, from 1795, was the predecessor of similar institutions in Prague (1811), Brussels (1813), Vienna (1817), Warsaw (1822), London (1822), St Petersburg (1862), and Berlin (1869).

A striking feature of violin-playing from the mid-nineteenth to the mid-twentieth centuries was the marked predominance of East Europeans. The phenomenon may possibly reflect the traditions of fiddle-playing among Jews and gypsies, and more probably the special status of music-making in politically repressed cultures. At all events, Niccolò Paganini (1782–1840) was for a long time the first and last of the 'greats' who was not either East European or Jewish or both. Joseph Joachim (1831–1907) of Vienna and Henryk Wieniawski (1835–80), a Pole from Lublin who helped launch the St Petersburg school, were founders of the magnificent line which ran through Kreisler, Ysaye, and Szigeti to Heifitz, Milstein, Oistrakh, Szeryng, and Isaac Stern. All played their 'Strads'. The 'Messiah' is one of the very few Stradivaris which, sadly, was destined to be seen but not heard. Modern craftsmen pay special attention to the choice of timber, variations in thickness and curvature, and effect of ageing.

none the less increased. The Socinians were expelled in 1658 for alleged collaboration with the Swedes. In 1718 all non-Catholics were barred from the Diet. In 1764 the Jews lost their Parliament, but not their *kahals* or local communes. Russian propaganda began to bemoan the plight of Poland's Orthodox, whose position was considerably easier than that of Catholics in Russia. Prussian propaganda inflated the alleged persecution of Lutherans.

The Roman Catholic Church settled into a routine that no longer sought to recover the Protestant lands. Much of its energies were directed abroad, especially to the Jesuit missions in South America, South India, Japan to 1715, China, and North America. The chain of twenty-one beautiful Franciscan missions in California, which were started by Fr. Junípero Serra (1713–84) and which ran from San Diego to San Francisco, have remained a spiritual solace in the surrounding wilderness to this day. In Europe the Vatican could not cope with the growing centrifugal tendencies of the Church provinces. One Pope, Innocent XI (1676–89), was driven in 1688 to excommunicate Louis XIV in secret for occupying Avignon in the *regalia* dispute. Another, Clement IX (1700–21), was pushed against his better judgement to issue the Bull *Unigenitus Dei filius* (1713) condemning Jansenism. The Bull, which was specifically directed against the *Réflexions morales* of Pasquier Quesnel, an Oratorian sympathetic to the Jansenists, caused a storm of protest dividing French opinion for decades. In the Netherlands in 1724 it led to schism within the Catholic ranks and the creation by the Archbishop of Utrecht of the Old Catholic Church of Holland. In Germany a movement started in 1763 by a tract of J. N. von Hontheim (Febronius) aimed to reconcile Catholics and Protestants by radically curtailing the centralizing powers of Rome. In Poland the Vatican lost effective control through political domination of the Church hierarchy by Russia.

In all these disputes the Jesuits, who showed themselves more papist than the Popes, became a growing embarrassment. Benedict XIV (1740–58), whose moderation won him the unusual accolade of praise from Voltaire, initiated an inquiry into their affairs. They were accused of running large-scale money-making operations, also of adopting native cults to win converts at any price. In 1759 they were banished from Portugal, in 1764 from France, and in 1767 from Spain and Naples. Clement XIII (1758–69) stood by the Society with the words *Sint ut sunt, aut non sint* (may they be as they are, or cease to be). But Clement XIV (1769–74), who was elected under the shadow of a formal demand by the Catholic powers for abolition, finally acquiesced. The brief *Dominus ac Redemptor noster* of 16 August 1773 abolished the Society of Jesus, on the grounds that it was no longer pursuing its founder's objectives. It took effect in all European countries except for the Russian Empire. It threw Catholic educational and missionary activities into chaos, opening major opportunities especially for secular schools and universities.

The horror of the age occurred in 1685, when Louis XIV revoked the Edict of Nantes and all of France's Huguenots were driven into exile (see below). But in general the pace of persecution was slackening. In many countries the laws of non-toleration were observed in the breach. Wherever nonconformists had survived, they now came into the open. In England a new label was coined—Latitudinarianism—to describe the strong body of opinion which favoured toleration for all Protestants. The Congregationalists or 'Independents' surfaced in 1662, initially on condition that their chapels were located at least five miles from any parish church. Following the remarkable career of George Fox (1624–91), the Society of Friends or 'Quakers' suffered numerous martyrdoms until gaining the right to worship, like other dissenters, from the Toleration Act of 1689. The General Body of Dissenters—Independents, Presbyterians, and Baptists—was organized in London in 1727. The Moravian Church re-emerged in Holland, in England, and in the experimental community of Herrnhut (1722) in Saxony. Eighteenth-century manners, as opposed to many eighteenth-century laws, favoured toleration. The climate was right for deists, for dissenters, even for religious jokers. 'They say', wrote Voltaire, 'that God is always on the side of the big battalions.' [MASON]

Various religious counter-currents appeared, in reaction to the growing inertia of the established Churches. In the Catholic world the Quietism of Miguel de Molinos (*c.*1640–97) caused real disquiet. Its founder, who taught that sin can only be avoided in a state of complete spiritual passivity, died in prison in Rome; and his book, the *Spiritual Guide* (1675), was condemned by the Jesuits as heretical. In the Lutheran world, the Pietism of P. J. Spener (1635–1705) caused similar ructions. Its founder, who proclaimed the universal priesthood of the faithful, instituted the practice of devotional circles for Bible-reading; and his book, *Pia Desideria* (1675), became the keystone of a long-lasting movement. The University of Halle was its centre.

In the Anglican world, the Methodism of John Wesley (1703–91) threatened to tear the Church of England apart. Wesley had created a spiritual Method for his 'Holy Club' of students at Oxford, and had visited Herrnhut. His lifetime of evangelism, touring the remotest parts of the British Isles, fired the neglected masses with enthusiasm. His rejection of episcopacy, however, was bound to cause a schism, and the first Methodist Conference assembled in London in 1785. His brother Charles Wesley (1707–88) was an Anglican hymn-writer of genius, whose magnificent cadences well expressed the changing tone of the times.

Methodism took particularly powerful root in Wales, where it is widely believed to have inspired not just a religious but a national revival.[3] The first Welsh Methodist Association, which met in January 1743, preceded the first equivalent meeting in England. Its Calvinistic theology was to lead in a direction more akin to Presbyterianism. At the same time, the Circulating Schools organized by the Revd Griffith Jones, Rector of Llanddowror; the magnificent Welsh hymns of William Williams (1717–91), 'Williams Pant y Celyn'; and an elevated preaching tradition started by Daniel Rowland (1713–90) of Llangeitho, the 'Jerusalem of Wales', forged the instruments which would ensure the survival of Welsh language and culture into modern times. No one who has heard a Welsh choir soaring in full harmony to the strains of *Llanfair, Cwm Rhondda*, or *Blaenwern* can fail to appreciate what national pride and spiritual uplift mean. Needless to say, the *hwyl* or fervour of the Welsh Methodists was diametrically opposed to the temper of the Enlightenment, which by then was the dominant trend in the leading intellectual circles of Europe.

In the Jewish world, the Hasidism of Baal Shem Tov (1700–60), the *Besht* of Międzybóż in Podolia, undermined the Polish rabbis much as Wesley was undermining the Anglican bishops. The *Hasidim* or 'Pious Ones' rejected the desiccated formalism of the synagogues, and set themselves apart in clannish communities ruled by hereditary *zaddiks* or 'holy men'. They were very distant in space and culture from Christian Methodism, but were close in temper. They rigorously adhered to orthodox Judaic laws of dress and diet, but, once again, the movement was marked by the fervour of the masses, by joyful music, by the revival of spirituality.

Equally prominent was a decided shift in Europe's social manners. People reacted against the strictures of the preceding age not so much by changing the laws as by ignoring the norms of taste and conduct which the religious authorities had once been able to impose. In sharp contrast to the Calvinist and Jesuit puritanism which still predominated *c.*1660, the following century saw both a sharp rise in artistic sensitivity and a sharp decline in moral restraints. The 'Age of Elegance' went hand in hand with an age of easy scruples. On the one hand the upper classes and their imitators took to the arts of graceful living as never before: luxury and refinement were seen everywhere in their dress, their palaces, their furniture, their music, their collections. At the same time, in all classes, there was a marked relaxation of social, and especially sexual, mores. With time, sexual licence became not just tolerated but ostentatious. After the long interval of the Reformations, everyone was free, if they wanted, to behave once again with abandon. For those whose health and pockets could afford it, excess in dressing, carousing, gourmandizing, and philandering was routine. People took pride in the perruque and the puffed petticoat, in the landscaped park, in painted porcelain and the powdered pudendum. This was the social climate which no doubt

---

EROS

I⊤ has been stated that 'he left no stern unturned'. Friedrich Augustus, Elector of Saxony and King of Poland, is said to be the father of some 300 children, including Maurice de Saxe, Marshal of France (1696–1750). His wonderful amours attested both to his catholic taste and his phenomenal stamina.¹ Apart from his wife, Eberdine of Bayreuth, he cultivated the favours of a covey of concubines—official, confidential, and top-secret. Maurice de Saxe was the son of the Swedish Countess Aurora of Konigsmarck; his half-brother, Count Rotowski, was the child of Fatima, a Turkish girl captured at Buda; his half-sister, Countess Orzelska, of Henriette Duval, daughter of a Warsaw wine-merchant. On the official list, the Countess d'Esterle was followed by Mme Teschen, Mme Hoym, Mme Cosel, Maria, Countess Denhoff, but not, exceptionally, by the ex-mistress of the British ambassador in Dresden. Friedrich Augustus would have been a great king if only his political ventures had been half as well-aimed as his spermatozoa.² (Spoil-sports estimate his progeny at eight.)³

---

helped promote the religious revivals. But it also enlarged the margin of intellectual tolerance which the *philosophes* of the Enlightenment were able to exploit. [**EROS**]

The Enlightenment, according to Kant, was the period in the development of European civilization when 'Mankind grew out of its self-inflicted immaturity'. More simply, one might say that Europeans reached 'the age of discretion'. The metaphor is a powerful one, with medieval Christendom seen as the parent and Europe's secular culture as a growing child conceived in the Renaissance. Childhood had been encumbered by the baggage of parental and religious tradition and by family quarrels. The key attainment came with 'the autonomy of reason', the ability to think and act for oneself. But the child continued to possess a number of strong family traits.

Perhaps the Enlightenment is best understood, however, by reference to the darkness which this 'light of reason' was trying to illuminate. The darkness was provided, not by religion as such, which was taken by the *philosophes* to be filling a basic human need, but by all the unthinking, irrational, dogmatic attitudes with which European Christianity had become encrusted. These attitudes, including bigotry, intolerance, superstition, monkishness, and fanaticism, were summed up in the most pejorative word of the age, 'enthusiasm'. The *Lumières*, as the French called the movement, were to be beamed on to a wide range of subjects: philosophy, science and natural religion, economics, politics, history, and education.

The particular intellectual habitat which fostered the growth of rationalism was not to be found everywhere. It required on the one hand the presence of both

Catholics and Protestants, whose rival dogmas set up a suitable clash of ideas, and on the other hand a measure of toleration within which a rational dialogue could be started. In the seventeenth century it was only found in three or four locations. Such conditions existed in Poland-Lithuania—where Jesuits mingled with Orthodox, Jews, and a number of radical sects. They existed to some extent in Switzerland, where an interchange of ideas was always possible between the Catholic and Protestant cantons. They existed in Scotland, and in England, where the broad Anglican tradition protected contrary points of view. But they existed above all in the Netherlands, where the native resources were supplemented by a long line of intellectual refugees, from J. J. Scaliger and René Descartes to Spinoza, Shaftesbury, Le Clerc, and Bayle. Leyden, the 'Athens of Batavia', Amsterdam, the 'Cosmopolis' of Europe, and The Hague were the main laboratories of the Enlightenment. Although Frenchmen were prominent from the start, and French was adopted as the *lingua franca*, France itself did not become the principal scene of activity until the mid-eighteenth century, when local conditions relaxed. Voltaire, one of the central figures, was forced to settle in Switzerland, or on the Swiss border.

The key concept—the *lumen naturale* or 'natural light of reason'—has been traced to one of Melanchthon's works, *De lege naturae* (1559), and via Melanchthon to Cicero and the Stoic philosophers. For this reason the translation of the text of the Stoics by Joost Lips (Lipsius, 1547–1606) at Leyden is seen as a landmark. Together with the fruits of the Scientific Revolution and the rational method of Descartes, it formed the core of an ideology which held centre-stage from the 1670s to the 1770s. It led to the conviction that reason could uncover the rules that underlay the apparent chaos of both the human and material world, and hence of natural religion, of natural morality, of natural law. In the arts, too, it led to the notion that strict rules and symmetrical patterns could alone give expression to the natural order with which all Beauty should be associated. Beauty was order; and order was beautiful. Here was the true spirit of Classicism.

The philosophy of the Enlightenment was primarily concerned with epistemology, that is, the theory of knowledge—or how we know what we know. Here, the basis for debate was supplied by three Britons: the Englishman John Locke (1632–1704), the Irishman Bishop George Berkeley (1685–1753), and the Scotsman David Hume (1711–76), sometime secretary of the British Embassy in Paris. As empiricists, they all accepted that the scientific method of observation and deduction should be applied to human affairs, and hence the precept of their contemporary, Alexander Pope:

> Know then thyself, presume not God to scan,
> The proper study of mankind is Man.[4]

Locke's famous *Essay Concerning Human Understanding* (1690) advanced the proposition that the human mind is blank at birth—a *tabula rasa*. All we know, therefore, is the fruit of experience, either through the senses, which process data from the external world, or through the faculty of reflection, which processes data from the mind's internal workings. Locke's proposition was developed in France by the Abbé Condillac (1715–80), whose *Traité des Sensations* (1754) used the analogy of an inanimate statue brought to life by the acquisition of its senses, and by Julien Offray de la Mettrie (1709–51), whose thoroughgoing materialism in *L'Homme machine* (1748) denied the existence of the spiritual altogether. Bishop Berkeley went to the other extreme, arguing that only minds and mental events can exist. Hume, whose *Treatise of Human Nature* (1739–40) pursues a rational inquiry into understanding, passions, and morals, ends up by denying the possibility of rational belief. Eighteenth-century rationalism concluded after all that irrationality may not be entirely unreasonable.

In the realm of moral philosophy, several strands of religious and intellectual thought led towards the ultimate destination of utilitarianism. Rationalists tended to judge moral principles by their utility in improving man's condition. The tendency is already present in Locke. Baron d'Holbach (1723–89), in some ways the most radical of the *philosophes*, advocated a hedonistic morality where virtue is that which causes the greatest pleasure. Later, happiness was viewed more as a communal than as an individual virtue. Social harmony became the goal, not just private well-being. In 1776 a young Jeremy Bentham (1748–1832) formulated the guiding principle: 'It is the greatest happiness of the greatest number that is the measure of right and wrong.'

The Enlightenment was not sympathetic to European Jewry. The Jews were regarded as a religious community, and their religion as unreasonable and obscurantist. Dryden, for one, did not spare the sarcasm:

> 'The Jews, a headstrong, moody, murmuring race,
> God's pampered people, whom, debauched with ease,
> No King could govern, nor no god could please.'[5]

In time, certain Jewish leaders grew similarly critical of themselves. They longed to escape from the constrictions of traditional Judaism. The end result was the Jewish Enlightenment, the *Haskalah*, which sought to reform the Jewish community from within (see p. 843).

Scientific knowledge, in the meantime, made great strides. The central giant of the period was Sir Isaac Newton (1642–1727), President of the Royal Society, who published his *Principia* in 1687. His Laws of Motion and Gravity provided the basis of physics, and hence of the working of the universe, for over 200 years. He invented differential calculus, which he called 'fluxions'. Appropriately enough for a father of the Enlightenment, he had conducted his first experiments in 1666 into the nature of Light, placing a glass prism behind a hole in the blind of his window in Trinity College, Cambridge:

'And I saw . . . that the light, tending to [one] end of the Image, did suver a Refraction considerably greater than the light tending to the other. And so the true cause of the length of that Image was detected to be no other, than that Light consists of *Rays differently refrangible* which . . . were, according to their degrees of refrangibility, transmitted towards divers parts of the wall.'[6]

It was a nice irony that the properties of light eventually gave Einstein the clues which eventually overthrew the Newtonian system. [$e = mc^2$] Newton, as a Unitarian, was debarred from many formal honours, but he did not miss out on fame and fortune. He even dabbled in alchemy. He described himself charmingly as 'a boy playing on the sea-shore . . . while the great ocean of truth lay all undiscovered before me'.[7] Pope wrote an epitaph intended for Newton's tomb in Westminster Abbey:

> Nature and Nature's laws lay hid in night;
> God said, Let Newton be! and all was light.

The exploitation of Newton's principles was assisted both by improvements in technology and by parallel advances in other sciences. The Royal Observatory (1675) at Greenwich developed superior telescopes; the British Admiralty, by offering a prize of £20,000, was given the chronometer. In mathematics the Leipziger Gottfried Leibniz (1646–1716) may well have discovered calculus independently before Newton did. In biology and, more specifically, in botany, the Swede Carl von Linne (Linnaeus, 1707–78), brought order from chaos in his system for classifying plants expounded in the *Systema naturae* (1735) and *Fundamenta botanica* (1736). In chemistry, fundamental steps were taken by Joseph Priestley (1733–1804), who explored the compound nature of air, by Henry Cavendish (1731–1810), who demonstrated the compound nature of water, and above all by Antoine-Laurent Lavoisier (1743–94), who finally discovered the workings of chemical reactions. [ELDLUFT][EULER]

The interest in the theory of knowledge, when added to the growing corpus of information, had a natural corollary in a mania for encyclopedias. Compendia of universal knowledge had been common enough in the Middle Ages; but they had fallen out of fashion. Early attempts to revive the genre included those of J. H. Alsted, published in Holland in 1630, and of Louis Moreri, published at Lyons in 1674. The father of the modern medium, however, is generally taken to be Pierre Bayle (1647–1706). The first folio of his *Dictionnaire historique et critique* appeared in Rotterdam in 1697. In England the genre was represented by the *Lexicon technicum* (1704) of John Harris FRS, and by the *Cyclopaedia* (1728) of Ephraim Chambers; in Germany by J. Hübner's *Reales Staats Zeitungs- und Conversations-Lexicon* (Leipzig, 1704) and by J. T. Jablonski's *Allgemeines Lexicon* (Leipzig, 1721); in Italy by G. Pivati's *Dizionario universale* (Venice, 1744); and in Poland by B. Chmielowski's *Nowe Ateny* (1745–6). A vast illustrated *Universal Lexicon* in 64 volumes and 4 supplements was published in Leipzig by J. H. Zedler between 1732 and 1754. In France, the great project of the *Encyclopédie* or *Dictionnaire raisonné des arts, des sciences, et des métiers*, undertaken by Denis Diderot (1713–84) and Jean d'Alembert (1717–83), was originally inspired by a French translation of Chambers. It appeared in Paris in 17 volumes of 16,288 pages between 1751 and 1765, with further supplements, illustrations, and indexes appearing up to 1782. It was programmatic, opinionated, anticlerical, and highly critical of the regime; and its editors were regularly harassed by officialdom. Yet it was a monument to

EULER

IN 1765 the Russian ambassador at Berlin was authorized to invite a one-eyed man to St Petersburg and not to spare the cost. Leonhard Euler (1707–83) accepted on condition that he receive the directorship of the Russian Imperial Academy, a vast salary of 3,000 roubles, a pension for his wife, and high appointments for his four sons. His conditions were met without demur. Five years earlier, when the Russian army had vandalized his farm at Charlottenburg, the Tsar had compensated him richly. For Euler was the supreme mathematical wizard of the age. By common accord, his only peer in the history of mathematics was C. F. Gauss (1777–1855), who was born in Brunswick ten years after Euler left Berlin.

It was said that 'Euler calculated as other men breathe, or eagles soar'. Son of a Swiss pastor and educated at Basle, he possessed a phenomenal memory. He could recite the whole of Virgil's *Aeneid* including the numbers of the lines and pages. He first went to Russia as a young man in the company of the Bernouilli brothers, before being 'head-hunted' by the agents of Frederick the Great. His output was as prolific as it was original. He wrote 886 scientific works and *c.*4,000 letters, at an average rate of two printed pages per day over five decades. The Russian journal *Commentarii Academiae Scientiarum Imperialis Petropolitanae* was still publishing the backlog of his articles forty-five years after his death. He discovered any number of theorems, invented the calculation of sines, completed the search for the numerical evaluation of pi, and posited the existence of transcendental numbers. 'Euler's Theorem' demonstrated the connection between exponential and trigonometric functions:

$$e^{ix} = \cos x + i \sin x$$

Euler's prestige brought the Russian Academy into the mainstream of European science. The brilliant school of mathematics at St Petersburg long outlasted him. But he was reluctant to talk about it. When pressed on the matter at Potsdam by Frederick the Great's mother, he replied, 'Madam, in that country they hang those who talk.'[1] Such however was Euler's authority that the symbols employed in his textbook *Introductio in analysis infinitorum* (1748) were to provide the basis for standard mathematical notation. He was instrumental in promoting for mathematicians a universal medium of communication of a type which, for the purpose of everyday life, Europeans never developed. (See Appendix III, p. 1243.)

the age. It aimed at nothing less than a summary of the whole of human know-ledge. The first edition of the *Encyclopaedia Britannica*, less distinguished but longer-lived, appeared in Edinburgh in 1768. In the meantime, Hübner's *Lexicon* had run into many editions and translations. Its copyright would eventually be bought in 1808 by the publisher F. A. Brockhaus (1772–1823), who used it as the basis for the most celebrated of all German encyclopedias.

Religious thought was profoundly influenced by rationalism—especially in the sphere of biblical scholarship. The initial problem was how to distinguish between the rival claims of Catholics and Protestants, both of whom gave scriptural back-ing to their dogmas. An early start had been made in *The Religion of Protestants* (1637) by William Chillingworth, an Oxford Fellow who had studied with the Jesuits at Douai and who, typically, was falsely accused of being a Socinian. The biggest advance was made by the French Oratorian Richard Simon (1638–1712), who applied the classical rules of French literary criticism to his *Histoire critique du Vieux Testament* (1678). Simon's book was attacked by Bossuet and placed on the Index, and all copies of the first edition destroyed. But the method survived.

In due course, reasoning about religion gave rise to an intellectual fashion for Deism. This was religious belief reduced to its minimal core: belief in a 'Supreme Being', in God the Creator, or in Providence. Its early manifestations surfaced in England in various shaky credos, notably the *De Veritate* (Paris, 1624) of Lord Herbert of Cherbury (1583–1648) and J. J. Toland's *Christianity Not Mysterious* (1696). It reached its peak in the 1730s, when Voltaire was in England, but was much diminished after the publication of *The Analogy of Religion* (1736) by Bishop Joseph Butler—of whose lasting influence Queen Caroline was once told: 'No Madam, he is not dead, but he is buried.' Deistic positions were reached in France in attempts to find the middle ground between traditional Christianity and the more extreme free-thinkers, such as Baron d'Holbach (1723–89) and Claude Helvetius (1715–71), who had begun to express openly Atheist opinions. Diderot, for example, writing the entries for his *Encyclopédie* on 'Christianity', 'Faith', and 'Providence', took a Deist stance. Voltaire, whose attacks on established religion were unrelenting, none the less sprang to defend the existence of God against the attacks of d'Holbach's *Système de la nature* (1770). Reflecting on the sky at night, he wrote: 'One would have to be blind not to be dazzled by this sight; one would have to be stupid not to recognise its author; one would have to be mad not to worship him.' 'Si Dieu n'existait pas,' he quipped, 'il faudrait l'inventer.'[8] (If God did not exist, He would have to be invented.)

The struggle of the *philosophes* against the authorities of Church and State inevitably created the impression that Catholicism and absolute monarchy were united in their blind opposition to all reason and change. Diderot has been cred-ited with the uncharitable comment about Salvation arriving when 'the last King was strangled with the entrails of the last priest'. He was only one step away from the simplified revolutionary vision of the universal war between progress and reaction. In due course the Catholic publicist Joseph de Maistre (1754–1821) accepted the same extreme position but from the opposite point of view, maintaining in his *Considérations sur la France* (1796) that rebellion and impiety are synonymous.

Rational economics stood high on the Enlightenment's list of priorities. The general notion of progress found expression in the particular idea of economic improvement. At the micro-level, gentlemen were absorbed by the rising science of estate management, convinced that their properties could not simply be put in order but could be transformed into thriving businesses. Land reclamation by the Dutch or on the Dutch model changed the face of several low-lying regions, from the fenlands of East Anglia to the delta of the Vistula. The enclosure movement gained speed, especially in England, threatening the peasantry but promising larger agrarian units suitable for commercial cultivation. Systematic stock-breeding, plant selection, soil nutrition, crop rotation, and drainage, as practised by 'Farmer George' at Windsor in the 1770s or by Thomas Coke of Holkham in Norfolk, was rewarded by dramatically improved yields. In those countries where serfdom prevailed, some enlightened landowners convinced themselves that their serfs would work more efficiently if freed from their obligations. Instances of voluntary emancipation can be found from France to Poland.

At the macro-level, mercantilism of the autocratic variety long held sway. Its great exponent was Jean-Baptiste Colbert (1619–83), minister to Louis XIV. State manufactories were started. Colonies were planted, taxation rationalized, ports, roads, and canals constructed, transport improved. The great Canal du Languedoc (1681) had its counterparts right across Europe, from the canalized Guadalquivir in Spain to the Eskilstuna Canal in Sweden, the Augustów Canal in Lithuania, and the great Neva–Volga complex in Russia.

Yet the conviction grew that economic life could not expand beyond a certain point unless shorn of artificial curbs and restrictions. This trend found early expression in the work of the Irish banker Richard Cantillon (d. 1734), who was quoted by Mirabeau senior in the highly popular work *L'Ami des hommes* (1756). But it gained currency with the economists or 'Physiocrats' associated with the *Encyclopédie*—François Quesnay (1694–1774), Jean de Gournay (1712–59), and J. P. Dupont de Nemours (1739–1817). The celebrated slogan 'Pauvres paysans, pauvre royaume' encapsulated the revolutionary notion that national prosperity could only be assured through the personal prosperity and liberty of all. Quesnay's disciple Jacques Turgot (1727–81) failed in the attempt to apply the movement's principles to practical government. But the Scots professor Adam Smith (1723–90), residing in Paris in 1765–6, made the close acquaintance of Quesnay's circle. It was a formative experience for the founder of modern economics. [**MARKET**]

Rationalist political theory was long associated with support for absolute monarchy, which accorded well with the classical spirit of order and harmony. It was seeking for the most efficient means of cutting through the maze of local and feudal privilege. Hobbes's conclusions, if not his argumentation, were not all that different from those of French divines such as the great J. B. Bossuet, Bishop of

Meaux (1627–1704), chief advocate of the divine right of kings. In the eighteenth century, however, the arguments changed. Locke's two *Treatises on Government* (1690) proposed that government should be subject to natural law, and opposed the hereditary principle. He demanded some form of neutral authority for settling disputes between ruler and ruled. Most importantly, whilst underlining the rights of property, he developed the idea of government through a social contract, and hence the principle of consent, the corner-stone of liberalism. Though he had little to say about the judiciary, he advocated the separation of powers, and the need for checks and balances between the executive and the legislative. These two last principles were most clearly formulated in *L'Esprit des lois* (Geneva, 1748) of Charles Louis de Secondat, Baron de Montesquieu (1689–1755), who drew his inspiration partly from Greek and Roman republicanism and partly from the English constitutional settlement of 1689:

In each state, there are three sorts of powers: the legislative power, the executive power over things dependent on the rights of the people, and the executive power relating to the civil law . . . All would be lost if the same man . . . were to exercise all three of these powers: the power of making laws, the power of putting public resolutions into effect, and the power of judging crimes.[9]

The theories of Locke and Montesquieu were widely disseminated by the *Encyclopédie*, especially in entries such as 'Political Authority' and 'Natural Liberty'. They encouraged democratic tendencies and, some would say, revolution.

Rationalist history-writing came to the fore. History moved from the mere relation of events in chronicles or diaries, and from the advocacy of the ruling church or monarch, to become the science of causation and change. Bossuet's so-called *Histoire universelle* (1681) or the Earl of Clarendon's *History of the Great Rebellion* (1704) still belonged to the old tradition, as did numerous Catholic and Protestant accounts of the religious wars. But in the eighteenth century several people turned their hand to history of the new sort. Bayle's *Dictionnaire* (1702) consisted of alphabetical entries on all the great names of history and literature, and examined with implacable scepticism the certainties and uncertainties in the received information about each of them. It showed that no historical fact could be accepted without evidence. Vico's *Scienza nuova* (1725) introduced the theory of history moving in cycles. Montesquieu's *Considérations* (1734) on the ancient world introduced the idea of environmental determinants, whilst Voltaire's studies of Charles XII or of Louis XIV introduced the factors of chance and of great personalities. Hume's treatise on *The Natural History of Religion* (1757) broke the sacred sod of religious history. All rejected the role of providence as an explanation for past events, and in so doing were returning to habits of thought not exercised since Machiavelli and Guicciardini. They were all susceptible to the new-fangled notion of progress, whose classic exposition was made at the Sorbonne by the young Turgot, in a long Latin discourse read in two parts on 3 July and 11 December 1750:

MARKET

D R ADAM SMITH (1723–90) was the ultimate absent-minded professor. He once brewed an infusion of bread and butter and pronounced it a very bad cup of tea. He became one of the sights of Edinburgh, where he was given to rambling the streets in a trance, half-dressed and twitching all over, heatedly debating with himself in a peculiar affected voice and careering along with his inimitable 'worm-like' gait. He once walked straight into a tanning pit in full discourse. Virtually unmarriageable, he always lived with his mother. It is nice to think that this charmingly chaotic character should have set about putting intellectual order into the workings of everyday life.[1]

Together with his friend David Hume, Smith was one of the stars of the Scottish Enlightenment in an era when English academic life slumbered. He was in close touch with Johnson, Voltaire, Franklin, Quesnay, Burke. When the elderly professor was received by the King's ministers, they all rose to their feet. 'We all stand, Mr Smith,' said William Pitt, 'because we are all your scholars.'

Smith's career started at the age of 28 with the Chair of Moral Philosophy at Glasgow, where he published his *Theory of Moral Sentiments* (1759). It was an enquiry into the origins of approval and disapproval. He entered the realm of economics by asking himself about the implications of human greed, and how self-interest could work for the common good. The 900 pages of *The Wealth of Nations* (1776) were essentially an extended essay in pursuit of that quest. It shattered the protectionist philosophy of mercantilism, which had reigned supreme in economic thought for 200 years. Smith's speculations led him to postulate the existence of 'society', in whose mechanisms all people participate, and to formulate the laws of 'the market'. He outlined the workings of production, of competition, of supply and demand, and of prices. He paid special attention to the organization of labour. This is shown in his famous description of a pin factory. Rationalized tasks and specialized skills enabled the workforce to produce 48,000 pins a day, where each of the workers might individually produce only two or three. He also stressed the self-regulating nature of the market, which, if unhindered, would foster social harmony. He identified two basic market laws—the Law of Accumulation and the Law of Population. 'The demand for men', he wrote rather shockingly, 'necessarily regulates the production of men.' His watchword was: 'Let the Market Alone.'[2]

The science of economics has been exploring the issues raised by Smith ever since. The trail leads from Ricardo, Malthus, and Marx, via Hobson, Bastiat, and Marshall, to Veblen, Schumpeter, and Keynes. In Smith's hands it was a branch of speculative philosophy; and its greatest practitioners have recognized the fragility of their conclusions. In the popular mind, however, economics has greater pretensions. It has moved into the void left by the decline of religion and the moral consensus; and it is increasingly seen as the main preoccupation of public policy, a panacea for social ills, the source even of private contentment. From being a technical subject, explaining human society in the way that medicine explains the human body, it threatens to become an end in itself, laying down goals, motives, incentives. Smith, the moralist, would have been appalled.

Nature has given all men the right of being happy . . . All the generations are linked to one another by a series of causes and effects which join the present condition of the world with all those that have preceded it . . . and the whole human species, looked at from its origins, appears to the philosopher as an immense whole, which, like an individual, has its infancy and its progress . . . The totality of humanity, fluctuating between calm and agitation, between good times and bad, moves steadily though slowly towards a greater perfection.[10]

Historians increasingly applied the social, economic, and cultural concerns of their own day to the analysis of the past. The doings of kings and courts no longer sufficed. Two great monuments of the age were William Robertson's *History of America* (1777) and Edward Gibbon's incomparable *Decline and Fall of the Roman Empire* (1788). Only one volume of the *History of the Polish Nation* (1780–) by Bishop Adam Naruszewicz saw the light of day, since the Empress Catherine's ambassador objected to a description of early Slav history in which the Poles were more prominent than the Russians.

On reflection, one has to doubt whether the sages of the Enlightenment were any more objective than the court and clerical historians whom they so mercilessly ridiculed. Gibbon's attacks on, say, monasticism, or Voltaire's ill-informed swipes at Poland, which he used as a whipping-boy to enliven his views on religious bigotry, replaced one form of bias by another. But in the process both the scope and reputation of historiography was greatly increased. In reality, the Enlightenment was full of contradictions. Its leading practitioners held a measure of agreement on aims and methods, but reached no consensus of views and opinions. The two most influential figures, Voltaire and Rousseau, were as different as chalk and cheese.

François-Marie Arouet (1694–1778), who had assumed the pen-name of Voltaire during a spell of imprisonment in the Bastille, was poet, dramatist, novelist, historian, philosopher, pamphleteer, correspondent of kings, and, above all, a militant wit. Born and educated in Paris, he spent much of his long life in various sorts of exile. His books, printers, and publishers were repeatedly condemned. He hovered on the outer fringes of political and social respectability, and eventually settled, symbolically, on the furthest frontier of France at Ferney, near

Geneva. He left Paris in disgrace at 32 and, apart from three uneasy years as historiographer royal at Versailles in 1744–7, he did not return until the age of 84. He spent six seminal years in England, three at the welcoming court of Stanisław Leszczyński at Lunéville in Lorraine, and three in Prussia with an admiring Frederick the Great. He was chased from Switzerland for comments about Calvin. At Ferney, 1760–78, where he held court to a constant crush of visitors, 'Europe's Inn-keeper' was hailed as 'Le Roi Voltaire'; and 'le seigneur du village' put his theories into practice: draining the marsh, running a model farm, building a church, a theatre, a silk factory, and a watch works. 'The refuge of forty savages has been turned into an opulent little town of 1,200 useful persons,' he noted with pride.

Voltaire's published works, which fill over 100 volumes, are addressed to the goals of tolerance in religion, peace and liberty in politics, enterprise in economics, intellectual leadership in the arts. The *Lettres anglaises* (1734), which talk admiringly about everything from the Quakers, Parliament, and the commercial spirit to Bacon, Locke, and Shakespeare, gave new food for thought to conventional Catholic circles on the Continent. The *Siècle de Louis XIV* (1751) gave the French a rich but critical view of their recent past. The philosophical novel *Candide ou l'optimisme* (1759) was written in response to Rousseau. It tells the story of the eager young Candide and his enlightened tutor, Pangloss, whose motto is 'all is for the best in the best of all possible worlds'. They set out into the world from the Castle of Thunder-ten-tronckh only to meet with every known form of disaster: war, massacre, disease, arrest, torture, treachery, earthquake, shipwreck, inquisition, and slavery. In the end they conclude, since the evils of the world are overwhelming, that all one can do is to put one's own affairs into order. Candide's closing words are 'il faut cultiver notre jardin' (we have to cultivate our own garden). The *Traité sur la tolérance* (1763), inspired by the appalling Calas affair in Toulouse, where a Calvinist father was broken on the wheel for allegedly opposing his son's conversion to Catholicism, was a cry from the heart. The *Dictionnaire philosophique portatif* (1764), a pocket-sized rival to the great *Encyclopédie*, is a *tour de force* of irony and satire. In addition there are a score of tragedies, a vast collection of polemical pamphlets, some 15,000 letters. He died in Paris, having seen his bust crowned on the stage of his latest play. 'They would come in the same numbers to see my execution,' he said. And he was still writing verse:

> Nous naissons, nous vivons, bergère,
> Nous mourons sans savoir comment;
> Chacun est parti du néant;
> Où va-t-il? . . . Dieu le sait, ma chère.

(We are born, we live, my shepherdess | How or why we die, it isn't clear; | Each one took off from nothingness; | Where to? . . . God knows, my dear.)[11]

'I die adoring God,' he proclaimed, 'loving my friends, not hating my enemies, but detesting superstition.'[12]

Jean-Jacques Rousseau (1712–78), born in Protestant Geneva, was still more of a wanderer than Voltaire. He possessed almost the same range of talents, as musician, novelist, and philosopher, and acquired a similarly formidable reputation. A runaway boy, who spent almost a decade on the open roads of Savoy and Switzerland, he was taken in, at the price of his conversion, by a Catholic lady living at Annecy. Largely self-educated, he made his way in the world as a tutor, composer, ballet-master, as a valet in Paris, as secretary of the French embassy in Venice. His liaison with a simple and uneducated girl, Thérèse Levasseur, and the fate of their five children, who were given in care to the Enfants Trouvés (Foundlings), was the source of much stress, of intellectual speculation, and possibly of his recurrent mental illness. He gained sudden celebrity in middle age by winning a prize from the Academy of Dijon for his *Discours sur les sciences et les arts* (1750), and by producing a popular opera, *Le Devin du village* (1752). Befriended by Diderot, he became by turns star and victim of the Parisian salons until he took once more to the road. Obsessed with a non-existent conspiracy against him, he was driven from refuge to refuge by fears of Voltaire's partisans and by his own inner insecurities: to Geneva, to Motiers in Prussian Neuchâtel, to an island in the Lac de Bienne, to England, to Bourgoin and Montquin in Dauphiné. His last years in Paris were spent editing his memoirs and the *Rêveries du promeneur solitaire* (1782). He died in the castle of Ermenonville.

Rousseau's contrary character used the methods of the Enlightenment to denounce the Enlightenment's achievements. The Discourse which made him famous argued that civilization was corrupting human nature. His second *Discours sur l'inégalité* (1755) painted an idyllic vision of primitive man and blamed prosperity for all the ills of political and social relations. It united both the radicals and the conservatives against him. The novel *Julie ou la nouvelle Héloïse* (1761), a love story set amid Rousseau's native Alps, forged an unprecedented link between passion, moral sentiment, and untamed nature. *Émile ou l'éducation* (1762), another prodigious success, outlines the upbringing of a child who is to avoid the artificial decadence of civilization. This child of nature was to learn from God-given experience, not from man-made books; to be happy, he must be skilled and free.

Du contrat social (1762) was truly revolutionary. Its opening sentence railed at the iniquity of the reigning order: 'L'homme est né libre, et partout il est dans les fers' (man is born free, and everywhere he is shackled). Its dominant ideas—the general will, the sovereign nation, and the Contract itself—pointed to solutions which would only be effectively defined, not by any ideal ruler, but by the interests of the governed. Whilst Voltaire appealed to the enlightened élite, here was Rousseau appealing to the masses.

Rousseau's *Confessions* (published 1782–9) analysed the author's extremely uncharming personality with great charm and candour. He makes an exhibition of his guilt and doubt. 'He beats his breast vigorously', wrote one critic, 'in the knowledge that the reader will forgive him.' This preoccupation with the contortions of his own psychology was reminiscent of a later age. Rousseau despised his fellow philosophers, especially Voltaire. He was all set to tell the Supreme Being on Judgement Day: 'Je fus meilleur que cet homme-là!' (I was better than that man over there!).[13]

Education was the sphere to which the ideas of the Enlightenment were most readily applicable. The Church held a virtual monopoly in the curricula of schools and universities. The influence of Renaissance humanism was long since diluted. In the Catholic world, Jesuit and Piarist schools for boys, and Ursuline schools for girls, were set in their ways. In France, pedagogy had ossified following the closure of both Huguenot and Jansenist schools. In the Protestant world, too, if Gibbon's memoirs of Oxford are to be believed, lethargy prevailed. 'The five years spent at Magdalen College', he recalled, 'were the five most idle and unprofitable years of my whole life.' Scotland's schools and universities were in much better shape, as were those in Prussia. The foundations of August Hermann Francke (1664–1727) at Halle and the *Realschule* in Berlin were laying the foundations both of vernacular and of technical schooling. None the less, the Enlightenment was pitted almost everywhere against a strongly entrenched religious tradition in education. D'Alembert's article in the *Encyclopédie* under 'College' raised an uproar:

All this means, is that a young man . . . leaves the college after ten years, with an imperfect knowledge of a dead language, with precepts of rhetoric and philosophy which he should endeavour to forget: often with impaired health . . . and more frequently with such a superficial knowledge of religion that he succumbs to the first blasphemous conversation . . .[14]

In the long run, under the influence of the Enlightenment religious teaching was separated from general education; modern subjects were introduced to supplement the classics; and, as in Bentham's long campaign for the University of London, higher education was divorced from ecclesiastical patronage. [COMENIUS]

Nothing, however, could rival the impact of *Émile*. Rousseau was not impressed by the methods of his fellow *philosophes*. 'Locke's great maxim was to reason with children, and that is the current vogue,' he wrote; 'but . . . I see no more stupid children than those who have been reasoned with' (*Émile*, bk. II). Instead, he advocated 'natural education' from birth to maturity, with book learning forbidden before adolescence. He exploded current assumptions about child development. The first educational manual in the Rousseauian spirit, J. B. Basedow's *Elementarwerk*, appeared in 1770–2; his first school, the Philanthropinium at Dessau, opened its doors two years later.

One of the boldest educational projects of the day, however, took place in Poland, where in 1772–3 very special circumstances gave rise to the National Education Commission, Europe's earliest ministry of state education. It coincided both with the political crisis of the First Partition, which provided the motivation, and with the dissolution of the Jesuits, who supplied much of the brain-power. Some years earlier the Polish reformers, desperate to escape from the Russian stranglehold on Poland, had approached Rousseau for his views; and his sympathetic *Considérations sur le gouvernement de Pologne* (1769) contained an all-important chapter on education. Rousseau recommended the creation of a single unified educational system in place of all existing institutions. He was taken at his word; and the last King of Poland, Stanisław August Poniatowski, put it

COMENIUS

WHEN Jan Amos Komenský died in Amsterdam on 15 November 1670, he was generally thought to have been the chief crank of a totally lost cause. He was the last bishop of the sect of Czech Brethren; he had been an exile for nearly fifty years; and his *grande œuvre*, setting forth a pansophic vision of universal peace and culture, remained unfinished. His prophecies regarding the overthrow of the pope, or the end of the world in 1672, had only excited ridicule.

Born in Moravia in 1592, Komenský had spent a lifetime fighting the tide. Widely travelled, and educated at Heidelberg, he had hoped to remain headmaster of the Brethren's school at Fulnek. But the Habsburg triumph in Bohemia drove him in 1621 to Poland; and the persecution of pro-Swedish Protestants in Poland in 1657–8 drove him on to the Netherlands. He spent much of his energies publicizing the fate of Bohemia, writing on pedagogics, or acting as an itinerant educational consultant. In this latter capacity, he paid extended visits to England, Sweden, and Transylvania.[1] He was even invited to be president of Harvard.

Yet Komenský's views were rather more coherent than his critics allowed. His passion for reforming education grew straight from the principles of the Czech Brethren, who nourished the Hussite tradition of reading the Bible in the vernacular. The need for language-teaching was obvious to someone from a multilingual province like Moravia, who had lived in a dozen countries. The obsession with a pacifist utopia was the natural product of a life hounded by war and religious conflict.

As a polyglot author, Comenius (as he was best known) established an international reputation. His early *Labyrinth of the World and Paradise of the Heart*, a sort of spiritual pilgrimage, was written in Czech. His *Janua Linguarum* or 'Gate of Languages', which started as a trilingual textbook in Latin, Czech, and German, ran to hundreds of versions, including Persian and Turkish. His *Orbis sensualium pictus* (1658) or 'World in Pictures', which pioneered the subject of visual learning, was equally popular. His collected pedagogical works, *Opera didactica omnia* (also 1658) far outweighed his ephemeral political publications. Komenský's legacy grew in stature with time, and attracted four distinct categories of admirer.

In religious matters, his name was honoured by those in the following century who revived the old sect of the Czech Brethren in the new form of the 'Moravian Church' (see p. 594 above).

In the era of the Czech revival, he was raised to the status of national saint. Palacký compiled his biography; Count Lützow popularized *The Labyrinth* round the world; and T. G. Masaryk saw him as the key figure in the history of Czech democracy and humanism. The first part of Masaryk's memoirs was entitled 'The Testament of Komenský'.[2]

Modern educational theorists have seen Comenius as one of the founding fathers of their discipline. His pupil-friendly textbooks inspired the
progressive methods of child-centred learning developed by Froebel,
Pestalozzi, or Montessori [**BAMBINI**]. Advocates of universal education
have quoted his texts as models before their time:

Not the children of the rich and powerful only, but boys and girls alike, rich
and poor, in all cities and . . . villages should be sent to school. . . . If any ask,
'What will be the result if artisans, rustics, porters, and even women become
lettered? I answer: none of these will lack the material for thinking, choosing,
following and doing good things. . . . Nor is it an obstacle that some seem to be
naturally dull and stupid . . . The slower and weaker the disposition of any man,
the more he needs assistance. . . .[3]

Every child who reads a comic, consults an illustrated textbook, or watches
a lesson on television, film, or video should hail Komenský as his mentor.

forward as the condition for submitting to the Partition. Poland's political
prospects were sinking; but its cultural survival could still be won. Over the next
twenty years the National Education Commission created some 200 secular
schools, many of which were to outlast the destruction of the Republic. New
teachers were trained. Textbooks in Polish language and literature, scientific subjects, and modern languages were written by ex-Jesuits. 'If in 200 years from now',
the King wrote in his diary, 'there are still people who call themselves Poles, my
work will not have been in vain.' Poland was indeed destroyed (see pp. 661–4, 719,
721–2), but its culture was not. The National Educational Commission was closed
down; but its ideals were carried over into the educational board of what became
the western region of the Russian Empire. Under the enlightened management of
Prince Czartoryski it survived until 1825, and educated the brightest generation of
Polish patriots and literati that ever learned poetry or pushed pen.[15]

From this one can see that the ideas of the Enlightenment were being used for
different purposes in different countries. In the Netherlands and in Britain, they
formed part of the repertoire of the liberal wing of the Establishment. They found
expression in the British Parliament in the speeches of C. J. Fox and Edmund
Burke. In the American colonies they were invoked by 'rebels' who defied that
British Establishment. In France, and to a lesser extent in Spain and Italy, they
inspired the intellectual circles who were opposing the Ancien Régime without
having the legal means to do so. In many parts of central and eastern Europe, they
were selectively adopted by the 'enlightened despots' who sought to improve their
empires much as private gentlemen sought to improve their serf-run estates.
Frederick II of Prussia or the Empress Catherine II in Russia certainly thought of
themselves as rational and enlightened, as did Charles III of Spain or Leopold,
Grand Duke of Tuscany, or his brother, Joseph II of Austria. But their relations
with their *philosophe* consultants was often that of absolute master and deferen-

tial client. In this regard, Voltaire's sycophancy was no less developed than his wit. He rarely said what he must have thought about Frederick's warmongering or Catherine's persecutions. Only Rousseau spoke his mind to Frederick. [**GOOSE-STEP**]

One can also see that the ideals of the Enlightenment survived the upheavals of the revolutionary crisis. Enlightened reformers of the pre-revolutionary era—such as the Baron von Stein (1757–1831) in Prussia, the Jewish convert Baron J. von Sonnenfels (1732–1817) in Austria, Stanisław Staszic (1755–1828) in Poland, or the Count von Montgelas (1759–1838) in Bavaria—were still active in 1815. Yet few of the revolutionaries who made their mark after 1789—Mirabeau, Danton, Condorcet, Robespierre, Saint-Just—had gained much prominence earlier. In this, Tom Paine was an exception, as in most things (see Chapter IX).

None the less, by 1778, when both Voltaire and Rousseau died, the Enlightenment was starting to run out of breath. Its influence was to be strong for many decades. Indeed, it had assured itself a place as a permanent pillar of modern European thought. Yet the rationalism which originally inspired it was losing its force of persuasion. Pure reason was felt to be inadequate to the task of understanding the world and of reading the auguries of upheaval.

Romanticism is a label which covers a multitude of sins. For the theoreticians of culture, the problem is so complex that some maintain there was not one Romanticism but several. But it refers to the titanic cultural movement which set in during the late eighteenth century in reaction to the waning Enlightenment. It was not associated in any way with formal religion. Indeed, it contained many features which may be considered at the very least non-Christian, if not actively anti-Christian. Yet its prime concerns were often directed to those spiritual and supernatural spheres of human experience which Religion also addressed and which the Enlightenment had neglected. In this sense, it is sometimes regarded as a reaction against the Enlightenment's overreaction against the preoccupations of the preceding Reformation and Counter-Reformation period. It may perhaps be better seen as the continuation and extension of certain strands of fashion and thought which, though always present, had little in common with the Enlightenment's ideals. These strands are often brought together under the headings of the 'Anti-Enlightenment' and of 'Pre-Romanticism'.

Discussions about the Anti-Enlightenment centre on philosophical themes leading from the Neapolitan G. B. Vico (1668–1744) to the three East Prussians Hamann, Kant, and Herder. Apart from its cyclical theory of history Vico's *Scienza nuova* (1725) paid great attention to mythology, and to the symbolic forms of expression used by primitive societies. These were subjects which most of the *philosophes* would have rejected as simply untutored. Both Vico and Herder grappled with the problem of how the human mind sifts and interprets the colossal mass of data which is required for establishing our knowledge of the past and present world. Both stressed the role of historical perspective. Both 'perceived . . . that the task of synthesising such heterogeneous material into a coherent

GOOSE-STEP

THE *Paradeschritt* or 'Parade March' of the Prussian Army was one of the
most unnatural and expressive movements ever invented for the
human body. Its foreign critics called it the goose-step. The lines of jack-
booted soldiers were trained to point their toes on every upward beat, raising their legs to a high horizontal position. In order to keep their balance,
they had to lean forward, swinging their arms like cantilevers, and holding
their chins in a characteristic jutting posture. Since every step required
enormous effort, the musical tempo had to be moderate to slow; and the
march was performed with a grim, deliberate air of latent menace. Fierce
facial expressions were an essential adjunct to the soldiers' exertions.

The body language of the goose-step transmitted a clear set of messages. To Prussia's generals, it said that the discipline and athleticism of
their men would withstand all orders, no matter how painful or ludicrous.
To Prussia's civilians, it said that all insubordination would be ruthlessly
crushed. To Prussia's enemies, it said that the Prussian Army was not
made up just of lads in uniform, but of regimented supermen. To the
world at large, it announced that Prussia was not just strong, but arrogant.
Here, quite literally, was the embodiment of Prussian militarism.[1]

The ethos of the goose-step contrasted very sharply with the parade-
ground traditions of other armies. The French Army, for example, took
great pride in the highly accelerated marching tempo of its light infantry,
which, with bugles blaring, exuded the spirit of *élan* or 'dash' that was so
much cultivated. The headlong charge of the Polish cavalry, who used to
stop one foot short of the commander's saluting base, demonstrates an
exhilarating mixture of horsemanship and showmanship. In London, the
magnificently slow Slow March of the royal Foot Guards, with its instant of
frozen motion in the middle of each stride, exuded a temper of serenity,
confidence, and self-control that was quintessentially British.

The career of the goose-step has been a long one. It was recorded in the
seventeenth century, and was still alive at the end of the twentieth. It was
a standard feature of all military parades in Prussia and Germany until
1945. It was exported to all the armies of the world which were trained by
Prussian officers, or which admired the Prussian model. In Europe, it was
adopted by the Russian Army, later by the Red Army and by all the Soviet
satellites. It was rejected by West Germany's Bundeswehr, but was kept in
being by the army of the German Democratic Republic until one month
before the DDR's collapse in November 1990. In 1994 it was still being performed in Moscow by the special squads of KGB troops who had been
high-stepping in slow motion round Lenin's mausoleum for the past 70
years.

picture demands gifts very different from those required for rational methods of investigation . . . above all, the gift . . . of a creative imagination'.[16]

J. G. Hamann (1730–88), who spent his life in Königsberg and Riga, is often dismissed as an obscure, lightweight philosopher, writing dense, disjointed (and untranslated) German prose in a scatter of minor pamphlets. But his critique of the Enlightenment, which developed Hume's line on irrationality, was well known to contemporaries and is highly rated by specialists. It is even claimed that Hamann 'lit a fuse which set off the great romantic revolt':

Hamann speaks for those who hear the cry of the toad beneath the harrow, even when it might be right to plough over him; since, if men do not hear this cry, if the toad is written off because he has been 'condemned by history' . . . then such victories will prove their own undoing.[17]

Of course, ideas do not permeate the cultural scene instantaneously. Several figures who were already active and mature in the 1770s and 1780s did not exercise any great influence until later. This is particularly true of Kant and Herder (see Chapter IX).

Many commentators, however, would insist on Rousseau's inclusion in this company, since Rousseau is often seen as the first Romantic rather than the last of the *philosophes*. (There is no good reason why he should not have been both.) Rousseau's view of nature as something benign certainly contradicted most of his contemporaries, who viewed it with hostility as something to be tamed and corrected. Rousseau's appeal to *sensibilité*, the cult of emotion, initiated yet another shift in European manners:

Having the tastes of a tramp, he found the restraints of Parisian society irksome. From him, the Romantics learnt a contempt for the trammels of convention—first in dress and manners . . . and at last over the whole sphere of traditional morals.[18]

Rousseau's love for his native Swiss Alps initiated a change in attitudes to the environment which until then was generally shunned in horror. Rousseau's cult of the common people, though accompanied by a sincere devotion to democracy, is sometimes seen as one of the roots of totalitarianism.

Discussions about Pre-Romanticism usually centre on literary themes connected with the School of *Sturm und Drang*—so-called after F. M. Klinger's play of the same name staged in 1777—and with the Theory of Symbols. Amidst that 'Storm and Stress' of the 1770s, Germany, long passive, was asserting itself against French rationalism, and European culture was passing into a new era. A major impact was made by Goethe's first novella, *The Sorrows of Young Werther* (1774), whose moody adolescent hero commits suicide. In writing the book, Goethe said that he had decided 'to surrender to his inner self '. It was a very unclassical decision.

Yet no one had a greater impact than a Scots schoolteacher from Kingussie called James Macpherson (1736–96), who pulled off one of the great literary forgeries of all time. He presented his *Fragments of Ancient Poetry* (1760), *Fingal* (1761), and *Temora* (1763) as the translated works of the legendary Gaelic bard, Ossian. As Dr Johnson realized, they were nothing of the sort. But their melancholic recital of Highland lore was immensely popular, not least in Germany, where Herder was a leading admirer. An Italian translation was said to be Napoleon's favourite reading.

Classical conventions came under attack in art also. In 1771, at the summer exhibition of the Royal Academy in London, the court painter Benjamin West (1738–1820) displayed a picture celebrating *The Death of General Wolfe*, who had been killed at Quebec twelve years earlier. To the scandal of the viewers, the scene was painted in contemporary dress. The dying general was shown in his regulation red army tunic. Joshua Reynolds, the senior artist of the day, took West on one side and lectured him on the convention of clothing all historic and moralistic scenes in the togas and laurels of antiquity. Paintings that defied the convention would lack the timeless, neutral setting which alone could ensure the transmission of their message. But it was to no avail: Realism had arrived. Whether or not Romanticism had arrived with it is a matter for conjecture.[19]

The French supremacy in Europe lasted for the greater part of 200 years. It began with the personal rule of the young Louis XIV in 1661 and lasted until the fall of Napoleon in 1815. Indeed, notwithstanding her defeat during the Napoleonic Wars, France was not definitively replaced as the single most powerful state of Continental Europe until her submission to Bismarck's Germany in 1871. For most of that time Paris was the unrivalled capital of European politics, culture, and fashion. [CRAVATE]

France's lengthy pre-eminence can be explained in part by the natural advantages of her large territory and population, and by the systematic nurture of her economic and military resources. It must be explained in part also by the disarray of major rivals: by the decay of Spain, by the ruin of Germany, by the divisions of Italy, by Austria's preoccupation with the Ottomans. It was certainly assisted by the extraordinary longevity of the ruling Bourbon kings—Louis XIV (r. 1643–1715), Louis XV (r. 1715–74), and Louis XVI (r. 1774–92)—who supplied a focus for unity and stability. In the end it was undermined by the growing tensions within French society, and by the appearance of new powers—notably Great Britain, the kingdom of Prussia, and the Russian Empire, none of which had even existed at Louis XIV's accession.

Like all great political organisms, France of the Ancien Régime passed through three distinct phases of growth, maturity, and decline. The first dynamic phase coincided with the central decades of Louis XIV in his magnificent prime, from 1661 to the end of the seventeenth century. The second phase saw France contained by the coalitions raised against her. It stretched from the last disillusioned years of Louis XIV to the death of Louis XV. The final phase coincided with the reign of Louis XVI. It saw the King and his ministers lose control of the mounting problems which led in 1789 to the outbreak of the greatest revolution that Europe had ever seen. For the French themselves, this was the era of *la gloire*.

CRAVATE

THE French word *cravate*, 'necktie', has been taken into almost every European language. In German, it is *krawatte*, in Spanish, *corbata*, in Greek, *gravata*, in Romanian, *cravata*, in standard Polish, *krawat*, in Cracow, eccentrically, *krawatka*. In English, it acquired the special meaning of 'a linen or silk handkerchief passed once or twice round the neck outside the shirt collar'.[1] In the standard French *Littré*, it is given two alternative meanings: '*1. Cheval de Croatie. 2. Pièce d'étoffe légère que les hommes et quelquefois les dames mettent autour du cou.*'[2] All sources agree that it derives from an old form of the adjective for 'Croat' or, as a Croat would say, *hrvati*.

Exactly how an East European adjective became permanently attached to one of the commonest items of European clothing is a matter for conjecture. One theory holds that Napoleon admired the scarves worn by captured Habsburg soldiers.[3] This is clearly a misattribution, since Littré cites Voltaire using the word long before Napoleon was born: 'Vous figurez-vous ce diable habillé d'écarlate? . . . Un serpent lui sert de cravate' (Do you see this devil dressed in scarlet? . . . He's wearing a snake in place of a cravate).[4]

Louis XIV is perhaps nearer the mark. Croat mercenaries in the French service at Versailles are the likeliest source of the fashion which spread all over the world. At all events, people who deny the influence of Europe's 'smaller nations' should remember that the Croats have the rest of us by the throat.

In Croatia, as it happens, men can choose to adorn their necks either with the native *masna*, or with the re-imported *kravata*.[5]

'S'agrandir', wrote Louis XIV to the Marquis de Villars on 8 January 1688, 'est la plus digne et la plus agréable occupation des souverains.'[20] (Self-aggrandisement is the most worthy and agreeable of sovereigns' occupations.)

Louis XIV, more than any other European monarch, has been taken as the supreme symbol of his age. Reigning for seventy-two years over Europe's most powerful nation, this *Roi Soleil*, this Sun King, was the object of a cult which coloured the opinions both of his courtiers and of later historians. Ruling over France from his magnificent palace at Versailles, as Philip of Spain had once ruled the world from the Escorial, he was credited with almost superhuman powers. He was, supposedly, the embodiment of the purest monarchy, the most perfect form of absolutism; the architect and inspiration of a model and uniform system of government; the moving spirit of economic and colonial enterprise, the dictator of artistic and intellectual taste, the 'Most Christian King' of a Catholic nation that brooked no religious deviation, the doyen of European diplomacy, the commander of the Continent's most formidable armies. The myth is not without substance. 'Le Grand Roi' was undoubtedly the monarch whom lesser princes loved to emulate. He stamped his personality on his surroundings, and his achievements were not inconsiderable. Yet no man could ever match up to so exaggerated an image. Whilst conceding the grandeur of the experiment, one must also try to see the man behind the royal mask, the suffering land of France beyond the glittering façade of Versailles.

The personality of Louis XIV cannot easily be separated from the theatrical performance which he felt to be an essential part of his trade. He grew up among the horrors of the Fronde, when the foundations of the modern French monarchy had been shaken to the core; and he felt instinctively that he was leader of a nation which longed for order and strong government. Hence the court of Versailles, which he designed and built, was not merely a piece of ostentation. It tied the nobles to the service of king and state. The spectacular royal balls, ballets, concerts, plays and hunts, the fêtes and the fireworks in the Grand Parc, all served to cement the subservience of his leading subjects, and to create a sense of national community. From the day in 1661 when, on Mazarin's death, he personally assumed the reins of government, he was playing out a role with a purpose. It was not for mere amusement that he appeared as the leading actor in the first great open-air fête of his reign, *Les Plaisirs de l'Île Enchanté* (see Plate 47). Louis inherited from his Spanish mother the love of etiquette; and he learned from Mazarin the art of secrecy and dissimulation. Possessed of a handsome and powerful physique, he combined remarkable energies and appetites with a temperament that swung from the gallant and generous to the mean and rancorous. As a horseman, huntsman, trencherman, and sexual athlete, he outclassed his enthusiastic entourage. Yet whilst wining and womanizing with gusto, he could be plotting the ruin of his companions or, as with the great Nicolas Fouquet in 1661, the arbitrary arrest of his leading minister. 'Le Grand Roi' was not above pettiness.

As the pupil of Richelieu and Mazarin, Louis had a firm grasp of the instruments that could increase his power. He inherited a huge, servile bureaucracy, a large standing army, a vast central treasury, and a subdued nobility. He further extended his control over a Gallican Church that was already subservient, destroyed the 'state-within-the-state' of the Huguenots, subordinated the provinces to his *Intendants*, and ruled without any form of central legislature. But his greatest talent was for publicity. Versailles was the symbol of an ideal which far outshone the facts of French reality. For Frenchmen and foreign visitors alike, the splendours of its ceremonies undoubtedly created the illusion that the *Roi Soleil* stood at the centre of a system of perfect authority. When Louis allegedly walked into the Palais de Justice and interrupted a judge with the comment, 'L'État, c'est moi', he may or may not have believed his witticism; but he certainly acted as if he did. Through his long series of flamboyant liaisons, from Louise de la Vallière to Mme de Maintenon, he flouted the moral code of the old *cabale de dévots*, creating a climate where the King's pleasure was law. Yet behind the façade the grand experiment of absolutism was fraught with failures. Versailles was not France; the King's will was widely defied. In a huge country, the means of avoidance were greater than the means of enforcement. The drive for uniformity, powerful though it was, could not iron out all the wrinkles. The Parlement and the provinces persistently jibbed. Louis's foreign wars brought more debt and humiliation than solid gains.

The government of France, therefore, cannot be understood through any formal analysis of its institutions. The long campaign to re-assert royal authority from the centre was not accompanied by the wholesale abolition of regional and municipal particularities. The great provinces of France remained divided between the *pays d'élection*, where royal officials exercised a large measure of direct control, and the *pays d'état*, which enjoyed a great degree of autonomy. Customary law operated in the north, codified Roman law in the south. Within each of the provinces, a mass of local *libertés, parlements, franchises,* and *privilèges* survived; and the nobles retained many of their traditional powers of jurisdiction in their own domains. It was essential, of course, that the central Assembly, or Estates General, should only survive in a condition of permanent suspension, and that the central Parlement in Paris should be schooled to register royal decrees without discussion. The vast army of some 50,000 royal officials, riddled with venality and corruption, pressed like a dead weight on the whole country, as slow to react to royal instructions as to the needs of their local subjects.

The King's main advantage lay in the absence of any major institution round which alternative centres of authority might have coalesced. Secure from concerted opposition, he was able to construct a small but extremely powerful complex of central organizations run by himself, together with a new network in the provinces which could override local objections. At the pinnacle, the King convened the *Conseil en Haut* (Supreme Council), where he discussed high policy two or three times every week with a small coterie of advisers. Louis made good an early boast to be his own chief minister. In the formative decade after 1661 he worked closely with the favoured triad of Le Tellier, Lionne, and Colbert. The formulation of advice and the execution of policy was entrusted to the Secretariats—initially *Étranger, Guerre, Marine,* and *Maison du Roi*—and to a series of secondary committees—the *Conseil Royal* for finance, the *Conseil Privé* for judicial decrees, the *Conseil de Conscience* for Religion, the *Conseil de Justice* for codifying the law.

For the enforcement of his decisions the King relied in the early days on special commissions, which would be sent out to regulate specific matters. But increasingly he relied on his *Intendants,* who were soon turned from mere inspectors of inquiry into permanent viceroys, each overseeing the financial and judicial affairs of their *généralités* or areas of competence. In the last resort he relied on the military reforms, which abolished the old noble levy and created a huge standing army entirely subordinated to royal command. This army was an instrument of internal as well as external policy.

The realities of French society bore little relation to the structures enshrined in the three traditional Estates. In theory, the Estates should have been autonomous, self-regulating communities. In practice, they were highly fragmented; they were deprived of any serious autonomy, and all were increasingly subordinated to royal control. The clergy (the First Estate) was alone in retaining its own organization, the quinquennial assemblies. But it was deprived of any corporate initiative by the King's patronage of over 600 leading abbatial and episcopal appointments, and by the glaring chasm of interest and outlook between high and low clergy.

The nobility (the Second Estate) had been tamed by Richelieu and disgraced by the failure of the Fronde. It was equally divided against itself. The grandees were turned into royal pensioners, boasting more titles than influence. Most of the old noble families depended increasingly on royal service, either in the *noblesse de robe*, through legal or administrative positions, or in the *noblesse d'épée*, through army commissions. Their influence was greatly diluted by the influx of a mass of upstarts and promotees—the *bourgeois gentilhommes* of whom Molière made such fun. Trouble-makers such as the petty nobles and robber lords of the remoter districts like the Auvergne found themselves brought violently to heel by hanging commissions.

As for the Third Estate, which contained everyone not included in the other two, it had no chance whatsoever of developing a sense of common purpose. The best hope of social advancement lay in buying a royal office or a patent of nobility. Least concern was shown for the peasants—the absolute majority of the population—who remained triple-taxed serfs, oppressed by their lord, their priest, and the royal officials. They lived on the verge of starvation. The academician La Bruyère called them 'animaux farouches'. They repeatedly described their own condition in terms of 'la Peur', the primordial fear of extinction. Their frequent, desperate, and ineffectual revolts were part of the rural landscape.

Economic policy constituted an important part of the Great Experiment. Under Jean-Baptiste Colbert (1619–83), the original 'homme de marbre' and a *bourgeois gentilhomme par excellence*, a systematic plan was conceived to put the finances, taxes, and commerce of the country onto a sound footing. This *Colbertisme* represented a specially *dirigiste* form of mercantilism, and is often considered a failure, especially in the later period. But it was the engine which made all the other projects of Louis XIV possible; and it can only be judged against the colossal demands made by the King's truly insatiable financial appetite.

In the financial sector, Colbert created the *Contrôle Général* (1665) through which all other subordinate institutions were supervised—the *Trésor de l'Épargne* (Treasury), the *Conseil Royal*, the *État de Prévoyance* and the *État au Vrai* (the annual forward estimates and balance-sheet), and the *Grand Livre* (the ledger of state accounts). From 1666 the Mint struck the handsome *louis d'or* and the silver *écu*, which maintained a stable value for nearly 30 years.

In the fiscal sector, the *Caisse des Emprunts* (1674) was created to raise money from state loans. The *Ferme Générale* (1680) was created to co-ordinate the collection of all taxes except for the notorious *Taille* or land-tax (which was left to the *Intendants*). After Colbert's death the budgetary deficit mounted, and a variety of expedients were tried, including the *capitation* or poll-tax in 1695, the *billets de monnaie* or paper money of 1701, and the *dixième* or state tithe of 1710.

In the commercial sector, Colbert introduced a régime which attempted to lock all private activity into state regulations, and to give priority to state enterprise, especially in manufactures and foreign trade. The *Code de la Draperie* (1669) or 'Textile Code' was an example of his mania for detailed regulation. The great Vanrobais textile factory at Abbeville, or the state Gobelin factory brought to Paris from Brussels, were monuments to his penchant for manufacturing. The various state trading companies—*des Indes Orientales* (1664), *des Indes Occidentales* (1664), *du Nord* (1669), *du Levant* (1670)—were monuments to his belief that the country's total wealth could only be increased by what was brought in from abroad. Colbert's enthusiasm for the navy, and for the construction of naval ports and state arsenals, derived from the common mercantilist dogma that foreign trade involved an international struggle over finite resources. Successful competition required military force. Significantly, France's principal industry—agriculture—received little attention, except as the object of regulated prices and the source of cheap food.

The mobilization of France's military resources required a sustained effort over several decades. Colbert himself laid great emphasis on the formation of a navy that could hold its own against the Dutch and the English. Apart from the traditional *chiourmes* or convict gangs which manned the galleys based at Toulon, he created a register of all the sailors and ships in the land, all liable to conscription. In twenty years he increased the ships of the line from 30 to 107, of which the four-masted *Royal-Louis*, armed with 118 canons, was the pride and joy. He founded the naval base of Rochefort, fortified the northern ports of Brest, Le Havre, Calais, and Dunkerque, and opened naval dockyards and naval academies.

For obvious reasons, however, France looked more to its land borders than to the sea. Louis XIV set foot aboard one of his warships on only one occasion. Under the *Bureau de guerre* of Colbert's chief rival, the ruthless war minister François Michel Le Tellier, Marquis de Louvois (1641–91), the main effort was devoted to the army. Louvois's bureaucrats took control of every detail. The old noble levy was abandoned and regimental structures revolutionized. New formations of grenadiers (1667), fusiliers (1667), and bombardiers (1684) were created. The traditional supremacy of the cavalry was handed to the infantry. Subjected to rigorous drill and training, armed with flintlock and bayonet, and dressed in fine uniforms, the new formations foreshadowed the practices of the eighteenth century. The artillery and the corps of engineers, once contracted out to civilians, were integrated into the overall command. Professional officers, trained in military academies and promoted on merit, were led by commanders of renown—first the old Turenne, then the young Condé and the dashing Maréchal du Villars. Massive barracks and arsenals were built in all the major cities. On the initiative of the celebrated siege-master, *ingénieur du roi* and *commissaire-général des fortifications*, Marshal Sébastien Le Prestre de Vauban (1633–1707), a magnificent chain of 160 fortresses was constructed along the northern and eastern frontiers.

The likes of Saarlouis, Landau, Neubreisach, and Strasbourg cost France even more than Versailles. The net result was a military machine that could only be stopped by the concerted strength of all France's neighbours. Its motto was *Nec pluribus impar* (a match for many). [**ELSASS**]

Religion stood necessarily near the centre of affairs. Louis XIV displayed little more than conventional Catholic piety, but he was guided by the tradition which demanded that *le Roi Très Chrétien* should be master in his own house, and that religious dissidence posed a threat to national unity. After his secret second marriage to Mme de Maintenon in 1685, he was strongly influenced by the advice of Jesuits. The overall result was one of considerable inconsistency and, as in other spheres, of striking contrast between the King's early and declining years. In 1669, when Molière's long-delayed anticlerical satire *Tartuffe* was finally performed, it received the royal applause; in 1680 it was banned.

For thirty years Louis was a true Gallican—packing the French bishoprics with the relatives of his ministers, authorizing the Declaration of the Four Articles (1682), and provoking in 1687–8 an open rupture with the Papacy. The Four Articles, the purest formulation of Gallican doctrine, were ordered to be taught in all the seminaries and faculties of France:

1. The authority of the Holy See is limited to spiritual matters.
2. The decisions of Church Councils are superior to those of the Pope.
3. Gallican customs are independent of Rome.
4. The Pope is not infallible, except by consent of the universal Church.

But then, distressed by his isolation from the Catholic powers, Louis turned tail. In 1693 he retracted the Four Articles, and for the rest of his life gave unstinting support to the ultramontane faction. His decree of 1695, handing the episcopate full control over the livings and property of the parish clergy, earned him the lasting opposition of the radicals. In the quarrel over Quietism, his decision to favour the bombastic Bishop Bossuet, 'the Eagle of Meaux', against the Quietists' champion, Bishop Fénelon, 'the Swan of Cambrai', offended both the aristocratic and the more spiritual elements. After all, it was Bossuet who had once enjoined Louis 'to be a god for his people'.

In his policy towards the Protestants, Louis passed from passive discrimination through petty harassment to violent persecution. At first, under Mazarin's tutelage, the King felt disinclined to disrupt a community that had demonstrated its loyalty throughout the wars of the Fronde. From the weavers of Abbeville to the great Turenne himself, the Huguenots were hard-working and influential. Unfortunately, breaches of the Edict of Nantes and the supposedly preferential treatment of the 'RPR' (*réligion prétendue réformée* or 'so-called reformed religion') were the two issues which united all wings of Catholic opinion. Hence from 1666 all Huguenot activities not specifically approved by the Edict were regarded as illegal. The first chapels were razed; a *caisse des conversions* or 'conversion fund' was created to reward the NCs (*nouveaux convertis*) at six livres per head. From 1679 a series of legal and military measures sought to extirpate Protestantism by force. In the vicious *dragonnades* of Poitou, Béarn, and Languedoc, where soldiers were billeted on all families refusing conversion, unspeakable atrocities were committed. Finally in October 1685, pressed by Louvois (Le Tellier), and the depraved Archbishop of Paris, Harlay de Champvallon, the King revoked the edict of toleration. Bishop Bossuet awarded him the epithet of the 'New Constantine'. Up to a million of France's most worthy citizens were forced to submit or to flee amidst a veritable reign of terror. Resistance in the Dauphiné and the Cévennes persisted for thirty years.

Similarly, in its treatment of the Jansenists, royal policy wavered between compromise and repression. Jansen's ideas were eagerly received by one wing of the French Church, and were widely disseminated through the works of the Abbé de St Cyran (1581–1643), of Antoine Arnauld I (1612–94), and, above all, of Blaise Pascal. Jansenist activities centred on the Cistercian convent of Port-Royal in Paris and on the ubiquitous Arnauld clan, who had strong connections at Court—with the King's cousin, Mme de Longueville, with the King's foreign minister, Simon Arnauld, Marquis de Pomponne (1616–99), with Racine, a former pupil of Port-Royal's school, even with Bossuet. But from the 1650s, when the 'Five Propositions' taken from Jansen's *Augustinus* were officially judged heretical, the Jansenists were treated as subversives. Pascal and others were forced to publish in secret. In 1661 a Formulation of Obedience denouncing the Propositions caused an open breach; and the sisters of Port-Royal, 'pure as angels, proud as demons', were rusticated to a new location at Port-Royal-les-Champs near Versailles. This first round of persecution ended in the strange *Paix de l'Église* (1668), which enabled the Jansenists to sign the Formulation whilst upholding their conscientious objections 'in respectful silence'. But further attacks were launched in concert with the campaign against the Huguenots. Arnauld *le Grand* was driven into exile at Brussels in 1679.

The decisive round followed the publication in 1693 of the *Réflexions* of the Oratorian Pasquier Quesnel (1634–1719). When the ensuing furore became entangled with the other feud between Bishops Bossuet and Fénelon over Quietism, the King resolved to act. In 1705 the Pope was persuaded to retract the compromise regarding 'respectful silence', and in 1713 the Bull *Unigenitus* comprehensively condemned the Jansenists and all their works. In the process the convent of Port-Royal was closed, its church destroyed, its cemetery razed. The remains of Pascal and Racine had to be rescued from their tombs by night. At a stroke, Louis turned a doctrinal squabble into a lasting confrontation between the reigning Establishment of Church and State and its intellectual critics. Here lay the true beginning of the French Enlightenment.

Nothing has been more schematized in the history books than the policy of Louis XIV to the arts. This 'Intellectual Absolutism' is sometimes described as a model where royal taste and patronage could determine the entire cultural life of an age. 'Classicism is made to appear as an official doctrine corresponding on the literary plane to the doctrines of monarchical order and religious unity which prevailed in the political and spiritual spheres.'[21] In the words of Nicolas Boileau

ELSASS

ONE day in 1670 the French army seized the Rhine bridge at Strassburg, and burned it. This was the signal that the French were not content with the part of Elsass acquired by the Treaty of Westphalia, and would not rest until Strassburg itself was theirs. At the time, Strassburg was the second city of the Holy Roman Empire, entirely German in character, its language the same Alemannic dialect spoken on the other side of the Rhine. But Louis XIV was implacable. Thanks to the dubious stratagem of the *Réunions*, Strassburg, or Strasbourg, would soon be absorbed, together with the whole of 'Alsace'. Though the local dialect would survive, the province would become the touchstone of French unity.[1] German restorations, in 1870–1918 and 1940–5, would not last.

On the other, eastern flank of the Empire, in Silesia, the great city of Breslau was ruled on behalf of the Austrian Habsburgs by the last prince of the Silesian Piasts. Silesia's origins were no more Austrian than Alsace was French. Silesia's first connections were Polish and, until 1526, Bohemian. Just as the native language and culture of Alsace were to resist every attempt to Frenchify them completely, so the Silesian Slavs would hold out against the waves of Bohemian Germans, Austrians, and Prussians who came to dominate their province over the centuries.[2]

On the other, eastern flank of Poland, in the province of Red Ruthenia, the great city of Lwów had been ruled by Poland for over 300 years. It was far more Polish than Strasburg was French or Breslau Austrian. Its Jewish community, too, had enjoyed great continuity. Yet the origins of Lwów or L'viv were not Polish but Ruthenian. In 1670, its career as a premier centre of Uniate, Ukrainian culture was in its infancy.[3] [**ÅYCZAKÓW**]

On the other, eastern flank of Ruthenia, the great city of Kiev on the Dnieper had just been conquered by Moscow (see p. 556). The Russian Orthodox Church was establishing its supremacy over central Ukraine, and launching the myth that Kiev was the cradle of Russian civilization.

Strassburg, Breslau, Lwów, and Kiev had more in common than they knew. All were cosmopolitan capitals of multinational provinces or countries, for whom exclusive national claims would prove particularly destructive. By 1945, each had been re-laundered many times. Alsace had changed hands between France and Germany four times over. Silesia (alias Śląsk or Schlesien) had been fought over regularly by Austria, Prussia, Germany, and Poland. Red Ruthenia (alias East Galicia, Western Ukraine, or eastern Małopolska) had been disputed by Austrians, Poles, and Ukrainians at least six times. Central Ukraine had been torn apart by Russians and Germans, Ukrainians and Poles, Reds and Whites, Nazis and Soviets, at least twenty times.

When Strasbourg was made capital of the Council of Europe in 1949, the Iron Curtain shut out the city's eastern counterparts. Indeed, since the German population of Breslau had been forced to leave, since Breslau had just become Wrocław through the mass influx of Polish refugees from Lwów, and since L'viv was swamped by an influx of Russians, resentments were running high. The internal frontiers of the Soviet bloc were every bit as impermeable as the Iron Curtain. The process of reconciliation, which started in the West, could not reach the whole of Europe for almost fifty years.

(1636–1711), the principal literary critic of the day, 'Un Auguste aisément peut faire des Virgiles' (an Augustus can easily create Virgils).

It is true, of course, that lavish royal patronage did provide a powerful stimulus in the direction of institutionalized uniformity. The Académie Française (1635), whose great Dictionary appeared in 1694, acted as the official guardian of the French language. The Académie de Peinture et de Sculpture, later the Beaux-Arts, put enormous powers into the hands of the King's painter, Charles Le Brun (1619–90). The Académie des Sciences (1666) pursued similar activities to those of the Royal Society in London. The Académie de Musique (1669) offered a similar platform for the talents of the King's musician, Jean-Baptiste Lully (1633–87), who wrote a score of operas. At the Beaux-Arts, which linked the artistic dictatorship of Le Brun with the organizational genius of Colbert, architects, decorators, engravers were mobilized into projects where harmony and order were the ruling passions. Above all, the royal Court commanded a concentration of cultural creativity with few parallels. In literature, 'the King's Four Friends'—Boileau, Molière, Racine, and La Fontaine—exercised an influence in their heyday which few writers have ever enjoyed. The Comédie-Française (1680) joined several existing troupes into one united, theatrical operation.

Yet on examination it becomes clear that the classical monopoly was more illusory than real. For one thing, the King's own taste was more eclectic than is often supposed. The classical mania for formulating artistic rules was certainly present, but the rules were not necessarily observed by everyone. For another, the 'Classical Parnassus' which reigned for perhaps twenty years was gradually undermined. From 1687 onwards French cultural life was absorbed by the furious quarrel of the *Anciens* and the *Modernes*. The façade of unity was cracked wide open, to expose a cultural landscape of variety and heterodoxy from which the parade of the giants has all too often diverted attention.

The foreign policy of Louis XIV was the best measure of his power and prestige. It rested on the most complete diplomatic service which Europe had ever seen—personally run by the King at Versailles—and on military forces which were only deployed in full after a long period of preparation. It led the continent of Europe into conflict. As a result, Louis XIV has been seen in some quarters as the first of a line of tyrants who have tried to conquer Europe by force, the precursor of Napoleon or Hitler. The coalitions ranged against him can be made to appear as the ancestors of the 'Allied Powers' of later centuries.

In reality, Louis's vision was rather limited. Despite later comment, he does not seem to have had any clear plan for attaining France's 'natural frontiers', let alone for overrunning the Continent. Though the caution of his early years was abandoned, his aims remained essentially dynastic and consolidatory. Having been linked by Mazarin to a Spanish Infanta, María Teresa, whom he married at Saint Jean-de-Luz in 1660 as part of the Treaty of the Pyrenees, he could not have avoided the problems presented by Spain's crumbling succession. His constant involvement in the Netherlands and on the Rhine was justified by a genuine fear of encirclement. His thirst for war and expansion can hardly be compared to that of his brother monarchs in, say, Sweden or Russia. His love for *la gloire* might have seemed entirely conventional had it not been backed by such threatening logistics. Of Louis's four major wars, the first two were confined to the Netherlands; the third was provoked by the *réunions*—Louis's campaign to acquire German territory by judicial subterfuge. The fourth arose directly from the failure of the ruling Spanish dynasty. Behind them all lay international rivalry over colonies and trade. [GROTEMARKT]

The War of Devolution (1667–8) derived from Louis's exploitation of a dynastic claim to Brabant. It began with a French invasion of the Spanish Netherlands; inspired a 'Triple Alliance' of England, Holland, and Sweden; and ended at the Peace of Aix-la-Chapelle with Louis in possession of twelve Belgian fortresses.

The Franco-Dutch War (1672–9) derived from Louis's determination to punish the Dutch for their interference in his previous campaign. It was thoroughly prepared diplomatically, with Holland's maritime rivals, England and Sweden, persuaded to switch their allegiance, and with Poland added to the French camp. It turned William III of Orange, Stadtholder of the United Provinces, into co-ordinator of the opposition. It began, as before, with a French advance into the Spanish Netherlands; but Condé's crossing of the Rhine roused the Empire; and Louis did not miss the chance to disrupt Spain's hold on the Franche-Comté. The Congress of Nijmegen (1678–9) saw Louis's diplomats holding the ring—appeasing the Dutch with commercial advantages, forcing the Spaniards to cede territory, imposing a settlement on the lesser powers.

By the policy of *réunions*, Louis suspended open warfare in favour of annexations arranged through elaborate but dubious legal process. Courts were established to try royal petitions laying claim to scores of cities and jurisdictions on the eastern border. Every favourable verdict led to immediate occupation of the district concerned. No less than 160 annexations were organized in this way in the 1680s, notably Strassburg (1681) and Luxemburg (1684). With the Empire preoccupied by the Turkish advance on Vienna, Louis had timed the operation well.

The Nine Years War (1689–97) occurred as the result of Louis's defiance of the League of Augsburg (1686), formed at the instigation of William of Orange to halt further French adventures. The French invasion of the Spanish Netherlands and of the Palatinate, where Heidelberg was devastated, initiated an exhausting series of sieges and naval battles. By the Treaty of Ryswick (1697) Louis was obliged to abandon most of his *réunions*, but not Strassburg. [ELSASS][GROTEMARKT]

The War of the Spanish Succession (1701–13) has some claim to be called 'the first world war'. It was fought in Germany, in the Netherlands, in Italy, in Spain, in the colonies, and on the high seas. It was brewing from the day in 1700 when Charles II of Spain died childless, and when Louis XIV decided to honour the late King's will and to neglect his own undertakings. It was unavoidable once Louis had presented the court with his infant grandson, Philippe d'Anjou, with the words 'Voici le Roi d'Espagne'. It brought together the most extensive and powerful of anti-French coalitions, which was managed on the military front by the triumvirate of Prince Eugene of Savoy, the Duke of Marlborough, and the Grand Pensioner Heinsius. The fighting began when Louis took the precaution of reoccupying the Dutch-held 'barrier fortresses' in the Spanish Netherlands. It carried on through siege and countersiege, on land and sea, until all parties were thoroughly drained. In 1709, after the 'very murdering' but indecisive battle of Malplaquet, which saved France from invasion, Marshal du Villars was said to have told his sovereign, 'One more victory like that for your enemies, Sire, and they will all be finished.'

The final outcome of the French wars, as enshrined in the twin treaties of Utrecht (1713) and Rastatt (1714), did not match the expectations of any of the principal combatants. France's ambitions were trimmed but not reversed. She kept many important gains, including Lille, Franche-Comté, and Alsace; and Philippe d'Anjou remained on the Spanish throne. The Dutch, like the French, were exhausted, but survived with the control of the barrier fortresses. Spain, which had lost out when allied to the anti-French coalitions, lost out again when allied to the French. The Spaniards' main purpose was to preserve the unity of their empire. They found that they provoked the very catastrophe which they had sought to avoid. The Austrians, who had sought to prevent the Spanish inheritance from falling to France, settled instead for a major share of the pickings, including the Spanish Netherlands, Milan, Naples, and Sardinia. It was the peripheral powers who proved the most obvious beneficiaries. Both the Hohenzollerns in Prussia and the House of Savoy were confirmed in their royal status. The former took Upper Gelderland on the Rhine and, with some delay, Swedish Pomerania; the latter took Sicily. The new United Kingdom of Great Britain (see below) gained immensely in status, confirmed in her control of Gibraltar and Minorca, of Newfoundland and other American lands, and of the Spanish colonial trade. The United Kingdom—no longer just England—now emerged as the foremost maritime power, as the leading diplomatic broker, and as the principal opponent of French supremacy.

From its high point early in the 1680s, therefore, Louis XIV's Great Experiment produced ever diminishing returns. The wars, the religious persecutions, the deaths of all the great personalities, were accompanied by failures of a more deep-seated nature. Both the French state and French society were showing signs of a

GROTE MARKT

I N 1695 the *Grote Markt* or *Grand'Place* of Brussels was reduced to cinders when one of France's more inept marshals, the Duke of Villeroi, bombarded the city with red-hot shot. In that one engagement, when the armies of Louis XIV advanced into the Spanish Netherlands, they destroyed sixteen churches, 4,000 houses, and a civic square which has been described as 'a perfect image in stone of our European political culture at its finest'.[1]

Laid out in the decades after 1312, when Brussels was granted its charter, the expanse of the Grote Markt had seen the jousting tournaments of the Dukes of Brabant and of Burgundy. On the south side, the Gothic City Hall supported a slender, soaring belfry 160 ft high, surmounted by a gilded statue of St Michael. Opposite, the Renaissance Maison du Roi had housed many dukes but never a king. On either flank rose the tall guild houses of the 'nine nations', among them the 'Bakers' Dome' of Le Roi d'Espagne, the statued façade of the Archers' House, La Louve, and the poop-shaped upper storey of the 'Boat-Builders'. In front of them, the cobbled pavement had witnessed the hanging of Egmont and Horn. In 1795 it would resound to Dumouriez's declaration of the French Republic, and in 1830 to skirmishes with Dutch troops. Nowadays, it is the setting for the annual Ommegang procession, headed by actors playing out 'the court of Charles V'. Otherwise it has been taken over by flower-sellers, the Sunday bird market and, until recently, by parking lots.

Brussels was handsomely restored under Austrian rule after 1713, and extensively renovated when it became capital of the Kingdom of Belgium in 1830. In the nineteenth century, linked by a 'pentagon' of boulevards, the new districts spread over the nearby hills. The Coudenberg received the royal palace, the government ministries, and the Parliament. The Koekelberg, in imitation of Montmartre, received the grandiose domed basilica of the Sacré-Cœur, completed only in 1970. The gleaming metallic molecule of the Atomium recalls the Universal Exhibition of 1958. The modern Cité de Berlaymont (1967) houses the headquarters of the European Commission, Zaventem the headquarters of NATO. Since 1971, Brussels-Bruxelles has formed a bi-lingual region within Belgium's three linguistic cantons—equal in legal status to its Flemish-speaking, French-speaking, and German-speaking counterparts. Originally a predominantly Flemish city, it now displays the most complicated linguistic patterns, including French, Turkish, and even English sectors..

Sentimental observers have seen Brussels as a fitting capital for the future Europe because it has supposedly overcome its own and its neighbours' nationalism. It has been described as the mouth of a 'tunnel of history', reaching back under the dark mountain of modern nationalism

to 'the wonderful model' of 'multicultural', 'polyphonic Burgundy'.[2] It may
be so. But extravagant intellectual pretensions do not fit the local style.
From his pedestal on a street corner just off the Grote Markt, the statue of
the *Manneken Pis*, the jovial 'Little Piddle Boy' (1619), who survived
Villeroi's bombardment, expresses the healthiest of opinions on all such
conceits.

long wasting disease. The state's finances, for example, passed into grave disarray.
By 1715 the Government's net income stood at 69 million livres, and expenditure
at 132 million; the public debt was variously computed at between 830 to 2,800
million.[22] More seriously, the mass of the French population was gaining little
benefit from a life of increasing deprivation: the scandalous exemptions of the
nobility continued; the middle classes, sorely wounded by the departure of the
Huguenots, were struggling to ease the burdens of state regulation; the peasants
toiled on the verge of starvation and without hope of relief. In the years of famine,
contemporary reports of their dire distress—of barefoot starvelings eking out a
subsistence on a diet of bark, berries, and beet—are supported by modern statistical studies of mortality and food prices. The long procession of provinces in
open and bloody revolt continued—Béarn (1664), the Vivarais (1670), Bordeaux
(1674), Brittany (1675), Languedoc (1703–9), Cahors (1709). Rural riots and outbreaks of château-burning were mercilessly punished with military repressions
and mass hangings. The façade still glittered, but the foundations were starting to
shake. When Louis XIV finally died, on 1 September 1715, the curtain fell to the
ringing words which began the funeral oration: 'Dieu seul, mes frères,' intoned
Bishop Massillon, 'Dieu seul est grand' (my brothers, God alone is great).

   France of the eighteenth century was entirely the child of Louis XIV's great but
flawed experiment. The intellectual ferment of the French Enlightenment was a
natural reaction against the political and social immobility of the Ancien Régime
which Louis had created. Both external and internal policy were devoted to the
maintenance of the status quo in all spheres. The innate conservatism of the system was bolstered by the initial shock of John Law's risky projects, which seemed
to discredit the very notion of change and reform. It was solidified by the minority (1715–23) of Louis XV, when the reins of government were held by a polished
but debauched Regent, the Duc d'Orléans, and by the young king's long subordination to his elderly tutor André, Cardinal de Fleury (1653–1743). The Regent
rashly restored the Parlement's right of remonstration against royal decrees—a
classic recipe for endless mischief without responsibility. The Cardinal supervised
an era of competent stability, marked only by diplomatic crises and a violent
resurgence of the controversy over Jansenism. The personal reign of Louis XV
(1723–74), who paid more attention to hunting women and stags than to governing the country, was one of debilitating stagnation. The perpetual financial crisis,
fuelled by recurrent wars, turned the clashes between court and Parlement into a

routine spectacle. The religious feuds between the ultramontanes, Gallicans, and Jansenists, which culminated in 1764 with the expulsion of the Jesuits, degenerated into a ritual round of spite and obscurantism. The chasm between court and people yawned ever wider. The most memorable personality of the age must surely be that of Jeanne Poisson, Mme de Pompadour (1721–64)—intelligent, influential, and totally helpless. She did what she could to relieve the King's unspeakable boredom, and is credited with that most telling of remarks, 'Après nous le déluge'. [**CORSICA**] [**DESSEIN**]

Louis XVI no doubt looked forward to a reign as long and as boring as that of his grandfather. He even saw the need for reform. But he was the first prisoner of the Ancien Régime. On the day that the Deluge broke, on 14 July 1789, his diary contained the entry which his grandfather had always used on days when there was no hunting—'Rien' (nothing).

In the British Isles the capital event of the period, the founding of the United Kingdom (1707), occurred as the culmination of complicated religious, dynastic, constitutional, and international conflicts. The Restoration of the Stuarts after the Civil War had ushered in an uneasy stand-off, and the reign of Charles II (d. 1685) survived two Dutch wars, the fraudulent Popish Plot of 1679, and two rebellions of Scottish Covenanters. Like his father, the King submitted unwillingly to government through Parliaments and did his best to circumvent them. His religious

---

CORSICA

IT is a moot point whether Napoleon Bonaparte was born a subject of the King of France. His elder brother, Joseph, was certainly not. The island of Corsica was sold to Louis XV by the Republic of Genoa in a deal that was not confirmed by the island's assembly until September 1770, when Napoleon was one year old. Napoleon's father had served as secretary to Pasquale Paoli, who had led the revolt against Genoa and who would lead another against the rule of the Jacobin Convention, before dying in England.

Corsica had a long history of self-government, the *terra di commune,* going back to the eleventh century. It survived under Pisan, Genoan, and French royal suzerainty, until suppressed by the French Republic.

Since 1793, Corse has been incorporated into metropolitan France as Département 90; but its individual character is very marked, and local separatism has always been present. The regional law of 1982 returned a measure of autonomy, but not enough to eliminate anti-French terrorism. The illegal Corsican National Liberation Front can be compared to the ETA of the Basque provinces in Spain or to the IRA in Northern Ireland.[1] Despite a widespread stereotype, terrorist-style nationalism is not confined to Eastern Europe or the Balkans.

policy steered a middle course between the extreme Protestant and Catholic factions. The return of the Anglican supremacy put limits on toleration. It was characterized in England by the Clarendon Code and Test Acts and in Ireland and Scotland by the reimposition of episcopacy. In foreign policy there was great dissension over fighting the Dutch on commercial grounds or supporting them on religious and strategic grounds. [LLOYD'S]

All these issues came to a head after 1685, when Charles was succeeded by his brother, James II (r. 1685–8 (1701))—a militant Catholic, an absolutist, and a client of Louis XIV. His accession was marked by two more unsuccessful rebellions—by the Duke of Argyll in Scotland and by the Duke of Monmouth in England. When the King tried to widen the toleration acts to include Catholics, the dominant Protestant and Parliamentary party in England—henceforth known as 'Whigs'—forced a showdown on their royalist opponents—henceforth known as 'Tories'. The spectre of civil and religious strife beckoned, though trimmers of every hue, like the Anglo-Irish Vicar of Bray, were ready to keep their positions at any cost:

> When royal James possessed the throne
> And Popery came in fashion,
> The Penal Laws I hooted down
> And signed the Declaration.
> The Church of Rome I found did fit
> Full well my constitution;
> And I had been a Jesuit
> But for the Revolution.
> And this is Law that I'll maintain,
> Until my dying day, Sir!
> That whatsoever King may reign,
> I'll be the Vicar of Bray, Sir![23]

James put his faith in mobilizing French support, and succeeded in fleeing abroad at the second attempt.

The Protestant victory was secured by the firm action of the Dutch Stadholder, William of Orange, the husband of James's daughter Mary, who was determined to stop England from falling into Louis's net. Landing at Torbay on 5 November 1688 with a powerful army of mercenaries, he cleared London of English troops without resistance, and established a position of unassailable strength. Only then did he summon the Convention Parliament which was to carry out the 'glorious' and 'bloodless' revolution and to offer him the English throne jointly with his wife.[24] Here was a resolution which suited all the main participants. The States General of the United Provinces, who paid for the operation, were content to see their Stadholder in a stronger position abroad than in the Netherlands. William was content to have greatly increased his resources for fighting the French. The English 'Whigs' were content to have a foreign king whom they could control more easily than the Stuarts.

In England, the 'Revolution' was confirmed by the Declaration and the Bill of

LLOYD'S

O N 18 February 1688 the *London Gazette* mentioned a coffee-house run by Edward Lloyd in Tower Street. Shortly afterwards Lloyd launched a weekly bulletin, the precursor of *Lloyd's List*, providing news about commerce and shipping. By so doing, he supplied both a meeting-place and an information service for all interested in the insurance business. Lloyd's would grow into the world's largest insurance association. Transferred to the Royal Exchange, it issued its first standardized policy in 1774. It was reorganized in 1811 [**TABARD**], its privileges confirmed by statute in 1888. It provides the point of contact between the syndicates of 'names', who subscribe the capital, and the firms of 'underwriters', who share out the cover on every policy issued.

The insurance business sells security. Its roots can be traced to the trading cities of medieval Italy, where the principle of 'mutuality', or risk-sharing, was clearly understood. It was one of the preconditions for the growth of commerce. Its acceleration in the eighteenth century reflects the wider growth of security in many other spheres.

Initially, the culture of insurance was the preserve of a tiny mercantile élite. [**MERCANTE**] But it steadily extended its frontiers—first into new areas of risk, such as fire, life, accident, and health; secondly into new social constituencies; and thirdly into new, less commercialized regions of Europe. By the mid-nineteenth century, governments were beginning to ponder the benefits of universal insurance schemes; and in 1888 the German government introduced a health and pension scheme for all state employees. By the late twentieth century the concept of 'social security', accessible to everyone by right, was a widely accepted ideal.

Insurance had far-reaching implications in the realm of social psychology. If chronic insecurity had encouraged traditional beliefs in religion and [**MAGIC**], the advance of material security was bound to have its effect on popular responses to the great imponderables of luck and death. In 1693 the Royal Society commissioned Edmund Halley to prepare a statistical report on 'The Degrees of Mortality of Mankind'. It was worried by a recent financial disaster resulting from annuities sold without reference to age. Halley found that the only suitable data came from Breslau (now Wrocław) in Austrian Silesia, where the registration of deaths included the age of the deceased. By analysing 6,193 births and 5,869 deaths in Breslau for the years 1687–91, he was able to draw up a table, showing the age cohorts of the population, the estimated population totals in each cohort, and the annual number of deaths at each age. From this he demonstrated the principle of life expectancy and the varying probabilities of death. Halley's 'Breslau Table' was the pioneer of all actuarial calculations. It robbed Providence of its monopoly on human mortality.

Rights and by another Toleration Act (which admitted Protestant dissenters but not Catholics). It was closely allied to new constitutional arrangements which shifted the balance away from the Crown and towards Parliament. In Ireland, it was achieved by bloody conquest and the triumph of 'King Billy' and his 'Orangemen' at the Battle of the Boyne on 1 (11) July 1690.* It perpetuated the Protestant supremacy in a largely Catholic country. In Scotland, it was sealed by the treacherous Massacre of Glencoe (1692)—where the murder of the Catholic Clan Macdonald by the English-backed Campbells marked the onset of a war to the death between Lowlands and Highlands. Internationally, it was accompanied by the engagement of England and Scotland in the League of Augsburg, and in all subsequent coalitions against Louis XIV.

The 'Glorious Revolution' of 1688–9, therefore, was not specially glorious nor revolutionary. It set out to save the political and religious Establishment from James's radical proposals; and it was brought to fruition through the only successful invasion of England since 1066. Yet in subsequent generations it would spawn a powerful myth. It lay at the root of a constitutional doctrine which came to be known as 'the English ideology', and which postulates the absolute sovereignty of Parliament. This doctrine holds that 'absolute despotic power', as the jurist Blackstone put it, had been transferred from the monarch to the elected Parliament. In theory at least, it gives Parliament the power to rule with all the lofty authoritarianism that was previously enjoyed by England's kings. In this it differs fundamentally from the doctrine of the sovereignty of the people, which most other European countries were to acquire from the example either of the USA or of revolutionary France, and which operates through a formal constitution governing all branches of the polity. It inevitably became the flagship not only of Protestant but also of English supremacy within Great Britain, since English MPs could always engineer a majority over the non-English members. It was destined to survive all the changes of subsequent centuries; 300 years later, it would still be offering one of the principal obstacles to Britain's entry into a united European Community.[25]

Dynastic complications rendered the ultimate outcome uncertain for 25 years. From 1701, Louis XIV formally recognized the claims of James Edward Stuart, the 'Old Pretender' or 'James III' (1688–1766), whilst the deaths of Mary (1694), of William III (1702), and of all 17 children of Queen Anne (r. 1702–14) rendered the Protestant Stuarts heirless. In the middle of the War of the Spanish Succession, no one needed to be reminded of the mischief which heirlessness could wreak; and the Act of Union (1707) between England and Scotland largely came about as a result of common frustration in London and Edinburgh at the welter of dynastic settlements being floated. As the price of its disbandment, the Scots Parliament was able to secure English acceptance of free trade between the two countries, English cash for settling Scotland's huge debts, English agreement to the separate

* 1 July 1690 (Old Style) = 11 July 1690 (New Style). Owing to confusion over the changed calendar, or perhaps over the Protestants' second victory of July 1690 at Aughrim, 'The Boyne' has come to be celebrated traditionally in Northern Ireland as a national holiday held on 12 July.

existence of Scots law and the Presbyterian Kirk, and the unwritten promise of English armed force against the rebellious Highlands (see Appendix III, p. 1285).

Henceforth, the 'United Kingdom of Great Britain' was to be ruled by a joint Parliament at Westminster; and a new 'British' nationality was to be superimposed on the older nations of the islands. Modern British identity derives from this time. English traditions were to be revered. Memories of Scotland's separate history were to be subverted. Britain entered the era of its greatest assertiveness, free from insular divisions. The choice of the Hanoverians as successors to the Stuarts, though hotly contested, was carried through. Thereafter, a monarchy which was neither English nor Scottish became a pillar of Britishness.[26] [GOTHA][MASON]

The Jacobite cause, which persisted for much of the eighteenth century, encompassed all that was lost in the events of 1688–1714. Apart from the personal fortunes of the Old Pretender and his son, Charles Edward Stuart, variously known as the 'Young Pretender', 'Bonnie Prince Charlie', and 'Charles III' (1720–88), it united all the wounded feelings connected with the defeated order. It mourned the demise of the old monarchies, of English Catholicism and its European connections, of the rights of the Scots and the Irish to control their own destinies. In England it commanded the sympathy of many High Tories, and of all who wept for the fugitives and exiles. It inspired two great risings—'the Fifteen' (1715), which saw the Jacobite armies march as far south as Lancashire, and the 'Forty-Five' (1745), which saw them reach Derby.

This latter occasion inspired the ultimate campaign to destroy the civilization of the Scottish Highlands. After the terrible disaster of Culloden Moor, on 16 April 1746, when the last great charge of the clansmen was cut down by the volleys of redcoat English and Lowland Scots, the life of the clans was suppressed forever. Their Gaelic language was proscribed, their native dress forbidden, their organizations banned, their leaders banished. The terrible Clearances, which allowed loyalist landowners to expel the inhabitants in favour of sheep, left more Gaels in North America than in Scotland. They gave the Highlands that haunting emptiness which unknowing tourists have admired ever since. [PHILIBEG]

Combined with the enclosure movement, which had been driving smallholders from the land in England for two centuries or more, the Clearances completed a purging process which was to give British society some of its most abiding characteristics. These purges deprived Great Britain of the peasants who formed the backbone of most other nations in Europe. They took away the social solidarity, the primitive democracy, and the sort of national consciousness which grows naturally from a peasant-based community. They meant that a sense of British nationality could only be projected downwards from the institutions of the state, especially from Crown and Empire, and could not grow upwards from the peasant family's traditional attachment to the soil. Henceforth the soil was largely the property of a narrow class of farmers and landowners. British society was divided into a well-endowed loyalist minority and a dispossessed majority, who would carry the half-remembered resentments of their disinheritance into the very bowels of the British class system.

MASON

O N St John Baptist's Day 1717, representatives from London's four existing freemasons' lodges met at the *Goose and Gridiron* alehouse to form a 'Mother Grand Lodge of the World' and to elect their first Grand Master. Though the minutes did not survive, historians of freemasonry do not question that the meeting took place, or that London's Grand Lodge was henceforth the nerve-centre of an international movement.[1]

The earlier history of freemasonry is murky. The story of a thirteenth-century papal bull creating a society of church-builders is pure fiction. Connections with the medieval *commecines* or *steinmetzen*, still more with an underground association of ex-Templars, are quite unproved. A report of 1723 contained the jingle:

> If history be no ancient Fable
> Freemasons came from the Tower of Babel.

The earliest reliable references point to seventeenth-century Scotland, and to contacts with England made during the Civil War. Elias Ashmole (1617–92), the antiquary, astrologer, and founder of the Oxford Museum, made a note of his own initiation in his diary:

1646 Oct 16, 4h 30' pm. I was made a Freemason at Warrington in Lancashire with Col. Henry Mainwaring of Cheshire. The names of those who were then of the Lodge: Mr Rich. Penket, Warden, Mr. James Collier, Mr. Rich. Sankey, Henry Littler, John Ellam, Richard Ellam, and Hugh Brew.[2]

The air of mystery surrounding freemasonry is deliberately cultivated. It is attractive to sympathizers, offensive to opponents. Non-initiates are left guessing about its rituals, its hierarchy, its pseudo-oriental jargon, its signs and symbols, and its purposes. The compass and square, the apron and gloves, and the circle on the floor are obviously designed to encourage belief in the movement's medieval guild origins. But it is the alleged oath of secrecy which has caused the greatest controversy. According to one account, the blindfolded initiate was asked:

'In Whom do you put your trust?' and answered, 'In God.' 'Where are you travelling?' and answered 'From West to East, to the Light.' He was then required to promise on the Bible, not to reveal the society's secrets 'under no less penalty than having my throat cut across, my tongue torn out, and my body buried in the rough sands of the sea . . .'[3]

Freemasonry has always acted essentially as a mutual benefit society, though the benefits are nowhere defined. Its enemies have often maintained that it is anti-feminist, since it does not admit women, and antisocial as well as anti-Christian, since its members supposedly help each other with political, commercial, and social contacts to the detriment of others. Freemasons have always stressed their opposition to atheism, their religious tolerance, neutrality in politics, and commitment to charitable works.

Freemasonry expanded dramatically in the eighteenth century. It recruited from the highest ranks of the British aristocracy, and became a lasting pillar of the monarchy. A lodge was founded in Paris in 1725 by expatriate Scots; thereafter it spread to every country of the Continent. It was established in Prague (1726), Warsaw (1755), even St Petersburg. By the time of the Napoleonic wars the network was sufficiently wide for stories to circulate about officers on opposing sides at Borodino or Waterloo giving each other the secret sign of recognition and holding their fire.

In the Catholic countries, freemasonry took an anti-clerical turn and played an important role in the radical Enlightenment.[4] Its members were often deists, philosophers, critics of Church and State. In Austria, for example, where the papal bulls denouncing it were not published, it was extremely active in the promotion of the arts until its suppression in 1795. In France, it contributed to the pre-revolutionary ferment. In the nineteenth century and beyond, it would be strongly associated with the cause of Liberalism.

The response of the Catholic Church was unequivocal. The Vatican regarded freemasonry as evil. From the Bull *In Eminenti* (1738) to *Ab Apostolici* (1890), the popes condemned it on six separate occasions as conspiratorial, wicked, and subversive. Loyal Catholics could not be freemasons, who were often classed in ultra-Catholic circles as a public enemy alongside Jacobins, Carbonari, and Jews. Totalitarian regimes of the twentieth century were still more hostile. Freemasons were consigned to concentration camps by both Fascists and Communists. In many parts of Europe they could only rebuild their activities after the fall of Fascism, or, in the East, after the collapse of the Soviet bloc.

Controversy about the role of freemasonry continues. But the most impressive document about freemasonry is its membership list, which is said to include, Francis I of Austria, Frederick II of Prussia, Gustav IV of Sweden, Stanisław-August of Poland, and Paul I of Russia; Wren, Swift, Voltaire, Montesquieu, Gibbon, Goethe, Burns, Wilkes, Burke; Haydn, Mozart, Guillotin, and Marat; Generals Lafayette, Kutuzov, Suvorov, and Wellington; Marshals MacDonald and Poniatowski; Talleyrand, Canning, Scott, Trollope, O'Connell, Pushkin, Liszt, Mazzini, Garibaldi, and Kossuth; Leopold I of Belgium, William I of Germany; Eiffel, Tirpitz, Scharnhorst, Masaryk, Kerensky, Stresemann, and Churchill; and all British kings except one from George IV to George VI. Which shows that the greatest of international secret societies was not completely secret.

PHILIBEG

IN 1727 the chief of the Clan Macdonnell of Glengarry entered the iron-smelting business. He leased the forest of Invergarry to a Quaker forgemaster from Barrow in Lancashire, Thomas Rawlinson, and raised the workforce to cut the timber and man the furnace. Rawlinson, who visited regularly, noticed that the clansmen's traditional attire, the long *breacon* or 'belted plaid', was hampering their labour. So, consulting the garrison tailor at Inverness, he designed a shorter, pleated, knee-length garment, which would soon be known as the *felie-beg*, the 'philibeg' or small kilt. In this way, the central item of Scotland's supposedly ancient Highland costume was invented by an Englishman.[1]

Soon afterwards the second Jacobite Rising was defeated; and the Westminster Parliament banned all Highland dress. For forty years the kilt could not be worn in public, except by the Highland regiments which the British Army was busy recruiting—the Black Watch (1739), the Highland Light Infantry (1777), the Seaforth Highlanders (1778), the Camerons (1793), the Argyll and Sutherlands and the Gordons (1794). In those same decades, whilst the Highland Society in London campaigned for the return of the kilt, male civilians in the Highlands took permanently to trousers. [NOMEN]

In 1822 George IV paid the first royal visit to Edinburgh since the Union. Sir Walter Scott, the novelist, acted as a master of ceremonies. The Highland regiments, who had covered themselves in glory at Waterloo, were paraded in full kilted splendour. All the clan chiefs of Scotland were urged to attend in 'traditional costume'. They, too, wore kilts, each in a distinctive tartan. Chequered plaid had been woven for centuries by a thriving industry, which supplied the 'trews' or tapered breeches of the well-to-do. But its colourful 'setts' or patterns had been loosely associated with regions, not with clans; and it had not been used by ordinary folk. The most famous of the setts, the black-and-green tartan of the Campbells, which would be given to the Black Watch, had been known in the trade as 'Kidd No. 155', after a Caribbean planter who ordered it for his slaves. Yet the Highland regiments and the gathering of 1822 combined to establish the custom of linking each sett with one particular clan name. They were greatly assisted by the later publication of a finely illustrated but spurious work, the *Vestiarium Scoticum* (1842), written by two charlatan brothers, the self-styled Sobieski-Stuarts, who held romantic court on the island of Eileann Aigas near Inverness.

The allocation of tartans completed a remarkable process of cultural invention which had been evolving over two centuries. In the first stage, after the founding of the Presbyterian colony in Ulster, the obviously Irish origins of Highland civilization were neglected, then repudiated. A new, exclusively Scottish history and literature were compiled, not least by the brilliant fake poetry of James Macpherson's 'Ossian'. Supposedly 'ancient and original' Highland customs, like the kilt, proved attractive, since they met the demand for an unambiguous national pedigree. In the final stage, which started with the Act of Amnesty (1786), masses of Highland refugees crowded into the Lowlands, and the new traditions were adopted by Scots of all ilks as a mark of their non-Englishness. This highly romantic game was abetted by Queen Victoria, who acquired the estate of Balmoral in 1848, and invented a Balmoral tartan for her own very un-Scottish consort and family.

The Macdonnells of Glengarry did not see the end of this revolution.[2] Originally a sept or sub-clan of the Clan Macdonald of Skye, once 'Lords of the Isles', their Gaelic name meant 'sons of Domhnull', the 'world ruler'. During intervals of their feud with the Mackenzies, they had always been prominent in the Catholic and Jacobite cause. A Macdonnell carried the standard of James II at Killiecrankie in 1689, and fought again at Sheriffmuir in 1715. His successor fought in the Forty-Five at the head of 600 clansmen, and was imprisoned in the Tower of London. But the sixteenth chief sold the ancestral lands and emigrated to New Zealand. Their red, black, dark green, and white tartan has all the signs of a simple and ancient sett. Whether it adorned the original Scottish kilt of 1727 is not known.

In the late nineteenth century, 'invented tradition' was mass-produced all over Europe.[3] When the German Socialists invented May Day (1890), when the Greeks restaged the Olympic Games (1896), when the Russians marked the founding of the Romanov Dynasty (1913), or the Scots instituted 'Burns Night'—the Lowlanders' answer to the kilt, the pipes, and the haggis—they were all seeking to endow their constituents with a common sense of identity.

Within the British Isles, Ireland was a country apart. Though its fate cannot be compared to the harrying of the Scottish highlands, the legacy of conflict was deep and bitter. Both Protestants and Catholics had suffered foul persecution during the religious wars. After 1691 the Protestant supremacy was bolstered by draconian penal laws which denied Catholics the right to office, property, education, and intermarriage. Ireland was excluded from the Union of 1707. It retained its own Parliament, but was still subject to the ancient 'Poyning's Law', which gave automatic control of legislation to the king's ministers in London. Unlike Scotland, Ireland was not allowed to benefit from free trade with England. Unlike Wales, it did not yet experience any sort of national or cultural revival. With the sole exception of Protestant Ulster, where Huguenot refugees started the prosperous linen industry, it did not participate directly in Britain's industrial revolution. A rising population made rural distress a fact of life. The famines of 1726–9 and 1739–41 foreshadowed the disaster of the 1840s. The ferocious 'Whiteboy' gangs first made their appearance in the countryside in 1761. A movement for reform led by Henry Flood (1732–91) and Henry Grattan (1746–1820) was eventually overtaken by the abortive rebellion of Wolfe Tone and his United Irishmen (1798), and by Ireland's forcible incorporation into the United Kingdom through the second Act of Union (1801).

Hanoverian Britain lasted for 123 years. The reigns of the four Georges—I (1714–27), II (1727–60), III (1760–1820), and IV (1820–30)—witnessed a truly constitutional monarchy presiding over the acquisition and the loss of an empire, over the world's first Industrial Revolution, and over the rise of unprecedented naval power which rendered Britain uniquely immune from the Continent's affairs. Such indeed were the differences between Britain and its Continental neighbours which arose during this period that many insular historians have been led to conceive of British and European history as separate subjects.

In retrospect, the most momentous event of later Hanoverian times is to be found in the loss of thirteen British colonies during the so-called 'American Revolution' of 1776–83. Of course, no one in 1776 could possibly have foreseen the full potential of the USA. The thirteen colonies still looked to be very fragile ventures, surrounded by the uncontrolled forces of nature in a largely unexplored continent. Even so, the prospects for the British Empire on the eve of the War of Independence were enormous by any standards. British naval power had already raised the very real possibility that the vast western and mid-western territories of Spain and France in America could be absorbed without serious opposition. (In 1803, the French were indeed obliged to sell their 'Louisiana'—effectively, the whole of the mid-West—for a song.) Shorn of their most attractive transatlantic possessions, however, the British were increasingly constrained to seek their further imperial fortunes elsewhere, especially in India and Africa.

At the time, the British government was blind to even the most immediate implications. John Hancock was right to sign the Declaration of Independence (1776) in large letters, so that King George could read it 'without his spectacles'. For Britain's Continental rivals, the American revolt provided an opportunity for short-term meddling. France and Spain assisted a cause which they would never have tolerated among their own colonists. Yet for all Europeans of conscience it raised issues of fundamental political principle, challenging the very foundations of the monarchies by which almost all of them were ruled. The seven articles of the Constitution to which it gave rise contain the clearest and most practical formulations of the ideals of the Enlightenment. They are short, secular, democratic, republican, rational; firmly grounded in the contract theory of Locke, in English legalism, in Montesquieu's thoughts on the division of powers, in Rousseau's concept of the general will. The Constitution was written in the name of 'We, the people of the United States', and has proved remarkably durable. Its irony lies in the fact that many of its leading authors, including Thomas Jefferson and George

Washington, were slave-owners, and that it was wrested from a country which was one of the most free and best-governed of the day.

Prior to the eighteenth century, Savoy had been a frontier province of the Holy Roman Empire. It straddled the ridge of the western Alps between the kingdom of France and the plain of Lombardy. Its ruling house, which claimed to be Europe's oldest ruling dynasty, was descended from the eleventh-century Count Umberto Biancamano, 'Humbert of the White Hand', whose family secured possession of territory on either versant of the Mont Cenis and the Grand St Bernard passes. Its western region—the francophone county of Savoy, including Chambéry, Annecy, and the massif of Mont Blanc—reached to the shore of Lake Geneva. Its eastern region, the Italian-speaking principality of Piedmont, including Aosta, Susa, and Turin, extended as far as the Ligurian riviera. After the rise of the Swiss Confederation the province was cut off from the main body of the Empire, and its rulers in Turin, when raised to the status of imperial dukes, were able to pursue a virtually independent existence. Like his predecessors, Duke Victor Amadeus II (r. 1675–1730) trod a delicate path between his powerful French and Habsburg neighbours. However, by deserting his alliance with Louis XIV at a critical point of the War of the Spanish Succession, he was rewarded by the Emperor with royal status, and the island of Sicily to boot. In 1720 he was obliged by the Austrians to exchange Sicily for the island of Sardinia, thereby ending his reign on the throne of a composite 'Kingdom of Sardinia' made up of Savoy, Piedmont, and Sardinia itself. This strange conglomerate, an archetypal product of dynastic politics, a 'Prussia of the south', was to turn a century later into the unlikely leader of the movement for Italian unification (see Chapter X).

Spain headed the long procession of countries which were fast losing their former political and economic standing. Under the Bourbon kings—Philip V (r. 1700–46), Ferdinand VI (r. 1746–59), Charles III (r. 1759–88), and Charles IV (r. 1788–1808)—it lost all pretensions to be a great power. Stripped of its Continental possessions except for Parma and Piacenza, and tied to a vast American empire of doubtful value, it stayed under the domination of the grandees, the Church, and the Inquisition. In Philip's reign alone, 700 *autos-da-fé* were staged. Some success was achieved in reorganizing the administration on French lines, in embellishing Madrid, and in encouraging cultural life through the Academy (1713). [**BASERRIA**] [**PRADO**]

Portugal likewise vegetated under the rule of indifferent monarchs and a militant Church. John V (r. 1706–50), known as 'The Faithful', was a priest-king, 'one of whose sons by an abbess became Inquisitor-General'. The reign of his successor, Joseph I (r. 1750–77), was shattered by the Lisbon earthquake, and restored by the energetic but short-lived reforms of Portugal's latter-day Colbert, Sebastão, Marquis of Pombal (1699–1782). Pombal probably never uttered the words most frequently attributed to him—'Bury the dead, and feed the living'—but from 1750 he dominated the country for a quarter of a century, reorganizing finance, edu-

---

BASERRIA

THAT the *baserria* or 'communal farmstead' formed the basis of a unique type of social organization in the Basque country is confirmed by the census records of Navarre from 1786. To overcome the succession crises which often beset the single peasant household [**GRILLENSTEIN**], the Diet of Navarre had confirmed the right of each farmstead to be run by two co-resident managerial couples. All the adult members of a farmstead, whether owners or tenants, were empowered to elect an heir or heiress in each generation who would succeed as soon as one of the managerial couples was disabled by death or retirement. The marriages and dowries of the managers and their offspring were also subject to communal approval. As a result, the *baserria* was remarkably stable in terms of ownership and management, as well as being economically self-sufficient. It was the 'true repository of Basque culture' in the face of growing urbanization and industrialization, the bedrock of the Basques' separate identity until the onset of rural depopulation in recent times. Culture, economy, and social organization were inseparable in a system which preserved one of Europe's oldest pre-Indo-European peoples through many centuries.[1]

---

cation, navy, commerce, and colonies. Maria I (r. 1777–1816), like her British contemporary, lapsed into insanity; and Portugal, like Britain, was to pass the whole of the revolutionary period under a regency. [**QUAKE**]

Eighteenth-century Italy was still divided, even if the lines of division were somewhat altered. The main rivalry now lay between the House of Savoy in Turin, the Austrian Habsburgs, holding Milan, and the Duchy of Tuscany. The re-establishment in 1738 of an independent Bourbon kingdom in Naples added some balance. All these territories benefited from the sound management of enlightened despots. Elsewhere, the old contrasts prevailed between the city republics such as Venice and the divine autocracy of the Papal States. The Vatican lost much of its room for political manœuvre when the Catholic powers were disunited in everything except their demand to suppress the Jesuits (see pp. 593–4). Three long papacies, those of Clement XI (1700–21), Benedict XIV (1740–58), and Pius VI (1775–99), could not check the Vatican's political effacement. Secular culture saw a marked revival; Italian language and literature were promoted by official academies in Florence and Rome. Science and scholarship flourished. Names such as that of L. A. Muratori the archivist (1672–1750) at Ferrara, Antonio Genovesi the economist (1712–69) at Naples, Cesare Beccaria the criminologist (1738–94) at Milan, or Alessandro Volta the physicist (1745–1821) at Pavia gained continental fame. They undoubtedly strengthened the bonds of a growing national cultural community. [**TORMENTA**]

QUAKE

ON 1 November 1755 the Portuguese capital, Lisbon, was wrecked by an earthquake. A tidal wave destroyed the quays and ships in the Tagus. Two-thirds of the city's buildings were razed or burned. Between 30,000 and 40,000 citizens lost their lives. The shocks were felt from Scotland to Constantinople.

The Lisbon earthquake was neither the first nor the last of Europe's disasters. Similar devastation had occurred in 1421, when the collapse of the Maas Polder drowned hundreds of low-lying villages in Holland, in December 1631, when an eruption of Mt Vesuvius killed some 18,000 people in Italy, or in 1669, when lava from Mt Etna buried the port of Catania in Sicily. The earthquake of 1356 wrecked Basle, whilst that of 28 December 1908 levelled both Messina and Reggio di Calabria, with a loss of 77,000. London's Great Fire (1666) had many counterparts. Visitations of plague and cholera did not cease until the end of the nineteenth century. [**SANITAS**]

Yet the quake of 1755 caused more than physical damage. It rocked the most cherished hopes of the Enlightenment. It shook the belief of the *philosophes* in an ordered, predictable world and in a benign, rational God. It brought ruin to just and unjust alike. As Voltaire himself was forced to admit: 'After all, the world does contain evil.'[1]

The United Provinces, like Portugal once a jewel in the Spanish crown, were still left with an overseas empire but with little influence over events nearer to home. At sea they had lost their maritime pre-eminence to the British; on land they were surrounded on all sides by the Habsburgs. The long-standing tug-of-war between the republican oligarchy and the House of Orange continued until 1815, when a hereditary monarchy was finally created. [**BATAVIA**]

Eighteenth-century Scandinavia entered centre-stage on only one occasion. Sweden's last throw for greatness under Charles XII (r. 1697–17) was an anachronism which ended in disaster (see below). With that exception, the Scandinavian countries settled down to an existence of inoffensive obscurity. In Denmark-Norway the four Oldenburg kings—Frederick IV (r. 1699–1730), Christian VI (r. 1730–46), Frederick V (r. 1746–66), and Christian VII (r. 1766–1808)—went some way to modernizing the country on enlightened lines. A zealous experiment in this direction, with 2,000 decrees passed in two years, ended abruptly in 1772 when the King's chief minister, J. F. Struensee, a Prussian, and presumed father of the Queen's child, was beheaded for *lèse-majesté*. In Sweden a long and strong reaction against royal absolutism gave prominence to a Diet whose stormy proceedings were given over to the laborious workings of its four estates, and the rivalry of the factions of 'Hats' and 'Caps'. The monarchy was greatly weakened by the abdication of Charles XII's sister, Ulrica Leonora, in favour of her hapless German husband, Frederick I (r. 1720–51), and in 1756 by the Prussian-inspired intrigues of his successor, Adolphus Frederick (r. 1751–71) of Holstein-Gottorp-Eutin. Its successful reassertion after the royal *coup d'état* of 1772 under Gustavus III (r. 1771–92) brought Sweden closer to the mainstream of contemporary politics and culture. This patriotic and accomplished young king, who had once stormed the salons of Paris, was to be assassinated in 1792 whilst trying to organize a league of princes against the French Revolution. [ELDLUFT]

Whilst Western Europe was preoccupied with the supremacy of France, the countries of Central and Eastern Europe had major preoccupations of their own. Within the lifetime of Louis XIV, Central Europe experienced two unexpected developments which seriously affected the history of the German states. One was the last great surge of the Ottomans, who in 1683 returned to the siege of Vienna. The other was provided by a further dramatic stage in the rise of Prussia, whose ambitions now stood to disrupt the entire region. Eastern Europe witnessed the decisive stage in the emergence of the Russian Empire, henceforth a military and political power of the first rank. Trapped in the middle of these rapid shifts, the old Republic of Poland-Lithuania first rallied to the rescue of Vienna, then slowly sank beneath the blows of her rapacious neighbours. Before the eighteenth century was out, the traditional power structure of Central and Eastern Europe had been transformed out of all recognition.

The Ottoman surge of the late seventeenth century was associated with an extended political crisis, which for thirty years put the grand viziership in the hands of the Köprülüs, a family of Albanian origin. It began in the 1650s amidst recriminations over Crete and the Venetian blockade of the Dardanelles, and was fuelled after 1660 by a disputed succession in Transylvania which placed the Porte in direct opposition to the Habsburgs. The Köprülüs saw war as a means for diverting the intrigues and resentments of the army, especially the corps of janissaries, against whom they had taken such drastic disciplinary measures. In 1672 they attacked the Polish province of Podolia, seizing the fortress of Kamieniets on the Dniester, until checked at Chocim by the Crown Hetman, John Sobieski. In 1681–2, in Hungary, they took the side of rebels led by Count Tököli and, after declaring Hungary to be an Ottoman vassal, advanced up the Danube towards Vienna.

The Siege of Vienna lasted for two months, from July to September 1683. It saw the poorly provisioned Austrian capital invested by a powerful army of 200,000 men equipped with a large siege train of heavy artillery. At a juncture when the German princes were fixated by the encroachments of Louis XIV on the Rhine, the Emperor had great difficulty responding to the danger on the Danube. As it was, the most effective assistance came from Poland, where Sobieski, now King and weaned from his early alliance with France, saw a Turkish war and Austrian subsidies as a solution to his own domestic problems. Having taken command of the relief force in early September, he prayed in the chapel on the

ELDLUFT

IN 1773 the Swedish pharmacist Karl Scheele (1742–86) discovered that air was a mixture of 'several airs', and that one of its components, which he called *eldluft* or 'fire air', held the secret of combustion.[1] In October of the following year, he sent his findings to Antoine Laurent Lavoisier (1743–94), the director of France's gunpowder and saltpetre monopoly. That same month Lavoisier gave lunch to the English dissenter and experimenter Joseph Priestley (1733–1804), and heard from him too how 'dephlogisticated air' caused lighted tapers to burn with incandescent flame.

Lavoisier, who directed the King's *Ferme Générale* or tax-farming system as well as the *Régie de Poudre*, had the time and money to indulge his passion for experimentation. He had already noticed that many substances gained weight when burned, and he knew that this effect was not compatible with the reigning theory of Phlogiston—an invisible (and imaginary) form of matter which most scientists, including Priestley, still believed in.

So Lavoisier designed an experiment which would measure the amount of 'fire air' that might be absorbed when quicksilver was burned in a closed flask.[2] He found not only that the heated quicksilver combined with fire air but also that further heating separated out the new compound into its component parts. Modern chemical notation would have described Lavoisier's experiment thus:

$$Hg + O = HgO \text{ (Mercuric oxide)}: HgO = Hg + O$$

Science had finally reached an understanding of the nature of chemical reactions, namely that substances could be coupled and uncoupled with others in a material world made up of simple elements and their compounds.

Lavoisier then addressed the task of giving simple names to the simple elements and compound names to compounds. Scheele's 'fire air', or Priestley's 'Dephlogisticated air', became *oxygenè*, Scheele's 'foul air', *hydrogène*. The compound of mercury and oxygen became 'mercuric oxide'. In 1787 Lavoisier helped publish a list of 33 elements with their new nomenclature. In 1789, he published his *Traité préliminaire de la Chimie*, the world's first chemical textbook.

Scheele was already dead, in all probability poisoned by the fumes of his own furnace. In 1791 Priestley was burned out of house and home by the Birmingham mob, for having welcomed the French Revolution. He fled to the USA. On 8 May 1794 Lavoisier met his death on the guillotine in the company of twenty-six other royal tax-farmers. The appeal judge was said to have remarked, 'The Republic has no need of savants.' The Chemical Revolution coincided almost exactly with its political counterpart. Both of them 'consumed their own children'.

heights of the Kahlenberg in the Vienna Woods. Then, in the mid-afternoon of the 12th, he ordered the attack: his winged hussars charged down the hill and rode straight for the centre of the Ottoman camp. At half-past five he was galloping through the enemy ranks amid scenes of panic, confusion, and slaughter. The following evening, he found time to write to his wife, Queen Marie-Louise, from the Grand Vizier's tent:

Only solace of my heart and soul, my fairest, most beloved Marysienka!

Our Lord and God, Blessed of all ages, has brought unheard victory and glory to our nation. All the guns, the whole camp, untold spoils have fallen into our hands . . . There is enough powder and ammunition alone for a million men . . . The Vizir took such hurried flight that he had time to escape with only one horse . . . [The camp is] as extensive as the cities of Warsaw or of Lwow within their walls . . . I have all the tents, and cars, *et mille autres galanteries fort jolies et fort riches, mais fort riches* . . . They abandoned their janissaries in the trenches, who were put to the sword during the night . . . They left behind a mass of innocent Austrian people, particularly women; but they butchered as many as they could . . . The Vizir had a marvellously beautiful ostrich . . . but this too he had killed . . . He had baths; he had gardens and fountains; rabbits and cats, and a parrot which kept flying about so that we could not catch it . . .[27]

When Sobieski posted the green standard of the Prophet to the Pope, he appended Charles V's comment after Mühlberg: 'Veni, vidi, Deus Vicit' (I came, I saw, God conquered).

The Ottoman retreat which began that day at Vienna continued by stages for the next 200 years. In the short term it inspired the leaders of the Holy League, organized by the Pope, to press on down the Danube into lands undisputed since crusading times. By the Peace of Carlowitz (1699) Hungary was returned to Austria, Podolia to Poland, Azov to Muscovy, and the Morea to Venice. In the long term it trapped the Ottomans' European provinces between a concerted pincer movement, with the Habsburgs holding the line of their Military Frontier on the western flank and the Russians advancing relentlessly round the Black Sea on the eastern flank. In this regard the Austro-Russian treaty signed in 1726 played a long-standing strategic role (see Appendix III, p. 1284).

The fortunes of the Ottoman wars swung back and forth. In 1739 Austria was made to disgorge all the gains, including Belgrade, achieved at the earlier Treaty of Passarowitz (1718). But three extended Russo-Turkish Wars—in 1735–9, 1768–74, and 1787–92—left the entire northern coast of the Black Sea in Russian hands. The decisive Treaty of Küçük-Kainardji (1774) gave the Tsar a protectorate over all the Sultan's Christian subjects, and commercial rights in the Ottoman Empire previously enjoyed only by the French. It marked the onset of the 'Eastern Question'. Much of the Balkans, however, remained under Ottoman rule. The eighteenth century was a period of slowly rising national expectations, often among people whose first instinct was to support the Ottoman authorities.

Greece was brought into the political arena partly through a growing degree of autonomy, partly through Russian intervention. A class of Greek officials grew up, together with Greek schools to educate them. The tribute of children (the *devşirme*) fell into abeyance after 1676. Greek society became more consciously Greek. The Venetian presence in Corfu and, from 1699, in the Morea strengthened links with the West. In 1769 a Russian fleet sent to the Mediterranean against the Ottomans promised deliverance to Greece. The extension of Russian commercial privileges to Greek merchants was an important step.

Serbia was affected by similar developments. The battles over Belgrade, and the Austrian occupation of 1711–18, when many Serb volunteers flocked to the Habsburg colours, showed that the Ottomans were not invincible. Serbia's Orthodox links with Russia were even closer than Greece's. The activities of 'Karađorđe' or 'Black George' Petrović (1767–1817), who served both with Turkish brigands and with a Habsburg regiment, culminated in the rising of 1804–13 that was to bring the first taste of independence. A second rising in 1815–17 under Karađorđe's assassin, Miloš Obrenović (1780–1860), was to pave the way for international recognition.

The two Romanian principalities, Moldavia and Wallachia, were ruled by the Porte through the medium of Phanariot Greeks—so-called from the Greek quarter of Phanar in Constantinople. The Phanariot regime, though corrupt and exploitative, encouraged immigration and Western cultural contacts. The Austrian seizure of Bukovina (1774) and still more the Russian occupations of 1769–74 and 1806–12 were catalysts of change. The notion of liberation from the Ottomans first gained ground among the dominant Greek minority.

Bulgaria suffered greatly from the passage of Ottoman armies, and from bands of deserters, known as *Krajlis*, who ravaged the countryside for decades. In 1794, one of the Krajli leaders, Pasvanoğlu, established himself at Vidin on the Danube in a virtually independent robber republic. Like the Serbs, the Christian Bulgars looked increasingly towards Russia.

Albania fell into the hands of local tribal chieftains. One such chief, Mehemet of Bushat, founded a dynasty *c.*1760, which ruled upper Albania from Scutari for several generations. Another, Ali Pasha of Tepelen, carved out a fiefdom centred on Joanina, which stretched from the Adriatic to the Aegean. [**SHQIPERIA**]

Crna Gora, which was known to the outside world by its Venetian name of 'Montenegro', was the only part of the Balkans to escape Ottoman rule. According to legend, when God created the earth a lot of rocks were left over; so He made Montenegro. Though the Turks occupied the capital, Cetinje, for short periods, they never held onto it. 'A small army is beaten', they said, 'and a large army dies of starvation.' From 1516 to 1696 Montenegro had been a theocratic state, ruled by monkish bishops. From 1696 until 1918 it was ruled by hereditary princes of the Petrović dynasty.

By the late eighteenth century, when the Balkan élites first began to dream about independence, they had been living under Ottoman rule for four to five centuries. The experience had left its mark. The Orthodox Church had made its accommodation long since, instilling in its subjects profoundly conservative and anti-Western attitudes. From the time of the Crusades, the Orthodox looked on the West as the source of a subjugation worse than that of the infidel. As a result,

SHQIPERIA

ALBANIA (*Shqiperia*, 'Land of the Eagles') can fairly claim to be the least familiar of all European states. Sailing down the coast in the 1780s, Edward Gibbon wrote of 'a country within sight of Italy which is less known than the interior of America'. Yet no country has suffered more from the whims of international politics.

The insurrection of 1911, which was to free Albania from Ottoman rule, accelerated the creation of the Balkan League made up of Albania's Christian neighbours. All the League's members, except Bulgaria, possessed territories containing important Albanian populations; and none was prepared to see a 'Greater Albania' in which all Albanians would have been united. The Treaty of London (May 1913), which ended the War of the Balkan League, recognized Albanian sovereignty. But it insisted on the delimitation of frontiers by an international commission, and the introduction of a Western-style monarchy. (See Appendix III, p. 1310.)

Albanian society was deeply divided both by social structure and by religion. The highland clans of the north, the Gheg, who lived by the law of the blood feud, had little in common with the lowlanders, or Tosk, of the south. Two-thirds of the inhabitants were Muslim. The remaining third was equally divided between Catholics and Orthodox. Important minorities included the Vlach-speaking pastoralists of the east, Italians in the coastal cities, and Greeks, who were accustomed to regard southern Albania as 'northern Epirus'. [GAGAUZ]

During the First World War Albania was invaded both by Serbia and by Greece. By the second Treaty of London (1915), with Italy, the Allied powers secretly promised to turn Albania into an Italian protectorate. The Albanian monarchy suffered a chequered fate. The first *Mpret* or King, Wilhelm von Wied (r. 1914) landed in March and fled in September. After the War, General Ahmet Zogu was established as State President of an Albanian Republic, only to have himself proclaimed King in 1926.

During the Second World War, Mussolini established the Italian protectorate promised a quarter of a century earlier. Albanian territory was extended to include the district of Kossovo; and Victor Emmanuel X was declared King. There was a brief German occupation in 1944–5.

The Albanian People's Republic was set up in 1946 by a group of communist Tosk partisans, who had gained wartime ascendancy thanks to Western support. Their leader, Enver Hodzha, resigned all interest in the Albanians living in Montenegro, Kossovo, and Macedonia, retreating into almost total isolation behind the pre-war frontiers. Two hundred years after Gibbon, tourists in the Adriatic were still sailing or flying past Albania with the same feelings of wonder and incomprehension.[1]

none of the great civilizing movements that shook the Western world—
Renaissance, Reformation, Science, Enlightenment, Romanticism—could effectively penetrate the Balkan countries. Political traditions owed little to rationalism, absolutism, or constitutionalism; kinship politics dominated at all levels;
nepotism lubricated by bribery was a way of life. 'Power is a trough,' ran the
Turkish proverb, 'and he who does not feed is a pig.' The border of the shrinking
enclave of what came to be called 'Turkey-in-Europe' formed one of Europe's
most deep-seated cultural fault-lines.

Once the Ottoman threat was repulsed, the fortunes of the Habsburgs revived.
Leopold I (r. 1658–1705) did not live to see the humbling of Louis XIV; but his
sons, Joseph I (r. 1705–11) and Charles VI (r. 1711–40), succeeded to an inheritance
greatly enlarged in Hungary, Italy, and the Netherlands. The principal political
crisis arose once again from a problem of succession, which caused the outbreak
of a major Continental war. Charles VI, like the Spanish namesake whom he had
once nominally succeeded, had no male heir. A narrow-minded bigot, he devoted
much of his life to enforcing religious conformity and, by the Pragmatic Sanction,
to ensuring the succession of his daughter, Maria Theresa. In the event, the imperial throne was seized on his death by Charles Albert, Elector of Bavaria, who as
Charles VII (r. 1742–5) briefly reigned with French collusion as the only non-
Habsburg emperor in 400 years. It then reverted to Maria Theresa's husband,
Francis I (r. 1745–65), Grand Duke of Tuscany, and their elder son, Joseph II
(r. 1765–90). In effect, in her various capacities as Empress-consort, Emperor's
mother, or Queen of Bohemia and Hungary, Maria Theresa (1717–80) held sway
in Vienna for 40 years. She was a woman of conscience and restraint, devoted
among other matters to agrarian reform and the relief of the serf-peasantry.
Joseph II, in contrast, was an impatient radical, 'a crowned revolutionary', a convinced anticlerical and opponent of noble privilege. Jozefism—the name given to
his policy of asserting state power against the traditional pillars of Church and
nobility—was one of the more thorough variants of enlightened despotism.
   In this period, Austria developed a bureaucratic system that is sometimes called
cameralism, that is, a system based on an élite caste of professional office-holders.
Together with an expanded and reorganized military system, it provided the
cement which was to keep the Habsburg monarchy going long after the demise of
the Empire in Germany. The University of Vienna possessed a special faculty for
the training of such civil servants, who passed straight into the higher echelons of
finance, justice, and education. (The University of Halle did the same for Prussia.)
These highly educated, well-paid, German-speaking and loyalist bureaucrats were
entirely dependent on the monarch's favour. They formed a solid buffer against
the divergent interests of the nobility, the Church, and the nationalities, and led
the drive for disinterested rationalization and reform.
   In this (as it proved) its terminal phase, the cohesion of the Holy Roman
Empire was greatly undermined by the separate dynastic policies of its leading
princes. Just as the Habsburg emperors could rely on their lands and possessions

beyond the Empire, so increasingly could the Electors. From 1697 to 1763 the
Wettins, Electors of Saxony, ruled as kings of Poland-Lithuania (see below). From
1701 the Hohenzollerns, Electors of Brandenburg, ruled as kings in Prussia (see
below). From 1714 the Electors of Hanover ruled as kings of Great Britain (see
above). Throughout the century the Wittelsbach Electors of Bavaria sought to
enlarge their fortunes through their traditional alliance with France. Because of
their varied connections, all the 'capital cities' of 'Germany'—Vienna, Dresden,
Berlin, Hanover, and München—assumed very different flavours. The last two
emperors—Leopold II (r. 1790–2), Grand Duke of Tuscany, and Francis II
(r. 1792–1806)—had little chance of saving their Empire from the revolutionary
deluge which destroyed it. [**FREUDE**]

Hungary, liberated from the Turks, fell victim to the despotic designs of its
Habsburg liberators. In 1687 the 700-year-old elective monarchy was abolished.
Hereditary Habsburg rulers turned the noble Diets into mere registers of royal
decrees. The ancient 'right of resistance' of the Magyar nobles was eliminated.
From 1704 to 1711 a widespread rebellion under Francis Rákóczi II succeeded in
exploiting the Habsburgs' preoccupations with Spain and with the Turks. Many
of the ancient liberties were restored first by the Peace of Szátmár (1711) and later
as the Magyars' price for acceding to the Pragmatic Sanction. Here were the basic
laws which prevailed until 1848. Hungary escaped the fate of neighbouring
Bohemia. Still, the compromise was not an easy one. Maria Theresa ruled after
1764 without recourse to the Hungarian Diet; whilst Joseph II rode roughshod
over all the constitutional formalities, omitting even to be crowned. In 1784, treating Austria and Hungary as one united state, he introduced German as the official
language. The storms of protest were defused by Leopold II, who in 1791 reconfirmed Hungary's separate status, together with the use of Latin and Magyar. The
deep conservatism of Hungarian life, centred on the patronage of the magnates
and the dietines of the counties, was strengthened by the repeated Turkish wars
and by the ethnic and religious divisions. It may well have been prolonged by
Maria Theresa's agrarian reforms which, in the so-called Urbarium of 1767, ended
the peasants' adscription to the land and reduced their revolutionary temper.
Her educational reforms, together with the founding of the University of Buda
and the Magyar literary revival at the turn of the century, laid the seeds of modern national consciousness. In due course, the groundswell of Magyar nationalism was to awaken corresponding reactions among the Slovak, Croat, and Jewish
minorities.

The rise of Prussia reached its critical momentum in the eighteenth century. It is
generally interpreted in the light of Prussia's later mission of unification in
Germany. In reality, it occurred through the relentless pursuit of dynastic policies,
which repeatedly divided the German world and which raised a kingdom possessing none of the characteristics of a latent national state. It was achieved
through the creation of an administrative machine of marvellous efficiency,
which enabled its rulers to maintain a standing army of disproportionate size. (In

terms of the ratio between professional soldiers and population, Prussia was thirty times more efficient than its neighbour, Poland-Lithuania.) The Prussian Excise (1680) made possible the upkeep of the Prussian army. The army was based on an aristocratic officer corps, and after 1733 on the cantonal system of peasant conscription. [**GOOSE-STEP**]

Under Frederick III (r. 1688–1713) and Frederick-William I (r. 1713–40), the 'drill-master of Europe', the Hohenzollerns followed the same unscrupulous path laid down by the 'Great Elector' (see Chapter VII). In 1700 their electoral vote was sold to the Habsburgs in return for recognition of their own claim to kingship. In 1728 their accession to the Pragmatic Sanction was bought by the cession of Berg and Ravenstein. Fleet footwork in the alliances of the Spanish Succession and the Great Northern War resulted in the important acquisitions of Stettin and Western Pomerania. Sweden was only the latest to learn that it was no less dangerous having Prussia as an ally than as an enemy. The inimitable 'Prussian spirit' grew from a mixture of loyalty to the dynasty, of arrogance born of military prowess, and of justified pride in cultural and educational advances. Halle received the first Prussian university in 1694; Berlin, invigorated by a major influx of French Huguenots and Austrian Protestants, received its Royal Academy of Arts (1696) and its Royal Academy of Sciences (1700). An edict of 1717 looked to the improvement of public education.

Under Frederick the Great (r. 1740–86) Prussia unleashed the forces so carefully garnered by his predecessors. From Frederick's opening sensation, the seizure of Austrian Silesia in 1740, war was the prime instrument of policy for a quarter of a century. Then, having brought his country to the brink of annihilation, Frederick turned to diplomatic brigandage, which in the first Partition of Poland finally brought the prize of a consolidated territorial base (see below). [**GROSSENMEER**]

Frederick's personality was one of the wonders of the age. It was formed under the lash of a brutal father, who had forced him in boyhood to watch the execution of his friend, Katte, and had imprisoned him for years in the fortress of Küstrin (Kostrzyn) on the Oder. Throughout the reign, the crash of cannon and the groans of the battlefield were mixed with the flights of the King's flute and the chatter of the *philosophes*. 'I was born too soon,' Frederick once said, 'but I have seen Voltaire.' German historians have not been alone in praising his merits. Lord Acton called him 'the most consummate practical genius' that ever inherited a modern throne.

The wars and battles of Frederick the Great fill many volumes. They are among classics of historic warfare. After the two Silesian wars, 1740–2 and 1744–5, which formed part of the wider War of Austrian Succession and earned him the undying hatred of Maria Theresa, he retained the fruits of his aggression. At Mollwitz, Chotusitz, Hohenfriedberg, Frederick carried the day. In 1745 he occupied Prague. In the Seven Years War he reached the heights of glory and the depths of despair. It began with his attack on Saxony. Through Lobositz, Rossbach, Zorndorf, Leuthen, Kolin, Kunersdorf, Liegnitz, and Torgau, he brilliantly exploited his interior lines of communication, and repeatedly evaded his enemies' attempts to bring their overwhelming numbers to bear. At Rossbach, he triumphed with trifling losses. At Kunersdorf, he survived amidst scenes of carnage. In 1762, with the treasury empty, British subsidies stopped, and the Russians poised to take Berlin, he was saved by the death of the Russian Empress and an unexpected truce. Once again, at the Treaty of Hubertusburg (1763), he kept his winnings intact. 'Hunde,' he had once railed, when his guards had hesitated, 'wollt ihr ewig leben?' (dogs, do you wish to live forever?).

Under Frederick-William II (r. 1786–97) Prussia began to take a different course. The new King even risked an alliance with Poland-Lithuania. But the logic of the revolutionary era and of Russian power brought him back into line. At the second and the third Partitions of Poland, Prussia acquired both Danzig and Warsaw. By 1795 Berlin found itself ruling over a country that was 40 per cent Slav and Catholic, with a large Jewish community. It was one of the most dynamic melting-pots of Europe. Had this situation developed without interruption, it is hard to imagine what course German and Central European history might eventually have taken. As it was, old Prussia was to be overwhelmed by Napoleon; and the new Prussia which appeared in 1815 was to be a very different beast indeed.

If Prussia exemplified the successful pursuit of power in a small country, Russia exemplified a similar phenomenon on a heroic scale in Europe's largest country. Frederick the Great himself was impressed. Of the Russians, he once remarked: 'It will need the whole of Europe to keep those gentlemen within bounds.'

In the 149 years which separated the deaths of Alexei Mikhailovitch in 1676 and of Alexander I in 1825, the Romanovs raised the fortunes of their country from that of a nascent regional power to that of the invincible 'gendarme of Europe'. Alexei, who had succeeded in the same decade as Louis XIV, was an obscure Muscovite prince of whom, at Versailles, little was even known; Alexander rode through Paris in triumph. During the intervening century and a half, scores of military campaigns were fought, largely with success; the Grand Duchy of Moscow was revamped as the 'Empire of all the Russias'; the territory of the state engulfed a string of neighbouring countries; society and administration were subjected to root-and-branch reforms; the whole identity of the state and ruling nation was remodelled. For all who revelled in this exhibition of power, all the people and policies who made the transformation possible were by definition good and, as Klyuchevsky wrote of Peter the Great, 'necessary'.

In autocracies the personality of the autocrat is no secondary factor, and in Russia two personalities stood out—those of Peter I (r. 1682–1725) and of Catherine II (r. 1762–96). Both were awarded the epithet of 'Great'; both were larger than life, in physical stature, animal energy, and determination; and both have been eulogized for their undoubted contribution to Russia's own greatness. In any overall judgement, however, whether about the ruler or the realm, one must wonder if size and brute strength alone can be taken as the test of greatness. Critics find no difficulty in finding traits that provoke shame rather than respect. Peter, in particular, was a moral monster. His lifelong participation in the

GROSSENMEER

IN 1785 Grossenmeer was a village in the Duchy of Oldenburg in north-west Germany, close to the border of the Netherlands and the newly acquired Prussian province of East Friesland. At that time it had a total population of 885, made up from 142 households, plus some 77 'paupers' or other casual residents. An analysis of the village's households reveals the following categories:

Household type	No.	%
1. Solitaries (e.g. widows)	2	1.4
2. Non-conjugal household (co-resident siblings)	1	0.7
3. Single-family households (parents and children)	97	68.3
4. Extended family units (several generations and relatives)	28	19.7
5. Multiple-family households (2 or more conjugal units co-resident)	14	9.9
Total	142	100

From this, it is evident that single-family households formed a clear major-ity (68 per cent), although extended and multiple-family households con-stituted a strong minority (30 per cent).

A senior scholar in the field chose this example to typify 'that ill-defined European area where households tended to have the characteristics we have called 'middle'. A 'Four-Region Hypothesis' was built on isolated examples of that sort. If Grossenmeer (1785) typified Europe's 'West-Central' or 'Middle' region, the Essex village of Elmdon (1861) was taken to typify 'the West', Fagagna (1870), near Bologna, 'the Mediterranean', and Krasnoe Sobakino (1849), in Russia, 'the East'. The geography is as sus-pect as the generalizing is grandiose.

The hypothesis was presented as the refinement of an older scheme, taken to be 'universally accepted', which had presumed to divide the tra-ditional European family into two still simpler types—'West' and 'East'. Grossenmeer was taken to be a variation on Elmdon, where no less than 73 per cent of households conformed to the simple type, whilst Fagagna was taken as a variation on Krasnoe Sobakino, where 86 per cent of house-holds were of extended or multiple type.[1]

Comparative social history is an extremely fruitful subject. But it is an absolute principle that like must be compared with like. To compare a vil-lage in pre-industrial Germany with one at the industrializing height of Victorian England is dubious. Yet to typify the whole of another 'ill-defined area' called 'Eastern Europe' on the basis of one serf-bound village in the depths of Russia is, for 'Western' scholars, alarmingly typical. Diversity schematized is diversity denied. [**ZADRUGA**]

Family history only came into its own in the 1970s. The English-language *Journal of Family History* dates from 1976. Hitherto, social scientists who studied family problems had apparently been 'indifferent to the historical dimensions', whilst social historians had been preoccupied with questions of class. Many scholars had assumed that a large, traditional, patriarchal form of household had existed in Europe since time immemorial, and hence that there was not much to study until the onset of modernization. The work of pioneers such as Frédéric Le Play (1806–82), whose *Organisation de la Famille* (1871) introduced a typology of families, was not widely known. Le Play posited three family types: the patriarchal extended family; the *famille souche* or 'stem-family', with three generational nuclei; and the unstable household unit or *cellule*, which only existed as long as the parents were raising children. Apart from genealogy, which had a very long genealogy, the systematic study of family problems in history had to wait for a hundred years.[2]

None the less, the variety of studies within the field has become very impressive. One can find studies of everything from wet-nursing techniques in medieval Iceland to bastardy in seventeenth-century England, or paternal authority in nineteenth-century Sardinia. There are several main lines of enquiry. One concerns the formation, structures, and disintegration of household units. [**BASERRIA**] Another centres on the statistical, biological, and sexual trends within the realm of family and kin. A third focuses on the problems of the individuals, of the sexes, and of the generations within the family unit—and hence on 'life-course analysis', on women, on labour patterns, on childhood, marriage, and old age. [**GRILLENSTEIN**] A fourth, anthropological focus highlights family customs, ceremonies, and rituals. A fifth is legal, examining the evolutions of family law and government policy. A sixth is economic, examining family budgets in varying agrarian, urban, or industrial contexts. All modern family problems, from single-parenting to unemployment, child discipline, and juvenile crime, have historical roots. Nor has genealogy been forgotten. What was once the passion of a noble élite has recently become the most popular of pastimes.[3]

To some extent, historians' interests reflect the nature of available sources. The households of the medieval nobility, for example, or of Renaissance merchants had long been accessible because both left copious records. [**MERCANTE**] The households of the peasantry or plebs were much less accessible. Yet the application of sociological and quantitative techniques [**RENTES**] and the exploitation of visual, literary, statistical, and oral sources has opened up a wealth of information. No period or location has escaped. Family history has universal appeal. For everyone has either been, or has missed being, the member of a family.

debaucheries of the *Sobor* of Fools and Jesters—an obscene and blasphemous Russian variant of the English Hell-fire Club—may conceivably be dismissed as eccentric bad taste. But his personal involvement in gross and sadistic tortures, first revealed during the mass maltreatment of the rebel *streltsy* in 1697, cannot be counted a foible, even by the standards of his own day. His quaint delight in model ships and tin soldiers must be contrasted with his colossal disregard for the immense human suffering which attended many of his projects—such as the building of St Petersburg. A Tsar who could watch his innocent son and heir racked to death in the afternoon before attending a ribald court party in the evening was not far from Nero, even if he did change Russia 'from non-being into being'.

Catherine, too, presents the historian with 'images of splendor contending with the specter of scandal'.[28] A German princess, born in Stettin as Sophia Augusta Frederica von Alhalt-Zerbst, she has few equals in the annals of grasping ambition. Her gross sexual licence was not in itself out of place, but must be judged repulsive when mixed with foul intrigue. The rumour that she died through the failure of a machine called 'Catherine's Winch' whilst trying to make love with a horse is notable only because people have been willing to believe it. More to the point, she seized the throne through a palace *putsch*, having incited the imperial guards to murder her husband, Peter III (r. 1761–2). She governed with the co-operation of a long line of ten official lovers—from Gregory Orlov, and Gregory Potemkin to Platon Zubov, 38 years her junior. In her favour, it can be said that she headed a civilian entourage practising persuasion more than terror. An indulgent biographer might conclude: 'she did for Russia what Louis XIV did for France before he became the prisoner of Versailles . . . autocracy [was] cleansed from the stains of tyranny . . . despotism turned into a monarchy.'[29]

Praetorian revolutions became a habit with the Romanovs, as with the Romans. Legal succession by the dynastic heir was a rarity. Catherine I (r. 1725–7), alias Skovorotska, a Latvian peasant girl and Peter's second consort, overthrew him on his deathbed. Peter II (r. 1727–30) succeeded through a forged will; the Empress Anne (r. 1730–40), Duchess of Courland, through a ploy of the Privy Council; Ivan VI (r. 1740–1), the infant Duke of Brunswick, through a scheme of Baron Biron; the Empress Elizabeth (r. 1741–61), sometime fiancée of a Bishop of Lübeck and *fréquentée* of the guards' barracks, through a straightforward *coup de force*; Alexander I (r. 1801–25), through the assassination of his father. Paul I (1796–1801), a would-be reformer-Tsar, was long held to be mentally unbalanced by official historiographers, obviously for being sane. When Paul insisted on exhuming the body of his murdered father, Peter III, and on reburying his parents in the cathedral of Peter and Paul, the aged Count Orlov was obliged to carry the imperial crown behind the coffin of the victim, whom he had killed 35 years before. This grisly act of reconciliation well symbolizes the fraud, fear, and violence which surrounded the court of St Petersburg and all its works.

Muscovy took its giant leap out of the shadows during the second or Great Northern War, 1700–21. This 20-year contest centred on the rivalry of Peter the

Great, who had set envious eyes on Swedish possessions at the head of the Baltic, and the youthful Charles XII of Sweden, who was eager to attack all his neighbours at once. It began in August 1700 with Charles's adventurous landing near Copenhagen and with Peter's disastrous attack on Narva, a Swedish fortress on the Gulf of Finland. But it was largely fought out on the intervening territory of Poland-Lithuania, whose King (Augustus, Elector of Saxony) had formed a private alliance with Peter. In the end, Poland-Lithuania was to be an even greater casualty than Sweden (see below).

After the initial clashes Charles XII took the initiative on the mainland. He first aimed to punish Peter's Saxon ally, and in 1704 succeeded in replacing Augustus on the Polish throne with a leader of the pro-Swedish faction, Stanisław Leszczyński. In so doing, he gave Peter the chance to grab the Swedish provinces of Livonia and Ingria, where in 1703 the foundation of the new city of St Petersburg was immediately proclaimed. In 1707 he turned east, counting on support from Livonia and from Mazeppa, Hetman of Ukraine. He was deceived on both scores. In the winter of 1708–9, harassed by peasant guerrillas, he was forced to abandon the original plan of a march on Moscow and to turn south. On 27 June 1709, at Poltava in Ukraine, he was comprehensively beaten and driven to take refuge in the Ottoman domains. The triumphant Muscovite armies swept westwards. Warsaw was occupied and Augustus II restored. The Baltic provinces remained in Muscovite hands. No shortage of vultures was found among the German princes to join Denmark and Prussia in preying on Sweden's more westerly possessions. Charles XII was killed in action in November 1718, besieging the fortress of Frederikshald on the Norwegian–Swedish frontier. A diplomatic congress held on the Åland Islands preceded the Russo-Swedish Treaty signed at nearby Nystadt (1721). Sweden was humbled. Peter was left the arbiter of the North, the proud possessor of his 'Window on the West'. In 1721 he promoted himself from the style of Muscovite 'Tsar' to that of Emperor—a title not generally recognized in his lifetime. [**PETROGRAD**]

As Muscovy assumed its imperial mantle, far-reaching reforms were imposed to turn the new Empire into a modern, Western state. In the eyes of Peter I, in particular, reform was equivalent to 'Westernisation'. The Tsar made two lengthy visits to Western Europe, in 1696–8 and in 1717, taking notes on the techniques of everything from naval construction to face-shaving. But it was the Great Northern War that served as Russia's taskmaster. First and foremost came the Tsar's demand for a standing army, and for the financial and social institutions required to support it. The old Muscovite state had been monstrously inefficient. A ragbag army, which melted away in winter, was consuming the produce of two-thirds of the population and, in bad years like 1705, up to 96 per cent of the state's revenues. By the end of Peter's reign a permanent force of over 300,000 trained men was supported by a poll-tax or 'soul tax', which had tripled revenue, by peasant conscription, and by the reorganization of the nobility.

Few stones were left unturned. A key statute, the *Preobrazhensky Prikaz* (1701), regulated the system of political police. Important changes were made by the division of the country into *guberniyas* or 'provinces' (1705); by the creation of a senate and of administrative colleges within the central administration (1711); by the introduction of municipal government (1718–24); by the state promotion of trade, industry, education, literature, science, and the arts. In 1721 the Patriarchate was abolished, subordinating the Russian Orthodox Church to the state-run Holy Synod. Priests were ordered to betray the secrets of the confessional. From 1722 the table of ranks tied an enlarged nobility into a hierarchical caste system wedded to state service and landed privileges. The creation of so many new institutions involved what one authority has called 'the partial dismantling of the Patrimonial State' and the first realization in Russia of the distinction between 'state' and 'society'.[30] This occurred even though no significant changes were made in the political sphere and the nobles themselves were held in abject servitude. They were subject to public flogging and *shelmovanie* (outlawry) for evading education or service. Most historians would now agree, in fact, that the Petrine reforms were not quite what contemporaries imagined. They did not act as a great unifying force; on the contrary, they divided the loyalties of the Tsar's subjects, especially in matters of religion and nationality. Equally, they were apt to introduce the form of Western institutions whilst ignoring the substance. Peter could not turn Muscovites into Europeans by ordering them to shave their beards and to dress in powdered wigs.

Catherine II cared more about the substance. Once again, despite the enlightened rhetoric, there was no tampering with the foundations of autocracy or serfdom. But her famous instruction to the legislative commission of 1766–8 aiming at a modern legal code, her centralizing and 'russifying' tendencies in provincial administration, and, above all, her acceptance of the 'freedom of the nobility' made lasting modifications to the system. The Charter of Nobility (1785), which confirmed an earlier decree granting limited rights of noble assembly and self-government in the provinces, complemented the table of ranks; and ancient restrictions on the sale of serfs as chattels were eased. The final product was a compromise, half-old, half-new: a hybrid whereby the autocratic monarchy was gradually rendered dependent on the service nobility which it had created, whilst the nobility could not transmit to central government the power which they wielded over the mass of the population in the localities. 'Paradoxically, by their insistence on the monopoly of political power, the Russian autocrats secured less effective authority than their constitutional counterparts in the West.'[31] The old Muscovite tyranny was at least consistent. The new Russian Empire contained the seeds of its own destruction. [EULER]

None the less, Russia's remorseless expansion continued (see Appendix III, p. 1277). A country that already possessed more land than it could usefully exploit kept on indulging its gargantuan appetite. In the west, Russia ate up the larger part of Sweden-Finland and of Poland-Lithuania. In the south, starting with Azov (1696), it swallowed up the whole of the Ottomans' Black Sea provinces and Crimea (1783), before moving against Persia, the Caucasus, and Central Asia. In the east, having crossed Siberia to the Pacific, from the 1740s it explored the shores of Alaska, where a permanent settlement was built on Kodiak Island in 1784.

Russian historians have rationalized their country's expansion in terms of 'national tasks' and 'the gathering of the lands'. In reality, Russia and its rulers were addicted to territorial conquest. Their land-hunger was the symptom of a pathological condition born of gross inefficiency and traditional militarism. It is highly ironic that the world's largest country needed an ever-growing supply of land and people to offset its sense of insecurity, to execute operations which others achieved with far smaller resources, and to reward the overblown machine which guarded the Romanovs' throne. Here, if ever, was an extreme case of *bulimia politica*, of the so-called 'canine hunger', of gross territorial obesity in an organism which could only survive by consuming more and more of its neighbours' flesh and blood. Every successful Russian officer needed an estate run by hundreds or thousands of serfs to support his family in the accustomed style. Of 800,000 such conquered 'souls' redistributed by Catherine II, no fewer than 500,000 came from Poland-Lithuania alone. Significantly, whilst the German nobility of the ex-Swedish 'Baltikum' were permitted to retain their privileges, the ex-Polish nobility of Lithuania and Ruthenia (Byelorussia and Ukraine) were not.

Within the expanding Russian empire, Ukraine upheld its separate identity for more than a hundred years. From 1654 to 1783 the 'Hetman State' of Ukraine was ruled, under Tsarist supervision, by the heirs of the Dnieper Cossacks who had first sought the Tsar's alliance against Poland. Their bid to break free under Hetman Mazeppa during the Swedish invasion of 1708–9 (see above) came to nothing. Their suppression coincided with the annexation of Crimea and the end of their usefulness as a buffer against Tartars and Ottomans. [RUS']

Thereafter, the historic distinction between Ruthenia and Russia was officially suppressed. Ukraine was renamed Malorossiya (Little Russia), and all traces of its separate traditions were erased. Its Cossacks were denied the same degree of autonomy granted to their Russian counterparts on the Don or the Kuban. Its rich lands were subjected to intense russification and colonization. The 'wild plains' of the south, Europe's last frontier, were settled with peasant immigrants, mainly Russians and Germans. The monopoly of the Russian Orthodox Church among the Slavs was enforced, as was the public use of the Russian language. Any remaining Uniates were removed. Russian immigrants began to change the complexion of the cities, especially Kiev, now presented as an ancient Russian city. Ukrainian, Polish, and Jewish culture steadily lost ground. The Ruthenian (Ukrainian) language, which survived in the countryside, was officially described as a Russian dialect. The magnificent new port of Odessa, founded in 1794 as capital of the province of 'New Russia', opened an outlet for the growing corn trade, a window to the south. [POTEMKIN]

The Republic of Poland-Lithuania was the principal European casualty of Russia's expansion. Indeed, the Republic's demise was the *sine qua non* of the Russian Empire's success. Like its former province of Ukraine, the Republic was the object first of Muscovite penetration and then of alternating periods of indirect and direct rule. Muscovite influence rose steadily after the death of Sobieski in 1696.

RUS'

O N 6 September 1749, in St Petersburg, the imperial historian, Dr
Gerhard Müller, rose to read a paper in Latin on 'The Name and
Origin of Russia'. He was to expound his theory that the ancient Kievan
state had been founded by Norsemen. But he was shouted down; his
patriotic Russian audience was not willing to hear how Russia had not
been founded by Slavs. After an official inquiry, Dr Müller was ordered to
abandon the subject and his existing publications were destroyed. (He at
least escaped the fate of the French scholar, Nicholas Fréret, who had
died that same year, and who had once been cast into the Bastille for writing that the Franks were not descended from Trojans.)[1]

Historians of Russia have been arguing about the 'Normanist' theory
ever since. Owing to state censorship, Russian history has been subjected
to a peculiar degree of political interference and teleological argument.
The story of the Kievan State has been made to serve the interests of modern Russian nationalism, or else, in reaction to the Russian version, the
interests of modern Ukrainian nationalism. It has proved impossible to
deny, however, that Norsemen were in some way involved. The name of
Rus' has been variously ascribed to 'red-haired' Vikings (cf. *russet* in
English); to *ruotsi*, a Finnish name for Swedes; to a Scandinavian tribe
called *Rhos*, unknown in Scandinavia; and even to a multinational mercantile consortium based at Rodez in Languedoc.

According to this last ingenious (and unlikely) hypothesis, Rodez Inc.
used Norse seamen to penetrate the Khazarian slave-market via the
Baltic–Dnieper route and, *c.* AD 830, to oust the rival Jewish Radaniya consortium, which had controlled the slave-trade from the Black Sea to North
Africa from Arles. Having established a 'kaganate' of Rus' over Khazaria,
the Rodezians supposedly changed from a ruling foreign élite centred on
T''mutorakan/Tamartarka on the Volga into the native princes of a predominantly Slav community centred on Kiev.[2] [**KHAZARIA**]

Where firm conclusions prove impossible, the re-examination of
sources is essential. Yet the most forbidding aspect of Kievan scholarship
lies in the vast range of its source materials. Apart from the Slavic and
Byzantine chronicles, scholars must examine Old Norse literature, comparative Germanic and Turkic (Khazarian) mythology, runic inscriptions,
Scandinavian and Friesian law codes, Danish and Icelandic annals, Arab
geographies, Hebrew documents, even Turkic inscriptions from
Mongolia. Archaeology, too, is vital. One rare element of hard evidence in
the puzzle lies with Arab coins that are found in hoards all over Eastern
Europe. [**DIRHAM**] The earliest mention of Kiev—in the form of QYYWB—
occurs in a Hebrew letter now in Cambridge University Library, which was
written by Jews in Khazaria to the synagogue of Fustat-Misr near Cairo.[3]

Yet from Dr Müller's time to 1991 the main obstacle to scholarship lay in the fact that no one in Russia or Ukraine was free to pursue independent research. The emergence of a free Ukraine, and of a free Russia, may or may not improve the academic climate. [**METRYKA**] [**SMOLENSK**]

In the course of the Great Northern War, it reached the stage where a Russian protectorate could be established in all but name. Then, after decades of turmoil between would-be Polish reformers and Russian-backed agents of the status quo, it moved towards the logical conclusion of the Partitions. Between 1772 and 1795, Russia led the feast in which the Republic was totally consumed.

John Sobieski (r. 1674–96) earned glory abroad whilst neglecting problems at home. The Siege of Vienna showed that the Republic was still a first-rate military power; but it was the final fling. Lithuania was left to stew in civil war; the Sejm was repeatedly broken by the *liberum veto*; the magnates went unpunished; central legislation and taxation ground to a halt. By the unratified 'Eternal Treaty' with Moscow in 1686, Ukraine was abandoned. The King spent his strength fighting for the Holy League, hoping to carve out a base for his son in Moldavia. Many years later, gazing at Sobieski's statue in Warsaw, a Russian Tsar was to remark: 'Here is another [like me] who wasted his life fighting the Turk'.[32]

The royal election of 1697 dashed all the Sobieskis' schemes. Jakub Sobieski did not gain the electors' confidence; the Austrian candidate was outbribed; the French candidate, the Duc de Conti, was shipwrecked off the coast of Danzig. Thanks to Russian gold and a timely conversion to Catholicism, the prize was won by Friedrich-August, Elector of Saxony, who took to the throne as Augustus II. The exiled Sobieskis had nothing left but to marry their daughter to the exiled Stuarts, who came to grief at the same time. Bonnie Prince Charlie had a Polish mother.

The Saxon period—under Augustus II (r. 1697–1704, 1710–33) and Augustus III (r. 1733–63)—is generally judged to be the nadir of Polish history. The Great Northern War, in which the Polish King, in his capacity as Elector of Saxony, was a leading combatant, brought endless disasters and divisions. Poland-Lithuania was fought over as the main theatre of operations between Swedes and Russians, each of whom was supported by a rival confederation of Polish nobles (see above). It was treated by the Saxon court as a counterweight to neighbouring Prussia and as a source of plunder. The Saxon army, when deployed in Poland, was immune to the protests of the Sejm. Its depredations led to the conflict between King and nobility which had much in common with the parallel conflict in nearby Hungary. This in turn gave an opening for direct Russian intervention.

After the Russian victory at Poltava in 1709, Augustus II only recovered his Polish throne with the aid of Russian troops. Thereafter he was seen as a double danger, both as a pawn of the Tsar and as an 'absolutist' in his own right. In

POTEMKIN

IN 1787 Field Marshal Prince Gregory Potemkin (1739–91), Governor of New Russia, organized a river journey down the Dnieper for the Empress Catherine and her court. His aim was to prove his success in colonizing the province, recently wrested from the Ottomans. To this end he assembled a number of mobile 'villages', each located at a strategic spot on the river bank. As soon as the imperial barge hove into sight Potemkin's men, all dressed up as jolly peasants, raised a hearty cheer for the Empress and the foreign ambassadors. Then, as soon as it turned the bend, they stripped off their caps and smocks, dismantled the sets, and rebuilt them overnight further downstream. Since Catherine was Potemkin's lover at the time, it is not possible to believe that she was ignorant of the ploy; the principal dupes were the foreign ambassadors. 'Potemkin Villages' has become a byword for the long Russian tradition of deception and disinformation.[1] Force and fraud are the stock-in-trade of all dictatorships. But in Russia Potemkinism has been a recurring theme.

On this subject, the views of a professional deceptionist may not be entirely irrelevant. According to a senior KGB defector, Western opinion has been skilfully and systematically duped ever since Lenin's NEP. The control of all information, combined with selective leaks and plants, enabled the Soviet security service to feed the West with an endless stream of false impressions. The 'de-Stalinization' of the 1950s was only a modified form of Stalinism. The 'Sino-Soviet split' of 1960 was jointly engineered by the CPSU and the CPC. 'Romanian Independence' was a myth invented for the convenience both of Moscow and Bucharest. Czechoslovak 'democratization' in 1968 was orchestrated by progressive elements in the KGB. 'Eurocommunism' was another sham. Even 'Solidarity' in Poland was run by Moscow's agents. Published in 1984, before Gorbachev's rise to power, this exposé of the KGB by an insider is obligatory reading for anyone pondering the ambiguities of *glasnost'* and *perestroika'*, or the mysteries of the 1991 'Putsch'. The problem is: when do professional deceivers stop deceiving?[2]

Apart from his 'villages', Prince Potemkin is most often associated with the battleship named after him, whose mutinous crew sailed out of Odessa during the Revolution of 1905. People inevitably wonder whether that mutiny, too, was a fake.[3] [**SOVKINO**]

The proponents of conspiracy theory hold that all historical events mask the designs of tricksters, plotters, and evil 'unidentified forces'. Their opponents suggest the opposite, that conspiracy and deception do not exist. Both are badly mistaken. [**PROPAGANDA**]

1715–16 open warfare broke out between the King and his opponents. For the Tsar, it was a heaven-sent opportunity. By acting as mediator, Peter the Great could save the Polish nobles from their Saxon king whilst imposing conditions that would reduce the Republic to dependence. At the 'Silent Sejm' or 'Dumb Diet' summoned to Warsaw in January 1717, the Russian army stood by as the following pre-arranged resolutions were passed without debate:

1. *The King's Saxon army was to be banished from the Republic.* (In other words, the King lost all semblance of an independent power base.)
2. *The 'golden liberties' of the nobility were to be upheld.* (In other words, through the preservation of the *liberum veto*, the central government of the Republic could be paralysed whenever convenient.)
3. *The armed forces of the Republic were to be limited to 24,000 men.* (In other words, Poland-Lithuania was to be rendered defenceless.)
4. *The armed forces were to be financed through allocations from a list of royal, ecclesiastical, and magnatial estates.* (In other words, they were put beyond the control of king or Sejm.)
5. *The settlement was to be guaranteed by the Tsar.* (In other words, the Tsar could intervene in Poland-Lithuania at any time, and could legally suppress any movement for Reform.)

Henceforth, to all intents and purposes the Republic of Poland-Lithuania became a Russian protectorate, a mere appendage to the Russian Empire, a vast buffer-state which sheltered Russia from the West but cost nothing to maintain. [EROS]

Under Augustus III the central government collapsed completely. The King had to be installed by a Russian army which had overturned the re-election of Stanisław Leszczyński, thereby sparking off the War of the Polish Succession; but he usually stayed in Dresden. The Sejm was regularly summoned, but regularly blocked by the *liberum veto* before it could meet. Only one session in 30 years was able to pass legislation. By an extreme example of the principle of subsidiarity, government was left to the magnates and to the provincial dietines. The Republic had no diplomacy, no treasury, no defence. It could enact no reforms. It was the butt of the *philosophes*. When the first volume of the French *Encyclopédie* was published in 1751, the prominent article on 'Anarchie' was all about Poland. [CAN-TATA][SZLACHTA]

The reforming party fled abroad, thereby starting the unbroken Polish tradition of political emigration. Stanisław Leszczyński, twice elected king and twice driven out by the Russians, took refuge in France. Having married his daughter to Louis XV he was given the Duchy of Lorraine where, at Nancy, as *le bon roi Stanislas* he could practise the enlightened government forbidden at home.

Stanisław August Poniatowski (r. 1764–95), the last King of Poland, was a tragic and in some ways a noble figure. One of Catherine the Great's earlier lovers, he was put in place with the impossible task of reforming the Republic whilst preserving the Russian supremacy. As it was, shackled by the constitution of 1717, he provoked the very convulsions which reform was supposed to avoid. How could one curtail the nobles' sacred right of resistance without some nobles' resisting?

CANTATA

I N October 1734, when the newly crowned King of Poland returned home at short notice, his music master had to compose an entire nine-part *Cantata Gratulatoria* in three days flat. The words were as baroque as the soaring music:

1. *Chorsatz*   *Preise dein Glücke, gesegnetes Sachsen*
     (Praise Thy Good Fortune, blessed Saxony)
4. *Rezitativ*   *Was hat dich sonst, Sarmatien, bewogen . . .?*
     (What has stirred thee, Sarmatia . . .?)
5. *Arie*   *Rase nur verwegner Schwarm . . .*
     (Bluster now, presumptuous swarm, in thine own bowels!)
7. *Arie*   *Durch die von Eifer entflammeten Waffen . . .*
     (To punish one's enemies with weapons inflamed by
       zeal . . .)
8. *Rezitativ*   *Lass doch, o teurer Landesvater, zu*
     (Grant then, O Father of our country, that the Muses may
       honour the Day when Sarmatia elected thee King.)
9. *Chorsatz*   *Stifter der Reiche, Beherrscher der Kronen . . .*
     (Founder of Empires, Lord of Crowns . . .)

The events which prompted the cantata have been long forgotten. But the music could be reworked into later compositions, and became immortal. No. 7 became No. 47 in the *Christmas Oratorio*. No. 1 now forms the 'Hosannah' of the B Minor Mass. For the King of Poland was also the Elector of Saxony, and his music master was Johann Sebastian Bach.[1]

How could one limit the Russians' right of intervention without the Russians intervening? How could one abolish the *liberum veto* without someone exercising the *liberum veto*? The King tried to break the vicious circle on three occasions; and on three occasions he failed. On each occasion a Russian army arrived to restore order, and on each occasion the Republic was punished with partition. In the 1760s the King's proposals for reform led to the war of the Confederation of Bar (1768–72) and to the First Partition. In 1787–92 the King's support for the reforms of the Great Sejm and the Constitution of 3 May (1791) led to the Confederation of Targowica and the Second Partition (see Chapter IX). In 1794–5 the King's adherence to the national rising of Tadeusz Kościuszko led to the final denouement. After the Third Partition, there was no Republic left over which to reign. Poniatowski abdicated on St Catherine's Day 1795, and died in Russian exile.

Throughout the terminal agony of the Republic, the Grand Duchy of Lithuania preserved its individuality. Its political weakness did not preclude a vigorous life which made it the source of four lasting traditions. Its capital city—Wilno-Vil'na-Vilnius—was a true cultural crossroads. The dominant Polish élite was doubly reinforced, first by the National Education Commission after 1773 and later by a regional board of education, based on the University of Wilno, which was to flourish under tsarist rule until 1825. Lithuania's Yiddish culture was to be strengthened when the Grand Duchy was made the basis for Russia's Jewish Pale of Settlement. The Lithuanian and Ruthenian (Byelorussian) peasantry, having preserved themselves from polonization, retained enough of their substance to withstand all the russifications of the future. Once absorbed by the Russian Empire, the Grand Duchy would never revive as an administrative entity. But its inhabitants would not completely forget their origins. They would participate in all the Polish risings of the nineteenth century. The Polish and Jewish traditions would hold out until the murderous era of Stalin and Hitler. The Lithuanian and to a lesser extent the Byelorussian traditions would survive hell and high water to reach independence in the 1990s. [**B.N.R.**][**LIETUVA**]

The international relations of the eighteenth century were concerned, above all, with the balance of power. All the general wars of the period were designed to maintain it (see Appendix III, pp. 1282–3). No one state felt strong enough to attempt the military conquest of the entire Continent; but relatively minor regional disturbances could provoke a chain reaction of coalitions and alliances to contain the perceived threat. Few matters of ideology or national pride were involved. Alliances could be rapidly permutated, and small professional armies could march swiftly into action to settle the disputes in tidy, set-piece battles. With the Concert of Europe in full operation, a series of diplomatic congresses could weigh out the consequences of the fighting and draw up the balance sheet of colonies, fortresses, and districts won or lost. Generally speaking, these wars served their purpose. No major redistribution of power and territory took place in Europe as the direct result of military conquest. Such adjustments that war did provoke—notably through the cession of Spanish territories at Utrecht or through Prussia's seizure of Silesia—cannot compare to the greatest of all the territorial redistributions of the era, the Partitions of Poland, which were arranged without recourse to war. [**DESSEIN**]

The three Partitions of Poland-Lithuania furnish the finest examples which European history can boast of peaceful aggression. Completed in three stages, in 1773, 1793, and 1795, they divided up the assets of a state the size of France. They were carried out by gangsterish methods, where the unwritten threat of violence underlay all the formal agreements and where the victims were forced to condone their own mutilation. Many contemporary observers, thankful for the avoidance of war, were conditioned to accept the partitioners' explanations. Many historians have accepted the view that the Poles brought disaster on themselves. It took a Burke, a Michelet, or a Macaulay to call a crime a crime.

The mechanism of the Partitions rested on two simple considerations: first, that a Russian army of intervention was required to suppress the Polish reform movement; and secondly, that a Russian advance into the Republic posed a threat to the Republic's other neighbours, Prussia and Austria. After the draining experience of the Seven Years War, Prussia in particular was in no condition to fight another war

DESSEIN

W HEN the second edition of the Duc de Sully's memoirs were prepared for publication in 1742, a great deal of re-editing was done. In particular, a large number of the Duke's scattered and often contradictory comments on foreign relations were simplified and consolidated into one single chapter entitled 'The Political Scheme commonly called the Grand Design of Henri the Great'. In this way, Sully's *Grand Dessein* was reconstructed, not to say invented, more than a century after his death. Critics have argued that it was a product more of the eighteenth than of the seventeenth century.[1]

It must be said that Maximilien de Béthune (1560–1641), Baron de Rosny and Duc de Sully, had little to do with foreign policy during his decade as Henri IV's chief minister. He had been Superintendent of the Royal Finances, Grand Voyer (from *viarius*, 'master of the roads') of France, Grand Master of Artillery and then of Fortifications, and Governor of the Bastille.[2] His thoughts on international relations date from his first years in retirement after 1610 and then, with major amendments, from the Thirty Years War. He had published them all, unsorted, in the two volumes of his *Mémoires des sages et royales œconomies d'estat* (1638).

Sully's immediate purpose was to reduce the preponderance of the Habsburgs. From this essentially opportunist purpose, however, he drew up a plan which envisaged both a new map of Europe and the machinery for maintaining a perpetual peace. The map was to consist of fifteen equal states that would be created by confining Spain to Iberia, by separating the House of Austria from the Empire, and by redistributing their possessions. The Spanish Netherlands, for example, were either to be divided between England and France or to be given to the United Provinces. Hungary was to be restored as an independent elective monarchy. The imperial throne in Germany was to be filled by open elections, and free from the monopoly power of any one dynasty. In the interests of perpetual peace, Sully planned a European League of Princes. The League was to be governed by a Federal Council, where the greater powers would hold four seats each and the others two, and where the chairmanship, starting with the Elector of Bavaria, would rotate. It would use its combined forces to settle disputes and to enforce policy.

The key concept behind both the new map and the new league was to be 'equilibrium of strength'. No power was to be strong enough to impose its will on the others. Europe was to be 'une république très chrétienne' and 'one great family'. Within its borders, it was to enjoy freedom of trade. Beyond its borders, it was to destroy the Turk and to undertake 'convenient' conquests in Asia and North Africa.

Fashioned by a statesman in irresponsible retirement, and refashioned by an eighteenth-century editor, the Grand Design has more than a smack of abstract theorizing. It may have been influenced by Émeric Crucé's *Nouveau Cynée* (1623), with its plan for a world-wide peace assembly to be chaired by the pope at Venice, which in turn may have owed something to the 'League of Perpetual Union' proposed by a Bohemian king as long ago as 1458 (see p. 428). It certainly belonged to the long tradition of theoretical writing from Dante's *De Monarchia* to Erasmus and Campanella. But popularized in the age of the 'balance of power', it attracted great attention. In the two centuries which separated its relaunch from the League of Nations and the European Community, its basic thoughts on international stability, on free trade, on pooled sovereignty, and on joint enforcement have not ceased to appeal. Above all, it recognized what many ignored, that peace is a function of power.[3]

against Russia. Instead, it was suggested that Prussian and Austrian interests could best be protected if, as the price of their acquiescence in Russian actions in Poland, they could be given territorial compensation. So, by general agreement of its neighbours, the defenceless Republic was to submit to the suppression of its reformers by Russian force, and to pay for the operation by the cession of huge tracts of territory. What was worse, the Republic had to listen in silence whilst its tormentors told the world of their generous and peaceful intentions.

In the first round, the point was reached in the late 1760s when the turmoil in Poland-Lithuania could no longer be contained. The King's proposals for limited reform had stirred up opposition on all sides. The Prussians had bombarded Polish customs posts on the Vistula, thereby ending all preparations for a modern fiscal system. The Russians had been stirring up a campaign against the alleged maltreatment of religious minorities in Poland, and had carried off the Polish bishops who protested. The Confederates of Bar, led by Casimir Pułaski (1747–79), had taken the field to oppose both the King and the Russians. In 1769 the Austrians had used the uproar to seize the thirteen towns of the district of Spisz. St Petersburg would be obliged to take drastic action as soon as its Turkish war permitted. Berlin saw the chance: Prussia would not oppose Russian intervention if granted the Polish province of Royal Prussia. Austria would agree if given a slice of southern Poland: 'The more she wept,' joked Frederick II of Maria Theresa, 'the more she took.' Russia would take most of 'White Ruthenia'.

The first Treaty of Partition was signed in St Petersburg on 5 August 1772. Legal niceties were observed throughout. The air was filled with homage to Poland's 'golden freedom'. Then the victim was persuaded to wield the knife. The King placed a motion in favour of the Partition before the Sejm. The one member to protest, Tadeusz Rejtan, who lay across the threshold of the Chamber to bar the King's entry, was later declared insane. The three treaties of secession between the Republic and each of the partitioning powers were completed on 7/18 September

1773. The one sovereign to protest was the King of Spain. 'I have partaken eucharistically of Poland's body,' was Frederick's comment, 'but I don't know how the Queen-Empress has squared her confessor.'

The First Partition bought several years of relative calm. Poland-Lithuania was absorbed with the labours of the National Education Commission (see above); and in 1775 the King was given permission to form the outlines of ministerial government. All the Confederates of Bar had been deported to Siberia or had fled abroad. Pułaski had gone off to America, where he founded the US Cavalry. Russia, Prussia, and Austria were busy absorbing their ill-gotten gains.

The century of the Enlightenment drew to its close with the spectacle of three enlightened despots taking concerted action to crush an enlightened reform movement. The assault on the Polish state was accompanied by much enlightened rhetoric; and the consequent 'rationalization of the map of Europe' was widely excused. 'Un polonais—', quipped Voltaire, 'c'est un charmeur; deux polonais—une bagarre; trois polonais, eh bien, c'est la question polonaise' (one Pole—a charmer, two Poles—a brawl, three Poles—the Polish Question).[33] [**METRYKA**]

Yet the basic problem remained. Poland-Lithuania was still a Russian captive, and the reformers were straining at the leash. If the King were to lose control, others would act for him. And as soon as they moved, the whole cycle of reform and repression would begin again. It began in 1787.

Monday evening, 29 October 1787, Prague. In the National Theatre of Count Nostitz in the old city (now the Tyl Theatre), Bondini's Italian opera company was presenting the première of *Il dissoluto punito*, 'The Rake's Reward'. The performance had originally been advertised for the evening of the 14th, under the title of 'The Guest of Stone', when it had been intended to entertain the Princess of Tuscany on the way to her wedding in Dresden. In the event, the score of the new opera had not been completed. According to one Václav Svoboda (Wenzel Swoboda), who played the double bass in the orchestra, the composer had sat up all the Sunday night of the 28th with a small army of copyists; and the score of the overture was delivered to the theatre with the ink still wet on the page.[34] But the players were not deterred. Cheering broke out when the composer took his bow at the front of the candlelit auditorium at 7 p.m. Two extended *forte* chords in D minor brought the uproar to a halt. Then the music sped away, *molto allegro*, into the fast chatter of the overture's opening bars.

Ouverture
Str. 2 Fl. 2 Ob. 2 Cl. 2 Bsn. 2 Hn. 2 Tr. Timp.

At the end of the overture the maestro turned to the orchestra and complemented them on their sight-reading: 'Bravo, Bravo, meine Herren, das war ausgezeichnet' (Bravo, Gentlemen, that was admirable).

The libretto, as printed in advance for the court, could be bought at the box-office in Italian only (40 kr. bound in gold paper, 20 kr. ordinary). The title-page read:

IL DISSOLUTO PUNITO. O sia Il D. Giovanni. Dramma giocoso in due atti. Da representarsi nel Teatro di Praga l'anno 1787. In Praga di Schoenfeld . . . La Poesia è dell'Ab Da Ponte, Poeta de' Teatri Imperiali di Vienna. La Musica è del Sig Wolfgango Mozzart, Maestro di Cap, dadesco.

The cast was: Giovanni—Luigi Bassi; Anna—Teresa Saporiti; Ottavio—Antonio Baglioni; Elvira—Caterina Micelli; Leporello—Felice Ponziani; Zerlina—Caterina Bondini (wife of the impresario); Commendatore—Giuseppe Lolli.[36]

Mozart's *Don Giovanni*, as it came to be known, was but the latest variant of a popular tale of seduction that had reached the status of a European myth. Don Juan, the *burlador* of Seville, had been played over two centuries both in Neapolitan carnival and in French fairground pantomime. It had been given literary form by Molina (1630), Cicognini (c.1650), Molière (1665), Corneille (1677), Goldoni (1736), and Shadwell (1776). It had been set to music, for ballet or stage drama, at Rome in 1669, at Paris in 1746, at Turin in 1767, at Cassel in 1770. In the decade before it reached Mozart it had inspired at least four full-blown operas—by Righini at Vienna (1777), by Albertini at Warsaw (1783), by Foppa/Guardi and Berlati/Gazzaniga at Venice (1787). Mozart's librettist, the Abbé da Ponte, had drawn heavily on Berlati's words; and the baritone who sang Ottavio in Prague had come post-haste from singing the same role to Gazzaniga's music in Venice.[37]

The basic plot was disarmingly simple. In the opening scene Don Giovanni kills the Commendatore, the angry father of Anna, his latest amorous conquest. After numerous intrigues, he is twice confronted in the closing scenes by the dead Commendatore's statue, which cries for vengeance as the sinner is swallowed by the fires of Hell. Da Ponte condensed the story into two matching acts, each built round the same dramatic structure:

ACT I	ACT II
Nos. 1–7	**Nos. 14–18**
SEPARATE EXPOSITION	SEPARATION OF ANTAGONISTS
[*Giovanni and 3 women*]	[*Giovanni disguised or absent*]
(Aria) Giovanni–Anna	Giovanni–Leporello
(Trio) Death of Commendatore	(Trio) Deceit of Elvira
(Duet) Anna–Ottavio	
Elvira misdirected to Leporello	Elvira misdirected to Leporello
(No. 4)	
Zerlina–Giovanni–Masetto	Giovanni–Masetto
Giovanni–Zerlina	Zerlina–Masetto
Nos. 8–10	**Nos. 19–21**
MIXTURE OF PERSONS &	MIXTURE OF PERSONS &
PASSIONS	PASSIONS
Collective antagonism	Antagonism directed at Leporello
Quartet	Sextet
[*Giovanni in background*]	[*Leporello escapes*]
Anna sees Giovanni's guilt	Ottavio sees Giovanni's guilt
Aria (No. 10)	Aria (No. 21)
	[*Graveyard Scene*]
Leporello's narrative	Giovanni's narrative
Aria (No. 11)	Duet (No. 22)
[*Giovanni's Garden*]	[*Anna's House*]
Aria (No. 12)	Aria (No. 23)
FINALE Entry of Masker	FINALE Entry of Elvira
Attempt on Zerlina	Retribution: the statue
Collective Antagonism	Collective Conclusion[38]

No synopsis, however, could do justice to the exquisite partnership of the score and the libretto, whose memorable moments have withstood any amount of repetition and parody. In Aria No. 4 ('Madamina, il catalogo è questo') Giovanni's servant boasts to Elvira of his master's prowess in gallantry:

> In Italy six hundred and forty,
> In Germany, two hundred and thirty-one
> A hundred in France, in Turkey ninety-one,
> While in Spain already a thousand and three! (*Mille e tre!*)[39]

In the delicious No. 7 ('Là ci darem la mano')—'the most perfect duet of seduction imaginable'—Giovanni wins the unsuspecting Zerlina without a trace of violence or deceit. His strong confident melody is picked up, played with by the soprano until both walk off arm in arm in a rapture of sheer delight:

Duettino Zerlina, D. Giovanni
Str. 1 Fl. 2 Ob. 2 Bsn. 2 Hn.

D. Giovanni: Là ci da-rem la   ma-no,   là mi di-rai di   si;

In the melodramatic graveyard scene (Act II, Scene 11) the players tremble as the Stone Guest declaims his eerie prophecy to the shattering accompaniment of trombones: 'By dawn you will have laughed for the last time':

Sestetto D. Anna, D. Elvira, Zerlina, D. Ottavio, Leporello, Masetto
Str. 2 Fl. 2 Ob. 2 Cl. 2 Bsn. 2 Hn. 2 Tr. Timp.

D. Elvira: So-la, so - la in bu - io   lo - co   pal - pi - tar
Vln. I II Vla.

After the finale, when Giovanni's doom is complete, the cast is left singing the none-too-convincing moral in chorus to a scintillating double fugue:

> Questo è il fin di chi fa mal
> E de' perfidi la morte alla vita è sempre ugual

(This is the end of the sinner's game | His life and death are just the same.)[42]

For the opera's second performance, in Vienna seven months later, Mozart and Da Ponte made a number of changes to suit a new cast and a new theatre. To accommodate some additions, they dropped Ottavio's Aria, No. 21(22) ('Il mio tesoro intanto'):

Aria D. Ottavio
Str. 2 Cl. 2 Bsn. 2 Hn.

Il mio te - so - ro in - tan - to

But the number was soon reinstated, and has remained an essential part of the standard repertoire ever since.

Mozart made two visits to Prague in 1787, both with his wife, Constanze. He was at the very peak of his career. During the first visit, in January and February, he presented his Symphony no. 38, 'The Prague' (K. 504), and later conducted a triumphant performance of *Le nozze di Figaro*. The reception was so favourable that he immediately signed a contract with Bondini for a new opera to be staged at the start of the next season. On his return to Vienna he gave some lessons to a seventeen-year-old pianist from Bonn called Beethoven. In May he was grievously stricken by the death of his beloved father and troubled by the settlement of the estate. Yet not a trace of his distress can be heard either in the *Divertimento* in F (K. 522) or in the delectable *Eine Kleine Nachtmusik* in G (K. 525) both of which were composed that summer.

Mozart's six-week trip to Prague with *Don Giovanni* can be traced both from his correspondence and from the local press. He left Vienna on 1 October, having just received the meagre proceeds of the auction of his father's chattels at Salzburg. He travelled again with Constanze, who was six months pregnant. The journey of *c*.150 miles took three days, since the *Praeger Oberpostamtszeitung* was already announcing his arrival on the 4th. 'The news has spread here that the opera newly written by [our celebrated Herr Mozart], *Das steinerne Gastmahl* will be given for the first time at the National Theatre.'[44] He took rooms in the Three Lions Inn at Kohlmarkt 20, and was joined four days later by his librettist Da Ponte, who stayed across the street at the Glatteis Hotel. The 13th, 14th, and 15th were taken up by the visit of the Princess of Tuscany, and by the last-minute decision to stage a German version of *Le nozze de Figaro* for her benefit. Mozart at this point was despondent. 'Everything dawdles along here,' he wrote to a friend, 'because the singers, who are lazy, refuse to rehearse on opera days, and the manager, who is anxious and timid, will not force them.'[45] The last week of the month was taken up by the sickness of various singers, and by the lack of an overture. But finally the première took place amidst universal applause. The *Oberpostamtszeitung* was ecstatic:

On Monday . . . the Italian Opera company gave the ardently awaited opera by Maestro Mozard [*sic*], *Don Giovanni* . . . Connoisseurs and musicians say that Prague has never yet heard the like . . . Everybody on the stage and in the orchestra strained every nerve to thank Mozard by rewarding him with a good performance. There were also heavy additional costs, caused by several choruses and changes of scenery, all of which Herr Guardosoni had brilliantly attended to. The unusually large attendance testifies to unanimous approbation.[46]

The opera was repeated on 3 November for Mozart's personal benefit. The Mozarts left Prague on the 13th, but not before several prominent Praguers had written lavish compliments in the composer's scrapbook:

> When Orpheus' magic lute out-rings
> Amphion to his lyre sings,
> The lions tame, the rivers quiet grow,
> The tigers listen, rocks a-walking go.
>
> When Mozart masterly music plays
> And gathers undivided praise,
> The quire of Muses stays to hear,
> Apollo is himself all ear.
>
> Your admirer and friend,
> Joseph Hurdalek
>
> Prague, 12 November 1787, Rector of the General Seminary[47]

Map 19.
Mozart's Journey to Prague, 1787

During their second trip to Prague the Mozarts stayed much of the time with their friends the Dušeks, in their Villa Bertramka at Smichov, where the final numbers of *Don Giovanni* were completed. Franz Dušek was a concert pianist; his wife, Jozefa, a soprano and long-standing friend with whom Mozart felt greatly at ease. Before leaving, Mozart was recommended for the sinecure of imperial *Kammermusikus.*

He arrived back in Vienna to find that the annual salary offered was only 800 gulden, the previous incumbent, Gluck, having died with a salary of 2,000. As always, his prestige outstripped his finances. On 27 December Constanze gave birth to their fourth child, a daughter who lived for six months. Mozart was coming to the end of a golden decade.

Mozart's collaboration with the Abbé Da Ponte marks a milestone in Europe's musical development. Their three productions—*Le nozze di Figaro* (1786), *Don Giovanni* (1787), and *Cosí fan tutte* (1790)—belong to *opera buffa,* one of the lightest and, supposedly, most ephemeral of genres; yet they have survived triumphantly. Together with Mozart's German operas *Die Entführung aus dem Serail* (1782) and *Die Zauberflöte* (1791), they form the earliest group of compositions to establish themselves within the standard repertoire of Grand Opera. Indeed, within that repertoire of some thirty items they are matched in quantity and unending popularity only by the operas of Wagner and Verdi. Da Ponte proved an ideal partner. A fugitive from his native Venice, where he had been born in the ghetto, he did not take his conversion and his holy orders too seriously. He wrote the text of *Don Giovanni* from the heart.[48] (See Appendix III, p. 1278.)

In the absence of sound-recording [**SOUND**], there have been several literary attempts to recapture the extraordinary ambience of Mozart's music-making. Sixty years after Mozart's death, for example, the poet Eduard Mörike (1804–75) did so by means of a short novella, *Mozart auf der Reise nach Prag* (1851). He recounts an imaginary encounter which the composer might well have had with the sort of cultivated people who made up his most enthusiastic audiences. Wolfgang and Constanze are travelling towards Prague through the pine-clad hills of the Bohemian forest when they spy the castle of the Counts von Schinzberg. Wolfgang is caught red-handed when he carelessly plucks a fruit from an orange tree in the castle's park. But he is rewarded with an invitation to dinner. After dinner he sits down to play at the piano and recounts, with musical illustrations, how he composed the finale of *Don Giovanni.*

Without more ado, he put out the candles in the two candelabra standing beside him, and that terrifying air—Di rider finirai pria dell'aurora—rang through the deathly stillness of the room . . . From distant starry spheres, the silver trumpet notes seem to fall through the blue night, to pierce the soul with the icy tremor of doom.

   Chi va là. Who goes there?

   Give an answer—One hears Don Giovanni demand.

Then the voice rings out afresh, monotonous as before, bidding the impious youth to leave the dead in peace . . .[49]

Nor have the Czechs forgotten the brief days when Mozart graced their country. A contemporary Czech poet uses an evening at the Villa Bertramka as a springboard for reflections on unattainable paradise:

> A když počal hrát
> a copánek mu poskakoval po zádech
> přestaly šumět i lastury
> a nasta vily svá rozkošná ouška . . .

(And when he began to play I and his pigtail to dance on his back I even the sea-shells ceased humming I and pricked up their delicate ears. I Why did they not lock the door then? I Why not unharness the horses from the coach? I He departed so soon.)[50]

The Prague which Mozart loved was reaching a peak of splendour that few European cities could rival. It was the second city of the Habsburg domains, and had recently undergone five or six decades of unparalleled architectural reconstruction. The elegant neo-classical Tyl Theatre, only four years old, where *Don Giovanni* was performed, was just one of many magnificent new public buildings. The Thun Palace (1727), now the British Embassy, where the Mozarts stayed during their first visit in 1787, was just one of a score of sumptuous aristocratic residences of recent date, including those of Colleredo-Mansfeld, Goltz-Kinsky, Clam-Gallas, Caretto-Millesimo, and Lobkowitz-Schwarzenberg. The basilica of St Nicholas (1755), where Mozart's *Mass in C* was performed in the week after his departure, was one of a dozen Baroque churches designed by the Diezenhofers, father and son. The Carolinum (completed 1718) housed the university complex, the Clementinum (completed 1715) the Jesuit church and library.

Most importantly, each of the city's four main historic centres had recently been enclosed, embellished, and united into a harmonious whole. Hradčany, Prague's ancient Castle Hill on the left bank of the Vltava, containing St Vitus' Cathedral (1344) and the Vladislavský Sàl (1502) of the Jagiellons, had been surrounded in 1753–75 by the high walls of Pacassi's imposing offices. The *Malá strana* or Lesser City, at the foot of Hradčany, was adorned by a new episcopal palace (1765). The ancient *Karlův Most*, or Charles Bridge (1357) which links the city's two sides, had been adorned along its 660-m length by a stunning series of religious and historical statues. The streets of the old city on the right bank, still dominated by the *Týnsky chrám* and the City Hall, had been revitalized by much renovation. They were enlivened, as always, by the hourly spectacle of the city clock where Christ and the apostles led a procession brought up in the rear by Death, the Turk, the miser, the fool, and the cock, and by the chimes of the Loretto carillon (1694). The Charter of United Prague had been granted by the Emperor Joseph II as recently as 1784.

The aristocrats whose residences graced the city and whose patronage ruled its music were the principal beneficiaries of Habsburg rule. They were largely drawn from German families who had benefited from the sequestrations of the native Czech nobility in the course of the Thirty Years War. The wealth of their estates in the prosperous Bohemian countryside supported the glitter of their life in town. By Mozart's time the majority of Czechs had been reduced to a headless, peasant nation, though a number of middle-class people, like the Dušeks, lived on the margins of Czech and German society.

The contrasts between rich and poor were extreme. During his first visit to Prague in 1771, when a sixth of Prague's population had died from famine, the Emperor Joseph II had been shocked:

How shameful are the cases which have occurred in this year's famine. People have actually died, and have taken the last sacrament in the street . . . In this city, where there is a rich Archbishop, a large cathedral chapter, so many abbeys and three Jesuit palaces . . . there is not a single proven case where any of these took in even one of the miserable wretches who were lying in front of their doors.[51]

Joseph II had no patience for the fossilized complacency of the Catholic Church. The Jesuit Order had been disbanded in the previous decade; and when he attained sole rule in 1780 he unleashed a flood of reforming decrees that threatened to undermine the most sacred pillars of the social order. Serfs were emancipated. Religious toleration was extended to Uniates, Orthodox, Protestants and Jews. Children under nine were forbidden to work. Civil marriage and divorce were permitted. Capital punishment was abolished. Freemasonry flourished. Wealth which derived from the secularization of ecclesiastical property was reflected in a spate of imperial and aristocratic architectural extravagance.

Prague's large Jewish community were sharing in the surge of prosperity. They had put the last of numerous expulsions behind them in 1744–5, and in the 1780s were reaping the fruits of the imperial *Toleranzpatent*. The Jewish quarter, renamed Jozefov in the Emperor's honour, shared in the city's extensive renovation. The medieval Old-New Synagogue and the Klaus Synagogue were both rebuilt. On the Jewish town hall, one modern clock showed the time in Latin numerals whilst another below it did so in Hebrew numerals. Prague's Jews were destined at a later date to supply the most dynamic element of Viennese Jewry.

Prague's freemasons, too, basked in the glow of imperial tolerance. They welcomed Mozart, who was a member of the Grand Lodge of Austria in Vienna, as one of their own. They represented the strong reaction that was running against the suffocating hold of the Catholic Church over all intellectual and cultural affairs.

Mozart thrived in the relaxed social climate of the 1780s, which the growth of the *opera buffa* reflected. He struck a neutral stance towards the morals of his day. But the Rake's 'Reward' is too melodramatic to be taken seriously; and the message of his next collaboration with Da Ponte, *Così fan tutte* (All the Women Are At It) was judged by some to be scandalously permissive. Lines about 'the gaping bottom of every sweet-watered vale' were not open to too many interpretations. Lorenzo Da Ponte himself, a converted Jew, had earned a reputation not far removed from that of his friend and fellow Venetian, Giovanni Casanova di Seingalt (1725–98). After a lifetime of spying, lechery, and fleeing from justice, Casanova was passing his final years as librarian to the Count Waldstein at Dux

(Duchcov) in northern Bohemia. He is known to have visited his publisher in Prague on 24 October 1787, and it is quite likely that he stayed on for *Don Giovanni*'s première. Some critics were to suggest that he was the model for the Don.

Gross libertinism had always been a strong undercurrent in the eighteenth century.[52] But given the official puritanism of Catholic Austria, it was no mean step to make sexual seduction the theme of public entertainment. It offended the moral guardians of Josephine Prague no less than it offends the guardians of feminist correctness today. Don Giovanni, after all, like Casanova, was a cynical philanderer for whom women were mere objects of desire. Casanova's own words are not irrelevant:

The man who loves . . . rates the pleasure which he is sure to give the loved object more highly than the pleasure which the object can give him in fruition. Hence, he is eager to satisfy her. Woman, whose great preoccupation is her own interest, cannot but rate the pleasure she will herself feel more highly than the pleasure she will give. Hence, she procrastinates . . .[53]

One of Mozart's greatest qualities, however, was to place himself above the passions of the world around him. His scores were blithe or sublime by turns, even when he was oppressed by the most agonizing pains of ill health, poverty, and bad fortune. His music, though composed in the world, was not of it. Though he was highly travelled, having spent twenty years touring the courts of Europe, there is not the slightest trace of the politics of his day.

In 1787 Europe was approaching the climacteric of its development over the previous two centuries. This was the year when the republican Constitution of the USA was signed, to the horror of Europe's monarchies, and when the American dollar began to circulate. In Britain, under the ministry of the Younger Pitt, world-wide imperial concerns were under discussion with the launching both of the impeachment of Warren Hastings, the first Governor-General of British India, and of the Association for the Abolition of the Slave Trade. In Russia, the Empress Catherine had just embarked on the latest of her campaigns against the Turks—to which end, in her new province of Crimea, she entertained her ally, the Emperor Joseph, Mozart's patron. In the Netherlands, the Stadholder William V had been expelled, and his wife taken hostage by the republican 'Patriot' party. As Mozart prepared to set out for Prague, the Prussian army was setting out for Holland to restore the Stadholder. The Vatican was fighting the secular tide: Pius VI (r. 1775–99) had been barred from sending a nuncio to Munich, and had been refused the customary feudal homage by the King of Naples. In Florence he was faced by a Grand Duke who had introduced Gallican rules into the Tuscan Church. In France, by the time that *Don Giovanni* was performed, both the Assembly of Notables and the Parlement of Paris had been convened and dismissed. The King of France had been convinced of the country's impending bankruptcy, and had resolved to summon the Estates-General, initially for July 1792.

Other events, of great importance for the future, took place virtually unnoticed. The first practical steamboat was demonstrated. In August, Horace Saussure made the first ascent of Mont Blanc. Man was mastering Nature.

With hindsight, the historian can see that Mozart's music was playing out many of the most doomed and decrepit elements of the Ancien Régime. No one knew at the time, but Joseph II was the penultimate occupant of the Holy Roman Empire. Doge Paolo Renier (r. 1779–89) was the 125th in the line of 126 doges of Venice. Bohemia's neighbour, Poland, had already entered the last decade of the last reign of its 51 sovereign kings and princes. Pope Pius VI was destined to die in a French revolutionary dungeon.

In the creative arts, as always, the traditional vied with the innovative. 1787 saw Jeremy Bentham's *Defence of Usury*, Goethe's *Iphigenie* in verse, and Schiller's *Don Carlos*. Fragonard, David, and Goya were at their easels, alongside Reynolds, Gainsborough, Stubbs, and Romney. Mozart's musical contemporaries included Haydn, Cherubini, and C. P. E. Bach.

Of course, it could be said that *Don Giovanni* was conceived as a brilliant, intuitive allegory of the judgement which awaited a corrupt and dissolute continent. If so, there is no such hint either in Mozart's correspondence or in the work itself. People had no awareness of impending catastrophe, least of all in France. The Marquis de Condorcet, for example, one of the most radical *philosophes* of the day, was certain of only one thing, that monarchy was impregnable.[54] An intelligent young Frenchwoman with musical inclinations recorded her impressions of Paris in that same era:

The musical gatherings [at the Hotel de Rochechouart] were very distinguished. They were held once a week . . . but there were rehearsals as well. Mme Montgeroux, a famous pianist of the day, played the piano; an Italian singer from the Opera sang the tenor parts; Mandini, another Italian, sang the bass; Mme de Richelieu was the prima donna; I sang the contralto, M de Duras the baritone; the choruses were sung by other good amateurs. Viotti accompanied us on the violin. We executed the most difficult finales in this way. Everyone took the greatest pains, and Viotti was excessively severe . . . I doubt if there exists anywhere the ease, harmony, good manners, and absence of all pretension which was to be found then in all the great houses of Paris . . .

Amid all these pleasures, we were drawing near to the month of May 1789, laughing and dancing our way to the precipice. Thinking people were content to talk of abolishing all the abuses. France, they said, was about to be reborn. The word 'revolution' was never uttered.[55]

IX

REVOLUTIO

A Continent in Turmoil, c.1770–1815

THERE is a universal quality about the French Revolution which does not pertain to any of Europe's many other convulsions. Indeed, this was the event which gave the word 'Revolution' its full, modern meaning: that is, no mere political upheaval, but the complete overthrow of a system of government together with its social, economic and cultural foundations. Nowadays the history books are filled with 'revolutions'. There have been attempts, for example, to turn England's Civil War into the 'English Revolution', and still more attempts to upgrade the Russian Revolution into the third round of a universal series. There's the Roman Revolution, the Scientific Revolution, the Military Revolution, the Industrial Revolution, the American Revolution, even, in recent years, the Sexual Revolution. Not all of them deserve the title.

But in 1789 there was reason to believe that changes were taking place which would affect people far beyond France and far beyond mere politics. Paris was the capital of a dominant power, and the centre of an international culture. The revolutionaries had inherited the Enlightenment's belief in the universal abstraction of man. They felt that they were acting on behalf of all people everywhere, pitting themselves against universal tyranny. Their most noble monument was not some parochial pronouncement on the rights of the French but a ringing declaration on the Rights of Man (see below). 'Sooner or later,' Mirabeau told the National Assembly,

the influence of a nation that . . . has reduced the art of living to the simple notions of liberty and equality—notions endowed with irresistible charm for the human heart, and propagated in all the countries of the world—the influence of such a nation will undoubtedly conquer the whole of Europe for Truth, Moderation and Justice, not immediately perhaps, not in a single day . . .

This was the sort of sentiment which has inspired the label of 'Europe's first Revolution' in place of something that was exclusively French.[1]

Foreigners shared the same vivid sense of involvement. A young English enthusiast, later to repent, was to write ecstatically: 'Bliss was it in that dawn to be alive.'

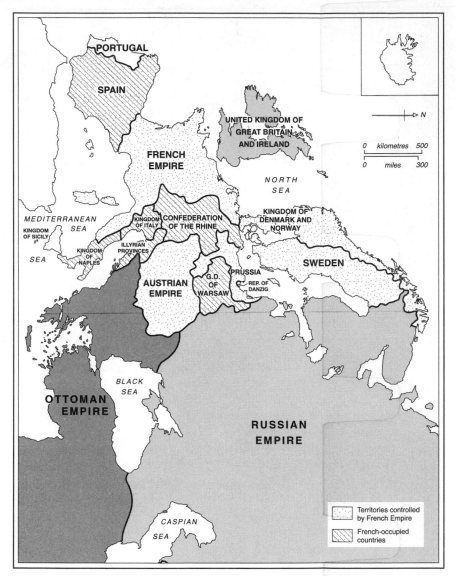

Map 20.
Europe, 1810

An elder statesman could bewail: 'The age of chivalry is gone. That of sophisters, economists and calculators has succeeded; and the glory of Europe is extinguished for ever.' 'Here and now', remarked the leading writer of the age having watched the Battle of Valmy, 'a new era in the world begins.'[2] Historians, whether for or against, have invariably resorted to strong words. Thomas Carlyle, appalled by what he dubbed 'sansculottism', called the French Revolution 'the frightfullest thing ever born of Time'.[3] Jules Michelet, harbouring the opposite feelings, began: 'I define the Revolution: the advent of the Law, the resurrection of Right, and the reaction of Justice.'[4]

The French Revolution plunged Europe into the most profound and protracted crisis which it had ever known. It consumed an entire generation in its tumults, its wars, its disturbing innovations. From the epicentre in Paris, it sent shock waves into the furthest recesses of the Continent. From the shores of Portugal to the depths of Russia, from Scandinavia to Italy, the shocks were followed by soldiers in bright uniforms with a blue, white and red cockade in their hats, and with 'Liberté, Égalité, Fraternité' on their lips. For its partisans, the Revolution promised liberation from the traditional oppressions enshrined in monarchy, nobility, and organized religion. For its opponents, it was synonymous with the dark forces of mob rule and terror. For France, it spelt the start of a modern national identity. For Europe as a whole, it provided an object lesson in the danger of replacing one form of tyranny with another. It began with hopes of limited peaceful change; 'it ended amidst promises of resistance to any form of change whatsoever'. In the short run, it met defeat; in the long run, in the realm of social and political ideas, it made, and continues to make, a major and a lasting contribution.

The pageant of the Revolution contains personalities and clichés that are known to every European schoolchild. The central parade of revolutionary leaders—Mirabeau, Danton, Marat, Robespierre, and Bonaparte—is complemented by the long line of their opponents and victims: by scenes of Louis XVI and Marie-Antoinette on the scaffold, of Charlotte Corday, the peasant girl who murdered Marat in his bath 'to save a hundred thousand men': of the *émigré* Duc d'Enghien, seized and executed on Bonaparte's orders. It is surrounded by a host of auxiliary figures of colour and enterprise—by radical Tom Paine, the exiled English philosopher who 'saw Revolution on two continents', by the inimitable Charles de Talleyrand-Périgord, *ci-devant* bishop, 'the irreverend Reverend of Autun', survivor supreme; by Antoine Fouquier-Tinville, the ice-cold prosecutor-general. In every European country it is accompanied by a vast gallery of heroes and villains, ranged for or against—in Britain by Nelson dying on the deck of HMS *Victory*, in Germany by Scharnhost and Gneisenau, in Austria by the patriot-martyr Andreas Hofer, in Poland by the noble Marshal Poniatowski riding his white horse to a watery grave, in Russia by the indomitable Kutuzov trudging doggedly through the snow. In European art and literature it is enriched by a series of unforgettable tableaux in words and paint, from Goya's *Desastres de la Guerra* or David's portraits of Napoleon to Stendhal's *La Chartreuse de Parme*,

Dickens's *A Tale of Two Cities*, Mickiewicz's *Pan Tadeusz*, or Tolstoy's *War and Peace*.

Any account of the revolutionary era must look successively at the causes, at the revolutionary events themselves, and at the consequences. Every chronological narrative must begin with the prelude of pre-revolutionary ferment. It must examine how moderate demands led to extreme changes, and how the conflict in France led to Continental wars. The crisis starts with the first waning of the Enlightenment in the 1770s, and closes with the Congress of Vienna which opened in 1814.

✦━━━✦

Prelude

The causes of the French Revolution are the subject of endless debate. One can distinguish the setting (which sometimes threatens to become the whole of previous history), the profound causes, or deep-laid sources of instability, and the immediate events or 'sparks' which ignited the barrel. The setting, in the last quarter of the eighteenth century, consisted of a generalized but deepening climate of unease right across Europe. The changes that generated the unease were not concentrated in France; but France was both a participant and a witness. France, facing political paralysis and financial stress, proved less capable of standing the stresses than her neighbours. 'The revolution [was] imminent in almost all of Europe. It broke out in France, because there the Ancien Regime was more worn out, more detested, and more easily destroyed than elsewhere.'[5]

On the political front, the major earthquake occurred across the Atlantic. Great Britain, which the *philosophes* had always regarded as the most stable and moderate of countries, was plunged into a war with its American colonists who, with French help, determined to break free of British rule. But the War of American Independence (1776–83) had important repercussions in Europe. For one thing, it pushed France's financial crisis towards the brink. It also made Frenchmen, and others, consider their own predicament: if poor old bumbling George III was to be classed as a tyrant, how should one classify the other monarchs of Europe? If the Americans could rebel against a 3*d.* duty on tea, what possible justification could there be for the massive imposts under which most Europeans groaned? If the USA had to be created because Americans had no representation in the British Parliament, what should all those Europeans think whose countries did not even possess a parliament? American constitutional thought was magnificently simple and universally relevant:

We hold these truths to be sacred and undeniable: that all men are created equal and independent, that from their equal creation they derive rights inherent and inalienable, among which are the preservation of life and liberty, and the pursuit of happiness.[6]

Europe's participation in the American Revolution is formally acknowledged with statues and monuments. The American factor in Europe's Revolution is not always acknowledged so readily. But in the dozen years which separated the

Declaration of Independence on 4 July 1776 from the inauguration of the first President, George Washington, on 29 April 1789, it was the creation of the USA which brought debates about modern government to a head.

Tom Paine (1737–1809), a Norfolk Quaker from Thetford, was the living link between Europe and America. 'Radical Tom' devoted himself to the American cause after being outlawed from England. His *Common Sense* (1776) was the most effective tract of the American Revolution; his *The Rights of Man* (1791) was to be one of the most radical responses to the French Revolution. He was to sit in the French Convention, and to escape the guillotine by a whisker. His *The Age of Reason* (1793), a deist tract written in firebrand prose, caused a scandal. 'My country is the world,' he wrote, 'and my religion is to do good.'

In Eastern Europe, the three great empires were digesting the first Partition of Poland (see Chapter VIII). There was relief that war had been avoided; but the clouds of propaganda could not conceal the facts of violence. What is more, in Poland-Lithuania itself the Partition only inflamed resentments against Russian hegemony. The strains of Polish Enlightenment were leading inexorably to a confrontation with the Tsarina. The Russian sphere of influence was moving in parallel with that of France towards a collision between the 'tyrants' and the 'friends of liberty'. It was no accident that the revolutionary era would eventually culminate in a titanic clash between France and Russia.

Beyond or beneath everyday politics, there were indications that deep forces invisible on the ordered surface of late eighteenth-century Europe were somehow getting out of control. One source of anxiety was technological: the appearance of power-driven machines with immense destructive as well as constructive potential. The second source was social: a growing awareness of 'the masses', the realization that the teeming millions, largely excluded from polite society, might take their fate into their own hands. The third source was intellectual: a rising concern both in literature and in philosophy with the irrational in human conduct. Historians are pressed to decide whether these developments were related phenomena: whether the so-called Industrial Revolution, the collectivist strand in social thought, and the beginnings of Romanticism were connected parts of one coherent process or not; whether they were causes of the revolutionary upheaval, or merely its companions and contributors.

The Industrial Revolution is a blanket term which is widely used to describe a range of technological and organizational changes that were considerably wider than the single best-known element: the invention of power-driven machinery. What is more, the term has come to refer, after immense historical debates, to merely one stage in a still more complex chain of changes—now called 'Modernization'—that did not begin to have its full effect until the following century (see pp. 764–82). Even so, there are a dozen elements of 'proto-industrialization' that must be taken into consideration; they include farming, mobile labour, steam power, machines, mines, metallurgy, factories, towns, communications, finance, and demography.

Scientific farming was one of the obsessions of the Enlightenment, and of the physiocrats in particular. From its initial, rationalizing stage, it progressed to the point where horse-driven (though not yet power-driven) machinery was creating the potential for greatly accelerated production. An English farmer from Hungerford, Jethro Tull (1674–1741), had advertised a machine-drill in his *Horse-Hoeing Husbandry*, published as long ago as 1703; the steel-tipped Rotherham ploughshare came on to the market in 1803. Over the intervening century, agricultural experimentation had raged. But progress was painfully slow; the average level of agricultural production was dictated, not by the tempo of innovations, but by the pace of the average farmer. [**CAP-AG**]

As farms increased their food production, more people could be fed from the produce of the same land. Men once used to work the fields could be released for other forms of employment. The rise in agricultural efficiency aided a rise in the birth rate, and stood to create a pool of surplus labour, at least in those countries where peasants were free to leave the land. Yet a supply of unskilled peasants provided only half an answer. Industry was to need skills as well as manpower. The most favoured locations would be found where artisan traditions were most developed.

Steam-power had been known since antiquity. But it had never been given any practical application until it was harnessed in 1711 by Thomas Newcomen (1663–1729) to a clumsy great engine for pumping flood-water from a mine in Devon. The steam-engine was immensely improved by James Watt (1736–1819), a Scots instrument-maker from Glasgow, who in 1763 was called in to repair a model of Newcomen's monster, and perfected the condenser. From then on, the different sorts of machinery to which the motive power of steam could be applied seemed limitless.

Machinery had been used ever since the water-mill and the printing-press. In the hands of the eighteenth-century clock-makers it had reached a high level of precision. But the prospect of a power source far more forceful than hand, water, or spring inspired a rash of inventions, all initially in the realm of textiles. Three Lancashire men, James Hargreaves (1720–78) of Blackburn, Richard Arkwright (1732–92) of Preston, and Samuel Crompton (1753–1827) of Hall'ith' Wood, Bolton, built respectively the spinning jenny (1767), the spinning frame (1768), and the spinning mule (1779). The jenny was suitable only for hand use in cottages; the frame and mule proved suitable for steam traction in factories. A new level of sophistication was reached in France with the silk loom (1804) of [**JACQUARD**].

Steam-power and machines, however, could not be put into widespread use unless coal—the most efficient fuel for raising steam—could be mined on a much expanded scale. This was achieved through a number of innovations, including underground pumps, Humphry Davy's safety lamp (1816), and the use of gunpowder for blasting. Machines, equally, which had to be made of hardened steel, could not be built in quantity unless the production of iron and steel could be expanded. This was achieved through a series of improvements, including those

---

JACQUARD

I N 1804 Joseph-Marie Jacquard (1752–1834), textile engineer of Lyons, perfected a loom which could weave cloth into any number of predetermined patterns, using sets of punched cards to control woof and shuttle. In textile history, Jacquard's loom was a major advance on the earlier inventions of Arkwright, Hargreaves, and Crompton. In the wider history of technology, it was an important step in the direction of automated machinery, the predecessor of all sorts of contraptions, from the pianola and the barrel-organ to punched-card data storage systems. Most significantly, perhaps, it established the dual principle on which computers would one day operate. The frame, and other working parts of Jacquard's loom, were the 'hardware', the sets of punched cards were the 'software'.[1]

---

introduced at the Carron ironworks in Scotland (1760) and Henry Cort's patents for the puddling and rolling of steel (1783–4).

The concentration of industrial workers under one roof, in a 'factory', long preceded the arrival of power-driven machinery. ('Factory' is a shortened form of 'manufactory', meaning 'production by hand'.) Silk factories, carpet factories, and porcelain factories had been common enough throughout the eighteenth century. But the installation of heavy plant, requiring constant servicing and regular supplies of fuel and raw materials, turned factory organization from an option into a necessity. The sight of the 'dark satanic mills'—vast, gaunt structures the size of a royal palace, set incongruously beside some little stream whose water they consumed, and belching forth pungent black smoke from a chimney the size of Trajan's Column—came first to the textile settlements of Lancashire and Yorkshire. The appearance of factories caused the sudden growth of new urban centres. The archetype lay in Manchester, capital of Lancashire's cotton industry. The first British Census of 1801 showed that Manchester had grown tenfold in a quarter of a century, from the proportions of a single parish to a town of 75,275 registered citizens. If population was drawn to new factory towns, it is also true that factories were drawn to the few large centres of existing population. Cities such as London or Paris, with a large pool of artisans and paupers, were attractive targets for employers seeking labour.

Inland communications were crucial; they had to be rendered as cheap and as effective as maritime trade. Huge loads of coal, iron, and other commodities such as cotton, wool, or clay needed to be moved from mines and ports to the factory. Manufactured goods needed to be delivered to distant markets. River, road, and rail transport were all involved. Once again, the greatest incentives arose in Britain. In 1760 the Duke of Bridgewater's engineer, James Brindley (1716–72), improved the scope of earlier canals by building a marvellous waterway that crossed Lancashire's River Irwell on the Barton Aqueduct (1760). In 1804, at

Merthyr Tydfil in South Wales, the Cornish engineer Richard Trevithick (1771–1833) coaxed a high-pressure steam locomotive into pulling coal wagons along a short railway. It proved more expensive than horses. In 1815 J. L. McAdam (1756–1836) gave his name (universally misspelled) to a system of road construction using a chipped-stone base and a tar surface.

Nothing could happen without money. Immense amounts of money were needed from investors willing to take immense risks to make immense but uncertain gains. Such money could only be forthcoming in countries where other forms of pre-industrial enterprise had accumulated a ready store of venture capital.

Demographic factors were also critical. It is not hard to understand the workings of the demographic motor where the processes of the Industrial Revolution generated an increase in population, and an increasing population encouraged the processes of the Industrial Revolution. The difficulty is to see how the motor was initially primed and fired. Certainly, in France, there was a long period of demographic impotence, where *la grande nation* of Europe, twenty million strong, proved incapable of increasing the population levels of the last three centuries. Great Britain, in contrast, enjoyed many advantages: prosperous farmers, mobile labourers, skilled artisans, ready supplies of coal and iron, an extensive network of trade, small internal distances, commercial entrepreneurs, a rising population, and political stability. It was decades before anyone else could begin to compete (see Appendix III, p. 1294).

Collectivism—the conviction that society as a whole may have rights and interests—was not well articulated in this period. It ran contrary to the individualism which had been strongly emphasized since the Renaissance and the Protestant Reformation. But it was an important development. It was implicit both in the idea of the modern state, which stressed the commonality of all its subjects, and in the discussions of the physiocrats and economists about the workings of the socio-political organism. It was explicit in Rousseau's concept of the general will, and was a cardinal principle with the utilitarians. It may well have been encouraged by the mobs and crowds in Europe's growing cities, by the sight of industrial workers pouring through the factory gates. At any rate, the power of the collective, whether ruly or unruly, could impress the imagination not just of philosophers but of generals, rabble-rousers, and poets.

Romanticism thrived on the growing tensions. After the initial inroads in Germany, the next generation was swelled by poets and publicists in England—notably by the trio of young Lakeland poets, Samuel Taylor Coleridge (1772–1834), William Wordsworth (1770–1850), and Robert Southey (1774–1843), and by the astonishing William Blake (1757–1827), poet, engraver, illustrator. German Romanticism was still productive. Goethe's friend, Friedrich von Schiller (1759–1805), published his historical dramas *Wallenstein* (1799), *Maria Stuart* (1800), and *Wilhelm Tell* (1804) at a time when Goethe had moved off in another direction. But by the time that Wordsworth climbed the cliffs at Tintern in 1798, it was the English Romantics who were taking the lead. Europe was already plunged into the horrors of war and revolution. Mankind seemed to be irrational to the point of self-destruction. The world was ever more incomprehensible. The untrammelled rule of logic and reason had come to an end:

> Ah! Well a day! What evil looks
> Had I from old and young!
> Instead of the cross, the albatross
> Around my neck was hung.[7]

* * *

> Oh rose, Thou art sick!
> The invisible worm
> That flies in the night
> Hath found out Thy bed
> Of crimson joy;
> And his dark secret love
> Doth Thy life destroy.[8]

Here, if ever, were Freudian verses almost a hundred years before Freud. [FREUDE]

Defiant young rebels were staking out the frontiers of Romanticism still further. In 1797 in Germany, Friedrich von Hardenberg (Novalis, 1772–1801) composed the mystical *Hymnen an die Nacht*, in which, like Dante for Beatrice, he sublimated his passion for a long-lost love. In 1799 Friedrich Schlegel (1772–1829), younger brother of the translator of Shakespeare, Dante, and Calderon, wrote the scandalous novel *Lucinde* which suggested that love of beauty should be the supreme ideal. In France, François-René Chateaubriand (1768–1843) published the *Essai sur les révolutions* (1797) and his *Génie du Christianisme* (1801) in the teeth of contemporary conventions. In 1812 in England, the outrageous Lord George Byron (1788–1824) published *Childe Harold's Pilgrimage*, which was to launch a Europe-wide cult.

Important, too, were the salons and centres which propagated the new ideas. The Jena circle of the Schlegel brothers was influential in Germany. But pride of place must go to Germaine Necker (Mme de Staël, 1766–1817), daughter of Louis XVI's chief minister and one of the most effective purveyors of romantic ideas. An author in her own right, Mme de Staël held court, first on the Rue du Bac in Paris and then in exile, to all the literati of the day. Her novel *Delphine* (1803) had feminist leanings; *Corinne* (1807) was a manifesto of passion; *De l'Allemagne* (1810) was a tract that made the world of German Romanticism accessible to France.

Reason was not tamed, however, until the philosophers themselves turned against it. Vico's earlier divergences from the Enlightenment were pursued in the unlikely setting of East Prussia. Immanuel Kant (1724–1804), undoubtedly a giant among philosophers, bridged the gap between Reason and Romanticism. A pietist, a bachelor, and a creature of pedantic routine, he was peculiarly insulated from the stirring events of his lifetime. He never once left the environs of his native Königsberg, and made himself all the more inaccessible by writing dense, contorted, professorial prose. ('Coleridge's Kantian phase', writes one commentator, 'did not improve his verse.'[9]) None the less, Kant's three Critiques

FREUDE

IN 1785, in the village of Gohlis near Leipzig, Friedrich Schiller composed *An die Freude*, 'Ode to Joy'. It was a paean to the spiritual liberation which overwhelmed him after a hopeless love affair and a winter of penury in Mannheim. It had political as well as personal overtones: a persistent rumour maintains that the original title was 'Hymn to Freedom':

Freude, schöner Götterfunken,	Joy, brilliant spark of the gods,
Tochter aus Elysium,	daughter of Elysium, heavenly being,
wir betreten feuertrunken,	we enter, drunk with fire,
Himmlische, dein Heiligtum.	your holy sanctuary.
Deine Zauber bindet wieder,	Your magic reunites
was die Mode streng geteilt;	what was split by convention,
alle Menschen werden Brüder,	and all men become brothers
Wo dein sanfter Flügel weilt.	where your gentle wings are spread.
Seid umschlungen, Millionen!	Be embraced, you millions!
Diesen Kuß der ganzen Welt!	This kiss for all the world!
Brüder—überm Sternenzelt	Brothers, above the starry canopy
Muß ein lieber Vater wohnen[1]	must surely dwell a loving father.

Seven years later the young Beethoven publicly stated his intention of setting the Ode to music. He was to brood about it for more than thirty years.

Beethoven conceived the idea of a grandiose 'German Symphony' some time in 1817. He felt that it might culminate in a choral finale. His early notes mentioned an *Adagio Cantique*, 'a religious song in a Symphony in the old modes . . . In the *Adagio* the text to be a Greek mythos (or) Cantique Ecclesiastique. In the *Allegro* a Bacchus festival'.[2] Only in June or July 1823 did he turn definitively to the Ode, and then with constant misgivings. During those years, bitter and despondent from advancing deafness, he triumphed over his adversity through the *Missa Solemnis* and the wonderful run of piano sonatas, Op. 109–11.

Yet the Symphony No. 9 (Choral) in D minor (Op. 125) was to scale the heights of intellectual invention and emotional daring still further. After a brief, whispering prologue, the first movement, *allegro ma non troppo*, is launched by the extraordinary sound of the whole orchestra playing the descending chord of D minor in unison. The second movement, *molto vivace*, 'the most divine of Scherzos', is punctuated by moments when the music stops completely, only to restart with redoubled energy. The third movement, *adagio*, is built round two intertwined melodies of great nobility.

The transition to the finale was contrived by bracketing a disjointed recital of the preceding subjects within two outbursts of the famous cacophony or 'clamour'. This, in its turn, is interrupted by the ringing appeal of the bass voice: *'O Freunde, nicht diese Toene!'* (Oh friends, no more of these tones! Let us sing something full of gladness!) Shortly, a new motif steals in from the wind section. Repeated in the triumphant key of D major, the key of trumpets, it is the simplest and yet most powerful of all symphonic melodies. In a line of fifty-six notes, it possesses only three which are not consecutive. It is the tune which will carry Beethoven's rearrangement of Schiller's stanzas:

The dazzling complexities which follow drive performers and listeners into the outer realms of effort and imagination. An augmented orchestra is joined by a full choir and four soloists. The quartet sings the theme with two variations. The tenor sings 'Glad, glad as suns through ether wending' to the strains of a military march with Turkish percussion. An orchestral interlude in double fugue leads to the thundering chorus 'Oh, ye millions, I embrace you!'. The soloists converse with the chorus over Schiller's opening lines before another double fugue pushes the sopranos to sustain a top A for twelve endless measures. The coda sees the soloists blending into a sort of 'universal round', a passage of florid polyphony, and a last dash into a diminished version of the main theme. At the end, the words 'Daughter of Elysium, Joy, O Joy, the God-descended' are repeated *maestoso* before the final, affirmative drop from A to D.[3]

Despite a commission from the London Philharmonic Society, 'the Ninth' received its first performance in the Theatre of the Kaerntnertor in Vienna on 7 May 1824. The composer conducted. Unhearing, he totally lost control; he was still conducting when the music ceased. He was turned round by one of the players so that he could *see* the applause.

Beethoven was always seen as a universal genius. During the Second World War, the opening bars of his Fifth Symphony were used to announce BBC broadcasts to Nazi-occupied Europe. A century and a half after his death, his rendering of *An der Freude* was adopted as the official anthem of the European Community. The words, which were taken to celebrate the universal brotherhood of Man, linked a pre-nationalist with a post-nationalist age. The melody was thought to fit the fervent hopes of a continent emerging from the cacophonous clamour of two world wars.

presented a body of ideas to which almost all subsequent philosophers claim to be indebted.

The *Kritik der reinen Vernunft* (Critique of Pure Reason, 1781) denies that rationalist metaphysics can be accepted as a perfect science like mathematics. It insists that every phenomenon existing outside time and space has its own inscrutable source of being. Each such source was called *das Ding-an-sich*, 'the thing-in-itself'. 'I had to abolish knowledge', he wrote apologetically, 'in order to make room for faith.' Reason is to be complemented by belief and imagination. The *Kritik der praktischen Vernunft* (Critique of Practical Reason, 1788) is a treatise of moral philosophy, elaborating Kant's theory of the 'categorical imperative'. It is sympathetic to traditional Christian ethics and stresses duty as the supreme criterion of moral conduct. The *Kritik der Urteilskraft* (Critique of Evaluation, 1790) is a treatise on aesthetics. It makes the famous distinction between *Verstand* (intellect) and *Vernunft* (reason) as instruments of judgement. Kant argues that art should serve morality and should avoid the portrayal of nasty objects. 'Beauty has no value except in the service of man.'

Kant was deeply interested in the philosophy of history. Like his contemporary, Gibbon, he was impressed by the 'tissue of folly', the 'puerile vanity', and the 'thirst for destruction' which filled the historical record. At the same time, he strove to find sense amidst the chaos. He found it in the idea that conflict was a teacher which would extend rationality from a few noble individuals to the conduct of all mankind. He wrote in his *Concept of Universal History* (1784), 'Men may wish for concord, but Nature knows better what is good for the species. [Nature] wants discord.' Kant's politics advocated republicanism. He welcomed the French Revolution though not the Terror, denouncing both paternal government and hereditary privilege. In *Zum ewigen Frieden* (On Perpetual Peace, 1795) he called for the creation of a *Weltbürgertum* or 'World Community' which would commit itself to universal disarmament and bury the Balance of Power. None of these views was particularly fitting for a subject of the King of Prussia.

[GENUG]

J. G. Herder (1744–1803), born at Mohrungen (Morąg), started his career as an enthusiastic reader of Rousseau, giving up a job at Riga in order to sail to France. He later settled in Weimar, under Goethe's patronage. His fertile mind produced a whole crop of original thoughts about culture, history, and art. He made an anti-rationalist contribution to the epistemological debate, propounding the idea that perception is a function of the total personality. In his *Ideen zur Philosophie der Geschichte der Menschheit* (1784–91), he developed Vico's cyclical concept of the birth, growth, and death of civilizations, but conceiving of progress as something much more complex than mere linear advancement. In his own estimation, however, his most important undertaking lay in a lifelong devotion to the collection and study of folklore and folksong, both German and foreign. Here was a subject that would play a central role not just in Romantic literature but in the whole story of national-consciousness (see pp. 816–17).

GENUG

WHEN Immanuel Kant died at Königsberg on 12 February 1804, his last word was *Genug* (Enough). Never a truer word is spoken than in death.[1]

Agrippina, Nero's Mother	AD 59	*'Smite my womb'*
Pierre Abelard, philosopher	1142	*'I don't know'*
Pope Alexander VI, Borgia	1503	*'Wait a minute'*
Chevalier de Bayard	1524	*'God and my country'*
Martin Luther	1546	*'Yes'*
King Henry VIII	1547	*'Monks, Monks, Monks!'*
François Rabelais	1553	*'I go to seek the great perhaps'*
Walter Raleigh	1618	(To the executioner) *'Strike, Man!'*
King Charles I	1649	*'Remember'*
Thomas Hobbes	1679	*'A great leap in the dark'*
Julie de Lespinasse	1776	*'Am I still alive?'*
Voltaire	1778	*'For God's sake, let me die in peace'*
Emperor Joseph II	1790	*'Here lies Joseph who was unsuccessful in all his undertakings'*
W. A. Mozart	1791	*'I was writing this for myself'*
Napoleon Bonaparte	1821	*'Josephine'*
Ludwig van Beethoven	1827	*'The Comedy is over'*
Georg Wilhelm Hegel	1831	*'And he didn't understand me'*
J. W. von Goethe	1832	*'More Light!'*
Nathan Rothschild	1836	*'And all because of my money'*
J. M. W. Turner, painter	1851	*'The sun is God'*
Heinrich Heine	1856	*'God will pardon me. It's his profession'*
Charles Darwin	1882	*'I am not in the least afraid to die'*
Karl Marx (asked for a last word)	1883	*'Go on, get out!'*
Franz Liszt	1886	*'Tristan'*
Emperor Franz-Joseph	1916	(singing) *'God Save the Emperor!'*
Georges Clemenceau	1929	*'I wish to be buried upright— facing Germany'*
Heinrich Himmler	1945	*'I am Heinrich Himmler'*
H. G. Wells	1946	*'I'm alright'*

All the arts responded to the shifting climate. In music, both Mozart and Haydn stayed devoted to the classical canon of orderly form, delicacy, and harmony. But Beethoven, who had quickly mastered the classical conventions, moved steadily on into the musical equivalent of revolutionary storm and stress. He had already reached it by the time of his Symphony no. 3, the 'Eroica' (1805), originally dedicated to Napoleon. Carl Maria von Weber (1786–1826), sometime opera-master at Dresden, was to become a stereotype of the Romantic artist. His first successful opera, *Die Waldmädchen* (1800), presented the touching story of a dumb girl communing with the mysteries of the forest. The melodic genius of Franz Schubert (1797–1828) was cut short, like his Unfinished Symphony, by disease and an untimely death, but not before he had compiled a matchless œuvre of over 600 songs. Alongside the acknowledged masters, there was a strong supporting cast of almost forgotten names such as J. K. Dussek (1761–1812), Muzio Clementi (1752–1832), M. K. Ogiński (1765–1833), J. N. Hummel (1778–1837), John Field (1782–1837), or Maria Szymanowska (1789–1831)—the latter unusual in her day as a female performer and composer.

In painting, the appeal of neo-classicism was only partially overtaken. The most influential of French painters, Jacques-Louis David (1748–1825), never ceased to address classical subjects. But Romantic pathos crept into even early pictures such as *Saint Roch* (1780), inspired by the plague at Marseilles; and it furnished an important element in his heroic portrayal of the Napoleonic saga. Yet the most radical innovations appeared elsewhere. In Germany, the portraitist P. O. Runge (1777–1810) sought 'symbols of the eternal rhythm of the universe'. In England, the animals of George Stubbs (1724–1806) passed from their classical pastures of utter calm and restraint to agitated scenes such as the much admired *Horse Attacked by a Lion*. J. M. W. Turner (1775–1851) took the first steps along the road which would lead him all the way to Impressionism. He visited Switzerland for the first time in 1802, and painted *The Reichenbach Falls*. From the start he was drawn to the tempestuous powers of Nature, especially at sea. His contemporary, the landscapist John Constable (1776–1837), brought a gentler temperament but no less talent to the study of Nature's moods. William Blake, as illustrator, entered the world of fantasy and the supernatural. His illustrations of Dante pointed to a Romantic taste that spread across Europe. In Spain, Francisco Goya (1746–1828), royal painter from 1789, found his *métier* recording all the nightmares and horrors of war and civil strife. 'The Sleep of Reason', he said about one of his pictures, 'engenders monsters.'[10]

For a long time historians sought the roots of the Revolution primarily in the intellectual and political conflicts of the preceding age. The *philosophes* were seen to have undermined the ideological foundations of the Ancien Régime, whilst the ministers of Louis XVI—Turgot, 1774–6, Necker, 1776–81 and 1788–9, Calonne, 1783–7, and Archbishop Loménie de Brienne, 1787–8—led France to national bankruptcy. Historians saw the calling of the Estates-General and the subsequent storming of the Bastille as the straightforward consequence of popular grievances, of excesses perpetrated by court, church, and nobility, and of reform pursued 'too little, too late'. Burke suspected a conspiracy of the 'swinish multitude'; Thiers, writing within memory of the Revolution, stressed the injustices of absolute government; Michelet stressed the miseries of 'the people'.

An important finesse to the debate was provided by Alexis de Tocqueville (1805–59). In his *Ancien Régime et la Révolution* (1856) he showed that the dynamic of reform and revolution was no straightforward matter. Many aspects of government were actually improving under Louis XVI, who had always been genuinely committed to reform. 'The social order destroyed by a revolution,' he wrote, 'is almost always better than that which preceded it; and experience shows that the most dangerous moment for a bad government is generally that in which it sets about reform . . .'[11] The slightest acts of arbitrary power under Louis XVI seemed harder to endure 'than all the despotism of Louis XIV.'[12]

More recent research has given precision to many of these assertions. It has revealed the role of the Paris Parlement in blocking the King's reforms, of the Parlement's pamphleteers in spreading the ideas of the *philosophes*, and of ideology as a force in its own right. One study even claims that Necker had succeeded in balancing the budget during his first ministry. This would suggest that the financial crisis following the War of American Independence, which precipitated the calling of the Estates-General, was the result not of systemic collapse but of simple mismanagement.[13]

At one stage in the debate, prime emphasis was placed on the economic and social problems which were judged to underlie the political upheaval. Marx had been an historical sociologist, who belonged to a vintage for whom the French Revolution remained the focus of all historical discussion; and many Marxists and quasi-Marxists followed suit. In the 1930s C. E. Labrousse published quantitative evidence both for cyclical agrarian depressions in late eighteenth-century France and for an acute food shortage and price catastrophe in 1787–9.[14] In the 1950s a long interpretative war between the followers of Lefebvre and Cobban only served to give prominence to their sociological preoccupations.[15] A consensus appeared to emerge about the primacy of 'bourgeois' interests. 'The revolution was theirs,' concluded Cobban, 'and for them at least it was a wholly successful revolution.'[16] 'The French Revolution', wrote another participant, 'constitutes the crowning point of a long social and economic evolution which made the bourgeoisie the mistress of the world.'[17] But then the bourgeois theory was challenged, and investigations shifted to the artisans and the sans culottes. Much of this class analysis retains a strong Marxian flavour, especially with those who deny any Marxist connections. In one view, the 'bagarre des profs' over the French Revolution 'has become the Divine Comedy of the modern secular world.'[18]

As always in a crisis, psychological factors were paramount. The King and his ministers did not have to be told that disaster loomed; but, unlike historians, they did not have 200 years in which to study it. Indeed, with no popular representation in place they had no reliable means of gauging public attitudes. Similarly, in the depths of a serf-run countryside, or of proletarian Paris, there was no means of regulating the waves of poverty-led fear and of blind anger. The combination of indecision at the centre and of panic amidst large sections of the populace was a sure recipe for catastrophe. Above all, violence bred violence. 'From the very beginning . . . violence was the motor of revolution.'[19]

There is much to be said for exploring the Revolution's international dimensions from the very earliest point.[20] When one considers the mechanisms which transformed generalized ferment into explosive revolution, political and military logistics have to be taken into the equation. There were several casks in the European cellar which were ready to blow their corks, and which actually did so. But in the case of the lesser casks, the corks could be swiftly replaced. It was only when one of the bigger barrels threatened to explode that the cellar as a whole was in danger. It is for this reason that historians have paid almost exclusive attention to events in Paris. Yet in terms of chronology and precedence, several other centres of ferment have to be brought into the reckoning. Extremely important, though not always mentioned, were developments in the Netherlands, first in the United Provinces and later in the Austrian Netherlands. Important, too, was the advanced disaffection of several French provinces, notably in the Dauphiné. Crucial for the whole of Eastern Europe was the meeting of the Great Sejm of Poland-Lithuania, bent on reform at all costs. Each of these stress-points acted to some degree on the others. Together, they showed that the revolutionary ferment had assumed transcontinental proportions before the explosion occurred.

In the United Provinces, the ancient conflict between the Stadholder and his opponents reached a new boiling-point in October 1787, when the Prussian army was invited in to maintain the status quo. The Dutch had suffered acutely from their adherence to armed neutrality during the American War of Independence, and from the resultant naval war with Great Britain. By the late 1780s old-established commercial and republican interests were in revolt against the Stadholder, Willem V (r. 1766–94), and his British and Prussian allies. They began to call themselves 'patriots' in the American style, and claimed to be the champions of the people against the princes. They caused an international outcry when in the course of their campaign against the government they kidnapped the Stadholder's consort, Wilhelmina. It was Wilhelmina's misfortune which spurred the Prussians into action and provided the pretext for the pacifications which followed in Amsterdam and elsewhere. But the appeal to force was not lost on those who were watching on the sidelines. It undoubtedly strengthened the resolve of the 'patriots' in the Austrian Netherlands, who were engaged in a trial of strength of their own; and it caught the attention of the French at the very time when relations between the monarch and his subjects were coming under intense scrutiny. French dissidents had looked to Holland as a haven of liberty ever since the days of Descartes. From 1787 the Dutch dissidents were looking again to France as the only realistic source of a rescue.

The Estates of Dauphiné met in the Salle du Jeu de Paume in the Château de Vizille, near Grenoble, on 21 July 1788. The meeting, which was illegal, had been conceived by local prominents as a means of defending the provincial parlement against the royal decrees which it had recently been ordered to register. It was the first assembly of its kind since 1628, when Richelieu had suspended many provincial institutions; and it was prompted by a riotous demonstration in support of the parlement which had taken place in Grenoble on 7 June. It started a process of escalating demands which anticipated many of the events in Paris a year later. The Parlement of Dauphiné had been defying royal authority for more than twenty years. Its refusal to legalize many of the King's demands for increased taxation had given it great local popularity. The decrees of May 1788, which aimed to break all such recalcitrant parlements and which provided for the banishment of offending magistrates, threatened to overthrow the comfortable stand-off of a whole generation.

A second meeting of the Dauphiné Estates at Romans in September 1788 was technically legal, since it coincided with authorized preparations for the Estates-General. But it saw the passage of a veritable provincial constitution. Apart from the election of deputies to the Estates-General, among them Lefranc de Pompignan, Archbishop of Vienne, it heard impassioned speeches on civic rights from its chairman, Judge J.-J. Mounier (1758–1806), the future Chairman of the Constituent Assembly, and from Antoine Barnave (1761–93), soon to be the author of the Jacobin Manifesto. It arranged for the doubling of the representation of its *Tiers État*, for joint debate of the three orders, and for individual voting. Each of these measures, when repeated in the Estates-General, was to turn a subservient body convened by the King into an independent assembly bent on implementing its own agenda. As the local guidebook proudly proclaims, '1788 est l'année de la Révolution dauphinoise.'[21]

The mini-revolution in Dauphiné caused ructions at the royal court. It provoked the resignation of the King's chief minister, Archbishop Loménie de Brienne, who had set in motion the convocation of the Estates-General but who was now refused permission to crush the rebel province by force. The way was thus opened for the return of Jacques Necker, the Swiss banker, who was recalled to rescue the King's finances. The events in Dauphiné dominated the deliberations of the (second) assembly of notables which was summoned to Versailles in November 1788 to advise on preparations for the Estates-General. The proposals of the dauphinois regarding the role of the Third Estate undoubtedly influenced the most radical pamphlet of the day. 'What is the Third Estate?' asked the pamphlet's author, the Abbé Sieyès. 'Everything. And what has it been until the present time? Nothing. And what does it demand? To become something.'[22]

In Warsaw, the assembly of the Wielki Sejm or 'Four Years' Diet' in October 1788 was conceived as part of a royal scheme to gain Russian approval for restoring the Republic's independence. It started a process of reform in Poland-Lithuania which ran parallel to developments in France until both were overtaken by coercion. Much had changed in recent years. Frederick the Great was dead, and the new King of Prussia was well disposed to his Polish neighbours. Russia was heavily engaged in campaigns against both Swedes and Turks. Austria under

Joseph II was preoccupied with the Netherlands. In 1787 Stanisław-August judged the moment ripe for an overture to the Empress Catherine. If the Empress would permit the Republic to raise a modern army, and the financial and administrative structures to support it, the King would immediately sign a treaty of alliance with Russia for common operations against the Turks. Russia and the Republic could then pursue their objectives in harmony. In May the King received the Russian Empress on the Dnieper near the royal castle of Kaniów. In this, the last meeting with his former lover, he learned little from Catherine. But it gradually emerged that the Empress, who also conferred with Joseph II, was not well disposed. In fact, she was determined to maintain the status quo at all costs. Polish aspirations were not to be accommodated.

Poland's Diet pressed on regardless with the internal aspects of the King's scheme. In October 1788 it began by declaring itself a confederation and subject to majority voting, thereby bypassing the *liberum veto* of its russophile members. It then proceeded to vote for the creation of a national army of 100,000 men, a step which had been blocked ever since the Russian-guaranteed constitution of 1717. It also backed a *rapprochement* with Frederick-William II of Prussia. Its activists were grouped round the anglophile King, who dreamt of a British-style monarchy, and a group of intellectuals—the Revd Hugo Kołłataj (1750–1812), Rector of the reformed Jagiellonian University, the Revd Stanisław Staszic (1755–1826), and Stanisław Małachowski (1736–1809), Speaker of the Sejm, who were all strong admirers of the American example. After three years of frenzied legislation, their brief moment of glory was to come in May 1791, when they pushed through their Constitution of Third May (see below).

In November 1788 the Estates of Brabant and Hainault took an equally momentous step. Infuriated by the torrent of reforms imposed by their overlord, the Emperor Joseph II, they voted to withhold the provinces' taxes. They had long felt aggrieved both on religious and on political grounds. As Catholics of the Spanish school, they could not easily accept the imperial decrees which had suppressed seminaries, pilgrimages, and contemplative orders; which had replaced episcopal by state censorship; and which had subjected the Church to direct taxation. Equally, as beneficiaries of privileges which had functioned since 1354, they could not bear the Emperor's lack of consultation. The cities of Brussels, Antwerp, and Louvain were jealously attached to their traditional right of veto over the deliberations of the Estates. Yet by making their stand at the time they did, they precipitated a constitutional crisis which would play itself out in the Austrian Netherlands one step ahead of the parallel crisis that was brewing in France. The Belgian 'patriots' hit the headlines in Paris in the same week that France's notables were heading for Versailles to advise on the agenda of the Estates-General. The Emperor tried to impose a new constitution on the Belgian Estates on 29 April 1789, exactly six days before France's Estates-General convened. When the Emperor's impositions were rejected by the State Council of the Austrian Netherlands, he determined to use force. The Austrian army invaded Brussels, dissolved the State Council, and abolished the *Joyeuse Entrée* on 20 June 1789. This was the self-same day when a defiant Estates-General, by taking the 'Tennis Court Oath', was setting the revolutionary process in motion in France (see below).

Brussels and Paris shared the same language. News travelled fast between them. The 'Belgian Revolt', which continued to run long after the Emperor's coup, was an essential component of the 'French Revolution'. Paris did not lead Brussels; Brussels led Paris.

The last week of April 1789 brought death to the streets of Paris. An exceptionally cold winter had added to the hardships inflicted by a bankrupt government, rising prices, and lack of work. Hunger stalked the poorer districts, and raids on bakeries were frequent. When a rich manufacturer called Réveillon dared to say in public that his workmen could live well off half the 30 sous per day which he paid them, his house in the Faubourg Saint-Antoine was surrounded. On the first day, the angry crowd demolished several buildings amidst cries of 'Vive le tiers!' and 'Vive Necker!'. On the second day, when soldiers of the Régiment du Royal-Cravatte were brought in, they were pelted with missiles; and someone fired a shot. The soldiers responded with volleys of musket-fire that left at least 300 dead. This was the news which awaited the members of the Estates-General when they converged on the capital at the weekend from all ends of France.

Revolution

In France, as in England 149 years before, the general crisis came to a head when a bankrupt King summoned a long-neglected Parliament to his aid. The expectation on all sides was that financial relief for the royal government would be granted in return for the redress of grievances. By prior arrangement, therefore, all the delegations elected by the provinces and cities came to the Estates-General armed with *cahiers de doléances* or 'catalogues of complaint'. These *cahiers* were intended by the King's ministers, and are widely used by historians, as a prime instrument for assessing the nature and proportions of popular discontent. Some of the complaints were less than revolutionary: 'that the master wig-maker of Nantes be not troubled with new guild-brethren, the actual number of ninety-two being more than sufficient.'[23]

The opening scene in Paris, on Sunday 4 May 1789, was painted in one of Carlyle's memorable word-pictures:

Behold . . . the doors of St. Louis Church flung wide: and the Procession of Processions advancing to Notre-Dame! . . . The Elected of France, and then the Court of France, are marshalled . . . all in prescribed place and costume. Our Commons 'in plain black mantle and white cravate'; Nobles in gold-worked, bright-dyed cloaks of velvet, resplendent, rustling with laces, waving with plumes; the Clergy in rochet, alb, or other best *pontificalibus*. Lastly comes the King himself, and the King's Household, also in the brightest blaze of pomp . . . Some fourteen hundred men blown together from all winds, on the deepest errand.

Yes, in that silent marching mass there is futurity enough. No symbolic Arc, like the old Hebrews, do those men bear; yet with them, too, is a Covenant. They, too, preside at a new era in the history of men. The whole future is there, and Destiny dim-brooding over it, in (their) hearts and unshaped thoughts . . .²⁴

Once summoned, however, the Estates-General proved impossible to control. The three orders of clergy, nobility, and Third Estate were supposed to meet separately, and to follow an agenda laid down by the royal managers. But the Third Estate, which had been granted double representation as in Dauphiné, soon realized that it could bend the proceedings to its own desires, if the three chambers were permitted to vote as one. The clergy and nobility, who included many sympathizers, offered no concerted opposition. So on 17 June, having invited the two other Estates to join them, the Third Estate broke the existing rules and declared itself to be the sole National Assembly. This was the decisive break. Three days later, locked out of their usual hall, the deputies met on the adjacent tennis court, *le jeu de paume*, and swore an oath never to disband until France was given a Constitution. 'Tell your master', thundered Count Mirabeau, to troops sent to disperse them, 'that we are here by the will of the people, and will not disperse before the threat of bayonets.' [GAUCHE]

Pandemonium ensued. At court, the King's conciliatory ministers fell out with their more aggressive colleagues. On 11 July Jacques Necker, who had received a rousing welcome at the opening of the Estates-General, was dismissed. Paris exploded. A revolutionary headquarters coalesced round the Duc d'Orléans at the Palais Royal. The gardens of the Palais Royal became a notorious playground of free speech and free love. Sex shows sprang up alongside every sort of political harangue. 'The exile of Necker', screamed the fiery orator Camille Desmoulins, fearing reprisals, 'is the signal for another St Bartholomew of patriots.' The royal garrison was won over. On the 13th a Committee of Public Safety was created, and 48,000 men were enrolled in a National Guard under General Lafayette. Bands of insurgents tore down the hated *barrières* or internal customs posts in the city, and ransacked the monastery of Saint-Lazare in the search for arms. On the 14th, after 30,000 muskets were removed from the Hôtel des Invalides, the royal fortress of the Bastille was besieged. There was a brief exchange of gunfire, after which the governor capitulated. The King had lost his capital.

At that point, at the centre of affairs, there was still hope of an orderly settlement. On the 17th, to much surprise, Louis XVI drove from Versailles to Paris and donned the tricolour cockade in public. In the provinces, in contrast, news of the fall of the Bastille triggered an orgy of attacks on 'forty thousand other bastilles'. Castles and abbeys were burned; noble families, indiscriminately attacked by hungry peasants, began to emigrate; cities declared for self-rule; brigandage proliferated. France was dividing into armed camps. It was the season of *la Grande Peur*, the Great Fear—a summer of unprecedented social hysteria fired by rumours of aristocratic plots and peasant atrocities across the country.²⁵

From then on, the Revolution acquired its own momentum, its rhythms dictated by tides of uncontrolled events. It passed through three main phases.

In the first, five-year phase, 1789–94, the French Revolution accelerated through ever-increasing degrees of radicalism until all the institutions of the previous social and political order had been swept away. For more than two years the National Assembly, the *Constituante,* laboured over the design of a constitutional monarchy. In one full night, 4–5 August 1789, thirty separate decrees abolished all the apparatus of serfdom and noble privilege. The Declaration of the Rights of Man (26 August 1789) was followed by the abolition of the provinces (December 1789) and the civil establishment of the clergy (June 1790). It appeared that stability and consensus might have been achieved when, on the anniversary of the fall of the Bastille, on 14 July 1790, the whole of France joined in a Grand Festival of Federation. In Paris, the King attended mass in the presence of the leaders of the assembly, and the commander of the National Guard, General Lafayette, swore a solemn oath of allegiance proffered by the Bishop of Autun, Talleyrand.

In the Austrian Netherlands, the revolution was moving still faster. In August 1789 the powerful Archbishopric of Liège was seized by 'patriots' in a bloodless coup. In August a patriotic army was raised by General de Mersch to confront the Austrians. In November demonstrations in Ghent ended in bloody massacres; and finally, in December, Brussels expelled its Austrian garrison. By the end of the year an independent Union of Belgian States had been declared. It lasted for thirteen months, before the re-entry of the Austrians in force in February 1791.

In France, the introduction of a consolidated Constitution (September 1791) called for elections which swept the original, moderate leaders aside. The new Legislative Assembly was much less sympathetic to the monarchy. It struggled to get a grip for twelve months until it, too, was overtaken by the declaration of a Republic and the opening of the Republic's National Convention. Then, in the summer of 1792, with France at war, the mainstream revolutionary movement was hijacked by root-and-branch radicals, who had earlier seized control of the municipal Commune of Paris. Hence, if the Estates-General and the National Assembly (1789–91) were dominated by Mirabeau's constitutionalists, and the Legislative Assembly (1791–2) by republican Girondins, the National Convention (1792–5) took its orders from Robespierre's extremist Jacobins.

The two dread years of Jacobin supremacy began during the invasion scare of 1792, when the Prussian army was thought to be in striking distance of Paris (see below). When the King dismissed his Girondin ministers in expectation of foreign rescue, popular resentments began to rise. In July, when the manifesto of the Duke of Brunswick announced his intention to liberate the King and to execute the whole population of Paris if the Royal Palace was touched, they boiled over. It was exactly the pretext which the Jacobins needed to declare 'the fatherland in danger', and to call for the abolition of the monarchy. Five hundred ardent Massilians marched to the support of Paris. On 10 August, with the Massilians in the van, the Tuileries was duly stormed and the King's Swiss Guard massacred. In September, with the Commune controlling the capital, thousands in the Paris prisons were butchered in cold blood; the King was deposed; and the Republic declared.

GAUCHE

FROM the earliest days of France's Estates-General, the nobles of the Court Party instinctively positioned themselves to the right of the King, whilst the Third Estate sat on the left. To sit on the right-hand of authority, as on 'the right-hand of God', was an established mark of privilege. As a result, 'the Right' became a natural synonym for the political Establishment, whilst 'the Left' was applied to its opponents. These divisions grew more marked after 1793 in the National Convention, where the Jacobins and their associates occupied benches in the left and upper sections of the chamber. They formed the revolutionary block of deputies on the '*Montagne*', which physically towered over the moderates of the '*Plaine*' below. The opposition of 'Left' and 'Right' has provided a basic metaphor for the political spectrum ever since.[1]

Yet the metaphor has its problems. It only works if the political spectrum is seen to be ranged along a straight line, with 'Left' and 'Right' separated by the conciliatory 'Centre' between them:

Reform————————Status quo————————Reaction
Extreme—Left—Centre-Left—CENTRE—Centre-Right—Right—Extreme
   Left   Right

In this scheme, the most successful politicians are likely to be those who command the consensus of 'the centre ground' with the help of either the moderate Left or the moderate Right.

Marxists, and other dialecticians, however, see the political spectrum not as unilinear, but as bi-polar. In their scheme, politics consists of a struggle where two opposite forces are fated to contend, and where one or the other will necessarily establish supremacy. In the long run, as in a tug-of-war, or with a pair of scales, the Centre cannot hold the balance indefinitely, and must always give way to 'Left' or 'Right'. The notion of a political order based on consensus, tolerance, compromise, restraint, or mutual respect for the law is a 'bourgeois illusion'.

LEFT————————————————————RIGHT
Progress   Regress

What the unilinear and the bi-polar schemes share is the dubious assumption that 'Left' and 'Right' are simple opposites.

The spatial arrangement of political assemblies, therefore, involves important considerations. The British House of Commons, for example, places the Government benches on the Speaker's Right in direct confrontation with the Opposition benches on the Speaker's Left. It accurately reflects the adversarial politics of the two-party system, putting ministers and shadow ministers face to face in their exchanges across the despatch box. This, too, is a dialectical concept, actively discouraging the activities of a third party and the spirit of coalition on which most Continental assemblies depend. It could not be adapted to the purposes of an assembly elected by proportional representation. The House of Lords, in contrast, which has to make provision for a substantial body of independent members on the 'cross benches', is arranged round three sides of an open rectangle. In the Supreme Soviet of the USSR, the massed rows of an undivided hall indicated the compulsory unanimity of all present (see Appendix III, p. 1334).

None the less, twentieth century experience has shown that the political Right could be every bit as radical as the political Left. In addition to opposing each other, the radical elements of Left and Right shared the ambition for overthrowing the democratic consensus. In this light, the realization dawned that political forces may best be aligned round a circular track. In this scheme, not only does Left oppose Right, but Totalitarianism opposes Democracy:

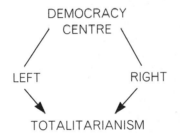

Given these considerations, it emerges that a horse-shoe or a semi-circle provides the most appropriate spatial arrangement for the multiple but competing interests within a democratic assembly. Such is the layout, not only for many national assemblies in Europe, from Warsaw to Paris, but also for the 'hémicercle' of the European Parliament at Strasbourg.[2]

On 20 September, the opening of the National Convention coincided exactly with the cannonade at Valmy which saved the Revolution from suppression from abroad. 22 September, the day when the Republic was proclaimed, was later judged to be the starting-point of the Revolutionary Calendar. [**VENDÉMIAIRE**].

In due course executive power was concentrated in two successive Committees of Public Safety—the first (April–July 1793), dominated by Danton, the second (July 1793–July 1794) by Robespierre. The Convention's independent initiatives were ended. The foreign war was prosecuted with vigour. The 'Counter-Revolution', in the Vendée and elsewhere, was mercilessly assaulted. A new

---

VENDÉMIAIRE

I N October and November 1793, France's National Convention voted to
introduce a Republican Calendar based on revolutionary principles. In
a series of decrees it was decided that the year should begin at midnight
on the autumnal equinox of 22 September, and that Year I of the
Republican era should be judged to have begun on the day of the
Proclamation of the Republic, 22 September 1792. The year was to be
divided into twelve equal months of thirty days, and each month into three
ten-day 'decades' (There were to be no more weeks, or Sundays.)

MONTHS: *Vendémiaire* (Month of Harvest); *Brumaire* (Month of Mist);
Frimaire (Month of Frost); *Nivôse* (Month of Snow); *Pluviôse* (Month of Rain);
Ventôse (Month of Wind); *Germinal* (Month of Seeds); *Floréal* (Month of
Flowers); *Prairial* (Haymaking Month); *Messidor* (Month of Reaping);
Thermidor (Month of Heat); *Fructidor* (Month of Fruits).

DAYS: 1, 11, 21, *primidi*; 2, 12, 22, *duodi*; 3, 13, 23, *tridi*; 4, 14, 24, quartidi; 5,
15, 25, *quintidi*; 6, 16, 26, *sextidi*; 7, 17, 27, *septidi*; 8, 18, 28, *octidi*; 9, 19, 29,
nonidi; 10, 20, 30, *decadi*. (See Appendix III, pp. 1288–9.)

When the system was put into operation, 1 January 1794 was officially
transformed into *Duodi* of the 2nd Decade, 12 Nivôse, Year II.

To keep in line with the natural year of 365¼ days, the calendar years
were organized into four-year groups called *franciades*; and each year was
allocated five complementary days, the *sans-culottides*. The fourth year of
each *franciade* received an extra 'leap day', the *Jour de la Révolution*.

The Republican Calendar was officially maintained for fourteen years;
but it was virtually abandoned after six. The Gregorian Calendar was in
widespread use again under the Consulate, long before it was formally
restored on 1 January 1806/11 Nivôse XIV.

Nothing was better calculated to disrupt the nation's sense of orientation than the change of calendar. Counter-revolutionaries tried to keep up
the old time. Revolutionaries tried to insist on the new. Historians have to
cope with both.

---

super-democratic Constitution providing for universal suffrage, for referenda,
and for an elected government was passed, but remained a dead letter. The
Committees of Public Safety in Paris maintained their grip on the whole country
through a network of subsidiary committees in every commune and department
in France. These committees, formed by the law of 21 March 1793 for regulating
foreigners, became instruments of unlimited dictatorial control.

The Revolution started to devour its own children. The Terror raged, consuming an ever-mounting tally of victims. Danton and his associates were denounced

and executed in April 1794, for questioning the purposes of the Terror. Robespierre, the chief terrorist, met denunciation and death on 28 July 1794, 10 Thermidor II. [**GUILLOTIN**]

The fate of the monarchy mirrored these developments. In October 1789, after a Women's March of protest to Versailles, Louis XVI had been brought with his family to their palace of the Tuileries in Paris. He was already the butt of indecent humour:

> Louis si tu veux voir
> Bâtard, cocu, putain,
> Regarde ton miroir
> La Reine et le Dauphin.

(Louis if you wish to see | Bastard, cuckold, and whore, | Look at your mirror | Your queen and your son.)[26]

In June 1791, after repudiating all concessions made since the days of the Tennis Court Oath, he had fled in disguise to the eastern frontier, only to be caught at Varennes in Champagne. Returned to Paris in disgrace, he then signed the first Constitution as prepared by the National Assembly, becoming the 'hereditary agent' of the people. In August 1792, when the Tuileries was stormed, he was arrested and 'suspended'. In September, he was deposed. On 21 January 1793 he was tried and executed as a traitor. On 16 October Marie-Antoinette suffered the same fate. The ten-year-old Dauphin, Louis XVII, was handed to plebeian foster-parents, and subsequently died from neglect and tuberculosis.

In Poland-Lithuania, events followed the same progression from constitutional reform to revolutionary terrorism. In the Constitution of 3 May 1791, in one short document of eleven clauses, all the obvious abuses of the old system, including the *liberum veto*, were abolished. The *Rzeczpospolita oboyga narodów*, the 'commonwealth of two nations' was established as a modern constitutional state. The monarchy was declared hereditary (though the King was an ageing bachelor). The bourgeoisie was admitted to the franchise previously limited to the nobility. The peasants were brought within the realm of public law, from which they had been excluded. Here was the first concrete success of peaceful reform, the first constitution of its type in Europe, formulated, passed, and published four months before its counterpart in France. It was the sort of advance which liberal reformers had been hoping for far and wide. In London, the enthusiasm of Edmund Burke knew no bounds. The Polish Constitution of Third May, Burke wrote 'is probably the most pure . . . public good which has ever been conferred on mankind':

The means were as striking to the imagination as satisfactory to the reason, and as soothing to the moral sentiments . . . Everything was kept in its place and order, but . . . everything was bettered. To add to this unheard-of conjunction of wisdom and fortune, this happy wonder, not one drop of blood was spilled, no treachery, no outrage . . . Happy people if they know how to proceed as they have begun.[27]

GUILLOTIN

DR JOSÈPHE-IGNACE GUILLOTIN (1738–1814) did not invent the guillotine. What he did was to urge France's National Assembly to adopt the humanitarian execution machine invented by his colleague Antoine Louis. The proposal was adopted in April 1792, in good time for the Jacobin Terror, thereby raising Guillotin to the status of an *eponym*—'a person after which something is (believed to be) named'.[1] The revolutionary years produced many such eponyms. Among them was Jean BIGOT, Napoleon's Minister for Religious Affairs, and the ultra-patriotic soldier Nicolas CHAUVIN, who sang 'Je suis français, je suis Chauvin'.

Many eponymous words have passed into the international vocabulary. Botany has been a fertile source, since scores of exotic plants were named after their discoverers. BEGONIA, which took its name from the botanist Michel Begon (d. 1710), was an early example, as were CAMELLIA, DAHLIA, FUCHSIA, and MAGNOLIA. The purple rock-plant AUBRIETIA was named after the French painter Claude Aubriet (1665–1742).

Physics has perpetuated the memory of its pioneers by allocating their names to universal units of measurement. The AMPERE, the metric unit of electric current, recalls André Ampère (1775–1836). Many others, from ANGSTROM to OHM, VOLT, and WATT fall within the same category.

Garments are a common source of eponyms. CARDIGAN and RAGLAN were both derived from British generals in Crimea. The fashionable LEOTARD derives from the acrobat Jules Léotard (1842–70). All wearers of PANT-ALOONS, PANTS, and PANTIES should remember the father of trouserdom, Pantaleone de' Bisognosi, who figured in the Commedia dell'Arte.

Food produced many examples. BECHAMEL sauce derives from a steward to Louis XIV. The SANDWICH, after John Montagu, 4th Earl of Sandwich (1718–92), was an eighteenth-century concoction. The nineteenth century gave rise to CHATEAUBRIAND steak, MADELEINE cake, and PAVLOVA, recalling respectively a marquis, a pastry-cook, and a prima ballerina. Smoking after dinner offers a reminder of the sometime French ambassador to Portugal, Jean Nicot (1530–1600).

Technical inventions often attracted the name of their inventors: hence SPINET and MANSARD, DIESEL, SHRAPNEL, and BIRO.

Many eponyms, however, are contested. Not all scholars accept that the painter Federigo Barocci (d. 1612) was the originator of the BAROQUE, nor that an Irish tearaway of Victorian London, Patrick Houlihan, was the original HOOLIGAN. But one thing cannot be contested: Europe's present is filled with the verbal shades of Europe's past.

Burke's welcome for the 'Polish Revolution' ought to be as well known as his denunciation of events in France. In Holland, the Leyden Gazette wrote: 'If there are miracles in this century, one has happened in Poland.'

The 'happy wonder' lasted for little more than a year. Russia was not prepared to tolerate a constitutional, let alone an independent, Poland on its doorstep. Just as Poland-Lithuania experienced the first round of revolutionary reform, it was also due to experience the first round of revolutionary war. As in France, the Polish reformers were driven from moderation to desperation. After the Constitution of 1791 was suppressed by Russian intervention and the Second Partition (see below), the national rising of 1794 took the field with still more radical proposals, only to see itself disintegrate amidst violence and terror. In France the revolutionary process was contained by its own internal reactions; in Poland it was destroyed by foreign force.

In the second phase, 1794–1804, which begins with Thermidor II, the French Revolution visibly halted in its tracks—to take breath and to take stock. Although executive instability continued, the blood-lust stopped. So, too, did the mania for legislation. (The National Convention passed 11,250 decrees in just over three years.) The revolutionaries had found a talent for war, and were absorbed in fighting their enemies. A series of political expedients were tried by politicians united only by the need to maintain order and to stem excess. After Robespierre's fall the Thermidorians ruled for 16 months. In November 1795, thanks to yet another constitution and yet another, two-tier, assembly, a five-man executive 'Directory' came into being. In September 1797 (18 Fructidor V), the Directors muzzled the assembly. In November 1799, thanks to the *coup d'État* of 18 Brumaire VIII by the Directory's most successful general, a three-man 'Consulate' was instituted, and confirmed by nation-wide plebiscite. In May 1802 the most successful general raised himself to the status of first Consul for life; in May 1804, to that of Emperor.

In the third, imperial phase, 1804–15, the Revolution found stability by locking itself to the cult of that general, the Empire's creator, Napoleon Bonaparte. The doubts and divisions which still remained in France were submerged under the titanic operations of his mission to conquer the world. Bonapartism turned revolutionary war and conquest into ends in themselves, and military requirements into an absolute priority. A pseudo-monarchy headed pseudo-democratic institutions; and an efficient centralized administration ran on a strange cocktail of legislative leftovers and bold innovation. Success or failure was handed to the gods of the battlefield. 'Success', said Napoleon, 'is the greatest orator in the world.'

Periodization arranged according to executive authority gives a slightly different result. In that case the phase of constitutional monarchy lasts from June 1789 to September 1792; the 'first Republic' from 1792 to November 1799; the dictatorship of Napoleon from '18 Brumaire' to 1815 (see Appendix III, pp. 1286–7).

The full range of revolutionary opinion became apparent in the early 1790s through the debates of the National Assembly and through the formation of political clubs.

The original constitutionalists, led by Count Honoré de Mirabeau (1749–91) and other liberal nobles such as General Lafayette, were responsible for the abolition of the absolute monarchy and of noble and clerical privilege. By the time of Mirabeau's (natural) death in April 1791, they were becoming a hard-pressed minority. They met in the club of the *Feuillants*, and after the King's flight to Varennes were left with the impossible task of delaying the demise of an unpopular monarchy. At one point Mirabeau had the idea of dedicating a monument to Louis XVI, the 'founder of French liberty'.

The Girondins took their name from a group of deputies from Bordeaux, capital of the Gironde, headed by the eloquent lawyer Pierre Vergniaud (1753–93), who came together in the Legislative Assembly. They were the centrists of the early years, willing to co-operate with the King's government but increasingly giving vent to democratic and republican sentiments. Their activities revolved round the salon of Mme Roland, and their influence reached its height in 1792, when they ran the King's last government and pioneered the transition to the Republic.

The Jacobins, in contrast, *la Société des Amis de la Liberté et l'Égalité*, were advocates of unlimited democracy, of revolutionary dictatorship and violence. They took their name from the site of their Club in a former Dominican convent on the Rue Saint-Honoré. (The Dominicans of Paris were known as 'Jacobins' because of their earlier residence on the Rue Saint-Jacques.) They formed a tiny, iron-hard clique—perhaps 3,000 persons who perfected the art of gripping the throats of 20 million. Their members ranged from the Prince de Broglie and a couple of dukes—the Duke d'Aiguillon and the young Duc de Chartres (the future King, Louis-Philippe)—to the rough-hewn Breton peasant, 'Père' Gérard. Gérard once told them, 'I had thought myself in Heaven among you, if there were not so many lawyers.' Their leaders included Georges Danton (1759–94), whom Carlyle called 'a Man from the great fire-bosom of Nature herself', Camille Desmoulins (1760–94), a firebrand journalist, who died beside him, Jean Marat (1743–93), the 'sick physician', editor of *L'Ami du Peuple*; Jérôme Pétion de Villeneuve (1756–94), sometime Mayor of Paris, Antoine Saint-Just (1767–94), known as 'the Archangel of the Terror' and as 'St John' for his servility towards Robespierre, and Robespierre himself.

Maximilien Robespierre (1758–94), the severe, the puritanical, the 'incorruptible advocate of Arras', was said to have refused a career as a judge before the Revolution rather than condemn a man to death. His power and influence assumed legendary proportions during the second Committee of Public Safety. He was the hero of the Paris mob, the devil incarnate to his opponents.

The Jacobins first surfaced in 1791, through the King's risky *politique du pire*, based on the idea of promoting his wildest opponents in the hope of taming the rest. After Pétion was appointed Mayor of Paris with the King's approval, they took an unshakeable hold on the capital's municipal government, the Commune.

Thereafter, having systematically eliminated their rivals and tamed the Convention, they decimated their own ranks until Robespierre alone remained alive. Danton's watchword was 'De l'audace, encore de l'audace, toujours de l'audace'. Saint-Just, attacking the monarchy, declared, 'One cannot reign innocently.' In proposing the redistribution of his enemies' wealth, he said: 'Happiness is a new idea in Europe.' Robespierre once asked the Convention, 'Citoyens, voulez-vous une Révolution sans révolution?' (Citizens, do you want a Revolution without revolution?) The associated Club of the Cordeliers, *la Société des Droits de l'Homme et du Citoyen*, whose membership overlapped with the Jacobins, met in a former Franciscan monastery in the Cordelier district of Paris. Their later leaders, the true *enragés* like J. R. Hébert (1757–94), were marked out for their militant atheism and the cult of reason. Hébert was executed on Robespierre's orders for 'extremism'. [GAUCHE]

If most of the Jacobins were professional lawyers and journalists, the majority of their active supporters were drawn from the anonymous proletarians of the Paris suburbs. These sansculottes contained elements that were still more radical than any of the groups and individuals that actually exercised power. They numbered among them Europe's very first communists, socialists, feminists. Organized in meeting-houses in each of the Paris 'sections', obscure formations such as the *Société Patriotique de la Section du Luxembourg* or the *Société Fraternelle des Deux Sexes du Panthéon-Français* exercised an influence that has not always been properly assessed. Indeed, in terms of revolutionary motive power they may well have been more effective than the bourgeois who are usually given the credit. They supplied many of the revolutionary commissars of the Jacobin period. They forged a lasting tradition which contested established authority in each of the 'revolutions' of the nineteenth century.[28]

Opposition to the Revolution came in many forms and from all quarters. It can be classified as political, social, ideological, and regional. Initially it focused on the royal court, where the 'ultras' led by the Count of Provence (later Louis XVIII) aimed to restore the status quo ante. They were joined by the majority of dispossessed nobles, and by the formidable array of *émigrés*, high and low. They opposed not only the republicans and Jacobins but also the constitutionalists: the court's contempt for General Lafayette, for example, knew no bounds. After 1790, when forbidden by the Pope to swear the oath of loyalty to the civil establishment, the clergy were forced either to submit or to defy. After 1792, when the Revolution took an atheistic and not merely an anticlerical turn, all Roman Catholics, and hence the great majority of the population, stood to be offended. This major source of counter-revolutionary feelings remained active until Bonaparte's Concordat with the Papacy in 1801. The peasant masses, who were given their freedom in 1789, were long thought to be among the main beneficiaries of revolution. It is now generally recognized, however, that a gulf of non-comprehension separated the peasant ethos from that of the revolutionary leaders in Paris. The peasantry soon turned against the oppressions of a republican regime which many thought worse than its predecessors.

Intellectual opposition to revolutionary ideas was not fully formulated until after the Restoration. But nothing could be more hostile than the *Considérations sur la France* (1796) of the Savoyard magistrate Josèphe de Maistre (1753–1821), who took revolutionaries to be servants of Satan. He also opposed the strand of enlightened universalism which had found its way into revolutionary thought. He wrote that he had often met Frenchmen, Italians, Germans, and Russians—'But as for Man, I've never met one in my life.' His contemporary, Antoine Rivarol (1753–1801), known as 'le Comte de Rivarol', who had written a famous discourse in praise of the French language, was forced to flee when he turned to counter-revolutionary pamphleteering. 'One does not fire guns against ideas,' he wrote.

Several French provinces remained staunchly royalist at heart, and repeatedly broke into open revolt. Royalist risings had to be suppressed even in Paris, notably on 13 Vendémiaire IV (1795). In some of the remoter departments, such as Le Gard, resistance continued right through to 1815.[29] The most determined resistance, however, was undoubtedly concentrated in the west. Popular fury had been rising there for several years, after an initially favourable reaction to the fall of the Ancien Régime. In 1792 many parishes supported the priests who refused to swear allegiance to the civil establishment. They were often rewarded by gangs of urban republicans who toured the countryside, smashing churches and assaulting the 'refractories'. In 1793 the same villages were hardest hit by the introduction of universal male conscription. They were specially offended by the exemptions that were frequently granted to the sons of republican administrators and professionals: it seemed that Catholic peasants were being ordered to die for an atheist Republic which they had never wanted in the first place. In May 1792 Danton was informed of a plot supposedly being hatched by the Marquis de la Rouairie in Brittany. The plot was nipped in the bud; but it was the precursor of two interrelated instances of mass rebellion, the rising of the Vendée and the wars of the Chouans, that were to grip the west for more than a decade.

The rising in the Vendée engendered civil warfare that lasted for nearly three years. It broke out in March 1793 at St Florent-sur-Loire, but soon spread throughout the villages of the *bocage*. It was started by peasants such as J. Cathelineau, a hawker from Pin-en-Mauges, and J. N. Stofflet, a gamekeeper from Monlévrier, who had refused the draft; but it soon passed under the command of the local gentry—the Marquis de Bonchamps, the Marquis de Lescure, 'Monsieur Henri' de La Rochejacquelin, General Gigot d'Elbée, the Prince de Talmont. The 'Royal and Catholic Army of Saints' was armed with scythes, pitchforks, and fowling-pieces. It marched under a white standard spangled with lilies and the device of 'Vive Louis XVII'. Its fighters wore a scapulary round their necks, together with the badge of the Sacred Heart and Cross in flames. They fought twenty-one pitched battles, triumphed on the bloody field of Cholet, captured Angers, laid siege to Nantes, and broke into the provinces of Maine and Anjou. Their desperate courage was caught in the orders of 'Monsieur Henri':

Si j'avance, suivez-moi! Si je recule, tuez-moi! Si je meurs, vengez-moi!'
(If I advance, follow me! If I retreat, kill me! If I die, avenge me!)

In October 1793 the Vendeans embarked on their most ambitious and (as it proved) their most foolhardy gambit. Some 30,000 armed men, followed by several hundred thousand civilians of all ages, crossed the Loire and wended their way towards the coast of Normandy. Their destination was the little port of Granville, where they had been led to believe that a British fleet and an army of *émigrés* would be waiting to greet them. But they were cruelly deceived: Granville was sealed. Rochejacquelin's attacks were beaten off; there was no sign of British ships. So the retreat began. As the columns straggled back along 120 miles of winter roads, they fell prey to every form of misfortune and violence. Refused entry to the towns, they had to fight every inch of the way. Fifteen thousand died in the streets of Le Mans. They perished of cold and hunger. They were mercilessly robbed, raped, and hunted down by roving Republican forces. Those who reached the Loire found the bridges blockaded and the boats burned. Their fighters were split up and killed. The defenceless civilians could then be massacred with impunity. The end came at Savenay near Nantes, two days before Christmas. General Westermann, a client of Danton, reported to the Convention:

The Vendée is no more . . . I have buried it in the woods and marshes of Savenay . . . According to your orders, I have trampled their children beneath our horses' feet; I have massacred their women, so they will no longer give birth to brigands. I do not have a single prisoner to reproach me. I have exterminated them all. The roads are sown with corpses. At Savenay, brigands are arriving all the time claiming to surrender, and we are shooting them non-stop . . . Mercy is not a revolutionary sentiment.[30]

The retreat of the Vendeans is known as 'la Virée de Galerne'. In the sheer scale of loss of life, it was not dissimilar to Napoleon's retreat from Moscow.

By then the heartland of the Vendée was being harried by General Kléber and a Republican army transferred from the Rhine. Throughout 1794 the 'infernal columns' of the Republic wreaked hateful revenge on the rebel villages. Tens of thousands were shot, guillotined, burned in their barns or their churches. At the harbour of Rochefort, several thousand non-juror priests were slowly starved to death on the decks of prison hulks. At Angers, thousands of prisoners were shot out of hand. At Nantes, thousands more were systematically drowned. Later, to contain resistance, a huge military fortress was planted in the centre of the troubled region with a garrison of 20,000. (First named Napoléon-Vendée when completed in 1808, it was renamed Bourbon-Vendée in 1815, and is now called Roche-sur-Yon.) Nearby, in the open fields, stands a cross to the memory of the last stand of the last commander of the Vendeans, the Chevalier de la Charette de la Contrie, who, expiring before the firing squad at Nantes, uttered one last cry of 'Vive le Roi!'. [**NOYADES**]

Thanks to the propaganda of the victorious Republic, 'Vendéeism' has been widely identified with peasant ignorance, religious superstition, and the rule of tyrannical priests. This picture is unfair. It is true that some of the Vendeans were

NOYADES

IN the spring of 1794, French Republican officers in Nantes had so many rebels from the Vendée to kill that they didn't know how to do it. They had unleashed the 'infernal columns'; they had starved and massacred their captives; and they had been shooting batches of prisoners by the thousand. But it was not enough. They then hit on the idea of drowning. Nantes was an Atlantic slave port; and a fleet of large, shallow hulks was to hand. By sinking a loaded hulk in the river at night, and then refloating it, they devised an efficient and inconspicuous system of reusable death chambers. These were the terrible *noyades*. Necessity proved the mother of invention in the technology of death.[1]

A century and a half later, Nazi officers in occupied Poland faced a similar problem. They had so many Jews to kill that they couldn't cope. They had unleashed the *Einsatzgruppen*; they had starved Jews in crowded ghettos: at Sobibór, they had driven their victims round the countryside in railway wagons packed with quicklime.[2] But it was not enough. Then they hit on gassing. Initial trials using carbon monoxide in mobile vans proved unsatisfactory. But early in 1941, experiments using capsules of Zyklon-B in sealed chambers, together with advice from the leading German designers of crematoria,[3] promised a vast increase in capacity. Within a year, the Nazi SS was able to embark on a programme of industrialized genocide in purpose-built facilities.[4]

An eye-witness from the death-camp at Treblinka would later describe the process for interrogators at the Nuremberg Tribunal:

[RAJZMAN] Transports arrived there every day; sometimes three, four or five trains filled exclusively with Jews. Immediately after their arrival, the people had to line up on the platform—men, women and children separately. They were forced to strip immediately . . . under the lashes of German whips. Then they were obliged to walk naked through the street to the gas chambers. *What did the Germans call that street?*
Himmelfahrtstrasse [the way to heaven].
Please tell us, how long did a person live after arrival?
The whole process of undressing and the walk down to the gas chambers lasted for the men eight to ten minutes, and for the women some fifteen minutes, because the women had to have their hair shaved off. . . .
Please tell us, what was the subsequent aspect of the station of Treblinka?
The Commander of the camp, Kurt Franz, built a first-class railroad station with signboards. The barracks where the clothing was stored had signs reading 'Restaurant', 'Ticket Office', 'Telegraph', and so forth . . .
A kind of make-believe station? . . . And tell us, how did the Germans behave when killing their victims?
They brought an aged woman with her [pregnant] daughter to this building. Several Germans came to watch the delivery . . . the grandmother begged to

be killed. But of course, the newborn baby was killed first, then the child's mother, and finally the grandmother. . . .
Tell us, witness, how many persons were exterminated in the camp on an average, daily.
On an average, from ten to twelve thousand persons daily.[5]

A view might conceivably be entertained that the Nazi gas-chambers reflected a 'humane approach', akin to that of a well-regulated abattoir. If the sub-humans had to die, it was better that they die quickly rather than in protracted agony. In practice, there is no evidence that Nazi logic knew any such considerations. The operation of the Nazi death-camps was characterised by totally heartless efficiency and gratuitous bestiality.

The 'death-factory' at Jasenovac in Croatia was operated by the Fascist Ustaša from 1942 to 1945. It became the object of intense propaganda in post-war Yugoslavia; and the official count of '700,000 victims, mainly Serbs' has since been called into question.[6] But there can be little doubt about the total absence at Jasenovac both of mercy and of modern technology. Sensational stories abound. But shooting or gassing might have been regarded as a blessed reprieve from death by mass clubbings, by immersion in boiling cauldrons, or by decapitation with handsaws.

driven *in extremis* to forms of mystical martyrdom, and also to excesses of their own. But their rebellion was not irrational. They had been subjected to many real assaults and humiliations, including the fashion for public mockery of religion. In any other country of Europe, their devotion to their traditional way of life would have been widely admired. Their moral integrity was well illustrated when the dying Bonchamps pardoned all his 5,000 prisoners. Their tragedy was to have taken up arms during the phase of extreme Jacobin fanaticism. Their enemies did not hesitate to employ genocidal measures, and then to cover the victims with calumny. Napoleon called them 'giants'. It has taken the best part of 200 years for France to come to terms with this terrible story of *populicide*, of *génocide franco-français.*[31]

The 'Chouanneries' of 1793–1801 shared many of the basic motives of the Vendée rising; and they overlapped with it geographically. On the other hand, they were much more widespread, embracing the greater part of Brittany, Normandy, and Anjou; and, since they took to guerrilla warfare, they were much more prolonged. The Chouans took their name from the *chat-huant* or 'catcalling' which was the favourite means of communication between peasant lads in the woods. Their first recognized leader, Jean Cottereau, a ranger from St Ouen-des-Toits near Le Mans, took the sobriquet of 'Jean Chouan'. To the Republican authorities they were simply 'brigands'; but they sustained three lengthy campaigns against all the forces which the Republic could muster.

The first campaign (October 1793 to April 1795) was sparked off by the passage of the Vendeans through western Normandy, where 5,000 Chouans joined their ranks. It was eventually suspended by a truce whereby the Directory ordered an end to the prosecution of non-juror priests. The second campaign (June 1795 to April 1797) began with a daring raid on a republican arsenal at Pont-de-Buis in Brittany. It promised to become a war of regular armies when a royalist force was landed from British ships on the nearby Quiberon peninsula. But General Hoche proved more than equal to his task: after annihilating the landing force, he gradually pacified the countryside by combining religious toleration with ruthless military measures. The third campaign (September 1797 to July 1801) was provoked by the Directory's decision to annul the electoral results in all the *départements* of the north and west where monarchist candidates had swept the board. It was marked by the renewed persecution of non-juror priests, and by a series of murderous local conflicts between Chouans and 'Bleus'. In 1799, under Georges Cadoudal (1771–1804) of Kerleano in Morbihan, the insurgents were able to co-ordinate their activities and briefly to occupy several cities, including Redon, Le Mans, Nantes, and St Brieuc. But their successes came to an end with the Consulship of Napoleon, who followed a similar strategy to that of Hoche. General hostilities ceased after the religious settlement introduced by the Concordat of 1801; but local bands of rebels continued to roam the backwoods until Cadoudal was caught and executed in 1804.[32] [CHOUAN]

No accurate account of the 'Counter-Revolution' can fail to take note of the rapidly shifting bench-marks. Constitutionalists who led the Revolution in 1789

CHOUAN

FOR most of the nineteenth and twentieth centuries, the local politics of the western region of the Département of the Sarthe, beyond Le Mans, was dominated by a solid right-wing, anti-republican tradition. It stood in marked contrast to the region to the east, dominated by an equally solid left-wing, anti-clerical and pro-republican block, *la zone rouge*, which in the 1960s was still voting Communist. The pattern could not be attributed to social, landholding, or religious factors. According to France's leading rural historian, it can only be explained by the lingering trauma of the revolt of the Chouans of 1793–9. This is all the more remarkable since the *cahiers de doléances* of 1789 show that the most militant protests against tithe and clergy emanated from the west, not the east. The conduct of the revolutionary Republic was apparently so extreme that it converted its original supporters into implacable enemies. Electoral behaviour in the Fifth Republic was still being influenced by the mistakes of the First. 'It is impossible', wrote Le Roy Ladurie, 'to explain the present by the present.'[1] If this is true of one department of France, how much more does it apply to Europe as a whole?

were already counted among the 'reactionaries' by 1792. One of the most determined waves of resistance, which sparked insurrections in Lyons, Marseilles, Bordeaux, and elsewhere in June 1793, was launched in support of the Girondins, who until recently had been the Jacobins' closest partners. Even the sansculottes, who won the right to a vote and to cheap bread, turned in time against their Jacobin patrons. Bonaparte, who was seen to have betrayed both the Bourbons and the Republic, attracted the hatred of both 'Whites' and 'Reds'. The explosion of an 'infernal machine' in Paris on 24 December 1800, which aimed to assassinate Bonaparte on his way to the opera, was the work of royalist *émigrés*, but it was used to justify the execution of Jacobin and republican opponents. Any unsuccessful opponent could be condemned as 'reactionary'. [ROUGE]

Violence is the one feature of the Revolution which its critics have always found most repulsive. It took many forms. Mob rule and lynching occurred from the start on 14 July 1789, when the heads of the Bastille's governor, du Launay, and of fellow victims were paraded round Paris on pikes. Wanton attacks against the persons and property of priests and nobles were commonplace. There were random massacres, such as the slaughter in the Paris prisons in September 1792; there were many assassinations, such as that of Marat; and there were terrible revenge killings, such as were perpetrated in Marseilles after the fall of the Jacobins. None of these events was unique. But two aspects of revolutionary violence had no precedent: one was the sheer scale of military casualties that arose from the use of mass conscript armies; the other was the cold-blooded reign of political terror unleashed by the Jacobins. In the realm of mass psychology, both these phenomena were connected to the vast energies which sent a despondent and bankrupt nation on a twenty-year spree of enthusiastic conquest. They were both avoidable.

The Reign of Terror was conceived by the (second) Committee of Public Safety and carried out as a deliberate instrument of policy. It was not confined to the destruction of the Revolution's active opponents. It was designed to create such a climate of fear and uncertainty that the very thought of opposition would be paralysed. Its twin weapons were to be found on the one hand in the Law of Suspects of Prairial and, on the other, in the Revolutionary Tribunal. The former required all citizens to denounce anyone who might be suspected of harbouring ill will towards the authorities. Linked to the Law of Maximum Prices, which turned the whole economic sphere into a source of potential crime, it exposed every French family to the possibility of sudden, baseless catastrophe. The latter law, which rarely issued anything but a summary death sentence, fed the guillotine with a constant supply of innocents. The total tally in Paris ran into tens of thousands. In the provinces, it was backed by military force. It is a sobering thought to realize that for every victim of the Terror killed in Paris there were ten who were killed in the Vendèe.

Yet the ethos of the Terror does not cease to amaze. It produced a climate of spies, informers, and unlimited suspicion. It produced the scenes of crowded tumbrils carting the condemned through hate-filled streets, of men and women facing death, alternately serene or wretchedly broken, of the ghoulish *tricoteuses*

ROUGE

THE tricolour of 1789 was made up from the white of France's royal standard and the red and blue ensign of Paris. It was destined to become the flag of the French Republic. The same colours, arranged horizontally, were adopted by the Batavian Republic in 1794, in succession to the similar but much older flag of the United Provinces.

But it was the red flag which the revolutionaries soon adopted. In Roman times, the red flag had signified war. Red was the colour of blood, fire, and magic. By tradition its modern career began in 1791, when the crowd attacking the Tuileries picked up a blood-soaked royal standard. Henceforth, 'red' and 'white' were the accepted colour codes for revolution and counter-revolution. Stendhal used the variant of *Le Rouge et le Noir* for his depiction of the struggle between the radicals and the clerical reaction under the Restoration.

The colour-coding of political movements has deep connotations. Red was taken up by Garibaldi's 'Thousand', by socialists, and most fervently by the Communists. Green, the colour of the land (and once of the Merovingians), was adopted by peasant parties, by Irish patriots, and much later by the environmentalists. 'True blue', once a Spanish epithet for aristocratic blood, suited British Tories and other conservatives. The Unionists preferred [**ORANGE**] and the Liberals yellow. The Nazis, from the SA uniforms, were first known as 'Browns'. Later, from the uniform of the SS, they were associated with black, which for others was the traditional European colour for evil, death, and piracy. In their concentration camps, they forced prisoners to wear colour patches according to the scheme of Red = political; green = criminal; black = antisocial; pink = homosexual; violet = Jehovah's Witness; brown = gypsy; yellow = Jew.[1]

Ambiguities abound. In Catholic symbolism, red stands for martyrdom and cardinals, white for purity and chastity, blue for hope and for the Virgin Mary, and black for grief, the Dominicans, and the Jesuits. In the age of racial consciousness and political correctness, 'black is beautiful'; 'whites' are as unwelcome as 'dead males', 'redskins' have to be changed to 'cardinals'; and the favourite metaphor is the rainbow.

knitting away beside the guillotine as severed heads dropped into the nearby basket. Through the dire extremity of the circumstances, it produced a large repertoire of grim humour. Danton, when asked for his name and abode, replied: 'I am Danton, a name tolerably well known. My abode is Le Néant [Annihilation]; but I shall live in the Pantheon of History.' Desmoulins, when asked for his age, said, 'My age is that of the *bon sansculotte* Jesus: a fatal age for revolutionaries.' He was 38. Louis XVI on the scaffold started an unfinished speech: 'I die innocent, and I forgive my enemies,' he began, 'I wish that my blood . . .' Danton, in the same straits, said, 'Danton, no weakness'; then: 'Executioner, show them my head; it's worth showing.' Robespierre, who had earlier taken a pistol shot through the jaw, could only shriek incoherently.

Many of the perpetrators of revolutionary violence, like Robespierre, met a violent death themselves. Westermann, the 'Butcher of the Vendée', died on the same scaffold as Danton. The Directory initiated trials which punished some of the more notorious sadists.

Legislative reform followed the same broad trends as the Revolution itself, passing through constitutional, republican, and imperial phases. The effect was immensely confusing. The institutions of the old order were abolished, and replaced by abortive or short-lived expedients, which the Empire then overturned or modified for its own purposes. The eventual offspring often consisted of strange hybrid creatures, neither *ancien* fish nor revolutionary fowl. Hereditary nobility, for example, was abolished in 1789, together with the other social estates. Under the Republic, all people were reduced to the one rank, *citoyen* or *citoyenne* (citizen). Bonaparte introduced the idea of advancement by merit, *la carrière ouverte aux talents*; and the Empire adopted a hierarchical system of new ranks and titles, an aristocracy of princes, dukes, and counts, based on state service. The *Légion d'Honneur* (1802) was Napoleon's own idea for an order of merit.

In religion, the civil establishment of the clergy (1790) turned all priests into salaried state officials, and sequestrated all Church property. The Republic persecuted the non-jurors, disestablished the constitutional Church, de-christianized public life by inventing its own secular Calendar and its own secular cults, such as the Worship of the Supreme Being in 1794 or the Theophilanthropy of 1796. Bonaparte, after humiliating the Papacy, officially reintroduced Roman Catholicism. The Concordat of July 1801 recognized it as the religion of most French people, whilst leaving Church appointments, salaries, and property at the disposition of the State. Pope Pius VII attended the Emperor's coronation at Notre Dame on 2 December 1804, but was too slow when Bonaparte placed the crown on his own head. Rightly or wrongly, Jean Bigot de Préamenau (1747–1825), Napoleon's minister of cults, gave his name to religious intolerance. [GUILLOTIN]

In education, the former monopoly of Church schools was broken. Under the Empire, the system of centralized state schooling based on the Ministry in Paris and on *lycées* in all major towns gave French life one of its most characteristic institutions.

In regional government, the old provinces were destroyed, together with their historic privileges and assemblies. The 83 smaller *départements*, or districts, of 1790, usually named after rivers or mountain ranges, were retained under the Empire and greatly increased in number. Their internal organization was remodelled by Napoleon, who set up the office of departmental Prefect.

In the economic sphere, the Revolutionary regimes worked their way through a long series of experiments. In 1790 the Constituent Assembly, having abolished the old revenues, was forced to invent a number of new land, income, and property taxes. It financed the nationalization of Church property by issuing the famous *assignats* or state bonds, which steadily deteriorated into a highly devalued form of paper money. In 1793 the Jacobins adopted an economic programme designed to meet the demands of a mass army, of the Terror, and of their own social ideology. Their doctrine of 'a single will' was applied to economics no less than politics, and produced a state-run armaments industry; rigorous price control through the Law of the Maximum, and the cancellation of all peasant debts. After 1795 the Directory looked increasingly to plunder and tribute as a substitute for economic policy. Napoleon added the outlook of an old-fashioned Colbertian mercantilist. Grandiose public projects were made possible by the priority given to the regular inward flow of cash.

Both the Republic and the Empire were opposed to free trade, and the long struggle with the British over the control of commercial shipping began during the first Coalition. In November 1806 Napoleon's Berlin Decree formally declared the British Isles to be in a state of blockade. 'I wish', he said, 'to conquer the sea by the power of the land.' The British response came in the Order in Council of 1807 forbidding all neutrals to trade with France, except under licence. This in turn provoked Napoleon's Milan Decree of December 1807, threatening dire retribution on anyone following the British rules. The resultant Continental System was enforced in all countries occupied by the French, and was made a condition for Napoleon's co-operation with other countries such as Denmark, Sweden, and Russia. It gave Europe its first taste of a united economic community; but it also generated much of the resentment which undermined the French position.

Taxation endured many vicissitudes. The old hated taxes and exemptions disappeared. The constitutional regime aimed at equitable and universal taxation for all; whilst the Jacobins excised the requirement whereby the franchise was limited to taxpayers. The Directory moved back towards a democracy of property-owners. Under the Empire, although centralized land taxes were more efficiently run, the tax burden, especially on the peasants, was enormous.

The torrent of legislation in the 1790s caused a log-jam which could only be sorted out by systematic review and codification. Work started by the Convention in 1792 culminated in the towering Civil Code (1804), soon to be renamed the *Code Napoléon*. The Code replaced the 360 local codes in force in 1789, and drove a middle path between the Roman law of the south and the customary law of the north, between the egalitarian principles of 1789 and the authoritarian, propertied reaction of the Directory. (Common law lost its place in the civil sphere.) The universal rights of citizenship, and of equality before the law, were confirmed. In family law, civil marriage and divorce were retained; but the equal division of property was limited to male heirs. Married women were judged 'incapable' of making contracts. This Code has profoundly influenced the social development of at least thirty countries.

In the long run the Revolution probably had its greatest impact in the realm of pure ideas. Much of this detailed legislation was due for further revision after 1815, or was applicable only in France. But many of the basic ideas, and ideals, remained in existence for all the world to contemplate, even where they found no immediate form of practical expression. Republicanism, for example, was defeated in France long before the restoration of the monarchy in 1814–15. But it remained alive to feed a tradition which reasserted itself in 1848–51, and took permanent hold of the country after 1871. Since monarchy was still the predominant mode of government in nineteenth-century Europe, the memory and example of the first French Republic of 1792–9 could not fail to offer powerful attractions.

The idea of revolution itself was irrepressible, even where particular revolutionary movements were repressed. Prior to 1789 most Europeans held a static view of the political and social order, where change could at best be limited and gradual. After 1789 everyone knew that the world could be turned upside down, that determined men could mobilize the social forces and psychological motors which underlay the surface of the most tranquil society. This realization aroused widespread panic and, in some quarters, hope. It also gave a powerful spur to the growth of the social sciences. Henceforth, revolution was to be distinguished from all lesser forms of rebellion, *jacquerie*, or *putsch*.

Counter-revolution, too, took flight. Henceforth, revolutionary creeds were to be balanced by their opposite numbers. Burke's *Reflections* (1790) in the English-speaking world and Goethe's in the German world were to have lasting influence. The theocentric *Considérations* (1796) of De Maistre, who saw the Revolution as the wrath of God, were to have a long progeny, stretching through the generations to Alexander Solzhenitsyn. All of them would share Burke's instinctive reaction against 'the antagonist world of madness, discord, vice, confusion, and unavailing sorrow'.

The concept of human rights, if not invented by the French revolutionaries, was certainly given its strongest modern impetus. The Declaration of the Rights of Man and the Citizen carried forward constructs contained in England's Bill of Rights of 1689 and the fundamental declarations surrounding the independence of the USA. Battered and bruised, it survived as a lasting monument to the early idealism of the Revolution. Passed on 26 August 1789, 'in the presence and under the auspices of the Supreme Being', it consisted of a Preamble, in the style of its American predecessor, and of seventeen Articles listing Mankind's 'natural, inalienable and sacred rights':

I. Men are born and remain free and equal in rights. Social distinctions can only be founded on public utility.
II. The purpose of every political association is the preservation of the natural and imprescriptible rights of men. These rights are liberty, property, and safety from, and resistance to, oppression.
III. The principle of all sovereignty resides in the nation. No body of men, and no individual, can exercise authority which does not emanate directly therefrom.
IV. Liberty consists in the ability to do anything which does not harm others.

    V. The Law can only forbid actions which are injurious to society . . .

    VI. The Law is the expression of the General Will . . . It should be the same for all, whether to protect or to punish.

    VII. No man can be accused, arrested, or detained except in those instances which are determined by law.

    VIII. The Law should only establish punishments which are strictly necessary. No person should be punished by retrospective legislation.

    IX. Every man [is] presumed innocent till found guilty . . .

    X. No person should be troubled for his opinions, even religious ones, so long as their manifestation does not threaten public order.

    XI. The free communication of thoughts and opinions is one of men's most precious rights. Every citizen, therefore, can write, speak, and publish freely, saving only the need to account for abuses defined by law.

    XII. A public force is required to guarantee the [above] rights. It is instituted for the benefit of all, not for the use of those to whom it is entrusted.

    XIII. Public taxation is indispensable for the upkeep of the forces and the administration. It should be divided among all citizens without distinction, according to their abilities.

    XIV. Citizens . . . have the right to approve the purposes, levels, and extent of taxation.

    XV. Society has the right to hold every public servant to account.

    XVI. Any society in which rights are not guaranteed nor powers separated does not have a constitution.

    XVII. Property being a sacred and inviolable right, no person can be deprived of it, except by public necessity, legal process, and just compensation.[33]

Social convention held that the 'Rights of Man' automatically subsumed the rights of women. But several bold souls, including Cordorcet, disagreed, arguing that women had simply been neglected. In due course the original Declaration was joined by new ideas, notably about human rights in the social and economic sphere. Article XXI of the revised Declaration of June 1793 stated:

Public assistance is a sacred obligation [*dette*]. Society owes subsistence to unfortunate citizens, whether in finding work for them, or in assuring the means of survival of those incapable of working.[34]

Slavery was outlawed in 1794. Religious toleration was guaranteed. [**FEMME**]

Naturally, the French version of human rights was greatly circumscribed by the dictatorial practices both of the Republic and of the Empire. After 1815 it continued to struggle against a strong, centralized, bureaucratic state. But its influence across Europe was far greater than the Anglo-Saxon version partly because French culture in general was more influential at this time and also because French soldiers had carried it all over the Continent in their knapsacks. Not for the first time did the agents of repression scatter the seeds of another liberation.

Geographical variations in the patterns of revolution are often missed. Paris, though dominant, was not France. In Toulon, which was occupied by an Anglo-Spanish naval force in 1793, the port and the city were the scene of bitter fighting between royalists and republicans. At Marseilles, Bordeaux, and Lyons also, extended civil wars were fought, with the Red Terror of the Jacobins being matched by the 'White Terror' of 1794–5. In many areas royalist sentiment would probably have commanded majority support if only it could have been effectively organized. In the event the revolutionaries carried the day, partly through their superior and centralized military capacity and partly through the outbreak of war, which effectively tied the defence of the Revolution to the defence of France. Nowhere is this coincidence of patriotic and revolutionary fervour more evident than in the *Chant de Guerre de l'Armée du Rhin* (1792), the 'Battle-Song of the Army of the Rhine' alias *La Marseillaise*, which was destined, eighty years later, to become the national anthem of the French Republic. [**STRASSBURG**]

The concept of the modern state, in the sense of a centralized administration applying common laws uniformly to all citizens over the whole territory, received an enormous boost. Its elements had been growing for centuries, and not only in France. But ferocious levelling by the Jacobins and the energetic dictatorship of the Empire made greater inroads into French particularism in twenty years than absolute government had done in so many decades. What is more, by sweeping aside the entire museum of antiquated state structures in Europe, from the Holy Roman Empire to the Republic of Venice, the revolutionary armies cleared much of the ground for the administrative reforms of the nineteenth century. Again, nationalism was not created whole by the French Revolution (see Chapter X); but both the ideology of the nation and the consciousness of nationality were immensely strengthened in all those countries where the old order was over-turned.

Militarism—the belief that military force is a valid and effective instrument of policy—inevitably gained ground. Eighteenth-century warfare possessed rather limited objectives; and the greatest of its practitioners won more territory through diplomacy than on the battlefield. The French revolutionary armies, in contrast, came together after 1792 at a juncture when mass conscript armies, a war economy, and the enthusiasm of a nation in arms, could deliver results on a completely different scale. Although their eventual defeat may also have demon-strated the limitations of militarism, their seemingly invincible progress for almost a quarter of a century showed how much war could accomplish. This was the legacy of Lazare Carnot (1753–1823), the military engineer and administrator who was hailed the 'organizer of victory' under the Committees of Public Safety, the Directory, the Empire, and above all, Bonaparte. 'War is a violent condition,' wrote Carnot; 'one should make it *à l'outrance* or go home.'

Revolutionary War, 1792–1815

The prospect that revolution would provoke first civil and then international war was present from the start. Despite the formal renunciation of wars of conquest by France's Constituent Assembly in May 1790, there was not a monarch who could listen in comfort to the cries of 'Mort aux Tyrans', 'Death to the Tyrants', which echoed ever more loudly from the streets of Paris. Equally, there was not a revolutionary who slept easily amidst the hostile plots of the *émigrés* and the

FEMME

OLYMPE DE GOUGES (1748–93), a butcher's daughter from Montauban, came to Paris as a young widow. Born Marie Gauzes, she refused to accept her married name, and invented her pen-name when she aspired to a literary career. She was writing plays and political pamphlets from the earliest days of the Revolution. Incensed by the exclusion of women from the Constitutional Assembly, she published *Les Droits de la Femme et du Citoyen* (1791) as a counterblast to the Rights of Man:

I. Woman is born free, and remains equal to man in rights . . .
II. The aim of all political associations is to preserve the natural and inalienable rights of Woman and Man. These are: liberty, ownership, safety, and resistance to oppression.
III. The principle of sovereignty resides in essence in the Nation, which is nothing other than the conjunction of Woman and Man.
IV. . . . The exercise of Woman's natural rights has no limit other than the tyranny of Man's opposing them.
V. The laws of nature and reason forbid all actions harmful to society . . .
VI. The law must be the expression of the General Will; all citizens, female and male, should concur in its formation. All citizens, being equal in its eyes, must be equally eligible for all honours, positions, and posts . . . with no distinction other than those of their virtues and talents.
VII. . . . Women obey the rigours of the law as men do.
VIII. No one may be punished except by virtue of a law which was promulgated prior to the crime, and which is applicable to women.
IX. Any woman found guilty will be dealt with in the full rigour of the law.
X. No one should be persecuted for fundamental opinions. Woman has the right to mount the scaffold; she must equally have the right to mount the rostrum.
XI. . . . Any citizen may freely say 'I am the mother of your child' without any barbarous prejudice forcing her to hide the truth.
XII. The guarantee of women's rights entails absolute service . . .
XIII. The contributions of Woman and Man to the upkeep of public services are equal.
XIV. Female and male citizens have the same right to ascertain the need for taxes.
XV. All women, united by their contributions with all men, have the right to demand an account of their administration from all public officials.
XVI. Any society in which rights are not guaranteed, and powers not separated, has no constitution.
XVII. Property is shared or divided equally by both sexes . . .[1]

This text, the founding charter of feminism, remained little more than a curiosity. After publicly daring to oppose Robespierre's Terror, its author met the guillotine.

Anne-Josèphe Thérouingue de Méricourt (1758–1817), 'the Amazon of Liberty', came to Paris from Liège to advocate a more militant brand of feminism. She held that women should fight for the Revolution, to which end she organized a ferocious legion of female militia. 'Needles and spindles', she wrote in *Les Françaises devenues libres* (1791), 'are not the only weapons which we know how to handle.'

Mary Wollstonecraft (1759–97) came to Paris from London, where in her *Vindication of the Rights of Man* (1791) she had attacked Burke's *Reflections*. Her *Vindication of the Rights of Women* (1792) enlarged on the rationalist position of Olympe de Gouges. She was married to the political writer William Godwin, and died giving birth to a daughter who grew up to be the wife of the poet Shelley.

The views of these radical feminist pioneers evoked little sympathy in leading revolutionary circles. Rousseau, who had set the tone, proposed a gender role combining the self-denying heroism of Roman matrons with a femininity that would encourage men to be more manly. The likes of de Gouges, Thérouangue de Méricourt, Mme Roland, Charlotte Corday, or Cécile Renaud no more impressed Robespierre than the March of the Women to Versailles had impressed the King. In June 1793, women were expressly excluded from citizenship.[2]

monarchists. The wilful flaunting of authority created a general climate of unease. In 1791 the Pope openly condemned the Revolution. The challenge was taken up on the one hand by the Girondin J.-P. Brissot, who called for a people's crusade against 'the despots', and on the other by the Emperor Leopold, Marie Antoinette's brother, who, after meeting the Prussian and Saxon monarchs at Pillnitz, called for a league of princes 'to restore the honour of his Most Christian Majesty'.

The rulers of Russia, Austria, Sweden, Prussia, Saxony, and Spain were all in favour of active intervention. Their plans were strongly encouraged by Catherine the Great, who expressed the view that 'the affairs of France were the concern of all crowned heads'. Their ringleader, Gustavus III, masterminded the ill-starred flight to Varennes. He was already receiving subsidies from Russia when he was assassinated at a masked ball in Stockholm on 16 March 1792. Yet their greatest obstacle lay in the ambiguous position of Louis XVI, whose public pronouncements contradicted his secret correspondence, and who was simultaneously opposing and co-operating with the Revolution. In the event, the divided counsels of Louis's would-be rescuers caused sufficient delay for the revolutionaries to take the initiative into their own hands. In April 1792, with the King's acquiescence, they declared war on Austria and Prussia. [**STRASSBURG**]

The descent into war must be traced to one of the most dire decisions of Louis XVI's *politique du pire*. In the spring of 1792 it so happened that the court party and the extreme radicals were both bending the King's ear in favour of war. The Queen wanted war so that the Revolution could be defeated by her brother's international

STRASSBURG

O N 24 April 1792 news reached the French army at Strasbourg that war had been declared against the First Coalition. That night, during revels in the house of the Mayor of Strasbourg, a Captain of Engineers from the Jura, Claude-Josèphe Rouget de Lisle (1760–1836), improvised both the words and the music of 'Le Chant de Guerre pour l'Armeé du Rhin' (The Battle Song for the Army of the Rhine). Its rousing stanzas would soon be sung wherever the revolutionary cause was in danger:

> Allons, enfants de la Patrie!
> Le jour de gloire est arrivé.
> Contre nous de la tyrannie
> L'étendard sanglant est levé. [*bis*]
> Entendez-vous dans les campagnes
> Mugir ces féroces soldats?
> Ils viennent jusque dans nos bras
> Égorger nos fils et nos compagnes
> Aux armes, Citoyens! Formez vos bataillons!
> Marchons, marchons!
> Qu'un sang impur abreuve nos sillons.

(Forward, children of the Fatherland! | The day of glory has arrived. | Tyranny's bloody standard has been raised against us. | [*Repeat*] Do you hear those ferocious soldiers bellowing in the countryside? | They are coming right into our embrace | To slaughter our sons and daughters. | To arms, citizens! Form up in your battalions! | Come on, let's march! | For poisoned blood is coursing through our furrows.)

To be sung in Strasbourg, the song had to be translated into German as the *Strassburgerlied*. By the summer, as *La Strasbourgeoise*, it had reached the Midi. On the evening of 22 June it was sung at a banquet in Marseilles by a medical student from Montpellier, François Miroir. It proved so seductive that it accompanied a battalion of volunteers from Marseilles all the way to Paris. When they entered the capital on 30 July, singing their song, it was immediately called 'The Hymn of the Massilians', or simply *La Marseillaise*. There is no doubt about its subsequent career. But there is some doubt whether that battalion of volunteers from the Midi could actually have spoken French.[1]

La Marseillaise quickened the step of the revolutionary armies as they marched round Europe. It was translated and sung in many languages, from Italian to Polish. It was formally adopted by a decree of the Convention on 26 Messidor III (14 July 1795), thereby initiating the custom of national as opposed to royal anthems (like 'God Save the King'). *La Marseillaise*, Napoleon used to say, was the Republic's greatest general.

As for Rouget de Lisle, he was arrested in 1793 for royalist sympathies; survived; and died in poverty. His monument stands in Lons-le-Saunier.

rescue force. The radicals wanted war so that the Brissotin faction might exploit a military triumph. So Louis took them at their word, spurning the advice both of his more moderate Girondin ministers and of the Jacobins. On 20 April 1792 ill-prepared French troops were ordered to cross the frontier and to invade the Austrian Netherlands. The results of Louis's gamble were not as any of its promoters had hoped. There was no immediate military confrontation. The Queen's rescue force was slow to materialize. The Brissot faction did not gain any lasting advantage, being overtaken during the summer by the Jacobins. Europe gradually lost all hope of a peaceful settlement. The King himself lost all credibility: his deposition was in progress before the first major battle took place at Valmy in September.

Russia alone showed no hesitation. The Empress Catherine was cramped by her Turkish war, which did not end until the Treaty of Jassy in January 1792. But after that she immediately turned her gaze to the West. Her contribution to the anti-revolutionary crusade was to be directed against the Polish Constitution, 'which she could not for one minute accept':

The Polish Constitution was in no sense Jacobinical. But to Catherine there was not, in spring 1791, much to choose between revolutionary Poland and revolutionary France . . . [She] sensed the revolutionary undercurrent in Poland . . . and she crushed the Revolution where she could most easily reach it.[35]

Summoning a bogus confederation of traitorous Polish notables to St Petersburg, and pressing the King of Prussia to drop his Polish sympathies or else, she ordered the Russian army to march at precisely the time that Louis XVI was ordering the French army to do the same. Thus the revolutionary wars began simultaneously in East and West. Twenty years were to pass before the initiators, France and Russia, were to meet in the decisive trial of strength.

The Russo-Polish War of 1792–3, therefore, was an integral part of the revolutionary panorama. It largely determined the balance of forces which were later to be waiting for Napoleon in the East. The outcome was not a foregone conclusion. Commanded by the King's nephew Józef Poniatowski, and by the veteran of the American wars Tadeusz Kościuszko, founder of West Point Academy, the fledgeling Polish army acquitted itself with distinction. A masterly victory was achieved at Zielence in Podolia on 18 June 1792, one month after Russian forces had crossed into Polish Ukraine. The Polish position continued to look tenable until surrounded by the Prussians from the rear. In the end, the matter was resolved by the King's capitulation rather than by force of arms. Joining the Russian-backed Confederation of Targowica to end the shedding of blood, Stanisław-August accepted the terms of the Second Partition, signed in St Petersburg on 4 January 1793, and undertook to put them into effect. Six months later the last Sejm of the Republic's history met at Grodno in Lithuania, under the shadow of Russian guns. Representatives of the nobility, threatened with sequestration, gave legal form to their country's humiliation. The Constitution of Third May, duly reviled, was annulled. Russia annexed a swathe of territory half the size of France. Prussia took Danzig (which promptly rebelled). [TOR]

TOR

THE *Brandenburger Tor* was built as one of the nineteen gates of Berlin's old walled city in 1793, the year that the Kingdom of Prussia entered the revolutionary wars. Its elegant Doric colonnade was modelled on the Propyleia in Athens. Surmounted by its *Auriga*—a group of giant bronze figures portraying 'the Chariot of Victory'—it was destined to preside over Germany's modern tragedies and triumphs. It saw Napoleon's grand entry into Berlin in 1806, and all the other military parades which crashed and boomed their way along the avenue of Unter den Linden for King, Kaiser, President, and Führer. In 1871, it welcomed the victorious troops returning from the Franco-Prussian War to a city still described as 'insanitary' and 'irreligious'—an event which spurred the first rebuilding of Berlin as Germany's imperial capital. In 1933, it hosted Chancellor Hitler. During the Battle for Berlin in April–May 1945, it stood on the dividing-line between the rival Byelorussian and Ukrainian 'Fronts' commanded by Marshals Zhukov and Koniev. On the day when two Russian sergeants from Zhukov's army planted a red banner atop the nearby Reichstag, its ruins received a red-and-white pennant from soldiers of the 1st Polish Army fighting under Koniev. In 1953, it towered over the fatal protest march of East German workers. From August 1961 until November 1989, it formed the captive centrepiece of The Berlin Wall.

Across the centuries, the *Auriga* has been seen as an unwitting weathercock of the political climate. In 1807 it was carried off to Paris. Restored in 1814, it was re-erected with the Chariot facing west. In 1945 it was destroyed only to be replaced in 1953 with new sculptures cast from the original moulds. This time the Communist authorities allegedly set the Chariot facing east. At all events, as the third rebuilding of Berlin began in 1991, in preparation for the government of a re-united Germany, the *Auriga* was firmly facing westwards. Its stance marked the condition, not only of relations between the two halves of Berlin, but of the two halves of Europe.[1]

Symbolic gestures in bronze or stone can be found in many places. In Zagreb, for example, the statue of the Croatian champion, General Jelacič, was first erected in the late 19th century with his accusing finger pointing unmistakably towards Budapest. In 1991, it was re-aligned to point towards Belgrade. In 1993, reports stated that it had been turned once more to point towards Knin, the capital of the self-styled Serbian Republic of Krajina.

In the West, the revolutionary wars grew into a titanic complex of conflicts engulfing almost the whole Continent. The campaign of 1792 gave France a thorough scare which spurred the revolutionary leaders first to depose the King and then to organize an open-ended war effort. The initial French incursion into Austrian territory was soon reversed by the advance of Prussian and Austrian columns into France. But the vigorous political manifesto of the Duke of Brunswick was not accompanied by vigorous military action. The Prussians moved so slowly that Goethe, who was travelling with the detachment from Weimar, had time to set up his experiments on the psychological effects of cannonballs. They were still in the Forest of Argonne, within twenty miles of the frontier, when, at the Battle of Valmy on 20 September 1792, they were repulsed by the famous 'revolutionary cannonade'. After that, war fed off the Revolution, and the Revolution fed off a successful war. Before the year was out the revolutionary armies were back in the Netherlands and had seized Savoy. They marched on and on and on, for nearly twenty years.

The progress of the revolutionary wars is often described in terms of the three great coalitions mounted against France in 1793–6, 1799–1801, and 1805–14. This is misleading, partly because each of the coalitions tended rapidly to disintegrate, and partly because fighting often continued in the intervals between the coalitions. The interests of the Continental powers which supplied the backbone of the coalitions' forces—Austria, Prussia, and Russia—did not always coincide with those of the coalitions' principal organizers, the British, and their great war minister, William Pitt the Younger (1759–1806). According to varying criteria, there were not just three but five, six, or seven coalitions. Britain's coalition partners repeatedly suffered invasion and occupation; the British, on their impregnable islands, did not. The conflict assumed important economic as well as military dimensions. On several occasions it spread beyond the confines of Europe, and showed signs of global, intercontinental strategy.

The First Coalition, 1793–6, demonstrated how difficult it was to hold the allies together. Russia made little contribution, being preoccupied with the digestion of Poland. Prussia dropped out in 1795 for the same reason. Austria was left exposed to devastating French attacks both in the Netherlands and in northern Italy. In 1795–6 Spain changed sides, and Britain was left alone, with only the navy staving off disaster. The French, whilst destroying the Counter-Revolution at home, began to manufacture revolutionary regimes abroad. The Batavian Republic (1794) in the Dutch Netherlands was the first of many. The French also began to field youthful generals of astonishing skill and energies. Of these, the first was General Lazare Hoche (1769–97), who conquered the Rhine, crushed the Chouans, and once set out to capture Ireland.

In the East, despite the Second Partition, Poland-Lithuania still refused to surrender. Early in 1794 Tadeusz Kościuszko returned from exile, and on 24 March, on the old Market Square of Cracow, read out the Act of Insurrection, 'for national self-rule . . . and for the general liberty'. In May he issued a manifesto granting

emancipation to the serfs. The victory of his peasant scythemen over a professional Russian army at Racławice (4 April) echoed the Vendeans' triumph at
Cholet. Yet in Warsaw and Wilno the mob went on the rampage. Popular courts
sentenced bishops, Russian agents, and confederates to death. Here at last was
open revolution: the monarchs had to act. Warsaw was besieged by Prussians in
the west. Two Russian armies advanced from the east. On 10 October, at
Maciejowice, a wounded Kościuszko fell from his horse, and was (wrongly)
reported as crying '*Finis Poloniae*'. Suvorov stormed Warsaw's eastern suburb of
Praga, and put the inhabitants to the sword. He sent a three-word report to St
Petersburg—HURRAH, PRAGA, SUVOROV, and received a three-word reply—
BRAVO FIELDMARSHAL, CATHERINE. [**METRYKA**]

On this occasion the Third Partition proceeded on the assumption that the
Poles and their Republic no longer existed; so, no consent was sought.
The Prussians took Mazovia and Warsaw and called it 'New South Prussia'. The
Austrians took another huge slice and called it 'New Galicia'. The Russians con-
tented themselves with a slice the size of England. The final treaty, signed in St
Petersburg, was followed by a secret protocol:

In view of the necessity to abolish everything which could revive the memory of the existence of the Kingdom of Poland . . . The high contracting parties are agreed . . . never to
include in their titles the name or designation of the Kingdom of Poland, which shall
remain suppressed as from the present and forever.[36]

By that time, with Bonaparte already on the march, no one in Western Europe
could spare a thought for the injustices of Poland's fate. Russia had established its
reputation as the most unbending opponent of revolution, the champion of
monarchy. The Poles had been cast in their role as the most obdurate opponents
of sound government. They were to supply the largest of numerous foreign contingents who fought in the French ranks throughout the revolutionary wars.

The Italian campaign of 1796–7 was launched by the Directory against the possessions of an Austria already isolated by the collapse of its coalition partners. It
was notable for the international début of General Bonaparte, one year younger
than Hoche. In the course of a few weeks the ragged French army on the frontier
of the Maritime Alps was transformed into an invincible force. 'Soldiers of the
Army of Italy', the youngster told them, 'I will lead you into the most fertile plains
in the world. You will find honour, glory and riches. Will you be wanting in
courage?' Within twelve months the whole of northern Italy was overrun.
Bonaparte's tactical mastery, first demonstrated on 10 May 1796 at the Bridge of
Lodi, delivered him strategic domination. Milan was liberated; Mantua was
reduced by siege; Austrian resistance was broken at Rivoli. The road was opened
into Carinthia, and Vienna itself was awaiting attack. [**GRILLENSTEIN**]

Bonaparte showed an interest in all matters contiguous to war. Revolts and
mutinies were repressed with swift and purposeful brutality. On entering the territory of the Duke of Parma, he demanded the instant surrender of all art treasures. This policy was to make the Louvre pre-eminent among art collections. On

METRYKA

IN 1795, after suppressing the Republic of Poland-Lithuania, the Russian army carried off the state archives of the conquered countries to St Petersburg. Their haul included the *Metryka Koronna* or 'Crown Register' of the Kingdom of Poland, containing copies of all acts, statutes, and charters issued by the royal chancery since the Middle Ages, together with similar collections from the Grand Duchy of Lithuania and the Duchy of Mazovia. Since the catalogues and indexes were also taken, no one in Warsaw knew exactly what was lost. Polish historians could not study the history of their country in the way that Prussians or Russians were doing throughout the nineteenth Century. The impression was created abroad that Poland's place in European history was as marginal as its role in the present.

Attempts to identify, to reconstitute, and, if possible, to recover Poland's lost archives have been in progress for 200 years. Some parts were returned after 1815, and more after the Treaty of Riga in 1921. Other parts were pieced together from copies scattered far and wide. The Soviet Army reappropriated everything of interest in 1945, and only released selected items in the 1960s. No independent researchers were ever allowed to search for themselves unsupervised through the Tsarist or Soviet archives.[1] [**LOOT**]

A detailed account of the fate of the Lithuanian Register, the *Metryka Litewska*, which dates from 1440, was only established by an American scholar in the 1980s. Working on an authorized survey of the Soviet archives for the benefit of Western scholars, and armed with a partial copy of the catalogues made in Warsaw by the invading Swedes in the seventeenth century, she painstakingly traced most of the constituent collections which Russian archivists had repeatedly relabelled, reassigned, and relocated.[2] Yet two centuries after it was stolen, the main part of the Lithuanian Register remained in St Petersburg. Appeals by the governments of Lithuania and Belarus' passed unheeded as the Russian Federation laid formal claim to all documents relating to 'the history of Russia' in the archives of the former RSFSR 'regardless of their place of preservation and their form of ownership'.[3]

Western historians have been trained to stress the principle of consulting documentary sources. This is sound advice wherever the documentary sources are accessible. They forget a still more important principle which the Russian authorities have well understood for centuries—namely, whoever controls the documents can also control their use and interpretation.

GRILLENSTEIN

IN 1797 a son was born to a family of peasant weavers in the village of Grillenstein, parish of Gmünd, in Austria's Waldviertel district. The name of the family is not given, but their life cycle has been reconstructed from the parish records (see Appendix III, p. 1292). In 1817, at the age of twenty, the son married a woman six years older than himself, and by December at the latest the newly-weds had a baby son of their own. At that point the household appeared to constitute a perfect example of the classic 'stem-family' as posited by Le Play—a patriarchal, three-generational unit headed by the 51-year-old grandfather. [**GROSSENMEER**]

Very soon, however, the picture changed. In the following year (1818), the grandfather went into retirement (*Ausnahm*), taking his wife and two unmarried teenage daughters with him and handing the headship of the household to his son. He continued to live somewhere on the farm for a further twelve years until, following his wife's death, he himself remarried and left.

From 1818, therefore, the household bore very little resemblance to the stem-family model. For a dozen years the son took charge, free of parental authority but with his retired parents in the background. His family was increased by the births of three more children, but afflicted by the deaths of his elder son (1821), his mother (1826), and his younger, newborn daughter (1827). After the departure of his father and unmarried sisters (1830), he could only cope with the losses by taking in a series of weavers and their families plus a number of servants. By 1841, when his eldest surviving child reached twenty-one, the household contained three separate, unrelated families—the head's family and the families of two older weavers, who had just replaced two single women and their illegitimate sons. One can imagine the troubles.[1]

This one example was chosen by historians who wished to demonstrate the danger of generalizing from standard sociological models whilst observing the dynamic changes which occur over time. The family life cycle, which reveals the ebb and flow of fortune, is a vital concept for understanding peasant life throughout Europe and throughout the ages.

entering into the negotiations preceding the Peace of Campo Formio (October 1797), he insisted on dictating the terms without reference to Paris. This sort of conduct was to give him the upper hand over the politicians at home.

The Egyptian campaign of 1798–9 was designed by the Directory to disrupt Britain's colonial and commercial supremacy. By establishing a French presence in the Middle East, it would have weakened British links with India and prepared the way for French domination of the whole Mediterranean. It began with the capture of Malta, and the landing of 40,000 troops at Alexandria. Despite the military defeat of the ruling Mamelukes, it was undermined by Admiral Nelson's destruction of the French fleet at Aboukir Bay (1799) and by a strategic alliance between Russia and the Ottomans. It was the predecessor of similarly abortive schemes to outflank the British in the Caribbean (1802), in America by the knockdown sale of Louisiana (1803), and even in Australia (1804). Nothing came to fruition, since the Royal Navy proved as invincible at sea as Bonaparte was on land. Bonaparte left Egypt in August 1799 to execute the Coup of 18 Brumaire, and to take the reins of power in France.

Nabulione Buonaparte (1769–1821)—like Hitler and Stalin—was a foreigner in the land which he came to dominate. He was born at Ajaccio in Corsica, one year after Louis XV had bought the island from Genoa. When he was sent to France for military education as a boy cadet, he had no personal wealth, no social connections, no competent command of the French language. He grew into a small, surly, assertive young man, with more than a hint of the native *vendetta* not far beneath his sallow skin. But France was 'a rebel mare', waiting to be tamed:

> O Corse à cheveux plats! Que la France était belle
> Au grand soleil de messidor!
> C'était une cavale indomptable et rebelle
> Sans frein d'acier ni rênes d'or.

(Oh, lank-haired Corsican! How fair was France | In the summer sun of Messidor! | She was a mare, rebellious and untameable, | With no steel bridle, nor reins of gold.)[37]

The 'lank-haired Corsican' owed everything to the Revolution, which had made him a general of artillery at the age of 24. He had personally watched the shambles at the storming of the Tuileries. But he then took French leave to help his brothers in Corsica, and might well have stayed if the family had not been driven out by the local troubles. In 1794, having served at Toulon with Robespierre's brother, he was briefly arrested by the Thermidorians, and applied in vain for a commission with the Ottoman Sultan. Yet in 1795 he was on hand in Paris during the royalist riots of October, when he saved the Convention with the timely 'whiff of grapeshot'.

After that, the once-suspect artilleryman could do no wrong. In 1796 he was given command of the ragged Army of Italy. He turned himself with equal speed into the master of his political superiors, correctly sensing that the fate of the government in Paris rested on good news from the battle-front. His support was openly courted by the faltering Directors, and his absence in Egypt during 1798–9 only strengthened his hand. The coup of 18 Brumaire, which made him the virtual dictator of France, was carried off without a hitch. It was the sort of feat which could only have been pulled off by a total outsider. From then on, through the consulships and the Empire, through the sea of blood of the forty battles which he claimed to have fought in self-defence, Napoleon never looked back. Surrounded by similar upstart marshals—Berthier, Masséna, Macdonald, Murat, Soult, and

Ney—and by similar brilliant ministers—Talleyrand, Gaudin, Fouché, and Clarke—he rode the French mare unerringly.

And when France had been bridled by its Corsican rider, he saddled her by the rules of Corsican kinship with the whole tribe of Bonapartes: with Joseph, King of Naples and Spain; with Lucien, Prince of Canino; with Louis, King of Holland; with Jerome, King of Westphalia; with Elisa, Pauline, and Caroline—duchess, princess, and queen. He only stumbled on his own dynastic path. His marriage with Joséphine de Beauharnais, a Créole from Martinique and the widow of an executed nobleman, produced no heir and ended in divorce. His Polish mistress, Maria Walewska, produced a son who was not recognized. His second wife, Marie-Louise of Austria, gave birth in 1811 to Napoleon II, King of Rome. By that time the clouds were gathering over 'the Sun of Messidor'. The first ruler of all Europe was already considering the invasion of Russia. According to Tocqueville, Napoleon was 'as great as a man can be without virtue'. [CORSICA]

The Second Coalition, 1799–1801, was made possible by a new Tsar, Paul I, who was eager to play a more active role. Suvorov's Russian army recovered most of Austrian Italy before Bonaparte reappeared to restore the balance. But Paul I was assassinated; the Continental allies lost heart; and again Britain was left facing France alone. The allies' Treaty of Lunéville (1801) was matched by Britain's Peace of Amiens (1802).

After the collapse of the second Coalition, Bonaparte could take stock from a position of strength. He made further conquests in Italy, including Piedmont, Parma, and Piacenza. He sent an unsuccessful expedition to crush the revolt of Haiti; he invaded Germany, provoking the demise of the Holy Roman Empire: and he began collecting the Armée de l'Angleterre at Boulogne. He even began to scheme once again for the strategic encirclement of his principal adversaries. On 30 March 1805 he wrote to the Shah of Persia:

Bonaparte, Emperor of the French to Feth Ali, Shah of the Persians, Greeting!

I have reason to believe that the Jinn who preside over the destinies of states wish me to support the efforts which you are making to uphold the strength of your empire.

Persia is the noblest country in Asia, France the premier empire of the West . . .

But there also exist upon the earth, empires . . . [where] men are by birth restless, greedy, and envious. Tired of their deserts, the Russians trespass on the fairest parts of the Ottoman realm. The English, who are cast on an island that is not worth the smallest province of your empire . . . are establishing a Power in India, that grows more redoubtable every day. Those are the states to watch and fear . . .[38]

Napoleon's high regard for the countries of Asia was not entirely insincere. During the Egyptian campaign, he had once said, 'Europe is a molehill. All great empires and revolutions have been in the Orient'.[39] But European affairs soon intervened.

The Third Coalition, 1805–14, Pitt's final diplomatic masterpiece, was organized with the intention of a decisive showdown. Yet the showdown was slow in coming. At sea, the British victory off Cape Trafalgar (21 October 1805) ensured the total naval supremacy which would deny the French any chance of invading Britain. On land, in contrast, Napoleon utterly destroyed each of his enemies in turn. In 1805 Austerlitz ensured the total defeat of Austria and the retreat of Russia; in 1806 Jena and Auerstadt ensured the total crushing of Prussia; in 1807 Eylau and Friedland ensured the total withdrawal of all Russian troops. Within 18 months Vienna, Berlin, and Warsaw were all occupied. By the time that Napoleon made his peace with Russia and Prussia, aboard a raft on the River Niemen at Tilsit (July 1807), Britain stood alone for the third time. [**SLAVKOV**]

SLAVKOV

S LAVKOV, 'place of fame', is a small town 15 miles east of Brno in Moravia. On 2 December 1805, under its German name of Austerlitz, it provided the setting for the 'Battle of the Three Emperors', the most dramatic of Napoleon's victories.

Napoleon, falling back before the advance of the combined forces of Austria and Russia, had drawn them on. Three allied columns marched against the French right in the dawn mists. 'Whilst they march to turn my right,' Napoleon had proclaimed, 'they present me with their flank.'

Marshal Davout, whose men had just covered the 90 miles from Vienna in 48 hours, held off the main attack throughout the day against four times their number. At 10 a.m. the mist lifted, and the famous 'soleil d'Austerlitz' began to shine. The French seized the commanding height of the Pratzen plateau, from which they could rake all sectors of the field with cannon and cut the enemy forces in two. After the French Imperial Guard repulsed their Russian counterparts, the retreat began. By breaking the ice on the lakes in the valley, the French artillery cut the main line of escape. Amidst 20,000 dead from 150,000, and as many prisoners, Napoleon savoured his finest hour. 'Il vous suffira de dire', he told the survivors, 'j'étais à Austerlitz.' (It will be enough for you to say: 'I was at Austerlitz'.)[1]

The battle was painted by Gros, Vernet, Callet, Gérard. It was exalted in poetry. But no description matches that of Leo Tolstoy in Book III of *War and Peace*:

When the sun broke through . . . and the fields and mist were aglow with dazzling light . . . he drew the glove from his shapely white hand, made a signal with it to his marshal, and ordered the action to begin.[2]

Nowadays Austerlitz, like Waterloo, is a railway station, serving France's south-west. Military historians are less concerned to recount the plans of the generals than the emotions and experiences of the soldiers.[3] None the less, it was the great battles which decided who was to be the master of all sorts of other things which constitute the past.

Britain's activities, however, were more than enough to keep the wars alive. Through the Royal Navy's blockade, Britain was waging commercial war against all the countries recruited to Napoleon's Continental System (see below). What is more, by sending an army to northern Spain in 1808, thereby opposing Napoleon's recent takeovers both of Spain and Portugal, she internationalized the civil wars of the Iberian Peninsula, creating an 'Iron Duke' from the young Arthur Wellesley, and an important diversion that Napoleon could never muster the time or resources to subdue.

One by one, and with painful delays, each of the members of the moribund Coalition began to revive. In 1808 parts of Italy joined Spain in rebelling against French rule. In 1809 Austria repudiated its agreement with Napoleon, only to be comprehensively crushed once more at Wagram (1809), within sight of Vienna. In 1810–12 Prussia started to stir, initially through secret, underground resistance. In the same period Russia grew tired of the French connection, fearful of Napoleon's plans for Poland-Lithuania, and irked, like everyone else, by the strictures of the Continental System. Napoleon was approaching the peak of his power. [**VIOLETS**]

In the twenty years from 1792 to 1812, the map of Europe, and the system of states, was widely remodelled. The French Revolutionary armies introduced territorial and political changes of three sorts.

VIOLETS

IN one year, 1810, Napoleon ordered 162 bottles of his favourite neroli-based cologne water from the parfumier Chardin. In a famous letter, he once begged Josephine not to bathe for two weeks before they met, so that he could enjoy all her natural aromas. When she died, he planted violets on her grave, and wore a locket made from them for the rest of his life.[1] He was an unabashed *odomane*.

Smell, 'the mute sense', 'the olfactory dimension', was present throughout history, though much ignored by historians.[2] According to one theory, the male sex drive is spurred by the female odour of 'herring-brine', and by the urge to swim back into the primordial ocean.[3] Natural perfumes, such as ambergris, castoreum, civet, and musk, formed one of the most expensive sectors of the luxury trade from ancient times. The Middle Ages were filled with perfumed rushes and with incense, by the 165 petals of the rosary, the Virgin's flower. The French Revolution was pervaded by the whiff of the open sewers of Paris, the twentieth century by the stench of corpses in the trenches and the camps, the age of modernism by industrial pollution and by the arrival of the first artificial aldehyde, Chanel No. 5, in 1922.

First, and at various times, they vastly extended the territory of France itself, by directly annexing large parts of the Netherlands, Germany, Switzerland, and Italy. By 1810 the 83 departments of the Republic had been increased to the 130 departments of the Empire, with a population of 44 million. To the series of Aisne, Allier, Aude . . . were added such novelties as 'Bouches de l'Elbe' (Hamburg), 'Simplon', and 'Tibre'. The Frenchness of the French Empire was diminishing with every annexation. (See Map p. 1291.)

Secondly, a whole panoply of new states was erected, each closely tied to France and each possessing its own model constitution and French-style administration. These states included the Batavian Republic (1795–1804), transformed into the Kingdom of Holland (1804–10), the Kingdom of Etruria (1801–5), the Confederation of the Rhine (1806–13), the Grand Duchy of Berg (1806–13), the Kingdom of Westphalia (1807–13), the Grand Duchy of Warsaw (1806–13), five Italian republics, and the so-called Kingdom of (northern) Italy (1805–14). [ILLYRIA]

Thirdly, after Napoleon's later conquests, a number of old-established states were allowed to survive, but with severely modified frontiers and with tightly controlled internal arrangements. These included Austria, Prussia, Spain, Naples, and Portugal.

The only parts of Europe to escape the revolutionary remodelling of Napoleon's enlightened despotism were the British Isles, Scandinavia, Russia, and the Ottoman domains. With those exceptions, the whole of Europe was subject to radical changes that swept away the traditional order, giving its people, however briefly, a taste for something entirely different. [BOUBOULINA]

The degree to which the local population either welcomed or initiated the changes is a matter of some complexity. In some places they obviously rejoiced. There were deep-rooted republican elements in Holland and in Switzerland, for example, who had sought French intervention in advance; and there were good reasons why certain cities such as Brussels, Milan, or Warsaw should have manifested great enthusiasm. Elsewhere, the reception of the French must be graded from mixed to hostile. Napoleon was strong on the rhetoric of liberation but weak on its practical application. The benefits of emancipation for the serfs, and of republican rule, had to be weighed against the burdens of increased taxation and of merciless conscription. In several countries, and in Spain in particular, the arrival of the French provoked vicious civil strife. Many people in Europe who supported the Revolution in theory found it to be immensely oppressive in practice.

The Napoleonic Netherlands led the way with France's foreign experiments. The Batavian Republic (1794) gave way for a Kingdom of Holland (1806) under Louis Bonaparte, before the whole of the Netherlands were directly annexed to the French Empire. Revolutionary ideas about the rights of nations affected Walloons, Flemings, and Dutch alike. They were due to surface in subsequent decades.

Napoleonic Italy took form over several years in the course of complicated swings of fortune. Bonaparte's initial arrangements of 1797 were overthrown by

ILLYRIA

Like many of the ephemeral creations of the Napoleonic Era, the Illyrian Provinces of 1809–13 continued to exert their spell long after their formal disbandment. Attached to the French-run Kingdom of Italy, they included a long section of the Adriatic coast from Trieste to Dubrovnik as well as important parts of Carinthia, Carniola, Istria, Slovenia, Slavonia, and Kraina. Their French governor resided in the capital city of Ljubljana (Laibach). The brief interval of freedom from Habsburg rule was sufficient to fire both a long-lasting 'Illyrist' movement among the Slovenes and Croats, and a long-running Italian irredentist campaign for the return of Trieste and Fiume (Rijeka). (See Appendix III, p. 1231)

After 1815, the special character of the region was underlined when Habsburg rule was restored within a separate 'Kingdom of Croatia-Slavonia'. This experiment came to an end in its turn amidst the troubles of 1848-9, when the Ban of Croatia, General Jelacic, took his army into battle against the forces of the Hungarian National Rising. With some delay Croatia was rewarded with extensive autonomy within the Habsburgs' Kingdom of Hungary.

'Illyrism' first gained momentum in the 1830s as a movement to protect all South Slavs in the Habsburg dominions from the mounting effects of foreign cultural domination.[1] It was strengthened by an attempt to impose Magyar as the official language of Croatia-Slavonia. From the mid-19th century, however, the national revival of the Slovenes based on Ljubljana, steadily diverged from that of the Croats based on Zagreb (Agram). The Slovenes, who found themselves after 1867 in the Austrian sector of the Dual Monarchy, cultivated and systematized their own distinct Slovenian language, which had possessed a fixed literary form since the Reformation.[2] The Croat leaders, in contrast, chose to join a group of Serbian cultural activists, and with them to create a common literary language known as 'Serbo-Croat'. They based it on the so-called 'shtokavsky' dialect, which uses *sto* as opposed to *ca* or *kaj* as the word for 'what'. At the same time, they fortified their separate national identity by emphasizing their attachment to Roman Catholicism (as opposed to Serbian Orthodoxy) and by writing Serbo-Croat in the Latin alphabet.[3] By 1918, both Slovenes and Croats had emerged as discrete but allied nationalities within the South Slav Movement. They both played a prominent role in the formation of the Yugoslav state[4] (see p. 979). [CRAVATE] [MAKEDON] [SARAJEVO]

After 1945, though the reconstructed Federation of Yugoslavia was completely subordinated to Tito's communists, Slovenia and Croatia aspired to autonomous status within the Federation alongside Serbia, Montenegro, Bosnia, and Macedonia. Slovenia, the smallest and wealthiest component, possessed a per capita GNP similar to that of Austria. In 1992, it led the field in gaining its independence. Croatia was less fortunate. Despite the support of the European Union, its declaration of sovereignty precipitated first a war with the Serbian-led rump of the Yugoslav Federation and then the violent fragmentation of Bosnia (see p. 1124). Only time will tell whether the fledgeling republics of Slovenia and Croatia will prove any less ephemeral than the long-forgotten Illyrian Provinces to which they had once belonged.

the Second Coalition, but were reinstated and extended in subsequent campaigns. Five local republics formed in 1797–9—the Cisalpine in Lombardy, the Ligurian in Genoa, the Parthenopaean in Naples, and the Republics of Lucca and Rome— were flagships of the revolutionary order. They were joined by other transient entities such as the Principality of Piombino and the Kingdom of Etruria, until merged after 1805 either into the French Empire or into the Kingdom of Naples or into the Kingdom of (northern) Italy created for Napoleon's stepson, Eugène de Beauharnais. The abolition of the Papal States, and the maltreatment of the Popes, was specially shocking to contemporary opinion, particularly in Catholic countries. Pius VI (1775–99), who condemned the Rights of Man, was deprived of his temporal powers, and died in French custody at Valence. Pius VII (1800–23), who had once declared that Christianity was not incompatible with democracy, ended up for five years under French arrest for excommunicating all (unnamed) 'robbers of Peter's patrimony'. The Napoleonic experience greatly enhanced national sentiments in Italy, whilst preparing a sharp confrontation between frightened conservatives and a new generation of liberals.

Germany, like Italy, was built and unbuilt several times during the revolutionary wars. In the 1790s major changes were afoot owing to Prussian gains from the last two Partitions of Poland. Under Frederick-William II (r. 1786–97), Prussia had even risked an alliance with Poland-Lithuania. But the logic of Russian power soon brought him back into line. By 1795, Berlin had acquired both Danzig and Warsaw, and found itself ruling over a population that was 40 per cent Slav and Catholic, with a very large number of Jews. One-fifth of Prussia's population were of immigrant origin. The brief reign in Warsaw of E. T. A. Hoffmann (1776–1822), did not pass without trace. The author of the *Phantasiestücke* (1814) or 'Fantastic Tales', as chief administrator of New South Prussia, was personally responsible for inventing the frequently fantastic German surnames for Europe's largest Jewish community. Had Prussia been allowed to develop without interruption, it is hard to imagine what course German history might have taken. As it was, old Prussia was overwhelmed by Napoleon, and the new Prussia, which reappeared in 1815 on a reconstructed territorial basis was a very different beast.

Napoleonic Germany emerged in consequence of determined French efforts to break up the Holy Roman Empire in the period after the Second Coalition. The

BOUBOULINA

IN 1801 a young widow from the island of Hydra near Athens married Demetrios Bouboulis, a shipowner from the neighbouring island of Spetses. Her father had been arrested by the Ottomans after the Russian-backed rebellion of Count Orlov, and she herself was to be connected with the secret *Philiki Etaireia* or 'Company of Friends' based in the Greek suburb of Phanari in Istanbul. She came from a group of islands where Albanian was spoken, but where the Orthodox Church gave a sense of Greek identity. When Bouboulis was murdered by pirates, Laskarina Bouboulina (1771–1825) became a wealthy businesswoman in her own right, and a prominent patron of the Greek national movement.[1]

During the war of independence, Bouboulina plunged into the fray in person. She built a battleship, the *Agamemnon*, which took part in many actions. Dubbed 'the Captain', she fearlessly rode her white horse onto the battlefields, dispensing bullets, food, and encouragement. At the siege of Naphlion, she led the force which blockaded the castle and massacred the Ottoman garrison. But she has not escaped criticism. Unsympathetic historians have suggested that this idol of bourgeois nationalism ordered Turkish and Jewish women to be slaughtered for their jewellery, and that she melted down the cannons of Naphplion for profit.

Greece's national struggle produced many stories of women's patriotism. The village of Souli in Epirus is specially venerated. After their menfolk were taken prisoner by the Ottomans in 1801, the women and children of the village gathered on the edge of a cliff to perform the dance of Zallongos. Each of the women led the swirling circle in turn, before leaping over the cliff to her death, till none were left. Modern Greek schoolgirls re-enact the dance, leaping off the stage onto a pile of mattresses, and singing the Zallongos song:

> Fish can't live on land,
> And flowers can't blossom on sand;
> The women of Souli can't understand
> Life without freedom.

National heroines like Bouboulina have many counterparts. Her Polish contemporary, Emilia Plater (1806–31), a noblewoman, died fighting the Russians disguised as a man. Such figures are now seen as a diversion from the main feminist concerns.

Bouboulina did not live to see Greek Independence. She was killed, not by Turks, but by an irate neighbour, who pushed a musket through his window during a row and shot her through the heart.

process began in 1803, with the secularization of the ecclesiastical states, and the reallocation of 112 other imperial cities and principalities to the benefit of Baden, Prussia, Württemberg, and Bavaria. In 1804 350 imperial knights lost their independent status, whilst several of the more important princes upgraded their titles. Francis of Habsburg assumed the rank of Emperor of Austria, whilst his colleagues of Bavaria and Württemberg declared themselves kings. In 1806 sixteen princes of southern and western Germany formed a Confederation of the Rhine which was duty-bound to provide Napoleon with military assistance. Their leader, the *Fürstenprimas*, was Karl Theodor, Freiherr von Dalberg (1744–1817), Archbishop of Mainz and Grand Duke of Frankfurt. Since all these developments contravened the constitution of the Holy Roman Empire, the Empire's standing was damaged beyond repair. Napoleon found no difficulty in arranging its final liquidation in August 1806. In that same year, following Jena, Prussia collapsed, the King retiring to Königsberg. Saxony joined the Confederation of the Rhine. In 1807, after the Peace of Tilsit, a Kingdom of Westphalia was carved out of Prussia's western possessions for Napoleon's brother Jérôme; and Danzig was turned into a Free City. The rest of Prussia, including Berlin, remained under French occupation. Apart from the Nuremberg bookseller J. W. Palm, shot by the French for his pamphlet 'On Germany's Deepest Humiliation', and the Prussian major of hussars, Ferdinand von Schill, who led his regiment in a premature revolt in 1809, there were few martyrs.

But the Napoleonic experience, by destroying so many older particularisms, prepared the ground for Germany's unified national identity. Napoleon had commented cynically that Germany was always in the process of 'becoming, not being'. But he did much to change matters. The University of Berlin, founded in 1810 during the French occupation, nourished the new thinking. Its first rector was the philosopher J. G. Fichte (1762–1814), author of the patriotic *Reden an die deutsche Nation* (1808). The 'War of Liberation' of 1813–14 proved specially exhilarating. The words of a song, 'Was ist das deutsche Vaterland?', written by the poet and historian Ernst Moritz Arndt (1769–1860), were on everyone's lips. Arndt, whose *Geist der Zeit* (1806) had first called for resistance, supposedly answered his own question: 'Germany is there wherever the German language resounds and sings hymns to God in Heaven.' In those same years the exiled Prussian Baron von Stein, who had visited St Petersburg and denounced Napoleon as 'the enemy of mankind', was inventing a precocious scheme for the federal union of the German peoples. 'Germany must assert itself', he wrote, 'in its strategic position between France and Russia.' Here was the kernel of the concepts both of *Gross Deutschland* and of *Mitteleuropa*. [CAUCASIA]

Napoleonic Spain descended into a quagmire of disorder. The original French expedition of 1807 merely aimed to punish Portugal for its British ties. But anger was aroused in Spain by the presence of French garrisons and by the imposition of Napoleon's brother Joseph on the Spanish throne. From then, the tribulations of the French party multiplied. With the Portuguese entrenched behind the lines of Torres Vedras and the British sallying forth from their base at Corunna,

CAUCASIA

THE notion that all the peoples of Europe belonged to one white race which originated in the Caucasus can be traced to a learned professor at Göttingen, Johann Friedrich Blumenbach (1752–1840). Though patently false, it was destined to have a long career.

Europeans brought up on the Bible and the classics had long been conditioned to look to the Caucasus for stories of their origins. The account of the Flood in the Book of Genesis states that 'the ark rested . . . upon the mountains of Ararat' (Genesis 8: 4)—Ararat being a biblical name for Armenia. The legends of the Golden Fleece and of Prometheus were both Caucasian. But the ethnic and racial composition of the peoples of the Caucasus is complicated in the extreme (see Appendix III, p. 1298). There is no reason whatsoever to look to them as a source of racial purity. None of the more prominent sub-types from the Caucasus, such as the so-called Armenoid group, are well represented elsewhere in Europe.

Blumenbach, a pioneer of comparative anatomy, and especially of craniometry or 'skull analysis', is generally credited with the invention of the 'five-race scheme'. It emerged from his study of an extensive skull collection that was published over a thirty-year period starting in 1798;[1] and it has passed into the realm of conventional wisdom. According to Blumenbach's system, Caucasians represent the European and the highest racial type within the human species. Whilst the professor was studying ethnology, he was supplied with a skull from the Caucasus region, and considered it the finest standard of the human type.[2] Given this background, it is extraordinary to find that some governments still use the Caucasian category in their formulation of social policy and statistics. In South Africa, the spurious concept of a white race informed the oppressive and discriminatory legislation of *apartheid* until 1991.

Apart from the white 'Caucasian race', Blumenbach identified a brown 'Malayan race', a yellow 'Mongolian race', a black 'Negro race', and a red 'American race'. His fivefold classification gained wider acceptance than the simpler white, brown, and yellow scheme of Baron G. L. Cuvier (1769–1852), another comparative anatomist working at the Collège de France.

Somewhat later, the colour-coded classification of races was augmented by the notion of a complete racial hierarchy, within which white-skinned peoples of European origin occupied the top position. This development was first promoted in the work of Victor Courtet (1813–67), although the most influential exposition was made in the *Essai sur l'inégalité des races humaines* (1855) by Joseph-Arthur, Comte de Gobineau

(1816–82). 'History shows', he wrote, 'that all civilisation derives from the white race, and that a society is great and brilliant only so far as it preserves the blood of the noble race that created it.' Interracial intercourse was equivalent to degeneracy. 'Peoples degenerate only in consequence of the various admixtures of blood which they undergo.'[3]

Gobineau, who wrote a history of Persia, was also responsible for propagating the mistaken coincidence between the 'white race', which he saw as the progeny of the ancient Aryans or 'Iranians', and the Indo-European linguistic family. In this way he turned the spurious Aryan label into a partner and a rival for the older but equally spurious Caucasian one.

'White', 'Caucasian', 'Aryan', and 'Europoid' all reflect the protracted search for an exclusive, and therefore non-existent, common denominator in the racial make-up of Europe's population. They form part of a wider vocabulary of doubtful terms including 'Black', 'Asian', 'Semitic', and 'Hispanic', where physical, geographical, and cultural criteria are hopelessly confused.

The great variety of physical types which exist within Europe's population has inspired many attempts to fix the boundaries of its constituent or regional subgroups. The flaxen-haired 'Nordic'[4] (adopted by Nazi ideology), the 'Ibero-Celtic', the 'Atlanto-Baltic' (which lumps the English with the Dutch and the north Germans), the 'Central European' (which includes both the majority of Germans and the majority of Russians), and the swarthy 'Indo-Mediterranean' can all be encountered in current reference works. These are only slightly less fanciful than the once fashionable practice of putting each modern nationality into its own racial group (see p. 817). Even so, phrases such as 'the Island Race', 'German genes', or 'Polish Blood' have not yet passed from popular parlance, not to mention the 'Daneskin' and the 'red-haired Irish', or the 'black dogs' and 'white ladies' with which European folklore abounds.

Modern genetic science has progressed far beyond the methods and conclusions of the nineteenth-century pioneers. In this, the crucial step came with the demonstration of the workings of DNA in 1953. Generally speaking, the advances have emphasized the overwhelming mass of genetic material which all members of the human race hold in common and the immense number of characteristics that are encoded in the genes.[5] In a series of declarations between 1956 and 1964, UNESCO condemned the principal racial myths that had prevailed since the days of Blumenbach and Gobineau.[6] Racial and kinship differences have not been discounted. But the field has been cleared for a greater emphasis on cultural, religious, and socio-economic factors, for sophisticated genetic analysis based on proven scientific principles, and for the final dismissal of the old obsession with skins and skulls.

with Madrid and many provincial centres in the hands of the opposition and much of the countryside in the grip of guerrilla warfare, the French found the costs of holding Spain steadily mounting. In 1808–9 flagging French fortunes were temporarily restored by Napoleon's personal intervention. But he had to leave; and every victory of his deputies, Soult and Masséna, only served to increase the complications. In 1812 the anti-French liberals, besieged in Cadiz, succeeded in passing a liberal Constitution for the restoration of a limited monarchy. In 1813 the pro-French party succeeded in restoring the original monarch, Ferdinand VII. But it was all rather superfluous: by then Wellington was well on his way to the conquest of the whole Peninsula. [**GUERRILLA**]

Napoleonic Poland was a land of fervent enthusiasms and deep disillusionment. Napoleon's arrival in December 1806, and the creation of the self-governing Grand Duchy of Warsaw, aroused great excitement; but the changes fell very short of the expected restoration of the late Republic. In 1809 the second defeat of

---

GUERRILLA

IN June 1808, laden with spoils after sacking Cordoba, the French General Dupont retreated towards Andujar and the passes of the Sierra Morena. He then found himself surrounded not only by the regular Army of Andalusia but also by armed bands of Andalusian peasants harrying his retreat from the rear. His surrender with 22,000 men gave notice that holding Spain would prove much more difficult than invading it.

Throughout the Peninsular War, the French Army faced two sorts of conflict—one, the main military campaigns against Spanish, Portuguese, and British formations, and the other, the *guerrilla* or 'little war' against roaming bands of peasants. The second form of warfare proved specially vicious. The guerrilla bands avoided open battle, specializing instead in ambushes, night raids, and surprise attacks on isolated outposts. They provoked the French into murderous, collective reprisals on civilians. And they bequeathed their name to all who have emulated their methods. They showed how small bands of determined fighters could contest the overwhelming force of a professional army.

The guerrillas of Napoleonic Spain have had many heirs, not least in the popular heroes of colonial wars and the backwood revolutionaries of Latin America. But they have had their disciples in Europe as well—in the Russian anarchists, in the partisans and *maquisards* of the Anti-Nazi Resistance Movement, and, with the IRA or ETA, in the 'urban guerrillas' of modern political terrorism.[1]

The only major dispute is one of precedence. In French historiography, the pride of place is not given to the Spanish guerrillas but to 'Jean Chouan' and his followers, that is, to Frenchmen who defied the might of the Republic more than a decade before French armies entered Spain.[2]

the Austrians delivered Cracow to the Duchy; but no help was forthcoming for the recovery either of Danzig or of Lithuania and the provinces absorbed by Russia. Polish volunteers served in every stage of the Revolutionary wars, from the legions of Italy in 1796. But vicious financial exactions symbolized by the so-called Bayonne Sums, and the constant toll of conscripts, dead, and *mutilés* swelled popular resentments. Napoleon never revealed his ultimate intentions for Poland, even in 1812, when he briefly controlled almost the whole of historic Polish territory. His legend fared better in the Romantic times after his death than during his lifetime. When his most faithful lieutenant, Marshal Poniatowski, spurred his charger into the waters of the Elster at the end of the 'Battle of the Nations', he was expressing the despair of an exceedingly deceived and weary people.

Great Britain, though free from French occupation, was shaken to its roots by the revolutionary wars. Indeed, whilst the external foe was repelled, there were moments when internal revolution loomed. In 1797–8 the coincidence of naval mutinies at Spithead and the Nore with the revolt of Wolfe Tone's United Irishmen was particularly menacing. Certainly the prosecution of almost constant war with France inhibited political reform. The Union of Great Britain with Ireland, for example, which came about in 1801 in consequence of Tone's defeat was marred by the postponement of promised Catholic emancipation for the best part of thirty years. At the same time the sense of British solidarity was greatly enhanced by the run of naval victories, and by the threats of French invasion, which on one occasion in 1798, in the remote extremity of Ireland, actually materialized. The prestige of Parliament was strengthened by the magnificent tussle between Pitt the Younger and his eloquent rival, Charles James Fox (1749–1806). All the while, Britain's commercial, colonial, and economic strength continued to accrue. The tally of French, Spanish, and Dutch colonial prizes grew longer and longer. At home, the General Enclosure Act (1801) greatly accelerated the tempo of social change. The Caledonian Canal (1803–22) was constructed despite the war. And in 1811 the first of the Luddite attacks on machinery took place, in Nottingham. In that same year the old King was finally declared permanently insane, and was succeeded by his son, the Prince Regent. The Regency, 1811–20, proved to be one of the most splendid intervals in British architecture, patronage, and high society.

Scandinavia, too, escaped the Revolution, but not the associated turbulence. Sweden was twice involved with wars against Russia. In 1788–90, after the naval victory at Svenskund, she came through unscathed. In 1808–9 she lost Finland and, in the ensuing débâcle, her King, Gustav IV Adolphus (r. 1792–1809). The constitution of 1809 introduced a limited monarchy, and one of Napoleon's ex-marshals, Jean-Baptiste Bernadotte (1763–1844), was invited to accept the throne as Charles XIV. He entered the anti-French coalition, participated in the war of liberation in Germany, and hived off Norway from Denmark. [NORGE]

Denmark, on the other hand, had desperately tried to maintain a policy of neutrality, which twice earned her ruthless retaliation from Britain. Under the great reformer C. D. F. Reventlow (1748–1827), the Danish Enlightenment achieved many things, including the emancipation of the serfs, Jewish civil rights, free trade, and a free press. But it did not save the country from her neighbours. In April 1801 the Danish fleet was sunk at Copenhagen on the occasion when Nelson reputedly put the telescope to his blind eye and refused the signal to desist. In September 1807 Copenhagen was invested by the British and forced to capitulate. After that the Danes went over wholeheartedly to the French connection, for which they were duly punished by Bernadotte and by the Congress of Vienna.

NORGE

A T the end of the Napoleonic Wars, when Denmark had clearly backed the losing side, Norway's leaders made their break from 400 years of Danish rule. On 17 May 1814 an assembly was convened at Eisvold, near Christiania, to declare Norway a sovereign, constitutional monarchy. The constitution was largely modelled on that of Spain (1812). The Danish governor of the country, Prince Christian Frederick, was unanimously acclaimed Norway's first king since 1389.

The assembly at Eisvold, however, had not reckoned either with Sweden or with the King of Denmark. Ever since their loss of Finland in 1809, the Swedes had sought to acquire Norway in compensation; and the Danish King had unilaterally conceded their claim. Moreover, the Swedish army, under the heir to the throne, Bernadotte, was already on the march to enforce the agreement. After a fortnight's war, the Norwegians were obliged to accept a bargain whereby they could retain their constitution, and their separate *Storthing* or parliament, but not their king, within a joint Suedo-Norwegian realm. This settlement was enshrined in an Act of Union and confirmed at the Congress of Vienna.

Henceforth, Norway's national movement was directed in the cultural sphere against Danish domination but in the political sphere against the union with Sweden. No amount of pressure could persuade the Norwegians to forgo their constitution; and ninety years of wrangles over foreign policy, over national flags, and, above all, over the powers of the Swedish king, soured the union. At one point the entire Norwegian cabinet was arraigned before the country's constitutional court, and the premier fined, for exceeding their rights. Finally, the Swedish government resigned itself to Norway's second declaration of independence. The Danish Prince Charles was unanimously elected king, and entered his capital on 25 November 1905. The King took the name of Haakon VI, and the capital returned to its ancient name of Oslo. With some delay, the will of the assembly of Eisvold had finally prevailed.[1]

The Balkans lay beyond the sphere of direct French influence. The only region to be held and administered by the French were the so-called Illyrian Provinces—mainly modern Slovenia and Croatia. [ILLYRIA] But the breath of revolutionary and national ideas blew into all corners. Greece was strongly affected. In 1799 the 'Septinsular Republic' was set up with Russian assistance [HEPTANESOS]; and when the larger part of the Parthenon frieze was carried off from Athens, there was an immediate outburst of national sentiment. [LOOT] In Serbia, two risings against Ottoman rule in 1804–13 and 1815–17 also received Russian support. In the Romanian principalities, the Russian occupation of 1806–12, and the consequent cession of Bessarabia, caused resentments which only served to fuel national feelings. [BOUBOULINA]

The Russian Empire under Alexander I (r. 1801–25), grandson of Catherine the Great, experienced one of the most liberal eras of its history. Alexander's father Paul I (r. 1796–1801) had bordered on insanity: his internal policy was moved by vicious whims such as the reintroduction of corporal punishment for nobles and civil servants, and his external policy by personal flights of fancy. He left the Second Coalition in 1799 because of his desire to possess the Order of Malta; and in 1801 broke with Great Britain for no sound reason. He was murdered by drunken officers. After that, Alexander settled down to the long confrontation with Napoleon. Guided by his boyhood companion and chief minister, Prince Adam Czartoryski (1770–1861), a Polish nobleman once taken hostage by Catherine, he took a serious and intelligent interest in the political and social problems of the day. He had broad visions for the reconstruction of Europe, and showed genuine concern for the advantages of a constitutional monarchy.[40] He incorporated Finland as an autonomous Grand Duchy; liberated the landless serfs of the Baltic provinces; and for a couple of decades turned the western region annexed from Poland-Lithuania into the scene of a liberal social and cultural experiment centred on the University and educational district of Wilno.[41] He was responsible for the foundation of a state school system, and of the (advisory) Council of State which remained a central organ of Tsarist government thereafter. Russia was hardly amenable to the application of radical ideas; but a generation of Russian soldiers who were brought into direct contact with Poland, Italy, and eventually Paris itself could not fail to be a source of ferment.

The Napoleonic Wars did not hinder Russia's territorial expansion eastwards. From 1801 the sixty-year conquest of the Caucasus began with the annexation of Georgia. In 1812, at the very time that Napoleon was approaching Moscow, a Russian expedition planted the tiny colony of Fort Ross on the coast of northern California—more than thirty years before American pioneers had reached the area.[42] [GAGAUZ]

With time, the strains of France's Continental System began to tell, as did the effects of the British blockade. They underlay the Tsar's alliance in March 1812 with Sweden, and the deployment by Napoleon of a *Grande Armée* of some 600,000 on the Tsar's western frontier. They equally provided the main bone of contention for the inglorious war of 1812–14 between Britain and the United

HEPTANESOS

I N March 1799 the French garrison on Corfu capitulated to a joint Russo-Turkish expeditionary force under Admiral Ushtakov. Corfu was the largest of the *Heptanesos*, the seven Ionian Islands, which the Treaty of Campo Formio had handed to France from the late Venetian Republic. (Its capture was the outcome of a rare example of Russo-Turkish co-operation inspired by Napoleon's invasion of Egypt.) Once established, the Russians shed their Ottoman allies and created a model 'septinsular republic' with its own parliament and a constitution (1803) designed by Tsar Alexander's chief minister, Prince A. J. Czartoryski.[1] The aim of their largesse was to outbid the 'revolutionary' French and to create the nucleus of a future Greek state. The arrangements lasted for only four years. The Ionian Islands reverted to French possession by the Treaty of Tilsit (see p. 733), only to be picked off one by one by the British Fleet from 1809 onwards.

The British regime proved rather less liberal than its Russian-sponsored predecessor. An imposed constitution gave overriding powers to the governor. A handful of notables ran both the consultatory assembly and the oppressive *colonia* system of landholding. During the Greek War of Independence, the main British aim was to frustrate the islanders' desire to join Greece. In 1848 and 1849, Cephalonia was the scene of agrarian revolts, which the Governor, Sir Henry Ward, suppressed with mass arrests, floggings, and executions. At the very time that Palmerston was condemning the Austrians as 'the greatest brutes that ever called themselves the undeserved name of civilized men', and when General Heynau was unceremoniously dumped into a London horse-trough, Governor Ward was described in the House of Commons as 'the bloody Heynau of the Ionian Islands'. But to no avail. It was a fitting prelude to Palmerston's rough handling of the Don Pacifico Affair.[2] Union with Greece was ruled out as late as 1859, on the advice of the British commissioner, W. E. Gladstone. But it was conceded in 1864 as a face-saving gesture in the general settlement with Greece. During the crisis Alfred, Duke of Edinburgh had been offered and had rejected the Greek throne. It was a nice irony that the British monarchy would eventually also concede the defunct title of Duke of Edinburgh to an exiled Greek prince born on Corfu.
[GOTHA]

LOOT

IN 1799, the British Ambassador to the Ottoman Porte, Lord Elgin, visited Athens and acquired the finest sections of the Parthenon Frieze. The Parthenon had been used as an arsenal: much of it had been demolished by an explosion: and no one was trying to repair it. Elgin could argue that his deal with the Ottoman authorities was both legal and public-spirited. But the Athenians objected. One of the Greek leaders opposed to Ottoman rule had warned against selling Greece's treasures to the 'Europeans'. 'After all,' he wrote later, 'that is what we fought for.'[1]

The 'Elgin Marbles' constitute one of the prize exhibits of the British Museum; and some people consider them part of the British Heritage.[2] (If large chunks of Stonehenge had been legally transported to Athens, one might equally consider them part of the 'Heritage of Greece'.)

Many European galleries and museums have been built on the proceeds of national or private loot. In the 17th century, the Swedes extracted vast quantities of art and valuables from Germany, Bohemia, and Poland. Napoleon was the Louvre's most ardent patron (see p. 722). Much of his archaeological loot from Egypt was looted in turn by the British. Much of the core collections of Russia's state libraries and museums was carried off from Poland. In the year that Lord Elgin was in Athens, General Suvorov's army was accompanied to Italy by trained teams of cultural procurers. Heavyweight political power has usually been accompanied by light fingers.

In the twentieth century, the Nazis were generally considered the master art thieves. Goering thought himself a connoisseur; and Hitler, the ex-art student, was planning the world's largest art centre in his home town of Linz. Cracow, Paris, Florence, Ghent, and Amsterdam, and many lesser centres, were comprehensively robbed. Trainloads of loot reached the Reich from the East. At the end of the war, thousands of Europe's greatest art treasures were found in a disused salt-mine at Alt Aussee in Austria.[3]

Nazi plunder, however, represents less than half the story. The Nazis had nothing to teach the Russians about looting. Fifty years after the war, hoards of old masters and other Nazi booty, which the Red Army had plundered from the German plunderers, started to come to light in Russia. The so-called golden 'Mask of Agamemnon' from Mycenae, for example, and the 16,000 items of 'Priam's Treasure' from Troy, once brought to Berlin by Schliemann, were all located in 1991 in Moscow.[4] Unknown except to the KGB and a handful of conservationists, these 'trophies' and 'special finds' had been secretly held for half a century in the Hermitage and the Pushkin Museum and the monastery at Zagorsk. For the most part they derived from private collections such as those of Herzog and Hatvany in

Budapest, of Franz Koenigs in Amsterdam, or of the Krebs Foundation in Mannheim. The talk was of a million works of art. The problem, as with the British Museum, was to persuade the Russian finders that finding is different from keeping.

Not that the other Allies were beyond suspicion. Berlin's collection of Mozartiana, which had been taken to Poland during the war for safety, did not return from the University Library in Cracow. In 1990, priceless items from the 'Quedlingburg Treasure', including a ninth-century illuminated German Bible in jewel-encrusted binding, were found in a Texas garage once owned by an ex-US Army lieutenant.[5]

Needless to say, the legal concept of 'cultural property', as enshrined in the Hague Convention of 1954, is a relatively recent innovation.[6]

States. American shipping was long trapped between the contradictory regulations of the British and the French; and in 1807 the boarding of the USS *Chesapeake* by a party from HMS *Leopard* gave grave offence. President Jefferson introduced his own regulations regarding 'peaceful coercion' and 'non-intercourse', but then gave way to the demands of the 'war hawks' of the Twelfth Congress. American forces failed to win any significant territory in Canada; and the British failed to reassert control over their former colonies. From a later perspective, it is ironic to reflect that the Continental System led both to the burning of the Executive Mansion in Washington, from 1814 known as the White House, and to the burning of Moscow.

The Russian campaign of 1812 was, as he later admitted, Napoleon's greatest mistake. He called it his 'Polish War', since most of the action took place on traditional Polish territory and since a successful outcome would inevitably have raised the question of restoring Poland-Lithuania. The frontier which the *Grande Armée* crossed on 22 June 1812 had only recently become the frontier of the Russian Empire. In the eyes of the local inhabitants, it was the historic border linking Poland with Lithuania. [MIR] Napoleon was faced with a clear choice between a political campaign, in which he could have used the army to liberate the serfs and to mobilize the anti-Russian sentiments of the population, or a purely military campaign, in which the outcome was left exclusively to the fortunes of war. He noticed that the Poles of Lithuania were rather different from the Poles of Warsaw. So, like Charles XII before him, and Hitler later, he chose to ignore local conditions and paid the price. Keeping all thoughts of the political future to himself, he pressed on through Lithuania to the heart of Muscovy. At Borodino, at the gates of Moscow, he suffered the most costly of all his victories. Moscow was occupied, but burned together with much of its stores. The Tsar simply refused to negotiate, and ordered his army to avoid any major engagement. In

GAGAUZ

SHORTLY after the Russian conquest of Bessarabia in 1812, the Tsar's new province attracted a wave of immigration. Among the migrants came a group of Balkan Christians known as *Gagauz*. They came from an area of what is now northern Bulgaria, and they settled in the district of Komrat, in what is now Moldavia. Their language belongs to the Ghoz branch of Turkic, and has counterparts in Central Asia. Their religious allegiance was to Slavic Rite Bulgarian Orthodoxy. It is an open question whether they left their ancestral homeland more from hope than from fear. A number of Gagauz communities, which were Moslem, stayed behind under Ottoman rule in Bulgaria.

There are two views about the earlier history of the Gagauz. One maintains that they were medieval Turks who had been partially bulgarized. The other holds that they were turkicized Bulgars, who kept their religion when they lost their language. Neither really fits the facts.[1]

The Gagauz were just one of several such minorities in eastern Europe who straddled the Christian-Muslim divide.[2] The Muslim Tartars of the Volga contained a baptised minority, the *Kryeshens*, who had adopted the religion of their Russian conquerors. The Chechens of the North Caucasus, though mainly Moslem, also included some Christians. The Abkhazians were in a similar position [**ABKHAZIA**]. Albanian Muslims, though a majority both in Albania and in Serbia's Kossovo province (see Appendix III, p. 1310), form an important minority in Macedonia. [**MAKEDON**] [**SHQIPERIA**]

On either side of the Rhodope Mountains, on the borders of Bulgaria and Greece, there lives a substantial community of Bulgarian-speaking Muslims known as *Pomaks*. They have outlying relations in parts of Macedonia and Albania. Their existence in Greece is not officially admitted. In 1876, it may have been the local Pomak militia rather than the professional Ottoman army which perpetrated what Mr Gladstone denounced as 'the Bulgarian Horrors'. If so, they were amply repaid amidst the horrors of the subsequent Balkan Wars. But they never left.[3]

In Bosnia, religion is the only criterion to divide the Bosnian Muslims from Orthodox 'Serbs' and Catholic 'Croats'. All speak the same 'Serbo-Croat' language, and all are Slavs. The Bosnian Muslims (44 per cent of the population in 1991) are often viewed by nationalistic neighbours as renegades who abandoned Catholicism or Orthodoxy in favour of the religion of the ruling Ottomans. In fact, it is likely that prior to adopting Islam many such Bosnian families had been Patarenes. [**BOGUMIL**]

In the late 20th century these little-known peoples repeatedly hit the European headlines. In the mid-1980s, Bulgaria's fading communist regime made a last desperate attempt to maintain control by launching an ultra-nationalist campaign called 'the Process for Rebirth'. Mosques were destroyed; and Bulgaria's Muslim minorities—Gagauz, Pomaks, and Turks—were forced to choose between changing their names or emigrating. Many chose to emigrate. In 1991, when Moldavia declared independence, the Gagauz of Komrat, by then some 200,000 strong, were reluctant to participate. The Chechens defiantly raised the standard of independence from Russia by proclaiming their own national republic in Grozny, whilst the Volga Tatars in Kazan prepared for 'Tatarstan'.

In 1992, amidst the rapid disintegration of Yugoslavia, the Government of Bosnia declared itself independent in the hope of maintaining the integrity of a multinational republic. It received international recognition, but no significant international aid or protection. The presence of Western charities and of token UN peace-keeping forces did nothing to restrain the orgy of land-grabbing, communal massacres, and 'ethnic cleansing' which ensued. A self-styled Serbian Republic of Bosnia based at Pale mirrored the self-styled Serbian Republic of Krajina based at Knin, which had been set up in the lands of the old Habsburg military frontier in Croatia. Within a year, Serbs representing 31 per cent of the population had seized 77 per cent of the territory. Sarajevo, like several other enclaves, was besieged. Croat attacks drove Muslims from mixed western districts like Mostar, whilst Serbs fled the Muslim-dominated districts in the centre. Perhaps a quarter of a million people perished. World leaders whistled whilst Bosnia burned. In the absence of decisive statesmanship, the dissolution of Communism was having the same sort of effect as the Ottoman retreat nearly two hundred years before.[4] [**SARAJEVO**]

November, with starvation pending, the retreat was sounded. The columns of the *Grande Armée*, stretched out over 500 miles, fell victim to the Russian winter, to marauding Cossacks, and to the unseasonal floods of the Berezina. Napoleon fled by sledge to Warsaw, and on to Paris. As for his men, of the 600,000 who had crossed the Niemen in June barely one in twenty survived to tell the terrible tale. As the Emperor once remarked, 'All empires die of indigestion'. [**MALET**] [**SPA-SIT'EL**]

The terminal campaigns of 1813 and 1814 were decided as much by logistics as by performance in battle. Although Napoleon's forces were comprehensively overwhelmed at the three-day 'Battle of the Nations' near Leipzig in October 1813, he continued to win the great majority of subsequent engagements. But he was facing the collective will of peoples whose sense of nationality he had helped to arouse, as well as the determination of the dynasts to restore their supremacy. The advance of the Russians, Prussians, and Austrians from the east, and of Wellington from the south, could not be stemmed. The toll of young French lives was inexorable. In those last two years Napoleon lost over a million men, even though he had failed to trap his foes into another concerted combat. The moment

MIR

IN July 1812, as General Platov withdrew into Byelorussia before the *Grande Armée*, his Cossacks placed barrels of gunpowder under the castle walls of Mir and blew them to pieces. Jerome Napoleon, King of Westphalia, used the place as his HQ for a few days on his way to Moscow. But on 10–11 November, when the Tsar's army returned, a desperate fight with the retreating French compounded the damage.[1]

Mir had long been one of the great fortresses of the Polish–Lithuanian borders, one of the most easterly feudal castles in Europe. Once a stronghold of the grand dukes of Lithuania, it passed into private hands in 1434. The massive fortifications were completed *c.*1500 under Jerzy I Illinicz, Marshal of Lithuania, and his son Jerzy II, a Count of the Holy Roman Empire. Five lofty bastions in red brick were joined by a battlemented wall. They were protected by a horseshoe barbican and surrounded by ditch and moat. From 1569, the central keep was turned by Prince M. K. Radziwiłł into a grand Renaissance palace in finished stone. Until 1812, it served with neighbouring Nieśwież as one of the Radziwiłłs' two principal seats.

In its long life Mir saw many military actions. It was plundered by the Teutonic Knights in 1395, twice raided by Tartars in the fifteenth century, captured by the Swedes in 1655, burned by Charles XII in 1706, and stormed by the Russians in 1794.

The great days of Mir came with Prince Karol Radziwiłł, 'Panie Kochanku' (1734–90), who restored the palace after the depredations of the Swedish wars. It was the 'key' property in a huge complex of estates worked by thousands of Byelorussian serfs. The Catholic church and the Greek Catholic (Uniate) church adjoined the Jewish synagogue and Tartar mosque. The annual horse-fair was run by a large community of gypsies whose 'king' was traditionally crowned by the Prince. In 1761 the palace hosted a stupendous orgy during a session of the Grand Duchy's Tribunal. In 1785 it saw a grand reception for the last King of Poland. Russian rule began at the Second Partition in 1793. The gypsies promptly migrated *en masse* to Moldavia. The Radziwiłłs left for their properties in Prussia. After 1812, only the ruins remained.

Mir lived on, however, immortalized by the epic poem, *Pan Tadeusz*, of Adam Mickiewicz. The poet had the palace of Mir in mind when he described Lithuania's 'Last Supper'. Filled with hope and goodwill at the prospect of liberation by Napoleon, the local nobles gathered for a dazzling banquet. Lords and ladies danced the *polonez*. They were entertained on the cymbals by Jankiel the Jew, 'who loved his country like a Pole'. At the end they raised their glasses to the old Polish toast, *Kochajmy Sie!* 'Let us love one another!'[2]

MALET

A T 3 a.m. on 23 October 1812, a man wearing the full dress uniform of an imperial general arrived at the Popincourt barracks in Paris and demanded an urgent interview with the Commandant of the National Guard. Introducing himself as General Lamotte, the new Military Governor, he announced that Napoleon had been killed in Moscow, that an emergency session of the Senate had declared a Provisional Republic, and that the National Guard must assemble forthwith in the Place Vendôme. Handing the Commandant a certificate of promotion, he ordered him to take charge of other units and then to secure the release of two state prisoners, Generals Guidal and Ladurie. His instructions were supported by an impressive file of decrees.

For several hours the plan proceeded smoothly. 'General Lamotte' did the rounds of the Paris garrison without opposition. So did General Ladurie. General Guidal settled for a good meal in a restaurant. But no fewer than thirteen senior officers took the orders of the non-existent Provisional Republic. The officer commanding the Luxembourg Palace, where the emergency session of the Senate had supposedly taken place, saw nothing amiss.

Things only went wrong when a large part of the National Guard was already drawn up in the Place Vendôme. At a private interview with General Hulin, whom Lamotte was replacing, 'Lamotte' was challenged to produce his own orders. Instead, he shot Hulin through the head. Shortly after, meeting another group of officers, he was recognized by a former comrade, who shouted, 'That's not Lamotte, it's Malet'. Overpowered, the chief conspirator was disarmed and unmasked.

Claude-François Malet (1754–1812), a native of the Jura, was a brigadier-general with strong Jacobin convictions. Long removed from active service, he had been held in detention for ill-concealed hostility to Napoleon. He had laid his plans with the help of a fellow detainee, the Abbé Lafon, an ultramontane royalist, who forged the documents. His wife hired the uniforms from a theatrical outfitter. The real Lamotte was a republican general living in exile in the USA.

Malet and Lafon had climbed the wall of their gaol at midnight. Malet went home to dress up, before heading for Popincourt. Lafon disappeared until after the Restoration. At the court martial Malet took sole responsibility, but could not save those who had fallen for his ruse. His last request was to give the order to his own firing-squad.[1]

The Malet incident revealed the truth about Napoleon's Empire. Malet had calculated correctly that the Empire's fate hung on one man's life. The minute that Napoleon was assumed dead, no one thought of the King of Rome or the Napoleonic succession. As a result, France was very nearly returned to the Republic with only one shot fired. 'Minor incidents' can have the potential to make major changes to the course of history.

came when the Emperor was told that the soldiers would fight no more. In April 1814, with the British, Russians, and Prussians encamped in Paris, Napoleon abdicated. The Revolutionary wars, and the Revolution, were over. Or so it appeared.

One might have thought that the result of the Revolutionary wars was plain enough. Yet in the eyes of the historian who studied the subject most exhaustively, the Allies did not achieve outright victory. 'The European coalition did triumph in the end over the French armies,' he wrote; 'yet one cannot say that France was defeated by the struggle.'[43] He was thinking no doubt of the maintenance of France's territorial integrity, of the continuing force of Revolutionary ideas, and of the surprises still to come.

Everyone accepted that the fate of a whole continent had been at stake. Napoleon loved to talk of 'Europe'. When he mentioned it at Tilsit, the Tsar had picked it up. 'Europe,' asked Alexander I, 'what's that?' Then he gave his own answer: 'Europe is us' (meaning, presumably, the ruling princes). In the spring of

---

SPASIT'EL

IN 1812, to celebrate Russia's salvation from Napoleon, Alexander I decreed that Moscow be adorned by a church dedicated to Christ the Saviour. The project was brought to fruition by a committee convened by Nicholas I. Works began on the riverside, close to the Kremlin, in 1837. The design, by Konstanty Ton, an architect of railway stations, envisaged a colossal cruciform basilica surmounted by five domes, a giant bronze cupola, and a soaring pinnacle cross. The interior was gilded with 422 kilograms of pure gold. The belfry housed the largest bells in Russia. The exterior was clad with sheets of Podolian marble and Finnish granite. After forty-five years' labour, the *Khram Khristusa Spasit'yel'ya* or 'Saviour's Temple' was consecrated in the presence of Tsar Alexander III on 26 May 1883.

On 18 July 1931 *Pravda* announced that a committee headed by V. Molotov had decided to build a 'Palace of the Soviets' beside the Moscow River. Five months later, the Saviour's Temple was dynamited. In 1933 Stalin commissioned a design by Yofon and Shchusev which envisaged an edifice 415 metres high, and six times more capacious than the Empire State Building. It was to be surmounted by a figure of Lenin three times taller than the Statue of Liberty, with an index finger 6 metres long.

The Palace was never built. The marble slabs from the demolished temple were used to decorate Moscow subway stations. After thirty years' delay, Nikita Khrushchev decreed that the hole by the river be turned into an open-air, all-weather swimming pool.[1] Inevitably, after the fall of Communism, plans reappeared to redevelop the site once again, and to restore the Saviour's temple to its former glory.

1814, when he was riding towards Paris, he said, 'I have come to reconcile France with Europe.' That reconciliation took rather longer than expected.

Wednesday, 20 April 1814, Fontainebleau. Napoleon Bonaparte, King of Elba, was bidding farewell to the Imperial Guard before leaving France for his new kingdom. In the lobby of the château he greeted the members of his remaining entourage, and the gaggle of Allied commissioners. From there he passed to the doorway at the head of the Horseshoe Staircase, whose marble balcony over-looked the spacious Courtyard of the White Horse. Some 5,000 troops of the Old Guard were drawn up. The senior officers stood at the front in a semicircle with the colour party and the orchestra. The carriages for his journey were waiting by the gate. As he appeared on the parapet, cavalry trumpeters sounded the *Fanfare de l'Empéreur*:

The standard which was paraded that day has survived in the Musée de l'Armée. It is a square tricolour with vertical stripes of blue, white, and red, embroidered in gold. The front border was adorned with the imperial emblems—two crowns in the top corners, two circles with the monogram 'N' on the sides, two eagles in the bottom corners, a sheaf surrounded by bees in the upper centre. The inscription reads: GARDE IMPÉRIALE—L'EMPÉREUR NAPOLÉON AU 1ᵉʳ RÉGI-MENT DES GRENADIERS À PIED. The reverse is covered with the regiment's battle honours: Marengo, Ulm, Austerlitz, Iéna, Eylau, Friedland, Eckmühl, Essling, Wagram, Smolensk, Moskowa, Vienne, Berlin, Madrid, Moscou. The honours of 1813–14—at Lutzen, Bautzen, Dresde, Hanau, Champubert, Montmirail, Vauchamps—were still to be added.

Napoleon's personal entourage had been reduced to under twenty men. It included General Drouot, 'the Sage of the Grand Army', who would one day pro-nounce the Emperor's funeral oration, General Bertrand, who would bring back the Emperor's ashes to France, and the Duke of Bassano, his foreign minister. The civilian staff included the aides-de-camp Belliard, Bussy, and Montesquion; and the Barons Fait and Lorgne d'Ideville and the Chevalier Jouanne, members of

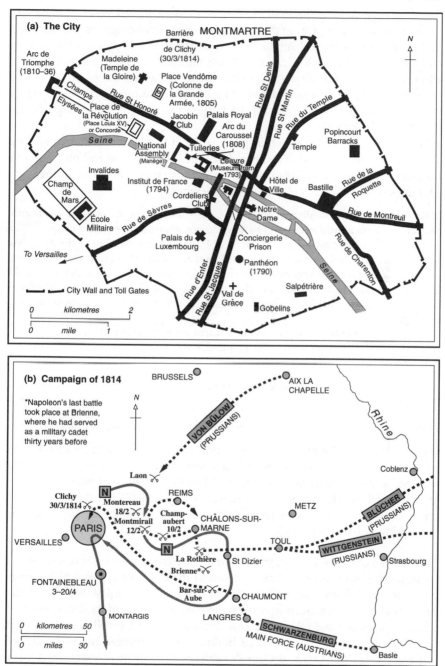

(a) The City

Barrière MONTMARTRE
de Clichy
(30/3/1814)

Arc de Triomphe (1810–36)

Madeleine (Temple de la Gloire)

Place Vendôme (Colonne de la Grande Armée, 1805)

Champs Elysées

Rue St Honoré

Place de la Révolution (Place Louis XV) or Concorde

Jacobin Club

Palais Royal

Arc du Caroussel (1808)

National Assembly (Manège)

Tuileries

Louvre (Museum from 1793)

Rue St Denis

Rue St Martin

Rue du Temple

Temple

Popincourt Barracks

Seine

Invalides

Champ de Mars

École Militaire

Institut de France (1794)

Cordeliers Club

Rue de Sèvres

Notre Dame

Hôtel de Ville

Bastille

Rue de la Roquette

Rue de Montreuil

To Versailles

Palais du Luxembourg

Conciergerie Prison

Panthéon (1790)

Rue d'Enfer

Rue St Jacques

Val de Grâce

Salpétrière

Seine

Rue de Charenton

City Wall and Toll Gates

Gobelins

0 kilometres 2

0 mile 1

(b) Campaign of 1814

*Napoleon's last battle took place at Brienne, where he had served as a military cadet thirty years before

BRUSSELS

AIX LA CHAPELLE

Rhine

VON BÜLOW (PRUSSIANS)

Laon

Coblenz

Clichy 30/3/1814

Montereau 18/2

REIMS

Champ-aubert 10/2

CHÂLONS-SUR-MARNE

METZ

BLÜCHER (PRUSSIANS)

Montmirail 12/2

PARIS

VERSAILLES

La Rothière

Brienne*

St Dizier

TOUL

WITTGENSTEIN (RUSSIANS)

Strasbourg

FONTAINEBLEAU 3–20/4

Bar-sur-Aube

CHAUMONT

MONTARGIS

LANGRES

SCHWARZENBURG

MAIN FORCE (AUSTRIANS)

Basle

0 kilometres 50

0 miles 30

Map 21.
Revolutionary Paris

the secretariat. Among the military staff was Count Kossakowski, commander of the *maison militaire*, Count d'Ornano, commander of dragoons, two colonels of the ordnance, Gourgaud and La Place, Col. Atthalin of the topographic service, and Col. Vauzovits (Wąsowicz), the Polish interpreter. The commander of the Old Guard, Marshal Lefebvre-Desnoëttes, Duke of Danzig, waited on horseback at the head of the cavalrymen who would accompany his carriage to Briare. Apart from him, none of the Marshals of the Empire was present, nor a single representative of the imperial family.

General Petit, heading the colour party, ordered the presentation of arms. The drums beat 'Aux Champs'. Napoleon descended the staircase and plunged into the midst of the assembled troops. The Emperor's exact words were not recorded, but General Petit was well placed to remember:

Officiers, sous-officiers, soldiers of my Old Guard! I am bidding you farewell. For twenty years, I have been pleased with you. I have found you always on the path of glory.

The Allied Powers have armed the whole of Europe against me. Part of the Army has betrayed its duties and France itself . . . With you and with other brave men, who have remained faithful, I could have carried on the war for another three years. But that would have made France miserable, and would be contrary to my declared aims. So, be faithful to the new sovereign which France has chosen. Do not abandon this dear *Patrie*, so long unhappy.

Do not regret my fate. I shall always be content if I know that you are content also. I could have died . . . But, no. I chose the honourable way. I shall write of everything that we have done.[45]

At this point General Petit raised his sword and shouted 'Vive l'Empereur', to a thunderous echo.

I cannot embrace you all, so I shall embrace your general. *Approchez, Général Petit . . .*

Having enveloped the general, he then said, 'Bring me the Eagle'. He kissed the hem of the standard three times with the words, 'Dear Eagle, may these kisses reverberate in the heart of all the brave.' Finally: 'Adieu, mes enfants.' 'Those grizzled warriors, who many a time had watched unmoved while their own blood ran, could not hold back their tears.'[46] Napoleon strode to the carriage, took his seat briskly, and was driven off.

The Château of Fontainebleau, 37 miles to the south-east of Paris, was Napoleon's favourite residence. Built by Francis I round the tower of a medieval hunting-lodge, it dated from 1528 and represented one of the earliest breaths of the Renaissance in France. Surrounded by the oaks and pines of its dense forest, it offered true escape and relaxation. Less forbidding than Versailles, it was free of the shades of anyone else's glory. Its buildings were arranged round a series of courtyards—la Cour Ovale, la Cour des Princes, la Cour de la Fontaine, la Cour des Offices, le Jardin de Diane. La Cour du Cheval Blanc, which has been known since the events of April 1814 as 'La Cour des Adieux', was realized under Louis XIII. The interior, which contained artistic treasures such as Rosso's frescos in the

Galerie François Ier, was designed with a touch of splendour, but not on a gigantic scale. The decorations and fittings, mainly of the sixteenth and seventeenth centuries, had been supplemented by Napoleon's own collection of Empire furniture. The château had been used as a gilded cage for Pope Pius VII, but had also seen the happiest days of Napoleon and Josephine. 'The Forêt de Fontainebleau is my English garden', he once said; 'I want no other.'[47] To leave it was no small wrench.

The Imperial Guard embodied the essence of two military terms—*corps d'élite* and *esprit de corps*. Formed in November 1798 as the Consular Guard, it was steadily expanded until it became an army within the army. In 1805 it numbered some 5,000 men from all four arms—infantry, cavalry, artillery, engineers. In 1809 it was split into the Old Guard, an élite of veterans within the élite, and the Young Guard, drawing on recruits and transferees. By 1813, at its height, it possessed nearly 60 different regiments, almost 50,000 men.

The Guard accepted only the finest applicants. They had to be 1.78 m (5 ft 10 in) tall, 25 years old, literate, and had to have fought in three campaigns. They were given resplendent uniforms, generous pay, special training, and top commanders with direct access to the Emperor. They had the right to be addressed as 'Monsieur' by all other soldiers. Every week when possible, their *Tondu*—the 'shorn one'—would inspect his *moustaches* and his *grognards*, his 'invincibles' and 'immortals'. In due course the core of veterans, 'the oldest of the Old', had served 17, 20, or even 22 years. Joking with the Emperor was accepted form. One trooper once called out to ask why he had not yet received the Légion d'Honneur. 'Why so?' 'Because I gave you a melon in the Egyptian desert!' 'A melon, *non, non . . .*' 'Yes, a melon, and eleven campaigns and seven wounds—at Arcola, Lodi, Castiglioni, the Pyramids, Acre, Austerlitz, Friedland . . .'. Before he had finished, he was a chevalier of the Empire with a payment of 1,200 francs. The Guard included many exotic foreigners. Two of the four regiments of 'grognards' were Dutchmen. There were whole 'Velite' formations of Italians. The cavalry included a regiment of scimitar-wielding Mamelukes, the German 'Lanciers de Berg', the Tartar Horse from Lithuania, and the three regiments of Polish Lancers, the 'truest of the true'.

For many years Napoleon had been notoriously reluctant to sacrifice his guardsmen in battle, except for lightning strikes at critical points. At Borodino he had held them back with the words: 'I will not have the Guard destroyed 300 leagues from Paris!' But then, in the later campaigns, as the supply of trained men dwindled amidst the floods of raw recruits, he spared them nothing. In the brilliant fighting retreat of 1814, they had marched and bled every step of the way.[48]

Napoleon had reached Fontainebleau three weeks before, still confident of defeating the allied armies. From his defensive position in Champagne, he had planned to turn in his tracks and to strike deep into the enemy's lines of communication. But marauding Cossacks had captured one of his couriers, and had discovered his

intention of 'drawing the enemy from Paris'.[49] In the last week of March, therefore, he found that the Russians, Prussians, and Austrians, instead of advancing
to fight him, had made a sudden concerted lunge against the weakly defended
capital. The Russians advanced on Romainville. The Prussians set up batteries on
Montmartre. The Austrians advanced up the Seine to Charenton. Two-hundred-
thousand allied troops surrounded the capital's defensive lines. The defenders
under Marshal Marmont, Duke of Ragusa, stood their ground. The gallant Duroc,
who had lost a leg in Russia, refused to surrender: 'I'll give up my positions when
you give me back my leg.' But the politicians had little stomach for a siege. The
citizens feared to share the fate of Moscow. Talleyrand had put out feelers to the
Tsar. Napoleon's brother Joseph left the city with the Empress on the 30th.

Racing back from St Dizier in his flying barouche, Napoleon covered the 120
miles in a single day. As on his lightning sleigh ride from Moscow two years
before, he was accompanied by his Foreign Minister, the loyal Caulaincourt. At 11
p.m. on the 31st, he was changing horses at the *Cour de France* inn at Juvisy-sur-
Orge, only eight miles from Notre Dame, when he met a French officer and heard
that Paris had capitulated. The news was premature. The Emperor set off on foot
in the direction of Paris; but then, meeting more men in retreat, he saw that he
was too late to intervene. He withdrew to Fontainebleau to regroup, arriving
exhausted at 6 a.m. Three days later, on 3 April, Palm Sunday, he reviewed the
Guard at Fontainebleau. 10,000 infantrymen and 4,600 sabres heard him say, 'In
a few days I shall march on Paris. Am I right?' They roared in approval. 'À Paris!
Vive l'Empereur.'

However, the reeling Emperor was soon forced to abandon all active plans. The
first blow was to learn that the Imperial Senate had approved a provisional government without him, and was proposing to restore the Bourbons. Then he
learned that Marmont's corps had defected, thereby rendering further resistance
almost impossible. The French language received a new verb—*raguser*, to betray.
The third blow was to hear from his marshals that they advised abdication in
favour of his infant son. Marshal Macdonald had told him that to draw the sword
against fellow-Frenchmen was unthinkable. Marshal Ney announced: 'The Army
will not march. The Army will obey its chiefs.'[50] The 'bravest of the brave' had lost
the will to fight. Finally, the Emperor found that the Allies would no longer accept
the terms of his first abdication, effected on 4 April. For a terrible week he writhed
under the growing realization that exile alone would suffice. The *dégringolade*, the
'disintegration', was complete.

The bitterest cup was handed him by his wife, Marie-Louise. Ignoring his tender and courageous letters, the Empress repaid all his earlier neglect and disloyal-
ties with interest. She responded with indecision, and then with callous disregard.
The initial assumption was that she would join him either at Fontainebleau, or
perhaps at some stage on their road to a shared exile. Then it was agreed that she
should travel to meet her father, the Emperor Francis, to plead her husband's
cause. It emerged that she had no such intentions. She was going to Vienna, but
to break with her husband for ever.

The Army had to be released from its oath of allegiance. The formula chosen by Marshal Augerau was specially wounding. 'Soldiers,' he declared, 'you are released from your oaths by the abdication of a man who, after sacrificing millions of victims to his cruel ambition, did not have the courage to die the death of a soldier.'[51] The tricolour was replaced by the white cockade.

The one fixed point in all these shifting sands lay with the Imperial Guard. On the night after the first abdication, they massed in the streets of Fontainebleau, torches in hand, to cries of 'Vive l'Empereur.' He had to order them to barracks. He also received a heart-warming letter from Count Wincenty Krasiński, the senior general of the Polish contingent. 'The marshals are deserting. The politicians betray you . . . But your Poles remain . . .'[52] But even the Polish regiments were divided. One-third of the *chevau-légers-lanciers* stayed on. But another third, mainly Frenchmen, broke up. The remaining 1,384 set off for Poland, led by the hero of Somosierra. Resplendent and perfumed on his black Arab charger, Kozietulski took leave of the emperor for the last time:

Sire, We lay at Your Imperial Majesty's feet the arms which no man could take from us by force . . . We have served as Poles the most amazing man of the century . . . Accept, Sire, the homage of our eternal loyalty . . . to an unfortunate prince.[53]

The politicking in Paris was led by Talleyrand, Chairman of the Senate, who emerged as the President of the Provisional Government. Talleyrand was behind the anonymous signals that had urged the Allied armies to attack; and he was now entertaining the Tsar in his own house. Royalist *émigrés* were streaming back, and the stock of the Bourbons was rising daily. The Comte de Provence (Louis XVIII), now 59 years old, was returning home. He had spent twenty-three years in exile, at Coblenz, Verona, Blankenberg, Calmar, Mittau in Courland, Warsaw, and the last five years in England. He was packing his bags at Hartwell in Buckinghamshire in the same week that Napoleon was packing at Fontainebleau. He was determined to underline his hereditary right by rejecting a constitution prepared by the Senate, but also to grant a liberal constitutional charter of his own making. Dubbed punningly *Louis des Huîtres*, 'the oyster-eater', from his gourmet reputation, he was a man of conciliation who had no intention of replacing the entire imperial establishment. Napoleon's marshals and ministers awaited the restoration with equanimity. The Russians were camped in the Champs Elysées. The Emperor Francis was at Rambouillet, Frederick-William of Prussia at The Tuileries. The Parisians went out to see the exotic sights—veteran Prussian grenadiers in pigtails, colourful Croats and Hungarians, Circassians in chainmail, mounted Bashkir bowmen.

As France wrestled with its ex-Emperor, the rest of Europe adjusted to the consequences of his fall. News in 1814 travelled slowly. Neither Wellington nor Soult were aware that Napoleon had already abdicated when they fought the last battle of the Peninsular campaign near Toulouse on 10 April. The imperial garrison on Corfu did not know about it until a British frigate called on them to surrender in June. Elsewhere, the main pieces of the Napoleonic Empire had already fallen apart. In the East, the Duchy of Warsaw had been occupied by the Russians for over a year. The Prussian and Austrian monarchies were resurgent. The Confederation of the Rhine had dissolved. In Switzerland, the old constitution had been revived. In Spain, Ferdinand VII had just been restored. In the Netherlands, William of Orange had just returned. In Scandinavia, Norway had just rebelled against its transfer from Denmark to Sweden. In Italy, the Napoleonic states had been overrun by the Austrians. Pope Pius was on his way back to Rome, where he would revive the Index and the Inquisition.

Britain, immune from the Continental fighting, was basking in the glow of the victorious Regency. Nash was rebuilding the Brighton Pavilion in fantastic pseudo-oriental style. The Prime Minister, Lord Liverpool, said of Napoleon, 'He will soon be forgotten.' Sir Walter Scott published the first of the Waverley novels. George Stephenson was perfecting the first effective steam locomotive at Killingworth Colliery near Newcastle. The English language later received from Mrs Margaret Sanger the term 'birth control'. The Marylebone Cricket Club opened its first season at Lord's. Popular discontent from the post-war recession was brewing. The war with the United States had died down, but had not yet been terminated.

In the arts, 1814 was a year when the Classical still vied with the rising Romantic. This was the year of E. T. A. Hoffmann's *Phantasiestücke*, his fantastic 'Tales'. In painting, Goya, Ingres, and Turner were all active. In music, the young Schubert wrote *The Erlking*; Beethoven completed his only opera, *Fidelio*. J. G. Fichte died; Mikhail Lermontov was born.

France's political crisis came to a head during Holy Week. Allied Commissioners arrived at Fontainebleau on 6 April to administer the revised act of abdication, which Napoleon duly signed.

The Allied Powers, having proclaimed that the Emperor Napoleon is the only obstacle to the re-establishment of peace in Europe, the Emperor Napoleon, faithful to his oath, declares that he renounces for himself and his heirs the thrones of France and of Italy, and that there is no personal sacrifice, even of life itself, that he is unwilling to make in the interests of France.[54]

Further negotiations led to the Treaty of Fontainebleau, concluded on the 11th, whereby Napoleon was to retain his title, a pension of 2 million francs, the Isle of Elba as his personal realm, and a personal staff and escort.

The British Commissioner, Sir Neil Campbell, spent many hours talking to the stricken Emperor at this time:

I saw before me a short active-looking man who was rapidly pacing the apartment like some wild animal with epaulets, blue pantaloons, and red topboots, unshaven, uncombed, with fallen particles of snuff scattered profusely over his upper lip and breast . . .[55]

They discussed Wellington's campaigns in the Peninsula. Then the Emperor reportedly said, 'Your nation is the greatest of all . . . I have tried to raise up the French nation, but my plans have failed. It is fate.'[56]

The ex-Emperor's psychological crisis came to a head when the negotiations were completed. He was convinced that he was deserted by his family as well as by the marshals. Giving command of the Guard to Marshal Ney, he had been assured: 'We are all your friends.' To which he replied bitterly, 'Aye, and Caesar's friends were also his murderers!' His messengers to the Empress had the greatest difficulty crossing the Allied lines. At Orléans, where the Young Guard stood at her side, the imperial paymaster was hiding the remains of the Emperor's treasure under a pile of horse manure in the bishop's stables. On the 11th, Napoleon ate a desultory evening meal with Caulaincourt, who had been acting as his go-between with the senators in Paris. He found that his valet had emptied the powder from the brace of pistols which he always kept by his bed. But he still had a phial of opiate that he had carried ever since his near-capture by Cossacks in Russia two years before. He retired to his room, and swallowed the contents. The poison had faded. It was strong enough to set him screaming from stomach cramps and convulsions, but not to kill him. Caulaincourt brought a doctor. The Emperor recovered by the morning. He said 'How difficult it is to die in one's bed!' (The secret was concealed until the publication of Caulaincourt's private memoirs in 1933.)[57]

On the 13th, Napoleon bade farewell to James Macdonald, Duke of Taranto, the last of his Marshals to stay by his side. The devoted Scotsman, son of an exiled Jacobite family, had joined Coulaincourt in the recent abdication talks with the Allied powers. He could not fail to notice that a Campbell had arrived as the Macdonald was about to leave. But his task was done. Napoleon presented him with the ceremonial sword of Murad Bey, a memento of the campaign in Egypt in 1799: 'Receive this in remembrance of me and of my friendship.'[58]

Preparations for the journey to Elba began as soon as the Treaty of Fontainebleau was signed. The Emperor was to be escorted to the south of France by the four Allied commissioners—Colonel Campbell, Count Shuvalov, Baron von Koller, and Count Trachsess von Waldburg. They were to travel via Lyons and Avignon to a port on the Riviera, where a British frigate would be waiting for the five-day passage to Elba. A team of grooms and wagoners were hard at work at the depot of Rosnières in the Forest of Fontainebleau, cleaning and greasing the eight carriages of the convoy, painting out the imperial armorials, packing stores into the twenty vehicles of the baggage train, preparing the 101 saddle and carriage horses that were needed. A hundred wagon-loads of the Emperor's furniture and personal effects were to follow later. The heaviest items would be sent in advance to Briare, in the south, where they would be joined by the Emperor and his escort at the end of the first day. The advance party moved off on the morning of the 14th down the Montargis road.

The selection of the escort was left to the Emperor. He was allowed a staff of thirty officers, and a garrison of 600 men. The cavalry detachment was formed under General Jerzmanowski from a squadron of Polish lancers into which a handful of Frenchmen and Mamelukes were also admitted. There was a crew of marines, an artillery battery with 100 gunners, and one infantry battalion made up from three companies of grenadiers and three of chasseurs. The men of the battalion were to be picked out in person at the final review.

On the last Saturday, Napoleon tried to settle accounts with the women of his life. To Josephine, he wrote:

In my exile, I will replace the sword with the pen . . . They've betrayed me one and all . . . *Adieu, ma bonne Joséphine.* Learn resignation as I have learned it, and never banish from your memory the one who has never forgotten you, and will never forget you.[59]

To Marie-Louise, his Empress, he used the formal *vous*:

My dear wife, Providence . . . has given its verdict against me. I congratulate you on the course you have taken . . . I hardly think that Destiny will bring us together again . . . Of all my punishments, my separation from you is the most cruel. I make only one reproach. Why not exercise the empire on my heart that motherhood conferred on you? You feared me, and you loved me . . .[60]

The letters were not sent. They were found in his desk at Fontainebleau some days later, unsigned.

After that, there was nothing left but to await the day of departure fixed for the following Wednesday. Napoleon recovered his spirits. He caused as much trouble as possible. He flew once or twice into his customary rages. And he spoiled the Commissioners' dinner, by telling his valet to announce his arrival at their table and making them stand, then remaining in his room.

As a soldier, Napoleon had contemplated death and oblivion many times. On one occasion he had questioned Marshal Ségur about what the people would say after he was gone. The minister recited a paean of grief and eulogy. 'Non,' said Napoleon, wringing his wrist in the Gallic fashion, 'ils diront "Ouf" ' (No, they'll just say 'Phew').[61]

On the Wednesday morning, Napoleon dressed simply for the farewell ceremony. He was the grand master of theatricality, and of timing. He had once explained that history was made up of time and space. 'One always has a chance of recovering lost ground,' he remarked, 'but lost time—never.' He must have savoured the chance to stage what historians were to dub the 'Last Supper' of Napoleonic iconography. According to conflicting accounts, he either wore the undress uniform of the Chasseurs de la Garde,—a cut-away tunic in green over white waistcoat and breeches,—or a blue tunic with blue pantaloons. At all events, he wore thigh-length boots, a dress sword at his side, on his breast the single star of the Legion, and on his head the legendary black hat with upturned brim at the rear. At 11 a.m. exactly, or by other accounts on the stroke of 1 o'clock, he made for the lobby and stepped out onto the head of the marble staircase.

There are many moments in history when it appears that an era has finished, that some long-established regime or system has finally passed away. These are dangerous moments for all concerned, not least for historians who wish to cut their subject into tidy periods. For regimes and societies and economies rarely die overnight as individuals do. Even in times of apparently cataclysmic collapse, the forces of continuity and inertia will always contend with the motors of change. Napoleon was not dead. He had not yet passed into legend. He had bid his Guard 'Adieu', but not for the last time.

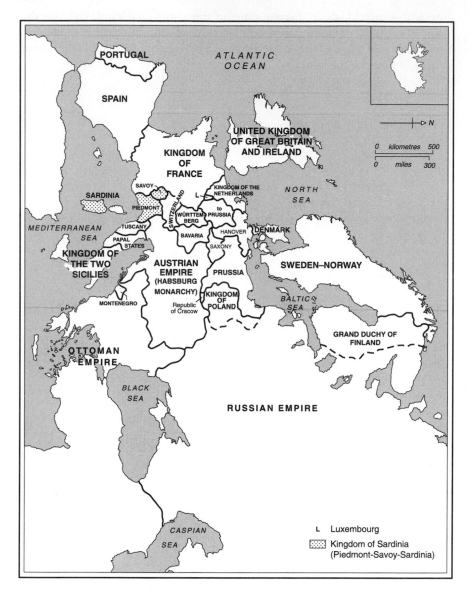

Map 22.
Europe, 1815

X

DYNAMO

Powerhouse of the World, 1815–1914

THERE is a dynamism about nineteenth-century Europe that far exceeds anything previously known. Europe vibrated with power as never before: with technical power, economic power, cultural power, intercontinental power. Its prime symbols were its engines—the locomotives, the gasworks, the electric dynamos. Raw power appeared to be made a virtue in itself, whether in popular views of evolution, which preached 'the survival of the fittest', in the philosophy of historical materialism, which preached the triumph of the strongest class, in the cult of the Superman, or in the theory and practice of imperialism.

Europeans, in fact, were made to feel not only powerful but superior. They were infinitely impressed by the unaccustomed 'forces' which surrounded them. They saw new physical forces, from the electric current to dynamite; new demographic forces which accompanied an unprecedented growth of population; new social forces which brought 'the masses' to the forefront of public concern; new commercial and industrial forces that thrived on the unparalleled expansion of markets and technology; new military forces that could mobilize millions of men and machines; new cultural forces which spawned 'movements' of mass appeal; new political forces which won unchallenged supremacy throughout the world.

Here, indeed, was Europe's triumphant 'power century'. Its leaders were in the first instance Great Britain, 'the workshop of the world', and in the later decades Germany, whose failure to find 'a place in the sun' helped reduce the whole edifice to ruins. Its losers and victims consisted of all the people and peoples who could not adapt, or could not compete—the peasants, the hand-weavers, the urban poor; the colonial peoples; the Irish, the Sicilians, and the Poles, who were forced to migrate in their millions; the three great empires of the East—Turkey, Austria-Hungary, Russia. The century began in the aftermath of one revolution, in France, and ended in the prelude to another revolution, in Russia. It began with one would-be master of all-Europe, Napoleon, proclaiming that Power was his mistress. It ended with another, Lenin, proclaiming: 'Communism is Soviet Power plus the Electrification of the whole country.'

It can be argued, of course, that the nineteenth century's experience of power was less than that of the twentieth century. After all, the potency of steam and electricity bears no comparison to that of nuclear fission. The marvellous speed of a railway train cannot compete with that of aeroplanes or intercontinental rockets. The oppressive capacity of imperialism and colonialism, great though it was, can hardly be likened to the totalitarian tyranny of fascism and communism. The point is that, for nineteenth-century man, power was the object of wonder and hope; for twentieth-century man, it became the object of suspicion. In the interval which separates the Industrial Revolution from Environmentalism, attitudes have been transformed. The benefits of electricity, when discovered in 1805, were not doubted; the benefits of nuclear power provoke anguished debates. Industrialization or colonialism were once seen as a great step foward for all concerned. They are now seen, at best, to have brought mixed blessings.

The psychology of power and speed has been changed out of all recognition. In 1830, when the world's first passenger train ran between Liverpool and Manchester, a senior British politician was knocked down and killed by the *Rocket*, which was travelling at 24 m.p.h.; despite ample warning, he had failed to comprehend the implications. In 1898, when motor vehicles were first allowed on to public roads in Britain, they were restricted to 4 m.p.h., so that a man might walk ahead with a red flag. Nowadays, no concern is shown by millions who cruise at 100 m.p.h. on the German autobahns, at 240 m.p.h. on the French TGV, or at 1,000 m.p.h. on Concorde. Since the nineteenth century power and speed have been made familiar; and familiarity has bred contempt.

Naturally, most Europeans did not realize how great was the power which had been put in their hands. The rash and the ambitious sought to exploit it to the full; the wise sought to use it with caution. The British, the early leaders, had little choice but to step warily in Continental affairs. So too did Otto von Bismarck, creator of the most powerful industrial and military unit of the age. The Iron Chancellor turned Germany into a great power, but not a universal menace. His best-known phrases about 'iron and blood' (1849) or 'blood and iron' (1886) were spoken about budgets and social affairs, not war. As the century's greatest statesman, he even grasped the limitations of statesmanship itself, not aspiring 'to control the current of events, only occasionally to deflect it'. 'In der Beschränkung zeigt sich erst der Meister', ran one of Goethe's epigrams (The master triumphs by holding back, or Genius consists of knowing when to stop).[1] Bismarck's successors did not practise such restraint.

Contrary to some expectations, Europe's brush with modern power revived its Christian culture. The 'Railway Age' was also the age of muscular Christianity. Engineers went out into the world in the company of missionaries. People who felt their own vulnerability in a fast-changing world hankered after earlier models of piety and discipline. Despite the mindless machines, and in line with the growing wave of Romanticism, they felt more need for divine reassurance, a greater readiness to accept the supernatural, an eagerness to experience 'the depth

of their being'. When they died, they were not averse to seeing their life as a journey on the 'Spiritual Railway':

> The Line to Heaven by Christ was made
> With heavenly truth the rails were laid,
> From Earth to Heaven the Line extends,
> To Life Eternal where it ends . . .
> God's Love the Fire, his Truth the Steam
> Which drives the Engine and the Train.
> All you who would to Glory ride
> Must come to Christ, in Him abide
> In First and Second, and Third Class
> Repentance, Faith, and Holiness . . .
> Come then, poor Sinners, now's the Time
> At any station on the Line,
> If you'll repent and turn from sin,
> The train will stop and take you in.[2]

The initial circumstances of nineteenth-century Europe were crucial. The forces
for change could only operate within the political and international framework
that came into being at the end of the revolutionary wars. And that framework
was given a very particular twist by the extraordinary events of 1815.

In February of that year, at the moment when the Congress of Vienna was failing to agree on a settlement, the revolutionary genie slipped once more from the
bottle. Napoleon escaped from Elba. In the subsequent 'Hundred Days', Europe
had to face the spectre of revolutionary war all over again. The shock was tremendous. If the political mood among the victorious powers in 1814 had been
cautious, in 1815 it became downright reactionary. It created a climate in the
subsequent decades where any sign of changes was instantly suppressed.

The *Cent Jours*, therefore, electrified Europe. Within three weeks of his lonely
landing at Antibes on 1 March, Napoleon had crossed the Dauphiné Alps, won
over Marshal Ney, who had been sent to 'bring him back in a cage', and entered
Paris in triumph, forcing Louis XVIII to flee. Within three months he had
reformed his army and left Paris to attack the forces of the Coalition which were
gathering on the northern frontier. His strategy was simple—to pick off the Allies
one by one before they could coalesce against him. On 16 June, at Loigny, he
defeated the Prussians, but did not prevent them from retiring in good order. On
18 June he confidently attacked the British at Waterloo near Brussels. But the 'thin
red line' of the Duke of Wellington resisted all the furious charges of the French
in a day of unrelenting slaughter; and Blücher's Prussian cavalry, riding over the
horizon in the late afternoon, swept the French from the field. Napoleon, after his
sixtieth set battle, was finally swept from the field of history. On 22 June he abdicated yet again; on 15 July, a fugitive at Rochefort, he surrendered to Capt.
Maitland of HMS *Bellerophon*. He was taken to Plymouth, and thence to the
remote island of St Helena. This time he didn't escape. Writing his memoirs, he

predicted that within ten years Europe would be either 'Cossack or republican'. When he died, 'it was not an event', Talleyrand said, 'only a news item'. [ECO]

Reconvening after Waterloo, the Congress of Vienna met in chastened mood. The representatives of the victorious powers could not be accused, as in the previous year, of 'dancing instead of making progress'. They were ready to risk nothing. They were determined, above all, to restore the rights of monarchy—the sacred institution considered most threatened by the Revolution. In so doing, they paid little attention to the claims either of democracy or of nationality. They resolved their differences by compensating the disgruntled at the expense of the defeated. A German Confederation of 39 states was to take the place of the Confederation of the Rhine and the Holy Roman Empire (see Appendix III, p. 1299). Prussia, which had been pressing for Alsace, Lorraine, and Warsaw, was given half of Saxony instead. Austria, which had lost its stake in the Netherlands, was given much of northern Italy. The United Provinces, which had lost the Cape of Good Hope, was given the Austrian Netherlands. Sweden, which had lost Finland, was given Norway. Russia was confirmed in its possession of Finland, Lithuania, and eastern Poland, and was given a separate kingdom of Poland round Warsaw, where the Tsar could be king. Britain contented itself with a bag of islands from Heligoland to Ceylon. A gaggle of antiquated monarchies was restored to Naples, Madrid, and Turin—but few of the old republics were allowed to revive. As Tsar Alexander remarked, 'Republics are not in fashion'. An exception was made for the Republic of Cracow, a city claimed by Prussia, Russia, and Austria and withheld from all of them.

The spirit of the settlement, therefore, was more than conservative: it actually put the clock back. It was designed to prevent change in a world where the forces of change had only been contained by a whisker. The Duke of Wellington's comment on Waterloo was: 'a damned nice thing, the nearest run thing you ever saw in your life'. Such was the feeling all over Europe. The issue between change and no change was so close that the victors felt terrified of the least concession. Even limited, gradual reform was viewed with suspicion. 'Beginning reform', wrote the Duke in 1830, 'is beginning revolution.' What is more, France, the eternal source of revolutionary disturbances, had not been tamed. Paris was to erupt repeatedly—in 1830, 1848, 1851, 1870. 'When Paris sneezes,' commented the Austrian Chancellor, Metternich, 'Europe catches cold.' French-style democracy was a menace threatening monarch, Church, and property—the pillars of everything he stood for. It was, he said, 'the disease which must be cured, the volcano which must be extinguished, the gangrene which must be burned out with a hot iron, the hydra with jaws open to swallow up the social order'.[3]

In its extreme form, as embodied by Metternich, the reactionary spirit of 1815 was opposed to any sort of change which did not obtain prior approval. It found expression in the first instance in the Quadruple Alliance of Russia, Prussia, Austria, and Britain, who agreed to organize future congresses whenever need arose, and then in a wider 'Holy Alliance' organized by the Tsar. The former produced the Congress of Aix-la-Chapelle (1818), which readmitted France to the concert of respectable nations. The latter produced the proposal that the powers should guarantee existing frontiers and governments in perpetuity.

All this was too much for the British government, which in advising the Prince Regent against the Holy Alliance had put him into the company of the Sultan and the Pope. By British standards, Lord Liverpool's government was unusually conservative: in its internal policies it was resisting reform on all fronts. But it could not allow the reactionaries of Europe to create the international equivalent of a steam-engine with no form of safety-valve. At each of the subsequent Congresses held at Troppau (1820), Laibach (1821), and Verona (1822), the British held strong reservations about the successive expeditions for crushing revolution in Naples, Greece, and Spain. On the critical issue of the revolt of Spain's South American colonies, the British Foreign Secretary, George Canning, joined the US President, James Monroe, in forbidding any sort of European intervention in the Americas. 'I called the New World into existence', he told the House of Commons in 1826, 'to redress the Balance of the Old.' In effect, he killed the Congress System stone dead. 'Things are getting back to a wholesome state,' he remarked shortly before his death. 'Every nation for itself, and God for us all.'

None the less, the short-lived 'Congress System' was important for setting the scene within which nineteenth-century Europe began its stormy career. Despite its failure to create any durable institutions—which had briefly promised to assume the mantle of some premature League of Nations—it set the climate of the conservative Continental order against which all subsequent reformers and revolutionaries had to contend. It delineated the international arena in which the five recognized powers—the Quadruple Alliance plus a reinstated France—were to operate against all upstarts and newcomers for the next century. Despite important modifications, it presided over a map of Europe that was not to change in its essentials until 1914–18.

From the starting-point of 1815 the century evolved through three clear stages, those of reaction (1815–48), reform (1848–71), and rivalry (1871–1914). In the first stage, the conservative fortress held out with varying success until it collapsed amidst the general revolutionary outburst of 1848. In the second stage, the powers reluctantly conceded that controlled reform was preferable to endless resistance. Important concessions were made on all fronts. Constitutions were granted, the last serfs emancipated. Two of the three leading contenders for national independence were allowed to achieve it. In the third and final stage, Europe entered a period of intense rivalry, aggravated by diplomatic realignments, military rearmament, and colonial competition. Forty years of unequalled peace could not restrain the growing tensions which in August 1914 were permitted to pass into open conflict. Europe's modern and modernizing societies, armed with modern weapons, recklessly entered a modern war whose slaughter made Napoleon's battles look like skirmishes.

'Modernization', not to be confused with Modernism,* is now the preferred sociological term to describe the complex series of transformations which communities undergo on their way from 'backwardness' to 'modernity'. Its starting-point is the traditional type of agrarian, peasant-based society, where the majority of people work on the land and produce their own food; and its destination is the modern type of urbanized and industrialized society, where most people earn their living in towns and factories. It consists of a chain of some 30 or 40 related changes, each link of which forms a necessary component in the total operation. It certainly includes and subsumes industrialization and 'the Industrial Revolution', which is now usually taken to be just one vital part, or one stage, of the overall process. 'No change in human life since the invention of agriculture, metallurgy, and towns in the New Stone Age has been so profound as the coming of industrialisation.'[4]

By general consent, modernization was first experienced in Great Britain—or rather in certain regions of Great Britain such as Lancashire, Yorkshire, the Black Country, Tyneside, Clydebank, and South Wales. But it was soon felt on the Continent, especially in locations on or near the great coalfields in Belgium, in the Ruhr, and in Silesia. From these areas of industrial concentration its effects were gradually felt in ever-widening circles, first in the ports, then in the capital cities, and eventually right across the countries which received the industrial stimulus. It could never be complete; but to varying degrees its effects were felt across the face of Europe. When they were felt overseas, either through the colonial end of imperial economies or through local initiative, they were seen as aspects of 'Europeanization'. In this way, modernization became the focal point not only of a world-wide economic system but equally of the distinction between 'developed' and 'developing' countries.

Modernization, above all, must be seen as a motor of change, not as the static sum of its component parts. This motor, or engine, needs first to ignite, then to accelerate, and finally to reach the critical point of 'take-off', when it passes into an entirely different mode of motion. (It can best be likened to the twentieth-century phenomenon of flying, although the example of the early nineteenth-century locomotive is perhaps more fitting.) There is the long period of preparation, when the boiler is lit and a sufficient head of steam accumulated; there is the dramatic moment of departure, when steam pressure is applied to the pistons and the wheels begin to move; there is the phase of consolidation, as the engine picks up speed amidst an array of groans and judders; and there is the glorious state of cruising, when it purrs sweetly along the track with maximum speed and efficiency.

Throughout the nineteenth century, most European governments were striving to foster the conditions that would take their countries from economic ignition to social 'take-off'. Some succeeded; some did not; some had no chance of success

---

* 'Modernism' is usually reserved for cultural as opposed to socio-economic trends. In the 19th c. it was used as a pejorative term by Catholic conservatives (see p. 797), but was later employed as a catch-all label for all avant-garde artistic movements (see p. 854).

in the first place. After Britain's lonely start, most of the countries of north-western Europe followed suit in the middle of the century—first Belgium and Holland, then Prussia, Piedmont, and France. By the end of the century Britain's lead was being rapidly overhauled by the superior resources and dynamism of a united Germany.

Most countries showed marked contrasts between modernized metropolitan regions and their outlying provinces. Within the United Kingdom, England began to look very different from the outlying highlands and islands. Highly developed regions began to appear along the Paris–Lyons–Marseilles axis in France; along the Lille–Liège–Rotterdam axis in the Low Countries; along the Rhineland–Ruhr–Berlin–Saxony–Silesia axis in Germany; in the Bohemia–Vienna–Budapest core of Austria-Hungary; in Lombardy within the united Italy. Provinces such as Ireland, Brittany, Galicia, or Sicily were highly underdeveloped. The Russian Empire, despite regional contrasts of the most extreme degree, was accelerating rapidly towards modernization in the last years before 1914.

Owing to differential developments both between states and within states, the existing economic contrasts within Europe were greatly accentuated. Indeed, in the course of the nineteenth century, two distinct economic zones emerged: an advanced, predominantly industrialized and modernized zone in the North and West, and a backward, industrializing but largely unmodernized zone in the South and East. The former participated in the 'worldwide maritime economy', still dominated by Great Britain, and like Britain was able to boost its performance by the acquisition of overseas colonies. The latter could only act as a dependent source of food, raw materials, and cheap migrant labour, and as a captive market for manufactured goods.

The one major discrepancy lay with Germany, which, though it became the most dynamic country of the industrialized zone, was prevented for reasons of politics and timing from acquiring a commensurate collection of colonies. As a result, once Germany was united in 1871, it forged close economic links with the countries of Eastern Europe, thereby compensating itself for its colonial failures. Whereas in former times the divide between Western and Eastern Europe had largely been religious and political in nature, it now assumed strong economic overtones.

Industrialization in Eastern Europe was confined to localized areas which stood out like islands in a sea of rural backwardness. Such islands grew up in northern Bohemia, in the triangle of Lodz–Warsaw–Dąbrowa, in the cotton mills of Nizhny Novgorod and St Petersburg, in the Donbass, and in the oilfields of Galicia, Romania, and the Caspian. What is more, these islands were not just geographically isolated: even at the end of the century, they generated insufficient momentum for driving the economy as a whole to the point of take-off. The consequences, both social and strategic, were considerable. The mass of the peasant population suffered mounting distress; they were freed from former obligations on the land but were given no adequate opportunity for betterment in the towns. They could benefit neither from modern agriculture nor from any significant degree of industrial employment. What is more, in a poor society, the state had to tax its poverty-stricken subjects mercilessly. Here were the makings of social and political revolt. Seeing this, and fearing the dynamism of Germany, the Western Powers decided to bolster their political *rapprochement* with Russia with a campaign for massive investment. In 1890–1914 French, British, and Belgian investment in Russia mounted mightily, fuelling a massive increase in Russia's railway mileage, industrial production, and foreign trade.

The question remains whether an all-European economy existed or not. The answer is probably not. But if it did—and those massive Western investments in Russia heralded growing economic integration—then the pivotal position clearly came to be occupied by Germany. By 1900 Germany combined a major stake in the industry and commerce of the West with a dominant role in the economics of the East.

Given the contrast between Germany's economic precocity and her political retardation, it is not surprising that modernization's leading theorists were both Germans. Yet Friedrich List (1789–1846), whose *National System of Political Economy* was published in 1841, derived very different conclusions from those of Karl Marx (see pp. 837–8). For Marx, the motor of change was to be found in the class struggle; for List, it was to be found in the economic policy of the state, which could foster development by protectionist tariffs and by heavy investment in infrastructure and education. List was the most coherent advocate of what others have called the 'Prussian road to capitalism'—an example which excited the imagination of many, especially in Eastern Europe, who longed to follow in Prussia's steps.[5]

At the time few Europeans bothered to ask the fundamental question why this modernization occurred in Europe rather than elsewhere. The answer would seem to lie in a particular *coincidence* of ecological, economic, social, cultural, and political circumstances, which other more ancient and highly sophisticated civilizations did not possess. The emphasis lies on coincidence—in other words, on 'the European miracle'.[6]

Seen in detail, the process of modernization can be broken down into an apparently endless chain of sub-processes and new developments, each interacting with the others. Apart from the dozen factors which contributed to the initial Industrial Revolution, some thirty others have to be taken into account as change fuelled change in the economic, social, cultural, psychological, political, and military spheres. (See Appendix III, p. 1293.)

Agricultural production benefited from the gradual introduction of machines, from McCormick's horse-drawn reapers (1832) to steam-driven threshers, and eventually to petrol-driven tractors (1905). The export of agricultural machinery was a major item in the trade between industrial and non-industrial regions. More machines meant fewer hands on the farm, and more people who could migrate to town and factory.

The mobility of labour was greatly increased during the Revolutionary wars, when serfdom was abolished in France, Italy, and Spain, and when millions of soldiers left their villages never to return. In Eastern Europe the emancipation of the serfs took place over several later decades. It caused much misery in Prussia in 1811–48, where brutal rentification of services often led to forcible clearances. It happened overnight in Austria in 1848, leaving a trail of unresolved disputes. It was effected in the Russian Empire by the *ukaz* of 1861, in the Kingdom of Poland by the *ukaz* of April 1864.

New sources of power were brought in to supplement 'King Coal', first with gas, then with oil, and later with the commercial use of electricity. Pall Mall in London had been illuminated by gas lights in 1813; and coal-gas was generally available in Britain for domestic and urban use from the 1820s. Oil was available from the 1860s. Oilfields were opened up in Europe at Borysław (Galicia), at Ploeşti (Romania), and at Baku on the Caspian. With time, the internal combustion engine (1889) was to prove as revolutionary as the steam engine. Electricity became widely available only in the 1880s, following Gramme's perfection of the dynamo (1869) and the construction by Deprez of high-tension transmission cables (1881). It could produce heat, light, and traction. The debut of 'la Fée Électricité' took place at the Universal Exhibition in Paris in 1900. At that time, 92 per cent of the world's energy still came from coal.

Power-driven machines and engines were applied to an ever-widening range of operations, from conveyor belts to steamboats. The critical developments, however, were those of machine tools—machines that manufactured machines—and of power tools, such as the steam-hammer or pile-driver, which eliminated the manual element from heavy operations. Henry Maudslay (1771–1831) of Woolwich, inventor of the metal lathe (1797), is sometimes seen as the father of the field.

Mining, for all the advances in pumping and safety, remained a labour-intensive industry. In 1900 as in 1800, millions of European coalminers crouched at the coalface, pick in hand, selling their health for a high wage and silicosis. Iron-mining was centred on the rich 'Minette' deposits in Luxemburg-Lorraine, in northern Spain, in northern Sweden, and at Krivoi Rog in Ukraine. Metallurgy made greater progress. A series of advances in blast-furnace design culminated in Sir Henry Bessemer's Converter at Sheffield (1856) and in Martin's open-hearth process at Sireuil (1864). The Railway Age was supplied with cheap, high-quality steel which, apart from rails, could be used for bridges, ships, building frames, munitions. In the 1880s advances in the theory and practice of allotropy brought a wide range of high-grade alloys on to the markets, with specialized uses in tool-making and artillery. Electro-metallurgy facilitated aluminium production. If the eighteenth-century ironmasters were the princes of the first Industrial Revolution, the steelmakers of the late nineteenth century, such as Schneider of Le Creusot or Krupp of Essen, were their true heirs apparent. Steel production became the key index of industrial power. (See Appendix III, pp. 1296–7).

Transport improved dramatically in speed, efficiency, and comfort. Roads entered a new era with John McAdam's stone and tar surface (1815), only fully utilized after the arrival of the motor car. Bridging acquired fresh dimensions with Telford's first suspension bridge at the Menai Straits (1819). Railways carried ever more passengers and freight ever more cheaply and faster. Overland travel time between Paris and St Petersburg was cut from 20 days in 1800 to 30 hours in 1900. Europeans were united by the romance and the utility of their railways. By the turn of the century, by far the densest network had been built in Belgium (42.8 km of track per 100 km^2 as compared to 19 km in the UK and 17.2 km in Germany). By far the most extensive provision had been made in Sweden (27 km per 10,000 inhabitants as against 12.2 km in Belgium). By far the worst provision had been made in Serbia (2.5 km per 10,000 as compared with 5.7 km in European Russia). [**BENZ**]

In aviation, the Montgolfiers' hot-air balloon, first tested on 5 June 1783 at Annonay near Lyons, made ballooning an important military skill throughout the nineteenth century. It was superseded by Count Zeppelin's dirigible airship (1900) and shortly afterwards by aeroplanes. In the 1890s Otto Lilienthal pioneered gliding in Germany, and in 1903 at Dayton (Ohio) the Wright Brothers achieved manned, petrol-driven flight. On 25 July 1909 Louis Blériot sensationally flew a monoplane across the English Channel in 31 minutes.

Communication systems improved in parallel. The creation of unified postal services made rapid correspondence available to all. Postage stamps made their appearance with Great Britain's 'Penny Black' on 1 May 1840. They were introduced in Zurich and Geneva (1843), in France and Bavaria (1849), in Prussia, Austria, and Spain (1850), in Sweden (1855), in Russia and Romania (1858), in Poland (1860), in Iceland (1873). The invention of the electric telegraph (1835), of the telephone (1877), and of radio (1896) rendered long-distance communication instantaneous. The most famous demonstration of the value of superior communication was staged on 19 June 1815, when Nathan Rothschild made a record killing on the London stock market, having used a special yacht to bring news of Waterloo many hours in advance of his rivals. Important improvements in international communications were effected by the International Postal Union (1874), the International Telegraph Union (1875), the International Bureau of Weights and Measures (1875), and the Central Bureau for Railway Traffic (1890). [**PHOTO**]

Capital investment multiplied in proportion to growing returns. Private firms reinvested growing profits; governments invested a growing proportion of rising taxation. A bottomless demand for capital exhausted the possibilities of private borrowing, and revived the potential for joint-stock companies (which in England and France, though not Scotland, had been curtailed since the Bubble disaster of 1720). From the 1820s the limited joint-stock company became familiar all over Europe. These *sociétés anonymes* (SA) or *Aktiengesellschaft* (AG) or 'Company Limited', with their shareholders and their AGMs, paid dividends to their investors whilst owing only limited liability to their creditors. Soon, through 'horizontal' mergers or 'vertical' contracts, they were combining themselves into ever-larger conglomerates—either consolidated trusts or confederated cartels. In Britain, where fears of monopoly were strong, trusts and cartels were slow

BENZ

I N 1885, Carl Benz of Mannheim (1844–1929) built a three-wheeled, self-propelled, petrol-driven *motorwagen*. Often billed as 'the first motor-car', it marked only the mid-point in two centuries of car history. A steam-driven vehicle built by Nicholas Cugnot (1725–1804) had earned the name of *automobile* as long ago as 1769. Steam carriages were in widespread service by 1850. Gas-driven cars were also tried. But it was the four-stroke, internal-combustion engines of Nikolaus Otto (1876), Gottlieb Daimler (1885), and Rudolf Diesel (1897) which really gave motor transport its future.

The original Benz tricycle is exhibited in the *Deutsches Museum* at Munich. It has two 80-spoke, solid-rimmed driving wheels connected to differential gears, and one forward guide-wheel steered by an upright handle. The engine, underneath a raised bench seat, had electric ignition. It developed less than 1 hp, but achieved a speed of 16 kph. There was no coachwork.[1]

European motorization was greatly assisted by André Michelin's pneumatic tyre (1888) and by American methods of mass production (1908). Motor cycles, lorries, and buses proliferated. The turn of the century welcomed major commercial firms such as Fabbrica Italiana di Automobilismo di Torino (FIAT, 1899) and Renault in Paris (1901). The Daimler-Benz 'Mercedes' of 1901 and the Rolls-Royce 'Silver Ghost' of 1906 set new standards of luxury and reliability. (Lenin owned a Rolls-Royce.) Two world wars slowed down growing car ownership, but increased the number of transport vehicles and of trained drivers. Popular motoring reached a landmark with Hitler's inauguration of the Volkswagen 'Beetle' in 1938. Motoring in Scandinavia was pioneered by Volvo of Gothenburg, and in Czechoslovakia by Skoda of Plzen. A Polski Fiat was built under licence in inter-war Poland. The era of general motorization reached Western Europe after 1950, and the Soviet bloc from the late 1960s.

The history of technology is bedevilled by claims about 'firsts', which often distort the essentially collaborative and cumulative nature of technological advance. Yet moments of qualitative change do occur. The difficulty is to identify them. When, for example, was the first powered flight? One can take one's choice between Launoy and Bienvenu's model 'bowstring' helicopter (1784), Henry Giffard's steam-powered airship (1852), the petrol-powered aeroplane (1890) of Clément Ader, whom it carried on a flight of 50 metres, or the experimental rockets of K. E. Tsiolkovsky. Most reference works prefer a flight at Kill Devil Hill (North Carolina) on 17 December 1903. But they refer to a different category, 'powered and controlled flight'.[2]

PHOTO

A N old barnyard at Chalons-sur-Sâone had the distinction of transmitting its image onto the world's first photograph. One day in 1826, Joseph Nicéphore Niepce succeeded in capturing the image on pewter plate after an exposure of eight hours. Thirteen years later Niepce's partner, Louis Daguerre (1789–1851), was able to market a photographic system which required an exposure of thirty minutes onto copper plates covered by light-sensitive silver chloride. The Daguerrotype launched a long process of evolution which led to the popular box camera, colour film, movies, sound movies, X-rays, infra-red and miniature photography, and, most recently, electronic camcorders.[1]

The impact of photography on peace and war cannot be exaggerated. It helped destroy the *raison d'être* of representational art. [**IMPRESSION**] It transformed people's visual consciousness of themselves and of the world around them. It put a powerful tool at the disposal of every branch of science and communications. Pictures of the Crimean War brought the realities of military conflict to the world's attention, just as family portraits revolutionized perceptions of social life. Photography also brought a new dimension to the historical record. Fifty years before sound could be recorded [**SOUND**], photographic collections began to amass real images of all aspects of the past. [**AUSCHWITZ**]

Yet the realism of photography was deceptive. The art of the retoucher in official Soviet photography, for example, was notorious. Stalin removed all traces of Trotsky's presence from the record; and Gorbachev's unsightly birthmark was removed as late as 1985. But even the honest photographer's arbitrary selection of angle, of the momentary snapshot, of light, tone, and texture, and, above all, of subject, leaves as much hidden as revealed. The camera, like the historian, always lies.

---

to develop. Many of the largest British companies, such as the steamship lines P. & O. or Cunard, appeared in the 1840s. But in France cartels were common. In united Germany there was little opposition to enormous trusts or *Konzernen* on the American model, which dominated each sector of the market.

Domestic markets were boosted by population growth, by the greater accessibility of population centres, by expanding affluence, and by the creation of entirely new sorts of demand. Among many newcomer industries the most important was the chemical industry, which grew from the separation of aniline dye stuffs (1856), the Solvay process of soda extraction (1863), and the production of artificial fertilizers. A barrage of exciting artificial materials then descended, including plastics, concrete, cellophane, celluloid, rayon, viscose, aspirin. German names were specially prominent among the chemical pioneers, notably Liebig, Hofmann, Bunsen, and Bayer. [MAUVE]

Foreign trade was boosted by the opening up of new continents, especially America and Africa, by the drive for colonies, by the hunger at home for raw materials, by the thirst abroad for an ever-greater range of manufactured goods. Foreign and domestic markets became interdependent. [JEANS]

Government policy towards modernization varied in accordance with a country's regime, its resources, and its relative position. Few could fail to see the benefits; but governments of poor countries, like Russia or Spain, vacillated between their shame of backwardness and their fear of dependence. Autocratic regimes like Russia could isolate themselves until a decision to accept foreign investment was taken. More liberal or more indecisive regimes, like Austria-Hungary, could not.

Once the Industrial Revolution was in motion, a long series of consequences ensued. In the purely economic sphere, the growth of the money economy turned self-sufficient peasants into wage-earners, consumers, and taxpayers, each with new demands and aspirations. Paper banknotes came into general circulation. A vast range of new skills and techniques in marketing, advertisement, and distribution was nurtured. The deluge of developments in science and technology took innovations away from the private inventor and into the realm of systematic, sponsored R. & D. The need for financial services great and small led to the proliferation of credit associations, savings banks, and insurance companies. The multiplication of commercial transactions encouraged the standardization of weights, measures, and currencies.

In the social sphere, urbanization on a massive scale brought a welter of new problems, a set of new social classes, and a crop of new public services. The latter included paved streets, city transport, street lighting, fire brigades, waterworks, gasworks, sewerage works; town-planning, hospitals, parks, and police. The old rural distinction between the nobles and the peasants was overtaken by the new urban distinction between the middle classes and the working classes. Just as the middle classes were conscious of strata within their ranks, with professional lawyers and doctors feeling much superior to traders and shopkeepers, so the working classes were channelled into hierarchies of their own. Wage-labourers formed an important sector of employees both on farms and in factories, and as 'navvies' on the ubiquitous construction projects. Domestic service in the large number of prosperous middle-class family houses provided a vital source of employment for both men and women. Employment in the new factories was thought more prestigious than self-employment in the older crafts. Skilled, well-paid specialists and foremen could feel themselves 'proletarian aristocrats' vis-à-vis the unskilled casuals and the urban poor. The concept of class based on flexible economic criteria was strongly opposed to the older groupings based on birth and legal privilege, and was a central feature of modern society.

The traditional European family household had always been thought to be large, complex, stable, and patriarchal. Modern research has challenged some of

MAUVE

SOMETIME in 1856 an 18-year-old student began experimenting in the back room of his home in the leafy London suburb of Harrow. The boy, later Sir William Henry Perkin (1838–1907), was trying to produce a synthetic form of the anti-malarial drug, quinine. Instead, by oxidizing aniline sulphate with potassium dichromate, he chanced on a new precipitate. When he dried it and extracted it in alcohol, he saw a brilliant colour which no one had ever seen before. It was the world's first synthetic dye. He called it 'Tyrian Purple'. French chemists later called it *mauveine* after the mallow flower or *mauve:*[1]

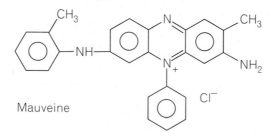

Mauveine

Two years later, when Perkin was already manufacturing mauveine commercially, another youngster from the Royal College of Chemistry, Johann Peter Griess, analysed the reaction which accounted for such startling results. He established that primary aromatic amines, like aniline, when treated with a mixture of hydrochloric acid and sodium nitrite, will give diazo compounds. These in turn react with phenolic compounds or aromatic amines to give intensely coloured products known as azo dyes. Aniline, for example, when treated with a mixture of hydrochloric acid and sodium nitrite, gives benzenediazonium chloride.[2] A key feature of this 'diazo-reaction', as of other dyes, lies in the presence in the molecule of so-called *chromophores*, that is, of groups of atoms which absorb light of a very specific wavelength and give the end product a unique colour.

Where mauveine led the way, other artificial colours followed in profusion: Magenta and Violet Imperial (1860), Bleu de Lyon (1862), Aniline Yellow and Aniline Black (1863), Dahlia Pink, Perkin's Green, and Manchester or Bismarck Brown (1864), Alizarin Red (1871), and London Orange (1875). When the British Post Office chose mauveine for printing the famous '1*d*. lilac' stamps of 1881, it was already falling from fashion. But the aesthetics of colour would never be the same again.

For colour constitutes one of the fundamental properties of matter, and hence of human reactions to the environment. In Europe, yellow has traditionally been associated with cowardice, red with anger, black with depression. Greens and browns are supposed to soothe, blues and reds to stimulate. Northern Europeans are thought to prefer subtle, subdued shades; the Mediterranean peoples revel in bright, primary colours.

The invasion of everyday life by unrestricted colour undoubtedly triggered a profound change. Prior to mauveine, all colours and pigments had to be extracted from natural materials. The root of the madder, *Rubia tinctorum*, was the standard source of reds. Thousands of tons of the plant had to be carted to every textile town. Indigo, which the Romans obtained from shellfish for their 'imperial purple', was the main source of blues: fustic or *annatto* of yellow. Some shades and colours, notably green, could only be achieved by double dyeing. A semi-artificial red called *murexide* was produced in France *c*.1850 by treating bird-droppings with nitric acid.

After mauveine, however, the supply of dazzling hues knew few bounds. By the late twentieth century the number of synthetic dyes produced commercially in Europe had risen to over 4,000.[3] Garish posters, gaudy clothes, and glamorous wallpaper—not to mention 'technicolor' films, colour photographs, and colour television—delight or disgust the post-industrial age in ways that the pre-industrials could not have imagined.

England's initial lead soon passed to Germany, where Friedrich Bayer (1825–80) founded his first aniline dyestuffs factory in a washhouse at Wuppertal-Barmen in 1863.[4] Bayer, BASF (Badische Anilin und Soda Fabrik), and Hoechst quickly turned Germany into the world capital of chemicals. By 1890, Germany's chemical industry was twenty times larger than Britain's.[5] The conglomerate of I.G. Farben, like Britain's ICI, was set up after the First World War.[5]

Synthetic dyes soon led scientists into fields unknown to the early dyemasters. By producing all the many categories of synthetic and semi-synthetic materials which have since been invented, modern chemistry has shattered the assumption that Nature or God alone could design the inner structure of substances. Synthetic dyes preceded the first semi-synthetic material—*Parkseine* or *Celluloid* (1862), and the semi-artificial fibre—*viscose* (1891). They foreshadowed the invention of synthetic drugs such as *phenacetin* (1888), *asprin* (1899), *salvarsan* (1910), *acriflavine* (1916), and *heroin*; the isolation of hormones such as *insulin* (1921) or *thyroxin* (1926), which were eventually synthesized; and the production of *chloramphenicol* (1950), the first synthetic antibiotic.

Chemistry became an art as well as a science. Its creations, which began to proliferate wildly after Baekeland's *Bakelite* (1907), Raschig's *amino-plastics* (1909), and of Ostromislensky's *polyvinyl chloride* or *PVC* (1912), have become an essential component of material life. Yet from the day in 1864 when the Empress Eugénie of France wore a gown in triphenylmethane green, synthetic products were shown to have aesthetic as well as practical qualities.

JEANS

'Gènes' is the French name for Genoa, and by extension for a traditional style of trousers worn by Genoese sailors. *Serge de Nîmes* was the name of a tough blue sailcloth, now corrupted to 'denim', traditionally woven in the French town. Levi Strauss (1829–1902) was a native of Bavaria who emigrated to New York at the age of fourteen and who joined his brothers in their business of supplying the prospectors and frontiersmen of the Californian Gold Rush. Some time in the 1860s Levi's company had the idea of matching the denim cloth with the Genoese trousers, and of strengthening the pockets and seams with brass horse-harness rivets. Thus was produced the most durable and universal item in the history of fashion design—a German immigrant using French materials and Italian style to invent an archetypal American product.

'Blue jeans' remained workaday clothing in North America for almost a century, before taking Europe (and the rest of the world) by storm in the 1960s, a prime symbol of 'Americanization'.[1]

---

the preconceptions about this 'classic family of Western nostalgia', and has shown that the small, simple household and the nuclear family were not exclusively modern inventions. Even so, it would be hard to accept that modernization did not have a profound effect on family structures. Certainly, it was the belief that modern life was destroying the stability of the family that motivated Frédéric Le Play (1806–82), the pioneer of family history and conceptualizer of *la famille souche* or 'stem family'.[7]

Women's circumstances were radically transformed. Traditional rural life had assured women of an equitable division of shared labour, and the presence of an extended family which eased the pressures of child-bearing and motherhood. Modern urban life turned the man into a primary 'breadwinner', and left the woman either as a lonely homemaker and domestic manageress or, in the case of the working class, as a thrice-burdened outworker, housekeeper, and parent. Not surprisingly, beyond the prim parlours of polite society lay a teeming underworld of prostitution, desperation, and early death.

Industrialization brought wave after wave of migration: first on a local or seasonal basis from village to factory; next on a regional basis from the countryside to the towns; and, from the 1850s onwards, on an international and an intercontinental basis to all the industrial cities of Europe and the USA. Unregulated migration brought in its turn urban overcrowding, vagrancy, housing shortages, homelessness, epidemics of typhus and cholera, unemployment amidst prosperity, persistent and irremediable poverty. With much delay, the worst epidemics, such as the Europe-wide outbreaks of cholera in 1830–5, 1847–8, 1853–6, 1865–7, 1869–74, 1883–7, and 1893–5, provoked a revolution in public and private hygiene and the institution of communal health services. [**SANITAS**] Medical progress eventually resulted in a startling drop in the death rate and in infant mortality.

Rising population, however, compounded the evils of overpopulation in the villages, and of sweatshops, child labour, inhuman working hours, female exploitation, and unspeakable sorrow in the slums. Organized crime thrived on poverty and the psychopathology of urban living. It spawned a new underclass of committed criminals, the new idea of professional police forces modelled on Scotland Yard, a new profession of detectives, a new rash of prison building, and, with *The Memoirs of Sherlock Holmes* (1894), a new literary genre—the crime thriller.

The terrible contrast between rich and poor has never been better described than by Benjamin Disraeli (1804–81), novelist and prime minister. In *Sybil* (1845) Disraeli wrote of 'Two nations between whom there is no intercourse and no sympathy; who are as ignorant of each other's habits, thoughts, and feelings as if they were . . . inhabitants of different planets'.[8] The description was accurate enough; but the accusation was not altogether fair. The nineteenth century also saw a huge explosion of private charities. [**CARITAS**]

In the cultural sphere, education vastly expanded its frontiers. Town dwellers could no longer function without basic literacy and numeracy: universal primary education became necessary for children of both sexes. Technical education was required for the army of fitters, technicians, and apprentices; higher scientific education for the corps of engineers and researchers. Government and business leaders called for secondary schools of a new type to train the executive cadres of the civil service, the colonial departments, and industry. Women's education was launched. Mass literacy, however, opened the way for new forms of mass culture: popular magazines, trash novels, romances, and whodunnits, comics, self-help almanacs, family reference works. Regular incomes created the possibility of new forms of leisure and recreation: musical associations, family holidays, tourism, mountaineering, and sport, football for the workers, golf for the bosses. [**RELAX-ATIO**][**TOUR**] The mania for physical pursuits, which was a product of cramped urban living, combined with the mania for education to create a number of hybrid youth movements such as the widespread 'Sokol' associations in central Europe or *Scouting for Boys* and *Guiding for Girls* (1908). Religious culture responded in tune. Literate children could not be expected simply to learn their catechism by rote. The church halls of urban parishes became the focal point of social, charitable, and temperance activities. In the Protestant countries evangelical fundamentalism, Sunday schools, and Bible-reading classes proliferated. In the Catholic countries the Church organized the first industrial parishes, worker-priests, and private Catholic primary schools. In the universities, with scholars struggling to comprehend the changing world about them, a whole new range of social sciences made their appearance—economics, ethnography, anthropology, linguistics, sociology. Each of the new disciplines were to have a profound influence on the recognized fields of study: philosophy, science, history, and literature.

SANITAS

IN 1829 the city of Orenburg in the Urals was hit by an unprecedented wave of cholera. In 1830 the same cholera hit Moscow. In 1831 it marched with the Russian Army against Poland before spreading to Hungary, Austria, and Prussia. It reached London in February 1832, Paris in March, Amsterdam in June, and thence spread to Scandinavia. The Spaniards tried to protect themselves behind a decree passing the death sentence on all non-quarantined immigrants. But in January 1833 cholera reached Oporto, and entered Spain through Portugal. Though no one knew it, Europe stood in the front line of the second of six pandemics of cholera that were to sweep repeatedly round the world for the next ninety years; and Russia was Europe's bacterial gateway.[1] [**EPIDEMIA**]

The effects of the pandemic were all the more deadly since its workings were not yet fully understood. *Cholera* is the old Greek word for 'gutter', and accurately described the violent intestinal flux that could empty out a sufferer's substance in a couple of days. Medical opinion is unsure whether earlier forms of this dysentery-like illness, under a variety of names, had in fact been the same. But the guilty agent was eventually identified in 1883 as a bacterium, *vibrio cholerae 01*, which infected the small intestine after being imbibed with contaminated water. First observed by British Army doctors in India, the launch-pad of all the pandemics, physicians eventually realized that it could best be prevented by a clean water supply and best treated by simple rehydration techniques. The initial outbreak of 1817–23 had moved eastwards round Asia. But all subsequent pandemics—in 1829–51, 1852–9, 1863–79, 1881–96, and 1899–1923—visited Europe with a vengeance. The second pandemic, which had raged for fifteen years in the USA, came round again for a final fling in Europe in 1847–51. In Britain 53,000 died in 1848, and a similar number died in France in 1849. In 1851 a statue was erected in Paris to implore God's mercy on cholera's helpless victims.

Help, however, was to hand. Cholera had the distinction of provoking Europe's first co-ordinated initiatives for public health, at both the national and the international level. In 1848 a General Board of Health was established in London to address the foul conditions and high death rates in Britain's burgeoning cities. Fortified by Disraeli's great Public Health Act (1875), which held all local authorities responsible for efficient sewage treatment, drainage, and water supply, it protected the United Kingdom most effectively. By the fourth pandemic, British losses of *c*.15,000 were only one-tenth of those experienced in Russia, Germany, Italy or Austria-Hungary. After the fifth pandemic, when Hamburg (1893) lost over 8,000 citizens, and Moscow and St Petersburg (1893–4) over 800,000, Britain could boast that it had already warded off its last indigenous case of cholera.

In 1851 Napoleon III took the initiative of convening the founding International Health Conference in Paris. Its purpose was to exchange information about the spread and prevention of disease, especially cholera. At the time neither Pasteur nor Lister had made the pioneering discoveries of bacteriology, but it led to a regular series of conferences on hygiene, and in 1907 to the International Health Organization in Paris, the forerunner of the WHO. By then, especially in Poland, *Choléra!* only remained as one of Europe's favourite swear-words.

Ironically, no sooner had Europe tamed cholera than an aberrant strain of influenza surpassed all of cholera's triumphs. Traced to an outbreak of swine fever in Iowa in January 1918, the influenza pandemic of 1918–19 sailed to Europe with the US army. Known as the *Blitzkatarrh*, the 'Flanders Grippe', and, through the infection of the King of Spain, as 'the Spanish Lady', it specialized in prime young adults, particularly women. During the terminal months of the First World War it devastated Germany, where influenza was not even a notifiable disease, paralysing the workforce of major cities, interrupting deliveries and troop movements. In three terrible peaks—July 1918, October 1918, and February 1919—it destroyed millions of Europeans, possibly 40 million world-wide. '[This pandemic] killed more humans in a couple of months than any scourge in history.'[2]

In the psychological sphere, urban and industrial life fostered attitudes that were entirely foreign to country dwellers. The factory hooter, the railway timetable, the need for punctuality and sobriety were all innovations that a peasant might find strange and irksome. Consumerism and compulsory thrift were complementary reactions of the fearful spender let loose on an unfamiliar market. Class-consciousness was born of anxious people uncertain of their status in a strangely mobile society. National consciousness was bred in newly educated generations who in their rural villages had never given a moment's thought to their identity or their language. Political consciousness was aroused in generations who were no longer helpless serfs and who could cultivate personal opinions about the rights and wrongs of political events. Indeed, national and political consciousness was often aroused most fiercely in those countries where a repressed population was deprived of free expression and a free vote. Lastly, there was the psychology of late nineteenth-century imperialism, where a whole generation of parvenu Europeans were taught to look down on other races and cultures in ways that secure and settled societies would not have embraced.

In the political sphere, governments faced new types of challenge. They were no longer addressing themselves to their own narrow élite but to a mass audience of taxpayers, holding a wide variety of views expressed with growing confidence and sophistication. They could not restrict political life indefinitely to the traditional male propertied caste; and they were increasingly faced with organized campaigns

CARITAS

I N 1818 the Netherlands *Maatschaapij van Weldadigheid* (Benevolent Society) opened a complex of labour colonies for the care of the unemployed. They conformed to a much older Dutch tradition for correcting the idle. [**BATAVIA**] One colony at Veenhuizen catered for up to 4,000 men convicted of begging. Another at Leyden catered for indigent women. Three 'free colonies' at Frederiksoord, Willemsoord, and Wilhelminasoord were designed to teach agricultural skills to voluntary inmates. In due course, they were funded by the state. Similar institutions came into being in Germany, Belgium, and Switzerland, often under military-style discipline.[1] They are examples both of the growing provision of social care in nineteenth-century Europe and also of growing regimentation. As with the workhouses introduced by the English Poor Law Amendment Act (1834), it was assumed that able-bodied recipients of charity would have to work.

Charity in various forms had been practised since ancient times. But the fundamental Christian principles were laid down by St Thomas Aquinas, who distinguished seven 'spiritual aids' and seven 'good works'. The former were listed as *consule* (counsel), *carpe* (sustain), *doce* (teach), *solare* (console), *remitte* (rescue), *fer* (pardon), and *ora* (pray); the latter as *vestio* (clothe), *poto* (to give water), *cibo* (feed), *redimo* (redeem from prison), *tego* (shelter), *colligo* (nurse), and *condo* (bury). From this, one could determine the classes of unfortunates to whom charity was to be extended. They included the bewildered, the weak, the illiterate, the bereaved, the oppressed, the criminal, the sinful, the stranger, the ragged, the hungry, the imprisoned, the homeless, the sick, the mad, and the dead. Christian teaching was emphatic: 'Faith, Hope and Charity: these three,' says St. Paul, 'but the greatest of these is Charity.'[2] For it is Charity meaning 'love for one's neighbour' that begets charity meaning 'generous giving'.

In medieval times, the burden of care had fallen on the Church, and was funded from the tithe. St Bernard launched the charitable tradition in monasteries, St Francis the tradition of social action within the community. Both had many successors. Royal, aristocratic, and municipal patrons were moved to found a widespread network of *maisons-Dieu* for the sick and infirm, of hospices for pilgrims, wayfarers, and strangers, of alms-houses for the deserving poor, and of leprosaria. A large city like London possessed a number of more specialized institutions, such as St Bartholomew's Hospital, St Mary's of Bethlehem, or 'Bedlam', for the insane, and St Mary's 'Converts' Inn' for Jewish converts expelled by their own community.[3] As elsewhere, prosperous merchants such as Sir Richard Whittington (d. 1423), sometime Lord Mayor, left generous endowments. [**LEPER**] [**MERCANTE**]

This medieval system began to fracture in the Reformation period, particularly in the Protestant countries. The dissolution of the English monasteries (1540) had social consequences with which the hard-pressed Elizabethan Poor Laws could not cope. Modern Europe was obliged to seek new solutions. As the population grew, charitable institutions became much larger and more specialized. Purpose-built veterans' homes, mental asylums, houses of correction, prisons, medical 'infirmaries', workhouses, labour colonies, and charity schools were multiplying fast in the eighteenth and nineteenth centuries. Liberal and humanitarian movements pressed for the abolition of slavery, torture, and of degrading conditions. The burden of funding and administration passed from the Church to parish and city councils, to private benevolent societies, and eventually to the state. [**PICARO**] [**TORMENTA**]

The expansion of charitable activities has usually been seen, in the Whig tradition, as evidence for the onward march of civilization. Some historians, however, have thought otherwise. They point out that, while the institutions of social care greatly expanded, they subjected the ever-growing army of inmates to ever-rising levels of repression. The recipients may not have feared the gross physical brutalities of times past, but rigorous regimes of psychological and moral coercion could rob them of their freedom, their dignity, and their individuality. Regimentation was on the rise across a wide spectrum of social life, on the military parade-ground, in the school classroom, in factories, in the hospital ward, in the workhouses. It was seen by its originators as the necessary price for efficiency.

But there may have been a darker side. One has to wonder whether the regimentation of the masses was not somehow connected with the drive towards more liberal political institutions. Unremitting labour was the fate of both the employed and the unemployed. And as Nietzsche remarked cynically: 'Work is the most efficient form of policing.' Political controls could only be relaxed when social controls were tightened.

This line of thought is implicit in the work of the French philosopher and historian Michel Foucault (1926–84). Himself a sado-masochist who died of AIDS, he was determined to explore extreme experiences, and he came to be an unsparing critic of modern social reform. His studies of the history of mental asylums, which locked the most vulnerable persons out of sight, or of sexual attitudes, which drove basic human drives into the realm of hypocrisy and taboo, caused him to pronounce modern times to be 'the Age of Repression'.[4] All social relationships are determined by power. 'Bourgeois society', he declared, 'was a society of blatant and fragmented perversion.'[5] He raises issues to which the inmates of those nineteenth-century labour colonies may have been quite sympathetic.

for universal male suffrage and later for women's suffrage. The majority of Europeans were enfranchised between 1848 and 1914. As a result, political parties sprang up, each with a mass following and each devoted to the interests of liberals, conservatives, Catholics, peasants, workers, or whatever. Governments had also to institute a wide range of specialized ministries and to run a bulging bureaucracy that had a mind and will of its own. They were employers on a grand scale, and were forced to consider the welfare of their employees with National Insurance and pensions. They had to reorganize local government to suit the needs of self-important cities and of freshly populated provinces, and hence to rethink the entire relationship between capital and periphery. They had to cope with a wide range of professional, commercial, and industrial associations—and, most particularly in the second half of the century, the trade unions—who claimed the right to act as pressure-groups long before they were formally integrated into political life.

Finally, in the military sphere, both generals and politicians had to contemplate conflicts where civilians and women would be recruited to the war effort, where conscript armies of unheard-of size would be mobilized, and where staff officers armed with railway timetables would marshal men armed with machine-guns onto ground that could be subjected to 20 tons of high-explosive shell-fire per square foot per hour. Of all the challenges, this was the one which by 1914 they were least equipped to face. Reflections on the implications of warfare did not lead Europeans to reduce their military establishments. Kant, in 1797, had issued the definitive moral condemnation. 'War', he wrote at the end of his *Metaphysics of Manners*, 'ought to have no place there.' But much more common was the assumption of De Maistre that war was 'the habitual state of the human species'. The treatise *On War* (1832), written by the Prussian general Karl von Clausewitz (1780–1831), was one of the most lucid and influential books of the century. 'War', he wrote, 'is the continuation of politics by other means.'

Recounting the onward march of modernization, it is easy to give the impression that the road was smooth and the direction obvious. But such an impression would be false. The territory was often hostile, the obstacles enormous, the accidents unremitting. For every entrepreneur there was an aristocrat who did not want the railway to cross his land; for every machine there was a dispossessed craftsman who wanted to smash it; for every fresh factory, abandoned villages: for every shining city hall, slums. Of every ten children born into that Europe of pride and progress, three or four died. Economic growth did not mount on a steady upward curve: the new capitalism was capricious. Violent booms alternated with sudden slumps; the first decade of peace after 1815 witnessed a prolonged recession throughout Europe. Later periods of recession occurred after 1848, and after 1871. All periods contained shorter cycles of advance and retreat. Wages and prices moved by fits and starts. In the past, economic crises had been caused by visible things like plague or famine. Now they were said to be caused by inexplicable things like over-production, market conditions, or monetary failure. Average material conditions were definitely improving; but for individual families they often spelt unfamiliar wealth or desperate penury. Materially, European society was better off; psychologically, Europeans were seriously disturbed.

None the less, the world created by European modernization was incredibly rich for its chief, middle-class beneficiaries—rich in material possessions, rich in variety, rich in culture and style, rich in new experiences. A university professor in Scotland in the 1880s might earn £600 annually, ten times the upper reaches of the working class and equivalent to the price of a six-bedroomed house. In 1890–1 the seventeen official nationalities of Austria-Hungary shared 215 registered spas and 1,801 newspapers and periodicals. 'La Belle Époque' was the time when people went waltzing, dined at the Café Royale, bought pictures by the Impressionists, lived in the luxury of Art Nouveau. 'A French politician like Édouard Herriot, mayor of Lyons, could speak excellent German, and hold his own on Wagner and Kant.' In 1895 Henry James, the American novelist living in Europe, acquired electric lighting; in 1896 he rode a bicycle; in 1897 he wrote on a typewriter. And that was in a period which a British Royal Commission had called 'the Great Depression'. Money was increasing in real value as prices gently fell. The poor, at least, could eat cheap food. Only the landowning aristocracy squeaked, appalled at their shrinking fortunes. There was no major war for more than forty years. 'It looked as if this world would go on for ever.'[9]

Demographic growth was one of the surest indicators of Europe's dynamism. In brute terms, the population rose from c.150 million in 1800 to over 400 million by 1914. The accelerating rate of increase was more than twice as great as in the previous three centuries (see Appendix III, p. 1294). Europeans were reminded of the implications from the start. In 1816 the English economist Thomas Malthus (1766–1834) published the final edition of his depressing *Essay on the Principle of Population*. He predicted that, while the production of food might rise arithmetically, the growth of population would proceed geometrically. If he had been correct, Europeans would have begun to starve to death within a few decades. Indeed, some thought that the Irish Potato Famine of the 1840s was a premonition of the general disaster. [FAMINE]

The British Isles, with a limited supply of arable land and a rocketing population, looked specially vulnerable. In the event, the general disaster never occurred. Such famines as did occur, as in Ireland, struck in the most backward rural districts of Europe, in Galicia and on the Volga, not in Europe's over-crowded cities. The point came in the 1870s when large amounts of grain began to be imported from North America. But several European countries, such as Ukraine and France, showed a healthy surplus, and food prices in 1870–1900 were falling everywhere. At no time did the overall situation become critical.

The dynamics of European demography came to be much better understood in the course of the century. Sweden had been exceptional in carrying out a general census as early as 1686; but every European government now began a regular series: France and Great Britain from 1801, the German Customs Union from 1818, Austria-Hungary from 1857, Italy from 1861, Russia from 1897. By the turn of the century sophisticated statistics were available for all countries. (In Eastern Europe they were far superior to much that the twentieth century produced.)

Europe's overall population gains were due to natural increase. The annual birth rate was highest early in the century, when death rates were also high; but in the 1900s it was still buoyant, up to 40 per 1,000 in many countries. With the help of medical advances, death rates were halved from c.40 to 20 per 1,000. With the curious exception of France, fertility and reproductive enthusiasm were much higher than ever before or since. The growth of cities was dramatic: by 1914 Europe had a dozen million-plus conurbations. London, Paris, Berlin, Vienna, St Petersburg, and Istanbul had reached that status earlier on; Glasgow, Manchester, Leeds, Liverpool, Birmingham, the Ruhr, Hamburg, and Moscow followed later. Another score of cities, from Madrid to Odessa, had passed the half-million mark. Numbers in the rural population remained fairly static in the developed countries, although their proportion plummeted. In Great Britain in 1900 they represented only 8 per cent, in Germany they stood at 40 per cent, having dropped from 75 per cent in 30 years. In the underdeveloped countries, where they could represent up to 80 per cent, as in Russia, they were rising alarmingly. Europe lost 25 million emigrants to the USA in the last quarter of the century. One-quarter of the population of Galicia emigrated in the two decades before 1914 (see Appendix III, p. 1294).

Historians disagree whether the stunning social and economic changes of the nineteenth century should be regarded merely as 'the background' to cultural life or its determinant. Marx, for example, was a determinist: 'in his view all forms of thought and consciousness are determined by the class struggle, which in turn is determined by the underlying economic relations.' (If this is true, then Marx himself was not so much an original thinker as the product of his time.) At the other extreme, there are those who maintain that culture has a life of its own. Nowadays, most people would at least accept the midway proposition that culture cannot be properly understood without reference to its political, social, and economic context.

Romanticism, which became a dominant intellectual trend in many European countries in the second quarter of the nineteenth century, is seen by some historians essentially as a reaction to the Enlightenment. By others it is seen as an emanation of attitudes generated by the Industrial Revolution and the Napoleonic Wars. Actually it was all of these things. The circumstances of its origins in the 1770s were closely connected indeed to the fading appeal of the Enlightenment (see Chapter IX). At the same time, the reasons for its mass appeal in the 1820s and 1830s were closely bound up with the experiences of a generation which lived through the revolutionary ordeal, which felt the impact of machines and factories, and which fumed after 1815 under the dead weight of the reactionary regimes. Romanticism found expression almost everywhere, even in Russia, treating the Catholic/Protestant and the Catholic/Orthodox divide with indifference. It affected all the arts, but especially poetry, painting, and music, and all branches of the humanities. It grew very strong in Germany. It was well represented in Britain, though the first British Romantics like Lord Byron were better received on the Continent than at home. After some delay, it appeared in force in France and Italy, as a counterweight to the deep-rooted traditions of classicism and rationalism. In Poland and in Hungary, where it was coloured by the agonies of national defeat, it became the dominant mode of thought.

The main tenets of the Romantic movement opposed everything which the Enlightenment had stood for. Where the Enlightenment had stressed the power of Reason, the Romantics were attracted by all in human experience that is irrational: by the passions, by the supernatural and paranormal, by superstitions, pain, madness, and death. Where the Enlightenment had stressed man's growing mastery over nature, the Romantics took delight in trembling before nature's untamed might: in the terror of storms and waterfalls, the vastness of mountains, the emptiness of deserts, the loneliness of the seas. Where the Enlightenment had followed the classical taste for harmony and restraint, and for the rules which underlay civilized conventions, the Romantics courted everything which defied established convention: the wild, the quaint, the exotic, the alien, the deranged. Where the Enlightenment had sought to expound the order underlying the apparent chaos of the world, the Romantics appealed to the hidden inner 'spirits' of everything that lives and moves. Where the Enlightenment was either unreligious or anti-religious, the Romantics were profoundly religious by temperament even where they scorned conventional Christian practice. Where the Enlightenment catered for an intellectual élite, the Romantics catered for the newly liberated and educated masses.
[**PARNASSE**][**RELAXATIO**]

The Europe-wide appeal of Romanticism can be illustrated in many ways, but nowhere better than in its poetry. John Keats (1795–1821) languished archaically before the charms of a medieval maiden:

> O what can ail thee, knight-at-arms,
> Alone and palely loitering?
> The sedge is withered from the lake,
> And no birds sing.[10]

Alphonse de Lamartine (1790–1869) revelled simultaneously in the beauties of the Lac du Bourget and in thoughts of eternity:

> Ô temps, suspends ton vol! et vous, heures propices,
> Suspendez votre cours!
> Laissez-nous savourer les rapides délices
> Des plus beaux de nos jours.

(Oh, Time, suspend your flight! And you, auspicious hours, | suspend your course! | Allow us to savour the fleeting delights | of our most beautiful days.)[11]

Giacomo Leopardi (1798–1837) sang the 'Night Song of a Wandering Shepherd of Asia':

PARNASSE

I N the summer of 1835, a walking-party which included the Hungarian pianist Franz Liszt and the French writer Georges Sand checked into the Hotel de l'Union in Geneva. Their comments in the hotel register said much about their good humour and about the outlook of their Romantic generation:

	Liszt	*Sand*
Place of birth	Parnassus	Europe
Residence	–	Nature
Occupation	Musician-Philosopher	–
Provenance	Doubt	God
Destination	Truth	Heaven
Date of passport	–	Infinity
Issued by	–	Public Opinion[1]

In 1835 the idea of 'Europe' was hardly less fantastic than that of 'Parnassus'.

> Pur tu, solinga, eterna peregrina,
> che sì pensosa sei, tu forse intendi,
> questo viver tereno,
> il patir nostro, il sospirar, ché sia;
> ché sia questo morir, questo supremo
> scolorar del sembiante
> e perir dalla terra, e venir meno
> ad ogni usata, amante compagnia . . .

(Yet, lonely, eternal wanderer, I who are so thoughtful, perhaps you understand I what this earthly life may be, I our suffering and sighing, I and what this dying is, this ultimate I fading of the features, I and perishing from the earth, and falling away I from every familiar, loving company.)[12]

Joseph, Freiherr von Eichendorff (1788–1857), recounted his favourite themes of *Lust* (desire), *Heimat* (homeland), and *Waldeinsamkeit* (forest loneliness) in his native Silesia:

In einem kühlen Grunde,	(In a cool and shady hollow
Da geht ein Mühlenrad,	The old mill wheel is turning.
Mein' Liebste ist verschwunden,	But my loved one has departed
Die dort gewohnet hat . . .	From where she once was dwelling.
Sie hat mir Treu' versprochen,	She promised to be my true love,
Gab mir ein'n Ring dabei,	And sealed it with a ring.
Sie hat die Treu gebrochen,	Now all her vows are broken,
Mein Ringlein sprang entzwei.	And shattered is the ring.

RELAXATIO

O N 14 July 1865 a young English illustrator and mountaineer, Edward Whymper, climbed the Matterhorn, or Monte Cervino, at the seventh attempt. On the way down from the 4,440 m (14,566 ft) pyramid of rock, which towers over Zermatt, four of Whymper's party fell to their deaths.[1]

This was by no means the first major alpine ascent. Mont Blanc had been climbed by Ferdinand de Saussure in 1799. But Whymper's tragic feat publicized the new sport of alpinism, and underlined changing attitudes to recreation. No more was sport to be the preserve of a leisured elite. Nor was it to be confined to the traditional pursuits of hunting, shooting, fishing, riding, 'taking the waters', and the Grand Tour. Europeans of all sorts were looking for new sports, new challenges, and new sources of physical fitness.

Less than two years earlier, the Football Association had been founded at a meeting in the *Freemasons' Tavern* in London on 26 October 1863. The aim was to standardize the rules of football, and to provide the framework for organized competition. (Representatives with other ideas about the game went off to found the Rugby Union.) Professional clubs soon followed; and the English Football League was created in 1888.[2]

Football of the FA's 'soccer' variety spread rapidly to the Continent. By the end of the century it had established itself as Europe's most popular sport and most frequented spectator entertainment. The International Federation of Association Football (FIFA) was founded in Paris in May 1904 by representatives from Austria, Belgium, Denmark, England, Finland, France, Germany, Hungary, Italy, The Netherlands, Norway, Sweden, and Switzerland. It was the most egalitarian of games. As the ancient proverb went: 'All are fellows at football.'[3]

Hör' ich das Mühlrad gehen:	When I listen to the mill wheel,
Ich weiss nicht, was ich will—	I lack all thought and will.
Ich möcht' am liebsten sterben,	The best course is to perish
Da wär's auf einmal still!	For then would all be still.)[13]

And Juliusz Słowacki (1809–49), intense and eloquent, celebrated the exalted inner life:

Kto mogąc wybrać, wybrał zamiast domu,
Gniazdo na skałach orła, niechaj umie
Spać gdy źrenice czerwone od gromu
I słychać jęk szatanów w sosen szumie.

(Whoever, having the choice, in place of a home, would choose I an eagle's nest on the cliffs, may he know how I to sleep though his eyes be reddened from the lightning I and to listen to the moaning of the spirits in the murmur of the pines.)[14]

In due course Romanticism elicited a reaction against its own heady success. The reaction took the form of a revival of the ideals of Classicism: in short, of Neo-classicism. Thereafter, the rival trends remained major influences throughout the century. Their rivalry was specially evident in architecture. Rival railway companies would build their terminal stations in contrasting styles: the London and North Western built Euston Station in elegant classic; the Midland Railway built the adjoining St Pancras Station in flamboyant Neo-gothic.

The Classical–Romantic mix was particularly fruitful in literature. The three giants of the age, Alexander Pushkin (1799–1837), Adam Mickiewicz (1798–1855), and J. W. Goethe, defy easy classification, exactly because their works fuse Classical and Romantic elements into an indivisible whole. Their masterworks— *Eugene Onegin* (1832), *Pan Tadeusz* (1834), and *Faust* (1808–32) were all verse-novels or verse-dramas, completed at almost the same moment. Their supreme mastery of language at a juncture when literacy was spreading rapidly gave their authors the status of national bards, making their lines and phrases an integral part of everyday communication. There is not a Pole who cannot recite 'Oh, *Litwo*, my homeland, you are like health . . .'; not a German who has not been bewitched by 'the land where the lemon-trees bloom'; no Russian schoolchild who has not been taught the lines of 'The Bronze Horseman' from St Petersburg:

> Природой здесь нам суждено
> В Европу прорубить окно,
> Ногою твёрдой стать при море.
>
> Люблю тебя, Петра творенье,
> Люблю твой строгий, стройный вид,
> Невы державное теченье,
> Береговой её гранит,
>
> Красуйся, град Петров, и стой
> Неколебимо, как Россия !
> Да умирится же с тобой
> И побеждённая стихия;

(Here we are destined by nature | To cut a window into Europe; | And to gain a foothold by the sea . . . I love you, Peter's creation, | I love your severe, graceful appearance, | The Neva's majestic current, | the granite of her banks . . . | City of Peter, stand in all your splendour, | Stand unshakeable as Russia! | May the conquered elements, too, make their peace.)[15]

Johann Wolfgang von Goethe (1749–1832), however, was not merely a national bard. He was an Olympian who bestrode almost all intellectual domains. The variety of genres in which he excelled, his awareness of a rapidly changing world, and the numerous evolutions through which his creativity passed gave him a claim to be the last 'universal man'. Born in Frankfurt-am-Main, educated in Leipzig and Strasburg, and resident for half a century in Weimar, he was poet, dramatist, novelist, philosopher, scientist, traveller, lawyer, administrator. His initial Romantic proclivities faded in the 1780s; his classical phase, strengthened by his friend Schiller, continued until *c.*1820. The vast psychological panorama of *Faust* embraced a lifetime's reflections on the human condition. When he died, he was the greatest personality of Europe's greatest cultural era, endlessly reaching for the unreachable:

> Alles Vergängliche
> Ist nur ein Gleichnis;
> Das Unzulängliche
> Hier wird's Ereignis;
> Das Unbeschreibliche,
> Hier ist's getan;
> Das Ewig-Weibliche
> Zieht uns hinan.

(All transient things | Are only a parable; | The inaccessible | Here becomes reality; | Here the ineffable is achieved; | The Eternal Feminine | Draws us on.)[16]

The later phase of Romanticism acquired a specially morbid flavour. It has been related to the tuberculosis from which many artists suffered, and to the opium which was routinely prescribed to cure it. A seminal figure was Thomas De Quincey (1785–1859), who ran away from Manchester Grammar School and who lived as a homeless stray before becoming an Oxford drug addict. His *Confessions of an English Opium Eater* (1822) exercised a formative influence on the American writer of the grotesque, Edgar Allan Poe, and on Baudelaire. The strange, mystical outpourings of Słowacki's last years belong to this same story,[17] as do the verses of Gérard Labrunie or de Nerval (1808–55), a schizophrenic, the 'super-Romantic', 'the most Romantic of them all':

> Où sont nos amoureuses?
> Elles sont au tombeau.

> (Where are our lovers, our girls? They are in their tomb.)[18]

In the apparent derangement, and the interest in visions and hallucinations, it is not difficult to see the early seeds of the Symbolism, Freudianism, and Decadence which were to form such important elements of Modernism (see below).

The Pre-Raphaelite Brotherhood was founded in 1848 in a house on Gower Street, London, by a circle of poets and painters who congregated round Dante Gabriel Rossetti (1828–82), the son of a Neapolitan exile. Despite Continental sources of inspiration, it remained an exclusively English movement, but archetypal of the age. Apart from the Rossetti brothers, its leading members included J. E. Millais (1829–96), W. Holman Hunt (1827–1910), Ford Madox Brown (1821–93), and Edward Burne-Jones (1833–98); and it found a champion in the critic John Ruskin (1819–1900). The group took its name from its members' common enthusiasm for the art of the Italian quattrocento, which fuelled their rebellion against contemporary academic painting. They were strongly exercised by the links between art and literature—D. G. Rossetti being the translator of both Dante and Villon—and applied their principles to everything from architecture and furniture to mosaics, tapestry, stained glass, and interior design. They cultivated what they took to be both the techniques and, above all, the spirit of late medieval art. They imitated the clarity of form and brightness of colour of iconographic painting; and they exuded a moral seriousness, often expressed in mystical religiosity. Among their most celebrated images would be Millais's *Ophelia* (1851) and Hunt's *The Light of the World* (1854). One of their later recruits was William Morris (1834–96), poet, primitive socialist, craftsman, printer, and designer. At Kelmscott Manor Morris hosted some of the Brotherhood's most inspired activities, long after the group as a whole had broken up.

That same era also saw the efflorescence of the novel across the Continent. Honoré de Balzac (1799–1850) and Charles Dickens (1812–70), born *en face* at Rouen and Portsmouth, were among the first to capture the popular imagination. But in time all the major novels were translated into all major European languages. Critics differ in their estimations; but the parade of the premier division should certainly include *I promessi sposi* (The Betrothed, 1825) by Alessandro Manzoni, Balzac's *Le Père Goriot* (1834), Dickens's *Oliver Twist* (1838), Mikhail Lermontov's *A Hero of Our Time* (1840), Charlotte Brontë's *Jane Eyre* (1847), W. M. Thackeray's *Vanity Fair* (1848), *Madame Bovary* (1857) by Gustave Flaubert, Victor Hugo's *Les Misérables* (1862), Leo Tolstoy's *Anna Karenina* (1877), Fyodor Dostoevsky's *Crime and Punishment* (1866) and *The Brothers Karamazov* (1880), and *Lalka* (The Doll, 1890) by Bolesław Prus. Through the analysis of social and psychological problems fiction had become a central feature of Europe's common culture. Authors adopted the convention of projecting their own most intimate observations into their fictional creations: Flaubert was reported to have said: 'Madame Bovary, c'est moi.'

In the realm of music, as in literature, the nineteenth century assembled a vast and varied corpus of works which greatly extended the repertoire founded by the classical and early Romantic masters. Johannes Brahms (1833–97), born in Hamburg, must surely be rated the central figure. He combined an intellectual concern for Classical form with a Romantic passion for lyricism and emotional intensity, thereby earning the title of 'true heir to Bach and Beethoven'. The succession of more obviously Romantic orchestral composers began with Hector Berlioz (1803–69), whose 'Symphonie Fantastique' (1831) broke all the existing rules. Berlioz relied heavily on Romantic literature for inspiration. It was said: 'Victor Hugo is a Romantic, but Berlioz is Romanticism itself.' The Romantic list continued with the languid Polish exile Frédéric Chopin (1810–49), the supreme master of the piano; with the indefatigable Hungarian virtuoso Franz Liszt (1811–86); with Robert Schumann (1810–56) and Felix Mendelssohn-Bartholdy (1809–47). It contained most of the names who are often classed as leaders of national schools (see pp. 819–20); and it continued later in the century with the magnificent Russians Anton Rubinstein (1830–94), Peter Tchaikovsky (1840–93), and Sergei Rachmaninov (1873–1943); with the German Protestant, Max Bruch (1838–1920) and the Swiss Jewish Ernest Bloch (1880–1959); and with a strong contingent of Austro-German neo-Romantics led by Anton Brückner (1824–96), Gustav Mahler (1860–1911), Richard Strauss (1864–1949), and the song-writer Hugo Wolf (1860–1903). Throughout the century, the French School produced a series of brilliant talents marked by great delicacy and originality, from César Franck (1822–90) and Camille Saint-Saëns (1835–1921) to Gabriel Fauré (1845–1924), Claude Debussy (1862–1918), and Maurice Ravel (1875–1937).

Grand opera, which married music to historical and literary drama, was a medium well suited to the Romantic style. Its success was driven by the rivalry of its three leading centres: the French opera, led by Charles Gounod (1818–93), Giacomo Meyerbeer (1791–1864), Georges Bizet (1838–75), and Jules Massenet (1842–1912); the German opera, launched by Mozart and Weber and culminating in the stupendous figure of Richard Wagner (1813–83); and the Italian opera, whose unequalled melodic traditions were promoted by Gioachino Rossini (1792–1868), Gaetano Donizetti (1797–1848), Giuseppe Verdi (1813–1901), and Giacomo Puccini (1855–1924). The genre variously known as *opéra comique*, operetta, or musical comedy also thrived, especially in the Paris of Jacques Offenbach (1819–80), the Vienna of Johann Strauss II (1825–99) and Franz Lehar (1870–1948), and the London of Gilbert and Sullivan. (See Appendix III, p. 1278).

The nineteenth century saw the rise of all the institutions which would turn the art of music into a major public enterprise—the conservatoires, the orchestral and choral societies, the purpose-built concert halls, the musical publishers, and the departments of musicology.

Philosophy in the Romantic era came to be dominated by the powerful speculations of G. W. F. Hegel (1770–1831), Fichte's successor at Berlin. Hegel was particularly un-Romantic in many of his attitudes, and as a professional philosopher saw himself in the line of the rationalists. On a tour of the Bernese Oberland he was moved to remark: 'The spectacle of these eternally dead masses gave me nothing but the tedious idea, *Es ist so* [That's what it's like].' On the other hand, the originality of many of his ideas attracted tremendous attention in a period of intellectual ferment; and he provided many distinguished pupils and critics, more rebellious than he, with a store of ammunition. Having brushed close to Napoleon in Jena in October 1806, on the day he finished his *Phenomenology of Mind* he wrote admiringly of the Emperor's 'World Soul'.

Two of Hegel's favourite ideas were to prove specially fertile. One of these was the Dialectic, the productive clash of opposites. The other was the *Geist* or 'Spirit', the essence of pure identity, which in his *Philosophy of History* he assigns to every political state and to each stage of developing civilization. The Dialectic, which Hegel confined to the realm of pure ideas, turned out to have many further applications which endowed the whole concept of progress with a dynamic and universal explanation. It seemed to make sense out of turmoil, to promise that good could emerge from conflict. The historical Spirit, on the other hand, which Hegel used for the glorification of the state, turned out to be a weapon in the hands of national movements struggling against the powers of the day. Hegel's views were intensely Germanocentric, and would seem to rationalize the Protestant and Prussian supremacy that was coming to the fore in his own lifetime. He praised war and military heroes, and gave the leading role in modern civilization to the Germans. 'The German spirit is the spirit of the new world. Its aim is the realization of absolute Truth as the unlimited self-determination of freedom.' Americans may or may not be flattered to learn that this po-faced purveyor of mystical metaphysics awarded America 'the final embodiment of the Absolute Idea, beyond which no further development would be possible'.[19] This may help explain the deep-seated Germanophile traditions in American academia.

Scientific thought provided one of the strands which furthered the traditions of the Enlightenment rather than of Romanticism. Pushed to extremes in the work of Auguste Comte (1798–1857), however, it led not just to the branch of philosophy called 'positivism' but to a new pseudo-religion replete with its own rites, dogmas, and priesthood. Comte held that all knowledge passed through three successive stages of development, where it is systematized according to (respectively) theological, metaphysical, and 'positive' or scientific principles. This 'Law of the Three States', first expounded in the *Système de politique positive* (1842), provides the key to his elaborate classification of the sciences and to his outline of a new 'science of society' which he presented in the *Philosophie positive* (1850–4). The discipline of 'social physics' would permit the reordering of human society along scientific lines. The corps of 'social engineers' was armed with the slogan: 'Savoir pour prévoir, prévoir pour prévenir' (To know in order to foresee, to foresee in order to prevent). Comte must be regarded as one of the fathers of modern sociology, which he placed at the top of the hierarchy of sciences. At the same time, by insisting on the necessity of institutionalized spiritual power and by launching what was in effect a scientific Church, he ended up in the paradoxical position of turning science into the object of a mystical cult. In the eyes of one of his critics, T. H. Huxley, Comte's positivism was equivalent to 'Catholicism minus Christianity'.

In this same period, science and technology forged ahead as never before. Although the nature of scientific discovery was perhaps less fundamental than that of Copernicus, Newton, or Einstein, whole new continents of knowledge were mapped out. Science moved into the forefront of public concern. The most distinguished names belong to the fields of physics, chemistry, medicine, and biology—above all, Faraday, Mendeleev, Pasteur, Mendel, Hertz, and Darwin. The list of major discoveries and inventions began to be counted not in the scores or hundreds but in thousands (see Appendix III, pp. 1272–3). With the exception of one or two Americans of genius, it was entirely dominated by Europeans. The Great Exhibition of 1851, which took place in London under the patronage of Prince Albert and whose profits were given over to the Science Museums and to the Imperial College of Science and Technology, attracted millions of visitors from all over the world. [ELEMENTA][GENES]

The growing scientific challenge to traditional religious assumptions

ELEMENTA

ON 1 March 1869 the Professor of Chemistry at St Petersburg University, Dmitri I. Mendeleev (1834–1907) was preparing to make a journey to Tver. Though preoccupied with the preparation of his textbook, *Osnovy Khimii* (Principles of Chemistry), he was also deeply involved in liberal schemes to apply science to everyday life in Russia, and he had accepted a commission to study peasant cheese-making methods. He had reached the point in his textbook where he was looking for a system to classify the chemical elements; and that day, he suddenly saw the benefit of ordering them in a table which listed them according both to their atomic weights and to common properties.

Nine years earlier, Mendeleev had attended the first International Chemistry Congress at Karlsruhe, where the Italian, Stanislao Canizzaro, had drawn his attention to a list of elements arranged by atomic weight. Since then he had been playing a kind of mental patience, laying out the elements both by atomic values and by suits of properties. He now combined Canizzaro's list with his own typological grouping. The result was a primitive version of the Periodic Table, and a provisional formulation of the Periodic Law: 'Elements placed in accordance with the value of their atomic weights present a clear periodicity of properties.' That month he read a paper at the Russian Chemical Society on 'An Attempt at a System of Elements Based on Their Atomic Weight and Chemical Affinity'. It appeared in a German journal in March 1871.

Prior to Mendeleev, the elements were only understood in piecemeal fashion. The ancients recognized ten real elements, but their thinking was confused by their parallel belief in the 'elemental forces' of earth, fire, air and water. Lavoisier knew 23 elements. Humphry Davy isolated sodium and potassium by electrolysis. By 1860, at Karlsruhe, Canizzaro had 60 elements on his list—exactly two-thirds of the 90 which occur in nature.

Mendeleev's findings did not gain much immediate support. They were rejected by leading British and German chemists, including Bunsen, with whom he had once worked at Heidelberg. The break came in 1875, when a Frenchman identified a new element called 'gallium'. Mendeleev was able to show that this was one of the six undiscovered elements whose existence, atomic weights, and properties he had been able to predict. To the surprise of the profession, the Russian theoretician had proved himself in advance of the empirical research. International fame and fortune followed. In Russia, however, Mendeleev's liberal opinions caused friction. In 1880 he failed to gain full membership of the Imperial Academy; and in 1890 he was forced to resign from the university. In his later years he served as a consultant on everything from gunpowder and icebreakers to weights and measures, aeronautics, and the petroleum industry.

Surprisingly, when Mendeleev learned of atomic structure, he felt the theory of radioactivity to be incompatible with his Periodic Law. In fact, it provided the ultimate confirmation of his great discovery. The electron count in the atom of each element is strictly related to its weight and properties. [**ELEKTRON**]

When Mendeleev died, his students carried a copy of the Periodic Table over his coffin. By then, it had become the accepted basis for the chemical classification of matter, the meeting-point of modern chemistry and physics. In 1955, one of nineteen artificial radioactive elements, created by bombarding einsteinium-253 with helium ions, was named in his memory. It is Mendelevium (Me^{101}).

culminated in a major dispute over Darwin's *Origin of Species* (1859) and the associated Theory of Evolution. Christian fundamentalists, schooled in the literal truth of the Book of Genesis, where God created the world in six days and six nights, saw no way to reconcile a theory that mankind had slowly evolved over millions of generations. It was odd that this particular row between science and religion did not break out much earlier. After all, the pioneering treatise of palaeontology, on the antiquity of fossils, had been written by the Dane, Nils Steno, as long ago as 1669. The first scientific computation of the age of the earth—G. Buffon's *Époques de la Nature*, which arrived at the figure of *c.*75,000 years—had been published in 1778; and the Nebular Hypothesis of Laplace, ascribing the origin of the universe to an expanding cloud of gas, had been in circulation since 1796. The French naturalist J.-B. Lamarck (1744–1829) had presented a theory of evolution based on the inheritance of acquired characteristics in 1809. Ever since Steno's time, scientific geologists had been locked in battle with the so-called 'diluvians', who ascribed all physical land forms to the effects of the Great Flood. [**MONKEY**]

Darwin's impact must be explained partly by the fact that scientific debates appealed by his time to a much wider audience, but mainly by the human aspect—the sensational news that all people were descended not from Adam but from the apes: from 'a hairy quadruped, furnished with a tail and pointed ears, probably arboreal in its habits'. Darwin had been collecting data on the formation of species ever since his voyage on HMS *Beagle* to South America and the Galapagos Islands in 1831–6; and his original flash of inspiration came after reading Malthus in 1838. More than twenty years passed before he was pushed into publishing his arguments in the *Origin of Species*, and more than thirty before he fully wrote them up in *The Descent of Man and Selection in Relation to Sex* (1871). Many particulars of Darwin's account of natural selection, otherwise known as 'the survival of the fittest', have been overtaken by later criticisms; but the main contention of evolutionism, that all living species of the plant and animal world

MONKEY

O N Saturday, 30 June 1860, seven hundred people crammed into an Oxford lecture room for a meeting of the British Association for the Advancement of Science. In theory, they had come to hear a paper by an American scholar, Dr Draper, on 'The Intellectual Development of Europe considered with reference to the views of Mr Darwin'. In fact they had come to watch a contest between the paper's two main discussants. On one side sat Samuel Wilberforce, Bishop of Oxford, a fierce adversary of the Evolution Theory, known as 'Soapy Sam'. On the other side, in Darwin's absence, sat Professor T. H. Huxley, palaeontologist, about to gain the label of 'Darwin's Bulldog'.

No one remembered Dr Draper's paper. But Bishop Wilberforce, who took the stand in jovial mood, ended his remarks by asking whether Mr Huxley 'claimed his descent from a monkey through his grandfather or his grandmother?' Huxley kept cool, and explained that Darwin's theory was much more than a hypothesis. 'I would not be ashamed to have a monkey as an ancestor,' he concluded, 'but I would be ashamed to be connected with a man who used great gifts to obscure the truth.'[1] A woman fainted amidst the uproar.

The meeting was a critical moment in the popular reception of modern science. It took place only one year after the publication of the *Origin of Species*, and two years after Darwin had read a joint paper 'On the Tendency of Species to Form Varieties: and on the Perpetuation of Varieties and Species by Natural Means of Selection'. Four years later, at a return match in the Sheldonian Theatre, Benjamin Disraeli could not resist a jibe in the style of 'Soapy Sam'. 'The question is this;' he said, 'Is Man an ape or an angel? My Lord, I am on the side of the angels!'

The subsequent career of Evolutionism is well-trodden history. One line of development fostered by Darwin himself came to be known as 'Social Darwinism'. It preached the ominous proposition not just that the fittest had survived but also that the fittest alone had a right to survive. Another line was concerned with the practical science of 'improving racial standards', i.e. of human breeding. This was pioneered by a series of English scholars headed by Sir Francis Galton (1822–1911), Professor at University College London, and came to be known as eugenics. Its later advocates included Galton's student and biographer, Karl Pearson (1857–1936), a statistician and Marxist, who founded a theory of 'social imperialism', and H. S. Chamberlain who publicized their ideas in Germany.

Francis Galton was responsible for some of the most influential research and pseudo-research of the age. His *Art of Travel* (1855) followed a pioneering expedition into the interior of South-West Africa, setting the fashion for African exploration. His *Meteorographica* (1863) launched the modern science of *meteorology*. As an early psychologist, he conducted the first studies on the behaviour of twins, and set up the world's first mental test centre. As an enthusiast for eugenics, he wrote a series of volumes on *Gregariousness in Cattle and Men* (1871), on *Inquiries into Human Faculty* (1883), and on *Natural Inheritance* (1889). Before that, he completed an extremely popular study of *Hereditary Genius: its Laws and Consequences* (1869). Applying statistical methods to the genealogies of a wide range of achievers from judges to wrestlers, he tried to show that 'talent and genius, and an inclination to moral traits, tend to run in families'. In a final section, he analysed 'The Comparative Worth of Different Races'. He graded the races on a scale from A to I, concluding that the ancient Greeks were 'the ablest race of which history bears record': that African negroes, despite outstanding individuals, could never attain the average grade of Anglo-Saxons: and that Australian aborigines were one grade beneath the negroes.[2] Darwin said that he had never read anything 'more original or interesting'; but he rejected eugenic science as 'utopian'. At Darwin's funeral in Westminster Abbey, Galton publicly called for the Abbey's Creation Window to be replaced by something more suited to Evolution.[3] The point is: Galton, the advocate of 'hereditary genius', was Darwin's cousin.[4]

have progressed through constant interchange with their environment and competition among themselves—quickly gained almost universal acceptance. With time, mainstream Christianity did not find difficulty in accepting human evolution as part of God's purpose. Social scientists adapted the evolutionary idea to numerous disciplines; and 'social Darwinism'—the notion that human affairs are a jungle in which only the fittest of nations, classes, or individuals will survive— was due to have a long career.

Indeed, the general conviction that scientific methods could and should be applied to the study of human as well as natural phenomena represented one of the characteristic changes of the age. Hence, in addition to economics and ethnography there appeared sociology, anthropology, human geography, political science, and eventually psychology and psychiatry. As the scope of the physical and social sciences expanded, the preserve of pure philosophy contracted until it was left with a handful of traditional fields—epistemology, logic, ethics, aesthetics, and political theory.

Religion was resurgent. It found expression in a rich corpus of theological writing, in the fervour of the masses, in the strengthening of Church dogma and organization. The new climate was formed partly in revulsion against the excesses of the revolutionary era and partly through the termination of many earlier forms of religious discrimination. The Enlightenment was reaching its term, but not before the principle of religious toleration was accepted. Discriminatory laws against Catholics dating from the seventeenth century were removed in most Protestant states. Protestants gained equivalent rights in most Catholic states. Judaism was readmitted in many places whence it had been excluded since medieval times. In Prussia, for example, a new national Church was created in 1817 through a merger of Lutheran and Calvinist elements; the Catholic Church was fully established by the Constitution of 1850. In Austria-Hungary, full religious toleration was guaranteed as part of the *Ausgleich* of 1867. In Great Britain, Roman Catholics were largely emancipated by Act of Parliament in 1829, and the Jews in 1888; though both continued to be excluded from the monarchy. In the Netherlands, similar measures were completed in 1853. In France, the Napoleonic Concordat remained in force until 1905, despite tension between Catholics and Republicans. Extreme French rationalists professed a zealotry of their own: at Limoges they staged a festival of mathematics to compete with the Feast of the Assumption.

In Russia, in contrast, the Orthodox establishment enforced severe restrictions on religious diversity. Although the Protestants of the ex-Swedish provinces of the Baltic, the native Christians of the Caucasus, and the Muslims of Central Asia enjoyed a large measure of autonomy, the Jews, Roman Catholics, and Uniates of the ex-Polish provinces were subject to state control, harassment, and discrimination. The Jews were legally required to reside in the so-called Pale of Settlement (see Appendix III, p. 1311), beyond which they could only live by special licence. The Roman Catholic Church was run via the so-called Holy Synod, and was deprived of all direct contact with the Vatican. St Petersburg refused all official ties with Rome until it succeeded in arranging the Concordat of 1849 on its own terms. The Uniates were forcibly converted to Orthodoxy, in the Empire in 1839 and in the ex-Congress Kingdom of Poland in 1875.

Theological debate was stimulated across Europe by three separate developments—by the interchange of Protestant and Catholic viewpoints that were now emerging from their isolation cages, by the profound interest of the Romantic period in exotic religions, especially Buddhism and Hinduism, and by the growth of scientific attitudes. In the course of the century, many theologians acquired an interdenominational and an international reputation. These included the Silesian Friedrich Schleiermacher (1768–1834), a Calvinist and professor at Berlin, the radical Breton abbé Hugues Lamennais (1782–1854), the Bavarian Catholic J. J. Ignaz von Dollinger (1799–1890), Rector at Munich, the Anglican convert to Roman Catholicism, John Henry Newman (1801–90), and the gloomy Dane Søren Kierkegaard (1813–55), whose works were not understood till decades after his death.

Schleiermacher, who was influential in the Prussian Union of Churches, brought theological rigour to an integrated view of human art and culture. His *Über die Religion* (1799) taught the Romantic generation that their outward contempt belied profound sympathies; his major work, *Der Christliche Glaube* (1821–2), is the standard summary of Protestant dogmatics. His *Kurze Darstellung*

(1811) or 'Brief Outline of Theology' was still being cited in 1989 as the best introduction to the subject.[20]

The Abbé Lamennais set out to reconcile the Church to those parts of the revolutionary tradition which he judged to be compatible with Christianity. Under the device of 'Dieu et Liberté', he gradually pushed Rome to disown him. Scandalized by the outcome of the Revolution of 1830, by the Vatican's betrayal of Catholic Poland, and by the Church's disinterest in social justice, he became a scourge of the Establishment. Faith was not to be confused with loyalty to the Church, nor patriotism with loyalty to the state. The titles of his books speak for themselves—*Paroles d'un croyant* (1833), *Les Affaires de Rome* (1836), *Le Livre du peuple* (1837), *L'Esclavage moderne* (1840). Lamennais's work has had a profound impact on the dissident tendency within European Catholicism, where a critical mind was no obstacle to profound belief.

Döllinger led the resistance to the doctrine of papal infallibility (see below). His *Der Papst und die Konzil* (1869) was described as 'the severest attack on the Holy See in a thousand years'. Newman, sometime Vicar of the University Church of St Mary the Virgin in Oxford, is particularly interesting, since his career illustrates the interaction between Protestants and Catholics. He came to prominence in the 1830s as a leader of the Tractarian or Oxford Movement within the Anglican Church. The polemical series of 'Tracts for the Times', which he prepared in the company of Edward Pusey (1800–82) and John Keble (1792–1866), sought to reconcile the Anglican and the Roman Catholic traditions. But attacks on his *Tract 90* (1841), which linked the Thirty-Nine Articles with the views of the early Church Fathers, destroyed his faith in Anglicanism and provoked his resignation. His *Apologia pro Vita Sua* (1864) examines his spiritual struggle with great candour. As he records, his entry into the Catholic fold occasioned much bleating. He later clashed with his fellow convert and cardinal, H. E. Manning (1808–92), on the issue of papal infallibility; but he did not push his dissent to the point of disobedience.

Kierkegaard's writings were aimed first at the philosophy of Hegel and secondly at the cosy practices of the Church of Denmark; but they penetrated far beyond, into intellectual regions otherwise unexplored. His *Fear and Trembling* (1843), *The Concept of Dread* (1844) and *Sickness unto Death* (1849) enter and explore the psychology of the unconscious. His *Unscientific Postscript* (1846) is often taken as the lead text of existentialism. All his works constitute a devastating offensive against rationalism. Subjectivity, according to Kierkegaard, is truth. 'The history of Christendom', he wrote, 'is the history of the subtle disregarding of Christianity.' In a passage strangely prescient of the tragedy of the *Titanic*, he once likened Europeans to the passengers of a great ship, passing the night in revels as they sailed towards the iceberg of doom.

In the course of these debates, theology and biblical scholarship began to adopt many of the methods and values of literary and historical criticism. The most daring foray in this direction, *The Life of Jesus* (1863) by Ernest Renan (1823–92), led to its author's suspension from the Collège de France. Even so, 'modernism' continued to make headway, especially when solemnly denounced by the hierarchy.

Religious fervour is not easily measured; but there is no doubt that the Christian faith now aroused greater passions among greater numbers of people than in the previous century. The general trend towards literacy strengthened religious as well as secular education; and missionary campaigns were targeted as much on the poor and lapsed souls of the new industrial towns as the pagans of distant continents. Especially in the Protestant countries, the Churches provided a measure of social leadership and social discipline that was previously unknown. The revivalist movements such as German Pietism or English Methodism now gripped whole districts, whole sections of society. In other countries, as in Ireland or parts of Poland, popular piety became associated with national resistance. Everywhere there occurred a great outpouring of religious art, often inspired and infused by medieval models. It found expression in the wave of Gothic church-building, in hymn-writing, in religious-minded art movements such as the Pre-Raphaelites in England or the Nazarenes in Germany, and in a great body of Church music. According to C. F. Schinkel (1781–1841), the Neo-Gothic architect, 'Art itself is Religion'. Composers from Berlioz to Franck worked to meet the demands for ever new settings of the Mass. [MISSA]

The Roman Catholic Church was by no means immune from the changes, though its reluctance to move with the times was manifest. The Catholic heartlands in Spain, Italy, Austria, Poland, and southern Germany were less immediately affected by industrialization and modernization. What is more, the higher echelons of the Catholic hierarchy had been shocked to the roots by the events of the revolutionary era, and were frozen into an ultra-conservative stance from which they did not begin to emerge until the 1960s. The Vatican was further frightened by the long rearguard action that was fought in Italy over the Papal States, which were suppressed in 1870. Ultramontanism returned to fashion, not least under pressure from the embattled French bishops and from the Jesuit Order, restored in 1814. [BERNADETTE]

Under Pius IX (r. 1846–78), whom Metternich had initially mistaken for a liberal, dogmas were adopted that exceeded the claims of the most assertive medieval Popes. In 1854 the doctrine of the Immaculate Conception of the Virgin was promulgated. In 1864 the Encyclical *Quanta Cura* asserted the Church's supremacy over all forms of civil authority, whilst the Syllabus expounded an extraordinary list of 'modern errors' including everything from civil marriage to religious toleration. In 1870, by the doctrinal constitution *Pastor Aeternus* passed by the General Vatican Council, the dogma of papal infallibility was introduced in matters of faith and morals. These positions were so extreme that the Papacy lost much respect both within and without the Church. A major conflict, the *Kulturkampf*, was provoked in Germany, and a number of Swiss, German, and Dutch clerics broke away to form the Old Catholic Church. Pius IX died in the Vatican Palace, stripped of all temporal powers, protesting he was 'a moral prisoner'. His loyal servants the Jesuits were expelled from Germany in 1872, from France in 1880. [SYLLABUS]

Under Leo XIII (r. 1878–1903), the 'Pope of Peace', the Church moved much

BERNADETTE

BETWEEN 11 February and 16 July 1858, in a grotto near the town of Lourdes in Bigorre, a malnourished, asthmatic waif, Marie-Bernarde Soubirous, saw a series of eighteen remarkable apparitions. She heard a rushing wind, then saw a beautiful young girl in a white dress and a blue sash, with golden roses at her feet. The apparition told Bernadette to pray, to be penitent, to build a chapel, and to drink of the fountain. On one occasion, it announced, in patois, that it was *immaculada concepciou*, 'the Immaculate Conception.' It let itself be sprinkled with holy water as proof against the Devil; and it showed itself capable of punishment and reward. Townspeople who blasphemed about it fell sick. Others who trampled the roses near the grotto found their property damaged. The water from the fountain proved to have healing powers.

At first, neither the civil nor the ecclesiastical authorities were impressed. They interrogated Bernadette at length, creating a large corpus of evidence; and they placed a barrier round the grotto. When they could restrain neither the locals nor the stream of visitors, they removed Bernadette to a convent at Nevers. In due course, they decided to join what they could not beat, building a huge basilica to receive the pilgrims, and a Catholic medical centre to test the claims of miraculous cures. Lourdes was to become the largest centre of Christian faith-healing in Europe.[1]

In Church History, St Bernadette (1844–79) belongs to the large company of Marian visionaries and Catholic devotionalists who upheld traditional religion against advancing secularism. Together with the consumptive St Thérèse Martin (1873–97), 'the Little Flower of Lisieux', whose autobiographical *History of a Soul* became a sensational best-seller, she helped to demonstrate the sanctity of the suffering believer. As such she was recruited for the French Church's struggle against its foes. She was canonized in 1933, eight years after St Thérèse.

In another respect, the case of Bernadette Soubirous suggests that the age of social modernization in which she lived was not quite so simple as conventionally portrayed. Historians have described the process whereby peasants were being steadily changed by state schooling and military service into uniform Frenchmen.[2] But the events of 1858 show other factors at work. Everyone in Lourdes, even the bishop, spoke patois. No one suggested that Bernadette was mad, or a devil-worshipper. She described no ordinary Madonna, and no Christ-child. She belonged to a timeless community, where water was venerated and where the rituals of washing, whether of clothes or of the dead and the newborn, was strictly woman's work. She lived in a region, where, though the bishop had been repairing Marian shrines, the caves and grottos of the Pyrenean wilderness were still held to be the haunt of fairies. She even called the apparition *petito demoisella*—a phrase sometimes used for 'fairy'. Her barefoot, lice-ridden body, her stubborn consistency, and, above all, the long hours on her knees in positions of ecstasy, proved very convincing. It has been suggested that her body language was acting as 'a non-verbal vehicle for social memory'.[3] Bernadette was conveying something which her neighbours took to be authentic.

closer to modern thinking on political and especially social issues. The Encyclical *Libertas* (1888) sought to affirm the positive aspects of liberalism, democracy, and freedom of conscience. Another, *Rerum Novarum* (1891), put the Church on the side of social justice, condemning the excesses of unrestrained capitalism and exhorting all states to promote the welfare of all their citizens. Under Pius X (r. 1903–14), however, the Encyclical *Pascendi Dominici Gregis* (1907) flatly denounced modernism as 'the résumé of all heresies', and seemed to raise the reactionary banner once again.

The Orthodox world saw changes principally in the sphere of national politics. As Ottoman power receded in the Balkans, separate autocephalous Churches were established in Greece, Serbia, Romania, Montenegro, and Bulgaria, each subject to its own synod or Patriarch. They provided an important focus for the developing identity of the Balkan nations. The Ecumenical Patriarchs of Constantinople correspondingly lost much of their previous prestige and influence. Repeatedly deposed by the Porte, they were particularly threatened by the pretensions of the Russian Orthodox Church, which increasingly claimed to exercise protection and patronage over all the Sultan's Orthodox subjects. The divisions between Christians proved hard to heal: there was no general wish for unity or intercommunion. The Russian Orthodox showed a certain interest in the Old Catholics; and at the Tsar's coronation in 1895 the first of a series of contacts were made with the Church of England. Yet the early stirrings of ecumenism were necessarily confined to the Protestant world. The Church Union of 1817 in Prussia brought Calvinists and Lutherans together. The British and Foreign Bible Society (1804), the YMCA (1844), and the YWCA (1855) were pioneering examples of interdenominational and international co-operation. Generally speaking, the Roman Catholic hierarchy stood aloof, until the scandal of competing missionary organizations in Africa and Asia eventually prompted action. The World Missionary Conference held in Edinburgh in 1910 gave rise to the International Missionary Council, one of two acknowledged sources of the subsequent ecumenical movement.

Politics in the nineteenth century centred on the fate of the monarchies whose supremacy was restored but then gradually undermined by the three great movements of the age—Liberalism, Nationalism, and Socialism. Generally speaking,

SYLLABUS

O N 8 December 1864 Pope Pius IX published the encyclical *Quanta cura* together with a 'Syllabus of the Most Important Errors of our Time'. The documents had been in the Vatican pipeline for more than fifteen years, and had been revised several times. They had already sparked a furore in 1862 when an anticlerical journal in Turin, *Il Mediatore*, had published a selection of their leaked contents.

The Syllabus is divided into ten thematic sections, each containing several clauses. Since the purpose is to expose errors, the Roman Church's position on any particular issue can be reached by prefacing the relevant clause with the words 'It is not true that':

Atheism and Absolute Rationalism
1. God does not exist.
2. Divine revelation can be used to oppose all science or philosophical speculation.

On Moderate Rationalism
Indifferentism
15. All religions and religious denominations are equal.

On Political Societies
18. All socialist, communist, secret, bible-reading, and clerico-liberal societies are permitted.

The Rights of the Church
24. The Church has no temporal power.
26. The Church can be denied the right to hold property.
28. Bishops may only promulgate apostolic letters by governmental consent.
30. The Church's rights derive from Civil Law alone.
32. The clergy's exemption from military service may be rescinded.
33. The Church may be denied the right to teach sacred doctrine.
37. National churches may be established free of papal control.

The Rights of the State
39. The State is the sole fount of social authority.
43. The State may rescind concordats unilaterally.
44. Civil Law is superior to Canon Law.
45. The State's right to determine educational policy is absolute.
46. The State may exercise ultimate control over seminaries.
49. The State may deny the Hierarchy free communication with Rome.
50. Lay bodies have the sole right to appoint or to depose bishops.
54. Kings and princes may be exempted from the laws of the Church.
55. The separation of Church and State is necessary.

Ethics
56. Human laws need not conform to natural or to divine law.
58. Only powers rooted in matter are to be acknowledged.
63. It is permissible to rebel against legitimate princes.

Christian Matrimony
66. Matrimony is not sacramental in nature.

67. The matrimonial bond is dissoluble, and hence divorce *sensu stricto* can be permitted by the State.
68. The State alone may define the impediments to matrimony.

The Pontiff's Temporal Powers

75. Faithful Catholics may dispute the Pontiff's temporal or spiritual powers.
76. The Church would benefit by relinquishing its temporal powers.

Liberalism

77. It is no longer expedient that Catholicism be the sole denomination.
78. Immigrants to Catholic countries should be entitled to the public exercise of all religions.
80. The Roman Pontiff can and should reconcile himself and harmonize with 'progress', 'liberalism', and 'modern civilization'.[1]

The origins of the Syllabus lay in the demands of Italian bishops for guidance in the maelstrom of debate surrounding the creation of the Kingdom of Italy. The Papacy was an active participant in the political struggle, and many of the clauses, though presented in universal terms, were dictated by very specific local conditions. This grave failing led to many misunderstandings. For example, the apparently blanket condemnation of all 'clerico-liberal' societies in Clause 18 was taken to be an attack on all enlightened clerics from Montalembert onwards. Its intention had merely been to curb that part of the clergy in Piedmont which was supporting government plans to dissolve the monasteries.

Reading the text carefully, it is clear that on the majority of issues the Vatican was simply reserving its position. By saying 'It is not true that the Pontiff should harmonize with modern civilization', the Syllabus was only stating the obvious: that the Church was guided by the timeless principles of its religion, and would not bow to fashionable slogans.

But the impression created was rather different. Several of the key clauses were lamentably drafted, and should not have been included. Once the double negatives had been bandied around in a hostile press, many people were convinced that the Roman Catholic Church was implacably opposed to all toleration, to all rational thought, to all forms of matrimonial separation, to all national self-determination, and to all forms of social charity.

On the political front, it is extraordinary in retrospect that the Vatican's lawyers could have lumped all socialists, communists, secret societies, independent bible-readers, and liberal clerics into the same ring of Hell. But that was a sign of the times. Other highly intelligent conservatives elsewhere in Europe thought in the same way. Fyodor Dostoevsky, arguably the greatest mind of the age, might have approved of Clause 18 as far as it went. Except, from his peculiarly Russian standpoint, he would have been tempted to add 'and all Roman Catholics'.[2]

despite some notable casualties, the monarchies survived intact. There were more ruling heads on sacred thrones in 1914 than a hundred years earlier. But they only survived by profoundly modifying the nature of the bond between rulers and ruled.

Liberalism developed along two parallel tracks, the political and the economic. Political liberalism focused on the essential concept of government by consent. It took its name from the *liberales* of Spain, who drew up their Constitution of 1812 in opposition to the arbitrary powers of the Spanish monarchy; but it had its roots much further back, in the political theories of the Enlightenment and beyond. Indeed, for much of its early history it was indistinguishable from the growth of limited government. Its first lasting success may be seen in the American Revolution, though it drew heavily on the experiences of British parliamentarianism and on the first, constitutional phase of the Revolution in France. In its most thoroughgoing form it embraced republicanism, though most liberals welcomed a popular, limited, and fair-minded monarch as a factor encouraging stability. Its advocates stressed above all the rule of law, individual liberty, constitutional procedures, religious toleration and the universal rights of man. They opposed the inbuilt prerogatives, wherever they survived, of Crown, Church, or aristocracy. Nineteenth-century liberals also gave great weight to property, which they saw as the principal source of responsible judgement and solid citizenship. As a result, whilst taking the lead in clipping the wings of absolutism and in laying the foundations of modern democracy, they were not prepared to envisage radical schemes for universal suffrage or for egalitarianism.

Economic liberalism focused on the concept of free trade, and on the associated doctrine of *laissez-faire*, which opposed the habit of governments to regulate economic life through protectionist tariffs. It stressed the right of men of property to engage in commercial and industrial activities without undue restraint. Its energies were directed on the one hand to dismantling the economic barriers which had proliferated both within and between countries and on the other to battling against all forms of collectivist organization, from the ancient guild to the new trade unions.

Liberalism is often categorized as the ideology of the new middle classes; and it certainly appealed to that wide and expanding social constituency which lay between the old privileged nobility and the propertyless industrial masses. Yet its appeal cannot be so closely confined. It also reached to a wide variety of interests that were not essentially social or economic in their motivation—to the widespread *Burschenschaften* or student associations of the 1820s, to freemasonry, to cultural dissidents, to educational and prison reforms, to aristocratic British Whigs and Polish magnates, even to groups such as dissident army officers in Russia, the 'Decembrists', who in 1825 dared to plot against the evils of autocracy.

Given England's precocious development, it is not surprising to find the most cogent exposés of liberalism in English writing. In economics, the *Principles of Political Economy* (1817) of David Ricardo (1771–1823) completed the work of the classical economists started by Adam Smith. Ricardo's disciples took practical action in the activities of the Anti-Corn Law League and in the campaigns of the Manchester School, the advocates of free trade headed by Richard Cobden (1804–65) and John Bright (1811–89). In political philosophy, the works of John Stuart Mill (1806–73) stand as the supreme monument to a tolerant and balanced brand of liberalism, where some of the starker principles of earlier advocates were refined and modified in the light of recent debates and experience. Mill defends *laissez-faire* economics, for example, but only if the power of capitalist employers is matched by the rights of employees' trade unions. He endorses the 'greatest happiness' principle of the Utilitarians—as proclaimed by his philosopher father, James Mill (1773–1836)—but only if happiness is not confused with pleasure. In his essay *On Liberty* (1859) he produced the standard manifesto of individual human rights, which should only be restricted where they impinge on the rights of others. 'The sole end where mankind is warranted . . . in interfering with the liberty of action of any of their number', he wrote, 'is self-protection.' In *The Subjection of Women* (1869) he made the clearest of arguments for the feminist cause, maintaining that there is nothing in the many differences between men and women that would justify their possession of different rights.

The central political drama over liberalism, however, was bound to be played out in France, the home of the frustrated Revolution and the scene of the most developed, honed, and diametrically opposed political opinions. French politics were characterized not merely by the entrenched positions of conservative Catholic monarchists and of radical anticlerical republicans. They were complicated by a number of paradoxical figures, such as the ex-Jacobin republican and 'Citizen-King', Louis-Philippe (r. 1830–48), or the would-be liberal and revolutionary turned Emperor, Louis-Napoleon (Napoleon III, r. 1848–70).

The result was a see-saw history of alternating conservative and liberal regimes interspersed with a series of violent revolutionary outbreaks. The Bourbon Restoration of Louis XVIII (r. 1815–24) and Charles X (r. 1824–30) was overthrown by the July Revolution of 1830. The July Monarchy of Louis-Philippe was overthrown by the Revolution of 23 February 1848. The short-lived Second Republic was overthrown by its original beneficiary, who proceeded to proclaim himself Emperor. The Second Empire (1851–70) was overthrown amidst the humiliation of the Franco-Prussian War, and the violence of the Paris Commune. The Third Republic, inaugurated in 1870, survived for 70 years; but it was marked by the extreme instability of its governments, by the extreme liveliness and futility of its public debates, and by the extreme animosity of the opposing camps. The notorious affair of Captain Dreyfus which gripped France between 1894 and 1906 was proof that the liberal and anti-liberal passions of the French had still not found a *modus vivendi*.

Similar swings of violent fortune prevailed in Spain, which served as a sort of laboratory of liberalism. An unbridgeable gulf yawned between the *exaltados* or 'extreme radicals' and the *apostolicos*, the extreme, Church-backed monarchists. From 1829 many of the latter supported the claims of the royal pretender, Don Carlos (d. 1855) and his heirs, who commanded a loyal following among the

Basques and Catalans. A succession of impoverished and debauched monarchs— Ferdinand VII (r. 1814–43), Isabella (r. 1840(3)–68), Alfonso XII (r. 1874–85)— bent to every breeze that blew. As a result, liberal constitutions were annulled as frequently as they were introduced—in 1812, 1820, 1837, 1852, 1855, 1869, 1876. Clerical intrigues, excesses, and civil war were the order of the day. After the brief reign of Amadeo, Duke of Aosta (r. 1870–3), a brief republic existed. After 1876, under Alfonso XIII (r. 1885–1931), the liberal centre was at last strong enough to maintain a constitutional monarchy until the 1920s. [PRADO]

Portugal endured an 80-year constitutional struggle that ended with the abolition of the monarchy. The constitutional Charter was granted in 1826, soon after Brazil had established its independence, and King Pedro had decided to stay on as Emperor of Brazil. But all manner of stratagems were used to obstruct the Charter's implementation. Until 1853 the absolutist court of Maria II and her two sons held sway. Under Carlos (r. 1889–1908), the *rotativos* or 'revolving ministries' of the Progressive and Regenerator Parties dominated the Cortes, and combined to exclude the growing body of republican sentiment. The reign culminated in a brief royal dictatorship, and in the assassination of the King and Crown Prince. The last King of Portugal, Manuel II (r. 1908–10), retired to England when the armed forces backed the revolution of 5 October 1910 and declared a Republic.

Each of France's 'Revolutions' had repercussions right across Europe. In 1830 the 'July days' in Paris sparked the August rising in Brussels, and the November rising in Warsaw (see below). In Paris, the sight of Lafayette at the head of the rebels led to the abdication of the reactionary Charles X and his *parti prêtre*, and the election of Louis-Philippe by the Chamber of Deputies. In Brussels, the seizure of the Hôtel de Ville and the failure of the Dutch army to restore order led to the election of Louis-Philippe's son, the Duc de Nemours, as prospective King of the Belgians. The Belgian provinces of the United Kingdom of the Netherlands had resented their subordination to Dutch interests ever since 1815. Belgian independence was acceptable to the Powers, who approved the creation of a model constitutional monarchy. But it was Leopold I of Saxe-Coburg (r. 1831–65) who emerged as King, not the Duc de Nemours. [GOTHA]

In February 1848 the head of revolutionary steam was much stronger than in 1830, and the rash of explosions spread to all the major states except for Britain and Russia. In this case trouble was already afoot in Switzerland from 1845, in the Republic of Cracow from 1846, and in Sicily from 1847. The overthrow of Louis-Philippe sent the signal which set almost all the major cities of Germany, Italy, Austria, and Hungary ablaze. The events of 1848–9 have been termed 'the Revolution of the Intellectuals', mainly on the strength of the weighty debates in the Vorparlament in Frankfurt and in the Slav Congress in Prague, and of the epoch-making publication of the *Communist Manifesto* (see below). In reality, it was a time when bloody actions spoke much louder than mere words. It was not only intellectuals who manned the barricades, even though poets such as Lamartine, Mickiewicz, or Sándor Petőfi plunged into the fray. Lamartine served as foreign minister in France's initial revolutionary government. Mickiewicz raised a legion of Polish exiles to fight for the Roman Republic. Petőfi died in a battle against the Austrians. In Paris, over 10,000 people died during the 'June days' when General Cavaignac's troops crushed the resistance of the workers, whose short-lived national workshops had been abolished. In Berlin and elsewhere, the monarchs tended to fire first and to discuss constitutions afterwards. In Italy, Sardinia launched a 'Guerra Santa' against Austrian rule in Lombardy. In Hungary, where the Habsburgs were dethroned and Kossuth proclaimed regent and dictator, two Russian armies and a year-long campaign were required to effect the restoration. In Italy, French, Austrian, and Neapolitan troops had to be called in to destroy the self-proclaimed Republics in Rome and Venice.

In the immediate reckoning, therefore, 1848 provoked a series of liberal disasters. Only one monarchy was toppled, and that in France, where President Louis-Napoleon moved swiftly to undermine the republican institutions that had brought him to power. Within three years the French, who had thrown out their King, were saddled once more with an authoritarian Emperor. Not one of Europe's new republics survived. Metternich, the symbol of the previous era, returned to Vienna from exile in London. New repressions, under new leaders, returned with him.

Yet before long 1848 came to be seen as a watershed in Europe's affairs. The reactionary régimes had triumphed, but only at such heavy cost that they could not bear a repeat performance. Constitutions that had been granted, imposed, and in some cases withdrawn were gradually reintroduced or widened. If the violent methods of the revolutionaries were rejected, the political and social reforms which they demanded were now given serious consideration. With some delay, monarchs realized that wise concessions to popular demands were preferable to endless repression. The basic liberal principle of government by consent steadily gained widespread acceptance. One by one over the next two decades, the victors of 1848 abandoned their frozen postures. National and constitutional aspirations came again to the fore. Even the autocratic empires of the East began to bend. In 1855, with the accession of Alexander II (r. 1855–81), the Romanovs set in motion a season of liberalization à la russe. In 1867, through the Ausgleich or 'Equalization Agreement', the Habsburgs finally addressed the long-standing desires of the Hungarians, setting up the dual Austro-Hungarian monarchy, Kaiserliche und Königliche, with which they had to live for the rest of their reigning days.

Economic liberalism, of course, was not necessarily tied to its political counterpart. The German Zollverein or Customs Union, for example, was initiated by Frederick-William III of Prussia in 1818, at a time when political liberalism was in sharp retreat. Originally intended for Prussian territories alone, it was steadily extended to all the states of the German confederation except Austria. By banning all internal tariffs, it created a growing zone of free trade within which Germany's infant industries could flourish. In 1828 two rival Customs Unions came into being, one based on Bavaria and Württemberg, the other on Saxony; but within four years these were absorbed. In 1852 Austria tried to break out of its isolation by proposing a customs union for the whole of Central Europe and northern

PRADO

SPAIN'S Royal Art Museum was opened to the public on Prado Avenue in Madrid on 19 November 1819. It owed its existence to the enthusiasm of King Ferdinand VII, recently restored to his throne, and to his second queen, Isabella de Braganza. It was managed by its first director, the Prince of Anglona, under the Council of Grandees. It was housed behind the Corinthian façades of a new building designed thirty years earlier by the architect Don Juan Villanueva as a museum of natural history. The initial exhibition displayed 311 paintings. It did not include the large number of masterpieces which had been captured by the Duke of Wellington six years earlier in the baggage of Joseph Bonaparte, but not returned.

The Museum's first catalogue was published in 1823 in French, since the Duke of Angoulême, and the latest French army of occupation, 'the sons of St Louis', had recently entered Spain to rescue the King from his subjects. It was renamed the National Museum in 1838, after merger with the Trinidad Collection taken from suppressed monasteries. It assumed the name Prado Museum in 1873, following the liberal revolt. It was closed during the Spanish Civil War of 1936–9, when many of its treasures were removed and exhibited in Geneva.

Spain's royal art collection goes back to John II of Castile (d. 1445), who is known to have bought pictures by Roger Van der Weyden. Its greatest benefactors were Charles V and Philip II, the patrons of Titian: Philip IV, who employed Velázquez: and Charles III, who in 1774 sequestered the entire property of the Jesuits. Despite severe losses through fire and the French, it grew into one of the world's prime collections, preserved in exceptional condition by the dry air of the Castilian plateau.

The glories of the Prado range over all the great names of the Italian, Flemish, German, Dutch, and French schools. Above all, it is the home base of the Spanish School—hence of El Greco (1541–1614), the Cretan who settled in Toledo; of the Sevillians, Diego de Velázquez (1599–1660) and Bartolomé Murillo (1618–82); of the Valencian, José de Ribera (1591–1652): and of the incomparable Francisco de Goya (1746–1828), who was Spain's most celebrated contemporary painter when the Prado was opened.

'Art galleries preserve the essence of man's creative genius.'[1] They provide perhaps the most accessible route into Europe's past, assailing the senses and arousing the imagination as no history book can do. The Prado stands at the top of a premier league of national galleries which includes the Louvre in Paris, the Rijksmuseum in Amsterdam, the Kunsthistorisches Museum in Vienna, the National Gallery in London, the Hermitage in St Petersburg, the Uffizi in Florence, and the Vaticano. They are supported by a second league of 'provincial' galleries and museums, Munich, in Cracow or in Oxford, often of surprising magnificence; by gal-in Minsk, Manchester, or Munich, in Cracow or in Oxford, often of surprising magnificence; by galleries dedicated to modern art; and by a supporting cast of obscure and devoted institutions from Cholet to Jędrzejów or Dulwich.

In 1784, when Ferdinand VII was born and the Prado building started, another European monarch was planning another public gallery. King Stanislaw-August of Poland had commissioned a dealer in London to assemble a selection of old masters to supplement his private collection in Warsaw. Then the Russo-Polish war and the partitions of Poland intervened. The King was deported to Russia, together with 2,900 of his pictures, which were destined to adorn Russian instead of Polish galleries. He never saw the paintings in London, which could not be paid for. They remained to form the core collection of the Dulwich Picture Gallery, which is one of those many minor treasure-houses that deserve to be better known.[2]

Italy. But the Prussians resisted. The accession of Hanover in 1854 made the Prussian victory complete, except for the recalcitrant cities of Bremen and Hamburg. The foundations of a united German economy, excluding Austria, had been laid at a juncture when prospects for political unification still seemed remote.

Judged by Continental standards of liberalism, Great Britain was both more and less advanced than its main rivals. On the one hand, Britain could fairly claim to be the home of 'the Mother of Parliaments', of the rule of law, of the Bill of Rights, and of free trade. British society was for long the most modernized and industrialized in Europe, and supposedly the most open to liberal ideas. On the other hand, British institutions were exceptional in never having experienced the shock of revolution or occupation. Prevailing political attitudes remained intensely pragmatic. The monarchy continued to reign according to rules and customs agreed in the late seventeenth century, as if the French Revolution had never happened. In Queen Victoria (r. 1837–1901) and her extensive family it found the ideal foil for parliamentary government, a force for stability, and a channel for discreet influence abroad. There were republican sympathies in Britain, but no serious move to abolish the monarchy or to introduce a constitution. [**GOTHA**]

Britain's ancient institutions were slow to reform. Radical reformers had to beat their heads on the gates, often for decades. The unreformed parliament, which survived till 1832, was a scandalous anachronism, like its French counterpart under the July Monarchy. The Corn Laws held out against Free Trade until 1846. Civil marriage and divorce only became possible in 1836 and 1857 respectively. The demands for universal suffrage first voiced by the Chartists in 1838–48 were never fully conceded. The Church of England was never disestablished, except in Ireland (1869) and in Wales (1914). The feudal privileges of the House of

GOTHA

THE Thuringian Duchy of Saxe-Coburg and Gotha was established in 1826, when the Duke of Saxe-Coburg-Saalfeld was obliged by divorce to exchange Saalfeld for Gotha. Together with Saxe-Altenburg, Saxe-Meiningen, and Saxe-Weimar-Eisenach, its eight tiny enclaves were ultimately destined to join the German Empire.

The Duke had two sons—Ernest (1818–93) and Albert (1819–61). His brother Leopold (1790–1865) had once been married to the heiress of the House of Hanover, Charlotte Augusta. His sister Louise, also married to a Hanoverian, was the mother of Princess Victoria (1819–1901), conceived at Amorbach in Franconia. The family's prospects greatly improved in 1830 when, like her deceased aunt before her, Victoria unexpectedly emerged as heir presumptive to the Hanoverian succession, and Leopold as King-elect of Belgium.

'Uncle Leopold' was the royal match-maker par excellence. Albert of Saxe-Coburg and Gotha was his nephew, and Victoria of Hanover his niece. In May 1836, he brought them together. They were both seventeen. They were to be 'the Father and Mother of Europe'.[1] (See Appendix III, pp. 1300–1.)

The House of Hanover, which in earlier times had used the titles of 'Lüneburg-Celle' and 'Braunschweig-Lüneburg', reigned simultaneously from 1714 as Electors (then Kings) of Hanover and Kings of the United Kingdom. Though resident in Britain, they had always taken German brides, whilst a *staathalter* or deputy ran their ancestral lands. Since the law of Hanover did not admit female monarchs, when Victoria ascended the British throne in 1837, Hanover passed to her father's brother and after that to Prussia. Albert and Victoria were married on 10 February 1840. They were blessed with nine children. As from 1858, the three eldest were married respectively to Frederick William of Hohenzollern, the future German Emperor; to Princess Alexandra of Denmark; and to the future Grand-Duke Louis of Hesse-Darmstadt.[2]

The Grand Duchy of Hesse-Darmstadt had enjoyed only middling rank until the Grand Duke's daughter Marie married Alexander II Romanov, the future Tsar of Russia, in 1841. Two of Marie's sons took wives from the family of Schleswig-Holstein-Sonderburg-Gluecksburg. Her daughter, also Marie, married Prince Alfred (1844–1900), Duke of Edinburgh, Admiral RN and the future Duke of Saxe-Coburg and Gotha. The Darmstadt–St Petersburg alliance was reinforced first by the marriage of Elizabeth of Hesse to a Russian Grand Duke and then by the marriage of Elizabeth's younger sister Alix to Nicholas II, the last Tsar.

The German family of Schleswig-Holstein-Sonderburg-Gluecksburg acquired the Danish throne in 1853. But they soon advanced further. Christian IX's eldest son, Frederick (1843–1912), was the progenitor of both the Danish and the Norwegian monarchies. His second son, William (1845–1913), was to marry a Russian Grand Duchess and, as George I, to found the Greek royal line.[3] His daughter Alexandra (1844–1925), wife of Edward, Prince of Wales, became British Queen. His second daughter, Marie (1847–1928), wife of Alexander III Romanov, became Tsarina.

Into this dense nexus of Germanic cousinage there stepped the supreme *arrivistes*—the Battenbergs.[4] The Hessian Counts of Battenberg had died out in the fourteenth century. But their title was revived in 1858 for the benefit of a morganatic union. Prince Alexander of Hesse (1823–88) had accompanied his sister Marie to Russia, and had served in the Tsarist cavalry. But eloping with an imperial maid of honour, Julia Hauke (1825–95), daughter of a murdered Polish general, he fled Russia and took a commission in Vienna. His morganatic bride, renamed Julia, Countess von Battenberg, gave her progeny their good looks and their surname. Her sister wrote children's stories. Her brother served in 1848 as commander of the Polish Legion in Tuscany.[5]

Alexander and Julia had four sons. No. 2 married a princess of Montenegro. No. 3 was enthroned, and dethroned, in Bulgaria. No. 4, Count Henry, married Albert and Victoria's youngest child, Beatrice. But it was the eldest son who scooped the kinship jackpot. Married to Queen Victoria's favourite granddaughter, Victoria of Hesse, Count Louis Battenberg (1854–1921) was a cousin on the paternal side both to Alfred, Duke of Edinburgh and to Tsar Alexander III, and brother-in-law to Empress Alix. Having joined the Royal Navy as a cadet, he worked his way up to be Admiral, Director of Naval Intelligence, and, at the outbreak of war in 1914, Britain's First Sea Lord. Unfortunately as a German, he was immediately forced to retire. By then, his elder daughter had become Queen of Sweden and his younger daughter, Alice, a Princess of Greece. His niece was Queen of Spain. His younger son, Louis (1900–79), known as 'Dickie', later Earl of Burma, was to follow him into the British Admiralty. In July 1917 the family name was changed once again, this time from Battenberg to Mountbatten. Their Romanov relatives were under arrest, and their relatives in the House of Saxe-Coburg-Gotha-Hanover-Teck were hurriedly renaming themselves 'Windsor'.

In time, Admiral Louis Mountbatten revealed the same match-making talents as Queen Victoria's Uncle Leo. His favourite nephew was a young exiled prince from Greece called Philip.[6] Amongst the Windsors, the

young Princess Elizabeth had unexpectedly emerged in 1937 as Britain's
heir presumptive. 'Uncle Dickie' brought them together. Prince Philip of
Schleswig-Holstein-Sonderburg-Gluecksburg (b. 1921), and Princess
Elizabeth of Windsor (b. 1926) were married in 1947. Both were descend-
ed in the same degree from the lines of Saxe-Coburg and Gotha,
Hanover, Hesse, and Denmark. Except for some relations of Elizabeth's
Scottish mother, neither had any modern English forebears. Both
changed their names twice. Philip had taken his uncle's adopted name of
Mountbatten. After his wife's Coronation as Elizabeth II in 1953, he and
his family reverted by an Order in Council to the Queen's maiden name
of Windsor. Skilful genealogists showed them to be descendants of
Plantagenets, Tudors, and Stuarts, even of Charlemagne, Egbert, and
King Alfred.

When the House of Windsor was created by deed poll in 1917, the republican H. G. Wells had called them 'alien and uninspiring'. But their cousin,
the German Kaiser, was less critical. In a rare flash of wit, he said that he
was off to the theatre to see a performance of *The Merry Wives of Saxe-
Coburg and Gotha.*[7]

Lords were not even trimmed until 1911. Religious toleration was never quite complete. The two-party system, which saw the ancient teams of Whigs and Tories
reclothed as Liberals and Conservatives, delayed the advent of a strong socialist
movement and of much social legislation. Under W. E. Gladstone (1809–98) and
Benjamin Disraeli (1804–81), who dominated the scene in the third quarter of the
century, and who both had liberal proclivities, domestic reforms were often overshadowed by the concerns of Empire. Wales remained an administrative part of
England. Scotland received its own Secretary of State, a second-rank minister, in
1885. Ireland never achieved Home Rule (see below). Though liberal policies were
followed with respect to the English-speaking dominions, there was little wish to
extend them to the colonies at large. The British loved to pride themselves on
their tolerance and liberalism; but much of their pride became outdated. In later
decades they lagged well behind France in domestic democracy, behind Germany
in social legislation, behind Austria-Hungary in nationality policy. [**RELAXATIO**]

The correlation between liberal politics and the growth of a powerful bourgeoisie has generated much historical comment, with special reference to the
contrasts between Britain and Germany. Attention has been focused on Britain's
success and Germany's failure in building a stable parliamentary system, and
hence on the differences of structure and ethos in their middle classes. Unlike
their British counterparts, the new German capitalists were seen to 'turn to the
state', supposedly shirking their democratic duty and submitting to the guidance
of enlightened but essentially illiberal ministers of the Prussian imperial service.
The thesis about Germany's *Sonderweg* or 'special path' was inspired at a much

later date by concern over the rise of Hitler, and by the weakness of German liberalism as shown by the 'collaboration of the capitalists' in the 1930s.[21] Prussia certainly set the example of a *Rechtsstaat,* which honoured legal forms but in which constitutions were subject to the authoritarian traditions of court, army, and bureaucracy. This has given German imperial government after 1871 the label of a 'façade democracy'. On the other hand, one has to remember that the German Empire was a federal state, where several of the kingdoms were much less authoritarian than Prussia.

In any case, a slightly wider sample of comparison might suggest that Germany's path was not so special after all. Sweden, for example, combined an expanding parliamentary system of the British type with an enlightened bureaucracy and a none-too-liberal capitalist class of the German type. Sweden's two-chamber parliament was organized at the instigation of liberal-minded bureaucrats in 1866. A capitalist bourgeoisie, which grew with rapid industrialization in the later decades, opposed the extension of the franchise, and did not involve itself with the Liberal Unity Party that took up the torch of liberal causes at the turn of the century. Swedish capitalists were no more interested in liberalism than their German partners. Swedish liberalism was inspired by a coalition linking state ministers, the non-capitalist *Bildungsbürgertum* or 'educated middle class', and even peasants, who together ensured the preservation of Sweden's evolving democracy.[22] [**NOBEL**]

Of all the major powers Russia was the most resistant to liberalism. Recurrent bouts of reform—after 1815, 1855, and 1906—produced impressive results in certain circumscribed spheres. After the establishment of a Council of State and the creation of state schooling under Alexander I, and the emancipation of the serfs (1861) under Alexander II, important degrees of autonomy were granted to the *mir* or peasant communes, to the *zemstva* or district councils, to the universities, and to the criminal courts. A legislative assembly or State Duma, with consultative powers, was eventually established at the second attempt. It operated in fits and starts between 1906 and 1917, and promised to set Russia definitively on the road to constitutionalism. Yet progress proved more apparent than real. No reforming Tsar was able to sustain a liberal course for long. Both Alexander II and Nicholas II seemed to be driven on to the liberal path by military defeats—the one by defeat in the Crimea and the other by the Russo-Japanese War and the subsequent 'Revolution' of 1905. Both were forced to reverse direction. Each bout of reform was brought to an end by *force majeure*—by the Decembrist revolt of 1825, by the Polish rising of 1863–4, and by the outbreak of the First World War. In each case periods of fierce reaction followed, when liberal forces were repressed. One hundred years after the Congress of Vienna, the Russian autocracy and its police regime remained essentially intact. Nothing had been done to dent the fundamental right of the Tsar-Autocrat to rescind any concessions made. What is more, Russia had frequently intervened to stop the march of liberalism abroad. Although Alexander III abandoned direct interventionism, the long-standing instinct had been for Russia to act as 'Europe's gendarme'. When Nicholas I heard during a palace ball in February 1848 that Louis-Philippe had been overthrown, he announced: 'Gentlemen, saddle your horses! France is a Republic.'

To a greater or lesser degree, therefore, the winds of liberalization blew through all the European monarchies. But their gusts were irregular and the effects ragged. European liberalism built up its head of steam during the reactionary decades after 1815, and made its greatest impact in the aftermath of the explosion of 1848. In the later part of the century, though liberals battled on, their uncompleted agenda was having to compete with the demands of Conservatism, Nationalism, Socialism, and Imperialism.

Conservatism began to crystallize as a coherent ideology in conjunction with liberal trends. It was not opposed to democracy or to change as such, and should not be confused with simple reactionary positions. What it did was to insist that all change should be channelled and managed in such a way that the organic growth of established institutions of state and society—monarchy, Church, the social hierarchy, property, and the family—should not be threatened. Hence its name, from the Latin *conservare*: 'to preserve'. Typically, its founding father, Edmund Burke (see above), had welcomed the French Revolution, before turning decisively against its excesses. Like the liberals, the conservatives valued the individual, opposed the omnipotent state, and looked for a reduction of central executive powers. Through this, they often turned out to be the most effective of would-be reformers, toning down the proposals coming from more radical points on the spectrum, and acting as the go-between with the ruling court. The leading practitioners of the conservative art in Britain were Sir Robert Peel (1788–1850) and his disciple, Disraeli. They had many admirers on the Continent. The ultimate distinction between liberal conservatives and moderate liberals was a fine one. In many democracies, the large area of agreement between them came to define the 'middle ground' of political life.

Nationalism, a collection of ideas regarding the nation, whose interests are taken to be the supreme good, has become one of the elemental forces of modern times. It received its greatest single boost from the French Revolution, and was crystallized by the social and political changes of nineteenth-century Europe. It has since travelled round all the continents of the globe. It came in two opposing variants. One of them, state or civic nationalism, was sponsored by the ruling establishments of existing states. The other, popular or ethnic nationalism, was driven by the demands of communities living within those states and against the policy of their governments. In this regard, some historians have contrasted the process of 'state-building' with that of 'nation-building'. The essential difference lay in the source of ideas and action. State nationalism was initiated 'at the top', among a political élite which sought to project its values downwards into society at large. Popular nationalism started 'at the grass roots', at the bottom, seeking to attract mass support before trying to influence or overthrow the existing order.[23] Another important distinction is made between peaceable cultural nationalism of the Herderian type, which is limited to the propagation or preservation of the culture of a national community, and aggressive political nationalism, which claims the right of self-determination to achieve the nation-state.[24] The nation-state is one where the great majority of citizens are conscious of a common identity, and share the same culture.

There are as many theories on the essence of nations as there are theorists. But the essential qualities would seem to be spiritual in nature. 'The nation is a soul,' wrote Renan, 'a spiritual principle. [It] consists of two things. One is the common legacy of rich memories from the past. The other is the present consensus, the will to live together . . .' In order to reach that consensus, many members of the nation will have to forget the oppressions and injustices which once divided them. 'L'oubli, the act of forgetting, and one might even say historical falsehood, are necessary factors in the creation of nations.'[25]

State nationalism, which was driven by the interests of the ruling élite, is well illustrated in the case of Great Britain, even better in that of the USA. In 1707, when the United Kingdom came into existence, there was no British nation. The people of the British Isles thought of themselves as English, Welsh, Scots, or Irish. Over the years, however, the propagation of the dominant English culture, and the promotion of its loyal Protestant and English-speaking servants, gradually consolidated a strong sense of overlying British identity. In the nineteenth century, when the liberal establishment came to favour mass education, non-English cultures were actively suffocated. Welsh children, for example, if they dared to speak Welsh, were punished with the Welsh 'Knot'. All 'Britons' were expected to show loyalty to the symbols of a new British nationality—to speak standard English, to stand up and sing the royal anthem, 'God Save Our Noble King' (1745), and to respect the Union Jack (1801). In this way the new British nation was successfully forged. Its older component nations, though not eradicated, were relegated to the status of junior and subordinate partners. (See Chapter VIII.)

Similarly, the US government was obliged to adopt an official national culture to replace those of its variegated immigrants. During the Civil War the US Congress allegedly voted for the compulsory adoption of English rather than German by the margin of one vote (though accounts of this disagree). Thereafter, before new citizens were allowed to swear loyalty to the 'Stars and Stripes', a knowledge of English was thought equal to a knowledge of the Constitution. The new, English-speaking American nation was forged under government sponsorship, especially by education. The adoption of the American version of English culture was put forward as the touchstone of success for all immigrant families.

One common characteristic of state nationalisms lies in their practice of equating the concepts of 'citizenship' and 'nationality'. In official British usage, nationality has been made to mean citizenship, that is, something granted by British law. In American usage, 'nations' have been equated with countries or political states. Such terminology only confuses the issues, perhaps deliberately. It is partly responsible for persistent errors, such as that which has regarded all inhabitants of the Russian Empire or the Soviet Union as 'Russians'; and it contrasts unfavourably with the practices of countries where citizenship has to be more precisely defined.[26] State nationalism accepts that governments determine nationality, whilst abhorring the idea that nations can forge states. As Lord Acton wrote: 'A State can sometimes create a nation, but for a nation to create a state is going against nature.'

Most European governments strove to strengthen the national cohesion of their subjects—by ceremonies, by symbolic art, by interpretations of history, above all by education and the promotion of a common culture. No nineteenth-century government planning to introduce universal primary education could avoid the crucial choice of language or languages in which the children were to be instructed. The Ottoman Empire, which had always granted autonomy to minority groups, was alone in never trying to enforce a common state culture. Austria-Hungary abandoned the attempt after 1867, overwhelmed by the contrary tides of popular nationalism.

Popular nationalism, which grew from the grass roots, was planted like so many acorns under the dynastic states and multinational empires of the era. Firmly grounded in Rousseau's doctrine of popular sovereignty, it assumed that the proper forum for the exercise of the general will was provided by the national or ethnic community, not by the artificial frontiers of the existing states. It created an elaborate mythology where the 'blood' of the nation was inextricably mixed with the 'soil' of the national territory. Hence, if Italians lived on the territory of half a dozen states from Switzerland to Sicily, it was assumed that justice for the Italian nation involved the abolition of those states, and their replacement by one united Italian kingdom. Of course, most down-to-earth nationalists realized that the existence of a fully fledged nation, fully conscious of a uniform national culture, belonged largely to the realm of dreams. Once the Italian state was established, many Italian leaders knew that they would have to follow the example of other governments and use the power of the state to consolidate the culture and consciousness of its citizens. As Massimo d'Azeglio remarked in the opening session of the parliament of a united Italy in 1861, 'Now that we have created Italy, we must start creating Italians.'

Much of the nineteenth-century debate on nationality was dominated by the conviction that the peoples of Europe could be divided into 'historic' and 'unhistoric' nations. The idea first appeared in Hegel. It was adopted by social Darwinists, who looked on the competition between nations as an evolutionary process, with some fitted for independent survival and others destined for extinction. With Marx, the economic factor came to the fore. Criteria and calculations naturally varied, and the list of potential nation-states differed widely. None the less, by the mid-nineteenth century a measure of consensus had been reached. It was generally assumed that the established Powers—France, Britain, Prussia, Austria, and Russia—possessed a historic destiny, as did the states whom the Powers already recognized—Spain, Portugal, Belgium, the Netherlands, Sweden, Denmark, and Greece—and the leading national contenders—the Italians, the Germans, and the Poles. Mazzini sketched a map of the future Europe containing twelve nation-states.

In reality, the concept of historicity was entirely subjective, not to say spurious. Three of the five Powers, whose admirers assumed that they were among the most permanent fixtures of the European scene, were destined to disappear within a century. Several countries, like Denmark or Great Britain, who liked to think of themselves as cohesive nation-states, were destined to learn that they were not. Many of the nations who felt that they had an iron-clad case for self-determination were due to be disillusioned. Here, the decisive factors turned out to be neither size, nor economic viability, nor valid historical claims, but political circumstance. The German nationalists, who had little chance when opposed by the might of Prussia, were assured of success as soon as Prussia changed heart. The hopes of the Italians were dependent on the active support of France. The Poles, whose historic statehood remained within living memory until the 1860s, had no outside support, and no luck. Politics alone decided that Greeks, Belgians, Romanians, and Norwegians might succeed, where for the time being the Irish, the Czechs, or the Poles could not. At first, the crumbling Ottoman Empire offered the most obvious prospects for change. The nationalities of the Tsarist and Habsburg empires, which were to produce the largest number of nation-states, did not come to the fore until the turn of the century.

[**ABKHAZIA**]

Nevertheless, nationalism did not only flourish where it was most likely to succeed: on the contrary, it thrived on deprivation and repression. One might almost say that the fervency of the national ideal increased in proportion to the improbability of its success. Throughout the century, committed national activists strove to arouse the consciousness of the people whom they wished to recruit. Poets, artists, scholars, politicians appealed to six main sources of information to construct the image of reality that was to inspire the faithful.

History was raked to furnish proof of the nation's age-long struggle for its rights and its land. Prehistory was a favourite subject, since it could be used to substantiate claims to aboriginal settlement. Where facts could not be found, recourse had to be made to myth or to downright invention. National heroes and heroines, and distant national victories, were unearthed to be praised. Anything of universal interest was ignored. Anything that reflected discredit on the nation, or credit on its foes, was passed over.

Language was reformed and standardized as proof of the nation's separate and unique identity. Dictionaries and grammars were compiled, and libraries collected, where none had existed before. Textbooks were prepared for national schools and national universities. Linguists set out to show that previously neglected vernaculars were every bit as sophisticated as Latin or Greek; that Czech or Catalan or Gaelic or Norwegian was every bit as efficient a means of communication as the existing state languages. The Norwegian case was specially interesting. A composite construct of peasant dialects called *nynorsk* or *landsmål* (New Norse or 'country language') was invented in order to challenge the established *riksmål* or *bokmål* (the 'state language'/'book language' of Denmark and Norway). The New Norse movement, which came to a head in 1899, saw itself as the necessary

ABKHAZIA

T HE Abkhazians are a small nation of less than a quarter of a million souls living on the Black Sea Coast some 300 miles east of the Crimea. Their chief city is Sukhum or Sukhumi. Their language and Moslem culture, which resemble those of the Circassians, have little in common either with the Russians to the north or the Christian Georgians to the east. They say that they live 'at the end of Europe'.

The site of a medieval kingdom, which flourished under Byzantine-Greek influence, Abkhazia has always occupied a vital location linking southern Russia with the Caucasus. Its conquest by the Tsars between 1810 and 1864 (see Appendix III, p. 1290) forced many natives to flee. From 1931, it became one of three nominally autonomous republics within the Georgian SSR; and a major influx of Russians and Mingrelian-Georgians turned the local population into an absolute minority in their own land. Stalin's police chief, Beria, who was himself a Mingrelian, deported the entire community of Pontic Greeks whilst initiating the brutal policy of georgianization.

Hence, when Georgia broke free from Moscow in 1991, the Abkhazians sought a measure of genuine self-rule from Georgia. Yet their conflict with Tiflis during the devastating Georgian civil war of 1992–3 only opened the way for the re-occupation of Abkhazia by Russian forces. As a foreign reporter was told by a Cossack ataman, the fate of peripheral territories like Abkhazia or the Kurile Islands would test Russia's greatness. 'These are ours—and that's the truth.'[1]

Discord among the ex-Soviet nationalities was fuelling an ugly brand of Russian nationalism. Voices in Moscow called for the re-conquest of Russia's 'near abroad'. For after Abkhazia, there waited several further targets for Russian intervention, including Tatarstan and Chechenia, and other non-Russian lands within the Russian Federation. Sooner or later, Russia would be forced to choose between its new-style democracy and its old-style imperialism.

partner to the drive for political independence. But like Gaelic in Ireland, it achieved only limited success. [NORGE]

Folklore, or *Volkskunde*, was mined for all it was worth. For one thing, it was thought to join the modern nation to its most ancient cultural roots; for another, its authenticity could not be easily checked. Unlike Herder, whose collection of *Volkslieder* (1778) had included songs from Greenland to Greece, nationalist scholars confined themselves to national folklore. In this connection, the work of the brothers Jakob (1785–1863) and Wilhelm Grimm (1786–1859) must be regarded as seminal. Their huge range included the *Über den altdeutschen Meistergesang*, the *Deutsche Sagen*, the *Deutsche Grammatik*, and the world-famous *Kinder- und*

Hausmärchen (1812–15), 'Grimms' Tales'. Their Serbian contemporary Vuk Karadzić (1787–1864) published a well-known collection of Serbo-Slavonic tales in addition to his grammar, his dictionary, and his reform of the Cyrillic alphabet. [KALEVALA]

Religion was mobilized to sanctify national sentiment, and in many instances to erect barriers between ethnic groups. For national Protestant or Orthodox Churches this form of separatism had long existed. But even the Roman Catholic religion could be turned against its universal mission, to separate Croats from Serbs, to keep Lithuanians immune from russification, or Poles from germanization. In some countries Christians looked on bemused as interest was revived in the rites and practices of the nation's pagan gods. Welsh Baptist ministers dressed up as Druids at the Welsh national *Eisteddfod*; the Germanic gods rode again on the stage and page of imperial Germany. [SHAMAN]

Racial theories exerted powerful attractions. The notion of a Caucasian race was invented in the late eighteenth century. The allied notion of the 'Aryan race' was first uttered in 1848 by a German professor in Oxford, Max Müller. Every nationality in Europe was tempted to conceive of itself as a unique racial kinship group, whose blood formed a distinct and separate stream. Extraordinary interest was devoted to ethnology, and to the study of 'racial types' that supposedly corresponded to each of the modern nations. In London, the Royal Historical Society sponsored a series of experiments on its Fellows showing that the brain-pans of those with Celtic names were inferior to those of Anglo-Saxon origin.[27] (There is no hope for the Davieses.) In Germany, the science of eugenics came up with similar results. Houston Stewart Chamberlain (1855–1927), an Englishman resident in Germany, narrowed the creative race from Aryans to Teutons. 'True history', he wrote, 'begins from the moment when the German with mighty hand seizes the inheritance of antiquity.' Or again, 'Whoever maintains that Christ was a Jew is either ignorant or dishonest.'[28] [CAUCASIA]

In Russia, the pan-Slav movement was loaded with racial overtones. Arguing for the unification of all Slav peoples under the aegis of the Tsar, it often assumed that political solidarity would emerge from the (non-existent) racial affinity of the Slavs. It enjoyed little resonance among Catholic Poles and Croats, who had both produced earlier versions of pan-Slavism, and who now countered with scientific papers showing that the Russians were really slavicized Finns.[29] It enjoyed its greatest currency amongst Serbs, Czechs, and Bulgars, all of whom looked to Russia for liberation. Russian nationalism, blended with pan-Slavism, exhibited unparalleled messianic fervour. Dostoevsky could wring an optimistic note from the most unpromising material:

Our great people were brought up like beasts. They have suffered tortures ever since they came into being, tortures which no other people could have endured but which only made them stronger and more compact in their misfortunes . . . Russia, in conjunction with Slavdom, and at its head, will utter to the world the greatest word ever heard; and that word will be a covenant of human fellowship . . . [For] the Russian national idea, in the last analysis, is but the universal fellowship of man.[30]

This was wishful thinking on a scale well suited to the country concerned.

KALEVALA

THE *Kalevala* or 'Land of Heroes' is generally regarded as the national epic of the Finns. It is a poem of some 50 cantos or 22,795 lines, published first in 1835 and in its second, definitive edition in 1849. It is a semi-literary epic compiled largely from authentic folklore. In fact it is, in large measure, the product of its main compiler, Elias Lönnrot (1802–84), who used classical models to transform and embellish the raw oral materials which he had collected among the peasants of eastern Finland and Russian Karelia. As such, it illustrates not only the legacy of Europe's pagan folklore but also the process whereby nineteenth-century activists drew on neglected popular sources to create a national consciousness. Herder (1744–1803) had established the idea that modern nations can only flourish when they possess a distinct cultural identity based on the vernacular language and on popular traditions. The *Kalevala* was a Herderian exercise *par excellence.*

In Lönnrot's time the Finns passed from rule by Sweden to that of Tsarist Russia, and were feeling the urge to dissociate themselves from the culture of their Swedish and Russian masters. The stories centre on Vainamoinen, the 'Eternal Sage' who presides over the land of Kalevala, leading it in the struggle against Pohjola, peopled by gods, giants, and unseen spirits:

Siitä vanha Väinämöinen,	Then the aged Vainamoinen
Laskea karehtelevi	Went upon his journey singing,
Venehellä vaskisella,	Sailing in his boat of copper,
Kuutilla kuparisella	In his vessel made of copper,
Yläisihin maaemihin	To the land beneath the heavens
Alaisihin taivosihin.	Sailed away to loftier regions.
Sinne puuttui pursinensa,	There he rested with his vessel
Venehinensä väsähyti.	Rested weary, with his vessel,
Jätti kantelon jälille,	But his kantele he left us,
Soiton Suomelle sorean,	Left his charming harp in Suomi,
Kansalle ilon ikuisen,	For his people's lasting pleasure,
Laulut suuret lapsillensa.	Mighty songs for Suomi's children.[1]

All the nations of Europe passed through the phase of compiling, romanticizing, and inventing their folklore. The republication of the Arthurian romances of Chrétien de Troyes and Sir Thomas Malory belonged to the same trend. Even the Americans wanted to participate; and Lönnrot's work exerted a strong influence on the *Hiawatha* (1855) of Henry Longfellow, who knew a German translation of *Kalevala* published in 1851 by a member of the Imperial Academy of Sciences in St Petersburg.

National epics such as the Finnish *Kalevala* or the Welsh *Mabinogion* held special significance for those nations whose drive towards a separate cultural identity was inhibited by political dependence. It is not surprising to find that both *Hiawatha* and the *Kalevala* had been translated into Polish by the 1860s.

SHAMAN

THE Shaman, or tribal 'medicine man', is a well-known figure among the native peoples of Siberia, and further afield among the Innuit and Amerindians. Folk healer, sage, and magician, he is a member of an immemorial profession whose potions, rituals, and proverbs give him unique authority. Dressed perhaps in a horned mask, and carrying the characteristic instrument of his trade, the drum, with which he communes with the spirits of wood, stone, and sky, he can be a force for good or for evil. He travels unseen to the other worlds, above and below, and brings mankind the wisdom of the Great Spirit. Shamanism has survived until modern times in many remote parts of Russia; but it is not entirely expected in Central Europe.[1] Women, too, can shamanize.

In Hungary, controversy over the origins of the Magyars raged throughout the nineteenth century. They were popularly thought to be related to the Huns. [CSABA] But scholars thought otherwise. One school looked to Iranian or Khazar forebears. Another, founded by Janos Sajnovits (1733–85), looked farther to the east. Since then, the Finno-Ugrian connection has been definitively proved by philologists, archaeologists, and anthropologists. A burial site at Bol'she Tigan on the Kama River, for example, discovered in 1974, has been confirmed as one of the major staging-posts before the Magyars moved off to the West. Similarly, modern research into Magyar folklore has revealed numerous traces of Shamanism, thereby underscoring the once unsuspected association with Siberia.[2]

All over Europe, every branch of art and literature was mobilized to illustrate and to embroider national themes. Poets sought to win the accolade of national bard or 'poet laureate'. Novelists developed a penchant for writing historical or pseudo-historical romances about national heroes and national customs. The Waverley novels of Sir Walter Scott (1771–1832) were the acknowledged model in this field, although earlier examples can be found. A novel called *Thaddeus of Warsaw* (1803) by Jane Porter (1776–1850), who fictionalized the life of Kościuszko, gained international celebrity. Painters and sculptors followed Romantic hankerings in the same direction. France's leading Romantic, Victor Hugo (1802–85), contrived to shine in all fields at once.

Musicians recruited the harmonies and rhythms of their native folk dance and folksong to elaborate distinctive national styles that became the hallmark of numerous 'national schools'. From the exquisite mazurkas and polonaises of Chopin and the Hungarian Rhapsodies of Liszt, a brilliant trail leads through the delights of the Czechs Bedřich Smetana (1824–84), Antonín Dvořák (1841–1904) and Leoš Janáček (1854–1928); the Norwegian Edvard Grieg (1843–1907), the Finn

Jan Sibelius (1865–1957), and the Dane Carl Nielsen (1865–1931); the Spaniards Isaac Albeniz (1860–1909), Enrique Granados (1867–1916), and Manuel de Falla (1876–1946); the Hungarians Béla Bartók (1881–1945) and Zoltán Kodály (1882–1967); the Englishmen Edward Elgar (1857–1934), Frederick Delius (1862–1934), and Ralph Vaughan Williams (1872–1958); and the famous Russian 'Five'—Cesar Cui (1835–1916), Mily Balakirev (1836–1910), Alexander Borodin (1833–87), Nicholas Rimsky-Korsakov (1844–1909) and Modeste Mussorgsky (1839–81). These national schools served to widen the social appeal of music. What is more, nations who were thwarted by the language barrier from further-ing their cause through literature could address the whole of Europe through the concert hall.

Interestingly, the abstract nature of music invited a wide range of reaction to the same scores. A composer like Chopin could appeal not only to listeners who were well attuned to his political message but equally to others who were totally oblivi-ous. There was no contradiction between the national and the universal aspects of his genius. The deliciously ambiguous emotional qualities of his bitter-sweet Polish melodies were woven into alternating moods of rousing protest and melan-cholic languor. For some, he translated Polish history into notes on the keyboard; for others, he conjured up poignancies of a purely personal and intimate charac-ter. As Robert Schumann said of perhaps the most famous piece by Chopin, the 'Revolutionary Étude', Op. 10 No. 12, it spoke of 'guns buried in flowers':

In the world of opera, national myths were yoked to stupendous sounds to form musical dramas of unequalled power. An audience which has watched and listened, riveted to their seats, during a performance of Mussorgsky's *Boris Godunov* or Wagner's *Ring* lose all concern for the rights and wrongs of history. National operatics is a field where the magnificence of the music only seems to be enhanced by the unlikeliness of the libretto. [NIBELUNG] [OPERA] [SUSANIN] [TRISTAN]

That the growth of nationalism was closely intertwined with the modernization of European society is undeniable. Indeed, some historians of the Marxist per-suasion go so far as to insist that the correlation was absolute. 'The basic charac-teristic of the modern nation and of everything connected with it', writes one of them, 'is its modernity.'[31] This sort of assertion spoils a good case by overstate-ment. Political oppression could be every bit as effective as socio-economic modernization in stimulating modern nationalism; and there are several instances of precocious national movements which were well developed long before modernization took hold. What the modernizing processes certainly did do was to change the nature of existing nationalisms, and to expand their social constituency beyond all previous limits. 'The Transformation of Nationalism' in the prime era of Europe's modernization after 1870 was a reality which few would want to refute.

Nationalism also underlined an important distinction between 'civilization' and 'culture'. Civilization was the sum total of ideas and traditions which had been inherited from the ancient world and from Christianity; it was grafted onto the native cultures of all the peoples of Europe from the outside, to form the common legacy. Culture (*Kultur* in the German sense), in contrast, grew from the everyday life of the people. It was made up from all that was specific to a particular nation: their native speech, their folklore, their religious deviations, their idiosyncratic practices. In earlier times, civilization had been extolled and culture despised. Nationalism now did the opposite. National cultures were extolled, and common civilization downgraded. The educated, multilingual, cosmopolitan élite of Europe grew weaker; the half-educated national masses, who thought of themselves only as Frenchmen, Germans, English, or Russians, grew stronger.

Theorizing about Nationalism has not abated with time. Among the ideas in vogue in the late twentieth century, one would have to consider the above-mentioned sociological link between Nationalism and Modernization: the psychological concept of the Nation as 'an imagined community', to which uprooted or newly educated individuals chose to belong: and the notion of 'Invented Tradition'—the mechanism whereby nascent nations created their own mythologies. It is interesting to note that each of these very contemporary ideas can be found in the writings of a little-known Polish socialist and social theorist, Kazimierz Kelles-Krauz (1872–1905).[32]

The passions of nationalism inevitably fuelled conflict. Almost all parts of Europe contained ethnic minorities whose popular nationalisms were bound to clash with the state-led nationalism of the authorities. In Britain there were three potential separatist movements; in the Russian Empire there were seventy. Even in the German Empire, which was remarkably homogeneous from the ethnic point of view, long-running conflicts emerged in the former Polish provinces, on the Danish border in Schleswig-Holstein, and in Alsace-Lorraine. [**ELSASS**] [**SLESVIG**] Important conflicts also arose between leaders of the national movements and leaders of liberal or socialist opinion who either disagreed with nationalism *per se* or objected to the priority given to national goals.

Russia was a case in point, where the imperial state-building of the Romanov dynasty came into conflict not only with the non-Russian peoples of the Empire but also with the popular nation-building sentiments of the Russians themselves. In the old Muscovite heartland, the 'Empire' lived uneasily alongside the 'Nation'. Imperial institutions based on the court, the nobility, and the bureaucracy operated like a foreign occupying power within a largely peasant society with which they had little in common. Emancipation of the serfs only postponed the frustrations of this peasant nation, whose life was based on the village commune and the Russian Orthodox Church. The failure of early nineteenth-century attempts to launch a vernacular Russian Bible, which could have served as the foundation-stone of a modern national culture, has been seen as crucial.[33]

As the decades passed, nationalism frequently assumed a more truculent tone. National movements which had started as part of the liberal crusade against reactionary dynasties became frustrated when their demands could not be fully realized. Hence in the last quarter of the century, the 'old liberating and unifying nationalism' frequently gave way to an intolerant strain of 'integral nationalism'. Talk began about the expulsion of minorities, and of the 'treason' of anyone not conforming to the nationalists' own dogmatic definition of their community. (It was in this negative sense that the term 'nationalism' entered general currency in the 1890s.) Germany was to be for Germans alone, 'Romania for the Romanians', Ruritania for the Ruritanians.

It was in imperial Germany, perhaps, that the ideas of *Blut und Boden* or 'blood and soil' took deepest root. But it was in France that integral nationalism found its most coherent advocates, in the writings of Maurice Barrès (1862–1923) and of Charles Maurras (1868–1952), co-founders in 1899 of the movement *Action Française*. For them, France was for Frenchmen alone, and for loyal, native-born, Catholic Frenchmen at that. Barrès, Deputy for the Moselle, spent his career fighting for the return of Alsace-Lorraine from Germany. His book *Les Déracinés* (The Uprooted, 1897) gave a label to the idea of rootless and hence worthless elements of society. It would soon be turned against the Jews, amongst others. *La Colline inspirée* (1913) advanced the notion that Catholicism and true Frenchness were inseparable. Maurras took a leading role as an anti-Dreyfusard, and later as a supporter of Pétain in Vichy France. His language became so extreme that in 1926 his writings were placed on the Catholic Index.

Integral nationalism affected all the national movements of the *fin de siècle*. In addition to Germany and France, it made a deep impact in Poland, where the National Democratic Movement of Roman Dmowski (1864–1939) was very characteristic of the trend. In Italy it was inherent in the activities of the irredentists, such as Gabriele D'Annunzio (1863–1938), who were trying to prise Trieste and South Tyrol from Austria. In Russia it led to the rejection of all who did not conform to the identification of Russianness with Orthodoxy. In Great Britain it could be observed among all who equated 'British' with 'English'. In Ireland it was represented both by the stance of many Protestant Ulstermen, who saw no place in Ulster for Catholics, and by the extreme tendency among Irish Catholic nationalists, who regarded all protestants and Anglo-Irish as agents of alien domination. Among Jews it could be observed in the wing of Zionism which saw Palestine not just as a refuge for oppressed Jews but as the land for a 'Jewish State', where non-Jews would have to live on sufferance.

Much depended on the political environment within which the various national movements were obliged to operate. Some political theorists have been tempted to place the 'moderate, humane, and liberating' forms of nationalism in Western Europe, and to lump the nationalisms of Eastern Europe into the intolerant, ethnic category.[34] This classification is patently unjust. There are many instances of intolerant, ethnic nationalism in Western Europe, from the IRA to the Flemish Fatherland Front. Many national movements in Eastern Europe have included both so-called 'Western' and 'non-Western' elements. The labels simply do not fit. What is true is that the autocratic empires of Eastern Europe inhibited nationalism of the liberal type, encouraging violent opposition from all sources. Whereas popular nationalism was given full rein in most parts of Europe in the fifty years after 1870, many of those peoples who found themselves under the control of the Russian Empire had to postpone their hopes of liberation for nearly a century. This delay was due more to the nature of successive Russian states than to the inherent characteristics of their captive peoples.

The Italian national liberation movement was in action for three-quarters of a century before its objective was achieved in 1871. It is known as *il Risorgimento*, 'the Resurgence', after a newspaper founded in 1847 in Turin by its most effective leader, Count Camillo di Cavour (1810–61), Prime Minister of Sardinia. But its origins lay among the secret independence societies, among them the famous Carbonari, who launched the abortive revolts in Naples (1820), Turin (1821), and Rome (1830), and the *Giovane Italia* or 'Young Italy' of Giuseppe Mazzini (1805–72). Mazzini, national revolutionary and prophet, spent much of his life in exile, in Marseilles, Berne, and London. He created a national ideology, roused his compatriots from apathy, and called on sympathetic rulers, like Charles Albert of Sardinia, to support them. 'A nation', he declared, 'is the universality of citizens speaking the same tongue.' In 1834 he founded an international branch of his campaign, Young Europe, which trained a network of conspirators for preparing democratic constitutions all over the Continent.

1848, the Year of Revolutions, brought Italy to the forefront of the eruptions sweeping Europe. Independent republics were proclaimed in Venice and Rome. Sicily and Naples turned on their Bourbon monarch, Ferdinand II. Charles-Albert launched a 'Holy War' on Austria, hoping to benefit from the revolt of Milan. All were crushed amidst the counter-attacks of General Radetzky and the merciless bombardments of 'King Bomba'. Mazzini's slogan, 'Italia farà da sé' (Italy will do it alone), had failed. His romantic associate Giuseppe Garibaldi (1807–82), who had fought both in Rome and in Venice, fled to South America.

Conditions improved a decade later. Cavour's Sardinia was converted to the Italian cause as the best means of dislodging the Austrians. After the fine performance of Sardinian troops in the Crimea, Napoleon III asked quaintly, 'What can I do for Italy?' and a Franco-Sardinian Pact was duly signed. France undertook to support Sardinia in the north against Austria, whilst continuing to defend the Papal States in the centre. Three wars later the game was complete. In 1859–60 the victories at Magenta and Solferino assured the success of the Franco-Sardinian attack on Austrian Italy; whilst the sensational private expedition of Garibaldi's 'Thousand' redshirts assured the fall of Sicily and Naples. Plebiscites in Parma,

Modena, and Tuscany all voted for Italy; France took Savoy and Nice; Austria still held Venetia; and with French help the Pope still ruled in Rome. But in May 1861 an all-Italian parliament at Turin proclaimed Victor Emmanuel II (r. 1849–78) King of Italy. In 1866, with Austria at war with Prussia, Italy contrived the cession of Venetia. In 1870, with France at war with Prussia, Italy seized the remainder of the Papal States and confined the Pope to the Vatican. Except for the Trentino (South Tyrol) and Istria, the Kingdom of Italy was complete. Cavour was dead; Garibaldi retired to the Isle of Caprera; Mazzini, the republican, still in exile, was heartbroken. (See Appendix III, p. 1304.) [**GATTOPARDO**]

The progress of the German national movement resembled that of its Italian counterpart in all essential respects. It began amidst the enthusiasm of the 'War of Liberation' of 1813–14 and the secret societies of the Restoration period. It met its greatest setback in 1848, when an all-German assembly was convened only to be disbanded. It reached its goal in 1871, when the King of Prussia was converted to the cause.

In the period before March 1848, known as the *Vormärz*, the futility of the German Confederation became self-evident. Its Diet declined into little more than a court of appeal. It was still preoccupied in settling debts from the Thirty Years War. The article of its constitution requiring each of the German princes to convene a parliament was observed or ignored at will. Liberal initiative was stifled by the princes' right to annul legislation and to call in outside assistance. In 1848–9 Germany was set alight, like France and Italy, with risings in Vienna, Berlin, Cologne, Prague, Dresden, Baden, and elsewhere. The national Vorparlament which met in St Paul's Church in Frankfurt drew up a constitution for a future German Empire. But it could not put any of its deliberations into effect. It was deeply divided by the question of Schleswig-Holstein. It could not decide whether Germany should be confined to German ethnic territory or should include all of the Austrian Empire, which was predominantly non-German. It offered the Crown to Frederick-William IV of Prussia, who turned down an honour 'that smelled of the gutter'. It broke up in July 1849 amidst recrimination and repression. (See Appendix III, p. 1303.)

Prussia's conversion to German reunification took place in the 1860s, largely as a means for breaking out of the German Confederation and the hopeless entanglement with Austria. In the early years of William I (r. 1861–88) Prussia's affairs had reached a very ambiguous condition. The authoritarian establishment had been strengthened by the military reforms of von Roon, whilst the *Landtag* elections had produced a liberal majority headed by the *Fortschrittspartei* of Waldeck. In 1862 Otto von Bismarck (1815–98) was appointed Premier to sort out the resultant crisis, if necessary by unconstitutional measures. His aim was to put Prussia 'in the saddle' in Germany, and Germany in the saddle in Europe. Immense friction was being caused by the joint Prusso-Austrian administration of Schleswig-Holstein. William I could not decide whether to lead the Confederation or to leave it to Francis-Joseph, as he did for the Frankfurt Furstentag in 1863. All these

GATTOPARDO

MAY 1860. '*Nunc et in hora mortis nostrae*. Amen.' The daily recital of the Rosary was over. For half an hour the steady voice of the Prince had recalled the Sorrowful and the Glorious Mysteries; other voices had interwoven a lilting hum from which, now and again, would chime some unlikely word; love, virginity, death. During that hum the whole aspect of the rococo drawing room seemed to change. Even the parrots spreading iridescent wings over the silken walls appeared abashed. Even the Magdalen between the two windows looked penitent . . .

Now everything returned to its usual order or disorder. Bendico, the Great Dane, came wagging his tail through the door by which the servants had left. The women rose slowly to their feet, their swaying skirts baring the naked, mythological figures painted all over the milky depths of the tiles. Only an Andromeda remained covered by the soutane of Father Pirrone, still deep in extra prayer . . .[1]

Don Fabrizio Corbera, Prince of Salina, was performing the ageless family rituals at his villa above Palermo. Sicily was passing through the uneasy interval between the abortive rising in Messina in April and Garibaldi's landing at Marsala on 11 May. The Prince, known from his coat-of-arms as 'the Leopard', was entering the twilight of the Bourbon monarchy, of feudal privilege, and of his own blighted emotional life.

Historical novels come in many categories. The cheap ones pillage the past to provide an exotic backdrop to unrelated fiction. Some use it as a neutral stage to impart conviction to the discussion of timeless issues. A few can enrich one's understanding both of history and of humanity. *Il Gattopardo* (The Leopard), published in 1958, was the posthumous work of Giuseppe Tomasi (1896–1957), Duke of Palma and Prince of Lampedusa. Rarely has a novelist shown such empathy, such historical sensitivity.

May 1910. Don Fabrizio's three maiden daughters still live at the Villa Salina. The relics of the family chapel have to be cast out, having been declared false by the Cardinal Archbishop. By chance, Bendico's fur, long preserved as a rug, is thrown out with them. As the carcass was dragged off, the glass eyes stared at her with humble reproach. What remained of Bendico was flung into a corner of the yard. During its flight from the window, its form recomposed itself for an instant; in the air there seemed to be a dancing quadruped with long whiskers, its right foreleg raised in imprecation. Then all found peace in a little piece of livid dust. *Poi tutto trovò pace in un mucchietto di polvere livida*.[3]

issues were settled by Bismarck's determination to create a new North German Confederation without Austria, and by the masterly use of limited war. In 1864 Prussia attacked and defeated Denmark for annexing Schleswig. In 1866, when Austria referred the Schleswig Question to the Confederation Diet, Prussia promptly walked out, attacking and defeating Austria and Austria's German allies. The lightning victory at Sadová, near Hradec Králové (Königgrätz), ensured Prussian supremacy, and the formation of the North German Federation. In 1870–1 Prussia attacked and defeated France. In the ensuing euphoria, Bismarck arranged for the Federation to admit the South German states and for William I to be proclaimed German Emperor. Germany was reunited; the conservative citadel was triumphant, and the liberals baffled. [**HERMANN**]

The Polish national movement had the longest pedigree, the best credentials, the greatest determination, the worst press, and the least success. It traced its origins to the anti-Russian confederations of the eighteenth century; and it bred an armed rising in every generation between the Partitions and the Second World War—in 1733, 1768, 1794, 1830, 1848, 1863, 1905, 1919, 1944. It nourished a precocious brand of nationalism which was already maturing in Napoleonic times. At heart this had little to do with economic rationale, everything with the will to preserve culture, identity, and honour.

The Polish risings of the early nineteenth century aimed to restore the crucified commonwealth of Poland-Lithuania. They were driven on by the mystical images of romantic poetry, by the conviction that Poland, 'the Christ of Nations', would have its 'Third Day':

> Hail, O Christ, Thou Lord of Men!
> Poland in Thy footsteps treading
> Like Thee suffers, at Thy bidding
> Like Thee, too, shall rise again.[35]

The principal actions were directed from the Congress Kingdom against Russia, although Poles from Austria and Prussia also took part. Sympathetic outbreaks occurred in Lithuania, Byelorussia, and Ukraine. In November 1830 a wild conspiracy, provoked by rumours of the Tsar's plan to dispatch his Polish army against Belgium, sparked a Russo-Polish war. The Tsar rejected the advice of a government in Warsaw taken over by the conservative Prince Czartoryski and refused all dialogue. So matters were left to the intransigents. On this occasion the professional Polish army had a real chance of victory, but was gradually outflanked and overwhelmed. In September 1831, when the Russians stormed the last emplacements near Warsaw, they found the corpse of General Sowiński still upright among the fields of dead and dying. The old Napoleonic officer had ordered his men to plant his wooden leg 'firmly in the Polish soil', so as not to bow to tyrants. The constitution of the Congress Kingdom was suspended. All insurgents were deprived of their freedom and their property. Ten thousand exiles found their way to France; tens of thousands more were marched to Siberia in chains.

HERMANN

THE *Hermannsdenkmal*, the monument to Arminius, stands on a lofty outcrop above the wooded slopes of the Teutoburgerwald near Detmold in Westphalia. It commemorates the victory in AD 9 of the Germanic chieftain Hermann, or Arminius the Cherascon, who somewhere nearby annihilated the invading Roman legions. A colonnaded pedestal supports a gigantic statue in beaten copper nearly 30 m in height. Ten times life size, Hermann frowns under his winged helmet as he brandishes a huge sword of vengeance over the plain below.

The monument took nearly forty years to build. Like the classical Temple of Walhalla (1830–42), built by the King of Bavaria on a bluff overlooking the Danube near Regensburg, it was conceived in a generation that remembered Napoleon and the wars of liberation. But it was not completed until Germany was united and German nationalism was assuming a more muscular form. The designer and prime mover of the project, Ernst von Bandel, had repeatedly failed to find the necessary finance. He finally succeeded by raising subscriptions from schools throughout the German empire. Hermann was unveiled in 1875, a fitting symbol of the Empire's new-found pride.

In the heyday of nationalism, every self-respecting nation felt honour-bound to find heroes suitable for commemoration; and public monuments served a definite social and educational purpose. The *Hermannsdenkmal* led the field in a special pseudo-historical genre that swept Europe.[1] In Germany it had several rivals, including the *Niederwaldsdenkmal* on the banks of the Rhine, the equestrian statue of Emperor William I on the Kyffhauser Mountain in Thuringia, and the *Völkerschlachtdenkmal* (1913), which was erected by a league of patriots in Leipzig on the centenary of the Battle of the Nations. In time and spirit, it closely resembles the statue to that most unparliamentary of kings, Richard Cœur de Lion, erected beside the Houses of Parliament in London, the Grunwald monument (1910) in Cracow, and the monument to Vercingetorix on the Plateau de Gergovie near Clermont-Ferrand.

Perhaps the ultimate in the political aesthetics of national sentiment can be found in the monument to Prince Llewellyn's dog, Gelert, which was erected at Beddgelert (Gelert's Grave) in North Wales in the 1790s.[2] The greater the pathos, the remoter the time, and the more the Romantic generation enthuse over these reminders of their roots.

Polish activities in 1848 were dampened by the fiasco of an intended general rising two years earlier, when the Republic of Cracow had sealed its fate by not controlling the revolutionaries. Thousands of nobles had been massacred in the surrounding Galician countryside by peasants abetted by Austrian officials. Poland's contribution to the 'springtime of other nations', therefore, was one minor disturbance in Posnania, two outbursts in Cracow and Lemberg, and a major contingent of exiles, headed by General Józef Bem, which fought for Hungary.

In January 1863, the Congress Kingdom erupted once more, frustrated by the contradictions of the 'Tsar Liberator', Alexander II. Whilst emancipating the serfs of his Empire, Alexander was not prepared to grant the Poles a constitution. Two years of patriotic demonstrations in Warsaw led by priests, pastors, and rabbis ended with the formation of a secret National Government. Sixteen months of fierce guerrilla warfare ended with the executions of the insurgent leaders on the walls of the citadel. On this occasion the Congress Kingdom itself was suppressed. Eighty thousand Poles made the terrible journey to Siberia—the largest of all political contingents in tsarist history.

In 1905 the torch of patriotic insurrection was taken up by the Polish Socialist Party. Waves of strikes and street battles in Warsaw and Lodz long outlasted the contemporary Russian revolt in St Petersburg. Huge conscriptions of sullen young men from the Polish provinces filled the ranks of the Russian army, fighting with no great conviction against the Japanese in Manchuria.

The persistent defeats of Polish nationalism fostered two important developments. Later generations of patriots often chose to work for their country rather than fight for it. Their concept of 'organic work' aimed to strengthen economic and cultural resources, and to curb all political demands beyond local autonomy. This became the standard strategy for all national movements whose military and diplomatic support was deficient. At the same time, 'integral nationalism' made its appearance in each of the nationalities of the Polish lands. Lithuanian, Byelorussian, Ukrainian, and Zionist Jewish nationalism each took a stance which effectively paralysed any sense of a common struggle. Dmowski's Polish nationalists fiercely contested Piłsudski's Polish independence movement. Its slogans demanding a 'Poland for the Poles' revealed deep anti-German, anti-Ukrainian, and antisemitic complexes.

Within the Russian Empire, important gradations could be seen in official attitudes to the rising tide of nationalism. Byelorussians and Ukrainians were simply not permitted to possess a separate identity. Poles, until 1906, were not permitted any form of political expression. Yet in the Grand Duchy of Finland, Finns enjoyed the autonomy of which many of their neighbours were deprived. The Baltic Germans, largely Lutherans, enjoyed the religious and cultural toleration that was denied the other inhabitants of the Baltic provinces. 'The prison of the nations' had many bars, and many holes in the wall.

The national question in Austria-Hungary was particularly recondite. The *Ausgleich* of 1867 was intended to moderate the problems; in practice it rendered them insoluble. There was no chance that the German-speaking élite could impose its culture throughout Austria, let alone extend it to the whole of the Dual Monarchy. After all, 'Austria was a Slav house with a German façade'. In practice the three 'master races'—the Germans, the Magyars, and the Galician Poles—were encouraged to lord it over the others. The administrative structures were so tailored that the German minority in Bohemia could hold down the Czechs, the Magyars in Hungary could hold down the Slovaks, Romanians, and Croats, and the Poles in Galicia could hold down the Ruthenians (Ukrainians). So pressures mounted as each of the excluded nationalities fell prey to the charms of nationalism. What is more, when Habsburg politics were complicated by the introduction first of the *Reichsrat* or 'Imperial Council' and eventually, in 1896, of universal suffrage, the three ruling groups could only maintain their supremacy by an endless game of deals and compromises. The Austrian Germans, who dominated the court and army, could only fend off the fiery Magyars by upholding the interests of ultra-conservative Polish aristocrats from Galicia. As a result, the Poles remained the most staunchly *Kaisertreu* element to the end. The Magyars were eternally dissatisfied; German opinion in Austria was increasingly drawn back to the old idea of a Greater Germany; and the Czechs in particular felt hopelessly trapped. Francis-Joseph I (r. 1848–1916), who described himself as 'the last monarch of the old style', ruled over a truly multinational state, where the imperial hymn could be sung in any one of seventeen official languages, including Yiddish. He was popular exactly because of his political immobility. Under the surface, the untreated ills were starting to fester. As one Prime Minister was ready to admit: 'It is my policy to keep all the nationalities in the Monarchy in a balanced state of well-modulated dissatisfaction.'[36] [GENES]

Europe was filled with national movements which do not feature in the textbooks. Many of the smaller communities willingly confined themselves to cultural tasks. In Provence, Frédéric Mistral (1830–1914) was able to organize the revival of Provençal language and culture and yet be elected to the French Academy. In Wales, the custom of an annual *Eisteddfod* or bardic meeting was revived in 1819 after centuries of abeyance. The pseudo-druidical ceremonies initiated at Llangollen in 1858 became an essential feature of the series. In Germany, Slavonic Polabs, Sorbs, and Kashubs, resurrected their ancient Slavonic cultures. The Polabs had survived in a tiny enclave round Lüchow near Hanover; a collection of their literature and a grammar-book were published with Russian assistance in 1871. The Sorbs of Lusatia, who numbered perhaps 200,000, established a *Maćica* or 'cultural society' at Budišyn (Bautzen) in 1847. The Kashubs of Pomerania did likewise.

Both constitutional and autocratic systems could prove hostile to national aspirations. In this respect the experience of the Irish and the Ukrainians is worthy of comparison; the political arithmetic was stacked against both of them.

The Irish participated in a prominent 'Western democracy'. From 1801, when the Union of Ireland and Great Britain was enacted, over fifty Irish MPs sat in the British Parliament at Westminster. It gave them all sorts of benefits except the one

GENES

IN 1866 Father Gregor Mendel (1811–84), abbot of the Augustinian monastery at Brno in Moravia, published the findings of his experiments into the propagation of the common green pea, *Pisum sativum*. For several years the abbot had been observing the peas in the monastery garden. By careful cross-pollination, and by concentrating on just a few specific characteristics such as height and colour, he was able to demonstrate definite patterns of inheritance in successive plant generations. He established the existence of dominant and recessive characteristics whose recurrence in hybrids he could empirically predict. His results were totally ignored. The 'Mendelian Laws of Inheritance', which form the starting point of modern genetics, were separately rediscovered in 1900 by three different biologists.[1]

Mendelism remained in the experimental stage for many decades. Although the presence of *chromosomes* in living cells was established early in the twentieth century, the mechanics of the *genes*, or 'unit-characters', as Mendel had called them, long defied the researchers. The significance of deoxyribonucleic acid (DNA) was not realized until 1944, and the double-helical spiral structure of the DNA molecule not demonstrated until 1953. In this regard, biology lagged well behind the corresponding advances in modern physics and chemistry.

In the mean time, a Soviet scientist claimed to have solved many of the fundamental problems. Trofion Denisovich Lysenko (1898–1976) rejected the chromosomal basis of heredity, arguing instead that inheritable changes could be induced in plants by environmental influences and by grafting. He published experimental results showing that the germination of wheat seed could be dramatically improved by subjection to low temperature. He even tried to make wheat plants produce rye seed. It was all a scam: his results had been falsified. But having persuaded Stalin that his theories would remedy the failures of Soviet agriculture, Lysenko shaped himself a dazzling career that flourished for three decades. Elected President of the Lenin Academy of Agricultural Science in 1938, he ordered millions of acres to be sown with grain treated by his methods. When the grain failed to sprout, the farmers were arrested for sabotage. Critics, including Russia's leading geneticist N. I. Vavrilov, were cast into the Gulag. Teachers had to present Lysenkoism as gospel. Soviet biology was blighted almost beyond repair. Lysenko received two Stalin Prizes, the Order of Lenin and the title Hero of the USSR.[2]

Western biologists treated Lysenko as 'illiterate'. In return, Lysenko derided all orthodox geneticists as 'reactionary decadents grovelling before Western capitalism'. Foremost among the targets of his scorn was Father Gregor Mendel.[3]

they most desired—control over their own affairs. But their political activities were incessant. The Catholic Association of Daniel O'Connell (1775–1847), which organized huge 'monster' public meetings for years, achieved religious toleration in 1829. Discontent was later kept on the boil by the sufferings of the Famine, by the injustices of successive Land Acts, and by the lack of political progress. The complacency of English Conservatives, the tenacious resistance of the Ulster Protestants, and the violent exploits of the Irish radical wing, which was represented by the Fenians (Irish Republican Brotherhood, from 1858) and by Sinn Fein (from 1905), made for political deadlock. In the Irish countryside the long-running war between government-backed landlords and the rebellious tenants of the Land League (1879) created a pervasive climate of fear. Even when C. S. Parnell (1846–91) and his Irish party at Westminster gained the support of Gladstone's ruling Liberals, three successive bills for Irish Home Rule were blocked in the House of Lords. The true cultural awakening of the Irish occurred late, in the 1890s, when the Irish Literary Theatre, the Gaelic Athletic Association, and the Gaelic League were all founded, 'On the necessity for de-anglicising the Irish People'. In 1900 Queen Victoria visited Dublin for the first time in forty years, rescinded the ban on 'the wearing of the green', and encouraged massive St Patrick's Day parades throughout the Empire. But it was too late for symbolic gestures. In 1912, when a fourth Home Rule Bill was prepared, both the Ulster Volunteers in Belfast and the National Volunteers in Dublin raised formidable armies. As Europe approached the Great War, Ireland stood on the brink of civil war. Ireland was indeed divided. Ulster, defiant, had no sense of Irishness. 'Ireland is not a nation,' said a future British prime minister, 'but two peoples separated by a deeper gulf than that dividing Ireland from Great Britain.'[37] Sinn Fein, which had always looked to the USA for support, now sought aid from Germany. [FAMINE][ORANGE]

The Ukrainians lived under two 'Eastern autocracies'. Once subjects of Poland, they were now subjects either of Russia or of Austria. An overwhelmingly peasant people, their level of national consciousness was necessarily low until the bonds of serfdom were severed in mid-century. Traditionally known as *Rusini* or 'Ruthenians', they now began to adopt the 'Ukrainian' label in reaction to the misleading and insulting designation of 'Little Russians', which tsarist officialdom had invented for them. (A Ukrainian simply meant a politically conscious Ruthene.) Their cultural awakening was greatly stimulated by the poetic writings of Taras Shevchenko (1814–61); their political awakening gathered pace in later decades. In Russia they were faced by a regime which refused to recognize their existence, regarding them as a regional Russian minority, and allowing them only one religion—Russian Orthodoxy. In Austria, where they enjoyed greater cultural and political freedom they preserved the Uniate Rite, and were slow to adopt the Ukrainian label. At the turn of the century, they organized Ruthenian schooling on a large scale. But there they were faced by a strong Polish community, which held the numerical majority in Galicia as a whole, including Lemberg. [UKRAINA]

FAMINE

BETWEEN 1845 and 1849 Ireland suffered one of Europe's worst natural disasters. The Irish potato famine caused a million deaths, drove over a million more to emigrate, and reduced the island's population of 8.2 million (1845) by at least a quarter. Although Ireland was an integral part of the United Kingdom, the most powerful state of the era, she received little effective relief. To some observers, it was the ultimate Malthusian apocalypse: to others, the culmination of centuries of misrule.[1]

The immediate cause of the disaster lay in the fungal blight *phytophthora infestans,* which decimated the potato crop in three successive years. The blight had been noted in the Isle of Wight a year before it crossed the Irish Sea in 1845. In England it was a minor nuisance, in Ireland the agent of death.

By the early nineteenth century, large sections of Ireland's rural population had become totally dependent on a 'potato culture'. A vegetable rich in vitamins and protein, it grew easily in the moist Irish earth. It sustained large numbers of poor people who were left with too much time for singing, dancing, drinking poteen, and telling stories. They had as many names for potatoes as the English had for roses. They called it the murphy, the spud, the tater, the pratie, and the 'precarious exotic'.

Potato dependency was the product of many disorders. In the six decades after 1780, Ireland experienced a demographic explosion—an increase of nearly 300 per cent as compared with 88 per cent in England and Wales. Yet, with the exception of Ulster, she experienced little industrialization to absorb the surplus numbers, though emigration to the USA and Australia began after the Napoleonic Wars. Most seriously, Irish society was clamped by a body of repressive legislation, which blocked many obvious solutions to her distress. Conditions on the land had been atrocious for longer than anyone remembered. Until 1829, Catholic Irishmen were not even allowed to buy land, and few had money to do so. Anglo-Irish landlords, often absentees, demanded high rents or deliveries in kind on pain of instant eviction. Evictions were enforced by the military, who customarily razed or 'tumbled' the houses of defaulters. Irish peasants had no security, and little incentive to work. They frequently murdered their persecutors, or joined the British army. In the words of the Duke of Wellington, 'Ireland was an inexhaustible nursery for the finest soldiers'. But it was also the home of squalor—with large ragged families living in mud huts with no furniture and the company of pigs. As a German traveller remarked: 'it seems that the poorest among the Letts, Esthonians and Finnlanders lead a life of comparative comfort'.[2]

A generous Irish historian writes that the initial policies of Sir Robert Peel's government 'were more effective than sometimes allowed'.[3] In 1846 prices were controlled, Indian meal distributed, and public works started to provide employment. But Peel's fall over Corn Law repeal ushered in a Whig ministry that did not believe in intervention. 'Rotten potatoes have done it all,' exclaimed the Iron Duke. Irishmen paid their rent, and ate nettles.

In 1847, 3 million public soup rations were served. But they did not stop typhus, or the crowds fleeing the countryside. In the district of Skibbereen in County Cork, where a dozen landlords took £50,000 in rent, there were corpses in the fields and children dying in the workhouse; and grain was still being exported under guard to England. Robber bands pillaged the country towns. 'What we have to contend with', said the Treasury Minister responsible for relief, 'is not the physical evil of the famine but the moral evil of the selfish, perverse and turbulent character of the people.'[4]

In 1848 the potato crop failed again, and the human exodus swelled to a flood. Ragged families garnered their last strength to walk to the ports. Landlords often paid for them to go. They collapsed on the roads, perished in the overcrowded steerage holds, and died in droves on the docks of New York and Montreal. They landed racked with fever, stomach cramps, and anglophobia.

The famine put an end to Daniel O'Connell's campaign to reject the Union. But it also killed any real hopes of reconciliation. And the exodus continued:

> A million a decade! Calmly and cold
> The units are read by our statesman sage.
> Little they think of a Nation old,
> Fading away from History's page:
> —Outcast weeds by a desolate sea
> Fallen leaves of Humanity![5]

This was not Europe's last famine. It was followed in 1867–8 by similar catastrophes in Finland and in Belgium. Nor was it on the scale of the Volga famine of 1921 or in the nature of the terror-famine in Ukraine of 1932–3 [**HARVEST**]. But it was shameful for where and how it happened. The British government's final relief measure, in August 1849, was to send Queen Victoria and Prince Albert on a state visit to Dublin.

In both empires, then, the Ukrainians had to contend with the fact that their homeland was inhabited by several other nationalities—Poles, Jews, and Russians—all of whom were hostile to Ukrainian nationalism. It was frustrating, to say the least. The potential membership of the Ukrainian nation was as numerous as the French or the English. Yet nowhere could they bring their numbers to bear. Like the Irish, they remained a stateless nation. Like the Irish, their activists began to look to Germany.

Balkan nationalism grew specially intense. The Ottoman Empire had always tolerated a large measure of religious and cultural autonomy, whilst extirpating political dissidence. Assimilation into the ruling Muslim culture, except in Bosnia, Albania, and parts of Bulgaria, was low. As a result, ready-made Christian nations were waiting to emerge as soon as Ottoman power receded. Typically, they enjoyed a long period of practical autonomy, subject to the presence of nominal Ottoman garrisons, prior to acquiring absolute sovereignty. They also tended to start life on a minimal territorial base, which failed to satisfy their aspirations, and which led to repeated conflicts with their neighbours. None of them possessed even the semblance of ethnic homogeneity. Greece won its formal independence in 1832, the Romanian principalities (Wallachia and Moldavia) in 1856, Montenegro in 1860, Serbia and Bulgaria in 1878. The Albanians, the only predominantly Muslim nation in the region, lacked the support of the Christian powers, and were kept waiting until 1913. (See Appendix III, p. 1302.) [SHQIPERIA]

The Greeks' experience was not felicitous, least of all with their monarchs. In seven reigns between 1833 and 1973, there were five abdications. The first King of the Hellenes, Otto I of Bavaria (r. 1833–62), a Catholic enthusiast for Germanic efficiency, proved more unpopular than the Ottomans. The second, George I (r. 1864–1913), was imported from Denmark to found an accident-prone dynasty. Nationalism and foreign kings did not mix. The Serbian experience was no happier: the blood feud between the rival dynasties of Karađorđević and Obrenović fuelled ten royal assassinations. Russian support aroused a strong reaction from Austria, especially since the Slavs of the Dual Monarchy were increasingly impressed by the Serbian example. Serbia's success in the Balkan Wars finally pushed Vienna into a show-down.

Unfortunately, the ethnic mosaic of the Balkans impeded the creation of stable national states. 'Balkanization' became a byword for political fragmentation, petty-minded nationalism, and vicious feuds. In the three Balkan wars of the early twentieth century, the Christian successor states fought no less eagerly among themselves than against the retreating Turks (see below).

Historians must also address the problem of why, in a continent brimming with popular nationalisms, a number of countries did not follow the general trend. Why, for example, did an effective national movement fail to develop in nineteenth-century Scotland? The Scots, after all, were exposed to intense modernization at an early date; and as junior partners within the United Kingdom they could easily have found early cause to resent English domination. But they did not. The answer must lie partly in the divisions between the Gaelic and the Lowland elements within Scottish culture, which impeded the growth of a common identity, and partly in the powerful attractions of British state nationalism. Like Cardiff or Belfast, Scotland's principal city, Glasgow, thrived mightily from the enterprises of the British Empire. Scotland's attachment to a successful Union would not decline until the Empire itself began to fade. The pioneer bard of Scottish nationalism, Hugh MacDiarmid (1892–1978), did not start to write until the 1920s. The key political tract of the movement, Tom Nairn's *Break-up of Britain*, was not published until 1977.[38]

In the meantime, one of the most prescient observers concluded that nationalism was no more than a phase. Speaking in 1882, Ernest Renan made the startling observation that no state or nation was eternal. Sooner or later all would be supplanted by something else, 'possibly a European confederation'. Metternich had once said, 'For me Europe has long held the essence of a fatherland.'[39] The hope was planted that such sentiments might some day return in more practical form.

Socialism, like Nationalism, was a collectivist creed. It opposed the exploiters and manipulators for the protection not just of the individual but of society as a whole. It took its name from the idea of fellowship or, in the modern idiom 'solidarity'—*socius* in Latin meaning 'companion'. It maintained that the poor, weak and oppressed could not be guaranteed a tolerable life except by the pooling of resources, by the equitable distribution of wealth, and by the subordination of individual rights to the common good. Unlike liberalism, it did not fear the modern state; on the contrary, it looked to the state as the arbiter and often as the prime mover of compassionate measures. Socialism was to be directed against oppressors both at home and abroad. The feeling of international solidarity made it the natural opponent of nationalism. Nineteenth-century socialism is generally considered to have drawn its strength from four separate sources: from Christian socialism, from the trade union movement, from the co-operative movement, and from the 'utopian' socialist theorists. (See Appendix III, p. 1308.)

Without ever using the label, Christian socialism had a centuries-old tradition. Christian doctrine had always urged service to the community and the renunciation of personal wealth. The Sermon on the Mount had been regularly invoked to justify collectivist economic schemes, from the practical workings of the monastic orders to the utopias of More, Campanella, Harrington, and Morelli. In the nineteenth century, Protestants generally showed the most initiative, through figures such as J. F. D. Maurice (1805–72), first principal of the Working Men's College (1854), Charles Kingsley (1819–75), Adolf Wagner (1835–1917), or the Kaiser's preacher, Adolf Stoecker (1835–99). The Oxford Movement also had a socialist streak, which came out in its 'missions' to city slums. The Roman Catholics were more inhibited until the publication of *Rerum novarum* in 1891. In Russia, the doctrines of the Orthodox Church, the collectivist traditions of the peasant communes, and existence of an all-powerful state all furnished fertile ground for the reception of socialist ideas.

The trade union movement grew out of the vulnerability of wage-labourers in the free-market economy. From the days of Dorset's Tolpuddle Martyrs, working men and women painfully won the right to form unions, to bargain collectively over pay and conditions, and to strike. The critical launch dates are seen as 1834 in Britain, 1864 in France, 1869 in Germany. By 1900 most European countries possessed an active labour movement. From the start, the trade unions adopted a variety of structures and ideologies. Apart from the non-ideological unions of the British type, there were 'horizontal' craft unions, which grew out of the old guilds, 'vertical' industrial unions, anarcho-syndicalist unions on the French or Spanish model, liberal workers' associations, pacifist 'yellow' unions opposed both to strikes and to war, and Church-based Christian unions. In many countries, as in Belgium, several different types of union worked alongside each other. In Russia, the initiative was taken by the Tsarist police, who decided to outflank various illegal organizations by forming official unions of their own. This experiment in 'police socialism' came to a bad end on 5 January 1905, when a demonstration headed by Father Gapon, a police agent, was fired on by the police. 'Bloody Sunday' launched the revolutionary outbreak of 1905; and Father Gapon was murdered. Russian trade unionism enjoyed barely one decade of independent existence before being suppressed by the Bolsheviks.

The formation of co-operatives, which sought to protect their members from the evils of big business, took place in three main sectors—manufacturing, consumption, and agriculture. In 1800 the experimental textile settlement of New Lanark Mills was set up in Scotland by the visionary Robert Owen (1771–1858). It guaranteed a ten-and-a-half-hour working day and sickness insurance, but did not outlast its founder. In 1844 the first consumers' co-operative, the Rochdale Pioneers, appeared in Lancashire. Agricultural co-operatives, which first emerged in Germany at the initiative of F. W. Raiffeisen (1818–88), were to have a broad future wherever peasant farmers were free to organize, and especially in Eastern Europe.

Socialist theorizing had been in progress ever since the 'Conspiracy of Equals' was organized in Paris in 1796 by François-Noël Babeuf (1760–97). Like Babeuf, who was executed by the Directory, all the founding theorists were French utopians. They included Claude Henri de Rouvroy, Comte de Saint-Simon (1760–1825), Charles Fourrier (1772–1837), Étienne Cabet (1788–1856), Louis Auguste Blanqui (1805–81), Louis Blanc (1811–82), and Pierre-Joseph Proudhon (1809–65). Saint-Simon, a Christian socialist who had been close to Comte, sought to mobilize science and technology for an ideal community governed by experts. His *Nouveau Christianisme* (1825) led to the foundation of a sectarian Church, model communes, and trials for immorality. Both Fourrier and Cabet established model co-operative settlements in the USA. Fourrier's *Théorie des Quatre Mouvements* (1808) envisaged a scientifically ordered society, free from all government, which would ascend through various stages of perfection on the road to 'Harmony'. (It is often regarded as the source of Marx's ideas on the stages of history and the withering of the state.)

Blanqui, known as 'l'Enfermé', 'the Interned', was a Babouvian class conspirator, who spent a total of 33 years in prison for persistently organizing insurrectionary cells against monarchy and republic alike. His seizure of the Hôtel de Ville in Paris for two days in 1839 was a disaster; but his followers played a leading role in the Commune of 1871. (He missed the event himself by being arrested the day before its outbreak.) His motto was 'Ni Dieu, ni maître' (Neither God, nor boss). Louis Blanc, in contrast, argued for the creation of egalitarian, worker-controlled, and state-funded workshops, where the workers were to contribute according to their ability and be paid according to their needs. The scheme outlined in *L'Organisation du Travail* (1839) was briefly put into practice during the Revolution of 1848, before its author was exiled in England. Proudhon was in some ways the most influential of them all. His attack on (excessive) private property in *Qu'est-ce que c'est la propriété?* (1840) was a sensation, especially when its most famous phrase, 'Property is theft', was quoted out of context. His *Philosophie de la Misère* (1846) provoked one of Marx's more trenchant retorts in *La Misère de la Philosophie*; whilst his *Ideé générale de la Révolution* (1851) described a future Europe free of frontiers, central governments, and state laws. Proudhon was the founder of modern anarchism, which soon led his followers into conflict with mainstream socialism; but his support for direct action by workers against the state became the corner-stone of French syndicalism.

French influences were strong in the thought of the early German socialists. Ferdinand Loslauer (Lassalle, 1825–64), a Silesian Jew, who was killed in a romantic duel after founding the first German socialist party, spent a formative period in Paris. The two inseparable exiles, Friedrich Engels (1820–95) and Karl Marx (1818–83), who met in Paris, based many of their arguments on study of the French Revolution. Their *Communist Manifesto* (1848) was well timed. 'A spectre is haunting Europe', it claimed, 'the spectre of communism. Let the ruling classes tremble . . . The proletarians have nothing to lose but their chains . . . Working men of all countries, unite!'

Marx and Engels were an odd pair. Expelled from Prussia for their radical journalism, they settled in England. Engels soon established himself as a prosperous capitalist, managing a cotton factory in Manchester. Marx eked out a penurious living in London, supported as a private scholar by a stipend from Engels. His life's work, *Das Kapital* (Capital, 3 vols., 1867–94) was the fruit of thirty years' lonely study in the Reading Room of the British Museum. It was a sustained exercise in speculative social philosophy, a rambling jumble of brilliant insights and turgid pedantry. It borrowed a number of disparate ideas current at the time, and reassembled them in the original combination of 'dialectical materialism'. Marx aimed to create the same sort of universal theory for human society that Darwin had done for natural history; and he had hoped to dedicate his first volume to Darwin. He took the subject of materialist history from Feuerbach, the class struggle from Saint-Simon, the dictatorship of the proletariat (which he soon rejected) from Babeuf, the labour theory of value from Adam Smith, the theory of surplus value from Bray and Thompson, the principle of dialectical progress from Hegel. All these components were put together in a messianic doctrine whose psychological roots are thought to lie in the Judaism which his family had deserted during his childhood. Marx was the Prophet; the Proletariat was the Chosen People; the socialist movement was the Church; the Revolution was the Second Coming; Communism was the Promised Land.[40]

Marx had little to do with practical politics. He helped found an International Working-men's Association, a phantom body later eulogized as 'the first International', for which he wrote a constitution and some fiery addresses. In his later years he attracted a substantial following among German socialists and their

Russian disciples, but not in Britain. When he died he was buried in Highgate Cemetery, in a tomb which faces that of Herbert Spencer, with the inscription: 'Philosophers have so far explained the world in various ways: the point, however, is to change it.' Engels wrote up the last two volumes of *Kapital* from Marx's notes, thereby completing a joint œuvre whose individual elements cannot always be disentangled. But he had ideas of his own. He was more familiar with social conditions than Marx, and more concerned with the practical implications of their theories. By expounding the 'withering of state power', his *Anti-Dühring* (1878) and *The Origins of the Family, Private Property and the State* (1884) gave great encouragement to active revolutionaries.

Latter-day commentators tend to be rather dismissive of Marxism's credentials. Marx, they say, was 'illustrative of liberal Europe', or 'a typical mid-19th century social theorist'.[41] They may be right; but they miss the point. The intellectual rigour of Marxism proved to be far inferior to its emotive power. The great majority who came to believe that Marx had provided a scientific basis for their dreams of social justice never gave a moment's critical thought to his writings. Marx had unwittingly provided them with yet another substitute religion.

The obvious social constituency for socialism was provided by the new working class. In practice, many workers steered clear; and almost all socialist organizations were dominated by middle-class intellectuals. The English Fabian society was archetypal. In Eastern Europe, where the fledgeling working class remained small, socialism was taken up either by internationalist conspirators, as in Russia, or, as in Poland, by that branch of the independence movement that wished to overcome the ethnic divisiveness preached by its nationalist rivals. Attempts to mobilize socialist movements with a mass following repeatedly foundered on the rocks of local interests, governmental repression, or intellectual frangipanery. In most countries, socialist parties of one sort or another struggled into existence, often after decades of frustration. It was the 1890s before a respectable parade of parties could be consolidated (see Appendix III, p. 1308). The most important, the German Social Democratic Party (SPD) was permanently established in 1890, after twelve years of banishment under Bismarck's anti-socialist law. It traced its origin to the Gotha Programme of 1875, and to the merger of Lassalle's association with various Marxist groups. The Erfurt Programme of 1891 was largely formulated by Karl Kautsky (1854–1938), and was openly Marxist. But it was soon modified both by the revisionist criticisms of Eduard Bernstein (1850–1932), who rejected the apocalyptic vision of socialism, and by the pragmatic inclinations of party leaders in the Reichstag.

The internationalist branch of the movement encountered similar difficulties. The 'First International' fell apart amidst recriminations between Marxists and anarchists. The 'Second International', which in 1889 succeeded in setting up a permanent secretariat in Brussels, was soon dominated by representatives of the SPD. It organized congresses, acted as a pressure group largely in the pacifist cause, and evaporated in 1914 when none of its national branches opposed the war. Its demise left the field deserted by all except the revolutionary Russian party, which was run by exiles like V. I. Ulyanov (Lenin, 1870–1924) and other like-minded conspirators.

The Russian revolutionary tradition was as old as the autocracy which fuelled it. Its first incarnation in the nineteenth century broke surface with the Decembrists of 1825—a fraternity of army officers influenced by French and Polish ideas. But in subsequent decades, under the guidance of Alexander Herzen (1812–70) and Nikolai Chernyshevsky (1828–89), it took on increasingly socialist, populist, and anarchist flavours. In the 1860s and 1870s Russian populism—*narodnichestvo* or 'the movement to the people'—saw starry-eyed idealists going out to the villages to convert the peasantry, only to be met with incomprehension. In 1879 the populists split into two wings, with one emphasizing agrarian and educational reform and the other, the *Narodnaya Vol'ya* or 'People's Will', advocating violence. A member of the latter assassinated Tsar Alexander II in 1881.

One key figure, P. N. Tkachev (1844–85), is often overlooked in Western accounts. Nor was he chosen for the later Bolshevik pantheon. Yet he was the true precursor of bolshevism. A 'Jacobin' among the Populists and an economic materialist, he provided the intellectual link between Chernyshevsky and Lenin. He spurned the education of the masses, calling instead for the training of a revolutionary élite. 'The question "What should be done?" should no longer concern us,' he wrote in the 1870s. 'It has long since been resolved. Make the Revolution!' He spent his later years in exile in Switzerland, where Lenin was to read his works avidly whilst denouncing him in public. There were no 'filial ties', but a definite fellow spirit.[42]

The history of Lenin's group well illustrates the impossible dilemmas forced on would-be socialists in a hostile setting. As exiles or illegals, they had no chance to practise the democratic methods of the German SPD, from whom their original inspiration was taken. As revolutionaries, they could appeal to a certain body of Russian opinion that would cheer on anyone promising to fight the Tsar. But as socialists, they were bound to conflict with other branches of the movement, notably the Social Revolutionaries or SRs, who were better attuned to the Empire's two largest constituencies, the peasants and the non-Russian nationalities. As Marxists, they had to concede that a genuine working-class revolution had little chance of success wherever, as in Russia, the working class was small; and as the group most devoted to conspiratorial methods, they were reluctant to organize an open, mass following. (Despite the name of *Bol'sheviki* or 'Majoritarians', which Lenin seized on at a suitable moment, they usually formed a minority, even within the Russian SDP.) Lenin rightly suspected, like Tkachev, that a disciplined minority could seize power without popular support. Yet in trying to justify such a strategy on socialist principles he was condemned from the outset to cloak it in fantasy. 'Mendacity is the soul of bolshevism.'[43] Put another way, Leninism was cargo-cult socialism—a weird and distant imitation of the original model. 'The Marxism which prevailed in the Russian Revolution', comments a critic who came to be highly regarded in post-Communist Russia, 'bore about as much relation to the original as the "Christianity" of T'ai Ping to that of Thomas

Aquinas.'[44] It has taken the best part of a century for this fact to be generally recognized.

Anarchism, though passing its infancy in the company of socialism, soon grew up to be incompatible. At the core of anarchist thought lies the contention that all forms of domination are hateful, that government is not just unnecessary but harmful. One early strand, which could be traced to the Anabaptists and Diggers of the seventeenth century,[45] came to fruition in England in the *Enquiry Concerning Political Justice* (1793) of William Godwin (1756–1836) and in the soaring vision of *Prometheus Unbound* written by Godwin's son-in-law, Shelley:

> The loathsome mask has fallen, the man remains
> Sceptreless, free, uncircumscribed, but man
> Equal, unclassed, tribeless, and nationless,
> Exempt from awe, worship, degree, the king
> Over himself . . .
> And women, too, frank, beautiful and kind . . .
> From custom's evil taint exempt and pure;
> Speaking the wisdom once they could not think,
> Looking emotions once they feared to feel
> And changed to all which once they dared to be,
> Yet being now, made earth like heaven . . .[46]

A second strand, in France, in the work and writings of Proudhon and his disciple, Anselme Bellegarrigue, centred on the doctrine of *mutualité* (mutualism). This held that the workers should avoid involvement in parliamentary politics, and should liberate themselves by direct action on the streets and in the factories.

A third strand grew from an extreme reaction against the extreme autocracy of the Russian Empire. It was nourished by two aristocratic Russian exiles, Mikhail Bakunin (1814–76) and Prince Peter Kropotkin (1842–1921). Bakunin, who once declared that 'the passion for destruction is also a creative urge', broke up Marx's First International. 'The Communists believe that they must organize the working class in order to seize power in states', he declared. 'Revolutionary socialists [meaning anarchists] organize in order to destroy states.' He was the inspiration of the collectivist variant of anarchism that took hold in the Latin countries. Kropotkin, a distinguished author and geographer, wrote *The Conquest of Bread* (1892), *Fields, Factories and Workshops* (1899), and *Mutual Aid* (1902) in his campaign for a communist society free from all central government.

A fourth strand, initially described in *Der Einzige und sein Eigentum* (The Individual and His Property, 1845) was launched by the Berlin journalist Max Stirner (1806–56). It stressed the absolute rights of the individual to freedom from institutional control. This proved attractive to numerous avant-garde artists and writers, from Courbet and Pissarro to Oscar Wilde. But it also shows why the anarchists' own principles ruled out any chance of an effective anarchist organization.

In practical terms, anarchism bore fruit in several directions. Revolutionary anarcho-syndicalists dominated workers' movements in France, Italy, and especially in Spain, where the *Confederacíon Nacional del Trabajo* (CNT) developed into a major popular movement. Their favoured weapon was the general strike, designed to paralyse all working institutions. Peasant anarchists wielded influence in scattered locations from Andalusia to Ukraine. Anarchism also inspired the birth of modern terrorism—what the early Italian militant, Enrico Malatesta, called the 'propaganda of the deed'. The idea was that sensational acts of murder or destruction would publicize injustice, break the resolve of government policy, and shatter the nerve of the ruling élite. The list of victims included Tsar Alexander II (1881), President Sadi Carnot of France (1894), Empress Elizabeth of Austria (1896), Premier Cánovas del Castillo of Spain (1897), and King Umberto I of Italy (1900). Nowhere did these violent preludes precipitate the peace and harmony which anarchists see as their ultimate destination.

Finally, and in diametric contrast, anarchism has inspired an important tradition of moral protest against all forms of coercion. Starting with Count Leo Tolstoy, the novelist, who felt that marriage was no less coercive than tsarism, the gospel of non-violence has attracted many dedicated followers, from Mahatma Gandhi in India to the Solidarity movement in Poland and to modern environmentalism.[47] Bellegarrigue's famous battle-cry, 'L'Anarchie, c'est l'ordre', is widely dismissed as a purely negative sentiment. But it contains a very serious moral constituent that underlies much of the modern concern about the mindless juggernauts of political and technological power. It is in this sense that anarchism has been classed as 'the most attractive of political creeds'.[48] It stood at the opposite end of the political spectrum from that of the one politician, Bismarck, who was as central to European politics as the anarchists were marginal.

Otto von Bismarck (1815–98) bestrode the Germany of the late nineteenth century much as the German Empire, which he designed, bestrode the rest of Europe. He, more than anyone else, was the architect of the European order which emerged from the turmoil after 1848, the year when he entered politics, and whose revolutions he detested. He was a man of immense contradictions both of personality and of policy. The 'Iron Chancellor', of fearsome countenance in *Reichstag* or diplomatic encounter, he was in private a hysteric, an insomniac, and, as recently revealed, a morphine addict. He was a landed Junker, wedded to his estates at Schonhausen and Varzin, who presided over Europe's mightiest programme of industrialization. He was an antiquated Prussian conservative and monarchist who despised his sovereign, who adopted the nationalism of the liberal opposition, and who gave Germany both universal suffrage and social insurance. He was a victorious militarist who was infinitely suspicious of the fruits of victory. He was the hero of so-called German unification who chose to keep Greater Germany divided. The key to his success lay in a marvellous combination of strength and restraint. He built up positions of great power, only to disarm his opponents with carefully graded concessions that made them feel relieved and secure. 'You can do everything with bayonets', he once said, 'except sit on them.'

Yet Bismarck's reputation is a mixed one. No one can deny his mastery of the political art; but many question his morality and his intentions. For German patriots and conservative apologists, he was the person who gave his country, and his continent, an era of unparalleled stability: one has only to see what conflicts arose after his downfall when Wilhelm II 'dropped the pilot'. For liberal critics, however, he was and remains, in the words of Isaiah Berlin, 'a great and an evil man'. They see him as an aggressor, who used war as a conscious instrument of policy (and, what is worse, succeeded); as a cheat, who introduced democratic forms in order to preserve the undemocratic Prussian Establishment; as a bully, who bludgeoned his opponents with the blunt instruments of state power—the Catholics with the *Kulturkampf,* the Poles with the Colonization Commission, the Social Democrats with proscription. He would not have denied it. He believed, no doubt, that minor surgery and small doses of nasty medicine were well justified if major diseases were kept at bay. To quote a rare admirer of a leftist persuasion: 'The history of modern Europe can be written in terms of three Titans: Napoleon, Bismarck, and Lenin. Of these three . . . Bismarck probably did the least harm.'[49]

European Jewry has played such a prominent role in modern times that its story has been the subject of all sorts of myths and misunderstandings, both sympathetic and hostile. The main lines, however, are clear. After the break-up of Poland-Lithuania, the only large state to have provided a safe haven in preceding centuries, three closely related developments took place. First, the Jews began a new era of migration. Secondly, they received full civil rights in most European countries. And thirdly, they rebelled in ever increasing numbers against the traditional restrictions imposed on them by their own community.[50]

Jewish migration was mainly set in motion after 1773 by the Partitions of Poland. Jews from the western districts of Poland, in Posen or Danzig, found themselves to be citizens of Prussia, and free to travel without restriction to Berlin, Breslau, and other German cities. Jews from Galicia, who became Austrian citizens, began to move to other Habsburg provinces, especially to Bukovina, Hungary, Bohemia, and Moravia, and at a later stage to Vienna. Jews living in the former Grand Duchy of Lithuania or in eastern Poland found themselves citizens of the Russian Empire, where they were required by law to inhabit the Pale of Settlement. (See Appendix III, p. 1311) But the law was often observed in the breach; and new, dynamic Jewish communities began to form in the great Russian cities, particularly in St Petersburg, Moscow, Kiev, and Odessa. Jewish migrants who left their homes in the ultra-conservative religious communities of historic Poland were subject to several new trends: to the *Haskalah* or 'Jewish Enlightenment', to assimilation, and to secular Jewish politics.

The scale and tempo of Jewish migration markedly increased in the second half of the nineteenth century. To some extent, the outflow can be explained by mounting demographic pressure and by the regular processes of modernization and urbanization. The Jewish population of Europe multiplied from about two millions in 1800 to about nine millions in 1900. But persecution, and still more the fear of persecution, were also factors. Under Alexander III (r. 1881–94), the Tsarist government sought to enforce the laws of the Pale. In the ensuing stampede, the distinction between migrants and refugees was often lost. Hundreds of thousands of Jews left Russia for good, heading for Western Europe and the USA. [**POGROM**]

Jewish migration was greatly assisted by the growing circle of European states where Jews enjoyed full civic rights. Here, the lead had been taken by revolutionary France, where on 27 September 1791 the Convention granted citizenship to all Jews swearing an oath of loyalty. The initiative had been taken by the Convention's President, the Abbé Gregoire (1750–1831), who regarded the equal treatment of Jews as part of his Christian duty. During the debate, the Marquis de Clermont-Tonnerre had made the famous distinction: 'The Jews must be refused everything as a separate nation, and be granted everything as individuals.'[51] Henceforth, the legal emancipation of Jews became a standard article of European liberalism, and was gradually introduced almost everywhere except for the Russian Empire. (See Appendix III, p. 1295.)

Yet Jewish emancipation was a double-edged operation. It required a fundamental change in the conduct and the attitudes both of the host societies and of the Jews themselves. It demanded the dismantling not only of the constraints imposed on Jews from outside but also of the 'internal ghetto' in Jewish minds. Modern concern with the roots of anti-Semitism sometimes overlooks the severity of the Jews' own laws of segregation. Observant Jews could not hold to the 613 rules of dress, diet, hygiene and worship if they tried to live outside their own closed community; and intermarriage was strictly forbidden. Since Judaic law taught that Jewishness was biologically inherited in the maternal line, Jewish women were jealously protected. A girl who dared to marry out could expect to be disowned by her family, and ritually pronounced dead. Extreme determination was needed to withstand such acute social pressures. It is not surprising that Jews who rejected their religion often turned to extreme alternatives, including atheism and communism.

The Haskalah, which first appeared in Berlin, was associated with the name of Moses Mendelsohn (1729–86) the prototype of Lessing's 'Nathan der Weise'. A natural outgrowth of the Enlightenment which had been at work in the Christian world for some time, it sought to modify the exclusively religious content of Jewish education, and to give Jews access to the mainstream of European culture. Its disciples, known as *maskilim* or 'men of understanding', found some adherents in the *shtetlakh* further east, especially in Galicia, where German-language Jewish secular schools began to open. A ban on the *maskilim* pronounced in 1816 by the Rabbi of Lemberg revealed the anxiety of Orthodox Jewish leaders.

In due course the limited educational ideals of the early Haskalah were extended. Some Jewish leaders began to advocate full-scale assimilation, whereby Jews were urged to participate in all branches of public life. This trend sought to confine Jewish practices to the private circles of family and synagogue, and to turn out Jews who were otherwise indistinguishable from their co-citizens. In so doing it broke many of the traditional taboos, and necessitated the foundation of

POGROM

IN April 1881 the town of Yelizavetgrad in Ukraine was the scene of an organized pogrom. It was the opening outrage in a wave of attacks over the next three years against Jewish communities in Kiev, Odessa, Warsaw, and Nizhni Novgorod. Frightened by the assassination of Tsar Alexander II, the Russian authorities did little to deter reactionary societies and town mobs from turning the Jews into a public scapegoat. *Pogrom* was an old Russian word meaning 'round-up' or 'lynching'. It was used to denote a co-ordinated assault by one ethnic group against another, and had been applied to many sorts of victims, including Armenians and Tartars. After 1881 it gained the special connotation of assaults on Jews.[1]

A second wave of pogroms occurred in 1903–6. Official propaganda made a point of associating Jews with revolutionary troublemakers. Forty-five people died in Kishinev (1903), 300 in Odessa (1905), and 80 in Białystok. In all, over 800 casualties were sustained in incidents across the Empire.

The third wave, in 1917–21, far exceeded all previous horrors. An initial massacre at Novgorod Severski was perpetrated by the Red Army, which had invented the slogan 'Beat the bourgeoisie and the Jews'. Ukrainian nationalist and Russian 'White' forces proved themselves still more merciless. Denikin's army flaunted the slogan *Biy zhyda, spassiy Rossiyu*, 'Thrash a Jew and save Russia'. 1,700 were killed at Proskirov (1919), 1,500 at Fastov (September 1919) and 4,000 at Tetiev. Total Jewish casualties exceeded 60,000. How far they were victims of civil war, or exclusively of antisemitism, is another matter.[2]

On the night of 22–3 November 1918, just after the Polish army had recaptured Lwów (Lemberg) from the Ukrainians (see p. 921), riots were sparked in several sections of the city, where the Polish soldiery claimed to have been fired on. In the ensuing bloodbath an estimated 374 persons lost their lives, 55 of them Jews. Three Allied missions disagreed about the causes. Could antisemitism have lain at the heart of a massacre where the great majority of the victims were Christians? None the less, the *Lembergerpogrom* was widely reported, and 'Pogroms in Poland' became one of the post-war headlines. The worst atrocities had been perpetrated elsewhere. But, not for the last time, Poland bore the brunt of the adverse publicity.[3] [**ŁYCZAKÓW**]

Reformed Judaism, a new denomination which appeared in Germany in 1825. Reformed Judaism sought to reconcile the principles of Jewish religion with the demands of life in a modern society; its adherents were not required to observe the same degree of rules and restrictions. It became the norm for the majority of migrant Jews in Western Europe and the USA, but did not affect the great mass of traditional Jewish communities in Central and Eastern Europe.

In Western Europe, and in some of the larger centres of the East, the combination of legal relaxations and of growing Jewish assimilationism created unprecedented opportunities. Jewish names appeared ever more frequently on the lists of financiers, lawyers, doctors, writers, scholars, artists, and politicians of the age. It was an era, in the words of one of its beneficiaries, Sigmund Freud, when 'every industrious Jewish schoolboy carried a Cabinet Minister's portfolio in his satchel'. Important landmarks were reached in Britain, for example, when in 1841 the City of London elected Baron Lionel de Rothschild as its (disqualified) Member of Parliament, and in 1868, when Disraeli emerged as Europe's first Jewish Prime Minister.

To be exact, Benjamin Disraeli (1804–81), Earl of Beaconsfield, grandson of a Sephardi immigrant from Venice, would have counted himself in the category of ex-Jews. Having been baptized with his entire family into the Anglican communion, he had broken for ever with Judaism, which, his father said, 'cuts off the Jews from the great family of mankind'. 'Yes,' he told his friends, 'I have climbed to the top of the greasy pole.'

Yet, as Disraeli's career well illustrates, the success of assimilation posed a threat to the very existence of a Jewish community. If all Jews had followed his example, all would soon have become ex-Jews. As a result, as migration and assimilation accelerated, a serious reaction set in. The onset of Jewish nationalism (Zionism), first in cultural and later in political form, was part of the Europe-wide nationalist trend; but it was boosted by anxieties born of specifically Jewish experiences. Cultural Zionism appeared in the work of the so-called Hebrew Revival, which succeeded in transforming Hebrew from a 'dead', liturgical language into a vehicle for modern literary and political usage. Its pioneers included the Galician satirist Józef Perl (1774–1839), the philologist I. B. Levinsohn (1788–1860) of Krzemieniec, the historian Nachman Krochmal (1785–1840) of Tarnopol, and the poet Jehudeh Loeb Gordon (1830–92) of Wilno, author of *Hakitzah Ammi* (Awake, my people). It was important in founding the brand of secular Jewish culture which was to be adopted a century later in Israel; but it enjoyed only marginal influence in Europe.

The opposing Yiddish Revival occurred at a slightly later date. In 1897, 90 per cent of Jews in the Pale and in Galicia still spoke Yiddish as their mother tongue. The Hasidim used it widely in written form, but only for religious purposes. At the turn of the century, Yiddish written in Hebrew characters was promoted by leaders opposed both to Zionism and to assimilationist education in Polish, Russian, or German. For 40 or 50 years it gave life to a thriving press, a lively collection of *belles-lettres*, and a secular school system supported in particular by the Bund. Its best known practitioners were I. L. Peretz (1852–1915) of Zamość and Isaac Bashevis Singer (1904–92), both of whom began their careers as Polish writers.

Political Zionism differed from other manifestations of European nationalism mainly in the fact that its sacred national soil lay outside Europe. Otherwise, it possessed all the characteristics of the other national movements of the day—a dedicated, visionary élite; a complex ideology based on nationalist interpretations of history and culture; a wide spectrum of political opinions; a mass clientele that still needed to be convinced; a full panoply of enemies; and, at the outset, no obvious chance of practical success. It began in the 1860s with the first attempts to send Jewish colonists to Palestine. One of the colonist associations, *Hoveve Zion* (Friends of Zion), obtained financial support in 1882 from Baron Edmund de Rothschild. Their first federal conference was held at Kattowitz (Katowice) in Silesia two years later; and a united World Zionist Organization (WZO) was created at the congress at Basle in Switzerland in 1897. The movement's founding fathers consisted largely of independent-minded Polish rabbis such as Zvi Hirsch Kalischer (1795–1874) of Thorn or Samuel Mohilever (1824–98) of Białystok. But leadership of the WZO fell to lay activists, headed by the Budapest-born journalist Theodore Herzl (1860–1904) and later by figures such as David Wolfson (1856–1914), a Cologne banker, and Chaim Weizmann (1874–1952), an academic chemist working in Manchester. Zionist ideology can be traced to Krochmal's *A Guide to the Perplexed* (1851), but received its most persuasive texts in the tract *Autoemancipation* (1882) written by Dr Leo Pinsker, a physician from Odessa, and in Herzl's *Der Judenstaat* (1896).

From the start, deep divisions separated the religious wing of Zionism, the *Mizrachi* or 'spiritual centre', from the dominant secular nationalists. Bitter differences also separated the socialist wing, based on the *Poalei Zion* (Workers of Zion) party of David Gruen, alias Ben-Gurion (1886–1973), who was born at Płock on the Vistula, from the integral Jewish nationalists, who duly emerged in the Zionist Revisionist grouping of Vladimir Jabotinsky (1880–1940). The one thing which they shared was the conviction that life for Jews in Europe was becoming less and less tolerable. For the time being the future of Zionism turned on three great imponderables—the fluctuating levels of antisemitism, the radicalization of the Jewish masses in Eastern Europe, and negotiations for a suitable tract of land. No Zionist could yet feel confident of an early solution. Negotiations for the acquisition of a Zionist homeland produced few results. Herzl's audiences with the Ottoman Sultan in 1901–2 did not bear fruit; and in 1903 the British offer of a land grant in the Kenyan highlands of East Africa split the WZO from top to bottom. This last experience strengthened the conviction that the Zionist dream could not be divorced from the historic 'land of Israel' in Palestine. No progress could be made on that front until the British conquest of Jerusalem in 1916, and the Balfour Declaration which followed.

Antisemitism in the sense of 'Jew-hatred' had been endemic throughout European history. Its causes have been classified as religious, economic, social, and cultural. But it is essentially a vicious psychological syndrome, where the stereotyping of Jews precedes accusations of conspiracy and treachery. It turned the Jewish community into the archetypal scapegoat for all sorts of ills. Its embers were always alight, bursting into flame and dying down in patterns that are not easily explained. In the late nineteenth century, however, it was fanned by the migrations which brought many Europeans into contact with Jews for the first time, by adverse social conditions, especially in the burgeoning cities, and by the rising tide of nationalism, which made many people less tolerant of ethnic and cultural diversity. It came to the surface in the Russian pogroms, in the Dreyfus Affair in France, and in the sinister invention of the 'Protocols of the Elders of Zion'.[52]

On the other hand, liberal opinion held that patience and education would eliminate the prevailing frictions. Well-integrated Jewish communities, such as that represented by the Anglo-Jewish Association in London, decried what they saw as the Zionists' desire to exaggerate antisemitism for political ends. In 1911 the view was expressed by the *Encyclopaedia Britannica*, for instance, that 'With the passing away of anti-Semitism, Jewish nationalism will disappear'.[53] It could not have been more mistaken. For both antisemitism and Jewish nationalism were due to increase. To a degree, they fed off each other. What could not have been easily predicted was that antisemitism, which was widespread in those countries, such as Russia, Poland, and Ukraine, where Jews were most numerous, would assume its most virulent form in Germany and Austria, where Jews were relatively few.

Radical Jewish politics thrived particularly among the Jewish masses of the East. Zionism was only one of the competing trends. Revolutionary communism, which condemned all forms of nationalism, including Zionism, gained a large number of Jewish, or rather ex-Jewish, recruits. They formed an important segment of the phenomenon which one of their number defined as 'the non-Jewish Jew'.[54] The socialist Jewish Workers' League or *Bund*, which aimed to improve conditions for Jews within the societies where they actually lived, opposed both Zionists and communists.

There remains the fascinating puzzle of why Europe's Jews should have made such a formidable contribution to all aspects of European culture and achievement. This development of the period aroused both envy and admiration, and has generated a wide variety of speculation. Jewish prowess undoubtedly touched the raw nerves of the last-ditch defenders of Europe's Christian civilization, and of those inadequates who felt threatened by the success of 'rootless cosmopolitans' and 'aliens'. In retrospect, however, it can reasonably be connected to the psychological drives mobilized in families struggling to overcome both the rejection of the closed Jewish communities which they had left and the suspicions of the predominantly Christian society where they strove to gain acceptance. It was clearly related, too, to the Jewish passion for education, which was rooted in the study of the Torah, but which could be easily redirected to the early acquisition of foreign languages, of legal qualifications, or of scientific expertise. It must also be related to the expanding frontiers of knowledge and communications, where people with international contacts stood at an advantage over their homegrown confrères. For talented individuals, the right measure of insecurity could prove positively beneficial. [$e=mc^2$] [WIENER WELT]

Most Jews, of course, did not either shine or thrive. Statistically, the greater part of European Jewry in the early twentieth century remained exactly what it was 100 years before—a scattered mass of poor, ultra-religious, rural communities huddled in the unchanging backwaters of the former Polish provinces. In many ways their outlook had less in common with their children who had migrated to the West than with the poor, ultra-religious, rural peasants among whom they had always lived. These downtrodden *Ostjuden* were the butt of much prejudice, not only from the locals but also from their fellow-Jews who had made the grade in Germany and Austria, and who had left the old Jewish world completely behind.[55]

European Imperialism in the late nineteenth century differed from earlier forms of the phenomenon in several important ways. It was part of a world-wide scramble for control of the last remaining countries suitable for exploitation. It was evident that the world's resources were finite: states which set up a colonial empire quickly stood to gain a permanent advantage; those who delayed might be excluded from the 'First Division' forever. In the two decades starting in 1875, over one-quarter of the land surface of the globe was seized by half-a-dozen European powers. Colonies were viewed as an integral part of the advanced industrial economies. The supply of raw materials, cheap labour, and semi-finished products was planned to maximize the benefit to the 'mother country'. There was a qualitative as well as quantitative leap in the intensity of exploitation. In the eyes of some, including the Marxists, the growing competition for colonial resources was bound to lead to international conflict. Lenin's *Imperialism as the Highest Form of Capitalism* (1916) was a typical work of this genre.

Political and economic imperialism was attended by a conscious cultural mission to 'europeanize' the colonies in the image of the mother countries. In this, Christian missionaries formed an important element, though their relationship to the political authorities and to the commercial companies was rarely a direct one. Unlike their predecessors, such as the Spanish missionaries in the Americas, they often saw their task in broad terms, encompassing medicine, secular education, administrative reforms, and technological innovation.

The imperial powers sought to exploit the military potential of the colonies. The introduction of colonial regiments to Europe was as strange as the earlier arrival of European soldiers overseas.

As the map of the globe rapidly filled up, the European imperialists were obliged to focus their attention on a shrinking range of targets. The Americans had already emerged from the colonial experience. Most of Asia had been subdued at an earlier stage. By the 1880s only Africa, Indo-China, China, and the Pacific Islands remained.

Important distinctions must be made in the various types of colony established.

WIENER WELT

BETWEEN 1848 and 1914 Vienna's population multiplied five times over, to c.2 million. Vienna's Jewish population increased thirty-five times, from 5,000 to 175,000, rising from c.1 per cent (1848) to c.9 per cent (1914).

Jews came to Vienna to escape from traditional Jewish life in the East, particularly from Bohemia and Galicia, and to receive a modern, secular education. For these reasons the number of Jews in Vienna's high schools, universities, and professions, was extremely high. In the peak years of 1881–6 they formed 33 per cent of the student body. In 1914 they accounted for 26 per cent of law students and 41 per cent of medical students. They reached 43 per cent (1910) in the teaching faculty. By 1936 62 per cent of Viennese lawyers were of Jewish origin, and 47 per cent of doctors.[1]

Numbers, however, were only part of the story. Thanks to their special circumstances, as rising professionals, Vienna's Jews formed a bulwark of the bourgeoisie. They were prominent patrons and activists in educational, cultural, and artistic charities. As a predominantly immigrant minority, anxious to establish their equality, they provided the backbone of liberal politics and of the socialist movement. As people who, in different degrees, had rejected their own culture, they were specially disposed to everything modern and innovative in the cultural world. Their experiences were a preview of a later wave of Jewish migration to America. 'The Jews of Vienna were only one of the major forces in the European avant-garde around 1900. But it was its Jews who made Vienna what it was in the realm of modern culture.'[2]

A selection of names might indicate the depth and variety of Jewish talent:

Music: Mahler, Schoenberg, Korngold, composers; Guido Adler, musicologist; S. Sulzer, liturgist; Ed Hanslick, critic; J. Joachim, violinist. *Philosophy*: T. Gomperz, L. Wittgenstein, and the *Wiener Kreis*; Frank, Hahn, Neurath. *Law*: J. Glaser, J. Unger, jurists; E. Steinbach and J. Ofner, social legislators; A. Loeffler, S. Türkel, criminologists. *Medicine*: Zuckerhandl, anatomist; Schenk, embryologist; Steinoch, physiologist; Gruber, hygienist; Landsteiner, haematologist; von Basch, pathologist; Pick, pharmacologist; Benedikt, neuropathologist; Karplus, neurologist; Freud and Adler, psychotherapists; Kassowitz, paediatrician; Klein, ophthalmist; Mandl, surgery; Halban, gynaecologist; Neuburger, medical historian. *Literature*: A. Schnitzler, J. Roth, S. Zweig, R. Beer-Hofmann, M. Herzfeld, writers; M. Szeps, M. Benedikt, T. Herzl, F. Austerlitz, editors and journalists; K. Kraus, critic. *Politics*: N. Birnbaum, Jewish autonomist; T. Herzl, Zionist; Eugenie Schwartzbach, educational reformer; Josephine von Wertheimstein, liberal hostess.

The relationship of Vienna's Jews to Judaism was not simple. A strong religious group supported the city's synagogues under their forthright Chief Rabbi, Moritz Güdemann (1835–1918). There were also Sephardi and Hasidic congregations. Yet many people seen as Jews would have thought of themselves more as 'ex-Jews'. Mahler was one of a large contingent who had converted to Catholicism. Freud was one of those who rejected all religion. 'I gladly and proudly acknowledge my Jewishness,' he wrote, 'though my attitude to any religion is critically negative.'[3]

One must also remember that the Jews did not form either the sole or the largest of Vienna's immigrant groups. Vienna received more Slavs and Hungarians than Jews, many of them on the lowest rung of the social scale. Considering Austrian anti-semitism at the turn of the century, one cannot overlook the generalized xenophobia of which it was part. As shown by Vienna's best known anti-semite, Adolf Hitler, the hatred of Jews was accompanied by, and often confused with, contempt for Slavs. The paranoia about 'Jewish Bolshevism' had deep Viennese roots.

Nor should one forget the Jews' own prejudices. Westernized Jews were tempted to look down on Jews from the East: 'The Frankfurt Jew despises the Berlin Jew; the Berlin Jews despise the Viennese Jew; and the Viennese Jew the Warsaw Jews.' All tended to look down on the Jews from Galicia, 'the lowest of all'.[4]

Even the Chief Rabbi could express dubious sentiments. Responding to a Catholic lady who asked him to read her pamphlet on anti-semitism, he replied in psychoanalytic vein, saying, among other things, that 'Christianity finds itself in the unsatisfactory role of a hermaphrodite':

The Christian kneels before the image of a Jew, wrings his hands before the image of a Jewess: his Apostles, Festivals and Psalms are Jewish. Most free themselves from [this contradiction] by Anti-semitism. Obliged to revere a Jew as God, they wreak vengeance on the rest of the Jews by treating them as devils . . .

You may say, dear Madam, that the Aryan people have emancipated the Jews. This is not the case. The Aryan people have emancipated themselves from the Middle Ages. This is one of the quiet and gradual influences which the Jewish Bible has exerted on mankind.[5]

The Chief Rabbi urged: 'Judaism bids me love and respect everyone.'

The bitter-sweet climate of Vienna mixed gall with gaiety. The Emperor had to hold the balance. When an openly anti-Jewish politician, Karl Lueger, was elected Lord Mayor in 1897, Francis-Joseph refused to confirm. Relenting after two days' reflection he accepted Lueger's appointment, whilst awarding a medal to Chief Rabbi Güdemann.

Britain held the largest of empires with a minimum of military force. It continued to rely heavily on native princes and on local troops. There were fewer British bureaucrats in Delhi, ruling an Indian population of 400 millions, than Austrian bureaucrats in Prague. All the larger territories settled by British immigrants were given self-governing dominion status—Canada in 1867, Australia in 1901, New Zealand and Newfoundland in 1907, South Africa in 1910. France, in contrast, followed a policy of closer integration. The Algerian and Tunisian départements were joined to France's metropolitan administration. French migration to North Africa, especially of Alsace-Lorrainers displaced by the Franco-Prussian War, was officially encouraged. This centralizing tradition was closer to Russia's than to Britain's. It caused immense problems when the time came for the links to be severed.

Africa, 'the Dark Continent', retained many of its geographical secrets until a surprisingly late date. European colonies had been planted on the northern coast from ancient times. But the source of the Nile, which watered the land of the Pharaohs, was not properly identified until 1888. Missionary explorers such as David Livingstone could still be lost in the 1870s for years on end. Contrary to European belief, Africa was devoid neither of organized government nor of ordered religion; and a huge variety of languages and cultures belied the idea that all Africans were Stone Age savages. However, the 'scramble for Africa' took place on the assumption that the land and the peoples were there for the taking. Such was the discrepancy in military technology that even the venerable kingdoms of West Africa could offer no more resistance than the Aztecs and Incas. Abyssinia was the only native empire to maintain its independence, perhaps because it adhered to Coptic Christianity.

China, which possessed the most ancient civilization in the world, also possessed an Emperor whom the European governments recognized. Formal colonization of the African type was not permitted; so leases of territory, and of trading concessions, became the order of the day. Such indeed was the value of the Chinese Imperial Government to Europeans that in 1901 it became the object of a joint European protectorate. This humiliating episode provided the impetus which led ten years later to the creation of the National Republic of China and the beginnings of modern Chinese history. [BOXER]

China's neighbour, Japan, was totally closed to outside influence until 1855; but so learned the essence of European ways that within a short time it was able to establish a colonial empire of its own, first in Korea and then in Chinese Manchuria. Japan's comprehensive defeat of Russia in the war of 1904–5, both on land and at sea, provided one of the sensations of the age, undermining many of Europe's most cherished delusions.

The Pacific Islands remained immaculate the longest. The final steps in the imperialist story saw Germany take Western Samoa (1898) and the USA take Hawaii (1900), whilst an Anglo-French condominium was established in the New Hebrides (1906).

If European imperialism, through 'europeanization', furnished one of the most

BOXER

A BOUT 2 p.m. on the afternoon of 14 August 1900, a multinational relief force fought its way into Peking after a ten-day march from Tientsin. It raised the siege of Peking's stockaded foreign quarter, which had been cut off from the outside world for the previous eight weeks.

China in the twilight of the Dowager Empress was gripped by the Boxer Rebellion—a xenophobic movement which was bent on expelling all 'foreign devils' and all their works. The Boxers, whose English name derived from their Chinese emblem—'the fist of righteous harmony'—were enraged by everything European, from railways to Christianity. They believed that the foreign legations exercised a nefarious influence over their own government. In their attempts to expel them they had not hesitated to murder European missionaries and diplomats, to massacre Chinese Christians, and to burn down much of the old city. They were aided by the collusion of at least part of imperial officialdom, and were joined by regular Chinese troops.

In European history, the China expedition of 1900 was unique in that it briefly united all the powers in a common enterprise. British, French, Germans, Italians, Russians, Americans, and Japanese joined forces to suppress the common threat. The defence of the foreign quarter was undertaken by a body of marines of various nationalities under the British Minister, Sir Claude Macdonald. The relief column, 20,000 strong, was led by General Sir Alfred Gaselee, and consisted of Russians, Americans, Japanese, and a brigade of the Indian army. A permanent expeditionary force of 20,000 German troops under Field Marshal Count von Waldsee arrived at the end of September, only to be promptly withdrawn.

For the solidarity of the Europeans broke down as soon as the immediate emergency was saved. Germany and Italy insisted on reparation claims far in excess of their partners. Russia refused to participate in moves to prosecute Chinese responsible for the massacres. Indeed, the Russian troops who had taken control of Manchuria had perpetrated large-scale massacres of their own. Britain and Germany interpreted the concluding convention in widely differing ways. Not for the first or the last time, all the participants demonstrated that European unity, if it existed at all, was best described as a flash in the pan.[1]

powerful formative experiences of the modern world at large, it also subjected Europe itself to a wide range of stresses and influences. It divided Europe's nations into those which had been proved *imperiumgültig* or 'empire-worthy' and those which had not, adding an extra tier onto the older category of 'historic' and 'unhistoric' nations. It gave a marked boost to the economies, and hence to the military potential, of those countries which had acquired empires, tipping the strategic balance in the favour of Western Europe. It greatly increased Europe's familiarity both with non-European cultures and with exotic 'colonial' products. In some cases, such as Britain, it made people more familiar with Tibet or Bechuanaland than with their European neighbours. Yet it also strengthened Europe's religious and racial prejudices, creating barriers and complexes that lasted as long as the empires themselves. Those prejudices were sufficiently extreme, for example, that in 1904 the city of Hamburg could exhibit a bevy of Samoan women in an enclosure of the local zoo.[56]

As predicted by the pessimists, colonial conflicts began to occur at the turn of the century. In 1898 Britain and France almost came to blows after their expeditionary forces came face to face at Fashoda in Sudan. In 1899–1902 Britain's war against the two Boer Republics in South Africa was complicated by Germany's support for the Boers. In 1906 and again in 1911, French moves to gain control of Morocco fired active German protests. But on no occasion did colonial rivalry result in all-out war. It certainly added to the sum total of resentments; but it could usually be defused by the sort of 'open-door policy' for commercial interests as adopted both in China and in Morocco.

Naval power was the key to imperial success. Battleships were related to the control of world-wide commercial interests in a way that land armies could never be. (The classic study, *The Influence of Sea Power upon History, 1660–1783* (1890), was written by a US admiral, Alfred Thayer Mahan.) The issue was brought very much to the fore in 1898. In that year, during the Spanish-American War, the US Navy stripped Spain of a string of its remaining colonies from Cuba to the Philippines. At the same time the German War Minister, von Tirpitz, took the strategic decision to launch a programme of shipbuilding and to challenge Britain's fleet of super-battleships. The arms race was on.

Late Imperial Russia was a magnificent beast. Its obvious defects were offset by a seemingly inexhaustible store of power and energy. It had been identified long since, by Alexis de Tocqueville and others, as the only power capable in the future of challenging the USA. It possessed the largest consolidated state territory on the globe, the largest population in Europe, and the world's largest army. It was Europe's chief source of agricultural exports and, with untold mineral resources, the chief recipient of external investment. Culturally, Russia had recently shot forward as one of the most glamorous stars of the European firmament. The Russian language, whose earlier literary traditions were limited, had grown to sudden maturity. Pushkin, Lermontov, Tolstoy, Dostoevsky, and Chekhov could be counted among the giants of world literature. In the hands of Mussorgsky, Tchaikovsky, Rimsky-Korsakov, Russian music was unsurpassed. The *Ballet Russe* and the Stanislavsky Theatre School were leaders in their field. Socially, Russia still rested on a backward peasant society of ex-serfs. But the lot of the peasants was improving; and nowhere did the Peasant Question receive more serious attention. The agrarian reforms of P. A. Stolypin in 1906–11 gave the peasants mobility and the means to buy land. In European eyes, much of Russia's backwardness was masked by the glittering court of the Tsar and by the stream of Russian aristocrats, merchants, artists, and professors who were thoroughly integrated into every aspect of European life. Politically, Russia was thought to be making serious liberal progress after 1905; the problem of the nationalities was largely submerged. Stability was required above all; internal crises had been repeatedly provoked by the side effects of external wars. What Russia needed to realize its enormous potential was an indefinite prolongation of the European peace. [CHERNOBYL]

Late imperial Germany was the country which felt the most cheated by the imperial experience. In many ways it was the model nineteenth-century state—modern, scientific, national, prosperous, and strong. But it has been likened to a magnificent machine with one loose cog—a machine that began to judder, to overheat, and, in its terminal explosions, to wreck the whole factory. Under Wilhelm II (r. 1888–1918), whose withered arm was seen as a mark of his country's flaws, it assumed an arrogant and a truculent air. Germany's mighty industrialization had occurred later than that of Britain and France. Political unification had only come about in 1871. As a result, the German colonial empire had not assumed the proportions which Germany's pride and prowess seemed to deserve. German ideas of *Lebensraum*, or 'living space', were first voiced in connection with her modest colonial swag. Objectively, Germany's disadvantage was more imagined than real: her economic penetration of adjacent areas in Eastern Europe more than offset the lack of distant colonies. Yet her psychological resentments ran deep. The Kaiser and his court did not see that peace was the key to Germany's eventual domination of Europe's political and economic scene. [*e=mc²*]

Modernism.   Europe's political unease was matched by many of the cultural trends of the *fin de siècle*, which are often subsumed under the omnibus term of Modernism. Modernism involved a series of fundamental breaks with tradition that went far beyond the usual ebb and flow of intellectual fashion. As one critic was to write, 'The aim of five centuries of European effort is openly abandoned'.[57] It affected all the arts, and is often correlated by theorists with other fundamental developments of the period, notably with Freudian psychology, Einstein's relativity, Frazer's anthropology, even with anarchist politics. Whether or not it was a direct reflection of political and social tensions, it was certainly accompanied by a deep feeling of malaise. [ARICIA][SOUND]

The brilliant and unstable German, Friedrich Wilhelm Nietzsche (1844–1900), Professor at Basle, articulated many of the era's most shocking thoughts. He once described the philosopher as a 'stick of dynamite'; and in *Thus Spake Zarathustra*

CHERNOBYL

'CHERNOBYL, *see* CZARNOBYL. A small town on the River Pripet in Ukraine, 20 versts from the confluence of the Dnieper, and 120 from Kiev. Inhabitants 6,483—Orthodox 2,160; Old Believers 566; Catholics 84; 'Israelites' 3,683. The castle of the estate, which is the property of Count Władysław Chodkiewicz, is charmingly set on a hill overlooking three rivers. The town lives from the river-trade, from fishing, and from growing onions.' [1]

The Polish *Geographical Dictionary*, from which the above extract is taken, was published in 1880 with a misleading title designed to beat the tsarist censorship. It contains an entry on every town and village that had ever belonged to the Polish Commonwealth. Chernobyl was a typical town of those vast territories which had once been part of Poland, and which were later to become part of the Russian empire and of the Soviet Union. Its Jewish inhabitants would have called it their *shtetl*. The Polish landowners, the Jewish townsfolk, and the Ruthenian peasantry had lived there side by side for centuries.

Chernobyl first appeared in a charter of 1193, described as a hunting-lodge of the Ruthenian Prince Rostislavitch. Some time later it was taken into the Grand Duchy of Lithuania, where it became a crown village. The castle was built for defence against marauding Tartars. In 1566, three years before the Grand Duchy's Ukrainian provinces were transferred to the Kingdom of Poland, Chernobyl was granted in perpetuity to a captain of the royal cavalry, Filon Kmita, who thereafter styled himself 'Kmita Czarnobylski'. In due course it passed by marriage to the Sapiehas, and in 1703 to the Chodkiewicz family. It was annexed by the Russian empire after the second partition of Poland in 1793.

Chernobyl had a very rich religious history. The Jewish community, which formed an absolute majority, would probably have been imported by Filon Kmita as agents and arendators (leaseholding managers) during the Polish campaign of colonization. Later on, they would have included Hasidic as well as Orthodox Jews. The Ruthenian peasantry of the district would have largely turned to the Greek Catholic (Uniate) religion after 1596, only to be forcibly converted to Russian Orthodoxy by the Tsars. The Dominican church and monastery was founded in 1626 by Łukasz Sapieha, at the height of the Counter-Reformation. In those days Chernobyl was clearly a haven of toleration. There was a group of Old Catholics, who opposed the decrees of the Council of Trent, just as the seventeenth century saw the arrival of a group of *raskolniki* or Old Believers from Russia. They all escaped the worst horrors of Khmyel'nytsky's rising of 1648–54, and that of 1768–9, when one of the rebel leaders, Bondarenko, was caught and brutally executed by

Chodkiewicz's hussars. The Dominican monastery was sequestrated by the Tsarist authorities in 1832, the church of the Raskolniki in 1852.

Since 1880, Chernobyl has seen many changes of fortune. In 1915 it was occupied by the Germans, and in the ensuing civil war was fought over by Bolsheviks, Whites, and Ukrainians. In the Polish–Soviet War of 1919–20 it was taken first by the Polish Army and then by the Red Cavalry. From 1921 it was incorporated into the Ukrainian SSR, and experienced the mass killings of Stalin's collectivization campaign and Terror-Famine. The Polish population was deported during the frontier clearances of 1936. The Jewish community was killed by the Nazis during the German occupation of 1941–4. Twenty years later, it was chosen as the site of one of the first Soviet nuclear power stations. From 1991, it was joined to the Republic of Ukraine. [**HARVEST**] [**KONARMIA**]

The *Great Soviet Encyclopedia* mentions none of these facts. A six-line entry talks only of a regional city of the Ukrainian SSR, which possesses an iron foundry, a cheese plant, a ship-repair yard, an artistic workshop, and a medical school.[2]

As it happens, the name of Chernobyl/Czarnobyl is taken from one of the Slavonic words for the wormwood plant (*artemisia*), which flourishes in the surrounding marshes. In the Bible, wormwood is used as a synonym for bitterness and hence for the wrath of God:

And there fell a great star from Heaven, burning as it were a lamp, and it fell upon the third part of the rivers, and upon the fountains of waters. And the name of the star is called Wormwood. . . . And many men died of the waters because they were made bitter.[3]

For anyone who takes their New Testament literally, the explosion at Chernobyl on 26 April 1986 was surely caused by the wrath of God.

(1883–4), *From the Genealogy of Morality* (1887), *The Twilight of the Gods* (1889), and *The Will to Power* (1901) he proceeded to explode received attitudes. He railed against Christianity, and democracy, and the accepted norms of morality. 'Morality', he explained, 'is the herd-instinct in the individual.' And 'religion is a world of pure-fiction'. Modern mankind was despicable. In its place, 'I teach you the Superman'. Ruling élites have always prevailed through violence. 'The blond beast, hungry for plunder and victory, is not to be mistaken.' Most daringly, he announced 'Gott ist tot' (God is dead), adding, 'there may still be caves in which his shadow will still be shown.' God's death was supposed to be a liberating event.

Nietzsche seemed to be preaching that life had no meaning beyond the mastery of the strong. He was seen by his enemies as the prophet of wickedness, and of

$e = mc^2$

ON 28 January 1896 Germany's Interior Ministry approved an unusual application for renouncing state citizenship. The applicant, resident in Switzerland, was only 16 years old. He had failed the entrance exam to the *Eidgenossische Technische Hochschule* in Zurich, and was studying at the cantonal school in Aarau. Born at Ulm and raised in Munich, the refugee student hated the regimentation of German schooling. He disliked his Catholic primary school, and fled his Gymnasium early. He felt very insecure after his family moved to Milan. Like many young ex-Jews, he was anti-religious, pacifist, and attracted by radical socialism. His one talent was with mathematics.

Finally admitted to the ETH, Albert Einstein (1879–1955) cut the lectures but conducted electrodynamic experiments of his own in the laboratories. He was friendly with Friedrich Adler, who later assassinated the Austrian Prime Minister in Vienna. When employed at the Swiss patent office in Berne in 1901–5, he continued to puzzle over the theoretical implications of work by Maxwell, Hertz, and Mach.

It is said that Einstein's hunch about the relativity of time and space was stimulated by daily tram-rides up the Kramgasse in Berne, where he imagined that he was travelling towards the clock-tower at the speed of light. Presuming that the light waves reflecting his image were moving at the same speed, he wondered for years whether or not he could have seen himself in the driver's mirror. At all events, in the principle of 'the relativity of simultaneity', he came to realize that Nature knows no instantaneous interactions. Whilst the speed of light is absolute, *c*.186,300 miles per second, intervals of time and space are relative. In 1905, in the *Annalen der Physik*, he published an article entitled 'Does the Inertia of a Body Depend Upon Its Energy Content?'. It contained the equation which would overturn classical physics and would lay the foundations for the nuclear age. Where e = energy, m = mass, and c = the speed of light, $e = mc^2$.

In due course, in addition to this Special Theory of Relativity, Einstein produced the General Theory of Relativity (1916), replacing Newton's Laws of Gravitation. It made a major contribution to quantum physics. He moved to the Kaiser Wilhelm Institute in Berlin in 1914, receiving a Nobel Prize in 1921.

In the days before his theories were shown to be correct, Einstein worried constantly. 'If Relativity proves right,' he once said, 'the Germans will call me a German, the Swiss will call me a Swiss, and the French will call me a great scientist. If Relativity is proved wrong, the French will call me a Swiss, the Swiss will call me a German, and the Germans will call me a Jew.'[1]

In 1933, when Einstein sought refuge in Paris from the Nazis, the Collège de France refused him employment because of his German citizenship, thereby obliging him to leave for the USA. Europe's most brilliant mind was lost to Europe.

SOUND

L ATE in 1888, or early in 1889, at his London home, the ageing poet Robert Browning was invited to recite some of his poetry for the benefit of Edison's 'perfected phonograph'. He started on his most popular verse:

> I sprang to the stirrup, and Joris, and he;
> I galloped, Dirck galloped, we galloped all three.
> 'God Speed!' cried the watch, as the gatebolts undrew;
> 'Speed!' echoed the wall to us galloping through.
> Behind shut the postern, the lights sank to rest,
> And into the midnight we galloped abreast.

> Not a word to each other, we kept the great pace
> Neck by neck, stride by stride, never changing our pace;
> I turned in my saddle, and . . . and . . .[1]

After a few lines he faltered, and confessed that he had forgotten the words written more than forty years before. Recovering, he said to applause that he would never forget the day when he had talked for Mr Edison's famous machine. This impromptu and undated performance gave rise to one of the very earliest sound recordings to have survived.[2]

In that same year the German, Emile Berliner, demonstrated his Gramophone, which in place of wax cylinders used discs that could be more readily copied. Manufactured by the toy firm Kammerer und Reinhardt of Waltershausen in Thuringia, the gramophone quickly became the basis of sound recordings for the mass market—a central feature of modern life.[3]

Recorded sound has transformed the world of music and of musical appreciation. For Mozart's bicentenary in 1991, for instance, it was possible to mount an exhibition demonstrating the evolution of the quality and variety of performed sound over the last 200 years. Visitors to Vienna's Neue Burg were equipped with stereo headphones that responded to infra-red signals as they moved from one 'sound zone' to another. They could listen to Leopold Mozart's own violin playing excerpts from his famous Primer published in the year of Wolfgang's birth, or compare the sounds of valveless horns and trumpets to those of modern brass instruments. They could listen to the extraordinary slow tempo of an early operatic recording from 1900, with Wilhelm Hersch singing the aria 'O Isis und Osiris', or watch as a computerized sonograph screen analysed the harmonic range of Edita Gruberova singing 'The Queen of the Night'. One could not hear Mozart himself, alas. But the least expert of listeners could tell how tremendously the performance of Mozartian scores has evolved over time. Here was Mozart's changing 'sound world' brought to life.[4]

Sound recording has revolutionized people's perception of their past in many ways. Before 1888, the historical record lacked one of its most vital dimensions: it was silent. Documents and artefacts are deaf and dumb. There is no trace of the roar of Napoleon's battles, the tempo of Beethoven's concerts, the tone of Cavour's speeches. After 1888, history received its soundtrack and has been immeasurably enriched.

The National Sound Archive of the British Library, which possesses Browning's flustered recital, is typical of scores of similar collections that now exist in every European country. The first such 'phonothèque' opened in Paris in 1910. Members of the International Association of Sound Archives (IASA) range from the vast collections of national broadcasting corporations to tiny local or private concerns. Apart from music, the main divisions relate to folklore, literature, radio, oral history, and dialectology.[5]

In Eastern Europe, Count Tolstoy was among the pioneers recorded for posterity. In 1910, the March issue of *Talking Machine News* commented: 'An order has been issued prohibiting the sale of Tolstoy's record in the Czar's territory. When will the Slavs rise up and do away with such narrow-mindedness?'[6]

cultivated irrationality. He was to philosophy what Kierkegaard had been to theology. Both were pioneers of existentialism. 'Christianity resolved to find that the world was bad and ugly,' declared Nietzsche, 'and has made it bad and ugly.'[58]
[FOLLY]

No less influential than Nietzsche was the bowdlerized version of his philosophy peddled by his sister. Elizabeth Nietzsche-Foerster (1846–1935), who led a party of 'Aryan' settlers to the colony of Nueva Germania in Paraguay in 1886, nursed her dying brother and appropriated his ideas. She befriended both Wagner and Mussolini, idolized the Nazis, and linked the name of Nietzsche with racism and antisemitism. A tearful Führer would attend her funeral.[59]

From the sociological point of view, Nietzsche's views may be seen as an intellectual's revulsion against the rise of mass literacy, and of mass culture in general. They were espoused by an international côterie of artists and writers, which wished to strengthen the barriers between so-called 'high culture' and 'low culture', and hence to preserve the role of the self-appointed aristocracy of ideas. In this, they formed a suitable partner for modernism in the arts, one of whose chief attractions lay in the fact that it was unintelligible to the person in the street. 'Mass culture generated Nietzsche in opposition to itself,' writes a recent critic, 'as its antagonist. The immense popularity of his ideas among early twentieth-century intellectuals suggests the panic that the threat of the masses aroused.'[60]

In retrospect, it is the virulence with which Nietzsche and his admirers poured contempt on 'the masses' that appears most shocking. 'Many, too many, are born,' spake Nietzsche's Zarathustra, 'and they hang on their branches much too

---

FOLLY

NIETZSCHE once complained that historians never write about the things which make history really interesting—anger, passion, ignorance, and folly. He can only have been referring to the German School. In Poland, for example, there has been a long tradition of analysing the past in terms of vices and virtues. Bochenski's classic work, *The History of Stupidity in Poland*, was published in 1842.[1] In 1985 the dissident historian Adam Michnik wrote his account of Polish resistance to Communism in terms of *The History of Honour*.[2]

Nowadays everyone has learned that the study of 'Mentalities' is central to the historian's trade. An American historian has demonstrated that Folly has marched through European history from beginning to end. The Trojans admitted the Wooden Horse; the Renaissance popes provoked the Protestant secession; the British government drove the American colonists to rebel . . .[3] Yet everyone can learn from mistakes. The old Polish proverb says *Polak mądry po szkodzie* (a Pole is wise when the damage is done). Blake said something similar in his *Proverbs of Hell*: 'If every fool would persist in his folly he would become wise.' Real folly consists of making the same mistake twice. One could write European history in those terms as well. [**ANNALES**]

---

long.' In *The Will to Power*, Nietzsche called for 'a declaration of war by higher men on the masses . . . The great majority of men have no right to existence.' In a private letter written in 1908, D. H. Lawrence, who had just discovered Nietzsche in Croydon Public Library, actually imagined a gas chamber for the painless disposal of superfluous people:

If I had my way, I would build a lethal chamber as big as the Crystal Palace with a military band playing softly, and a cinematograph working brightly; then I'd go out in the back streets and main streets and bring them in, all the sick, the halt, the maimed; I would lead them gently, and they would smile a weary thanks; and the band would softly bubble out the Hallelujah Chorus.[61]

This gem, thirty-three years before Auschwitz, came out of Edwardian England. So, too, did the deeper thoughts of H. G. Wells (1866–1946), seer, socialist, author of *The Time Machine* (1895) and *The War of the Worlds* (1898), and one of the most popular and prolific writers of the age. In his *Anticipations* (1902), he showed himself an enthusiastic advocate of eugenics, the science of improved human breeding which demanded the elimination of the weak, the inferior, and the undesirable. 'And how will the New Republic treat the inferior races', he asked, 'the black . . . the yellow men . . . the alleged termite of the civilised world, the Jew?'[62]

The important point to remember, of course, is that 'the masses', as reviled by their detractors, did not and do not exist. 'Crowds can be seen; but the mass—the sum of all possible crowds, [is] the crowd in its metaphysical aspect . . . a metaphor . . . [which] turns other people into a conglomerate . . . [and] denies them the individuality which we ascribe to ourselves and to people we know.'[63]

In this same era, the challenge of Marxism spawned intellectual debates which far transgressed the narrow bounds of politics. For example, early readings in historical materialism provided the spur for the 'Philosophy of Spirit' developed by the Neapolitan writer Benedetto Croce (1866–1952). Croce's work in *Aesthetics* (1902), in *Logic* (1905), and in *The Theory of Historiography* (1917) was accompanied by historical studies of Naples, of modern Europe, and of contemporary Italy. Rejecting both metaphysics and religion, he stressed the role of human intuition and the importance of history as the study of evolving spirit. His journal *Critica*, founded in 1903, gave a platform for his ideas for half a century. Later in life, Croce was to become the intellectual leader of opposition to Italian fascism.

Sigmund Freud (1856–1939), an Austrian physician, was founder of the theory and practice of psychoanalysis. His work exercised a profound influence not only on the nascent medical sciences of psychology and psychiatry, but on all branches of the humanities concerned with the workings of mind and personality. Starting from hypnosis, he explored the unconscious processes whereby the human mind defends itself against external and internal pressures. In particular, he revealed the role of sexuality in the life of the unconscious and of repression in the formation of neuroses. The publication of *The Interpretation of Dreams* (1900) brought in many followers who were soon to form the International Psychoanalytical Association. Dissension ensued, however, especially when one of Freud's early associates, Carl Jung (1875–1961), launched the concept of 'collective psychoanalysis' in *The Psychology of the Unconscious* (1912), together with the distinction between introvert and extrovert personalities. In *Civilisation and its Discontents* (1930) Freud argued that the repression of desire required by life in developed societies made happiness virtually impossible. He was driven by the rise of the Nazis to flee to England in 1938. By that time psychoanalysis had many strands and many critics; but it had established a new, uneasy dimension in people's perception of themselves: 'The Ego is not the master in its own house.'[64]

Decadence, as an artistic movement, can be regarded as an outgrowth of late Romanticism. It was born of the desire to explore the most extreme experiences of human sensuality. In the process, despite endless scandals, it furnished some of the most creative masterpieces of European culture. Its links with Romantic precursors can be traced through Charles Baudelaire (1821–67), who had translated both De Quincey and Poe into French. Baudelaire's collection *Les Fleurs du Mal* (1857) was later seen as the manifesto of poetical symbolism, a style seeking to find hidden 'correspondences' of order and beauty beneath the ugly surface of reality:

> La Nature est un temple où de vivants piliers
> Laissent parfois sortir de confuses paroles;
> L'homme y passe à travers des forêts de symboles
> Qui le regardent avec des regards familiers.

(Nature is a temple where living columns | now and then release confused words; | There Man passes amongst forests of symbols | which watch him with familiar glances.)[65]

In his 'Invitation to the Voyage', he sets out for an imaginary paradise, 'where everything is order and beauty, delectation, calm and bliss'—*Là, tout n'est qu'ordre et beauté, | Luxe, calme et volupté.* Baudelaire's successors, especially Paul Verlaine (1844–96) and Arthur Rimbaud (1854–91) achieved poetical effects which were the linguistic counterparts of the images of the Impressionist painters, whom they were among the first to admire:

> Les sanglots longs
> Des violons
>   De l'automne
> Blessent mon cœur
> D'une langueur
>   Monotone.

(The long sobbings | Of the violins | Of autumn | Wound my heart | With their languorous | Monotony.)[66]

> A noir, E blanc, I rouge, U vert, O bleu: voyelles
>
> (Black A, white E, red I, Green U, blue O—vowels)[67]

The Decadents paid dearly for their defiance. Verlaine expressed the view that 'decadence implies . . . the most sophisticated thoughts of extreme civilization'. But few of his contemporaries agreed. Baudelaire was heavily fined and humiliated for the 'offence to public morals' supposedly contained in his poems. Verlaine was imprisoned, having eloped with Rimbaud and shot him during a quarrel. In 1893 a German writer in Paris decried the drugs, the homosexuality, the pornography, the hysteria, and 'the end of an established order that has satisfied logic and fettered depravity for thousands of years'. 'The prevalent feeling', wrote Max Nordau, 'is that of imminent perdition and extinction.'[68] In England, Oscar Fingall O'Flahertie Wills Wilde (1854–1900), author of several brilliant comic dramas, notably *The Importance of Being Earnest* (1895), spent two bitter years in Reading Gaol for homosexual offences. Much of the work of his collaborator, the erotic illustrator Aubrey Beardsley (1872–98), was unpublishable, as was that of Algernon Swinburne (1837–1909), poet, critic, and Old Etonian flagellant. The mood of these aesthetes was totally at odds with the preoccupations of most sections of society, where religious observance, social betterment, and temperance were at their height. [BAMBINI][TOUR]

Modern painting broke forever with the representational art which had prevailed since the Renaissance, and which photography had now rendered obsolete. The moment of departure came in 1863, when Édouard Manet (1832–83) in a fit of

BAMBINI

O N 6 January 1907 a one-room nursery school opened its doors in Rome's slum suburb of San Lorenzo. It was equipped with child-size furniture, with a cupboard full of puzzles and learning games, and with no qualified teacher. It was provided for the children of working parents who would otherwise abandon them on the streets during the daytime. It was called *La Casa dei Bambini*, 'the Children's House'.

The founder of the school, Dr Maria Montessori (1870–1952), was a woman well in advance of her time. She was a feminist who advocated equal pay for equal work, a qualified doctor, and director of an institute for retarded infants. Secretly, she was also the mother of an illegitimate boy, Mario Montessori, who was later to run the Association Montessori Internationale in Amsterdam.

The *Montessori Method*, published in 1910, preached the principles of child-centred education. Children want to learn. Children can teach themselves. Children have five senses and must explore them all. Children must have the freedom to choose what to learn and when. All they need is a place free from intimidation, proper equipment, and encouragement. These ideas were anathema to most of the educators of the day, who favoured 'chalk and talk', religious instruction, ferocious discipline, and a rigid syllabus and timetable. 'Education is not acquired by listening to words,' Dr Montessori told them, 'but by experiences in the environment.'[1]

Some of Montessori's ideas can still raise a frown. She believed that children hate sweets, and love silence. She insisted that writing should precede reading. But her central conviction, that the needs of the child are paramount, became the cornerstone of modern, progressive pedagogics. Hundreds of her schools were opened across Europe, and in the USA. In Fascist Italy and in Nazi Germany they were closed down.

In many ways, Montessori followed in the steps of two earlier pioneers—the Swiss J. H. Pestalozzi (1746–1827) and the Thuringian Friedrich Froebel (1782–1852). Froebel's first *Kindergarten* or 'Children's Garden', set up at Burgdorf near Berne in 1837, was the true ancestor of the *Casa dei Bambini*. Montessori's ideas on child psychology were in turn developed by the Swiss educationalist, Jean Piaget (1896–1980).[2]

TOUR

A T 2.15 pm on 1 July 1903, some sixty cyclists set off from a starting-line near the café of Réveil-Matin in the Parisian suburb of Montgéron. They were heading for Lyons, over 467 km of ill-made roads, on the first of six designated stages of the first *Tour de France*. They were expected to ride night and day. Nineteen days later, Maurice Garin was acclaimed the winner when he entered the Parc des Princes, having covered a total of 2,430 km at an average road speed of 26.5 km per hour. He was riding a machine with dropped handlebars, and wore knee-length stockings, plus-fours, a polo-neck sweater, and a flat cap with earflaps. His prize was 6,125 Fr.F.—the equivalent of £242. With the exception of the war years, the race has been contested every July ever since.[1]

Europe's most protracted and most popular sporting event arose from the conjunction of several modern phenomena—the concept of leisure and recreation; the organization of mass (male) sport; targeted technology—in this case cable brakes, cycle gears, and rubber tyres; and the competition of mass-circulation newspapers.

The immediate origins lay in the rivalry of two Parisian weeklies, *L'Auto* ('The Motor Car') and *Le Vélo* ('The Bicycle'). The publisher of *L'Auto*, Henri Desgrange, who was trying to break into the cycling market, had been successfully sued for changing his paper's name to *L'Auto-Vélo*. The Tour was his response. He never looked back. He saw the circulation of *L'Auto* multiply dramatically whilst *Le Vélo* dwindled into obscurity. He remained patron and sponsor of the Tour until his retirement in 1936.

The Tour took final form over a period of years. The route, in particular, varied. For five years, from 1906, it was extended to include Alsace; but permission was withdrawn by the German government when roadside crowds began singing the *Marseillaise*. In the mountains, it was directed over the Col de Tourmalet (2,122 m) in the Pyrenees, and the terrifying Col du Galibier (3,242 m) in Savoy, where contestants had to carry their machines over unmade tracks. From a maximum length over 5,000 km, it settled down in the 1930s to a more modest length *c*.3,700 km, undertaken in 30 daily stages. The idea of a bright-coloured jersey to identify the race leader was adopted in July 1913, when Desgrange dashed into a wayside store and bought the first *maillot jaune*.

After the First World War, the Tour assumed international proportions. Belgian, Italian, and Spanish riders frequently gained the laurels. Champions such as Eddie Merckx or Jacques Anquetil had a following as great as any sports stars. In July 1991, watched by 22 million spectators, the 79th Tour was won by the Basque from Spain, Miguel Indurain, with an average speed of 39.504 km/h.[2] In 1994, the 82nd Tour saw Indurain winning for an unprecedented fourth time in a row over a course which took the riders across the Channel to England. And Indurain would live to ride again.

exhibitionism exhibited *Le Déjeuner sur l'herbe* at the 'Salon des Refusés' in Paris. From then on a dazzling succession of labels had to be invented to keep track of the trends and groupings which were incessantly experimenting with genre, technique, colour, and form. The original Impressionists, Monet, Pissarro, Sisley, Renoir, Cézanne, and Degas, so named after Monet's *Impression, Sunrise* (1874), were followed by the Pointillists (1884) led by Seurat, the Neo-impressionists (1885), the Nabis (1888) of Serusier and Bonnard, the Synthetists (1888) inspired by Gauguin, and the Expressionists (1905) pioneered by Ensor, Van Gogh, and the German Brücke Group. After them came the Orphists, the Fauves (1905), headed by Matisse, Dufy, and Vlaminck, the Cubists (1908) of Braque and Picasso, the Futurists, the Black Cat and the Blue Rider Group (1912). By 1910 or 1911, in the work of Vassily Kandinsky (1866–1944), a Russian settled in Germany, painting approached the stage of pure abstractionism. [IMPRESSION]

In architecture and design, the Continent-wide wave of Art Nouveau 'seceded' from prevailing standards and practices. The earliest example was Victor Horta's Tassel House (1893) in Brussels. But its monuments could be found at every point between the Glasgow School of Art (1898) of C. R. Mackintosh, the factories of Peter Behrens in Germany, and a string of Austro-Hungarian railway stations from Carlsbad to Czernowitz. The Secessionshaus (1898) in Vienna was built by J. Olbrich in what was called the *Jugendstil* for exhibiting the works of breakaway artists. It bears the inscription: 'DER ZEIT IHRE KUNST: | DER KUNST IHRE FREIHEIT' (Art for its time; freedom for Art).

In music, Debussy and Ravel explored musical impressionism. Then, with Schoenberg, Hindemith, and Webern, the avant-garde abandoned the basic harmonies and rhythms which had reigned since the Middle Ages. [TONE]

In literature, the Decadents' defiance of social and sexual mores was overtaken by intellectual radicalism of a still more profound order. First the Frenchman Marcel Proust (1871–1922) and the Irishman James Joyce (1882–1941), then Franz Kafka (1883–1924), a German Jew from Prague, overturned accepted views concerning the reality of the world, and the means whereby human beings perceive it. They were the literary partners of Freud and Einstein. [COMBRAY]

The year 1913 saw the appearance of the first volume of Proust's *À la recherche du temps perdu* and of Kafka's first stories. The première of Stravinsky's *Sacre du Printemps* caused a riot in Paris. One publisher in Dublin tore up Joyce's manuscripts for fear of libel, whilst others took their courage in their hands with D. H. Lawrence's *Sons and Lovers* and Apollinaire's *Alcools*. The first light of day fell on Max Ernst's *Landscape (Town and Animals)* and on Kokoshka's *Self-portrait*. Most European artistic ventures, like most of European society, still clung to tried and traditional forms; but in the world of Modernism, the fashion was to tear apart the very foundations of conventional culture.

International relations had remained remarkably stable throughout the nineteenth century. Europe continued to be dominated by the five Great Powers that had organized the Congress of Vienna; and no general conflict had occurred

IMPRESSION

IN the 1860s, Claude Monet and Auguste Renoir liked to paint together. They wanted to see how each would capture a different effect from the same scene, and to compare their results. One of their favourite haunts was the suburban riverside of Bougival, beyond St Cloud, near Paris.

Monet's *La Seine à Bougival* dates from 1869 (see Plate 67). He appears at first to have chosen the mundane, not to say banal, scene of people strolling over a bridge in the evening sunlight. Yet he was trying to achieve an entirely novel effect: he was not painting the world as he thought it was or ought to be, i.e. realistically or idealistically; he was painting the impression which the world made on him. Another canvas of his, *Impression: Lever du soleil* (1874), was to lend its name to a movement which was deliberately and unashamedly subjective. Monet paid a high price for pursuing his own stubborn course. For years he sold no pictures. To his contemporaries his work seemed either worthless or outrageous. Once, when he left Paris to visit his new-born son, creditors seized the contents of his studio and sold them off for a pittance. He attempted suicide.[1]

The Impressionists were interested in three matters. First, they sought to explore the foibles of the human eye which contrives to see certain things and not to see others. For this reason, they were intent on constructing an imprecise or selective image. Monet's deliberately blurred brush strokes at Bougival produced blotchy waves, lop-sided windows, fuzzy leaves, and messy clouds.

Secondly, they were fascinated by the wonderful workings of light. Monet had served for a couple of years with the Chasseurs d'Afrique, and had seen the extreme effects of desert light in the Sahara. He would later conduct a series of systematic experiments with light by painting the same subjects over and over again. His twelve studies of the façade of Rouen Cathedral, each one bathed in the different light of a different time of day, did much to convince the public of the method in his madness.

Thirdly, they were delving into the complex variations in the sensibility and receptivity of the artist's own mind. This was the key to the epoch-making impetus which they gave to modern art.

It is sometimes considered that modern art, and Impressionism in particular, was reacting against the realistic imagery made possible by photography. [PHOTO] In fact, nothing could be more selective and transitory than the image registered by light entering a camera lens for a fraction of a second at a specific exposure and a specific angle. The Impressionists were intensely interested in photography. They often used it in their preparatory studies. Cézanne, for instance, used snapshots both for his landscapes and his self-portraits.[2] However, the camera, though selective like the human eye and very responsive to the play of light, has no mind. And it is in the realm of the human mind that modern artists really came into their own. For that reason, they ultimately reached their goal, which, in Cézanne's words, was to make themselves 'more famous than the old masters'.

between them since 1815. The wars which did break out were limited both in time and scope. There were international police actions, where one of the Powers could intervene to suppress revolutionary outbreaks that could not be controlled locally. Such were repeated French interventions in Spain and in Italy, or Russian interventions in Poland and Hungary. There were regional conflicts, notably in Italy, in Germany, and in the Balkans. There were various colonial wars overseas. But there was nothing to match the scale of the Napoleonic Wars before 1815 or the Great War which began in 1914. Europe's energies were for long directed

COMBRAY

EUROPE is full of locations redolent of time past. But there is none to equal the village of Illiers, near Chartres. For Illiers was the place which provided Marcel Proust with his boyhood vacations, and which he was to recreate in his mind as 'Combray'.

Of all the literary masters, Proust was the supreme timesmith—and hence a writer of special interest to historians. He was convinced that the past never dies, and that it can be recaptured by art from the deepest levels of subconscious memory. Hence, a banal incident such as the crumbling of cake into a cup of tea could trigger the recall of places and events thought lost for ever. More exactly, it could trigger the recall not just of similar banalities in the past but of worlds of emotion and experience with which they were inextricably connected.

For this reason, Proust spent the nineteen years from 1903 to 1922 immured in a fumigated, cork-lined room in Paris, isolated from the world in an attempt to bring the past back to life. And much which he resurrected, together with the myriad thoughts and anxieties of his youth, was to be found at Illiers—'la maison de Tante Léonie', 'la rue de l'Oiseau-Flèche', 'le Parc de Tansonville', 'le côté de chez Swann':

These are not at all the sort of places where a great man was born, or where he died, and which one visits to pay him homage. These are the places which he admired, which he asked to provide him with thought, and which still stand guard over that thought . . .[1]

Generally speaking, the spirit of the past is best preserved in small intimate museums. One can still feel the shade of Charles Dickens in his house on Doughty St, London WC1; one can visit the life of the young Karl in the Marxhaus, preserved by the SPD in face of much adversity at Trier; and one can still imagine oneself stretched out on Freud's red velvet couch in his house at Bergstrasse 19 in Vienna. But the ultimate pilgrimage in search of lost time can only be directed to that very ordinary village in the Eure-et-Loir, now suitably renamed in Proust's honour 'Illiers-Combray'.

either inwards, to the tasks of internal change, or outwards to fresh imperialist conquests across the globe. Only two intractable problems possessed the capacity to upset the international order. One of them was the accelerating rivalry between France and Germany. The other was the so-called 'Eastern Question'.

Franco-German rivalry could be traced to the division of Charlemagne's Empire; but its modern emanations were rooted in the Revolutionary Wars. Frenchmen remembered the two German powers, Prussia and Austria, as the invaders of 1793 and 1814–15. Prussians and Austrians remembered France as the occupier of 1805–13, against whom their modern existence had been won and defined. For several decades after 1815 a defeated France and a divided Germany were indisposed to brawl. Yet the old animosities seethed under the surface. By 1840 France was once again demanding the frontier of the Rhine, and raising a storm of German protest reflected in the patriotic songs of the day, 'Die Wacht am Rhein' and the 'Deutschlandlied'. In 1848 France was seen, once again, as the source of Germany's internal unrest. By the 1860s, when France was launched into the self-confident adventures of the Second Empire and Prussia was asserting itself in Germany, both powers were frightened by the other's aggressive posture. Bismarck engineered the perfect pretext through the Ems Telegram. As it proved, he engineered the event whose consequences would destroy the balance.

The Franco-German War of 1870–1, the third of Bismarck's lightning wars, caused an even bigger sensation than Sadová. It was actively sought by the French, who were itching to teach the Prussians a lesson. But they found themselves facing a coalition of all the German states, whose forces were better armed, better organized, and better led. France's military supremacy, which had lasted since Rocroi in 1643, was annulled in less than two months. The first cannon-shot was ceremoniously fired on 1 August 1870 by the Emperor Napoleon's son, to cries of 'À Berlin'. After that, one mighty German thrust surged across the frontier, and encircled the main French army at Metz. Another French army, marching to the relief of Metz with the Emperor at its head, marched straight into a finely laid trap near Sedan. In the immortal words of General Bazaine on the eve of almost certain defeat: 'Nous sommes dans le pot de chambre, et demain nous serons emmerdés'[69] (We are in the chamber pot, and tomorrow we shall be covered in it). Surrounded on all sides, and battered at arm's length by an enemy that had learned to refrain from frontal assaults, the French resisted Krupp's steel guns for some hours before capitulating. The Emperor was taken prisoner, abdicated, and eventually took refuge in England. France fought on for eight months; but with Paris besieged, starving, and crumbling from the Prussian artillery, the government of the Third Republic was forced to sue for a humiliating peace. In May 1871 it submitted, consenting to cede Alsace-Lorraine, to pay huge reparations, and to accept German occupation for two years.

Prussia's crowning victory had several long-term consequences. It facilitated the declaration of a united German Empire, whose first Emperor, William I (r. 1871–88), King of Prussia, was acclaimed by the princes of Germany assembled at Versailles. It served notice that the new Germany would be second to none in military prowess. In France, it provoked the desperate events of the Paris Commune, and it fuelled the passions of anti-German hatred that were to call ever more insistently for revenge.

The 'Eastern Question', as it came to be called, grew from two related and apparently unstoppable processes—the continuing expansion of the Russian Empire and the steady retreat of the Ottomans. It gave rise to the independence of the Balkan nations, to the Crimean War (1854–6), and to a chain of complications which eventually sparked the fatal crisis of 1914. The prospect of Ottoman collapse loomed ever more starkly throughout the century. For the Russians, this was entirely desirable. The re-establishment of Christian power on the Bosporus had formed the ultimate goal of tsarist policy ever since the myth of the Third Rome was formulated. Possession of the Straits would fulfil Russia's dream of unrestricted access to warm water. As Dostoevsky remarked in 1871, in triumphant expectation: 'Constantinople will be ours!' For the other Powers, the demise of the 'Sick Man of Europe' held a host of dangers. Britain feared for its lines of communications to India. Austria felt threatened by the emergence of a gaggle of Russian-sponsored states on her south-eastern border. Germany felt threatened by the rise of the only land power whose military capacity might some day overtake her own.

Russia's compulsive expansion continued at a rate which for the period 1683–1914 has been calculated on average, perhaps conservatively, at 55 square miles per day.[70] But it did not always threaten Europe directly. Following the gains of the Napoleonic period, the main thrusts were now directed against what Russians sometimes called the 'Middle South' in the Caucasus and Central Asia, and against China and Japan. Europe, however, was not immune from the Bear which constantly probed the limits of tolerance. Russia's involvement in the Greek War of Independence sounded the alarm bells, and her gains at the Treaty of Adrianople (1829) were restricted to a small corner on the Danube delta. Both in 1831 and 1863, Russian violation of Poland's nominal independence evoked vigorous protests from Britain and France. But it was not unwelcome to Berlin and Vienna, which had Polish territories of their own to hold down. So nothing was done. Russia's advance into the Danubian principalities in 1853 provoked an immediate military response from Austria and the onset of the Crimean War (see below). After that, St Petersburg understood that direct annexations in Europe could be costly, and that parts of her empire were vulnerable to attack from adversaries with superior naval power. The decision was taken to withdraw from North America; and in 1867 Alaska was sold off to the USA for a trifling $8 million. Real estate was more easily acquired elsewhere. In 1859, after half a century of brutality and devastation, the conquest of the mountain tribes of the Caucasus was completed, and their Chechen hero, Shamil, captured. In 1860 the Amur and Maritime provinces were acquired from China, in 1864 Turkestan from Persia, in 1875 Sakhalin and the Kuriles from Japan. All these gains would later be denounced by the losers as the fruit of 'unequal treaties'. In 1900 the Russian occupation of Manchuria provoked conflict and defeat in the Russo-Japanese

War (1904–5). In 1907 the division of Persia into British and Russian spheres of influence ended several decades of Britain's fears over Central Asia whilst raising suspicions about Russia's designs on the Persian Gulf.

The Crimean War (1853–6) took place when Britain and France decided to assist the Porte in efforts to defend the Danube principalities and to resist Russian claims of protection over the Ottomans' Christian subjects. Austria immediately occupied the principalities, and the Western powers, aided by Sardinia, sent a punitive expedition to the Crimea. Despite nasty trench warfare, cholera, and appalling losses, the Allied siege of Sebastopol finally succeeded. The Peace of Paris (1856) neutralized the Black Sea, imposed a joint European protectorate over the Ottoman Christians, and guaranteed the integrity of both the Ottoman Empire and the principalities. [**ABKHAZIA**]

None the less, the Russians were back in the Balkans within twenty years. On this occasion, the opening was provided by simultaneous revolts in three Ottoman provinces—in Bosnia, Herzegovina, and Bulgaria. Military intervention by Serbia and Montenegro, diplomatic meddling by Austria, and the murder of 136 Turkish officials in Bulgaria elicited a ferocious Ottoman response. In May 1876 over 20,000 peasants were slaughtered in the notorious Bulgarian Horrors. In London, Gladstone raged: 'Let the Turks now carry away their abuses in the only possible manner, namely by carrying off themselves.' In Constantinople, two successive sultans were overthrown. In St Petersburg, the Tsar felt duty-bound to protect the Balkan Christians. Two international conferences were convened to impose conditions on the new Sultan, Abdul Hamid II the Damned (r. 1876–1909), who baffled them all by promises of a parliamentary constitution. In April 1877 Russian armies invaded Ottoman territory on the Danube and in Armenia. Their advance was long delayed by stout Turkish resistance on the Balkan passes; but by January 1878 the Cossacks were threatening the walls of Constantinople. By the Treaty of San Stefano (1878) the Porte was obliged to accept the Tsar's stiff terms, including the creation of an independent 'Greater Bulgaria' of alarming proportions (see Appendix III, p. 1245).

The Congress of Berlin, 13 June–13 July 1878, was convened to satisfy British and Austrian demands for the revision of the San Stefano Treaty and the curtailment of Russian ambitions. It was a grand diplomatic occasion, the last when all the European Powers could meet to settle their differences on equal terms. With Bismarck in the chair as the self-styled 'honest broker', it marked united Germany's supreme status in Europe; and it drew the sting of the war fever, which filled the London music halls:

> We don't want to fight, but by jingo if we do,
> We've got the ships, we've got the men, we've got the money too.
> We've fought the Bear before, and while Britons will be true,
> The Russians shall not have Constantinople![71]

In many respects, however, the Congress exemplified the most cynical aspects of the European power game. None of the Balkan peoples was effectively represented. None was treated with consideration: Bosnia and Herzegovina were handed over to Austrian occupation; Bulgaria was split in two, and excluded from the Aegean; Serbia, Montenegro, and Romania, patronizingly confirmed in their independence, were all refused the pieces of territory which they thought most important. The Powers, in contrast, simply helped themselves: Russia, denied the Straits, took Bessarabia from her Romanian ally; Britain took Cyprus from her Ottoman client; Austria took the Sanjak of Novi Bazar; Disraeli left Berlin claiming 'Peace with Honour'. Not surprisingly, the Balkan nations were soon seeking their own, often violent solutions. The Powers abandoned the Concert, and sought security in bilateral treaties and alliances. The brakes were removed from the pursuit of national interest at all levels.

Land forces still provided the key to Continental politics. So long as this held true, it was possible to discern that Germany and Russia would be bound to play the preponderant roles in any generalized conflict. Of the five European Powers, three had serious military defects. Britain possessed a mighty navy but no conscript army. France was suffering a catastrophic fall in the birth rate that seriously threatened the supply of conscripts. The Austro-Hungarian army was technically and psychologically dependent on Germany.

The formation of two opposing diplomatic and military blocs took place over three decades. At first, Britain and France were kept apart by colonial rivalry, Britain and Russia by mutual suspicions over central Asia, Russia and France by tsarist–republican animosities. So for a time Bismarck was free to construct a system that would protect Germany from French revenge. In 1879 he forged the Dual Alliance with Austria, in 1881–7 the *Dreikaiserbund* of Germany, Austria, and Russia, from 1882 the Triple Alliance of Germany, Austria, and Italy, in 1884–7 and 1887–90 the two 'reinsurance treaties' with Russia. Yet the logic of Europe's two most intense political passions—France's loathing for Germany and Russia's longing for the Straits—was sure to assert itself. France was bound to seek escape from the web which Bismarck had so brilliantly woven; and Russia was bound to chafe at the check on her Balkan ambitions. Hence, in the years after Bismarck's dismissal, Russia's relations with Germany cooled: and the Tsar looked for new partners. In 1893, with French banks already investing heavily in Russian concerns, the Franco-Russian Alliance was signed between Paris and St Petersburg. At a stroke, France escaped from isolation, regained her confidence, and threatened Germany from both sides. In 1904, France settled her differences with Britain, and entered the *Entente Cordiale*. In 1907, after the Anglo-Russian agreement over Persia, the way was finally opened for the Triple Entente of France, Britain, and Russia.

At the time, it may have seemed that Europe's diplomatic kaleidoscope had thrown up just another temporary constellation. Both the Triple Alliance and the Triple *Entente* were essentially defensive in nature; and there were still several loose ends. Both Britain and Germany, for example, were still hoping to reach an accommodation, despite their differences. In fact, with the West and East combining against the Centre, the Powers had manœuvred themselves into a strategic configuration whose stresses were to be played out for the rest of the twentieth century. Almost without noticing, Europe had divided itself into two massive armed camps; and there was no 'honest broker' left. (See Appendix III, p. 1312)

Developments in military technology remained sluggish through much of the century, though important organizational and logistical changes took place. Railways revolutionized the existing methods of transport, mobilization, and supply. The work of the General Staffs was redesigned on the Prussian model in order to deal with the permanent flow of conscripts. But apart from their rifled percussion muskets, the armies of the Crimea were much like those of Austerlitz. The effect of rifled barrels was felt only gradually, first in the Prussian Dreyse needle gun of 1866, then in the superior French *chassepot* rifle and the Krupp breech-loading cannon of 1870. In naval design, steam-driven and armour-plated warships came into vogue. Yet the thorough exploitation of modern machines and modern chemicals had to await the advent in the 1880s of high explosives, the machine-gun, and long-range artillery. [**NOBEL**]

Despite the absence of major engagements after 1871, it is not true to say that military theorists failed to consider the impact of the new weapons. One writer, the Polish railway magnate Jan Bloch, argued in *La Guerre future* (1898) that offensive war had ceased to be a viable proposition. The reaction of most generals was to demand the supply of more troops.[72] As the numbers multiplied, and battlefield prognosis promised stalemate, the realization dawned that mobilization procedures might provide the key to victory. General mobilization was judged more threatening than mere declarations of war. Yet there were few signs of urgency. In the heyday of imperialism, Europe's armies were much more likely to be facing spear-carrying tribesmen than each other.

None the less, a growing awareness of the potential for large-scale conflict gave rise to the science of geopolitics. The tentacles of imperial power circled a globe that was now criss-crossed by world-wide communications. It was only to be expected that military and political strategists should begin to think in global terms. In his seminal lecture 'The Geographical Pivot of History' (1904), Halford Mackinder (1861–1947), Oxford's first Professor of Geography, remarked that there was no more virgin territory into which the empires could expand. So competition over existing resources was bound to intensify. The progress of that competition would be constrained both by the distribution of population and by the configuration of the continents. In a sensational map entitled 'The Natural Seats of Power', he marked out Eurasian Russia as the location of the world's supreme natural fortress. This 'heartland' was ringed by an 'inner crescent' of semi-continental powers from Britain to China, and by an oceanic 'outer crescent' linking the Americas with Africa, Australasia, and Japan. In the first instance, his aim was to warn the Western powers against a possible conjunction of Russia with Germany. At a later stage, when advocating the creation of a belt of strong new states to keep Russia and Germany apart, he coined the famous formula:

> Who rules eastern Europe, commands the Heartland;
> Who rules the Heartland, commands the World-island;
> Who rules the World-Island, commands the World.[73]

NOBEL

IT is a supreme irony that the world's most prestigious prizes for achievement in physics, chemistry, literature, medicine, and, above all, peace should have been funded from the profits of armaments. Alfred Bernhard Nobel (1833–96) was a Swede who grew up in St Petersburg, where his father had founded a torpedo works. Trained as a chemist, he returned to Sweden to work on the improvement of explosives. After first producing nitroglycerine, he then invented dynamite (1867), gelignite (1876), and ballistite (1889), the precursor of cordite gunpowder. The family firm grew immensely rich from their manufacture of explosives and from their development of the Baku oilfields. Always a man of pacifist views, Nobel founded the five prizes which bear his name by testamentary bequest. In the first nine decades of the Nobel Peace Prize, and presumably because Europe had urgent need for peacemakers, the great majority of prizewinners were Europeans:

1901 J.-H. Durant	1930 Archbishop Nathan
Frédéric Passy	Söderblom
1902 Élie Ducommun	1933 Carl von Ossetzky
Charles-Albert Gobat	1937 Sir Edgar Cecil
1903 William Randall Cremer	—
1905 Bertha von Suttner	1946 Emily Balch
1907 Ernesto Moneta	J. R. Mott
1908 K. P. Arnoldson	1949 Lord Boyd Orr
Fredrik Bajer	1951 Léon Jouhaux
1909 Auguste Beernaert	1952 Albert Schweitzer
Baron P. d'Estoumelles	1958 Fr. Dominique Pire
1911 Tobias Asser	1959 Philip Noel-Baker
A. H. Fried	1961 Dag Hammarskjöld
1913 Henri L. Fontaine	1962 Linus-Carl Pauling (U.S.A.)
—	1968 René-Samuel Cassin
1920 L.-V. Bourgeois	1971 Willy Brandt
1921 Karl Branting	1974 Sean Macbride
Christian Lange	1976 Elizabeth Williams
1922 Fridtjof Nansen	Mairead Corrigan
1925 J. Austen Chamberlain	1979 Mother Teresa
1926 Aristide Briand	1982 Alva Myrdal
Gustav Streseman	1983 Lech Wałęsa
1927 F. E. Buisson	1986 Elie Wiesel
Ludwig Quidde	1990 Mikhail Gorbachev

Of all the recipients, only two, both Germans, were made to suffer for their support of peace. Ludwig Quidde (1858–1941) had been jailed for opposing German rearmament. Carl von Ossetzky (1889–1939), leader of the German peace movement, died in a Nazi concentration camp.

Mackinder's ideas were destined to be taken very seriously in Germany, as they were, in the subsequent era of air power, in the USA.

In the first dozen years of the twentieth century, the long European peace still held. But fears began to be expressed about its fragility. Franco-German rivalry, recurrent Balkan crises, antagonistic diplomatic blocks, imperialist frictions, and the naval arms race all combined to raise the temperature of international relations. One alarm sounded in Bosnia in 1908, another at Agadir in 1911. Whilst all the Powers professed a desire for continued peace, all were preparing for war. [EULENBERG]

The Bosnian crisis indicated where Europe's most likely flash-point lay. Austria-Hungary annexed Bosnia in 1908 without a shred of legal justification, having occupied and administered the country for the previous thirty years by international mandate. But Kaiser Wilhelm declared that he would fight at Austria's side 'like a knight in shining armour'; and the Powers felt unable to intervene. Austria's *démarche* robbed Belgrade of its hopes of a Greater Serbia, and served notice on Russia about further meddling. It was also a factor in the revolt of the 'Young Turks' who in 1908–9 took over the Ottoman government, throwing themselves into a programme of nationalism and modernization. Above all, it convinced the Balkan states that their differences could only be settled among themselves and by force.

In 1912–13 three regional wars were fought in the Balkans. In May 1912 Italy attacked the Ottoman Empire, seizing Rhodes, Tripoli, and Cyrenaica. In October 1912, with the Porte diverted by a rising in Albania, the Balkan League of Montenegro, Serbia, Bulgaria, and Greece took the offensive against the Ottomans in Macedonia. In June 1913 Bulgaria attacked Serbia to start the Balkan War of Partition. On each occasion, international conferences were held and treaties were signed. Albania emerged as a sovereign state, but Macedonia did not. Austrian gambling paid off. Germany's influence in Turkey greatly increased. Russian ambitions remained unsatisfied. The Eastern Question stayed unresolved (see Appendix III, p. 1309). [MAKEDON][SHQIPERIA]

In a climate of growing unease, serious thought was given to the task of minimizing international conflict. In the absence of government leadership, a number of private initiatives gave rise to agencies such as the Institute of International Law (1873), the Inter-parliamentary Union (1887), and the Nobel Committee. After a long period of gestation which began in 1843, when the first Peace Congress had been held in London, an International Peace Bureau began to operate regularly from 1891 out of Berne in Switzerland, co-ordinating national branches and organizing meetings. Pacifist opinions were given publicity from various quarters including the Swiss jurist J. K. Bluntschli (1808–81), the German Bertha von Suttner (1843–1914), the Austrian A. H. Fried (1864–1921), the French socialist Jean Jaurès, and the English economist Norman Angell (1873–1967). Angell's *The Great Illusion* (1910) argued that the economic interest of nations had rendered war redundant. [NOBEL]

Yet the most successful appeal for action came from the Tsar of Russia.

Following his intervention, two massive peace conferences assembled at The Hague in 1899 and 1907 to discuss disarmament, the arbitration of international disputes, and the rules of land warfare. Practical results were not lacking. The International Court of Justice came into being in 1900, and the Hague Convention in 1907. A maritime conference assembled in London in 1908–9.

But pacifism enjoyed general support neither among the citizens nor the politicians of the leading states. The ethos of unrestrained state power was deeply rooted. As Field Marshal von Moltke had written in response to Bluntschli:

Perpetual peace is a dream, and not even a beautiful dream. War is part of God's order. Without war, the world would stagnate and lose itself in materialism. In it, Man's most noble virtues are displayed—courage and self-denial, devotion to duty, willingness to sacrifice oneself, and to risk life itself.[74]

Similar sentiments were voiced in France and Britain. Jaurès would be murdered on 31 July 1914 on the grounds that pacifism was treason.

At the same time, the generals were coming to recognize that the destructiveness of a future war would far exceed anything previously known, and that the Powers would embark on it at their peril. In his last address to the Reichstag in May 1890, the ageing Moltke issued a grave warning:

If this war were to break out, no one could foresee how long it would last nor how it would end . . . Gentlemen, it could be a Seven Years' War; it could be a Thirty Years' War; and woe to the man who . . . first throws the match into the powder keg.[75]

As a result, the military staffs of Europe were torn between the prevailing spirit of militarism and the growing counsels of prudence. They then followed the most dangerous of all courses. They accelerated their preparations for war, assembling huge arsenals and training vast conscript armies, whilst carefully avoiding conflict for decade after decade. The cauldron of rivalries, fears, and hatreds steadily raised an explosive head of steam.

The cauldron's lid was eventually blown off by another assassination, a month before that of Jaurès. On 28 June 1914 the heir to the throne of Austria-Hungary, Archduke Francis-Ferdinand of Austria-Este, was paying an official visit to the Bosnian capital, Sarajevo. Accompanied by his morganatic Czech wife, Sophie, Duchess of Hohenberg, he had disregarded all warnings, having deliberately timed his visit to coincide with the Serbian National Festival of *Vidovdan* (St Vitus' Day), the anniversary of the Battle of Kossovo (See Chapter VI). In Serbian eyes, it was a calculated insult. In consequence, the crowds which lined the streets of Sarajevo concealed a group of young assassins sent by one of the secret Serb societies opposing Habsburg rule, the Black Hand.

In the morning, the Archduke's car, a Gräf und Stift (1910) 28 h.p., took an unexpected route; and the visitors arrived safely for lunch at the city hall, where Sophie received a delegation of Muslim ladies. A bomb had been thrown, but the explosion caused no injuries and a man was arrested. After lunch, however, the Archduke's driver took a wrong turning. In his efforts to change direction, he

EULENBERG

O N 23 October 1907 the case of *Moltke* v. *Harden* opened in a Berlin court. It was the first of six highly publicized trials known collectively as 'the Eulenburg Affair'. It exposed a widespread homosexual network in the Kaiser's immediate entourage.

In Germany, as elsewhere, male sodomy was illegal. Paragraph 175 of the penal code punished 'unnatural vice' between men with 1–5 years' imprisonment. General Kuno von Moltke had sued the editor of the journal, *Die Zukunft* (The Future), Maximilian Harden, for publishing material which ridiculed two high-ranking courtiers named only as 'Sweetie' and 'the Harpist'. Moltke claimed that he and his friend, Philip, Prince von Eulenburg, had been libelled. Lurid details were aired in open court, especially by Eulenburg's ex-wife and by a soldier called Bollhardt. But the key evidence came from Dr Magnus Hirschfeld, a professional sexologist. Latent homosexuality, he explained, was not in itself illegal, though the practice of sodomy was. The court accepted Harden's defence that the plaintiff's homosexuality was manifest, but that no breach of Paragraph 175 had been implied.[1]

The political implications were grave. Moltke was the military commandant of Berlin. Eulenburg, sometime ambassador to Vienna, was especially close to the Kaiser and openly aspired to the Chancellorship. Both Harden and Hirschfeld held liberal views, and opposed the Kaiser's foreign policy. Both were campaigning for the repeal of Paragraph 175, and both were Jews. The imperial establishment felt itself to be under attack from treasonable elements.

In later rounds of the scandal Chancellor von Bulow sued another liberal editor, Adolf Brand; the chief of the Kaiser's military secretariat, Count von Huelsen-Haeseler, dropped dead in the Kaiser's presence dressed in a tutu in the middle of a drag act; and the Moltke/Harden case was twice retried. The Potsdam garrison was shaken by a series of courts martial for sodomy, and by a rash of associated suicides. (The tight white breeches and thigh-length boots of the cuirassiers had been singled out in court as specially provocative.) Harden's legal costs were secretly refunded by the imperial chancellery. Eulenburg was ruined. Despite a lifetime of licence, he protested his innocence. But he was condemned on charges of perjury, and only avoided arrest through a stream of feigned illnesses and legal postponements that continued to 1918.

Germany was not alone in its experience of salacious scandals with political overtones. In that same era, Britain was rocked both by the trial of Oscar Wilde and by the tragedy of Sir Roger Casement, who was executed for treason.[2] In the 1920s, however, when Germany was humiliated by national defeat, the scars of the earlier sexual scandals ran deep. The circle of homosexuality–treason–Jewry was further implanted in the popular mind by a chain of associations which started with the murder of the finance minister, Walter Rathenau, a homosexual Jew, in 1922. In his memoirs, the Kaiser himself linked the catastrophe of the Great War to a conspiracy of 'international Jewry' first revealed by Harden's accusations. Historians have linked the events of 1907–9 to the Kaiser's increasing reliance on his generals, and to their policy of pre-emptive attack.[3]

The Nazi Party, whose propaganda fed on such matters, was peculiarly hostile to homosexuals. Dr Hirschfeld's Institute of Sexology was demolished by a Nazi mob as early as May 1933. The Gestapo decimated Berlin's large homosexual community through a series of raids immediately before the Olympic Games in 1936. The lot of the 'Pink Triangles' in the concentration camps must be placed high on the list of Nazi crimes.[4] Paragraph 175 was finally abolished in 1969.

reversed the open vehicle and its passengers right up to a spot beside another conspirator, a 19-year-old consumptive student, Gavrilo Princip. Fired at point-blank range, the bullets of Princip's revolver mortally wounded the imperial couple. Francis-Ferdinand murmured 'Sopherl, Sopherl! Sterbe nicht! Bleibe am Leben für unsere Kinder!' (Sophie dear, don't die! Stay alive for our children!) But Sophie was dead. And her husband died within the hour. They would be buried at the dead of night in the chapel of their house at Arstetten on the Danube. Their car, and their blood-soaked clothing, would be preserved at the Army Museum in Vienna.[76] [**KONOPIṆTE**]

Within four weeks, the gunshots of Sarajevo brought Europe's diplomatic and military restraints crashing to the ground. Ultimata, mobilization orders, and declarations of war ricocheted round the chancelleries. Vienna wanted action against Serbia, and was given *carte blanche* by Berlin. On 23 July an ultimatum was delivered to Belgrade, demanding Austrian participation in the pursuit of the assassins. The Serbian government prevaricated, and ordered partial mobilization. On the 25th, Russia's Imperial Council decided to give support to Serbia, but failed to consult either Britain or France about it. On the 28th, Austria-Hungary officially declared war on Serbia. Thereon Russia mobilized, prompting Germany to issue ultimata first to Russia and then to France. Thanks to the war-plan of General Schlieffen, the German General Staff needed to be assured that they would not be trapped by a simultaneous attack on two fronts. The die was cast. When the two ultimata evoked no response, the Kaiser followed his generals' advice that the safety of the Reich permitted no delay. On 1 August Germany declared war on Russia, and on the 3rd on France. On the latter date, since German troops had crossed the Belgian frontier on their way into France, the British government sent an ultimatum to Berlin. The five European powers were

KONOPIŠTE

THE castle of Konopište (formerly Konopischt) lies deep in the pine-woods of central Bohemia. In the 1890s, when it served as the favourite hunting-lodge of Archduke Francis Ferdinand, it was fitted out in sumptuous leather and mahogany. It housed the Archduke's enormous collection of game trophies. It was, and still is, an elegant charnel-house, crammed with everything from elephants' tusks to reindeer antlers. It later appealed as a rest home for the Nazi SS, who chose to paint it black.

Archduke Francis-Ferdinand is remembered for four things. First, by morganatically marrying a Czech Countess, Sophie von Chotek, he was obliged to surrender his children's rights of succession. Secondly, with Sophie's approval, he was 'a determined champion of the narrow (Catholic) bigotry that, in Austria, went under the name of religion'.[1] Third, he wanted to transform the Dual Monarchy into a federation of equal nations. Fourthly, by scorning advice to steer clear of Bosnia in the summer of 1914, he helped lay the fuse which detonated the First World War.

Francis-Ferdinand's assassination was the third in a series of family killings. He had become imperial heir twenty-five years earlier through the death of his cousin Rudolf. Rudolf had been deeply disturbed by the conflicting influences of an ultra-traditionalist father, the Emperor Francis-Joseph, and of a wilful and wayward mother, the Empress Elizabeth. Passionately anti-clerical, he had once written in a notebook: 'Are we higher spirits or animals? We are animals . . .'[2] He shot himself and his lover of seventeen days, Maria Vetsera, at another Habsburg shooting-lodge, at Mayerling in Austria in 1889. The Empress Elizabeth was stabbed to death by an anarchist in Geneva in 1898.

Few sources stress Francis-Ferdinand's passion for hunting. Yet he scoured the globe for species to kill with a zeal that far exceeded the social demands of his day. He was an early adept of the machine-gun, and would have all the animals of the forest driven into his sights. Two of his trips to Poland sufficed to bring the European bison to the point of extinction. He ordered the remains of his victims to be carefully preserved. At Konopište their bodies were stuffed and mounted under glass in their thousands; their heads hung on the walls; their teeth, meticulously repaired by the imperial dentist, packed into row upon row of display cabinets.

The Archduke left Konopište with his wife on 23 June 1914, heading for Sarajevo. When he was killed, the Emperor was said to have breathed a sigh of relief. 'God permits no challenge,' he muttered to his aide-de-camp; 'a Higher Power has re-established the order which I had no longer been able to maintain.'[3] This epitaph is generally thought to refer to the Archduke's morganatic marriage. It might equally apply to the wilful slaughter of helpless creatures.

embarking on the general war which they had studiously avoided for ninety-nine years.

Monday, 3 August 1914, The Foreign Office, Whitehall, London sw1. The British Foreign Secretary was looking from his study onto a peaceful summer's evening. Sir Edward Grey was responsible for the international relations of the largest Empire in history. Austria was fighting Serbia. Two days ago, Germany had declared war on Russia and France had mobilised; German troops had occupied Luxemburg, and were poised to attack Belgium; Russian troops had entered East Prussia. But Britain was still at peace. After a long speech in the House of Commons, Sir Edward had just helped the Prime Minister, Henry Asquith, to draft an ultimatum to be sent to Berlin if Belgium were invaded. It must have been 8 or 9 p.m., for he remembered the lamplighter turning up the gaslamps in the courtyard below. He turned to a friend who was with him and who later recalled his words: 'The lamps are going out all over Europe. I doubt that we shall see them lit again in our lifetime.' The scene is one of the most famous in British history, described in numberless textbooks. The words are cited in almost all anthologies of quotations.[77]

Unfortunately, Sir Edward's memoirs did not entirely confirm the story:

My recollection of those three days, August 1, 2 and 3, is one of almost continuous cabinets and of immense strain; but of what passed in discussion very little remains in my mind . . . There was little for me to do; circumstances and events were compelling decision. . . .

A friend came to see me on one of the evenings of the last week—he thinks it was on Monday, August 3rd. We were standing at a window of my room in the Foreign Office. It was getting dusk, and the lamps were being lit in the space below . . . My friend recalls that I remarked on this with the words, 'The lamps are going out all over Europe: we shall not see them lit again in our lifetime.'[78]

What exactly transpired is rather puzzling. It is strange that a metaphor about lamps being extinguished should have been prompted by the sight of lamps being lit. Grey's most meticulous political biographer makes no mention of the scene.[79] What is more, on the very eve of war, when diplomacy was supposedly at its most intense, the man at the eye of the storm had 'little to do'. He had time to receive a friend, and to have a conversation of such little consequence that he could not remember the details.

That same evening, Berlin was facing the realization that its diplomats had just committed Germany to a war on two fronts and with no committed allies. In the Reichstag the Chancellor, Bethmann Hollweg, had blamed it all on Russia: 'Russia has thrown a firebrand into our house,' he declared. In St Petersburg, where Germany's declaration of war had been received two days previously, the Tsar and his generals had already set the steamroller in motion. In Paris the French were reeling under Bethmann's unlikely accusation that a French plane had bombed Nuremberg. In Vienna, where the Austrian Government had been pursuing its

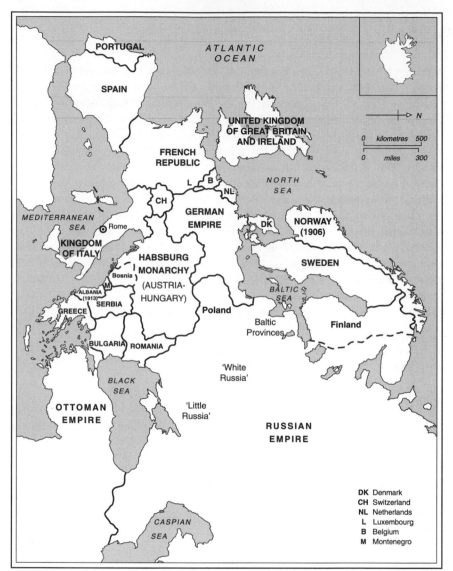

Map 23.

Europe, 1914

attack on Serbia for the past week, the Emperor-King and his ministers were in no hurry to join another war against Russia. In Rome the third partner of the Triple Alliance was lying low. Only in Belgrade could one actually hear the sound of the guns.

In the interminable debates about the causes of the Great War, the diplomatic system of the early twentieth century has often been made a prime culprit. It has been frequently asserted that the dice were weighted in favour of war through the logic of the two opposing blocs, the Alliance and the *Entente*. Vast political and economic forces had supposedly created a 'geopolitical consensus' in which both sides agreed about the necessity of supporting their allies and the dire consequences of inaction. This consensus allegedly tied the diplomats' hands, driving them inexorably along the fatal road from a minor Balkan incident to a global conflagration. This contention needs to be examined. The Central Powers were bound in advance by the Triple Alliance. Germany was indeed obliged to assist its Austrian ally, if Austria had been attacked. But Austria had not been attacked, and Vienna was not able to invoke the terms of the existing treaties. The assassination at Sarajevo could not be construed as an act of war against Austria, especially after Belgrade's conciliatory response to the Austrian ultimatum. What is more, Germany was painfully aware that her third ally, Italy, would never take up arms in defence of Austria unless absolutely forced to do so. Austria's determination to punish Serbia, therefore, and her request for German approval cannot be attributed to the requirements of the Triple Alliance.

In the case of the Triple *Entente*, the chain of obligations was still looser. The *Entente* was not an Alliance. Russia and France were indeed obliged by treaty to assist each other if attacked; but they were painfully aware that the third member of the *Entente*, Great Britain, was not formally obliged to take up arms in their defence. What is more, since none of the *Entente* Powers was formally allied to Belgrade, an Austrian attack on Serbia could not be construed as a *casus belli*. In particular, there was no Russo-Serbian treaty in force.[80] By the Treaty of 1839, Britain was committed to uphold the independence of Belgium. But that was an old obligation which long preceded the undertakings of the *Entente*. Despite appearances, therefore, the diplomatic system of 1914 left the governments considerable room for manœuvre. It did not oblige Germany to support Austria in all circumstances, or Russia to support Serbia, or Britain to support Russia and France. Almost all the key decisions were justified in terms of 'honour' or 'friendship' or 'fear' or 'expediency', not of treaties. In which case it is appropriate to look less at the diplomatic system and more at the diplomats.

Sir Edward Grey (1862–1933), later Earl Grey of Fallodon, was a quintessential English gentleman. Handsome, modest, and retiring, he was imbued with the spirit of patriotic service. G. B. Shaw mischievously called him a 'typical British Junker'. He was descended from a county family in Northumberland which came to prominence first through the exploits of a soldier forebear on the battlefield of Minden in 1759, and later through the whiggish 2nd Earl, a sponsor of the Great

Reform Bill of 1832. The family was best known from the perfumed brand of Indian tea which was named in the 2nd Earl's honour. Sir Edward himself was just old enough to remember the Franco-Prussian war. When at the age of 8 he asked his father which side Britain favoured, he was told: 'The Germans'. He was sent with his two brothers to board at Winchester, before proceeding via Balliol College, Oxford, to an impeccable career as Liberal MP for North Berwick, Under-Secretary at the Foreign Office 1892–5, and Foreign Secretary in Asquith's Liberal Government from 1906 to 1916.[81]

Grey's lifestyle was simplicity itself. He was deeply devoted to his wife, Dorothy, with whom he shared a passion for nature and to whom he corresponded, when separated, on every single day of their marriage. With her he remodelled the estate at Fallodon, creating an extensive wildfowl reserve. He was an habitual angler and bird-watcher, and an accomplished poetical scholar. When working in London, it was part of his sacred routine to catch the 6 o'clock train from Waterloo every Saturday morning, and to spend a weekend's fishing near his cottage at Itchen Abbas in Hampshire. 'He would much rather catch a 3 lb trout on the dry fly than make a highly successful speech in the House of Commons.'[82]

Grey was destined to write at length about these simple joys. He published books on fly-fishing, on the waterfowl at Fallodon, and on Wordsworth's *Prelude*:

> That serene and blessed mood
> In which . . .
> . . . we are laid asleep
> In body, and become a living soul.
> With an eye made quiet by the power
> Of harmony, and the deep power of joy,
> We see into the life of things.

As a guest lecturer in America, he once chose the subject of 'Recreation'. He recounted the story how, as Foreign Secretary, he had entertained the ex-President, Theodore Roosevelt, whom he had taken on a twenty-hour trip through the Hampshire countryside. The visitor was a keen ornithologist with a fine ear for birdsong. Grey was greatly impressed when Roosevelt unhesitatingly picked out the call of a gold-crested wren—the only member of the species that is common to England and America. 'We are listening today', he had said, 'to songs which must have been familiar to races of men of which history has no record.'[83]

Grey was not the typical imperialist or globe-trotting diplomat. Unlike his two brothers, one of whom was killed in Africa by a lion and the other by a buffalo, he saw little of the British Empire. Though he read French, he spoke no foreign languages; and, with the exception of Continental vacations, he knew no foreign countries well. He was deeply imbued with the spirit of the 'splendid isolation' of the 1890s, when he had first entered foreign relations. He saw no reason why Britain should become unduly involved in Europe's affairs. His watchwords were 'No commitments' and 'Our hands must be free'. In 1914, at 52, Grey's personal life was blighted. His wife had been killed in a carriage accident eight years before. He communed with nature alone, and with failing eyesight. He could not read papers easily: he had cataracts and deteriorating damage to the retina. But for the pressure of business, he would have gone in the summer of 1914 to consult an oculist in Germany.

Grey's views on Germany were not hostile. He was not really hostile towards anything. But he felt uneasy about German ambitions. Contrary to talk of colonial rivalry, and of Germany's desire for 'a place in the sun', he judged that the Kaiser's ambitions were directed elsewhere. 'What Germany really wanted', he wrote after the war, 'was a place in a temperate climate and a fertile land which could be peopled by her white population . . . under the German flag. We had no such place to offer.'[84] He did not approve; on the other hand, German designs on Eastern Europe did not pose a threat to the British Empire.

Most of the news in the month following Sarajevo had little to do with the European crisis. On the afternoon that the Archduke was shot, Baron de Rothschild's Sardanapale won the Grand Prix de Paris by a neck. Britain's calendar for July 1914 was filled with the usual summer announcements:

2   Death of Joseph Chamberlain.

3   At Christie's, Corot's *Le Rond des Nymphes* realized 6,600 guineas.

4   Harvard won the Grand Challenge Cup at Henley Regatta.

7   A statue to Victor Hugo unveiled at Candide Park, Guernsey.

9   The Anglican Church admitted women to parochial councils.

11   London–Paris–London Air Race won in 7 hrs 13 mins 6 sec.

12   Diventis, Switzerland: 1,300th anniversary of St Sigisbert.

16   Gravesend Parish Church: the US Ambassador unveils stained-glass windows commemorating the Indian princess Pocahontas.
      Georges Carpentier (France) defeats 'Gunboat' Smith (America) in the White Heavyweight Boxing Championship of the World.

24   Failure of the Conference on Irish Home Rule.

26   The Scottish Borderers' Regiment fires on a crowd at Howth following an Irish gun-running incident.

31   Jean Jaurès, French socialist leader, was murdered in Paris.
      On 1 August Sir Ernest Shackleton's Expedition sailed for Antarctica.[85]

The first sign of real trouble in London came on 31 July, when the Stock Exchange was closed and the bank rate raised to 8 per cent. On Sunday, 2 August, 'prayers for the nation' were offered in all churches and chapels of the United Kingdom. Ominously, on 3 August Cowes Regatta was cancelled.

Grey's performance during the crisis of 1914 attracted both praise and scorn. Winston Churchill, First Lord of the Admiralty, was an admirer:

[Grey] plunged into his immense double struggle a) to prevent war, and b) not to desert France should war come. I watched . . . his cool skill . . . with admiration. He had to make the Germans realise we were to be reckoned with, without making France or Russia feel that we were in their pocket.[86]

The *Manchester Guardian*, Britain's leading Liberal paper, strongly disagreed. Having expected Britain to stay neutral, it was horrified when war was declared. 'For years', it cried, '[Grey] has been holding back the whole truth.'[87]

David Lloyd George, Chancellor of the Exchequer, was also very critical. At the start of 1914 he had argued for a reduction in arms expenditure, believing that Anglo-German relations were 'far more friendly than for years past'. 'Grey was the most insular of our statesmen,' he later wrote. 'Northumberland was good enough for him . . .' And he pointed to what he considered the fatal flaw: 'Had he [Grey] warned Germany in time of the point at which Britain would declare war . . . the issue would have been different.'[88]

In Germany, similar criticisms were expressed in harsher language. Many believed that Grey was 'the bungler', 'the wily hypocrite', 'the chief architect of the war', who dragged Germany down. Even those Germans who appreciated Grey's goodwill judged him severely. '[Sir Edward] imagined that he was steering his ship with a sure hand, unaware that other hands were on the wheel.' He was 'a man with two sets of human values . . . a double morality'.[89]

After the war Grey did not mention collective guilt, still less the faults of the diplomats. Instead, he recounted an anecdote about Japan. 'We used to be a nation of artists,' a Japanese diplomat once told him; 'but now . . . we have learned to kill, you say that we are civilized.'[90]

Sir Edward's road to war began very late—in the last week of July. On the 25th he travelled as usual for a weekend's fishing at Itchen Abbas—'with unflappable sang-froid . . . or with culpable disregard of duty'.[91] At that stage, 'he had no thoughts of war.' His initial sympathies had lain with Austria, and to him things only seemed to slide when Austria spurned Serbia's conciliatory stance. He was convinced that the powers would 'recoil from the abyss'; that Britain was bound to support France if war came; that Britain, however, should give no pledge it could not fulfil; and, therefore, that we (the British Government) 'must address ourselves to Germany'. On the 26th, after dining with Viscount Haldane, he talked with an informal German emissary, Ballin, who reported back that Britain would stay neutral unless Belgium was completely 'swallowed'. On the 27th he proposed an international conference, but found that the proposal was not taken up.

On the 31st, when Germany and Russia were both mobilizing, Grey had still made no positive commitments to anyone, though he had rejected a German proposal for a non-aggression treaty (see below). On Saturday, 1 August, since he had cancelled his trip to Hampshire, he dined at Brooks's Club, where he was seen playing billiards. On the 2nd he attended a Sunday Cabinet meeting, an unheard-of event, where ministers came to no definite conclusion about the consequences of a German invasion of Belgium. Several ministers, including Morley, the Lord President, and John Burns, President of the Board of Trade, gave notice of resigning if Britain did not stay neutral.

Sir Edward's timetable on 3 August started with another morning Cabinet. At 2 p.m., after lunch, he went to the Foreign Office to meet the German

Ambassador, Prince Lichnowsky, who informed him that the invasion of Belgium was imminent, and asked in return for the drift of Sir Edward's speech due within the hour. Grey declined to divulge this, then he crossed the street to the Palace of Westminster and at 3 p.m. rose to speak:

Last week, I stated that we were working . . . to preserve the peace of Europe. Today . . . it is clear that the peace of Europe cannot be preserved. Russia and Germany at any rate have declared war.

Sir Edward explained that Britain still possessed the freedom to decide its policy. Britain was not a party to the Franco-Russian Alliance, and 'did not even know [its] terms'. However, in outlining the factors which would determine British action, he started by expressing sympathy for the predicament of the French. 'No country or Government has less desire to be involved in war over a dispute between Austria and Serbia than France. They are involved in it through an obligation of honour . . . under a definite alliance with Russia.' In listing Britain's interests, he made special mention of the English Channel and the Anglo-Belgian Treaty of 1839. From this he concluded that Britain's 'unconditional neutrality' would not be an acceptable stance. Thanks to the Navy, Britain did not stand to suffer much more by entering the war than by standing aside. But British prestige would be severely damaged if the 'obligations of honour and interest' were disregarded. He was confident that Britain would not flinch from its duty:

If, as seems not improbable, we are forced to take our stand on these issues, then I believe . . . that we shall be supported by the determination, the resolution, the courage and the endurance of the whole country.[92]

Though the language was vague, Sir Edward had finally told the world that Britain's continuing neutrality was conditional on Germany withdrawing the threat to Belgium and the Channel ports.

After his speech Sir Edward was approached by Winston Churchill, who said, 'What next?' 'Now we shall send them an ultimatum to stop the invasion of Belgium within 24 hours.'[93] In the Prime Minister's office in the Commons, Asquith was visited by his wife. 'So it's all up?' she said. 'Yes, it's all up.' 'Henry sat at his writing table, leaning back, pen in hand . . . I got up and leant my head against his. We could not speak for tears.'[94]

In 1914 Britain's defences depended almost entirely on the Fleet. Neither the First Lord of the Admiralty nor the First Sea Lord, Prince Louis Battenberg, had favoured war. But Prince Louis had stopped the Fleet's dispersal after the summer's manœuvres, and on 2 August he had recommended full naval mobilization.[95] Churchill concurred. In the early hours of the 3rd, at his Admiralty desk, Churchill received a letter from his wife, who wrote that 'it would be a wicked war'. He replied:

Cat-dear, It is all up. Germany has quenched the last hopes of peace by declaring war on Russia, and the declaration against France is momentarily expected.

I profoundly understand your view. But the world has gone mad, and we must look after ourselves and our friends ... Sweet-Cat, my tender love, Your devoted W. Kiss the kittens.[96]

After talking to Grey, Churchill sent a note to the Prime Minister: 'Unless forbidden to do so, I shall put Anglo-French naval disposition into force to defend the Channel.'[97]

Tuesday 4 August was a day of waiting in London. News arrived in the morning that German troops had crossed the Belgian frontier in force. Britain's ultimatum to Berlin was dispatched at 2 p.m., demanding a reply within the day. Asquith wrote to his intimate confidante, Venetia Stanley: 'Winston, who has put on all his warpaint, is spoiling for a sea fight ...'[98] Two German ships, the *Goeben* and the *Breslau*, were steaming through the Mediterranean bound for Turkey. The British were confident of catching them.

The ultimatum expired, unanswered, at 11 p.m.—midnight in Berlin. Fifteen minutes later the Cabinet convened at 10 Downing Street. The scene was later described by David Lloyd George in a private letter to Mrs Asquith:

Winston dashed into the room radiant, his face bright, his manner keen, one word pouring out on another how he was going to send telegrams to the Med., to the North Sea, and God knows where. You could see he was a really happy man.[99]

At which point the Admiralty sent the signal to all ships of the Fleet: 'Commence hostilities at once with Germany.' Contrary to the inclination of its leading politicians, Britain had abandoned peaceful neutrality. The decision transformed a Continental war into a world-wide conflict.

Britain's declaration of war put the final seal on the biggest diplomatic disaster of modern times. It completed the most dire of the scenarios which the diplomats had been contemplating over the previous month. It was the fourth such declaration in line—the first by Austria, the second and third by Germany. Britain was the only *Entente* Power to take the initiative in going to war.

Four weeks earlier, when Vienna had demanded satisfaction from Belgrade over the assassination at Sarajevo, analysts could have foreseen that the European crisis could be resolved in one of four different ways. It might conceivably have been settled without war, as had happened in 1908 after the Bosnian affair. On the other hand, it might have produced a local war limited to Austria and Serbia. Thirdly, if the Great Powers did not show restraint, it might have sparked the Continental war for which both the current diplomatic alliances and the plans of the General Staffs had been designed. In this case Germany and Austria would have been pitted against Russia and France, and Britain would have remained neutral. Lastly, God forbid, it was just possible that Britain would become directly involved and that the controlled Continental war would be expanded into a totally uncontrolled global conflict. For this reason the diplomatic relations between London and Berlin were of greater import than those between Europe's other capitals. Vienna was the key to a local war, Berlin to the Continental war, London to global conflict.

Any competent student could have listed the reasons why Britain's involvement raised very special complications. From the strategic point of view, Britain's assets were spread right round the globe, and their fate would not just affect the interests of the European states. From the political point of view, the British Empire in 1914 was still judged the world's greatest power, and war against Britain would be seen as a bid for world supremacy. From the economic point of view, Britain was still the capital of world finance. Though her technical and industrial strength was no longer the equivalent of Germany's, she could mobilize colossal resources. From the diplomatic point of view, the lofty 'lords of Albion' had never known defeat. They were noted for their ineffable self-confidence, for their obstinate sense of righteousness, and for their perfidy.

Most importantly, from the purely military point of view, Britain represented a wild card, a spoiler, a participant whose impact was completely unpredictable. Thanks to naval supremacy, the British Isles could not be eliminated even by the most decisive of Continental campaigns. At the same time, Britain only possessed what the Kaiser was to call 'a contemptibly small army',* which could not play a major role on the Continent until gradually expanded by conscription. The British Government enjoyed the exceptional luxury of a position where sudden defeat did not come into the reckoning, and where a protracted war would see British military capacity steadily rising over a period of two or three years.

These facts had clear consequences. If the Continental campaigns went well for France and Russia in the early stages, Britain's participation might well tip the balance in favour of a decisive victory. If things went well for the Central Powers, however, Berlin and Vienna could not count on any such favourable outcome. Even if the French and Russian armies were defeated in the first shock, the Central Powers, like Napoleonic France, would still be left facing a defiant and impregnable Britain, which would use all its wiles to mount new coalitions against them. If the initial fighting were inconclusive, Britain would be better placed than anyone to build up its relative strength in later phases. Unlike Germany, Britain had no chance of winning a Continental campaign; but she could not be easily defeated. In short, whatever happened, Britain had the capacity for ruining the prospects for the quick 'limited war' of which all German generals dreamed.

There was much talk at the time of militarism. Colonel House, the American, who visited Berlin in 1914, was shocked by the bombastic displays. Yet all the Powers cultivated a degree of military pomp and swagger; the differences were at best those of style. In all countries in 1914, unlike 1939, the military ethos was closely bound by a code of honour. A German observer remarked bitterly, 'Militarism in the United Kingdom is regarded [by the British] as of God, and militarism in Germany as of the devil.'[100] Military technicalities were in play as well. One concerned the control of the English Channel. The British and French naval staffs had agreed in advance that the French fleet should be concentrated in

---

* The Kaiser's comment was wrongly translated and widely publicized in Britain as 'a small, contemptible army'—hence the chosen nickname of the British Expeditionary Force, 'The Old Contemptibles'.

the Mediterranean, whilst the Channel should be patrolled by the Royal Navy. This meant that British neutrality during a Franco-German campaign in Belgium would automatically give German warships a free run of the French and British coasts. Another important detail concerned mobilization procedures. German provisions envisaged a preparatory stage called 'a state of imminent war', to be followed by a second stage in which full mobilization could be completed almost immediately. In effect, a German declaration of *Kriegsbereitschaft* was equivalent to other countries' declarations of general mobilization.

These were the matters to which Germany's diplomats, led by their Chancellor, Bethmann Hollweg, were required to turn their minds before forcing a showdown.

Theobald von Bethmann Hollweg (1856–1920) was an archetypal Prussian civil servant. Learned, polite, and earnest, he had spent his entire life in the upper echelons of the state bureaucracy. He was descended from a banking family from Frankfurt, which had moved to Berlin and been ennobled two generations back. They came to prominence through Theobald's grandfather, Moritz August, a law professor who had distinguished himself in the liberal opposition to Bismarck's regime. Theobald himself was just too young to have served in the Franco-Prussian War, which his grandfather had abhorred. He was sent with his brother, Max, to board at the Fürstenschule Pforta, before proceeding via legal studies at Strasburg and Leipzig to success in the formidable civil service examinations. As a *primus omnium* at school, and with a Ph.D. in jurisprudence in his late twenties, he was perfectly prepared for a lightning ascent of the bureaucratic career ladder—*Oberpräsidialrat* at Potsdam, *Regierungspräsident* at Bromberg (Bydgoszcz), *Oberpräsident* or 'Provincial Governor' of Mark Brandenburg, Minister of the Interior in 1905, Vice-Chancellor in 1907, Imperial Chancellor and Prime Minister of Prussia from 1909. From then until July 1917 he was responsible for all civilian policies, domestic and foreign, of Europe's most powerful state.[101]

Bethmann Hollweg was not the typical Junker. He inherited a fine landed estate at Hohenfinow east of Berlin, but the *Rittergut* was bought by his grandfather, not rooted in family tradition. He had served in the local regiment, the 15th Uhlans, but only for one year after leaving school. He came to be deeply attached to Hohenfinow—a three-storey red-brick pile set at the end of a long linden avenue amid 7,500 acres on a bluff overlooking the Oder. He adopted the motto *Ego et domus mea serviemus domino* (My house and I shall serve the Lord). But as a young man he had lived through years of restless, romantic wanderlust, reading poetry and rambling round the Eifel and the Siebengebirge with bohemian friends. He was embarrassed by his brother, who fled to sell real estate in Texas rather than face the state exams. He once stood for election to the Reichstag in the local constituency; but the narrow vote in his favour was overruled by the electoral commission on a technicality; and he never ventured into popular politics again. He married a somewhat unconventional girl, Martha Pfuel-Wilkendorf, who remarked, when he was offered the highest office in the Reich, 'Theo, dear, you can't do that!'[102]

Bethmann's personality was anything but simple. He was a creature of routine, taking a hard morning's horse ride at 7 a.m. even in Berlin. But his orderly habits did not make for efficiency or decisiveness. He was extremely articulate and well informed; but he had a fatal tendency for procrastination, and repeatedly committed gaffes which a smarter politician would have avoided. He was particularly ill at ease in the military establishment which surrounded the Kaiser; yet he was also terrified of the Social Democrats, who held great sway in the subservient democratic sector of German politics. Much of the inside information about his chancellorship derives from the diary of his personal assistant, Kurt Riezler, who worked alongside him admiringly throughout the crisis of 1914. Riezler noted: 'His cunning is as great as his bungling.'[103] His biographer talks of his 'aggressively defensive self-consciousness'.[104]

Bethmann owed his position partly to his seniority in the civil service and partly to the belief that he could hold the middle ground between the conservatives and the radicals. By German standards he was a very moderate conservative: in foreign policy he had frequently gone on record to state his commitment to peace, and to warn against the dangers of militarism. For this he was the *bête noire* of the Pan-German League, who often called for his dismissal.

His guiding principle was supposedly *Weltmacht und kein Krieg,* 'World power but no war'. In the previous November he had reprimanded the Crown Prince for his lack of restraint: 'To rattle the sabre at every diplomatic entanglement . . . is not only blind but criminal.'[105] Pondering the prospects shortly after Sarajevo, he had confided to Riezler, 'Any general conflict [will lead] to a revolution of all existing conditions.'[106] Two weeks later, he had personally protested to the Kaiser about the bombastic statements of the Crown Prince and certain sections of the Press.

In July 1914, at the age of 58, Bethmann's personal life had been blighted by the death of his wife only two months earlier. He travelled back and forth between Hohenfinow and Berlin alone, or with Riezler. Bethmann's feelings towards England were very friendly. His son Ernst, who was to be killed in the war, had been a Rhodes scholar at Oxford in 1908. Everything he said or wrote before the crisis underlined his wish and expectation for Anglo-German *rapprochement.*

Bethmann's performance attracted little admiration, except from his immediate associates. Riezler admired his fortitude under pressure, and compared his 'scruples' to the 'icy hypocrisy' of Grey. 'The Chancellor is a child of the first half of the nineteenth century,' he noted, 'and the heir to a more idealistic culture.'[107] Yet the Kaiser was brutal: when things began to go wrong in mid-July and Bethmann offered to resign, the Kaiser apparently said, 'It's you that have cooked this soup, and now you're going to eat it.'[108] Albert Ballin, President of the Hamburg–Amerika Line and the informal go-between with London, was no more sympathetic. A friend of Bethmann's predecessor as Chancellor, he called Bethmann 'Bülow's revenge', and talked of his 'torpor', his 'passivity', his 'lack of initiative', his 'enormous ineptitude'. 'Bethmann', he said, 'was an uncommonly articulate man . . . who did not realise that politics is a dirty business.'[109] Von

Bülow, the former Chancellor, pointed to what he considered the fatal flaw: 'It would have been quite enough to have told Vienna [after Sarajevo] that we definitely refused our authorisation of any breach between Serbia and Austria-Hungary.'[110]

In England, the criticisms of Bethmann were merciless. Popular sources recounted not only his 'half-heartedness' and 'indecision' but also his 'essentially Prussian conceptions of political morality'. It was generally believed that Bethmann conducted German foreign policy unaware that the wheel of state was really in the hands of the military.[111] After the war, Bethmann was to make a strong point of collective guilt. 'All nations are guilty,' he insisted in his *Memoirs*. 'Germany, too, bears a large part of the blame.'[112]

Bethmann's road to war began in the first week of July. Owing to the Foreign Minister's absence on honeymoon, Bethmann took personal charge of German diplomacy from the start. He constantly protested his determination to avoid an international conflict. On the morning of 5 July he was summoned by the Kaiser to advise on Austria's request for assistance in its quarrel with Serbia. Two contradictory decisions were taken—one to refrain from a direct response, and the other to assure Francis-Joseph that Germany would not desert him. In the afternoon he attended a meeting of the Kaiser's military advisers, where the opinion prevailed that Russia would not intervene and that Serbia should be punished, 'the sooner the better'. This encouraged Bethmann to tell the Austro-Hungarian Ambassador:

Vienna has to judge what has to be done to clarify Austria's relations with Serbia. [None the less], in this undertaking it can count safely on Germany's support of the Monarchy as an ally and a friend—whatever the decision.[113]

Here was the notorious 'blank cheque' for Austria's war against Serbia.

Back at Hohenfinow on the evening of the 8th, Bethmann talked to Riezler 'on the verandah under a starry sky'. He explained the dangers of a general conflict. He then said that inaction was the worst policy of all. He was obsessed by fears of Russia: 'The future belongs to Russia, which grows and grows, looming above us as an increasingly terrifying nightmare.'[114] At bottom, therefore, the Chancellor agreed with those more outspoken generals who said that Germany's position could only suffer from delay. Six days later, on the 14th, though nothing special had happened, Riezler reports the Chancellor as saying, 'Our position is desperate . . . This action is a leap in the dark and as such a most serious duty.' It would seem that Bethmann had already resigned himself to 'the calculated risk' of a Continental war.[115]

In the third week of July Bethmann began to suspect that his gamble was ill-conceived. None of the requisite pieces of the puzzle was falling into place. He advised the Kaiser to prolong his Baltic cruise in order to maintain a show of normalcy. When his advice was refused he tendered his resignation, and his resignation was refused as well. According to Riezler, the Chancellor was in fatalist mood, and was sensing that public opinion favoured war—'an immense if undirected drive for action in the people'.[116] With this in mind he took two practical steps. He stopped the Minister of Interior from arresting the assorted socialists, Poles, and others on its list of *Reichsfeinde* or 'unreliable elements'; and in a secret meeting with the Social Democrat leader he informed the Opposition of the gravity of the situation. Both these steps had the effect of disarming popular opposition to the war.

On the 29th, when Russia responded to Austria's attack on Belgrade with partial mobilization, Bethmann at last paid serious attention to the possibility of a general conflict. He proposed a neutrality agreement to Great Britain, guaranteeing the integrity of France's metropolitan territory. In the night, contrary to his previous line, he bombarded Vienna with 'World on Fire' telegrams advising mediation. Neither produced any effect. As a result, Germany was facing war with Russia without having secured Austrian support. Berlin was committed to help Vienna, but Vienna might not help Berlin. The Alliance was in total disarray.

The moment of decision was reached on 30 July. The Kaiser took fright from the telegrams coming out of St Petersburg. In the margin of one of them he scrawled a note about 'the war of extermination against us'.[117] Berlin was convinced of its 'encirclement'. At 9 p.m. Bethmann met with the military leaders, von Moltke and von Falkenhayn. They took the decision to declare 'a state of imminent war', thus automatically starting the countdown to the outbreak of a general Continental war in the first days of August. And they did so without any knowledge of Russia's full mobilization or of Belgian and British intentions. From that point on, barring retractions, the die was cast.

In the two key decisions of 5 July and 30 July, there is little evidence to suggest that the generals forced through a warlike line contrary to Bethmann's advice. It is true that in the last resort the Kaiser possessed the traditional Prussian *Kommandogewalt* or 'power of command' over both generals and ministers. But the Chancellor never put himself in a position where it might have been used against him. He did not stumble into war; he was party to the decisions which provoked it.[118] The one thing to say in mitigation, and often ignored by Allied historians, is that Russia had mobilized with the same rashness as Germany.

Henceforth, for the Chancellor, the main consideration was to pin the blame on the *Entente*. At 11 p.m. on the 30th he learned that Russia's general mobilization was in train, and used the information to justify his prior decision taken in the dark. On the 1st Bethmann declared war on Russia, whilst demanding impossible assurances from Paris that France should abandon the Franco-Russian alliance. Ballin was privy to the scene in the garden-room of the Kanzlerspalais, where Bethmann was frantically driving the clerks to complete the drafting of the declaration. 'Why such haste to declare war on Russia, Your Excellency?' he asked. 'If we don't, we shan't get the socialists to fight.'[119] On the 2nd the German Ambassador in Brussels was ordered to take a letter from a sealed envelope, prepared seven days before by von Moltke. The letter demanded that Belgium accept German protection against a (non-existent) French attack. On the 3rd, Germany declared war on France.

On the afternoon of 3 August, at the same time that Grey was addressing the Commons, Bethmann addressed the Reichstag with his speech about the Russian 'firebrand'. 'A war with Russia and France has been forced upon us,' he declared. Echoing Grey's words about determination and resolution, Bethmann said: 'The entire German nation . . . is united to the last man.'[120]

On the 4th, German troops invaded Belgium. In mid-afternoon Bethmann heard from the Wilhelmstrasse that the British ultimatum had arrived. In his Speech from the Throne, the Kaiser spoke calmly of 'drawing the sword with a clear conscience and clean hands'.[121] But Bethmann was livid. When the British Ambassador called to take his leave, the walls of the Kanzlerspalais reverberated to the strains of an unprecedented tirade of recriminations. Shouting in French, the Chancellor harangued the Ambassador for a good twenty minutes:

This war is only turning into an unlimited world catastrophe through England's participation. It was in London's hands to curb French revanchism and pan-Slav chauvinism. Whitehall has not done so, but rather repeatedly egged them on . . . All my attempts [for peace] have been wrested from me. And by whom? By England. And why? For Belgian neutrality. Can this neutrality, which we violate from necessity, fighting for our very existence, really provide the reason for a world war? . . . Compared to the disaster of such a holocaust, does not this neutrality dwindle into a scrap of paper? Germany, the Emperor and the Government are peaceloving. The Ambassador knows that as well as I do. We enter the war with a clear conscience. But England's responsibility is monumental.[122]

The Ambassador broke into tears. Diplomacy had come to an end.

Oddly enough, Bethmann's phrase about the 'scrap of paper'—*un chiffon de papier*—does not appear in the Ambassador's original summary of the tirade. Like Grey's words about 'the lamps going out', there must be some doubt whether it was uttered at that fateful meeting.[123]

The emotions of those summer days found their best expression in places often far removed from the haunts of diplomats.

In Paris, on 3 August Marcel Proust drove to the Gare de l'Est with his brother, a medical officer *en route* for Verdun, then returned to the Boulevard Haussmann after midnight to write to his agent. 'Millions of men are going to be massacred in a War of the Worlds, like that of Wells.'[124]

In England, Virginia Woolf was spending the Bank Holiday at Rodmell, near Lewes in Sussex. At 4 p.m. on the 3rd she wrote to Vanessa Bell. 'Dearest, Would it be possible for you to let us have half the rent—£15—before we go away? . . . The postman brought rumours that two of our warships are sunk—however, we found . . . that peace still exists . . . I do adore Thee.'[125]

The young poet Rupert Brooke, who had dined the previous week at 10 Downing Street with the Asquiths and Churchill, dashed off a letter to Gwen Darwin, now Mrs Raverat:

Everything's just the wrong way round. I want Germany to smash Russia to fragments, and then France to break Germany. Instead of which I'm afraid Germany will badly smash

France, and then be wiped out by Russia. France and England are the only countries that ought to have any power. Prussia is a devil. And Russia means the end of Europe and any decency. I suppose the future is a Slav Empire, world-wide, despotic and insane.[126]

D. H. Lawrence was on holiday with three friends in the Lake District:

I had been walking in Westmoreland, rather happy, with water-lilies twisted round my hat . . . and I pranked in the rain, [whilst] Kotilianski groaned Hebrew music—*Ranani Sadekim Badanoi* . . . Then we came down to Barrow-in-Furness, and saw that war was declared. And we all went mad. I can remember soldiers kissing on Barrow station, and a woman shouting defiantly to her sweetheart: 'When you get at 'em, Clem, let 'em have it' . . . — and in all the tram-cars 'War—Messrs Vickers Maxim call in their workmen' . . .

Then I went down the coast for a few miles. And I think of the amazing sunsets over flat sands and a smoky sea . . . and the amazing vivid, visionary beauty of everything heightened up by immense pain . . .[127]

In Germany and Austria the excitement ran equally high. Thomas Mann was at Bad Tölz in Bavaria, wondering when the *Landsturm* would call. Declining to act as witness at his brother Heinrich's wedding, he recorded his current feelings:

Shouldn't we be grateful for the totally unexpected chance to experience such mighty events? My chief feeling is a tremendous curiosity—and, I admit it, the deepest sympathy for this execrated, indecipherable, fateful Germany, which, if she has not hitherto unqualifiedly held 'civilisation' as the greatest good, is at any rate preparing to smash the most despicable police state in the world.[128]

In Vienna, rumours were rife that the Papal Nuncio had been refused access to the Emperor. Pius X was said to be heartbroken by his failure to preserve the peace. (He died on 20 August.) Vatican documents later showed the rumours to have been false: the Papal Secretary of State approved of imperial policy.

Vienna was in aggressive mood. The Chief of Staff, General von Hoetzendorff, had asked his German counterpart six months earlier, 'Why are we waiting?' He was now doubly incensed by the delays. Even the sceptical Hungarian Prime Minister, Count Tisza, had been won over. 'My dear friend,' he told the Belgian ambassador on 31 July, 'Germany is invincible.'[129]

The poet Stefan Zweig, who would later condemn the war, was moved by the crowds of patriotic demonstrators. He had just cut short a seaside holiday at Le Coq, near Ostend, and had arrived home on the last Orient Express to run. 'You may hang me from a lamp-post', he had told a Belgian friend, 'if ever the Germans march into Belgium.' He had then watched German military trains rolling to the frontier at Herbesthal:

As never before, thousands and hundreds of thousands felt what they should have felt in peacetime, that they belonged together, [acknowledging] the unknown power which had lifted them out of their everyday existence.[130]

Zweig was fearing service on the Eastern Front. 'My great ambition . . . is to conquer in France,' he confessed, 'the France that one must chastise because one loves her.' He would soon print a public farewell to friends in the enemy camp: 'I shall not try to moderate this [widespread] hatred against you, which I do not feel myself, [but which] brings forth victories and heroic strength.'[131]

On 3 August, as Zweig arrived at Vienna's Westbahnhof, Lev Davidovich Bronshtein—Trotsky—departed. He had seen the same demonstrations, had seen the confusion of his socialist colleagues in the offices of the *Arbeiterzeitung*, and had been warned about internment. He immediately took train to Zurich, where he began to pen *The War and the International*—a work where he mobilized famous phrases such as 'the self-determination of the nations' and 'the United States of Europe' for his vision of a socialist future.[132]

Lenin, in contrast, lay low in his refuge at Poronin, near Zakopane in Galicia, confident that the opposition of the German Social Democrats would prevent a major conflict. When he heard that his German comrades had voted for war credits, he was reported to exclaim, 'From today I shall cease being a socialist and shall become a communist.'[133] In nearby Cracow, the university year had just finished. Graduating students, many of them reserve officers, were leaving to join their regiments—some to fight for the Emperor-King, some for the Kaiser, and some for the Tsar.

In St Petersburg, the court of Nicholas II was coming to terms with the fateful decisions of previous days. The Tsar had ordered full mobilization on Thursday 17/30 July, apparently without consulting the Minister of War. The resultant German ultimatum had been left unanswered. St Petersburg heard of Germany's declaration of war on the Saturday, and had followed suit on the Sunday. Monday 21 July/3 August, therefore, was the first full day at war. At 7 p.m. military censorship came into force. The newspapers announced that 'the nation must accept the paucity of information released, content in the knowledge that this sacrifice is dictated by military necessity'.[134] That day, the Tsar visited Moscow, and gave a speech in the Great Palace of the Kremlin. Their Imperial Majesties went to pray in the chapel of Our Lady of Iveron, an icon which celebrated Russia's earliest religious links with Mt Athos.

The optimists in Russia put their faith in the *Bol'shaya Voennaya Programma*, the 'Great Military Programme', which had been launched early in 1914 and which aimed, among other things, to cut the imperial army's mobilization time to eighteen days. As the British military attaché reported, their hope was that 'the Russians would be in Berlin before the Germans were in Paris.' The pessimists, headed by Pyotr Durnovo, the Minister of the Interior and Director of Police, felt a strong sense of foreboding. Durnovo had reported to the Tsar in February that if the war went badly 'a social revolution in its most extreme form will be unavoidable'.[135]

At Vevey in Switzerland, Romain Rolland, musicologist, novelist, and star of the international literary set, watched aghast as his friends succumbed to war fever. Furious at the stance of the Vatican, he claimed that Europe had lost all moral guidance since the death of Tolstoy, whose biography he had just written:

3–4 August. I'm devastated. I would like to be dead. It is horrible to live in the middle of this demented humanity, and to be present, but powerless, at the collapse of civilization. This European War is the greatest catastrophe in history, for centuries. [It's] the ruin of our holiest hopes for human brotherhood. . . . I'm almost alone in Europe.[136]

The outbreak of war in 1914 provoked more ponderings on the subject of historical causation than any other modern event. Many people were led to believe that a catastrophe of such titanic proportions must have been determined by causes of a similarly titanic scale. Few imagined that individuals alone were to blame. Huge works were written about the war's 'profound causes'. Indeed, historians were still arguing these issues out when a second world war gave them even more food for thought.

The word 'titanic' is not irrelevant. Shortly before the First World War, Europe had been shocked by a huge maritime disaster which all the experts had said could not happen. On 15 April 1912 the largest steamship in the world, the White Star liner SS *Titanic* of 43,500 tons, struck an Atlantic iceberg on her maiden voyage and sank with the loss of 1,513 lives. Given the vessel's size, it was obvious that an accident would have unprecedented consequences. On the other hand, there was no reason to relate the causes of the disaster to its scale. Two committees of inquiry pointed to very specific features of the particular ship and the particular voyage. These included the design of the hull, the provision of lifeboats, the unusual state of the Arctic ice, the excessive speed, the northerly course set by Capt. Smith, and the lack of co-ordinated action during the one and three-quarter hours following the initial collision with the iceberg. Historians of shipwrecks clearly have to inquire why the *Titanic* sank, but also why so many other huge ships have been able to cross the Atlantic in perfect safety.[137]

The analogy with wars is not entirely out of place. Historians of wars have to enquire not only why peace failed in 1914, but also why it held in 1908 or in 1912 and in 1913. The more recent experience of the 'Cold War' has shown, despite the potential for colossal disaster, that armageddon does not necessarily flow from the dynamic of two rival military and political blocs.

No one did more to provoke discussion of these issues than the wiseacre of Magdalen College, A. J. P. Taylor. For the generations involved, war history had been heavily coloured by emotions and moral overtones fired by the death of millions; and it took a man of monumental irreverence to challenge conventional attitudes. Addressing the events of 1914, Taylor named the persons who appeared to have caused the war single-handed: 'The three men who made the decisions, even if they, too, were the victims of circumstances, were Berchtold [the Austrian Foreign Minister], Bethmann Hollweg, and the dead man, Schlieffen.' As an incurable germanophobe, he said nothing about Sir Edward Grey.[138]

In another brilliant essay on the military logistics of 1914, Taylor approached an extreme position where the very notion of causation seemed redundant: 'It is the fashion nowadays to seek profound causes for great events. But perhaps the war that broke out in 1914 had no profound causes . . . In July 1914, things went wrong. The only safe explanation is that things happen because they happen.'[139]

Elsewhere, he reverted to the more convincing standpoint, which explains the great catastrophes of history in terms of a fatal combination of general and specific causes. The 'profound causes', on which other historians had laid such stress, were shown to be an essential element both of the pre-war peace and of the breakdown of peace. Without the 'specific causes', they were of little consequence:

The very things which are blamed for the war of 1914—secret diplomacy, the Balance of Power, the great continental armies—also gave Europe a period of unparalleled peace . . . It's no good asking 'What factors caused the outbreak of war?'. The question is rather 'Why did the factors that had long preserved the peace of Europe fail to do so in 1914?'[140]

In other words, there had to be a spark to ignite the keg of gunpowder. Without the spark, the gunpowder remains inert. Without the open keg, the sparks are harmless.

To illustrate the point, Taylor might well have chosen the case of the *Titanic*. Instead, he chose the analogy not of ships but of motor cars. By so doing, he emphasized the dynamic element common to most variants of catastrophe theory, where events are seen to be moving inexorably towards the critical point:

Wars are much like road accidents. They have a general and a particular cause at the same time. Every road accident is caused in the last resort by the invention of the internal combustion engine . . . [But] the police and the courts do not weigh profound causes. They seek a specific cause for each accident—driver's error, excessive speed, drunkenness, faulty brakes, bad road surface. So it is with wars.[141]

XI

TENEBRAE

Europe in Eclipse, 1914–1945

THERE are shades of barbarism in twentieth-century Europe which would once have amazed the most barbarous of barbarians. At a time when the instruments of constructive change had outstripped anything previously known, Europeans acquiesced in a string of conflicts which destroyed more human beings than all past convulsions put together. The two World Wars of 1914–18 and 1939–45, in particular, were destructive beyond measure; and they spread right across the globe. But their main focus lay unquestionably in Europe. What is more, in the course of those two war-bloodied generations, the two most populous countries of Europe fell into the hands of murderous political regimes whose internal hatreds killed even more tens of millions than their wars did. A rare voice of conscience said early on that something vile was happening:

> Why is this age worse than earlier ages?
> In a stupor of grief and dread
> have we not fingered the foulest wounds
> and left them unhealed by our hands?
>
> In the west, the fading light still glows
> and the clustered housetops glitter in the sun,
> but here Death is already chalking the doors with crosses,
> and calling the ravens, and the ravens are flying in.[1]

Future historians, therefore, must surely look back on the three decades between August 1914 and May 1945 as the era when Europe took leave of its senses. The totalitarian horrors of communism and fascism, when added to the horrors of total war, created an unequalled sum of death, misery, and degradation. When choosing the symbols which might best represent the human experience of those years, one can hardly choose anything other than the agents of twentieth-century death: the tank, the bomber, and the gas canister: the trenches, the tombs of unknown soldiers, the death camps, and the mass graves.

Consideration of these horrors, which overshadow all the life-giving

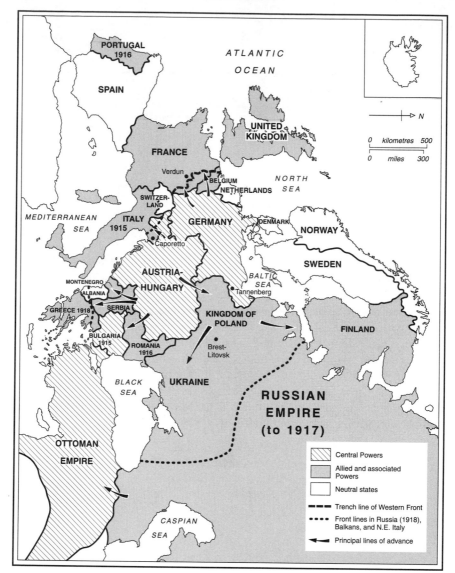

Map 24.
Europe during the Great War, 1914–1918

achievements of the era, prompts a number of general remarks. In the course of the horrors, Europeans threw away their position of world leadership: Europe was eclipsed through European folly. In 1914 Europe's power and prestige were un-rivalled: Europeans led the field in almost any sphere one cared to mention—science, culture, economics, fashion. Through their colonial empires and trading companies, European powers dominated the globe. By 1945 almost all had been lost: the Europeans had fought each other to the point of utter exhaustion. European political power was greatly diminished; Europe's military and eco-nomic power was overtaken; European colonial power was no longer sustainable. European culture lost its confidence; European prestige, and moral standing, all but evaporated. With one notable exception, every single European state that entered the fray in 1914 was destined to suffer military defeat and political annihi-lation. The one country to avoid total disaster was only able to survive by surren-dering its political and financial independence. When the wartime dust finally settled, the European ruins were controlled by two extra-European powers, the USA and the USSR, neither of which had even been present at the start.

On the moral front, one has to note the extreme contrast between the material advancement of European civilization and the terrible regression in political and intellectual values. Militarism, fascism, and communism found their adherents not only in the manipulated masses of the most afflicted nations but amongst Europe's most educated élites and in its most democratic countries. Such was the distortion of worthy ideals that there was no shortage of intelligent men and women who felt compelled to fight 'the War to end War', to join the fascists' genocidal crusade for rescuing 'European civilization', or to excuse the commu-nists' pursuit of peace and progress through mass murder. When the moment of truth arrived in 1941, Allied leaders fighting for freedom and democracy did not hesitate to enlist one criminal in order to defeat another.

On the historiographical front, one has to take account of the fact that the European horrors were committed within the span of living memory, and that subjective, political, and partisan opinions continue to dominate popular accounts. The history of all great conflicts always tends to be rewritten by the vic-tors, who maximize the crimes and follies of the vanquished whilst minimizing their own. Such, after all, is human nature. In both World Wars, it so happened that victory was achieved by similar coalitions headed by the 'Western powers' and by their strategic ally in the East; and it is their version of the period which continues to dominate post-war education, media, and history books. This 'Allied version' was first given official credence after 1918, when representatives of the defeated nations were obliged to confess to their own exclusive war guilt. It was cemented after 1945, when an Allied tribunal applied itself exclusively to the war crimes of the enemy. Any public attempt to judge the Allied Powers by the same means or standards was politically impossible. Official war museums from Lambeth to Moscow and Washington continued to present a one-sided view of the evils and the heroism. The captured archives of the losers were fully accessible in all their gruesome detail; key archives on the winning side remained firmly closed. Fifty years on, it was still too early for a fair and objective balance sheet to be drawn up.

On the interpretational front, many years passed before some historians began to ponder the unity of the 'European civil war'. People who lived through the two World Wars were often impressed by the discontinuities. The 'soldiers' war' of 1914–18 was thought to be very different from the 'people's war' of 1939–45. Anyone involved in the feud between communism and fascism was encouraged to think of the two movements as simple opposites. Now, with the benefit of hindsight, it is increasingly clear that the successive conflicts formed part of one dynamic process: the two World Wars were separate acts of the same drama. Above all, the main contestants of the Second World War were created by the unfinished business of the First. By entering into military conflict in 1914, the European states unleashed the mayhem from which were born not one but two revolutionary movements—one of which was crushed in 1945, the other left to crumble in the dramatic events of 1989–91 (see Chapter XII).

Faced by German expansionism, and then by the twin hydras of communism and fascism, the democratic Western Powers could only survive by calling in the USA—first in 1917–18 and then in 1941–5. After 1945 they relied very largely on American muscle to withstand the challenge of a bloated Soviet empire. Only in the 1990s, with Germany reunited and the Soviet empire in a state of collapse, could the people of Europe resume the natural course of their development so rudely interrupted in that beautiful summer of 1914.

In this scenario, therefore, the years between 1914 and 1945 appear as the time of Europe's troubles, which filled the space between the long peace of the late nineteenth century and the still longer peace of the 'Cold War'. They may be likened to the slipping of a continental plate, and to the resultant season of earthquakes. They encompass the initial military quakes of 1914–18, the collapse of four empires, the outbreak of communist revolution in Russia, the emergence of a dozen new sovereign states, the armed truce of the inter-war decades, the fascist take-overs in Italy, Germany, and Spain, and then the second, general military conflagration of 1939–45.

At the heart of the troubles lay Germany, Europe's newest, most dynamic, and most disgruntled nation-state. The fault-line of the earthquake zone ran along Germany's eastern border. Germany harboured few designs against Western Europe. But in Eastern Europe she faced both the temptation of relatively weak and poor neighbours and, in Russia, the challenge of the only European country large enough to contest German military strength. Hence, from the start, the major duel over Europe's future lay between Germany and Russia. It was a duel which in the hands of totalitarian revolutionaries was destined to become a fight to the death. From the start, the Western democracies were cast in the role of spoilers, essentially uninterested in the fate of east Europeans, but determined to stop the growth of any overweening Continental power which might eventually turn against the West. This constellation of forces governed European politics for the rest of the twentieth century. It underlay the fighting of the two World Wars and, but for the invention of nuclear weapons and the involvement of the Americans, would probably have produced a third.

In the event, the era of open and general conflict was somehow confined to those 30 blood-soaked years. It began and ended, quite appropriately, in the German capital, Berlin. It began on 1 August 1914, in the imperial Chancellery, with the Kaiser's declaration of war on Russia. It ended on 8 May 1945, in the Soviet field HQ at Berlin-Karlshorst, where a third act of capitulation finally concluded Germany's acts of unconditional surrender.

The First World War in Europe, 1914–1921

The Great War, which began in August 1914, was widely expected to last for three or four months. It was going to be over by Christmas. Conventional wisdom held that modern warfare would be more intense than in the past, but more decisive. Whichever side could gain the upper hand in the early stages would have the means for a swift victory. In the event, the fighting lasted not for four months but for more than four years. Even then it was not decisive: the 'Great Triangle' of military-political power blocs was not resolved until 1945, and in some respects not until 1991. (See Appendix III, p. 1312.)

In their initial configuration, the geopolitical structures of the Great Triangle were somewhat tentative. The Western Allies (Britain and France) were severely handicapped by the fact that France alone possessed a large standing army. They had to pass two precarious years before their full potential could be realized. They held on, first, by tempting Italy to join the Allied camp in May 1915; secondly, by the steady military build-up in Britain and the British Empire; and thirdly, by the entry of the USA in April 1917. Britain's Asian associate, Japan, which declared war on Germany on 23 August 1914, did not play any part in the European conflict. The Allies' main partner, imperial Russia, was thought to be handicapped by clumsy mobilization procedures, by a vast network of internal communication, by doubts over its industrial capacity, and by divided counsels over strategic aims. Yet Russia mounted an early offensive. She eventually collapsed, not through lack of shells or soldiers, but through political and moral decay.[2]

The Central Powers (Germany and Austria-Hungary) could benefit from all the advantages of consolidated policy and interior lines of communication. They lost one associate through Italy's desertion, but gained an unexpectedly resilient ally in the Ottoman Empire, which was obliged to take sides in November 1914 from fear of Russia. In 1914 they were terrified by the prospect of a war on two fronts. They need not have worried: they were to prove themselves capable of sustaining major campaigns in eight theatres of operations—on the Western Front, in Belgium and France; on the Eastern Front, against Russia; in the Balkans; in the Levant; in the Caucasus; in Italy; in the colonies; and at sea.

The war aims of the combatants had not been articulated by the outbreak. The

Central Powers started the war with defensive and deterrent purposes in mind. They aimed to prevent Austria being undermined, to break the encirclement of Germany, as they saw it, and to forestall French and Russian claims. Yet they were quick to formulate a catalogue of demands. They planned to transfer the eastern provinces of Belgium (Liège and Antwerp) to Germany, and parts of Serbia and Romania to Austria; to increase the German colonial collection, in order to undermine the British and the Russian Empires; and to establish political and economic hegemony over 'Mitteleuropa', including Poland. Only the Ottomans aimed merely to survive.

The *Entente* Powers took up arms because they were attacked, hence their incurable sense of moral superiority. Yet Serbia hoped to drive the Austrians from Bosnia, France aimed to recover Alsace-Lorraine, Britain was soon looking for colonial and financial compensation, and Russia harboured extensive plans for aggrandizement. In September 1914 the Russian General Staff published a 'Map of the Future Europe' which was remarkably similar to the one which was realized in 1945.[3] In addition Russia extracted a secret promise from its allies for post-war control of the Straits. Italy aimed to gain the *irredenta*.

Several countries contrived to stay neutral. Spain, Switzerland, the Netherlands, and the three Scandinavian countries maintained their neutrality throughout, and prospered from it. Bulgaria was pulled into the war in September 1915, Romania in August 1916, Greece in June 1917. China, despite Japan's seizure of the Chinese enclaves leased to Germany, attacked by Japan, entered the war on the Allied side in 1917. Others were less reluctant to fight. Several hundred members of Piłsudski's Polish Legion opened up the Eastern Front by marching across the Russian frontier near Cracow on 6 August 1914. They were carrying cavalry saddles in the hope of finding mounts. They aimed to demonstrate that Poland was still alive after a century and more of Partition. They wisely retreated when Cossacks approached, and were incorporated into the Austrian army.

Military strategy and tactics, as always, were based on the lessons of recent wars. The Franco-Prussian War and the Boer War had proved the vulnerability of infantry attack. The solution was thought to lie in three areas—in the use of massed artillery as the primary offensive arm against battlefield positions, in the use of railways for the rapid deployment of attacking forces, and in the use of cavalry for encirclement and pursuit. On the Eastern Front these assumptions did not prove ineffective. But in the West, where fortified trench-lines came into being, it took thousands of abortive operations before the superiority of the concrete blockhouse over the high-explosive shell was even suspected. Despite the manifest advantages of defence over attack, the generals were slow to revise their assumptions. Aircraft, whose engines were weak and unreliable, could only be used for reconnaissance, artillery guidance, and aerial combat. In the majority of locations, where there were few metalled roads, horsepower remained indispensable. At sea, submarine torpedoes proved more lethal than the 15-inch guns of the Dreadnoughts.

On the Western Front, the German army very nearly pulled off a shock assault before the war of attrition set in. Whilst the central German thrust plunged into the heart of Champagne, the German right wing rode off on a huge wheeling arc through northern France. Aiming to repeat the triumph of 1870, they moved on Paris from three directions. They were briefly held by the Belgians at Liège, and by the British Expeditionary Force at Ypres. [**LANGEMARCK**] The central German forces were delayed by the cellars of Épernay. But by the first week of September 1914 the French capital was facing disaster. At the very last moment, General Joffre impressed 600 Renault taxis to ferry all available French reserves to the line of the Marne. The German centre had just too little momentum; the German right was just too far away. So the line fell back. In October and November the Front stabilized along the whole length of a double trench-line running from Switzerland to the Channel (see Map 24).

For the next three years the line hardly moved. Both sides expended men and materials in titanic proportions to straighten out the occasional salient, or to achieve a breakthrough. But every 'push' was to no avail. Never had European blood been spilled in such profligate quantities. In the three battles of Ypres, at Vimy Ridge, on the Somme, and, above all, at Verdun the loss of life could on occasion be counted in tens of thousands per hour or hundreds per square yard. Here was a mindless tragedy which no one had foreseen, and which no one knew how to stop. The planned German retreat to prepared defensive positions between Arras and Soissons in February 1917 was a rare act of rationality. Inevitably, the public finger was pointed at the impotent generals. Of the British army, it was said, 'They were lions led by donkeys.' [**DOUAUMONT**]

On the Eastern Front, which ran through the heart of Poland, the Central Powers enjoyed much greater success and the hell of unbroken trench warfare was avoided. In August 1914 two Russian army groups crossed the frontier, one entering East Prussia in the north, the other penetrating deep into Galicia in the south. Seeing that the 'Russian steamroller' was meant to move slowly, this was a considerable achievement. But then fortunes changed: in the Battle of the Masurian Lakes in September, Hindenberg and Ludendorff totally destroyed Russia's northern armies, thereby avenging the German failure on the Marne. Russia's southern group was halted on the outskirts of Cracow. In the winter of 1914–15 indecisive battles were fought both on the German/Russian frontier near Łódź and on the Hungarian border in the Carpathians. But then in May 1915, at Gorlice in Galicia, German troops managed to do what proved impossible in the West: they broke through enemy lines, and fanned out into the plain beyond. In August they occupied Warsaw, and retook Lvov. In the autumn they entered Lithuania, and were poised to cross the mountains into Romania. [**PETROGRAD**]

With the Russian Empire facing invasion along a 1,000-mile front, the Tsar took personal command of his forces in the field. In January 1916, Brusilov's counter-offensive drove back deep into Galicia, laying an 18-month siege to the fortress of Przemyśl. But the toll was tremendous; and there it ended. In Romania, the Germans took Bucharest in December. In 1917 the main German and Austrian advance restarted, moving steadily into the Baltic provinces, Byelorussia, and

LANGEMARCK

LANGEMARCK is a small village five miles to the north of Ypres in Belgium. Like all the villages in that district, it possesses a war cemetery filled with the dead from successive Anglo-German battles over the Ypres salient in 1914–17. In outward appearance it is indistinguishable from scores of others. Indeed, the long-overgrown grave of 25,000 unidentified German soldiers bears no comparison to the imposing monument at the nearby Menin Gate, where the names of 40,000 unidentified British casualties are inscribed. Yet, in the opinion of a leading military historian, 'It is, in a real sense, the birthplace of the Second World War.'[1] For, unbeknown to many modern visitors, Langemarck shelters the last resting-place of the comrades of a young Austrian volunteer whom Providence spared for still greater deeds.

Hitler, an unsuccessful art student and draft-dodger from the Austrian army, had listened with rapture in a Munich crowd to the declaration of war on 1 August 1914, and had immediately signed up for service in the German Army. He was assigned to the 16th Bavarian Reserve Infantry (List) Regiment, and arrived on the Western Front in October, just in time for the first Battle of Ypres. In this way he became a witness to the terrible *Kindermord*, the 'Massacre of Innocents', where tens of thousands of half-trained German recruits, mainly eager university students, were cut to pieces by the steady firepower of professional British soldiers. It was the first great slaughter of Germans, amply revenged, no doubt, at Passchendaele and on the Somme. Hitler never forgot it.

Hitler's 'supreme experience' in the trenches, where for four years he lived the charmed life of a courageous *Meldegänger* or 'regimental runner', undoubtedly fired the pathological drive of his subsequent career. Tormented by the fate of his dead and mutilated comrades, and by a huge German sacrifice that led only to defeat, he set out to avenge their deaths; to humiliate Germany's conquerors in their turn; and to make Germans feel once again proud, superior, hateful, ruthless. His vow of vengeance struck a common chord in millions of wounded German hearts.

Langemarck, therefore, symbolizes the essential psychological link between the First World War and the Second, between the slaughter of Ypres and Verdun, and that of the London Blitz, Warsaw, and Stalingrad.

DOUAUMONT

O N 25 February 1916, on the fourth day of the German offensive against
Verdun, the troops of the Crown Prince seized the stone and concrete fortress of Douaumont. The fort lay 6 km from their starting-point on
the circumference of the salient, and half-way to the centre of the city. For
the next eighteen months it would be the focal point of a battle which in
duration and intensity has no equal. Flanked to the west by the Fort de
Vaux, it commanded the right bank of the Meuse and looked across to the
hills of the left bank, especially to Côte 304 and to Le Mort-Homme. For the
German attackers, it formed the pivot of a giant pincer operation fed by
fourteen railway lines along a 130-mile arc. For the French defenders, it
formed the terminus of the *voie sacrée*, the narrow corridor which brought
reinforcements through the evacuated city from Bar-le-Duc. Shelled night
and day, mined from below, and constantly rocked by explosions, its ruins
and tunnels were the scene of hand-to-hand combat and of whole companies buried alive. The moonscape was steadily churned into a cold stew
of mud, masonry, and human remains. It was regained by the French on
24 October, contested by the Germans until August 1917, but not
definitively relieved until the American offensive of St Michel in
September 1918. Pétain's words proved true. 'Courage,' he had promised;
'On les aura.'

Verdun claimed some 800,000 lives—forty times the population of the
city. It is for the French memory what the Somme and Ypres were for the
British and Caporetto for the Italians, or what Stalingrad would be for
the Russians. For the Germans, it implied what all their military failures
would do—titanic, futile sacrifices.

On the seventieth anniversary of the battle in 1986, the French President
and the German Chancellor participated at Verdun in a ceremony of reconciliation. Their hands were linked in a gesture which few other leaders
of Europe's warring nations have been able to achieve.

By then, much of the devastated landscape had been reclaimed by veg-
etation. But the vast ossuary at Douaumont, with its tower of four crosses,
guards the remains of 130,000 unidentified soldiers of both armies who
rest in the common granite tombs. A memorial centre, equipped with
exhibits, guidebooks, and video shows, attempts to communicate what a
veteran once called the 'incommunicable'. On the site of the disappeared
village of Fleury-devant-Douaumont, a Madonna adorns the façade of a
memorial chapel. She is Notre Dame de l'Europe.[1]

PETROGRAD

IN 1914 the name of Russia's capital, Sankt Petersburg, was changed to the more patriotic-sounding Petrograd. As with the British royal family of Hanover-Saxe-Coburg, which was changed to Windsor, a name of German origin was thought inappropriate during the war against Germany. But Petrograd was to last for only one decade before it gave way in its turn to Leningrad. [**GOTHA**]

St Petersburg had grown into one of Europe's most magnificent cities. In addition to the classical palaces and government buildings, the banks of the Neva housed a major port and commercial centre, a brilliant cultural community, an expanding industrial district, and a huge garrison. The spirit of the community of two million citizens was captured in the statue of the Bronze Horseman presented to the city by Catherine the Great in honour of her predecessor, Peter.

At the time of the first name-change, the city's future dedicatee was exiled in Switzerland with no hope of an early return. He was no pacifist; and his statement on *The Tasks of Revolutionary Social Democracy*, where he called for an 'international civil war' to exploit the conflict, envisaged the defeat of Tsardom. All his leading supporters in Russia were arrested on suspicion of treason. At their trial they were defended by a liberal lawyer, Alexander Kerensky, who must later have rued his choice of clients.[1]

Under Soviet rule, Petrograd/Leningrad was to be subjected to the most extreme of experiences. Spurned by the Bolsheviks, who had moved the capital to Moscow, it was repeatedly seen by Stalin as the conspiratorial nest of a non-existent opposition; it lost a significant part of its population first in the Revolution and again in the Purges. In 1941–4, it endured a 1,000-day siege on the edge of the German–Soviet frontline, and in conditions of indescribable cold, hunger, and starvation lost up to a million inhabitants.[2] Although state officials and the military secured the means to fight on for three years, the Soviet authorities either could not or would not evacuate or supply the civilian population. The result was a daily mix of Coventry and the Warsaw Ghetto. Descriptions of carousing in the Party House, alongside corpses in the streets and scientific workers dead at their laboratory benches, only add to the tally of inhumanity.[3]

After each ordeal Leningrad was replenished by a fresh influx of immigrants. The 'Hero City' became a symbol of the human capacity for regeneration. Yet in 1991, on the eve of the Soviet collapse, the question of its name arose for the third time. To the horror of Communist veterans, the citizens' referendum decided neither for Leningrad nor for Petrograd but for Sankt Petersburg.

Ukraine. With internal revolution compounding Russia's military failure, it was a matter of fine judgement whether the Central Powers could destroy the Empire of the Tsars before it collapsed of its own accord. It is often said that the Russian army suffered excessive casualties; in reality the Russians lost a lower percentage of their population than other combatants. The key statistics refer to prisoners of war. For every 100 tsarist soldiers who fell in battle, 300 surrendered. The comparable figure for the British army was 20, for the French 24, for the Germans 26. The soldiers of the Tsar had little will to fight.[4]

Meanwhile, in the Balkan theatre, superior Austrian forces steadily gained the upper hand. They occupied Belgrade (October 1915), Montenegro, and Albania (1916). A heroic Serbian retreat across the mountains to the Dalmatian coast provided the stuff of legend. In 1915 the Serbs were corralled into Macedonia, where Bulgaria joined the Austrian attack. But the Macedonian Front held, partly through French support via Thessalonika. Merciless Western pressure on Greece forced the collapse of the government, and ended Greek neutrality. [FLORA]

In the Mediterranean, the Western Powers enjoyed naval supremacy, and several attempts were made to compensate for the stalemate in France. On 25 April 1915 a British force landed at Gallipoli on the Dardanelles. The aim was to seize Constantinople, to establish direct contact with Russia, and, in the words of the First Lord of the Admiralty, Winston Churchill, to attack 'the soft underbelly' of the Central Powers. The plan was brilliantly conceived, but ended in tragedy. The movements of the expeditionary force, which contained the heroic Anzac Division from Australia and New Zealand, had been betrayed in advance. The Turks were waiting on the cliff-tops, commanded by an energetic young officer called Kemal Pasha. After that, the Western Powers confined their activities to the Ottoman periphery. A young English visionary, T. E. Lawrence, single-handedly led the tribes of the Arabian peninsula into revolt. The French established themselves in Lebanon. In 1916 General Allenby advanced into Palestine from the British base in Egypt, riding into Jerusalem on Christmas Day. The British also entered Mesopotamia. They captured Baghdad after a humiliating reverse in March 1917, and pressed on into Persia. Both Arabs and Zionist Jews took heart from the British victories. On 2 November 1917 the British Foreign Minister, Arthur Balfour, was persuaded to issue a declaration accepting the principle of a Jewish National Home in Palestine. In the Caucasus, Russians and Ottomans struggled back and forth over the mountainous Armenian border region. The fighting provided the backdrop to the Ottoman Government's reprisals against its Armenian subjects. [GENOCIDE]

In Italy, battle was joined with the Austrians in difficult alpine terrain on the edge of the lands which the Italians were claiming as their own. In eleven colossal battles on the River Isonzo, the fighting was no less sacrificial than in the West. Half a million men died at Caporetto (September–December 1917). Italy's casualties were on the same scale as Britain's. Her magnificent recovery from the brink of disaster greatly weakened the Central powers. The Austrian army was broken

FLORA

L ATE in August 1914, the 35-year-old daughter of a Suffolk clergyman, Flora Sandes, arrived with seven companions in the Serbian town of Kragujevac. Some fifty miles from Belgrade, Kragujevac was the main base for Serbian forces fighting for their capital city against the Austro-Hungarian offensive. Flora's group preceded several British, French, Russian, and American medical teams appointed by the Serbian Relief Fund. In mid-April 1915 they were joined by Mrs Mabel St Clair Stobart, a formidable dame who had raised a Women's Sick and Wounded Convoy Corps during the recent Balkan wars. She now came up from Salonica, in command of a 70-strong field hospital staffed entirely by women, except for her husband, John Greenhalgh, their treasurer. She collected her casualties with a special 'flying column', which she led on horseback. Over 600 British female volunteers were active in Serbia.

Of all the women's wartime organizations, the British women's medical services were undoubtedly among the most professional. Known as the Scottish Women's Hospitals (SWH), after their founder, an Edinburgh surgeon called Elsie Inglis, they set out to prove that women could cope with the most stressful and responsible of enterprises. In due course they sent fourteen fully equipped hospitals to all the Allied fronts except those controlled by the British army. Mrs St Clair Stobart had worked in Cherbourg and in Antwerp before sailing for Serbia. Dr Inglis died in November 1917 after a year in Russia.[1] Female surgeons were still a novelty in those years, especially in military hospitals. A French journalist, who once asked to watch Dr Inglis at work, emerged looking green and yelling: 'C'est vrai, elle coupe!' (It's true, she's cutting!)[2]

In October 1915, when the Austrians and Bulgarians broke through, the Serbian army could escape only by a winter trek over the mountains to the Albanian coast. That terrible march through mud, snow, hunger, frostbite, typhus, and gangrene cost 40,000 lives. The Stobart Unit marched with them.

Of all the volunteers, Flora Sandes (1879–1961) went furthest in her career of gender inversion. She joined the Serbian infantry, survived the trek to Albania, fought in combat, was severely wounded, and was decorated for bravery. She ended the war with an officer's commission. She later married a Russian *émigré*, settled in Belgrade, defied the Gestapo, and only returned to England in widowhood.[3] She was following a well-worn East European tradition, observable from Russia and Poland to Albania, where women in hard times stand in for their decimated menfolk.

One source for the British women's determination lay in the attitudes of their own government. When Elsie Inglis offered the services of the SWH to the War Office in August 1914, she was told: 'My good lady, go home and sit still.'[4]

in Italy. The Italian sacrifice, largely discounted by her allies, left a deep sense of wounded pride.

In the colonies, every outpost of the combatant powers felt bound to uphold the cause of the mother country. There was a remote campaign between the French and the German Cameroons. The British seized German East Africa (Tanganyika) and German South-West Africa. In this unequal contest the weaker German party generally proved the more resourceful. The German force in East Africa under General Paul von Lettow-Vorbeck (1870–1964) survived intact until the Armistice.

At sea, the war ought in theory to have produced a series of almighty contests between the bristling fleets of battleships. In practice, the French fleet betook itself

---

GENOCIDE

O N 27 May 1915, the Ottoman Government decreed that the Armenian population of eastern Anatolia should be forcibly deported. The Armenians, who were Christians, were suspected of sympathizing with the Russian enemy on the Caucasian Front, and of planning a united Armenia under Russian protection. Some two to three million people were affected. Though accounts differ, one-third of them are thought to have been massacred; one-third to have perished during deportation; and one-third to have survived. The episode is often taken to be the first modern instance of mass genocide. At the Treaty of Sèvres (1920), the Allied Powers recognized united Armenia as a sovereign republic. In practice, they allowed the country to be partitioned between Soviet Russia and Turkey.[1]

Adolf Hitler was well aware of the Armenian precedent. When he briefed his generals at Obersalzburg on the eve of the invasion of Poland, he revealed his plans for the Polish nation:

Genghis Khan had millions of women and men killed by his own will and with a gay heart. History sees him only as a great state-builder . . . I have sent my Death's Head units to the East with the order to kill without mercy men, women, and children of the Polish race or language. Only in such a way will we win the *lebensraum* that we need. Who, after all, speaks today of the annihilation of the Armenians?[2]

The term 'genocide', however, was not used before 1944, when it was coined by a Polish lawyer of Jewish origin, Rafał Lemkin (1901–59), who was working in the USA. Lemkin's campaign to draw practical conclusions from the fate of Poland and of Poland's Jews was crowned in 1948 by the United Nation's 'Convention for the Prevention and Punishment of Genocide'.[3] Unfortunately, as the wars in ex-Yugoslavia have shown, the Convention in itself can neither prevent nor punish genocide.

to the Mediterranean, whilst the German fleet, after one inconclusive engagement with the Royal Navy off Jutland (31 May 1916), betook itself to port. The British, who could nominally claim command of the seas, could not cope with German submarines operating from Kiel and Bremerhaven which sank over 12 million tons of Allied shipping. The British blockade, which practised unrestricted submarine warfare in the North Sea, contributed to serious food shortages in Germany. But Britain also faced acute deprivation. The sinking of the civilian liner *Lusitania* by submarine U20 on 7 May 1915, and Germany's subsequent extension of unrestricted submarine warfare into the Atlantic (1917), were instrumental in ending American neutrality.

In the third year of war the strains began to be reflected in politics. In Dublin, the Irish Easter Rising (1916) had to be suppressed by force. In London, regular party government was overturned by the formation of Lloyd George's coalition War Cabinet (December 1916). At that same time, in Austria-Hungary the death of Francis-Joseph struck a note of deep foreboding. The first wartime meeting of the Reichsrat (May 1917) broke up amidst Czech demands for autonomy and rumours of a separate peace. In France, an epidemic of mutiny provoked a prolonged crisis that was eventually brought under control by the combined efforts of the new commander, Marshal Pétain, and the new Premier, Georges Clemenceau. In Germany the Kaiser's Easter message in 1917 proposed democratic reforms; and in July all parties of the Reichstag who had voted for war credits in 1914 now voted for a peace of reconciliation. On the Eastern Front, after the failure of moves for a separate peace with Russia, the Central Powers restored a puppet Kingdom of Poland in Warsaw. The kingdom had no king, and a regency council with no regent. It had no connection with the Polish provinces in Prussia, in Austria, or east of the Bug. Its formation was soon followed by the dissolution of Piłsudski's Polish Legions, who refused to swear allegiance to the German Kaiser. In Russia, there was revolution. In the USA, there was war fever. [COW-ARD] [LILI]

Austria's young *Friedenskaiser* (Peace Emperor) personally led one of several sets of secret negotiations with the Allied Powers. In the spring of 1917, in Switzerland, he twice met with his brother-in-law, Prince Sixtus of Bourbon-Parma, a serving Belgian officer, who acted as the go-between with Paris and London. He was ready to make territorial concessions to Italy, and accepted French claims to Alsace-Lorraine. But he did not convince either the Italians or the French of his ability to influence Berlin, and was forced to grovel before the German Emperor when Clemenceau eventually made the contacts public. From that point on, the fate of the Habsburg monarchy was tied to the military fortunes of Germany; and all hope for the peaceful evolution of the nationalities in Austria-Hungary was dashed.[5]

The entry into the war of the USA, which occurred on 6 April 1917, came after many American attempts to promote peace. The 28th President, Thomas Woodrow Wilson (1856–1924), an East Coast liberal and a Princeton professor, had been re-elected in November 1916 on the neutrality ticket; and his envoy,

---

COWARD

A T 6 a.m. on 18 October 1916, at Carnoy on the Western Front, Private Harry Farr of the West Yorkshire Regiment was shot dead by a British firing squad. A volunteer with six years' service, not a conscript, he had twice been withdrawn from the front line suffering from shell-shock. On the third occasion he had been refused treatment at a medical station, since he had no wounds, and, after resisting the sergeant escorting him to the trenches, was arrested. He repeatedly said, 'I cannot stand it'. At the court martial, the general commanding XIV Corps said that the charge of cowardice seemed 'clearly proved'. This was confirmed by Commander-in-Chief Douglas Haig.

In due course Farr's widow, Gertrude, received a letter from the War Office: 'Dear madam, We regret to inform you that your husband has died. He was sentenced for cowardice and was shot at dawn on 16 October.' She received neither a war widow's pension nor an allowance for her daughter. But she did receive a message via her local vicar, from the regimental chaplain: 'Tell his wife he was no coward. A finer soldier never lived.' She lived to be 99 and to read the papers of the court martial, which were not released by Britain's Public Record Office until 1992.

Private Farr was one of 3,080 British soldiers sentenced to death by court martial in 1914–18, mainly for desertion, and one of 307 who were not reprieved. In rejecting the plea of mercy in a similar case, Douglas Haig minuted: 'How can we ever win if this plea is allowed?'[1]

In the Second World War, some 100,000 British soldiers deserted, but none was shot. Recaptured deserters from the Red Army or from the Wehrmacht were not so lucky.[2]

Colonel House, had visited all the European capitals. As late as January 1917 Wilson's State of the Union speech was calling for 'peace without victory'. But America's maritime economy was mortally threatened by German submarines; and Germany's clumsy scheme to recruit Mexico, as revealed in the Zimmerman Telegram of February 1917, finally removed all doubts. Wilson's idealism openly confronted the secret diplomacy of the British and French. His Fourteen Points (January 1918) lent coherence and credibility to Allied war aims. He was strongly attached to the principle of national self-determination, equitably applied. Thanks to the musical soirées given at the White House by Ignacy Paderewski, he put Polish independence on the agenda.

Taken together, however, the changes of 1917 aroused great anxiety in the Allied camp. For the time being, the entry of the USA was more than offset by the chaos in Russia. The *Entente* was gaining a partner with great potential whilst losing its most powerful partner in the field. Twelve months would pass before the weight

LILI

SOME time in 1915, somewhere on the Eastern Front in the middle of Poland, a young German sentry was dreaming of home. Hans Leip imagined that two of his girlfriends, Lili and Marlene, were standing with him under the lamp by the barrack gate. He whistled a tune to cheer himself up, invented a few sentimental lines, then promptly forgot them. Twenty years later, in Berlin, he remembered the tune, and added some verses, merging the two girls' names into one. Set to music by Norbert Schultz, it was published in 1937. Inter-war Berlin was one of the great centres of cabaret and popular songs. But *The Song of a Lonely Sentry* met no success.[1]

In 1941, when the German Army occupied Yugoslavia, the powerful transmitter of Radio Belgrade was requisitioned by the military. Amongst its stock of second-hand disks was a pre-war recording of Hans Leip's song. By chance, Belgrade's nightly music programme could be heard beyond the Balkans in North Africa, both by Rommel's men and by the 'desert rats' of the British Eighth Army. This time, the voice of Lale Andersen, floating on the ether under the starlit Mediterranean sky, bewitched the listening soldiers. The words were soon translated into English, and recorded by Anne Shelton. After the siege of Tobruk, when a column of British prisoners passed through the lines of the *Afrika-Korps,* both sides were singing the same tune:

1. Lili Marleen

Vor der Kaserne, vor den
    grossen Tor
Stand eine Laterne, und steht
    sie noch davor.
So wolln wir uns da wiedersehen,
bei der Laterne wolln wir stehn
Wie einst Lili Marleen.

Underneath the lantern by the barrack
    gate
Darling, I remember, how you used to
    wait.
'Twas there you whispered tenderly,
That you lov'd me; you'd always be,
My Lili of the lamplight, My own Lili
    Marlene.

When the USA joined the war, *Lili Marlene* was taken up by Marlene Dietrich. It was to cross all frontiers.[2]

Les Feuilles mortes was composed in the wartime Paris of 1943, where *Lili Marlene* was on everyone's lips. Its bitter-sweet words were written by

Jacques Prévert, its haunting melody by Joseph Kosma. Its theme of separated lovers might again have matched the mood of millions. But the Jean Gabin film for which it had been commissioned was cancelled; and the song was never issued. By the time it was rediscovered after the war, the social and political climate had changed; and the English words had lost the original flavour:

2. Feuilles Mortes

C'est une chanson, qui nous ressemble	The falling leaves drift by the window
Toi tu m'aimais, et je t'aimais.	The autumn leaves of red and gold.
Nous vivions tous les deux ensemble	I see your lips, the summer kisses,
Toi qui m'aimais, moi qui t'aimais.	The sun-burned hands I used to hold.
Mais la vie sépare ceux qui s'aiment,	Since you went away, the days grow long,
Tout doucement, sans faire de bruit.	And soon I'll hear old winter's song.
Et la mer efface sur le sable	But I miss you most of all, my darling,
Les pas des amants désunis.	When autumn leaves start to fall.

Where were the waves on the seashore, and the lovers' footprints lost in the sand? But in the 1950s *Autumn Leaves* was unstoppable.[3]

In the post-war era, popular songs headed the tide of American culture—good, bad, indifferent—which was to sweep over Europe. The transatlantic sound of Anglo-American songs was destined for dominance. But it is well to remember that in many parts of Europe, in Naples, in Warsaw, in Paris, and in Moscow, the native idioms preserved their excellence:

---

1. Не слышны в саду даже шорохи,
    Всё здесь замерло до утра.
    Если б знали вы, как мне дороги ⎱ 2 раза
    Подмосковные вечера.   ⎰

3. Что ж ты, милая, смотришь искоса,
    Низко голову наклоня?
    Трудно высказать и не высказать ⎱ 2 раза
    Всё, что на сердце у меня.   ⎰

(Not even the garden rustle is heard.
Silence has fallen till the light.
If only you knew how dear to me
Are these suburban Moscow nights.
So why, my sweet, do you hang your
                                   head,
Look aside, and stand apart?
It's hard to speak, and not to speak,
Of all that weighs on my heart.)[4]

---

of American manpower and industrial production could be felt. In the mean time, as Russian resistance declined, the Central Powers could transfer an increasing share of their resources from East to West. The outcome of war was seen to depend on a race for time between the effects of mobilization in the USA and the effects of revolution in Russia.

The Russian Revolution of 1917 consisted of several interwoven chains of collapse. The two political eruptions—the February Revolution which overturned the tsarist monarchy and the second, October Revolution or coup which installed the Bolshevik dictatorship—were attended by upheavals reaching to the very depths of the Empire's social, economic, and cultural foundations. They were also accompanied by an avalanche of national risings in each of the non-Russian countries which had been incorporated into the Empire, and which now took the chance to seize their independence.

The effects on the prosecution of the War were dramatic. In mid-February 1917 the last of the Romanovs still stood at the head of Europe's largest war-machine. Within twelve months the Romanovs had been extinguished; their Empire had disintegrated into a score of self-ruling states; and the Bolshevik rulers of the central rump territory had pulled out of the war for good. Following an armistice agreed at Brest-Litovsk, all effective Russian participation in the war ceased from 6 December 1917. German policy, which had been supporting both the aspirations of the separatists and the machinations of the Bolsheviks, scored a triumph of unparalleled proportions.

The disintegration of the Russian Empire must be seen not simply as one of the effects of the Revolution but also as one of its causes. The Russian Tsar had been losing the allegiance of his non-Russian subjects long before the appearance of the Bolshevik dictatorship definitively confirmed their desire for a separate existence. When the Polish provinces were lost due to the German advance in 1915, the Empire's leading Polish politician, Roman Dmowski, turned his back on Russia once and for all. Henceforth he was to work for Polish independence under the auspices of the Western Powers. A Polish National Committee was set up under his chairmanship in Paris in August 1916. In Lithuania, the *Taryba* or National

Council was set up under German auspices in September 1917. In Finland, an independent republic had to fight for its existence, with German help, from mid-1917 to May 1918. In Ukraine, the national movement came to the fore as soon as imperial power weakened. A Ukrainian Republic was formed in Kiev in November 1917. By the so-called 'Bread Treaty' of 9 February 1918, it was able to gain recognition from the Central Powers in return for grain contracts. In the Caucasus, the independent Transcaucasian Federation came into being at the same time.

Faced with this spontaneous wave of separatism, successive Russian governments in Petrograd had little choice but to bow before the storm. The Provisional Government declared itself to be in favour of the independence of the nationalities in April 1917. The Bolsheviks and others followed suit. In reality, despite the rhetoric, the Bolsheviks had no intention of conceding independence to the nationalities. As soon as they seized power in Petrograd, the chief Bolshevik commissar for the nationalities, an obscure Georgian revolutionary known as J. V. Stalin, began organizing branches of the Bolshevik Party in each of the emerging republics, fomenting trouble against each of the fledgeling national governments. Bolshevik policy aimed to restore the defunct Russian Empire in new communist guise. From the start, they sought to impose a centralized Party dictatorship behind a façade of cultural autonomy and nominal state structures. Here lay one of the principal sources of the so-called 'Russian Civil War' (see below).

The Revolution in Petrograd, therefore, was addressed to the central government of a state that was already in an advanced state of decomposition. The immediate cause lay in a crisis of management in the tsarist court. The Tsar himself was absent at the front, floundering in his ill-judged determination to conduct the war in person. The Duma was ignored; and the Tsar's ministers were left at the mercy of a paranoiac 'German' Tsarina and her mountebank confidant, the so-called 'mad monk', Gregory Rasputin (1872–1916). When urgent wartime business regarding inflation, food shortages, and army supply was neglected, members of the innermost tsarist circle rebelled. Rasputin was murdered by Oxford-educated Prince Felix Yusupov, son of the richest woman in Russia and husband of the Tsar's niece. In other circumstances, the event might have gone down in history as a petty court intrigue. As it was, it added the last ounce of accumulated resentment that broke the stays of the entire system. For beyond the confines of court politics lay tens of millions of the Tsar's voiceless subjects—disaffected intellectuals, frustrated constitutionalists, confused bureaucrats, workers without rights, peasants without land, soldiers without hope either for life or for victory. The glittering shell of tsarism stayed upright till the last second, then fell like a house of cards.

The chain of events which led from Rasputin's murder on 17 December 1916 to the Bolsheviks' seizure of power ten months later was extremely tortuous and entirely unplanned. In late February the arctic winter, which had contributed to a breakdown of food supplies, changed suddenly to premature spring sunshine. Thousands of strikers and demonstrators poured on to the streets of Petrograd calling for peace, bread, land, and freedom. On 26 February, on Znamensky Square, a company of the Imperial Guard fired the first fatal volley. The next day 160,000 peasant conscripts of the capital's garrison mutinied and joined the rioters. The Tsar's generals prevaricated. The Duma dared to appoint a Provisional Government without him, whilst representatives of various socialist factions convened the Petrograd Soviet or 'Council of Workers' and Soldiers' Deputies'.

In this way there arose the *dvoyevlas'tye* or 'Dual Power', where the Duma had to compete with the Petrograd Soviet. Each side took momentous decisions. On 1 March the Soviet issued its unilateral Order No. 1, which called on every military unit to elect a soviet of its own. At a stroke, the authority of the officer corps was ruined throughout the Army. On 2 March the Provisional Government issued an 8-point programme calling for the installation of elected officials in local government and for the replacement of the state police by a people's militia. At a stroke, the authority of the police and of local officialdom was undermined throughout Russia. The Russian Empire fell apart 'by telegraph'. That night, Nicholas II abdicated.

For a time an uneasy alliance between the constitutional liberals within the Duma and the moderate socialists within the Soviet—mainly Mensheviks and Socialist Revolutionaries (SR), both opposed to the Bolsheviks—kept the Dual Power on an even keel. Here the central figure was Alexander Kerensky (1881–1970), a socialist and a lawyer, who was a member both of the Provisional Government and of the Soviet. But their policy of continuing the war was highly unpopular. They only succeeded in stoking the climate of ceaseless discontent which was to prove so favourable to more radical elements. The Provisional Government declared its intention of calling universal elections for a Constituent Assembly, which could then put Russian democracy on to a permanent footing. This gave the Bolsheviks their timetable: to stand any chance of ruling Russia, they had to take control of the soviets and overthrow the Provisional Government before the Constituent Assembly could meet. [**FATIMA**]

Prior to Lenin's return to Petrograd in April, the Bolsheviks played only a minor role in the revolutionary events. But a deteriorating situation in the spring and summer created a fertile environment for disciplined subversives. On three occasions, in April, in June, and in July, they tried to exploit their growing influence in the Petrograd garrison, seeking to transform street demonstrations into armed insurrections. On the last occasion, the Provisional Government actually ordered the Bolshevik leaders' arrest on charges of high treason, having learned of their German contacts. Lenin was forced to take refuge in the countryside. In August and September, however, the Government was paralysed by its conflict with the army under General Lavr Kornilov. Kornilov's abortive *putsch* gave Lenin the respite to plan a coup of his own.

When Lenin slipped back into Petrograd early in October, Kerensky's government was isolated and thoroughly discredited. The army was disaffected; the soviets were divided. Bolshevik plans aimed to neutralize the main Petrograd Soviet by calling a parallel Congress of Soviets crammed with Bolshevik delegates

FATIMA

O N 3 May 1917, at the height of the First World War, Pope Benedict XV appealed to the Blessed Virgin Mary for a sign in the cause of peace. Ten days later, three illiterate children reported a vision of Our Lady outside the village of Fatima in Portugal. They heard her say that she was 'the Lady of the Rosary', that the advent of Antichrist was at hand, and that a chapel of prayer should be built on the site. Some time afterwards one of the children, Lucia dos Santos, revealed that the Virgin's prophecy had referred to Russia:

'I shall come to ask for the consecration of Russia to my Immaculate Heart. If my requests are heard, Russia will be converted, and there will be peace. If not, she will spread her errors through the entire world, provoking wars and persecution of the Church . . . But in the end, my Immaculate Heart will triumph.'[1]

The Marian cult was often associated with anti-Communism, especially during the Spanish Civil War. In 1942 Pius XI initiated the Feast of the Immaculate Heart of Mary. On 13 May 1981 Pope John Paul II, who played a prominent personal role in the downfall of Communism, was struck down by a would-be assassin's bullet in Rome. He prayed to Our Lady of the Rosary, recovered, and joined the pilgrimage to Fatima.[2]

Practising Christians must still wrestle with the mysteries of prophecy. Visions of the Virgin, first recorded with that of Elizabeth of Schonau (1164), have persisted throughout modern times. They include La Salette (1846), Lourdes (1854), Pontmain (1871), Knock in Mayo (1879), Banneux in Belgium (1933), and Medjugorje in Bosnia (1981). The apparitions at Medjugorje, near Mostar, which continued to attract thousands, were not authenticated by the Catholic hierarchy. They were all the more disturbing for seemingly having occurred on the site of wartime massacres, foreshadowing the Bosnian horrors of 1992–3.[3] [BERNADETTE] [MADONNA]

---

from the provinces. Simultaneously the Soviet's key Military-Revolutionary Committee, now under Bolshevik control, was briefed to supply the necessary soldiers, sailors, and armed workers, for purposes which the Soviet itself had not approved. Trotsky took command. [SOVKINO]

On the night of 25 October the plan was activated. Bolshevik pickets surrounded all government buildings. There was no reaction. On the morning of the 26th, at 10 a.m., Lenin issued a press release:

To the Citizens of Russia

The Provisional Government has been deposed. Government authority has passed into the hands of the organ of the Petrograd Soviet . . . the Military-Revolutionary Committee, which stands at the head of the Petrograd proletariat and garrison. The task for which the

SOVKINO

O N 24 October 1917 the cinemas of St Petersburg were showing *The Silent Ornaments of Life*—a psychological drama centring on the complex relations of a Prince Obolensky with the gentle Claudia and the scheming Nelly. The very next day power was seized by the Bolsheviks. They had a very different, and very definite, view of cinematic art. 'Of all the arts,' wrote Lenin, 'for us the cinema is the most important.' Cinema was an instrument not to entertain but to propagandize the masses. In 1919, therefore, Lenin signed a decree transferring the photographic and cinematographic industry to the People's Commissariat for Education. In due course a 'Society of Friends of the Soviet Cinema' was founded by none other than Felix Dzierzhynski, head of the political police.[1]

Russian cinema had made its debut shortly after silent movies were launched by Louis Lumière in the Grand Café in Paris on 28 December 1895. There were Russian film directors, Russian newsreels, Russian film studios, and Russian film stars, such as the super-cool Vera Kholodnaya. The first Russian feature film was an historical drama, Drankov's *Sten'ka Razin* (1908). After the February Revolution 1917 there was a brief flutter of sensational films about contemporary politics, such as *Grisha Rasputin's Amorous Escapades*. Under the Bolsheviks, all such frivolity was to cease.

The Bolsheviks made no secret of their plans for turning cinema into an arm of the Party. In order to do so, they first had to destroy the existing institutions. In *Kino-Fot* (1922), the poet Mayakovsky wrote lines as if by order of the agitprop department:

> For you, a cinema spectacle
> For me, almost a *Weltanschauung*!
> The cinema—purveyor of movement
> The cinema—renewer of literature
> The cinema—destroyer of aesthetics
> The cinema—fearlessness
> The cinema—a sportsman
> The cinema—a sower of ideas.
> But the cinema is sick. Capitalism has covered
>   its eyes with gold . . .
> Communism must rescue the cinema from
>   speculators.[2]

After years of chaos, the State Cinema Board, Sovkino, did not really begin to operate until the mid 1920s. Even then, it was not the expected success until subordinated to thoroughgoing Stalinist planning in the 1930s.

Much of Soviet cinema history was taken up either by socialist realism or by the heroics of the Second World War. But there were shafts of light amidst the gloom—one of them connected with the brilliant productions of 'The Thaw' in the 1960s, when Bondarchuk's *War and Peace* or Kalatozov's *The Cranes are Flying* were released, others with directors of genius, notably Eisenstein.

Sergei Eisenstein (1898–1948), son of the chief architect of Riga, belonged to that part of gilded Tsarist youth who threw in their lot with the Bolsheviks. Apart from his technical brilliance, he had a clear idea of his objectives, the most important of which was to convey the irresistible tide of history. He completed only six films; in every one, the human collective is to the fore.

In his first film, *Strike* (1925), Eisenstein portrayed the passion of a work-force as it awakes to its own sense of power. He also caricatured the bosses in the manner of 'Krokodil'. In *Battleship Potemkin* (1926), which embellished a true incident from the 1905 Revolution, he concentrated on the emotions of the ship's crew and the oppressions of the common people. The tableau of the Odessa Steps, where a regiment of Cossacks slaughter innocent protesters, must be one of the most famous set-pieces in cinema history. In *October* (1927) he celebrated the tenth anniversary of the Bolshevik coup, once again by highlighting the role of the masses in such inspiring (but imaginary) scenes as the storming of the Winter Palace (see p. 920). In *Old and New* (1929) he examined the communal life of the peasantry.

When Eisenstein returned to Russia after several years abroad, he addressed more distant history. His *Alexander Nevsky* (1938) was a prophetic study of the coming conflict with Germany. The tableau of the medieval battle on the ice, where grotesque Teutonic Knights drown *en masse* from the weight of their own armour, was an uncanny allegory of Stalingrad, five years before the event. To have directed a film of *Ivan the Terrible* (1945) while Stalin was still alive and watching—he was an eager movie buff—was a measure of Eisenstein's unrivalled standing.

Eisenstein's films prove that great art is not incompatible with overt propaganda. Indeed, as with religious art, when the message is unambiguous, the audience can concentrate on the skill by which it is being conveyed. At the Brussels Film Festival of 1958, *Battleship Potemkin* was voted No. 1 on the list of the world's twelve best films. [**POTEMKIN**]

---

people have been struggling has been assured—the immediate offer of a democratic peace, the abolition of the landed property of the landlords, worker control over production, and the creation of a Soviet Government. Long live the Revolution of Workers, Soldiers and Peasants![6]

Practically every word in the declaration was false or misleading. But it made no difference. As Lenin and Trotsky had correctly calculated, there was no one in the capital with the will to oppose them. The government ministers still huddled in the Winter Palace, waiting for a rescue that would never come. The imperial army was nowhere in sight. At 9 p.m. Bolshevik sailors on the cruiser *Aurora* fired one blank salvo at the Winter Palace. Some 30 shells were fired from the Peter and Paul Fortress, of which two found their target around 11 p.m. Most of the government guards just left; the mob moved in when they saw that no resistance was offered. The 'storming of the Winter Palace' was a later fiction. At 2.30 a.m. the Ministers surrendered. That was the moment when the Bolsheviks seized power in Petrograd. They did not intend to stop there. At a brief appearance that morning at the Congress of Soviets, Lenin hailed 'the worldwide socialist revolution'. It was nothing of the sort. It was not even a rising of the Petrograd socialists. In the original draft of the declaration of the 26th, Lenin had ended with the slogan 'Long Live Socialism'. But he crossed it out.

This is not to deny that Lenin and his Bolsheviks were revolutionaries of a most thoroughgoing kind. Once in power, they set about tearing up the old Russia root and branch. Under Lenin in 1917–21, and even more under Stalin from 1929 onwards, they reconstructed almost every aspect of Russian life. But they did it by coercion from above; and in defiance of Russia's mainstream radical and socialist movements. Their methods had little in common with the spontaneous revolution from below which filled their textbooks.

Bolshevik actions in the immediate aftermath of the coup were summarized in the three famous 'decrees' which Lenin submitted to the Congress of Soviets in the evening of 26 October. None of them was quite what they purported to be. The Decree on Peace was, in effect, a private appeal to the Powers to accept a three-month armistice. The Decree on Land ordered the transfer of private landed property to the village communes. It had been lifted from the programme of the SRs, and was entirely inconsistent with the previous (and later) Bolshevik line, which supported the transfer of land to state ownership. The Decree on Government, which created the *Sovnarkom* or 'Council of People's Commissars', chaired by Lenin, was proclaimed subject to approval by the future Constituent Assembly. On each and every score, Lenin was indulging in sophistry. The international peace, which was realized by the December armistice and by the Treaty of Brest-Litovsk with Germany on 3 March 1918, was used for launching all-out war on the Bolsheviks' opponents at home. The granting of land to the peasants was a well-timed tactic that calmed the rage of Russia's most numerous class at a critical moment. It would soon be followed by an all-out 'War on the Village', when the Bolsheviks enforced their state monopoly over prices and the food trade.

The gesture to the Constituent Assembly was pure opportunism. The Bolsheviks let the country-wide elections for the Assembly proceed, as envisaged by the Provisional Government. The elections duly took place in the second half of November; and Bolshevik candidates polled 24 per cent of the vote. In this, the one and only free election in Soviet history, a clear victory went to the SRs, who took 40.4 per cent. But no such detail was going to deter Lenin. He allowed the Constituent Assembly to meet on 5 January 1918, then simply closed it down.

Between 3 and 4 a.m. on the 6th, the Chairman of the Assembly and leader of the SRs, Victor Chernov (1873–1952), was trying to pass a law for the abolition of landed property when he was tapped on the shoulder by a sailor, the commander of the Bolshevik Guard. 'I have been instructed to inform you that all those present should leave the Assembly Hall,' the sailor announced, 'because the guard is tired.'[7] From that point on, Russia was condemned to a conflict in which more Russians would die than on the Eastern Front (see Appendix III, p. 1320).

The final year of the Great War, 1918, opened with the Central Powers planning a war-winning offensive, and ended with them in full retreat. The Eastern Front had been closed down; and the mountainous Italian Front was deadlocked. So everything turned on the Western Front. From March to July, the German command poured in their remaining reserves. They were not unsuccessful. On the British sector, they pushed forward some 35 miles south of Amiens. In the centre, they advanced once more to the Marne. But they broke neither the line nor the will of the Allies. In July, at the second Battle of the Marne, Pétain's 'elastic defence' showed that the attackers did not possess the critical mass of offensive superiority. Then, on 8 August, on 'the Black Friday of the German Army', 456 British tanks surged through the line, winning back 8 of the lost 35 miles in one day. One week later, the German and Austrian emperors were told by their generals that the war must be ended. In September and October, in the eastern sector, American strength could at last make itself felt, first at Saint-Mihiel, where the largest salient of the Front was eliminated, and later in the Argonne. The German line never broke; the Germans did not feel defeated. But on 3 October they were sufficiently hard pressed to convey the offer of an armistice to President Wilson. [HATRED]

October 1918 was a remarkable month. The smell of peace did more to destroy the Central Powers than four years of fighting had done. The news from the minor fronts was bad. An Allied attack in Macedonia had succeeded, and Bulgaria had just collapsed. In Palestine, the British had finally achieved a competent battlefield victory at Megiddo near Mt Carmel; and the Ottomans were suing for peace. In Italy, after a last abortive push on the Piave, the Austro-Hungarian army had ceased to struggle. Everyone in Europe knew that the advantage lay with the *Entente*, that peace feelers were out, that further resistance would only prolong the agony. Whenever they could, the troops took matters into their own hands. The idle German and Austrian garrisons in the East were riddled with *Soldaten-räte* mimicking the Russian soviets. The Austrian army fell apart through the desertion of Czech, Polish, Croat, Hungarian, and indeed German regiments, who simply decided to go home. Everyone was claiming their national independence. On 20 October, when a German-Austrian assembly was convened in Vienna to prepare an Austrian Republic, the game was obviously up. The Emperor Charles, and 500 years of Habsburg rule, became irrelevant overnight. Proclamations of independence were issued by several hitherto unknown states: Czechoslovakia (28 October), Yugoslavia (29 October), Hungary (1 November), and, in Lemberg, the West Ukrainian Republic (1 November). [ŁYCZAKÓW]

HATRED

O N 3 August 1918 the Archbishop of Canterbury, Randall Davidson, preached at St Margaret's, Westminster, before King and Queen, ministers, and both Houses of Parliament. Many in the congregation would have known that the Archbishop had repeatedly protested in private about the morality of the Government's wartime policy. Many must have been discomfited by what he now said in public. 'There is a form of wrath which may degenerate into a poisonous hatred running right counter to the principles of a Christian's creed,' he said in his soft Scot's voice. 'As pledged disciples of a living Lord and Master who died upon the Cross for all who hated Him, we have to see to it that the spirit of hate finds no nurture in our hearts.'[1] At his side, the Archbishop's chaplain and his later biographer, was Revd George Bell (1883–1958), the future Bishop of Chichester. Given the lead, the chaplain was to blossom into Protestant Europe's leading exponent of 'Christian Internationalism'.[2]

Bishop Bell was an unlikely internationalist. He spoke no word of a foreign language. But he possessed a firm command of Christian principles, and the courage to express them. In the post-war years he came under the close influence of Archbishop Nathan Söderblom of Uppsala, a Swedish Lutheran who had once been professor at Leipzig. In 1919 he attended the Wassenaar conference in Holland, which discussed war guilt; and in 1925, he helped organize the Stockholm conference on Christian 'Life and Work', which sowed the seed of the later World Council of Churches.

In the early 1930s, as chairman of the Universal Christian Council for Life and Work (UCCLW), Bell was faced with the problem of German churches under pressure from the Nazis. In 1935 he insisted on a public resolution of protest; wrote a strong letter to Reichbishop Muller on behalf of the 'Confessing Church', and received an indignant von Ribbentrop in person at Chichester. Bell's meetings of the UCCLW at Novi Sad (1933) and Fano (1934) paved the way for the Oxford conference of 1937, which united several ecumenical groups and, recognizing the totalitarian challenge of both Nazism and Communism, saw the start of the Oxford Group for Moral Rearmament.

As war loomed, Bishop Bell fearlessly spoke his mind. In June 1939, at Oxford University, he spoke on 'God above Nation', denouncing the 'flagrant' insistence on state sovereignty and 'the havoc wrought by collective egoism'.[3] In November, he published 'The Church's Function in Wartime':

The Church fails to be the Church if it forgets that its members in one nation have a fellowship with its members in every nation. [The Church] must . . . condemn the infliction of reprisals or the bombing by the military forces of its own nation. It should set itself against the propaganda of lies and hatred. It should be ready to encourage a resumption of friendly relations with the enemy nation. It should set its face against any war of extermination or enslavement, and any measures directly aimed at destroying the morale of a population . . .[4]

These principles were not popular, not least with HM Government or with his diocesan congregation. But they were followed up by speeches in the House of Lords against the Internment of Aliens (August 1940), against 'obliteration bombing' (9 February 1944), and against the use of the atomic bomb. [**ALTMARKT**] On the Allied Bombing Offensive, he used no euphemisms:

It is no longer defence, military and industrial objectives which are the aim of the bombers. But the whole town . . . is blotted out. How can there be discrimination in such matters when civilians, monuments, military and industrial objects all together form the target?[5]

In July 1942 the Bishop undertook a dangerous flight to Stockholm to meet members of the Christian resistance from Germany. His appeal to the allied powers on their behalf was to be rejected. But it was to George Bell that Pastor Bonhoffer would smuggle out his last message from his death-cell in a Nazi prison. 'Tell him', it read, 'that . . . with him I believe in the principle of our universal Christian brotherhood, and that our victory is certain.'[6]

'Christian Europe' was always uppermost in Bell's thoughts on the future. Of the authors of the bombing offensive he had asked: 'Are they [alive] to the harvest they are laying up for the future relationships of the peoples of Europe?' In a post-war broadcast to Germany in 1945, he appealed to 'the spirit of Europe':

Today, one of the principal goals . . . should be the recovery of Christendom. We want to see Europe as Christendom . . . No nation, no church, no individual is guiltless. Without repentance, and without forgiveness, there can be no regeneration.[7]

These ideas held the foreground in the early phase of the post-war European movement before it was hijacked by economists (see pp. 1064–6). George Bell played a proper and prominent part in the founding of the World Council of Churches, which took place in the Concertgebouw in Amsterdam on 22 August 1948—almost exactly thirty years after Archbishop Davidson's Westminster sermon.

ŁYCZAKÓW

O N 24 November 1918 three young people were buried in a special military sector of the Catholic cemetery at Łyczaków in the suburbs of Lwów (L'viv). Zygmunt Menzel, aged 23, Jozef Kurdyban, aged 19, and Felicja Sulimirska, aged 21, had all been killed in fighting between Poles and Ukrainians for the former capital of Austrian Galicia. It was the first of several thousand burials which brought the bodies of the Polish dead from temporary graves in parks and squares, and the starting-point for the 'Cemetery of the Defenders of Lwów', the *Campo Santo* of the 'Young Eagles'.[1] The grave of the youngest would be that of Antoś Petrykiewicz, killed in action, aged 13.

Like any of the great urban cemeteries of nineteenth-century Europe, Łyczaków was already a remarkable historical and artistic repository. Like Père Lachaise in Paris or Highgate in London, its sylvan setting guarded the ornate mausolea of the families who had enlivened the growth of a major city. Two separate plots contained rows of simple crosses marking the graves of soldiers from the Polish risings of 1830 and 1863.

The military cemetery at Łyczaków had its counterparts in hundreds of locations after the Great War, especially in Belgium and northern France. Constructed in 1919–34, in the period of Polish rule, it was dominated by an elevated *arc de triomphe* flanked by stone lions and a semicircular colonnade. The central arch was surmounted by the inscription MORTUI SUNT UT LIBERI VIVAMUS (they died so that we might live free); the lions held shields carrying the city's motto, SEMPER FIDELIS (always faithful) and TOBIE POLSKO (To Thee, Poland). Behind the graves stood an arcaded crypt flanked by steps leading to a rotunda chapel. The ensemble was decorated by evergreen shrubbery and lit by bronze lampstands. Individual monuments were raised in memory of the Posnanian volunteers, the French infantry, and American pilots who lost their lives defending the city against the Bolsheviks in 1919–20. [**DOUAUMONT**] [**LANGEMARCK**]

If the origins of Łyczaków were unremarkable, its fate was not. In the years of Soviet annexation after 1945, the cemetery was vandalized and devastated. The crosses were uprooted, the inscriptions profaned, the monuments defaced, the chapel turned into a stonemason's workshop. Guarded by fierce dogs, the overgrown site could only be visited at the risk of arrest. Its decline was documented in secret; visitors were not supposed to look beyond the vast Soviet War Memorial built alongside. Restoration work, at the request of the Warsaw government, did not begin until 1989.

In Western Europe, existing cemeteries generally survived the Second World War intact. Yet all over Eastern Europe, German, Jewish, Polish, Lithuanian, and Ukrainian cemeteries fell under the Communist campaign of oblivion. They were an obstacle to the rewriting of history. In the struggles of 1918–19, the defeated Ukrainians suffered similar casualties to those of their Polish foes. Yet the Ukrainian military cemetery in Lwów was honoured and tended throughout the years of Polish rule. Under Soviet rule, it was obliterated.

In 1991, as the chief metropolis of western Ukraine, L'viv became the second city of the independent Ukrainian Republic. The defeated dreams of 1918–19 were revived. The hopes of the young Poles buried at Łyczaków were finally dashed. [**ELSASS**]

The peace disease spread rapidly into Germany; and demands for peace turned rapidly into demands for the head of the Kaiser. The imperial fleet mutinied in port at Wilhelmshaven. Socialist revolution broke out in Munich on 7 November, and in Berlin on the 9th, when the formation of a German Republic was proclaimed. On the 10th, having abdicated some days previously, Kaiser Wilhelm and the Crown Prince departed for exile in the Netherlands. In their very last throw, German military intelligence released their most dangerous Polish prisoner, Joseph Piłsudski, and put him on a train to Warsaw. He arrived on the morning of the 11th, supervised the disarming of the German garrison, and, to the chagrin of the Western Allies, took over the reins of an independent Poland.

In the end, therefore, like Russia the Central Powers were brought down more by political collapse than by outright military defeat. The German army, victorious in the East, was still intact in the West; it was never driven back onto German territory. But it had parted company with the political authorities that gave it orders. Armistice negotiations took place from 8 November onwards at Réthondes-sur-Aisne, near Soissons. Agreement was soon reached on the basis of Wilson's 14 points plus 18 extra Allied demands. The latter concerned the evacuation of occupied territory, the creation of a neutral zone in the Rhineland, the surrender of Germany's fleet, heavy armament, and transport, the payment of reparations, and the annulment of the treaties of Brest-Litovsk and Bucharest. The Allies were insisting on capitulation terms so severe that they could dictate the terms of peace. The agreement was signed in a parked railway carriage at 3 a.m. on the 11th, to come into force six hours later. The guns fell silent at the eleventh hour of the eleventh day of the eleventh month.

Over 10 million soldiers were dead—overwhelmingly, young married men or bachelors (see Appendix III, pp. 1328–9). Casualty rates were specially high among junior officers. They were called the 'lost generation', *les sacrifiés*. The burden of their war service, of their loss, and of their injuries had to be borne by their families, especially by the womenfolk. Women during the war had been conscripted into jobs left vacant by the soldiers. They worked in the munitions factories, in offices, and in many occupations previously closed to them—as tram-drivers, managers, or journalists. For many girls this opened the road to social liberation, as symbolized by the fashion for short, 'bobbed' hair and for smoking in public.

In the industrialized countries at least, European women moved out of the protective custody of their homes and families as never before. The change was reflected in the widespread advance of women's suffrage. But the social and psychological cost was enormous. The lost generation of young men was matched by an abandoned generation of young widows and lonely spinsters, whose life-chance of a partner had disappeared with their loved ones in the mud of the trenches. The demographic damage, and the imbalance of the sexes, was to have lasting effects.

Statistics are not so comprehensible as the experience of individual families. On 5 September 1918, Second Lieutenant Norman Davies, aged 18, of Bolton, Lancashire, and of 11 Wing, 48 Fighter Squadron RAF, crashed in practice in a Bristol fighter near Saint-Omer, on his second day in France. His CO's report showed greater concern for the loss of the machine than for that of the pilot.[8] On 11 November 1918 the Bolton family, also of Bolton, celebrated the end of the war. On the 12th they received the 'King's telegram' announcing, with regret, that their eldest son, Private James Bolton, aged 19, of 11 Battalion, East Lancashire Regiment, had died several minutes before the Armistice. Millions of French, German, Italian, Austrian, and Russian families suffered in the same way.

Europe was full of war refugees—principally from Belgium, from Galicia, and from Serbia. On top of that came the biggest pandemic visited on Europe since the Black Death. The 'Spanish flu' killed more Europeans than the War did, including Private Bolton. [**EPIDEMIA**] Europe became the subject of a vast external relief effort. The International Red Cross and the American Relief Administration faced a task, especially in Eastern Europe, of unprecedented proportions.

To say that Europe was at peace, however, was an exaggeration. Western Europe had won some respite; but there were huge areas of Central and Eastern Europe where all established order had broken down. A score of independent states had been born, every one at odds with its neighbours (see Map 25). The largest of them, Soviet Russia, was at war with most of its citizens and with all of its neighbours, and was acting as the *provocateur* to all sorts of revolutionary events elsewhere. Thus, while the victorious allies strove to make peace where they could, much of the Continent continued to be engulfed in raging conflict. 'The War of the Giants has ended,' wrote Churchill, 'the wars of the pygmies begin.' Geopolitically, the Great Triangle had been flattened to the point where only the Western Powers remained intact. Russia had been knocked out by the Central Powers, and the Central Powers by the West. Yet Russia and Germany were both breathing; unlike Austria-Hungary and the Ottoman Empire, they were not total casualties. In November 1918 the Western Powers were granted no more than a breathing-space within which a stable European order might be built 'whilst Russia and Germany slept'. Unfortunately, the peace-making efforts of the Western Powers were seriously flawed from the start.

The Peace Conference, which deliberated in Paris throughout 1919, was organized as a congress of victors, not as a general assembly of the European states. Neither Soviet Russia nor the German Republic was represented; and the other successor states were only admitted in their capacity as clients and petitioners. All the major decisions were taken by the Council of Ten, its successor, the Council of Four— Clemenceau, Lloyd George, Wilson, and sometimes Orlando of Italy—or, from January 1920, by the standing Conference of (Allied) Ambassadors. This in itself was sufficient to create the impression of a *Diktat* or 'imposed settlement'. Despite the high-flown pretensions of the organizers, the Peace Conference did not take responsibility for many of Europe's most urgent problems. It confined itself to the task of preparing treaties for signature by the ex-enemy states. Its reluctance to recognize the disintegration of the Russian Empire, whose interests it sought 'to hold in trust', had specially baleful consequences. The half-baked policy of Allied Intervention in Russia, which was half-heartedly pursued with half-measures throughout 1919, played straight into the hands of the Bolsheviks (see pp. 931–2 below).

Although the Wilsonian ideal of national self-determination was widely endorsed, it was not applied either consistently or fairly. The victorious Allies saw no reason to discuss the aspirations of their own subject nationalities, such as the Irish, still less the wishes of colonial peoples. They encouraged far-reaching territorial changes at the expense of their ex-enemies, whilst discouraging demands at the expense of their own side. The Czechs, for example, whose demands encroached on Austria and Hungary, were fully supported in their claims to the medieval 'lands of St Wenceslas' (see Appendix III, p. 1317). The Poles, whose demand for the restoration of the frontiers of 1772 was incompatible with the restoration of the Russian Empire, were roundly condemned for 'small-power imperialism'. For every satisfied customer there were two or three disgruntled ones.

The Western Powers showed little sense of solidarity among themselves. The Americans suspected the British and French of imperialist designs. The British suspected the French of Napoleonic tendencies. Both the British and the French suspected the strength of America's commitment. Their fears were amply confirmed when the US Congress failed to ratify both the Treaty of Versailles with Germany and American membership of Wilson's pet project, the League of Nations (see below). Allied diplomacy greatly underestimated the problem of enforcement. It was one thing for the politicians to make grand decisions in Paris. It was quite another for the decisions to be upheld in distant parts of Europe where the Western Powers had little influence and no control. Assorted inter-Allied Commissions gave temporary relief to assorted trouble-spots. But the League of Nations was born toothless. The USA turned its back on the settlement; the British demobilized; France shrank from policing the Continent single-handed. It was only a matter of time before those offended by the settlement began to guess that they might challenge it with impunity.

Of course, the Peace Conference worked its way through an astonishing amount of business. Five major treaties were put into effect. A dozen new states were given international recognition. A score of territorial awards were made. A batch of plebiscites were organized and administered. Much of Europe was given a basis for the new start which so many desired. Nor is it fair to say that the

spirit of vengeance reigned supreme. As the Conference progressed, the tone softened. Lloyd George, the most flexible of the 'Big Three', arrived in January amidst
cries of 'Hang the Kaiser!' but later took the lead in seeking the road of accommodation. The creation of the Free City of Danzig, for which he received no
thanks, was an example of his moderating influence. There is no denying the vin-
dictiveness which underlay the war guilt clauses, the principle of reparations,
which set out to bill Germany for the entire cost of the war, and the one-sided
plans for disarmament. At the same time, despite Clemenceau's intransigence,
there was a growing sense that Allied demands must be tailored to the limits of
German tolerance. [**SLESVIG**]

Yet the resultant international climate was far from healthy. The mix of
vengeance and cynicism portrayed by the victorious Allies did not augur well.
Eastern Europe, the original source of conflict, was still unregulated. No sooner
was the ink of the treaties dry than all sorts of people set out to revise them.

Most of the wars which erupted in 1918–21 were fuelled by disputes of a purely
local nature. Whole encyclopaedias have been filled with the rights and wrongs of
obscure localities which made the news, from Allenstein to Zips. Yet four of the
wars had wider implications. These were Russian Civil War, the Hungarian Civil
War, the Polish–Soviet War, and the Graeco-Turkish War. On each occasion, the
inability of the Western Powers to exercise a benign influence on the Eastern part
of Europe was amply demonstrated.

The 'Russian Civil War' of 1918–21 is arguably the victim of a misnomer. In reality, it was a series of civil wars and a series of international wars all rolled into one.
It consisted of two main strands. One strand centred on a contest for control of
the central Russian government, and was fought out between the Bolshevik 'Reds'
and an assortment of their 'White' challengers. All the participants in this part of
the proceedings aspired to the reconstitution of the Russian Empire in one form
or another. A second strand involved a succession of conflicts between Reds or
Whites on the one side and the independent republics of the former tsarist borderlands on the other. All the republics were fighting for the preservation of their
new-found sovereignty. But that was not all. The Reds fielded local formations in
each of the republics in addition to the central reserves based in Moscow. The
Whites, too, fielded several separate armies. Numerous foreign forces intervened.
The governments of the national republics were frequently confronted by local
rivals; and there were a number of 'loose cannon', such as the Czech Legion of ex-
prisoners of war who in 1918 seized the Trans-Siberian Railway. As a result, the
mêlée in most areas took the form of a multi-sided free-for-all. [**B.N.R.**]

In Ukraine, for example, which constituted one of the most valuable prizes,
eleven armies took to the field. The forces of the Ukrainian Republic, which was
formed in January 1918, were divided between supporters of the initial *Rada* or
'National Council' and those of the subsequent Directory. The German army of
occupation on the Eastern Front had stayed on until February 1919 in order to

give aid to Ukraine's independence. The 'Red Army' of Ukraine had strong backing among Russian workers in the Donbass region, and was supplemented by units from the central Bolshevik command in Moscow. General Denikin's 'Russian Volunteer Army', backed by a French force, landed in Odessa; its successor, Baron Wrangel's 'White Army', camped in Crimea. Piłsudski's Polish army defeated the forces of the West Ukrainian Republic in early 1919, before advancing on Kiev in April 1920 in alliance with the Ukrainian Directory. The peasant guerrillas of the anarchist, Nestor Makhno, took over a broad region of central Ukraine. The Ukrainian capital, Kiev, changed hands fifteen times in two years. To reduce such a kaleidoscope to the binary struggle of Reds versus Whites is simplification pushed to absurdity (see Appendix III, p. 1315).

The course of events was no less complicated than the *ordre de bataille*. But seen from the Bolsheviks' point of view in the centre, there were two successive phases, each with its own priorities. The first phase, which occupied the whole of 1918 and 1919, saw the Whites advance on Soviet Russia from all sides—General Yudenich from the West in Estonia, Admiral Kolchak from the East in Siberia, General Denikin from the South in Ukraine. The Bolsheviks were desperately strained to hold the Muscovite heartland and to repel each advancing army in turn. The second phase, which began in the winter of 1919–20, saw the 'Red Army' take the offensive, pursuing each of the retreating Whites before moving on to crush each of the national republics in turn.

The critical moment occurred in November 1919, when Denikin had reached Tula, only 100 miles south of Moscow, and the Poles stood not much further away, to the west near Smolensk. One concerted push might well have spelled the end of the Bolshevik regime. But Piłsudski's emissaries received no satisfactory answer about Denikin's attitude to the independence of Poland. So the Poles stood still, and began to negotiate with Lenin. Denikin hesitated fatally, until swept from his positions by the Red cavalry, hotfoot from their victory at the siege of Tsaritsyn. In his memoirs, Denikin was to blame Piłsudski for the Bolsheviks' final victory.[9]

After that, having secured the centre, numerous Red armies fanned out in all directions, carrying all before them. Their reconquest of the republics in the European part of the former Empire reached its term in 1921, when a Bolshevik force overthrew the Menshevik regime in Georgia (see Appendix III, p. 1314).

The Bolsheviks' victory, which confounded the military experts, must be attributed to the divisions of their enemies, to the talents of Leon Trotsky, Commissar for War and the 'Russian Carnot', to the strategic advantage of internal lines of communication, and to the utterly ruthless measures of their 'war communism'. The Bolshevik regime was unwelcome to all the major classes of Russian society, including the peasants, to all the major groupings of the political spectrum from reactionary monarchists to liberals and socialists, and to all the non-Russian nationalities. But the outbreak of civil war—which Lenin himself provoked—provided the pretext for suspending all existing institutions and for wiping out all social and political opposition. The *Cheká* or 'Extraordinary Commission' of

SLESVIG

O N 10 July 1920, King Christian X rode on a white horse across the Danish frontier to reclaim the district of *Sónderjylland* ('South Jutland' or 'North Schleswig'), which had recently been awarded to Denmark by popular plebiscite.[1] Thus ended one of the most bitter and protracted territorial disputes of modern Europe.

The neighbouring provinces of Schleswig and Holstein, situated at the base of the Jutland peninsula, had long formed the borderlands between Germany and Denmark. Historically, Schleswig—or 'Slesvig' in Danish—had been a Danish fief whilst Holstein had belonged to the Holy Roman Empire. The ancient 'Eider Stone' embedded in the city gate at Rensburg marks the Empire's traditional frontier. Although the population was ethnically mixed, Danish-speakers predominated in the north and German-speakers in the centre and south. (See Appendix III, p. 1305.)

The 'Schleswig-Holstein Question' had first raised its head in 1806, when the French awarded both provinces to Denmark. The award was confirmed by the Congress of Vienna, but was subsequently rendered ambiguous when Holstein was declared a member of the German Confederation. It was a recipe for trouble. In an age of growing nationalism, the 'autochthonous Germans of the northern marches' demanded their secession from Denmark. Patriotic 'Danes on the Eider' rallied to resist them. Nationalist claims soon became embroiled with the struggles to establish constitutional government. In 1848 Prussian troops occupied Schleswig-Holstein in response to appeals from the German-dominated provincial assemblies. They were eventually forced to withdraw after both Britain and Russia threatened counter-measures. Prussia had its eyes on the naval port of Kiel.[2]

A further crisis was precipitated in November 1863, when Frederick VII of Denmark died without male heir, having just approved a joint constitution for 'Denmark-Schleswig'. Saxon and Hanoverian troops promptly moved in to secure Holstein. In 1864, amidst growing uproar, Prussia and Austria agreed to take joint action, establishing a six-year period of joint occupation of both provinces for the examination of all problems. These dispositions were overtaken by the Austro-Prussian War of 1866. The Prussians' victory enabled them to take sole control of the occupied lands, and then to annex them outright. Arrangements to hold a plebiscite, and to ease the position of people opting for Danish citizenship, were not honoured.

Danish national pride was greatly aroused by the wars of 1848–51 and 1863–4. The fortifications of the Dannevirke Line had seen heavy fighting; and points of fierce resistance, such as Dybbol Mill, were to become national shrines. Still more persistent were resentments caused by the maltreatment of the Danish 'optants', and by crude policies of germanization pursued, as in Prussian Poland, in the 1880s and 1890s.

The Schleswig plebiscites of 1920 were instigated under Allied auspices in accordance with the Treaty of Versailles. In the northern district, they showed a 92 per cent majority for Denmark; in Flensburg and central Schleswig, a 75 per cent vote for Germany. The agreed frontier has lasted ever since.

Lord Palmerston once said that only three people understood Schleswig-Holstein—'the Prince Consort, who was dead; a German professor, who had gone mad; and himself, who had forgotten all about it'. After 1920, the whole of Europe was free to follow Palmerston's example, though many similarly intractable disputes remained elsewhere. For every territorial conflict settled at that time, several new ones were created.

revolutionary police (forerunner of the OGPU, NKVD, and KGB) was organized by the Polish nobleman Felix Dzierżyński (1877–1926) with a ferocity that made Robespierre look faint-hearted. It struck down all 'class enemies', real or imagined, from the ex-Tsar and his family, murdered on Lenin's orders at Ekaterinburg in July 1918, to unnumbered multitudes of nameless victims. The militarization of all branches of the economy, including labour, transport, and production, enabled the Bolsheviks to take over all enterprises and trade unions, and to shoot all dissenters for 'counter-revolutionary sabotage'. Popular support rarely came into the reckoning, except when the Bolsheviks could appeal to patriotic Russian sentiment against the presence of foreign 'interventionists'. In April 1920, when the Poles helped the Ukrainians to retake Kiev, all ideological pretence was cast aside. Lenin called for the defence of Holy Russia, and Trotsky for the enlistment of all ex-tsarist officers. Extreme necessity was the mother of extreme invention.

Foreign intervention in Russia has been exaggerated. On the face of it, a terrible array of ill-intentioned outsiders had poked their noses into Russia's distress. The regular German army was left over from the World War in the *Oberost*. The volunteer German army of the 'Baltikum' tramped round Latvia and Lithuania, the Polish irregulars of General Bulak-Balakhovich round Byelorussia; regular Polish troops appeared in the *Oberost* as soon as the Germans withdrew. British expeditionary forces landed at Murmansk and at Batum in Georgia; the French occupied Odessa; Americans and Japanese controlled Vladivostok and the Far East. It was an easy trick for Soviet propaganda to turn these foreigners into a concerted conspiracy of evil capitalists, hired to destroy Russia. There was no such conspiracy. The Allied governments were mainly concerned to hold the Russian Empire together; they had nothing to do with the presence of the Germans, and especially of the Poles, who expressly defied Allied advice to stay out. The Allied expeditions were despatched to guard the munitions which had earlier been sent to Russian ports for the benefit of the Provisional Government. Their sympathies undoubtedly lay with their former Russian allies whom the Bolshevik coup had overthrown and who were now begging for help. But they never sent the men or the money to conduct serious military operations. They withdrew when everyone could see that their presence was handing a major propaganda success to the Bolsheviks. By then the damage was done; Soviet history books beat the nationalist drum on this point for decades.

Western history books have their own peculiarities. The collapse of the Russian Empire is rarely discussed along the same lines as the parallel collapse of the Austro-Hungarian or Ottoman Empires. Except for Poland, Finland, and the three Baltic States, which were all recognized by the Peace Conference, the national republics that broke free from Russian control are not given the same status as those which broke away from the Central Powers. Few historians seem to regard Soviet Russia's reconquest of Ukraine or the Caucasus as anything other than an internal 'Russian' event. It is still more unfortunate that the creation of the Soviet Union, which began in December 1922, is often thought to have involved a mere change of name. In this way the lengthy process of decomposition of the Empire, and the five-year labours of the Bolsheviks to replace it, can be passed over in silence. Crucial distinctions between 'Russia', 'the Russian Empire', 'Soviet Russia' (RSFSR), and 'the Soviet Union' (USSR) only entered general discourse when the Bolsheviks' handiwork started to fall apart 70 years later. [**B.N.R.**]

The scale of the Russian Civil War is equally overlooked. Yet if the victims of the fighting, of the White and Red Terrors, and of the terrible Volga Famine are all added together, the total number of deaths would not be lower than the mortality on all fronts of the Great War.[10]

The collapse of the Habsburg Empire was attended by a number of serious conflicts, but none more serious than in Hungary. The Soviet Republic of Hungary lasted for five months, from March to August 1919. Many European communist parties were founded at that time; but Budapest was the only city outside Russia where a communist regime managed to take power for any length of time. The short career of the first 'Hungarian Revolution' is very instructive. It was given its chance when the initial, liberal government of independent Hungary resigned in protest against the punitive nature of the peace settlement. Most Hungarians were appalled by the prospect of losing both Slovakia and Transylvania, which they saw as cradles of their civilization. The communist leader, Béla Kun (1886–?1939), a Jewish ex-prisoner of war freshly returned from Russia, exploited the nationalist fever. The Hungarian communists took power with the support both of the social democrats and the old officer corps, promising to drive the Slovaks and the Romanians from the disputed lands. In June 1919 a Hungarian army actually invaded Slovakia. At the same time a new Constitution was passed by delegates of workers' and soldiers' councils on the Soviet model, and radical reforms were decreed. All industry was nationalized; church property was confiscated; priests and peasants were subjected alike to compulsory labour.

B.N.R.

UNTIL recently, most Western historians were totally unaware of the Byelorussian National Republic (BNR), which was proclaimed in Miensk (Minsk) on 25 March 1918. Indeed, most Westerners were unaware that Byelorussia or *Belarus'* was anything other than a district of Russia.[1] Before 1918, squeezed between Poland and Russia, Belarus' had never known a separate political existence. Once known to the outside world as 'White Ruthenia', it had formed a major part of the Grand Duchy of Lithuania, but had been submerged since the Partitions in the Tsarist Empire where it was renamed 'White Russia' (see pp. 655, 663).

German support during the First World War greatly strengthened the country's separate national consciousness. In 1914–15 Byelorussian schools, bookstores, newspapers, and publishers began to operate in Vilna (Wilno) and Minsk. On 1 January 1916, a decree signed by Field Marshal von Hindenburg recognized Byelorussian as an official language in territories occupied by the German army. In 1916–17 Byelorussian theatres, seminaries, pedagogical institutes, and eventually political parties were free to organize.

The initiative was taken by a democratic socialist grouping, the *Hramada*. A Byelorussian National Congress assembled in Minsk in December 1917, only to be dispersed by the Bolsheviks. But the further advance of German forces in February 1918 expelled the Reds, and enabled the locals to take charge. The BNR, which was pledged to the welfare of all nationalities—Ruthenian, Polish, Jewish, Lithuanian, and Tartar—functioned until the end of the year. It was forcibly suppressed in 1919 by the return of the Red Army, which created first a joint Lithuanian–Byelorussian SSR and then a Byelorussian SSR.

During the Polish–Soviet War of 1919–20 (see pp. 934–7) most of Byelorussia was occupied by the Poles. The Treaty of Riga (1921) partitioned the country without reference to the population's wishes. Under Soviet rule, the eastern sector was subject to repressions whose recipients regard them as 'genocide'.[2] The horrors continued in 1939–45 through Nazi murders and Stalinist deportations. But the memory of the BNR lived on. In 1992, when the Republic of Belarus' was restored, the visiting doyen of the European Parliament expressed the firm conviction that Belarus' had every right to be a candidate for future membership of the European Community.[3] He was rather more sanguine on this point than many of the local population, whose administrative and managerial class had been almost completely sovietized and russified. The appalling modern history of Belarus' had ensured that it was far more dependent on Russia than any of the other ex-Soviet republics.

At this point Hungary awoke to the monster it was feeding. Strikers were met by bullets. Armed peasant risings faced mass executions. A group of dissident officers formed at French-occupied Szeged. They were joined by Nicholas Horthy de Nagybánya (1868–1957), a former Habsburg admiral, and a government was created. The Romanians exploited the situation, and it was a Romanian army that entered Budapest in August and brought the Hungarian Soviet Republic to an end.

The Red Terror was now answered by a White Terror. Indiscriminate vengeance was wreaked on Kun's followers, especially communists and Jews. In 1920 Horthy was declared Regent, and instituted a dictatorship that lasted for 24 years. Two attempts by the ex-Emperor Charles to recover his Hungarian throne were rebuffed, as were attempts by the parliament to shake off military control. Although the 'Fascist' label was not yet used, and may not be entirely appropriate, Admiral Horthy is sometimes counted as 'Europe's first Fascist'. Not for the last time, however, an extreme communist adventure had provoked a strong anti-communist reaction (see Appendix III, p. 1318).[11]

The Polish–Soviet War of 1919–20 had implications for the whole of Europe. Contrary to the Bolshevik version of events, it was *not* organized by the *Entente*; it was *not* part of Allied intervention in Russia; and it did *not* begin with Piłsudski's attack on Kiev in April 1920. Of course, a territorial dispute did exist. But the main source of conflict lay in the Bolsheviks' declared intention of linking their Revolution in Russia with the expected revolution in Germany, and hence of marching through Poland. This course of action was quite explicit in early Bolshevik ideology, and was a necessary step if the Soviet experiment in Russia was to be brought into line with Marxist doctrine.

The Bolsheviks first thought of marching across 'the Red Bridge' to Germany in the winter of 1918–19. At that time they ordered the Red 'western army' to probe the Polish borderlands. However, such were the demands of the civil war that the necessary million-strong strike force could not be assembled until a year later. Trotsky always expressed caution; and despite public utterances about the 'infantile disease of leftism', it was Lenin who became the enthusiast for revolutionary war.[12] Regular fighting between Poles and Soviets began in February 1919, almost by accident, and continued for 20 months. It started when the German army evacuated the intervening area of the *Oberost*. Polish and Soviet forces were drawn into the vacuum from either side. The initial clash took place in Byelorussia at 6 a.m. on the morning of 14 February, when a Polish cavalry patrol disturbed a Bolshevik encampment at breakfast. At the time, Piłsudski was hoping to organize a federation of all the border republics, from Finland to Georgia. His scheme was repeatedly spiked by Poland's dispute with Lithuania. But by August 1919, having taken both Wilno and Minsk, he was standing on Poland's historic frontiers. He was tempted to help Denikin (see above), but in the event opened negotiations with the Bolsheviks.

For the Poles, the problem lay in the discrepancy between Bolshevik slogans and Bolshevik deeds. All the time that Lenin was making extravagant speeches about peace with Poland, the Red Army's strike-force on the Berezina was steadily growing. So the Poles waited. In January 1920 Piłsudski made a foray across the frozen Dvina to confirm the independence of Latvia. Then he received the signal which he most feared: the command of Soviet forces on the Polish front had been given to the most successful Red general, the young Mikhail Tukhachevsky (1893–1937), conqueror of Siberia and theorist of revolutionary warfare. Convinced that the Bolsheviks' long-postponed offensive was about to be launched, Piłsudski patched up a belated alliance with one of the Ukrainian factions and struck the Bolsheviks at their weakest point, in the south. The Poles and Ukrainians marched into Kiev, and were welcomed as liberators. Tukhachevsky's preparations were interrupted. In the West, people who understood neither the politics nor the geography took up the Bolshevik shout of 'Hands off Russia'.

The campaign of 1920 was no border skirmish. It was a vast war of movement, which inspired the young adviser to the French military mission in Warsaw, Col. Charles de Gaulle, to formulate his new ideas on modern warfare. Up to a million men on either side marched the best part of a thousand miles and back in six months. The arrival of the Red cavalry drove the Poles out of Ukraine in May–June. Their commander boasted of 'clattering through the streets of Paris before the summer is out'. On 4 July Tukhachevsky finally launched his offensive with the order: 'To the West! Over the corpse of White Poland lies the road to world-wide conflagration.' The speed of his advance was phenomenal. In mid-August his cavalry reached the bend of the Vistula near Thorn, only five days' march from Berlin. Dzierżyński stood by in the rear, ready to assume power in Poland with a 'Polish Revolutionary Committee'. Lenin cabled him to shoot more landlords. In Warsaw the papal legate, the future Pius XI, prepared to brave the hordes of Antichrist in person. Volunteers, including many Jews, flocked to defend their homeland. The Western governments despatched several generals, but no reinforcements. [**KONARMYA**]

The 'Miracle on the Vistula' occurred on 15–16 August. Piłsudski had secretly prepared a counter-attack from the southern flank. Tukhachevsky had failed to protect his extended lines of communication. When Piłsudski struck, five Soviet armies were decapitated. Three of them were annihilated; another took refuge in East Prussia. The rout was complete. On 31 August in the south, in the 'Zamosc Ring', the Red cavalry finally met its match. In the last great cavalry battle of European history, 20,000 horsemen charged and counter-charged in full formation, until the Polish uhlans carried the day. The Red Army had lost its first war. Lenin sued for peace. An armistice was signed on 10 October, the Treaty of Riga on 18 March 1921.

The wider significance of the Polish victory has not always been appreciated. Poland's independence was secured, and with it the Versailles settlement. The British Ambassador to Berlin, who had viewed some of the action near Warsaw from his Rolls-Royce coupé, summed it up in Gibbonian tones:

KONARMYA

IN the summer of 1920 Izaak Babel' (1894–1941) was serving on the Polish front as a war correspondent of Yug-ROSTA, the South Russian Press Agency. He was attached to Budyonny's 1st Red Cavalry Army, whose political commissar was J. V. Stalin (see p. 959). He later wrote up his experiences in *Konarmiya* (Red Cavalry, 1926), a masterful collection of short stories which throb with the immediacy of historical realism:

Crossing the River Zbrucz

The Divisional Commander reported that Novograd-Volhinsk had been captured at dawn. The Staff advanced from Krapivno, and the noisy rearguard of our train was stretched out all along the eternal road which Nicholas I once built from Brest to Warsaw on the bones of peasants . . .[1]

In this, the first paragraph of the first story, the reader might be forgiven for imagining that real events were being reported as they really happened.

Anyone familiar with the Polish–Soviet war, however, must soon smell a rat. There was a town called Novograd-Volhinsk, of course. In 1920 it was the headquarters of Semeon Petlura's Ukrainian Directory. Yet it lies not on the Zbrucz but on the Slucz; and it was captured not by the 1st Cavalry but by the Soviet 14th Army. There was indeed a high-road from Warsaw to Brest built by serfs under Nicholas I. But it lay 200 miles beyond Novograd, and could not possibly have been cluttered by the rearguard. . . .

Numerous such examples show that Babel' was not simply making mistakes. He was deliberately jumbling dates, names, places, and events in order to create a precisely calculated effect. He was engaged in a form of literary collage, whose appearance is often more 'historical' than history itself. 'He is quite content to burgle history, so long as the resulting haul is artistically satisfying.' The same can be said for his cult of violence. *Red Cavalry* is written in a special brand of 'faction', which is not historically accurate.[2]

Yet, taken in isolation, many of the facts can be verified. In *Squadron Leader Trunov* Babel' tells the story of a macho Cossack commander who went out one day to shoot down one of the American volunteer pilots who were fighting for the Poles. The memoirs of the American 'Kościuszko Squadron', under Col. Cedric E. Fauntleroy, agree exactly with Babel''s account. They relate how a foolhardy Soviet machine-gunner kept firing at the American planes from an unprotected clearing, and how one of them peeled off, executed a low-level run, and shot him to pieces.[3]

In the long run, Babel' fared no better. The author who perhaps did most to spread the fame of the Red Army died in Stalin's Gulag.

If Charles Martel had not checked the Saracen conquest at Tours . . . the Koran would now be taught at the schools of Oxford. . . . Had Piłsudski and Weygand failed to arrest the triumphant march of the Soviet Army at the Battle of Warsaw, not only would Christianity have experienced a dangerous reverse, but the very existence of western civilisation would have been imperilled.[13]

Yet the impact on the Bolsheviks was equally great. The defeat of 1920 killed their strategic hopes of linking up with a revolutionary Germany. They were forced to retreat from internationalism. Soviet Russia had no option but to turn itself into the base for what Stalin was soon to call 'socialism in one country'. Lenin retreated quickly from his leftist fervour. War communism was abandoned. In the same week in March 1921 that peace was signed with Poland, Lenin introduced his tactical compromise with capitalism—the New Economic Policy, known as NEP.

What is more, once Byelorussia and Ukraine were partitioned with Poland, the Bolsheviks were free to reorganize their state on federal lines. The formation of the USSR—which consisted initially of Soviet Russia, Soviet Byelorussia, Soviet Ukraine, and the Soviet Caucasus—could not have been undertaken until the Polish war had settled the fate of the borderlands. In reality, the Poles had won no more than a breathing-space: the Soviets' advance into Europe had been repulsed, but not abandoned (see Appendix III, p. 1316).

The final collapse of the Ottoman Empire can hardly have come as a surprise. Yet the Western Powers held no contingency plans. They had once thought of installing their Russian allies on the Straits; but they were not going to grant such a favour to the Bolsheviks. So Greece, with Allied approval, moved into a vacuum.

In August 1920 the Treaty of Sèvres was signed by a rump Ottoman government with little authority. An Allied fleet held Istanbul. The Italians occupied the southern coast; the French, Cilicia; separatist Kurds and Armenians held large regions in the east. The Greeks held both Thrace and Smyrna (İzmir). They had long memories of Constantinople, torn from Christendom in 1453; and they had genuine fears about the large Greek population of Asia Minor. So, when the last Ottoman parliament failed to ratify the Treaty, the Supreme Allied Council in Paris invited the Greeks 'to restore order in Anatolia'. They had not counted on Kemal Pasha.

In the previous two years, Kemal had surfaced at the head of a Turkish national movement dedicated to the creation of a national republic based on a modern, secular society. His HQ was in Ankara, in the Turkish-speaking heartland. The hero of Gallipoli, he was the sworn enemy of the Sultan, the mosque, and the veil. A war against foreign invaders was exactly what he needed. In this light, the outcome of the Graeco-Turkish campaigns of 1920–2 was fairly predictable. The lonely Greek force marched up onto the Anatolian plateau, until held on the River Sakarya. Kemal roused the Turks to defend their native soil. In 1922 the Greek retreat turned into a rout: Smyrna fell; the Greek forces were driven into the sea.

The great majority of Greeks from Asia Minor, where their ancestors had lived for three millennia, together with the Pontic Greeks of the Black Sea littoral, were expelled. For them, this was 'the Great Catastrophe'. Most of them would be exchanged for the Turkish population of northern Greece, which was expelled at the same time. In the process, Kemal established himself as *Ghazi Pasha* or 'Warrior Lord', and eventually as *Atatürk*, the 'Father of the Turks'; and the Sultan was deposed.

Allied intervention in Turkey offered a more blatant case of foreign interference than that in Russia. But the effect was the same. It stimulated what it was supposed to restrain. The Republic of Turkey established exclusive control of its national territory. The imposed Treaty of Sèvres had to be replaced by the negotiated Treaty of Lausanne (1923). Greece and Turkey undertook to organize an extensive exchange of population; and the demilitarized Straits were handed over to yet another International Commission.[14] At which point the chain of conflicts generated by the Great War finally ground to a temporary halt. [SOCIALIS]

The Inter-War Period

In the inter-war period, which conventionally begins on Armistice Day in November 1918 and ends on 1 September 1939, Europe never escaped the shadow of war. The 1920s were passed amidst the after-shocks. The 1930s were passed in the growing conviction that a second quake was brewing. At the time there were statesmen and historians, including Churchill, who argued that lack of decisive action against the peace-breakers would inevitably lead to a renewal of conflict. In theory, their warnings proved to be correct; but they ignored both the political and the military realities. The Western democracies, horrified by the losses of 1914–18, could not be galvanized into action at the first sign of trouble. Also, their experiences with limited 'fire-brigade' operations were dispiriting. Allied intervention in Russia had shown that the West possessed neither the will nor the resources to control the Bolsheviks. French occupation of the Ruhr was to show that Germany could not be coerced by measured means. From then on, most military staffs were convinced that it had to be full-scale war or nothing. And full-scale war could not be prepared overnight.

What is more, if Russia and Germany could not be restrained separately, there was no chance of restraining them if they chose to work together. This nightmare was first glimpsed in April 1922, when German and Soviet delegates attending an Inter-Allied economic conference at Genoa decided to take an unscheduled train ride along the riviera to Rapallo, and to sign a German–Soviet trade treaty without reference to their outraged Allied hosts. In itself, the Rapallo incident was not crucial; but it revealed the central weakness of the Allies' victory: it revealed that Moscow and Berlin in concert could defy the West with impunity. Often unspoken, it underlay all of Europe's peacetime deliberations until the nightmare finally turned to reality.

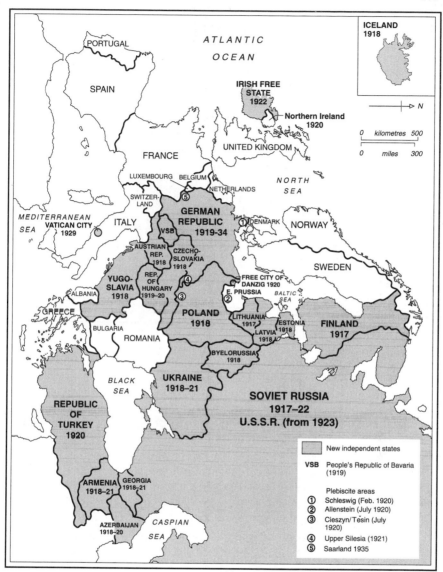

Map 25.

The New Europe, 1917–1922

SOCIALIS

I N the spring of 1920, the election results obliged the King of Sweden to invite a socialist to head the government. But he did so reluctantly. He called in the leader of the Social Democratic Workers' Party, Karl Hjalmar Branting (1860–1925), and said that he could become prime minister so long as there was 'no socialism, no disarmament, and no constitutional change'. For a socialist party which had demanded defence cuts to finance social welfare, and which had demanded a republic, these were tough conditions. But the deal was struck; and Branting formed a coalition cabinet. The first step had been taken in the governmental career of a . party whose record of office was to be unequalled in the democratic world.

The *Sveriges Socialdemokratiska Arbetarparti* had been founded over thirty years before, in 1889. Closely modelled on the German SPD, it forgot its initial flirtation with Marxism and moved instead towards the parliamentary path and to a programme of social reform, redistribution of wealth, and state intervention. Like the British Labour Party, it possessed strong links with the trades unions, including block membership by affiliation; and it was well organized at the local level in workers' communes. Its electoral muscle consisted mainly of Sweden's new class of industrial workers, with an important leaven of middle-class and intellectual support. It gained a foothold in the Riksdag in 1896, and scored a landslide electoral success in 1914. By 1920 Branting commanded the largest single party in both houses of parliament.

Sweden's system of proportional representation, which had been introduced in 1909 together with universal male suffrage, made it difficult for any one party to win a clear majority. Four democratic parties—the Conservatives, Liberals, Peasants', and Socialists—participated in the main forum, and coalition or caretaker ministries were a frequent occurrence. A small Communist Party was also represented. Prior to the constitutional reform of 1952, it was possible for parties to run electoral cartels to increase their representation.

The SSDA's rise to power and influence passed through several phases. In the 1920s Branting headed three coalitions—in 1920, 1921–3, and 1924–5(6). He once lost out through an unemployment bill, and once through his drive for defence cuts. He never formed a majority government.

From 1932 Branting's successor, Per Albin Hansson, began to give the SSDA the look of a permanent ruling party. With one brief interval, he was to control Swedish government for fourteen years. The ministry of 1936–9 was a 'Red–Green Coalition' with the Peasant Movement, and that of 1939–45 a multi-party wartime coalition of national unity.

After the war, the Social Democrats gained such a hold that they could transform Sweden in their own image. Tage Erlander held office for twenty-three years from 1946. Sweden's prosperity was as high as its taxation and its standards of state-sponsored health, education, and social security.[1] A brief period of conservative rule separated the two socialist ministries of Olaf Palme (1969–76, 1982–6). The SSDA fortress did not crumble until 1988—after an unparalleled run of over half a century. And despite the King's fears in 1920, the Swedish monarchy outlasted the socialists.

As for Socialism sitting uneasily in one of Europe's richest countries, the paradox was more apparent than real. Socialist ideas can only be effectively applied where there is a substantial productive surplus to distribute and a democratic government to ensure equitable distribution. Indeed, they worked ever less efficiently in Sweden as the gap between available resources and popular aspirations narrowed. Yet in countries where the surplus is meagre, or the government dictatorial, or both, the workers in a collective economy are vulnerable to exploitation and the ruling elite hoards all the benefits. Such was the case in the Soviet Union, 'the world's first socialist state', which was not truly socialist either in spirit or in practice.

The limitations of the Western Powers were also made apparent in the wider world beyond Europe. Major problems of the Pacific, of China, and of global maritime power had to be settled at the Washington Conference of 1921–2, not at the Peace Conference in Paris. The Washington Naval Agreement (1921) set limits to naval tonnage in the ratios of USA 5 : Britain 5 : Japan 3 : France 1.5 : Italy 1.5. In the Gondra Treaty of 1923, the USA made its dispositions in Latin America without involving its former European partners. The centre of gravity of world power was shifting. Europe was no longer the sole master of its fate.

The legacy of the Peace Conference was not what its organizers would have wanted. Germany was gravely wounded, but not reconciled. The infant German Republic was extremely fragile. Its National Assembly, which met in permanent session at Weimar throughout 1919, was run by a coalition dominated by social democrats. Its representatives only signed the Treaty of Versailles under the express threat of coercion. Emotional ceremonies were staged to bid farewell to the Germans excluded from the Reich. Berlin, which had already experienced the left-wing rising of January 1919, when Rosa Luxemburg was murdered, now saw the right-wing Kapp *Putsch* of March 1920, and in August the approach of the Red Army. One cannot say what would have happened if Tukhachevsky had reached his destination. But by driving the Poles from disputed towns and handing those towns over to local Germans, he had betrayed his intention of playing the German card and of overthrowing the Versailles settlement. Three-hundred thousand armed *Freikorps* members were still on the loose. 'Red Saxony' was held by communists, Bavaria by ultra-conservatives talking of secession. Germany was one step from chaos.

The spectre of social upheaval stalked the land. The violent hostility of the German left and the German right was growing. In 1922 the Jewish Minister of Reconstruction, Walter Rathenau, was assassinated. Radical socialists fed on mass unemployment and the dire effects of hyperinflation. Radical nationalists fed on the humiliation of the war guilt clauses, on resistance to reparations, and on Allied occupation of the Rhineland. A new variety of desperado, seeking to fuse the grievances of both Left and Right, surfaced after 1920 in the National Socialist German Workers' Party (NSDAP). Their leader, Adolf Hitler, reached the headlines on 8–9 November 1923, in the abortive fiasco of the 'Beer-cellar *Putsch*' in Munich.

For a time, however, a modicum of confidence was restored in Germany by Gustav Stresemann (1878–1929), sometime Chancellor and, from 1923, Foreign Minister. Stresemann allowed the German military to evade the disarmament clauses through secret co-operation with the Soviets. But he won Western approval by suppressing the communist governments in Saxony and Thuringia, and by restoring reparation payments. He then persuaded the Allies that the battle over reparations was harming Europe's economy. In 1924, under the Dawes Plan, he negotiated a loan from the USA of 800 million marks backed by gold, which assured the recovery of German industry. In 1925, at Locarno, in exchange for a guarantee of the Franco-German frontier, he obtained Germany's rehabilitation as a member of the international community, and in 1926 her admission to the League of Nations. In 1927 the last Inter-Allied Commissions were withdrawn. In the glow of improved relations with the West, few people cared to notice that Germany's eastern frontiers, and Germany's eastern policy, had been left open to revision.

In the realm of international finance, confusion reigned for years. Thanks to the arrangements of the wartime *Entente*, Britain and France were owed colossal sums, principally by Russia, whilst they themselves owed still greater sums, principally to the USA. The reparations plan incorporated into the Treaty of Versailles sought to make Germany pay the entire costs of the war, so that Allied governments could then pay off their war debts. But the plan proved unworkable: the sums involved could not be properly calculated; Germany refused full payment; the Soviet Government refused to recognize the debts of the Tsar; and the USA refused to consider rescheduling. So alternative arrangements had to be made. Already at the Peace Conference a British delegate, J. M. Keynes, had published stringent criticism of the prevailing approach. In his *Economic Consequences of the Peace* (1919) he argued that support for the economic recovery of Germany was a precondition for the recovery of Europe as a whole, and that punitive reparations would harm the enforcers. His ideas met strong political opposition, partly because he seemed to be recommending preferential treatment for Germany over Germany's alleged victims. But it gradually came to be realized that recovery must have priority.

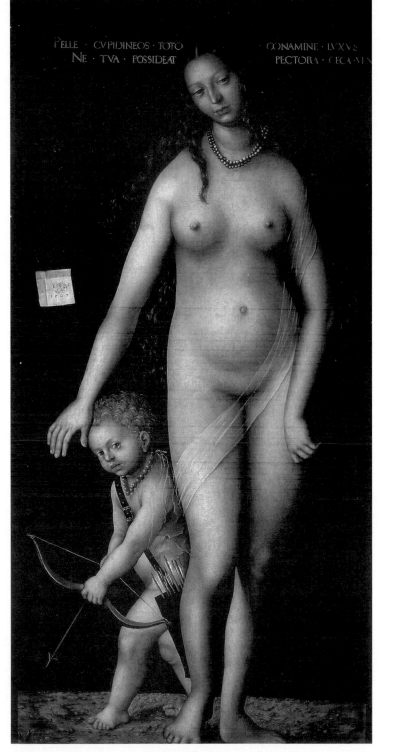

PELLE · CVPIDINEOS · TOTO   CONAMINE · LVXVS
NE · TVA · POSSIDEAT   PECTORA · CECA · VEN

38. Venus

39. Perspective

40. Allegory

41. Columbus lands at San Domingo, 1493

42. Luther enters Worms, 1521

43. Dream of Empire

44. Vision of Past Glory

45. The Board of Governors

46. Moscow Holiday

47. Sun King as Paterfamilias

48. Trouserless Philosopher

49. Master of the Continent

50. Lords of the Sea

51. Infanta in Pink

52. Reader and Listener

53. Mother

54. Summer

55. Royalist

56. Republican

57. The Children's Friend

58. Knight in Shining Armour

59. Eternal Wanderer

60. Dynamo

61. No Surrender

62. Free Hellas

63. Musical Evening

64. Concert of Europe

65. Rural Poverty

66. Industrial Grime

67. Impressionist

68. Primitive

69. Surreal

70. Europe Deceived

71. Europe Divided

72. Europe in Torment

Reparations initially fixed at 269 million German Goldmarks payable over 42 years, i.e. to 1962, were successively reduced. In 1921 the British made a move by promoting an Anglo-Soviet Trade Treaty, thereby breaking the boycott of the Bolsheviks. Having pressed for a reduction of German reparations to 132 billion Goldmarks, they acquiesced in the French threat to occupy the Ruhr if the reduced payments were not met. In 1922 they proposed the cancellation of *all* war debts, alternatively the limitation of British repayments to the USA to £33 million per annum over 63 years, i.e. to 1985. In 1923, having fuelled Germany's hyper-inflation by their demands, the French occupied the Ruhr to no good effect. In 1924, under the Dawes Plan, moderation at last prevailed. Germany was to pay reparations at a moderate rate until 1929, then at 2,500 million Reichsmarks per annum. An Allied loan of 800 million RM was to facilitate the next instalment. But even this proved impossible. In 1929, under the Young Plan, Germany was told to pay 34,500 million GM annually over 58 years, i.e. to 1988, on a mortgage secured against the German state railways. In 1932, at the Lausanne Conference, Germany was invited to make one final payment of 3,000 million RM—which was not achieved. By that time the whole business had become irrelevant. Germany had been receiving more by way of US loans than she was paying in reparations. In any case, as from 24 October 1929, the day of the Great Crash on the New York Stock Exchange, the world economy was moving into depression; and all US loans to Europe were suspended.

Inter-war politics were dominated by the recurrent spectacle of liberal democracies falling prey to dictatorship. The Western Powers had hoped that their victory would usher in an era modelled in their own image. After all, at the start of the Great War the European Continent contained 19 monarchies and 3 republics; at the end, it consisted of 14 monarchies and 16 republics. Yet the 'Democratic Revolution' soon proved illusory. Hardly a year passed when one country or another did not see its democratic constitution violated by one or other brand of dictator. It cannot be attributed to any simple cause, save the inability of the Western Powers to defend the regimes which they had inspired. The dictators came in all shapes and sizes—communists, fascists, radicals, and reactionaries, left-wing authoritarians (like Piłsudski), right-wing militarists (like Franco), monarchs, anti-monarchists, even a cleric like Father Tišo in Slovakia. The only thing they shared was the conviction that Western democracy was not for them (see Appendix III, p. 1320). [**EESTI**]

Of the two new states to come into existence between the wars, one, Ireland, was a national republic, the other, the Vatican state, an apostolic dictatorship. The Irish Free State was established in 1922, initially as a sovereign dominion of the British Empire. Millions of Irishmen had loyally served in the British army during the Great War. But opinion in 1918 was still split by the prospect of Home Rule. Ulster prepared once again to defend the Union by force, and in 1920 was turned into an autonomous province of the UK. The predominantly Catholic southerners prepared for independence. They succeeded, but only after two

EESTI

IN 1923 one of the first offices of Count Coudenhove-Kalergi's Pan-European League was opened in the capital of Estonia, Tallin. Outside the office door was a brass plate with the inscription PANEUROPA UNION ESTONIA. Seventeen years later, when the Soviet Army invaded Estonia, the plate was hidden by members of the League. In 1992, during the visit to Estonia by the doyen of the European Parliament, Dr Otto von Habsburg, it was brought out of hiding and presented to him. It was the symbol of Estonia's hidden aspirations, invisible to the outside world for half a century. 'Don't forget the Estonians!', said Dr von Habsburg; 'they are the best of Europeans.'[1]

At the time, admirers of the Soviet Union were saying that the Baltic States were too tiny to be viable, sovereign countries. Similar things were said about the new-born republics of Yugoslavia. The point is: Estonia, or Latvia, or Slovenia, or Croatia, would be extremely vulnerable if left in isolation. But as members of the European Community they would be every bit as viable as the Grand Duchy of Luxembourg or an independent Wales or Scotland. After all, Estonia is nearly twenty times larger than Luxembourg, and is four times as populous. In a united Europe, every small country can find its place alongside the former great powers.

vicious wars—one against a British paramilitary police force, the 'Black and Tans', the other a civil war amongst themselves. The dominant personality, and many times Premier, Éamon de Valera (1882–1975), was a half-Cuban Catholic born of an Irish mother in New York. The Free State declared itself the Republic of Éire in 1937, severing all formal ties with Great Britain in 1949.

The Vatican State, which was almost as papist as Éire, was created in 1929 in pursuance of the Lateran Treaty signed by Mussolini's Italy and Pope Pius XI. It covered 44 hectares (*c.*100 acres) on the right bank of the Tiber in central Rome. Its population of perhaps 1,000 resident souls was to be ruled by the absolute authority of the Pope. Its creation ended 60 years of the Pope's 'captivity' since the suppression of the Papal States in 1870.

Despite the victory of the Western democracies, the most dynamic political product of the Great War lay in the anti-Western, anti-liberal, and anti-democratic monster of totalitarianism. The term was coined by Italian fascists to describe their own aspirations. But it was taken up from 1928 to encompass the common denominator of both fascism and communism. After the suppression of Soviet Hungary, Soviet Russia (1917–22) and its successor, the USSR (from 1923), long remained the sole communist state. Its example was immensely influential. The main fascist regimes emerged in Italy (1922), Germany (1933), and Spain (1936).[15]

The concept of totalitarianism was rejected both by communists and by fascists, that is, by the totalitarians themselves. It was destined to become a political football in the era of the Cold War, and it has enjoyed only mixed fortunes among Western academics and political theorists.[16] It has failed to attract those who demand tidy, watertight models, or who identify political phenomena with social forces. It is anathema, and abominable 'relativism', to anyone who holds either communism or fascism to be uniquely evil. On the other hand, it is strongly supported by those Europeans who have had practical experience of both communism and fascism at first hand. Communism and fascism were never identical: each of them evolved over time, and each spawned variegated offspring. But they had much more in common than their practitioners were prepared to admit. The features which they shared form a long list. A seminal study on the subject talks in terms of 'a six-point syndrome'.[17] But six points are not enough:

Nationalist-Socialist ideology. Both communism and fascism were radical movements which developed ideologies professing a blend of nationalist and socialist elements. During the 1920s the Bolsheviks gradually watered down their inter-nationalist principles, whilst adopting the characteristic postulates of extreme Russian nationalism. Under Stalin, the ideological mix was classified as 'National Bolshevism'. The German Nazis modified the socialist elements of their ideology over the same period. In both cases the socialist-nationalist or nationalist-socialist blend was stabilized at the same moment, in 1934.

At the conscious level, communists and fascists were schooled to stress their differences. On the other hand, when pressed to summarize their convictions, they often gave strikingly similar answers. One said, 'For us Soviet patriots, the homeland and communism became fused into one inseparable whole.' Another put it thus: 'Our movement took a grip on cowardly Marxism, and extracted the [real] meaning of socialism from it. It also took Nationalism from the cowardly bourgeois parties. Throwing both together into the cauldron of our way of life, the synthesis emerged as clear as crystal—German National Socialism.'[18] It is not for nothing that people treated to such oratory were apt to think of communists as 'red fascists' and of fascists as 'brown communists'.

Pseudo-science. Both communists and fascists claimed to base their ideologies on fundamental scientific laws which supposedly determined the development of human society. Communists appealed to their version of 'scientific Marxism' or historical materialism, the Nazis to eugenics and racial science. In neither case did their scientific methods or findings find widespread independent endorsement.

Utopian goals. All totalitarians cherished the vision of a New Man who was to create a New Order cleansed of all present impurities. The nature of the vision varied. It could be the final, classless stage of pure communism as preached by the Marxist-Leninists: the racist, Jew-free Aryan paradise of the Nazis: or the restoration of a pseudo-historical Roman empire in Italy. The building of the

New Order was a task which justified all the sacrifices and brutalities of the present. [UTOPIA]

The dualist party-state. Once in power, the totalitarian party created organs within its own apparatus to duplicate and to oversee all other existing institutions. State structures were reduced to the status of conveyor belts for executing the Party's wishes. This dualist dictatorial system was much more pervasive than that implied by the familiar but misleading term of the 'one-party state'. (See Appendix III, p. 1321.)

The Führerprinzip *or 'Leader Principle'.* Totalitarian parties operated on strict hierarchical lines. They exacted slavish obedience from their minions, through the unquestioning cult of the Party Leader, the fount of all wisdom and beneficence—the *Führer,* the *Vozhd',* the *Duce,* the *Caudillo* or the 'Great Helmsman'. Lenin shunned such a cult: but it was a centrepiece both of Stalinism and of Hitlerism.

Gangsterism. Many observers have noted the strong similarity between the conduct of totalitarian élites and that of professional criminal confraternities. Gangsters gain a parasitical hold over a community by 'protecting' it from the violence which they themselves generate. They habitually terrorize both their members and their victims, and eliminate their rivals. They manipulate the law and, whilst maintaining an important façade of respectability, use blackmail and extortion to take control of all organizations in the locality.

Bureaucracy. All totalitarian regimes required a vast army of bureaucrats to staff the bloated and duplicated organs of the party-state. This new bureaucracy offered rapid advancement to droves of opportunist individuals of any social origin. Entirely dependent on the Party, it arguably formed the only social constituency whose interests the regime had to consider. At the same time, it included a number of competing 'power centres' whose hidden rivalries gave rise to the only form of genuine political life in existence.

Propaganda. Totalitarian propaganda owed much to the subliminal techniques of modern mass advertising. It employed emotive symbols, *son et lumière,* political art and impressive architecture, and the principle of the 'Big Lie'. Its shameless demagoguery was directed at the vulnerable and vindictive elements of society uprooted by the tides of war and modernization. [PROPAGANDA]

The Aesthetics of Power. Totalitarian regimes enforced a virtual monopoly in the arts, propagating an aesthetic environment which glorified the ruling Party, embellished the bond between Party and people, revelled in heroic images of national myths, and indulged in megalomaniac fantasies. Italian Fascists, German Nazis, and Soviet Communists all shared a taste for portentous portraits of the Leader, for oversized sculptures of musclebound workers, and for ostentatious public buildings of ultra-grandiose proportions.

The dialectical enemy. No totalitarian regime could hope to legitimize its own evil designs without an opposite evil to contend with. The rise of fascism in

Europe was a godsend for the communists, who otherwise could only have justified themselves by reference to the more distant evils of liberalism, imperialism, and colonialism. The fascists never ceased to justify themselves in terms of their crusade against Bolshevism, the communists through 'the struggle against fascism'. The contradictions within totalitarianism provided the motor for the hatreds and conflicts which it promoted.

The psychology of hatred. Totalitarian regimes raised the emotional temperature by beating the drum of hatred against 'enemies' within and without. Honest adversaries or honourable opponents did not exist. In the fascist repertoire, Jews and communists headed the bill; in the communist repertoire, fascists, capitalist running dogs, 'kulaks', and alleged saboteurs were mercilessly pilloried.

Pre-emptive censorship. Totalitarian ideology could not operate without a watertight censorship controlling all sources of information. It was not sufficient to suppress unwanted opinions or facts; it was necessary to prefabricate all the data that was permitted to circulate.

Genocide and coercion. Totalitarian regimes pushed political violence beyond all previous limits. An elaborate network of political police and security agencies was kept busy first in destroying all opponents and undesirables and later in inventing opponents to keep the machinery in motion. Genocidal campaigns against (innocent) social or racial 'enemies' added credence to ideological claims and kept the population in a permanent state of fear. Mass arrests and shootings, concentration camps, and random murders were routine.

Collectivism. Totalitarian regimes laid stress on all the sorts of activity which strengthen collective bonds and weaken family and individual identity. State-run nurseries, 'social art', youth movements, party rituals, military parades, and group uniforms all served to cement high levels of social discipline and conformist behaviour. In Fascist Italy, a system of Party-run Corporations was established to replace all former trade union and employers' organizations and in 1939 to take over the lower house of the national assembly.

Militarism. Totalitarian regimes habitually magnified the 'external threat', or invented it, to rally citizens to the fatherland's defence. Rearmament received top economic priority. Under party control, the armed forces of the state enjoyed a monopoly of weapons and high social prestige. All offensive military plans were described as defensive.

Universalism. Totalitarian regimes acted on the assumption that their system would somehow spread across the globe. Communist ideologues held that Marxism-Leninism was 'scientific' and therefore universally applicable. The Nazis marched to the refrain 'Denn heute gehört uns Deutschland, | Und morgen die ganze Welt' (For today it's Germany that's ours, and tomorrow the whole wide world.) [LETTLAND]

Contempt for liberal democracy. All totalitarians despised liberal democracy for its humanitarianism, for its belief in compromise and co-existence, for its commercialism, and for its attachment to law and tradition.

Moral nihilism. All totalitarians shared the view that their goals justified their means. 'Moral Nihilism', wrote one British observer, 'is not only the central feature of National Socialism, but also the central feature between it and Bolshevism.'[19]

The concept of totalitarianism stands or falls on the substance of these points of comparison between its principal practitioners. Its validity is not affected by the various intellectual and political games for which it has subsequently been used.

However, communism and fascism obviously differed in the sources of their self-identity. Communists were wedded to the class struggle, the Nazis to their campaign for racial purity. Important differences also lay in the social and economic sphere. The fascists were careful to leave private property intact, and to recruit the big industrialists to their cause. The communists abolished most aspects of private property. They nationalized industry, collectivized agriculture, and instituted central command planning. On these grounds, communism must be judged the more totalitarian branch of totalitarianism. [**GAUCHE**]

Of course, one has to insist that the 'total human control' sometimes claimed on behalf of totalitarianism is a figment of someone's imagination. Totalitarian utopias and totalitarian realities were two different things. Grand totalitarian schemes were often grandly inefficient. Totalitarianism refers not to the achievements of regimes but to their ambitions. What is more, the totalitarian disease generated its own antibodies. Gross oppression often inspired heroic resistance. Exposure to bogus philosophy could sometimes breed people of high moral principle. The most determined 'anti-communists' were ex-communists. The finest 'anti-Fascists' were sincere German, Italian, or Spanish patriots.

From the historical point of view, one of the most interesting questions is how far communism and fascism fed off each other. Before 1914, the main ingredients of the two movements—socialism, Marxism, nationalism, racism, and autocracy—were washing around in various combinations all over Europe. But communism crystallized first. Its emergence in 1917 occurred well in advance of any coherent manifestations of fascism. The communists, therefore, must be rated the leaders, and the fascists the quick learners. The point is: can chronological precedence be equated with cause and effect? Was fascism simply a crusade for saving the world from Bolshevism, as many of its adherents maintained? What exactly did the fascists learn from the communists? It is hard to deny that Béla Kun gave Horthy's regime its *raison d'être*. The Italian general strike of October 1922, dominated by communists, gave Mussolini the excuse for his 'March on Rome'. It was the strength of the communists in the streets and voting booths of Germany which frightened the German conservatives into handing power to Hitler.

But that is hardly the whole story. The fascists, like the communists, were notorious fraudsters: one should not take their pronouncements too seriously.

Benito Mussolini (1883–1945), sometime ex-editor of the socialist newspaper *Avanti* (Forward), author of a pseudo-Marxist work on the class struggle (1912), embezzler and street brawler, had little commitment to political principle. He had no qualms about using his squads of *Fascisti* first to help the nationalists' brutal seizure of Fiume in 1920, to support Giolitti's liberal bloc in the general election of 1921, and later to murder the Socialist leader, Matteotti. He declared himself in favour of constitutional monarchy, for example, shortly before overthrowing it. One need not search for ideological consistency in such tactics: he was simply seeking to exploit the mayhem which he had helped to unleash.

The same must be said of Mussolini's extraordinary, and extraordinarily successful, behaviour in October 1922. Having first contributed to the chaos which produced the general strike, he then cabled the King with an ultimatum demanding to be made Prime Minister. The King should have ignored the cable; but he didn't. Mussolini did not seize power; he merely threatened to do so, and under the threat of further chaos Italy's democrats surrendered. 'The "March on Rome"', writes the leading historian of Italy, 'was a comfortable train ride, followed by a petty demonstration, and all in response to an express invitation from the monarch.'[20] Years later, when Mussolini's regime was in dire trouble, Adolf Hitler insisted on saving him. 'After all,' the Führer was reported as saying, 'it was the Duce who showed us that everything was possible.'[21] What Mussolini showed to be possible was the subversion of liberal democracy, and a second terrible round of Europe's 'total war'.

The tone of international relations was set by the almost universal abhorrence of war. On the surface at least, 'non-aggression' was obligatory. In twenty years, a large number of non-aggression pacts were signed (see Appendix III, p. 1322). For those states who intended no aggression, such pacts were irrelevant. For those intending aggression they provided excellent cover: both Hitler and Stalin were fond of them.

The creation of the League of Nations must be counted among the achievements of the Peace Conference. The Covenant of the League came into force on 10 January 1920, the same day as the Treaty of Versailles, into which it had been incongruously incorporated. It sought to provide for the settlement of disputes by arbitration and consent, and for the use of collective force against aggressors. It envisaged an annual General Assembly, where each member state had an equal vote, an executive Council, and a permanent Secretariat, all based in Geneva. The League also took over the International Court of Justice at The Hague, and the International Chamber of Labour. The General Assembly first convened in November 1920, and met every year thereafter until 1941. It dissolved itself in April 1946, when the residual operations were transferred to the United Nations Organization in New York.

The work of the League started too late to affect the immediate settlement of the Great War, and was hobbled by the non-participation of the powers who might have rendered it effective. At no time in the 21 years of its operation were all three of Europe's power centres properly represented. Of the Western Powers, France alone played a full part. The USA, the League's original sponsor, stayed away; and Great Britain failed to sign the fundamental Geneva Protocol (1924) on the pacific settlement of disputes. Germany only participated from 1926 to 1933, Italy from 1920 to 1937. The Soviet Union was admitted in 1934, and expelled in 1940. An important initiative was taken by France and the USA in 1928 to plug some of the League's obvious failings. The Briand–Kellogg pact for the renunciation of war was eventually signed by 64 states, including the USSR. But it was never incorporated into the League's own rules. Hence, whilst the League advocated military or economic sanctions against aggressor states, it did not possess the means to enforce its own sanctions. As a result, it played a major role in the management of minor issues and a negligible role in the management of major ones.

Thanks to the ambivalent attitudes of the Western Powers, the League was not empowered to challenge the general European Settlement which the former thought they had put into place in 1919–20. A fatal ruling determined that demands for Treaty revision could not be accepted as a 'dispute' under the terms of the Geneva Protocol. The principle of unanimity, which governed voting in the Assembly and the Council, ensured that no decision could ever be taken contrary to the wishes of the Powers. The crucial Disarmament Conference did not meet until 1932, by which time rearmament was well advanced in the USSR and was soon to be launched in Germany.

Overall, therefore, the sponsors of the League deprived it of the means to observe its high ideals. It ran the colonial Mandates Commission for Palestine and Syria. It administered the Free City of Danzig, the Saarland, and the Straits Commission. It mediated between Turkey and Iraq over Mosul, between Greece and Bulgaria over Macedonia (1925), and, unsuccessfully, between Poland and Lithuania over Wilno (1925–7). It could not cope with the Japanese invasion of Manchuria (1931) or the Italian invasion of Abyssinia (1936). Through no fault of its own, it was completely out of its depth when the major powers of Europe began to unsheath their claws in the late 1930s.

The most active statesman in the field of European peace and co-operation was undoubtedly Aristide Briand (1862–1932). A reforming socialist born at Nantes, Briand had been ten times France's Premier; but the most expansive phase of his career was reached in 1925–32, when he served as Foreign Minister. He was specially energetic in the pursuit of Franco-German reconciliation. He was the chief architect of the Locarno Pact; he forged the Kellogg–Briand pact for the renunciation of war; and he made proposals for European union. His noble ideals, and their lack of success, were typical of the times.

Briand's proposals for European union had few immediate consequences. But they are important for all who seek the seeds of policies which eventually bore fruit twenty years later. They were first raised in a speech to the Assembly of the League on 5 September 1929:

'I think that among peoples constituting geographical groups, like the peoples of Europe, there should be some kind of federal bond . . . Obviously, this association will be primarily economic, for that is the most urgent aspect of the question . . . Still, I am convinced that this federal link might also do useful work politically and socially, and without affecting the sovereignty of any of the nations belonging to the association . . .'[22]

The key phrases were 'geographical groups', 'primarily economic', and 'sovereignty'.

A more detailed Memorandum was presented in May 1930. This document spoke of 'the moral union of Europe', and outlined the principles and mechanics whereby it might be achieved. It insisted on 'the general subordination of the economic problem to the political one'. It envisaged a Permanent Political Committee for executive decisions, and a representative body, the European Conference, for debate. In the immediate term, it called on the 27 European members of the League to convene a series of meetings to study a wide range of related issues, including finance, labour, and inter-parliamentary relations. From January 1931, Briand chaired a subcommittee of the League which examined members' responses to the Memorandum. Of these, only the Dutch reply was prepared to accept that European union involved an inevitable reduction of sovereignty.

As it proved, 1931 was the terminal year both for Briand and for his ideas. His initial speech on European union had been closely followed by the Wall Street crash. Discussions on his Memorandum coincided with the first electoral success of the German Nazis. Briand's European schemes were overtaken by his chairmanship of the Manchurian Committee, which, after much deliberation, issued a verbal reprimand to Japan for the invasion of China. In Asia, Japan flouted the League and reaped the rewards of aggression. In Europe, 'the spirit of Locarno' was sick. Stresemann was dead; Briand himself ailed, and resigned. Briand's death elicited an impassioned tribute from Britain's Foreign Secretary, Austen Chamberlain. Briand 'was proud of his country, and jealous of her prerogatives,' he said. 'But his pride was only content when France stepped out like a goddess, leading the other nations in the paths of peace and civilisation. There is no-one of his stature left.'[23] It was a rare demonstration of Anglo-French solidarity.

In this atmosphere, an alternative plan for European security was advanced by Fascist Italy. Mussolini proposed a four-power pact of Britain, France, Germany, and Italy. It represented a cynical return to the bad habits of the Concert of Europe, and would have dropped all pretence about the equal standing of states. It unashamedly attempted to mobilize the 'West' against the dangers of the 'East'—that is, against the squabbles of the successor states, and the potential expansion of communism. It found a measure of favour in the British Foreign Office; but it did not appeal to the Quai d'Orsay, which preferred to stick to existing arrangements. Apart from the Munich Conference, its provisions remained a dead letter.

Europe's cultural life was deeply affected by the hangovers of war, which heightened the questioning of traditional values and accelerated existing centrifugal trends. The tone of anxiety and pessimism was set by Oswald Spengler's *Der Untergang des Abendlandes* (The Decline of the West, 1918), a specifically German view of 'Western civilization'. The advent of communism excited many Western intellectuals, for whom the defiant utopian stance of the Bolsheviks in Russia proved unusually fascinating. Active communist politics was for the few; but *marxisant* opinions were much in fashion. The long stream of Moscow-bound pilgrims, for whom the most murderous regime in European history could do no wrong, offers one of the stranger spectacles of mass delusion on record.[24] Fascism, too, was to recruit its academic and cultural collaborators. Some individuals, such as G. B. Shaw, managed to fawn on dictators of all hues. Visiting the USSR in 1931, he remarked: 'I wish we had forced labour in England, in which case we would not have two million unemployed.' His opinion of Stalin after a personal meeting was: 'he is said to be a model of domesticity, virtue and innocence'.[25] In retrospect, books such as the Webbs' *Soviet Communism: A New Civilisation* (1935) look simply fatuous; but they pandered to the genuine anxieties of the post-war generation whilst serving to hold the world in ignorance about Soviet realities. The lack of moral integrity among politically pressured intellectuals, as described in Julien Benda's *La Trahisón des clercs* (1927), was a recurring theme. It would have been more convincing if Benda himself had not tried to justify Stalin's show trials. The Spanish social philosopher José Ortega y Gasset saw totalitarianism as a sign of the threat from mass culture. In his *Rebelión de las Masas* (Revolt of the Masses, 1930), he warned that democracy carried the seeds of tyranny by the majority.

In religious thought, the conservative Catholic hierarchy took a stronger line against communism than did the Protestant churches. But in 1937 Pius XI's twin encyclicals, *Mit brennender Sorge* and *Divini Redemptoris*, ruled that both Nazism and communism were incompatible with Christianity. At the same time, modernist Catholic philosophers such as the neo-Thomist Jacques Maritain (1882–1973) sought to update the Church's social thought. Interdenominational religious debate was stimulated by the Jewish theologian Martin Buber (1875–1965), sometime Professor at Frankfurt, and by the Swiss, Karl Barth (1886–1968), whose influential *Die kirchliche Dogmatik* (1932) sought to reinstate Protestant fundamentals.

In literature, the post-war sense of devastation and disorientation was eloquently conveyed in T. S. Eliot's marvellous *Waste Land*, in Pirandello's play *Six Characters in Search of an Author* (1920), and in the 'stream of consciousness' texts of James Joyce's novels *Ulysses* (1923) and *Finnegans Wake* (1939). The year 1928 marked the creation both of D. H. Lawrence's unpublishable *Lady Chatterley's Lover*, a bold attack on English sexual mores, and of Berthold Brecht's *Dreigroschenoper* (Threepenny Opera), the best-known product of a politically left-wing and unconventional artistic milieu in pre-Nazi Berlin. In that same era the novelist Thomas Mann (1875–1955), who had made his name before the war with *Buddenbrooks* (1900) and *Death in Venice* (1911), took the lead in protecting German culture from the ill repute of German politics. He published more novels, such as *Der Zauberberg* (The Magic Mountain, 1924), which explored the dubious legacy of Wagner and Nietzsche, before emigrating and becoming the epitome of 'the good German' in exile. In Russia, a brief interval of literary freedom in the 1920s gave space to the powerful talents of the revolutionary poets Alexander Blok (1880–1921) and Vladimir Mayakovsky (1893–1930). The advent of Stalinism divided Soviet writers into servants of the Party, such as Gorky and Sholokov, and persecuted dissidents, such as Osip Mandel'shtam (1891–1938) or Anna Akhmatova (1889–1966). The memoirs of Mandel'shtam's widow, Nadzezhda, *Hope Against Hope*, could not be published until the 1960s; but they provide the most eloquent testimony to Russian culture in the catacombs. In Central Europe, premonitions of totalitarianism hang over Kafka's *The Castle* (1925) and *The Trial* (1926), over Karel Čapek's allegorical drama *The Insect Play* (1921), over Witkiewicz's novel *Insatiability*, as in the work of the Romanian Lucian Blaga (1895–1961) and the Croat Miroslav Krleža (1893–1975). Kafka's anti-hero 'K', who is arrested on charges which he can never discover, is eventually killed by two men in opera-hats to the words 'Like a dog'. Stanisław Witkiewicz (1885–1939), known as 'Witkacy', painter and mathematician as well as writer, is now acknowledged as the pioneer of the Theatre of the Absurd. Barely known in his lifetime outside Poland, he was destined to commit suicide on the day the Red Army joined in the invasion of the Nazi Wehrmacht. Nothing gained such popular acclaim, however, as the memoirs of a Swedish doctor on Capri, Axel Munthe, whose *Story of San Michele* (1929) was translated into forty-one languages. [**INDEX**]

[**WASTE LAND**]

In the social sciences, the so-called 'Frankfurt School' exerted a huge influence in a very short time. Opened in 1923 and closed by the Nazis in 1934, the Institut für Sozialforschung at Frankfurt sheltered a circle of intellectuals working at the interface of philosophy, psychology, and sociology. Figures such as Max Horkenheimer (1895–1973), Theodor Adorno (1903–69), and Karl Mannheim (1893–1947) felt that modern science had yet to find effective methods for analysing human affairs and assisting their progress. Radical and left-wing, but opposed to all ideologies, including Marxism, they rejected conventional logic and epistemology, whilst fearing the evils of technology, industrial society, and piecemeal reform. Their search for a free-floating 'critical theory', conditioned but not determined by the times, was to impress a whole generation of social scientists both in the USA and in post-1945 Europe. The best-known fruit of their general research was the joint work by Horkheimer and Adorno, *Die Dialektik der Aufklärung* (The Dialectic of the Enlightenment, 1947).[26] [**ANNALES**]

In art, traditionalist styles continued to disintegrate. After Symbolism, Cubism, and Expressionism came Primitivism, Dadaism, Suprematism, Abstractionism, Surrealism, and Constructivism. The leading experimenters included the Russian exile Vasily Kandinsky (1866–1944), a Jewish exile, Marc Chagall (1889–1985), the left-wing Catalan exile Pablo Picasso (1881–1973), the Italian exile Amedeo Modigliani (1884–1920), the Swiss Paul Klee (1879–1940), the Austrian Oskar Kokoschka (1886–1980), the Frenchman Jean Arp (1887–1966), and the Spaniard

WASTE LAND

T. S. ELIOT'S *The Waste Land* appeared in 1922, the work of an American who had settled in Europe. The original draft began: 'First we had a couple of feelers down at Tom's place.' The published version began:

> April is the cruellest month, breeding
> Lilacs out of the dead land, mixing
> Memory and desire, stirring
> Dull roots with spring rain.

Eliot's 433-line poem, largely written in Switzerland, was inspired by the legend of the Holy Grail, and was composed from a string of arcane literary allusions and fragments. The overall effect resembled a ramble through the relics of a shattered civilization.

The final section deals, among other things, with the decay of Eastern Europe:

> Who are those hooded hordes swarming
> Over endless plains, stumbling in cracked earth
> Ringed by the flat horizon . . .

A note refers to a quotation from the Swiss novelist Hermann Hesse: 'Beautiful at least is that eastern half of Europe which is travelling drunk after the Holy Grail on the road to Chaos, singing like Dmitri Karamazov.'

The poem concludes:

> London Bridge is falling down, falling down, falling down.
> *Poi s'ascose nel foco che gli affina*
> *Quando fiam ceu chelidon.*—O swallow, swallow
> *Le Prince d'Aquitaine à la tour abolie.*
> These fragments I have shored against my ruins
> Why then Ile fit you. Hieronymo's mad againe.
> Datta. Dayadhvam. Damyata.
>   Shantih shantih shantih

'Various critics', Eliot explained later at a Harvard lecture, 'have done me the honour to interpret the poem in terms of criticism of the contemporary world . . . To me . . . it was just a piece of rhythmic grumbling.'[1]

ANNALES

VOLUME 1, number 1 of the journal *Annales d'histoire économique et sociale* was dated Paris, 15 January 1929.[1] A short preface 'To our readers' was signed by the two directors, Lucien Febvre (1878–1956) and Marc Bloch (1886–1944). It expressed the belief that the new review would 'make its mark in the sun'. Four main articles were published: Gustave Glotz on the price of papyrus in Greek antiquity; Henri Pirenne on the education of medieval merchants; M. Baumont on German industrial activity since the last war; and G. Méquet (Geneva) on the population problem in the USSR. A second section on 'Scientific Life' contained various news items, together with a technical description of *plans parcelaires*, or 'sketch-plans of landed property', by Bloch and an outline of the career of Max Weber by Maurice Halbwachs. A review section carried a dozen essays covering topics varying from Sicilian slavery to Welsh economic history. The back cover carried advertisements for the 'Collection Armand Colin', the journal's principal sponsor, and for the 22-volume *Géographie universelle* of Paul Vidal de la Blache and L. Gallois.

Annales was to launch not just a journal but a school of history of unrivalled authority. Its aims were to break the dominance of established fields, and to broaden historical studies by techniques and topics drawn from the social sciences. Not just economics and sociology, but psychology, demography, statistics, geography, climatology, anthropology, linguistics, and medical science were all to have their place. Special emphasis was to be laid on the interdisciplinary approach.[2]

The intellectual pedigree of *Annales* is revealing. Febvre met Bloch at the University of Strasbourg. He had made his name through a regional study of the Franche-Comté. Bloch was working on French rural history. Neither felt attracted to the historical stars of the day such as Renouvin, the diplomatic historian, or Fustel de Coulanges, the apostle of documentary research. Both had come under the influence of very different masters. One of these was Émile Durkheim (d. 1917), pioneer sociologist. The second was the Belgian, Henri Pirenne (1862–1935), author of problem-centred studies on medieval democracy and 'the social history of capitalism'. The third was Paul Vidal de la Blache (1845–1918), professor at the École Normale Supérieure and the founder of human geography. It was Vidal who had inspired Febvre and Bloch to go out into the countryside in search of new sources and perspectives on the past.[3]

Most revealing, perhaps, was the professional sin against which the original directors of *Annales* were preparing to do battle. It was the sin of specialization. Historians were concentrating their efforts ever more narrowly behind their own *cloisonnements* or 'dividing walls'. The appeal was unambiguous:

'Nothing would be better if all legitimate specialists, whilst carefully tending their own gardens, would take the trouble none the less to study the work of their neighbours. Yet the walls are so high that very often the view is blocked. It is against these formidable divisions that we see ourselves taking our stand.'[4]

If the menace was recognizable in 1929, It was to grow inexorably in the decades which followed.

Salvador Dali (1904–89). France was their Mecca. Their eclectic inventiveness matched their longevity. Klee painted abstractions in pure colour; Dali painted disturbing Freudian dreamscapes; Arp dropped pieces of paper onto the floor.

In music, the neo-Romantic and Modernist styles launched before the war both found new advocates in the Russians Stravinsky, Prokofiev, Shostakovich, and Rachmaninov, in the Pole Karol Szymanowski (1882–1937), and the Hungarian Béla Bartok (1881–1945). The prominence of East Europeans, both as composers and as instrumentalists, emphasized the cultural bonds which overarched the growing political divide. [STRAD] The German Carl Orff (1895–1982) distinguished himself both in composition and in the realm of musical education. His popular secular oratorio, *Carmina Burana* (1937), set medieval poems to strong, deliberately primitive rhythms. [TONE]

In architecture and design, the German Bauhaus was founded at Weimar by Walter Gropius (1883–1969) and closed down by the Nazis. It drew its inspiration from Expressionism and Constructionism in turns, and pioneered functional methods. Its stars included Itten, Moholy-Nagy, Kandinsky, and Klee.

Except in music, where international barriers were most permeable, the East European contribution to the cultural avant-garde remained long and widely unrecognized. A number of groups or individuals gained renown either through migrating to the West, like the Romanian sculptor, Constantin Brancusi (1876–1957), or through state-sponsored Soviet exhibitions in the 1920s which brought attention to figures such as Kazimierz Malewicz (1878–1935), Pavel Filonov (1882–1946), Vladimir Tatlin (1885–1953), or Alexander Rodchenko (1891–1956). Naturally, the full acceptance of the avant-garde proceeded slowly everywhere. But in Eastern Europe the advent of fascism and the still longer reign of communism drove non-conformist culture into the shadows for half a century. The 'Osma Group' of early Czech Cubists, for example, centred on painters such as Antonin Prochazka (1882–1945) or Bohumil Kubista (1884–1918), was known only to the most specialized experts. The importance of the pioneer Lithuanian symbolist Mikalojus Ciurlionis (1875–1911) or of Władysław Strzemiński (1893–1952), theorist and practitioner of Constructivism, or the strength of the Jewish presence, was not revealed until exhibitions planned in the 1990s.[27] The cultural unity of a politically divided Europe was much deeper than was realized at the time.

TONE

IN 1923 Arnold Schoenberg completed his *Serenade*. It was the first piece composed entirely by the rules of dodecaphony or 'twelve-tone serialism'. Dodecaphony was the chosen medium of the pioneering school of atonal music.[1]

Ever since the Middle Ages, the twelve keys, in major or minor mode, had formed a fundamental element of European musical grammar; and the eight-note octave of each key presented composers with the pool of notes from which to build their melodies, chords, and harmonies. In dodecaphony, in contrast, the traditional keys and octaves were abandoned in favour of a basic set or 'row' of notes using all points of the twelve-point chromatic scale. Each set could begin at any pitch on any point in the scale, and could be arranged in inversions and regressions, giving 48 possible patterns to every series. The resultant music was filled with previously unknown intervals and combinations of notes and was, to the unaccustomed ear, excruciatingly discordant. It represented a break with the past as radical as abstract, non-representational art, or non-grammatical 'stream-of-consciousness' prose. Its principal practitioners after Schoenberg were Berg, Webern, Dallapiccola, Lutyens, and Stravinsky.

Atonality, however, was not the only way of deconstructing musical form. The Parisian 'Six', who took Erik Satie (1866–1925) as their master, and who included Artur Honegger (1892–1955), Darius Milhaud (1892–1974), and Francis Poulenc (1899–1963), experimented with *polytonality*, that is, using two or more keys simultaneously. Paul Hindemith (1895–1963) extended tonal harmony by exploiting harmonic series. Olivier Messiaen (1898–1993), organist of St Sulpice, developed complex rhythms inspired by oriental music, melodies based on bird-song, and musical tones matched to visual colours. Henryk Górecki (b. 1933) sought inspiration in medieval harmonies and in free time. Harrison Birtwhistle (b. 1934) turned Renaissance monody to new uses. Anthony Burgess (1917–93) wrote 'post-tonal' music alongside criticism and fiction.[2]

Both Messiaen and Górecki were Catholic believers, seeking modernist methods to recapture old effects. The former's *Quattuor pour la fin du temps* (1941), written during wartime imprisonment in Silesia, and the latter's phenomenally popular Symphony No. 3 (1976), also motivated by wartime experiences in Silesia, reflect a special sensitivity to time and mood. They appealed to a wider musical audience than the cerebral dodecaphonists ever could.[3]

Nevertheless, the growing prominence of Modernism should not conceal the fact that the strongest influences on inter-war European culture came from two other directions—from technological change and from America. The impact on popular consciousness of radio, of the Kodak camera, of affordable gramophones, and above all of the cinema was immense. Thanks to Hollywood, Charles Chaplin (1889–1977), an orphaned entertainer from London's East End, probably became the best-known person in the world. Many of his films, such as *City Lights* (1931), *Modern Times* (1935), or *The Dictator* (1939), contained clear social and political messages. Other Europeans re-exported by the silver screen included the Swede Greta Garbo, the German Marlene Dietrich, and the Pole, Pola Negri. American imports of the era included popular motoring, Walt Disney's animated cartoons (1928), jazz, and popular dance music. Much of young Europe danced its way from war to war to the strains of ragtime, the Charleston, and the tango.

In the socio-economic sphere the modernization of European society surged ahead, but in highly irregular patterns. The demands of the war had given a strong stimulus to heavy industry and to a wide range of technological innovation. Yet the peace began amidst the widespread disruption of markets, trade, and credit. Despite the great potential for development, especially in new sectors such as oil and motorization, the industrialized countries faced the threat of post-war recession and mass unemployment, and of accompanying social protest.

The struggle for women's rights was barely started, let alone won. In Great Britain, for example, Constance Gore-Booth (Countess Markiewicz, 1868–1927), who had once been condemned to death for her part in the Easter Rising, had the distinction of being both the first female British MP elected and the first female Irish Cabinet Minister.[28] But the movement for women's suffrage, which had been founded during the childhood of its most devoted activist, Emmeline Pankhurst (1858–1928), did not achieve success in Britain until the year of her death. The pioneer of birth control, Marie Stopes (1880–1958), who opened the UK's first birth-control clinic in 1921, was also a professional palaeontologist employed by Manchester University. [CONDOM]

The peasant societies of Eastern Europe were faced by the problems of rural overpopulation, by dwindling opportunities for migration, by a drastic fall in agricultural prices, and by the dearth of capital investment, both local and foreign. In all these matters the economic paralysis of Germany and the unnatural isolation of the Soviet Union caused untold disruption beyond their borders. No sooner had a measure of stability been restored than the whole of Europe was hit by the Great Depression.

The countries of East Central Europe, trapped between Germany and the USSR, faced very special difficulties. Whilst struggling to establish stable political regimes, Poland, Czechoslovakia, Hungary, and the Baltic States were forced to carry the economic consequences of the collapse of the empires. Semi-industrialized but still largely agrarian in character, their infant economies started life under the multiple burdens of hyperinflation, post-war industrial recession, and rural distress. Łódź, for example, the largest textile city in the region, suffered a 75 per cent drop in production between 1918 and 1939, when its traditional Russian market was closed. Peasant societies were increasingly polarized by conflicts between conservative landowning interests and radical peasant parties, by the impositions of new government bureaucracies and foreign-based enterprises, and by class and ethnic protests. In this light, the great advances made in education and the elimination of illiteracy, in parcelling out of the large estates, and in urban development command much respect—not least because later regimes were to deny that any such progress had been made.

The greatest ever experiment in planned modernization took place from 1929 onwards in the Soviet Union. It was so radical and so ruthless that many analysts would maintain that this, and not the events of 1917, constitute the real Russian Revolution.[29] It was made possible by the rise to supreme power of Joseph Stalin, General Secretary of the CPSU since 1922.

Iosif Vissarionovich Dzhugashvili (1879–1953), alias 'Koba', alias 'Stalin', is the clearest example in history of a pathological criminal who rose to supreme power through the exercise of his criminal talents. In *The Guinness Book of Records* he holds the top place under 'mass murder'. He was born in the mountain village of Didi-lilo, near Gori in Georgia, the son of a drunken father and of a devout, abandoned mother. Georgians say that he was an Ossetian. At all events, he was not a Russian, though he was sent to be educated in a Russian Orthodox seminary. He was expelled, but not before he had imbibed the paranoiac nationalism of a Russian Church which, in Georgia, was an alien creed. He drifted into revolutionary politics, in the seedy area where the political and the criminal undergrounds overlapped. He made his name in the Bolshevik Party in 1908, when he staged the most spectacular armed robbery in tsarist history, ambushing the Tiflis mail-coach and leaving the scene with a haul of gold. He was repeatedly arrested and exiled to Siberia, whence he repeatedly escaped. This circumstance created the suspicion, first voiced by Trotsky, his most jaundiced biographer, that he was an agent of the Tsarist secret police, the *Okhrana*. He arrived in Petrograd early in 1917 after the latest of his escapes, and, with no qualifications in journalism or Marxism, assumed the editorship of *Pravda*. In the revolutionary years he was Lenin's choice as Commissar for the Nationalities, and built up a circle of loyal accomplices, notably at Tsaritsyn (later renamed Stalingrad), who followed his fortunes thereafter. His most dangerous moment came in Poland in August 1920 when, as political commander of the South-west Front he had ignored orders to link up with Tukhachevsky and was held responsible by a Party tribunal for the ensuing disaster. As usual, he could not be nailed; but he never forgot it. (Seventeen years later, the death warrant of Tukhachevsky and of four other associates from 1920 was signed by three generals who had all served on Stalin's South-west front.)

Stalin became General Secretary of the Party during Lenin's first illness, and he survived Lenin's belated advice to have him removed. According to Trotsky, he poisoned Lenin to prevent further enquiries. Thereafter, with the *Cheka* and the Party Congresses in his practised hands, there was no stopping him. He proceeded with a masterful display of cunning and cynicism. He outmanœuvred all his senior rivals, setting them up on policy issues which he coolly adopted for himself or used to discredit them. It took him five years to ruin Kamenev, Zinoviev, and Bukharin, and seven to ruin Trotsky. He then set about killing them. He had no family life. He drove his second wife to suicide. He lived like a hermit in one room of the Kremlin, attended by his daughter, Svetlana Alliluyeva, whose memoirs are a prime source. He slept all day and worked all night with his cronies, endlessly playing the gramophone and watching silent movies, and visiting his dacha for relaxation. He rarely emerged, and made few speeches. On his annual trip to Georgia he travelled in one of five identical trains, each of the others carrying a 'double' to lessen the risk of assassination. He need not have bothered. He lived out his natural term. Later, though he spoke no foreign language except Russian, he proved himself as skilful in diplomacy as in home tyranny and in war management. When he was finally struck down, he was the unchallenged master of a superpower.

In looking for superlatives to describe Stalin's chief rival, an American officer in Petrograd had once called Trotsky 'A four-kind son-of-a-bitch, but the greatest Jew since Jesus Christ'.[30] Yet Stalin's record was to make Trotsky's achievements look like the small change of history. And Trotsky saw it coming: already in 1924 he was correctly predicting that 'the gravedigger of the Party of the Revolution' would take over:

The dialectics of history have already hooked him and will raise him up. He is needed by all of them, by the tired radicals, by the bureaucrats, by the nepmen, by the kulaks, by the upstarts, by all the sneaks that are crawling out of the upturned soil of the revolution . . . He speaks their language, and knows how to lead them. Stalin will become the dictator of the USSR.[31]

As a manipulator of political power, Stalin has every claim to be judged the greatest man of the twentieth century. He once said, modestly, 'Leaders come and go, but the People remain.'[32] In fact, under his guidance the people had to come and go and the Leader remained. The only person whose evil can be compared to his own was another small man with a different moustache, whom he never met, and who was not so successful.

Once Stalin was firmly in the saddle, the tempo of Soviet life began to whir. Lenin's NEP had done much to restore social and economic equilibrium; but it did nothing to further communist ideals or to equip the Soviet Union for modern warfare. So, confident in his command of unlimited coercion, Stalin plunged into a breakneck programme which was designed to forge a first-class industrial and military power within a decade. Its ambitions were breathtaking; yet in terms of human life its destructiveness outdid any other disaster in European history, even the Second World War. Its apologists, who still thrive in distant universities, are apt to maintain that 'omelettes can't be made without breaking eggs'.[33] But

Stalin was breaking the people whose lives he was supposedly improving; and in the end the omelette proved inedible. There were six main interlocking elements: central planning, accelerated industrialization, rearmament, collectivized agriculture, ideological warfare, and political terror.

Stalinist planning methods exceeded anything previously attempted anywhere. The State Planning Commission, Gosplan, was empowered to draw up Five-Year Plans that determined every detail of every branch of economic activity—production, trade, services, prices, wages, costs. Every enterprise, and every worker, was given 'norms' that were to be fulfilled without discussion. Since the Soviet state was a monopoly employer, all workers became 'slaves of the Plan'. Indeed, since the Party insisted on the ethos of 'socialist emulation', that is, forcing workers to outdo their norms in the manner of the legendary coalminer Alexei Stakhanov, over-fulfilment of the Plan was regularly demanded. The Five-Year Plans of 1928–32, 1933–7, and 1938–42 set unprecedented targets for economic growth and productivity of labour. Industrialization was to be achieved in exchange for a marked reduction in consumption. In practice, this meant 'work harder, eat less'. Industrial growth rates were set at over 20 per cent per annum. Total crude industrial output rose astronomically: in 1928 the index stood at 111 per cent of the 1913 level, in 1933 at 281 per cent, in 1938 at 658 per cent. Absolute priority was given to heavy industry—steel, coal, power, and chemicals. Quantity reigned supreme over quality. Falsified statistics became the object of an official cult whose central temple stood in the Permanent Exhibition of Economic Achievement in Moscow.

Rearmament was not announced, though the military-industrial complex was evidently the chief beneficiary of the changes. A separate and secret military-industrial sector was supplied with its own favoured factories, personnel, and budget. (The very existence of that separate budget was denied until 1989.) From 1932 onwards the Red Army was able to invite its German partners to participate in training and manoeuvres using the most modern equipment, including tanks, war-planes, and parachute troops.

The collectivization of agriculture, postponed in 1917, was now put into effect with utter disregard for the human cost. The aim was to ensure that the state took full control of the food supply at a period when a large part of the rural labour force was being drafted into the new industrial towns. In the ten years 1929–38, 94 per cent of the Soviet Union's 26 million peasant holdings were amalgamated into a quarter of a million *kolkhozy* or state-owned 'collective farms'. After 70 years of emancipation, the Russian peasant was returned to serfdom at the point of a gun. All who resisted were shot or deported. A fictional social enemy, the *kulak* or tight-fisted peasant, was invented in order to justify the murders. An estimated 15 million men, women, and children died. Agricultural production dropped by 30 per cent. Famine, both natural and artificial, stalked the land.

Stalinist ideology, as instituted in the 1930s, involved the adoption of numerous official fictions which were then enforced as the absolute and incontrovertible truth. These fictions had little to do with serious political philosophy, and took a radical turn away from Lenin's internationalist Marxism. They included: the role of Stalin as 'the best disciple' of Lenin; the role of communists as the chosen leaders of the people; the role of the Great Russians as 'elder brothers' of the Soviet nationalities; the status of the Soviet Union as the crowning achievement of 'all patriotic and progressive forces'; the function of the Constitution as a source of democratic power; the unity of the Soviet people and their love for the communist system; the 'capitalist encirclement' of the USSR; the equitable distribution of wealth; the joyous freedom of learning and art; the emancipation of women; the solidarity of workers and peasants; the justness of 'the people's wrath' against their enemies. Many of these fictions were enshrined in Stalin's *Short Course* (1939) on the history of the Communist Party of the Soviet Union (CPSU), the bible of the faithful. Soviet scholars, educators, and legislators were obliged to propagate them for fear of their lives; Western scholars were not.

The cult of Stalin's personality knew no bounds. All the country's foremost poets and artists were conscripted to the chorus:

> Thou, bright sun of the nations,
> The unsinking sun of our times,
> And more than the Sun,
> For the Sun has no wisdom . . .[34]

In religious matters, Stalinism followed the established atheist line. State education was militantly anti-religious. In the 1920s and 30s the Orthodox Church was mercilessly attacked, churches destroyed, and priests killed. Later, the emphasis shifted more towards manipulation: during the Second World War, Stalin would call for the defence of Holy Russia and reopen the churches. Mature Stalinism contained a strange symbiosis of state atheism and Orthodox patriotism.

The main instruments of coercion and terror—the *Cheka* (OGPU/NKVD/KGB), the *Gulag*, or network of state concentration camps, and the dependent judiciary—had been refined during the early Bolshevik period. In the 1930s they were expanded to the point where the manpower of the security agencies rivalled that of the Red Army, and the camps contained up to 10 per cent of the population. By 1939 the Gulag was the largest employer in Europe. Its prisoner-employees, the *zeks*, who were systematically starved and overworked in arctic conditions, had an average life expectancy of one winter. Innocent victims were rounded up in their homes and villages; others were charged with imaginary offences of 'sabotage', 'treason', or 'espionage', and tortured into confession. The usual sentences consisted either of summary execution or of fixed periods of imprisonment or exile, such as 8, 12, or 25 years, from which very few could emerge alive. Show trials of the most prominent victims were staged for the benefit of publicity. They also served to mask the nature and scale of the main operations. Such was the paralysing fear that gripped the largest state in the world for three decades that most of the concrete information about the Terror was successfully suppressed. [**VORKUTA**]

VORKUTA

I F space in history books were allotted in proportion to human suffering, then Vorkuta would warrant one of the longest chapters. From 1932 until 1957, this mining town on the Pechora River, in Russia's Arctic, stood at the centre of Europe's most extensive complex of concentration camps. In Stalin's 'Gulag Archipelago', the *Vorkutlag* ranked second only to Kolyma in north-eastern Siberia, whose entrance gates were surmounted by the slogan: 'LABOUR IS A MATTER OF HONOUR, COURAGE, AND HERO-ISM.' At the time of the *zek* rebellion in 1953, Vorkuta held some 300,000 souls. Over the years, more human beings perished there than at [AUSCHWITZ]; and they died slowly, in despair. But few history books remember them.[1] There are many eye-witness reports from Vorkuta, several of them published in English;[2] but few people have read them. There is even a detailed guidebook to over 2,000 'facilities' of the Soviet Gulag written by a Jewish survivor in the 1970s. His account was barely noticed.[3] In addition to the familiar categories of camps, prisons, and *psikbol'nitsa* or 'psychiatric prisons' [DEVIATIO], it contains a section on 'death-camps'. These were installations like those at Paldiski Bay (Estonia), Otmutninsk (Russia), and Cholovka (Ukraine), where prisoners were forced to work without protection on tasks such as the manual cleaning of atomic-powered submarines or the underground mining of uranium. Death from radiation was only a matter of time.[4] (See Appendix III, p. 1330.)

At the height of the Glasnost era, local people started digging in the Kuropaty Forest near Minsk in Belarus'. They knew that it sheltered the remains of men, women, and children killed during the Great Terror fifty years before. They uncovered several circular pits, each containing a mass grave for *c*.3,000 bodies. They could see that scores, if not hundreds more such pits lay under the pines. But in 1991 they were ordered to stop. They planted a cross by the roadside, and left the secrets of the forest intact.[5]

In 1989 the Russian 'Memorial' organization, which devotes itself to discovering the truth about Stalinist times, unearthed a pit at Chelyabinsk in the Urals dating from the 1930s. It contained 80,000 skeletons. Bullet holes in skulls told an unambiguous story. These were not victims who had been worked to death in the Gulag. 'People were taken out of their flats', said the local photographer, 'and shot with their children at this place.'[6]

One was entitled to ask; how many more such sites did the immensity of Russia conceal?

The three phases of the Stalinist Terror succeeded each other in a rising tide of brutality and irrationality. The preliminary terror was directed against carefully selected targets. Its victims were mainly second-rank figures—the ex-Menshevik managers of the pre-1929 Gosplan, internationalist Marxist historians, the Byelorussian intelligentsia, and the minor associates of major figures. Lenin's widow, Krupskaya, was warned that she wasn't 'irreplaceable'. The Peasant Terror or 'anti-kulak drive' mushroomed after 1932, as peasants resisted collectivization or slaughtered their livestock in protest. No clear definition of a kulak was available, though poorer peasants were urged to denounce their more prosperous neighbours. The Terror-Famine 1932–3 was a dual-purpose by-product of collectivization, designed to suppress Ukrainian nationalism and the most important concentration of prosperous peasants at one throw. [**HARVEST**]

The Political Terror or 'Purges' began in earnest in December 1934 with the murder of S. M. Kirov, the Party leader in Leningrad. From that starting-point, it spread out in ever-widening circles until it engulfed the leadership of the CPSU, including officers of the Red Army and of OGPU itself, and eventually the entire population. Since every victim was required to denounce ten or twenty 'accomplices' and their families, it was only a matter of time before the numbers involved were being counted in thousands and, in the end, in millions. The initial purpose was to destroy all the surviving Bolsheviks and everything they stood for. But that was only a beginning. Participants in the XVIIth Party Congress of 1934, the 'Congress of Victors', meekly hailed Stalin's triumph over the 'opposition', only to find themselves accused and decimated in turn. After the three main show trials of Zinoviev (1936), Pyatykov (1937), and Bukharin (1938), the sole Bolshevik leader left alive was Trotsky, who survived in his fortified Mexican refuge until 1940. But the full fury of the indiscriminate *Yezovshchina*, the Terror of N. I. Yezhov, Stalin's chief hangman, was still to be unleashed. Such was the dynamic of the infernal machine that early in 1939 Stalin and Molotov were signing lists of several thousand named victims each morning, whilst every regional branch of the security police was scooping up far greater quotas of random civilian innocents. The Terror did not take a pause until at the XVIIIth Congress of March 1939 Stalin coolly denounced Yezhov as a degenerate; and it did not stop completely until the *Vozhd'* himself expired.

For many decades, opinion in the outside world was unable to comprehend the facts. Prior to the documentary writings of Alexander Solzhenitsyn in the 1960s, and the publication of painstaking research by a few courageous scholars, most people in the West thought that stories of the Terror were much exaggerated. Most sovietologists sought to minimize it. The Soviet authorities did not admit to it until the late 1980s. Stalin, unlike Hitler, did not pay the price of public exposure. The total tally of his victims can never be exactly calculated; but it is unlikely to be much below 50 millions.[35]

Without doubt, Stalinism was the child of Leninism; on the other hand, it acquired many specific characteristics which were not important in Lenin's lifetime. Trotsky classified the change as the 'Thermidorian Reaction', and it greatly

HARVEST

'A QUARTER of the rural population, men, women and children, lay dead or dying' in 'a great stretch of territory with some forty million inhabitants', 'like one vast Belsen'. 'The rest, in various stages of debilitation', 'had no strength to bury their families or neighbours'. '(As at Belsen), well-fed squads of police or party officials supervised the victims.'[1]

In 1932–3, as part of the Soviet collectivization campaign, the Stalinist regime had unleashed a man-made terror-famine in Ukraine and the neighbouring Cossack lands. All food stocks were forcibly requisitioned; a military cordon prevented all supplies from entering; and the people were left to die. The aim was to kill Ukrainian nationhood, and with it the 'class enemy'. The death toll reached some 7 million.[2] The world has seen many terrible famines, many aggravated by civil war. But a famine organized as a genocidal act of state policy must be considered unique.

The writer Vasily Grossman would later describe the children:

Have you ever seen the newspaper photos of the children in German camps? They were just like that; their heads like heavy balls on thin little necks, like storks . . . and the whole skeleton was stretched over with skin like yellow gauze . . . And by spring, they no longer had faces at all. Instead they had bird-like heads with beaks—or frog heads—thin white lips—and some of them resembled fish, mouths open . . . These were Soviet children and those who were putting them to death were Soviet people.[3]

The outside world was not informed. In the USA a Pulitzer Prize was given to the *New York Times* correspondent, who spoke freely in private of millions of deaths but published nothing.[4] In England, George Orwell complained that [the terror-famine] had 'escaped the attention of the majority of English russophiles'.[5]

The historian who eventually brought convincing proof to the event struggled to convey its enormity. He wrote a book of 412 pages, with about 500 words per page, then stated in the Preface: 'about twenty human lives were lost, not for every word, but for every letter in this book.'[6]

complicates all debates on Soviet and Communist history. The central fact to remember is that Stalinism was the mode within which Soviet Communism stabilized, and which provided the foundations of Soviet life in the USSR until 1991. For this reason it is Stalin's version of Communism, not Lenin's, that must be addressed whenever any general assessment of the system is to be made. (See Appendix III, p. 1321.)

As it happened, 1929, the year of Stalin's revolution in the USSR, was also the year of crisis in the capitalist world. Historians have wondered whether the two events were not somehow linked, perhaps through the rhythms of post-war economic adjustment. At all events, on 24 October 1929, 'Black Thursday', the prices of shares on the New York Stock Exchange suddenly collapsed. Panic set in; banks recalled their loans; and, before anyone could control it, the Great Depression was rolling round all the countries with whom the USA did business. It was a back-handed compliment to the extent of American influence in the world economy. In the USA itself, the sudden end to the easy credit of the 'roaring twenties' caused a massive wave of bankruptcies, which in turn caused an accompanying wave of unemployment. At the height of the 'Slump', in 1933, one-third of the American labour force was out of work; the steel industry was working at 10 per cent of its capacity; food stocks were destroyed because hungry workers could not afford to buy them; and 'poverty raged amidst plenty'.

In Europe, which was struggling to pay its war debts, often from dwindling reserves of gold, the effects of the Slump were felt with little more than a year's delay. In May 1931 Austria's leading bank, the *Kreditanstalt* of Vienna declared itself insolvent; in June the USA had to accept a moratorium on all debts owed by European governments; and in September the Bank of England was forced to take sterling off the gold standard. Confidence, the corner-stone of capitalism, was breaking down. Within a couple of years business had lost its way, and 30 million workers had lost their jobs. By 1934 the USA had a new, dynamic President, Franklin D. Roosevelt, whose New Deal programme of government-funded works was to haul America back to prosperity. 'The only thing we have to fear,' he said, 'is fear itself'. But Europe had no Roosevelt, and no New Deal. Recovery was as slow as the Slump was sudden.

The effects of the Depression were psychological and political as well as purely economic. Everyone from banker to bellboy was perplexed. The Great War had brought death and destruction; but it had also brought a purpose to life and full employment. Peace appeared to bring neither. There were men who said that life amidst the danger and comradeship of the trenches was preferable to life on the dole. Others said that Spengler's gloomy broodings about Europe returning to a Dark Age were correct. The anxieties brimmed over into violence on the streets: left-wing battle squads pitched into right-wing gangs in many European cities. It was the season for charlatans, adventurers, and extremists. [**MOARTE**]

In Germany, the rise of Hitler and his Nazi Party was unquestionably connected to the Great Depression. But the connection was not a simple one. The Nazis did not march on Berlin at the head of an army of unemployed; there was no 'seizure of power'. Hitler did not have to topple a weakened government as the Bolsheviks did, nor threaten the head of state, like Mussolini. He came to power through par-ticipation in Germany's democratic process, and at the invitation of the lawful authorities. It is beside the point that he and his ruffians were anything but democrats or constitutionalists at heart.

German politics were specially vulnerable to the Depression, whose effects were poured into a cup of insecurity already full to the brim. The rancour of defeat still lingered. The street battles of extreme left and extreme right were ever-present.

Democratic leaders were mercilessly squeezed both by the Allied Powers and by voters' fears. The German economy had been tortured for a decade, first by reparations, then by hyperinflation. By the end of the 1920s it was exceptionally dependent on American loans. When Stresemann died in October 1929, several days before the Crash, it took no genius to forecast turbulence ahead. None the less, the turbulence which ensued in 1930–3 was accompanied by several unusual and unforeseen circumstances.

In those years, the Nazis took part for the first time in a rash of five parliamentary elections. On three successive occasions they increased both their popular vote and their list of elected deputies. On the fourth occasion, in November 1932, their support declined; and they never won an outright majority. But in a very short time they had established themselves as the largest single party in the Reichstag. What is more, the rising tide of street violence, to which Nazi gangs greatly contributed, took place in a much-changed international setting. In the early 1920s, Communist-led strikes and demonstrations were overshadowed by the apparently limitless power of the *Entente*. German industrialists and German democrats knew exactly whom to call in if the Communists ever tried to take over. But in the early 1930s Britain, France, and the USA were in no better fettle than Germany; and the Soviet Union was seen to be modernizing with remarkable energy. With the communists claiming almost as many votes as the Nazis, Germany's conservative leaders had much-reduced means to keep the red menace at bay.

Somewhere in German political culture there also lurked the feeling that general elections could be supplemented by a national plebiscite on specific controversial issues. Given the chance, Hitler would not miss it. In the chaos of crumbling Cabinets, one of the transient ministers invoked emergency presidential powers. In September 1930, in the interests of democracy, one minority Chancellor persuaded President Hindenburg to activate Article 48 of the Weimar Constitution. Henceforth, the German president could 'use armed force to restore order and safety' and suspend 'the fundamental rights of the citizen'. It was an instrument which others could exploit to overthrow democracy.

The sequence of events was crucial. The storm raged for three years: deepening recession, growing cohorts of unemployed, communists fighting anti-communists on the streets, indecisive elections, and endless Cabinet crises. In June 1932 another minority Chancellor, Franz von Papen, gained the support of the Reichstag by working with the Nazi deputies. Six months later, he cooked up another combination: he decided to make Hitler Chancellor, with himself as Vice-Chancellor, and to put three Nazi ministers out of twelve into the Cabinet. President Hindenburg, and the German right in general, thought it a clever idea: they thought they were using Hitler against the Communists. In fact, when Hitler accepted the invitation, suitably dressed in top hat and tails, it was Hitler who was using them.

Less than a month later, and a week before the next elections, a mysterious fire demolished the Reichstag building. The Nazis proclaimed a Red plot, arrested

MOARTE

IN 1927 the Legion of the Archangel Michael was formed in Bucharest by Corneliu Codreanu. Together with its paramilitary wing, the Iron Guard, it grew into one of Europe's more violent Fascist movements. In 1937 it secured a substantial share of a large right-radical vote, and in 1940–1, in alliance with General Antonescu's army, it briefly commanded Romania's 'National Legionary State'. In February 1941, having rebelled against its military allies, it was suppressed.

The Legion's ideology expounded a peculiar variation on the theme of 'Blood and Soil', giving a special place to 'the bones of the ancestors'. In resurrecting Romania's fortunes it claimed to have created one national community of the quick and the dead. Party rituals centred on a death cult. Meetings began with a roll-call of fallen comrades, whose names were greeted with the shout of 'Present'. Earth from the tombs of saints was mingled with the 'blood-soaked soil' of Party battlefields. Grandiose ceremonies attended the exhumation, cleaning, and reburial of the corpses of Party martyrs. The exhumation of 'the Captain', Codreanu, murdered in 1938, constituted the grandest event of the Legion's months in power. Nazi planes flew overhead, dropping wreaths on the open tomb. Codreanu's death was one among hundreds of political murders in Romania in the late 1930s, when the Legion's death squads fought a running battle with the King's political police. Codreanu was garrotted, shot in the head, and disfigured by acid, before being buried in secret under seven tons of concrete.

In Romania, Serbia, and Greece, Orthodox belief maintains that the soul of the deceased cannot depart until the flesh has decomposed. For this reason, families traditionally gather three to seven years after the first burial and exhume the skeleton, which is then lovingly cleaned and washed in wine before committal to eternal rest. It is also believed that certain categories of corpse are unable to decompose. The Orthodox service of excommunication contains the phrase 'May thy body never dissolve'. In cases of murder and suicide, the tormented souls are thought to remain indefinitely trapped in the grave. In the district of Maramures, a ceremonial 'Wedding of the Dead' is held to placate them.

In certain regions of Romania, folk tradition further holds that a trapped soul can take flight between sundown and cock-crow. Especially on St Andrew's Day (30 November) and on St Michael's Eve (8 November), the reanimated corpse returns to haunt the world, slipping through keyholes to take sexual favours from its sleeping victims and to suck their blood. To guard against such visitations, peasants will lead a black stallion into the graveyard. Wherever it shies from stepping over a grave, they drive a great stake through the suspect corpse, to pin it down. From the earliest ethnographic studies, it is well known that this is vampire country.[1]

Political scientists have concluded that Romanian Fascism was just a nasty variety of the genre, with special interests in anti-semitism and necrophilia. The anthropologist would conclude that it mobilized deep-rooted religious and folk traditions. In December 1991, as soon as the Communist dictatorship collapsed, a new 'Movement for Romania' emerged, with Codreanu as its hero.[2]

communist leaders, won 44 per cent of the popular vote in the frenzied, anti-communist atmosphere, then calmly passed an Enabling Act granting the Chancellor dictatorial powers for four years. In October Hitler organized a plebiscite to approve Germany's withdrawal from the League of Nations and from the Disarmament Conference. He received 96.3 per cent support. In August 1934, following the President's death, he called another plebiscite to approve his own elevation to the new party-state position of 'Führer and Reich Chancellor' with full emergency powers. This time he received 90 per cent support. Hitler was in control. In the final path to the summit, he did not breach the Constitution once. The personal responsibility for Hitler's success is easily pinpointed. Four years after the event, Hitler received his former partner, von Papen, at Berchtesgaden. Hitler said: 'By making me Chancellor, Herr von Papen, you made possible the National Socialist Revolution in Germany. I shall never forget it.' Von Papen replied, 'Certainly, my Führer.'[36]

Hitler's democratic triumph exposed the true nature of democracy. Democracy has few values of its own: it is as good, or as bad, as the principles of the people who operate it. In the hands of liberal and tolerant people, it will produce a liberal and tolerant government; in the hands of cannibals, a government of cannibals. In Germany in 1933–4 it produced a Nazi government because the prevailing culture of Germany's voters did not give priority to the exclusion of gangsters.

Adolf Hitler (1889–1945) was an Austrian who became the master of all Germany as no German had ever been. He had been born at Braunau on the Bavarian frontier, the son of a customs official, and had grown up with the stigma of his father's bastardy (for this reason, unkind acquaintances sometimes called him 'Schickelgrüber'). His early life had been painful and, in career terms, disastrous. He had some artistic ability, but failed to follow the requisite courses, and drifted round Vienna's twilight doss-houses as a part-time decorator and postcard artist. Introverted, resentful, and lonely, he was well versed in the social pathology of German Vienna's anti-Slav and antisemitic *demi-monde*. Having fled to Munich, he welcomed the First World War, which came as a blessed relief to his personal misery. He served with courage, was twice decorated with the Iron Cross (second class and first class), survived when his comrades died, and was gassed. He ended the war in a military hospital, profoundly embittered. [**LANGEMARCK**]

Hitler's post-war political career filled the void of the early failures. His party, the NSDAP, had adopted a brew of commonplace racism, German nationalism, and vulgar socialism which proved attractive first to drifters like himself and later to millions of voters. On the soap-boxes and street-corners of defeated Germany, he found the gift for oratory, or demagoguery, which would carry him to the heights. He learned to modulate the pitch and tempo of his voice, to gesticulate, to wrap his face in winning smiles and blazing fury, and so to captivate an audience that the substance of his words was almost immaterial. His skill, which would soon be magnified by searchlights, loudspeakers, and musical choruses, can only be likened to that of revivalist preachers or of latter-day popstars, whose pseudo-hypnotic performances induce mass hysteria. His emotional intensity uncannily matched the feelings of a humiliated nation. He played on people's fears, ranting against the 'Jewish–Bolshevik conspiracy' and the Allies' 'stab in the back'. His one and only attempt to seize power was a total fiasco. The 'Beer-Cellar *Putsch*' of November 1923 taught him to stick to 'legal means'—that is, to mass rallies, electoral procedures, and political blackmail. His trial, where he railed impressively at the judges, made him a national figure: and his two years in the Landsberg gave him the leisure to write his rambling memoirs, *Mein Kampf* (My Struggle, 1925–6), which became a best-seller. *Ein Volk, ein Reich, ein Führer* was exactly what the majority of Germans wanted to hear. He promised to make Germany great again, in a 'Third Reich' that was to stand a thousand years. To be precise, he kept it in being for twelve years and three months. 'In the Big Lie', he had written, 'there is always a certain force of credibility.'

In his private life, Hitler remained withdrawn, and unmarried until his final hours. He loved animals and children, and kept a homely mistress. In contrast to his companions, many of whom were swaggering louts, he was well-groomed and polite. He has never been linked to personal violence, although he clearly gave the (unrecorded) orders for genocide. But his heart was filled with hate. He was given to quoting Frederick II, whose portrait hung in his study to the end: 'Now that I know men, I prefer dogs.'[37] His one passion was architecture. In the 1920s he built himself a magnificent mountain chalet, the *Berghof*, perched on a peak near Berchtesgaden. Later, he revelled in grandiose plans to rebuild the ruins of Berlin or to turn his native Linz into the art centre of Europe. Western commentators have built Hitler up into an 'evil genius'. 'Evil' is accurate, 'genius' doubtful.

[BOGEY]

Once at the helm, Hitler moved swiftly to eliminate rivals and opponents. He had to crush the socialist wing of the NSDAP, which had considerable popularity, and which had been calling for the 'second, socialist revolution' to follow his own success. On the night of 30 June 1934, 'the Night of the Long Knives', he called in the Party's new élite guard, the SS 'Blackshirts', to cut down the Party's older formation of stormtroopers, the SA 'Brownshirts'. All the Führer's immediate rivals were killed at a stroke—Ernst Röhm, the SA leader, Gregor Strasser, the Party's leading socialist, General von Schleicher, the Nazis' leading ally in parliament. Having banned the German Communist Party in 1933, he then dissolved all the other parties. Assuming Hindenburg's office of Commander-in-Chief, he won the army to his side and proceeded to remove unreliable elements.

Hitler arrived with no grand economic design. After all, Germany did not need to be modernized as Russia did. But he soon gained a feel for collectivist economics, and was offered a ready-made scheme by Dr Hjalmar Schacht, President of the Reichsbank. His initial industrial backers were demanding action, and he guessed that action would generate confidence and employment. Schacht's plan combined Keynesian financial management with complete state direction of industry and agriculture: the trade unions were replaced by a Nazi labour front; strikes were outlawed. The new deal, like its American counterpart, aimed at full production and full employment through a state-funded work creation programme. The flagship projects included the building of the German Autobahns (1933–4), the launching of the Volkswagen (1938), and, above all, rearmament.

The relationship between Nazism and German industry provides a most contentious issue. One standard interpretation, much favoured by communist scholarship, posited 'the primacy of economics'. According to this, the interests of big business determined not only short-term political policy, aimed at the destruction of the German left, but long-term strategic policy as well. Germany's expansion to the East was supposedly motivated by German industry's demands for raw materials, secure oil, and cheap labour. A contrary interpretation has posited the 'primacy of politics'. In this view, Hitler soon threw off the tutelage of the industrialists and developed the state-owned sector as a counterweight to private industry. As from 1936, the introduction of a Four-Year Plan, the replacement of Schacht as chief economic adviser, and the promotion of the state-owned steel corporation, the Reichswerke Hermann Göring, all pointed in that direction. A compromise interpretation argues on the basis of the shifting alliances of a 'polycratic power centre' made up of the NSDAP, army, and industry.[38] Rearmament was important for psychological and for political reasons. The German armaments sector, which had been artificially constrained, could recover very quickly; Krupps' turnover began to improve dramatically from 1933. But rearmament also healed Germany's wounded pride; and it won over the army, which in 1935–6 was able to reintroduce conscription. Hitler had no precise plans for using his rearmed forces. But it was convenient to let people think that the gun under his coat was loaded.

Agriculture was not a subject that interested the Nazis. They came up with a scheme for the formation of co-operatives. But the main thrust was to guarantee state-fixed prices, and hence the farmers' security.

Nazi ideology, to put it mildly, was not very sophisticated. Unlike Stalin, Hitler did not inherit a corpus of party thought which could be bent to his own purposes. His one and only work, *Mein Kampf* (1925), which was to find its way onto the bookshelf of almost every German family, contained only two or three consistent ideas, and nothing original. Most important was the chain of argument which led from the supposed existence of the *Herrenvolk* or 'master race' to the supposed German right to *Lebensraum* or 'living space' in the East.

Hitler took a hierarchy of races for granted. He divided mankind into 'culture-founders', 'culture-bearers', and 'culture destroyers'. 'The bearers of human

BOGEY

SOON after the German Army occupied Austria in March 1938, Adolf Hitler is said to have ordered the commander of Wehrkreis XVII to demolish the village of Dollersheim by 'target practice'. The inhabitants were evacuated, and all the buildings of the village, including the cemetery, were duly reduced to rubble by artillery. The point behind this savage operation seems to have been that both Hitler's father and paternal grandmother, Maria Anna Schicklgruber, were buried at Dollersheim, and that Hitler had recently learned the facts of his father's early life. According to a Gestapo report, the young Fräulein Schicklgruber had conceived Hitler's father when working as an unmarried domestic servant in a rich Jewish household. The implications, from Hitler's point of view, were disturbing.

From this, and many other indications, there is reason to believe that Hitler suffered from intense feelings of repressed guilt, shame, and self-hatred about his origins, his blood, his body, and his personality. One is not obliged to take the conflicting evidence at face value to conclude that Hitler is a prime subject for 'psycho-history'.[1]

Particularly interesting, and possibly crucial to the Führer's wartime state of mind, was his rampant hypochondria. From 1936 to 1945 he placed total faith in a dubious physician, Dr Theo Morell, who treated him with constant massive doses of glucose, vitamins, stimulants, appetizers, relaxants, tranquillizers, and sedatives, usually by direct intravenous injections. Hitler's obsession with flatulence addicted him to a huge daily diet of anti-gas pills based on atropine and strychnine. Morell's rivals unsuccessfully reported to the Gestapo that Morell was poisoning the Führer by stealth.[2]

Soldiers can be intuitive. Sometime during the Second World War, marching to the magnificent beat of 'Colonel Bogey', someone in the British Army composed the immortal refrain:

'itler — 'as only got one ball;
Goering's two are far too small.
'immler — is rather sim'ler,
But Gerballs—'as no balls—at all.[3]

The point here is that twenty years later, when the Soviet authorities released the text of a supposed autopsy report on the late Führer's corpse, it stated that 'the left testicle was missing'.[4] The report bore traces of a KGB plant, and was not supported by other witnesses. But some historians have taken it seriously. Since congenital monorchidism is rare, they have concluded that Hitler must have mutilated himself by self-castration.[5] The mystery was not resolved by the opening of the KGB files in the 1990s.[6]

Yet the observations do not stop with the physical evidence. Numerous aspects of Hitler's conduct hint at something hideous beneath the demure exterior. He permitted no talk in his presence about even mildly sexual matters. He had a deep fear of incest. He professed revulsion about 'filth' of all sorts. Although the evidence is contradictory, his sex life was either totally sublimated or disgustingly perverse.

At every stage, Hitler's brilliant openings were paralysed by a pervasive sense of failure. And he repeatedly flirted with suicide. In his love of polit-ical ritual, he indulged in a range of pseudo-religious Catholic parodies. Above all, he felt constantly impelled to say that history, or the German nation, or God, or whatever, had found him *würdig*—'worthy'. The infer-ence has to be that the cauldron of self-hatred which seethed within him fuelled the overt hatred which he then projected onto Jews, Slavs, com-munists, homosexuals, and gipsies, and eventually onto Germany herself.

Needless to say, self-mockery is a healthier mechanism than self-praise. In the First World War, the British had marched to another mag-nificent refrain, sung to the lugubrious hymn tune of 'Greenland's Icy Mountains':

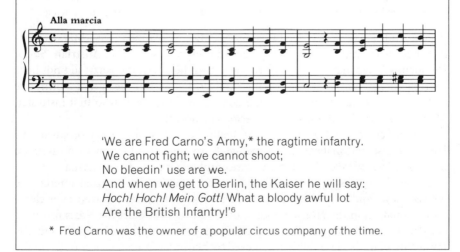

'We are Fred Carno's Army,* the ragtime infantry.
We cannot fight; we cannot shoot;
No bleedin' use are we.
And when we get to Berlin, the Kaiser he will say:
Hoch! Hoch! Mein Gott! What a bloody awful lot
Are the British Infantry!'[6]

* Fred Carno was the owner of a popular circus company of the time.

cultural development' today were 'the Aryans'. 'The mightiest counterpart to the Aryan is the Jew.' The Jews were the *Todfeind*, the mortal enemy. He did not care to define the Aryans, nor to establish a hierarchy of nations within the Aryan race. His chapter on the subject starts with the observation that some things are so obvious that they don't need explaining.[39] Hitler also believed in 'the iron logic' of 'racial purity'. 'In every mingling of Aryan blood with that of lower people', he observed, 'the result was the end of the cultured people.' 'All great cultures of the past perished . . . from blood-poisoning.'[40] Hitler believed that the health of a nation was dependent on the value of its national territory. 'Only an adequately large space on this earth assures a nation freedom of existence.' 'The foreign policy of the folkish state must . . . create a healthy relation between the nation's population and the quantity and quality of its soil.'[41]

Since Germany's neighbours already possessed land in abundance, either in the colonies or, in Russia's case, through the conquest of the steppes, Germany could only compete by seizing the adjacent lands to the East. 'We stop the endless German movement to the South and West, and turn our gaze towards the land in the East.'[42] German expansion into Poland and Ukraine would give her the strength not only to fight Russia but also to check France, also 'the mortal enemy'. Hitler believed that Germany was fighting at a disadvantage in its struggle to exist. 'Germany is no world power,' he wailed. 'Germany will either be a world power, or there will be no Germany.'[43]

Overt racism was accompanied by a collectivist creed which has often been described in vague terms such as 'the herd instinct', but which has distinct Marxist overtones. Of his own debt to the Marxism of the pre-war SPD, Hitler once said:

I had only to develop logically what social democracy failed in . . . National socialism is what Marxism might have been if it could have broken its absurd ties with a democratic order . . . Why need we trouble to socialise banks and factories? We socialise human beings.[44]

Recent studies have shown that the young Hitler was familiar with Marxist writing, and was impressed by the flag-waving rallies of the Austrian Social Democrats.[45] He may have absorbed more than he knew: the Nazis did not have a strong intellectual tradition, but their reticence does not mean that a primitive sort of socialism lay beyond their horizons. It was the Nazis who first instituted May Day as a national festival for (German) workers.

Nazi policies were deduced very rationally from these few shaky propositions. Hitler's racist nationalism led immediately to the introduction of antisemitic measures. Jews were excluded from state employment and from German citizenship; Jewish traders were officially boycotted; marriage and sexual intercourse between Jews and non-Jews was forbidden. These measures received their clearest formulation in the Nurnberg Laws of 1935. From the start the Nazis favoured euthanasia, the killing of the mentally and genetically handicapped, and the rewarding of multiple childbirth achieved by heroic German motherhood. On the social plane, the Nazis were contemptuous of all the existing hierarchies—aristocracy, officer corps, professions, and guilds. The ranks of the Nazi Party-State were thrown open to everyone who was prepared to serve without shame or dissent. Offices were filled by the advancement in every German town and village of the most vulgar, unqualified, and grasping elements. Their idols were the failed chicken farmer, Heinrich Himmler, who ran the SS, or the overweight ex-pilot, Reichsmarschall Hermann Göring, who could no longer squeeze into a cockpit.[46] Here was another close counterpart to the ethos of the burgeoning Stalinist bureaucracy of the USSR.

Nazism, like Stalinism, was strong on official fictions. Nazi propaganda peddled many strange notions. Hitler was the new Frederick or the new Bismarck. The Nazis were successors to the Germanic gods or the Teutonic Knights. The Third Reich was the natural heir to the Holy Roman Empire and to the Hohenzollerns. The German people, united and free, knew unbounded love for their homeland, unlimited joy in their learning and art, untrammelled pride in their emancipated women, unstinting wrath against traitors and enemies . . . It was all rather familiar. The cult of Hitler's personality knew no bounds. The Führer was the embodiment of all that is beautiful, wise, and good.

Most Nazi leaders were unbelievers; Hitler himself was a lapsed Catholic. Their rituals owed more to the parody of ancient Germanic paganism than to any modern religion. So they had a major problem in defining their relationship with a German nation that was still predominantly Christian. As often as not, they ignored the theoretical issues. But to pacify the Catholics, Hitler signed a Concordat with the Vatican in July 1933, confirming the autonomy of the German See in return for the hierarchy's renunciation of political involvement. The compromise encouraged some Catholic prelates, such as Archbishop Innitzer of Vienna, to express sympathy for Nazi aims. But it did not prevent the Vatican from ordering *Mit brennender Sorge* (1937), which denounced Nazi ideology, to be read in all Catholic churches in Germany. To manage the Protestants, Hitler announced the creation in 1935 of a state-controlled Union of Protestant Churches. There was also an attempt to found a new movement for 'German Christians', where the swastika embraced the cross, under Reichsbishop Dr Müller. In November 1933 these pseudo-Christian Nazi surrogates staged a demonstration in Berlin to the honour of 'Christ the Hero'. In the end, religion and irreligion had to co-exist as best they could.

In the field of coercion and terror the Nazis were fast learners. Their 'Brownshirts' and 'Blackshirts' had a solid grounding in common fraud, blackmail, and thuggery. On the other hand, at the head the German *Rechtsstaat*, they did not have 500 years of the Muscovite *oprichniki* behind them. The structures of social control were less complete than in the USSR. There was no state monopoly in employment; there was no collectivized countryside; and there were no party cells or commissars in the Wehrmacht until 1944. All of which goes some way to explain the Nazis' special style, where studied bestial ferocity had to compensate for structural weaknesses. A high level of well-publicized brutality was required, simply because more refined instruments of control were often lacking.

The security organs of the Reich never assumed the monstrous proportions of their Soviet counterparts. Both the Party Guard, the *Schutzstaffeln*, and the *Gestapo*, the 'Secret State Police', were used by the Party to supplement existing military and police forces. But neither was given the same range of competence invested in the NKVD. One concentration camp was opened at Dachau, near Munich, in 1934; but the number of prisoners was dropping in the late 1930s. Nazi-run People's Courts and People's Judges increasingly absorbed the work of the traditional judiciary. But wholesale terror was not the norm. In Germany itself, Nazi violence stayed within predictable parameters. Germans who conformed could expect to survive. Some 500,000 German Jews were persecuted and expelled; the *Kristallnacht* of 1938, when Jewish synagogues and shops were smashed, caused vast damage and apprehension. But it does not appear that 'the Final Solution' was planned in advance. At no point prior to the outbreak of war did the Reich possess the facilities or the modern death technology which it subsequently employed. It is an open question how far the Nazis emulated the Soviet terror machine, which was both older and larger than theirs.

Political scientists worry too much about the theoretical classification of Nazism. Some, after Arendt, accept that it was a member of the totalitarian family; others, after Nolte, think of it as one of the 'three faces of Fascism'; others prefer to leave it as a movement *sui generis*.[47] It was one, none, or all of these things, according to the criteria one chooses. Less than fifty years after the last Nazi fell from grace, many analysts are still strongly swayed by personal rancour, by political bias, or by the victors' syndrome. Suffice it to say, if personal views are permitted, that Nazism was the most repulsive movement of modern times. The ideals of its utopia were no less ugly than the realities of its Reich.

Europe, wracked by the Depression, was in poor shape to meet the challenge posed by Stalin and Hitler. The Western Powers were absorbed with their own affairs. The USA was absent. The states of East Central Europe were weak and divided. At the very time that the idea of collective security was mooted, Europe's attention was diverted by the Civil War in Spain.

Britain at the end of the Great War had retreated into its island and imperial concerns. There were crises enough in Ireland, in India, and in Palestine. Despite the formation of two Labour governments, labour troubles multiplied at home. The General Strike of May 1926, the launching of the communist *Daily Worker* (1930), the Labour Party's expulsion of its own leader, Ramsay MacDonald, for forming a National Government (1931), and the creation of Sir Oswald Mosley's British Union of Fascists (1932), all took place to the background of unemployment rising to 3 million. The Conservative Government headed first by Stanley Baldwin and then by Neville Chamberlain was elected in 1935 on promises of stability and good management. Its principal headache prior to the Munich Crisis lay in the young King's love affair with an American divorcee and his subsequent abdication. All the while, a remarkable series of social and technological advances were taking place: the initiation of the BBC (1922), of family planning (1922), of full women's suffrage (1928), and of paperback books (1935); the invention of television (1926), penicillin (1928), and the jet engine (1937). The British generation which came to maturity after the Great War felt that they had lived through enough stresses; the last thing they wanted to worry about was storm clouds on the Continent.

France could not withdraw from the Continent. In the 1920s French policy gave priority to building security, partly by the hard line towards Germany and partly through the 'Little Entente' in the East (see below). But then the emphasis shifted. The 1930s saw the heyday of French Algiers and French Saigon, whilst at home the Depression brought labour issues to the fore. Édouard Daladier (1884–1970), a radical socialist, twice served as Premier, whilst shifting coalitions and the Stavisky scandal (1934) aroused widespread disillusionment. Political opinion polarized, with the Parti Communiste Français and Action Française both vociferous. A whole stereotype of allegedly static French attitudes came to be associated with the name of André Maginot, Minister of War 1929–32 and constructor of a vast line of fortifications along the eastern frontier. This was not entirely fair. It is not true, as the British were later to charge, that the French army was unwilling to fight; but in the absence of any significant British force, it did not relish the task of fighting Germany single-handed; and it was locked into organizational plans that impeded early offensive action.

Scandinavia in the 1930s was fortunate in lying beyond the sphere of strategic tensions. Sweden was hard hit by recession in the iron trade, but responded under the Social Democrats by organizing the most comprehensive system of social welfare in the world. [SOCIALIS]

East Central Europe, in contrast, lay in the eye of the gathering storm. With Hitler on one side and Stalin on the other, its leaders had every right to be nervous. Security arrangements made by the French in the 1920s had several serious loopholes. The concept of the *cordon sanitaire*, which began as a belt of states holding off Soviet Russia, was not pursued with any consistency. The 'Little Entente', which joined Czechoslovakia, Romania, and Yugoslavia in a co-operative system designed for the containment of a resurgent Hungary, did not include Poland—the largest country of the region—and from 1934 was matched by an independent Balkan Pact of Romania, Yugoslavia, Greece, and Turkey. The Western Powers had no high reputation for decisiveness. When Warsaw had been attacked by the Red Army in 1920, they sent a flurry of unsolicited military missions, but no military reinforcements. In 1934, when Marshal Piłsudski took soundings in Paris about a preventative war against Nazi Germany, he elicited no response. The Western Powers never quite decided whether their policy in Eastern Europe was to be based on the new states, like Poland, or on the congenial post-Bolshevik Russia, which never materialized. From 1935, when their fear of Hitler outgrew their dislike of Stalin, they turned to a hyena to tame a wolf.

In East Central Europe, the international crisis of the 1930s inevitably affected internal affairs. The communist parties, usually illegal, had little popular support except in Czechoslovakia; but they acted as an important irritant, provoking nationalist elements to react. Hitler, when he wasn't inciting the German minorities in Poland, Czechoslovakia, and Romania, encouraged other nationalistic elements to emulate him. In the process dictatorships were strengthened, military budgets soared, the political role of the officer class increased; nationalism and ethnic conflicts of all sorts intensified.

In Poland, for example, the vicinity of Stalin and Hitler could be sensed on every hand. Marshal Piłsudski, who signed a non-aggression pact with the USSR in 1932 and another with Germany in 1934, sought an even-handed stance summed up in his 'doctrine of two enemies'. The Polish Communist Party, which had opposed Poland's independence in 1918–20, had adopted an internationalist and Trotskyite leaning. Its exiled leadership, largely Jewish, was liquidated *en masse* during Stalin's purges. At the other extreme, the National Democratic movement spawned a fascistic offshoot, the *Falanga*, which was also banned. Militant nationalistic organizations sprang up in each of the national minorities. The Ukrainian OUN—a radical offshoot of the older UWO organisation—indulged in common terrorism and provoked brutal pacifications of the peasants. Zionism made rapid headway in the Jewish community, where 'revisionist' groups such as *Betar* spawned militants such as Menachem Begin or Yitzak Shamir, who would shine elsewhere. A Nazi Fifth Column was organized among the German minority. The activities of all these groups fuelled the fires of mutual hatred. After Piłsudski's death in 1935, the so-called 'Government of Colonels' strove to check the centrifugal forces by forming a Camp of National Unity (OZON). But they found that the main opposition parties joined forces against them. General Sikorski joined Paderewski in Switzerland in the anti-government Morges Front. Priority was given to belated military reform and, in a state economic plan, to rearmament. The Foreign Minister, Colonel Józef Beck, trod an even-handed course which displeased the Western Powers, who wanted him to co-operate with Stalin. Towards his lesser neighbours, however, he thumped the nationalist drum. He set his eyes on the district of Zaolzie (Polish Cieszyn), which had been forcibly seized by the Czechs in 1919. And in early 1939 he sent a brusque ultimatum to Lithuania demanding an end to the state of undeclared war. Violent incidents were few; but the threat of violence was abroad.

Poland's Jewish community—still the largest in Europe—lived out its last summers. In the late 1930s apprehension about the future was growing, especially when waves of Jewish refugees and expellees arrived from Germany. Various forms of petty harassment, in education, municipal laws, and employment, were on the rise, but there was nothing to compare with the rampages of the Nazis. For anyone who has seen the pictures and documents of those years, the image is one of a vibrant, variegated communal life. The Jewish *kahals* enjoyed full autonomy. Jewish parties of many hues were free to operate. There were Jewish film stars, Jewish boxing champions, Jewish women MPs, Jewish millionaires. To say, as is sometimes done, that Polish Jewry was 'on the edge of destruction' is true enough; but it is to read history backwards.[48]

Czechoslovakia had a reputation for democracy that was stronger abroad than among the country's own German, Slovak, Hungarian, Polish, and Ruthenian minorities. Exceptionally for the region, it was highly industrialized, it had a genuine communist movement, and it looked to Russia for moral support. During the long presidency of the great T. G. Masaryk, who retired in 1935, it held together.

The 'Kingdom of Serbs, Croats, and Slovenes' changed its name to the Kingdom of Yugoslavia in 1929. It had no common history, language, or religion. It had come into being on the initiative of Slovenes and Croats from Austro-Hungary, who urged the Serbian establishment to admit them and then came to resent Serbian domination. The Serbian monarchy and army played the central role, particularly after the establishment of a unitary royal dictatorship in 1929. In Catholic Croatia, the national party of Stefan Radić gained the upper hand in local affairs that had been impossible under Hungarian rule, only to find its voice blocked in Belgrade. Slovenia prospered quietly under its leader, Father Korošec, the original convenor of the Yugoslav National Council. Macedonia simmered. The climate of violence was heightened by the murder of Radić (1929) and then of King Alexander (1934). The democratic Serb opposition began to make common cause with the Croats. But time was short: 'Yugoslavia is a necessity,' wrote one observer, 'not a pre-destined harmony.'[49] (See Appendix III, p. 1319.) [SARAJEVO]

In the Mediterranean the main shock-waves were generated by Fascist Italy. Mussolini, who liked to talk in ancient Roman style of 'Mare Nostro' (Our Sea), was determined to become the regional power. Having eliminated the active opposition, who abandoned the parliament after the murder of a socialist deputy, he had a free hand. His designs were expedited by a pliant King and by the stage-managed organs of a streamlined 'corporate state'. In the 1930s he looked further afield: Italian troops were sent to Abyssinia, to Spain, and, in March 1939, to Albania. The League of Nations recommended sanctions, the British and the French threatened reprisals, but nothing was actually done. Mussolini thrived by baiting Austria over South Tyrol. Prior to the 'Pact of Steel' of 22 May 1939, and the consequent Rome–Berlin Axis, he liked to flaunt his independence from Germany.

Civil strife had been festering in Spain for at least twenty years. The Spaniards met added misfortune by unleashing a civil war at a juncture when communist–fascist rivalry was moving to its peak throughout Europe. As a result, the military insurrection of 1936 attracted the attention of Hitler and Stalin. Spain was turned into a laboratory for Europe's nastiest political practices. Three years of agony culminated in the resounding defeat of democracy. The roots of the conflict lay deep in Spain's unstable history, in a polarized society, and in an intractable land problem. Over half of the land belonged to barely 1 per cent of the population. The mass of peasants lived on tiny holdings or on starvation wages. The small working class was badly hit by the Depression. The Roman Catholic Church, dominated by an ultra-reactionary hierarchy, was deeply involved in economic affairs as a major landowner and as the controller of many enterprises from the Banco Espíritu Santo to the Madrid tramways. An army whose ratio of

SARAJEVO

WHOEVER lies awake in Sarajevo hears the voices of the Sarajevo night. The clock on the Catholic cathedral strikes the hour with weighty confidence: 2 a.m. More than a minute passes—seventy-five seconds to be exact—and only then does the Orthodox church chime its own 2 a.m. A moment later the tower clock on the Bey's Mosque strikes the hour in a hoarse, faraway voice; and it strikes 11, the ghostly Turkish hour. The Jews have no clock, so God knows what time it is for them . . . Thus division keeps vigil, and separates these sleeping people, who wake, rejoice, and mourn, feast and fast by four different calendars . . .

Bosnia is a country of hatred and fear. And the fatal characteristic is that the Bosnian is unaware of the hatred which lives within, shrinks from analysing it—and hates anyone who tries to do so. Yet there are more people ready in fits of subconscious hatred to kill and be killed than in other much bigger lands . . . It is hatred acting as an independent force: hatred like a cancer consuming everything around it.

And by a strange contrast, it can also be said that there are few countries with such firm belief, so much tenderness, such loyalty and unshakeable devotion. But in secret depths hide entire hurricanes of compressed and maturing hatreds awaiting their hour. The relationship between your loves and your hatred is the same as between your high mountains and the invisible geological strata beneath them. You are condemned to live on deep layers of explosive which are lit from time to time by the very sparks of your loves.

In countries like Bosnia, virtue itself often speaks and acts through hatred. Those who do believe and love feel a mortal hatred for those who don't, or who believe and love differently. (The most evil and sinister-looking faces can be met in greatest numbers at places of worship—at monasteries and dervish tekkes.)

On every occasion you will be told: LOVE YOUR BROTHER, THOUGH HIS RELIGION IS OTHER, IT'S NOT THE CROSS THAT MARKS THE SLAV, and RESPECT OTHERS' WAYS AND TAKE PRIDE IN YOUR OWN. But there has been plenty of counterfeit courtesy since time immemorial. Under cover of these maxims, old instincts and Cain-like plans may only be slumbering. They will live on until the foundations of material and spiritual life are completely changed. And when will that time come, and who will have the strength to carry it out?

In some Maupassant story, there is a dionysiac description of spring which ends with the remark that on such days there should be a warning posted on every corner: CITOYENS! THIS IS SPRING—BEWARE OF LOVE!

Perhaps in Bosnia, too, people should be warned . . .[1]

These paragraphs are contained in a work that is classed as fiction. They enshrine the imagined reflections of an emigrant, who left Bosnia in 1920. They were composed in 1946 by Ivo Andrić (1892–1975), child of Travnik, student of Zagreb, Vienna, and Krakow, sometime prisoner of the Habsburgs, pre-war Yugoslav diplomat, and Nobel laureate.

Is it really fiction? 'Much of [Andrič's work] is set in Bosnia,' his editor explains, 'and is closely dependent on this setting. He roots his stories in a specific geographical and historical context.'[2] In other words, an important element of the stories is *not* fiction. Andrič paints the psychological landscape of Bosnian society with the same precision that he reports the sounds of the Sarajevo night. These descriptions can be treated as invaluable historical documents.

At that same time, in 1946, an experienced welfare officer was working for UNRRA in Sarajevo. She presented the opposite opinion. 'It is only by working together that people can get over their hatreds,' she wrote. 'Now is a good time. Everything that is young is thinking the right way . . . Now we don't care—is he Moslem, is he Catholic, is he Orthodox? Now it is brotherhood and unity.'

---

officers to men was unusually high was a bastion of ultramontane and monarchist sentiment. The result was a peculiarly obtuse and resistant social fortress composed of priest, squire, and officer, which habitually obstructed any reforms that touched their interests. Social protests were desperate, vicious, and anticlerical. Anarchists were prominent among both the rural labourers of the south and the workers' unions of Barcelona. There were separatist provinces in Catalonia, in the Basque country, and, to some extent, in Galicia. In Morocco, where the long war against the Riffs ended in 1925, the army ruled supreme. In 1930–1 the latest lurch of the political seesaw brought the downfall of the military dictator, General Primo de Rivera, a lengthy interregnum, the *Dictablanca*, the abdication of King Alfonso, and finally the declaration of the Second Republic.

The five years of constitutional government from 1931 to 1936 brought mayhem out of chaos. In 1931 the Primate, the Archbishop of Toledo, was exiled for denouncing the Republic. In 1932 an abortive *pronunciamiento* was launched by the generals. In 1933 the landowners of the south kept peasants off the land rather than accept reform. Legislation introducing state schools and divorce, and separating Church from State, could not be implemented. Agrarian reform was reversed and sequestrated land returned to its former owners. In 1934 a determined strike by miners in Asturias grew into a separatist rising which was broken only with massive bloodshed. In the elections of February 1936 the left-wing *Frente Popular* or 'Popular Front' of republicans, socialists, Catalans, and communists carried the day. But by then the central government was losing control. Recalcitrant peasants were occupying the great estates. Workers were organizing one general strike after another. The Catalans were claiming autonomy. Political murders and church-burning proliferated. 'We are present today' said the outgoing Catholic Prime Minister, 'at the funeral service of democracy.' The country was becoming ungovernable.

On 18 July 1936 the Generals struck for a second time. General Francisco Franco (1892–1975) crossed to Tetuán from his command in the Canaries and issued a manifesto. Spain was to be saved from Red revolution; the army in North Africa would not hesitate to use its Moorish troops. 'The Crusade against Marxism', as one republican sympathizer put it, 'was to be undertaken by Moors against Catholics.'[50]

At the outset, the political spectrum in Spain was extremely wide and complicated. In the Cortes, the Popular Front was opposed by a right-wing coalition, including the *Acción Popular* or 'People's Action' and the Fascist *Falange Española*, recently founded by Primo de Rivera's son. On the left, the Communist Party hold only 16 out of the Front's 277 seats, compared to 89 for the Socialists headed by Largo Caballero and 84 for Manuel Azaña's Left Republicans. Inexorably, however, the strains of civil war boosted the fortunes of the two most violent and radical extremes. The *Falange* was destined to become the main political instrument of the army. The communists were destined to dominate the beleaguered Republic. Franco said, and possibly believed, that he was fighting to forestall Bolshevism. His slogan was *Fe ciega en la victoria* 'Blind Faith in Victory'. It was beside the point that the communist menace was exaggerated, what counted was that many Spaniards feared it.

The pattern of political and geographical support became very complex. When Franco's army command proclaimed its insurrection in Morocco, it rebelled against the Government of the Spanish Republic in Madrid, headed at the time by Azaña. The army could count on garrisons in each of the main cities of the mainland, on the paramilitary squads of the *Falange*, and, in some areas, on the ultra-Catholic formations, the *Requetes*, left over from the Carlist era. Generally speaking, they could count on the political support of the Catholic hierarchy, of the larger landowners, and of all who gave priority to the restoration of law and order. From an early stage they received military assistance from Portugal, from Nazi Germany, and from Fascist Italy. Portugal offered secure bases. The warplanes of the German Condor Legion provided air superiority. Early in 1937 Italian troops occupied the Balearic Islands, and the southern coast round Málaga.

The Government, in contrast, had few professional troops to call its own. In time, it trained and fielded a regular force; but it had to rely heavily on the armed militias of various left-wing unions—the socialist PSOE, the anarchist FAI, the Marxist but anti-Stalinist POUM, the UGT and the communist-run CNT. Generally speaking, it could count on the political support of the peasants in the countryside, of workers in the towns, of anticlericals everywhere, and of all who gave priority to constitutional government. From an early stage they received assistance from abroad: tanks, planes, munitions, and advisers from the USSR, and in the International Brigades a flood of perhaps 50,000 foreign volunteers. In the later stages, in 1938–9, it has to be said that the nightmare painted by Fascist propaganda *did* materialize. Under Dr Negrín, the Government did fall under the influence of hard-line communists, and its security agency, the Military Investigation Service (SIM), into the direct control of the Soviet GPU. The Spanish Republic's gold, transferred to Odessa for safe keeping in September 1936, was never returned. [**ADELANTE**]

The fighting was long, fragmented, and often confused (see Appendix III,

ADELANTE

IN September 1936, Comintern's propaganda chief in Western Europe advised Moscow to form a series of International Brigades to fight for the Spanish Republic. The idea had originated with Maurice Thorez of the Parti Communiste Français, who remembered the 'International Legion of the Red Army' which had fought in the Russian Civil War.[1]

From the start, therefore, though the Brigades were presented as the spontaneous action of volunteers, they were thoroughly subordinated to the Communist movement. They operated outside the regular command of the Spanish Republican Army; all their senior military and political staff were Communist appointees; and all recruits were vetted by Soviet agents. Their slogans were 'Spain—the graveyard of European Fascism', *No pasarán* ('They will not pass'), and *Adelante*, 'Forward'.

The principal recruiting office in Paris was headed by Jozip Broz, alias 'Tito', the future dictator of Yugoslavia. It organized a 'secret railway', using false passports to send recruits to the Spanish frontier and thence to the Brigades' main base at Albacete in La Mancha.

In Europe of the Depression there was a large pool of manpower to draw on—unemployed workers, refugees from the Fascist states, rebel intellectuals. Of the 50,000 who served, the biggest contingents were raised by the Confédération Générale du Travail in France, by Polish miners' organizations in Belgium and the French département of Le Nord, and by left-wing German exiles. Eighty per cent of them were working men. There was also a nucleus of foreign volunteers already serving at the front. These included German, Italian, French, and British 'columns' (see Appendix III, p. 1325). Their leaders included Carlo Rosselli, a socialist who had escaped from a Fascist gaol in Italy, and Hans Beimler, a German escapee from Dachau.

The intellectual recruits were few, but vocal. They answered the call, often without knowing the implications:

> Many have heard it on remote peninsulas,
> On sleepy plains, in the aberrant fisherman's islands,
> Or the corrupt heart of a city;
> Have heard and migrated like gulls or the seeds of a flower.[2]

The military leadership of the Brigades was not experienced in warfare. The commander-in-chief, André Marty, a Catalan sailor from Perpignan, had led a mutiny in the French fleet off Odessa in 1919. The chief military adviser, Col. Karol Swierczewski, alias 'Walter', was a Polish officer from the Soviet security service, and a professor at the military academy in Moscow. The inspector-general, Luigi Longo, and the chief political officer, Giuseppe di Vittorio, were Italian Communists. The one commander to show real talent was Lazar Stern, alias 'General Kléber', an Austrian Jew from Bukovina, who had gone over to the Bolsheviks as a POW in

Russia. He, like many such comrades, would be shot on Stalin's orders on his return to Russia.

The courage of the men was not in doubt. They lived in squalid conditions and were subject to ferocious discipline, including executions, for the slightest offence. They fought with desperate courage. At the siege of Madrid in November 1936, for example, the British battalion lost one third of its effectives. At the Jarama, the same unit suffered 375 casualties out of 600 men.[3] Worst of all, the Brigades were used to suppress the communists' erstwhile socialist and anarchist allies by brute force.

By the end of 1938, the Kremlin agreed to pull the Brigades out. About 12,000 departed, leaving some 6,000 Germans with nowhere to go. A farewell parade in Barcelona on 15 November, held under portraits of Negrin, Azaña, and Stalin, was addressed by 'La Pasionaria':

You are history . . . You are legend . . . We will not forget you. And when the olive tree of peace puts forth its leaves again, and mingles them with the laurels of a victorious Spanish Republic . . . come back![4]

Thanks to later developments, when the Western powers adopted the anti-Fascist cause, the career of the International Brigades in Spain attracted much favourable publicity. In fact, they were always outnumbered by the foreigners fighting for Franco. The latter included some Fascist regulars, some idealistic volunteers, and some, like the Irish Brigade of General O'Duffy, blatant adventurers. To see the overall picture, one has to compare the recruits raised by the Communists in 1936–7 with those attracted by the Fascists both in Spain and in the Second World War [**LETTLAND**].

p. 1324). Ragged and vicious local confrontations were more common than sustained campaigns or set-piece battles. Behind the lines, massacres of prisoners and civilians were perpetrated by both sides. The strategic layout was not simple. After the initial exchanges, when army garrisons in Madrid and Barcelona were shelled into submission, the Government held most of the country except for the northwest at Corunna and the extreme south at Seville. But once the army had re-established itself along the Portuguese frontier, and captured the central fortress of Toledo, it could gradually envelop the Government strongholds on the north coast and in the corridor linking Madrid and Valencia. The Army Junta established itself at Burgos, with HQ at Salamanca; the Government at Valencia. Outstanding events included the year-long nationalist siege of Oviedo, the German bombing of Guernica in April 1937, the lunging operations for control of the Ebro and the strong point of Teruel in 1938, and, in 1939, the terminal sieges first of Barcelona (January) and then of Madrid (March). In Barcelona, 'the wildest city in Europe', where Catalans and anarchists were opposed to any form of Spanish government, whether Red or White, the tragedy ended with frightful massacres perpetrated by both the defeated communists and their erstwhile anarchist allies. In Madrid, where the rump Council of Defence of the Popular Front eventually renounced the communists, it ended with the rebels' triumphal entry on 29 March. At the victory parade, Franco could at last voice his slogans with conviction: 'Hay orden en el país' (there is order in the country) and 'España, una, grande, libre' (Spain is one, great, and free). Republican leaders fled. Thousands of refugees poured over the Pyrenees.[51] Spain lay firmly in the Fascists' grip for 40 years. [**FARAON**]

Franco's victory over 'the Spanish people', as his opponents put it, was frequently attributed to his superior armaments and foreign help. But the truth was not so simple or so palatable. The 'Spanish people' were not all on one side, and neither were all of Spain's 'anti-democratic' forces. It is hard to say whether the Spanish Republic was more discomfited by its nationalist enemies or by the totalitarian elements within its own ranks. Franco could unite his supporters; the Republic's supporters could not organize a united or effective democracy.

For Spain, the Civil War was a tragic lesson in the fruits of fratricidal hatred. Estimates of casualties range from 400,000 to a million.[52] For Europe, it was yet another object lesson in the mechanisms whereby disciplined minorities can take control of countries which let them breed. Also, since Western sympathies were strongly behind the defeated Republic, it greatly magnified fears of a general fascist menace. By the same token, it diminished fears of the 'Red Bogey'. Thanks to Franco's unwelcome success, public opinion in the Western democracies entered the 'anti-fascist' mode which was to characterize its priorities for the duration. Franco strengthened the West's resolve to stand up to Hitler and Mussolini, whilst lowering its sensitivity to Stalin. After March 1939 it was hard for any politician in the West to argue that communism was as great a menace as fascism.

FARAON

GENERAL Franco's mausoleum, at Cuel de Moros in the Valley of the Fallen near Madrid, was built after his victory in 1939. It consists of a grandiose underground basilica, larger than the nave of St Peter's, which is approached through a tunnel hewn through the granite and lined with the tombs of the Civil War dead. On the exterior it is surmounted by 'the largest Christian symbol ever erected'—a stone cross 492 ft high and weighing 181,740 tons.[1] It was constructed by the slave labour of ex-POWs, branded with the letter 'T' for *trabajador* or 'worker', who toiled for two decades between the work-site, the quarries, and compulsory church services in the nearby Escorial. They were officially employed by the 'Board for the Redemption of Penalties through Labour'—a name reminiscent of Nazi slogans. Visiting the site in 1940, a Nazi officer was said to have remarked, 'Who does [Franco] think he is—a new Pharaoh?'

Ironically enough, Franco's victory came too late to arrest the general drift of events. If fascism had triumphed in Spain in 1937 or 1938, it is conceivable that the West would have been aroused to the danger in time to nip Hitler in the bud. It is conceivable that the whole sorry story of appeasement could have been avoided. As it was, in the three years that the Civil War in Spain dragged on, the dictators grew from strength to strength, and the chance for collective security was missed.

'Collective security' was one of several abortive brain-children of the Western Powers, especially of the British, who were past masters at getting somebody else to do the fighting for them. Discussions went back to late 1933, when Hitler first pulled Germany out of the League of Nations. Before then, since the Soviet Union did not impinge on the West directly, Western anxieties had remained low. But the prospect of Nazi Germany on the loose in central Europe brought the danger rather nearer home. The obvious solution was for London and Paris to revive the strategic triangle of the Great War, and to recruit the Soviet Union as a counterweight to Germany. It was a move which the British in particular had been hoping to make since 1917. There was something of a public-relations problem, of course, in that Western politicians had been given to bad-mouthing Soviet communism; but it was not beyond the ingenuity of diplomats to explain that the Soviet regime was now entering a constructive phase, or that Stalin was more democratic than Lenin and Trotsky. Hence, in the middle of the most enormous campaigns of mass killing in European history, Stalin was made respectable and brought into the fold of the peaceful nations. Hitler's representative walked out of the League on 14 October 1933; Stalin's representative, Maxim Litvinov, moved in on 18 September 1934.

From Stalin's point of view, *rapprochement* with the West offered several advantages. It would increase trade, and with it the import of technology. It would improve the USSR's image, whilst keeping the Nazis guessing. It would give Moscow's loyal communist parties abroad the chance to win acceptance and, by entering the Popular Fronts—as in Spain—to penetrate democratic parliaments and unions. Again there was a public-relations problem, since the Stalinists were given to calling democratic politicians everything from 'bourgeois exploiters' to 'lackeys of international imperialism'; but this did not mean that Stalin had to abandon his discreet relations with Berlin, or the possibility of an eventual deal with Hitler. For the time being, he could keep all options open.

In the years that followed, the Nazis reacted to the fumblings of the West with thinly disguised contempt. Their every step spelled disaster for the Versailles settlement. In July 1934 they almost brought off a coup in Austria, where they murdered the Chancellor, Dr Engelbert Dolfuss, whose Fatherland Front had organized a one-party but anti-Nazi state. In 1935 they celebrated the Saarland's accession to the Reich, through a plebiscite envisaged by the Treaty, then promptly reintroduced conscription, reconstituted the Luftwaffe, and renounced the disarmament clauses. In March 1936 they openly defied the Treaty by reoccupying the demilitarized zone in the Rhineland. In 1937 they pulled out of the British-backed Non-Intervention Committee that was trying to keep foreign forces out of Spain, and signed the Anti-Comintern Pact with Italy. In March 1938 Hitler engineered the *Anschluss* or 'merger' with Austria, proclaimed the Greater German Reich, and drove to Vienna in triumph (see Appendix III, p. 1323).

Throughout this period Hitler was boasting of, and exaggerating, the scale of German rearmament. He kept quiet about the fact that he had already told his staff to prepare for war. [HOSSBACH] This does not mean that he had prepared a timetable for the events which ensued; on the contrary, the major conflict for which German industrialists and generals were preparing was not envisaged before 1942. In the mean time Hitler would be engaged in the tactics of bluff and threat, in what has aptly been called the policy of 'peaceful aggression'. He felt that he could get what he wanted either without war or at most by localized conflict. To this end, in the spring of 1938 he began to make noises about the intolerable oppression of Germans in the Sudetenland of Czechoslovakia. By that time the Western leaders could not fail to notice that Nazi Germany was bent on expansion, and that collective security was not producing concrete results. So, at the instigation of the new British Prime Minister, Neville Chamberlain, they embarked on appeasement. Chamberlain was acutely aware that renewed war in Europe would undermine Britain's fragile economic recovery and her imperial position overseas.

Appeasement, despite its later reputation, need not necessarily have been a policy of abject surrender. It contained elements both of realism and of magnanimity; certainly, in the form that favoured negotiations with Germany, it rejected the cynicism revealed in earlier Franco-British dealings with Italy. As Chamberlain well knew, the Hoare–Laval Pact of December 1935, which simply sought to acquiesce in the Italian attack on Abyssinia, had been disowned both in London and Paris, and had led to the downfall of its inventors. What is more, twenty years after the Great War, liberal opinion largely accepted that German grievances over their minorities in Eastern Europe deserved discussion. Many also agreed with the MacDonald Plan of 1933, which had proposed a balance of armaments in Europe in place of the indefinite prolongation of Allied supremacy. The generals advised that there were only two ways of effective Allied intervention against eventual German aggression in the East. Yet co-operation with Stalin's Red Army was fraught with dangers; and direct action against Germany in the West could only be undertaken by starting the full-scale war whose avoidance was so heartily desired. All in all, it was not dishonourable for Chamberlain to seek out 'Herr Hitler' in Germany, or to seek a resolution of the Sudeten question. It was not the fact of negotiation that was at fault, only the skills and priorities of the negotiators. Chamberlain went as a lamb into the lion's den, woefully ignorant of the 'faraway country' whose fate hung in the balance. Nor should one imagine that the history of appeasement was confined to the policy of the Western Powers towards Hitler. It has an even longer chapter in their relations at a slightly later date with Stalin. Democratic governments who neglect the moral fundamentals negotiate with dictators at their peril.[53]

The Munich Crisis, as it came to be called, unfolded in September 1938 on terms set by Hitler and never seriously challenged. It was concerned with Germany's

HOSSBACH

O N 5 November 1937, from 4.15 to 8.30 p.m., a conference was held in the Reich Chancellery in Berlin. It was attended by a group of leading German dignitaries, including Goering, Neurath, and Raeder, and was addressed by Hitler on the subject of 'opportunities for the development of our position in the field of foreign affairs.' The contents of his speech, the Führer melodramatically announced, were, in the event of his death, to be regarded as his last testament. They are known from a memorandum written up by Hossbach, the man who took the minutes:

The aim of German policy was to secure and preserve the *Volksmasse*, the racial community and to enlarge it. It was a question of space . . . German policy had to reckon with two hate-inspired antagonists, Britain and France, to whom a German colossus . . . was a thorn in the flesh.

Germany's problem could only be solved by means of force, and this was never without risk . . . There still remain the questions of 'when' and 'how'. In this matter, there were three cases to be dealt with:

Case 1: the period 1943–5. After this date only a change for the worse, from our point of view, could be expected . . . If the Führer was still living, it was his unalterable determination to resolve Germany's problem of space by 1943–5 at the latest.

Case 2: If internal strife in France . . . should absorb the French completely, then the time for action against the Czechs had come.

Case 3: If France is so ambivalent in war with another state that she cannot proceed against Germany . . . our first objective, if embroiled in war, must be to overthrow Czechoslovakia and Austria simultaneously . . .

Poland—with Russia at her rear will have little inclination to engage . . .

Military intervention by Russia was, in view of Japan's attitude, more than doubtful . . .

It was to be assumed that Britain—herself at war with Italy—would decide not to act against Germany . . .[1]

The Hossbach Memorandum has featured more than any other document in controversies over the origins of the Second World War. It was produced by Allied prosecutors at the Nuremberg Trial, and was used to accuse Goering and others for their part in planning the war 1939–45. However, the significance of the Memorandum was greatly deflated when a British historian demonstrated that the Memorandum did not support the views of the Allied prosecutors at Nuremberg. On the contrary, it showed that in November 1937 the Nazis had no concrete plans for war, and that Hitler had no clear assessment of the developing situation. It showed the Führer ranting rather vaguely about the possibility of a very limited war sometime before 1943–5:

Hitler's exposition was in large part day-dreaming . . . He did not reveal his innermost thoughts . . . The memorandum tells us what we know already, that Hitler (like every other German statesman) intended to become the dominant Power in Europe. It also tells us that he speculated how this might happen. His speculations were mistaken. They bear hardly any relation to the actual outbreak of war in 1939. A racing tipster who only reached Hitler's level of accuracy would not do well for his clients . . .[2]

A. J. P. Taylor's analysis was all the more surprising since it came from a historian noted for his germanophobia.

Outraged critics denounced Taylor's alleged disregard for 'historical context' and for the dynamics of Nazi expansionism. In mid-December 1937, they insisted, the German Army's directives were changed to envisage military aggression against Austria and Czechoslovakia. They took this change as justification for their interpretation of the Memorandum, and the conference, as marking 'the point where the expansion of the Third Reich ceased to be latent and became explicit'.[3] They failed to notice that German military aggression against Austria and Czechoslovakia did not materialize any more than any of the Führer's other faulty scenarios.

In effect, by overturning the 'almost universal view that Hitler planned the Second World War', Taylor was wrongly accused of trying to absolve Hitler from blame. What Taylor successfully demonstrated was the strange combination in the Führer's make-up of a general aggressive intent and an inability to formulate systematic war plans.

Almost thirty years later, one of the striking features of the debate about the origins of the Second World War may be seen in the absence of any mention of Stalin, or of the dynamic interplay of German and Soviet policy. All the participants, including Taylor, confined themselves to a discussion of Germany's intentions. None thought it worthwhile to comment on the intentions of the USSR. Historians were faced with the locked doors of Soviet archives. If a Soviet equivalent of the Hossbach memorandum exists, it has never yet seen the light of day. There is no way of knowing whether Stalin did or did not speculate about war in a similar way to Hitler. So, in the absence of documentary evidence about Stalin's intentions, most commentators have preferred to assume that there is nothing to discuss.

The long tradition of documentary-history writing, therefore, has fostered two opposite extremes. One is to say, in effect: if no documents can be examined, then nothing happened. The other view, well expressed in 'Taylor's Law' as formulated by Taylor's detractors, says: documents do not signify anything. Both extremes are equally pernicious.

designs on France's ally Czechoslovakia. Yet France took a back seat; the Czechoslovak government was excluded from the main discussions; and no thought was given to keeping Czechoslovakia's defences viable. The negotiations were supposed to draw a line on German expansion to the East. Yet they proceeded without the participation of the two most interested parties, namely Poland and the USSR. They were supposed to impress on Hitler the risk he was running. Yet the Western negotiators did not lay their strongest cards on the table. As Hitler rightly sensed, the more outrageous aspects of his contentions were not going to be tested. This, plus Chamberlain's limitless gullibility, determined the outcome. 'In spite of the hardness and ruthlessness of his face,' Chamberlain mused of Hitler, 'I got the impression that here was a man who could be relied on.'[54]

Chamberlain made three visits to Germany. At Berchtesgaden, on 15 September, he received a demand from Hitler for the secession of the Sudetenland—positively 'the Führer's last demand'. He promised to have it examined. At Godesberg, on the 23rd, he was faced by an unexpected ultimatum for the evacuation and annexation of the Sudetenland within five days. This was rejected by the British Cabinet, and by all concerned. France and Germany began to mobilize. At Munich, on 29–30 September, Chamberlain met the Führer for the final confrontation in the company of Daladier and of Mussolini, who had suggested the meeting. He handed over a memorandum accepting the substance of the (unacceptable) Godesberg ultimatum. With the help of his distinguished colleagues, he then gave an ultimatum to the Czechs, huddled in an adjoining room, pressing them to accept the unacceptable themselves or to pay for the consequences. His final contribution was to underline the Allied guarantee of a rump Czechoslovakian state, shorn of its magnificent frontier fortifications, and to draft a declaration on Anglo-German friendship. He alighted from his plane waving a paper which he claimed to bring 'Peace in our time'. He did so in the same spirit which underlay the British Foreign Office's advice to the England football team that same year—to give the Nazi salute at the start of their match against Germany in Berlin.

Chamberlain's three rounds with Hitler must qualify as one of the most degrading capitulations in history. Under pressure from the ruthless, the clueless combined with the spineless to achieve the worthless. Chamberlain had no need to concede any part of the Führer's demands without making cast-iron arrangements for Czechoslovakia's security; but he did. Beneš, the Czechoslovak President, had no right to sign away his country's integrity with nothing more than a personal protest; but he did. The outcome was to be summarized by Churchill in the House of Commons:

'£1 was demanded at the pistol's point. When it was given, £2 was demanded at the pistol's point. Finally the Dictator consented to take £1. 17s. 6d., and the rest in promises of goodwill for the future . . . We have suffered a defeat without a war.'[55]

Elsewhere, Churchill wrote that Britain had a choice 'between shame and war'; 'we have chosen shame, and we will get war'. Within six months the remnant of Czechoslovakia disintegrated, and Hitler entered Prague.

Munich undoubtedly marked the crucial psychological moment in inter-war diplomacy. It did not yet make war inevitable; what it did do was to sow the confusion in which two fatal assumptions were born. First, it convinced Hitler, and probably Stalin too, that further peaceful aggression would bring further cost-free dividends. Secondly, it created the impression in the West that talking to the Nazis had been a mistake. In the next round of the game, where the map ensured that Poland would be threatened, Munich ensured that Hitler and Stalin would seek to aggress by peaceful methods; that the West would seek to deter without negotiating; and that the Poles would seek to avoid the fate of Czechoslovakia at all costs. This was the deadly recipe.

In any number of European history books, 1939 is the year when 'the world went again to war', or words to that effect. In all chronologies except those once published in the USSR, it marks the 'outbreak of the Second World War'. This only proves how self-centred Europeans can be. War had been on the march in the world for eight years past. The Japanese had invaded Manchuria in 1931, and had been warring in central China since 1937. From August 1938 they were embroiled in fighting on the Mongolian frontier against the Soviet Red Army. As part of this conflict, Japan had joined Germany and Italy as one of the Axis Powers. What happened in 1939, therefore, was simply the addition of Europe to the existing theatres of war. It gave a second, European dimension to campaigns which hitherto were summarized, to quote the Japanese slogan, as 'Asia for the Asiatics'. In this sense, it turned a regional war into a global one. It has also been called 'Hitler's War'. This too is inaccurate.

By 1939 general rearmament was greatly adding to the strains. All the powers were rearming. Two years before, on Churchill's insistence, Britain had taken the decision to expand and to re-equip the RAF. This was the decision which would ensure her survival. At the same time France had created a new Ministry of Defence, and had nationalized the great Schneider–Creusot concern. This was a sign that European governments were preparing for a protracted conflict in which industrial strength would be every bit as decisive as trained men. On this score, specialist studies indicated the dramatic changes which had occurred in the last decade.

	USA	UK	France	Germany	USSR
Production (1938) (1932 GNP = 100%)	153	143	108	211	258
Relative manufacturing strength (World output = 100%) 1929	43.3	9.4	6.6	11	5
1938	28.7	9.2	4.5	13.2	17.6
Military expenditure (1933–8) (£ million)	1,175	1,201	1,088	3,540	2,808
Relative war potential (1937) (World = 100%)	41.7	10.2	4.2	14.4	14.0[56]

Estimates no doubt varied. But the British figures underlined several stark facts. The totalitarian powers had suffered from the Depression much less than the Western democracies had. Their military expenditure was twice as great as that of all the Western Powers put together. Their 'relative war potential'—which was a calculation based on the ability to translate industrial strength into military power through indices such as machine-tool levels—was roughly equal, and was separately equivalent to that of Britain and France combined. Italy hardly entered the reckoning. The RWP of Japan, was put, somewhat derisively at 3.5 per cent. All the other countries in the world added up to barely 10 per cent.

It took no genius to draw the conclusions: Stalin and Hitler were already in possession of war machines that far outstripped anything else in Europe. If the USA remained aloof, the Western Powers would be hard pressed to contain either Stalin or Hitler. If Stalin and Hitler joined forces, the West would be powerless to stop them. All eyes were, or should have been, on Stalin and Hitler, and on the unhappy countries trapped between them. Everything else was secondary.

Stalin's intentions in 1939 were governed by factors which are not always fully discussed. Professional historians, since they never gained access to the documentation, have often pretended that the subject does not exist. But it is not impossible to reconstruct its outlines. Generally speaking, the internal revolution of the USSR was reaching a plateau of relative stability, and the *Vozhd'* could look forward with confidence to more active foreign involvement. The most vulnerable years of the first Five-Year Plans and Collectivization had been passed; the Great Terror was drawing to a close; and a rearmed Red Army could already be rated as one of Europe's mightiest formations. However, two important inhibitions remained. The last phase of the Purges, which had been directed against the officer corps, was still incomplete; in 1939 the killing of the old military cadres was still in progress. And the Red Army was still engaged against the Japanese in Mongolia. Stalin, forever cautious, calculating, and secretive, was unlikely to commit himself to a major adventure in Europe until the new army cadres were trained and the Japanese conflict had been resolved. His obvious objective in the first instance was to lure Germany into a war with the Western Powers, whilst the USSR garnered its strength.[57]

Hitler's position was not so cramped. He had recently gained full control of the Wehrmacht, and he had no military commitments. He now held the offices of both War Minister and Commander-in-Chief. He had cut out all opposition in the General Staff; and after the dismissal of Dr Schacht had taken direct control of German industry. His protégé in Spain was poised for victory, and his own triumph at Munich had wrecked the defence plans of his Eastern neighbours. His minions were stirring up trouble all along the line—in Klajpėda (Memel) in Lithuania, in the Free City of Danzig, in Poland's German community, and in Slovakia, where a local nationalist movement was looking to Berlin for assistance. He had no definite war plans for the coming season; but as he pored over the outspread map in front of the plate-glass window of the 'Eagle's Nest' at

Berchtesgaden, it must have seemed that Europe was full of opportunities. On which miserable prey would the Eagle choose to swoop?

Early in 1939 Hitler's preference was still for some sort of deal with Poland. Three weeks after Munich he had called the Polish Ambassador to Berchtesgaden and had outlined the possibilities. It was the culmination of long preparations which had taken Göring on several hunting trips to the Polish forests, and which had led communist propaganda to assume that a Nazi–Polish alliance was already in existence.[58] Hitler's proposals centred on the idea that if the Poles would cede their rights in Danzig, and permit the building of the Berlin–Königsberg auto-bahn across Polish territory, they could join in a favourable political and economic association directed against the Soviet Union. The unspoken threat did not have to be spelled out. If the Poles were foolish enough to refuse, then Hitler would take Danzig anyhow and might seek a political and economic realignment with the USSR, directed against Poland. One has to assume that Hitler's well-known racial and ideological prejudices would have led him to expect an early acceptance. After all, since the Polish colonels had to contend with the largest Jewish community in Europe, and since Poland was fiercely anti-communist, it must have seemed to him that Poland and Nazi Germany were natural partners.

Unfortunately, neither Hitler nor those who advised him knew much about Poland's mettle. They did not know that Polish nationalism was every bit as hos-tile to Germany as to Russia. They did not know that Polish colonels could feel defensive about their handling of the Jewish Question, especially when foreigners interfered. Above all, they did not understand that the response of Marshal Piłsudski's heirs would be completely different from that of Chamberlain and Beneš. The colonels were not going to bow and scrape to an ex-Austrian ex-corporal. Their instinct was to fight, and to go down fighting. Every single Polish official who had to deal with Nazi and Soviet threats in 1939 had been reared on the Marshal's moral testament: 'To be defeated, but not to surrender, that is victory.'[59]

So the Führer was kept kicking his heels. The weeks passed; Poland pointedly opened 'trade and friendship talks' with the USSR; Berlin's proposals were left unanswered. On 21 March 1939, a week after the collapse of Czechoslovakia, the Polish Ambassador was called in again and told that the Führer was furious at the lack of progress. On 28 March Germany renounced the non-aggression pact with Poland. Nazi propaganda switched to the Danzig problem, and complained of the intolerable oppression of the German minority in Poland. On 31 March Poland received from Great Britain an unsolicited Guarantee of its independence. Hitler's response, on 3 April, was to issue confidential directives for planning the seizure of Danzig and for possible war with Poland. [SUSANIN]

In the mean time, prize after prize fell into the Führer's lap. On 10 March the autonomous Slovak Government was declared deposed by the central Czechoslovak authorities in Prague; and the offended Slovak leader, Father Tišo, appealed to the Führer for protection. Then the Czechoslovak President begged for an interview at Berchtesgaden. After a terrible drubbing before the plate-glass

SUSANIN

ON 26 February 1939 the Bolshoi Theatre in Moscow resounded to a lavish revival of Russia's most popular opera. Glinka's *A Life for the Tsar* (1836) had lain dormant since the Bolshevik Revolution; and a brief production of it in 1924, under the title of *For Hammer and Sickle*, had not prospered. But re-equipped with a politically correct libretto and yet another title, *Ivan Susanin*, it could now recover the vast popularity of pre-revolutionary decades.[1] It was the clearest sign that the Party's line had shifted to embrace traditional Russian nationalism.

Glinka's opera had been an ideological creature from the start. Described as a 'patriotic, heroic-tragic opera', it had been composed in the aftermath of the Polish Rising of 1830–1, reflecting the composer's 'determination to embody state ideology in symbolic sound'.[2] The libretto is set in the year 1613, at the moment when the founder of the Romanov dynasty was struggling to bring order from the chaos of the Time of Troubles (see p. 557). In the best tradition of 'rescue opera', it tells the tale of a good Russian peasant, Susanin, who saves the Tsar from the clutches of the dastardly Polish invaders. In this, it closely follows a patriotic textbook, *Russian History for the Purposes of Upbringing* (1817), compiled by the composer's brother.

Glinka's aesthetic concept was to use the dichotomy of Russian heroes and Polish villains throughout the spectacle. There are two sets of leading characters, two alternating choruses—Polish and Russian: two contrasting scenographic and musical styles. The faceless Poles are characterized by excess, singing and dancing exclusively in a formal collective to the melodies of the *polonez*, the *mazurka*, and the *krakowiak*. The Russians sing either charming folk-songs or romantic lyrics in the fashionable 'Italo-Russian style'. Nothing is spared to stress the political message.

After Susanin's murder, the epilogue reaches a climax with the scene of Mikhail Romanov's triumphant entry into Red Square. Here the music changes to that of a sacred 'hymn-march', the words to those of a super-patriotic anthem:

> Slav'sya, slav'sya, nash ruskiy Tsar',
> Gospodom danniy nam Tsar-gosudar.
> Da budet bessmyerten tvoy tsarskiy rod.
> Da im blagodenstvuyet russkiy narod.

(Glory be to our Russian Tsar, | To our God-given Tsar-Ruler. | May thy imperial clan be deathless! | May the Russian nation grant them blessing.)

In the 1939 production the anthem was duly modified:

> Slav'sya, Slav'sya ty Rus' moya!
> Slav'sya ty, russkaya nasha zemlya!

> Da budet vo veki vekov silna
> Lyubimaya nasha rodnaya strana.
>
> (Glory be to Thee, my Rus' | Glory to Thee our Russian land | May our beloved native country | For ever and ever be strong.)
>
> The power of opera harnessed to nationalism is most frequently discussed in relation to Wagner. But with Glinka the connection is still more explicit. Indeed, sensitivity to Russian nationalism determined where and when the opera could be staged. In Tsarist Russia it became the automatic choice for the opening night of each operatic season in Moscow and St Petersburg. By 1879 it had attained its 500th performance. It was staged in Prague, in Czech, in 1866; in Riga, in Latvian, in 1878; and at the German Theatre in Posen, Prussia, in 1899. But it never found an audience in Warsaw or Cracow. Most significantly, in February 1940, on the first anniversary of its revival in Moscow, it received its première under Nazi auspices in Berlin.

window, and one of Hitler's most histrionic performances, during which the unconscious visitor had to be revived by injections, President Hácha meekly accepted that the break-up of his country was unavoidable. Bohemia and Moravia were to be turned into a Nazi Protectorate; Slovakia was to be a sovereign republic; Sub-Carpathian Ruthenia was to be ceded to Hungary. Hitler drove in triumph into Prague, as he had driven to Vienna, without a shot being fired. On the 21st German troops seized Lithuanian Memel. This was the point at which Chamberlain finally grasped the truth that Hitler was *not* 'a man of his word'. The British Guarantee of Poland, an act of bluff taken from a position of weakness, was the product of his belated realization. To cap it all, the Hungarians seized Ruthenia without anyone's permission. On Good Friday, 2 April, the Italian army invaded Albania. Europe was already at war.

Faced with a specific commitment to Poland, the Western Powers now sought to put some practical measures into place. In April and May an inter-Allied mission visited Warsaw. It established a firm understanding that, in the event of a German attack on Poland, the task of the Polish army was to hold back the Wehrmacht whilst an Allied counter-attack was prepared in the West. General Gamelin was quite specific: on the fifteenth day after mobilization at the latest, 'le gros de nos forces', 'the bulk of our forces', would be thrown across the Franco-German frontier. Another military mission was sent to Moscow, to discuss co-operation with the Red Army. Long before they sailed on 5 August on a slow boat to Leningrad, in blissful ignorance of the main play, Hitler and Stalin had decided to settle the Polish Crisis on their own.

A Nazi–Soviet *rapprochement* was in the offing from the first week of May, when one of Stalin's closest henchmen, Molotov, emerged as Commissar for Foreign Affairs. Molotov's Jewish predecessor, Litvinov, who had an English wife, Ivy, was closely connected with the West and with the ailing policy of collective security. His last throw, for an Anglo-Soviet defensive alliance, had fallen on stony ground. Molotov was appointed with a view to reactivating the line to Berlin. Direct negotiations began in Moscow in June under the cover of 'trade talks'.

Once Stalin and Hitler had cast their suspicions aside, and their representatives had began to talk, they must rapidly have realized the scale of the opportunity. Given the indecisions of the West, Poland was the only serious obstacle to the prospect of dividing up Eastern Europe between them. With such a glittering prize in view, neither Hitler nor Stalin can have worried too much about the later prospect of Russia and Germany fighting over the spoils. Nor can they have cared to guess the long-term reactions of the West. Given Stalin's blessing, Hitler reckoned that he could deal with Britain and France single-handed and greatly strengthen Germany in the process; and Stalin was more than content to let him try. Given Hitler's blessing, Stalin reckoned that he could clean up the states of Eastern Europe single-handed, and greatly strengthen the USSR in the process. They probably both believed that it was better to solve Europe's problems before the USA, whose present military expenditure was less than Great Britain's, was alerted to the dangers. The opportunity had to be grasped; it might not recur. One week after the British mission made its leisurely way to Moscow, Herr von Ribbentrop flew smartly in from Berlin.

In those summer days, when the weather was as sunny as the political forecast was grim, Hitler's ebullience grew. His rearmament record, which had increased the Wehrmacht's front-line divisions from 7 to 51 in three years, excelled that of the Kaiser's army in the decade before 1914. He felt sure that the West could be fooled as usual, that the ungrateful Poles could be punished in isolation. With the great Stalin thinking the same way as himself, he was ready for limited war, without knowing whether war would be needed. He had little inclination to listen to the whingeing Western diplomats, nor to those in his own camp, like Göring or Mussolini, who wanted to prolong the peace. At a military conference on 23 May he had ranted on about *Lebensraum* in the East and the inevitability of war sooner or later. On 14 June he had set a timetable for his generals to be ready in eight weeks' time. On 22 August, when the eight weeks were up, he told another conference at the Berghof that 'War is better now'. His notes ran: 'No pity—brutal attitude—might is right—greatest severity.'[60]

The final piece of the preparations fell into place the very next day. On 23 August the news broke from Moscow that those mortal enemies, Nazi Germany and the Soviet Union, had followed up their recent trade agreement with a pact of non-aggression. What is more (though no one outside Moscow or Berlin was to know for certain until the Nazi archives were captured six years later), the Ribbentrop–Molotov pact had been supplemented by a secret protocol:

Moscow, 23 August 1939

On the occasion of the Non-Aggression Pact between the German Reich and the USSR, the undersigned plenipotentiaries . . . discussed the boundaries of their respective spheres of influence in Eastern Europe. These conversations led to the following conclusions:

1. In the event of a territorial and political rearrangement in the areas belonging to the Baltic States (Finland, Estonia, Latvia, Lithuania), the northern boundary of Lithuania will form the boundary of the spheres of influence of Germany and the USSR. In this connection, the interest of Lithuania in the Vilna area is recognised by each party.

2. In the event of a territorial and political rearrangement of the areas belonging to the Polish state, the spheres of influence of Germany and the USSR shall be bounded approximately by the line of the rivers Vistula, Narew, and San. The question of whether the interests of both parties make desirable the maintenance of an independent Polish State, and how such a state should be bounded, can be definitely determined in the course of further political developments. In any event, both Governments will resolve this question by means of a friendly agreement.

3. With regard to Southeastern Europe, attention is called by the Soviet side to its interest in Bessarabia. The German side declares its disinterest in these areas.

4. This protocol shall be treated by both parties as strictly secret.

For the Gov't of the German Reich Plenipotentiary of the Gov't of the USSR
'J. VON RIBBENTROP' 'V. MOLOTOV'[61]

Hitler and Stalin had carved up Eastern Europe into spheres of influence. Their so-called 'pact of non-aggression' was the perfect blueprint for aggression.

Neither party had a good word for the Western Powers. Ribbentrop was confident that Germany could deal with the French army. As for Great Britain, 'The Reich Foreign Minister stated that . . . England was weak and wanted others to fight for its presumptuous claim to world domination. Herr Stalin eagerly concurred . . . [but he] further expressed the opinion that England, despite its weakness, would wage war craftily and stubbornly.'[62]

The German–Soviet pact is often described as Hitler's licence for war. This is true, but it is only half the story; for the pact was equally Stalin's licence for war. From the moment the ink was dry, each of the signatories was free to assault its neighbours without hindrance from the other. Which is exactly what both of them did.

The Wehrmacht was due to march on 24 August; but the Führer, in one of his fits of nerves, failed to give the final order. He was also curious to see if a second Munich was possible. The Nazi press was publishing stories about Poles castrating Germans; and Göring was urging him to contact London. On the 25th the British Ambassador was summoned and handed a set of unlikely proposals. A Swedish friend of Göring's was sent to talk directly with Whitehall. But then Chamberlain missed his cue by guaranteeing Poland's independence once more in a formal Anglo-Polish Treaty. After that, the diplomats were wasting their time: there could be no second Munich. Hitler issued Directive No. 1 for the conduct of war against Poland at 1 p.m. on the 31st. [GENOCIDE]

The outbreak of the Polish campaign was stage-managed in best Nazi style. There was no declaration of war. Instead, SS Sturmbannführer Alfred Helmut

Naujocks received orders to round up a detachment of convicts, code-named *Konserven* or 'Tin Cans', and to take them to a German radio station at Gleiwitz in Silesia close to the Polish frontier. The studio was duly stormed by men dressed in Polish uniforms, and a rousing Polish chorus was broadcast to the sound of pistol shots. Once outside, the Tin Cans were mown down by the machine-guns of their SS minders, and their blood-soaked bodies were dumped where they would soon be found by the local police. The first casualties of the campaign were German convicts killed by German criminals. Before the night was out, the Nazi news service was announcing that the Polish Army had launched an unprovoked attack on the Third Reich.[63]

The Second World War in Europe, 1939–1945[64]

The invasion of Poland which began on 1 September 1939 did not mark the start of fighting in Europe. It had been preceded by the German attack on Lithuania in March 1939 and by the Italian invasion of Albania in April. But it transformed a series of essentially local wars into the setting for world-wide conflict. By involving the USSR, which was already engaged against the Japanese in Mongolia, it established the link between the European and the Asian theatres of operations. In theory Japan belonged to the Nazi system of alliances, even when the Nazi–Soviet pact put a clamp on the anti-Comintern club. But the fact that Japan, the USSR, Poland, Germany, and the Western Powers were all enmeshed in the web of conflict makes the best argument for contending that a Second World War had really begun.

The Red Army's role in Poland remained uncertain until the confrontation with Japan was resolved. The decisive Soviet victory at Khalkin-gol on 28 August, achieved by the armour of an unknown general called Zhukov, seems to have been the precondition for an active Soviet policy in Europe. It was perhaps no accident that Stalin delayed his entry into Poland until a truce was signed in Mongolia on 15 September, and Zhukov's divisions could return across the Urals.[65]

The German–Soviet Pact had created a new geopolitical framework in Europe. The Great Triangle was now turned round, with the Western Powers (Britain, France, and Canada) facing a combination of the Centre and the East (see Appendix III, p. 1312). The Triangle was not quite complete, however, since the Western Powers and the USSR both avoided direct confrontation. This meant that the West would close its eyes to Stalin's aggressions, so long as Stalin would limit his anti-Western activities to propaganda and to logistical support for Germany.[66] None the less, the German–Soviet Pact transformed the European scene. It enabled Germany and the USSR to destroy Poland and to re-establish the common frontier which had existed throughout the nineteenth century. After that, it permitted them to clear away all the minor states which cluttered their path. In the slightly longer term, it gave Hitler the chance to attack the West with Stalin's support and encouragement.

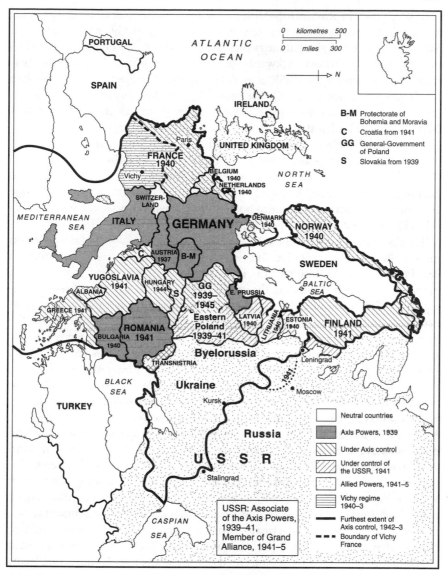

Map 26.

Europe during the Second World War, 1939–1945

In later years the Ribbentrop–Molotov pact was to be justified on the grounds that it gave the Soviet Union time to construct its defences. Given what happened two years later, the argument looks plausible; but this could be yet another classic case of reading history backwards. In 1939 there was indeed a possibility that Hitler would turn on the USSR after defeating the West; but this was only one contingency, and not necessarily the most likely or the most immediate one. At least three other scenarios had to be considered. One was the possibility that Germany would be defeated in the West, as in 1918. Another was the prospect that Germany and the West would fight each other to a bloody stalemate, after which the USSR could emerge as the arbiter of Europe without firing a shot. This was Goebbels's view of the Soviet game. 'Moscow intends to keep out of the war until Europe is . . . bled white,' he noted. 'Then Stalin will move to bolshevize Europe and impose his own rule.'[67] A third possibility was that Stalin would use the interval of Hitler's western war to prepare and launch an offensive of his own.

Thanks to the closure of the relevant Soviet archives, historical knowledge on these matters remains tentative. But two indications are important. First, there is very little evidence to show that the Red Army gave priority after August 1939 to preparing defence in depth. On the contrary, it favoured a theory of revolutionary attack. Stalin had often stressed that communism was not the same as pacifism; speaking to cadets in 1938, he stressed that the Soviet state would take the military initiative whenever required. Secondly, studies of the Red Army's dispositions in the early summer of 1941 suggest that the two previous years had been spent creating a distinctly offensive posture.[68] They go a long way to explaining the disaster which then overtook it (see below). In that case, one would have to conclude that Stalin entered his pact with the Nazis, not to win time for defence, but to outplay Hitler in the game of calculated aggression.[69]

What is certain is that the German–Soviet Pact led Europe into events which no one could have foreseen. In the first phase, 1939–41, whilst the pact still held, Nazi and Soviet adventures proceeded apace in each of their designated spheres. The Red Army met with varied fortunes; but the Wehrmacht's stunning conquest of Western Europe came more swiftly than the most starry-eyed German general could have imagined. In the second phase, 1941–3, the Nazi war-machine was thrown into the East. The German–Soviet war constituted the central military contest whereby Europe's fate would be decided. The Western Powers, reduced to the control of one embattled island, could only exert a peripheral influence. In the final phase, 1943–5, the Soviet Army in the East combined with growing British and American forces in the West to ensure Germany's downfall.

The Nazi–Soviet Partnership (September 1939–June 1941). Thanks to the secret protocols of the German–Soviet pact, many participants in the opening campaign of the Second World War entered the fray on false premisses. The Western Powers thought that they had guaranteed an ally under threat from Nazi aggression; in fact, they had guaranteed an ally which was to be attacked by the Soviet Union as well as the Third Reich. The Poles thought that their task was to hold off the German advance for fifteen days until the French crossed the German frontier in the West; in fact, they faced the impossible task of holding off both the Wehrmacht and the Red Army on their own. The French launched no offensive; the British limited their assistance to dropping leaflets over Berlin.

In this constellation Poland's invaders enjoyed every possible advantage. The German Command possessed roughly the same 60 divisions as its Polish adversary; but, thanks to the occupation of Czechoslovakia, it had Poland surrounded from three sides at once. It enjoyed a decisive superiority, both in mechanical forces and in air power, which would inflict a hundred Guernicas on Poland in the opening days. Above all, it could confidently launch its Panzer divisions deep into Polish territory, secure in the knowledge that its Soviet partners would take any Polish counter-measures in the rear. The Soviet Command held the trump card. Declining any joint timetable with the Germans, the Soviet generals could watch and wait until Poland was stretched on the German rack before marching in to deliver the *coup de grâce*. In the Polish campaign of September 1939, therefore, military operations were overshadowed by politics and treachery. The Poles did their duty, fighting on for five weeks against hopeless odds. The Western Powers declared war on Germany, but declined to confront the Soviet Union, even when Soviet complicity became evident. Nor did they intervene in the fighting. The British could not, and the French would not. French mobilization procedures had been designed to prepare for a long war: they required all front-line divisions to be stripped down to the status of temporary cadres, during a long period of reorganization which precluded any immediate offensive operations. So Hitler and Stalin had everything their own way.

At dawn on 1 September, German columns stormed into Poland from the north, the west, and the south. The Polish defence lines close to the frontier were circumvented. Warsaw was surrounded from the 9th. The civilian population was subjected to unprecedented bombardments. A German fifth column was operating behind the lines. Nazi Einsatzgruppen appeared in the rear, shooting resisters, stragglers, and Jews. Screaming Stuka dive-bombers destroyed railways, roads, and bridges, together with the refugees that crammed them. Warsaw, half-reduced to rubble, dug in for a long siege. The Polish army regrouped in the south-east for the defence of Lwów, whilst mounting a determined counter-attack in the centre on the Bzura. On the 15th a Nazi communiqué falsely announced that Warsaw had fallen. (It held out for two more weeks.) But Stalin may have thought that he was losing out. The blow was struck on the 17th, when Red Army troops poured over the eastern frontier. They sowed total confusion by their own false communiqués about saving Poland from the Nazis. In fact, they drove straight to the agreed demarcation line on the River Bug, and to the southern frontier with Romania and Hungary to seal it off. The Germans and Soviets held a joint victory parade in Brześć (Brest-Litowsk) before fixing the details of their victory.

The German–Soviet Treaty of Friendship, Co-operation, and Demarcation signed on 28 September reached much further than the pact of five weeks before.

It redrew the demarcation line, putting Lithuania into the Soviet sphere in exchange for a slice of central Poland. And it contained yet another secret protocol which envisaged joint action against Polish 'agitation'. These measures were put into place as Warsaw finally surrendered. The Polish Government had escaped into exile. Large numbers of Polish troops took to the woods, or fled abroad. The final capitulation took place on 4 October, the day when Hitler arrived in Warsaw to receive the salute of his admiring legions. Everything to the east of the Bug was taken by the Soviets.

Hitler's thoughts at this juncture were recorded by his faithful propaganda chief:

The Fuehrer's verdict on the Poles is damning. More like animals than human beings, completely primitive and amorphous. And a ruling class that is an unsatisfactory result of a mingling between the lower orders and an Aryan master-race. The Poles' dirtiness is unimaginable. Their capacity for intelligent judgement is absolutely nil . . .

The Fuehrer has no intention of assimilating the Poles . . . Had Henry the Lion conquered the East . . . the result would certainly have been a strongly slavicised race of German mongrels. Better the present situation. Now we know the laws of racial heredity and can handle things accordingly.[70]

The double occupation of Poland brought two laboratories of totalitarianism into being side by side. For two years the Nazi and Soviet vultures feasted on Poland's fallen body undisturbed. In the German zone the Western districts were annexed to the Reich, and subjected to an intense regime of racial screening and germanization. All other districts were thrown into a so-called General Government of Poland under SS and military rule. This 'Gestapoland', subject neither to Polish nor to German law, became the ultimate test-bed of Nazi ideology. It was the only part of occupied Europe where, in pursuit of their eastern *Lebensraum*, the Nazi planners had the time to apply their racial policies with full vigour to the whole population. After Himmler's first inspection, the aged and mentally handicapped were seized from the hospitals, orphanages were raided for boys and girls suitable for the stud programme of the *Lebensborn* organization;[71] and concentration camps were organized at Auschwitz and Majdanek to deal with the Resistance. In an act of cold-blooded genocide, the so-called *AB-Aktion*, some 15,000 Polish intellectuals, officials, politicians, and clergy were selected for shooting or for consignment to concentration camps. As from late 1939, Poland's large Jewish community was ordered into designated ghetto districts, which were then gradually walled, locked, and totally segregated; Jewish councils, supported by a Jewish police force, were recruited to run the ghettos under Nazi supervision.[72]

[**AUSCHWITZ**]

In the adjoining Soviet zone, phoney referenda were staged to justify the claim that 'western Byelorussia' and 'western Ukraine' had opted for annexation. This 'GPU-land', which remained cordoned off from the rest of the USSR, was scourged by the full force of the Stalinist terror. Some forty categories of people, from policemen to philatelists, were selected for instant arrest and deportation. By the summer of 1941 between 1 and 2 million individuals had been transported either to the Arctic camps or to forced exile in Central Asia. The Terror was directed not only at all former Polish state officials, down to village teachers and foresters, but equally at all communal organizations of Byelorussians, Ukrainians, and Jews. The peoples who had supposedly been 'liberated from Polish rule' were scourged as mercilessly as everyone else. In an act of cold-blooded genocide, some 26,000 Polish prisoners of war—mainly reserve officers, and hence intellectuals, officials, politicians, and clergy—were taken from their camps and shot in a series of massacres known under the collective name of Katyń. On the frontier bridge over the Bug at Brest, people entering the USSR met others, including Jews, who were seeking haven in the Reich. 'Where on earth are you going?' exclaimed an SS-officer on one occasion; 'we are going to kill you.'[73]

The full extent of co-operation between the SS and the NKVD in these years has never been properly established. The Nazi files went missing; and Soviet archives remained closed. Even so, a high-ranking Soviet liaison officer was attached to SS HQ in Cracow right up to 1941. Nazi and Soviet delegations attended joint conferences; prisoners were exchanged; Nazi and Soviet propaganda worked in unison, and at full blast. As from 24 August the Soviet press reversed its previous policy, and took to quoting the *Völkischer Beobachter* as a credible source of information. *Pravda* announced that 'German–Soviet friendship is now established forever'.[74] [**KATYŃ**]

The impotence of the Western Powers undoubtedly gave encouragement to Hitler and Stalin. What a French politician dubbed the *drôle de guerre* or 'phoney war' was only droll for those not directly involved. In the 20 months after the fall of Poland, 13 European countries were due to be overrun—8 by Hitler, 5 by Stalin. Stalin took the lead by sending the Red Army into Finland on 30 November 1939.

The 'Winter War' of 1939–40 revealed serious deficiencies in the Red Army, whilst testing the tolerance of the Western Powers to the limit. For five months, well-motivated Finnish troops held off the Soviet invader. In the early months they inflicted bloody slaughter on clumsy Soviet attempts to storm the Mannerheim Line. Soviet tactics and equipment were made to look inferior; Soviet policy was condemned for blatant aggression. When the League of Nations expelled the USSR, the Western Powers could no longer pretend, as with Poland, that Stalin's depredations were somehow more legitimate than Hitler's. In the spring, as the Red Army prepared for an overwhelming assault, the British Government was obliged to consider Finnish pleas for aid and assistance via Narvik and the Lapland railway. There was even a scheme to bomb the Baku oilfields in retaliation for Soviet supplies to Germany. Squadrons of British bombers, repainted with the swastika emblem of the Finnish air force, were standing by when news of a Finno-Soviet Treaty saved London from its dilemma. Finland was to remain independent and neutral, though forced to cede a large tract of eastern territory, in Karelia. The German General Staff can hardly have missed the implications about the USSR's apparent weakness.

The Finnish campaign exposed the vulnerability of German interests in Scandinavia, notably in the Swedish iron ore exported via Narvik. Hitler struck on

KATYŃ

O N 5 March 1940, Stalin signed an order authorizing the NKVD to shoot over 26,000 Allied prisoners-of-war. The prisoners, who had been captured during joint German-Soviet operations in Poland the previous September, were being held in three separate Soviet camps—at Kozielsk, Oshtakovo, and Starobielsk. They were nearly all Polish reserve officers— doctors, lawyers, professors, engineers, policemen, priests, and one woman—who had been separated out from a much larger pool of POWs in the USSR. They were driven in small groups to secret killing-grounds, bound and blindfolded, shot in the head, and buried in mass graves. The operation was concluded on 6 June.

During those same months, in pursuance of a secret clause in the German-Soviet Treaty of Friendship and Demarcation, the Nazi SS and Soviet NKVD were co-operating closely. Hidden from the outside world, both occupying powers conducted a series of parallel massacres and deportations.[2] Whilst the West was transfixed by the 'Phoney War', their Polish allies were being systematically and cynically murdered.

In 1941, when the Nazi-Soviet Pact collapsed and Stalin signed an alliance with the exiled Polish Government, the Poles sought news of their missing officers. In one exchange in the Kremlin, Stalin told General Sikorski that they must have fled. 'But where could they flee to?' 'Well, to Manchuria for instance.'[3]

In April 1943, during the outbreak of Warsaw's Ghetto Rising, the Nazi authorities in Poland released a newsfilm showing the bodies of *c.*4,500 murdered Polish officers unearthed in the Katyń Forest near Smolensk (they had found the victims taken from Kozielsk). They said it was a Soviet crime. The Soviets said that it was a Nazi provocation. The exiled Polish Government appealed to the International Red Cross for an enquiry. For this, they were denounced as 'Fascist collaborators' by the Kremlin, which promptly withdrew diplomatic recognition. One international commission which visited the site in 1943 under German auspices supported the German claims. A second commission in 1944, under Soviet auspices, supported Soviet claims.[4]

The Katyń Massacres presented a major embarrassment for British policy. Whilst playing host to the Polish Government, London was deeply committed to the alliance with Stalin. An official but unpublished British report had concluded that Soviet guilt was a 'near certainty'. But the superior moral purpose of the Allied cause could be put at risk. So every effort was made to suppress the facts. Official agencies encouraged belief in the Soviet version. War censorship kept contrary accounts out of circulation.[5] The situation was summarized in confidential SOE files: 'The official line in the UK has been to pretend that the whole affair was a fake . . . Any other view would have been distasteful to the public, since it could be inferred that we were allied to a power guilty of the same sort of atrocities as the Germans.'[6]

More surprisingly, little honest information was forthcoming in peacetime. The Katyń murders were raised by Soviet prosecutors at the Nuremberg Tribunal; but the charges against Germans were soon dropped, and the case was not pursued. Throughout the Cold War, Polish emigrés in London were prevented from erecting a public memorial; and British officers were forbidden to attend the annual services of remembrance. Despite the unequivocal findings of a US Congressional Committee in the 1950s, a British Foreign Office minister was still proclaiming in 1989 that the rights and wrongs were unclear. In 1990–1, when Soviet responsibility was confirmed by President Gorbachev in part, and then by President Yeltsin in full, the British War Crimes Act was carefully designed to exclude Allied criminals from its purview. Several of the alleged NKVD murderers were reported alive and well in Russia.[7]

In the USSR and in communist-ruled Poland, 'Katyń' remained a non-subject for exactly fifty years.[8] A major Soviet memorial to Nazi barbarity was erected at a nearby Byelorussian village called Khatyń, to which millions of visitors were taken in a calculated policy of disinformation. *The Black Book of Polish Censorship* classed Katyń as an event which could not be mentioned, even to blame the Nazis.[9] Possession of the *Lista Katyńska*, a roll-call of the victims published abroad, was a criminal offence.[10]

Throughout that half-century, 'Katyń' offered a litmus test for the professional honesty of historians and their grasp of the realities of the Grand Alliance. It was by no means the most extreme of Soviet acts of violence. But it was the issue *par excellence* which forced commentators to choose between the growing weight of evidence and the self-serving statements of the victorious Western and Soviet governments. Those who chose to tell the truth stood to be dismissed as 'unscientific'.[11]

9 April 1940. Denmark was quickly overrun, and Norway invaded shortly afterwards. An Allied expeditionary force sent to Narvik was repelled with heavy loss. This was the first occasion on which British intelligence chose to withhold life-saving information rather than betray their knowledge of the Nazis' Enigma Code, whose secrets had first been penetrated by the Poles.[75] Henceforth, Scandinavia lay firmly under German control. Denmark retained its King and government; Norway was handed over to a native collaborator, Vidkun Quisling; Sweden was to retain its neutrality, so long as the iron ore continued to flow. Here were signals that German policy in the West was to be incomparably more lenient than in the East.

By the early summer of 1940 the Nazi war machine was ready for its assault on the Western alliance. It was essential to strike while German morale was high, and before British rearmament delivered results. The campaign was based on three related strategies—an operation in the Low Countries to clear the lines, the major land operation against France, and an air operation against Britain to neutralize the Royal Navy and to keep the Allies apart. Once again, German performance exceeded all expectations. From the merciless bombing of Rotterdam on 10 May to the surrender of Belgium on the 28th, the conquest of the Low Countries took 18 days. From the crossing of the French frontier on 14 May to the fall of Paris on 16 June, the defeat of France took less than five weeks.

The fall of France was one of those bone-chilling events which mark the end of an era. France had been regarded as a major military power for three centuries. The victory of 1918 was supposed to have redeemed the disaster of 1870. Yet the French army, with British and Polish support, was now knocked out by the Nazi Wehrmacht in less time than Germany and Russia together had taken to knock out Poland. 1940 showed that 1870 was no aberration. The German invaders held no overall numerical superiority, not even in armoured vehicles; but their panzer divisions waged this second Blitzkrieg with great dash and vigour. The impregnable Maginot Line, which did not reach into Belgium, was simply bypassed; and the panzers drove a steel column between the British in the north and the main French grouping in the centre. When the outflanked French forces withdrew, they were pursued by an opponent moving with far greater speed and firepower. At Arras, a brigadier called Charles de Gaulle led the only significant armoured counter-attack. But the confusion was universal. The BEF was totally beaten, and stranded on the dunes of Dunkirk. The 51st (Highland) Infantry sold itself dearly on the cliffs of Sainte-Valérie-en-Caux. Death, capture, or evacuation were the only alternatives.

By mid-June, when Paris was facing a repeat of the terrible siege of 70 years before, the French political establishment snapped. Unlike their Polish counterparts, who had refused to treat with invaders, the French leaders took the initiative in proposing a settlement. Marshal Pétain, the hero of Verdun, sent an underling to the symbolic carriage of Compiègne to sign the capitulation. France was to be disarmed; 2 million French soldiers were to be interned for work in the Reich; an autonomous government, based at Vichy in Auvergne, would be allowed to rule the southern half of the country, on condition that Alsace-Lorraine was returned to Germany, and northern France subjected to German military occupation. When Hitler came to receive the salute of his legions on the Champs-Élysées, he was master of Europe from the Pyrenees to the Pripet. A few assorted British, Polish, and Free French forces had scrambled back across the Channel; and a new defiant English voice, Churchill's, speaking in execrable French, crackled over the air waves: 'Une nation qui produit trois cents sortes de fromage ne peut pas périr.' General de Gaulle declared: 'France has lost a battle, but not the war.' [EMU]

Compared to the mighty conquest of France, the German air offensive against Britain must have seemed a secondary matter. But it proved to be one of the

EMU

I N the summer of 1940 the German Reichsbank drew up plans for making
the Reichsmark the common currency of an economic union throughout
German-occupied Europe. Since the Nazis never succeeded in establishing a stable political order, the plans remained a dead letter.

A second attempt at monetary union was made thirty years later, under
the auspices of the European Commission. Post-war arrangements based
on the gold-backed US dollar were ailing; and the currencies of the
Common Market, especially the Deutschmark, were uncomfortably strong.
First the Barre report of 1969, then a committee headed by Pierre Werner
of Luxembourg, drew up plans for full EMU (European Monetary Union) by
1980. In the meantime, a mechanism nicknamed 'the Snake' was to hold
the exchange rates of member currencies in line both with each other and
with the dollar. The system was quickly disarmed by the USA's abandonment of the dollar's gold standard in 1971 and by the Common Market's
acceptance of Great Britain, which soon left the Snake. Only five of a possible nine currencies held to a much-modified Snake in the 1970s.[1]

The third attempt was launched in 1977 by a speech from the British
President of the European Commission, Roy Jenkins. His initiative bore
fruit two years later, with the introduction of the EMS (European Monetary
System) together with a new exchange rate mechanism (ERM) and its own
supporting currency, the *écu* (see p. 1086). The system was greatly
strengthened in the 1980s by France's policy of the *franc fort* linked to the
DM, and by the Single European Act (1986), which attracted the pound
sterling into the ERM. All seemed to be going well until the reunification
of Germany in 1990, and the fateful decision to exchange the worthless
East German Ostmark at parity with the Deutschmark. After that, high
German interest rates put weaker currencies at a disadvantage, forcing
them either to devalue beneath the permitted limits or to float outside the
system completely. By August 1993 only the DM and the Dutch guilder
remained within the narrow band of the ERM, described by earlier proponents of the Maastricht Treaty as the 'glide-path to EMU' (see pp. 1126–7).

In 1940–5, despite Germany's military victories, a subordinate Reichsbank
was never strong enough to put its monetary plans into operation. After
1969, an independent Bundesbank was always strong enough to put its
own immediate priorities first. One can only conclude that economic plans
conceived in the absence of an effective political framework are always
doomed to failure.

Nazis' costliest failures. Entrusted to Reichsmarschall Göring, it consisted of a mounting crescendo of nightly bombing raids against ports and factories, the so-called 'Blitz', and of accompanying air battles aimed at gaining supremacy over southern England and the Channel. It used a large fleet of 1,330 Heinkel and Junkers bombers, operating from bases in northern France and supported by packs of Messerschmitt and Focke-Wolf fighters. It was planned as the prelude to 'Operation Sealion', the invasion of Britain, whose details, including the arrest of some 1,100 prominent personalities, were well advanced. It was opposed by RAF fighter squadrons equipped with Hurricanes and Spitfires, roughly 10 per cent of which were manned by Polish, Czech, and Free French pilots. (The top ace proved to be a Czech pilot flying with the Polish 303 Squadron.) The raid on Coventry, which missed the tank factories but levelled the cathedral and 500 houses, was a minor event compared to the subsequent exploits of the RAF over Germany. But in Allied lore it became one of the prime symbols of Nazi barbarism. The Battle of Britain, which was fought over four months, culminated on 15 September—a day when the RAF's reserves were almost depleted but when Göring reluctantly decided that the Luftwaffe's still greater losses could no longer be sustained. The air offensive, and the invasion of Britain, were postponed *sine die*. 'Never in the field of human conflict', Churchill told the Commons, 'has so much been owed by so many to so few.' After the débâcle of Dunkirk, this was Britain's 'Finest Hour'.

Britain's victory in the air was crucial on three scores. It gave the Allied cause an impregnable base, where the vastly superior land forces of the Continent could never be brought to bear. Secondly, by turning Britain into 'the world's most unsinkable aircraft carrier', it secured a platform for the sensational growth of Allied air power—the decisive element of the war in the West. Thirdly, on the diplomatic front, it gained a breathing-space within which the latent alliance of the English-speaking world could mature. Churchill, who became Prime Minister on 7 May at the height of the French crisis, had strong American connections and a strong determination to involve the Americans as soon as possible. But in autumn 1940 Britain represented the last foothold of the Allied cause in Europe. Without the preservation of Great Britain by the RAF, the USA could never have intervened in the European War. As it was, American assistance kept Great Britain financially and psychologically afloat during 'the darkest days'. In September 1940, old US destroyers were traded for the American rights to build military bases on British islands in the Caribbean. This was extended in March 1941 in the wider principles of the Lend-Lease Bill. Germany had good reason to complain.

The war at sea was not resolved so quickly. Germany mounted a determined challenge to Britain's naval supremacy, with a line of ultra-modern 'pocket battleships' and a growing fleet of U-boats. The first round saw the British veteran, *Royal Oak*, sunk at her berth in Scapa flow, and the German *Graf Spee* harried to her doom in the River Plate. Then the *Bismarck* and the *Tirpitz* took to sea. The former, having destroyed her pursuer, HMS *Hood*, with one spectacular shot, was disabled by an aerial torpedo, then sunk by the pack. The latter was chased into a Norwegian fiord. As in the First World War, however, Germany's chief effort was put into the submarine campaign. After the French ports of Brest and Nantes fell into Nazi hands, the 'Battle of the Atlantic' raged for three years (see below).

In the Mediterranean, Allied interests clashed with those of the Axis powers over control of North Africa and the Suez Canal. Matters were brought to a head in May 1940, when Mussolini declared war and invaded the French Alps. The Italian base in Tripoli was surrounded by the British in Palestine and Egypt and by the French in Tunis and Algiers; and it soon required the dispatch of a German *Afrika Korps* for its sustenance. The 2,000-mile shipping lane between Gibraltar and Alexandria was only protected by Britain's half-way station at Malta, which heroically survived unending blockade and bombardment. Yet the most tragic action of the early years took place between the Western Powers. When Paris fell to the Nazis, Britain demanded the surrender of the entire French fleet, a large part of which was berthed in the Algerian base of Mers-el-Kabir. When the French admiral declined, on 3 July 1940 the Royal Navy executed a merciless order to destroy all the French ships and their crews at anchor. Attention then turned to the Libyan desert. Faced with the advance of the *Afrika Korps* on one side and with growing Jewish terrorism in Palestine on the other, Britain's hold on Egypt remained precarious until the victory at the second battle of El Alamein on 23 October 1942. Anglo-American forces landed in Morocco and Algeria in the following month.

In the mean time, with Hitler preoccupied in the West, Stalin renewed his aggressions in the East. After the Finnish fiasco, he reverted to what the *New York Times* had aptly described as 'playing the hyena to Hitler's lion'. This time his targets lay in the three Baltic States, and in parts of Romania, which he conveniently seized whilst the world was diverted by the fate of France.

In the Baltics, the Soviet Union had mounted a concerted campaign of subversion. Then, in June 1940, communist cells in Estonia, Latvia, and Lithuania were activated to call for Soviet 'assistance'. Moscow demanded the admission of the Red Army on the pretext of Soviet security interests. In the ensuing uproar, the governments collapsed; the Red Army marched in; pre-packaged plebiscites were staged with foregone results; and the Stalinist Terror set to work with unrivalled ferocity. Amongst the massacres and the deportations, an arrangement was reached to transfer the entire German population of the Baltic States to areas of German-occupied Poland. It is hard for Westerners to grasp, but from the viewpoint of Tallinn, Riga, or Vilnius, the growing possibility of a Nazi advance felt like blessed liberation from Liberation. In the case of Romania, Stalin counted more on direct German help. Romania's fragile freedom depended largely on the continued export of oil to Germany. So when Moscow made demands and Berlin advised compliance, there was no easy way for Bucharest to refuse. On 27 June 1940, ten days after the Baltic States, the Romanian provinces of Bukovina and Bessarabia were grabbed amidst fanfares of their 'reunion with the Soviet

fatherland'. Romania, humiliated, was left smarting for revenge. [**MOLDOVA**]
[**TSCHERNOWITZ**]

By the autumn of 1940 the benefits of the Nazi–Soviet partnership could be weighed; and it was obvious that Hitler was gaining more than Stalin. The industrial and strategic value of France, the Low Countries, and Scandinavia was much greater than that of the Soviet conquests. Though the Führer was held off by the wily Franco, whom he had met at Hendaye, the Fascist bloc commanded the greater part of the Continent. What is more, Germany had made its colossal gains at minimal cost: a protracted contest with the West had been avoided. From Stalin's point of view, Hitler's success was beginning to look menacing. After France, there were only two destinations left for German expansion: one was the traditional Russian hunting-ground in the Balkans; the other was the Soviet Union itself.

The tensions surfaced when Molotov visited Berlin in November 1940. He behaved with excruciating crudity, emitting a torrent of tactless demands. One assumes that he had been ordered to test the limits of German tolerance. When the Führer admitted that Germany was engaged in 'a life and death struggle' with Britain, Molotov said, 'Yes, Germany is fighting for its life and Britain for Germany's death.' Both sides suspected that the partnership was doomed. It is not known exactly what instructions Stalin gave to the Red Army; but on 18 December Hitler issued Instruction 21 for the preparation of Operation Barbarossa.

The Balkan crisis of April 1941 had its roots in Mussolini's blunders. The Italian troops who had advanced from Albania into northern Greece were being mauled by the doughty Greeks; and the Duce was in need of another German rescue. Apart from that, the royal Yugoslav Government was being hounded from within and without. After the Regency had tried to sign an agreement with Germany, it was deposed by the military. When the Wehrmacht moved in, the country fell apart. After 11 days of fighting, the Germans were left in occupation of a huge and hostile territory. The Yugoslav Government fled into exile in London. Croatia declared itself an independent republic. Hungarians, Bulgarians, and Italians all took chunks of the carcass. Underground armies proliferated. The terrible *Ustaši* or Croat 'insurrectionaries' were set on ethnic cleansing of their Serbian minority, deploying the full fascist repertoire of death camps and mass executions. The royalist Četniks, who led the Yugoslav resistance, were increasingly opposed by a rival communist movement led by Josip Broz, 'Tito' (1892–1980). The fierce determination of the Yugoslav partisans to kill the invaders was only exceeded by their proclivity for killing each other. [**NOYADES**]

Further south, in Greece, the Germans carried all before them. Athens was occupied; a British force which had tried to hold Crete was overwhelmed by the end of May.

Stalin's reaction to the Balkan crisis showed no signs of solidarity with Hitler. One day before the German attack, on 5 April, he had signed a treaty of friendship with Yugoslavia. On 13 April he signed a vital neutrality pact with Japan. The

MOLDOVA

FIVE young harvesters are sitting on a rug, eating their lunch on a rise amidst the golden cornfields. A girl in a bright red headscarf has spread out the newspaper on her knees, and is reading to her smiling companions. They are sharing a flagon of wine or water, a bowl of bread or rice, and a huge red water-melon. Acres of standing wheat and sheaves roll down to the green valley and to the wooded hills beyond. In the foreground a gleaming green motorcycle is parked; in the distance a combine is reaping. The location, as indicated by the pattern of the rug, is Moldavia (now Moldova). The date could be any time after 1940, when Moldavia was annexed to the USSR. The painting, by Alexei Vasilev, is called 'They are talking about us in *Pravda*'.[1] (See Plate 70.)

This is hardly great art. But the technique is competent; and the effect is pleasant to the eye. Without indulging any crude political gesture, Vasilev has succeeded in mobilizing all the main elements of Socialist Realism—or 'revolutionary romanticism' as Zhdanov called it—as decreed by the Party authorities in 1934. He produces a picture which, to quote Stalin's phrase, is 'national in form, and socialist in content'. The *narodnost'* or national spirit of the work is implicit in the link between these Moldavian peasants and their admirers in Moscow. Its *partiinost'* or 'devotion to the party' is explicit in their delight at the mention of their work in the Party paper. Its *klassovost'* or 'class-consciousness' is underlined by their peasant clothes and physical labour. Its *ideinost'* or 'ideological character' is manifest in their optimistic and politically correct attitudes. Its *tipichnost'* or 'representative message' comes over loud and clear: happy workers plus modern machinery make for high productivity and the welfare of the masses. It is overtly socialist, and it looks quite realistic.

The fact is, all the most important realities of life in the Soviet Union have been systematically falsified. In reality, the Moldavian peasantry had recently been robbed both of its land and its culture. They were forced to live and work in collectives, whose surplus was taken away by the Soviet state. Thousands upon thousands had been driven to their death in the Gulag, or shot as so-called saboteurs. Their language had been arbitrarily transferred to the Cyrillic alphabet, so that Soviet-educated children could no longer read pre-war Romanian or Moldavian literature. They were denied all contact with the western half of their province in Romania, which they were told was a foreign country. They were beaten, beggared, and bullied. And the world was told they were stunningly content.

For the impartial viewer, the question posed is this: how much aesthetic value can art retain when, in human and moral terms, its principal purpose is fraudulent?

TSCHERNOWITZ

T HE Soviet army's entry into northern Bukovina in June 1940 was the
first step in the destruction of a civilization. Conquered by Austria
from the Ottomans in 1775, this corner of old Moldavia had passed a century and a half as the furthest outpost of the Habsburg realms. It was then
taken over for twenty years by Romania. Its capital city,
Tschernowitz/Cernati, on the Prut, was the centre of a polyglot, multi-
denominational, hierarchical society where the imperial German culture
of *Mitteleuropa* had lain like a transparent sheet over the rich layers of local
Jewish, Romanian, Polish, and Ruthenian life. After fifty years of Soviet
levelling it has been left, as Chernovtsy, a drab provincial backwater of
Ukraine.

Old Bukovina has vanished. But it can still be glimpsed through the nostalgia of an exile who returned in the last months of Soviet rule, having
been raised in the 1920s amidst 'futile attempts to maintain the dignity of
a German ruling class in the border marches of a defunct empire':

The old houses are still painted in an Austrian egg-yolk yellow, alternated with
an imperial Russian pea green. But the Bukovinian melting-pot has gone . . .
all have been killed or repatriated, and their places taken by stolid, cabbage-
eating Ukrainians. The wild, colorful, murderous variegation . . . has been
replaced by the sub-Stalinist uniformity of Chernovtsy. The market in the
city square, where 'under a fragrant cloud of garlic' Jews, Armenians,
Lipovanians, and Germans haggled for sheepskins, sharp cheese, rotgut, and
tobacco, cooking oil and cowdung, is now a concrete-covered parade ground,
hung with a gigantic billboard of Lenin. The cosmopolitan border world of
Austria-Hungary and tsarist Russia has been transformed into 'an immense

---

USSR was clearing the decks for major action in Europe. On 15 May, Zhukov is
known to have suggested that the Red Army forestall the Wehrmacht by attacking first and disrupting German preparations..

From Yugoslavia, the German battle divisions were transported to the Reich's
eastern borders. In early June 1941, the backwoods and byways from East Prussia
to Romania were filled with the bustle of German bivouacs and the revving of
tank engines. Every Polish peasant, and most of the world's intelligence services,
knew that Hitler was preparing to attack the Soviet Union. The only person who
didn't appear to know was Stalin, who ordered that border provocations should
be avoided at all costs.

In the absence of the necessary documentation, the circumstances have never
been clarified. Conventional wisdom has usually held either that Stalin could not
comprehend the depths of Hitler's treachery or that he was playing for time to
complete his defences. Neither seems likely. One did not have to be an expert to
realize that the German war machine had nowhere to go but eastwards. Hitler's
earlier thinking had foreseen all-out war in 1942 or 1943; but he had now to decide

either to follow the momentum of success or to call a halt and risk losing the initiative. For the ex-corporal and his gang of adventurers there was hardly a moment's hesitation; their urge was to ride on to glory or to *Götterdämmerung*.

As for Stalin, the master of secrecy, one can only speculate. However, as the Germans would soon discover, the Soviets had not been idle. Huge military concentrations had been repositioned in vulnerable forward areas; the warplanes of the Soviet air force stood exposed on forward airfields; frontier cordons had been withdrawn; roads and bridges had been repaired to facilitate the movement of heavy traffic. The Red Army's stance was one of imminent attack. Everything points to the probability that Stalin had been acting dumb in order to conceal his preparations for a surprise offensive against the Reich.[76] If so, he was beaten to the draw. The Wehrmacht struck at dawn on 22 June.

The Nazi Supremacy in Europe (June 1941–July 1943). Operation Barbarossa, which took the German army deep into the Soviet Union, launched the central military and political play of the Second World War in Europe. It opened up the front which was to account for 75 per cent of German war casualties, and which must be judged the main scene of Hitler's ultimate defeat. It came astonishingly close to total success, and for two or three years vastly extended the territory of the Nazis' New Order. The offensive of 1941 carried the Wehrmacht to the gates of Moscow; the offensive of 1942 led them to the Volga and the Caucasus (see Map 26).

The initial attack of June 1941 had spectacular results. One hundred and fifty-six divisions, consisting of over 3 million men, crossed the Ribbentrop–Molotov line and caught the Red Army entirely out of position. The Soviet air force was destroyed on the ground in a couple of days. Whole Soviet armies were surrounded, and vast numbers of prisoners taken. Panzer columns raced forward at unprecedented speed. In the Baltic States, in Byelorussia, and Ukraine they were cheered as liberators. German soldiers were greeted by local peasants offering the traditional welcome of bread and salt. In Lwów, where the retreating NKVD had massacred many thousands of its political prisoners, a public demonstration openly declared for Ukrainian independence. By December, despite the lack of winter equipment, forward German units had entered Russia and laid siege to Leningrad. They caught the Moscow Kremlin in their binoculars, before (on the same day as Pearl Harbor) Stalin's secret reserve of fresh Siberian divisions arrived to drive them back. [SMOLENSK]

In 1942 the German Command chose to direct its advance along the southern steppes. Their priority was to seize the good black earth of Ukraine, and the distant oil of Baku. Yet they were meeting ever more effective resistance; and the retreating Soviets had stripped the land bare. The industrial areas were empty; the factories had been dismantled and removed to points east, and the working population evacuated; the great dam of Dniepropetrovsk, pride of the Five-Year Plans, had been dynamited. German soldiers scaled Mount Elbruz. When the second winter set in, they were approaching the Volga at Stalingrad.

SMOLENSK

IN July 1941 the Wehrmacht captured Smolensk with such speed that the local Communist Party house and all its contents fell into German hands. The Smolensk archives contained detailed files on all aspects of communist activity since the Revolution, including Stalin's purges and the Great Terror. Carried off to Germany, they were duly captured for a second time in 1945 by the American army, and taken to the USA. They were far smaller than the vast collections of Nazi documents which fell into American hands and which would form the core of the American-run Document Centre in Berlin. But the Soviet authorities had never granted free access to their state archives, let alone to secret Party records. So the windfall from Smolensk had inestimable value. Historical studies based on its files penetrated the fog of Soviet propaganda and Western theorizing, and provided one of the first authentic glimpses into the true nature of communist rule.[1]

Many Sovietologists and Soviet apologists, however, were not happy. Having framed their fantasies in the knowledge that little or no primary evidence was available, they had no wish to confront hard facts. Hence, when the scholar who first analysed the Smolensk archives concluded that Stalin had perpetrated 'an almost continuous purge' in the 1930s, he was promptly denounced. 'This view', the arch-apologist could glibly declare, 'is weakly supported by the available primary evidence.'[2] Such sophistry often passed for science until the fall of the Soviet Union.

Archives have always attracted those who wish to manipulate the writing of history. In 1992 the Russian authorities revealed the existence of the so-called *Osobii Arkhif* or 'Special Archive', which the Soviet regime had kept separate from all other records. Its full contents were still to be determined; but in addition to the Goebbels diaries, they certainly included such items as the records from France's Sûreté Nationale and from Poland's pre-war *Dwójka* or 'Military intelligence', even the papers of the British Expeditionary Force (1940) and of the Grand Duchy of Luxembourg. It was said to contain all the missing collections of the Nazis' RSHA (Reich Security Main Office). Apparently, Nazi archive-hunters had put their swag from all over Europe into various castles and cellars in Poland and eastern Germany, only to see it looted in turn by the Red Army. The Soviets repaid the loss of the Smolensk archive many times over. [METRYKA]

Still more intriguing is the possibility that parts of the captured Nazi archives were falsified after they fell into communist hands. In Warsaw, for example, the post-war communist Security Office (UB) inherited the contents of the city's former Gestapo secretariat. Armed with the appropriate registers, codes, stationery, blank report forms, and official seals, it

was a simple matter to amend the records. The UB had little difficulty providing documents to show that Poland's resistance movement, the Home
Army, had been run by Nazi collaborators.[3]

For fifty years, therefore, historians' views of the mid-twentieth century
have been given a one-sided slant by the one-sided nature of the documentation.[4] But in the 1990s the hidden treasures of the ex-communist
world were starting to restore the balance. In Germany, as the files of the
East German Stasi were yielding their secrets, the Nazi files of the Berlin
Document Centre were being prepared for transfer to the Federal
Government. In Washington, congressional hearings were held to challenge the move.[5] For, as the victors of the Second World War were only too
well aware, 'Power brings knowledge, and knowledge power'.

The German advance to the Volga extended the territory under Hitler's control
by an area equal to all the Nazi conquests in Western Europe. It gave him the
Lebensraum of which he had dreamed. The lawless zone beyond the Reich now
stretched out for more than 1,000 miles. The Nazis, it transpired, had no intention of consulting the wishes of the inhabitants. There were to be no independent
republics—only military government in the front-line regions, and Reichs-
kommissariats run by the SS in the 'Ostland' and Ukraine. The national movement in Ukraine, which in 1917–18 had been given full German support, was to
be crushed. Through wilful stupidity, the Nazis spurned all the chances to win
the population to their side. Through sheer arrogance, they turned their largest
asset into an unbearable burden. Their savagery knew no bounds. They gave their
new subjects no option but to resist. One hundred peasants were to be executed
for every German soldier killed by 'bandits'. Villages were routinely razed, and
their inhabitants murdered. Nazi officials felt free to massacre people at will. As
in Poland, the population was screened, assigned to racial categories, and issued
with ration cards and work permits according to their classification. Where Jews
were not killed outright, they were cast into ghettoes. The Slavonic nations, whose
élites were slated for annihilation, were regarded as fit only for a pool of uneducated slave workers. Several million men and women were sent to the Reich for
forced labour. With the growth of all categories of 'undesirables', the Nazi network of prisoner-of-war and concentration camps was greatly expanded. Since
Soviet prisoners of war were granted no rights, some 3–4 million men were
allowed to perish in open enclosures. The East was treated as a fund for unlimited
human and material exploitation. In three years, the population of Ukraine
dropped by 9 million.

Yet the Nazis' self-styled 'Crusade for Civilization' was able to attract consider-
able support. Large contingents were sent to the Eastern Front by Romania,
Hungary, and Italy. Romania took charge of Odessa and the district of
'Transnistria'. General Franco's crack 'Blue Division' was sent from Spain. In the

Baltic States, existing army and police units were transferred to German service. Recruits and volunteers flocked in from almost all the occupied countries. Some of these, especially among Soviet prisoners of war, were volunteers in name only, having been given a choice between service or starvation. But many others, especially from Western Europe, joined willingly. General Vlasov, a former Soviet officer, commanded the million-strong Russian Liberation Army. A Cossack Brigade attracted many pre-war exiles. Even the Waffen-SS recruited large numbers of foreigners. [LETTLAND]

Holocaust. In conjunction with their occupation of the Eastern *Lebensraum*, the Nazis launched their largest and most systematic campaign of racial genocide. What they characteristically labelled 'the Final Solution of the Jewish Question' has since been called the 'Holocaust' or, in Hebrew, the Shoah. It was an attempt to exploit modern industrial technology to kill every Jewish man, woman, and child in Europe, simply for being Jews. Its starting-point is obscure. No direct order from the Führer has been unearthed, although his ultimate responsibility is incontestable. There is every reason to suppose that Hitler took precautions to conceal his involvement and to avoid the bad publicity which had arisen from leaks about the earlier Euthanasia Campaign.[77] Europe's Jews were to be the prime, though not the sole target for the Nazi programme of racial murders.

After several years of prudent restraint, Hitler had returned in 1938–9 to the extreme language of his early career. In a broadcast on 30 January 1939 he made a 'prophesy' that if the Jews precipitated another war, then the effect would be the *Vernichtung*, destruction, of all Jews. Yet prior to July 1941, despite high mortality in the Nazi-built ghettos of occupied Poland, there had been no move towards wholesale slaughter. Indeed, vague talk had continued about the dispatch of Jews to distant destinations and about the sensitivities of the neutral USA. Yet on 31 July 1941 Göring ordered the chief of the RSHA (Reich Security Main Office) to prepare 'the Final Solution'.[78] Some time shortly beforehand, he must have received express instructions from the Führer. All hesitations were to be cast aside. The policy was annihilation. 'Resettlement' became an official euphemism for genocide. As the German armies advanced into the heart of the former tsarist Pale, the notorious *Einsatzgruppen* reappeared, rounding up Jews by the thousand, driving them to pits and gulleys and shooting them *en masse*. One such action, at the chasm of Babi Yar near Kiev, would involve the shooting of 70,000 victims.

In January 1942 SS chiefs, including Adolf Eichmann, the head of the RSHA's IV-B-4 Jewish Section, held a one-day conference at a villa on the Wannsee near Berlin to co-ordinate technical and organizational arrangements. Decisions were taken to accelerate experiments with Zyklon-B gas; to create a number of dedicated death camps, at Chelmno, Belzec, Sobibór, and Treblinka; to expand the Nazi concentration camps in occupied Poland, notably KL Auschwitz II-Birkenau; to consult the best German firms regarding crematorium design and 'surplus disposal'; to draw up the timetables and rolling-stock for international

LETTLAND

L ATVIANS had no special love for Germany. Germans had formed a ruling caste in the Baltic States since medieval times, and had been loyal servants of tsarist Russia. Yet such was the effect of the massacres and deportations of Soviet rule in 1940–1 that the arrival of the Wehrmacht promised blessed relief.

The Germans encountered little opposition, therefore, when they started to raise Latvian military formations as soon as they entered Riga on 1 July 1941. At first, ex-Latvian army and police units and ex-Soviet Army deserters were reorganized under German command. 'Auxiliary Security Police', later renamed *Schutzmannschaft* or 'Schuma', were used for front-line service, for guard, labour, and fire-fighting duties, and for 'special operations'. (The last euphemism turned out to include the murder of Jews under SS-guidance.) In 1942 a conscription decree greatly increased the numbers, whilst facilitating the formation both of low-grade *Hilfswillige* or 'Hiwi' units and of a regular 'Latvian Legion'. From 1943, swelled by volunteers, the Legion was to feed the main recruitment drive for three Latvian divisions of the Waffen-SS (see Appendix III, pp. 1326–7). The men swore an oath 'to struggle against Bolshevism' and 'to obey the commander-in-chief of the German armed forces, Adolf Hitler'. Their language of command was Latvian, and they wore arm-shields bearing the name Latvija. They fought at Leningrad, and in the German retreat all the way to Berlin.[1]

At a meeting with the Reichsführer-SS in 1944, the chief of staff of the Latvian Legion recorded Himmler's updated vision of the Nazi Order:

The present demands that every SS-officer, regardless of nationality . . . must look to the whole living space of the family of German nations. [*He then singled out those nations which he regarded as belonging to the German family: the Germans, the Dutch, the Flemish, the Anglo-Saxons, the Scandinavians, and the Baltic peoples.*] To combine all those nations into one big family is the most important task at present. It is natural in this process that the German nation, as the largest and strongest, must assume the leading role. [But] this unification has to take place on the principle of equality . . . [Later] this family . . . has to take on the mission to include all Roman nations, and then the Slavic nations, because they, too, are of the white race. It is only through unification of the white race that Western culture could be saved from the danger of the yellow race.

At the present time, the Waffen-SS is leading in this respect because its organisation is based on equality. The Waffen-SS comprises not only German, Roman and Slavic but even Islamic units . . . fighting in close togetherness. Therefore it is of great importance that every Waffen-SS officer gets his training at the same military college. . . .[2]

Nazi internationalism only came to the fore in the final phase of the war when Germany was standing on the brink of defeat. It does not feature prominently in accounts of Fascist ideology. Nor do the reasons why so many Europeans fought for it. One forgets that the Nazis published a journal called *Nation Europa*.

railway transports; and to recruit auxiliary formations. If one did not know the object of the exercise, one could be forgiven for mistaking it for the AGM of German abattoirists: 7–8 million 'units' were designated for processing. The problem was to collect them, transport them, and dispose of them as quietly and as efficiently as possible. [**NOYADES**] From then on, the Final Solution proceeded without interruption for three years—town by town, ghetto by ghetto, district by district, country by country. In 1942–3 it concentrated on the largest single category—the 3 million Jews of occupied Poland. In 1943–5 it spread to the Balkans, to the Low Countries, to France, and to Hungary. In the end it achieved perhaps 65 per cent of its target. It was only brought to a halt when the facilities were overrun by the Allied armies.

In due course the horrific dimensions of humanity *in extremis* have become well known through a mass of memoirs and documentary material. A bright young Jewish girl recorded her daily thoughts as she lay in hiding at 263 Prinsengracht in Amsterdam.[79] The head of the *Judenrat* or Jewish Council in Warsaw recorded the agonizing dilemmas which he faced trying to serve both his own people and the Nazis.[80] The death-cell autobiography of a former death-camp commandant revealed a conscientious and sentimental man completely impervious to moral reflection:

In Auschwitz, I truly had no reason to complain that I was bored . . . I had only one end in view, to drive everyone and everything forward so that I could accomplish the measures laid down.

I had to watch coldly as mothers with laughing or crying children went to the gas-chambers . . . I had to stand for hours on end in the ghastly stench . . . I had to look through the peep-holes . . . and watch the process of death itself.

My family, for sure, were well provided for at Auschwitz. When I saw my children playing happily, or observed my wife's delight in our youngest, the thought would often come over me, how long will our happiness last?[81]

Some have used the imaginative insights of fictional literature to approach these lower realms.[82] But the most moving testimony comes from those who simply sought to preserve their humanity. [**RESPONSA**]

Discussions about contemporary attitudes have centred on the alleged passivity of Jews and the alleged complacency of Gentiles. Both accusations are overstated. Mindful of the inspiring example of Janusz Korczak, a well-known Polish writer who calmly accompanied a group of orphans on their last journey from the Ghetto, a surviving combatant has said: 'To go quietly was also heroic.'[83] Another recalls the inaction of his own Jewish family when neighbours were removed for the gas-chambers.[84] Jews participated in the underground partisan movement, sometimes in separate units; and armed risings took place in several ghettos. In Warsaw, the heroic Ghetto Rising erupted on 19 April 1943 to oppose the final clearance. It lasted for three weeks, until all but eighty of the fighters were killed. Its leader, Mordecai Anielewicz, committed suicide with the last group of friends in the final redoubt on Mila Street.[85] At Treblinka, a determined break-out led to the successful escape of 300 inmates. [**KATYŃ**]

RESPONSA

ON 3 October 1943 a boy was saved from a *Kinderaktion*, which killed large numbers of Jewish children in the Nazi-built ghetto of Kaunas (Kowno) in Lithuania. The man who had saved the boy asked his rabbi whether the boy might be brought up as his own son. The rabbi offered words of comfort, but the answer was 'No'. The boy must always be taught to honour his own father and mother.[1]

In the vast literature of the Jewish Holocaust, few items can compare in their moral grandeur to the rabbinical responsa from the ghettos of Nazi-occupied Europe. Answering queries about the religious dilemmas of their flock was one of the rabbis' central duties; and it was their custom to keep a register of the questions asked and the replies given. Several such registers exist, but none more moving than that of Rabbi Ephraim Oshry of Kaunas, a survivor, who pieced it together after the war. Even the briefest selection of contents reveals a community on the brink of extinction that was still intent on leading a principled existence:

- Can Jews try to save themselves by obtaining a forged certificate of (Christian) baptism? *It is absolutely forbidden.*

- Is it permissible for a pregnant woman to seek an abortion in the ghetto? *Yes, because without the abortion both mother and child will be killed.*

- Is a woman in the ghetto, whose husband has disappeared, entitled to be released from the usual rules governing remarriage? *No.*

- May a Jew in the ghetto commit suicide? *It is better to receive burial after suicide than to be cremated after extermination.*

- Can an apostate Jew wearing a cross be buried in holy ground? *Yes, but at a little distance from the other burials.*

- Can a child born from extramarital fornication receive the *pidyan haben* ritual of the first-born? *Yes.*

- What should be done with the garments of murdered Jews? *According to religious law, blood-stained garments must be buried; but unstained garments may be given to the children of the victims.*[2]

It has been said that responsa issued under the duress of the Holocaust exhibit undue lenience. That is a matter for expert judgement. But anyone can recognize a desire to combine the rigour of the Jewish law with the duty of compassion. In August 1941, for example, German soldiers had filled the synagogue at Slobodka with dead cats and dogs, before ordering a group of Jews to tear up the Torah scrolls on top of the carcasses and to set fire to the building. When Rabbi Oshry was asked how atonement might be obtained, the persons concerned were starving. His response was clear but gentle: 'they should fast in atonement, if they can.'[3]

Much comment has been expended on the charge of the alleged 'passivity' of Europe's condemned Jews. In some circles Jews driven to collaborate have even been branded as 'war criminals'.[4] The Hasidic view certainly was that 'God's face is covered' during times of persecution, and that devout Jews should accept their fate.[5] Non-Hasidic rabbis did not follow such a firm rule, although there was a long tradition of respecting the law of the land. The Chief Rabbi of Athens destroyed the membership lists of his congregation, enabling many to survive. The Chief Rabbi of Salonika did not do so, and most of his flock were killed.

The real point is that decisions, whether to co-operate or to resist, were taken on the basis of positive moral principle. Even where no action was taken, the evidence does not lie on the side of moral passivity or indifference. It is impossible to deny that individuals could commit all manner of treachery. But the counter-examples are legion. A team of Jewish doctors in the Warsaw ghetto determined to turn their misery to good use and to conduct a scientific study of the symptoms and progress of their own starvation. Hidden in a buried milk churn, their study survived to be published in post-war Warsaw.[6]

In the Nazi death-camp at Sachsenhausen, a Jewish member of a *Sonderkommando*, which was carrying out the physical work of extermination, recognized the rabbi of his own congregation on the ramp. The rabbi's one request was that the *luz*, the top vertebra of his backbone, be salvaged. (In Jewish belief, the *luz* is the core round which the body will reform in the afterlife.) So the man cut the bone from the rabbi's corpse, and was last seen vowing to bury it in holy ground in Jerusalem after the war.[7]

Gentile attitudes were not uniform. Most people, living themselves in the shadow of terror, did nothing; a few assisted in the genocide. Yet many showed compassion. A poet felt anguish at the sight of a children's playground beside the Ghetto Wall in Warsaw which reminded him of the lonely death of Giordano Bruno:

> I thought of the Campo di Fiori
> in Warsaw by the sky carousel
> one clear Spring evening
> to the strains of a carnival tune.
> The bright melody drowned
> the salvos from the ghetto wall,
> and couples were flying
> high in the cloudless sky.
>
> . . .
>
> Those dying here, the lonely
> forgotten by the world,
> our tongue becomes for them
> the language of an ancient planet.

Until, when all is legend
and many years have passed,
on a new Campo di Fiori
rage will kindle at a poet's word.[86]

A thoughtful Catholic intellectual has written of the moral involvement even of those who took no practical part.[87]

Europe's response to the Holocaust touched the depths of depravation and the heights of heroism. In the eye of the storm, in occupied Poland, the chances of saving the segregated Jews were never very great. Critics from more fortunate countries do not always realize how a totalitarian regime drives everyone in its power to varying degrees of complicity. Unfree people should not be judged by the criteria of free societies. Even so, there were individuals, the so-called *szmalcownicy* or 'greasers', who did sell fugitive Jews (and members of the Resistance) to the Gestapo. There were others who risked their lives, and those of their families, to hide and protect the fugitives. In 1943 the Polish Resistance set up the *Żegota* organization to help save Jews.[88] Perhaps 150,000, or 5 per cent, survived by hiding in barns and cellars, in convents, on false papers, or in the woods.[89] [**BATT-101**]

Elsewhere, in less extreme circumstances, Europeans showed everything from noble sacrifice to apathy. In Copenhagen, where King Christian rode out into the streets in sympathy wearing a Star of David armband, most of Denmark's 300 Jews were able to escape. In Romania, where the army and police killed hundreds of thousands of Jews on their own account, the government none the less jibbed at handing over Romanian Jews to the Nazis. In France, where the Vichy regime operated its own execrable concentration camps, as at Le Vernet, the local *milice* took the lead in collecting Jews. They made a distinction between 'alien' Jewish refugees and 'native' French Jews, only 8 per cent of whom lost their lives. The French Protestant Churches registered their protest, and the French Resistance took steps to disrupt the deportation trains. In Holland, despite a determined Resistance movement, most Jews were lost. In Hungary, which stayed free of Nazi occupation until 1944, a resourceful Swedish diplomat, Ralph Wallenberg, organized many Jewish escapes. He was due to disappear, for his pains, under Soviet detention. Local Zionist leaders were charged with striking deals at others' expense. Even in the German-occupied Channel Islands, Jews were handed over. Jews were generally safest in Fascist Italy, in Italian-occupied Yugoslavia, in Fascist Spain or Portugal.[90] [**TAIZÉ**]

The lack of demonstrative protest from the Vatican was the subject of much subsequent controversy. Pius XII's detractors believe that he was indifferent to the Jewish tragedy. His defenders claim that he was torn by fears of reprisals against German Catholics, and by a desire to maintain 'impartiality' between the evils of Fascism and Communism.[91] He certainly did little for the millions of Catholics killed by the Nazis.

The exact Jewish death-toll will never be known. An estimate of 5.85 million was made for the Nuremberg Tribunal. It is unlikely to be very inaccurate. In

BATT-101

IN the early hours of 13 July 1942, the men of the German Reserve Police Battalion 101 were roused before dawn at the Polish village of Józefów, and driven to the nearby town of Otwock. They were not told what awaited them. On arrival, they were ordered by their SS officers to seize all the able-bodied Jewish males in the town, and to shoot all the Jewish women, children, and elderly. That day, they killed about 1,500 persons, the first instalment of the Battalion's estimated total of over 83,000 victims.

In 1962–72, 210 ex-members of Battalion 101 were examined by West German prosecutors, who prepared detailed files on them. They had all been non-Party, middle-aged, largely working-class conscripts from Hamburg, one of the least Nazified cities in Germany. They were the most ordinary of Germans. Almost all expressed revulsion at their wartime duties; and many claimed to be innocent of direct killing. But the great majority took part. 'It was easier for them to shoot':

In every modern society, bureaucratisation and specialisation attenuate the sense of personal responsibility of those implementing official policy. The peer group exerts tremendous pressure on behaviour and sets moral norms. If the men of Reserve Police Battalion 101 could become killers under such circumstances, what group of men cannot?[1]

For obvious reasons, little is known about Jews who were placed in a similar moral position to that of Battalion 101. Very few survived. Yet it was standard practice for the SS to employ Jewish policemen in the ghettos and to recruit Jewish *Sonderkommandos* for the worst tasks in the death-camps. Carel Perechodnik was one such recruit. He was an educated man, who joined the Jewish police force in the Otwock ghetto in the hope of avoiding death and feeding his family. He obeyed Nazi orders, and lived quite well. With the help of non-Jewish friends, he escaped to 'the Aryan side', where he lived long enough to write his memoirs. The memoirs are called *Am I a Murderer?* [2]

For anyone unfamiliar with Eastern Europe, the activities of the communist political police which flooded Poland in 1944–5 are still harder to believe. Popular knowledge in the country has always insisted that the notorious communist Security Office (UB) contained a disproportionate number of Jews (or rather ex-Jews), and that their crimes were heinous. But few hard facts were ever published, and the stories remained unsubstantiated. Recent disclosures, however, have broken the taboo. They are all the more convincing since they were made by a Jewish investigator on evidence supplied by Jewish participants, and in the spirit of Jewish redemption. The study deals with the district of Upper Silesia, and in particular with the town of Gliwice (Gleiwitz). It concludes that in 1945 every single commander and three-quarters of the local agents of the UB were of Jewish origin; that ex-Nazi camps and prisons were refilled with totally innocent civilians, especially Germans; and that torture, starvation, sadistic beatings, and murder were routine. The number of deaths inflicted by the communist regime on the German population is estimated at 60–80,000. In this light, it is difficult to justify the widespread practice whereby the murderers, the victims, and the bystanders of wartime Poland are each neatly identified with specific ethnic groups.[3]

round terms, the total was made up of c.3 million Jews from pre-war Poland, c.2 million from the USSR, and c.1 million from other countries. There may be some overlap between the Polish and the Soviet categories, since in 1939 the eastern part of Poland was annexed to the USSR. But no responsible estimates have brought the total below 5 million.[92] In quantitative terms, this figure may be compared with estimates of c.8.7 million Soviet and c.3.5 million German military losses, and of civilian losses among Ukrainians, non-Jewish Poles, Byelorussians, and Russians each of which ran into several millions.[93] [**BUCZACZ**]

For many years after the War, two round figures enjoyed wide circulation: 'six million' Holocaust victims overall, and 'four million' dead in Auschwitz. The first figure, though somewhat high, is likely to stand. The second figure was impossible. Auschwitz received two people who were later proclaimed Christian saints. The Blessed Edith Stein was a Jewish convert to Catholicism, captured by the Nazis in Holland. Father Maximilian Kolbe was a Catholic priest who gave his life to save a married inmate from death. Fifty years later, pain was still being caused by attempts to find appropriate ways of commemorating the multinational and multi-confessional character of the victims.[94]

At the time, one of the main problems lay in the fact that the outside world could not be made to grasp the enormity of what was happening. As early as September 1940 a courageous officer of the Polish Underground, Witold Pilecki (1901–48), had succeeded in penetrating Auschwitz I. He spent two years organizing secret resistance cells inside the camp, before escaping.[95] Yet the information gathered was not judged credible outside Poland. When the Polish Government in Exile in London published a report on the fate of Poland's Jews, a leading Jewish member of the Government committed suicide in desperation at the feeble response.[96] When a Polish courier visited Washington to give an eye-witness account of the death camps, he was countered by the chilling words of Chief Justice Frankfurter: 'We don't say that you're lying, but . . .' American Jews were no more spurred to action than anyone else.[97] When the proposal was eventually made to bomb the approaches to Auschwitz, the Allied Powers found reasons to refuse.[98] Stalin had killed his millions in the 1930s without significant world reaction. Hitler was able to do the same in the 1940s until outsiders saw the evidence with their own eyes. [**AUSCHWITZ**]

The Holocaust has inspired a vast corpus of literature. Its leading historians are

TAIZÉ

ONE day in August 1940, soon after the fall of France, a 25-year-old theology student from Switzerland wandered into the little Burgundian town of Cluny. He was writing a thesis on pre-Benedictine monasticism. He was less interested in the ruins of the monastery than in the vague possibility of founding a monastic community himself. He was the son of a Protestant pastor from the district of Neuchâtel, until recently a confused agnostic. He saw a sign 'House for Sale in Taizé', cycled the 10 km up the valley, and bought the house in the half-empty village. He was Roger-Louis Schutz-Marsauche.[1]

Wartime Taizé lay close to the demarcation line between the German-occupied and the Vichy zones. The self-appointed monk lived there inter-mittently and alone. For two years he devoted himself to sheltering Jewish refugees until the Gestapo carried his guests away. In September 1944, after the Liberation, he returned again, and took to sheltering German prisoners of war. The villagers reacted violently, and one of the prisoners, an ailing Catholic priest, was killed. At the war's end Roger was joined by his sister, Geneviève, and together they provided a home for twenty rural orphans. Seven more 'brothers' arrived. As non-Catholics, they had to apply for special permission to use the deserted parish church. When per-mission was granted in 1948, it bore the signature of the Papal Nuncio, Cardinal Roncalli.

The Community of Taizé defies classification. It has no formal rule, and belongs to no denomination. It is inspired by the Beatitudes in their purest form—Joy, Simplicity, Mercy, by the service of youth, by the mission of re-conciliation, and by a powerful idea, which is the subject of Brother Roger's book, *The Dynamic of the Provisional* (1965). It is instantly recog-nizable from the unique 'Taizé Sound'—the sound of energetic young voices singing the simplest of words and melodies in rhythmic, incanta-tory, four-part harmony.

Once the Church of Reconciliation was built on the nearby hill in 1962, it became the focus of a world-wide movement, of two-way traffic devoted to the perpetual 'Council of Youth', and the 'pilgrimage of trust on earth'. Eighty white-robed brothers manned a spiritual generator which reached out to all continents. Missions set out for Asia, Africa, Latin America, New York. Wherever there were human divisions, the spirit of Taizé sought to heal them. Initially shunned both by the World Council of Churches and by the Vatican, it won them both over. In Europe it found the support of the Orthodox Patriarch of Constantinople and of the then Archbishop of Cracow. In the 1980s it breached the Iron Curtain, when its European meetings moved on from St Peter's and St Paul's to East Berlin and to Warsaw.

Contemporary European Christianity has produced a number of inspirational figures who have transcended all existing barriers. One was Agnes Gonxha Bojaxhiu (b. 1910, Skopje), an Albanian nun better known as Mother Teresa of Calcutta.[2] Another was a Dutchman, Father Werenfried van Straaten, founder of 'Aid to the Church in Need'.[3] A third such person, of simple heart and unsimple name, is without doubt Brother Roger. 'One passes through Taizé', said John Paul II, 'as one passes a spring of water.'

nearly all Jewish scholars who believe fervently in its uniqueness. They reject 'the oecumenical nature of evil'[99] just as they reject the old question: 'Why do you come with your special Jewish sorrows?'[100] Even so, much variety of emphasis prevails. Elie Wiesel is credited with turning the term 'Holocaust' to its present usage.[101] Lucy Dawidowicz argued for the premeditated nature of the Nazis' genocidal programme.[102] Raul Hilberg saw the Holocaust as the culmination of two millennia of Christian antisemitism.[103] Yehudah Bauer constructed a stark landscape of Nazi 'murderers', Jewish 'victims', and Gentile 'bystanders'.[104] Martin Gilbert compiled a heart-rending compendium of individual experiences.[105]

Dissentient voices betray little uniformity. Non-Zionist witnesses, such as Marek Edelman, the last living leader of the Warsaw Ghetto Rising, have been pilloried for opposing the dominant Zionist viewpoint.[106] One scholar maintained that the Holocaust arose from unforeseen circumstances in 1941.[107] Another tried to show that the Jewish tragedy should be judged within the wider context of the Nazi Terror in general.[108] A group of dubious publicists centred on the *Journal of Historical Review* has sought to maintain either that the 'gas chamber stories' were a hoax, or that the statistics were vastly inflated. The liveliest debate which they provoke concerns their own right to be tolerated.[109] Other critics complain that 'the Holocaust industry' has exploited Jewish suffering for political ends.[110] The film-maker Claude Lanzmann won less than universal acceptance for his evocative film *Shoah* (1984), which many people mistook for documentary history.[111] For passions still rage. The last word has still to be spoken.

No European country was more scarred by the Holocaust than Poland. Jewry's thousand-year Polish abode virtually came to an end. An important element in Poland's population and culture had been torn out. Future generations of Polish citizens would have to bear not only the degrading memory of atrocities perpetrated in their homeland but also a humiliating legacy of recrimination, misinformation, and moral confusion. Only those who were both Polish and Jewish could fully comprehend the trauma. 'The paths of the two saddest nations on this earth have parted for ever.'[112] [**BUCZACZ**]

The German attack on the USSR rapidly transformed the world's diplomatic alliances. Since August 1939 the Centre and the East of Europe's threefold power

AUSCHWITZ

O N 31 May 1944, a British 'Mosquito' reconnaissance plane of 60 Photo Squadron took off from an airbase at Brindisi in southern Italy. Its mission was to fly some 900 miles to German-occupied Poland and to photograph a synthetic fuel factory in the town of Oświęcim (Auschwitz). By chance, since the South African crew left the camera running, the final frames of their film shot at 27,000 feet caught the first ever bird's-eye view of the two nearby SS-concentration camps of Auschwitz I and Auschwitz II-Birkenau.[1]

Many such pictures were subsequently obtained by Allied reconnaissance flights. One photograph taken over Auschwitz-Birkenau from a lower altitude on 25 August 1944 was sharp enough to show a line of new arrivals being marched under guard from the railway ramp towards the open gate of Crematorium No. 2. The trains in the siding, the roof vents of the gas chamber, the chimneys of the furnaces, and groups of prisoners are all visible.[2] Later pictures, in December, showed that the dismantling of the crematoria had already begun.

Aerial photography is a valuable tool in several branches of historical research. It is widely used by archaeologists, by urbanologists, and by landscape analysts. In this case, it supplied a convincing item in the proof of a genocidal campaign that post-war 'revisionists' have sought to deny.

Partial knowledge of the Nazi death-camps had been available in the West since late 1942, when the exiled Polish Government in London published information supplied by its underground couriers. Despite this, the Allied Powers did not see fit to take action.[3] The identification of Auschwitz II as the 'unknown destination' to which Jews from all over Europe were being deported, was only confirmed from the accounts of five escapees in July 1944.[4]

From then on, repeated appeals were made by Zionist groups who hoped that the murders might be disrupted by bombing the camp installations and railway tracks. The appeals fell on deaf ears. Air force officers insisted on the priority of their military and industrial targets. One official of the British Foreign Office minuted: 'a disproportionate amount of time . . . is wasted . . . on these wailing Jews.'[5]

The fate of the aerial intelligence pictures is no less instructive than their contents. The films were flown back from Italy for processing and interpretation at RAF Medmenham in Buckinghamshire. There, since the directors of the operation were only interested in the synthetic fuel factory, the last frames on the reels were not checked out. The historic photographs of 31 May and 25 August 1944 were found thirty years later in the archives of the US Defense Intelligence Agency—unprinted.[6]

Auschwitz was liberated by the Soviet Army on 27 January 1945. Yet the Western Governments' urgent requests for detailed information brought no further news until an ambiguous telegram arrived from Moscow on 27 April. It mentioned 'investigations at Auschwitz' which showed that 'more than four million citizens of various countries had been killed'.[7] This figure, if applied to the victims of Auschwitz alone, was not compatible with statistics produced by Allied prosecutors at Nuremberg.[8] But it was allowed to pass into conventional wisdom. Not until the collapse of Communism in 1990 did the State Museum at Oświęcim feel free to release a more credible estimate of 1.2–1.5 million victims,[9] of whom probably c.800,000–1.1 million were Jews.

Between the extremes of credulity and incredulity, it took exactly fifty years for an approximation of the truth to emerge about one of contemporary history's most intensively researched topics. 'After Auschwitz', Theodor Adorno said, 'poetry is no longer possible'. It seems that historians, too, lost their faculties.

structure had been partners. They were now mortal enemies. This opened the way for the remnant of the third power centre, Great Britain, to join the Soviet Union and to rebuild a new version of the diplomatic system of the First World War. The West would now combine with the East to hold the Centre, before bringing in the USA to tip the balance. The Great Triangle was resurrected. For Churchill, a life-long anti-communist, this meant 'speaking well of the Devil himself'. For Stalin, it offered the only possible source of assistance. An Anglo-Soviet Treaty of Mutual Assistance was signed in Moscow on 12 July 1941. The German–Soviet pact was formally annulled. Stalin was even persuaded to swallow his pride over Poland, and to sign an alliance with Britain's other ally, the Polish Government in London. The Soviet–Polish military convention of July 1941 was followed by a political treaty. An 'Amnesty' was to be granted for the millions of innocent Polish deportees and prisoners in the USSR; and a new Polish army was to be formed in the depths of Russia. The command was given to General Anders, freshly released from the dungeons of the Lyubianka. It was the start of a famous Odyssey.[113]

The crucial step, however, was still to come. Without the USA, the Allied Powers amounted to little more than a club for invalids. Churchill and Roosevelt signed the Atlantic Charter on 11 August, establishing eight common principles. These included:

First—their countries seek no aggrandizement, territorial or other. . . . Third—they respect the right of all peoples to choose the form of government under which they will live . . . Eighth—they believe that all of the nations of the world, for realistic as well as spiritual reasons, must come to the abandonment of the use of force.[114]

But the US Congress was still unwilling to enter the war. The Soviet Government had retired to Kuybyshev on the Volga; its first service to the Allied cause was to join the British in a joint occupation of Persia. Fortunately for London and Moscow, the Japanese proved more persuasive than the Allies. When Japanese bombers attacked the US Pacific Fleet at Pearl Harbor on Hawaii on 7 December 1941, they 'awoke the slumbering giant'. Their action had no direct connection with the war in Europe; yet it changed American attitudes overnight. America's war-shyness evaporated; the Congress voted lavish war credits; and the hands of the President were untied. It was not part of the Japanese plan; but they had unwittingly unlocked the doors of the Grand Alliance. 'The Big Three'—the war-winning trio of Churchill, Stalin, and Roosevelt—were in business.

The Germans, of course, felt cheated. They had sought no quarrel with the USA, if only the President would stop helping the British. In any case, they were counting on finishing the war before the Americans could intervene. So Berlin opted for bravado: Hitler declared war on the USA in a speech to the Reichstag on 11 December 1941.

In its way, the emergence of the Grand Alliance was every bit as shocking as that of the Nazi–Soviet partnership two years earlier. Every principle of the Anglo-Saxon democracies was contradicted by the Soviet system. Nor was it just a matter of forgetting Stalin's past crimes. The Western leaders had to close their minds to the fact that Stalin continued to kill perhaps a million of his own people every year throughout the war. But when Stalin was weak and Hitler was strong, Stalin had to be helped. By Stalin's standards, the Western democracies were every bit as nauseating and 'anti-socialist' as the Führer. But with the Wehrmacht at the gates of Moscow, the helping hand of the West had to be accepted; ideological niceties did not enter the reckoning. Though the anti-Nazi alliance was to be wrapped in the verbiage of freedom, democracy, and justice, the Big Three were bound together by cynical convenience.

For the time being, the Grand Alliance could do little to challenge German hegemony in Europe. The immediate tasks were to secure their lines of communication, to limit Germany's further advance, to damage Germany's war industries, and to construct the basis for offensive action in the future. To these ends the Anglo-Americans combined to fight the Battle of the Atlantic; they planned a vast campaign of aerial bombing; and they undertook to supply the Soviet Union with war material. Everything depended on the Red Army's ability to avoid collapse, on Britain's ability to preserve its island fortress, and on the Americans' ability to muster their colossal resources for simultaneous wars in the Pacific and in Europe. [**OXFAM**]

The Battle of the Atlantic secured the sea lanes which guaranteed Britain's life-line to the USA and the USA's gateway to Europe. 21,194,000 tons of Allied shipping, 77,000 British sailors, and 70 per cent of all German U-boats were to be lost before the seas would be cleared of raiders. The U-boats' bases were invulnerable: the abortive British raid on St Nazaire in March 1942 highlighted the contrast between the Allies' mastery of the sea with Germany's supremacy on land. Anti-

OXFAM

THE Oxford Committee for Famine Relief began its career in the University Church of St Mary the Virgin on 5 October 1942. Its immediate purpose was to alleviate distress caused by the war in Greece. It was by no means the sole agency devoted to international humanitarian relief: the International Red Cross had been operating out of Geneva since 1863, when it was formed by Henri Dunant as a result of horrors witnessed at the Battle of Solferino. In the First World War campaigns had been organized to assist war victims in Belgium, Serbia [**FLORA**], and Galicia. In 1918–21 the American Relief Administration (ARA) provided enormous assistance, especially in Eastern Europe, as did UNRRA after 1945. Almost all the combatant countries, including Germany, had operated some form of relief agency. Yet Oxfam had several advantages. Like the IRC, it was independent of government policy. Also, being based in one of the Allied states, it did not cease to function at war's end. Thirdly, being British, it had ready access via the Empire to all the continents. It was well placed when the focus for international relief shifted away from Europe.[1]

The history of the relief agencies inevitably reflected Europe's changing position in the world. Post-war affluence created a huge economic discrepancy between 'North' and 'South' at the very time that the 'West' was confronting 'the East'. The USA was more preoccupied with politics than previously; the Soviet bloc was not involved in humanitarian issues; and the UN was somewhat constricted by member governments. So an important role was left to private organizations from post-imperial Europe such as Oxfam, Save the Children, CAFOD (Catholic Fund for Overseas Development), and Médecins Sans Frontières. The North–South Commission (1978–83) and the associated Brandt Report established the target figure of 1 per cent of GNP whereby the wealthier nations should aim to assist the 'Third World'. But in 1992–3 the disasters in ex-Yugoslavia emphasized the fact that Europe's own agonies were far from finished.

---

submarine measures, including the convoy system, aerial patrols, and sonar, took months and months to be deployed. Allied shipping losses peaked in March 1943, immediately before the U-boats met their own catastrophe. The sinking of 41 U-boats in conjunction with Convoy ONS-5 forced Admiral Dönitz to withdraw his submarines from the Atlantic for good.

As from the first 1,000-bomber raid on Cologne on 31 May 1942, the Allied bombing offensive rose steadily to a mighty crescendo. It has been strongly criticized both on practical and on moral grounds. Precision bombing, such as the famous 'Dam-Buster Raid' on the reservoirs of the Ruhr Basin or the elimination of the Nazis' heavy-water plant at Telemark in Norway, had clear objectives. But the wholesale destruction of German cities by fire-bombing, and the attempt to terrorize the civilian population, did not achieve the expected results. In the years between 1941 and 1945, 1.35 million tons of high explosive were dropped on the Reich by the endless waves of Lancasters, Halifaxes, and Flying Fortresses. Counter-measures absorbed a great deal of Germany's dwindling resources. But the Nazis' war industries were never halted; and German civilians, like their British counterparts under the Blitz, rallied to the national cause. One enormous raid on Hamburg in May 1943 caused a fire-storm that killed 43,000 innocents. Another on Dresden may have wreaked destruction approaching that of the atomic bombs dropped on Japan. [**ALTMARKT**]

Western operations to supply the Soviet Union, which gathered pace from 1941, were rarely acknowledged by the beneficiaries. The Royal Navy took on the hazardous assignment of leading Arctic convoys to Murmansk. Many seamen and ships and the best part of one whole convoy, the PQ17, were lost without trace. The USA organized huge overland transports into Russia from the Persian Gulf. American aid to the USSR under the Lend Lease Scheme was estimated at 7 per cent of Soviet military production and $2.8 billion in non-military supplies.

Allied political plans took shape round the Atlantic Charter and the Washington Pact of 1 January 1942, whereby the twenty-six states at war with the Axis Powers undertook not to sign a separate peace. These states formed the kernel which grew in the space of four years into the United Nations, the successor to the League.

As soon as the Grand Alliance started its work, the Anglo-Americans were pressed by Stalin to open a second front in Europe. Almost the whole of the German war machine was concentrated in the East; and it was entirely reasonable for Stalin to ask his allies to share the burden. He himself possessed larger reserves of trained manpower than he revealed to anyone—which is one reason why the Red Army consistently exceeded German estimates of its capacity. Even so, there was a huge disproportion between the 150 German divisions which the Red Army had to face and the 4 assigned to the only other front then operating, in North Africa. The Anglo-Americans, however, had no easy means to oblige. Their air power drew the Luftwaffe away from the Volga at a crucial moment; and they eventually took a larger number of Axis prisoners in Africa than were taken at Stalingrad. But they could not project their strength onto the European mainland. Every single Continental port was in enemy hands, and a vast Atlantic wall of coastal defences was under construction in northern France. An abortive raid on Dieppe showed what fearsome obstacles awaited any major Allied landing force. Neither the British nor the Americans possessed trained reserves. Stalin was told that a major offensive would be launched in the West in 1943; it did not materialize until June 1944. Before that, the only relief which the Anglo-Americans could bring to the main land war was on the southern periphery, in Italy.

The hard-fought Italian campaign developed from the Allies' growing strength throughout the Mediterranean. Contrary to expectations, the British held on to Malta and the sea route to Suez; and Anglo-American landings on the western extremities of North Africa spelled mortal danger for the *Afrika Korps*. Operation Torch soon had the Axis bottled up in Tunisia, whence in May 1943 they were obliged to withdraw completely. Thereafter it was a relatively simple step for the Allies to cross the Sicilian Straits, and to attack the toe of the Fascist boot.

The invasion of Sicily began on 10 July 1943, when British and American troops landed simultaneously on the southern and eastern shores. German reinforcements arrived too late to prevent the rapid conquest of the whole island. From Sicily, the Allies jumped across to Calabria in September and began the arduous task of pushing northwards up the mountainous peninsula; in all, the task was to take them nearly two years. Yet the Allied toehold in southern Italy was to have important consequences. Once a major base was established at Brindisi, it permitted the projection of Allied air power onto a wide range of destinations throughout Central and Eastern Europe, including Poland and Yugoslavia. It forced the German Command to commit ill-spared divisions to the occupation of southern France. Most importantly, it provoked the collapse of Mussolini's regime. On 25 July 1943 Marshal Badoglio persuaded the King of Italy to dismiss the Duce and to accede to Allied overtures. The Duce was saved from arrest on the Gran Sasso in a sensational rescue by German paratroopers, and lived again to rule a German-sponsored Republic of Northern Italy from Milan. But the first major crack in the Axis fortress could not be concealed.

Meanwhile, on the Eastern Front, the gigantic German–Soviet War was moving to its climax. Having survived the disaster of 1941, the Soviet regime moved to tap the great reservoir of Russian patriotism. Stalin reopened the Orthodox churches which he had all but annihilated, and appealed like Lenin before him for the defence of Holy Russia. What seemed impossible at any time before 1941, millions of men went willingly to their deaths with 'Za Stalina' (For Stalin) on their lips. The Red Army's prodigal use of its expendable manpower amazed and, to a degree, demoralized the German soldiery. Waves of infantry were used to assault fixed positions with no sign of artillery support. Through fields of mounting corpses, the hordes of ill-clothed and ill-armed 'Ivans' kept coming and coming, till the German machine-guns overheated and the gunners lost stomach for the slaughter. It was an accepted fact of the contest that the Soviet side could sustain casualties of three or four to one and still carry the day. The Red Army's sacrifices were helped by the wilderness and the weather, and by the T-34, the best tank of the war. A brilliant military team led by Marshal Zhukov maximized the advantages of space and numbers.

In 1942 the Wehrmacht was drawn on and on. The constant series of local German successes concealed the fact that the elusive Soviet enemy was not now being trapped or encircled, and that the long lines of communication were growing ever longer. By the early autumn, as the weather deteriorated, neither the Volga nor the Caspian had been reached; and a dangerous salient was developing on the approaches to Stalingrad. A tactical withdrawal might have remedied the situation. But the Führer adamantly refused. Hitler must take the sole blame for the fateful order which told General von Paulus to hold his ground at all costs.

The Germans' momentum eventually took them to the right-bank suburbs of 'Stalin's city'. Yet they were entering the head of a noose. Day after day, Zhukov's forces inched round the German flanks, until, in one sudden movement, von Paulus was finally surrounded. Three months of desperate hand-to-hand fighting in icy, deserted ruins preceded von Paulus's surrender on 2 February 1943. Stalingrad cost over one million lives. It was the largest single battle of world history. The invincible Nazi colossus was shown to be fallible.

News of Stalingrad flashed round the world, giving heart to anti-Nazi resistance movements all over Europe. Before Stalingrad, Resistance leaders had only been able to indulge in small-scale sabotage, or to run the clandestine escape lines for Allied airmen and prisoners. After Stalingrad, they began to dream of liberation.

In Western Europe, resistance was relatively uncomplicated. Prompted by the broadcasts of the BBC, and by the skulduggery of the British Special Operations Executive (SOE), devoted cells of courageous men and women planned the sabotage and diversions which would eventually help the advance of the Allied armies. In Denmark, where the Nazis had hoped to create a model protectorate, the Resistance forced the Germans in August 1943 to declare martial law. In Norway, too, the Nazis abandoned the attempt to rule through the pro-Fascist government of Vidkun Quisling. Their one and only shipment of heavy water from the Norsk-Hydro Plant was sunk in the Tinnsjo fiord by Norwegian saboteurs. In the Netherlands they were less disturbed, having penetrated the Dutch Resistance in a brilliant project called the *Englandspiel*, the 'English Game'. In Belgium, France, Italy, and Greece, the resistance was increasingly influenced by communist elements. The French resistance came to life after 1942 with the German occupation of the Vichy Zone, where large numbers of patriots took to the *maquis*. At the same time the Italian partisans, whose achievements were still greater, concentrated their activities in the northern zone ruled by Mussolini, whom they eventually captured and killed.

Yet nowhere was popular defiance more determined than in tiny Luxemburg. In the plebiscite of October 1941, only 3 per cent of Luxemburgers voted for joining the Reich. Later, they organized the only effective general strike against Nazi rule, whilst sustaining a ceaseless campaign of obstructions and propaganda.

In Eastern Europe, Resistance was more problematical. German policies there were far harsher. Despite very different political colorations, the leading formations of the Underground—the democratic Polish *Armia Krajowa* (Home Army, AK), the undemocratic Ukrainian Insurrectionary Army (UPA), and the Serbian *Četniks*—were all caught in a painful political trap, where the pursuit of national freedom demanded resistance to Stalin as well as to Hitler. Co-operation with the advancing Red Army, or with communist partisans, who did not recognize the principle of 'bourgeois independence', involved at best abject surrender, more usually imprisonment and death. [BUCZACZ]

In Poland, for example, the largest and most senior of Europe's Resistance movements faced an almost impossible task. It came into being in late 1939, when it treated both the Nazis and the Soviets as occupation forces. Its main formation, the *Armia Krajowa* (AK), was a loose federation of ill-assorted groups. Its authority was respected by the numerous Peasant Battalions (BCh), but not by the semi-fascist (but violently anti-German) National Armed Forces (NSZ) or by the communist People's Guard (GL). It had proper, if slight, relations with the Jewish Fighting Organization (ZOB) in the ghettos—and bloody confrontations with the Ukrainians, the Soviet partisans, and the gangs of deserters, fugitives, and bandits with whom it shared the woods. It organized and ran an impressive 'Secret State'—with clandestine intelligence, diversionary, educational, judicial, and political branches. But it did not survive the Soviet 'Liberation'. Its democratic leaders ended up in a Moscow show trial. Honourable men, like the unbroken General Okulicki, the AK's last Commander, deserve to stand amongst the heroes of the Allied cause. Instead, amidst the shameful silence of their comrades in the West, they were consigned to obscurity, dishonour, and an early grave.[115]

In Yugoslavia, the problem was solved by a controversial and, some would say, disreputable decision of the Anglo-Americans. Yugoslavia, unlike Poland, lay outside the sphere of direct Soviet influence. But in 1943 it came within range of Allied support from Italy. London and Washington chose to back Tito's communists. Thereafter, Tito's rivals, the *Četniks*, were heaped with every form of calumny. Their leaders, including Mihajlović, would eventually be executed by Tito's courts for 'treason'.

Such developments well illustrate the facile definitions of 'resistance' and 'collaboration' which prevailed in Anglo-American circles. Nations who have never experienced foreign invasion rarely comprehend its complications. Of course, some people in continental Europe chose to serve the invaders from base motives of personal gain. Others, like Leon Degrelle's Rexist Movement in Belgium, acted in accordance with principles developed before the war. But many were moved to collaborate in order to exert a moderating influence and to limit the harm done. In France, after Pétain's fateful meeting with Hitler, the policy of collaboration may or may not have been misguided. But it was coined for reasons of patriotic necessity.

In the broad expanse of Europe that was successively occupied both by Soviets and by Nazis, the element of choice was largely absent. Both totalitarian regimes sought to enforce obedience through outright terror. For most ordinary civilians, the prospect of serving the Soviets posed the same moral dilemmas as serving the fascists. The only course of principled action for patriots and democrats was the suicidal one of trying to oppose Hitler and Stalin simultaneously.

After Stalingrad, the news from the Eastern Front continued to be disheartening for Berlin. In the spring of 1943, the Red Army moved to the general offensive for the first time in two years. In the opening stages of five mighty campaigns that would carry them all the way to Berlin, Stalin's confident marshals began to roll back the Nazi enemy. On the open steppe near Kursk in July, the Germans' strategic tank-force was smashed. Their capacity for large-scale attack was broken. The tide, to use Churchill's metaphor, had turned.

BUCZACZ

'THE DEACONRY OF BUCZACZ. In 1939, this district was inhabited by 45,314 Poles. Among its 17 parishes, Barycz numbered 4,875, Buczacz 10,257, Koropiec 2,353, Kowalówka 3,009, Monasterzyska 7,175 . . . In Barycz, a couple of Polish families were murdered by Ukrainians in 1939 . . . One of the Biernackis had a leg severed . . . But the main attack took place on the night of 5–6 July 1944, when 126 Poles were killed. Men, women and children were shot, or hacked to death with axes. The "Mazury" ward of the town was burned down. The attackers were armed with machine guns and shouted "*Rizaty, palyty*" (kill, burn). The survivors fled to Buczacz, where they survived the winter in terrible conditions, in ex-Jewish houses without doors or windows . . .

The [Catholic] parish of Nowostawce, though sparsely inhabited, contained three Greek-Catholic parishes within its bounds. The ratio of Poles to Ukrainians was 2 : 3. In 1939 co-existence was still possible. But conditions worsened after the German Occupation. In 1944, when the German–Soviet front line passed through, nothing but ruins remained . . .

The vicar of Korościatyn reported an attack on his village on 28 February 1944. 78 persons were shot, smothered or axed in the vicarage cellar . . . Some ninety people had perished in an earlier attack in 1943. Then typhus carried off a further fifty. A curious thing occurred. The village had thirteen so-called "wild marriages". All of them died except one.

In Koropiec, no Poles were actually murdered. But it was reported that the Greek-Catholic pulpits resounded to calls regarding mixed Polish–Ukrainian marriages: "Mother, you're suckling an enemy—strangle it." '[1]

Forty years after the event, the Roman Catholic Church in Poland was still trying to document the wartime 'ethnic cleansing' perpetrated in the former eastern provinces of Galicia and Volhynia. Estimates of casualties range from 60,000 to 500,000.[2]

Buczacz, or Buchach, was one of scores of districts which shared a similar fate. It lay in the Archdiocese of Lwów which covered all of Red Ruthenia (East Galicia) and beyond. Its pre-war population was made up of Ukrainians, Poles, and Jews. All three communities were scourged by Soviet repressions at the start of the war. Then the Jews were killed by the Nazis and their local collaborators. After that, the Poles were attacked by Ukrainians. Finally, the returning Soviets destroyed anyone and everyone connected with independent organizations.

Ethnic cleansing in wartime Poland was started in 1939–41 both by the Nazis, who cleared several western regions for German resettlement, and by the Soviets, who deported millions from the East. After 1941, it was taken up by small factions of the Polish underground, who sought to drive out Ukrainians from central Poland, and on a far larger scale by the Ukrainian Insurrectionary Army (UPA), who terrorized Poles. In 1945, the communists completed the cleansing of Poles from Ukraine and, through 'Operation Vistula', of Ukrainians from their homes in 'People's Poland'.

At Potsdam, Allied policy approved the expulsion of all Germans from east of the Oder (see p. 1047).

The UPA came into being in October 1942 to initiate an exclusive, nationalist Ukraine and to oppose the growing bands of Soviet partisans infiltrated behind German lines. (Its commander, General Roman Shukevich, 'Chuprynka', fought on until captured in 1950.) However, when the rising communist tide had been stemmed neither by the Wehrmacht nor by the formation of the SS Galizien, the Ukrainian underground adopted desperate solutions. Western Ukraine was heading for the return either of Soviet or of Polish rule. The more radical elements then decided to wipe out their most vulnerable adversaries, namely Polish civilians.[3] They had no compunction in killing anyone who opposed them:

11 March 1943. In the Ukrainian village of Litogoszcz (Volhynia), Ukrainian nationalists murdered a Polish school teacher whom they had abducted. Together with this Pole they murdered several Ukrainian families who opposed the massacre.[4]

In a conflict with strong religious undercurrents, the clergy were selected for bestial treatment:

Revd Ludwik Włodarczyk from Okopy was crucified; Revd Stanisław Dobrzański from Ostrówka was beheaded with an axe; Revd Karol Baran was sawn in half in Korytnica; Revd Zawadzki had his throat slit . . .[5]

In post-war Eastern Europe, all war crimes were officially ascribed to the Nazis. Victims from areas like Buczacz were lumped together in the 'Twenty Million Russian War Dead', or otherwise hidden by silence.[6] The multinational dimensions of the tragedy were not appreciated. All nationalities have been guilty of publicizing their own losses, and of ignoring others, although one sometimes meets accounts of shared suffering:

Between May and December 1942, more than 140,000 Volhynian Jews were murdered. Some who had been given refuge in Polish homes were murdered together with their Polish protectors in the spring of 1943, when, of 300,000 Poles living in Volhynia, 40,000 were murdered by Ukrainian 'bandits'. In many villages, Poles and Jews fought together against the common foe.[7]

But no overall, even-handed survey of wartime genocide has been undertaken. Attempts to establish Polish or Catholic losses, for example, inevitably sideline Jewish and Ukrainian losses. They stress the role of Jewish and Ukrainian collaborators in the Soviet service, or of Ukrainian units under German command. They are not concerned with the activities of Silesian Poles in German *Schupo* units, nor with the Polish co-operation with the Soviet Army. It is not part of their brief to count the UPA's Jewish and Ukrainian victims. Any exercise which looks at one side alone is bound to generate distortions.

Buczacz, incidentally, was the home town of Simon Wiesenthal, Nazi-hunter extraordinary.[8]

The Triumph of the Grand Alliance (July 1943–May 1945). From mid-1943 the Grand Alliance held the upper hand in almost every sphere. The Reich, though fighting hard, was under siege. The Soviets held the initiative on land. The Anglo-Americans held mastery of sea and air. The combined resources of American industrial strength, of Russian manpower, and of the British Empire could not be matched by Hitler's shrinking realm. There was still no Second Front beyond Italy, and no sign of serious opposition inside Germany. Save for the *Wunderwaffen* or 'wonder weapons' which were supposed to reverse the Führer's fading fortunes, the demise of the Reich grew ever more likely.

Despite exaggerated rumours, the intense competition over weapon development was real enough. It focused on jet engines, on rocketry, and on the atomic bomb. German scientists won two of the three contests outright. A prototype of the jet-powered Messerschmitt 262 flew in 1942. The *Vergeltung* or 'revenge' rockets, the V1 and V2, were developed at Peenemunde on the Baltic, and targeted on London from June 1944. But the race for the atomic bomb was won by the Allies' Manhattan Project in distant New Mexico. Its success, in July 1945, came too late for the European war.

For the Allies, the most acute problems lay in the realm of political and strategic co-ordination. To this end, three personal meetings of the 'Big Three' were organized—at Teheran (December 1943), at Yalta (February 1945), and at Potsdam (June 1945). Three major issues underlay their discussions—the definition of war aims, the priorities of the Pacific and the European War, and the plans for post-war Europe. On war aims, the Grand Alliance decided to insist on the unconditional surrender of the Reich. This was done partly in deference to Stalin's suspicions about a Second Front, partly in recognition of the mistakes of 1918. The effect, whilst binding the Alliance together, was to give the Soviet Union a licence for its totalitarian designs in the East. Once the Western leaders had renounced the possibility of withdrawing from the conflict, they surrendered the strongest lever for moderating Soviet conduct.

The clash of priorities between the war against Germany and the war against Japan was especially acute for the Americans, who alone were carrying a major share in both conflicts. It was to come to a head at Yalta. The Soviets had observed strict neutrality towards Japan since 1941, and were not likely to change their position until the European war was over. The British, in contrast, were deeply involved in the Japanese war. Their fragile lines to the Far East were stretched very thin, and great reliance had to be placed on the independent war effort of the dominions, especially of Australia and New Zealand. Singapore had fallen, dramatically, at an early stage. Thereafter, Britain's participation was confined to Burma (where the Japanese sphere lapped the borders of British India) and to auxiliary support for the Americans.

Plans for the future of Europe never reached full agreement. The Western Allies excluded Stalin from considerations about Western Europe, starting with Italy, and Stalin pressed on regardless with his own dispositions in the East. An important exception lay in the so-called 'Percentages Agreement' which Churchill discussed with Stalin during his visit to Moscow in October 1944. It was never formally adopted; but there is some reason to think that both sides regarded it as a working guideline for the Balkans. Pulling half a sheet of paper from his pocket, Churchill is said to have written down a short list of countries and alongside it a series of percentages representing the expected balance of Western and Russian influence. After puffing on his pipe, Stalin is said to have placed a neat blue tick against the following:

	Russia	Others
Romania	90%	10%
Greece	10%	90%
Yugoslavia	50%	50%
Hungary	50%	50%
Bulgaria	75%	25%[116]

The 'naughty document', as Churchill called it, has not survived in the public section of Britain's Public Record Office, and its existence has been questioned. What it meant in practice, however, is that Greece was marked down as the sole country on the list where Western influence was supposed to prevail. And that is what happened.

Poland was the one country whose future could not be agreed even in unofficial outline. Its plight is often seen as the source of the later Cold War. Poland, like France, was a member of the original alliance of 1939. Its Government in London was fully recognized, its soldiers, sailors, and airmen were serving with distinction under both British and Soviet command. In April 1943 Stalin used the pretext of the Nazis' revelations about Katyń to sever relations with the Polish Government. At the same time, in Moscow, he recognized the ineptly named Union of Polish Patriots, the core of a Soviet puppet regime. In July the Polish Prime Minister and Commander-in-Chief, General Sikorski, the one Polish politician enjoying universal confidence, was killed in an air crash at Gibraltar. From then on the Polish tragedy moved to its nemesis. Soviet propaganda was demanding a return to the Ribbentrop–Molotov frontier, now conveniently referred to as the Curzon Line. On no sound authority, the population of eastern Poland were said to be clamouring for union with the USSR; and a Polish Government 'friendly' to Soviet interests was said to be essential. These claims bore no close examination; but Western opinion, whose admiration for the magnificent Soviet war effort knew no bounds, was well disposed to believe them. So, as the Red Army rolled ever deeper into Poland, the Western powers pressed their wretched Polish allies to concede.

Teheran lay at the mid-point of the wartime air route between London and Moscow; and it was there from 28 November to 1 December 1943, that Roosevelt, Churchill, and Stalin held their first meeting. They made sufficient progress to ensure the continued prosecution of the war. They agreed on the urgency of opening the Second Front in France, and on the post-war independence of Iran. But they disagreed quite violently over Poland. During a blazing row between

Eden and Molotov, President Roosevelt 'slept in his chair'. The Western leaders conceded that Poland's territory should be moved bodily to the West at Germany's expense, to compensate for Stalin's claims; but they kept it secret from the Poles. The occasion was hardly auspicious—but it achieved enough to restore confidence in the prospect of a joint Allied assault on the Reich in the coming year.

The Red Army's offensives of 1943–5 sustained a masterly drum-beat that kept the Wehrmacht constantly reeling. They began in the middle of the Baltic States, Byelorussia, and Ukraine and ended with the siege of Berlin. They were organized in a series of huge forward leaps, in which colossal concentrations of men and material would be massed in front of the Germans' over-stretched lines, then unleashed in an irresistible flood. The second such offensive, after Kursk, was aimed at the Dnieper, which was defended by the Germans with a wide zone of scorched earth. The third, launched in January 1944, was aimed at the distant Vistula. The fourth, beginning in August 1944, turned south into the Balkans and was aimed at the Danube. The fifth, in January 1945, was aimed at the Oder and beyond.

In each of these movements, the basic tactic was to surround and to envelop the points of resistance. Once a defensive fortress was cut off and isolated, it could safely be left for destruction at a later date. In this way, several German armies were cut off in Courland and left undefeated till the end of the war. Major German fortresses in the East, such as Breslau, were still intact when Berlin fell. The main thing was to prevent the Wehrmacht from preparing a counter-blow, and hence to harry, to harass, and to maul. The Russians knew war on the steppes: aggression usually paid off, fixed defence could usually be outflanked. As the Plain narrowed, the Wehrmacht's temptation to stand and fight grew stronger. Three such choke-points occurred at the Dukla Pass in the Carpathians, in the battle for Budapest, and at the line of the Pomeranian Wall. Here Soviet and German blood was spilled in profusion.

The reputation of the Red Army—renamed the Soviet Army in 1944—went before it. Given the memories of 1939–41, it was often regarded as an alien force even in the Soviet Union. In the Balkans, it was received at best with mixed feelings. In Germany, where the troopers were encouraged to murder and rape, it provoked panic. The first German village to be freed from the Nazis was martyred. Pictures of German women crucified on barn doors were circulated by the Nazis to stiffen resistance. Instead, in the winter of 1944–5, the mass of the German population took flight.

The Soviet drive into central Europe was one of the grandest and most terrible military operations of modern history. One of the soldiers in its ranks, who was himself arrested at the front, wrote of 'the Juggernaut of Comintern' crushing all beneath its wheels.[117] For, if the Soviet Army brought liberation from the hated Nazis, it also brought subjugation to Stalinism. With it came looting, rape, common violence, and official terror on a horrific scale. For those who saw it, it was an unforgettable sight. As the battered German formations pulled back, wave after wave of liberators passed through. First came the front-line troops, alert, well-clothed, heavily armed. Next came the second-class units and punishment battal-ions, who marched with ammunition but no food. Behind them the flotsam of the front—stragglers, camp followers, walking wounded, refugees trapped between the lines. At the back rolled the cordon of the NKVD in their smart uniforms and American jeeps, shooting all who failed to keep going. Finally there came 'the hordes of Asia', the endless supply columns riding on anything that would move westwards—broken-down trucks, hijacked peasant carts, ponies, even camels. The contrast between the red-eyed, bandaged, and weary German soldiery and the endless truck-loads of fresh-faced Slavonic and Asiatic lads told its own story.

The Soviet advance into the Balkans in August 1944 had important political consequences. Romania changed sides, and took the field against her erstwhile Nazi patrons; Hungary was occupied by the German army to prevent Budapest from following Bucharest's example. In Bulgaria, the royal government was top-pled in September. In Yugoslavia, Tito's partisans joined up with Soviet troops and freed Belgrade in October. In Greece and Albania, both of which lay beyond the line of Soviet occupation, the communist underground made preparations to take over. At which point, in December, the Soviets ran into the obstinate defence of Budapest; and the advance came to a halt until the New Year.

In the West, the Second Front was finally opened on 6 June 1944, D-Day, when British, Canadian, Polish, and American troops landed on the beaches of Normandy. Operation Overlord undoubtedly involved the greatest technical feat of the war. It demanded the safe disembarkation of hundreds of thousands of men and their weapons on a heavily fortified coast, whose defenders had been preparing the reception for four years. It succeeded because good planning was matched by good luck. Deception measures, which included the bombing of false targets in the Pas-de-Calais, confused the German Staff about the location of the landings. Hitler, whose hunch about Normandy had been correct, was overruled. Air supremacy ensured close support on the beaches and, still more importantly, the interdiction of the Germans' powerful armoured reserve. The technological marvels included the huge floating dockyards called 'Mulberry Harbours' that were towed into position off the Normandy coast, and Pluto (Pipeline Under The Ocean) which guaranteed an unlimited supply of petrol. A change in the weather, which produced the biggest Channel storm for 25 years, ensured that the German commander, General Rommel, went home for the vital weekend.

Rommel's opponent, US General Dwight D. Eisenhower, knew that he would only be allowed one throw of the dice. The start was twice postponed. With the favourable moon fast on the wane, 156,000 men, 2,000 warships, 4,000 landing craft, and 10,000 warplanes were held on the alert for days. But then, amidst great trepidation, the order was given. In the middle of the night, in the subsiding gale, American paratroopers of the 82nd and 101st Airborne Divisions jumped into the middle of the German lines. One of them, from Kansas, feigned death as he hung suspended from the spire of the Sainte-Mère Eglise. Further west, at 'Pegasus Bridge', the first British soldier on French soil, Sgt. Jim Wallwork, silently landed his Horsa glider at 00.16 hrs within 30 yards of the target, knocking himself unconscious on impact. D Company of the 2nd Oxford and Bucks Light Infantry then shot their way across the bridge, captured the lock on the Orne Canal, entered the café of M. et Mme. Gondrée, and spoke the words of Liberation: 'It's all right, chum.'[118]

Then, in the grey dawn, the steel doors of the landing craft were thrown open and the main force waded ashore onto five code-named beaches. Seventy-three thousand men of the US 1st Army hit Utah and Omaha; 83,000 men of the Second British and First Canadian armies stormed on to Gold, Juno and Sword. The shocked German defenders lay low in their bunkers, bombarded by heavy shells from unseen warships and mercilessly strafed from the air. Only at 'bloody Omaha' did they manage to raise a screen of fire to pin the attackers down. There, the Texas Rangers heroically scaled the cliff under fire, only to find that the gun position on the top had been dismantled. But the setback was local. D-Day worked. In addition to their toehold in Italy, the Allies had won their fingerhold in France. The Reich could now be pincered from all sides.

Overlord, however, was slow to develop. When the Wehrmacht recovered from its surprise, resistance was fierce. The Americans could not take Cherbourg, the principal port of the invasion coast, for three weeks. The British, who should have entered Caen on the evening of D-Day, fought their way in on D + 34 (9 July). But the logistics outmatched anything that was seen in the East. Reinforcements poured into the Mulberries; the petrol flowed smoothly through Pluto. When the Americans finally broke through to the rear, the Germans had nothing to do but run. Caught at Falaise in an ever-shrinking gap, they ran the gauntlet amidst scenes of slaughter. After that, the Allies' road was clear for the race to Paris and the drive for the Rhine.

After two years of defeats, the German Army finally reacted against Hitler. On 20 July 1944, at the Führer's eastern HQ, his *Wolfschanze* near Rastenburg in East Prussia (now Kętrzyn in Poland), an attempt was made to assassinate him. A bomb was left in a briefcase under the heavy oak table of the conference room. It exploded in the Führer's presence; he escaped, badly shaken, with a damaged arm. It had been planted by Col. Claus von Stauffenberg, a member of the Moltkes' aristocratic Kreisau Circle. Its failure, and the horrible fate of the plotters, whose slow deaths on meat-hooks were filmed for the Führer's enjoyment, discouraged other attempts. Large volumes are written about the German Resistance. The role of noble individuals and small groups, such as Pastor Bonhoeffer or the 'White Rose', is beyond question. But the fact is that they did not achieve their goals.[119]

By the time of the bomb plot, Germany's immediate neighbours in Poland and France were both eagerly awaiting their freedom. The Soviet army was approaching the eastern suburbs of Warsaw. The American army was working its way round the western suburbs of Paris. Both cities were filled with various groups of resistance fighters directed mainly from London; both were straining at the leash to rise against the Nazi oppressor. In Warsaw they were led by the underground AK, in Paris by the Free French.

Paris rose on 19 August. Despite poor intelligence, the idea was to mount attacks inside the city and accelerate the Americans' final push. Parts of the French Resistance worked with the American Command, which had recognized their value in the battles since the Normandy landings. Assailed from all quarters, the German garrison pulled back—and the Americans struck. General Leclerc's French armoured division, fighting under American command, was given the honour of spearheading the advance. The German garrison surrendered, having ignored the Führer's order to leave no stone standing. On 25 August, with snipers still active, General de Gaulle walked magnificently erect down the Champs-Élysées. The cathedral of Notre-Dame celebrated a great Te Deum. Despite the heavy loss of civilians, the population rejoiced. France's pre-war Third Republic was restored; Paris was free.

Warsaw had risen on 1 August, almost three weeks before Paris. The plan was to co-ordinate attacks inside the city with the Soviets' final push. But the Varsovians were not to share the Parisians' success. The intelligence of the Polish Resistance was poor; and they found too late that the Soviet Command was not going to help. The Soviet generals had used the Polish Underground in all the battles since crossing the Polish frontier. But Stalin did not recognize independent forces; and he had no intention of letting Poland regain its freedom. Assailed from all quarters, the German garrison had began to withdraw. But then the Soviets suddenly halted on the very edge of the city. Foul treachery was afoot. Moscow Radio, which had called on Warsaw to rise, now denounced the leaders of the rising as 'a gang of criminals'. Two German panzer divisions moved forward; and the garrison was given time to receive massive reinforcements from the most vicious formations of the Nazi reserves. General Berling's Polish army, which was fighting under Soviet Command, was withdrawn from the Front for defying orders and trying to assist the rising. Berling himself was cashiered. Western attempts to supply Warsaw by air from Italy were hamstrung by the Soviets' reluctance to let their planes land and refuel. Street by street, house by house, sewer by sewer, the insurgents were shelled, gunned, and dynamited on one bank of the Vistula, whilst Soviet soldiers sunbathed on the opposite bank. In one of several orgies of killing, in the suburb of Mokotów, Nazi troops massacred 40,000 helpless civilians in scenes reminiscent of the liquidation of the Warsaw Ghetto in the previous year. Weeks after the liberation of Paris, the Warsaw insurgents were still fighting on. They surrendered after sixty-three days, on 2 October, when their commander, General Bór, walked into German captivity.[2] Their only consolation was to be granted combatant status. Despite the sacrifice of 250,000 of its citizens, Warsaw remained unfree. Poland's pre-war Republic was not restored. There was no Te Deum in the destroyed cathedral of St John. The remaining population was evacuated. In his fury, Hitler ordered that no stone of the rebel city was to be left standing. The demolition proceeded for three months, whilst the Soviet army, with its committee of Polish puppets in tow, watched passively from across the river. They did not enter Warsaw's empty, silent, snow-bound ruins until 17 January 1945.

Despite the Normandy landings, the Western Allies encountered many set-backs. In Italy, Rome fell the day before D-Day, but only after the Allied armies had been bottled up for months at Monte Cassino. One week after D-Day the London blitz was resumed, with the dispatch first of the V1 flying bombs, the 'doodlebugs', and in September of the V2. An American landing on the French Riviera in August was poorly conceived and developed slowly. In the north, Brussels was freed amidst great rejoicing on 3 September. But the British scheme, under Operation Market Garden, to jump ahead and seize the Rhine bridges at Arnhem was a costly disaster. In the centre, in December, in the 'Battle of the Bulge', the Americans had to absorb the weight of the Wehrmacht's last major armoured counter-attack in the Ardennes. At Bastogne, where the 101st Airborne was called on to surrender, the resources of the German Staff and their translators were finally overpowered by the American reply of 'Nuts'. In the Mediterranean, the British army re-entered Greece in October, only to find itself with a civil war on its hands. Churchill did not hesitate to assist the government in Athens against communist attacks. Before it fell, the Reich was allowed to totter on the brink.

The terminal conquest of Germany in January to May 1945 took place amidst scenes never before experienced. In the West, British and American bombers were steadily reducing every major German city to hecatombs of rubble and corpses. Nazi officials vainly planned their last stand in the Alpine redoubts of Austria and Bavaria. In the East, millions of desperate German refugees were trekking west-wards through the winter. Tens of thousands perished in the sinking of the *Wilhelm Gustloff* and other mercy ships, or on the deathly trail across the ice-bound waters of the Frisches Haff. The Führer's last throw was to draft all German males above 14 into the so-called *Volkssturm*. Most of those schoolboys, invalids, and veterans were to die from the Soviet policy of killing anyone in German uni-form. The compulsory evacuation of major cities such as Danzig or Breslau, and of concentration camps such as Auschwitz, were accompanied by death marches. German life in the East was coming to an end. [**DONHOFF**]

Zhukov's offensive against Berlin was launched on 12 January 1945 from a range of some 400 miles. The Red Army cleared Poland when the Western allies were still well short of the Rhine. The fall of Budapest in mid-February permitted a two-pronged lunge which had Vienna as well as Berlin in its sights. In early March the Americans had a fortunate break, when German sappers failed to blow the last remaining bridge across the Rhine, at Remagen. Soon General Patton would come riding triumphantly out of this Western bridgehead even faster than Zhukov out of the East; his men would eventually meet up with the Soviets in the Torgau in Saxony on 23 April. The British, with Canadian and Polish support, had liberated the Netherlands, and were far advanced along the northern Plain. Berlin was cut off by a ring of Russian steel. From his bunker beneath the bomb-blasted debris, the Führer watched the Reich's defences crumble.

When the Big Three met again at Yalta in Crimea from 4 to 11 February 1945,

DÖNHOFF

MARION, Countess Dönhoff was born in 1909 at the family palace of Friedrichstein, twenty miles from Königsberg in East Prussia. The seventh child of a numerous brood, she followed the timeless routine of the semi-feudal East European aristocracy, unaware that their time was running out.

Friedrichstein in the 1900s still offered its residents all the beauties of nature and the benefits of privilege. Set amidst the lakes and forests and the sharp seasons of the East, it drew its children into a blissful round of horses, picnics, and libraries, of tutors, loving nannies, and distinguished guests. Marion's mother, once a lady-in-waiting to the Empress at Potsdam, ran the house with a taste for the rigid etiquette and social hierarchy of the Kaiser's court. She trained the servants to address her with 'Most humbly, good morning, Your Excellency'. Marion's father, Karl August, an easy-going globetrotter and sometime diplomat at the German embassies at St Petersburg and Washington, was a member of both the hereditary Prussian Senate and the elected German Reichstag. The style was one of public opulence, private austerity, and Lutheran piety.

The Dönhoffs, like many German noble families, had moved to the East in the Middle Ages. Their original home was at Dunehof on the Ruhr in Westphalia. Their second, also Dunehof, was set up in 1330 near Riga in Livonia, where they remained for eighteen generations. That senior Livonian branch of the family, usually known as Denhoff, became prominent Polish magnates—palatines, hetmans, starostas, and cardinals. The Prussian, Protestant Dönhoffs were descended from the Livonian Magnus Ernst von Dönhoff, sometime Polish ambassador to Saxony and Brandenburg, who settled near Königsberg in 1620. His son, Friedrich, bought the main estates by the Pregd in 1666. His grandson, Otto Magnus, governor of Memel and Prussian ambassador at the Treaty of Utrecht, built the pile of Friedrichstein in 1709–14.

Wars and disasters were taken in their stride on the Prussian frontier. In the Great Northern War, 40 per cent of East Prussia's population died of plague. The revolutionary wars saw the entailing of the estate in 1791, the arrival of the French in 1807, the emancipation of the serfs in 1810, and the arrival of Kutuzov in 1813. In the First World War, having escaped from the Russian advance of August 1914, it greeted its saviour, Field Marshal von Hindenburg, in person.

At first the war of 1939 looked just like any other. Yet by the winter of 1944–5 it was clear that some final and total nemesis was at hand. Unlike any of its predecessors, the advancing Soviet army was intent on eradicating the Germany of East Prussia once and for all. With all the adult males of her family dead, either killed on the Eastern Front or executed after the bomb-plot against Hitler, Marion Dönhoff had been left administering the estates of Friedrichstein and Quittainen alone. One night in January 1945 she mounted her horse, joined the flood of westbound refugees, and rode 1,000 miles in two months, all the way to Westphalia. (She paused only once, to stay with Bismarck's daughter-in-law at Varzin in Pomerania.) The 600-year Eastern adventure of the Dönhoffs had come full circle. Friedrichstein, deserted, was annexed to the RSFSR.

The fate of Friedrichstein and of the Dönhoffs was repeated hundreds of times over right across Europe. The destruction which the Bolsheviks meted out to Russia's own aristocracy in 1918–21 awaited the landed proprietors of every country which the Red Army entered, either in 1939–40 or in 1944–5. The old German families of Prussia, Bohemia, and the Baltic States were cast into the same abyss which engulfed the Polish families of Lithuania, Byelorussia, and Ukraine, and the Magyars of Slovakia and Croatia. Indeed, not just the aristocrats but entire populations of all classes were removed. The Soviet scourge destroyed not just privilege but centuries of culture.[1]

At least Marion Dönhoff survived. After the war she worked as a journalist in Hamburg, becoming editor of *Die Zeit* in 1968 and its publisher in 1973. When she wrote her memoirs, she mused on the futility of revenge:

'I also do not believe that hating those who have taken over one's homeland . . . necessarily demonstrates love for the homeland. When I remember the woods and lakes of East Prussia, its wide meadows and old shaded avenues, I am convinced that they are still as incomparably lovely as they were when they were my home. Perhaps the highest form of love is loving without possessing.'[2]

the end was already close. Regarding Germany, they agreed on the establishment of four separate Allied occupation zones, on the destruction of the Reich's military-industrial capacity, on the prosecution of war criminals, and on the need to guarantee Germans no more than 'minimum subsistence'. Regarding Poland, they agreed that there should be 'free and unfettered elections', and that a Provisional Government should draw its members both from Stalin's Lublin Committee and from the London Poles. On Japan, which worried the ailing Roosevelt most, they agreed that the USSR should enter the Pacific war two to three months after the end of hostilities in Europe. A secret protocol empowered the Soviets to reoccupy the Kurile Islands. These arrangements did not have the force of an international treaty; they were the private working guidelines of the Allied Powers. [**KEELHAUL**]

Just as doctors will debate the exact moment of human death, in heart, brain, lungs, or limbs, so it is with bodies politic. In the case of the Third Reich, the siege of Berlin ensured suffocation; the suicide of the Führer on 30 April prevented all chance of recovery; the general surrender of 8/9 May marked the last twitch. The Nuremberg Tribunal of 1946 may be likened to the coroner's court.

The siege of Berlin, as foreseen at Yalta, was left to the Soviet Army. The terminal phase lasted for three weeks from 20 April. Zhukov poured in reserves without counting the cost; he was probably to lose more men in this one operation than the US army lost in the whole of the war. As the noose tightened, various Nazi officials slipped out. Hitler's deputy, Martin Bormann, left—never to be seen again. One of the last planes to take off disappeared with a cargo of Nazi archives. Berlin sold itself dearly: it was the Warsaw Rising in reverse. Eventually, Soviet soldiers hung the Red flag atop the shattered Reichstag.

In his bunker at the junction of the Wilhelmstrasse and Unter den Linden, the Führer lost all contact with outside events. 'If the war is to be lost,' he had remarked, 'the nation will also perish.'[120] His orders were transmitted into an unresponsive vacuum. On 29 April he went through a form of marriage with Eva Braun, who had declined the offer of escape. On the 30th the newly-weds died in a poison and pistol-shot suicide pact. They thereby avoided the fate of Mussolini and his mistress, who the previous day had been strung up by the feet in Milan. When the Hitlers died, the Russians were 200 yards away. The Führer left orders for the burning of the bodies in a petrol pit, and a brief will and testament:

It is untrue that I, or anyone in Germany, wanted the war in 1939. It was desired and instigated solely by those international statesmen who were either of Jewish descent or who worked for Jewish interests . . . I die with a happy heart, aware of the immeasurable deeds of our soldiers at the front . . . Above all, I charge the leaders of the nation . . . to scrupulous observation of the laws of race, and to merciless opposition to the universal poisoner of all peoples, international Jewry.[121]

The last remains of the Führer and his wife were buried by the KGB in east Germany, and eventually incinerated by them in 1970. Two fragments of a skull said to be Hitler's were produced from the ex-Soviet archives in 1993.

'Victory in Europe', or VE Day, followed in the second week of May. For the Nazis it meant annihilation, the vengeance of their gods; for the German nation it spelled total defeat. General Montgomery accepted the submission of a German delegation in his tent on the Lüneburg Heath; General Eisenhower accepted the formal capitulation at his base near Reims; Marshal Zhukov did the same at his HQ at Karlshorst. The moment of Germany's unconditional surrender was fixed for midnight on the 8th (GMT). This was 5 a.m. on the 9th (Moscow Time).

As always, the declaration of peace did not quite match the reality. The Allied Powers were still at war in the Pacific. In the desert of New Mexico, the scientists were still working feverishly for the first atomic test. In Europe, pockets of fighting continued. A German army cornered in Prague was finished off by elements of Vlasov's RLA, who had vainly changed sides in the hope of a reprieve. Pockets of local resistance against the Soviet takeover continued in Eastern Europe and the western USSR until the 1950s.

KEELHAUL

IN February 1945, Major Denis Hills, an officer of the British Eighth Army in Italy, was given command of a POW camp at Taranto containing 8,000 men of the 162 Turkoman Infantry Division, classified as 'repatriates'. His charges had been conscripted into the Red Army, been captured on the Eastern Front by the Germans, and had endured starvation and cannibalism under arrest before volunteering for service with the Wehrmacht. Having sailed with them to Odessa, whither they were transported under the terms of the Yalta Agreement, he had no doubts that all such Soviet repatriates were being sent home to be killed.[1]

In subsequent assignments, Hills repeatedly faced the age-old dilemma of a soldier whose conscience did not match his order. In the case of the SS *Fede*, which was trying to leave La Spezia for Palestine with an illegal shipload of Jewish emigrants, he advised his superiors that regulations should be waived to let them sail—which they did. 'I had wished to extinguish a small glow of hatred before it grew into a flame.'[2]

During Operation Keelhaul (1946–7), Hills was given 498 ex-Soviet prisoners for screening in a camp at Riccione. His orders were to repatriate to the USSR (1) all persons captured in German uniforms, (2) all former Red Army soldiers, and (3) all persons who had aided the enemy. By inventing spurious categories such as 'paramilitaries' and by privately urging people to flee, he whittled down the number of repatriates to 180. When they left, the Russian leader of the group told him: 'So you are sending us to our deaths . . . Democracy has failed us.' 'You are the sacrifice', Hills replied; 'the others will now be safe.'[3]

In the case of Ukrainians from the Waffen-SS Galicia Division held at Rimini, Major Hills was one of several British officers who personally rebuffed the demands of the Soviet Repatriation Commission. When the Division was reprieved, he was sent a letter from the division's CO, thanking him 'for your highly humane work . . . defending the principles in the name of which the Second World War has been started'.[4] According to international law, the Galicians were Polish, not Soviet citizens.

Hills admitted that he 'bent the rules'.[5] Shortly afterwards, he was court-martialled and demoted on a charge of unseemly conduct, having been caught doing cartwheels and handsprings at dawn in the city square of Trieste.

The Allied policy of forcibly repatriating large numbers of men, women, and children for killing by Stalin and Tito has been called a war crime. In the Drau Valley in Austria, where in June 1945 British troops used violence to round up the so-called Cossack Brigade and their dependants, it provoked mass suicides. But it was well hidden until a report written by Major

Hills came to light in the USA in 1973, and the opening of British archives. Solzhenitsyn called it 'The Last Secret'. It only reached the wider public through books published thirty and forty years after the event.[6]

More recently, an unusual libel trial in London awarded £1.5 million damages against Count Nikolai Tolstoy, author of *The Minister and the Massacres*, who had written of an official British conspiracy and cover-up. The plaintiff was not the minister accused of ordering the handover of the Cossacks, but a British officer who, faced with the same problem as Hills, had pursued a different policy. He did not receive a penny of his award, as the defendants fought on in the European courts.[7]

Individual responsibility is always hard to prove. But the moral principle is unequivocal. If 'obeying orders' could be no defence for Adolf Eichmann, it can be no defence for Allied officers.

Six weeks later, at Potsdam, from 17 July to 2 August, the Big Three met for the last time. Of the wartime leaders Stalin alone survived, suspicious that the capitalist powers might turn against him. Contrary to all predictions, Churchill was defeated in Britain's post-war election, and replaced in the middle of the conference by the socialist Clement Attlee. Roosevelt had died before the fall of Germany; he was succeeded by his no-nonsense Vice-President, Harry Truman. Differences among them were so great that the original idea of organizing a Peace Conference was shelved. When Truman arranged for a melodramatic announcement of the successful American A-bomb test, Stalin did not even blink.

So Potsdam stuck to practical matters. Germany was to be given an Interallied Council to co-ordinate the administration of its four occupation zones. Austria was to be restored to its independence. France was to be given back Alsace-Lorraine, and Czechoslovakia the Sudetenland. Poland was to be given a frontier on the Oder–Neisse line, whether the Poles wanted it or not. All Germans living east of the new frontiers were to be expelled. All the Nazi leaders who had fallen into the Allied net were to stand trial before an International War Crimes Tribunal. Beyond that, the Allies could agree on little; and they did not try.

By which time, the processes of reconstruction and forgetting were in full swing:

> After every war
> someone has to clear up.
> For things won't find their right place
> on their own.
>
> Someone has to heave
> the rubble to the roadsides
> so the carts piled high with corpses
> can pass by.

Photogenic it certainly isn't;
and it takes years.
All the cameras have gone off
to other wars.

Those who knew
what this was all about
must make way for those
who know little, or less than a little,
or simply nothing.[122]

Friday, 19 October 1945, Nuremberg.[123] The city was occupied by the US Army. An American colonel had taken command of the city prison which stood immediately behind the Palace of Justice on the Fürtherstrasse. Of the 24 named defendants in the 'Trial of German Major War Criminals', 21 were locked in their cells. It was the day when they were due to be served with their indictments.

The task of serving the indictments had fallen to a young British major, a former prisoner of war, who spoke fluent German. As he entered the cell-block just before 2 p.m. he saw three tiers of cells, each with a small window grille in the door. A guard was lolling at every door, peering through the grille. On the upper floors the open balconies were covered with wire netting. The twenty-second defendant had recently committed suicide. The event was to be witnessed by a dozen men. The major was shown into the block by the commandant of the prison and by a master-sergeant who carried the keys. Behind them walked the General Secretary of the International Military Tribunal with his interpreter, two American soldiers carrying documents, an officer of the US security staff, the prison psychologist, notebook in hand, and the prison's Lutheran chaplain. A handful of 'snowdrops'—American military policemen in their characteristic white helmets—brought up the rear.

The indictments, freshly translated from English into German, were bulky documents. The cover-page read: 'The United States of America, the French Republic, the United Kingdom of Great Britain and Northern Ireland, and the Union of Soviet Socialist Republics against . . .', followed by a column of 24 names, headed by that of Goering. There were four counts—conspiracy in common, crimes against peace, war crimes, crimes against humanity. Each of the accused was to receive two copies, which outlined both the general charges and the particular counts on which he was accused. Anglo-American practice required that the indictments be served in person.

The young major, though a law graduate, had no particular experience of such duties. When he saw the wire netting his thoughts turned to one of his wartime companions, a Belgian airman captured by the Gestapo, who had leapt to his death from exactly such a balcony in the prison at Suresnes. Though he had been working for the Tribunal for several months, the major had only just arrived in Nuremberg, and he had never met any of the prisoners face to face:

Map 27.

Post-War Germany, after 1945

'I looked towards the high window at the far end of the prison. The spiral stairs to the upper rows of cells were in silhouette against the bright autumn sun. There was that eternal silence, only the menacing sound of keys . . .

The silence continued until we reached a cell near the end of the row. The guard on duty saluted. I noticed that he was armed with a revolver and a blackjack . . . As the cell was unlocked, I braced myself to meet [the prisoner, who] rose unsteadily to his feet. . . .

I was surprised to find my voice.

'Hermann Wilhelm Goering?'

'*Jawohl.*'

'I am Major Neave, the officer appointed by the International Military Tribunal to serve upon you a copy of the indictment in which you are named as a defendant.'

Goering's expression changed to a scowl, the look of a stage gangster, as the words were interpreted. I handed him a copy of the indictment which he took in silence. He listened as I said, 'I am also asked to explain to you Article 16 of the Charter of the Tribunal.'

A copy in German was handed to him.

'If you will look at paragraph (c). You have the right to conduct your own defence before the tribunal, or to have the assistance of counsel.'

My words were correct and precise. Goering looked serious and depressed as I paused. 'So it has come,' he said. . . .

'You can have counsel of your own choice, or the tribunal can appoint one for you.'

It was evident that Goering did not understand . . . Then he said, 'I do not know any lawyers. I have nothing to do with them.' . . .

'I think that you would be well advised to be represented by someone.' . . .

He shrugged his shoulders.

'It all seems pretty hopeless to me. I must read this indictment very carefully, but I do not see how it can have any basis in law.' . . .

Some hours after I left Goering's cell, Dr. Gilbert, the prison psychologist, asked him to autograph a copy of the indictment. Goering wrote, 'The victor will always be the judge and the vanquished the accused.'[124]

In this way, the fundamental dilemma of the Nuremberg Trials found expression even before the trials began.

Europe in the autumn of 1945 was functioning at the lowest level of subsistence. The victorious Allies had divided a devastated Germany into four zones of occupation, and were struggling to maintain a united front. The Western countries liberated by the Anglo-Americans—France, Italy, Belgium, the Netherlands—were picking up the strands of their pre-war existence. The Eastern countries liberated by the Soviets were finding that liberation was joined to a new form of subjugation. Great Britain, the only combatant country to have avoided occupation, had recently chosen a socialist government which was realizing that victory was no safeguard against a marked decline in status. There was no single state in Europe, like the USA, which was both victorious and unscathed. A handful of neutrals, from Spain to Sweden, were free to exercise a degree of real independence.

Several countries had already staged trials to punish wartime acts that were now considered criminal. In Oslo, Quisling was tried and executed in September: in Paris, Laval suffered the extreme penalty on 9 October. In Moscow, the trial of

Polish underground leaders had taken place in June; public opinion in the West was not fully aware that the defendants in this case were neither fascists nor collaborators, but heroic allies whose only crime had been to fight for their country's independence. Western governments had preferred to press privately for lenient sentences rather than protest publicly.

Nürnberg (Nuremberg), one of Germany's most ancient and most German cities, had been reduced to a sea of rubble, having been subjected to eleven mass bombing raids. Then, when two SS divisions decided to make it the scene of their last stand, it had been mercilessly shelled into submission by American heavy artillery. Home of the medieval Meistersingers and of Tannhäuser, of Albrecht Dürer and of Veit Stoss, it had been chosen in the previous century as the home of the German Museum, a magnificent collection of German national art and history. In the 1930s it had been chosen as the venue for Hitler's most dramatic Nazi rallies. It had now been chosen for the Trials partly for its symbolic value, partly because its imposing Palace of Justice had miraculously survived the bombing. To hold the trials in Nuremberg was to emphasize the Allied view that the root of Germany's evil lay not in Prussian militarism (as was the view in 1918) but in the very nature of the Germans' national identity. The setting of the trial seemed designed to teach a history lesson far deeper than the offences of the individual defendants.

Nuremberg's special contribution to the Trials, however, was to be found in the person of defendant no. 8, Julius Streicher (b. 1885), who had ruled the city as Nazi Gauleiter from 1933 to 1940. He was serving his second time in the cells behind the Palace of Justice, having once been arrested for molesting a boy prisoner during one of his official visits. He was a blatant sexual pervert, as his jailers were able to observe, and a lifelong Jew-baiter whose speciality lay in linking sex with anti-semitism. In his crusade against 'race pollution' he had invented a spurious biochemical theory, whereby the albumen of Jewish semen was capable of permanently 'infecting' any woman with whom it came into contact. As the editor of *Der Stürmer* he waged a constant campaign to protect German maidens from Jewish seducers—a cause which he later gave pseudo-scientific cover in the journal *Deutsche Volksgesundheit aus Blut und Boden*. He was the main instigator of the Nuremberg Laws which forbade all sexual intercourse in Germany between Jews and non-Jews. In 1938, on Kristallnacht, he had made a speech urging the rioters to follow the glorious example of the medieval pogroms that had been perpetrated in the city. As an early recruit to the NSDAP, he was one of the few Nazi leaders to address the Führer as *du*. But he overstepped the mark when he publicly asserted that Göring's daughter had been conceived by artificial insemination. The infuriated Reichsmarschall had instigated a commission of inquiry that uncovered such gross corruption that Hitler himself could not save his Gauleiter from instant retirement.

The Allied decision to stage a war crimes trial had not been lightly reached. Churchill had been against it, as had Henry Morgenthau, the Secretary of the US Treasury. In the absence of legal precedents, they argued that it would be better to shoot the Nazi leaders by summary execution. Their opinion was overruled: the Allied governments had committed themselves to the principle of war crimes trials by the Declaration of St James (January 1942) and the Moscow Declaration (November 1943); and the established policy had too much support to be discarded. Of the Big Three, Roosevelt and Stalin were both in favour. As a result, the trial had to take place. They were necessary both as 'a sincere but naïve attempt to apply the rule of law'[125] and to demonstrate the limitless power of the victors. Stalin had used show trials as an instrument of his political victory inside the Soviet Union; and there is no reason to think that he would have missed the opportunity for a similar show of strength after his great international victory. Stalin, after all, was the chief beneficiary, since in any equitable settlement he might easily have found himself in the dock.

The International Military Tribunal was created in consequence of the Potsdam Agreements. Its Charter was published on 8 August 1945, two days after the Hiroshima bombing. The Nuremberg Trials were planned as the European counterpart to similar trials against Japanese leaders that were due to take place in Tokyo.

Once the indictments were served, the opening of the Nuremberg Trials was set for 20 November 1945. From then, the Trials proceeded through 403 open sessions in the main courtroom of the Palace of Justice until the final sentences of the judgment were read more than ten months later, on 1 October 1946. The four Allied judges, under their Chairman, Sir Geoffrey Lawrence QC, sat on one side with their deputies. The 21 defendants present, who all pleaded not guilty, filled the benches of the dock opposite, under strict military guard. The four Allied prosecutors—an American, a Briton, a Frenchman, and a Soviet—shared the middle ground with their deputies and assistants, with the crowd of defending German counsel, and with a mass of clerks, translators, and interpreters. A raised public gallery had been built in one lateral wing of the courtroom. The proceedings were conducted and recorded in English, German, French, and Russian. At any one time, therefore, the majority of participants would be listening to simultaneous translations on headphones.

In addition to those present, Martin Bormann, Hitler's deputy, was tried *in absentia*, as were eight defendant organizations charged with collective criminality: the SS, the SD, the SA, and the Gestapo: the 'leadership corps of the NSDAP', the Reich Cabinet, the General Staff, and the High Command of the German Armed Forces. Proceedings against Gustav Krupp, the industrialist, were dropped on account of the defendant's incapacity. In all, the prosecution produced over 4,000 documents, 1,809 affidavits, and 33 live witnesses. They also showed films, and introduced a number of grisly exhibits including 'human lampshades' and the heads of men mounted on wooded stands like those of stags. The defence produced 143 witnesses, together with hundreds of thousands of affidavits. The corpus of the Trials, published in 1946, ran to 43 volumes.[126]

The opening speeches of the prosecution made lofty appeals to the highest moral principles, whilst betraying some sensitivity to the legal uncertainties. Justice Robert H. Jackson admitted that the Tribunal was 'novel and experimental'. Sir Hartley Shawcross appealed to the 'rule of law', M. de Menthon to 'the conscience of the peoples'. General Rudenko spoke of 'the sacred memory of millions of victims of the fascist terror' . . . and 'the conscience of all freedom-loving peoples'. Jackson probably made the best case by arguing from the inadmissibility of inaction. 'Civilisation asks whether law is so laggard as to be utterly helpless to deal with crimes of this magnitude . . .'[127]

Within their limited terms of reference, the Trials were conducted with great decorum and circumspection. Lord Justice Lawrence set an example to the judges by extending every courtesy to the defence, and by acidly reprimanding the prosecution where necessary. The only time when the proceedings became unruly was when Jackson lost control of Göring during cross-examination. Blanket verdicts were never likely, acquittals always possible.

The strongest testimony was presented on the counts of war crimes and crimes against humanity. Here the evidence against the Nazi party men was damning, especially when derived from their own records. The death-camps of the Final Solution, the unspeakable horrors of pseudo-medical experiments, mass atrocities of unprecedented proportions were comprehensively documented in a manner leaving little margin for error. The weakest testimony was offered on the counts of common conspiracy, and on points where it was easy for the defence to plead normal practice of sovereign states. It was hard to prove that Hitler's 'secret meetings' with his colleagues constituted evil intent, or that rearmament was in itself inspired by aggressive motives. Direct comparisons with Allied conduct, however, were not permitted. The defence could not raise the failings of the Versailles settlement or of the Allied bombing offensive, nor the subject of Soviet atrocities. 'We are here to judge major war criminals,' Lord Justice Lawrence insisted, 'not to try the prosecuting powers.' Attempts to discuss conditions in Allied internment camps or the forcible expulsion of Germans, which was in progress at the time, were cut short. 'The Defence is attempting to introduce breaches of International law by the Allies,' reported *The Times* on 8 May 1946, 'but [the prosecutor] made the point that if this were accepted, he would be obliged to bring evidence of rebuttal, which would needlessly prolong the trial.'[128]

The subject of the Katyń massacres was initially raised by the Soviet prosecutor. When the defence lawyers were able to show that many of the prosecutor's facts were false, the Soviet team promptly dropped the accusations. [**KATYŃ**]

Eyewitnesses to the Trials recalled many moments of drama and irony. There was the symbolic scene of the wild-eyed Hess sitting in the dock reading Grimms' *Fairy Tales*. Another minor sensation occurred in November when the Soviet prosecution team was joined unannounced by Andrei Vyshinsky, the chief Soviet delegate to the United Nations, best remembered as Stalin's chief prosecutor in the Purge trials of the 1930s. Many observers commented on the eerie contrast between the fate-laden climate of the courtroom and the merry flow of pink gins in the bar of the Grand Hotel next door.

The American security staff provided two psychiatrists and one psychologist for the defendants' welfare. As part of his duties, the psychologist prepared tests for the defendants' IQ ratings:

Schacht, 143; Seyss-Inquart, 140; Göring, 138; Dönitz, 138; von Papen, 134; Raeder, 134; Frank, 130; Fritzsche, 130; von Schirach, 130; Ribbentrop, 129; Keitel, 129; Speer, 128; Jodl, 127; Rosenberg, 127; von Neurath, 125; Funk, 124; Frick, 124; Hess, 120; Sauckel, 118; Kaltenbrunner, 113; Streicher, 106.[129]

The sentences, when they came, caused some surprise. Schacht, the banker, Fritzsche, the propagandist, and von Papen, the sometime Vice-Chancellor, were acquitted on all counts. So, too, were the Reich Cabinet, the General Staff, and the High Command. Dönitz, von Neurath, von Schirach, Speer, and Hess received prison sentences varying from 10 years to life. Göring was branded 'the leading war aggressor' and convicted on all four counts. He and ten others were sentenced to death by the rope. The Soviet prosecutor entered a dissenting opinion on all the acquittals and prison sentences. Each of the prisoners reacted in his own way to the prospect of hanging. Jodl said bitterly 'That, I didn't deserve.' Ribbentrop said, 'I won't be able to write my beautiful memoirs.' Hans Frank said, 'I deserved it and expected it.'[130] When the psychologist asked Hess what sentence he had been given, Hess replied 'I've no idea. Probably the death penalty. I didn't listen.'[131] Göring cheated the hangman by killing himself with a cyanide pellet concealed in a dental crown.

Ten executions were carried out in the gymnasium of the prison block on 16 October 1946. Most of the condemned died with patriotic words on their lips. Frank shouted, 'Deutschland über alles'. Streicher said, 'Heil Hitler. Purim 1946. The Bolsheviks will hang you all,' then commended himself to his wife. Rumour held that the US army executioner botched his job, causing lingering deaths, and that the bodies were cremated at Dachau. The five remaining convicts were transported to Spandau Jail in Berlin, where the four-power administration was to continue until the strange death of Hess in 1987.

A wide range of criticisms was levelled against the trials from the outset. On the purely political front, fears were expressed that the defendants would be turned into martyrs. This did not happen, either in Germany or elsewhere. The head of repugnance built up by the Trials' revelations was large enough to offset any counter-currents of sympathy. If there was a general consensus, it held that the crimes of the Nazis outweighed any element of rough justice that was meted to individuals. Many lawyers, however, were gravely worried by the *ex post facto* nature of the indictments. *Nulla poena sine lege.* Dissenting voices did not accept Jackson's contention that the Tribunal was contributing to 'the growth of international law'.[132] They were also scandalized by the court's lack of independence. For the Allied Powers to supply both the judges and the prosecutors on terms and in an arena dictated by themselves made for bad legal practice, and for poor publicity. 'While clothed with forms of justice,' objected Senator Robert Taft, '[the trials] were in fact an instrument of government policy, determined months before at Yalta and Teheran.'[133] A widespread opinion, especially among the Allied military, held that honourable German officers like Admiral Dönitz should not have been put in the same dock as active Nazis like Göring or Streicher. When Dönitz was released in 1956, several hundred distinguished Allied veterans, headed by US Admiral Nimitz, contributed to a volume of regrets.[134]

To those who could resist the emotions of the times, it was scandalous that the Western press and government agencies often encouraged the notion of collective guilt. All the defendants were routinely labelled as 'criminals' long before the verdicts were pronounced. Most seriously of all, the fact that the Nuremberg trials were limited to offences committed by the defeated enemy erected an insuperable obstruction to any general and impartial investigation into war crimes or crimes against humanity. It created the lasting impression in public opinion that such crimes could not by definition be committed by agents of the Allied Powers.

For historians, the Nuremberg Trials are of interest both as a historical event in their own right and as an exercise in examining the past through legal methods. Their advocates were convinced that 'we discovered the truth'.[135] Their critics maintain that less than half the truth was discovered. To be precise, the Nuremberg Trials confirmed beyond all reasonable doubt the reality of Nazi crimes. They also documented the role played by Germany in the origins and conduct of the Second World War, not always in the light demanded by the prosecutors. At the same time, by isolating the German factor from all others, they were bound to construct a biased and, in the last resort, an untenable analysis. Equally, by knowing omissions, they encouraged the erroneous view that there was little more to discover. The historical material which was marshalled in the indictments, and then in the preamble to the final judgment, was intended for 'throwing light on matters of interest to the International Military Tribunal'. Yet it was so blatantly selective that even the most fervent opponents of Nazism could despair. To mention the Nazi–Soviet pact, for example, but only in the category of treaties violated by the German Reich, was grossly misleading. 'The published indictment', wrote a leading historian on the day that the document was served in the cells, 'reads like history written by non-historians.'[136]

The Nuremberg Trials were the source both of huge quantities of valid historical information and of manifest historical distortions. Bolstered by the public attitudes which they encouraged in the West, and by the Soviet censorship, which used the findings as gospel, they became the bastion of a particular 'Allied Scheme of History' that would prevail for fifty years (see Introduction). Not until Solzhenitsyn in the 1960s, and *Glasnost'* in the 1980s, did public opinion begin to realize that the Nuremberg prosecutors were masters no less of concealment than of unmasking. Andrei Vyshinsky demonstrated the fact when, in a rare moment of honesty, he proposed a toast at a Nuremberg reception: 'Death to the Defendants!'.[137] As usual, his Western partners did not understand Russian. They drank the toast without hesitation, then asked what it meant afterwards.

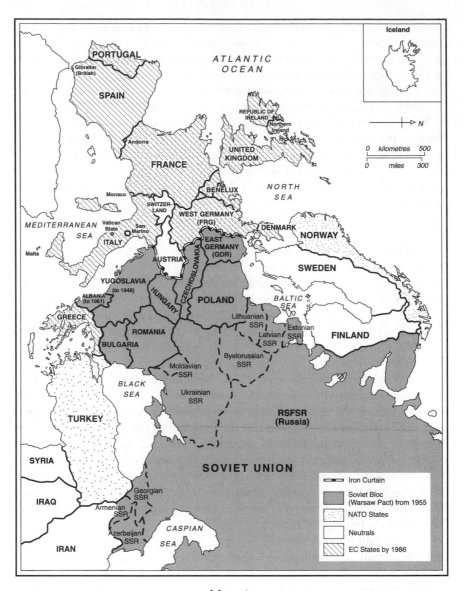

Map 28.
Europe Divided, 1949–89

XII

DIVISA ET INDIVISA

Europe Divided and Undivided, 1945–1991

THERE is a strong sense of futility about Europe in the second half of the twentieth century. The vast sacrifices of the Second World War did not generate security: the Continent was soon divided into rival political and military blocs whose energies were squandered for nearly fifty years. Immense resources were poured into unproductive tasks, especially in the East; there were few countries who could maintain a neutral stance; and the construction of European unity was repeatedly postponed.

The mood of futility was well caught in the post-war circle of Jean-Paul Sartre and the philosophers of existentialism. It faded soon enough in most Western countries, but surfaced again with the peace movement and the anti-nuclear protesters of later decades. In Eastern Europe it belied the optimism of official propaganda, and remained a dominant note in people's inner lives until the 'Refolution' (revolution by reform) of 1989–91.

Fortunately, for those who wished to heal the wounds, the division of Europe helped to stimulate the strong European movement which had been planted before the war, and which now grew up in the West. First as a moral campaign for reforming international relations, and later in the realm of economic cooperation, it fostered a new sense of community. In the Council of Europe (from 1949) and in the EEC and its associated bodies (from 1956), it founded a complex of institutions, which were designed to expand as more and more European countries were welcomed into the fold. Even so, the alternative prospect of an all-European communist camp was not effaced for many decades.

In the event, the West proved itself to be immeasurably more dynamic than the East. With the assistance of the USA, Western Europe rapidly emerged from the post-war ruins and set a course for unrivalled prosperity. Inspired by the example of West Germany's *Wirtschaftswunder*, the original members of the European Economic Community had little difficulty in publicizing the benefits of their cause. Membership doubled from six in 1956 to twelve in 1983, with many applications pending. Whilst the Kremlin coped ever more ineptly with its muscle-bound empire, the rapid process of decolonization in Asia and Africa liberated West Europe's imperial powers for a new future in an integrated Europe. Under the leadership of NATO, West Europe's defences held firm against a Soviet threat that grew ever less credible. By the late 1980s the European movement seemed to be moving towards maturity at the very time that Soviet communism was climbing onto its death-bed.

Despite the divisions, however, the concept of Europe was no less alive in the East than in the West. Soviet tyranny was very effective in promoting the European ideal by default. Citizens of the former Soviet bloc were mightily impressed by Western Europe's food mountains; but there is every reason to believe that their aspirations to rejoin 'Europe' had a spiritual as well as a material dimension. 'Europe has two lungs,' declared a Slavonic Pope; 'it will never breathe easily until it uses both of them.'[1]

Europe's wasted years fall neatly into three periods. They began in the immediate post-war era (1945–8), when Allied unity was lost. They continued through four decades of the Cold War (1948–89); and they drew to a close with the astonishing reign in Moscow of Mikhail Gorbachev (1985–91). Overall, they may be said to have begun on VE Day, 9 May 1945, and to have ended with the final disbandment of the Soviet Union in December 1991. By that time, almost all of Europe's peoples were free to determine their own destiny.

◁━━━▷

The End of the Grand Alliance, 1945–1948

The division of Europe was implicit in the state of affairs at war's end. As Stalin correctly predicted, the social and political systems of East and West were destined to follow the positions of the occupying armies. Yet the division of Europe did not crystallize immediately. At first the victorious Allies were preoccupied with the immediate problems of refugees, resettlement, and reparations; and they were obliged to co-operate in the joint administration of Germany and Austria. Stalin acted cautiously, following different policies in different capitals. The Americans, too, were very slow to reveal their intentions.

Unlike 1918, there were no urgent demands for a general Peace Conference. There was no German government with whom a new Treaty might be signed; and Stalin in particular had no wish to renegotiate the massive gains which he had already secured. In consequence, the only Peace Conference to be held was the one which met at Paris in July–October 1946 to settle the affairs of five lesser defeated states—Italy, Romania, Bulgaria, Hungary, and Finland. Proceedings were fixed by the Allied Council of Foreign Ministers, who virtually dictated the terms of the settlement. All the defeated states were obliged to cede territory. Italy lost the whole of her African empire, but not South Tyrol. All had to pay enormous indemnities, totalling $1,250 million, mainly to the USSR and to Yugoslavia. In the teeth of Soviet opposition, the Conference insisted on establishing the Danube as an international waterway, and Trieste as a free port under the United Nations.

Trieste, the sole European territory to be openly disputed after the Second World War, remained in a high state of tension for seven years. Zone A, including the port and city, was secured by British troops; Zone B, to the east, was held by the Yugoslavs. This partition was finally accepted by Italo-Yugoslav agreement in October 1954. (See Appendix III, p. 1313.)

Post-war Europe was faced with tidal waves of refugees. Both the Nazis and the Soviets had resorted to mass deportations and slave labour. Many survivors were now set free. There were 9 million such displaced persons (DPs) in Germany alone. They lived in primitive, overcrowded camps, often in barracks recently vacated by prisoners of war. The largest numbers came from countries recently occupied by the Red Army, to which, fearing retribution, they steadfastly refused to return. They were administered by UNRRA (the UN Refugee Relief Administration) and slowly dispersed, first as European Voluntary Workers to various industrial centres in Western Europe and later by emigration schemes to Canada, USA, Australia, and South America. The last emigrants did not leave until 1951–2.

Military personnel were also stranded in huge numbers. The Western Powers had difficulty making provision even for units that had fought on the Allied side. General Anders's Polish army, for example, which had fought its way into northern Italy, contained several hundred thousands of men, and dependants, whose homes had been seized by the USSR. In 1946 they had all to be brought to Britain, where they were added to the Polish Resettlement Corps (PKRP) for retraining and assimilation.[2] Ironically enough, they were joined in Britain by ex-members of the Waffen SS *Galizien*, who had also found their way to Italy and who, as citizens of pre-war Poland, were not handed over to the mercies of the Soviet authorities. Most ex-Wehrmacht personnel were not so lucky. German prisoners of war captured by the Soviets were transported to the Gulag, where they shared the fate of ex-Soviet prisoners of war from Germany. (The remnants were repatriated in 1956.)

The Western Allies were aware of communist barbarities towards people returning from abroad. But they generally held to a policy of forcible expulsion for all persons, both civilian and military, whose return was demanded by Stalin. The first transports of ex-slave labourers captured by the British Army in Normandy sailed in secret from Liverpool to Murmansk in October 1944. Serious resistance was provoked in Austria in the Spring of 1945 when many Soviet citizens chose mass suicide before repatriation. Hundreds of thousands, notably the Cossack Brigade and large numbers of Croats, were handed over to almost certain death before the practice was stopped.[3] [**KEELHAUL**] Not that the Anglo-Americans could necessarily boast about the treatment of POWs in their own charge. One study of American policy in 1945–6 has claimed that German prisoners held in western Europe were administratively reclassified in order to bypass the Geneva Convention, and that a significant proportion may have died from neglect.[4]

The population exchanges envisaged at Potsdam took effect from the autumn of 1945. At least 9 million German expellees were driven from their homes in Czechoslovakia and Poland. Defenceless refugees became the prey of local revenge. The Communist security services used former Nazi camps as collection centres. Maltreatment was routine. The death toll was counted in tens of thousands. Miserably overcrowded transports were sent straight through to the British and American zones of Germany. The resultant *Vertriebene verbände* or provincial 'associations of expellees' were to become a potent anti-communist force in post-war politics. Their successful absorption was the first of West Germany's many miracles.[5]

Compensatory population movements took place further East. The empty city of Königsberg, renamed Kaliningrad, was repopulated by the Soviet military as an enclave of the Russian Soviet Federative Socialist Republic. Some 2–3 million Poles were allowed to migrate westwards from provinces annexed by the USSR. The empty city of Breslau, for example, renamed Wrocław, was largely taken over by Poles driven out of the city of Lwów, who arrived complete with their university, their mayor and corporation, and their national museum. Both in Poland and in Czechoslovakia, the former German territories provided a ready source of housing and employment for the poorest internal migrants.

Given the fiasco after the First World War, the Western Powers decided not to press Germany for punitive reparations. The Soviets, in contrast, set out to extract the maximum. The official Soviet demand stood at $20 billion. But they did not wait for inter-Allied negotiations to fail: from the earliest days of occupation, Soviet reparation squads set about dismantling and removing industrial plant, railway lines, power stations, livestock, and rolling stock. The Soviet looters, private and collective, drew no distinction between Germany and lands designated for administration by Poland or Czechoslovakia.

Across Europe, people wanted to settle accounts with wartime collaborators. In some cases, it was undertaken by legal process. Pierre Laval, Vidkun Quisling, William Joyce (Lord Haw-Haw), and Father Tiso were among those sentenced and executed. The aged Marshal Pétain, though sentenced to death, lived out his remaining years on the Île d'Yeu. Proceedings were most thorough in the Netherlands, where some 200,000 suspected collaborators were detained, and in Belgium, where, of 634,000 detained, 57,000 were sentenced. This compares with 9,000 trials and 35 death sentences in Austria. Often enough, though, the populace took matters into their own hands. In Italy, thousands of fascists were simply lynched or shot by partisans. In France, in a wild wave of retribution, at leaast 10,000 were killed, often on the flimsiest of accusations. In West Germany, once the Nuremberg trials of major war criminals were over (see pp. 1048–54), denazification proceeded slowly; criminal trials began in the late 1950s. Sporadic trials of SS officers, employers of slave labour, and concentration camp personnel continued through the 1960s. But most of the big fish had swum off: 9 million ex-Nazis were too many to deal with.

In Eastern Europe, the Communists used the purge of collaborators as a pretext for eliminating their own opponents. A few prominent Nazis and collabora-tors were made an example of: Hoess, the Commandant of Auschwitz, was tried and hanged in Poland in 1946. On the other hand, many of the rank and file were able to survive if they agreed to change sides. Bolesław Piasecki, head of the Polish fascist Falanga, for example, emerged from a Soviet jail in 1945 as head of the communist-sponsored pseudo-Catholic organization PAX. Meanwhile the vast majority of East European politicals who were consigned in droves to the Soviet Gulag or to other communist prisons under the label of 'fascists' or 'collaborators' were nothing of the sort. It was not uncommon for Nazi war criminals to share their cells with the flower of the anti-Nazi resistance.[6] Nazi concentration camps, such as Buchenwald, were reopened by the KGB in order to repress a new gener-ation of inmates.

Somehow, amidst the chaos, the ex-Reich had to be administered. Austria was immediately hived off. Germany, disarmed, diminished, and demilitarized, was divided into five parts—four occupation zones, plus Berlin, which was also split into four sectors (see Map 27, p. 1049). Since it was agreed at Potsdam that there should be no central German government, a clutch of ministries required to restart eco-nomic life had to be organized under the direct supervision of the Inter-Allied Control Commission (ICC). All aspects of local administration were subordinated to committees chaired by British, American, French, or Soviet officers. For the first two winters priority had to be given to mere survival. Germany's cities had been reduced to rubble; roads, railways, and bridges had to be rebuilt. Fifty million people, one-fifth of them refugees, had somehow to be fed and housed.

German politics, however, did revive, in the first instance in the Soviet zone. A communist initiative group headed by Walter Ulbricht (1893–1973) arrived from Moscow almost before the fighting had stopped. When local elections in December 1945 suggested that the socialists of the Soviet zone held an advantage, the communists openly assaulted them, arresting their leaders and withholding ration cards. The results of the only free election in the Soviet zone were ignored; a forced merger was pushed through between communists and socialists. Already in April 1946 the resultant Socialist Unity Party (SED) was under Ulbricht poised for the creation of a one-party state. In these circumstances, the three nascent all-German parties, which began to operate in 1945 under Allied proposals for Germany's 'democratic transformation'—the SPD of Dr Kurt Schumacher, the Christian Democratic Union (CDU) of Dr Konrad Adenauer, and the Free Democratic Union—were only able to function freely in the three Western zones.

Communist machinations were particularly blatant in Poland. Ever since 1943 the Western powers had closed their eyes to the crucifixion of their Polish ally [KATYŃ]; and at Yalta they had handed Poland to Stalin on a plate. The results were disastrous. In the wake of the Moscow Trial of June 1945 (see p. 1050–1), members of the wartime Resistance were arrested *en masse*; non-communist par-ties were mercilessly harassed; a vicious civil war was fought with the remnants of the underground; and the 'free, unfettered elections' promised at Yalta were repeatedly postponed. The country was run by an NKVD officer, Bolesław Bierut

(1892–1956), who was masquerading as a 'non-party' leader. The one representative of the London Poles to participate was powerless. The results of a dubious referendum held in June 1946 were drowned amidst news of a dastardly pogrom perpetrated with official connivance at Kielce. The elections, when finally held in January 1947, were so manifestly fraudulent that the US Ambassador in Warsaw promptly resigned in protest.[7]

Yet Stalin's overall intentions were far from clear at this stage. If the conduct of the communists was bad in Poland and Yugoslavia—where Tito had crushed his opponents in a bloodbath of revenge—it was not so bad in Czechoslovakia, the West's favourite son. Beneš and his Foreign Minister, Jan Masaryk (1886–1948), were still at the head of affairs. The Czech communists had a popular following; and they seemed to be responsible partners in the ruling coalition. Elsewhere in Eastern Europe the political situation was confused. Republican constitutions were adopted in Hungary, Bulgaria, and Albania in 1946, and in Romania in 1947. But the disappearance of the last Balkan monarchies, who all had German connections, did not cause much grief. A general increase in communist influence, as in France and Italy, was taken as a natural reaction against the fascist era. There was no sign of a fixed Soviet blueprint.

Stalin's caution is easily explained. The Soviet Union was still in surprisingly good odour with Western opinion, especially in the USA. It had suffered appalling devastation, and desperately needed an interval of respite. The Soviet Union had annexed 272,500 square miles of foreign territory, with an extra population of 25 millions, and needed time to purge and prepare them for the Soviet way of life. Most importantly, the Soviet Union did not yet possess the atomic bomb. On this score alone, any physical confrontation with the Americans would be premature. The most sensible approach was to wait and see whether the Americans would carry out their promise to withdraw their troops from Europe or not.

American counsels were long divided. There was a strong lobby in Congress which held that the Soviet threat was much exaggerated and that Europeans should be left to sort out Europe's problems. The contrary view, held by President Truman, agreed with the closing words of Churchill's Fulton speech: 'our Russian friends . . . admire nothing so much as strength.' For two years, therefore, US policy hung in the balance. The advocates of engagement had to fight every inch of the way. Their determination was gradually strengthened by the insulting nature of Soviet propaganda, by the subversive activities of Soviet sympathizers, by the obstructiveness of Soviet administrators in Germany, by the Soviets' refusal to accept America's economic proposals, and by British advice. They finally won the day after the strategic decision forced on President Truman by the crisis in Greece in the spring of 1947. In the background, American concern was heightened by news of communist advances in China.

The communist parties of Western Europe were greatly strengthened by the victory over fascism. They were particularly active in France, Belgium, and Italy, where their role in the Resistance was widely admired and where one-quarter of the electorate supported them. After the fiasco of a failed communist coup in Brussels in November 1944, their strategy was to participate in parliamentary and governmental coalitions. But then in 1947 a wave of orchestrated strikes in Italy, and in the French mines, destroyed the reigning harmony. Stalin's Western cohorts were seen to be damaging the progress of democracy and economic recovery. Relations between Western and Soviet administrators in Germany went from moderate to bad, and from bad to worse. There was no common language; Berlin remained split into mutually hostile sectors. In mid-1946 the Western Powers sought to realize the united German economic space as envisaged at Potsdam. The Soviets refused to participate. Thereon the three Western zones went their own way, assisted by a German Economic Council formed under Anglo-American auspices in June 1947.

Until 1947, both Persia and Greece had been managed by the British. But suddenly, pressured by other major crises in India, Egypt, and Palestine, the bankrupt British decided that they could no longer cope. In Persia, the parliament had decided to reject an arrangement which would have seen Soviet forces retire from the northern region in return for huge deliveries of oil. In face of possible Soviet retaliation, American advisers were brought to Teheran. A new source of Soviet–American confrontation was in the making. In Greece, the civil war was reopened in May 1946. Communist rebels pressed southwards from bases in Albania, Yugoslavia, and Bulgaria. Britain's costs for defending the royal government in Athens soared; London appealed to Washington for financial aid. Instead of preparing its withdrawal from Europe, the USA was being asked to shoulder the burden of resistance against communist expansion. A decisive shift in global power was about to occur.

President Truman's response was unequivocal. In applying to Congress for $400 million economic aid for Greece and Turkey, he spelled out the principles of a firm new policy. 'It must be the policy of the United States', he declared, 'to help free peoples who are resisting subjugation by armed minorities or outside pressure.' This Truman Doctrine of 12 March 1947 marked America's voluntary acceptance of the leadership of the free world. It put an end to prolonged indecision, and ensured that American troops would remain in Europe for the duration. Truman's stance towards communism came to be known as 'containment'—a fresh version of the pre-war *cordon sanitaire*. It coincided closely with an analysis entitled 'The Sources of Soviet Conduct', anonymously published in July 1947 by the experienced diplomat George Kennan. It called for 'adroit and vigilant application of counterforce . . . corresponding to the shifts and manœuvres of Soviet policy'. It was purely defensive, and far from the Third World War which some hotheads had advocated.[8]

At this juncture the USA produced a generous economic scheme to complement its policy of increased political involvement in Europe. On 5 June 1947, at a Harvard Commencement speech, Truman's Secretary of State, General George Marshall, unveiled plans for a European Recovery Program. 'It is logical', he declared, 'that the United States should do whatever it is able to do to assist in the return of normal economic health in the world, without which there can be no political stability and no assured peace.' In contrast to the 1920s, the USA was offering to finance Europe's recovery in the interests of the common good. The Marshall Plan ran for four years, from 1948 to the end of 1951. It dispensed a total of $12,500 million to 16 participating members. To manage the funds, it required the establishment of the Organization for Economic Co-operation and Development (OECD), which insisted that recipients increase production, expand trade, and make 'counterpart contributions' of their own. Although one-quarter of Marshall Aid was earmarked for Britain and one-fifth for France, it was made available to allies, neutrals, and ex-enemies alike. It has no peer in the history of enlightened self-interest.

The USSR condemned Marshall Aid as a capitalist ruse. Moscow refused to participate, and ordered the countries which it controlled to do likewise. As a result, the hardening political divide was reinforced by a marked economic divide. The 16 countries of Western Europe who benefited from Marshall Aid were able to forge ahead; the USSR and its dependants were cast into self-imposed isolation.

The European movement could trace its roots right back to the seventeenth century (see Introduction, p. 10; Chapter XI, pp. 949–51). But the ambitions of the national states had ruined every practical enterprise in that direction. Europeans had to drink the bitter dregs of defeat and humiliation before the dreams of the early idealists could be realized. They had to lose their empires, and their hopes of empire, before governments would give priority to living with their neighbours.

The moral dimensions of the post-war European movement are not always remembered. One strand was centred on the survivors of the anti-Nazi resistance movement in Germany, for whom international reconciliation assumed prime importance. For them, the Declaration of Guilt formulated by Pastor Martin Niemöller, at the Stuttgart Conference of the German Evangelical Church in October 1945, was an act of great moment. Another strand was centred in France on a number of radical Catholic organizations inspired by the doyen of pacifist protest, Marc Sangnier (1873–1950), whose Gratry Society looked back in direct line to the Abbé Lamennais. Sangnier had been fighting for 30 years for 'un nouvel état d'âme international', 'a new international state of mind'. He was the guru of Robert Schuman, and exerted a strong influence on policy in the French zone of occupation in Germany. A European Union of Federalists held a founding conference for some 50 activist groups at Montreux in August 1947. Other, specifically Anglo-Saxon strands were to be found in the pre-war Oxford Group of Lionel Curtis, founder of the Royal Institute of International Affairs, and in the actively anti-communist Movement for Moral Rearmament.

In 1945, however, the immediate problem lay with the intentions of the British and American Governments. London and Washington were politically supreme in Western Europe. They could easily have taken the lead in the formation of new European institutions, or indeed in opposing them. They did neither. In the field of international co-operation they looked principally to the United Nations;

politically, they were preoccupied by the growing confrontation with Stalin. They had no special vision for Europe.

The lack of intent, however, was not immediately evident. Churchill's personal involvement in the early post-war years boded well for official British support. Only later did it become apparent that the ruling British Labour Party did not share his views. The most that it did was to encourage the discussions which was to lead to the Council of Europe (see below). A Labour Party pamphlet entitled *European Unity* (1950) stressed that 'no iota of British sovereignty' was negotiable. The Americans, too, exuded goodwill. The OECD, which acted as the conduit for Marshall Aid, seemed to be a first step in the direction of European integration. Only in 1949–50, when Marshall Aid was running down, did the limits of American as well as of British interest become clear.

The first person of stature to identify the direction in which Europe was moving was Winston Churchill. Rejected by the British electorate in July 1945, Europe's most admired war leader had leisure to reflect. 'What is Europe?' he wrote. 'A rubble heap, a charnel house, a breeding-ground for pestilence and hate.' In 1946, in two landmark speeches that were to prove prophetic, he expressed views that were not very popular at the time. On 5 March, at Westminster College in Fulton (Missouri), with President Truman at his side, he spoke of 'the Iron Curtain':

From Stettin on the Baltic to Trieste on the Adriatic, an iron curtain has descended across the continent. Behind that line, lie all the capitals of the ancient states of central and eastern Europe—Warsaw, Berlin, Prague, Vienna, Budapest, Belgrade, Bucharest, and Sofia. . . . This is certainly not the liberated Europe which we fought to build up.[9]

Churchill rejected the likelihood of an early Soviet attack on the West, but he believed that Moscow was intent on 'indefinite expansion'. He called for 'timely action' of the sort that had been lacking ten years earlier against Nazi Germany. US opinion was 'almost universally hostile'.[10] In London, *The Times* bristled with disapproval, announcing that 'Western Democracy and Communism have much to learn from each other'.[11]

On 19 September, in Zurich, Churchill appealed for 'a kind of United States of Europe'. Time, he said, might be short; the spread of atomic weapons might soon reinforce existing divisions. The first step had to be a partnership between France and Germany. 'If we are to form a United States of Europe . . .', he declared, 'we must begin now.'[12] The future of the 'European family' depended on 'the resolve of millions to do right instead of wrong'. So the appeal was not economic or political, but moral. *The Times* sniffed at this 'outrageous proposition'. 'Even in Western Europe,' it commented, 'there is little to suggest that the unity so much spoken of . . . is on the way.' The founder of the pre-war European movement, Count Coudenhove-Kalergi, was one of the few to congratulate Churchill. 'Now that *you* have raised the European question,' he wrote, 'the governments can no longer ignore it.'[13]

In this period, Churchill's strategic vision postulated a 'fraternal association' of three interlocking circles made up of the British Commonwealth, the 'European Union', and the United States. Britain was to act as 'the vital link between them all'. He correctly identified the competing interests which were to cause tremendous strains in the ensuing decades by pulling British foreign policy in three different directions at once.

Churchill's views made him the natural choice for chairing the Congress of Europe which was privately organized in The Hague on 7–10 May 1948. Some 800 eminent invitees were asked to ponder the problems of European disunity. A strong German delegation attended, with Konrad Adenauer at their head. The cultural commission was chaired by the exiled Spanish minister and writer Salvador de Madariaga. In their debates, they recognized the principle of 'supranationality': the need for states to surrender part of their sovereignty in the interests of common institutions. Churchill's statement enshrined the loftiest ideals:

We must proclaim the mission and the design of a United Europe whose moral conception will win the respect and gratitude of mankind, and whose physical strength will be such that none will dare molest her tranquil sway . . . I hope to see a Europe where men and women of every country will think of being European as of belonging to their native land, and wherever they go in this wide domain will truly feel 'Here I am at home'.

De Madariaga waxed equally eloquent:

This Europe must be born. And she will, when Spaniards say 'our Chartres', Englishmen 'our Cracow', Italians 'our Copenhagen', and Germans 'our Bruges' . . . Then Europe will live. For then it will be that the Spirit which leads Europe will have uttered the creative words: FIAT EUROPA.[14]

The Congress was undoubtedly carried away by the force of its own enthusiasms. But the final communiqué called for practical steps such as the creation of a European Assembly and a European Court of Human Rights; and a liaison committee was formed to keep the Congress aims alive. This latter body was destined to adopt the name of 'European Movement', of which it was indeed the progenitor. Apart from Churchill, its honorary presidents were Schuman (France), De Gasperi (Italy), and Spaak (Belgium). They had now to see whether any of the ruling governments might adopt their ideas. Given the truculence of the USSR, it was obvious that they could only hope for support from the governments of the West (see below).

By the end of 1947, therefore, Churchill's Iron Curtain was becoming a reality. Three events removed all lingering doubts: the creation of Cominform; the February coup in Prague; and the Berlin Blockade.

Meeting in the Polish mountain resort of Szklarska Poręba in October 1947, communist delegates from the USSR, Eastern Europe, France, and Italy founded the Communist Information Bureau. Its purpose was to co-ordinate the strategies of fraternal parties. To the outside world, it looked suspiciously like a revival of Comintern, an instrument of subversion, the harbinger of a new ideological offensive.

The Communist coup in Prague took place on 25 February 1948. The Czech communists had been sharing power with the socialists for two years; but their fears of a rising socialist vote meant that their own influence might soon decline. Their involvement in a genuine democratic system equally meant that they could not gain supremacy by manipulation, as in neighbouring Poland; so they resorted to force. Armed workers and militiamen appeared on the streets. Red Army garrisons were rumoured to be preparing for action. Non-communist politicians were arrested, and their parties dissolved. Jan Masaryk was thrown to his death from his ministry window. Klement Gottwald, the communist boss, said 'it was like cutting butter with a sharp knife'. President Beneš, pliant as ever, did not resist. For the second time in ten years, Eastern Europe's most promising democracy had been subverted without a shot fired in its defence. Western opinion took fright. Fearing a Soviet attack, five West European countries formed a 50-year alliance providing for economic and military co-operation. The Brussels Treaty of 17 March 1948, signed by Britain, France, and the Benelux group, was the precursor of the new security alignments now congealing.

The final blow fell in Germany. The German Economic Council was preparing its new plan. The key proposals envisaged a radical currency reform, involving the exchange of ten old Reichsmarks for one new Deutschmark, and a new central bank—the Bank Deutscher Länder (the ancestor of the Bundesbank). The Soviet commissioner, Marshal Sokolovsky, would have none of it. On 20 March 1948 he and his aides marched out of the Allied Control Commission, never to return. The Grand Alliance was finished.

Stalin had reached the point where restraint was no longer paying dividends. Soviet diplomacy had failed both to persuade the Americans to leave Europe and to prevent the growing integration of Germany's Western zones. With active American assistance, Western Europe could only grow in strength. So the time had come for the Russian bear to growl. The Soviet Army could not risk a direct assault; but it could demonstrate its hold on the vulnerable, and highly symbolic, city of Berlin. On 1 April 1948 Soviet patrols began interfering with traffic in the corridor between Berlin and the Western zones, but to no effect. On 18 June the D-Mark and the BDL Bank were introduced. This, from the communist viewpoint, was an act of aggression; on the 24th Soviet troops sealed off Berlin completely, to save their zone from invasion by the Deutschmark. The German capital was under blockade, and would remain so for 15 months. The Cold War had begun.

Western Europe, 1945–1985

Post-war Western Europe is easily defined: it consisted of the countries which were not occupied by the Soviet Army, and which did not fall under communist control. These countries belonged, however, to two distinct groups. One was made up of neutrals, who stayed outside the various military and economic associations of the era; the other, larger group was made up of those who became members either of the North Atlantic Treaty Organization (NATO) or of the European Economic Community (EEC), or both (see Appendix III, p. 1335).

Western Europe was also distinguished by the fact that in 1945 it was still the home base of the world's colonial empires. Indeed, with the exception of the USA and the Soviet Union, whose imperialisms did not conform to the traditional type, there were no imperial powers that were not West European. Germany had been stripped of its overseas colonies in 1919. Italy suffered the same fate in 1946. But the British, the Dutch, the French, the Belgian, and the Portuguese Empires were largely intact. The dissolution of these empires in the early post-war decades constituted a fundamental element in the changing European scene. Decolonization was a necessary precondition for the emergence of a new European Community of equal, democratic partners.

During and immediately after the Second World War, many European imperialists had hoped that they would be able to keep, or to reconstitute, their empires. 'I have not become His Majesty's First Minister', said Churchill, 'in order to preside over the liquidation of the British Empire.' But he did.

There were many reasons why, by 1945, the maintenance of Europe's empires had become virtually impossible. First and foremost, the élites of the colonial peoples, many of them educated in Europe, had learned the nationalism and democracy of their masters and were now vociferously demanding independence. The links between the colonies and the home countries had weakened during the war. There were no longer the resources available to restore them by force; nor was there the will to perpetuate the rule of one race over another. The USA, on whom Western Europe now depended, was resolutely opposed to old-style colonialism; and so was the United Nations. Imperialism was no longer either viable or respectable. The main question was whether the imperialists would bend to the wind of change or try to stand against it. Nothing better reveals the gulf between Eastern and Western Europe at this stage. At the very time that the Soviet Union was extending and consolidating its empire over the peoples of Eastern Europe, the imperial governments of Western Europe were desperately seeking means to dismantle theirs. For some reason, these twin aspects of European imperialism are rarely discussed under the same heading.

The process of decolonization was immensely complex, and many of the complications derived from conditions beyond Europe. But each empire possessed its own ethos; each possessed a variety of territories ranging from self-governing dominions to colonies and trusteeships; and each wielded very different degrees of military force. Except for Britain and Portugal, all the imperial powers had been defeated and occupied during the war, and started from a position of weakness.

The British Empire, which occupied an area roughly 125 times larger than Great Britain, was already in an advanced state of transformation. All of the 'white dominions' had been fully independent since 1931; and many other crown possessions were being prepared for self-rule or native administration. Of 250,000 employees of the British Colonial Office in 1945, only 66,000 were from Britain. The test case was India, a subcontinent of 400 million people where Gandhi's campaign of non-violent resistance had attracted world-wide attention. The post-war British Labour Government decided to grant India unconditional independence. On 15 August 1947 the last Viceroy took the salute in Delhi as the Raj saw the British flag lowered for the last time. India, Pakistan, Burma, and Ceylon all arose as independent states. There was an orgy of intercommunal massacres between Muslims and Hindus, but nothing aimed directly at the British.

Several of the smaller dependencies caused much greater trouble. In May 1948 Britain returned the mandate of Palestine to the UN after years of violence both from Zionist terrorists and from Arab rebels. In Malaya, the communist insurgency lasted from 1948 to 1957; in Cyprus, the war against Eoka from 1950 to 1960; in Kenya, the Mau-Mau campaign from 1952 to 1957; in Egypt, the struggle culminating in the Suez Crisis from 1952 to 1956; in Southern Rhodesia (Zimbabwe), the emergency over white UDI from 1959 to 1980. Elsewhere in Africa, a procession of peaceful acts of independence started with that of Ghana in 1956 and Nigeria in 1960. At the end of the process, almost all of Britain's former colonies had joined the British Commonwealth, a voluntary association originally founded for the self-governing dominions. South Africa left in 1961, Pakistan in 1973. The residual administrative functions of the Commonwealth Office had been transferred in stages to the Foreign Office (FCO) by 1968. Preferential Commonwealth tariffs were terminated in 1973. The dissolution of the world's largest empire was essentially complete within a quarter of a century.

The Dutch Empire, 55 times larger than the Netherlands, was closed down at one blow. The Dutch East Indies were never effectively resecured by the Dutch after the Japanese occupation of 1941–5. The Republic of Indonesia was confirmed in 1950.

The French Empire, 19 times larger than France, expired in agony. Many inhabitants of the colonies possessed full French citizenship; and several north African departments, with large French populations, formed an integral part of metropolitan France. Humiliated during the war, French governments felt obliged to assert their authority, and wielded enough military power to make their ultimate defeat very costly. Tunisia and Morocco were safely disentangled by 1951, as were the Levantine mandates in Syria and Lebanon. But in Indo-China an eight-year war was fought against the Viet-Cong, until the disaster of Dien Bien Phu in May 1954 forced Paris to hand over to an incautious Washington. In Algeria, another vicious eight-year war against the FLN, which destroyed the Fourth Republic on the way, ended with General de Gaulle's dramatic concession of Algerian independence in May 1962. Preoccupied by the Algerian war, France had already set its other African colonies free.

The Belgian Empire, 78 times the size of Belgium, collapsed in 1960, when the Congo sought to follow the example of its ex-French neighbours. The move was quite unprepared. The secession of Katanga caused a civil war which claimed the lives of thousands, including those of the Soviet sponsee, Patrice Lumumba, and the UN Secretary-General Dag Hammarskjöld.

The Portuguese Empire survived longest. Angola, which itself was 23 times larger than Portugal, broke away in 1975, together with Mozambique and Goa.

All the ex-colonies in Europe but one were set free. The Dodecanese were returned to Greece by Italy in 1945. Malta was given independence from the British in 1964. Only a clutch of small colonial dependencies clung on, including Gibraltar, which faced threats of a Spanish takeover, the Falkland Islands (British), the source of the Anglo-Argentine war of 1983, and the Marquesas Islands (French), the site of France's nuclear testing. Hong Kong (British) was due to revert to China in 1997, Macao (Portuguese) in 1999.

The effects of decolonization were almost as profound on the ex-imperialists as on the ex-colonies. The former imperial powers were reduced to the same standing as other sovereign states in Europe, thereby rendering eventual union less problematical. They lost many traditional economic benefits, especially cheap raw materials and captive colonial markets. Yet they also shed the burden of defending and administering their distant possessions. They each maintained strong cultural and personal links with the Asian and African peoples, who could now send floods of voluntary immigrants to join the 'old country's' labour force. In the post-imperial decades, far more people from the Caribbean or the Indian subcontinent came to Britain, and Muslims to France, than ever came previously. Imperial race problems were imported with them.

The decolonization of the West was watched in Eastern Europe with a mixture of surprise and envy. Official propaganda found difficulty in celebrating the national liberation movements of distant continents without giving ideas to their own subjects. Ordinary citizens wondered why so much publicity was given to the Arabs, the Vietnamese, and the Congolese. The intelligent ones wondered why decolonization should not also apply to them. For this, they had to await the era of Mikhail Gorbachev (see below).

Once the Truman doctrine had been enunciated, it was necessary to create formal institutions for co-ordinating US involvement in Europe's defence and security. The Berlin blockade only emphasized the urgency. The foreign ministers of nine West European countries joined the US and Canada in a treaty founding NATO on 4 April 1949.

In a sense, NATO may be seen as a replacement for the former Grand Alliance; it was centred on the same Anglo-American partnership dating from 1941. In the first instance, it joined the Anglo-Americans to the signatories of the earlier Brussels Treaty, together with Italy, Portugal, Denmark, Iceland, and Norway. It was later expanded to include Greece and Turkey (1952), West Germany (1955), and Spain (1982). It was run by a political committee, the North Atlantic Council, based in Brussels, with its own Secretary-General. Its regional military commands, with air, land, and sea forces, covered the Atlantic routes between North America and Europe, and the full length of the Iron Curtain from the North Cape to the Black Sea. It was the prime instrument for the 'containment' of the USSR, which was now perceived as the principal threat to European peace. Its mission lasted for 40 years, and was carried out with indisputable success.

NATO's first task was to break the Berlin blockade—which it did, quite literally, with flying colours. Relying on superior air power, relays of British and American transport planes undertook to supply a city of 2 million souls with all the fuel, food, and raw materials they needed. The airlift required 277,264 flights; at its height, one fully laden aircraft was touching down at Tempelhof Airport every minute. Every day 8,000 tons of supplies dropped out of the sky. By the end, dozens of east-facing air-strips had been constructed across Western Germany, where the popularity of the Western Powers soared. The Soviets could only watch in silent fury, until they lifted the blockade on 12 May 1949.

By that time, preparations for the creation of a separate West German Republic were well advanced. The previous July, in Frankfurt, the Allied commanders had presented recommendations to the premiers of the regional Länder, calling for the creation of a constituent council and the drafting of a federal constitution. Reluctant German leaders had been tempted to hold out for a united Germany; but the Berlin blockade removed their hesitations. The *Grundgesetz* or Basic Law was passed in the week that the blockade ended; elections were held in August. Konrad Adenauer took his place as the first federal Chancellor with a one-vote majority. The Bundesrepublik, with its capital at Bonn, took its place as Western Europe's most populous sovereign state.

It was perhaps inevitable that the Soviets would respond in kind. The German Democratic Republic (DDR) provided a formal framework for the existing dictatorship of the SED, and was instituted in October 1949, with its capital in (East) Berlin. West Berlin, still occupied by the Western Allies, remained an enclave of disputed status, a loophole through which thousands of refugees continued to seek freedom in the West. The memory of a united Germany receded ever more rapidly into the past.

Political life in Western Europe was restarted on the basis of a universal commitment to liberal democracy and a widespread belief in the absolute sovereignty of the nation-state. Monarchies survived in Scandinavia, the Low Countries, and in Britain, but only as national totems. There was much interest in Anglo-American democracy and, in the early post-war years, great admiration for the Soviet Union. Revulsion against fascism inhibited the nationalist wing of opinion, boosted parties seeking social reform, and made communism respectable. Proportional representation, and government by multi-party coalitions, were most common. Spain and Portugal had not been involved in the war, and were the only countries where pre-war fascism persisted. Three general trends can be observed: the rise of Christian Democracy, the tribulations of socialism, and the decline of communism.

Christian Democracy, which before the war had often possessed confessional and clerical overtones, now made a fresh start free of ecclesiastical patronage, often in the hands of former left-centre Catholics. It had a 'left wing' connected with Catholic trade unions, and a 'right wing' that was not; party brokers managed the middle ground. In Italy, the Democrazia Cristiana (DC), headed at first by De Gasperi, was deeply riven by factions, but gradually edged its way to forming a national establishment. In France, the Mouvement Républicain Populaire (MRP) was created in 1944 under Georges Bidault and the Schuman brothers, but suffered from rivalry with the main-line Gaullist Rassemblement du Peuple Français (RPF). In West Germany, the CDU of Dr Adenauer slowly emerged as the major political force. Adenauer was an old-time conservative, fond of the motto 'No Experiments'. But his partnership with Ludwig Erhard, a proponent of the social-market economy, was a winning combination. Exceptionally, the Dutch 'Catholic People's Party' remained a confessional grouping. Exceptionally, Great Britain possessed no Christian Democratic tradition at all.

European socialism was especially prone to fragmentation, and frequently suffered from communist competition. Post-war social democracy shed its pre-war emphasis on the class struggle, pressing instead for human rights and social justice within the capitalist system. The Italian Socialists of Pietro Nenni manœuvred in the middle ground between the DC and the powerful communists. In France, the PSF of Guy Mollet moved away from its pre-war dogmatism, but did not enjoy much success until the era of François Mitterrand in the 1970s and 1980s. In West Germany too the SPD, whose Godesberg Programme of 1959 broke with its proletarian traditions, remained in opposition until the late 1960s. Once again the British Labour Party, a 'broad church' of very variegated tendencies, was something of an odd man out.

West European communist parties, initially prominent, declined rapidly after 1948. They normally took instructions and financial support from Moscow. They had a strong intellectual wing which ill matched the proletarian base, and which gradually disintegrated as the enormity of Stalin's crimes was revealed. They only remained powerful in Italy and France, where they regularly polled 20–25 per cent, forming a solid bloc which rallied all other parties against them. In Italy, they played an effective role in local government, administering bourgeois cities like Bologna with success. In France, they eventually achieved a brief moment of 'cohabitation' with the socialists in 1980–1, before falling away for good.

Post-war French politics were marked by the fundamental divide between the Fourth Republic (1946–58), which emerged from the Liberation, and the subsequent Fifth Republic. They were strongly influenced by the towering figure of Charles de Gaulle, who returned in triumph as Premier in 1944–6, retired in disgust for twelve years, reigned as President 1958–69, and left an enduring legacy after his death. De Gaulle, though a democrat, was an advocate of a strong executive, and a jealous guardian of French sovereignty—anti-British, anti-American, and, initially, both anti-German and anti-EEC. The Fourth Republic was blighted by *immobilisme*, 'political paralysis', caused by the attacks of communists and extreme right—the Poujadistes—and by a succession of fleeting, unstable coalition governments. On average, it saw a new prime minister every six months. It was temporarily rescued after 1947 by the success of the Gaullist RPF, which acted as a patriotic force for unity, but was destroyed by the effects of Indo-China, the Suez Crisis, and the Algerian War. The Fifth Republic came into being in 1958, when de Gaulle was recalled from Colombey-les-Deux-Églises to quell the revolt of army officers in Algeria, which had all the makings of a military coup that could have spread to Paris. It introduced a powerful presidency, which was independent of the National Assembly and controlled the formation of governments. There was a major crisis in the summer of 1968, with sensational street-fighting between police and demonstrators in Paris; but it passed. Under de Gaulle's successors, Georges Pompidou, 1969–74, Valéry Giscard d'Estaing, 1974–81, and the socialist François Mitterrand from 1981, it found both stability and rising prosperity. The failures of the Fourth Republic turned many French politicians into committed European federalists. The assertiveness of the Fifth Republic led to great friction with the European Commission (see below) and, in 1966, to France's withdrawal from NATO's integrated military command.

In 1962–3, however, General de Gaulle took a decision of lasting importance. He decided not only to make Franco-German reconciliation the corner-stone of French policy but also to give it institutional substance. Touring West Germany, he congratulated German youth for being 'the children of a great people', contrasted 'Germany's great crimes and great miseries', and praised Germany's 'treasures of courage, discipline and organization'. He restored German self-respect. By the Élysée Treaty of January 1963, signed with Chancellor Adenauer, he established a 'special relationship' which no other European nations possess. Henceforth, a comprehensive programme of Franco-German co-operation in foreign affairs, defence, education, and youth, cemented by regular meetings of heads of state, provided the only consistent source of leadership in Western Europe.[15] [**DOUAUMONT**]

Post-war Italian politics have long displayed the same shortcomings as France's Fourth Republic, without ever producing a de Gaulle to mount a rescue. After the abolition of the monarchy in 1946, continuity was built on a strong consensus against a return to fascism, on the entrenchment of the Christian Democrats, who shared in all post-war governments, and on the vitality of municipal and regional politics. The consistency of state policy contrasted remarkably with the instability of cabinets. The polarization between the anti-Catholic and anticlerical left, dominated by Communists, and the conservative right has generated considerable violence. The terrorism of the Red Brigades culminated in the murder of a Prime Minister in 1978, and in the counter-terror which killed many people in the Bologna bombing of 1980. There were important divergences between the prosperous north, especially Turin and Milan, and the backward, Mafia-ridden south, which seemed impervious to reform. The Italian economy was slow to recover from the war, but made rapid strides within the EEC. Economic success offset political weakness. Italy was an active member of NATO, providing the bulwark of the Southern Front in the Mediterranean and the base of the American Sixth Fleet in Naples. Domestic political weakness has strengthened Italian adherence to European federalism.

After 1949 West German politics were, frankly, unexciting—which was perhaps a sign of their efficacy. Seventeen years of the CDU's supremacy under Adenauer and Erhard gave way in 1966 to three years of coalition government, to a long period of dominance by the SPD under Willy Brandt (1969–74) and Helmut Schmidt (1974–82), then again, after 1982, to the CDU, under the chancellorship of Dr Helmut Kohl. The Constitution created a Bundesbank independent of the federal government, whilst reserving wide powers to the regional governments of the Länder (some of which pre-dated the Bundesrepublik). The central authorities in Bonn enjoyed the freedom to concentrate on their internal co-ordinating role and on foreign affairs. In the federal parliament the proportional representation of the Weimar system was amended to minimize the disruptive influence of fringe parties. Trade unions, remodelled on British advice, turned out to be more effective than in Britain itself. Though Germany was to rearm after joining NATO, defence policy remained very dependent on American leadership. The *Wirtschaftswunder* or 'Economic Miracle' of the 1950s (see below) brought stability and prestige as well as prosperity, greatly assisting in the country's rehabilitation. Adenauer moved step by step, trading German partnership for Allied concessions. West Germany gained sovereign status in 1952, full membership of NATO in 1955, membership of the EEC in 1956, membership of UNO in 1973. After that, the political scene was enlivened or disturbed by the well-publicized activities of the anti-nuclear peace movement, of the environmental 'Greens', and, for a time, of the Baader–Meinhof terrorist gang. Decades of confrontation with East Germany were modified after 1970 by the Ostpolitik (see below), and crowned with success in 1990 through reunification. For years, West Germany was described as an economic giant and a political pygmy. This was not entirely just; but the burden of history undoubtedly inhibited an assertive stance, and it predisposed many Germans to the idea of European union. Critics worried about what could happen if Germany's prosperity faded. 'The German Dictatorship has failed,' a historian wrote in 1969, 'but German democracy has not yet been secured.'[16] Similar worries would recur again after reunification.

Post-war British politics had to cope with a country whose traditional identity was quietly disintegrating. They were governed by the swings of the two-party Westminster system, by the stop-go performance of the economy, and, above all, by Britain's long search for a post-imperial role. In July 1945 the dramatic election victory of the Labour Party introduced an extensive welfare state and a mixed economy, where evenly matched private and nationalized sectors competed. In the next half-century, three Labour governments ruled for a total of 17 years, three Conservative governments (up to 1992) for over 30. Thanks to the near-dictatorial powers of the parliamentary majority, each government's programme tended to be reversed by its successor. The over-mighty position of the trade unions, for example, which had been encouraged by the Labour governments, was overturned by the fierce anti-union policies of the Conservatives in the 1980s. Attempts by assorted 'third parties' to stop the sterile duel—by the Liberals, by the Social Democrats in the early 1980s, and by the Liberal Democrats—repeatedly failed. The unsteady performance of the economy created a climate of declining confidence. The long monetarist reign of Margaret Thatcher (1979–90) chose an authoritarian book-keeping style to bring discipline to all spheres that the government could reach. The effect, perhaps unintended, was to create an unusual degree of centralized power, which all but eliminated the voice of local government and the regions. Many British institutions had remained undisturbed for longer than anyone could remember; and a succession of disgraceful or divisive episodes in the City of London, the police, the royal family, and the Church of England heightened the sense of authority in decline. British society was increasingly polarized: the relative prosperity of the new 'enterprise culture' was matched by the decay of the inner cities and their despairing underclass, by falling standards in education, and by juvenile crime. The cohesion of the state was also being shaken: an initial surge of national separatism in Wales and Scotland in the 1970s was checked by referenda, which upheld the status quo. But from 1969 a virtual civil war in Northern Ireland required a strong military presence and brought provincial self-government to an end. Scottish separatism revived in reaction to the Anglocentric stance of successive Conservative governments. By the time that the strong hand of Mrs Thatcher left the helm, there was a widespread awareness of British democracy in crisis.

As the Empire sank from view, however, Britain's principal dilemma lay in the need to choose between her precarious 'special relationship' with the USA and the prospect of closer links with her European neighbours. The natural inclination was to get the best of both worlds: to give unstinting support to the USA and to NATO, and to join the European Community as well. With luck, the British could combine maximum economic benefits with a minimal loss of sovereignty and historic ties. General de Gaulle spotted this ploy, and blocked it. After his death, British entry to the EEC was successfully negotiated. But in the late 1980s the old dilemma returned; sooner or later, the British would be forced to make their choice. British diehards feared that the United Kingdom might lose its soul; their critics argued that internal problems could only be solved in the European context.[17] Amidst the confusion, some people wondered whether the United Kingdom would live to celebrate its tercentenary.

France, Italy, West Germany, and Great Britain—each with populations over 50 million—were by far the largest states of Western Europe. The smaller countries could best exert an influence by joining regional associations. Belgium, the Netherlands, and Luxemburg had co-ordinated their policies informally ever since the war; they completed the Benelux Economic Union in 1958. Riven by ethnic discord, Belgium turned itself in 1971 into a federalized union of three autonomous provinces—Flanders, Brussels, and Wallonia. In Scandinavia, Denmark, Norway, and Iceland, all members of NATO, joined Sweden and Finland, both neutrals, in the Nordic Council, formed in 1953. In their internal politics, various brands of social democracy predominated. Generally speaking, the smaller the state the greater was its stake in eventual European union.

European fascism, though peripheral, was slow to disappear. The Salazar regime in Portugal was not overturned till 1974. Franco's regime survived in Spain until the Caudillo's death in 1975. In Greece, deeply divided by the conflict in Cyprus, a junta of colonels seized power between 1967 and 1974. Spain's transition from fascism to democracy presented relatively few problems. A programme of economic reform dating from the early 1960s had steadily removed many discrepancies. The revival of the monarchy in the person of King Juan Carlos provided a crucial source of political leadership; and there was a strong public consensus in favour of Spain's accession to West European institutions. American support was also a factor. As a result, though negotiations between Brussels and Madrid were long and at points precarious, 141 sessions were sufficient for Spain to gain entry to the EEC in 1983, one year after joining NATO. Contrary to the gloomier predictions, the integration of a supposedly backward economy proved virtually trouble-free.

The cultural life of Western Europe was conditioned by the climate of political liberalism, by great advances in technology and the mass media, especially television, and by a tidal wave of American imports. The overall effect was seen in the loosening of conventional restraints and, to some degree, in the reduction of national particularities. Freedom of the arts and sciences was taken for granted. Pluralism of views was the norm.

In philosophy, the existentialism of Martin Heidegger (1889–1976) and Jean-Paul Sartre (1905–80) came into fashion after the war, whilst in the English-speaking world the followers of Ludwig Wittgenstein (1889–1951), an Austrian on the Cam, thought that logical positivism had rendered all other philosophy redundant. In France, the devotees of Jacques Derrida (b. 1930) and his method of deconstruction imagined that all rationalist thought could be taken apart, and shown to be meaningless. Marxism was modish in intellectual circles for twenty or thirty years, leading to what has been called 'the Great Confrontation' between Marxist intellectuals, fed on Gramsci, Lukács, and Bloch, and their critics. The most devastating critique came from the Polish ex-Marxist, Leszek Kołakowski (b. 1927), whose *Main Currents of Marxism* (1978) served both as a handbook and as an obituary to the movement. European feminism received its modern manifesto in *The Second Sex* (1949) of Simone de Beauvoir. Sartre had written: 'Hell is other people.' His partner, de Beauvoir, wrote: 'You are not born a woman; you have to become one.' [LAUSSEL]

Growing respect for science, a very American trait, affected all branches of study. The social sciences—psychology, economics, sociology, political science—exerted a profound effect on all the older disciplines. Perhaps the most fruitful alternatives to the arid trends of the time, however, were supplied by the Austrian-born Karl Popper (1902–94). Popper's *Logic of Scientific Discovery* (1934) overturned reigning assumptions about the scientific method. He argued, after Einstein's example, that no knowledge was absolute or permanent, and that hypotheses were best established by searching for proof of their wrong-headedness. His *Poverty of Historicism* (1957) demolished the pretensions of social science to formulate laws governing historical development. His *Open Society and*

Its Enemies (1945) served to justify the liberal democracy which he would live to see triumph all over Europe.

In the arts, the tide eventually turned against the disintegrating tendencies of modernism; and the 'post-modernist' blend of old and new gained ground. International festivals such as those at Salzburg, Bayreuth, or Edinburgh broke down national barriers.

The communications media proliferated. In an age of almost total literacy, a free press flourished. Quality papers such as *The Times, Le Monde, Corriere della Sera*, or *Frankfurter Allgemeine Zeitung* were joined by popular news magazines, gutter-press tabloids, and from the 1960s by legalized pornography. Cinema, radio, and sound technology greatly extended the mass audience and created new art forms such as *musique concrète*. Nothing, however, could compare in the scale of its impact with television—whose general broadcasting began in France in December 1944, in Britain in 1946, in West Germany in 1952.

American influences were felt in almost every sphere, especially in Hollywood films, dance music, and popular dress. Youth fashions and 'pop culture', where adolescents dressed in unisex jeans jived and minced in imitation of film idols or rock stars, became entirely transatlantic and cosmopolitan. In a world conditioned by unrestrained commercial advertising, fears began to be expressed that 'the media was the message', in other words, that people could be conditioned to believe anything. American English—the language of NATO, science, and 'pop' alike—could not be resisted as the main vehicle of international communication. 'Franglais' was officially condemned in France; but the teaching and, increasingly, the use of English came to be accepted as an educational and cultural priority in all West European countries. Mindless materialism, however, came to be regarded as the most insidious of American imports. It may have been very unfair to blame the USA for reducing Europeans to the level of economic animals; but Willy Brandt was expressing widespread feelings in this regard when he asked, 'Do we all want to be Americans?'

Post-war social life was much more relaxed and egalitarian than previously. The war had acted as a great leveller: the old hierarchies of class, profession, and family origins did not entirely disappear; but people became more mobile, and rising standards of living ensured, as in America, that wealth and income should be the main criterion of status. Motorization proceeded apace, as did the mass adoption of domestic appliances. By the 1970s an absolute majority of West European families, including the working class, possessed a motor car, a washing-machine, and a refrigerator, and could travel abroad for summer holidays on the Mediterranean beaches. East Europeans could only watch with envy. At the same time, the Common Agricultural Policy (CAP) of the European Community, which dispensed huge subsidies, served to redistribute wealth from the town to the countryside. Starting from the 1960s, several million peasants were transformed into relatively prosperous farmers. Primitive villages, especially in France, Germany, and northern Italy, were rapidly modernized and mechanized.

A number of structural changes made a deep impression on social attitudes. The 'Welfare State'—which provided a wide range of services such as Britain's National Health Service (1948), West Germany's model pension scheme, or France's massive HLM projects for cheap housing—removed many of the traditional anxieties about ill health, unemployment, homelessness, and old age. But it also served to create a form of psychological dependence where people could relapse into torpor, expecting to be coddled by the state from cradle to grave. It certainly did not eliminate the problems of poverty, which in a generally affluent society were particularly bitter. Rising wages turned the masses into 'consumers', pressured to become big spenders by aggressive advertising and by social emulation. Consumerism certainly fuelled the economy; but it turned material advancement into the goal, not the means; it threatened to reduce politics to a debate about the supply of goods; and it taught young people that possessions alone brought fulfilment. Since it put a dazzling supply of desirable goods before people's eyes, it was a more effective form of materialism than that which communist propaganda was advocating in the East.

The 'sexual revolution' of the 1960s, facilitated by general access to the contraceptive pill, rapidly destroyed conventional mores. It eliminated the social shame of extramarital sex, bastardy, homosexuality, divorce, and unmarried cohabitation. In most countries it was accompanied by the de-closeting of homosexuals, by the decriminalization of consensual sodomy in private, by the relaxation of laws on pornography and obscenity, and by the widespread legalization of abortion. There were considerable variations in the tempo of change, with Denmark in the van and Ireland in the rear. And there was a strong reaction, especially in Catholic circles, where fundamental values of marriage, family, and human love were thought to be under threat.

Religious life experienced a serious decline. Wartime horrors and post-war materialism destroyed many people's faith. Church-going ceased to be a social convention, and was left to the private inclination of families and individuals. Semi-deserted churches, lacking both congregations and regular clergy, could be encountered not only in city centres and industrial suburbs but also in rural areas. Protestant England and Catholic France were both badly hit. For the first time in 1,500 years Christianity was becoming a minority belief.

One response lay in ecumenism. From 1948 the World Council of Churches, with headquarters in Geneva, brought together the main Protestant and Orthodox Churches with the aim of voluntary co-operation. Its high ideals were not always immune from low politics.

At first the Roman Catholic Church stayed aloof. In the 1950s, a minor French experiment of 'worker-priests' working in industry was suppressed by the Vatican. But the elevation of Cardinal Roncalli, a man of radiant humanity, as Pope John XXIII (1958–63) marked the turning towards comprehensive reform. His Encyclical *Pacem in Terris* was addressed, exceptionally, to people of all faiths. *Mater et Magistra* showed concern for world social welfare. His convocation of the 21st Ecumenical Council of the Universal Church, known as 'Vatican II', launched the most radical change of direction since the Council of Trent.

Vatican II, whose four sessions lasted from October 1962 to December 1965, has been labelled 'the end of the Counter-Reformation'. In the battle between conservatives and liberals, many of the proposed reforms were diluted or rejected: the declaration absolving Jewry from accusations of deicide was passed in modified form; the proposals favouring modern methods of birth control was scotched. But the powers of the Curia were clipped; the obligatory Tridentine Latin Mass was to be replaced in the Roman rite by vernacular liturgies; the laity were given greater responsibility; restrictions on intermarriage were relaxed; and the seal of approval was given to ecumenism. Most importantly, a new, open, flexible spirit took flight.

Among several new Catholic bodies, Opus Dei attracted growing attention. Founded in 1928 by a Spanish priest, Mgr José-María Escrivá de Balaguer (1902–75), it seized on the special role given by Vatican II to the laity. When its founder moved with record speed towards canonization, it was seen by its critics as a sinister and irrational force within the Church. To its adherents, it was a blameless movement for spiritual regeneration, especially of youth.

The momentum generated by John XXIII was maintained by his two principal successors. Paul VI (Cardinal Montini, 1963–78) was the first Pope to leave Italy since Napoleon had deported Pius VII. His Encyclical *Humanae Vitae* (1968), which reaffirmed the ban on contraception, dismayed the liberals, but his pilgrimage to Constantinople and Jerusalem, where he embraced Orthodox leaders, was a milestone. Limited approaches were made to Anglicans and Lutherans. John Paul II (Cardinal Karol Wojtyła, elected 1978) added immense charm and energy to the agenda. Actor, linguist, and globetrotter extraordinary, he took the Papacy to the world. In May 1981, in St Peter's Square, he survived an assassination attempt by a Turkish terrorist, possibly hired by the KGB. Implacably hostile to 'liberation theology', birth control, and clerical indiscipline, he was in some respects a fierce traditionalist. His suspension of the Swiss theologian Professor Hans Küng (b. 1928), who had questioned the dogma of papal infallibility, worried many Catholic intellectuals; and his assertion of the Church's teaching on moral philosophy, as summarized in *Veritatis Splendor* (1993), offended the 'relativists' in the field. Yet his horizons were broad and compassionate. In the West he entered the Anglican den at Canterbury; and he pleaded in person for peace in Ireland. In the East, he played a vital role in his native Poland, undermining communism by sheer force of personality and his support for human rights. He succoured persecuted Lithuanians and Uniate Ukrainians; he declared his respect for the Orthodox. For the captive peoples of the Soviet bloc, he proved to be the steadiest beacon of hope shining from the West. Notwithstanding the resistance of the Russian Orthodox, who boycotted his Synod of European Bishops (1991), he aimed to bring East and West together. He was deeply committed to the unity of Europe that was Christian.

Contrary to expectations, the population of Western Europe grew more rapidly after the war than before it (see Appendix III, p. 1332). Affluence did not inhibit population growth. Wartime losses were rapidly restored by the ten-year post-war baby boom. The population of the 16 OECD countries rose from 264 million in 1940 to 320 million by 1966, and to 355 million by 1985. The country with the highest per capita income, Switzerland, also achieved the highest birth rate: in 1950–85 the Swiss population almost doubled. France's recovery was particularly striking: having remained stable at around 40 million for almost a century, the French population reached 55.2 million in 1985, thereby closing the gap on Britain and Italy. West Germany soon established itself as the largest single country (61.1 million in 1985) with the largest GDP. Birth rates generally fell again after the 1960s, causing characteristic 'troughs' and 'bulges' in subsequent generations. But death rates also fell steadily. This affected age structures. Refugees and immigrants accounted for a significant part of the increase in Germany, France, and Britain. Whereas pre-war Europeans were predominantly middle-aged, post-war Europeans included growing cohorts of elderly and retired. There was a dramatic decline in the size of the agrarian population, which had dropped to only 17 per cent overall in the EEC by 1965.

Western Europe's greatest success story lay in the realm of economic performance. The speed and the scale of economic resurgence after 1948 was unprecedented in European history, and unmatched in any part of the world except Japan. It was so unexpected and spectacular that historians cannot easily agree on its causes. It is far more easily described than explained. It clearly owed much to the start provided by Marshall Aid, to continuing interplay with the USA, and to the climate of liberal democracy, which greatly favoured unfettered enterprise. It must also be examined in conjunction with advances in science and technology, radical changes in agriculture, power, transport, and industrial relations.

Marshall Aid was essentially a pump-priming exercise, which supplied the cash to sustain European trade and industry after the initial post-war upsurge faltered. But it was not interested in the design of the pump. To use another metaphor, it was a blood transfusion which gave the economies of the OECD the strength to manage their own recovery. Several of the largest American firms invested in Western Europe at an early stage. Dupont, General Motors, and later IBM all helped to create transatlantic competition. In due course many of the larger European multinationals—Royal Dutch Shell, BP, EMI, Unilever—were well able to repay the compliment.

Contemporary economic theory and practice is very much the product of Euro-American interaction. The Keynesian revolution in macroeconomics had already established that government intervention had a vital role to play in nourishing the business climate, maintaining full employment, and managing recurrent crises through adjustments of money supply, interest rates, currency, and taxation. In due course the monetarist reaction against Keynes set in under the inspiration of Milton Friedman. Western Europe participated from the start in the international monetary system created in July 1944 under Anglo-American auspices at the Bretton Woods conference, where Keynes had led the British delegation. The resultant institutions, the International Monetary Fund (IMF) and the World Bank, both run by the United Nations, have strong European involvement, and to some extent compete with other purely European bodies. In Western Europe, as in the USA, it was taken for granted that democratic politics were a necessary adjunct to the effective management of a successful market economy.

Science and technology moved into an era when they were promoted by huge state and international funds. CERN, the European Centre for Nuclear Research (1953), and ESRO, the European Space Research Organization (1964), were among the major projects. National budgets no longer sufficed for expensive operations such as aircraft production. Modern agricultural techniques only reached the greater part of Western Europe in the 1950s. In 1945 British farmers were exceptional in using tractors; by 1960 even the smallest Continental smallholders did so. All manner of mechanization, artificial fertilizers, and intensive methods followed. Britain and West Germany remained food importers, but Denmark, France, and Italy became massive exporters. From the 1960s, Western Europe was embarrassed by colossal surpluses—the notorious 'butter mountains', 'wine lakes', and gargantuan 'grain hills' of the CAP. Power generation moved steadily away from the traditional coal to oil, natural gas, hydroelectricity, and nuclear fuels. France, in particular, made vast investments in hydroelectricity and nuclear power stations. The discovery of North Sea oil and gas off Scotland and Norway in the 1970s reduced dependence on foreign imports.

The infrastructure of transport was expanded beyond all recognition. State railway networks were electrified and rationalized. In the case of the SNCF's *Train de Grande Vitesse* (TGV), introduced in 1981, France moved into the era of supertrains equalled only in Japan. The German autobahns were systematically extended; they served as the model for magnificent autostrade, autoroutes, and motorways elsewhere. Tunnels under the Alps or under the Channel (1993) and stupendous bridges, such as the Europabrücke in Austria, closed the missing links in a unified network. International waterways with huge capacity linked the Rhine with the Rhône, Rotterdam with Marseilles. The Europoort near Rotterdam, the largest in the world, was the focus of the ambitious Rhine Delta Plan of reclamation and flood control completed in 1981. Air travel progressed to the point where no West European businessman needed to think twice about doing a day's work in any European city of his choice, and returning the same evening.

Post-industrial economies ceased to rely on the quantitative production of heavy industry. The service sector proliferated, as did the new retail structures of supermarkets and department stores. European iron and steel, after a famous boom in the 1950s, gave way to electronics, plastics, and sophisticated machinery.

Here were the components for the mighty economic motor which began to accelerate as soon as Marshall Aid had primed it. With only two minor pauses, one in 1951–2 caused by the Korean War and another in 1957–8, every major index showed a relentless upwards trajectory. The *Economic Survey for Europe*, published in 1951, predicted a 40–60 per cent growth in industrial production by the end of the decade. The targets were surpassed in under five years. By 1964 industrial output was more than two-and-a-half times that of 1938. Over 1948–63, average yearly growth of GDP was 7.6 per cent in West Germany, 6 per cent in Italy, 4.6 per cent in France, 2.5 per cent in the UK. West European trade was still growing faster than world trade, of which it accounted for some 40 per cent.

West Germany's *Wirtschaftswunder* or 'Economic Miracle' lay at the heart of Western Europe's resurgence. Contrary to popular misconceptions, West Germany did not exceed the performance of all its rivals. Italy's *miracolo* was hardly less spectacular; and Germany did not generate the Continent's highest standard of living. But thanks to the sheer size and central location of the West German economy, it was vital to everyone else's success. Its psychological impact was enhanced because the starting-point had been so low. Its author, Dr Erhard, spurned government planning of the sort preferred in France and Italy, though certain key sectors were nationalized. The rest was left to efficient organization, heavy investment, sound training, and hard work. The figures spoke for themselves: in 1948–62 West Germany's foreign trade grew by an annual average of 16 per cent; West German car ownership soared from 200,000 in 1948 to 9 million in 1965; in the same period, 8 million new housing units were constructed—enough to house a minor nation. Unemployment fell dramatically, bringing in a wave of *Gastarbeiter* or 'guest workers', especially from Turkey and Yugoslavia. Foreign investment in West Germany reached the point in 1961 when the government took active steps to discourage it. Industrial production (1958 = 100) showed how West Germany, having sustained the greatest damage from the war, travelled the furthest afterwards:

	1938	1948	1959	1967
West Germany	53	27	107	158
France	52	55	101	155
Italy	43	44	112	212
Great Britain	67	74	105	133
USA	33	73	113	168
Japan	58	22	120	347[18]

As matter for comparison, the GNP of West Germany was larger at $115 billion than that of all East European members of the Soviet bloc combined.

Western Europe's triumphant economic recovery inevitably set minds ticking. If each of the national economies had prospered so well on their own, how much more might they prosper in unison, if all the manifold barriers between national states were removed? Here was the germ of an idea which would give the faltering movement for European union a new source of vitality. It would appeal not only to those who saw economic unification as a limited end in itself but also to those who saw it as an instrument for advancing a more fundamental political process.

Not surprisingly, once the Anglo-Saxons had declined to take the lead, the European mantle fell primarily on the French. Unlike the Germans and Italians, the French had been restored to their place in the victorious coalition; at the same time they resented the secondary role allotted to them. In these circumstances, the less nationalist wing of the dominant Gaullist movement found itself facing a historic opportunity. On 20 July 1948 a strong statement in favour of European unification was made by the outgoing French Foreign Minister, Georges Bidault. After that, Monnet, Schuman, and Pleven would all rise to the challenge.

Jean Monnet (1888–1979), an economist, had started his career as the head of his family's brandy business in Cognac. From 1920 to 1923 he was Deputy Secretary-General of the League of Nations; and in 1940 he gave Churchill the idea of a Franco-British union. In 1947–9 he headed France's National Economic Plan, which he pursued under a number of ministries. He believed fervently in full-scale European union—political and military as well as economic. His goal was to be achieved step by step by what was called 'functionalism', that is, by steadily transferring an ever-increasing number of *fonctions*, or 'spheres of activity', from national to supranational control. He was the heir to Aristide Briand, and has been called 'the Father of Europe'. Robert Schuman (1886–1963), a Catholic Lorrainer, was a leading disciple both of Sangnier and of Monnet. Before the war he had been a long-serving Deputy. During the war he had fought in the Resistance, and was imprisoned. After the war he became a founding member of the Catholic MRP, of which Sangnier was honorary President. In the musical chairs of the Fourth Republic, he was twice Prime Minister. At the critical moment, in 1948–50, he stood at the head of the French Foreign Ministry, the Quai d'Orsay. René Pleven (1901–), a member of the wartime Forces Françaises Libres, was twice France's Prime Minister. He was the leader of the ex-Gaullist faction which deviated from de Gaulle's own path.

The French group found ready partners in Paul-Henri Spaak (1899–1972) and in Alcide De Gasperi (1881–1954), Schuman's partners from the original Liaison Committee (see above). The former was a socialist, who held office in Belgium as Foreign Minister, Finance Minister, or Prime Minister almost continuously from 1938 to 1966. In 1946 he had been President of the first UN General Assembly. The latter, a Christian Democrat, was a bilingual South Tyroler, who served as Premier in successive Italian coalitions from 1945 to 1953. Like Spaak, he was a strong supporter of NATO. Together they formed a formidable team, which set out to force the pace.

In August 1949 the Council of Europe started business in Strasburg. Its minimalist mandate, which was to promote European unity by debate, publicity, and research, was determined by British reservations. It had no executive powers. Its 11 original members, including Great Britain, soon swelled to 18. It was run by a Committee of Ministers meeting in private, and by a public Consultative Assembly. Its commissions on crime, human rights, cultural and legal co-operation did useful work, as did the European Court of Human Rights over which it presided. But its vision was geared to a vague and distant future. Within a year of Strasbourg welcoming the Council, the far more ambitious Schuman Plan was unveiled in Paris.

The strategy of the activists was to press for maximum proposals in the hope that a modicum of the programme would be accepted. They had to operate within a Western alliance still dominated by Washington and London, and had to be seen to complement existing arrangements in NATO, the OEEC (later OECD), and the Council of Europe. None the less, the Schuman Plan of May 1950 proposed a far-reaching package of economic, military, and political institutions. It called for an economic organization co-ordinating the iron and steel industry and for a European army, which together would form the foundation for a United States of Europe. And it was prepared in secret, without advance consultation with London. In the event, the economic element took flight whilst the military and the political elements were shelved. Henceforth, the three strands of European unification were destined to progress along separate tracks and at different speeds.

The main strength of the Schuman Plan lay in its appeal to Franco-German reconciliation. It appeared at a juncture when the Bundesrepublik stood on the brink of spectacular economic expansion, but when it was still politically isolated. Chancellor Adenauer, a Rhinelander, had lived all his life in the shadow of Franco-German wars; and he shared Schuman's liberal and democratic Catholicism. The prospect of harmony between France and Germany provided the fund of agreement which no one could reasonably oppose. Once rolling, it gathered momentum.

The European Coal and Steel Community (1951–67) was the first-born child of the Schuman Plan. It was designed to prevent the reappearance of a separate military-industrial base in each member country; and its first president was Jean Monnet. Its founding treaty, signed in May 1951, brought together 'the Six'— France, Germany, Italy, and Benelux. They agreed to operate free trade in coal and steel, to abide by common regulations governing manufacture and competition, and, in the event of 'manifest crisis', to control prices and production. It was a manifest success. Britain did not participate.

The military strand encountered severe obstacles. The Pleven Plan (1950) floated a modified version of the military clauses of the Schuman Plan; but it still encountered the forthright denunciation of de Gaulle. Complicated negotiations dragged on for four years. The British were in no mood to weaken NATO; the French came out against a compromise organization, the European Defence Community (EDC). An eventual outcome was found in the Western European Union (1955), a deliberative body with few independent powers, which came into being just in time to experience the chaos of the Suez Crisis.

The Messina Conference of 1955 marks the moment when the European movement turned to economic integration as the leading element in its strategy. The political strand was not making progress; members decided that a strong and successful economic community would open up the surest path for pursuing their long-term political goals. They were to hold to this course for more than 30 years. The two treaties signed in Rome (25 March 1957) embodied the determination of the Six to extend the success of the ECSC into all sectors of their commercial and economic life. They gave rise to the European Economic Community (EEC), otherwise known as the Common Market, which came into official effect on 1 January 1958 and also to Euratom. The main aims were to remove all internal tariffs, to formulate a common external trade policy, to harmonize transportation, agriculture, and taxation, to eliminate barriers to free competition, and to encourage the mobility of capital, labour, and enterprises.

In order to pursue these aims, four new bodies were created: the Council of Ministers, which was to control and authorize all policy decisions; a subordinate Executive Commission in Brussels, with a Permanent Secretariat and numerous directorates for proposing policy; the European Court of Justice; and a European Parliament sitting alternately in Strasbourg and Luxemburg. Once again, the venture prospered. Internal tariffs were abolished by 1968. The Common Agricultural Policy (1962), thanks to vast subsidies and despite the protests of manufacturers, brought a new lease of sturdy life to millions of farmers. The introduction of Value Added Tax (VAT) in 1967 raised important revenues which could be used to spread the community's growing wealth into deprived social sectors and backward regions. The first President of the European Commission, Professor Walter Hallstein (West Germany), guided its fortunes from 1958 to 1967. Among his successors were Roy Jenkins (UK) and, from 1985, Jacques Delors (France). Whatever the criticisms of the EEC—and there were many—it was demonstrably true that its members were waxing more prosperous than the countries which stayed out. 'Anyone who does not believe in miracles in European affairs', remarked Professor Hallstein, 'is not a realist.'

The European Free Trade Area (EFTA, 1958–) was created in response to the EEC by the so-called 'Outer Seven', led by Britain, who had not been parties to the Treaty of Rome. Its interests were confined to the commercial sector; and its long-term future was constantly clouded by the likelihood of defection to the EEC. It played a valuable role until 1973, when Britain and Denmark left EFTA to join the EEC.

Britain's membership of the European movement proved a bone of contention that rankled for more than 40 years. The UK Government did not participate in the ECSC in 1951, and dropped out of negotiations preceding the Treaty of Rome. The inhibitions were both psychological and practical. Not having suffered the sobering humiliation of national defeat, many Britons still harboured illusions of sovereignty and self-sufficiency. They also possessed very real commitments to the Commonwealth—including the thorny matter of Commonwealth commercial preference. In the political sphere, they gave priority to relations with the USA and to membership of NATO. In 1961 and 1967 under Macmillan and Wilson, they twice applied to join the EEC, only to meet the shocking rebuff of de Gaulle's veto. Throughout the decade before the Treaty of Rome, de Gaulle was in retirement and France's European policy had rested with milder men. But de Gaulle's return to power coincided with the launching of the EEC. Conflict was unavoidable. The General was still nursing resentments about the alleged betrayal of French interests first by the British in wartime and then by the leaders of the Fourth Republic. He held strong views about 'l'Europe des Patries', a 'community of nation-states'; and he insisted on reinstating what he saw as France's sovereign rights. The results were seen in his vetoes against Britain's entry, and then in a long-running battle against the European Commission—'the Emperor versus the Pope'. French representatives boycotted proceedings in Brussels until they forced through the Luxemburg Compromise (1966)—an arrangement whereby members were permitted to disregard the rules of the Treaty of Rome on majority voting in matters of supreme national concern.

The first two decades of the EEC were crowned by a number of important financial developments. The European Monetary System (EMS), which began in 1979, tied the currencies of member states into the framework of an exchange rate mechanism (ERM) which was designed to dampen previous fluctuations. It was conceived by its authors as the initial stage on the long road to European monetary union (EMU). The appearance of the European Currency Unit (ECU) promised later moves towards a single currency. The European Social Fund and the European Development Fund were both designed to redistribute wealth into areas of social or regional deprivation.

The Community's economic success ensured a steady stream of new applicants. In 1973, under Edward Heath, the UK was admitted at the third attempt, together with Denmark and Ireland. A British referendum (1975) confirmed the permanence of UK membership. The Six became the Nine. In 1981, the admission of Greece turned the Nine into the Ten. In 1986, after lengthy negotiations, Spain and Portugal were admitted: the Ten became the Twelve. For the first time, the Community embraced three 'developing economies', and, in the case of Greece, an East European country with no contiguous frontier.

Yet the military and political strands of European union remained stalled. In the early 1980s the Atlantic alliance was reactivated by the assertive Reagan–Thatcher duet; and the value of NATO was emphasized by the controversy over Soviet and American missiles. The political and international role of the EEC was peripheral. Its institutions, which were designed to fit a small Community of Six, were increasingly strained by the expanding business of the Twelve. In due course, one of the leading Europeans would call the Community 'a growing man still walking around in babyclothes'.[19] There seemed little chance that the EEC could soon break out of its narrowly economic concerns.

One would like to think, however, that the creation of the Twelve had given birth to something qualitatively new. Europe had seen any number of alliances between the rich and powerful, any number of visions based on selective membership of the privileged 'West'. But now the point appeared to have been reached at which the European Community was changing itself into a voluntary association of equal nations—rich and poor, East and West, great and small. The main criteria for entry, apart from being European was that applicants should have shed the nationalistic, imperialist, and totalitarian traditions of the past. Only time would tell whether the change was permanent.

The Neutral States

Neutrality has been a feature of the European scene throughout the twentieth century. Eleven neutral states existed in 1945; four countries which had avoided involvement in one or both World Wars also declined to be drawn into the post-war military blocs; two countries achieved neutral status in the early post-war years. There was a high correlation between neutrality and affluence; and most neutrals did not make haste to join the European Economic Community.

Switzerland, for whom neutrality was a way of life, thrived mightily. It had steeled itself to resist German invasion during the war, and saw a marked rise in population afterwards. It benefited greatly from the proximity of northern Italy and southern Germany, both regions of massive post-war economic growth, whilst continuing to play a special role in banking and in tourism. It welcomed numerous multinational companies and international agencies, from Bayer chemicals to UNESCO. Rhaeto-Romanic was raised to the status of a national language, alongside Swiss German, French, and Italian, and the French-speaking Jura was made a special canton. The defence budget was high, and universal male conscription remained in force to support the national militia. Swiss women had no vote until after the (all-male) referendum of 1980. Switzerland shunned the Council of Europe till 1963; its association with the EEC was limited to a free-trade agreement signed in 1972.

Thanks to Switzerland, several adjoining territories have claimed the status of free customs zones. These include the German enclave of Büsingen, the Italian districts of Campione d'Italia, Livigno, and Val d'Aosta, and, since 1815, the French département of Haute-Savoie.

Sweden had prospered from neutrality in wartime, and continued to do so in peacetime. It was the centre-piece of the regional Baltic Council, but remained aloof from both NATO and the EEC even when its Scandinavian partners joined. The long rule of Social Democracy carried on to the elections of 1989. Especially under its premier, Olaf Palme, who was murdered in 1986, Sweden took the lead in a number of initiatives involving Third World, refugee, and environmental issues.

Franco's Spain remained a political pariah so long as the Caudillo lived. Indeed, the extraordinary longevity of both Franco and Salazar held Iberian politics in a time-warp until the mid-1970s. The anachronistic survival of fascism served to offset anti-communist opinion in Western Europe, especially in France. With Portugal a member of NATO, Spain agreed to receive American bases, but rejected any greater involvement. Mass tourism, however, militated against total isolation. The re-establishment of the constitutional monarchy in 1975 opened the way for EEC membership, and for the remarkable economic resurgence of the 1980s. Basque terrorism in the north-west, Catalan separatism in Barcelona, and the intractable dispute with Great Britain over Gibraltar all complicated the Spanish revival.

The Republic of Ireland had survived the threat of British occupation during the war, and left the Commonwealth at the end of it. But economic dependence on the United Kingdom remained a reality: Ireland had little alternative to following in Britain's contorted wake in negotiations with the EEC. Political life centred on the privileged position of the Catholic Church, on the endless conflict with Northern Ireland, and on the rivalry of the two main parties, Fianna Fáil ('Soldiers of Destiny') and Fine Gael ('Race of Gaels'). The Irish Constitution treated the counties of British Ulster as an integral part of the Republic. But the Irish Republican Army (IRA) was regarded as an illegal organization on both sides of the border; and relations between London and Dublin were not a major obstacle to a settlement.

Finland, which had joined the German attack on the USSR (see p. 1013), escaped Soviet occupation, though further territory, notably Viipuri (Vyborg) and Petsamo, had to be ceded at the armistice of 1944. In 1947, however, a peace treaty confirmed the country's limited sovereignty in return for the lease of the Porkkala naval base. Henceforth, Finland was obliged to observe strict neutrality, to reduce its armed forces, and to pursue a foreign policy concordant with Soviet interests. After that, the economy boomed, and Helsinki became one of Europe's most elegant and expensive cities—a western showpiece on the doorstep of Leningrad. 'Finlandization' was a status which many Soviet-occupied countries coveted, but none, except Austria, ever obtained.

Austria benefited from the Allied fiction that it had been the Nazis' first victim. Divided, like Germany, into four occupation zones, the Republic succeeded in regaining full sovereignty on the basis of a *Staatsvertrag* or 'state treaty' (1955) signed by all four occupying powers. The conditions included strict neutrality, plus the maintenance in perpetuity of Vienna's vast Soviet war memorial. The restoration of independence was followed by a period of unprecedented prosperity, similar to that in neighbouring Switzerland, and of relative détente. Politics was dominated by the nicely balanced rivalry of the Socialist Party, which held the chancellorship under Bruno Kreisky (1970–83), and the conservative People's Party. In 1986 an international campaign to discredit the Austrian President, Kurt Waldheim, formerly Secretary-General of UNO, did not harm him; but it served as a reminder of Austria's past. Austria's frontiers contained several aberrations. Thanks to a treaty of 1868, the two districts of Jungholz and Mittelberg form part of the Bavarian customs area. The provinces of Vorarlberg and Tyrol enjoyed free trade with the Alto Adige and Trentino in Italy.

Seven European principalities, the last survivors of numerous historic mini-states, were too small to exercise an active role in international relations; but each has been well able to exploit its eccentric position.

San Marino (founded in the fifth century AD, territory 62 km², population 23,000) claimed to be Europe's oldest state. Recognized as independent in 1631, it hugs the slopes of Monte Titano, near Rimini, and is entirely surrounded by Italian territory. It functioned after the war as a tax haven for rich Italians, ruled by a local government dominated alternately by communists and Christian Democrats.

The Grand Duchy of Liechtenstein (founded 1719, territory 157 km², population 27,000) had ceded its foreign policy to Switzerland. In 1980, at $16,440 it had the highest per capita GNP in Europe. It is the last surviving constituent of the Holy Roman Empire.

The Principality of Monaco (territory 150 ha, population c.30,000) was a self-governing protectorate of France occupying a tiny enclave on the Riviera, east of Nice. Its modern status emerged in 1861; it had previously been a possession of Spain (from 1542), France (from 1641), and Sardinia (from 1815). Its constitution put government into the hands of the Grimaldi family. Its income depended heavily on the casino at Monte Carlo.

Andorra (territory 495 km², population c.43,000), high in the eastern Pyrenees, has preserved its autonomy since 1278, when it was placed under the joint protection of the Bishop of Urgel and the Comte de Foix. In recent times the powers of the latter were exercised by the Prefect of the Ariège on behalf of the President of the French Republic. It lived from tourism, especially skiing, and from duty-free trade.

The Isle of Man (territory 518 km², population 65,000 in 1986) and the Channel Islands (of Jersey, Alderney, Guernsey, and Sark—territory 194 km², population c.134,000 in 1981) were both British dependencies with English connections dating from the Norman Conquest. They were never formally joined to the United Kingdom. Both were wealthy tax havens. The Dame of Sark was still contesting her prerogatives with Westminster in the 1960s. In the 1990s the 'parliament' of the Isle of Man was courting a showdown by failing to follow England's example in legalizing private homosexual acts between consenting adults.

Gibraltar was the only British dependency outside the British Isles to join the EC. In this it followed the French Overseas Departments of Guadeloupe, Martinique, Réunion, and Guiana. All other British and French colonies, like the autonomous Danish regions of [FAROE] and Greenland, remained outside the EC.

The Vatican City (territory 44 ha, estimated population 1,000 in 1981) was Europe's last autocracy. Its ruler, the Pope, exercised the same unlimited governance over this latter-day papal state as over the Roman Catholic Church, of which it was the headquarters. Its nearest counterpart was the 'theocratic republic' of [ATHOS], which has enjoyed autonomy within Greece since 1926.

These survivals serve as a reminder that variety and tradition play a prominent part in European life. Europe has not been entirely submerged by power politics.

Eastern Europe, 1945–1985

'Eastern Europe' in the post-war era had two distinct meanings. It could reasonably be taken to refer to any part of the Continent which lay on the Soviet side of the Iron Curtain. In this sense, it included the European countries which had been incorporated into the Soviet Union and others which had not. More usually, however, it was used as a synonym for the satellites of the USSR in 'East Central' and 'South-Eastern' Europe, as distinct from the USSR itself.

In the last analysis, these distinctions carry only limited weight. None of the states organized on Leninist lines, whether as so-called 'people's democracies' or as republics of the Soviet Union, were supposed to enjoy any significant measure of independence. All were designed as façades for the exercise of the dictatorial prerogatives of the Soviet-led communist movement. By any definition, therefore, the post-war history of Eastern Europe can only take the policies of the CPSU as its starting-point, before moving to examine the ever more dyslectic translation of Moscow's wishes by Moscow's ever more wayward dependants.

Prior to the terminal decline after 1985, the post-war history of the Soviet Union fell into three periods. The first (1945–53) was taken up by the last years of the Great Stalin. The second (1953–64) was dominated by so-called de-stalinization, during the rise and fall of Nikita Sergeevich Khrushchev. The third (1964–85), later labelled 'the Age of Stagnation', was initiated and inspired by Leonid Il'ich Brezhnev. Taken together, those four decades witnessed one of the grand illusions of modern history. The Soviet Union had emerged from the Second World War as the greatest military power in Europe; and it proceeded to turn itself into one of two global superpowers. To all outward appearances it was unimaginably strong, an impregnable fortress armed with the world's largest arsenal of nuclear weapons. At the same time, its internal processes were decomposing at an unprecedented rate; its body was riddled with the political equivalent of cancer. History is full of giants with feet of clay—the old Russian Empire was a prime example—but here was an armoured dinosaur which was dying on its feet. And no one saw its distress—neither Western sovietologists nor, until much too late, the Soviet leaders themselves. With a number of honourable exceptions, both groups spent most of those 40 years admiring the Soviet Union as a paragon of health and progress.

Stalin's last years brought no relief to the long night of fear and suffering. Speculation that age and victory would mellow him proved unfounded. The same old gang of Stalin's pre-war cronies clung to power. The same mixture of terror, propaganda, and collective routine kept the Soviet peoples down. The gulag kept up the same regular motions of mass arrests and slave labour. There is strong evidence to suppose that Stalin, having discovered the so-called 'Doctors' Plot', was preparing yet another great Purge when he died.

In those years the Soviet Empire expanded to its greatest extent. It did so through military conquest and through political surrogates who created political, economic, and social clones of the Soviet model. Shortly after the occupation of Eastern Europe, the major advance came with the victory of the communists in China. Mao Zedong had written that 'Power grows from the barrel of a gun'; and he triumphed in 1949 without the direct intervention of Moscow. He held somewhat different ideological views from the Soviets, and was well aware that Stalin had originally backed his arch-enemy, Chiang Kai-shek. But for the time being he was content to be a loyal member of the Soviet camp. For a dozen years, Moscow stood at the head of a movement which controlled the world's most populous nation as well as the world's largest state. The so-called 'Socialist Camp' contained half of humanity.

Great store was placed on growing Soviet influence with the ex-colonial peoples. In the era of decolonization, Moscow saw itself as the natural patron and beneficiary of all national liberation movements. Its strongest links were forged with Vietnam, the Arab world, and Cuba.

All available resources were thrown into the military aspects of nuclear science. At Mayak in the Urals, and elsewhere, teams of cosseted slave scientists laboured to produce the Soviet 'bomb'. An atomic device was successfully tested on arctic Novaya Zemlya in 1949, a hydrogen device in 1953. After that, the period of America's nuclear monopoly had passed. By the time that Stalin died, the Soviet Union had confirmed its status as a superpower.

Stalin died on 5 March 1953 after suffering a stroke at his dacha in Kuntsevo. In his death-throes he was left lying on the floor for 24 hours. No Kremlin doctor who valued his own life was going to save Stalin's. The Politburo members kept vigil at his bedside in turns:

As soon as Stalin showed signs of consciousness, Beria threw himself on his knees, and started kissing Stalin's hand. When Stalin lost consciousness again, Beria stood up and spat . . . spewing hatred.[20]

News of Stalin's death caused tens of millions to weep.

De-stalinization meant exactly what the term implies. It removed those features of the Soviet regime which were directly connected with Stalin himself—the cult of personality, the *edinonachalie* or 'one-man rule', and the practice of random mass terror. It initiated an interval known, after Ehrenburg's novel, as 'the Thaw'. When Beria was gunned down at the very first Politburo meeting, the collective leadership of his colleague-assassins was able to trim the power of the NKVD—now reorganized as the KGB. But they kept the dictatorial machine intact. They lightened the climate of fear, but introduced no significant measure of democratization or liberalization. The Soviet system retained its totalitarian character. Over three years, the collective leadership gave way to the personal supremacy of Khrushchev.

The ebullient Khrushchev was perhaps the least obnoxious of Stalin's creatures. He was typical of the proletarian opportunists who had made their way up the Party apparatus in the worst years of the Terror. He had a black record as Stalin's boss in Ukraine; a late recruit to literacy, he was a cultural philistine of the crudest sort. Yet he had a rough peasant charm—especially when beating the table with his shoe at the United Nations. And he was surrounded by high hopes. Khrushchev's sensational 'Secret Speech' to the XXth Party Congress in March 1956 must be seen in context. It set the precedent where every Soviet leader would ritually denounce his predecessor as a criminal; and its highly selective revelations of Stalin's crimes were carefully matched to the needs of the Party. It concealed much more than it revealed, and by minimizing Soviet criminality earned him an exaggerated reputation for honesty. It belongs to the evolving Soviet genre of 'openness' that ran from Stalin's own revelatory speeches to Gorbachev's feats 30 years later.

Khrushchev's reign was notable for three signal developments. Misunderstandings over the policy of 'Different Roads to Socialism' led to great tensions throughout Eastern Europe, to open conflict in Hungary, and to the fateful split with China. Developments in military science and the launching of Sputnik, the first earth satellite, led to intense rivalry with the USA and to the Cuban missile crisis of 1963. The quantitative achievements of the Soviet economy led Khrushchev to boast that the Soviet Union would overtake the West within 20 years: 'We will bury you.' Khrushchev's adventurism thoroughly scared the comrades; in October 1964 he was removed in a Kremlin coup and sent into live retirement.

Leonid Brezhnev, another Russian from Ukraine, dominated the Soviet bloc for two long decades. He has been blamed as the man who allowed the USSR to revert to 'neo-Stalinism', and to 'stagnate'. In time, he may come to be seen as the leader who understood the system best, who prolonged its life for as long as was possible. He was, above all, a cautious and canny *apparatchik*, who realized the consequences of tampering with a faulty machine. His brief experience of liberalization during the Prague Spring convinced him, quite rightly, of the unreliability of his closest allies and the need for the Brezhnev Doctrine (see below). His brief dalliance with economic reform at home, associated with his chief partner, Alexei Kosygin, convinced him that the risks were greater than the gains. His personal knowledge of Ukraine must have convinced him that the slightest relaxation of the nationality issue could only spell trouble. His pursuit of *détente* with the West, which combined an aggressive military stance with the careful delimitation of spheres, produced a stable arrangement that seemed to guarantee the international position of the USSR in perpetuity.

Brezhnev could not fail to notice how the USSR had been built. But he also understood—as his successors did not—that eliminating the lies and the coercion must inevitably dissolve the fabric of the building. So Brezhnev sat tight. What his detractors were to denounce as 'stagnation' could be seen as the peace and stability for which he and his generation had longed. The most one could do was to calibrate the force and the fraud to tolerable proportions. Unlike Stalin, he did not kill people in millions; unlike Khrushchev, he did not go in for 'hare-brained schemes'; unlike Gorbachev, he did not destroy the system with which he was entrusted.

One of the great ironies of the era became apparent when successive General Secretaries showed signs of a variety of wasting diseases that perfectly symbolized the Soviet condition. By the late 1970s stability was slipping into inertia. Brezhnev's speech slurred and his movements slowed to the point where jokers claimed that he was a corpse maintained on a life-support machine. His death turned inertia into paralysis, as ailing successors argued the contrary merits of reform and inaction. Yuri Andropov (1982–3), an exponent of reform, died of cancer before reforms could be started. Konstantin Chernyenko (1983–5), a victim of emphysema, had no intention of starting anything.

The Soviet political dictatorship, which reached maturity after Stalin's death, did not conform to its popular image abroad. It was supported by the largest 'secret police' in the world, by the Gulag, by an aggressive brand of pre-emptive censorship, by a vast arsenal of tanks and security forces. But these were not the primary instruments of oppression: the dictatorship relied above all on the dual structures of the party-state, that is, on the civilian organs of the Communist Party and their control over the parallel institutions of the state (see Appendix III, p. 1321). There was no branch of human activity which was not subordinated to the relevant department of the state. There was no branch of the state which was not governed by orders from the relevant 'committee' of the Party. Whatever was going on, be it in the most august of ministries or in the lowliest of local farms, factories, or football clubs, it could only be legal if organized by the state; and it could only be organized if approved by the Party.

The plight of the individual citizen was dire. Since state law and state judges were subject to the universal principle of Party control, anything which the Party disliked could be promptly and legally suppressed, without effective right of appeal. Since all human needs were supplied by state monopolies, any person who chose to defy the Party's wishes stood to be rendered destitute on the spot, or, as the jargon had it, to be given their 'wolf's ticket'. Recalcitrant individuals and their families could be routinely deprived of their residence permits, their ration cards, their identity papers, and hence their access to employment, housing, education, and health care. Once the Party's bureaucratic dictatorship was in place, the more violent instruments of oppression did not need to be invoked except against exceptionally courageous and resourceful dissidents. In theory at least, there simply was no place for private initiative, individual judgement, or spontaneous social action. In normal circumstances, it was virtually impossible to organize a strike, to form a private society, or to publish unauthorized information. News of popular uprisings, such as that at Novocherkassk in 1962, which led to huge massacres, could be concealed for decades.

Party control over state institutions was exercised by an elaborate array of laws, levers, structures, and psychological taboos. Party control was enshrined in law. The only important clause of the Soviet Constitution was the one which proclaimed 'the leading role' of the Party. This simple device ensured that all other clauses of the Constitution, and all other Soviet laws, were subject to the interpretation of the Party and its officials. By outside standards, they were not laws at all. The Party rule-book was a much more efficacious document than the Soviet Constitution. The *nomenklatura* system ensured that every appointment, from the State Presidency to the chair of the village council, was exclusively filled by the Party's nominees. Each Party committee reserved the right to draw up lists of posts at its level in the state and Party hierarchy, and of suitable candidates to fill them (including lists of Party-approved 'non-Party' persons). As a result, Party members would generally hold one position in the Party apparatus and a second one in some state institution. The *nomenklatura* of the Party's Central Committee secured all appointments in the ministries, and in the supreme commands of the armed forces and the KGB.

The management of all state institutions was further restricted by Party control exercised 'from without and from within'. The nominal heads of all state institutions—ministers, generals, ambassadors, leaders of delegations, all directors of factories, schools, or institutes—were formally obliged to accept instructions from a parallel Party committee. They were the servants of more powerful Party secretaries operating behind the scenes. At the same time, they had to bow to the day-to-day supervision of the primary Party organization, or 'Party cell', made up of all Party members within the ranks of their own personnel. As a result, ministers *qua* ministers did not really run their ministries; army commanders did not command their units; managers did not manage their firms.

Everything depended on the efficient transmission of the Party's orders. Party discipline ensured that the decisions of the 'higher organs' were enforced right down the line. Party members were sworn both to obedience and to secrecy (not least about the contents of the rule-book). They were trained to anticipate and to execute the wishes of their superiors without question. Open debate was discouraged; discussion was limited to the means whereby higher decisions could be implemented.

These realities were so alien to the experience of democracies that it is easy to understand why political scientists could be so easily misled. All explanations to outsiders have to begin with the warning that Western concepts and Western terminology simply did not apply. The ruling Communist Party, for instance, was *not* a political party; it was a political army which had been transformed into the executive branch of government. The Soviet state was no more than the administrative agency of the Party. The so-called Soviet Government, i.e. the Council of Ministers, was not the government, since it was subordinate both to the Party's Politburo and to the Party's Secretariat. The chief executive of the system was not the President of the USSR or his Prime Minister, but the Party's General Secretary (who was free to appoint himself President or Prime Minister if he so wished). The Supreme Soviet or state legislative assembly was not supreme, since it could only register statutes prepared in advance by the Party's Central Committee. State elections, above all, were not elections, since there was no element of choice. Citizens were compelled by law to endorse the lists of Party nominees.

In a very real sense, therefore, the Soviet Union never really existed, except as a facade for Party power. It was the grandest communist front organization in history. That is why, when the CPSU eventually collapsed, the USSR could not possibly exist without it.

An important shift of political power took place in the Brezhnev era, largely unnoticed. In return for absolute loyalty to the policies of the centre, Brezhnev was ready to let the Party bosses of the 14 non-Russian republics of the USSR run their affairs without interference. The Soviet republics were turning almost imperceptibly into national fiefdoms, where Moscow's writ ran ever more uncertainly. Brezhnev's regional baronies did not enjoy the same latitude as the East European satellites: they were prominently represented in the Politburo, and were an important pillar of the conservative order. But their emergence helps to explain why their centrifugal trajectory could accelerate so surprisingly and so rapidly when the signals from Moscow grew confused.

The Soviet armed forces, though enormous and very prestigious, were deprived of all capacity for independent action: the Party left nothing to chance. It was not sufficient that all military officers were trained in Party-run academies, that they could only obtain promotion by joining the CPSU, or that they could issue no orders without the counter-signature of a *politruk* or 'political director' working alongside them. The entire fabric of the military hierarchy was run by agents of *Glavpolit*, the Main Political-Military Department, whose senior members included the most important marshals of the General Staff and whose juniors filled key positions throughout the lower echelons. As a matter of routine, rocket forces were not given control over their own warheads, parachute forces did not control their transports, tank forces did not possess their own ammunition or fuel.

The Soviet armed forces comprised four main components—the strategic nuclear forces, the air forces, the army, and the navy. At their height they contained perhaps 10 million men. According to the wishes of their masters, they were designed to be the most formidable, or the most impotent, force imaginable. From 1955, when the Warsaw Pact was formed in belated response to NATO, the Soviet military became enmeshed in yet another layer of bureaucracy. They retained absolute control over the running of the Pact, whose HQ was in Moscow, not Warsaw.

The scale and organization of the Soviet security forces bore little resemblance to counterparts elsewhere. To call them 'the secret police' was a travesty. The KGB was the equivalent of the CIA, the FBI, and the US Coast Guard rolled into one, with many other functions to boot. Apart from foreign intelligence, its various directorates ran the Gulag, the *Glavpolit*, the civilian militia, and the system of censorship. Its principal mission, however, was to keep itself informed of everything and everyone, and to root out 'unreliable elements' by all means available. Its uniformed officers, with their sky-blue epaulettes, could be encountered in every Soviet town. They commanded a vast horde of informers, thugs, and secret agents hidden within the population, and a duplicate army of up to a million crack internal troops trained to police the army, to watch the borders, to man the camps, to quell disorder, and to protect the Party élite. As their most public and sacred duty, they mounted guard on Lenin's mausoleum. Their headquarters in the Lyubianka in central Moscow looked out on a statue of Feliks Dzierżyński, their founder. It contained the most feared dungeons in all Russia.

Soviet society, officially classless, was dominated by a growing gulf between the Party élite and the rest of the population. Once the Purges stopped, the members of the *nomenklatura* were able to entrench their position, to purloin state property for their own use, and to grow rich and powerful from patronage. The higher echelons were allocated luxury flats and dachas, expensive limousines, exclusive access to closed stores, Western currency, and foreign travel. They were, as Milovan Djilas declared as early as 1957, the 'New Class'—the proprietorial caste. The collectivized peasants, in contrast, suffered deprivations worse than those of the serfs. Until the 1970s they possessed neither social security benefits nor personal identity papers. The industrial workers were told that they had inherited the earth; they toiled in expectation of the improved housing, wages, and safety which never materialized. The intelligentsia—which in the official definition represented a professional stratum of 'brain workers'—enjoyed high prestige but low incomes. Despite the fact that several professions, such as medical doctors, were predominantly female, Soviet women received little relief from conditions that their sisters in the West would not have tolerated. As in Nazi Germany, the official ethos encouraged heroic child-bearing; abortion was the only form of family planning to be widely available. 'Developed socialism' was, by European standards, very underdeveloped.

Not surprisingly, earlier Soviet demographic trends started to falter, especially in European Russia. In the 1950s and 1960s the Soviet population recovered from the traumatic losses of the Stalin years, rising from 178.5 million (1950) to 262.4 million (1974); and there was a spectacular rise in the size and number of large cities. But the hardships of Soviet urban living were not conducive to carefree reproduction. By the 1980s both the birth rate and life expectancy were falling. Thanks to sustained growth in the central Asian republics, the dominant Russian nationality was declining. Even if the official figure of 52 per cent in 1979 was accurate, the Russians were poised to fall into an absolute minority.

The Soviet economic system held to the basic methods and priorities laid down by Stalin—central command planning, militarization, heavy industry. Its fundamental failures were long concealed behind the screen of falsified statistics. Five-Year Plans continued to give the illusion of continuing quantitative success even when growth rates inevitably slowed and targets failed to be met. Global results still looked impressive right up to 1980:

USSR: Selected indices of production

	1945	1950	1960	1970	1980
Steel (million tonnes)	12.3	27.3	65.3	116	148
Coal (million tonnes)	149	261	510	624	716
Oil (million tonnes)	19	40	148	353	603
Electricity (million kw hrs.)	43	91	292	741	1,294
Automobiles (000)	75	363	524	916	2,199
Industrial Group A (Capital goods 1913 = 1)	15	27.5	89.4	213.8	391.4
Industrial Group B (Consumer goods 1913 = 1)	2.7	5.7	15	30	49.8
Grain (million tonnes)	47	81	126	187	189
Cows (million head)	30	25	34	39	43[21]

Not till the early 1980s did the truth begin to dawn that global production figures were next to irrelevant, and that the Soviet Union's rivals were forging far ahead in almost every sector.

Unknown to the public or the outside world, the privileged military and nuclear sector was consuming over 30 per cent of Soviet GNP—at least five times more than was officially admitted. At the same time, the overblown communist shibboleth of heavy industry continued to pour out unwanted iron, steel, and crude chemicals. The result was an economy which produced tanks, rockets, and aircraft in huge quantities but which could not support the basic needs of the population. All the most important elements of the civilian economy were woefully neglected. Soviet agriculture produced low-grade food in huge amounts; but was incapable of delivering it to the family table. The USSR became a net importer of grain, whilst domestic supplies relied increasingly on the collective farmers' back gardens (50 per cent of food derived from 3 per cent of arable land). Science and technology remained far behind the state of the art in the civilian sphere. Soviet conditions proved specially inimical to computerization and to the free flow of information outside the central bureaucracy. Motorization, which began in a big way in the 1960s with the purchase of a licence from Fiat to build Lada cars, was hampered by the absence of supporting services, especially modern roads. The service sector in general was no more than nascent. The consumer sector remained starved of goods. Subsidized prices in food and housing guaranteed a subsistence standard of living whilst nourishing a vigorous black market. The infrastructure remained woefully inadequate. After 70 years of progress, the Soviet Union had not built a single all-weather road link from west to east. The single-track trans-Siberian railway remained a solitary lifeline to the Far East. Aeroflot, the world's largest airline, was also the most overworked. The riches of Siberia could not be properly exploited. The more commands emitted by Moscow, the feebler the response. Notwithstanding Comecon, the East European satellites moved from being net contributors to being a net burden. Soviet export earnings were unhealthily dependent on gold and oil. By the early 1980s the combination of uncontrolled military spending and the diminishing returns of domestic performance spelled the onset of a systemic crisis requiring urgent treatment.

Environmental protection was not a serious possibility. Primitive industrial methods and the pressures of quantitative planning left no room for ecological considerations. Even where environmental laws were passed, there was little chance that lowly elements of the bureaucracy could enforce them against the interests of the Party's main productive drive. In the totalitarian party-state, there was place neither for an independent environmental agency nor for grass-roots activism. As a result, the Soviet Union systematically created Europe's most scandalous examples of neglect and of persistent pollution. Blighted cityscapes, dead rivers, toxic air, dying forests, unmonitored radiation hazards, and declining health indices were all suppressed in the fog of habitual secrecy. Only the explosion of a nuclear reactor at Chernobyl in Ukraine in April 1986, which bathed half of Europe in fall-out, alerted the world to the dangers at a very late stage.

Soviet culture was rendered schizophrenic by state censorship, which unwittingly divided all activities into official and unofficial spheres. Artists could only perform or publish if they belonged to one of the party-run associations. Their work could be categorized as the blatantly conformist, the trimmed, and the courageously defiant. Official culture centred on the principles of so-called Socialist Realism, which were laid down in 1934 and reformulated in 1946 by Andrei Zhdanov. [**MOLDOVA**] This style presented Soviet life in an idealized, compulsorily joyful, and essentially mendacious fashion. Some important deviations were permitted in the decade after Stalin's death. Khrushchev on the one hand permitted the publication of Alexander Solzhenitsyn's *One Day in the Life of Ivan Denisovich* (1962)—a grim picture of the Gulag. On the other, he excoriated Moscow's first exhibition of modern art, calling it 'the lashings of a donkey's tail'. Thaw soon passed into refreeze. A handful of talented artists preserved a margin of independence on the fringe of toleration; but most of the great works of the era, from Boris Pasternak's *Doktor Zhivago* (1957) or Alexander Zinoviev's and Solzhenitsyn's major novels, had to be published illegally abroad. Many masterpieces did not see the light of day for 20 or 30 years.

Paradoxically, Soviet repressions generated a genuine thirst for independent high culture, a hunger for spiritual and aesthetic values which most free countries do not know. The immorality of official policy generated its own moral antibodies. With time, the most determined opposition hardened in the most educated circles of an increasingly educated society. (By 1979, 10 per cent of Soviet citizens possessed higher education.) 'Whether he wants it or not,' Vladimir Bukovsky once said, 'a Soviet citizen is in a state of permanent inner dialogue with the official propaganda.'[22] One of the earliest rebels was Andrei Sakharov, father of the Soviet H-bomb; one of the most eloquent was the Christian poet and prisoner Irina Ratushinskaya (b. 1954):

> And the sad tale of Russia
> (Maybe we are only dreaming?)
> Makes room for Mashka Mouse, and us and the radio set,
> On the clean page, not yet begun,
> Opening this long winter
> On tomorrow.[23]

Religious life in the USSR was kept to a minimum by systematic persecution. The Soviet state was officially atheistic; Khrushchev in particular launched militantly anti-religious campaigns; the religious education of children constituted a criminal offence. The Muslims of Tatarstan and Central Asia were the least active, and the least troubled. But the Russian Orthodox Church was shackled hand and foot. Its clergy were state pensioners, its hierarchy supervised by the KGB. The Uniate Church in Ukraine, banned in 1946, survived only in the catacombs. The Roman Catholic Church survived only in Lithuania, its clergy decimated by assaults and deportations. With time, numerous Protestant and fundamentalist sects, especially Baptists and Adventists, came to be well represented. Judaism attracted harassment as soon as it showed signs of revival in the 1970s. In the decay of the Soviet ethos, the religious factor cannot be overrated.[24]

There have been many attempts to characterize the essential qualities of Soviet communism. Many outsiders have stressed the gulf between theory and practice—as if the theory were genuine and the practice faulty. Yet there is a rich literature to show how intelligent communists came to realize that the theory itself was fraudulent. Leninist, Stalinist, and post-Stalinist communism always paid tribute to Marx and Engels. But they bore the same relation to intellectual Marxism that South Sea 'cargo cults', which worshipped American presidents as gods, bore to American democracy. From a very early stage, communism had no more serious goal than keeping itself in existence. Its heart was mendacity.[25]

In most essential respects, the eight East European countries that were incorporated into the Soviet bloc (but not into the Soviet Union) followed a similar pattern of development to the USSR itself. Poland, Hungary, Czechoslovakia, East Germany, Romania, Bulgaria, Yugoslavia, and Albania all passed through phases characterized by stalinization (after 1948), and de-stalinization (at various points after 1953). Most of them were subsequently subjected to 'normalization', that is, the reimposition of Brezhnevian norms after an episode of open defiance. Most of them belonged to the Soviet Union's military 'alliance', the Warsaw Pact, or to the Soviet Union's parallel economic organization, CMEA or Comecon. All of them were ruled by communist dictatorships which had learned their trade under Soviet tutelage, which justified their existence by reference to the same Leninist ideology, and which, with two exceptions, continued to owe allegiance to Moscow.

Of course, there were important variations and important synchronic dissonances. In the mid-1960s, for example, there were some countries like Czechoslovakia which had not yet reached de-stalinization, whilst others, like Hungary, had already passed through both de-stalinization and normalization. Generally speaking, since their exposure to Soviet methods was shorter—40 years in Eastern Europe as opposed to 70 years within the Soviet Union—the degree of 'sovietization' was much lower. Historians disagree over whether to emphasize the differences or the similarities. The fact remains, however, that the historical experience of those eight countries in the four post-war decades was tied to that of the Soviet Union and was fundamentally different from that of Western Europe. They were all subsumed in the category of 'People's Democracies', which by no stretch of the imagination could be described either as popular or as democratic.

In the first, Stalinist phase (1945–53), all the countries of Eastern Europe were forced to accept the type of system then prevalent in the USSR. In the immediate post-war years Stalin had insisted on close control only in the Soviet zone of Germany, in Poland, and in Romania. Elsewhere, whilst building communist influence, he had not insisted on rigid conformity. But from 1948 discipline was tightened: all chinks in the Iron Curtain were to be sealed in response to the

Truman Doctrine. All the main features of late Stalinism were to be ruthlessly enforced wherever they did not already exist. Cohorts of Soviet 'advisers' and specialists were integrated into the local apparatus to ensure standardization and obedience.

In this new galaxy, Stalin remained 'the sun of unsurpassed radiance'. But in each of the countries a string of lesser suns, of little local Stalins, was put into orbit. Bierut, Gottwald, Rákosi, Ulbricht, Georghiu Dej, Zhivkov, Tito, and Enver Hoxha were all Moscow-trained Stalinist clones. To call them 'puppets' was to flatter.

Yugoslavia was the only country where obedience to Moscow was rejected at an early stage. Josip Broz, or Tito (1892–1980), a Croat, was in the unique position of having spent the war in his own country, of possessing ties with the Western Powers, and of setting up his regime without Soviet assistance. He was a Stalinist, with a nasty record of repressions. His multinational federation, dominated by Serbia, was closely modelled on the Soviet Union dominated by Russia, with all nationality problems effectively suppressed. The Federated People's Republic of Yugoslavia had come into being in 1945. Its Constitution, defining the powers of the ruling League of Yugoslav Communists and of the six constituent republics, had been functioning since January 1946. But Tito had built an independent base, and was not inclined to take orders. He did not favour collectivized agriculture, and he was interested in workers' self-management. So, when criticized by Cominform, he made no effort to mend his ways. In June 1948 he and his party were expelled; for several years they lived under the threat of Soviet punishment. They remained what many believed impossible, both communist and independent—proof that there was life after defying Stalin. Belgrade made its peace with Moscow during Khrushchev's visit in 1955. But it never joined either the CMEA or the Warsaw Pact. Having left the Soviet bloc, it was free to take a prominent lead in the movement of non-aligned states.

East Germany joined the Soviet bloc as Yugoslavia was leaving it. Political affairs in the Soviet zone had been conducted on the hopeful assumption that foundations were being laid for a united communist Germany. The failure of the Berlin blockade and the declaration of the Federal Republic showed that such hopes were false. The German Democratic Republic (DDR) was formally constituted on 7 October 1949, five months after the FRG. As in Poland, the DDR's constitution arranged for the ruling communist party (SED) to work in conjunction with a number of satellite parties operating within the communists' Front of National Unity. The first elections gave the Front a vote of 99 per cent. The Soviet occupation forces reserved important powers for themselves. The collectivization of agriculture was delayed until 1953, since the SED had only just implemented a massive land reform in favour of peasant ownership. The principal problem lay in the constant haemorrhage of escapees: for a dozen years, anyone could reach West Berlin by taking the U-bahn train from Friedrichstrasse to the Tiergarten. Over those dozen years, 1949–61, thousands of people availed themselves of the opportunity. The DDR was the only state in Europe with a declining population.

The Council for Mutual Economic Assistance (CMEA), better known as Comecon, was founded on 8 January 1949 in Moscow, where its Secretariat remained. The founding members were joined by Albania (1949), the DDR (1950), Mongolia (1962), and Cuba (1972). At this stage, its main function was to assist in the theory and practice of 'building socialism' by Soviet methods.

It is an open question how far the People's Democracies were formally integrated into Soviet structures. But it would have been uncharacteristic if their dependence had been left to chance. The main clues must be found in the inimitable mechanisms of inter-party controls. If 'socialist internationalism' meant anything, it meant that the CPSU could control the affairs of the fraternal parties, who in turn controlled the republics for which they were responsible. The International Department of the CPSU's central Secretariat was specially entrusted with this vital task; and each of its 'bureaux' were charged with overseeing the internal affairs of a particular country. Through its channels, all the leading posts in the fraternal parties could be subordinated to the *nomenklatura* system of the 'higher organs' in Moscow; and Soviet agents could be placed at will into key positions throughout the bloc. In effect, the Soviet Politburo could appoint all the other politburos. The KGB could run all the other communist security services, and *Glavpolit* all the General Staffs of the emerging People's Armies. For several years after 1945 Stalin did not wish his clients to have large military forces of their own; and expansion did not begin until after 1948. Soviet military advisers exercised such direct control that the need for a formal military alliance to match NATO did not yet arise.

The most obvious sign of Stalinism taking hold was seen in the series of purges and show trials that smote the leadership of the fraternal parties after June 1948. Stalin put the East European comrades through the same 'meat-grinder' that he had once used on the CPSU. In Warsaw, the founding congress of the PZPR in December 1948 saw the grovelling self-criticism of Władysław Gomułka, before charges of 'national deviation'. In Sofia, Traichov Kostov, the Deputy Prime Minister, was tried and executed on charges of Titoism. In Tirana, Koci Dzodze was sentenced to death for allegedly plotting to give Albania to Yugoslavia. In Budapest, the Foreign Minister, László Rajk, was tried and executed. In Prague, after years of slurs and test trials, the finger was pointed directly at General Secretary Rudolf Slánský. At Slánský's trial in November 1952, in which 11 of 14 defendants were Jewish, charges of Zionism were added to the more usual ones of Titoism, Trotskyism, anti-Sovietism and foreign espionage.

In the second, post-Stalinist phase (1953–68), the Soviet satellites worked their way towards a stage that has been variously labelled as 'national communism' or 'polycentrism'. Each of the fraternal parties was to claim the right to fix its own separate 'road to socialism'. The CPSU reserved the right to intervene by force if the gains of socialism were in danger. 'Gains of socialism' was a codeword for communist monopoly power and for loyalty to the Kremlin.

In the climate of uncertainty fostered by the in-fighting of Moscow's collective leadership, the more courageous elements took matters into their own hands. On 17 June 1953 workers in East Berlin staged demonstrations that threatened open rebellion. They were mercilessly crushed by Soviet tanks. A similar outburst occurred in Plsen in Czechoslovakia. Popular protest still lay beyond the pale of the tolerable. In Poland, the Party quietly dropped several keystone policies. Forcible collectivization was halted; the hated Soviet-run Ministry of Security was replaced; jailed Party leaders, and the jailed Primate, were released. A communist poet was allowed to publish a *Poem for Adults* which daringly stated that life was less than perfect:

> They ran to us shouting
> 'Under Socialism
> A cut finger doesn't hurt.'
> But they felt pain.
> They lost faith.
>
> . . .
>
> There are overworked people . . .
> There are Polish apples unavailable for children . . .
> There are girls forced to tell lies . . .
> There are people slandered and spat on,
> assaulted on the streets
> by common hoodlums undefined by the law . . .[26]

The Warsaw Pact came into being on 14 May 1955. The armies of the People's Democracies had been growing for seven years; and the point had been reached where the native officer corps had to assume greater responsibility. Thanks to the integrated political structures, the Warsaw Pact was not a genuine alliance of free and equal partners; none of the members' armies had the capacity for independent action. But there were obvious military advantages in standardized weaponry and joint training; and a strong gesture was made to national pride. A strong signal was sent to NATO against the admission of West Germany.

The critical year proved to be 1956. Khrushchev's Speech at the XXth Congress inevitably propelled a shock-wave right across Eastern Europe. The fraternal parties had to come to terms with Stalin's crimes against them. The Polish delegation, for example, which leaked the proceedings to the Western press, learned that the entire leadership of the pre-war Polish communist movement had been murdered on imaginary charges. Bierut died of a heart attack on the spot. By the summer, developments were reaching boiling point. Popular unrest welled up, as the old guard of the ruling parties was rocked by demands of would-be reformers. In Poznań, in June, 53 workers were killed when the Polish army fired on demonstrators carrying banners demanding 'Bread and Freedom' and 'Russians Go Home'. In October, first in Warsaw and then in Budapest, two fraternal parties took the momentous step of changing the composition of their politburos without first clearing their choice in Moscow.

Khrushchev's management of the East European crisis was facilitated by its coincidence with the presidential election in the USA and with the Suez Crisis. The Western Powers were distracted by their differences over the Middle East; the USSR was left with a free hand in Warsaw and Budapest.

On Sunday 21 October an apoplectic Khrushchev flew into Warsaw unannounced. He found the city ringed with Polish commandos in full battle gear and the Polish leadership steadfast in its support for Władysław Gomułka. (Later rumour held that the Polish army had planned to break through East Germany into NATO lines.) Two days of talks showed that Gomułka's 'Polish Road to socialism' was not inimical to basic Soviet interests, and that open warfare with his largest, and reputedly most courageous, ally was not exactly desirable. So Khrushchev backed down—agreeing that Gomułka's election as General Secretary should stand, and that Marshal Rokossowski and his advisers should be withdrawn. For a spell, Gomułka basked in the glow of being Poland's one and only popular communist leader.

In Budapest, events took the fatal turn which might so easily have afflicted Warsaw. Khrushchev was anxious that his generosity to the Yugoslavs, and now to the Poles, should not be construed as a sign of general weakness. The suppression of Hungary posed fewer military problems than action in Poland. And the Hungarian comrades, unlike the Poles, were deeply divided. On the night of 23–4 October, at the exact moment that the Polish crisis was defused, the Hungarian Party's Stalinist Secretary and security chief, Ernő Gerő, Rákosi's successor, called for Soviet military intervention to save him from dismissal. Hungary was battered into submission in less than a month. At first it seemed that an accommodation would be reached. The Soviet Army retreated from the capital; the Soviet Ambassador, Yuri Andropov, abandoned Gerő and approved his replacement by János Kádár—a loyal communist who, like Gomułka, had suffered Stalinist persecution. This seemed to check the progress of Imre Nagy, the leader of the Party's reformist faction, who had emerged as Prime Minister. The Soviet Army's final departure was said to be under negotiation. Khrushchev was making a second visit to Tito at Brioni. But then Nagy admitted several non-communists into his government, breaking the communist monopoly. The release of the Primate, Cardinal Mindszenty, sparked enthusiastic demonstrations, followed by ugly attacks on the hated security police. On 2 November popular pressure pushed the Government into appealing for assistance from the United Nations, and announcing Hungary's withdrawal from the Warsaw Pact. At dawn on the 4th, Soviet armoured divisions poured back into Budapest without warning. For ten days, heroic youths fought the tanks with their bare hands. Blood flowed copiously. Nagy took refuge in the Yugoslav embassy, which he left on a Soviet safe-conduct, only to be promptly arrested. In due course, after incarceration in Romania, he and 2,000 followers were shot. Hundreds of thousands of refugees flooded into Austria. The final toll of casualties reached similar proportions. Hungary was left in the hands of Andropov's client, Kádár, and a 'revolutionary government of workers and peasants'.

Hungary's national rising left an indelible stain on the Soviet record. It showed the world that communism was impervious to popular demands. It destroyed the lingering sympathies of many leftists, ruined the future for communist parties in the West, and greatly increased the tensions of the Cold War. In the Soviet bloc itself, it offended Mao Zedong, who favoured national variants of communism, and who had tried to intercede on behalf of Gomułka and Nagy. It also provided the impetus for a new general economic strategy, of which the victors of Budapest, Andropov and Kádár, were among the chief proponents. But its lessons were not learned by everyone. Czechoslovakia had to go through a similar ordeal before the rules of the post-Stalinist game were fully understood.

The Sino-Soviet split, when it came in 1960, had direct repercussions in only one European country, Albania. Like the Chinese, the Albanian comrades had important reservations about de-stalinization. What is more, since they had been cut off by Tito's break with Stalin and did not possess a frontier with the rest of the bloc, they were shielded from Soviet intervention. So they took the 'Chinese Road': Tirana shifted its loyalties from Moscow to Peking. It remained fully Stalinist, totally collectivized and atheized, utterly isolated, and at odds with all its neighbours. Nothing was to change until 1990. 'The only religion in Albania', declared Enver Hoxha, 'is being an Albanian.' [**SHQIPERIA**]

The new Soviet economic strategy of the 1960s was adopted partly in imitation of the EEC and partly in recognition of the shortcomings of existing Stalinist methods. One development was to raise the profile of the CMEA as the co-ordinator of joint planning. The CMEA allocated specialized tasks to each member country, and put great store on the dissemination of modern science and technology. This satisfied everyone, except Romania. But the main pilot scheme was launched in Hungary. Andropov, now head of the CPSU's International Department, and Kádár both realized that the reign of terror which followed the Hungarian rising had created an opening for intelligent economic experimentation. Economic reform could proceed without the threat of political turbulence. 'Goulash communism' would cure well-fed citizens of their dreams of liberty. The main idea was to introduce limited market mechanisms into a system still controlled by the state, and to encourage enterprise, especially in agriculture, by relaxing controls on compulsory deliveries and land ownership. Results came swiftly: by the mid-1960s Hungary's prosperity was leading people to forget its political misery. Budapest was a city of thriving restaurants, groaning shelves, and no politics. 'Kadarization' seemed to offer an attractive compromise between communism and capitalism, especially to Western economists with no political sense.

Three countries failed to react to the developing trends—each for different reasons.

The German Democratic Republic was the most unnatural of all the People's Democracies. Its rigid ideological conformism and excessive pro-Sovietism were fostered by the Stasi, a security apparatus of fearful reputation. It was blighted by the continuing division of Berlin, by the presence of nearly 40 divisions of Soviet occupation troops, above all by the steady exodus of its citizens. On 13 August 1961 all the crossings between East and West Berlin were sealed. For the next 28 years the Berlin Wall turned the DDR into a cage, the most visible symbol of communist oppression in Europe. All thoughts of a united Germany were dropped in favour of a theory that East Germany was inhabited by a separate nation with separate traditions. Great efforts were made to force the pace of heavy industrialization, and to win international recognition through massive state sponsorship of Olympic sport. By the time that Ulbricht gave way as General Secretary to Erich Honecker in 1971, a *modus vivendi* was about to be reached with West Germany. Yet the spirit of the 1950s lingered on in the DDR for 30 years. 'We so love Germany,' said one French minister with no little irony, 'we prefer there to be two of them.'

Romania jibbed against all the changes, but never forced an open breach. Nicolae Ceausescu (1918–89), who became General Secretary of the Romanian League of Communists in 1965, pursued a line that was as eccentric as it was disreputable. As *Conducător* he created a neo-Stalinist cult of personality and a brand of nepotistic despotism that was well described as 'socialism in one family'. He invented a constitution announcing Romania's arrival in the highest 'socialist' stage of development, whilst keeping his people in fear and beggary. His dreaded *Securitate* made the KGB of the epoch look like real gentlemen. He gained a minimum of diplomatic leverage by balancing between Moscow and Peking; and he gained a measure of (undeserved) Western admiration by recognizing Israel and by staying on the margins of the CMEA and the Warsaw Pact. He stayed at Buckingham Palace, with his own taster, and, on the advice of the Foreign Office, was knighted by the Queen of England. Romania has been aptly called the North Korea of Eastern Europe—a closed country acutely aware of its inferiority, excessively proud of its dubious record, and instinctively given to acting as mediator between other Mafia gangs.

Bulgaria competed with East Germany for the laurels of grim immobility. Industrialization started late, as did the state's exploitation of tourism and the wine trade. The Party leader, Todor Zhivkov, held the country on its slavishly pro-Soviet course from 1954 to 1990.

Czechoslovakia resisted de-stalinization until January 1968. The rule of Antonin Novotny, General Secretary since Gottwald's death in 1953, paid no attention to political relaxation in Poland on one side or to the economic reforms in Hungary on the other. He was finally overturned by a coalition in the Politburo of Slovaks disgruntled with Czech dominance and Czechs eager for systemic reform. The new leader, Alexander Dubček (1927–93), was a mild-mannered Slovak communist, the only General Secretary in the history of the bloc to be endowed with smiling eyes. True to character, he declared for 'socialism with a human face'.

The Prague Spring burst into bud with intoxicating vigour. Dubček and his team were planning the imposition of reforms from above. But they suspended censorship at an early stage, and the populace was brought into the frenzy of joyful debate. They were the first communist planners to realize that psychological incentives had to be mobilized if reforms were to really prosper. In their April programme they foresaw a stronger role for the State National Assembly. Nineteen years later, when Mikhail Gorbachev's spokesman was asked what was the difference between the Prague Spring and Gorbachev's programme of *perestroika*, he answered 'nineteen years'. The Czechoslovak experiment struggled against the odds for barely seven months. At first, it seemed that an accommodation could be reached. The Soviet comrades expressed concern over alleged excesses, such as the freedom of the media. The Czechoslovak Government affirmed its commitment to socialism, its friendship for the USSR, and its determination to stay in the Warsaw Pact. Yet in July threatening Warsaw Pact manœuvres were held throughout the country, and a personal meeting between Brezhnev and Dubček and their politburo members was held at the frontier village of Černá-nad-Tisou. After that, the manœuvres were halted and the troops withdrawn.

At dawn on 21 August 1968, half a million soldiers drawn from all the Warsaw Pact countries except Romania poured back into Czechoslovakia without warning—Poles alongside grey-uniformed East Germans from the north, Hungarians and Bulgarians from the south, Soviet divisions via Poland and Ukraine in the east. The surprise and the saturation were overwhelming; resistance was minimal. Dubček was flown to Russia in chains; the reforms were halted. Czechoslovakia's frontiers were to be permanently guarded by the Warsaw Pact. In due course Dubček was replaced by Gustáv Husák, an old-timer who, like Gomułka and Kádár, had kept the faith despite bitter personal memories of Stalinism. When it was all over, Brezhnev spelled out the Soviet position at a summit meeting of bloc leaders in Warsaw in November 1968. The Brezhnev Doctrine stated in the clearest terms that Moscow was obliged by its socialist duty to intervene by force to defend the 'socialist gains' of its allies. East Berlin (1953), Budapest (1956), and Prague (1968) were all of a piece. There had been no fundamental progress. The members of the Soviet bloc were not sovereign states.

The invasion of Czechoslovakia was far less brutal than the suppression of the Hungarian Rising. But it unfolded on the world's television screens; and its impact on world opinion was enormous. It was condemned by several communist Parties. China called it 'barefaced fascist power politics', Yugoslavia called it 'illegal occupation', Romania 'a flagrant violation of national sovereignty'. It promised an unending ice age in Europe. Few people who heard it would forget the crackling voice from the last free broadcast from Radio Prague: 'Please remember Czechoslovakia when we are no longer in the news.'

In the third, Brezhnevian phase (1968–85), the Soviet bloc saw the norms laid down by the Brezhnev Doctrine progressively challenged by a growing tide of intellectual, social, and eventually political protest. All the levers of power were in the hands of the communist authorities; so opposition had to find new, non-violent channels. The principal exemplar of 'normalization' was Czechoslovakia. The principal challenger was Poland.

Czechoslovak normalization was a sorry spectacle indeed. Husák used all the petty tyranny of the Party's social controls to destroy the soul of the Prague Spring. There were no shootings or show trials, but the despair of the young student Jan Palách, who burned himself to death in public, caught the national mood.

Ex-ministers and academics were sent to work in the most menial jobs— Dubček worked as a forestry inspector. Police harassment was universal. Prague, Europe's most beautiful city, was also the most depressed. A decade passed before a lonely band of dissidents around the playwright Václav Havel put their names to 'Charter 77'—a declaration of human rights.

Compartmentalization was a central feature of the Soviet bloc in its later stages. Despite continuing lip-service to 'socialist internationalism', the bloc was divided up into a series of watertight compartments. National communism encouraged conditions where each country, whilst closely connected to Moscow, was effectively insulated from the others. The cordon separating Poland from Lithuania or Ukraine or, after 1968, from Czechoslovakia was every bit as severe as the Iron Curtain itself. The arrest of the *Taternicy*—a group of athletic dissidents backpacking with banned literature over the snowy ridges of the Tatra mountains— well illustrated the state of affairs. East Europeans were often more familiar with life in Western Europe or the USA than with their immediate neighbours.

The Polish People's Republic (PRL) displayed an unusual number of idiosyncrasies. It was the largest of the Soviet satellites, with an army larger than that of Great Britain. Both structurally and psychologically it was the least sovietized. The Polish peasantry had successfully resisted collectivization; the Polish Bar had resisted the communist monopoly; the Polish intelligentsia had largely avoided Marxism. The pseudo-pluralism of the Front of National Unity permitted a margin of non-Party politics. Most importantly, the Roman Catholic Church under its formidable Primate, Stefan Cardinal Wyszyński (1901–81), never submitted, as elsewhere, to political control. By an agreement of December 1956 the Church hierarchy was granted full autonomy, so long as Party rule was not openly subverted. The calculation of the Party's sociologists had presumably been that the rapid modernization which was turning Poland into an industrial power would rapidly undermine religion. In fact it was the Church which kept the loyalty of the new proletariat, which in turn undermined the Party.

Poland's cycle of opposition and normalization occupied a quarter of a century. Gomułka passed rapidly from national hero to crabbed old boss. In the mid-1960s he repressed the Marxist intellectuals, in March 1968 the students, in 1970 bloody workers' protests in the Baltic ports. In 1968 the challenge of an ultranationalist faction within the Party, whose bid for power had targeted the Jewish element in the Party apparatus, grew into a generalized and shameful 'anti-Zionist campaign', provoking the exodus of almost all of Poland's remaining Jews. In the 1970s the ten-year reign of Edward Gierek adopted a strategy of '*bigos* communism' funded by excessive Western loans. A brief interval of prosperity preceded renewed austerity, mass protests, and, in the Workers Defence

Committee (KOR), the formation of a consolidated intellectual and workers' opposition, the precursor of 'Solidarity'. In June 1979 the visit of a Polish Pope created a moral climate pregnant for change.

The Solidarity trade union grew from a group of determined strikers in the Gdańsk shipyards in August 1980. It was led by an unknown, unemployed electrician on his 'wolf's ticket', Lech Wałęsa. It swelled into a nation-wide social protest, millions strong. Dedicated to non-violence, it did not fight the communists; it simply organized itself without them. The only independent organization in the Soviet bloc, it won the formal right to strike and to recruit members. Party members defected in droves. Within a year, Solidarity threatened to topple the existing order without even trying. From Moscow's viewpoint, it had to be suppressed. A non-communist workers' movement was anathema. The ailing Brezhnev put the Soviet Army on alert, then left the job to the Polish army. On the night of 13 December 1981, aided by deep snow, General Wojciech Jaruzelski executed the most perfect military coup in modern European history. In a few hours, 40–50,000 Solidarity activists were arrested; all communications were cut and military commissars took over all major institutions. Martial law paralysed the country. In 1982, having imposed stability, Jaruzelski introduced the first stage of economic reform. The victory of communist 'normalization' appeared complete. In reality, it was the hollowest of victories. Within seven years, Jaruzelski would be at the end of his tether. History must give the Poles the principal credit for bringing the Soviet bloc to its knees.

Despite appearances, Jaruzelski's emergence in Poland could later be seen as the first emanation of a reforming trend that was about to break surface in Moscow itself. This trend, which in due course would acquire the Russian name of *perestroika* or 'restructuring', was founded on the realization that the system was profoundly sick. Significantly, it came out of the KGB, the only body which had the means to know what was really happening. Jaruzelski had served for 25 years as head of the Polish army's military-political department. He was necessarily a client of the man who ran the KGB throughout the 1970s. He was 'playing John the Baptist' to Andropov's other protégé, Mikhail Gorbachev. With Gorbachev's collusion, he was destined to turn Poland into 'the laboratory of *perestroika*'.

By the early 1980s the internal operations of the Soviet bloc were no longer achieving their goals. Forty years of corrosion had sapped their strength. On the surface, everything was in place; underneath, little was working well. In the age of the inter-continental ballistic missile (ICBM), the territory of the Warsaw Pact could no longer serve as an effective security buffer. In the age of high oil prices, the CMEA was draining more from the USSR than it was putting in. In the age of television, the gulf in living conditions between East and West was evident in every home. As Solidarity showed, the workers had no respect for the 'workers' state'. Important sectors of the Communist élite were losing the will to rule. One of Jaruzelski's closest aides had chosen the patriotic course of feeding the CIA over a decade with the biggest flood of operational documents from the Warsaw Pact in the history of espionage.[27]

It is the career of Yuri Andropov, however, which provides the key to the extraordinary change of direction which preceded and then precipitated the collapse of the Soviet system. As ambassador in Budapest, Andropov had been co-author of the strategy of substituting economic for political reform. As head of the international department of the CPSU he must have known that the costly revolts which had beset Hungary, Czechoslovakia, and now Poland could spread to the Soviet Union. As head of the KGB during the era of *détente* (see p. 1115), he was the person best placed to see the glaring contrast between external strength and internal decay. In the 1970s Andropov had waged a cunning and flexible campaign of persecution against Soviet dissenters. He had no need to use mass terror; instead, he curtailed their access to the population at large, whilst consigning the obdurate to psychiatric hospitals or to foreign exile. He countered the growing disaffection of Soviet Jewry by giving them preferential access to emigration. As the files passed over his desk, he could only have wondered why the finest talents in the land had no love for communism. The list was a long one: Solzhenitsyn the political novelist, Nureyev the dancer, Rostropovich the cellist, Sakharov the physicist, the indomitable Bukovsky, a biologist, Andrei Amalrik, the mathematician who had written, after Orwell, *Will the Soviet Union Survive until 1984?* These people must necessarily have figured prominently in Andropov's long talks with the bright young Party Secretary from Stavropol who attended him at the nearby spa where he stayed to treat his kidneys.

Andropov's penchant for reform, however, was repeatedly baulked. The Soviet Politburo was packed with guardians of the *status quo*. Gorbachev was brought in from Stavropol in 1979 only to be given the thankless task of running Soviet agriculture. Andropov did not reach the top until his own terminal illness was upon him. His death gave the Brezhnevites a final lease of inaction. Despite Amalrik's prediction, 1984 came and went; the Soviet Empire survived unreformed.

East–West Relations: The Cold War in Europe, 1948–1989

From start to finish, the Cold War was focused on Europe. Its dynamic developed from the collapse of the 'Great Triangle' of European Powers, which had left the victorious Western Allies face to face with a victorious Soviet Union (see p. 1312). It grew from the inability of the wartime allies to reach agreement on the independence of Poland, on the future of Germany, and on the division of Europe as a whole. There can be some debate as to when exactly it began; but it came to a head through the American commitment to Europe, as expressed in the Truman Doctrine and the Marshall Plan of 1947, and through subsequent expressions of Soviet disapproval. It was clearly in progress during the Soviet blockade of Berlin in 1948–9 which led to the formation of NATO; and it did not end until the Iron Curtain in Europe was breached 40 years later. None the less, it is important to stress that the Cold War soon overreached its European focus. There was always an Asian component; and there was a strong inner logic resulting from Soviet–American rivalry which turned it into a truly global confrontation.

The Asian component developed over disagreements parallel to those that occurred in Europe. In this case the Soviet Union entered the scene in August 1945, when the Soviet army was thrown into the final campaign of the Pacific War against Japan. The Yalta Agreement had made provision for the Soviets to occupy the Kurile Islands as the price for Stalin's participation. But no one at Yalta had foreseen the sudden and total collapse of Japan, brought about by the US atomic bombs dropped on Hiroshima and Nagasaki. In the event, the Soviets were given an altogether unexpected bonus. They rapidly occupied Manchuria, whence they carried off 600,000 men of the Kwantung army into the Siberian camps. In addition to the main Kurile chain, they seized four northern Japanese islands, hitherto regarded as part of Hokkaido, renamed them the 'Lesser Kuriles', and turned the Sea of Okhotsk into a strategic Soviet lake. What is more, they openly championed the cause of communist revolutionaries in China and Korea, to which they now had direct access. In China, they were taking sides against America's long-standing client, Chiang Kai-shek, who had been part of the Grand Alliance throughout the war with Japan. By the time that Mao Zedong entered Beijing in 1949, a 'Bamboo Curtain' was rising in the Far East to match the Iron Curtain in Europe.

The globalization of the Cold War took place in the course of the 1950s. In its geopolitical aspect, this was the natural outcome of a confrontation that pitted one power which dominated the land mass of Eurasia against another which could project land, sea, and air forces to all parts of the world. In its political, economic, and ideological aspects it reflected the rivalry of one bloc with pretensions to the worldwide patronage of communist-led revolution and another wedded to democracy, capitalism, and free trade. It was fuelled by the contemporary process of decolonization, which left a string of unstable, ex-colonial countries open to wars by proxy, and where, as in the oil-rich Middle East, valuable resources presented irresistible temptations. It was finalized in the late 1950s by the invention of ICBMs, which put the whole earth within the range of constant surveillance and instant nuclear attack. Henceforth, the cities of the Russian and American heartlands found themselves in the front line no less than Taiwan or Berlin.

In the military field, the Cold War passed through several distinct phases. In the 1950s, when the USA held a decisive lead both in its nuclear arsenal and in the means of airborne delivery, the Soviets could not risk a major clash. At the Moscow meeting in January 1951, whilst the Americans were tied down in Korea, the leaders of the Soviet bloc were apparently given orders by Stalin to prepare for the Third World War. But the plans were never put into effect.[28] First Britain (1952) then France (1960) developed independent nuclear capacity; and NATO professed a doctrine of 'overwhelming retaliation'. Two communist proxy wars were fought—one against an American-led UN force in Korea in 1950–1, the other in Indo-China, where defeated French troops gave way to the Americans in 1954. Europe, though bristling with weapons in two armed camps, did not erupt.

In the late 1950s the game changed. Thanks to the Sputnik (1958) and the U2 incident (1960), the Kremlin was able to demonstrate that its rocketry had more than closed the technological gap. The superpowers poured vast resources into the 'Space Race' and into the deployment of earth satellites and ICBMs. Although the USA won the competition to put a man on the moon, there was no certainty where the true military advantage lay. The USSR seemed to be building a remorseless superiority in nuclear, conventional, and naval forces. But the advent of 'tactical' and later of 'battlefield' nuclear weapons, coupled with NATO's new doctrine of 'flexible response', rendered any purely quantitative calculations redundant. Pressure on the European theatre was somewhat relieved by the knowledge that the main exchange of ICBMs, if it happened, would be directed over the North Pole. Stalemate was reached at maximal levels of military spending. The offensive doctrines adopted by the Warsaw Pact were not put into practice; the vastly expanded Soviet Fleet was not put to the test; massive rearmament proceeded alongside repeated and much feebler attempts at disarmament. But once again the European conflict stayed cold.

In the 1980s another turn of the screw was reached with the deployment of a more deadly generation of weapons, notably Soviet SS-20s, and American Pershing 2 and Cruise missiles. In 1983 President Reagan's announcement of the multi-billion-dollar Strategic Defence Initiative (SDI), commonly known as 'Star Wars'—a space-based anti-ICBM defence system—openly challenged Moscow to a race that simply could not be run. Each side possessed the kilotonnes to destroy the planet many times over; neither side could possibly use them. Advocates of the nuclear deterrent believed strongly that their point was being made. Their opponents—who could only speak freely in the West—believed with equal passion that the military planners, like Dr Strangelove, had gone mad. But the *Pax atomica* held.

With some slight delay, the political rhythms of the Cold War usually followed military developments. Tensions were highest in the late 1950s, since both sides could pursue their cause with convictions unsullied by failure. They reached their peak in the Cuban missile crisis of October 1962. In the 1960s, despite numerous alarms, both sides lost their expectations of a simple victory. International communism was all but paralysed by the Sino-Soviet split which in 1969 came close to a pre-emptive nuclear strike against Beijing; the mighty USA was immensely disheartened by its inability to coerce the diminutive state of Vietnam; and NATO was profoundly disrupted by de Gaulle. In the 1970s, therefore, both Soviets and Americans felt sufficiently contrite to give greater emphasis to the process that was cleverly labelled *détente*. The initial Strategic Arms Limitation Talks (SALT) at Vienna were soon joined by political discussions leading to the Helsinki Final Act of 1975. In the 1980s tensions rose again after the Soviet invasion of Afghanistan (1979)—the Kremlin's Vietnam—and the declaration of martial law in Poland (1981). At all stages, in fact, one could observe a subtle mixture of threats and relaxations. There were early moments of *détente* in the coldest years of confrontation, and frigid intervals in the so-called era of *détente*. Certainly in

Europe, where no open warfare occurred in four decades, it is probably less accurate to talk of the Cold War than, in a French commentator's phrase, of the 'Hot Peace'. It was a fever which rose and fell many times.

Economic relations could never reach their potential levels. The West was reluctant to sell advanced technology of military value. The American COCOM list grew to contain many thousands of forbidden commercial items. The East, for its part, believed strongly in economic self-sufficiency, preferring backwardness to dependence on capitalist imports. By the late 1970s Soviet harvest failures regularly caused panic purchases of vast quantities of US grain, whilst 50 per cent of Soviet oil production was earmarked for loss-making trade within the CMEA.

Cultural relations remained conservative in scale and content. Tours by the Bolshoi Ballet and the Red Army Choir, or the Mazowsze folk dance ensemble, were exchanged for visits by various western orchestras or the Royal Shakespeare Company. The Soviet bloc countries set great store by the Olympic Games, where their state-sponsored athletes performed very well. Sport was used as a political instrument, most openly by the US boycott of the Moscow Games in 1980, and Soviet retaliation at Los Angeles in 1984.

Diplomatic relations were beset by obstacles of all sorts. The Security Council of the UN was paralysed for 40 years, most frequently by the Soviet veto. The war of spies reached grotesque proportions: Western intelligence was penetrated at the highest levels by Soviet recruits in Britain, and by East German agents in Bonn. In the 1950s, in the era of Senator Joseph McCarthy, reasonable fears about the activities of communist agents in the USA caused a totally unreasonable witch-hunt. Successive American embassies in Moscow were so riddled with bugging devices that they had to be abandoned. There was no trust.

The origins of *détente* go right back to the start of the Cold War. Stalin once offered to permit the reunification of Germany in return for American disengagement. At the Geneva meeting in 1955 when President Eisenhower met Stalin's successors, the West was surprised again by far-reaching Soviet proposals for disarmament. 1959 saw Khrushchev at Camp David, and Macmillan, in Cossack hat, in Moscow. But the developing dialogue was withered by the U2 incident, by the second Berlin crisis, and, most severely, by the discovery of Soviet missiles in Cuba.

The U2 was a high-altitude American spy-plane, supposedly immune to attack. In 1960 a flight from Turkey was shot down over the Volga. Eisenhower was foolish enough to deny the existence of all such operations until Khrushchev produced the pilot and the damning evidence of his duties.

The Berlin crisis of 1961 had been brewing for years. The stream of refugees from East to West was gathering pace. Ten thousand crossed in the last week of July 1961 alone. The Kremlin had repeatedly threatened to sign a unilateral treaty with the DDR, and to terminate the rights of four-power occupation. The Soviets held overwhelming local military superiority. But the West made no move. Then, on 13 August 1961, the Wall was built. The young President Kennedy was being tested as never before. Privately relieved that the Wall had lessened the chances of a second Berlin blockade, he did not react militarily; instead, he staged a propaganda coup. Standing beside the Wall, he shouted defiantly in his inimitable Boston drawl, 'Ich bin ein Berliner'.*

The Cuban crisis of the following October brought the Cold War to the brink. Kennedy had come out of the Berlin crisis, and his earlier meeting with Khrushchev in Vienna, convinced of his failure to impress Moscow with America's determination. Next time, he had to give proof of firmness. He increased US commitments to South Vietnam. When aerial photography revealed the presence of Soviet missiles in Cuban silos only 90 miles off the coast of Florida, he decided that the Kremlin must be forced to back down. The only question was how. Washington rejected a surgical air strike in favour of putting Cuba into quarantine. For a week the world held its breath; then the Soviet missiles were withdrawn. The USA undertook to withdraw its own missiles from Turkey, and refrain from invading Cuba.[29]

Disarmament talks dragged on for decades. The Geneva offer foundered over Soviet refusals to allow inspection. In 1963 the Moscow Agreement banned nuclear testing in the atmosphere, but only after enormous damage had been caused to the global environment. The Nuclear Non-Proliferation Treaty of the same year, proposed by Britain, was designed to maintain the monopoly of the four existing nuclear powers and, in particular, to exclude China. It failed on all counts, except as a temporary brake. The first round of Strategic Arms Limitation Talks (SALT I) reached an interim conclusion in 1972 after four years. SALT II ground along until blocked by the US Congress in 1980. The further stage of trying to negotiate an absolute reduction in the size of military arsenals, as opposed to limiting their rate of increase, proceeded from the mid-1970s onwards. Talks on Mutual Balanced Force Reduction (MBFR), concerning conventional armaments, were located in Belgrade for fifteen years. The Strategic Arms Reduction Talks (START), concerning nuclear weapons, were located in Madrid from 1982. Thirty years of inter-governmental talking proved as impotent as the series of popular campaigns against nuclear weapons which attracted considerable support in the West in the early 1960s, and again in the early 1980s.

Direct European involvement in Cold War diplomacy inevitably took second place to the main US–Soviet confrontation. But it gradually asserted itself from the mid-1950s onwards. In 1957, with Soviet agreement, Poland presented the UN with the Rapacki Plan for a nuclear-free zone in central Europe, and in 1960 the Gomułka Plan for a nuclear freeze in the same area. Nothing much ensued. In 1965 the Polish Catholic bishops published an open letter to their counterparts in Germany, stating their readiness 'to forgive and to be forgiven'. This courageous initiative, denounced as traitorous by the communist governments, pointed a clear way forward through the moral fog of fear and hatred.

* Meaning 'I am a doughnut'. He should have said, 'Ich bin Berliner'.

Soviet policy in Eastern Europe played heavily on the German bogey, and communist propaganda made huge efforts to keep wartime germanophobia alive. In West Germany the strident voice of the expellees carried considerable weight with Christian Democrat governments; and the unregulated fate of their Eastern homelands only served to keep passions simmering. The prevailing political climate only began to thaw in the late 1960s, largely through the good offices of the German Churches, who thereby prepared the way for the *Ostpolitik* of Chancellor Willy Brandt.

The *Ostpolitik* or 'Eastern Policy', launched in 1969, was based on consistent short-term, mid-term, and long-term objectives. In the immediate situation, Brandt sought to break the deadlock in East–West relations which had set in after the invasion of Czechoslovakia. Ever since the full recognition of the Federal Republic, West Germany had pursued the so-called Hallstein Doctrine, refusing to deal with any government (except the USSR) which dealt with the DDR. The result had been almost total isolation from all of Germany's Eastern neighbours. After breaking the ice, Brandt then sought to establish a *modus vivendi* with the DDR, and with other members of the Soviet bloc. Over 10, 20, or perhaps 30 years, he hoped that growing intercourse between Western and Eastern Germany would soften the regime in East Berlin, and lead to eventual reconciliation. On the first two scores the *Ostpolitik* undoubtedly gained its objectives. On the third it had the opposite effect from that intended. Indeed, it is not certain that Brandt ever really expected Germany to be reunited. During his retirement, he admitted: 'Reunification is the lie of German political life.'

None the less, Willy Brandt's appearance on the international scene had a very considerable impact. Eastern Europe had not been conditioned to the idea of a German Chancellor who was a socialist with manifestly peaceful intentions. Born the illegitimate son of a Lübeck salesgirl, Brandt (Herbert Frahm, 1913–92) overcame every possible social disadvantage. Having lived in Norway during the war, and fought the Nazis, he had impeccable democratic credentials. What is more, as the Mayor of West Berlin from 1957 to 1963, he had gained a reputation for staunch resistance to communism. When he appeared in Moscow in August 1970, therefore, 25 years after the defeat of the Wehrmacht, he made a great impression. That December in Poland, where he fell to his knees before the memorial to the fighters of the Warsaw Ghetto, he made an emotional gesture that was long remembered. In East Berlin, his overtures could not be resisted. Within three years, he had forged a German–Soviet Treaty of Co-operation (1970), a German–Polish Treaty (1970) which drew the sting of Germany's lost territories, and in 1973 a treaty of mutual recognition with the DDR. The Iron Curtain and the Berlin Wall were not breached; indeed, they were given a new lease of life. The German problem had not been solved; but it had been fixed in a stable framework of minimal intercourse. Brandt's conservative opponents accused him of giving away Germany's birthright. 'One cannot give away something which has already been *gambled* away,' was his reply.

Historians will always debate whether West Germany's *Ostpolitik* served to prolong the division of Europe or whether, through humiliating compromise, it set the course which eventually led to reunification. The two interpretations are not, in fact, exclusive. It certainly set the tone for the next decade. By ending the boycott of the DDR, it involved the Federal Government in a great deal of expense with no visible return, and a large number of shady operations—such as the scandalous trade in political prisoners, which East Berlin sold off for royal ransoms. By defusing the threat-laden atmosphere of the late 1960s, it opened the way for 'the era of *détente*'.

Détente is a diplomatic term of the choicest ambiguity. For those who so wish, it can mean 'relaxation' or 'a mild spell of weather'. It is also the French word for the trigger of a gun. In the context of the 1970s it obviously signified the release of pressure; but whether that release was to have a benign or a deadly effect was entirely open to conjecture.

Apart from Bonn's *Ostpolitik* and the progress of SALT I, an important spur to *détente* must be found in distant China. In 1972 the American President, Richard Nixon, visited the ageing Chairman Mao, thereby 'playing the China card'. The bipolar structure of the Cold War was transformed into a new, triangular configuration made up of the Soviet bloc, China, and the West. The Soviet leaders, resigned to an uneasy stalemate with Beijing, felt constrained to stabilize their position in Europe. After all, 30 years after the triumph of Stalingrad the Soviet Union was still having to live without a formal settlement on its Western flank. Discussions started in 1970 and culminated in the Helsinki Conference on Security and Co-operation in Europe (CSCE), which ran on from 1973 to 1975.

From the Soviet viewpoint, the Helsinki Final Act took the place of the German Peace Treaty that never was. From the Western viewpoint, it marked a recognition that Soviet dominance of Eastern Europe could not be ended by force, and a decision to make the Soviets buy stability at a high political price. Basket One of the negotiations, on security issues, ended with an agreement to guarantee Europe's existing frontiers, except for peaceful changes by mutual consent. Basket Two contained measures for extending economic co-operation. Basket Three contained an agreement to promote a wide range of cultural and communication projects, and to guarantee human contacts. This was the political price-tag. From the day that the Final Act was signed in 1975, the regimes of the East had to choose between respecting their citizens' rights or being exposed for breaking their solemn undertakings.

The Helsinki Final Act was criticized by many as a capitulation to the Soviet conquest of Eastern Europe. At the same time, it gave formal encouragement to political dissent throughout the Soviet bloc. In Poland, it gave an early boost to KOR, the predecessor of Solidarity; in Czechoslovakia, to the Charter 77 group led by Václav Havel; and in the Soviet Union, to numerous 'Helsinki Watch Committees'. It was totally ignored by Andropov's KGB; but it was taken very seriously by the American administration of President Carter, who, in view of constant Soviet violations, saw no reason to disengage from Europe.

At the end of the 1970s three new faces appeared in the West. In 1978 a Slavonic Pope ascended the throne of St Peter, endowed with a vision of reuniting Christian Europe. In 1979 a woman of great fortitude moved into 10 Downing Street. She was soon to be dubbed, by the Kremlin, 'the Iron Lady'. In 1980 a retired film actor entered the Oval Office of the White House. The 'Great Communicator' was soon to call the Soviet Union 'the evil empire'. These three personalities breathed a new spirit into East–West relations. All three opposed communism on moral principle; all three were hugely popular in Eastern Europe—more so than in the West; all three looked unhappy with the accommodations of the previous decades. Reagan and Thatcher honed the twin-track policy of NATO, which held out the palm of peace whilst strengthening its military shield.

By the 1980s, hard experience had shown that the West had been suffering from three persistent illusions. It had been the vogue among political scientists to talk of 'convergence'—the idea that time would draw the political and economic systems of East and West closer together. This was pure make-believe. The gap was widening with every day that passed. It had also been judged appropriate to 'differentiate' between communist regimes according to their degree of subservience to Moscow. This policy had given the greatest favours to the most repressive of regimes, like that of Ceausescu. *Détente* had fostered a hypothesis that has been called 'ornithological'. The conduct of the communists, it was argued, was dependent on the good conduct of the West. Beastly comments in Western capitals would only encourage the 'hawks'; kindness would encourage the 'doves'. In practice, no such pattern emerged. No one had been subjected to such harsh words as Jaruzelski, yet he turned to reform. No one was offered so many sweeteners as Honecker—and Honecker remained as hawkish as ever. The fact is, the communists did not respond to kindness. As one of the earliest critics of *détente* had argued in his *Theses on Hope and Hopelessness*, raising the tension of East–West relations was a dangerous ploy; but it was the only strategy which held out a promise of ultimate success.[30]

In the midst of these divided counsels there appeared a new star in the East. In March 1985 Mikhail Sergeevich Gorbachev (b. 1931) emerged as the fourth General Secretary of the CPSU in three years. He was chosen by the Party apparatus, and had no democratic credentials. Yet, as a person, he was completely different; and he was the first Soviet leader to be untainted by a Stalinist record. He was affable, quick-witted, and spoke without notes. Here at last was a man, as Mrs Thatcher was quick to announce, 'with whom we can do business'.

Gorbachev's early months in office were taken up by reshufflings of the Politburo, by the ritual denunciation of previous leaders, and by an ominous campaign against corruption. But the style had obviously changed. The world waited to see if the content would change with it. Foreign policy offered a Soviet leader the most room for manœuvre. It was reasonable to assume, if Gorbachev moved, that he would first make a move on East–West relations.

The initial meetings between Gorbachev and Reagan were not specially productive. The newcomer was taking the old 'Star Warrior's' measure. But the burden of military spending was no secret; long preparations for a treaty on the reduction of Intermediate-range Nuclear Forces (INF) preceded the summit scheduled at Reykjavík, Iceland, for December 1987. Suddenly, in the middle of the talks at Reykjavík, Gorbachev struck without warning. He proposed a sensational 50 per cent cut in all nuclear weapons. Reagan reeled, recoiled, and regretted. The INF was signed; but the ultra-cautious, ultra-suspicious encounters of the past were over. This General Secretary seemed intent on stopping the Cold War in its tracks.

Shortly afterwards, an extraordinary incident served to puncture the balloon of East–West tensions. Air defence had been the burning military issue of the decade: it was the issue behind Cruise, and behind Star Wars itself, and it was costing multi-billions. Each side was terrified that the missiles and bombers of the other would find their target without response. The Soviet Union had attracted enormous opprobrium for building an unauthorized anti-IBM radar station at Krasnoyarsk, and for shooting down a South Korean passenger flight, KAL 007, which had strayed into Soviet air space. Yet all the expert anxieties of the world's military planners were cut down to size by the prank of a German schoolboy. On 28 May 1987, 19-year-old Matthias Rust piloted a tiny private monoplane up the Baltic from Hamburg, crossed the Soviet frontier in Latvia, flew at treetop level under the most concentrated air defences in the world, and landed on the cobblestones near Moscow's Red Square. Single-handed, he made the whole Cold War look ridiculous.

By the time of the Malta Summit in December 1989, Presidents Bush and Gorbachev felt free to announce that the Cold War had ended.

Integration and Disintegration, 1985–1991

For two or three years after Gorbachev's appearance, the main contours of Europe's political landscape remained untouched. In Western Europe the American presence was still a determining factor; and the horizons of the EEC were still confined to the economic sphere. In Eastern Europe people were still being shot for trying to cross the Iron Curtain. All the old immovables still held office—Honecker, Husák, Kádár, Ceausescu, Zhivkov, Hoxha. The 'Other Europe' was still 'the last colonial empire in existence'.[31] Even Gorbachev maintained a granite exterior. In November 1987 he presided over the 70th anniversary celebrations of the Bolshevik Revolution in traditional style. As late as May 1988 he was promoting the Orthodox millennium in Kiev in a spirit of Russian nationalism of which Stalin himself would have approved.

Yet Europe, both East and West, was fast approaching the brink of unforeseen transformations. As the clouds of the Cold War lifted, new, exciting vistas could be glimpsed on many fronts. Within two years of Gorbachev's disarmament offensive at Reykjavík, the Soviet Union had relinquished its grip on its satellites.

Within three years, political union was moving up the agenda in Western Europe. Within four years, the Soviet Union itself evaporated. As Western Europe integrated, Eastern Europe disintegrated.

No single individual, or individuals, can claim the credit for upheavals on such a scale. But two men found themselves promoted to positions at the centre of the swirling tides. One was Gorbachev; the other was the new President of the European Commission, Jacques Delors. Their enemies would say that both lacked a sense of realism—the reformer in pursuit of the unreformable, the integrator in charge of the unintegratable.

Jacques Delors (b. 1925), formerly French Finance Minister, presented the outward appearance of an archetypal technocrat. Born in Paris, he was at once a practising Catholic and a socialist, but had never visited the USA. But he was also a man with a mission, a true disciple of Monnet and Schuman, whose wider vision had lain dormant for 30 years. His opponents called him a Euro-fundamentalist. 'Europe will not be built at a stroke or according to a single plan,' Schuman had once remarked; 'it will be built through concrete achievements.' This summed up the Delors approach exactly. The principal instrument for his ambitions was the Single European Act (SEA). Two terms of office, 1985–9 and 1989–92, would be sufficient to see it through from conception to realization.

In the formal sense, the Single European Act could be regarded as nothing more than the contents of its text—an elaborate programme for the total abolition of barriers to trade and mobility within the EEC. As presented in 1985 and adopted by member states in 1986, its 282 chapters set out a long list of humdrum measures which would lead to a single unified market of 320 million customers by the end of 1992. It envisaged the removal of internal frontiers, free business competition, the standardization of consumer protection, the equalization of living standards, the mutual recognition of professional qualifications, the harmonization of VAT and other indirect taxes, and unified guidelines for television, broadcasting, and telecommunications. Article 148 introduced the principle of qualified majority voting in the executive Council of Ministers. Members' votes were to be weighted in the ratio of West Germany, France, Italy, and Britain (10 each), Spain (8), Belgium, Netherlands, Greece, Portugal (5 each), Denmark and Ireland (3 each), and Luxemburg (2). An effective majority was to require 54 of the 72 votes, or 75 per cent.

However, it was not hard to foresee that the SEA could be used as the Trojan Horse for more comprehensive plans. Once launched, there was every opportunity to argue that the single market could not be made viable without the abolition of still more barriers. This is indeed what happened: a chain reaction of demands set in for further financial, political, legal, and social integration. After two decades of very modest advance, the tempo of the EEC was quickening: the catch-word in Brussels was 'ça bouge' (it's moving). In 1987, as a sign of the times, the Community officially adopted the flag of the Council of Europe. Twelve golden stars on a deep blue ground no longer symbolized the starry ideals of Strasbourg. They now stood for the twelve member states in an expandable circle of perfect union.

The European Commission issued a growing flood of directives. Taken separately, these directives often looked petty. One concerning the obligatory dimensions of the European condom (whose size the Italian Government apparently sought to reduce) was not the sole butt of ribaldry. Taken together, they formed an avalanche moving in a consistent direction. After the Council's acceptance of the free movement of capital, in June 1988 the Commission issued a directive for reviving the process of Economic and Monetary Union.

When the Commission's intentions became apparent, its critics pressed the alarm button. Margaret Thatcher had accepted 'Project 1992' with reluctance. In a speech to the College of Europe in Bruges on 20 September 1988, she now attacked the prospect of a 'European superstate', and of 'an identikit European personality' with passion. On another occasion her strident protests of 'No! No! No!' recalled de Gaulle's performances 20 years before. She won the sympathy both of the 'Little Englanders' and of conservative Americans who feared the growth of an anti-American 'Fortress Europe'. But she misjudged the mood of her own Party, which removed her in a 'Cabinet Coup' in November 1990.

At this point the tide seemed to be turning fast in the Commission's favour. The disintegration of the Soviet bloc was transforming the political and economic landscape. German reunification led to unease (not least in Germany itself) about Germany's disproportionate influence. With no common policy, there was a danger that Europe as a whole would begin to drift.

In this climate, yet another wave of initiatives swept the Community. A Belgian memorandum of March 1990 set out the fourfold objectives of Subsidiarity, Democracy, Efficiency, and Coherence. A month later, a Franco-German letter raised the issues of common foreign, security, justice, and police policies. At that year's Madrid summit, Delors spoke of 'an embryo European Government' within five years. The further enlargement of the Community, and the strengthening both of the European Parliament and of European security, all reached the agenda. Enlargement plans were directed at several categories of entrant. By 1991 the Community was proposing to admit the remaining EFTA countries to the Common Market (though not yet to full membership), to grant associate status to three post-communist states, and to finalize the admission of Austria, Sweden, Finland, and Norway within three years. Applications for full or associate status were pending from a number of extra-European states such as Turkey and Israel. The Twelve stood fair to become the Twenty or even the Thirty.

One reason why the member states welcomed the Commission's initiative lay in their understanding of the principle of subsidiarity. This principle, borrowed from the practices of Catholic Canon Law, stated that the central organs of the Community should only be concerned with the most essential areas of policy, leaving everything else to 'subsidiary levels of government'. National governments were eager to insist that everything else was going to be left to them. But subsidiarity, if extended, could also be used to link Brussels directly with regional or local authorities, and to bypass the national level of government. Definitions were urgently required.

The more rigorous advocates of political union made no secret of their dislike of the nation-state. In addition to all its historic sins, the nation-state was now seen to be 'too small to cope with the big issues, and too big to cope with the small ones'. There was some reason to fear that the Community might be turned, like the UN, into a club of governments. It was certainly consistent to argue that European democracy could not progress until the Community's own Parliament was upgraded against the separate assemblies of member states.

It was in this context that debates about the 'regions' of Europe came to the fore. Any strengthening of the central organs of the Community automatically encouraged centrifugal tendencies within the member states. The rise of Brussels was bound to be followed by the rise of Edinburgh, of Milan, of Barcelona, and of Antwerp. Regional interests could be identified both within and between member states. Within the decentralized Federal Republic of Germany, for instance, the governments of the *Länder* enjoyed far-reaching autonomy. France, too, once the bastion of centralism, had recently strengthened the competence of its 22 regions. (In Britain, by contrast, where regional 'devolution' had been rebuffed and local government diminished, the opposite trend prevailed.) The concept of 'Euroregions' came into being to bridge the gap between the Community and its Eastern neighbours. Italy mooted the creation of a 'Pentagonale' of five countries in the Adriatic hinterland; Germany, Poland, and the Scandinavian countries discussed the possibility of future regions of co-operation on either side of the Baltic.

Political uncertainties strengthened centrifugal pressures within member states. In Spain, the long-standing discontents of Catalans and Basques were controlled but not fully satisfied. In Italy, a Lombard League was reborn with the aim of 'liberating' the north from the burdens of the *Mezzogiorno*. In Britain, the Scottish Nationalists were drawing their second wind: an independent Scotland looked a better risk inside the European Community than outside it.

In practice, though, everything remained to be played for. The Community was still debating whether it should be geographically enlarged before it was constitutionally 'deepened'. Delors preferred 'Deepen first, enlarge later'. His critics thought this a ruse for keeping the community small, Western, and controlled by the Commission. Even so, by the time that the leaders of the Twelve were due to meet at Maastricht in Limburg in December 1991, the momentum was still accelerating. To this end, the Commission was preparing to present a massive Treaty on European Union designed to amend and expand the Treaty of Rome. The 61,351 words of its text were to mark 'a new stage in the process of European integration'. It mapped out pathways towards 'economic and monetary union', 'a single and stable currency', a 'common citizenship', and 'a common foreign and security policy'.[32] But it said nothing about enlargement, nothing about the transformation of Europe as a whole. Conceived by a Commission still preoccupied with purely Western concerns, Maastricht in no way prepared Europe for the avalanche that was about to break in the other half of the Continent.

Meanwhile, as Delors flourished, Gorbachev flashed, floundered, and flopped. His analysis of the Soviet crisis can be deduced from his subsequent actions.

Much of it was explicitly stated in his book, *Perestroika* (1989). It was a sorry catalogue. Further expansion of the Soviet arsenal did not promise greater security. Military spending had reached levels which precluded any improvement in civilian living standards. Indeed, the Soviet economy could no longer sustain established patterns of expenditure. Communist planning methods had failed, the technology gap with the West was widening every day. The Party was corrupt and dispirited; the young were turning their backs on communist ideology; the citizenry had lost patience with empty promises. Soviet society was beset by apathy. Soviet foreign policy was in disarray. The war in Afghanistan, like all the other revolutionary struggles, was a bottomless drain; Soviet hegemony in Eastern Europe paid no dividends. Gorbachev's strategy lay first in defusing the Cold War climate of fear and hatred on which the old system had thrived, and then, having cleared the air, to move on to the trickier problems of internal reform. On the external front he was brilliantly successful. On visits to the USA and to West Germany, he was hailed as a conquering hero. Gorbymania raged. Notwithstanding his continuing support for traditional communist subversion in Western countries, he was eager to welcome President Reagan to Moscow.

Gorbachev's internal policies were encapsulated in two programmatic buzzwords that went round the world. *Perestroika*, 'restructuring', envisaged the injection of market principles into economic management and of non-Party interests into political life. *Glasnost'* was wrongly translated as 'openness'. It was, in fact, a standard Russian word for 'publicity', the opposite of 'silence' or 'taboo'. It was initially intended as a goad for the Party comrades to propose solutions to problems whose very existence had hitherto been denied. Gorbachev set out to stimulate debate; and for this, it was essential that outspoken views should not be punished. So the Party began to talk, and then the media, and eventually the public. For the first time in their lives, Soviet people found that censorship and the police were not going to be used against them. With some delay, therefore, *Glasnost'* did turn into openness, in an unprecedented, unrestrained, unstoppable torrent of argument. The strongest stream within that torrent was the near-universal denunciation of communism.

Very soon, therefore, General Secretary Gorbachev found himself in an anomalous position. In spite of his liberal reputation in the West, he was a convinced communist who wanted to humanize and revitalize the system, not to dump it. He stood for 'democratization', not democracy. Like Brezhnev before him, he arranged to be given the office of state 'President'—as if he were the equivalent of the American President. Yet he never faced the electorate, and never sought to relinquish his main, unelected office of Party leader. His six years of reform, therefore, could never proceed beyond half- or quarter-measures. He supplemented the central Party organs with a new Congress of hand-picked People's Deputies; but he never granted free elections. In the economic sphere he toyed repeatedly with marketization, but rejected all the more radical plans. He refused to decollectivize agriculture or to desubsidize prices; he delayed the legalization of private property. As a result, the planned economy started to collapse in conditions where the market economy could not start to function. On the nationality issue, he encouraged the republics to state their demands, then refused to grant them.

Gorbachev was a political tactician of consummate skill, coaxing the conservatives and restraining the radicals; but he did not win any substantial degree of public confidence. In the eyes of the ordinary Russian, he was *tipicheskiy komunisticheskiy aktivist*—a typical Communist activist. Gorbachev, and his Western admirers, seemed to grasp neither the elementary features of the Soviet system which he was running nor the unavoidable consequences of Soviet history. They ignored the implications of removing coercion from a machine that had known no other driving force. They abandoned the Party's dictatorial powers, the spine of the body politic, and were surprised when the limbs stopped responding to the brain. They underestimated the effects of decades of Party indoctrination which rendered the majority of administrators incapable of independent thought. They persisted in thinking of the Soviet Union as a natural, national entity—*moya strana* ('my country'), as Gorbachev was still calling it in 1991. Above all, they misjudged the effect of Glasnost on the suppressed nationalities, for most of whom freedom of expression was equivalent to demands for independence. Tinkering was the worst possible course of action.

Much ink has still to be spilled on the causes of communism's collapse. Political scientists inevitably put their emphasis on systemic political causes, economists on the failings of the economy. It may be that equal attention should be paid to the everyday lives of ordinary people. There are some excellent anthropological studies of East Europeans struggling with the absurdities of life under communism. It now seems that a generation which had lost the pervasive fear of the Stalinist era suddenly decided that enough was enough. As the Party bosses lost the will to enforce their authority, millions of men and women simply lost the inclination to obey. Communist society was as rotten at its grass roots as it was at the top.[33] Independent culture, especially religion, played a greater role than is often supposed. Artists and believers were often the only people who could imagine a world without communism. The rest were like the inhabitants of a submerged planet in a science fiction story which the censors had failed to spot. They had been trained with great difficulty to live under water; when the water began to subside, they had forgotten how to breathe in the open air.[34]

Once again, in this final round, the earliest cracks in the edifice appeared in Poland. Material conditions were deteriorating; renewed strikes loomed. Desperate ministers turned to the leader of the banned Solidarity union, Wałęsa. It was an admission of political bankruptcy. Early in 1989 they called round-table talks to discuss power-sharing with the illegal opposition. The result was an agreement whereby Solidarity would compete for a limited number of parliamentary seats. The elections produced a sensation: Wałęsa's people swept the board in every constituency where they competed. Many prominent communists were unable to get themselves re-elected, even where they were the sole candidates:

voters simply crossed them off the ballot. In this most recently 'normalized' of 'communist countries', communist authority was fast approaching zero.

In June 1989 China showed the world what demons lurked beneath the skin of communists facing popular wrath. Gorbachev, on an official visit to Beijing, witnessed the protests though not the massacre. He could not fail to draw conclusions. Later, when visiting East Berlin for the 40th anniversary of the state, he let it be known that the DDR could not count on the use of Soviet troops. There was to be no Tiananmen Square in Europe. The Brezhnev Doctrine had died before anyone noticed.

In August Poland's bewildered communists invited Solidarity to form a government under their own continuing communist constitutional and state presidency. Tadeusz Mazowiecki, a devout Catholic, was accepted as Premier. He took his seat in the Council of the Warsaw Pact. The Soviet bloc was no longer a bloc. Hungary was engaged in its own roundtable talks. Regular demonstrations were being organized by the Protestant Churches of East Germany.

The decay was well advanced, therefore, when the avalanche began to slip in the autumn of that *annus mirabilis*. In Budapest, on 23 October, on the 33rd anniversary of the Hungarian national rising, the Hungarian People's Republic was abolished. The Hungarian communists admitted the Opposition into the parliament, whilst turning themselves into a social democratic party. Still more astonishingly, in Berlin on 9 November 1989, East German border guards stood idly by as crowds on both sides of the Berlin Wall demolished it with gusto. The DDR government had lost the will to fight. In Prague, on the 17th, a student demo went wrong: a demonstrator was reported killed by the police. But then, a week later, Havel and Dubček appeared together on a balcony in Wenceslas Square before the adoring crowds; and a general strike soon finished off the unresisting authorities. The 'velvet revolution' was complete. The sharpest of foreign observers on the spot was moved to utter the much-repeated quip: 'In Poland it took ten years, in Hungary ten months, in East Germany ten weeks, and in Czechoslovakia . . . ten days.'[35] Finally, over Christmas, a bloody uprising in Bucharest, where the hated Securitate defended itself to the death, culminated in the grisly execution of the Ceausescus.

Gorbachev's role, though honourable, has been exaggerated. He was not the architect of East Europe's freedom; he was the lock-keeper who, seeing the dam about to burst, decided to open the floodgates and to let the water flow. The dam burst in any case; but it did so without the threat of a violent catastrophe.

In 1990, the practical consequences of the previous year's crash began to work themselves out. First the CMEA, then the Warsaw Pact, ceased to function. One after another, the ruling communist parties bowed out. Every new government declared itself for democratic politics and a free market economy. With varying degrees of haste, treaties and timetables were drawn up for the phased withdrawal of Soviet troops. In Germany, the drive for reunification accelerated. The organs of the DDR simply evaporated. The West German parties began to campaign in the East, and a general election was won by Chancellor Kohl. In October the

Federal Republic formally absorbed the citizens, territory, and assets of East Germany. The fires of freedom spread far and wide on the westerly wind. Bulgaria and Albania ignited, as did the constituent republics of Yugoslavia and the Soviet Union. Slovenia and Croatia, Estonia, Latvia, Lithuania, and Chechenia all declared their independence, as yet unrecognized. Bosnia and Macedonia, Armenia, Georgia, Moldavia, and Ukraine were poised to follow suit.

The pulverization of the Yugoslav Federation was specially vicious. Democratic elections had brought militant nationalists to the fore both in Serbia and in Croatia. In Belgrade, the Federal State Council was overtaken by the designs of a Serbian leadership stoking the passions of a 'Greater Serbia'. When in August 1990 the Serbs of Knin in Croatia rebelled against Zagreb, the stage was set for the open wars, which erupted the following Spring. After a miserable rout in Slovenia, the Serbian-led Yugoslav army launched its assault on Croatia. Panic and intercommunal violence rapidly gripped several parts of a disintegrating state, where ethnic minorities were as common as compact majorities. Just before his death, Tito had sighed: 'I am the only Yugoslav.'[36] It was not true. But, with the genie of ethnic violence on the wing, it was all but impossible for supranational 'Yugoslav' policies to be asserted. [**CRAVATE**] [**ILLYRIA**] [**MAKEDON**] [**SARAJEVO**]

Only in Poland did the pace slacken. The country which had been the first to loosen the communist yoke was the last to cast it off. The Mazowiecki Government gave priority to economics. In December 1990 Wałęsa pushed his way to the presidency after losing a quarter of the votes to a stooge of the ex-security service. Liberation from a parliament still dominated by communists took ten months more. According to the old stereotypes, the Polish Revolution was rather un-Polish.

The reunification of Germany was undertaken impetuously, not to say thoughtlessly. No one questioned the propriety of reunification. 'What belongs together', said Willy Brandt, 'is now growing together.' But when the ex-DDR became part of the Federal Republic, it was automatically joined to the European Community with no questions asked; and, contrary to the advice of the Bundesbank, the O-Mark was exchanged for the D-Mark at the rate of one for one. Little thought was given to the political and financial costs for Germany or for Germany's neighbours. The Government in Bonn took it for granted that East Germans, being Germans, would welcome the imposition of the institutions of the Federal Republic, and that the West Germans, being Germans, would pay for it cheerfully. The prospect dawned that a united Germany might not be so interested in Europe as a disunited Germany had been. As public opinion grew more anxious and self-centred, the Federal Government felt obliged to reassert its commitment to European integration. 'In a symbolic act of profound significance, the same Article 23 of the Basic Law under which German unification had been achieved was amended . . . so that the Federal Republic, instead of being open "for other parts of Germany", was now committed to "the realisation of a united Europe".'[37]

Decommunization proved a thorny problem in all post-communist countries.

The prevailing laws, though lacking legitimacy, could not be abandoned whole-sale. The communist *nomenklatura*, now declaring undying devotion to demo-cracy, could not be dismissed *en masse*. The ex-secret policemen could not be easily unmasked. Germany was rocked by the exposure of thousands and thou-sands of Stasi informers; Poland reopened investigations into political murders; in Romania, the new regime was actually opposed to decommunization. Czechoslovakia was alone in passing its *Lustracni zakon*, or 'Verification Law', which sought to exclude corrupt or criminal officials.

The legacy of Soviet-type economies was dire. Despite initial successes, such as the currency reform and the conquest of hyperinflation under Poland's Balcerowicz Plan (1990–1), it became painfully clear that no overnight remedy was to hand. All the former members of the bloc faced decades of agonizing reorgan-ization on the way to a viable market economy.[38] In the mean time, their prob-lems could be used to exclude them from the European Community.

Everywhere, the social attitudes engendered by communism persisted. Embryo civil societies could not rush to fill the void. Political apathy was high; petty quar-rels ubiquitous; residual sympathy for communism as a buffer against unemploy-ment and surprises was greater than many supposed. The decades 'under water' had conditioned the masses to disbelieve all promises and to expect the worst. The cynical idea that someone loses if someone else is gaining was all but ineradicable. No one could have guessed the dimensions of the devastation.

The fact that communism died without a fight did not ease the pain which it left behind; there was no catharsis. One participant complained of 'the impossi-bility of epiphany in peacetime'. Another remarked: 'I'm happy to have lived to see the end of this disaster; but I want to die before the beginning of the next one.'[39]

The second stage of the avalanche, in the Soviet Union, began to slide in 1991. Economic reform had made no appreciable progress; material conditions were deteriorating. Over the winter, Gorbachev had drawn closer to the Communist Party apparatus. Several of his colleagues resigned in protest against the impend-ing reassertion of dictatorship. Most ominously, the national republics were lin-ing up to follow the example of the Baltic States, where national and Soviet authorities governed in parallel. In Moscow itself the city council elected a demo-cratic mayor, whilst the Government of the RSFSR elected a democratic presi-dent, Boris Yeltsin. Yeltsin began to distance Russia from Gorbachev's Soviet Kremlin. Armenia and Azerbaijan were at war over Nagorno-Karabakh. In Georgia, where Gorbachev had earlier sanctioned the use of deadly force, the revolt against Moscow was finalized. In Vilnius, where Soviet troops had also killed civilians, the Lithuanian parliament despaired at the lack of outside sup-port. The Kremlin was moving to replace the USSR with a much looser union of sovereign republics. The new union treaty was set to be signed on 20 August.

The abortive Moscow coup of 19–22 August 1991 was launched to stop the Union Treaty, and thereby to preserve the residual power of the CPSU. It precipitated the disaster which it was supposed to prevent. The plotters were in no sense 'hardliners': they were committed to the limited form of *perestroika* which they had good reason to believe was Gorbachev's own preference. Indeed, they clearly believed that Gorbachev himself would acquiesce. As a result, they made none of the provisions which competent putschists make. In fact, it was not really a coup at all; it was the last twitch of the dying dinosaur's tail. On Sunday 19 August, seven nervous apparatchiks appeared in a row on Soviet television and announced the formation of their emergency committee. They were obeyed by the Party's organs and media. They had timed their action to coincide with Gorbachev's last day on vacation in Crimea. When he refused to deal with their emissary, they had nothing else to propose. Yeltsin, unarrested, clambered onto a tank in front of the Russian Parliament and breathed defiance. No move was taken to disperse his supporters; the tanks on the streets had no ammunition and no orders. After three days, the plotters simply climbed into their limousines and drove off. The attempted coup proved beyond doubt that the system was brain-dead. The Soviet communists were still in control of the world's most formidable security apparatus; but they could not bring it to perform the simplest of operations.

For a time, Gorbachev did not grasp what had happened. He flew back from Crimea still talking about the future of the Party and of *perestroika*. He was brutally brought back to reality by Yeltsin, who made him read out the names of the plotters to the Russian parliament. They were Gorbachev's men every one. Gorbachev's credit was exhausted. He resigned as General Secretary just before Lenin's Party dissolved itself. On 5 September 1991 the Soviet Congress of Deputies passed its last law, surrendering its powers to the sovereign republics of the former Union. On 24 October 1991 Gorbachev issued a last decree, splitting the Soviet KGB into its component parts. He was left stranded as the figurehead president of a ghost state.

Nothing better illustrated the realities of the Soviet collapse than the fate of Sergei Krikalyev, a Soviet cosmonaut who was fired into space in May 1991. He was still circling the earth at the end of the year for want of a decision to bring him back. He had left a Soviet Union that was still a superpower; he would return to a world from which the Soviet Union had disappeared. His controllers at the Baikonur Space Centre found themselves in the independent republic of Kazakhstan.

December 1991 was a month of decision at both ends of Europe. It started on 1 December with a referendum in Ukraine, where 91 per cent of the people, including the great majority of the Russian minority, voted for independence. The Republic of Ukraine was second in Europe in territory, fifth in population.

On the 9th and 10th at Maastricht, the twelve leaders of the European Community met to consider their scheme for comprehensive European union. Having banished the dreaded 'f-word',* the British Prime Minister inserted a

---

* To British ears, *federalism* was coloured by American, as opposed to German or Continental, usage, and was taken to be a codeword for a centralized United States of Europe.

monetary opt-out clause, refused to sign the social chapter, persuaded his partners to reconfirm the role of NATO, and claimed a famous victory. Fears were
expressed that 'variable geometry' and a 'two-speed Europe' were in the making.
Yet the great bulk of the Treaty's provisions were accepted. The leaders initialled
agreements which provided that citizenship of the Union would be given to all
citizens of member states (Title II, 8–8e), that members should follow a common
economic policy (II, 102–109m), that EMU and a European Central Bank (ECB)
were to be achieved by 1999 within a joint banking system (II, 105–108a), that the
European Parliament should be given powers of co-decision with the Council of
Ministers (II, 137–138a, 158, 189–90), that an advisory Committee of the Regions
was to be established (II, 198a–c), that common foreign and security policies were
to be pursued (VI), and that subsidiarity should leave most Community action 'to
Member States' (II, 3b). They accepted detailed chapters on education, culture,
health, energy, justice, immigration, and crime. Outside the Treaty, they also
confirmed recognition of the three Baltic States, but not Croatia or Slovenia. It
was all suspiciously easy. All that remained was ratification. It would not be long
before merchants of doom would be predicting the Treaty's demise.[40]

That same weekend, President Gorbachev was making a last vain attempt to
summon the heads of the Soviet Republics to Moscow. Unbeknown to him, however, the leaders of Russia, Byelorussia and Ukraine were already negotiating in a
forest hunting-lodge near the Polish border. At 2.17 pm on 8 December they signed
a declaration stating that 'the USSR had ceased to exist'. Next day they announced
the creation of a Commonwealth of Independent States. The CIS was a convenient
cover behind which the core of the strategic arsenal could be kept under a single
command whilst most other Soviet institutions were quietly buried. By the end of
the year, the peaceful passing of Europe's last empire was complete.

Some small steps were taken to bridge the East–West divide. NATO established
a Joint Co-operation Council to which former Warsaw Pact members were invited. The European Community signed treaties of association with Poland,
Hungary and Czecho-Slovakia. A joint European Bank of Development and
Reconstruction was opened in London. Food and financial aid was sent to the ex-
Soviet Union, and peace-keeping missions to ex-Yugoslavia. Yet the steps were
exceedingly small. The EC was still blocking agricultural imports from the East,
throttling trade. Except for German investment in East Germany, Western investment in the former East was minimal. No co-ordinated foreign policy was forth-
coming; no effective action was taken to contain the looming wars in Croatia and
Bosnia; no dynamic leadership emerged. The gulf between 'White Europe' and
'Black Europe' still gaped.

Events moved so fast after 1989 that few observers had the leisure to reflect on
the interdependence of Western and Eastern Europe. The habits of a lifetime led
people to assume that East was East and West was West. Western statesmen
were preoccupied with the cultivation of their own gardens; they did not readily notice that the explosion which had demolished their neighbours' house had

blown away their own fence and gable. 'They leaned against the Wall in comfort,' a Hungarian had written, 'not knowing that the Wall was made of dynamite.'[41]

For 40 years the Iron Curtain had provided the framework for political and economic life in the West as well as the East. It had defined the playing-field for Marshall Aid, for NATO, for the EEC, for Germany's Federal Republic, for Western Europe's economic success. It had been extremely convenient, not just for the Communists but also for Western bankers, planners, and industrialists, whose efforts could be directed to the easy part of Europe. It was specially advantageous for the protectionist element within the EEC, and hence for the distortions of the CAP. In short, it was one of the factors which threatened to turn Western Europe into a short-sighted and self-satisfied rich man's club, careless of other people's welfare. It was responsible for attitudes mirroring the Brezhnev Doctrine, where 'the gains of capitalism' had to be defended at all cost, where Western statesmen dreamt of perpetuating their isolation indefinitely. In the long run, Europeans would have to face the choice either to rebuild their village in unison or to reinvent the Iron Curtain in a new guise.

In reality, the events of East and West in Europe were closely connected. The success of the European Community, as seen from the East, had been a potent factor in the failure of the Soviet bloc. The success or failure of the post-communist democracies would condition the fate of European Union. Moscow's retreat from Eastern Europe and from critical regions such as that of oil-rich Baku would create new arenas where the new Russia might feel compelled to resist expanding Western firms and institutions.

To some, the common denominator seemed to lie in the universal attachment to liberal democracy and free market economics. The Western victory appeared to be so complete that one academic gained instant fame by asking whether the world had reached 'the End of History'.[42] Nothing could have been further from the truth: Europe was locked in an intense period of historical change with no end in view.

In the eyes of one ex-statesman, the revolution of 1989–91 had given rise to three Europes. 'Europe One' consisted of the established democracies of Western Europe. 'Europe Two' coincided with the Visegrád Triangle of Poland, Hungary, and Czecho-Slovakia plus Slovenia. These four post-communist countries had reason to hope that they could join the European Community with no greater obstacles than those overcome in the previous decade by the post-fascist countries of Spain, Portugal, and Greece. 'Europe Three' comprised the remaining countries of the former Soviet bloc, whose European aspirations would have to await the twenty-first century.[43]

Yet declarations of goodwill could not of themselves bring results. The priority given to economic considerations was suffocating the wider vision. Any rigid insistence on economic convergence was bound to delay the Community's enlargement, perhaps indefinitely. On the other hand, any major enlargement was bound both to involve extensive costs and to strengthen the case for institutional reform. If Germans could resent the costs of integrating seventeen million fellow Germans, other member states of the Union were unlikely to welcome the sacrifices required for integrating ever more new entrants. If governments were to face difficulties over ratifying the Maastricht Treaty, they would encounter much greater problems implementing it.

As the march towards further enlargement and integration proceeded, therefore, resistance was bound to intensify. In a forum of potential confrontation between the Community and its sovereign members, the status of the European Court would become a critical issue. A 'Europe of Sixteen' or a 'Europe of Twenty' could not be managed by the structures that had sufficed for 'The Six' and 'The Twelve'. The European Union would steadily grind to a halt if it did not reform its governing institutions as part of the drive towards widening and deepening.

According to one pessimistic observer, Europe would only be persuaded to integrate further if faced by extreme catastrophe—that is, by scenes of genocide, by mass migration, or by war.[44] By the same line of reasoning, monetary union would only be achieved through the collapse of the existing monetary regime: and political union through the manifest failure of political policies. 'Europe One' might only be driven to accept 'Europe Two', if 'Europe Three' reverted to form.

In December 1991 neither integration in the West nor disintegration in the East had run their course; yet very few Europeans could remember a time when so many barriers were down. The frontiers were open, and minds were opening with them. There were adults too young to remember Franco or Tito. One had to be nearing 30 to recall de Gaulle or the Prague Spring, 50 the Hungarian Rising or the Treaty of Rome, 60 the end of the Second World War. No one much under retirement age could have any clear recollections of pre-war Europe. No one much under 90 could have active memories of the First World War. Centenarians were the only persons alive to have known those golden days at the turn of the century before the great European Crisis began.

Count Edward Raczyński (1891–1993) belonged to this last rare company. He was born in Zakopane, on the border of Austria and Hungary, to a Polish family which possessed large estates in Prussia. Their palace in Berlin had been demolished to make way for the Reichstag. He had studied in Austrian Cracow, at Leipzig, and then at the London School of Economics. He had served as Polish Ambassador to the League of Nations and from 1933 to 1945 at the Court of St James. He later became President of Poland's Government-in-Exile. He could never go home. But on 19 December 1991 he was honoured on his 100th birthday in the Embassy which Britain's alliance with Stalin had forced him to surrender forty-six years before. Newly married, he was one of the very few indefatigable Europeans to have seen off the European Crisis from start to finish—if finished it was.

Map 29.

Europe, 1992

14 February 1992, Summertown. In the beginning, there was no book. Now the last words are rolling onto the last pages. The desk beside the window of the top studio is dimly lit by the dawn. The night frost has left patches of damp on the roof that glistens through the glass. Clouds amble over the dark skyline towards the brightening band of pale yellow. The leafless apple trees of the old Thorncliffe Orchard straggle through the gloom towards the next row of red-brick Victorian houses. A solitary crow stands sentinel on the tip of the highest beech, as on a thousand such dawns since 'The Legend of Europa' was written. For once, the foul fumes of the Oxford Automobile Components factory are blowing elsewhere. The family slumbers on towards school-time.

The family connections of this house span half of Europe. One side of the family is firmly attached to this offshore island, to Lancashire and, further back, to Wales. The other side was rooted in the eastern parts of old Poland, which spent most of the last hundred years either in Austrian Galicia or in the Soviet Union. After education in Oxford and in Cracow, the two principals of the house met on the Boulevard Gergovia in Clermont-Ferrand, in the city of Blaise Pascal, who might well have been amused by such an infinitesimal probability. These happy accidents inevitably colour one's sense of history. Time and place in the writing of history are sovereign. Historians are a necessary part of their histories.

Today is the feast-day of SS Cyril and Methodius, the co-patrons of Europe. Prayers at the Jesuit church of St Aloysius 'celebrate the origins of the Slavonic peoples . . . May their light be our light.' The rosary is recited 'in the intention of the peoples of eastern Europe'. The priest explains, eccentrically, that Cyril and Methodius were apostles of the Poles, Czechs, and Hungarians (see Chapter V).

School-time. This week at Squirrel School, the headmistress has been talking at assembly about the needy children of Albania.

The morning's newspapers have nothing to say about SS Cyril and Methodius. The *Independent* leads with 'UN Troops for Croatia'. The *Guardian*'s 'Europe' supplement leads with an extended report on shopping in Murmansk. Yesterday's *El País* from Madrid leads with the formation of joint Franco-Spanish brigades to fight the Basque organization ETA; it has just recruited 'Mikailo Gorbachov' as a monthly columnist. In *Le Monde*, three pages of North African news predominate. *De Telegraaf* from The Hague gives its top spot to a problem with NATO's low flying F-16 fighters. The front page of *Süddeutsche Zeitung* from Munich is taken up with the affairs of the federal finance ministry. *Gazeta Wyborcza*, two days in the post from Warsaw, is preoccupied with the Constitutional Tribunal and its rejection of a statute on pensions passed by the communist-run parliament. The *Oxford Times* writes a leader about its own letter column, which is headed by a communication from the Anglican Bishop of Oxford on the priestly ordination of women.[45]

The only major story of historical interest appears on the front page of the *Corriere della Sera*, under the headline 'Massacrateli' ordine di Lenin'. Moscow is the growth-point of knowledge about modern European history. A correspondent in Moscow, quoting *Komsomolskaya Pravda*, lists hitherto secret documents from the archive of the Institute of Marxism-Leninism. They reveal the Bolshevik leader's personal insistence on revolutionary atrocities. On 11 August 1918, for example, Lenin wrote to the Comrades at Penza:

The rising of the five Kulak regions must be met with merciless repression . . . There's need to make an example. 1) Hang not less than 100 Kulaks, rich ones, blood-suckers, . . . 2) Publish their names. 3) Take all their food away. 4) Pick hostages according to yesterday's telegram. Do everything so that the people will see, tremble, and groan for miles and miles around . . . PS. Search out hard people. Lenin.[46]

These flourishes do not come from the correspondence of Hitler, comments the *Corriere*. So it's true. Bolshevik barbarity did not start with Stalin.

The week's home news has been dominated by mean pre-election wrangles, mainly about money. Abroad, one could choose between the travails of the French President, the future of the ex-Soviet nuclear arsenal, the conviction of a world boxing champion, or a decision of Ireland's Constitutional Court to deny abortion to a 14-year-old rape victim. The President of the European Commission has submitted proposals for a larger budget—'to match the Age of Maastricht'. The British tabloids have greeted this last item with derision. Under the headline 'No, Jacques, It's Not All Right', the editorial of the *Daily Mail* comments: 'Such Euro-largesse could so easily find its way into the pockets of shady contractors, or under the mattresses of colourful, but lazy, characters, basking in the Mediterranean sun.'[47] *Le Monde* analyses the phenomenon: 'La Grande-Bretagne se mobilise contre les "eurocrates"'.[48]

Above all, there is the 16th Winter Olympics at Albertville and Courchevel in Savoy. The 'blue ribbon' event, the men's combined downhill and slalom skiing, has been won by an Italian, Josef Pollg.

The *European*, which claims to be the only all-European newspaper, has recently lost both its crooked publisher and its hero in the Kremlin. This week's lead story, 'Italy Faces the Wrath of Europe', reports on Rome's poor record in implementing EC directives. The business section slams opposition from 'American isolationists' to a $10 billion IMF scheme for stabilizing the Russian rouble.[49]

In late morning, as predicted, it has started to rain. The papers' weather maps illustrate the range of their readers' interest. *The Times* publishes three weather maps—two larger ones for the British Isles (less the west of Ireland), for a.m. and p.m., and one centred on the mid-Atlantic. *Le Monde* has two weather maps for Europe, and one for France. The *Corriere* has one for Europe from the Atlantic to the Crimea, another for Italy. The *SZ* has three spacious maps, all for the whole of Europe, providing detailed information from a score of weather stations bounded by Reykjavik, Luleå (Sweden), Lisbon, and Athens. *Gazeta Wyborcza* has no weather map, but lists the previous day's temperatures from selected European capitals—Rome and Lisbon (13 °C), London (10 °C), Athens (9 °C), Vilnius, Riga, Tallinn, and Minsk (+1 °C), Kiev and Prague (+1 °C), and Bucharest (+3 °C). Varsovians do not know what the temperature is in Moscow.

The *European* splashes out with the largest of all weather maps, in colour. It marks the new republics, including Slovenia, Croatia, Belarus, and Moldavia, but not Russia, which is wrongly equated with the CIS. The accompanying list of 'European road works' mentions nothing further east than the A9–Bad Dürrenberg crossroads near Leipzig. So it's true: they don't mend roads in Eastern Europe.

Such is the tangle of daily information from which future historians will have to make sense.

Today is St Valentine's Day. By tradition, it is the day when birds begin their mating; so it also became the day when human lovebirds exchange suitable signals. *The Times* publishes page after page of cryptic, and frequently ungrammatical, messages:

AGATHA AARDVAARK, All my love Hector Tree. . . . ARTEMIS, Not only Hesperus entreats Thy Love, Algy. . . . CHRISTIANE, Un vraie couscous royale. Je t'aim infiniment, King. . . . MENTEN, Blue Seas in Basalt Rocks. . . . MOONFACE loves Baby Dumpling and Smelly. . . . POOPS, Ich bin deiner, bist du meine? Wirst du sein mein Valentine?[50]

Several papers give contradictory explanations of the origins of St Valentine's Day. One version says that the medievals adopted the Roman festival of Lupercalia; Lupercal or 'the wolf's lair' was the cave where Romulus and Remus had been reared by the she-wolf and where Romans would later smear themselves in goats' blood in the hope of parenthood. Neither of the two Roman martyrs called Valentine can be held responsible for the pagan frolics.

Today is also the tricentenary of the Massacre of Glencoe. It turns out that only 38 persons were killed. 'In the context of clan history,' says Lord Macdonald of Skye, 'the numbers involved were minimal.' So there are still Macdonalds enough to march with the pipes to the Glen of Weeping. In any case, as *The Times* reports, the Campbells were acting 'as agents of the Westminster government'. Now that's a topical note. Last week's *Die Zeit* devoted a major feature article to the roots of Scotland's separate identity; it was accompanied by a photo of a huge graffito from Glasgow, 'Brits Out Now'.[51]

Writing to music is a practical habit. BBC Radio 3 helps the ink to flow. At 07.35 the first paragraphs were started to Bach's Concerto for oboe d'amore, BWV 1055. The morning papers were accompanied by Rachmaninov's Piano Concerto No. 3. St Valentine's Day was suitably preceded by Tchaikovsky's symphonic fantasia, *Francesca da Rimini*. At 2 p.m. the Katowice Brass was missed, but Beethoven's Eighth is giving strength to the afternoon. Today, there is a good balance between West and East. For once, BBC 3 is not playing Janáček.

It is an irony that historians, who study the past, are invariably pressed to predict the future. It helps to have followed the drift of events, but not much.

To the west, across the ocean, the USA has surely reached the peak of its power. It looks to be heading for trouble with its debt, for trouble with its allies, and for trouble from the 'diversity' of its own citizens. It has specially intransigent problems with Japan, whose economic prowess has wounded America's pride. It is drifting away from Europe, to which it is no longer bound by the chains of the late Cold War. Vice-President Quayle in London this week, protesting to the contrary, did protest too much.

To the north, in Scotland, the independence movement has started to roll again. This week, an absolute majority of Scots expressed a preference for changing the country's status. They possess the power to destroy the United Kingdom, and thereby to deflate the English, as no one in Brussels could ever do. They may make Europeans of us yet.

To the south, in the heartland of the present European Community, both the French and the Germans are feeling the strain. France is beset by the weight of Muslim immigrants from North Africa, by the nationalist backlash of M. Le Pen, and by a socialist presidency that has outstayed its welcome. Germany is reeling under the costs of reunification. In their distress, both governments have turned to closer European union for comfort and support. This week, a television programme on 'The Germans' showed the German Chancellor quoting Thomas Mann, who longed 'not for a German Europe, but for a European Germany'. The Germans may lose their enthusiasm if they have to lose their Deutschmark.

To the east, the map of Europe is still in flux: a new state seems to be established every month. There is much talk of the dangers of nationalism. Where does it come from? It would be more convincing if it targeted the larger and more dangerous nationalisms, not the petty ones. Not that the dangers do not exist. The three Baltic States are afloat in a sea of troubles. Poland, Hungary, and Czecho-Slovakia are aiming at full membership of the EC by the end of the decade. Czechs and Slovaks may be heading for a divorce. Romania, Bulgaria, and Albania have nowhere to go. The Yugoslav Federation must surely split up soon. Slovenia and Croatia, like Belarus', Ukraine, and Moldavia, should prove viable, if left in peace. The Commonwealth of Independent States, however, is unlikely to survive; and in its present form the Russian Republic looks no more healthy than the CIS. It is still a vast artificial amalgam, twice the size of the USA, with a very uneven economic infrastructure and no political cement. Its leaders can hardly hold it together by democracy and a prayer. They may have a chance if Moscow allows the Far Eastern Region to drift in the direction of autonomy and Japanese investment, and if Siberia is encouraged to develop its own resources with foreign help. European Russia, as always, has too many people and too many soldiers, and not enough to feed them. The Russians have drawn on their exceptional powers of stoic endurance through two years of Soviet collapse; but they may not do so indefinitely. If democratic Russia does not prosper, it will start to fragment still further. In that case, autocratic Russia will try to reassert itself with a vengeance.

The collapse of the Soviet Empire is certainly 'the greatest, and perhaps the most awful event' of recent times. The speed of its collapse has exceeded all the other great landslides of European history—the dismemberment of the Spanish dominions, the partitions of Poland, the retreat of the Ottomans, the disintegration of Austria-Hungary. Yet it is hardly an event which calls for the historian to sit on the ruins of the Kremlin, like Gibbon in the Colosseum, or to write a requiem. For the Soviet Union was not a civilization that once was great. It was uniquely mean and mendacious even in its brief hour of triumph. It brought death and misery to more human beings than any other state on record. It brought no good life either to its dominant Russian nationality or even to its ruling élite. It was massively destructive, not least of Russian culture. As many thoughtful Russians now admit, it was a folly that should never have been built in the first place. The sovereign nations of the ex-Soviet Union are picking up the pieces where they left off in 1918–22, when their initial flicker of independence was snuffed out by Lenin's Red Army. Almost everyone agrees: 'Russia, yes. But what sort of Russia?'[52]

The most obvious fact of the Soviet collapse is that it happened through natural causes. The Soviet Union was not, like ancient Rome, invaded by barbarians or, like the Polish Commonwealth, partitioned by rapacious neighbours, or, like the Habsburg Empire, overwhelmed by the strains of a great war. It was not, like the Nazi Reich, defeated in a fight to the death. It died because it had to, because the grotesque organs of its internal structure were incapable of providing the essentials of life. In a nuclear age, it could not, like its tsarist predecessor, solve its internal problems by expansion. Nor could it suck more benefit from the nations whom it had captured. It could not tolerate the partnership with China which once promised a global future for communism; it could not stand the oxygen of reform; so it imploded. It was struck down by the political equivalent of a coronary, more massive than anything that history affords.

The consequences of so massive a shock were bound to affect the whole of Europe. It was an open question whether the peoples of the ex-Soviet Empire could continue to reorder their affairs with a minimum of blood and hate. That the collapse occurred so peacefully was proof that it was ripe to happen; but the national warriors who took the field in the Caucasus and in Yugoslavia had many potential imitators. Not surprisingly, the countries of Western Europe had reacted to the Soviet collapse with excessive caution. Governments were slow to assist the struggling republics. Some, in the name of misplaced stability, were eager to keep the Soviet Union and the Yugoslav Federation alive. They were in a phase of confusion, and of half-measures bungled by competing agencies.

Paradoxically, the threat of anarchy in the East may well act as a spur to closer union in the West. Last year, Albanian refugees sailed across the Adriatic in their tens of thousands, and tried to force their way into Italy. Hordes of Russian, Ukrainian, and Romanian tramps and traders are pouring into Poland, just as Poles recently poured into Germany and Austria. Germany's wonderful capacity of absorption is under the severest strain, not only from millions of unemployed East Germans but also from thousands of legal asylum-seekers, whose presence cannot be popular. If scenes of disorder were to be repeated on a larger scale, and

in Central Europe, the sense of urgency in Western capitals would be wonderfully enhanced. So far, the consolidation of the European Community has been proceeding at the pace of the slowest. A strong blast of cold air from the East might
quicken the pace.

Much depends on developments in America. So long as the USA remains
strong and relatively prosperous, the status quo in Western Europe is unlikely to
change suddenly. NATO will be preserved, and the European Community will
evolve by measured steps. If and when the USA moves into crisis, however, the
countries of Europe would draw together for common protection. An Atlantic
gale from the west could have the same effect as a cold east wind.

Europe, like nature itself, cannot abide a vacuum. Sooner or later, the European
Community in the West and the successor states in the East must redefine their
identities, their bounds, and their allegiances. Somehow, at least for a time, a new
equilibrium may be found, perhaps in a multilateral framework. Regional groupings such as the Baltic Council, the *hexagonale*, and some form of ex-Soviet club
or clubs, could all play their part. But somewhere between the depths of Russia
and the heart of Europe a new dividing line will have to be established—hope-
fully along a border of peace.

'Europe, yes. But what sort of Europe?' The old Europe, which existed before the
Eclipse, has passed away. With the poet, one can regret its passing and its ancient,
clear-cut walls:

> Fileur éternel des immobilités bleues,
> Je regrette l'Europe aux anciens parapets![53]

But one cannot bring it back. The present 'Europe', a creature of the Cold War, is
inadequate to its task. The moral and political vision of the Community's founding fathers has almost been forgotten.

Europe is not going to be fully united in the near future. But it has a chance to
be less divided than for generations past. If fortune smiles, the physical and psychological barriers will be less brutal than at any time in living memory. Europa
rides on. *Tremulae sinuantur flamine vestes.*

NOTES TO CHAPTERS

THE LEGEND OF EUROPA

1. See Chapter 1, note 15.
2. Ovid, *Metamorphoses*, ii. lines 862 ff. translated by A. D. Melville (Oxford, 1986), p. 50.
3. More correctly, 'tit for tat'. Herodotus, *The Histories*, Book 1.2.
4. Ovid, *op cit.* ii, line 875.
5. Possibly from the Assyrian word, *Ereb*, meaning 'the West'.

INTRODUCTION

1. Henryk Batowski, *Kryzys dyplomatyczny w Europie, 1938–39* (Warsaw, 1962); *Ostatni tydzień pokoju i pierwsze tygodnie wojny*, 2nd edn. (Poznań, 1969); *Europa zmierza ku przepaści* (Poznań, 1989); see also his *Niedoszła "Biała Księga" z roku 1940: rozprawa zródłoznawcza* (Cracow, 1993); and '17 September 1939: Before and After', *East European Quarterly*, 27/7 (1993), 523–34.
2. *L'Évolution de l'humanité*, ed. Henri Berr (Bibliothèque de Synthèse Historique) (Paris). J. Vendryes, *Le Langage: introduction linguistique* appeared in 1921, H. Verin, *La Gloire des ingénieurs* in 1993.
3. From Juliusz Słowacki, *Journey to the East* (1836), trans. by Norman Davies, rather better than in *Heart of Europe* (Oxford, 1984), p. xi.
4. *The Cambridge Mediaeval History*, ed. J. B. Bury, H. M. Gwatlin *et al.* (8 vols., Cambridge, 1936–9).
5. *Handbuch der europaischen Geschichte*, ed. T. Schieder (7 vols., Stuttgart, 1968–79).
6. *Periods of European History*, ed. Arthur Hassall (9 vols., London, 1897–1936).
7. e.g. *The Fontana History of Europe* (400–1945), General Editor J. H. Plumb (15 vols., London, 1963–); *The Library of European Civilisation*, General Editor Geoffrey Barraclough (London, 1965–); *A General History of Europe, from the Decline of the Ancient World to 1945*, General Editor Denys Hay (11 vols., London, 1968–).
8. John Bowle, *A History of Europe: A Cultural and Political Survey* (London, 1979), 589.
9. See Anthony Seldon, *Contemporary History: Practice and Method* (Oxford, 1988).
10. Walter Raleigh, *A Historie of the World*, in his *Works* (London, 1829). Raleigh prudently confined his history to the ancient Greeks and Romans.
11. H. A. L. Fisher, *A History of Europe* (London, 1936).
12. Eugen Weber, *A Modern History of Europe: Men, Cultures, and Societies from the Renaissance to the Present* (New York, 1971).
13. Kenneth Clark, *Civilisation: A Personal View* (London, 1969).
14. Jacob Bronowski, *The Ascent of Man* (London, 1973).
15. Michael Andrews, *The Birth of Europe: Colliding Continents and the Destiny of Nations* (London, 1991).
16. Fernand Paul Braudel, *La Méditerranée et le monde méditerranéen à l'époque de Philippe II* (Paris, 1949), trans. as *The Mediterranean and the Mediterranean World* (London, 1973); see also William McNeil, *The Rise of the West: A History of the Human Community* (Chicago, 1963); and Immanuel Wallerstein, *The Modern World System* (New York, 1974).
17. A. Low-Beer, 'Empathy in History', *Teaching History*, 55 (Apr. 1989), 8 ff.; J. Cairns, ibid. 13 ff.; also K. Jenkins and P. Brickley, 'Reflections on the Empathy Debate', ibid. 18 ff.

18. See David Lehman, *Signs of the Times: Deconstruction and the Fall of Paul de Man* (New York, 1991); reviewed by Louis Menand, 'The Politics of Deconstruction', *New York Review of Books*, 21 Nov. 1991.

19. Apocryphal. On my mischievous master, see Adam Sisman, *A. J. P. Taylor* (London, 1994).

20. Claude Delmas, *Histoire de la civilisation européene* (Paris, 1969), 127, 'il n'y a pas une Vérité, mais autant de vérités que de consciences.'

21. Norman Davies, Preface to *God's Playground: A History of Poland* (Oxford, 1981), vol. i, p. vii.

22. Lord Acton, quoted by Geoffrey Parker, *The Thirty Years' War* (New York, 1984), p. xv.

23. 'It is part of my creed that the only Poetry is History, could we tell it right'; Thomas Carlyle, letter to Ralph Waldo Emerson, 12 Aug. 1834, in *The Correspondence of Emerson and Carlyle*, ed. J. Slater (New York, 1964), 105.

24. See Gertrude Himmelfarb, 'Telling It as You Like It: Post-modernist History and the Flight from Fact', *TLS*, 16 Oct. 1992, 12–15.

25. Ibid. 15.

26. Voltaire, *Le Siècle de Louis XIV*, quoted by Denys Hay, *Europe: The Emergence of an Idea* (Edinburgh, 1957), 123.

27. Edmund Burke, from *Letters on a Regicide Peace* (1796), quoted by Hay, *Europe*, 123.

28. William Blake, 'The Ancient of Days' (Urizen Creating the Finite Universe), frontispiece to *Europe a Prophecy* (1794), British Museum; reproduced in *William Blake*, ed. Vivian de Sola Pinto (London, 1965), pl. 4.

29. John of Trevisa, translating Bartholomew the Englishman's Latin Encyclopaedia; quoted by R. Barber, *The Penguin Guide to Mediaeval Europe* (London, 1984), 30.

30. George F. Kennan, *Siberia and the Exile System* (New York, 1891), i. 420–2; quoted by Benson Bobrick, *East of the Sun: The Epic Conquest and Tragic History of Siberia* (New York, 1992), 267–8.

31. See Hay, *Europe*, 125; also Egbert Jahn, 'Wo befindet sich Osteuropa?' *Osteuropa*, 5 (May 1990), 418–40.

32. See W. H. Parker, 'Is Russia in Europe? The Geographical Viewpoint', in *An Historical Geography of Russia* (London, 1968), 27–9.

33. T. S. Eliot, *Die Einheit der Europaeischen Kultur* (Berlin, 1946); also published as 'The Unity of European Culture' in an appendix to *Notes towards the Definition of Culture* (London, 1948), esp. 122–4.

34. Henri Janne, *Europe's Cultural Identity* (Strasburg, 1981).

35. Quoted by Margaret Shennan, *Teaching about Europe* (London, 1991), 241.

36. Jean Monnet, quoted by Anthony Sampson, *The New Europeans* (London, 1968), 6; see also Mia Rodriguez-Salgado, 'In Search of Europe', *History Today*, 42 (Feb. 1992), 11–16.

37. See J. Tazbir, *Myśl polska w nowożytnej kulturze europejskiej* (Warsaw, 1986), 101–5.

38. L.-P. Ségur, *Tableau historique et politique de l'Europe de 1786 à 1806*, quoted by J. Fabre, *Stanislas-Auguste Poniatowski et l'Europe des lumières* (Paris, 1952), 8.

39. Dostoevsky, 8 June 1880. For a full discussion see Milan Hauner, *What Is Asia to Us? Russia's Asian Heartland Yesterday and Today* (New York, 1990), esp. pt. i, 'Russian Ideology and Asia: Historians and Geographers'.

40. Alexander Blok, 'The Scythians', in Cecil Kisch, *Alexander Blok: Prophet of Revolution* (London, 1960), 152–3.

41. René Albrecht-Carrié, 'Two Special Cases: England and Russia', in *The Unity of Europe: An Historical Survey* (London, 1966), 24–7.

42. Timothy Garton Ash, *The Uses of Adversity: Essays on the Fate of Central Europe* (New York, 1989; 2nd rev. edn. London, 1991); also G. Schopflin and Nancy Wood (eds.), *The Search for Central Europe* (Oxford, 1989); and J. Le Rider, *La Mitteleuropa* (Paris, 1994).

43. *Heart of Europe* is the title of an appeal for the fate of occupied Belgium (London, 1915); of a short history of Poland by Norman Davies (Oxford, 1984); of a guidebook to Prague by Bohomir Mraz (London, 1988); of a Hungarian art exhibition at the National Gallery of Scotland (Edinburgh, 1992); and of J. P. Stern's collected essays on German literature and ideology (London, 1992).

44. Hugh Seton-Watson, 'What Is Europe, Where Is Europe? From Mystique to Politique', 11th Martin Wight Lecture, delivered at the Royal Institute of International Affairs, 23 Apr. 1985; *Encounter*, 65/2 (July–Aug. 1985), 9–17.

45. Ibid. 14.

46. Ibid. 16.

47. Ibid. 17.

48. Dimitri Obolensky, 'Hugh Seton-Watson, FBA', *Proceedings of the British Academy*, 78 (1987), 631–41.

49. Douglas Johnson, 'What is European History?', *UCL History Newsletter*, 8 (University College London) (Dec. 1991), 9–10.

50. F. Guizot, *The History of Civilisation in Europe* (London, n.d.), 32.

51. George Burton Adams, *European History: An Outline of Its Development* (London and New York, 1899), 6.

52. Terne L. Plunkett and R. B. Mowat, *A History of Europe* (Oxford, 1927), preface, p. vii.

53. Rudyard Kipling, 'The Ballad of East and West', in *The Definitive Edition of Kipling's Verse* (London, 1949), 234–8.

54. Kipling, 'Recessional: June 22, 1897', in *The Oxford Book of English Verse* (Oxford, 1939), 1069.

55. Martin Bernal, *Black Athena: The Afroasiatic Roots of Classical Civilization* (2 vols., London, 1987–91). [**BLACK ATHENA**]

56. Molefi Kete Asante, *Afrocentricity* (Trenton, NJ, 1988), 6, 11. Afrocentrists can be particularly scathing about American black leaders like W. E. B. Du Bois who worked for integration and assimilation. 'Educated at the University of Berlin and at Harvard, the citadel of western images in America, Du Bois was steeped in the traditions of European scholarship. . . . Working from a Eurocentric vision, he participated in the philosophical currents of Western Europe, and therefore reflected the same mental flow as Darwinism, Marxism, and Freudianism. These rather materialistic approaches to life viewed conflict as the driving force behind progress' (ibid. 16–17).

57. See George James, *Stolen Legacy* (San Francisco, 1976), which maintains that European philosophy and creative thought derive from Africa.

58. S. Amin, *Eurocentrism* (London, 1989); V. Lambropoulos, *The Rise of Eurocentrism: anatomy of interpretation* (London, 1993).

59. Jacques Ellul, *Trahison de l'occident* (Paris, 1975), 217.

60. Edward Said, *Orientalism* (London, 1978).

61. In his *History of Western Civilization: A Handbook* (see n. 64 below), W. H. McNeill uses 'Western Civilization' interchangeably with 'the Civilization of Western Europe', 'European Civilization', 'our civilization', and 'European History'. He makes two main divisions: 'Classical Civilization' and, from AD c.900, 'European Civilization', the latter identified with 'Western Christendom' (pp. v–vii, 243–8).

62. Maurice Keen, *The Pelican History of Mediaeval Europe* (London, 1969), 9.

63. Ibid. 12.

64. W. H. McNeill, *History of Western Civilization: A Handbook,* 6th edn. (Chicago, 1986), 672. 1st edn. 1949—a companion to the 9-vol. *University of Chicago Readings in Western Civilization.*

65. J. Mortimer Adler, 'Great Books, Past and Present', in his *Reforming Education: The Opening of the American Mind,* ed. G. van Doren (New York, 1988), 318–50; see also Harold Bloom, *The Western Canon: The Books and School of the Ages* (New York, 1994).

66. J. Plamenatz, 'Two Types of Nationalism', in E. Kamenka (ed.), *Nationalism: The Nature and Evolution of an Idea* (New York, 1976), 23–36.

67. Ibid. 29–30.

68. Eric Hobsbawm, 'The Return of Mitteleuropa', *Guardian,* 11 Oct. 1991. [**WIENER WELT**]

69. Halford Mackinder, *Democratic Ideas and Reality* (London, 1919), and esp. 'The Round World and the Winning of the Peace', *Foreign Affairs,* 21 (1943), 595–605. See Chapter X, n. 73.

70. In this, Dr Plamenatz (see n. 66 above) was not alone. See Chapter X, n. 23.

71. See 'The Stanford Mind', *Wall Street Journal,* 22 Dec. 1989, and 'Stanford's Image', *San Jose Mercury News,* 17 Mar. 1991; also 'Travels with Rigoberta: Multiculturalism at Stanford', in Dinesh D'Souza, *Illiberal Education: The Politics of Race and Sex on Campus* (New York, 1991), 59–93.

72. See Allan Bloom, *The Closing of the American Mind* (New York, 1987).

73. Stanford University, General European Program, 1987–8: 'Europe I' (Prof. J. Brown), 'Europe II' (Prof. J. Diefendorf), 'Europe III' (Prof. J. J. Sheehan).

74. Quoted by George Gordon, 'The Land Where You Can't Tell Wrong from Rights', *Daily Mail,* 21 June 1991.

75. Allan Bloom, *The Closing of the American Mind,* op. cit.

76. D'Souza, *Illiberal Education,* op. cit.

77. Adler, *Reforming Education,* op. cit.

78. Goethe, 'Talismane', from the *West–Ostlicher Divan* (1815), in *Goethe: Selected Verse,* ed. David Luke (London, 1964), 233.

79. A. J. P. Taylor, *English History, 1914–45* (Oxford, 1965).

80. Hugh Gaitskell, in the House of Commons, 1962; quoted by Keith Robbins; see n. 98 below. Lord Tebbitt in the House of Lords in 1992 improved on Gaitskell's gaffe, talking of '1000 years of British parliamentary history'; quoted by Prof. David Cannadine at the Anglo-American Historical Conference, University of London, 30 June 1994.

81. University of London: School of History and Institute of Historical Research, *Syllabus and Courses, 1992–3* (The White Pamphlet) (London, 1992).

82. Jonathan Israel, 'History in the Making', *Independent,* 28 Dec. 1992. See also Conrad Russell, 'John Bull's Other Nations', *TLS,* 12 Mar. 1993.

83. David Cannadine, 'British History; Past, Present, and Future', *Past and Present,* 116 (Aug. 1987), 180. Dissenting opinions were published in 119 (May 1989).

84. See BBC *Newsnight,* 17 Sept. 1991, on 'J. R. Tolkien's Heritage'; also H. Carpenter, *J. R. R. Tolkien: A Biography* (London, 1992).

85. As of 1992. By 1993–4, the Honours School of English Language and Literature at Oxford was offering two course variants, one of which was the 'Special Course in English Language and Early English Literature'. 'Old English Literature' and 'Old English Translation' were still set papers for all candidates for Honour Moderations and Preliminary Examinations in English. *University of Oxford Examination Decrees and Regulations,* Oxford 1993, 31–3, 71–2, 177–87. 'The Examination in the School of

Modern History shall always include 1) The History of England ... 2) General History during some period ... 3) a special Historical subject ...' The requirement for a knowledge of compulsory non-English texts had been dropped (ibid. 49, 257 ff.).

86. Jean-François Baque, 'Car chaque enfant meurt à son rang: le patriotisme en chantant', *Historama*, 89 (July 1991), 64–6.

87. V. Ogilvie, 'Teaching Without Nationalistic Bias', *The Times*, 7 June 1947; G. M. Trevelyan, 'Bias in History', *History*, 32/115 (1947), 1–15; Paul Kennedy, 'The Decline of Nationalistic History in the West, 1900–70', *Journal of Contemporary History* (1973), 77–99.

88. Tadeusz Korzon, *Historya Nowożytna, Tom I do 1648 roku* (Cracow, 1889), 1–2.

89. Korzon's volume initiated a series planned to cover four periods of Modern History: i, Renaissance; ii, Reformation, 1517–1648; iii, Balance of Power, 1648–1789; and iv, Revolution, 1789–1815. In his judgement, *historya najnowsza* or 'Contemporary History' took over from Modern History in 1815. Thereafter, the historian's task was reduced to collecting material for later analysis (pp. 2–4).

90. Special credit in this field must go to the Eckert Institute in Brunswick, which embodied UNESCO's efforts to revive pre-war schemes for eliminating national bias from history-teaching. See *Georg Eckert Institute for International Textbook Research: An Outline of the Institute's Development, Tasks and Perspectives* (Braunschweig, 1947); also n. 107 below.

91. K. V. Bazilevich *et al.*, *A History of the USSR* (3 vols., Moscow, 1947–8).

92. e.g. the Oxford Syllabus for GCE A-Level History (1992) required candidates to take two papers from a list of seven 'Outline' and seven 'Special' papers. The Outline Papers cover limited periods such as 1066–1273, 1603–1715, or 1895–1964, and are subdivided into so-called 'British' and 'General' sections (in effect, into English and West European plus Russian). Each contains 'Nominated Topics', such as 'The Peasants' Revolt' or 'The Thirty Years War'. The Special Papers address subjects such as 'Government in Early Tudor England, 1509–53' or 'Nazism and the Third Reich, 1919–45'; University of Oxford Delegacy of Local Examinations, *General Certificate of Education 1992: Regulations and Syllabuses* (Oxford, 1990), 49–72.

93. D. Iredale, *Discovering Local History* (Aylesbury, 1977); C. Phythian Adams, *Rethinking English Local History* (Leicester, 1987); also E. Hinrichs, *Regionalitaet: der 'kleine Raum' also Problem der internationaler Schulbuchforschung* (Frankfurt, 1990).

94. See M. G. S. Hodgson and E. Burke (eds.), *Re-thinking World History: Essays on Europe, Islam, and World History* (Cambridge, 1993).

95. Élie Halévy, *L'Histoire du peuple anglais au XIXème siècle* (1913–26), trans. as *History of the English People in the Nineteenth Century* (6 vols., London, 1949–52); Denis Mack Smith, *Italy: A Modern History* (1959), trans. as *Storia d'Italia dal 1861 al 1958* (2 vols., Milan, 1966); Hugh Kearney, *The British Isles: a history of four nations* (Cambridge, 1989).

96. Christopher Dawson, *The Making of Europe* (London, 1932). See also C. Scott, *A Historian and His World: A Life of Christopher Dawson, 1889–1970* (London, 1984).

97. Richard Coudenhouve-Kalergi, *Pan-Europa* (Vienna, 1924; New York, 1926); Pierre Renouvin, *L'Idée de fédération européenne dans la pensée politique du XIXe siècle* (Oxford, 1949); Salvador de Madariaga, *L'Esprit de l'Europe* (Brussels, 1952); R. Albrecht-Carrié, *The Unity of Europe: a historical survey* (London, 1966).

98. Keith Robbins, 'National Identity and History: Past, Present, and Future', *History*, 75/245 (Oct. 1990), 369–87, being the presidential address to the Historical Association Conference in Cheltenham, Apr. 1990.

99. Jenny Wormald, 'The Creation of Britain: Multiple Kingdoms or Core and Colonies?', *TRHS*, 6th ser., iii (1993), 194.

100. See Norman Davies, 'Stalin's History Lesson', *Spectator*, 6 Aug. 1988.

101. L. Brezhnev, Speech at Bad Godesberg, W. Germany, 23 Nov. 1981.

102. M. Gorbachev, *Perestroika: New Thinking for Our Country and the World* (London, 1987), 191–5: 'We are Europeans' (p. 191); 'The home is common, but each family has its own apartment, and there are different entrances' (p. 195).

103. See G. W. Blackburn, *Education in the Third Reich* (Albany, NY, 1985).

104. Such, apparently, was the fate of Tiny Rowland, later Chairman of Lonrho and proprietor of the *Observer*, who in 1941 was arrested and interned under Section 18B of the Act relating to 'British-born persons with leanings towards Fascism'; 'All Well That Ends Well', *Observer*, 23 May 1993.

105. Norman Stone, 'The Evil Empire: Heroes and Villains', *Sunday Times*, 1 Sept. 1991.

106. David Cesarani, *Justice Delayed* (London, 1992).

107. *Against Bias and Prejudice: The Council of Europe's Work on History Teaching and History Textbooks* (Council of Europe Report, Strasbourg, 1986).

108. Margaret Shennan, op. cit. p. 53, esp. the chapters 'Europe and the Time Dimension' and 'Europe's Cultural Identity'.

109. Jean-Baptiste Duroselle, *Europe: A History of Its Peoples* (London, 1991), 'Epilogue', 411–15.

110. See Adam Zamoyski, 'An Historic Case of Euro-fudge', *Sunday Telegraph*, 6 Nov. 1988. J. Nicholas, 'Half-truths about Half of Europe', *Guardian*, 25 Oct. 1991.

111. 'Quand un livre scandalise la Grèce', *Libre Belgique*, 26 Apr. 1990; 'La prima Storia Europea offende tutti i 12', *La Stampa*, 4 Nov. 1990; C. M. Woodhouse, in *Kathimerini* (Athens), 3 June 1990.

112. Academician M. V. Sakellariou, letter to the Greek Deputies of the European Parliament, 18 Mar. 1990.

113. *Kathimerini*, 30 Sept. 1990.

114. Jacques Montaville *et al.*, *Histoire de l'Europe* (Paris, 1992). See Julian Nundy, 'History Leaves Britain Behind', *Independent on Sunday*, 19 Jan. 1992.

115. Benedikt Anderson, *Imagined Communities: Reflections on the Origin and Spread of Nationalism*, 2nd edn. (London, 1991); quoted by G. Varouxakis in *UCL History Newsletter*, 8 (Dec. 1991), 22–4.

116. Prof. Marc Raeff, in 'What Is European History?', *History Today*, 36 (Jan. 1986), 46–50.

117. Professor Marc Ferro, ibid.

118. Dr. Eva Haraszti, ibid.

119. Prof. Immanuel Wallerstein, ibid.

120. A. J. P. Taylor, ibid.

CHAPTER I

1. Charles Louis de Secondat, Baron de Montesquieu, in *Considérations sur les causes de la grandeur des Romains* (1734); also 'On the Difference of Men in Different Climates', *De l'Esprit des lois* (1748), trans. as *The Spirit of Laws* (London, 1878), xiv. 2.

2. P. Vidal de la Blache, *Principes de géographie humaine*, ed. E. de Martonne (Paris, 1921), trans. as *Principles of Human Geography* (London, 1926); also *La Personnalité géographique de la France*, being the introduction to his *Tableau de la géographie de la France*, English trans. (Manchester, 1941); F. Braudel, *L'Identité de la France* (Paris,

1985). Montesquieu wrote that Britain was 'a nation so distempered by the climate to have a disrelish of everything, nay even of life' (Esprit des lois).

3. Luigi Luca Cavalli-Sforza in *Scientific American* (1991), as reported by S. Connor, 'On the Origin of Speeches', *Independent on Sunday*, 10 Nov. 1991.

4. Dr Steve Jones, BBC Reith Lectures 1991, published as *The Language of the Genes: Biology, History and the Evolutionary Future* (London, 1993).

5. See Introduction, nn. 42, 43, and 68; also J. Szucs, 'Three Historical Regions of Europe', in *Történelmi Szemle* (Budapest), 24 (1981), 313–69, published as *Les Trois Europes* (Paris, 1985); H. C. Meyer, *Mitteleuropa in German Thought and Action, 1815–45* (The Hague, 1955); and O. Halecki, *The Borderlands of European Civilization* (New York, 1952).

6. See Braudel, *La Méditerranée* (see Introduction, n. 16).

7. Robert Fox, *The Inner Sea: The Mediterranean and Its People* (London, 1991).

8. See David Kirby, *Northern Europe in the Early Modern Period* (London, 1990); also J. Fitzmaurice, *The Baltic: A Regional Future?* (London, 1992).

9. Neil Ascherson, *Black Sea*, p. 267 (London and New York, 1995).

10. Ellsworth Huntington, *Civilization and Climate* (1915; 3rd edn., New Haven, Conn., 1924); *The Mainsprings of Civilization* (New York, 1945).

11. Arnold J. Toynbee, *A Study of History* (1934), abridged (London, 1960), 151.

12. Michael Anderson, *The Birth of Europe*, op. cit. 97.

13. C. Stringer and R. Grun, 'New Light on Our Shadowy Ancestors', *Independent on Sunday*, 1 Sept. 1991.

14. W. J. Perry, *The Growth of Civilization* (London, 1925), 34.

15. See Barry Cunliffe, 'Aegean Civilization and Barbarian Europe', in *The Roots of European Civilization* (Chicago, 1987), 5–15; also J. Howell, 'The Lake Villages of France', ibid. 42–53.

16. See Gerald S. Hawkins, *Stonehenge Decoded* (London, 1970).

17. Colin Renfrew, *Archaeology and Language: The Puzzle of Indo-European Origins* (London, 1987).

18. Marija Gimbutas, in G. Cardona *et al.* (eds.), *Indo-European and Indo-Europeans* (Philadelphia, 1970), 54; quoted by Renfrew, *Archaeology and Language* 17.

19. As suggested by Jones, *The Language of the Genes*.

20. On European onomastics, see G. Semerano, *Le origini della cultura europea: rivelazioni della linguistica storica* (Florence, 1984).

Cnossos, 1628 BC

21. See Jacquetta Hawkes, 'The Grace of Life', in *The Dawn of the Gods* (London, 1968), 73–156, where 'the feminine spirit of Minoan life' is contrasted with 'the masculine Achean spirit' of later times.

22. Sir Arthur Evans, *The Palace of Minos: A Comparative Account of the Early Cretan Civilization* (4 vols., London, 1921–36), i. 17. See also S. Horwitz, *Find of a Lifetime* (London, 1981), and A. C. Brown, *Arthur Evans and the Palace of Minos* (Oxford, 1981).

23. On the Anemospelia sacrifice, discovered in 1979, see Peter Warren, 'The Minoans and Their Gods', in Barry Cunliffe, *Origins*, op. cit. 30–41.

24. Gerald Cadogan, 'A Theory That Could Change History', *Financial Times*, 9 Sept. 1989.

CHAPTER II

1. Eliza Marian Butler, 'The Myth of Laocoön', in *The Tyranny of Greece over Germany* (Cambridge, 1935), 43–8.

2. *The Oxford Book of English Verse* (1939), Nos. 632, 614, 608.

3. Maurice Bowra, *Ancient Greek Literature* (Oxford, 1933), 9; Walter Savage Landor, quoted ibid.; J. C. Stobart, *The Glory That Was Greece: A Survey of Hellenic Culture and Civilization* (1911; rev. edn. London, 1933), introduction.

4. Gilbert Murray, *The Legacy of Greece* (Oxford, 1922), Introduction.

5. From Aeschylus, *The Persians*, in D. Grene and R. Lattimore (eds.), *Complete Greek Tragedies* (Chicago, 1959), i. 232–3.

6. George Grote, *History of Greece* (London, 1907), xii. 303.

7. From Jules Michelet, *Histoire Romaine* (1834), bk. ii.

8. Rainer Maria Rilke, 'Die Sonette an Orpheus', *The Penguin Book of German Verse*, ed. L. Forster (London, 1957), 403–4.

9. Bernard Williams, quoted by Oliver Taplin, *Greek Fire* (London, 1989), 170.

10. Sappho, quoted ibid. 141.

11. Glycon, trans. Peter Jay; see *The Greek Anthology: A Selection in Translation*, ed. Jay (London, 1990).

12. Simonides, 'On the Spartans at Thermopylae', of which there are innumerable translations. See Earl of Cromer, *Paraphrases and Translations from the Greek* (London, 1903), no. 33.

13. Quotations by, respectively, Oliver Taplin, George Steiner, and Friedrich Nietzsche, *The Birth of Tragedy* (1872): in Taplin, 'Outstaring the Gorgon', in *Greek Fire*, 36–61.

14. *Antigone*, 332 ff., in Sophocles, *The Theban Plays*, trans. E. F. Watling (London, 1947), 135–6.

15. Sir Ernst Gombrich, *The Story of Art* (Oxford, 1952), 52.

16. Ibid. *passim*.

17. K. J. Dover, *Greek Homosexuality* (London, 1978).

18. See David M. Halperin, 'Sex Before Sexuality: Pederasty, Politics, and Power in Classical Athens', in M. B. Duberman *et al.* (eds.), *Hidden from History: Reclaiming the Gay and Lesbian Past* (New York, 1989; London, 1991), 37–53.

19. See John Boswell, 'Revolutions, Universals, and Sexual Categories', ibid. 17–36.

20. Thucydides, from 'Pericles' Funeral Speech', *The Peloponnesian War*, trans. Rex Warner (London, 1954), ii. 4.

21. Dithyramboi, Fragment 76, *The Works of Pindar*, ed. L. R. Famell, (London, 1932) iii, 171

Syracusae, Year 1, Olympiad 141

22. See M. Finley, 'Five Tyrants', in *Ancient Sicily: To the Arab Conquest*, vol. i of a *History of Sicily* written with D. Mack Smith (1968), abridged C. Duggan (London, 1986).

23. Livy, *History of Rome*, xxiv. 34 (Loeb Library).

24. After ibid.

25. From Plutarch, *Marcellus*, xv (after Loeb).

26. ibid. xix. 3.

27. Ch. M. Danov, 'The Celtic Invasion and Rule in Thrace in the Light of Some New Evidence', *Studia Celtica*, 10/11 (1975–6), 29–40.

CHAPTER III

1. Cato, *De Re Rustica*, 1.

2. Quoted by, among others, the Venerable Bede, and by Edward Gibbon, *Decline and Fall of the Roman Empire*, ch. 17.

3. Reginald Blomfield, in R. W. Livingstone (ed.), *The Legacy of Greece* (Oxford, 1924), 406.

4. From Thomas Babington Macaulay, 'Horatius', in *The Lays of Ancient Rome* (1842); W. H. Henley (ed.), *Lyra Heroica* (London, 1921), 147–63.

5. Appian, *Romaika*, bk. 132, quoted by B. H. Warmington, *Carthage* (London, 1964), 260.

6. Rudyard Kipling, 'A Song to Mithras' (Hymn of the XXX Legion, AD *c*.350), in *The Definitive Verse of Rudyard Kipling* (London, 1940; repr. 1989), 523–4.

7. *Aeneid*, vi. 851–3.

8. W. De Burgh, *Legacy of the Ancient World* (London, 1936), ch. ii, 'The Reception of Roman Law'.

9. Gibbon, *Decline and Fall*, ch. 9.

10. Virgil, *Georgics*, ii. 490; iii. 284; *Eclogues*, xi. 32; i. 66; *Aeneid*, i. 362.

11. See Gilbert Highet, 'Vergil', in *Poets in a Landscape* (London, 1959), 55–81.

12. Horace, *Odes*, ii. 3; *Ars Poetica*, 139; *Epistles*, 11, 2, 45; *Odes*, xxx. 1.

13. Ovid, *Ars Amatoria*, ii. 107.

14. Theodor Mommsen, *The History of Rome*, English trans. (London, 1890), iv. 90.

15. Ronald Syme, *The Roman Revolution* (Oxford, 1939), p. vii.

16. Ibid. 11.

17. Ibid. 201.

18. Suetonius, *The Twelve Caesars*, trans. Robert Graves (London, 1957), on Augustus, 51–108.

19. Ibid. 149–79.

20. Ibid. 209.

21. Ibid. 223.

22. Ibid. 285.

23. Gibbon, *Decline and Fall*, ch. 3.

24. Ibid.

25. Adapted from J. B. Bury, *A History of the Roman Empire from Its Foundation to the Death of Marcus Aurelius* (London, 1908), 438–48.

26. *The Meditations of the Emperor Marcus Aurelius Antoninus*, trans. Robert Graves (London, 1955), iii. 21.

27. Ibid. vi. 50, 48.

28. Gibbon, *Decline and Fall*, ch. 10.

29. Ibid. ch. 15.

30. See G. Vermes, *Jesus and the World of Judaism* (London, 1983); D. Flusser, *Judaism and the Origins of Christianity* (Jerusalem, 1988); and M. Baigent and R. Leigh, *The Dead Sea Scrolls Deception* (London, 1991).

31. With thanks to the Al-Shalom Reformed Synagogue, Glencoe, Ill.

32. Irenaeus, *Adversus Heraeses*, III. iii. 1–2, quoted by J.-B. Duroselle, *Histoire du catholicisme* (Paris, 1949), 8.

33. Gibbon, *Decline and Fall*, ch. 16.

34. C. P. S. Clarke, *A Short History of the Christian Church* (London, 1929), 69; also J. F. Bethune-Baker, *An Introduction to the Early History of Christian Doctrine* (London, 1903). There are, in fact, two different formulas of the Nicene Creed—the shorter version issued at Nicaea in 325 and a longer version, also known as the Niceno-Constantinopolitan Creed, possibly drawn up at the General Council of 381. See World Council of Churches, *Confessing One Faith . . . : the Nicene–Constantinopolitan Creed* (Geneva, 1991).

The Bosporus, 4 November 1079 AUC

35. Jacob Burckhardt, *The Age of Constantine the Great* (1852), trans. M. Hadas (New York, 1949), 343–53.
36. Eusebius of Caesarea (*c.*260–340), *Vita Constantini,* quoted by Burckhardt, *Constantine the Great,* 231. See also *The Essential Eusebius,* trans. Colm Luibhaid (New York, 1966).
37. Gibbon, *Decline and Fall,* chs. 14, 16.

CHAPTER IV

1. See Mortimer Wheeler, *Rome Beyond the Imperial Frontiers* (London, 1954).
2. Salvian of Marseilles, *c.*440, quoted by Jacques Le Goff, *Mediaeval Civilization, 400–1500* (Oxford, 1988).
3. Simeon Potter, *Language in the Modern World* (London, 1960), ch. 7, 'The Indo-European Family'. See also Harold Goad, *Language and History* (London, 1958).
4. G. Labuda, *Źródła, sagi, i legendi do najdawniejszych dziejów Polski* (Warsaw, 1961) contains studies of Alfred the Great, the Gotho-Hunnic Wars, the *Widsith,* and the *Chanson de Roland.* See also J. Otto Maenchen-Helfen, *The World of the Huns* (Berkeley, Calif., 1973).
5. Gibbon, *Decline and Fall,* ch. 42. For the 4,600 villages, he quotes 'a curious MS fragment of the year 550 in the library at Milan' (n. 11). On the subject of *panicum milium* he comments: 'In the wealth of modern husbandry, our millet feeds poultry, not heroes' (n. 12).
6. Ibid. ch. 30.
7. Ferdinand Lot, *La Fin du monde antique et le début du Moyen Âge* (Paris, 1951), 3; also 'Le Régime des castes', 115 ff.
8. Charles Oman, *The Dark Ages, AD 476–918* (6th edn., London, 1919), 29.
9. Lot, *La Fin du monde antique,* 311.
10. Oman, *The Dark Ages,* 207.
11. See Dimitri Obolensky, *The Byzantine Commonwealth: Eastern Europe, 500–1453* (London, 1971).
12. *Koran,* sura 5, verse 3.
13. Steven Runciman, *A History of the Crusades* (Cambridge, 1953), i. 3.
14. From the *Shorter Encyclopaedia of Islam,* ed. H. A. R. Gibb and J. H. Kramers (London, 1961), 16, 491.
15. Gibbon, *Decline and Fall,* ch. 35.
16. *La Chanson de Roland,* cxlix. 2000–9; *The Song of Roland: The Oxford Text,* trans. Roy Owen (London, 1972), 76.
17. Henri Pirenne, *Mediaeval Cities: Their Origins and the Revival of Trade* (Princeton, NJ, 1925), 27; also his *Mahomet and Charlemagne* (London, 1939).
18. Gibbon, *Decline and Fall,* ch. 23.
19. *Historiae Ecclesiasticae Francorum,* ii. 27, trans. J. H. Robinson in *Readings in European History,* i (Boston, 1904), 51.
20. Bede, *A History of the English Church and People,* trans. Leo Shirley-Price (London, 1955), i. 27, p. 76.
21. Ibid. i. 30, pp. 86–7.

Mons Iovis, *c.*25 November AD 753

22. C. Bayet, 'Remarques sur le caractère et les conséquences du voyage d'Étienne III en France', *Revue historique,* 20 (1882), 88–105.

23. J. N. D. Kelly, *The Oxford Dictionary of Popes* (Oxford, 1988), 91–2.

24. Abbé L. Duchesne (ed.), *Le Liber Pontificalis: texte, introduction et commentaire* (Paris, 1884), 440 ff.; *Étude sur le Liber Pontificalis* (Paris, 1877).

25. J. M. Wallace-Hadrill (ed.), *The Fourth Book of the Chronicle of Fredegar with Continuations* (London, 1960).

26. *Liber Pontificalis,* 447.

27. Ibid.

28. *The Fourth Book of the Chronicle of Fredegar,* 104.

29. Ibid. 109.

CHAPTER V

1. Thomas Hobbes, *Leviathan,* 4, 47.

2. Quoted by Donald Bullough, *The Age of Charlemagne* (London, 1965), 13.

3. Ibid. ch. 4, 'A Court of Scholars and the Revival of Learning'.

4. Oman, op. cit. p. 382.

5. Shakespeare, *Macbeth,* v. v. 19–28.

6. F. L. Ganshof, *Qu'est-ce que la féodalité?* (Brussels, 1944); trans. as *Feudalism* (London, 1952), p. xx.

7. Hugh Trevor-Roper, *The Rise of Christian Europe* (London, 1966), 96.

8. Lynn White, Jr., *Mediaeval Technology and Social Change* (Oxford, 1961), 14–28.

9. A 9th-cent. investiture described in the 12th cent. *Chanson de Saisnes,* or *Saxenleid,* of Jean Bodel of Arras; quoted by Ganshof, *Feudalism,* 126; see Jacques Le Goff, 'The Symbolic Ritual of Vassalage', in *Time, Work, and Culture in the Middle Ages* (Chicago, 1980), 237–87.

10. C. Seignobos, *The Rise of European Civilization* (London, 1939), 128.

11. N. Brussel, *L'Usage général des fiefs en France* (1727), i. 3; quoted by J. H. Robinson, *Readings in European History* (Boston, 1904), i. 178.

12. Eric Fromm, *The Fear of Freedom* (London, 1942), 34.

13. Marc Bloch, 'Les Deux âges féodaux', in *La Société féodale: la formation des liens de dépendance* (Paris, 1949), 95–7.

14. P. Skwarczyński, 'The Problem of Feudalism in Poland', *Slavonic and East European Review,* 34 (1956), 292–310.

15. F. Tout, *The Empire and the Papacy, 918–1273* (London, 1921).

16. C. W. Previté-Orton, *Shorter Cambridge Mediaeval History* (Cambridge, 1952), i. 368.

17. From Liutprand, *Antapadoseos, vi,* in *Monumenta Germaniae Historiae,* quoted by Robinson, *Readings in European History,* i. 340–3.

18. See Zbigniew Dobrzyński, *Obrządek Słowiański w dawnej Polsce* (3 vols., Warsaw, 1989).

19. *Relacja Ibrahim Ibn Jakuba z podróży do krajów słowiańskich w przekładzie Al Bekriego,* ed. T. Kowalski (Cracow, 1946); quoted by Davies, *God's Playground,* i. 3–4.

20. See Otto Hoetzsch, *The Evolution of Russia* (London, 1966), 17.

21. *The Rubáiyát of Omar Khayyám,* trans. Edward Fitzgerald (1859; ed. G. F. Maine, London, 1954), quatrains 1, 11, 49.

22. See H. F. B. Lynch, *Armenia: travels and studies,* 2 vols. (London, 1901, repr. 1990); also M. Chahin, *The Kingdom of Armenia* (London, 1987).

23. Shota Rustaveli, trans. M. J. Wardrop as *The Man in the Panther Skin* (London, 1912). On Georgia see W. E. D. Allen, *A History of the Georgian People . . . to the Russian Conquest* (London, 1932); D. M. Lang, *The Last Years of the Georgian Monarchy,*

1652–1832 (London, 1957); and R. G. Suny, *The Making of the Georgian Nation* (London, 1988).

24. Henri Pirenne, *Economic and Social History of Mediaeval Europe* (New York, 1956), 51.
25. J.-B. Duroselle, *Histoire du catholicisme*, 55.
26. From *The Confession of Golias* composed by Hugh, a follower of Archbishop Reinald of Cologne and known as 'the Archpoet'; text in M. Manitius, *Die Gedichte des Archpoeta* (Munich, 1913), 24–9; quoted by Charles Homer Haskins, *The Renaissance of the Twelfth Century* (Cambridge, Mass., 1927), 182.
27. Bernard de Ventadour, quoted by R. Pernoud, *Aliénor d'Aquitaine* (Paris, 1965), trans. Peter Wiles as *Eleanour of Aquitaine* (London, 1967), 102.
28. Jean, Sire de Joinville, *Livre des saintes paroles et bons faits de notre roi, Saint Louis*, quoted by A. Lagarde and L. Michard, *Le Moyen Âge* (Paris, 1962), 123–32.
29. Gibbon, *Decline and Fall*, ch. 48.
30. Jacques Le Goff, *La Civilisation médiévale de l'Occident* (Paris, 1965), 98.
31. Norman Cohn, *The Pursuit of the Millennium* (London, 1970), 61, 64.
32. See Jonathan Riley-Smith, *The Feudal Nobility and the Kingdom of Jerusalem, 1174–1277* (London, 1973).
33. Ernle Bradford, *The Great Betrayal: Constantinople 1204* (London, 1967).
34. *The Oxford Book of Prayer*, ed. G. Appleton (Oxford, 1985), no. 217.
35. Edmund Holmes, *The Albigensian or Catharist Heresy* (London, 1925); republished as *The Holy Heretics: The Story of the Albigensian Crusade* (London, 1948). See also J. Madaule, *The Albigensian Crusade* (London, 1967); Z. Oldenbourg, *Massacre at Montségur* (London, 1961).
36. Eric Christiansen, *The Northern Crusades: The Baltic and the Catholic Frontier, 1100–1525* (London, 1980), 53.
37. Ibid. 92.
38. Ibid. 85.
39. *The Travels of Marco Polo the Venetian*, introduction by John Masefield (London, 1908), 413.
40. White, *Mediaeval Technology and Social Change*, 40.
41. Georges Duby, *The Early Growth of the European Economy: Warriors and Peasants from the Seventh to the Twelfth Century* (London, 1974).
42. Jean Gimpel, *The Mediaeval Machine: The Industrial Revolution of the Middle Ages* (London, 1977), 100. [There was a charioteer's strike in Rome under Nero.]

Schiedam, AD 1265

43. J. G. Kruisheer (ed.), *Oorkondenboek van Holland en Zeeland tot 1299* (Maastricht, 1992), iii. 1305.
44. Ibid. 1528.
45. W. G. Brill (ed.), *Rijmkronik van Melis Stoke* (Utrecht, 1885), iv. 55–6.
46. See N. Denholm-Young, *Richard of Cornwall* (Oxford, 1947).
47. T. Wright (ed.), *The Political Songs of England from the Reign of King John to that of Edward II* (London, 1839), 69.
48. Ibid. 59–63.
49. P. A. Meilink (ed.), *Het Archief van de Abdij van Egmond* (The Hague, 1951), ii, 'Regestenlijst 889–1436', no. 83 (1265) 13 July.
50. Lord Bryce, *The Holy Roman Empire* (London, 1875), 213.
51. See W. G. Heeres *et al.* (eds.), *From Dunkirk to Danzig: Shipping and Trade in the North Sea and the Baltic, 1350–1850* (Hilversum, 1988).

52. G. J. Renier, *The Criterion of Dutch Nationhood: An Inaugural Lecture at University College, London, 4 June 1945* (London, 1946), 16–17.

CHAPTER VI

1. Johan Huizinga, *The Waning of the Middle Ages* (1924; London, 1955), 30.
2. Ibid. 10.
3. Ibid. 26.
4. 'The Advent of the New Form', ibid. 334.
5. R. Lodge, *The Close of the Middle Ages* (London, 1920), 496.
6. Steven Runciman, 'The Rising Sultanate', in *The Fall of Constantinople, 1453* (Cambridge, 1965), 31.
7. Quoted by Richard Pipes, *Russia under the Old Regime* (London, 1975), 62.
8. See Gabriel Jackson, *The Making of Mediaeval Spain* (London, 1972).
9. Bryce, op. cit., p. 238.
10. Dante Alighieri, *Inferno*, vi. 49–50, 74–5.
11. As related by Simonde de Sismondi, *Histoire des républiques italiennes du Moyen Âge* (Geneva, 1807–8), iii. 129.
12. Petrarch, 'Di pensier in pensier', in *The Penguin Book of Italian Verse*, ed. George Kay (London, 1958), 116.
13. Dante Alighieri, *Paradiso*, xxvii. 22–7, 55–60.
14. Robert Burns, 'Scots wha hae' (Bruce Before Bannockburn), in *Poems and Songs of Robert Burns*, ed. J. Barke (London, 1955), 629.
15. Declaration of Arbroath, 6 Apr. 1320, English translation; see G. F. Maine, *A Book of Scotland* (London, 1950), 81–2. On Scottish history, J. D. Mackie, *A History of Scotland* (2nd edn., London, 1978); W. Moffat, A. M. Gray, *A History of Scotland* (Oxford, 1989).
16. Quoted by Philip Ziegler, *The Black Death* (London, 1970), 66.
17. W. Rees, 'The Black Death as Recorded in English Manorial Documents', in *Proceedings of the Royal Society of Medicine*, xvi. 2, p. 4; quoted by Ziegler, *The Black Death*, 197.
18. P. D. A. Harvey, *A Mediaeval Oxfordshire Village: Cuxham* (Oxford, 1965), 135.
19. Ziegler, *The Black Death*, 239.
20. H. Pirenne, *Economic and Social History of Mediaeval Europe* (London, 1936), 200.
21. Quoted by George Holmes, *Europe: Hierarchy and Revolt, 1320–1450* (London, 1975), 131–2.
22. See R. B. Dobson, *The Peasants' Revolt of 1381* (London, 1983).
23. Charles d'Orléans, 'En regardant vers le pais de France', in *Oxford Book of French Verse* (Oxford, 1957), 30–1.
24. Shakespeare, *King Richard the Second*, ii. i. 40–50.
25. See D. Keys, 'Very Civil War and Unbloody Battles', *Independent*, 23 Dec. 1989.
26. See Richard Vaughan, *Valois Burgundy* (London, 1975), 129, 175, 191–3.
27. Ibid. 169–70. Destroyed in 1793, it was turned into the site of the departmental lunatic asylum.
28. Michał Giedroyć, 'The Arrival of Christianity in Lithuania, i: Early Contacts (Thirteenth Century)'; 'ii: Baptism and Survival (1341–87)', *Oxford Slavonic Papers*, xviii (1985), 1–30; xix (1986), 34–57.
29. P. Rabikauskas, 'La cristianizzione della Samogizia, 1413–17' in *La cristianizzione della Lituania: colloquio internazionale di storia ecclesiastica (1987)* (Rome, 1989).
30. V. H. H. Green, *Mediaeval Civilisation in Western Europe* (London, 1971), 4.

31. Green, op. cit. 98–9.

32. From H. von Treitschke, *History of Germany* (1879), ii; quoted by J. Sheehan, *German Liberalism in the Nineteenth Century* (London, 1982), 37.

33. Huizinga, *The Waning of the Middle Ages*, 248.

34. Friedrich Heer, *Mittelalter* (1961), trans. as *The Mediaeval World: Europe from 1100–1350* (London, 1962), 251–3.

35. Steven Runciman, *The Fall of Constantinople: 1453* (Cambridge, 1965), 131.

36. Ibid. 37.

37. Gibbon, *Decline and Fall*, ch. 68.

38. See Felipe Fernández-Armesto, 'Spain Repays Its Debt to the Jews', *European*, 19–25 Mar. 1992.

39. Emma Klein, 'The Sultan Who saved the Sephardim', ibid.

40. For the conventional view of Columbus, see J. H. Parry, *The Age of Reconnaissance: Discovery, Exploration and Settlement, 1450–1650* (London, 1963).

Moscow, AD 1493

41. See *The Orthodox Liturgy, being the Divine Liturgy of S. John Chrysostom and S. Basil the Great according to the use of the Church of Russia*, trans. P. Thompson *et al.* (London, 1939), from which all the following quotations, except for the Gospel reading, derive.

42. The Old Church Slavonic text uses the terms 'Ierod Tsr′′' and 'Tsr′ Iudeiskyi'; from *Gospoda Nashego Iesusa Khrista Novyi Zavyet na Slavyanskom i Ruskom Yazykakh* (The New Testament of Our Lord Jesus Christ in the Slavonic and Russian Languages), parallel texts (St Petersburg, 1823), 23.

43. See Dimitri Strémooukhoff, 'Moscow the Third Rome: Sources of the Doctrine', *Speculum* (Jan. 1953), 84–101; repr. in M. Cherniavsky, *The Structure of Russian History: Interpretative Essays* (New York, 1970), 108–25.

44. See J. L. I. Fennell, *Ivan the Great of Moscow* (London, 1961).

45. R. G. Howes, *Testaments of the Grand Princes of Moscow* (Ithaca, NY, 1967), 267–98.

46. Fennell, *Ivan the Great*, op. cit. 122.

47. Strémooukhoff, 'Moscow the Third Rome', *passim.*

48. Ibid. 113, esp. n. 46.

49. 'Testament of Ivan III', in Howes, *Testaments.* See also G. Vernadsky, *Russia at the Dawn of the Modern Age* (vol. iv of G. Vernadsky and M. Karpovich, *History of Russia*), (New Haven, Conn., 1959), ch. 3.

50. Fennell, *Ivan the Great*, 146.

51. Strémooukhoff, 'Moscow the Third Rome', 115.

52. Ibid. *passim.*

53. Dimitri Obolensky, 'Russia's Byzantine Heritage', *Oxford Slavonic Papers*, i (1950), 37–63.

54. Fennell, *Ivan the Great.*

55. Vernadsky, *Russia at the Dawn of the Modern Age*, ch. 3.

56. Fennell, *Ivan the Great*, preface, pp. v ff.

57. Dimitri Obolensky, 'Italy, Mount Athos and Muscovy: The Three Worlds of Maximos the Greek' (Raleigh Lecture, 1981), *Proceedings of the British Academy*, lvii (1981); repr. in *Six Byzantine Portraits* (Oxford, 1988), 201–19.

58. Ibid. 160.

59. Élie Dennisoff, *Maxime le Grec et l'Occident* (Paris, 1942), 423.

CHAPTER VII

1. See Keith Thomas, *Religion and the Decline of Magic: Studies in Popular Beliefs in Sixteenth and Seventeenth Century England* (London, 1971).
2. Herbert Weisinger, 'The Attack on the Renaissance in Theology Today', *Studies in the Renaissance*, 2 (1955), 176–89.
3. See Jacob Burckhardt, *The Culture of the Renaissance in Italy* (London, 1878).
4. Bert S. Hall (ed.), *On Pre-modern Technology and Science* (Los Angeles, 1976).
5. Walter Pater, *The Renaissance* (1873; repr. New York, 1959), 72.
6. Johan Huizinga, *Erasmus of Rotterdam: with a selection from his letters* (London, 1952).
7. Erasmus, Preface to New Testament (1516). *Prefaces to the Fathers, the New Testament, and On Study*, facsimile edn. (Menton, 1970); H. P. Smith, *Erasmus: A Study of His Life and Place in History* (New York, 1923).
8. Erasmus, *In Praise of Folly*, trans. and ed. Betty Radice, in *Collected Works* (Toronto, 1974–), xxvii. 2, 120 ff.
9. Ibid. 148.
10. *Adagia*, ibid. 31–4; see also Erasmus, *Proverbs or Adages . . . Englished by R. Taverner*, facsimile edn. (Gainsville, Fla., 1956).
11. Étienne Gilson (1937), Reinhold Niebuhr (1941), and Nicholas Berdyaev (1931), quoted by Weisinger, 'The Attack on the Renaissance', 176 ff. See also W. K. Ferguson, *The Renaissance in Historical Thought* (Boston, 1948).
12. Michelangelo Buonarroti, in G. Kay (ed.), *The Penguin Book of Italian Verse* (London, 1958), 172–3.
13. Leopold von Ranke, *The History of the Popes, their Church and State, and especially of their conflicts with Protestantism* (1834–6), trans. E. Foster (London, 1847), i. 38.
14. Charles Drelincourt, d. 1669; quoted by Albert-Marie Schmidt, *Jean Calvin et la tradition calvinienne* (Paris, 1957), 169.
15. In 1622, by Pope Gregory XV; quoted by John Padberg, 'The Jesuit Question', *Tablet*, 22 Sept. 1990.
16. Quoted by Fisher, *A History of Europe*, 557.
17. Ranke, *History of the Popes*, i. 266.
18. Herbert Butterfield, in *The Origins of Modern Science, 1300–1800* (London, 1947).
19. Ibid. It is curious that the historian who in *The Whig Interpretation of History* (1931) so brilliantly exposed the teleological tendencies of political historiography should have argued for 'the strategic line in the development of science'.
20. P. M. Harman, *The Scientific Revolution* (Lancaster, 1983), 17.
21. Quoted by A. W. Crosby, Jr., *The Columbian Exchange: Biological and Cultural Consequences of 1492* (Westport, Conn., 1972), 11.
22. Ibid.
23. See ibid.; also Kirkpatrick Sale, *The Conquest of Paradise* (New York, 1991).
24. See J. Larner, 'The Certainty of Columbus', *History*, 73/237 (1988), 3–23, for a summary of the changing historiography; also Garry Wills, 'Man of the Year', *New York Review of Books*, 22 Nov. 1991.
25. 'Where Did Columbus Discover America?', *National Geographic Magazine*, 170/5 (Nov. 1986), 566A with maps.
26. Yen Chung-ping, in *Historical Research* (Beijing) (1977), quoted by Larner, 'The Certainty of Columbus'; also Simon Wiesenthal, *Sails of Hope* (New York, 1973).
27. J. Manzano, *Colón y su segreto: el Predescubrimiento* (Madrid, 1982).

28. David Henige, *In Search of Columbus: The Sources for the first Voyage* (Tucson, Ariz., 1991).

29. See J. A. Levensen (ed.), *Circa 1492: Art in the Age of Exploration* (Catalogue to an Exhibition at the National Gallery, Washington DC) (New Haven, Conn., 1992).

30. Jacques Attali, *1492* (Paris, 1991), pt. i: 'Inventer l'Europe', 15 ff.

31. See Eugenio Garin (ed.), *Renaissance Characters* (Chicago, 1991).

32. Martín Goncalvez de Cellerigo, *Memorial de la política necesaria* (1600); quoted by H. Kamen, *The Iron Century: Social Change in Europe, 1550–1660* (London, 1976), 79.

33. See J. H. Hexter, 'Storm over the Gentry', in *Reappraisals in History* (Chicago, 1979), 117–62.

34. Kamen, *The Iron Century*, 89–135.

35. With special thanks to Dr Robert Frost. See M. Roberts, 'The Military Revolution, 1550–1660' in M. Roberts (ed.), *Essays in Swedish History* (London, 1967), 195–225; also G. Parker, 'The Military Revolution: A Myth?', in *Spain and the Netherlands, 1559–1659: Ten Studies* (London, 1989).

36. See J. H. Shennan, *Government and Society in France, 1461–1660* (London, 1968).

37. Hobbes, *Leviathan* (1651), ed. J. Plamenatz (London, 1962), 143.

38. Thomas Mun, *Englands Treasure by Foreign Trade* (1622); quoted by Charles Wilson, *Mercantilism* (London, 1958), 11–12.

39. An expression of H. Wiesflecker, *Maximilian I: die Fundamente des habsburgischen Weltreiches* (Vienna, 1991).

40. Otto von Habsburg, *Charles V* (Paris, 1967; London, 1970), p. xii.

41. See R. J. W. Evans, *The Making of the Habsburg Monarchy, 1550–1700: An Interpretation* (Oxford, 1979); also his 'The Imperial Vision', in G. Parker (ed.), *The Thirty Years War* (New York, 1987), 83 ff.; and 'Culture and Anarchy in the Empire, 1540–1680', *Central European History*, 18 (1985), 14–30.

42. R. J. W. Evans, *Rudolf II and His World: A Study in Intellectual History* (Oxford, 1973); also Robert Grudin, 'Rudolf II of Prague and Cornelius Drebbel: Shakespearean archetypes?' *Huntington Library Quarterly*, 54/3 (1991), 181–205.

43. J. H. Elliot, *Imperial Spain, 1469–1716* (London, 1963), 13.

44. Ibid. 14.

45. Ibid. 249.

46. J. Ortega y Gasset, quoted by Elliot, *Imperial Spain*, 249.

47. Geoffrey Parker, *The Army of Flanders and the Spanish Road, 1567–1659* (Cambridge, 1972).

48. Paul Kennedy, *The Rise and Fall of the Great Powers: Economic Change and Military Conflict, 1500–2000* (New York, 1988), 61.

49. Quoted by J. Huizinga, 'The Spirit of the Netherlands', in P. Geyl (ed.), *Dutch Civilisation in the Seventeenth Century and other essays* (London, 1968), 101.

50. See Charles Wilson, *The Dutch Republic and the Civilisation of the Seventeenth Century* (London, 1968).

51. S. R. Gardiner, *History of the Great Civil War, 1642–49* (London, 1886–9), i. 168.

52. Conrad Russell, 'The Slumbering Hatreds of the English', *Independent*, 18 Aug. 1992. See his *The Causes of the English Civil War* (London, 1990).

53. Sigismund Herberstein (1581), quoted by R. Pipes, *Russia under the Old Regime*, 85.

54. C. Veronica Wedgwood, *The Thirty Years War* (London, 1957), 460.

55. C. R. Friedrichs, 'The War and German Society', in Parker (ed.), *The Thirty Years War*, 208–15.

56. Wedgwood, *The Thirty Years War*, 440.

Rome, AD 1667

57. Timothy Kitao, *Circle and Oval in the Square of St Peter's: Bernini's Art of Planning* (New York, 1974), 'The Last Revision', 49–52; also figs. 67–74.
58. See Torgil Magnuson, *Rome in the Age of Bernini* (Stockholm, 1982).
59. Ibid. i. 360.
60. See Oreste Ferrari, *Bernini* (Florence, 1991).
61. Filippo Baldinucci, *Vita del Cavaliere Gio. Lorenzo Bernino* (Florence, 1682), trans. C. Enggass as *The Life of Bernini* (University Park, Penn., 1966), 80, 74; the source for all quotes and anecdotes below relating to Bernini's life.
62. John Milton, *Paradise Lost*, Bk. I, ll. 1–6, in *The Poetical Works of John Milton* (Oxford, 1952), I. 5.

CHAPTER VIII

1. *Shorter Oxford English Dictionary*, quoted by J. Lively, *The Enlightenment* (London, 1966), p. ii.
2. Alexander Pope, *An Essay on Criticism*, ii. 162–5; *An Essay on Man*, I. x. 9–14; *The Poetical Works*, ed. H. F. Cary (London, n.d.), 53, 224.
3. See Wyn Griffith, 'The Growth of Radicalism', in *The Welsh* (London, 1950), 20–43.
4. *Essay on Man*, ii. 1; *Poetical Works*, 225.
5. Dryden, *Absalom and Achitophel* (1681), i. 45–8.
6. Quoted by Bronowski, *The Ascent of Man*, 226.
7. Ibid. 236.
8. 'Voltaire's Deism', in Lively, *The Enlightenment*, 43–5.
9. *L'Esprit des Lois*, XI. vi.
10. Anne Robert Jacques Turgot, 'Discours aux Sorbonniques', in *Œuvres de Turgot*, ed. G. Schelle (Paris, 1913), i. 205, 215–16. See also D. Dakin, *Turgot and the Ancien Regime in France* (New York, 1972).
11. Voltaire, 'Stances à Mme Lullin, de Genève' (1773), in *Contes en vers et poésies diverses* (Paris, 1936), 163–4.
12. Voltaire's 'Declaration' of 1778, text in app. 497, *Complete Works* (Oxford, 1987–), quoted by R. Pomeau (ed.), *Voltaire en son temps* (Oxford, 1994), v, 'La Fin'.
13. On Rousseau's loathing for Voltaire, see his letter of 17 June 1760, in Voltaire's *Correspondence and Related Documents* (Oxford, 1968–77), cv, no. D8986.
14. Quoted by James Bowen, *A History of Western Education* (London, 1981), iii. 182.
15. See Norman Davies, 'The Cultural Imperative', in *Heart of Europe*, 262–8; Daniel Beauvois, *Lumières et société en Europe de l'est: l'université de Vilna et les écoles polonaises de l'empire russe* (Paris, 1977); and his *Szkolnictwo polskie na ziemiach litewskoruskich, 1803–32* (Lublin, 1991); on the Romantic generation, see C. Miłosz, *History of Polish Literature* (2nd edn., Berkeley, 1969), chapter vii, 'Romanticism', 195–280.
16. Isaiah Berlin, *Vico and Herder: Two Studies in the History of Ideas* (London, 1976), p. xxvi.
17. Berlin, in *The Magus of the North: J. G. Hamann and the Origins of Modern Irrationalism* (London, 1993); quoted by M. Rosen, 'The first Romantic?', *TLS*, 8 Oct. 1993.
18. Bertrand Russell, *History of Western Philosophy* (London, 1946), 702.
19. Simon Schama, *Dead Certainties (Unwarranted Speculations)* (London, 1991).
20. Quoted by H. Méthivier, *Le Siècle de Louis XIV* (Paris, 1950), 63.
21. R. Hubret, quoted by Méthivier, *Louis XIV*, 112.

22. Compare R. Briggs op. cit. p. 220 with Méthivier, *Louis XIV*, 95.

23. From 'The Vicar of Bray' (early 18th cent.), in Ernest Newton, *The Community Song Book* (London, 1927), 24–5. The song is usually said to be inspired by the career of Revd Simon Symonds, who kept his position from Cromwell's time to that of George I.

24. See Jonathan Israel (ed.), *The Anglo-Dutch Moment: Essays on the Glorious Revolution and Its World Impact* (Cambridge, 1991).

25. Neal Ascherson, 'The Spectre of Popular Sovereignty Looms over Greater England', *Independent on Sunday*, 18 Nov. 1990.

26. See Linda Colley, *Britons: Forging the Nation, 1707–1837* (New Haven, Conn., 1992); also Colin Kidd, *Subverting Scotland's Past: Scottish Whig Historians and the Creation of an Anglo-British Identity, 1689–c.1830* (Cambridge, 1993).

27. *Listy do Marysieńki*, ed. L. Kukulski (Warsaw, 1973), ii. 214–19, trans. B. Mazur; quoted by Davies, *God's Playground*, i. 484–6. See also Davies, *Sobieski's Legacy* (M. B. Grabowski Lecture, 1984) (London, 1985).

28. J. T. A. Alexander, *Catherine the Great: Life and Legend* (Oxford, 1983), 329.

29. Isabel de Madariaga, *Russia in the Age of Catherine the Great* (London, 1981), 587–8.

30. Pipes, *Russia Under the Old Regime*, 112–38.

31. Ibid. 115.

32. Quoted by Davies, *Sobieski's Legacy*; passim.

33. See E. Rzadkowska (ed.), *Voltaire et Rousseau en France et en Pologne* (Warsaw, 1982).

Prague, 29 October 1787

34. From the *Recollections* of Wilhelm Kühe, quoted by J. Rushton, *W. A. Mozart, Don Giovanni* (Cambridge, 1981), 124–5.

35. Ludwig von Köchel, *Chronologisch-thematisches Verzeichnis samtlicher Tonwerke Wolfgang Amadé Mozarts* (Salzburg, 1862), 591 [K. 527].

36. Rushton, *Mozart*, 67.

37. See Jonathan Miller (ed.), *The Don Giovanni Book: Myths of Seduction and Betrayal* (London, 1990).

38. After Rushton, *Mozart*, 47.

39. Köchel 591, 527/Ouverture.

40. Köchel 592, 527/7.

41. Köchel 593, 527/20.

42. Köchel 594, 527/26.

43. Köchel 593, 527/22.

44. H. C. Robbins (ed.), *The Mozart Compendium* (London, 1990), 299.

45. Emily Anderson (ed.), *The Letters of Mozart and His Family*, rev. edn. (London, 1985), no. 550, Mozart to Baron von Jacquin, pp. 911–12.

46. Robbins, *Mozart Compendium*, 303–4.

47. Ibid. 304.

48. See Andrew Steptoe, *The Mozart–Da Ponte Operas: The Cultural and Musical Background to 'Le Nozze di Figaro', 'Don Giovanni', and 'Così fan tutte'* (Oxford, 1983). Later in life Da Ponte migrated to New York, becoming Professor of Italian Literature at Columbia College.

49. Eduard Morike, *Mozart auf der Reise nach Prag*, introd. by M. B. Benn (London, 1970); also *Mozart's Journey to Prague*, trans. L. von Loewenstein-Wertheim (London, 1957).

50. Jaroslav Seifert, 'Na Bertramce', from the Collection *Halleyova Kometa* (Prague, 1967), 82–7 (trans. R. Pynsent).

51. Joseph II's 'Journal of a Journey across Bohemia' (1771) quoted by E. Wangermann, *The Austrian Achievement 1700–1800* (London, 1973), 93.
52. Roy Porter, 'Libertinism and Promiscuity', in Miller, *The Don Giovanni Book*, 1–19.
53. Giacomo Casanova, *The History of My Life* (1826), trans. W. R. Trast (London, 1967), 71; quoted by Steptoe, *The Mozart–Da Ponte Operas*, 207.
54. See J. Bouissonouse, *Condorcet: le philosophe dans la révolution* (Paris, 1962).
55. *Memoirs of Madame de la Tour du Pin*, ed. abridged, and trans. Felice Harcourt (London, 1985), 94–5.

CHAPTER IX

1. Mirabeau 25 Aug. 1790, quoted by Albert Sorel, *L'Europe et la révolution française* (Paris, 1885), i. 554. See Norman Hampson, *The First European Revolution, 1776–1815* (London, 1969).
2. Wordsworth, *Prelude*, xi. 108; Burke, *Reflections*; Goethe at the Battle of Valmy, 1792.
3. Thomas Carlyle, *The French Revolution* (1837), ed. A. R. H. Hall (London, 1930), 205.
4. J. Michelet, *History of the French Revolution*, ed. G. Wright (Chicago, 1967), 17.
5. Sorel, *L'Europe et la révolution française*, i. 1 V.
6. Thomas Jefferson, first draft of the Declaration of Independence, 1775. Cf. the final text, *In Congress, July 4 1776, the unanimous declaration of the thirteen united states of America* (facsimile, Washington, DC, 1960).
7. S. T. Coleridge, 'The Rime of the Ancient Mariner' (1797), 139–42, in *Complete Poetical Works*, ed. E. H. Coleridge (Oxford, 1912), 191.
8. William Blake, 'The Rose', in *Poetical Works*, ed. J. Sampson (Oxford, 1905), 123.
9. Russell, *History of Western Philosophy*, 705.
10. F. Claudon, *Encyclopédie du romantisme* (Paris, 1980), 48.
11. Alexis de Tocqueville, *The Ancien Régime and the French Revolution* (London, 1966), pt. iii, ch. 6, 196; also Whitney Pope, *Alexis de Tocqueville: His Social and Political Theory* (London, 1983).
12. de Tocqueville, *L'Ancien Régime et la révolution française* (1856) (Paris, 1953), pt. ii, ch. 1, 223–4.
13. R. D. Harris, *Necker: Reform Statesman and the Ancien Regime* (San Francisco, 1979). See Norman Hampson, 'Update: The French Revolution', *History* (1989), 10–12.
14. C. E. Labrousse, *Esquisse du mouvement des prix et des revenus en France au XVIIIème siècle* (Paris, 1937).
15. G. Lefebvre, *Quatre Vingt-Neuf* (1939), trans. as *The Coming of the French Revolution* (Princeton, NJ, 1947); *La Révolution française* (1958), trans. as *The French Revolution from the Origins to 1793* (London, 1962); Alfred Cobban, *The Social Interpretation of the French Revolution* (Cambridge, 1964).
16. Ibid. 173.
17. Albert Soboul, *Les Sans-culottes parisiens en l'an II* (Paris, 1962), 1.
18. See M. Browers, 'Can We Stop the French Revolution?', *History*, 76/246 (1991), 56–73; also Conor Cruise O'Brien, 'The Decline and Fall of the French Revolution', *New York Review of Books*, 15 Feb. 1990, being a review of F. Furet and M. Ozouf, *A Critical Dictionary of the French Revolution* (Cambridge, Mass., 1990).
19. Simon Schama, *Citizens: A Chronicle of the French Revolution* (London, 1989).
20. See T. C. W. Blanning, *The Origins of the French Revolutionary Wars* (London, 1986).
21. R. Avezou, *Petite histoire du Dauphiné* (Grenoble, 1946), 85.
22. Abbé Emmanuel de Sieyès (1748–1836), *Qu'est-ce que le Tiers État?* (Jan. 1789).

23. Carlyle, op. cit., p. 35.

24. Ibid. 29.

25. G. Lefebvre, *La Grande Peur de 1789* (1932); trans. as *The Great Fear of 1789: Rural Panic in Revolutionary France* (New York, 1973).

26. Source unverified.

27. Edmund Burke, from *An Appeal from the Old to the New Whigs* (London, 1791), 127–8; text published as appendix to Norman Davies, 'The Languour of so Remote an Interest: British Attitudes to Poland, 1772–1832', *Oxford Slavonic Papers* (new series), 16 (1983), 79–90.

28. See R. B. Rose, *The Making of the Sans-culottes: Democratic Ideas and Institutions in Paris, 1789–92* (Manchester, 1983).

29. See Gwyn Lewis, *The Second Vendée: The Continuity of Counter-Revolution in the Department of the Gard, 1789–1815* (Oxford, 1978).

30. C. Dufresne, 'La Virée de Galerne', *Historama*, 20 (1991), 56 ff.

31. See J. de Viguerie, *Christianisme et Revolution* (Paris, 1986); G. Babeuf, *La Guerre de Vendée et le système de dépopulation* (Paris, 1987); S. Reynald, *Le Génocide franco-français* (Paris, 1986), and *Juifs et vendéens: d'un génocide à l'autre: la manipulation de la mémoire* (Paris, 1991); J.-C. Martin, *Les Guerres de Vendée au Musée d'Histoire de Cholet* (Cholet, 1990); also *Une guerre interminable: la Vendée deux cents ans après* (Nantes, 1985); Charles Tilly, *The Vendée* (London, 1964).

32. See D. Sutherland, *The Chouans: The Social Origins of Popular Counter-Revolution in Upper Brittany* (Oxford, 1992). [GUERRILLA]

33. E. Blum (ed.), *La Déclaration des droits de l'homme et du citoyen* (Paris, 1902), 3–8; trans. J. H. Stewart, *A Documentary Survey of the French Revolution* (New York, 1951), 113–15.

34. Quoted by Geoffrey Best, 'The French Revolution and Human Rights', in G. Best (ed.), *The Permanent Revolution* (London, 1988), 105.

35. de Madariaga, *Russia in the Age of Catherine the Great*, 420–1, 423, 451.

36. Quoted by Davies, *God's Playground*, i. 542.

37. From André Barbier, 'L'Idole' (1831); quoted by P. Gehl, *Napoleon For and Against*, rev. edn. (London, 1964), 31.

38. After J. M. Thompson (ed.), *Napoleon's Letters* (Oxford, 1934), no. 87.

39. J. C. Herald, *The Mind of Napoleon: a selection from his written and spoken words* (New York, 1955), no. 64.

40. Quoted by Milan Hauner, 'Německá střední Europa?' (A German Central Europe?) *Lidové noviny* (Prague), 30 Oct. 1993.

41. Daniel Beauvois, *Société et lumières à l'Europe de l'est: l'université de Vilna et les écoles polonaises de l'empire russe* (Paris, 1977), also W. H. Zawadzki, *A Man of Honour: Prince Adam Czartoryski as Statesman of Russia and Poland, 1801–30* (Oxford, 1993).

42. J. Miller, 'California's Tsarist Colony', *History Today*, 42 (Jan. 1992), 23–8; K. T. Khlebnikov, *Colonial Russian America: Khlebnikov's Reports, 1817–32* (Portland, Oreg., 1976); P. A. Tikhmenev, *The History of the Russian American Company* (Seattle, 1978).

43. Sorel, op. cit. i, 1.

Fontainebleau, 20 April 1814

44. 'Fanfare de l'Empéreur'; Henri Lachouque, *Napoléon et la Garde Impériale* (1957), trans. A. S. Brown as *Anatomy of Glory* (London, 1978), 795.

45. Ibid. 712–15.

46. Armand, Marquis de Caulaincourt, *Mémoires* (1933) (see n. 53 below); quoted by D. Chandler, *The Campaigns of Napoleon* (London, 1967), 1003.

47. Herald, *Mind of Napoleon*, no. 176.

48. Lachouque, op. cit. The *grognards*, or 'grumblers', was the nickname of the Imperial Guard's 1st Regt of Grenadiers à Pied.

49. R. F. Delderfield, *Imperial Sunset: The Fall of Napoleon, 1813–14* (London, 1969), 219.

50. Ibid. 245.

51. Louis Cohen, *Napoleonic Anecdotes* (London, 1925), no. 209.

52. J. M. Thompson (ed.), *Napoleon's Letters*, op. cit.

53. Lachouque, *Napoléon et la Garde Impériale*, 415.

54. Chandler, *The Campaigns of Napoleon*, 1002.

55. Quoted by Felix Markham, *Napoleon and the Awakening of Europe* (New York, 1965), 127.

56. Ibid. 127.

57. Caulaincourt, *Mémoires*, English trans. (London, 1935).

58. Delderfield, *Imperial Sunset*.

59. Charles de la Roncière (ed.), *The Letters of Napoleon to Marie-Louise* (London, 1935), 265.

60. Ibid. 266.

61. Louis Cohen, *Napoleonic Anecdotes*, no. 143.

CHAPTER X

1. Quoted by A. J. P. Taylor, 'Bismarck: Man of German Destiny', in *Europe: Grandeur and Decline* (London, 1967), 80.

2. From the tombstone of William Pickering and Richard Edger, who both died 24 Dec. 1845; South Porch, Ely Cathedral.

3. A. Palmer, *Metternich* (London, 1972), 15: 'Revolution became for him the supreme bogey.' See also L. B. Namier, 'Metternich', in *Vanished Supremacies: Essays on European History, 1812–1918* (London, 1958).

4. Eric Hobsbawm, *Industry and Empire* (London, 1969), 21–2.

5. See Roman Szporluk, *Communism and Nationalism: Karl Marx versus Friedrich List* (Oxford, 1989).

6. See E. L. Jones, *The European Miracle: Environments, Economies, and Geopolitics in the History of Europe and Asia* (Cambridge, 1981).

7. See Peter Laslett, 'The History of the Family', an introduction to *Household and Family in Past Times* (Cambridge, 1972), 1–89; on Le Play, ibid. 16–23.

8. B. Disraeli, *Sybil, or the Two Nations* (1845) (London, 1925), 67.

9. Norman Stone, 'The Great Depression', in *Europe Transformed: 1878–1919* (London, 1982), 20–42.

10. Keats, 'La Belle Dame Sans Merci', *The Oxford Book of English Verse* (1939), no. 640.

11. Lamartine, from 'Le Lac', *The Oxford Book of French Verse* (1907), no. 236.

12. Leopardi, from 'Canto notturno di un pastor dell'Asia', *The Penguin Book of Italian Verse* (London, 1958), 279–85.

13. Joseph von Eichendorff, 'Das Zerbrechenen Ringlein' (The Broken Ring), in L. Reiners (ed.), *Der ewige Brunnen*, Beck Verlag, 1992.

14. Słowacki, from 'Beniowski', translated by Norman Davies, more accurately than in *Heart of Europe* (Oxford, 1984), 243. These lines are inscribed on the tomb of Józef Piłsudski in the Rossa Cemetery, Vilnius, Lithuania.

15. A. Pushkin, from the Prologue to 'The Bronze Horseman (1833)', *The Penguin Book of Russian Verse*, ed. D. Obolensky (London, 1962), 111–15. Pushkin's words echo the lines of the exiled Mickiewicz, with whom he had once stood before the statue of Peter the Great 'under one coat'. See A. Mickiewicz, 'Pomnik Piotra Wielkiego', from 'Dziadów Części III Ustęp' (1832), *Wybór Pism* (Warsaw, 1950), 308–9.

16. Chorus Mysticus, from *Faust*, pt. ii, 12, 104–end; *Goethe: Selected Verse*, ed. David Luke (London, 1964), 355.

17. See Maria Korzeniewicz, *Od ludowości ironicznej do ludowości mistycznej: przemiany postaw estetycznych Słowackiego* (Wrocław, 1981).

18. de Nerval, the opening lines of 'Les Cydalises', *Oxford Book of French Verse*, no. 276. See R. Sabatier, *La Poésie du XIXe siècle*, i: *Les Romantismes* (Paris, 1977), 221–52.

19. Quoted by B. Russell, 764–5.

20. See B. A. Gerrish, *A Prince of the Church: Schleiermacher and the beginnings of modern theology* (London, 1984); K. W. Clements, *Friedrich Schleiermacher: Pioneer of Modern Theology* (London, 1987).

21. See James Sheehan, *German Liberalism in the Nineteenth Century* (London, 1978).

22. See D. Blackbourn and G. Eley, *The Peculiarities of German History: Bourgeois Society and Politics in Nineteenth Century Germany* (Oxford, 1984); see also Madeleine Hurd, 'Sweden and the German Sonderweg', paper presented to the 8th International Conference of Europeanists, Chicago, 27–9 Mar. 1992.

23. These definitions are not too dissimilar from those preferred by A. D. Smith in *Theories of Nationalism* (London, 1971), where the proponents of state nationalism are associated with the 'lateral aristocratic ethnos'. See also Hans Kohn, *Nationalism: Its Meaning and History* (Princeton, NJ, 1965); Louis Snyder, *The Dynamics of Nationalism* (New York, 1964), and *Varieties of Nationalism: A Comparative Study* (New York, 1976); Elie Kedourie, *Nationalism* (Oxford, 1966); Ernest Gellner, *Nations and Nationalism* (Oxford, 1983); P. Alter, *Nationalism* (London, 1989); A. D. Smith (ed.), *Ethnicity and Nationalism* (Leiden, 1992). (See n. 31 below.)

24. N. Gardels, 'Two Concepts of Nationalism: An Interview with Isaiah Berlin', *New York Review of Books*, 21 Nov. 1991.

25. Ernest Renan, from *Qu'est-ce qu'une nation? Conférence faite en Sorbonne le 11 mars 1882*, in *Œuvres complètes* (Paris, 1947), i. 887–906.

26. See Hugh Seton-Watson, *States and Nations: An Enquiry into the Origins of Nations and the Politics of Nationalism* (London, 1977).

27. J. F. Palmer, 'The Saxon Invasion and Its Influence on Our Character as a Race', *Transactions of the Royal Historical Society*, N.S., ii (1885), 173–96.

28. H. S. Chamberlain, *Die Grundlagen des neunzehnten Jahrhunderts* (1899), quoted by W. and A. Durant, 'Race and History', in *The Lessons of History* (New York, 1968), 26–7.

29. See H. Paszkiewicz, *The Origins of Russia* (London, 1954); also 'Are the Russians Really Slavs?' *Antemurale*, 2 (Rome, 1955).

30. F. M. Dostoevsky, *The Diary of a Writer*, trans. B. Basol (London, 1949), 565–6, 632.

31. Eric Hobsbawm, *Nations and Nationalism since 1780* (Cambridge, 1990), 14.

32. Timothy D. Snyder, 'Kazimierz Kelles-Krauz: a political and intellectual biography'. D.Phil. thesis, Oxford University, 1995.

33. With acknowledgement to a paper 'Empire and Nation in Russian History' read by Professor Geoffrey Hosking at St Antony's College, Oxford, 3 May 1992.

34. See Louis L. Snyder, *The New Nationalism* (New York, 1968), 55 (see also Introduction, n. 66 above); Yael Tamir, *Liberal Nationalism* (Princeton, NJ, 1993).

35. Kazimierz Brodziński, quoted and translated by Norman Davies, *Heart of Europe*, 202.

36. Count Eduard von Taafe und Ballymote (1833–95). 'Not only did Taafe not find an answer to the riddle, he did not even look for one'; C. A. Macartney, *The Habsburg Empire, 1790–1918* (London, 1969), 615.

37. Bonar Law, 1912. *Encyclopaedia Britannica*, 11th edn. (New York, 1911), 554; R. Kee, *The Green Flag: a history of Irish Nationalism* (London, 1972).

38. C. M. Grieve (Hugh MacDiarmid), 'A drunk man looks at the thistle' (1926), 'The annals of the five senses' (1930), in *Collected Poems* (London, 1978); T. Nairn, *The Break-up of Britain: crisis and neonationalism*, 2nd edn. (London, 1981); *The Enchanted Glass: Britain and its monarchy* (London, 1988). See also N. MacCormick (ed.), *The Scottish Debate: essays on Scottish Nationalism* (Oxford, 1970); G. Bryan, *Scottish Nationalism: an annotated bibliography* (Westport, Conn., 1984).

39. Renan, 1882 (see n. 25 above).

40. See Isaiah Berlin, *Karl Marx: His Life and Environment*, 4th edn. (Oxford, 1978); Angus Walker, *Marx: His Theory and Its Context*, 2nd edn. (London, 1989).

41. From A. J. P. Taylor, introduction to *The Communist Manifesto*, trans. S. Moore (Harmondsworth, 1967).

42. Quoted by Tibor Szamuely, *The Russian Tradition* (London, 1974), 292. See Deborah Hardy, *Petr Tkachev: The Critic as Jacobin* (Seattle, 1977).

43. Professor Kołakowski reports that he has made the statement so often that he forgets where exactly he wrote it. See his *The Main Currents of Marxism: Its Origins, Growth, and Dissolution* (Oxford, 1978).

44. Robert Conquest, introduction to Szamuely, *The Russian Tradition*, p. ix.

45. See G. Woodcock, *Anarchism: A History of Libertarian Ideas and Movements* (London, 1963), 'The Family Tree', 35–55.

46. Percy Bysshe Shelley, *Prometheus Unbound* (1819), III. iii. 131–5, 154, 157–61.

47. Peter Marshall, *Demanding the Impossible: A History of Anarchism* (London, 1991).

48. A. J. P. Taylor, 'The Wild Ones', *Observer*, 25 Oct. 1964, being a review of James Joll, *The Anarchists* (London, 1964).

49. Taylor, 'Bismarck', 90.

50. See F. Malino and D. Sorkin, *Jews in a Changing Europe, 1750–1870* (Oxford, 1990); P. Johnson, *A History of the Jews* (London, 1987).

51. Quoted by C. Jelen, *Le Point* (Paris), 1, 163 (1994), 45.

52. See Heinz-Dietrich Loewe, *The Tsars and the Jews: Reform, Reaction, and Antisemitism in Imperial Russia, 1772–1917* (Chur, 1993); F. Raphael, *The Necessity of Antisemitism* (Southampton, 1989); R. Wistrich, *Anti-zionism and Antisemitism in the Contemporary World* (Basingstoke, 1990); Douglas Johnson, *The Dreyfus Affair* (London, 1966); N. Cohn, *Warrant for Genocide: The Myth of the Jewish World-Conspiracy and the Protocols of the Elders of Zion* (London, 1967).

53. *Encyclopaedia Britannica*, xxviii. 989.

54. Isaac Deutscher, *The Non-Jewish Jew and other essays* (London, 1968).

55. J. Wertheimer, *Unwelcome Strangers: East European Jews in Imperial Germany, 1890–1914* (Oxford, 1987); S. E. Aschheim, *Brothers and Strangers: The East European Jew in German and German Jewish consciousness, 1800–1923* (Madison, Wis., 1988).

56. *Hundert Jahre Jahrhundertwende* (Berlin, 1988), 155.

57. Herbert Read, in *Art Now* (1933), quoted in *The Oxford Companion to English Literature*, ed. Margaret Drabble (1985), 658.

58. See J. P. Stern, *A Study of Nietzsche* (Cambridge, 1979); S. Aschheim, *The Nietzsche Legacy in Germany* (Oxford, 1992).

59. See Ben Macintyre, *Forgotten Fatherland: The Search for Elizabeth Nietzsche* (London, 1992).

60. John Carey, *The Intellectuals and the Masses* (London, 1992), 4. See 'Extreme Prejudice', *Sunday Times, Books* 28 June 1992, 8–9.

61. Quoted by Carey, *The Intellectuals and the Masses*, 12.

62. Michael Coren, 'And the Inferior Swarms Will Have to Die', *Independent*, 2 Jan. 1993: a flyer for his *The Invisible Man: The Life and Liberties of H. G. Wells* (London, 1993). *Anticipations* is not mentioned in the entry on Wells in *The Oxford Companion to English Literature*.

63. Carey, *The Intellectuals and the Masses*, 21.

64. See J. Miller, *Freud: The Man, His World, and His Influence* (London, 1972).

65. Baudelaire, from the sonnet 'Correspondences', *Oxford Book of French Verse*, no. 305.

66. From Verlaine, 'Chanson d'automne', ibid. no. 345.

67. Rimbaud, from 'Voyelles', ibid. no. 362.

68. Max Nordau, *Degeneration* (1892–3), quoted by R. C. Mowat, *Decline and Renewal: Europe Ancient and Modern* (Oxford, 1991), 12–13.

69. Quoted by Michael Howard, *The Franco-Prussian War: The German Invasion of France, 1870–1* (London, 1962), 208. von Moltke preferred 'We have them in a mouse-trap'; ibid. 207.

70. Ewa M. Thompson, 'Russophilia', in *Chronicles* (Oct. 1994), 32–5.

71. Music-hall song by G. W. Hunt, popularized in 1878 by Jas. MacDermott; *The Concise Oxford Dictionary of Quotations* (Oxford, 1964), 112.

72. See Michael Howard, *War in European History* (Oxford, 1976), 97–106.

73. From Halford Mackinder, *Democratic Ideas and Reality* (1919), quoted by C. Kruszewski, 'The Geographical Pivot of History', *Foreign Affairs* (Apr. 1954), 2–16; 'The Geographical Pivot of History' (25 Jan. 1904), *Geographical Journal* (Apr. 1904), 421–44 (repr. London, 1969). See B. B. Bluet, *Halford Mackinder: a biography* (College Station, TX, 1987).

74. H. von Moltke, *Gesammelte Schriften und Denkwurdigkeiten* (Berlin, 1892), v. 194.

75. Quoted by Michael Howard, 'A Thirty Years' War: Two World Wars in Historical Perspective', *Transactions of the Royal Historical Society*, 6th ser., 3 (1993), 171. Cf. Adolf Hitler before the Reichstag, 21 May 1935: 'Whoever lights the torch of war in Europe can wish for nothing but chaos.'

76. Joachim Remak, *Sarajevo: The Story of a Political Murder* (London, 1959); L. Popelka, *Heeres-gesichtliches Museum* (Vienna, 1988), 50–1. Francis-Ferdinand's two sons, Max and Ernst von Hohenberg, died in Nazi custody in 1938 at Dachau.

Whitehall, 3 August 1914

77. D. C. Browning (ed.), *Everyman's Dictionary of Quotations and Proverbs* (London, 1951), no. 1792; *The Concise Oxford Dictionary of Quotations*, 113; A. and V. Palmer, *Quotations in History: A Dictionary of Historical Quotations* (Hassocks, 1976), 97.

78. Viscount Grey of Fallodon, *Twenty-five Years, 1892–1916* (London, 1925), ii. 10, 20.

79. Keith Robbins, *Sir Edward Grey: A Biography of Lord Grey of Fallodon* (London, 1971).

80. See B. Jelavich, *Russia's Balkan Entanglements, 1800–1914* (Cambridge, 1991), esp. 248–75. The Tsar's Manifesto of 3 Aug. made no reference to Russia's diplomatic obligations to Serbia, only to the common 'faith', 'blood', and 'historical traditions of the Slav peoples'; ibid. 275.

81. See G. M. Trevelyan, *Grey of Fallodon* (London, 1937).

82. See Sidney Buxton, *Edward Grey: Bird Lover and Fisherman* (London, 1933).

83. 8 Dec. 1919, Harvard Union; Viscount Grey, *Recreation* (London, 1920).

84. Grey, *Twenty-five Years*, i. 121.

85. From 'Chronicle' in *The Annual Register, 1914* (London, 1915).

86. W. S. Churchill, *World Crisis*, quoted by Trevelyan, *Grey of Fallodon*, 200–4.

87. *Manchester Guardian*, 4 Aug. 1914.

88. David Lloyd George, *War Memoirs*, quoted by Trevelyan, *Grey of Fallodon*, 69, 254.

89. See Hermann Lutz, *Lord Grey und der Weltkrieg*, trans. as *Lord Grey and the World War* (London, 1926), esp. 193–4.

90. Grey, *Twenty-five Years*, i. 57.

91. Robbins, *Sir Edward Grey*, 290.

92. Grey, *Twenty-five Years*, ii. 10–18.

93. Martin Gilbert, *Winston S. Churchill*, iii (1914–16) (London, 1971), 3 Aug. 1914.

94. J. Spender and C. Asquith, *The Life of Lord Asquith and Oxford* (London, 1932), ii. 93.

95. B. Connell, 'Prince Louis of Battenberg', in *Manifest Destiny* (London, 1953), 44–5. [GOTHA]

96. Gilbert, *Churchill*, iii, ch. 1, 'A Really Happy Man', 25–6.

97. Ibid.

98. Ibid. 30, 4 Aug. 1914.

99. Ibid. 31.

100. Lutz, *Lord Grey and the World War*, 156.

101. See K. H. Jarausch, *The Enigmatic Chancellor: Bethmann Hollweg and the Hubris of Imperial Germany* (New Haven, Conn., 1972).

102. Ibid. 70.

103. K. H. Jarausch, 'The Illusion of Limited War: Bethmann Hollweg's Calculated Risk, July 1914', *Central European History* (Atlanta), 2 (1969), 48–78.

104. Jarausch, *Enigmatic Chancellor*, 149.

105. 15 Nov. 1913, Bethmann to the Crown Prince, quoted by Jarausch, 'The Illusion of Limited War'.

106. 8 July 1914, ibid.

107. Jarausch, *Enigmatic Chancellor*, 149.

108. Prince Bernhard von Bülow, *Memoirs, iii: 1909–19* (London, 1932), 161—not a friendly witness.

109. L. Cecil, *Albert Ballin: Business and Politics in Imperial Germany, 1888–1918* (Princeton, NJ, 1967), 122 ff.

110. Von Bülow, *Memoirs*, iii. 159–60.

111. *Encyclopaedia Britannica*, 12th edn. (London, 1922), xxx. 453–4.

112. Quoted by Jarausch, 'The Illusion of Limited War'.

113. Ibid. 54.

114. Ibid. 58.

115. Ibid. 75–6.

116. 27 July 1914, ibid.

117. A. and V. Palmer, *Quotations in History*, no. 1751.

118. This is the thesis of Fritz Fischer, *Griff nach der Weltmacht* (1969), trans. as *War of Illusions: German Policies from 1911 to 1914* (London, 1972). For the crucial sequence of events on 29–30 July, see 492–8.

119. Von Bülow, *Memoirs*, iii. 163.

120. Fischer, *War of Illusions*, 511.

121. Palmer, *Quotations in History*, no. 1752.

122. Jarausch, 'The Illusion of Limited War', 71 ff.

123. The phrase 'a scrap of paper' certainly accords with Bethmann Hollweg's sentiments on Belgian neutrality as confirmed that same day by his speech to the Reichstag. But the earliest documentary source for his use of the particular form of words would seem to be the British Ambassador's report written four days later. From there it was taken up by all the standard reference works. Sir E. Goschen to Sir Edward Grey, London, 8 August 1914, HMSO, *Collected Diplomatic Documents Relating to the Outbreak of the European War* (London, 1915), no. 160, p. 111; Speech of the Imperial German Chancellor before the German Reichstag, on 4 Aug. 1914, ibid. 436–9; Palmer, *Quotations in History*, 18; *Everyman's Dictionary of Quotations* (London, 1951), no. 215.

124. Marcel Proust, *Correspondence*, ed. P. Kolb, iii (1914) (Paris, 1985), no. 16.

125. *The Letters of Virginia Woolf* (London, 1976), ii. no. 708.

126. C. Hassall, *Rupert Brooke: A Biography* (London, 1964), 454–5.

127. *The Letters of D. H. Lawrence*, ed. J. T. Boulton (Cambridge, 1981), ii. no. 851, to Lady Cynthia Asquith, 30 Jan. 1915.

128. *The Letters of Thomas Mann, 1889–1955*, ed. R. and C. Winston (London, 1970), i. 69–70, to Heinrich Mann, 7 Aug. 1914.

129. Count Carlo Sforza, 'Tisza, the Magyar', in *Makers of Modern Europe* (London, 1930), 65.

130. D. A. Prater, *European of Yesterday: A Biography of Stefan Zweig* (Oxford, 1972).

131. Ibid.

132. See Isaac Deutscher, *The Prophet Armed: Trotsky 1879–1921* (Oxford, 1954).

133. Robert Service, *Lenin: A Political Life*, 2nd edn. (Basingstoke, 1991), ii, ch. 2, 'Storms before the Storm', 34–71.

134. Quoted by A. Solzhenitsyn, *August 1914* (London, 1971), 59 ff.

135. F. A. Golder, *Documents of Russian History* (New York, 1927), 3–23; quoted by R. Pipes, *The Russian Revolution, 1899–1919* (London, 1990), 211.

136. R. Rolland, *Journal des années de guerre, 1914–19*, ed. M. R. Rolland (Paris, 1952).

137. Michael Davie, *The Titanic: the full story of a disaster* (London, 1986); G. J. Marcus, *The Maiden Voyage: a complete and documentary history of the Titanic disaster* (London, 1988); A. Rostron, *The Loss of the Titanic* (Westbury, 1991).

138. A. J. P. Taylor, 'The Outbreak of the First World War', in *Englishmen and Others* (London, 1956).

139. Taylor, quoted by Paul Kennedy, 'Profound Forces in History', in C. J. Wrigley (ed.), *Warfare, Diplomacy and Politics: Essays in Honour of A. J. P. Taylor* (London, 1986), abridged in *History Today*, 36 (Mar. 1986), 11.

140. Taylor, 'The Outbreak of the First World War': *Struggle for Mastery in Europe* (Oxford, 1954), chapter xxii.

141. Taylor, quoted by Kennedy, 'Profound Forces in History' (*History Today*), 12.

CHAPTER XI

1. Anna Akhmatova (1889–1966), *Selected Poems*, trans. and introd. S. Kunitz with M. Hayward (London, 1989), no. 16, 'Chem khuzhe etot vyek pryedshetvuyushikh?' (1919), 70.

2. See Norman Stone, *The Eastern Front* (London, 1975); also A. Clark, *Suicide of the Empires: The Battles on the Eastern Front, 1914–18* (London, 1971).

3. K. Rosen-Zawadzki, 'Karta Buduszczej Jewropy', *Studia z dziejów ZSRR i Srodkowej Europy* (Wrocław, 1972), viii. 141–5, with map.
4. R. Pipes, *The Russian Revolution, 1899–1919* (London, 1990), 419.
5. J. and J. Bogle, *A Heart for Europe: The Lives of Emperor Charles and Empress Zita of Austria-Hungary* (Leominster, 1990), chs. 7, 8.
6. Pipes, *The Russian Revolution*, 492.
7. Ibid. 553.
8. RAF Casualty Reports, 1–10 Sept. 1918, Public Record Office, London—Air 1/858/204/5/418 (opened 1969).
9. See Adolf Juzwenko, *Polska a 'Biała' Rosja* (Poland and the Russian 'Whites'), Wrocław 1973 (with French summaries).
10. See David Footman, *The Civil War in Russia* (London, 1961). On the demographic statistics of Soviet history, see n. 35 below.
11. See R. L. Tokes, *Bela Kun and the Hungarian Soviet Republic, 1918–19* (New York, 1967); I. Volges, *Hungary in Revolution, 1918–19: Nine Essays* (Lincoln, Nebr., 1971).
12. See Norman Davies, 'The Missing Revolutionary War', *Soviet Studies*, 27/2 (1975), 178–95; also *White Eagle, Red Star: The Polish–Soviet War, 1919–20* (London, 1972).
13. Lord D'Abernon, *The Eighteenth Decisive Battle of World History* (London, 1931), 8–9.
14. See P. B. Kinross, *Ataturk: The Birth of a Nation* (London, 1964); Alan Palmer, *Kemal Ataturk* (London, 1991); M. Llewellyn-Smith, *The Ionian Vision: Greece in Asia Minor, 1919–22* (London, 1973); M. Houspian, *Smyrna 1922: The Destruction of a City* (London, 1972).
15. See Walter Lacqueur (ed.), *Fascism: A Reader's Guide* (Berkeley, Calif., 1976).
16. See Hannah Arendt, *The Origins of Totalitarianism* (London, 1986), first published as *The Burden of our Time* (1951); also Leonard Shapiro, *Totalitarianism* (London, 1972).
17. See Carl Friedrich, 'The Unique Character of Totalitarian Society', in *Totalitarianism* (Cambridge, Mass., 1954); also C. Friedrich *et al.*, *Totalitarianism in Perspective: Three Views* (New York, 1969).
18. Vyacheslav Molotov, 6 Nov. 1939, and Hermann Göring, 9 Apr. 1933.
19. Hugh Seton-Watson, in *The Imperialist Revolutionaries* (London, 1961).
20. Denis Mack Smith, 'The March on Rome', *Mussolini* (London, 1981), 52 ff.; see also Adrian Lyttleton, *The Seizure of Power: Fascism in Italy, 1919–29* (London, 1987).
21. Mack Smith, 'The March on Rome', 240, described Mussolini as 'one of the few people whom [Hitler] really liked'.
22. Quoted by R. Albrecht-Carrié, *The Unity of Europe: An Historical Survey* (London, 1966), 223–4.
23. Retranslated from the French; *Dictionnaire Quillet* (Paris, 1935), i. 602.
24. P. Hollander, *Political Pilgrims: Travels of Western Intellectuals to the Soviet Union, China and Cuba, 1928–78* (New York, 1981); also S. Margulies, *The Pilgrimage to Russia: The Soviet Union and the Treatment of Foreigners, 1924–37* (Madison, 1965).
25. Michael Holroyd, 'Fellow Traveller', extract from *George Bernard Shaw: A Biography* (London, 1991); *Sunday Times*, 15 Sept. 1991.
26. See P. Slater, *The Origin and Influence of the Frankfurt School* (London, 1977).
27. See *Europa, Europa: das Jahrhundert der avantgarde in Mittel- und Osteuropa*, an exhibition at the Kunst- und Ausstellungshalle der Bundesrepublik Deutschlands, Bonn, 27 May–16 Oct. 1994, directed by Ryszard Stanisławski and Christoph Brockhaus; catalogue (Bonn, 1994), 4 vols.

28. S. O'Faolain, *Constance Markievicz* (London, 1934); also Anne Haverty, *Constance Markievicz: An Independent Life* (London, 1988).

29. Sheila Fitzpatrick, *The Russian Revolution, 1917–32* (Oxford, 1982).

30. Col. Robins, 1918, quoted by Isaac Deutscher, *The Prophet Armed: Trotsky 1879–1921* (Oxford, 1954); also by A. J. P. Taylor, 'Trotsky', in *Englishmen and Others* (London, 1956), 135.

31. L. B. Trotsky, *Stalin: An Appraisal of the Man and His Influence* (1941; new edn. London, 1968).

32. In 1936; quoted by John Maynard, 'The Two Disciplines', in *The Russian Peasant and Other Studies* (London, 1942).

33. See Alec Nove, *Was Stalin Really Necessary? Some Problems of Soviet Political Economy* (London, 1964); also J. Arch Getty, *The Origins of the Great Purges: The Soviet Communist Party Reconsidered* (Cambridge, 1988).

34. Alexis Tolstoy; quoted by Trotsky, *Stalin*, op. cit.

35. For decades, many historians counted Stalin's victims in 'hundreds' or 'thousands', whilst others, such as Solzhenitsyn, talked of 'tens of millions'. Since the collapse of the USSR, the highest estimates have been vindicated. See R. Conquest, *The Great Terror: A Re-assessment* (London, 1992); also Conquest's review of the semi-repentant 'revisionists' (J. Arch Getty and R. T. Manning (eds.), *Stalinist Terror: New Perspectives* (Cambridge, 1993)), in *TLS* Feb. 1994. Yet no precise statistical breakdown has been produced. Studies based on 'the demographic gap' of *c.*27 million for 1941–5, for example, make no distinction between Soviet citizens killed by the Nazis and those killed by the Soviet regime itself. No proper analysis of losses in the USSR by nationality has been forthcoming. See Norman Davies, 'Neither Twenty Million, nor Russians, nor War Deaths', *Independent*, 29 Dec. 1987; also M. Ellman, 'On Sources: A Note', *Soviet Studies*, 44/5 (1992), 913–15.

36. Quoted by A. J. P. Taylor, 'Hitler's "Seizure of Power"', in *Englishmen and Others*, 139–53.

37. Alan Bullock, *Hitler: A Study in Tyranny*, rev. edn. (London, 1964), 773.

38. Ian Kershaw, *The Nazi Dictatorship: Problems and Perspectives of Interpretation*, 2nd edn. (London, 1989), 42–60. See also Tim Mason, 'The Primacy of Politics: Politics and Economics in National Socialist Germany', in H. A. Turner (ed.), *Nazism and The Third Reich* (New York, 1972), 175–200.

39. Adolf Hitler, *Mein Kampf*, trans. R. Manheim (London, 1969), introd. by D. C. Watt, ch. 11, 'Nation and Race'.

40. Ibid. 260.

41. Ibid. 587.

42. Ibid. 598.

43. Ibid.

44. Quoted by D. Thompson, *Europe since Napoleon* (London, 1966), 727.

45. George Watson, 'Hitler's Marxism', in *The Idea of Liberalism: Studies for a New Map of Politics* (London, 1985), 110–25.

46. See R. Grunberger, *A Social History of the Third Reich* (London, 1971); also T. Childers, *The Nazi Voter: The Social Foundations of Fascism in Germany* (London, 1983).

47. See Kershaw, *The Nazi Dictatorship*, 18–41.

48. Cf. Celia Heller, *On the Edge of Destruction* (New York, 1977), with L. Dobroszycki and B. Kirschenblatt-Gimblett (eds.), *Image Before my Eyes: A Photographic History of Jewish Life in Poland, 1864–1939* (New York, 1977–8). For a fine period piece, see Lewis

Namier, 'The Jews in the Modern World' (1934), in *In the Margin of History* (London, 1940).

49. From Lewis Namier, 'Yugoslavia', in *Facing East* (London, 1947), 66–82, a review of Rebecca West's wonderful travelogue, *Black Lamb and Grey Falcon* (London, 1942).

50. Arthur Koestler, *Spanish Testament* (London, 1937); see also his *Darkness at Noon* (London, 1968).

51. See D. W. Pike, *In the Service of Stalin: The Spanish Communists in Exile, 1939–45* (Oxford, 1993).

52. Hugh Thomas ventures a figure of 500,000 including c.200,000 military deaths and c.245,000 victims of political repressions; *The Spanish Civil War*, 3rd edn. (London, 1977), 270, 925–7.

53. Geza Jeszenszky, Foreign Minister of Hungary, 'The Lessons of Appeasement: Central Europe between NATO and Russia', lecture at SSEES, University of London, 6 Dec. 1993.

54. Keith Feiling, *A Life of Neville Chamberlain* (London, 1946), 367.

55. See M. Gilbert, *Winston Spencer Churchill*, v: *1922–39* (London, 1976), chs. 47, 48, 'The Worst of Both Worlds' and 'A Defeat without a War'.

56. After H. C. Hillman, *The Comparative Strength of the Great Powers* (London, 1939). See also Paul Kennedy, 'The Politics of Appeasement', in *The Realities behind Diplomacy: Background Influences on British External Policy, 1865–1980* (London, 1985).

57. For an intelligent discussion of this necessarily speculative subject, see Ernst Topitsch, *Stalin's War: A Radical New Theory of the Origins of the Second World War* (1985), trans. A. and B. E. Taylor (London, 1987).

58. This piece of misinformation found its way into many Western textbooks, e.g. M. L. R. Isaac, *A History of Europe, 1870–1950* (London, 1960), 241, where the Poles are described as 'Germany's much vaunted ally'.

59. See Norman Davies, *Heart of Europe: A Short History of Poland* (Oxford, 1984), 'The Military Tradition', 239–43.

60. Quoted by Bullock, *Hitler*, 527.

61. *Nazi–Soviet Relations, 1939–41: Documents from the Archives of the German Foreign Office*, ed. R. J. Sonntag and J. S. Beddie (Washington, DC, 1948), 78.

62. Memorandum of a conversation between Ribbentrop, Molotov, and Stalin, 23–4 Aug. 1939, *Nazi–Soviet Relations*, 74.

63. US Chief of Counsel for Prosecution of Axis Criminality, *Nazi Conspiracy and Aggression*, vi (Washington, DC, 1948), 390–2, quoting Naujocks's own deposition at the Nuremberg Tribunal.

64. For up-to-date encyclopedic information on the Second World War, see Ian Dear and M. R. D. Foot *et al.* (eds.), *The Oxford Companion to the Second World War* (1995).

65. Alvin D. Coox, *Nomon-han: Japan against Russia, 1939* (Stanford, Calif., 1985).

66. See A. Read and D. Fisher, *The Deadly Embrace: Hitler, Stalin and the Nazi–Soviet Pact, 1939–41* (London, 1988).

67. 16 June 1941; *The Goebbels Diaries*, ed. F. Taylor (London, 1982), 414.

68. See Victor Suvorov, *Icebreaker: Who Started the Second World War?* (London, 1990).

69. R. C. Raack, 'Stalin's Plans for World War Two', *Journal of Contemporary History*, 26 (1991), 215–27.

70. *Goebbels Diaries*, 16.

71. J. Wnuk, *Losy dzieci polskich w okresie okupacji hitlerowskiej* (Warsaw, 1980); see also C. Henry and M. Hillel, *Au nom de la race* (Paris, 1974), trans. as *Children of the SS*

(London, 1976); Richard Lukas, *Did the Children Cry? Hitler's War against Jewish and Polish Children, 1939–45* (New York, 1994).

72. Jan T. Gross, *Polish Society under German Occupation, 1939–44* (Princeton, NJ, 1979); Richard Lukas, *The Forgotten Holocaust: The Poles under German Occupation* (Lexington, Ky., 1986); also M. Broszat, *Nationalsozialistische Polenpolitik, 1939–45* (Frankfurt, 1965). On the Nazi-built ghettos in occupied Poland, see L. Wells, *The Janowska Road* (London, 1966); L. Dobroszycki (ed.), *The Chronicle of the Łódź Ghetto* (New Haven, Conn., 1984); A. Lewin, *A Cup of Tears: A Diary of the Warsaw Ghetto* (Oxford, 1988); A. Tory, *Surviving the Holocaust: The Kovno Ghetto Diary* (New York, 1990).

73. Norman Davies and Antony Polonsky, *The Jews in Eastern Poland and the Soviet Union, 1939–45* (London, 1991), introd. See also J. T. Gross, *Revolution from Abroad: The Soviet Conquest of Poland's Western Ukraine and Western Byelorussia* (Princeton, NJ, 1988); Keith Sword, *The Soviet Takeover of the Polish Eastern Provinces, 1939–41* (Basingstoke, 1991); Irena and J. T. Gross, *War Through Children's Eyes: The Soviet Occupation of Poland and the Deportations, 1939–41* (Stanford, Calif., 1981); and Anon. [Zoe Zajdlerowa], *The Dark Side of the Moon* (preface by T. S. Eliot) (London, 1946).

74. 30 Sept. 1939. See Ewa M. Thompson, 'Nationalist Propaganda in the Soviet Russian Press, 1939–41', *Slavic Review*, 50/2 (1991), 385–99.

75. J. Garliński, *Intercept: The Enigma War* (London, 1979); also R. Wojtak, 'The Origins of the Ultra-secret Code in Poland, 1937–38', *Polish Review*, 23/3 (1978).

76. See Suvorov, *Icebreaker*: op. cit. A large part of the Soviet air force, for example, was located in vulnerable forward positions.

77. Alan Bullock, 'Hitler and the Holocaust', lecture, Logan Hall, University of London, 14 July 1993.

78. Göring to Heydrich, 31/7/1941. Text in R. Hilberg, *The Destruction of the European Jews* (London, 1961), 262.

79. *The Diary of Anne Frank: The Critical Edition* (London, 1989).

80. R. Hilberg *et al.* (eds.), *The Diary of Adam Czerniakow, 1939–42* (New York, 1979).

81. After Rudolf Hoess, *Commandant of Auschwitz: The Autobiography of Rudolf Hoess* (London, 1959), 144–57.

82. Prominent items include Primo Levi, *If This Is a Man* (1956), *The Truce* (1963), *If Not Now, When?*; Jerzy Kosiński, *The Painted Bird* (1966), *The Devil Tree* (1973); Leon Uris, *Mila 18* (1961), *QB VII* (1971).

83. See Hanna Kral, *Zdążyć przed Panem Bogiem: rozmowy z Markiem Edelmanem*, trans. as *Shielding the Flame* (New York, 1986); review by Norman Davies, *New York Review of Books*, 20 Nov. 1986; also 'Poles and Jews: An Exchange', ibid. 9 Apr. 1987.

84. Isaak Shahak, 'The Life of Death: An Exchange', *New York Review of Books*, 29 Jan. 1987, 45–50.

85. See M. Edelman, *The Ghetto Fights* (New York, 1946); Y. Zuckerman, *A Surplus of Memory: A Chronicle of the Warsaw Ghetto Rising* (New York, 1993).

86. From 'Campo di Fiori', Warsaw 1943; Czesław Miłosz, *Collected Poems, 1931–87* (London, 1988).

87. Jan Błoński of the Jagiellonian University, Cracow, 'The Poor Poles look at the Ghetto', in *Polin*, ii (1987), 321 ff., the translation of an article which first appeared in *Tygodnik Powszechny* (Cracow), 11 January 1987.

88. Irene Tomaszewski and T. Werbowski, *Żegota: the rescue of Jews in wartime Poland*

(Montreal, 1994); T. Prekerowa, *Konspiracyjna Rada Pomocy Żydom w Warszawie, 1942–45* (Warsaw, 1983); W. Bartoszewski and Z. Lewin (eds.), *Righteous among Nations: How Poles Helped the Jews, 1939–45* (London, 1959); also K. Iranek-Osmecki, *He Who Saves One Life* (New York, 1971).

89. See Bruno Szatyn, *A Private War: Surviving in Poland on False Papers, 1941–45* (Detroit, 1985); N. Tec, *When Light Pierced the Darkness: Christian Rescue of Jews in Nazi-occupied Poland* (New York, 1985); Thomas Keneally, *Schindler's Ark* (London, 1982); also the true life story of Solomon Perel, as portrayed in Agnieszka Holland's film *Europa, Europa* (1990) videorecording by Channel 4 Television (London, 1991).

90. See Istvan Deak in 'Who Saved Jews? An Exchange', *New York Review of Books*, 25 Apr. 1991, 60–2, a continuation of earlier discussions starting with Deak's 'The Incomprehensible Holocaust', ibid. 28 Sept. 1985.

91. S. Friedlander, *Pius XII and the Third Reich* (London, 1966); J. D. Holmes, *Pius XII, Hitler and the Jews* (London, 1982); also R. G. Weisbord, *The Chief Rabbi, the Pope, and the Holocaust* (London, 1992).

92. A high estimate of 5.957 millions was produced by Jakub Lestchinsky, a low estimate of 5.1 millions by Raul Hilberg, *The Destruction of the European Jews*, rev. edn. (New York, 1985), 767, 670. A detailed appendix in the *Encyclopaedia of the Holocaust*, ed. I. Gutman (New York, 1990) provides a minimum estimate of 5.596 millions and a maximum estimate of 5.86 millions: iv. 1797–1802. From this, the median estimate would work out at 5.728 millions. There can be no definitive figure. But various historians using similar methods reach similar conclusions (see Appendix III, p. 1328).

93. The total of excess wartime deaths within the USSR is now estimated at 26–7 millions. See S. Maksudov, 'Losses Suffered by the Population of the USSR, 1918–58', in R. Medvedyev (ed.), *The Samizdat Register II* (London, 1981). Figures above 27 million, which began to appear in the 1990s, appear to relate not to wartime deaths but to projections of demographic losses, including those of post-war generations that were never born. The breakdown of such figures, however, is highly problematical. One may reasonably assume that the heaviest civilian casualties during the war were incurred in regions most heavily contested by the Nazis and Soviets, i.e. Ukraine, Byelorussia, and eastern Poland. See n. 35 above. One must equally be wary about dubious definitions of territory, chronology, and causes of death. See M. Ellmann, S. Maksudov, 'Soviet deaths in the Great Patriotic War: a note', *Europe–Asia Studies*, vol. 46, no. 4 (1994), 671–80.

94. Jean Paul II, *Maximilien Kolbe: Patron de notre siècle difficile* (Paris, 1982); W. Herbstrath and B. Bonowitz, *Edith Stein: A Biography* (London, 1985); W. T. Bartoszewski, *The Convent at Auschwitz* (London, 1990).

95. See Józef Garliński, *Fighting Auschwitz: The Resistance Movement in the Concentration Camp* (London, 1970); also M. R. D. Foot, *Six Faces of Courage* (London, 1978), 105–19. Piłecki was executed by the communist security service on 25 May 1948. His own account, suppressed for fifty years, was published as *Raport Witolda*, ed. A. Cyra (Warsaw, 1991). Polish communist propaganda wrongly stated that resistance inside Auschwitz was run by J. Cyrankiewicz, a post-war prime minister.

96. Jan Karski, 'The Tragedy of Szmul Zygelbojm', *Poland*, May 1987, 43–50, extracts from *Story of a Secret State* (Boston, 1944); see also David Engel, *In the Shadow of Auschwitz: The Polish Government in Exile in London and the Jews, 1939–42* (London, 1987).

97. See D. S. Wyman, *The Abandonment of the Jews: America and the Holocaust, 1941–45* (New York, 1984); also R. Bolchover, *British Jewry and the Holocaust* (Cambridge, 1993).

98. M. Gilbert, *Auschwitz and the Allies* (London, 1981).

99. Lucy S. Dawidowicz, 'The fate of the Jews under National Socialism was unique'; 'The Jews: A Special Case', in *The Holocaust and the Historians* (Cambridge, Mass., 1981), 11 V. Discussions on the unique character of the Holocaust centre less on the historical event itself than on the motives of those who oppose all forms of comparison. According to Sir Isaiah Berlin, for example, 'If uniqueness of a phenomenon is examined . . . , we mustn't rush to the conclusion that it's unique before we have compared it to other events which in some ways resemble it. That is what's happening to the Holocaust . . . It has a conspicuously political motive.' in G. Thomas (ed.), *The Unresolved Past: a Debate in German History*, chaired and introduced by Ralf Dahrendorf (London, 1990), pp. 18–19.

100. Rosa Luxembourg, in relation to antisemitism at the turn of the century: 'Why do you come with your special Jewish sorrows? I feel just as sorry for the wretched Indian victims of Putamayo.' Quoted by Dawidowicz, 'The Jews: A Special Case', 4.

101. See I. Abrahamson (ed.), *Against Silence: The Voice and Vision of Elie Wiesel* (New York, 1985).

102. Lucy Dawidowicz, *The War Against the Jews, 1933–45* (London, 1975).

103. R. Hilberg, *The Destruction of the European Jews*.

104. Yehudah Bauer, *The Holocaust in Historical Perspective* (London, 1978). This line is developed in Raul Hilberg, *Perpetrators, Victims, Bystanders: The Jewish Catastrophe, 1939–45* (London, 1992).

105. Martin Gilbert, *The Holocaust: The Jewish Tragedy* (London, 1986).

106. L. Dawidowicz, 'The Curious Case of Marek Edelman', *Commentary* (New York), 83/3 (March, 1987), 66–9. See M. Edelman, *The Ghetto Fights* (New York, 1946), a non-Zionist view by the last surviving leader of the Warsaw Ghetto Rising.

107. Arnold J. Meyer, *Why Did the Heavens Not Darken? The 'Final Solution' in History* (London, 1988).

108. Lukas, *The Forgotten Holocaust*: also R. C. Lukas (ed.), *Out of the Inferno: Poles Remember the Holocaust* (Lexington, Ky., 1989).

109. Arthur R. Butz, *The Hoax of the Twentieth Century* (Richmond, Va., 1976), also P. Rassinier, *The Holocaust Story and the Lies of Ulysses* (Costa Mesa, Calif., 1978); see also Noam Chomsky, 'All Denials of Free Speech Undercut a Democratic Society', *Journal of Historical Review*, 7/1 (1986), 123–7; also his 'Thought Control in the USA', *Index on Censorship*, 7 (1986), 2–23, and subsequent correspondence.

110. Paul Findley (ed.), *They Dare to Speak Out: People and Institutions Confront Israel's Lobby* (Westport, Conn., 1985).

111. C. Lanzmann, *Shoah: An Oral History of the Holocaust (The Complete Text of the Film)* (New York, 1985); numerous reviews included T. Garton Ash, 'The Life of Death', *New York Review of Books*, 19 Dec. 1985; J. Karski, 'Shoah (Zaglada)', *Kultura* (Nov. 1985), 121–4; J. Turowicz, 'Shoah w polskich oczach', *Tygodnik powszechny* (Cracow), 10 Nov. 1985; P. Coates, 'A Ghetto in Babel', *Encounter*, 49/1 (1987); and the collection *Polish Americans Reflect on Shoah* (Chicago, 1986).

112. Rafał Scharf, 'In Anger and in Sorrow', *Polin: A Journal of Polish–Jewish Studies*, 1 (1986), 270.

113. Władysław Anders, *An Army in Exile: The story of the Polish Second Corps* (London, 1947; repr. Nashville, 1981).

114. 'Declaration of Principles known as the Atlantic Charter, made public 14 August 1941'; J. A. S. Grenville, *The Major International Treaties, 1914–73: A History and Guide with Texts* (London, 1974), 198–9.

115. 18–21 June 1945. *Trial of the Organisers, Leaders, and Members of the Polish Diversionist Organisation, Moscow* (London, 1945). See Z. Stypułkowski, *Invitation to Moscow* (New York, 1962).

116. Gilbert, *Churchill,* vii: *1941–5* (London, 1986), 991–3.

117. A. Solzhenitsyn, *Prussian Nights: A Narrative Poem,* trans R. Conquest (London, 1977), esp. 41–3, 49–53.

118. S. E. Ambrose, *Pegasus Bridge: 6 June 1944* (London, 1984). At midnight on 5/6 June, Pegasus Bridge was guarded by two Polish conscripts, one of whom, Pte. Vern Bonck, was reported leaving for the Benouville brothel. The 'Ox and Bucks' were relieved next day by Lord Lovat's commandos headed by a bagpiper.

119. Peter Hoffmann, *The History of German Resistance, 1933–45* (London, 1988); see also T. Prittie, *Germans Against Hitler* (London, 1964); F. R. Nicosia (ed.), *Germans against Nazism* (New York, 1990); D. C. Large, *Contending with Hitler: Varieties of German Resistance* (Cambridge, 1991).

120. To Albert Speer, 19 Mar. 1945; Bullock, *Hitler,* 774.

121. Ibid. 794–5.

122. Wisława Szymborska, stanzas from 'Koniec i początek' (Beginning and End), to be published in English translation. Presented by Stanisław Baranczak, in 'The Most Pressing Questions are Naïve Ones', Conference on Contemporary Polish Literature, SSEES, University of London, 22–5 Mar. 1993.

Nuremberg, 19 October 1945

123. An earlier Polish version of this section was published in *Gazeta Wyborcza* (Warsaw), 3–4 Apr. 1993, under the excellent title 'Prawda ujawniona, i prawda ukryta' (Truth Revealed and Truth Concealed).

124. Airey Neave, *Nuremberg: A Personal Record* (London, 1978), 73–85. The author was killed in 1979 by a bomb placed by Irish terrorists in the House of Commons car park.

125. Ibid. 26.

126. International Military Tribunal, Nuremberg, *The Trial of German Major War Criminals: Documents and Proceedings,* ed. L. D. Egbert (Nuremberg, 1947–9), vols. i–xlii.

127. International Military Tribunal, Nuremberg, *Speeches of the Chief Prosecutors* (London, 1946).

128. *Manchester Guardian,* 23 Mar. 1946, *The Times,* 8 May 1946; quoted by A. and J. Tusa, *The Nuremberg Trial* (London, 1983), *passim.*

129. Quoted by Neave, *Nuremberg,* 331.

130. M. Bloch, *Ribbentrop* (London, 1992), 454.

131. Tusa and Tusa, *The Nuremberg Trial,* 472.

132. See R. K. Woetzel, *The Nuremberg Trials in International Law* (New York, 1962).

133. See R. A. Kirk, *The Political Principles of R. A. Taft* (New York, 1967).

134. H. K. Thompson and H. Strutz (eds.), *Doenitz at Nuremberg: A Reappraisal* (Torrance, Calif., 1983).

135. Neave, *Nuremberg,* 26.

136. Lewis Namier, *Manchester Guardian,* 19 Oct. 1945; quoted by Tusa and Tusa, *The Nuremberg Trial, passim.*

137. Ibid. According to the American interpreter, Vyshinsky's exact words were: 'I propose a toast to the defendants. May their paths lead straight from the courthouse to the grave'; Telford Taylor, *Anatomy of the Nuremberg Trials: A Personal Memoir* (London, 1993), 211.

CHAPTER XII

1. A favourite metaphor of John Paul II, e.g. in his Apostolic Letter *Euntes in mundum* (1988), on the millennium of Kievan Rus'.
2. See Keith Sword *et al.*, *The Formation of the Polish Community in Great Britain, 1939–50* (London, 1989).
3. Nikolai Tolstoy, *Victims of Yalta* (London, 1977).
4. James Bacque, *Other Losses: An Investigation into the Mass Deaths of German prisoners . . .* (New York, 1989), a thesis vehemently contested by G. Bischoff and S. Ambrose (eds.), *Eisenhower and the German POWs: Facts Against Falsehood* (Baton Rouge, La., 1993), reviewed in *History*, 79/255 (1994), 186.
5. Krystyna Kersten, 'The Transfer of the German Population from Poland, 1945–7', *Acta Poloniae Historica*, 10 (1964), 27–47; Alfred M. De Zayas, *Nemesis at Potsdam: The Anglo-Americans and the Expulsion of the Germans*, rev. edn. (London, 1979), and *The German Expellees: Victims in War and Peace* (London, 1993); John Sack, *An Eye for an Eye: The Untold Story of Jewish revenge on Germans, 1945* (New York, 1993).
6. See Kazimierz Moczarski, *Rozmowy z katem* (1974), trans. as *Conversations with an Executioner* (London, 1978).
7. Arthur Bliss Lane, *I Saw Poland Betrayed* (New York, 1947); Stanisław Mikołayczyk, *The Rape of Poland: The Pattern of Soviet Domination* (London, 1949); Jan Ciechanowski, *Defeat in Victory* (London, 1968). On the Kielce Pogrom, see T. Wiącek, *Kulisy i tajemnice pogromu kieleckiego 1946r* (Cracow, 1992).
8. George Kennan, *Foreign Affairs* (July 1947), under the pseudonym 'Mr X'.
9. Gilbert, *Churchill*, viii. 200.
10. Ibid.
11. *Times*, 6 Mar. 1947.
12. Gilbert, *Churchill*, viii. 265–7.
13. Ibid. 267.
14. Ibid. 355. For statements at the Hague Congress, see Anthony Sampson, *The New Europeans: A Guide to the Workings, Institutions, and Character of Contemporary Western Europe* (London, 1968), 4–5.
15. Neal Ascherson, 'The Special Relationship that will Survive all Tiffs', *Independent on Sunday*, 21 Feb. 1993.
16. K. D. Bracher, *Die deutscher Diktatur* (1969), trans. as *The German Dictatorship* (Harmondsworth, 1970).
17. Anthony Sampson, *The Essential Anatomy of Britain: Democracy in Crisis* (London, 1992).
18. After Walter Laqueur, *Europe since Hitler* (London, 1967), 194.
19. Dr Otto von Habsburg, *The Economist*'s Charles Stransky Memorial Lecture, London 20 Sept. 1993.
20. 'The Last Testament', in Strobe Talbot (ed.), *Krushchev Remembers* (Boston, 1974), 284.
21. See Laqueur, *Europe since Hitler*, 'The Soviet Economy', 231 ff.
22. Quoted by Geoffrey Hosking, *A History of the Soviet Union* (London, 1985), 405.
23. Irina Ratushinskaya, *Grey Is the Colour of Hope*, trans. A. Kojevnikov (London, 1989), 229.
24. Michael Bourdeaux, *The Role of Religion in the Fall of Soviet Communism* (London, 1992).

25. Adam Ważyk, 'Poemat dla dorosłych' (A poem for adults), *Nowa Kultura* (Warsaw), 21 Aug. 1955; quoted by Davies, *God's Playground*, ii. 582–3.

26. On the Prague Spring, see H. Gordon Skilling, *Czechoslovakia's Interrupted Revolution*, (Princeton, NJ, 1976).

27. Col. Ryszard Kukliński: as reported in *Washington Post*, 27 Sept. 1992; *Gazeta Wyborcza*, 28 Sept. 1992.

28. As reported by the Czech ex-Politburo member Karel Kaplan in *Panorama* (May 1977): see 'Stalin's Secret Council of War', *The Times*, 6 May 1977; also 'Secrets from the Prague Spring', *Time*, 9 May 1977.

29. George Ball, 'JFK's Big Moment', *New York Review of Books*, 13 Feb. 1992.

30. L. Kołakowski, 'Tezy o nadziei i o beznadziejności', *Kultura* (Paris), June 1971, trans. as 'Hope and Hopelessness', *Survey*, 17/3(80) (Summer 1971), 37–52.

31. Jacques Rupnik, *The Other Europe* (London, 1988), p. xv.

32. *The Treaty on European Union: including the protocols and final act with declarations, Maastricht 7 February 1992* (London, 1992); text published by *Sunday Times*, London, 11 Oct. 1992.

33. Slavenka Drakulic, *How We Survived Communism and Almost Laughed* (London, 1992); Janine Wedel, *The Private Poland* (New York, 1986).

34. Stanisław Lem, in Stanisław Barańczak (ed.), *Breathing Under Water and other East European essays* (Cambridge, Mass., 1992), 1–6.

35. Timothy Garton Ash, *We the People: The Revolutions of '89 witnessed in Warsaw, Budapest, Berlin and Prague* (Cambridge, 1990), 78. See also David Selbourne, *The Death of the Dark Hero: Eastern Europe, 1987–90* (London, 1990).

36. To the Governor of Steiermark; after von Habsburg, Charles Stransky Lecture, *passim*.

37. Timothy Garton Ash, *In Europe's Name: Germany and the Divided Continent* (London, 1993), 385.

38. See E. and J. Winiecki, *The Structural Legacy of the Soviet-type Economies* (London, 1992).

39. Arpad Goncz, quoted by Garton Ash, op. cit., 60.

40. Conor Cruise O'Brien, 'A Grave marked Maastricht', *The Times*, 30 Apr. 1992.

41. Gyorgi Konrad, in *Antipolitics* (London, 1982).

42. Francis Fukuyama, 'The End of History?' in *The National Interest* (1989); also 'The End of History Is Still Nigh', *Independent*, 3 Mar. 1992.

43. Zbigniew Brzeziński, speaking at Bologna, Feb. 1992; see J. Moskwa, 'Brzeziński o trzech Europach', *Nowy świat*, 3 Mar. 1992.

44. Prof. Ken Jowitt (UC Berkeley) at the International Security Conference, Yale University, 2–4 Apr. 1992.

Summertown, 14 February 1992

45. *Independent*, 14 Feb. 1992; *Guardian*, 14 Feb. 1992; *El Pais*, 13 Feb. 1992; *Le Monde*, 13 Feb. 1992; *De Telegraaf*, 13 Feb. 1992; *Suddeutsche Zeitung*, 13 Feb. 1992; *Gazeta Wyborcza*, 12 Feb. 1992; *The Oxford Times*, 14 Feb. 1992.

46. *Corriere della Sera*, 13 Feb. 1992.

47. *Daily Mail*, 13 Feb. 1992.

48. *Le Monde*, 14 Feb. 1992.

49. *European*, 13–19 Feb. 1992.

50. *The Times*, 14 Feb. 1992.

51. Alan Hamilton, 'Scots Recall an Ancient Act of Treachery', *The Times*, 14 Feb. 1992, 16; *Die Zeit*, 7 Feb. 1992, Reiner Luyken, 'Schotten, erhebt euch! Reisst der Nationalismus nun auch Grossbritannien in Stücke?'

52. *Polska tak, ale jaka?* (Poland, yes, but what sort of Poland?) is an old tag from the 19th cent., when Poland had been destroyed. Now it's Russia's turn.

53. (Eternal wanderer of the unmoving azure, | I miss Europe with its ancient ramparts); from Arthur Rimbaud, 'Le Bateau ivre', in *Poésies: Une saison en enfer; Illuminations* (Paris, 1973), 97.

NOTES TO CAPSULES

ABKHAZIA   1. Yutaka Akino, *The Last Scenario of Gamsakhurdia* (December 1993). Institute of East–West Studies (Prague, 1994); also Neal Ascherson in the *Independent*, 17 July 1994. Ascherson's *Black Sea* (1995) contains a chapter on Abkhazia.

ADELANTE   1. Hugh Thomas, *The Spanish Civil War*, 3rd edn. (London, 1977), 452 ff.   2. From W. H. Auden, 'Spain 1937', quoted by Thomas, *The Spanish Civil War*, 460.   3. See F. Graham, *The Battle of Jarama, 1937: The Story of the British Battalion of the International Brigades* (Newcastle, 1987).   4. Thomas, *The Spanish Civil War*, 853.

AGOBARD   1. Allen Cabaniss, 'Agobard of Lyons' in P. Quennell (ed.), *Diversions in History* (London, 1954), 41–51.   2. *Monumenta Germaniae Historica: Epistolae*, iii. 159; quoted by Christopher Dawson, *The Making of Europe* (London, 1932), 257.

ALCHEMIA   1. R. J. W. Evans, 'Rudolph and the Occult Arts', in *Rudolph II and His World: a Study in Intellectual History, 1576–1612* (Oxford, 1973), 196–242.   2. M. Rady, 'A Transylvanian Alchemist in London', to be published in the *Slavonic and East European Review*.   3. Evans, op. cit. 199.   4. J. Bronowski, *The Ascent of Man* (London, 1970).   5. See F. Sherwood Taylor, *The Alchemists* (London, 1952); J. Read, *Through Alchemy to Chemistry: a procession of ideas and personalities* (London, 1957).   6. William Shakespeare, *Sonnet 33*.

ALCOFRIBAS   1. Lucien Febvre (1942), trans. as *The Problem of Unbelief in the Sixteenth Century: The Religion of Rabelais* (Cambridge, Mass., 1982).   2. M. Bakhtin, *Rabelais and His World* (Cambridge, Mass., 1968).

ALPI   1. L. Pauli, *The Alps: Archaeology and Early History* (London, 1980). 2. R. Blanchard, *Les Alpes et leur destin* (Paris, 1958); also P. P. Viazzo, *Upland Communities: Environment, Population and Social Structure in the Alps since the Sixteenth Century* (Cambridge, 1989).

ALTMARKT   1. *Jewish Encyclopedia* (New York, 1903), iv. 658 and references. 2. Arthur Harris, *Bomber Offensive* (London, 1947); D. Saward, *Bomber Harris: the story of Marshal of the Royal Air Force, Sir Arthur Harris* (London, 1984).   3. See D. Irving, *The Destruction of Dresden*, rev. edn. (London, 1971); also Gordon Musgrove, *Operation Gomorrah: the Hamburg Firestorm Raids* (London, 1981).   4. Ibid. 195 ff.   5. Ibid. 218–26. 6. Norbert Burger, Lord Mayor of Cologne, 'The Memorial for Sir Arthur Harris: A Summary'; also 'Bomber Harris: A Tactless Choice', *Financial Times*, 2–3 May 1992.   7. *Suddeutsche Zeitung*, 23 November 1994, as reported in the *Daily Telegraph*, 24 November 1994.

ANGELUS   1. Commemorative tablet in the nave of Saint-Pierre, Saintes (Charente Inférieure).

ANNALES   1. *Annales d'Histoire Économique et Sociale*, revue trimestrielle, tome premier, année 1929, No. 1 (Paris, 1929).   2. See P. Burke, *The French Historical Revolution and the 'Annales' School* (Cambridge, 1990).   3. M. Aymar, 'L'Évolution de l'historiographie braudélienne', Lecture, 15 Nov. 1990, Maison Française, Oxford.   4. *Annales*, 1 (1), 1–2.

ANNO DOMINI 1. 'Dionysius Exiguus', in *Encyclopaedia Britannica*, 11th edn. (1910–11), vii. 285. 2. 'Calendar', ibid. iv. 987–1004. 3. S. V. Utechin, *Everyman's Concise Encyclopaedia of Russia* (London, 1961), 85.

APOCALYPSE 1. Rev. 21: 4–6.

AQUILA 1. J. E. Cirlot, *Diccionario de simbolos tradicionales*, trans. as *A Dictionary of Symbols*, 2nd edn. (London, 1971), 91–3. 2. Adrian Frutiger, *Signs and Symbols: Their Design and Meaning* (London, 1989), 247. 3. W. Leaf and S. Purcell, *Heraldic Symbols: Islamic Insignia and Western Heraldry* (London, 1986), 70–1.

AQUINCUM 1. T. Cornell and J. Matthews, *Atlas of the Roman World* (Oxford, 1982), 143. 2. Klara Poczy, *Aquincum Polgárvárosa* (Budapest, n.d.).

ARCHIMEDES 1. See Heinrich Dorrie, *Triumph der Mathematik* (Wurzburg, 1965), trans. as *100 Great Problems of Elementary Mathematics: Their History and Solution* (New York, 1965), nos. 1, 38, 56; also T. L. Heath, 'Mathematics and Astronomy', in G. Murray (ed.), *The Legacy of Greece* (Oxford, 1921), 122–5; also E. J. Dijksterhuis, *Archimedes* (Copenhagen, 1956).

ARICIA 1. James G. Frazer, *The Golden Bough: the Roots of Religion and Folklore* (First Edition), 2 vols. (London, 1890), i. 6. 2. Ibid. i. 210. 3. Ibid. i. 211–12. 4. Ibid. ii. 370. 5. Ibid. ii. 370. 6. Ibid. ii. 370–1.

ATHLETES 1. See M. I. Finley and H. W. Pleket, *The Olympic Games: The First Thousand Years* (London, 1976). 2. See H. A. Harris, *Greek Athletes and Athletics* (London, 1964). 3. Pindar, Nemean 6.1–7. Trans. C. M. Bowra. 'Men and Gods', ode in the honour of Alcimidas of Aegina, winner in the boys' wrestling at the Nemean Games; in *Greek Literature: An Anthology*, chosen by Michael Grant (London, 1977), 104. 4. 2 Tim. 4: 7. 5. A. Krawczuk, *Ostatnia Olimpiada* [The Last Olympiad], (Wrocław, 1976); R. D. Mandell, *The first modern Olympics* (Berkeley, 1976).

ATHOS 1. Sotiris Kadas, *Mount Athos: An Illustrated Guide to the Monasteries and their History* (Athens, 1979). See also P. Sherrard, *Athos: The Mountain of Silence* (Toronto, 1970). 2. Father Maximos, *Human Rights on Mount Athos: An Appeal to the Civilised World* (Welshpool, 1990). 3. Richard North, 'Doctrinal Divisions among the Monks of Athos', the *Independent*, 17 July 1990.

AUC 1. J. J. Bond, 'The Roman Calendar', in *A Handy-book of Rules and Tables for verifying dates with the Christian Era* . . . (London, 1869), 1–6, 195–6 (repr. Llanerch, 1991).

AUSCHWITZ 1. US Defense Intelligence Agency, Strategic Bombing Survey. Record Group 373: Mission 60 PRS/462, Can D1508, exposure 3055, to Can D1510, exposure 5020. Quoted by Martin Gilbert, *Auschwitz and the Allies* (London, 1981), 216, 249. 2. Ibid. fig. 28, and pp. 331–2. 3. See Jan Karski, *The Story of a Secret State* (London, 1944); also D. S. Wyman, *The Abandonment of the Jews: America and the Holocaust, 1941–45* (New York, 1984). 4. Gilbert, *Auschwitz and the Allies*, ch. 21. Witold Piłecki, who had escaped from Auschwitz I in 1942, had no direct knowledge of Auschwitz II-Birkenau. (See Chapter XI, n. 95.) The five Jewish escapees of 1944 raised the alarm after making their way to Slovakia. 5. Ibid. and 312. 6. See D. A. Brugioni and R. G. Poirer, *The Holocaust Revisited: A Retrospective of the Auschwitz-Birkenau Extermination Complex* (Washington, 1979). Reference from Gilbert, *Auschwitz and the Allies*, 249 n. 7. Gilbert, *Auschwitz and the Allies*, 337. 8. See Ch. XI, note 29. Given a total of *c.*6 million Jews killed overall, including *c.*2 million on Soviet territory and *c.*2 million in other Nazi ghettos and camps in occupied Poland, it is impossible to reach the figure of 4 million for Auschwitz alone. Testimony supplied to the Nuremberg Tribunal by the former commandant of Auschwitz, Hoess, suggested a total of 2.5 million deaths in the camp. **9.** In 1970 Dr Józef Garliński, a former inmate, made a calculated estimate of 2 million deaths in the camp. (See Chapter XI, n. 95.) In 1983 another former prisoner, the French researcher G. Wellers, reached a figure of 1,471,595. Dr Franciszek Piper's figures, as prepared for the State Museum at Oświęcim, were published in the *New York Times*. F. Piper, *Ilu ludzi zginęło w KL Auschwitz? Liczba ofiar w świetle źródeł i badań, 1945–90* (Oświęcim, 1992).

BALETTO   **1.** Iain Fenlon, 'The origins of the seventeenth century staged ballo', in I. Fenlon, T. Carter (eds.), *Studies in Italian Opera, Song, and Dance, 1580–1740* (Oxford, 1995); A. Bland, *A History of Ballet and Dance in the Western World* (London, 1976); A. Haskell, *Ballet Russe: the age of Diaghilev* (London, 1968).

BAMBINI   **1.** M. Pollard, *Maria Montessori* (Watford, 1990), 35. See also Rita Kramer, *Maria Montessori* (Oxford, 1978), and James Bowen, *A History of Western Education*, iii: *The Modern West* (London, 1981), 394–402. **2.** On the tradition of progressive education see *Friedrich Froebel: a selection of his writings* (Cambridge, 1967); G. L. Gutek, *Pestalozzi and Education* (New York, 1968); J. Piaget, *Science of Education and the Psychology of the Child*, trans. D. Coltman (New York, 1971).

BARBAROS   **1.** Edith Hall, *Inventing the Barbarian: Greek Self-definition through Tragedy* (Oxford, 1989). **2.** Neal Ascherson, *Black Sea* (London & New York, 1995), 49.

BARD   **1.** *King Henry IV*, Part 2, IV. iii; *The Taming of the Shrew*, II. i. See F. G. Stokes, *Who's Who in Shakespeare* (London, 1924), 124.

BASERRIA   **1.** W. A. Douglass, 'The Basque Stem-Family Household: Myth or Reality?', *Journal of Family History*, 13 (1) (1989), 75–89.

BATAVIA   **1.** S. Schama, *The Embarrassment of Riches: An Interpretation of Dutch Culture in the Golden Age* (Fontana, London, 1987), 15–24, 'The Mystery of the Drowning Cell'. **2.** Ibid. 6. **3.** Ibid. 289.

BATT-101   **1.** Christopher Browning, *Ordinary Men: Reserve Police Battalion 101 and the Final Solution in Poland* (New York, 1993); quoted by Alan Bullock, 'The Evil Dream', *TLS*, 5 Feb. 1993, 3. **2.** C. Perechodnik, *Czy ja jestem mordercą?* (Warsaw, 1993), ed. with notes and commentaries by Pawel Szapiro. See Leszek Kołakowski, 'International Books of the Year', *TLS*, 3 Dec. 1993. **3.** John Sack, *An Eye for an Eye: The Untold Story of Jewish Revenge Against Germans in 1945* (New York, 1993), endorsed by Anthony Polonsky, Professor of East European Jewish History, Brandeis University. Similar testimony was provided by Jakub Berman, head of Poland's post-war communist Security Office (UB), interviewed in 1981. See T. Torańska, *Oni: Stalin's Polish Puppets* (London, 1983).

BAUME   **1.** *Guide Michelin: Jura, Franche-Comté* (Paris, 1990), 56–7. **2.** René Locatelli, Pierre Gresser *et al.*, *L'Abbaye de Baume-les-Messieurs* (Dole, 1978), 24–31. **3.** Ibid. 234.

BENZ   **1.** *Deutsches Museum von Meisterwerken der Naturwissenschaft und Technik: Guide Through the Collections* (Munich, 1988), 92–3. **2.** D. Cardwell, *The Fontana History of Technology* (London, 1994).

BERNADETTE   **1.** With special acknowledgement to R. Harris, 'Evidence and Devil's Evidence', seminar paper, University of Oxford Faculty of History, 24 May 1993. See also R. Laurentin, *Lourdes: dossiers des documents authentiques* (Paris, 1957); F. Duhoureau, *Saint Bernadette of Lourdes: a saint of the Golden Legend* (London, 1934).

2. Eugene Weber, *Peasants into Frenchmen, the modernization of rural France, 1870–1914* (London, 1977). **3.** Harris, 'Evidence and Devil's Evidence', *passim*.

BIBLIA **1.** Compiled from entries under 'Bible', 'Codex', 'Ulfilas', etc. in *New Catholic Encyclopedia* (Washington, DC, 1967), *The Oxford Dictionary of the Christian Church*, ed. F. L. Cross (Oxford, 1957), and E. A. Livingstone, ed., *The Concise Oxford Dictionary of the Christian Church* (Oxford, 1977).

BLACK ATHENA **1.** Martin Bernal, *Black Athena: The Afroasiatic Roots of Classical Civilization* (2 vols., London, 1987–91). See M. Levine, 'The Challenge of Black Athena', *Arethusa* (Fall 1989); also Jasper Griffin, in *New York Review of Books*, 15 June 1989.

BLARNEY **1.** For modern Irish history, see Roy F. Foster, *Modern Ireland 1600–1972* (London, 1988). **2.** *Shorter Oxford English Dictionary* : 'blarney, sb 1819, a cajoling tongue and the art of flattery', hence *v.*, 'to use flattering speech'.

B.N.R. **1.** V. Kippel and Z. Kippel (eds.), *Byelorussian Statehood: Reader and Bibliography* (New York, 1988). **2.** Symon Kabysh, 'Genocide of the Byelorussians', in *Genocide in the USSR: Studies in Group Destruction* (New York, 1958), 77–88. [**VORKUTA**] **3.** As reported by Otto von Habsburg, Charles Stransky Memorial Lecture, London, 20 Sept. 1993.

BOGEY **1.** R. G. L. Waite, 'Adolf Hitler's Guilt Feelings', *Journal of Interdisciplinary History*, 1 (1970–1), 229–49. **2.** David Irving, *The Secret Diaries of Hitler's Doctor* (London, 1983). **3.** From the oral tradition, with many variants. Prof. M. R. D. Foot, historian of SOE, confirms that this immortal ditty is of wartime vintage. **4.** L. Bezymenski, *The Death of Adolf Hitler: Unknown Documents from the Soviet Archives* (New York, 1968). ('Bezymenski' is probably a Russian pseudonym meaning 'nameless'.) **5.** Waite, 'Hitler's Guilt Feelings', 236 ff. The subject of the Führer's allegedly abnormal anatomy may ultimately derive from a secret disinformation campaign launched by SOE in the Arab countries in 1941: *Independent*, 5/6 Sept. 1994. **6.** After 'Fred Karno's Army', from Joan Littlewood, *Oh What a Lovely War!* (Theatre Workshop, London, 1976).

BOGUMIL **1.** See Steven Runciman, *The Mediaeval Manichee: A Study of the Christian Dualist Heresy* (Cambridge, 1947; repr. 1984). **2.** Euthymius Zigaberius, *Dogmatic Panoply*, quoted by Runciman, 76. **3.** See V. H. H. Green, *Medieval Civilization in Western Europe* (London, 1971), 179–80.

BOUBOULINA **1.** *The Great Greek Encyclopaedia*, 'PIRSOS' (Athens, *c*.1980), 75.

BOXER **1.** See H. Keown-Boyd, *The Fists of Righteous Harmony: A History of the Boxer Uprising in China* (London, 1991); A. H. Smith, *China in Convulsion* (Edinburgh, 1901).

BRIE **1.** Patrick Ronce, *The French Cheese Book* (London, 1989), 299, 340. **2.** Hugh Johnson, *World Atlas of Wine* (London, 1971), 60–1. Corton or 'Curtis Ottonis' received its modern name after the later Emperor, Otto I; *The Great Book of Wine* (Lausanne, 1970), 65–6. **3.** Ronce, op. cit. 3–7.

BRITO **1.** Bede, *History of the English Church and People*, i. 10. **2.** See B. R. Rees, *Pelagius: A Reluctant Heretic* (Woodbridge, 1988); St Prosper of Aquitaine, *The Call of All Nations* (Westminster, Md., 1952).

BUCZACZ **1.** Wincenty Urban, *Droga krzyżowa Archidiecezji Lwowskiej, 1939–45* (The Way of the Cross of the Archdiocese of Lwów) (Wrocław, 1983), 52–5. **2.** The figure of 60–80,000 is given by Jan T. Gross, *Polish Society Under German Occupation* (Princeton,

NJ, 1979). The Polish (Communist) Commission for the Investigation of Crimes Against the Polish Nation suggested a figure of 300–400,000. See M. Terles, *Ethnic Cleansing of Poles in Volhynia and Eastern Galicia* (Toronto, 1993), 32, 36. The alleged admission of President Krawchuk of Ukraine that 'Ukrainian chauvinists murdered around one half million Poles in the Eastern Borderlands' (ibid. 70) has not been substantiated, and appears to derive from a forgery. **3.** Ryszard Torzecki, *Polacy i Ukraińcy: Sprawa ukraińska w czasie II Wojny Światowej na terenie II Rzeczypospolity* (Warsaw, 1993), esp. ch. 6, 'Wojenna tragedia', also Wiktor Poliszczuk, *Gorzka prawda: zbrodniczość OUN–UPA* (unpublished typescript, Toronto, 1993). **4.** Terles, *Ethnic Cleansing*, 16–17. **5.** Z. Zieliński (ed.), *Życie religijne w Polsce pod okupacją, 1939–45* (Katowice, 1992), 500. **6.** See Norman Davies, 'Neither Twenty Million, Nor Russians, Nor War Dead', the *Independent*, 29 Dec. 1987. **7.** Martin Gilbert, *Atlas of the Holocaust* (London, 1982), 82. **8.** 'In Lieu of a Self-Portrait', in Simon Wiesenthal, *Justice Not Revenge* (London, 1989); also Alan Levy, *The Wiesenthal File* (London, 1993).

BUDA **1.** Martyn Rady, *Mediaeval Buda: a study of municipal Government and Jurisdiction* (Boulder, 1985). **2.** Henry Bogdan, *Histoire de Hongrie* (Paris, 1966), 14. **3.** Lovag Zsuzsa, *The Hungarian Crown and other regalia* (Hungarian National Museum), Budapest, 1986. **4.** 'Inamissible. Now rare, 1649– . Not liable to be lost.' *SOED*.

C14 **1.** H. Y. Göksu *et al.* (eds.), *Scientific Dating Methods* (Luxembourg, 1991): also S. Bowman, *Radiocarbon Dating* (London, 1990). **2.** A. Gob, *Chronologie du mésolithique en Europe* (Liège, 1990), nos. 0217, 2279, and 1816. **3.** L. Picknett, C. Prince, *The Turin Shroud: the shocking truth revealed* (London, 1994); R. Hoare, *The Turin Shroud is genuine: the irrefutable evidence* (London, 1994).

CABALA **1.** See Bernhard Pick, *The Cabala: Its Influence on Judaism and Christianity* (La Salle, Ill., 1913).

CADMUS **1.** See M. Bernal, *Cadmean Letters: The Transmission of the Alphabet to the Aegean Before 1400 BC* (Winona Lake, Minn., 1990).

CANTATA **1.** W. G. Whittaker, *The Cantatas of J. S. Bach* (Oxford, 1959), 659–74. **2.** Norman Davies, *God's Playground*, op. cit. ii. 505–7.

CANTUS **1.** Russian notation, 12th–13th centuries; from Armand Machabey, *La Notation musicale* (Paris, 1952). **2.** *Ut queant laxis* from the Gregorian *Liber Usualis* and in modern transcription. See Alec Harman, *Mediaeval and Early Renaissance Music* (Man and His Music, pt. 1) (London, 1988), 3 and pl. iii. **3.** See Deryck Cooke, *The Language of Music* (Oxford, 1959; paperback 1985). **4.** J. Gayard, *La Méthode de Solesmes* (Paris, 1951).

CAP-AG **1.** R. Brenner, 'Agrarian Class Structure and Economic Development in Pre-industrial Europe', *Past and Present*, 70 (1976), 30–75. **2.** *Past and Present*, 78, 79, 85, 97 (1975–81). **3.** Immanuel Wallerstein, *The Modern World-System: Capitalist Agriculture and the Origins of the European World-Economy* (New York, 1974). With special acknowledgement to Martyn Rady, 'Core and Periphery: Eastern Europe', a paper presented at the Mid-West Slavic Conference (c.1992). **4.** Wallerstein, *The Modern World-System*, 99. **5.** R. Brenner, 'The Origins of Capitalist Development: A Critique of Neo-Smithian Marxism', *New Left Review*, 104 (1977), 25–92. See also R. A. Denemark and K. P. Thomas, 'The Brenner–Wallerstein Debate', *International Studies Quarterly*, 32 (1988), 47–65.

CARITAS **1.** *Encyclopaedia Britannica*, 11th edn. (1912), vol. xiii, 593–4, under 'Drente'. **2.** Ibid. vol. v, 876, under 'Charity and Charities'. **3.** See R. M. Clay, *The Mediaeval Hospitals of England* (London, 1909). **4.** Michel Foucault, *Historie de la folie*

(1961), *Histoire de la Sexualité* (1976), *Surveiller et punir* (1975), trans. as *Discipline and Punish: the birth of the prison* (Harmondsworth, 1991). **5.** Foucault, *Discipline and Punish, passim.*

CATACOMBI **1.** See J. Stevenson, *The Catacombs: Rediscovered Monuments of Early Christianity* (London, 1978).

CAUCASIA **1.** J. F. Blumenbach, *Collectionis suae cranorum diversarum gentium . . .* (Göttingen, 1798–1828). **2.** Revd E. Cobham Brewer, *The Dictionary of Phrase and Fable* (1870; repr. New York, 1978), 229. **3.** L. Poliakov, *The Aryan Myth: A History of Racist and Nationalist Ideas in Europe* (New York, 1974), esp. 233 ff.; J. Boissel, *Gobineau: Un Don Quichotte tragique* (Paris, 1981). **4.** See Madison Grant, *The Passing of the Great Race* (New York, 1916). **5.** For the most recent, popular, and brilliant survey of the subject, see Steve Jones, *The Language of the Genes: Biology, History, and the Evolutionary Future* (London, 1994). **6.** See Ashley Montague, *Statement on Race: An Annotated Elaboration of . . . the Statements on Race Issued by UNESCO* (New York, 1972).

CEDROS **1.** Russell Meiggs, *Trees and Timber in the Ancient Mediterranean World* (Oxford, 1982).

CHASSE **1.** Gaston Phoebus, repr. as *The Hunting Book* (Geneva, 1978). See *Musée International de la Chasse: Château de Gien, Summary of the Collection* (Gien, Loiret, n.d.). **2.** Marcin Kromer, *Polonia* (1577), quoted by Norman Davies, *God's Playground* (Oxford, 1981), i. 249. **3.** See Raymond Carr, *English Fox-Hunting: A History* (London, 1986).

CHASTITY **1.** Rom. 7: 22–4; 8: 6. **2.** 1 Cor. 7: 9. **3.** Peter Brown, *The Body and Society: Men, Women, and Sexual Renunciation in Early Christianity* (New York, 1988), 446–7.

CHERNOBYL **1.** *Słownik geograficzny Królewstwo Polskiego i innych krajów słowiańskich* (A Geographical Dictionary of the Kingdom of Poland and of Other Slavonic Countries), ed. F. Sulimierski, B. Chłebowski, W. Walewski (Warsaw, 1880), 'Czarnobyl', i. 750–4. **2.** *The Great Soviet Encyclopaedia*, 3rd edn. (Moscow, 1978), vol. xxix, 'Chernobyl'. **3.** Rev. 8: 10, 11.

CHERSONESOS **1.** See M. Rostovtzeff, *Iranians and Greeks in South Russia* (Oxford, 1922). **2.** D. Obolensky, 'Crimea and the North before 1204', *Archeoin Pontou* 35 (1978), 123–33. **3.** G. A. Koshalenko *et al.*, *Antichnye Gosudarstva Severnogo Prichernomor'ya* (Moscow, 1984); Alexander L. Mongait, *Archaeology in the USSR* (Moscow, 1955, London, 1961), chapter 6, 'Classical Cities on the North Coast of the Black Sea.' **4.** Neal Ascherson, *Black Sea* (London, 1995), 12–48. **5.** R. Conquest, *The Nation Killers: the Soviet Deportation of Nationalities*, London, 1970).

CHOUAN **1.** E. Le Roy Ladurie, 'The "Event" and the "Long Term" in Social History: The Case of the Chouan Uprising' (a review of P. Bois, *Paysans de l'ouest* (Paris, 1972), in *The Territory of the Historian* (Chicago, 1979), 111–32.

CODPIECE **1.** Lois Banner, 'The Fashionable Sex, 1100–1600', *History Today*, 42(4) (1992). **2.** A. Junke and E. Stille, *Zur Geschichte der Unterwaesche, 1700–1960* (Illustrated Catalogue to an Exhibition at the Historical Museum) (Frankfurt a.M., 1988).

COMBRAY **1.** From 'Itinéraire proustien,' in Syndicat d'Initiative, *Illiers-Combray* (Illiers-Combray, 1989). See R. Hayman, *Proust: a biography* (London, 1990); L. Hodgson (ed.), *Marcel Proust: the critical heritage* (London, 1989); Sheila Stern, *Swann's Way* (Cambridge, 1989).

COMENIUS 1. *Comenius, 1592–1670: European Reformer and Czech Patriot* (Catalogue to an Exhibition at the Bodleian Library, Oxford, 1992), notes by R. J. W. Evans. See also M. Spinka, *The Incomparable Moravian* (Chicago, 1943). 2. T. G. Masaryk, *Svetová revoluce, za války i ve válce, 1914–18* (Prague, 1925); trans. as *The Making of a State: Memories and Observations, 1914–18* (New York, 1969). 3. From J. A. Comenius, *The Great Didactic,* 2nd edn. (London, 1910), 66–9: see also J. E. Sadler, *J. A. Comenius and the Concept of Universal Education* (London, 1966).

COMPOSTELA 1. See B. Tate, *Guià del Camino de Santiago* (Santiago); W. Starkie, *The Road to Santiago: pilgrims of St James* (London, 1957); H. Davies, *Holy days and holidays: the mediaeval pilgrimage to Compostela* (Lewisburg, PA, 1982); also James Bentley, *The Way of St James: a pilgrimage to Santiago de Compostela* (London, 1992).

COMPUTATIO 1. See J. B. Geisbeek, *Ancient Double-Entry Book-Keeping: Lucas Pacioli's Treatise* (Denver, 1914; repr. Osaka, 1975); also R. G. Brown and K. S. Johnston, *Pacioli on Accounting* (New York, 1963). 2. See P. L. McMickle and R. G. Vangermeersch, *The Origins of a Great Profession: Catalogue to an Exhibition of Rare Accounting Books and Manuscripts from the Montgomery Collection* (Memphis, 1987). 3. M. F. Bywater and B. Yamey, *Historic Accounting Literature: A Companion Guide* (London, 1982).

CONCLAVE 1. J. N. D. Kelly, *The Oxford Dictionary of Popes* (Oxford, 1988), 327.

CONDOM 1. Aetius, quoted by M. K. Hopkins, 'Contraception in the Roman Empire', *Comparative Studies in History and Society*, 8 (1965–6), 124–51. 2. P. Ariès, 'Sur les origines de la contraception en France', *Population*, 3 (1953); see P. P. A. Biller, 'Birth Control in the West in the 13th and 14th Centuries', *Past and Present*, 94 (1982), 3–26. 3. See J. T. Noonan, *Contraception: A History of Its Treatment by Catholic Theologians and Casuists* (Cambridge, Mass., 1966). 4. Deposition of Beatrice de Planissoles, quoted by E. Le Roy Ladurie, *Montaillou* (London, 1980), 172–3. 5. See A. McLaren, *Birth-Control in Nineteenth Century Britain* (London, 1978). 6. A. Nikiforuk, *The Fourth Horseman* (London, 1991), chapter 6. 7. Christina Hardyment, 'Marie Stopes and Germaine Greer . . .', paper read at the Alistair Horne Fellowship Symposium, St Antony's College, Oxford, June 1993. 8. Ibid.

CONSPIRO 1. S. Hutin, *Les Sociétés secrètes*, 11th edn. (Paris, 1993). See also G. Falzone, *La Storia de la Mafia* (1973), translated as *Histoire de la Mafia* (Paris, 1973); R. Catanzaro, *Men of Respect: a social history of the Sicilian Mafia* (New York, 1992).

CORSICA 1. Dorothy Carrington, *Napoleon and His Parents: On the Threshold of History* (London, 1988); *Granite Island: A Portrait of Corsica* (London, 1962); also P. Arrighi, *Histoire de la Corse* (Paris, 1947); R. Ramsay, *The Corsican Time-Bomb* (Manchester, NH, 1983).

CORVINA 1. C. Csapodi and K. Csapodi-Gárdonyi, *Biblioteca Corviniana 1490–1990* (catalogue of the exhibition) (Budapest, 1990); reviewed by H. R. Trevor-Roper, 'Reunion in Budapest', *New York Review of Books*, 19 July 1990.

COWARD 1. 'Campaign to Pardon Troops Hits Setback', The *Independent*, 16 Aug. 1993. See also J. Putkowski and J. Sykes, *Shot at Dawn* (London, 1989). 2. 'Deserters', in *Oxford Companion to the Second World War* (Oxford, 1995).

CRAVATE 1. *Oxford English Dictionary* Compact Edition (1970), i. 1144. 2. É. Littré, *Dictionnaire de la langue française* (Paris, 1966), ii. 1094. 3. The *Independent*, 3 July 1991. 4. *Louis XIV*, 16. Littré, *Dictionnaire.* 5. R. Filipovic, *Englesko–Hrvatski ili Srpski*

Rjecnik, 8th edn. (Zagreb, 1977); M. Benson, *An English–Serbocroatian Dictionary* (Cambridge, 1990). Filipovic favours *kravata,* Benson *masna.*

CRUX 1. A. Frutiger, *Der Mensch und Seine Zeichen* (Dreieich, 1989), trans. as *Signs and Symbols: Their Design and Meaning* (London, 1989), 276–7. 2. Frutiger, op. cit., pp. 276–7. 3. 'Tamgas and Tribal Signs' in W. Leaf, S. Purcell, *Heraldic Symbols: Islamic Insignia and Western Heraldry* (London, 1986), 76–82. 4. Tadeusz Sulimirski, *The Sarmatians* (London, 1970), discussed by Ascherson, *Black Sea,* op. cit. 230–43. 5. Władysław T. Bartoszewski, *The Convent at Auschwitz* (Bowerdean Press, London, 1990).

CSABA 1. Arpad's Tale, 'The Skyway of the Warriors', after Kate Seredy, *The Good Master* (Budapest), trans. into English (London, 1937), 92–6.

DANNEBROG 1. B. Rying, *Denmark: History* (Copenhagen, 1988), 39.

DANUVIUS 1. See C. Magris, *Danube: a sentimental journey from the source to the sea* (London, 1989). 2. Dimitrie Radu, *Pasarile din Delta Dunarii* (Birds of the Danube Delta) (Bucharest, 1979). 3. See A. Demangeon, L. Febvre, *Le Rhin: problèmes d'histoire et d'économie* (Paris, 1935).

DASA 1. John D. Barrow, *Pi in the Sky: Counting, Thinking and Being* (Oxford, 1992), 60–3. 2. C. Kephart, *Sanskrit: its origin, composition and diffusion* (Strasburg, VA, 1949); also K. Srinivasachari, *Learn Sanskrit in Thirty Days* (Madras, 1987). 3. See G. Flegg, *Numbers: Their History and Meaning* (London, 1983); A. Lillo, *The Ancient Greek Numeral System* (Bonn, 1990).

DEMOS 1. Peter France, *Greek as a Treat,* programme 3, BBC Radio 4, 12 May 1993. 2. See R. K. Sinclair, *Democracy and Participation in Athens* (Cambridge, 1988), and E. M. Wood, *Peasant-Citizen and Slave* (London, 1988), both reviewed in P. Cartledge, 'The First Popular Government', *TLS,* 6–12 Jan. 1989. 3. T. G. Masaryk, inaugural address, 23 Dec. 1918.

DESSEIN 1. C. Pfister, 'Les "Œconomies Royales" de Sully et le grand dessein de Henri IV', *Revue historique,* 56 (1894), 304–39. 2. D. J. Buisseret, *Sully and the Growth of Centralised Government in France, 1598–1610* (London, 1968). 3. See F. H. Hinsley, *Power and the Pursuit of Peace* (Cambridge, 1967), 24 ff.

DEVIATIO 1. Thomas Szasz, *The Manufacture of Madness: A Comparative Study of the Inquisition and the Mental Health Movement* (London, 1971). 2. P. Reddaway (ed.), *Uncensored Russia: The Human Rights Movement in the Soviet Union* (London, 1977); S. Bloch, *Russia's Political Hospitals: The Abuse of Psychiatry in the Soviet Union* (London, 1977); S. Bloch and P. Reddaway, *Soviet Psychiatric Abuse: The Shadow over World Psychiatry* (Boulder, Colo., 1985); Vladimir Bukovsky, *To Build a Castle: My Life as a Dissenter* (London, 1978).

DIABOLOS 1. N. Forsyth, *The Old Enemy: Satan and the Combat Myth* (Princeton, NJ, 1987); reviewed by G. Steiner, *TLS,* 1–7 Apr. 1988.

DING 1. Kirsten Hastrup, *Culture and History in Mediaeval Iceland: An Anthropological Analysis of Structure and Change* (Oxford, 1985). 2. S. Lindal, 'Early Democratic Traditions', in E. Allardt (ed.), *Nordic Democracy: Ideas, Issues and Institutions* (Copenhagen, 1981).

DIRHAM 1. *The Risālah of Ibn Fadlān,* (trans. and introd. J. E. McKeithen (Ph.D. thesis, Indiana Univ., 1979), quoted by T. S. Noonan, 'The Impact of the Silver Crisis in Islam upon Novgorod's Trade with the Baltic', in *Oldenburg-Wolin-Staraja Ladoga-*

Novgorod-Kiev: Handel und Handlesverginbungen im südlichen und östlichen Ost-seeraum während des frühen Mittelalters (Kiel, 1987), 411–47. **2.** T. S. Noonan, 'Dirhams from Early Mediaeval Russia', *Journal of the Russian Numismatic Society* (USA), 17 (1984–5), 8–12. **3.** M. Sternberger, *Die Schatzfunde Gotlands der Wikingerzeit* (Lund, 1947). **4.** After I. Andersson, *History of Sweden* (London, 1962), 18. Andersson's translation of 'Rus' as 'Swedes' is acceptable in this period.

DOLLAR **1.** See D. R. Cooper, *Coins and Minting* (Princes Risborough, 1983), 10–16. **2.** J. Hans, *Maria-Teresien Taler: zwei Jahrhunderte* (Leiden, 1961).

DÖNHOFF **1.** See Roman Aftanazy, *Dzieje rezydencji na dawnych kresach Rzeczpospolitej* (The History of the Great Houses in the Former Borderlands of the Polish-Lithuanian Commonwealth) (11 vols., Wrocław, 1991), illustrated. **2.** Marion Dönhoff, *Kindheit in Ostpreussen* (Berlin, 1988); trans. as *Before the Storm: Memoirs of My Youth in Old Prussia* (New York, 1990), 204.

DOUAUMONT **1.** *Voir et comprendre Verdun: Champ de bataille, environs* (Drancy, 1981); *Ouverture à la visite du champ de bataille* (Fleury-devant-Douaumont, n.d.). See Alistair Horne, *The price of glory: Verdun 1916* (London, 1993).

$e = mc^2$ **1.** See J. Schwartz, *Einstein for Beginners* (Exeter, 1979), 2—a quotation which appears in various forms. See M. White and J. Gribbin, *Einstein: A life in Science* (New York, 1993); reviewed by R. Dinnage, 'Man of Science Agog', *TLS*, 17 Dec. 1993.

ECO **1.** From Plato's *Critias*; quoted by Clive Ponting, *A Green History of the World* (London, 1991), 76–7. **2.** Genesis ix. 1–3: God's promise to the sons of Noah; Psalm viii. 5–6; Psalm cxv: 16. **3.** Hazel Henderson, *Creating Alternative Futures* (1978), quoted by Ponting, 159. **4.** See Sven Forshufvid, *Assassination at St. Helena* (Vancouver, 1978); B. Weider and D. Hapgood, *The Murder of Napoleon* (London, 1982).

EESTI **1.** At the Charles Stransky Memorial Lecture, London, 20 Sept. 1993; also letter from Dr von Habsburg, 28 Sept. 1993. See also E. Uustalu, *A History of the Estonian People* (London, 1952); R. Taagepera, *Estonia: Return to Independence* (Oxford, 1993).

EGNATIA **1.** *The Oxford Dictionary of Byzantium* (Oxford, 1991), i. 679. See also R. Chevallier, *Roman Roads* (Berkeley, Calif., 1976).

EIRIK **1.** Quoted by Magnus Magnusson and H. Pálsson, *The Vinland Sagas* (London, 1965), 24–5. **2.** See Helge Ingstad, *Westward to Vinland* (New York, 1969). **3.** S. E. Morison, *The European Discovery of America*, i, *The Northern Voyages*, AD 500–1600, ch. 3, 'The Norsemen and Vinland' (O.U.P.) (New York, 1971), 32–80. **4.** R. A. Skelton, T. E. Marston *et al.*, *The Vinland Map and the Tartar Relation* (New Haven, Conn., 1965). See also J. H. Parry, 'The Vinland Story', in *Perspectives in American History*, i (1967), 417–33; M. A. Musmanno, *Columbus Was First* (New York, 1966). **5.** Texts in Magnusson's translation, *The Vinland Sagas*. **6.** Morison, *The European Discovery of America*, i. 61. **7.** On John Davys, see R. Hakluyt's *Principal Navigations and Voyages . . . of the English nation*, A. S. Mott (ed.) (Oxford, 1929).

EL CID **1.** R. Fletcher, *The Quest for El Cid* (Oxford, 1989); C. Smith, *The Making of the 'Poema del Mío Cid'* (Cambridge, 1983). **2.** M. H. Keen, *The Outlaws of Mediaeval Legend* (London, 1961); J. C. Holt, *Robin Hood* (London, 1989); R. B. Dobson and J. Taylor, *Rymes of Robyn Hood: An Introduction to the English Outlaw*, rev. edn. (London, 1989). **3.** Juraj Janosik (*c.*1688–1713). See 'Legenda Tatr', *Literatura polska: Przewodnik Encyklopedyczny* (Warsaw, 1984), 553.

ELDLUFT   1. With acknowledgement to the Open University programme 'Oxygen', broadcast on BBC2, 26 Sept. 1992.   2. As illustrated in J. Bronowski, *The Ascent of Man* (London, 1970), 146–7.

ELEKTRON   1. See V. W. Hughes, H. L. Schultz, *Atomic and electron physics* (London, 1967); G. Leon, *The Story of Electricity* (New York, 1983).

ELEMENTA   1. See J. Hudson, *The History of Chemistry* (Basingstoke, 1992); W. H. Brock, *The Fontana History of Chemistry* (London, 1992).

ELSASS   1. F. L. 'Huillier, *Histoire de l'Alsace* (Paris, 1947); G. Livet, *L'Europe, l'Alsace, et la France* (Colmar, 1986).   2. E. Birke, *Silesia: A German Region* (Munich, 1968); W. J. Rose, *The Drama of Upper Silesia: A Regional Study* (Battleborough, Vt., 1935); K. Popiolek, *śląskie dzieje* (Warsaw, 1981); W. B. Goldstein, *Tausend Jahre Breslau* (Darmstadt, 1974).   3. Rose Bailly, *A City Fights for Freedom: The Rising of Lwów, 1918–19* (London, 1958); West Ukrainian Press Agency, *The Problem of Eastern Galicia* and *The Eastern Galician Question* (Vienna, 1920); L. Podhorodecki, *Dzieje Kijowa* (Warsaw, 1982).

EMU   1. See Stephen George, *Politics and Policy in the European Community* (Oxford, 1985), Ch. 9, 'Economic and Monetary Union'.

EPIC   1. From Stephanie Dalley, *Myths from Mesopotamia: The Creation, the Flood, Gilgamesh, and Others* (Oxford, 1989).   2. Homer, *Odyssey*, I. i.   3. See Stephanie West, *Assurbanipal's Classic*, a review of Dalley, and of Maureen G. Kovacs, *The Epic of Gilgamesh* (Stanford, Calif., 1989), *London Review of Books*, 8 Nov. 1990, 23–5.

EPIDEMIA   1. See C. D. Gordon, 'The Huns', in *The Age of Attila* (Ann Arbor, Mich., 1966), 55–111.   2. A. Nikiforuk, *The Fourth Horseman* (London, 1991), ch. 5, 'The Smallpox Conquest'.   3. Ibid. 14.

EPIGRAPH   1. *CIL* xii. 7070; quoted by R. Bloch, *L'Épigraphie latine* (Paris, 1952), 59.   2. *CIL* vi. 701; quoted by Bloch, *L'Épigraphie latine*, 83.   3. *CIL* xiii. 3, fasc. 2, 10021; quoted by Bloch, *L'Épigraphie latine*, 102. See also D. Feissel *et al.*, *Guide de l'épigraphiste* (Paris, 1986).

EROS   1. K. L. von Pollnitz, *Le Saxe galante, or The Amorous Adventures of Augustus of Saxony . . . translated by a Gentleman of Oxford* (London, 1750).   2. Norman Davies, *God's Playground: A History of Poland* (Oxford, 1981), i. 493–5.   3. In Cambridge.

ETRUSCHERIA   1. Quoted by M. Finley, 'The Etruscans and Early Rome', in *Aspects of Antiquity* (London, 1968), 115.   2. 'The Etruscans and Europe', Galéries du Grand Palais, 15 Sept.–14 Dec. 1992, in *Le Petit journal des grandes expositions*, 237 (Paris, 1992).   3. D. H. Lawrence, *Etruscan Places* (1927), quoted by Finley, 'The Etruscans and Early Rome', 100.

EULENBURG   1. James D. Steakly, 'Iconography of a Scandal: Political Cartoons and the Eulenburg Affair in Wilhelmian Germany', in M. B. Dubermann *et al.* (eds.), *Hidden from History: Reclaiming the Gay and Lesbian Past* (New York, 1989; London, 1991), 233–63. 2. B. Inglis, *Roger Casement* (London, 1973); H. O. Mackey, *The Crime Against Europe: The Writings and Poetry of R. Casement* (Dublin, 1958); Richard Ellmann, *Oscar Wilde* (London, 1987).   3. M. Baumont, *L'Affaire Eulenberg et les origines de la Guerre Mondiale* (Paris, 1933); quoted by Steakley, 'Iconography of a Scandal', 235.   4. E. J. Haeberle, 'Swastika, Pink Triangle, and Yellow Star: the Destruction of Sexology and the Persecution of Homosexuals in Nazi Germany', in Dubermann *et al.* (eds.), *Hidden from History*, 365–82.

EULER   1. Petr Beckmann, *A History of PI* (New York, 1971), 147–57.

FAMINE 1. Cecil Woodham-Smith, *The Great Hunger: Ireland 1845–49* (London, 1962), 91. 2. Ibid. 19. 3. Roy Foster, *Modern Ireland: 1600–1972* (London, 1988), 325. 4. Quoted by A. Nikiforuk, 'The Irish Famine', in *The Fourth Horseman* (London, 1991), 123. 5. From Lady Wilde, 'The Exodus', in C. Morash (ed.), *The Hungry Voice: Poetry of the Irish Famine* (Dublin, 1989), 219; S. Cronin, *Irish Nationalism: a history of its roots and ideology* (New York, 1980).

FARAON 1. *The National Monument of the Santa Cruz de Valle de los Caldos: a tourist guidebook* (Madrid, 1961).

FAROE 1. L. K. Schei and G. Moberg, *The Faroe Islands* (London, 1991), ch. 5, 'Political Awakening'.

FATIMA 1. J. Delaney, *A Woman Clothed in the Sun* (Dublin, 1991), 194. See also M. De la Sainte Trinité, *The Third Secret of Fatima* (Chulmleigh, 1986). 2. See T. Tindale-Robertson, *Fatima, Russia, and Pope John Paul II* (Chulmleigh, 1992). 3. See M. Parham, 'With God on Our Side', *Independent Magazine*, 4 Dec. 1993; also the quarterly *Medjugorje Messenger* (London, 1986–).

FAUSTUS 1. Goethe, *Faust*, pt. ii, ll. 12,073–5. 2. *The Oxford Companion to German Literature*, 173.

FEMME 1. Translated for *Wollstonecraft, Women, and the French Revolution*, an exhibition at University College, London, 1992. 2. See Sara E. Melzer and Leslie W. Rabine (eds.), *Rebel Daughters: Women and the French Revolution* (Oxford, 1992).

FIESTA 1. Federico de Cesco, *Viva Europa: Die Hundert schönsten Volksfeste* (Zurich, n.d.).

FLAGELLATIO 1. C. Bertelli, 'The Flagellation', in *Piero della Francesca* (New Haven, Conn., 1991), 115–26; C. Ginzburg, *The Enigma of Piero: The Baptism, the Arezzo Cycle: The Flagellation* (London, 1985); K. Clark, *Piero della Francesca* (London, 1969). 2. R. Wittkower and B. A. R. Carter, 'The Perspective of Piero della Francesca's "Flagellation"', *Journal of the Warburg and Courtauld Institutes*, 16 (1953), 292–302. 3. Bertelli, 'The Flagellation', 115–16. 4. John Pope-Hennessy, *The Piero della Francesca Trail* (23rd Walter Neurath Lecture) (London, 1993), 10; also his 'Whose Flagellation?', *Apollo*, 124 (1986), 162–5. 5. Alison Cole, *Perspective* (London, 1992). 6. See Michael Woods, *Perspective in Art: A Drawing Tutor* (London, 1984). 7. Cole, *Perspective* 24. 8. J. Berger, *Ways of Seeing* (London, 1972); also *The European Way of Seeing* (London, 1972).

FLAMENCO 1. With thanks to Sra. Jozefina Del Carmen Boyd. 2. Quoted by James Woodall, *In Search of the Firedance: Spain through Flamenco* (London, 1992), 149.

FLORA 1. See Monica Kippner, *The Quality of Mercy: Women at War, Serbia 1915–18* (Newton Abbot, 1980), 223. 2. Ibid. 34. 3. See Julie Wheelwright, *Amazons and Military Maids* (London, 1989) which contains a chapter on Flora Sandes. 4. Kippner, *The Quality of Mercy*, 30.

FOLLY 1. Aleksander Bocheński, *Dzieje głupoty w Polsce* (repr. Warsaw, 1947). 2. Adam Michnik, *Z dziejów honoru w Polsce: wypisy więzienne* (Paris, 1985). 3. Barbara Tuchman, *The March of Folly: From Troy to Vietnam* (London, 1984).

FREUDE 1. F. von Schiller, 'An die Freude', in L. Reiners (ed.), *Der ewige Brunnen* (Munich, 1992), 910 ff.; F. von Schiller, *Ode to Joy* (Paisley, 1987). 2. G. Grove, *Beethoven and his Nine Symphonies* (London, 1898), 326–7. 3. Ibid. 309–400; Ralph Hill (ed.), *The Symphony* (London, 1949), 113–17.

FUTHARK   **1.** See R. A. Page, 'Rune-Masters and Skalds', in J. Campbell-Graham, *The Viking World* (London, 1989), 155–71. **2.** N. Pennick, 'Figure and Sequence', in *Games of the Gods: The Origin of Board Games in Magic and Divination* (London, 1988), 75. **3.** Tacitus, quoted ibid. 91. **4.** Pennick, *Games of the Gods*, 95–100: see also R. A. S. Macalister, *The Secret Languages of Ireland* (Cambridge, 1987); D. McManus, *A Guide to Ogham* (Maynooth, 1991); R. R. Brash and J. R. Allen, *Ogham Monuments in Wales* (Llanerch, 1992).

GAGAUZ   **1.** See W. Zajączkowski, *Język i folklor u Gagauzów w Bulgarii* (Kraków, 1966). **2.** See H. T. Norris, *Islam in the Balkans: religion and society between Europe and the Arab world* (London, 1993). **3.** T. J. Winnifrith, 'The Pomaks', in *Shattered Eagles, Balkan Fragments* (London, 1995), 82–98. **4.** R. J. Donie, J. V. A. Fine, *Bosnia and Hercegovina: a tradition betrayed* (London, 1994).

GAT-HUNTER   **1.** Clive Gamble, 'Hunter-gatherers and the origin of states', in J. A. Hall (ed.), *States in History* (Oxford, 1968); see also R. B. Lee, I. De Vore (eds.), *Man the Hunter* (Chicago, 1968).

GATTOPARDO   **1.** Giuseppe Tomasi di Lampedusa, *Il Gattopardo* (Milan, 1958); trans. Archibald Colquhoun as *The Leopard* (London, 1960), 11. **2.** Ibid. 29. **3.** Ibid. 223.

GAUCHE   **1.** See J. van Clove, R. E. Frederick, *The Philosophy of Right and Left: incongruent counterparts and the nature of space* (London, 1991). **2.** N. Nugent, 'The European Parliament', in *The Government and Politics of the European Community* (3rd edn.) (London, 1994).

GENES   **1.** P. J. Bowles, *The Mendelian Revolution* (London, 1989); C. F. Meyer, *The Genesis of Genetics: The Growing Knowledge of Heredity Before and After Mendel* (Rome, 1953); C. Stern, *The Origin of Genetics: A Mendelian Source Book* (London, 1966). **2.** Zhores Medvedev, *The Rise and Fall of T. D. Lysenko* (1967; trans. New York, 1969); D. Joravsky, *The Lysenko Affair* (Cambridge, Mass., 1970). **3.** See J. S. Huxley, *Soviet Genetics and World Science* (London, 1949).

GENOCIDE   **1.** G. J. Libaridian, *A Crime of Silence: the Armenian Genocide* (London, 1985); D. M. Lang, *The Armenians: a people in exile* (London, 1981); C. J. Walker, *Armenia: survival of a nation* (London, 1990); S. L. Sonyel, *The Ottoman Armenians, victims of great power diplomacy* (London, 1987); R. Hovannisian (ed.), *The Armenian Genocide: history, politics, and ethics* (London, 1991); R. Melson, *Revolution and Genocide: on the origin of the Armenian genocide and of the Holocaust* (London, 1992). **2.** From the notes of Admiral Canaris, 22 August 1939, quoted by L. P. Lochner, *What about Germany?* (New York, 1942), 2. The passage is sometimes misquoted as if it referred to the Final Solution. With acknowledgement to Dr Mark Levene. **3.** R. Lemkin, *Axis Rule in Europe: Laws of Occupation, Analysis of Government, Proposals for Redress* (New York, 1944). See also 'Genocide', *Encyclopaedia Judaica* (Jerusalem, 1971), vol. 7, 410.

GENUG   **1.** After G. Brandreth, *Famous Last Words and Tombstone Humor* (New York, 1989).

GESANG   **1.** Martin Luther, 'Ein' feste Burg ist unser Gott', in *Der ewige Brunnen: ein Handbuch deutscher Dichtung* (Munich, 1979), 971; see also F. Blume, *Protestant Church Music: a history* (London, 1975). **2.** Translated by Thomas Carlyle, *The English Hymnal with Tunes* (Oxford, 1933), no. 362. **3.** Thrasybilos Georgiades, 'The German Language and Music', in *Music and Language: The Rise of Western Music as Exemplified in Settings of the Mass* (Cambridge, 1982), 49–58. **4.** 'Tallis's Canon', a shortened form of the melody by Thomas Tallis (1505–85) from T. Ravenscroft's *Psalter* (1621), words by Thomas Ken

(1637–1710). See M. Baughen (ed.), *Hymns for Today's Church* (London, 1982), no. 274. See also E. H. Fellowes, *English Cathedral Music* (London, 5th edn., 1969).

ĠGANTIJA 1. J. D. Evans, *Prehistoric Antiquities of the Maltese Islands* (London, 1971). 2. B. Blouet, *The Story of Malta*, 3rd edn. (London, 1981).

GHETTO 1. 'Ghetto', in *Encyclopaedia Judaica* (Jerusalem, 1970), vii. 542–6. 2. Gershon Hundert, *Jews in a Polish Private Town: The Case of Eighteenth Century Opatów* (Baltimore, 1992).

GONCALVEZ 1. B. Davidson, *Black Mother* (Boston, 1961); rev. edn. *The African Slave Trade* (Boston, 1980), 53–4. 2. Ibid. 55. 3. Ibid. 67–9, 101–3. 4. Ibid. 163. 5. 'How Many?', ibid. 95–101.

GOOSE STEP 1. See P. J. Haythornthwaite, *Frederick the Great's Army* (London, 1991); also Gordon Craig, *The Politics of the Prussian Army, 1640–1945* (Oxford, 1955).

GOTHA 1. E. Scheeben, *Ernst II: Herzog von Sachsen-Coburg und Gotha* (Frankfurt, 1987); J. Van der Kirstie, *Dearest Affie: Alfred, Duke of Edinburgh and Duke of Saxe-Coburg and Gotha, 1840–1900* (Gloucester, 1984). 2. R. R. James, *Albert, Prince Consort: A Biography* (London, 1985); S. Weintraub, *Victoria: A Biography of a Queen* (London, 1988); T. Aranson, *Heart of a Queen: Queen Victoria's Romantic Attachments* (London, 1991). 3. A. S. Gould Lee, *The Royal House of Greece* (London, 1948). 4. Brian Connell, *Manifest Destiny: A Study in Five Profiles of . . . the Mountbatten Family* (London, 1953); M. Kerr, *Admiral Louis of Battenberg* (London, 1934); R. Hough, *Louis and Victoria* (London, 1974). 5. *Polski Słownik Biograficzny* (Wrocław, 1960–1), ix, 'Hauke'. 6. Anthony, Lord Lambton, *The Mountbattens* (London, 1989). 7. Richard Tomlinson, 'Trying to be Useful', the *Independent on Sunday*, 19 June 1994; extracts from *Divine Right: The Inglorious Survival of British Royalty* (London, 1994).

GOTHIC 1. J. Ruskin, *The Nature of Gothic* (1892; repr. Portland, Oreg., 1975), 5. 2. See A. Saint, 'Building in the Holy Town', *TLS*, 9–15 Mar. 1990, a review of A. Erlande-Brandenburg, *La Cathédrale* (Paris) and R. Recht (ed.), *Les Bâtisseurs des cathédrales gothiques* (Strasburg, 1989).

GOTTHARD 1. Ian Robertson, *Switzerland*, Blue Guide (London, 1989), 230, 304–5. 2. Suvorov monument. Personal visit.

GRECO 1. David Holton (ed.), *Literature and Society in Renaissance Crete* (Cambridge, 1991); A. Embiricos, *La Renaissance Crétoise*, 2 vols. (Paris, 1960–7). 2. C. T. Dimaras, *A History of Modern Greek Literature* (London, 1972).

GRILLENSTEIN 1. R. Sieder and M. Mitterauer, 'The Reconstruction of the Family Life Course: Theoretical Problems and Empirical Results', in R. Wall *et al.* (eds.), *Family Forms in Historic Europe* (Cambridge, 1983), 309–45.

GROSSENMEER 1. Peter Laslett, 'Family and Household as Work Group and Kin Group: Areas of Traditional Europe Compared', in R. Wall *et al.* (eds.), *Family Forms in Historic Europe* (Cambridge, 1983), 513–63. 2. Peter Laslett, 'Introduction: The History of the Family', in Laslett and Richard Wall (eds.), *Household and Family in Past Times: Comparative Studies in Size and Structure of the Domestic Group over the Last Three Centuries* (Cambridge, 1972). 3. J. Valynseele, *La Généalogie: histoire et pratique* (Paris, 1991). See also Genealogical Society of the Church of Jesus Christ of Latter-day Saints, *Finding Aids to the Microfilmed Manuscript Collection . . .* (Salt Lake City, 1978–83).

GROTE MARKT   1. Jacques Darras, 1989 Reith Lectures, 1, 'The Time Traveller', from *Beyond the Tunnel of History* (BBC Radio 4), *Listener*, 23 Nov. 1989.   2. Reith Lectures, 2, 'The Golden Fleece', *Listener*, 30 Nov. 1989.

GUERRILLA   1. Robert Moss, *Urban Guerrillas: the new face of political terrorism* (London, 1972).   2. A. Racineux, 'Les Chouans: une armée de l'ombre', *Historama*, no. 89, July 1989, 12–19.

GUILLOTIN   1. After Martin Manser, *Dictionary of Eponyms* (London, 1988), 120.

HANSA   1. T. Lindner, *Die deutsche Hanse: ihre Geschichte*, 4th edn. (Leipzig, 1911); Hugo Yrwing, *Visby: hansestad pae Gotland* (Stockholm, 1986).   2. Fritz Grotemeyer, 'Warenzug hansischer Kaufleute' (1942), in *Die Hanse: Lebenswirklichkeit und Mythos, Ausstellungskatalog des Museums für Hamburgische Geschichte*, Bd 2 (Hamburg, 1989), 623; also Carsten Prange, *Auf zur Reise durch Hamburgs Geschichte—A Journey through Hamburg's History* (Hamburg, 1990).

HARVEST   1. Robert Conquest, *The Harvest of Sorrow: Soviet Collectivisation and the Terror Famine* (London, 1986), 3.   2. Ibid. ch. 16, 'The Death Roll'.   3. Vasily Grossman, *Forever Flowing* (New York, 1972), quoted by Conquest, *The Harvest of Sorrow*, 286.   4. S. J. Taylor, *Stalin's Apologist: Walter Duranty, the New York Times' Man in Moscow* (Oxford, 1990).   5. Conquest, *The Harvest of Sorrow*, ch. 17, 'The Record of the West'.   6. Ibid. 'Preface', 1.

HATRED   1. G. Bell, *Archbishop Davidson* (London, 1935), ii. 756–70.   2. K. Slack, *George Bell, 1883–1958* (London, 1972).   3. In G. Bell, *The Church and Humanity* (London, 1946), ch. 22, 'God Above Nation', 201–10.   4. Ibid. 22–31.   5. Ibid. ch. 14, 'Obliteration Bombing'. See also M. Czesany, *Allierten Bombenterror: der Luftkrieg gegen die Zivilbevölkerung Europas, 1940–5* (Leoni, 1987).   6. D. Bonhoffer, *Letters and Papers from Prison*, E. Bethge, ed. (New York, 1967), quoted by Slack, *George Bell*, 97.   7. Bell, *The Church and Humanity*, ch. 19, 'Christianity and the European Heritage', 177–82.

HEJNAŁ   1. With thanks to Professor Jacek Woźniakowski, art historian and, in 1991, Lord Mayor of Cracow.   2. Gaspard de Marval, *Le Guet de la cathédrale*, Postface by Oliver Freeman (Chapelle-sur-Moudon, 1992).

HEPTANESOS   1. W. H. Zawadzki, *Man of Honour: A. Czartoryski, Statesman of Russia and Poland* (Oxford, 1993).   2. 'Great Britain and the Ionian Islands, 1848–51: A Case of Bad Publicity', *European History Quarterly*, 17(2) (1987), 131–44.

HERMANN   1. See George Mosse, *The Nationalisation of the Masses: political symbolism and mass movements in Germany* (Ithaca, 1991).   2. Professor Rees Davies of Aberystwyth writes: 'The story and the monument [of Beddgelert] belong to the 1790s . . . The "inventor" was an immigrant into the area, David Pritchard—no doubt wanting to attract more visitors to this part of Wild Wales. He was, I think, the local publican. It was a typical, Romantic, Ossian, Iolo Morganwg sort of story . . .'; private letter, 16 May 1994.

HEXEN   1. Hugh Trevor-Roper, *The European Witch-Craze of the Sixteenth and Seventeenth Century* (London, 1990), 84.   2. Ibid.   3. *Księgi Miejskie Kaliskie* (1612), quoted by B. Baranowski, *Procesy czarownic w Polsce XXVII i XVIII wiekach* (Łódź, 1952). Recent estimates put the total number of victims at c.50,000.

HOLISM   1. *Das Buch von der Gebärung* (c.1520), 3.3; in *Paracelsus: Essential Readings*, sel. and trans. Nicholas Goodrick-Clarke (Wellingborough, 1990), 59.

HOSSBACH 1. 'The Hossbach Memorandum', in *Documents on German Foreign Policy 1918–45* (London, 1949), ser. D, i. 29–30. 2. A. J. P. Taylor, *The Origins of the Second World War* (London, 1963), 168–72. 3. T. W. Mason, in E. M. Robertson (ed.), *The Origins of the Second World War* (London, 1971), 114. See also F. H. Hinsley, *Power and the Pursuit of Peace: Theory and Practice in the History of Relations Between States* (Cambridge, 1963), esp. 328–34.

HYSTERIA 1. Quoted by Mary K. Lefkowitz in 'The Wandering Womb', *Heroines and Hysterics* (London, 1981), 15–16. See also L. Dean-Jones, *Women's Bodies in Classical Greek Science* (Oxford, 1994). 2. Lefkowitz, 'The Wandering Womb', 12. 3. E. Shorter, *A History of Women's Bodies* (London, 1982).

IKON 1. See J. Baggley, *Doors of Perception: Icons and their spiritual significance* (London, 1987). 2. See N. P. Kondrakov, 'Iconography of the Boguroditsa', in *The Russian Icon* (Oxford, 1927). 3. G. Ramos-Poquí, *The Technique of Icon Painting* (Tunbridge Wells, 1990). 4. Stefania Hnatenko, *Treasures of Early Ukrainian Art: Religious Art of the 16–18th Centuries* (Ukrainian Museum) (New York, 1959); S. Hordynsky, *The Ukrainian Ikon from the XII to the XVIII centuries* (Toronto, 1973). 5. Suzanne Martinet, *La Sainte-Face de Laon et son histoire* (Laon, 1988). 6. Maxim Gorky, *Childhood* (Penguin Classics, London, 1966), pp. 61–4.

ILLYRIA 1. See D. Gelt, *The Slovenians from the Earliest Times* (Victoria, 1983); E. M. Despalatović, *L. Gaj and the Illyrian Movement* (New York, 1973); J. Punk *et al.*, *A Brief History of Slovenia* (Ljubljana, 1994); S. Gazi, *A History of Croatia* (New York, 1973); R. W. Seton-Watson, *The Southern Slav Question and the Habsburg Monarchy* (New York, 1911); J. Pogonowski, *Iliryzm i Słowianszczyzna* (Lwów, 1924).

ILLYRICUM 1. See J. Wilkes, *The Illyrians* (Oxford, 1992); also 'The Provinces of the Empire', T. Cornell, J. Matthews, *Atlas of the Roman World* (Oxford, 1982), 118–66.

IMPRESSION 1. Herman Wechsler, *Lives of Famous French Painters* (New York, 1962), 103–8. 2. Ibid. 16.

INDEX 1. N. Parsons, *The Book of Literary Lists* (London, 1985), 207–13. 2. See J. Vernaud and A. Bennett, *An Index to INDEX ON CENSORSHIP, 1972–88* (London, 1989). 3. *New Catholic Encyclopedia* (Washington, DC, 1967).

INFANTA 1. Quoted by Philippe Ariès, *Centuries of Childhood: A Social History of Family Life* (London, 1979), 15. 2. Prado, Madrid: Coello, *The Infanta Isabella* (1579), Cat. 1137; Velasquez, *The Infanta Margherita of Austria* (1659), Cat. 1192. See S. N. Orso, *Velazquez, los Barrachos, and Painting in the Court of Philip IV* (Cambridge, 1993). 3. Ariès, *Centuries of Childhood*, ch. 5, 'From Immodesty to Innocence'.

INQUISITIO 1. See F. E. Dostoyevsky, *The Brothers Karamazov* (1880) trans. D. Magarshack (Harmondsworth, 1958); also *The Grand Inquisitor*, trans. S. Koteliansky, intro. by D. H. Lawrence (London, 1935). 2. See Eduard Wasiolek, *Dostoyevsky: the major fiction* (Boston, 1964); Judith Gunn, *Dostoyevsky: dreamer and prophet* (Oxford, 1990); J. Frank, *Dostoyevsky* (Princeton, 1979–), 3 vols.; W. J. Leatherbarrow, *Dostoyevsky: The Brothers Karamazov* (Cambridge, 1992). 3. Quoted by A. B. Gibson, *The Religion of Dostoyevsky* (London, 1973), 187. 4. Quoted by Gunn, op. cit. 5. John 12: 24.

IONA 1. Ellen Murray, *Peace and Adventure: The Story of Iona* (Glasgow, 1987). See also T. O. Clancy, G. Marcus, *Iona: the Earliest Poetry of a Celtic Monastery* (Edinburgh, 1995).

JACQUARD 1. See S. Augarten, *Bit by Bit: An Illustrated History of Computers* (London, 1984).

JEANS 1. See Joanna Brogden, 'Strauss, Levi', in *Fontana Biographical Companion to Modern Thought* (London, 1983), 734.

KALEVALA 1. With special acknowledgement to Prof. M. A. Branch. See also F. J. Oinas, *Studies in Finnic folklore: homage to the Kalevala* (Mäntä, 1985).

KATYŃ 1. NKVD to Comrade Stalin, 5 March 1940, nr 794/5, Central Committee Archives of the CPSU. Document released by President Yeltsin, and published in *Gazeta wyborcza* (Warsaw), nr 243 (1016), 15 Oct. 1992. 2. See J. T. Gross, *Polish Society under German Occupation, 1939–45* (Princeton, 1979); R. Lukas, *The Forgotten Holocaust* (Lexington, KY, 1986). 3. Conversation with Stalin in the Kremlin, 14 November 1941. S. Kot, *Conversations with the Kremlin and Despatches from Russia* (London, 1963), 112–43. 4. Detailed studies summarizing the case prior to Moscow's confession of guilt included *The Crime of Katyń: Facts and Documents* (Polish Cultural Foundation, 1948), trans. (London, 1965); J. Mackiewicz, *The Katyn Wood Murders* (London, 1951); J. Czapski, *The Inhuman Land* (London, 1951); J. K. Zawodny, *Death in the Forest: The story of the Katyn Forest Massacre* (Notre Dame, 1962); Louis Fitzgibbon, *Katyn: Crime without parallel* (London, 1971); *Despatches of Sir Owen O'Malley to the British Government* (London, 1972); M. Dąbrowski (ed.), *KATYN, 1940–1990: Documentary Exhibition Commemorating the Fiftieth Anniversary* (Polish Institute and Sikorski Museum, London, 1990). 5. Philip C. Bell, 'The Katyn Graves Revealed' in *John Bull and the Bear: British Public Opinion, Foreign Policy and the USSR, 1941–5* (London, 1990). See also C. S. and S. A. Garrett, 'Death and Politics: The Katyn Forest Massacre and American Foreign Policy', *East European Quarterly*, 20/4, Jan. 1987, 429–46. 6. As reported in *The Times*, 10 June 1995. 7. Nicholas Bethell, 'The Cold Killers of Kalinin', the *Observer*, 6 Oct. 1991. Further studies published after the Soviet confession of guilt include: Allen Paul, *Katyń: the Untold Story of Stalin's Polish Massacre* (New York, 1991), and Vladimir Abarinov, *The Murderers of Katyn*, trans. from the Russian (Hippocrene, New York, 1993). 8. See the illegal publication by J. Łojek, *Dzieje sprawy Katynia* (Warsaw, 1983). 9. *The Black Book of Polish Censorship* (Directives of the Polish State Censorship for 1976) (London, 1977). 10. A. Moszyński (ed.), *Lista Katyńska* (The Katyn List) (London, 1977). 11. See Ewa Haraszti Taylor, *A Life with Alan* (London, 1987), 221.

KEELHAUL 1. Denis Hills, *Tyrants and Mountains: a Reckless Life* (London, 1992), 103–8. 2. Ibid. 120–4. Hills was rewarded by being caricatured in Leon Uris's novel *Exodus*, and the subsequent Hollywood film based on the incident, as the man who tried to *stop* the ship from sailing. 3. Ibid. 130. 4. Ibid. 136. 5. Ibid. 137–40. 6. See Nicholas Bethell, *The Last Secret: Forcible Repatriation to Russia, 1944–47* (London, 1974); Nicholas Tolstoy, *Victims of Yalta* (London, 1978); Nicholas Tolstoy, *The Minister and the Massacres* (London, 1986). 7. A. Cowgill, T. Brimelow, C. Booker, *The Repatriation from Austria in 1945: the Report of an Enquiry*, 2 vols. (London, 1990); reviewed by J. Jolliffe, 'The Riviera of Hades', *Spectator*, 20 Oct. 1990; D. Johnson, 'Macmillan: a vindication that came too late', *The Times*, 19 Oct. 1990; R. Harris, 'Here's a way out for every war criminal', *Sunday Times*, 21 Oct. 1990.

KHAZARIA 1. Quoted by O. Pritsak, 'The Khazar Kingdom's Conversion to Judaism', *Harvard Ukrainian Studies*, 2 (1978), 271; also in Pritsak, *Studies in Mediaeval Eurasian History* (London, 1981). 2. Arthur Koestler, *The Thirteenth Tribe: The Khazar Empire and Its Heritage* (London, 1976).

KONARMYA   **1.** I. Babel', *Konarmiya* (Moscow, 1928), 5.   **2.** N. Davies, 'Izaak Babel''s "Konarmiya" Stories, and the Polish–Soviet War', *Modern Language Review*, 67 (1972), 845–57.   **3.** K. M. Murray, *Wings over Poland* (New York, 1932).

KONOPIŠTE   **1.** Count Carlo Sforza, 'The Man Who Might Have Saved Austria', in *Makers of Modern Europe* (London, 1930), 32–43.   **2.** Ibid. 27.   **3.** Ibid. 20.

KRAL   **1.** See H. Spanke, *Deutsche und französische Dichtung des Mittelalters* (Stuttgart, 1943).   **2.** W. Kootz, *Frankfurt: City Guide* (Frankfurt, n.d.), 9–12.

LANGEMARCK   **1.** John Keegan, 'When the guns fell silent: the Belgian battlefield where the seeds of German revenge were sown', *Daily Telegraph*, 11 Nov. 1988. That one grave site contains a similar number of men to that of all US military deaths during the Vietnam war. (See Appendix III, p. 1326.)

LAUSSEL   **1.** Monica Sjoo and Barbara Mor, *The Great Cosmic Mother: Rediscovering the Religion of the Earth* (San Francisco, 1987), 84. On Stone Age religion, see G. Rachel Levy, *The Gate of Horn* (London, 1948).   **2.** R. Graves, *White Goddess: a Historical Grammar of Poetic Myth* (London, 1966); also *The Greek Myths* (London, 1955), 2 vols.   **3.** Neal Ascherson, *Black Sea* (1995), 111–17.   **4.** W. I. Thompson, *The Time Falling Bodies Take to Light: Mythologies, Sexuality and the Origins of Culture* (New York, 1981), 102; quoted by Sjoo and Mor, op. cit. 79.   **5.** See Riane Eisler, *The Chalice and the Blade: Our History, Our Future* (Centre for Partnership Studies, Pacific Grove, Ca.) (New York, 1988).

LEONARDO   **1.** Jean Mathé, *Leonardo's Inventions* (Geneva, 1980).   **2.** After D. Wallechinsky *et al.*, *The Book of Lists* (New York, 1977), and C. M. Cox, *Genetic Studies of Geniuses* (Stanford, Calif., 1926).

LEPER   **1.** Quoted by S. N. Brody, *The Disease of the Soul: Leprosy in Mediaeval Literature* (Ithaca, NY, 1974), 80–1.   **2.** Ibid. 66–7.   **3.** *Chronicle of Lanercost*, quoted by R. M. Clay, *Mediaeval Hospitals of England* (London, 1909), 56.   **4.** Eilhart, L 4276–9, quoted by Brody, 180.   **5.** James A. Michener, *Hawaii* (New York, 1959).

LESBIA   **1.** Judith C. Brown, *Immodest Acts: The Life of a Lesbian Nun in Renaissance Italy* (New York, 1985).   **2.** Lillian Faderman, in *Signs: A Journal of Women in Culture and Society*, 12(3) (Spring 1987), 576.

LETTLAND   **1.** A. Silgailis, *Latvian Legion* (San José, Calif., 1986).   **2.** After ibid. 245–50.

LEX   **1.** H. F. Jolowicz, *The Roman Foundations of Modern Law* (Oxford, 1957); A. D. E. Lewis (ed.), *The Roman Law Tradition* (Cambridge, 1994).

LIETUVA   **1.** H. H. Bender, *A Lithuanian Etymological Index* (Princeton, NJ, 1921), 5.   **2.** V. Ambrazas *et al.*, *Grammatyka litovskogo yazika* (Vilnius, 1985), 5.   **3.** See J. Biddulph, *Lithuanian: A Beginning* (Pontypridd, 1991).

LILI   **1.** R. Lax and F. Smith, *Great Song Thesaurus*, 2nd edn. (Oxford, 1985).   **2.** Hans Leip, 'Lili Marleen', in *Der ewige Brunnen: ein Hausbuch deutscher Dichtung*, ed. L. Reiners (Munich, 1979), 502. The original English title was '*My Lili of the Lamp-light*'. See 'The Saga of Lilli Marlene'.   **3.** *Les Feuilles Mortes* (Autumn Leaves); words by J. Prévert, music by J. Kosma, English lyrics by Johnny Mercer.   **4.** *Podmoskovnye Vechera* (Moscow Nights), *c.*1958; words by M. Matusovsky, music by V. Solovyov-Sedi; C. V. James (ed.), *Russian Song-Book* (Oxford, 1962), i. 31.

LLANFAIR   **1.** Melville Richards, 'Ecclesiastical and Secular in Mediaeval Welsh Settlement', *Studia Celtica*, 3 (1968), 9–19. On Welsh History see John Davies, *Hanes Cymru*

(1990), trans. as *A History of Wales* (London, 1993).   **2.** Ward Lock's *North Wales* (Northern Section), 14th edn. (London, n.d. *c.*1948), 193. The name combines and improves on three genuine Welsh village names: LLANFAIR PWLLGWYNGYLL and LLANDYSILIO (Anglesey) and LLANDYSILIOGOGO (Cardiganshire). Letter from Professor Rees Davies of Aberystwyth, 16 May 1994.

LLOYD'S   **1.** A. Brown, *Hazard Unlimited: From Ships to Satellites: 300 years of Lloyd's of London* (Colchester, 1987).   **2.** Edmund Halley, in *Mortality in Pre-industrial Times: The Contemporary Verdict: Edmund Halley et al.*, J. H. Cassedy, ed. (Farnborough, 1973); also R. Schofield *et al.*, eds., *The Decline of Mortality in Europe* (Oxford, 1991).

LOOT   **1.** 'I once had two wonderful statues, a woman and a young man, both so perfect that one could see their veins. They were taken when Poros was destroyed, and some soldiers were going to sell them to the Europeans in Argos. . . . But I took the soldiers aside and talked to them. "Even if they give you ten thousand thalers, you should not let them be taken out of our homeland. That is what we fought for."' After H. A. Lidderdale, ed., *The Memoirs of General Makriyannis* (Oxford, 1966).   **2.** W. St. Clair, *Lord Elgin and the Marbles* (Oxford, 1967); C. Hitchens *et al.*, *The Elgin Marbles: should they be returned to Greece?* (London, 1987).   **3.** Charles de Jaeger, *The Linz File: Hitler's Plunder of Europe's Art* (Toronto, 1981); Lynn Nicholas, *The Rape of Europe* (London, 1994).   **4.** M. Bailey, 'Nazi Art Loot Discovered in Russia', *Observer*, 24 March 1991.   **5.** Wm. H. Honan, 'New Facts and Lawsuits in the tale of art thefts from German Church', 'Stolen Treasure' and 'Inventory in Texas Case Turns up New Works', *New York Times*, 25 June, 30 June, 10 September 1990.   **6.** E. Aleksandrov, Z. Stankov, *The international legal protection of cultural property* (Sofia, 1979); Australian Association of Humanities, *Who Owns the Past? a Symposium* (Melbourne, 1985); B. Walter, *Rueckfuehrung von Kulturgut in internationalen Recht* (Bremen, 1988); J. Greenfield, *The Return of Cultural Treasures* (Cambridge, 1989).

LUDI   **1.** See D. P. Mannix, *Those About to Die* (London, 1960).   **2.** Ibid. 29.   **3.** From the *English Prayer Book* (1662).

LUGDUNUM   **1.** A. Pelletier, *Histoire de Lyon: Des origines à nos jours* (Roanne, 1990).   **2.** F. Braudel, *The Identity of France*, i, *History and Environment* (New York, 1988), 288–91.   **3.** Paul Vidal de la Blache, *Tableau de la géographie de la France*, pt. 1 of E. Lavisse, *Histoire de la France* (Paris, 1911), i. 8.

ŁYCZAKÓW   **1.** See S. S. Nicieja, *Comentarz Obrońców Lwowa* (Wrocław, 1990).

MADONNA   **1.** José Maria de Sagarra, *The Monserrat* (Barcelona, 1959).   **2.** S. Z. Jabłoński, *Jasna Góra: ośrodek kultu maryjnego* (Lubin, 1984); Z. Różanów *et al.*, *The Cultural Heritage of Jasna Gora* (Warsaw, 1974).   **3.** J. Brun, *Rocamadour: historique, description, excursions* (Saint-Cere, Lot, 1927).   **4.** Guide Michelin, *Auvergne* (Clermont, 1980), 87.   **5.** With due acknowledgement to Alex Boyd.   **6.** Marina Warner, *Alone of All Her Sex: The Myth and the Cult of the Virgin Mary* (London, 1976).

MAGIC   **1.** H. S. Cronin, 'The Twelve Conclusions of the Lollards', *English Historical Review*, 22 (1907), 298, quoted by Keith Thomas, *Religion and the Decline of Magic* (London, 1971), 58.   **2.** Ibid. 485–90.   **3.** See David Cannadine, *Rituals of Royalty: Power and Ceremonial in Traditional Societies* (Cambridge, 1987).

MAKEDON   **1.** M. Andronikos, *Verginia: The Royal Tombs* (Athens, 1984).   **2.** E. Kofos, 'National Heritage and National Identity in 19th and 20th Century Macedonia', *European History Quarterly*, 19 (2) (1989), 229–68.   **3.** 'Writers Campaign for Greek Scholar', the *Independent*, 13 May 1994.

MALET   1. Godfrey LeMay, 'The Conspiracy of General Malet', in P. Quennell (ed.), *Diversions of History* (London, 1954), 52–68.

MARKET   1. See R. J. Heilbroner, 'The Wonderful World of Adam Smith', in *The Worldly Philosophers: The Lives, Times, and Ideas of the Great Economic Thinkers*, 6th edn. (London, 1991), 42–74.   2. Adam Smith, *An Inquiry into the Nature and Causes of the Wealth of Nations* (1776).

MARSTON   1. Sir G. N. Clark, 'Marston', in *The Victoria History of the County of Oxford*, v, ed. Mary D. Lobel (Oxford, 1957), 214–21.   2. Jennifer Sherwood and Nikolaus Pevsner, *The Buildings of England: Oxfordshire* (London, 1974), 699–700. See also J. Sherwood and J. Piper, *A Guide to the Churches of Oxfordshire* (Oxford, 1989).   3. W. E. Tate, *The Parish Chest: A Study of the Records of Parochial Administration in England* (Chichester, 1983).   4. From 'Elegy in a Country Churchyard' (1750), by Thomas Gray, written at Stoke Poges, Buckinghamshire.

MASON   1. See F. L. Pick and C. N. Knight, *A Pocket History of Freemasonry*, rev. edn. (London, 1992); also Stephen Knight, *The Brotherhood: The Secret World of the Freemasons* (London, 1984); J. J. Robinson, *Born in Blood: The Lost Secrets of Freemasonry* (London, 1990).   2. Ibid. 45.   3. Knight, chapters 1 and 2, 'Origins' and 'Metamorphosis', 15–24.   4. See Margaret Jacob, *The Radical Enlightenment* (London, 1981).

MASSILIA   1. Marcel Pagnol, *Marius* (Paris, 1946), ii. vi.   2. J.-L. Bonillo, *Marseille: ville et port* (Marseille, 1992).

MATRIMONIO   1. D. B. Rheubottom, ' "Sisters First": Betrothal Order and Age at Marriage in Mediaeval Ragusa', *Journal of Family History*, 13 (1988), 359 ff.   2. F. W. Carter, *Dubrovnik (Ragusa): A Classic City-State* (London, 1972); Z. Zlatar, *Between the Double Eagle and the Crescent: The Republic of Ragusa and the Origins of the Eastern Question* (Boulder, Colo., 1992).   3. J. Haynal (1965); discussed by P. Laslett, 'Family and Household as Work Group and Kin Group', in P. Wall *et al.* (eds.), *Family Forms in Historic Europe* (Cambridge, 1983), 513–63.   4. See D. Herlichy, *Mediaeval Households* (Cambridge, Mass., 1985).   5. 'When Beauty Is Destroyed, God suffers', *Financial Times*, 10 Feb. 1992.

MAUVE   1. *An Outline of the Chemistry and Technology of the Dyestuffs Industry* (ICI Dyestuffs Division) (London, 1968), 10.   2. Ibid. p. 7.   3. 'The Amazing Chemistry of Colour', *Crosslink* (Newbury), vol. 2, no. 1 (1990), 4–6.   4. *The Bayer Tapestry: An Unfolding History from 1863* (Newbury, n.d.); *100 Years Research and Progress: Bayer Pharma 1988* (Bayer AG) (Leverkusen, 1988), p. 4.   5. D. W. F. Hardie and J. D. Pratt, *A History of the Modern British Chemical Industry* (Pergamon, Oxford, 1966), pp. 68–70.

MENOCCHI   1. Rounding the Cornice of Pride in Purgatory, Virgil turns to Dante: *O superbi cristiani!* . . . (Oh proud Christians! . . . do you not see that we are worms, whose insignificance lives but to form the angelic butterfly, that flits to judgement naked of defence?); *Purgatorio*, x. 121–6.   2. Carlo Ginzburg, *The Cheese and the Worms: The Cosmos of a Sixteenth-Century Miller* (London, 1982), 57.

MERCANTE   1. Iris Margaret Origo, *The Merchant of Prato: Francesco di Marco Datini* (London, 1957), 336–8.   2. See F. Bensa, *Francesco di Marco da Prato* (Milan, 1928).   3. Usance meant the customary interval between delivery and payment. Between Florence and Barcelona it was 20 days.   4. File 1145; Origo, *The Merchant of Prato*, 146–7.   5.

Francesco to Margherita, 5 Apr. 1395; File 1089; Origo, *The Merchant of Prato*, 136. **6.** Fernand Braudel, *Afterthoughts on Material Civilisation and Capitalism* (Baltimore, 1979), 57. **7.** Ibid. ch. 2, 'The Market Economy and Capitalism'.

METRYKA 1. See A. Tomczak, *Zarys dziejów archiwów polskich* (Toruń, 1982); R. C. Lewandowski, *Guide to the Polish Libraries and Archives* (Boulder, Colo., 1974). **2.** Patricia Grimsted, *The Lithuanian Metrica in Moscow and Warsaw: Reconstructing the Archives of the Grand Duchy of Lithuania* (Cambridge, Mass., 1986); also her *Handbook for Archival Research in the USSR* (Washington, DC, 1989). **3.** A. E. P. Zaleski, 'Some New Archival Sources for the Study of Recent Polish History', MA thesis (SSEES, University of London, 1994), 5–6.

MEZQUITA 1. Rafael Castejón, *La Mezquita Aljama de Cordoba* (Madrid, n.d.). **2.** Adam Hopkins, 'Of Castles and Castanets', *The Independent on Sunday,* 16 May 1993.

MICROBE 1. Z. Swięch, *Klątwy, Microby i Uczeni* (Warsaw, 1989).

MIR 1. F. Sulimirski *et al.*, *Słownik Geograficzny Królestwa Polskiego* (Warsaw, 1885), 485–8. **2.** See also 'Mir' in Roman Aftanazy, *Dzieje rezydencji na dawnych kresach Rzeczypospolity* (Warsaw, 1991). **3.** A. Mickiewicz, *Pan Tadeusz*, xii.

MISSA 1. Thrasybulos Georgiades, *Musik und Sprache* (1974), trans. as *Music and Language: The Rise of Western Music as Exemplified in Settings of the Mass* (Cambridge, 1982), 7. See also J. Harper, *The Forms and Orders of the Western Liturgy from the Tenth to the Eighteenth Century* (Oxford, 1991). **2.** W. Mellers, *Romanticism and the Twentieth Century* (*Man and His Music, pt. iv*), rev. edn. (London, 1988), 1011.

MOARTE 1. See M. V. Riccardo, *Vampires Unearthed: The Vampire and Dracula Bibliography . . .* (New York, 1983). **2.** With acknowledgement to Rebecca Haynes, 'Vampirism, the Cult of Death and the Romanian Legionary Movement', seminar paper presented at SSEES, University of London, 10 June 1993. See Z. Barbu, 'Rumania', in S. J. Woolf (ed.), *European Fascism* (London, 1968), 146–66; also C. Z. Codreanu, *For My Legionaries* (Madrid, 1977).

MOLDOVA 1. Aleksei Vasilev, *They are talking about us in Pravda* (1951), oil on canvas 99 × 156 cm, in M. C. Down *et al.*, *Soviet Socialist Realist Painting, 1930s–1960s*, pl. 28 (catalogue of the exhibition 'Engineers of Human Souls', Oxford Museum of Modern Art, Jan.–Mar. 1992).

MONKEY 1. William Irvine, *Apes, Angels and Victorians: The Story of Darwin, Huxley and Evolution* (New York, 1955), chapter i. **2.** F. Galton, *Hereditary Genius: an Inquiry into its laws and consequences*, 2nd edn. (London, 1892; repr. 1950), pp. 325 ff. **3.** Irvine, p. 280. **4.** D. W. Forrest, *Francis Galton: the Life and Work of a Victorian Genius* (London, 1974).

MONTAILLOU 1. E. Le Roy Ladurie, *Montaillou: Cathars and Catholics in a French Village, 1294–1324*, trans. B. Bray (London, 1980), 276. **2.** Ibid. 212.

MORES 1. Norbert Elias, *Über den Prozess der Zivilisation: soziogenetische und psychogenetische Untersuchungen* (Basle, 1939), i; trans. as *The History of Manners* (Oxford, 1978), 68 ff. **2.** Ibid. ch. 2, vii, 'On Spitting'. **3.** Ibid. 129. **4.** Ibid. 85–162. **5.** Ibid.

MOUSIKE 1. After A. Isacs and E. Martin (eds.), *Dictionary of Music* (London, 1982), 247–8 (mode), 337–8 (scale).

M U R A N O   1. L. Zechin, *Vetro e vetrai di Murano: studi sulla storia del vetro* (Venice, 1987); also M. Dekówna, *Szkło w Europie wczesnośredniowiecznej* (Wrocław, 1980).

N E Z   1. Desmond Morris *et al.*, *Gestures: Their Origins and Distribution,* 'The Nose Thumb' (London, 1979), a survey confined to Western Europe, 25–42.   2. See J. Bremmer and H. Roodenburg (eds.), *A Cultural History of Gesture* (Oxford, 1993).

N I B E L U N G   1. W. Huber, *Auf der Suche nach den Nibelungen* (Gütersloh, 1981), 20.   2. H. and M. Garland, *The Oxford Companion to German Literature,* 2nd edn. (Oxford, 1986), 664–7.

N I K O P O L I S   1. See Barbara Tuchman, *A Distant Mirror: The Calamitous Fourteenth Century* (London, 1978).

N O B E L   1. E. Bergengen, *Alfred Nobel: the Man and his Work* (London, 1962); N. K. Stahle, *Alfred Nobel and the Nobel Prizes* (Stockholm, 1986).

N O M E N   1. James Gow, *A Companion to School Classics* (London, 1888), 166 ff.   2. Neal Ascherson, 'Do me a favour, forget my name . . .', the *Independent on Sunday*, 4 Sept. 1994.   3. See *Pamiętniki Filipka*, ed. W. Zambrzycki (Warsaw, 1957), 115 ff.; quoted by Norman Davies, *Heart of Europe*, 245–7.

N O M I S M A   1. E. Junge, *World Coin Encyclopaedia* (London, 1984), 15.   2. See Jean Babelon, *La Numismatique antique* (Paris, 1949).

N O R G E   1. See G. Opstad *et al.*, *Norway* (London, 1991).

N O S T R A D A M U S   1. Nostradamus, Prophecies i. 35. See E. Cheetham, *The Prophecies of Nostradamus* (London, 1973).   2. Prophecies x. 39.   3. Ibid. i. 3.   4. Ibid. i. 63.

N O V G O R O D   1. F. M. Thompson, *Novgorod the Great: Excavations at the Mediaeval City* (London, 1967), 58. See also M. Brisbane (ed.), *The Archaeology of Novgorod, Russia: Recent Results from the Town and Its Hinterland* (Lincoln, 1992).   2. Ibid. 63.   3. On the destruction of Novgorod and the slaughter of 60,000 citizens see I. Grey, *Ivan the Terrible* (London, 1964), 178–82.

N O Y A D E S   1. See J. Brooman, *The Reign of Terror in France: Jean-Baptiste Carrier and the Drownings at Nantes* (York, 1986).   2. See Jan Karski, *The Secret State* (London, 1944).   3. R. Hilberg, 'Origins of the Killing Centers', *The Destruction of the European Jews* (New York, 1985), 221–38.   4. J. C. Pressac, *Auschwitz: Technique and Operation of the Gas Chambers* (New York, 1989).   5. Paraphrased from *International Military Tribunal* (Nuremberg, 1946), viii. 324–9.   6. Lyubo Boban, 'Jasenovac and the Manipulation of History', *East European Politics and Societies,* 4 (1990), 580–93.

O E D I P U S   1. Betty Radice, *Who's who in the Ancient World: a Handbook to the Survivors of the Greek and Roman Classics* (London, 1973), 'Oedipus', pp. 177–8.

O M P H A L O S   1. F. Poulsen, *Delphi* (London, 1920), 29.   2. See H. W. Parke, *The Greek Oracles* (London, 1967), 'Delphic Procedure', 72–81.   3. H. W. Parke and D. E. W. Wormell, *The Delphic Oracle* (Oxford, 1956). Vol. ii, *The Oracular Responses,* contains an exhaustive and critical study of all the oracle's known utterances, which, however, are not translated from the Greek.   4. Parke, *The Greek Oracles,* 34.

O P E R A   1. *New Grove's Dictionary of Music and Musicians,* ed. Stanley Sadie (London, 1992), XII. 514–34. See also R. Parker (ed.), *The Oxford Illustrated History of Opera* (Oxford, 1994).

ORANGE 1. Françoise Gasparri, *La Principauté d'Orange au Moyen Âge* (Paris, 1985). 2. See C. V. Wedgewood, *William the Silent* (London, 1944); Marion Grew, *The House of Orange* (London, 1947); H. H. Rowen, *The Princes of Orange: Stadholders in the Dutch Republic* (Cambridge, 1988). 3. See C. Fitzgibbon, *Red Hand: The Ulster Colony* (London, 1971); Tony Gray, *The Orange Order* (London, 1972).

OXFAM 1. M. Black, *Oxfam: the first 50 years* (Oxford, 1992); F. Jean, *Life, Death, and Aid: the Médecin sans Frontières Report . . .* (London, 1993).

PALAEO 1. D. C. Greetham, *Textual Scholarship: An Introduction* (London, 1992); B. Bischoff, *Latin Palaeography: Antiquity to the Middle Ages* (Cambridge, 1990); T. J. Brown, *A Palaeographer's View: Selected Writings* (London, 1993). 2. C. Hamilton, *The Hitler Diaries: Fakes That Fooled the World* (Lexington, Ky., 1991).

PANTA 1. See Michele d'Avino, *Pompeii prohibited* (Edizioni Procaccini, Naples, n.d.); M. Grant *et al.*, *Erotic Art in Pompeii: the secret collections of the National Museum of Naples* (London, 1975). 2. 'Oh, [my] rampant son, how many women have you fucked?' *Corpus Inscriptionum Latinarum* (*CIL*) vol. iv, no. 5213. 3. '[In case you hadn't noticed], Ampliatus, Icarus is buggering you.' ibid. no. 2375. 4. 'Restituta, drop your tunic, I beg you, [and] show [your] hairy pud', ibid. no. 3951. 5. 'Weep girls, sod [—] . . . superb cunt, farewell . . . Ampliatus . . . so many times . . . This also I fookie fookie . . .', ibid. no. 3932. 6. 'Thrust slowly' (with illustration), ibid. no. 794. 7. 'Here Messius fucked nothing.' ibid. (from the House of Amando).

PAPESSA 1. J. N. D. Kelly, *The Oxford Dictionary of Popes* (Oxford, 1988), appendix, 329–30; also J. Morris, *Pope John VIII—An English Woman: Alias Pope Joan* (London, 1985).

PAPYRUS 1. On Derveni, see S. G. Kapsomenon, *Gnomon,* 35 (1963), 222–3; *Archaeoll. Deltion,* 14 (1964), 17–25; also Eric Turner, *Greek Papyri: An Introduction* (Oxford, 1980). 2. E. G. Turner, *Greek Papyri, an introduction* (Oxford, 1968; repr. 1980); *Greek Manuscripts of the Ancient World* (Oxford, 2nd edn. 1987).

PARNASSE 1. After Ronald Taylor, *Franz Liszt: Man and Musician* (London, 1986), 46.

PASCHA 1. E. A. M. Fry, *Almanacks for Students of English History: being a series of 35 almanacks arranged for every day upon which Easter can fall . . . 500–1751 AD (OS), 1751–2000 AD (NS)* (London, 1915). 2. C. Wesley, 'Christ the Lord is Risen Today', *Hymns Ancient and Modern,* rev. edn. (London, 1950), no. 141.

PETROGRAD 1. R. J. Service, *Lenin: a political life* (London, 2nd edn. 1991). 2. See Harrison Salisbury, *The 900 Days' Siege of Leningrad* (New York, 1969). 3. Ruth T. Kamińska, *Mink Coats and Barbed Wire* (London, 1979).

PFALZ 1. See Leo Hugot, *Aachen Cathedral: A Guide* (Aachen, 1988); Erich Stepheny, *Aachen Cathedral* (Aachen, 1989).

PHILIBEG 1. Hugh Trevor-Roper, 'The Highland Tradition of Scotland', in T. Ranger and E. Hobsbawm (eds.), *The Invention of Tradition* (Cambridge, 1983), 15–42. 2. See Robert Bain, *The Clans and Tartans of Scotland,* 5th edn. (Glasgow, 1976), 164–5. 3. Ranger and Hobsbawm, *The Invention of Tradition,* 263–307.

PHOTO 1. Brian Coe, *The Birth of Photography: The Story of the Formative Years, 1800–1900* (London, 1976).

PICARO 1. Bronisław Geremek, *Świat Opery Żebraczej: obraz włóczęgów i nędzarzy w literaturach XV–XVII wieku* (The World of the Beggar's Opera: Tramps and Beggars in the literature of the 15th–17th Centuries) (Warsaw, 1989); *Poverty: A History* (Oxford, 1994). 2. Ewa M. Thomson, *Understanding Russia: The Holy Fool in Russian Literature* (London, 1987).

PLOVUM 1. Lynn White Jr., 'The Agricultural Revolution in the Early Middle Ages', in *Mediaeval Technology and Social Change* (Oxford, 1962), 39–78, with superlative footnotes.

POGROM 1. 'Pogrom', in *Encyclopaedia Judaica* (Jerusalem, 1971), xiii. 694–702. 2. See J. D. Clier, *Pogroms: Anti-Jewish Violence in Modern Russian History* (Cambridge, 1991); I. M. Aronson, *Troubled Waters: The Origins of the 1881 Anti-Jewish Pogroms in Russia* (Pittsburgh, 1990). 3. Norman Davies, 'Great Britain and the Polish Jews, 1918–20', *Journal of Contemporary History*, vol. viii/2, 1973, 119–42.

POTEMKIN 1. J. Dreifuss, *The Romance of Catherine and Potemkin* (London, 1938). 2. Anatoliy Golitsyn, *New Lies for Old: The Communist Strategy of Deception and Disinformation* (London, 1984), 412. 3. H. Marshall, *Sergei Eisenstein's 'Battleship Potemkin'* (New York, 1978).

PRADO 1. F. J. Sanchez Canton, *The Prado* (London, 1959), 7. 2. See *Treasures of a Polish King: Stanislaus August as Patron and Collector* (Catalogue to the Exhibition, Dulwich Picture Gallery, London, 1992).

PRESS 1. S. H. Steinberg, *Five Hundred Years of Printing* (London, 1955), 23. 2. Ibid. 177–8. 3. See Francis Robinson, *Technology and Religious Change: Islam and the Impact of Print*, inaugural lecture at Royal Holloway and Bedford New College, University of London, 4 Mar. 1992.

PROPAGANDA 1. J.-M. Domenach, *La Propagande Politique* (Paris, 1955), 55. See also Z. Zeman, *Nazi Propaganda* (Oxford, 1973); F. C. Barghoorn, *Soviet Foreign Propaganda* (Princeton, 1964). 2. Stephen Koch, *Double Lives: Stalin, Willi Munzenberg and the Seduction of the Intellectuals* (New York, 1994), 12. 3. Sidney Hook, *Out of Step* (New York, 1987), 491–6, quoted by Koch, 77.

PROSTIBULA 1. J. Rossiaud, *La Prostitution Médiévale*, trans. as *Medieval Prostitution* (Oxford, 1988); L. L. Otis, *Prostitution in Mediaeval Society: The History of an Urban Institution in Languedoc* (Chicago, 1989). 2. L. Roper, *The Holy Household: Women and Morals in Reformation Augsburg* (Oxford, 1989).

PUGACHEV 1. See Oliver Figes, *Peasant Russia, Civil War: the Volga Countryside in Revolution, 1917–21* (Oxford, 1989). 2. See Paul Avrich, *Russian Rebels, 1600–1800* (New York, 1972); also J. Y. Alexander, *Autocratic Government in a national crisis: the imperial Russian government and Pugachev's Revolt, 1773–75* (Bloomington, Ind., 1961); A. Bodger, *The Kazakhs and the Pugachev Uprising in Russia, 1773–4* (Bloomington, 1988). 3. E. Hobsbawm, *Primitive Rebels: studies in archaic forms of social movement* (Manchester, 1971); also R. H. Hilton, *Bondmen made free: mediaeval peasant movements and the English rising of 1381* (London, 1973); D. Mitrany, *Marx against the Peasant* (Chapel Hill, 1951). 4. Theodore Shanin, *Peasants and peasant societies: selected readings* (Oxford, 2nd edn., 1987); *Defining peasants: essays concerning rural societies* (Oxford, 1990). 5. *Journal of Peasant Studies*, 1, no. 1 (1973–4), 1–3. 6. E. Le Roy Ladurie (1969), trans. as *The French Peasantry, 1450–1660* (Aldershot, 1987). 7. Y. M. Berce, *Croquants et nu-pieds: les soulève-*

ments paysans en France du XVIème au XIXème siècle (Paris, 1974). **8.** R. Mousnier, *Peasant Uprisings in Seventeenth Century France, Russia and China* (London, 1971). **9.** R. Pillorget, *Les mouvements Insurrectionnaires de Provence entre 1596 et 1795* (Paris, 1975). **10.** L. Sciascia, *La Corda Pazza* (Turin, 1970), 390.

QUAKE **1.** T. D. Kendrick, *The Lisbon Earthquake* (London, 1956); J. Noses, *O terramote de 1755: British Accounts* (Lisbon, 1990).

RELAXATIO **1.** Edward Whymper, *The Ascent of the Matterhorn* (1880) (reprinted London, 1987); *Scrambling Amongst the Alps*, 5th edn. 1890 (reprinted Exeter, 1986); see also P. Bernard, *The rush to the Alps: the Evolution of Vacationing in Switzerland* (Boulder, Colo., 1978). **2.** J. Walvin, *The People's Game: a social history of British football* (London, 1975); B. Butler, *The Football League, 1888–1988* (London, 1987). **3.** J. Mercier, *Le Football* (Paris, 1971); P. Soar, M. Tyler, *The Story of Football* (Twickenham, 1986).

RENTES **1.** E. Le Roy Ladurie, P. Couperie, *Annales*, July 1970, translated as 'Changes in Parisian Rents', in *The Territory of the Historian* (Chicago, 1979), 61–78.

RESPONSA **1.** Rabbi Ephraim Oshry, *Mi-Maamakkim*, III. i. 11; in Rabbi Dr H. J. Zimmels, *The Echo of the Nazi Holocaust in Rabbinic Literature* (London, 1975), pt. 3, 'An Anthology of Responsa', pp. 253–353, s. 24, 'Adoption'. **2.** These paraphrased examples are taken either from Zimmels, *The Echo of the Nazi Holocaust*, or from 'Religious Leadership during the Holocaust', a seminar paper read by Rabbi Hugo Gryn at SSEES, Univ. of London, 30 Apr. 1992. **3.** Oshry, *Mi-Maamakkim*, I. i. **4.** *The Holocaust: The Victims Accuse. Documents and Testimony on Jewish War Criminals* (Brooklyn, NY, 1977). 'If there is such a thing as spiritual pornography, this would fit it' (Hugo Gryn). **5.** See Pesach Schindler, *Hassidic Responses to the Holocaust in the Light of Hassidic Thought* (Hoboken, NJ, 1990). **6.** Dr Milejkowski *et al.*, *Recherches cliniques sur la famine exécutées dans le ghetto de Varsovie* (Warsaw, 1946). **7.** Letter of 9 Dec. 1993 from Rabbi Hugo Gryn.

REVERENTIA **1.** See Peter Brown, *Relics and Social Status in the Age of Gregory of Tours*, Stenton Lecture 1976 (Reading, 1977). **2.** Patricia Morison, 'An Exquisite Gothic Treasure Trove', *Financial Times*, 3 Sept. 1991.

ROMANY **1.** Jules Bloch, *Les Tsiganes* (Paris, 1969), 7–16. A Franciscan pilgrim reported seeing a community of cave-dwellers, probably gypsies, near Candia in Crete in 1322; ibid. 16. **2.** See Angus Fraser, *The Gypsies* (Oxford, 1992); also G. Puxon, *Roma: Europe's Gypsies* (London, 1987). **3.** Matthew Arnold, from 'The Scholar-Gipsy', *Oxford Book of English Verse, 1250–1918*, no. 760, p. 914.

ROUGE **1.** E. J. Haeberle, 'Swastika, Pink Triangle and Yellow Star: The Destruction of Sexology and the Persecution of Homosexuals in Nazi Germany', in M. Duberman *et al.* (eds.), *Hidden from History* (London, 1991), 365–79.

RUFINUS **1.** Nicholas Barker, *The Oxford University Press and the Spread of Learning: An Illustrated History, 1478–1978* (Oxford, 1978), 2–4. **2.** *Why We Are at War: Great Britain's Case, with an appendix of original documents*, by Members of the Oxford Faculty of Modern History (E. Barker, H. W. C. Davis, C. R. L. Fletcher, Arthur Hassall, L. G. Wickham Legg, F. Morgan) (Oxford, 1914); as recorded in the OUP archives, and with acknowledgement to Dr H. Pogge von Strandmann.

RUS' **1.** N. Freret, *Mémoire sur les origines des francs* (Paris, 1714). **2.** Omeljan Pritsak, *The Origins of Rus'* i (Cambridge, Mass., 1981), ch. 1. **3.** Norman Golb and Omeljan Pritsak (eds.), *Khazarian Hebrew Documents of the Tenth Century* (Ithaca, NY, 1982), ch. 1, 'T-S (Glass) 12.122—the Kievan Letter'.

SAMOS   1. Guy de la Bédoyère, *Samian Ware* (Princes Risborough, 1988).   2. J. Dechelette, *Les Vases céramiques ornées de la Gaule romaine* (Paris, 1904); H. B. Walters, *Catalogue of Roman Pottery . . . in the British Museum* (London, 1905); M. Durand-Lefebvre, *Marques de potiers gallo-romans trouvées à Paris* (Paris, 1963); J. A. Stansfield and Grace Simpson, *Central Gaulish Potters* (Oxford, 1958); A. C. Brown, *Catalogue of Italian Terra Sigillata in the Ashmolean Museum* (Oxford, 1968); P. Petru, *Rimska keramika v Slovenji* (Ljubljana, 1973).   3. Stansfield and Simpson, *Central Gaulish Potters*, chronological table, 170.

SAMPHIRE   1. Jane Renfrew, *Food and Cooking in Prehistoric Britain: History and Recipes* (London, 1985), 35, after R. Philips, *Wild Food* (London, 1983).   2. Ibid. 36, after Mrs Beeton.   3. Ibid. 38, after M. B. Stout, *The Shetland Cookery Book* (Lerwick, 1968).

SANITAS   1. Dhiman Barua and Wm. Greenough III (eds.), *Cholera* (New York, 1992), ch. 1, 'The History of Cholera'.   2. A. Nikiforuk, op. cit., 154. See also F. R. van Hartesfeld, *The Pandemic of Influenza, 1918–19* (Lampeter, 1992); R. Collier, *The Plague of the Spanish Lady* (New York, 1974).

SARAJEVO   1. Adapted from 'A Letter from 1920' (*Pismo iz 1920g*) by Ivo Andrič, trans. Lenore Grenoble, in *The Damned Yard and Other Stories*, ed. Celia Hawkesworth (London, 1992), 107–19.   2. Ibid. 7.   3. Francesca Wilson, *Aftermath* (London, 1947), 'Sarajevo'.

SCHOLASTIKOS   1. From *The Philogelos or Laughter-lover*, trans. by A. Eberhard (Berlin, 1869) and into Polish by J. Łanowski (Wrocław, 1965).   2. See S. West, 'More Very Old Chestnuts', *Omnibus*, 20 (Sept. 1990).

SHAMAN   1. Nevill Drury, *The Elements of Shamanism* (Longmead, Dorset, 1989).   2. Aleksander Nawrocki, *Szamanizm i Węgrzy* (Warsaw, 1988).

SHQIPERIA   1. S. Pollo, A. Puto, *The History of Albania* (London, 1981); James Pettifor, *Albania* (London, 1994).

SINGULARIS   1. Montaigne, *Essais* (1580): quoted by Alain Laurent, *Histoire de l'individualisme* (Paris, 1993), 27.   2. See Colin Morris, *The Discovery of the Individual, 1050–1200* (London, 1972).   3. Margaret Thatcher; see *Margaret Thatcher in Her Own Words* (Harmondsworth, 1987).   4. R. Hughes, *The Culture of Complaint: The Fraying of America* (London, 1993); and David Selbourne, *The Principle of Duty: An Essay on the Foundations of Civic Order* (London, 1994).

SLAVKOV   1. D. Chandler, *Austerlitz 1805: Battle of the Three Emperors* (London, 1990).   2. Leo Tolstoy, *War and Peace*, trans. Rosemary Edmonds (London, 1957), vol. I, book 1, ch. xiv, p. 317.   3. John Keegan, *The Face of Battle* (London, 1978).

SLESVIG   1. Bent Rying, *Denmark: History* (Copenhagen, 1981), ii. 332.   2. See W. Carr, *Schleswig-Holstein, 1815–48: A Study in National Conflict* (Manchester, 1963); *The Origins of the War of German Unification* (London, 1991).

SMOLENSK   1. Merle Fainsod, *How Russia Is Ruled: Smolensk under Soviet Rule* (Harvard, Mass., 1953).   2. J. Arch Getty, *The Origins of the Great Purges: The Soviet Communist Party reconsidered, 1933–38* (Cambridge, 1988), 203.   3. See Jacek Kuroń, *Wiara i wina: do i od komunizmu* (Warsaw, 1990), 324–5. The author, a leading member of the Solidarity movement, was jailed by the communist regime in the 1960s, when he shared a prison cell with a Gestapo officer of wartime vintage.   4. Norman Davies, 'The

Misunderstood War', *New York Review of Books*, 9 June 1994. **5.** Gitta Sereny, 'Giving Germany Back Its Past', the *Independent on Sunday*, 15 May 1994.

SOCIALIS **1.** Nils Andrén, *Modern Swedish Government* (Stockholm, 1961).

SONATA **1.** W. Mellers, *The Sonata Principle* (London, 1988), 655; W. S. Newman, *The Sonata in the Classic Era* (New York, 1972).

SOUND **1.** Robert Browning, 'How They Brought the Good News from Ghent to Aix', *Collected Works* (London, 1896), i. 250–1. **2.** Brian Rust, *Discography of Historical Records on Cylinders and 78s* (London, 1979), 41. (It is possible that it was preceded by Edison's recording of W. E. Gladstone on 22 November 1888.) **3.** See *Revolutions in Sound: A Celebration of 100 years of the Gramophone* (British Library exhibition and catalogue, London, 1988). **4.** *Die Klangwelt Mozarts* (exhibition of the Kunsthistorisches Museum, Vienna, 1991–2). **5.** See Grace Koch, *International Association of Sound Archives (IASA), Directory of Member Archives*, 2nd edn. (Milton Keynes, 1982). **6.** Quoted by Rust, *Discography*, 277.

SOVKINO **1.** N. Zorkaya, *An Illustrated History of Soviet Cinema* (New York, 1991). **2.** Quoted by R. Taylor, *The Politics of the Soviet Cinema, 1917–29* (Cambridge, 1979), 39.

SPASIT'EL **1.** Ryszard Kapuściński, 'The Temple and the Palace', in *Imperium* (London, 1994), 95–108.

SPARTACUS **1.** R. Orena, *Rivolta e rivoluzione: il bellum di Spartaco* (Milan, 1984). **2.** W. D. Phillips, *Slavery from Roman Times to the Early Transatlantic Trade* (Manchester, 1985); C. W. W. Greenidge, *Slavery* (London, 1958). **3.** W. Z. Rubinsohn, *The Spartacus Uprising and Soviet Historical Writing* (Oxford, 1987).

SPICE-OX **1.** Marcel Détienne, *Les Jardins d'Adonis* (Paris, 1972), trans. as *The Gardens of Adonis* (Hassocks, 1972), ch. 4, 'The Spice Ox', 37–59.

STATE **1.** See Rein Taagepera, 'Growth and Decline of Empires since 600 AD' (unpublished paper, University of California at Irvine). **2.** Norbert Elias, *Uber den Prozess der Zivilisation* (Basle, 1939), ii. **3.** Charles Tilly, *Coercion, Capital and European States, AD 990–1990* (Oxford, 1990). **4.** Paul Kennedy, *The Rise and Fall of Great Powers: Economic Change and Military Conflict, 1500–2000* (London, 1988). **5.** Richelieu, *Testament politique*, quoted by J. H. Shennan, *The Origins of the Modern European State, 1450–1725* (London, 1974).

STRAD **1.** D. Boyden, *The Hill Collection* (Ashmolean Museum) (Oxford, 1969), No. 18, 'Le Messie'. **2.** W. E. Hills, *The Salabue Stradivari* (London, 1891).

STRASSBURG **1.** See G. Gardes, *La Marseillaise, ou les paradoxes de la gloire* (Lyons, 1989); F. Robert, *La Marseillaise* (Paris, 1989).

SUND **1.** C. E. Hill, *Danish Sound Dues and Command of the Baltic* (Durham, NC, 1926).

SUSANIN **1.** A. Loewenberg, *Annals of Opera, 1597–1940* (London, 1978), 784–6. **2.** S. Sadie (ed.), *The New Grove Dictionary of Opera* (London, 1992), ii. 1261–4.

SYLLABUS **1.** This paraphrase is based on the much larger one in the *New Catholic Encyclopedia* (Washington, DC, 1967), xiii. 854–6. **2.** On Dostoyevsky's political views, which regarded socialism, anarchism, terrorism, and Roman Catholicism as closely related, see [**INQUISITIO**].

SYPHILUS   1. See Claude Quétel, *A History of Syphilis* (Cambridge, 1990).   2. Quoted by Nikiforuk, *The Fourth Horseman*, op. cit. 91.   3. L. Baumgartner and J. F. Fulton, *A Bibliography of the Poem 'Syphilis sive morbus Gallicus' by Girolamo Fracastro of Verona* (London, 1935) also G. Eatough, *Fracastro's Syphilis*, (Leeds, 1984).

SYROP   1. See R. H. Bainton, *The Hunted Heretic: The Life and Death of Michael Servetus* (Boston, 1953).   2. J. Bossy, *Giordano Bruno and the Embassy Affair* (New Haven, Conn., 1992).

SZLACHTA   1. Norman Davies, 'Szlachta: The Nobleman's Paradise', in *God's Playground* (Oxford, 1981), vol. i, ch. 7. See also A. Goodwin (ed.), *The European Nobility in the Eighteenth Century* (London, 1953); also M. J. Bush, *Rich Noble, Poor Noble* (Manchester, 1988).

TABARD   1. Eric Delderfield, *Inns and Their Signs: Fact and Fiction* (Newton Abbot, 1975); also Dominic Rotheroe, *London Inn Signs* (London, 1990).

TAIZÉ   1. J. L. Gonzalez Balado, *The Story of Taizé*, 3rd edn. (London, 1988); Rex Brice, *Brother Roger and his community* (London, 1978).   2. J. Playfoot (ed.), *Mother Theresa: My life for the poor* (Yarmouth, 1986); E. Egan, *Such a Vision of the Street* (London, 1985); P. Porter, *Mother Theresa: The Early Years* (London, 1986); N. Cahwla, *Mother Theresa* (London, 1992); Sue Shaw, *Mother Theresa* (London, 1993).   3. See 'Aid to the Church in Need', *Mirror*, bi-monthly (Antwerp, 1992–).

TAMMUZ   1. M. Lambeth, *Discovering Corn Dollies* (Aylesbury, 1987). See also 'Demeter and Proserpine' and 'Lityerses: The Death of the Corn-spirit', in James Frazer, *The Golden Bough* (London, 1890), ch. 3, sects. 8, 9.   2. See D. Harris and G. C. Hillman, *Foraging and Farming: The Evolution of Plant Exploitation* (London, 1988); M. N. Cohen, *The Food Crisis in Prehistory: Overpopulation and the Origins of Agriculture* (New Haven, Conn., 1977); P. J. Ucko and G. W. Dimbleby, *The Domestication and Exploitation of Plants and Animals* (London, 1969).   3. J. Percival, *The Wheat Plant* (London, 1921).

TAXIS   1. See S. MacCormack, *Art and Ceremony in Late Antiquity* (Berkeley, Calif., 1981).   2. Leipzig Univ. Library 28.   3. See J. P. Bury, 'The Ceremonial Book of Constantine Porphyrogennetos', *EHR* 22 (1907), 209–27; also A. Vogt, *Constantin Porphyrogenète: le livre des cérémonies* (Paris, 1935–40).   4. See D. M. Nicol, '*Kaiseralbung*: The Unction of Emperors in Late Byzantine Ritual', *Byzantine and Modern Greek Studies*, 2 (1976), 37–52.

TEICHOS   1. *Oxford Dictionary of Byzantium* (1991), i. 519–20; see also A. van Millingen, *Byzantine Constantinople: The Walls of the City and Adjoining Historical Sites* (London, 1899).

TEMPUS   1. E. Bruton, *The History of Clocks and Watches* (London, 1979), 34–5. **2.** See G. J. Whitrow, *Time in History: Views of Time from Prehistory to the Present Day* (Oxford, 1989).

TEREM   1. See Nancy S. Kollmann, 'The Seclusion of Elite Muscovite Women', *Russian History*, 10 (1988), 170–87.   2. Augustin von Mayerburg, *Iter in Moscoviam . . .* (1661), quoted by Lindsey Hughes, *Sophia: Regent of Russia, 1657–1704* (New Haven, Conn., 1990), 17. (Winner of the Heldt Prize for Women's Studies, 1992.)   3. Ibid. 264–5. This unflattering description was printed in Foy de la Neuville's *Relation curieuse et nouvelle de Moscovie* (Paris, 1698), but had been added to the original manuscript, possibly by a hostile editor during Peter's reign.

THRONOS   1. See A. C. Mandel, 'The Seated Man: Homo Sedens', in *Applied Ergonomics*, 12(1) (1981); also published separately (Copenhagen, 1981).

TOLLUND   1. Seamus Heaney, 'The Tollund Man', *New Selected Poems, 1966–87* (London, *1990*), 31–2.   2. 'Iceman of the Alps comes in from the cold . . .', *Sunday Times*, 29 Sept. 1991; also F. Spencer, *Piltdown: a scientific forgery* (London, 1990).

TONE   1. G. Perle, *Twelve-Tone Tonality* (London, 1977); M. Hyde, *Schoenberg's Twelve-Tone Tonality* (Ann Arbor, Mich., 1982); S. Milstein, *Schoenberg: Notes, Sets, Forms* (Cambridge, 1992).   2. R. R. Reti, *Tonality, Atonality, Pantonality: A Study of Some Trends in Twentieth Century Music* (London, 1958).   3. P. Griffiths, *Olivier Messiaen and the Music of Our Time* (London, 1985); B. M. Maciejewski, *H. M. Górecki: His Music and Our Times* (London, 1994).

TOR   1. See A. Reissner, *Berlin, 1675–1945: The Rise and Fall of a Metropolis* (London, 1984); A. Read, D. Fisher, *Berlin; the biography of a city* (London, 1994).

TORMENTA   1. Norbert Elias, *History of Manners*, 203–4.   2. After Michel Foucault, *Surveiller et punir: Naissance de la prison* (Paris, 1975), 9–11, quoting contemporary accounts.   3. C. Phillipson, *Three Criminal Law Reformers: Beccaria, Bentham, Romilly* (London, 1923); *Cesare Beccaria and Modern Criminal Policy*, International Congress, 1988 (Milan, 1990); J. H. Langbein, *Torture and the Law of Proof: Europe and England in the Ancien Regime* (Chicago, 1977).   4. See G. R. Scott, *A History of Torture* (London, 1994); J. H. Burgess and H. Danelius, *The UN Convention against Torture* (London, 1988).

TOUR   1. Serge Douay, 'Tours et Détours du Tour de France', *Historama*, 89/July 1991, 58–63; see also G. Watson, *The Tour de France and its heroes* (London, 1990); G. Nicholson, *The Rise and Fall of the Tour de France* (London, 1991).   2. *Independent*, 27 July 1992.

TRISTAN   1. John Manchip White, 'Tristan and Isolt', in P. Quennell (ed.), *Diversions in History* (London, 1954), 138–46.   2. Gabriel Bise, *Tristan and Isolde: From a Manuscript of 'The Romance of Tristan'* (15th century) (Fribourg–Geneva, 1978).   3. *Povest'e Tryschane* (1580), Raczyński Library, Poznań (MS 94): trans. Z. Kipel as *The Byelorussian Tristan* (New York, 1988).   4. From the *Morte D'Arthur*, quoted by White, 'Tristan and Isolt', 146.   5. G. Phillips and M. Keaman, *King Arthur: The True Story* (London, 1992).   6. See G. Ashe, *The Quest for Arthur's Britain* (London, 1968).   7. Tennyson, *Idylls of the King*, 'To the Queen', ll. 62–6; in R. W. Hill (ed.), *Tennyson's Poetry* (New York, 1971), 431.

TSCHERNOWITZ   1. Michael Ignatieff, 'The Old Country', *New York Review of Books*, 15 Feb. 1990, reviewing Gregor von Rezzori, *The Snows of Yesteryear: Portraits for an Autobiography* (New York, 1989).

UKRAINA   1. Taras Shevchenko, '*Zapovit*' (Testament, 1845) in *Song out of Darkness*, selected poems translated by Vera Rich (London, 1972), p. 85 (modified). See D. Čyževsky, *A History of Ukrainian Literature* (Littleton, Colo., 1975); G. Grabowicz, *Toward a history of Ukrainian literature* (Cambridge, Mass., 1981).   2. D. Doroshenko, *A Survey of Ukrainian History* (Winnipeg, 2nd edn. 1975); R. Szporluk, *Ukraine, a brief history* (Detroit, 1982); R. Magocsi, *Ukraine: a historical atlas* (Toronto, 1985); O. Subtelny, *Ukraine: a history* (Toronto, 1988).

USKOK   1. Catherine Wendy Bracewell, *The Uskoks of Senj: piracy, banditry, and holy war in the sixteenth century Adriatic* (Cornell, Ithaca, 1991).

USURY   1. See J. Shatzmiller, *Shylock Reconsidered: Jews, Moneylending and Medieval Society* (Berkeley, Calif., 1989), reviewed in *New York Review of Books*, 36/21–2 (18 Jan. 1990).   2. K. B. McFarlane, 'Loans to the Lancastrian Kings: The Problem of Inducement', *Cambridge Historical Journal*, 9 (1947–9), 57–68.

UTOPIA   1. Sir Thomas More, *Utopia*, trans. Raphe Robynson, 1552 (Cambridge, 1879) (17th repr., 1952).   2. See Isaiah Berlin, *Against the Current: Essays in the History of Ideas* (Oxford, 1979); also H. Hardy (ed.), *The Crooked Timbers of Humanity: Essays in the History of Ideas* (London, 1991).   3. Vercors, *Le Silence de la mer, et autres récits* (Paris, 1951), 19–43.   4. K. Moczarski, *Rozmowy z katem*, trans. as *Conversations with an Executioner* (London, 1974).

VALTELLINA   1. See Geoffrey Parker, *The Army of Flanders and the Spanish Road, 1567–1659* (Cambridge, 1972). On Sfurzat wine, see G. Dalmass, 'The Wines of Italy', *The Great Book of Wine* (Lausanne, 1970), 221.

VENDANGE   1. See E. Le Roy Ladurie, *Histoire du climat depuis l'an mille* (Paris, 1967), trans. as *Times of Feast, Times of Famine: A History of Climate Since the Year 1000* (New York, 1971); H. Lamb, *Climate, History and the Modern World* (London, 1982); also Sir Crispin Tickell, 'Climate and History', Radcliffe Lecture (Oxford, 1994).   2. Le Roy Ladurie, *Times of Feast, Times of Famine*, ch. 2.   3. Ibid. ch. 3, 'Problems of the Little Ice Age'.

VENDÉMIAIRE   1. H. Morse Stephens, *Revolutionary Europe, 1789–1815* (London, 1936), app. vi: 'Concordance of Republican and Gregorian Calendars', 374–5.

VINO   1. J.-F. Gautier, *Histoire du Vin* (Paris, 1992). See also H. Warner Allen, *A History of Wine* (London, 1961).   2. Gautier, op. cit. p. 99.   3. Hugh Johnson, *World Atlas of Wine* (London, 1971), p. 191.

VIOLETS   1. D. Ackerman, 'Smell', in *A Natural History of the Senses* (London, 1990), 3–63.   2. See Alain Corbin, *The Foul and the Fragrant: Odours and the French Social Imagination* (Leamington Spa, 1986).   3. S. Ferenczi, *Thalassa: A Theory of Genitality* (1938; repr. London, 1989).

VLAD   1. M. Cazacu, 'Il Potere, la Ferocitá, e le Leggende di Vlad III, Conte Dracula', *Storia* (Firenze), iii, no. 15, 10–16; see also C. Leatherdale, *The Origins of Dracula: the background to Bram Stoker's Gothic masterpiece* (London, 1987); A. Mackenzie, *A journey into the past of Transylvania* (London, 1990); S. Pascu, *A History of Transylvania* (Detroit, 1982).   2. John Foxe, *The new and complete Book of Martyrs, or an universal history of martyrdom*, revised & corrected (London, 1811–17).

VORKUTA   1. See Paul Hollander, 'Soviet Terror, American Amnesia', *National Review*, 2 May 1944, 28–39.   2. J. Scholmer, *Vorkuta* (London, 1954); Edward Buca, *Vorkuta* (Constable, London, 1976); also Bernard Grywacz, interviewed by Caroline Moorhead, 'Out of the Darkness', *Independent Magazine*, 26 Jan. 1991.   3. Avraham Shifrin, *The First Guidebook to the Prisons and Concentration Camps of the Soviet Union* (Seewis, GR, Switzerland, 1980), 2nd edn. (London, 1981); on Vorkuta, pp. 203–9. See also R. Conquest, *Kolyma: the Arctic Death Camps* (London, 1978).   4. Shifrin, op. cit. 31–5.   5. Personal visit, Oct. 1991.   6. '80,000 ghosts return to haunt Moscow', the *Independent*, 6 Sept. 1989.

WASTE LAND 1. T. S. Eliot, *The Waste Land: A Facsimile and Transcript of the Original Drafts with the Annotations of Ezra Pound*, ed. Valerie Eliot (London, 1971), 5, 135, 145, 148, 1.

WIENER WELT 1. Stephen Beller, *Vienna and the Jews 1867–1938: A Cultural History* (Cambridge, 1989), esp. 34–7. **2.** Ibid. *passim.* **3.** Martin Freud, 'Who Was Freud?', in J. Fraenkel (ed.), *The Jews of Austria: Essays on Their Life, History and Destruction* (London, 1967), 197–211. **4.** Joseph Roth, quoted by R. S. Wistrich, *The Jews of Vienna in the Age of Franz-Joseph* (Oxford, 1990). **5.** Rabbi Güdemann to Kamilla Theimer, 19 Dec. 1907, quoted by J. Fraenkel, 'The Chief Rabbi and the Visionary', in Fraenkel, *The Jews of Austria*, 115–17.

XATIVAH 1. See David Hunter, *Papermaking: The History and Technique of an Ancient Craft* (London, 1947); also J. Dąbrowski and J. Siniarska-Czaplicka, *Rękodzieło papiernicze* (The Papermaking Craft) (Warsaw, 1991), with extensive English summaries.

ZADRUGA 1. Maria Todorova, 'Myth-Making in European Family History: The Zadruga Revisited', *East European Politics and Society*, 4(1) (1991), 30–69.

ZEUS 1. M. J. Price, 'The Statue of Zeus at Olympia', in P. Clayton and M. J. Price, *The Seven Wonders of the World* (London, 1988), 59–77.

APPENDIX I

LIST OF CAPSULES

APPENDIX II

NOTES ON PLATES AND ACKNOWLEDGEMENTS

SECTION 1   (*between pages* 430–1)

1. EUROPA'S RIDE. *Il ratto dell'Europa.* Hellenistic fresco from 'the House of Jason', Pompeii. First quarter of the 1st century AD. Both Greeks and Romans treasured the legend of Europa. Museo Nazionale, Naples.

   Photo: Anderson/Alinari 23469.

2. GATHERERS AND HUNTERS. A composite drawing based on palaeolithic cave art from Teruel and Cogul (Lerida), Spain. Male and female figures combine to present an evocative reconstruction of a sophisticated social order frequently dismissed as that of 'cavemen'.

   Drawing by Danyon Rey 1993.

3. MINOAN FISHERMAN. 2nd millennium BC, National Archaeological Museum, Athens.

   Photo: National Archaeological Museum, Athens.

4. PRINCE OF KNOSSOS. Late Minoan. Minoan Crete was unfortified, and possessed no warrior caste. Heraklion Museum.

   Photo: Ancient Art & Architecture Collection.

5. SYMPOSION—A BANQUET. Greek vase-painting by the Brygos painter (490–480 BC). The 'symposium' provided the setting both for eating, drinking, and love-making and for serious conversation. The men reclined on couches in the oriental fashion. Women and boys did not attend except for the purposes of entertainment.

   Photo: British Museum BM E 60.

6. ETRUSCHERIA. Mural from the Tomb of the Banquet, Tarquinia (*c.*470 BC). See [**ETRUSCHERIA**].

   Photo: Hirmer Fotoarchiv BM E 60.

7. ARCADIAN IDYLL. *Et in Arcadia ego* (1639–43), Nicholas Poussin, bought by Louis XIV in 1683. In the Classical Tradition, Arcadia was the land of pastoral bliss. In Poussin's famous development of an idea by Guercino, a group of pensive shepherds and nymphs examine the tomb of Daphnis, who died of love, thereby discovering that 'Even in Arcadia, I (Death) am to be found'. Louvre.

   Photo: © RMN.

8. SABINE RAPE. *Les Sabines* (1796–9) by Jean-Louis David. As recounted by Livy and Ovid, one of the favourite tales of early Rome tells how King Romulus organized a festival at the Circus Maximus in order to ensnare the women of the neighbouring Sabine tribe. David's heroic rendering shows Roman matrons intervening to stop the

bloodshed on a background reminiscent of the Bastille. It earned him the label of 'the Raphael of the Sansculottes'. Louvre.

Photo: © RMN.

9. DEATH OF SIEGFRIED. An episode from the 5th-century Legend of the Nibelungen: Julius Schnorr von Carolsfeld (1794–1872): *Hagen ermordet Siegfried (Hagen killing Siegfried)* (1845). Hagen surprised Siegfried drinking at the spring, and pierced his magical protection. Munich was the capital of King Ludwig II of Bavaria, patron of Richard Wagner, who popularized the nationalistic revival of pagan Germanic folklore. Koenigsbau, Munich. See [**NIBELUNG**].

Photo: AKG, London.

10. ATTILA INVADES ROME, AD 452. Ulpiano Checa y Sauz (1860–1916), *The Fall of Rome* (1891). Many pictures of this genre, which lionize the barbarian heroes, say as much about the nineteenth-century revolt against classical taste as about ancient history.

Photo: © Hulton Deutsch Collection.

11. EASTERN ORTHODOXY. Christ Pantakrator flanked by the Emperor Constantine IX Monomachos (r. 1042–55) and the Empress Zoe at the time of the Church Schism (1054): 11th-century mosaic. The Byzantine tradition stressed the union of spiritual and temporal authority. Hagia Sophia, Istanbul.

Photo: Foto Fabbri.

12. WESTERN MONASTICISM. St Benedict and the Abbey of Monte Cassino, founded c.529. 11th-century miniature. The first great Western monastery, founded by Europe's Patron Saint, survived intact until 1944.

Vatican Photographic Archive. Vat. Lat. 1702 IIr.

13. CONSTANTINE'S DONATION. The medieval legend that the Pope's temporal powers were donated by the Emperor Constantine I, illustrated in a fresco (AD 1246). The legend was unmasked as a papal forgery during the Renaissance. San Silvestro, Rome.

Photo: Foto Fabbri.

14. THE SLAVONIC LITURGY. Alphonse Mucha, *Zavedeni slovanska liturgie* (1910). A late Romantic view of an event in the 9th-century mission of SS Cyril and Methodius to Moravia: the first of Mucha's series illustrating scenes from Czech history. City Gallery, Prague.

Photo: State Gallery, Prague.

15. CATHOLIC PIETISM. Enguerrand Quarton, *La Pietá de Villeneuve-les-Avignon* (1444–66). An expressive representation of the Virgin Mary's 'Lamentation of Christ' from 15th-century Provence. Louvre.

Photo: © RMN.

16. ST AUGUSTINE. *St Augustin et les patrons de Marchiennes* (12th-cent.) miniature. Bibliothèque Municipale, Douai.

Photo: Photo Giraudon.

17. ST CHARLEMAGNE. A. Dürer, *Karl der Grosse* (1512).
Germanisches Nationalmuseum, Nuremberg.

18. ST MATTHEW. A full-page illumination on folio 25h of the Lindisfarne Gospels
(late 7th century, Northumbria).
British Library, BL Cott. Nero Div. 25v.

19. SS JOHN THE BAPTIST AND JEROME. By Masolino, *c.*1383. National Gallery,
London.
Photo: Bridgeman Art Library.

20. MATKA BOSKA 'The Mother of God'. (14th-century.) The Black Madonna of
Częstochowa, Poland, an icon of Byzantine origin or possibly a copy ordered by King
Władysław Jagiełło. See [**MADONNA**].
Photo: Polish Cultural Institute, London.

21. ST JOHN THE THEOLOGIAN. The dictation of the Gospel to Prokhor (Italo-
Cretan School, early 17th century). Crete, which was ruled by Venice until 1669, saw an
inimitable blending of Orthodox and Catholic styles. See [**GRECO**].
Photo: Sotheby's, London.

22. ST. LUKE—ICON PAINTER. According to Orthodox tradition, the first icon
was painted by St Luke, when he drew the Virgin Mary from life. (17th-century icon
from the Church of St Luke, Opachka, Pskov, Russia: restored.)
Photo: Church of St Luke, Pskov, Russia.

23. BOGORODICA. The Virgin of Pelagonitissa: a Serbian icon of the Holy Mother
and Child (14th-century) from Skopje, Macedonia.
Photo: AKG, London.

24. HOMAGE TO OTTO III. The four lands of Europe—Slavonia, Germany, Gaul,
and Italy—offering homage to an Emperor who sought to re-unite East and West. Otto
III's Gospels, Bamberg (*c.* AD 1000).
Photo: Staatsbibliothek, Marburg.

25. ENGLAND CONQUERED. The Death of King Harold at Hastings, AD 1066. Detail
from the late 11th-century *Tapisserie de la Reine Mathilde*, known in English as the
Bayeux Tapestry. The 58 panels of this early example of strip cartoon art relates the
Norman version of events, including King Harold's alleged treachery and Duke
William's consequent claim to the English throne.
Photo: Michael Holford.

26. WENDISH CRUSADE. L. Tuxen, *The Fall of Svantevit* (1894). The destruction of
the pagan idols of the Slavs during the Wendish Crusade (12th century). Such scenes
attended the 'advance of civilization' in Europe from Caesar's felling of the druidical
grove at Marseilles to the final baptism of the Lithuanians in 1386. Fredericksborg,
Copenhagen.
Photo: Fredericksborg, Copenhagen.

27. TRUCE IN THE RECONQUISTA. 12th-century miniature from *El libro de Juegos de Ajedrez*. A Christian and a Moslem warrior play chess. Escorial, Spain.

Photo: Arxui Mas.

28. TRISTAN'S LAST SONG. Miniature (*c.*1410) from the *Roman de Tristan*. From its origins in 6th-century Cornwall to Wagner's opera of 1859, the tragic love story of Tristan and Isolde was recounted in numberless versions. See [**TRISTAN**].

Photo: Austrian Nat. Library, Vienna, MS 2537.

29. IRON PLOUGH. 'March' from *Les Trés Riches Heures du Duc de Berry* (early 15th-century). The heavy horse-drawn plough was the principal instrument of the medieval 'Agricultural Revolution'. Musée Condé, Paris. See [**PLOVUM**].

Photo: Photo Giraudon.

30. SCENT OF THE STAG. 'Tracking' from Gaston de Foix, *Le Livre de la Chasse* (late 14th-century). Until recent times, the art of hunting was a mainstay of Europe's diet and nourishment. Bibliothèque Nationale, Paris. MS Français, 616 fol. 57v. See [**CHASSE**].

Photo: Bibliothèque Nationale, Paris.

31. DANTE IN LOVE. H. Holiday, *Dante and Beatrice* (1883). A popular representation of the moment on the banks of the Arno in Florence which was to inspire Europe's greatest poem. Beatrice Portinari, who died in 1290, was adopted by Dante as his spiritual guide through Paradise.

Photo: Walker Art Gallery, Liverpool, no. 3125.

32. BARTOLOMEA IN A DILEMMA. 'Dioneo's Tale' from Boccaccio's *Decameron*: 15th-century miniature. The neglected wife of a Pisan judge, Bartolomea, goes off on pilgrimage, where she is seduced by the pirate, Paganino da Nare (*left*). On reflection, however, she chooses to live with the pirate (*right*).

Photo: Bibliothèque de l'Arsenal, Paris. Arsenal 5070 fol. 91v.

33. ST FRANCIS BLESSES THE BIRDS. Fresco (1295–1300) by Giotto. The patron saint of animal lovers, St Francis was also a social radical whose devotion to poverty and non-violence challenged many of the reigning assumptions of the medieval world. Church of San Francesco, Assisi.

Photo: AKG, London.

34. KING CASIMIR GREETS THE JEWS. Wojciech Gerson (1831–1901), *Kazimierz Wielki i żydzi* (*c.*1890). This late Romantic painting celebrates the expansion of Europe's largest Jewish community at the time of the Black Death, when large numbers of Jews took refuge in Poland from persecution in Germany. Museum Narodowe, Warsaw.

Photo: H. Romanowski, Museum Narodowe, Warsaw.

35. PICARO. Hieronymus Bosch, *The Vagrant*. Rural poverty, vagrancy, and fugitive serfs constituted one of the perennial social ills of late medieval and early modern Europe. See [**PICARO**].

Photo: Museum Boymans van Beuningen, Rotterdam.

36. MARCO POLO. Marco Polo the Venetian sets sail for China from the Grand Canal, AD 1270. Miniature, *c.*1400. Europe's voyages of discovery began long before the age of Columbus.

  Photo: Bodleian Library, Oxford. MS Bod. 264 f. 218.

37. WESTERNER AS EASTERNER. Jean-Etienne Liotard, *Portrait de Richard Pococke* (*c.*1738–9). The British Ambassador to the Sublime Porte painted in Ottoman dress, overlooking the Bosporus.

  Photo: © Musée de l'Art et d'Histoire, Geneva.

SECTION 2   (*between pages* 942–3)

38. VENUS. Lucas Cranach, *Venus restraining Cupid* (1509). Cranach's full frontal female nude crowned the long process of artistic defiance, initiated by Donatello's bronze *David* (*c.*1434), which broke the medieval taboo against nudity, thereby reviving interest in the human body. Hermitage Museum, St Petersburg.

  Photo: Bridgeman Art Library.

39. PERSPECTIVE. Piero della Francesca, *The Flagellation* or *The Dream of St Jerome* (*c.*1460). A profoundly enigmatic work by an artist experimenting both with technical innovations and visual symbolism. Galleria Nazionale, Urbino. See [**FLAGELLATIO**].

  Photo: Bridgeman Art Library.

40. ALLEGORY. Antoine Caron (1521–99), *L'Empéreur Auguste et la Sibylle de Tibur* (*c.*1575). In an attempt to reconcile the paganism of the Ancient World with Christianity, Caron portrays the Roman Sibyl prophesying to the Emperor Augustus about the Immaculate Conception and the Birth of Christ. Louvre. From the court of Henri III.

  Photo: Photo Giraudon.

41. COLUMBUS LANDS AT SAN DOMINGO, 1493. F. Kemmelmeyer, *The First Landing of Christopher Columbus* (1800–5). An evocation of a moment now described not as a 'discovery' but as an 'encounter'.

  Photo: National Gallery of Art, Washington.

42. LUTHER ENTERS WORMS, 1521. R. Siegard, *Die Rede Martin Luthers von dem Reichstag in Worms*. A reconstruction of the scene on the day which was to split Catholic Europe, and launch the Reformation.

  Photo: Stadtarchiv, Worms.

43. DREAM OF EMPIRE. El Greco, *The Adoration of the Name of Jesus* (*c.*1578): an autographed version of a larger picture in the Escorial, Spain, known as *The Dream of Philip II*. The kneeling figures of the King of Spain, the Pope, and the Doge of Venice embody the ultra-Catholic mission of the Holy League whose forces defeated the Turks at Lepanto in 1571, thereby saving Europe from the jaws of Hell.

  Photo: National Gallery, London.

44. VISION OF PAST GLORY. J. Matejko (1838–93), *Bathory at Pskov* (1872). A nostalgic Romantic painting recalling the occasion in 1582, when the King of Poland received the submission of the Russian *boyars*.

  Photo: Royal Castle, Warsaw.

45. THE BOARD OF GOVERNORS. Frans Hals, *Regentessen Dude Mannenhuis* (*The Regentesses of the Old Men's Almshouse*) (1664). A portrait of corporate pride showing the lady governors of a Dutch charitable organization. A parallel portrait of *The Regents* bears the same date.

Photo: © Frans Halsmuseum, Haarlem.

46. MOSCOW HOLIDAY. A. P. Riabushkin (1861–1904), *A Seventeenth Century Moscow Street on a Holiday* (1895). This lively scene from old Moscow shows a cross-section of Muscovite society, from the haughty black-bearded *boyar* to the blind beggar, wending their way home from church through the muddy streets.

Photo: SCR Photo Library.

47. SUN KING AS PATERFAMILIAS. J. Nocret (1615–82), *Louis XIV en famille* (*c.*1680). Louis XIV participated in all the masques and galas of the Court, in this scene putting his entire family into classical dress. Musée de Versailles.

Photo: © RMN.

48. TROUSERLESS PHILOSOPHER. Jean Huber (1721–86), *Le Lever de Voltaire* (*c.*1770). Voltaire changing from his nightclothes whilst dictating to a secretary: one of a series of intimate scenes from Ferney, painted by Voltaire's Swiss friend and savant. Musée Carnavalet.

Photo: Giraudon.

49. MASTER OF THE CONTINENT. A. J. Gros, *Napoléon à Eylau* (1808). One of the less sycophantic portrayals of a Napoleonic battle scene, this one at Eylau (Iława) in East Prussia, 8 February 1807. Louvre.

Photo: © RMN.

50. LORDS OF THE SEA. C. van Wiermigen, *Het ontploffen van het Spaanse admiraalschip* (*The explosion of the Spanish Admiral's Flagship, 25 April 1607*). Dutch naval supremacy, which underpinned the successful Revolt of the Netherlands against Spain, was not seriously challenged until the rise of England's Royal Navy in the later 17th-century.

Photo: © Rijksmuseum, Amsterdam.

51. INFANTA IN PINK. Diego Velazquez, also attributed to Mazo, *Infanta Margarita* (1664). A child portrayed as a miniature adult. Other versions of the same portrait can be found in Vienna and in Kiev. Prado, Madrid.

Photo: Bridgeman Art Library.

52. READER AND LISTENER. Hubert Gravelot, *Le Lecteur* (*c.*1740). Marble Hill House.

Photo: English Heritage.

53. MOTHER. J. Rembrandt, *The Artist's Mother* (1639). Neeltje Willemsdochter van Zuydhoeck painted by her son in the last year of her life.

Photo: Kunsthistorisches Museum, Vienna.

54. SUMMER. G. Arcimboldo, *Estate* (1573). One of four such pictures ordered by the Emperor Maximilian II as a gift for the Elector of Saxony. In a later series of 'composed heads' Arcimboldo used the Emperor Rudolph as model. Louvre, Paris.

Photo: © RMN.

55. ROYALIST. P. N. Guerin, *Henri de La Rochejacquelein* (1817). A heroic portrait of the Vendéan leader painted after the Restoration.

Photo: Musée de Cholet.

56. REPUBLICAN. A. Cambron, *La République* (1798). A personification of republican France painted one year before Napoleon's coup d'état and a whole generation before similar images attracted the name of 'Marianne'.

Photo: Musée de Montaubon.

57. THE CHILDREN'S FRIEND. This picture of Stalin embracing a young admirer at the Communist Party Congress of 1938 at the height of the purges was widely reproduced by Soviet propaganda agencies. It even inspired a public statue erected in Moscow. The girl, Gelya Sergeyevna, learned much later that her father had been shot on Stalin's orders, and that her mother had been cast into the Gulag for enquiring about his fate.

Photo: David King.

58. KNIGHT IN SHINING ARMOUR. H. Lanzinger, *Adolf Hitler als Ritter* (c.1939). The Nazis' search for *Lebensraum* in the East was often seen as a continuation of the medieval *Drang nach Osten* and the campaigns of the Teutonic Knights.

Photo: AKG, London.

59. ETERNAL WANDERER. C. D. Friedrich, *Wanderer above the clouds* (1818). The supreme image of the Romantic spirit.

Photo: © Elke Walford, Hamburger Kunsthalle.

60. DYNAMO. J. M. W. Turner, *Rain, Steam and Speed* (1844). A pioneering example of Impressionism, and the supreme image of the nineteenth century's obsessions both with Nature and with Mechanical Power.

Photo: National Gallery, London.

61. NO SURRENDER, 1831. W. Kossak (1856–1942), *Sowiński on the Ramparts of Wola* (1922). Facing the Russian assault on Warsaw, the Napoleonic veteran, General Józef Sowiński, ordered his men to fix his wooden leg in the ground, resolving never to bow down to tyrants.

Photo: Museum Wojska Polskiego, Warsaw.

62. FREE HELLAS. Ch. Perlberg, *Popular festivities at the Olympeion in Athens, 1838*. This scene from the newly independent Kingdom underlines both Greece's Classical heritage and her legacy of four centuries of Ottoman rule.

Photo: National Historical Museum, Athens.

63. MUSICAL EVENING. J. Danhauser, *Liszt am Flugel* (1840). From the left: Alfred de Musset (or Alexandre Dumas), Victor Hugo, Georges Sand, N. Paganini, Gioacchino Rossini, Marie d'Agoult. Nationalgalerie, Berlin.

Photo: Bildarchiv Preussischer Kulturbesitz.

64. CONCERT OF EUROPE. A. von Werner, *The Congress of Berlin* (1881). From the left: Count Karolyi (Austria), Prince Gorchakov (Russia), Benjamin Disraeli (Britain), Count Andrassy (Hungary), Chancellor von Bismarck (Germany), Count Shuvalov (Russia), Mehmet Ali (Ottoman Empire). Staatlichen Museum, Berlin.

Photo: AKG, London/Berlin.

65. RURAL POVERTY. J.-F. Millet, *Les Glaneuses* (*The Gleaners*) (1857). The summer countryside of Normandy seen by a master of French realism.

Photo: Bridgeman Art Library.

66. INDUSTRIAL GRIME. L. S. Lowry (1887–1976). Though painting in the mid-20th-century, the Lancashire artist evoked a quaint and anachronistic vision of the early industrial landscape, which had all but disappeared.

Photo: Bridgeman Art Library.

67. IMPRESSIONIST. Claude Monet (1840–1926), *The Seine at Bougival* (1869). An experimental study of suburban Paris painted by a young Monet taking his first cautious steps into Impressionism. See [**IMPRESSION**].

Photo: The Currier Gallery of Art, Manchester, New Hampshire.

68. PRIMITIVE. Henri Rousseau (1844–1910), *War* (1894). One of the vivid, dream-like images of 'Le Douanier' Rousseau, instinctively produced by a naïve artist in the era of Freud's discovery of the subconscious and in the middle of the great European peace. Musée d'Orsay, Paris.

Photo: Bridgeman Art Library.

69. SURREAL. P. Blume, *The Eternal City* (1937). A dislocated vision of Rome from the years when Mussolini sought to build a new Roman Empire and when Eliot's *Waste Land* suggested that European civilization had been shattered. See [**WASTE LAND**].

Museum of Modern Art, Guggenheim Fund, New York.
© Estate of Peter Blume/DACS, London/VAGA, New York 1997

70. EUROPE DECEIVED. A. Vasilev, *They are Writing About Us in Pravda* (1951). A practitioner of Stalinist 'Socialist Realism' presents an idyllic imaginary scene from a collective farm in Moldavia. In reality, Moldavia's population had been purged and repressed after the Soviet invasion of 1940, and the peasantry collectivized by force. Private Collection. See [**MOLDOVA**].

Photo: Museum of Modern Art, Oxford.

71. EUROPE DIVIDED. Sigmar Polke, *Watch Tower with Geese* (1987–8). An image of the Iron Curtain painted two years before its collapse by a German who had himself escaped across 'the Wall' in 1953. On the left, in the East, a concentration camp: in the West, floating consumer *kitsch*.

Photo: © 1994 The Art Institute of Chicago. All Rights Reserved.

72. EUROPE IN TORMENT. Marc Chagall (1889–1985), *White Crucifixion* (1938). The central symbol of Christian Europe is overlain with Jewish imagery: painted by a Russian Jewish exile to Western Europe on the eve of the Second World War.

© 1993 The Art Institute of Chicago. All Rights Reserved; © 1994 DACS, London.

APPENDIX III

HISTORICAL COMPENDIUM

Geological and Historical Time

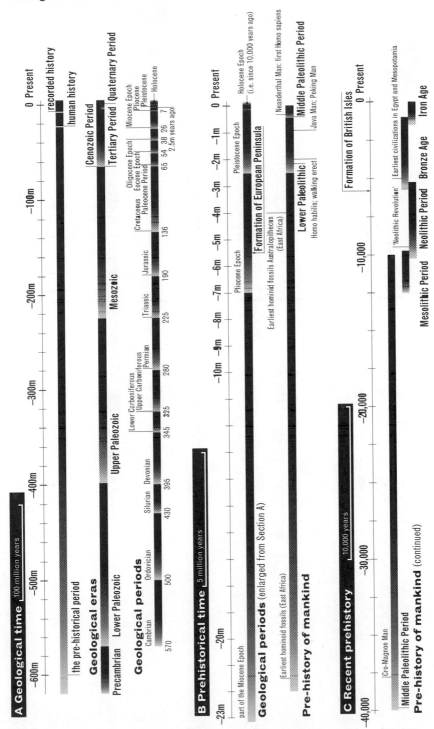

A Geological time — 100 million years

Present 0
recorded history
human history
the pre-historical period

Geological eras
Precambrian · Lower Paleozoic · Upper Paleozoic · Mesozoic · Cenozoic Period · Tertiary Period · Quaternary Period

Geological periods
Cambrian | Ordovician | Silurian | Devonian | Lower Carboniferous | Upper Carboniferous | Permian | Triassic | Jurassic | Cretaceous | Paleocene Period | Eocene Epoch | Oligocene Epoch | Miocene Epoch | Pliocene | Pleistocene | Holocene

570 · 500 · 430 · 395 · 345 · 325 · 280 · 225 · 190 · 136 · 65 · 54 · 38 · 26 · 7 · 2.5m years ago

−600m −500m −400m −300m −200m −100m 0 Present

B Prehistorical time — 5 million years

part of the Miocene Epoch
Earliest hominoid fossils (East Africa)

Geological periods (enlarged from Section A)
Pliocene Epoch
Earliest hominid fossils Australopithecus (East Africa)
Formation of European Peninsula
Pleistocene Epoch
Homo habilis; walking erect | Lower Paleolithic
Java Man; Peking Man | Middle Paleolithic Period
Neanderthal Man: first Homo sapiens
Holocene Epoch (i.e. since 10,000 years ago)

Pre-history of mankind

−23m −20m −10m −9m −8m −7m −6m −5m −4m −3m −2m −1m 0 Present

C Recent prehistory — 10,000 years

Cro-Magnon Man
Middle Paleolithic Period
Mesolithic Period
'Neolithic Revolution'
Neolithic Period
Formation of British Isles
Earliest civilizations in Egypt and Mesopotamia
Bronze Age
Iron Age

Pre-history of mankind (continued)

−40,000 −30,000 −20,000 −10,000 0 Present

Ancient Mediterranean Civilizations: Periodization

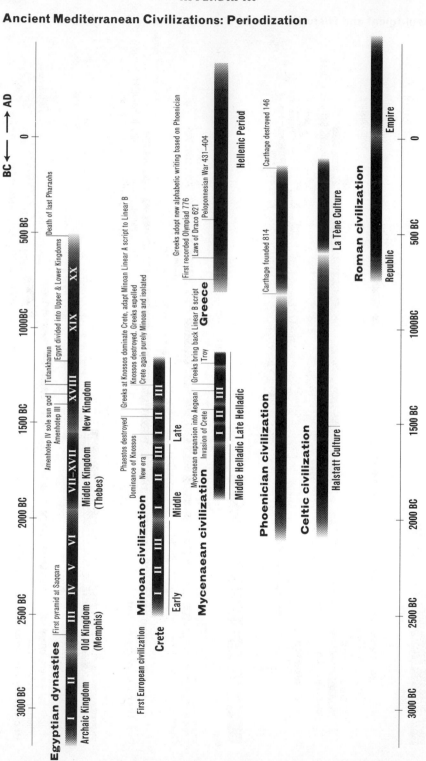

Minoan Scripts

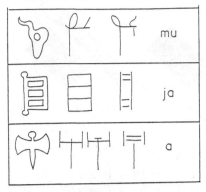

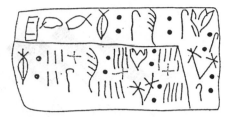

a. The evolution of Aegean writing (left to right): hieroglyphic, Linear A, Linear B, sound value.

b. Stage I: 'pictographic' or 'hieroglyphic', from *c.*2000 BC: a hieroglyphic tablet from Phaistos, Crete.

J. Chadwick, *The Decipherment of Linear B* (Pelican), 1961

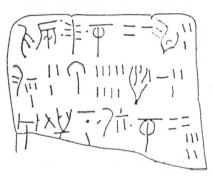

c. Stage II/1: Linear A (undeciphered), from +1750 BC: tablet from Hagia Triada no. 114

J. Chadwick, *The Decipherment of Linear B* (Pelican), 1961

d. Stage II/2: The Cypriot syllabary: fragment of a clay tablet from Enkomi, *c.*1200 BC

J. Chadwick, *Linear B and Related Scripts* (London, British Museum Publications, 1987)

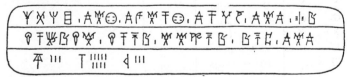

e. Stage III: Linear B, found both on Crete and in Mycenaean Greece. Like modern Japanese *kanji* and *kana*, it contained a mixture of pictographic and syllabic signs. Linear B tablet from Pylos, with proto-Greek transliteration and English translation.

'*Hiereia echei-que, euchetoi-que etonion echeen theon, ktoinoochons-de ktionaon kekeimenaon onata echeen. (Tossonde spermo) WHEAT 3–9–3.*'

'This the priestess holds, and solemnly declares that the god has the true ownership, but the plot-holders the enjoyment, of the plots in which it is laid out. (So much seed) 3³⁄₆₀ units.'

Leonard Cottrell, *The Bull of Minos* (Athens, 1982)

European Alphabets

Hebrew	Phoenician	Ancient Greek Ionic	Ancient Greek Chalcidic	Ancient Greek (Minuscules)	Name	Modern Greek	Imperial Latin	Glagolithic (Dalmatian)	Modern (Russian)
א ב	✕ ۹	A	A	α	alpha	A		Ⰰ Ⰱ	А Б
		B	B			B		Ⰲ	В = v
ג ד ה ו ז ח ט י כ ל מ נ ס ע פ צ ק ר ש ת	⅂ Δ Ⴈ Y I	Γ Δ E	Γ Δ E	β γ δ ε	beta gamma delta epsilon	C D E F	Ⰳ Ⰴ Ⰵ	Г = g Д Е
			F=w						
	Ⅎ H ⊗ Z Ӿ	Z H Θ I K Λ M N Ξ Θ Π	Z ⊟ ⊕ I K Ʌ ᛗ N O Γ Q	ζ η θ ι κ λ μ ν ξ ο π	zeta eta theta iota kappa lambda mu nu xi omicron pi	G H I K L M N O P	Ⰸ Ⰹ Ⰺ Ⰻ Ⰼ Ⰽ Ⰾ Ⰿ Ⱀ Ⱁ	И К Л М Н О П
	Ρ Ϙ W ✝	P Σ T Y Φ X Ψ Ω	Q P Σ T Y Φ X Ψ	ρ σ τ υ φ χ ψ ω	rho sigma tau upsilon phi chi psi omega	Q R S T V X	Ⱃ Ⱄ Ⱅ Ⱆ Ⱇ Ⱈ Ⱉ	Р С Т У Ф Х
						Y* Z*	Ⱋ	З

Glag.	Russ.	Glag.	Russ.	Glag.	Russ.
Ⱋ	Щ = shch	Ш	Ш = sh	Δ	Я = ya
Ⱌ	Ц = ts	Ⱖ	Ы = i		Ь = soft sign
Ⱍ	Ч = ch	Ⱓ	Ю = yu		Ъ = hard sign
				Ⱖ	Ж = zh

* Introduced after 100 BC for foreign words only.
Imperial Latin did not distinguish between I and J, or V and U.
There was no W.

Crossing the Alps: The St Gotthard Pass and the Valtellina

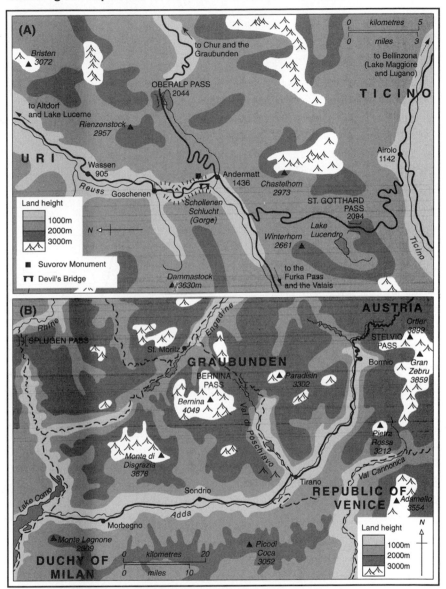

(A) The St Gotthard Pass; (B) The Valtellina (17th century)

Phenology and *Sägesignatur*: Indices of Historical Climatology, 1530–50

Vendange

Consolidated mean dates of the
wine harvest in NE and Central France:
number of days after 1 September
(after Le Roy Ladurie)

Sägesignatur

Mean thickness of oak rings in the
Western Rhineland, in 1/100 mm
(after Hollstein)

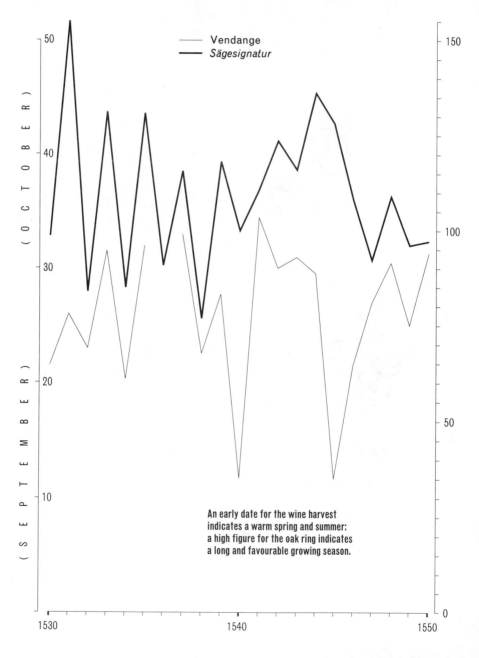

—— Vendange
—— *Sägesignatur*

An early date for the wine harvest
indicates a warm spring and summer:
a high figure for the oak ring indicates
a long and favourable growing season.

Spice-Ox: The Pythagorean Classification of Foods

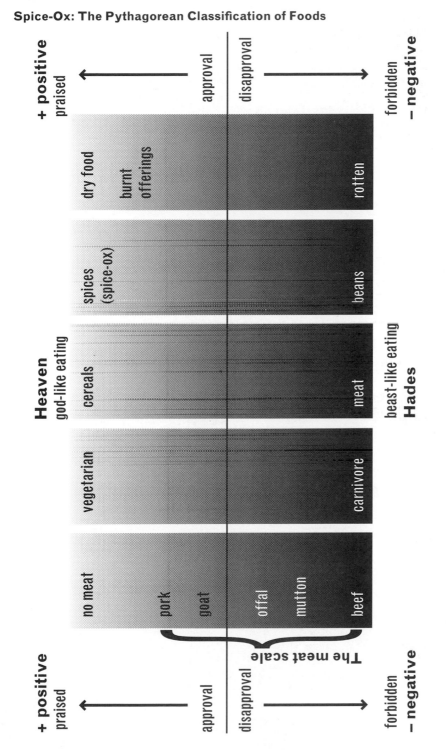

Ancient Greek Colonies, with their Contemporary Locations

PARENT CITIES. Achaea (A); Megara (M); Corinth (C); Locris, Athens, Chalcis, Eretria. (Ionia)*; Lesbos, Phocæa, Samos, Miletus, Thera, Rhodes**.

SPAIN
Mainake* (Malaga)
Alonae*
Saguntum*
Hemereoskopeion*
Taraco* (Tarragona)
Emphoriae* (Amporias)
Aphrodisias*

FRANCE
Agathe* (Agde)
Avennio* (Avignon)
Massilia* (Marseille)
Olbia*
Athenopolis*
Antipolis* (Antibes)
Nicaea* (Nice)
Herculis Monoeci*
   (Monaco)
Alalia* (in Corsica)

ITALY
Pithecusa* (Ischia)
Cyme*
Neapolis* (Naples)
Laus Pompeii
Posidonia (A)
Elea*
Pixus
Terina
Hipponium (A)
Medina
Rhegium (A)
Locri (A)
Scylletium (A)
Croton (A)
Sybaris (A)
Metapontum
Siris
Taras** (Tarento)
Hydruntum
Callipolis
Ancona (Ancona)

(SICILY)
Zancle
Panormus (Palermo)
Messania* (Messina)

Lipara
Naxos
Catana (Catania)
Megara Hyblaea (M)
Syracusa (C)
Camarina (C)
Gela**
Acragas** (Agrigento)
Himera*
Selinus (M)
Lilybaeum

EASTERN ADRIATIC
Tragyrium
Epetium
Issa
Pharos
Lissus
Epidamnus (C) (Durres)
Apollonia (C)

GREECE
Corcyra (C) (Corfu)
Leucas (C)
Ambracia
Mende*
Potidaea (C)
Olynthos
Torone*
Acanthos
Stagiros
Amphipolis
Neapolis
Crenides
Thasos*
Abdera
Lemnos
Chios

TURKEY (in Europe)
Ainos
Kardia
Elaious
Madytos
Sestos
Tiristasis
Bisanthe
Heraion*

Perinthos*
Selimbria (M)
Byzantion (M) (Istanbul)

BULGARIA
Mesembria (M) (Nesebar)
Apollonia Pontica*
   (Sozopol)
Odessus* (Varna)

ROMANIA
Cruni*
Kallatis*
Tomoi* (Constanta)
Histria*

MOLDOVA
Tyras* (Belgorod)

UKRAINE
Ophiusa*
Olbia*

(CRIMEA)
Chersonesus*
Theodosia*
Kimmerikon*
Akra*
Nymphaion*
Tiritake*
Pantikapaion*

RUSSIA
Tanais* (Azov)
Phanagoria*
Hermonassa*
Gorgippia*
Pityus*

ABKHAZIA
Dioskourias* (Sukhumi)

GEORGIA
Guenos*
Phasis* (Poti)
Bathys Limen* (Batumi)

TURKEY (Asia Minor)
Trapezous* (Trabzon)
Kerasous*
Kotyora*
Amisos* (Samsun)
Sinope* (Sinop)
Heraclea Pontica (M)
Chalcedon (M)
Astakos (M)
Kios
Kyzikos*
Artaka
Abydus (M)
Assus
Atarneos
Cyme
Smyrna (Izmir)
Ephesos
Miletus
Halicarnassus
Patara*
Phaselis*
Side*
Corcesium*
Nagidus*
Calenderis*
Soli*
Cytorus*

CYPRUS
Lapethos
Salamis
Amathus
Curium
Paphos

EGYPT
Milesiorum Castellum
   (Alexandria)
Naucratis

LIBYA
Paliouros
Apollonia**
Cyrene**
Barca**
Tauchira**
Euhesperides**

The Roman Emperors, 30 BC–AD 1453

JULIO-CLAUDIAN DYNASTY

31 BC–AD 14	Augustus
14–37	Tiberius
37–41	Caligula
41–5	Claudius I
54–68	Nero
68	Galba
	Otho
69	Vitellius
69–79	Vespasian
79–81	Titus
81–96	Domitian
96–8	Nerva
98–117	Trajan
117–38	Hadrian
138–61	Antoninus Pius
161–80	M. Aurelius*
161–9	Lucius Verus*
180–92	Commodus
193	Pertinax
193	Dedius Julianus
193–211	S. Severus
211–17	Caracalla*
211–12	Geta*
217–18	Macrinus
218–22	Heliogabalus
222–35	Alex. Severus
235–8	Maximinius
238	Gordian I
238	Gordian II
238	Balbinus*
238	Pupienus*
238–44	Gordian III
244–9	Philippus
249–51	Decius
251	Hostilianus
251–3	Gallus
253	Aemilianus
253–60	Valerian*
260–8	Gallienus*
268–70	Claudius II
270–5	Aurelian
275–6	Tacitus
276	Florianus
276–82	Probus

282–3	Carus
283–5	Carinus*
283–4	Numerianus*
284–305	Diocletian*
286–305	Maximian*
305–6	Constantius I*
305–10	Galerius*
306–12	Maxentius
308–13	Maxinus
308–24	Licinius (E)
305–37	Constantine I
337–40	Constantine II
337–50	Constans*
337–61	Constantius II*
361–3	Julian
363–4	Jovian
364–75	Valentinian I
364–78	Valens (E)
375–92	Valentinian II*
375–83	Gratian* (W)
379–95	Theodosius I
395–423	Honorius* (W)
395–408	Aroadius (E)
408–50	Theodosius II
421	Constantius III*
425–55	Valentinian III
450–7	Marcian (E)
455	Petronius (W)
455–6	Avitus (W)
457–61	Majorian (W)
457–74	Leo I (E)
461–5	Libius (W)
467–72	Anthemius (W)
472	Olybrius (W)
473–4	Glycerius (W)
474	Leo II (E)
474–5	J. Nepos (W)
474–91	Zeno (E)
475–6	Romulus Augustus (W)
491–518	Anastasius I
518–27	Justin I
527–65	Justinian I
565–78	Justin II
578–82	Tiberius II
582–602	Maurice
602–10	Phocas

HERACLIAN DYNASTY

610–41	Heraclius I
641	Constantine III*
641	Heracleonas*
641–8	Constans II
668–85	Constantine IV
685–95	Justinian II
695–8	Leontius
698–705	Tiberius III
705–11	Justinian III
711–13	Philippicus
713–15	Anastasius II
716–17	Theodosius III

ISAURIAN DYNASTY

717–41	Leo III
741–75	Constantine V
775–80	Leo IV
780–97	Constantine VI
797–802	Irene
802–11	Nicephorus I
811	Stauracius
811–13	Michael I
813–20	Leo V
820–9	Michael II
829–42	Theophilus
842–67	Michael III

MACEDONIAN DYNASTY

867–86	Basil I
886–912	Leo VI
912–13	Alexander
913–19	Constantine VII
919–44	Romanus I
944–59	Constantine VII
959–63	Romanus II
963	Basil II
963–9	Nicephorus I
969–76	John I
976–1025	Basil II
1025–8	Constantine VIII
1028–34	Romanus III
1034–41	Michael IV
1041–2	Michael V

1042	Zoe and Theodora
1042–55	Constantine IX
1055–6	Theodora
1056–7	Michael VI
1057–9	Isaac I
1059–67	Constantine X
1067–8	Michael VII
1068–71	Romanus IV
1071–8	Michazel VII
1078–81	Nicephorus III

COMNENIAN DYNASTY

1081–1118	Alexius I
1118–43	John II
1143–80	Manuel I
1180–3	Alexius II
1183–5	Andronicus I
1185–95	Isaac II
1195–1203	Alexius III
1203–4	Alexius IV
1204	Alexius V
1204–22	Theodore I
1222–54	John III
1254–8	Theodore II
1258	John IV

PALAEOLOGAN DYNASTY

1258–82	Michael VIII
1282–1328	Andronicus II
1328–41	Andronicus III
1341–76, 1379–91	John V
1376–9	Andronicus V
[1390	John VII]
1391–1425	Manuel II
1425–48	John VIII
1448–53	Constantine XI

* Joint Emperor; (W) Western Emperor; (E) Eastern Emperor

The Popes, Patriarchs of Rome

Peter, St, d. AD 64
Linus, St, c.66–c.78
Anacletus, St, c.79–c.91
Clement I, St, c.91–c.101
Evaristus I, St, c.100–c.109
Alexander I, St, c.109–c.116
Sixtus I, St, c.116–c.125
Telesphorus, St, c.125–c.136
Hyginus, St, c.138–c.142
Pius I, St, c.142–c.155
Anicetus, St, c.155–c.166
Soter, St, c.166–c.174
Eleutherius, St, c.174–89
Victor I, St, 189–98
Zephyrinus, St, 198/9–217
Callistus I, St, 217–22
[Hippolytus I, St, 217–35]
Urban I, St, 222–30
Pontian I, St, 230–5
Anterus, St, 235–6
Fabian, St, 236–50
Cornelius, St, 251–3
[Novatian, 251–8]
Lucius I, St, 253–4
Stephen I, St, 254–7
Sixtus II, St, 257–8
Dionysius, St, 260–8
Felix I, St, 269–74
Eutychian, St, 275–83
Gaius, St, 283–96
Marcellinus, St, 296–?304
Marcellus I, St, 306–8
Eusebius, St, 310
Miltiades, St, 311–14
Silvester I, St, 314–35
Mark, St, 336
Julius I, St, 337–52
Liberius, 352–66
[Felix II, St, 355–65]
Damasus I, St, 366–84
[Ursinus, 366–7]
Siricius, St, 384–99
Anastasius I, St, 399–401
Innocent I, St, 401–17
Zosimus, St, 417–18
Boniface I, St, 418–22
Celestine I, St, 422–32
Sixtus III, St, 432–40
Leo I, St, 440–61

Hilarus I, St, 461–8
Simplicius, St, 468–83
Felix III (II), St, 483–92
Gelasius I, St, 492–6
Anastasius II, 496–8
Symmachus, St, 498–514
[Lawrence, 498–9; 501–16]
Hormisdas, St, 514–23
John I, St, 523–6
Felix IV (III), St, 526–30
[Dioscorus, 530]
Boniface II, 530–2
John II, 533–5
Agapitus I, St, 535–6
Silverius, St, 536–7
Vigilius, 537–55
Pelagius I, 556–61
John III, 561–74
Benedict I, 575–9
Pelagius II, 579–90
Gregory I, St, 590–604
Sabinian 604–6
Boniface III, 607
Boniface IV, St, 608–15
Deusdedit (later Adeodatus I) St,
    615–18
Boniface V, 619–25
Honorius I, 625–38
Severinus, 640
John IV, 640–2
Theodore I, 642–9
Martin I, St, 649–53
Eugene I, St, 654–7
Vitalian, St, 657–72
Adeodatus II, 672–6
Donus, 67 3
Agatho, St, 678–81
Leo II, St, 682–3
Benedict II, St, 684–5
John V, 685–6
Conon, 686–7
[Theodore, 687]
[Paschal, 687]
Sergius I, St, 687–701
John VI, 701–5
John VII, 705–7
Sisinnius, 708
Constantine, 708–15
Gregory II, St, 715–31

Gregory III, St, 731–41
Zacharias, St, 741–52
Stephen (II), 752
Stephen II (III), 752–7
Paul I, St, 757–67
[Constantine, 767–8]
[Philip, 768]
Stephen III (IV), 768–72
Hadrian I, 772–95
Leo III, St, 795–816
Stephen IV (V), 816–17
Paschal I, St, 817–24
Eugene II, 824–7
Valentine, 827
Gregory IV, 827–44
[John, 844]
Sergius II, 844–7
Leo IV, St, 847–55
Benedict III, 855–8
[Anastasius Bibliothecarius, 855]
Nicholas I, St, 858–67
Hadrian II, 867–72
John VIII, 872–82
Marinus I, 882–4
Hadrian III, St, 884–5
Stephen V (VI), 885–91
Formosus, 891–6
Boniface VI, 896
Stephen VI (VII), 896–7
Romanus, 897
Theodore II, 897
John IX, 898–900
Benedict IV, 900–3
Leo V, 903
[Christopher, 903–4]
Sergius III, 904–11
Anastasius III, 911–13
Lando, 913–14
John X, 914–28
Leo VI, 928
Stephen VII (VIII), 928–31
John XI, 931–5
Leo VII, 936–9
Stephen VIII (IX), 939–42
Marinus II, 942–6
Agapitus II, 946–55
John XII, 955–64
Leo VIII, 963–5
[Benedict V, 964]

Antipopes in square brackets.

John XIII, 965–72
Benedict VI, 973–4
[Boniface VII, 974, 984–5]
Benedict VII, 974–83
John XIV, 983–4
John XV, 985–96
Gregory V, 996–9
[John XVI, 997–8]
Silvester II, 999–1003
John XVII, 1003
John XVIII, 1003–9
Sergius IV, 1009–12
Benedict VIII, 1012–24
[Gregory (VI), 1012]
John XIX, 1024–32
Benedict IX, 1032–44, 1045,
   1047–8
Silvester III, 1045
Gregory VI, 1045–6
Clement II, 1046–7
Damasus II, 1048
Leo IX, St, 1049–54
Victor II, 1055–7
Stephen IX (X), 1057–8
[Benedict X, 1058–9]
Nicholas II, 1058–61
Alexander II, 1061–73
[Honorius (II), 1061–4]
Gregory VII, St, 1073–85
[Clement III, 1080, 1084–1100]
Victor III, 1086–7
Urban II, 1088–99
Paschal II, 1099–1118
[Theoderic, 1100–1]
[Albert or Adalbert, 1101]
[Silvester IV, 1105–11]
Gelasius II, 1118–19
[Gregory (VIII), 1118–21]
Callistus II, 1119–24
Honorius II, 1124–30
[Celestine (II), 1124]
Innocent II, 1130–43
[Anacletus II, 1130–8]
[Victor IV, 1138]
Celestine II, 1143–4
Lucius II, 1144–5
Eugene III, 1145–53
Anastasius IV, 1153–4
Hadrian IV, 1154–9
Alexander III, 1159–81
[Victor IV, 1159–64]
[Paschal III, 1164–8]
[Callistus (III), 1168–78]

[Innocent (III), 1179–80]
Lucius III, 1181–5
Urban III, 1185–7
Gregory VIII, 1187
Clement III, 1187–91
Celestine III, 1191–8
Innocent III, 1198–1216
Honorius III, 1216–27
Gregory IX, 1227–41
Celestine IV, 1241
Innocent IV, 1243–54
Alexander IV, 1254–61
Urban IV, 1261–4
Clement IV, 1265–8
Gregory X, 1271–6
Innocent V, 1276
Hadrian V, 1276
John XXI, 1276–7
Nicholas III, 1277–80
Martin IV, 1281–5
Honorius IV, 1285–7
Nicholas IV, 1288–92
Celestine V, St Peter, 1294
Boniface VIII, 1294–1303
Benedict IX, 1303–4
Clement V, 1305–14
John XXII, 1316–34
[Nicholas (V), 1328–30]
Benedict XII, 1334–42
Clement VI, 1342–52
Innocent VI, 1352–62
Urban V, 1362–70
Gregory XI, 1370–8
Urban VI, 1378–89
[Clement (VII), 1378–94]
Boniface IX, 1389–1404
[Benedict (XIII), 1394–1417]
Innocent VII, 1404–6
Gregory XII, 1406–15
[Alexander V, 1409–10]
[John (XXIII), 1410–15]
Martin V, 1417–31
[Clement (VIII), 1423–9]
[Benedict (XIV), 1425]
Eugene IV, 1431–47
[Felix V, 1439–49]
Nicholas V, 1447–55
Callistus III, 1455–8
Pius II, 1458–64
Paul II, 1464–71
Sixtus IV, 1471–84
Innocent VIII, 1484–92
Alexander VI, 1492–1503

Pius III, 1503
Julius II, 1503–13
Leo X, 1513–21
Hadrian VI, 1522–3
Clement VII, 1523–34
Paul III, 1534–9
Julius III, 1550–5
Marcellus II, 1555
Paul IV, 1555–9
Pius IV, 1559–65
Pius V, St, 1566–72
Gregory XIII, 1572–85
Sixtus V, 1585–90
Urban VII, 1590
Gregory XIV, 1590–1
Innocent IX, 1591
Clement VIII, 1592–1605
Leo XI, 1605
Paul V, 1605–21
Gregory XV, 1621–3
Urban VIII, 1623–44
Innocent X, 1644–55
Alexander VII, 1655–67
Clement IX, 1667–9
Clement X, 1670–6
Innocent XI, 1676–89
Alexander VIII, 1689–91
Innocent XII, 1691–1700
Clement XI, 1700–21
Innocent XIII, 1721–4
Benedict XIII, 1724–30
Clement XII, 1730–40
Benedict XIV, 1740–58
Clement XIII, 1758–69
Clement XIV, 1769–74
Pius VI, 1775–99
Pius VII, 1800–23
Leo XII, 1823–9
Pius VIII, 1829–30
Gregory XVI, 1831–46
Pius IX, 1846–78
Leo XIII, 1878–1903
Pius X, St, 1903–14
Benedict XV, 1914–22
Pius XI, 1922–39
Pius XII, 1939–58
John XXIII, 1958–63
Paul VI, 1963–78
John Paul I, 1978
John Paul II, 1978–

Source: J. N. D. Kelly, *The Oxford Dictionary of Popes*, Oxford, 1988.

Palaeography

(*a*) Roman majuscule (Virgil, 4th–5th cents. AD). (*b*) Roman minuscule, mixed uncials (*Pandects*, 6th–7th cents.). (*c*) Lombardic or Beneventan cursive (Lectionary, Monte Cassino, 1058–87). (*d*) English pointed insular (*Anglo-Saxon Chronicle*, c.1045). (*e*) Carolingian minuscule, Latin (10th cent.). (*f*) *Littera fractura*, Gothic script (14th cent.). (*g*) Gothic rotunda (Horace, Cremona, 1391). (*h*) Greek papyrus (Timotheus, *Persae*, 4th cent. BC).

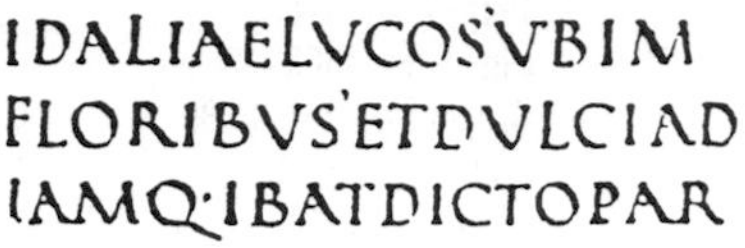

IDALIAELVCOSVBIM
FLORIBVS'ETDVLCIAD
IAMQ·IBATDICTOPAR

a.

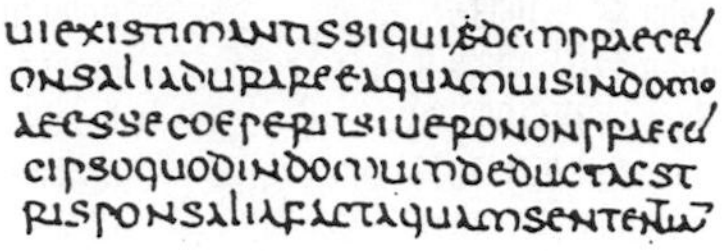

b.

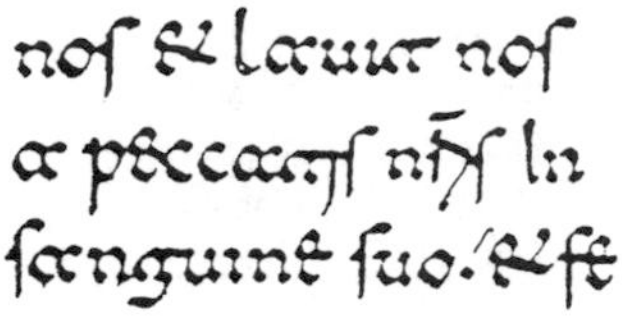

c.

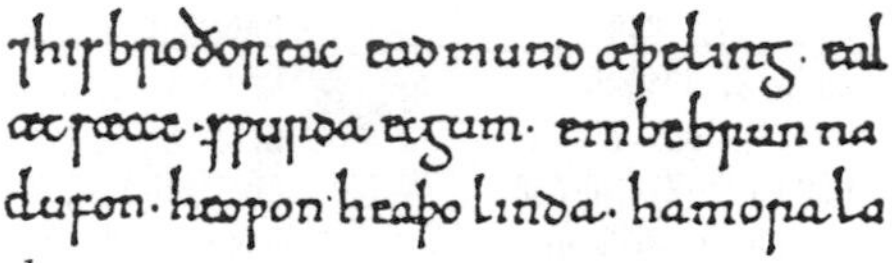

d.

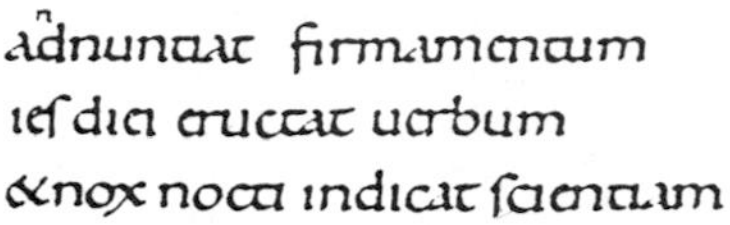

adnunciat firmamentum
iesdia eructat uerbum
&nox nocti indicat scientiam

e.

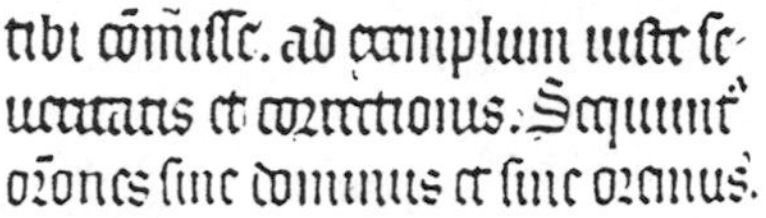

f.

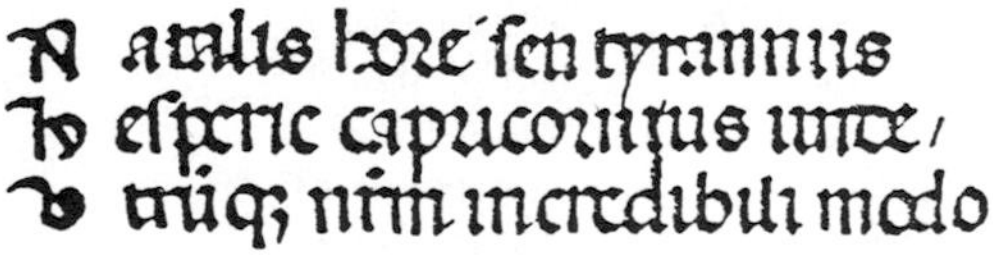

g.

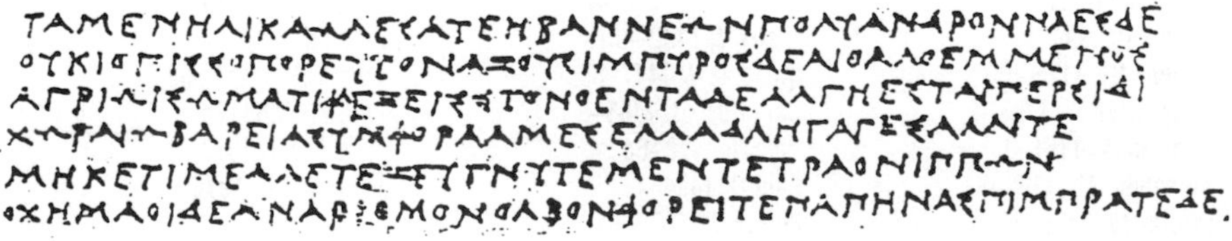

h.

(*i*) Greek 'biblical uncial' (1 Cor. 12; *Codex sinaiticus*, *c.*AD 350 ; after C. H. Roberts). (*j*) Greek cursive minuscules (*Iliad* vi, BM Townley MS, *c.*1255). (*k*) Glagolithic (Kiev Missal: 9th-cent. translation of a 7th-cent. Roman rite). (*l*) Bulgarian Cyrillic (*Savinna Kniga*, 11th cent., preserved at Pskov, Russia). (*m*) Serbian Cyrillic (15th cent. MS, Belgrade; after R. Auty). (*n*) Ottoman chancellery script (accounts from Podolia, late 17th cent., after D. Kołodejczyk).

i.

j.

k.

l.

m.

n.

Eagles and Crosses

Top row, left to right. (**a**) Double-headed Roman Eagle under a single crown, symbolizing the creation of the Eastern and Western Empires (after an inscription in Athens, 4th century AD). (**b**) Late Byzantine Eagle, from the throne of Sophia Palaeologos, Grand Duchess of Moscow, *c*.1470. (**c**) Charlemagne's Eagle, embroidered in silk on his cloak (9th century, after Frutiger). *Centre:* (**d**) The 'Small Coat-of-Arms' of the Russian Empire, 1914: crowned imperial double-headed black eagle holding orb and sceptre, with the arms of the city of Moscow in escutcheon and surmounted by the Romanov crown. The eagle's wings carry the arms of the Tsar's assumed titles (*dexter*: Kazan, the white eagle of Poland, Taurida and Kiev, Novgorod and Vladimir; *sinister*: Astrakhan, Siberia, Georgia, and Finland). *Bottom row, left to right.* (**e**) The 'Small Coat-of-Arms' of the Austrian Empire, 1915: crowned imperial double-headed black eagle holding orb and sword, with the red-white-red shield of Austria in escutcheon, ensigned by the Habsburg Crown. (**f**) Arms of the Albanian People's Republic, 1944. (**g**) Arms of the Kingdom of Spain, 1947: a black eagle bearing in escutcheon a crowned shield quartered with the arms of Castile and Leon, Aragon and Navarre, supported by a yoke, the pomegranate of Granada, and a sheaf of arrows, and surmounted by the slogan of the Falanga, 'One, Great, and Free'.

a.

b.

c.

d.

e.

f.

g.

1st row (left to right): Crux capitata, Crucifixion Cross or Latin Cross; *Crux decussata* or St Andrew's Cross; Greek Cross; St Peter's Cross; Cardinal's Cross or Cross of Lorraine; Templars' Cross or Disc Cross. *2nd row:* Papal Cross; Triple Cross; Orthodox Cross; Cross of Jerusalem; Germanic Cross; Heart Cross. *3rd row:* Cross of the Crusades; Gamma Cross; Sword Cross; Anchor Cross of Faith; Anchor Sign (Cross of Christ with the Virgin Mary's Crescent); Cloverleaf Cross. *4th row:* Chi-Rho sign (monogram of Christ); Cross of St John or Maltese Cross; Celtic Cross (Christian Cross within the Sun); Alpha Cross; Omega Cross; Leaf Cross. *5th row:* Resurrection Cross; modified Maltese Cross; Arrowhead Cross; Teutonic or Iron Cross; Polish Anchor Cross (*Polska walczy*, 'Poland fights'); Runic Circle Cross. *6th row:* Pagan Sun Cross; Runic Lightning Cross; clockwise *Gammadion, Fylfot,* or 'Swastika', signifying bad luck; anti-clockwise swastika, signifying good fortune. (After Frutiger.)

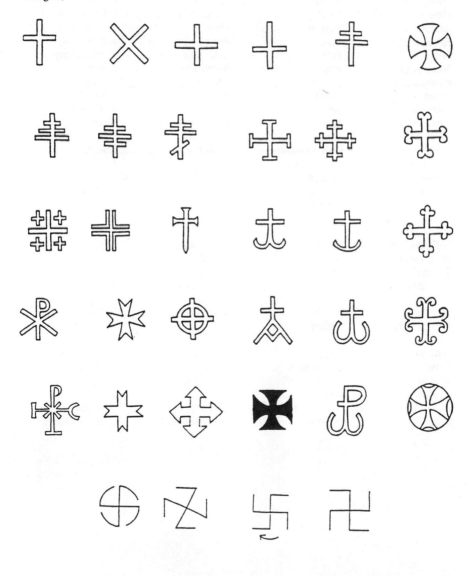

'The Great Books Scheme': The Chicago Canon of Western Civilization.

A list of authors proposed by Mortimer J. Adler, in 'Great Books, Past and Present', an Epilogue to G. van Doren (ed.), *Reforming Education: The Opening of the American Mind* (New York, 1988), 318–50.

Homer	Shakespeare	C. Lyell	B. Russell
Aeschylus	Galileo	A. Comte	Santayana
Sophocles	Kepler	Balzac	E. Gilson
Herodotus	W. Harvey	de Tocqueville	J.-P. Sartre
Euripides	Hobbes	J. S. Mill	J. Ortega y Gasset
Thucydides	Descartes	Darwin	Max Planck
Hippocrates	Milton	Dickens	Einstein
Aristophanes	Molière	C. Bernard	N. Bohr
Plato	Pascal	Kierkegaard	E. Schrodinger
Aristotle	Huygens	Marx	J. H. Woodger
Epicurus	Spinoza	George Eliot	J.-H. Poincaré
Euclid	Locke	H. Melville	T. Dobzhansky
Archimedes	Racine	Dostoevsky	G. Sorel
Apollonius	Newton	Flaubert	Trotsky
Cicero	Leibniz	Ibsen	Lenin
Lucretius	Defoe	Tolstoy	W. Sumner
Virgil	Swift	J. W. R. Dedekind	Max Weber
Plutarch	Congreve	M. Twain	R. H. Tawney
Tacitus	Bishop Berkeley	W. James	T. Veblen
Nicomachus	Montesquieu	Nietzsche	J. M. Keynes
Epictetus	Voltaire	G. Cantor	
Ptolemy	Fielding	Freud	*1945–1977*
M. Aurelius	Johnson	D. Hilbert	A. Camus
Galen	Hume		G. Orwell
St Augustine	Rousseau	*1900–1945*	T. Pynchon
St Thomas Aquinas	Sterne	G. B. Shaw	Solzhenitsyn
Dante Alighieri	Adam Smith	James Joyce	S. Bellow
Chaucer	Kant	Proust	S. Beckett
Machiavelli	Gibbon	T. Mann	Wittgenstein
Erasmus	Boswell	Joseph Conrad	Heidegger
Copernicus	Lavoisier	Faulkner	M. Buber
Thomas More	Goethe	D. H. Lawrence	W. Heisenberg
Luther	Dalton	T. S. Eliot	J. Monod
Rabelais	Hegel	Kafka	R. P. Feynman
Calvin	Jane Austen	Chekhov	S. Hawking
Montaigne	von Clausewitz	O'Neill	A. Toynbee
W. Gilbert	Stendhal	Henry James	C. Lévi-Strauss
Cervantes	Schopenhauer	Kipling	F. Braudel
Bacon	Faraday	J. Dewey	E. Le Roy Ladurie
		A. N. Whitehead	

Ancient Illyricum and Napoleon's Illyrian Provinces

| Illyrian Provinces 1809–13 | – – – Roman provincial boundaries |

0   kilometres   150
0   miles   100

Modern names of Roman cities:

Aquincum (Buda)
Aspalathos (Split)
Dyrrachium/Epidamnus (Dürres)
Emona (Ljubljana)
Lindia (Linz)
Naissus (Nis)
Ovilava (Weils)
Raetinium (Bihac)
Savaria (Szombathely)
Scodra (Shkodra)

Scupi (Skopje)
Senia (Senj)
Singidunum (Belgrade)
Sirmium (Metrovica)
Siscia (Sisak)
Siscia Segestia (Zagreb)
Tergiste (Trieste)
Vindobona (Vienna)
Zara (Zadar)

From AD 395, an enlarged dual Prefecture of Illyricum was created from the provinces of Pannonia, Dalmatia, and Macedonia: capitals Sirmium and Salonica

Proto-Indo-European*

West   **East**

Celtic   **Germanic**   **Hellenic**   **Italic**   **Anatolian**

Goidelic   **Brythonic**

Anglo-Frisian   **East Germanic**   **Scandin-avian**

Romance   **Tocharian**

Balto-Slavonic   **Armenian**   **Albanian**   **Indo-Iranian**

Slavonic   **Baltic**

Iranian   **Dardic**   **Indic**

Goidelic:
Erse
Gaelic
Manx*
Old Irish*

Brythonic:
Welsh
Breton
Cornish*
Gaullish*

Anglo-Frisian:
Frisian
Anglo-Saxon*
Middle English*
English
Scots
Pidgin

East Germanic:
Gothic*

Scandinavian:
Old Norse*
Icelandic
Faroese
Norwegian
Danish
Swedish

High German
Old High German*
Middle High German*
Standard Hochdeutsch
Yiddish

Low German
Platdeutsch
Dutch (Nederlands)
Vlaamsch (Flemish)
Afrikaans

German

Hellenic:
Classical Greek*
Hellenistic Koiné*
Modern Greek
Demotic

Italic:
Latin*

Romance:
Classical Latin*
Vulgar Latin*

Portuguese
Galego

Castilian Spanish
Catalan

French
Romanz
Oecitan/Provençal
Québecois
Acadian
Old French*

Italian
Neapolitan
Sicilian
Sardinian
Dalmatian*

Romanian
Moldavian

Rheto-Romance
Ladin
Friulian

Anatolian:
Hittite*

Slavonic:
Proto-Slavonic*

Baltic:
Ancient Prussian*
Lithuanian
Latvian

Iranian:
Avesta*
Pharsee
Kurdish
Baluchi
Pushtu
Ossetian

Dardic:

Indic:
Sanskrit*
Prakrit*
Pali*
Hindustani
Hindi
Urdu
Gujurati
Bengali
Punjabi
Bihari
Marathi
Rajasthani
Sindi
Oriya
Singhalese
Romany

Non-Indo-European Languages spoken in Europe

Basque
Maltese
Etruscan*

Finno-Ugrian
Finnish
Estonian
Lapp
Karelian
Cheremiss
Mordvin

Hunnic*
Mongol
Tartar
Magyar
Permian
Ostyak

Altaic
Turkish
Tartar

North Caucasian
Abkhaz
Chechen
Avar

South Caucasian
Laz
Mingrelian
Georgian

* = language no longer spoken

The Indo-European Languages

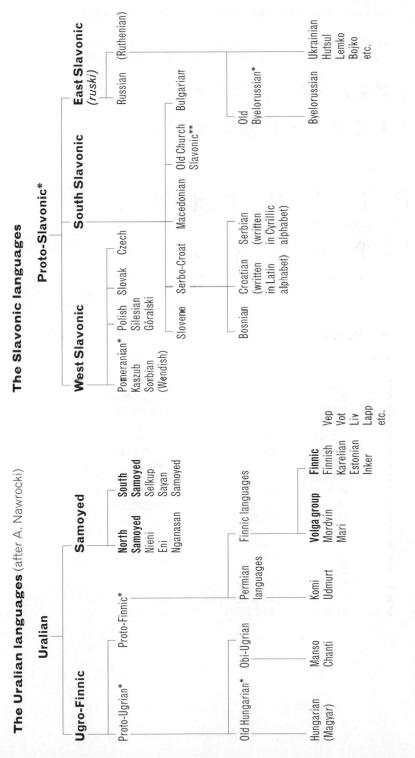

The Uralian languages (after A. Nawrocki)

The Slavonic languages

The Slavonic and Uralian Language Groups (after A. Nawrocki)

* = language no longer spoken

** = Liturgical language

Runes and Oghams

(*a*) The 33-sign Northumbrian Rune-stave containing earlier 24- and 29-sign staves common in England.

(*b*) The 18-sign Armanen Rune-stave, a modern reconstruction of the most ancient Germanic runic system; and (*below*) possible divinatory connotations (after N. Pennick).

a.

Fa	Ursache	Thor	Os	Rit	Ka	Hagal	Not	Is

Ar	Sig	Tyr	Bar	Laf	Man	Yr	Eh	Gibor

b.

The Armanen Runes

number	letter	name	symbol	connotation
(1)	F	FA	CATTLE	Wealth
(2)	U	UR	PRIMAL OX	Creative Power
(3)	Th	THURS	THORN TREE	Lightning/Sudden change
(4)	A	OS	MOUTH	Wisdom
(5)	R	RAD/RIT	WHEEL	Journey
(6)	K	CEN/KA	PINE-TORCH	Fire/Regeneration
(7)	H	HAGAL	HAIL	Delay
(8)	N	NOT/NYD	—	Caution
(9)	I	IS	ICE	Inertia
(10)	Y	AR	SERPENT	Necessary Evil
(11)	S	SIG/SIGEL	SUNBEAM	Light/Victory
(12)	T	TYR	ARROWHEAD	Success
(13)	B	BAR	BIRCH	Purity/Rebirth
(14)	L	LAF	WATER	Lifeforce
(15)	M	MAN	MAN	Humanity
(16)	—	YR	YEW, BOW	Skill
(17)	Kh	EH	CHALICE (Inverted)	Death
(18)	G	GA/GIBOR	ODIN'S SPEAR	Axle, Fulcrum

(*c*) The Basic Irish Ogham-stave.
(*d*) An Irish 'Bardic Alphabet'; and (below) possible divinatory connotations (after N. Pennick).

B L F   S N H D T C Q M G Ng ST R   A O U E I Ea Oi Ui Ia Ao

c.

A   B   C   D   E   F   G   H   I   K   L   F

M   N   O   Q   P   S   T   U   Y   A' I'

d.

The Irish Ogham Alphabet: the *beithe-luis*

letter	*tree*		*bird*		*colour*	*dates*
B	beithe	*birch*	besan	*pheasant*	White	24 Dec.–20 Jan.
L	luis	*rowan*	laoha	*duok*	Light Grey	21 Jan.–17 Feb.
N	nion	*ash*	naoscach	*snipe*	Transparent	18 Feb.–18 Mar.
F	fearn	*alder*	faoileán	*gull*	Crimson	19 Mar.–14 Apr.
S	saileach	*willow*	seabhac	*hawk*	Fire	15 Apr.–12 May
H	(h)uath	*hawthorn*	(h)adaig	*night crow*	Earth	13 May–9 Jun.
D	dair	*oak*	dreoilin	*wren*	Black	10 Jun.–7 Jul.
T	tinne	*holly*	truit	*starling*	Grey	8 Jul.–4 Aug.
C	coll	*hazel*	corr	*crane*	Brown	5 Aug.–1 Sept.
M	muin	*vine*	meantán	*titmouse*	Motley	2 Sept.–29 Sept.
G	gort	*ivy*	géis	*mute swan*	Blue	30 Sept.–27 Oct.
Ng	(n)getal	*broom*	(n)gé	*goose*	Green	28 Oct.–25 Nov.
R	ruis	*elder*	rocnat	*rook*	Blood-red	26 Nov.–23 Dec.
A	ailme	*pine*	airdhircleog	*lapwing*	Piebald	Winter Solstice, 1
O	onn	*furze*	odoroscrach	*cormorant*	Dun	Vernal Equinox
U	úr	*heather*	uiseóg	*skylark*	Resin	Summer Solstice
E	edad	*poplar*	ela	*whistling swan*	Red	Autumn Equinox
I	iúr	*yew*	illait	*eaglet*	White	Winter Solstice, 2

B = Birchday/Sunday; S = Willowday/Monday; T = Hollyday/Tuesday; N = Ashday/Wednesday; D = Oakday/Thursday; Q = Appleday/Friday; F = Alderday/Saturday

After C. J. Marstrander *et al.* (eds.), *Dictionary of the Irish Language* (Dublin, 1913–76), 4 vols.

The Christianization of Europe

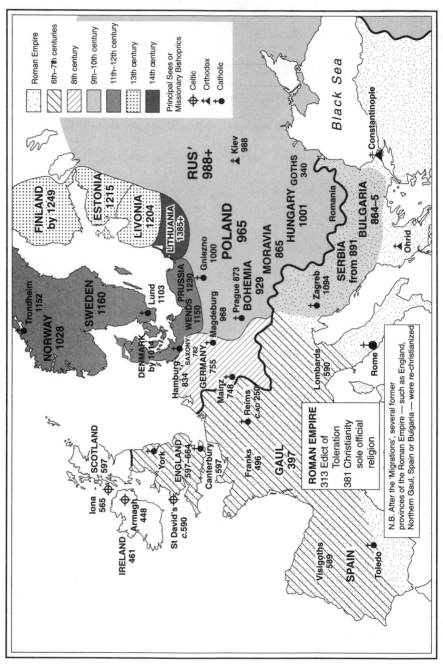

Legend:
- Roman Empire
- 6th–7th centuries
- 8th century
- 9th–10th century
- 11th–12th century
- 13th century
- 14th century

Principal Sees or Missionary Bishoprics
- ⊕ Celtic
- ⚔ Orthodox
- † Catholic

Black Sea

† Constantinople

⚔ Kiev 988

RUS' 988+

FINLAND by 1249

ESTONIA 1215

LIVONIA 1204

LITHUANIA 1385+

POLAND 965

HUNGARY 1001

GOTHS 340

Romania

BULGARIA 864–5

Gniezno 1000

† Prussia 1230

WENDS 1150

Prague 873

BOHEMIA 929

MORAVIA 865

Zagreb 1094

SERBIA from 891

⚔ Ohrid

Trondheim 1152

SWEDEN 1160

† Lund 1103

NORWAY 1028

DENMARK by 1014

SAXONY 782

Hamburg 834

GERMANY 755

Magdeburg 968

Mainz 748

Reims c.AD 250

Lombards 590

● Rome

SCOTLAND 597

York

ENGLAND 597–664

Canterbury 597

Franks 496

GAUL 397

Iona 565

Armagh 448

St David's c.590

IRELAND 461

Visigoths 589

SPAIN

† Toledo

ROMAN EMPIRE
313 Edict of Toleration
381 Christianity sole official religion

N.B. After the 'Migrations', several former provinces of the Roman Empire — such as England, Northern Gaul, Spain or Bulgaria — were re-christianized

The Byzantine Empire

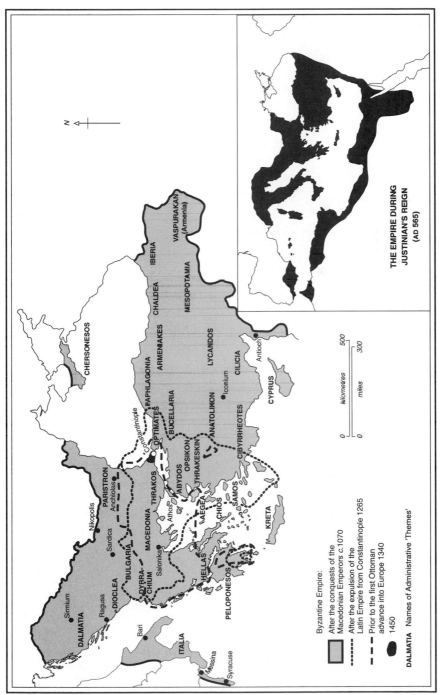

Byzantine Empire:

After the conquests of the
Macedonian Emperors c.1070

After the expulsion of the
Latin Empire from Constantinople 1265

Prior to the first Ottoman
advance into Europe 1340

1450

DALMATIA   Names of Administrative 'Themes'

THE EMPIRE DURING
JUSTINIAN'S REIGN
(AD 565)

Europe's Cultural Circles: an Interpretation (after M. Shennan)

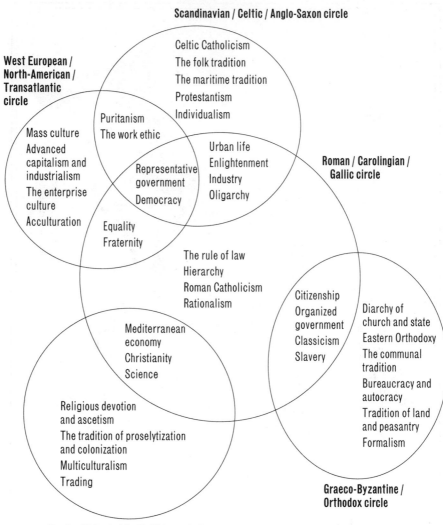

Scandinavian / Celtic / Anglo-Saxon circle

**West European /
North-American /
Transatlantic
circle**

Celtic Catholicism
The folk tradition
The maritime tradition
Protestantism
Individualism

Puritanism
The work ethic

Mass culture
Advanced
capitalism and
industrialism
The enterprise
culture
Acculturation

Urban life
Enlightenment
Industry
Oligarchy

**Roman / Carolingian /
Gallic circle**

Representative
government
Democracy

Equality
Fraternity

The rule of law
Hierarchy
Roman Catholicism
Rationalism

Mediterranean
economy
Christianity
Science

Citizenship
Organized
government
Classicism
Slavery

Diarchy of
church and state
Eastern Orthodoxy
The communal
tradition
Bureaucracy and
autocracy
Tradition of land
and peasantry
Formalism

Religious devotion
and ascetism
The tradition of proselytization
and colonization
Multiculturalism
Trading

**Graeco-Byzantine /
Orthodox circle**

Iberian / Islamic / North African circle

The Frankish Empire, AD 800–77

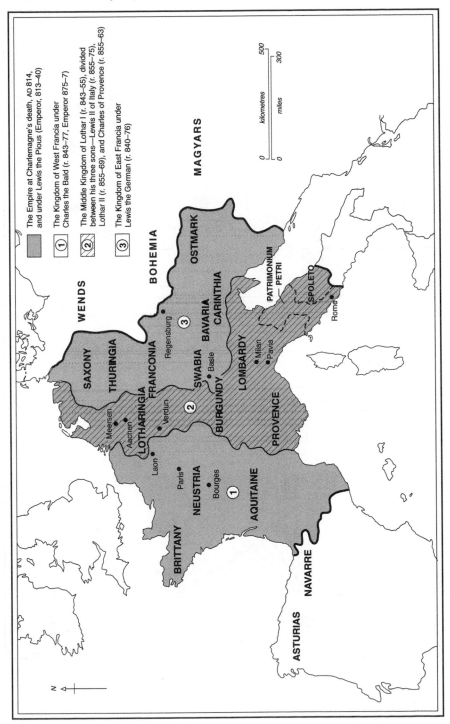

The Empire at Charlemagne's death, AD 814, and under Lewis the Pious (Emperor, 813–40)

(1) The Kingdom of West Francia under Charles the Bald (r. 843–77, Emperor 875–7)

(2) The Middle Kingdom of Lothar I (r. 843–55), divided between his three sons—Lewis II of Italy (r. 855–75), Lothar II (r. 855–69), and Charles of Provence (r. 855–63)

(3) The Kingdom of East Francia under Lewis the German (r. 840–76)

500 kilometres

300 miles

MAGYARS

OSTMARK

BOHEMIA

WENDS

CARINTHIA

PATRIMONIUM PETRI

SPOLETO

SAXONY

THURINGIA

BAVARIA

Regensburg

SWABIA

FRANCONIA

Basle

LOMBARDY

Milan

Pavia

Rome

LOTHARINGIA

Meersen

Aachen

Verdun

BURGUNDY

PROVENCE

Laon

Paris

Bourges

NEUSTRIA

AQUITAINE

BRITTANY

NAVARRE

ASTURIAS

N

Khazaria at its Greatest Extent, *c.* AD 900

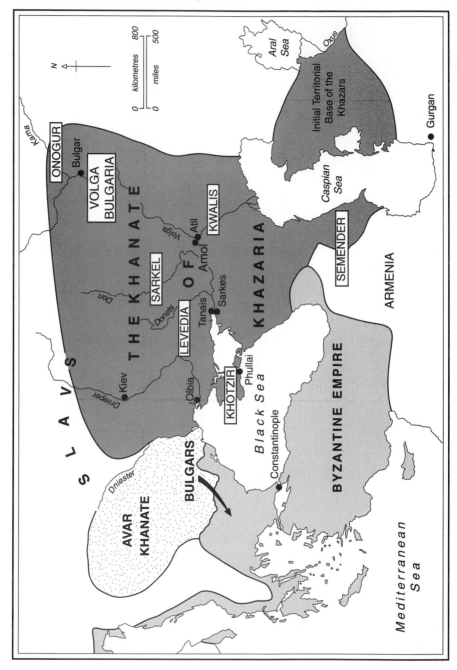

The Christian *Reconquista* in Iberia, 850–1493

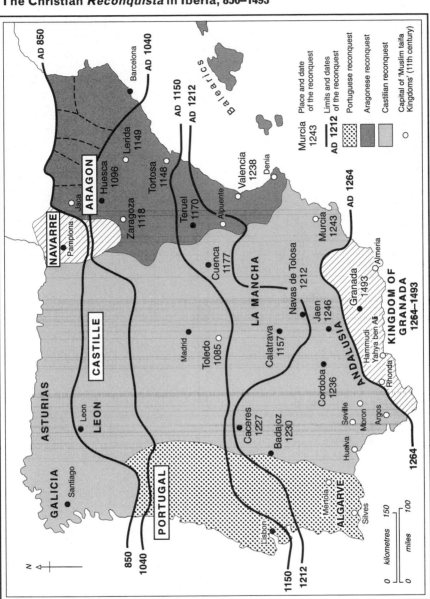

Murcia 1243 — Place and date of the reconquest

AD 1212 — Limits and dates of the reconquest

Portuguese reconquest

Aragonese reconquest

Castilian reconquest

○ Capital of 'Muslim taifa Kingdoms' (11th century)

AD 850
AD 1040
AD 1150
AD 1212
AD 1264

Barcelona
Lerida 1149
Huesca 1096
Tortosa 1148
Valencia 1238
Denia
Teruel 1170
Alpuente
Zaragoza 1118
Jaca
ARAGON
NAVARRE
Pamplona
Cuenca 1177
Murcia 1243
Almeria
Navas de Tolosa 1212
LA MANCHA
Jaen 1246
Granada 1493
KINGDOM OF GRANADA 1264–1493
Madrid
Toledo 1085
Calatrava 1157
Cordoba 1236
Hammudi Yahya ben Ai
Rhonda
ASTURIAS
Leon
LEON
CASTILLE
ANDALUSIA
Caceres 1227
Badajoz 1230
Seville
Moron
Argos
Huelva
GALICIA
Santiago
PORTUGAL
Mertola
ALGARVE
Silves
Lisbon

850
1040
1150
1212
1264

N

Balearics

0 kilometres 150
0 miles 100

Numerals and Mathematical Notation

(1) *Numerals:* (*a*) Phoenician (1st millennium BC), based on Egyptian hieroglyphic numerals, and similar to the Minoan system. (*b*) Greek (from 350 BC), a literal system, and a close counterpart to Hebrew numerals. (*c*) Roman. (*d*) North Indian (Sanskrit, 1st millennium AD). (*e*) Eastern Arabic (10th cent.). (*f*) Iberian Arabic (11th cent.). (*g*) Renaissance calligraphic. (*h*) Modern standard printed numerals. (*i*) Contemporary seven-bar digital. (After F. Cajori, A. Frutiger.)

1	2	3	4	5	6	7	8	9	10	20	100

(2) The Origins of Standard Mathematical Notation: A Selection.
(After Cajori.)

Sign		Date	Probable first use
L	latus, square root	—	Roman
½	fractional line	1202	Leonardo da Pisa, *Liber abbaci*
%	per cent	1425	Italian commercial usage
+	(et) plus	1489	J. Widman, *Behennde und hubsche Rechnung auf*
−	minus	1489	*allen Kaufmanschaften*
p̃	plus	1494	Luca Pacioli, *Summa de arithmetica* (Venice)
m̃	minus	1494	
M	multiplicatio	1544	M. Stifel, *Arithmetica integra* (Germany)
D	divisio		
=	equality	1557	R. Recorde, *Ground of Artes* (Oxford)
•	decimal fraction	1585	Simon Stevin, *La thiende* (Antwerp)
±	plus/minus	1626	J. Girard (France)
×	multiplication	1631	W. Oughtred, *Clavis mathematica* (London)
∷	proportion	1631	
∽	difference	1631	
>	greater than	1631	T. Harriot, *Artis analyticae praxis* (London)
<	less than	1631	
x^2	powers	1634	P. Herigone, *Cursus mathematicus* (Paris)
∞	infinity	1655	J. Wallis, *De sectionibus conicis* (Oxford)
∼	similar	1655	
÷	division	1659	J. H. Rahn, *Teutsche Algebra* (Nuremberg)
∴	therefore	1659	
:	ratio	1669	V. Wing, *Astronomica britannica* (London)
√	square root	1669	
π	pi	1706	W. Jones, *Synopsis palmariorum matheseos*
( )	aggregation	1726	J. Herman, *Commentarii*, i (St Petersburg)
e	logarithm base	1736	L. Euler, *Mechanica*, i
E	Euler's Number	1736	
C	Euler's Constant	1736	L. Euler, *Commentarii* (St Petersburg)
∫	summa, number theory	1750	L. Euler, *De numeris amicalibus*
Σ	summation	1755	L. Euler, *Institutiones calculi differentialis*
≡	congruence	1801	F. Gauss, *Disquisitiones arithmeticae*
∵	since, because	1805	*Gentleman's Mathematical Companion*

The Growth of the Royal Domain in France, to 1547

PICARDY
AND
FLANDERS
to 1483

Calais

ARTOIS
(Arras to 1494)

BRABANT

LUXEMBOURG

Rouen

Reims

**NORMANDIE
1453**

Paris
ILE DE
FRANCE

**CHAMPAGNE
1453**

LORRAINE

**BRETAGNE
1497**

**MAINE
1453**

**ANJOU
1482**

**BLOIS
1453**

Orléans

**FRANCHE-COMTÉ
1678**

Dijon

**TOURAINE
1482**

**BERRY
1416**

**BOURGOGNE
1477**

**POITOU
1416**

SAINTONGE

**MARCHE
1531**

**BOURBON
1523**

**PÉRIGORD
1453**

**LYONNAIS
1312** Lyon

SAVOY

LANGUE D'OÏL
LANGUE D'OC

N

Bordeaux

**AUVERGNE
1523**

**DAUPHINÉ
1349**

**GUYENNE
(AQUITAINE)
1453**

Comtat
Venaissin
(to Papacy)

Toulouse

**PROVENCE
1491**

Marseilles

**GASCOGNE
1453**

**LANGUEDOC
1271**

NAVARRE

0   kilometres   250

0   miles   150

ARAGON   ROUSSILLON

The Capetian royal
domaine 987

- - - - Linguistic frontier

——— Frontier 1547

Greatest extent of
English control during
100 Years War (1429)

NORMANDIE Ancient Provinces of
France with dates of their
recovery or acquisition by
the French Crown

Bulgaria, Medieval and Modern

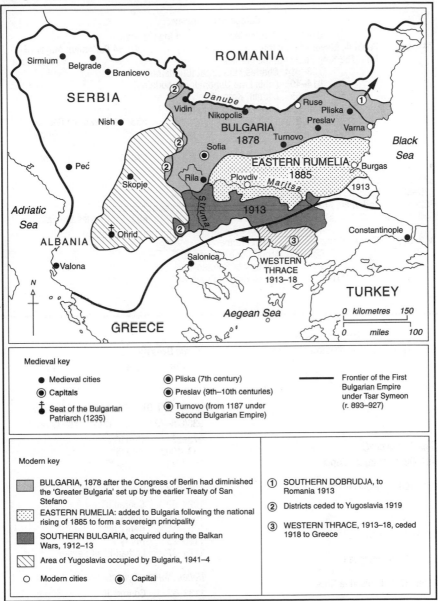

Medieval key

- **Medieval cities**
- ◉ **Capitals**
- ✝ **Seat of the Bulgarian Patriarch (1235)**

- ◉ Pliska (7th century)
- ◉ Preslav (9th–10th centuries)
- ◉ Turnovo (from 1187 under Second Bulgarian Empire)

— Frontier of the First Bulgarian Empire under Tsar Symeon (r. 893–927)

Modern key

BULGARIA, 1878 after the Congress of Berlin had diminished the 'Greater Bulgaria' set up by the earlier Treaty of San Stefano

EASTERN RUMELIA: added to Bulgaria following the national rising of 1885 to form a sovereign principality

SOUTHERN BULGARIA, acquired during the Balkan Wars, 1912–13

Area of Yugoslavia occupied by Bulgaria, 1941–4

○ Modern cities   ◉ Capital

① SOUTHERN DOBRUDJA, to Romania 1913

② Districts ceded to Yugoslavia 1919

③ WESTERN THRACE, 1913–18, ceded 1918 to Greece

German Emperors and Kings of France

Carolingian Dynasty

	d741	Charles Martel, Duke of the Franks

741–68 Pepin III, Mayor of Neustria
    from 752 King Pepin I of the Franks

741–54 Carloman, Mayor of
                    Austrasia

	768–814	Charles I the Great (Charlemagne*)
	814–40	Louis I the Debonair of Aquitaine*
	840–55	Lothair, King of Italy*
	855–75	Lewis II, King of Italy*

855–76 Lewis the German of
                    Bavaria, King of
                    Germany
876–82 Lewis the Saxon

875–7	Charles II le Chauve, King of Neustria*
877–9	Louis II, King of France
879–82	Louis III, King of France
882–4	Carloman, King of France

882–5   Charles the Fat*

	891–4	Wido of Spoleto*
893–928	Charles III the Simple, King of France
	887–99	Arnulf, King of Germany*
	896–9	Lambert of Spoleto*
	901–5	Lewis, King of Provence*

KINGDOM OF FRANCE

928–54	Louis IV d'Outremer, King of France
954–85	Lothair, King of France
986–7	Louis V, le Faineant, King of France

Capetian Dynasty

987–96	Hugues Capet
996–1031	Robert le Pieux
1031–60	Henri I
1060–1108	Philippe I
1108–37	Louis VI le Gros
1137–80	Louis VII
1180–1223	Philippe-Auguste
1223–6	Louis VIII
1226–70	Louis IX, St.

Saxon Dynasty

918–36	Henry I, the Fowler, King of Germany

HOLY ROMAN EMPIRE

936(62)–73	Otto I,* The Great
973–83	Otto II*
983–1002	Otto III*
1002–24	Henry II*

Salian or Franconian Dynasty

1024–39	Conrad II*
1039–56	Henry III*
1056–1106	Henry IV*
1106–25	Henry V*
1125–37	Lothair II* of Saxony

Hohenstauffen Dynasty

1138–52	Conrad III
1152–90	Frederick I Barbarossa*
[1177–80	Rudolf of Swabia]
[1081–8	Hermann of Luxemburg]
1190–7	Henry VI*
1198–1218	Otto IV* of Brunswick (Guelph)
[1198–1208	Philip of Hohenstaufen]
1211–50	Frederick II*
[1246–50	Henry Raspe of Thuringia]
[1247–56	William of Holland]

* Crowned Emperors   [ ] = anti-Emperors, or unconfirmed electees

KINGDOM OF FRANCE

HOLY ROMAN EMPIRE

1250–4	Conrad I
[1257–72	Richard of Cornwall]
[1257–75	Alfonso X of Castile]
1273–91	Rudolf I of Habsburg

1270–85	Philippe III le Hardi
1285–1314	Philippe IV le Bel

1292–8	Adolph of Nassau
1298–1308	Albert I of Habsburg
1308–13	Henry VII* of Luxemburg

1314–16	Louis X
1316–22	Philippe V

1314–47	Lewis IV* of Wittelsbach
	= Matilda of Habsburg
[1314–30	Frederick the Fair of Habsburg]

Valois Dynasty

1322–8	Charles IV
1328–50	Philippe VI
1350–64	Jean Le Bon
1364–80	Charles V le Sage
1380–1422	Charles VI le Simple

1346–78	Charles IV* of Luxemburg
[1349	Gunther of Schwartzburg]
1378–1400	Wenceslas of Luxemburg
1400–10	Rupert of the Palatinate
1410–37	Sigismund* of Luxemburg
[1410–11	Jobst of Moravia]

1422–61	Charles VII le Bien Aimé

Habsburg Dynasty

1438–9	Albert II
1440–93	Frederick III

1461–83	Louis XI
1483–98	Charles VIII

1493–1519	Maximilian I*

1498–1515	Louis XII

1519–56	Charles V*

1515–47	Francis I

1556–64	Ferdinand I*
1564–76	Maximilian II*
1576–1612	Rudolf II*

1547–59	Henri II
1559–60	Francis II
1560–74	Charles IX
1574–89	Henri III

1612–37	Ferdinand II*
1637–57	Ferdinand III*
1658–1705	Leopold I*
1705–11	Joseph I*
1711–40	Charles VI*
1742–5	Charles VII* of Bavaria
1745–65	Francis I* of Lorraine = Maria
	Theresa, Habsburg
1765–90	Joseph II*

Bourbon Dynasty

1589–1610	Henri IV

1610–43	Louis XIII

1643–1715	Louis XIV

1790–2	Leopold II*
1792–1806	Francis II* (Francis I)

1715–74	Louis XV

Habsburg Emperors of Austria

1804–35	Francis I*
1835–48	Ferdinand I*

1774–93	Louis XVI
1793–5	Louis XVII

1848–1916	Francis-Joseph I*

Napoleonic Empire

1804–15	Napoleon I*

Bourbon Restoration

1814–24	Louis XVIII
1824–30	Charles X
1830–48	Louis-Philippe

1916–18	Charles I*

Hohenzollern Emperors of Germany

Napoleonic Restoration

1852–70	Napoleon III*

1871–88	William I* of Prussia
1888	Frederick III*
1888–1918	William II*

European University Foundations, 1088–1912

Bologna	1088	Catania	1434–44	Besançon	1691
Paris	c.1150	Barcelona	1450	Halle	1693
Oxford	1167	Glasgow	1451	Breslau	1702
Salerno*	1173	Valence	1452	Dijon	1722
Palenzia	c.1178	Greifswald	1456	Camerino	1727
Reggio	1188	Freiburg	1457	Göttingen	1733
Vicenza	1204	Basel	1459	Erlangen	1743
Cambridge*	1209	Ingolstadt	1459 (1472)	Moscow	1755
Salamanca	1218–19	Nantes	1460	Ljubljana	1774
Padua	1222	Bourges	1463	Zagreb*	1776
Naples	1224	Bratislava (Pressburg)	1465	Palermo*	1779
Vercelli	1228	Genoa*	1471	Lemberg (Lwów)	1784
Toulouse	1229	Trier	1452 (1473)	Kharkov	1804
Piacenza	1248	Saragossa	1474	Kazan	1804
Valladolid	c.1237	Mainz	1476	Lille	1808
Seville	1254	Tübingen	1476	Lyons	1808
Arezzo*	1255	Uppsala	1477	Rennes	1808
Montpellier*	1289	Copenhagen	1475 (1479)	Berlin	1810
Lisbon	1290	Palma	1483	Christiania (Oslo)	1811
Macerata	13th cent.	Aberdeen	1495	Genoa*	1812
Lerida	1300	Frankfurt/Oder	1498	Ghent	1815
Rome	1303	Alcala	1499	Liège*	1815
Avignon	1303	Valencia	1500	Warsaw	1816
Orléans	1306	Wittenberg	1502	Bonn	1818
Perugia	1308	Avila	1504	St Petersburg	1819
Coimbra	1308	Marburg	1527	Madrid	1822
Treviso	1318	Granada	1531	London	1826
Cahors	1332	Königsberg	1544	Munich*	1826
Angers	1337	Jena	1558	Zurich*	1832
Grenoble	1339 (1542)	Geneva	1559 (1876)	Durham	1832
Pisa	1343	Olomouc	1570	Bern*	1834
Prague	1347	Leiden	1572	Brussels*	1834
Perpignan	1350	Oviedo	1574 (1608)	Kiev	1834
Huesca	1354	Helmstedt	1575	Athens	1837
Sienna*	1357	Vilnius	1578	Messina	1838
Pavia	1361	Altdorf*	1578	Munster*	1843
Kraków	1364 (1400)	Edinburgh	1582	Queen's Belfast	1850
Vienna	1365	Graz	1586	Marseille	1854
Orange	1365	Dublin	1592	Iasi	1860
Pecs (Fünfkirchen)	1367	Cagliari	1596	Bucharest	1864
Erfurt	1379	Harderwijk	1600	Odessa	1865
Heidelberg	1385	Giessen	1607	Cluj	1872
Cologne	1388	Groningen	1614	Czernowitz	1875
Buda (Ofen)	1389	Rinteln	1621	Amsterdam	1877
Ferrara	1391	Strasbourg*	1621	Stockholm	1877
Barcelona	1401 (1450)	Salzburg	1623	Manchester	1880
Wurzburg	1402	Dorpat	1632	Birmingham	1880
Turin	1404	Utrecht	1634	Fribourg	1889
Aix-en-Provence	1409	Sassari	1634	Lausanne*	1891
Leipzig	1409	Pest (Tyrnau) Nagyszembat	1635	Wales*	1893
St Andrews	1411	Abo (Helsinki)	1640	Constantinople	1900
Rostock	1419	Bamberg	1648	Leeds*	1904
Dole	1422	Durham	1657 (1837)	Liverpool*	1904
Louvain	1425	Kiel	1665	Sofia*	1904
Poitiers	1431	Lund	1666	Belgrade*	1905
Caen	1432	Innsbruck	1672	Bristol	1909
Bordeaux	1441	Modena*	1683	Debrecen*	1912

Main source: L. Jílek (ed.), *Historical Compendium of European Universities* (Geneva, 1983).
* University founded from an older institution   (dates) in brackets indicate refoundations.

The Partitions of Kievan Rus'

Lithuania absorbed the whole of Western Rus'(Ruthenia), including Kiev, following the Mongol invasions, but was obliged to surrender Ukraina to Poland in 1569.

Moscow assumed hegemony over the eastern parts of Rus' from the 14th century onwards, following the conquest of western Rus' (Ruthenia) by Lithuania. In the first stage Moscow aimed to conquer all the other principalities in the region, notably Novgorod.

Ladoga

NOVGOROD

Pskov

to MUSCOVY

TVER

VLADIMIR

Bulgar

VILNIUS

POLOTSK

to LITHUANIA

MOSCOW

Minsk

SMOLENSK

RYAZAN

NOVGOROD-SEVERSKY

WARSAW

Kursk

Volga

TUROV

to UKRAINA

POLAND   KIEV

L'viv

PEREYASLAV

Don

HALICZ
(Galicia)

The Kingdom of Poland was in personal union with Lithuania from 1385 under the Jagiellonian kings. From 1569, it took over the southern parts of Rus' (Ukraina) at the time of the formation of the Polish-Lithuanian *Rzeczpospolita* or Republic.

Dnieper

CRIMEA

Black Sea

	Maximum extent of the Kievan State (10th–13th centuries)
	Early medieval principalities
	Seat of Orthodox Metropolitan

In the second stage Moscow's ambition was to conquer all the lands of Rus'. This process lasted from 1667 (Kiev) to 1945 (Western Ukraine).

| 0 | kilometres | 400 |
| 0 | miles | 250 |

Timekeeping in History: a graph illustrating the rate of increase in the accuracy of timekeeping that has occurred since the invention of the first mechanical clock around AD 1300

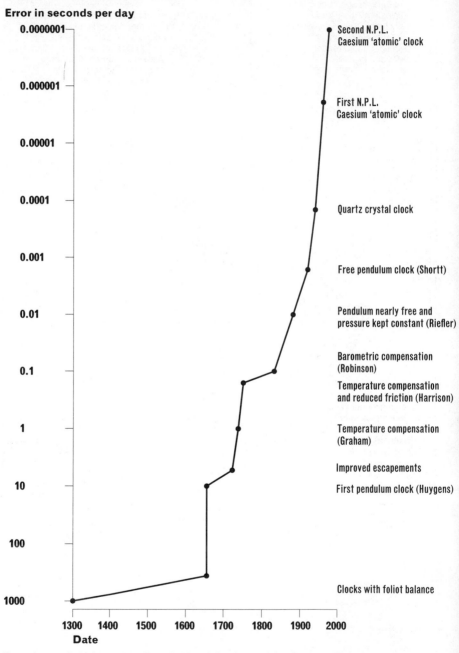

Based on a chart devised by F. A. B. Ward, formerly of the Science Museum, London.

The Kingdom of Aragon and Its Overseas Possessions

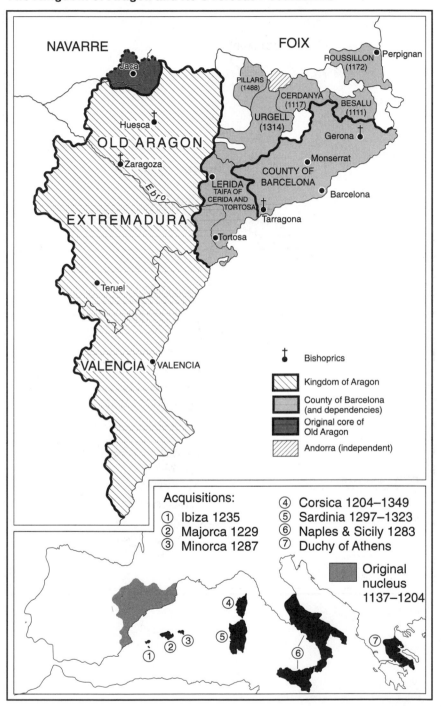

NAVARRE

FOIX

ROUSSILLON
(1172)

Perpignan

Jaca

PILLARS
(1488)

CERDANYA
(1117)

BESALU
(1111)

URGELL
(1314)

Gerona

Huesca

OLD ARAGON

Zaragoza

Monserrat

COUNTY OF
BARCELONA

Ebro

LERIDA
TAIFA OF
CERIDA AND
TORTOSA

Barcelona

EXTREMADURA

Tarragona

Tortosa

Teruel

VALENCIA   VALENCIA

✝ Bishoprics

Kingdom of Aragon

County of Barcelona
(and dependencies)

Original core of
Old Aragon

Andorra (independent)

Acquisitions:

① Ibiza 1235
② Majorca 1229
③ Minorca 1287

④ Corsica 1204–1349
⑤ Sardinia 1297–1323
⑥ Naples & Sicily 1283
⑦ Duchy of Athens

Original
nucleus
1137–1204

The Plantagenet Realm, *c.*1170

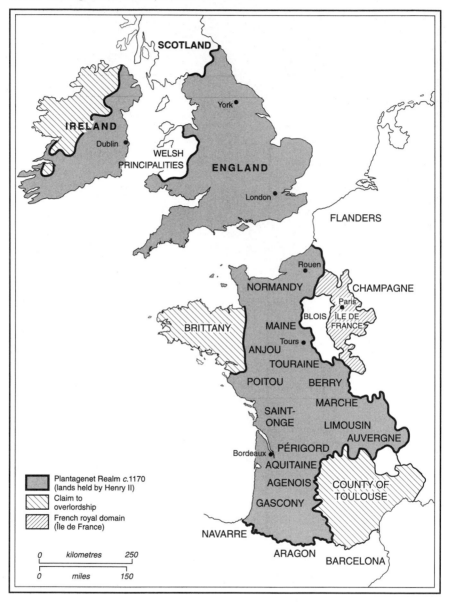

Plantagenet Realm *c.*1170
(lands held by Henry II)

Claim to
overlordship

French royal domain
(Île de France)

0   kilometres   250

0   miles   150

SCOTLAND

YORK

IRELAND

Dublin

WELSH
PRINCIPALITIES

ENGLAND

London

FLANDERS

Rouen

NORMANDY

CHAMPAGNE

Paris

BRITTANY

MAINE

BLOIS ÎLE DE
FRANCE

Tours

ANJOU

TOURAINE

POITOU

BERRY

MARCHE

SAINT-
ONGE

LIMOUSIN

AUVERGNE

PÉRIGORD

Bordeaux

AQUITAINE

AGENOIS

COUNTY OF
TOULOUSE

GASCONY

NAVARRE

ARAGON   BARCELONA

The Roads to Santiago de Compostela

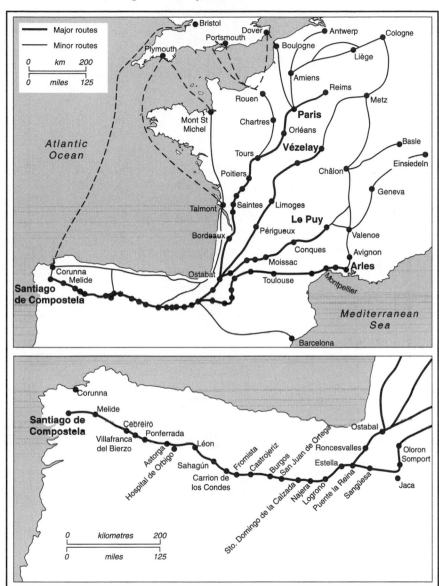

Major routes

Minor routes

0   km   200

0   miles   125

Bristol
Dover
Antwerp
Portsmouth
Cologne
Plymouth
Boulogne
Liège
Amiens
Reims
Metz
Rouen
Paris
Basle
Mont St
Michel
Chartres
Orléans
Einsiedeln
Atlantic
Ocean
Vézelay
Tours
Châlon
Geneva
Poitiers
Le Puy
Talmont
Saintes
Limoges
Valence
Bordeaux
Périgueux
Avignon
Conques
Moissac
Arles
Corunna
Ostabat
Montpellier
Melide
Toulouse
Santiago
de Compostela
Mediterranean
Sea
Barcelona

Corunna
Melide
Santiago de
Compostela
Cebreiro
Ponferrada
Ostabal
Villafranca
del Bierzo
Léon
Astorga
Castrojeriz
San Juan de Ortega
Hospital de Orbigo
Fromista
Burgos
Roncesvalles
Oloron
Somport
Sahagún
Estella
Carrion de
los Condes
Sto. Domingo de la Calzada
Najera
Logrono
Puente la Reina
Sangüesa
Jaca

0   kilometres   200

0   miles   125

The Principality of Orange and the *Comtat Venaissin*

LANGUEDOC

LANGUEDOC, annexed by France 1271

COMTAT DE VENASQUE (VENAISSIN), a fief of Provence centred on the Plain of Vaucluse, leased to the Papacy in 1229, and granted in perpetuity in 1274. Thereafter, to 1791, an element of the Papal States. Principal centres: Venasque, later Carpentras.

Montdragon (to the Archbishopric of Arles)

PRINCIPALITY AND BISHOPRIC OF ORANGE (1274–1713), an enclave within the Venaissin, was originally a fief of Provence, which became practically independent from 1274, when the surrounding Comtat was ceded to the Papacy. It was held by the dynasties of Baux (1173), Châlons-Arlay (1415), and Nassau. The rights of the family of Orange-Nassau, Stadholders of Holland, were confirmed by the Treaty of Cateau-Cambrésis, violated by Louis XIV's seizure of Orange in 1673, and terminated by the Treaty of Utrecht. From 1713, France held the territory of Orange, whilst the heirs of William III kept the title.

COMTAT D'AVIGNON
A dependency of Provence, and later of the Venaissin. 1309–76 the seat of the Papacy, to which, in 1348, it was sold in freehold and added to the Venaissin.

DAUPHINÉ

DAUPHINÉ— bought by the Kingdom of France, 1349

Les Baronnies

Baronnie de Sault

Baillie d'Apt

France →|← Empire (to 1481)

PROVENCE

COUNTY OF PROVENCE : capital AIX. A county of the Kingdom of Arles and of the Holy Roman Empire until annexed by France in 1481. It passed from the Counts of Toulouse to the Counts of Barcelona, and eventually to the Angevins. René d'Anjou (r. 1434–), 'Good King René', presided over Provence's golden age. 1501 Parlement d'Aix instituted. 1529 Edict of Villers-Cotterets: French language imposed. NW Provence, on the Rhône, contained three separate administrative units—Orange, Venaissin, and Avignon.

Montélimar · Valouse · Montbrison · Valréas · Pierrelatte · Eygues · Ouvèze · Gigondas · Suzette · Mont Ventoux 1551m · **ORANGE** · Courthézon · Carpentras · Châteauneuf-du-Pape · Venasque · **COMTAT VENAISSIN** · Villeneuve · Nesque · Avignon · Coulon · Beaucaire · Cavaillon · Bonnieux · Tarascon · Durance · Arles · Aix · Aigues Mortes · **Camargue** · *Mediterranean Sea*

0 kilometres 20 · 0 miles 15

The Republic of Venice: *Terra Firma* and the Venetian Empire

(*a*) Venice's *Terra Firma*; (*b*) The Venetian Empire

Lithuania, Medieval and Modern

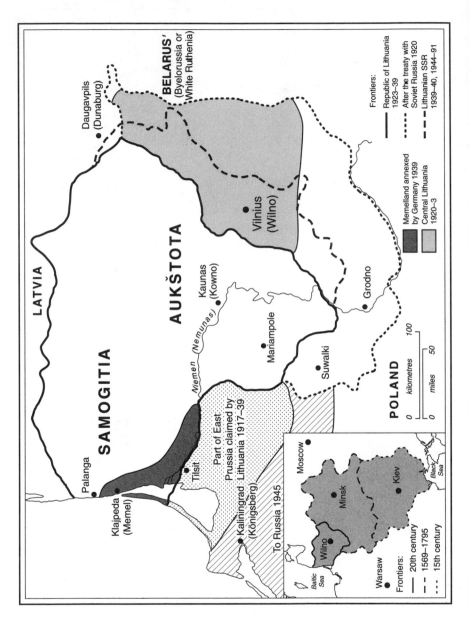

The Growth of the Swiss Confederation, the *Eidgenossenschaft*, 1291–1815 (simplified)

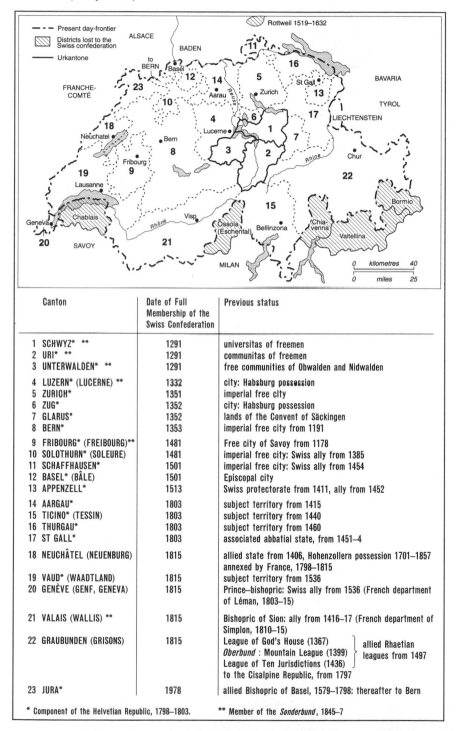

Canton	Date of Full Membership of the Swiss Confederation	Previous status
1 SCHWYZ* **	1291	universitas of freemen
2 URI* **	1291	communitas of freemen
3 UNTERWALDEN* **	1291	free communities of Obwalden and Nidwalden
4 LUZERN* (LUCERNE) **	1332	city: Habsburg possession
5 ZURICH*	1351	imperial free city
6 ZUG*	1352	city: Habsburg possession
7 GLARUS*	1352	lands of the Convent of Säckingen
8 BERN*	1353	imperial free city from 1191
9 FRIBOURG* (FREIBOURG)**	1481	Free city of Savoy from 1178
10 SOLOTHURN* (SOLEURE)	1481	imperial free city: Swiss ally from 1385
11 SCHAFFHAUSEN*	1501	imperial free city: Swiss ally from 1454
12 BASEL* (BÂLE)	1501	Episcopal city
13 APPENZELL*	1513	Swiss protectorate from 1411, ally from 1452
14 AARGAU*	1803	subject territory from 1415
15 TICINO* (TESSIN)	1803	subject territory from 1440
16 THURGAU*	1803	subject territory from 1460
17 ST GALL*	1803	associated abbatial state, from 1451–4
18 NEUCHÂTEL (NEUENBURG)	1815	allied state from 1406, Hohenzollern possession 1701–1857 annexed by France, 1798–1815
19 VAUD* (WAADTLAND)	1815	subject territory from 1536
20 GENÈVE (GENF, GENEVA)	1815	Prince–bishopric: Swiss ally from 1536 (French department of Léman, 1803–15)
21 VALAIS (WALLIS) **	1815	Bishopric of Sion: ally from 1416–17 (French department of Simplon, 1810–15)
22 GRAUBUNDEN (GRISONS)	1815	League of God's House (1367) / *Oberbund* : Mountain League (1399) / League of Ten Jurisdictions (1436) } allied Rhaetian leagues from 1497 / to the Cisalpine Republic, from 1797
23 JURA*	1978	allied Bishopric of Basel, 1579–1798; thereafter to Bern

* Component of the Helvetian Republic, 1798–1803.   ** Member of the *Sonderbund*, 1845–7

Medieval Serbia and Bosnia

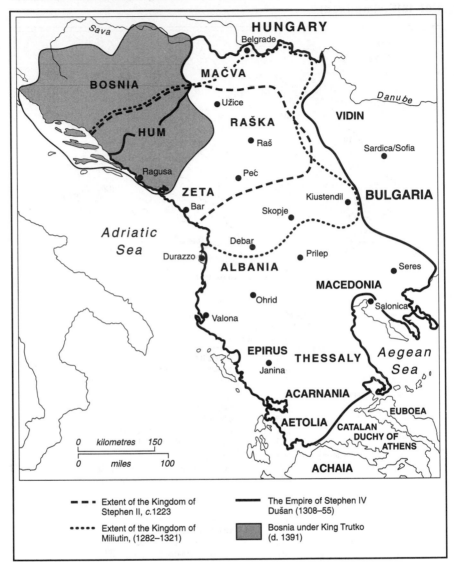

Extent of the Kingdom of Stephen II, c.1223

Extent of the Kingdom of Miliutin, (1282–1321)

The Empire of Stephen IV Dušan (1308–55)

Bosnia under King Trutko (d. 1391)

The Growth of the Ottoman Empire in Europe, 1355–1683

NEMÇE (AVUSTURYA)

LEHISTAN

MOSKOVA

Viyana

Podolya (1672–99)

Ukrayna

Budin

① ③

BUĞDAN 1456

Yedisan

Azak

Hirvatistan

MACARISTAN

Mohacs 1526

ERDIL

②

Bucak

KIRIM 1476

BOSNA 1463–

Saray Belgrat

EFLAK

Bükres

Silistre

Kefe

Çerkez

Hersek

SIRBISTAN 1389

BULGARISTAN 1393

Black Sea

GÜRCİSTAN

KARADAG

Kossovo 1389

Sofya

Varna 1444

ARNAVUTLUK 1461–

RUMELI

Makedonya

Istanbul

Trabzon

ERMENİSTAN

Otranto 1480

Selánik

Bursa

Sivas

Epir

Lepanto 1571

İzmir

ANADOLU

YUNANISTAN 1460–

Atina

Karaman

Mora

RODOS 1522

GIRIT 1669

KIBRIS 1571

kilometres 300

miles 200

Mediterranean Sea

① Royal Hungary (to Habsburgs, from 1529)

Ottoman Realm 1355

Battlefields

② Ottoman Hungary (1529–1697)

Ottoman Realm 1481

Habsburg military frontier after 1697

③ Transylvania

Maximum extent of Empire 1682–3

RUMELI BEYLERBEYLİĞİ (Lordship of Lordships of RUMELI)
ANADOLU BEYLERBEYLİĞİ (Lordship of Lordships of ANATOLIA)

MACARISTAN	— Hungary	SIRBISTAN	— Serbia	EFLAK	— Wallachia
HIRVATISTAN	— Croatia	BULGARISTAN	— Bulgaria	KIRIM	— Crimea
KARADAG	— Montenegro	GIRIT	— Crete	GÜRCİSTAN	— Georgia
ARNAVUTLUK	— Albania	ERDIL	— Transylvania	ERMENİSTAN	— Armenia
YUNANISTAN	— Greece	BUĞDAN	— Moldava	KIBRIS	— Cyprus

Fifteenth-Century Burgundy

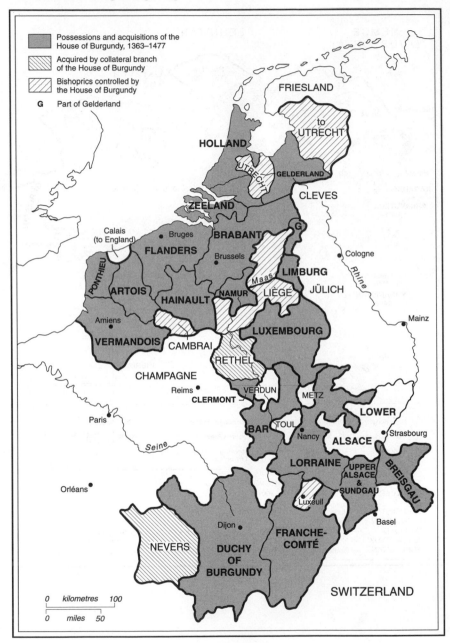

Dynastic Consortia in East Central Europe, 1273–1526

Holy Roman Empire	Bohemia	Hungary	Poland	Key

↓ Arpad Dynasty   ↓ Piast Dynasty

Holy Roman Empire

Rudolf I von Habsburg * (1273–91)

Adolf of Nassau (1292–8)

Albert I

Henry VII* (1308–13)

Lewis of Bavaria Wittelsbach * (1314–47)

Charles IV * (1347–78)

Vaclav (Wenzel) * (1378–1419)

(Sigismund ** 1410–19)

Sigismund * (1419–37)

Albert II* (1438–9)

Frederick III (1440–93)

(Maximilian ** 1486–93)

Maximilian (1493–1519)

(Charles 1516 – **)

Charles V 1519–56

Bohemia

Vaclav II (Wenzel) 1278–1305 (Wenceslas Wenzel)

Vaclav III 1305–6

Rudolf 1306–7

Henry of Carinthia 1307–10

John of Bohemia 1310–46

Charles 1346–78

Vaclav IV (1378–1419)

Sigismund (1419–37)

Albert 1437–9

Ladislas Posthumous 1453–57

George of Podiebrady 1458–71

Wladyslaw Jagiellonczyk 1471–1516

Louis 1516–26

Hungary

Andrew III

Vaclav III 1301–5

Otto von Wittelsbach

Carobert of Anjou 1308–42

Louis of Anjou 1342–82 (Lajos the Great)

Maria 1382–7

Sigismund 1387–1437

Albert 1437–9

Wladyslaw 1440–44

Ladislas 1445–57

Matthias Corvinus Hunyadi 1458–90

Wladyslaw Jagiellonczyk 1490–1516

Louis 1516–26

Ferdinand von Habsburg 1526–56

Poland

Vaclav III 1300–5

Wladyslaw Lokietek 1320–33 (Wladyslaw I)

Kazimierz I 1333–70 (Casimir the Great)

Louis of Anjou 1370–82

Jadwiga 1382–6

Jagiello of Lithuania 1386–1433 (Wladyslaw II)

Wladyslaw III of Varna 1433–44

Kazimierz Jagiellonczyk 1445–92

Jan Olbracht 1492–1501

Alexander 1501–6

Sigismund I 1506–48

Key

Habsburg

Premyslids

Wittelsbach

Luxembourg

Anjou

Jagiellon

* Holy Roman Emperor

** King of the Romans

The Jagiellonian Realm to 1572, and the *Rzeczpospolita* after 1572

☐	Fiefs of Poland or of Poland-Lithuania
❶	Duchy of Prussia, 1525–1657
❷	Duchy of Mazovia, 1351–1529
❸	Siewierz, to the Bishop of Cracow
❹	The Thirteen Towns of Spisz (Zips), 1413–1769
❺	Moldavia, 1387–1497
❻	Lembork & Bytów 1637–57
❼	Courland and Semigalia, 1561–1773
❽	Livonia (Inflanty), 1561(82)–1621(60)
❾	Smolensk, Seversk, Chernigov, 1619–67

— Jagiellonian Realm at its greatest extent *c.*1500

- - - Rzeczpospolita at its greatest extent 1634–5

0   kilometres   300

0   miles   200

Paris *Rentes*, 1420–1787

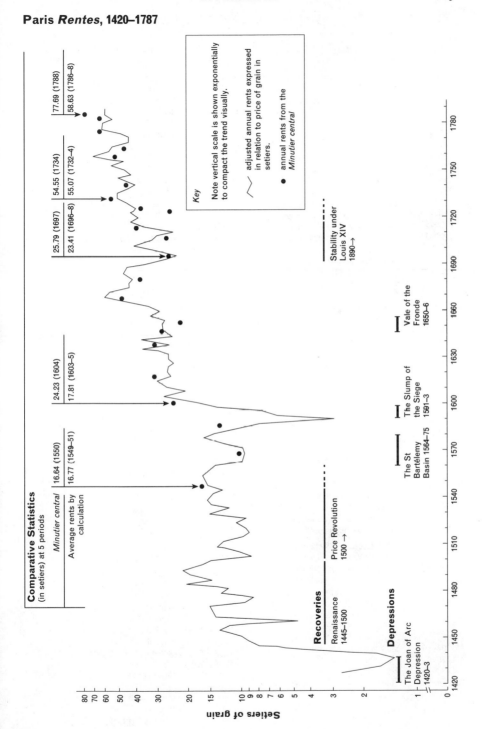

Poland, Rus', Muscovy and Russia: Princes, Kings, Tsars, Emperors

POLAND

Piast Dynasty

9th cent.?	Piast
pre-965–91	Mieszko I
992–1025	Bolesław I (the Brave)*
1025–37	Mieszko II*
1038–58	Casimir I (the Restorer)
1058–79	Bolesław II (the Generous)*
1079–1102	Władysław Herman
1102–38	Bolesław III (the Wry-mouthed)
1138–46	Władysław II (the Exile)
1146–77	Bolesław IV (the Curly) of Mazovia
1173–7	Mieszko III
1177–94	Casimir II (the Just) of Sandomierz
1194–1202	Meszko the Elder, of Wielkopolska
1202–27	Leszek the White, of Sandomierz
1228–31	Władysław III (Spindleshanks) of Wielkopolska
1231–8	Henry I Brodaty of Silesia
1238–41	Henry II of Silesia
1241–3	Konrad I Mazowiecki
1243–79	Bolesław V of Sandomierz
1279–88	Leszek (the Black)
1288–90	Henry IV of Silesia
1290–1300	Przemysl I Wielkopolski
1300–5	Vaclav II (King of Bohemia)
1305–6	Vaclav II (King of Bohemia)
1306–33	Władysław I* (the Elbow-high)
1333–70	Casimir III* (the Great)

Angevin Dynasty

1370–82	Louis of Anjou* (King of Hungary)
1384–6	Jadwiga (Hedwig) of Anjou* (1386–99, co-monarch)

Jagiellonian Dynasty

1386–1434	Władysław Jagiełło*
1434–44	Władysław III* of Varna (King of Hungary)
1444–92	Kazimierz IV of Jagiellonczyk*
1492–1501	Jan Olbracht (John Albert)*
1501–6	Alexander*
1506–48	Zygmunt Stary (Sigismund I)*
1548–72	Sigismund II Augustus*

Elected Kings of the Rzeczpospolita

1573–4	Henry de Valois of France*
1576–86	Stefan Bathory* of Transylvania
1587–1632	Sigismund III* Vasa of Sweden
1632–48	Władysław IV* Vasa
1648–68	Jan Kazimierz Vasa*
1669–73	Michał Korybut Wiśniowiecki*
1674–96	Jan III Sobieski*
1697–1704	Augustus II Wettin* of Saxony
1704–10	Stanisław Leszczyński*
1710–33	Augustus II Wettin*
1733–63	Augustus III Wettin*
1764–95	Stanisław-August Poniatowski*

KIEVAN RUS'

Rurikid Dynasty

c.862–79	Rurik, Prince of Novgorod
880–	Oleg, Prince of Kiev
912–45	Igor
945–69	Olga, St
969–80	Sviatoslav
980–1015	Vladimir, St (Volodymyr)
1019–54	Yaroslav the Wise
1113–25	Vladimir Monomakh of Rostov
1155–7	Yuri Dolgorukii of Kiev
1157–74	Andrei Bogoliubskii of Vladimir & Suzdal
1178–1202	Igor of Sever
1240–63	Alexander Nevskii, of Novgorod & Vladimir
1235–65	Daniel Romanowicz, of Halich

MUSCOVY

(Rurikid) Grand Dukes of Moscow

1305–40	Ivan I Kalita
1350–89	Dmitri Donskoi
1389–1425	Vassili I
1425–62	Vassily II
1462–1505	Ivan III

Tsars of 'Moscow and All-Russia'

from 1473	Ivan III (the Great)
1505–33	Vasili III
1533–84	Ivan IV (the Terrible)
1584–98	Feodor I
1598–1605	Boris Godunov
1605	Feodor II
1605–6	Dmitri I
1606–10	Vasili Shuiski
1608–10	Dmitri II

Romanov Dynasty

1613–45	Mikhail Romanov
1645–76	Alexei
1676–82	Feodor III
1682–9	Ivan V
1689–1725	Peter I (the Great)

Emperors of Russia

from 1721	Peter I (the Great)
1725–7	Catherine I
1727–30	Peter II
1730–40	Anne
1741–61	Elizabeth
1761–2	Peter III
1762–96	Catherine II (the Great)
1796–1801	Paul
1801–25	Alexander I**
1825–55	Nicholas I**
1855–81	Alexander II**
1881–94	Alexander III
1894–1917	Nicholas II (†1918)

* crowned King; ** also King of Poland

Early Modern Political Systems

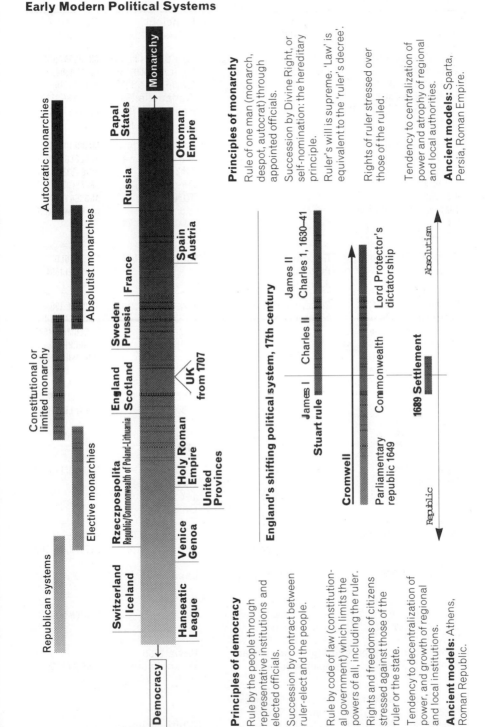

Principles of democracy

Rule by the people through representative institutions and elected officials.

Succession by contract between ruler-elect and the people.

Rule by code of law (constitutional government) which limits the powers of all, including the ruler.

Rights and freedoms of citizens stressed against those of the ruler or the state.

Tendency to decentralization of power, and growth of regional and local institutions.

Ancient models: Athens, Roman Republic.

Principles of monarchy

Rule of one man (monarch, despot, autocrat) through appointed officials.

Succession by Divine Right, or self-nomination: the hereditary principle.

Ruler's will is supreme. 'Law' is equivalent to the 'ruler's decree'.

Rights of ruler stressed over those of the ruled.

Tendency to centralization of power and atrophy of regional and local authorities.

Ancient models: Sparta, Persia, Roman Empire.

	Principal contestants	Principal battles	Peace treaties
The Italian Wars 1494–1518 Seven French expeditions 1494–8, 1499–1500, 1500–1, 1502–3, 1508–10, 1511–15, 1511–15	Successive French Kings from Charles VIII to Francis I v. Successive coalitions from initial League of Venice to Papal Leagues	Fornovo 1495 Novara 1500 Garigliano 1503 Agnadello 1509 Ravenna 1512 Marignano 1515	GRANADA 1500 LYONS 1504 NOYON 1516 FREIBURG 1516 LONDON 1518
Franco-Imperial Wars 1512–59 Five wars initially in continuation of the preceding Italian Wars: 1521–5, 1526–9, 1536–8, SIS 1542–4, 1555–9	France v. Empire and the Empire's successive allies	Pavia 1525 Sack of Rome 1527 Aversa 1528 Turin 1537	MADRID 1526 BARCELONA 1529 NICE 1538 CRESPI 1544 ANDRES 1546 CATEAU-CAMBRÉ- 1559
German Wars of Religion	Emperor v. Protestant Princes Schmalkaldic League	Muhlberg 1547	FRIEDWOLD PASSAU 1551
French Wars of Religion 1562–1629 Nine civil wars ending with the Edict of Nantes, plus two later Huguenot revolts: 1562–3, 1567–8, 1568–70, 1572–3, 1574–6, 1577, 1580, 1587–9, 1589–98 1622 1622–3, 1627–9	Protestant Huguenots v. Catholic League	Dreux 1562 St Denis 1567 Jarnac 1568 Coutras Ivry 1590 Siege of Paris 1589–93	AMBOISE 1563 LONGJUMEAU 1568 ST GERMAIN 1570 LA ROCHELLE 1573 MONSIEUR 1576 BERGERAC 1577 FLEIX 1580 VERVINS 1598 MONTPELLIER ALAIS 1629
Spanish Wars 1502–1659 War of Naples 1502–3 North Africa 1562–3 Revolt of the Netherlands 1566–1648 The 'Amada', 1588 Mediterranean Wars Flanders War 1598–9 Valtellina 1622–6 Mantuan Succession 1627–31 [Spanish involvement in Thirty Years War] French War 1648–59	Spain v. Portugal Spain v. France Spain v. Barbary States Spain v. United Provinces England Spain and Empire v. Ottomans Spain v. France Spain v. France Spain v. France Spain v. France	(Division of New World) Terranova Garigliano Tunis Haarlem 1572 Antwerp 1576 Lepanto 1571 Amiens Pavia 1655 Valenciennes 1656	TORDESILLAS 1494 1609–12 WESTPHALIA 1648 MONZON 1626 PYRENEES 1659
Thirty Years Wars 1618–48 Bohemian War 1618–23	Empire & Catholic Princes & Spain v. Protestant Princes &	White Mountain	

	their allies (esp. Denmark, Sweden, & France)	1620 Lutter 1626	LÜBECK 1629
Danish War 1624–9			

	Principal contestants	Principal battles	Peace treaties
[Edict of Restitution 1629] Swedish War 1630–5		Breitenfeld 1631 Lützen 1633 Nordlingen 1634	PRAGUE 1635
French War 1635–48		Wittstock 1635 Rocroi 1643	WESTPHALIA 1648

England's Wars

Tudors'Scots Wars 1469– 1502, 1511–43	England v. Scotland in alliance with France	Flodden 1513 Solway Moss 1542	'PERPETUAL PEACE' 1502 GREENWICH 1543
Anglo-French Wars 1512–18, 1522–5, 1544–6, 1557–64, 1627–30	England v. France	Spurs 1513	LONDON 1518 ARDRES 1544 TROYES 1564
Spanish War 1564–1630 N'lands Campaign 1585–7	England v. Spain	Zutphen 1587 Armada 1588	
Anglo-Irish Wars 1598–1603, 1651–4	Expeditions of Mountjoy, Essex & Cromwell		
'English Civil War' 1642–6	Scots intervention 1644–6, 1647–51		
Three Anglo-Dutch Wars 1652–4, 1664–7, 1672–4	England v. UP		BREDA 1667 WESTMINSTER 1674

Sweden's Wars

Wars of Independence 1500–23	Denmark v. Sweden & Norway		
Five Danish Wars 1563–70, 1611–13, 1657–60, 1675–9	Sweden v. Denmark		STETTIN 1570 KNÄRED 1613 COPENHAGEN 1660
Two Muscovite Wars 1560– 92, 1614–17	Sweden v. Moscow	Eslorua	LUND 1679 STOLBOVA 1617
Three Polish Wars 1598– 1611, 1617–29, 1655–60	Sweden v. Polish Vasas	Kirkholm 1605	STUMSDORF 1629
[Swedish involvement in Thirty Years War 1630–48]			OLIVA 1660

Poland's Wars

Moldavian War 1497–9			
Six Muscovite Wars 1500–13, 1561–9, 1577–82, 1610–19, 1632–4, 1654–67	Poland-Lithuania v. Moscow	Smolensk 1511 Livonia Pskov 1582	ZAPOLYA 1582 DYLINO 1619 ANDRUSOVO 1667
Swedish Wars 1598–1611, 1617–29, 1655–60	Polish Vasas v. Swedish Vasas	Cecora 1620 Chocim I 1621	OLIVA 1660
Two Ottoman Wars 1620–1, 1671–6		Chocim II 1672	BUCZACZ 1674 ZURAWNO 1676

N.B. The complex of Livonian Campaigns between 1561 and 1592, which involved, *inter al.*, Poland, Sweden, Denmark, and Muscovy, might reasonably be considered 'The First Northern War'.

Ottoman Wars

Danube Campaigns 1481–1512			
Three Hungarian Wars 1521–47, 1551–62, 1573–81	v. Habsburgs	Mohacs 1526 Vienna 1529 Rhodes 1522	
Mediterranean Wars & Venetian Wars 1569–72, 1648–69	v. Venice & Catholic Powers	Siege of Malta 1565 Lepanto 1571 Siege of Crete 1648–69	

The Rise and Fall of European States, 1493–1993

Termination of the sovereignty or of the separate existence of states present in 1493

Aragon, Kingdom	1516
Astrakhan, Khanate	1556
Bohemia, Kingdom	1526
Burgundy, Duchy	1579
Castile, Kingdom	1516
Crimea, Khanate	1783
England, Kingdom	1707
Florence, Republic	1532
France, Kingdom	1792
Genoa, Republic	1797
Georgia, Kingdom	1801
Golden Horde, Khanate	1502
Holy Roman Empire	1806
Hungary, Kingdom	1526
Ireland	1801
Kazan, Khanate	1552
Lithuania, Grand Duchy	1569
Livonia	1561
Milan, Duchy	1535
Moldavia, Principality	1859
Moscow, Grand Duchy	1721
Naples, Kingdom	1860
Navarre, Kingdom	1516
Ottoman Empire	1920
Papal States	1870
Poland, Kingdom	1569
Portugal, Kingdom	1580
Scotland, Kingdom	1707
Teutonic State	1525
Union of Colmar	1523
Venice, Republic	1797
Wallachia, Principality	1859

Date of formation of the sovereign states present in 1993

Albania, Republic	1913
Andorra, Principality	1278
Armenia, Republic*	1918 (1991)
Austria, Republic	1918 (1945)
Azerbaijan, Republic	1918 (1991)
Belarus', Republic*	1918 (1991)
Belgium, Kingdom	1830
Bosnia, Republic	1992

Bulgaria, Kingdom	1878
—— Republic*	1946 (1989)
Croatia, Republic	1941 (1992)
Cyprus, Republic	1960
Czech Republic*	1992
Denmark, Kingdom	1523
Estonia, Republic*	1918 (1991)
Finland, Republic	1917
France, Republic	1792 (1871)
Georgia, Republic*	1918 (1991)
Germany, Federal Republic*	1949 (1990)
Greece, Kingdom	1829
—— Republic	1973
Hungary, Regency	1918
—— Republic*	1946 (1989)
Iceland, Republic	1944
Ireland, Free State	1922
—— Republic	1949
Italy, Kingdom	1860
—— Republic	1946
Latvia, Republic*	1918 (1991)
Liechtenstein, Principality	1866
Lithuania, Republic*	1918 (1991)
Luxembourg, Grand Duchy	1890
Macedonia, Republic	1992
Malta, Republic	1964
Moldova, Republic	1991
Monaco, Principality	1297
Netherlands, Kingdom	1648
Norway, Kingdom	1905
Poland, Republic*	1918 (1989)
Portugal, Kingdom	1640
—— Republic	1910
Romania, Kingdom	1877
—— Republic*	1947 (1989)
Russia, Republic*	1917 (1991)
San Marino, Republic	1631
Slovakia, Republic*	1939 (1992)
Slovenia, Republic	1992
Spain, Kingdom	1516 (1976)
Sweden, Kingdom	1523
Switzerland, Confederation	1648
Turkey, Republic	1923
Ukraine, Republic*	1918 (1991)
United Kingdom	1707
Vatican State	1929
Yugoslavia, Federal Republic	1945

* States which lost all but nominal sovereignty for a period under Soviet domination.

Renaissance Italy

AUSTRIA

VALAIS
GRISONS
TYROL

HUNGARY

SAVOY
and
PIEDMONT

MILAN
(to Spain)
Bergamo

VENICE

Croatia

Verona
Brescia
Cremona

Padua

Turin
MONT-
FERRAT

Man

Milan

GENOA

Reggio
Modena
P

Ferrara
F

Genoa

B
Bologna

OTTOMAN
EMPIRE

M

Lucca
Pisa

L

Florence

FLORENCE

Rimini

Siena
SIENA

PAPAL
STATES

CORSICA
(to Genoa)

Perugia

Aquila

Adriatic Sea

Rome

SARDINIA
(to
Spain)

KINGDOM
OF
NAPLES
(to Spain)

Bari

Naples

Taranto

Tyrrhenian Sea

Palermo

Messina

KINGDOM
OF
SICILY
(to Spain)

B	Bologna
M	Modena
L	Lucca
P	Parma
F	Ferrara
Man	Mantua

MALTA
(to Knights of
St John from 1523)

0   kilometres   200
0   miles   150

The Habsburg Dominions in Europe after 1519

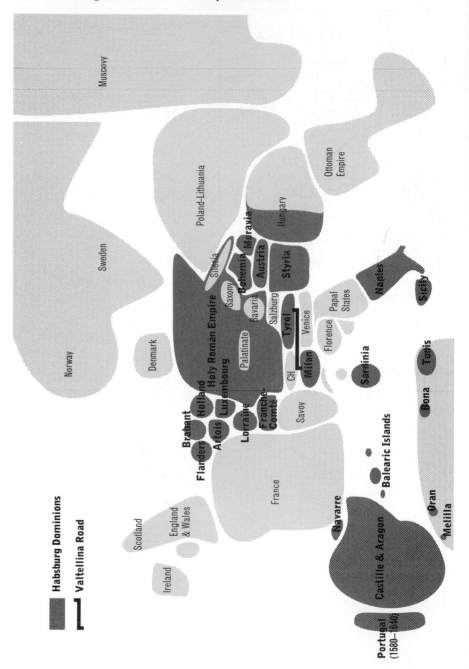

Habsburg Dominions

Valtellina Road

Muscovy

Ottoman Empire

Poland-Lithuania

Sweden

Hungary

Bohemia Moravia

Silesia

Austria

Styria

Saxony

Naples

Sicily

Norway

Bavaria

Salzburg

Papal States

Denmark

Holy Roman Empire

Tyrol

Venice

Florence

Tunis

Palatinate

Milan

Sardinia

Bona

Brabant

Holland

CH

Luxembourg

Artois

Lorraine

Franche-Comté

Savoy

Balearic Islands

Flanders

Oran

France

Navarre

Melilla

Scotland

England & Wales

Castille & Aragon

Ireland

Portugal (1580—1640)

The Price Revolution in Sixteenth-Century Spain

1 Shipping in the port of Seville, 1506–1600

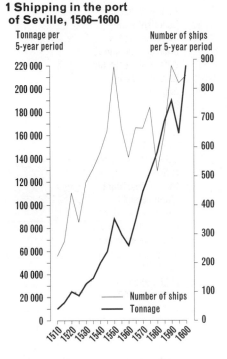

Tonnage per 5-year period

Number of ships per 5-year period

— Number of ships
— Tonnage

2 Importation of precious metals (gold and silver) into Spain, 1500–1600

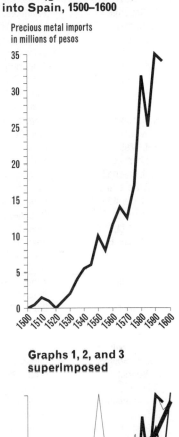

Precious metal imports in millions of pesos

3 Commodity prices 1500–1600

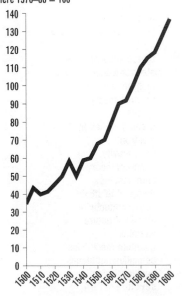

Commodity price index where 1570–80 = 100

Graphs 1, 2, and 3 superImposed

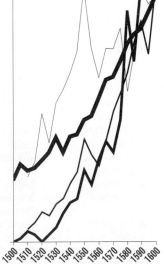

a) Scientific Discoveries and b) Technological Inventions, 1526–1951: A Selection

a)

P. A. Paracelsus	Basle, 1526	theory of disease
M. Kopernik	Frombork, 1543	heliocentrism
W. Harvey	London, 1628	blood circulation
R. Descartes	Amsterdam, 1644	analytical geometry
G. Leibniz	Leipzig, 1666	differential calculus
I. Newton	Cambridge 1666	laws of gravity
A. von Haller	Bern, 1757	neurology
H. Cavendish	London, 1766	hydrogen
K. Scheele	Uppsala, 1771	oxygen
S. Hahnemann	Leipzig, 1796	homeopathy
E. Jenner	London, 1796	vaccination
E.-L. Malus	Strasburg, 1808	polarization of light
B. Courtois	Paris, 1811	iodine
A.-J. Fresnell	France, 1815	frequency of light
J. J. Berzelius	Stockholm, 1818	atomic weight
H.-C. Oersted	Copenhagen, 1819	electromagnetism
G. Ohm	Cologne, 1827	electrical resistance
M. Faraday	London, 1831	electrical induction
J. von Liebig	Giessen, 1831	analysis of elements
R. Brown	London, 1831	cell nucleus
F. Runge	Berlin, 1833	phenol anilin
R. A. Kolliker	Zurich, 1841	spermatozoon
C. J. Doppler	Prague, 1842	acoustics
R. Remak	Berlin, 1852	segmentation of cells
W. Perkin	London, 1856	aniline dye
C. Darwin	London, 1859	theory of evolution
G. R. Kirchhoff	Heidelberg, 1859	spectral analysis
I. Semmelweis	Budapest, 1861	asepsis
G. Mendel	Brno, 1865	genetics
J. Lister	Glasgow, 1867	antisepsis
D. I. Mendeleev	St Petersburg, 1869	periodic table
E. Fischer	Munich, 1875	hydrazine: biochemistry
L. Pasteur	Paris, 1881	bacteriology
R. Koch	Berlin, 1882	tuberculosis bacillus
H. Hertz	Karlsruhe, 1888	electromagnetic waves
E. von Behring	Berlin, 1892	diphtheria serum
H. Lorentz	Leiden, 1895	electron theory
W. Röntgen	Wurzburg, 1895	X-rays
H. Becquerel	Paris, 1896	uranium radiation
J. J. Thompson	Cambridge, 1897	elektron
P. and M. Curie	Paris, 1898	radioactivity
M. Planck	Berlin, 1900	quantum theory
T. Boveri	Wurzburg, 1904	chromosomes
A. Einstein	Zurich, 1905	theory of relativity
H. K. Onnes	Leiden, 1911	superconductivity
E. Rutherford	Manchester, 1911	atomic structure
K. Funk	Cracow, 1911	vitamins
W. Heisenberg	Copenhagen, 1925	quantum mechanics
A. Fleming	London, 1928	penicillin: antibiotics
O. Hahn	Berlin, 1938	nuclear fission
Crick and Watson	London, 1951	structure of DNA

b)

J.Lippershey	Middleburg, 1608	telescope
Z. Janssen	Amsterdam, 1609	microscope
E. Torricelli	Rome,1643	mercury barometer
T. Savery	England, 1698	steam pump
G. Fahrenheit	Amsterdam, 1718	mercury thermometer
Jethro Tull	Hungerford, 1731	agricultural machinery
J. Watt	Birmingham, 1769	steam engine condenser
S. Crompton	Bolton, 1779	spinning mule
J. and J. Montgolfier	Annonay, 1783	hot-air balloon
C. Chappe	Paris, 1791	aerial telegraph
A. Volta	Bologna, 1800	electric battery
J.-M. Jacquard	Lyons, 1804	automated machinery
R. Laennec	Paris, 1816	stethoscope
C. Macintosh	Glasgow, 1823	waterproof fabric
G. Stephenson	Stockton, 1825	passenger railway
T. Telford	Menai Straits, 1825	suspension bridge
N. Niepce	Chalon-sur-Saône, 1826	photography
B. Fourneyron	Paris, 1827	turbine
C. Babbage	Cambridge, 1834	mechanical calculator
S. Bauer	Kiel, 1850	submarine
L. Foucault	Paris, 1852	gyroscope
H. Giffard	Paris, 1852	steam-powered airship
H. Bessemer	St Pancras, 1857	blast furnace: steel
J. Reis	Friedrichsdorf, 1861	telephone
A. Nobel	Stockholm, 1867	dynamite
W. von Siemens	Berlin, 1867	dynamo
N. Otto	Cologne, 1876	internal combustion engine
E. Berliner	Germany, 1877	microphone
C. von Linde	Munich, 1877	refrigerator
W. von Siemens	Berlin, 1879	electric locomotive
H. S. Maxim	London, 1883	machine-gun
G. Daimler	Connstatt, 1884	petrol engine
Daimler and Benz	Mannheim, 1885	motor car
R. Mannesmann	Düsseldorf, 1885	seamless pipes
H. Goodwin	London, 1887	photographic film
C. Ader	France, 1890	aeroplane
W. Maybach	Connstatt, 1892	carburettor
A. L. Lumière	Lyons, 1895	cinematograph
R. K. Diesel	Berlin, 1895	diesel engine
V. Poulsen	Copenhagen, 1898	magnetic sound-recording
F. Zeppelin	Berlin, 1900	dirigible airship
G. Marconi	London, 1901	radio transmitter
K. E. Tsiolkovsky	Moscow, 1903	rocketry
Bréguet-Richet	France, 1907	helicopter
British Army	Cambrai, 1915	military tank
J. Logie Baird	London, 1924	television
H. Geiger	Kiel, 1928	Geiger counter
F. Whittle	Cranwell, 1930	jet engine
Air Ministry	Dover, 1940	radar
Wilkes and Renwick	Manchester, 1946	EDSAC, computer
Power Ministry	Calder Hall, 1956	nuclear power station

Sources: Various. N.B. The subject of Historical Inventions is subject to historical invention.

Works and Authors Banned by the Papal Index, 1559–1952: A Selection

1559	Abelard	*opera omnia*
	Boccaccio	*Il Decamerone*
	Calvin	*opera omnia*
	Dante	*De Monarchia*
	Erasmus	*opera omnia*
1624	Luther	German Bible
1633	Descartes	selected works
1645	Sir Thomas Browne	*Religio Medici*
	Montaigne	*Essais*
1700	Locke	*Essay on Human Understanding*
1703	La Fontaine	*Contes nouvelles*
1734	Swift	*Tale of a Tub*
1738	Swedenborg	*Principia*
1752	Voltaire	*Lettres philosophiques*
1755	Richardson	*Pamela*
1759	Diderot	*Encyclopédie*
1763	Rousseau	*Émile*
1766	Rousseau	*Du contrat social*
1783	Gibbon	*Decline and Fall of the Roman Empire*
1789	Pascal	*Lettres provinciales*
1791	de Sade	*Justine; Juliette*
1792	Paine	*Rights of Man*
1806	Rousseau	*La Nouvelle Héloïse*
1819	Sterne	*A Sentimental Journey*
1827	Kant	*Critique of Pure Reason*
1834	Casanova	*Mémoires*
	Hugo	*Notre-Dame de Paris*
		Les Misérables
1836	Heine	*De l'Allemagne; Reisebilder*
1841	Balzac	*opera omnia*
1836	Dumas	all romances
1864	Flaubert	*Madame Bovary*
		Salammbô
1894	Zola	*opera omnia*
1911	d'Annunzio	selected works
1914	Maeterlinck	*opera omnia*
1922	France	*opera omnia*
1937	Darwin	*On the Origin of Species*
1939	Stendhal	*opera omnia*
1948	Descartes	*Méditations*
1952	Gide	*opera omnia*

Source: N. Parsons, *The Book of Literary Lists* (London, 1985), 207–13; in turn from A. L. Haight, Banned Books (1955).

The Revolt of the Netherlands, 1584–1648

Legend:

- United Provinces (The Dutch Republic, from 1648)
- Spanish Netherlands (1648–1713), Austrian Netherlands (1713–94)
- Frontier of 1579
- Archbishopric of Liège
- Territories ceded by Spain to France under Louis XIV
- Approximate linguistic frontier

GRONINGEN
Groningen
FRIESLAND
DRENTHE
HOLLAND
Haarlem
Amsterdam
OVERIJSSEL
Leiden
The Hague
UTRECHT
GELDERLAND
Rotterdam
Brill
ZEELAND
THE GENERALITY
Breda
Rhine
Ostend
Bruges
Antwerp
LIÈGE
HOLY ROMAN EMPIRE
Dunkirk
FLANDERS
Ghent
BRABANT
Maastricht
Brussels
LIMBURG
DUTCH
WALLOON
Liège
Lille
NAMUR
ARTOIS
HAINAULT
Arras
Cambrai
CAMBRAI
LUXEMBOURG
FRANCE
Luxembourg
GERMAN
FRENCH

0   kilometres   100
0   miles   50

The Prussian Agglomeration, 1525–1871

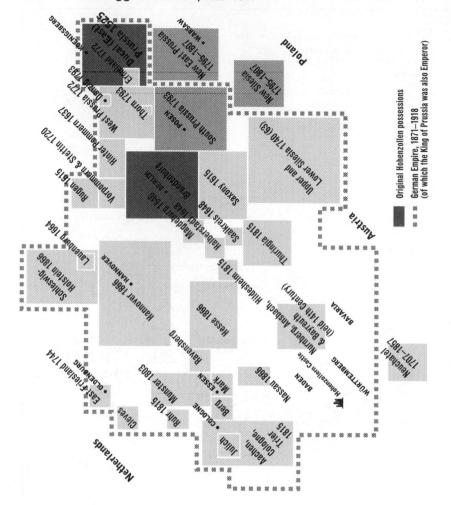

Original Hohenzollen possessions

German Empire, 1871–1918
(of which the King of Prussia was also Emperor)

Russia's Expansion into Europe, 1552–1815

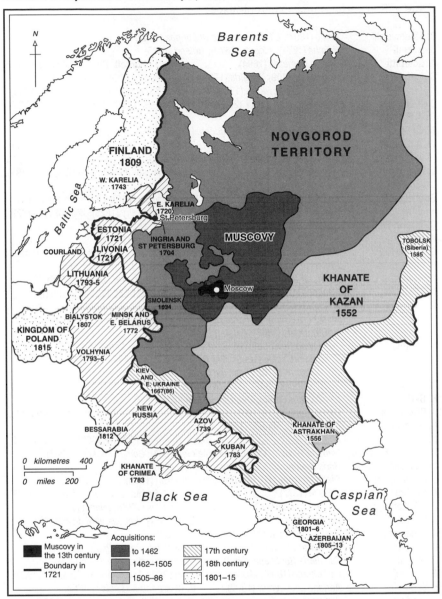

N

Barents
Sea

NOVGOROD
TERRITORY

FINLAND
1809

W. KARELIA
1743

Baltic Sea

E. KARELIA
1720
St.Petersburg

ESTONIA
1721

INGRIA AND
ST PETERSBURG
1704

MUSCOVY

COURLAND

LIVONIA
1721

TOBOLSK
(Siberia)
1585

LITHUANIA
1793-5

SMOLENSK
1634

Moscow

KHANATE
OF
KAZAN
1552

BIALYSTOK
1807

MINSK AND
E. BELARUS
1772

KINGDOM OF
POLAND
1815

VOLHYNIA
1793-5

KIEV
AND
E. UKRAINE
1667(86)

NEW
RUSSIA

BESSARABIA
1812

AZOV
1739

KHANATE OF
ASTRAKHAN
1556

KUBAN
1783

0   kilometres   400

KHANATE
OF CRIMEA
1783

0   miles   200

Black Sea

Caspian
Sea

GEORGIA
1801-6

AZERBAIJAN
1805-13

■ Muscovy in the 13th century	Acquisitions:	
— Boundary in 1721	to 1462	17th century
	1462–1505	18th century
	1505–86	1801–15

The Standard Repertoire of Grand Opera, 1609–1969
(Date of first performance in parentheses)

C. Monteverdi	*Orfeo* (1607); *L'Incoronazione di Poppea* (1642).
J.-B. Lulli	*Psyche* (1671); *Alceste* (1674); *Roland* (1685).
A. Scarlatti	*Pirro e Demetrio* (1694). H. Purcell *Dido and Aeneas* (1696).
G. F. Handel	*Agrippina* (1709); *Rinaldo* (1709); *Giulio Cesare* (1724); *Rodelinda* (1725); *Orlando* (1733); *Alcina* (1735); *Berenice* (1737); *Xerxes* (1738); *Semele* (1744).
J.-P. Rameau	*Hippolyte et Aricie* (1732); *Les Indes galantes* (1735); *Castor et Pollux* (1737).
G. B. Pergolesi	*La Serva Padrone* (1733).
W. C. Gluck	*Orfeo et Eurydice* (1767); *Alceste* (1767); *Iphigenie en Aulide* (1774).
W. A. Mozart	*Idomeneo* (1781); *Il Seraglio* (1782); *Le Nozze de Figaro* (1786); *Don Giovanni* (1787); *Così fan tutte* (1790); *Die Zauberflöte* (1791); *Clemenza di Tito* (1791).
L. Cherubini	*La Medée* (1797). D. Cimerosa *Il Matrimonio Segreto* (1792).
L. van Beethoven	*Fidelio* (1814).
G. Rossini	*Italiana in Algeri* (1813); *The Barber of Seville* (1816); *La Cenerentola* (1817); *Gazza Ladra* (1817); *Semiramide* (1823); *Comte Ory* (1828); *William Tell* (1829).
C.-M. von Weber	*Der Freischutz* (1821); *Oberon* (1826).
V. Bellini	*La Sonnambula* (1831); *Norma* (1831); *I Puritani* (1835).
G. Donizetti	*L'Elisit d'Amore* (1832); *Lucia di Lammermoor* (1835); *Don Pasquale* (1843).
H. Meyerbeer	*Robert le Diable* (1931); *Les Huguenots* (1836); *L'Africaine* (1864).
M. Glinka	*A Life for the Tsar (Ivan Susanin)* (1836); *Ruslan and Ludmila* (1842).
G. Verdi	*Nabucco* (1842); *I Lombardi* (1843); *Macbeth* (1847); *Rigoletto* (1851); *Il Trovatore* (1853); *La Traviata* (1853); *Simon Bocanegra* (1857); *Ballo in Maschera* (1859); *La Forza del Destino* (1862); *Don Carlos* (1869); *Aida* (1869); *Otello* (1887); *Falstaff* (1893).
R. Wagner	*The Flying Dutchman* (1843); *Tannhäuser* (1845); *Lohengrin* (1850); *Tristan und Isolde* (1865); *Der Ring des Nibelungen—Das Rheingold* (1869); *Die Walküre* (1870); *Siegfried* (1876); *Gotterdämmerung* (1876)—*Die Meistersinger* (1868); *Parsifal* (1882).
H. Berlioz	*Les Troyans* (1855); *Béatrice et Bénédict* (1862).
J. Offenbach	*Orphée aux Enfers* (1855); *La Vie Parisienne* (1866); *Tales of Hoffmann* (1881).
C. Gounod	*Faust* (1859); *Mireille* (1864); *Roméo et Juliette* (1867).
A. Thomas	*Mignon* (1866). G. Bizet *The Pearl Fishers* (1863); *Carmen* (1875).
N. Rimsky-Korsakov	*Ivan the Terrible* (1873); *Snow Maiden* (1881); *Golden Cockerel* (1907).
M. P. Mussorgsky	*Boris Godunov* (1874); *Khovanshchina* (1886).
J. Strauss, Jnr.,	*Die Fledermaus* (1874); *Der Zigeunerbaron* (1885).
E. Chabrier	*L'Etoile* (1877). C. Saint-Saëns *Samson and Delilah* (1877).
P. I. Tchaikovsky	*Eugene Onegin* (1878); *The Queen of Spades* (1890); *Iolanta* (1891).
L. Delibes	*Lakmé* (1883). C. Debussy *Pelléas et Mélisande* (1902).
J. Massenet	*Manon* (1884); *Werther* (1892); *Thais* (1894).
B. Smetana	*The Bartered Bride* (1886). A. Borodin *Prince Igor* (1890).
P. Mascagni	*Cavalleria Rusticana* (1890). R. Leoncavallo *I Pagliacci* (1892).
G. Puccini	*La Bohème* (1895); *Madame Butterfly* (1900); *Tosca* (1904); *Turandot* (1926).
F. Cilea	*Adriana Lecouvreur* (1902). G. Charpentier *Louise* (1900).
L. Janáček	*Jenufa* (1904); *The Cunning Little Vixen* (1924); *Katya Kabanova* (1921).
R. Strauss	*Salome* (1905); *Elektra* (1909); *Der Rosenkavalier* (1911); *Ariadne auf Naxos* (1912); *Intermezzo* (1924); *Arabella* (1933); *Capriccio* (1942).
B. Bartok	*Bluebeard's Castle* (1911). M. de Falla *La Vida Breve* (1915).
M. Ravel	*L'Heure Espagnole* (1911); *L'Enfant et les sortilèges* (1925).
S. Prokofiev	*The Love for Three Oranges* (1919); *War and Peace* (1945).
P. Hindemith	*Cardillac* (1926); *Harmonie der Welt* (1957).

The Colonization of Ireland (Seventeenth Century)

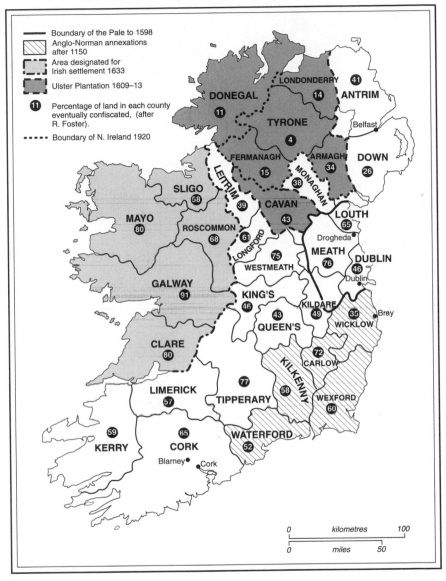

Boundary of the Pale to 1598

Anglo-Norman annexations after 1150

Area designated for Irish settlement 1633

Ulster Plantation 1609–13

11 Percentage of land in each county eventually confiscated, (after R. Foster).

Boundary of N. Ireland 1920

LONDONDERRY **41** ANTRIM

DONEGAL **11**   **14**

TYRONE **4**   Belfast

FERMANAGH **15**   ARMAGH **34**   DOWN **26**

MONAGHAN **38**

SLIGO **58**   LEITRIM **39**   CAVAN **43**   LOUTH **65**

MAYO **80**   ROSCOMMON **68**   **61**   Drogheda

LONGFORD **75**   MEATH **76**   DUBLIN **46**   Dublin

GALWAY **91**   WESTMEATH

KING'S **46**   KILDARE **49**   **35**   Bray

QUEEN'S **43**   WICKLOW

CLARE **80**   KILKENNY **72**   CARLOW

77   **58**   WEXFORD **60**

LIMERICK **57**   TIPPERARY   WATERFORD **52**

59   **65**   CORK

KERRY   Blarney   Cork

0   kilometres   100

0   miles   50

Grand Opera continued from opposite page.

A. Berg	*Wozzeck* (1925).
I. Stravinsky	*Oedipus Rex* (1927); *The Rake's Progress* (1951).
A. Schoenberg	*Moses and Aaron* (1932).
D. Shostakovich	*Lady Macbeth of Mtzensk* (1936).
F. Poulenc	*Les Mamelles de Tirésias* (1947); *Les Dialogues des Carmelites* (1957).
B. Britten	*Peter Grimes* (1945), *Billy Bud* (1951); *Turn of the Screw* (1954); *A Midsummer Night's Dream* (1960); *Death in Venice* (1973).
W. Walton	*Troilus and Cressida* (1954).
M. Tippett	*Midsummer Marriage* (1955); *King Priam* (1961).
K. Penderecki	*The Devils of Loudun* (1969).

Germany during the Thirty Years War, 1618–48

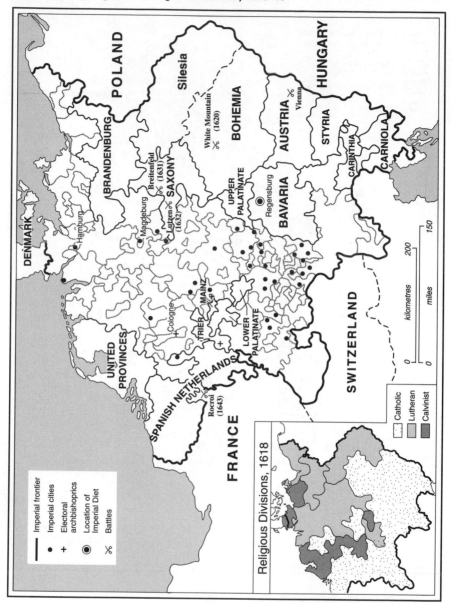

The Franco-German Frontier in Lorraine and Alsace

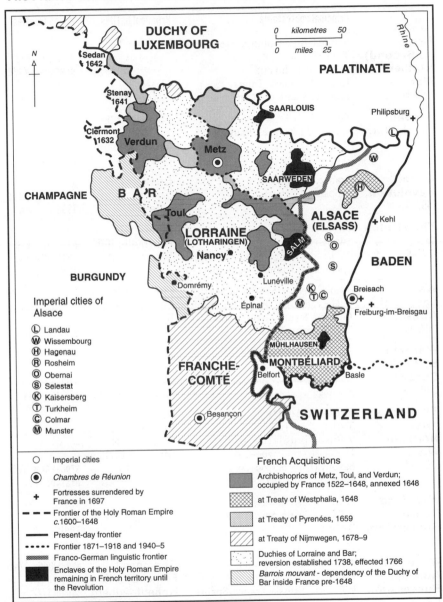

N

DUCHY OF LUXEMBOURG

0 kilometres 50
0 miles 25

Rhine

Sedan 1642

PALATINATE

Stenay 1641

SAARLOUIS

Philipsburg

Clermont 1632

Verdun

Metz

L

SAARWEDEN

W

CHAMPAGNE

B A R

Toul

H

ALSACE (ELSASS)

Kehl

LORRAINE (LOTHARINGEN)

Nancy

SALM

R O

S

BADEN

BURGUNDY

Domrémy

Lunéville

Breisach

Imperial cities of Alsace

Épinal

Freiburg-im-Breisgau

L Landau
W Wissembourg
H Hagenau
R Rosheim
O Obernai
S Selestat
K Kaisersberg
T Turkheim
C Colmar
M Munster

K T C

M

FRANCHE-COMTÉ

MÜHLHAUSEN

MONTBÉLIARD

Belfort

Basle

Besançon

SWITZERLAND

○	Imperial cities
◉	*Chambres de Réunion*
+	Fortresses surrendered by France in 1697
– – –	Frontier of the Holy Roman Empire c.1600–1648
——	Present-day frontier
•••••	Frontier 1871–1918 and 1940–5
▨	Franco-German linguistic frontier
■	Enclaves of the Holy Roman Empire remaining in French territory until the Revolution

French Acquisitions

	Archbishoprics of Metz, Toul, and Verdun; occupied by France 1522–1648, annexed 1648
	at Treaty of Westphalia, 1648
	at Treaty of Pyrenées, 1659
	at Treaty of Nijmwegen, 1678–9
	Duchies of Lorraine and Bar; reversion established 1738, effected 1766
	Barrois mouvant - dependency of the Duchy of Bar inside France pre-1648

Europe's Wars, 1648–1789: A Selection

	Principal contestants	Principal battles	Peace treaties
First (or Second) Northern War, 1655–60	Sweden, Brandenburg, 1656-7, Transylvania v. Poland-Lithuania, Russia, Denmark, Tatars, Empire, Brandenburg 1657-60	Warsaw 1655 Siege of Czestochowa 1655–6 Warka 1656	ROSKILDE 1658 COPENHAGEN 1660 OLIVA 1660 KARDIS 1661
Second Dutch War, 1664–7	England v. United Provinces, France	Lowestoft 1665 The Downs 1666 North Foreland 1666	BREDA 1667
War of Devolution, 1667–8	France, Portugal v. Spain	Charleroi 1667 Lille 1667	AIX-LA-CHAPELLE 1668
Third Dutch War, 1672–9	France, England (1672–4), Sweden (1675–9) v. The Emperor, United Provinces, Spain, Brandenburg, Denmark	Seneff 1674 Fehrbellin 1675 Stromboli 1676	NYJMEGEN 1679 FONTAINEBLEAU 1679
War of the League of Augsburg, 1689–97	France, Savoy (1696–7), James II v. The Emperor, United Provinces, England, Spain, Savoy (until 1695), Brandenburg, Bavaria	Fleurus 1690 Beachy Head 1690 La Hougue 1692	RYSWIJK 1697
War of the Spanish Succession, 1701–13	France, Spain, Bavaria v. the Emperor, United Provinces, England, Savoy, Prussia, Portugal	Blenheim 1704 Ramillies 1706 Oudenarde 1708 Malplaquet 1709	UTRECHT 1713 RASTADT 1714
Third or 'Great Northern War', 1700–21	Sweden, Poland (1705–9), Turkey (1710–11) v. Russia, Prussia (1715–20), Denmark (1700, 1709–20), Saxony (1700–6, 1709–20), Hanover (1715–20)	Narva 1700 Kliszów 1702 Poltava 1709 Stralsund 1715	STOCKHOLM 1720 NYSTADT 1721
War of the Polish Succession, 1733–5	Saxony, Austria, Russia v. France, Spain, Sardinia, Prussia, Bavaria		TURIN 1733 VIENNA 1735
War of the Austrian Succession, 1740–8	Austria, Britain, Holland, Hanover, Saxony, Sardinia v. Bavaria, Prussia, France, Spain, James III	Dettingen 1743 Fontenoy 1745 Hohenfriedberg 1745	NYPHENBURG 1741 BRESLAU 1741 BERLIN 1742 WORMS 1743 WARSAW 1745 AIX-LA-CHAPELLE 1748
Seven Years War, 1756–63	Saxony, Austria, France, Sweden, Russia (until 1762) v. Prussia, Britain, Hanover	Grossjägersdorf 1757 Rossbach 1757 Zorndorf 1758	WESTMINSTER 1756

	Principal contestants	Principal battles	Peace treaties
Seven Years War (continued)		Minden 1759 Kunersdorf 1759 Leignitz 1760 Torgau 1760	STOCKHOLM 1757 PARIS 1763 HUBERTSBURG 1763
War of American Independence, 1774–83	Britain v. USA, France, Spain, & 'Armed Neutrality'	Bunker Hill 1775 Saratoga 1777 Flamborough 1779 Cape St. Vincent 1780 Yorktown 1781 Minorca 1782	 VERSAILLES 1783
War of the Bavarian Succession, 1778–9	Austria v. Prussia, France 'Kartoffelkrieg' 'The Potato War'		TESCHEN 1779
Ottoman Wars in Europe, 1671–1812	Podolian War 1671–6 v. Poland-Lithuania Viennese Campaign 1683 v. Empire, Poland War of the Holy League 1684–99 v. Empire, Poland, Venice, and Russia from 1689 Moldavian Campaign 1710–11 v. Russia Serbian War 1714–18 v. Venice, Austria Austro-Turkish War 1736–9 v. Austria, Russia Russo-Turkish War 1768–74 v. Russia Crimean War 1778–84 v. Russia, Austria from 1781 Russo-Turkish War 1787–92 v. Russia Austro-Turkish War 1788–91 v. Austria Russo-Turkish War 1806–12 v. Russia	 Siege of Vienna Buda 1686 Belgrade 1688 Azov 1696 River Pruth 1711 Peterwardein 1716 Belgrade 1717 Azov 1736 Belgrade Akerman 1769 Chesmé 1770 Ochakov 1788 Belgrade 1789	BUCZACZ 1672 ZURAWNO 1676 CARLOWITZ 1699 PRUTH 1711 PASSAROWITZ 1718 BELGRADE 1739 KUCHUK-KAINARDJI 1774 CONSTANTINOPLE 1784 JASSY 1792 SISTOVA 1791 BUCHAREST 1812
Wars of the Polish Partitions, 1768–95	War of the Confederation of Bar 1768–72. Polish Confederates v. Russia, Prussia, Austria War of the Second Partition 1792–3 Poland v. Russia, Prussia, and Confederates of Targowica War of Poland's National Rising 1794–5. Polish Insurrectionaries (T. Kościuszko) v. Russia, Prussia, Austria	Siege of Czestochowa 1771–2 Zieleńce 1792 Dubienka 1792 Racławice 1794 Maciejowice 1794	TREATY OF THE FIRST PARTITION 1772 TREATY OF THE SECOND PARTITION 1793 TREATY OF THE THIRD PARTITION 1795

The 'Eastern Question': Ottoman Decline, 1683–1920

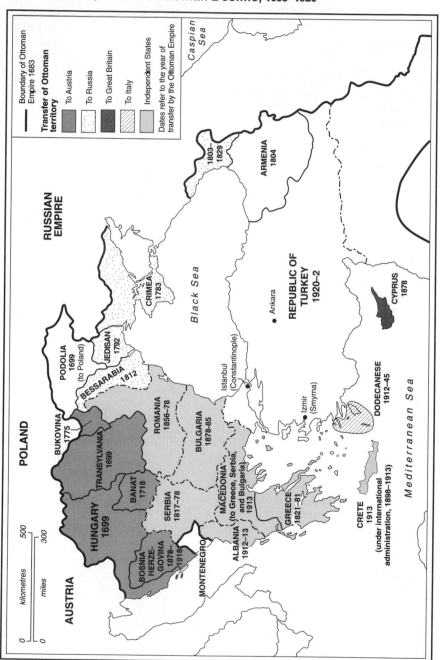

The Formation of the United Kingdom, 1707–1922

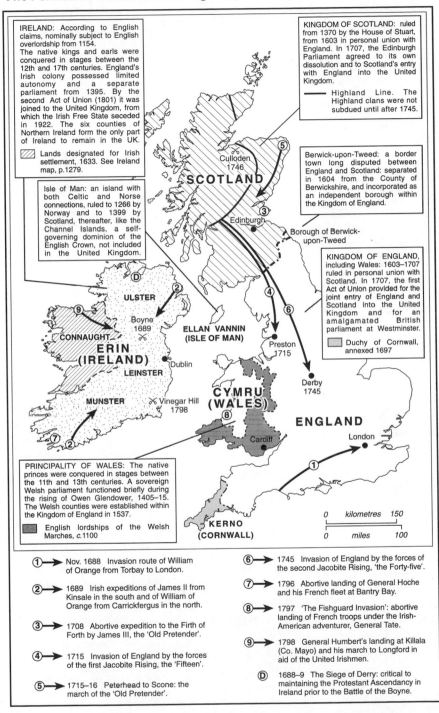

IRELAND: According to English claims, nominally subject to English overlordship from 1154.
The native kings and earls were conquered in stages between the 12th and 17th centuries. England's Irish colony possessed limited autonomy and a separate parliament from 1395. By the second Act of Union (1801) it was joined to the United Kingdom, from which the Irish Free State seceded in 1922. The six counties of Northern Ireland form the only part of Ireland to remain in the UK.

Lands designated for Irish settlement, 1633. See Ireland map, p.1279.

Isle of Man: an island with both Celtic and Norse connections, ruled to 1266 by Norway and to 1399 by Scotland, thereafter, like the Channel Islands, a self-governing dominion of the English Crown, not included in the United Kingdom.

KINGDOM OF SCOTLAND: ruled from 1370 by the House of Stuart, from 1603 in personal union with England. In 1707, the Edinburgh Parliament agreed to its own dissolution and to Scotland's entry with England into the United Kingdom.

Highland Line. The Highland clans were not subdued until after 1745.

Berwick-upon-Tweed: a border town long disputed between England and Scotland: separated in 1604 from the County of Berwickshire, and incorporated as an independent borough within the Kingdom of England.

KINGDOM OF ENGLAND, including Wales: 1603–1707 ruled in personal union with Scotland. In 1707, the first Act of Union provided for the joint entry of England and Scotland into the United Kingdom and for an amalgamated British parliament at Westminster.

Duchy of Cornwall, annexed 1697

PRINCIPALITY OF WALES: The native princes were conquered in stages between the 11th and 13th centuries. A sovereign Welsh parliament functioned briefly during the rising of Owen Glendower, 1405–15. The Welsh counties were established within the Kingdom of England in 1537.

English lordships of the Welsh Marches, c.1100

SCOTLAND
Culloden 1746
Edinburgh
Borough of Berwick-upon-Tweed

ULSTER
Boyne 1689
CONNAUGHT
ERIN (IRELAND)
Dublin
LEINSTER
MUNSTER   Vinegar Hill 1798

ELLAN VANNIN (ISLE OF MAN)
Preston 1715

Derby 1745

CYMRU (WALES)
Cardiff

ENGLAND
London

KERNO (CORNWALL)

| | 0 | kilometres | 150 |
| 0 | miles | 100 |

(1)→ Nov. 1688 Invasion route of William of Orange from Torbay to London.

(2)→ 1689 Irish expeditions of James II from Kinsale in the south and of William of Orange from Carrickfergus in the north.

(3)→ 1708 Abortive expedition to the Firth of Forth by James III, the 'Old Pretender'.

(4)→ 1715 Invasion of England by the forces of the first Jacobite Rising, the 'Fifteen'.

(5)→ 1715–16 Peterhead to Scone: the march of the 'Old Pretender'.

(6)→ 1745 Invasion of England by the forces of the second Jacobite Rising, 'the Forty-five'.

(7)→ 1796 Abortive landing of General Hoche and his French fleet at Bantry Bay.

(8)→ 1797 'The Fishguard Invasion': abortive landing of French troops under the Irish-American adventurer, General Tate.

(9)→ 1798 General Humbert's landing at Killala (Co. Mayo) and his march to Longford in aid of the United Irishmen.

(D) 1688–9 The Siege of Derry: critical to maintaining the Protestant Ascendancy in Ireland prior to the Battle of the Boyne.

Chronology of the French Revolutionary Era 1789–1815

Events in France, 1789–1815

1789	5 May	The Estates-General meets
	20 June	Tennis Court Oath: National Assembly
	14 July	storming of the Bastille
	4/5 August	abolition of the feudal order
	27 August	declaration of the Rights of Man

1790	12 July	Civil Constitution of the Clergy

1791	20 June	The Flight to Varennes: King's arrest
	3 September	Constitution: constitutional monarchy

1792	20 April	declaration of war on Austria
	10 August	storming of the Tuileries
	20 September	National Convention: republic declared, monarchy abolished. Girondin supremacy

1793	21 January	execution of Louis XVI
	2 June	fall of the Girondins; installation of 'Revolutionary Government'
	July	Committee of Public Safety; Terror begins; Jacobins' Constitution of Year I; War against the Vendée Rising

1794	27/28 July	fall of Robespierre (9 Thermidor); the 'Thermidorian Reaction'
	September	abolition of the revolutionary tribunal

1795	5 March	Peace of Basle
	17 August	Constitution of Year III; Directory created

1796/7		campaign in Upper Italy

1797	4 September	coup d'état of 18 Fructidor; rise of Bonaparte
	October	Annexation of Belgium: Cisalpine Republic

1798/9		campaign in Egypt

1799		beginning of 2nd War of the Coalition
	9 November	coup d'état of 18 Brumaire; dissolution of the Directory; Bonaparte's Constitution of Year VIII; Consulate created; Napoleon elected First Consul

1801		Concordat with the Papacy
	9 February	Peace of Lunéville

1802	27 March	Peace of Amiens
	2 August	Constitution of Year X; Bonaparte Life Consul; Annexation of Piedmont

1803		The 'Armée de l'Angleterre' camps at Boulogne

1804	21 March	promulgation of Code Napoléon
	2 December	Constitution of Year XII; French Empire created

1805		Napoleon, King of Italy
	August–Dec.	War of the Third Coalition

France's Wars, 1792–1815

1792–1797
War of the First Coalition
Membership
- from 1792: Austria, Prussia (to March 1795)
- from 1793: Britain, the Netherlands (to 1795); Spain (to June 1795); Portugal, Naples, Sardinia, the Papal State (to 1796)

Principal battles
Valmy (20 September 1792); Neerwinden (18 March 1793); Lodi (10 May 1796)
Treaties
Basle (5 March 1795); Campo Formio (17 October 1797)

1799–1802
War of the Second Coalition
Membership
Britain, Austria (to 9 February 1801); Russia (to 22 October 1799); Turkey, Naples, Portugal (to June 1801)
Principal battles
Pyramids (21 July 1798); Aboukir (Battle of the Nile) (1 August 1798); Marengo (14 June 1800); Hohenlinden (3 December 1800)
Treaties
Lunéville (9 February 1801); Amiens (27 March 1802)

1805
War of the Third Coalition
Membership
Britain, Austria, Russia, Prussia, Naples, Sweden
Principal battles
Ulm (20 October 1805); Trafalgar (21 October 1805); Austerlitz (2 December 1805)
Treaties
Schönbrunn (12 December 1805); Pressburg (26 December 1805)

1806		Joseph Bonaparte, King of Naples; Confederation of the Rhine; Holy Roman Empire abolished
	September	War of the Coalition
	November	proclamation of the Continental System
	21 November	Berlin Decree: Continental System proclaimed
1807		Jerome Bonaparte, King of Westphalia; Grand Duchy of Warsaw created
	July	Treaty of Tilsit: Franco-Russian Accord; Occupation of Portugal
1808	May	Bayonne Talks: Re-organisation of Spain
	27 September to 14 October	Congress of Erfurt
1808/9		campaign in Spain
1809		Illyrian Provinces created Annexation of Rome and Papal States
	April	beginning of 5th War of the Coalition
	14 October	Peace of Schönbrunn
1810		Annexation of Holland and North Germany Bernadotte, Prince Royal of Sweden
1812	24 June to December	Russian Campaign: Napoleon's 'Polish War'; collapse of the Grand Army in Russia
1813		German Campaign: 'War of Liberation' begins
1814	31 March	capitulation of Paris
	6 April	Napoleon's first abdication: exile to Elba
	24 April	Restoration of Louis XVIII
	30 May	Treaty of Paris I: frontiers of 1792 re-instated
	4 June	Royal Charter restores constitutional monarchy
	September	Congress of Vienna convened
1815	6/7 March	Napoleon lands at Cannes; The '100 Days' begin
	May to June	campaign in Belgium
	9 June	Napoleon's second Abdication: exile to St. Helena
	22 June	Final Act of the Congress of Vienna
	20 November	Treaty of Paris II: foreign occupation, reparations

1806–1807
War of the Fourth Coalition
Membership
Britain, Prussia, Russia, Saxony
Principal battles
Jena and Auerstedt (14 October 1806);
Prussian Eylau (8 February 1807);
Friedland (14 June 1807)
Treaties
Posen (December 1806);
Tilsit (7–9 July 1807)

1808–15
Peninsular War

1809
War of the Fifth Coalition
Membership
Britain, Austria
Principal battles
Aspern (22 May 1809); Wagram (5 July 1809)
Treaties
Schönbrunn (14 October 1809)

1812
Russian War
Principal battles
Smolensk (18 August 1812); Borodino
(7 September 1812); crossing of the
Berezina (26–28 November 1812)

1813–1815
War of the Sixth Coalition
Membership
Russia, Prussia (from March 1813), Britain
(from June 1813), Austria (from August
1813), Sweden, Spain, Portugal
Principal battles
Leipzig (16–19 October 1813);
Tolentino (3 May 1815); Ligny
(15 June 1815); Waterloo (18 June 1815)
Treaties
Paris I (30 May 1814); Vienna (9 June 1815);
Paris II (20 November 1815)

The French Revolutionary Calendar, Years I–VIII (1792–1800)

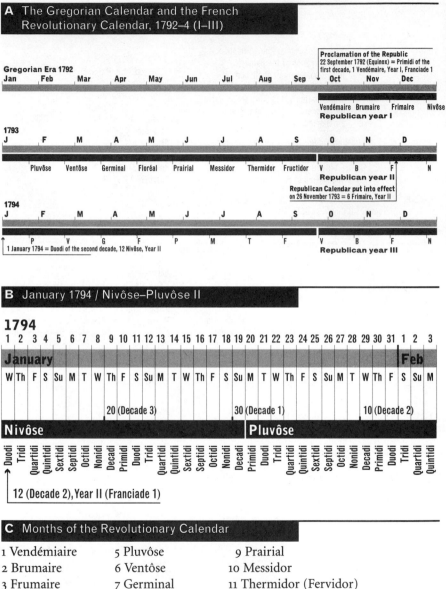

A The Gregorian Calendar and the French Revolutionary Calendar, 1792–4 (I–III)

B January 1794 / Nivôse–Pluvôse II

C Months of the Revolutionary Calendar

1 Vendémiaire	5 Pluvôse	9 Prairial
2 Brumaire	6 Ventôse	10 Messidor
3 Frumaire	7 Germinal	11 Thermidor (Fervidor)
4 Nivôse	8 Floréal	12 Fructidor

Sources: H. Morse Stephens, *Revolutionary Europe 1789–1815* (London, 1936), pp. 374–5, J. J. Bond, *A Handy-book of Rules and Tables*, (London, 1869), pp. 102–12.

D The Republican Era, years I–VIII

Jan	Feb	Mar	Apr	May	Jun	Jul	Aug	Sep	Oct	Nov	Dec

1792　　　　　　　　　　　　　　　　　　　　　　　　a

Year I
Ven　Bru　Fri　Niv

1793　　b
Plu　Ven　Ger　Flo　Pra　Mes　The　Fru
Year II
V　B　F　N

1794　　　　　　　　　　　　c
Plu　Ven　Ger　Flo　Pra　Mes　The　Fru
Year III
V　B　F　N

1795　　　　d　　　　　　　　　　　　　e
Plu　Ven　Ger　Flo　Pra　Mes　The　Fru
Year IV
V　B　F　N

1796
Plu　Ven　Ger　Flo　Pra　Mes　The　Fru
Year V
V　B　F　N

1797　　　　　　　　　　　　　　f
Plu　Ven　Ger　Flo　Pra　Mes　The　Fru
Year VI
V　B　F　N

1798
Plu　Ven　Ger　Flo　Pra　Mes　The　Fru
Year VII
V　B　F　N

1799　　　　　　　g
Plu　Ven　Ger　Flo　Pra　Mes　The　Fru
Year VIII
V　B　F　N

	Event	Revolutionary Calendar	Gregorian Calendar
a	Proclamation of the Republic	1 Vendémiaire I	22 September 1792
b	Execution of Louis XVI	2 Pluvôse I	21 January 1793
c	Fall of Robespierre	9 Thermidor II	27 July 1794
d	Constitution of Year III	14 Germinal III	3 April 1795
e	Insurrection of Vendémiaire	13 Vendémiaire IV	5 October 1795
f	Revolt of Fructidor	18 Fructidor V	4 September 1797
g	Bonaparte's Coup d'Etat	30 Prairial VII	18 June 1799

The Crimea, with Russian Colonization of the Black Sea Coastland

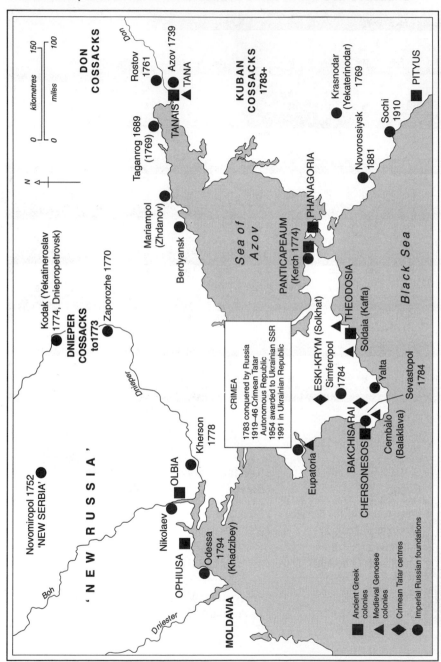

CRIMEA
1783 conquered by Russia
1919–46 Crimean Tatar
Autonomous Republic
1954 awarded to Ukrainian SSR
1991 in Ukrainian Republic

Ancient Greek colonies

Medieval Genoese colonies

Crimean Tatar centres

Imperial Russian foundations

The French Empire, 1812

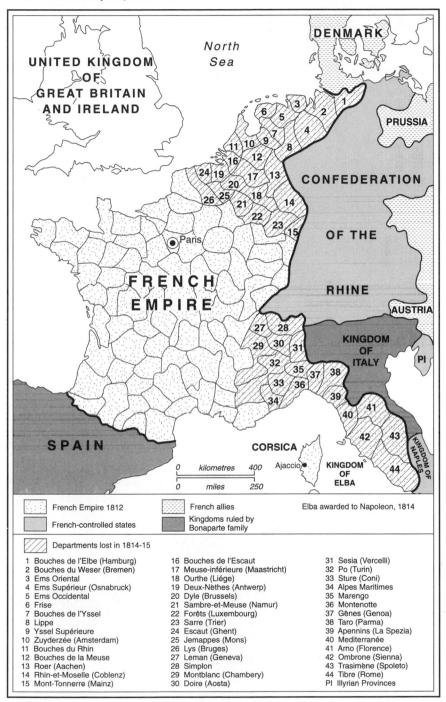

Departments lost in 1814-15

1 Bouches de l'Elbe (Hamburg)
2 Bouches du Weser (Bremen)
3 Ems Oriental
4 Ems Supérieur (Osnabruck)
5 Ems Occidental
6 Frise
7 Bouches de l'Yssel
8 Lippe
9 Yssel Supérieure
10 Zuyderzée (Amsterdam)
11 Bouches du Rhin
12 Bouches de la Meuse
13 Roer (Aachen)
14 Rhin-et-Moselle (Coblenz)
15 Mont-Tonnerre (Mainz)

16 Bouches de l'Escaut
17 Meuse-inférieure (Maastricht)
18 Ourthe (Liége)
19 Deux-Nèthes (Antwerp)
20 Dyle (Brussels)
21 Sambre-et-Meuse (Namur)
22 Forêts (Luxembourg)
23 Sarre (Trier)
24 Escaut (Ghent)
25 Jemappes (Mons)
26 Lys (Bruges)
27 Leman (Geneva)
28 Simplon
29 Montblanc (Chambery)
30 Doire (Aosta)

31 Sesia (Vercelli)
32 Po (Turin)
33 Sture (Coni)
34 Alpes Maritimes
35 Marengo
36 Montenotte
37 Gènes (Genoa)
38 Taro (Parma)
39 Apennins (La Spezia)
40 Mediterranée
41 Arno (Florence)
42 Ombrone (Sienna)
43 Trasimène (Spoleto)
44 Tibre (Rome)
Pl Illyrian Provinces

Grillenstein: The Life Course of an Austrian Peasant Household, 1810–42

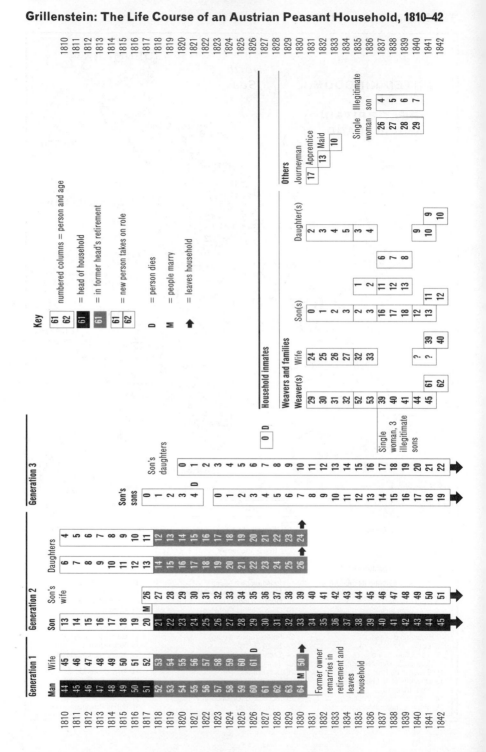

Modernization: The Component Processes

(The Industrial Revolution)

 1. Scientific and mechanized agriculture
 2. Mobility of Labour: enclosures, emancipation of the serfs
 3. New sources of power: coal, steam, gas, oil, electricity
 4. Power-driven machinery
 5. Heavy industry: mining and metallurgy
 6. Factories and factory towns
 7. Improved transport: canals, roads, railways, flight
 8. Communications: post, telegraph, telephone, radio
 9. Capital investment: joint-stock companies, trusts, cartels
10. Expanding domestic markets: new industries, internal trade
11. Foreign trade: import and export, colonies
12. Government policy
13. Demography: rapid population growth and its consequences

14. The money economy: wages, prices, taxes, paper money
15. Marketing skills: advertising, stores, sales distribution
16. Science and technology: research and development
17. Financial services: credit, savings banks, insurance
18. Standardization of weights, measures, and currencies

19. Urbanization: town planning, public services
20. New social classes: middle classes, domestics, 'workers'
21. Transformation of family structures: 'the nuclear family'
22. Women: dependency and subordination
23. Migration: local, regional, international
24. Public health: epidemics, hygiene, medical services
25. Poverty: unemployment, vagrancy, workhouses, slums
26. Exploitation: child labour, female labour, sweatshops
27. Organized crime: police, detectives, criminal underclass
28. Private charities

29. Education: primary, technical, scientific, executive, female
30. Literacy and mass culture
31. Leisure: organized recreation and sport
32. Youth movements
33. Religious trends: fundamentalism, temperance, worker priests
34. Social sciences: economics, anthropology, ethnography, etc.

35. Collectivism: industrial and urban psychology
36. Consumerism
37. Class consciousness
38. National consciousness
39. Political consciousness

40. Extension of the electorate: universal suffrage, suffragettes
41. Political parties with mass constituencies
42. State-run welfare: pensions, social insurance, benefits
43. Elaborate social legislation
44. Expansion of the civil service: state bureaucracy
45. Reorganization of local government
46. Political associations and pressure groups: trade unions
47. Imperialism
48. Total war: conscript armies, mechanized warfare, home front

European Demography, 1800–1914

1 European population by country

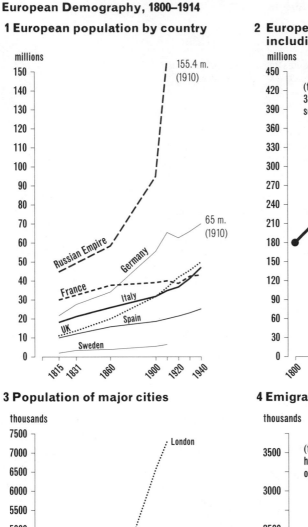

millions

155.4 m.
(1910)

65 m.
(1910)

Russian Empire

Germany

France

Italy

UK

Spain

Sweden

2 European population including European Russia

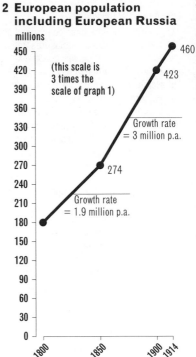

millions

460

423

(this scale is 3 times the scale of graph 1)

Growth rate = 3 million p.a.

274

Growth rate = 1.9 million p.a.

3 Population of major cities

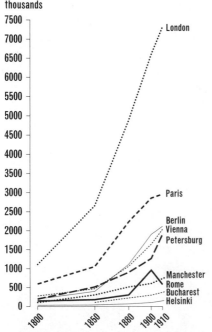

thousands

London

Paris

Berlin
Vienna
Petersburg

Manchester
Rome
Bucharest
Helsinki

4 Emigration from Europe

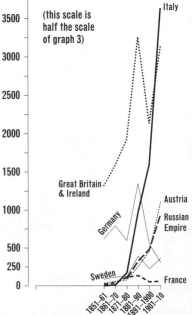

thousands

Italy

(this scale is half the scale of graph 3)

Great Britain & Ireland

Germany

Austria

Russian Empire

Sweden

France

Indices of Liberalization, 1791–1948

Country	State constitutions		Universal male suffrage	Women's suffrage	Jewish emancipation*
France	1791 1830 1848	1852 1875 1946	1848 1852 1870	1944	1791
Poland	1791 1815	1921	1918	1919	(1809) 1921
Sweden	1809		1909	1919	1838 1870
Spain	1812		1890		
Norway	1814		1898	1912	1851
Netherlands	1814		1896	1946	1796
Portugal	1821		1910		
Belgium	1831		1893	1948	1831
Greece	1844 1864			1952	1830
Switzerland	1848		1848 1874	1971	1866
Italy	1861(71)			n.a.	1945
Piedmont/ Sardinia	1848		1912	—	1870
Austria	1849		1907	—	
Hungary	1867		1907	— n.a.	1867
Denmark	1849		1915		1814 1849
Prussia	1850		1850	n.a.	1812
German Empire	1871		1871	1919	1871
Romania	1864		n.a.	n.a.	1919–1923
Ottoman Empire	1876		1908	1934	
Great Britain	—		1884	1928	1871
Ireland	1922		1922	1922	—
Jugoslavia	1921		1921	1946	—

n.a. data not available   — does not apply   * removal of all limitations on Jewish civil rights

Selected Indices of Industrialization, 1800–1914

Output of coal (■ = 10,000,000 metric tonnes)

	Austria	France	Germany	UK	Sweden	Italy	Russian Empire
1815	95,000	882,000	1,300,000	18,200,000	—	—	—
1850	877,000	4,434,000	5,100,000	50,200,000	26,000	34,000	300,000
1875	4,471,000	16,957,000	47,800,000	135,400,000	64,000	117,000	1,700,000
1900	10,990,000	33,404,000	142,650,000	228,800,000	252,000	480,000	16,160,000
1913	16,460,000	40,844,000	277,330,000	292,000,000	364,000	701,000	36,050,000

Output of pig iron (■ = 1,000,000 metric tonnes)

	Austria	France	Germany	UK	Sweden	Italy	Russian Empire
1815	—	—	—	310,000	—	—	123,000
1850	155,000	406,000	210,000	2,285,000	142,000	—	228,000
1875	303,000	1,448,000	1,759,000	6,467,000	351,000	28,000	428,000
1900	1,000,000	2,714,000	7,550,000	9,104,000	526,000	24,000	2,937,000
1913	1,758,000	5,207,000	16,761,000	10,425,000	730,000	427,000	4,641,000

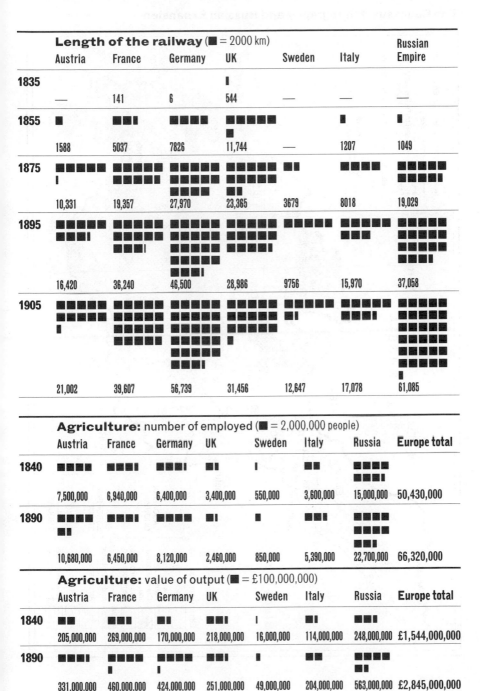

Length of the railway (■ = 2000 km)

	Austria	France	Germany	UK	Sweden	Italy	Russian Empire
1835	—	141	6	544	—	—	—
1855	1588	5037	7826	11,744	—	1207	1049
1875	10,331	19,357	27,970	23,365	3679	8018	19,029
1895	16,420	36,240	46,500	28,986	9756	15,970	37,058
1905	21,002	39,607	56,739	31,456	12,647	17,078	61,085

Agriculture: number of employed (■ = 2,000,000 people)

	Austria	France	Germany	UK	Sweden	Italy	Russia	**Europe total**
1840	7,500,000	6,940,000	6,400,000	3,400,000	550,000	3,600,000	15,000,000	50,430,000
1890	10,680,000	6,450,000	8,120,000	2,460,000	850,000	5,390,000	22,700,000	66,320,000

Agriculture: value of output (■ = £100,000,000)

	Austria	France	Germany	UK	Sweden	Italy	Russia	**Europe total**
1840	205,000,000	269,000,000	170,000,000	218,000,000	16,000,000	114,000,000	248,000,000	£1,544,000,000
1890	331,000,000	460,000,000	424,000,000	251,000,000	49,000,000	204,000,000	563,000,000	£2,845,000,000

The Caucasus: Ethnography and Russian Expansion

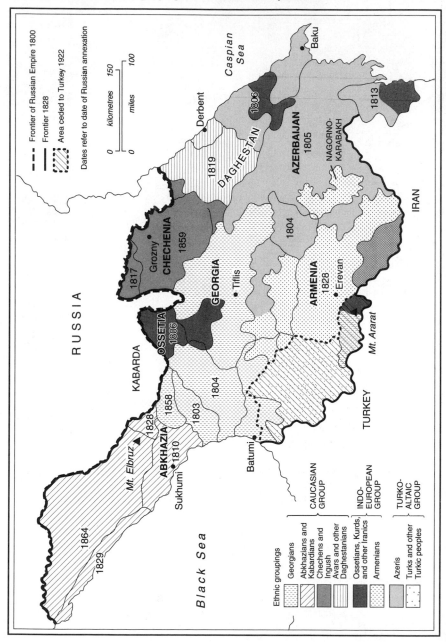

Germany: The Confederation and the Empire, 1815–1918

DENMARK

N. SCHLESWIG
(to Denmark
1920)

Königsberg

EAST
PRUSSIA

Danzig

to
Poland
1920

Hamburg   MECKLENBURG

NETHERLANDS

OLDEN-
BURG

⊙ Berlin

BRUNSWICK

P R U S S I A

Posen

RUSSIAN
EMPIRE

Essen

Breslau

BELGIUM

WESTPHALIA

Leipzig

Eupen and
Malmédy
(to Belgium)

Cologne

HESSE

THURINGIAN
STATES

SAXONY

UPPER
SILESIA

Kattowitz

BOHEMIA

PALA-
TINATE

ALSACE

BAVARIA

AUSTRIA

Strasbourg

WÜRTTEM-
BERG

BADEN

Munich

⊙
Vienna

HUNGARY

FRANCE

SWITZERLAND

| 0 | kilometres | 200 |
| 0 | miles | 150 |

| Territories lost in 1918–21 | •••• Boundary of North German Confederation 1867 |
| — — Boundary of German Confederation 1815 | —— Boundary of German Empire, 1871–1918 |

Queen Victoria (1819–1901) and her Relatives

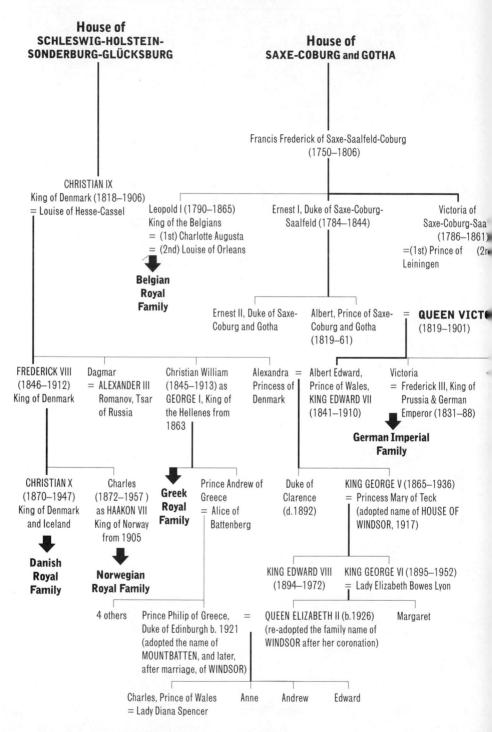

House of
SCHLESWIG-HOLSTEIN-
SONDERBURG-GLÜCKSBURG

House of
SAXE-COBURG and GOTHA

Francis Frederick of Saxe-Saalfeld-Coburg
(1750–1806)

CHRISTIAN IX
King of Denmark (1818–1906)
= Louise of Hesse-Cassel

Leopold I (1790–1865)
King of the Belgians
= (1st) Charlotte Augusta
= (2nd) Louise of Orleans

Ernest I, Duke of Saxe-Coburg-
Saalfeld (1784–1844)

Victoria of
Saxe-Coburg-Saa
(1786–1861)
=(1st) Prince of   (2n
Leiningen

Belgian
Royal
Family

Ernest II, Duke of Saxe-
Coburg and Gotha

Albert, Prince of Saxe-
Coburg and Gotha
(1819–61)

= **QUEEN VICT**
(1819–1901)

FREDERICK VIII
(1846–1912)
King of Denmark

Dagmar
= ALEXANDER III
Romanov, Tsar
of Russia

Christian William
(1845–1913) as
GEORGE I, King of
the Hellenes from
1863

Alexandra =
Princess of
Denmark

Albert Edward,
Prince of Wales,
KING EDWARD VII
(1841–1910)

Victoria
= Frederick III, King of
Prussia & German
Emperor (1831–88)

German Imperial
Family

CHRISTIAN X
(1870–1947)
King of Denmark
and Iceland

Charles
(1872–1957)
as HAAKON VII
King of Norway
from 1905

Greek
Royal
Family

Prince Andrew of
Greece
= Alice of
Battenberg

Duke of
Clarence
(d.1892)

KING GEORGE V (1865–1936)
= Princess Mary of Teck
(adopted name of HOUSE OF
WINDSOR, 1917)

Danish
Royal
Family

Norwegian
Royal Family

KING EDWARD VIII
(1894–1972)

KING GEORGE VI (1895–1952)
= Lady Elizabeth Bowes Lyon

4 others

Prince Philip of Greece,
Duke of Edinburgh b. 1921
(adopted the name of
MOUNTBATTEN, and later,
after marriage, of WINDSOR)

=

QUEEN ELIZABETH II (b.1926)
(re-adopted the family name of
WINDSOR after her coronation)

Margaret

Charles, Prince of Wales
= Lady Diana Spencer

Anne   Andrew   Edward

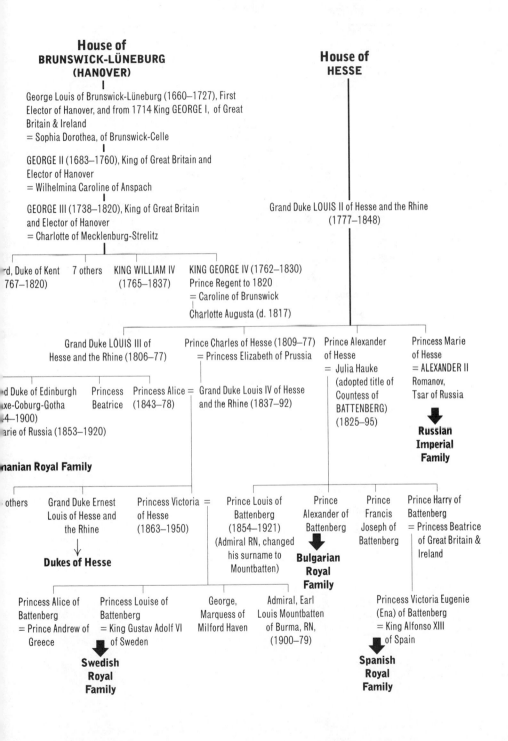

House of BRUNSWICK-LÜNEBURG (HANOVER)

George Louis of Brunswick-Lüneburg (1660–1727), First
Elector of Hanover, and from 1714 King GEORGE I, of Great
Britain & Ireland
= Sophia Dorothea, of Brunswick-Celle

GEORGE II (1683–1760), King of Great Britain and
Elector of Hanover
= Wilhelmina Caroline of Anspach

GEORGE III (1738–1820), King of Great Britain
and Elector of Hanover
= Charlotte of Mecklenburg-Strelitz

House of HESSE

Grand Duke LOUIS II of Hesse and the Rhine
(1777–1848)

...d, Duke of Kent   7 others   KING WILLIAM IV   KING GEORGE IV (1762–1830)
767–1820)   (1765–1837)   Prince Regent to 1820
                                                    = Caroline of Brunswick
                                                    Charlotte Augusta (d. 1817)

Grand Duke LOUIS III of   Prince Charles of Hesse (1809–77)   Prince Alexander   Princess Marie
Hesse and the Rhine (1806–77)   = Princess Elizabeth of Prussia   of Hesse   of Hesse
                                                                        = Julia Hauke   = ALEXANDER II
...d Duke of Edinburgh   Princess   Princess Alice = Grand Duke Louis IV of Hesse   (adopted title of   Romanov,
...xe-Coburg-Gotha   Beatrice   (1843–78)   and the Rhine (1837–92)   Countess of   Tsar of Russia
...4–1900)   BATTENBERG)
...arie of Russia (1853–1920)   (1825–95)   **Russian
                                                                                          Imperial
...nanian Royal Family   Family**

...others   Grand Duke Ernest   Princess Victoria =   Prince Louis of   Prince   Prince   Prince Harry of
            Louis of Hesse and   of Hesse   Battenberg   Alexander of   Francis   Battenberg
            the Rhine   (1863–1950)   (1854–1921)   Battenberg   Joseph of   = Princess Beatrice
                                                        (Admiral RN, changed   Battenberg   of Great Britain &
            Dukes of Hesse   his surname to   **Bulgarian   Ireland
                                                        Mountbatten)   Royal
                                                                          Family**

Princess Alice of   Princess Louise of   George,   Admiral, Earl   Princess Victoria Eugenie
Battenberg   Battenberg   Marquess of   Louis Mountbatten   (Ena) of Battenberg
= Prince Andrew of   = King Gustav Adolf VI Milford Haven   of Burma, RN,   = King Alfonso XIII
Greece   of Sweden   (1900–79)   of Spain

**Swedish   **Spanish
Royal   Royal
Family**   Family**

The Expansion of Greece, 1821–1945

SERBIA

BULGARIA

Black Sea

Adriatic Sea

Edirne (Adrianople)

Constantinople

Alexandropolis (Dedeagatch)

⑤

ITALY

ALBANIA

Thessalonika

④

IMBROS

CORFU   Janina   Trikkala

③

LIMNOS

LESBOS

TURKEY

Missolonghi

④

CHIOS

Athens

Smyrna (Izmir)

Patras

①

ZAKINTHOS

②

Navarino (1827)

⑥

RHODES

④   Heraklion

| 0 | kilometres | 200 |
| 0 | miles | 150 |

① 1832 Peloponnese

② 1863 Ionian Islands (from Britain)

③ 1881 Thessaly

④ 1913 Macedonia, Eastern Aegean, and Crete

⑤ 1919 Western Thrace (from Bulgaria)

⑥ 1945 Dodecanese (from Italy)

Occupied by Greece 1920–2

CYPRUS—claimed by the Greek Enosis Movement from 1945; Independent Republic, 1960–74; 1974, Republic of Northern Cyprus established by Turkish invasion.

Nicosia

Springtime of Nations: The Revolutions of 1846–9

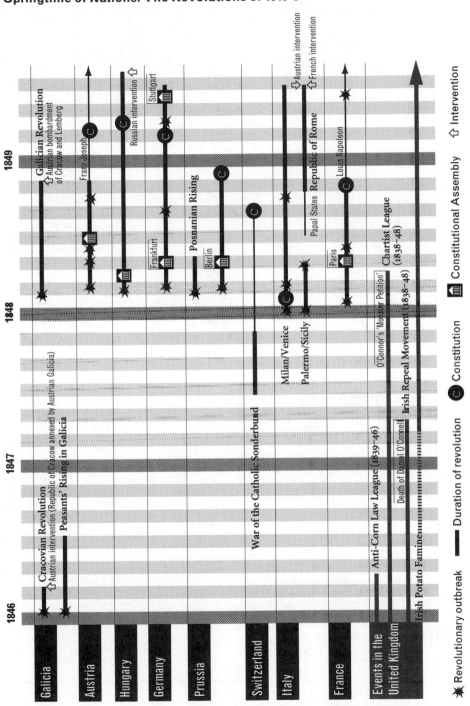

The Unification of Italy, 1859–70

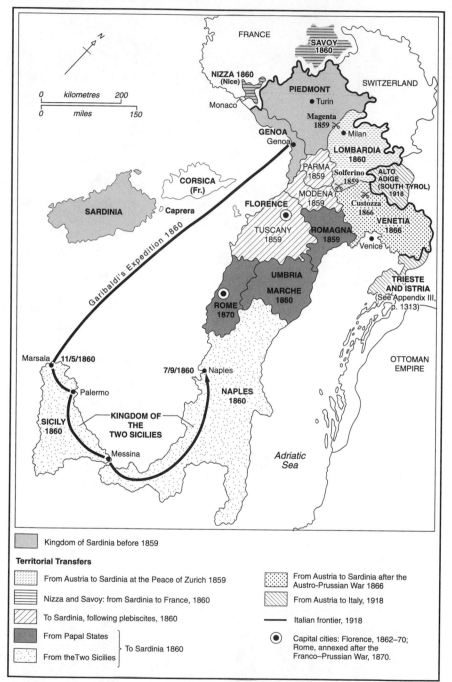

FRANCE

SAVOY
1860

NIZZA 1860
(Nice)

PIEDMONT   SWITZERLAND

● Turin

Monaco   **Magenta**
                          1859 ✕
                                   ● Milan
GENOA
Genoa ●   **LOMBARDIA**
                          1860
                    PARMA
                    1859   **Solferino**   **ALTO**
                              1859   **ADIGE**
                                        (SOUTH TYROL)
                    MODENA   **1918**
FLORENCE   **1859**
                              Custozza
SARDINIA   *Caprera*   ●   **1866**
                                      VENETIA
                    TUSCANY **ROMAGNA** **1866**
                    1859   **1859**
                                   Venice

                    UMBRIA
                                        TRIESTE
                    MARCHE   **AND ISTRIA**
                    1860   (See Appendix III,
              ROME   p. 1313)
              1870

kilometres
miles

CORSICA
(Fr.)

Marsala   **11/5/1860**   **7/9/1860** ● Naples   OTTOMAN
                                                             EMPIRE
● Palermo   **NAPLES**
                                   1860
SICILY   **KINGDOM OF**
1860   **THE**
             TWO SICILIES
              ● Messina   *Adriatic*
                                           Sea

0   *kilometres*   200
0   *miles*   150

Garibaldi's Expedition 1860

Territorial Transfers

Kingdom of Sardinia before 1859

From Austria to Sardinia at the Peace of Zurich 1859

Nizza and Savoy: from Sardinia to France, 1860

To Sardinia, following plebiscites, 1860

From Papal States
                        } To Sardinia 1860
From the Two Sicilies

From Austria to Sardinia after the
Austro-Prussian War 1866

From Austria to Italy, 1918

——— Italian frontier, 1918

⊙   Capital cities: Florence, 1862–70;
    Rome, annexed after the
    Franco–Prussian War, 1870.

Slesvig (Schleswig) and Holstein

N

SCHLESWIG/SLESVIG: Province of mixed Danish and German population—ruled by Denmark with Holstein, 1815–64. Chief city—Flensburg

HOLSTEIN—Duchy of the Holy Roman Empire. Ruled by Denmark from 1400, and with Schleswig, from 1815–64. Chief city—Kiel.

SCHLESWIG AND HOLSTEIN were conquered by Prussia in 1864, jointly administered by Prussia and Austria 1864–7, and annexed by Prussia in 1866. From 1945, Schleswig-Holstein is a Land of the German Federal Republic

PLEBISCITE AREA (1920) N. Schleswig (S. Jutland) voted 75% for inclusion in Denmark. The southern zone, including Flensburg, voted 81% for Germany

Frontier from 1920

HELIGOLAND. 1807–90 ruled by Great Britain. 1892 incorporated into the Prussian province of Schleswig-Holstein

Aalborg

JYLLAND
(JUTLAND)

Kattegat

Esbjerg

COPENHAGEN

SJAELLAND
(ZEALAND)

Odense

FYN

S.
JYLLAND
(N. SLESVIG)

Doppel

Sonderburg

LOLLAND

Flensburg

Glucksburg

SCHLESWIG

Schleswig

Rensburg

KIEL

HELIGOLAND

Kiel Canal

HOLSTEIN

Lübeck

MECKLENBURG

Cuxhaven

HAMBURG

0   kilometres   50

0   miles   25

The Growth of Romania, 1861–1945

① 1861 Ţara Românească, 'the Romanian Land'
(Wallachia and Moldavia)

② 1878 Dobrogea (Dobrudja)

③ 1913 S. Dobrogea from Bulgaria, lost 1945

④ 1918 Basarabia (Bessarabia) (see box), lost 1944

⑤ 1919 Bucovina (Bukovina) (see box), lost 1944

⑥ 1920 Transilvania (Transylvania), from Hungary

⑦ Transnistria; occupied by Romania, 1941–4

——— Boundary 1920   – – – Present-day
boundary

BESSARABIA, now MOLDOVA. In Russian
Empire 1812–1917; in the Moldavian SSR
1940–1, 1944–91; in Romania 1918–40,
1941–4; independent since 1991.

BUCOVINA (BUKOVINA) In Austria until 1918,
in Ukraine 1918–19, 1940–1, since 1944; in
Romania, 1919–40.

The Dual Monarchy: The Nationalities of Austria-Hungary, 1867–1918

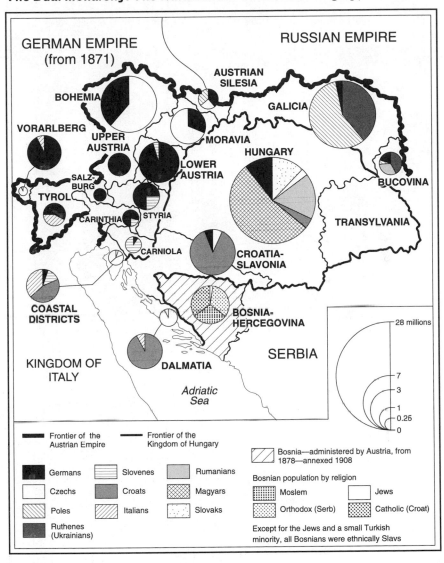

GERMAN EMPIRE
(from 1871)

RUSSIAN EMPIRE

AUSTRIAN
SILESIA

BOHEMIA

GALICIA

VORARLBERG

UPPER
AUSTRIA

MORAVIA

LOWER
AUSTRIA

HUNGARY

SALZ-
BURG

BUCOVINA

TYROL

CARINTHIA

STYRIA

TRANSYLVANIA

CARNIOLA

CROATIA-
SLAVONIA

COASTAL
DISTRICTS

BOSNIA-
HERCEGOVINA

28 millions

KINGDOM OF
ITALY

DALMATIA

SERBIA

7

3

Adriatic
Sea

1

0.25

0

Frontier of the
Austrian Empire

Frontier of the
Kingdom of Hungary

Bosnia—administered by Austria, from
1878—annexed 1908

Germans

Slovenes

Rumanians

Bosnian population by religion

Czechs

Croats

Magyars

Moslem

Jews

Poles

Italians

Slovaks

Orthodox (Serb)

Catholic (Croat)

Ruthenes
(Ukrainians)

Except for the Jews and a small Turkish
minority, all Bosnians were ethnically Slavs

The Pedigree of Socialism

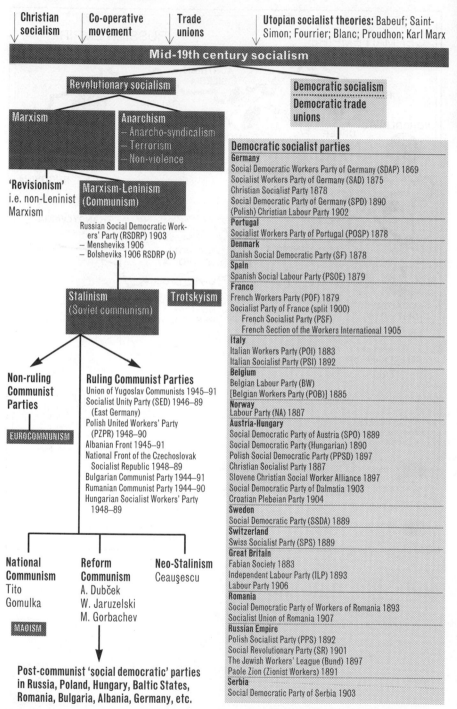

Christian socialism | Co-operative movement | Trade unions | Utopian socialist theories: Babeuf; Saint-Simon; Fourrier; Blanc; Proudhon; Karl Marx

Mid-19th century socialism

Revolutionary socialism

Democratic socialism
Democratic trade unions

Marxism

Anarchism
– Anarcho-syndicalism
– Terrorism
– Non-violence

Democratic socialist parties

Germany
Social Democratic Workers Party of Germany (SDAP) 1869
Socialist Workers Party of Germany (SAD) 1875
Christian Socialist Party 1878
Social Democratic Party of Germany (SPD) 1890
(Polish) Christian Labour Party 1902

'Revisionism' i.e. non-Leninist Marxism

Marxism-Leninism (Communism)

Russian Social Democratic Workers' Party (RSDRP) 1903
– Mensheviks 1906
– Bolsheviks 1906 RSDRP (b)

Portugal
Socialist Workers Party of Portugal (POSP) 1878
Denmark
Danish Social Democratic Party (SF) 1878
Spain
Spanish Social Labour Party (PSOE) 1879
France
French Workers Party (POF) 1879
Socialist Party of France (split 1900)
  French Socialist Party (PSF)
  French Section of the Workers International 1905

Stalinism (Soviet communism)

Trotskyism

Italy
Italian Workers Party (POI) 1883
Italian Socialist Party (PSI) 1892
Belgium
Belgian Labour Party (BW)
[Belgian Workers Party (POB)] 1885
Norway
Labour Party (NA) 1887
Austria-Hungary
Social Democratic Party of Austria (SPO) 1889
Social Democratic Party (Hungarian) 1890
Polish Social Democratic Party (PPSD) 1897
Christian Socialist Party 1887
Slovene Christian Social Worker Alliance 1897
Social Democratic Party of Dalmatia 1903
Croatian Plebeian Party 1904

Non-ruling Communist Parties

EUROCOMMUNISM

Ruling Communist Parties
Union of Yugoslav Communists 1945–91
Socialist Unity Party (SED) 1946–89
  (East Germany)
Polish United Workers' Party
  (PZPR) 1948–90
Albanian Front 1945–91
National Front of the Czechoslovak
  Socialist Republic 1948–89
Bulgarian Communist Party 1944–91
Rumanian Communist Party 1944–90
Hungarian Socialist Workers' Party
  1948–89

Sweden
Social Democratic Party (SSDA) 1889
Switzerland
Swiss Socialist Party (SPS) 1889
Great Britain
Fabian Society 1883
Independent Labour Party (ILP) 1893
Labour Party 1906
Romania
Social Democratic Party of Workers of Romania 1893
Socialist Union of Romania 1907

National Communism
Tito
Gomulka

MAOISM

Reform Communism
A. Dubček
W. Jaruzelski
M. Gorbachev

Neo-Stalinism
Ceauşescu

Russian Empire
Polish Socialist Party (PPS) 1892
Social Revolutionary Party (SR) 1901
The Jewish Workers' League (Bund) 1897
Paole Zion (Zionist Workers) 1891
Serbia
Social Democratic Party of Serbia 1903

Post-communist 'social democratic' parties in Russia, Poland, Hungary, Baltic States, Romania, Bulgaria, Albania, Germany, etc.

Macedonia: The Partition of 1913

RUSSIA

AUSTRIA-HUNGARY

BOSNIA

SERBIA

MONTENEGRO

ROMANIA

BULGARIA

ITALY

ALBANIA

Skopje

Salonica

Constantinople

OTTOMAN EMPIRE

GREECE

Smyrna (Izmir)

Crete

Boundaries after the Treaty of Bucharest (August 1913)

Aspirations

Serbia 1912   — · —

Bulgaria 1912   — — —

Greece 1912   ·····

Montenegro 1912

Greater Albania

The Jewish Pale in the Russian Empire, to 1917

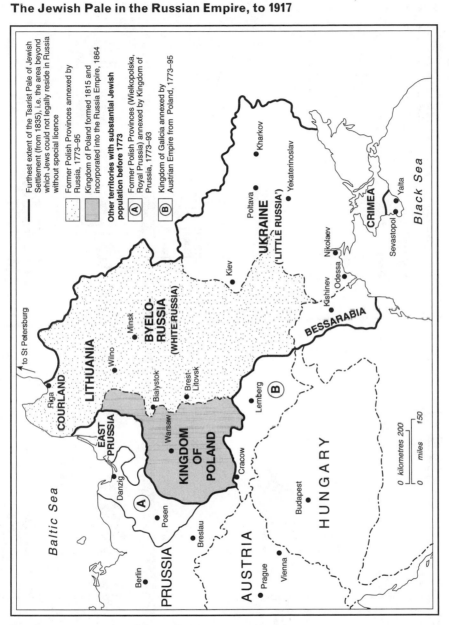

Furthest extent of the Tsarist Pale of Jewish Settlement (from 1835), i.e. the area beyond which Jews could not legally reside in Russia without special licence

Former Polish Provinces annexed by Russia, 1773–95

Kingdom of Poland formed 1815 and incorporated into the Russia Empire, 1864

Other territories with substantial Jewish population before 1773

(A) Former Polish Provinces (Wielkopolska, Royal Prussia) annexed by Kingdom of Prussia, 1773–95

(B) Kingdom of Galicia annexed by Austrian Empire from Poland, 1773–95

Black Sea

Kharkov

Yekaterinoslav

Poltava

UKRAINE ('LITTLE RUSSIA')

CRIMEA

Yalta

Sevastopol

Kiev

Nikolaev

Odessa

Kishinev

to St Petersburg

Minsk

BYELO-RUSSIA (WHITE RUSSIA)

BESSARABIA

LITHUANIA

Wilno

Riga

COURLAND

Bialystok

Brest-Litovsk

Lemberg

(B)

EAST PRUSSIA

Warsaw

KINGDOM OF POLAND

Cracow

HUNGARY

Baltic Sea

Danzig

(A)

Posen

Breslau

Budapest

PRUSSIA

Berlin

AUSTRIA

Prague

Vienna

0 kilometres 200

0 miles 150

The 'Great Triangle': European Power Centres, 1914–91

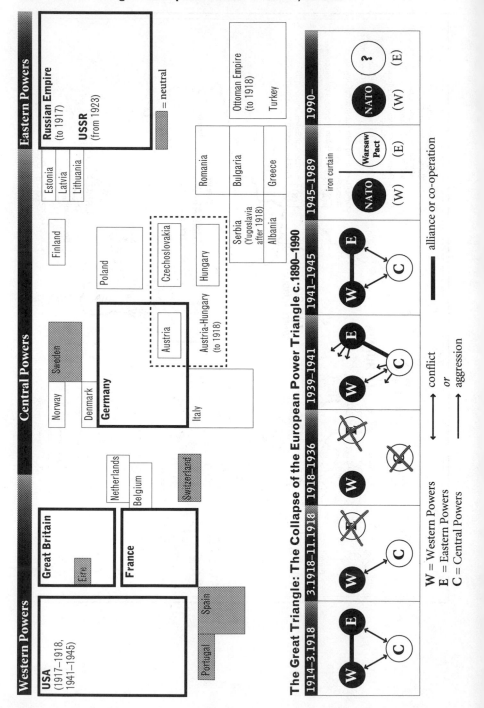

The Italo-Slav Borders, 1939–92

Villach
(Beljak)
AUSTRIA
Klagenfurt
(Celovec)
Tarvisio
(Trbiž)
Jesenice
▲ Triglav
N

ITALY

Ljubljana
(Laibach)

Udine
(Videm)
Gorizia
S L O V E N I A

Monfalcone
(Trzic)
Postojna
(Postumia)

Trieste
(Trst)

Piran
(Pirano)
C R O A T I A
Motovun
(Montona)
Rijeka (Fiume)
Poreč
(Parenzo)

Italo-Yugoslav boundary
as of 1 September 1939
Frontier since Italian
Peace Treaty of 1947
Present-day frontier between
Slovenia and Croatia
Free territory of Trieste
1945–7

KRK
(VEGLIA)

0   kilometres   80

0   miles   50

Pula
(Pola)

CRES
(CHERSO)

(a) 1939–92
Italy's North-
Eastern
Frontier

ITALY
Ljubljana
Zagreb
Fiume
SERBIA
C R O A T I A

Areas occupied by
Italy during World
War 2
Zadar
Areas annexed to
Italy 1941–5

(b) Italian
Occupation
Zones,
1939–44

A d r i a t i c   S e a

MONTENEGRO
Dubrovnik
KOSOVO
0   kilometres   150

0   miles   100
Kotor (Cattaro)
ALBANIA

The Expansion of Soviet Territory in Europe, 1917–45

Soviet Russia 1918

States joined with Soviet Russia to form USSR 1922

Annexed 1939

Annexed 1940

Annexed 1945

| 0 | kilometres | 500 |
| 0 | miles | 300 |

SOVIET RUSSIA (RSFSR—from 1917)

In 1917–18, all the non-Russian lands of the former Tsarist Empire, plus Siberia and the Don and Kuban Cossacks, seceded. With the exception of Poland and Finland, they were all reconquered by the Red Army either at the end of the Civil War in 1919–21 or during the currency of the Nazi–Soviet Pact in 1939–41.

NORWAY

SWEDEN

FINLAND

W. Karelia

Karelia

Leningrad

ESTONIA

Baltic Sea

LATVIA

LITHUANIA

Kaliningrad/ Königsberg

Moscow

SOVIET RUSSIA (RSFSR)

POLAND

BYELO- RUSSIA

EASTERN POLAND

Sub-Carpathian Ruthenia (1945)

Kiev

CZECHO- SLOVAKIA

UKRAINE

Don and Kuban Cossacks

HUNGARY

BUKOVINA

BESSARABIA

Caspian Sea

ROMANIA

Crimean Tatar Autonomous Republic, 1919–46

YUGOSLAVIA

GEORGIA

AZER- BAIJAN

BULGARIA

Black Sea

ARMENIA

TURKEY

The Republic of Ukraine, 1918–91

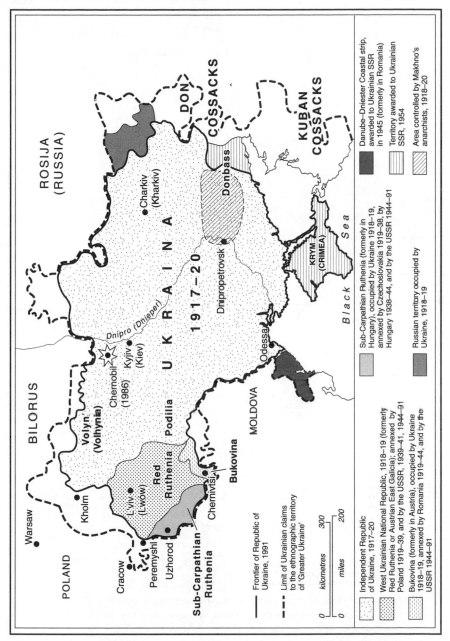

Legend:

— Frontier of Republic of Ukraine, 1991

– – – Limit of Ukrainian claims to the ethnographic territory of 'Greater Ukraine'

Independent Republic of Ukraine, 1917–20

West Ukrainian National Republic, 1918–19 (formerly Red Ruthenia or Austrian East Galicia); annexed by Poland 1919–39, and by the USSR, 1939–41, 1944–91

Bukovina (formerly in Austria), occupied by Ukraine 1918–19, annexed by Romania 1919–44, and by the USSR 1944–91

Sub-Carpathian Ruthenia (formerly in Hungary), occupied by Ukraine 1918–19, annexed by Czechoslovakia 1919–38, by Hungary 1938–44, and by the USSR 1944–91

Russian territory occupied by Ukraine, 1918–19

Danube–Dniester Coastal strip, awarded to Ukrainian SSR in 1945 (formerly in Romania)

Territory awarded to Ukrainian SSR, 1954

Area controlled by Makhno's anarchists, 1918–20

Poland, 1921–45

0 kilometres 200
0 miles 150

Baltic Sea

N

LATVIA
• Riga

LITHUANIA

Kaliningrad
(Königsberg) • **RUSSIA**

Gdańsk
(Danzig)

Olsztyn
(Allenstein)

Szczecin

Białystok •

• Wilno
(Vilnius)

BELARUS

Poznań
(Posen)

Warsaw •

Bug

Lublin •

Brześć
(Brest) • Pińsk

GERMANY

Wrocław
(Breslau) •

Vistula

UKRAINE

Cracow •

Lwów
(L'viv)

Katowice

Zaolzia

CZECH REPUBLIC

SLOVAKIA

Poland's former eastern provinces annexed by USSR, 1939, and as so-called 'Recovered Territories' in 1945.

Germany's former eastern provinces awarded to Poland as so-called 'Recovered Territories' 1945.

The northern sector of former East Prussia annexed by RSFSR in 1945

District of Wilno (Vilnius),1920–3 nominally independent as 'Central Lithuania':1923–39 incorporated into Poland; since 1945 in Lithuania.

The former Eastern Galicia: 1918–19 established as the 'West Ukrainian Republic', 1919–39 in Poland; 1939–41 and 1945–91 in Ukrainian SSR: since 1991 in Republic of Ukraine.

Zaolzia District (the Western part of the former Duchy of Austrian Silesia), annexed by Poland from Czechoslovakia 1938–9.

Districts of pre-war Poland incorporated into the Reich, 1939–45.

Plebiscite Areas, 1919–21.

- - - - - Riga Line (March 1921) fixed by the Treaty of Riga between Poland and Soviet Russia.

— — Molotov–Ribbentrop Line (September 1939) revived as the so-called 'Curzon Line' (1943–5).

——— Oder–Western Neisse Line (July 1945) imposed by the Potsdam Conference.

Czechoslovakia, 1918–92

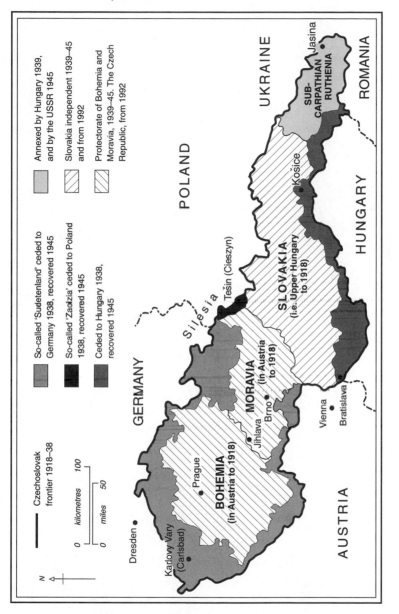

Hungary, 1918–45

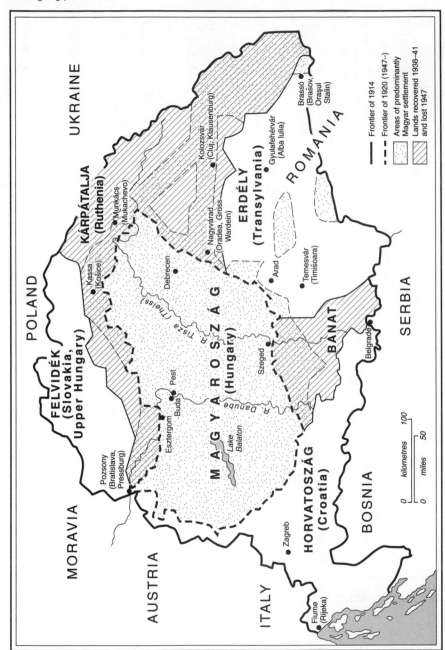

Frontier of 1914
Frontier of 1920 (1947–)
Areas of predominantly Magyar settlement
Lands recovered 1938–41 and lost 1947

The Growth of Serbia (1817–1913) and of Yugoslavia (1918–45)

In October 1918, the 'Kingdom of the Serbs' was expanded to form the 'Kingdom of the Serbs, Croats, and Slovenes'. The name of the state was changed in 1931 to the 'Kingdom of Yugoslavia'. Broken up and occupied by its neighbours 1941–4, the country was reconstituted in November 1945 as the 'People's Federal Republic of Yugoslavia' consisting of Serbia, Croatia, Slovenia, Bosnia and Hercegovina, and Macedonia. There were two autonomous regions within Serbia—Vojvodina and Kosovo. In 1992, the Yugoslav Federation disintegrated once more, leaving Serbia and Montenegro as its only members after all the other ex-Yugoslav republics had declared their independence.

The Dictatorships of Inter-War Europe, 1917–39

	Duration	Dictator(s)	
Soviet Russia and USSR	25.10.17 o.s [7.11.17]–1991	Lenin (to 1924) J. V. Stalin 'Vozhd' (to 1953)	Bolshevik coup d'état, totalitarian, Communist/Party State. Terror.
Hungary	21.3.19–9.1919 1919–44	Bela Kun Admiral Horthy	Soviet Communist Republic. Terror. Proto-fascist dictatorship. Terror.
Italy	28.10.22–1943	Benito Mussolini	Fascist takeover: constitutional monarchy replaced by 'corporate state'. All opposition parties disbanded, 1926.
Bulgaria	8/9.6.23–1944	Aleksandr Tsankov	Military coup d'état: authoritarian regime, dissolution of opposition: from 1934, royal dictatorship of Boris III.
Spain	23.9.23 –20.1.30	General Miguel Primo de Rivera	Authoritarian regime in agreement with King Alfonso XIII, military directorate: suspension of the constitution.
Turkey	29.10.23–1938	Gazi Mustaf Kemal Pasha	Personal dictatorship, one-party national state.
Albania	1.25–1940	Ahmed Zogu (became king 1928)	Authoritarian regime, first presidential then royal.
Poland	12.5.26–1939	Marshal Joseph Pilsudski	Military coup d'état: left-wing military regime: 'Sanacja' dictatorship, operating behind a parliamentary façade.
Portugal	28.5.26–1975 from 1932	Manuel de Oliveira A. Salazar	Authoritarian regime, dissolution of parliament, constitution suspended.
Yugoslavia	1.29–1941	King Alexander	Coup d'état: royal dictatorship.
Lithuania	19.9.29–1940	Antónas Smetona	Nationalist one-party state.
Romania	9.6.30–1941	King Carol II	Coup d'état, royal dictatorship.
Germany	30.1.33–1945	Adolph Hitler, 'Führer'	Nazi electoral success: one party state introduced through 'emergency powers'. Terror.
Austria	3.33–1937	Engelbert Dollfuss	Dictatorship by the semi-fascist 'Father-land Front', rule by emergency decree.
Estonia	12.3.34–1940	Konstantin Päts	Authoritarian regime, state of emergency, rule by decree, parliament dissolved.
Latvia	15.5.34–1940	Karlis Ulmanis	Authoritarian regime, a government of national unity, parliament dissolved.
Greece	10.1935–1941	General J. Kondilis General I. Metaxas	Authoritarian military-royal regime, dissolution of parliament.
Spain	9.36–1975	General Francisco Franco, 'Caudillo'	Military Fascism: totalitarian regime. Terror.

The Dual System of Communist 'Party-States'

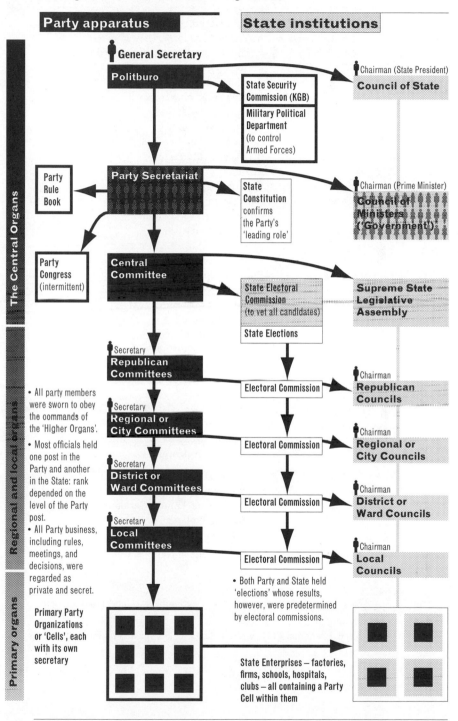

Party apparatus

State institutions

General Secretary

Politburo

Chairman (State President)
Council of State

State Security
Commission (KGB)

Military Political
Department
(to control
Armed Forces)

Party
Rule
Book

Party Secretariat

Chairman (Prime Minister)
**Council of
Ministers
('Government')**

State
Constitution
confirms
the Party's
'leading role'

Party
Congress
(intermittent)

**Central
Committee**

State Electoral
Commission
(to vet all candidates)

**Supreme State
Legislative
Assembly**

State Elections

The Central Organs

Secretary
**Republican
Committees**

Electoral Commission

Chairman
**Republican
Councils**

• All party members
were sworn to obey
the oommands of
the 'HIgher Organs'.

• Most officials held
one post in the
Party and another
in the State: rank
depended on the
level of the Party
post.

• All Party business,
including rules,
meetings, and
decisions, were
regarded as
private and secret.

Secretary
**Regional or
City Committees**

Electoral Commission

Chairman
**Regional or
City Councils**

Secretary
**District or
Ward Committees**

Electoral Commission

Chairman
**District or
Ward Councils**

Regional and local organs

Secretary
**Local
Committees**

Electoral Commission

Chairman
**Local
Councils**

• Both Party and State held
'elections' whose results,
however, were predetermined
by electoral commissions.

Primary organs

**Primary Party
Organizations
or 'Cells', each
with its own
secretary**

State Enterprises – factories,
firms, schools, hospitals,
clubs – all containing a Party
Cell within them

Key
= Lines of executive command

Inter-War treaties of Non-Aggression and/or Neutrality, 1925–39

1925	USSR–TURKEY.	Paris, 17 December 1925, renewed 1929, 1931.
1926	USSR–GERMANY.	Berlin, 24 April 1926, renewed 1931.
	USSR–AFGHANISTAN.	Pahgman, 31 August 1926, renewed 1931.
	USSR–LITHUANIA.	Moscow, 28 September 1926.
1927	USSR–LATVIA.	Riga, initialled 9 March 1927.
	USSR–PERSIA.	Moscow, 1 October 1927.
1928	GREECE–ROMANIA.	Geneva, 21 March 1928.
	ITALY–TURKEY.	Rome, 30 May 1928.
	GREECE–ITALY.	Rome, 23 September 1928.
1929	GREECE–YUGOSLAVIA.	Belgrade, 27 March 1929.
1930	GREECE–TURKEY.	Ankara, 30 October 1930.
1932	USSR–FINLAND.	Moscow, 21 January 1932.
	USSR–POLAND.	Moscow, initialled 25 January 1932, signed 25 July 1932, renewed 5 May 1934.
	USSR–LATVIA.	Riga, 5 February 1932.
	USSR–ESTONIA.	Moscow, 4 May 1932.
	USSR–FRANCE.	Paris, 29 November 1932.
1933	USSR–ITALY.	Rome, 2 September 1933.
	ROMANIA–TURKEY.	Ankara, 17 October 1933.
	TURKEY–YUGOSLAVIA.	Belgrade, 27 November 1933.
1934	GERMANY–POLAND.	Berlin, 26 January 1934.
1939	PORTUGAL–SPAIN.	Madrid, 18 March 1939.
	GERMANY–USSR.	Moscow, 23 August 1939.

General Pacts

1925   THE LOCARNO TREATIES, 16 October 1925. (1) Treaties of Guarantee of the Franco-German and the Belgian-German Frontiers. (2) Arbitration Treaties between Germany and France, Belgium, Czechoslovakia, and Poland. (3) Treaties of Mutual Guarantee by France, Czechoslovakia, and Poland.

1928   TREATY FOR THE RENUNCIATION OF WAR AS AN INSTRUMENT OF NATIONAL POLICY (The Briand–Kellogg Pact), Paris, 27 August 1928: signed by Australia, Belgium, Canada, Czechoslovakia, France, Germany, Great Britain, India, Ireland, Italy, Japan, New Zealand, Poland, South Africa, USA.

   GENERAL ACT FOR THE PACIFIC SETTLEMENT OF INTERNATIONAL DISPUTES: General Assembly of the League of Nations, Geneva, 26 September 1928.

1933   LONDON CONVENTIONS DEFINING AGGRESSION:
   3 July, Afghanistan, Estonia, Latvia, Persia, Poland, Romania, Turkey, USSR.
   4 July, Lithuania, USSR.
   5 July, Greece, Romania, Turkey, Yugoslavia, USSR (joined by Finland, 23 July 1933).

1934   BALKAN PACT OF MUTUAL GUARANTEE, Athens, 9 February 1934: signed by Greece, Romania, Turkey, Yugoslavia.

The Rise of Nazi Power, 1933–43

The Spanish Civil War, 1936–39

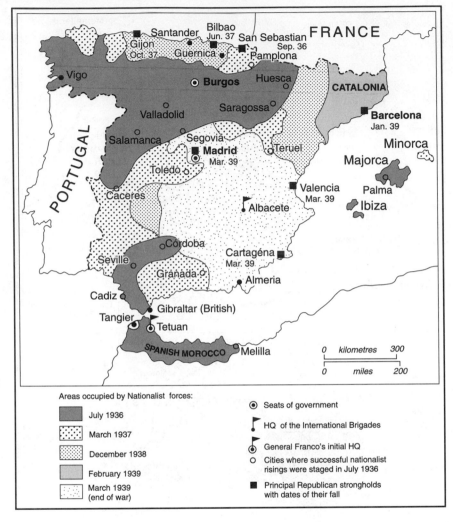

Areas occupied by Nationalist forces:

- ▓ July 1936
- ▒ March 1937
- ▒ December 1938
- ▒ February 1939
- ⬚ March 1939 (end of war)

- ◉ Seats of government
- ⌐ HQ of the International Brigades
- ⌐ General Franco's initial HQ
- O Cities where successful nationalist risings were staged in July 1936
- ■ Principal Republican strongholds with dates of their fall

The International Brigades in Spain, 1936–9

Formed	No.	Name	Battalions	Principal initial composition
Oct. 1936	**XI**	Hans Beimler (later Thaelmann)	1 Edgar André 2 Commune de Paris (later transferred to IB XIV) 3 Dombrowsky (transferred to IB XII)	German Franco-Belgian Polish
Nov. 1936	**XII**	Garibaldi	1 Thaelmann (transferred to IB XI) 2 Garibaldi 3 André Marty	German Italian Franco-Belgian
Dec. 1936	**XIII**	–	1 Louise Michel (transferred to IB XIV) 2 Chapiaer (transferred to IB 129) 3 Henri Vuillemin (transferred to IB XIV) 4 Mickiewicz (Palafox)	Franco-Belgian Balkan French
Dec. 1936	**XIV**	Marseillaise	1 Nine Nations Battalion (transferred to IB XI.2) 2 Domingo Germinal 3 Henri Barbusse 4 Pierre Brachet	 Spanish Anarchist French French
Dec. 1937	**XV**	Lincoln-Washington	1 Dimitrov (transferred to IB 129) 2 British 3 Lincoln, Washington 4 Sixth of February (transferred to IB XIV)	 British USA French
June/July 1937	**'150'**	–	1 Rakosi 2 – (transferred to IB XIII)	Hungarian
	'129'	–	1 Masaryk 2 Dajakovich 3 Dimitrov	Czechoslovak Bulgarian Yugoslav/Albanian
	– (attached to the 86th Brigade)		Col. Morandi Battalion	Mixed

The Waffen-SS Divisions, 1933–45

Number	Designation	Name	Formation	Recruitment
I	SS-PD	Leibstandarte Adolf Hitler	1933–	SS Panzer Regt. 1
II	SS-PD	Das Reich (initially Deutschland)	1939	SS Verfügungsgruppe (Special task force)
III	SS-PD	Totenkopf	1939	Totenkopfverbände (KL guards); Politische Bereitschafte (Political Readiness Group)
IV	SS-PgD	Polizei	1939	Militarized Police
V	SS-PD*	Wiking (initially Germania)	1940	Nordland Regt. (Danes and Norwegians); Westland Regt. (Flemings/Dutch; Finnish Battalion)
VI	SS-GbD**	Nord	1941	Kampfgruppe 'Nord'
VII	SS-FGbD**	Prinz Eugen	1942	Balkan Volksdeutsche recruits
VIII	SS-KD	Florian Geyer	1941	SS Totenkopf Reitenstandarte
IX	SS-PD	Hohenstaufen	1942	German conscripts
X	SS-PD	Frundsberg	1943	German conscripts
XI	SS-FPgD*	Nordland	1943	Norwegian and Danish Legions; SS Wiking
XII	SS-PD	Hitlerjugend	1943	17-year-old Hitler Youth volunteers
XIII	WGbD der SS*	Handschar	1943	Bosnian Muslims
XIV	WGD der SS*	Galizien (Ukrainische 1)	1943	West Ukrainians
XV	WGD der SS*	(Lettische No. 1)	1943	Latvian Legion
XVI	SS-PgD	Reichsführer-SS	1943	SS Escort Battalion
XVII	SS-PgD	Götz von Berchlingen	1943	Wehrmacht (France)
XVIII	SS-PgD**	Horst Wessel	1944	Hungarian Volksdeutsche +
XIX	WGD der SS*	(Lettische No. 2)	1944	Latvian Legion
XX	WGD der SS*	(Estnische No. 1)	1943	Estonian Legion
XXI	WGbD der SS*†	Skanderbeg	1944	Albanian Muslims
XXII	FKD der SS**	Maria Theresa	1944	Hungarian Volksdeutsche + Veterans of SS-VIII
XXIII	WGbD der SS*†	Kama (Kroatische No. 2) (disbanded)	1943	Croatians and Bosnian Muslims
XXIII	FPgD der SS*	Niederland/Nederland	1944	Dutch Legion
XXIV	WGbD†	Karstjäger	1943	Karstwehr Security Battalion (Italy)
XXV	WGD der SS*†	Hunyadi (Ungarische No. 1)	1944	Hungarians
XXVI	WGD der SS*†	(Ungarische No. 2)	1944	Hungarlans

Number	Designation	Name	Formation	Recruitment
XXVII	SS-FGD*†	Langemarck (Vlanderen 1)	1944	Flemish Legion
XXVIII	SS-FGD*†	Wallonien	1944	Walloon Legion
XXIX	SS-FGD*	(Russische No. 1) (disbanded)	1944	Kaminski Brigade; ex-Soviet POWs
XXIX	WGD der SS*†	(Italienische No. 1)	1945	Ex-Italian Army
XXX	WGD der SS*	(Russische No. 2)	1944	Ex-Soviet POWs
XXXI	SS-FPgD**†	Böhmen-Mähren	1944	Bohemia and Moravia
XXXII	SS-FPgD*	30 Januar	1945	Courland
XXXIII	WKD der SS*†	(Ungarische No. 3) (disbanded)	1944	Hungarians
XXXIII	WGD der SS*	Charlemagne (Französische No. 1)	1944	*Légion Volontaire Française*
XXXIV	SS-FGD*†	Landstorm Nederlands	1944	Dutch volunteers
XXXV	SS-GD†	Polizei (No. 2)	1944	(As SS-IV)
XXXVI	WGD der SS	—	1944	Dirlewanger Brigade
XXXVII	SS-FKD†	Lützow	1944	
XXXVIII	SS-GD†	Nibelungen	1945	Bad Tölz Cadet School
XXXIX	GbD der SS†	Andreas Hofer	1945	formation incomplete
XL	SS-FPgD†	Feldherrnhalle	1945	formation incomplete
XLI	WGD der SS*†	Kalevala (Finnische No. 1)	1945	formation incomplete
XLII	SS-D†	Niedersachsen	1945	formation incomplete
XLIII	SS-D†	Reichsmarschall	1945	formation incomplete
XLIV	SS-D†	Wallenstein	1945	formation incomplete
XLV	SS-D†	Warager	1945	formation incomplete

Miscellaneous SS Units:
† Legion of St George (1940), British volunteers; SS-Fallschirmjäger (SS Parachute Brigade (penal); SS-Panzer Abteilung 'Hermann von Salza'; Begleit Battalion-Reichsführer (SS escort battalion); Wachtbattalion-Adolf Hitler (Führer's bodyguard).

* Units composed mainly of non-German troops.
** Units composed mainly or partly of East European *Volksdeutsch* troops.
† Units always below divisional strength. NB. Designations were prefixed either with 'SS-' (for units fully integrated into all the SS organizations) or with 'der SS' (for non-integrated units).

Abbreviations: SS: Schutzstaffeln; PD: Panzer Division; PgD: Panzergrenadier Division; GbD: Gebirgs (Mountain) Division; KD: Kavallerie (Cavalry) Division; F: Freiwillinge (Volunteer); WGD: Waffen Grenadier Division; WGbD: Waffen Gebirgs Division.

Sources: A. J. Barker, *The Waffen-SS at War* (London, 1982), app.: 'SS Divisions, 1940–5', 121–2; B. Quarrie, *Hitler's Samurai: The Waffen-SS in Action* (London, 1983), ch. 2, 'The Growth of the Waffen-SS'; G. H. Stein, *The Waffen-SS: Hitler's Elite Guard at War, 1939–1945* (Ithaca, NY, 1966).

Europe's Estimated Death Toll, 1914–45

1 Military losses during the First World War
(by states, killed in action or dead of wounds) (not including USA)

Allied Powers

Russian Empire	1 700 000
France	1 357 800
Britain & Empire	908 371
Italy	650 000
Romania	325 706
Serbia	70 000
Belgium	13 716
Portugal	7 222
Greece	5 000
Montenegro	3 000
sub-total	**5 040 815**

Central Powers

Germany	1 773 700
Austria-Hungary	1 200 000
Turkey	325 000
Bulgaria	87 500
sub-total	**3 386 200**

Total (estimate)	**8 427 015**

2 Military losses during the Second World War
(by states, killed in action or dead of wounds) (not including USA)

Allied Powers

Soviet Union	* 8 – 9 000 000
Yugoslavia	305 000
Britain	264 443
France	213 324
Poland	123 178
Greece	88 300
Belgium	12 000
Czechoslovakia	10 000
Netherlands	7 900
Norway	3 000
Denmark	1 800
sub-total	**10 026 945**

Axis Powers

Germany	3 500 000
Romania	300 000
Italy	242 232
Hungary	200 000
Finland	82 000
Bulgaria	10 000
sub-total	**4 335 232**

Total (estimate)	**14 362 177**

* This figure includes 3–4 million Soviet POWs killed during Nazi captivity or on repatriation to the USSR.

3 Civilians killed during the Second World War
(by states)

Allied Powers

	minimum	maximum
Soviet Union	** 16 000 000	19 000 000
Poland	*** 5 675 000	7 000 000
Yugoslavia	1 200 000	
France	350 000	
Greece	325 000	
Czechoslovakia	215 000	
Netherlands	200 000	
Britain	92 673	
Belgium	76 000	
Norway	7 000	
Denmark	2 000	

Axis Powers

Germany	780 000	
Hungary	290 000	
Romania	200 000	
Italy	152 941	
Bulgaria	10 000	
Finland	2 000	

Total (estimate)	**27 077 614**

** This huge number, which is based on post-war demographic short-falls, not on recorded deaths, conceals several categories listed in Table 5. It is only partly attributable to the German Occupation. It also ignores the breakdown by nationality, never officially disclosed, where the heaviest losses were sustained by Ukrainians, Byelorussians, Russians, Poles, Balts, and Jews.

*** The lower figure does not allow for Polish citizens obliged to adopt Soviet citizenship in 1939.

4 The Holocaust: the genocide of Jews by the Nazis, 1939–45
(by states of origin, minimum and maximum estimates)

	minimum	maximum
Poland	2 350 000	3 000 000
Soviet Union	1 500 000	2 000 000
Germany & Austria	218 000	240 000
Hungary	200 000	300 000
Romania	200 000	300 000
Netherlands	104 000	110 000
Czechoslovakia	90 000	95 000
France	60 000	65 000
Greece	57 000	60 000
Yugoslavia	55 000	60 000
Belgium	25 000	28 000
Italy	8 500	9 500
Luxembourg	2 800	3 000
Norway	700	1 000
Denmark	less than 100	

Totals (estimate)	**4 871 000**	**6 271 500**
average	c.5 571 300	

5 Categories of people killed in Soviet Russia and the Soviet Union 1917–1953 (excluding war losses, 1939–45)

(after R. Medvedev, R. Conquest)

	minimum	maximum
Civil War & Volga Famine, 1918–22	3 000 000	5 000 000
Political repressions in the 1920s	tens of thousands	
Forced collectivization and 'dekulakization' after 1929	10 000 000	14 000 000
Ukrainian Terror-Famine, 1932–3	6 000 000	7 000 000
Great Terror (1934–9) and Purges	1 000 000	
Deportations to the Gulag, to 1937	10 000 000	
Shootings and random executions, 1937–9	1 000 000	
Deportations from Eastern Poland, Baltic States, and Romania, 1939–1940	2 000 000	
Foreign POWs: Poles, Finns, Germans, Romanians, Japanese	1 000 000	
Deportations to the Gulag, 1939–45	7 000 000	
Deportations of nationalities: Volga Germans, Chechens, Ingush, Crimean Tatars, etc.	1 000 000	
Post-war screening of repatriates and inhabitants of ex-occupied territory	5 000 000	6 000 000

Gross total (median estimate)　　　　　　*c.***54 million**

NB. Several of these categories overlap.

6 Principal categories with Europe's death toll (1914–1945)

⚰ = 1 million deaths

Total civilian losses in Europe in WW2	⚰⚰⚰⚰⚰⚰⚰⚰⚰⚰⚰⚰⚰⚰⚰⚰⚰⚰⚰⚰⚰⚰⚰⚰⚰⚰⚰⚰⚰⚰⚰⚰⚰⚰⚰⚰
Soviet citizens killed during WW2	⚰⚰⚰⚰⚰⚰⚰⚰⚰⚰⚰⚰⚰⚰⚰⚰⚰⚰⚰⚰⚰⚰⚰⚰⚰⚰⚰⚰⚰⚰⚰⚰⚰⚰⚰
Victims of the Soviet Gulag	⚰⚰⚰⚰⚰⚰⚰⚰⚰⚰⚰⚰⚰⚰⚰⚰⚰⚰⚰⚰⚰⚰⚰⚰⚰
Military losses WW2	⚰⚰⚰⚰⚰⚰⚰⚰⚰⚰⚰⚰⚰⚰⚰⚰
Collectivization and dekulakization losses	⚰⚰⚰⚰⚰⚰⚰⚰⚰⚰⚰⚰
Military losses WW1	⚰⚰⚰⚰⚰⚰⚰⚰
Losses during Russian Civil War	⚰⚰⚰⚰⚰⚰⚰
Ukrainian Terror-Famine	⚰⚰⚰⚰⚰⚰
Jewish Holocaust	⚰⚰⚰⚰⚰⚰
Poland's losses, 1939–1945	⚰⚰⚰⚰⚰⚰
Total US and UK losses during WW2	⚰
Total civilian losses in Europe in WW1	⚰⚰⚰⚰⚰

(chiefly in Austrian Galicia, Russian Poland, Serbia, Belgium, and N. France)

Warning Except for the Military losses during WW1 and the Jewish Holocaust, none of these estimates have been satisfactorily researched or substantiated. They can only be used as general indicators of the scale of the losses involved.

The Gulag Archipelago: Soviet Concentration Camps and KGB prisons
(after Avraham Shifrin, c.1980)

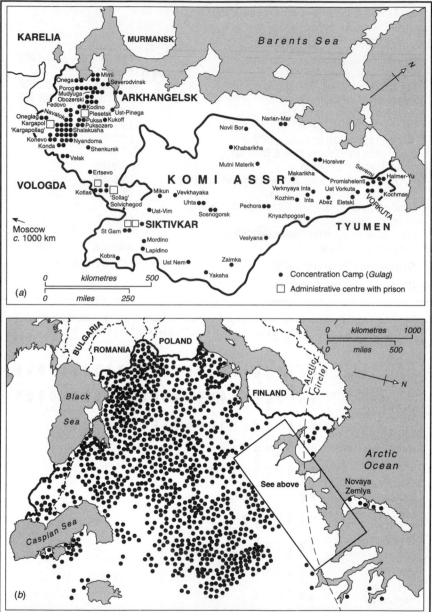

(a) In Arctic Russia; (b) In the European part of the USSR

The Baltic Countries, 1993

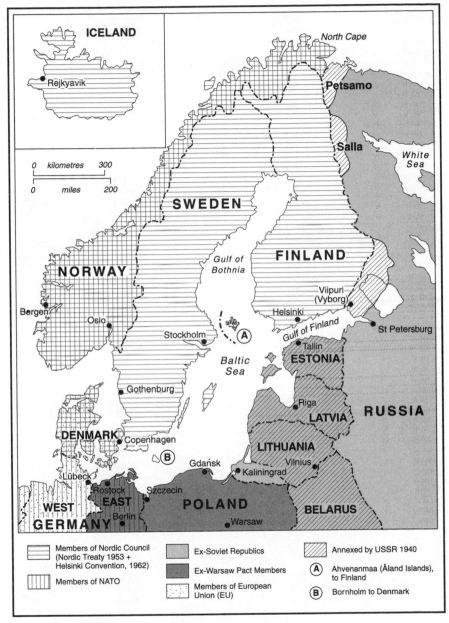

Legend:

- Members of Nordic Council (Nordic Treaty 1953 + Helsinki Convention, 1962)
- Members of NATO
- Ex-Soviet Republics
- Ex-Warsaw Pact Members
- Members of European Union (EU)
- Annexed by USSR 1940
- (A) Ahvenanmaa (Åland Islands), to Finland
- (B) Bornholm to Denmark

Europe, 1992: Assorted Statistics

Country	Territory (sq. miles)	Population Density (per sq.m.)	Population (m.)	GDP ($ bn.)
European Union				
Belgium	11,781	851	10.025	218.7
Denmark	16,629	311	5.17	142.1
France	211,207	272	57.372	1324.9
Germany	137,352	587	80.569	1775.1
Greece	50,944	202	10.3	79.2
Ireland	27,136	131	3.547	48.8
Italy	116,303	497	57.782	1223.6
Luxembourg	908	374	.340	10.4
Netherlands	15,963	951	15.178	320.4
Portugal	35,553	277	9.846	83.9
Spain	194,884	175	34.085	573.7
UK	94,226	614	57.848	1040.5
European Free Trade Area				
Austria	32,374	244	7.884	184.7
Finland	130,119	39	5.042	109.6
Iceland	102,819	3	.260	6.6
Norway	125,181	34	4.286	113.1
Sweden	173,648	50	8.678	245.8
Switzerland	15,941	433	6.905	240.5
Ex-Soviet Bloc				
Czech Rep.	30,343	342	10.383	25.3
Hungary	35,969	284	10.202	30.7
Poland	120,725	318	38.365	75.3
Slovakia	18,917	283	5.346	10.2
Albania	11,101	301	3.338	1.0
Bulgaria	42,823	209	8.952	11.9
Romania	91,699	249	22.865	24.9
Cyprus	3,578	200	.715	7.1
Malta	122	2,950	.360	2.6
Ex-Yugoslavia				
Bosnia	19,741	221	4.366	
Croatia	21,824	219	4.784	8.6
Macedonia	9,928	205	2.039	5.06
Montenegro	5,332	120	.639	
Serbia	34,107	287	9.792	
Slovenia	7,817	258	2.017	14.4
(Yugoslavia, to 1991)	(98,766)	(239)		
Ex-USSR				
Belarus'	80,150	129	10.346	32.2
Estonia	17,413	89	1.554	5.9
Latvia	24,500	107	2.617	8.9
Lithuania	25,174	149	3.754	10.1
Moldavia	13,000	335	4.359	9.5
Russia	6.591m.	23	148.920	479.5
(in Europe)	c.1.3m.	92!	120!	
Ukraine	232,046	225	52.1	121.9
EUROPE: TOTAL	3,639,001 sq.m.!	c.190	694.01!	8626.6#
EU	912,886	375	342.062	6841.3
USA	3,618,770	70	252.18	5689.2
Japan	142,811	871	124.45	3707.9

GDP ($ per capita)	GDP (purchasing power parity)	Higher education (% pupils/population 20–4 aged)	Medical care (people per physician)
21,815	18,170	37	321
27,485	17,768	32	448
23,093	18,665	40	421
22,032	16,310	33	710
7,689	8,417	29	340
13,758	12,427	26	410
21,176	17,521	31	552
30,588	24,771	33	496
21,110	17,023	34	444
8,521	9,736	18	575
16,831	14,731	34	360
17,987	16,300	25	870
23,427	18,005	33	333
21,737	15,025	47	322
25,385	17,067	25	960
26,388	17,785	43	503
28,324	16,496	33	355
34,830	22,159	28	1,441
2,437	6,923	18	389
3,009	5,297	15	740
1,963	4,081	22	416
1,908	5,224	18	389
229	—	7	2,070
1,329	4,770	31	340
1,089	2,307	9	n.a.
9,930	—	15	754
7,222	—	11	500
			636
1,800			471
2,481			463
			493
7,150	8,098		512
3,110			250
3,830			204
3,410			195
2,710			222
2,170			249
3,220			214
2,340			229
11,933!#			
20,000			
22,560			
29,794			

! = estimate   # includes the whole of the Russian Federation

Sources: OECD Main Economic Indicators, December 1993; IMF IFS, December 1993; DOTS 1993 Yearbook; World Bank Atlas, 1994

Parliamentary Assemblies

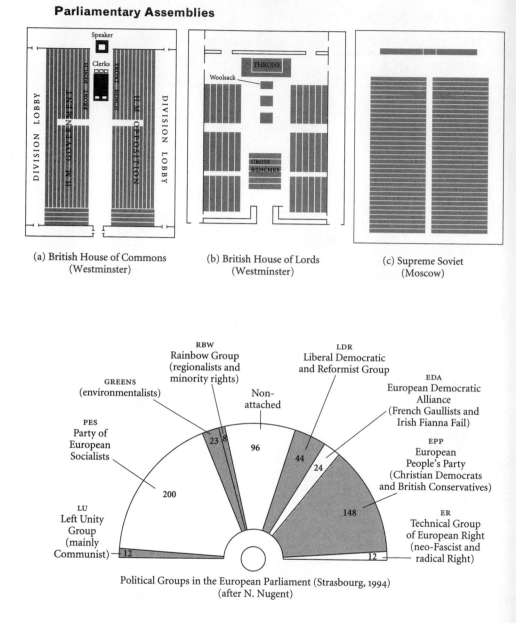

(a) British House of Commons
(Westminster)

(b) British House of Lords
(Westminster)

(c) Supreme Soviet
(Moscow)

Political Groups in the European Parliament (Strasbourg, 1994)
(after N. Nugent)

See also pp. 696–7.

Europe 1995: Membership of Five International Organizations*

	C of E[1]	NATO[2]	WEU[3]	EU[4]	CSCE[5]
Founded	1949–50	1949	1954	1957	1975
Function	Co-operation in legal and cultural affairs and human rights	Defence	European Defence	Economic, social, and political integration	Confidence-building measures
HQ	Strasbourg	Brussels	Brussels	Brussels	Prague
Total membership (1995)	33	16	10	15	53
Albania	G	PfP			CSCE
Andorra	C of E			STr	
Armenia		PfP			CSCE
Austria	C of E			EU	CSCE
Belarus	G	PfP			CSCE
Belgium	C of E	NATO	WEU	EU	CSCE
Bosnia	G				
Bulgaria	C of E	PfP	A	A	CSCE
Croatia	G				CSCE
Cyprus	C of E			A	CSCE
Czech Republic	C of E	PfP	A	A	CSCE
Denmark	C of E	NATO	Ob	EU	CSCE
Estonia	C of E		A	A	CSCE
Finland	C of E	PfP	Ob	EU	CSCE
France	C of E	NATO	WEU	EU	CSCE
Georgia		PfP			CSCE
Germany	C of E	NATO	WEU	EU	CSCE
Greece	C of E	NATO	WEU	EU	CSCE
Hungary	C of E	PfP	A	A	CSCE
Iceland	C of E	NATO		EEA	CSCE
Ireland	C of E		Ob	EU	CSCE
Italy	C of E	NATO	WEU	EU	CSCE
Latvia	G	PfP	A	A	CSCE
Lithuania	C of E	PfP	A	A	CSCE
Luxembourg	C of E	NATO	WEU	EU	CSCE
Macedonia	G				Ob
Malta	C of E			A	CSCE
Moldova	G	PfP			CSCE
Monaco				STr	CSCE
Netherlands	C of E	NATO	WEU	EU	CSCE
Norway	C of E	NATO		EEA	CSCE
Poland	C of E	PfP	A	A	CSCE
Portugal	C of E	NATO	WEU	EU	CSCE
Romania	C of E	PfP	A	A	CSCE
Russia	G	PfP			CSCE
San Marino	C of E			STr	CSCE
Slovakia	C of E	PfP	A	A	CSCE
Slovenia	C of E	PfP		A	CSCE
Spain	C of E	NATO	WEU	EU	CSCE
Sweden	C of E	PfP	Ob	EU	CSCE
Switzerland	C of E			STr	CSCE
Turkey	C of E	NATO			CSCE
Ukraine	G	PfP			CSCE
United Kingdom	C of E	NATO	WEU	EU	CSCE
Vatican State					CSCE
Yugoslav Federation (Serbia & Montenegro)					Suspended
Canada		NATO			
USA		NATO			

Key
C of E = Full member; A = Associate status; G = Guest member; EEA = Member of European Economic Area only; PfP = Member of Partnership for Peace; Ob = Observer status; STr = Special Treaty status
* *Source: Independent*, 5.12.94   [1] Council of Europe (including Court of Human Rights)
[2] North Atlantic Treaty Organisation   [3] Western European Union
[4] European Union (formerly European Economic Community) including the European Court
[5] Conference on Security and Co-operation in Europe

SELECTIVE INDEX

(**Bold** page numbers refer to the Capsules)

EIRIK

ATLANTIC OCEAN

N

IONA PHILIBEG

MARKET

FAMINE

BLARNEY

LLANFAIR

BARD
MAGIC   MARSTON
MONKEY OXFAM

London
HATRED SOUND
LLOYD'S TABARD
MASON UTOPIA
MAUVE

TRISTAN

CARITAS

LANGEMARCK
REVERENTIA INFANTA

COWARD

GROTE MARKT

Paris
ANNALES   RENTES
DESSEIN   ROUGE
FEMME   TORMENTA
GOTHIC   TOUR
GUILLOTIN VENDÉMIAIRE
IMPRESSION VIOLETS
MALET

COMPOSTELLA

FATIMA

NOYADES CHOUAN CRAVATE PFALZ
                GAUCHE EPIDEMIA
         COMBRAY BRIE   EPIC
ALCOFRIBAS   DOUAUMONT   PRE

ANGELUS

CABALA

ELSASS
STRASSB

SINGULARIS LAUSSEL BAUME HOLISM FA
                    PHOTO   DAN
SAMOS   CODPIECE

PRADO
FARAON

BASERRIA

AGOBARD   PARNASSE WASTEL
JACQUARD SYROP
LUGDUNUM

BERNADETTE   TAIZÉ RELAXATIO GOTT
                   ALPI   VALT

GONCALVEZ
QUAKE

CHASSE   ORANGE   LEPER
MONTAILLOU PROSTIBULA

FLAMENCO   ADELANTE

MADONNA NOSTRADAMUS BALLETTO
         MASSILIA BRITO JEANS STRAD
SYPHILUS USURY   TEMPUS
                        SONATA

INQUISITIO
PICARO

MEZQUITA
GUERRILLA

EL CID
XATIVAH

LEONARDO
LESBIA
MERCANTE

CORSICA

FLA

Ancient Rome   Rome   ETRUSC
AUC   ANNO DOMINI
AQUILA   BAMBINI
ARICIA   CANTUS
CATACOMBI CONCLAVE
CONDOM   INDEX   SPA
LEX   PAPESSA   PA
LUDI   PROPAGANDA
NOMEN   SYLLABUS

MISCELLANEOUS

BOXER   NEZ
C 14   OPERA
CAP-AG   PALAEO
CHASTITY   PASCHA
CRUX   PLOVUM
DASA   SAMPHIRE
DEVIATIO   SPICE-OX
DIABOLOS   STATE
FOLLY   TAMMUZ
GAT-HUNTER VENDANGE
MISSA

GATTOPAR

ARCHIMED

ĠGANTIJA

MEDITERRA
SEA

To locate the capsules in the
text, see Appendix I, p. 1203